DICTIONARY OF THE ECUMENICAL MOVEMENT

Edited by

Nicholas Lossky

José Míguez Bonino

John Pobee

Tom Stransky

Geoffrey Wainwright

Pauline Webb

WCC Publications, Geneva

William B. Eerdmans Publishing Company, Grand Rapids

First published 1991 in Switzerland by
WCC Publications
World Council of Churches
150 Route de Ferney, 1211 Geneva 2, Switzerland
ISBN 2-8254-1025-X

in Great Britain by
Council of Churches for Britain and Ireland
Inter-Church House, 35-41 Lower Marsh, London SE1 7RL, England
ISBN 0-85169-225-7

and in the USA by
Wm. B. Eerdmans Publishing Co.
255 Jefferson Ave. SE, Grand Rapids, Mich. 49503
ISBN 0-8028-2428-5

Printed in the United States of America

Contents

The Editors

Nicholas Lossky (Russian Orthodox Church) is professor of English intellectual history at the University of Paris-Nanterre, of church history at the Orthodox Theological Institute of St Sergius in Paris, and director of the Institut supérieur d'études œcuméniques at the Catholic Institute in Paris. He is the author of *Lancelot Andrewes (1555-1626): le prédicateur* (1986, ET 1991).

José Míguez Bonino (Argentine Evangelical Methodist Church) is emeritus professor of systematic theology, the Higher Evangelical Institute of Theological Studies (ISEDET), Buenos Aires. He was a president of the World Council of Churches from 1975 to 1983. Among his books in English are *Doing Theology in a Revolutionary Situation* (1975), *Room To Be People* (1979) and *Toward a Christian Political Ethics* (1983).

John S. Pobee (Church of the Province of West Africa — Anglican) is professor of New Testament at the University of Ghana, currently on leave of absence to serve as associate director of the WCC's Programme on Ecumenical Theological Education-Bossey. He is a member of the Anglican-Roman Catholic International Commission and president of the International Association of Mission Studies. His books include *The Theme of Persecution and Martyrdom in the Letters of St Paul* (1985) and *Church and State in Ghana 1949-1966* (1989).

Tom Stransky (Roman Catholic), a staff member of the Vatican Secretariat for Promoting Christian Unity from 1960 to 1970 and past president of the Paulist Fathers, is a member of the Joint Working Group between the Roman Catholic Church and the World Council of Churches, and rector of the Tantur Ecumenical Institute for Theological Studies, Jerusalem.

Geoffrey Wainwright (Methodist Church of Great Britain) is professor of systematic theology at Duke University, Durham, NC, USA, and chairman of the World Methodist Council's committee on ecumenism and dialogues. His books include *Doxology* (1980) and *The Ecumenical Moment* (1983) as well as the editing of *The Study of Liturgy* (1978), *The Study of Spirituality* (1986) and *Keeping the Faith* (1988).

Pauline Webb (Methodist Church of Great Britain), a lay preacher, was organizer of religious broadcasting in the World Service of the BBC. A vice-moderator of the WCC's central committee from 1968 to 1975, she was a member of the WCC's Communication Committee from 1983 to 1991. In Britain, she co-chairs the World Conference on Religion and Peace, and is president of the Society for the Ministry of Women in the Church.

The Editorial Board

Preface

The appearance of the *Dictionary of the Ecumenical Movement* is a tribute to a massive amount of work on the part of those who have organized, written and edited it. It may also be seen as a kind of parable of ecumenism.

Writers and editors from a wide range of contexts and Christian traditions — chosen for their familiarity with how the 20th-century ecumenical movement has unfolded and for their engagement in the diversity of issues on the agenda of the churches as they grow together towards unity — have worked together to create a resource whose scope and usefulness go far beyond what any individual could produce.

The unique gifts which each of these people has brought to this project remain. Alongside accounts of the events of the ecumenical past, readers will often find personal insights into and visions of the ecumenical future. Far from seeking to eliminate the diversity of perspectives of its many contributors, the *Dictionary* acknowledges the richness and strength this represents for the ecumenical movement.

Strenuous efforts have been made to ensure that this is an up-to-date account of ecumenical reality. Inevitably, however, that reality will continue to unfold: hard-won advances, disappointing setbacks and, as always, the surprises of the Spirit. The months and years to come will move some of the discussions and assessments in these pages beyond what the writers could have described or foreseen. That, too, mirrors the reality of ecumenism: it is a *movement*, unfinished, on the way, ever changing, broadening and deepening the understandings and commitments and dreams whose origins are portrayed in these entries.

The energy of the ecumenical movement has always been the creative visions, solemn covenants, courageous engagements and fervent prayers of countless women and men, churches and groups. But the ecumenical story is also one of meetings and reports and documents, programmes and declarations and statements, theological convergences and pastoral guidelines. As this movement has, by God's grace, grown and expanded, the amount of written material with which one must be acquainted in order effectively to build on the past would fill a good-sized library. For those without ready access to such documentary resources, this *Dictionary of the Ecumenical Movement* will be indispensable; even for those who have such access it will provide a reliable starting point for their explorations.

It is, therefore, with joy and gratitude that I commend this new work, confident that it will prove useful to anyone interested and involved in the ecumenical movement and hopeful that it will, in its way, stimulate a continuing passion for the unity we seek.

Geneva
Week of Prayer for Christian Unity 1991

Emilio Castro
General Secretary
World Council of Churches

Introduction

If church history continues to be written future historians will almost certainly regard the ecumenical movement as one of the most remarkable features of Christianity in the 20th century. To a degree never witnessed before, Christianity became a worldwide religion, spread over the whole inhabited earth. And an unprecedentedly large number and range of Christian communities, hitherto separated by doctrinal and institutional factors, set about a serious process of consultation, co-operation, communion and even union among themselves, inspired by the prayer of the Lord that his followers "be one", "so that the world may believe" (John 17:21).

A hundred years is a long time for the duration of any "movement" in history. Memories fade, and apparently secure results get forgotten. As the century draws to a close, it seems wise to draw together a record of this period, while many of the participants who have devoted the greater part of long adult lives to the cause of Christian unity are still present in the flesh. There is, moreover, much work still to do: several traditionally controversial issues remain unsettled among the churches; new questions arise for the Christian faith as a global culture develops with its own characteristics in economics, geopolitics, the religious field, science and technology, information and communication; the kingdoms of this world have not yet become the kingdom of God and of his Christ (Rev. 11:15). To take stock of the past, to interpret the present, and to look forward into a third millennium of Christian existence are therefore indispensable exercises. This dictionary is intended as a contribution to these ends.

In its beginnings, the modern ecumenical movement was largely the work of Christians in Protestant churches, Reformation and Free, who were committed, in the words of John R. Mott around the turn of the century, to "the evangelization of the world in this generation". Then, and increasingly, the Orthodox churches began to play a significant part, notably in the sequel of the Ecumenical Patriarchate's proposal, after the first world war, for a "league of churches". After initial suspicions, and then cautious beginnings after the second world war, the Roman Catholic Church at the Second Vatican Council recognized that other Christians, by baptism and faith in Christ, enjoy "a certain, though imperfect, communion with the Catholic Church", and that their churches and ecclesial communities are "not without significance in the mystery of salvation" — so that finally the way was open for Orthodox and Protestants on their side to take the Roman Catholic Church seriously as an ecumenical partner. By enlisting contributions from Protestants, Orthodox and Roman Catholics, the dictionary seeks to show how the ecumenical movement has been perceived and lived within various confessional perspectives.

Much of the history of the ecumenical movement has to be focused on the World Council of Churches, for this has been since its foundation in 1948 the institution in which the earlier "Faith and Order" and "Life and Work" movements coalesced, and since 1961 the evangelism and mission represented by the former International Missionary Council. Further ramifications have brought into the purview of the WCC such matters as adult and theological education, medical care, international law and politics, social ministries, public media, and dialogue with people of other living faiths and ideologies. The Roman Catholic Church, which numbers the majority of Christians among its adherents, is not a member of the WCC but is engaged at many levels with its work. Rome has also conducted bilateral dialogues with several of the other "world Christian communions" through their respective organizations, and most of these other communions have in turn conducted such dialogues with several respective partners among their own number. This "classical" ecumenism has its critics within all camps, but most notably among Evangelicals who actively oppose some tendencies within the larger movement, and among Pentecostals who tend to ignore it. More recently, there are some promising signs of change in these directions; and for their part, the WCC and the long-established world Christian communions need the contributions of the Evangelical and Pentecostal visions. The dictionary gives perhaps most attention to studies and activities sponsored by the WCC, but it also devotes considerable space to the ecumenical interests of the Roman Catholic Church and of other Christian families, and it seeks to take account of criticism addressed to classical ecumenism.

At its best, the ecumenical movement has been a search for unity in the truth as it is found in Jesus (Eph. 4:21), and into which the Holy Spirit leads (John 16:13). It has not been a matter, on the one hand, of creating a super-orthodoxy uniformly formulated or, on the other, of doctrinal compromise or indifferentism. Rather, the churches have together searched the scriptures, the venerable Tradition of the church, and the belief and practice of the contemporary communities with the aim of reaching a "common expression of the apostolic faith today" (to adopt the title of a Faith and Order study). The dictionary contains many articles on doctrinal themes, showing how the churches have converged in their teachings on God, Christ, the Holy Spirit, the church, redemption and salvation, grace and faith, the word and the sacraments, and the last things, while indicating also the continuing bones of contention in such matters as pastoral authority and the constitution of the ordained ministry.

At its best, the ecumenical movement has embodied a search for the will of God in every area of life and work. It has been a matter neither of a pretentious "building of the kingdom" nor of a quietism that remains unmoved by the world's needs. Rather, the churches have sought to engage in the studies and action for the furtherance of "justice, peace and the integrity of creation" (to use the title of the programme set out by the Vancouver assembly of the WCC in 1983). The dictionary contains many articles on social, political, legal, cultural and ethical issues from perspectives within the Christian faith.

At its best, the ecumenical movement has sought to discern, proclaim and participate in the Triune God's eternal and constant purpose for humankind and the mission of God to the world. It has not been a matter either of weakening witness to Jesus Christ or of refusing the truths that can be found outside the institutions of Christianity. Rather, participating churches, whether members of the WCC or not, have "confessed the Lord Jesus Christ as God and Saviour" and looked to "fulfill together their common calling to the glory of the one God, Father, Son and Holy Spirit" (to use the words of the membership basis of the WCC). The dictionary contains many articles on aspects of evangelism and mission, of worship and prayer, of education and renewal in the churches, of care for the needy and the place of the poor in church and society, of witness to the powers that be, and of communication to the world and dialogue with those of other faiths and outlooks.

In the nature of the case, the ecumenical movement is a movement of people. It was the vision of committed individuals that led to the formation of the WCC. Once the Council was established it was led and served by men and women from many parts of the world. The dictionary must commemorate them and all others who contributed to major ecumenical developments. But any list that is drawn up of such architects and pioneers of 20th-century ecumenism is bound to be incomplete and appear arbitrary. The editors are aware that theirs is, and they hope that the biographical sketches that are included in the dictionary will be seen as a few standing for the many.

Ecumenism exists at global, regional and local levels. As a contribution to the sharing of information throughout the churches, the dictionary contains not only articles of direct universal interest but also descriptions of ecumenical relations and activities in the several regions of the world. Moreover, our contributors have been encouraged to include, with inevitable selectivity, examples from very local situations.

Under the ecumenical umbrella, many special interests are at work: liturgists, ecologists, feminists, and several more. Much more often than not, the writers asked to contribute to the dictionary on these subjects have been chosen from among those sympathetic to the respective causes.

Articles in the dictionary are of several kinds. The longest type survey a major doctrinal theme, an entire area of activity; through manifold cross references in the body of the article (marked by an asterisk at the first occurrence) and a final listing of the principal related articles, they direct the reader to detailed items in the debate or to matters of related interest. Articles in the medium range look at more restricted but still weighty topics. Many of the shorter articles provide for quick reference on a precise question. The indexes provide a further grid through which to read about a chosen issue, conference or institution. The bibliographies have favoured publications in English, while not neglecting studies in other languages for which there is no English equivalent; they are not exhaustive, and the items they contain have often been chosen precisely because they yield further bibliographical information.

The editors themselves have learned once more what it means to engage in team work. After seeking advice on contents and authorship from a widely representative larger board, the six co-editors corporately established the list of articles and of contributors to be invited. Then each editor took under his or her wing a batch of entries matching some of their own respective interests and competences. Very roughly speaking, Nicholas Lossky has attended to the Eastern churches and some of the dogmatic concerns close to Orthodox hearts; José Míguez Bonino to the area of church and society and to matters of moral theology; John Pobee to geographical and cultural variety and to issues in theological education; Tom Stransky to institutional histories and to matters of specifically Roman Catholic concern within the ecumenical movement; Geoffrey Wainwright to doctrinal issues in faith and order and to the dialogues among the world Christian communions; Pauline Webb to mission and evangelism, communication and renewal. Each editor, however, has had the opportunity to make suggestions of detail for all the articles. Much of the minute biographical and bibliographical research has been done by Ans J. van der Bent, on the basis of suggestions from contributors and editors, and he also compiled the indexes. The services of the WCC Library and the Language Service have been invaluable.

The in-house production in Geneva has been ensured by the experienced staff of the Publications Department of the WCC, with Jan Kok at the helm. The technical editing has been in the unrivalled hands of T.K. Thomas and Marlin VanElderen, with the competent help of Craig Noll. The illustrations were chosen by Miriam Reidy. The entire process has been administered with unfailing grace and efficiency by Joan Cambitsis. The six editors undersigned wish to express their deep gratitude to all these colleagues and friends for their sustained collaboration over some four years as well as thanking each and every contributor, whether their texts came promptly and with joy, or had to be wheedled out of them as they pursued their busy lives, or were supplied to meet some sudden emergency of a missing entry. May the Lord reward your labours of faith, hope and love.

Nicholas Lossky   *José Míguez Bonino*   *John S. Pobee*
Tom F. Stransky   *Geoffrey Wainwright*   *Pauline Webb*

Notes for the Reader

.The arrangement of entries in the Dictionary is alphabetical. However, readers seeking information on a particular topic may find it useful to begin their search by referring to the detailed index of subjects or, in the case of a person, the index of names.

Cross references are also included in the entries themselves. An *asterisk* in the text refers the reader to a substantial (though not necessarily major) mention of a word to which an entry elsewhere corresponds. At the end of many articles, *"see also"* sends the reader to other entries closely connected in their main themes.

There are *no cross references to personalities*; here readers may consult the index of names.

Some *overlapping of information* in articles related to allied subjects has been retained to allow readers to find all the basic information on a specific subject in one article, without having to refer to others.

Quotations are short, and have been used only where they support a particular line of argument. The use of *footnotes* has been avoided: references to works cited in the bibliographies are indicated by the name of the author(s) or title of book(s) in brackets in the text. Other references, also in brackets, give author's name, title of work, and year of publication.

Bibliographies with entries include mainly English works. Where these are translations from other languages, this is indicated by "ET". Some titles have been included because they themselves contain useful bibliographies. Older references are cited if they are still considered to be basic works.

In the *biographical sketches*, only the person's major writings are cited.

Articles about sub-regions (e.g. South Asia) are alphabetized under that region (i.e. "Asia: South"). In a few cases, a single country constitutes a "sub-region"; other than these, there are no entries for individual countries.

Particularly in the regional entries, *information of a general nature*, which can be found in encyclopedias and other reference works, has not been included.

The editors have used *inclusive language* as much as they felt possible and certainly in cases where a text has been translated from another language. Some authors have maintained the traditional use of the pronouns "he/him/his/himself" when referring to God; others have avoided this use.

An effort has been made during the final stages of production to bring entries up to date (including the addition of a brief entry on the WCC's seventh assembly in February 1991); but it is obvious that the practical possibilities for doing this are limited. For example, nearly all of the entries were written before the union of the two Germanys, and many references to the Federal Republic of Germany and the German Democratic Republic have been maintained.

The *list of contributors* gives the title and position of authors as known at the time of publication. The identifying sentence is followed by the title(s) of the article(s) written by that author. (Contributions by the six editors are included in this list.)

The editors believe that this *Dictionary of the Ecumenical Movement* will be a useful and reliable reference tool for many years to come. They would be grateful to be notified by users of any errors which may have found their way into the text, as well as to receive suggestions for improvements in succeeding editions. These should be sent to the Publications Editor, World Council of Churches, P.O. Box 2100, 1211 Geneva 2, Switzerland.

ABORTION. Throughout the Old Testament numerous passages attest to the sacredness of human life within the womb (Job 31:15; Isa. 44:24, 49:1,5; Jer. 1:5; Ps. 127:3). In contrast, references to abortion are extremely rare. The most important such text is Ex. 21:22-23; even here, however, the reference is indirect. The text stipulates that if a miscarriage results from men quarrelling, the guilty party shall be fined; if, however, the woman herself is killed, the assailant shall "give life for life". According to the talmudic interpretation of this passage, feticide — unlike homicide — is not a capital offence, since the fetus does not become a person prior to its emergence from the womb. Before birth the fetus is an organic part of the mother. While abortion is thus distinguished from murder or homicide, the former is always a matter of extreme moral gravity in Jewish thought; when abortion is permitted, it is generally justified on grounds of compassion for the mother.

There are no explicit references to abortion in the New Testament. Nevertheless, the early church consistently condemned it in opposition to widespread abortion and infanticide in the Greco-Roman world. Christians found indirect support for their stand in the Septuagint translation of Ex. 21:22-23, which — unlike the Masoretic text — made a distinction between a "formed" and an "unformed" fetus and on this basis made even the accidental destruction of a "formed" fetus a capital of-

fence. Tertullian held that the fetus is fully human from the moment of conception. Abortion was morally permissible, he believed, only when necessary to save the life of the mother. Augustine distinguished between the destruction of an "animated" and an "unanimated" fetus. Although he condemned abortion at any stage, he did not consider it homicide prior to animation (quickening).

In the 13th century Thomas Aquinas, following Aristotle, held that the infusion of the rational soul occurred about the 40th day following conception for males and about the 80th day for females. Aquinas's doctrine of infusion of the soul — like Augustine's earlier teaching concerning animation — provided the basis for a distinction in moral gravity between an earlier and a later abortion. Such a distinction was officially dropped by the Catholic church in the 19th century. In 1869 Pope Pius IX extended excommunication as the penalty for abortion to include the abortion of any embryo. In 1917 the new code of canon law required that all aborted fetuses must be baptized, clearly implying that the unborn fetus is fully human from the time of conception. This position was re-affirmed by Vatican II (*Gaudium et Spes*, 1965, 51) and by Pope Paul VI (*Humanae Vitae*, 1968).

Luther and Calvin held that the fetus is both body and soul from conception. Both opposed abortion at any stage. During their formative years and well into the 20th century, the major branches of Protestantism were closely aligned with Catholicism in this regard. Subsequently, however, many Protestants, as well as some Catholics, have begun to reinterpret the traditional Christian teaching concerning abortion in the light of a number of deep-rooted cultural changes, including in particular: new attitudes towards authority,* the growth of cultural pluralism,* a revolution in sexual morality, feminism,* and dramatic new reproductive technologies (see **bioethics**).

Theologians and churches have responded to these movements in a variety of ways which can best be understood in terms of a continuum. On the one hand, many Protestants continue to defend a strongly anti-abortion stance represented by Catholic moral theology. Representatives of this group generally support anti-abortion legislation and defend the fetus's right to life. At the opposite end of the spectrum, members of a second group advocate both the legal and the moral right of the woman to decide whether or not to have an abortion. A third group occupies the broad middle ground between these polar positions. While they differ widely among themselves, those who embrace this position believe that abortion may sometimes be morally justified. For them, abortion is not morally neutral; neither is it murder. While it is always evil, it is sometimes justifiable as the lesser evil or, alternatively, as the most responsible option available. In this view, primary responsibility for the abortion decision rests with the woman.

The WCC has not made any significant statement about abortion beyond recognizing that it presents a serious ethical problem and that most churches are opposed to it (Salonika 1959, Louvain 1971, Nairobi 1975). In the context of a discussion on family planning and population policies, the WCC's Christian Medical Commission rejected the use of abortion as a means of population control (Zurich 1973).

In the abortion debate it is important to distinguish clearly between the moral and legal issues involved. Support for the right of a woman to choose an abortion does not in itself imply moral approval. Closely related to the question of a woman's right to choose is the issue of public funding of abortion for the poor. Those who support such funding do so on grounds of social justice.

In addressing the abortion issue, the churches are confronted with the need to seek ways to alleviate the underlying causes and to provide alternatives to abortion through family planning, adoption and financial assistance. The most basic challenge to the churches is to nurture a fundamental respect for human life, including that of the unborn, both among their members and in society at large (see **life and death**). This respect — rather than the enactment of either restrictive or permissive legislation — is a prerequisite for the goal of preventing abortion without coercing women.

E. CLINTON GARDNER

E. Batchelor, Jr, ed., *Abortion: The Moral Issues*, New York, Pilgrim, 1982 • S. Callahan & D. Callahan eds, *Abortion: Understanding Differences*, New York, Plenum, 1984 • B.W. Harrison, *Our Right to Choose: Toward a New Ethic of Abortion*, Boston, Beacon, 1983 • F. Rosner & J.D. Bleich eds, *Jewish Bioethics*, New York, Hebrew Publishing Co., 1979.

ABRECHT, PAUL. B. 9.12.1917, Cincinnati, OH. Joining the staff of the WCC in 1949 as secretary for the Study Programme on Christian Action in Society, Abrecht was director of the Department (later Sub-unit) on Church and Society, 1954-83. He organized three ecumenical study projects: "The Responsible Society" (1949-54), "The Common Christian Responsibility towards Areas of Rapid Social Change" (1955-61), and the inquiry on "The Future of Humanity and Society in a World of Science-based Technology" (1969-79). He was also responsible for the organization and follow-up of the world conference on Church and Society (Geneva 1966). Secretary of the Ecumenical Commission on European Co-operation, later the Committee on the Christian Responsibility for European Co-operation, 1950-62, Abrecht was greatly influenced by the Oldham-Visser 't Hooft emphasis on ecumenical "study" of controversial social questions and enlisted talented Christian laypersons from economic, political, industrial and scientific disciplines to contribute to ecumenical social thinking. Born of a Baptist family, Abrecht received higher education in economics at the University of California. He pursued theological studies at Berkeley Baptist Divinity School and also studied Christian ethics under

Reinhold Niebuhr and John Bennett at Union Theological Seminary. He edited *Background Information* (1959-69) and *Anticipation* (1969-83). He was guest editor of *Fifty Years of Ecumenical Social Thought*, a special issue of *The Ecumenical Review* (April 1988). He wrote *The Churches in Rapid Social Change* (London, SCM, 1961), and *Church and Society: Ecumenical Perspectives* (= *The Ecumenical Review*, 37, 1, 1985) was published in his honour.

ANS J. VAN DER BENT

ACADEMIC ECUMENICAL SOCIETIES.
Such societies include the professional bodies which concentrate specifically on ecumenical themes, e.g. Ecumenical Association of Third World Theologians,* Ecumenical Association of African Theologians, North American Academy of Ecumenists, and Societas Oecumenica (European Society for Ecumenical Research). Also more than 50 national and regional associations of theological schools, e.g. North East Asia Association of Theological Schools, the Association of Theological Institutes in the Middle East, and in Latin America the Asociación de Seminarios e Instituciones Teológicas, face issues in a manner that is necessarily ecumenical.

ANS J. VAN DER BENT

ACADEMIES, LAY.
Lay academies are church-affiliated conference centres where individuals and social groups meet for encounter, dialogue, research and reflection-for-action. The oldest "academy" was founded in 1917 at Sigtuna near Stockholm by the Swedish bishop Martin Lidquist, but most of such institutes came into being in Europe following the second world war, many of them established between 1945 and 1955. A European association of academy directors was established in 1956 including about 45 member centres in Finland, France, Netherlands, Switzerland and the United Kingdom. At present the Ecumenical Association of Academies and Laity Centres in Europe includes some 90 centres in 16 European countries. The majority are Protestant, but there are also a dozen Roman Catholic and two Greek Orthodox member centres.

The term "academy" was used in Germany, where in 1945 the first European institute was opened at Bad Boll by Bishop Theophil Wurm, one of the heads of the Confessing Church. The term expressed the original working philosophy of such centres: "dialogue on the world's agenda". It derives from the Greek philosophic tradition, where Plato is said to have *educated* his students *in dialogue* while walking in the forest *akadēmeia*. The initiative for establishing academies grew out of the historic experiences of the German churches, which had failed to prepare themselves and their members to resist the ideological and political trends of fascism and Nazism and to render a prophetic witness. Academies were thus supposed to serve as centres of education — originally for laypeople but later for "the whole people of God" in order to awaken their conscience in political and social matters towards a "spirituality for combat". Daily worship, Bible studies and theological discourse have always been basic elements in their conferences, seminars, workshops and consultations. Hospitality and sharing have also remained vital elements in the process of education and communication, predominantly led by lay experts from various fields.

Partly independently, partly through the sharing of experiences, insights and resources, lay academies also emerged in Asia, Africa and North America. In Asia they began working during the later 1950s and early 1960s in Japan, South Korea, Taiwan, Hong Kong, Indonesia and India. In the 1960s Africa followed with centres in South Africa, Lesotho, Benin, Nigeria, Cameroon, Tanzania, Kenya, Zambia, Ethiopia and Madagascar. The centres developed a plurality of concepts and programmes. They call themselves "Christian academies", "ecumenical centres", "institutes for the study of church and society", etc. According to their contextual social challenges, their programmes focus on issues arising from industrialization, nation-building and urban-rural problems as well as on intercultural and inter-religious dialogue. An African association and an Asian association have also been formed.

Together with the European association they formed the World Collaboration Committee for Christian Lay Centres, Academies and Movements for Social Concern (WCOLC).

This came as a result of the first world conference of lay academies organized by the WCC (unit III) in 1972 at the Orthodox Academy in Crete. WCOLC is co-ordinated by the WCC Sub-unit on Renewal and Congregational Life (RCL). Since 1980 a North American Retreat Directors' Association (NARDA) has operated in the US and Canada, representing their centres in WCOLC, which also regularly co-operates with centres in Latin America, the Caribbean, the Pacific and the Middle East. Some 600 centres around the world are related to RCL, which in conjunction with WCOLC seeks: (1) to encourage communication within the network through the interchange of information and experience; (2) to develop programmes such as international studies, research, training courses, staff exchange, etc.; (3) to offer consultative and advisory services on personnel and programmes within the network; (4) to develop relations with other agencies whose concerns converge with those of the WCOLC network.

Following Vatican II, growing co-operation between unit III of the WCC and the Vatican Consilium de Laïcis led to a significant world conference on "New Trends in Laity Formation" jointly organized by the two agencies in 1974 at Assisi. Beginning in 1976, WCOLC has organized world courses for leaders in lay training (CLLT), which has become a regular annual project sponsored jointly by RCL and the regional associations.

The mission of the laity* has figured prominently on the ecumenical agenda from the very beginning. One of the institutional first-fruits was the foundation of the Ecumenical Institute at Bossey.* Its first director, Hendrik Kraemer, wrote the influential book *A Theology of the Laity*. Suzanne de Diétrich developed a specific Bible study model ("in one hand the Bible, in the other the newspaper") which became prominent in the work of lay academies. The WCC's Evanston assembly (1954) emphasized the role of the laity, which was confirmed at New Delhi (1961), where the ecumenical study on "The Missionary Structure of the Congregation"* was initiated. Lay academies have played a vital role as instruments for the churches to put this mission into action. A document from the Crete consultation (1972) states: "Our task is liberation and social transformation... our centres have a great opportunity to become places where there is a creative 'doing of theology'... We also have a responsibility in the further training and re-orientation of the ordained ministry and leadership of the church." In pursuing these aims, lay academies widely followed the principles of "Oldham's method", thus continuing and deepening the concerns of Life and Work through dialogue and confrontation (see **study as an ecumenical method**). They have become prominent agencies for ecumenical learning through relating local and regional concerns with global perspectives and challenges. Within and through their global network they contribute creatively to the ecumenical dialogue of cultures.

WERNER SIMPFENDÖRFER

AFRICA. Africa, the second largest continent, offers a tremendous variety and diversity of climates, natural vegetation, cultures and human as well as natural resources. The human resources include Caucasoids, Hamites and Negroids, who live in 50 countries, each with a unique history. The principal religions are African Traditional Religions (ATR), Christianity and Islam. These have not lived in watertight compartments but have interacted with each other, principally because traditional African thought and religions tend to absorb religious ideas from other religions. Pluralism and diversity mark the African context as a whole, within a sub-region and even in the same locale. This fact itself prescribes an ecumenical task — how to avoid violence and unnecessary strife, to seek unity without loss of identity and integrity, and to cherish mutual respect and support in spite of diversities and differences.

The creation of nation states out of congeries of tribes has made more evident Africa's brokenness. The new tribalism and tensions between neighbouring nations and tribes plague the new states. Neither the African politicians in power nor the Organization of African Unity (OAU) has been able to forge a unity of Africans across differences of tribe, race and gender. The OAU was established in 1963 as a symbol of unity and mutuality and as an instrument of the new order in Africa, but after some 25 years it is still struggling to find its identity and proper place and simply has not had the energy to solve such problems. The task is made more difficult because the churches which claim to be committed to reconciliation* are themselves tribal churches, and they fail to translate their rhetoric into action. For example, in the 1980s the Methodist Church of Ghana was in the throes of a struggle between the Fante and the Ga. The central issue was, Which tribe would the president of the conference come from?

South Africa is a special story. Its government, in the name of the ideology* of apartheid,* divides the nation along racial lines and consigns all but whites to a life of misery and poverty. Racism* is the principal ecumenical issue here and has brought the churches at home and the world church together to fight this system.

The history of Christianity in Africa. Africa's history has been much influenced by the North in cultural development, economics, politics and religion. Belgian, British, French, German and Portuguese colonialism* has left indelible marks on the political and economic organizations and ideologies, with varying implications for church-state* relationships, a vital ecumenical issue in Africa. In some countries, the Christian missions in colonial times appeared to be ecclesiastical fronts of the North Atlantic colonial incursions. This encounter with the North was a mixed blessing. It brought Africa into contact with modernity and a bigger world, but it also contributed to Africa's underdevelopment.

Christianity, of course, was in Africa long before colonialism. North of the Sahara it was present in the Maghrib, Roman North Africa, by A.D. 180, and in Egypt in earliest times. Egyptian Christianity is said to go back to St Mark and grew into a mighty and dynamic force, with its famous catechetical school in Alexandria. It produced theologians such as Clement, Origen, Dionysius of Alexandria, and the great Athanasius. Today, in the face of Islam, the Egyptian church is relatively small. Similarly, Islam all but wiped out the Christianity of the Maghrib, which produced martyrs like Perpetua and Felicitas and thinkers such as Cyprian of Carthage and Augustine of Hippo. Here one finds today only a straggling band of Christians. It fell before Islam partly because it was a church bitterly divided, between Donatists and Catholics.

That division was symptomatic of the deeper problem that Christianity never truly engaged the native Berbers. Rather, it imposed a Latin culture on them and insufficiently emphasized spirituality in the Berber culture, whose world-view included a spiritual and religious epistemology and ontology. In the process, Christianity created ill will in the Berbers, who consequently opened the gates to the Muslims. That story points to a missiological and ecumenical issue. Must the people of Africa become Europeans to be adjudged Christian? Must the African be Christianized, or must the Christian faith be Africanized? This issue continues today in pleas for African and black theologies and in the discussion of indigenization (see **theology, African**). There can be no reconciled church as long as a faith captive to an alien culture* is imposed on a local people.

In Africa south of the Sahara, Christianity came in fragmented form in the 19th and 20th centuries from the churches of Europe and America. The denominationalism* of the Northern countries was transported to the South, even though the original causes of division have not been part of the experience of Africans. Beyond fragmentation, there was often no love lost between sister churches. In Portuguese Africa (Mozambique and Angola) Roman Catholics held a privileged position because of their intimate connection with the Portuguese colonial administration, and they used this to the disadvantage of Protestants. Anglicanism in British colonies, though not officially established as in England, still had an advantage over other denominations.

Furthermore, the missions, partly as a result of comity ("denominations by geography"), resulted in tribal churches, compounding the divisiveness of the society composed of nations welded from collections of loosely knit tribes. In Uganda, for example, political parties have been co-extensive with the Protestant-Roman Catholic divide: the Uganda People's Congress, which is Protestant, particularly Anglican, is nicknamed United Protestants of Canterbury, while the Democratic Party, being Roman Catholic, is nicknamed *Dini ya Papa* (the religion of the pope). Acrimony, divisiveness and hostility have been the result of differences in belief, doctrine and sacramental practice, with far-reaching consequences for national political life.

Christian missions were influenced by a crusader mentality. The missionaries to Africa viewed Africans as having no valid religious insights at all. They also held to a kind of social Darwinism, the idea that peoples of the tropics conducted their business so badly that peoples of the temperate zone had a divine right to manage their affairs for them, including exploiting their resources. For such reasons Christianity as represented by historic churches looked foreign and oppressive — a sore for African Christians and a whipping boy for African politicians. African Instituted Churches* represent a response to the foreignness and oppressiveness of historic churches, providing "a place to feel at home". These churches are at once a renewal* movement in the church and a further fracturing of the *una sancta*. Such dynamics mean that the quest for the selfhood of the African churches, the tabernacling of the Word in Africa, is a key issue in ecumenism. Africa desires its rightful place in the oikoumene, a place that respects and responds to the identity and integrity of Africa, as well as its hopes and fears.

Christian missions often introduced Western education and health care in Africa, or at least they have been much involved in it. Consequently, churches and ecumenical efforts in Africa have expended considerable energies and resources on the institutions of social services. To that extent, ecumenism looks like the transfer of material resources from the churches of the North to the churches of the South. As Africa goes from crisis to crisis, besieged by famine and drought, floods and violations of human dignity through dictatorships, the ecumenical movement's valid involvement in social services has loomed much larger than it should, thus producing a jaundiced impression of ecumenism.

On the other hand, through this involvement in social services, the Christian conscience has spread beyond the Christians themselves. The church has consequently become "a third race", a new culture. In places it may be the only force besides the political party in power. Since many of the politicians have been raised in the stables of the church, they are often not unsympathetic to the churches. The net effect is that churches have become influential, though often not sensitive to the pluralism* of society and the consequent need for tolerance of others and for

dialogue between diverse religions and cultures (see **dialogue, interfaith**).

In the last decades of the 20th century, Christianity is most buoyant in Africa and growing faster there than in other continents. To that extent, the future of world Christianity may well depend on how African Christianity develops. Already ecumenical circles seek and treasure the insights of African Christians, as do churches of the North.

Islam in Africa. Not only Christianity is important and fast-growing in Africa; Islam also has a history of rich involvement there. It was in Africa south of the Sahara before Christianity ever arrived. Through trade, principally across the Sahara along the gold, ivory and slave routes, Islam was in West Africa in the middle ages, leading to the establishment of the Ghana, Mali and Songhai empires. On the east coast of Africa, long before the Portuguese appeared there, the Arabs had established commercial and connubial relations with the Bantus from Sofala to Somalia, leading to the rise of Islamized African communities called *habashi*s. Statistically, Islam has maintained a strong presence in the population of Africa, at present only slightly less than that of Christianity, as the following table indicates.

MAJOR AFRICAN RELIGIONS, 1900-2000

Date	Population (millions)	Christianity	Islam	ATR
		(percentage of total pop.)		
1900	108	9	32	59
1970	346	41	41	18
1980	457	44	42	14
2000	804 (est.)	49	42	9

Source: D. Barrett ed., *World Christian Encyclopedia*, Oxford, Oxford UP, 1982.

Christianity and Islam are the two religious heavyweights in Africa. They are also rivals because both religions have become imperialized. In the 4th century Christianity had become the official religion of particular nations and empires such as Armenia, Assyria, Byzantium and later still Belgium, Portugal and Britain. Islam too, soon after the Prophet's death in 632, became identified with the caliphate, which ruled a vast empire that stretched from the western Mediterranean to central Asia. Thus the two major religions became rivals.

Muslims have widely criticized Christianity for corrupting itself into a Western religion, thus becoming unfaithful to the simple teaching of a semitic prophet. The rivalry led to the crusades from the 11th to the 13th centuries. Consequently, the Qur'an's respect for 'ahl-al-kitab, the people of the book — Jews and Christians — largely disappeared, Christians in some countries were marginalized as minority communities (e.g. Copts in Egypt) and subjected to social legislation, and they closed in upon themselves.

The ecumenical perspectives of both the Qur'an and the Bible have been compromised because their socio-political teachings were subjected to the interests of particular empires and nations. A key issue for African ecumenism centres on relationships between Christians and Muslims in places such as northern Nigeria, Sudan and Gambia. The issues are how to recognize the legitimate place for Christians and other non-Muslims in predominantly Muslim societies, and what it means today for a Muslim to call Christians and others 'ahl-al-dhimma, people of protection, who have full rights to the protection of the Islamic state.

The issue needs to be addressed also where Muslims are minorities in predominantly Christian societies. Several African nations (e.g. Ghana) have found a solution by declaring themselves secular nations, despite evidence of vibrant religiosity of one type or another. The practical question remains as to how Muslims and Christians can live together so that they show they worship the one God,* the Creator, and respect freedom of conscience* and religion.

Ecumenism in Africa. We may speak of three kinds of ecumenism in Africa. First is the unstructured and natural ecumenism which is often co-extensive with the nuclear and extended family.* Not infrequently in the same family there is a Christian, an adherent of ATR and even a Muslim. Their different religious affiliations do not make them opt out of their family obligations and involvements. The rites of passage — birth, puberty, marriage, death — bring the family together, transcending religious affiliations. The divisions of religions and churches are shown at these points of the life-cycle to be alien and unnatural impositions on Africans. But there is the other side: this "natural ecumenism"

excludes those outside the kin group, which is the proto-typical group. Thus the unstructured ecumenism has only limited ecumenical significance.

Second is enforced ecumenism. The harsh circumstances of Africa, including natural disasters and political dictatorships, force churches and religions to come together to work for survival. The dictatorship of Kwame Nkrumah of Ghana (1957-66) forced the Protestant churches and Roman Catholics to work together to seek the dignity and peace of the people. In Uganda in 1973, when dictator Idi Amin Dada banned 28 Christian denominations for alleged subversive activities, some of the groups came together under the wings of the Anglican church. In the face of the lawlessness of the government, Roman Catholics and Muslim leaders sent a joint memorandum to Amin in 1976, documenting their claim that the regime was responsible for the killing, disappearance and flight of hundreds of thousands of Christians. The co-operation of the South African Council of Churches and the Catholic bishops' conference of Southern Africa to fight apartheid is yet another example.

There is, however, another type of enforced unity. In 1970 President Mobutu of Zaire forced all the Protestant churches into a United Protestant Church, the Eglise du Christ au Zaïre (ECZ), which is the only Protestant church the state recognizes. The ECZ, however, displays internal diversity because its member churches (communautés) maintain their previous ecclesiastical traditions, structures and fraternal ties. Such enforced ecumenism is of limited value because the basic differences remain untouched. When the pressure is taken off, the separate groups generally revert to denominationalism.

Third is structured ecumenism, which has consciously or unconsciously taken its impetus from the Edinburgh conference of 1910 and the modern ecumenical movement. A good illustration of this ecumenism is the creation of Christian councils in Africa (at present, there are 22). Ghana's Christian Council, for example, was set up in 1929 to foster and express the unity* of the church, to uphold the principles of comity among the churches, to enable member churches to consult together concerning their Christian witness* and service, and to promote study of social and cultural changes in the national life as they affect the task of the church. Similarly the Uganda Joint Christian Council was founded in 1963 to assist churches to come together to listen to the voice of Christ and of the Holy Spirit, a voice of love, forgiveness and understanding. In Uganda, this council has become the visible expression of the desire of Ugandan Christians to forget the past and to work together for a better future.

As a result of their togetherness in the councils, church union discussions were begun. Some have been successful, as with the United Church of Zambia; others have failed, as in Ghana and Nigeria. Such councils and negotiations have been the brainchild of European missionaries and have been influenced by the experience of the united Church of South India. The model has been the European Protestant ecumenical orthodoxy which was fashionable in the 1930s but is not perhaps suitable for the present time. The councils, however, locked into social services, have become development agencies and thus are losing their strictly ecumenical raison d'etre.

Other expressions of the ecumenical spirit in Africa are Bible societies, churches' medical associations, ecumenical study groups (as in Kampala), and Christian literature associations which promote joint publication, distribute literature, and encourage local writers. Zambia has Multimedia of Zambia, which prepares Bible study materials and coordinates Bible study groups. In Malawi, a Christian service committee of the churches includes both Protestants and Roman Catholics for the purpose of integral human development, motivating the churches and their members for full social obedience to Christ through service. Other such examples of ecumenism are the Mindolo Ecumenical Foundation and joint or united theological colleges (Trinity College in Ghana; Trinity College, Umuahia, Nigeria; United Theological College, Zomba, Malawi; Protestant Faculty of Theology, Yaoundé, Cameroon), which were designed to foster ecumenism through training together persons for different denominations. These institutions largely appear to be in crisis because members seem not to have as much commitment to them as to their own denominational colleges and Bible schools.

Two more examples need special mention: associations of theological schools and the Islam in Africa Project, now called Project for Christian-Muslim Relations in Africa. Africa currently has ten national or sub-regional associations of theological schools. For the most part their constituencies encompass Protestant and Roman Catholic seminaries, Bible institutes, university departments of religious studies and other programmes of theological studies. The associations sponsor conferences and institutes and publish Bible commentaries and studies in Christian education and church history which take the African context seriously. Such efforts foster ecumenical perspectives and spirit. Six continentwide associations foster co-operation between church-related institutions of theological education and ministerial formation.

Theological education in Africa is so conscious of the pluralism of society that it is more inclined to pursue curricula of religious studies than of divinity, which is typically sectarian and almost exclusively devoted to Christian theology. Even those which retain divinity in their nomenclature still take religious pluralism seriously. These departments of religious studies introduce students to the entire religious aspect of human life, with all its personal, social and philosophical involvements as well as serious engagement with indigenous African religions, the scriptures* and the historical development and theologies of the main religions in Africa. Above all, these departments seek to bring together persons of different faiths in fruitful human encounter, in a symbiosis of persons and subjects of study.

The Project for Christian-Muslim Relations in Africa was founded in 1960 as a channel for expressing the concerns and responsibilities of churches in Africa in their relationships with Muslims. It reflects the challenge of the large-scale movement of people and ideas across communal and international frontiers and brings the insight of faith and commitment to bear on shared ideals and common failings. The project has studied the undefined forces which motivate and inspire committed people to engage in mutual sharing and exchange and is thus an important ecumenical agency.

There are several continentwide, regional ecumenical bodies. The All Africa Conference of Churches* (AACC) was inaugurated in 1963 at Kampala as a pan-African organization of co-operation. Over the years, despite problems of mismanagement, the AACC has become a working instrument of ecclesiastical co-operation and political influence as well as a public expression of the maturity which Protestant Christianity seeks. But even the AACC labours under the legacy of history, principally the multiplicity and poverty of the local churches and the formidable language divide between French, English and Portuguese. The AACC's organizational structure is based on WCC structures, as is its style of operation. Now it is struggling to find its own identity as an African ecumenical body.

Evangelicals* founded the Association of Evangelicals of Africa and Madagascar (AEAM) in 1966. Although AEAM is not known for its openness to non-evangelicals, this group is a seminal embodiment of ecumenism in that its membership includes people from various denominations who co-operate and share fellowship. In local areas, however, its churches often function as para-churches. The AEAM too needs to find its African identity because it is influenced heavily by its moneyed supporters from the North.

There is also a pan-African Roman Catholic organization, the Symposium of Episcopal Conferences of Africa and Madagascar (SECAM), which was inaugurated by Pope Paul VI in 1969 in Uganda. Its secretariat is in Accra, Ghana. SECAM has considered some ecumenical themes, such as human rights in various African countries.

Ecumenism in Africa is taking its own course and shape, with denominational consciousness still much in evidence. Mostly it takes the form of occasional celebrations of unity at assemblies, but it is also expressed in meaningful practical co-operation at the national and international levels. One can be critical and point out that in international ecumenism, African churches are at a disadvantage

The 400-year-old church of Debre Berhan Selassie, Gondor, Ethiopia (WCC photo)

because the ecumenical structure and style they must work with are very alien to most of them. The agenda is often not theirs, and even when it is, Africans are often addressed in a paternalistic manner. Some of the structures, such as the councils of churches, do not seem to reach the grassroots, and the funds for ecumenical projects often come from overseas. But there are also some bright spots. In the 1980s, for example, the Pretoria Council of Churches (RSA), especially under the leadership of Rev. Nico Smith, has been revitalized as an instrument for uniting local churches in their action in society as a whole, as in the black townships. That council is motivated by a clear vision of the need for Christian unity and united social action, identifying needs of people such as those imprisoned without trial, bringing pressure to bear on the authorities and arranging legal representation. It has developed a strategy involving field workers who visit homes of those in distress and need.

Equally significant is the koinonia in RSA, an experiment in integration and reconciliation through the sharing of meals together in one another's houses in a country where it is not normally possible for persons of different races to share communion. Such koinonia is fostering bonds between churches and races, creating a deep sense of religious commitment and political awareness.

African ecumenism is fragile and has shortcomings. Nevertheless, the ecumenical efforts are an index of the growing consciousness of the church in Africa, of a shared identity as Christians, despite differences of language and denomination, and of the celebration of unity, common faith and commitment in spite of diversity.

JOHN S. POBEE

C.G. Baëta, The Relationships of Christians with Men of Other Living Faiths, Legon, University of Ghana, 1971 • A. Chepkwony, The Role of Non-Governmental Organizations in Development: A Study of the National Christian Council of Kenya, 1963-1978, Uppsala, Studia Missionalia Uppsaliensia, 1987 • H.B. Hansen, Mission, Church and State in a Colonial Setting, Uganda 1890-1925, London, Heinemann, 1984 • B. Hearne, Seeds of Unity, Kampala, Gaba, 1975 • O. Kalu, Divided People of God: Church Union Movement in Nigeria, 1875-1966, New York, NOK, 1974 • J. Mugambi, J. Mutiso-Mbinda & J. Vollbrecht, Ecumenical Initiatives in Eastern Africa, Nairobi, AACC/AMECEA, 1982.

AFRICAN INSTITUTED (INDEPENDENT) CHURCHES.

The AIC represent a variety of expressions of Christian faith. The name African Independent Churches, one given them by others, stressed the fact that they have broken away from the historic churches (e.g. the Church of the Lord [Aladura] broke away from the Church Missionary Society in Nigeria). Hence they are also called separatist churches. But since even historic churches in Africa are also independent at least juridically from their mother churches, this description is confusing and inadequate. They include spiritual or Pentecostal churches, which have a preoccupation with the Spirit and with experiencing Pentecost anew, offering a range of techniques for the emotional enhancement of religious experience (e.g. Musama Disco Christo Church, which broke away from the Methodist Church of Ghana). The Ethiopian movement emphasizes the importance of Africans controlling their own affairs in both religious and secular spheres. Zionist churches (e.g. The Christian Catholic Apostolic Holy Spirit Church in Zion, founded between 1917 and 1920 by Daniel Nkonyane) are primarily interested in the adaptation of Christian teaching and liturgy to the indigenous cosmology and ways of worship; they stress expressive and emotional phenomena and cater to the strong preoccupations of Africans with fears of witchcraft.

The foregoing names have led scholars to give interpretative names to the AIC, such as Witchcraft Eradication Movement, precisely because of the preoccupation with exorcism by the power of the Holy Spirit,* and messianic movements. These messianic movements are built around a leader who fills the role of a messianic leader and in their patterns of social action serve both as compensation for thwarted social aspirations and as an agency of socialization. Interestingly enough, such leaders do not normally claim the title of messiah. Perhaps the only exception is Limba, founder of the Church of Christ in South Africa. Prophetic movements are so called because they are built on a strong leader, a prophet. This is possible in part because of the scarcity of leadership, which encourages persons with initiative to claim authority. They are also called apostolic churches, probably because some of them, like the Church of the Twelve Apostles of Ghana, have apostles in their ecclesiastical polity. *Syncretistic movements* is a name given them because these churches are seen as mixing Christian beliefs with traditional African customs and ethos. Similarly, their designation as *naturistic movements* highlights the mixture of Christian belief and traditional African cosmology. Finally, their own self-designation is *African Instituted Churches*, which stresses the fact that they were founded and are led by Africans. These varied names are not mutually exclusive; two or more descriptions may apply to a given church.

The phenomenon of the AIC represents a number of things. First, the AIC is "a place to feel at home". Western missionary practices by and large were negative about African culture and alienated Africans from the gospel dressed up in European garb. To that extent, the AIC represent an indigenizing movement in Christianity. They in effect protest against the verbal and cerebral mode of Western Christianity, which is often out of the reach of people's comprehension and experience. Instead, the AIC offer a celebrative religion in which considerable use is made of symbols, music and dance. Thus they represent cultural renaissance in reaction to the cultural imperialism by the mission work of the historic churches.

Second, while Western churches emphasize Christology, the AIC make the Holy Spirit the focus of belief and practice. While they firmly believe in the person of Jesus Christ,* the AIC appear more at home with the Holy Spirit, especially as Christ has ascended into heaven. But their affirmation of the Holy Spirit is not just along the lines of sanctification* as in Methodism but also in terms of the experience of the Spirit as power made manifest in healing, exorcism, glossolalia and mission. Since Africans traditionally have a spiritual and religious epistemology and ontology, this emphasis on the Spirit is a way of asserting the Spirit as continuous and yet discontinuous with the many spirits of their heritage. The emphasis also represents an experiential supernaturalism which seeks for and believes in the promise of Christ to send his Spirit. To that extent, the phenomenon is a protest against the tendency of the historic churches to institutionalize every manifestation of the Spirit.

Third, the AIC represent a radically biblicist movement. Taking off from the Protestant claim that the Bible is an open book for individual interpretation, the AIC have seen the Bible as a source to legitimate a wide variety of basic Christian patterns, often of special relevance to local conditions or of special appeal to local people. Thus in Southern Africa the biblical stories regarding the bondage of Israel have become a paradigm for their circumstances. Old Testament pronouncements regarding polygyny (e.g. Solomon) and taboos are very much of interest to them. The importance of dreams, visions and trances as media of the revelation* of God (see, e.g., Gen. 40; Matt. 1:18-24) are stressed as in the Bible. The penchant for such visitations represents the mysticism of the AIC, an experience of the divine on earth.

Fourth, the churches of the West and their daughter churches in Africa have the stamp of individualism, which characterizes society after the industrial revolution. That, of course, goes against the ethos of African societies, which proverbially view life in communitarian terms. The AIC thus act as a surrogate tribe or an auxiliary to it, creating a self-selected community (e.g. Holy Apostles of Aiyetoro in Nigeria). This sense of community is manifested in pilgrimages to their holy cities, mutual aid in resources, and their sharing together of a common vocabulary.

From the foregoing, it can be argued that the AIC represent a renewal movement, particularly in terms of effective evangelism,* better communication of the gospel than was received from the churches founded from the West. For them, particularly the Pentecostalists, glossolalia is a supernatural way by which God wishes the so-called heathens to be converted to Christianity. Indeed, the expectation of a speedy parousia of Christ is a reason for Pentecostal missionary engagement.

The historic churches, at best, have been suspicious of the AIC, regarding them as a heathenization of Christianity. Not surprisingly the AIC have rarely found a place in the ecumenical movement; the WCC currently includes only two such AIC: the Church of the Lord (Aladura) from Nigeria, which claims a membership of over 1 million, and Eglise du Christ sur la terre par le prophète Simon Kimbangu (EJCSK, Church of Christ on Earth

Church members dramatize the life of Simon Kimbangu, Zaire (WCC/John Taylor)

by the Prophet Simon Kimbangu), or Kimbanguist Church, which claims a membership of 5 million.

Relationships between the historic churches and the AIC are not easy, despite the encouraging signs like the presence of two AIC in the WCC. In the Republic of South Africa the Interdenominational National Ministers endeavours to unite ministers of historic churches and those of the AIC. However, there are some real difficulties. For example, several AIC leaders, because of poor education, are unable to participate in the business of regional ecumenical bodies because of the language used (English or French). On the other hand, AIC leaders complain that they are seldom, if ever, elected to executive positions in these bodies. Ecumenism for the AIC is a different model in that the base of ecumenicity is the masses of people who unite in prayer, not the institutional leaders. For the time being, ecumenical relations between historic churches and the AIC are limited to co-operation in specific ventures.

JOHN S. POBEE

M. Assimeng, *Saints and Social Structures*, Tema, Ghana Publishing, 1986 • C.G. Baëta, *Prophetism in Ghana*, London, SCM, 1962 • D.M. Barrett, *Schism and Renewal in Africa: An Analysis of Six Thousand Contemporary Religious Movements*, Nairobi, Oxford UP, 1968 • P. Makhubu, *Who Are the Independent Churches?*, Johannesburg, Skotaville, 1988 • M.-L. Martin, *Kimbangu: An African Prophet and His Church*, Oxford, Blackwell, 1975 • J.S. Pobee, "Religion and Politics in Ghana, 1972-1978", *Journal of Religion in Africa*, 17, 1987 • B.G.M. Sundkler, *Bantu Prophets in South Africa*, London, Oxford UP, 1961 • B.G.M. Sundkler, *Zulu Zion and Some Swazi Zionists*, Uppsala, Gleerup, 1976 • H. Turner, *Church of the Lord, Aladura*, Oxford, Clarendon, 1967 • F. Welbourn, *East African Rebels*, London, Oxford UP, 1962 • F.B. Welbourn & B.A. Ogot, *A Place to Feel at Home*, London, Oxford UP, 1968.

AIDS. AIDS (acquired immune deficiency syndrome) is a newly recognized disease caused by infection with the human immune-deficiency virus (HIV). Infection with HIV is transmitted from person to person in three fundamental ways: (1) through sexual intercourse, (2) through blood, and (3) from mother to infant. HIV transmission through sexual intercourse involves sexual penetration and can occur from any infected person to his or her sexual partner(s). Worldwide, heterosexual transmission (woman to man, man to woman) is more common than homosexual transmission. HIV transmission through blood can involve blood transfusions (if the blood has not been screened), blood products (only those used for persons with hemophilia have been implicated; these can now be made essentially safe from HIV contamination), and re-use of contaminated injection equipment or other skin-piercing instruments (e.g. shared needles or syringes in intravenous drug use or re-use of unsterilized needles in providing health care). Finally, HIV transmission from infected mother to infant involves spread before, during or shortly after birth. Fortunately, HIV does not spread in other ways; specifically, HIV does not spread through food, water, coughing, sneezing, contacts at work or school, insects, toilets, swimming pools or telephones.

The geographical origin of HIV is not known. However, it is clear that during the mid-to-late 1970s, HIV began to spread worldwide. By 1981, when the disease AIDS was first recognized in the US, the virus was already present in five continents and was spreading. By mid-1988, the World Health Organization (WHO) estimated that between 5 and 10 million people worldwide had been infected with HIV.

When HIV infects a person, the genetic material from the virus enters the genetic material of some of the host cells. Therefore, HIV infection may be considered lifelong. The infected person is very likely to remain healthy for several years after initial HIV infection. However, the HIV gradually damages the host's immune system. When the immune system becomes severely depleted, the infected person becomes susceptible to infections which would normally not be a problem. These infections are called opportunistic because they take advantage of the weakened host immune system. Some malignancies can also take advantage of this situation, and some problems may be directly caused by the effect of HIV itself. An HIV-infected person who develops severe immune-system damage with accompanying opportunistic and life-threatening infections or malignancies has AIDS. However, other health problems can occur in HIV-infected people who do not have full-blown AIDS. Current information suggests that about 50% of HIV-infected people develop AIDS within the first ten years after they are infected. What will happen later to those who have not developed AIDS is as yet unknown, but most predictions are pessimistic.

As of March 1989, a total of 142,000 AIDS cases were reported officially to the WHO from 145 countries. However, WHO estimates the actual number of AIDS cases worldwide from the mid-1970s until the end of 1988 to be about 375,000. During the period 1989-91, an *additional* 700,000 AIDS cases are expected to emerge from the 5-10 million people infected already with HIV worldwide. Therefore, the numbers of people with AIDS will likely increase substantially during the next few years.

The challenges of HIV infection and AIDS are global. Each society confronts the difficulties of helping people change their sexual behaviour and alter or prevent altogether their drug-injecting behaviour. An AIDS vaccine is highly unlikely for at least five years. Although progress is being made in AIDS treatment (zidovudine [AZT] is of some benefit), treatment of AIDS remains very complex, expensive and inadequate.

To face this global challenge, WHO developed the Global AIDS Strategy, focusing on the need to prevent HIV infection, to reduce the personal and social impact of HIV infections and to unify national and international efforts against AIDS. Prevention of HIV requires information and education programmes, linked with specific health and social services, within a socially supportive climate of non-discrimination. The protection of the rights and dignity of HIV-infected persons, including those with AIDS, is a central feature of the strategy. Important changes in risk behaviours are now beginning to be reported from areas where information/education, relevant services and non-discrimination have been linked together.

The care of HIV-infected people and those who live with them is critical for individual and public health. Compassion and a non-judgmental approach are essential, for the world is fighting a virus, not people.

The WCC has played a vital role in protecting the rights and dignity of infected people, in diminishing stigmatization and discrimination, and in helping to care, humanely and equitably, for people who are infected. Technology alone will not be enough to prevent and control HIV/AIDS, the challenge of which is, above all, social and personal.

JONATHAN M. MANN

ALEXIS (SIMANSKY), patriarch of Moscow and all Russia. B. 9.11.1877, d. 17.4.1970. From 1945 to 1970, Alexis was patriarch of the Russian Orthodox Church. After studies first in law and then in theology, he became a monk in 1902, a priest in 1903, and bishop of Tikhvin in 1913. Following his exile from 1922 to 1926, he became leader of the diocese of Novgorod in 1926, metropolitan of Leningrad in 1933 and patriarch in 1945. In 1943 he discussed with Stalin a *modus vivendi* between church and state. After long negotiations the Russian Orthodox Church joined the WCC in 1961. Alexis was the only patriarch who sent observers to the Second Vatican Council.

ANS J. VAN DER BENT

ALIVISATOS, HAMILKAR SPIRIDONOS. B. 17.5.1887, Lixourion, Greece; d. 14.8.1969, Athens. An Orthodox layman, Alivisatos was a member of the WCC central committee from 1948 until his death. He was on the Faith and Order* commission and was vice-chairman of the committee on "intercommunion"* preparing for the Lund conference, 1952. He took part in Stockholm 1925 and Lausanne 1927 and attended later major ecumenical meetings. After studies in Athens which led to a doctorate on John Chrysostom in 1908, he studied church history in Berlin and Leipzig under Karl Holl and Adolf von Harnack; in 1918 he became professor of canon law and pastoral theology in Athens. The renewal of the church, the training of priests and the social commitment of Christians were his major concerns. In 1936 Alivisatos organized the first international congress of Orthodox theology in Athens, of which he became president. He frequently criticized the WCC for its one-sided Protestant outlook and pleaded for a more active participation of the Orthodox churches in the ecumenical movement. He was active in the ministry of education and as state representative with the holy synod.

ANS J. VAN DER BENT

ALL AFRICA CONFERENCE OF CHURCHES. The AACC constitution contains the following preamble and statement of basis: "Believing that the purpose of God for the churches in Africa is life together, in a common obedience to him for the doing of his will in the world, the churches and the national councils of Africa subscribing hereto have constituted the All Africa Conference of Churches as a fellowship of churches for consultation and co-operation within the wider fellowship of the universal church... The All Africa Conference of Churches is a fellowship of churches which confess the Lord Jesus Christ as God and only Saviour according to the scriptures and therefore seek to fulfill together their common calling to the glory of the one God, Father, Son and Holy Spirit." That statement is very much like that of the WCC basis. It is thus a pan-African organ of co-operation, a Protestant symbol of unity* that provides something of a common sense of direction for the African churches.

Such an all-Africa organization became possible only in the years after the second world war, when African nationalism gathered momentum. Gold Coast became the first black African nation (besides Liberia and Ethiopia) when it assumed the name Ghana at its independence in 1957. In the next ten years many more nations became independent of European nations. In March 1990 the last colony, Namibia, became independent. Such political developments could not but affect things in the religious sphere, for Christianity had been seen as yet another aspect of the colonial front.

As these developments were taking place in Africa, the WCC also sought to address issues of war and injustice by witness, study and service rooted in faith commitment. But in an age of nationalism, the WCC could not operate directly in Africa. It thus became clear that what was needed was a regional Christian agency, especially as intergovernmental regional associations and programmes were assuming increasing significance.

And so in 1958 a conference in Ibadan, Nigeria, considered how the churches could best meet the challenges of African nationalism and impending nationhood. One result of the conference was to set up a provisional committee under the chairmanship of Sir Francis Akanu Ibiam, a Nigerian, to prepare for the first AACC assembly, which took place in Kampala, Uganda, in 1963.

Kampala adopted a constitution, appointed the Ghanaian-born S.H. Amissah as its first general secretary, and located the AACC secretariat at the Mindolo Ecumenical Foundation in Kitwe, Zambia, whence it was transferred in 1965 to Nairobi. At this point two other bodies were incorporated into the AACC — the African Sunday School Curriculum Project and the Ecumenical Programme for Emergency Action in Africa.

Currently the structure of the AACC includes a general secretariat which comprises the general secretary, an office of international affairs, information and linguistic services, public relations, and finance and administration. The selfhood of the church unit includes evangelism and Christian education, women's work, youth work, and interfaith and human resources development. The refugee and emergency unit provides general assistance through national Christian councils, leadership development, employment and self-help projects, education and training, awareness building, and emergency service and emergency preparedness. Research and development consultancy deals with programmes and projects for development, partnership in development, situating development in the framework of African history and community, development exchange (experience sharing), development education and special projects. The communication training centre is concerned with consultations, radio broadcasting, audiovisual aids, creative arts and personnel training. The structure is programme oriented, with the staff travelling to work with church and community leaders in identified areas of greatest need.

One of the success stories of the AACC has been its training centre, later renamed the AACC communication centre. AACC set up Broadcasting Audiovisual Services, which has accepted students from all over Africa, including some government employees, for courses in broadcasting, script-writing, photography, and related areas. Another accomplishment was its role in assisting in the Addis Ababa negotiations of 1972, which led to the reconciliation of warring factions in the Sudan.

The AACC as an ecumenical body links up with other ecumenical bodies like the WCC and councils of churches overseas and partner churches and agencies in other areas of the world. But financially, at any rate, it is too dependent on overseas partners. Of course,

the poverty of African churches affects the ability of local churches to face up to their financial responsibilities. African churches are to some extent in the grip of a dependency syndrome that they need to break.

Africa is a vast continent. A pan-African organization can be effective only in relation to the local church,* which the AACC conceives of as its vital cell. Local Christian councils are therefore very important to the AACC. For example, since 1989 the national councils of Southern Africa and the AACC are together responsible for co-ordinating the emergency work of the sub-region. Similar developments are in process in eastern and northern Africa, central and western Africa. These are efforts at regionalization of the AACC so as to bring the ecumenical movement face to face with local needs and innovative solutions.

But on a continent riddled with linguistic divisions, tribal divisions which are even reflected in churches, and ideological differences, there is particular concern that regionalization does not degenerate into regionalism. For that reason the AACC has been working at all-Africa events such as a women's event in Lomé (1989), a youth and students' event (1990), and a lay and ordained leaders' event (1991) to explore the church's mission for today. At these meetings the hope is that the diverse peoples of Africa will share information from their respective spiritual and cultural resources, learn from each other's knowledge and experiences, identify common problems and participate in finding possible solutions.

NAT IDAROUS and JOHN S. POBEE

The Church in Changing Africa: Report of AACC, New York, IMC, 1958 • Drumbeats from Kampala, London, Lutterworth, 1963 • Follow Me — Feed My Lambs, Nairobi, AACC, 1982 • R. Sakala & N.N. Nku, You Shall Be My Witness: Official Report of the Fifth AACC General Assembly, Nairobi, AACC, 1988 • The Struggle Continues, Nairobi, AACC, 1975.

ALLEN, ROLAND. B. 29.12.1868, England; d. 9.6.1947, Kenya. Allen was an Anglican missionary to China and proponent of reforms in missionary principles and practices which would focus on establishing independent and indigenous churches. His major books, *Missionary Methods: St Paul's or Ours?* (1912) and *The Spontaneous Expansion of the Church and the Causes Which Hinder It* (1927), argued that not allowing new Christians to run their own churches was in effect to deny the power of the Holy Spirit. Churches would grow in God's own time as a "spontaneous" process; meddling and control — especially financial — by missionaries would only hinder this process. Allen's missiology has been especially influential in the development of the Three-Self (self-governing, self-supporting, self-propagating) movement in Chinese Protestantism. See David Paton ed., *Reform of the Ministry: A Study in the Work of Roland Allen* (London, Lutterworth, 1968).

ANS J. VAN DER BENT

AMNESTY INTERNATIONAL. AI is an international human rights* organization and movement which works to ensure that the 1948 United Nations Universal Declaration of Human Rights is respected. AI seeks the release of non-violent prisoners and fair and prompt trials for all political prisoners. It campaigns against torture* and the death penalty and is involved in refugee* work and in human rights education.

In 1961 the British lawyer Peter Beneson published an "Appeal for Amnesty" on behalf of political prisoners. Originally planned to run for two years, the appeal received such wide support that in 1963 the more permanent secretariat of Amnesty International was set up in London. The scope of its work developed rapidly, at first mostly in Europe and North America, later in other continents. In 1977 AI won the Nobel peace prize and in 1978, the UN human rights prize.

AI's constitution clearly defines its mandate and working principles. AI does not take a stance on the political intentions and objectives of the governments it addresses regarding their observance of human rights. It campaigns for political prisoners regardless of their political convictions or religious beliefs, ethnic origin, sex, colour or language.

Strict rules govern financing in order to safeguard AI's independence. It accepts no financial support from governments. The donations from its members and supporters may not exceed a stipulated amount. Money raised

by the sale of materials or received from bequests or fines from lawsuits also funds the work. AI does not accept donations designated for specific countries, but only contributions for its overall human rights work.

AI tries by all means at its disposal to draw public attention to those people whose rights are being violated. Its work is directed first and foremost to governments, reminding them of the obligations they themselves have undertaken to protect human rights (through conventions, declarations, etc.) and pressuring them to observe human rights by publicizing cases of human rights violations. AI's research department at the international secretariat in London makes reliable information rapidly available. The secretariat "adopts" a prisoner before he or she is allocated to a national AI group, which then works for the immediate and unconditional release of the prisoner if he or she has not used or advocated violence.

Other AI means for effective protection of human rights are: publication of an annual report on the development of human rights, country by country; campaigns against the use of torture and the death penalty, against extrajudicial executions and against the "disappearance" of persons; international campaigns concerning specific countries; urgent actions where people are under acute threat through human rights violations; and limited financial help to some prisoners or to their families.

AI has formal international relations with the UN, UNESCO, the Council of Europe, the Organization of African Unity and the Organization of American States; it co-operates also in regional human rights work. Within AI there has been a long-running discussion on how to achieve respect for human rights by organizations and groups which function virtually as the state in that they control a territory or an area.

AI's work is strongly influenced by political developments. The East-West detente in Europe in the late 1980s has led to the formation of new national AI sections in Central and Eastern Europe. At the same time, human rights are ceasing to be used as a propaganda weapon in the East-West conflict. It may be that in the 1990s AI's policy and work will be more strongly determined by the human rights aspects of the unjust North-South relations.

Increasing worldwide in the 1980s have

been conflicts between nationalities and disputes of an ethnic nature, with a consequent increase in serious human rights violations. The 1990 AI report has defined this development as its central challenge.

VOLKMAR DEILE

Annual *Amnesty International Report*, London.

ANATHEMAS. An anathema is a formula pronouncing a ban and so excluding sinners from the fellowship of the church and delivering them up for punishment by God.

In the Old Testament *herem* means something which is under the ban or intended as a sacrifice. It is withdrawn from human use and delivered over to God irrevocably. In the New Testament the word *anathema* can mean an offering (Luke 21:5), a curse (1 Cor. 12:3), a curse called down on oneself (Rom. 9:3), and above all a curse by which someone is excommunicated and hence cut off from Christ: if anyone "should preach to you a gospel contrary to that which we preached to you, let him be accursed" (Gal. 1:8). And "if any one has no love for the Lord, let him be accursed" (1 Cor. 16:22). Here Paul probably is using a sacral formula of condemnation taken over from Judaism, in order to express complete separation from Christ, spiritual death and final condemnation.

With the synod of Elvira (around 300) the anathema became a formula of excommunication in the linguistic usage of the church. It added a solemn curse to excommunication,* thus increasing its gravity. In 343 the synod of Gangra produced for the first time the formula "If anyone... anathema." The anathema later became an intensified form of excommunication: while simple excommunication *(excommunicatio minor)* meant only a bar on receiving the sacraments and exclusion from the fellowship of the saints, the anathema meant a complete separation from the church as the Body of Christ.

In dogmatic pronouncements, positive statements of the right doctrine are juridically protected by an accompanying rejection of the opposing position. Most often this is conveyed through the use of the formula *si quis dixerit... anathema sit* (If anyone says... let them be excluded). This was the form adopted, for instance, by the council of Trent* in its confrontation with the Reformation, which it condemned as heretical. Here it should be noted that in the Reformation period the concept of heresy* had not yet been so sharply outlined and legally defined in the sense of false doctrine. Any separation from the one church and any opposition to its authority was regarded as heresy. At Trent not every anathematization was directed against a false teaching. Infringement of church regulations on discipline were also anathematized, and those who supported these were excluded from the fellowship of the church.

In so far as an anathema relates to ecclesiastical regulations, it can of course be revoked (see H. Denziger, *Enchiridion Symbolorum* 1811). With an anathema condemning a false teaching, the first question must be historical: what was it directed against? In many instances, individual sentences torn out of their context, or even mere misunderstandings, were condemned. Doctrines which today are not advanced by the other church were repeatedly anathematized. The formula *si quis dixerit... anathema sit* opens up ecumenical opportunities in all these instances. It does not assert that anyone is actually teaching a position that has been declared to be wrong; the anathema does not excommunicate anyone by name. Thus the study of the joint theological commission of German Catholics and Protestants entitled "Lehrverurteilungen — kirchentrennend?" (Condemnations of the Reformation era: do they still divide?, K. Lehmann and W. Pannenberg eds) reached the conclusion that almost without exception the doctrinal condemnations of the 16th century no longer apply to the other church and cannot continue to legitimate excommunications dating from the Reformation period. Those censures which still apply even today have in the interval come to be seen within such a broad framework that the commission concluded that they need not divide the church.

In a common declaration issued by Pope Paul VI and Patriarch Athenagoras on 7 December 1965, the mutual excommunications of 1054 were "erased from the memory" of the church, a step that has not yet led to the restoration of communion* between Rome and Constantinople. In the Leuenberg concordat of 1973, European Lutherans and Reformed included in their establishment of mutual pulpit and altar fellowship the declaration that the mutual condemnations of the 16th century "no longer apply to the contemporary doctrinal position of the assenting churches".

See also **church discipline, excommunication**.

PETER NEUNER

ANGLICAN COMMUNION. The Anglican communion, as described by the Lambeth conference of bishops of 1930, is "a fellowship, within the one holy catholic and apostolic church, of those duly constituted dioceses, provinces or regional churches in communion with the see of Canterbury". These churches "uphold and propagate the catholic and apostolic faith and order as it is generally set forth in the Book of Common Prayer". They are "particular or national churches and, as such, promote within each of their territories a national expression of Christian faith, life and worship". "Anglican" refers not to language or culture but to common ancestry in the Church of England. Today, on account of the varied courses taken by Prayer Book revision, one has to omit the reference to the Book of Common Prayer, but in other respects the description stands.

The Anglican communion began its separate life in the reign of the English king Henry VIII (d.1547). In 1533-34 the Church of England defied the pope and unilaterally asserted its autonomy under God as a local expression of the universal church. This step hardly altered the outward appearance of the church; the old mass, for instance, remained its central liturgy throughout Henry's reign. But the principle of autonomy was an explosive force which led to more profound and extensive changes.

In the reigns of Edward VI (1547-53) and of Elizabeth I (1558-1603), the Church of England followed largely Protestant ways and separated itself from the Church of Rome in doctrine and ethos as well as in structure. The cornerstones of this settlement were the Book of Common Prayer and the Thirty-Nine Articles of Religion, which rooted the church in the life of the one nation, brought the whole country (in theory) into the one liturgical usage, and stamped an Anglo-Saxon literary style upon Anglican worship for future generations. The changes, of course, were originally intended only for the one Anglo-Saxon nation of England.

How did this singular development become a worldwide "communion"?* From the same period, a parallel church in Ireland also became separated from Rome and reformed by monarchical decrees, though the bulk of the Irish people refused to separate themselves from the pope. Another independent Episcopal church developed in Scotland by the late 1600s — not established by law as the Church of England was. During the 18th century this church devised its own eucharistic rites and thus demonstrated its substantial independence from the Church of England, while it retained profound family ancestries, resemblances and ties in common with that church.

From 1633 onwards, the bishop of London had charge of all Church of England congregations beyond the shores of Britain, whether in the American or other colonies, or on the continent of Europe. No bishop of London ever visited such overseas congregations. Thus when in 1776 the American colonies declared their independence from England, the Church of England congregations there faced a crisis. The church in America suffered severe setbacks in the immediate post-war years because of its former association with the British crown and the number of clergy and prominent laity who had been loyalists during the war. Nevertheless, the church soon established its own separate identity. No longer wanting to be viewed as still under the British through the bishop of London, they also did not want lose the principle and practice of episcopacy* for the sake of being American.

Thus, the Connecticut clergy elected Samuel Seabury to be their bishop, and sent him to London for consecration in 1783. The archbishop of Canterbury could not legally give consecration without exacting an oath of loyalty to George III. Not wanting to swear loyalty to the king, Seabury was consecrated instead in 1784 in Aberdeen by three Scottish bishops who had no state connection. Seabury was the first Anglican bishop consecrated for service outside the British Isles.

In 1789 the American Anglicans formed a general convention. The convention modelled its church constitution on the new civil one, authorized a separate prayer book, and declared themselves the autonomous "Protestant Episcopal Church in the United States". ("Episcopal Church" has now become the official alternate name.) And so came to be another adult member of the communion. In 1910 this US church's general convention initiated a commission to bring about a world-wide conference of "all Christian commun-ions" for "questions of faith and order", and later sent delegations to Europe and the Mid-dle East to issue invitations, which in 1927 resulted in the first Faith and Order confer-ence.

Slowly Anglicans in other nations or col-onies followed the American pattern. They were settlers on plantations or belonged to companies with private chaplains, or they were the evangelistic result of Anglican vol-untary overseas missionary societies of clergy and laity, such as the Society for Promoting Christian Knowledge (1699), the Society for the Propagation of the Gospel (1701), and the Church Missionary Society (1799).

The growing Anglican communities asked the Church of England for bishops. They were consecrated for Nova Scotia (1787) and for other Canadian provinces soon after, and then for Calcutta (1814), Jamaica (1824), Australia (1836), New Zealand (1841), and various parts of Africa from 1853 onwards. Because they were ministering in English colonies, these bishops and their dioceses were viewed as in some respects part of the Church of England, though their structural and organiza-tional problems were very complex. In New Zealand the first bishop, Selwyn (1841-68), held a synod of church people, though such a move was impossible in England itself. In South Africa in the early 1860s Gray, the bishop of Cape Town, attempted to depose the bishop of Natal, Colenso, for heresy.* Colen-so appealed to the judicial committee of the Privy Council in London, which in 1865 con-firmed him in his episcopate.

At this Colenso decision, agitation arose in the Anglican churches around the world. The church in Canada proposed a common confer-ence "of the members of our Anglican com-munion" to consider common problems; the archbishop of Canterbury would convene it. From this came the first Lambeth conference in 1867, with 76 bishops in attendance (Lam-beth palace is the archbishop's residence in London). The conference took great care not

only to tiptoe around the case of Colenso (who was not invited) but also to ensure that the status of the proceedings was not that of a deliberative synod, but only of a consultative conference.

Since 1867 Lambeth conferences have been held every ten years, except for interruption by the two world wars. The conference's authority is still only consultative, not legisla-tive or executive. The archbishop of Canter-bury issues the invitations, and thus he decides in doubtful cases who are proper members. To this day, over against this con-sultative character of the Lambeth con-ferences, the self-governing churches of the Anglican communion individually enjoy an autonomy comparable to that which the Church of England claimed for herself at the Reformation.

Since the second world war more and more autonomous provinces (or churches, like the Church of England, with more than one pro-vince within it) have been created; today there are 29. In recent years inter-Anglican struc-tures or agencies have appeared: at present, the Anglican Consultative Council* and the biennial primates' meeting in addition to the Lambeth conferences.

It is very difficult to measure the strength of the Anglican churches. In England, because of the state establishment of the Church of England, all the baptized are traditionally viewed as Church of England persons *unless* they themselves indicate otherwise. This mea-sure would indicate 20-30 million members, far more than the number who worship on Sundays (attendance is well under 1 million). In other provinces, a roll of members may reflect actual church strength more accurately. Similarly, the ratios of bishops to congrega-tions, bishops to clergy, and bishops to lay worshippers vary enormously, and one can gain no good comparison of strength from the numbers of bishops. But overall, the com-munion has over 600 active bishops, and perhaps 60 million active or semi-active wor-shippers.

The Anglican communion faces grave questions of unity, identity and calling. The lack of central decision making means, e.g., that the ordination of women* to the presbyt-erate or episcopate is approved and practised in one part of the communion and not in another. Liturgical revision is pursued on a province-by-province basis. Reunion with other Christian denominations, which is in theory central to the calling of Anglicans, seems to throw up great trouble when it actually becomes imminent. And the communion still wrestles with a problem of its cultural conditioning which arises from its original provenance in England, its conservatism in relation to distinctively Anglo-Saxon ways, and its continued role for the see of Canterbury. Within it Catholic and Reformed (and charismatic) understandings of Christianity and the church* live alongside each other, now in tension, now in some kind of fusion, but rarely truly resolved.

COLIN BUCHANAN

S. Sykes & J. Booty eds, *The Study of Anglicanism*, London, SPCK, 1988.

ANGLICAN CONSULTATIVE COUNCIL.

The Anglican communion* has never had a substantial central secretariat or an over-arching authoritative assembly, but it has increasingly seen a need for stronger international bonds. After the 1958 Lambeth conference, an "executive secretary of the Anglican communion" was appointed, answerable to the archbishop of Canterbury. The 1968 Lambeth conference formed a federal agency, the Anglican Consultative Council (ACOC), and the executive secretary then became its secretary-general. With its central offices in London, the ACOC includes one bishop, one presbyter, and one layperson from each of the 29 autonomous churches of the communion. Convened under the presidency of the archbishop of Canterbury, the ACOC meets about every two years, each time in a different part of the world. Its public reports usually advocate broad policies in respect of reunion, political and social affairs, or other matters of general concern to the communion, such as the ordination of women.* The ACOC has no authority over the autonomous churches. A number of the member churches provide its small budget. At the 1988 Lambeth conference, unlike that in 1978, the archbishop of Canterbury invited the ACOC members to participate with the bishops. At this conference the unity and identity of the communion was under consideration, and the role of the ACOC, especially in relation to the develop-

ing primates meeting, received close scrutiny. But its focal character as a federal agency remains clear.

COLIN BUCHANAN

ANGLICAN-LUTHERAN DIALOGUE.

Two main factors prompted Anglican-Lutheran convergence. First, the worldwide expansion of both traditions brought them into new local contact. Second, this mutual rediscovery fitted well with the ecumenical strategy expressed by the 1888 Lambeth Quadrilateral.*

Phase 1: 1909-39. In 1909 the first official Anglican-Lutheran dialogue occurred in Uppsala between the Church of Sweden and the Anglican communion. Discussion centred mainly on the fourth point of the Lambeth Quadrilateral concerning ministry and succession (see **apostolicity, episcopacy**). The findings were accepted by the Lambeth conference in 1920 and the Swedish bishops in 1922. Anglicans declared that the Swedish church had a true succession of bishops and an orthodox doctrine of the ministry, and that its clergy should be allowed to preach in Anglican churches. Both sides approved eucharistic hospitality and agreed to participate mutually in consecrating bishops.

Similar dialogue was held in 1933-34 by the church of Finland and in 1936-38 by the churches of Latvia and Estonia with the Church of England. Although episcopal succession had been briefly interrupted in Finland and Latvia, it was now decided to restore a common episcopal ministry. On this assurance eucharistic hospitality was approved. Anglo-Scandinavian theological conferences began in 1929 and still meet biennially.

Phase 2: 1947-82. In 1947 dialogue began between the Church of England and the churches of Denmark, Iceland and Norway, whose episcopal succession had been interrupted at the Reformation. Mutual eucharistic hospitality ensued in the 1950s. In 1964 theological conferences began between the Church of England and the Evangelical Church in Germany (Federal Republic), including Lutheran, Reformed and United churches.

In 1968 the executive committee of the Lutheran World Federation* (LWF) and the Lambeth conference agreed to launch an international dialogue. This began in 1970, and its first-fruits were the 1973 Pullach report, which registered substantial agreements on sources of authority, the church,* the word and sacraments,* apostolic ministry and worship. Differing convictions were recorded about the historic episcopate. After this, regional Anglican-Lutheran dialogues developed separately in Europe and the USA.

The European commission met during 1980-82 and added further substantial agreements on justification,* baptism,* eucharist,* spiritual life and liturgical worship, ordained ministry and episcopacy,* and the nature of the church. These findings were published as the 1983 Helsinki report. It claimed that no serious obstacles remained in the way of full communion* and recorded similarities of stance towards witnessing to the gospel in modern Europe. It recommended joint Anglican-Lutheran celebration of the eucharist and occasional mutual participation in presbyterial and episcopal ordinations. Anglo-Scandinavian pastoral conferences began in 1977 and continue biennially.

Lutheran-Episcopal dialogue (LED) in the USA began in 1969-72 and continued in 1976-80. The Missouri Synod took part but did not endorse the conclusions. In 1982 the three bodies which later formed the Evangelical Lutheran Church in America agreed with the Episcopal Church to recognize each other as churches in which the gospel was preached, to encourage common action between congregations, and to establish interim sharing of the eucharist (see **intercommunion**).

Phase 3: 1983 onwards. These regional achievements were summarized in the 1983 Cold Ash report by a joint working group. This acknowledged the helpful influence of multilateral Faith and Order* discussions and bilateral dialogue* with the Roman Catholic Church. It defined the goal of full communion and described the stages by which this could be reached. It recommended setting up a permanent body to foster mutual relations, the Anglican-Lutheran International Continuation Committee, which started work in 1986.

It also requested a consultation on episcope ("oversight"), the chief remaining obstacle to progress. This gathering occurred in 1987 at Niagara, when a fresh approach was taken by viewing episcope in the light of the church's mission* and of the ministry of the whole people of God.* The 1988 Niagara report showed how seriously episcope was regarded at the Reformation and urged that responsible solutions adopted at times of emergency should be evaluated positively. It saw succession as consisting not primarily in an unbroken chain of ordinations but in maintaining the presiding ministry of a church standing in continuity of apostolic faith. It summarized Anglican-Lutheran doctrinal agreements to date and posed key questions about the reform and renewal of the episcopal office. Anglican churches were challenged to recognize the authenticity of Lutheran ministries, and Lutheran churches to conform to the Nicene canon requiring that a bishop be consecrated by at least three bishops. The Niagara report set out practical steps for realizing full communion. This report was received by the LWF executive committee and the Lambeth conference in 1988 and commended to member churches for action. A translation into Swahili was commissioned.

Regional dialogues continued. In the USA a third round of LED occurred in 1983-87, and its report on the implications of the gospel was published in 1988. The Church of England held new talks in 1987-88 with the Evangelical Church in both German republics, culminating in the Meissen statement; in 1989 it began updating its ecumenical agreements with the Nordic and Baltic churches.

DAVID TUSTIN

Anglican-Lutheran Relations: Report of Joint Working Group at Cold Ash, London, ACC, and Geneva, LWF, 1983 • C.H. Lyttkens, *The Growth of Swedish-Anglican Intercommunion between 1833 and 1922*, Lund, Gleerups, 1970 • *Niagara Report: Consultation on Episcope 1987*, London, ACC, and Geneva, LWF, 1988 • *On the Way towards Visible Unity: Meissen Statement 1988*, London, Church of England, 1988.

ANGLICAN-METHODIST RELATIONS.

In 1988 the bishops of the Lambeth conference recognized "with regret that there is no international theological dialogue between the Anglican communion and the World Methodist Council" and requested "the Anglican Consultative Council to initiate conversations with the WMC with a view to the beginning of such a dialogue". In 1989 the executive committee of the WMC welcomed this opening and authorized its ecumenical officers to explore the possible nature and themes of such dialogue.

The historical background in Anglican-Methodist relations is complex. Methodism started as a movement of evangelical, sacramental and moral renewal* within the Church of England. Its chief organizer, John Wesley (1703-91), professed continuing allegiance to the Church of England; but the para-ecclesial structures he created made an eventual separation almost inevitable, and after Wesley's death British Methodism developed into distinct denominations, spread throughout the land, though not so numerous in membership as the mother church. In North America, with the independence of the United States and the breaking of political and ecclesiastical ties to the British crown, Wesley's people very soon constituted themselves as the Methodist Episcopal Church (1784), and the new denomination came to outnumber the Protestant Episcopal Church (i.e. the Anglican body in the USA).

Throughout the 19th century, missionaries and emigrants from both Britain and America established Anglican and Methodist churches in other parts of the world, and in the 20th century some of these churches have engaged in union negotiations and plans, usually with Christians of other traditions also. In the Church of South India (1947) and the Church of North India (1970), Methodists (of British provenance) and Anglicans united in episcopally ordered bodies with Christians of Presbyterian, Congregationalist and (in North India) believer-baptist traditions; some provinces of the worldwide Anglican communion, however, have been hesitant about establishing full fellowship with these new churches.

In England, a two-stage plan for Anglican-Methodist unity — a growing together through a period of intercommunion, to precede full organic union — was approved by the Methodist conference but twice failed to achieve sufficient majorities in the assemblies of the Church of England (1969 and 1972). The main obstacle was the method and understanding by which British Methodism would "take episcopacy into its system", i.e. acquire a ministry recognized by the Church of England to be in the "apostolic succession" it claims for itself. In 1982 a proposed "covenant" — this time including also the United

Reformed Church and the Moravian Church — broke down on largely similar grounds, although the Church of England declared itself satisfied with the doctrinal assurances it had received from Methodism in connection with the earlier plans.

In the USA, Methodists and Anglicans have largely lacked the "special relationship" which has sometimes been felt to obtain in England. But the Episcopal Church (i.e. Anglican), the United Methodist Church and three black Methodist denominations participate in the wider Consultation on Church Union.*

GEOFFREY WAINWRIGHT

J.M. Turner, *Conflict and Reconciliation: Studies in Methodism and Ecumenism in England, 1740-1982*, London, Epworth, 1985.

ANGLICAN-ORIENTAL ORTHODOX DIALOGUE.

The five historic Oriental Orthodox churches are the Armenian, the Coptic, the Ethiopian, the Syrian, and the Indian. All were separated from the great church, some as early as the fourth ecumenical council of Chalcedon* (451). They were largely ignored by Roman Catholic and Byzantine Christianity until "rediscovered" between the 16th and 18th centuries by European Catholic missionaries who sought to unite them to the papacy. In the 19th century Protestant missionaries built hospitals, colleges and schools in an attempt to win the Oriental Orthodox for the churches of the Reformation. The Anglican relationship to these churches is somewhat different; in friendships extending over more than a century, Anglicans have tried to support rather than to absorb them.

A sixth church, the Catholic Assyrian Church of the East, broke its official relationship with the churches to the west of it at the council of Ephesus (431). Once numbering millions of faithful, the Assyrian church is now, through persecution, reduced to less than a million members. Here again the Anglican church was called to make a unique contribution in the 19th century, through the work of the archbishop of Canterbury's Assyrian mission, which was sent to Kurdistan at the repeated request of the people themselves, not to draw them from their church and customs, but to give them the means of restoring that old church once more to a state of efficiency.

Reports and resolutions of the Lambeth conferences record that the period between 1908 and 1920 was clearly a high-water mark in relations between Anglicans and Oriental Orthodox. However, for a variety of reasons, impetus was then lost on both sides. The way was re-opened between 1982 and 1988 when the archbishop of Canterbury, Robert Runcie, and the other primates of the Anglican communion requested Bishop Henry Hill of Canada to make a number of semi-official visits, in some cases more than twice, to the heads of all the Oriental churches in their homelands; and to the Catholicos Patriarch of the Assyrian Church of the East, who is now resident in the USA.

In July 1983 during the Vancouver assembly of the WCC, with the co-operation of Paulos Mar Gregorios, metropolitan of Delhi (of the Syrian Orthodox Church of India), a meeting was arranged between representatives of all the Oriental churches and Anglicans from England, Scotland and Canada, with the archbishop of Canterbury in the chair. Such was the enthusiasm of the meeting that the Oriental Orthodox, and the Assyrians who were also present, accepted an Anglican invitation to attend a theological forum in Great Britain, set for autumn 1985.

When the forum was convened in St Albans, 7-11 October 1985, it was under the presidency of the Rt Rev. Samir Kafity, Anglican bishop in Jerusalem. The discussions revolved around friendship and practical aspects of co-operation which were later reaffirmed at the Lambeth conference of 1988: "(1) the development of dialogue on matters of common theological interest and concern; (2) the establishment of theological scholarships mainly for post-graduate study for students who have completed their basic training in their own institutions and the possibility that some Anglican students spend some time in Oriental Orthodox theological institutions and monasteries as part of their regular training for the ministry; (3) the hope that theological seminaries of the Oriental Orthodox churches can be assisted especially in the building up of libraries, in the supply of new books, and in subscriptions to scholarly journals, with journals and magazines published by the churches of the two communions being ex-

changed on a more systematic basis; (4) the need for regional co-ordinating bodies for promoting understanding and co-operation among the churches especially in the USA and Canada, in the Middle East, in Australia and New Zealand, and in the United Kingdom".

Runcie, in his address at the conclusion of the St Albans forum, said to the Oriental Orthodox: "Your churches are at the interface of some of the greatest issues facing the world today. Christianity and Islam face each other, and there is an increasing stridency in the followers of the Prophet which makes dialogue more difficult than in former years. In India there is a wider encounter with other faiths as well as the new phenomenon of a third-world secularism. In Ethiopia the church seeks to play its part in the alleviation of one of the greatest famines in modern times. In that country and also in Armenia the church must find a way of working alongside a theoretically Marxist and atheist state. In Lebanon we see the tragedy of the disintegration of a state in the pressures of competing ideologies and neighbouring powers. Anglicans salute your courageous witness. I hope this forum will mark the beginning of a more co-ordinated Anglican sense of solidarity with you as brothers in the faith. And I believe we are one in faith."

Archbishop Runcie had further meetings with the patriarchs of these churches, most notably with Coptic pope Shenouda III, when on 10 July 1987 they signed a common declaration of the Nicene faith. They touched on past misunderstandings of the incarnation* of our Lord, "who is perfect in his divinity and perfect in his humanity in a real and perfect union without mingling or commixture, without confusion or change, without division or separation. His divinity did not separate from his humanity for an instant. He who is God eternal and invisible became visible in the flesh, and took upon himself the form of a servant."

The Lambeth conference of 1988, in affirming present progress, welcomed the presence of more Oriental Orthodox observers than at any previous Lambeth conference, thus regaining the momentum of the conferences of 1908 and 1920; it also expressed the desire "that in view of the importance of Anglican-Oriental Orthodox relations, the Anglican Consultative Council* enter into

consultation with the relevant Oriental Orthodox authorities with a view to the forum
being upgraded to a formally organized commission" (Resolution 5:9).

HENRY HILL

H. Hill ed., *Light from the East: A Symposium on
the Oriental Orthodox and Assyrian Churches*, Toronto, Anglican Book Centre, 1988.

ANGLICAN-ORTHODOX
DIALOGUE. There were a few mostly
individual contacts between Anglicans and
Orthodox from the 16th century to the 19th.
Although the two churches were largely ignorant of each other, there was no legacy of
mutual hostility. After the first world war
contacts became more official as the Ecumenical Patriarchate sent a delegation to the Lambeth conference of 1920, a pan-Orthodox delegation attended that of 1930, and in 1931 a
joint doctrinal commission met to discuss the
differences between the two churches. It was
agreed that the basis of any eventual communion* between them should be a union of
faith.* Anglicans had earlier pressed for intercommunion* and recognition of Anglican ordinations, which Orthodox had insisted could
come only after doctrinal agreement.

Agreed statements on the mystery of holy
orders (see **ordination**), the eucharist,* holy
tradition (see **Tradition and traditions**), justification* and other matters were drawn up at
the Bucharest conference of 1935 between
Anglican and Romanian Orthodox theologians. The Romanian Orthodox Church subsequently joined other Orthodox churches
which had earlier provisionally recognized
Anglican ordinations.

The developing theological dialogue was
interrupted by the second world war. Then in
1956 an Anglican-Russian Orthodox theological conference was held in Moscow. When
Archbishop Michael Ramsey visited Ecumenical Patriarch Athenagoras in 1962, the two
leaders agreed to begin setting up a joint
doctrinal commission. From 1966 to 1972 the
two sides met separately to prepare the dialogue.

Anglican-Orthodox joint doctrinal discussions began in 1973. Annual meetings of three
sub-commissions followed. The work of this
first phase of the official dialogue was drawn

together in the Moscow agreed statement of
1976. The titles of its seven sections indicate
the subjects covered, on which a measure of
agreement was recorded: (1) the knowledge of
God, (2) the inspiration and authority of scripture, (3) scripture and Tradition, (4) the authority of the councils, (5) the filioque*
clause, (6) the church as the eucharistic community, and (7) the invocation of the Holy
Spirit in the eucharist.

Symbolically significant was the agreement
among the Anglican members that for historical and canonical reasons the filioque should
not be in the Nicene Creed.* The first section
recognized the difficulties caused for some
Anglicans by such traditional Orthodox terms
as "divinization", and by the distinction between the essence and energies of God, although agreement on the underlying truths
was acknowledged. The fourth noted the traditional Anglican emphasis on the first four of
the ecumenical councils,* compared with the
Orthodox insistence on the equal importance
of all seven. Anglicans agreed that the veneration of icons* was not to be rejected but held it
could not be required of all Christians.

In 1977 the dialogue ran into trouble over
the ordination of women* to the priesthood,
which the Orthodox members realized was
now a reality in Anglicanism rather than a
possibility. A special meeting was held in
1978 at which the Orthodox made clear their
opposition to the ordination of women, hoping to influence the forthcoming Lambeth
conference in any decision it reached. They
were disappointed by the outcome of the conference. Some of them felt strongly that the
discussions should now be seen only as an
academic and informative exercise, and no
longer as an ecclesial endeavour aiming at the
ultimate union of the two churches. But a
series of visits to the Orthodox churches
undertaken in 1979 by the Anglican co-chairman revealed that the Orthodox churches as a
whole wished the dialogue to continue. A
steering committee that year agreed that the
full commission should continue its work.

In 1980 the second phase of the discussions
began. Its work was summed up in the Dublin
agreed statement of 1984. It contained three
main sections, each with several sub-sections:
(1) the mystery of the church: approaches to
the mystery, the marks of the church, communion and intercommunion, wider leader-

ship within the church, witness, evangelism and service; (2) faith in the Trinity, prayer and holiness: participation in the grace of the holy Trinity, prayer, holiness, the filioque; (3) worship and Tradition: paradosis-Tradition, worship and the maintenance of the faith, the communion of saints and the departed, icons.

The statement revealed a useful measure of agreement, although it was clear that further work was needed on several issues, among them the way in which the two churches conceived of the unity* and holiness* of the church.* The Orthodox regarded the Orthodox church as the one true church of Christ, which is not and cannot be divided. The Anglicans saw divisions as existing within the church. The Orthodox could not ascribe sinfulness to the church, while Anglicans saw the struggle between grace and sin to be a characteristic of the church on earth. The statement included an epilogue, summarizing points of agreement and disagreement, and those requiring further exploration. The discussions so far had shown that, specific issues apart, Anglicans as Western Christians had a different approach in general to that of Orthodox.

The commission did not meet again in full until 1989. Meanwhile a new Orthodox co-chairman had been appointed, Metropolitan John (Zizioulas) of Pergamon, and the membership of the commission had been reduced. In spite of further difficulties caused for the Orthodox by the consecration of the first woman bishop in the Episcopal Church (USA) and the varieties of interpretation among some Anglicans of basic Christian beliefs, the Ecumenical Patriarchate and most of the other Orthodox churches remained firmly committed to the dialogue. The reconstituted commission met in June 1989 in New Valamo in Finland. Its title was altered to International Commission for Anglican-Orthodox Dialogue. After fruitful discussion the meeting drew up a programme for the third phase of the dialogue, concentrating on ecclesiology and beginning with an examination of its roots in the doctrine of the Trinity* and in Christology.

HUGH WYBREW

Anglican-Orthodox Dialogue: The Dublin Agreed Statement 1984, London, SPCK, 1984 ● K. Ware & C. Davey eds, *Anglican-Orthodox Dialogue: The Moscow Agreed Statement*, London, SPCK, 1977.

ANGLICAN-REFORMED DIALOGUE. Theologically, both Anglicans and the Reformed are indebted to such Reformation figures as Martin Bucer, Peter Martyr and John Calvin. Historically, if some parts of the two communions have had little contact with each other, elsewhere they have known one another perhaps only too well. In any case, the problems and opportunities of present-day relationship, between Anglicans and Reformed (Presbyterians and Congregationalists) are profoundly marked by British history.

The Church of England remains the church "by law established", and its Articles of Religion (1562) acknowledge the monarch as the temporal head of the church. The 16th-century political conviction was that national unity would be cemented by religious uniformity; but to the separatist precursors of Congregationalism, the state church was antichrist, the monarch having no proper authority over the worship and ordering of Christ's church (see **church and state**). Some 17th-century Independents, like their Presbyterian counterparts, did not object to the establishment of religion, provided the polity was of their favoured kind. After the Cromwellian era, the English monarchy was restored in 1660, and between that date and the passing of the act of uniformity in 1662 almost one-fifth of the clergy (including 172 Congregationalists and over 1,700 Presbyterians) left, or were ejected from, their livings. They refused to give their "unfeigned assent and consent" to the Book of Common Prayer, to submit to re-ordination if they had been non-episcopally ordained, and to abjure the solemn league and covenant (1643). The fact that the act of uniformity did not apply to the "foreign reformed churches" in England did not go unnoticed.

The toleration act of 1689 accorded limited and conditional freedom to many Dissenters. Over the next 200 years, the social and other disabilities suffered by Nonconformists were gradually removed, and calls for the disestablishment of the Church of England began to subside. However, the theological questions remain: Who are the church? How are the "crown rights of the Redeemer" to be secured in his church? What is the proper relationship between church and state? Since there are Reformed establishments of varying kinds in

Scotland and some of the Swiss cantons, and Lutheran ones elsewhere, these questions are of some general ecumenical significance.

Among other traditional difficulties between Reformed and Anglicans are the Reformed opposition in some quarters to confessional subscription (by no means necessarily a cover for heterodoxy) and the Reformed resistance to the insistence upon episcopal ordination (see **episcopacy, ordination**), with which is often coupled a deep suspicion of sacerdotalism (see **priesthood**). While many Reformed churches value the *pastor pastorum*, they fear the sectarianism which attends the elevation of questions of church order* above the gospel. The Anglicans are variously puzzled and appalled by the diverse theologies and ecclesiologies, and by the propensity to secession, displayed by the Reformed family. The Reformed may appear as less than serious about the catholic heritage of faith* and its symbols, as taking liberation to the point of licence, as inadequately sacramental, and, in doctrine, as varying from the cerebral (whether conservative or liberal) to the innocent or the perverse. (On this last point, Anglicans risk a *tu quoque*.)

Nevertheless, Anglicans and Reformed have managed to co-operate in the Religious Tract Society (1799), the British and Foreign Bible Society (1804), the Evangelical Alliance (UK 1846, USA 1867) and, more recently, in local and regional councils of churches* and in the WCC. They have united — with others also — in the Churches of South (1947) and North (1970) India; they have entered into a covenant* in Wales, though the covenant proposed by the (English) Churches' Council for Covenanting failed (1982). There have been Anglo-Scottish Anglican-Presbyterian conversations and, within Scotland, conversations including also the Methodists, although none of these has led so far to union. Anglican-Reformed union negotiations have failed in Nigeria, Ghana, Sri Lanka, the Sudan, Canada, Australia and New Zealand.

God's Reign and Our Unity (1984) is the report of the international dialogue (1981-84) sponsored by the Anglican Consultative Council* and the World Alliance of Reformed Churches.* The report analyzes the obstacles to union between the two families, sets the traditional ecclesiological problems within the context of the common call to mission,* and concludes with nine specific, challenging recommendations, including the advocacy of reciprocal communion* as a means to unity,* where visible unity is seriously sought. The report raises, but does not treat in detail, the questions of establishment and of the ordination of women* to the ministry (where practice varies in both communions). To date the report has prompted more favourable comment than widespread action.

ALAN P.F. SELL

God's Reign and Our Unity, London, SPCK, 1984 • J. Huxtable, *A New Hope for Christian Unity*, London, Collins, 1977 • A.P.F. Sell, "Dubious Establishment? A Neglected Ecclesiological Testimony", *Mid-Stream*, 24, 1, 1985.

ANGLICAN-ROMAN CATHOLIC DIALOGUE.

The contemporary Anglican-Roman Catholic dialogue must be understood against the background of the break in communion* in the 16th century between what were to be known as the Roman Catholic Church (RCC) and the Church of England. This break in communion came about over a period of time, and the reasons for it are complex, both historically and theologically.

Among the cluster of events which consolidated the break was the act of supremacy of Henry VIII in 1534, which confirmed the king and his successors as "the only supreme head on earth of the Church of England, called *Anglicana Ecclesia*". A revised version of this act was passed by Elizabeth I in 1559 declaring the queen to be "the only supreme governor of this realm, and of all other of her highness's dominions and countries as well in all spiritual and ecclesiastical things or causes as in temporal". This legislation deprived the pope of any jurisdiction in the Church of England. Important also was the publication in 1552 of an English ordinal which was to be used for consecration of bishops, priests and deacons. The decisive event on the part of Rome was the promulgation in 1570 of the bull *Regnans in Excelsis* by Pope Pius V, which excommunicated Queen Elizabeth and absolved her subjects of allegiance to her.

This series of events and their manifold repercussions led to an almost complete estrangement between the RCC and the Church of England which lasted until the 20th century. The most momentous event for relations during the intervening period was the promulgation in 1896 by Pope Leo XIII of the apostolic letter *Apostolicae Curae*. This letter focused the reasons for the estrangement and also specified the issues that had to be faced between Roman Catholics and Anglicans when relations gradually warmed and theological dialogue began. *Apostolicae Curae* solemnly ratified the practice which had consistently been maintained of unconditionally ordaining Anglican clergymen who wished to be priests in the RCC. The letter judged Anglican ordinations to be "absolutely null and utterly void". The core of the position presented by Leo XIII was that the 1552 ordinal embodied an understanding of the ordained ministry which was in conflict with the teaching of the Catholic church, since it deliberately excluded all reference to the sacrificial nature of the eucharist* and of the priesthood.* This rendered the ordinal defective both in its form and intention, so that ordinations in which it was used were invalid. *Apostolicae Curae* elicited a response from the archbishops of Canterbury and York in 1897 in which they stated that the intention of the Church of England in its ordinations was precisely to confer the ministry that was instituted by Christ.

The period since *Apostolicae Curae*, however, has witnessed a slow but sure development in contacts and exchanges between the two communions. Between 1921 and 1925 a series of meetings between Catholics and Anglicans was held in Malines, Belgium, under the presidency of the archbishop, Cardinal Mercier. These conversations were initiated by the English Anglican layman Lord Halifax and their substance communicated to Pope Pius XI and archbishop Davidson of Canterbury. In 1932 the archbishop of Canterbury's council for foreign relations was set up, and officials from this office began to visit Rome, some of them being received in the Vatican by Mgr G.B. Montini, the future Pope Paul VI. From 1950 onwards unofficial meetings of distinguished Anglican and Roman Catholic scholars took place both in England and on the continent. The first visit to Rome by an archbishop of Canterbury was made by Archbishop Geoffrey Fisher to Pope John XXIII in 1960.

The major change in Anglican-Roman Catholic relations, however, took place during the Second Vatican Council* (1962-65), at which Anglican observers were present throughout. Vatican II developed the theological principles which gave the RCC a clear dogmatic basis for its ecumenical relations with other Christians. After the Council one of the first ecumenical initiatives was with the Anglicans, who now formed a worldwide communion of independent provinces, united in the fact of their communion with the archbishop of Canterbury. Archbishop Michael Ramsey of Canterbury visited Pope Paul VI in 1966, and together they set up the Anglican-Roman Catholic International Commission (ARCIC), whose brief was "a serious dialogue which, founded on the gospels and on the ancient common traditions, may lead to that unity in truth, for which Christ prayed".

The first commission (ARCIC-I) met between 1970 and 1981 and addressed itself to those matters which were historically divisive between Anglicans and Roman Catholics and which figured in the negative verdict on Anglican orders made by Leo XIII, namely eucharist and the ordained ministry, together with the question of authority* in the church. The purpose of the dialogue was to reach agreement in faith which would establish "unity in truth". The fruits of the dialogue were published in 1982 in the final report of ARCIC-I. This report comprised statements on eucharistic doctrine, ministry and ordination,* and authority, together with elucidations. On eucharist and ministry and ordination, the commission claimed to have reached "*substantial* agreement" in the sense of unanimous agreement "on matters where it considers that doctrine admits no divergence". They claimed to have reached a "degree of agreement" on authority. The claimed agreements on eucharistic doctrine and ministry and ordination were especially significant, since the judgment of *Apostolicae Curae* was based precisely on there being a conflict between Catholics and Anglicans on these matters in the 16th century, which was reflected in the ordinal of 1552.

The final report was duly submitted to the authorities of the RCC and the Anglican communion for their evaluation. The Anglican communion gave its verdict at the 1988 Lambeth conference, which recognized "the agreed statements of ARCIC on *Eucharistic*

Doctrine, Ministry and Ordination and their *Elucidations* as consonant in substance with the faith of Anglicans and believes that this agreement offers a sufficient basis for taking the next step forward towards the reconciliation of our churches grounded in agreement in faith". The authority statements were recognized "as a firm basis for the direction and agenda of the continuing dialogue on authority". In 1982 the Vatican Congregation for the Doctrine of the Faith published its reaction to the final report in the form of a set of *Observations*, intended as "its own contribution to the dialogue". The final official Catholic response was expected during 1990.

Events moved on, however, and of particular significance was the historic visit of Pope John Paul II to Canterbury in 1982 at the invitation of Archbishop Robert Runcie. The pope and the archbishop prayed together in Canterbury cathedral and, in a joint declaration, set up a second commission (ARCIC-II) "to examine, especially in the light of our respective judgments on the final report, the outstanding doctrinal differences which still separate us" and "to study all that hinders the mutual recognition of the ministries of our communions".

ARCIC-II convened in 1983 and thus began its work before the authorities on either side had given a final response to ARCIC-I. Its first report, "Salvation and the Church", an agreed statement on the doctrine of justification,* was published in 1987. The task of studying the question of "mutual recognition of ministries" came increasingly to be dominated by the question of the ordination of women.* By the time of the 1988 Lambeth conference, six provinces of the Anglican communion had ordained women to the priesthood. In February 1989 the Anglican (Episcopal) church in the USA ordained the first woman bishop. This whole issue has caused great controversy and division within the Anglican communion. It likewise profoundly affected the task of seeking reconciliation of ministries between the Catholic Church and the Anglican communion.

In the autumn of 1989, Archbishop Runcie paid an official visit to Rome at the end of which he and Pope John Paul II made a common declaration which, among other things, pinpointed the problem posed to Ang-

lican-Roman Catholic relations by this development: "The question and practice of the admission of women to the ministerial priesthood in some provinces of the Anglican communion prevents reconciliation between us even where there is otherwise progress towards agreement in faith on the meaning of the eucharist and the ordained ministry." It would be a distortion, however, to see ecumenical relations between the Roman Catholic Church and the Anglican communion exclusively in terms of the problems associated with this issue. The Roman Catholic Church and the Anglican communion have entered into a new relationship that looks to the future and seeks increasingly to overcome the estrangement of the past. Archbishop Runcie was the fourth archbishop of Canterbury to visit Rome in modern times. The pope and the archbishop prayed together, bore witness to the faith they hold in common and frankly discussed their differences. This spirit of hope and attitude of openness are reflected in many countries. National Anglican-Roman Catholic commissions seek to develop closer relations within the particular circumstances of each country. Most important of all are those changes that have taken place in local situations where Anglicans and Roman Catholics have come together in a new spirit of friendship, collaboration, and prayer.

KEVIN McDONALD

B. Pawley & M. Pawley, *Rome and Canterbury through Four Centuries: A Study of the Relations between the Church of Rome and the Anglican Church 1539-1981*, London, Mowbray, 1981 • *Salvation and the Church: An Agreed Statement by the Anglican-Roman Catholic International Commission ARCIC II, with Commentary and Study Guide*, London, Church House, 1989 • J.W. Witmer & J.R. Wright eds, *Called to Full Unity: Documents on Anglican-Roman Catholic Relations 1966-1983*, Washington, US Catholic Conference, 1986 • *Women Priests, Obstacle to Unity? Documents and Correspondence, Roma and Canterbury 1975-1986*, London, Catholic Truth Society, 1986.

ANOINTING OF THE SICK.

ANOINTING OF THE SICK. Two passages in the New Testament speak of anointing the sick: the apostolic ministry of healing (Mark 6:13) and the presbyterial rite of anointing (James 5:14-15). Prayers for blessing oil for this purpose are found in the early liturgical sources of both the Eastern and Western churches: the *Apostolic Tradition* of Hippolytus (215), the prayer book of Serapion (c.350), the Gelasian and Gregorian sacramentaries.

Virtually all the Eastern churches anoint the sick with oil. The rituals for administration are usually based on the Eastern Orthodox *Euchologion* and when fully implemented are very elaborate, involving seven priests, a deacon, a choir and a representative congregation. The mystery of "prayer oil" *(euchelaion)* intends the spiritual, physical and mental healing of the sick person.

For the first 800 years in the Western church, anointing with oil was used as a rite for the sick. The bishop was expected to bless the oil; the oil once blessed could be applied by presbyters or by laypeople. Pastoral changes during the Carolingian era and the subsequent theological speculation of the scholastics served to transform the rite into a sacrament for the dying called extreme unction ("last anointing").

The reformers of the 16th century repudiated this practice, since it lacked a dominical command of institution. According to John Calvin and Martin Bucer, anointing the sick belonged to the gift of healing of apostolic times, which was not communicated to later generations; furthermore, the extreme unction of their day scarcely resembled the anointing advised by James. The single exception was the optional rite of anointing retained in the first Anglican Book of Common Prayer of 1549, which in the wake of criticism was deleted from the office of the visitation of the sick in the 1552 prayer book and never restored until this century.

For the Church of England, the convocations of Canterbury (1935) and York (1936) officially approved services for the "administration of holy unction and the laying on of hands". The Authorized Alternative Services (1983) also includes anointing within its ministry to the sick. Anointing of the sick has also for some time been incorporated into the prayer books of other churches of the Anglican communion, most notably the American (1928 and again in the 1977 revision), Scottish (1929), South African (1954) and Canadian (1962, 1983).

At the Second Vatican Council* the Roman Catholic Church initiated a development which has led to the recovery of the original tradition of anointing. The 1972 *Ordo unctionis infirmorum eorumque pastoralis curae*, to be translated and adapted by the local churches of the Roman communion, envisions anointing as a sacrament* to be administered to those whose health is seriously impaired by sickness or old age. The priest is to anoint the forehead and hands with olive or other vegetable oil, while using a new prayer formulated from the epistle of James, the teaching of the council of Trent,* and the earlier *Rituale Romanum* of 1614. One of the most successful of the post-Vatican revisions, the anointing is frequently celebrated within a communal service now sanctioned by the new code of canon law.

Finally, the anointing of the sick is also provided for in the Book of Occasional Services, a companion to the Lutheran Book of Worship (1982); in the Book of Worship of the United Church of Christ (1986); and in the renewal of baptism for the sick and dying found in the supplemental liturgical resource 2 of the Presbyterian Church in the USA (1985). All anointing rites surveyed seem to be cast in the format of a visitation for the sick, which also includes a ministry of the word, confession and absolution, the laying on of hands, intercessory prayers for the sick, and sometimes holy communion afterwards.

CHARLES W. GUSMER

C.W. Gusmer, *And You Visited Me: The Sacramental Ministry to the Sick and the Dying*, rev. ed., New York, Pueblo, 1989 • C. Ortemann, *Le sacrement des malades*, Paris, Chalet, 1971.

ANTHROPOLOGY, AFRICAN. Our understanding of who we are as human beings is inextricably bound up with our experience (in my case, that of a Christian woman from Africa). The core of this statement on what it means to be human is my belief in the oneness of the human family and the sacredness of the human. I do not provide a systematic theological anthropology, only my theological intuitions.

The Hebrew scriptures point to human beings as having a direct link with God. We are created beings, and our Creator is the God who also made the heavens and the earth. We are therefore an integral part of God's creation. Since we humans have stewardship of

the earth, we have come to see the interdependence of all creation and our responsibility for ensuring that every created being is
named and respected. The Hebrew scriptures
have attributed this position of responsibility
to humans out of the belief that we are made
in the image of God. One task of Christian
theology is to interpret Gen. 1:26-27 — What
does it mean, and what does it require of us?

In Africa, many myths explain human origins. For the Akan, e.g., all human beings are
children of God, none is a child of the earth.
There is no explanation of how we came into
being, but the belief is firm that God called us
into being. The Yoruba have a more elaborate
myth in which a divine agent of God moulds
our bodies, and we are then brought to life by
the act of God, breathing into us individually.
In all the myths, the message is clear: human
beings have a special place in creation and
special links with God, which demands a
special relationship of responsibility to other
human beings and the rest of creation. We are
akin to God, whom we cannot see, or rather
who cannot be seen in this dimension of
being.

The living essence in ourselves, that which
we call soul (in different African languages,
known as *okra, chi, ori*, etc.), is also of the
spirit dimension of life, that which we do not
see. Africans believe this to be the principle
that links us to God and gives us a divine
aspect, but we do not develop a dual system to
enable the separation of body and soul that
Christian theology tends to generate. We are
our bodies, and these bodies with souls make
us human beings. Our make-up as beings in
relation to God and akin to God confers on us
a dignity which is to be scrupulously guarded.
This affirmation is fundamental to Christian
anthropology, as it is to African anthropology. Our dignity is associated with our immor-
tal life-essence, the soul, and in the African
Traditional Religion all is done to prevent or
remove self-hatred and self-disgust. Disgrace
is not meant for human beings. The dignity of
the individual person also demands that we
put people above structures and that we recognize, accept and celebrate the diversity of
persons and cultures that make up humanity.
The dignity of the individual demands a view
of humanity in which the particular is elevated
to the universal plane and not one in which the
universal is particularized.

In addition to this basic perception of the
human, Africa's religion posits the existence
of destiny for each individual. There is a
unique programme of life for each one,
chosen or given in the pre-mundane world and
which unfolds in the life we live here. This
destiny is carried in the soul and may be
modified through religious rites usually for
the shalom of the person. This factor of African religion has no parallel in Christian anthropology and serves to underline our dependence on the spirit dimension of existence,
the interaction of the two dimensions, as well
as the continued link between the human family that we experience fully and the family we
relate to only in the spirit.

Persons in community. Humanity is
linked chronologically. Between the "departed", the living and the unborn there is a
mutual answerability. We are accountable to
God and the generations on each side of us for
what we do on and to the earth. We are
persons in community. Africans define the
unity of humanity in terms of ethnic groups,
just as biblical language provides for tribes
and nations. The important factor, however,
is humanness *(muntu, nipa)*, which includes
the whole race, male and female, and ensures
hospitality and protection for the stranger.
Today's Western Christian anthropology
struggles to promote this humanness across all
the barriers that human beings continue to
create.

The tribal mentality prevails in all human
communities, giving all the liberty to classify
strangers as hostile or inferior. When we meet
strangers, we have to make deliberate moves
to extend humanity to them through the offering of friendships and covenants (Dickson &
Ellingworth, 110). If Christian anthropology
is to be relevant to African spirituality, it will
have to take a holistic approach and work for
the preservation of the unity and wholeness of
humanity. African myths of creation highlight
the community aspect of being human and
therefore focus on solidarity. They give an
important place to corporate personality and
mutuality to counter individualism, domination, oppression and economic exploitation,
hence promoting a sense of social consciousness.

There is a dialectical element in the struggle
to attach equal importance to selfhood and
community. We desire to be surrounded by

our community and to be accepted, but the urge to be our unique selves is also ingrained and nurtured by this same community. What African anthropology rejects is the crass individualism that Western culture has fostered as essential to Christianity and the authoritarianism it promotes by its top-down structures and patriarchalization of all human relations. When Christian anthropology teaches the inferiority of flesh and the superiority of spirit and goes on to set an antagonism between them in the human body, this relationship affects the rest of human thought and action, creating hierarchies of being, which leads to the marginalization of all that is deemed inferior (Moore, 124-26). Christian anthropologies thus require what may be described as the politics of truth. Liberation theology, e.g., seeks to enact historically the Christian truth about human beings. The faith affirmations of the sacredness and unity of humanity from a theological perspective have to be demonstrated by practice.

The relational aspect of being human remains underdeveloped in standard classical Christian anthropology (see **anthropology, theological**). Being human in any world-view involves cultivating and enjoying humanizing relations. When human relations nurture truth, justice and mutual understanding, we put some content into the Christian word "love", and compassion is able to bloom as a human quality reflecting our kinship with God. Our affirmation of self is meaningful only when we affirm the humanity of others and enable them to think for themselves (Moore, 130).

Life and death* are intertwined in human experience, but whereas the theological anthropology of Christianity makes physical death the result of human sin,* the African attributes it to the distance between God and humanity. When we sin, we do not necessarily die physically, but we distance ourselves from the presence of God. Our relations to God directly affect our relations to other human beings. As a result, the distance from God becomes alienation from other human beings, and a chain of sinning and being sinned against is set in motion. This cycle of

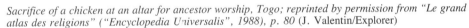

Sacrifice of a chicken at an altar for ancestor worship, Togo; reprinted by permission from "Le grand atlas des religions" ("Encyclopedia Universalis", 1988), p. 80 (J. Valentin/Explorer)

sin is experienced as death — the apparent absence of God.

Christian anthropology starts us off as perfectly good human beings, the very image of God, and then leads us to a fall occasioned by our rebellion against God, followed by rejection of the humanity of others. The dignity, honour and worth of humankind according to Gen. 1 and Ps. 8 are replaced by our repudiation of the sacredness of human life. Our lives individually and as a community of humans universally fall short of what they could be. African anthropology tries to re-instate our dignity and worth by promoting the sense of belonging and the solidarity of the human race in time (past, present and future) as well as in space. There is a struggle to strengthen us in our desire for community, to enable all to affirm their humanity as individuals and to affirm the humanity of others who constitute the community.

African religion has not set up a salvation myth in which the death of a Christ becomes the salvific event for all human beings. The struggle to be human is firmly located in the belief that God wishes it so, and the original goodness of humanity continues to be stimulated by God through each human being and through the community effort to humanize and to remain human. The need for fullness of life, described in both tangible and intangible needs of life such as are found in Matt. 25:31-46 and Matt. 4:4-6:25, is universally felt. The story of salvation in African religion is an attempt to humanize through religious demands and through a theocentric view of life but does not set up a one-person saviour. At this point the Christian claim on who the human is parts company and begins its own internal debate on total or partial fallenness and on human depravity as we experience it. "Being human", says Peter Sarpong, "involves cultivating and enjoying humanizing relationships of love, truth, justice, mercy and kindness." The absence of this is both a cause and a result of our fallenness, i.e. our being less than human.

The fallen human race. African Christian theologians under the influence of Western theology debate the extent and impact of sin on the divine image in the human being, but more relevantly they deal with the causes of evil as experienced in Africa. These explorations take them into African beliefs in the

sources of evil: divine beings whose moral demands on humans have been ignored, human beings (e.g. witches) who have become evil in the way they use their spiritual powers. They call attention to the direct source of death and dehumanization arising out of human irresponsibility. These theologians discuss the difference between sin and guilt, they speak of conscience and destiny, but all agree that human sin affects God, the ancestors, the whole spirit world, and not just the individual who sins. Sin equally affects the whole human community. It is an offence against one's neighbour, alive or dead, says J.S. Mbiti (Dickson & Ellingworth, 168). In this area the hermeneutical connection between Hebrew scriptures and African Traditional Religion becomes a fertile source of imagery for African Christian anthropology. Discussions of the evidence of human fallenness range from personal morality to classism, sexism* and racism.* All that is judged to be contrary to God's intention for the human being and human community demonstrates our fallenness from our status of beings made in God's image and the disruption of our relations with God and with other beings. It manifests itself in the demonization of "the other", in attributing powers of witchcraft to one's self or to others, and even in harbouring malice against others and whatever else generates guilt feelings.

Sin therefore is to a certain extent contextual and is often defined as related to power and its misuse. Sinfulness becomes manifested as power without justice, love, mercy and grace; it can operate against self and "the other" including against God. The distinction between societal evil and individual sin does not play a major role in this construct. Sin in the traditional religion affects God, the ancestors and the whole spiritual world; it affects total health, physical and relational; and in African culture it is countered by taboos, rituals and regulations. The Christian concept of original sin that demands a belief in "grace alone" does not operate in Africa's autochthonous religion.

Rather than a fall caused by original sin, the African belief goes in the direction of defining sin as disruptive energy: all that offends one's neighbour, living or dead; all ideological legitimization of that which diminishes the humanity of the other; the legitimization of hierarchies and structures that have disruptive effects on relationships. Sin is present wherever and whenever we separate unity and peace from the demands of justice. All barriers to community have to be exorcised, as they are seen to be the result of sin.

Redeemed and restored. Christian anthropology stipulates that the remedy for guilt, sin and death is to be found in Christ — specifically, in his death and resurrection. In African religion the reality of sin is not disputed, but redemption* and restoration demand more direct and immediate activity of the sinner than popular Christian preaching would lead one to think. The need for exorcism, sacrifice and purification rites goes with the immediacy of sin and the urgency to counter its effects. This I believe is what has led to the predominance of the cross in the preaching of salvation in Africa.

Sickness rather than death is what is seen in Africa as dehumanizing; physical death, being inevitable, is not seen as a result of sin. Death does not put an end to the self-expression of an individual, so funeral rites simply affirm the transition from this dimension of existence to the other; they become a means of renewing the bonds of the living as well as what binds the living to the generations that have passed through death to the other dimension. The "blood of Jesus" as a salvific principle is one that Africans can associate with. Our struggles against Western colonialism* and racism affirm for us the necessity for "blood sacrifice". It is with blood that Africa regains its land and dignity and humanity for its peoples. "Redeemed by the blood of Jesus" therefore strikes an immediate chord.

What exactly Christianity has to do with the redemption of African personality and restoration of dignity to the African is a debatable point. If Christ is preached as bringing back values of sacredness into human life and the full humanity of all, then a reconciled humanity can be defined as human communities in which the quality of life is theocentric, one that operates on the basis of the presence of the divine image in each and every person. Our restoration through Christ is to God and to our mutual acceptance of the humanity of all. The question of worth and dignity is one located in the sacred value of human life.

Christian anthropology's preoccupation with the fundamental corruption of human nature has a tendency to be debilitating. To concentrate on human weakness is to legitimize the status quo. We shall be saying human beings are too lazy to think or act, not that we are too helpless to take up our mats and move. The need to deliberate more on the meaning of life and the barriers to community and to peace with justice become aspects of Christian anthropology that our contemporary world has to face diligently. Human nature may be ill, but it is not dead. When death comes, we go to our rest; when we are ill, however, we fight to retain our humanity. A totally corrupt image of God cannot be seen to be divine.

Humanity is sick and fights to retain its self-understanding as being in the image of God. What is at stake in redemption as an immediate experience is the humanity of all. Basil Moore says: "My humanity is deficient when I live in total ignorance of yours." This at its core may signify a refusal to accept the image of God in others and even may be more fundamentally an atheistic view of human being. The concept of fallen humanity plunges us into a vicious circle, out of which we cannot step unless we are plucked out by the hand that made us. Here we come face to face with the issue of the nature of human freedom.

Western thought focuses attention on destiny and well-being, the individual and the race, nature and freedom. The quest for self-knowledge is an intellectual exercise. Debates are rife over the differences and relations of reason and imagination, knowing and being. The human is divided up, and the community is seen as made up of individuals, or at best groups with competing interests, and the human being is divided into spiritual and material. The African world integrates all but seems to fear the idea of an autonomous individual. Autonomy implies acting as a moral agent. To be able to be critical, one has to be autonomous. Neither perspective on the human being is able to produce the freedom in Christ that Paul talks about. When one looks at the various hierarchies created by human sub-groups and societies, one is faced with a formidable panorama of brokenness that cries for restoration and seems to demand mediatorial roles.

We are limited in the understanding of our humanity, but if we take the African traditional line, we could say we are limited beings whose fullness is being revealed to us as we interact in society and with nature.* Christian theology would say, "whose fullness has been revealed to us in Christ". We have been granted the privilege of seeing true human life. Jesus Christ is this life, life so potent that it breaks through death. If this is the major key, then all Christians (all humans) can attempt to live playing the minor key — defeating the death structures around us. This would signify something of our restoration in Christ. Restoration comes to us as we acknowledge the tiny sparks and acts of goodness, for it is these that confirm for us that God is in our humanity, God is in our midst sharing our suffering as we strive to burst the shell that covers the divine image in us. When we live for others, we reveal a little bit of the God who in human form lived for us. We believe that in this is our experience of restoration to our true being and our participation in the family (the kindom) of God.

This family is a reality in which we live, even if imperfectly, while awaiting our final restoration. It is in this light that we need to see our humanity.

See also **theology, African**.

MERCY AMBA ODUYOYE

R. Alves, *A Theology of Human Hope*, Washington, DC, Corpus Books, 1969 • *Bulletin of African Theology*, 4, 1984 • D.S. Cairns, *The Image of God in Man*, London, SCM, 1983 • K. Dickson & P. Ellingworth eds, *Biblical Revelation and African Beliefs*, London, Lutterworth, 1966 • D. Jenkins, *What Is Man?*, London, SCM, 1970 • P.K. Jewett, *Man as Male and Female*, Grand Rapids, MI, Eerdmans, 1976 • E. Moltman-Wendel and J. Moltman, *Humanity in God*, London, SCM, 1983 • B. Moore ed., *Black Theology: The South Africa Voice*, London, Hurst, 1973 • P. Teilhard de Chardin, *L'avenir de l'homme* (ET *The Future of Man*, New York, Harper & Row, 1964).

ANTHROPOLOGY, THEOLOGICAL.

In the broadest sense, the word "anthropology" is used for a wide range of studies which have for their subject matter the human being, as viewed in one aspect or another. "Theological anthropology", traditionally called the "doctrine of man", is the study of the human being in relation to God* or in the light of a particular theological or religious context. In Christianity, many theologians

have maintained that we do not know God "in himself" but in his relation to us, so that all Christian theology is concerned with the human as well as the divine, so much so that Karl Barth said that "theology would be better called 'theanthropology'".

Christian anthropology has its roots in the Bible, particularly in the teachings about creation* and incarnation.* According to the biblical doctrine of creation, the universe is dependent for its being on a more ultimate reality, namely, God. This is true also of the human being, who is part of the creation. So perhaps the first truth we learn about the human reality is its finitude — it is not self-originating, and its meaning must be sought beyond itself. Yet although the human being belongs to the creation and thus stands over against God, humanity is accorded a quite special place in the creation, for in creating the human race, God was aiming to bring into being a creature "in his own image" (Gen. 1:27). There has been much debate as to what this "image" is — some have seen it as dominion, others as rationality, others as freedom or even a limited share in the divine creativity. Or the word "spirit" may be used to express this reflection of the divine in the human, where "spirit" is understood as the capacity to reach out beyond actuality to new possibilities. Karl Rahner, for instance, writes: "Man is spirit, because he finds himself situated before being in its totality, which is infinite." So we have to ask whether there is a contradiction here. The human being is said to be finite, yet reaches out towards the infinite!

The same contrast appears in the alternative story of the creation in Gen. 2. There God creates the man "of dust from the ground", so that humanity is very definitely described as part of the finite creation. Yet it is immediately added that God "breathed into his nostrils the breath of life". Although it would be a mistake to read this in any pantheistic way, it does imply that God has imparted to the human being a special gift that makes the difference between the human and the non-human creation — one that may be called "spirit". So from the beginning there has been in humanity, if not a contradiction, then at least a polarity — the finitude of the dust conjoined with a reaching out for the infinite.

In speaking of this polarity, we are acknowledging that in humanity there is a duality, but not a dualism. The duality is represented in the Genesis story by the "dust from the ground" contrasted with the "breath of life", and this may be understood as a whole series of polarities — finitude contrasted with the desire for the infinite, reason contrasted with passion, individuality with sociality, the anxiety that comes from death-awareness with the hope that reaches even beyond death, the acceptance of responsibility with the experience of moral impotence, and so on. These violent polarities in the human being have been taken by some philosophers to mean that the human being is an accidental product of the world process, hopelessly involved in internal conflicts, a "useless passion", in the notorious phrase of Jean-Paul Sartre. But it can equally well be argued that these polarities are themselves part of the meaning of being created "in the image of God", for God too has been visualized as a "coincidence of opposites" (Nicholas of Cusa), though it has been held that in God the opposites are reconciled in a perfect unity. It can also be argued that it is the very presence of polarities in the human being that makes possible human transcendence, the plasticity of human nature which is not fixed like the nature of an inanimate object but can move to different and, we may hope, higher levels of being.

The duality (or, better, polarity) in the human being as portrayed in the biblical teaching is quite different from the dualism which we find in Gnosticism and Manichaeanism and some modern Eastern religions. In the dualistic view, a human being is compounded of two quite different substances — a material body and an immaterial soul or spirit. The body is held to be evil or, in any case, of inferior worth, while the soul alone constitutes the truly human element. This view in turn usually (though not always) leads to an ascetic mode of life. But on the biblical view, the material world including the body is good and deserving of care. The fall of human beings into sin* is not the contamination of pure spirit by an alien matter but the fall of the unitary psychosomatic human being. But it must be acknowledged that Christian theology has always been somewhat confused on these matters. While the creation stories and likewise the teaching about resurrection* imply that the body is an original and authentic constituent of a full human being, there have

been subsidiary and apparently incompatible beliefs about the "implanting" and the immortality of the soul as a substantial entity distinct from the body.

Related to the duality or polarity that is characteristic of human life is the matter of sex — human beings are either male or female. The sexual difference is not, of course, distinctive of humanity, for the great majority of living organisms are sexually differentiated. But from the point of view of *theological* anthropology, it is not the universal biological characteristics of sexuality that are of interest. Rather, we take note of the important point that when God carried out his intention of forming a creature in his own image, he did not create a solitary individual human being, but a human couple. "So God created man in his own image, in the image of God he created him; male and female he created them" (Gen. 1:27). Among modern theologians, Karl Barth has best brought out the significance of these words. From the first, the human being has been a being-in-relation, or, as the matter can also be expressed, there has never been an "I" without a "Thou". Sexuality is understood here as the primordial form of sociality. Now if humanity is made in the image of God and if this image requires for its manifestation not just a solitary human being but human beings in community, then this suggests that individuality and sociality, which occur as polarities in every human being and are often in tension with one another, are mysteriously united in the infinite being of God. The insight is already present in the Genesis story, though it was only many centuries later that it came to be theologically formulated in the Christian doctrine of the Triune God (see **Trinity**).

There are other interesting points to be gathered from these early chapters of Genesis, but we must move on to one which is of fundamental importance, namely, the teaching that this human community speedily fell into sin. The very plasticity of human nature, the fact that it is capable of transcendence and of growing into the image and likeness of God, implies ineluctably that it must also be capable of regression and of falling away from its possibilities. Ironically, the temptation to which the human couple succumbs is "You will be like God" (Gen. 3:5). The human race was destined for partnership with God in building up the creation but was not satisfied with this finite share in the image of likeness but sought rather to become what in modern times Nietzsche called the *Übermensch* (superman) who dispenses with God and claims the universe as his own. So in spite of all the tremendous claims that the theological anthropology of the Bible makes for humanity, it declares that this greatest work of creation has been flawed, that our actual humanity fails to coincide with the image or archetype which the Creator intended and made possible. A Christian anthropology therefore must always stand opposed to all facilely optimistic views that think of the human race as embarked on an inevitable progression towards a utopian society to be devised by their own cleverness and to philosophies which claim that the human race has within itself the resources for its own salvation.* Any view which ignores the universality of sin in human affairs is unrealistic.

Yet the same plasticity of humanity assures the possibility of repentance and renewal. At the centre of Christianity is the doctrine of incarnation, of the Word made flesh, and this is at the same time the re-creation of humanity. Again Barth is worthy of study, for in expounding his theological anthropology, he focuses attention on Jesus Christ* as the "true man". The history of sin is the clue to answering the question, "Who or what is man?"

There have, of course, been quite sharp differences on anthropology during the course of Christian history, but these differences have not been so extreme that there is no possibility of reconciliation. Friedrich Schleiermacher claimed that there are two views of humanity so extreme that they must be excluded from Christian theology — that men and women are so good that they have no need of salvation, or so bad that they are incapable of receiving salvation. But there are many possible positions between these extremes.

The Augustinian-Calvinist position has laid great stress on human sinfulness, even on "total depravity". This teaching has been influential chiefly, though not exclusively, among Protestants, who, in turn, have accused Roman Catholics of leanings towards Pelagianism or at least towards synergism. But in practice many theologians follow a middle course. It is interesting to note that in the earlier part of the 20th century there was strong emphasis on sin, whereas from about 1960 onward that theme has been muted, and we hear more of hope and transcendence. The reasons for this change are not clear, but they do seem to indicate that what is at stake is a difference of emphasis rather than something more fundamental.

Another difference (though this one is most clearly to be seen as between Western and Eastern Christianity) is between world affirmation and world renunciation. We have seen that the doctrine of creation pronounces the material world and the body to be the work of God and fundamentally good. But it may be asked whether the churches of the West with all their affluence have come to overprize the material. The churches of the East have been more ready to acknowledge the temptations of worldly well-being, and they provide for the West a warning "sign of contradiction".

But there is also at the present time a large measure of convergence on the anthropological question. This is because there has emerged since the time of the Enlightenment a new secular interpretation of the human reality (see **secularization**). It is in opposition to this view that Christian theologians of different traditions have been forced to draw together. The most threatening feature of this secular anthropology is its treatment of the human being as a part of nature,* to be studied in the same way as one studies any natural phenomenon. This has curiously contradictory consequences. On the one hand it leads to a diminution of our respect for men and women as persons, for it excludes such "mythological" ideas that they may be created in the image of God, and it has no categories for dealing with what personalist philosophers have called the I-Thou relation. Yet if this view has demeaned humanity in some respects, it has exaggerated its status in others, for in leaving God out of account, it pushes humanity into the place which Nietzsche had claimed for the "superman", who takes over control from the God who is no more. Many secular thinkers have revolted against this absorption of human beings into the realm of natural phenomena (e.g. the existentialists), and quite naturally they have had an attraction for theologians. The early Marx too was seeking a more human role for the workers in industrial societies, but this phase passed, and the collapse of Marxism in Eastern Europe today is in large measure due to its failure to protect the values of personal life. Thus a major challenge to the churches today is to work out together a convincing anthropology which will be true to the Christian faith and at the same time will meet the deepest needs of men and women for self-understanding.

See also **anthropology, African**.

JOHN MACQUARRIE

K. Barth, *Kirchliche Dogmatik* (ET *Church Dogmatics*, III/2, Edinburgh, Clark, 1960) • K. Barth, *Die Menschlichkeit Gottes* (ET *The Humanity of God*, London, Collins, 1967) • J. Macquarrie, *In Search of Humanity*, London, SCM, 1983 • W. Pannenberg, *Anthropologie in theologischer Perspektive* (ET *Anthropology in Theological Perspective*, Edinburgh, Clark, 1985) • J. Plamenatz, *Karl Marx's Philosophy of Man*, Oxford, Oxford UP, 1964 • R.L. Shinn, *Man: The New Humanism*, Philadelphia, Westminster, 1968.

ANTISEMITISM. Antisemitism cannot be ignored in the framework of interfaith dialogue;* it is central to the confrontation between Christianity and Judaism (see **Jewish-Christian dialogue**). Viewed historically, one must distinguish between the anti-Judaism existing within the New Testament (see Rosemary Radford Ruether and Charlotte Klein) and the xenophobia and anti-Jewish agitations found in antiquity — the texts of Manetho, Tacitus, Martial, Juvenal and Apion, for example. Moreover, hatred of Jews and their "king", as evidenced in the Roman occupation army in Palestine, indicated a non-religious bias even when this was fanned by religion.

None of this background is comparable with the modern antisemitism (a term coined by Wilhelm Marr in 1879), which ultimately culminated in the Nazi holocaust. Contemporary declarations by Christianity in this area often respond to both aspects of this past, recognizing the religious dimension, with its problems of rivalry and contradictory beliefs, which was joined to an irrational hatred of the Jews. These declarations have attempted to change both dogma and attitudes within Christianity in an attempt to move closer to their Jewish neighbours; Vatican II and the 1980 declaration of the German Protestant church synod in the Rhineland are examples of this new attitude. Yet one cannot understand Christianity and its development, particularly its relationship to others and to its component parts, without examining the Christian relationship to antisemitism.

Antisemitism must be translated as "Judeophobia" or "Jew hatred", which can reach paranoid levels. In its full pathological dimension, it identifies the Jews with the devil and sees Judaism as a devilish creed to be hated and despised. Within the early Christian community, the early antagonism congealed into the fear and hatred of the "Christ-killer"; and the epithet "blood libel" was added to this. Pagans had once charged Christians with killing children and using their blood for the rituals they attended in the catacombs and their secret assemblies. Later, Christians claimed that the Jews needed the blood of Christian children for their *mazzot* on Passover, thus linking the passions of the Easter period with the concept of unleavened bread which becomes the Host. These days, ecumenical "Passover Easter" study sessions confront this problem, but even in 1990 a "blood libel" accusation in Eastern Europe was reported in the media.

Interfaith dialogue brings together groups who are prepared to examine their prejudices. In time, it may reach into the unconscious level Freud explored, where Jews are not evil for evil actions but for forcing the Christian to accept the moral demands of the Jew Jesus. Jesus must be loved; Jews can be hated (see George Steiner's *In Bluebeard's Castle*). And one must also be aware that among some Christians the conversion* of the Jew used to rank high among the priorities for evangelism. During the Nazi period, these hidden feelings made Christianity particularly susceptible to the racialist doctrine of a total war against the Jews, which used Luther and other Christian teachers by quoting selectively from them. Dietrich Bonhoeffer and Martin Niemöller showed that believing Christians could resist, and the priests who entered the concentration camps evidenced true Christian faith; but the silent majority betrayed Christianity as much as their neighbour, the Jew. Acknowledging this guilt seems essential in a situation of interfaith dialogue examining the past. The first WCC assembly condemned antisemitism as "sin against God and man" and called upon the churches to denounce it as "absolutely irreconcilable with the profession and the practice of the Christian faith". Several statements of a similar nature have been issued by the Council itself and a number of its member churches. The "Ecumenical Considerations on Jewish-Christian Dialogue", received and recommended to the churches for study and action by the WCC central committee in 1982, provides detailed guidelines for Jewish-Christian dialogue and takes a strong stand against antisemitic theological perspectives.

In Islam, the Jewish rejection of Muhammad led to Jewish subjection within the Islamic state, but not to an agenda of killing the Jews, even though the current confrontation between Muslims and Jews in the Near East has changed the earlier mood of a shared life. Islam has not only come to stress earlier anti-Jewish texts of its tradition but has politicized its antisemitism and has used all weapons, including Nazi texts and forgeries like "The Protocols of the Learned Elders of Zion", in order to wage war against the Jews. A limited dialogue continues, as seen in the "Jewish-Christian-Muslim Standing Committee in Europe", which holds its annual "trialogue" in Bendorf, Federal Republic of Germany, and enters into open discussion, which at least clarifies the issues.

In the end, antisemitism must be recognized as a virulent, endemic illness which lives on within Europe and the rest of the world. Often, it is generated through a political situation which then turns into a religious dispute. The recent confrontation at Auschwitz, where a Carmelite convent was erected so that the nuns could pray for the victims, was a case in point. The place of killing millions of Jews and others had become a "Tomb of the Unknown Soldier", and much secular antisemitism fought against the notion of recognizing in any special way the martyrdom of the Jews in that killing place. The decent piety of the nuns ignored the anguish of the Jewish community, and it took a long time for some mutual understanding to emerge. And yet, if an ecumenical centre of prayer some distance from Auschwitz replaces the convent, this incident may yet give us the clearest insight into antisemitism and its role in the encounters between religions.

ALBERT H. FRIEDLANDER

H. Croner ed., "Rheinland Declaration of 1980", in *More Stepping Stones to Jewish-Christian Relations* *(1975-1983)*, New York, Paulist, 1985 ● C. Klein, *Anti-Judaism in Christian Theology*, Philadelphia, Fortress, 1978 ● H. Maccoby, *The Sacred Executioner*, New York, Thames & Hudson, 1982 ● R. Ruether, *Faith and Fratricide*, New York, Seabury, 1974 ● G. Steiner, *In Bluebeard's Castle*, New Haven, CT, Yale UP, 1971 ● *The Theology of the Churches and the Jewish People*, WCC, 1988 ● J. Trachtenberg, *The Devil and the Jews*, Philadelphia, Jewish Publication Society of America, 1966.

APARTHEID. The National party of South Africa was elected to power in 1948 in a white minority election on a platform of apartheid (lit. "apartness") as a basis for protecting white power and privilege. The relationship between apartheid as a political ideology entrenched in law and earlier forms of racial segregation is a complex one. South African history is the story of initiatives by whites to exclude others from having rights in a common society. For example, the land act, as the foundation stone of the entire apartheid system, became the law in 1913, restricting blacks (who constitute over 80% of the population) to 13% of the land surface.

The theological controversy around apartheid is commonly traced back to the debate in the Nederduitse Gereformeerde Kerk (NGK) in 1829. The synod of that church found it to be theologically wrong that "persons of colour" should be prevented from sharing in holy communion with whites. Then, in 1857, the synod ruled that "as a result of the weakness of some", segregation should be permitted.

Support for segregation and apartheid within the Afrikaans Reformed churches developed into an involved ideology in subsequent decades. The 1974 report of the NGK, *Human Relations and the South African Scene in the Light of Scripture*, provides explicit biblical and theological legitimation of apartheid. This contributed directly to the declaration of heresy against this church by the World Alliance of Reformed Churches (WARC) in 1982. A revised document, entitled *Church and Society*, was published in 1986. It moves away from the theological white nationalism of the Verwoerdian-Vorster era of apartheid, but it fails to move the NGK towards the complete eradication of apartheid either in church or in society.

Member churches of the South African Council of Churches and others like the Roman Catholic Church have rejected apartheid on theological grounds but often have been implicated (if only by default) in the practice and implementation of it. At the world level, several churches have also rejected apartheid, declaring it a sin in its persistent disobedience of the word of God, a heresy (WARC 1982), a *status confessionis* (Lutheran World Federation 1977). After the Cottesloe* consultation (1960), the NGK withdrew from the WCC, which has issued several resolutions of condemnation of apartheid as "a sin which, as a fundamental matter of faith, is to be rejected as a perversion of the gospel" (central committee 1980). On a practical level the WCC, through its Programme to Combat Racism,* has implemented and recommended to the member churches and to social institutions measures such as disinvestment (1972), discouraging of white immigration to South Africa (1972), refusal of bank loans (1974), and the application of comprehensive sanctions (1980). The Roman Catholic Church has also expressed its rejection and, as part of ecumenical national councils, has participated in such direct anti-apartheid actions. But there can be no doubt that the brunt of the struggle against apartheid is shouldered by the people in South Africa and by their lay and religious leaders.

See also **racism, Rustenburg**.

CHARLES VILLA-VICENCIO

J. De Gruchy & C. Villa-Vicencio eds, *Apartheid Is a Heresy*, Cape Town, David Philip, 1983 • R. Ormond, *The Apartheid Handbook*, Harmondsworth, Penguin, 1985 • *PCR Information*, 23, 1986 • B. Sjollema, *Isolating Apartheid*, WCC, 1982 • C. Villa-Vicencio, *Trapped in Apartheid*, Maryknoll, NY, Orbis, 1988.

APOSTASY. The word comes from the Greek *apostasia* and means publicly relinquishing one religion for another. Apostates are therefore people who abandon their faith. Among the biblical authors "apostasy" is used specifically in the sense of falling away from one's religion, rejecting one's faith. Thus Antiochus Epiphanes seeks to get the Jews to apostatize by forcing them to sacrifice to idols (1 Macc. 2:15). The apostle Paul is accused of apostasy by the Jews (Acts 21:21). The apostasy of those who are not true Christians will precede the coming of the antichrist (2 Thess. 2:3 and also 1 Tim. 4:1; Heb. 3:12). When Christians were persecuted by the Roman em-

pire, the church knew of many instances and types of apostasy: *sacrificati* (who acquiesced in sacrificing to idols), *traditores* (who handed over the sacred books to the persecutors), *thurificati* (who acquiesced in burning incense before the images of the false gods or of the emperor), *libellatici* (who obtained false certificates testifying that they had taken part in the worship of idols), *acta facientes* (who contrived to be mentioned in the public records as having renounced their faith). In the 4th century a notable instance of apostasy was that of Constantine the Great's nephew, Emperor Julian, who was known as "the Apostate" (361-63).

Apostasy in the early church led to very severe penalties in canon law.* Clergy who had apostatized because of human fear were repudiated by the church. Clergy who disowned their clerical status as such lost it; if they repented, they were received back as laity. Those who had apostatized and had forced others to do so were excommunicated (see **excommunication**) for ten years if they were of the laity. According to Basil the Great's canon 73, those who had repented after apostatizing had to remain among the penitents ("mourners") for the rest of their lives and were re-admitted to communion* only just before their death. Later apostates were punished by the confiscation of their property, exile and sometimes death.

Abandonment of a Christian confession for another religion has also been called apostasy. In the past such a move took those who brought this guilt upon themselves to the stake. Leaving one religion for another is still regarded as the offence of apostasy by the church one has left and is therefore liable in canon law to penalties, which are all the more strict because the transfer can also be regarded as heresy* if there are significant doctrinal differences between the confession left and the body joined. When there is a return to the church that has been left, rites of reconciliation* are accompanied by rituals for the abjuration of heresy.

The churches permit apostates to be reconciled with their faith. The rites vary, depending as a rule on whether the apostate is a minister of the church, a religious, or a layperson. But most often the public penalties of former days have been replaced by others within the church courts. In the Orthodox church, apostates who have repented, just like heretics and schismatics, are anointed with holy chrism during the ceremony by which they return to the church. It should be noted that at the present time, when Christians are seeking a return to unity,* practices such as proselytism* represent barriers which are sometimes insurmountable on the way towards this unity.

See also **schism**.

ALEXIS KNIAZEFF

APOSTLES' CREED. Since the early centuries of the Christian era the creed* known as the Apostles' Creed has been the confession of faith (or symbol) professed in the Western churches by those receiving baptism.* Adolf von Harnack and Hans Lietzmann traced it back to the 2nd-century church of Rome. However that may be, it is already found in outline by the end of the 2nd century, for instance in the writings of Irenaeus (*Against Heresies* 1.10.1). Well attested in Rome, Milan and Aquileia, in Dalmatia and in Africa at the end of the 4th century, it received its final form *(textus receptus)* some time between the 7th and 9th centuries.

From the beginning of Christianity the content of the profession of faith* at baptism has been regarded as belonging to the heart of the apostolic Tradition* (see **Tradition**). In the 3rd century, the Syriac *Didascalia* (6.12) attributes the formulation of the rule of faith to the apostles; and at the end of the 4th century, Ambrose of Milan (*Letters* 42.5; *Explanation of the Creed* 2-3) and Rufinus of Aquileia (*Commentary on the Apostles' Creed* 3) regard the baptismal creed of the Roman church as the work of the apostles, hence its name. This text was adopted by the Western churches as the profession of faith at baptism. The Eastern churches had formulations of the baptismal creed very similar to the Apostles' Creed. The Nicene Creed,* received by the churches of East and West, is similar in structure to the Apostles' Creed, but has an important addition on the divinity of Christ, made by the council of Nicea* (325), and another on the equality of the Holy Spirit* in relation to the Father and the Son, made by the council of Constantinople* (381).

The Apostles' Creed is Trinitarian in pattern, i.e. it is structured upon the persons of the Father, the Son and the Holy Spirit. The central, Christological part dealing with the work of Christ is the most developed. The mention of the Holy Spirit is followed by the reference to the church,* in which the Spirit is at work, and to certain essential points of the Christian faith. The Apostles' Creed does not claim to be an exhaustive statement of the Christian faith, any more than does the Nicene Creed or the other confessions of faith. It says nothing about scripture, for example, or explicitly about the eucharist,* ministry,* or justification.* These points of the Christian faith are taken for granted here as being derived directly from scripture. As they were not the subject of controversy in the early church, they required no further explanation.

As compared with the Nicene Creed, the Apostles' Creed has ten distinctive features. (1) Unlike all the Eastern creeds, it affirms the faith in the Father, in Jesus Christ his Son, in the Holy Spirit, and in the church without stressing their oneness (see 1 Cor. 8:6; Eph. 4:5-6). (2) It distinguishes between conception through the Holy Spirit (Matt. 1:18; Luke 1:35) and birth through the Virgin Mary. (3) It affirms that Christ descended into hell (see Phil. 2:10-11; Rom. 10:7; Acts 2:24; 1 Pet. 3:19), thus indicating the universality of the salvation* effected by Christ. (4) It proclaims that Christ is risen "from the dead" (Luke 24:46). (5) It underlines the divinity of the glorified Christ, stating that he is seated at the right hand of God, the Father Almighty (Matt. 26:64 par.). (6) It particularly highlights faith in the holiness of the Spirit, and hence the divinity of the Spirit, by repeating at the start of this third section the opening affirmation of the creed, "I believe...". (7) It professes the church as holy (see **holiness**) and catholic (see **catholicity**), expressing by the use of this second adjective the belief that, animated by the Holy Spirit, the church alone is established for the salvation in Christ of all human beings (see Eph. 1:22-23, 3:10-11). (8) It mentions belief in "the communion of saints", i.e. among Christians who are all members of the one Body of Christ (see 1 Cor. 10:16-17). (9) Whereas the Nicene Creed affirms that we "look for the resurrection of *the dead*", the Apostles' Creed, countering the Gnostic heresy, has always stated "the resurrection of the *body*" (Luke 24:39; John 6:51-56; Acts 2:30 [Western text]; 1 Cor. 15:36-39). (10) The statement of belief in the Holy Spirit is followed without transition by belief in the church, in the communion of saints,* the forgiveness of sins, the resurrection* of the body, and the life everlasting, thereby making it clear that all these are manifestations of the Spirit: the entire life of the church and of the Christian believer, right up to its final consummation, is under the influence of the Holy Spirit.

The Apostles' Creed has a special ecumenical value. In the Lambeth Quadrilateral* of 1888, the Anglican communion deliberately added it to the four fundamental articles of Chicago (1886) "as the baptismal symbol", while considering the Nicene Creed "as the sufficient statement of the Christian faith". The Lausanne Faith and Order conference of 1927 placed the Apostles' Creed alongside the Nicene Creed as the common expression of the Christian faith. It recognized that although the Eastern Orthodox church gives no place to the Apostles' Creed in its rites, it agrees with its teaching. This was repeated at the Edinburgh conference (1938), and then at the third assembly of the WCC at New Delhi (1961). Traditionally the baptismal symbol of the Roman Catholic Church, the Apostles' Creed has also since Vatican II* been introduced as an alternative to the Nicene Creed in the celebration of the eucharist.

See also **baptism, creeds, faith, Nicene Creed**.

EMMANUEL LANNE

J.N.D. Kelly, *Early Christian Creeds*, London, Longman, 1981 • E. Lanne, "The Apostolic Faith as Expressed in the Apostles' Creed, Especially Compared with the Nicene Creed", in *The Roots of Our Common Faith: Faith in the Scriptures and in the Early Church*, H.-G. Link ed., WCC, 1984 • A.M.G. Stephenson, *Anglicanism and the Lambeth Conferences*, London, SPCK, 1978 • L. Vischer, *A Documentary History of the Faith and Order Movement*, St Louis, MO, Bethany, 1963.

APOSTOLIC TRADITION.

"Tradition"* is a dynamic concept and presupposes a double movement, of receiving and transmitting. The apostolic Tradition is the gospel, the word and event of salvation,* entrusted by Jesus to the disciples he had chosen as its witnesses so that they in turn might hand it on with authority* (see Matt. 28:18-20; Acts

1:21-22). The term "tradition" lies at the heart of 1 Cor., where it refers to the teaching transmitted by Paul to the church in Corinth (11:2), especially concerning the Lord's supper (11:23) and the event of Christ's death and resurrection (15:3) (see **common confession, creeds, eucharist**). Paul, the last to be favoured with an appearance of the risen Christ (15:8), had himself "received" the apostolic witness which he "handed on" to the Corinthians (15:3-7). What Paul received and transmitted was the gospel (15:1); it was also the meaning and manner of celebrating the Lord's supper (11:20,24-26), the central act of the life of the community Paul had founded at Corinth. The context of 1 Cor. 11 shows that the apostolic Tradition has a "centre" — the gospel of the saving passion of the Lord (11:23-26; cf. 15:1-8) — and a broader context of practices which the apostle bases on the mystery of Christ (11:2-16).

In the pastoral epistles, we do not find the terminology of "tradition", but the idea itself is everywhere implicit. Once again the gospel is the centre of the message (1 Tim. 1:15-18, 3:16-4:6) and connected with it, the context of ecclesial life, though with a new emphasis. False teachings oppose the gospel transmitted by the apostle. This authentic apostolic Tradition is referred to three times as a deposit — "that which has been entrusted" (1 Tim. 6:20; 2 Tim. 1:12,14) — associated with the idea of keeping or guarding, and fairly close to the Jewish idea of tradition (Ceslaus Spicq). But what is transmitted and guarded is, above all, the gospel. The organization of the church and the norms handed down by Paul for this purpose are meaningful only in reference to the transmission of the unique gospel (see **church order, church discipline**).

The tradition of the church. From the sub-apostolic age onwards, works like the *Didache* (Teaching of the twelve apostles) formulate the norms of Christian and ecclesial life as apostolic Tradition. The spread of the Gnostic heresy in the course of the 2nd century led the mainstream church to define the apostolic Tradition in more precise terms. The Gnostics appealed to secret traditions of the apostles. From then on the churches sought to establish which were the writings of apostolic origin that could and should be read in congregations. In this way the "canon"* of the New Testament came to be formed. At the same time, however, norms emerged for interpreting these writings correctly in harmony with the prophecies contained in the Jewish scriptures which foretold the Christ and his work of salvation (see **hermeneutics**).

Around the year 180, in a work entitled *Against Heresies*, Irenaeus of Lyons established rules for discerning the authentic Christian message in opposition to the errors of the Gnostics. From the beginning (1.10.1) he insists that the church throughout the world has had a single and unique rule of faith,* the articles of which constitute the substance of what would become the baptismal creed (see **creeds**), "for although the languages of the world are dissimilar, yet the import of the Tradition is one and the same" (1.10.2; see **catholicity**). The sole content of the Tradition is the preaching of the apostles deposited in the scriptures, interpreted by the bishops instituted in the churches by the apostles (3.3.1; see **teaching authority, episcopacy**). This interpretation goes beyond a simple exegesis of the prophecies recorded in the Old Testament or of the NT writings, for, as already in Paul's case, the reading of scripture in accordance with the apostolic Tradition has concrete implications for the life of the churches and the behaviour of the Christian. In opposition to the secret traditions the heretics claimed to have received from the apostles, Irenaeus asserts the public character of the Tradition and denounces all forms of esotericism. This Tradition is not necessarily written, for the "barbarians who believe in Christ... having salvation written in their hearts by the Spirit without ink... carefully preserve the ancient Tradition" (3.4.2).

This concept of Tradition was repeated and developed by Christian theologians and polemicists after Irenaeus (Tertullian, Hippolytus, Origen). Some of them listed the unwritten traditions in force in ecclesial life deriving from the apostles (Tertullian, *Concerning the Crown* 3-4; Hippolytus in his *Apostolic Tradition*, where ecclesiastical organization derives from the apostles by tradition; the Syriac *Didascalia*; and church orders based on these writings). At the beginning of the 5th century a principle was formulated which is rooted in this conception of the intimate bond between the heritage of the apostles, scripture (as read in the universal tradition of the church) and ecclesial life:

namely, the normative character of the life of prayer of the universal church for the faith (see **lex orandi, lex credendi**).

Written tradition and unwritten secret tradition. With Basil of Caesarea (d.379), there is an appreciable development in the concept of apostolic Tradition. Although one of the arguments used in anti-Gnostic controversy was the refusal to admit that the apostles had transmitted secret teachings to which only the initiated had access, Basil distinguishes between the tradition of the *kerygma* (preaching), which was open to all, even to the unbaptized, and that of the dogma (doctrine; see **dogma**), reserved for the initiated, i.e. to those partaking of the sacraments* (*On the Holy Spirit* 27.66). According to the bishop of Caesarea, this distinction derives from the apostles and fathers, who from the beginning arranged all that concerns the churches. In fact, these unwritten secret traditions mainly concerned the rites, formulas and prayers used in the celebration of baptism* and the eucharist.* Basil was alone in his day in developing a theory of the secret: he distinguished between traditions of two kinds (*kerygmata* and *dogmata*) but affirmed that "both have the same force for the faith".

The council of Nicea II, the reformers, the council of Trent. At the council of Nicea II (787), the reverence offered to the holy images was legitimized by the Tradition of the church. This Tradition comprises both written and unwritten elements. The written tradition is the gospel but also the writings of the holy fathers, whereas the holy images and the veneration accorded to them, e.g. to the book of the gospels and to the cross, belong to the unwritten tradition. In practice, Christian antiquity, especially the Greek and Oriental, did not always see clearly the distinction between scripture, commentaries on it, and the various traditions which constituted the fabric of the church's life. The Tradition appeared to it rather as a living continuity with the church of the apostles and fathers, with scripture at its heart.

A clear distinction of the kind implied above between scripture and the traditions began to establish itself in the West in the 12th and 13th centuries with the desire for a life in accordance with the gospel *sine glossa*, with the scholastics, then with John Wycliffe and Jan Hus, who, in the name of scripture and the

"The Last Supper", by the contemporary Japanese artist Sadao Watanabe

pure gospel, rejected those traditions which contradicted them and identified the apostolic Tradition with scripture (see **Tradition and traditions**). They had thereby laid the foundations for the principle which was to become one of the pivots of the Reformation, first with Luther and then with Calvin: that of *sola scriptura*, on the basis of which every tradition was rejected which appeared not to be founded directly on the canonical text of scripture. Calvin does indeed frequently cite the fathers, but he does so in order to explain the pure gospel which the apostles deposited in writing as "sure and genuine scribes of the Holy Spirit" (*Institutes* 4.8.9).

Reacting to this position, in 1546 the council of Trent* affirmed that "the truths and rules" of the gospel are preserved "in [all] the written books" of the OT and NT "and in the unwritten traditions, which, received by the apostles from the mouth of Christ himself or from the apostles themselves, have come down to us in the Catholic church in unbroken succession" (H. Denziger, *Enchiridion Symbolorum*, 1501). The council refused to set scripture in opposition to the apostolic Tradition but wished at the same time to maintain the position of Basil and Nicea II. Post-Tridentine theologians often misinterpreted this, believing that in juxtaposing scripture and oral traditions, the council was pointing to two sources of the Christian revelation.* Some subsequently went so far as to assert that truth is "partly" in scripture and "partly" in the unwritten traditions.

Scripture and Tradition in the contemporary ecumenical movement. Only in the second half of the 20th century did we begin to emerge from the blind alley of four centuries' conflict between Protestants and Catholics, thanks partly to a better acquaintance with the history of the church and partly to ecumenical contacts with Orthodoxy. Eastern Orthodox teaching, already mentioned in connection with Nicea II, remained in fact a living reality in the churches of the East. These, in particular, attach great importance to the teachings of the councils and the fathers on the one hand, but also to the celebration of the liturgy, on the other, as living and authoritative witnesses to the apostolic Tradition. The participation of the Orthodox in the work of the Faith and Order* commission of the WCC and in the debates of Vatican II* as active observers helped to get the dialogue moving again.

The fourth world conference of F&O in Montreal (1963) produced a report on "Scripture, Tradition and the Traditions" which, by starting from the Tradition of the gospel (the *paradosis* of the *kerygma*; see **Tradition and traditions**), considerably transformed the approaches to the problem.

In November 1962 the Second Vatican Council rejected a draft text entitled "The Sources of Revelation" and then drafted and promulgated another text entitled "The Word of God" (the constitution *Dei Verbum*). This text outlines the central place of scripture in the life of the church, the relationship (concordance) between scripture and Tradition, and the role of the magisterium* (the teaching of the bishops, councils and the pope) in the authentic interpretation of the word of God.* The originality of this text lay in its recalling that the apostolic Tradition had preceded the scriptures of the NT (para. 7), and that the apostolic Tradition embraces the whole life and faith of the church and is continued in the church (para. 8). Scripture and Tradition, "flowing out from the same divine wellspring, come together in some fashion to form one thing and move towards the same goal. Sacred scripture is the speech of God as it is put down in writing under the breath of the Holy Spirit. And Tradition transmits in its entirety the word of God which has been entrusted to... the successors of the apostles so that, enlightened by the Spirit of truth, they might faithfully preserve, expound and spread it abroad by their preaching. Thus it comes about that the church does not draw her certainty about all revealed truths from the holy scriptures alone. Hence, both scripture and Tradition must be accepted and honoured with equal feelings of devotion and reverence" (para. 9). In no way, however, is Tradition a "source" of revelation independent of scripture.

That the problem of the Tradition has largely been settled is recognized in the dialogue between the Christian communions since Montreal and Vatican II (Anglican-Lutheran 1972, paras 32-44; Anglican-Orthodox 1976, paras 9-12; 1984, paras 47-52 and 90-92; Anglican-Roman Catholic 1981, para. 2; Disciples-Roman Catholic 1981, paras 46-56; Lutheran-Roman Catholic 1972, paras 14-34;

1980, paras 62-65; 1984, para. 57; Reformed-Roman Catholic 1977, paras 25-30). Following the official responses of the churches to the Lima document on *Baptism, Eucharist and Ministry*,* further clarifications are under way on the relationship between church and word of God, scripture and Tradition.

See also **apostolicity, Tradition and traditions**.

EMMANUEL LANNE

Y. Congar, *La tradition et les traditions* (ET *Tradition and Traditions in the Church*, London, Burns & Oates, 1966) • H. Meyer & L. Vischer eds, *Growth in Agreement: Reports and Agreed Statements of Ecumenical Conversations on a World Level*, WCC, 1984 • P.C. Rodger & L. Vischer eds, *The Fourth World Conference on Faith and Order: Montreal 1963*, London, SCM, 1964 • G. Tavard, *Holy Writ or Holy Church? Crisis of the Protestant Reformation*, London, Burns & Oates, 1959.

APOSTOLICITY. Although the concept of apostolicity is not found explicitly in the New Testament, the basic range of ideas it expresses appears in such passages as Acts 2:42 ("And they devoted themselves to the apostles' teaching and fellowship, to the breaking of bread and the prayers"), John 20:21 ("As the Father has sent me, even so I send you") and Eph. 2:20 ("built upon the foundation of the apostles and prophets, Christ Jesus himself being the cornerstone"). Together with unity,* holiness* and catholicity,* it is one of four concepts traditionally regarded as marks or essential qualities of the church.*

Although some Protestants explicitly reject the notion of (Roman) catholicity, all churches claim to be apostolic in the broad sense of the word. Apostolicity is not an essentially contested concept to the same extent as catholicity is. Nevertheless, to the extent that the apostolic succession of bishops, guaranteed (as has often been claimed) by the laying on of hands, is treated as a necessary condition of both catholicity and apostolicity, there is still a sharp contrast between many Protestants, on the one hand, and the Roman Catholic Church, the Orthodox churches, the Anglican communion and some Lutheran churches, on the other, all of which do have bishops and also claim to have preserved the apostolic succession intact. Many Protestants stress instead their faithfulness to the pure doctrines and biblically legitimated practices of the original apostles as the main (if not the sole) criterion of genuine apostolicity.

The uncontroversial aspects of apostolicity were summarized by a WCC Faith and Order consultation at Chantilly in January 1985 as part of the study "Towards the Common Expression of the Apostolic Faith Today". The church is *apostolic* (1) in that it recognizes its fundamental identity with the church of Christ's apostles, as presented in the NT; (2) in its faithfulness to the word of God lived out and understood in the apostolic tradition, guided by the Holy Spirit throughout the centuries and expressed in the creeds; (3) by its celebration of the sacraments instituted by Christ and practised by the apostles; (4) by the continuity of its ministry (whether in the apostolic succession or otherwise is not specified here because it is dealt with elsewhere; see further below), initially taken up by the apostles, in the service of Christ; (5) by being a missionary church which, following the example of the apostles, will not cease to proclaim the gospel to the whole of humankind until Christ comes again in glory. The trend in current ecumenical thinking is to see the basis of what is now called "our unity in the apostolic faith" in the Old and New Testaments, the Apostles' Creed* and the Nicene Creed,* and in the two dominical sacraments of baptism* and the eucharist,* all as interpreted primarily by the classical ecumenical councils.*

In addition to the problems posed by the historic episcopate and the apostolic succession guaranteed by the laying on of hands, a number of other issues also arise with respect to the content of the "apostolic faith", e.g. which councils are indeed ecumenical (and should therefore be received by the whole of the undivided church); whether the two Marian dogmas do or do not belong to the basic apostolic tradition; and whether the filioque* clause should or should not be included in the classic credal statements of the church.

The concept of apostolicity through the ages. "Apostolicity" is derived from the Greek verb *apostellein*, to send out (on an errand or a mission). As a basic concept, apostolicity is intimately related both to the message and to the bearers of the message. The original messengers were the apostles

mentioned in the NT. There were also Jewish emissaries who taught in the synagogues and collected taxes to support the rabbis. In late Judaism, however, the task of the *shaliach* was not transferable to others, because theirs was an ad hoc ministry. The Jewish *shaliach* did not have an explicit ecclesiastical status, so his role cannot be regarded as an ecclesiastical office. His authority was precisely defined by the one who sent him and ended when he had accomplished each mission.

Likewise, Jesus was sent by the Father. In turn, Jesus called, commissioned and sent out his own disciples to proclaim the coming of the kingdom of God* and to teach the radical ethic of the kingdom. After Jesus' death and resurrection, however, the main task of the apostle was to proclaim that Jesus had indeed risen from the dead. Paul uses the noun "apostle" to denote those sent out by local churches (e.g. Titus in 2 Cor. 8:23). In the primitive church, there were more apostles than the original twelve called by Jesus, e.g. the successor of Judas, and Paul himself. Peter was often regarded as the first of the apostles: hence the development of a Petrine ministry in the Roman Catholic Church (see **primacy**).

Although it is sometimes argued that the apostolic ministry of the original eye-witnesses was unique and not directly transferable to successors, few Christians would deny that the church is apostolic in the sense that it is built upon the foundation of the original apostles (to the extent that it proclaims their message and performs the same essential tasks). In this sense, the notion of apostolicity is "absolutely basic to the church's comprehension of itself", as J.N.D. Kelly insists (*One in Christ*, 1970). Furthermore, the second generation of Christian teachers and evangelists (appropriately called the apostolic fathers) believed they were acting "in the manner of an apostle", as Ignatius claimed in the 2nd century. Nevertheless, Ignatius did not claim that he was acting in an official capacity or by virtue of an explicitly apostolic status; indeed, he clearly states that he was *not* acting "as an apostle" (*Letter to the Trallians* 3.3).

In other words, the quality or attribute of apostolicity is primarily an attribute or quality of the whole church. Its ministry is apostolic because the church itself is (or should be) apostolic. Its teachings are apostolic because, as Justin tells us, they are the "memoirs" of the apostles (e.g. *First Apology* 66.3). The church is, therefore, apostolic to the extent that it participates in the original mission which Jesus entrusted to his own disciples. Those whom Jesus originally commissioned and sent out were commanded not only to teach all nations but also to baptize them in the name of the Father, the Son and the Holy Spirit (Matt. 28:19). They were also commanded to commemorate the Lord's death "until he comes", i.e. by celebrating the eucharist in remembrance of Jesus.

But if apostolic ministry involves the right kind of proclamation and the right kind of sacraments, what is the right kind of teaching and sacraments? To counteract heretics and schismatics, lists of authoritative writings circulated, showing which scriptures had been produced by the original apostles or were believed to have originated from an apostle. In this way, the principle of a canon* of scriptures eventually emerged. Apostolic teachings were also officially codified in the form of creeds* such as the Nicene Creed and

the Apostles' Creed. The latter was not (as was once believed) composed by the original apostles, but its common name does illustrate the point that authoritative witness is indeed supposed to be apostolic.

Derivation from the original apostles thus became an essential criterion of what is genuinely apostolic. It is not surprising, therefore, that in the disputes with heretics and schismatics at the end of the 2nd century, Irenaeus and Tertullian began to stress not only the continuity of authentic Christian teaching with the original apostolic preaching but also the historical links in the processes of tradition which, eventually, go right back to the original apostles. Irenaeus states that "those who were appointed bishops in the churches by the apostles and those who have been their successors down to our own day" not only possess "true knowledge" but also preserve "the ancient structure of the church throughout the world, and the character of the Body of Christ according to the successions of the bishops to whom they entrusted the church which is in every place" (*Against Heresies*

Ordination, Armenian Apostolic Church (WCC/John Taylor)

3.3.1 and 4.52.2). Hence the importance which came to be given to Tradition* — the process of handing on the original apostolic message — and to the authoritative interpretation of the original message, whose meaning was now the subject of theological dispute. The process of interpretation also generated traditions, i.e. authoritative interpretations of the original message. Authentic interpreters could trace their line of succession right back to the original apostles, while ecumenical councils were also regarded as authentic interpreters of the same apostolic tradition. Succession lists were soon drawn up in order to demonstrate which bishops were indeed entitled to claim that their sees were apostolic. The so-called apostolic succession by laying on of hands thus came to be seen as a guarantee of authoritative apostolic teaching and validly performed sacraments.

While Tertullian had insisted that every local church founded by an apostle or *sharing in the same apostolic faith* is indeed an "apostolic church", in the writings of Cyprian, Jerome and Augustine (for example) the apostolate and the episcopate are virtually identified.

During the Reformation,* the intervening accumulation of "innovations" seemed to many Protestants to contradict the traditional assumption that only the faith and practice of the *original* apostles is authentically apostolic. The criterion "by scripture alone" was thus applied in order to determine which doctrines were pure and which practices were genuinely apostolic. It was no longer believed that apostolic succession could guarantee the purity and the continuation of apostolic faith and practice — hence the rejection of both apostolic succession and the office of bishops, since which time, episcopacy, ministry and ordination have been controversial issues between many Protestants and the episcopal churches. The question of whether apostolic faith and practice could legitimately "develop", which was raised again by Newman in the 1840s, also became a crucial ecumenical issue.

Apostolicity in recent ecumenical thinking. As previously stated, an ecumenical consensus presently exists upon a wide range of issues relating to the apostolicity of the church. Although there is substantial progress on the issue of development of doctrine and the precise relationship between apostolic witness and apostolic succession, it cannot yet be claimed that all of these issues have been finally resolved. Development of doctrine has been discussed primarily by Anglicans, Lutherans and Roman Catholics, especially in the US. The obvious questions are: What are the precise criteria of legitimate and illegitimate developments? And who decides what the criteria should be? Such questions cannot easily be answered as long as either the NT church or the classic conciliar period is regarded as absolutely normative. There is as yet no consensus on the disputed question of the relationship between continuity and change in the Christian church, except for the impossibility of simply repristinating whatever is regarded as *the* normative period.

This particular issue, however, has been placed in a new context by the growing realization that apostolicity is a process with both a historical and an eschatological dimension. Even if the structures of "apostolic ministry" which soon developed in the early church have indeed been preserved intact, the *fullness* of church unity, holiness, catholicity and apostolicity will not be realized until the advent of the kingdom of God. This recognition relativizes the previous assumption that particular churches have been perfect societies in the past or are perfect at this present moment (perfect in this case meaning *ecclesiologically* correct, as distinct from morally perfect — a rather different matter). No single church is invulnerable to criticism; all, therefore, need to change. "Normative periods" can no longer simply be appealed to in order to unite divided churches or to realize the fullness which unity, holiness, catholicity and apostolicity ultimately seem to require. The notion that the church has ever been undivided and completely perfect (in an ecclesiological sense) is increasingly regarded as a historical myth.

The relationship between apostolic witness and apostolic succession has been discussed primarily in the F&O section of the WCC, especially in the process which produced the Lima text of 1982 on *Baptism, Eucharist and Ministry* (BEM).* Basically, the solution now offered to the still-divided churches assumes that what has traditionally been called apostolic succession does not necessarily guarantee faithfulness to apostolic faith and practice, though the recovery of the traditional threefold ministry (including bishops) could properly be regarded as a sign that apostolic continuity has been preserved in practice. The role of charismatic and prophetic leadership is also stressed. In the first place, however, it is the Holy Spirit that keeps the church "in the apostolic tradition until the fulfilment of history in the kingdom of God" (M34). Most important, it is "the apostolic tradition of the church as a whole" which is now regarded as the "primary manifestation of apostolic succession", though the ministerial succession (by laying on of hands) is also treated as "an expression" of both the permanence and the continuity of the original apostolic mission. The orderly transmission of the ordained ministry not only emphasizes the vocation of the minister but also expresses the continuity of the church throughout history. Ministerial structures which do not serve the apostolic faith ought to be reformed (M35).

While it is explicitly stated that apostolic continuity has been preserved in churches which did not retain "succession through the episcopate" (M37), it is also hoped that non-episcopal churches will accept "episcopal succession as a sign, though not a guarantee, of the continuity and unity of the church" (M38). In other words: "The church as the Body of Christ and the eschatological people of God is constituted by the Holy Spirit* through a diversity of gifts or ministries. Among these gifts a ministry of episcope is necessary to express and safeguard the unity of the body. Every church needs this ministry of unity in some form in order to be the church of God, the one Body of Christ, a sign of the unity of all in the kingdom" (M23). Finally, in order to proceed to the mutual recognition of ministries, it will be necessary for those churches which have preserved episcopal succession to recognize the apostolicity of non-episcopal churches and their ministers; while churches which lack episcopal succession are invited to strengthen and deepen their own apostolic continuity by recovering what is called "the sign of the episcopal succession" (M53).

See also **apostolic Tradition, catholicity, episcopacy, faith, ordination, teaching authority, unity**.

PETER STAPLES

Baptism, Eucharist and Ministry, WCC, 1982 ● "Catholicity and Apostolicity: The Report of the World Council of Churches-Roman Catholic Joint Theological Commission", *One in Christ*, 6, 1970 ● R.P.C. Hanson, *Groundwork for Unity: Plain Facts about Christian Ministry*, London, SPCK, 1971 ● H.G. Link ed., *One God, One Lord, One Spirit: On the Explication of the Apostolic Faith Today*, WCC, 1988 ● H.J. Urban & H. Wagner eds, *Handbuch der Ökumenik*, vol. 3, part 1, pp.142-69, Paderborn, Bonifatius, 1986.

ART IN THE ECUMENICAL MOVEMENT. Art as a medium of ecumenical communication was not much evident in the initial period of the ecumenical movement. The main medium of expression was verbal, either delivered at ecumenical meetings or written and printed as reports and study materials.

Theological emphasis on the proclamation of the word of God enforced the trends in biblical preaching and Bible study in the pre-television era. However, even in the earlier period, coming out of involvement in mission fields, there were some pioneers who made the arts once again relevant. Daniel J. Fleming published *Each with His Own Brush: Contemporary Christian Art in Asia and Africa* (1938), and Arno Lehmann introduced artistic expressions of Christian faith in the third world in his books *Die Kunst der jungen Kirchen* and *Afroasiatische Christliche Kunst* (1957 and 1966).

In the assemblies and major ecumenical conferences, the presence of the members of the Orthodox churches who brought their colourful altar icons* not only carried a traditional continuity but also awakened the artistic sensitivity of many participants. The Uppsala assembly (1968) broke the dominating verbal way of communication and added stimulation with the Czech puppet film *Homo Homini* and the dramatic presentation led by Olov Hartman.

The Nairobi assembly (1975) was not only filled with the sound of African drama and music but also enriched by the powerful African artworks related to the theme "Jesus Christ Frees and Unites", which were exhibited in various parts of the Kenyatta conference centre where the assembly met. There were also enlarged reproductions from *Christian Art in Asia*. One of the striking artworks, in terms of artistic challenge, was brought by the Brazilian sculptor Guido Rocha, "The Tortured Christ", which vividly depicted the agonizing cry of people under oppression and in captivity.

As preparation for the Vancouver assembly (1983), a set of 14 pictures was published to promote the discussion of the theme, "Jesus Christ — the Life of the World". Artistic symbols and images were taken more seriously at the Vancouver assembly than at previous ecumenical gatherings. It included the setting aside of a native arbour, "a sacred meditative area among the trees". Also a 15-metre totem pole was raised on the campus of the University of British Columbia, later permanently located in the grounds of the Ecumenical Institute at Bossey, as a reminder of the spiritual quest through the ages and also showing concern for the land claims of all native peoples. There was a major Asian Christian art exhibition, supervised by Yushi Nomura, containing 50 original works by 22 Asian artists. There was also a film festival and a children's art exhibition on assembly themes. The most significant fact of the Vancouver assembly in terms of Christian art was that it treated art not as a side show but as a central part of the life of the assembly. In fact the whole experience of worship in a tent was an occasion of celebration, utilizing all the gifts of God, including visual art and music. With the aid of a film on Andrey Rublyov's famous 15th-century icon of the Trinity, the assembly was led in a meditation on the Triune God, the ultimate ground for both the unity of the church and the renewal of the human community.

In 1978 the Christian Conference of Asia* sponsored the first consultation at Bali for Asian Christian artists, which resulted in the formation of the Asian Christian Art Association. Since then it has published a quarterly, *Image: Christ and Art in Asia*.

Various fascinating African Christian artworks were compiled by Josef Franz Thiel. On the world level, two books written by Hans-Ruedi Weber show the ecumenical relationship between Christian faith and the visual arts.

MASAO TAKENAKA

M. Takenaka ed., *Christian Art in Asia*, Tokyo, Kyo Bun Kwan, 1975 ● J.F. Thiel, *Christliche Kunst in Afrika*, Berlin, Reimer, 1984 ● H.-R. Weber, *On a Friday Noon: Meditations under the Cross*, WCC, 1979 ● H.-R. Weber, *Immanuel: The Coming of Jesus in Art and the Bible*, WCC, 1984.

ASCETICISM. Christian asceticism is as old as the church. We find warrant for it in the account of the temptation of Jesus in the desert. There we find all the elements later used in the ascetic traditions: the isolation of the desert, a harsh, disheartening environment which puts one entirely at God's mercy and in which it is not possible to escape God's presence; fasting, which indicates that we seek to live by God alone, and not by what we can do ourselves; meditation on scripture, the key to distinguishing between spirits (1 Cor. 12:10); temptation; and the power of the Spirit, which guides the soul safely on its path despite all the promptings of the Enemy. This path is the opposite of the path of pride, violence and self-glorification — in fact it is the way of the cross in the footsteps of Jesus.

This way of following Christ was experienced first in the very earliest centuries of the church during persecutions. Its ideal is martyrdom,* undergone not arrogantly but with forgiveness for the persecutors. After the peace of Constantine in the 4th century, the monastic life embraced a new way of following Christ (intended to be just as radical), with self-denial and an opening of oneself to the mercy of God through all of everyday life.

Some of the desert fathers and those who followed their example subjected themselves deliberately to great sufferings to renew the power of the spirit over the body and so come closer to the angels, who are bodiless spirits and see God. But sometimes the only purpose of that suffering was to enable them to be one with the suffering Christ and show him the genuineness of their love.

Their search for an austerity which would detach them from the attractions of the flesh and the refinements of civilization soon led them to chastity, which called for complete commitment to the age to come, to poverty and effective care for the poor, and finally to obedience to a chosen or simply accepted guide.

Another line of tradition in Eastern and Western monasticism is the quest for purity of heart and continuous prayer, two aspects of the same mystery. Purity of heart removes everything that stands in the way of the pursuit of love towards God and one's fellow human beings. It comes even more from our experience of God's mercy than from extended efforts at self-purification. It develops through setting a watch over the heart against proud and vain thoughts, doubts, grudges, desires for revenge or domination. It also progresses through compassion for all God's creatures, through a desire for the salvation of souls, including if possible the souls of the damned in the hell which is theirs.

Constant prayer would make it possible to have real contact of the whole person with God, because it harmoniously eliminates the conflict between head and heart. This prayer is the antidote to every kind of modern depression and to the grip of ideologies and systems, as well as to the childish, credulous sentimentality which might distort our faith. If that faith remains living and true, our common enterprises as Christians of different churches will have their source very close to God and will be safe from rivalries, discouragements and activism; and perhaps together we shall then be able to discover fruitful solutions to the problems of our day, including the divisions among Christians.

As followers of Christ, we are called to remain in company with God, in the radiance of his splendour, to reject pride and hatred, to consider others as greater than we are, always to hope* and to impart hope, to devote ourselves to serving the poor and to being witnesses in this world of a merciful and forgiving God. Our prayer life should be like a great retreat and should detach us from comfort, the consumer society, prejudices, and collective selfishness, so that together we may listen to the word of God* and, in the face of temptations, discover the way Christ marks out for us today. "If anyone would come after me, let him... take up his cross daily and follow me" (Luke 9:23).

See also **mysticism**.

SUZANNE ECK

ASIA: CHINA. Nestorian Christianity was introduced into China in the 8th century. It disappeared with the demise of non-Chinese hegemony because the majority of its adherents were not ethnic Chinese. In the 13th century John of Mountecorvo, a Roman Catholic, attempted mission but had no lasting results. In the 16th century the Italian Jesuit Matteo Ricci was more successful due to the missionary practice of accommodation, an attempt at interfaith dialogue* and adoption of indigenous Chinese forms of worship, customs and culture.* Ricci was ahead of his time; his method soon led to the rites controversy between the Vatican and the Jesuits and the banning of Jesuit activity in 1702 by the pope. The significance of this story is that it raised for the first time the principle of missionary indigenization. That issue continues to influence discussions, whether Roman Catholic or Protestant.

In 1807 a Protestant missionary Robert Morrison was sent out by a society that was at the time non-denominational. Indeed, the largest of all societies in terms of missionary personnel, the China Inland Mission, now the Overseas Missionary Fellowship, has always been non-denominational. In the numerous areas where CIM worked, the churches it set up were not allied to a Western denomination except in West China, where the Anglican CIM workers were concentrated. In the late 19th century, beginning about 1873, an independent movement with Chinese leadership was much in evidence. It was part of a movement which coincided with the tumultuous years before the founding of the People's Republic in 1949. That movement is represented by such indigenous churches as the Little Flock (1924), the True Jesus Church (1917), the Jesus Family (1926) and independent gospel halls. Such groups were mostly biblicist and ethnicist in orientation and tended to be highly critical of the theologies and polities of the missions-related denominations. Today, as earlier, the inheritors of the independent church tradition are the most reluctant ecumenists.

The foregoing occurred within the larger story of the struggles of Chinese people — the moral and political bankruptcy of the Ch'ng dynasty, the humiliations of the unequal treaties with Western colonial powers, the republican revolution, the partition of China by the warlords, the desperate and unsuccessful attempts at reform, the anti-Christian movements, massive famine and starvation, the complete breakdown of social and political fabrics, the Japanese invasions, the founding of the People's Republic and the regimentation of life under communist rule.

None of these circumstances could encourage ecumenism. The situation is further compounded by the popular perception of Protestantism and Catholicism as two different religions, one worshipping the King Above (Shang Di), the other the Heavenly Lord (Tian Thu). The conditions for ecumenicity were, at the best, limited.

Nevertheless, there have been significant, if sporadic, signs towards oneness and ambitious, if ambiguous, attempts at unity.* There were missionary conferences in 1877, 1890 and 1907, comity agreements and co-operation in publishing of Bibles, tracts and other literature. Co-operation in education, especially at the university level but also secondary and theological education, began very early and was seminal in forming the church leaders who after liberation led the church unity movement. The influence of the YMCA* and the YWCA* was always a unifying factor. After liberation the leadership which the people provided was absolutely determinative in many ways, not least ecumenically. Other pre-liberation expressions of ecumenical life included relief programmes and the more than occasional joint evangelistic programmes and campaigns, where there was common planning in the cities and much exchange of preachers. In the 1940s the relief programmes produced the first working contacts between Protestants and Catholics, one step towards unity.

Against this background the beginning of the ecumenical movement in China is earlier than the founding of the National Council of Churches (NCC) in 1922. NCC included perhaps half of the Protestant Christian bodies, mainly the more liberal ones. There were however, some non-theological reasons for some not joining the NCC, e.g. the deep hesitation of the Chinese to centralize power.

The Church of Christ in China was formed in 1927. It was a united church composed of Presbyterians, Congregationalists, Methodists and Baptists. It became the largest church in China, with about 120,000 members.

When the WCC was founded in 1948, four Chinese churches were present. Indeed, T.C. Chao, a noted theologian at Yenching University, was elected one of the six presidents. Chao, however, resigned in 1952 in protest against the WCC's approval of UN intervention in the Korean war. This proved to be the last major act of participation in the WCC for over 30 years, though at the time of writing, there are rumours of a Chinese return to the WCC.

Worship at a meeting point in Shanghai (WCC/ Peter Williams)

In 1949, the communists came forcibly to power. They drastically reduced the number of churches throughout the country and sent pastors and priests to farms and factories. But there were two other developments: the founding of the Three-Self Patriotic Movement and the Catholic Patriotic Association (CPA). The former was conceived in 1951 but formed in 1954 as the only legitimate umbrella grouping for Protestant activities. The parallel CPA held its first national congress in 1957. Both movements were formed at the behest of the government and not as expressions of ecumenicity. However, denominations did not die out immediately with the founding of the two movements because most of them existed formally until the cultural revolution (1966). Ties with foreign churches were severed in 1951, with the outbreak of the Korean war, but even before that, church workers and Buddhist and Taoist clergy were being "laicized", and some were imprisoned. In any case, with the founding of the Three-Self Patriotic Movement, Chinese Protestantism entered a post-denominational period.

The formation of the CPA meant that the government had decided to split the RCC. Pope Pius XII, on the other hand, also forced the issue as to which side the Roman Catholics must take, under pain of excommunication. We currently have CPA and an RC underground church which consecrated 50 bishops, thus compounding the delicate situa-

tion between the two. Neither side has declared the other schismatic.

From 1966 to 1976, under the cultural revolution, organized religious life was impossible. Church premises were taken over, and
public worship was stopped, forcing Christians to meet in homes. The cultural revolution and other anti-religious campaigns, however, had positive influences on human ecumenical relations. Personal contacts and
friendships born in prison among Catholics
and Protestant clergy have helped to change
the previous mutually hostile images. Contacts established in the working meetings of
religious leaders by the bureau of religious
affairs have also helped, and with Buddhist
and Muslim leaders as well. But formal Roman Catholic-Protestant conversations are
still non-existent, though in Hong Kong, for
practical reasons, informal talks occur. The
house church* movement, which has always
been a part of Chinese Christianity, assumed a
new and all-important role. New communities
of faith, consisting of Christians from different traditions, came into being all over the
country.

In 1980 another important stage of the story
of China began, as the nation opened its door
to the world once again. Public worship resumed, first with the ethnic Koreans in Shen-
yang and a few churches in Shanghai. The
Three-Self Patriotic Movement met for the
first time in 20 years. In this first meeting,
two major decisions of historic dimension
were made. It announced the formation of the
China Christian Council, which would henceforth be responsible for the pastoral and
theological needs of the churches. Also, it
acknowledged the legitimacy of the house
churches. "All Christians, whether worshipping in church premises or at homes, (should)
share in the same mind, looking towards
Jesus."

Since then the China Christian Council
(CCC) has helped reclaim, restore and re-
institute over 5,000 congregations, set up 14
Bible schools and a seminary, and established
other support ministries. There is now a common hymnal, a common catechism* as a common offering to the churches. Ties with overseas churches both mainline and evangelical,
and with ecumenical organizations, have also
been re-established. But the invitation to the
Lausanne-in-Manila congress on world evan-

gelization failed to materialize. There is
as yet no resumption of membership in any
international Christian body. However, in
1989, the CCC officially sent a delegation to
the WCC world mission conference in Texas,
USA. In 1981 an official delegation of the
CCC, led by Bishop K.H. Ting, had met with
the leadership of the Christian Conference of
Asia in Hong Kong. Soon afterwards, official
contacts with the WCC began.

In 1984, the Amity Foundation was
formed, inspired and led by Christians. Given
the principle of self-support of the Chinese
churches, the Amity Foundation was seen as a
new instrument to facilitate Christian involvement in China's modernization, particularly in
the fields of education, health and social
work. The foundation has received much personnel and financial support from both within
and without China. With the help of the
United Bible Societies,* it built a printing
plant which has since turned out 1 million
copies of much-sought-after Bibles.

At about the same time, intensive effort
was made by the CCC towards a united
church. Although there was a great deal of
Christian support, the attempt was finally
dropped or postponed due to a strong minority
opposition. The Christians of the Little Flock
tradition recognize the local church* as the
only genuine form of the church. While they
have participated in the CCC, they could not
envisage being part of a nationwide church.
The choice was either to go ahead and form a
united church without the dissenters or to
shelve the idea. The latter option prevailed. A
contributing factor was the traditional suspicion many Chinese Christians harbour towards the idea of the episcopacy.*

Despite the difficulties, the decade since
1979 has probably been the most encouraging
and fruitful period for Chinese Christianity in
a century. Faith* is taking root. Witness* is
maturing. The churches are growing. And a
spirit of ecumencity is slowly but clearly taking hold within China.

In June 1989, the army brutally crushed the
pro-democracy demonstrations in Beijing,
and similar protests were suppressed in the
major cities in China. In many cases, Christians had been involved in the popular movement for democracy. Since then, the religious
affairs bureau has taken a more direct administrative role in religious activities, impos-

ing a tighter rein on the churches. At the same time, interest in the Christian faith and participation in Sunday services have increased visibly among the urban population. The days ahead will be difficult for the churches but not without cause for confidence.

For future ecumenical development, one of the most interesting factors is the effect Hong Kong's return to China will have. In 1997, Hong Kong will become a special administrative region of China. Relations between the churches in the city and on the mainland will be watched closely by the rest of the world.

See also **Christian Conference of Asia**.

RAYMOND FUNG

R. Fung, *Households of God on China's Soil*, WCC, 1982 • Wing-hung Lam, *Chinese Theology in Construction*, Pasadena, CA, William Carey Library, 1983 • A.S. Lazzarotto, *The Catholic Church in Post-Mao China*, Hong Kong, Holy Spirit Study Centre, 1982 • B. Whyte, *Unfinished Encounter, China and Christianity*, London, Collins Fount, 1988.

ASIA: NORTHEAST. This entry covers Japan, Korea and Taiwan; a separate entry deals with China.*

Japan. Although Japanese imperial court chronicles report a visit by Nestorian Christians in 736, there is no record of their activities in Japan. The first missionary to Northeast Asia was Francis Xavier in 1549, but in the 17th century the Catholic church disappeared from Japanese history not only because of severe persecution but also because of rivalry between the Jesuits and other orders. Japanese ports were closed to foreigners in the 17th century, except for Dutch traders, who were considered anti-Catholic and allowed into Nagasaki; they did not engage in mission work.

The first Protestant missionaries to Japan came in 1859 and believed in co-operation in mission. The first Japanese Protestant church was founded in Yokohama, in affiliation with Presbyterian and Reformed missionaries, as the Japan Christian Catholic Church. They sought to work with US Congregationalist missionaries to create united churches, but the Congregationalists rejected the plan for union; and as other missionaries arrived, foreign denominations were transplanted onto Japanese soil.

The spirit of unity stayed alive in evangelistic and educational work, including the Sunday school and Kingdom of God movements. A federation of Christian churches in Japan was formed in 1911, and the National Christian Council of Japan was organized in 1948. Although Protestant churches were eager for unity on the eve of the second world war, the formation of the United Church of Christ in Japan came about because of pressure from the militarist government, which sought uniformity of Christians in the interest of wartime co-operation.

After the war, Anglicans, Lutherans, Unitarians and other denominations left the United Church; and parts of the Baptist church, Salvation Army and other churches also became separate denominations. Remaining in the United Church were other Baptists, most Presbyterian-Reformed, Methodists, Congregationalists, Disciples, Evangelical United Brethren and some others.

During the next 40 years, the United Church repented of its collaboration with the militarist government and strengthened its inner unity. Although it is now financially independent, its schools and other institutions continue to employ many foreign fraternal workers in the conviction that this ecumenical presence is important for Christian education.

Many Japanese Christians have been ac-

A local congregation in Seoul worships in the street (WCC/Peter Williams)

tively involved in the work of the Christian Conference of Asia (CCA) and the WCC. Among the ecumenical issues they are concerned with are the plight of the burakumin and other minority groups in Japan such as Koreans and the Ainu (see **minorities**), the controversies around emperor worship and Shintoism as a state religion, and interfaith dialogue.*

Korea. Protestant Christianity was introduced to Korea in 1884 by US Methodist and Presbyterian missionaries. When Japan colonized Korea in 1910, the churches were persecuted for their leadership in the independence movement. After the second world war, the country was divided at the 38th parallel. The churches in South Korea grew rapidly, with some of their leaders taking important roles in the democratization of the country. The Presbyterian Church, however, has divided into numerous smaller denominations, most of them conservative and remaining outside the National Council of Churches, which co-ordinates ecumenical efforts in the country.

The NCC has provided significant leadership both nationally and internationally, working as it does in close co-operation with the CCA and the WCC. Through the difficult years of the people's struggle against dictatorship, the NCC and the churches were a rallying point for democratic forces in the country. The influence of the church among students and intellectuals was to a large extent due to the stand it took against militarism* and state control. A number of church leaders were in the forefront of the pro-democracy movement and suffered years of imprisonment. The CCA Urban Rural Mission involvement led to the organization of workers, often exploited in the name of national development. The emphasis on indigenization led in the 1960s to the birth of minjung theology.* The reunification question is high on the ecumenical agenda.

Christians in North Korea were long isolated from the outside world. Beginning in the late 1970s, the (North) Korean Christian Federation has had some contact with foreign Christians, which accelerated in the mid-1980s and led to a series of meetings with South Korean church leaders on the re-unification of the country. In 1988 Protestant and Roman Catholic church buildings were built in Pyongyang, the first since the independence of Korea.

Taiwan. During the 16th and 17th centuries, Portuguese and Dutch occupied some parts of Taiwan but did not leave much Christian impact. Catholicism was re-introduced into Taiwan in the 18th century.

In 1865 the British Presbyterian Mission began work on the island, and it was soon followed by Canadian Presbyterians. Since that time, the Presbyterian Church in Taiwan has accounted for the majority of the Protestant population, although after the Nationalist Chinese retreated to Taiwan, other denominations began missions there.

During the 1970s the Nationalist government forced the Presbyterian Church to withdraw its membership in the WCC, but this was later restored, and the church is actively engaged in ecumenical work. An ecumenical co-operative committee, whose membership includes the Roman Catholic Church as well as Protestant churches and organizations, co-ordinates ecumenical relationships.

See also **Christian Conference of Asia**.

TOSH ARAI

K.T. Cho ed., *Comparative Chronology of Protestantism in Asia, 1799-1945*, Tokyo, International Christian University, 1984 • D. Hoke ed., *The Churches in Asia*, Chicago, Moody, 1975 • K.S. Latourette, *A History of the Expansion of Christianity*, vol. 6, New York, Harper, 1944 • T.K. Thomas ed., *Christianity in Asia*, vol. 1, Singapore, CCA, 1979.

ASIA: SOUTH. The countries that lie south of the Himalayas — India, Pakistan, Bangladesh, Sri Lanka, Nepal and Bhutan — are here taken as belonging to South Asia. Afghanistan also is often included. While there are many general features and common factors among these countries, even within this sub-region of Asia the diversity is considerable. All are located within the tropical or sub-tropical zone, though there are significant differences in climate among and within them.

An oft-noted characteristic common to South Asian countries is the influence of religion.* Three religions — Hinduism, Islam and Buddhism — dominate the scene. There are minority religions also, including Christianity. Generally the religious orientation of the people pervades every sphere from social and economic life to science, literature and art. The traditional way of life is largely determined by ritual and belief.

The people of South Asia are predominantly agricultural. More than 90% of them live in villages, whereby they depend on traditional forms of agriculture for their livelihood. The basic economic conditions of the countries are similar. All are very poor, and in general the largest are the poorest. Social and economic inequalities are extreme and are usually most pronounced in the poorest countries. There are considerable differences among the individual countries, but poverty and inequality are universal.

For many generations, change has come slowly. Society is characterized by a hierarchical social system with a large number of caste* groupings. The joint family* is another basic institution in the societies of South Asia. In spite of some perceptible changes in traditional cultures, in general South Asia continues to be rural and conservative.

The countries have a common cultural heritage. Several possess a wealth of ancient textual literature. There is considerable similarity, reflecting common traditions in music and dance, rituals, customs and modes of worship.

Most of the countries of South Asia share a common colonial past under the British. Independence accelerated a revolution of rising expectations, but the lot of the vast majority has not improved since independence, while disparities have widened. The general religious outlook appears to have acted as a force for social inertia and against modernization ideals which have been officially accepted.

A South Asian Association for Regional Co-operation was established in 1975, composed of Bangladesh, Bhutan, India, the Maldives, Nepal, Pakistan and Sri Lanka. It has formed several economic, cultural and technical committees to provide for inter-regional technical assistance.

In 1988 there was an ecumenical development in Christianity of significance for the whole of the sub-region. At the 1988 Lambeth conference the united churches of South India, North India, Pakistan and Bangladesh, which were in full communion with the see of Canterbury, were received into "full membership". In other words, while the united churches of Asia belong to Asia, they also belong to a wider oikoumene, just as the ecumenical

giants from that part of the oikoumene, such as D.T. Niles and Bishop V.S. Azariah, made significant contributions to the ecumenical movement as a whole.

Afghanistan. Landlocked Afghanistan, known originally as Ariana, was formed as a separate state by Ahmed Shah Durrani in 1747. The last king of Afghanistan, Zahir Shah, reigned from 1933 to 1973 when the monarchy was overthrown by a coup. In April 1978 another coup brought communists to power, leading to fighting between traditionalist Muslim rebels and the Afghan army and then Soviet military intervention at the end of 1979. In early 1988 a UN-sponsored agreement was reached for the withdrawal of Soviet forces.

The principal languages of Afghanistan are Pashtu and Dari. The majority of Afghans are Muslims of the Sunni sect. There are minority groups of Hindus, Sikhs, etc. According to the constitution, "Muslims are free to practise religious rites, as are members of other religions, provided they pose no threat to Afghan society". Afghanistan is essentially a tribal society. Agriculture is the mainstay of the economy.

Christians are not a significant minority. However, there are issues of ecumenical concern. There is obviously the matter of inter-religious relations, especially between the majority Muslim population and small religious groups. There is the unfolding drama of relationships between religious groups and a Marxist government. In this regard it may be noted that the government makes attempts to win over Islamic groups. But perhaps more important is the matter of human rights infringement. In September 1989 the government admitted to holding 2,125 political prisoners. Some of them had been sentenced by special revolutionary courts which did not conform to international standards. There have also been extra-judicial executions by Afghan security forces and Soviet troops.

Bangladesh. The People's Republic of Bangladesh is surrounded by Indian territory except for a short southeastern frontier with Burma and a southern coast facing the Bay of Bengal. The present-day Bangladesh was formerly East Pakistan, formed after the partition of British India in 1947. Though it began with parliamentary democracy at the time of independence, a series of military coups resulted

Agricultural worker in India (WCC/John Taylor)

in military government which, in spite of some parliamentary processes, has remained virtually unchanged. With the exception of a few small city states, Bangladesh is the most densely populated country in the world. In terms of average income, it is also among the world's poorest countries. Poverty is as much an economic issue as a religious and ecumenical one.

Ninety-five percent of Bangladeshis speak Bengali; 85% are Muslims, and there are small minorities of Hindus, Buddhists and Christians. With a recent constitutional change Islam has become the state religion of Bangladesh. Obviously the ecumenical issue in this country is one of religious co-existence and tolerance.

India. The Republic of India forms a natural sub-continent, having a territorial unity bounded by the Himalaya mountain range to the north and the seas in the west and the east. India, "the jewel of the British Empire", became independent in 1947 and has since maintained a parliamentary form of democracy. The sheer size of the country contributes to the difficulty of national consolidation, but the achievements in terms of national unity, in spite of the various centrifugal forces, are remarkable.

The official language is Hindi, with English as an associate language. There are 16 regional languages and many other local languages. Religiously, 83% are Hindus and 11% Muslim (the second largest Muslim population in the world). There are about 2.5% Christians and smaller percentages of Sikhs and Buddhists. Cultural and religious pluralism is a major ecumenical issue.

India presents much diversity and many contradictions. There has been significant economic growth, but with its vast population (second only to the People's Republic of China) the country remains among the 20 poorest. On the basis of aggregate gross national product, India ranks among the 15 largest economies in the world.

Nepal. Nepal is a landlocked country in the Himalaya mountain range, with India to the east, south and west and the People's Republic of China to the north. It is a constitutional monarchy with the executive power vested in the king, who presides over the national assembly. It is a mountainous country, and the terrain is generally inhospitable. It is among the least-developed countries in the world. Poverty is a major issue.

Nepali is the official language; 95% of the population are Hindus, and Buddhists and Muslims constitute the rest. Religious pluralism is an ecumenical issue.

Pakistan. The Islamic Republic of Pakistan was founded in 1947 by Quaid-e-Azam Mohammed Ali Jinnah. Today 97% of the population are Muslim. Bordered by India on the east, Afghanistan and Iran on the west, it was formed by the partition of the former British Indian empire into the independent states of India and Pakistan. Not only was the new country split into two wings, east and west, separated by over 1,000 miles of Indian territory, but also many vital arteries were severed in the process. The national language is Urdu.

Pakistan has been subjected to religious and sectarian clashes between Shias and Sunnis, between Mohajirs, on the one hand, and Sindkhis, Pathans and Punjabis, on the other. These clashes have been manipulated by politicians, religious leaders and bureaucrats to their respective ends. Thus the nation has divided horizontally and vertically.

In the 11-year-rule of General Zia, which ended in August 1988, the period was dominated by strenuous Islamization, armed forces and US presence. The US presence was to ensure that Pakistan became the conduit for the US supply of arms to Afghan Mujahideen who had rebelled against the Soviet-backed Afghanistan government. Thus the US meddled in the internal affairs of Pakistan.

Given the involvement in Afghanistan, militarization and militarism were inevitable.

But in the process, the armed forces bolstered the tyrannical rule of Zia, resulting in widespread violations of human rights with consequent scars. Besides, partly as a result of the militarization of Pakistan, the economy of the nation has considerably declined.

Committed to the Islamization of Pakistan, Zia invoked the penal aspects of Islamic jurisprudence but ignored the socio-economic aspects of Islam. In the name of the sharia, there were public floggings, cutting off of hands and stoning to death. It did, however, mean discrimination against and victimization of minorities such as Hindus and Christians. The introduction of Hudood Ordinance and laws relating to the "Diyat" and "Qisas" discriminated against women and minorities. And though the founder of Pakistan gave assurances of safety to minorities, such groups continued to be marginalized. In that context, the established churches generally did not speak against injustice or give leadership in the community. A few Christian leaders spoke up and gained the support of progressive sections of the majority community. Such occasions became rare opportunities for meaningful Muslim-Christian dialogue* in struggle as well as for churches to exercise their prophetic ministry. Christian leaders and Christian politicians have united with Hindus to campaign against the system of separate electorates (1985), which has compartmentalized minorities in terms of the national electorate, reducing them to second-class categories as well as reneging on the rich tradition of Islam.

Sri Lanka. Until 1972 called Ceylon, Sri Lanka consists of one large island and a few smaller islands situated in the Indian Ocean, close to the southern tip of India. It is a multiracial nation. In 1981 Sinhalese composed 74% of the total population of 14.85 million, Tamils 18% (two-thirds are Sri Lankan Tamils, one-third Indian Tamils), with Malays and Burgers among the other 8%. Significant is the fact that 92% of the North and 68% of East are Tamil. Religiously too the country is pluralistic. Buddhists (mostly Sinhala) are in the majority, followed by Hindus (mostly Tamils), Muslims, and Catholics and "Christians" (i.e. Protestants). This distinction reveals the division in Christianity, which was compounded by the lack of love between the Portuguese, who introduced Roman Catholicism, and the Dutch, who first brought in Protestantism. Today there are also Methodists, Anglicans and others who came in with the British who held the island until its independence in 1948.

An ethnic conflict between the majority Sinhalese and the minority Tamils has escalated since 1983, and a political settlement has proven elusive. Some of the factors in this tragedy are the attempt to build a nation on the Sinhalese Buddhist culture, resentment of Tamils (who in some regions have economic clout), as well as a fear of Tamils as the bridgehead of Indian imperialism in Sri Lanka. Thus the ecumenical issue includes race relations, living with religious pluralism, violence and refugees resulting from the violence, some of which is state directed. In 1983 there were some 200,000 Tamil refugees alone. In the process, Christian groups have suffered for their alleged support of or sympathy with the minority groups. For example, on 9 April 1983 the Roman Catholic Church of Our Lady of Refuge, Jaffna, was bombarded for alleged complicity with the Tamils.

Secular and religious ecumenical groups have sprung up to search for peace and justice in the nation, including the Movement for Inter-Racial Justice, and the Council for Communal Harmony through the Media. On the side of religious ecumenism may be mentioned Pravidi Handa (the voice of the clergy), which includes Christian and Buddhist religious leaders, working together for peace and justice. In 1983 there was formed the Committee for Rational Development, composed of Sinhalese, Tamils, Muslims and Burgers of different political persuasions to assist in finding solutions to contemporary social problems on the basis of strengthening democratic institutions and encouraging rational process in society.

See also **Christian Conference of Asia**.

NINAN KOSHY

M. Azariah, *Mission in Christ's Way in India Today*, Madras, CLS, 1989 • S. C. Neill, *The Story of the Christian Church in India and Pakistan*, Grand Rapids, MI, Eerdmans, 1970 • G. Robinson ed., *Sharing and Living: A Study on the Ecumenical Sharing of Resources in India*, Arasaradi Tamilnadu Theological Seminary, 1983 • *The Sri Lanka Search for a Liberating Spirituality*, Colombo, Ecumenical Institute for Study and Dialogue, 1989 • M. Zachariah, *The Christian Presence in India*, Madras, CLS, 1981.

ASIA: SOUTHEAST. Geographically, Southeast Asia corresponds to the Indo-Chinese peninsula, which includes the countries of Cambodia, Laos, Malaysia, Singapore and Vietnam. However, ecumenical use of the term includes also the countries of Burma, Indonesia, the Philippines, and the Crown Colony of Hong Kong. Except for Thailand, these countries all came under Western colonial domination between the 16th and the 20th centuries. Colonial domination in most cases provided easy access to Southeast Asia's teeming populations by Christian missions, thus ensuring the churches they planted both social prestige and power for the duration of the colonial era. And yet, Christian missions in most Southeast Asian countries were not able to make profound and massive penetrations into their vast populations, owing perhaps to the previous hold of other religions upon them. These other religions, primarily Buddhism and Islam, have penetrated deeply into the cultural psyche of the peoples of Southeast Asia in a way that makes it difficult for any new religion to make much impact. Culture* and religion* have blended together in a way that has resisted massive conversions. And the way Christianity came to this part of the world, deeply ensconced as it was in an evangelical-eschatological world-view and in a pietistic-moralistic ethos, obscured to an extent the meaning of the gospel. On the other hand, there were many stories of love and sacrifice on the part of Christian missionaries, which allowed the gospel to find powerful expression within Southeast Asian culture.

The Philippines is somewhat of an exception to the foregoing description, as it never came under the full sway of any of the major religions. Its spiritual culture therefore offered no resistance to Christianity. When the Philippines finally launched a revolution against Spain, its revolutionary leaders had the sophistication to make a distinction between the gospel and those who sought to abuse it.

In terms of numbers, Christianity is a minority religion in Southeast Asia. The only country where Christianity is predominant is the Philippines, about 85% of whose population is Christian. Indonesia's huge population is overwhelmingly Muslim, though Christianity exerts an influence disproportionate to its numbers, perhaps because of a highly educated group of Christians who found themselves in influential positions when it had wrested its independence from the Dutch. Pancasila, the state ideology of Indonesia, is tolerant of the existence of other religions and does not overtly restrict evangelistic activity. Malaysia, on the other hand, is an Islamic state which prohibits Malaysians from converting to Christianity. Myanmar (Burma) and Thailand are overwhelmingly Buddhist countries and pose no restrictions on evangelism politically and socially, although their peculiarly tolerant spirit resists the conversion* experience. Singapore has many faiths — Islam, Christianity, Hinduism, Buddhism, Confucianism and Shintoism — and religion is tolerated as long as it remains privatized. Vietnam, Laos and Kampuchea are predominantly Buddhist societies with some Christian presence.

After the second world war, a strong pressure for self-determination swept through Asia. Sensing that foreign domination would no longer be tolerated by the peoples of Asia, the colonial powers granted independence to their colonies, but only after ensuring that they would enjoy favourable terms in trade relations with their former colonies. Such arrangements plus the imposition of Western democratic structures that were not sufficiently rooted in the culture and traditional power structures of the countries in the region gave rise to complex socio-political problems that sometimes give the impression that the peoples of these countries are not quite capable of self-governance. Most of Southeast Asia except the city state of Singapore, the Crown Colony of Hong Kong, and Taiwan have not been able to achieve economic stability for the simple reason that the economies remained dependent on the old imperial powers. The old colonial masters had established an elite who immediately saw that they could wield enormous powers — and gain great wealth in doing so — by serving the interests of their former masters rather those of their own people. This practice created a socio-political dynamic that spawned more problems than it could deal with, increased the gap between the rich and the poor, and unwittingly provoked radical movements that favoured communism.

In the late 1960s, Southeast Asia, like most under-developed areas, plunged into national development programmes which in a way were of a piece with the dependent-economy syndrome fostered by the powerful countries of the West. And though a few Southeast Asian societies were able to pull themselves out of poverty — notably Singapore, Hong Kong and Taiwan — most of them were pushed down deeper into it by the development process. As a consequence, Southeast Asian populations have become restive and have worked to dismantle socio-political structures subservient to the West, thus plunging their populations into the East-West ideological conflict. Thus some of the Southeast Asian societies have become, in varying degrees, highly conflictual societies as two contradictory ideological forces push their peoples in internecine conflict.

This is the cultural and socio-political context in which the young churches in Asia live and witness. Not surprisingly, the churches themselves have not been exempt from ideological polarization. Some churches claim an apolitical stance in the social and political maelstrom they find themselves in, and a few self-consciously situate themselves within the ideological conflict; others simply see their mission as one of rendering service to the

Vietnamese grandfather and child (WCC/Helmut Reuschle)

poor* and of remaining in solidarity with them.

The ecumenical regional body in the area, the Christian Conference of Asia (CCA), has played a theologically avant-garde role. It sees its mission as the inculturation of the gospel in Asian cultures, engagement in dialogue (see **dialogue, interfaith**) with the living faiths in the region, the proclamation of the gospel in a holistic way, expression of solidarity with the poor in their struggle for justice and human dignity, and the search for the unity* of the church through acts of diakonia* and a deeper understanding of its various symbols. The CCA has taken the lead in doing contextual theology in Asia, in developing new forms of worship and spirituality, in grappling with the complex realities of poverty, injustice, and religiosity, and in developing an Asian identity for the church.

It is increasingly difficult to witness to the gospel of justice, truth and freedom in the Southeast Asian context due to the emergence of authoritarian governments which impose peace and order on their terms. The CCA was expelled from Singapore in 1988 by the Lee Kuan Yew government because its acts of solidarity with the poor were interpreted by the government to be a threat to its national security. Conditions in other Southeast Asian countries, though not as politically unreceptive as in Singapore, are also characterized by ideological conflicts where either part may find some CCA activities repulsive. The peoples of this Asian region are still in the process of struggling for a genuine democratic society, and that search is often thwarted by the ideological forces in the region. One of the urgent tasks of the CCA is the search for a theological as well as a political vision that can transcend the current ideological tension and participate in the Asian task of breaking from the bonds of economic, political and cultural domination of the West, and create a church and a people that are truly Asian.

See also **Christian Conference of Asia**.

LEVI V. ORACIÓN

V. Fabella ed., *Asia's Struggle for Full Humanity*, New York, Orbis, 1980 ● *People against Domination: A Consultation Report on Peoples' Movements and Structures of Domination in Asia*, Singapore, CCA, 1981 ● *Religions and Ideologies in the Asian Struggle, Assembly Proceedings*, Asia Regional Fellowship, 1987.

ASSOCIATION OF INTERCHURCH FAMILIES.

Founded in 1973 in England, the AIF was formed for the mutual help and support of members of interchurch families, that is, families resulting from marriages between committed members of their respective churches, usually a Roman Catholic and a Christian of another communion. It also welcomes clergy, relatives, godparents, and all involved with the pastoral welfare of such families. The AIF is run by those who are themselves partners in interchurch marriages.

There are now sister associations in Scotland, north and south Ireland and several countries in Europe. International conferences have been held every two years since 1980, with couples from Britain and Ireland, France, Finland and Australia, as well as clergy who minister to interchurch families in the USA and New Zealand.

The AIF is pastorally concerned for mixed marriages in which denominational differences have been a factor in weakening the Christian commitment of one or both of the partners. One can find interchurch couples at every point on the ecumenical scale, which runs from competition, through co-existence to co-operation and commitment on the way to full communion. AIF members would probably find themselves somewhere in the area of co-operation or commitment. Partners at the "competition" stage often feel that their differences are too painful and potentially destructive to their marriage to risk open discussion of religious belongings. And those at the co-existence stage may be accepting the churches simply as a set of co-existing "clubs", each with its own static life-style and rules, so that the partners have little incentive to work for church unity.*

The AIF believes that interchurch couples are in a unique position of responsibility for the promotion of Christian unity. Their marriage is a living, day-to-day meeting point between the churches. Interchurch families are the smallest of the ecumenical communities in which Christians of different traditions are living and working together. In their marriages they "live the hopes and difficulties of the path to Christian unity" (Pope John Paul II to interchurch families, York, 1982).

Like other Christian families, the interchurch family is a "domestic church", but the difference is that it belongs to the one church of Christ through belonging to both communions of the partners, who intend to call upon the resources of both churches in their work of evangelizing and teaching their children. This perspective has become possible only because the churches have set themselves on a course of convergence towards that unity which Christ wills for his church.

It is a difficult path. These families are often living at a stage on the way to Christian unity which is further ahead than that of their churches as a whole. This is why they constantly make representations to their church authorities, asking for consideration of their deeply felt need for eucharistic sharing (see **intercommunion**) and for shared celebrations of baptism* for their children.

The AIF raises the underlying questions of "double belonging" or dual membership for the children, if not the parents, of interchurch families. The 1986 report sums up the ecumenical concern. First, double belonging concerns the whole ecumenical movement and not just interchurch families; when we become involved in interchurch relations and get to know a church other than our own, we come by degrees to share more and more in its life and to belong to it; this double belonging is an immediate aim of the ecumenical movement. Second, while the churches are not yet in full communion* with each other, it is impossible for participants in the ecumenical movement and for interchurch couples to have the same relationship with a church other than their own.

See also **mixed marriage**.

RUTH REARDON

J. Coventry, *Mixed Marriages between Christians*, London, CTS, 1981 • M. Finch & R. Reardon, *Sharing Communion: An Appeal to the Churches from Interchurch Families*, London, Collins Liturgical, 1983.

ASYLUM.

The word "asylum" is derived from the Greek *asylon*, a place of refuge. In current history it is primarily used in connection with the plight of refugees.* One of the basic problems of refugees who have fled their countries is their lack of legal protection, as they can no longer count on their own governments to protect them.

The 1948 Universal Declaration of Human Rights confers on individuals a right "to seek and enjoy" asylum. But in spite of other international instruments (the 1951 convention relating to the status of refugees, the 1967 declaration on territorial asylum), the right of asylum is not recognized by international law as an individual human right. The right to grant or to refuse asylum is the prerogative of each state.

Historically asylum has had the meaning of sanctuary. In early civilizations, the tradition of religious protection was well known; only temples and altars under the protection of a deity could provide refuge. The Old Testament tells how God commanded Moses to create six cities of refuge so that a person who unintentionally committed a murder might escape blood vengeance (Num. 35:9-15; Deut. 4:41-43 and 19:4-13). In the Christian church of the 4th century, bishops often provided sanctuary. This privilege continued to exist, though in ever more restricted forms, until the establishment of national states in the 16th century.

Since the early 1980s, asylum issues have been high on the agenda of the ecumenical movement. A major ecumenical consultation on asylum was held in Zurich in May 1986, where participants struggled to find appropriate church response to refugees with inadequate legal protection.

One of the ways in which churches, especially in Western countries, have been involved in asylum is through offering of church asylum. This implies sheltering refugees in church buildings as well as providing refuge in church congregations. Most widely known is the sanctuary* movement in the USA, which began in 1982 with the sheltering of Salvadoran refugees who were not granted asylum by the US government. By providing shelter and protection, churches and congregations not only accepted responsibility for the immediate legal and physical needs of that refugee but also challenged the premises of US foreign policy.

In the course of the 1980s a rapidly growing number of churches and other religious communities in Western Europe have started sanctuary actions, in direct response to the increasingly restrictive asylum policies and practices adopted by Western governments. By upholding the rights of refugees and protecting those threatened by deportation to countries with oppression and civil war, these churches respond to the biblical call for solidarity with the powerless and the persecuted. The sanctuary actions are also seen in the context of the churches' struggle for justice through challenging national laws and practices that are deemed to be in violation of international legal commitments.

There is no legal basis for sanctuary actions, and sanctuary workers may therefore violate the law, risking fines and even imprisonment. This has already happened in the US.

The British Council of Churches made a policy statement which called for a fundamental review of the UK immigration policy, law and practice, giving a number of concrete suggestions to that effect. The statement then continues: "Failing measures such as these to overcome the current difficulties, sanctuary movements and other efforts to protect threatened individuals and families are likely to increase. The council believes that it is inappropriate that it should give support to evasion of the UK immigration laws. Where, after a full exploration of an impending deportation, Christians believe that fear of persecution is well-founded, there is a serious threat to family life and/or there is the possibility of gross injustice, and they decide to challenge the law, the council is clear that they can claim no special privileges with regard to the consequences of their action. The council nevertheless fully understands the dilemmas involved and respects the courage and integrity of those who stand with and support vulnerable and fearful people in their search for a safe and secure future."

Sanctuary is a movement at the local level. It has created tensions within congregations but has sharpened the awareness of the churches about crucial asylum questions. It has stirred up extensive debates at all levels of the churches on the legal, political and theological issues involved, including church-state* relations.

GEERTRUIDA VAN HOOGEVEST

ATHANASIAN CREED. This document, also known as *Quicumque Vult*, from its opening words, is an outline in Latin of Trinitarian and Christological theology (including the filioque*). It is a didactic poem rather than a creed. In its preface and conclusion it is stated that belief in the truths it asserts is necessary for salvation.* The text includes a series of anathemas.*

The Athanasian Creed has no connection with Athanasius of Alexandria. It is a product of the Western church, indebted to the thought of Ambrose, Augustine and Vincent of Lérins, and was probably composed in southern Gaul or Spain. Scholarship in the early 20th century argued for a date between 381 and 428. Many authorities, influenced by the work of J.N.D. Kelly, now place the document after 428. It is likely that it was composed in the late 5th or the 6th century. The synod of Autun in the 7th century refers to it as "the faith of St Athanasius". By the next century it was accepted in the liturgical books of the Western church, and by the 13th century it was valued as the third *symbol*. The Eastern churches seem to have become acquainted with it during the filioque controversies.

In the Carolingian period the Athanasian Creed entered the breviary and from there passed into the Anglican tradition for feast days. The Book of Common Prayer of the Church of England contains it before the litany. In the Book of Common Prayer of the Episcopal Church in the USA, it is included among the "historical documents". Lutherans have retained it as a statement of faith in the Book of Concord of 1580, and it appears in the Lutheran Book of Worship in the USA. In other churches of the continental Reformation this creed never assumed much importance. It has appeared, without the filioque clause, in the service books of the Greek and Russian Orthodox churches since the 17th century.

The Athanasian Creed is neither a doxological creed, nor is it a narrative confession of faith. It is an intellectual and theological exposition. Attempts have been made to remove it from the official books of some churches. Such actions have been motivated by the unpopularity of the anathemas in the text. Today the Athanasian Creed plays neither theologically nor liturgically a very great role in the churches. It is not regarded as an ecumenical resource, as is the Nicene Creed* of 381.

WILLIAM G. RUSCH

A.E. Burn, "The Authorship of the *Quicumque Vult*", *Journal of Theological Studies*, 27, 1925-26 • J.N.D. Kelly, *The Athanasian Creed*, London, Black, 1964.

ATHEISM. The Greek word *atheos* (without God) is unknown in the Bible, both in the Septuagint and in the New Testament, with a single exception: in Eph. 2:12 it is used to describe the darkness in which gentile Christians lived before their conversion; they were "without God in the world". In general Greek usage, "atheist" described one who denied the recognized gods or otherwise deviated from prevailing religious customs. Frequently the term was used in all its ambiguity as a tool in religious or political polemics. Thus not only Epicurus, a materialist, but also Socrates, a thinker with a philosophical faith, could be accused of atheism. Accordingly, Jews and Christians were often regarded as *atheoi* by their pious contemporaries.

In the modern sense of a general denial of God, or godlessness, the term first crops up in European thought in the 16th and 17th centuries. It became an extremely complex and equivocal term. Several different senses can be identified: *theoretical* atheism, arising out of an irreligious world-view (e.g. among the materialistic thinkers of the French Enlightenment, such as Paul-Henri Holbach, or in the German League of Monists [Monistenbund] and other free-thinking circles); unformulated *practical* atheism, as an abandonment of any activity related to God (though without necessarily denying God in theory); *programmatic* atheism, a struggle against religion considered as alienation and demeaning (Ludwig Feuerbach, Friedrich Nietzsche); *political* atheism, with the aim of liberating humanity from exploitation by throne and altar (Marx, Lenin), and of course soon with the ideological intention also of controlling the citizens' souls in totalitarian fashion by enforced elimination of the "uncertainty factor 'God'" (Stalinism and neo-Stalinism); *psychologically motivated* atheism, which sees religion as an illusion in which the "oldest, strongest and most imperious desires of humanity" (Freud) are projected; *existential* atheism, due to the experience of suffering or the will for unlimited freedom (Albert Camus, Jean-Paul Sartre); and finally, as an extreme form of atheism, the nameless and featureless secular approach which dismisses the quest for meaning. There is also the *theological* concept of atheism which distances itself critically from traditional theism in order to be able to "believe in God atheistically" (the "God is dead" school).

In its many guises atheism today has become both a challenger and a partner of theology and the church and must be taken seriously. This is something relatively new. During the greater part of church history it was assumed that humanity had an almost natural piety. This view can be seen in the Bible, where the real challenge to Israelite and NT faith was "gentile" religiosity as a belief in *gods*, not the absence of a God or gods. Right up to modern times this was the rule in the history of religion and culture, as the atheist was if anything a curious exception. In the last few centuries the world has changed in this respect for theology and the church, especially in industrial societies. The process of secularization* has led to secularism and the entrenchment of this world within its own bounds on the basis of the "dogma of immanence": on this view our cosmos and our history have no transcendence. For more and more people atheism seems a more natural option for existence than does religion. Here a distinction must be made between an atheism that is "methodological" and one that is part of a world-view. It is one thing to consider that God never appears within his creation* as a tangible object of scientific study and that we therefore should carry on as if God did not exist; it is another to turn this principle into a philosophical dogma and advocate a "scientific atheism" as a philosophical system or basic existential attitude.

In view of the reductionist tendency in atheistic thinking (eliminating or re-interpreting the "vertical" dimension of human existence), Christian theology and the church must engage critically with atheism. This debate, however, has often been conducted with a lack of relevance and not in the spirit of the gospel. Without any careful distinctions, the word has been used as a term of abuse to describe and censure not merely explicit denial of God but any deviation from established doctrine. The struggle against atheism has used not merely arguments but every kind of repression, including political and physical means. This response has ignored the fact that atheism arises not always as a purely arbitrary act but also in response to shortcomings in church theory and practice.

This is why ecumenical thinking today is striving for an attitude to atheism which is sensitive to different nuances. Although Vatican II,* in harmony with previous encyclicals, still condemns atheism because it "casts man down from the noble state to which he is born" (*Gaudium et Spes* 21), it reveals itself as self-critical in regard to how atheism comes about, and open to the need that "all men, those who believe as well as those who do not, should help to establish right order in this world where we all live together". And the Faith and Order study document *One God, One Lord, One Spirit* (1988) emphasizes that "contemporary atheism may today be challenging believers to purify their notion of God".

Thus in its encounter with atheism the oikoumene today is moving "from anathema to dialogue". Here experiences from Eastern Europe are instructive and encouraging. The question of God and attempts to give a credible answer to it have in no way been superseded and settled in an ideologically and programmatically atheistic society. In the course of the Christian-Marxist dialogue, it came to be recognized even among a good number of atheists that "God is not completely dead" (Vítezslav Gardavsky). And the Christians came to see that the gospel holds good for atheists too (see Josef Hromádka, "Gospel for Atheists").

See also **faith, God**.

JAN MILIC LOCHMAN

V. Gardavsky, *Gott ist nicht ganz tot* (ET *God Is Not Yet Dead*, Harmondsworth, Penguin, 1973) ● J.L. Hromádka, *Die marxistische Religionskritik und der christliche Glaube* (ET *The Christian Faith and the Marxist Criticism of Religion*, Edinburgh, St Andrew, 1970) ● H. Küng, *Existiert Gott?* (ET *Does God Exist? An Answer for Today*, Garden City, NY, Doubleday, 1980) ● F. Mauthner, *Der Atheismus und seine Geschichte im Abendlande*, Berlin, 1920-23, reprinted, Hildesheim, G. Olms, 1963 ● J. Turner, *Without God, without Creed: The Origins of Unbelief in America*, Baltimore, Johns Hopkins UP, 1985.

ATHENAGORAS I (Aristokles Pyrou).

B. 25.3.1886, Tsaraplana (northwest Greece, then under Turkish domination); d. 6.7.1972, Istanbul. Athenagoras was ecumenical patriarch of Constantinople (1949-72) and leading figure in the contemporary development of the Orthodox church and the ecumenical movement.

After studies in Halki, Pyrou became a

monk and deacon, adopting the name of the 2nd-century apologist Athenagoras, who sought the Logos in the wisdom and poetry of the "heathen". In Macedonia during the Balkan wars (1912-13) and the first world war he came face to face with human diversity, acquired a knowledge of Islam and learned firsthand about atrocities and revolutions. After serving as secretary to the holy synod, he became metropolitan of Corfu in 1923. When Mussolini occupied the island, he intervened as "ethnarch" (defender of the community), and when Asiatic Greece collapsed under the Turks, he saw to it that the refugees had food, care and work.

In 1931 Athenagoras was named archbishop of the Greek church in America, then torn by political dissensions imported from Greece and swollen in numbers by refugees from Asia Minor. He instituted biennial meetings of clergy and laity (the latter in the majority) to define the main directions of pastoral work. A friend of Presidents Roosevelt and Truman, he supported their social policy; and when he was elected ecumenical patriarch in 1949, the US looked to him to foster Greco-Turkish reconciliation in the face of communism. Six years later he was placed in a disappointing and dangerous situation when Turkish nationalists launched pogroms against the Greek Orthodox in Cyprus.

Athenagoras determined to "set aside all the cares of the world" to serve Christian unity by gathering together all the Orthodox churches in conciliar fashion. He secured the position of the Greek church in the WCC despite continuous obstacles and supported WCC membership for Eastern European churches, ratified at New Delhi (1961).

Convinced that dialogue between Orthodoxy and the Christian West must also include the Roman Catholic Church, Athenagoras devoted himself to transforming relations that had long been marked by distrust and ignorance. Learning of Pope Paul VI's pilgrimage to Jerusalem in December 1963, Athenagoras proposed that leaders of *all* confessions gather there "to ask in common and fervent prayer... on our knees, with tears in our eyes and in a spirit of unity... that for the glory of the holy name of Christ and for the well-being of all humanity the way may be opened to the complete restoration of Christian unity".

Although the time was not ripe for such a meeting, the pope did agree to meet the patriarch, and on 5 and 6 January 1964 they exchanged blessings and the kiss of peace after reading Jesus' prayer in John 17. Thus began a "loving dialogue" between Rome and Constantinople and a genuine friendship between the two men, recorded in their posthumously published letters and declarations (see **Orthodox-Roman Catholic dialogue**). On 7 December 1965, during the Second Vatican Council, in which Orthodox observers took part, the anathemas* of 1054, which had symbolized the separation of Eastern and Western Christendom, were abrogated. In July 1967 Paul VI went to Istanbul and in a gesture of reparation knelt at the very place in St Sophia where the Roman delegates had brought the anathema.

At the same time the patriarch undertook to undo the estrangement among the Orthodox churches brought about by the system of "autocephalous" churches and aggravated by religious nationalism. After a 1950 encyclical failed to revitalize Constantinople's disputed rights as the primatial see, he began patiently and realistically to work out the idea of primacy as a sacrificial offer of service. He proposed (but never imposed) initiatives, travels and meetings (including pan-Orthodox conferences in the 1960s) which finally led to a consensus not so much primatial as a display of a universality and communion.

In October 1967 Athenagoras made a successful journey to bring together and consult with the Balkan daughter churches of Constantinople. Amidst enormous popular enthusiasm in Belgrade, Bucharest and Sofia, he preached the union of Orthodoxy in the service of Christian unity. Although the Soviet government compelled the Moscow patriarchate to sidestep the coming of Athenagoras, he nevertheless consulted it. With the agreement of all the canonical Orthodox churches, he then undertook to go to Western Europe in October-November 1967 as a "pilgrim for unity".

He began with Paul VI in Rome, where he celebrated a service of peace and forgiveness, venerated the tombs of Peter and Paul and received young people in an unforgettable service at St Paul beyond the Walls. Next he went to the ecumenical centre in Geneva, where he described Western Christianity as a

Athenagoras I (WCC/John Taylor)

fragmented whole which might be helped to reconstitute itself through a disinterested and peace-making Orthodox presence. Finally he was welcomed in London by the Anglican archbishop of Canterbury Michael Ramsey.

Athenagoras's vision was of an evangelical, eucharistic and conciliar church in which the various confessions would meet as "sister churches"* on the basis of the apostolic faith "in faithfulness to the traditions of the fathers and the inspiration of the Spirit", and around an axis of universal agreement, a renewed Roman primacy,* a "presidency of love" no longer above the church but in the centre of its fellowship and in its service. He distrusted abstract theological speculation designed to prove oneself right by discrediting others. Above all he wanted to translate ideas into the language of experience, holiness and service.

A preoccupation of Athenagoras was re-establishing eucharistic fellowship, which he saw not only as a confirmation of a re-established unity of the faith* but also as an anticipation of that unity, through the force of love, so that differences could be investigated, not simply by looking forward to the eucharist,* but under its light (see **communion, inter-communion**).

In June 1968 a pan-Orthodox conference at Chambésy near Geneva (where Athenagoras was determined to set up an Orthodox centre, a place where there was freedom and ecumenical contacts) resolved to call a council for

aggiornamento (updating), which would be prepared by a whole series of conferences. For Athenagoras the realist, this apprenticeship to conciliarity* mattered more than the council itself.

The patriarch's last years were difficult. Hardening of Soviet policy after the 1968 invasion of Czechoslovakia brought intense conflicts between Moscow and Constantinople, paralyzing the preconciliar process. The crisis of faith that shook the Western churches and a corresponding increase in fundamentalism in Orthodoxy, in which the most moderate theologians could not accept the patriarch's views on intercommunion, increasingly isolated him.

Athenagoras then tried to begin a dialogue in depth with Islam, as well as encouraging the reconciliation of Chalcedonian and pre-Chalcedonian Orthodox (see **Oriental Orthodox-Orthodox dialogue**) and outlining a deep and simple spirituality for people of today. He emphasized Christianity not as law but as creative inspiration ("knowing how to live"), the fellowship or communion of individuals and the miracle of living creatures, and the humble illumination of everyday life through the presence-in-absence of the unknown who has become our secret Friend and through the church, witnessing and praying for all and influencing the development of the universe and humanity through the attractive force of Christ's resurrection.

OLIVIER CLÉMENT

The letters of Paul VI and Athenagoras (in Greek, *Tomos Agapes*) were published in English in *Towards the Healing of Schism*, E.J. Stormon ed., Mahwah, NJ, Paulist, 1987 • *Apostolos Andreas* (review of the Ecumenical Patriarchate, Istanbul), 1951-64 • O. Clément, *Dialogues avec le Patriarche Athénagoras*, 2nd ed., Paris, Fayard, 1976 • S.C. de Medicis, *Athenagoras 1er, l'apport de l'Orthodoxie à l'oecuménisme*, Lausanne, L'Age d'Homme, 1968 • B. Ohse, *Der Patriarch Athenagoras von Konstantinopel. Ein ökumenischer Visionär*, Göttingen, Vandenhoeck & Ruprecht, 1968.

AUSTRALIA. The Christian churches came to Australia with European settlement in 1788. For the first 20 years or so, the Church of England was the only denomination holding regular worship. When Irish settlers began to arrive, the Roman Catholic Church was established, and the first public mass was celebrated in 1820. As other settlers came from England and Scotland, they brought their churches with them, as well as their denominational structures and prejudices.

Early church history in Australia was characterized by competitiveness rather than co-operation. There was strong antagonism between Protestant and RC churches. The latter feared the established power of the former, while the Protestants were suspicious of RC religious practices. The mutual prejudices were reinforced by strong nationalist feelings between the Irish and English and Scottish settlers. The bitter divisions were aggravated further by arguments over privileges relating to land grants and education, the latter being closely tied to the parish churches. Class divisions, too, separated RCs and Protestants. Many RC settlers came to Australia to escape hardships of the Irish famine and so were disadvantaged economically and socially, while the Protestant clergy associated with the gentry.

There were divisions within each of the established churches: between low- and high-church Anglicans; between the Presbyterian churches from England and those from Scotland; between Wesleyan and Free Methodists, and numerous other splinter groups within each denomination. There were divisions also among the churches of the various state colonies. The early 19th century brought with it more denominations, including the Baptist and Lutheran churches, the Society of Friends and the Churches of Christ. The Salvation Army entered Australia in 1880. The first church of the Orthodox tradition, the Greek Orthodox Church, was established in 1897. As frontier townships grew throughout Australia, churches vied with each other to establish parishes, build churches and entice the population into their congregations.

There were few signs of co-operation among the churches until the second half of the 19th century, when three colonial councils of churches were formed in New South Wales, Victoria and South Australia. Their formation was stimulated by a felt need for a united front among the churches against gambling, alcohol and the decline in church attendance, and for the strict observance of Sunday, the recognition of God in the draft constitution and the inclusion of the Bible in the curricula of government schools.

One of the early forms of co-operation was the Sunday School Union in the mid-19th century, but it was mainly in the student and missionary areas that organizational expression was given first to ecumenical activity. The Australian Student Christian Union (ASCU) was formed in 1896. With its links with the World Student Christian Federation, the ASCU gave students an experience of belonging to international and interdenominational Christian communities. The YWCA and YMCA were significant, too, in fostering an ecumenical climate around this time.

In 1901 Australia became one nation with a federal parliament and a national constitution. Just as the fragmentation of the churches in Australia reflected the fragmentation of the country into state colonies or settlements, so too did the move to unite the country encourage union within the churches.

Within this national and theological climate, in 1901 the Presbyterian, Methodist and Congregational churches began their 70-year path to union. As early as the 1870s there had been plans for a union of the Anglican, Congregational, Presbyterian and Methodist churches, but these did not come to fruition. In 1924 a proposal for union among the Congregational, Presbyterian and Methodist churches failed to receive sufficient support within the Presbyterian church.

International events, too, were influencing the Australian scene. Several Australians participated in the world missionary conference at Edinburgh in 1910. On their return, united missionary councils were formed in New South Wales and Victoria. During a major missionary conference in Melbourne in 1926, these were replaced by the National Missionary Council of Australia.

The beginnings of a national council of churches received a direct impetus in the context of overseas ecumenical developments in 1946, when representatives from the Anglican, Baptist, Congregational, Methodist and Presbyterian churches, the Churches of Christ, the Salvation Army and the Society of Friends held the inaugural meeting of the WCC (Australian section). Building on the enthusiasm of the delegates returning from the first assembly of the WCC in Amsterdam in 1948, the Australian Council for the WCC was formed. In 1960 this became the Australian Council of Churches (ACC).

In 1950 the re-settlement of refugees from war-torn Europe became the major programme of the new council. Margaret Holmes, who was already working with the Student Christian Movement to assist German evacuees from Britain to settle in Australia, established the first re-settlement office in her home in Kew, Victoria. Two years later, with the active support of the Anglican archbishop of Sydney, H.W.K. Mowll, Elsie Needham opened a re-settlement department in Sydney. In July 1954 another office was opened in Brisbane.

Work among refugees and migrants has been a major role of the ACC from its inception. Almost 100,000 people have been assisted in the re-settlement programme. The ACC has been influential in government and migration policies and has carried out education programmes in the churches and in the community.

The waves of migration to Australia in the last three decades brought with them a growth of the number of Orthodox churches in Australia. The Greek Orthodox Church became a member of the council in 1958. Eight churches of the Eastern and Orthodox traditions are among the present 13 member churches of the ACC.

The year 1960 also saw the first national church conference in Australia. Held at Melbourne university, the conference gathered delegates and observers from 14 denominations. Following this conference, Australian Frontier was formed. For the next 20 years this organization brought together people from various walks of life and organizations to work on problematic areas in society. The national conference led also to the formation of the interchurch trade and industry mission, an ecumenical chaplaincy agency in the industrial workplace.

Following a national strategy consultation in 1964, the ACC sponsored a study-action programme in 1966 which involved more than 2,000 local churches in the Church and Life movement. For thousands of Australian Christians, this proved their first in-depth encounter with Christians of other denominations in their local area. It was a stimulus to local ecumenical co-operation.

In 1954 a fresh start was made in union discussions among the Congregational, Presbyterian and Methodist churches. A brief basis of union was prepared in 1957. Meanwhile, co-operation was going ahead in many areas, particularly in education, mission and service programmes. From 1963 Anglican and Churches of Christ sat with the joint commission.

A revised basis of union was presented to the negotiating churches in 1971. After a sequence of voting arrangements, the Uniting Church in Australia was inaugurated in 1977, an effective union between the Congregational, Presbyterian and Methodist churches, although some Congregational and Presbyterian parishes did not join. (It should be noted, too, that two branches of the Lutheran churches were re-united in 1966.) Following the founding of the Uniting Church, the ACC appointed a task group to prepare proposals for covenanting* for unity. These were studied by the churches over the next four years but did not come to fruition.

With the impetus of the Second Vatican Council,* a new link was formed between the ACC and the RCC with the formation of the Joint Working Group (1967). Over the ensuing seven years the following issues were studied: ecumenism and baptism (1968), the eucharist (1969), ministry (1970), Christian marriage and pastoral responsibility (1971), authorities in moral behaviour (1972), and the person in church and society (1974). In 1976 the group produced a popular statement on "Common Witness and Evangelism" which was widely distributed. Roman Catholic dioceses are members of some of the state ecumenical bodies. There has been continued close co-operation with the RCC and the ACC, particularly in the area of aid and development, and in the issuing of joint social statements.

In 1949 the ACC launched a Christmas Bowl Appeal so that help could be given to churches in places "with which none of our separate denominations have direct contact". It raised A$30. Since then the ACC has acted on behalf of its member churches in channelling over $3 million annually for emergency relief, support of refugees, and development projects.

In 1970 a national conference, focusing on world development and the responsibility of the Australian churches, was held in Sydney under joint ACC-RCC sponsorship. This was followed by a national study programme in

1972 involving thousands of Christians across Australia. Since its inception, the member churches have seen the ACC as a vehicle for their common prophetic witness. In the early years this effort focused on subjects as diverse as the white Australia policy, unemployment, the visit of Elvis Presley to Australia and the introduction of television. In the late 1960s Australia's involvement in the Vietnam war and compulsory national service proved controversial for the churches. In 1968 the ACC issued a well-researched and highly respected report on "Conscientious Objection to Military Service".

In recent years the ACC's work on national issues has become more analytical of injustices within Australian society. The publication in 1977 by the Commission on Church and Society of a study "How Lucky Are We?" contributed to this analysis.

The integration of the National Missionary Council into the ACC in 1965 brought with it an active and growing concern for the welfare of Aboriginal Australians and their struggle for land rights,* a concern which has been at the forefront of the council's interests since that time. A commission on Aboriginal development was established in 1970, and in the

following years lengthy submissions on Aboriginal affairs and land rights were made to the Australian government.

In 1981 the ACC invited the WCC's Programme to Combat Racism* to come to Australia. The international visitors wrote a comprehensive and challenging report which made a good impact on the churches, community and governments. A subsequent decision (1982) by the ACC to encourage its member churches not to participate in Australian bicentennial events planned for 1988 unless satisfactory land rights had been granted placed the rights of Aboriginals well and truly on the agenda of Australian churches.

The ACC has provided a platform for those whose voices are not normally heard. At a migrant women's speak-out in 1982, some 150 migrant women were able to communicate in their own languages. In 1986 the holding of hearings on peace and justice in nine centres around Australia enabled many groups to testify to their own experiences of injustice and to their concerns for peace. The ACC's commission on the status of women has done important work on the feminization of poverty and domestic violence.

Australia has had difficulties in finding its

Roman Catholic worship service in Northcote, Australia (Joint Board of Christian Education, Melbourne)

place in the international arena. It represents the North in the South; it is both colonized and colonizer; it is geographically in the Pacific, but culturally not of the Pacific. Yet there is a growing awareness of its place in the Asia-Pacific region. The ACC is a founding member of, and played a significant role in, the establishment of the East Asia Christian Conference, later the Christian Conference of Asia.* Similarly, it helped to bring together the churches in the Pacific to form the Pacific Conference of Churches,* in which it has observer status.

Against the background of the ACC and the negotiations for organic church unity,* many other ecumenical gains have been made. There have been significant advances in the area of theological education. Colleges of divinity at major universities involve RC as well as Anglican, Orthodox and Protestant churches. United faculties take responsibility for ministerial training. There is ecumenical co-operation in religious education in schools and in the churches.

Much interchurch activity occurs through ministers' fraternals, industrial and hospital chaplaincies. Para-church groups, the charismatic movement and social action bring people together across denominational boundaries. Traditional ecumenical events such as the Week of Prayer for Christian Unity* and the World Day of Prayer* continue to be celebrated. The publishing of an Australian hymnbook in 1977 was an important cultural and ecumenical development.

Historical ties still link some churches more to the overseas churches from which they have come than to other denominations in the same area. Divisions within some denominations reflect early colonial history. New sources of division such as moral conservatism, women's ordination* and political polarization of the wider society are reflected within and among the churches. The word "ecumenism" is often used cheaply to describe any level of co-operation or interchurch activity. While in some ways the momentum for ecumenism seems to have slowed and there are many signs of retreat into denominational boundaries, the 20th-century ecumenical movement, with impetus from the WCC and the Second Vatican Council, has created a certain minimum of expectations for ecumenical relationships.

Churches which were largely Anglo-Celtic in formation and membership are being challenged in new ways by the multicultural nature of Australian society. New religious movements among Aboriginal Christians may prove to be another significant challenge to denominational isolationism.

The decision of the WCC to accept the invitation from the Australian churches to hold the seventh assembly in Canberra in 1991 offers the Australian churches a unique opportunity for the revival of ecumenism.

JEAN SKUSE

C.M.H. Clark, *A History of Australia*, 6 vols, Melbourne, Melbourne UP, 1962-87 • F. Engel, *Australian Christians in Conflict and Unity*, Melbourne, Joint Board of Christian Education of Australia and New Zealand, 1984 • M. Hogan, *The Sectarian Strand*, Sydney, Penguin, 1987 • M. Porter, *Land of the Spirit? The Australian Religious Experience*, WCC, 1990.

AUTHORITY. The word "authority" comes from Latin *augere*, cognate with Greek *auxanein*, which means "to cause to grow, to increase, to enlarge". Growth is therefore the original meaning underlying the word "authority". Under the various senses it bears, etymology uncovers a dynamism that produces, promotes and completes the bond which unites people (G. Fessard, *Autorité et bien commun*, 1969). If, then, authority is needed and exercised among human beings, it is because they do not at once realize and achieve what they are to become on the personal and social plane. Each human being's desire is universal, which inevitably poses the problem of the progress of each with the co-existence of all. No social life can be established or maintained without some form of authority. The origins of societies of very different kinds show that at the basis of all authority lies a de facto power, employed either for the better (the "charism" of the born leader, the natural ancestor of the "saint"*) or for the worse (brutality of the gang leader, tyranny of violence), which has in any case a tendency to turn into juridical power. The de facto becomes the de jure; institutional structures develop and regulate the common will to live. Paradoxically, the goal of authority is its own disappearance; the authority of parents and educators ceases when the child in its turn has become a free and responsible person. In the case of a society, the common good is never perceived or achieved by all so fully that authority can cease. The goal remains asymptotic. As long as it has not been reached, authority appears as the necessary mediator of the common good of the group.

In a Christian perspective, the ultimate ground of all authority is the sovereignty of God (Rom. 13:1), who wills the good of his creatures. God, however, also wills their salvation,* i.e. wills that humanity grow in life towards eschatological fulfilment. God therefore sent his Son in a humanity like ours in order to manifest and exercise his saving authority in human terms, in a visible and historical way. Of his own free choice, Jesus falls in with the anthropological laws that govern the genesis of all authority.

The basis of authority in the church. Jesus appears as a charismatic leader who makes an unheard-of claim to authority (Matt. 7:29; Mark 1:22,27; Luke 4:32), sets his own word above that of Moses (Matt. 5:21-48, 19:8-9), claims authority to forgive sins (Matt. 9:1-8; Luke 7:48-49), commands with power unclean spirits, the sea and the winds (Luke 4:36; Matt. 8:27), calls on people to leave everything and follow him (Matt. 4:18-22, 9:9) and claims a unique relation with God, whom he declares to be his own Father (Matt. 11:27; Luke 10:22), designating himself as the Son. That authority is questioned by his contemporaries (Matt. 21:23-24 par.), but it compels recognition from those who follow him and is acknowledged as rightful authority in the light of Jesus' death and resurrection.* The risen Jesus can then send his disciples on mission* in the name of the total authority that has been given him in heaven and on earth (Matt. 28:18). Johannine reflection sees Jesus as having received from the Father authority to execute judgment (John 5:27) and power to give life (John 17:2). Jesus' authority is exercised for the sake of the growth of the kingdom,* the common good of humanity of which it is the channel. The Revelation to John celebrates the Son as the Lamb sacrificed and victorious, on whom all authority and power has been conferred (Rev. 5:12).

Jesus gathered round him a community of disciples; after the ordeal of his passion, that community re-assembles once again through faith* in his resurrection and the strength of the Spirit received at Pentecost.* In the primitive church every baptized person has the responsibility, and as it were the authority, to bear witness to the truth of the message and to serve in the name of Christ both inside and outside the community. Within that communal group, the special authority of the twelve chosen by the Lord and bearing witness to his resurrection is confirmed. They have received the official mission to proclaim the gospel to every creature. The group of apostles is joined by Paul in virtue of the singular grace* he received of seeing the risen Christ. The authority of the twelve, of the apostles and ministers who assist them in their task, is lived in an atmosphere of close fellowship with the community. According to Jesus' words, it is an authority of service (Mark 10:43-45), which must not follow the model of the political structure of secular society (Luke 22:25-26). This authority is based on the bond of the apostles with Jesus (in this sense it is a de jure authority); in its turn it is the basis of a ministry which consists in preaching the word, prayer and worship, and maintenance of the church community in a fellowship of faith and love. Paul claims this authority for himself (2 Cor. 13:10); it includes if necessary the duty of reproof (Titus 2:15). In another order of ideas, Paul commends obedience to the civil authorities because they are established by God (Rom. 13:1-3).

All Christian churches consequently acknowledge the authority and sovereignty of Christ over his church in the power of his Spirit. That authority is that of the gospel, which Origen identified with Christ himself and which is a power of salvation for the believer. It is attested in the scriptures, the authentic formulation of the word of God,* which demand, both from the church as a gathered community and from every Christian, the adherence of faith and obedience. Any authority exercised in the church can only be in the service of that faith and obedience.

Dispute about authority. The question of authority was one of the earliest matters of dispute between the churches. This is not surprising, for separations always involve questioning the legitimacy of the authority of the existing church. Between East and West the dispute was more about the way authority functions in the church (more synodical, collegial and communal, more respectful of local freedoms in the East; more centralized, personalized and "authoritarian" in the West). In the 16th century the conflict about authority assumed strictly doctrinal significance. It is connected with the deep ecclesiological divergence which still exists between certain confessions, and with different conceptions of the nature of the ordained ministry (see **ministry in the church**). The reformers — the Lutherans in particular — in the name of justification* by faith and the incapacity of human beings to co-operate in any way in their salvation, did indeed acknowledge the existence and necessity of human authority for the good order of the church,* the correct proclamation of the gospel and the right administration of the sacraments.* They did not accept, however, that the church in these domains is the administrator of an authority derived from God himself, for the sake of the salvation of human beings.

The Roman Catholic Church (RCC), on the other hand, and also the Orthodox churches, even if authority assumes a different form with them, hold that an authority of that kind is given to them by the will of Christ. The divergence was so great in the West that the challenge of that authority led on the Roman Catholic side to a stiffening and strengthening of the authority principle, together with increasing Roman centralization, so much so that in the late 19th century it was possible for that church to be styled a religion of authority in contrast to the Reformation churches now understood as religions of the Spirit, of conscience* and liberty.*

This divergence finds concrete expression in the way the structure of the church is understood, and especially in the role assigned to the episcopal ministry, the ministry of "superintendence" and pre-eminently the ministry of authority in the church. The divergence extends to the three chief domains of this ministry: proclamation of the word, sacraments, government and maintenance in communion.*

The RCC considers that the ministry of the word includes not only the task of preaching it but also the authority to interpret the scriptures correctly, in order to maintain the community in the truth of faith. The ministry therefore constitutes a magisterium (see **teaching authority**), which is exercised in regard to the scriptures, without standing above them. This magisterium pertains to the bishops in communion with the pope, acting either separately or assembled in a council. When an irrevocable and solemn decision is taken by a council, this is considered to be infallible (i.e. free from error, see **infallibility/indefectibility**), for the council is an organ of expression for the infallibility of the whole church, that which rests on the "supernatural sense of the faith which characterizes the people as a whole... from the bishops down to the last member of the laity" (*Lumen Gentium* 12). The First Vatican Council defined that the pope, as bishop of Rome, in virtue of his responsibility to maintain unanimity in faith among the churches, can on certain precise conditions himself commit the infallibility of the whole church.

The Orthodox churches share the ideas of episcopal magisterium and of infallibility (or, more exactly, inerrancy) but are loath to separate this exercise of authority from the "general consciousness" of the church (the *synaisthesis*, the Greek equivalent of the Latin *sensus fidelium*; see **consensus fidelium**), the primordial seat of Christian authority. For this reason the Orthodox link the infallibility of councils more with their reception* — it is discerned after the event and cannot be guaranteed beforehand. The Reformation churches generally reject the idea of an ecclesial magisterium in the name of the principle that scripture is its own interpreter and always produces anew its own correct interpretation. Doctrinal authority in the church is simply human and is judged by its fidelity to "the sovereign authority of the holy scriptures".

The RCC claims for the ministers of the word and the sacraments an authority of a sacramental nature (often denoted by what has now become an ambiguous term, "power"), received by ordination,* which places them in the apostolic succession (see **apostolicity**). Ordained ministers thus act in the name of Christ and of the church, for the sacraments are acts of Christ, celebrated in the church by the power of the Spirit who is invoked. The Orthodox churches share this fundamental conviction. For the Reformation churches, the authority of ministers belongs above all in the place of ecclesial investiture, for the ultimate basis of all ministry is, most often, baptism.*

Finally, the RCC holds that its ministers have received an authority of jurisdiction (referred to in Matt. 16:18 and 18:18) over the members of the Christian people, which is exercised in the order of faith and life, in the service of their salvation. That authority is likewise necessary to the maintenance of communion among local and particular churches. That is why the councils of Florence (1439) and Vatican I* declared that the primacy* of the bishop of Rome confers on him a power of universal jurisdiction over pastors and faithful. The Orthodox churches, who share an analogous conception of jurisdiction, have historically always rejected this Catholic doctrine of the Roman primacy as extraneous to their tradition and to the practice of earlier centuries. The Reformation churches remain alien to the idea of jurisdiction, which attributed to the church an instrumental role in the domain of salvation.

The Anglican communion has always sought to be a *via media*, but its "comprehensiveness" covers in fact a very complex situation. It includes trends close to the Roman Catholic conception (high church) and others close to Reformation ecclesiology (evangelical).

Ecumenical understanding of authority. Contemporary ecumenical discussions have devoted considerable attention to the question of authority in the church, examining it mainly in relation to the theme of ministries (see **ministry in the church**), which still constitutes at the present time a crucial item for ecumenical progress. Before summarizing results, the chief dialogues and relevant documents may be listed.

International dialogues: To be mentioned here are the Anglican-Roman Catholic International Commission (ARCIC) "Authority in the Church I" (Venice 1976), "Authority in the Church I: Elucidation" (Windsor 1981), "Authority in the Church II" (Windsor 1981); the Lutheran-Roman Catholic International Commission, "The Ministry in the Church" (1981, esp. sec. 3); the International Commission between the Roman Catholic Church and the World Alliance of Reformed Churches, "The Presence of Christ in Church and World" (1977, esp. sec. 2, "Doctrinal Authority in the Church"); the Methodist-Roman

Catholic dialogue, in its reports of Denver (1971, paras 99-118), Dublin (1976, paras 106-107), Honolulu (1981, paras 35-38) and Nairobi (1986, paras 61-75); the Anglican-Lutheran dialogue, Pullach (1972, paras 17-50); the Anglican-Orthodox dialogue, Moscow (1976, paras 1-18) and Dublin (1984, paras 21-30, 47-52, 90-92, 104-106); and Faith and Order, *BEM* (Lima 1982, esp. M15-16,19-25). The Roman Catholic-Orthodox International Commission will shortly tackle the question of authority.

National dialogues: Here we may mention from the USA volumes 5 and 6 of Lutherans and Catholics in Dialogue: *Papal Primacy and the Universal Church* (P.C. Empie et al. eds) and *Teaching Authority and Infallibility in the Church* (P.C. Empie et al. eds, Minneapolis, Augsburg, 1974 and 1978). The French Groupe des Dombes* has produced "Episcopal Ministry" (1976, esp. n.32-49) and "The Ministry of Communion in the Universal Church" (1985) in *Pour la communion des Eglises: L'apport du Groupe des Dombes, 1937-1987* (Paris, Centurion, 1988).

The immense advances achieved in regard to the nature, basis and meaning of ministry and ministries in the structure of the church also represent progress on the question of authority, in particular as regards ordination, apostolic succession of ministry treated within the apostolicity of the whole church, the ecclesiological reference of the episcopal ministry, its symbolic function in the service of Christ's action for his church, and the traditional significance of the threefold ministry.* Openness, no doubt qualified and still hesitant, to the idea of the sacramentality of the church holds out serious hope that the fundamental difficulty referred to earlier concerning the nature of the instrumentality of the church in relation to salvation may be overcome.

Another area of progress is that of dialogue on scripture* and Tradition (see **apostolic Tradition, canon, Tradition and traditions**), scripture and magisterium.* The whole state of the question has been completely transformed here since it has come to be recognized, on the one hand, that the composition of the New Testament belongs to apostolic church Tradition and the constitution of the canon to post-apostolic church Tradition and, on the other hand, that Tradition essentially consists in the transmission of the message of scripture and does not constitute another source alongside it. Convergence is also emerging in regard to recognition of the authority of the creeds* and councils* of the so-called undivided church. As regards the magisterium proper, a conciliatory formula might be along the following lines: whereas the Reformation churches have one-sidedly maintained the church's sole obedience to scripture, while the RCC has laid no less one-sided emphasis on the authority of the magisterium, to such an extent as to seem to suggest that the magisterium is self-sufficient, a dialectic approach capable of integrating the two points of view would be to recognize that the authority of the church is a *norma normata* (a secondary norm) that is bound by obedience to the *norma normans* (primary norm) of scripture and yet is truly a norm that, with the assistance of the Holy Spirit, provides in its most solemn pronouncements a guarantee of fidelity to scripture.

The dialogue which has advanced furthest towards agreement on the problem of authority is certainly the ARCIC. Its first Venice document (1976) starts from the Christian authority which is at work in the church through the action of the Holy Spirit. It underlines the importance of the authority of holiness, then acknowledges the authority attached to the episcope of the ordained ministry, which is exercised conjointly with the community in a "permanent process of discernment and response". It considers the authority which serves communion between churches in conciliar relations and even tackles the question of primatial, regional and universal authority (Roman primacy). It also deals with authority in matters of faith (see **teaching authority**), a point where it gives an important place to the doctrine of reception. The Windsor document (1981) studies four particularly thorny topics: the interpretation of the Petrine passages in scripture, divine right, jurisdiction, and infallibility. Although complete agreement has not yet emerged, particularly on the last point, the whole bearing of the question has been considerably clarified, and noteworthy advances made; this dialogue points the way forward towards the full reconciliation and conversion which each tradition must be able to accomplish.

The exercise of authority in the church also assumes concrete form which varies with cultures and historical epochs and which always to some extent reflects ways in which authority is exercised in civil society. This non-theological factor, extremely important as regards the image the churches present to one another and to the world, must also be subject to conversion. Each tradition has a tendency particularly to emphasize one of the three aspects — personal, collegial and communal — whose complementarity was recognized at the 1927 Faith and Order conference in Lausanne (cf. BEM, M26 and comm.). In a movement of ecumenical conversion, each confession owes it to itself to restore to a due place in its life and organization the aspect or aspects that it has a tendency to obscure.

See also **church discipline, church order, infallibility, primacy, teaching authority**.

BERNARD SESBOÜÉ

J. Robert Dionne, *The Papacy and the Church: A Study of Praxis and Reception in Ecumenical Perspective*, New York, Philosophical Library, 1987 • P. Hégy, *L'autorité dans le catholicisme contemporain: Du Syllabus à Vatican II*, Paris, Beauchesne, 1975 • J.M. Todd ed., *Problems of Authority: An Anglo-French Symposium*, London, Darton Longman & Todd, 1961.

AZARIAH, VEDANAYAGAM SAMUEL.

B. 17.8.1874, Tinnevelly, South India; d. January 1945, Dornakal. Azariah, a champion of ecumenism among the younger churches, served as YMCA secretary for a period. With a few others he founded the Indian Missionary Society of Tinnevelly in 1903, and later went as a missionary to work in the territories of the Nizam of Hyderabad, today part of the state of Andhra Pradesh. In a provocative address at Edinburgh 1910, he strongly criticized the unequal partnership between Western missionaries and their indigenous colleagues. He was consecrated bishop of Dornakal in 1912, the first Indian to become a bishop of the Anglican church. During the period of his services, the diocese registered phenomenal growth in numbers and activities. He was chairman of the National Christian Council of India, an influential participant in the International Missionary Council, and one of the leaders in the movement which issued in the Church of South India in 1947. He was present at

Lausanne 1927, Oxford 1937, and Tambaram 1938. Azariah was an evangelist, a man of prayer, a tireless teacher, and an able administrator. He wrote *South Indian Union* (Madras, CLS, 1936) and *Christian Giving* (London, Lutterworth, 1965). See Carol Graham, *Azariah of Dornakal* (London, SCM, 1946), J.Z. Hodge, *Bishop Azariah of Dornakal* (Madras, CLS, 1946), and Stephen Neill, *Brothers of the Faith* (New York, Abingdon, 1960).

ANS J. VAN DER BENT

B

BAËTA, CHRISTIAN GONCALVES KWAMI.

B. 23.5.1908, Keta, Ghana. Vice-chairman of the International Missionary Council* in 1958 and later its last chairman, Baëta superintended the merger of IMC and WCC in 1961. He served on the Commission of the Churches on International Affairs, and on the WCC central and executive committees, 1961-68. After his ordination in 1936, he became synod clerk of the Evangelical Presbyterian Church, 1945-49, and was chairman of the Ghana Christian Council and of the Ghana church union negotiations committee. He was a member of the legislative council of the Gold Coast, 1946-50, and later served on the constitutional assembly which after Nkrumah's overthrow prepared the way for a return to civilian rule in 1969. He has written *Prophetism in Ghana* (London, SCM, 1963) and *The Relationships of Christians with Men of Living Faiths* (Accra, Ghana Universities Press, 1971). See *Religion in a Pluralist Society: Essays in Honour of C.G. Baëta*, J.S. Pobee ed. (Leiden, Brill, 1976).

ANS J. VAN DER BENT

BAM, BRIGALIA HLOPHE.

B. 21.4.1933, Tsola, South Africa. Bam is deputy general secretary of the South African Council of Churches. She was executive secretary of the WCC Women's sub-unit, 1967-80, and staff moderator of unit III (Education and Renewal). After her term with the WCC, she served on the staff of the World YWCA. Previously she was programme secretary of the World Affiliated YWCA in South Africa, 1958-67, and a member of the All Africa Conference of Churches general and executive committees, 1963-68. She served in NGO conferences on the UN decade for women as resource person and speaker and has organized several international and national ecumenical conferences. She studied social work at Johannesburg and sociology at the University of Chicago.

ANS J. VAN DER BENT

BAPTISM.

Together with faith* in Christ, baptism administered in the name of the Holy Trinity — Father, Son and Holy Spirit — is regarded by almost all Christian communions as the basis of the Christian life and membership of the one church* of Christ. Unity* in baptism should thus be for all such disciples of the Lord Jesus the mark by which they recognize each other as members of the Body of Christ. The importance attached by Christians and their churches to baptism — lately reflected in the Lima text (*Baptism, Eucharist and Ministry**) and the responses to it — derives from the teaching of the New Testament and the practice of the first Christian community.

The evidence of the NT and the first Christian community. We may consider

75

here four different aspects of early Christian baptism.

Significance: Together with the proclamation of the gospel, with which it is closely linked, the act of baptism is presented in the NT as an essential mission,* entrusted by the risen Christ to his disciples so that all human beings might share in the salvation* he came to bring (Matt. 28:19; Mark 16:16; Acts 2:38, 10:47-48; Rom. 6:3-6). In John's gospel, the Lord affirms the necessity of baptism for entry into the kingdom of God:* "Unless one is born of water and the Spirit, he cannot enter the kingdom of God" (John 3:5). As at the baptism of Jesus (Mark 1:9-11 and par.), so too the baptism received by the disciples from the Lord closely connects the rite with the Holy Spirit* (Mark 1:8 and par.; Acts 2:38) and implies faith, which is itself a gift of the Holy Spirit (Mark 16:16; Acts 8:37 [Western text]; Rom. 6:8). Through the Spirit, the baptized person becomes a son or daughter in the Son, an adopted child of the heavenly Father (Rom. 8:15-17; Gal. 4:5-7; Eph. 1:5), a child of God (John 1:12). Buried with Christ in baptism, the baptized person has died to sin,* partakes of the life and resurrection of the Lord (Rom. 6:3-11; Col. 2:12) and, with other baptized persons, becomes a member of Christ's Body (1 Cor. 12:12-13). For the baptized, this means a new birth (John 3:5). This rite of baptism is a mystery or sacrament* because it was instituted by the Lord as a visible and effective sign of the regeneration of those receiving it and of their incorporation in the church as the Body of Christ. The responses to BEM show the churches to be largely agreed on this meaning of baptism just outlined.

The baptismal rite: Baptism is a washing with water accompanied by a word (cf. Eph. 5:26). This "word" can be understood as a confession of faith in the Father, the Son and the Holy Spirit (see **Trinity**), mentioned in all baptismal rituals back to Matt. 28:19 (cf. *Didache* 7.1). Jesus was baptized by John in the Jordan. During the first centuries the Christian tradition kept to the practice of baptizing in running water, usually channelled into a pool or basin known from earliest times as a baptistery. In any case, the rite had to be performed with water, even still water, as became customary in most churches very early on (already accepted in the *Didache* 7.2).

BEM declares that "baptism is administered with water in the name of the Father, the Son and the Holy Spirit" (B17).

Gift of the Spirit: The gift of the Spirit which accompanies the baptismal rite seems to have been mentioned variously from very early times, as attested in the Acts of the Apostles. The apostles Peter and John come to Samaria so that the Spirit might "fall" on those evangelized and baptized by Philip (Acts 8:16-17). In the case of the Ethiopian eunuch (8:29-38), however, and above all of Saul (9:18-19), the Spirit appears to have been given prior to baptism. During the "Caesarean Pentecost", Peter baptizes Cornelius and his household because they have just received the Holy Spirit (10:45-48, 11:15-17). This variety ultimately lies behind the observation in BEM that "Christians differ in their understanding as to where the sign of the gift of the Spirit is to be found" (B14).

Communion: The NT provides no clear evidence of newly baptized persons participating immediately in the eucharistic celebration after receiving the baptism with which the gift of the Spirit is linked (cf. 1 Pet. 2:2-3), but all the baptismal orders of the patristic church attest the participation of newly baptized persons or neophytes in the eucharist* following their baptism (esp. in the case of the paschal vigil). As full members of the church, the Body of Christ, they partook of the Lord's supper along with their brothers and sisters (cf. John 6:53). Linked in this way with the gift of the Spirit and the eucharistic meal, baptism constituted a single, if complex, unity regarded as "initiation" into the mysteries. In several places BEM hints at the restoration of that unity where it has been lost (e.g. B14 comm., E19 comm.).

Baptismal customs. Historically, the church has exhibited both uniformity and diversity in its practice of baptism.

The ancient custom: The first detailed rite of Christian initiation is found in the document identified with the *Apostolic Tradition* of Hippolytus of Rome (c. A.D. 217), which reports customs which were certainly earlier: a catechumenate including instruction, scrutinies, prayers and exorcisms; then the baptism of infants and adults, almost certainly in the night between Saturday and Easter Sunday. This rite began with the signation of the candidates and prayer over the water, over the oil of thanksgiving and over the oil of exorcism. The candidates renounced Satan and were anointed with the oil of exorcism. They were dipped three times in the water with the confession of faith (see **common confession, creeds**) in the form of questions and responses. After the water baptism there was a first anointing of the newly baptized ones with the "oil of thanksgiving" by a presbyter. Then the bishop laid hands on them to "make them worthy of being filled with the Holy Spirit" and again anointed them with the oil of thanksgiving. He then marked them with the sign of the cross and gave them the kiss of peace, after which they joined in the eucharistic celebration with all the faithful and received the communion in the body and blood of Christ.

The anointings: When and how the practice of ritual anointing was introduced into the baptismal rite is uncertain (see **chrismation**). There is not much evidence for it in the NT (perhaps 1 John 2:20,27; 2 Cor. 1:22; also Mark 14:3-8 and par., 16:1 and par.), but theologically it rests on the Christian's participation in the anointing of Jesus the Messiah or Christ (cf. Isa. 61:1-2 = Luke 4:18-19; 2 Cor. 2:15); moreover it was the custom in antiquity for baths to be preceded by anointings with oil for detergent purposes and to be followed by anointings with aromatic and invigorative oils. These were given a spiritual significance in Christian practice.

Diversity of customs: The sequence of rites in Hippolytus appears to have influenced the baptismal practices of most of the churches in subsequent centuries, even though the twofold post-baptismal anointing is attested in the Roman tradition only. The early Syrian tradition, however, conferred the gift of the Spirit before the water baptism and for long knew nothing of any post-baptismal anointing with the "oil of thanksgiving", called chrism or *myron*, i.e. aromatic oil. The same was the case in Constantinople down to the mid-5th century, as John Chrysostom and Proclus (d.446) testify. It also appears that a laying on of hands as sign of the gift of the Holy Spirit was not universal. The spread of the custom of post-baptismal chrismation in connection with the gift of the Holy Spirit appears to have been linked to the conflict with Messalianism and also to the use of chrismation in the reconciliation of heretics. Moreover, the dif-

fusion throughout the Christian world of the Mystagogic baptismal homilies and catecheses of such well-known bishops as Basil, Cyril of Jerusalem, Ambrose of Milan, John Chrysostom and Theodore of Mopsuestia, helped to produce not only a more uniform theology but also a more uniform symbolism and practice of baptism.

Generalization of baptism and divergent customs: With the mass entry of pagans into the church from the 4th century onwards, a difference between East and West emerged and was reinforced by the reaction against Pelagianism. It was not always possible for the bishop to preside at baptism. Moreover, baptism came to be administered systematically to newborn infants. In the churches of the East, the post-baptismal anointing conferring the gift of the Holy Spirit was performed by the priest immediately after the baptism but with *myron* consecrated by the bishop. In the churches of the West, Rome, under Innocent I (A.D. 416), reserved this gift of the Holy Spirit to the imposition of hands and the anointing performed by the bishop, while the priest continued to perform an initial anointing with chrism. In the West, therefore, the gift of the Spirit conferred by the bishop was deferred to a later date, eventually making it possible for persons baptized in infancy later to renew, in the presence of the bishop and the church, the profession of faith that had been made on their behalf in baptism. Because of the dominical precept concerning the necessity of eucharistic communion for participation in eternal life (St Augustine, Innocent I), communion came to be given prior to the gift of the Spirit by the bishop. It was, however, only in fairly recent times that this custom of eucharistic communion prior to the gift of the Spirit conferred by the bishop became general in certain countries. Despite usages to the contrary, the Roman Catholic Church has retained in principle the sacramental sequence of baptism, anointing for the gift of the Holy Spirit and eucharistic communion, as do the Orthodox and pre-Chalcedonian churches, and it is always in this sequence that it now administers them in the case of adult baptism.

*Chrismation and confirmation:** Essentially, the gift of the Spirit is linked to Christian baptism. In the "Catholic" churches, however, a specific rite marks this gift: the imposition of hands and/or anointing with chrism or *myron*. Different practices followed by churches in East and West in the administration of infant baptism have led on the two sides to different theological emphases. The churches of the East have kept the celebration of baptism, confirmation/chrismation and eucharistic communion as an indivisible whole even for infants. Their emphasis has thus been not so much on the personal commitment of faith which is in principle presupposed in these sacraments but rather on the single whole they together constitute. On the other hand, the churches of the West, because of reserving confirmation/chrismation for the bishop, have usually allocated the rites of baptism, confirmation and communion to different times in a person's life and, since the middle ages, have come to attach considerable importance to the ratification by the Christian of the commitment of faith made for him or her in infant baptism. The churches of the Reformation, abolishing the rite of anointing, have retained from confirmation the personal commitment of Christians which "confirms" the promise made by other Christians for them in infant baptism. Among the Protestant churches, the heirs to the Anabaptist or Baptist traditions of the 16th century are unable to attach any significance to the baptism of an infant too young to make a personal commitment of faith and are themselves willing to baptize only at a later age, while "(re-)baptizing" those who have received infant baptism.

Theological issues underlying different baptismal practices. A controversy arose in the 3rd century between Rome and the churches of Africa led by Cyprian of Carthage (d.258) over the worth of *baptism conferred outside the full communion of the church*. According to the Roman position and its later refinements, if baptism was correctly administered with water in the name of the Father and of the Son and of the Holy Spirit with the intention of doing what the church does, the personal status of the ministrant is only of secondary importance. Baptism administered outside the institutional bounds of the church can therefore be recognized as valid and even to some degree efficacious. Taking its cue from this theology, the Roman Catholic Church, along with many churches of the East, accepts the baptism of Christians of other churches and recognizes this baptism

as an important element in the ecclesial communion* which continues to unite Christians in some measure, despite their divisions. The Second Vatican Council strongly emphasized this position (*Unitatis Redintegratio* 3-4, 22-23; *Lumen Gentium* 15).

Cyprian, however, and with him the bishops of Roman Africa, affirmed that outside the church there can be no gift of the Holy Spirit or any sacrament. The rigidity of this position has in one way or another been abandoned by almost all the churches. Basil of Caesarea (d.379) regarded the baptism given by certain Christians outside the great church as a special case. From Basil's position, all the Orthodox churches have inherited an attitude towards the baptism of other churches which is often reserved. Some Orthodox churches recognize this baptism only "by economy",* i.e. while seldom administering baptism to such Christians requesting admission to the Orthodox church, they refrain from official comment on the value of baptism conferred outside the Orthodox communion. Despite this, all the Orthodox churches now recognize that the practice of baptism with water in the name of the Blessed Trinity by other churches is a decisive factor for the recognition of them as true Christian brothers and sisters and for co-operation with them in the quest for the visible unity of all Christ's disciples.

A related question is that of *the ministrant of baptism*. For the vast majority of churches, the ministrant of baptism should be an ordained minister or at least a baptized Christian. The Roman Catholic Church holds that, in an emergency, any human being *(quicumque homo)* can administer baptism, even one who is not baptized or even a Christian. The Orthodox churches do not accept this position.

But if the baptism administered by the other churches is in some way recognized, how is it possible to refuse to allow Christians from these same churches *participation in the eucharist*, which is the completion of baptismal initiation? The eucharist as such does not require an act of faith different from that of baptism. The reply offered by churches which recognize the baptism of other Christians but are unable to admit them to the eucharist is that the eucharist is the visible expression of the fullness of the community's faith in worship and as such can be shared only by those who are fully and visibly integrated into this community by complete communion in faith, sacraments and discipline.

The problem of *the restriction of baptism to adults only*, as those who are able to assume full responsibility for their faith, has hardly progressed on the theoretical side since the 16th century. Recent meetings between Mennonites and Lutherans in France have shown that the principles remain unchanged on both sides, apart from regret at the harshness of the condemnations of the past (see the Augsburg confession, arts 9,12,14,16-17) and the desire for and possibility of dialogue on both sides. The increasing frequency of adult baptism in all the churches will in all probability also help to settle this question. Meanwhile, BEM seeks to make the most of existing agreements by affirming that "baptism is both God's gift and our human response to that gift... Both the baptism of believers and the baptism of infants take place in the church as the community of faith" (B8 and 12).

The *"baptism of the Spirit"*, which Pen-

tecostalists see as the foundation of the Christian life, poses problems for other Christian communions. Useful clarifications have been achieved though without settling all the basic questions.

The ecumenical significance of the common baptism. Under the combined pressure of the Orthodox churches and then of the Roman Catholic Church and the Second Vatican Council, the Faith and Order commission attached increasing importance in the 1950s and 1960s to a common recognition of baptism by all the churches. Recognition of value to all correctly administered baptisms in other Christian communions amounts already to recognition of a measure of ecclesiality in the community administering such baptisms; it means recognizing a fundamental community of faith in Christ as unique Lord and Saviour, in the Trinity of the Father who sent his Son for the salvation of the world and bestowed the Holy Spirit, who enables us to call on the Father. It is also recognition of a certain degree of communion in the one Body of Christ, the church. Many of the dialogues

A baptism in Ghana (Ulrich Schweizer)

between the Christian communions have dealt specifically with the question of baptism. In 1987 the Roman Catholic and Orthodox churches produced a document devoted solely to this theme: "Faith, Sacraments and the Unity of the Church".

The challenge of the tension-laden words of BEM remains: "The inability of the churches mutually to recognize their various practices of baptism as sharing in the one baptism, and their actual dividedness in spite of mutual baptismal recognition, have given dramatic visibility to the broken witness of the church... The need to recover baptismal unity is at the heart of the ecumenical task" (B6 comm.); "When baptismal unity is realized in one holy, catholic, apostolic church, a genuine Christian witness can be made to the healing and reconciling love of God. Therefore, our one baptism into Christ constitutes a call to the churches to overcome their divisions and visibly manifest their fellowship" (B6).

EMMANUEL LANNE

Baptism, Eucharist and Ministry, WCC, 1982 • A. de Halleux, "Foi, baptême et unité", *Irénikon*, 61, 1988 • G. Kretschmar, "Die Geschichte des Taufgottesdienstes in der alten Kirche", in *Leiturgia*, vol. 5, K.F. Müller & W. Blankenburg eds, Kassel, Johannes Stauda, 1971 • E. Lanne, "La contribution du Cardinal Béa à la question du baptême", in *Simposio Card. Agostino Bea (16-19 dicembre 1981)*, Rome, 1983 • M. Thurian & G. Wainwright, *Baptism and Eucharist: Ecumenical Convergence in Celebration*, WCC, 1983 • G. Wainwright, *Christian Initiation*, London, Lutterworth, 1969.

BAPTISM, EUCHARIST AND MINISTRY (the "Lima text").

At Lima, Peru, in January 1982 the WCC Faith and Order commission gave final form to a text entitled *Baptism, Eucharist and Ministry* that, often under the acronym BEM, has since attracted an attention unprecedented in the history of the modern ecumenical movement. The commission believed it had recognized and formulated "a remarkable degree of agreement" in

three areas where many points had been controversial among the churches.

The meaning of baptism* was expounded as "participation in Christ's death and resurrection", "conversion, pardoning and cleansing", "the gift of the Spirit", "incorporation into the body of Christ" and "the sign of the kingdom". On knotty problems concerning the relation of faith,* water baptism and the Spirit, the Lima text declared that "baptism is both God's gift and our human response to that gift... The necessity of faith for the reception of the salvation embodied and set forth in baptism is acknowledged by all churches"; it emphasized that "both the baptism of believers and the baptism of infants take place in the church as the community of faith"; and, while noting that "Christians differ in their understanding as to where the sign of the gift of the Spirit is to be found", it claimed general agreement that "Christian baptism is in water and the Holy Spirit".

The eucharist,* or Lord's supper, is seen as "a gift from the Lord", and it is said that every Christian receives the "gift of salvation through communion in the body and blood of Christ". The "meaning of the eucharist" is expounded according to a Trinitarian and credal pattern as "thanksgiving to the Father", "anamnesis or memorial of Christ", "invocation of the Spirit", "communion of the faithful" and "meal of the kingdom". The text speaks of "Christ's real, living and active presence in the eucharist", which is "the living and effective sign of Christ's sacrifice, accomplished once and for all on the cross and still operative on behalf of all humankind".

The section on ministry* begins with "the calling of the whole people of God" and locates the ordained ministry within that context. The ordained ministry is seen as a reminder "of the dependence of the church on Jesus Christ, who is the source of its mission and the foundation of its unity". As an element within the broader reality of an "apostolic Tradition" that is transmitted in many ways, the "episcopal succession" is proposed as "a sign, though not a guarantee, of the continuity and unity of the church"; and it is claimed that "the threefold ministry of bishop, presbyter and deacon may serve today as an expression of the unity we seek and also as a means for achieving it".

The preparatory history. The Lima text

marks the outcome of a long history of study and dialogue. The milestones of that history were four world conferences (Lausanne 1927, Edinburgh 1937, Lund 1952, Montreal 1963) and ten plenary meetings of the Commission on F&O (from Chichester 1949 to Lima 1982, by way of Bristol 1967 and Accra 1974, which marked important stages in the development of BEM). There has been an increasingly universal church representation in the process, with steadily growing involvement of Orthodox and, after the Second Vatican Council, of Roman Catholic theologians.

The history of BEM must be divided into two periods, corresponding to two different styles of working. The first period, from Lausanne to Bristol, developed in two stages: the period of *doctrinal comparisons* among churches intent on defining their own identity (from Lausanne to Lund) and that of common effort to *build on* the biblical and Christological bases (from Lund to Montreal). With a prelude at Aarhus (1964), where the themes of eucharist and ministry were taken up again in the light of Montreal, the second period really got under way at Bristol. That meeting resumed work on the relation between scripture and Tradition* and took up again the systematic study of the eucharist, but above all it recognized that a sort of "ecumenical tradition" had evolved in the course of the various world conferences and plenary commission meetings of F&O. This tradition can be identified in the various final reports adopted by the delegates of the different churches.

Baptism and the eucharist were the subject of theological discussions in the ecumenical movement from the very outset. No important F&O conference ever took place without at least some reference to these two sacraments.* A common understanding of baptism was one of the main preoccupations between the world conferences on F&O in Lund and in Montreal. The results of the study carried out during those years were presented in the report "One Lord, One Baptism" (1961) and were favourably received by the Montreal conference.

The study on baptism was resumed in 1967 at Bristol. A first consultation in early 1968 produced a short analytical study of the subject which was discussed and commented on by a large number of regional groups. A second international consultation took place two years later at Revnice, Czechoslovakia, to discuss certain problems in greater detail. The findings of all this work were assembled in the report submitted to the Commission on F&O at its meeting in Louvain (1971) entitled "Baptism, Confirmation and Eucharist".

The special study of the eucharist had been started a little earlier. A series of consultations led to the report "The Holy Eucharist", which was discussed by the Commission on F&O in Bristol. At the request of the fourth assembly of the WCC (Uppsala 1968), efforts were focused on the question of intercommunion.* A consultation held in Geneva in 1969 produced the report entitled "Beyond Intercommunion".

In the course of this work a proposal was made to compile two documents bringing together the agreements on baptism and the eucharist achieved in the ecumenical movement. Several attempts were made, and finally two texts were submitted to the Commission on F&O at Louvain: "Ecumenical Agreement on Baptism" and "The Eucharist in Ecumenical Thought". At the commission's request, the WCC executive committee decided a few weeks later to send the two documents to all the member churches for their reactions and comments (Sofia, September 1971). In the light of the responses received from the churches, the texts were then amended and again submitted to the F&O commission at its meeting in Accra in 1974.

In response to the discussion at the fourth world conference in Montreal, a study on ministry was undertaken. This progressed in several stages. The first-fruits were presented to the Commission on F&O at its meeting in Louvain in the report "The Ordained Ministry". The commission considered that substantial progress had been made and requested that the work be continued. As a result of this new mandate, an international consultation was organized in Marseilles in 1972. The text produced by this meeting was distributed to a large number of groups and theologians, with a request for their reactions and comments. In the light of their responses, the text was revised at a second consultation in Geneva at the end of 1973 before being submitted to the F&O commission at its meeting in Accra. At its meeting in Berlin, the WCC central committee decided that the three texts should be published and communicated to the member churches (see the historical note in *One Baptism...*, pp.58-61).

The first drafts drawn up by Max Thurian from 1967 onwards, to serve as a basis in this search for convergences, consisted essentially in quotations from the official reports, organized around an intelligible theological structure. First came the text on the eucharist (1967), then the one on baptism (1968) and finally that on ministry (1972). A large number of theologians invited by Lukas Vischer, then director of the F&O secretariat, attended a succession of meetings to discuss these themes and to correct and complete the embryo BEM texts. After Accra (1974), the document was sent to the churches for their reactions. The evaluation of the amendments proposed by the churches (150 letters were received in Geneva) enabled a smaller steering group to bring the BEM text closer to the final form that it would receive at Lima in 1982.

The members of the BEM steering group were Vitaly Borovoy (Orthodox), Nils Ehrenström (Lutheran), Bert Hoedemaker (Reformed), Anton Houtepen (Roman Catholic), Max Thurian (Taizé), Emilianos Timiadis (Orthodox), Lukas Vischer (Reformed), Geoffrey Wainwright (Methodist). A number of experts were also involved in the work of the steering group, among them Nikos Nissiotis and John Zizioulas (Orthodox), Emmanuel Lanne and Jean Tillard (Roman Catholic), Günther Gassmann and Harding Meyer (Lutheran), and Günter Wagner (Baptist).

The nature of the BEM process. The ecclesiological conviction underlying the composition of BEM is that when the churches, through their representatives, are gathered together by the WCC, they are no less churches than when making their decisions individually. Indeed, when a church is validly represented at a responsible ecumenical gathering, its tradition and witness are enriched by the contribution of the other churches gathered there. The sharing of the truth in love illumines and reveals the fundamental nature of each. This ecumenical action of the Spirit in the churches has forged what may justifiably be called an ecumenical tradition. This ecumenical tradition, guided by the Holy Spirit, is the fruit of a common "reading" by the various churches of holy scripture and of

Communion elements for the Lima liturgy, Vancouver 1983 (WCC photo)

the great Tradition interpreting God's word, with a view to rediscovering the visible unity* willed by Christ.

It is important to be clear about the authority of the Lima text. It is intended as a theological service to the churches in ecumenical dialogue. It is in no way a complete dogmatic statement claiming to be the perfect solution to the doctrinal differences that have developed between the churches in the course of history. The churches remain entirely free to accept, correct or reject the text.

In the interests of a good (objective and generous) reception* of the document by the churches, it may be useful to mention a few ways of receiving it which would be neither too immediately critical nor too hastily authoritarian. With other texts on the same subjects, but with its special character as a broad-based ecumenical document, it could be a useful instrument in *catechesis*.* It could help pastors to give believers a sound basis for their faith. For the rebuilding of Christian unity it is indispensable that the people of God should hold a strong, simple faith. This document is a valuable expression of ecumenism at this level. A second area where the Lima text can be extremely useful is in the field of *theological education* in seminaries or faculties, in the training of the church's future ministers. Apart from providing a sound basis of theological reflection, the document can also help to promote a healthy ecumenical attitude. It may also inspire *liturgical reform** in the churches, where new worship texts may have to be composed. Lastly, the Lima document can serve as a basis for reflection for local groups engaging in ecumenical dialogue, especially those for *confessionally mixed households*. Thus, without wishing to impose itself dogmatically, the Lima convergence text may be received in a live way by the churches as a means of strengthening the common faith of Christian believers.

The responses of the churches. By the middle of 1990, BEM had been translated and published in 35 languages, and the F&O secretariat had received responses from 190 churches (including the Roman Catholic Church), which together represent the vast majority of the more than 1,100 million Christians in the world. Reactions were also received from several councils of churches and numerous groups of theologians. The churches were asked to say how far they could "recognize in this text the faith of the church through the ages", what consequences they could draw from it for their relations particularly with other churches that "also recognize the text as an expression of the apostolic faith", what guidance they could take from the text for their life and witness, and what suggestions they could make for incorporation of BEM material into the ongoing project of F&O, "Towards the Common Expression of the Apostolic Faith Today". An examination of the various responses, published in the series *Churches Respond to BEM*, will enable each church to measure the degree of convergence in the faith and the steps that still need to be taken in dialogue to arrive at full visible unity.

Meanwhile, at its plenary meeting in Budapest in August 1989, the F&O commission prepared a brief message to the churches to accompany a full report on the BEM process and responses. This 1990 report contains an analytical description of the churches' responses to each section of BEM, proposes some initial clarifications that were called for

or suggested by the responses, and sketches possibilities for further work on three issues of a more general kind that were recurrently raised by the churches: the relation of scripture and Tradition, the nature of sacrament and sacramentality (including the relation of word and sacrament) and the need for common perspectives on ecclesiology.

See also **apostolic Tradition, baptism, chrismation, church, common confession, communion, confirmation, eucharist, Faith and Order, Lima liturgy, ministry in the church**.

MAX THURIAN

Baptism, Eucharist and Ministry, WCC, 1982 • *Baptism, Eucharist and Ministry 1982-1990: Report on the Process and Responses*, WCC, 1990 • *One Baptism, One Eucharist and a Mutually Recognized Ministry*, WCC, 1975, text of Accra • M. Thurian ed., *Churches Respond to BEM*, 6 vols, WCC, 1986-88 • M. Thurian ed., *Ecumenical Perspectives on BEM*, WCC, 1983 • M. Thurian & G. Wainwright eds, *Baptism and Eucharist: Ecumenical Convergence in Celebration*, WCC, 1984 • G. Wainwright, "The Lima Text in the History of Faith and Order", *Studia Liturgica*, 16, 1986.

BAPTIST-LUTHERAN DIALOGUE.
Baptists and Lutherans trace their origins to the Reformation. Baptist roots are located in the Anabaptist wing of this 16th-century movement. Anabaptists rejected infant baptism* and stressed conscious conversion* before baptism by immersion. They were denounced and persecuted by the followers of Luther, Zwingli and Calvin. More recent Baptist origins are identified in the English separatist movement of the 17th century and in the work of John Smyth, who taught the baptism of adult believers as the basis of the gathered church.

Lutheran beginnings are found in the teaching of Luther and of the Lutheran confessions, the latter brought together in the Book of Concord of 1580. Lutherans stressed as the chief article of the Christian faith justification* by grace* through faith;* they rejected the view that faith can be a prior condition for baptism.

After the Reformation, there were few formal relations between Baptist and Lutheran churches. However, in the 20th century many Baptist and Lutheran churches joined the WCC and regional and national councils of churches and encountered each other in the ecumenical movement.

The first international theological conversation between representatives of the Lutheran World Federation* and the Baptist World Alliance* began in 1986. Its aim was to clarify differences, convergences and agreements in thought and practice. Baptists were concerned about condemnations of their positions and practices in the Lutheran confessions; Lutherans, about Baptist reluctance to recognize infant baptism. The second meeting, in 1987, took up faith, discipleship and baptism. In 1988 the next session discussed the nature of the church. The fourth, and final, meeting in 1989 prepared a statement on authority for preaching and teaching, and on the condemnations.

National dialogues have taken place in the USA from 1979 to 1981, in the Federal Republic of Germany from 1980 to 1981, and in the German Democratic Republic from 1982 to 1983. All these dialogues have focused on the theology of baptism and the condemnations. Recurring problems were the relation between belief and baptism, believer's baptism and infant baptism, and the understanding of church and sacraments.

Significant differences remain between the Baptist and Lutheran traditions, but the international and national discussions have resulted in greater understanding. The participants have been able to recognize each other's churches as true churches that live from the gospel. Topics for future conversations will probably include the authority of scripture, the place of creeds* and confessions, and the nature of the church.*

WILLIAM G. RUSCH

"Lutheran-Baptist Dialogue", *American Baptist Quarterly*, 1, 1982 ● G. Rothermundt, "Ein Dialog beginnt: Die baptistisch-lutherischen Gespräche seit 1979", *Ökumenische Rundschau*, 36, 3, 1987 ● "Schlussbericht des Gespräches zwischen dem Bund Evangelisch-Freikirchlicher Gemeinden in Deutschland und der Vereinigten Evangelisch-Lutherischen Kirche Deutschlands", *Texte aus der VELKD*, 17, 1981.

BAPTIST-REFORMED DIALOGUE.

The Baptist World Alliance* and the World Alliance of Reformed Churches* sponsored a dialogue from 1973 to 1977. Prepared through official contacts in the preceding years, it was grounded in a centuries-long relationship.

The Swiss reformers rejected and persecuted the Anabaptist movement, so called by its opponents because the practice of baptizing believers on profession of faith was, from the Reformed point of view, doing "over again" *(ana-)* what had been done once for all in infant baptism.* The Baptist churches trace their direct descent not from the Swiss movement (today represented by the Mennonites) but from independent churches in England; but the Swiss and English groups together believed that they were not doing anything over again, since in their view infant baptism, whatever its intention, was quite other than New Testament baptism.

Yet Baptists and Congregationalists as one type of Reformed Christians were drawn together by suffering common persecution as radicals. They saw themselves as seeking to renew the local church,* on a NT model, as the place of Christ's rule over his people. In England John Bunyan pleaded that differences over baptismal teaching and practice ought not to divide Christians.

A review of these two interacting tendencies in church history was a main theme of the dialogue and led to positive conclusions, including the recommendation of a dual practice, whereby Christian parents could choose either to present their children for infant baptism or to seek a service of thanksgiving and of dedication to their parental task, leaving to the children the decision to request baptism when they were able to do so on their own profession of faith.* Such a dual practice had already been offered, independently of the dialogue, in some Reformed and United churches.

In 1982 the responses of the churches to the report of the dialogue were evaluated in a short consultation. The responses did not agree concerning a dual practice. Some see it as a positive step in mutual recognition of well-grounded convictions, a recognition that each practice is supported by the evidence of some strands of scripture and tradition. Others see a dual practice as an uneasy compromise. Despite this continuing disagreement, the dialogue has emphasized a common inheritance which owes much to the Calvinist understanding of systematic theology; it shares also an insistence upon lay participation in church government and is resistant to the focusing of authority in a personal episcope (see **church order**).

The Baptist-Reformed dialogue has a particular place in the whole series of bilateral dialogues* because it is a dialogue of the "radical" Reformation with the "classic" Reformation. Reformed churches and more recently Baptist churches have engaged in dialogue with those who stand, in the range of traditions, more on the wing of clerical authority and who emphasize the sacramental (i.e. the Anglican, Lutheran, Orthodox and Roman Catholic). The Baptist-Reformed dialogue has ensured both that the common radicalism of these churches has not been forgotten in the wider debate and that Reformed churches do not face only in one direction in their search for visible unity.*

MARTIN H. CRESSEY

Baptists and Reformed in Dialogue, Studies for the World Alliance of Reformed Churches, no. 4, Geneva, WARC, 1984 • L.A. Creedy, "Baptism in Church Union Negotiations", *Mid-Stream*, 9, 2-3, 1970-71.

BAPTIST-ROMAN CATHOLIC INTERNATIONAL CONVERSATIONS.

The first international Baptist-Roman Catholic conversations took place 1984-88, co-sponsored by the Commission on Baptist Doctrine and Interchurch Cooperation of the Baptist World Alliance* and the Vatican Secretariat (now Pontifical Council) for Promoting Christian Unity.* The overall theme of the discussions was "Christian Witness in Today's World". Goals included mutual understanding of convergences and divergences between Baptists and Catholics, establishment of relations and communication for mutual and self-understanding, identification of possibilities and difficulties for common witness, and addressing existing prejudices.

Previous Baptist-Catholic contacts on different levels included collaboration on social issues, theological contacts of scholars, e.g. in Faith and Order settings. In the USA the Bishops' Committee for Ecumenical and Interreligious Affairs (BCEIA) co-sponsored dialogue with the American Baptist Churches between 1967 and 1970. The BCEIA and the Department of Interfaith Witness of the Southern Baptist Convention have jointly organized several series of conversations between Southern Baptist and Catholic scholars since 1978.

In the international conversations, the overall theme and the first session on "Evangelism/Evangelization: The Mission of the Church" (West Berlin 1984) set a missiological direction for subsequent sessions on Christology, conversion/discipleship (Los Angeles 1985), the church (New York 1986), religious freedom, evangelism vs proselytism (Rome 1987). The final report of this series, developed at Atlanta, Georgia, USA (1988), gives a "common statement" which placed the findings in the context of fostering common witness.*

Setting a firm Christological foundation, the report states that "our common witness" rests on shared faith* in the centrality of Christ as revelation* of God and sole mediator between God and humankind, a faith in Christ that is proclaimed in the New Testament and expressed in the first four ecumenical councils.* This common faith should be the basis for discussion of remaining differences. Referring to conversion/discipleship, the report notes that the mystery of Christ can ultimately be grasped only in faith and in the practice of Christian discipleship through faith and love.

Regarding the church,* these conversations explored, as have other dialogues, the biblical notion of koinonia* and found "koinonia of the Spirit" (Phil. 2:1) a helpful description of a common understanding of the church. For Baptists, koinonia is expressed principally in local congregations gathered voluntarily under the lordship of Christ (see **local church**). They avoid structures which threaten individual freedom and local autonomy. For Roman Catholics, the koinonia which the Spirit effects in the local congregation is simultaneously koinonia with other local churches in the one universal church, expressed in spiritual and institutional bonds. These differences and the relationship of Spirit to structures need further discussion (see **church order**).

Concerning witness in the world, both Baptists and Catholics respond to the great commission (Matt. 28:16-20) through evangelism* or evangelization. Baptists prefer the term "evangelism" and emphasize free personal response of individuals to the gospel.

Catholics apply the term "evangelization" to the "first proclamation" of the gospel to non-believers and in the wider sense to the renewal of humanity, witness and related factors. Study is needed to clarify the use of these terms, to help promote further common witness.

In a penitential spirit both Catholics and Baptists confess that competition and bitterness among missionaries have been stumbling blocks for those to whom the gospel is proclaimed. Distinguishing evangelism/evangelization from proselytism,* they confess that both have been guilty of proselytism in its negative sense and lament that division and strife between Christians "can be such a scandal that non-believers may not be attracted to the gospel". Both need greater vigilance in respecting religious liberty.*

Issues for further dialogue include approaches to theological authority and method; relationships between faith, baptism, and Christian witness; the role of Mary. The report ends by urging Baptists and Catholics to find concrete ways to offer common witness.

JOHN A. RADANO

C. Ghidelli, "Ecumenismo in crisi? Una testimonianza", *Rivista del Clero Italiano*, December 1988 • *Review and Expositor*, 79, 2, 1982 • *Southwestern Journal of Theology*, 28, 2, 1986 • "Summons to Witness to Christ in Today's World: A Report on the Baptist-RC International Conversations, 1984-88", *Information Service*, Pontifical Council for Promoting Christian Unity, 72, 1990.

BAPTIST WORLD ALLIANCE. The BWA is the worldwide fellowship of Baptist believers. Formed in 1905 in London, the BWA, like other Christian World Communions,* is a result of the desire for greater denominational unity that was emerging from the missionary movement at the end of the 19th century.

Although originally seen only as a movement for fellowship, since 1945 the BWA has adopted a number of programmes whereby Baptists can support one another. Composed of 138 member bodies, called conventions or unions, Baptists work in more than 145 countries. There are 35 million baptized believers in BWA member bodies, with a community of at least 65 million.

The purpose of the alliance is stated in the preamble of the BWA constitution: "The Baptist World Alliance, extending over every part of the world, exists as an expression of the essential oneness of Baptist people in the Lord Jesus Christ, to impart inspiration to the fellowship, and to provide channels for sharing concerns and skills in witness and ministry. This Alliance recognizes the traditional autonomy and independence of churches and general bodies."

Five divisions carry out the work of the BWA: Baptist world aid, communications, evangelism and education, study and research, promotion and development. Three departments carry on significant work for men, women and youth.

The BWA has six regional fellowships of Baptist conventions: All-African Baptist Fellowship, Asian Baptist Federation, Caribbean Baptist Fellowship, European Baptist Federation, North American Baptist Fellowship, and Union of Baptists of Latin America. Each regional fellowship relates to the BWA through a regional secretary who lives in the area.

Every five years the BWA sponsors a Baptist world congress, attended by thousands from all continents. These congresses set the theme and programmes of the alliance for the next five years. Every Baptist member body can send council members, who have equal voice and vote.

DENTON LOTZ

BAPTISTS. The modern Baptist movement began in 17th-century England. Separatists, unable to "purify" the Church of England, broke from the puritans and advocated separation from the state church (see **church and state**). Among these separatists was a group who became convinced that infant baptism* was contrary to scripture. In 1607, to avoid persecution, a group led by John Smyth and Thomas Helwys left Gainsborough, England, and sailed for Amsterdam, where freedom of religion was flourishing.

In Holland, after further study of scripture, the whole congregation rejected their infant baptism and were baptized as believers in 1608. Helwys eventually became the leader of part of the group, and in 1611 with ten others he returned to London to establish the first Baptist church on English soil.

During their stay in Holland these early Baptist believers had contact with the Mennonites, who had also become convinced of the scriptural basis for believer's baptism. The Mennonites and others were accused of rebaptism and thus were called Anabaptists. The Anabaptists rejected the charge of rebaptism because they did not believe infant baptism to be scriptural baptism. Although not directly related to this movement, Baptists count Anabaptists as part of their spiritual history.

Thus one must see the rise of the Baptist movement in the context of this 17th-century movement. The Reformation in Europe had led to the rediscovery of the Bible. Many former Catholic priests were even more radical than the German reformer Martin Luther in calling for reform. These "radical reformers" saw the danger of the union of church and state. They called for separation not only from the church but from the state! Many such as Balthasar Hubmaiaer of Waldshut, Switzerland (1528), Felix Manz and Conrad Grebel of Zurich (1526) were persecuted, and some were killed for their convictions. Throughout the history of the church other Nonconformists also opposed state control and infant baptism; e.g. the Waldensians of Italy go back to the 12th century and represent this tradition.

Baptists, with Mennonites and other Anabaptists, were part of the 16th-century spiritual movement for renewal, separation of church and state, believer's baptism, and a purified and conscious commitment as an adult to personal belief in Jesus Christ as Lord and Saviour. Out of the small group of Baptists in 17th-century England, a worldwide movement has developed. Today there are 35 million Baptist believers in 145 countries around the world. If one includes children and the larger community of worshippers, they would number at least 65 million, making the Baptists one of the largest Protestant groups in the world.

Baptist beliefs. In common with Christians around the world, Baptists hold the apostolic faith as expressed in the Apostles' Creed.* Although Baptists have many "confessions of faith", they hesitate to sign or quote a creed* because of their great concern for the freedom of the individual. The following is a list of some Baptist beliefs, shared by many other churches, but yet the combination of which makes them very distinctively Baptist.

Religious freedom for all: In 1612 Helwys wrote bravely against the king: "Our Lord the king is but an earthly king...: for men's religion to God is betwixt God and themselves; the king shall not answer for it, neither may the king be judge between God and man. Let them be heretics, Turks, Jews or whatsoever, it appertains not to the earthly power to punish them in the least measure." Baptists defend religious freedom and liberty for all people in every country. The American Baptist Roger Williams wrote in the 1650s: "Man hath no power to make laws to bind conscience." Having suffered much religious persecution, Baptists are anxious to defend the rights of all peoples and religions.

Separation of church and state: Following on the doctrine of religious freedom is the natural corollary of the separation of church and state. A.C. Underwood said of the Anabaptists: "They stood for a complete separation of church and state. They denied the right of the state to compel belief or regulate religion and therefore exercised their own discipline over their members, by the democratic action of each congregation, and excommunicated all who were guilty of grave moral offences." This doctrine is perhaps one of the greatest contributions to unity* and the ecumenical movement. The separation of church and state encourages the movement for unity among the churches. Otherwise, there would have been entanglements of governments trying to control efforts towards unity.

Open communion: Many of the more credal churches do not allow Christians of other traditions to participate in their celebration of the Lord's supper (see **communion, euchar-ist, intercommunion**). Generally, Baptists belong to that part of the world church that has only the requirement of personal faith and trust in the Lord Jesus Christ. In 1673 John Bunyan, the English Baptist writer, wrote: "The church of Christ hath no warrant to keep out of the communion the Christian that is discovered to be a visible saint of the word, the Christian that walketh according to his own light with God."

Emphasis on local congregation of believers: One cannot speak of a single national or world Baptist church. There are thousands of

Baptist congregations around the world which are gathered into conventions or unions of Baptist churches. It is the Baptist belief that the local congregation is the Body of Christ in that area, but it does not reserve the right to call itself the church of any region or any country, or of the world (see **local church**). Nevertheless, individual Baptist congregations form themselves into district associations, state and national conventions to enhance their missionary endeavours. The Baptist World Alliance* (BWA) is the world expression which unites Baptists in 145 countries for fellowship and witness.

Morgan Patterson, president of Georgetown College, Kentucky, summarizes well the Baptist way: (1) the essence of the Christian faith is spiritual, personal, and voluntary; (2) the scriptures are uniquely inspired and authoritative; (3) the church is composed of committed believers; (4) salvation is provided by the grace of God and is available to everyone through repentance and faith; (5) all believers are priests, with no intermediary other than Christ himself; (6) the scriptures command the observance of two ordinances, baptism and the Lord's supper, which are understood to be basically symbolic in meaning; (7) baptism is properly performed by the biblical mode of immersion; (8) the authority for the administration of the church is in the hands of the congregation; (9) religious freedom should be given to all to enable each person to respond to the leadership of the Holy Spirit; (10) the separation of church and state best guarantees liberty of conscience for every citizen.

The following significant Baptists have worked for unity: John Bunyan, writer of *Pilgrim's Progress*, called for unity and did not want any bar to participation in the Lord's supper. William Carey, great missionary to India in 1793, is called the father of modern missions, and has been referred to by Ernest Payne as father of the ecumenical movement. As early as 1810, Carey called for an ecumenical meeting of all Christians, although not until 1910 in Edinburgh did his "pleasant dream" take place. Billy Graham, world evangelist, represents the strong Baptist concern for world evangelization. All of his meetings are interdenominational and demonstrate a strong expression of evangelical ecumenism. Martin Luther King, Jr, carried on the strong tradition of Walter Rauschenbusch and the social gospel. Baptists believe that the Christian faith has as its mission a call for justice and human rights for all.

The list is long of outstanding Baptists who have contributed to the world missionary movement and wider witness of the Christian church. Besides those named above, one could mention Johann Oncken, John Clifford, Adoniram Judson, Lottie Moon, Charles Haddon Spurgeon, Lott Carey, J.H. Shakespeare, Ernest Payne and Jimmy Carter.

Baptists and unity. Baptists are eager for co-operation in mission* and evangelism,* but because of their congregational polity they are wary of structural integration (see **church order**). Some Baptists are unhappy with the present expression of the WCC, which they think has become too political. Nevertheless, 16 Baptist conventions or unions are members of the WCC, only a small percentage of the 138 Baptist groups in the BWA. If we analyze the numerical membership of the Baptist conventions in the WCC, however, a different picture emerges: about 45% of the 35 million Baptists in the world belong to member churches of the WCC. Baptists in the WCC feel a responsibility for keeping alive the missionary concern out of which grew the WCC. Of the more than 45,000 Protestant missionaries from the USA, only 8,000 come from churches holding membership in the WCC. A large portion of the rest come from Baptist backgrounds.

An early theme of the ecumenical movement was "mission *and* unity". Baptists represent this strain within the ecumenical movement, whether expressed in the WCC or in the evangelical ecumenical movement of the Lausanne congress (see **Lausanne covenant**). Recent debate which emphasizes "mission and doctrine" sounds divisive to Baptist ears. Where there is need for co-operation for evangelism and mission, Baptists will be involved. Where there is a call for structural unity or doctrinal unity, Baptists, mindful of their heritage, will be hesitant to join.

DENTON LOTZ

W.H. Brackney, *The Baptists*, Westport, CT, Greenwood, 1988 • H.L. McBeth, *The Baptist Heritage*, Nashville, TN, Broadman, 1987 • R.G. Torbet, *History of the Baptists*, Valley Forge, PA, Judson, 1963.

BAROT, MADELEINE.

B. 4.7.1909, Chateauroux, France. Barot was a leading figure in the ecumenical youth, student and women's movements, as well as in the French Protestant aid organization CIMADE,* especially in its work with internees during the second world war.

Born into a Protestant family, Madeleine Barot became fervently involved in the Student Christian Movement while at the University of Paris. Studies in history and library science did not dampen her enthusiasm, which was always characterized by ecumenical concern and the desire to anchor Christian witness firmly in reality.

Appointed archivist at the French School in Rome in 1935, she witnessed first-hand the advance of fascism and Nazism in Europe. During these years, under the influence of the Confessing Church* in Germany, the World Student Christian Federation was playing a significant role in equipping an entire generation, including Barot, to respond to the Nazi occupation of France.

At this time Protestants from Alsace and Lorraine were being evacuated to the south of France, away from the German frontier. When the joint committee of French Protestant youth movements was challenged by Suzanne de Diétrich to come to the aid of these people, the inter-movement committee for aid to evacuees, CIMADE* (Comité inter-mouvement auprès des évacués), was born. Barot was named its general secretary in May 1940 on her return from Italy, which had joined the war on the side of Germany. The dreadful condition of foreigners marshalled in camps and their fear of being handed over to the Nazis was just becoming known. Barot immediately installed a CIMADE team in the vast internment camp at Gurs, near the Pyrenees, convinced that one ought to live alongside those whom one is seeking to help.

As the number of CIMADE teams working under Barot grew, they sought to support internees not only materially but also spiritually and culturally. When the deportation of political activists, gypsies and, above all, massive numbers of Jews began in 1942, CIMADE joined the resistance and worked clandestinely to help many to escape across the borders into Spain and Switzerland (in the latter case in close liaison with the WCC in

Madeleine Barot (WCC/Peter Williams)

process of formation and its general secretary, W.A. Visser 't Hooft). Many parishes answered CIMADE's appeal, hiding Jews on the run.

In 1945, after the liberation, two tasks confronted CIMADE and the churches in an exhausted France: reconstruction, with the resettlement of displaced persons, and reconciliation with the Germans. Evaluating its own role under the new circumstances, CIMADE accented relations with foreigners, uprooted people and refugees, as well as ecumenism, organizing encounters of Protestants, Catholics and Orthodox. Barot however was convinced that by remaining independent of the churches, CIMADE and similar movements could take greater risks and initiatives. At the world Christian youth conference in Oslo in 1947, Barot (who had chaired part of a similar conference in Amsterdam in 1939) emphasized how much post-war young people were looking for a new, more community-focused life-style for the Christian world.

Like many others during the war, Madeleine Barot had shown that women are able to take on very significant responsibilities. At a time when the need for renewal of the church was evident, the post-war years clearly raised the issue of the place of women; in that connection Barot was called to the WCC's Department on the Co-operation of Men and Women in Church and Society, which she directed from 1953 until 1966. Unafraid to face the many delicate discussions to which underlying theological differences gave rise during those years — particularly the question of the place of women in the ordained ministry — Barot also devoted much of her time to promoting the preparation of women for various ecumenical responsibilities.

Later she was appointed to the WCC's department on development education, thus tackling different educational needs. The influence of the world conference on Church and Society (Geneva 1966) and the changes in perspective it produced, together with the dynamic unleashed in the Roman Catholic Church by the Second Vatican Council, led to the establishment of the joint body SODEPAX,* in which also Barot played an enthusiastic part.

Her years in Geneva enriched a wide-ranging network of contacts throughout the world, and after her retirement in France, she placed this at the disposal of the French Protestant Federation, the ecumenical anti-torture organization ACAT and, once again, CIMADE.

ANDRÉ JACQUES

A. Jacques, *Madeleine Barot*, WCC, 1991.

BARROW, NITA. B. 15.11.1916, Barbados. Barrow was a president of the WCC, 1983-91, and associate director of the WCC Christian Medical Commission in 1971 and its director, 1975-81. Her responsibilities included advising church-affiliated health institutions throughout the world on all developments in health care. She was among the first to study and work with alternative forms of health care for the underprivileged. She served as president of the YWCA and as president of the International Council for Adult Education, and was permanent representative and ambassador of Barbados at the United Nations. She is presently governor-general of Barbados. In 1985 she served as convener of the forum in Nairobi which marked the close of the United Nations Decade for Women. Barrow graduated from the University of Toronto School of Nursing and from Columbia University, New York.

ANS J. VAN DER BENT

BARTH, KARL. B. 10.5.1886, Basel, Switzerland; d. 10.12.1968, Basel. As a leading theologian, Barth had a decisive influence on the course of Protestantism in the 20th century, but remained a critical challenger of the ecumenical movement. He believed that authentic unity of the church would come about only if the church dared to be itself and to leave behind all self-righteous manifestations of power. Although from the early 1930s onwards he became a friend to W.A. Visser 't Hooft, Pierre Maury, and other ecumenical leaders, he missed a clear repudiation of natural theology in the Life and Work* movement, an attitude of uncompromising support for the Confessing Church* in Germany struggling against National Socialism, and an ecumenical reception of the Barmen declaration. He addressed Amsterdam 1948, inverting the theme to "God's Design and Man's Disorder", and participated in the meetings of the Committee of 25, which worked on the theme "Christ — The Hope of the World" for the Evanston assembly in 1954. For a long time critical also of the Roman Catholic Church, he showed an openness towards the movement of *aggiornamento* within Vatican II, warning the churches of the Reformation not to lag behind in their efforts towards renewal (see his *Ad Limina Apostolorum*, 1967). He lifted the dialogue between Protestantism and Roman Catholicism to a higher level. At the time of Uppsala 1968, Barth addressed a local congregation in Basel and asserted: "Anyone who says 'Yes' to Christ must say 'No' to the division of the churches."

Before he became professor of theology at Basel (1935-62), Barth was professor at Göttingen (1921), Münster (1925) and Bonn (1930). No other Protestant theologian of this century has produced so many works which were translated into so many languages. His *Commentary on Romans* (1919) led later to the development of dialectical theology. The formulation of confessional theology in the Barmen declaration was largely Barth's work. Between 1932 and 1967 he wrote 13 volumes of his *Church Dogmatics*. His message was that God's sole revelation* is in Jesus Christ* and that the word of God is his one and only means of communication with human beings. Since humanity is utterly dependent on divine grace,* all its boasted cultural achievements are rooted in sin.* See *Bibliographie Karl*

Barth, Hans Markus Wildi comp. (Zurich, Theologischer Verlag, 1984), Eberhard Busch, *Karl Barth* (Philadelphia, Fortress, 1976; orig. in German) and W.A. Visser 't Hooft, "Karl Barth and the Ecumenical Movement", *The Ecumenical Review*, 32, 2, 1980.

ANS J. VAN DER BENT

BEA, AUGUSTIN. B. 28.5.1881, Riedböhringen, Baden, Germany; d. 16.11.1968, Rome. Bea was president of the Secretariat for Promoting Christian Unity,* 1960-68, and presided over the drafting of three documents of the Second Vatican Council: Declaration on the Relationship of the Church to Non-Christian Religions, and Declaration on Religious Freedom. His personal influence in preparing the Dogmatic Constitution on Divine Revelation was considerable. His ecumenical achievements in the cause of Christian unity stemmed directly from his talents for friendship and his interest and competence in biblical studies. Already in 1935, with the express approval of Pius XI, his participation in the Old Testament congress of Protestant scholars at Göttingen established a precedent for future Roman Catholic collaboration in common projects concerning the Bible. He served on many Roman congregations, including the Pontifical Biblical Commission and the Congregation for the Doctrine of the Faith, was confessor to Pius XII, 1945-58, and was chairman of the committee for the revision of the Latin psalter. In 1959 he was created a cardinal deacon. Together with W.A. Visser 't Hooft he received in 1966 the peace prize of the Frankfurt Book Fair. During the last years of his life he intensified contacts with the WCC, the Orthodox churches, and the Christian World Communions, in particular the Lutheran World Federation, the Methodist World Council and the Anglican communion.

After two years of study in Freiburg, Bea entered the Society of Jesus in 1902 and was ordained in 1912. He taught Old Testament in the German seminary at Valkenburg, Holland, 1917-21. He was influential in the founding of Sophia University, Tokyo. In 1924 he took charge of Jesuits in Rome assigned to graduate studies and taught in the Pontifical Biblical Institute, of which he was rector, 1930-49. He was the editor of *Biblica*

for 20 years and wrote numerous works translated into several languages, including: *L'unione dei Cristiani* (ET *The Unity of Christians*, London, Chapman, 1963) and *Der Ökumenismus im Konzil* (ET *Ecumenism in Focus*, London, Chapman, 1969). See Stjepan Schmidt, *Augustin Cardinal: Der Kardinal der Einheit* (Vienna, Styria, 1989).

ANS J. VAN DER BENT

BEAUDUIN, LAMBERT. B. 5.8.1873, Rosoux-lès-Waremme, Belgium; d. 11.1.1960, Chevetogne. Beauduin was a pioneer in the 20th-century liturgical and ecumenical renewals of the Roman Catholic Church. Ordained in 1897, he joined the Aumôniers du Travail, a society of priests for the care of working men. In 1906 he entered the Benedictine abbey of Mont-César at Louvain. Convinced as both a scholar and a pastor that "the liturgy should be democraticized", he helped to organize the annual liturgical weeks which began in 1909, established the periodical *La vie liturgique* (since 1911 *Les questions liturgiques*), and wrote the manifesto of the liturgical movement, *La piété de l'Eglise* (1914). In 1921 he became professor of theology at San Anselmo in Rome, when he further developed his interest in the liturgies of the Eastern churches.

In response to Pius XI's 1924 request that the Benedictine congregations mediate the work of reunion between East and West, in 1925 Beauduin founded the monastery "of Union" at Amay-sur-Meuse, which moved in 1939 to Chevetogne.* In 1926 he founded the journal *Irénikon*. He had joined Cardinal D.J. Mercier in the later Malines (Belgium) conversations between Roman Catholics and Anglicans (1921-26). In a 1925 memoir he formulated the then controversial: "the Anglican church united to Rome, not absorbed".

The bold views of Dom Lambert in liturgy and ecclesiology shocked many Catholics. In 1928 he had to leave Amay, and three years later he was condemned before a Roman tribunal and sent to the abbey of En-Calcat in southern France. He was able to return to Chevetogne in 1951. As papal nuncio to Paris (1945-53), Angelo Roncalli (in 1958, Pope John XXIII) became a friend of Beauduin, and later said of the "condemned" monk of 1931: "The true method of working for the

reunion of the churches is that of Dom Beauduin." See L. Bouyer, *Dom Lambert Beauduin, un homme d'Eglise* (Tournai, Casterman, 1964), and S. Quitsland, *A Prophet
Vindicated* (New York, Paulist, 1973).

TOM STRANSKY

BELL, GEORGE ALLEN
KENNEDY. B. 4.2.1883, Norwich, England; d. 3.10.1958, Canterbury. The first
moderator of the WCC central committee and
a leading British ecumenist from the 1920s
through the 1950s, Bell has been called "the
paradigm of creative dissent". The eldest of
seven children, he was educated at Westminster School and Christ Church, Oxford.
After study at Wells Theological College,
under H.L. Goudge, he became a curate at
Leeds parish church. In 1914 he became
chaplain to Randall Davidson, archbishop of
Canterbury, who believed ecclesiastical
statesmanship to be "the art of the possible".
Bell later wrote a magnificent life of Davidson (1935).

At the first post-war meeting of the World
Alliance for Promoting International Friendship through the Churches,* Bell came under
the influence of Nathan Söderblom. He acted
as a secretary at the Lambeth conference of
1920, was one of the initiators of the "Appeal" and thereafter edited the four volumes of
Documents on Christian Unity, essential sources for the ecumenical historian. At 41, Bell
became dean of Canterbury, where he fostered the arts and the use of drama, including
John Masefield's *Coming of Christ* and T.S.
Eliot's *Murder in the Cathedral*, in Christian
worship. In 1929 he became bishop of
Chichester.

Bell's ecumenical work blossomed in the
area of Life and Work,* with Stockholm 1925
as the conference which brought his skills to
prominence. As a member of the commission
on church and state (1935), he wrestled with
what he thought the bankruptcy of social purpose in the church. His theological acumen
revealed itself after Stockholm in organizing
Anglo-German theological conferences at
Canterbury (1927) and Eisenach (1928),
which resulted in the symposium *Mysterium
Christi* (1930). Concern for peace and arbitration were also characteristic of Bell at this
time.

Hitler soon set Bell's agenda. Bell not only
warned against the Nazis but forged links with
Christians in Germany, especially the founders of the Confessing Church* like Bonhoeffer, to whom he was a true spiritual father.
Bell, as chairman of Life and Work, supported the Confessing Christians in forthright
resolutions at Fanø in 1934. Refugees, especially the so-called non-Aryan Christians,
other victims of Nazism and German internees
in Britain were a ceaseless concern. The later
Interchurch Aid and Refugee Service (now
Christian Aid) owed much to Bell, who sponsored the Christian Council for Refugees in
1938.

The most dramatic episode in Bell's career
was his meeting in Stockholm in May 1942
with Hans Schönfeld and Dietrich Bonhoeffer, who convinced Bell of viable opposition
to Hitler. Bell gave detailed information (a
mark of the enormous trust put in him) to
Anthony Eden, who did not act on it, but
Eden had little room for manoeuvre and could
not appear to be responding to "peace feel-
ers". The resistance issued in the debacle of
the Hitler "bomb plot" of 20 July 1944.

Bell never feared being in a minority. His
keen sense of justice to non-Nazi Germans led
to his speaking out in the House of Lords in
1944 in opposition to "area bombing" of German cities as incompatible with the doctrine
of the just war. His aversion to mass destruction is supported by evidence that neither
German industry nor morale was broken by
bombing, but this was not clear at the time.
Air Chief Marshall Harris thought he could
win the war without an invasion of Europe.
The loss of RAF personnel was heavy, as was
the threat of the German V1 and V2 rockets.
Bell appeared to some insensitive to the
realities of total war. In this matter he was
supported by A.C. Headlam, who had opposed him on Nazism and on proposals for a
WCC. Many thought Bell should have succeeded Temple as archbishop of Canterbury,
but he was not a popular speaker and Temple
clearly favoured Fisher.

Bell was prominent in the reconstruction of
relationships with the German churches after
war and a witness with Gordon Rupp and
W.A. Visser 't Hooft to the Stuttgart declaration* of October 1945, when the Council of
the German Evangelical Church spoke of
"solidarity of guilt". In England Bell was

George Allen Kennedy Bell (WCC photo)

secretary to the Anglican panel in conversations with the Free Churches after Lambeth 1920, was episcopal secretary at Lambeth 1930, a keen advocate of the South India scheme and joint chairman of the first round of negotiations between the Church of England and the Methodist Church (see **Anglican-Methodist relations**).

Few did more to facilitate the launching of the WCC. After being chairman of the central committee from 1948 to 1954, he was honorary president until his death. His last sermon was preached at the tenth anniversary of the Amsterdam conference. In 1958 he was awarded the order of merit of the Federal Republic of Germany but died before receiving it.

Bell saw the church* as the instrument of the kingdom,* the "sustaining, correcting, befriending opposite of the world". The statement of the Oxford conference of 1937 was very much Bell's stance, moulded by his incarnational Anglicanism. The aims of the ecumenical movement were "to secure that the church declares and maintains its vital interest as the body of the incarnate Lord in the community itself, in public as in private conduct, in the social, national and international affairs of men". *His Christianity and World Order* (1940) and *The Kingship of Christ* (1954) encapsulate his theological stance.

A fitting epitaph is the scene in April 1945, when Bonhoeffer, before execution, cried out: "Tell him [Bell] that for me this is not the end but the beginning... With him I believe in the principle of our universal Christian brotherhood, which rises above all national interests."

JOHN MUNSEY TURNER

Among the works of Bell are *Christian Unity: The Anglican Position*, London, Hodder & Stoughton, 1948; *Christianity and World Order*, Harmondsworth, UK, Penguin, 1940; *The Church and Humanity 1939-1946*, London, Longmans, 1946; *The Kingship of Christ: The Story of the WCC*, Harmondsworth, UK, Penguin, 1954; *Documents on Christian Unity*, 4 vols, London, Oxford UP, 1924-58 • See also R.C.D. Jasper, *George Bell, Bishop of Chichester*, London, Oxford UP, 1967 • K. Slack, *George Bell*, London, SCM, 1971 • W.A. Visser 't Hooft, *The Ecumenical Review*, 11, 2, 1959.

BERDYAEV, NICOLAS. B. 6.3.1874, Kiev; d. 23.3.1948, Paris, France. Involved in the study programme of the Life and Work* movement, in the Russian Student Christian Movement in exile and in the Oxford conference in 1937, Berdyaev attempted to persuade the educated class of his nation and abroad to give up its disregard of religion and to resume active participation in the life of the church. His numerous writings had a deep influence on Western Christianity and broadened the understanding of Orthodox thought and literature. Originally a sceptic, of Marxist leanings, he found his way back to the Orthodox faith after the revolution of 1905. He was brought to trial by the church in 1914 for his non-conformist position in religious matters and was saved from sentencing only by the onset of the Russian revolution. From 1922 onwards he lived as an émigré in Paris, where he interpreted the Christian religion in the light of modern intellectual interests, expounding a "spiritual Christianity" which has no need of doctrinal definitions. Often referred to as a "Christian existentialist", he was indebted for some of his ideas to Jacob Böhme, Immanuel Kant, Friedrich Nietzsche and Fyodor Dostoevski. Among his books are *Freedom and the Spirit* (London, Centenary, 1935), *The Destiny of Man* (London, Bles, 1937) and *The Meaning of History* (Cleveland, OH, Meridian, 1962).

ANS J. VAN DER BENT

BERKHOF, HENDRIKUS.

B. 11.6.1914, Appeltern, Gelderland, Holland. Berkhof was a member of the WCC central committee, 1954-75, and had a major part in the Faith and Order* study on "God in Nature and History", 1963-68. He addressed Uppsala 1968 on "The Finality of Jesus Christ", another Faith and Order study. He served as pastor in Lemele, 1938, and in Zeist, 1944, and was on the staff of the Institute "Church and World" at Driebergen, 1950. From 1960 onwards, he was professor of dogmatics and biblical theology at the University of Leiden. Several of his works are fruits of his ecumenical reflections and include *The Doctrine of the Holy Spirit* (Richmond, VA, John Knox, 1964), *Christus de zin der geschiedenis* (ET *Christ the Meaning of History*, London, SCM, 1966) and *Christelijk Geloof* (ET *Christian Faith*, Grand Rapids, MI, Eerdmans, 1979).

ANS J. VAN DER BENT

BIBLE, ITS ROLE IN THE ECU-MENICAL MOVEMENT. A particular type of Bible study has marked the ecumenical movement from its beginning. Its mood was expressed in a telegram sent by 500 Japanese students to a North American student conference in 1889, stating simply: "Make Jesus King!" This movement among students had started in Asian, North American and European student hostels, where young people from different churches gathered for prayer and Bible study, receiving a new vision of Christ's purpose for the oikoumene, the whole inhabited earth. Bible study not only served their own religious needs but led to Christian commitment, especially to missionary service abroad across cultural and denominational frontiers. In 1895 the telegram from Japan became a decisive factor in the creation of the World Student Christian Federation (WSCF),* which in turn served the ecumenical movement in all continents as the training ground for future leaders.

Ecumenical Bible study. There are many ways of studying the Bible: listening to and praying the biblical message in the context of liturgical celebration, preaching expositorily on biblical passages, analyzing biblical texts scientifically, seeking guidance through personal biblical meditation, choosing proof-texts for supporting doctrinal or socio-political creeds. All these and other ways of using (and often, alas, misusing) the Bible can be found in the ecumenical movement. Nobody has influenced the particular character of ecumenical Bible study more deeply than Suzanne de Diétrich. Her way of enabling successive generations of young people to study the scriptures, first in the service of the WSCF and later at the Ecumenical Institute in Bossey, near Geneva, made a strong impact on the movement, especially from the 1930s to the 1960s.

A few random examples highlight four characteristics of such ecumenical Bible study. The section of the conference on Faith and Order in Edinburgh 1937 which dealt with "The Church of Christ and the Word of God" states that the testimony given in holy scripture "affords the primary norm for the church's teaching, worship and life". This does not mean that all must have the same doctrinal understanding of biblical authority. It does imply, however, that all are ready to be guided, questioned and corrected by the biblical message in their various doctrinally and culturally conditioned situations. A small incident during a discussion at the WCC assembly in Amsterdam (1948) made this priority clear. A participant insisted that the Bible must be understood in the light of the later creeds. Irritated by this, Karl Barth closed the book of confessional statements from which the speaker had argued and put his Greek New Testament on top of it. The Bible is the primary norm.

The Bible was given to the churches so that they may discover their vocation in today's world. Ecumenical Bible study is therefore not an end in itself, nor can its impact and value be measured by the number of Bible quotations used. Rather, it is a continuing discipline and training for biblically informed thinking, acting and worshipping in the situations of today, which often appear to have no precedent. When the Ecumenical Institute was inaugurated in 1946, W.A. Visser 't Hooft wrote: "The programme of the Institute has three basic subjects: the Bible, the world and the universal church." In most gatherings at Bossey, Bible study indeed played an important role, attempting to discern the Christian vocation as churches face the challenge arising, e.g. from modern industrial society, new scientific discoveries or the religious and cultural pluralism of contemporary societies. Another instance of relating God's word with the modern world is found in the four small paperbacks called *Word for the World*, commissioned by the WCC assembly in Uppsala. For each day of the year there is a biblical meditation on the left-hand page, while on the right appear questions raised and insights gained in the ecumenical movement. The authors represent all major Christian confessions and five continents. The agenda of the oikoumene is here confronted with the biblical message.

Because of this essential relationship between the present world and God's word, ecumenical Bible study becomes an enterprise of the whole people of God. All have something to contribute — those who through their exegetical studies have a special knowledge of biblical texts in their original context and those who through their involvement in today's struggles of faith gain special insights into the biblical message for the present-day context. Small groups are the best setting for this. There the full participation of all becomes possible, doubts and critical questions can be frankly raised and Bible study then often leads to spontaneous worship and corporate involvement in biblically informed action. In the decades after the second world war, this type of participatory Bible study occurred in ecumenical work camps. In more recent times church base communities are typical examples of such groups and communities.

Searching for God's word together in the way described above leads to conversion and commitment. In the ecumenical movement quite different forms of involvement are thus triggered. Through common worship and biblical meditation during the Week of Prayer for Christian Unity,* many Orthodox, Catholics and Protestants were led to a deeper commitment to local church unity. Bible study was a major motivation for missionary commitment in the former Student Volunteer Movement; it provides the same motivation today in the costly involvement of groups in urban-rural mission.

Much less known are the biblical roots of the controversial WCC Programme to Combat Racism (PCR).* Ecumenically, all the right words about the sin of racism had been said from the WSCF conference in Peking in 1922 onwards. What more could be done? In the programme of the Uppsala assembly, no session on this topic had originally been planned. The assassination of Martin Luther King, however, who was to have preached at the opening worship, and events in Southern Africa led the organizers to squeeze in a discussion on racism during a free afternoon at the assembly. On the evening before that memorable session, a Swedish group had presented a challenging dance drama on Amos. The next day the assembly was confronted with a modern Amos, when the black American novelist James Baldwin spoke: "At this moment in the world's history it becomes necessary for me, for my own survival, not to listen to what you say but to watch very carefully what you do, not to read your pronouncements but to go back to the source [i.e. the Bible] and to check it out myself." It was partly the "coincidence" between the play on Amos and the prophetic challenge based on the Bible by James Baldwin which led to the establishment of the PCR. No wonder that one who was much involved in this new programme testified: "The word of God *happened* to us!"

Common biblical texts, translations and studies. Scholars from all Christian confessions have for many centuries worked together with Jewish scholars to establish the most accurate possible original Hebrew and Greek text of the Bible. As more ancient manuscripts are discovered, the process of reconstruction of the oldest and most reliable version of the Bible must continue. The ecumenical significance of this highly specialized scholarly work is seldom recognized.

Bible societies and their federation in the United Bible Societies (UBS), created in 1946, have often pioneered in interconfessional co-operation and transcultural work, where others lagged behind (see **Bible societies**). This is especially true of the co-operation between Christians of what is inadequately called evangelical and ecumenical persuasions. The UBS was also the first international Christian organization to assist the Amity Foundation (created by the China Christian Council) in a major project: the installation of a modern printing press in Nanjing, which since 1987 has been printing Bibles and educational material for the rapidly growing number of Christians in China.

Bible study in Oaxtepec, Mexico (WCC photo)

Since the Second Vatican Council the co-operation between the UBS and the Roman Catholic Church has increased. Thus in 1968 the Vatican Secretariat for Promoting Christian Unity and the UBS published jointly the "Guiding Principles for Interconfessional Cooperation in Translating the Bible". A revised version of this document was published in 1987. Protestant Bible translations are increasingly being used by Catholics and vice versa, and the number of joint translations is increasing.

Undoubtedly the most important of these common enterprises is the "Traduction oecuménique de la Bible" (TOB). With the full support of their respective church authorities, Protestant and Roman Catholic biblical scholars of the French-speaking world worked in interconfessional teams for translating, introducing and annotating all books of the Bible. To a lesser extent the Orthodox church and Orthodox biblical scholars also collaborated in this venture. In 1972 the New Testament and three years later the Old Testament with the deutero-canonical books (the Apocrypha) were published, both in a one-volume UBS version with abbreviated notes and in a much larger integral version with extensive introductions and annotations. With the TOB the French-speaking world has now a unique tool for ecumenical Bible study.

Such interconfessional Bible translation and annotation would have been impossible without the growing collaboration and mutual

correction among biblical scholars. They now use not only the same original text of the Bible but also essentially the same tools and methods of research. In several countries this close collaboration between biblical scholars has led to a similar collaboration for Bible study at the local church level. Study outlines and resource material are written and tested by interconfessional teams before they are jointly published, and the study enablers are trained in ecumenical seminars.

Such joint efforts can be extended to regional and world levels, if in the future the working relationship between the UBS, the World Catholic Federation for the Biblical Apostolate and the WCC is strengthened. Such a development might well become instrumental for a major ecumenical breakthrough in the coming decades, because in ecumenical Bible study not only do Christians from different confessions and cultural backgrounds meet with one another, but they also come into the presence of the living God, who challenges their disunity and lack of faith, giving courage and vision for renewal and joint mission.

According to the scriptures. When the WCC was founded in 1948, Bible study had become such an integral part of ecumenical thinking, action and worship that it was not felt necessary to mention this in the constitution, or even in the WCC basis. Soon, however, several churches asked that the content of the basis be spelled out more clearly. In 1953 the Church of Norway made the official proposal to add "according to the holy scriptures" to the basis. This proposal was inspired by the Reformation doctrine of *sola scriptura*. When an expanded version of the basis was accepted in 1961, the wording had been changed accordingly. The explanatory note specifies that this phrasing, "used by the apostle Paul on a number of occasions, has found a place in the ancient creeds and in later confessions and directs attention to the authority the scriptures possess for all Christians". What the revised basis expresses is therefore not one particular confessional understanding of biblical authority but the common ancient Christian acceptance of the Bible as the primary norm.

The Evangelical Alliance, a Protestant pioneer movement for church unity, had stated in its basis of 1846 that persons wanting to belong to the alliance must maintain "the Divine Inspiration, Authority, and Sufficiency of the Holy Scriptures" as well as "the Right and Duty of Private Judgment in the Interpretation of the Holy Scriptures". A much fuller authoritative statement on the role and interpretation of the Bible was made by the Second Vatican Council in 1965, when the Dogmatic Constitution on Divine Revelation was promulgated, a document of deep ecumenical significance. For the whole of the ecumenical movement, no similar authoritative statement exists. While Orthodox, Catholics and Protestants all recognize the scriptures as the primary norm, no full consensus has been reached on how this authority is to be understood and how the scriptures are authoritatively interpreted. However, a long study process was initiated by the WCC on exactly these questions. This led to a series of reports pointing to important convergences.

The first major inquiry which the study division of the WCC (then still in process of formation) undertook from 1946 onwards dealt with the theme "From the Bible to the Modern World". This study led to the Wadham College statement on "Guiding Principles for the Interpretation of the Bible" (1949). It strongly emphasizes the unity of the Bible and reflects the biblical theology which characterized ecumenical discussions in the 1940s and 1950s. The Commission on Faith and Order pursued this study and accepted in Montreal (1963) the report on "Tradition and traditions".* The Tradition (capital *T*) of the

gospel, testified in the scriptures, is distinguished from the various traditions (small *t*) which developed in the process of transmission. The report acknowledges that scripture itself is the result of this process of transmission, and it emphasizes the role which culture plays in the transmission of faith. This conclusion led to an examination of "The Significance of the Hermeneutical Problem for the Ecumenical Movement". Its report was presented to F&O in Bristol in 1967. It addresses the problem of theological pluralism in the Bible, which "reflects the diversity of God's actions in different historical situations and the diversity of human response to God's actions".

The report on "The Authority of the Bible", accepted by F&O in Louvain in 1971, is the most substantial statement arising from this study process. It examines how biblical authority relates to the present human experience. This approach leads to the rejection of a purely dogmatic definition of scriptural authority. What the Bible reports are not "bare facts" but interpreted events, whose authority proves itself to be authoritative in the life of the church. The report also deals with the question of the inspiration of the Bible and asks what is canonical within the canon.* This study process was concluded by an examination of "The Significance of the Old Testament in Its Relation to the New" (Loccum 1978), where the unity of the Bible is again strongly affirmed, but not in the sense of just one, all-embracing biblical theology. The complementarity between the two Testaments and the specificity of each are analyzed. The report also lists a whole series of new questions which need further ecumenical exploration. One of these was taken up in a consultation on "The Authority of Scripture in the Light of New Experiences of Women" (Amsterdam 1980).

The Bible in the life of the WCC. It would be presumptuous to claim that the whole life of the WCC is guided by God's word. The early leaders of the Council had been part of the biblical renewal in the 1940s and 1950s, strongly influenced by the remarkable ecumenical Bible studies at the world conferences of Christian youth in Amsterdam (1939) and Oslo (1947). The fact remains, however, that during the initial period of the WCC, ecumenical Bible study continued mainly at the Ecumenical Institute, during meetings of the ecumenical youth organizations and in training courses on the ministry of the laity, but it had no place in more official programmes such as those of the first two WCC assemblies. It must also be acknowledged that when the Bible is quoted in WCC documents, the danger of proof-texting is not always avoided. Nor have the insights gained in the above-mentioned study process on the authority and interpretation of the Bible become fully operative in the life of the WCC.

From the beginning, working relationships were established with the UBS. In the leadership of the two organizations there is considerable overlap, and in several WCC assemblies the work of the UBS was presented in special sessions. Moreover, from 1951 to 1968 UBS study secretaries — Arthur Mitchell Chirgwin, Edwin Hanton Robertson and Gerrit H. Wolfensberger — worked in Geneva under a joint committee with the WCC. Thus a study on "The Place and Use of the Bible in the Life of the Churches" was undertaken which led to a series of surveys. This collaboration with the UBS (which was totally financed by the Bible societies) could easily have become an alibi for the WCC to initiate no work for helping its member churches to live "according to the scriptures". However, at New Delhi in 1961 the experiment was made to have six sessions of participatory Bible study on the main theme in the three sections of the assembly. The report states that "many participants in the assembly found these periods of corporate Bible study to be among the most rewarding hours in the entire programme".

Encouraged by this experience, all the following assemblies reserved much time for such corporate reflection on God's word. In Uppsala (1968) participatory Bible studies were first held in the plenary and subsequently in the six sections of the assembly. In Nairobi (1975) the assembly participants divided into numerous small groups for Bible study and discussion, an attempt which received such a good response that even more time was set aside for small-group work in Vancouver (1983). Also world mission conferences (Mexico City 1963, Bangkok 1972-73, Melbourne 1980 and San Antonio 1989) as well as many other small and large WCC meetings provided substantial time for corporate Bible

study. In the WCC staff weeks of meetings at the Ecumenical Centre in Geneva, Bible study has become a regular feature.

The joint UBS/WCC study produced a statement on "The Bible in the Ecumenical Movement" which was received by the Uppsala assembly. Commending this statement, the assembly asked that means be developed "by which the World Council could more effectively help the member churches to encourage the distribution, reading and study of the Bible by their members". Therefore popular Bible study resources for use in local congregations were prepared on the themes of the last four assemblies, and this material has been translated into or adapted in many language areas in different continents. These resources were widely used by groups who thus in their own local situation participated in the global process of discerning God's will. The study material on "Images of Life" in connection with the Vancouver assembly was published in more than 30 different language editions, and the reactions received show that there is a great need for similar resources to serve local ecumenism. In response to the demand the WCC Publications office has made a great effort to publish books which stimulate ecumenical Bible study and biblical meditation.

The growing awareness of the role of the Bible for the ecumenical movement led in 1971 to the creation of a small Biblical Studies Secretariat (BSS), which until 1988 was directed by H.-R. Weber. Initially the BSS had mainly a consultative function, helping to strengthen the biblical orientation of various WCC programmes and pursuing studies on how various cultures influence the interpretative process. Because of increasing requests from member churches, national councils and theological education centres, the main emphasis of BSS work then changed, concentrating instead on the training of ecumenical Bible study enablers. BSS was thus involved in the leadership of over 100 national and regional residential training courses, organized by the inviting bodies in all regions of the world except the Middle East. This training combines the teaching of biblical theology with exercises in a variety of Bible study methods: historical-literary analysis of texts; story-telling and drama; biblical meditation by using visual art, fantasy and mime; transforming biblical passages into songs, prayers and liturgical celebrations. What has been learned in different confessional and cultural milieus is thus transmitted to Bible-study enablers around the world.

Much work is still to be done. Ecumenical reflection about the authority and interpretation of the Bible needs to be continued, taking account especially of the experience of women and theologies developing outside the North Atlantic world. The Orthodox churches are relatively little involved in the corporate ecumenical search for living "according to the scriptures", though they can both contribute to it and learn from it. Through the work of BSS an informal worldwide network of enablers for ecumenical Bible study is growing which needs to be strengthened by a continuing exchange of experience and resources. This means that the working relationship between the WCC, the UBS and the World Catholic Federation for the Biblical Apostolate must develop further. The discipline of corporate Bible study in ecumenical groups, meetings and assemblies has to be maintained in order that the ecumenical movement may indeed live and witness "according to the scriptures".

See also **canon; exegesis, methods of; hermeneutics; New Testament and Christian unity; Old Testament and Christian unity; scriptures; word of God.**

HANS-RUEDI WEBER

J. Crawford & M. Kinnamon eds, *In God's Image: Reflections on Identity, Human Wholeness and the Authority of Scripture*, WCC, 1983 • S. de Diétrich, *Le renouveau biblique, hier et aujourd'hui*, Neuchatel, Delachaux & Niestlé, 1969 • "Ecumenism and the Bible", *The Student World*, 49, 5, 1956 • E. Flesseman-van Leer ed., *The Bible: Its Authority and Interpretation in the Ecumenical Movement*, WCC, 1980 • "The Role and the Place of the Bible in the Liturgical and Spiritual Life of the Orthodox Church", in *Orthodox Thought*, G. Tsetsis ed., WCC, 1983 • R.C. Rowe, *Bible Study in the World Council of Churches*, WCC, 1969 • W.A. Visser 't Hooft, "The Bible and the Ecumenical Movement", *Bulletin of the United Bible Societies*, 56, 1963 • H.-R. Weber, *Experiments with Bible Study*, WCC, 1983 • *Word for the World*, London, Bible Reading Fellowship, 1970.

BIBLE SOCIETIES. Bible Societies are non-denominational organizations whose purpose is to translate, produce and distribute the Christian scriptures* in languages that people can understand at prices they can afford. In 1989 there were 110 Bible Society offices throughout the world linked through membership of the United Bible Societies. During 1989 they distributed some 15 million Bibles, 12 million New Testaments, and 500 million booklets and leaflets with portions of scripture.

The modern Bible Society movement began in 1804 with the founding of the British and Foreign Bible Society (BFBS). By confining itself to the distribution of the Bible only, "without note or comment", it hoped to enlist the support of Christians of all denominations. It inspired the formation of supporting branches in the United Kingdom, and of affiliated or independent societies overseas. By 1820 there were societies in France, Germany, the Netherlands, Scandinavia, Russia, Switzerland, Greece, Malta, Canada, the USA, the West Indies, South Africa, India, Ceylon, Malaysia and Australia. Their members were drawn from Anglican, Lutheran and Reformed churches and in some countries also from the Orthodox churches (Greece, Russia) and the Roman Catholic Church (Malta, Russia, Germany). Bible editions were published in translations approved by the various churches and according to their respective canons.

This fully interconfessional phase was short-lived: pressure from Protestant supporters of the BFBS, especially in Scotland, forced it to abandon publication of the deuterocanonical (apocryphal) books in 1826. Not all societies, however, accepted this decision. At the same time, successive popes began to issue attacks on Bible Societies as instruments of Protestant proselytism* and publishers of corrupted Bibles. Although the societies continued to provide a field for joint work by Anglicans and Protestants, by the middle of the 19th century co-operation with Roman Catholics and Orthodox was extremely limited.

After the Apocrypha controversy the BFBS increasingly sent its own representatives to establish agencies overseas. The American Bible Society (ABS), founded in 1816, developed work in areas where US missionaries were serving, notably the Middle East, China, Japan and South America. In 1861 the Bible Societies in Scotland joined together to form the National Bible Society of Scotland and soon had agents in Africa and the Far East. The Netherlands Bible Society (NBS), founded in 1814, concentrated its overseas work mainly in Indonesia. The societies worked closely with Protestant missionaries and aided the development of Protestant churches, not only in non-Christian areas, but also in traditionally Catholic and Orthodox countries.

After the first world war the societies began to look for ways of co-ordinating their work through "comity" agreements, through joint agencies in some areas and by setting up an international co-ordinating body, which finally came into existence as the United Bible Societies (UBS) in 1946. Since then, the larger societies have withdrawn from direct control of work in other countries and encouraged the development of autonomous national societies. The UBS provides information and technical assistance to all member societies and administers a world budget through which the richer societies support the less rich.

In 1804 it was reckoned that the Bible or some part of it had been translated into 67 languages. Largely through the work of the Bible Societies, that number rose to 200 by 1850, to 500 by 1900 and to 1,000 by 1950. In the main the societies published translations made by missionaries and local Christians, sometimes giving financial assistance to translators as well as specialist advice. The NBS was unique in sending out linguists to study indigenous languages and make Bible translations. The Württemberg Bible Society in Stuttgart (founded 1812) made a notable contribution through the publication of scholarly texts: Eberhard Nestle's Greek New Testament (1898, revised by Kurt Aland, 1979), Gerhard Kittel's Hebrew Old Testament (1937, revised by Karl Elliger and Wilhelm Rudolph, 1977), Alfred Rahlfs's Septuagint (1935), and Robert Weber's Vulgate (1969). The UBS called on an international group of scholars to produce a new edition of the Greek New Testament (1966, 3rd ed. corrected 1983) and handbooks giving exegetical and linguistic help to translators.

A movement of biblical renewal in the Roman Catholic Church was given an increased impetus by the Second Vatican Council, which stated that "easy access to sacred scripture should be provided for all the Christian faithful" (Constitution on Divine Revelation, 1965). In turn, the Bible

Societies began to re-affirm their original desire to serve all the churches by providing the Bible in the form that each communion required. Restrictions barring the publication of the Apocrypha were removed by the ABS in 1964 and the BFBS in 1966. Of the 527 UBS translation projects current in 1989, 155 had Roman Catholic participation. Also working in close liaison with the UBS is the World Catholic Federation for the Biblical Apostolate, which has co-operated in formulating a number of mutually agreed position papers, the most important of which was "Guiding Principles for Interconfessional Co-operation in Translating the Bible" (1968, updated in 1986).

An increasing number of Bible Societies have Roman Catholics on their boards and as staff members. Relations with the Orthodox churches are also close, with Orthodox staff and board membership in some countries, and UBS assistance, e.g., in providing printing paper for the Romanian and Armenian Orthodox church presses. The Bible Societies, meeting in council in Chiang Mai, Thailand, in 1980, pledged their "openness to assist every Christian church with scripture publications that support, deepen and intensify the church's life and mission", thus echoing the vision of one of the first secretaries of the BFBS in 1818, of a Bible Society that "studies to unite the Christian world, by distributing among them, according to their respective versions, the common standard of their faith and their practice." Consistent with this goal, the UBS maintains a close working relationship with the WCC.

Bible translating and publishing agencies not linked to the UBS include the Gideons, the International Bible Society, Living Bibles International, the Scripture Gift Mission, the Trinitarian Bible Society, the World Home Bible League and Wycliffe Bible Translators. Through the work of all these agencies, some portion of the Bible had, by the end of 1989, been published in 1,928 languages and dialects.

KATHLEEN CANN

W. Canton, *History of the British and Foreign Bible Society*, 5 vols, London, Murray, 1904-10 • J. Roe, *History of the British and Foreign Bible Society*, London, British & Foreign Bible Society, 1965 • *UBS Bulletin*, nos 144-45, 1986, on the history of the UBS.

BIBLIOGRAPHIES. The growth of the modern ecumenical movement has been accompanied by an increasingly rich store of bibliographic resources, some of which are listed here.

Bibliographies. Besides the bibliographies of the ecumenical movement listed below, extensive listings appear in *A History of the Ecumenical Movement*, vol. 1: *1517-1948*, Ruth Rouse & Stephen C. Neill eds, 3rd ed., WCC, 1986; and vol. 2: *1948-1968: The Ecumenical Advance*, Harold E. Fey ed., 2nd ed., WCC, 1986.

Classified Catalogue of the Ecumenical Movement, 2 vols, Boston, G.K. Hall, 1972, 1st supp., 1981; contains the major holdings of the WCC library in Geneva.
The Ecumenical Movement: A Bibliography Selected from the ATLA Religion Database, Chicago, American Theological Library Association, 1983; author and subject index.
International Ecumenical Bibliography (Internationale ökumenische Bibliographie), *1962-77*, 16 vols, Munich, Kaiser; Mainz, Matthias-Grünewald, 1967-83.
Répertoire bibliographique des institutions chrétiennes, Strasbourg, Centre de recherche et de documentation des institutions chrétiennes (CERDIC), 1968-; annual volumes indexed by computer.

Handbooks and encyclopedias. Several works list WCC-related churches, consultations, reports and various other aspects of the ecumenical movement.

Ans J. van der Bent, *Six Hundred Ecumenical Consultations, 1948-1982*, WCC, 1983.
Ans J. van der Bent, *Vital Ecumenical Concerns: Sixteen Documentary Surveys*, WCC, 1986.
Handbook of Member Churches: World Council of Churches, Ans J. van der Bent ed., rev. ed., WCC, 1985.
Index to the World Council of Churches Official Statements and Reports, 1948-1978, WCC, 1978.
Ökumene Lexikon: Kirchen, Religionen, Bewegungen, Hanfried Krüger, Werner Löser & Walter Müller-Römheld eds, 2nd ed., Frankfurt am Main, Otto Lembeck, 1987.

Ökumenische Theologie: Ein Arbeitsbuch, Peter Lengsfeld ed., Stuttgart, Kohlhammer, 1980.
Orientierung Ökumene: Ein Handbuch, Im Auftrag der Theologischen Studienabteilung beim Bund der Evangelischen Kirchen in der DDR, Hans-Martin Moderow & Matthias Sens eds, Berlin, Evang. Verlagsantalt, 1979.
World Christian Encyclopedia: A Comparative Study of Churches and Religions in the Modern World, AD 1900-2000, David B. Barrett ed., Nairobi, Oxford UP, 1982.

Major current ecumenical journals and serial publications. The following publications provide additional information about all aspects of the ecumenical movement. All of these are included in the holdings of the WCC library.

Catholica — Vierteljahresschrift für Ökumenische Theologie, Munich, 1932-.
CCIA Background Information, Geneva, 1975-.
CCPD Documents, Geneva, 1983-.
Christian Century: An Ecumenical Weekly, Chicago, 1884-.
Christianity and Crisis, New York, NY, 1941-.
Communio Viatorum, Prague, 1958-.
Concilium, Edinburgh, 1965-.
Dialogo Ecuménico, Salamanca, 1966-.
Ecumenical Press Service, Geneva, 1933-.
Ecumenical Review, Geneva, 1948-.
Ecumenical Trends, Garrison, NY, 1972-.
Ecumenism, Quebec, 1965-.
Ecumenist: A Journal for Promoting Christian Unity, Ramsey, NJ, 1962-.
Episkepsis, Chambésy-Geneva, 1970-.
Information Service, Secretariat for Promoting Christian Unity, Rome, 1967-.
International Bulletin of Missionary Research, Ventnor, NJ, 1950-.
International Review of Mission, Geneva, 1912-.
Irénikon, Chevetogne, 1926-.
Istina, Paris, 1954-.
Journal of Ecumenical Studies, Philadelphia, 1964-.
Kosmos in Oecumene, 's-Hertogenbosch, 1962-.
Materialdienst der ökumenischen Zentrale, Frankfurt, 1959-.

Mid-Stream: An Ecumenical Journal, Indianapolis, IN, 1961-.
Oecuménisme, Quebec, 1965-.
Ökumenische Rundschau, Frankfurt, 1952-.
Ökumenisches Forum, Graz, 1977-.
One in Christ: A Catholic Ecumenical Review, London, 1965-.
One World, Geneva, 1974-.
PCR Information: Reports and Background Papers, Geneva, 1979-.
Pro Mundi Vita Bulletin, Brussels, 1964-.
Proche Orient Chrétien, Jerusalem, 1951-.
Renovación Ecuménica, Salamanca, 1974-.
Saamhorig, Amersfoort, 1976-.
Sobornost, London, 1935-.
Una Sancta, Freising, Bavaria, 1947-.
Unité chrétienne, Lyons, 1949-.
Unité des chrétiens, Paris, 1975-.
Wereld en Zending, Amsterdam, 1972-.
WSCF Journal, Geneva, 1979-.

WCC library. The WCC library in Geneva, established in 1946, has over 50,000 titles of printed ecumenical literature. Since 1986 the library has provided a computer service to churches, ecumenical bodies and individuals in any part of the world. The computer system is multilingual and compatible with other equipment commonly used in many countries. Thus, institutions can have direct on-line access to the data bank in Geneva and can place their book orders by electronic mail. In 1989 the WCC's documentation service was integrated into the library. Those who have no access to a computer can consult the extensive updated bibliography on the ecumenical movement in the second edition of *A History of the Ecumenical Movement, 1948-1968*.

The library also houses the archives of the 20th-century ecumenical movement: Faith and Order, since 1927; Life and Work, 1925-48; the International Missionary Council, 1910-61; the World Alliance for Promoting International Friendship through the Churches, 1906-48; the World Student Christian Federation, since 1920; the World Council of Christian Education and Sunday School Association, 1907-71; the German church struggle and relations between Geneva and the Confessing Church in Germany, 1933-45; the world conferences of Christian youth, 1939-52; the World Council of Churches "in process of formation", 1938-48; the WCC since 1948, including (1) correspondence and files

of the general secretariat; (2) complete files of the first six assemblies; (3) records of the central and executive committee meetings; (4) documents of WCC divisions, departments and secretariats, and of WCC units and sub-units from 1971 onwards; the Joint Working Group and SODEPAX; national and regional conferences and councils of churches. The WCC archives contain some 3 million documents (A.J. van der Bent, "Historia Oecumenica", *The Ecumenical Review*, 35, 3, 1983). Students and scholars have direct access to most of the records.

ANS J. VAN DER BENT

BILHEIMER, ROBERT S.
B. 28.9.1917, Denver, CO, USA. Bilheimer was programme secretary in the WCC New York office, involved in the organization of Evanston 1954, and was associate general secretary and director of the WCC Division of Studies, with responsibility for organizing the New Delhi assembly, 1954-63. Before his ordination in the Presbyterian Church in the USA in 1945, he was administrative secretary of the newly founded, New York based World Student Service Fund, 1940-41, and associate secretary of the Student Volunteer Movement for Foreign Missions, 1941-45. He served as national secretary of the Interseminary Movement, 1945-48, and in 1947 became assistant to the general secretary of the WCC, responsible for the final preparations of Amsterdam 1948. He has written *What Must the Church Do?* (New York, Harper, 1947) and *The Quest for Christian Unity* (New York, Association Press, 1952), and edited *Faith and Ferment: An Interdisciplinary Study of Christian Beliefs and Practices* (Minneapolis, Augsburg, 1983). His latest book, *Breakthrough* (WCC, 1989), is an insightful personal account of the ecumenical movement.

ANS J. VAN DER BENT

BIO-ETHICS. The scope of bio-ethics includes all questions of right and wrong in decisions or behaviour which arise in the scientific study and control of organic life. Biology, biochemistry and biotechnology are the life sciences within which bio-ethical questions arise. These have particular reference to medical practice: hence, biomedical ethics. But they refer also to modes of research in molecular genetics and the technical application of genetic knowledge to fields beyond medicine, such as agriculture, animals and pharmacology.

The beginning of the new era of bio-ethics can be dated to 1953 with the discovery of the structure and chemical codes of the deoxyribonucleic acid (DNA) molecule. In 1973 researchers announced that the 3,000 million units of the human DNA, comprising 100,000 genes, were susceptible to manipulation, or engineering, which changes the very nature of cells. Using much simpler organisms, such as bacteria, fruit flies or mice, researchers opened new possibilities for enhancing human health and economy. However, they also created difficult problems for theology, ethics, ecology and social policy.

For theology, new meaning is given to the doctrine of divine creation,* both original and continuing. The wonder of life has become ever more wonderful as scientists explain the genetic nature of all organisms, human and non-human, and their evolutionary relationships and continuities. The biological uniqueness and free will of humans, as traditionally viewed, are thus called into question.

Ethical issues are intensified, or newly introduced, by modes of assisted reproduction, genetic screening, abortion,* treatment or non-treatment of newborns, gene therapy and care of handicapped persons. Ecological problems are caused by the ambiguities of value in engineering transgenic animals and plants, creating bacteria for specific purposes, and possibly disrupting the balances of ecosystems necessary to all life on earth. Social policies and laws are needed to assure that medical services of a genetic nature, along with all kinds of sophisticated devices and treatments, are accessible in a democratic way; that human and animal subjects are protected; and that risks to human health and safety are minimized by regulation.

Social policies and laws are needed to assure that medical services of a genetic nature, and all kinds of sophisticated devices and treatments, are accessible in a democratic way, particularly in relation to the concerns of women, minorities and third-world peoples, whose right to be involved in decision-making processes has been particularly emphasized by the ecumenical movement. Human and animal subjects should be protected, and risks to human health and safety minimized by regulation.

The WCC. The WCC began considering some of these developments in 1968 with a consultation on human experimentation, held at the Ecumenical Institute, Bossey. Beginning in 1970, the Sub-unit on Church and Society convened several conferences of scientists, theologians and policy-makers to discuss genetics and the quality of life. The findings of the consultation held in Zurich in 1973 constituted the biological and bio-ethical agenda for the world conference on "Faith, Science and the Future" in Cambridge, Massachusetts, in 1979. The report of the conference emphasized five points. First, it warned against the ideology of eugenics based upon false theories of biological inequities of human worth and implemented by coerced genetic selection. Second, it recommended genetic counselling for prospective parents and pre-natal diagnosis for pregnant women but rejected "cost-benefit" reckoning as a determining factor for abortion. Here and elsewhere in WCC discussions, abortion has been a very sensitive issue because of divided opinions over its moral legitimacy and its unique pertinence to women's rights. Third, contraception was accepted by the report, as well as artificial insemination by the husband's sperm (AIH); but the use of donated sperm or ova outside of the marital union (AID) was questioned. Fourth, it accepted therapy for monogenic diseases by gene replacement in the body (somatic) cells of humans but rejected the modifying of sex (germ) cells in vitro. Finally, the report urged churches to seek justice and equity in the allocation of all medical resources, especially those involving new genetic techniques.

The momentum of the Cambridge conference led to a small consultation in the Netherlands in 1981 on "Ethical and Social Issues in Genetic Engineering and the Ownership of Life Forms". In a general context of concern for social and economic problems engendered by genetic science, the participants defended the integrity of human life and of the person against the reducing of human life to chemical-physical processes. Manipulations of germ-line cells, or the mixing of human and non-human DNA, could result in producing something less than human, they said. They advocated regulatory control of recombinant DNA technology at all institutional levels, especially when such would lead to monopolizing plant seeds, hybridizing human embryos for experimentation or preparing new organisms for biological warfare.

Recommendations were made for continuing efforts to study and clarify these kinds of issues within the WCC and in co-operation with other churches outside the council and with various international organizations.

Some churches took up particular biotechnological issues during the 1980s, but lack of funds and staff made it impossible for the WCC to carry the international ecumenical discussion further until 1989, when the central committee referred a report on biotechnology to the churches and approved a set of recommendations.

The report, which set the issues of biotechnology within the context of a theology of creation, treated six areas: human genetic engineering, reproductive technologies, intellectual property (patenting of life), environmental effects, military applications and impact on the third world.

The recommendations called for prohib-

The "transgenic mouse", patented in 1988 (Keystone)

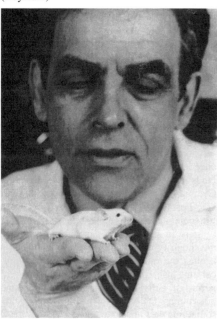

ition of genetic testing for sex selection, commercialized child-bearing and the commercial sale of ova, embryos and sperm, patenting of animal life-forms, and use of genetic engineering as part of biological or chemical warfare research. Warning of the dangers of the use of genetic testing for "involuntary social engineering", experiments involving the human germline, embryo research and release of genetically engineered organisms into the environment, the WCC also called for further reflection and international controls in these areas.

The Roman Catholic Church. Deep differences between the Roman Catholic teaching on procreation and the teachings or views of Protestant communions have prevented the full involvement of all these churches in studies of bio-ethics. Individual Catholics have participated in WCC conferences, however. And at least one bilateral dialogue has dealt with the difficult question of abortion: that between the RCC and the Reformed churches, 1976-79. In 1986 the American dialogue on terminal care and death began between the RCC and the United Methodist Church.

Many consultations among Roman Catholics have resulted in formal pronouncements from the Vatican on certain bio-ethical issues. Pope John Paul II has spoken frequently about them. The Second Vatican Council* declared a categorical prohibition of "murder, genocide, abortion, euthanasia or wilful self-destruction" (*Gaudium et Spes* 27). The encyclical *Humanae Vitae* by Pope Paul VI (1968) clearly forbade contraception (see **birth control**). And a series of exhortations, declarations and instructions from the Congregation for the Doctrine of the Faith specified inhibitions against abortion (1974), euthanasia (1980) and artificially assisted reproduction (1987). However, papal statements on biotechnology and genetic intervention have been negative only in respect to putting human subjects at undue risk.

Ongoing developments. In the US an ecumenical coalition prompted the federal government to make a study of the possible dangers of genetic engineering. A letter was addressed to President Carter in 1980 by the officers of the National Council of the Churches of Christ (NCCC), the US Catholic Conference and the Jewish Synagogue Council, expressing strong concerns. This resulted in the government's publication of *Splicing Life* (1982), which has become a standard of thinking on the subject. In 1986 the NCCC adopted a lengthy policy statement on "Genetic Science for Human Benefit", which gives theological reasons for considering the promises as well as the dangers of biotechnology. A large group of Protestant evangelicals, known as the American Scientific Affiliation, is also committed to the study of bio-ethical problems.

With the proliferation of centres for research and teaching in the fields of bio-ethics and medical ethics, as well as the formation of ethics committees in hospitals, it is evident in many countries that persons having religious commitment and theological expertise are playing prominent roles. There is an implicit ecumenism expressed in these institutions which is also revealed in the rapidly growing number of books and journals devoted to ethics in the life sciences.

Any survey of the vast field of bio-ethics is doomed to be rendered obsolescent by the accelerated findings of scientific research. The science-fiction character of certain procedures and techniques changes to fact within a decade, and soon these methods of assisting procreation, treating diseases or extending life's longevity become routine. One thinks readily of in vitro fertilization, cardiac surgery and organ transplants, pharmaceuticals, intensive care units and artificial organs for human bodies.

What does Christian faith have to do with all these scientific and technological developments? Discussions within the broad ecumenical movement of churches reveal the main concerns and contributions which Christianity offers. There is unyielding commitment to the enhancement of human life and the protection of the integrity and dignity of all persons. Beyond the humanistic motive is the ultimate belief in the divine creation of each human being in the image of God and in the divine purpose to redeem each one from sin* and death through the salvific work of Jesus Christ (see **salvation**). It is this faith, rather than a theory of vitalism or a philosophy of human rights, which is the basis for maintaining the sanctity of human life.

Belief in the divine creation and redemption of human beings carries with it the mandate of responsibility to God for one's own life and for others' lives and for the created order itself. The WCC's emphasis upon "the integrity of creation" is a reminder of human obligation before God. For Christians, then, bio-ethics implies a particular, strong sense of fidelity to the perceived will of God, however debatable such perceptions may be.

The breadth and diversity of the ecumenical movement are such as to remind people of differing points of sensitivity about bio-ethical concerns. In countries of the northern hemisphere, where technical development is advanced, ethical interest usually focuses on scientific laboratories and the modern hospitals. For the majority of humankind, however, bio-ethical problems are limited to basic areas of primary health care. "Equal access" and "cost containment" for high-tech medicine are unreal questions where sheer survival and the struggle for political and economic self-dependence are uppermost.

The universal church and the many churches of Jesus Christ have a special role in the human venture of finding healing and wholeness of life in freedom and fulfilment. All the emerging issues of bio-ethics are thus of concern to the whole Christian community.

See also **life and death**.

J. ROBERT NELSON

P. Abrecht & C. Birch eds, *Genetics and the Quality of Life*, Potts Point, Australia, Pergamon, 1975 • P. Abrecht ed., *Faith and Science in an Unjust World*, WCC, 1980 • *Biotechnology: Its Challenges to the Churches and the World*, WCC, 1989 • *Manipulating Life*, WCC, 1982 • A.C. Varga, *The Main Issues in Bioethics*, New York, Paulist, 1984 • H.-R. Weber ed., *Experiments with Man*, WCC, 1969.

BIRTH CONTROL. Although birth control refers in a general sense to all measures to regulate birth (including intercourse only on days when the woman is biologically incapable of conceiving), the term is normally used for artificial measures of contraception (use of pills, condoms, intra-uterine devices, contraceptive foam). It is on this latter sense that Christian ethical debate has centred.

Historical background. The ability to love without producing children is a fundamental distinction between human beings and animals. Animals reproduce at specific periods marked by the rut or heat; women and men *procreate*, something completely different psychologically and culturally, even if very similar biologically. Here it is no longer instinct that triggers mutual attraction but a host of feelings and fantasies as well as family and social conventions. There is evidence from civilizations of the distant past of human beings looking for prescriptions making sexual love possible without the risk of conceiving an unwanted child. There is no question of this having been an erotic perversion.

Yet for thousands of years women and men accepted (and usually wanted) all the children nature gave them through fruitful sexual intercourse. Children were seen as a blessing from God. The infant death rate was high; and many births were needed to ensure a few survivors.

The Bible offers no explicit guidance in this area but does have some significant suggestions. The Old Testament has nothing to say in favour of birth control. Its comments are all against it, among them the scandalous story of Onan and Tamar (Gen. 38). From the time of the patriarchs, Israel wanted children at any price to keep hold of the inheritance of the founding fathers and, some say, to see the promised Messiah. For them there was no greater spiritual misfortune or social shame than to be a childless widow or an infertile woman. Moreover, Israel was a very small people, constantly threatened by its neighbours with slavery and deportation, genocide and extinction.

Nevertheless, we do find pointers in the Bible. The animals reproduce abundantly "according to their kinds", but humanity has been created in the very image of God, free and loving. Why, then, should human beings not also be free and loving in their sexual lives, rather than linking sexuality exclusively with reproduction? Many biblical passages speak of love without speaking of children (e.g. Gen. 2:23-24; the prophet Hosea; the Song of Songs; Eph. 5:21-33).

With the New Testament and the coming of the Messiah, those who cannot have children — widows and eunuchs — are fully rehabilitated. Children are a blessing, a gift of God, and no longer a religious necessity. Now all live under the new covenant,* and no longer under the first, old covenant.

The contemporary situation. The rapid development in this century of generally safe and widely available methods of contraception has increased possibilities to liberate women and couples from conceiving unwanted children and the attendant anxiety. At first, the churches saw in this several risks: that of disobeying God, the actual giver of children, by artificial intervention in the natural mystery of procreation; that of a family selfishness which rejected the prolific nature of life; and that of growing immorality as sexual relations became free of the danger of conception. Increasingly, these timid reactions were at odds with the aspirations of couples and above all of women, scientific possibilities and social needs.

Since the 1930s church opinion on the subject of birth control has generally divided into two groups. On the one side, first the Anglican church, then all Protestant churches except the most conservative, have approved, supported and favoured the use of contraceptives. On this issue, Orthodox churches are divided among themselves, according to where they are situated.

Churches approving the use of contraceptives have sought to be sensitive to the needs and difficulties of couples who felt obliged by religious tradition either to produce too many children or to abstain completely from sexual intercourse. They would agree that the Bible does not legalistically enjoin a high birth rate, and that its portrayal of children as a blessing from God does not mean that they are an inescapable fate. And the churches have worked educationally to ensure that contraception does not cheapen sexuality, for while methods change, personal affection and long-term attachment do not.

On the other hand, the official teaching of the Roman Catholic Church has consistently opposed contraception by artificial means, a teaching reiterated several times since 1930. Although the Second Vatican Council discussed the issue (1964), Pope Paul VI reserved to himself the final decision after a full review by a commission appointed by his predecessor, John XXIII. A report by the majority of that commission favoured a change in the traditional Catholic position, but Paul VI, in his encyclical* *Humanae Vitae*, wrote that "the church, calling men back to the observance of the norms of the natural law as interpreted by constant doctrine, teaches that each and every marriage act must remain open to the transmission of life". Besides this reasoning from natural law,* the encyclical argued that artificial contraception has such consequences as conjugal infidelity, general lowering of morality, corruption of youth and loss of respect for women.

The appearance of the encyclical drew a vigorous negative response in some Catholic quarters. While accepting its teaching as authoritative, a number of European and North American bishops conferences noted the primacy of conscience, the need to be understanding and forgiving and the judgment that Catholics who sincerely cannot follow its teaching are not thereby separated from the love of God. Subsequent surveys have generally indicated a high percentage of non-compliance with its teaching among Catholics.

The question of birth control also arises in connection with the issue of population explosion.* Several factors lead to rapid increase in the number of children in many countries: infant mortality rates have declined with the spread of medical knowledge and hygiene, and old traditions, such as that which forbade sexual relations while a mother was breastfeeding her child (sometimes as much as three years), have been abandoned. For many peasants, agricultural subsistence requires labour; with no capital to hire workers, they continue to have children in order to work the land and survive. Because the decline in child mortality has not been accompanied by global economic and political changes, there are many countries in which adequate food, health care and education are not available for the growing number of children.

The relationship of artificial means of birth control to population policy is an extremely controversial issue, particularly in countries with a high Roman Catholic population. A WCC report in 1973 rejected "insistence on effective population limitation as a condition of aid" to countries and argued against a "focus only on population policy in order to change social and economic conditions. It is necessary to change social and economic conditions to make population policy effective."

Ecumenical perspectives. So great is the difference among the churches here that when the opinion of the public is sought on what divides churches, many would no longer answer in terms of theological issues like baptism, eucharist or ministry, but in terms of contraception, abortion* and divorce*. The sixth report (1990) of the Joint Working Group* between the WCC and the Roman Catholic Church mentioned "permanent married love and procreation" among its examples of ethical issues on which "there is not enough serious, mature, and sustained ecumenical discussion".

Is ecumenical reconciliation possible on this point? My impression is that on this issue the vast majority of Roman Catholics have the same reactions as Protestants, but that the magisterium* is afraid to reverse its many previous public condemnations of contraception. At the same time, we may add that the danger for Protestants is to accept every scientific and social novelty without sufficiently indicating what is genuinely unacceptable, namely the dissociation of sexuality not from the capacity to reproduce but from human love. We must therefore watch out for the limitations of science when it is tempted to experiment in detachment from emotional considerations.

ANDRÉ DUMAS

Fruitful and Responsible Love, Middlegreen, St Paul, 1979 ● M.S. Webb, *Family Planning*, New York, Friendship, 1972 ● K.H. Wrage, *Children, Choice or Chance*, Philadelphia, Fortress, 1969.

BLAKE, EUGENE CARSON.

B. 7.11.1906, St Louis, MO, USA; d. 13.7.1985, Stamford, CT. Blake was general secretary of the WCC, 1966-72. Earlier he was a member of the central and executive committees, 1954-66, chairman of the WCC finance committee, 1954-61, and chairman of the Division on Interchurch Aid, Refugee and World Service, 1961-66. His proposal in 1960 for church union, made in a sermon at Grace Cathedral, San Francisco, developed into the Consultation on Church Union.* President of the National Council of Churches of Christ in the USA (NCCC), 1954-57, Blake continued as a member of its general board until 1966. He was stated clerk of the United Presbyterian Church in the USA (until 1958, the Presbyterian Church in the USA) and was a delegate to the WCC assemblies in 1954 and 1961, to the general councils of the World Presbyterian Alliance in 1948, 1954 and 1959, and to the Faith and Order conferences Lund 1952, Oberlin 1957 and Montreal 1963.

After studies at Princeton Theological Seminary, he served as assistant pastor in New York City, 1932-35 and as pastor in Albany, NY, 1935-40, and Pasadena, CA, 1940-51. He taught at Forman Christian College, Lahore, India (now Pakistan), 1928-29. Blake was an ardent advocate of the civil rights movement, particularly through his chairmanship of the NCCC's commission on religion and race. In 1963 he was jailed for leading an anti-segregation demonstration. He spoke publicly against US involvement in the Vietnam war. He served on President Johnson's National Advisory Council for the War on Poverty, and was a trustee of various universities and institutes. In retirement Blake was active in several areas, including the work of Bread for the World, a US Christian anti-hunger lobby. He had remarkable administrative skills, which guided the WCC during the time when its structures required re-alignment and revision. He wrote *The Church in the Next Decade* (New York, Macmillan, 1966). See R. D. Brackenridge, *Eugene Carson Blake: Prophet with Portfolio* (New York, Seabury, 1978), and also *The Ecumenical Review*, 38, 2, 1986.

ANS J. VAN DER BENT

BLISS, KATHLEEN. B. 25.7.1908, London; d. 13.9.1989. Bliss was a main speaker at Amsterdam 1948, where she was chairperson of the committee on the laity. In a preliminary draft of the assembly message, she wrote, "We intend to stay together", a sentence widely quoted since then. She was a member of the central and executive committees, 1954-68, and was moderator of the Commission on Integration of the WCC and the World Council of Christian Education. She served on the British Council of Churches, 1942-67, and was general secretary of the Board of Education of the Church of England, 1957-66. Bliss studied theology at Cambridge and was lecturer in religious studies at the University of Sussex, 1966-73. She was the editor of *The Christian News-Letter*, 1945-49, and wrote *The Service and Status of Women in the Churches* (London,

SCM, 1963) and *The Future of Religion* (Harmondsworth, Penguin, 1969).

ANS J. VAN DER BENT

BOEGNER, MARC. B. 21.2.1881, Epinal, France; d. 19.12.1970, Strasbourg, France. Boegner was a member of the WCC provisional committee, 1938-48, and then a president of the WCC, 1948-54. He was president also of the Protestant Federation of France, 1928-61, the Reformed Church of France, 1938-50, the Comité inter-mouvements auprès des évacués, 1945-68, and the French Student Christian Movement, 1920-39. Participating in Oxford 1937 and Edinburgh 1937, he was one of the founders of the WCC. After studying law and theology, he was ordained in 1905 and then was pastor at Aouste-sur-Sye, 1905-11, professor at the College of the Evangelical Missionary Society, 1911-18, and pastor at Passy (Paris), 1918-54. During the second world war, he courageously intervened for Jews and refugees. From 1962 he was a member of the French Academy. Boegner greatly promoted the ecumenical movement in France and abroad. He was an observer at the Second Vatican Council and in 1965 addressed the gathering in Geneva when Cardinal Bea announced the creation of the Joint Working Group.* His writings include *Le problème de l'unité chrétienne* (Paris, Editions "Je sers", 1947) and *L'exigence oecuménique* (ET *The Long Road to Unity: Memories and Anticipations*, London, Collins, 1970). See R. Mehl, *Le Pasteur Marc Boegner* (Paris, Plon, 1987).

ANS J. VAN DER BENT

BONHOEFFER, DIETRICH.
B. 4.2.1906, Breslau, Prussia; d. 9.4.1945, Flössenberg, Bavaria. Executed in the last days of the second world war in a vengeful act of cruelty by the Nazi regime, which he had contested since Hitler came to power in 1933, Bonhoeffer as a young man played a minor but highly significant part in the international relationships of German Protestants with the ecumenical organizations of the 1930s. After his death, however, the spiritual and theological inspiration of his last years, shining through his *Letters and Papers from Prison*

and the great biography by his close friend Eberhard Bethge, have proved to be of worldwide and lasting significance for many of the leaders and the issues in the continuing ecumenical movement.

Born into a large and influential family of intellectuals and professionals in Berlin, Bonhoeffer was a successful theological student and quickly embarked on an academic career. Travels and study opportunities in Rome, Barcelona and New York opened him to other cultures, and the fire of Karl Barth's Christ-centred theology drew him into a passionate opposition to much in his own church, which flowered in a lifelong commitment to the Confessing Church.* Appointed in 1931 as one of three part-time youth secretaries for the World Alliance for Promoting International Friendship through the Churches* and for the Ecumenical Council for Life and Work,* he spent 1933-35 as pastor of one of the German congregations in London, devoting most of his energy to the many questions in the early stages of the Confessing Church and coming to know Bishop George Bell of Chichester, for whose prophetic leadership against Nazism Bonhoeffer provided much of the material and inspiration.

From 1935 he was in charge of an unofficial, later illegal, theological seminary of the Confessing Church in Pomerania, whose innovations in spirituality and community living are reflected in *The Cost of Discipleship* and *Life Together*. When this activity was totally proscribed, American friends invited him in June 1939 to the USA, but he was at once unhappy there and returned to Germany in August in order to face the dark days ahead among his own people. Family members then invited him into the demanding double life of a secret agent in the counter-espionage service, where a plot against Hitler was being prepared. This enabled him to visit W.A. Visser 't Hooft and Hans Schönfeld in Geneva, as well as church leaders in occupied Norway, and to meet Bishop Bell in Stockholm to appeal for British support for the plotters. He was arrested in April 1943 and spent the remaining two years of life outwitting the interrogators, impressing his warders and fellow prisoners with a deeply Christian demeanour, and writing the poems, letters and fragments of his *Ethics* that are his finest memorial.

Much in the subsequent fascination with his legacy has focused on many-layered phrases such as his advocacy of radically new Christian responses to "a world come of age" or his practice of a "secret discipline" of meditation and prayer. His friends have witnessed to the growth in less than 40 years of a remarkably rich and mature Christian, able to face with open mind and heart even the deepest ambiguities of human existence, while radiating single-mindedly the love that stems from the Creator who has been willing to accept death on a cross in order that all may live.

MARTIN CONWAY

BOROVOY, VITALI. B. 18.1.1916, Byelorussia. Representative of the Russian Orthodox Church at the WCC, 1962-66 and 1978-85, Borovoy was a member and assistant director of the Secretariat for Faith and Order,* 1966-72, and currently is a member of the WCC central committee and the Faith and Order standing committee. He was an observer at the Second Vatican Council, 1962-65, a member of the Joint Working Group* of the WCC and the RCC, 1965-72, and of the annual meeting of the Christian World Communions,* 1962-85. Educated at Vilna Theological Seminary and Warsaw University, he was ordained in 1944 and became vice-dean of the Minsk Theological Seminary, 1944-54, professor of ancient church history at the Leningrad Theological Academy, 1954-62, and dean of the Moscow Patriarchal Cathedral and professor of Byzantine church history at the Moscow Theological Academy, 1973-78. Since 1985, he has served as deputy chairman of the department for external church relations of the Moscow patriarchate and professor of the history of the Western churches at the Moscow Theological Academy. His articles have appeared in several ecumenical journals, and his essays in ecumenical anthologies.

ANS J. VAN DER BENT

BOSSEY, ECUMENICAL INSTITUTE OF. At the initiative of W.A. Visser 't Hooft and the WCC provisional committee, the Ecumenical Institute of Bossey was founded in 1946 as an ecumenical training centre, with emphasis on laity and youth. Visser 't

Hooft foresaw that reconciliation and reconstruction after the second world war would require both "the renewal of the church" and "the penetration of Christian convictions in all realms of life". Located in the foothills of the Jura mountains, about 20 km. from Geneva, the institute has served over 15,000 participants, in seminars and conferences, from a wide range of churches and ecumenical bodies, cultures and nations. WCC member churches and the Roman Catholic Church sustain and use the facilities, including its permanent staff and other nearby WCC personnel.

In 1952 the institute began a graduate school of ecumenical studies — a five-month programme recognized by the theology faculty of the University of Geneva. Many institute students now hold key ecumenical responsibilities in churches and organizations.

Directors contributed to the present shape, direction and methodology of the institute. A lay mission scholar, H. Kraemer (1946 and 1948-55) and Suzanne de Diétrich (1946-55), a lay biblical scholar and educator, laid the basis for a biblical and world-oriented Christian witness. H.-H. Wolf (1955-66), of Germany, enlarged the range of participants. N.A. Nissiotis (1966-74) gave Eastern Orthodoxy more visibility and stressed interdisciplinary ecumenical research and debate between theology and other sciences. The African theologian J.S. Mbiti (1974-78) enlarged intercultural dialogue, mainly with Africa and Asia. Karl Hertz (1978-83) secured a more solid and widespread financial support and independence, while Adriaan Geense (1983-88) oriented the institute to a changing world ecumenical scene.

Ecumenical learning through the action-reflection method and the sensitive "equipping" of lay and clergy leaders for local ministries remain the institute's aim. This process of "doing theology" is achieved through study, worship and community living in an interconfessional, international and intercultural setting.

ALAIN BLANCY

"Christianity and Culture: 40 years of the Ecumenical Institute", *The Ecumenical Review*, 39, 2, 1987.

BRASH, ALAN ANDERSON.
B. 5.6.1913, New Zealand. Brash was deputy

general secretary of the WCC and staff moderator of unit II, 1974-78, and earlier was general secretary of the National Council of Churches in New Zealand (NCCNZ), 1947-52, 1956-64. He served as interchurch aid secretary for mission and service of the East Asia Christian Conference, 1957-68, interim Asia secretary of the WCC Division of Interchurch Aid, Refugee and World Service, 1965, interim director of the Division of World Mission and Evangelism, 1966, director of Christian Aid, London, 1968-70, and director of WCC Inter-church Aid, Refugee and World Service, 1970-74. He was a delegate to Oxford 1937 and Edinburgh 1937 and has attended all WCC assemblies except Evanston 1954. He published popular reports on Amsterdam 1948 and New Delhi 1961. Brash was moderator of the Presbyterian Church of New Zealand, 1978-79, and first regional secretary of the NCCNZ, 1979-84.

ANS J. VAN DER BENT

BRENT, CHARLES HENRY.
B. 9.4.1862, Newcastle, Ontario, Canada; d. 27.3.1929, Lausanne. Brent studied at Trinity College, Toronto, and was ordained priest in 1887. From 1888 to 1891 he served a parish in Boston; in 1901 he became the Protestant Episcopal bishop of the Philippines, where he energetically combatted the opium traffic. In 1909 he was president of the opium conference at Shanghai, and in 1923 represented the USA on the League of Nations Narcotics Committee. He was elected bishop of Western New York in 1917, and in 1926-28 was in charge of the Episcopal churches in Europe. On returning from the world missionary conference at Edinburgh in 1910, he spoke of the need for unity at the general convention of the Protestant Episcopal Church, and of his own conviction that a "world conference on Faith and Order should be convened".

Throughout the rest of his life Brent exercised a profound influence on the Faith and Order* movement, even as he also participated in the world mission and Life and Work* movements, and in the World Alliance for Promoting International Friendship through the Churches,* travelling widely and addressing numerous gatherings. His appreciation of traditions other than his own opened many doors of friendship to him. Brent was pre-eminently a man of prayer. When the first world conference on Faith and Order met at Lausanne in 1927, Brent was its president. He wrote *The Mount of Vision* (London, Longmans, Green, 1918). See *Things That Matter: The Best of the Writings of Bishop Brent* (New York, Harper, 1949) and A. Zabriskie, *Bishop Brent, Crusader for Christian Unity* (Philadelphia, Westminster, 1948).

ANS J. VAN DER BENT

BRETHREN. The Brethren came into being in the late summer of 1708 near Schwarzenau, Germany. Five men and three women, all religious refugees, were baptized in the river Eder. One among them, chosen by lot, baptized Alexander Mack, their leader and first minister; Mack then baptized the rest. All eight had been influenced by the radical living of German pietistic renewal as well as by descendants of the 16th-century Anabaptists, the Mennonites.

From the beginning, Brethren embodied a high doctrine of the church as a close-knit community whose life together is a means of grace,* not a loose association of like-minded believers. Brethren members who are baptized are the church. Creeds, liturgies, official hierarchies, and buildings do not "make" the church the church. Rather, the church is manifest when members come together for worship or work dedicated to "the glory of God and our neighbours' good".

Brethren stress obedience to the teachings of Jesus and conformity to the life of early Christian communities. They practise adult baptism* by immersion, celebrate the love feast (with foot washing according to John 13, a common meal, and the bread and cup), greet one another with the "holy kiss", anoint for healing, reconcile conflict according to Matt. 18:15-17, and teach non-resistance.

Religious persecution and economic hardship in Germany were among the problems that pushed the Brethren across the Atlantic, the last group in 1729. They first settled in Pennsylvania, soon spread along the Atlantic seaboard, then moved westwards by the mid-19th century.

The late 19th century was a time of church schism* and splintering that resulted in a number of Brethren bodies: the Old German Baptist Brethren, the Brethren Church, the Fellowship of Grace Brethren, the Dunkard Brethren, and the Church of the Brethren (the largest). In 1973 M.R. Zigler arranged a historic meeting of members of these bodies, "just to shake hands". More meetings followed, giving rise to the comprehensive three-volume *Brethren Encyclopedia*.

Although the Brethren prospered and grew in their new country, they retained a certain isolation from American society. The American revolution deepened this isolation. As a people committed to non-resistance, they could not in good conscience either bear arms against the British or swear an oath of allegiance to the new government. Brethren were accused of treason, severely fined, and often brutally mistreated. During the civil war and the first world war, Brethren were fined and imprisoned for refusing to bear arms. Just before the second world war, the Church of the Brethren worked closely with Mennonites and Friends to provide a service programme for their young men as an alternative to military conscription.

The Church of the Brethren began an organized response to needy peoples when collections for famine relief in Armenia were taken up in 1917. During the 1930s, a number of service opportunities developed, such as the sending of relief workers to Spain during its civil war. A heifer project provides farm animals for places of need; it is now an ecumenical service programme.

A Brethren Service Committee (1939) focused during the second world war on civilian public service, a co-operative programme of the Brethren, Mennonites, and Friends with the federal government. This programme provided civilian work of national importance for conscientious objectors to war. Brethren facilities at New Windsor, Maryland, are an ecumenical service centre, with offices for Church World Service, Lutheran World Relief, Christian Rural Overseas Programme, and Interchurch Medical Aid. Other Brethren-sponsored agencies also became ecumenical, and many Brethren joined ecumenical agencies as staff workers during the 1940s through the 1960s.

The Brethren have a strong missionary spirit, inspired especially by the great commission in Matt. 28:19-20. This spirit led to the development of home missions from the earliest beginnings; interests in missionary activity outside the USA developed in the mid-19th century. The major Brethren missionary areas were in India, China, Nigeria, Puerto Rico, Ecuador, Indonesia and Sudan.

In 1955 a new foreign mission policy refocused mission from "parenting" to "indigenization", initiating the process of passing leadership into local hands. In 1978 a Latin American mission strategy, "misión mutua en las Américas", emphasized ecumenical planning, solidarity with the oppressed, and mutuality in mission. Work has begun on a mission philosophy to guide the church during the 1990s.

Among the Brethren bodies, the Church of the Brethren is the only one to be involved in the conciliar expressions of the 20th-century ecumenical movement. In 1941 the Church of the Brethren joined the Federal Council of Churches in America (now the National Council of the Churches of Christ), and the WCC in 1948. The Church of the Brethren has participated vigorously in the work of these councils, always contributing an unusually large number of leaders and dollars to the NCCC and WCC in proportion to its size.

Church of the Brethren membership has declined significantly during the past 25 years to 164,680 in 1983, and the membership is aging, with a median age of 54. As the past and present of the Church of the Brethren have depended on service rather than size, so does its future. For as a servant people, the enduring calling for Brethren is to give birth to and let go of programmes for ministry and mission, so that the whole Body of Christ and all God's people may be blessed.

MELANIE A. MAY

D.F. Durnbaugh ed., *The Brethren Encyclopedia*, 3 vols, Philadelphia, Brethren Encl., 1983-84 ● D.F. Durnbaugh, *Church of the Brethren: Yesterday and Today*, Elgin, IL, Brethren, 1986.

BUDDHIST-CHRISTIAN DIALOGUE.
Buddhist-Christian encounter, particularly through the monastic and the mystical, stretches back to the early years of Christianity. Our concern here is the more recent 20th-century movement in which Buddhist-Christian encounter has taken the form of planned dialogue sessions and joint explorations into the spiritual life and social action. In this, it must be seen in the wider context of dialogue with Asian religions (see **dialogue, interfaith**), shaped, according to Aloysius Pieris, by Western Christianity's loss of power, the awareness that Asia's religions were powerful and destiny-shaping forces, and increasing contact with the living practices of these religions through Westerners travelling east and Eastern religions coming west.

Vatican II* also encouraged the movement in its statement that the Catholic church "rejects nothing which is true and holy" in other religions. Specific mention was made of Buddhism as teaching a path by which humans "can either reach a state of absolute freedom or attain supreme enlightenment by their own efforts or by higher assistance".

A great 20th-century pioneer was Thomas Merton. Yet he was, in fact, following the ancient tradition of dialogue through monasticism and mysticism in his plea for an international and inter-religious monastic, spiritual encounter. His death, on the second day of the 1968 Bangkok meeting of "L'aide à l'implantation monastique" (AIM), served to stimulate further interest in his vision. In 1973, in Bangalore, AIM brought together Christian and non-Christian monks, one result of which was the planning of a series of East-West spiritual exchanges between Zen and Christian monks.

Parallel to this, Christians were reaching out in new ways towards Buddhism in several Asian countries. In Japan, H.M. Enomiya Lassalle and J. Kachiri Kadowaki, Jesuits, were delving into the richness of Zen. In 1967 the first of what became the annual Japanese Zen-Christian colloquia was held. In Sri Lanka a group of priests including Aloysius Pieris, Michael Rodrigo, Antony Fernando (Catholic), Lynn de Silva (Methodist) and Yohan Devananda (Anglican) were studying Buddhism under Buddhists and searching for new forms of Buddhist-Christian community living and dialogue. In Thailand, Sr Theodore Hahnenfeld and Fr Edmond Pezet were part of the same wave; similar ventures can be cited in other countries.

In the 1970s, academic research into religious pluralism* grew. New institutions were formed such as the Ecumenical Institute for Study and Dialogue in Sri Lanka (formerly the

Centre for Religion and Society), and new initiatives were taken by established ones. Significant for Buddhism and Christianity was the East-West religions project, started in 1980 by the University of Hawaii department of religion, with international and ecumenical dimensions. The following international Buddhist-Christian conferences have resulted: Buddhist-Christian renewal and the future of humanity (Honolulu 1980), paradigm shifts in Buddhism and Christianity: cultural systems and the self (Hawaii 1984), Buddhism and Christianity: towards the human future (Berkeley 1987). From them have come regional initiatives: a Japan chapter of the project (1982) and the North American Buddhist-Christian theological encounter group under Masao Abe and John Cobb (1983). Of particular significance was the 1987 conference, which drew 800 people from 19 countries and gave birth to the Society for Buddhist-Christian Studies to co-ordinate and enable worldwide encounter.

In Europe, an important international Buddhist-Christian dialogue was held in Austria in 1981, convening Western theologians and their Asian Buddhist counterparts to discuss the theme of salvation, individual and social. Other European encounters, less international in scope, have also been held, e.g. Karma Ling Institute, France (4th dialogue held in 1988); De Tiltenberg, The Netherlands (1988, on the theme of suffering, enlightenment, salvation and social responsibility).

In Eastern Asia, an important development was when institutions in eight countries formed themselves into a network of Christian organizations for inter-religious encounter: Inter-Religio. Included were the Tao Fong Shan Ecumenical Institute (Hong Kong), the Driyarkara Institute of Philosophy (Indonesia), the Institute for Oriental Religions (Japan) and the Inter-religious Commission for Development (Thailand). Buddhist-Christian dialogue is a central component in Inter-Religio's work.

Durwood Foster, of the Pacific School of Religion, spoke about three central issues emerging from the 1984 Hawaii meeting: emptiness or God; existence as suffering or good; the ultimate goal of life as nirvana or God (*Buddhist-Christian Studies*, 7, 1987). The Berkeley conference offered topics such as liberation theology* and Buddhism, Ko-

rean minjung theology* and Buddhism, religion and violence, agape and compassion, sunyata and *kenosis*, women in Buddhism and Christianity. Philosophical topics alternated with social and political concerns. The latter were dominant in two international 1988 conferences. The first, held at the Institute for Oriental Religions (Japan), was entitled "Wisdom and Compassion: The Message of Buddhism and Christianity for Our Times". The theme of the second, in Seoul, sponsored by the WCC, was "Buddhist and Christian in the Search for Peace and Justice". The final declaration from this meeting stresses the injustice of poverty,* the nuclear threat, ecological disturbance and worldwide violence. It states that personal and social transformation had to go together, implying the Buddhist-Christian action which must take place beyond the conference table in shared spirituality and struggle.

Many of the above conferences stressed the need for joint action in a world of crisis. There is no doubt that this is occurring. Yet, in some contexts, there is still mistrust: for instance, where the legacy of colonialism and the missionary enterprise makes any Christian move suspicious, illustrating the fact that political and social contexts mould the nature and possibilities for dialogue. One key maxim is that of Michael Rodrigo, pioneer of Buddhist-Christian dialogue: "Only after a dialogue of life is there dialogue of prayer and then of religious experience."

ELIZABETH J. HARRIS

Buddhist-Christian Studies, annual, East-West Religions Project, University of Hawaii • *Dialogue*, Ecumenical Institute for Study and Dialogue, Colombo, Sri Lanka • *Inter-Religio Newsletter*, Nanzan Institute for Religion and Culture, Tokyo, Japan • A. Pieris, *Love Meets Wisdom: A Christian Experience of Buddhism*, Maryknoll, NY, Orbis, 1988 • *Society for Buddhist-Christian Studies Newsletter*, Berkeley, CA, Graduate Theological Union.

BÜHRIG, MARGA. B. 17.10.1915, Berlin. A president of the WCC, 1983-91, Bührig has been deeply involved in its initiatives on "Justice, Peace and the Integrity of Creation". Since 1946 she has been engaged in ecumenical women's work in Switzerland and Germany, and since 1954 in the worldwide ecumenical movement through the WCC Department for Co-operation of Men and Women in Church, Family and Society. She was co-president of the Women's Ecumenical Liaison Group (WCC and Consilium de Laicis, Vatican), 1968-72, director of Boldern Academy (near Zurich), 1971-81, and president of the Ecumenical Association of Academies and Laity Centres in Europe, 1976-82. In 1939 she received a doctorate in German literature and modern history from the University of Zurich, where she also studied theology. She has written *Die Frau in der Schweiz* (Bern, Paul Haupt, 1969), "Discrimination against Women", in *Technology and Social Justice*, R. H. Preston ed. (London, SCM, 1971), and *Spät habe ich gelernt, gerne Frau zu sein: Eine feministische Autobiographie* (Stuttgart, Kreuz, 1987).

ANS J. VAN DER BENT

BULGAKOV, SERGIUS. B. 16.6.1871, Livny, Russia; d. 12.7.1944, Paris. Dean of the Russian Orthodox Theological Institute of St Sergius, Paris, 1925-44, Bulgakov had considerable intellectual influence in the West through his participation in the ecumenical movement, of which he was a warm but frequently a critical supporter. He was actively involved in the Anglo-Russian Fellow-

ship of St Sergius and St Alban (England). He strove to give a comprehensive interpretation of all the main traditional Christian doctrines in the light of the doctrine of "sophia", the holy wisdom. Since he viewed Mary as the most perfectly created image of the uncreated sophia, he criticized the Faith and Order conference at Lausanne in 1927 for neglecting the veneration of the mother of God. His teaching was condemned by the Moscow patriarchate in 1935, largely perhaps on political grounds.

Bulgakov wanted to enter the priesthood, but became a religious and philosophical sceptic under the influence of G.W.F. Hegel and active in Marxist political movements. Disillusioned after the 1905 revolution, Bulgakov slowly retraced his steps to the church. In 1917 he was an active member of the All-Russian Church Council and was elected to the Supreme Church Board. In 1918 he was finally ordained to the priesthood. Expelled from Russia in 1923, he left for Prague, where he became professor of political economy at the Russian Graduate School of Law, and then settled in Paris in 1925. His chief works are *The Orthodox Church* (London, Centenary, 1935) and *La sagesse de Dieu* (Lausanne, L'Age d'Homme, 1938).

ANS J. VAN DER BENT

CAMPUS CRUSADE FOR CHRIST.

In 1951 William R. Bright, 31, left the business world to found, at the University of California at Los Angeles, an evangelical interdenominational organization, Campus Crusade for Christ. CCC soon expanded beyond the university world to include work with high school students, athletes, business and professional people, local churches, families, prisoners and others. Stressing discipleship and evangelism through one-on-one personal contact, CCC staff and programmes are found in more than 100 countries.

At the centre of CCC's identity is an evangelistic tool known as *The Four Spiritual Laws*, by which the gospel of Jesus Christ and the invitation to follow him as Lord and Saviour are explained in simple terms. More than 1,500 million copies of the 16-page wallet-size booklet have been printed. It is not unusual to find Protestant congregations using their own version of the booklet. In some areas of the world, including Mexico and the Philippines, the Roman Catholic renewal movement has adapted and incorporated *The Four Spiritual Laws* in its Christian life programme.

Since 1979, CCC has used the film *Jesus* in mass evangelization. This film, a spin-off of a project related to CCC known as "The New Media Bible" (an audiovisual rendering of scripture), follows the life of Christ as told in the gospel of Luke. Currently available in 160 languages, *Jesus* has been viewed by more than 330 million people, with tens of millions indicating a decision to follow Jesus Christ.

CCC is spearheading "New Life 2000", an ambitious effort to share the gospel worldwide, with the goal of helping introduce at least 1,000 million people to Jesus Christ by the year 2000.

ROBERT T. COOTE

CANON.

The word "canon" derives from the Greek *kanōn*, a straight stick, measuring rod, or ruler (cf. Latin *regula*); hence, a standard or norm. At the end of the 2nd century, Irenaeus, Tertullian and others spoke of the "rule of faith" or "canon of truth", meaning the heart of the gospel as expressed in summary forms similar to the creeds.* From the 4th century onwards, conciliar decisions on doctrine and discipline were designated canons (see **ecumenical councils**). "Canon law" is the way most churches regulate their life (see **canon law, church discipline**), and monastic rules may also be called canons. In the liturgy of the Roman (Catholic) church, the "canon" of the mass is a normative eucharistic prayer.

Ecumenically, the most widespread use of "canon" occurs in connection with the scriptures of the church. Verbally, such usage goes back only to the 4th century, but the fact and idea of a "collection of authoritative writings" (intrinsic authority) or even an "authoritative collection of (such) writings" (extrinsically recognized authority) has been present to Christianity since its beginnings. To the scriptures of Israel — which it claimed for its own — the earliest church added writings that told the story of Jesus the Christ and recorded the preaching, teaching and life of the primitive Christian community. The question of *which* writings were to be properly so treated arose acutely in the mid-2nd century. The catholic "canon" established itself over against, on the one hand, the reductionism of Marcion (whose own canon comprised only a doctored Luke and a mutilated *corpus paulinum*) and, on the other hand, the pullulation of apocryphal gospels, acts and apocalypses that were largely Gnostic in character and, perhaps, the more recent oracles that the Montanists considered as further revelation. Positively put, the catholic canon consisted of those writings which had been accepted for reading in the worship of the church and, in the case of the "New Testament", were held to be derived from an apostle or his surrogate (e.g. Mark writing for Peter, or Luke writing on the authority of Paul).

There was no conflict between such writings and authentic tradition. Indeed the scriptures were intrinsic to the tradition — a vehicle for transmitting the Christian message and faith. While preaching, catechesis, sacramental rites, episcopal teaching, and the confession of martyrs and everyday saints were also instruments of the Tradition, a special role and value attached to the scriptures — shown, for example, in the care given to protecting them in times of persecution — as the permanent legacy of the original witnesses and of inspired writers who had been normatively guided by the same self-consistent Spirit as indwelt the believing community. According to an ecumenically influential formula of Oscar Cullmann: in establishing the principle of a canon, "the church, by an act of humility, submitted every later tradition that she would elaborate to the higher criterion of the apostolic tradition fixed in the holy scriptures" (*La tradition*, 1953). Thus the canonical scriptures of Old and New Testament constitute, for the continuing life of the church, the decisive written testimony to God's history with Israel, the incarnation of the Son, and the mission of the Spirit. In times of doctrinal and ecclesiastical controversy, however, there has been conflict over their interpretation and over

their operative relation to the other vehicles of tradition.

At the fourth world conference on Faith and Order (Montreal 1963), a remarkable convergence was registered between Protestants and Orthodox on Tradition (the "great *T*radition", which is to be distinguished from the particular ecclesiastical "*t*radition*s*", even if these are its channels) as the "*paradosis* of the *kerygma*", the handing on of the message, "the Tradition of the gospel" — with the scriptures as a privileged and normative element within the Tradition. As "the Tradition in its written form", the scriptures have "a special basic value" and serve as "an indispensable criterion" for distinguishing "faithful transmission" (Montreal 1963, paras 38-76). At the same time Vatican II, in line with the historical work of J.R. Geiselmann on the limits of the formula of the council of Trent* concerning "scriptures and *(et)* unwritten traditions", rejected a draft text on "the two sources of revelation" and adopted instead the constitution *Dei Verbum*, which was much closer to Yves Congar's systematic notion that the scriptures and the oral-practical tradition of the church are diverse modes — themselves interactive — of transmitting one and the same gospel.

Thus there has been growing ecumenical agreement on the *sufficiency* of the scriptures, even if varying emphases continue to reflect historical controversies. The Protestant principle of *sola scriptura* was first erected against some practical and doctrinal tradition*s* that were tolerated or even endorsed by the pastoral authorities of the medieval West but that in the reformers' eyes contradicted the original gospel and faith. Understood absolutely, "scripture alone" implies that the Bible is self-interpreting, at least under the Holy Spirit's direct guidance; but in fact the "living voice of the gospel" *(viva vox evangelii)* is always mediated by preachers who actively expound — and therefore *interpret* — what they take to be the scriptural message within a variable cultural context. While continuing to insist on the primacy of the scriptures, ecumenically minded Protestants recognize that the church has willy-nilly a "teaching office" — and the issue is as to where such a magisterium is lodged (bishops, synods, professors, pope...). The Roman Catholic tradition has always recognized more openly the need for a teaching office and has been more willing to admit the fact of later "explication" or "development" of what was latently or germinally present in the apostolic faith recorded in the scriptures (not only as regards, say, the full formulation of the doctrine of the Trinity but also, controversially, the Marian dogmas and the "Petrine office" itself). On its side, however, Vatican II has insisted that the magisterium remains subservient to the apostolic witness (*Dei Verbum* 7-10).

While not all problems have yet found an ecumenical solution with regard to the sufficiency of the scriptures in relation to Tradition, it is possible that the more explosive question now concerns the *integrity* of the canonical scriptures. Although Christian churches differ somewhat over the extent of the OT (see **Old Testament and Christian unity**), they are officially just about unanimous over the composition of the NT, i.e. those 27 books whose precise listing is first found in the festal letter for 367 of Athanasius (see **New Testament and Christian unity**). Nevertheless, three recurrent or newly arising issues may prove disruptive.

One issue is the relation between the OT and the NT. If we adopt, say, the historical categories of "promise and fulfilment" or the theological categories of "law and gospel", the question in each case remains that of the kind and extent of continuities and discontinuities between the Testaments. Answers affect not only the relations between Christianity and Judaism but also wider matters in the understanding of the history and nature of salvation.* These issues have been present since the beginning of Christianity and, after the rupture of church and synagogue, do not appear to have been directly church-divisive before the Reformation (and even in the 16th century the soteriological arguments were not primarily framed directly in terms of the relations between the Testaments). Today these issues probably belong, among Christians, to the realm of theological controversy rather than to strictly doctrinal conflict or institutional separation between the churches. Yet an explosive potential remains over the history and nature of salvation when, for example, the nature and practice of the Christian mission* is at stake vis-a-vis (in different ways) Jews, people of other faiths, or the irreligious.

Second, given the dimensions and the diversity of the Bible, it is not surprising that Christians have looked for a substantive "centre" of the scriptures. If, say, "that which advances Christ" (*was Christum treibt*, Luther) is taken as an interpretative principle, then Christians can fairly easily agree on the point. When, however, to stay with the example, Lutherans further define "justification through faith alone" as the "canon within the canon", other Christians will put forward other candidates for the job (e.g. the motifs of "covenant" or "liberation" or "kingdom of God"). In striking harmony with the ancient "rule of faith" or "canon of truth", the current Faith and Order project "Towards the Common Expression of the Apostolic Faith Today" is taking the Nicene Creed* as its "theological basis and methodological tool" as it seeks to present a faith that is roundly and thoroughly biblical to our time and world. The question remains whether different "interests" (justificationists, liberationists, pietists, liturgists, etc.) can be contained within this more complex hermeneutical grid that is needed to catch the full range of the scriptural material and neglect or dismiss none.

A third issue affecting the integrity of the canon concerns the use of "historical criticism" in exegesis (see **exegesis, methods of**). Modern biblical scholarship has sought to "get behind" the inherited text to earlier stages in the transmission of the material and even to "what really happened". The historical-critical approach is legitimated by an incarnational faith that takes human history* seriously, and it does not of itself — despite many of its more sceptical practitioners — exclude the occurrence and perception of divine presence and action within that history. It can in fact help to make clear that the interpretation of events is part of history itself, so that words and deeds are "revelation"* only when they are received as such; and thus the way is open for the Christian community to accept certain writings — precisely on account of their interpretation of events — as "correct records" of God's operation in and through Christ. Historical research has proved valuable ecumenically, in that it has shown the scriptures to be a privileged part of such an earlier and continuing Tradition that perceives, receives and transmits the gospel of Jesus Christ (see Montreal 1963). Yet while historical exegesis may help to illuminate the earliest stages in that process, the faith cannot be made to depend upon particular scholarly reconstructions and speculations (hypotheses that enjoy varying degrees of probability) concerning what preceded and surrounded the scriptural writings. Otherwise there would be as many churches as there are scholars.

Spiritual and ecclesial dissatisfaction with the uncertainty and fluctuation in the "results" of modern NT scholarship has more recently prompted some within the academic profession of exegesis to adopt a more "canonical" hermeneutics. While *historical* investigations are not abandoned, greater attention is now focused in a more *literary* way upon the final text of scripture as the church has received it (with the question of manuscript and textual variants rightly seen as a relatively minor one for most substantial purposes). Abiding by the decisions of the church(es) concerning the extent of the canon, exegetes seek to understand and interpret a particular passage or book in light of its place and function within the Bible as a whole. The flat, univocal reading of the scriptures that characterizes fundamentalism can be avoided by a recognition of differences in literary genre (not everything is intended as "historical reporting", and history itself, as we saw, is a complex notion) and by allowing some passages to complement and even correct others (though the "canonical" school is less likely to scent "contradictions" within the scriptures than some historical critics or the most ardent advocates of a single "canon within the canon"). The way is still open, for example, for the careful detection of "trajectories" within the biblical material such as a mixed group of Protestant and Roman Catholic scholars in the United States found ecclesiastically promising in their work published as *Peter in the New Testament* (1973) and *Mary in the New Testament* (1978). Since the "canonical" method is in greater harmony with the way in which the scriptures have actually been read in the liturgical, homiletical and devotional life of the church, its practice also opens up the possibility of dialogue with past interpretations of the scriptures and thus a more integral relation between scripture and the continuing, enveloping Tradition. Herein resides perhaps its greatest ecumenical potential.

In the contemporary secular West, the whole notion of a literary, artistic, cultural canon — which was in any case a much looser notion than that of a scriptural canon within the church — has recently come under strain, even to the point of dissolution in the eyes of some. Excisions of the offending, the hegemony of a single and narrow hermeneutical principle, the addition of matter believed to have been neglected — all has been attempted without a communal consensus. Perhaps the nearest proposal for dealing with the scriptural canon in a similar way occurs in, say, the work of Rosemary Ruether: after rejecting any interpretation of the messiahship of Jesus that might offend a Jew (*Faith and Fratricide*, 1974, where 1 Cor. 1:23 goes unmentioned), Ruether proposes "whatever promotes the full humanity of women" as the criterion for taking or leaving scriptural material and looks to add from "pagan resources" what is otherwise missing (*Sexism and God-Talk*, 1983). Such proposals, however, present a wide variety of theological difficulties, and are thus unlikely to bring Christian unity closer.

See also **exegesis, methods of; hermeneutics; inspiration; scripture; scriptures; teaching authority; Tradition and traditions; unity; word of God**.

GEOFFREY WAINWRIGHT

R.E. Brown, "The Gospel of Peter and Canonical Gospel Priority", *New Testament Studies*, 33, 1987 • H. von Campenhausen, *Die Entstehung der christlichen Bibel* (ET *The Formation of the Christian Bible*, Philadelphia, Westminster, 1972) • B.S. Childs, *Introduction to the Old Testament as Scripture*, Philadelphia, Fortress, 1979 • B.S. Childs, *The New Testament as Canon*, Philadelphia, Fortress, 1985 • E. Käsemann ed., *Das Neue Testament als Kanon*, Göttingen, Vandenhoeck & Ruprecht, 1970 • B.M. Metzger, *The Canon of the New Testament*, Oxford, Clarendon, 1987.

CANON LAW. Canon law states the rules for institutional ecclesiology, which reconciles normative ecclesiological principles — taught as dogma* — with the ecclesiological maxims that touch the lives of the people of God in practice. According to this canonical approach, true ecumenism requires two encounters — one covering the behaviour of church members as Christians, and the other relating to the dogmaticians of the various churches. The history of these two encounters shows that the problem of the institutional church is structural and ecumenical, and might be stated as follows: *If the gospel is to be preached and experienced, does it call for institutionalism in Christian life?* With this question in mind, we may look briefly at the main stages in the history of the German Lutheran churches as an example of the path taken by the Reformation churches in their institutional history.

In the socio-political situation of that day, it became urgently necessary to transfer episcope (oversight, or the *ius episcopale*) to the temporal prince, because of the radical Lutheran idea of original sin,* on the one hand, and the combination of the Thomist view of the non-sacramental nature of the episcopacy* with Luther's advocacy of the priesthood of all believers, on the other. This established the fundamental principle that any legal organization is contrary to the essence of the church, and this principle generally made itself felt in the five following stages of church-state relations: (1) between the 16th century and the middle of the 17th century — the church was governed by the sovereign princes of the territory (*Landesherrliches Kirchenregiment*, supreme ecclesiastical authority of the regional sovereign); (2) between the mid-17th century and 1848 — the church was organically incorporated in and served the state (*Staatskirchentum*, the system of the state church); (3) from 1848 till just before 1919 — the churches administered their own internal affairs, and the state now had the right to inspect and supervise them only in matters of external order (*Staatskirchenhoheit*, the system of state church sovereign rights); (4) between 1919 and 1933 — the church made agreements with the state in the Weimar Republic (parallel to the Roman Catholic concordats) made possible through the constitutional process separating church and state; and (5) between 1933 and 1945 — during the Third Reich the Protestant churches contended with the implantation of Nazi ideology in a German national people's church which was to be the religious mainspring of the state (*Kirchenkampf*, struggle between church and state).

On the eve of the *Kirchenkampf* the tragedy of German Protestantism arose from its failure to create for itself a church law that would embody the content of the Protestant faith, because it had always left it to the state to receive its legal structure. Since then, German Protestantism has been re-discovering itself as its structures have come to be distinguished from those of the state. By way of comparison, we may say (in J. Hoffmann's terms) that while the Roman Catholic Church is able to remain itself throughout the variety of its relations with the state (thanks to the institutional objectivization it worked out for itself through its canon law), the German Protestant churches are progressively discovering themselves in the actual evolution of these relations. The effort that Lutheran churches spent on re-integrating the institution of episcopacy in line with a practice like that of the RCC allows differences between the two to persist: Lutheran bishops are not legislators, they have no magisterium,* they do not belong to a higher order than the pastor, and they are not directly installed as pastors.

Between 381 and 1453 in the Orthodox churches, the church was sometimes absorbed by the state (Emperor Leo VI, for instance, represented himself as an external bishop, convening and presiding at councils and promulgating degrees and appointing bishops and patriarchs); however, entrusting this function of supervising the church to the emperor did not plunge the system into Caesaro-papism. On the other hand, in the Russian church, Caesaro-papism found its best expression in the *Spiritual Regulation* of Peter the Great (25 January 1721). He subjected the church to the state and suppressed the patriarchate of Moscow, replacing it by a synod of which the czar was the supreme judge. He thereby destroyed the reality of the episcopate: the church was no longer governed only by the bishops, and the synod became a body with power over the church and no longer within the church; church law and the church as an institution had their source sacramentally no longer in the episcopal office but in the secular order of the state. In 1917 the Russian church was to re-establish the patriarchate of Moscow, and in coping with the atheist state, it has since then — and by analogy with the state principle of socialization — gradually re-discovered the sacramental basis of canon law, first giving expression to this in the synod of 1961.

Today the Orthodox Church of Russia, while declaring the law of the state to be canonical, has re-affirmed the special nature of the law of communion* (the law of grace as koinonia*) over against the secular right of association. On the local level and in its relations with the Ecumenical Patriarchate of Constantinople, it tackles difficult questions similar to those experienced by the Oriental Catholic churches in their own context, namely: What room has to be made for political and national principles in the organization of the church? How are the rights of the Ecumenical Patriarchate to be defined in relation to those of the autocephalous sister church over its own members, especially in the diaspora? What is the specific nature of the unity of the Orthodox churches? Recent work done by the Joint Roman Catholic-Orthodox theological commission has, however, happily re-introduced the idea of the sacramental basis of church law, re-discovering in particular the sacramental character of episcopal jurisdiction and the Trinitarian eucharistic basis of the local church.*

Within the restricted scope of this article it is enough to follow the course of the recent institutional history of the RCC, starting simply with the *Codex Juris Canonici* of 1917. The theory underlying this code regards the church as a specific type of "perfect" society, so intended and founded by Christ and requiring law* by its very nature as a society.* The church was thus seen in terms of means and ends, and the ecclesiology of the codex expressly favoured an individualist idea of the Christian life and of salvation.* In it Christians as individuals were confronted with a hierarchy that was regarded as extrinsic, and the fact that the church is a fellowship that is Trinitarian in its structure could not be institutionally expressed in the codex — it forgot the law of grace.*

Vatican II brought with it significant shifts. For the ecclesiology of the perfect society, essentially one of inequality, it substituted reciprocity in dignity and common action for the upbuilding of the Body of Christ among all members of the church. And then it re-discovered the sacramental basis of the episcopate — the basis for the power of order and of jurisdiction; structurally it restored the importance of synodal practice at all church levels.

The code of the Roman church promulgated in 1983 is a compromise between that of 1917 and the contributions of Vatican II: in it the people of God is the fundamental

visible reality of the church as *communio*, or fellowship, where the members find themselves for the first time given rights and duties. Within certain limits the laity* are called upon to participate widely in ministries contributing to the achievement of the church's mission;* synodal practice is implemented in new collegial structures, often of a consultative nature. Ecumenical concern has meant the opening up of various RC structures and institutions to the possibility of exchange and co-operation with their non-Roman Catholic equivalents.

To sum up generally: a fundamental ecumenical experience has been the re-discovery of canon law both as intrinsic to the Trinitarian *communio*, which gives the church a structure as a confessing church, and also as expressing itself in sacramental processes with an instituting function: because institutional law gives expression to the statute or law of grace, it is primary — whereas law as legislation setting up norms comes only second. The "inductive" type of approach makes the local church a primary element of the church, it restores the process of "reception"* of the laws to its rightful place and it makes it possible for custom and jurisprudence to re-discover their legitimate creative capacity; it is an approach which cannot dispense with the gains from ecumenical exchanges among the people of God. Finally, if theologians and specialists in the social sciences are actively associated in working out church law, the various churches will then have more opportunities to develop an awareness both of the worldwide environment in which they live together and of the fundamental unity of their mission to proclaim the gospel as the 20th century draws to its close.

See also **church discipline, law**.

SAÏD ELIAS SAÏD

The Book of Church Order: The Reformed Church in America, New York, Reformed Church in America, 1989 • *Church Law and Polity in Lutheran Churches: Reports of the International Consultations in Järvenpää (1970) and Baastad (1977)*, Geneva, LWF, 1979 • *Constitution and Regulations: And the Basis of Union: And Standing Orders and Rules of Debate*, Melbourne, Uniting Church Press, 1990 • J. Provost & K. Walf eds, *Canon Law-Church Reality*, Edinburgh, Clark, 1986 • L. Vischer, "Reform of Canon Law: An Ecumenical Problem", *The Jurist*, 26, 1966.

CAPITALISM. The word "capital" is found in early economic thought as a description of one of the three principal factors of production, the other two being labour and land. It has generated two particular areas of debate: the economic return attributable to capital and the question of the ownership of capital.

In the neutral sense of the word, "capital" (as a factor input — certainly in its physical sense of plant and machinery) exists in all economic systems. However, the historical debate over economic return and ownership has led to the word "capital", or more especially its derivative "capitalism", being used as a term to describe those forms of economic systems in which most capital is privately owned, in which a return on capital (profit) for the owners of capital is accepted and in which the pricing mechanism is widely used to balance supply and demand in the market (hence also the use of the term "market capitalism"). Although there are many variants of the capitalist system, these characteristics broadly separate the system from command economies, in which the distribution of income and allocation of resources is determined either by a local or a central planning mechanism without significant recourse to the market mechanism.

The economic, social and environmental consequences of this system, both within market capitalist societies and outside them, since the economies of the rest of the world (particularly the southern hemisphere) are crucially inter-related with them, have been a constant concern at successive assemblies of the WCC. They have also been examined in closer detail in various Church and Society conferences. More recently the issues have been examined in the context of the development* debate led in the main by the Commission on the Churches' Participation in Development.

Although the form of the critique has changed emphasis over time, it has largely centred on three areas of criticism and judgment: (1) a view of the capitalist system as a whole in relation to the claims of other systems based on alternative political precepts such as communist/socialist systems; (2) an assessment of the workings of the capitalist system itself to see whether the system creates injustices or impedes human development, whether the objectives of the system are ade-

quate and the means used to achieve them are fair, and whether the wider social consequences are acceptable; (3) a judgment of the capitalist system against the background of wider social, cultural and environmental issues; e.g. whether the system, which is largely determined by economic ideology, conflicts with wider social values; whether its operation is fair and just to the third world; whether the workings of the system respect the environment; and finally whether it is possible to formulate a new international economic order less open to criticism.

The first assembly report (Amsterdam 1948) drew attention to the conflict between Christianity and capitalism. It argued that capitalism tended to subordinate what should be the primary task of any economy — the meeting of human needs — to the economic advantages of those who had most power over its institutions. It also argued that capitalism tended to produce inequalities and encouraged a practical form of materialism (particularly in Western countries, in spite of their Christian background) by placing the greatest emphasis on success in making money. Finally, it drew attention to the way in which the people of capitalist systems suffered from such catastrophes as mass unemployment. The report concluded that, like communism, laissez-faire capitalism made promises that it could not redeem. Capitalism falsely claimed that by putting emphasis on freedom, it could be presumed that justice would follow as a by-product of free enterprise.

The second assembly report (Evanston 1954) raised the question of the appropriateness of the capitalist system as a model for third-world development. However, its main attention was focused on formulating a critique of the Western system itself. On the whole supportive of the system, it stressed that the church should be ready to welcome new initiatives in state control and industrial organization. The importance of efficient production and fair distribution was underlined, and the sins of waste and laziness were mentioned. The report criticized the existence of monopolies but recognized the contribution of the skilled executive and the virtues of responsible initiative and hard work. It also stressed the need to associate work with human dignity. Evanston warned against the accumulation of riches for their own sake, pressed for equity in distribution, underlined the need for the system to care for the handicapped, urged more responsibility on the part of trade unions and drew attention to the need for national policies to be aware of the international consequences of their actions.

The third assembly report (New Delhi 1961) stressed the need to see economic development as a process to create freedom (from hunger, etc.) but questioned whether freedom could be achieved in an economic model built around large-scale organizations. It warned against the danger of the Western capitalist systems creating the concept of an anonymous person and against the risks associated with technology (particularly in destroying freedom). Questioning the objectives of the present dynamic economies, New Delhi argued that the pursuit of maximum production for maximum consumption was no longer acceptable. Objectives based on that principle distorted and debased ethical values and created a society unable to cope with life other than that revolving around work. It also challenged the role of the welfare state in Western capitalist economies. Although recognizing that the welfare state had justifiably grown out of the failures of earlier capitalism, it questioned whether there was now too much security.

The fourth assembly (Uppsala 1968) took an optimistic view of capitalism in the sense of affirming the benefits offered by technology and economic growth but, pessimistically, referred to the failure of development programmes so far. It argued for an alternative framework based on the admission that the capitalist system had not yet come to terms with technology and had failed to construct workable transfer mechanisms for creating growth in the third world. The importance of the fourth assembly was in its special emphasis on the problems of development, as distinct from the problems inherent within the capitalist system itself.

The fifth assembly (Nairobi 1975) took as its main concern the way in which growth-oriented and affluent capitalist societies unduly dictated the fate of much of the rest of the world, largely by forcing it to adopt similar methods and objectives and similar ethical standards. It thus underlined again the failure of development policies and criticized capitalism for its bad effects in the third world,

especially its built-in tendency to exploit others, leading to the uneven distribution of resources. It contended, too, that while the previous means of this exploitation had been colonialism, it was now taking place through the operations of transnational corporations.

Nairobi also considered proposals for a new international economic order as an alternative way of ordering both national and international economic structures and systems. However, it questioned whether such a new order could be introduced without radical change at national levels. It also referred to the argument for limits to growth and particularly emphasized the need to pursue the ideas revolving around the appropriate technology movement. It also raised the issue of the stewardship of nature.* (It must be remembered that this assembly took place in the aftermath of the 1973-74 oil price crisis.)

The sixth assembly (Vancouver 1983) took as its principal area of judgment of the capitalist system the need to demonstrate a concern for the poor;* the need for the church to identify itself with the poor in setting its ecumenical priorities; and the need to learn from the poor, particularly by identifying with a simpler life-style. The report set out four key criticisms of the present economic order. The first was to call the rich to repentance to free them from slavery to possessions. It denounced the concentration of goods in the hands of the few. It criticized the arms race as a principal cause of the gap between the rich and the poor, and it commended to all the task of drawing value insights from poor communities. The report also had much to say about technology,* arguing that it could be destructive both socially and environmentally and could be a means of domination. It also argued that new technologies tended to encourage consumerism, were being applied without any context of overall planning, were used to support harsh economic policies and, more particularly, brought society to a point where important moral and ethical issues were being raised, particularly within the field of biotechnology.

This general concern thus expressed through the reports of all six assemblies was also articulated in the major conferences; in particular the 1937 and 1966 Church and Society conferences and the conference on "Faith, Science and the Future" in 1979.

The conference on "Church, Community and State" (Oxford 1937) listed a number of key criticisms of capitalist countries. First, the ordering of economic life had tended to enhance acquisitiveness and set up false standards of economic and social success. Second, capitalist countries created indefensible inequalities of opportunity for education, leisure and health. The existence of economic classes was seen as an intolerable obstacle to human fellowship. Third, centres of economic power had been formed which were not responsible to any organ of the community and thus presented a tyranny over human lives. Finally, the only forms of employment open to many (or the absence of any employment whatsoever) prevented many men and women from finding a sense of Christian vocation* in their daily lives.

The Church and Society conference (Geneva 1966) welcomed the fact of scientific and technological development as an expression of God's creative work by which men and women were helped to be free from unnecessary toil and poorer countries could be aided. However, it criticized market capitalist economies because of their inability to take adequate account of the long-range needs of society, to grasp the advantage of large-scale rationalization and to regulate supply and demand where the market was insensitive to price changes. The capitalist system relied too heavily on the market for income distribution; it was weak at dealing with the production and allocation of public goods. The report also raised other issues such as ethical problems of consumption, the problems of controlling incomes to avoid inflation, the adjustment of working patterns to meet changing technologies and a concern over the adverse consequences of affluent life-styles.

The conference on "Faith, Science and the Future" (MIT, Cambridge, USA, 1979) presented a substantial critique of the market capitalist system. It attacked the notion of positive economics, which attempts to explain economic behaviour on the basis of a limited number of economic considerations such as revealed choice by individual consumers, free markets in which these choices can be satisfied and the maximization of profits as a primary tool for allocating resources efficiently. The critique argued that while positive economics recognized that goals were required for the system, it assumed either that these were externally given or that they were

Capitalism in Peru (Sebastião Salgado)

embodied in the choices of individuals in the market place. The criticisms of this approach were that it took too narrow an analytical frame and focused too heavily on the individual as the key agent. The latter concept was not thought to be adequate from a Christian point of view, which would rather emphasize the concept of person, the difference being the recognition in the Christian view of the individual's social responsibilities. Moreover, positive economics seemed to move inevitably towards emphasis on continuous growth, increased production and capital accumulation. A perspective from political economy, which offered a broader view of economics and linked economic analysis with wider social goals, was commended as a better basis of evaluation.

Analyses, comment and judgment along the three broad lines of criticism set out earlier can be found in each of the respective reports, although it would be true to say that there has been a major shift in emphasis, particularly towards the third set of issues in recent times. A more general point that can be made — with the benefit of hindsight provided by a review of this nature — is that the respective reports reveal a close relationship between the emphasis given to particular issues by the ecumenical movement and the topicality of wider secular issues of public concern at the time. For example, the concern in the assembly reports of the 1960s over the functioning of the welfare state and a stress on the importance of economic growth reflected the principal issues of debate in the period now commonly regarded as the heyday of post-war economic growth and social democratic planning. In the 1970s in reaction to the two oil crises, the ecumenical debates concentrated on the problems of finite and depleting resources and raising issues such as sustainability for the world economic and ecological systems. Later reports also reflected the pessimism created by the failure of the post-war development movement to evolve a method of closing the gap between the rich and poor countries of the world.

See also **development; economics; growth, limits to; property; socialism**.

OWEN NANKIVELL

P. Abrecht ed., *Faith and Science in an Unjust World*, vol. 2: *Reports and Recommendations*, WCC, 1980 • *The Churches Survey Their Task*, London, Allen & Unwin, 1937 • P.F. Drucker, *The New Society: The Anatomy of the Industrial Order*, New York, Harper, 1950 • M.M. Thomas & P. Abrecht eds, *Christians in the Technical and Social Revolutions of Our Time*, WCC, 1967.

CARIBBEAN. Although the Caribbean can boast of a history which predates the exploits of Christopher Columbus in the late 15th century, the historical antecedents for the contemporary situation lie in the period of European mercantile expansion and the colonial societies which were created by Europe for its own economic advantage. The historical developments from conquest and exploitation, through economic and industrial prosperity (based on slavery, indentured labour and colonial domination), provide the real context for an understanding of the place of religion in Caribbean history and the significance of ecumenical endeavours by Christian churches.

Religion came to the Caribbean in different ships and from different ports. African religions came with the slaves; various Christian persuasions (mainly Catholicism and Anglicanism, and some Methodism) accompanied the slave-owners and planters. The Moravian faith was introduced first into the Danish islands (Virgin Islands) and later to some British colonies. It was mainly a missionary venture to the slave population and the freed lower classes. Whether it was the Roman Catholic Church in the French Antilles (Guadeloupe, Martinique, French Guyana) or the Church of England in the British Antilles (e.g. Jamaica, Barbados, Antigua), the major Christian bodies were mainly "ecumenical" in their role as chaplains for the status quo, as providers of as much education as the socio-economic system required for its maintenance, and as principal agents of social containment and rigid stratification. This was a common religious agenda in the 17th to the 19th centuries of Caribbean religious history. Variations from this religious preoccupation were generally submerged, politically ineffective, or minimally organized. No significant bodies emerged to alter radically the social context of Caribbean life in the last century.

Several social and religious factors have combined to make the 20th century a new period for Caribbean ecumenical activity. The expansion of educational opportunities, the effects of migration within the region as well as to Europe and North America, the influx of newer religious bodies (mainly of the Pentecostal type), and the increased missionary activities of extra-regional agencies all created a new climate for a different ecumenical agenda. The gradual emancipation of the lower classes, their participation in the political process, and the growing assumption of leadership in the established churches by Caribbean people have contributed much to a new understanding of the role and mission of the church in the Caribbean. Initiatives by mission boards and ecumenical bodies in Europe and North America generally also played a significant role in forging a joint Christian identity and in addressing youth and women's concerns, theological education, family life education, human rights, and regional integration. The Caribbean Conference of Churches (CCC), inaugurated in Kingston, Jamaica, on 13 November 1973, has been the foremost instrument of Caribbean ecumenism during the 20th century and has placed special emphasis on the role of communications in the regional process, trained several persons in communication skills, and embarked on a number of effective programmes of regional education and communication. Its most successful programme has been the publication of *Caribbean Contact*, a monthly newspaper which has consistently provided a critical analysis of the social, economic, political and religious issues of the region. This publication has not infrequently been the cause for uneasy concern on the part of the political powers in the Caribbean.

Much of the funding for ecumenical work in the Caribbean is generated from the outside. The major portion of it is specially designated for the support of community projects and programmes towards the amelioration of poverty, unemployment, and other depressing social conditions. Projects in agriculture, fishing, appropriate technology, and local arts and crafts are funded throughout the region, and efforts at developing community leaders are often pursued by means of scholarships. Regional programmes generally cannot be supported by regional resources in the Caribbean. The future of the regional ecumenical agenda will therefore be circumscribed by the continuing goodwill of extra-regional part-

ner agencies. It is not likely that any significant advances in growth into union between regional churches will precede similar occurrences by their counterparts in Northern Atlantic countries.

The CCC was in the making before 1973. Two important precursors to the organization were the Caribbean Committee on Joint Christian Action (CCJCA) and the Christian Action for Development in the Eastern Caribbean (CADEC). The CCJCA itself developed out of a consultation held in Puerto Rico in 1957 under the sponsorship of the International Missionary Council.* A major first step in the development of ecumenism in the region, that consultation has been described as "the first broadly ecumenical Christian assembly that had ever met in the Caribbean".

After its formation, the CCJCA functioned as the primary ecumenical structure in the Caribbean and was instrumental in developing CADEC, a programme for the social and economic development of the Leeward and Windward Islands and Barbados. In 1971 CADEC organized the Caribbean ecumenical consultation for development, held at Chaguaramas, Trinidad and Tobago. This major meeting of Caribbean church leaders and consultants analyzed the social, economic and political conditions of the region to determine what role the church might play in Caribbean development.

This consultation was epochal. It marked an important shift in the work of the Caribbean churches. Development* came to be seen as part of the mission of the church to the region. To be sure, some members of the constituencies represented at Chaguaramas showed an ambivalence as to whether this activity was legitimately part of the church's mission, but their representatives at Chaguaramas were infused with an optimism that was infectious. The outcome of the consultation profoundly influenced the orientation and thrust of the CCC, which was inaugurated two years later with 18 churches as founding members, among them the Antilles Episcopal Conference of the Roman Catholic Church (RCC).

The membership also spanned the four major languages of the Caribbean — Dutch, Spanish, French and English. Membership in 1990 stands at 34 from 37 countries. The CCC's mandate sprang from the conviction that the renewal of the Christian community is an instrument for the total human development of Caribbean people. Involvement in the daily struggle for human dignity, liberation* and hope* was therefore basic to this renewal.

Two features of Caribbean ecumenism since the 1970s — the participation of the RCC and the involvement of churches from Cuba — are worth remarking on. The Antilles Episcopal Conference (AEC) of the RCC, which in the 1970s included only the English- and Dutch-speaking dioceses of the region, participated fully in the Chaguaramas consultation on development and was a founding member of the CCC. Subsequently, the French-speaking dioceses (in Martinique, Guadeloupe and Cayenne), which hitherto had been linked directly to the RCC in France, became full members of the AEC without severing their links with France. At this writing the Spanish-speaking dioceses (in Cuba, Dominican Republic and Puerto Rico) still stand outside the AEC. In the French-speaking Caribbean, where Catholicism predominates and Protestantism hardly exists, ecumenism as it is understood and lived in the English- and Dutch-speaking countries is unknown. For this reason the RCC values its links with the CCC, as these help to reduce the isolation of French-speaking Catholics from the rest of the region.

It was the vibrant ecumenical movement which led the way in ending Cuba's isolation from the rest of the Caribbean imposed by the US government in the tense years of the 1960s after Cuba declared itself the first socialist state in the American hemisphere. Member churches of the Cuban Council of Churches participated in the Chaguaramas consultation and subsequently joined the CCC. Four Caribbean governments (Barbados, Guyana, Jamaica, and Trinidad and Tobago), following the lead given by the churches, formally recognized the government of Cuba and established diplomatic relationships with it.

The CCC came into being at a time when optimism over the future was high in the region. Some Caribbean countries had begun to develop a strong pride in the sovereignty political independence had brought. National development was being perceived in terms of five- and ten-year development programmes. New regional institutions were emerging to respond to the challenges of the new day. The

heads of governments meeting became formalized. A Caribbean Free Trade Area came into being; so too did the Caribbean Development Bank and the Caribbean News Agency.

As the 1960s shaded into the 1970s, Caribbean societies and economies were registering impressive strides. Gross domestic product doubled in some countries; per capita incomes increased. Progressive social legislation was enacted. National insurance schemes were introduced, and higher education was emphasized. Then came the crisis of the 1970s and the 1980s fuelled by the oil crisis and the consequent international price inflation and currency instability. Caribbean economies were put out of joint, and their development was severely affected. The crisis had its impact on the life of the churches in the region, no less than on the CCC.

In this respect, the ecumenical scenario in the Caribbean reflects many of the general trends in other parts of the world. Caribbean representatives make their contribution to the global search for "justice, peace and the integrity of creation". But much will depend on the will of coming generations to seek God's gift of unity* in the conviction that "the renewal of the Christian community is an instrument for the total human glorious liberty of all God's people in the Caribbean and development of Caribbean people".

See also **Caribbean Conference of Churches**.

KORTRIGHT DAVIS

J. Braithwait ed., *Handbook of Churches in the Caribbean*, Barbados, CADEC, 1973 • R.W.M. Cuthbert, *Ecumenism and Development*, Barbados, CCC, 1986 • K. Davis, *Mission for Caribbean Change*, Frankfurt, Lang, 1982 • D. Mitchell ed., *New Mission for a New People*, New York, Friendship, 1977 • D. Mitchell ed., *With Eyes Wide Open*, Barbados, CADEC, 1973 • *The Right Hand of God*, Kingston, CCC, 1976 • *Workers Together with Christ*, Georgetown, CCC, 1978.

CARIBBEAN CONFERENCE OF CHURCHES.

The CCC was inaugurated at an ecumenical service in St Luke's Anglican (Episcopal) Church in Kingston, Jamaica, on 13 November 1973. At that service delegates from 37 churches signed the instruments. The formation of the CCC was preceded by years of negotiations, some of them intraconfessional. A few confessions could not in the end

Inaugural assembly of the Caribbean Conference of Churches (WCC/John Taylor)

agree to join as confessions. For example, Baptists in Jamaica subscribed, while no other convention or union of Baptists did. The Anglicans and Roman Catholics subscribed on a Caribbean-wide basis.

Other negotiations were interconfessional at the level of councils of churches and ministers' fraternals. These bodies as such did not become members, but where councils were vibrant, the churches in membership with them were more eager to join.

"Ecumenical" and Caribbean-wide church relatedness is not a new feature, since the administration of the region as colonies demanded to a large extent co-operative approaches and integration. Religious as well as political policy was designed to be integrative.

The chief executive organ of the CCC is the general assembly, which meets once every five years. It is composed of representatives of the member churches who have voting rights. But to the meetings are also invited fraternal bodies, consultants, and others interested in the council's work. When the assembly is not in session, the continuation committee acts in an executive capacity. This committee is appointed by the assembly according to the bylaws of the constitution. It consists of 20 members and meets normally

twice a year between assemblies. Since the general secretariat is housed in Barbados, the easternmost Caribbean island, regional co-ordinators have been located in Jamaica, Antigua, and Trinidad and Tobago.

The most widely known section of the CCC is the Christian Action for Development in the Eastern Caribbean (CADEC), which began as a development arm in the eastern Caribbean but now covers the whole region. CADEC makes loans and grants funds for development projects. The criterion for the evaluation of a project is the true development of a person or group so that self-authentication and independence might be achieved on a lasting basis.

Communication must cover a wide region and is of high priority within the CCC. Two organs have been developed: the monthly newspaper *Contact*, which comments on issues of regional importance, and a radio programme called "Caribbeat", broadcast over 14 regional stations and giving information on cultural and educational events. The CCC studies are also at the service of the churches. A monthly newsletter called *Christian Action* reports on church and church-related events.

The CCC also runs a documentation centre, with a wide range of Caribbean publications — nearly 1,000 volumes on topics like appropriate development, technology, tourism, church and society, women, youth, religion, government and politics. This centre provides archival and research services and is open to students.

Since the CCC is composed of 34 member churches in 33 Caribbean countries and functions in four major language areas, the issue of education is crucial. A textbook on Christian education called *Fashion Me a People* is designed for use in the churches and, where possible, in the public education system at primary and secondary levels. Related to it is a scholarship programme which addresses the problems of trained personnel in the region. It works in co-operation with the WCC scholarships programme.

The objectives of the CCC are the same as those of the WCC. It is committed to an ecumenism which will also assist in the improvement of the social and economic well-being of the poor. Its programmes are thus focused on uplifting the underprivileged both spiritually and economically. It analyzes the problems of poverty and under-development in the region, identifying the contributing causes, assessing the capacity of communities to provide solutions from their own resources and helping with funding and training where necessary.

The preamble to the CCC constitution states: "We, as Christian people of the Caribbean, separated from each other by barriers of history, language, culture, class and distance, desire because of our common calling to Christ to join together in a regional fellowship of churches for inspection, consultation and co-operative action. We are deeply concerned to promote the human liberation of our people and are committed to the achievement of social justice and the dignity of man in society. We desire to build up together our life in Christ and to share our experience for the mutual strengthening of the kingdom of God in the world." To achieve these objectives, apart from encouraging participation in joint worship and theological endeavour, the conference conducts through its agencies national surveys, arranges consultations, and collaborates in efforts with governmental and non-governmental organizations and develops strategies of awareness through television, radio and education programmes.

In 1983 the mandate and rationale of the

CCC programme strategy was reformulated as the "promotion of ecumenism and social change in obedience to Jesus Christ and in solidarity with the poor".

The CCC has taken many initiatives in the areas of theology and Christian education, holistic development, youth and women's concerns, family life, human rights and communications. All these initiatives started from the assumption that, despite the divisiveness of a long colonial heritage, there is an authentic, unifying Caribbean identity through which Caribbean people must articulate their understanding of God's will for them and make their response to it.

HORACE RUSSELL

CARITAS INTERNATIONALIS. CI is a Roman Catholic confederation of 120 national Caritas organizations. Its primary mission is to assist the Roman Catholic Church as a whole to incarnate charity and justice in the world. This action ranges from emergency aid to long-range development; from health and social services for individuals to community organization; from rural outreach to urban centres; from social rehabilitation to prevention, planning and legislative advocacy.

Each national organization is autonomous; in many countries, it is subdivided into diocesan- and parish-based organizations that work in close collaboration with the local bishops. The national Caritas organizations, in turn, receive their mandate from the national episcopal conferences. At the same time, Caritas collaborates closely on all levels with religious communities, Catholic lay movements, and others who sponsor similar socio-pastoral services in the community.

The general secretariat is headquartered in the Vatican, with three principal functions: spreading information within and outside the Caritas network, in order to deepen commitment and improve actions in charity and justice; coordination among CI members, especially in projects of emergencies and development; international representation of CI members and their joint interests before intergovernmental and other international religious and social service organizations (e.g. UNESCO, Food and Agriculture Organization, International Labour Office, Council of Europe).

Since Vatican II,* CI has promoted ecumenical collaboration. It was a founding member of the Churches' Drought Action in Africa and of the International Ecumenical Committee for Refugees. On the national and local levels, Caritas organizations often work together with other church partners to provide for essential needs, promote integral human development, and advocate on behalf of the voiceless and disenfranchised.

GERHARD MEIER

CASTE. Caste is a social grouping that is peculiar to Indian society. *Varna* and *jati* are two Sanskrit terms, both translated in English as "caste", that are used for this phenomenon. *Varna* (lit. "colour") refers to the classic fourfold division of the traditional society into Brahmins (priests), Kshatriyas (rulers and warriors), Vaisyas (merchants and peasants) and Sudras (workers and servants). This pattern, although present in all the descriptions of the caste system, does not fully explain the existence of many thousands of small groups, or *jatis* (from Sanskrit root *jata*, meaning "born"), each with its own assigned position in relation to the rest of the groups.

The origin of caste is unknown, and the ambiguity of the term makes understanding of the system and phenomenon difficult. A close link between caste and occupational differentiation is quite obvious. Each sub-grouping is assigned a particular job in the village. Inextricably bound up with the system of caste are the concepts of ritual purity and pollution. Some jobs are considered "impure", e.g. scavenging, handling dead animals and working with leather. The sub-castes engaged in these are considered impure and consequently contact with them is thought to pollute a higher-caste person. However, caste is not just based on occupation. It is more complex than race or class, though it shares some of the features of both. Religion provided some legitimation to the caste system. Mythologies picture the origin of humankind in terms in which caste differentiations are implicit. Rigid prescriptions about food, dress, behaviour, occupation and social distance for each caste enforced in the name of religion and ritual fortified and perpetuated these divisions. The doctrines of karma and rebirth, linking the faithful performance of one's caste duty in one's life to the possibility of upward mobility in successive births, has tempered the severity of the caste system and in a sense justified caste practices in the popular Hindu mind.

Caste, thus, is a hierarchical system legitimized by tradition and religion, but in effect it functions as a social mechanism by which the dominant groups maintain their power and authority in the village. A harsh concomitant of this system is the marginalization of a section of the population as "casteless" — the "untouchables" who have been exploited for ages in Indian society. Although the inhuman aspects of the caste system are undeniable, in the traditional society it did provide a sense of security and a source of a stable order.

From the time of India's independence, its leaders have introduced many legislative, administrative and social measures to end discrimination based on caste. Modern education, secular jobs and migration to urban centres have weakened the caste system in recent times. Inter-dining and other forms of social intercourse between castes are now fairly common, although intercaste marriages are still rather rare. But caste consciousness and caste as an identity principle continue to be strong among Indian people. Instances of violence by upper castes against lower castes are not uncommon. Caste is a nexus of associative relationships which are reshaped by cultural, religious, psychological and economic factors, and there is no sector of life in India, private or public, that it does not permeate.

Caste has become one of the principal organizing clusters for the collective struggle of people for their rights, with caste considerations having much influence in politics and caste itself being politicized. In a democracy, where numbers count, smaller sub-castes are merged into larger units and act as pressure groups. While the higher castes are organizing to consolidate their power, the lower castes and untouchables are using their caste base for militant struggles for justice.

Gandhi used the term "Harijan" (lit. "people of God") for untouchables and lower-caste people, but many of them reject it, calling themselves *dalit*. Dalit Christians have developed their own liberation theology — Dalit theology — and have been organizing themselves to secure greater recognition in church and society. One of the incentives for conversions to Christianity, Islam and to a lesser extent to Buddhism was the desire to escape caste-based discriminations. However, the caste ethos is so pervasive that it has made inroads even into other religions such as Islam and Christianity. All the main religious divisions of India have in some way been affected by status evaluation based upon the pollution concept. The church itself is not free from caste divisions. In the state of Kerala, for instance, there have been separate churches for converts to Christianity from lower castes. Such divisions adversely affect the fellowship in the church.

The Christian Institute for the Study of Religion and Society (Bangalore, India) has done several studies on caste and its manifestations in the church and in the society at large. These studies have shown that there are several new trends in caste relationships as a result of the system's adaptability and that caste has deeply influenced the life of the churches in many part of India.

The WCC studies on race and ethnic relations in the 1960s did not deal with the issue of caste. In the 1970s, with the launching of the Programme to Combat Racism,* the WCC showed some interest in the issue, but it was not followed up. The sixth assembly (Vancouver 1983) included caste oppression as part of the "web of oppression and injustice", along with racism, sexism and class domination, in the assembly issue, "Struggling for Justice and Human Dignity".

K.C. ABRAHAM

M.G. Castairs, *The Twice Born*, London, Hogarth, 1968 • C. von Fürer-Haimendorf ed., *Caste and Kin in Nepal, India and Ceylon*, Bombay, Asia Publishing, 1966 • J. Maliekal, *Caste in India Today*, Madras, Centre for Social Action, 1980.

CASTRO, EMILIO. B. 2.5.1927, Montevideo, Uruguay. General secretary of the WCC, 1985-, Castro has been active in a wide range of church and ecumenical activities. He has served, for example, as professor of contemporary theological thought at the Mennonite Seminary, Montevideo, 1959-64, chairman of the Fellowship of Christians and Jews, Uruguay, 1962-66, vice-president of the Christian Peace Conference, 1964-68, and a member of its working committee, 1968-69,

co-ordinator of the Commission for Evangelical Unity in Latin America (UNELAM), 1965-72, executive secretary of the South American Association of Theological Schools, 1966-69, president of the Evangelical Methodist Church of Uruguay, 1970-72, chairman of the Agency for Christian Literature Development, 1970-72, and director of the Commission on World Mission and Evangelism, 1973-83. He studied at Union Theological Seminary, Buenos Aires, 1944-50, and was ordained by the Evangelical Methodist Church of Uruguay in 1948. Under a WCC scholarship Castro pursued post-graduate work in Basel in 1953-54 under the guidance of Karl Barth. He received a doctoral degree from the University of Lausanne in 1984. In Bolivia he was pastor of the General Methodist Church, La Paz, 1954-56, and then pastor of the Central Methodist Church, Montevideo, 1957-65. He attended the WCC assemblies in 1961 and 1968, the Life and Mission conference of the World Student Christian Federation in Strasbourg, and the 1966 Church and Society conference in Geneva. His writings include *Amidst Revolution* (Belfast, Christian Journals, 1975), *Freedom in Mission. The Perspective of the Kingdom of God: An Ecumenical Inquiry* (WCC, 1985), and *When We Pray Together* (WCC, 1989).

ANS J. VAN DER BENT

CATECHESIS. This word, used in the New Testament only in its verbal form, describes the oral teaching about the faith.* Later, it came to be applied to the specific teaching given to those preparing for baptism* (catechumens) or recently admitted into membership of the church.* It includes the essential elements of the doctrine, liturgy and life of the church: the Apostles' Creed,* commandments, sacraments* and prayers (esp. the Lord's prayer). As the practice of infant baptism became more common, the institution of catechesis disappeared, but slowly a special instruction for children developed. It led finally to the codification of such instruction in books known as catechisms,* especially at the time of the Reformation, e.g. Luther's small catechism (1529), the Heidelberg catechism (1563), and in turn the catechism of the council of Trent (1566). Within Orthodoxy there was *The*

Orthodox Confession of the Catholic and Apostolic Eastern Church (mid-17th century). Some of these catechisms are still in use today. Many churches have felt a need, however, for modern catechisms that would meet more directly the needs and questions of both children and adults.

Catechesis can be a means of perpetuating the division among the churches but can also contribute to the growth of their unity* and communion.* The synod of bishops (Rome 1977) on catechesis in our time insisted that catechesis has to create and foster a true desire for unity* and has to facilitate involvement in the ecumenical movement. This is no longer debated in churches which strive for unity and common witness.* The ecumenical dimensions of such catechesis could mean a teaching which enables one "to understand better those Christians who belong to other churches or ecclesial communities while also preparing them for dialogue and fraternal relations with them" (synod of bishops). Or it could involve a teaching which emphasizes agreements and a common witness (instead of particular denominational understandings of faith) and which fosters active involvement in the ecumenical movement (see **ecumenical learning**).

Various churches now have such common catechetical programmes for Sunday and day schools which aim to bring to the fore agreements and not disagreements, a common witness and not a divided witness. Distinctions are being made strictly for interpreting church history rather than for characterizing the present situation. But this common catechetical material is not in all cases a sign of growing mutual understanding, acknowledgment and collaboration of churches which have been separated for centuries. In some cases it is rather the result of pressure from a government or society or a common Christian witness (e.g. in Kenya ard Ghana). Others are unofficial statements of faith in catechetical form like the *Common Catechism: A Christian Book of Faith* (1975), by Roman Catholics and Protestants. How far the agreement reached in *Baptism, Eucharist and Ministry** will have consequences for the teaching of the churches and for their catechesis of baptism or eucharist is still uncertain.

See also **catechisms**.

ULRICH BECKER

Apostolic Exhortation Catechesi Tradentae of His Holiness Pope John Paul II to the Episcopate, the Clergy and the Faithful of the Entire Catholic Church on "Catechesis in Our Time", Rome, 1979 • U. Becker, "Catechetical Implications", in *Ecumenical Perspectives on Baptism, Eucharist and Ministry*, M. Thurian ed., WCC, 1983 • U. Becker, "Ecumenical Dimensions of Catechesis", *The Ecumenical Review*, 32, 1980 • Y. Nomura ed., *Together in Faith: A Collection of Models of Common Catechetical Programmes*, WCC, 1978 • L. Vischer & J. Feiner eds, *The Common Catechism: A Christian Book of Faith*, London, 1975.

CATECHISMS. In the first centuries of the church, the term "catechism" referred to the process or method of instruction for catechumens on their way to baptism;* later it was extended to encompass religious instruction in general, making the term largely co-extensive with "catechesis".* In the 16th century, however, "catechism" became identified almost exclusively with manuals of instruction in the basics of the Christian faith. In book form, the catechism became the primary instrument of religious education. Short catechetical summaries of faith are as old as the church, and some manuals were certainly used for catechizing in the middle ages, but it was not until the time of the Reformation (and the invention of the printing press) that catechisms proper flourished.

History, nature, use. There were attempts at manuals for instruction prior to Martin Luther's catechisms, such as the *Children's Questions* of the Bohemian Brethren (1502), and the *Catechismus* of Andreas Althamer (1528), the first book actually to carry the title "Catechism". But it was the two classic catechisms of Luther (small catechism, 1529; large catechism, 1530) which broke the floodgates for the proliferation of these catechetical manuals. The context of Luther's catechisms was clearly homiletical: they grew out of his preaching and were supposed to be used for and in connection with the sermon. These two catechisms themselves became the basis of many others. Reformed catechisms followed soon after, among them those of Martin Bucer (1537), John Calvin (1537, 1541-42), and Heinrich Bullinger (1561).

With the number of catechisms, the subject matter included in them also grew steadily: the core material of the catechisms (largely taken over from the traditional basics of instruction in the Christian faith) consists of the creed, the ten commandments, the Lord's prayer, and teachings on the sacraments — for the Roman Catholic tradition the Hail Mary has to be added. In this material one can easily detect core texts of the church's doctrine, worship and life. Catechisms, however, grew beyond these core doctrinal, doxological and ethical texts and rapidly became more and more detailed. The catechetical material is presented in question-and-answer form (Bullinger's reformed catechism of 1561 already contained nearly 300 questions, Joseph Deharbe's famous *Catholic Catechism* of 1847 contained 750), with the catechist usually asking and the catechized responding. The material was to be learned by heart. Catechisms could be either a book of instruction for the catechized or a manual for the catechist.

Some catechisms of the Reformation are also clearly designed as confessions of faith and doctrinal statements. As such they can actually become part of the confessional documents *(Bekenntnisschriften)* of a particular tradition, as is the case with the Heidelberg catechism of 1563 (Luther's two catechisms were also included in the Book of Concord of 1580). A similar status is enjoyed by the two Westminster catechisms, compiled by the Westminster assembly (1643-53). The shorter catechism has been in regular use among Presbyterian, Congregationalist and Baptist churches. The Anglican church included a catechism in the Book of Common Prayer. It was printed before the confirmation service and used in the preparation for confirmation.

In the Roman Catholic Church, catechisms flourished in the 16th century in response to the challenges of the Reformation. Especially the catechisms of Peter Canisius and of Robert Bellarmine enjoyed a wide reception. In 1566 the *Catechismus Romanus*, written under order from the council of Trent,* was published as an instrument for teaching in the hands of parish priests.

As the number of catechisms and their subject matter grew, apologetics began to play an increasingly important part. Catechisms became more and more consciously confessional, spelling out in detail the particular confessional identity of one ecclesial tradition over against others. Not infrequently, catechisms came to be simplified compendia of scholastic theology. The emphasis lay clearly

on intellectual adherence to a set of doctrinal propositions. (That catechisms, nevertheless, were used not only for religious instruction can be seen by the fact that some of them contained ABC primers or Latin grammars.) Despite the "confessionalism" of most catechisms, some ecumenical borrowing did take place: the Jesuit Edmond Auger, for example, modelled his 1563 catechism consciously on Calvin's catechetical work.

With Christianity's entry into non-Western countries, European catechisms were often simply directly transplanted. In some cases, translations into indigenous languages came within the first generation of mission work: the third council of Lima, e.g., in 1582-83 provided for a translation of a catechism into Quechua and Aymara, the indigenous languages of the region. In the early period of Jesuit missionary outreach in Japan, adaptations in content and language style to the Japanese culture were attempted — while at the same time a Latin guidebook for catechists was published under the title *Catechismus christianae fidei in quo secta japonenses confutantur*. Catechisms were never without culturally conditioned presuppositions (and weaknesses): in the USA, the Anglican "catechism to be used by the teachers in the religious instruction of persons of colour" from 1837 taught slaves very clearly that their state was ordained by God and that they should be content in it.

Both in Europe and the New World, catechisms were the prime instrument of religious education for nearly 400 years. With the introduction of compulsory education in the 18th and 19th centuries, the main use of catechisms came to be within the religious education in schools, the method of learning still being that of memorizing and reciting the text. The Eastern churches, however, generally remained without catechisms, except under Western influence (see e.g. the catechism of Metropolitan Platon of Moscow, d.1812).

Current situation. The rethinking of catechesis and the renewal in catechetical methods in the 20th century led to a new approach and orientation in the nature and use of catechisms. This century has seen the end of the traditional scholastic compendium catechism, while at the same time witnessing a veritable flood of new catechisms which are taking into account the anthropological foundations and the cultural context of faith as well as the biblical-narrative core of the *depositum fidei* and the liturgical life of the church. Most catechisms have moved away from the standard question-and-answer format to a more narrative, participatory and situation-oriented approach. Catechisms now also take directly into account the age group they are addressing and its psychological make-up, by adapting both the structure of the content and the pedagogical techniques to the respective audience. Catechisms for children, for example, will now generally employ very simple language and use a variety of images, stories and songs.

A clear signal of newness was sent out with the publication of the so-called Dutch catechism in 1966. This Roman Catholic catechism for adults is structured around two foci: the concrete situations and questions of life, and the witness of faith. A dialogic approach, relating human experience and the good news, seems to have found acceptance in many catechisms over a broad range of ecclesial traditions. To name but two examples: the German *Evangelischer Gemeindekatechismus* of 1979 (and its US-American edition *Evangelical Catechism* of 1982) begins with human experience and moves from there to information, reflection, discussion and personal appropriation. Included in this catechism are pictures, meditative texts, prayers and songs which come from a variety of ecclesial, geographical and cultural backgrounds. *Vamos Caminando* (the English sub-title calls it *A Peruvian Catechism*) is yet more situation-oriented. It starts with reflections on the daily life of campesinos in the northern Andes of Peru with a clear view towards liberating conscientization. It evidences a great appreciation for the local cultural context and emphasizes its importance in the growth of faith. Examples of catechisms such as these two are numerous. Especially in non-Western contexts, the structure of new catechisms is often governed by basic life themes rather than doctrinal concerns. There are, however, also catechisms which move in a more conservative direction: the revised catechism of the British Methodist church, for example, maintains the traditional question-and-answer format. The new World Catechism of the Roman Catholic Church will take its structure from the traditional division into doctrine, sacraments, and commandments; it is intended as a reference book for national and diocesan catechisms.

An ecumenical Protestant-Catholic venture was edited by J. Feiner and L. Vischer under the title *Neues Glaubensbuch* in 1973, but catechisms have on the whole not been a favourite area of ecumenical initiative. With the growth of ecumenical commitment, polemics against other churches have, however, been eliminated from almost all catechisms. The apologetic and polemical emphasis has also given way to a renewed concentration on the basics of Christian doctrine, worship and life. (There are, of course exceptions to this: see e.g. the recent edition of A. Makrakis's *The Sacred and Holy Catechesis of the Orthodox Church as Taught by the Holy Spirit and His Solemn Instruments from the Day of Pentecost to the Last Ecumenical Council*, 1885, 2nd ed. 1969).

Future directions. Maybe one of the concrete outcomes of the Faith and Order convergence document *Baptism, Eucharist and Ministry** and the study "Towards the Common Expression of the Apostolic Faith Today" could be something like an "Ecumenical Base Catechism" which would serve as a model and reference book for denominational catechisms. There are, however, some fundamental questions related to the very nature of catechisms which need answering in relation to such a venture. Catechisms are instruments for the transmission and explication of the faith.* For most ecclesial traditions, they do not belong to the symbols of faith themselves. They also clearly presuppose a book culture. This raises problems which cannot be ignored: in primarily oral cultures, say in Africa or in black churches in North America, with their clearly established patterns of oral teaching, the catechism may not be the most helpful tool for the faithful transmission of the gospel. In a *post*-book culture, as we begin to find it in certain sub-cultures of the West, the catechism may not be a helpful tool either — for very different reasons. The question facing the churches, one not yet answered, is, What will best serve the transmission of the faith in the diversity of the one-church-to-be in the ages to come?

TERESA BERGER

J. Feiner & L. Vischer eds, *Neues Glaubensbuch: Der gemeinsame christliche Glaube* (ET *The Com-*

mon Catechism: A Christian Book of Faith, London, Search, 1975) ● H.-G. Link ed., Apostolic Faith Today: A Handbook for Study, WCC, 1985 ● H.-G. Link ed., One God, One Lord, One Spirit: On the Explication of the Apostolic Faith Today, WCC, 1988.

CATHOLIC CONFERENCE FOR ECUMENICAL QUESTIONS.

In application of the 1949 Vatican Letter of the Holy Office Ecclesia Catholica, which permitted Catholic experts, approved by their local bishops, to participate in discussions "on faith and morals", two Dutchmen — Johannes Willebrands and Frans Thijssen — travelled through Europe to enlist Catholic theologians, historians, biblical scholars, liturgists and missiologists in taking seriously Protestant and Orthodox ecumenical efforts, especially WCC faith and order issues. With the approval of Rome, they founded the Catholic Conference for Ecumenical Questions (CCEQ) — at that time, Europe's only transnational organization of Roman Catholic scholars.

With a fluctuating list of 70-80 scholars, the CCEQ held study meetings in Fribourg (Switzerland, 1952), Utrecht (1953), Mainz (1954), Paris (1955), Chevetogne (1957), Paderborn (1959), Gazzada (1960), Strasbourg (1961), and its final one again in Gazzada (1963). Between those meetings, an executive committee co-ordinated activities and relations with the WCC and different authorities in Rome. The president was Willebrands, and his contact person in the Vatican was designated by Pius XII — the Jesuit Augustin Bea.

The WCC's general secretary, W.A. Visser 't Hooft, met often in confidence with his fellow Dutchman Willebrands. The WCC was able to turn to the CCEQ for advice, reports and studies. For example, the CCEQ prepared documents on the major themes of the Evanston (1954) and New Delhi (1961) WCC assemblies.

From this network of scholars came the original staff of the Secretariat for Promoting Christian Unity,* with Willebrands as the secretary, and most of its original body of consultors. Many CCEQ members were among the key drafters of several Vatican II documents, e.g. Yves Congar, Charles Moeller, Gustave Thils, Jérôme Hamer, Balthasar Fischer, Karl Rahner, Johannes Feiner, Maurice Bévenot, Pierre Duprey and Emmanuel Lanne.

TOM STRANSKY

CATHOLICITY.

Like the term "Christianity", "catholicity" is still an "essentially contested concept". It has been claimed exclusively by Roman Catholics, some of whom have believed in the past that Roman was a fifth "mark" of the church in addition to the four traditional ones, i.e. one, holy, catholic and apostolic; Cardinal Bellarmine (1542-1621) thought that the term "catholic" had been a synonym for "Roman" since at least the 12th century. On the other hand, Luther wanted to replace "catholic" with "Christian" in the translations of the classical Christian creeds,* as if the word had been spoiled by Rome's departure from classical catholicity in introducing innovations not legitimated by the scriptures. The quality of catholicity has also been claimed by Anglo-Catholics as well as the advocates of Reformed Catholicity (e.g. in the Netherlands Reformed Church in the 1950s). The advocates of Reformed Catholicity in Protestant circles have been criticized as "Romanizers"; while puritans, evangelicals and liberals alike have argued that Roman "catholicity" is "a legalistic religion in which divine authority was falsely claimed for human ecclesiastical regulations". Eastern Orthodoxy tends to understand the concept of catholicity in terms of the "fullness" of life received by way of the apostolic and patristic church. At the first assembly of the WCC in 1948, fundamental differences were noted between member churches which were "Catholic" and those which were "Protestant". Whereas the former emphasized "the visible continuity of the church in the apostolic succession of the episcopate", the latter stressed "the initiative of the word of God* and the response of faith,* focused on the doctrine of justification* sola fide (by faith alone)".

To remove "catholicity" from the sphere of ecclesiastical politics and theological dispute which has been its main context for about 1,000 years, it is necessary to understand more precisely how this concept has been used in the past and to see how it is being redefined and re-applied in the ecumenical process today.

A historical analysis of the concept of catholicity. The adjective "catholic" is derived from the Greek adverbial phrase *kath' holou* which means "in general", "universal", or "on the whole". It is the opposite of what is particular, individual or partial. It also denotes "completeness" (the sense preferred by the Orthodox churches). Other than in Acts 4:18 (where it appears in the negative expression "not to speak *at all*"), the term is not used in the New Testament: hence the reluctance of Christians who reject non-biblical doctrines and non-biblical concepts to use it in practice. For most Christians, however, its use is legitimated by its occurrence in the Apostles' Creed* and the so-called Nicene Creed.*

As early as the 2nd century the term was used to distinguish between the catholic epistles (which were addressed to the *whole* of the church) and letters written to individuals or to local churches. The catholic church was also conceived to be co-extensive with the whole of the world (the oikoumene): "the whole catholic church throughout the inhabited world" (*Martyrdom of Polycarp* 8.1). "Catholicity" almost always carried with it a qualitative meaning, and a normative sense attaches to it: "Wherever Christ Jesus is, there is the catholic church" (Ignatius, *Letter to the Smyrnaeans* 8.2). As early as about 150 it meant truly orthodox with respect to doctrines and beliefs. "Catholic" now denoted the one true church, as opposed to all other heretical or schismatic bodies (see **heresy, schism**). This notion was further strengthened during the conflicts with the Gnostics and Donatists.

All of these nuances can be found together as early as 350, e.g. in the Catechetical Lectures of Cyril of Jerusalem (lecture 18): "The church is called catholic because it is spread throughout the world, from end to end of the earth; also because it teaches universally and completely all the doctrines which man should know concerning things visible and invisible, heavenly and earthly; and also because it subjects to right worship all mankind, rulers and ruled, lettered and unlettered; further because it treats and heals universally every sort of sin committed by soul and body, and possesses in itself every conceivable virtue, whether in deeds, words or in spiritual gifts of every kind."

Universal extension, soundness of doctrine, adaptation to the needs of all sorts and conditions of men and women, together with moral and spiritual perfection — all are combined here to demonstrate what the complex concept of catholicity entails. A similar statement is found in the *Commonitorium* of Vincent of Lérins (before 450): "Within the catholic church itself the greatest care must be taken that we hold that which has been believed everywhere, always, and by all. For this is truly and properly catholic, as the very force and effect of the word declares, which includes all things with practical universality. But this will be found precisely in this way, if we follow that which is universal, that which is ancient, and that about which there is consent."

Here, the notion of development of doctrine (which Newman subsequently applied to legitimate later Roman Catholic doctrinal innovations) is not entirely excluded, because there must also be progress in understanding, in knowledge, in wisdom. In the middle ages, however, there was little development with respect to the notion of catholicity, as these comments of Thomas Aquinas on the Apostles' Creed demonstrate: "The church is catholic, i.e. universal, first with respect to place, because it is everywhere in the world... Secondly, the church is universal with respect to the state of men, because no one is rejected, whether master or slave, male or female... Thirdly, it is universal with respect to time. For some have said that the church should last until a certain time, but this is false, because the church began from the time of Abel and will last until the end of the world... [But] after the close of the age it will remain in heaven."

However, Roman Catholics began to emphasize that "whoever does not agree with the Roman church is not to be considered Catholic" (a proposition stated explicitly by Pope Gregory VII in 1075). This position later allowed "Protestant" and "Catholic" to develop into antitheses when Protestants no longer agreed with Catholics, especially in Protestant circles which believed Roman Catholicism to be the cult of the antichrist and in Reformed churches which abandoned such traditional structures as episcopacy.* The Orthodox churches also contested communion* with Rome as a criterion of catholicity, although some became "Uniate churches" by accepting the universal jurisdiction of the pope. Anglicans and some Lutherans, however, continued to accept the classical catholicity of the early church, while insisting that the Reformation was also necessary. Thus Melanchthon's *De Appellatione Ecclesiae Catholicae*: "It is one thing to be called Catholic, something else to be really Catholic. Those are truly called Catholic who embrace the doctrine of the truly Catholic Church, i.e. that which is supported by the witness of all time, of all ages, which believes what the prophets and apostles taught, and which does not tolerate factions, heresies and heretical assemblies. We must all be Catholic, i.e. embrace this word which the rightly thinking church holds, separate from, and untangled with, sects warring against that Word."

Despite the schisms between East and West, Rome and the Reformation, a number of moderates in most Protestant groups and in the mainstream of Counter-Reformation Catholicism continually strove to re-unite the divided churches by retrieving the classical understanding of catholicity before agreement with the see of Rome developed into a criterion of genuine catholicity and before Christianity was equated with the position adopted by the Roman Catholic Church (RCC). A statement of the irenic position is found in an Anglican report on "Catholicity" (1947): "In our divided Christendom we do not believe that any existing institution or group of institutions gives a full and balanced representation of the true and primitive catholicity. It is the recovery of the principles of that catholicity which is our quest."

It was quite impossible, however, to reunite divided churches as long as the RCC continued to insist that full communion with an unreformed papacy and agreement with the whole of Roman Catholic teaching were acid tests of genuine catholicity. For example, when Anglo-Catholics such as Edward Pusey began to advocate a dialogue with Rome in the middle of the 19th century, the holy office issued the following declaration in 1864: "No other church is Catholic except that which is built on the one individual Peter, and which grows up into one body closely joined and knitted together in the unity of faith and love." The response of the RCC to the ecumenical appeals of the patriarch of Constantinople as of the Anglican episcopate in 1920 and to the

first meetings of Life and Work and Faith and Order in 1925 and 1927, as well as to the semi-official conversations between Anglicans and Roman Catholics at Malines/Mechelen in Belgium in the early 1920s, was negative (as is shown by the encyclical *Mortalium Animos* of 6 January 1928). Nevertheless, it is evident that at least some Roman Catholics were already willing to enter into a dialogue with non-Catholics in order to re-unite divided churches. The main question was, When could such unofficial and semi-official contacts become official? And when would the RCC itself respond positively to the ecumenical imperative? This was eventually a two-sided process, because many Protestants were still unwilling to engage in ecumenical dialogue with the RCC before it had given clear indications that it was also willing to reform itself. This did not happen until the Second Vatican Council.

Meanwhile, important developments were already taking place in both the RCC and the Protestant churches. In 1928, for example, Karl Barth published an essay on the relationship between Catholicism and Protestantism ("Roman Catholicism: A Question to the Protestant Church"), in which he argued that Protestantism must allow itself to be critically questioned by Roman Catholicism. Barth believed that Roman Catholics, unlike liberal Protestants, had not abandoned the substance of the Christian faith. If forced to choose between Friedrich Schleiermacher, Albrecht Ritschl and Ernst Troeltsch, on the one hand, and Roman Catholicism on the other, Barth would choose the latter. Nevertheless, Roman Catholicism had failed to make the church subservient to the word of God. Like Protestant modernism, Roman Catholicism had ultimately made the church dependent upon itself. Paul Tillich would argue that "the Protestant principle" must ultimately be united with "Catholic substance". On the Roman Catholic side, moreover, Louis Bouyer argued in the late 1950s that the positive principles of the Reformation (such as the primacy of divine grace, the justifying power of faith, the unique mediation of Christ in the process of salvation* and the total sovereignty of God) could indeed be interpreted in a Catholic sense.

Catholicity in conciliar and post-conciliar ecumenism. The Second Vatican Council nuanced the Counter-Reformation understanding of Catholicism in a remarkable way. In *Lumen Gentium* (8) catholicity is no longer assumed to be Roman Catholicity pure and simple. Catholicity is treated now primarily as an attribute of the church of Christ. It *subsists in* the RCC. The fullness of catholicity can be obtained only in full communion with Rome. But this does not imply that churches not in communion with Rome have not preserved at least some of the essential qualities of catholicity.

It is explicitly stated in the Decree on Ecumenism (13 and 17) that essential features of Catholicism have been preserved in churches such as the Anglican communion and Orthodoxy. The entire heritage of the Orthodox churches "belongs to the full catholic and apostolic character of the church". It is also admitted that divisions in the church "prevent the church from effecting the fullness of catholicity", which makes it difficult for the church to express its "full catholicity". Furthermore, the manifold variety of local churches "with one aspiration" (i.e. which share the same purpose) constitutes evidence for the catholicity of the undivided church. Legitimate differences no longer impede full catholic unity: indeed, they actually "enrich and strengthen it" (*LG* 13 and 23). On this basis, A. Dulles has stated that Vatican II conceives catholicity in the mode of "reconciled diversity".* The main question now is whether practice will eventually confirm the theory.

In 1968 a joint theological commission of 18, half of whom were Roman Catholics and the other half representatives of the WCC, produced a document on "Catholicity and Apostolicity" in which the most important emphases are upon pneumatology and Christology. The church attains catholicity to the extent that it expresses the truth and charity of Christ and the Holy Spirit. The full manifestation of catholicity, moreover, will not occur until the return of Christ in glory, which also adds an important eschatological dimension to the notion of catholicity. Four aberrations were signalled: the restriction of communion to certain races, nations or social classes; the formation of sects or parties within the body of the church; denominational pride to the detriment of others; and the misuse of the concept of catholicity in order to legitimate

doctrines and practices which are not congruent with the Christian identity.

This is consistent with the report presented to the WCC's fourth assembly (Uppsala 1968) on "The Holy Spirit and the Catholicity of the Church". The gulf between Catholic and Protestant is now much less apparent than it was in 1948 at Amsterdam. Catholicity is defined as "the quality by which the church expresses the fullness, the integrity, and the totality of life in Christ". It is argued here that catholicity cannot be separated from the notions of unity, holiness, and apostolicity. There must also be a balance between continuity and renewal. Finally, in the ecumenical process, the church of Christ might achieve an even broader catholicity. "The purpose of Christ is to bring people of all times, of all races, of all places, of all conditions, into an organic and living unity in Christ by the Holy Spirit under the universal fatherhood of God. This unity is not solely external; it has a deeper, internal dimension, which is also expressed by the term 'catholicity'. Catholicity reaches its completion when what God has already begun in history is finally disclosed and fulfilled."

No one suggests, though, that Christians should simply wait passively until the second coming or until the end of time in order to create the right kind of catholicity in this world of space and time.

See also **apostolicity, church, unity**.

PETER STAPLES

Catholicity: A Study in the Conflict of Christian Traditions in the West, report to archbishop of Canterbury by E.S. Abbot and others, Westminster, Dacre, 1947 ● "Catholicity and Apostolicity: The Report of the World Council of Churches-Roman Catholic Joint Theological Commission", *One in Christ*, 6, 1970 ● A. Dulles, *The Catholicity of the Church*, Oxford, Oxford UP, 1985 ● P.W. Fuerth, *The Concept of Catholicity in the Documents of the World Council of Churches, 1948-1968*, Rome, Anselmiana, 1973 ● E. Schlink, "The Holy Spirit and the Catholicity of the Church", *The Ecumenical Review*, 21, 1969.

CENTRAL AMERICA. For years ecumenism in Central America has not been a living experience, largely due to the type of Protestantism in Central America and the political convulsions that have racked the region since the 1960s. Even the present decade is marked by acute polarization, which has generated a religious mentality in which ecumenical thinking and any talk of unity are considered heterodox.

A conservative ideological background in both society and church has blocked the acceptance of the presuppositions of the various ecumenically oriented movements, especially as the avant-garde organizations clearly question the social and ecclesiastical status quo. Because the conservatives, especially with the support of North American Protestantism, are more concerned with perpetuating their own institutions than with church co-operation, any ecumenical endeavour is considered dangerous, and the very word "ecumenical" is taboo.

In Central America the WCC, seen as the instigator of ecumenism, is known more by what its detractors say against it than by whatever its sympathizers say in its favour. In such an ideologically repressive situation, anything having to do with ecumenicity is automatically eliminated from the agenda of most of the churches. Indeed in the eyes of the religious conservatives, Central American ecumenism is synonymous with communism.

Three attitudes towards the ecumenical movement are discernible. First is outright

opposition because the WCC is perceived as doctrinally deviant and politically leftist. This may be the majority position. Another attitude is openness to ecumenical issues, while carefully avoiding involvement in ecumenical activities or even using the word "ecumenical". These are the evangelical and socially "progressive" churches which are trying to protect those small spaces for co-operation and unity that have been won with considerable effort. Meanwhile, they are attempting to re-educate their congregations towards a better understanding of Christian unity. An excellent example of this effort is a pamphlet published by the Baptist Association of El Salvador. A third attitude is that of the official representatives and functionaries of regional and national ecumenical organizations. They proceed with their business with little concern for what the very conservative churches think about them.

The anti-ecumenical attitudes of the Protestant missions are in part in reaction to the historic churches. They were also influenced by their experience of mission fields such as Asia and Africa. The decision of the Edinburgh conference of 1910 to exclude Latin America from the legitimate fields for Prot-

Mothers of missing persons in El Salvador (WCC/Peter Williams)

estant mission was at variance with the vision of the evangelical and revivalist churches in the USA. To further their missionary strategy towards Latin America, these churches worked towards greater co-operation among themselves. Their efforts came to a culmination in the Panama congress of 1916. However, actions did not match the rhetoric. The extreme individualism (and messianic self-awareness) of 19th-century US Protestant missions worked rather towards intensifying the differences. With few exceptions, their doctrinal tenets caused them to disparage the Catholic church for obscurantism and thus to paint the region in sombre colours: Latin America was a land of darkness and its people ignorant; what these countries needed was "the light of the Protestant gospel".

Catholic-Protestant dialogue. If by ecumenism we mean a meeting of minds between the various confessions, then ecumenicity is non-existent in Central America. It has taken place neither at the ecclesiastical level nor by the initiative of the national evangelical alliances. Both the Catholic and the Protestant hierarchies have proceeded with their separate agendas, maintaining an ideological intolerance that has excluded the possibility of any kind of intrafaith dialogue.* The Roman Catholic Church, because of historical precedence, claims the right to control the religious needs of the people. Protestant churches consider themselves sent by God to re-evangelize the people with a purer and more practical gospel. These conflicting starting points account for Roman Catholic attempts to destroy the early Protestant movement in Central America as well as for the pugnacious attitude of many Protestant missionaries.

This anti-ecumenical spirit was encouraged by the liberal (anti-clerical) political parties, which saw in the Roman Catholic Church the greatest obstacle to progress and development. Hence they brought to Central America the first Protestant missionaries in 1891 (from the Presbyterian Board of Mission), who began to work among Spanish speakers in Guatemala. During the close of the 19th century and the early part of the 20th, the political ambitions of the liberal parties were abetted by the expansionist dreams of mission agencies.

The late 1960s and early 1970s saw various short-lived ecumenical and evangelical co-operative movements. On the ecumenical side, the best known was the Unión Evangélica Latinoamericana (UNELAM), whose first secretary was Emilio Castro. It was the forerunner of the Latin American Council of Churches (CLAI). The most successful evangelical movement was the Evangelism in Depth programme of the Latin America Mission, with headquarters in Costa Rica. For periods of about a year in each case, virtually every Protestant church and agency in Nicaragua, Costa Rica, Guatemala and Honduras worked together in a concerted programme of "saturation evangelism". From there the programme moved to several South American countries and to other parts of the world. However, there was never a willingness by the participating churches to engage in dialogue with the Catholic church.

After a period of stand-off since Vatican II,* relations with the Catholic church have begun to worsen in recent years. For the most part, non-dialogue continues to be the rule in an era when Catholicism is losing ground and the Protestant churches and groups are growing. This same phenomenon, however, has contributed to the polarization within Protestantism itself.

Not everything has been negative. Outstanding Catholic and Protestant leaders have taken the risk to step across the boundaries of prejudice to engage in dialogue. Two early exponents of ecumenical dialogue were R. Kenneth Strachan, director general of the Latin America Mission and the founder of Evangelism in Depth, and Augusto Cotto, a Baptist pastor in El Salvador. In 1964 Strachan discussed mission and evangelism with the staff of the WCC and its Commission on World Mission and Evangelism in the pages of the *International Review of Mission*. He also met with Catholics in a televised debate on Vatican II. More recently, other noteworthy Central American Protestants have taken similar risks. Outstanding in the Catholic church was Archbishop Oscar Romero. He did not hestitate to engage in dialogue with Baptists, Lutherans and other Protestants who shared his concern over the political crisis in El Salvador.

Some efforts at intra-Protestant dialogue have been encouraged by the Confraternidad Evangélica Latinoamericana (CONELA) as

well as by CLAI. Although neither of them
has been notably successful in incorporating
Central American churches into their respective fellowships, CLAI is gaining increasing
acceptance in the region, in spite of the de-
famatory campaign waged against it. CLAI's
more recent success can be attributed to its
presence among grassroots congregations in a
wide spectrum of churches in the region.
Meanwhile, CONELA, in spite of its conservative agenda, is a long way from uniting Central American Protestants.

Unity amid tragedy. The ecumenical
spirit has sprung to life in Central America,
paradoxically, in the midst of death. It is
significant that the human suffering caused by
natural disasters (hurricanes and earthquakes)
has given rise to signs of true ecumenicity.
While some of this response has been ephemeral, much has endured, in every Central
American country. Chief among them is
CEPAD, which was born before the after-
shocks of the 1979 Managua earthquake had
ceased. Something like this happened with
CEDEN in Honduras, after the devastation of
hurricane Fifi in 1974. CONCAD's birth in
Guatemala was due also to the disastrous
earthquake of 1976. In Costa Rica, towards
the end of 1988, hurricane Joan brought about
a degree of ecumenical participation that
would have otherwise seemed impossible.

More recently, the political turmoil in El
Salvador has opened up ecumenical spaces
where both Protestants and Catholics work
together. Here, as well as in Guatemala, permanent peace committees, with wide interfaith representation, have been formed to encourage national dialogue. In Panama the Roman Catholic Church participates officially
alongside Methodist, Lutheran and Episcopal
clergymen in what is the region's only truly
ecumenical forum.

But perhaps the most significant ecumenical advances are being made among basic
Christian communities, or church base communities,* where peasant Christians from every conceivable tradition worship and pray
together and seek to understand their situation
in the light of scripture. There are said to be as
many as 200 of these groups in Guatemala
alone. The movement is also spreading in El
Salvador.

Ecumenical agencies that have been influential in South America have generally not
been too significant in Central America. One
reason may be that their agenda is too far
ahead of the churches. These movements are
largely directed from outside, and local participation in their activities, for the most part,
does not represent church bodies. It may be
too early to evaluate the impact of homegrown
ecumenical agencies; several, however, are
worthy of mention. The Junta Evangélica de
Servicio Social, long since suppressed by the
army, was founded in Guatemala by lay
theologian Julia Esquivel. The Seminario Bíb-
lico Latinoamericana and the Departamento
Ecuménico de Investigación, both of Costa
Rica; the Eje Ecuménico and the Centro In-
terinstitucional de Estudios Teológicos in
Nicaragua; the Comisión Cristiana de Desar-
rollo in Honduras; and the conference of
evangelical churches of Guatemala are only a
few of the many ecumenical agencies in the
region.

Church unity does not seem to be of interest
when it is presented in theoretical terms. It
becomes relevant only in the face of human
tragedy and need — when we are forced to set
aside our theological differences and prejudices for the sake of a total Christian witness.

ARTURO PIEDRA

Go In Peace, Leave Us In Peace, Quito, CLAI,
1987 • *Kairos: Central America. A Challenge to the
Churches of the World*, New York, Circus, 1989 •
A. Langerak ed., *When Christians Meet: Across
North-South Barriers. The Affluent Church Meets
Central America*, San José, CELEP, 1989 • *Life
Amid Death in Central America*, New York,
NCCCUSA, 1983 • J. Nelson-Pallmeyer, *The Poli-
tics of Compassion*, Maryknoll, NY, Orbis, 1986 •
The Road to Damascus: Kairos and Conversion,
London, Catholic Institute for International Rela-
tions, 1989.

CHAKKO, SARAH. B. 13.2.1905,
Trichur, South India; d. 25.1.1954, Lucknow, North India. Chakko was an ecumenical youth and student movement leader, first
chair of the WCC's Commission on the Life
and Work of Women in the Church, and
first woman on the WCC presidium (1951-
54).

Born in a Syrian Orthodox family, Sarah
Chakko studied history at Queen Mary's, a
government women's college in Madras,

Sarah Chakko (WCC photo)

taught for two years in a London Missionary Society high school, then earned a master's degree at Presidency College in Madras and was appointed to teach at Isabella Thoburn College, an ecumenical school under US Methodist auspices in Lucknow. In 1937 she undertook further study in the US at the University of Chicago and the University of Michigan. She was named principal of Isabella Thoburn in 1945.

Active in the Student Christian Movement of India, Burma and Ceylon, she attended student conferences in Java in 1933 and in San Francisco in 1936, and was part of an Indian SCM team that visited university students in China in 1946. She also served on the national committee of the YWCA of India, Burma and Ceylon and was a vice-president of the World YWCA.

When G. Bromley Oxnam asked Chakko to be a delegate to the WCC's first assembly in Amsterdam, she wrote back to say that she was not a Methodist (although she worshipped in a Methodist church in Lucknow). When he told her she was being invited to represent not the Methodists but the "younger churches", she reminded him that the church to which she belonged was some 1,600 years old. After Amsterdam — where she presented the report of the study committee on women — she took a leave of absence from her academic duties

and during 1950 and 1951 worked full-time on behalf of the WCC's new Commission on the Life and Work of Women in the Church, arranging meetings and discussion groups and travelling widely through North America, Europe and the Middle East.

Though her health was impaired, she continued after her return to Lucknow in 1951 to attend and address international conferences and to make official visits to churches abroad, always encouraging a wider ministry for women. When T.C. Chao resigned as president of the WCC in 1951 because of the central committee's declaration on the Korean war, she was asked to succeed him, "in recognition of her exceptional service to the whole ecumenical movement". At her invitation, the WCC central committee met at Isabella Thoburn College in January 1953.

Named as a Syrian Orthodox delegate to the second assembly (Evanston 1954), she had begun to take an active part in preparations for it; but at the end of January 1954, as she sat down to rest during a basketball game with some students, she died of a heart attack.

SUSANNAH HARRIS-WILSON

M.L. Slater, *Future-Maker of India: The Story of Sarah Chakko*, New York, Friendship, 1968 • H. Thomä, *Sarah Chakko — eine grosse Inderin*, Stuttgart, Evang. Missionsverlag, 1955.

CHALCEDON. The 5th century received from the 4th century a Christological heritage that was not completely thought through. The problem was to interpret more precisely the basically common belief in the incarnation* of God in Jesus Christ, after Arianism had been conquered (the true divinity of the Son was proclaimed at Nicea in 325) and Apollinarianism overcome (according to the council of Constantinople in 381, Jesus Christ is fully human, with body and intellectual soul). One main Christological school was particularly careful to ensure the unity of God and human being in Christ (esp. in Alexandria, but also partially in Syria); the other school emphasized the unity of divinity and humanity and the distinction between the two (thus Gregory of Nazianzus and the Antiochenes, such as Diodore of Tarsus, Theodore of Mopsuestia).

A special problem was posed by the

expression and use of the principal concepts *hypostasis* and *physis*, or "person" and "nature". In 428-29 this problem resulted in the first major Christological crisis in the Eastern church. Nestorius wanted to emphasize that the two natures in Christ are unmixed, but this view was interpreted by Alexandria as a doctrine of two hypostases, or two persons. Through the intermediary of Apollinarians, Cyril of Alexandria received texts which circulated under the name of 4th-century fathers (e.g. Pope Julian and Pope Felix, Gregory Thaumaturgus and Athanasius). Those texts included the characteristic formula of the Apollinarians: "the one nature *(mia physis)* of the incarnate God-Word". Cyril took over this *mia physis* formula as the criterion of orthodox Christology in the struggle against Nestorius. At the council of Ephesus in 431, Nestorius was condemned for rejecting the council of Nicea and confessing the doctrine of two persons, although he too tried in different conceptual language (albeit in an infelicitous manner) to express his loyalty to Nicea and to the true unity of divinity and humanity in Christ. The Antiochenes were especially scandalized by the anathemas of Cyril (see the third letter to Nestorius), in which they saw the doctrine of heretical monophysitism.

The appearance of the archimandrite Eutyches brought about the second major crisis of Christology. Eutyches misinterpreted the *mia physis* formula of Cyril by saying that while Jesus Christ is consubstantial with the Father because of his divinity, he is not consubstantial with us because in him there is only one *physis*. At a synod convened in 448 by Patriarch Flavian of Constantinople, Eutyches was condemned.

The reaction came at the second council of Ephesus (449) under the leadership of Patriarch Dioscorus I of Alexandria (ruled 444-51; d.454), where Flavian was condemned and deposed together with Theodoret of Cyrus, and Eutyches was rehabilitated. Now the schism was imminent. From the Roman side, in 448 Pope Leo had written his famous tome to Flavian, which caused particular offence because of the formula *agit enim utraque forma* ("each nature works what is proper to itself"; see Grillmeier, I [rev. ed.], 535-36).

The council of Chalcedon (451). In 450 Emperor Theodosius II, who favoured Patriarch Dioscorus, died. His place was taken by Emperor Marcian, who in 451 convened in Chalcedon, near Constantinople, the largest synod of the ancient church (there are about 450 signatures to the definition of faith).

Divisive elements in the definition of Chalcedon: Besides the deposition of Patriarch Dioscorus, the main scandal to the Alexandrian school was (1) the composition of a new formula of faith, which was seen as contradicting the prohibition of Ephesus 431 against such new compositions; (2) the acceptance of the formula "one *hypostasis* in two natures" and the rejection of the Cyrillian-Alexandrian expression "from two natures"; and (3) the use of divisive terminology: whereas Alexandria adhered to the synonymous use of the terms *physis* and *hypostasis* for the teaching of the incarnation, Chalcedon, with Antioch, Constantinople and Rome, accepted the distinction of the two concepts in this area of incarnation just as in the doctrine of the Trinity. There was no attempt to analyze the concepts.

Unifying elements: The Chalcedonian definition is based on those of Nicea of 325 and of Constantinople of 381. Up to today, these symbols have formed the most widely accepted doctrinal bond among Christian churches. Second, Cyril's Letter of Union *(Laetentur)* of 433 was acknowledged and used by Chalcedon, together with the symbol composed in 431 by the Antiochenes and later supplemented, although the latter had been modified in a theologically significant way by Cyril in his explanation of it (Grillmeier, I, [rev. ed.], 499-500). Such acknowledgments continued to keep the peace of 433 between Cyril and the Antiochenes. Third, general agreement was accorded to Cyril's formula: "one and the same [Son and Lord Jesus Christ], perfect in divinity, the same also perfect in humanity, truly God and truly human, the same with a rational soul and body, consubstantial with the Father as to his divinity, the same consubstantial with us as to his humanity; like us in all things except for sin". The characterization of the unity by the four expressions "without confusion, without change, without division, without separation" also found general agreement. Finally, the chief expression which continued to give scandal to the monophysites — "one *hypostasis* (person) in two natures" — was in fact demonstrably gained through a close interpretation of the main statements of Cyril by Basil of Seleucia (so André de Halleux). Basically a synthesis of Cyril, Antioch and Leo I was arrived at, but unfortunately this fact was not recognized at the time.

After Chalcedon. In the 5th and 6th centuries, the adherents of the *mia physis* formula, especially after its impressive interpretation and passionate defence by Severus of Antioch, bitterly opposed Chalcedon. Attempts at reconciliation, like the Henoticon of Emperor Zeno (482), failed. Under the Emperors Justin and Justinian a Chalcedonian revival took place, partially affected by violence. But the attempts at reconciliation through dialogue (with Severians in 532, with Nestorians in 561-62) also miscarried, just as the second council of Constantinople (553) could not win over the anti-Chalcedonians. Alexandria remained anti-Chalcedonian, despite imperial attempts to install Melkite patriarchs. The Syrians developed their own (Jacobite) hierarchy. Incapacity for dialogue and the lack of a method for analyzing different systems of language led to consolidation of the misunderstandings and hardening of the fronts.

Since 1971 ecumenical consultations between theologians of the non-Chalcedonian Oriental Orthodox churches and the Roman Catholic Church have been held by the Pro Oriente* foundation, Vienna. In 1974 began the official joint commission of the Catholic Church and the non-Chalcedonian Coptic Orthodox Church. The main points of agreement are summarized in the declaration on Christology of this commission during its meeting in Vienna in 1976 and partly reflected in the general formula on Christology, signed on 12 February 1988 by Pope Shenouda III and Pro-nuncio Moretti at the St Anba Bishoy monastery (see **Oriental Orthodox-Roman Catholic dialogue**). Following unofficial preparatory conversations since 1964, an official joint commission for theological dialogue between Orthodox and the non-Chalcedonian Oriental Orthodox churches met successfully in 1985, 1989 and 1990 (see **Oriental Orthodox-Orthodox dialogue**).

ALOYS GRILLMEIER
and THERESIA HAINTHALER

P. Gregorios, W.H. Lazareth & N.A. Nissiotis eds, *Does Chalcedon Divide or Unite? Towards Convergence in Orthodox Christology*, WCC, 1981 • A. Grillmeier, *Christ in Christian Tradition*, I (rev. ed.) and II/1, London, Mowbray, 1975 and 1987 • A. de Halleux, "Actualité du néo-chalcédonisme. Un accord christologique récent entre Orthodoxes", *Revue théologique de Louvain*, 21, 1990 • R.V. Sellers, *The Council of Chalcedon: A Historical and Doctrinal Survey*, London, SPCK, 1953.

CHANDRAN, JOSHUA RUSSELL. B. 6.5.1918, Kadamankuly, South India. Vice-moderator of the WCC central committee, 1966-68, and president of the Asian Christian Peace Conference, Chandran has represented the Church of South India (CSI) at various ecumenical meetings and committees. He was convener of the Union Negotiations Committee of the CSI, secretary of the Joint Council of the Church of North India, the Church of South India and the Mar Thoma Church, and founder-president of the Christian Union of India. Joining the United Theological College (UTC) in Bangalore in 1950, he became its first Indian principal in 1954. Later he was professor at Union Theological Seminary, 1964-65, the Louisville Theological Seminary, KY, the Episcopal Theological Seminary, Cambridge, MA, 1972, and the Pacific Theological College, Suva, Fiji, after retiring from the UTC. He served as president of the Senate of Serampore College, 1968-71, and of the Ecumenical Association of Third World Theologians.* His studies were in India, Oxford (England), Union Theological Seminary, New York, and the Chicago University Divinity School. He wrote *Political Outlook in India Today*, with M.M. Thomas (Bangalore, Committee for Literature on Social Concerns, 1956). See *A Vision for Man: Essays on Faith, Theology and Society in Honour of J.R. Chandran*, S. Amirtham ed. (Madras, Christian Literature Society, 1978).

ANS J. VAN DER BENT

CHARISM(ATA). A charism is a manifestation of divine grace, a gift bestowed irrespective of merit or spiritual maturity, a spiritual gift or endowment sometimes called a "gift of the Spirit" granted by the Triune God to individuals for the enhancement of the life, worship and service of the people of God.* By extension, those who receive such charismata are sometimes called charismatics. In modern social theory the term "charisma" has been extended further to describe a quality of personality which enables an individual to attract the confidence of others in such a way as to enable that person to become a leader or authority figure.

The Greek term for "grace" *(charis)* lies behind the late and rarely used diminutive *charisma*, its plural *charismata* and the Anglicized version "charism". *Charisma* appears in the LXX as a variant reading only at Sir. 7:33 and 38:30, and at Ps. 30:20 (Theodotion). While it is used by a few other writers, among them Philo, its meaning is most heavily influenced by New Testament usage. Except for its use in 1 Pet. 4:10, it appears only in the Pauline corpus (16 times). Post-NT secular usage typically conveys the meaning of "favour" or "benefit".

In Rom. 6:23, Paul uses the term broadly to describe the generous gift of eternal life granted by God in Jesus Christ (cf. 5:15-16). Rom. 11:29 describes the benefits of God's covenant with Israel in terms of charismata. But 1 Cor. 12:4-11 is the *locus classicus* for the most frequent definition of the term in the NT. The passage occurs within 1 Corinthians 12-14, chapters addressed to the subject of *pneumatika*, meaning "spirituals" or "spiritual things", hence "spiritual gifts". In one sense, the term "charismata" is used synonymously with *pneumatika*, although the nuance conveyed by each term points in opposite directions. "Pneumatika" was a Corinthian term used to describe phenomena such as speaking in tongues, words of knowledge, and prophecy, by which "spirituality" was measured. The ability to speak in tongues had limited value in the community (1 Cor. 14:4-19), knowledge could lead to inflated egos (1 Cor. 8:1), and even prophecy needed to be tested (1 Cor. 14:29-32,37-38; 1 Thess. 5:19-22). Paul's designation of these same phenomena as charismata points not to alleged spirituality on the part of those who exercised these gifts but rather towards the graciousness of the Triune God who supplies them "to each one individually as he wills".

Within 1 Corinthians 12 at least three lists of charisms may be found (vv.8-10,28, and 29-30). Rom. 12:6-8 provides yet another.

The overlap of certain charismata mentioned in these lists with those mentioned in Eph. 4:11 suggests that in Pauline thought the terms *dōrea* and *dōma* are also synonymous with "charismata".

Variations in the number of gifts and the sequence in which they appear suggest that there is no normative catalogue and no attempt to communicate the relative value of these charisms in relation to any others, other than what is explicitly stated in the biblical text. The appearance of *charisma* in 1 Pet. 4:10 is consistent with Pauline usage, although the examples given are suggestive of categories (speaking and serving) rather than of specific charisms. Indeed, 1 Cor. 12:8-10 lists several "speaking" gifts (e.g. utterances of wisdom, utterances of knowledge, prophecy, tongues, and the interpretation of tongues). On the other hand, Rom. 12:7-8 appears to emphasize various "serving" charismata (e.g. service, contribution, giving of aid, and acts of mercy). Other charismata include faith, healings, miracles, the ability to distinguish or discern spirits (1 Cor. 12:8-10), apostles, teachers, helpers, administrators (1 Cor. 12:28), and exhortation (Rom. 12:8). Paul viewed celibacy as a charism (1 Cor. 7:7-8) and pointed towards martyrdom (1 Cor. 13:3) as a charism, a perspective especially dear to Christians persecuted in the patristic period.

The range of charismata may be extended if one looks at the empowering role of the Spirit within the whole of scripture. Hence, such activities as Bezalel's craftsmanship (Ex. 31:3, 35:31-33), Samson's ability to judge Israel (Judg. 15:14-15, cf. also 3:10, 6:34, 11:29), the Spirit's enablement to provide counsel (Isa. 11:2), even certain musical abilities as is evidenced by the close relationship between Israel's musicians and prophetic guilds, may ultimately qualify as charisms.

It is significant that all Pauline discussions of charismata lie within the context of the metaphor in which the church is depicted as the Body of Christ (Rom. 12:4-8; 1 Cor. 12:4-31; Eph. 4:4-16). His concern is that charismata be understood as gracious bestowments upon individuals (indicative of diversity), given according to God's sovereign will, but that their purpose is to meet the needs of the one Body (indicative of unity*). The tension between unity and diversity is mediated by love (1 Cor. 13), and the purposes for which these charisms have been given are the common good (1 Cor. 12:7), care for one another (vv.25-26), upbuilding and encouragement and consolation (1 Cor. 14:3), and edification (v.5). Gifts are also viewed as being given to the church in the form of persons (e.g. apostles, prophets, evangelists, pastors and teachers, Eph. 4:11-14), so that the saints may be equipped for the work of ministry. The proper exercise of all Spirit-bestowed charisms ultimately is intended to bring glory to God through Jesus Christ (1 Pet. 4:10-11).

The appearance of certain charismata within the history of the church has been both divisive and unifying at times. Debates have raged over issues of whether certain gifts continue or have ceased to appear within the church (Augustine, Benjamin Warfield), what constitutes decent and orderly use of certain gifts (contexts seem to vary), how gifts are to be discerned by the community of faith (the role of experience in relation to rationality), the relationship between nature and grace in the appearance of these gifts (Aquinas; natural endowments, talents, or spontaneous interventions), the legitimate limits of experience (fanaticism, fervency or rigidity) and the limits of authority (clergy vs laity) in the use of these gifts. Still the subject has contributed greatly to grassroots ecumenism.

In the late 19th century several historical streams came together to produce the 20th-century phenomenon called Pentecostalism. Restorationist tendencies which longed for a return of the church to her NT glory, a quest for the "apostolic faith" including its experiences and charisms, the divine healing movement, and a shift by many from post- to pre-millennial perspectives, all contributed to a mood of expectancy towards the appearance or re-appearance of more spectacular charisms. The result was the Pentecostal movement, derogatorily nicknamed the "tongues" movement because of its emphasis upon the gift of tongues as evidential of Spirit baptism.

Charismatic renewal, a related movement since the 1960s within the historic churches of East and West, has brought to the attention of the whole church the range of charismata available to the church. The appearance of such phenomena as prophecy, healing, and speaking in tongues among Christians in the historic churches has enabled previously sectarian Pentecostals to look more favourably upon the historic church. It has also enabled them more openly to recognize the role of the Spirit in the whole church through less spectacular gifts. Many within the historic churches who have recently experienced some of the more spectacular charismata now look more favourably upon the newer Pentecostal churches. Continued discussion between these groups is bound to enhance hopes for greater unity within the whole church.

See also **grace, Holy Spirit, ministry in the church, Pentecostals**.

CECIL M. ROBECK, Jr

A. Bittlinger ed., *The Church Is Charismatic*, WCC, 1981 • D. Gee, *Spiritual Gifts*, rev. ed., Springfield, MO, Gospel Publishing, 1980 • J. Koenig, *Charismata: God's Gifts for God's People*, Philadelphia, Westminster, 1978 • L. de Lorenzi ed., *Charisma und Agape, I Kor. 12-14*, Rome, St Paul's outside the Walls, 1983 • K. McDonnell, *The Charismatic Renewal and Ecumenism*, New York, Paulist, 1978 • F.A. Sullivan, *Charisms and Charismatic Renewal*, Ann Arbor, MI, Servant Publications, 1982.

CHARISMATIC MOVEMENT. The expression "charismatic movement" (or "charismatic renewal") refers to the movement of persons and groups who confess the availability of a personal pentecostal experience of the Holy Spirit,* often accompanied by speaking in tongues, and the appropriation of the spiritual gifts listed in 1 Cor. 12:8-10 (see **charism(ata)**). Participants commonly see the charismatic movement as a second wave of the Spirit. It extends the first wave of the Pentecostal movement (see **Pentecostals**) but differs in its refusal to organize into separate Pentecostal denominations and in its generally less dogmatic formulation of the core experience of the baptism in the Holy Spirit.

As with all grassroots eruptions, the boundaries of the charismatic movement are hard to delimit. Its original naming by J. Stone and H. Bredesen in 1963 had in view the occurrence of pentecostal experience and phenomena within the historic denominations. But by 1975 there were signs, especially in North America and Great Britain, of newly emerging groups of Christians outside the historic churches who claimed the same spiritual experience but who clearly were not Pentecostals. These so-called non-denominational groupings generally understood themselves as part of the worldwide charismatic movement.

By the 1980s, some independent networks had espoused an ideal of "restoration": the present outpouring of the Spirit is for the restoration of the New Testament church. For them, restoration is a distinct movement which builds on and goes beyond the charismatic movement. The 1980s have also seen the rapid spread of John Wimber's "signs and wonders" message in many evangelical* milieus which had been closed to the charismatic movement, teaching that Holy Spirit power in healing and deliverance is the basis for effective evangelism.* Peter Wagner has labelled this "the third wave", distinct from the Pentecostal and charismatic movements. This trend may be another mutation of the charismatic movement; it emphasizes acceptance of pentecostal experience, while it modifies Pentecostal doctrine.

For several decades indigenous Christian movements with pentecostal-type phenomena have arisen in Africa. These have not been seen by themselves or by charismatics as part of the charismatic movement, however, despite important phenomenological and spiritual similarities.

Characteristics. The charismatic movement is characterized by vibrant praise, new power to minister and witness, contemporary hearing of the Lord, revived interest in eschatology, and the giftedness of each Christian. Charismatic worship praises God, with an emphasis on the lordship of Jesus, in songs, choruses and simultaneous vocal praise. The charismatic movement's impact on the wider church can be seen in increased emphasis on congregational praise and a vast dissemination of new songs of varied quality.

The charismatic movement is experienced as new power for the Body of Christ. Believers yield themselves to the risen Christ in being baptized in the Spirit. As a result, they experience new power in the preaching of the word, in evangelism, in intercession and in deliverance from evil. Charismatics emphasize the God-given equipping of the local church, the spiritual gifts of 1 Cor. 12:8-10, the ministries of Eph. 4:11 and the whole armour of God in Eph. 6:10-20.

Participants claim the abilities to hear the Lord and to speak his contemporary word in prophecy and other utterances. This revelatory work of the Holy Spirit in the Christian remains one of the less-examined aspects of the charismatic movement (see **revelation**).

The spread of the charismatic movement regularly gives rise to a heightened "end-times" consciousness. Occasionally this takes the form of predictions of an imminent end; more commonly, it leads to a re-discovery of the prayer "Maranatha, come, Lord Jesus".

While not rejecting ordained ministry, the charismatic movement has a fundamentally egalitarian streak in its emphasis on the spiritual giftedness of every participant. This dimension challenges received patterns of clericalism, both Catholic and Protestant.

Ecumenical dimensions. The charismatic movement can be seen as a re-capturing on a larger scale of ecumenical elements which had been in some origins of the Pentecostal movement but later were eclipsed. In this perspective, the Holy Spirit was poured out to revive all the (Protestant) churches. In the 1930s this original vision was revived in France through the ministry of Louis Dallière, a Reformed pastor in the Ardèche and founder in 1946 of the *Union de prière*.

In the 1950s, sporadic outbreaks of pen-

Combined meeting of charismatic churches in Sydney, Australia (WCC photo)

tecostal phenomena occurred outside the Pentecostal denominations: in circles which pray for revival (Anglicans and Methodists in Great Britain); among those who seek a deeper spiritual life (Baptists in Brazil); in circles which re-discover divine healing (Episcopalians in the USA, Reformed in the Netherlands, Anglicans in Great Britain); and in milieus which promote a less cerebral view of the human person (Camps Farthest Out, USA). Only in the 1960s did these preliminary strands coalesce into one recognizable movement. Its interchurch character attracted attention.

In this process, significant roles were played by the Pentecostal David Du Plessis, the American Episcopalian Dennis Bennett, and the English Anglican Michael Harper. For many grassroots Christians, participation in charismatic prayer meetings was their first experience of fellowship across church boundaries.

As the charismatic movement spread across the churches, most of its first informal structures took an ecumenical form. In the Netherlands, the quarterly *Vuur* (1957) developed an editorial board of several church traditions. In the USA the quarterly *Trinity* (1961-66), though with a strong Episcopalian base, served charismatics from many Protestant churches. In Britain, the Fountain Trust (1964-80), established by Harper to serve the charismatic movement in all churches, served as a model for charismatic service agencies in Australia (Temple Trust) and New Zealand (Christian Advance Ministries).

The advent of Roman Catholic charismatic renewal in 1967 dramatically advertised the movement's ecumenical character and potential. Catholics, more than other charismatic-movement Christians, interpreted their pentecostal experience in ecumenical terms. They saw it as a providential result of the renewal thrust and ecumenical openings of the Second Vatican Council.* The advent of the charismatic movement among Catholics increased its publicity and, particularly in North America, inaugurated a phase of expanding denominational conferences with an ecumenical dimension.

Continental ecumenical gatherings for leaders in the charismatic movement began in 1972 in both Europe and Latin America. The European charismatic leaders conference merged in 1988 with the leaders' groups, formed by Harper, to organize the Acts 1986 ecumenical conference in Birmingham, England.

The charismatic movement among Catholics spurred the rise of covenant communities, mostly led by laypeople. Several major communities are ecumenical in composition, such as the Word of God community, Ann Arbor, Michigan; the Mother of God community, Gaithersburg, Maryland; the Emmanuel community, Brisbane, Australia; the Chemin neuf community in Lyons, France; the Alleluia community, Augusta, USA. The covenant communities, whether interconfessional or all Catholic, involve married people and single, ordained and unordained, in a shared life-style based on the new life in the Holy Spirit. They exercise a major role of leadership and formation, particularly in France, the Philippines, Colombia, Australia, Malaysia and the USA. The interconfessional communities are strong witnesses to the ecumenical character of the charismatic movement.

The rapid spread of Catholic charismatic renewal led many charismatics in other traditions to integrate the charismatic movement into church life. The 1970s saw a proliferation of denominational service agencies in North America, a process followed worldwide by Catholics in the 1970s and in the 1980s by Anglicans and Protestants in Britain and Scandinavia. Ireland was the only country to establish an ecumenical national service committee, though this was later abandoned in the face of Catholic pressures.

The increased orientation of the mainline charismatic movement towards church renewal* has not notably accelerated positive responses from denominational authorities. Catholic episcopal conferences have been among the most positive; they recognize the charismatic movement among other organized movements and encourage clerical participation and discernment. Many Protestant churches have been slower in welcoming the charismatic movement, though gradually it is finding acceptance in many countries. Official church reactions up to 1980 have been gathered in Kilian McDonnell's three volumes.

In parts of the third world, Catholic hierarchies have imposed tighter organization on the charismatic movement, often superseding lay leadership and clergy. In Latin America this reaction has been associated with fear and distrust of Protestant charismatics and Pentecostals, and in Africa with concern about losses to indigenous independent churches with charismatic characteristics. Denominational tendencies in North America and Europe have caused some diminution in ecumenical thrust and fellowship, but the charismatic movement's original ecumenical vision continues to inspire many, as shown in the mammoth gatherings at Kansas City (1977), Strasbourg (1982) and New Orleans (1987).

Points of contention. Like all more spontaneous movements which appeal to the initiative and freedom of the Spirit, the charismatic movement has had its history of tensions, divisions and conflict. Five issues recur most frequently.

Theology of baptism in the Spirit: While charismatics commonly posit this foundational experience as a "second blessing" after primary Christian initiation, Catholics and Protestants interpret "baptism in the Spirit" in different ways. Evangelicals commonly differentiate it from conversion-regeneration, though charismatics with a Reformed Calvinist theology are most opposed to a distinct post-conversion reception of the Holy Spirit. Catholics often explain baptism in the Spirit as a coming to conscious experience of those graces which sacramental baptism* has already conferred. Neither interpretation sufficiently recognizes the role of preaching a fuller message in Spirit baptism. Most charismatics do not accept the majority-Pentecostal doctrine of "initial evidence", i.e. that baptism in the Spirit has to be attested by the physical sign of speaking in other tongues. However, many charismatics do expect glossolalia to accompany baptism in the Spirit, a feature that has caused concern to some church authorities.

Spiritual power versus holiness: Most charismatics understand baptism in the Spirit as power for ministry and service. However, some (Mother of God community in Maryland, Bethany fellowship in Minneapolis, and the Mary sisters in Darmstadt) see this grace primarily in terms of new depth of relationship with the persons of the Trinity,* from which new power flows. This discussion echoes earlier debates within the Holiness and Pentecostal movements and is likely to intensify in the wake of serious scandals among prominent independent leaders.

Discipleship and apostleship: As in the Pentecostal movement, the charismatic movement has seen an association between the rediscovery of the spiritual gifts of 1 Cor. 12:8-10 and the ministry gifts of Eph. 4:11. Some circles, mostly non-denominational, believe God is restoring the proper order of the church under apostles, prophets, evangelists, pastors and teachers. A tension exists in the charismatic movement between those who espouse this view of restoration and those who operate within traditional patterns of ministry and teaching. Many charismatic congregations have adopted pluralist patterns of church leadership with teams of elders. This development has led some local churches (e. g. some prominent British Baptist congregations) out of their parent denominations. Some networks emphasize church authority. They teach the need for each Christian to be "discipled" by accepting the directive authority of a pastor for all major life-decisions. The discipleship teaching, associated in the 1970s with Christian Growth Ministries of Fort Lauderdale, Florida, and *New Wine* magazine, and with Juan Carlos Ortiz from Argentina, has been vehemently opposed by some Protestant charismatics as a betrayal of cherished Reformation principles.

Scripture and prophecy: The claim that God speaks also today as in New Testament times has caused controversy, particularly among those concerned to uphold the unique authority of holy scripture. The widespread evangelical unease about the charismatic movement is rooted more in this fear that contemporary experience is exalted above scripture than in "second-blessing" difficulties. This unease may be lessening as charismatic congregations and groups demonstrate their biblical loyalty, but this issue raises theological questions about the relationship between biblical and post-biblical times which are similar to the long-standing debates concerning scripture and Tradition.

Personal and social transformation: The charismatic movement has re-inforced emphasis on personal conversion, and charismatics have often been uneasy with emphases which focus on structural reform. Some charismatic leaders recognize the need to overcome any charity-justice dichotomy, an ideal recommended in *Charismatic Renewal and Social Action*, by Cardinal Suenens and Dom Helder Camara (1980).

PETER HOCKEN

A. Bittlinger ed., *The Church Is Charismatic*, WCC, 1981 • L. Christenson, *Welcome, Holy Spirit*, Minneapolis, Augsburg, 1987 • M. Hebrard, *Les nouveaux disciples dix ans après*, 1987 • P. Hocken, "Charismatic Movement", in *A Dictionary of the Pentecostal and Charismatic Traditions*, G. McGee & S. Burgess eds, 1988 • P. Hocken, *One Lord, One Spirit, One Body*, Exeter, Paternoster, 1987 • K. McDonnell, *Presence, Power, Praise*, 3 vols, Collegeville, MN, Liturgical Press, 1980 • R. Quebedeaux, *The New Charismatics II*, San Francisco, Harper & Row, 1983 • J.R. Williams, *The Gift of the Holy Spirit Today*, Durango, CO, Logbridge-Rhodes, 1980.

CHEVETOGNE. This Benedictine monastery in Belgium has been committed since its foundation in 1925 to the healing of Christian divisions, especially the schisms* between the church of Rome and the churches of the East. In 1924 Pope Pius XI requested the Benedictine congregations to foster this aim through prayer and studies. In response Dom Lambert Beauduin (1873-1960) founded a new priory at Amay-sur-Meuse, and in 1939 the "monks of unity" moved to their present site at Chevetogne.

But Dom Beauduin faced such crises of ecclesiastical accusations against the monastery's approach and methods that in 1928 he resigned as prior, and in 1930 he went into virtual exile in France until his return to Chevetogne in 1951. The monastery itself survived, including its quarterly *Irénikon* (1926), judged by many to be too open to ecumenical ideas.

Among the more notable of the Chevetogne monks are Clement Lialine (1901-58), who gave attention to the WCC in its formation stages and had friendly contacts with W.A. Visser 't Hooft and other early WCC leaders; Olivier Rousseau (1898-1984), who re-inforced the institutional and spiritual structures at Amay-Chevetogne to withstand the accusations against the monastery; Pierre Dumont (1901-70), most personable specialist in Greek Orthodoxy; Emmanuel Lanne, a drafter of Vatican Council II's Decree on Ecumenism and the first Roman Catholic vice-moderator of the WCC Faith and Order* commission.

The monastery has two groups of monks, one of the Latin rite and the other of the Byzantine (Greek and Slavonic). They celebrate simultaneously the daily liturgies in the two churches of the monastery. Since 1943 Chevetogne has sponsored conferences on critical ecumenical themes, with internationally known specialists. The monastery has a hostel for guests, a library of over 100,000 volumes, and a publishing house for works on history, ecclesiology, liturgy and spirituality. The monks are also responsible for directing the pontifical Greek college in Rome.

TOM STRANSKY

CHILDREN. The church has from its very beginning concerned itself with children, including them in its ministry and its service through such activities as infant baptism, children's communion, children's catechism, Sunday school, religious instruction and confirmation classes. Churches have taken responsibility for the nurture, guidance and welfare of children, not leaving these only to parents and society. Churches and missionary societies were often the first to care for orphans and abandoned and disabled children and to set up institutions for them: orphanages, schools, homes, centres, nurseries and hospitals.

When women and men opened schools on Sunday in the latter half of the 18th century in Britain, they were primarily motivated by a concern for destitute and illiterate children as victims of the industrial revolution. This in turn stimulated the provision of day school education for all children, so that Sunday schools could concentrate more and more on competent Christian education. What was started in Britain became in the 19th century a worldwide movement which led in 1907 to the formation of the World Sunday School Association. In 1947 it changed its name to the World Council of Christian Education* (WCCE).

Ecumenically the church's concern for children was lodged in the WCCE. Although pioneer ecumenical conferences discussed "education in relation to the Christianization of national life" (Edinburgh 1910) and "church, community and state in relation to education" (Oxford 1937), the child was not really a theme as such. Within the WCC, it was only with the integration of WCCE in 1972 that the long tradition and experience of work with children was taken up. It was finally recognition of and participation in the International Year of the Child in 1979 which presented a timely opportunity for the ecumenical movement to make visible its concern for the child today, and to give it the priority it deserves: "for the suffering of children today is such as to provoke our anger, and the love of our Lord Jesus for the little ones such as to provoke our penitent compassion" (WCC report on the International Year of the Child).

More recently, many efforts have been concentrated in the ecumenical movement on a new theological understanding of childhood (initiated by the British Council of Churches' 1976 report on *The Child and the Church*) and on a new role for children in the community of faith (cf. the 1980 ecumenical conference in Evian on "Children as Active Partners in the Congregation", jointly organized by the WCC and the Lutheran World Federation). Not the child's transformation to adulthood but the adult's transformation to childhood determines Jesus' words about the child (Mark 9:33-37 par. and 10:13-16 par.). A theological re-evaluation of the category of the child as a significant factor in understanding the Christian way of existence has begun, which has opened eyes anew to children's particular way of living and believing and to their fundamental needs and interests.

Acceptance of such insights has led many churches to re-appraise their work with children and to change traditional patterns of church and congregational life. Envisaged is a community of faith in which adults and children, old and young, share experiences and learn from one another. A high point of such intergenerational learning was at the sixth assembly of the WCC (Vancouver 1983), when children from all over the world were present at the Bible studies, the worship services (leading some of them), a peace-and-justice event and an international day camp.

All attempts at a re-appraisal of the church's work with children must bear in mind the twofold task of ministry with children (child's nurture in faith, etc.) and advocacy for children (political, international, legal, etc.). The story of children's woes and trials in today's world is endless; already in May 1974 UNICEF declared a "world emergency for children". Many basic needs of children, not to mention their essential human rights, remain unfulfilled.

The churches in the ecumenical movement have realized that the battle is on and that they are to be in it. There is a wide field for them, committed to implementing God's promise to children, to engage themselves or to join in with others in advocating the needs and the rights of children, in churches, homes, societies, and also in schools and in a variety of learning processes.

ULRICH BECKER

U. Becker, "The Child in Theology and Church", *The Ecumenical Review*, 31, 1979 • *The Child in the Church*, London, BCC, 1976 • *International Year of the Child and the World Council of Churches*, WCC, 1978 • G.E. Knoff, *The World Sunday School Movement*, New York, Seabury, 1979 • G. Müller-Fahrenholz ed., *...and Do Not Hinder Them: An Ecumenical Plea for the Admission of Children to the Eucharist*, WCC, 1982 • K.E. Nipkow, "Verantwortung für Kinder und ökumenisches Lernen, Pädagogische Schwerpunkte in Vancouver", *Ökumenische Rundschau*, 33, 1984 • *Strategies for Children in the 1990s: A UNICEF Policy Review*, New York, Unicef, 1989 • H.R. Weber, *Jesus and the Children*, WCC, 1979 • *When I'm Grown Up I'm Going to Change Things*, children at the sixth assembly of the WCC, WCC, 1985.

CHRISMATION. Chrismation is the anointing or sealing in the post-baptismal rites of the Eastern and Oriental churches in which the presider (either bishop or priest) anoints the newly baptized on the forehead, eyes, nostrils, ears and mouth (and in some rites on as many as 36 places) with consecrated chrism.

In its origins the rite was probably pre-baptismal and eschatological in character involving the images of the seal on the foreheads of the redeemed in Revelation (7:2-8, 9:4, 14:1, 22:4) and the first-fruits of salvation* in 2 Cor. 1:21-22 and Eph. 1:13-14, 4:30. By the end of the 3rd century, the chrismation was post-baptismal and more pneumatic. As baptismal rites developed, there was an increasing tendency to identify one particular moment in the liturgy as the point at which the Holy Spirit* is given rather than the more ancient understanding, according to which the activity of the Holy Spirit was acknowledged throughout the rite. The chrismation occupies this place in Eastern and Oriental baptismal liturgies.

While apologists for the Eastern and Oriental rites have often suggested that chrismation is the equivalent of confirmation in the Roman rite, it would be more accurate to say that it parallels the first post-baptismal anointing of that rite and that the Eastern and Oriental churches do not have a liturgical equivalent to confirmation.

See also **baptism, confirmation**.

DAVID R. HOLETON

L.L. Mitchell, *Baptismal Anointing*, London, SPCK, 1966 • A. Schmemann, *Of Water and the Spirit*, Crestwood, NY, St Vladimir's Seminary, 1974.

CHRISTIAN CONFERENCE OF ASIA.

The East Asia Christian Conference (EACC), now called the CCA, was the first institutionalized expression of regional ecumenism. Its origins may be traced back to the meeting of the International Missionary Council* (IMC) at Tambaram in 1938, or even to earlier world meetings where Asian delegates expressed the need for their churches to work towards greater unity in life, partnership in mission and autonomy in administration. At Tambaram, for the first time in world meetings, Asian participants formed the majority, and some of them wanted the IMC to set up an Asian office. Years later, in 1945, the IMC committee in Geneva considered a proposal from the Chinese and Indian national councils urging the formation of an East Asia regional committee, in order "(1) to promote and give expression to the spirit of Christian unity among the churches of East Asia; (2) to promote fellowship and mutual helpfulness among Christians in East Asia through conferences, exchange of delegations and such other measures as may be agreed upon; (3) to promote a sense of the responsibility of the churches in East Asia for the Christian witness and for the building up of the churches in this area; (4) to deepen the unity of the churches in East Asia with the world church; (5) to bring to the life of the world church the distinctive contribution of the churches in East Asia".

Following a decision taken in 1947 by the joint committee of the IMC and the WCC to set up an East Asia regional office, the first meeting of Asian church leaders was held in Bangkok in 1949. Its theme was "The Christian Prospect in Eastern Asia". It led to the appointment, two years later, of Raja B. Manikam from India as East Asia secretary. In 1956, at a joint consultation of the newly formed Asia Council on Ecumenical Mission, the IMC and the WCC, it was resolved to call together a meeting of representatives of Asian churches and national councils so that they could decide for themselves what form regional ecumenism should take in Asia.

Prapat, Indonesia, was the venue of that meeting, held in 1957. Its theme was "The Common Evangelical Task of the Churches in East Asia". It decided to create the EACC and appointed a core staff team, consisting of D.T. Niles from Ceylon, U Kyaw Than from Burma and Alan Brash from New Zealand, to organize the new ecumenical body. The Prapat meeting is generally considered as the first EACC assembly, although the inaugural (now reckoned as the second) assembly was held only two years later, in 1959, at Kuala Lumpur, Malaysia. Present at that meeting were representatives from 34 churches and 14 Christian councils from Asian countries and from Australia and New Zealand. The theme was "Witnesses Together". The inaugural declaration said: "Believing that the purpose of God for the churches in East Asia is life together in a common obedience to him for the doing of his will in the world, the East Asia Christian Conference is hereby constituted."

It is instructive to recall the themes of EACC/CCA assemblies. The third and fourth assemblies were held in Bangkok. The third (1964) addressed the theme "The Christian Community within the Human Community", affirming Christian identity but not over against the identities of other religious communities, and thus recognizing the need to be involved in the common search for truly human communities. The fourth (1968) had a biblical theme: "In Him All Things Hold Together". At the fifth assembly, which met in Singapore in 1973, the theme was "Christian Action in Asian Struggle"; it affirmed the need to be involved in the common struggle against poverty and injustice. The sixth assembly (1977) met in Penang, Malaysia, and its theme was "Jesus Christ in Asian Suffering and Hope". The theme of the seventh assembly (Bangalore 1981) was "Living in Christ With People"; the eighth (Seoul 1985) met around the theme "Jesus Christ Sets Free to Serve"; the theme of the ninth assembly (Manila 1990) was "Christ Our Peace: Building a Just Society". Asian Christian themes have moved from a preoccupation with the Christian prospect to an affirmation of Christian presence and common struggle, a change that tells its own ecumenical story.

The 1973 assembly marked a new phase in the life of the regional body. It received a new name — the Christian Conference of Asia. It was given a new structure and a new team to head its general secretariat. It saw the beginning of a more centralized administrative set-up. The CCA had previously maintained a small office in Bangkok, with a number of its large staff, many part-time, working out of their home countries; now the number was considerably reduced, and most of them moved to Singapore, where the CCA was based till 1987.

In December that year the CCA was "dissolved" by the Singapore government and the expatriate staff "expelled" from the country. The government claimed that the CCA had breached its undertaking "not to indulge in any political activity or allow its funds to be used for political purposes". The government action was soundly condemned by churches and other ecumenical bodies. Since then, CCA has been working from offices in Osaka (Japan), Hong Kong (where its Urban Rural Mission [URM] and International Affairs operations were based for several years), Manila, and Chiang Mai (Thailand).

The CCA constituency which includes 95 churches and 15 national councils, is spread over a vast area from Japan in the north to Pakistan in the west and New Zealand in the southeast. It works with nine programme committees, each responsible for a cluster of related concerns: youth, women, URM, theology, mission and evangelism, international affairs, education, development and service, and communications. According to its constitution, the CCA is "an organ of continuing co-operation among the churches and national Christian bodies in Asia within the framework of the wider ecumenical movement". Its functions are set forth as follows: (1) develop

effective Christian response to the challenges of the changing societies of Asia; (2) explore opportunities and promote joint action for the fulfilment of the mission of God in Asia and throughout the world; (3) encourage Asian contributions to Christian thought, worship and action throughout the world; (4) develop mutual awareness, fellowship and sharing among the churches in the region and relationships with other regional conferences and the WCC; (5) promote common study and action in such fields as evangelism, service, social and human development and international relations; (6) stimulate initiatives and experiments in dynamic Christian living and action.

D.T. Niles, U Kyaw Than, Yap Kim Hao from Malaysia and Park Sang Jung from Korea have served as CCA general secretaries. John Victor Samuel from Pakistan is the present general secretary.

The chief communication organ of the CCA is the monthly magazine *CCA News*. The annual observance of the Sunday before Pentecost* as Asia Sunday recalls the inauguration of the CCA on the eve of Pentecost in 1959 and celebrates the relatively new sense of solidarity among the churches in Asia.

Those who worked for the creation of a regional ecumenical body in the early years had three main motives. First, they hoped that Asian Christians would develop closer and more regular contacts with one another. Second, they wanted the churches to develop contextual theologies and ways of witness which would address the fast-changing social, religious and political situations of their nations and remain in dialogue with one another. Third, they wanted Asian churches to involve themselves more effectively in ecumenical thinking and action at the global level.

The first of these hopes has been realized. Asian Christians now meet in Asia, and not only in London, New York and Geneva. The increasing co-operation between the Federation of Asian Bishops Conferences and the CCA augurs well for the future. In the area of contextual theology and witness too there have been significant gains, though the churches, as churches, have not always appropriated the new insights. A number of the study centres and people's movements that emerged during the last few decades have close links with the CCA, and they have been addressing the two basic realities of Asian existence — endemic material poverty and pervasive religious and ideological pluralism. Finally, ecumenical interaction between the regional and the global levels has been limited. Nor is there much evidence of dialogue among the various regions. That dialogue is crucial for the future of the ecumenical movement.

TOSH ARAI and T.K. THOMAS

CHRISTIAN LITERATURE.

For around 300 years in Europe Christian literature has been regarded by the churches as an important means of providing the tools of evangelism* and education.* In Britain in 1698 five Anglican laymen set up the Society for Promoting Christian Knowledge (SPCK), which is still committed to literature and education on a worldwide scale and which has over 200 prayer book translations to its credit. In 1799 a group of Anglican and Free Church laymen followed with the Religious Tract Society (RTS), which in 1935 amalgamated with its daughter societies (the Christian Literature Society, India and Africa, and the Christian Literature Society for China) to become the United Society for Christian Literature (USCL), though not before it had published in over 200 languages for missionary purposes and distributed millions of magazines among soldiers, sailors and prisoners of war. In 1804 several of those who were active with RTS went on to found the British and Foreign Bible Society for the printing and distribution of the Bible at home and abroad. This pattern remained almost unchanged in Britain until the early 1960s. In 1942 the Committee for Christian Literature of the Foreign Missions Conference in North America joined with Frank C. Laubach's World Literacy Committee to become the Committee on World Literacy and Christian Literature, known informally as Lit-Lit.

In Asia and Africa Christian literature was very much in the hands of the missionaries and the emerging churches. At first it was imported from Europe. Then local production began and printing presses were set up in church headquarters and mission compounds in capital cities. Basic needs were recognized: the need for literacy and education combined with books in the local language and reflecting local culture. Some missionaries were

themselves writers and wanted to encourage their students and converts also to write and publish. This led to the need for distribution and so began the custom of using a colporteur, the forerunner of the book bicycle and today's more sophisticated bookmobile.

It is worth recalling that in several places Christian literature played a pioneering role. The need to have Christian literature often led to the development of alphabets and grammar, of a prose style and the growth of printing; it had its impact on journalism, the development of secular literature, even on politics and culture.

The major change that came in the post-war period coincided with changed relationships between churches overseas and mission boards in Europe. In some cases publishing houses and bookshops which had originated in the church had acquired a certain commercial independence and there were good reasons for keeping it that way. Most of them needed training and professionalism, but what they needed most of all was capital.

A British initiative came with the setting up of the Archbishop of York's Fund for World Literature in 1964, followed immediately by the Feed the Minds (FTM) campaign, in which the Archbishop of York's Fund, the Bible Society, SPCK, USCL and the British Missionary Societies combined to raise funds for Christian literature, partly for their own programmes and partly to provide the British contribution to the WCC-sponsored Christian Literature Fund* (CLF) in consultation with the Supporting Literature Agencies Consultation (SLAC). When the FTM campaign ended in 1967, having raised £530,000, SPCK, USCL and the Conference of British Missionary Societies stayed together as FTM with SLAC, which became the Joint Action for Christian Literature Overseas until 1983, when mainstream British churches joined with the missionary societies (including USCL) to re-construct Feed the Minds. In the USA Lit-Lit became a formal part of the National Council of Churches. In Europe the International Committee for Christian Literature for Africa, based in London, had considerable influence in getting people to think on development lines while first the CLF and subsequently the World Association for Christian Communication* formed a further unifying (though not a uniting) force for literature concerns.

During the 1960s and 1970s there was much re-thinking on the meaning and role of Christian literature. The traditional identification of Christian literature with missionary literature was challenged in many parts of the world. Partly through the contributions of the CLF, which later became the Agency for Christian Literature Development, there was increasing emphasis on literature that was indigenous and contextual. A more inclusive understanding of Christian literature emerged during this period. The Bible itself was recognized as a compendium of Christian literature, containing poems and stories, history and prophecy, sermons, visions, songs and letters.

In the third world publishing and distribution have become the preserve of the local churches or specialized Christian agencies with national leadership. Some have weathered the storms of missionary withdrawal better than others but many have continued to turn for support to their former church links or to one of the literature agencies, most of which have continued not only to provide funds but also to encourage training and development.

ALEC GILMORE

W.K.L. Clarke, *A History of the SPCK*, London, SPCK, 1959 • S.G. Green, *The Story of the Religious Tract Society for One Hundred Years*, London, 1899 • G. Hewitt, *Let the People Read*, London, 1949 • F.C. Laubach, *Thirty Years with the Silent Billion*, London, Lutterworth, 1961; and *Forty Years with the Silent Billion*, Old Tappan, NJ, Revell, 1970 • J.G. Williams, *Hungry World*, London, 1961.

CHRISTIAN LITERATURE FUND.

The CLF was launched out of a concern among some of the Western missionary agencies and specialist literature societies for the production and distribution of Christian literature in the third world. After exploratory conferences in Asia and Africa, a report to the WCC's Commission on World Mission and Evangelism at Mexico in 1963 led to the birth of the CLF, sponsored by the WCC, with an interchurch and international committee. Two years later the fund was officially launched with a five-year mandate. After a mid-term

review (1968), it was followed in 1970 by the Agency for Christian Literature Development (ACLD), which merged with the World Association for Christian Communication* (WACC) in 1975.

The major aim was the growth of a thriving, well co-ordinated, indigenous Christian literature in each country that would be of high quality, self-sustaining and capable of spontaneous growth. At least 25% of the fund was to go for training, and this was intended to include top-level personnel in publishing, printing and distribution as well as regional and local workshops for writers, translators and salespersons. A further important element was the setting up, training and organizing of literature committees. Christian literature was then further defined to include literature for development, relating the whole gospel to the whole person, and so strong was the emphasis on indigenous and creative writing that even translations were regarded as "a second best", though the records state that "translation of Christian classics was permitted".

The committee was representative of many countries but had autonomy. It had a fixed schedule for five years but was not an operating agency; instead it had capital funds of US$500,000 from agencies of the church in many countries in order to carry out its mandate. Supporting countries were Canada, Federal Republic of Germany, the Netherlands, New Zealand, Denmark, the USA, Australia, Sweden and the UK. Apart from the Bible societies, the main church mission boards and councils, the specialist literature societies were Lit-Lit (Committee on World Literacy and Christian Literature, USA), SPCK (Society for Promoting Christian Knowledge, UK) and USCL (United Society for Christian Literature, UK).

The first large grant in 1965 went to Argentina for writer training. From 1965 to 1968 grants and allocations totalled US$1,886,577, and at the end of the mandate more than $2.5 million had been disbursed in addition to further sums by many participating societies. The original intention was to support 15 major projects of $100,000 each and a further 30 smaller projects of $20,000. In the event, the largest grants made were between $30,000 and $60,000 (16), with 66 for $20,000 or less.

The real contribution of the CLF, however, could not be assessed in terms of dollars and was summarized in an evaluation report as "the effect of a world-based committee, inspiration to local planning within a regional strategy for long-term development, making definitive the work of a publisher, and the existence of an uncommitted fund". In 1970 the CLF gave way to the ACLD to continue the work, but by now other changes were taking place. Literature was increasingly seen in relation to other forms of communication, and the WACC was an obvious ally. Closer links were formed, and the ACLD became the print media development unit of the WACC in 1975.

See also **Christian literature**.

ALEC GILMORE

The Bethel Consultation on Christian Literature, London, SPCK, 1963 • *Christian Communication in the South-West Pacific*, Dodoma, Tanzania, Central Tanganika Press, 1965 • *Literature and the Gospel: The Work and Aims of the Christian Literature Fund*, Lausanne, CLF, 1968 • F. Shacklock, *World Literacy Manual*, New York, Friendship, 1967.

CHRISTIAN PEACE CONFERENCE.

After the Bandung (Indonesia) conference in 1955, which began to gather nations which considered themselves non-aligned within the blocs dominated by the USA and the USSR; and after the aborted uprising in Hungary (1956), Europe found itself still in the grip of the cold war.* The world remained solidly divided into the two power blocs. The organized ecumenical movement was to a large extent dominated by political and social ideas coming from the West. There was no platform where Eastern European churches, church groups and individuals could come together to discuss the most urgent global political issues, especially the ever-present threat of a nuclear catastrophe, and to address such issues as Christians and not only as loyal citizens of their countries. In this atmosphere the idea of the Christian Peace Conference (CPC) was born.

In the autumn of 1957 two Protestant theological faculties in Czechoslovakia (Prague and Bratislava) came together to discuss a plan of convening the first CPC meeting in June 1958. The leading personalities were Josef Hromádka and Bohuslav Pospisil (both related to the Comenius Theological Faculty in Prague). Inspiring them was the original idea of Dietrich Bonhoeffer, who as early as 1934 had called for such a peace council. From the outset it was made clear that the CPC would not compete with the WCC but would complement its activities. The beginning was small and unassuming. The concept found a positive echo among Western church people and theologians, although in the early years in Prague, Westerners present did not match the Eastern leaders in rank and influence.

The first three CPC meetings in 1958-60 and the first All Christian Peace Assembly in 1961 concentrated mostly on the division between the East and the West and on the issues stemming from the continuing cold war. The 1961 assembly brought together 600 participants from 42 countries, including three delegates from the People's Republic of China who spoke bitterly of the *pax Russo-Americana*. The term "peace" was discredited because it was ideologically loaded. However, theologians such as Hans Joachim Iwand, Heinrich Vogel, Helmut Gollwitzer and Ernst Wolf understood that the question of peace in the presence of nuclear arms had acquired a new quality and had become a relevant theological issue. The basic focus in the initial stage was the struggle against atomic catastrophe, the ban of nuclear weapons and the effort to ease the cold war. Later the scope included the study of justice, freedom, new developing countries, the German question, governmental manipulation of the churches, disarmament, and the peace service of youth. Unsuccessful efforts were made to secure the cooperation of the Roman Catholic Church.

The second assembly (1964) represented a major breakthrough. The participants from Latin America, Africa and Asia directed the CPC thinking towards third-world issues and shaped the CPC into a truly worldwide movement. The urgent needs of developing countries, the question of revolution, and the growing unrest among students and young people became an integral part of the CPC agenda. The term "theology of revolution" was first coined in the CPC youth commission. The CPC contributed substantially to the Geneva conference on Church and Society (1966) and its impact.

The third assembly (1968) was marked by Czechoslovakian developments. The Communist Party came under the leadership of Alexander Dubcek, who was developing a programme for "socialism with a human face". The invasion by five socialist states on 21 August 1968 stopped the innovative experiment and had far-reaching consequences also for the CPC. Its president, Hromádka, wrote a memorandum which condemned the action of the five countries. The delegates from the Soviet Union produced a counter-memorandum. The stormy session of the CPC working committee in Massy (early October 1968) initiated a protracted crisis which led to dismissal of the general secretary, Jaroslav Ondra. A few weeks later, Hromádka also resigned. Some CPC representatives tried to silence the dissenting voices. This led to another crisis symbolized by the walkout of a number of Western and third-world participants in early 1970. So the CPC was dangerously weakened, and in some countries it never recovered from the events of 1968-69.

The 1971 assembly was designed to overcome the latent crisis and to elect new governing bodies, eliminating the dissenters. Regrettably, in the 1970s the CPC had at times defended the policies of one power bloc. The theological work so important in the initial stage became sterile or even neglected. On the other hand, the CPC effort found a good echo in the southern hemisphere. The CPC was able to start important regional work in Asia (1975), in Africa (1977) and in Latin America (1978). Also the work of women's groups and their contribution to the feminist cause are worth mentioning. The CPC work would not have been possible without the participation and financial support of the churches in Central and Eastern Europe, especially the Russian Orthodox Church. Being located in Prague, the headquarters and the leadership of the CPC were vulnerable to the massive interference by communist governments in the organization's inner life.

The 1978 and 1985 assemblies became rallying points for many Christians from around the world, thus influencing the thinking and life of churches and individual Christians not only in Europe but altogether in around 90 countries (including Vietnam and North Korea). The CPC has contributed towards creating an atmosphere in which the programme for justice, peace and the integrity of creation* could emerge as a major theme in the ecumenical movement.

The recent radical changes in Central and Eastern Europe question CPC's raison d'etre, its structures and decision-making process. The legacy of its first president calls the CPC to repentance. As were peace and nuclear arms in the 1950s, global economic justice has become, among Christians, tomorrow's great theme. Given the CPC's past burden and faltering credibility, the question remains whether it will be able to recuperate and deal effectively with this issue.

MILAN OPOCENSKY

God Calls: Choose Life! The Hour Is Late. Christians in Resistance to the Powers of Death. On the Path to Peace and Justice for All, Prague, CPC, 1985.

CHRISTIAN WORLD COMMUN-IONS.

From the second half of the 19th century onwards, various confessional movements have come into being with the aim of leading churches of a particular confession and tradition in various countries out of their isolation and uniting them into one international confessional body. The first confessional associations were the Seventh-day Adventists (first world conference in 1863), the Anglicans (first Lambeth conference in 1867), the Reformed (the World Alliance of Reformed Churches was established in 1875) and the Baptists (Baptist World Alliance in 1905). The Lutherans began the process of consultation in 1923, when the Lutheran World Conference met for the first time, and launched the Lutheran World Federation in 1947. After the second world war the other confessions also established their own international organs.

The term "Christian World Communions" (CWCs) came into common use only in 1979. In 1967, a meeting of secretaries of such bodies adopted the term "World Confessional Families" (WCFs), but this designation proved to be not entirely satisfactory. Several communions of churches (Orthodox, Anglican and others) do not understand themselves as a particular confession, that is, as churches marked by ties to particular creeds. They are also built on different ecclesiological assumptions. The forms of "structured visible expressions" of confessional organizations, moreover, vary greatly. The Lutheran World Federation has many employees and a large annual budget. Other confessional communions are represented by small organizations.

Since 1957 the conference of secretaries of the CWCs has met annually (except for 1960, 1961 and 1975). The following communions and groups of churches have participated in this annual gathering: Anglican, Baptist, Christian Church (Disciples of Christ), Eastern Orthodox, Lutheran, Mennonite, Methodist, Old Catholic, Oriental Orthodox, Pentecostal, Presbyterian and Reformed, Religious Society of Friends, Salvation Army, General Conference of Seventh-day Adventists and united churches. Since 1968 the Vatican Secretariat for Promoting Christian Unity* has been regularly represented at the conference, thus keeping the question of the relationship between the CWCs and the Roman Catholic Church on subsequent agendas. The fact that an important network of interconfessional conversations has developed in recent years, in which the RCC is involved at the world level, reveals how seriously this church is taking the role of the various CWCs (see **dialogue, bilateral**).

The conference has discussed various concerns, including the place and task of confessional families in the ecumenical movement, national loyalties as a help or hindrance to world fellowship, bilateral dialogues, the relationships between Bible societies and CWCs, religious liberty and human rights.

Self-understanding. In the course of CWC conferences two attempts have been made to formulate the raison d'etre of the CWCs. The "working definition" of a 1962 meeting reads: "These bodies have this in common: (1) that their member churches share together not only the general tradition which is common to all Christian churches, but also specific traditions which have grown out of spiritual crises in the history of the church; (2) that they desire to render witness to specific convictions of doctrinal or ecclesiological character which they consider to be essential for the life of the whole church of Christ." In 1967 was added: "Each World Confessional Family consists of churches belonging to the same tradition and held together by this common heritage; they

are conscious of living in the same universal fellowship and give to this consciousness at least some structured visible expression."

Although both of these attempted definitions emphasize important points, neither has been wholly satisfactory. Three theological aspects, however, have continued to dominate the life of the CWCs and determine their work: (1) a concern for legitimate diversity within the one catholic church and the one apostolic faith; (2) a concern for the historical continuity of Christian faith and life; (3) a concern for Christian fellowship as universal, transcending national, ethnic, and cultural barriers and boundaries.

The East Asia Christian Conference assembly at Bangkok (1964) asked Asian Christians to answer three questions. Do the world confessional organizations rest on a theological principle, or do they simply gather churches because of common history? Even where world confessional organizations are seeking to preserve for the universal church some fundamental insight into an aspect of Christian truth, is this best done by an organization built around that truth? Are the confessions and doctrines which are the historical basis of these world confessional organizations living realities among the people in these confessional families?

Still other problems have been raised in various parts of the world. CWCs are in danger of rigidifying confessional differences and divisions which the ecumenical movement tries to overcome. The question as to whether the way to unity necessarily passes through the CWCs rather than through the WCC as a community of all confessional churches has not been answered. Another problem is whether bilateral conversations and agreements between the various CWCs are as conclusive as the multilateral efforts of the Faith and Order* movement, although the WCC has to reckon with the confessional loyalty of its member churches. In the realms of witness and service, the efforts of the CWCs often duplicate the worldwide activities of the WCC.

United churches, which have come into existence from the 1920s onwards, and independent or indigenous churches, especially in Africa, have tended to view the claims of CWCs as a hindrance to the community of the church "in each place" to seek fellowship with

Eighth assembly of the Lutheran World Federation, Curitiba, Brazil (WCC/Peter Williams)

other local churches (see **unity of "all in each place"**). Some united churches, such as the Church of North India and the Uniting Church in Australia, still have relationships with respective CWCs. Other united churches have largely cut their confessional ties. F&O invited united churches and churches engaged in union negotiations to several consultations (Bossey 1967, Limuru 1970, Toronto 1975, Colombo 1981 and Potsdam 1987). At the Toronto consultation united churches decided not to create a world organization of united churches.

CWCs and the WCC. A 1973 consultation on "Concepts of Unity and Models of Union", sponsored by the F&O commission at Salamanca, Spain, urged the CWCs "to clarify their understanding of the quest for unity by co-operating with the WCC". To overcome the tensions and conflicts which have often arisen in the past, the Nairobi assembly (1975) made a number of suggestions. Co-operation with the confessional families should be co-ordinated with the relevant regional ecumenical organizations. There should be an effort to agree mutually on "the unity we seek" and "the witness we bear in the

world". The findings of the bilateral discussions should be effectively applied to the work of the WCC. A useful instrument for this purpose is a forum sponsored by the F&O commission, but closer contacts should also be developed with other sectors of the WCC as well.

Representatives of the conference of secretaries of the WCFs met in Geneva with representatives of the WCC in 1978 to consult on mutual relationships. Three themes were discussed: the unity of the church, common witness and collaboration, and the appropriate form mutual relationships should take.

In 1979 the WCC central committee called for exploration of ways in which CWCs might assist the WCC in communicating with member churches which belong to the respective CWCs and encouraged the general secretary to explore maintaining and strengthening liaison with CWCs interested in building closer overall relationships, making maximum use of existing constitutional provisions for CWC involvement in developing WCC policies.

The Vancouver assembly (1983) recognized the ecumenical importance of the CWCs and of the conference of secretaries of CWCs as partners in the quest for the full visible unity of the church. It urged both to seek clarity as to the goal of the unity which Christians seek within the one ecumenical movement and to identify steps in achieving that goal. It also expressed the hope that a new series of ad hoc meetings of the forum on bilateral conversations would give specific attention to the reception of the report on *Baptism, Eucharist and Ministry** and to its relations to the bilateral dialogues among CWCs. The question of the relationship between the three concepts of unity — organic union,* conciliar fellowship (see **conciliarity**) and reconciled diversity* — remains crucial (see **unity; unity, models of; unity, ways to**).

See also **dialogue, multilateral**.

ANS J. VAN DER BENT

N. Ehrenström & G. Gassmann, *Confessions in Dialogue: A Survey of Bilateral Conversations among World Confessional Families, 1959-74*, 3rd ed., WCC, 1975 • H. E. Fey, "Confessional Families and the Ecumenical Movement", in *A History of the Ecumenical Movement*, vol. 2: *1948-1968*, 2nd ed., WCC, 1986 • Y. Ishida, H. Meyer & E. Perret, *The History and Theological Concerns of World Confessional Families*, LWF report, August 1979 • M. Kinnamon & T. F. Best eds, *Called to Be One in Christ: United Churches and the Ecumenical Movement*, WCC, 1985 • J. F. Puglisi & S.J. Voicu, *A Bibliography of Interchurch and Interconfessional Theological Dialogues*, Rome, Centro Pro Unione, 1984.

CHURCH. At a lucid moment in the difficult and continuing study on "The Unity of the Church and the Renewal of Human Community", it was recognized in the WCC Faith and Order* commission that "in a divided Christianity, the existing churches" have "varying understandings of the nature, identity and boundaries of the church. The churches' differences come to expression in several ways: their perceptions of the character of the church as both the body and bride of Christ and a historic reality; the role they attribute to the institutional element that is necessary for any form of ecclesial life; the place they accord to the church in the saving activity of God; the sense in which the church itself may be said to be sacramental in character; the weight they attach to ecclesiology in their doctrinal schemes. Most concretely, the

existing churches differ as to the persons and communities which are to be reckoned as belonging to the church" (*Faith and Renewal: Stavanger 1985*, 194-95).

It is in fact fairly easy for the churches to agree in describing *what the church is* and stating *what the church is for:* it is "people of God", "Body of Christ", "community of the Holy Spirit", privileged with anticipating God's kingdom in its worship *(leitourgia)* and meanwhile charged with proclaiming the gospel to the world (*martyria*, witness) and serving the needy among humankind *(diakonia)*. A text of this kind, entitled "The Calling of the Whole People of God", is found in the first five paragraphs of the ministry section of *Baptism, Eucharist and Ministry** (1982) and has met with great approval in the responses of the churches to the Lima document. But when the church shifts from being the subject of the sentence to the predicate, it is much more difficult for the churches to agree in identifying *who are the church*. Different views on the identity of the church, on where the church is concretely to be found, are linked to differences as to its unity* and mission* — and therefore after all also to its nature (what the church is) and its relationship to the world and the human community in which it is placed (what the church is for).

A historical and systematic typology of ecclesiologies. Looking at the history and present state of Christianity, it is possible to detect some eight different intuitions or perceptions as to the identity, nature, unity and mission of the church. These arose in a rough historical sequence, although each has interacted with its predecessors and successors, and all are present today, although often in mixed form. The following are ways in which the fellowship of the church — the sacrament* of whose beginning is baptism* and continuance is eucharistic communion (see **communion, eucharist**) — has been defined and located.

1. In the view associated with Cyprian of Carthage (d.258), there is only one church, the "ark of salvation", and its institutional and spiritual boundaries coincide. Any who fall away, whether into heresy* (failure of faith) or schism* (failure of love), lack the Holy Spirit* and drop into an ecclesiological void. The sacraments of the delinquent party are counterfeits; and when individuals are con-

verted to the catholic church, they receive baptism (not re-baptism, since what they received in the other body was not in fact baptism at all).

The Orthodox and the stricter type of Baptists remain closest to this view. In the Anglican-Orthodox dialogue, the Orthodox maintained that their church "is the one true church of Christ, which as his body is not and cannot be divided" (Dublin 1984, 9). The strength of this view in its pristine form resides in its witness to the ontological realism of God's self-gift to "the one undivided historical church": "We are not merely moving towards unity, but rather our very existence derives from the inseparable union between the three persons of the Holy Trinity given to us as a historical event on the day of Pentecost" (Nikos Nissiotis). Its difficulty, especially apparent in an ecumenical age, lies in giving an account of the *prima facie* presence of faith* beyond the bounds of one's own community. In an exercise of "economy",* the Orthodox have not always required baptism of those coming to them from at least certain other would-be Christian communities, while insisting that this is not a general recognition of the baptisms performed there in the absence of conversion to Orthodoxy.

2. According to a view indebted to Augustine (d.430), outside baptisms may be valid (at least in the sense that a convert will not be re-baptized, on the grounds that, whoever baptizes, "it is Christ who baptizes"), but they will not be "fruitful" before conversion to the true church. This view has the advantage of acknowledging Christ's sovereignty over his sacraments, while retaining the importance of the ecclesial connection for their benefits; but it involves the problem of a gap, both notional and temporal, between "validity" and "efficacy". Historically, the Augustinian position is characteristic of Rome. The council of Trent* anathematized any who should deny that baptism performed in water in the name of the Trinity* with the intention of doing what the church does was true baptism; but in cases where the persons baptized belonged to communities holding beliefs judged contrary to Roman doctrine, such baptisms could hardly be more than merely valid, since their efficacy for salvation would be immediately cut off by the anathemas* attaching to heresies and schism.

3. A view that elements of the faith persisted, even savingly, outside one's own community eventually led some to the detection of "traces of the church" *(vestigia ecclesiae)* beyond their own institution. The classic Protestant reformers, and particularly perhaps Calvin (no doubt on a predestinarian base), were willing to recognize that there were Christians present within the unreformed Roman communion, which has not been left entirely without the means of grace (*Institutes* 4.2.11-12). Despite the bull *Unam Sanctam* of 1302, in which Pope Boniface VIII declared in face of "the Greeks" as well as of political resistance in the West that "it is altogether necessary to salvation for every human creature to be subject to the Roman pontiff", the Roman church maintained an intermittent dialogue with the "Eastern churches" (with the ecclesial designation apparently acquiring increased substance from Leo XIII onwards, until indeed the designation by Paul VI of Constantinople as a "sister church" appears to transcend the *vestigia ecclesiae* model).

Eventually, and clearly from the 19th century onwards, Rome from its standpoint counted Protestants among the "separated brethren", with an increasing emphasis on the family ties that still joined them to Rome across the division. Vatican II declared that, by virtue of their baptism and the faith in Christ thereby signified, such individuals enjoy "a certain, though imperfect, communion" with the Roman Catholic Church (*Unitatis Redintegratio* 3). Even their communities that stem from the Reformation are "not devoid of meaning and value in the mystery of salvation" (*ibid.*; cf. 19-23). The scriptures and the rites, as well as the faith, hope and love, that are found outside the Roman Catholic Church, belong by rights, however, to the "one church of Christ", which, according to *Lumen Gentium* 8, "subsists in" the Roman Catholic Church. The interpretation of Vatican II's *subsistit in* is controversial even among Roman Catholic theologians; but it is in any case clear that other Christians and their communities have difficulty with the notion that they need the mediation of the Roman Catholic Church in order to be (part of) the church of Christ, and consequently with any interpretation of Vatican II's idea that elements of the faith outside Roman bounds properly "lead back" to the unity *with* the RCC in terms of a restored unity *in* the RCC.

4. While the Protestant reformers did not abandon the institutional aspect of the church, a stronger emphasis was placed, particularly perhaps on the Lutheran side, upon the church as "event". When the Augsburg confession declares in article 7 that "the church is a gathering of believers in which the gospel is purely preached and the sacraments are administered according to the gospel", the direction of thought among Lutheran interpreters is less likely to be that of the church celebrating the word and the sacraments than that of word and sacraments constituting the congregation. This more punctiliar or episodic view of the church has the advantages of dynamism and of allowing for repeated correction of the church by God; but it has difficulty in concretizing a pastoral and teaching office for the sake of the continuity or identity of the believing fellowship in time and space.

5. A "branch theory" of the church has been most characteristic of Anglicanism. It may be as early as the prayer of Bishop Lancelot Andrewes (1555-1626) for "the church catholic: Eastern, Western, British". Certainly the 19th-century Oxford movement and its aftermath thought in terms of the Greek, Latin and Anglican churches (see William Palmer's *Treatise on the Church of Christ*, 1838). This model retains or revives something of the "substantialist" or "institutionalist" aspects of the Cyprianic. But it differs in holding that schism is, even if only temporarily, "internal" to the church. It may, in the end, prove to be the way by which at least the two "sister churches" of Rome and Constantinople find reconciliation between themselves.

6. Protestant pietism of the 17th and 18th centuries was the seedbed for a more subjective ecclesiology. Christianity appears as a religion of the heart, in which fellowship consists in a warm personal relationship with Christ and with the brothers and sisters. The church consists of "true believers everywhere", and even though outward circumstances and differences over non-essentials "may prevent", as Wesley put it in his sermon on a "Catholic Spirit", "an entire external union", they do not preclude a "union in affection". This view is characteristic of many who in recent times have been called evangelicals. It may serve as a valuable reminder that

institutional unity without spiritual unity would be a mere facade; its weakness is that it tends to acquiesce too easily in visible *disunity*.

Avery Dulles has wondered whether the one-sided emphasis on the church as a "spiritual community" does not underlie "the repeated statements in WCC literature that the aim of the ecumenical movement is to manifest, rather than to bring about, the oneness of Christ's church" (in *Theological Studies* 33, 1972). Certainly the New Delhi 1961 description of the unity which is both God's will and gift, for which we must both work and pray, speaks of its "being made visible as..." Yet this very formulation makes clear that classical ecumenism is not content with a merely "invisibilist" unity.

7. The great rise of Protestant missions in the 18th and 19th centuries brought an evangelistic model of the church into prominence. A sacramental symptom is the practice of what Methodists in particular, in an exaggeration of Wesley's notion of the Lord's supper as a "converting ordinance", call "open communion". In the 1950s and 1960s, this vision acquired a renewed eschatological intensity in the advocacy by the Dutch missiologist J.C. Hoekendijk of a sacramental banquet totally "open to the world": "Communion as an eschatological sacrament is the representation of the kingdom in the *world*; it is impossible to lock up the kingdom in the church, it is equally impossible to make this sacrament of the kingdom a purely churchly event." The attractiveness of this ecclesiology resides in its perception of the inviting character of the gospel and the welcoming nature of the church. The danger is that, since by receiving communion one becomes henceforth part of the proclaiming community, the identity of that body and its message may be obscured or lost through the immediate aggregation of persons who do not yet have the depth of understanding and commitment signified by baptism and the profession of faith.

8. With the Life and Work* movement, the last ecclesiological vision to be listed believes that "service unites". This pragmatic, or "secular" (Avery Dulles), approach finds Christian unity pre-eminently expressed in a diaconal ministry amid the needy of the world. Collaborators for justice* and peace* may celebrate their fellowship, as happened in

places in the 1960s, with a holy meal on the march or on the barricades. The sacrament here helps to keep the Christological inspiration present to the participants and should in turn bring home to all Christians the social and ethical implications of their faith. The main problem with this view is that it minimizes the doctrinal and institutional components of Christianity.

Shifts in ecclesiological methodology. Only when, by virtue of this or a similar typology, the institutions claiming to be church are deliberately aware of the diversity in their starting points is it possible to go beyond bland re-affirmations concerning the church as "people of God", "Body of Christ", and "community of the Holy Spirit" that leave the problem of a divided Christianity intact. In the light of an awareness of their own starting points and those of the others, however, the churches are enabled to examine afresh the scriptural and traditional images with a view to re-discovering the nature, tasks and concrete location of the church. As part of a joint hermeneutical endeavour, conducted with a readiness for self-criticism and a willingness to look at others sympathetically, the churches now need to ask again where the agreed "marks of the church" are concretely to be found. Are they recognizable in my own community? In which other communities are they recognizable? What do these discernments mean for the restoration of fellowship, communion and unity?

Ecclesiology in fact became a hot topic in both bilateral and multilateral dialogues and relationships in the 1980s. It is often said that the world conference on F&O at Lund in 1952 marked the end of "comparative ecclesiology" and the transition to a method whereby all ecumenical partners would focus together upon the Christological, Trinitarian, salvation-historical centre and source of the church. This concentration was valuable. But the convergences it produced — as most notably in the Lima text on *Baptism, Eucharist and Ministry* — then make it necessary, precisely in so far as they appear to bring the possibility of unity closer, to integrate again, now in a more hopeful light, the questions raised by comparative ecclesiology. If so many of the churches' responses to BEM ask ... 's ecclesiological implications, it is on ... only its presuppositions but

also its possible consequences. The preface to BEM itself put to the churches the question of "the consequences your church can draw from this text for its relations and dialogues with other churches, particularly with those churches which also recognize the text as an expression of the apostolic faith". Concurrently, the international bilateral dialogues* among Christian World Communions* have recognized that as progress is registered towards agreement in the faith, so the presently divided communities, as carriers of that faith, are by that very fact coming *ecclesially* closer to one another and so need a doctrine of the church that holds open the prospect of mutual recognition and eventually unity.

Ecclesiology in the bilateral dialogues. One of the first bilateral dialogues to give explicit attention to ecclesiology was that between the Orthodox and the Old Catholics (Chambésy 1977, Bonn 1979, Zagorsk 1981). In a section on "the boundaries of the church" (Bonn, 27-31), each party affirms, despite their present lack of communion with each other, that "from the day it was founded right down to our own days, the true church, the one, holy, catholic and apostolic church, has gone on existing without any discontinuity wherever the true faith, worship and order of the undivided church are preserved unimpaired" (29). To take account, no doubt, at least of their own situation vis-a-vis each other, the mixed commission tentatively asserts that "since it is impossible to set limits to God's power,... it can be considered as not excluded that the divine omnipotence and grace are present and operative wherever the departure from the fullness of truth in the one church is not complete and does not go to the lengths of a complete estrangement from the truth" (30).

The Orthodox-Roman Catholic dialogue began with a treatment of "The Mystery of the Church and of the Eucharist in the Light of the Mystery of the Holy Trinity" (Munich 1982): "The church exists in history as a local church... in a given place" (2.1), but it is already "eschatological" (2.2). "There is a 'Jerusalem from on high', which 'comes down from God'; a communion which is at the foundation of the community itself", so that "the church comes into being by a free gift, that of the new creation" (2.1). The church "manifests itself when it is assembled", most fully in the eucharist (2.1). The eucharist includes "the proclamation of the word to the assembly, and the response of faith given by all" (2.2). "Each eucharistic assembly is truly the holy church of God, the Body of Christ, in communion with the first community of the disciples and with all who throughout the world celebrate and have celebrated the memorial of the Lord" (3.1). There are two conditions for a local church to be "truly within the ecclesial communion": first and fundamentally, "the identity of the mystery of the church lived by the local church with the mystery of the church lived by the primitive church"; and then, "mutual recognition today between this local church and the other churches... Each should recognize in the others through local particularities the identity of the mystery of the church." This mutual recognition depends on "communion in the same kerygma, and so in the same faith", and on "the will for communion in love and in service, not only in words but in deeds" (3.3). The subsequent stages of the Orthodox-Roman Catholic dialogue on faith, sacraments and order (Bari 1987; Uusi Valamo 1988) have worked towards achieving the conditions of such mutual recognition among the local churches of their respective communions.

In the 1984 Dublin statement between Orthodox and Anglicans on "the mystery of the church", the Orthodox re-affirm their own identity with the one true church of Christ; but "at the same time they see Anglicans as brothers and sisters in Christ who are seeking with them the union of all Christians in the one church" (9). The two parties "are not agreed on the account to be given of the sinfulness and division which is to be observed in the life of Christian communities. For Anglicans, because the church under Christ is the community where God's grace is at work, healing and transforming sinful men and women, and because grace in the church is mediated through those who are themselves undergoing such transformation, the struggle between grace and sin is to be seen as characteristic of, rather than accidental to, the church on earth" (99); consequently, "we disagree in our view of the relationship between the church's basic unity and the present state of division between Christians. The Anglican members see our divisions as existing within the church, while the Orthodox members believe that the Orthodox church is the one true church of Christ, which as his Body is not and cannot be divided" (100).

In the Anglican-Roman Catholic dialogue, ARCIC I in the introduction to its *Final Report* (1982) revealed that the implicit leitmotif in its earlier texts on eucharist, ministry and authority had been "the concept of koinonia (communion)" in its Trinitarian, Christological and ecclesiological aspects: "Koinonia with one another is entailed by our koinonia with God in Christ. This is the mystery of the church" (intro., 5). This then set the context for the first statement of ARCIC II, on "Salvation and the Church" (Llandaff 1986). Ecclesiologically, the most lapidary formulation in that text is the declaration that "the church is called to be, and by the power of the Spirit actually is, a *sign, steward* and *instrument* of God's design. For this reason it can be described as *sacrament* of God's saving work" (29). This is, first, an attempt to deal with the tension which ARCIC I's co-chairmen had already recognized in 1976 between the ideal and the actual, a tension which affects the ecclesial life of both churches as well as the relations between them. The Llandaff text writes further to this point: "The credibility of the church's witness is undermined by the sin of its members, the shortcomings of its human institutions, and not least by the scandal of division. The church is in constant need of repentance and renewal so that it can be more clearly seen for what it is: the one, holy body of Christ. Nevertheless the gospel contains the promise that despite all failures the church will be used by God in the achievement of his purpose: to draw humanity into communion with himself and with one another, so as to share his life, the life of the Holy Trinity" (29).

Second, the language of the Llandaff text about the church as "sign, steward and instrument" (29) — "of what it has received" (27) — is an attempt to overcome the historic Reformation controversy concerning "the role of the church in the process of salvation": "As well as believing that Catholics did not acknowledge the true authority of scripture over the church, Protestants also felt that Catholic teaching and practice had interpreted the mediatorial role of the church in such a way as to derogate from the place of Christ as 'sole mediator between God and man' (1 Tim. 2:5).

Catholics believed that Protestants were abandoning or at least devaluing the church's ministry and sacraments, which were divinely appointed means of grace; also that they were rejecting its divinely given authority as guardian and interpreter of the revealed word of God" (7). Now the church is jointly affirmed to be both "evangelized and evangelizing, reconciled and reconciling, gathered together and gathering others" (28).

Ecclesiology is now recognized to be the "lodestone" (André Birmelé) of the international Lutheran-Roman Catholic dialogue, which had in fact begun with "The Gospel and the Church" (Malta 1972). As interpreted in Birmelé's very detailed study of the continuing dialogue, there still remains "a basic difference" concerning "the nature of the instrumentality of the church in the transmission of salvation" (which we saw ARCIC identifying as a Reformation controversy). According to Birmelé, this difference remains divisive because it is not fully covered by "the even more fundamental... broad consensus" on the gospel and salvation in Jesus Christ: the problem is that ecclesiology is, in the Catholic view, integral to a sufficiently complete agreement on the matter in hand, whereas Lutheranism permits a variety of ecclesiologies, since the doctrine of the church is not itself a (primary) part of the gospel.

In the dialogue between the Lutheran World Federation and the World Methodist Council, the partners have been able to reach a mutually satisfying agreement on "The Church: Community of Grace" (1984). The leading statement is this: "The church is the community of Jesus Christ called into being by the Holy Spirit. Those who respond in faith to the gospel of Christ, proclaimed in word and sacrament, are brought into a new relationship with God and with one another" (28). The joint commission recommended that the member churches "take steps to declare and establish full fellowship of word and sacrament" (91), while admitting the need for further study on "forms of unity" (88). Concurrently, the World Methodist Council is conducting the ecclesiological phase of its dialogue with the Roman Catholic Church under the rubric of koinonia: "Because God so loved the world, he sent his Son and the Holy Spirit to draw us into *communion* with himself. This *sharing* in God's life, which re-

sulted from the mission of the Son and the Holy Spirit, found expression in a visible *community* of Christ's disciples, the church" (Nairobi 1986, 1).

Dialogues involving the World Alliance of Reformed Churches have emphasized the location and role of the church in the world. This was already the case of the first dialogue with the Roman Catholic Church, "The Presence of Christ in Church and World" (1970-77), and the same perspective is pursued in "Towards a Common Understanding of the Church" (1983-89). The Anglican-Reformed International Commission's report on "God's Reign and Our Unity" (1984) sees the church as "a pilgrim people called to a journey whose goal is nothing less than God's blessed kingdom embracing all nations and all creation, a sign, instrument and foretaste of God's purpose 'to sum up all things with Christ as head' (Eph. 1:10). It is only in this missionary and eschatological perspective that the question of unity is rightly seen" (14): "The church is thus a provisional embodiment of God's final purpose for all human beings and for all creation. It is an embodiment because it is a body of actual men and women chosen by God to share through the Spirit in the life of Christ and so in his ministry in the world. It is provisional in a double sense: only part of the human family has been brought into its life, and those who have been so brought are only partly conformed to God's purpose. If they were fully conformed, they would be fully reconciled to one another. The quest for unity is one aspect of the church's acting out of her unceasing prayer: 'Your kingdom come'" (30).

The "theological conversations sponsored by the World Alliance of Reformed Churches and the Baptist World Alliance" (1973-77) have shown an awareness that the issue of the nature and conditions of baptism was "central to the ecclesiological question, confronting the whole ecumenical movement, on the nature and understanding of the church" (intro.). "The Reformation tradition", which includes the baptism of infants, "emphasizes the community of salvation and thus the thought of the church as also a mixed body (*corpus permixtum*, see Matt. 13:24-30,47-50)... The Baptist tradition emphasizes the aspect of mission and the thought of the church as 'gathered believers' committed to the task of proclaiming the gospel to each individual (see Matt. 28:16-20)" (8). The place and role of the church in the world are clearly at issue again here. Baptists and Reformed were able to note some practical convergences between them, e.g. the "dual practice" in some Reformed churches whereby "believer's baptism is as legitimate as infant baptism", and "the important fact that many Baptist churches admit other Christians, baptized as infants, to the Lord's supper on the basis of their personal faith in Christ and when they are in good standing with their own churches, a practice which is a de facto recognition of their Christian status" (17).

Ecclesiology in Faith and Order after BEM. Taking up the questions and requests of the churches in their responses to BEM, the WCC F&O commission at Budapest 1989 resolved to undertake a major ecclesiological study which would integrate at least some aspects of the projects on "The Unity of the Church and the Renewal of Human Community" ("the church as mystery and prophetic sign") and "Towards the Common Expression of the Apostolic Faith Today".

A preliminary sketch proposes making koinonia* a major, though not exclusive, category: "Koinonia in the life of the Father, the Son and the Holy Spirit (see John 14:17; 1 John 1:2-10; 2 Pet. 1:4; 1 Cor. 1:9; 2 Cor. 13:13) is the life centre of all who confess Jesus Christ as Lord and Saviour. They share and participate in the gospel and in the apostolic faith, in suffering and in service (2 Cor. 8:4; Rom. 15:26; Acts 2:32). This koinonia is lived in Christ through baptism (Rom. 6) and the eucharist (1 Cor. 10-11) and in the community with its pastors and guides (Heb. 13). Koinonia means in addition the participation in the holy things of God and the communion of saints of all times and places (*communio sanctorum* in the double sense of the word). Each local Christian community is related in koinonia with all other local Christian communities with whom it shares the same faith. In this koinonia they live the catholicity of the church... Such a koinonia is not an inward-looking group of believers, but a missionary community sent into the world to bear witness to God's love for humanity and creation" (*Baptism, Eucharist and Ministry, 1982-1990: Report on the Process and Responses*, p.150). It is hoped that this would allow the integration — into "a convergent vision on the nature, unity and mission of the church" — of different, but potentially complementary, key

Baptist church in Nyagahinka, Rwanda (WCC/Peter Williams)

conceptions and images that all belong to the common biblical heritage but have been particularly emphasized by different Christian traditions:

The church as gift of the word of God (creatura verbi): "The koinonia of the church is centred and grounded in the word of God testified in the scriptures, incarnated in Jesus Christ and visible among us through the living voice of the gospel in preaching, in sacraments and in service. All church institutions, forms of ministry, liturgical expressions and methods of mission should be submitted to the word of God and tested by it. The *pleroma* of God's creative word is never exhausted in the church's institutions."

The church as mystery or sacrament of God's love for the world: "The church as koinonia is the church of the living God (see 1 Tim. 3:15), not a human association only. It lives in permanent communion with God the Father through Jesus Christ in the Holy Spirit and is not merely the historical product of Jesus' ministry. Because of its intimate relation with Christ himself as the head of the Body, the church is to be confessed according to the apostolic faith as one, holy, catholic and apostolic. Therefore the visible organizational structures of the church must always be seen in the light of God's gift of salvation in Christ. The word and the sacraments of Jesus Christ are forms of God's real and saving presence for the world. As such, they express the church's participation in the mystery of Christ and are inseparable from it."

The church as the pilgrim people of God: "A third aspect of the understanding of the church as koinonia stresses the provisional and incomplete character of the church in its present form, its hope and despair, its suffering and compassion, its shame and glory, its being still a mixed reality of sinners and saints. The church is a community of justified sinners in search of the kingdom of God, struggling as they serve the world to be obedient to the commands and promises of Christ as expressed in the sermon on the mount. It is a community of pilgrims who have already received a foretaste of that fulfilment for which they are longing."

The church as servant and prophetic sign of God's coming kingdom: "The church is also a servant people for God's coming kingdom, 'the sign held up before the nations'. As a first-fruit of the kingdom, the church takes sides with the weak, the poor and the alienated. This is for the sake of involving all its members in a personal appeal to seek first of all the kingdom of God by being itself, as a collective whole, an instrument for the liberation of people in distress. An ecumenically conceived ecclesiology, therefore, must not be self-centred, triumphalist or complacent, but should direct the churches' service to the world, to justice, peace and the integrity of creation" (*ibid.*, p.151).

From division, through reconciliation, towards the kingdom. All the bilateral and multilateral reflections on ecclesiology recognize, and try to give an account of, a number of tensions that may in fact be variants of a single tension: between the ideal and the actual, the believed and the empirical, the already and the not yet. The four "notes" of the church — its unity,* holiness,* catholicity,* and apostolicity* — all labour under that tension: there is need for reconciliation and a manifest unity; there is an imperative to the conquest of sin and a growth in holiness; there is room for many forms of the true faith in a harmonious catholicity; there is a test of apostolicity to be applied to all intended embodiments of the gospel message.

According to the Toronto statement* of 1950, no church is required to give up its own ecclesiology for membership in the WCC. Ecclesiological dialogues, whether under the auspices of the WCC or not, show churches discovering the presence of Christian faith and life beyond their own boundaries, struggling to formulate an account of that fact which may in effect gradually modify their respective ecclesiological theories, and reflecting on the conditions and means of bringing all acknowledged Christians and their divided communities into the unity which the gospel entails. The Methodist-Roman Catholic report of Nairobi 1986 judges that "as we reflect on a re-united church, we cannot expect to find an ecclesiology shaped in a time of division to be entirely satisfactory". Nevertheless, "our explorations towards a more adequate ecclesiology have begun and are helping us to give proper recognition to each other's ecclesial or churchly character. They will also assist in overcoming our present state of division" (22). Not even an ecumenically formulated ecclesiology may be perfect, yet it remains the task of the ecumenical movement to fashion a faithful doctrine of the church that will best allow for the recognition of the Christian reality wherever it is found, for the reconciliation of those who have been divided, and for the life henceforth in a church that is seeking that perfection of unity, holiness, catholicity and apostolicity which will mark the completed kingdom of God.*

See also **apostolicity; catholicity; church and world; church as institution; church discipline; church order; communion; holiness; images of the church; intercommunion; koinonia; local church; Toronto statement; unity; unity, models of; unity, ways to.**

GEOFFREY WAINWRIGHT

A. Birmelé, *Le salut en Jésus Christ dans les dialogues oecuméniques*, Paris, Cerf, 1986 • C. Davey, "The Doctrine of the Church in International Bilateral Dialogues", *One in Christ*, 22, 1986 • Dombes, Groupe des, *L'Espirit Saint, l'Eglise et les sacrements*, Taizé, Presses de Taizé, 1979 • A. Dulles, "The Church, the Churches, and the Catholic Church", *Theological Studies*, 33, 1972 • R.N. Flew ed., *The Nature of the Church: Papers Presented to the Theological Commission Appointed by the Continuation Committee of the World Conference on Faith and Order*, London, SCM, 1952 • A. Houtepen, "Towards an Ecumenical Vision of the Church", *One in Christ*, 25, 1989 • H. Küng, *Die Kirche* (ET *The Church*, London, Burns & Oates, 1968) • G. Limouris ed., *Church, Kingdom, World: The Church as Mystery and Prophetic Sign*, WCC, 1986 • H. Meyer & L. Vischer eds, *Growth in Agreement*, WCC, 1984 • L. Newbigin, *The Household of God*, London, SCM, 1953 • D. Papandreou, "Die Frage nach den Grenzen der Kirche im heutigen ökumenischen Dialog", in *Oecumenica et Patristica*, Stuttgart, Kohlhammer, 1989 • F.A. Sullivan, "'Subsistit in': The Significance of Vatican II's Decision to Say of the Church of Christ Not That It 'Is' but That It 'Subsists in' the Roman Catholic Church", *One in Christ*, 22, 1986 • G. Thils, *Histoire doctrinale du mouvement oecuménique*, 2nd ed., Paris, Desclée de Brouwer, 1963 • J. Willebrands, "Vatican II's Ecclesiology of Communion", *One in Christ*, 23, 1987 • J. Zizioulas, *L'être ecclésial* (ET *Being as Communion*, Crestwood, NY, St Vladimir's Seminary, 1985).

CHURCH AND STATE. Liberal democracies see the state as an instrument of society. If a nation's constitution is democratic, should all religions be equal before the law? Is an "established" or "national" church compatible with such equality? "Established" means any church whose doctrines, worship and discipline are supported in some way by civil law. "National" signifies a church which is independent of ecclesiastical control from outside the state. This dual relationship has long existed in most Eastern Orthodox churches, and the system began to occur in Western Europe with the rise of nation states and the growth of the Reformation.

The British Isles reveals four models of relationship. In *England* the Church of England is "by law established"; that is, it has recognized civic primacy, with the monarch as its supreme governor; its principal bishops are part of the legislature as members in the House of Lords; church law is incorporated in the law of the realm; and parliament has the final veto on doctrine and worship, though its power has been drastically limited (Worship and Doctrine Measure, 1974).

Apologists claim that this establishment of the Church of England enables pastoral coverage for all its faithful, builds on the "folk religion" of the past, and aids the church in its role as a critical and befriending counterbalance to the state from within rather than from outside positions of power. On the other hand, the non-established or dissenting churches have had to fight for their status and still suffer from the establishment's "effortless assumptions of superiority". They view the establishment of the largest of the fragments into which the Western church divided at the Reformation to be an injustice both to other ecclesial bodies and to those who are not Christians. They assert that a church's national character is a matter of how it understands its ecclesial calling and does not depend on the status which the state gives or allows.

Furthermore, some Anglicans see in the establishment that the church is vulnerable to state control against its interests. Conflict of interest and interference with doctrines and practices can occur, even more so since parliament is now composed largely of non-Anglicans. This could happen, the critics say, on the issue of the ordination of women* to the priesthood and episcopate.

More radical Christians see establishment as morally indefensible; it inhibits prophecy. Christianity is not a civic or folk religion but demands an active and total allegiance to Christ. Reunion negotiations, especially the

Anglican-Methodist scheme (1955-72), deemed some form of disestablishment inevitable.

Such systems, with variations, are still found in Norway, Sweden and Denmark (Lutheran), in Finland (Lutheran and Russian Orthodox), and in Greece (Greek Orthodox).

In *Scotland*, the Church of Scotland, whose polity is Presbyterian, is established but autonomous. "As a national church representative of the Christian faith of the Scottish people, it acknowledges the distinctive call and duty to bring the ordinances of religion to the people of Scotland through a territorial ministry." This national recognition is linked with spiritual independence. Nevertheless, smaller churches can feel marginalized as did the Methodist synod when it rejected reunion. But cultural and national factors loomed large here also.

In *Eire*, until the 1980s, the state acknowledged the primacy of the Roman Catholic Church, the majority church, with its freedom in moral and religious education. Clashes have occurred over legal issues such as abortion and artificial methods of contraception.

Some Latin American countries have total separation of church and state. Others have had concordats (public treaties between the Vatican and the secular state), in which the rights of the Roman Catholic Church and its faithful are protected. Some of these treaties and/or national constitutions reserve certain privileges to Roman Catholic faithful, and in a few, at least until the Second Vatican Council, the civil rights of religious freedom for other Christian churches were severely curtailed, if not denied.

In *Wales* and *Northern Ireland* the Anglican churches are disestablished. Ecumenism in Wales is expressed nationally by a Covenant (1975) between Anglican and non-Episcopalian churches concerning ministry, worship, mission and education, a position not yet achieved in England. The Anglican church in Wales has been more closely identified with Welsh culture since its disestablishment, while the Welsh non-episcopal churches have endured sharp decline associated with social and economic factors.

Recently, the concept of a neutral, pluralist state with no dominant religious ideology has clashed with more traditional ideas of a confessional state — Christian, Islamic or, increasingly in India, Hindu. In the late 1950s and 1960s the concept of the secular state received a great deal of attention in ecumenical circles in India and elsewhere. With the rise of Islamic states in many parts of the world (and recent developments in Fiji) there is perhaps need for the ecumenical movement to take up once again a serious study of the secular and theocratic options.

The issues of church-state relationships are raised more sharply in Europe. Here the long-term consequence of the principle *cuius regio eius religio* (each ruler determines the religion of his people), of the Reformation and of later wars of religion was the suppression or diminution of dissent, with consequent hardening of conflict between the Christian majority and the minority, and between Christian and non-Christian. In France the 19th-century battles over education culminated in the separation of church and state in 1905. In Germany there were the two political episodes of a culture struggle: first, under the founder of the German Reich (1871-1918), Bismarck (1871-90), involving the papacy; second, under Hitler when the Confessing Church* (1934-45) decried the state "German Christian Church", and was prepared to defy the Nazi state, even subvert it. The Barmen declaration (1934) is often seen as a paradigm, a manifesto of the priority of the word of God over any state-inspired ideology.

The classic questions of political thought — what is the state? why should I obey it? — are raised in the sharpest form in South Africa, though clear lines blur because of the long cultural tensions between "Boer" and "British" churches, as well as between the black, white and coloured. The 1985 Kairos document* asserts that all church life must be politicized, since "the church cannot collaborate with tyranny".

In many parts of the world critical dissent is growing, and it is by no means confined to technically "dissenting" churches. So in 1968 the Medellín (Colombia) conference of Latin American Catholic bishops set out what they considered to be the biblical doctrine of a "preferential option for the poor", and this position, later supported in principle by Pope John Paul II, is one causing tension within churches and between them and the Latin American regimes. Church base communities* are raising the aspirations of the poor* as did Methodism in 18th-century England.

What of church relationships with states which profess and support a Marxist-Leninist ideology? In the German Democratic Republic the Evangelische Kirche (Lutheran) sought "critical solidarity", while providing its churches space for discussion and dialogue. Can there be true democracy without alternative policies and free discussion? The harsher forms of Leninism are now disappearing, except in Albania and in post-Maoist China, though even in these countries there are signs of change.

The churches now have a powerful role in the extraordinary post-1989 changes in Eastern Europe. In the USSR too, the Leninist-Stalinist state is fading, the state that had sought to domesticate and undermine the Russian Orthodox Church, with worship in the churches tolerated but outreach prohibited. The churches are becoming a focus of societal renewal in parts of the Soviet empire. The dissident churches, such as the Baptists and the Ukrainian Catholics, are likely to receive civil toleration, in contrast to the pressures and persecution under Lenin, Stalin and Khrushchev.

As the 1900s draw to an end, every imaginable interpretation of Jesus' answer to the question about payment of taxes (Mark 12:13-17) has thus been found in the worldwide fellowship of the church.

JOHN MUNSEY TURNER

B.R. Bociurkiw ed., *Religion and Atheism in the USSR and Eastern Europe*, New York, Macmillan, 1975 • *Church and State: Opening a New Ecumenical Discussion*, WCC, 1978 • J. Habgood, *Church and Nation in a Secular Age*, London, Darton, Longman & Todd, 1983 • E. Norman, *Christianity in the Southern Hemisphere*, Oxford, Oxford UP, 1981 • J.M. Turner, *Conflict and Reconciliation*, London, Epworth, 1985 • A. Wilkinson, *Dissent or Conform?*, London, SCM, 1986.

CHURCH AND WORLD. Fundamental to a biblical understanding of the relation between the church and the world is the Old Testament profile of the calling of Israel among the nations. The background of this calling is the divine concern for the world as a whole (creation,* restoration); the experiment of the covenant* is the election of one people out of and for the sake of "all nations". The self-understanding of the New Testament community of believers in Jesus Christ — the people of God, the Body of Christ, the temple of the Spirit — presupposes this profile: the community is seen as a new form of the covenant among the nations and as the sign of the coming restoration. This position of the church determines its relation to the world: there is much hatred and hostility (a specific emphasis in the gospel of John and also in Paul's references to principalities and powers), but there is also a basic solidarity in suffering and hope (Rom. 8). The world is seen in the perspective of its createdness and fallenness, its relation to God (where the Greek word *kosmos* is used), or in the perspective of its impermanance, its contrast with the "age to come" (the Greek *aiōn*). All these various elements are implied in the NT concept of mission.* A vision of the church which is true to these biblical emphases will somehow integrate a reference to the "cosmic" context of creation and eschaton, a sense of a particular and distinct calling, and the basic conviction that it is in the life of the world that the signs of the kingdom* have to be made manifest.

Historical profiles. In the history of Christianity this basic biblical conviction has taken on different forms, institutionally and theologically.

Eastern (Orthodox) Christianity tends to interpret the nature of the church as a reflection of the mystery of the Trinity.* This mystery is celebrated in the eucharistic liturgy, and this celebration includes the whole created world ("the liturgy is the cosmos becoming ecclesia"). In this tradition, the term "mission" does not refer in the first place to particular activities which the church upholds in the world, but to the self-presentation of the Christian community as a "living icon of Christ". Because of this emphasis, a basic tension between the church and the institutions of culture* and politics is not a matter of principle.

In Western Christianity, the relation between church and world has developed in a more political-institutional way: there is a tension here between faith* and culture, religion and society,* church and state.* Augustine's *City of God* is of paradigmatic significance in this tradition. In the course of post-Reformation history, at least four models have become distinguishable.

The Roman Catholic model emphasizes

synthesis and continuity in the relation between the community of the people of God and the whole created world; in the encompassing framework of the divine law,* there is no ultimate contradiction between the fundamental tendencies in the life of the world and the revelation* which the church represents, although there is a duality: church and worldly institutions have distinct responsibilities.

The Lutheran model (sometimes called the doctrine of the two kingdoms; the relation of this doctrine to Luther's teaching is disputed) sees a fundamental distinction between the realm of faith and church community, and the realm of public responsibility — on the basis of a basic discontinuity between human sinfulness and divine grace.* There are two ways in which God deals with humankind: organizing human life by restricting evil, and gathering a community on the basis of the gospel of justification.* When these are confused, the nature of salvation* itself is obscured.

The Calvinist model assumes a constructive tension between gospel and world: the world is being sanctified and transformed, both in individual lives and in social structures; the institutions of public life have a function of their own to perform in the encounter of revelation and human life. This model has occasionally stimulated ideals of a "Christian commonwealth".

The model of the radical reformation sees a basic antithesis between worldly powers and the community of those who choose to follow the alternative of the gospel. The antithesis leads sometimes to virtually complete withdrawal of the church from the world, sometimes to creative forms of witness* on the basis of an attitude of non-resistance.

The development of Christianity in North America gives the impression of a melting pot in which all the available alternatives begin to look alike. The most important feature of this melting pot is disestablishment; separation between church and state is axiomatic, and all churches are "free" — including those which by tradition and conviction would opt for a form of establishment. At the same time, religion as such has an important function in culture and in public life, and many churches consider themselves as the guardians and representatives of this function. The interplay between these two factors — disestablishment

and public function — has decisively influenced the conception of the church-world relation in North America.

Churches in the so-called third world are heir to one or more of the earlier models of the relation between church and world. Nevertheless, new elements are beginning to influence not only actual missionary practice but also theological reflection. One is the minority position of the church in a context in which other religious traditions are dominant or at least alive and present; another is the fact that in many countries a new sense of national and cultural identity has grown in a struggle against Western dominance. A basic solidarity of Christians with nation* and culture goes hand in hand, therefore, with a sense of competition with other religions. The way in which missions and ethics are conceived is largely influenced by this predicament.

Theological reflection on the position and the calling of the church in the midst of and over against the realities of the world, in the wide frame of reference of creation and eschaton, comes out of this historical plurality; this reflection will therefore have to deal with the strengths and weaknesses of the various options. There may be common convictions about the missionary task or political responsibility of the church, but behind these, widely divergent interpretations of the biblical structure may be hidden. These divergences are clearly due in part to historical developments, but they are also obviously connected to differences in fundamental conviction about human nature, sin,* reconciliation* and redemption.* The relation between church and world does not constitute an isolated topic; in dealing with it, one addresses issues like the meaning of revelation and the nature of salvation.

The ecumenical movement. The growth of the ecumenical movement presupposes important changes in the experience of the relation between church and world: the development of global networks of social and economic life, the force of secularization* which stimulates this development and meanwhile has become a dominating feature of Western culture, two world wars, the process of decolonization,* and the emergence of many diverse liberation* movements. More specifically Christianity is beginning to experience the effects of cultural diversity and the influence of worldwide economic and ideological developments within itself. A rethinking of the church-world relation — more particularly, the nature of mission, the relation between general human history* and "history of salvation", the relation of church, kingdom of God and humankind — has become necessary now that the "unity of humankind"* has become a pressing issue. Various ecumenical involvements, such as the fight against racism,* the struggle against poverty,* the promotion of inter-religious dialogue* and critical reflection on the relation of women and men (see **women in church and society**), emphasize this necessity.

Important contributions of 20th-century theology have been instrumental in the development of this process of rethinking. Henri de Lubac and Karl Rahner have helped to transform the traditional Roman Catholic conception of nature* and super-nature and to define the church as the pioneer and sacrament* of a dynamic of grace* which pervades the whole of humankind. Karl Barth and Dietrich Bonhoeffer have helped to break through a paralyzing thinking in terms of two realms by emphasizing the absolute priority of God's "mission" and the concreteness of worldly obedience to this mission. Johann Baptist Metz and Jürgen Moltmann have opened the eyes of many to the destructive effects of a "political religion" which legitimizes a bourgeois narrow-mindedness with an appeal to an unworldly gospel. Liberation theologians, such as Gustavo Gutiérrez, José Míguez Bonino and Juan Luis Segundo, have radicalized this approach by linking theological reflection to the praxis of involvement in the historical struggle for the poor.* The cosmic aspects of Christology have been rediscovered by Asian theologians to the benefit of constructive thinking about inter-religious dialogue. And process theologians have consistently emphasized the open-endedness of human history and of God himself as involved in this history. On the strength of these and other contributions, and in the context of an unprecedented secularization — a loss of social and cultural support for the Christian faith which is both threatening and liberating — many Christians are rediscovering the nature of the church-in-mission and the relevance of a creation- and eschaton-oriented faith for the actual problems of humankind.

An impression of the harvest of this rethinking of the church-world relation can be gained by looking at a few important statements and documents from recent ecumenical history. One of the most important products of the Second Vatican Council was the Pastoral Constitution on the Church in the Modern World, *Gaudium et Spes* (1965). Its analysis of the problems of global society may not reach the level of later insights into issues of justice, peace and the integrity of creation, but its theological structure has been very influential. The order of creation and the order of salvation are seen in close relation to each other; the humanity of humankind is both the purpose of creation and the challenge of the gospel; the church is the sacrament, the sign, of the unification of the whole of humankind in God. For the church this implies an awareness of its position in history and its character as a pilgrim people and a readiness to cooperate with many "worldly" movements which are serving the same purpose of humanity.

Crucial for ecumenical reflection on the nature of mission was the 1952 world mission conference of the International Missionary Council in Willingen (Federal Republic of Germany). Various lines of thinking converged here: a biblical-eschatological vision of the relation of mission and kingdom of God, an effort to link the mission of the church to the signs of Christ's presence in secular history, and a battle against church-centrism in mission in favour of a "worldly" concept of salvation. Willingen helped to prepare the ground for the central role of the concept of *missio Dei* (God's mission), which places the centre of gravity of all mission in God's plan of salvation for the whole world, rather than in efforts of expansion of the church or of Western culture.

The WCC study on "The Lordship of Christ over the World and the Church" (1957, 1959) was a careful effort to summarize the Protestant thinking on the church-world relation in a period of awakening social responsibility. It tried to take up in a more dynamic fashion the traditional dualistic way of speaking about the negative situation of the fallen world and about the positive purpose of God. The world and the church are destined to become the one kingdom of God, each in its own way: the church's calling is to be a critical sign of salvation history among hostile powers, but in positive appreciation of what is given in creation.

Two reports of the WCC Department of Studies on Evangelism which greatly influenced the Uppsala assembly (1968) attempted to deal with the experience of secularization in a theologically constructive way ("The Church for Others" and "The Church for the World" — a quest for structures for missionary congregations, 1967). The relation between God and world is the decisive framework here for the definition of the "ex-centric position" of the church; the familiar sequence God-church-world should be changed into God-world-church.

The study document "God in Nature and History", presented to the Faith and Order commission at its Bristol meeting (1967), is an effort to deal with the difficulties which the development of modern science (see **science and technology**) and the experience of universal history present to the Christian faith. It seeks to show that the biblical and the modern world-views, although not identical, are not totally incompatible; that technology is rooted in the desacralization of nature, which is an aspect of biblical thinking, and can therefore be approached with an open mind; that creation and salvation are (decisive) moments in a history of God with humankind, which includes nature and is aimed towards consummation.

At its Stavanger meeting (1985) the F&O commission received a document called "The Church as Mystery and Prophetic Sign", intended as a statement of theological orientation in the study on "The Unity of the Church and the Renewal of Human Community". The document describes the relation between church and world in an eschatological perspective, i.e. in light of the kingdom of God, which is related to both church and world in judgment and grace. The church is seen as that part of humanity which acknowledges the truth of the coming kingdom. That is the church's inalienable identity; but this identity implies the recognition that what is gathered, reconciled and renewed in the church is in fact "world": what takes place in the church refers back to the world and forward to its final redemption. Both aspects of the church — "mystery" and "prophetic sign" — must be understood in this eschatological framework.

Taken together, these examples show that the ecumenical experience has generally led to a more positive appreciation of "the world" and simultaneously to a more dynamic interpretation of the role of the church vis-a-vis the whole of humankind. A rediscovery of OT notions as well as of the cosmic significance of Christ may have contributed to this involvement. Meanwhile, more radical questions with regard to the survival of humankind and the sustainability of life on the planet are likely to stimulate further thinking on creation and eschaton and might ultimately lead away from the Christocentric missionary paradigm which has tended to dominate ecumenical thinking until recently.

See also **church and state, creation, eschatology, unity of humankind**.

LIBERTUS A. HOEDEMAKER

H. Küng, *Die Kirche* (ET *The Church*, London, Burns & Oates, 1968) • J. Moltmann, *Kirche in der Kraft des Geistes* (ET *The Church in the Power of the Spirit*, New York, Harper, 1977) • H.R. Niebuhr, *Christ and Culture*, New York, Harper, 1951 • H.R. Niebuhr, *The Social Sources of Denominationalism*, New York, Holt, 1929 • E. Troeltsch, *Die Soziallehren der christlichen Kirchen und Gruppen* (ET *The Social Teachings of the Christian Churches*, New York, Macmillan, 1931) • G.F. Vicedom, *Missio Dei, Einführung in eine Theologie der Mission*, Munich, Kaiser, 1958.

CHURCH AS INSTITUTION.

The institutional nature of the church* has been the subject of WCC studies from both theological and sociological perspectives. The Theological Commission on Christ and the Church (1952-63) described the church as at once "essential and provisional" and (following Barth) as "event and institution", while the study on institutionalism (1955-63) stressed that the church was not just a divine-human community (koinonia*) but a historical institution, similar in structure to other social institutions. A later study on spirit, order and organization (1964-71) focused on the activities of the Spirit in transforming the forms and structures of church life; and one on the missionary structure of the congregation (1962-67) pointed out that church structures can help or hinder its missionary purpose (see **mission**). Protestant churches engaged in reshaping inherited structures drew insights from this study, as also increasingly from the sociology of organizations, although these insights were often applied half-heartedly and sometimes without due regard to theological considerations.

A similar debate arose within the Roman Catholic Church after Vatican II,* which in *Lumen Gentium* put primary emphasis (following Yves Congar) on the church as the people of God,* yet also retained the traditional view of the church as a divine institution manifest in history through the Catholic hierarchy. The resulting ambiguity, together with uncertainty regarding the limits of permissible change, led to a tension between more traditional and more radical views of the church as institution. After the anti-institutional fervour of 1968, many Catholics were led to distance themselves from "the institutional church" and to set up church base communities* (CBCs, also known as basic Christian communities) both in Europe and most notably in the third world. During the 1970s, small Christian communities emerged in Protestant churches as well — some (like the CBCs) with a socio-political commitment, others with a more personal or charismatic orientation — and appealed to many (especially younger) Christians dissatisfied with the institutionalized character of the larger churches. In Latin America the rapid growth of CBCs accompanied the development of liberation theology,* not so much in opposition to existing church structures as in the gaps left by a thinly spread diocesan system.

While some European observers see the institutional church as doomed, others (like the Catholic Karl Rahner and the Reformed theologian Jürgen Moltmann) believe that "double strategies" of church reform are necessary, both from below and from above. The Brazilian theologian Leonardo Boff encountered the opposition of the Vatican when he asked bluntly: Can the institutional church be converted? Boff himself believes that it can, that there is "a new way of being church" — one that is more flexible and more lightly institutionalized. Many third-world Christians would agree with him; European CBCs have come to the same conclusion.

Gerd Theissen has recently shown that the original Jesus movement, like other protest groups, inevitably became institutionalized on its transference to Hellenistic culture. A similar process is visible today in many Pentecos-

tal and charismatic churches. Some commentators point to a possible shift in the other direction, as "old-line Protestant churches" in the West begin to relinquish their establishment character and are revitalized by contemporary movements critical of hierarchies and bureaucracies. To contrast such movements with "the institutional church" is both inexact and confusing. Ian Fraser, Christian Duquoc and Moltmann, among others, in different ways insist, like the earlier studies, that the church is *both* movement *and* institution, and that what must above all be avoided is a church institution which seeks to wield power and to control its members.

See also **church, church discipline, church order**.

STEVEN G. MACKIE

L. Boff, *Igreja, Carisma et Poder* (ET *Church, Charism and Power: Liberation Theology and the Institutional Church*, London, SCM, 1985) • C. Duquoc, *Des Eglises provisoires: essai d'ecclésiologie œcuménique* (ET *Provisional Churches: An Essay in Ecumenical Ecclesiology*, London, SCM, 1986) • M. Fraser & I. Fraser, *Wind and Fire: The Spirit Reshapes the Church in Basic Christian Communities*, Dunblane, Scottish Churches' Council, 1986 • P.S. Minear ed., *Faith and Order Findings: The Final Report of the Theological Commissions to the Fourth World Conference on Faith and Order, Montreal, 1963*, London, SCM, 1963 • M.A. Thung, *The Precarious Organization: Sociological Explorations of the Church's Mission and Structure*, The Hague, Mouton, 1976.

CHURCH BASE COMMUNITIES.

CBCs, or grassroots Christian communities, denote a new pastoral experiment or, rather, a new comprehensive church movement that sprang up in Latin America and has spread worldwide since the 1960s. They consist of groups of Christian laypeople, generally poor, who meet regularly (once a week or fortnightly) in private houses or on communal premises to hear and ponder the word of God,* to nourish a spirit of fraternal community and to undertake activities of Christian commitment in the world.

CBCs are especially widespread in Brazil, Chile and Bolivia, as well as Central America and Mexico. In Africa they are found in Zaire, Zambia, Tanzania, Cameroon, Malawi, Uganda, Kenya, Rwanda, Burundi and Burkina Faso. In Asia they are present in the

Philippines, India and Malaysia. Western Europe has a significant CBC movement, especially in Spain, Italy, Germany, Netherlands and Belgium. Nor are they absent from Eastern Europe: Hungary and Poland have their CBCs, and they even exist in the Soviet Union, as well as in China, the USA and Canada.

The internal structure of CBCs varies considerably. Some consist of elementary groups of 10 to 15 called biblical circles, evangelization groups or fraternal encounters, which meet usually on their own initiative in their homes. Others initially form a community of families (15 or more) and meet in a chapel or communal premises. Both types have (1) coordination, linking and promoting the advance of the whole community; (2) a programme of activities, including worship, formation, festivities and celebration of the sacraments; (3) organization of the various services (lay ministries), such as care of the sick, catechesis, liturgy and administration of baptism. Springing up and developing within the ambit of parishes, CBCs maintain with them a relation of communion and renewal.

The constitutive elements of every CBC are (1) the Bible,* heard and shared jointly and related to the life of the people; (2) the community, united and organized in its various services; and (3) the concrete commitments which the community undertakes in the line of justice and solidarity (social charity).

These elements make it clear why CBCs are called *communities* (because they are primary groupings in which relations of deep fraternal communion* prevail), *church*, or ecclesial (because they are actually religious, and specifically Christian groups, which meet in church on the basis of the word of God), and *base*, or basic (because they constitute elementary associations — as it were, church cells or miniature churches). In fact their starting point is the "basic" constituents of the church: word, faith, baptism, fraternal charity, service of others, etc., so that they constitute the base or basis of the church, which is the laity. This primary ecclesiological sense of the term "base" means "of the people", "popular". In fact the CBCs spring from the poor strata of the population and for that reason are generally found in the countryside and on the outskirts of towns.

Origins and development. Various social and religious factors influenced the emergence of CBCs in Latin America in the 1960s. This period was known in Latin America as the decade of development.* It was a time of great economic progress and enormous social vitality, particularly on the popular level. That vitality, stimulated from above by populist governments, found expression in extremely varied social movements: trade unionism, basic education, communal organization, technical assistance and general human advancement. The triumph of the Cuban revolution (1959), with its repercussions on the continent, served to hasten the process of popular ferment. This was the soil in which the CBCs took root. The end of the "development illusion" and the emergence of a different social consciousness (dependence*/liberation*) at the end of the decade, as well as the rise of military regimes, did not hinder but rather promoted the advance of CBCs.

In the historical climate just described, how did the church react? The elements involved were complex, but the following stand out. First, the crisis and breakdown of traditional pastoral practice centred on the parish and clergy, which was no longer able to reach the Catholic masses of the Latin American continent. This breakdown acted as a sort of "negative cause", as a challenge, and prompted positive reactions in the direction of what eventually became CBCs. Second, the emergence of the social pastoral action of the church united activists of Specialized Catholic Action and prophetic bishops such as D. Larrain (Talca, Chile), D. Hélder Camara (Recife, Brazil) and others. Then, the powerful drive for church renewal of Vatican II brought added justification and powerful impulses to the nascent popular pastoral movement. Fourth, the Latin American bishops' conference (CELAM) in its assemblies at Medellín (1968) and Puebla (1979) formally confirmed the existing experiment of the CBCs and re-launched it on a continental scale. Finally, the 1974 synod of bishops of the Catholic church, the results of which were embodied by Paul VI in *Evangelii Nuntiandi* (1975), recognized CBCs as a valid type of enterprise throughout the church (no. 58 in the document).

Subsequently in the midst of this cultural, social and ecclesial ferment, thanks to the initiative of some priests, focal points of church creativity sprang into life all over the

Church base community in Ecuador (Sebastião Salgado)

continent and in the third world generally, at first in the still indeterminate form of popular groups, where concern for human advancement combined with the aim of religious formation, which developed into clearly defined CBCs. In Brazil, which was in the vanguard of this process, the first CBC may be identified as that of St Paulo do Potengi (diocese of Natal, northeast Brazil), in the early 1960s, led by Mgr Expedito of Medeiros. The emergency plan of the Brazilian bishops' national conference, drawn up in 1962 on the recommendation of John XXIII in the light of the then-existing experiments, itself launched the idea of CBCs as an innovative and promising pastoral project. The General Pastoral Plan, 1966-70, drawn up in 1965, presents the CBCs as a pastoral priority on the national level.

It is significant, however, that in recent times the "communitarian principle" has become increasingly widespread — and not only in the churches. One of its chief sources continues to be a reaction against the anonymity of modern mass societies, perhaps most expressively kindled and symbolized by the 1968 revolution. This had its counterpart within the churches to the extent that they, too, represented rigid mass institutions. In the

first world this desire for personal involvement through the medium of the community indubitably represents the most powerful factor in the communitarian phenomenon. That relatively independent factor was subsequently reinforced in church circles by the influence of the CBCs of the third world. In Africa and Asia the process seems to have been similar. Internal factors, among them African tribal culture and the social situation of religious minorities in Asia, were reinforced by the example of the Latin America CBCs, thus stimulating the emergence of their own CBCs. The CBCs are nothing but a particular expression of the phenomenon of communitarianism, though a new and significant one, particularly in church terms. In every case where people meet together, whoever they may be socially and wherever they are, in order to take up responsibility for their own faith and the demands it makes, a church base community has come into being.

CBCs and the institutional church. The CBCs are offspring of the institutional church. The pastoral agencies of the church itself — priests, sisters or laity — in most cases initiated them and continue to run them.

The process of developing relations between CBCs and the institutional church runs through various stages, generally as follows. At first the CBCs spring up in the margins of the institutional church, among the masses whom the church's pastoral ministry cannot reach. There is then a real process of ecclesiogenesis, i.e. a birth of the church, but now in new patterns: lay, popular, participatory, biblical, evangelical, prophetic, liberating. Subsequently, as they grow, the CBCs make their way into the domain of the existing institutional church. They become present and influential in liturgy, catechesis and meetings. Then comes a period of more or less painful conflict with the institution, for the "new way of being the church" (as the CBCs define themselves) clashes with the traditional way and with its centralizing tendency. Finally, if things go right (as has usually happened in Latin America), this new way is accepted by the church authorities. From then on, it tends to predominate in the structuring and general activities of the local community — parish, diocese, region and even country. Even so, traditional forms of church organization (i.e. a type of clerical church, sacramentalist and socially uncommitted) continue to exist, often scarcely modernized.

The ecclesiological status of the CBCs is actually no longer that of a church movement, but rather of *the whole church in movement*. The CBCs are not in themselves a new type of church. They represent, rather, a comprehensive project or idea of the church, a new dynamic — in fact a "new mode of being" (new, that is, in comparison with the traditional type, not with the New Testament ideal). The new church model, formed around the axis of the CBCs, comprises the whole force of the renewal and innovation which is emerging in the church institution: renewal of the *traditional parish* and its activities: catechesis, liturgy, sacraments, ordained ministries, etc.; emergence of *new pastoral services*, both internal and external in scope, such as pastoral concern for the sick, for children, for Indians, for blacks, for workers, for human rights; rescue of *popular religion* and piety with its festivities, pilgrimages, novenas, etc.; creation of new *church movements* such as those serving youth, women, industrial workers and farmers; finally, creation and strengthening of independent *popular movements*: associations, trade unions and parties. All this is what constitutes the church of the poor or people's church, of which the CBCs are not merely a part but the living tissue.

Bible reading in the CBCs. The cornerstone of the CBCs is the word of God. Members come together in order to hear it, thus constituting an ecclesia, i.e. the assembly of those called together by the word. What primarily and specifically constitutes the CBCs is therefore not friendship or even the struggle for survival or social change but the word which gives rise to faith. In the CBCs the word of God is received directly in the Bible, its prime witness, and not in secondary witnesses such as catechism, documents of the magisterium or some particular theology, not even the theology of liberation.

In the CBCs the Bible is always read face to face with the actual life of the people. This is the Bible/life method, a procedure that obviates any spiritualizing fundamentalism. It sets the word in the real living conditions of the people: a struggle for survival and for social change. Bible and life are linked in a hermeneutical circle: the Bible leads to vital commitment, and vital commitment to better understanding of the Bible. The opposite danger, of making a political tool of the Bible, does exist, but more for the middle-class activist than for the people, who possess a deep sense of God and sincere respect for religious things.

We must also note that Bible reading in the CBCs is done in a communal, i.e. participatory way. Furthermore it is an extremely flexible and creative reading, rather like the *sensus spiritualis* (spiritual sense) of the fathers, only here it is very "material".

It may be said that the CBCs express and transmit the great hunger and thirst for the word of God felt by the religious and disinherited masses of the third world. The re-appropriation of the Bible by them is leading to renewal of the church and transformation of society in accord with the purposes of the Spirit, who inspired the sacred books.

CBCs and social commitment. The CBCs are communities committed to striving for justice. Dedication to social transformation — i.e. the dimension of liberation — is constitutive of this new church experience/movement. This dimension does not always appear from the beginning in the way it does when a CBC owes its existence to a particular social conflict. But it is present from the start at least in the form of openness and interest. It is the actual growth of the community, on the basis of the dynamic relation between gospel and life, which leads to the real creation and deepening of social commitment. In fact such commitment develops in various stages: (1) mutual help within the community and with the neighbourhood; (2) participation in struggles in the place of residence or perhaps in associations; (3) entry into the world of work, with its trade union and other campaigns; (4) finally, party-political involvement in various degrees.

In this sense the CBCs in Latin America have been seedbeds of many popular organizations and continue to provide them with active participants and support. Nevertheless the CBCs know that their specific function is not to organize the social struggle, except on a secondary level. Thus they endeavour to bring into existence and to strengthen, alongside and linked with themselves, independent popular agencies such as associations, trade unions and parties. The CBCs have evangelization as their own specific and permanent function, but always in the perspective of liberation and therefore adapted to the demands of each historical moment.

This element of social commitment may create problems, such as that of the radical secularization of militants originating in the CBCs but deviating from them, or the temptation of "neo-Christendom", the impression sometimes given by CBCs that they can transform society on their own, or the notion that the social question will be solved the day when everyone is like them.

CBCs and ecumenism. CBCs are of particular ecumenical significance by the mere fact that they re-create the church on the pattern of the early church and not as a reproduction of the prevailing type of church. By their essential or elementary character they emphasize not the denominational (in Latin America, typically Catholic) aspects but rather the common Christian elements: baptism, the centrality of faith in Jesus Christ, the sacred scriptures, the Lord's supper, charity, witness, etc. This is not a case (as is sometimes suggested) of Protestantizing the Catholic church, for this would be to fall back into the domain of denominationalism. Rather, the CBCs are striving to get nearer to the one and undivided church, like the apostolic church.

In consequence, while preserving their origin and denominational identity (demonstrated by communion with their own church through their own pastors), the CBCs have achieved an original kind of ecumenical activity. This is marked by two distinctive features. First, it is built around charity (practice) and not around faith (doctrine). In other words, the Christian poor meet in the same struggles, where they get to know and esteem one another and only subsequently come to pray together and to discuss their respective religious convictions. Second, the ecumenical practice of the CBCs is at the church-base level among simple believers and therefore not in the upper reaches of hierarchy and theology. Simple believers, especially if they are poor, are more genuine and free in regard to ecumenical dialogue.

If, however, many Catholics and Protestants — the "historic" Christians — feel at home in the style of "basic Christianity", there is also resistance, opposition and competition on the part of many sects because of their biblical fundamentalism and political conservatism. There is also some of the traditional anti-Protestant prejudice of Catholic circles in the CBCs.

Conclusion. The process has scarcely begun of forming a new church model (not a new church), i.e. a participatory and liberating church model, of which the CBCs are the living cells and embodiment. The journey is a long one and full of conflicts, precisely because it is new and historic. Nevertheless everything indicates that the way has been found. It is a matter now of going ahead, at the impulse of the Spirit.

CLODOVIS BOFF

L. Boff, *Ecclesiogenesis*, Maryknoll, NY, Orbis 1986 • *Concilium* 104, 1975, and 164, 1981 • G. Cook, *The Expectation of the Poor: Latin American Ecclesial Communities in Protestant Perspective*, Maryknoll, NY, Orbis, 1985 • M. Fraser & I. Fraser, *Wind and Fire: The Spirit Reshapes the Church in Basic Communities*, Dunblane, Basic Communities Resource Centre, 1986 • *Good News from the Poor: Basic Communities in the Third World*, London, Catholic Institute for International Relations, 1985 • T. Highton & G. Kirby, *The Challenge of the House Churches*, Oxford, Latimer, 1988 • J. O'Halloran, *Living Cells: Developing Small Christian Communities*, Maryknoll, NY, Orbis, 1984.

CHURCH CALENDAR. The idea of a liturgical calendar must not be confused with that of the civil (solar) calendar. The point of the latter is to count the days in relation to the tropical solar cycle with its four seasons: spring, summer, autumn and winter. These four seasons are defined by the four phases through which the earth passes as it goes round the sun. We have the spring equinox (when day and night are equal), the summer solstice (the longest day), the autumn equinox (when day and night are equal) and finally the winter solstice (the shortest day and longest night). Thus in a good solar calendar we can know the dates which correspond to the four phases just mentioned, which may be described as cosmic events.

The purpose of the liturgical calendar is entirely different from that of the (solar) civil calendar. The liturgical calendar is not concerned with the tally of days. The church uses the civil calendar which science has already fixed and gives it a liturgical content. The criterion for this content is the light which at one point of time is eclipsed by the darkness and at another makes the darkness disappear. Thus the sun becomes, as it were, an icon of God, and the darkness becomes a symbol of death. In this scheme of thinking, cosmic events (i.e. the two equinoxes and the two solstices) have a liturgical meaning which represents the struggle of light with darkness. For example the winter solstice (when the day begins to become longer) corresponds to the nativity of Christ (in the northern hemisphere); the spring equinox (when the day begins to be dominant) corresponds to the annunciation and also to Easter, etc.

In Julius Caesar's day (46 B.C.), a solar calendar was introduced in the Roman empire. It is called the Julian (or Old Style) calendar. It has 365 days in the year, and every fourth year an additional day (29 February) is added to ensure that the calendar dates correspond to the sun. As a result of the inaccuracy of this correction, the calendar falls behind the sun by one day every 128 years. In practical terms this means that around the time of the first council of Nicea (325), which defined the principle for dating Easter, the spring equinox, which was on 25 March in 46 B.C., fell on 21 March. Thus the calendar date of 25 March had fallen behind the cosmic event it was supposed to reflect.

In 1582 the calendar date corresponding to the spring equinox had become 11 March (10 days behind the situation in the 4th century). The church of Rome under Pope Gregory XIII then decided to correct the calendar again. By eliminating ten calendar dates (5-14 October 1582 inclusive), the date of the spring equinox was restored to 21 March (instead of 11 March), as it had been in the 4th century. And to prevent the calendar's falling behind in the future, it was decided to eliminate the 29th day of February three times in every period of 400 years. The calendar thus corrected is known as the Gregorian (or New Style) calendar.

At present the Julian calendar is at odds with solar time by 13 days, and the spring equinox, instead of occurring on 21 March, which is still the ostensible date for it, actually falls on 8 March. On the other hand, the Gregorian calendar agrees with the sun and will continue to do so for a very long time. It lags behind the sun by around one day for every 3,323 years instead of 128 years in the Julian calendar.

As to the fixed liturgical cycle, i.e. liturgical events with fixed calendar dates, two practices are followed in the Orthodox church. The majority follow the New Style, the others the Old. Thus Christmas is fixed for December 25; and if the Russian Church, for example, appears to celebrate the feast at the present time on 7 January (New, or Gregorian, Style), this day is in fact 25 December according to the Old, or Julian, Style.

The movable (paschal) cycle is not fixed for specific dates of the solar calendar but depends on the date of Easter — "the feast of feasts" — which changes from year to year in accordance with the principle worked out in 325 at Nicea. It was decided to celebrate Easter on a Sunday chosen in relation to the sun and the moon, the "two great lights" (Gen. 1:16). First comes the spring equinox, corresponding to the point in the year when the day (the sunlight) begins to triumph over night. Next comes the full moon, when the "lesser light" is on the dark side of the earth (that away from the sun) to "rule [or illuminate] the night" (Gen. 1:16), and thus the earth is simultaneously lit on both sides. Finally, the first Sunday after this phenomenon becomes Easter Day.

According to a 4th-century document by an author from Asia Minor, "Une homélie anatolienne sur la date de Pâques en l'an 387", the Nicene formula for the date of Easter — the feast of Christ's resurrection — is regarded as having a direct link with the "week of creation". The "week of redemption" is only its fulfilment.

The spring equinox recalls the first day of creation (Gen. 1:5). The full moon is the fourth day, when "God made the two great lights, the greater light [the sun] to rule the day, and the lesser light [the moon] to rule the night" (Gen. 1:16). Finally, the first Sunday, corresponding in this context to the eighth day, follows both Friday, the sixth day (the creation of human beings and their fall), and Saturday, the seventh day (on which God rested and which the Christian church regards as Christ's descent "to the dead", or "into hell", prior to his resurrection).

In practice the formula for dating Easter is applied by waiting, in the first place, for the day of the spring equinox. Counting from it, the first full moon (which might fall at the equinox itself) is the paschal moon (the Old Testament Passover), and thus the first Sunday following that full moon is the Christian Easter Day.

To make it easier to apply the paschal formula, the Christian church began quite early to compile paschal tables giving the date of Easter for relatively long periods. In about the 7th century, paschal tables appeared covering a period of 532 years in conformity with the Julian calendar. These tables were regarded as perpetual; i.e. at the end of that period of 532 years, everything should begin again in the same order.

The Orthodox church has used these tables right up to the present. According to them, 21 March Old Style should always be the day of the spring equinox. According to the New Style that day is already 3 April, i.e. 13 days later than the actual spring equinox.

For Western Christians, the necessary correction was introduced into these tables after the Gregorian reform in 1582, so that the festival of Easter depends on the actual spring equinox. This is the only reason for the difference between Western and Eastern Christians as to the date of Easter. The idea that the Orthodox supposedly reckon the date from the Jewish Passover, which Western Christians do not, is a serious misunderstanding. The full moon of the Nicene formula happens in fact to coincide always with the OT Passover.

All the full moons occurring between 21 March and 3 April (New Style) are paschal moons for the Western Christians but not for the Orthodox. In this case the Orthodox Easter will come after the second full moon — making a difference of four or five weeks in the dates.

It may be hoped that in their quest for unity, Christians will come to agree on a calendar as close as possible to the solar system and that this will enable them to celebrate all the great festivals of the liturgical year together, especially Easter, the "Feast of Feasts", by applying together the principle adopted at Nicea I.

See also **Easter, Pentecost**.

NICOLAS OSSORGUINE

"Report of the Consultation on a Fixed Date for Easter", *The Ecumenical Review*, 22, 2, 1971.

CHURCH DISCIPLINE. In a characteristic sense, "church discipline" (French, *discipline ecclésiastique*; German, *Kirchenzucht*) is the term used above all in Reformed churches and some communities of the radical Reformation for that procedure by which God's word is applied by particular exhortation to individual members and, more specifically, to cases that fall under the provisions of Matt. 18:15-18, whereby faults in the congregation are to be treated first by way of fraternal conversation, then by a small group (usually pastors and elders), and finally, if still necessary, before the whole church. To the true preaching of the gospel and the obedient administration of the sacraments, Calvin and many Reformed confessions added "right order" or "the exercise of discipline" as a third mark by which the church on earth can be recognized (Calvin, *Institutes* 4.1.1,22; 4.10.27-32; 4.11.1-5; 4.12.1-21; Belgic confession, 29; Scots confession, 18). According to the Westminster confession, "church censures are necessary for the reclaiming and gaining of offending brethren; for deterring of others from the like offences; for purging out of that leaven which might infect the whole lump; for vindicating the honour of Christ, and the holy profession of the gospel; and for preventing the wrath of God, which might justly fall upon the church, if they should suffer his covenant, and the seals thereof, to be profaned by notorious and obstinate offenders" (30:3).

Combining the concerns that figured in the so-called church orders of the early centuries (from the *Didache* onward), church discipline in a broader sense covers in their entirety the regulation, standards and pattern of the spiritual and moral life of Christians and their communities. It always takes some juridical form (see **canon law**), but it also involves pastoral care and looks for faithful observance on the part of all believers. All would-be Christian communities in fact practise an ecclesial discipline of one kind or another. But they differ over the *proper* discipline, over which elements in it should be attributed to "divine law" and which to merely "human law" within the church (often as the question of the variability or invariability of particular disciplinary dispositions), over whether and when the juridical order should be understood as advisory guideline or as binding law (Lukas Vischer), and over the importance they attach to discipline in relation to other features of church life; they differ in the relative rigour or laxity with which they put their discipline into practice; and amid the vicissitudes of political history, they have differed over the appropriate relation between church discipline and civil law.

The most fundamental matter in church discipline concerns the requirements for entry into, and continuance in, the ecclesial community. Baptism is almost always a necessary, but seldom the sufficient, condition of church membership. Thus the British Methodist church regards both baptism and the Lord's supper to be of "divine appointment and perpetual obligation", and abstinence for long from the communal means of grace could lead to the removal of a member's name from the rolls on grounds of having "ceased to meet". The (Anglican) Church of England requires that "every parishioner shall communicate at least three times in the year, of which Easter to be one". To be a Roman Catholic, one must belong to a local church whose bishop is in communion with the see of Rome. In practically all would-be Christian bodies, a member may for various fail-

ings suffer varying degrees of suspension or even exclusion from communion (see **excommunication**).

The ecclesial community makes certain requirements of faith and morals. It is expected that one will continue in the faith to which one has been summoned and invited by the preaching of the gospel, the faith in which one was baptized and which finds eucharistic expression in the celebration of the Lord's supper. That is why the search epitomized by Faith and Order's project "Towards the Common Expression of the Apostolic Faith Today" is a vital part of the restoration and achievement of church unity: unity is impossible without agreement in what is commonly "necessary and sufficient" to the Christian faith. Similarly, all churches cherish certain moral expectations of their members. Yet in this case, a curious reticence is noticeable in ecumenical dialogues, both multilateral and bilateral, concerning the treatment of ethical teaching. The international Methodist-Roman Catholic dialogue was a modest pioneer in daring to mention issues of home and family life (Denver 1971, paras 69-78; cf. Dublin 1976, para. 39), while the tripartite Lutheran-Reformed-Roman Catholic statement on "The Theology of Marriage and the Problem of Mixed Marriages" (1977) went somewhat further.

Almost all churches assign to "pastors and teachers" (Eph. 4:11), however named, a special role in the maintenance of church discipline. They are to instruct all members in the faith; "in them", as *Baptism, Eucharist and Ministry** puts it, "the church seeks an example of holiness and loving concern" (M12); and they are usually the ones principally entrusted with the ministry of encouragement, admonition, and (where necessary) rebuke and even excommunication. Their duties call for their own fidelity to Christian doctrine in faith and morals as their church receives and perceives it, and for their own acceptance of ecclesial discipline. None of this responsibility should be seen in terms of a personal superiority in faith or practice on the part of an ordained ministry; it is rather a functional necessity for the edification of the church and all its members. In Calvin's words: "Thus the body of Christ is built up; thus 'we grow up in every way into him who is the Head' and grow together among ourselves" (*Institutes*

4.3.2). Discipline subserves the church in its primordial responsibilities of worship (leitourgia), witness (martyria) and service (diakonia).

Clearly, different versions of ecclesial discipline reflect basic options and guiding perspectives in the areas of Christology, pneumatology, and the understanding of the gospel and of the church. The legal structure of the Roman Catholic Church emphasizes Christ the legislator, and both Orthodox and Protestant critics have considered this an overemphasis. The more sacramentally and pneumatologically inspired concept of the Orthodox churches can nevertheless leave their canonical order "fixed" at an early stage of the Tradition that has difficulty in accommodating to changes in the social and cultural context. Lutherans make a sharp distinction, even opposition, between law and gospel, and other Christians have feared there a resulting antinomianism. Calvinists and Methodists have allowed a "third use of the law" as serving the sanctification* of believers, and the danger here is of hypocrisy for the sake of outward observance. "Enthusiastic" communities have exalted spontaneity in ways that threaten to divorce the Spirit from the word of God* and the great Tradition.*

Although there will probably always be variety in the detailed translation of the faith into practice, particularly as historical circumstances differ, yet the attainment and recognition of consensus* in major doctrines should have the result of bringing the disciplines of the churches within recognizably common bounds of principle. In turn, work on current disciplinary differences could help the churches in their search for a common expression of the faith.

See also **canon law, church, church order, excommunication**.

GEOFFREY WAINWRIGHT

H. Dombois, *Das Recht der Gnade*, vol. 1, 1969; vol. 2, 1974; vol. 3, 1983; Witten, Luther Verlag • S.L. Greenslade, *Shepherding the Flock: Problems of Pastoral Discipline in the Early Church and in the Younger Churches Today*, London, SCM, 1967 • M. Jeschke, *Disciplining the Brother: Congregational Discipline according to the Gospel*, Scottdale, PA, Herald, 1972 • M. Plathow, *Lehre und Ordnung im Leben der Kirche heute*, Göttingen, Vandenhoeck & Ruprecht, 1982 • L. Vischer, "Reform of Canon Law: An Ecumenical Problem", *The Jurist*, 26, 1966.

CHURCH GROWTH. From the inception of the church, reports on its progess have frequently included reference to its numerical size (e.g. Acts 2:41). A goal of missionary outreach was the winning of new adherents to the faith (see **mission**). Debates about missionary strategy surrounding the work of outstanding figures such as Francis Xavier, Robert de Nobili, Matteo Ricci, John Eliot or David Livingstone focused on the most effective means of adding converts rather than whether or not growth of the church was a legitimate goal. In the 19th century the goal of mission was defined to be the establishment of an "indigenous church" which aimed at self-propagation or growth.

The term "church growth" has become a technical term since the 1950s and is now identified with a particular missiological approach. Donald A. McGavran, who served in India with the US Disciples of Christ missionary society, published *The Bridges of God* and *How Churches Grow*, in which he critically evaluated the traditional missionary approach and forcefully advocated a radical overhaul.

Like Rufus Anderson and Henry Venn in the 19th century and Roland Allen in the early 20th, McGavran attacked the "mission station" mentality. He argued that missions ought to respect the social unit — ethnic clan, class, caste — in which the individual is most at home and seek to win groups to Christ. He refined this concept as the "homogeneous unit principle" (HUP). Observing that the degree of responsiveness varies from one group to another, McGavran argued that missions should place priority on responsive groups. He called for a re-orientation of missions and offered a strategy based on people groups. He advocated thoroughgoing scientific research. In 1961 McGavran founded the Institute of Church Growth at Eugene, Oregon, which merged in 1965 with the School of World Mission of Fuller Theological Seminary in Pasadena, California, with McGavran as dean.

McGavran built on a tradition of research and evaluation in various parts of the world conducted by the Survey Application Trust (World Dominion) and national Christian councils in a number of countries. He himself had participated in some of these surveys in India in the 1930s in collaboration with J. Waskom Picket and others.

McGavran sought from the beginning to get a hearing for his concerns in ecumenical circles, but the climate was not favourable. In 1950 J.C. Hoekendijk had published a highly influential article in the *International Review of Missions (IRM)*, "The Call to Evangelism", in which he roundly criticized ecclesiocentric mission. Hoekendijk called for the abandonment of church planting as a goal of mission. By the early 1960s this line of thought had gone even further in the direction of what was called the "secular gospel".

In 1963 the department of missionary studies of the WCC convened a "Consultation on Church Growth" at Iberville, near Montreal, with McGavran participating. The October 1963 *IRM* carried a report: "Growth: A Test of the Church's Faithfulness". The official Iberville statement was not published in *IRM* until 1968. In 1965 *IRM* published an article by McGavran, "Wrong Strategy: The Real Crisis in Mission". This elicited strongly negative reactions in WCC circles. The July 1968 issue featured seven articles by an international panel of writers critical of McGavran's viewpoint and two by those that were sympathetic. McGavran was criticized for his emphasis on numerical growth as the primary criterion of mission, his inadequate ecclesiology and the fact that his approach was "a faulty American strategy".

Among non-conciliar Protestants there had been a revival of emphasis on the "indigenous church" ideal after the second world war, and McGavran's ideas found an enthusiastic reception in these circles. Since the 1960s the movement has been identified largely with conservative Protestants. Church growth has been a major force in their missiology since 1965. That is not to say it has not had its critics even among those sympathetic to its goals. While not dismissing church-growth thinking, conservative Protestants have offered theological critiques of the HUP (a position that McGavran himself subsequently abandoned), the overweening emphasis on pragmatism, the unsatisfactory exegetical foundation and the ideological pitfalls inherent in such a system. In this connection criticism has been forthcoming from the non-Western world, including South Africa and Latin America.

See also **evangelism, mission**.

WILBERT R. SHENK

D.A. McGavran, *Understanding Church Growth*, Grand Rapids, MI, Eerdmans, 1970 • D.A. McGavran ed., *The Conciliar-Evangelical Debate: The Crucial Documents, 1964-1976*, South Pasadena, CA, William Carey, 1977 • W.R. Shenk ed., *Exploring Church Growth*, Grand Rapids, MI, Eerdmans, 1983 • W.T. Thomas, "Growth: A Test of the Church's Faithfulness", *International Review of Missions*, 52, 1963 • C.P. Wagner, *Our Kind of People*, Atlanta, GA, John Knox, 1979.

CHURCH MUSIC. Any music used in or associated with Christian worship can be considered church music. Both presently and historically, there is a great variety of musical forms, styles and performance practices in the various Christian churches. Such differences in musical practice may indicate underlying differences in theological emphasis, since the music used in Christian worship reflects a church's interpretation of its liturgy.* (Likewise, similarities may indicate ecumenical agreement or convergence on theological issues.) Much of the significant diversity stems from two factors: (1) an emphasis on different liturgical functions of music, especially those concerning its relationship with the words of the service; (2) differing interpretations of the liturgy, which lead to different requirements for its performance.

Liturgical functions. The church has generally regarded music as an essential part of the liturgy because it supports the liturgy's purpose: praise of God. Most churches agree that this means that the music must in some way be surbordinated to the larger aims of the liturgy; however, they have differed widely in their attempts to provide acceptable music. For example, in most Eastern Orthodox churches, the liturgy is primarily chanted and generally unaccompanied by instruments: vocal music is considered normative, since the words of the liturgy keep the function of the music clear. In contrast, the role of music has gradually changed in Western liturgies. While it has often consisted entirely of vocal music, Western churches gradually accepted instruments starting in the 8th century and deemphasized chant (cultivating polyphony) from the 12th century on.

In all churches, musical practices and the liturgy have interacted in two important ways. First, music has influenced the interpretation of liturgical texts and actions. Even in a largely chanted service, music indicates how a text is to be performed and understood, by punctuating the text through melodic formulas and cadences; by emphasizing words through melisma, or repetition; and by organizing the length and balance of each section of the liturgy. Changes in musical style alter the delivery of the texts and have often been considered disruptive of the liturgy, consequently causing conflict. For example, as early as the 4th century, a melodic style of chanting imported from the East caused considerable controversy as it spread through Western churches. According to Augustine, the problem was that the music could detract from the words by calling attention to itself. Such tensions between words and music have been heightened in the West by the development of functional harmony, which aims at relatively autonomous musical forms, making words dispensable or interchangeable. However, these forms have not been found necessarily incompatible with the supporting of words, as the widespread popularity of the accompanied hymn suggests. In practice, even purely instrumental music has generally been tied to words or liturgical actions: substituting for words, as in the *alternatim* practice of the late middle ages; referring to words, as in the Lutheran chorale prelude; or highlighting an important action, as in the baroque elevation toccatas.

Second, changes in liturgical style and content can lead to a sense of musical deficiency. For instance, the translation of liturgies into various vernaculars has provoked changes as diverse as the growth of divergent families of Byzantine chant and the development of the Lutheran chorale. More recently, the Second Vatican Council's emphasis on the vernacular and the transplanting of various Eastern churches to the West have led to the creation of many new or adapted vernacular settings.

Performance practice. Most churches agree that the liturgy requires the active participation of all those assembled; however, there is little agreement about how such participation should be reflected in church music. For instance, in Eastern churches there is a predominantly sung liturgy, but the singing parts are mostly taken by ministers, cantors or choirs; congregational participation largely consists of (active) listening. In contrast, in the West, the churches of the Reformation have historically emphasized congregational singing.

Differences in the performance of the liturgy stem from the fact that churches emphasize various traditional models of worship. The New Testament offers two influential examples: the model of heavenly worship (Rev. 4-5) and the model of the community gathered to remember the Lord Jesus (1 Cor. 3 and 11-14). It would be fair to say that the Eastern churches have tended to emphasize the former, while the Western churches have swung between the two, currently tending to emphasize the latter.

Most churches would tend to agree that it is the relationship between the two models that needs to be expressed in the liturgy. The predominantly congregational music of the West and the predominantly ministerial music of the East may both be in need of re-discovering a balance which the history of church music could suggest. For instance, in the 4th century the liturgy included specialized musical ministries exercised by the priest and cantors, as well as congregational participation. These two performance practices were commonly interpreted by the church fathers as reflecting the two music metaphors implicit in the word *symphonia:* musical harmony (the balance between various musical elements and performers), and musical agreement (most fully realized in unison congregational singing). Both metaphors stress a unity which reconciles all diversities, but if both are to be realized fully, some sort of variety in musical roles may still be necessary.

The ecumenical investigation of the history of liturgy has led to a number of insights relevant to this issue, which are reflected in the revised liturgies of both Roman Catholics and Protestants. From its origins, at the abbeys of Solesmes and Maria Laach, the modern liturgical movement* has gone hand in hand with a renewed appreciation of chant. One indication that musical practice is responding to these recoveries is the increasing use of responsorial psalm forms in both Protestant and Roman Catholic churches. In North America, the question of congregational singing is also being raised more frequently in Orthodox publications.

Although the musical practices of the churches continue to indicate unresolved theological and social tensions, they may also indicate important resources for mutual enrichment. The Western churches would profit greatly from examining the wider range of interaction between text and music which can be observed in the largely chanted services of the Eastern churches; this might enable the West to recover what is useful of its own chant tradition. The East might also offer some insights into the question of the proper ministerial role of the choir. The Eastern churches could attend to the successful balancing between congregational singing and professional musical ministry in the Protestant and Roman Catholic traditions.

Both in the East and the West, church music from the southern hemisphere deserves to receive greater attention than it does at present. Some areas, particularly in Latin America and Africa, are discovering their own musical voice for worship. Music indigenous to local cultures is increasingly being recognized as a meaningful aid to worship. The rhythms of Africa and Latin America and the variety of melodies from Asia provide enriching possibilities for musical expression within the liturgy. All churches could profit from a continuing discussion about and greater use of the wide diversity of music available now for liturgical use.

See also **hymns; lex orandi, lex credendi; worship in the ecumenical movement.**

WILLIAM T. FLYNN

F. Blume, *Protestant Music: A History*, New York, Norton, 1974 • K. Fellerer ed., *Geschichte der katholischen Kirchenmusik*, 2 vols, Kassel, Bärenreiter, 1972 • J. von Gardner, *Russian Church Singing*, Crestwood, NY, St Vladimir's Seminary, 1980 • J. McKinnon, *Music in Early Christian Literature*, Cambridge, Cambridge UP, 1987 • D. Power, M. Collins & M. Burnim eds, *Music and the Experience of God*, Edinburgh, Clark, 1989.

CHURCH ORDER. There is much diversity in structure or polity, but three basic patterns of church order have dominated since the 16th century: congregational, presbyterial and episcopal. Episcopal polity is the most widely used, being characteristic of Roman Catholic, Orthodox and Anglican traditions. Presbyterial or congregational structures are more prominent among churches that emerged out of the Protestant Reformation* or later divisions.

All three polities may claim New Testament antecedents. A congregational structure would have suited the so-called house churches formed by early missionaries like Paul, who refers several times in his letters to churches in the homes of persons he knew (Rom. 16:5; 1 Cor. 16:19; Col. 4:15; Philemon 2). The church at Corinth probably employed a congregational structure. A presbyterial pattern, where leadership is exercised by presbyters (also called overseers, episcopoi) and deacons, seems to have gained wide currency during the last half of the 1st century. Paul saluted "bishops and deacons" at Philippi (Phil. 1:1). Acts and the pastoral epistles, both perhaps dating from the late 1st century, envisioned apostolic appointment of presbyters "church by church" or "city by city" (Acts 14:23; Titus 1:5). In 1 Tim. 4:14 Paul referred to a "council of elders", or *presbyterion* (see **presbyterate**).

Monarchical episcopacy,* or rule by a single bishop, did not develop until the 2nd century, but a kind of prototype for it may be found in the primitive community of Jerusalem. Parallels between the structure of this community and that of the Jewish community at Qumran are striking. James, brother of Jesus, stood at the head, like the Qumran *mebaqqer*, or "superintendent" (episcopos?). The Twelve, including the "three pillars" (see Gal. 2:9), formed a kind of council like the Council of Twelve — including or in addition to three priests — at Qumran. Beyond these were the presbyters and the "many" in both communities (Acts 15:2,4,6,22,23).

Progress towards the threefold order (bishop, presbyters, deacons) moved at different paces in different places. According to J.B. Lightfoot, the twofold order of presbyter-bishops and deacons prevailed in most churches by the end of the 1st century. Within the church of a city (polis), whatever the number of congregations, one of the presbyter-bishops probably served as chair of the *presbyterion*. A number of factors — the demands of an expanding constituency, threats of schism and heresy, a natural inclination to clarify authority — probably encouraged a permanent presidency. When this happened, the term "episcopos" was reserved for the presiding presbyter-bishop and the term "presbyter" for others.

Judging from the urgency of the plea of Ignatius of Antioch to "do nothing without the bishop!" (*Letter to the Philadelphians* 3.2), the church of Asia Minor had not yet fully secured the tripartite order at the time he passed their way en route to Rome c.110-15. Indeed, Ignatius left his own flock in some kind of turmoil (see his *Letter to the Philadelphians* 10.1; *to the Smyrnaeans* 11.1; and *to Polycarp* 7.1). Rome, always conservative, moved still more slowly to accept the monarchical episcopate.

Concern for the indigent, need for additional assistance, and desire to include as many persons as possible in the ministry of the church led to the development of "minor orders" not part of the threefold ministry: subdeacons, widows, deaconesses, exorcists, porters, readers, acolytes and others. These varied widely from church to church.

In line with Pauline missionary strategy, the polis-church served as the primary unit in the development of Christian polity. Polis-churches extended their reach to surrounding villages and the countryside. Quite naturally, the bishop of the polis-church considered himself the bishop of areas evangelized by his church. Accordingly, Ignatius called himself bishop of both Antioch and Syria (see his *Letter to the Romans* 2.2). Claims often overlapped, necessitating the establishment of certain lines of jurisdiction. At Nicea in 325 bishops accepted the Roman dioceses and provinces as the units recognized by the church. Parish units did not develop until around 400 or after, perhaps first in Gaul. Heads of churches in provincial capitals gained special recognition as metropolitans (in the East) or archbishops (in the West).

From an early date certain churches held more eminent places and came to be designated patriarchates. Jerusalem did so for a time by virtue of its importance in Christian origins, then faded out of the picture after the Bar Kochba revolt (132-35) but recovered some of its pre-eminence after Constantine's conversion opened the way for Christians to return. The council of Nicea in 325 officially restored to the Jerusalem church some of its status. Antioch gained prominence as a result of its special role in the early Christian mission led by Paul and Barnabas. Rome had a natural advantage as the capital of the empire, and the martyrdoms of Peter and Paul there further enhanced its standing. When Constantine shifted the capital from Rome to Byzan-

tium in 330, he brought the latter immediately into the limelight; yet it never succeeded in taking the place of Rome. At Constantinople in 381 the bishops listed it second after Rome as "the New Rome". Several other large cities such as Alexandria, Ephesus, Carthage and Caesarea gained prominence at one time or another, but of these only Alexandria, perhaps as the centre of Christian learning in the 3rd century and after, attained the title of patriarchate in the early church.

Rome held a certain prestige almost from the beginning, but the extent to which it exercised authority over churches outside Italy is debated. The theory that the bishop of Rome was Peter's successor appeared first in Tertullian (*Prescription* 32). Damasus (366-84) established clerical right of appeal to Rome. Pope Leo I (440-61), however, shaped the theory of Roman primacy* based on succession from Peter, which claimed for Rome full power over the whole church. The power vacuum created by the barbarian invasions allowed Rome to implement the theory in the West in ways it could not in the East.

Church order changed little during the middle ages either in East or West. The Protestant Reformation, however, led to radical changes. Although Luther emphasized that clergy differ from laity* only in function, he did not make far-reaching changes. Calvin and more radical reformers wanted to return to the order set by primitive Christianity but disagreed among themselves as to what the pattern was. Anglicans steered a middle course under guidance of the church fathers and not too far from the Orthodox and Roman Catholic models (except for rejection of Roman hegemony over the Church of England).

Episcopal polity, whether Roman Catholic, Orthodox, Anglican or Lutheran, usually is conceived in terms of a diocese over which a bishop presides with the assistance of other clergy. The bishop is the chief pastor, worship leader and teacher. Priests (presbyters) serve as the bishop directs in pastoral, liturgical, or other duties, normally in a parish, a sub-unit of the diocese. Some churches have virtually dispensed altogether with the diaconate,* but where it exists it usually supplements the priesthood. Today many episcopal churches still recognize a number of "offices" for which persons are not ordained. Ordination* to the priesthood is believed to confer special grace for the performance of certain sacramental functions and thus to distinguish clergy and laity.

In the Roman Catholic Church bishops exercise authority only in union with the Roman pontiff, who "has full, supreme and universal power over the whole church, a power which he can always exercise unhindered... Together with their head, the Supreme Pontiff, and never apart from him, the bishops have supreme and full authority over the universal church; but this power cannot be exercised without the agreement of the Roman Pontiff" (*Lumen Gentium* 22).

Presbyterial polity, preferred especially by churches of the Reformed/Presbyterian tradition, is less tied to a territorial understanding of the church and stresses instead the relative independence of the ministerial "college". In this model the ordained clergy belong to presbyteries, which supply leadership to congregations grouped under them. The clergy — originally pastors, elders, teachers and deacons, according to Calvin's scheme — lead in word (preaching), sacrament (baptism and Lord's supper) and exercise of discipline. Local synods and national assemblies attended by both clerical and lay delegates wrestle with issues of common interest and exercise varying degrees of authority over the smaller units.

Congregational polity operates on the assumption that power lies with people gathered voluntarily for worship, education, discipline and fellowship. Co-operation between congregations is also voluntary and varies widely — from complete independence to an order similar to the presbyterial. Many congregational traditions such as Baptists have abandoned almost all traditional offices and developed structures like those employed by modern business corporations. Although they may retain names such as pastor or deacon, authority may rest with an executive board and various committees entrusted with a variety of responsibilities: personnel, nominations, education, worship, ministry, outreach, etc. The prevailing social model obviously affects all three major types, but it has greater impact on the congregational one than on the others because of its limited commitment to a defined structure.

The Lima text on *Baptism, Eucharist and Ministry** (1982) recognizes that certain features of the episcopal, presbyterial and congregational systems all have an appropriate place in the order of a reunited church, where ministry should have "personal, collegial and communal" dimensions (M26-27, with comm.).

See also **church discipline; laity/clergy; ministry in the church; ministry, threefold**.

E. GLENN HINSON

J.J. von Allmen, *Le saint ministère selon la conviction et la volonté des Réformés du XVIᵉ siècle*, Neuchâtel, Delachaux & Niestlé, 1968 • R.E. Brown, *Priest and Bishop: Biblical Reflections*, Paramus, NJ, Paulist, 1970 • H. von Campenhausen, *Kirchliches Amt und geistliche Vollmacht in den ersten drei Jahrhunderten* (ET *Ecclesiastical Authority and Spiritual Power in the Church of the First Three Centuries*, London, Black, 1969) • R. Dunkerley ed., *The Ministry and the Sacraments*, London, SCM, 1937 • T.W. Manson, *The Church's Ministry*, London, Hodder & Stoughton, 1948 • E. Schweizer, *Gemeinde und Gemeindeordnung im Neuen Testament* (ET *Church Order in the New Testament*, London, SCM, 1961).

CHURCHES, SISTER. The current use of "sister churches" in ecumenical discourse, in particular between Eastern Orthodox and Roman Catholics, restores an ancient church expression. "Your elect sister", in 2 John 13, seems to be the only biblical text which calls a Christian community sister. Clement of Rome and Ignatius of Antioch (1st-2nd centuries) witness to the family relations between local churches. Later the theological foundations of these relations become explicit: common apostolic origins, communion in faith and hope, believers calling one another "brother" or "sister", and mutual hospitality (Irenaeus and Tertullian, 2nd-3rd centuries). Emerging at the time of the first great councils (4th-5th centuries) were large geographical spheres of church administration, and responsible for them were bishops, especially those who became patriarchs of the more important centres. The bishops who represented their churches were brothers of one another, colleagues, *sylleitourgoi*, and they ensured the sisterly relations between their churches.

Later development saw a double movement: in the West one accented the primacy of the local church of Rome; in the East one gave a predominant role to Constantinople, and the ancient patriarchs recognized its privileged place. To a large extent this divergent evolution resulted in the gradual dissolution and final rupture of communion* between the Greeks and the Latins. The explicit term "sister churches" appears in two letters in which the Byzantines protest against a certain will of Rome to annul their authority and present itself as "mother and teacher". In reaction to this, Patriarchs Nicetas of Nicomedia (1136) and John X Camateros (ruled 1198-1206) affirmed that the church of Rome is only the first among "sisters", equal in both dignity and origin.

In the 20th century Patriarch Athenagoras (1949-72) was the first to use "sister churches" to describe the relation between his church of Constantinople and the church of Rome (1963). Pope Paul VI (1963-78) gave the term its official status in his formal letter to the same patriarch, *Anno Ineunte*, on the occasion of the pope's visit to Constantinople, July 1967: "For centuries we lived this life of 'sister churches', and together held the ecumenical councils." Paul VI based the expression on the relationship of children of the same Father who share in a common life, through the Son in the Holy Spirit — made explicit in baptism,* then "united more closely by the priesthood and the eucharist, in virtue of the apostolic succession". This relationship concerns not only persons but also the churches.

This papal declaration recognizes fully the ecclesial character of the Orthodox church and envisages that the relations between the church of Rome and the Orthodox church could follow another model than that of the authority which Rome now exercises in the Roman church. In 1964 the Second Vatican Council's Decree on Ecumenism recognized the legitimacy of the Eastern churches' theological, spiritual and canonical traditions and described the nature of the family relations as that "which ought to exist between local churches, as between sisters" (n.14).

In October 1967, at the end of Patriarch Athenagoras's visit to Rome, he and the pope issued a common declaration which considered their meeting as playing "a part in helping their churches to make a further discovery of themselves as sister churches". Although the term has since become customary to desig-

nate relations between the Catholic and Orthodox churches, one is far from having drawn from it all the theological and practical conclusions.

In 1970 Pope Paul VI, on the occasion of the canonization of the 40 English martyrs, used the expression as a future hope for Catholic-Anglican relations: "There will be no seeking to lessen the legitimate prestige and the worthy patrimony of piety and usage proper to the Anglican church when the Roman Catholic Church... is able to embrace her ever beloved sister in the one authentic communion of the family of Christ: a communion of origin and of faith, a communion of priesthood and of rule, a communion of the saints in a freedom of love of the spirit of Jesus."

See also **Orthodox-Roman Catholic dialogue**.

FRANS BOUWEN

J. Meyendorff, "Eglises-soeurs: Implications ecclésiologiques", and E. Lanne, "Eglises-soeurs", *Istina*, 20, 1, 1975 • E.J. Stormon ed., *Towards the Healing of Schism*, New York, Paulist, 1987.

CIDSE. Coopération internationale pour le développement et la solidarité (CIDSE) is a Roman Catholic federation of 14 RC organizations for development,* located in Europe and North America. It includes the Catholic Fund for Overseas Development (England), Catholic Relief Services (USA), Entraide et fraternité (Belgium), Misereor (Germany) and Organisation catholique canadienne pour le développement et la paix (Canada). Its general secretariat is in Belgium.

CIDSE co-ordinates more than 6,000 projects each year, including efforts with partners in Africa, Asia and Latin America. It seeks to enlighten public opinion in the industrialized countries and to represent their concerns to United Nations organizations (e.g. UNESCO, FAO, ILO) and to the World Bank.

Its revenues, around $330 million each year, come from national collections among RCs and from governments and multilateral organizations, in particular the European communities. It has close contacts with the WCC, Caritas Internationalis,* International Coalition for Development Action, and other agencies.

TOM STRANSKY

CIMADE. CIMADE (Comité inter-mouvement auprès des évacués — inter-movement committee for aid to evacuees) was set up by Protestant youth movements in October 1939. The idea was to send teams to live among the French evacuees from Alsace. In 1940, after the Nazi invasion, CIMADE worked to alleviate the distressing situation of foreigners assembled in internment camps under inhuman material and psychological conditions. Madeleine Barot, then appointed as general secretary under the president, Marc Boegner, managed to get CIMADE teams into the camps. The year 1942 brought the beginning of mass deportations, particularly of Jews, and it became necessary to go underground in the resistance, doing whatever possible to help those most at risk to flee to Spain or Switzerland. In this effort CIMADE had the help of the WCC, then in formation, and many parishes.

After the liberation, CIMADE, still headed by Barot and Boegner, was involved in helping resettle persons displaced by the war. On this occasion it worked with Swiss churches, which donated temporary huts, and with so-called fraternal workers — volunteers delegated by their churches to help in the post-war reconstruction work, as an act of witness to the gospel. Later the teams also contributed to the efforts for reconciliation with the Germans by setting up temporary reception centres in Germany. CIMADE also took some more ecumenical initiatives, such as organizing training conferences involving Roman Catholics, Orthodox and Protestants.

At this time CIMADE gradually affirmed its identity as an organization independent of the churches but related to them. Its defined purpose was to show active solidarity with refugees, migrant workers and oppressed peoples: "CIMADE is one form of the service which the churches seek to render to humanity in the name of the gospel of liberation. It works in relation with the World Council of Churches, the French Protestant Federation and the Orthodox Church and co-operates with various lay and Roman Catholic bodies."

Waves of uprooted people arrived in France from Eastern Europe, Africa and the Mediterranean countries, then from Latin America and the Caribbean and Southeast Asia and, more recently, from Africa and the Middle East. The work done by the teams has changed to meet the needs of each successive group. The reception and support given to the refugees is marked by the desire to respect their adherence to their own beliefs until such time as they can return home.

This effort to work in partnership also involves undertaking legal defence of foreigners and migrant workers and combating all forms of discrimination, including racism.* Today, now that it is clear that many people who came to France expecting to stay for only a short time are actually there to stay, their integration has become an important element in CIMADE'S work. Because one of the main causes of migration continues to be underdevelopment and unequal living conditions, CIMADE has been developing a third branch of its work and extending its activities to partners in the countries of the South, anxious to take their own destiny in hand. CIMADE now has working links with some 30 countries.

CIMADE'S activities beyond France's borders are of necessity complemented by work "at home" in France itself to make people more aware of the structures of inequality. Whether in relation to human rights* in France, or the structures of injustice and exploitation elsewhere, CIMADE always tries to tackle the root causes of the situations which challenge Christian responsibility. This calls for constant reflection and review in the light of changing situations. Such reflection makes it possible to go beyond giving personal help, necessary as this always is, to the level of dealing with the structures which cause marginalization and exploitation.

CIMADE recently celebrated its 50th year of service. As CIMADE continues its efforts, its direct involvement in the reality of tragic situations and injustice means that when it speaks to the political authorities, to society at large and to church members, calling on them to work unceasingly for justice and the defence of outcasts, its voice is unmistakably authentic.

ANDRÉ JACQUES

CIVIL RELIGION. The idea of civil religion goes back to the Enlightenment and to Rousseau's book *The Social Contract*. This concept, with its four simple dogmas about the existence of God,* the life to come, the reward of virtue and the punishment of vice, and the exclusion of religious intolerance, had both a polemical and emancipatory character in contrast to the spirit of established churches and theology. Civil religion became a form of widely accepted religious beliefs that were private, personal, civil and inward. Within the ecumenical movement this complex religious phenomenon was initially stimulated by the analysis made by the American sociologist Robert N. Bellah, who wrote: "Few have realized that there actually exists alongside of and rather clearly differentiated from the churches an elaborated and well-institutionalized civil religion in America. This religion — perhaps better this religious dimension — has its own seriousness and integrity and requires the same care in understanding that any other religion does."

Between 1981 and 1987 the Lutheran World Federation (LWF) Department of Studies co-ordinated an ecumenical interdisciplinary study on civil religion in 52 countries. The following working definition was used: "Civil religion consists of a pattern of symbols, ideas, and practices that legitimate the authority of civil institutions in a society. It provides a fundamental value orientation that binds a people together in common action within the public realm. It is religious in so far as it evokes commitment and, within an overall world-view, expresses a people's ultimate sense of worth, identity, and destiny. It is civil in so far as it deals with the basic public institutions exercising power in a society, nation, or other political unit. A civil religion can be known through its observance of rituals, its holidays, sacred places, documents, stories, heroes, and other behaviour in or analogous to recognized historical religions. Civil religion may also contain a theory that may emerge as an ideology. Individual members of a society may have varying degrees of awareness of their civil religion. It may have an extensive or limited acceptance by the population as long as it serves its central function of legitimating the civil institutions."

Churches, universities, seminaries, experts and institutions were asked by the LWF to prepare local and national studies, and the LWF organized several area and continental conferences and a final meeting for general evaluation. According to the findings of the LWF, civil religion is not a "religion" like Christianity, Buddhism or Islam but rather a certain — sometimes overt and sometimes hidden — socio-political orientation that borrows and interprets for its own purposes a given religious framework. Every socio-political system can produce a civil religion by which it will legitimate its way of life, understanding of history, beliefs, values, and regulations in relation to other socio-political systems. It is important to differentiate but not separate the following four aspects of civil religion: (1) religiosity as folk-church or folk religious tradition (e.g. communities and individuals struggling for identity and hungering for transcendence); (2) the relationship between church, religion and state, as defined by the constitution, legislation, the national anthem and the idea of a "neutral" state; (3) the relationship between church, religion and nation, which includes national or tribal elements of religiosity and the role of religion in the process of nation building; (4) the relationship between church, religion and the deep structure of basic values, as reflected in the values of the constitution and the educational structures.

Governments and people in authority have always used religion in order to legitimate or safeguard their own position. The privileged church or religion used its music or liturgy to support social and civil institutions, which in turn guaranteed favoured treatment for that church or religion. Any community will sooner or later produce its own civil religion, and every society harbours certain forms of civil religion, although of course they differ and depend on the background and the elements that have shaped the development of the country. In the process of integrating and uniting a given society with the help of many kinds of myths, ceremonies and ideologies, civil religion must provide the sense of a common past, present and future in the transmission and interpretation of a society's values and goals and make them appear to be right, necessary and, indeed, the only possible ones. A further element can be the mobilization of people for common tasks and responsibilities. For example, in Indonesia the Pancasila (or the five pillars) represents an attempt to provide a framework of unity for religion and peoples through belief in one supreme God, just and civilized humanity, the unity of Indonesia, a democracy led by the wisdom of deliberations among representatives, and social justice for the whole of Indonesia.

Any theological evaluation of civil religion must remember that the church is always involved in the process of civil religion. At its best, civil religion can create social order and national or group cohesion, and at its worst it can become a kind of idolatry. The church can sometimes use civil religion as a point of contact *(Anknüpfungspunkt)*; at other times the church should stand in prophetic judgment over it.

See also **church and state, religion**.

BÉLA HARMATI

R.B. Bellah, *The Broken Covenant: American Civil Religion in Time of Trial*, New York, Seabury, 1975 • *The Church and American Civil Religion*, New York, Lutheran World Ministries, 1986 • B. Harmati ed., *The Church and Civil Religion in Asia*, Geneva, LWF, 1985 • B. Harmati ed., *The Church and Civil Religion in the Nordic Countries of Europe*, Geneva, LWF, 1984 • H. Kleger & A. Müller eds, *Religion des Bürgers: Zivilreligion in Amerika und Europa*, Munich, Kaiser, 1986 • R. Schieder, *Civil Religion: Die religiöse Dimension der politischen Kultur*, Gütersloh, Mohn, 1987.

COLD WAR. The term "cold war" is used to designate the ideological, political and economic struggle for power between the two super-powers, the Soviet Union and the United States, each being the centre of a group of allies. It has had worldwide repercussions, causing the nations not wishing to be involved to form a non-aligned bloc. The period began soon after the second world war when the Soviet Union gained control of Eastern Europe, beginning with Poland in 1945. This was strongly opposed by the US and its allies. There was a parallel situation in the case of the Soviet control of Manchuria. While overt military conflict between the super-powers was prevented in these cases, the cold war can be blamed for regional wars in Korea, Vietnam, Afghanistan and other places.

The cold war had very destructive effects within some countries: e.g. in the US, Latin American countries, and South Africa, where reactionary forces used the label "communist" to discredit as subversive any significant efforts to change society for the sake of greater justice. Churches related to the ecumenical movement, social action groups within them,

and the WCC itself have often been victims of such attacks.

The response of the ecumenical community to the cold war was illustrated by the Amsterdam assembly of the WCC in 1948. There were plenary addresses reflecting both sides in the cold war, one by the US statesman John Foster Dulles and another by Joseph Hromádka, a Czech theologian and Christian leader in Eastern Europe. The assembly's corporate thinking of more lasting influence was expressed in the reports of its sections, which tended to transcend the cold war, to criticize economic institutions of both sides, and especially to try to keep the cold war from becoming a "holy war".

The Russian Orthodox Church joined the WCC in 1961, and its representatives participated in the discussion of the issues of the cold war. They did not support communism as an ideology, though they showed sympathy for socialistic aspects of the Soviet economy and they often defended Soviet foreign policy. Their presence helped to prevent the non-communist majority in the WCC from using it as a forum for direct attacks on the Soviet Union. The Council was often attacked in the US and some other Western countries for being one-sided in its criticism of capitalist countries. Official criticism of communism was indeed muted — in the interest of preserving the freedom of Christians in communist countries and of ensuring their continued ecumenical participation.

In the 1980s the cold war was modified by such factors as the increasing diversity among communist countries and the rapidly growing realization that the use of nuclear weapons by the super-powers in a war, which could not be expected to be limited, would be suicidal for both. Also, it became clear that the nuclear arms race was a threat to all humanity and to the natural environment on which life depends.

In the late 1980s "new thinking", perestroika (restructuring) and glasnost (openness) promulgated by Mikhail Gorbachev touched off rapid changes in both the Soviet Union and its Central and Eastern European allies. By late 1989 and early 1990, with constitutional changes allowing for multi-party systems in which communist parties no longer had a dominant role and moves towards German reunification removing one of the cold war's most potent symbols, it had become common to speak of the end of the cold war.

Initial ecumenical response to these developments, cautious because of the speed of change, welcomed the new liberties and accompanying opportunities for Central and Eastern European churches, but warned against the dangers of "triumphalist claims" for capitalism, increased conflict with ethnic and other minorities, and "Eurocentrism" diverting ecumenical attention and aid from the problems of the countries of the third world.

JOHN C. BENNETT

COLLEGIALITY. In modern Roman Catholic teaching, collegiality in its technical sense is officially described in the document of Vatican Council II* on the church: "Together with its head, the Roman pontiff, and never without this head, the episcopal order is the subject of supreme and full power over the universal church" (*Lumen Gentium* 22). This college of bishops, "in so far as it is composed of many, expresses the variety and universality of the people of God, but in so far as it is assembled under one head, it expresses the unity of the flock of Christ" (*LG* 22). All bishops, by virtue of their episcopal consecration and their communion among themselves and with the head of the college, the bishop of Rome, have a corporate or collegial responsibility for the unity of faith* and communion* of the universal church* and for its mission* "to teach all nations and to preach the gospel to every creature" (*LG* 24).

Whatever authority the pope and the bishops enjoy, it is always to be exercised through the faithful preaching of the gospel, the administration of the sacraments, and loving governance. They collaborate thereby in the Holy Spirit's work of unity: "in the confession of the one faith, in the common celebration of divine worship, and in the fraternal harmony of the family of God" (Decree on Ecumenism 2).

Since all power in the church is that of Christ in the Spirit, and thus truly vicarious, Vatican II wrestled with how to explain the bishops' power as coming from Christ while still maintaining good order and structure in the church. And since the agents of supreme power are multiple (i.e., the pope and the rest of the bishops in full communion with him),

the issue of their relationship in the exercise of authority is crucial. Otherwise that power which is intended for the unity of the church could seem to lead to disunity.

Although collegiality was hotly debated in Vatican II, Karl Rahner and other scholars claim it offered nothing new that went beyond canon law (1917), or even the understanding of Vatican I* (1870). Others see significant shifts. All would admit that one of the most urgent internal problems of the RCC today, one with direct ecumenical consequences, is the need to develop further the articulation of collegiality in both theological theory and ecclesial practice, for the sake of both the local and the universal church.

Since Vatican II at least three major schools of thought have defined the relation between the pope and the other bishops in terms of supreme authority. The first focuses solely on the pope. No act of supreme authority can take place without his direct involvement, even if he joins himself to other bishops in an ecumenical council such as Vatican II. The second view sees two different modalities in which the unifying power of Christ can be legitimately exercised as the supreme authority: the pope, in his own right and not involving the college of bishops, or in his acting together with them in a collegial act. Thus, there are two subjects of supreme authority, although they are inadequately distinct. The third view places the role of the college of bishops, as that of the first college of the apostles, as more central in the plan of salvation. The college alone is the subject of supreme power. When the pope freely acts by himself, he is still exercising the supreme power that Christ gave the apostolic college, a college that Christ designated Peter to head but not to replace or duplicate.

In this debate, one must place collegiality within the Vatican II understanding of the worldwide communion of the people of God* and of the local (diocesan) churches* in which they live, for the church is at once local and universal. Bishops are rooted in these particular churches in which they minister. In the universal church as "a communion of churches", the relationship of these churches to one another "is the foundation of the office *(munus)* that one bishop has in regard to others, whether as pope, patriarch, metropolitan, etc." (James Provost).

Indeed, episcopal-papal collegiality should be understood as "a means whereby the contemporary disciples of Christ, the successors of the apostolic church, are enabled to keep alive the tradition and memory of Christ and avoid subjection to domineering lords (1 Pet. 5:3) because they all are the communion of 'the many brothers of his Son' (Rom. 8:29)" (Robert Kress).

Vatican II spoke also of "the collegial spirit", what many now call affective collegiality, that is, the attitudes and motives of mutual interaction and collaboration in decision making within the college of bishops and their structural expressions (e.g. national and regional episcopal conferences, the international synod of bishops, the college of cardinals, the Roman curia, etc.). In a more derived meaning, Catholics now use "spirit of collegiality" for attitudes and structures in the local church or diocese through presbyterial and pastoral councils, relations between bishop-clergy-religious-laity, etc.

Collegiality, biblically understood and historically developed, has understandably entered the Roman Catholic ecumenical debate. Can the idea of collegiality bear fruit for the communion of churches in the ecumenical movement? Could its broad interpretation at least constitute a base of agreement between the churches? How can the pope exercise a ministry which is acceptable to other churches? How does collegiality relate to conciliarity* and lead to a future "council truly ecumenical"?

Such topics have appeared in the official RCC bilateral dialogues with the Orthodox and Anglicans (and the RCC-Lutheran dialogue in the USA). The questions are appearing in Faith and Order studies, with an impetus from the 1982 *Baptism, Eucharist and Ministry** report, especially BEM's section on the continuity of the apostolic Tradition and the episcopal succession as a servant, symbol and guardian of the continuity of the apostolic faith and communion. Indeed, collegiality is a major item on the agenda of what is more starkly emerging as an unavoidable broader question of the 1990s — what and for what is the Christ-given authority* in and of his one church? Where is that authority, and how should it be exercised?

See also **conciliarity, episcopacy**.

TOM STRANSKY

Y. Congar, "Le problème ecclésiologique de la papauté après Vatican II", in *Ministères et communion ecclésiale*, Paris, Cerf, 1971 ● R. Kress, "Collegiality", in *The New Catholic Encyclopedia*, vol. 17 (supplement), New York, McGraw-Hill, 1978 ● J. Provost, "The Hierarchical Constitution of the Church", in *The Code of Canon Law: A Text and Commentary*, New York, Paulist, 1985 ● K. Rahner, "On the Relationship between the Pope and the College of Bishops", in *Theological Investigations*, vol. 10, New York, Herder & Herder, 1977 ● D. Stanley, "The NT Basis for the Concept of Collegiality", *Theological Studies*, 25, 1964.

COLONIALISM. An examination of official church statements from the end of the 19th century shows how slow the Christian churches were to recognize the implications of colonialism. It is not until long after the end of the second world war that the term "colonialism" begins to appear in church documents. While the peoples of Asia and Africa had been busy for years organizing nationalist and freedom movements, not to mention armed movements for national liberation, practically nothing of this activity appears in official ecclesiastical texts. It is not until after the war that a certain number of explicit references are found, and even then often in a very watered-down form.

Colonialism is not mentioned in any of the great social encyclicals.* Yet the anti-colonialist movements were born long before the end of the last century and were even organizing international conferences like the one held in Brussels in 1925. The first explicit allusion on the side of the Roman Catholic Church (RCC) dates from the Second Vatican Council. In the case of the WCC we have to wait until the Evanston assembly in 1954 and the New Delhi assembly in 1961 for a relatively concrete treatment of the problem. These ecclesiastical statements, however, are generally short on social analysis and reflect a very optimistic view of colonialism. The 1967 papal encyclical *Populorum Progressio*, for example, makes the following statement: "It must certainly be recognized that colonizing powers have often furthered their own interests, power or glory, and that their departure has sometimes left a precarious economy, bound up for instance with the production of one kind of crop whose market prices are subject to sudden and considerable variation.

Yet while recognizing the damage done by a certain type of colonialism and its consequences, one must at the same time acknowledge the qualities and achievement of colonisers who brought their science and technical knowledge and left beneficial results of their presence in so many underprivileged regions. The structures established by them persist, however incomplete they may be; they diminished ignorance and sickness, brought the benefits of communications and improved living conditions."

How are we to explain this lack of awareness and of historical objectivity in judging the situation? Here are one or two suggestions.

The history of missions and its parallels with colonialism. There were two main stages in colonialism: mercantilism and industrial capitalism.

Mercantile colonialism (15th to 18th centuries): This stage was organized by the monarchies of Portugal and Spain and subsequently by those of the nations of northern Europe, such as the Netherlands, England and France. In the nations of southern Europe like Portugal and Spain, mercantile colonialism was seized on by a power which was establishing the balance between the feudal aristocratic class and the merchant class.

Since the feudal ideology, which was religious, continued to dominate, the mercantile enterprise was given a legitimation of the same sort. At the same time, the RCC saw in this mercantile activity a possibility of evangelism,* at least of evangelism as understood in this period. So it was that the ventures of the kings of Portugal and Spain were regularly legitimized by a succession of papal bulls issued throughout the entire mercantile period. It is also true that not a few missionaries, particularly from religious orders (e.g. the Dominicans in Santo Domingo, the Jesuits in Paraguay, and even some bishops), fought against the brutality of the conquest and tried to develop a different understanding and practice of evangelization. But their testimony, sometimes heroic, was not able to modify seriously the course of events or change the policies of a church subject to the patronage power of the state and generally allied to the interests of the colonizers.

In return for this legitimation, the effort of evangelism received material and political assistance from the royal power. Evangelism was seen, on the one hand, as one of the best means of establishing tacit agreements with the local populations or of domesticating slaves and, on the other hand, as a task incumbent also on lay Christians in the exercise of power.

The colonialism of industrial nations: This new type of colonialism concentrated mainly on the discovery and exploitation of raw materials for industrial development and the marketing of manufactured goods. The large Indies companies of the Netherlands, France, Sweden and Britain paved the way for this stage of colonialism. The new type of colonialism gradually found itself competing and warring with the more traditional powers, which continued to engage in mercantile colonialism — hence the wars between Britain and Holland, on the one hand, and Spain and Portugal, on the other, and the eventual conquest of the respective colonies in Latin America, Asia and Africa. The colonialism of this stage no longer claimed the same religious legitimation as that which prevailed in the mercantile period. Adopting a much more pragmatic approach and making use of the colonial governments, capitalism provided the churches, both Catholic and Protestant, with support to encourage the arrival of missionaries in the colonized territories, entrusting them with educational and medical missions extremely useful to the colonial enterprise of the day. Support for the work of missions was thus never interrupted, even when the European governments adopted a hostile attitude towards certain churches in their own countries.

The emergence of nationalist, anti-colonialist and anti-imperialist movements (see **liberation, struggles for**): Originating in the colonized nations, these movements were directed against the Western countries. In Latin America, this phenomenon dates back to the beginning of the 19th century. The holy see refused to recognize the new nations and long remained loyal to Spain, thus endangering the organization of local churches during a long period. Members of the lower-ranking clergy joined the nationalist movements, which at that time represented the emancipation of a local middle class rather than of the ordinary people. These movements, however, played an important historical role.

In Asia, strong nationalist movements, based on traditional cultures and religions, began to develop from the beginning of this century: in India with the Hindu movements; in Sri Lanka, Burma, Vietnam and Laos with the Buddhist movements; in most of the Arab countries, Iran, Malaysia, Indonesia, in the part of British India corresponding to present-day Pakistan and Bangladesh, with Islamic movements.

The Christian churches were alarmed by these movements and to the end resisted national emancipation, preferring to maintain their links with the colonizing powers. Only a few churches adopted a truly national position; only a few isolated voices were raised, usually in lay intellectual circles. There were exceptions, notably in Indonesia and Korea, the latter country having been colonized by the Japanese.

Generally speaking, the Reformation churches had less difficulty in severing connections with the colonial power, since these connections were usually less direct. An exception to this rule was the Anglican church in British India; given its character as an established state church, it tended to take its cue more often than not from government colonial

policy, though the same also applied when that policy was one of decolonization. All this helps to explain the fact that in Asia a number of political leaders after independence were Christians with a nationalist bias but were at the same time exponents of the capitalist ideology characteristic of the West.

In Africa, the movement for independence after the second world war was rather sudden, and the local clergy adopted positions more explicitly emancipatory in character. In Roman Catholicism, this was the case with a number of local episcopates, even when the latter were predominantly white. This stance is attested, for example, by the pastoral letters of bishops in Tanganyika in 1953, in Madagascar in 1953 and in Cameroon in 1955, of the bishops of French West Africa and of Togo in 1955 and of the bishops of Madagascar in 1956. It should also be noted that a number of anti-white emancipation movements were led by Africans who had founded independent churches or religious movements such as Kimbanguism in the Belgian Congo (Zaire).

The case of Portuguese colonialism was particularly distressing. The RCC did not dissociate itself from the colonial war waged by

Statue to the colonialists, Windhoek, Namibia (epd-bild/Neetz)

Portugal right up to 1974. The concordat between the holy see and the Portuguese government was still in force, and the holy see never renounced it. Only a tiny number of priests and lay Catholics joined various leaders of the Protestant churches in identifying themselves with the nationalist movement.

It is clear, then, that the Christian churches had a largely blinkered ecclesiastical and proselytizing vision of what was happening and lacked the critical distance for an objective analysis. They were almost completely unrepresented in the critique of colonialism which had developed in the West, largely inspired by socialist movements and later by a Marxist analysis, and played hardly any part in the movements within the colonized nations which for the most part preached a cultural emancipation inspired by the traditional religions. It was only later, particularly in the struggles in Southern Africa, that some churches, following the leadership of the WCC, were able to overcome the colonialist mentality and establish a positive relation with liberation movements, often led by people from the local churches. But it is necessary to recognize that these relations were violently criticized in the West.

In the positions adopted at the end of the colonial era, the Christian churches put the emphasis mainly on their tasks in the new situation of national sovereignty and the importance of the autonomy of the local churches rather than on critical appraisal of the colonial past. This was the standpoint expressed, for example, at the Uppsala assembly of the WCC in 1968.

A Eurocentric vision. Another feature of church documents is their deep conviction of the superiority of the civilized values which "Christian" Europe brings to the "non-civilized" peoples. From the 15th to the 16th centuries, this was the justification for the struggle against Islam. The absolute conviction that Christianity was necessary for the salvation* of all human beings and that it was essential to spread it by all legitimate — or what were deemed legitimate — means found expression in its alliance with the mercantile colonial enterprise. The notion of European cultural superiority and the blessings of European civilization together constituted a particularly important ideological basis during the period of colonialism by the industrial nations, and the Christian churches were the main vehicle for this ideology.

Even after the attainment of independence by the former colonized countries, church documents still remained close to the old way of thinking, as can be seen, for example, from the allocution of Pope Pius XII of 24 December 1955. A critical distance in this area is found only in certain positions adopted by the WCC, notably in 1961 at the third assembly in New Delhi.

The post-colonial era. The churches were very quick to draw a veil over the colonial era and at the same time in many cases to adopt a more concrete and courageous attitude to the problems of the post-colonial era. In *Pacem in Terris*, Pope John XXIII spoke of the relationships between the young peoples and the old peoples. The self-determination of the new nations was a theme at the Uppsala assembly. The encyclical *Populorum Progressio* tackled the theme of development and did not hesitate to condemn economic imperialism. Various documents of the WCC and especially of its Programme to Combat Racism* have spoken of the phenomenon of neo-colonialism. The capacity for analysis was gradually developed within the churches. It must be acknowledged, however, that the official documents show little in the way of self-criticism as to the role played in colonialism by the churches themselves, whatever the personal devotion and heroism shown by individual missionaries. Nor are there any critiques of colonialism as such, of its economic and political roots and the domination resulting from it.

See also **decolonization, imperialism**.

FRANÇOIS HOUTART

C. Alix, "Le Vatican et la décolonisation", in *Les Eglises chrétiennes et la décolonisation*, Marcel Merle ed., Paris, Colin, 1967 ● *The Problem of Colonies*, New York, Federal Council of the Churches of Christ in America, 1938.

COMMON CONFESSION. From its very beginning, the organized ecumenical movement has aimed at attaining a common confession of the same apostolic faith.* As early as 1927, the first world conference on Faith and Order at Lausanne received this resolution unanimously: "Notwithstanding the differences in doctrine among us, we are united in a common Christian faith, which is

proclaimed in the holy scriptures and is witnessed to and safeguarded in the ecumenical
creed, commonly called the Nicene, and in
the Apostles' Creed, which faith is continuously confirmed in the spiritual experience of
the church of Christ" (4.28).

Perhaps such a declaration was at that stage
too optimistic for the ecumenical movement
as a whole. The "basis" prepared for the
constitution of the WCC, adopted at Amsterdam (1948) and revised in a more Trinitarian
direction at New Delhi (1961), was indeed a
provisional and minimal criterion of faith for
admission to membership. But it was not yet
the common confession required and sufficient for the unity* of the church and the
"unity in one faith" which is the explicit goal
pursued by the WCC and its F&O commission.

From Lausanne onwards, F&O has studied
ways for making a common confession and
the problems which hinder the reception* of a
common confession of faith. Its world conference at Montreal in 1963 studied the relation
of scripture, Tradition and traditions and,
within that context, the relation of scripture
and creeds.* After Montreal, studies were
undertaken on the councils of the early church
and their hermeneutical significance, and on
the possibility of a genuinely universal council, which would be able to receive such a
common confession. In 1967, at the F&O
commission's meeting in Bristol, the proposal
for a study on a common confession of faith
was deemed to be unripe for the time being.
Emphasis was laid, after the Uppsala assembly (1968) and the Louvain meeting of the
commission (1971), on the contextual pluralism* of credal witness and of "accounts of
hope". On the basis of material collected from
all parts of the world, F&O issued, at its
meeting in Bangalore (1978), a "Common
Account of Hope" (see **hope**). It was followed directly by a proposal for a study on the
"Common Confession of the Apostolic Faith
Today", in order to implement more fully the
exhortation of the Nairobi assembly (1975):
"We ask the churches to undertake a common
effort to receive, re-appropriate and confess
together, as contemporary occasion requires,
the Christian truth and faith, delivered
through the apostles and handed down
through the centuries. Such common action,
arising from free and inclusive discussion

under the commonly acknowledged authority
of God's word, must aim both to clarify and to
embody the unity and the diversity which are
proper to the church's life and mission"
(Nairobi, 2.19).

A joint consultation of F&O together with
the Joint Working Group between the Roman
Catholic Church and the WCC produced in
1980 an important study document, "Towards
a Confession of the Common Faith". Here the
issue of the plural, and sometimes contradictory, character of confessional traditions
among the churches is taken up: "Since their
divisions the churches have each given themselves either conciliar decrees or confessions
to which they attach a real authority. But this
authority always remains subject not only to
the authority of scripture but also to that of
those universally received documents which
concern the centre of the faith and which the
church holds from the period that may be
deemed its building period."

In spite of those differences, however, the
churches within the ecumenical movement
have to meet the aspirations and hopes, the
doubts and fears of people in various contexts.
Confidence could be restored between older
and younger churches, and between older and
younger church members, only if "the faith of
the church through the ages" was expressed in
such ways that it met the longings and desires
of people in modern societies without destroying the trust and faith as it is held by older
people or by the older churches.

Time-bound expressions of faith must always be measured by the *regula fidei* (rule of
faith) transmitted through the centuries. To
face the hermeneutical task, the Lima meeting
of F&O in 1982 proposed a study project in
three stages, under the title "Towards the
Common Expression of the Apostolic Faith
Today". It aimed at three interdependent
goals: (1) recognition of the Nicene Creed (in
the version of 381, i.e. without the filioque*
clause) as *the* ecumenical creed of the church,
(2) explanation of that creed for the sake of
contemporary understanding and establishing
confidence concerning its meaning in the service of unity, and (3) finding ways to express
that same common faith today.

Recognition of the Nicene Creed — without the addition of the filioque clause —
seems a real possibility now, provided that an
ecumenical explanation becomes a sufficient

basis for mutual trust. Such explanation is developing now within the F&O commission, and a first draft was published in 1987, entitled "Confessing One Faith". After further work, it will be shared with the churches at a F&O world conference, planned for 1993. This explanation sets out the biblical sources of the articulations of faith used in the creed of 381 and then treats them in relation to questions being asked about them today. At the Budapest commission meeting of F&O in 1989, it was requested that the explanation should deal also with the 4th-century setting in which the creed was formulated, in order to understand better the creed's hermeneutical dynamics with regard to the scriptures and to its own contemporary context.

Recognition and explanation of the Nicene Creed, however, must not replace the search for new confessions of faith as they are provoked today by situations of persecution, of church union negotiations, or of urgent socioeconomic, political or ideological threats. Several such examples of "credal witness in context" have been collected and published by the WCC in the series "Confessing Our Faith around the World". Among this material, some modern confessions of faith that have been made on an authoritative level could enrich the variety of credal expression and ought to be communicated within the ecumenical community as concrete evidence that we are "listening to what the Spirit has to say to the churches". Reception and fraternal correction of such confessional formulas would then become a real sign of koinonia* and conciliar fellowship. An ecumenical "Book of Confessions" would then become an enriching possibility for dialogue and exchange of spiritual experiences.

Important problems that are still to be solved in the explanation of the ancient creeds and the reception of contemporary expressions of faith relate to the understanding of creation* and redemption,* the images and names of God,* the challenge of atheism,* the dialogue with other faiths (see **dialogue, interfaith**), the doctrine of the incarnation* and the resurrection* of the Son of God, the activity of the Holy Spirit* in church* and world, and the right understanding of the gospel of "the kingdom of God".* More important, however, is the question of how the churches could discover together "how to *live*

the faith in such a way that it will meet the aspirations on which people and persons set their hopes together, and how to proclaim this faith unanimously by overcoming its divisions" *(Towards a Confession of the Common Faith)*.

See also **common witness, creeds, faith, Nicene Creed**.

ANTON HOUTEPEN

Confessing One Faith: Towards an Ecumenical Explication of the Apostolic Faith as Expressed in the Nicene-Constantinopolitan Creed (381), WCC, 1987 • *Confessing Our Faith around the World*, vols 1-4, WCC, 1984-86 • A. Houtepen, "Bekenntnisse der Kirchen — Bekenntnisse der Ökumene. Einheit und Vielfalt, Tradition und Erneuerung im christlichen 'Bekennen'", *Una Sancta*, 40, 1985 • H. Küng & J. Moltmann eds, *An Ecumenical Confession of Faith?*, New York, Seabury, 1978 • H.G. Link ed., *The Apostolic Faith: A Handbook for Study*, WCC, 1985 • H.G. Link ed., *The Roots of Our Common Faith*, WCC, 1984 • C.S. Rodd ed., *Foundation Documents of the Faith*, Edinburgh, Clark, 1987 • *Towards a Confession of the Common Faith*, WCC, 1980.

COMMON WITNESS. By common witness is meant the witness* that the churches, even while separated, bear together, especially through joint efforts, by manifesting whatever divine gifts of truth and life they already share and experience in common. "Common witness" has become a popular expression since the early 1970s. In the Protestant origins of the ecumenical movement, a limited understanding of common witness had been conveyed by other words, such as "co-operation", "united ministries" and "joint mission".

Early co-operation. Co-operation marked a few Protestant missions from their beginnings in the early 18th century. For example, in 1710 the Anglican-based Society for Promoting Christian Knowledge began supplying personnel and funds to the Danish-Halle mission in India, which Lutherans were staffing.

In the 19th century, Christians across denominational lines formed associations, notably Bible and tract societies, and some mission groups were working for common policies and effective home-base collaboration. Co-operation in health and education ministries led to union institutions, e.g. in India and in China. At least there was common witness to basic Christian convictions about helping people in need and sharing the same gospel.

By so-called comity arrangements, various mission groups, whether of the churches or independent of them, divided new territories into spheres of operation. Although comity led to "denominationalism* by geography", there was at least common witness to lessen wasteful duplication of resources and to keep at a distance obvious variant forms of worship and polity which could scandalize non-Christians and hinder witness to the basic gospel message which Christians share.

The Edinburgh conference in 1910 stimulated co-operation in other lines, especially in the gradual spread of interdenominational "home base" and "foreign" federations; after the first world war, many of these developed into national Christian councils.

Some Protestant bodies in conscience rejected the very principle of such co-operation, e.g. Missouri Synod Lutherans, Seventh Day Adventists and certain Baptist groups. Until the 1960s, the Roman Catholic Church (RCC) and most of the Orthodox churches also refused to co-operate. The Roman Catholic (RC) and Orthodox refusals were based on ecclesiological self-understanding, on the pastoral judgment of "not confusing the faithful" by apparent compromise of revealed truth, and on the anxiety over legitimizing and even increasing what they judged to be Protestant proselytism* among their vulnerable flocks.

On the other hand, Protestants and Orthodox questioned RC understandings and policies on religious freedom.* The RCC seemed to demand free exercise of religion when Catholics are in a minority in any nation, and at the same time to refuse and deny the same freedom when Catholics are in a majority. If one could trust RC ecumenical "moves" towards co-operation with other Christians, the RCC should state "clearly and authoritatively that it will respect the liberty of other believers, even if it has the power or the occasion to do otherwise, and that it condemns intolerance, persecution and discrimination on grounds of religious liberty" (A.F. Carillo de Albornoz, WCC secretary for religious liberty, 1964).

The pre-condition of common witness. In hindsight, one thus sees that consensus over religious freedom and proselytism (or false witness) was a pre-condition for the acceptance of authentic common witness

among all the churches. The New Delhi WCC assembly in 1961 approved the report on Christian witness, proselytism and religious liberty. The report's clarifications eased the entrance of certain churches, the Orthodox in particular, into the active life of the WCC — itself a "privileged" instrument and sign of common witness.

The official RC entrance into the ecumenical movement was signalled in several documents of the Second Vatican Council (1962-65), especially those on the church, on ecumenism and on religious freedom. Based on the ecclesiological conviction that "real but imperfect communion" already exists between the churches, the Decree on Ecumenism pleaded: "Before the whole world, let all Christians profess their faith in God, our Redeemer and Lord. United in their efforts, and with mutual respect, let them bear witness to our common hope." The decree called for "co-operation among Christians", for it "vividly expresses that bond which already unites them, and sets in clearer relief the features of Christ the Servant".

Furthermore, in its religious freedom declaration, Vatican II insisted that no individual or community may be forced to act against conscience* or be prevented from expressing belief in teaching, worship or social action.

The expression "common witness" appears extensively for the first time in the 1970 document of the WCC/RCC Joint Working Group* "Common Witness and Proselytism". The same group further elaborated its reflections in the 1982 study "Common Witness". Since the early 1970s, "common witness" seems to be dominating other expressions in ecumenical vocabulary, such as "collaboration" or "common mission".

Implications of common witness. Clarifications and ecumenical implications of common witness include several aspects.

First, Christian witness is the continuous act by which a Christian individual or community proclaims, in deed and word, God's saving deeds in history. Christ calls each disciple wholly to be his witness but does not demand each to be a witness to the whole of him. Only the church,* the community of all disciples, in its many-splendoured variety, is a witness to the whole incarnate counsel of God. This continual witness includes the whole life of the church: personal and communal worship,

Closing worship at Kirchentag, Düsseldorf
(WCC/Peter Williams)

responsible service, and proclamation of the good news. The church is prodded to persevere in such witness by the "cloud of witnesses" (Heb. 12:1), especially of those who suffered for the faith, even unto death (see **martyrdom**).

Second, common witness, as it is now used, applies to the historical situation of the real but imperfect communion* between the churches in their search for the full visible communion of the one church of Christ. Common witness will always remain imperfect until there is full communion in faith, sacramental life and teaching authority,* and in the exercise and recognition of all the Spirit's charisms* given "for the common good" (1 Cor. 12:7), "for building up the body of Christ" (Eph. 4:12).

Third, even while still lacking that full communion, the churches nevertheless acknowledge that proclaiming the saving deeds of God is their central task, and this should be the burden of their common witness. They all find in the one gospel their motivation, their purpose and their content for common witness. The churches give common witness whenever and however they express the gifts of faith, hope and love according to God's word, e.g. in Christian marriage and family life, Sunday worship, acts of compassion and forgiveness, selfless service to those in material and spiritual need, the promotion of social and economic justice, the explicit invitation to hear Christ's call to God through him and his church, and the very silence of a prison cell or of a civilly restricted but still serving, waiting, praying church.

Thus, common witness is broader than cooperation or joint efforts. In fact, Christians give common witness when they acknowledge and respect the shared gifts of grace, truth and love in all the churches, rejoice in their exercise, and praise and thank God, always wonderful in his works and worthy of all praise.

Fourth, common witness is heightened whenever the churches and their members jointly carry out shared Christian responsibilities: prayer (common celebrations which mark the Week of Prayer for Christian Unity* or highlight the great Christian festivals or other occasions of local significance); reading, studying and praying through the Bible; the translation, production and distribution of Bible editions; Christian catechism texts, especially for the young; theological reflection on classically dividing issues (bilateral and multilateral dialogues*); approaches to local, national or international civil authorities to make known to them Christian witness in political matters where human rights and dignity as well as spiritual and moral values are at stake; and direct evangelism.

The range and diversity of interchurch organizations for joint action and other forms of co-operation run from councils of churches at various levels, to joint working groups, service councils and committees, and study and action groups of every kind. One should expect further forms to appear as renewed faithfulness to mission impels Christians towards unity, as they already try to proclaim a message of hope and peace in a broken world.

Finally, common witness has limits because of different, even contradictory, understandings of the revealed content of the faith regarding worship (e.g. eucharistic sharing), faith (e.g. authority in and of the church) and personal and social ethics (e.g. abortion, active homosexuality, women's rights in the church). In fact, certain ethical issues rise high like flags, and transdenominational coalitions form to wave a particular flag. They often take opposite sides, and each side claims it is faithful to the gospel and is expressing common witness.

Such situations and experiences, rather than create standstills in the ecumenical movement, should further press Christians "to find the right ways to proclaim together to all peoples the good news of the kingdom of God" (Pope John Paul II) and to pray and work for that true common witness in the full visible communion of the one church of Christ, who is "the faithful and true witness" (Rev. 3:14).

See also **common confession, communion, evangelism, mission**.

TOM STRANSKY

G. Anderson & T. Stransky eds, *Mission Trends*, no. 2, New York, Paulist, 1975 • *Common Witness*, WCC, 1982 • *Mission and Evangelism: An Ecumenical Affirmation*, WCC, 1983 • Vatican Secretariat for Promoting Christian Unity, "Ecumenical Collaboration at the Regional, National and Local Levels", in *Doing the Truth in Charity*, T. Stransky & J. Sheerin eds, New York, Paulist, 1982 • WCC/RCC Joint Working Group, "Common Witness and Proselytism", *The Ecumenical Review*, 23, 1971.

COMMUNICATION. The word "communication" by its very definition is central to the ecumenical movement. Its literal root meaning is "bound together in one". It refers to the bond that is forged when information is imparted, when ideas and thoughts are exchanged, when cultures are shared and when people or places normally treated as separate entities are brought into close relationship with one another. Communication lies at the heart of the churches' commission to make known the message of the gospel and supremely describes that act of sharing together in the gifts of grace when Christians "communicate" in the holy sacrament (see **eucharist**).

"I would call communication the fundamental human fact", wrote the Dutch theologian Johannes de Graaf, "because communication is the essential divine fact. The nature of the Triune God is the communication of the Father, the Son and the Holy Spirit in that holy *perichōrēsis* of love, out of which results the creation and in which the creation rests."

The church has consequently from the earliest days been concerned about the means of communication and has frequently been the pioneer in the development of new media, though often expressing ambivalent views about the potentiality or perils inherent in them. Thus, though the invention of printing in the 15th century was first used to disseminate the holy scriptures, it was regarded with suspicion by those who feared that this would put into common possession writings once safeguarded by religious teachers and scholars and might lead to misinterpretation and debasement of their worth. Similarly, as drama developed in the churches of medieval times as a way of communicating the gospel among illiterate people, the players were eventually driven out of the sanctuaries and had to perform in the streets instead.

The same ambivalence has been apparent in the churches' attitudes towards the mass media of communication that have developed in the 20th century, although in many cases their pioneers were people of good conscience and Christian intent. It is said that Samuel Morse, the inventor of telegraphy, for example, declared as his hope that it might be used to make known "not so much the price of pork, as what God hath wrought". The first public radio broadcast was made to ships at sea by the Canadian inventor Richard Fessenden, who began the transmission with a reading from St Luke's gospel. Broadcasting House, the headquarters of the British Broadcasting Corporation, was dedicated at the outset to the glory of God. Yet the churches were slow to see the new opportunity for Christian communication presented by these mass media. Nor were they immediately aware of the impact that electronic methods of transmission would eventually have upon the whole of society, affecting the way people send and receive messages and shaping new patterns of perception.

The value of the media to the churches. Pope Pius XII (1939-58) was one of the first church leaders in the 20th century to speak positively about the potential value of the mass media. While sharing the anxieties of his predecessors about the debasing of values in the secular press, he pursued the thesis that the media in themselves were not inherently good or evil but that the abuse of them reflected the sickness in human society. He emphasized that they should be used to propagate Christian teaching.

Similarly, the earliest statements of the WCC on the theme of mass communication concentrated on their value as tools to be used by the churches in their own task of evangelism* and particularly emphasized the importance of safeguarding the right to the freedom of religious expression. At the first WCC assembly in Amsterdam, the principle was enunciated that "the right to determine faith and creed becomes meaningful when man has the opportunity of access to information... This right requires freedom from arbitrary limitation of religious expression in all means of communication, including speech, press, radio, motion pictures and art." The assembly urged that further research into the effect of these media should be undertaken.

Warning notes about the perils inherent in using mass media as a means of evangelism were sounded at the Evanston assembly, where it was stated: "When the gospel is secularized, vulgarized or diluted into an easy alternative to facing the demand of God for a personal response, it does much harm." But the assembly emphasized the important role of communication in publicizing the ecumenical movement itself and gave a mandate to the communication department of the WCC to "make known the activities of the WCC through the church and secular press and other media. It should also serve the churches by providing them with news about the life of their sister churches."

Inter Mirifica. The first major council of a church to address communication as an area of Christian concern in itself was the Second Vatican Council* in its Decree on the Instruments of Social Communication, known as *Inter Mirifica*. This was one of the earliest documents approved by the Council and was given little discussion. Later it was generally regarded as too slight a commentary on what was becoming a major issue. But as Pope Paul VI remarked later, it was "not of small value" in that it stressed the need for everybody to develop "an upright conscience on the use of these instruments", particularly with regard to the purveying of information and the portrayal of human morality. "Within human society", the decree declared, "exists a right to information about affairs which affect men individually or collectively." But such information should be "honourable and appropriate". The stress, however — as at the early WCC assemblies — was mainly on the value of the media in the fulfilment of the church's own task. "The church claims as a birthright the use and possession of all instruments which are necessary and useful for the formation of Christians and for every activity undertaken on behalf of man's salvation."

The practical outcome of the Vatican decree was that it recommended that national offices should be everywhere established for "affairs of press, motion pictures, radio and television". Such offices would have "the special obligation of helping the faithful to form a true conscience about the use of these media and of fostering and co-ordinating Catholic activities directed to this end". Following the re-organization of the Roman curia in 1989, the new Pontifical Council for Social Communications is concerned with all media: written, cinema, radio and television.

Commentators on the decree criticized its clerical and paternalistic tone, and its failure to take account of the expertise of professional journalists among the church's laity. It had insisted that "on religious shepherds devolves the task of so training and directing the faithful that by the help of these instruments [of communication] they may pursue their own salvation and fulfilment". It seemed to claim the right of the church to possess the communication media for its own purposes while exercising control over all other uses.

Archbishop Andrea Pangrazio, quoted in the Italian Catholic weekly *Ave Maria* in January 1965, took a more prophetic view. "A mass society has come into being which has given itself a mass culture. The intellectual is contemptuous of it and rejects it, but the fact remains that this mass culture contains real human values: a thirst for knowledge and truth, a need to communicate these with every means and with all speed so that people may be in communication with each other and finally a cultural heritage accessible to all and offered as a gift. These values must find their own theological interpretation so that a new humanism can be realized."

The Uppsala statement. Out of a similar concern that the churches did not seem to be taking the media seriously enough and were failing to recognize the quantum leap that was taking place in the whole field of communication, a group of professional journalists and broadcasters met with an ecumenical group of theologians for a consultation convened by the WCC at Bossey (1965). This was the first international conference under church auspices to consider the relationship of theology to mass communication. It stressed that with the advent of radio and television, the patterns of human perception were being changed, in that the printed word was no longer the main way in which people were receiving and transmitting messages. While recognizing that the churches had a pastoral responsibility towards all who used the media, it emphasized especially the role of professional journalists and the wide impact of their work on society as a whole.

The outcome of the consultation was a major statement prepared for the Uppsala assembly of 1968 on the church and the media of mass communication. Optimistic in tone, it reflects the theological mood of the 1960s in its affirmation of the presence of God in the secular world of the media, claiming that the world of communication is a theatre of the Holy Spirit's operation and that the mass media are tools which could help to forge a new, universal human society. "The media can enrich human life considerably," it stated. "As never before, they make it possible for people to share experience with the hope that they may grow in awareness, understanding and compassion. The media provide some of the bone structure for a responsible world society. The sufferings of others are swiftly known and may be quickly alleviated. The crucial issues of our time are discussed before all people. Minority views can be given a public airing. New proposals and plans can be openly debated. Cultural treasures can be circulated en masse in what can be described as 'museums without walls'. Moribund traditions can become living knowledge. It is possible that senses which have lain dormant as a result of the development of a primarily verbal or literate culture may be quickened. The media can do these things but there is no guarantee that they will."

Within the Uppsala assembly itself much use was made of visual and aural means of communicating the concerns of the various sections. Films, songs, drama, exhibitions of graphic art were prominent foci of attention, all presented with the kind of professional expertise the statement had emphasized. "The preaching of the good news of Christ", it had said, "should not be confused with poor techniques, cheap advertising methods and presentations designed as propaganda for our own groups. The presentation of the gospel requires respect for the freedom of the audience and the integrity of the media."

The recommendations arising out of the Uppsala statement began by acknowledging that the churches had been tardy in taking the communication media seriously and urged that the WCC should initiate studies in this area, a mandate given subsequently to the department of communication. This led to considerable discussion later about the place of the department in the whole structure of the WCC. Was it to be regarded mainly as a service department, fulfilling the mandate expressed at Evanston for providing efficient communications to serve the churches and the ecumenical movement, or should it have a programme in its own right, concerned with the need for the more wide-ranging studies recommended at Uppsala? For a short time the department was located in the Unit on Education and Renewal, but later it reverted to a direct relationship with the General Secretariat, charged mainly with the responsibility of meeting the communication needs of the whole Council.

Communio et Progressio. The optimistic note of the Uppsala statement was sounded too by Pope Paul VI in a pastoral instruction he issued in 1971 entitled *Communio et Progressio* (The means of social communication). This stressed the need for a more positive and affirmative attitude to the media. The pope saw modern developments as making it possible to multiply the contacts within human society and to deepen social consciousness, which would contribute to the growth of human unity. In a vivid simile, he compared the availability of the mass media to the provision of a round table which could give the whole human family an opportunity to participate in dialogue and fellowship with one another.

During the 1970s the regional offices concerned with communication set up after the Second Vatican Council were beginning to make their impact. In Latin America the issue of communication was given prominent attention at the third general conference of Latin American bishops (Puebla 1979). This conference reflected on the results of monitoring the media that had gone on in their own region and had both positive and negative judgments to make. "We recognize that the media of social communication are factors for communion. They contribute to the integration of Latin America and to the expansion and democratization of culture. They also contribute to the entertainment of people. They increase people's capacity for perception and sensory acuteness through auditory and visual stimuli."

But the report went on to denounce the control and ideological manipulation of the media exercised by political and economic power groups. "They seek to maintain the status quo or even to create a new order of dependence and domination, or else they seek to subvert the existing order and to create one that is the very antithesis of it. Exploitation of passions, feelings, violence and sex for consumeristic purposes constitutes a flagrant violation of individual rights."

The ecumenical dimension of the media. Meanwhile, ecumenical commentators were stressing the potential of the mass media as a democratizing influence, putting information, education and entertainment within the reach of all. In a paper written for the *Christian Broadcaster*, the journal of the World Association for Christian Broadcasting, Albert van den Heuvel, at that time director of communication at the WCC, commended the role of the media in extending a sense of universalism over against the nationalism of the time and in serving ecumenism by unmasking the inefficiency of the denominational structures of the churches. He suggested that the development of mass methods of communication was providing the one stable factor in a mobile society, even describing the media as "the breviary of modern man" and claiming that they showed signs of "messianic quality". He showed how the "communication theologians" — Karl Barth, Roger Mehl, Jacques Ellul — had written about communication as being of the very essence of the divine-human relationship but had used the word only within the context of interpersonal relationships and had not seriously addressed the question of the media of social communication. This theological dimension was sounded in the WCC central committee in 1972 in the report of the Sub-unit on Communication. "Often the churches have been content to talk about communication as technique without realizing that communicative techniques are always developed within a theoretical framework and betray deep theological or ideological presuppositions. It is high time that the churches accept the need to give to the theological reflection on communication the place of importance which is necessitated by the crises of

communication they experience within and among themselves... Are we too harsh when we accuse the churches of still thinking mainly in terms of *using* the media? The well-being of the media for mass communication, their proper structures, the code of professional ethics, their purpose and the ministry in a technological society are not given the attention which their importance requires."

Throughout the 1970s the issue of communication began to appear on the agenda of many ecumenical consultations. In 1971 the Lima meeting of the Sub-unit on Education discussed the growing use of mass media as tools of instruction. The committee on Society, Development and Peace (SODEPAX) emphasized the role of the media in disseminating news of the developing world. At its consultation in Montreux, the Commission on the Churches' Participation in Development saw the important role of social communication in seeking to change society's structures, commending it as a powerful alternative to violent confrontation. At St Polten in 1974 the Commission of the Churches on International Affairs drew attention to the danger of selec-

Press conference, National Council of Churches in the Philippines (WCC/Peter Williams)

tive presentation of world affairs in the Western-dominated news media. The particular question of the image of women portrayed in the media was the subject of a conference in Vienna and was introduced in a vivid audiovisual presentation at the opening of the conference on sexism at Berlin in 1974.

At the Nairobi assembly (1975) it became clear that budgetary constraints had restricted the activities of the department of communication to its primary task of serving the communication needs of the WCC itself, and the larger questions concerning the theology and ethics of communication did not surface. The development of the electronic media was mentioned only in the context of the work of the church and even then in a somewhat dismissive way. "Never before has the church universal had at its disposal such a comprehensive set of means of communication as we have today — literature, audiovisuals, electronic media. While we need to improve our use of such media, nothing can replace the living witness in words and deeds of Christian persons, groups and congregations who participate in the sufferings and joys, in the struggles and celebrations, in the frustrations and hopes of the people with whom they want to share the gospel. Whatever 'methodologies' of communication may seem to be appropriate in different situations, they should be directed by a humble spirit of sensitivity and participation." No doubt, such statements were influenced by scepticism about the glittering showmanship of the increasingly popular "tele-evangelists", who were using television in America to reach mass audiences and draw them to what has been described as an electronic church.

Communication problems. Meanwhile the WCC itself had become embroiled in much controversy in the media about its own programme and purpose. Largely through the debates aroused by the Programme to Combat Racism (PCR)* the Council became a focus of attention in press, radio and television in the Western world. A great deal of the time of the department of communication was taken up in interpreting the Council's action both to the churches and to the secular media. The PCR by the very nature of its action-oriented programme had vigorously communicated the nature of the struggle in which it was engaged.

Another communication problem internal to the WCC has been the problem of language. Inherited Babel does not make easier the task of those who seek to enter into a post-Pentecost community. As the membership of the Council has grown in extent, the number of people whose native tongue is not one of the working languages used by the Council has also grown, and the need for greater recognition and inclusion of the main languages of the southern and eastern regions of the world as well as of the northern and western has become clamant. But the limitation of resources does not make possible the extension of the department of communication's present language service. The question of language remains of crucial importance in the development of good ecumenical communication.

The emphasis put at Nairobi on the value of person-to-person encounter as the best means of communication found concrete expression in preparations for the sixth assembly (Vancouver 1983), when team visits were organized, whereby delegates to the assembly were encouraged to travel and to communicate with their counterparts in churches in other countries and cultures. In the Roman Catholic community too the value of travel and of personal encounter, enhanced by the co-operation of the mass media, has become a highlight of the papal tours to all parts of the world.

The search for credible communication. The "media malaise", as it has been described, grew during the 1980s. The need for deeper reflection on how the media themselves are shaping as well as reflecting modern society and extending their influence in a global network has become an even more urgent task. At a consultation in Versailles in 1981, representatives of the WCC, the World Association for Christian Communication,* the Lutheran World Federation and three Roman Catholic agencies met to discuss their common concerns. It was determined that the focus of attention should still be primarily on church-related communication in the widest sense. A discussion paper was circulated among some 400 churches, media institutes and individuals involved in the media. Under the title "The Search for Credible Christian Communication", the paper was described as "an invitation to the churches to join a journey towards a new understanding of their communication opportunities in the 1980s". It noted that "the churches exist to communicate" and observed: "How well we succeed is the measure of our mission and our Christian credibility."

The paper went on to sketch out a wider context for the discussion, pleading for Christians to develop a greater awareness of the influence of the media on the whole of life. It recognized the injustice of the present international order, whereby the tools of mass communication are owned and for the most part wielded by the powerful nations or commercial interests of the Western world. The paper raised many fundamental questions, the responses to which were intended to form the basis of debate at Vancouver in 1983, where the issue of communication figured in the programme in its own right as one of eight sections set before the delegates.

The report emerging from that section at Vancouver was, in contrast to the Uppsala statement of 15 years before, more critical in its assessment of the mass media and their impact on modern society. While recognizing that "credible communication serves the cause of justice and peace", it did not support the demand for a New World Information and Communication Order, whereby people would "affirm their own values, assert their own cultures and determine their own priorities. Their demands for such a new order have been largely ignored." The Vancouver report suggested criteria by which people should judge the credibility of what they see and hear, questioning the content, the style, the opportunity for dialogue and the appropriateness of the media themselves. To these it added criteria which might be raised from a Christian viewpoint. The gospel of Christ, it asserted, reverses the values so often pervading the modern media of communication.

The section report, while raising these pertinent questions, was felt to be short on both analysis and prescription. It becomes evident that there is still much profound work to be done in all the churches if they are to address adequately the fundamental theological and ethical issues raised by the escalation of electronic communication, now the most rapidly growing industry of our times. The more extensive the outreach of the mass media, the more intensive has become their ownership, so that they have become tools in the hands of great powers in the commercial, political and industrial world. The question of the values and life-style which they purvey universally, the effect upon regional and indigenous cultures, the ethical issues raised by the content of modern communication and the means of expressing it, the debate about censorship and the principle of freedom of information, and above all theological reflection on what mass communication means for a faith which at its very heart is communication between God and the human soul are all matters of vital importance to the agenda of the ecumenical movement as a whole.

Many of these issues were taken up at the first world congress (Manila 1989) of the World Association for Christian Communication (WACC), a forum which at an international level, and also in its many regional organizations, brings together practitioners in the field of communications, theologians and social scientists whose special study is the influence of the media in society. Other ecumenical organizations giving special attention to the development of the media of communication are the Roman Catholic Unda* (from the Latin word meaning "wave"), which specializes in radio and television, and OCIC (Organisation catholique internationale du cinéma) which is particularly concerned with films. These two organizations encourage excellence in the Christian use of the media by making annual awards for the best productions, judged on an international basis. There is an ever-increasing collaboration between the Catholic agencies and the WACC.

Each year, the Pontifical Commission for Social Communications promotes a World Communications Day, when the pope speaks to the people about the message and mission of the church in relation to the media of communication. The churches' role, he said in his 1988 address, is to insist on "the values which constitute the grandeur of the human being". Mass communications could be a means whereby the human race might realize its deep aspiration towards solidarity as well as its sense of belonging to one human family, "an aspiration often disowned or disfigured, but indestructible because it is sculpted in the human heart by the same God who has created in it the need for communication and the capacity to develop it on a planetary scale".

PAULINE WEBB

J. Bluck, *Beyond Neutrality*, WCC, 1983 • J. Bluck, *Christian Communication Reconsidered*, WCC, 1989 • *Communio et Progressio*, Pope Paul VI, pastoral instruction, 1971 • W. Fore, *Television and Religion*, Minneapolis, Augsburg, 1987 • L. Jorgenson, *The WCC and Communication*, WCC, 1982 • C. Morris, *God in a Box*, London, Hodder & Stoughton, 1984.

COMMUNION. Among the many traditional conceptions of the church,* one of the most ancient and enduring is that of a communion of human persons with the Triune God (see **Trinity**) and, consequently, with one another in God. This communion, though fundamentally spiritual, is effected, nourished and certified by adherence to common expressions of the faith,* by participation in the same sacraments* and, some would add, by submission to a single collegially unified pastoral leadership.

In patristic times the Greek term "koinonia" (and its Latin equivalent, *communio*) referred to a whole set of ecclesial bonds. Each particular church was seen as a group of faithful in communion with their own bishop (see **episcopacy**) and, through the bishop, in communion with the faithful of other local churches.* The universal fellowship was both a communion of persons (the "communion of saints"*) and a communion in sacred things, especially in sacraments.

In the early centuries communion was effected and expressed in a great variety of ways. For example, the bishop of Rome had the custom of sending particles of the bread consecrated at his own altar (the *fermentum*) to the titular churches of the city. Unconsecrated hosts were sent over great distances to be used for the eucharist. Bishops of major sees would send lists of approved and orthodox bishops in their own region to bishops of distant lands. Christian travellers would be furnished with *tesserae* (letters of communion), entitling them to hospitality in the churches they visited. The most fundamental sign of communion was admission to the eucharist* — as celebrant or concelebrant, in the case of clergy, or as communicant, in the case of laity.

When one bishop established communion with another, he entered into communion, at least nominally, with all the bishops recognized by the second bishop. When a bishop was out of communion with the principal churches, and especially with Rome, he and his faithful were to that extent "excommunicated".

Excommunication* was not yet viewed as a canonical penalty imposed by a superior authority but seen rather as a suspension of communion between fellow bishops. Communion would be denied in various degrees for various offences ranging from heresy* at worst, through schism,* down to lesser infractions of good order. A person who was in some respects excommunicated — e.g. from the eucharist — might be in communion in other respects, such as participation in non-eucharistic prayers.

Gradually, in the middle ages, the church became more centralized, especially in the West, where it took on the appearance of a monarchy under the sovereignty of the bishop of Rome. With the increased codification of canon law,* the church was seen in predominantly juridical terms, as the spiritual counterpart of the holy Roman empire. Excommunication came to be viewed as a penalty imposed from above, involving a denial of churchly status to those who were, so to speak, cut off from the body. From the Roman point of view, any individual or community outside its communion was to that extent outside of the church.

This juridical type of ecclesiology continued to dominate in Roman Catholic theology until the mid-20th century. With the rise of the ecumenical movement, however, there was an increasing readiness among the participants, including the Roman Catholic Church, to attribute some true churchly status to bodies of Christians with whom one's own church was not in communion. Thus the conditions were ripe for a revival of the patristic theology of communion.

In Roman Catholicism, Vatican II* (1962-65) was a major contributor to this revival. Following the lead of Catholic theologians well versed in patristic literature, the Council adopted, in many key texts, a *communio* ecclesiology. The Catholic church described itself as a communion of particular (or diocesan) churches, each of which, being a communion, was a distinct realization of the mystery of the church (e.g. Constitution on the Sacred Liturgy 41). The member churches, while maintaining their individual character, were linked to one another in a fellowship of charity and truth. As bonds of union the Council referred to communion in the same faith, the same sacraments, and the same structured fellowship. The bishops were charged with presiding over the communion of their own churches and keeping those churches in communion both synchronically with the other churches and diachronically with the church of previous ages. The bishops were seen as mutually joined to one another in a collegial fellowship, or hierarchical communion, over which the bishop of Rome presided in charity and truth.

In its Decree on Ecumenism, Vatican II took the position that all baptized Christians were in some degree in communion with one another and with the Catholic church, but that the lack of full participation in the same professions of faith, the same sacraments and the same societal structures were obstacles to that full communion which should flow from baptism. Thus the present ecumenical situation, as described by the Council, was one of communions in imperfect communion with one another and with the Catholic church. The goal of the ecumenical movement was seen as the establishment or restoration of full communion among separated Christian groups.

The ecumenical vision of Vatican II has been consistently maintained by the highest Roman Catholic authorities since the Council. Pope Paul VI and Cardinal Jan Willebrands, the president of the Secretariat (now Council) for Promoting Christian Unity, repeatedly spoke of the desirability of restoring full communion with "sister churches"* such as the Orthodox churches of the East. Paul VI, followed by John Paul II, described the Orthodox churches as being in "almost complete" communion with Rome (Paul VI, letter to Patriarch Athenagoras, 8 February 1971; John Paul II, address for Week of Prayer for Christian Unity, 17 January 1979). The extraordinary synod of bishops of 1985, reviewing the work of Vatican II, re-affirmed an ecumenism of communion: "We bishops ardently desire that the incomplete communion already existing with the non-Catholic churches and communities might, with the grace of God,

come to the point of full communion" (final report, 2.C.7).

A similar theology of communion is accepted by many other Christian bodies. In dialogue statements representatives of the Orthodox and Roman Catholic churches have been able to agree that "the church is a communion of believers living in Jesus Christ and the Spirit with the Father. It has its origin and prototype in the Trinity, in which there is both distinction of persons and unity based on love, not subordination" (USA consultation, 4 December 1974). The International Joint Commission for Theological Dialogue between the Catholic Church and the Orthodox Church declared in its Munich statement on "The Church, the Eucharist and the Trinity" (July 1982): "The one and unique church finds her identity in the koinonia of the churches." In its Bari statement on "Faith, Sacraments and the Unity of the Church" (June 1987), the same commission stated: "The human person is integrated into the Body of Christ by his or her koinonia (communion) with the visible church, which nourishes this faith by means of the sacramental life and the word of God, and in which the Holy Spirit works in the human person" (see **Orthodox-Roman Catholic dialogue**).

Anglicanism has traditionally defined itself as a fellowship of local and regional churches in communion with the see of Canterbury. The Lambeth conference of 1930 depicted the Anglican communion as "eagerly awaiting the time when the churches of the present Anglican communion will enter into communion with other parts of the catholic church not definable as Anglican... as a step towards the ultimate reunion of all Christendom in one visibly united fellowship". The national ecumenical consultation of the Episcopal Church, USA, in its Detroit report of 5-6 November 1978, declared: "The visible unity we seek is one eucharistic fellowship, a communion of communions, based upon mutual recognition of catholicity." The final report of the Anglican-Roman Catholic International Commission in 1982 stated in its introduction that the concept of koinonia was fundamental to all its statements.

Lutheranism has historically looked upon itself as a confession, but this confessional consciousness does not exclude the idea of communion. Lutheran commentators have

Pope Paul VI and Patriarch Athenagoras I (WCC/John Taylor)

discussed the question of pulpit and altar fellowship in the context of a well-articulated ecclesiology of communion; and the new constitution of the Lutheran World Federation,* adopted in 1990, defines the LWF as "a *communion of churches* which confess the Triune God, agree in the proclamation of the word of God and are united in pulpit and altar fellowship".

In its statement "Facing Unity", the Roman Catholic-Lutheran Joint Commission (1984) proposed a gradual process of achieving a structured fellowship. The statement takes its departure from the assertion that the church is by its very nature a *communio* subsisting in a network of local churches (no. 5). The statement also calls attention to the Union of Florence (1442) as one possible model for church union without merger or absorption. Communion is seen in "Facing Unity" as involving three dimensions: fellowship in confessing the same apostolic faith, fellowship in sacramental life and fellowship in ministry and service.

The WCC at its New Delhi assembly (1961) made use of the concept of koinonia to explain the meaning of the "one fully committed fellowship", which the member churches accepted as the goal for which they should work and pray. The assembly warned, however, that this fellowship did not imply "a rigid uniformity of structure, organization, or government". The Nairobi assembly (1975) approved a new constitution in which the purpose of the WCC was described, in the first instance, as "to call the churches to the goal of visible unity in one faith and one eucharistic fellowship expressed in worship and in common life in Christ, and to advance towards that unity in order that the world may believe". The "conciliar fellowship" envisaged at Nairobi may be seen as a version of what has been here described as communion.

Because the theology of communion admits of many degrees and modalities, it is not possible to state in simple terms which churches are in communion with one another. Churches that are still divided to some extent in doctrine and polity have sometimes chosen to express their mutual proximity by establishing "interim eucharistic fellowship", such as that which is encouraged in the Consultation on Church Union* in the USA. Other churches that are very close to each other in doctrine, styles of worship and ecclesial polity have seen fit to refrain from eucharistic sharing until all barriers between them have been overcome. Thus eucharistic fellowship, although it is of great importance in the concept of communion, should not be used as the exclusive criterion.

The term "full communion" is used with various nuances. From Roman Catholics it normally signifies not only doctrinal and sacramental agreement but submission to the same system of pastoral rule. Some ecumenical statements, however, use the term to designate a relationship of "pulpit and altar fellowship", together with commitment to mutual respect and consultation in teaching and decision making, among communions that "become interdependent while remaining autonomous" (Anglican-Lutheran Joint Working Group, Cold Ash, Berkshire, England, 1983). Occasionally "full communion" is interpreted as a synonym for "intercommunion" among churches of different confessional families (*Lutheran-Episcopal Agreement: Commentary and Guidelines*, New York, Division for World Mission and Ecumenism, 1983).

According to the perspective adopted in this article, ecclesial communion is a complex notion that includes not only eucharistic fellowship but also agreement regarding the necessary doctrines of faith, sharing in the full sacramental life of worship and affiliation with the same socially structured community. Christians who believe that a unified pastoral office is essential to the church will regard acceptance of the same body of leaders as necessary for full communion. Wherever any one of these elements is present, even minimally, communion exists to some extent, but "full communion" requires the total verification of all the elements.

See also **church, church discipline, excommunication, intercommunion, koinonia**.

AVERY DULLES

P. Avis, *Christians in Communion*, London, Chapman Mowbray, 1990 • E.L. Brand, *Toward a Lutheran Communion: Pulpit and Altar Fellowship*, Geneva, Lutheran World Federation, 1988 • *Facing Unity: Models, Forms and Phrases of Catholic-Lutheran Fellowship*, Geneva, Lutheran World Federation, 1985 • L. Hertling, *Communio: Church and Papacy in Early Christianity*, Chicago, Loyola UP, 1971 • K. McDonnell, "Vatican II (1962-1965), Puebla (1979), Synod (1985): *Koinonia/Communio* as an Integral Ecclesiology", *Journal of Ecumenical Studies*, 25, 3, 1988 • J.R. Wright ed., *A Communion of Communions: One Eucharistic Fellowship. The Detroit Report and Papers of the Triennial Ecumenical Study of the Episcopal Church, 1976-79*, New York, Seabury/Crossroad, 1979 • J.D. Zizioulas, *Being as Communion: Studies in Personhood and the Church*, Crestwood, NY, St Vladimir's Seminary, 1985.

COMMUNION OF SAINTS.

In some of the ancient eucharistic liturgies of the church, at the time of communion the celebrant turns to the people with the words "holy things for holy people", words which are sometimes now translated "the gifts of God for the people of God". These words speak of a sharing in holy gifts by holy people, a sharing created by the grace of our Lord Jesus Christ, by the love of God the Father and by the communion of the Holy Spirit (see **Trinity**). This communion is not broken by death, for by his death Christ has destroyed death. It is a communion which fulfills the loving purposes of the Father from all eternity, bringing all together into a unity which preserves all the richness and diversity which God has placed in his creation.

In time the all-inclusive phrase *communio sanctorum* — a sharing of holy people in holy things — came to refer especially to the sharing of life and love across the barrier of death which exists between all who are in Christ and in the Spirit. We are at one with the saints in heaven, and they are at one with us. Questions have been raised about this doctrine, however, and differences surfaced, particularly at the time of the Reformation. What is the situation of those who have died? Are they already either in heaven or in hell and so beyond the reach of our prayers? Or are we still bound together with them in mutual prayer and intercession? Should we pray for them and ask for their prayers? How far should the churches officially recognize and proclaim certain of their departed members as saints, a practice common to Roman Catholics and Orthodox, and not unknown among Anglicans? Does such a recognition undermine the faith that all God's people are called to be saints?

Most, if not all, Reformation theologians maintain that we should not address the saints directly, and that if we pray for them our prayer should take the form of a simple commendation of them into the hands of God. To pray to the saints, in this perspective, is to make a confusion in the nature of prayer. Prayer is that which is addressed to God alone. Christ alone is Mediator and Intercessor. This does not mean that the doctrine of the communion of saints is repudiated. In hymnody in particular there is sometimes a strong affirmation that the saints are worshipping with us. But in much of the Protestant world, little is said on this subject.

The Eastern Orthodox tradition is very different in this respect. The church's faith in the unity of heaven and earth across the barriers of death finds exuberant expression in prayers and hymns, in the veneration of relics and icons, in the commemoration of the departed in church and at home. We are at one with them. They pray for us, we pray for them. At the heart of the communion of saints there stands the dearest of them all, Mary the mother of God, always praying for the human race.

The practice and theology of the Roman Catholic Church is in many ways very similar, not least in the central place given to Mary. In some areas, at least in the past, lines have been more sharply drawn. It was commonly taught, e.g., that whereas we have a duty to pray for the souls in purgatory, they are not able to pray for us. But in Catholicism as in Orthodoxy, the veneration of the saints and prayers for the departed have an essential place in the official liturgy of the church, no less than in the faith and devotion of the people.

Is this not a point where mutual correction and enlightenment is possible? The Reformation insistence on the centrality of Christ in Christian faith and worship is universally accepted. The saints should lead us to him and not divert us from him. But the Catholic and Orthodox affirmation of our solidarity with the departed gives vivid expression to our faith in the resurrection* of Christ, which breaks the power of death, and to our faith in the transforming power of God, which works wonders in the lives of his servants, men and women of flesh and blood like ourselves.

See also **communion, life and death, martyrdom**.

A.M. ALLCHIN

P.-Y. Emery, *L'unité des croyants au ciel et sur la terre*, Taizé, Presses de Taizé, 1962.

COMMUNITY OF WOMEN AND MEN IN THE CHURCH. The CWMC study goes back to Berlin 1974, to the "Sexism in the 1970s" consultation sponsored by the WCC Sub-unit on Women in Church and Society. Recommendations from that consultation were forwarded to the Faith and Order* commission meeting some months later in Accra, Ghana. At Accra, the F&O commission agreed to "undertake a study of the theological and practical aspects of the community of men and women in the church". The study was to deal with theological issues such as the Christian concept of God,* the authority of scripture* with reference to present-day situations, the fullness of diakonia* as it affects the relationship of men and women, the ordination of women* and the "language, symbols and imagery of scripture and churches today as they influence men-women relationships".

At the fifth assembly (Nairobi 1975) F&O affirmed that integral to the unity* of the church is that women be free to live out the gifts God has given to them, to respond to their calling, to share fully in the life and witness of the church. Also at Nairobi, the Sub-unit on Women in Church and Society agreed to collaborate with F&O to "ensure active continuation" of the community study, leading to an international consultation.

At the 1976 central committee, the study was lodged in the F&O commission in collaboration with the Sub-unit on Women. In January 1978 the programme was staffed. The study's international consultation was held in Sheffield, England, in 1981, and its findings and recommendations were reported to the 1981 Dresden central committee and to the 1982 Lima meeting of F&O. The Lima meeting marked the end of the community study as a special WCC programme, but the issues which it raised continue to receive attention.

The pre-history of the study can be traced to the first F&O meeting in Lausanne (1927) and to a pre-Amsterdam assembly study entitled "The Service and Status of Women in the Church", not published until 1952. In 1978 the community study was given a twofold task: to integrate these two parallel tracks of WCC concern about the roles and status of women in the church and to create a methodology that would make this possible.

Using an experience-based method of theological reflection, the CWMC developed a study book of questions and invited church and Christian groups around the world to participate. Starting with an initial publication of 3,000 copies in English, German and French, it was re-published in these languages and translated into about a dozen other languages, ending up with an estimated 65,000 copies in distribution around the world, mostly as a result of local initiatives by women's church and ecumenical organizations, by official church and ecumenical agencies, and by some seminaries.

Subsequently, the office received several hundred local group reports, which were carefully sifted, studied and used in the preparation of the Sheffield consultation. Supplementing these grassroots reports were regional meetings in Africa, Asia, Latin America, the Middle East, Europe and North America. Because many more reports arrived from the Euro-Atlantic area than from other areas, the method of regional reports was pivotal for gaining the range and depth of regional differences, yet finding commonalities regarding women's experiences in the churches. In addition, responding to the specific concerns of F&O with respect to ordination of women, interpretation of scripture and issues of theological anthropology (including the Virgin Mary), four specialized consultations were held on these subjects drawing on the theological and interdisciplinary expertise of women and men from WCC member churches and the Roman Catholic Church, but still using an experience-based methodology.

Roman Catholics were involved in the study as participants in local groups, in the regional and specialized consultations and as official observers and consultants at Sheffield. All groups, from grassroots to Sheffield, were encouraged to be 60% women and 40% men in order to redress the imbalance of decision making in many churches where women's participation had been 10% or less; issues of race, class and minority status were always considered, but not always present in the balance.

At the Vancouver assembly in 1983, it was recommended that the insights of the community study be appropriated and translated into a variety of the Council's programmes. From 1983 to the present the results of this translation can be seen in many areas, such as the Decade of the Churches in Solidarity with Women programme, all dimensions of F&O work (renewal; baptism, eucharist and ministry; unity; and apostolic faith), and the participation of more women in decision-making areas of the Council's work.

The community study process contributed to the ecumenical movement, and especially to F&O, the impulse for a new constituency, extending its mostly male ranks to include more women theologians, thus honouring a request by women participants at Lausanne in 1927. Theologically, learning from the account of hope* study of 1974, its inductive method began, not with what is the hope within us, but the prior question — what is the pain that inspires and prompts the hope? For women the starting point was the suffering of exclusion, being underestimated, silenced or unheard. Getting in touch with this pain and the emptying of the self *(kenosis)* which ensued was the dialogic starting point, meeting point and end point of the study. Using this process at every consultation, including Sheffield, these meetings became ecclesial events, glimpses and foretastes of church life. In the words of the Sheffield letter, women and men learned "how deep are the emotions involved in any reflection on our being as women and men", "how hard it is to address and envision God in ways that respect the Christian understanding of personhood rather than suggesting male superiority", "how great is the need for education" on these issues and "how radical may be the changes needed".

See also **women in church and society**.

CONSTANCE F. PARVEY

T.F. Best ed., *Beyond Unity-in-Tension: Unity, Renewal and the Community of Women and Men*, WCC, 1988 • T.F. Best ed., *The Search for New Community*, WCC, 1987 • J. Crawford & M. Kinnamon, *In God's Image: Reflections on Identity, Human Wholeness and the Authority of Scripture*, WCC, 1983 • S. Herzel, *A Voice for Women: The Women's Department of the World Council of Churches*, WCC, 1981 • M.A. May, *Bonds of Unity: Women, Theology and the Worldwide Church*, Atlanta, Scholars Press, 1989 • C.F. Parvey ed., *The Community of Women and Men in the Church: The Sheffield Report*, WCC, 1983 • C.F. Parvey ed., *Ordination of Women in Ecumenical Perspective*, WCC, 1980 • B. Thompson, *A Chance to Change: Women and Men in the Church*, WCC, 1982.

CONCILIARITY. Although the whole history of the church is punctuated by councils or synods, conciliarism and the theory of conciliarity did not appear until the late middle ages, at the time of the great schism in the Western church, when two popes each laid claim to legitimate authority. The controversy could be settled only by a council. In the decree *Haec Sancta*, the council of Constance in 1415 declared that "being lawfully assembled in the Holy Spirit, constituting a general council and representing the Catholic church militant, this synod has its power directly from Christ. All persons of whatever rank or dignity, even a pope, are bound to obey it in matters relating to faith and the end of the schism." This conciliar doctrine was based on earlier theological and canonical tradition. However, from the time of the council of Florence (1438-39), it was strongly contested and later came to symbolize what was known as Gallicanism (1682), which was opposed by the First Vatican Council (1870) (see **Vatican Councils I and II**).

At the council of Constance the laity, the non-episcopal clergy, and the religious had been present in large numbers, and many of them had been entitled to speak and vote through the nations, princes and universities they represented. From the outset, in most of the Reformation churches, the laity played an active part in the synods alongside the pastors. This is also the case today in the Anglican communion. As to the Orthodox, most churches also have, in addition to the synod of bishops, wider councils at which the laity are entitled to speak and vote. Nevertheless, only the bishops have the authority to decide in matters of the faith. Their doctrinal decisions, however, must be "received" by the whole people of God (see **reception**).

It should also be noted that, when the encyclical of the Orthodox patriarchs (1848) affirmed that "the preservation of the faith resides in the whole body of the church", the Russian thinker Aleksey Khomyakov saw in this text the foundation of his doctrine of conciliarity known as *sobornost** (from the Slavonic word *sobor*, meaning "council", and the adjective *sobornaja*, which translates the word "catholic" in the Nicene Creed). *Sobornost*, according to Khomyakov, is the specific mark of the Orthodox church which, through the action of the Holy Spirit, unites all the faithful in freedom, harmony and love and so ensures the infallibility of the church (see **indefectibility/infallibility**). This concept of *sobornost* has, however, been criticized in that it compromises the explicit authority of the bishops in the councils.

Since 1960 ecumenical reflection on conciliarity has been prompted by the event of Vatican II (1962-65) and by the need to clarify the significance of the WCC and the goal of unity* which it is intended to serve. The Uppsala assembly (1968) suggested that the member churches should "work for the time when a genuinely universal council may once more speak for all Christians and lead the way into the future". Faith and Order took up this suggestion at Louvain (1971) and started a study on conciliarity understood as "the coming together of Christians — locally, regionally or globally — for common prayer, counsel and decision, in the belief that the Holy Spirit can use such meetings for his own purpose by reconciling, renewing and reforming the church by guiding it towards the fullness of truth and love" (*Louvain 1971*, 226). The Salamanca consultation (1973) declared: "The one church is to be envisioned as a conciliar fellowship of local churches which are themselves truly united. In this conciliar fellowship, each local church possesses, in communion with the others, the fullness of catholicity, witnesses to the same apostolic faith, and, therefore, recognizes the others as belonging to the same church of Christ and guided by the same Spirit." This description, adopted and refined by the WCC at Nairobi (1975, sec. 2), is now being developed by F&O in its continuing work on the nature and goal of unity.

See also **ecumenical councils; *sobornost*; unity, models of**.

EMMANUEL LANNE

"Conciliarity and the Future of the Ecumenical Movement, Commission on Faith and Order, Louvain 1971", *The Ecumenical Review*, 24, 1, 1972 • "Councils, Conciliarity and a Genuinely Universal Council", *Study Encounter*, 10, 2, 1974.

CONFERENCE OF EUROPEAN CHURCHES. The CEC is the regional ecumenical organization covering the whole of Europe, both East and West. Comprising some 120 member churches in 26 European countries, CEC is both in association with the WCC and a non-governmental organization recognized by the United Nations Economic and Social Council.

The project of bringing the churches of Europe into conversation with each other developed in the deep divisions and acute tensions in Europe after the second world war. This was the period of the so-called cold war,* which developed dangerously in Europe in the mid-1950s. With profound international separations and perilous tensions the order of the day, a small group of church leaders from both Eastern and Western Europe, most of them friends from the pre-war period, began to consult together about the possibility of contributing to the establishment of a true peace by bringing into conversation churches in European countries separated by highly differing political, economic and social systems. Building on the basis of a few already-existing bilateral structures for reconciliation between the churches, the exploratory conversations began in the early 1950s, but it was only in 1957, at Liselund, Denmark, that a first real preparatory meeting could be convoked.

The first full assembly, simply described as "a conference of European churches", was held in Nyborg Strand, Denmark, in January 1959. In 1960 and again in 1962 two more assemblies were held at Nyborg Strand, and the assemblies began to be known as Nyborg I, II, III, etc. At first these assemblies represented nothing more than a very loose association of the churches concerned, but at the Nyborg IV assembly (1964), with the adoption of a constitution, a decisive step was taken towards the formation of a regional conference of churches, such as was already happening in other parts of the world. Important for this assembly was also its setting, for it took place at sea, aboard the MV *Bornholm*, as the only possible answer to last-minute visa problems. The Nyborg V assembly (1967) at Pörtschach, Austria, prepared the way for the replacement of the existing part-time executive secretariat by a full-time general secretariat as from 1 April 1968. Subsequent assemblies were held in Nyborg Strand (1971), Engelberg, Switzerland (1974), Crete (1979), and Stirling, Scotland (1986). With the assembly of 1974 (Nyborg VII), it became clear that, due to the growth in size of the assemblies, it would no longer be possible to return to Nyborg Strand, and those of 1979 and 1986 were designated simply assembly VIII and IX.

According to its constitution, CEC exists "to discuss questions concerning the churches in Europe and to assist each other in the service which is laid upon the churches in the contemporary... situation". In this activity churches of the Anglican, Protestant, Old Catholic and Orthodox traditions, from all parts of Europe, play their part. Although the Roman Catholic Church is not a member, since 1964 a steady pattern of co-operation has developed and, under the guidance of a Joint Committee CEC/Council of Roman Catholic Bishops' Conferences in Europe (CCEE), has made significant progress, particularly since the first European ecumenical encounter between CEC and CCEE in 1978.

Two meetings perhaps indicate an up-to-date development of CEC. In the mid-1980s there was a much larger CEC/CCEE ecumenical encounter at Lago di Garda on "Common Witness". Even more significant was the May 1989 Basel meeting on "Justice, Peace and the Integrity of Creation". At that meeting there was an increased presence of Eastern European churches, represented particularly by the Orthodox. It was the most representative church meeting in Europe ever, and one of the most impressive instances where the church exercised its prophetic role. It took place a few months before the walls between Eastern and Western Europe began to crumble.

After relying, in a first stage, upon frequent assemblies, developments in structure have followed the diversification of activities and the increase in membership. Thus, although the assemblies from the mid-1960s onwards have become less frequent, there has been a steady growth in study groups, whose work has formed the basis for consultations on a variety of subjects, with an average participation of some 50 delegates. In order to handle these growing activities there has been a small extension of special secretariats, alongside the general secretariat.

The first to be established was a study secretariat, which was followed by a secretariat with the joint tasks (later separated) of the administration of finance and interchurch service. Interchurch service now also co-ordinates the work of the European churches' working group on asylum and refugees. Then came a churches' human rights programme for the implementation of the Helsinki Final Act (established at first as a joint activity with the National Council of the Churches of Christ in the USA and the Canadian Council of Churches), which has now become an autonomous CEC peace, justice and human rights programme. More recently a communication service has been integrated into the general secretariat. Between assemblies the whole work is overseen by an 8-member presidium and a 27-member advisory committee meeting together annually.

In the accomplishment of these tasks there is close co-operation between CEC and other ecumenical organizations both at the world and regional levels, especially with the WCC — which provided the part-time staff who initially serviced the CEC. CEC is, nevertheless, completely autonomous and self-supporting; the European members of the WCC are not necessarily identical with those of CEC.

Among the conditions, peculiar to the European situation, which CEC has to face and which determine its priorities are the long history of separation and enmity between the churches, much of it originating in Europe; the relationships between church and culture* and church and state;* the co-operation of very large and very small churches, and of ancient and comparatively new churches; European responsibility in the divisions and tensions of the contemporary international situation; and European responsibility towards the developing nations.

See also **Europe**.

GLEN GARFIELD WILLIAMS

CONFESSING CHURCH. The formation of the Confessing Church *(Bekennende Kirche)* and the German church struggle *(Kirchenkampf)* relate to the German Third Reich, 1933-45. The political religion of National Socialism inspired also various so-called German Christians. They aimed to produce a synthesis between nationalist ideology and Christianity. Some favoured a German Christian national church. The "new deeds of God of 1933" and Adolf Hitler as saviour of the German people were incorporated into its standards and proclamation.

The contamination of the German church by such thinking, the luring of church youth into the Hitler youth movement, the notorious church elections of July 1933 (which the German Christians had won), and the new regime's interference in church affairs (Hitler's nomination of Ludwig Müller as the imperial bishop of the newly combined German Evangelical Church, anti-semitic laws, offences against church constitution and life) sparked off the so-named German church struggle.

Opposition groups formed, such as the emergency alliance of pastors led by Martin Niemöller and theologians inspired by Karl Barth and his Theologische Existenz Heute (May 1933). They joined to form in a "confessional community". Its leaders came together at Barmen in May 1934 as the first Confessing Church synod, despite Nazi and German Christian threats. In declaring itself to represent the only legitimate German Evangelical Church, it proclaimed the Barmen theological declaration. Its starkly worded six "evangelical truths" rejected the false doctrine that the church should and could claim for itself the tasks of the state as an organ of the state (see **church and state**). The declaration identified a deep-seated disease in the life of church and society: placing one's trust in life's realities rather than in God's grace; deriving God's word from history, reason and desires rather than in Jesus Christ, the one Word of God whom one is to hear, trust and obey; no other source of revelation is valid. Thus, the Confessing Church struggle was about the true church and a false church.

The evolution of the struggle was marked by the state's attempt to settle the church question on its own authority, by power plays and divisions within the Confessing Church, by the state's dismissal of Barth from his professorship at the University of Bonn, by the arrest of Niemöller and by the prohibition of theological education. While preparing the Final Solution, Hitler strategically observed peace with the churches during the 1939-45 war. Evangelical groups of pietist and revivalist tradition generally supported Hitler. The Roman Catholic Church arrived at a treaty with him (concordat of 1933), but it did express concern over state idolatry, racism and the initial holocaust. Confessing Church members were at work in German-occupied countries, in the Netherlands, Norway (led by Bishop Eivind Berggrav of Oslo) and France (led by Pastor Mark Boegner). Thus a European Confessing Church was arising.

The ecumenical significance of the Confessing Church appears at various levels. The WCC "in formation", by electing members of the Confessing Church, such as Dietrich Bonhoeffer, into its provisional committees, indicated where it saw the true church at work; it also initiated studies on "Church, Nation and State". The provisional WCC could not publicly speak up for the Confessing Church; and the Nazi state forbade ecumenical contact abroad. Nevertheless, Visser 't Hooft and Bishop George Bell of Chichester acted on behalf of the "other Germany" — the Confessing Church and the resistance movements. Bonhoeffer's "whoever parts knowingly from the Confessing Church, separates himself from salvation" placed the ecumenical movement before the question of its own ecclesial quality.

The 1945 Stuttgart "confession of guilt" *(Schuldbekenntnis)* enabled the German church in post-war reconstruction to participate in the ecumenical movement and to be accepted by the churches elsewhere (see **Stuttgart declaration**). This was possible because of the Confessing Church's ecumenical relations during the war and the assistance which church and interchurch groups had given to German war victims. Confessing Church leaders also served as WCC leaders. Niemöller, for example, was a member of the central committee 1948-61, and president 1961-68.

Today one evokes the Confessing Church as a model for situations where the confrontation between church and state is strong and the political oppression particularly painful (e.g. South Korea, South Africa, Latin America). Bonhoeffer is often quoted as an outstanding example of Christian witness and martyrdom.* The Barmen declaration became a model statement of Christian freedom and obedience and has inspired texts such as "A Message to the People of South Africa" (1968) and the Kairos document* about the South African situation (1985). Finally, the Barmen declaration is still a model for churches in search of witness in social and political matters, although its theological perspec-

tive seems highly problematic for contextual theologies in Africa, Asia and Latin America. The questions it raises are controversial: To what extent can religious, political and socio-economic conditions determine theological statements and the Christian confession? And how do a theology of the word of God* and a theology of history* relate to each other?

See also **fascism, totalitarianism**.

KLAUSPETER BLASER

K. Blaser, "The Barmen Declaration and Its Present Theological Context", *The Ecumenical Review*, 36, 1984 • E.C. Helmreich, *The German Churches under Hitler: Background, Struggle and Epilogue*, Detroit, Wayne State UP, 1979 • A. Lindt, *Das Zeitalter des Totalitarismus: Politische Heilslehren und ökumenischer Aufbruch*, Stuttgart, Kohlhammer, 1981.

CONFIRMATION. In its origins, confirmation is the second post-baptismal anointing of the Roman liturgy, in which the bishop anoints the newly baptized on the forehead with chrism and imposes his hand on them, giving thanks for the gifts of the Holy Spirit (see **baptism**). It is a liturgical expression of the reality that "in God's work of salvation, the paschal mystery of Christ's death and resurrection is inseparably linked with the pentecostal gift of the Holy Spirit" (*Baptism, Eucharist and Ministry,* * B14).

While originally an integral part of the Roman baptismal rite, confirmation became separated in time from the rest of the baptismal liturgy because it was reserved to bishops alone, who were no longer able to be present at every baptism. By the 9th century the rite had come to be called confirmation and began to be given a theology of its own, independent of its baptismal roots. This theology emphasized the images of "strengthening" and "confirming to fight" and drew heavily on medieval images of chivalry.

During the middle ages the rite was administered as soon as possible after baptism (by one, two or three years of age) and only in the 16th century generally came to be reserved for candidates who had attained the age of reason (seven years). In the contemporary Roman Catholic rite it is administered at the time of baptism to all those aged 14 or older (by either the bishop or the priest presiding) and is closer in form to chrismation* of the

Eastern and Oriental churches than to its medieval predecessor. Those baptized as infants are not confirmed until a later time, often early adolescence.

In the churches of the Reformation, confirmation was given an entirely new meaning. Rejecting the medieval understanding of confirmation as a completion of baptism, it instead became a completion of catechesis.* Beginning with the 15th-century Bohemian Brethren, a rite developed in which young adolescents, after a period of intensive catechesis, made a public profession of their faith.* Through Erasmus, this new practice came to be known and adopted by reformers of the 16th century, for whom a rite of catechesis appealed to their renaissance concern for education. In this second, catechetical form it found a place in a number of Reformation churches (Anglican, Lutheran) but was totally rejected by others. In some Reformed churches confirmation was introduced in the 19th and 20th centuries only as a rite of admission to communion after a period of intensive catechesis.

Because there is a common word for two or more quite distinct liturgical practices and because the theologies given to confirmation often relate to the churches' contemporary theological understanding of baptism, the place of confirmation in the life of the churches is being questioned increasingly. It seems to be an area where ecumenical agreement cannot be achieved easily.

See also **baptism, chrismation**.

DAVID R. HOLETON

G. Austin, *The Rite of Confirmation: Anointing with the Spirit*, New York, Pueblo, 1985 • D. Holeton, "Confirmation in the 1980s", in *Ecumenical Perspectives on Baptism, Eucharist and Ministry*, M. Thurian ed., WCC, 1983 • A. Kavanagh, *Confirmation: Origins and Reform*, New York, Pueblo, 1988.

CONFLICT. Conflicts have been a recurring feature in the life of the church and in the history of nations, as even a cursory reading of the New Testament shows. Sometimes they have been resolved by the recognition of different doctrinal, liturgical or moral views co-existing with greater or lesser tension in the same community or in different communities; sometimes they have led to division. The roots of conflict have been seen as either doctrinal or moral (see **apostasy, heresy, schism**).

In modern times we have been much more conscious of the psychological and social dimensions of conflicts in the religious field. In a famous letter written in 1949, C.H. Dodd called the attention of the WCC to "non-theological factors" in church conflicts. This awareness led to studies on institutionalism (see **church as institution**) and to the attempt to relate the issue of conflict and unity in the church with that of conflict and community among humankind (see **unity of humankind**)

In recent decades, however, social, international and ideological conflicts have increasingly forced the churches and the ecumenical movement to take positions in matters that involved theological, ethical and social issues. In extreme cases, like Nazism in Germany (see **Confessing Church**) or apartheid,* churches have found conflicts irreconcilable. In other cases, they have had to admit that differing points of view can claim legitimacy and have to be kept in tension (e.g. in questions of violence and non-violence,* pacifism,* just war*).

Sometimes churches have raised conflictive issues through documents that try to provide a theological framework but leave the question open for discussion (e.g. the United Methodist "In Defence of Creation", 1986, or the US Roman Catholic bishops' "Letter on the Economy", 1986). In a similar way but with more precise limits, a Vatican "Instruction" on liberation theology tries, first, to set limits to the admissible interpretation and, then, to define lines for a positive understanding of the issue of freedom and liberation.

In recent years social scientists have described typical forms of conflict. They have distinguished between conflicts that occur within a shared set of values and those that represent ultimately incompatible options, and they have considered different ways of containing and resolving conflict and the positive significance of conflict for social life. Some of these studies have been fruitfully used to understand the dynamics of conflict in the early church. But neither churches nor the ecumenical movement has, on the whole, taken advantage of insights from such studies to deal with their internal conflicts or with those that emerge in their relation with society.

JOSÉ MÍGUEZ BONINO

O. Maduro, *Religion and Social Conflicts*, Maryknoll, NY, Orbis, 1982 • J. Rex, *Social Conflict. A Conceptual and Theoretical Analysis*, London, Longman, 1981.

CONGAR, YVES. B. 13.4.1904, Sedan, France. French ecclesiologist and one of this century's most influential and consistently pioneering Roman Catholic ecumenists, Congar entered the Dominican order, was ordained in 1930, and then taught at Le Saulchoir near Paris. His 1937 *Chrétiens désunis* marked the first carefully argued shift in RC theology of ecumenism developed and recognized in Vatican Council II (1962-65). As a French army officer in the second world war, he spent five years in a German prisoner-of-war camp; in this crucible of shared suffering he experienced a unity of faith and charity far deeper than the "Protestant" and "Catholic" labels of cellmates.

After the war Congar became a leader and mentor of the French church's flowering renewal in theology, missionary and pastoral practice, e.g. the priest-worker movement, and the missionary parish. Under Vatican threats that the French Dominicans would be dissolved, in February 1954 he and some confreres obediently went into exile, forbidden to teach and, for Congar, to have contacts with Protestants. After quiet writing in Jerusalem and Cambridge, Congar was assigned to Strasbourg, still under suspicion but more or less left alone. This dark decade he described as a time of "active patience". He was a member of the Catholic Conference for Ecumenical Questions* under Johannes Willebrands's leadership, and was enlisted in the early drafting of the WCC's Toronto statement* and in reflecting on Faith and Order papers.

Pope John XXIII rehabilitated Congar by personally placing him on the preparatory theological commission for Vatican II. And during the Council he directly helped to draft critical documents, such as those on the church, the church in the modern world, revelation, religious freedom, missionary activity and ecumenism.

Although inflicted already in the mid-1930s by a chronic and painful neurological disease, Congar seemed indefatigable. When not lecturing to groups ranging from parish workers to international scholars, he spent 12-13 hours a day at his desk. By 1967 over 1,000 entries of books and articles appear in Congar's bibliography, and over 300 since then, until in 1985 his illness made such scholarly research almost impossible.

Besides *Chrétiens désunis*, Congar's pivotal works on ecclesiology are *Vraie et fausse réforme dans l'Eglise* (1950), *Jalons pour une théologie du laïcat* (1953), *Tradition et traditions* (1960), and *Je crois en l'Esprit Saint* (1979-80). One can place his other books and hundreds of articles on the history of ecclesiology around these major works. He considered Christ, Mary and the church; laity and the relation of the church to the world; the local church; the Eastern churches; collegiality and the papacy; evangelization; ecumenism and the future of the church; and prepared commentaries on Vatican II documents.

Congar's careful studies restored a historical understanding of the RCC as "a living, collective, organic personality faithful to revelation recorded uniquely in scripture and summoned to constant renewal... History ran through the narratives of the Hebrew and

Yves Congar (WCC photo)

Christian scriptures, and history insisted that the church be both the same and different for various ages and cultures" (T. O'Meara). His last and culminating work, in three volumes, is on the Holy Spirit,* source and image of church unity, who makes possible tradition to be indeed living in prompting renewal and growth. The ecumenical movement is a movement of the Spirit, and no generation should make an idol of any stage.

He bluntly claimed that the logical refutation and canonical separation in most of post-Reformation RC apologetics did not do justice to the intent and insights of the reformers, most of which should be incorporated into the entire church to be more church. And he insisted that the Eastern Orthodox tradition on the church's mystery, the sacraments, government, monasticism and pieties offers "a complementarity" with the Western tradition; although both differ on the level of tangible and historic expression, "the two constructions of the mystery are experienced by the same faith" (1982).

Congar's personal journey never gave way to defeatism, and as he could write at the age of 80: "Whatever we have to... say, as sublime as it is, it is really not worth much unless it is accomplished by a praxis, by real action, by concrete service and love."

TOM STRANSKY

Y. Congar, *Diversités et communion*, Paris, Cerf, 1982 • Y. Congar, *Une passion: l'unité: Réflexions et souvenirs 1929-73*, Paris, Cerf, 1974 • J.-P. Jossua, *Le père Congar*, Paris, Cerf, 1967 • T. O'Meara, "Ecumenist of Our Times. Yves Congar", *Mid-Stream*, January 1988.

CONGREGATIONALISM. Congregationalism understands the church to be God's gathering of saints, called by the Spirit through the word; as such it is both local and visible, catholic and eternal, and subject in all things to Christ as head. The local church meeting, comprising professed believers, calls its officers (normally minister[s] and deacons), orders its worship and witness under the word, and is normally, though not universally, associated with sister churches in regional and international fellowship. The polity is shared by Baptists, some Pentecostalists, and others, but this entry focuses on the Congregationalists themselves.

The 16th-century harbingers of Congregationalism were separatist Puritans in England who despaired of adequate church reformation under any establishment, whether episcopalian or presbyterian. Under persecution many of them fled to Holland, whence, in 1620, some sailed as pilgrims to the New World. Other exiles returned to England in 1640. Their ranks were swollen when, in the wake of the Cromwellian era, the monarchy was restored in 1660. Between that date and 1662, some 172 Congregational ministers were ejected from their livings. Not until the toleration act of 1689 were dissenters given limited and conditional religious freedom.

The spread of Congregationalism to many parts of the world was the result of the evangelical awakening of the second half of the 18th century and its child, the modern missionary movement. Colonial expansion played its part, and 19th-century revivals in Czechoslovakia, Sweden and Finland further increased the Congregational family. The International Congregational Council (ICC) first met in London in 1891, secured its constitution in 1948, and united with the World Presbyterian Alliance (WPA) to form the World Alliance of Reformed Churches* in 1970.

Doctrinally, Congregationalists have traditionally been orthodox Trinitarians (see **Trinity**) and (*pace* the Dutch Remonstrants) Calvinists. From the 18th century onwards they have been subject to the moderating influences of evangelical Arminianism and, to a much lesser extent (except locally, e.g. in New England) to Unitarianism. They observe the dominical sacraments.*

Though for the most part shunning subscription to creeds* and confessions, Congregationalists have confessed their faith* in a variety of ways: in formal declarations (classically, the Cambridge [New England] Platform, 1646-48; the Savoy Declaration of Faith and Order [doctrinally a revision of the Westminster confession, with additions on Congregational church order], 1658); in local church covenants; in personal testimonies on reception as church members; at the ordination and induction of ministers; and in their hymns — supremely those of Isaac Watts (1674-1748) and Philip Doddridge (1702-51).

Although Congregationalism's raison d'etre is ecclesiological, internal variety is not precluded; some, for example, are more open to advisory synods than others. In England, the home missions and county unions were roughly contemporary with concerted foreign missionary activity; the Congregational *Union* of England and Wales was proposed in 1831 and formed in 1832; but only in the 20th century did the idea that mutual co-operation and episcope were not only useful but right become sufficiently widely espoused as to enable the formation of the nationally covenanted Congregational *Church* in England and Wales (1966) — an unbiblical anomaly, tolerable given the divided church.

Because of their inherent catholicity* (to be a member of the local church is to be a member of the church catholic), many Congregationalists have been ecumenically inclined. The charter of the (largely Congregational) London Missionary Society (1795) was both noble and practical in disavowing any intention of propagating a particular church polity. The ICC/WPA union of 1970 remains the only merger of its kind to date. Congregationalism has given such leaders to the ecumenical movement as Leslie E. Cooke, A.E. Garvie, Norman Goodall, Douglas R.F. Horton and Henry Smith Leiper. Congregationalists went into transconfessional church unions in Canada (1925), South India (1947), the Philippines (1948), Zambia (1964), North India (1970) and Australia (1977); and into Reformed unions in the USA (1957), Jamaica and Grand Cayman (1965), and England and Wales (1972, with the further union with the Reformed Association of Churches of Christ in 1981). Transconfessional union has ever proved too much for some, and there remain such sorrows as the failure in 1988 of the Congregational Union of Scotland to secure the majority required to allow it to unite with the United Reformed Church in the UK.

Like all polities, Congregationalism, so vulnerable in human hands, is prone to defacement. Freedom under Christ can degenerate into "freedom to do and believe as we like". When the polity is misconstrued as democratic rather than Christocentric, the objective becomes "one person, one vote and government by the majority", rather than the mind of Christ and unanimity in him. The advocacy of local autonomy can be a pretext for (sometimes financially motivated!) isolationism.

The ecclesiology of earthed sainthood is undermined theologically when the biblical-Calvinistic distinction upon which it rests — i.e. that there is an eternally significant gulf between those who are Christ's and those who are not — is eroded by more genial, relativistic doctrinal stances. The idea of the covenant people of God has been threatened by post-Enlightenment individualism (not least in its evangelical-awakening form, whereby the church can come to be regarded as the aggregate of saved, atomistic souls), whence flows religious consumerism. The reduced emphasis upon regeneration and personal testimony, coupled with the increased emphasis upon infant baptism as the point of entry into the church, raises the question of the *process* of Christian initiation; while the increasing participation of children in the Lord's supper poses an important question to those who have traditionally required both profession of faith and the acceptance of church-governmental responsibility (e.g. attendance at church meetings) prior to participation in the supper qua sacrament of the (professed and enrolled) church.

Further challenges are posed by societal change, or lack of it. The classical Congregational order could not be imposed upon hierarchical societies. In socially mobile environments it can be difficult to keep track of the saints, especially when they wish to be elusive; and in some areas the Congregational church, being the only neighbourhood church, functions as a quasi-parish church. In contexts which are tolerant to the point of being unprincipled, "godly discipline under the gospel" is all but a relic of the past.

Perils, pitfalls and lapses in practice notwithstanding, those of the Congregational way make affirmations of profound ecumenical significance: Christ alone is Lord of the church, and church order* must reflect this fact. Christian profession entails locally rooted church membership; one cannot be a Christian "in general". The church which hears the word and receives the bread and wine must go on (church meeting) to seek the mind of Christ for its witness* and mission.* Since the church catholic comprises all whom God calls, the sectarian spirit, whether inspired by establishment, sacerdotal, theological or "issue-oriented" considerations, is strenuously to be resisted.

See also **Anglican-Reformed dialogue,
church discipline, church order**.

ALAN P.F. SELL

G.G. Atkins & F.L. Fagley, *History of American
Congregationalism*, Boston, Pilgrim, 1942 • Con-
gregational Church in England and Wales, *A Decla-
ration of Faith*, Hull, Independent Press, 1967 •
P.T. Forsyth, *Faith, Freedom and the Future*, London, Independent Press, 1955 • R.T. Jones, *Congregationalism in England, 1662-1962*, Hull, Independent Press, 1962 • A.P.F. Sell, "Confessing the
Faith in English Congregationalism", *Journal of the
United Reformed Church History Society*, 4, 1988 •
A.P.F. Sell, *Saints: Visible, Orderly and Catholic:
The Congregational Idea of the Church*, Princeton,
NJ, Princeton UP, 1986 • W. Walker, *The Creeds
and Platforms of Congregationalism*, Boston, Pilgrim, 1960.

CONSCIENCE. The term "conscience"
derives from *conscientia*, the Latin translation of *syneidēsis*. It means one's knowledge
of oneself as judging and acting which accompanies one's judgments and actions. The
relevance of this knowledge is brought out by
the following sequence of questions: What
have I done? Who was I when I acted in such
and such a way? Who do I want to be? The
concept captures the notion that every morally relevant action of a person puts one into a
relation to oneself and thus concerns that
person's identity. Consequently, the judgments of conscience bear on (1) a person's
planning of future actions, and (2) his or her
critique of past decisions to act in a particular
way.

Unlike other animals, a person* not only
recognizes the goals of possible actions but
also develops opinions or attitudes towards
them. The fact that one is acting in a particular
way is the result of a decision and thus based
on reasons, rather than causes. Consequently,
the implied maxim of moral action "do good
and avoid evil!" turns out to be equivalent to
the rule "follow reason!"

Thomas Aquinas describes the possession
(habitus), i.e. the (possibly implicit) knowledge, of this first principle of morality with
the Greek term *synderesis* (translated as
"original conscience" or "Urgewissen"). Nobody can fail to possess this principle. He
distinguishes from it the particular moral
judgments of our conscience *(conscientia)*,
which are applications of — but not deduc-

tive derivations from — the principle to our
past and future decisions to act in a particular
way. Although later reflection can show this
application to be defective, Aquinas insists
that the judgment was binding at the time it
was made.

This two-tier interpretation of conscience as
synderesis and *conscientia* is also evident in
Immanuel Kant. On the one hand, he calls it
"the application of our actions to the law in
us"; on the other, he talks of it as the practical
reason that judges itself. Because the same
person cannot be both the accused and the
judge, conscience for Kant "has to be thought
of as a subjective principle of responsibility
for one's actions before God".

On the basis of concepts taken from the
social psychology of G.H. Mead, Niklas
Luhmann interprets conscience as a reflection
on the consistency of our biographical development. This interpretation is compatible
with the older ones if Luhmann's (formal)
concept of a (logically) consistent life is filled
with the qualitative notions associated with
the expression "good life". Considering that
judgments of conscience concern a person's
biography and identity, it is not suprising that
they are accompanied by strong emotional
reactions. This phenomenological observation
need not, however, lead one to suppose that
persons have a special, possibly irrational
faculty that is responsible for these judgments.

No Hebrew word in the Old Testament
quite corresponds to the meaning of *syneidēsis*. In the LXX this word is used only
twice, in late books that bear Greek influence
(Eccles. 10:20 and Wis. 17:10). The word is
also absent from most of the New Testament,
but rather frequently used (some 30 times) by
Paul, Hebrews and the epistles of Peter. It is
perhaps relevant to point out that recent research suggests that its NT use probably goes
back to popular usage in Hellenistic Greek
rather than to the philosophical use by the
Stoics and others. In most cases "conscience"
is seen as a critical organ, a sort of court of
appeal that judges actions, rather than as a
legislator. This latter function, however, is
not absent in Paul. Frequently the word is
used with an adjective (good, bad, clear,
blemished). The conscience can be misguided
by sin,* and therefore it is not an infallible
judge (1 Cor. 4:4), but it can be cleansed by

faith* through the redeeming work of Christ (Heb. 9:14, 10:22).

In theology, conscience may be interpreted as articulating the voice of God.* The legitimacy of this interpretation is based on the fact that conscience judges on a matter of absolute character, a person's own identity. The reverse argument, however, would not hold. Martin Luther discards the term *synderesis* as unbiblical and retains only the meaning of "conscience" as "judgment on our actions". With his insistence that the Christian can have a "good conscience" only through faith, he strips the concept from the moral context which had dominated its theological use and locates it exclusively in the religious sphere.

LUDGER HONNEFELDER
and RUDOLF TEUWSEN

CONSCIENTIOUS OBJECTION. At

least as early as Deuteronomy (20:5-8), legislation prescribing who must participate in war has provided that certain categories of persons should be exempted. Medieval canon law* called for priests, religious and penitents to be excluded. Sometimes rulers have accorded exemption to minorities (Jews, Mennonites) on the grounds of other services they rendered to the regime. Others have excluded some of their subjects of whose loyalty they were unsure. Since modern states have adjusted to religious pluralism,* providing legal protection for the rights of conscience,* it has become possible to call states to respect the rights of individuals or communities whose faith convictions lead them to refuse military service on moral grounds.

This development has recently come to be designated as conscientious objection. That governments ought to recognize conscientious refusal to serve in war was stated by the WCC central committee in 1951 and confirmed in 1953. The same call was stated by Vatican II (*Gaudium et Spes*, 79). The Federal Republic of Germany is the only nation where such exemption is constitutionally protected.

Recognition of the rights of a conscientious objector is usually conditioned upon the individual's being willing to render some alternative service to the nation. The state's claim to judge what counts as authentic religious or philosophical "conscience" necessarily runs risks of arbitrariness.

No nation has yet found a way to respect those who conscientiously reject a *particular* war or weapon on grounds of discrimination guided by the just war* tradition.

JOHN H. YODER

CONSENSUS. The question of the meaning of consensus for the true unity* of the church* has become the subject of intensive theological and ecclesiological reflection in the ecumenical movement, particularly in recent years. Yet essentially it is as old as the ecumenical movement itself. To ask about the unity of the church is inevitably to raise the question of the kind of consensus necessary for unity. To give some idea of the issues involved here, four sets of general observations may be made.

Implications of the word "consensus". The word "consensus" may be used in various senses. On the one hand, it can mean the agreement that characterizes a particular community — the fundamental convictions, attitudes and behaviour common to the members of that community, the validity of which is generally unchallenged. On the other hand, the word can mean agreement in the form of a specific accord or joint statement.

This distinction is important. The consensus which makes community possible and sustains it is far more fundamental and comprehensive than anything that can be expressed in specific agreements and declarations. It rests on common experiences, on certain commonly acknowledged authorities, on customs evolved over a period of time. It is expressed in a variety of ways — in stories, songs, rites and other communal actions. Consensus in the narrower sense is the attempt to understand the agreement that is rooted in the life of the community, to interpret it and express it in appropriate ways.

The two senses of consensus are intimately related and mutually interactive. Without the preliminary agreement of the community (*consentire*), explicit agreements and statements are inconceivable. Conversely, interpretations and formulated statements can help to strengthen and deepen the basic consensus of the community and perhaps even guide it in new directions.

If we ask about the consensus that characterizes the church, our starting point has to be the fact that the church understands itself as a community which has *its origin and its raison d'etre in Jesus Christ*. It did not constitute itself but was called into being on God's initiative. It is the church so long as it reflects this fundamental understanding in its life, its prayers, its words and its action. The content of the consensus that characterizes the church is therefore God's gracious gift in Jesus Christ. It is first and foremost accord with Jesus Christ, the head of the Body, and only afterwards, and on that basis, agreement among ourselves.

This raises the difficult question of the relationship between truth and community. How can consensus reflect the truth of the gospel and at the same time represent the common convictions of the church as a human community? The accord with Jesus Christ may be watered down by certain compromises made for the sake of "unity". But the fellowship among us can equally be placed at risk if too great a value is put on certain theological statements. The church has always been exposed to these twin dangers in its efforts to achieve genuine consensus.

In society* and church alike, consensus is never something static but is *a constantly evolving process*. New historical experiences create new conditions. Questions arise that call for answers. Things which once stood unchallenged are suddenly called in question, and the consensus has to be established all over again. This is not an easy challenge for any community. The danger is that it may shy away from the task and simply keep invoking the existing consensus. But that consensus may eventually be so undermined by such refusal to face up to the challenge that it collapses and the community crumbles with it.

The consensus has to be renewed in each new generation, and also when the composition of the community changes for other reasons. To be genuinely valid, a consensus has to be supported by the whole community. This problem is particularly acute in the church today. The missionary movement has made the church a worldwide community. How do things stand with the consensus that holds this worldwide community together? Does it really accommodate the experiences of the young churches? Or does it actually represent only part of the oikoumene?* The church as a worldwide community today faces

the difficult task of broadening the base of its inherited consensus.

If the church wants to tackle this task in earnest, it requires *appropriate structures*. The community must be able to keep revising its understanding of what binds it together. It is no mere chance that throughout the ages the church has gathered in representative assemblies. Only as a conciliar fellowship can the church be and remain the church. It has to live in a constant process of exchange. It has to face up to the questions asked of it and, when necessary, to take decisions to settle the issues. Councils are instruments which have often helped the church to "tune in" to what for it is the fundamental truth.

The possibility of consensus. Christianity today is divided into numerous traditions and communities. How can they arrive at a consensus which will allow them to see themselves as one fellowship? The ecumenical movement works on the assumption that, despite all their divisions and differences, the churches are bound together by a fundamental consensus. They confess their faith in Jesus Christ, and this confession obliges them to assume at least the possibility of fellowship with one another. The goal pursued by the ecumenical movement is to bring to light the fundamental consensus that binds the churches together and to make them consciously aware of it. By so doing, it confronts them with their common confession* of faith* and obliges them to examine how far their respective interpretations can withstand comparison with it. Where have they become one-sided, rigid and exclusive with the passage of time? Where has the truth been betrayed? Where has legitimate diversity been suppressed? Where has the fundamental consensus been blotted out by disobedience and self-righteousness? The task of the ecumenical movement is not to create consensus but rather, in a conciliar process, to rediscover and make effective the consensus that is given in us in Christ.

Consensus in church history. Every confessional tradition is likewise held together by a particular consensus. Each has its specific teaching, its particular spirituality, forms of worship and internal organization. This consensus forms a whole which cannot be resolved into individual elements. Moreover, every confessional tradition has its idea of the kind of consensus that is necessary for true church unity. The fact that the churches bring differing conceptions of consensus into conversations is one of the things that makes understanding more difficult to achieve.

Some may insist that the consensus which holds the church together remains essentially unchanged throughout the ages. The Orthodox church maintains that the original Tradition* has developed in its midst through the power of the Holy Spirit. It has represented across the centuries *the* consensus which marked the church of Jesus Christ from the very beginning. Unity can only come about as others likewise let themselves be permeated by this consensus. The Roman Catholic Church lays no less a claim to have preserved the original truth in unbroken continuity and free of inner contradictions: what the church's magisterium today describes as consensus may perhaps seem like a new interpretation, but in substance it is claimed to be what "has been believed by all at all times and in all places".

The Reformation* led to radically new perspectives. In view of the church's decadence the prevailing consensus had to be called in question. Genuine consensus can be achieved only when the church heeds the word of God* as it is attested in holy scripture and allows itself to be guided by it. Consensus is formed not by tradition but by the church's following its Lord and "heeding no other voice". Therefore, true consensus may on occasion be represented by only a small flock.

At the same time, the consistent following of God's word opened the way for a new conception of unity, namely the view that agreement on the essentials of the faith was sufficient for true unity. So long as churches agree that Jesus Christ is the sole source of salvation,* they can admit differences in many spheres in regard to both doctrine and order. This path has been trodden again and again since the consensus of Sandomir (1570), which linked different Protestant groups together in a federative union, up to the Leuenberg agreement (1973), which declared church fellowship among the Lutheran, Reformed and United churches in Europe.

This conception, however, inevitably raised the question of what constituted the nucleus on which agreement must prevail. The Protestant churches have given various answers to this question over the centuries.

Whereas for the reformers the essential thing was the message of forgiveness, later generations tried to define what was central in a series of dogmatic theses or rational statements about God and the human being. In the age of pietism and revival, attention focused on the experience of salvation.

There has been no lack of attempts to reconcile the contradictory concepts of consensus. In the 17th and 18th centuries, for example, the idea of the *consensus quinquesaecularis* was discussed — i.e. the suggestion that, on the strength of the tradition of the supposedly undivided ancient church, the churches should come together. The Lambeth Quadrilateral* of the Anglican communion took this idea up in a new way.

Consensus within the ecumenical movement. In the ecumenical movement various concepts of consensus have been used over the years. The 19th-century movements such as the Evangelical Alliance continued the Protestant idea of agreement on essentials: they called on Christians of all (or at least all Protestant) traditions to come together for exchange and common witness on the basis of a confession of faith which synthesized the indispensable core of the gospel. In the first half of the 20th century different concepts of consensus were pursued by three movements. The *International Missionary Council** held the conviction that the decisive consensus comprised the common affirmation of the church's missionary task. If the churches faced up to the urgency of this mission,* they would also be brought together. Arguments about questions of doctrine, initially at least, were therefore deliberately set aside and postponed. The *Faith and Order** movement, in contrast, set itself the task of gradually working out, in patient conversations, the agreement in doctrine and order that is necessary for church unity. The same concept underlay the discussions on union which have led to the formation of a number of united churches, particularly in North America, Asia and Africa. The *Life and Work** movement held the view that the churches can come together only at the level of action. While the churches were divided at the level of doctrine and would in all probability remain so in the foreseeable future, at the level of action they were confronted with challenges to which they could respond only by referring back to the original tradition. As they faced up to these challenges, they might be brought to confess the gospel together in a new way. The consensus that was formed simply on the level of action might develop into a common confession of faith. In this respect the experience of the Confessing Church* in Germany at the time of the Third Reich broke new ground. The response to the challenge of that time revealed a consensus which was not incorporated in that form in any of the established confessional traditions.

The founding of the WCC in 1948 led beyond these three approaches. A simple idea underlay this step: conversations, the exchange of ideas and occasional meetings are not enough. If a fundamental consensus is to be formed among the churches, they must begin to share their life together. The WCC gives the churches the chance to come together in a fellowship of exchange and common witness, based on their common confession of "Jesus Christ as God and Saviour", but without relinquishing their distinctive identity. The three concepts of consensus previously followed in the three separate movements are now linked together. *Within* the fellowship into which they have entered, the churches are trying to extend the consensus on doctrine and order, to fulfill their missionary task and to respond in action to the challenges of the times. The WCC lives in the hope that their common experience and common efforts will form the basis on which a consensus will gradually grow and allow the churches one day to declare full fellowship with one another.

The consensus within the WCC has gradually been deepened over the decades. The basis was expanded by a reference to the Trinity* (1961), and while for the moment no definition was given of "the unity we seek", the assemblies in New Delhi (1961) and Nairobi (1975) adopted extensive texts on the goal of unity. Following the Nairobi assembly, which described unity as a conciliar fellowship, the F&O commission was able to reach agreement on what kind of consensus was necessary for unity: consensus in the apostolic faith; in baptism, eucharist and ministry; and on structures making possible common deliberation and decision (Bangalore 1978). The work on both the church's confession of faith and on its understanding of bap-

tism, eucharist and ministry were initial steps in this direction.

More important still, perhaps, is the consensus it has been possible to achieve in the WCC as regards the response to certain challenges of the contemporary world, e.g. the common responsibility for the poor countries, the struggle to combat racism,* defence of human rights,* the community of women and men* in the church. At the same time the debates on these issues admittedly also caused some profound tensions. The consensus reached at the level of the WCC met with resistance and rejection in some churches. In coming to terms with new issues, the WCC has to work through exactly the same difficulties as individual churches (e.g. think of the debate on the ordination of women* in the Anglican communion).

The Roman Catholic Church attaches particular importance to bilateral talks (see **dialogue, bilateral**) between the different confessional traditions. Since it decided in favour of active participation in the ecumenical movement during the Second Vatican Council, a network of bilateral conversations with almost all the confessional traditions has developed. The aim of these conversations is to determine the degree of consensus in teaching, worship* and church order.* To what extent does consensus exist? To what extent do different statements ultimately mean the same thing? How far is mutual recognition possible? The bilateral dialogues of recent decades have undoubtedly contributed to bringing the churches closer together. The partial consensus noted in the talks has come to symbolize the lively relations between the churches. But at the same time the limits of the bilateral conversations must be recognized. With the exception of the Lutheran-Reformed conversations in Europe (Leuenberg 1973) none of these dialogues has so far led to full communion* being declared between two traditions. The results so far are no more than instruments which can help in formulating an acceptable consensus.

How can a comprehensive consensus be achieved? It is obvious that the consensus necessary for unity has to be built up by various means at once. Above all, it is becoming increasingly clear that a valid consensus has to be implanted in the minds of ordinary church members *(sensus fidelium)*. Consensus cannot be worked out at the level of official representatives alone. This aspect has not been sufficiently considered in the ecumenical movement up till now. Attention needs to be given to the experience which members of different churches have had and continue to have in the ecumenical movement, for a tradition is growing up here which can lead to a common interpretation.

See also **church; conciliarity; consensus fidelium; dialogue, intrafaith; teaching authority**.

LUKAS VISCHER

R. Groscurth ed., *What Unity Implies*, WCC, 1969 • P. Lengsfeld ed., *Ökumenische Theologie*, Stuttgart, Kolhammer, 1980 • H. Meyer & L. Vischer eds, *Growth in Agreement: Reports and Agreed Statements of Ecumenical Conversations on a World Level*, WCC, 1984 • C.-S. Song ed., *Growing Together into Unity*, Madras, CLS, 1978 • M. Thurian ed., *Ecumenical Perspectives on Baptism, Eucharist and Ministry*, WCC, 1983.

CONSENSUS FIDELIUM. It is largely through the influence of Cardinal Newman that the concepts *sensus fidelium* and *consensus fidelium* have been revived. What they express is an essential feature of ecclesial life, namely the implementation of the *sensus fidei*.

Sensus fidei (the instinct of faith). The *sensus fidei* is the consequence of the presence in the church of the Spirit, who inspired the prophets, Christ and the apostles. It may be described as a kind of instinctive discernment or "spiritual sense" by which Christians whose lives are faithful to the gospel are enabled to perceive intuitively what accords with the word of God* and what does not. We may think of a musician whose ear spontaneously recognizes the perfect note. Although Christians may often be unable to provide a rational explanation, they know that their discernment "rings true".

This *sensus* is in every Christian inasmuch as he or she participates in the life of the ecclesial body as a full member. Possession of it comes through membership in the community of all the baptized, upon which it is formally bestowed; and its presence in each individual instantiates the supernatural sense of the faith inherent in the whole body (*Lumen Gentium* 12).

Sensus fidelium (the mind of the faithful). The *sensus fidelium* follows as the consequence of the *sensus fidei*. It is the expression of the latter by the community of the faithful and always reflects the contemporary social and historical background. It is not the sum total of the spiritual idiosyncrasies of the baptized but rather their manner of affirming the conscience of the Body of Christ in response to the constantly changing situation. The truth that has been revealed and remains unchanged must nevertheless be interpreted afresh to meet new needs; and the *sensus fidelium* perceives what is appropriate or necessary, in the light of important developments in the realm of human affairs, so that the gospel may remain a living reality through all the fluctuations of successive generations. The *sensus fidelium* is equally perceptive of any strands of untruth which may permeate certain attitudes, movements or facile concessions to changing values in the world. Clearly, it is not to be obtained by a majority vote, for there is no element of democracy involved. However, if an impressive number of Christian faithful speak out on their own for or against a certain opinion or decision, the profound significance of their views should be recognized and their ideas given serious consideration by all those who hold authority or exercise an official teaching role (see **teaching authority**).

Throughout the course of history the corporate perception of the *sensus fidelium* has been sought and expressed within an institutional setting by means of synods at all levels convoked for this purpose. The Orthodox church, for example, has remained firmly committed to this procedure, and the churches issuing from the Reformation also give it an important place. The canonical legislation of the Roman Catholic Church attests to its continuing importance, and it has been infused with new life and strength by diocesan synods since Vatican II.*

Consensus fidelium (the agreement of the faithful). The expression *consensus fidelium* has several meanings. When used as a synonym of the *sensus fidelium*, following the example of Newman, it expresses the communal perception of the baptized. On some occasions it has the more precise connotation of an agreed statement by the faithful in response to questions previously brought to their attention by ecclesiastical authorities or by public opinion (Pius XII's consultation of Catholics concerning the assumption of Mary illustrates the former, and the Christian condemnation of racial prejudice and violations of liberty the latter).

A careful study of Tradition reveals a third and more important use of the term. It denotes also the reception* by the ecclesial community of the decisions and, above all, the definitions of faith issued by councils or other hierarchical bodies. In so doing, the church, as the community of the faithful, recognizes its own good in the judgments and accordingly accepts them as its own.

By circulating the Lima document (*Baptism, Eucharist and Ministry**) among the churches, the Faith and Order commission has set in motion a procedure along these lines. The ecumenical movement will bear real fruit only to the extent that, having elucidated the desire for Christian unity and put forward proposals for agreement, it can lead Christians to a consensus* on the essential truths of the faith and on the structures necessary to bring about ecclesial communion.

See also **communion, communion of saints, consensus**.

J.-M.R. TILLARD

J.H. Newman, *On Consulting the Faithful in Matters of Doctrine*, The Rambler, July 1859 (J. Coulson ed. 1961) • J.-M.R. Tillard, *Eglise d'églises*, Paris, Cerf, 1987 • J.-M.R. Tillard, *Foi populaire et foi savante*, Paris, Cerf, 1976 • H. Vorgrimler, "From *sensus fidei* to *consensus fidelium*", in *The Teaching Authority of the Believers*, J.B. Metz & E. Schillebeeckx eds, Edinburgh, Clark, 1985.

CONSTANTINOPLE, FIRST COUNCIL OF.

The first council of Constantinople was convened by the Roman emperor Theodosius I to bring an end to the Arian dispute, which had continued after the condemnation of Arianism at Nicea (325), and to deal with various new heretics who emerged during this 4th century as a result of this dispute. It lasted from May to July 381 and was attended by 150 bishops, all of them Easterners, including many great saintly fathers, such as Gregory the Theologian, Amphilochius of Iconium, Gregory of Nyssa, Cyril of Jerusalem, Nectarius of Constantinople, and a good number of moderate Arianiz-

ers under the leadership of the saintly Meletius of Antioch, who presided at the council but died during its proceedings. It was accepted by the fourth ecumenical council of Chalcedon (451) as the second ecumenical council, especially because of its positive work in reconciling the moderate Arians around Meletius to the Nicene position and in expanding the original doctrines of the Nicene Creed in the light of new needs. The theological work of the council is summed up in the so-called Nicene-Constantinopolitan (or simply Nicene) Creed,* but modern scholars have propounded a variety of opinions as to the precise connections of this creed, on the one hand, with the deliberations of the council and, on the other hand, with the original creed of Nicea.

The creed as it stands re-affirms the doctrine of the consubstantiality (the *homoousios*) of the Son to the Father and adds certain new clauses, especially to the third article concerning the Holy Spirit.* The council also issued seven canons which succinctly represent the contents of its proceedings. Canon 1 stresses the necessity of retaining the faith of the council of Nicea and its creed and condemns the following heretics: Eunomians and Eudoxians (who denied the consubstantial Trinity* and supported a sort of tritheism), semi-Arians and Pneumatomachians (who denied the true godhead of the Holy Spirit), and Sabellians, Marcellians and Photinians (who were unitarians and had an inadequate doctrine of the Trinity). Canon 2 restricts the movements of bishops to their own dioceses. Canons 3 and 4 deal with the church of Constantinople; the former grants the status of seniority of honour to the bishop of Constantinople next to that of the bishop of Rome, because Constantinople is New Rome, and the latter nullifies the irregular ordination of Maximus the Cynic to the throne of Constantinople and of those who had been ordained by him. Canon 5 accepts as Orthodox certain Trinitarian statements of the churches of Rome and Antioch. Canon 6 deals with procedures for adjudicating accusations against bishops, and, finally, canon 7 specifies the manner of receiving heretics who repent into the Catholic church. This council also dealt with the canonical ordination of bishops to the thrones of Constantinople, Antioch and Jerusalem, and with the processes for electing and ordaining their bishops.

GENNADIOS LIMOURIS

J.N.D. Kelly, *Early Christian Creeds*, 3rd ed., London, Longman, 1972 • I. Ortiz de Urbina, *Nicée et Constantinopel: Histoire des conciles oecuméniques*, vol. 1, Paris, Orante, 1963 • A. Ritter, *Das Konzil von Konstantinopel und sein Symbol*, Göttingen, Vandenhoeck & Ruprecht, 1965.

CONSULTATION ON CHURCH UNION.

COCU came into being in 1962, the result of a sermon preached by Eugene Carson Blake (later general secretary of the WCC) in late 1960. By the late 1960s it had grown to include nine US communions (including three predominantly black churches). The stated purpose of this organism was to explore the establishment of a church that was truly catholic, truly evangelical, and truly reformed.

During the period 1962-68 growing theological agreement in areas such as ministry* and the sacraments* was reached in COCU. From 1968 to 1970 a plan of union was written, envisioning a new ecclesial body, including institutional merger. An ambitious study process was undertaken throughout the US.

But by 1973 it was clear that this type of union was not acceptable to the member churches. Thus, through the 1970s insight and experience were gained in various types of unity in local settings, such as sharing of the eucharist* among several congregations and joint mission* for covenanted periods among contiguous bodies. The theological insights of black Christians, women, and persons with disabilities were sought, and a theology commission worked from the mid-1970s to 1984 to develop an acceptable theological agreement. This COCU *Consensus* was agreed upon in 1984, and by late 1989 all nine member churches had officially found it an "expression in the matters with which it deals, of the apostolic faith, order, worship, and witness of the church". Another important development of the late 1970s was the official recognition by each church of the baptism*/membership of the others.

Since 1979 a second form of unity was developed, inasmuch as the traditional union proposed in 1970 had not been accepted. It is called covenanting* and, on its own interpretation, incorporates the primary foundation stones of "conciliar fellowship" as affirmed at the Nairobi assembly (1975). A definitive statement of covenanting was agreed upon by the 17th plenary of COCU (1988). This proposal is being voted upon by the member communions of COCU for possible implementation in the mid-1990s. Covenanting also incorporates COCU's continuing concern to address church-dividing practices such as racism* and sexism;* in its own experience COCU has been living out the unity* of the church in the context of the unity of humankind.

The elements of covenanting are confessing the faith* as one people (accepting the *Consensus*), embracing inclusiveness of persons as a sign of wholeness, mutually recognizing members in one baptism and each other as churches, mutually recognizing ordained ministers, celebrating the eucharist together, engaging together in Christ's mission, and creating a means of deciding and acting together. The intention of covenanting is to enable organic unity without organizational merger and while providing for much diversity in retaining the ethos of each communion.* Covenanting, when inaugurated, would bring into being a "communion of communions" of the COCU churches, under the name "Church of Christ Uniting".

See also **covenanting; unity, models of; unity, ways to**.

GERALD F. MOEDE

Churches in Covenant Communion: The Church of Christ Uniting, Princeton, NJ, COCU, 1989 • G.F. Moede ed., *The COCU Consensus*, Princeton, NJ, COCU, 1985 • G.F. Moede, *Oneness in Christ: The Quest and the Questions*, Princetown, NJ, COCU, 1981.

CONSUMERISM.

Since the early part of this century, Christian social teaching has emphasized the moral dangers inherent in modern economic life because of the way it focuses human endeavour on getting wealth, leading to what the English economist R.H. Tawney called "the Acquisitive Society". From the earliest Life and Work conference to the present day, ecumenical statements on social issues have repeatedly warned against this spiritual danger: "When the necessary work of society is so organized as to make the acquisition of wealth the chief criterion of success, it encourages a feverish scramble for money, and a false respect for the victors in the struggle, which is as fatal in its moral consequences as any other form of idolatry" (Oxford 1937).

However, the ability of the rich industrial countries to produce greater wealth has not dampened the desire, stimulated by ever more seductive advertising, to consume more and more. "Consumerism" is now the phrase commonly used to describe this readiness to accept the ideology* of seeking happiness in the abundance of possessions. The result is that nearly all members of the modern industrial society are "rich", but not in the biblical sense of the word. In this regard Evanston (1954), in its statement on social questions, emphasized the broader implications for modern times of the biblical warnings about the dangers to the rich: "In our day those warnings must be applied to the temptations facing everyone in a rich society. The tendencies to create unlimited wants, to over-emphasize material values and to appeal to motives of social pride, envy and lust, stimulated by irresponsible salesmanship and advertising, are dangerous and need curbing."

In later years the sight of rich societies gorging themselves and living in material abundance while the great majority of the world's population continued to live at bare subsistence or below subsistence levels has shocked many churches into a greater awareness of the moral responsibilities facing the rich countries, especially since a considerable part of this abundance comes from the exploitation of the resources and the labour of the poor countries.

This new moral dimension of consumerism has been much discussed in Christian social thought since Uppsala (1968). From this standpoint consumerism is more than a question of excessive individual consumption. Contemporary ecumenical ethics has cited consumerism as one sign of what is spiritually and morally wrong with the Western affluent society. Liberation* in this sense means freedom from a world-view in which people are captive to all the promises of wealth, comfort and greed which the modern Western consumption-oriented society encourages people

to live by. In his writing in the 1960s, the heretical Marxist Herbert Marcuse emphasized the need "to subordinate the development of the productive forces to creating solidarity for the human species, for abolishing poverty and misery beyond all national frontiers and spheres of interest" (*One-Dimensional Man*, 1964).

Liberation theologians like Gustavo Gutiérrez accepted this view as part of the basic step which the encounter with Christ "gives to the historical becoming of mankind on the way towards total communion". Hence he rejects "developmentalism", which involves copying and applying the values and the economic goals of production-oriented capitalist societies. He therefore posits the need for "liberation from the domination exercised by the great capitalist countries".

Ecumenical social thought in the 1970s and 1980s follows closely this critique of the capitalist system. Nairobi (1975) speaks of the need to question Western-style development, and "the growing weariness with consumerism in affluent societies", especially in view of warnings about the depletion of natural resources. It warns of the "fatal tendency" in modern life to let "having gain the rule over being... Thus having becomes pathological and demonic." The corruption of obsessive having is called "consumerism: the need to consume conditioned by external motivation". In this regard "Christ calls us to a proper asceticism". This view led to a proposal for the socialization of the production and distribution of goods and services.

By 1989, in view of the collapse of socialism in many countries, there was not as much certainty about the moral superiority of this approach. There was a new awareness of the merits of the market economy which promotes industrial progress and demands a measure of personal responsibility in making economic choices. It is not just that socialist economies have, like market economies, wasted resources and exploited labour. Where economic life is directed by a political party which assumes it knows what people should consume, everything depends on the moral insights of that political party. There is no evidence that decisions taken by such political bodies, once they have power, are necessarily more wise and responsible than those taken within the "free-market" system, where that system has been supervised and guided by governments under democratic control.

The creation of political and economic structures and institutions to restrain conspicuous consumption and the preoccupation with the acquisition of wealth continue to confront highly productive (rich) societies today. The success of new governmental strategies will depend on groups like churches in helping to create a new understanding of what responsible consumption means in a world with limited and very unevenly distributed resources.

See also **development, poverty, science and technology**.

PAUL ABRECHT

The Churches Survey Their Task, London, Allen & Unwin, 1937 • *The Consumer Goods Society*, London, BCC, 1978 • *The Evanston Report*, London, SCM, 1955 • *The First Assembly of the WCC*, London, SCM, 1949 • D. Paton ed., *Breaking Barriers: Nairobi 1975*, London, SPCK, 1976.

CONVERSION. The general religious use of the term in English, French or German means "converting or being converted to a religion, a belief, or opinion". A specific concept of conversion, however, developed in the course of the pietistic, Methodist and revival movements beginning in the 17th century. Counteracting the emphasis on doctrine and formal membership in the church of Protestant orthodoxy, the concept of conversion stressed the need for a personal dedication to Christ, implying a clear decision for him. In the view of some, the particular moment of such a decision, rather than baptism,* came to be regarded as the starting point of one's Christian biography.

In the course of the Protestant missionary movement, the concept of conversion received a new reference and prominence. William Carey, one of its fathers, in 1792 defined the aim of mission* as "conversion of the heathens". In consequence a double meaning came into use: conversion as the heart of mission, standing for a personal acceptance of faith by each individual; and the conversion of a group, tribe or people as the general goal of the missionary enterprise.

The importance of conversion for Protestant mission was the reason that conversion became a topic on the ecumenical agenda. The context was the integration of the International Missionary Council* and the WCC: while the Orthodox emphasized the questions of mission and unity* and mission and church,* attention was drawn to all that conversion stands for as an effort to draw in more strongly the evangelistic tradition of the missionary movement. The WCC proposed a study of conversion published in the workbook for the Uppsala assembly (1968). That ecumenical study and the discussion process connected with it contributed to a recovery of the biblical meaning of conversion and to a wider meaning of the term.

Recovering a biblical understanding meant going back to the Old Testament roots. There the term *shub* refers to the prophetic call addressed to the people of Israel to return to the covenant* relationship with God. Hence conversion has here a collective meaning challenging Israel to re-orient itself within the given relationship. In the NT two words appear: to turn around from a wrong way *(epistrephein)* and to think anew radically *(metanoein)*. The first is addressed to disciples after following Jesus for years (to Peter in Luke 22:32) and can be used of the conversion of Saul to the Christ-believer Paul at Damascus (Acts 9) or of Israel (2 Cor. 3:16) or of heathen (Acts 15:3). The latter is sparsely used but is central for the message of Jesus, summarized as "the kingdom of God is at hand; repent" (Mark 1:15 and par.). The Johannine writings speak of re-birth.

In summary, we find no closely defined concept of conversion in the NT which would lend itself to a doctrinal or ideological use. However, conversion is always linked with the kingdom of God* rather than with entry into the church or a mere individual decision. Conversion always means a re-orientation to God and to fellow persons at the same time. In the words of Lesslie Newbigin, conversion is "a turning round in order to participate by faith in a new reality which is the true future of the whole creation. It is not, in the first place, either saving one's soul or joining a society. It is these things only secondarily" ("Conversion to God and Service to Man"). Thus the ecumenical Bible study process helped to overcome not only a narrow understanding of pietistic Protestant missionary usage but also a restricted understanding of conversion as "repentance".

The intention to further an interchange between the evangelical and other traditions in the ecumenical movement was partially achieved. For instance, in 1967 a theme number of *The Ecumenical Review* included a theological discussion with such diverse contributors as the Orthodox Nikos Nissiotis, Billy Graham, Bishop E.R. Wickham, Letty Russell, Christoph Barth and Emilio Castro. Yet a growing estrangement between the WCC and conservative evangelicals could not be avoided during those years.

The debate in section 2 on "Renewal in Mission" at Uppsala in 1968 failed to reconcile theological differences. In 1974 the separate World Evangelization Congress took place at Lausanne, emphasizing a concept of evangelism* in line with the traditional understanding of conversion. In the WCC an ecumenical affirmation on mission and evangelism was adopted in 1982 which redefines the understanding of mission. It retains the reference to conversion as a prominent point, describing it as a personal decision to accept the saving power of Christ and to enter into his discipleship, but it warns of a narrow delineation and includes a transpersonal, collective significance (paras 10-13). Also the call to conversion is seen as part of the missionary task together with engagement for justice* and dialogue with persons of other faiths (see **dialogue, interfaith**).

Although the freedom to change one's religion is specifically mentioned in the UN Declaration on Human Rights, laws restricting or prohibiting conversion have been passed in some areas. In many other societies, conversion may result in total ostracism of the convert. In its response to the Lima document *Baptism, Eucharist and Ministry*,* the Church of South India points to the problem that "making public declaration of one's commitment to Christ as Lord and Saviour" may be understood as becoming "separated from the community and lost to the culture".

The ecumenical discussion indirectly exposed the Western individualistic anthropology, deeply connected with the traditional concept of conversion. Accordingly, third-world theology and progressive Western trends made little use of it or gave it a very different emphasis as conversion to the world or conversion of structures. On the other hand, it stimulated an inter-religious discussion on parallel phenomena of conversion in different religions and even a common approach between Christians and Marxists (see M. Machovec, *The Ecumenical Review*, 1968).

In the discussion of the Roman Catholic Church, conversion was and is a side issue. When taken up (e.g. in 1967 by the "Semaine de missiologie" at Louvain), conversion has meant the transition from one Christian church to another. However, on this point ecumenical consensus (including the Roman Catholics) has been reached that the term "conversion" should not be applied to a change of membership between different churches.

See also **proselytism, renewal**.

PAUL LÖFFLER

"Conversion to God and Service to Man", workbook for assembly committees, Uppsala, WCC, 1968 ● *International Review of Mission*, 72, 287, 1983 ● *Religion and Society*, 13, 4, 1966.

COTTESLOE. The Cottesloe consultation met, from 7 to 14 December 1960, in a suburb of that name in Johannesburg. The gathering was in response to the crisis generated by the Sharpeville massacre, which took place on 21 March of the same year: 20,000 people had converged on the Sharpeville police station in support of the campaign to defy pass laws on what was to become a decisive day in South African history; 60 people were killed, and a further 180 persons were injured. Two weeks later, on 8 April, the African National Congress and the Pan Africanist Congress were banned under the hastily enacted unlawful organizations act. Repercussions echoed around the world, and Robert S. Bilheimer, then associate general secretary of the WCC, visited South Africa in the latter part of April to assess the situation on behalf of the Council. As a result of the visit it was agreed that a consultation should take place between representatives of the WCC and South African member churches as a basis for formulating an appropriate Christian response to the crisis at hand.

The consultation statement issued by the delegates had far-reaching implications for the church and society in South Africa, although it cannot be regarded as in any way radical. Much of it was based on a preparatory document drafted by Nederduitse Gereformeerde Kerk (NGK) theologians.

The document regarded the prohibition of racially mixed marriages as without scriptural warrant but admitted they were inadvisable in practice. It further suggested that there could be "no objection in principle to direct representation of coloured people in parliament". Regarding apartheid* and the church, Cottesloe resolved that "no one who believes in Jesus Christ may be excluded from any church on the grounds of his colour or race" and that the "spiritual unity among all men who are in Christ must find visible expression in acts of common worship and witness, and in fellowship and consultation on matters of common concern". Most churches around the world took such observations as self-evident. The Nederduitsch Hervormde Kerk (NHK) had, however, a clause which excluded blacks from membership, and the NGK a policy of segregated churches (these situations remain in these churches).

The NHK rejected the consultation statement and subsequently withdrew its membership from the WCC. The majority of the NGK representatives accepted the statement. However, under pressure from Hendrik Verwoerd, then prime minister, the NGK rejected the statement and re-affirmed its theological justification for government policy, and later that year the two synods of that church (the Cape Province and the Transvaal) which had been members of the WCC withdrew their membership. The process of moving into increasing ecumenical isolation by the white Afrikaans Reformed churches had started. It would come to a head with the declaration of the theological justification of apartheid as heresy and with the suspension of the membership of both the NGK and the NHK by the World Alliance of Reformed Churches* at the meeting of its general council in Ottawa in 1982.

See also **apartheid**.

CHARLES VILLA-VICENCIO

Cottesloe Consultation: The Report of the Consultation among South African Member Churches of the World Council of Churches, 7-14 December 1960 at Cottesloe, Johannesburg, Johannesburg, 1961 • A.H. Luckhoff, *Cottesloe*, Cape Town, Tafelberg, 1978 • C. Villa-Vicencio, *Between Christ and Caesar: Classic and Contemporary Texts on Church and State*, Grand Rapids, MI, Eerdmans, 1986.

COUNCILS OF CHURCHES: LOCAL, NATIONAL, REGIONAL.

A council is a voluntary association of churches, within a defined geographic area, which without compromising the distinctive identity and authority* of its members enables their sharing in common reflection and action on matters of Christian unity,* faith* and ethics,* and in programmes of common Christian witness* and service (see **diakonia**).

Councils are among the most pervasive and significant expressions of the ecumenical movement. They vary greatly in size, number of members and staff, and scope of programme, and the terminology used of them is inconsistent. Historically local and national councils have included co-operative missionary organizations, interchurch or non-denominational Christian organizations such as the YWCA or Bible Society, or Christian "action groups" working on specific issues such as world hunger; such broadly based bodies are properly (though not always in practice) termed "Christian councils" or "Christian federations" rather than councils of churches (see **federalism**). Because councils are, properly speaking, the *churches* joining together in reflection and action, the tendency today is to emphasize the unique authority and role of the councils' member churches, with other bodies having associate membership or observer status. Most regional councils refer to themselves as "conferences" of churches; their membership may include also national councils and other Christian bodies. Finally, the term "local" may refer to any level from suburb or town to federal state, while "regional" indicates a large, culturally coherent geo-political area such as Africa, Latin America or the Pacific.

Councils exist as servants of their members and have no authority apart from that granted them by their member churches. For national and regional councils these are autonomous, usually national, churches; for local councils, congregations or city or state denominational structures. The various levels of councils are structurally independent; they do not form a hierarchy in which local councils are "branches" of their national councils, which in turn make up the regional ecumenical bodies.

Modern councils must be distinguished from the "ecumenical councils"* of the ancient church. These were authoritative decision-making bodies, among churches which understood themselves to be one, on matters of doctrine and practice; modern councils are organs for consultation and joint programming among the still-separated churches. (In French and German the first meaning of the English word "council" is indicated by the terms *concile* and *Konzil* respectively, the second by *conseil* and *Rat*.)

The origin and development of modern councils. Several essential elements of modern councils were heralded by Philip Schaff in his address on "The Reunion of Christendom" to the World's Parliament of Religions in Chicago in 1893; he called for a "federal or confederate union" between churches, each retaining its independence "in the management of its internal affairs" but recognizing the others as having "equal rights", and all "co-operating in general enterprises" in areas of evangelism, apologetics, social services, and social and moral reform.

The earliest national council-like structure appears to have been the Protestant Federation of France, formed in 1905; this added the dimension (crucial to councils in difficult cultural and political situations) of providing a channel for the churches' common action to preserve freedom of religious expression, and "to uphold with public authorities, where necessary, the rights of the churches in the federation". The formation of a council in Puerto Rico in 1905 is also reported.

The modern council with the most extensive programme and largest staff was also founded in this era: the Federal Council of the Churches of Christ in America, which came into existence in 1908 on the basis of a constitution drawn up at the Inter-Church Conference on Federation in New York in 1905. Its constitution was typical of those of many later councils both in setting careful limits to the council's activities and in seeking actively to promote the "spiritual life and religious activities of the churches", as well as allowing for "the recommending of a course of action in matters of common interest". By 1910 the council included 31 denominations and encompassed the majority of American Protestants. It was succeeded in 1950 by the National Council of the Churches of Christ in the USA, which subsumed not only the Federal Council but also some seven other national

religious bodies (such as the National Protestant Council of Higher Education and the United Council of Church Women), and whose member churches included some 32 million Christians.

Many national councils around the world are rooted in the efforts begun in the first three decades of this century to strengthen the identity and independence of missionary-founded churches. Often this built upon previous co-operation between mission agencies and enjoyed the strong support of the International Missionary Council* (IMC) (indeed, John R. Mott considered his greatest contribution to the IMC to have been enabling the formation of these national Christian councils). The IMC was also important in providing the newly formed national councils with access to international ecumenical structures.

For example, in India in 1922 the National Missionary Council became the National Christian Council of India, Burma and Ceylon, with the requirement that 50% of the churches' representatives be nationals of their countries. In Japan a federation of churches, continuing impulses from the Conference of Federated Missions in 1902, led in 1922 to the formation of the National Christian Council, which soon became a member of the IMC. The need for a common Christian voice in dealing with governments sometimes provided a powerful impetus towards the formation of councils. Thus in Indonesia a "missions consulate" had been established in 1906 to represent virtually all Protestant mission bodies in the Netherlands Indies in their relations with the state, and this proved to be the forerunner of the National Council of Churches in Indonesia, founded in 1950.

The number of national councils has grown steadily from only 2 in 1910 to 23 in 1928 and at least 30 by 1948, including 9 in Asia, 3 in Africa and the Near East, and 5 in Latin America. It is estimated that today there are some 90 national councils, including almost 25 in Africa, more than 15 in Asia, 10 in the Caribbean and Central America, almost 20 in Europe, 2 in North America, 4 in Latin America and 8 in the Pacific.

Local councils of churches exist in virtually every town or rural area with a sizable Christian population. They have often developed to provide a more formal structure for existing co-operation among local church leaders, or from the initiative of laypersons who, impatient with denominational divisions, have sought broader forms for fellowship and co-operation with other Christians. Such councils have played a vital role in enabling — and sometimes legitimizing — contacts across confessional lines; indeed, for the "average" Christian "ecumenism" probably means the Week of Prayer observance, or the "interchurch food pantry", sponsored by the local council of churches. And far more than national or regional councils, local councils have offered opportunities for lay ecumenical leadership. The number of such councils can only be estimated. Already in 1949 the US alone claimed 181 local councils with paid leadership, and more than 660 with voluntary leadership, as well as some 40 state councils; today the number of local councils around the world must be in the tens of thousands.

Regional councils exist in all the major geo-political areas of the globe except for North America (where there are only the national councils of Canada and the US). Their principal aims include helping their members shape a common Christian response to issues of regional concern, and serving as a bridge between churches and national councils in the region and global issues and organizations.

Many regional councils also have roots in the contacts fostered by the missionary and Christian youth movements in the early decades of this century. Thus on the basis of encounters through the World Student Christian Federation in 1907 and 1921, Asian Christians called at a WSCF meeting in Peking in 1922 for a regular "international conference in the Far East... to promote co-operation" and mutual understanding. In response an East Asia regional committee of the IMC was eventually proposed; but what Asian Christians themselves wanted was rather "an East Asia *conference*, whereby representatives of the church can share their experience and concern, join in meditation and prayer and make common plans for participating more fully in the life of the ecumenical church". Such a conference met first in Bangkok in 1949; from its second meeting in 1957 in Prapat, Indonesia, its three secretaries worked each from their home countries of Burma, New Zealand and Ceylon, and in 1959 the East Asia Christian Conference

(EACC) held its inaugural assembly in Kuala Lumpur, Malaysia. In recognition of its true scope its name was changed in 1973 to the Christian Conference of Asia (CCA); with staff dispersed in several countries and its general secretary presently located in Japan, it now includes some 101 member churches and 15 national councils encompassing an area from Korea in the north to New Zealand in the east to Pakistan in the west.

Similar stories, coming to fruition more recently, can be told within the distinct cultural and historical circumstances of the other regions. The All Africa Conference of Churches (AACC, inaugurated in 1963 and with offices in Nairobi) has focused on issues of worship and evangelism, the search for a Christian family life in the African context, and indigenization of the gospel (sponsoring in 1966, for example, a first consultation of African theologians on biblical revelation and African belief). The Pacific Conference of Churches (founded in 1966 and headquartered in Suva, Fiji) has emphasized themes of education, citizenship, and the relation of gospel to culture; while the Caribbean Conference of Churches (founded in 1973 and based in Barbados, West Indies) has focused upon "the decisive action of God in Christ in terms of [Caribbean] culture, experience and needs", and the search for both unity and renewal among the churches. The Latin American Council of Churches (CLAI, founded in 1982 and based in Quito, Ecuador) culminates a long history of co-operation among Protestant missions and then indigenous churches; it has supported its members especially in evangelism and in their search as Christians for "a system based on justice and brotherhood". The Middle East Council of Churches (founded in 1974 and now based in Cyprus) has emphasized promoting understanding and co-operation among its member churches and providing links with the global ecumenical family. The special calling of the Conference of European Churches (founded in 1959 and headquartered in Geneva), has been helping the churches rebuild sustaining relationships across bitter lines of political and ideological division and enabling their common participation in the spiritual and material rebuilding of a Europe (both East and West) shattered by the second world war.

Regional councils have also been an important factor in indigenizing the church and developing a Christian identity rooted in local culture. Thus retiring EACC general secretary, D.T. Niles, in his inaugural John R. Mott lecture in 1959 on the theme of "A Church and its 'Selfhood'", spoke of the EACC as an expression of the "growth of the church in Asia into selfhood... the instrument of our resolve to be churches together here in Asia". And — voicing their sense of "coming of age" over against the Western missionary agencies which had "planted" them — he called this regional council "the means by which we [Asian churches and Christians] enter into a meaningful participation in the missionary task of the church".

Membership, organization and programme of councils. Most councils began as pan-Protestant organizations (though there are striking early examples of Orthodox membership, such as the four Eastern Orthodox bodies which entered the Federal Council in the US in 1940). Councils today typically encompass the classic "ecumenical Protestants" (from Brethren through Methodists,

Disciples and Presbyterians to Lutherans and Anglicans) and the Orthodox. There is often a significant presence of churches whose members are predominantly from minority groups (for example, the black-led churches, with their Caribbean roots, within the former British Council of Churches). Many councils today are making serious efforts to include a broader range of members, particularly from the Pentecostal and evangelical churches.

The formal basis for membership in most councils reflects the Christocentric orientation of the Protestantism of the first half of this century, broadened by a Trinitarian allusion and by references to the scriptures and to the churches' divine calling to common witness and work. The following statement (used by national councils in such diverse countries as Zambia, Tonga and Austria) is typical: "The council is a fellowship of churches which confess the Lord Jesus Christ as God and Saviour according to the scriptures and therefore seek to fulfill together their common calling to the glory of the one God, Father, Son and Holy Spirit" (see **WCC, basis of**).

Fifth general assembly of the All Africa Conference of Churches, Lomé, Togo (WCC/Guidon Musa, Kenya)

Other themes may be mentioned, such as the churches' imperative to work for unity (as in the basis of the Council of Churches of Malaysia).

Two negative principles have helped councils to encompass churches with very diverse theological, ecclesiological and cultural profiles. The first is that its membership does not imply that a church accepts the doctrinal positions — or even the full ecclesiological status — of other member churches: councils exist precisely to help the *divided* churches understand one another and work together. Second, its membership does not commit a church to specific statements and actions taken by the council: the churches retain their autonomy of judgment and action in each case. (In practice the process for shaping public statements and determining their status remains among the most complex and difficult issues faced by councils.)

Roman Catholic membership was out of the question before the recognition, heralded by Vatican II, of other churches as being in some sense "ecclesial communities". Roman Catholic participation is defined by the text *Ecumenical Collaboration at the Regional, National and Local Levels*; this insists that initiating "formal doctrinal conversations" is the prerogative of the churches themselves in their "immediate and bilateral contacts", that procedures for making public statements must leave room for member churches to define their own distinctive positions, and that representatives of churches "should be clearly aware of the limits beyond which they cannot commit the[ir] church without prior reference to higher authority". Within these limits, there is clear approval for the fullest possible Roman Catholic involvement in councils. The decision whether to join rests with the "highest ecclesiastical authority in the area served by the council" (for national councils, the episcopal conference); in reaching this decision there "must necessarily be communication" with the Pontifical Council for Promoting Christian Unity* in Rome.

Recently this has been an area of dramatic ecumenical growth. In 1971 there was Roman Catholic membership in 11 national councils; this had increased by 1975 to 19 and by 1986 to no fewer than 33, including membership in councils in the regions of the Pacific, Africa, Europe and the Caribbean. In addition Roman Catholics are members of three regional conferences of churches (the Caribbean, the Pacific and, as of January 1990, the Middle East).

It remains true, however, that councils related to the ecumenical movement incorporate only a portion of the churches within their area. (It is estimated, for example, that the AACC — with its 117 member churches and 19 associate Christian councils in some 38 countries — encompasses only about 35% of African Christians.) In many parts of the world Pentecostal, evangelical and fundamentalist churches have declined membership, from the fear that they will inevitably be associated with council statements or actions with which they disagree; or from a general distrust of the ecumenical movement, which they see as being too "progressive"; or from the conviction that councils tend towards the creation of a "super-church", so that membership will inevitably compromise their own freedom of judgment and witness (see **criticism of the ecumenical movement**). Often such churches form their own organs for agreed forms of Christian witness and action.

Councils have adopted many forms of governance. Typically there is a general assembly, meeting every one to three years to set broad programmatic guidelines; a governing board of church representatives meeting every year or two for detailed programmatic and personnel oversight; an executive committee; and steering committees in such areas as faith and order, evangelism, world service and family life. Council staffs range from a few volunteers to 100 or more full-time ecumenical professionals. Councils are usually financed by contributions from their member churches; sometimes significant funds are received from government or other secular sources in support of "community service" programmes. Most councils feel that they receive insufficient support to provide the programmes and services which many of their member churches ask from them.

Council programmes and activities vary greatly. Virtually all councils seek to promote common worship and spiritual life among their members. A few councils in the most affluent countries conduct extensive national and even international operations — having, indeed, a larger programme and staff than some of their member churches. Others with more limited material resources work in specific areas. Many councils emphasize programmes of aid or relief in the face of natural disasters, or the continuing social disasters of chronic poverty and unemployment, drug abuse or juvenile delinquency. Councils have been particularly effective in promoting common witness where a divided Christian voice would be less than effective (e.g. the prison or hospital chaplaincy programmes of many councils). Many councils actively encourage evangelism (though its practice is understood to be the prerogative of the churches themselves); and many have extensive publishing programmes, particularly of worship materials and Christian analyses of local issues. Some councils promote interfaith dialogue, helping their churches relate responsibly to other faith communities; others are called upon to represent their member churches in dealings with the government. Sometimes councils feel duty-bound to speak out in support of human rights, or to criticize unjust social structures; such prophetic witness often has its price (the most dramatic recent example being the expulsion in 1987 of the CCA from Singapore).

Some councils have dealt more zealously with the divisions of society than with the theological and cultural divisions among their own member churches. In recent years, however, many councils have given more attention to the "difficult" questions of faith and order, and to helping members discuss their differences in the areas of doctrine, church order and moral teaching. This has been an important point of contact with the broader ecumenical movement, as many councils have used the WCC's Faith and Order text *Baptism, Eucharist and Ministry* as a basis for their work in this area.

Councils have developed extensive contacts with one another for sharing of information and for mutual support. Regional councils have sought close working relationships with the WCC; and many national councils have sought "associate council" status with the WCC since this was established at its second assembly in 1955. For its part the WCC has sponsored two international consultations for national councils of churches — in 1971 and in 1986 (the last gathering 120 representatives from some 70 national councils around the world) — and, with the Roman Catholic Church, held an important consultation in 1982 on the ecclesiological significance of councils.

Enduring issues and future challenges facing councils. Councils at all levels face certain enduring issues. First is *the nature of their relationship to their member churches*: do the councils exist only to serve the churches, enabling their more effective witness in certain carefully defined areas; or must they sometimes lead the churches, calling them prophetically back to the search for unity, common witness and service? The churches have an essential and legitimate concern for their unique ecclesial status, and the councils must remain their servants. But should the churches cling to their present structures and divided identities, then is it not the councils' duty — precisely *as* their faithful servant — to challenge the churches to a deeper and more costly ecumenical commitment?

This is closely related to a second issue, that of the *ecclesiological significance of councils of churches* (see **church**). Recent ecumenical discussion has placed this squarely within the context of the churches' search for unity.* At the first international consultation of national councils in 1971 it was emphasized that theological work for unity is not an "extra" beside the practical work of councils, but is "the real basis for their common witness and action"; and that councils, although they lack an independent ecclesiological status, are nonetheless "instruments" enabling crucial ecclesiological developments to occur among their member churches. The 1982 consultation on the ecclesiological significance of councils emphasized their role as instruments of the churches' "irreversible" commitment to unity: they are "interim expressions of unity" shared by churches already committed to each other and to their common search for unity.

Councils, then, offer an environment in which churches and ecclesial communities "provide each other with the means to grow together towards full ecclesial status, each helping the other to acquire what it lacks"; in their "communion of mission, witness and prayer the full *koinonia* [of the churches in a truly conciliar state] is seen in profile and forecast". This means that membership in a council "expresses a commitment to practise some real measure of mutual recognition and reconciliation at every level of church life". This ascribes to councils a real, though carefully limited, ecclesiological significance, one unthinkable only 15 years ago. But it must be noted that such a purely "instrumental" understanding does not satisfy many Christians, who have experienced their foretaste of unity through the life and work of councils rather than — if not in spite of — the structures of their still-divided churches.

A third issue confronting councils is the *continuing search for a truly adequate form* for their life and work. In the past 15 years several national councils have entered adventurous schemes of re-organization. In Canada, Britain, Aotearoa/New Zealand and, most recently, in Australia one major aim has been to enable the fuller participation of the Roman Catholic Church. In the US the need to re-align programmatic and financial aspects of the council's life seems to have been the decisive factor.

The re-organizations under way in Britain and in Aotearoa/New Zealand may well yield creative new insights for councils of churches. The new ecumenical scheme in Britain (with the Council of Churches for Britain and Ireland as the co-ordinating body for regional ecumenical instruments in England, Scotland, Wales and Ireland) was initiated in September 1990 as the result of the broadly inclusive process "Churches Together in Pilgrimage". This had been launched in 1985 as a positive response to the failure of several church union schemes, and under the pressure of the positive experience of many Christians worshipping and working together across denominational lines in local ecumenical projects. It is rooted in the resolve of the churches to move (in the words of Roman Catholic Cardinal Basil Hume) "quite deliberately from a situation of co-operation to one of commitment to each other". Given this, the new ecumenical instrument need not be a force "outside" the churches, but an expression of their own will towards unity; and thus there could be a shift, as expressed by Archbishop of Canterbury Robert Runcie, from "ecumenism as an extra which absorbs energy" to "ecumenism as a dimension of all that [the churches] do which releases energy, through the sharing of resources".

The new Conference of Churches in Aotearoa/New Zealand, inaugurated in March 1987, raises a fourth issue confronting councils: *the proper participation* of the whole people of God** in their life and work. This was a major theme at the second international consultation of national councils (1986), which went so far as to refer to an "imperative towards participation" and to identify as an "urgent challenge" the need "to create a context within which their member churches may challenge each other [towards] fuller participation... in their *koinonia* of confession, worship and action". This challenge has been taken up boldly in Aotearoa/New Zealand; its new ecumenical body has sought a much greater participation of persons normally under-represented in church decision-making structures, particularly laypersons, women and youth, and has committed itself to inclusive and participatory styles of work, to consensus styles of decision making, and to a decentralized structure.

The results and implications of these new ventures are not yet clear. The British scheme has been very successful in expressing the churches' desire for unity, and their understanding of councils as servants of their members (to the point that the new council should not issue public statements in its own right at all, but only "enable" the churches themselves, when they agree, to speak a common word). This raises the question of how independent a council *must* be in order to maintain its own identity, and to challenge its members should their enthusiasm for unity falter. The new body in Aotearoa/New Zealand has been very successful in expressing the desire of the people of God for fuller participation (to the point that its first three presidents were all laypersons, and its first three co-general secretaries women). This raises the question of how independent a council *can* be and still maintain sufficient contact with its members' traditional structures to be taken seriously by them.

The future of councils is at once uncertain and full of hope. They are dependent upon the ecumenical enthusiasm and commitment of their members and their (often shrinking) financial means. They may face unclear or even conflicting expectations about their identity and role. They may become frustrated at what seems the snail's pace of the churches towards unity.

Yet councils are an essential expression of the ecumenical movement. Ecclesiologically speaking, they embody (in however imperfect a form) the divided churches' calling to be *together* the church in each place. Practically speaking, they enable the divided churches to reflect together on issues which divide them, and to work together day-by-day. They will remain necessary as long as the churches remain divided, for they provide a precious "space" in which the churches' *common* life, reflection, witness and work is "normal", and it is their continuing state of *division* which is the problem. They confirm the words of the great ecumenical pioneer J.H. Oldham, who wrote in 1922 of the nascent national Christian councils around the world: "If our unity is real, and we have a common purpose, these must express themselves through some visible organ."

See also **church, conciliarity, ecumenical councils, local church, local ecumenism**.

THOMAS F. BEST

A. van der Bent, "National and Regional Councils and Conferences of Churches", in *Handbook of Member Churches of the World Council of Churches*, A. van der Bent ed., WCC, 1985 • T.F. Best ed., *Instruments of Unity: National Councils of Churches within the One Ecumenical Movement*, WCC, 1988 • M. Conway, "Kirchen- und Christenräte", in *Ökumene Lexikon: Kirchen, Religionen, Bewegungen*, H. Krüger, W. Löser & W. Müller-Römheld eds, Frankfurt-am-Main, Lembeck & Knecht, 1987 • *Directory of Christian Councils*, 4th ed., WCC, 1985 • "Rethinking the Role of Christian Councils Today: A Report to Churches and Councils", *The Ecumenical Review*, 23, 4, 1971 • R. Rouse, "Movements of Formal Ecclesiastical Co-operation", in *A History of the Ecumenical Movement*, vol. 1: *1517-1948*, R. Rouse & S. C. Neill eds, 3rd ed., WCC, 1986 • F. Short, "National Councils of Churches", in *The Ecumenical Advance: A History of the Ecumenical Movement*, vol. 2: *1948-1968*, H.E. Fey ed., 2nd ed., WCC, 1986 • H.-R. Weber, "Out of All Continents and Nations: A Review of Regional Developments in the Ecumenical Movement", in *The Ecumenical Advance*, Fey ed.

COUTURIER, PAUL-IRÉNÉE.

B. 29.7.1881, Lyons, France; d. 24.3.1953, Lyons. Couturier was a French priest and worker for Christian unity. In 1932, when he was staying at the priory of Amay-sur-Meuse (Chevetogne*), an introduction to the work of Cardinal Mercier aroused his interest in the ecumenical movement. The following year he in-

troduced a triduum, or three-day period of prayer, for church unity at Lyons, followed in 1934 by an octave of prayer, 18-25 January. From 1939 the octave was observed throughout the world as the "Annual Prayer for Christian Unity" (see **Week of Prayer for Christian Unity**). He arranged interdenominational conferences at the monastery of La Trappe des Dombes (see **Groupe des Dombes**) and at Présinge, which influenced the creation of the Taizé* community. He was engaged in a vast correspondence in connection with his ecumenical work, produced and distributed innumerable tracts on prayer for unity, and was in close touch with leaders of the WCC. His efforts are continued by the interconfessional association Unité chrétienne (Lyons). Couturier was ordained priest in 1906 and joined the Institute des Chartreux at Lyons, where he remained until 1951. During the 1920s he came in touch with Russian refugees in the area and learned much of their spiritual background. In the 1930s he greatly contributed to Anglican-Roman Catholic contacts. See M. Villain, *Oecuménisme spirituel: Les écrits de l'Abbé Paul Couturier* (ET *The Life and Work of Abbé Paul Couturier*, Haywards Heath, UK, Holy Cross Convent, 1959) and G. Curtis, *Paul Couturier and Unity in Christ* (London, SCM, 1964).

ANS J. VAN DER BENT

COVENANT. This central biblical word first appeared in ecumenical vocabulary in the message of the first assembly of the WCC in 1948. After a brief greeting to the churches, the message stated: "We bless God our Father, and our Lord Jesus Christ, who gathers together in one the children of God that are scattered abroad... Here at Amsterdam we have committed ourselves afresh to him, and have covenanted with one another in constituting this World Council of Churches. We intend to stay together. We call upon Christian congregations everywhere to endorse and fulfill this covenant in their relations with one another. In thankfulness to God we commit the future to him" (assembly report, 9).

The idea of churches covenanting together had not been a familiar part of the ecumenical call to renewal* and unity.* Indeed, the word does not appear in the *History of the Ecumenical Movement: 1517-1948* except for the above quotation. Nor does it appear in the second volume of this history.

Earlier usage. At the very beginning of the Christian era, a deterrent to using the word "covenant" may have been that for the Roman authorities a covenant meant an illegal secret society, which the Christian community was already considered to be. It may also be conjectured that the great Eastern and Western churches, after recognition by Constantine, would not want to emphasize the covenant character of the church in view of their close links with the state. Of course, it was long accepted, from the formation of the canon* of the scriptures, that the two parts of the Bible were originally the old and new covenants ("testament" being a Latin translation of the word *berith* in Hebrew and *diathēkē* in Greek).

With the Reformation and the availability of the Old and New Testaments (covenants) in the hands of the people, "covenant" became a rallying point for reform and radical obedience to the word of God. Peasants in Germany banded themselves into associations called by the general title of *Bund* (covenant), and their leather-laced shoe *(Bundschuh)* became their symbol of protest. The peasants were encouraged by Thomas Münzer with his preaching on the covenant of the elect, but their rebellion was brutally suppressed in 1524-25. In 1531 the Protestant princes and free cities combined to form the Smalcald league, or covenant *(Bund)*, to preserve their freedom of belief and practice, by force if necessary. With John Calvin, covenant *(foedus* or *alliance)* became, in close association with the doctrine of predestination, a major theological category in the history and understanding of salvation.

In 17th-century Britain an important segment of the Church of Scotland adopted the word "covenant" as a protest against the determination of Charles I of England to impose episcopacy and a new liturgy on the Reformed Kirk. In 1638, a group of their leaders made a national covenant for the defence and preservation of "the true religion, liberties, and laws of the kingdom". Each pledged to behave "as beseemeth Christians who have renewed their covenant with God". The rebellion of 1640 in England led, among other things, to convening the Westminster assembly, which produced a Solemn League and Covenant whose purpose was to preserve reformed religion in England, Scotland and Ireland "according to the word of God and the example of the best reformed churches".

In 1648 the Dutch theologian John Cocceius, in *Doctrine of the Covenant and Testaments of God*, sought to change the emphasis of Calvinism on the unilateral decrees of God by drawing attention to the divine covenant of grace* prefigured in the OT and fully revealed in the NT, whereby every repentant sinner may share in the covenant grace. During the latter part of the 17th century a new piety developed among the puritans, who regarded themselves as people who were bound to God individually and corporately, and who, especially on new year's day, would renew their covenant with God and pledge to be more devoted in worship and the reading of the word of God, to employ their time wisely, and to seek opportunities for doing good to others.

John and Charles Wesley were heirs to this puritan tradition. John Wesley notes in his journal on Christmas day 1747 that he rejoiced in God his Saviour with a gathered company of believers, and during the following days, "I strongly urged the wholly giving up of ourselves to God, and renewing in every point our covenant that the Lord should be our God". Around that time Wesley began the practice of the covenant service in the first Sunday of the year. It has developed into a liturgy which has been celebrated by Methodists and has also, during the past 40 years, been used at ecumenical meetings as an affirmation of God's covenant of grace and our participation in it in all dimensions of our existence.

One active member church of the WCC is called the Mission Covenant Church of Sweden. Starting in 1855 as a congregation, it became a denomination in 1878 as "a free association of committed believers in local fellowship".

Another use of the word "covenant" has not enhanced its popularity. "Covenant" was a legal term since the middle ages for an agreement or promise made under seal to do or refrain from doing things, or to lease or renew lease of land. The term carried a certain solemn commitment about it. After the first world war, the 26 articles agreed in the Treaty of Versailles formed the covenant of the League of Nations. It constituted a firm undertaking by the signatory states to maintain international peace and security, to promote international co-operation, and to act collectively when the territorial integrity and political independence of member states were threatened or violated. In the event, the USA, the leading state at the time and the best guarantor of the covenant, withdrew its membership. The invasion by Japan of Manchuria in 1931 was unchallenged. Germany left the league in 1933. Italy invaded Ethiopia in 1935, but while condemning Italy, the member states did little to deter Italy. The Spanish civil war began in 1936. The way was set for the second world war and the demise of the League of Nations. "Covenant" became such a word of ill repute that, when the United Nations was formed, the former "covenant" was now named "charter". But in 1966 the UN assembly re-introduced the word "covenant" by adopting, under the rubric of the Universal Declaration of Human Rights, two international covenants — one on economic, social and cultural rights, and the other on civil and political rights. The further fact that many nations either took a long time to ratify or have not ratified these covenants has encouraged a perception that there is a certain cynicism or at best disinclination to be committed to meeting obligations internationally. It is therefore not surprising that some of these unhappy associations of the word "covenant" have predisposed most church traditions not to employ it in expressing their commitment to God in Christ and their relations to one another.

The biblical and theological renewal of the 1930s and 1940s highlighted the central and comprehensive character of God's liberating work and covenant with Israel fulfilled in the covenant made in Christ through his ministry and death for the redemption of the world. In 1933 Walther Eichrodt published the first volume of his *Theology of the Old Testament*. In the preface to a later edition (1957) of the book, he re-affirmed his conviction: "As an epitome of the dealings of God in history the 'covenant' is not a doctrinal concept, with the help of which a complete corpus of dogma can be worked out, but the characteristic *description of a living process*, which was begun at a particular time and at a particular place, in order to reveal a divine reality unique in the whole history of religion." Eichrodt's col-

league in the University of Basel, Karl Barth, published in 1945 the first part of volume 3 of his *Church Dogmatics* on "The Doctrine of Creation". The central section of this half-volume is entitled "Creation and Covenant". Barth's thesis was that "the purpose and therefore the meaning of creation is to make possible the history of God's covenant with man, which has its beginning, its centre and its culmination in Jesus Christ. The history of this covenant is as much the goal of creation as creation itself is the beginning of this history." He goes on to say that "in the Christian concept of the creation of all things the question is concretely one of man and his whole universe as the theatre of the covenant of grace; of the totality of earthly and heavenly things as they are to be comprehended in Christ (Eph. 1:10)." This same scriptural text provided the theme of the inaugural assembly of the WCC: "Man's Disorder and God's Design", which Barth rightly pointed out in his address to the assembly should be "God's Design and Man's Disorder".

Ecumenical use of "covenant". The message of the WCC second assembly (1954) invoked the covenant in a paragraph addressed directly to each congregation: "Six years ago our churches entered into a covenant to form this Council, and affirmed their intention to stay together. We thank God for his blessing on our work and fellowship during these six years. We enter now upon a second stage. To stay together is not enough. We must go forward. As we learn more of our unity in Christ, it becomes the more intolerable that we should be divided. We therefore ask you: Is your church seriously considering its relation to other churches in the light of our Lord's prayer that we may be sanctified in the truth and that we may all be one? Is your congregation, in fellowship with sister congregations around you, doing all it can to ensure that your neighbours shall hear the voice of the one shepherd calling all into the one flock?" (*Evanston Report*, 2).

The call to go beyond staying together to going forward and growing together was seen as an expression of the covenant relationship of the churches which God has established in Christ through the power of the Holy Spirit. The accent is clearly on the churches being obedient to their call in all its manifold dimensions.

The third WCC assembly (1961) did not use explicitly the word "covenant", although it attempted to give a vision of the unity which Christ wills for his church on earth to be "one fully committed fellowship". In his report to the assembly, the general secretary, W.A. Visser 't Hooft, posed the question of how the local congregations in each place can become "unitable". He asked: "For what is the use of deep convictions and imaginative plans about unity which arise at the level of world meetings, if our church members are indifferent, lukewarm or even hostile with regard to unity? There is as yet an immense task to be performed by all of us together to prepare our churches spiritually for action towards unity."

In November 1964 there was a first British conference on Faith and Order in Nottingham. This conference made the following resolutions: "United in our urgent desire for one church renewed for mission, this conference invites the member churches of the British Council of Churches, in appropriate groupings such as nations, to covenant together to work and pray for the inauguration of union by a date agreed amongst them... Since unity, mission and renewal are inseparable, we invite the member churches to plan jointly so that all in each place may act together forthwith in mission and service to the world" (*Unity Begins at Home*, 77-78).

This spontaneous suggestion of covenanting came up against the history of the word in the great conflicts of the 17th century regarding Scottish covenanters and the puritans. So the phrase "an act of commitment" was later substituted for "covenant". However, six churches in Wales continued to have a joint covenant committee and to discuss "the implications of covenanting". The discussions which were carried on in the British Isles have not produced any major breakthrough, apart from union of Reformed churches in England. But a significant number of joint congregations have demonstrated the will to live and witness together on the local level.

At the fourth WCC assembly (1968), the section on "The Holy Spirit and the Catholicity of the Church", while not using the word "covenant", expressed its substance. It articulated "a fresh understanding of the unity of all Christians in all places. This calls the churches in all places to realize that they belong together and are called to act together. In a

Detail, Hadassah Hospital Synagogue window, Jerusalem, by Marc Chagall

time when human interdependence is so evident, it is the more imperative to make visible the bonds which unite Christians in universal fellowship" (*Uppsala Report*, 17). More explicitly, the WCC fifth assembly (1975) formulated the first of three guidelines for future WCC programmes as follows: "All programmes of the WCC should be conceived and implemented in a way which enables the member churches to grow towards a truly ecumenical, conciliar fellowship. In this respect, the programmes of the WCC should become living expressions of the covenant relationship among the churches within the WCC and foster growth towards fuller unity. These programmes should challenge the churches beyond the brokenness of our human situation as well as beyond the partial, incomplete character of our ecumenical efforts towards deeper sustained and sustaining relationships" (*Breaking Barriers, Nairobi 1975*, 297).

The clearest instance of discussions on church unity or "conciliar fellowship of local churches" where "covenant" has emerged strongly is in the latest phase of the Consultation on Church Union* (COCU) in December 1988. COCU arose from a challenge to the US churches in December 1960 to explore the establishment of "a united church, truly catholic, truly reformed, and truly evangelical". The present scheme which is proposed by and to nine churches is entitled: "Churches in Covenant Communion: The Church of Christ Uniting". The whole document is written as a covenant act and process. An explanatory pamphlet says: "It begins at a moment in time when church representatives stand together before God and the world and make promises to each other. It continues as a process of growing daily into deeper understanding and spiritual unity. God has made covenant with us in Jesus Christ, and has drawn us to God by cords of saving love. In grateful response to God's covenant with us, we make covenant with one another to live henceforth, not as strangers or competitors, but as one community in Christ — just as our Saviour prayed that we should. Covenanting is not an interim step towards eventual church union, because covenanting is itself a valid form of church union, though differing from the more traditional forms."

The novelty of this plan is that while the nine churches will maintain their structures and traditions, what is intended is "to focus the energy of the churches' shared life upon the local communities of now separated congregations". To further this process, there will be covenanting councils — local, regional and national — whose aim will be "to nurture and encourage our deepening unity in Christ".

In the ecumenical movement and among the churches the covenant has been mentioned in terms of God's new covenant in Christ, which demands that, according to the WCC basis,* the churches "seek to fulfill together their common calling to the glory of the one God, Father, Son and Holy Spirit". And that common calling is to renewal, unity, mission and service. At the WCC sixth assembly (1983), one of the priority areas for WCC programmes which was articulated was: "To engage member churches in a conciliar process of mutual commitment (covenant) to justice, peace and the integrity of all creation... The foundation of this emphasis should be confessing Christ as the life of the world and Christian resistance to the demonic powers of death in racism, sexism, caste oppression, economic exploitation, militarism, violations of human rights, and the misuse of science

and technology." It is, however, curious that the word "covenant" was put in parenthesis.

The fact is that there has been much debate about the use of the concept of covenant both during and in the years following the assembly. Nevertheless, the world convocation on "Justice, Peace and the Integrity of Creation" in March 1990 made several major affirmations "in responding anew to God's covenant". The convocation proposed as an "act of covenanting" examples of faithful action required for promoting justice, peace, and the integrity of creation. It said: "They translate the response to God's covenant into acts of *mutual* commitment within the covenant community. The building of links of solidarity around specific issues and concerns, of networks of communication and support, is the most urgent priority for action today. This underlines the fact that the human response to God's covenant is a corporate act."

Biblical foundation. It is clear that ecumenical thinking is still at an initial stage concerning the relation between covenants given by God, the human acceptance of them, and, within that context, covenants made among human beings themselves. What, then, is the biblical foundation for an act of covenanting in response to God's covenant? The word "covenant" in the OT, *berith*, is related to various languages in the ancient Near East and has the general meaning of a strong reliable bond or treaty. There is abundant evidence that covenants were a normal feature of international relations, as demonstrated by Hittite records of the second millennium before Christ. But nothing has been discovered of people making covenants with their gods or vice versa. Only in the Bible is "covenant" used to describe the relations between God and humanity, and especially between God and Israel, old and new. God is always the true subject of covenants and lays down the conditions of the covenant, which are based on God's character as holy, righteous and merciful.

In the OT record, three covenants which God makes can be mentioned in the order in which they appear in scripture. The first is God's covenant with Noah before and after the flood which destroyed nearly all creation as a result of human corruption and violence on the earth. This primeval story speaks of God's everlasting covenant with the whole creation, the rainbow being the visible sign of God's grace (Gen. 6-9).

The second covenant is God seeking to create a people bound in faith and obedience, starting with the call to Abraham to go out to a land which he will be shown. "And I", says God, "will make of you a great nation, and I will bless you... and by you all the families of the earth shall be blessed" (Gen. 12:2-3). God later says to him: "I am God Almighty; walk before me, and be blameless... Behold, my covenant is with you, and you shall be the father of a multitude of nations" (Gen. 17:1,4). This is the promise of the new humanity which exists by the blessing, shared empowerment and life in community.

The third covenant is the centrepiece of God's revelation to the people of Israel. When God rescued the people from Egypt and accompanied them through the wilderness, we read that Moses went to the mountain where he heard the word of the Lord: "Thus you shall say to the house of Jacob, and tell the people of Israel: You have seen what I did to the Egyptians, and how I bore you on eagles' wings and brought you to myself. Now, therefore, if you will obey my voice and keep my covenant, you shall be my own possession among all peoples; for all the earth is mine, and you shall be to me a kingdom of priests and a holy nation. These are the words which you shall speak to the children of Israel" (Ex. 19:3-6).

This covenant with the people includes God's claim not only on them but also on all the earth. The content to the covenant is given in the book of the covenant (Ex. 20-23), and particularly in the ten commandments (Ex. 20:1-17). There are four basic features about these commandments.

First, they are the proclamation of a fact. The people's existence derives solely from the Lord, Yahweh, the One who has been present with them, hearing their cry and liberating them from slavery in Egypt, and leading them in the desert so that through the struggle and learning God's way they may become a people ready for God's service. That is the foundation and living reality of the covenant. Second, God demands that the consequence of this fact is having no other gods, i.e. not giving their allegiance to other powers or ideologies or styles of life. There must be no graven images or representations of God other than the constant awareness that they, like all

human beings, bear the image and likeness of God. Nor must they try to manipulate God, for this is taking God's name in vain. Third, the covenant calls for the celebration of sabbath, which enables people to pause and recollect their place before God in creation and the possibilities for a rhythm of respecting the identity of all creatures and the interdependence with them under God. And that includes the sabbath and Jubilee years, when the land is rested, prisoners and slaves are freed, the poor, the widows and strangers have a chance to share the fruit of the land, and all things have the state of shalom, of the imbalances being put right (Ex. 23:10-11; Lev. 25). Fourth, part of the very centre of the covenant is the solemn call to respect and maintain the integrity of all persons in the community as well as living creatures.

Faith in the one God remains faith only as it is practised in the way which is unfolded, and that means all realms of life. Faith is ethics, and ethics is faith. Faith means faithfulness to all that God demands in the covenant, which involves our relations with God, humanity and the rest of creation. It is this undivided character of faith and ethics which is sealed by the act of the covenant — the bond, obligation, disposition, commitment. The people offer their allegiance to keep the covenant, and blood is offered up to God and sprinkled on the people, as a symbol of life offered which binds them together as a people to be witnesses in word and deed to the peoples of the world.

The subsequent history of this covenant people is the long drama of how they kept the covenant and renewed it from time to time (Deut. 31:9-13), and especially how they broke it, with disastrous consequences for themselves and for creation (e.g. Isa. 24:4-6). The prophets testified to the failure of Israel to live up to the covenant teaching. It was Jeremiah who saw that God would have to make a new covenant in which everyone, whatever the rank or age, being forgiven, would know God and walk with God in a relationship of responsible faithfulness in their whole life and in creation (Jer. 31:31-34).

This new covenant is fulfilled in Jesus Christ.* It is he who comes and calls people to make a radical change of mind and attitude and to believe the gospel of the kingdom of God* in righteousness, reminding the people that they cannot serve God and mammon (Mark 1:15; Matt. 6:24,33). It is he who embodies the covenant. And in the dread hour of betrayal, he shares the paschal meal with his disciples: "This is my body which is for you... This cup is the new covenant in my blood" (1 Cor. 11:24-25; see **eucharist**). And, indeed, in the presence of the destroying powers of the world at the cross, his blood is poured out for the life of the world. In communion* with him in his body and blood, we offer our body and blood for the life of the world. We are therefore an inseparable part of God's covenant to continue Christ's eucharistic ministry in creation* for justice and peace. And we do so with Christ's new commandment that we love one another (John 13:34-35). And our competence for doing this comes from God, who has made us competent to be servants of a new covenant, not in the written code (of the old covenant) but in the life-giving Spirit, in whose presence there is freedom (2 Cor. 3:4-6,17). And this freedom in the Spirit means that we are part of a new creation in Christ entrusted with the ministry of reconciliation* (2 Cor. 5:17-20).

Thus we cannot speak of the covenant as though it were solely a matter of God's unmerited grace. So it is, but it requires of us constant, loyal commitment in the daily realities of our existence. And because we are members one of another in the worldwide Body of Christ, the church,* our commitment must be a mutual one carried out in a continuous process of having counsel together on ways in which we can be obedient to our covenant God. "Now may the God of peace, who brought again from the dead our Lord Jesus, the great shepherd of the sheep, by the blood of the eternal covenant, equip you with everything good that you may do his will, working in you that which is pleasing in his sight, through Jesus Christ, to whom be glory for ever and ever" (Heb. 13:20-21).

See also **covenanting, New Testament and Christian unity, Old Testament and Christian unity**.

PHILIP POTTER

K. Barth, *Church Dogmatics: The Doctrine of Creation*, III/1, Edinburgh, Clark, 1958 • U. Duchrow, *Global Economy: A Confessional Issue for the Churches?*, WCC, 1987 • *The Ecumenical Review*, esp. 38, 3, 1986 • D.J. Hall, *Imaging God*, Grand Rapids, MI, Eerdmans, 1986.

COVENANTING. Covenanting is a concept of visible church unity* that seeks to be responsive to the diversity of traditions within the unity Christ gives to and wills for the church. As a modified expression of organic union (see **union, organic**), it calls the churches to unite in "sacred things" *(communio in sacris)* — faith,* baptism,* eucharist,* ministry,* and mission* — without organizational unity. In covenanting, each church maintains, for the present and as long as each church shall decide, its ecclesiastical structures, traditions, forms of worship, and systems of ministerial placement. Nevertheless, in a solemn act the churches ask God through the Holy Spirit to create out of their separated life a new ecclesial community committed to common mission in the world.

The first serious initiative towards covenanting as a model of reconciling divided churches came in Wales. The British conference on Faith and Order, held at Nottingham in 1964, had passed a resolution calling the member churches of the British Council of Churches, "in appropriate groupings such as nations, to covenant together to work and pray for the inauguration of union by a date agreed amongst them". Responding to the Nottingham call, six Welsh churches formed the Joint Covenant Committee, whose efforts produced three documents: "The Call to Covenant" (1966), "Covenanting in Wales" (1968), and specific proposals in "Covenanting for Union in Wales" (1971). On 18 January 1975, the Anglican Church in Wales, the Presbyterian, the Methodist and the United Reformed churches made solemn covenant in worship "to work and pray in common obedience to our Lord Jesus Christ, in order that by the Holy Spirit we may be brought into one visible church to serve together in mission to the glory of God the Father". The Welsh pattern is one of mutual recognition and common mission based on seven "recognitions", namely of the same faith, of the same calling of God to serve all humanity, of already being in the one church of Jesus Christ, of common baptism and membership, of ordained ministries, of patterns of worship and sacramental life that are "manifestly gifts of Christ", and of the same concern for church government. Since the covenanting act in 1975, the formation of a united church in Wales came closer with the publication of two consensus reports:

"The Principles of Visible Unity in Wales" (1980) and "Ministry in a United Church: From Recognition to Reconciliation" (1986).

In England the covenanting process began in 1973, when the United Reformed Church invited all Christian churches in England to develop a new approach to visible unity. Their Churches' Unity Commission eventually articulated a proposal for covenanting in "Visible Unity: Ten Propositions" (1976). Five churches — Anglican, Disciples of Christ, Methodist, Moravian and United Reformed — then constituted the Churches' Council for Covenanting, whose major document "Towards Visible Unity: Proposals for a Covenant" (1980) became the hope for a united church. The English covenant shared similarities with the Welsh, including full recognition of each other as churches, the placement of their unity in the wider context of all churches, mutual recognition of each other's baptism and members, receiving members of the covenanting churches at the eucharist, acceptance of one another's ministries as "true ministries of word and sacrament in the holy catholic church", and commitment to common ordinations in the future using a common ordinal. Additional dimensions were to include, following the lead of the Faith and Order* commission of the WCC, the development of processes of joint decison making and a respect for the rights of conscience* and freedom of thought and action. The drama of covenanting ended in England, however, when the churches voted in 1982. The Methodists, the Churches of Christ (Disciples of Christ), and the United Reformed voted affirmatively. The Church of England failed to win final approval when the proposals missed by only a few votes to secure the required two-thirds majority in the house of clergy of the general synod.

The covenanting concept was endorsed during this same period in several commonwealth countries, usually after an impasse had been reached on plans of structural union. Activity, mostly short-lived, took place in Ghana, Ceylon (now Sri Lanka), Southern Rhodesia (Zimbabwe), and New Zealand. None produced lasting fruits, especially as Anglicans turned away from intimate ecclesial relations with Protestants and became preoccupied with possible reconciliation with the Roman Catholic Church.

Learning from their Welsh and English brothers and sisters, the US churches in the US Consultation on Church Union* (COCU) developed another variation of covenanting. The nine churches of COCU — Episcopal, Disciples, Presbyterian, United Methodist, African-American Methodists (AME, AME Zion, and CME), United Church of Christ, and Community Churches — have based their proposals for a united future on two documents: "The COCU Consensus" (1984), and "The Churches in Covenant Communion: The Church of Christ Uniting" (1989). The latter document proposes eight elements of covenanting: claiming unity in faith, mutual recognition of each others' members in one baptism, mutual recognition of each other as churches, commitment to become an inclusive church, mutual recognition and reconciliation of ordained ministry, establishing regular eucharistic fellowship, engaging together in mission and evangelism, and formation of councils of oversight.

While definitely not duplicating the various continuing denominational structures, the "councils of oversight", varying in composition and operation from place to place, are to exercise leadership in the covenanting process "as member churches move forward year by year into deeper unity in Christ". The plenary bodies of these nine churches will be deciding the destiny of covenanting for church union in the US.

As its brief history reveals, covenanting is not a magic formula. In some instances and places it is as yet unachievable; in a few places it goes forward with promise and hope. Like all other models of unity, the decisions necessary to sustain it are often affected more by historical burdens and non-theological factors than by the adequacy of this concept, which seeks to bind divided churches in an undeniable, visible unity as a sign of God's unity in Jesus Christ for the whole world.

See also **covenant; union, organic; unity, models of; unity, ways to**.

PAUL A. CROW, Jr

P.A. Crow Jr, "The Covenant as an Ecumenical Paradigm", *Seminary Bulletin* (Austin, TX), 96, March 1981 • P.A. Crow, Jr, "Reflections on Models of Christian Unity", *Mid-Stream*, 27, 2, 1988 • P. Hocken, "Covenants for Unity", *One in Christ*, 25, 1-3, 1989.

CRAGG, ALBERT KENNETH. B.

8.3.1913, Blackpool, England. Cragg has been assistant professor at the American University of Beirut, 1942-47, professor of Arabic and Islamics, Hartford Seminary, CT, 1951-56, study secretary of the Near East Council of Churches, 1956-66, and visiting professor at the Union Theological Seminary, New York, 1965-66, the University of Ibadan, Nigeria, 1968, and Virginia Theological Seminary, 1984. Ordained priest in 1937, he was assistant bishop to the archbishop of Jerusalem, 1970-74, and assistant bishop, diocese of Chichester, 1973-78. He has contributed significantly to interfaith understanding. Editor of *The Muslim World*, 1952-60, among his books are *The Call of the Minaret* (New York, Oxford UP, 1956), *The Dome and the Rock* (London, SPCK, 1964), and *Muhammed and the Christian* (Maryknoll, NY, Orbis, 1984).

ANS J. VAN DER BENT

CREATION.

The Judeo-Christian tradition confesses that the world is God's creation. Implicit in this confession are a number of fundamental themes, most of which recur explicitly or as assumptions in the literature of the ecumenical movement. Among these, the following may be named:

Purposeful: To designate the world as creation is to deny that it is either random or value-neutral. While the Tradition does not find its redemptive principle within creation as such, it does assume the purposefulness of the created order.

Contingent, yet distinct: The creation is wholly dependent upon its Creator, yet it is not an emanation; and in relation to God it is both "other" and internally comprehensive.

In essence, "good": Despite its forthrightness with respect to evil, the Tradition insists upon the essential goodness of creation as the work of God. ("This world", declared the WCC at Evanston, "disfigured and distorted as it is, is still God's world. It is his creation, in which he is at work, and which he sustains in being until the day when the glory of his new creation will fully appear.")

Made out of nothing: The dogma *creatio ex nihilo*, officially formulated at the fourth Lateran council of 1215 (though appearing as early as 2 Macc.), denies the assumption of pre-existent matter and therefore, at least in theory, curbs the persistent "religious" temptation to attribute evil to materiality.

Reflecting divine commitment: That the world is God's own work suggests the continuing commitment of the Creator to creation. While this implication of creation theology has frequently been neglected or underdeveloped, it is a rudimentary assumption of biblical faith, is foundational for the doctrines of providence and *creatio continua* and is confirmed by the central affirmation of Christian faith — the incarnation of the Word. In its deliberations and documents, the WCC has frequently drawn upon this assumption (e.g. "God has not abandoned this world... He rules and over-rules its tangled history... The world in which we... live is the world that God has loved from all eternity in Jesus Christ" [Evanston]).

Confessional: Belief in creation is not based upon scientific observation or philosophical speculation. As in the historic creeds, the epistemological presupposition of all creation theology is faith* in God.

Problems associated with the doctrine. Like every area of Christian teaching, the doctrine of creation is attended by inherent or acquired ideas and practices which must be regarded as problematic. A responsible theology must be aware of the real and potential distortions which result from such problems as the following three.

Especially in the 19th and 20th centuries, in reaction to modern methods of scriptural analysis as well as the impact of the natural sciences, *biblical literalism* has marred the discussion of creation. Taking the Genesis creation sagas as literal accounts of the world's beginnings, many Christians (esp. in North America) have entered into conflict with the advocates of other theories, notably the theory of evolution (see **creationism**).

This approach is linked with a second recurring problem, namely the tendency to consider creation *an event rather than a process*. Moreover, the event in question is pictured as a *past* event — something which occurred long ago, at the beginning of time, and was almost immediately distorted by "the fall". While such conceptualization sustains a theoretical confession of creation, it is almost wholly lacking in existential import. Beyond that, when combined with a strong emphasis upon "personal salvation" (as is frequently the case), it easily leads to the third problematic area:

Some have tended to regard salvation* as salvation *from* the world. Although Christological and Trinitarian theology links creation and redemption, there has always been a temptation in and around Christendom to "spiritualize" the doctrine of redemption and thus to supersede creation. This is historically associated with Gnostic and other forms of world denigration, yet its roots are deeper than these influences, involving perhaps the most subtle form of sin* — the abhorrence and rejection of our creaturehood.

A "new" problem: anthropocentrism. The theological emphases of the WCC have demonstrated a consistent sensitivity to the problems just enumerated. Ecumenical Christianity generally has fostered responsible scholarship with respect to biblical interpretation; it has been open to process theology and other modern schools of thought, including modern physics, which have helped to replace static with dynamic views of the universe (e.g. the Uppsala report states that "the Living God [is] the creative force within everything that is constantly renewing all things"), and above all it has accentuated the world as the locus of God's redemptive activity, thus combating the otherworldliness of much conventional religion.

Within the past decade or two, however, another problematic dimension of the Christian concept of creation has surfaced in a conspicuous way, and a cursory examination of WCC literature will demonstrate that it has not been adept at anticipating the consequences of certain of its assumptions in this and cognate areas of theology. In the light of contemporary threats to the natural world, it appears that Christianity in general has concentrated so wholeheartedly upon the well-being of the *human* creature that it has fostered a civilization whose "manifold crisis" (C.F. von Weizsäcker), in part, is its apparently inevitable propensity to befoul and destroy its natural environment.*

Many contemporary environmentalists have in fact (with historian Lynn White, Jr) accused the Judeo-Christian tradition of containing "the historical roots of our ecological crisis", accentuating, as it seems to do, the "dominion" of the human being over all of nature. While as historical analysis such an explanation must be deemed simplistic, it cannot be taken lightly by contemporary Christians. One must at least ask whether, a little earlier in the century, some Christians were not too eager to celebrate modern secularity and Western technology.

Secularism reduces the natural order to a one-dimensionality devoid both of mystery and meaning. In their haste to accentuate human dignity and responsibility and to avoid, once more, the hint of pantheism, Christian theologians have sometimes failed to discern the dangerous overtones of their affirmation of secularity. Read against the backdrop of present-day concern for the environment, a statement like the following (from the preparatory essays for the 1966 Geneva conference on Church and Society) reinforces the need for theology to be vigilant with respect to the negative aspects of its own positive pronouncements: "The biblical story... secularizes nature. It places creation — the physical world — in the context of the covenant relation and does not try to understand it apart from that relation. The history of God with his people has a setting and this setting is created nature. But the movement of history, not the structure of the setting, is central to reality. Physical creation even participates in this history; its timeless or cyclical character, so far as it exists, is unimportant. *The physical world, in other words, does not have its meaning in itself.* There are no spirits at work in it which can help or harm mankind. It is the creation of God alone and is the object of his manipulation" (Harvey Cox ed., *The Church amid Revolution*).

The secular mentality offers no opposition to the technological society. It is not surprising, therefore, that the same mood which permitted WCC and other Christian agencies to celebrate "the secular city" simultaneously regarded Western technology (see **science and technology**) uncritically, sometimes indeed in almost salvific terms — and did so on the basis of a type of creation theology. E.g.: "The traditional Christian doctrine of creation is an obvious basis for the view that God acts in and upon nature. It teaches that nature is both to be dominated by man and to be offered to man's contemplation and awe... Nature is under both the providence of God and the mastery of men... We cannot and we must not speak of nature apart from human perception in the historical development of knowledge, since man gives meaning to nature, as the only being called by God to name, to keep, and to use nature; as such, he is the crown of creation. In this sense the comprehension of nature is theologically anthropocentric... Jewish and Christian theology... has thus freed men for their critical examination of natural phenomena. They can proceed with scientific and technical research and development without fear of being impious or guilty of desecration. It is this de-deification or de-sacralization of nature which is one basic starting point of true science and of its results in technology" (*Christians in the Technical and Social Revolutions of Our Time*, 1967).

The same document does go on to speak of human "stewardship" of nature;* yet in making the language of stewardship almost synonymous with that of mastery, it evokes a posture which seems calculated to confirm the worst suspicions of scientists and environmentalists who link technocracy and Christian anthropocentrism: "'Subdue the earth and have dominion,' God says to man (Gen. 1:28). What does this mean? Does God give man the vocation of controlling or dominating the world which he puts at man's disposal? Yes. Moreover, God puts no limit upon man's dominion or control over nature except that it has to be fulfilled under God's lordship: it is man's *mastery* and God's *lordship*. Man is responsible to use his stewardship of nature to make possible a fuller human life for all mankind; in this way he regains his original God-given destiny for which Christ dies and has risen... Man is both the master and the steward of nature" (*ibid*, 198).

In a similar vein, the deliberations at the third assembly (New Delhi 1961) seemed prepared to embrace the technological mind-set — or at least to see no negating potentiality within technology itself: "For Christians, who recognize that Christ is Lord of the mind, so that all that has been rightly discovered belongs to us, there cannot conceivably be any kind of choice between science and religious faith. For science is essentially a method of discovering facts about nature and ordering them and interpreting them within a conceptual pattern. Pure science is concerned with the body of knowledge thus acquired; technology with the useful application of this scientific knowledge and technique. The nature that scientists investigate is part of God's creation; the truth they discover is part of God's truth; the abilities they use are God-given. *The Christian should welcome scientific discoveries as new steps in man's dominion over nature.*"

While the anthropological and technological optimism of such pronouncements has usually been qualified in WCC circles by such unavoidable aspects of the Tradition as the doctrine of human sin ("sin corrupts men... We need God's forgiveness for our misuse of his resources"), the Council, like most other Christian bodies, has heretofore seldom if ever exercised a critical regard for its possible over-emphasis upon the *human* creature or (more to the point) explored the Judeo-Christian tradition for its positive and independent valuation of *extra-human* creation.

"The integrity of creation". The recognition of this neglect has inspired — and in turn been stimulated by — the decision of the Vancouver assembly (1983) "to engage member churches in a conciliar process of mutual commitment (covenant) to justice,

"The Logos envisioning the human being" (also known as "God creating the birds envisages Adam in his mind"), 13th-century sculptured relief, cathedral of Chartres, France (Photo Houvet, Chartres)

peace and *the integrity of creation*"* (JPIC). Although the churches have to date devoted more attention to the first two aspects of this theme, exploration of the integrity of creation has been expedited by the growing urgency of the multifaceted crisis of the environment as well as the recognition, on the part of many Christian scholars, that the Tradition *does* have important contributions to make to the search for new and better human attitudes towards the earth and its myriad creatures.

Meeting in Amsterdam in 1987, a small group of scientists and theologians reflected on this facet of the JPIC theme and achieved remarkable unanimity both in their assessment of the problem to which it is addressed ("the disintegration of creation") and the pertinence of (regularly neglected) dimensions of the Christian Tradition for "reintegrating God's creation". Their report draws upon the biblical metaphor of stewardship, but in contradistinction to the above reference it assumes the solidarity of the human "steward" with all the creatures for whom the steward is responsible, and it deplores the language of mastery: "The elevation of the human to the status of mastery... not only ignores the most rudimentary *theology* of the biblical Tradition, which attributes sovereignty to God *alone* (Calvin), but it bypasses as well the Tradition's most salient *anthropology*, which confesses on the one hand the permanent *accountability* of the human creature... and on the other is consistent in attributing human *pretension* to sovereignty to rank sin and disobedience."

Later, a major consultation in Granvollen, Norway, produced similar conclusions: "The drive to have 'mastery' over creation has resulted in the senseless exploitation of natural resources, the alienation of the land from people and the destruction of indigenous cultures. It ignores the experience of oppressed peoples like the blacks and women who suffer under its weight. It also undermines other highly developed systems of scientific, religious and philosophical thought. For example, Western medicine as it developed and spread over the world began to supplant indigenous systems of medicine which have a more holistic approach to health care and healing."

For the first time in any consistent manner, such documents demonstrate the church's readiness to consider the creation for its own sake and not only as the setting for the human drama. There is even a sense in which the human creature is a late and perhaps a reluctant participant in a creational glory which precedes and vastly transcends its own consciousness: "Creation came into being by the will and love of the Triune God, and as such it possesses an inner cohesion and goodness. Though human eyes may not always discern it, every creature and the whole creation in chorus bear witness to the glorious unity and harmony with which the creation is endowed. And when our human eyes are opened and our tongues unloosed, we too learn how to praise and participate in the life, love, power and freedom that is God's continuing gift and grace" (Granvollen, 16).

Future perspectives. Clearly, the question ecumenical Christianity will have to address in this area of theology is whether the biblical and traditional bases of the faith are able to sustain a "theology of nature" which can function both *critically* — as a prophetic critique of the rampant technocratic manipulation and rape of the natural order — and as a *source of vision and courage* for the development of alternative conceptions of the relation between God, humanity, and extra-human creation. To achieve this, it will be necessary for Christians to overcome the abiding ambiguity about the world which has tempted them to distinguish too sharply between nature and grace,* secular and sacred, creation and "new creation", and to entertain doctrines of salvation which in effect bypass this world. Creation can no longer be treated as a mere preliminary to the gospel story. In a context comprising enormous threats to the future of the planet, the hope of the gospel must be articulated as the redemption of creation itself. In making "the integrity of creation" one of the three, fundamentally inseparable facets of its programme, the WCC has demonstrated its determination to do just that.

See also **anthropology, theological; church and world; history; justice, peace and the integrity of creation; providence; salvation; secularization; sin**.

DOUGLAS JOHN HALL

G. Altner ed., *Ökologische Theologie: Perspektiven zur Orientierung*, Stuttgart, Kreuz, 1989 • K. Barth, *Kirchliche Dogmatik III* (ET *Church Dogmatics*, vol. 3: *The Doctrine of Creation*, Edinburgh, Clark, 1958) • E. Brunner, *Dogmatik II* (ET *Dogmatics*, vol. 2: *The Christian Doctrine of*

Creation and Redemption, London, Lutterworth, 1952) • L. Gilkey, *Maker of Heaven and Earth*, New York, Doubleday, 1959 • D.J. Hall, *Imaging God: Dominion as Stewardship*, Grand Rapids, MI, Eerdmans, 1986 • J. Moltmann, *Gott in der Schöpfung* (ET *God in Creation: An Ecological Doctrine of Creation*, London, SCM, 1985) • R. Niebuhr, *The Nature and Destiny of Man*, New York, Scribner, 1953 • H.P. Santmire, *The Travail of Nature: The Ambiguous Ecological Promise of Christian Theology*, Philadelphia, Fortress, 1985 • J. Sittler, *Essays on Nature and Grace*, Philadelphia, Fortress, 1972.

CREATIONISM. Though all Christians are creationists in the sense of believing that God created the universe, the term "creationism" in recent usage generally refers to the belief that, contrary to theories of naturalistic or theistic evolution, the world was created in the relatively recent past in six 24-hour days and suffered a universal flood as described in the biblical account in Genesis.

After the publication of Darwin's *Origin of Species* in 1859, many Christians — including conservative Protestants — gradually came to accept some form of theistic evolution. Following the first world war, however, fundamentalists in the United States, led by William Jennings Bryan, pressed to ban the teaching of biological evolution in the schools. This movement climaxed in the famous Scopes "Monkey Trial" of 1925. Negative publicity in the national press dealt a serious blow to the anti-evolution movement and led to its gradual demise.

In its narrow contemporary form, creationism, or "creation science", was developed primarily by Henry Morris. Morris and like-minded fundamentalists, following the lead of George McCready Price (1870-1963), seek scientific evidence for a young earth and a worldwide flood. Hence, contrary to many earlier fundamentalists, such as Bryan, who allowed for an old earth and perhaps even some evolution of lower life-forms, creation scientists deny all biological evolution. Dissatisfied with the increasing acceptance of theistic evolution in the American Scientific Affiliation, an organization of fundamentalist and evangelical scientists founded in 1941, Morris founded the Creation Research Society in 1963, which helped spawn a number of related organizations. Beginning in the 1970s, creation scientists promoted legislation, sometimes with temporary success, to require US public schools to give equal time to "scientific creationism" as a balance to the teaching of biological evolution. Many other Christians, including mainline Protestants, many evangelicals, and Roman Catholics, opposed such legislation and attempts to limit the term "creationism" to a literalistic reading of Genesis. Though generated principally in the US, creationism has been spread around the globe by its adherents.

See also **evangelicals, fundamentalists**.

BRADLEY J. LONGFIELD

E. Barker, "Let There Be Light: Scientific Creationism in the Twentieth Century", in *Darwinism and Divinity: Essays on Evolution and Religious Belief*, John Durant ed., Oxford, Blackwell, 1985 • G.M. Marsden, "A Case of the Excluded Middle: Creation versus Evolution in America", in *Uncivil Religion: Inter-religious Hostility in America*, R.N. Bellah & F.E. Greenspahn eds, New York, Crossroad, 1987.

CREEDS. For the restoration of the full communion* of Christians, a common confession of the faith* will be an essential prerequisite. From the very beginning of the modern ecumenical movement, with the Chicago-Lambeth Quadrilateral (1888),* it has been recognized that the classic creeds, notably the Apostles'* and the Nicene* creeds, are the most common ecumenical formulation and the most appropriate. While the WCC is not authorized by its member churches to compose or propose a creed to the churches, present studies "Towards the Common Expression of the Apostolic Faith Today" hope to assist the churches in their pilgrimage towards full reconciliation.* This article treats the definition and use of creeds, their role in the ecumenical movement and issues being addressed today in connection with them.

Before the text of the New Testament itself was received, and as these texts were being brought together in the early church, short formulations were in use. These formulations were used as elements in initiation and instruction and occasionally as authentication of orthodoxy (see 1 Cor. 12:3; Phil. 2:11; Rom. 10:9; 1 John 4:2-3,15). Such formulations sometimes take the shape of spontaneous acclamations, or *homologia*; in other cases they take the form of summaries of elements affirmed to be essential for Christian initiation or evangelical witness. They represent a personal testimony of continuity with the faith of the apostles and communion with the church* into which one was being baptized. Often they bear the character of prayers or hymns.

The structure of these creeds as they emerged in the liturgical practice of the church was Trinitarian. While the formulas may have differed from local church to local church, their character and content were rather consistent. The word "symbol" is often used for these early creeds.

In the patristic period, after the reception of the biblical canon* and the liberation from persecution, creeds of initiation became useful vehicles for a common confession of faith. This function was particularly important in the early councils (325, 381, 431, 451). Later councils likewise put forward affirmations as formulations, and then criteria, for the authentic confession of the apostolic faith. Confessions, or confessional statements of the faith, gained particular importance during the period of the Reformation,* when they served the functions of clarification and differentiation, on the one hand, and of uniting one of the confessing parties, on the other.

In some branches of the Reformation, covenants* became the primary mode of formulating the faith in a similar fashion to creeds and confessions. These covenants are rooted in the experience of confession found in the Hebrew scriptures and play a credal function in congregations and churches. In elements of the free church and pentecostal traditions, the confession "no creed but the scripture" is used. Careful scrutiny of the worship, preaching and hymnody of these communities reveals both a series of fundamental affirmations and often a test of orthodoxy, which is no less specific and not necessarily any more biblical than those of churches affirming the Nicene Creed.

The early use of the creeds belongs to the rites of Christian initiation. It was from these baptismal formulas that the early church drew the formulations put forth in the early councils. The purpose of the creeds, as they came into the life of the early conciliar fellowship, was to provide common affirmations that also excluded anything judged to be an unacceptable formulation of the apostolic faith. Their

formulation as a contextual expression of the biblical faith, in this time and this place, and their use to bind the ecumenical family together in affirmations about the Trinity* and incarnation,* precede any use that was later made of them as tests of orthodoxy or impositions by secular authorities.

From the earliest times, credal differences have featured in the church divisions that give urgency to the ecumenical movement. The formulations of Chalcedon (451)* were rejected by the Armenians, Syrians and Copts, giving rise to a schism between churches now spoken of as Oriental Orthodox* and the rest of the Christian world. The Western insertion of the phrase "and from the Son" (filioque*) into the Nicene Creed — adopted, only after long resistance, by the Roman church probably in the year 1014 — has been an element in the continuing schism* between East and West. Certain of the Free churches and Quakers have considered the "imposition" of creeds a church-dividing issue. For others there has developed a lack of trust as to whether the content of the creeds is really affirmed by those who confess them liturgically.

The classic creeds, once formulated, also came to function as theological summaries and as such to supply the outline of theological treatises. Therefore the Nicene Creed and, in the West, the Apostles' Creed formed the backbone around which much of systematic theology was built. Their familiarity as the normal doxological affirmation in worship* helped them to serve admirably as the synthetic focus for theological reflection. In a similar fashion, in areas of fresh evangelization, they became the framework for catechetical instruction. While their normal use was that of evangelical witness (see **evangelism**), prayer and teaching, they were also used as instruments of social control and ecclesiastical scrutiny where the state* was engaged as the instrument for ensuring orthodoxy.

Since the Reformation, the ecumenical role of the classic creeds has been affirmed by both sides of the Reformation schism. Both Luther and Calvin were insistent on the credal basis of their confessional reforms, and the Anglican Articles of Religion and Book of Common Prayer are clear about their credal orthodoxy. However, the interpretation of these creeds and the role of the church in interpreting them, as with the role of the church in

interpreting scripture, continue to be an element of ecumenical discussion only gradually
moving towards resolution.

In the 19th century, the World's Evangelical Alliance* and the Anglican bishops at
Lambeth made the role of the credal affirmations central to the call for reconciliation and
common evangelical collaboration. In the history of the Faith and Order movement, credal
discussions have taken a central place from
the very beginning. With the work leading up
to the New Delhi assembly (1961), building
on the Toronto statement (1950),* the WCC
has incorporated central elements of the
Nicene affirmation into its own basis* of
membership (notably the Trinitarian formula
"Father, Son and Holy Spirit", and the phrase
"according to the scriptures").

In various bilateral discussions and specifically in church union negotiations, the classic
credal affirmations and their use in worship
have been an important element in progress
towards reconciliation. Discussions with non-
credal churches have likewise begun to show
a common ground in the Trinitarian faith
which is affirmed by these communities,
though not often in the liturgical and confessional forms utilized by the classic Orthodox,
Protestant, Anglican and Roman Catholic
churches. These affirmations are being taken
most seriously, as the non-credal churches
themselves reassess the usefulness of these
classical formulations in a new context. Often
the history of the rejection of credal formulations does not lie in their content so much as
in their use by states for coercion or by ecclesiastical institutions not judged to be serious about their content.

Throughout history, but especially since the
Reformation, from time to time churches and
individuals have seen fit to put forth their faith
in confessional statements adapted to the
times in which they live. These are often done
out of a sense of crisis, as in the confessions
of the Reformation. Occasionally they have
become ways of clarifying the faith of a community and producing unity. Among Protestants, those in the Reformed tradition have
been more prone to produce new confessions
than other Christians.

In recent centuries the ethical context has
been of particular importance in eliciting confessions or creeds, as with Hitler's Germany
or apartheid* in South Africa. If one notes the

history of the 4th and 5th centuries closely,
the ethical and social vigour is no less present
in these earlier affirmations than in the ones
closer to our time. Likewise, the doxological
and orthodox character of many of the contemporary formulations engendered by the
ethical urgency of the gospel stands up well
when compared with the classic formulations.

As the churches join the pilgrimage towards
that unity* to which they are called in the
gospel of Jesus Christ, unity of confession
will be essential if a true conciliar fellowship
is to be realized. The different approaches to
creeds, their relationship to church fellowship
and to authority, the means whereby we recognize the apostolic faith in a creed, the
means whereby we recognize one another as
churches authentically confessing this apostolic faith, the sufficiency or adequacy of any
formulations of the faith, and the limits of
diversity in the interpretation of these formulations will all be elements to be considered in
fidelity to God's will for Christian unity.

See also **baptism, common confession,
consensus, consensus fidelium, teaching
authority**.

JEFFREY GROS

H. Bettenson ed., *Documents of the Christian
Church*, London, Oxford UP, 1963 • H. von Cam-
penhausen, "Das Bekenntnis im Urchristentum",
Zeitschrift für die neutestamentliche Wissenschaft,
63, 1972, and 66, 1975 • *Confessing Our Faith
around the World*, 4 vols, WCC, 1980-86 • J.N.D.
Kelly, *Early Christian Creeds*, London, Longmans,
1972 • J.H. Leith, *Creeds of the Churches*, Atlanta,
John Knox, 1982 • H.-G. Link ed., *Apostolic Faith
Today: A Handbook for Study*, WCC, 1985 • H.-G.
Link ed., *One God, One Lord, One Spirit: On the
Explication of the Apostolic Faith Today*, WCC,
1988 • D.K. Ocvirk, *La foi et le credo: Essai
théologique sur l'appartenance chrétienne*, Paris,
Cerf, 1985 • C.S. Rodd ed., *Foundation Docu-
ments of the Faith*, Edinburgh, Clark, 1987 • J.
Stevenson, *Creeds, Council and Controversies*,
London, SPCK, 1966.

CRITICISM OF THE ECUMENICAL MOVEMENT AND OF THE WCC.

In
the second half of the 20th century, the WCC
has become the most visible international expression of the ecumenical movement. No
wonder, then, that ever since its foundation in
1948, the WCC has been the target of constant
criticisms, both inside and outside of its constituencies. In fact, the WCC often is the focal

point for criticisms of the ecumenical movement itself: its vision and motivations, its intermediate goals, its activities and its institutional forms.

Some of these criticisms are based on deliberate or unintended caricatures and judgments shaped from a distance. Other criticisms are made more accurately and reflect a critic's differing theological, ecclesiological or even political convictions. Others point to discrepancies, if not contradictions, between intentions and facts.

For several decades, more and more Christians from various confessional, geographical, cultural and political backgrounds have met in a bewildering variety of ecumenical forums. As their agendas cover almost every divisive issue in church and in society, agreements, convergences and differences ultimately come into sharper relief. A position which favours or claims one point of view may provoke objections within the constituencies or even from people who are not affiliated with any church but feel confident to prescribe what the church should say or do.

For the purposes of our discussion here, we may divide criticisms of the ecumenical movement and the WCC into four general categories: theological, ecclesiological, political and institutional.

Theological criticism. The main flaw in the present ecumenical movement, some contend, is the juxtaposition of so many varied theological visions, often flawed and limited, of what ecumenism is. As a result there is a potpourri of criteria by which each draws up a long list of ecumenical advances and breakthroughs, standstills and setbacks. An ecumenical "success" for one is considered a "failure" by another (e.g. consider the differing reactions to the introduction of women priests into the church, or of inclusive language into the Bible and liturgy).

Although no church equates church unity* with a uniformity that goes beyond revealed essentials, some nevertheless fear that too many are pressing for a future church so monolithic, quasi-totalitarian and well organized that the free, unsolicited promptings of the Holy Spirit* and the exercise of the Spirit's diverse gifts throughout the grassroots will be stifled by the weight of the uniform institution — "a multinational religious corporation like Coca-Cola, with the same

bottle, the same slogan, the same management techniques in every culture".

Other critics question the underlying motivation, which they cynically see as based on political expediency in the face of dwindling congregations — and funds. Or more radically, the push towards the reunion of denominations is seen not as the product of evangelistic outreach, fervently held doctrinal convictions, and biblical spirituality, but more often the result of scepticism about the real value of weary denominational systems; it is considered "a response to this sense of being about to become extinct, rather than to any zeal for union as such" (Malcolm Muggeridge, 1970).

The search for unity, one hears, is covering a multitude of sins by soft-pedalling theological barriers in favour of organizational unity based on co-operative social action. A persistent emphasis on what already unites the churches papers over, through study documents, what theologically really separates or should separate them. Church unity is exalted at truth's expense. A Scottish critic (1988) fervently calls the ecumenical movement "the greatest disaster to affect the Christian church this century. It has reduced the professing churches of this country to a collection of bloodless, spineless and boneless organizations, which can hardly raise a whimper on the side of Christ and his truth."

In 1948, a few months before the WCC's first assembly, delegates of 58 conservative evangelical, mostly fundamentalist, churches formed the International Council of Christian Churches,* in order "to stand against the WCC". Though small in numbers, the ICCC continues to reflect widespread extreme conservative Protestant charges against the WCC: its theological error in failing to uphold biblical infallibility; its communist influence and infiltrations ("confusion plus communism"); its betrayal of Protestantism through acceptance of Orthodox membership and close co-operation with the Roman Catholic Church ("buy the truth and sell it not").

Other critics of councils of churches in general, and the WCC in particular, focus on serious discrepancies between good intentions and actual results in holding together in balanced tension major theological items on the Christian agenda. In the WCC, the tension between the "doctrinal" faith-and-order issues and "social" life-and-work concerns more often favours the latter over the former. Faith and Order* theologians may enjoy the platform, but in fact their audience is rather limited.

The WCC intended that the 1961 integration of the International Missionary Council would place the missionary task, especially direct evangelism,* into the very centre of WCC life. Indeed, several statements balance mission-in-unity and unity-in-mission, such as the 1982 central committee's "Mission and Evangelism: An Ecumenical Affirmation". But critics claim that WCC programmes, even its Commission on World Mission and Evangelism, in fact minimize or even ignore the explicit verbal proclamation of the gospel to the millions who have never been challenged to accept Jesus Christ as Lord and personal Saviour. This questioning of the WCC commitment to direct evangelism takes on a new dimension with growing WCC involvement in interfaith dialogues.* Does not the very fact of such dialogues dull the edge of Christian witness and lead even to "religious syncretism"? This line of thinking has led many evangelical Christians, in member or non-member churches or in para-church groups, to remain aloof from the WCC and to support other world mission forums, such as the Lausanne Committee for World Evangelization.*

Furthermore, some critics link this de-emphasis of direct evangelism with the "liberal theology" which they claim dominates the WCC. Such theology is said to have too optimistic a view of human nature; a view of sin* that focuses too much on the subtle evils embedded in the institutions and structures of society, and not enough on downright sinful persons; and too uncritical a faith in the ever-progressing human potential for bringing in the kingdom of God.*

Even in F&O studies, what one regards as strength in convergences, another regards as weakness. Some churches in the Reformation tradition see in the 1982 WCC document *Baptism, Eucharist and Ministry** a "catholicizing" tendency which they say subordinates the word to the sacraments or so emphasizes the special ministry of the ordained that the ministry of ordinary believers is belittled. On the other hand, Orthodox members complain that too many theological concerns and approaches are essentially Western Protestant or Latin Roman Catholic and thus foreign to the Eastern traditions, e.g. grace and sacrament, faith and works, creation and redemption.

Ecclesiological criticism. Never-ending discussions of the nature of the WCC as a vehicle or instrument of church unity have always been complex and generally inconclusive. Some charges re-appear, despite WCC disavowals from its early years. For example, it is said that the WCC seems to be a "super-church", or that the authority of its statements and public declarations carries more weight than "the wisdom of their contents", or that membership implies the acceptance of a specific doctrine concerning the nature of church unity. Some attack the WCC basis* as such. It is not credal, it does not specify enough of the non-negotiable elements of the Christian faith. Or even though every member church must express agreement with the basis, never has the WCC tried to verify this assent of any member. This double vagueness is the root of the "separatist" argument: affiliation with the WCC is a biblically prohibited alliance with "unbelievers".

Others criticize the fundamental structure of WCC membership. They come typically from traditions which stress that the Body of Christ becomes one and visible "from below" as local congregations gather around the word and sacrament, whereas most international confessional and ecumenical structures, including the WCC, presume national churches as the basic building blocks of church unity. (This national structure, claim some in the "historic peace churches", is why the WCC has never taken a theologically consistent stand against war in any modern form.)

Some argue that the WCC's structure as a council of churches prevents it from acknowledging the prophetic contribution to social justice, peace, and mercy works of Christian communities and movements, whether confessional or transdenominational. Yet others claim that the WCC, as most other ecumenical bodies, employs too many "prophets" — elite lobbyists of single causes who are inexperienced in congregational life and in direct church governance — and not enough "pastoral, priestly, churchly" types. This composition of staff creates the image of being too far ahead of the average laity, clergy and hierarchy and of writing them off too easily.

Demonstration at Vancouver 1983 (WCC photo)

Political criticism. Already in 1948 the Orthodox church of Russia and several Orthodox churches which followed its lead decided not to join the WCC. (Many did so later, in 1961.) Its real aim, they had declared, was the composition of an "ecumenical church" with political power rather than "the reunion of the churches by spiritual ways and means". Continuing objections to WCC political stands often accompany charges that the WCC has increasingly subordinated concerns of church unity to immediate social, political and economic issues. Such negative, even contradictory reactions to WCC political involvement go back to the very first assembly. Negative comments on capitalism* prompted the *Wall Street Journal* to call the critique Marxist inspired. But the assembly's equally severe criticism of communism inspired Marxist interpretations of ecumenism as "an ideological struggle to integrate modern theology and bourgeois ideology within the ecumenical framework, testifying to the deepening crisis in contemporary social thought and bourgeois society's inner life" (see Yuri Kryanev, 1983).

The charge that WCC public statements tilt "leftward" is common, especially in Western circles. Such criticisms became strident in the late 1970s and early 1980s with widely publicized charges that many ecumenical bodies were giving money from unwitting church members to radical revolutionary and often violent Marxist causes and even to armed groups. Especially controversial were 1978 grants by the WCC Programme to Combat Racism* to armed movements which were trying to topple the white minority rule in Rhodesia (now Zimbabwe). Two bodies withdrew their WCC membership — the Presbyterian Church of Ireland and the Salvation Army (which also cited other reasons).

From the other side of the political spectrum, in 1961 Beijing's *People's Daily* called the integration of the IMC and the WCC a "new strategy of American imperialistic missionary enterprise"; this interpretation reflected an estrangement which dates back to the 1950 WCC central committee's commendation of the United Nations' "police action" in Korea. Political leaders in Hungary accused the WCC of encouraging the 1956 popular uprising. Soviet media attacked the WCC's human rights stand at the fifth assembly (1975). In the 1980s Brazilian landowners who were exploiting Indian lands described WCC support for the land rights of the Indian population as a conspiracy with Western interests to deny Brazil's sovereignty over its own country. And in the tangle of Middle Eastern politics, all sides have criticized the WCC, often blaming it for activities of Christian groups, in and outside the region, with which the Council has no connection whatever.

A more general objection is that ecumenical bodies such as the WCC exhibit "selective indignation" in political stands, including human rights violations. For example, "hard" on USA military support in El Salvador but "soft" on USSR troops in Afghanistan; or explicit on apartheid* in South Africa but silent on tribal conflicts in black Africa. Some propose that ecumenical bodies should refrain from public statements on international issues. They try too quickly to analyze conflicts and propose solutions; their "instant expertise" smacks of Christian arrogance. And in fact, these proposals claim, it is impossible to maintain a totally balanced stance that is comprehensively forthright about the flaws and wrongdoings of all governments, political parties and movements.

Institutional criticism. As the ecumenical movement has evolved, some observers say that institutionalization has diminished the original vision into a blur and somewhat frozen the movement. Ecumenical bodies have unwittingly become structured status quos;

they satisfy the majority of the members, including the leaders, who prefer the autonomy of denominations to church unity, yet who want to be "ecumenical" in some activities with some members. The main structural flaw, say these observers, is not in ecumenical bodies but in the member churches, which are not structured to receive the full service of, say, national councils or the WCC. Furthermore, membership in such councils is no guarantee that authentic ecumenical thinking, attitudes and practices deeply affect the majority of Christians. In fact, they do not, even in those churches that pioneered the movement decades ago. Ecumenical bodies are pastorally to help a minority movement grow, not to comfort the majority in cosy indifference or adamant standstills.

On the other hand, committed Christians do criticize large ecumenical structures, such as the WCC, in order to help them achieve stated goals. Airing differences can be a ministry of healing in a forum for churches from so many different confessional, cultural, political, social, economic and linguistic contexts.

Some complain that the large ecumenical structures are still too much under the control of the professionally church-engaged. High-level visits and fact-finding tours, summit conferences and confidential conversations (called dialogues) eventually produce conclusions that all other Christians should accept or else be labelled "unecumenical" — games that are all too familiar in politics. Others point out that in the face of so many human needs, the WCC too reflexively adds new programmes to its already heavy agenda. This overload overcomplicates the organization with little coordination among staff, and programmes have little chance of being digested by wider constituencies, which already have enough on their pastoral plates.

Finally, critics charge that the numerous international conferences absorb too much staff time and energy and cost too much money for what such gatherings in fact accomplish. If their more permanent effects are documents, these are too long, either too rhetorical or too technical, appealing to a very limited audience, even if it would like to take advantage of them.

TOM STRANSKY

B.B. Beach, *Ecumenism, Boon or Bane?*, Washington, DC, Herald, 1974 • "Critical Voices",

in *And So Set Up Signs*, WCC, 1988 • Y. Kryanev, *Christian Ecumenism*, Moscow, Progress, 1983 • E.W. Lefever, *Amsterdam to Nairobi*, Washington, DC, Georgetown University Ethics and Public Policy Center, 1979 • C. McIntire, *Servants of Apostasy*, Collingswood, NJ, Christian Beacon, 1955 • P. Staples, "Towards an Explanation of Ecumenism", *Modern Theology*, 1988, 5.

CULLMANN, OSCAR. B. 25.2.1902, Strasbourg, France. Cullmann's ecumenical interests are evident in his study on the place of Peter in the early church (*Peter, Disciple — Apostle — Martyr*, London, SCM, 1953). Observer at the Second Vatican Council and active in developing relations between Protestants and Roman Catholics in Europe, he believed that every Christian confession embodies a permanent spiritual gift which it should preserve, nurture, purify, and deepen, and which should not be given up for the sake of homogenization. He was especially concerned in developing a theory of *Heilsgeschichte* (history of salvation), which he expounded in *Christ and Time* (Philadelphia, Westminster, 1950). According to Cullmann, what is most distinctive in the New Testament is its view of time and history.* Running through the whole course of world history there has been a relatively narrow stream of sacred history (see **salvation history**). This special history, the midpoint of which is Jesus Christ, provides the clue to the understanding of general history, which is linear in form and runs from creation to consummation.

Cullmann studied at Strasbourg and Paris, and in 1930 became professor at Strasbourg. From 1938 he was a professor at Basel, and after 1948 simultaneously professor in the Protestant Faculty of Theology in Paris. He also lectured at the Ecole de hautes études of the Sorbonne in Paris and the Waldensian Seminary in Rome. His writings include *Katholiken und Protestanten* (ET *Catholics and Protestants*, London, Lutterworth, 1960), *Heil als Geschichte* (ET *Salvation in History*, London, SCM, 1967) and *Einheit durch Verschiedenheit* (ET *Unity through Diversity*, Philadelphia, Fortress, 1986). See *Neues Testament und Geschichte: Oscar Cullmann zum 70. Geburtstag*, H. Baltensweiler & B. Reicke eds (Zurich, Theologischer Verlag, 1972).

ANS J. VAN DER BENT

CULTURE. The issue of the relations between Christianity and culture is not new. The fledging Christian community in Antioch had to face it. It had to do with the Mosaic practice of circumcision for gentile Christians. Between some Jewish Christians who asserted circumcision to be essential for salvation* and Paul and Barnabas who opposed it, "no small dissension and debate" broke out (Acts 15:2). The case was brought to Jerusalem, where the first Christian council was held to settle the matter. The outcome was an apostolic letter sent to the gentile Christians in Antioch conveying the decision "to lay upon you no greater burden than these necessary things: that you abstain from what has been sacrificed to idols and from blood and from what is strangled and from unchastity" (15:28). The issue of circumcision was resolved, but that of "food offered to idols" was not, as Paul's letter to Christians at Corinth was to show later (1 Cor. 8:1).

As Christianity spread from Jerusalem, Judea, Samaria and to the ends of the earth (see Acts 1:8), the question of circumcision receded into the background and finally disappeared. But the question of "food offered to idols" came to the foreground and has not ceased to engage the mind of the Christian church down the centuries. For generations of Christians the phrase "food offered to idols" came to stand for idolatry, and idolatry stood for religions other than Christianity. From time to time the Christian church also found itself under hostile socio-political systems in which the power of "Caesar" is divinized and takes the pseudo-religious form of idolatry. In the minds of Christians, then, idolatry, whether in its religious or pseudo-religious form, is identified with religious beliefs and cultural practices alien to the Christian faith.

Christ and Culture, an influential work by American theologian H. Richard Niebuhr, should be understood against this background. In the history of Christianity Niebuhr discerns five ways or types by which the Christian church addresses itself at different times to the complex problem of the relations between the Christian faith and cultures, namely, Christ against culture, the Christ of culture, Christ above culture, Christ and culture in paradox, and Christ the transformer of culture. While a typology such as this helps us to have a better understanding of the issues involved in the

problem, there is a danger of reductionism, reducing the ways in which Christianity encounters cultures to Niebuhr's five types. Although this is not what was intended by Niebuhr, his typology has restricted thinking Christians, not least those in the third world, from taking a fresh look at the problem and coming up with new insights. A new Christian theology of cultures is called for.

The negative view of Protestant neo-orthodox theologians towards culture and religion is well known. Karl Barth's pronouncement on religion* as unbelief (*Church Dogmatics*, I/2), taken out of context, serves to deepen the suspicion of the Christian church towards the world of cultures and religions outside the sphere of its influence. It was Hendrik Kraemer, a Dutch missiologist, who did much to translate this neo-orthodox theological view into missiological formulation of the relations between Christianity and other religions. This is evident in the prominent theological role he played at the world missionary conferences held in Jerusalem in 1928 and in Tambaram (Madras) in 1938.

Then came the second world war, which plunged the world into the unprecedented destruction of human lives and civilization. It also marked the beginning of the end of Western colonial culture in Africa and Asia (see **colonialism**). Emerging from the war were newly independent nations preoccupied with the terrifying task of nation-building (see **nation**). Inevitably, there was resurgence of the indigenous cultures and religions — resurgence that often went hand in hand with a strong sense of nationalism. One thing became abundantly clear: a world under the sole influence of Christian religion and culture could never have existed, and Christianity had to face other cultures and religions asserting themselves with new vigour. A quest for new relations between Christianity and cultures had to begin, particularly in Africa and Asia.

In the West, a theology of culture developed by Paul Tillich, a German-American theologian, re-defined the issue of relations between Christianity and culture on the broader basis of religion and culture. After discerning three forms of culture (autonomous culture, heteronomous culture and theonomous culture), he identified theonomous culture as an expression of an ultimate concern and coined the now-famous dictum, "religion is the substance of culture, and culture the form of religion". This theological approach to religion and culture, while correcting the excessiveness of the neo-orthodox position and opening up the possibility of correlating religion and culture theologically, may result in subsuming all cultural activities under the religious rubric, leading to a new conflict between Christianity and cultures endowed with other religious values than those of the Christian church.

It is at this point that Christian theology must turn to behavioural sciences, especially anthropology, for a broader understanding of culture. It has to be acknowledged that scholars differ in their understanding of what culture is, but the working description of it offered by the English anthropologist Edward Tylor (1832-1917) still is useful. According to Tylor, "culture or civilization, taken in its wide ethnological sense, is that complex whole which includes knowledge, beliefs, art, morals, law, custom, and any other capabilities and habits acquired by man as a member of society" (*Primitive Culture*, 1871). Culture, it is evident, is closely related to religion. But it has to do with religion not in

a narrow sense of doctrine, teaching, or institution, but with the complex whole of life in which religion plays a critical and dynamic, but not the only, role. It is within this expanded framework of culture that relations between Christianity and cultures must be reconstructed theologically.

This is the central concern that underlies most of the theological efforts undertaken outside traditional Western theology in recent years, especially in Asia and Africa. These efforts are expressed in different but related ways. *Indigenization* first came to be widely advocated. The Christian gospel must take roots in the soil to which it has been transported. To use a metaphor popularized by D.T. Niles, an Asian theologian from Sri Lanka, the Christian gospel must cease to be a "potted flower" without roots in the alien soil. The movement towards indigenization gained momentum in the 1950s and the 1960s and enabled churches in the third world to shed their foreignness. But the change was largely of a structural and political nature. It was assumed that the Christian gospel would remain unchanged in the process of indigenization. Theologically, it was on the whole a

Methodist church choir, near Gweru, Zimbabwe (WCC/Peter Williams)

matter of finding parallel indigenous religious and philosophical language and ideas and expressing the Christian truth in those terms.

Closely related to the indigenization model is the emphasis on *contextualization*, or the careful study of the "fit" between the Christian Bible, the gospel, and the various cultural and religious settings to which Christian faith addresses itself. It was carried out with much zeal and insight, mainly in the area of theological education. It was indebted to the WCC's Theological Education Fund, later called Programme for Theological Education, for initiative and inspiration in the late 1960s and the early 1970s. Its director then was Shoki Coe, an energetic theological educator from Taiwan who did much to focus attention on the relation between the text and context in theological schools and seminaries. Although there was no surprising breakthrough, the contextualization model encouraged innovative theological education in the third world and firmly put cultures in the forefront of continuing theological efforts.

It became obvious in the efforts of indigenization and contextualization that Christian theology could not go about reconstruction of the relations between Christianity and cultures single-handedly. It must be open to the findings and insights of colleagues in other fields of study and research, particularly behavioural sciences and history of religions. It is not surprising that from the mid-1970s terms such as "acculturation" and "inculturation" came to be a part of theological language, in both Protestant and Roman Catholic circles. *Acculturation*, to put it simply, is to adapt Christian practices to local culture: the clergy in the pulpit wearing traditional clothing, using indigenous music and traditional instruments in worship service, incorporating local architectural ideas and styles into church buildings, developing Christian arts in relation to indigenous art forms. This, obviously, is a great step forward, although it still remains tentative for most established churches in Africa and Asia, heavily conditioned as they are by their Western mentors. But the acculturation process is bound to develop more and more in the years to come.

The question is whether these traditional cultural forms and expressions adapted into the practice of Christian faith are only the means to make Christianity appear less for-

eign, or whether they also lead to interactions between Christianity and cultures on a much deeper theological level. The latter seems to be the case. *Inculturation* deals more with this deeper matter of the theological understanding of different cultures. It is no longer just the question of forms and styles but one of theological relations between Christian faith and cultures. As Mercy Amba Oduyoye, theologian from Ghana, puts it: "How can one be African and Christian at the same time? In this area we meet, for example, questions about the rites of passage, naming and other initiation ceremonies, as they confront Christian baptism and confirmation" *(Hearing and Knowing)*. This is a soul-searching question for Christians not only in Africa but in Asia also. It is the most urgent and most difficult question that will engage the serious minds of Christians and churches in the third world in the next decade.

At the heart of these and other theological efforts to wrestle with the question of relations between Christianity and cultures is the concept of *incarnation*. If the divine has taken human form not only in Judeo-Christian cultures but in cultures that are African, Asian, Latin American or secular Western, do we not have to admit that there are already theological meanings embedded in these cultures? Do we not have to train our Christian theological minds to perceive God's judgment and salvation working through men, women and children in their own cultures? Cultures will then open new theological horizons that give us glimpses of the depth and breadth of the mystery of God,* the Creator and Saviour of all nations and peoples.

See also **history, inculturation, Jesus Christ, salvation history, uniqueness of Christ**.

CHOAN-SENG SONG

A.J. Chupungco, *Cultural Adaptation of the Liturgy*, Ramsey, NJ, Paulist, 1982 • C.H. Kraft, *Christianity in Culture*, Maryknoll, NY, Orbis, 1979 • H. Richard Niebuhr, *Christ and Culture*, New York, Harper, 1951 • L. Sannah, *Translating the Message: The Missionary Impact on Culture*, Maryknoll, NY, Orbis, 1989 • J. Segundo, *The Liberation of Theology*, Maryknoll, NY, Orbis, 1975 • A. Shorter, *Towards a Theology of Inculturation*, London, Chapman, 1988 • C.S. Song, *The Compassionate God*, Maryknoll, NY, Orbis, 1982 • P. Tillich, *Theology of Culture*, Robert C. Kimball ed., New York, Oxford UP, 1959.

DANIÉLOU, JEAN. B. 14.5.1905,
Neuilly-sur-Seine, France; d. 20.5.1974,
Paris. Daniélou was an influential theologian
whose interests included ecumenism, missiology and the Christian attitude towards communism. He was a member of the editorial
board of *Etudes* and, together with Henri de
Lubac, edited the series *Sources chrétiennes*.
He had a particular interest in biblical theology and the sacramental theology of the church
fathers and tried to approach Marxism from a
Christian vision of history based on biblical
inspiration and marked by an eschatological
orientation. In 1929 he entered the Jesuit
order and in 1944 was appointed professor of
Christian origins of history at the Catholic
Institute in Paris; later he was made a cardinal. Daniélou influenced several decrees issued by the Second Vatican Council. He
wrote *Essai sur le mystère de l'histoire* (ET
The Lord of History, London, Longmans,
1958), *L'Eglise face au monde*, with Jean
Bosc (Geneva, La Palatine, 1966), *Pourquoi
l'Eglise?* (Paris, Fayard, 1972) and *Christianisme et religions non-chrétiennes* (Paris,
Cercle Sant-Jean-Baptiste, 1980), and was co-editor of *The Catholic-Protestant Dialogue*
(Baltimore, Helicon, 1960).

ANS J. VAN DER BENT

DEBT CRISIS. The foreign debt crisis,
which is a heavy burden on many countries in
Africa, Latin America, the Caribbean, Asia
and the Pacific, began to be apparent towards
the end of the 1970s. Among the underlying
causes the following may be mentioned: First,
the price of raw materials on world markets
stagnated and in many cases declined. Second, the international financial instability began to make itself felt at the end of the 1960s.
In 1971, in response to the first concerted
measures taken by the Organization of Petroleum Exporting Countries, President Nixon
suspended US currency laws. At that point
currency exchange rates began to fluctuate.
Third, as a result of the US administration's
action and the resulting increase in the mass of
dollars in circulation, the banks in the more
developed market-economy countries adopted
an aggressive policy. They offered loans on
very favourable terms to third-world countries, assuming that development* would be a
natural consequence of good management of
the debt. Consequently, from 1973 to 1979
many countries in Africa, the Caribbean and
Latin America, as well as some Asian countries, doubled and even tripled the amount of
their foreign debt.

Fourth, from the end of the 1970s, as a
result of the instability of the international
financial system, interest rates on dollar loans
soared to astounding levels, in some cases
even tripling. This produced an imbalance
between the rate of economic growth in the
indebted countries and the amount they had to
pay out to service the debts incurred. Bank
interest — often calculated as compound in-

terest — raised the amounts owed by many countries to levels which simply cannot be paid. Rescheduling of the payment of this interest led in turn to further increases in the debts. Fifth, a considerable share of responsibility for this situation lies with the authorities of the indebted countries themselves. In many cases they contracted debts for projects which did not deserve priority, thereby adding to the sums owed. Moreover, even when the money received in loans was spent on investments to encourage development, it was often drained away from the debtor countries back to the lending banks through the process of capital flight.

It is clear that for many countries the foreign debt has become unpayable. At the end of the 1980s, the interest due represented an intolerable burden. The adjustment programmes demanded by the International Monetary Fund (IMF) and the World Bank will not provide a satisfactory solution (although the IMF programmes do take a little more acount of the situation of the poor in each country and tend to offer easier terms than does the World Bank). These programmes are in general extremely rigid both in their economic approach (with the financial aspect being given priority over the necessary structural changes) and as regards the time period allowed for adjustment. Unfortunately, the social cost is extremely high, above all for the poorest sections of society.

The WCC's Advisory Group on Economic Matters (AGEM), at a working session in Geneva (1984), spoke of the need to reform the international financial system. On the one hand, this calls for a restatement of goals and values, stressing the priority of equality, justice and sustainability. To this end, the AGEM also proposed that the churches should endeavour to formulate clearly "an international moral and ethical order. Two basic principles are at the core of the search for this order: (1) international responsibility for all the world's people; (2) universality in the approach to finding and funding solutions to the world's financial problems." Clearly, this approach to the problem has to be based on an economic order which gives priority to justice (see **economics**), at both national and international levels. At the same time, the AGEM affirmed the need for systematic reforms which would include changes in the relations

and modus vivendi of the IMF, the World Bank and national governments. These and further complementary measures would make it possible to overcome the existing stalemate.

In July 1985, on the basis of these studies, the central committee of the WCC called for creditors to cancel the debt.

See also **development**.

JULIO DE SANTA ANA

R.H. Green ed., *The International Financial System: An Ecumenical Critique*, WCC, 1985 ● C. Mulholland, *Ecumenical Reflections on Political Economy*, WCC, 1988.

DECOLONIZATION. In the 20th century, decolonization in Africa and Asia has entailed different strategies of resistance, each rooted in certain cultural patterns:

Primary forms of resistance. In the *chronological* sense it means resistance by the people at the very time of European penetration and conquest. Many African and Asian societies fought colonialism* as it arrived. Resistance ranged from the Ashanti wars in Ghana to the Matabele wars in Zimbabwe, from the struggle against the British in Afghanistan to the early struggles against the Dutch in Java. Primary resistance in the *cultural* sense means resistance on the basis of indigenous fighting symbols, regardless of chronology. The Mau Mau did it as late as the 1950s on the basis of Kikuyi values and related religious beliefs, and although they were militarily defeated by the British, they were politically triumphant in the sense that they broke white settler political power. The Maji Maji war in Tanganyika (mainland Tanzania) was primary resistance in an intermediate sense between chronology and pure culture: chronologically it occurred quite early, but it was also inspired culturally by indigenous beliefs. The movement was militarily crushed, but it influenced the Germans to formulate less repressive imperial policies.

Islamic forms of resistance. African primary resistance in the chronological sense was, at least in symbolism, sometimes Islamic rather than purely indigenous, usually sounding the clarion call of the *jihad* (struggle in the name of God), a theme that has persisted in Afghanistan and parts of the Arab world. This tradition in religious terms manifested itself in Africa and Asia: in the Nile valley it was influential as Mahadiyya opposition to British penetration. The fear of jihads influenced British colonial policies in Muslim areas. It is arguable that it is responsible for the decision to let northern Nigeria enjoy substantial autonomy during the colonial period and for the policy of indirect rule in Africa. Missionary education was also discouraged in Muslim areas for similar reasons. Some caution was also shown by France in the policies towards Muslim colonial subjects. In North Africa opposition to European imperial rule was often re-inforced by some pan-Islamic sentiment. In Egypt it took the form of nationalism becoming increasingly secular in the 20th century. In British India, Islamic sentiment in favour of creating a separate country (Pakistan) awakened some worry about Islamic militancy in other parts of the empire and in African Christian nationalists like Nhamdi Azikiwe and Kwame Nkrumah, but the fact is that West Africa has not experienced separatist Islam of a magnitude comparable to Pakistan.

Indian-inspired forms of resistance. While some colonial nationalists worried in the 1930s and 1940s about religious tension such as was affecting India, distant colonial subjects were also often impressed by the achievements of the Indian nationalist struggle for independence. One Indian leader was particularly influential: Mahatma (Mohandas) Gandhi. Nkrumah used Gandhian ideas as basis for his strategy of "positive action" in the early 1950s. Kenneth Kaunda of Zambia was also Gandhi's disciple and for a time was opposed to violence in all its forms and advocated the strategy of non-violent resistance of "soul force" (or *satyagraha*) more compatible with his Christian faith. African opposition to armed struggle was evident at the All-African People's Conference held in Accra, Ghana, in 1958, where the Algerians — then at war with France — found it difficult to get pan-African endorsement for their struggle. The obstinacy of white colonial rule in Southern Africa and the stubborn Portuguese insistence that the colonies were part of metropolitan Portugal helped to radicalize and militarize anti-colonial struggles.

Christian and Western-inspired forms of resistance. The top leaders of African independence struggles were disproportionately Western-educated or educated in Christian missionary schools and colleges. Nkrumah, Senghor, Nyerere, Kenyatta, Mugabe, Awololo, Banda, Kaunda, Houphouet-Boigny are notable examples. The West (Europe and North America) inspired African and Asian resistance through the following "transmission belts": Western education, including Christian mission schools, Christianity as a social and political force, Western political ideologies (nationalism, liberalism, socialism*), Afro-Asian alliance with metropolitan political parties or organizations, Western military technology adopted and adapted by liberation movements. Again, the top political leaders in Asian and African liberation movements came disproportionately from among the more culturally Westernized natives: Sukarno (Indonesia), Jawaharlal Nehru (India), Nelson Mandela (South Africa), Kwame Nkrumah (Ghana), Ahmed Ben Bellah (Algeria) and Robert Mugabe (Zimbabwe).

Decolonization and the second world war. These forms of resistance were profoundly affected by the second world war. Politically, imperial control was being weakened by the declining of the imperial powers themselves, breaking the old mystique of imperial invincibility. Japan, on the other hand, played havoc with Burma, Indonesia, Vietnam and the Philippines. African nationalists were watching these developments with rising hopes and aspirations for African liberation. India was restive. Never before had so many ordinary Asians and Africans tried so hard to understand conflict in such remote places as Dunkirk and Rangoon, Pearl Harbor and El Alamein. Not a few "natives" were servicemen experiencing combat, learning new skills and acquiring new aspirations. On the other hand, the war was also increasing temporarily Europe's need for the products of the colonies. The seeds were being sown for the deeper incorporation of the colonies into Western capitalism. In other words, while politically the war weakened imperial control and prepared the way for the disintegration of the empires of France and Great Britain, economically it helped to integrate the colonies more firmly into the global capitalist system as the economies of the periphery were made to serve more systematically the war needs of the centre. Culturally it broadened Africa's exposure to alien influences and later resulted in the imperialist building of higher educational institutions for the colonies. Militarily it initiated more firmly the idea of recruiting colonial soldiers and setting up colonial armies equipped with modern weapons, with the well-known consequences of both military dependency and the tensions of civil-military relations in the former colonies.

See **colonialism; liberation, struggles for; revolution**.

ALI A. MAZRUI

N. Miller & R. Aya, *National Liberation: Revolution in the Third World*, New York, Free Press, 1971 • J. Mittleman, *Out from Underdevelopment: Prospects for the Third World*, New York, St Martin's, 1988 • A.W. Singham & S. Hune, *Non Alignment in an Age of Alignment*, London, Zed, 1986.

DECREE ON ECUMENISM. This document of Vatican II (see **Vatican Councils I and II**) is the most official charter of the Roman Catholic Church's active participation in the one ecumenical movement. The council promulgated the decree *Unitatis Redintegratio* on 21 November 1964. The decree has three chapters.

Chapter 1 unfolds the Catholic understanding of the fundamental invisible and visible unity* of the Lord's "one church and one church only" as the expression of the undivided Trinity.* This church "subsists in" the Roman Catholic Church but is not co-extensive with it, because "outside its visible borders", i.e. in other Christians and their communions, exist "elements and endowments which together build up and give life to the church itself". The division among Christians indeed "openly contradicts the will of Christ, scandalizes the world and damages... the proclamation of the gospel". Nevertheless, there already is *real* communion* between Christians because of what God has done and does to and through them, but an *imperfect* one because of what they have done and continue to do to each other — "a real but imperfect fellowship" between all Christian communions.

These ecclesiological positions shape the fundamental shift in Roman Catholic understanding of Christian relations and underlie the guidelines, methods and helps for Catholic participation in "the restoration of unity". The shift is from a former ecclesiology of self-sufficiency and the church model of "return", to that of incompleteness and the need for one another in the one but still-divided household. Ecumenism deals not with foreign, but with domestic relations. It is not a return to the past but a common search for future reconciliation.*

In the practice of ecumenism (ch. 2), the whole church is involved, laity and clergy alike. Ecumenism demands both the "continual reformation" of the pilgrim church as well as the continual conversion of each Catholic. In fact, "the very soul of the ecumenical movement is the change of heart and holiness of life", along with private and public prayer for unity and with occasional joint worship. A loving understanding of each other's communion through dialogue (see **dialogue, intrafaith**), an ecumenically oriented formation in theological studies and a common search into the word of God* will foster mutual understanding and esteem. And to express the bond which already unites Christians to the Servant Lord and to one another, common witness* is strongly encouraged through co-operative action, especially in social matters.

Chapter 3 describes the two principal historical divisions in the Christian family, those in the East and those in the West. With regard to the Eastern churches, one must bear in mind the special features of their origin and growth, which resulted in a mentality and historical development different from that in the West. The Eastern liturgical and monastic traditions, Eastern spiritualities and church disciplines, and "complementary rather than conflicting" theological formulations should be respected, for they contribute to the comeliness of the one church and to its mission.* Prayer, dialogue, and co-operation in pastoral work are the means for restoring full communion.

Among the Christian communions in the West, the decree proposes a programme for dialogue. The commitment to Christ as Lord and Saviour, the loving reverence for holy scripture, the baptismal liturgy and celebration of the Last Supper, the apostolic witness to the gospel in social action — all form points of agreement as well as disagreement among Catholics and their Anglican and Protestant brothers and sisters in Christ.

The decree ends with a plea for God's blessings on the ecumenical movement, born of God's Spirit and resting in hope on God's continuing guidance.

See also **church, Roman Catholic Church**.

TOM STRANSKY

A. Bea, *The Way to Unity after the Council*, London, Chapman, 1967 • *The Ecumenical Review*, 17, 2, 1965 • B. Leeming, *The Vatican Council and Christian Unity*, London, Darton, 1966 • T. Stransky, *Decree on Ecumenism*, translation, notes and commentary, New York, Paulist, 1966 • G. Thils, *Le décret sur l'oecuménisme*, Tournai, Casterman, 1965.

DENOMINATIONALISM. Denominationalism denotes a pattern of religious structuring and of ecclesial diversity that appeared in the modern, Western world under conditions of religious pluralism,* disestablishment, toleration and religious liberty.* As a state of dividedness and as the object of corrective endeavours on the part of 20th-century ecumenism, denominationalism has been portrayed negatively, as the "moral failure" of the church (H. Richard Niebuhr). With more sympathy, one might recognize in denominations and denominationalism a form of religious order and organization peculiarly expressive of the social and cultural life of democratic capitalism.* That recognition comes easier as the vitality and salience of denominationalism recede. In its heyday, denominationalism and related forms of voluntarism seemed to be actually constitutive of democratic society. Diversity took different forms at earlier points in the church's life and will doubtless assume a different aspect in the future. Such a perspective on denominationalism invites perhaps some reconsideration of ecumenism. Modern ecumenism may also need to be construed less in moral terms as an onslaught against schism* and more as an expression of the church's *unity** appropriate to the same set of social conditions as those in which denominations express the church's *diversity*.

Denominationalism patterns vary geographically, reflecting the social-cultural landscape, the political configurations, and the route taken in each country. In the Anglo-Saxon world, denominationalism bears the marks of its origins in the 17th-century religious maelstrom out of which modern Britain emerged. The theological languages of the Reformation(s) gave urgency, even ultimacy, to causes and social groupings. British society fractured into religious parties. The fracturing itself set the terms for later British denominationalism and that of Britain's colonies.

The habits of mind and heart that characterize denominationalism, that give its peculiar colouration, also derived from the 17th century and particularly from Puritanism. Reformed theology put a high premium upon conceptualizing God's order for the world and actualizing order in church and state.* Puritan parties re-inforced that mandate for structure with eschatological urgency. In the face of an imminent end, they felt driven to build God's new order. Detailed blueprints for the structural order of the church they discovered in the Bible. So Presbyterians, Independents, Separatists, Baptists, Quakers and a myriad of radical groups sought to build God's order. These groups carried the mandate for order throughout the Anglo-Saxon world, thereby providing an essential ingredient in denominationalism, i.e. purpose. Each group cherished its order as God's own, planted it wherever it went, and viewed other ecclesiological expressions as a betrayal of God's will.

Such presumption bred intolerance, fanaticism, war and regicide. It also bred the reactions that we know as the Glorious Revolution and the Enlightenment and credit with the invention of toleration. Such tolerance, or acceptance of other religious bodies, was another essential for denominationalism. And to a certain extent, the Enlightenment and political liberalism did provide the social conditions for religious groups to recognize one another's legitimacy. However, that vital achievement derived its positive content from one strand of Puritanism, namely the Independents. Committed to the ecclesial sufficiency of the local gathered community (see **local church**), the Independents worked out for themselves and ultimately for a larger Protestant community a conception of the church's unity that transcended the manifest plurality of churches (see **congregationalism**). The key notion was that schism did not apply to the mere fact of division but rather to attitudes and relationships, specifically to the want of love between Christian groups that put brothers at enmity with one another. On that premise, groups could recognize one another as legitimate, as part of the church, even though differing on non-essentials. That posture guided the attitudes towards one another of the groups bred or nurtured by pietism and thus suffused the whole evangelical wing of Protestantism.

Other constructions of unity-amid-diversity would eventually reinforce that puritan/pietist one and imbed themselves in the folkways and laws of Western states. The US, in particular, made denominationalism seem almost constitutional. The federal amendments proscribing establishment of religion, providing for separation of church and state, and guaranteeing religious freedom and corresponding legislation on the state levels did seem to envelop the existing religious pluralism in political sanctity. But other factors as well made denominationalism into what Tocqueville recognized as the first of American political institutions. The public theology derived from New England puritanism and the missionary imperialism of revivalistic Protestantism drove denominations into the quest for a Christian America, a quest that re-oriented denominational attention away from internal preoccupations and towards the amelioration of the moral and spiritual conditions of the American people. The denominationalism that resulted constituted what scholars have recognized as a voluntary establishment of religion, an extremely ironic but nevertheless highly visible establishment despite disestablishment. Well into the 20th century, so-called mainstream Protestant denominations and denominationalism functioned as the structure or skeleton for the American civil religion.*

That skeletal function depended upon the diversity that denominationalism permitted, even blessed. The unitive purposes of denominations and denominationalism went hand in hand with intense competitiveness and social divisiveness. Denominations facilitated division of church and society along ethnic, sectional, radical, economic and linguistic lines. It was this "compromise" of the church that Niebuhr pronounced as the sin of denominationalism.

By the final third of the 20th century, that form of denominationalism seemed to be crumbling, a casualty of the many developments that rendered mainstream Protestant hegemony implausible — the social and political maturity of Judaism and Catholicism, the waning plausibility of a missionary conception of the world, the self-critique typified by Niebuhr and known as neo-orthodoxy, the increased secularization* of American society, the more "civil" tone of civil theology, the political strength of the Protestant right and, of course, ecumenism. Many mainstream Protestants (and increasingly Catholics as well) found in ecumenism the purpose, vision and unity that denominationalism and a Christian America had once provided. Abandoned by the mainstream, both denominationalism and the quest for a Christian America have prospered among conservative and evangelical Protestants. The future of denominationalism and of its relation to democratic society remains an interesting question.

See also **federalism**.

RUSSELL E. RICHEY

J.A. Beckford, "Religious Organization: A Trend Report and Bibliography", *Current Sociology*, 21, 2, 1973 ● H.R. Niebuhr, *Social Sources of Denominationalism*, Hamden, CT, Shoe String, 1954 ● R.E. Richey ed., *Denominationalism*, Nashville, TN, Abingdon, 1977.

DEPENDENCE. The debate on development* inevitably raised the question of the need for strategies aimed at overcoming underdevelopment. And analysis of the material conditions of the underdeveloped countries in its turn made it possible to understand that the problem of economic growth cannot be separated from that of domination. The situation of the great majority of the underdeveloped countries is the result of a historical process which in general was decisively influenced by colonialism.* For the majority of former colonies, the achievement of political independence has not set them on the path of development.

In many instances the situation even became worse. The new nations (see **third world**), despite their new political sovereignty, generally continued to be dominated by external factors, i.e. to be in a state of dependence. This is understood to mean "the situation of underdevelopment, which socially implies a kind of domination... In extreme cases this situation presupposes that the decisions affecting production or consumption in a given economy are made in terms of the dynamics and the interests of the developed economies. The economies based on colonial enclaves represent a typical example of this extreme situation" (F.H. Cardoso and E. Faletto).

The theory of dependence stresses that this linkage of domination and dependency takes place within the process of capitalist development, with its associated social structuring (see **capitalism**). It follows that dependence brings an expansion and intensification of tensions between capital and labour (1) by alienating the immediate producers from their products, especially in the case of those who work in rural areas; (2) by concentrating excess production in private capital; (3) by concentrating and centralizing the ownership of the means of production in private capital; (4) by increasing the number of unemployed people; and (5) by giving new impetus to the development of productive resources.

The fundamental problem is that capitalistic growth is a process which involves the whole of society in the same way. Capitalist development in a region and in an economic sector has a destructive effect on the forces already existing, on the production relations in that region and sector, and also in the regions and sectors which depend on it. It is therefore a destructive process which in turn creates new tensions. Thus for instance an imbalance occurs between industrialized countries and others which provide them with raw materials, promoting the power of the former while weakening the latter. This inequality in turn has repercussions within the society of the countries subjected to domination, causing serious social confrontations and general instability.

The theory of dependence was formulated chiefly as a criticism of the developmentalism of the 1950s and early 1960s. In the 1960s it was claimed that economic growth would result from a process of investment to which domestic savings and international aid would contribute. Those who formulated the theory of dependence emphasized that the impact of this investment would not yield the results claimed unless the problem of structures was tackled. The view of the developmental theorists was that the social well-being of the countries on the periphery would come about through the processes of reform and modernization: the model for growth had already been given through the success obtained by the more industrialized countries. Those who framed the theory of dependence, however, stressed that this assumption ignored the historical conditions which had led to the growth of the strong and the economic weakening of the impoverished. The development of some, therefore, meant the underdevelopment of the others and vice versa.

This view of economic and social reality contributed decisively to the initial analyses that led to the proposals enunciated by liberation theology,* especially in Latin America and the Caribbean. Gustavo Gutiérrez pointed out that "the poor countries are becoming ever more clearly aware that their underdevelopment is only the by-product of the development of other countries... Moreover, they are realizing that their own development will come about only with a struggle to break the domination of the rich countries." This perception sees the conflict implicit in the process. Development must attack the root causes of the problems, and among them the deepest is economic, social, political and cultural dependence of some countries upon others — an expression of the domination of some social classes over others. Attempts to bring about changes within the existing order have proved futile. Only a radical break from the status quo — i.e. a profound transformation of the private property system, access to power by the exploited class, and a social revolution that would break this dependence — would allow for the change to a new society.

The novelty of dependence theory does not lie in recognizing domination. Rather, the theory makes it possible to understand the effects of economic domination today on the various social classes and the state. The specific nature of the economic situation over the last 20 years is due to transnational interests, which are directly influencing the internal situation of the various countries and favouring the creation of an industrial and financial economy in the periphery. It absorbs the dominant classes in the dependent nations, aiming thereby to reduce the consequences of a typically colonialist kind of economic exploitation. The contrast between centre and periphery thereby gains in intensity in dependent societies. It has found expression in the continual series of acute social conflicts in the countries of Africa, Asia, Latin America, the Caribbean and the Pacific.

See also **development, economics, third world**.

JULIO DE SANTA ANA

H. Assmann, J. de Santa Ana, G. Casalis et al., *To Break the Chains of Oppression*, WCC, 1975 • A.G. Frank, *Capitalism and Underdevelopment in Latin America*, New York, Monthly Review, 1967 • G. Gutiérrez, *A Theology of Liberation*, Maryknoll, NY, Orbis, 1973.

DEVANANDAN, PAUL DAVID.

B. 9.7.1901, Madras; d. 10.9.1962, Dehra Dun, India. An ordained minister of the Church of South India, Devanandan was a speaker at New Delhi 1961. He was literature secretary of the Indian YMCA and was associated with the work of the East Asia Christian Conference and the Committee for Literature on Social Concerns. The last five years of his life he was director of the Christian Institute for the Study of Religion and Society in Bangalore. He studied at Madras University and the Pacific School of Religion, Berkeley, and obtained his PhD in religion from Yale University. A teacher in theology, philosophy and religion, he was William Paton lecturer at Selly Oak, Birmingham, Henry Luce visiting professor at Union Theological Seminary, New York, and Teape lecturer at Cambridge University. Many leaders of the churches and Christian institutions in India looked to him for personal guidance and counsel. He had many friends among adherents of other faiths and was a pioneer in the area of interfaith dialogue.* He wrote *Christian Concern in Hinduism* (Bangalore, Christian Institute for the Study of Religion and Society, 1961) and *Christian Issues in Southern Asia* (New York, Friendship, 1963). With M.M. Thomas he was editor of the journal *Religion and Society*.

ANS J. VAN DER BENT

DEVELOPMENT.

DEVELOPMENT. The idea of "development" became prominent after the second world war. The term, originally synonymous with "growth", often has been criticized as inadequate to express fully the reality of promoting human well-being through societal transformation. Various factors contributed to the increasing use of the notion of development after 1945. One prominent factor was the emergence, between 1946 and 1970, of approximately 50 nations to sovereign independence, most of them in Africa or Asia, starting with India in 1947 and Indonesia in 1949. Another precipitating factor was a revolution of rising expectations closely associated with political freedom, new technology and increasing appreciation for the marvels of science (see **science and technology**). Contributing to this revolution was a radically changing understanding of human and civil rights and a new commitment to social justice not only for nations but also for individuals and groups within a nation. Perhaps of lesser significance, but not to be under-estimated, was the remarkable success of the US Marshall Plan for the recovery of war-torn nations, as well as the cold war,* which led to a competition between super-power blocs to enlarge their spheres of ideological, political and economic influence.

Perhaps no title reveals the early understanding of development better than Walter Rostow's *Stages of Economic Growth*. Too simply stated, Rostow's argument was that nations could reach a stage of "take-off" towards economic and social prosperity if sufficient technical skills, financial support, and economic organization were made available. While Rostow's view relied heavily on long-run market forces, his thesis was compatible with both socialist and capitalist views of development. Both relied heavily on capital formation, development of human technical skills, industrialization and infrastructure enhancemant. Some 300 years of Western history and 40 years of Soviet history seemingly confirmed the scientific validity of Rostow's view. When the newly politically independent nations found themselves shackled to economic dependencies, coupled with a paucity of other key ingredients in Rostow's prescription for development, the stages of growth theory became even more convincing. But as later sections of this article will demonstrate, there has been progressive disaffection, especially among some Christian ethicists, with the assumptions implicit in this notion of development.

Early involvement in development. It was natural for the churches, who already had a long tradition of mission* and service pro-grammes among the poor, to become involved in the development agenda. The existence of thousands of church-sponsored schools, col-leges, hospitals, rural-development schemes and other projects to improve human life al-ready had forced upon the churches many important questions about the purposes and efficacy of their work. What should be the relationship between mission and service? What is the relationship between charity or relief, and the promotion of longer-term human welfare? Is there any end to charity unless development is also achieved?

In the mid-1950s the ecumenical churches embarked on influential studies of what hap-pens to individuals, communities and chur-ches under conditions of "rapid social change". Growing attention to the reality and problems of the poorer countries was sym-bolized in the fact that just after the comple-tion of these studies of rapid social change, an assembly of the WCC was held for the first time in a third-world nation, India. (In this article "third world"* does not refer to a third-class denotation, as is sometimes argued; it originates in the use of this term by a French social scientist, for whom the phrase *tiers monde* meant neither the first-world market economies nor the second-world Marxist economies, but a third-force group of nations which had particular characteristics and sets of problems, including, for most, grinding poverty.*)

A watershed in the ecumenical debate about development occurred at the 1966 Geneva conference on the churches' relationship to the "social and technological revolutions of our time". Influenced more strongly than ever before by leading speakers from the third world, the case for systemic political and cultural transformation was dramatically ar-gued, a transformation in which the churches would be called upon to play more than a palliative role. The nature of the church's role was vigorously debated. Many tended to jux-tapose mission and service, contending that mission, i.e. proclaiming the gospel, was the primary task of the churches, with service a strictly ancillary function. Some stressed charity and relief rather than systemic de-velopment, either because the churches were perceived to be ill-equipped to engage in sys-temic transformation, or because systemic de-

velopment required a kind of political or eco-nomic ideological commitment in which the churches should not engage.

Although the debate was not completely resolved, by 1968 at the Uppsala assembly it was clear that for most people the issue was not *whether* the churches should be involved in socio-economic development but *how*. In fact, so strong was the Uppsala commitment to development that the WCC immediately began a process which led to the overt in-stitutionalization of this commitment through the establishment in 1970 of the Commission on the Churches' Participation in Develop-ment (CCPD). The Uppsala assembly had also approved plans for a Joint Commit-tee on Society, Development and Peace (SODEPAX*), which was established in 1968. In the early 1970s SODEPAX was seen as an instrument for wide-ranging collaboration be-tween the WCC and the Roman Catholic Church. This dream never materialized fully, in part because of differing emphases in the analysis of development and what the chur-ches should do to promote it. After the first period, the SODEPAX mandate was redefined, with a reduced staff and programme, and at the end of 1980 it was terminated.

Under the aegis of the CCPD, the debate about the purposes, nature and processes of development became a focused agenda for the ecumenical churches. In the initial debates about development within the ecumenical churches, the Rostow understanding of de-velopment was fairly broadly accepted im-plicitly. In fact, some argued that the basic function of the churches was to generate financial resources to give to secular agencies and technical specialists, with full confidence that the latter could achieve development through their own emphases. In the debates of the early 1970s, the issue seemed to be more the moral question of how to generate the will and material resources for sacrificial giving than the problem of defining goals and methods of fostering development. The Ros-tow conception of development was also im-plicit in the composition of the first 25-person commission, largely composed of technical experts in social analysis, management, or technical development matters. It included persons who served on UN specialized agen-cies. Programmatically, also, emphasis was on technical economic considerations and the mobilization of greater capital and human resources.

Rejection of earlier views of development. It soon became apparent that the churches would not settle for the widespread secular paradigm for development, nor would they relinquish their own distinctive, often experimental, programmes. Formative for ecumenical thinking during the early years was Sam Parmar, an Indian professor of economics. Already in his thinking, which stressed economic growth, self-reliance and social justice, lay the seeds for fundamental questioning of the Rostow model. A first agenda for the churches was to test their existing mission work to see whether they promoted these three goals enunciated by Parmar and fully endorsed by the ecumenical churches. Clearly there were shortcomings, and alternative operational models were sought.

A common ecumenical development fund was established to generate more funds, to which churches and other organizations were asked to contribute 2% of their annual budget. A serious commitment to sharing power and decision making was implemented by transferring much more power to "recipient" groups to establish their own priorities and monitor their own progress. Emphasis was put on comprehensive development efforts rather than exclusively on individual sectors like population planning, health schemes, farming co-operatives, etc. And financial support, formerly often on a year-to-year basis, was committed for longer periods of time to enhance planning and fundamental development.

All of these institutional changes implied changing understandings of the churches' roles in promoting development, but it was only in the mid-1970s that a conscious assessment of the idea of development itself became a prominent feature. The widely adjudged failure of the first UN Development Decade (1960-70) and the active involvement of third-world persons in the debate about development led to a radical questioning in the 1970s of the notion of development itself. Much of the initial challenge came from Latin America, but questions also came from Africa and Asia. Significant in this intensified questioning was the emergence of the "limits-to-growth" debate, coupled with the oil supply crunch in Western nations in 1973, which dramatically challenged the assumption that

more is always better, even if more for all people were possible.

In church circles this questioning of the very idea of development had theological as well as sociological, political and economic roots, and major shortcomings of the concept of development were identified as follows. First, the traditional understanding of development focused too narrowly on economic development per se and paid too little attention to non-economic factors in social transformation, such as cultural and religious divisions.

Second, in parallel fashion, real social transformation was to be measured by what happens to *people* in the social change process, while the traditional notions of development tended to emphasize more abstract economic or political objectives. In fact, the notion of people-centred development soon was to become the distinctive feature of the ecumenical understanding of development.

Third, many discussions on development, such as the Pearson commission's influential report *Partners in Development*, appeared to assume a too facile harmony of interests between the rich and the poor, while the real situation often was a conflict between the haves and the have-nots, at least in the short term. One should not assume a harmony of interests, or that the rich will see it in their own interest to promote the well-being of the poor. To some extent, it was argued, the structures which promote the prosperity of the affluent at the same time perpetuate the subservience of the poor. While some saw a direct one-to-one relationship between enrichment and impoverishment, others were content to argue that there is sufficient relationship between the two that one cannot speak glibly of partnership in development.

Fourth, the typical measurements for development were increasingly attacked as inadequate. "Gross national product" and "per capita income" were defective because improvements in aggregate prosperity almost always obscured the real situation: the poor sectors of the population typically receive a disproportionately modest part of the bigger pie (or none at all). Disparities between the rich and the poor,* between and within countries, often became larger rather than smaller. Without justice it is impossible to speak of development. Pope Paul VI argued that justice is the new name for peace, and justice is essential to development.

Fifth, as a consequence, ecumenical reflection increasingly led to the conviction that in the name of development many national and international economic structures were perpetuating or even re-inforcing structures of injustice. Rather than a benign collaboration between the rich and the poor, with a slow evolutionary and developmental process, authentic development often is conflictual and revolutionary (see **revolution**). Development traditionally presupposed the primacy of order, predictability and rationality, but such emphases simply reified and re-inforced the status quo. Thus many prominent ecumenical ethicists gradually rejected "development" altogether and chose instead to speak of "liberation". The idea of liberation* seemed to reflect better a holistic understanding of development rather than one focusing only on material and societal factors; it made it easier to connect issues of material well-being with deeper psychological and religious values and concerns.

Furthermore, it was argued, "liberation" was more a biblical concept, and many rooted their understanding in the Hebrew exodus from slavery in Egypt. While accepting liberation as more fully expressive of many faith affirmations, some warned that to jettison the idea of development entirely, in favour of liberation, would tend to marginalize Christians from the broader development debate, thereby tacitly encouraging the churches to escape into theological analysis without taking seriously hard economic and political questions.

Sixth, given the enormous strain on the environment, which growth models of development implied, and in the face of increasingly visible signs of the earth's limited resource and absorptive capacities, many began to question whether even the ideals of development were suitable goals. The question increasingly was not whether the goals were attainable but whether the goals were desirable. The persistent question became whether human relationships and affinity with the natural world were being not only undermined in practice but lost sight of in principle. The MIT conference (1979) was an attempt by theologians and scientists to reflect together on issues of "faith, science and the future", in which scientific and technological values were seriously questioned.

Finally, a cardinal feature of traditional development theory was that prosperity should be generated at the "top" of centres of strength, and that from these centres of strength prosperity would radiate ever more fully towards the periphery of society. This centrifugal radiation, or trickle down, worked better in theory than in practice. Experience and not a few studies showed that trickle up was more likely the case than trickle down, draining further the resources from the poor to the already relatively better off. To rely heavily on trickle down seemed at best inefficient, at worst a hoax upon the poor.

Participation of the people. Two key emphases had become central to ecumenical thinking about development and liberation in the mid-1970s. One was the crucial role of "participation".* Following the logic of the liberation argument and the example of the Hebrew people's escape from slavery in Egypt, it was argued with increasing cogency and vehemence that people should be the subjects of history* rather than the pawns moved about in other people's shaping of history; that justice should be not merely distributive but participatory. Thus a society could not be considered developed, even moving towards development, when those who are governed do not have a share in determining where their society is headed. The popular notion of development encouraged concentration of power rather than its distribution. This sentiment was eloquently expressed by the ecumenical community in the mid-1970s, in its theme of development as struggle towards a "just, participatory and sustainable society". Because justice had been so long associated only with distributive justice, this formula reflected a conscious insistence upon including "participation" as a visible element in the vision of an emergent society.

In a parallel and even more central way, the second dominant idea about development and liberation in the mid-1970s was that of "the people". For it was not simply participation in general that emerged as a priority, but participation by the marginalized and oppressed people who had too often been written off. C.I. Itty, director of CCPD, captured this change graphically in his report to the commission in 1977: "Development is essentially a people's struggle in which the poor and oppressed should be the main protagonists, the active agents and immediate beneficiaries. Therefore, the development process must be seen from the point of view of the poor and oppressed masses who are the subjects and not the objects of development. The role of the churches and Christian communities everywhere should be essentially supportive." Itty went on to argue that this notion of development has direct consequences for the way the churches should pursue development. "In situations where the poor accept their lot of poverty and misery in passive resignation, the churches should assist the masses to recognize the roots of their plight, to acquire a new awareness of themselves and the possibilities for changing their situation. In situations where the poor and oppressed are organizing themselves for the struggle, the churches should manifest their solidarity with them and provide supportive means for the struggle."

This commitment to solidarity with the poor has been controversial. Who are the poor? Which poor? Do the poor really have wisdom about the direction society should take and what methods are best to get there? Are Christians to endorse every strategy adopted by poor people? What is the relationship between poverty and righteousness? Is the church to abandon the rich and middle class? And what are the practical implications for the churches as they try to promote development? One programmatic consequence has so far been much greater attention by the churches to the development of networks of people or people's movements rather than to the building of institutions or the encouragement of projects from outside a local situation.

The logic of experience and analysis, intentionally testing and contributing to one another, led quite naturally to this emphasis on people's participation. This "praxis", or dialectical interaction between theory and practice, has been a dominant motif in recent ecumenical understanding of development. There has emerged a concomitant concern that analysis and action not become so preoccupied with the local or micro-situation that the impact of the macro-level economic, political and cultural forces is ignored. The practices of giant transnational corporations,*

many of them with more financial clout than the nations in which they are working, do have profound influence upon a local economy. A rich nation's aid and trade decisions do significantly affect a poor nation's or region's ability to meet the needs of the people. The General Agreement on Tariffs and Trade and the International Monetary Fund, as well as a cluster of UN agencies, do strongly affect the local possibilities.

Seeing the whole picture. Thus, while giving primary attention to people's participation in movements for justice and human dignity, ecumenical thought about development also gives considerable attention to macro-level factors. Prominent among these have been recent studies on the role of transnational corporations, analyses of the tendencies of technology to concentrate power, critiques of the information and communication industries and how they have been used to exert enhanced control over the weak, assessments of how Western-style medicine has often created unneccessary dependencies of the poor on health professionals and the pharmaceutical industry. More recent studies show how the enormous debt of poorer countries distorts national priorities in favour of export and the further impoverishment of the poor. Recent ecumenical reflection on development, therefore, struggles to combine analysis and action which take into account both macro-level forces and micro-level initiatives and realities.

More than ever before, in the 1980s there emerged a consciousness of the integral connections between all of the major justice questions facing the world family. Racism* is deeply connected with economic injustice; sexism* constitutes an incredibly resistant barrier to social development; ecological disaster compounds pressures upon the poor and makes justice more difficult to achieve; militarism* and the enormous costs of "security" exact their disastrous toll on human and financial resources; consumerist values insidiously exert their corrosive effect on humanistic and justice values; population pressures exacerbate environmental degradation, etc. The list of complex interdependent forces is seemingly endless.

In the final analysis the issues are so huge and complex that some contributors to the development debate have warned against two

A display in the market place about health programmes, Pucarani, Bolivia (WCC/Peter Williams)

powerful temptations: either to ignore the issues altogether, or to be physically overwhelmed by trying to resolve them all at once. The current ecumenical response to the interlocking character of all these issues, and their negative impact on prospects for the justice and dignity of the poor, is to work towards a comprehensive vision of what society ought to be under the rubric of "justice, peace and the integrity of creation".* Not understood as a blueprint for society, this theme nonetheless attempts to provide a normative conceptual framework for keeping all fragmented issues dynamically related.

Notwithstanding the very significant strides of the past two decades, especially in the realm of understanding more fully the nature and problems of development, the mood today in the poorer countries often is quiet — and sometimes not-so-quiet — exasperated desperation. Caught in those desperate living conditions, many people argue that it is euphemistic to talk about development at all. They argue that things are not improving; in fact in vast areas of the world they are deteriorating further. In the face of the debt crisis, environmental degradation, lack of food, dearth of elementary health care, repres-

sion by those in control, paucity of even basic education, the dominant concern is simply to survive. The revolution of rising expectations has, in many parts of the world, been replaced by a resignation to lowered expectations. Perhaps the greatest achievement of the period from 1960 to 1980 was the arousal of the common people to the belief, the hope, that they did not have to live in dire poverty and tacit oppression, that they were called to a different possibility. Many believed that this could happen peacefully, with the goodwill and collaboration of those who controlled society. Perhaps the greatest achievement of the development concept was that it sowed this hope in the people. In the 1990s that dream, belief, expectation is struggling to survive among the poor, even while it remains a popular idea among people of liberal persuasion who are still determined to foster development.

The issue of development has become a major preoccupation of the churches, but the churches have not been uncritical participants in the broader debate about the goals and methods for promoting development. They have challenged fundamental assumptions and conceptions, and they have called into question many existing patterns for trying to achieve development at both the macro- and micro-levels. Not least significant, they have continuously explored the possible implications of these new insights for their own theories and actions. The pressures for justice, dignity and ecological sanity guarantee that, despite their complexity, the issues of development will remain a compelling challenge conceptually as well as practically.

See also **debt crisis; economics; growth, limits to; people**.

RICHARD D.N. DICKINSON

R. Dickinson, *Poor, Yet Making Many Rich*, WCC, 1983 • C. Elliott, *The Development Debate*, London, SCM, 1971 • C. Furtado, *Development and Underdevelopment*, Berkeley, Univ. of California Press, 1964 • D. Goulet, *The Cruel Choice*, New York, Atheneum, 1978 • R. Laurentin, *Liberation, Development and Salvation*, New York, Orbis, 1969 • J. de Santa Ana ed., *Towards a Church of the Poor*, WCC, 1978 • *To Break the Chains of Oppression*, WCC, 1975.

DIACONATE. The primary model for the diaconate is the serving aspect of the ministry of Christ himself, especially his statement: "I am among you as one who serves" (Luke 22:27). A form of serving ministry alternative to that of the apostles was established in Acts 6, which reached more types of people. The first gentile Christian church, in thankfulness for receiving the gospel, reciprocated with diakonia (service) when the Jerusalem church was in need. Later Paul bound together the Greek churches with the mother church through the practice of diakonia. By the time of Philippians and 1 Timothy some serving ministers were definitely known as deacons; Luke may have had this in mind when he was writing. An increasing number of biblical scholars have concluded that Phoebe served as a deacon (see Rom. 16:1). Some of the enrolled widows of 1 Tim. 5 would have been the most obvious candidates for the women deacons of 1 Tim. 3:11.

By the 2nd century, the early deacons were linked most closely with their bishop and together performed the church's social-caring ministry. The deacons' teaching work was centred on baptismal preparation. They linked together bishop and people in the liturgy and in social care. Rome limited its deacons to seven; they then became the administrators of

7 (later 14) areas of the city. Their heavy work-load led to subdeacons. Eventually the 14 areas gave their titles to the cardinal deacons (abolished in the 19th century). The golden age of the male diaconate was the 3rd and 4th centuries in the East.

Women deacons ministered to women and children, especially in the sexually segregated churches and households of the East, and in women's monasteries. Their liturgical duties were connected with the baptism of women and involved taking communion to the housebound; their social-serving duties included chaperoning interviews between laywomen and male clergy. According to canon 15 of Chalcedon, 40 was the minimum age for ordination. Scholars differ concerning whether canon 19 of Nicea means that deaconesses (called so for the first time in that document) were lay, or whether the Paulianist "deaconesses" had never been ordained. The golden age for women in the diaconate was the 4th through 7th centuries in the East; best documented is Chrysostom's mentor, Deacon Olympias of Constantinople. As part of financial stringency after the great fire there, parishes were restricted to six women deacons, and the cathedral staff was limited to 100 male and 40 female deacons. In Syria there were special canons for abbesses who were deacons; by the 14th century, knowledge of the diaconate of abbesses ceased, but traces remained in the Orthodox Euchologium and in the ordination of abbesses in the West. Women deacons occurred in at least the late 4th through 6th centuries in the West, probably as a result of Byzantine influence, but tended to be barred by synods.

For many centuries the difference between the minumum age for the diaconate and the minimum age for the presbyterate ensured that most clergymen served as deacons for several years, and some served so all their lives. Some head or arch deacons proceeded directly to the episcopacy (Thomas Becket) and even to the papacy (as late as Gregory the Great).

The development of the sacerdotal presbyterate led to rivalry. Increasingly the diaconate was regarded as a transitional stage on the way to the more highly prized priesthood. A transitional diaconate in turn led to a less qualified diaconate which retained its liturgical roles but lost its administrative and social-serving roles.

In the 19th century there was a revival of a social-serving diaconate beginning with Fliedner's deaconesses at Kaiserswerth and Wichern's deacons. The Kaiserswerth deaconesses remained single and usually lived communally in a motherhouse, were sent out to their work of nursing or teaching, and received pocket money. The deacons were trained by their brotherhood, could marry, and often worked as house fathers in institutions. After training and probation, both were blessed by the pastor of their brother- or sisterhood. Another life-style developed at Zehlendorf and Herrenberg, whereby the institution trained diaconia sisters who then worked for salaries, especially as district nurses; in return for a percentage of income, the institution provided in-service training, pastoral guidance, and retirement opportunities. German cultural contacts and missionary work spread these forms throughout the world. The German examples and similar 19th-century social needs evoked parish deaconesses — some lay and some ordained — in the various Anglo-Saxon churches. Some formed sisterhoods. Churches of the Reformed tradition tended to elect lay deacons to do financial or pastoral work in parishes.

After the second world war, changes in the large hospital-based institutions with which the deaconesses were bound was causing them stress. By the 1960s there were married Germanic deacons of either sex living a style of life similar to the diaconia sisters; they had been commissioned by their church, held both social-serving and theological qualifications, and often served as parish workers or as youth leaders in parishes. By the 1970s many Anglo-Saxon deaconesses had gained liturgical duties.

The study of the liturgy and ministry of the early church, the call of individual social workers and teachers, and the writings of Josef Hornef and Karl Rahner led in 1964 to the restoration of the permanent diaconate in the Roman Catholic Church, with married men eligible.

Although in the 1970s some officials in various Protestant churches thought of laicizing or even abolishing the diaconate, more and more now agree that having deacons as authorized leaders brings into focus and stimulates the diakonia of all believers. The diaconal movement has spread to several provinces of the Anglican church. They, as well as the Roman Catholic Church, now have both transitional and permanent deacons, some for particular ministries. Many Protestant churches are now restructuring their diaconal ministries. Worldwide there are at least 50,000 men and women authorized for lifelong diaconal ministry. More recently some Oriental and Orthodox churches are beginning to think about their diaconates and about the diakonia appropriate for women.

There is a wealth of new literature on the diaconate and such explicit statements as those found in *Baptist, Eucharist and Ministry*:* "Deacons represent to the church its calling as servant in the world. By struggling in Christ's name with the myriad needs of societies and persons, deacons exemplify the interdependence of worship and service in the church's life" (M31).

The ecumenical working group, Koinonia-Diakonia, includes people from Diakonia* (the World Federation of Diaconal Associations and Sisterhoods), the International Diaconate Centre (Roman Catholic), the European Conference of Deacons, various Orthodox churches, and the Commission on Inter-Church Aid, Refugee and World Service and Faith and Order sub-unit of the WCC. It works on the theology of the diaconate ecumenically and encourages local ecumenical meetings of members of the diaconate and local ecumenical diaconal projects.

See also **diakonia; ministry in the church; ministry, threefold**.

TERESA J. WHITE

J.M. Barnett, *The Diaconate: A Full and Equal Order*, New York, Harper, 1981 • *Deacons in the Ministry of the Church*, a report to the House of Bishops, Church of England, London, 1988 • "Distinctive Diaconate Bibliography (Ecumenical, 1859-1989)", *Distinctive Diaconate Study*, 22, London, St Andrew's House, 1990 • G. Swensson ed., *The Churches and the Diaconate: In the Ecumenical and International Perspective*, 1985.

DIAKONIA. The term "diakonia" derives from the Greek verb *diakonein*, to serve. A related form is *diakonos*, servant (male or female). The present article considers, first, "diakonia" or service as a permanent activity of the church throughout its history, rather like the church's "leitourgia" (worship) and "martyria" (witness); and second, "Diakonia" as the name of a modern international oganization for co-ordinating the service ministries of the churches. A separate article is devoted to the "diaconate"* as an order of ministry in the churches (see **ministry, threefold**).

I. THE DIAKONIA OF THE CHURCH

Diakonia, or the "responsible service of the gospel by deeds and by words performed by Christians in response to the needs of people", is rooted in and modelled on Christ's service and teachings. Because Christ has served us, we as Christians do our diakonia. The intimate link between the service of God and the service of humankind is said by *Baptism, Eucharist and Ministry** to be exemplified for the whole church by the ministry of "deacons", which is traditionally both liturgical and social (M31).

The Old Testament law provided a variety of ways to alleviate the sufferings of the poor,* and the prophets often spoke as advocates of the widows and orphans. The early Jerusalem church practised a form of communism: those with possessions sold them to benefit those who were in need. When the first gentile church (at Antioch) heard of the need at Jerusalem, it responded with diakonia as a thank offering for receiving the gospel from Jerusalem. Paul deliberately encouraged the gentile churches to contribute to the Jerusalem church (2 Cor. 8). In addition to the general diakonia of all believers, bishops and deacons soon became entrusted with the administration of diakonia as agents of the diocesan parish.

Elements of the tradition. In some periods of Christian history, Christian care has been outstanding and pioneering and greatly impressed the pagan or indifferent neighbour. In the ancient churches, the funds used for the care came from the whole congregation and were collected at the eucharist.* In the church at Rome the male deacons, and in the Eastern church in Syria and in Greece both men and women in the diaconate were key administrators of practical care in the name of the church.

By the 3rd century the church at Rome had over 1,500 registered widows and recipients of alms. The whole city was divided into seven administrative districts, or *diaconiae*, under the care of seven deacons, such as Lawrence, whose duties included oversight of the catacombs. Instead of the Roman state distributing bread, the deacons were doing it. The apostate Emperor Julian was extremely impressed by the care the Christians provided for one another.

In Syria the monk-bishop Rabbula built a hostel, arranged for a female deacon and nuns to provide care for the women in need, and then arranged for a male deacon and monks to provide for men. "Diakonia" as an institution to care for the sick and poor spread from Syria throughout the Byzantine empire.

Bishop John Chrysostom and his staff of deacons (e.g. Olympias) exercised widespread responsibility for the social and spiritual welfare of the people. At the height of their ministry, the deacons of the Eastern churches were involved in social care, liturgical-pastoral care, teaching, administrative-juridical duties, and burial diakonia. Emperor Justinian stressed philanthropy as the most important attribute of his office and of the state; he claimed his philanthropic legislation was all-embracing, involving not only the capital but also the provinces. He established separate residential institutions to care for the various types of people in need. During his reign many institutions to care for poor pilgrims in Jerusalem were established; through the pilgrims the idea of hospices reached the Western church.

In both East and West, the documentation preserves the activities of the official institutions and tells us little of the diakonia of the ordinary laity.* Both Basil and Benedict expected monks to practise diakonia; each guest was to be received like Christ. The monasteries tended mainly to provide food for the poor at their gates; this feeding of the poor became part of the Maundy Thursday ritual. The Hospitallers specialized in their own forms of diakonia, and their name is still attached to ambulance care in Great Britain. The Beguines cared not only for themselves and their children but at times for orphans and other ill women as well. When suppressed, their houses often became municipal orphanages.

When the diaconate came to be used only as a transitional office to the priesthood, the duties of deacons became more limited to the formal liturgical ones. During the course of the medieval period, the responsibility for the care of the poor shifted from the bishop to the rector or vicar of the parish. This meant that the situation was dealt with mainly on an ad hoc and local basis. Systematization developed the scheme of the seven corporal and the seven spiritual works of mercy based on Matt. 25:34-46; their illustration in art indicates the widespread diakonia practised by the laity.

The crisis of the black death greatly increased the need for care and depleted the carers by about 50%. Changes in ways of life and economy added to the difficulties. By the 16th century, the system was no longer able to cope with the needs. In England the breakdown of the medieval provisions resulted in the Poor Law, by which the parish gave minimal relief to residents only through a poor rate levied on all householders.

Luther and Calvin reminded the church that the deacons of the early church cared for the poor. Luther recommended deacons "to keep a register of poor people and care for them". Calvin stressed that not liturgy but the collection of alms from the faithful and their distribution to the poor was the proper function of a deacon, which was put into practice in some Reformed churches. The most extensive social concern was shown by the radical reformers and institutionalized by the Mennonites and others. The 1662 ordinal of the Church of England directed the deacon to search out the sick and poor of the parish and inform the curate so that "by his exhortation they may be relieved with the alms of the parishioners, or others".

Meanwhile in the Roman Catholic Church (RCC) new forms of religious orders, especially those inspired by St Vincent de Paul, specialized in various aspects of diakonia. Under Turkish rule the Greek church found itself severely restricted from public diakonia, as more recently have several other Orthodox churches under various communist governments. In some countries laissez-faire capitalism led to extreme hardship under the new industrial conditions; sometimes a feared "means test" was used to assess whether one was among the "deserving poor".

19th-century social reformers. Both Christian and secular interests tackled the problem in the 19th century. In Hamburg the threat of revolution and social hardship led Wichern to form the Innere (or "Home") Mis-

sion and to train deacons. At Kaiserswerth-on-the-Rhine the social conditions of women and children led Fliedner to found a training institution for deaconesses to be sent to nurse and teach in parishes. The 19th-century deacon and deaconess movement understood evangelization and social care to be a unity and developed large diaconal institutions to care for the sick, epileptic, handicapped, elderly, etc.

The secular and Christian social reformers made many people conscious of the plight of their neighbours. Public charities increased, and secular movements produced a philanthropy not tied to any religion or denomination (e.g. the Red Cross). Meanwhile the idea of the professional social worker began to emerge.

Post-second world war. The second world war and its aftermath challenged all philanthropic agencies and especially the relief agencies. In 1966 a world consultation on interchurch aid,* refugee and world service was called by the WCC at Swanwick, UK. To the prevailing concept of social relief work and service, the Swanwick consultation added the idea of social advancement or social action. Service to refugees developed into interchurch aid. The WCC began to help in the co-ordination of the help coming from such regional and national Christian agencies as Hilfswerk, Christian Aid and Nordic Aid.

In 1967 the WCC, the International Federation of Innere Mission and Diakonie, and Diakonia* established a diakonia desk for research and action attached to the interchurch aid unit. Swanwick contributed to the formation of the WCC unit II, Justice and Service. In 1971 the diakonia desk was integrated into a new portfolio and became part of the Commission on Inter-Church Aid, Refugee and World Service (CICARWS); this made it more difficult for the members of the diaconates to contribute to discussions about diakonia. CICARWS contributed to the preparation for Nairobi 1975 and put more stress on justice.

Within the WCC, diakonia is particularly the concern of unit II, the largest unit of the WCC, with over 100 staff. And within Justice and Service, diakonia is especially the concern of the CICARWS commission. Questions concerning the theology of diakonia and of the relationship of diakonia to the churches belong more properly to Faith and Order.

In Western Europe from the 1960s to the 1980s, as various governments have taken on more responsibility for social security, some churches left diakonia in the hands of the social services and welfare and have seen their role as one of only "plugging the gaps". Christian socialism has found itself in dialogue with or locked into combat with many other forms of socialism. Some churches have established "boards of social responsibility" which try to influence government policy and thus practise prophetic diakonia. In Eastern Europe, Christians were asking: "What does it mean to be a Christian in a socialist and communist state? What is left for the churches to do?" Others would equally ask: "What does it mean to be a Christian in a capitalist state?" Does it mean evangelizing the government as well as those in private companies? In the global village, is diakonia to be exercised only towards the Christian neighbour, or is it for all?

There has been major criticism of the "new missionaries of the interchurch aid empire". Some have charged them with making the same mistakes and putting almost the same pressures on developing nations that international aid does. This viewpoint would prefer a local sharing of resources (Paulos Gregorios, *The Meaning and Nature of Diakonia*, 3-5).

Vancouver 1983 reported: "The 'liturgy after the Liturgy' is diakonia. Diakonia as the church's ministry of sharing, healing and reconciliation is of the very nature of the church. It demands of individuals and churches a giving which comes not out of what they have, but what they are... Diakonia constantly has to challenge the... self-centred structures of the church and transfer them into living instruments of the sharing and healing ministry of the church" (3.4.3). Vancouver recommended "that the churches initiate new models of diakonia rooted in the local congregation as it is confronted by increasing brokenness as a result of poverty, unemployment, marginalization and consumerism" (3.4.21).

CICARWS has tried to enable practical partnerships which involve people as well as funds. Europe now is a new mission field which needs to receive spiritual help from the third world. CICARWS has sponsored large

consultations and has serviced small groups such as the Koinonia-Diakonia working group (see **diaconate**).

The WCC's Larnaca consultation (1986) discussed current issues such as worldwide regression to parochialism, hunger, debt, armaments expenditure (and other non-productive or counter-productive investment of resources), racism, and uprooted and displaced people. It noted that diakonia can exist on various levels: emergency, prevention, rehabilitation, development and change. It stressed that the form that diakonia will take should be shaped by local needs. For the future, Larnaca suggested (1) renewal of philanthropic diakonia, (2) diakonia and development for justice and human rights and dignity, (3) diakonia for peace between people, (4) diakonia and church unity in the service of society, and (5) diakonia and interreligious understanding for common involvement in justice and peace.

The churches now. The individual churches vary immensely in their degree of articulation of diakonia (very few even use the term) and in their practice. The specific form of diakonia may vary not so much according to the church which practises it but according to the culture in which it is exercised. There is also great variation concerning who has primary responsibility for diakonia: the central ministers (bishops or special officials), local presbyters, deacons, professional social workers, or laity? A recent Finnish Evangelical Lutheran Church study states: "Diaconal work is not merely the actions of certain church employees or active members, but it arises from the very centre of faith." The Orthodox made a major contribution to the consultation at the Orthodox Academy of Crete and now are considering the best ways of using new opportunities.

The custom of the diaconate exercising social care has continued or been revived in some churches. In the Federal Republic of Germany, church tax helps to support separate evangelical and Catholic diaconal institutions. The Diakonisches Werk of the Evangelical churches in Germany employs 260,000 staff in 18,000 institutions. The churches have government help to cover costs; sometimes this partnership works smoothly, and sometimes there are conflicts. In Württemberg the churches supply about half of the district nurses. Young people give a "diaconal year". Unlike the situation in most other countries and churches, diakonia is no longer a foreign word in Germany (*Called to Be Neighbours*, 64). In some Scandinavian countries each parish is obliged to have a deacon or deaconess authorized by the church to visit those in need. The Finnish Evangelical Lutheran Church reports a decreased participation by diaconal workers in health care and increased participation in counselling. In the Dutch Reformed Church, the elected deacons collect offerings and use them for projects at home and abroad.

The theoretical basis in the RCC is mainly found in the various papal encyclicals (see **social encyclicals, papal**). The re-structuring of the religious congregations has greatly affected its diakonia. Fewer religious and more lay professionals are now involved in the diminished institutional work, and religious are taking on new forms of work (e.g. AIDS* ministry). Caritas* is the largest Catholic aid agency.

The restored permanent diaconate of the RCC and the distinctive diaconate in some of the Anglican churches are becoming more aware of a role in regard to advocacy for people in need and working for change which will produce justice for them as well as pastoral and emergency care. In many Anglican churches there is stress on studying root causes and trying to influence those in power. In England, *Faith in the City* has led to an exciting growth in church-based community work projects. But can changes in the church's response keep up with the changes in the welfare state? Our world is an interactive system so complex that it becomes virtually impossible to be sure of the outcome of any course of action. The churches themselves "share the same problems and internal tensions" as their societies, and they "can only to a very limited extent stand over against their social settings and judge them from an external standpoint" (Lambeth 1988).

By the late 1980s most social welfare provisions were in danger of failing to cope. In several countries, the governmental authorities were asking voluntary agencies to take on the new tasks at the very time when they were facing acute funding difficulties or when, as in England, accumulated resources which some churches had developed had often been absorbed by the public sector.

We can ask: Is any state more likely than any other to subordinate its own ideology, structure, system, and institutions to the welfare of individual people? Is any faith or any church more likely than any other to subordinate its own ideology and institutions to the welfare of individual people? How do we think about the welfare of every person in a world of *limited* resources? The churches of Eastern Europe are avid to do now what they have been restricted from doing. But is the re-staffing of institutions the best approach?

Old problems increase in scope. What can churches do to ease the plight of the 10 million refugees and the 20 million people living as aliens outside their countries of nationality? Ad hoc responses to emergencies vie for money and staff with long-term evaluation and remedying of causes. Where should the priority be put? On the global scale not only the catastrophes but also the recognition of long-term needs seem to be growing more rapidly than various capitalist-type insurances, socialist-type governmental social-security provisions, or communist-type more direct governmental provisions can respond to adequately.

New questions arise. What is the role of diaconal institutions for those people who desire liberation from institutions? How does one reconcile local grassroots people's participation with professionalization? Can local mutual sharing be effective in time of a major disaster? Will a given irrigation project prove to be another ecological nightmare? When some speak of diakonia as "reconciliation and healing", are they in danger of widening diakonia to include all aspects of the Christian faith? Can our churches do more to perform their diakonia together rather than separately?

What should be the diakonia of the local congregations? Locally, nationally, and globally, what proportion of our church resources should go to emergency aid, prevention, rehabilitation, development, and political change? Should one church specialize in emergency aid and another in changing governmental policy? Should our churches practise complementary diakonia?

See also **ministry, threefold**.

TERESA J. WHITE

Called To Be Neighbours, WCC, 1987 • "Christianity and the Social Order", in *The Truth Shall*

Make You Free: The Lambeth Conference 1988, London, Church House, 1988 • D.J. Constantelos, *Byzantine Philanthropy and Social Welfare*, New Brunswick, NJ, Rutgers UP, 1968 • Koinonia-Diakonia Working Group, *Koinonia-Diakonia*, WCC, 1985 • W. Liese, *Geschichte der Caritas*, 2 vols, Freiburg, Herder, 1922 • B. Tierney, *Medieval Poor Law: A Sketch of Canonical Theory and Its Application in England*, Berkeley, Univ. of California Press, 1959.

II. THE ORGANIZATION DIAKONIA

Diakonia as an organization became part of the ecumenical movement beginning in 1946-47, in the years before the foundation of the WCC. After the second world war, deaconess associations felt a need to form a close-knit federation. Thanks to Dutch initiative, an international conference was held in 1946 for the purpose of exploring possibilities. An interim committee was appointed to work out a plan for an international organization. After much study, prayer and consultation, this committee met in Riehen, Switzerland, in April 1947 and produced a proposal which formed the basis of the constitution for Diakonia, an ecumenical, international federation of diaconal associations and sisterhoods. It was adopted by the delegates of the various countries at a conference in Copenhagen in October 1947. In the beginning a conference was held every two years for the consideration of mutual concerns. From 1951 to 1975 Diakonia met every three years; at present the federation holds such conferences every four years.

The constitution of Diakonia was adopted at Utrecht in 1946, revised at Edinburgh in 1966 and rewritten as the Constitution of the World Federation of Diaconal Associations and Sisterhoods, in Manila in January 1979. Diakonia performs its task in cooperation with the WCC. The aims of Diakonia are to further ecumenical relationships between diaconal associations in various countries, to reflect on the nature and task of diakonia in the New Testament sense and to further the understanding of it, to strengthen a sense of community among the associations and sisterhoods, to render mutual aid and to undertake common tasks.

Diakonia presently comprises about 50 organizations from 30 countries. It has three working groups: Kaire, which encourages an ecumenical spiritual experience that embraces both contemplation and service; Koinonia/Diakonia, which reflects on the meaning and understanding of diakonia/diaconate and its practical consequences in churches and parishes; and Diak-Aid, a programme for mutual aid and exchange of personnel.

See also **diaconate**.

INGA M. BENGTZON

DIALOGUE, BILATERAL. In the 16th century and later, bilateral dialogues, i.e. religious conversations between two parties only, were a usual method of overcoming or of avoiding church division. At the time of the Reformation, there were such bilateral religious conversations (between Catholics and Lutherans, Lutherans and Anglicans, and Reformed and Lutherans); in the beginning of our century too such dialogues took place, e.g. between Anglicans and Roman Catholics (1921-26), Anglicans and Orthodox (1930ff.), Anglicans and Old Catholics (1931), and Lutherans and Reformed (1947ff.). Then for a time bilateral dialogues receded into the background. Multilateral ecumenical encounters and dialogues strongly prevailed, particularly in the realm of the WCC.

In the 1960s, however, there was a new emphasis on and a sudden surge of bilateral dialogues. Today, there is a widespread network of bilateral dialogues on both international and national levels, in which almost all churches and church traditions are involved. Thus, bilateral dialogues have again become a main focus within the modern ecumenical movement.

Two factors especially contributed to this development. The multilateral encounters of the early ecumenical movement and later within the WCC, particularly its Faith and Order* commission, had both theologically and spiritually prepared the ground for a more direct encounter between the individual churches. In addition it happened that, with Vatican II,* the Roman Catholic Church officially entered the ecumenical movement, a church which, by its strong sense of identity and universality, developed a natural preference for bilateral dialogues. Other churches, particularly those which themselves have a fairly strong sense of identity and worldwide coherence in doctrine, worship and practice, took up the dialogue with the Roman Catholic Church and subsequently also among themselves.

Apart from their bilateral method, most such dialogues have two features. First, they are *official* church dialogues in that they are officially authorized by the respective church authorities who appoint the delegates and to whom the results must be directly submitted. Second, they are mainly concerned with *doctrinal matters* (esp. authority* in the church, eucharist,* ministry,* ecclesiology), the aim being to overcome the church-divisive divergences inherited from the past and reach agreements on these issues sufficient for the establishment of closer fellowship.

This bilateral form of dialogue has gained renewed emphasis for three reasons. First, the bilateral approach allows for thorough and detailed study of the specific issues which separate two traditions and, at the same time, makes it possible to bring out more effectively the elements which, despite separation, the traditions have in common. Second, the official nature of the dialogue helps in reaching results which carry at least a certain amount of authority and thereby contributes to the process of receiving the dialogue results in the churches (see **reception**). Third, the emphasis on doctrinal matters results from the conviction that the theological divergences rooted in the historical heritage of the churches are still operative today and must be overcome if an authentic and lasting church fellowship is to be established.

A disadvantage of bilateral dialogues may be the danger of isolating the individual dialogues from each other and of losing sight of the indivisibility of the ecumenical movement. In order to counteract this danger, there have been five forums on bilateral dialogues (1978, 1979, 1980, 1985 and 1990). At the same time this point demonstrates that bilateral dialogues and multilateral dialogues are not to be seen as alternatives but that both types of ecumenical dialogue have their specific tasks and, therefore, are in need of close interrelation.

See also **dialogue, intrafaith**; **dialogue, multilateral**.

HARDING MEYER

N. Ehrenström & G. Gassmann, *Confessions in Dialogue: A Survey of Bilateral Conversations among World Confessional Families, 1959-1974*, WCC, 1975 ● G. Gassmann, "Nature and Function of Bilateral and Multilateral Dialogues and Their Inter-relation", *Mid-Stream*, 25, 3, 1986 ● H. Meyer & L. Vischer, *Growth in Agreement: Reports and Agreed Statements of Ecumenical Conversations on a World Level*, WCC, 1984 ● Reports of the "Forum on Bilateral Conversations", WCC, 1981 and 1985.

DIALOGUE, INTERFAITH.

The struggle to comprehend the relationship between Christianity and other religious traditions has been an important issue from the beginnings of the church.* Christian faith* was born in a Jewish milieu. Inevitably it soon came into contact with the Greco-Roman world. When persons who were not of Jewish origin became Christians, controversy erupted over the basis of their common life in a religious community made up of Jews and Gentiles (Acts 15; Gal. 2). In his letter to the Romans, Paul seeks to clarify theologically the relationship between the Jewish religious tradition and the Christian faith, which by then were beginning to be seen as two distinct religious groupings. Writing to the Corinthians, Paul gave pastoral advice to people who had become followers of Christ but had partners in marriage who continued to remain in another religious tradition (1 Cor. 7:12-16).

The writings of the early church also show that there were divergent schools of thought on how to understand and relate to religious life that was not based on Christian convictions. The history of Christianity is also the history of Christian relationships, for the most part conflictual, with other faith traditions. In this survey we confine ourselves to the period of the modern ecumenical movement and to the development of the concept and practice of interfaith dialogue inspired by and structured within it.

Historical background. The world missionary conference at Edinburgh in 1910 is commonly accepted as marking the beginning of the modern ecumenical movement. This conference called on the 1,200 delegates gathered from the missionary societies and so-called younger churches (from which there were only 17 delegates) to bring about the evangelization of the world in that generation.

The question of Christian understanding of and relationship to other religious traditions became one of the important issues of that conference, and the section that dealt with the missionary message in relation to non-Christian religions was, by common consent, the finest of all reports produced at Edinburgh. It spoke of the Christian encounter with the religious traditions of Asia, for example, as being of the same order as the meeting of the New Testament church with Greco-Roman culture, demanding fundamental shifts in Christian self-understanding and theology. The evangelistic thrust of the conference, however, was predominant in the overall Edinburgh message.

The Edinburgh discussions stimulated scholarly interest both in comparative religion and in exploring the Christian relation to other faith traditions. An influential book of the period was J.N. Farquhar's *The Crown of Hinduism*, which argued that Christ fulfilled the longings and aspirations of Hinduism. By the time of the next international missionary conference (Jerusalem 1928), there was considerable controversy within the missionary movement over the approach to other religious traditions. The growth of liberal Protestantism, mainly in the USA, troubled some European thinkers, who saw in it arguments, however tentative, in support of a universal religion. There was also deep concern that what was considered "syncretistic thinking" with regard to Asian religions was undermining the importance and urgency of Christian mission.*

Jerusalem 1928 met, however, under the cloud of rising secularism in both East and West, and that issue dominated the meeting (see **secularization**). While asserting that the Christian gospel provided the answers to a troubled world, the conference affirmed the "values" in other religions and called on all believers to join hands with Christians in confronting the growing impact of secular culture. But some participants could not agree with the positive affirmations of other faiths and maintained that the Christian gospel was unique among religious traditions. Thus, even though the message was unanimously accepted (partly because of the drafting skills of William Temple), the Christian attitude to other faiths became a highly controversial issue shortly after the Jerusalem meeting.

At the heart of the post-Jerusalem dispute was the *Report of the Commission of Appraisal of the Laymen's Foreign Mission Enquiry*, edited by W.E. Hocking. This report was critical of the exclusive attitude of Christians towards other faiths and claimed that the challenge to the Christian faith came not from other faiths but from anti-religious and secular movements. This approach produced so much controversy and debate that the leadership of the missionary movement called upon Hendrik Kraemer, the well-known Dutch missionary and missiologist working then in Java, to write a book on the biblical and theological basis of the Christian attitude to other faiths. Kraemer's *The Christian Message in a Non-Christian World* became the preparatory study book for the 1938 international missionary conference in Tambaram, Madras, India.

Kraemer, following Karl Barth, insisted that the biblical faith, based on God's encounter with humankind, is radically different from all other forms of religious faith. Admitting that God's will shines through, albeit in a broken way, in the all-too-human attempts to know God in all religious life, Kraemer maintained that the only true way to know the revealed will of God is by responding to the divine intervention in history in Christ. Both Barth and Kraemer emphasized the uniqueness of the revelation* in Christ and considered Christianity as a religion to be as human as any other. But neither could avoid giving, at least by implication, a unique place to Christianity in so far as it had become the vehicle through which this unmatched revelation of God is lived and proclaimed.

Even though Kraemer made a lasting impact on Tambaram and subsequent missionary thinking, there were many dissenting voices. A.G. Hogg, H.H. Farmer, T.C. Chao and others challenged Kraemer's view that the gospel was in discontinuity with other religious traditions. They witnessed to what they were convinced was a "two-way traffic" between God and the human soul in the religious life and experience of others. It was inconceivable to them that God had no witnesses among the nations of the earth. All participants agreed on the special revelatory character of the Christ event, but many had difficulty with Kraemer's view of religions as "totalitarian systems" of human thought and practice.

Although the Tambaram report leaned heavily towards Kraemer's views, it noted that "Christians are not agreed" on the revelatory character of other religious traditions. It also noted that it was "a matter urgently demanding thought and united study" within the ecumenical movement.

Post-Tambaram developments. Not long after Tambaram, Europe became embroiled in the second world war, and other concerns demanded the attention of the missionary movement. Once the war was over, the International Missionary Council* (IMC) turned its attention again to Christian relations to other faith traditions. But now it was a different world. Nationalism was sweeping through the newly independent states in Asia and Africa, and with it came a revival of religious traditions. The churches, awakened to the need to express their unity in a world shattered by war, had come together in Amsterdam in 1948 to form the WCC. Both the IMC and the WCC's Department on Evangelism were eager to follow up on the unfinished Tambaram debate on other faiths.

One of the strategies adopted was to set up a number of study centres around the world that would address the question in concrete historical situations. Another was a long-term joint study on "The Word of God and the Living Faiths of Men", which sought to take the discussion beyond Tambaram and the continuity-discontinuity polarity.

A great deal of attention was focused on Asia, where outstanding work on the issue was carried out by people such as Paul Devanandan, D.T. Niles and Sabapathy Kulendran. Devanandan's address to the New Delhi assembly of the WCC (1961) challenged the churches to take seriously the experience of the younger churches in the newly independent countries, where they had to work and struggle together with peoples of different religious traditions in nation-building.

It was in this context that the concept of dialogue emerged as a way of speaking about Christian relations with people of other faith traditions and became part of the New Delhi assembly statement. At this assembly the IMC was integrated into the WCC as the Division (later Commission) on World Mission and Evangelism (CWME).

Members of five faiths (a Buddhist, Hindu, Christian, Jew and Muslim) take part in a panel at the world consultation "Diakonia 2000—Called to Be Neighbours" (WCC/Michael Dominguez)

The concept of dialogue received further consideration at the first meeting of the CWME at Mexico City in 1963. A more significant discussion took place at the assembly of the East Asia Christian Conference (now Christian Conference of Asia) at Bangkok in 1964. Its statement on "Christian Encounter with Men of Other Beliefs" incorporated much of the rethinking in Asia in relation to other faiths. This was an important contribution to ecumenical thinking on other faiths, at many points taking the debate beyond the Tambaram controversy.

Given the importance of clarifying these issues, a conference was convened in Kandy, Sri Lanka, in 1967. This meeting was in many ways a landmark in the development of interfaith dialogue. Not only did it mark the beginning of serious interest in interfaith dialogue in the WCC, but it was also the first time Roman Catholic consultants of the Vatican Secretariat for Non-Christians were part of the discussion. Kenneth Cragg challenged, in a fundamental way, the Barth-Kraemer attitude to religions that had so dominated Protestant thinking during the previous decades.

Developments within the Roman Catholic Church. There were some significant differences between the Protestant and Roman Catholic traditions in their general theological orientation towards other religions. The Protestant missions tended to place enormous emphasis on Christology and on the need to respond to the message of the gospel as a way to salvation.* While the attitude to other faiths had not always been negative, it had tended to be neutral at best on the question of salvation outside a response to Christ. This gave rise to a sense of urgency to bring the message of the gospel to the nations of the world.

Roman Catholic theology placed greater emphasis on ecclesiology. Salvation is a free gift of God offered in Christ to one who has faith in Christ. One expresses this faith by being baptized and becoming part of the church, which was instituted by Christ to carry on his saving work. The church is the sign and sacrament of the saving work of Christ that is available to all humankind.

Within this overall concept, Roman Catholic theology could provide for the possibility of salvation to those who had not explicitly become members of the church.

Building mainly on the issue of the salvation of those who had lived before the ministry of Jesus, and those who had had no opportunity to hear the message, Roman Catholic theology developed the idea of "implicit faith" or "faith by intention", so that no one was "lost" simply because he or she was born at a particular time or place which made it impossible to become part of the historical expression of the church. Salvation offered in Christ is mysteriously available to all who seek to fulfill the will of God; it is possible to be incorporated into the sacrament of the paschal mystery, the church, by intention.

These thoughts were developed in the 1960s by two prominent Roman Catholic thinkers, the French cardinal Jean Daniélou and the German theologian Karl Rahner. In so doing they spelled out the theological implications of some of the positive developments that took place on the question of other faiths at the Second Vatican Council.

The Roman Catholic Church (like many churches within the WCC, and the WCC itself) has had a long history of relating to the Jewish people. During the Vatican Council it was decided that such an attitude should be extended to the followers of other religions as well. In keeping with this, Pope Paul VI established a special secretariat for relationships with non-Christians, naming Cardinal Paolo Marella as its first president. The papal encyclical *Ecclesiam Suam* emphasized the importance of positive encounter between Christians and people of other faith traditions.

The Vatican II Declaration on the Relationship of the Church to non-Christian Religions (*Nostra Aetate*), promulgated on 28 October 1965, spelled out the pastoral dimensions of this relationship. Other key Vatican II documents, including the Dogmatic Constitution on the Church (*Lumen Gentium*) and the Decree on the Church's Missionary Activity (*Ad Gentes*), had contained important comments that pointed to a dialogic attitude towards people of other religious traditions.

Although Vatican II did not develop clear theological positions on other religions, it did, by opening up the issue in the direction of interfaith dialogue, mark a new phase in the relationships of the Roman Catholic Church, in all parts of the world, with people of other faiths.

The Kandy meeting (whose preparatory

material included *Nostra Aetate* and parts of *Lumen Gentium*) not only clarified some of the issues but also affirmed dialogue as the most appropriate approach in interfaith relations. Although its findings were not communicated officially to the Uppsala assembly (1968), their impact was very much felt in the discussions. After the assembly the CWME called on Stanley J. Samartha to pursue with greater intensity the study on "The Word of God and the Living Faiths of Men".

A turning point in the development of this study was the convening of the first multifaith dialogue under WCC auspices. Hindu, Buddhist, Muslim and Christian participants came to Ajaltoun, Lebanon, in 1970, not only to consult about inter-religious dialogue, but also actually to engage in it.

Two months later, a WCC consultation in Zurich evaluated theologically the experience of dialogue in Ajaltoun and produced a report that became the fundamental document on the basis of which the WCC central committee, meeting in Addis Ababa in 1971, created a new Sub-unit on Dialogue with People of Living Faiths and Ideologies, with Samartha as its director.

The dialogue controversy. The establishment of the Vatican Secretariat for Non-Christians and the WCC sub-unit on dialogue heightened the visibility of interfaith dialogue in the life of the churches. The secretariat published materials promoting interfaith dialogue and encouraged closer collaboration between Christians and others in local situations. The WCC dialogue sub-unit organized bilateral dialogue meetings with Jews, Muslims, Hindus and Buddhists and sought to clarify the meaning and significance of interfaith dialogue.

Basically, interfaith dialogue was understood as an encounter between people who live by different faith traditions, in an atmosphere of mutual trust and acceptance. Dialogue did not require giving up, hiding or seeking to validate one's own religious conviction; in fact, the need for being rooted in one's own tradition to be engaged in a meaningful dialogue was emphasized, as were common humanity and the need to search in a divided world for life in community. Dialogue was seen not only as a way to become informed about the faiths of others but also as a means of rediscovering essential dimensions of one's own faith tradition. The benefits of removing historical prejudices and enmities as well as the new possibilities for working together for common good were recognized and affirmed.

Within this general framework individual theological explorations have yielded a variety of points of view. Some see dialogue primarily as a new and creative relationship within which one can learn about and respect others but also can give authentic witness* to one's own faith. Others see it as an important historical moment in the development of religious traditions and claim that each of the faith traditions in dialogue is challenged and transformed by the encounter with others. Still others view dialogue as a common pilgrimage towards the truth, within which each tradition shares with the others the way it has come to perceive and respond to that truth.

Within the Christian tradition, the practice of dialogue has raised questions about the theological assumptions about other faiths at the heart of Christian mission. The suspicion of interfaith dialogue among some Christians surfaced in the open controversy at the WCC's fifth assembly (Nairobi 1975), where the sub-unit made its first report to an assembly and where, for the first time, five persons of other faiths were invited to a WCC assembly as special guests. They participated in the discussions of section 3 on "Seeking Community", where the dialogue issue was debated. Plenary discussion on the report of this section highlighted the deep disagreement within the church on the issue of dialogue. Some felt that dialogue would lead to the kind of syncretism so feared at the 1928 Jerusalem meeting. Others wanted to defend the uniqueness and finality of the revelation in Christ and feared that the dialogue enterprise compromised that faith. Still others saw in interfaith dialogue a threat to mission, which they saw as fundamental to the being of the church itself. As in Tambaram, voices, especially from Asia, defended dialogue as the most appropriate way for the church to live in a pluralistic world. The assembly referred the report back to the drafting group, which added a preamble to meet the hesitations expressed at the plenary.

But Nairobi made clear the urgent need to clarify further the nature, purpose and limits of interfaith dialogue and to give more detailed attention to issues of syncretism, indigenization, culture,* mission, etc. Evaluating the debate, the WCC central committee authorized a major theological consultation to pursue further the questions raised at the assembly. The meeting, on the theme "Dialogue in Community", in Chiang Mai, Thailand, in 1977, aimed to clarify the Christian basis for seeking community with others and to draw up guidelines for Christian communities in pluralistic situations, in order that they might become communities of service and witness, without compromising their commitment to Christ.

The statement of the consultation dealt with such issues as: What is community? What are the marks of Christian community? Why should one be involved in dialogue? Is dialogue a betrayal of Christian mission? The meeting affirmed that dialogue is not a betrayal of mission or a "secret weapon" of proselytism but a way "in which Jesus Christ can be confessed in the world today". The Chiang Mai meeting led to the formulation of "Guidelines for Dialogue", adopted by the WCC central committee in 1979 and commended to the churches for study and action.

Within the Roman Catholic Church, there were problems similar to those within the WCC. All agreed on the need to develop positive and friendly relations with people of other faiths and on the value of interfaith dialogue for mutual understanding and collaboration. But the plenary commission of the secretariat also had to draw up guidelines that dealt with the purpose and goals of dialogue so that it was seen within the overall convictions of the church; the relationship of dialogue to mission remained a persistent problem also in Roman Catholic discussions. In general, dialogue and mission have been affirmed as legitimate activities of the church. The initial guidelines sought to avoid placing dialogue at the service of mission, a view that some advocated both within the Roman Catholic Church and the member churches of the WCC. The statement on dialogue within the Vatican underwent many revisions owing to the disagreement within the church on the theological basis of dialogue.

A plenary meeting of the consultants in February 1984 came up with a version which was officially accepted and issued by Pope John Paul II under the title "The Attitude of the Church towards the Followers of Other Religions: Reflections and Orientations on Dialogue and Mission". The statement, like the preamble to the Nairobi report, stressed the missionary vocation of the church, even as it sought to exhort Christians to be in a relationship of dialogue with others. Significantly, the pressure to clarify the dialogue-mission relation further was so great that, not long after the proclamation of this statement, the secretariat had to begin work on a document that specifically dealt with "Dialogue and Proclamation".

Dialogue in the churches. While the theological issues continue to be discussed, dialogue activities have been more and more accepted at the local level. A number of churches have expanded their desks on ecumenical affairs to include an interfaith component. Some churches and councils have created staff positions to promote interfaith dialogue. There has been an increase in the number of local and international interfaith councils. Interest in interfaith prayer was further kindled by the call issued by Pope John Paul II to leaders of all religious communities to come together in Assisi in 1986 to pray for peace, an event that attracted media attention.

Interfaith dialogue today takes place at many levels. There is the continuing dialogue of life in all pluralistic situations. There is intentional dialogue, or discourse, where persons come together to share and converse on specific issues. There are academic dialogues and what are called spiritual dialogues, emphasizing prayer and meditation. The Zen and the Benedictine monasteries, for example, exchange monks each year to learn from each other's meditative practices. In India there are weekend live-in sessions where people of diverse traditions come together for exposure to each other's prayer life and to participate in common devotions. There is a proliferation of books and articles on interfaith dialogue and the challenge of pluralism.*

Dialogue as a continuing ecumenical concern. Evidence of the overall impact of the programme on dialogue was clear at the WCC's sixth assembly (Vancouver 1983). The number of guests of other faiths had gone up to 15, four of whom participated in the presentations to plenary sessions. Interfaith dialogue was an integral part of the assembly's extensive visitors' programme. In the section on "Witness in a Divided World", there was no serious disagreement on the need for interfaith dialogue. There was, however, much controversy over the theology of religions, with a number of participants challenging a statement in the report that spoke of God's hand active in the religious life of our neighbours. Whether other religious traditions are vehicles of God's redeeming activity became a hotly debated issue.

Evaluating the experience of Vancouver, the dialogue sub-unit identified the issue of the theology of religions as an important issue for sustained study. The process of opening a discussion was begun with the launching of a study project in the churches: "My Neighbour's Faith — and Mine: Theological Discoveries through Interfaith Dialogue". The four-year study, which involved the use of a study booklet which was translated into 18 languages, was intended to raise the awareness of plurality in the churches and to explore how Christians today may look theologically at other traditions of faith. Preparations for the WCC's seventh assembly (Canberra 1991) include a major consultation on the theology of religions. The WCC world conference on mission in San Antonio, USA, in 1989 had for the first time at a mission conference consultants from other faiths, and the question of Christian relation to other faiths was one of the major issues discussed.

Within the ecumenical family interfaith dialogue will continue to remain a profoundly important, if controversial, issue. The challenge it brings to the ecumenical movement is far-reaching. It summons the church to seek a new self-understanding in its relation to other religions. It requires it to look for deeper resources to deal with the reality of plurality, and it calls the church to new approaches to mission and witness.

See also **God, mission, religion, salvation, syncretism, uniqueness of Christ.**

S. WESLEY ARIARAJAH

Guidelines on Dialogue with People of Living Faiths and Ideologies, WCC, 1979 • P.J. Griffiths ed., *Christianity through non-Christian Eyes*, Maryknoll, NY, Orbis, 1990 • S.J. Samartha ed., *Faith in the Midst of Faiths*, WCC, 1977 • S.J. Samartha ed., *Living Faiths and the Ecumenical Movement*, WCC, 1971 • R.B. Sheard, *Inter-religious Dialogue in the Catholic Church since Vatican II: An Historical and Theological Study*, Queens Town, Canada, Edwin Mellen, 1987.

DIALOGUE, INTRAFAITH. "Dialogue" has become a fashionable term, and correspondingly it lacks semantic clarity. It sounds civilized and reassuring, for it indicates an effort to fight with the weapons of the mind or even to let contrasting positions stand. In the broadest political context dialogue is the opposite of an attitude in which conflict is waged with weapons of devastating power. For this reason the threat to break off dialogue — e.g. in the statement "we have nothing more to say to each other" — has such a menacing sound. Frequently the end of dialogue is the beginning of armed conflict. If we enter into dialogue, however, hostilities come to an end.

In church usage the term "dialogue" is applied in various sets of relationships. It is applied, for instance, to the relation between Christianity and world-views which are not religious, especially Marxism. The Vatican has published documents on "Dialogue with Non-believers". Dialogue characterizes also the relation to non-Christian religions. Then, too, discussions between Christian churches have been described as the way "from polemics to dialogue". The Orthodox churches have described their opening up to the churches of the West as a "dialogue of love" which is intended to lead to a "dialogue of truth".

Lack of clarity in our understanding of dialogue increases when the meaning of this term is considered in the context of the philosophy of dialogue and personalism. Is dialogue a form of behaviour intended to solve problems, or a metaphor for mutual dependence in the age of pluralism? Is dialogue an expression of human openness from which the truth question is excluded, or is it the opposite — is it in fact a method which occurs only in discourse and which is to be used for deciding about the truth of propositions?

In view of this varied and often not very exact use of the word, Lukas Vischer expressed doubts in 1969 about whether the term was still appropriate as a way of describing the relation of the Christian churches to each other. According to him, "the word 'dialogue' is quickly losing the magic it had till quite recently, and there is even some uneasiness about its use. For what is it that the churches are doing when they converse together? Have these conversations become a means of preserving the churches in their present condition and actually protecting them against full fellowship? They are in dialogue. What more is needed?" (*The Ecumenical Review*, 1970).

The view of interchurch dialogue presented here bases our understanding of dialogue on *communio* as the structure of the church and so makes dialogue fruitful for tackling ecumenical problems (see **communion, koinonia**).

A basis in *communio* as the structure of the church. Dialogue is a mark of the church,* which exists as a fellowship of churches. Nowadays there is no longer any dispute among the confessions that the church occurs first of all as the local church* and that the criteria which make a church the church are met in the local situation. These criteria are the proclamation of Christ's message (see **word of God**), the celebration of the sacraments,* Christian love (agape, caritas) and (for churches with an episcopate) the true (episcopal) ministry (see **ministry in the church**). These local churches cannot stand in mutual isolation if they wish to remain faithful to their Christian mission and message — i.e. they are members of a fellowship.

This *communio* of the churches is achieved differently in different Christian traditions. For the churches that have bishops, the highest representative of the universal church is the ecumenical council,* in which the bishops bear witness to the faith* of their churches, while regional synods express and embody the *communio* regionally at their own geographical level. In non-episcopal churches too the idea of "conciliar fellowship" is alive (see **conciliarity**). In it the local churches are linked together in a network of exchanges, proclamation and criticism, and common efforts to find the right Christian path to follow. In this fellowship of local churches or among their representatives, the universal church is built up as *communio*. The Roman Catholic Church also took up this idea in Vatican II, seeing the church no longer as a rigid, monolithic world church but as a fellowship of churches each contributing a part to the whole. In this *communio* structure and in the mutual interdependence of the local churches and their representatives, dialogue finds its basis as an element of the church's nature.

Individual local churches are also *communio* and also achieve fulfilment in dialogue. In all the confessions there are structures and forms of organization which are intended to ensure exchanges between the different functions, ministries and charisms.* These structures and forms make dialogue possible between ministers, church authorities, theologians and "laity". In this fellowship of different gifts and tasks, the Christian congregation achieves its proper form and can proclaim its message in faithfulness to its origins and with relevance to the situation.

This dialogue, as a realization of the *communio* structure of the church, also determines the relation of the Christian confessions to each other. In this dialogue the degree of fellowship already existing between the churches is realized, and a situation is sought in which the still-divided churches of today become churches which are parts within the one universal church or mutually recognize each other as part-churches and thus build up the universal church.

Dialogue and understanding. The churches realize their *communio* structure in dialogue, and in this way their various functions, tasks and charisms and the different forms they have taken in time and space have a mutually fertilizing and stimulating effect. Such benefit occurs through their attempt to understand each other; dialogue contributes to (mutual) understanding. This process of understanding takes place at a given time between individuals in the churches, between different Christian traditions and between confessions in conflict or tension with each other; but it also takes place across time, in relation to the past. The common factor in all these different efforts at understanding is that they are directed towards human beings or groups whose worlds are unfamiliar to me initially but which I presume have something to say to me and a meaning for my own self-understanding. But if the other party is in the first instance unfamiliar to me, how can I understand at all? My immediate horizon is the sphere within which I do my understanding. A text written long ago or uttered by someone who shapes his or her life within a circle of meaning unfamiliar to me has its own, and different, horizon. My position is not that of my opposite number but is in my own particular world. I have my particular horizon, not that of the other person.

In the process of understanding, we are attempting first of all to incorporate the unfamiliar world in our own horizon. We therefore think initially that we shall find a confirmation of everything we already knew and wanted — congenial things that fit in with our own pre-understanding. But the unfamiliar world will simply not be disclosed in this way. Rather, understanding takes place because a strange world initially strikes us precisely as strange. Pre-eminently it was Hans-Georg Gadamer who drew attention to this fact. Initially I think I understand, but I have still not got beyond the circle of my own pre-understanding and prejudice at that stage. Unfamiliar things and people who live differently do not seem at first to be a problem, and everything makes some kind of sense on my own terms. Here I am still continuing to understand only myself. But the more I concern myself with a text or with people or with a church, the clearer it becomes that I no longer understand. Only on the collapse of my own pre-understanding do I begin to understand and another world becomes comprehensible to me in (so to speak) its own terms. So long as everything seems to be free of problems, I am working only on the basis of my own preconceptions. The first stage in any understanding is when something becomes unfamiliar and is not understood. This stage in dialogue cannot be skipped.

In understanding, I must recognize the unfamiliar horizon but must also hold on to my own horizon, which is just as necessary for dialogue as the unfamiliar. After all, it is I who am seeking to understand, and this means that I am not simply absorbed into the unfamiliar world. I have to live within my own horizon of understanding. In dialogue, which is meant to lead to understanding, my self-understanding is made new. The aim of the dialogue is a fusion of the horizons — of my own and the unfamiliar horizon. In understanding I remain myself, and yet as an unfamiliar world opens up to me, I become another. A new world thus discloses itself to me, and my own self-understanding assumes a new form. The person who is engaged in understanding changes, and one's horizon expands. Thus dialogue opens up the future and freedom to act. New worlds and possibilities for action open up for me in the act of understanding. Understanding demands that I should take my own and the unfamiliar horizon equally seriously; and when the two horizons fuse, the aim is achieved.

Interchurch dialogue. All churches have conducted dialogue, constantly striving better to understand their ministers, theologians, fellow Christians, doctrinal traditions, and above all the biblical proclamation, and thus better to preach the Christian message and to put it into practice more fully and thoroughly. Since the age of the church fathers, dialogue has been a means of improving the formulation or implementation and exposition of Christian doctrine. Behind the medieval disputations, which flourished for the last time at the Reformation, lay the awareness that everyone is needed and must make his or her contribution if the truth is to be discovered. The rules of disputation at the medieval universities were meant to systematize dialogue and guarantee at the same time that the parties to the dialogue listened to each other and learned from each other — and did not simply try to confute each other. But from the time of the Reformation, the churches carried on dialogue only with those they have regarded as standing on the same ground as themselves ecclesially. It was, so to speak, only half a dialogue, which did not seek to understand the unfamiliar horizon but deliberately excluded it. Even in the ancient church, dialogue was not a stylistic medium for disputations with pagan philosophy. Medieval scholasticism did not argue with heretics. In that direction no common basis was seen that could have facilitated and justified a dialogue, and the religious discussions of the Reformation were used not to contribute to understanding the other but to demonstrate their error. From then on, a fusion of horizons transcending confessional boundaries was excluded as the point of the process of understanding, for there was in fact no desire to learn or to change. This meant that a basic presupposition for any dialogue whatever was missing.

This curtailment of dialogue to half-measures defined by confessional boundaries meant that the churches inevitably became partisan and gradually defined themselves in opposition to rival churches. In every Christian tradition *one* particular element was emphasized in a special way and was regarded as the *differentia* of one's own church as opposed to the other confession. The term "Prot-

The archbishop of Milan and the metropolitan of Leningrad and Novgorod, co-presidents of a recent European ecumenical assembly in Basel, Switzerland (WCC/Peter Williams)

estantism"* came to be used in a primarily critical way, and the protest against, or criticism of, everything Roman Catholic became the distinctive feature which characterized the Reformation churches. After the council of Trent,* the basis of self-understanding among Roman Catholics came to be the rejection of the Reformation, and catechisms* incorporated the idea of "not being Protestant" as Roman Catholic teaching. The resulting antagonisms have continued to have their aftereffects right up to the present. The "church of the word" was now opposed to "the church of the sacraments", the "church of the clergy" to that of the "priesthood of all believers", the "church of authority" to that of the "freedom of a Christian man". And the resulting differences were not infrequently elevated into the specific confessional identity — the "Protestant principle" or the "fundamental Catholic option". Each side identified itself by its protest against the other or against the picture one had constructed of the other. The wall of separation between them served as a means of defining their own standpoints. The separation became a system of co-ordinates within which their own position was fixed.

To overcome such one-sidedness and re-

gain the fullness of witness, the churches of each individual tradition do not need to disavow it but need to understand it and change themselves in a fusion of horizons. Only the tradition which is still unfamiliar, and dialogue with it, can provide what is lacking in the various confessionally blinkered views of doctrine and structure in church and devotional life, or can balance one's own bias by other elements in tension with it. The churches need dialogue and the fusion of their horizons that occurs in the process of understanding so that they will not truncate the gospel and so that men and women today may be able to discover a meaning to their existence and a way of structuring their lives and world through encounter with the full Christian revelation.

Consequences for the oikoumene. Dialogue presupposes both common elements and divergences. Where there is no common basis, no dialogue takes place. At best there are two-way monologues which serve to create barriers, not understanding. Dialogue requires the other to be genuinely other and calls for a readiness to listen to the other and learn from the other.

Dialogue assists self-discovery. Thus the churches need dialogue to become genuinely

Christian and credible. Because of the division of the Christian world, each of the churches has become partisan and has lost credibility and the power to persuade. Ecumenical dialogue is a means of enabling them to disclose to each other what each of them has repressed and cannot acquire again in its own strength. Through ecumenical dialogue the churches will become more credible witnesses for Jesus' cause than they are at present.

Understanding means changing ourselves — in a fusion of horizons. I emerge from a dialogue changed from what I was when I entered into it. "Reception"* is not a later recognition of what has been agreed but an inherent dimension of understanding itself. If I am not ready for input in this way, then I have not been in dialogue. In dialogue I cannot predict how and in what direction this change will take place. Dialogue is therefore always hazardous. If churches exclude a change of this kind, they are not conducting a dialogue, even if they are talking to each other.

My own position is just as indispensable for dialogue as my partner's. Only if I as myself come with my ideas and convictions and contribute what is my own to the conversation can I carry on a dialogue. Dialogue does not mean a surrender but an encounter of different horizons. It would serve no one's purpose if we were willing in advance to discard our own convictions for the sake of a false irenic approach. "Fusion of horizons" presupposes the existence of the two horizons. Abandonment of our own position is no way to conduct dialogue.

It is part of the process of mutual understanding that initially we become detached from ourselves and can no longer easily understand and accept some things. This is where dialogue inevitably becomes difficult. We are all too easily tempted to accept the other only within the limits of our own horizon. And then if someone belonging to another confession acts in a way that does not correspond to the knowledge I already have, that person is often regarded as being dishonest and insincere. Mutual accusations of dishonesty, which have by no means been overcome in interconfessional relations, seem the most dangerous way of misunderstanding others and claiming to have the truth ourselves. In dialogue, too, I must grant that the

other can be different and can react differently from what I expect. Without this acceptance of unfamiliarity and clarification of misconceptions, oikoumene would remain superficial and bogged down in an initial, facile stage of understanding.

Controversy and argument are also part of dialogue and can contribute to an enlargement of the horizon for both parties. This controversy is not the same thing as polemics, which does not seek to understand others or learn anything from them. As long as the readiness exists to let the other tell us something, to listen to his or her arguments and to acquire something of value for our own form of Christian life and doctrine from the way the others structure their Christianity, a controversy can be wholly fruitful for dialogue and can promote the credibility of the Christian churches.

See also **dialogue, bilateral; dialogue, interfaith; dialogue, multilateral;** and the various articles on particular interfaith and intrafaith dialogues.

PETER NEUNER

H.G. Gadamer, *Wahrheit und Methode* (ET *Truth and Method*, London, SCM, 1979) • B. Lonergan, *Method in Theology*, London, Darton, Longman & Todd, 1971 (under "conversion", "dialectic").

DIALOGUE, MULTILATERAL.

From the beginning of the modern ecumenical movement, bilateral and multilateral dialogues have been conducted side by side. Bilateral dialogues* enjoy the advantage of allowing the two parties to concentrate on the particular issues that have divided them or the common ground that still or already joins them. If the problems can be settled or mutual recognition achieved, official action towards the restoration or establishment of closer unity* may follow quite expeditiously, e.g. the Leuenberg concordat of 1973 (see **Lutheran-Reformed dialogue**) between European Lutherans and Reformed, or the Bonn accord of 1931 between the Anglicans and Old Catholics, or even the various church unions between Methodist and Reformed denominations beginning with the United Church of Canada in 1925. This piecemeal approach, however, takes place within the broader ecumenical movement, whose complexity is ensured by the fissiparous history of Christendom that it seeks to mend. The wider context calls forth multilateral dialogue(s).

While a few multilateral church unions have taken place at a national or regional level (notably the Church of South India, 1947, and the Church of North India, 1970), at the universal level the WCC has been the principal locus and instrument of the churches for multilateral dialogue. In particular, Faith and Order* has supplied the forum for the most sustained and cumulative treatment of doctrinal matters. The furthest development up to now has been embodied in "the BEM process" (see *Baptism, Eucharist and Ministry*). This experience allows one to note the following factual characteristics of multilateral dialogue in the ecumenical movement.

A certain common ground is needed for dialogue. This has been minimally provided by the membership basis of the WCC (see **WCC, basis of**). While member churches may retain their own ecclesiology (see **Toronto statement**), to join the fellowship of the WCC implies the provisional judgment that one's fellow members are at least plausible partners in a common effort to serve the Triune God (see **Trinity**). It is worth noting that the Roman Catholic Church (since 1968), as well as some other churches not in membership with the WCC, has official representatives on the F&O commission.

The interchurch dynamics of multilateral dialogue vary with the issues under discussion. It is not always easy to say who stands to one's "right" or to one's "left", who holds the "higher" or "lower" churchmanship. Having confronted the intricate diplomacy of seating arrangements at Amsterdam 1948, the Russian-American Orthodox theologian Alexander Schmemann liked ever after to say that he belonged with the Quakers on some matters rather than with his ostensibly nearer neighbours among the Old Catholics or the Anglicans. While "reunion all-round" was the mocking title of a pamphlet by the then Anglican satirist Ronald Knox in 1914, at the Lambeth conference of 1988 Archbishop Robert Runcie called for "an all-round ecumenism". Most churches have in fact discovered in and through multilateral dialogue that there are worthwhile relationships to be cultivated in all directions.

Progress may be slow, and great patience

required, as the attempt is made to clarify the manifold positions of the churches, to develop a convergence from many different starting points, and to keep the greatest possible number of the participants in a state of positive engagement for the furthest possible advance. The reward will be the maturity which is widely recognized in the Lima text, which resulted from 55 years of attention to questions of baptism, eucharist and ministry in F&O.

The multilateral dialogues have profited from, and perhaps contributed to, the more diffuse and sometimes less official movements which have drawn scholars and church people from a very wide spectrum together in the 20th century. At the academic level, some agreement has been attained in exegetical methods (see **exegesis, method of**) and hermeneutical principles (see **hermeneutics**). At the pastoral level, most churches have been affected by the liturgical movement.* BEM would have been unthinkable without the "biblical theology" of the mid-third of our century and the recovery of patristic perspectives on worship and the sacraments.

Multilateral dialogue helps to "keep the churches honest" in what they affirm with various particular partners in their respective bilateral dialogues. It would, for instance, be wrong to play up the question of episcopal succession in discussion with one body while playing it down with another. Less suspiciously put, multilateral dialogue encourages the churches to develop positions which are both internally consistent and simultaneously mindful of their effect on all interlocutors. Positive signs are the "borrowings" of material which take place between multilateral dialogues and the various bilaterals. Under the auspices of F&O and the officers' conference of Christian World Communions,* five forums (1978, 1979, 1980, 1985 and 1990) have enabled the tendencies and results of the various bilateral dialogues to be compared multilaterally.

Multilateral dialogue tends to focus on central themes of the Christian faith,* since these are shared by the greatest range of partners, and it is on these that it is most important to find agreement in confession and interpretation. It is significant that the current F&O study "Towards the Common Expression of the Apostolic Faith Today" takes the Nicene

Creed* as its "theological basis and methodological tool". At the same time, multilateral dialogue allows even a single church to put on the agenda for universal attention a matter whose importance may not be widely perceived, or which others might have chosen to avoid; so that the reduction of agreement to a few uncontroversial commonplaces is less of a risk.

Multilateral dialogue corresponds to the fact that, in many ways, the churches in the 20th century have faced common tasks in a common world. The churches have needed and enjoyed mutual support among as many as they can each recognize, at least *prima facie*, to be responding to the same call to worship the Triune God (leitourgia), to proclaim the gospel of Christ (martyria), and to serve the needy among humankind (diakonia).

See also **dialogue, bilateral; dialogue, intrafaith; Faith and Order**.

GEOFFREY WAINWRIGHT

G. Gassmann, "Nature and Function of Bilateral and Multilateral Dialogues and Their Inter-Relation", *Midstream*, 25, 1986 ● M. Kinnamon, *Truth and Community: Diversity and Its Limits in the Ecumenical Movement*, Grand Rapids, MI, Eerdmans, 1988.

DIASPORA. The term "diaspora" is a Greek word meaning dispersion, dissemination (the Hebrew equivalent is *galuth*). It applies to the situation of the Jews scattered in various places around the world, living as separate communities in foreign and sometimes hostile environments. As such, this term is never applied by biblical writers to the situation of the Christian church; the three New Testament occurrences of the word (John 7:35; James 1:1; 1 Pet. 1:1) clearly pertain to the Jewish diaspora (including Jewish Christians). The related verb "scatter, disperse" *(diaspeiresthai)* is used twice in the NT to indicate the result of the first persecution against the disciples of Jesus of Nazareth (Acts 8:1-4, 11:19). Another verb *(diaskorpizein)* conveys the idea of dispersion, conceived as a (temporary) curse, not as the manifest destiny of the Christian church (Matt. 26:31 and the oft-quoted John 11:52). Whereas the Old Testament as a rule sees the dispersion as a curse which will come to an end in the days of the Messiah, when the whole people of God will be gathered in one place, the NT generally insists that the gathering of the children of God which is the work of Jesus Christ breaks barriers that separate those living "far off" and those "near" (Eph. 2:13). In patristic literature all mention of the dispersion of the church worldwide supports the idea of the geographical catholicity* of the church (Irenaeus, *Against Heresies* 1.10.1 and 3.11.8). The ecumenical discussion about the biblical origin of the (modern) theology of the diaspora has definitely been marked by the contribution of the Dutch biblical scholar Willem Cornelis van Unnik in 1959, acknowledged by Hans-Ruedi Weber in that same year but still widely ignored.

The Jewish diaspora was originally thought of as the counterpart of the homeland; after the disasters of A.D. 70 and 135, the Jewish people became practically homeless. Following the terrible experience of annihilation (Shoah) before and during the second world war, the situation of the Jews completely changed with the foundation of the new state of Israel in 1948. This event has been acclaimed by many Christians as fulfilment of prophecies and as reinforcement of the old covenant. It includes theological and non-theological realities. The special bond with the land of Israel is maintained, although the majority of Jews live in the diaspora. The Jewish-Christian dialogue* has to wrestle with differing appreciations of the meaning of the diaspora and of the promised land.

Many factors have led to the multiplication of denominational or confessional diasporas in modern times. Nearly all Christian churches have large or small affiliated groups scattered in various places, sometimes without any active connection with the "home base" of the mother church, which in its turn may have disappeared from its original place. Schisms, reformation movements, political upheavals and demographic explosions, as well as human mobility and voluntary emigration, have led to many Christian "diasporas". Protestant diasporas in Roman Catholic countries after the Peace of Augsburg (1555), the dispersion of the French Huguenots after the Revocation of the Edict of Nantes (1685), the exile of Armenians after 1915, the emigration of Orthodox Russians after 1917, the continuing flow of immigrants to the Americas and increasingly to Western Europe — all these historical developments create new diasporas. In a sense missionary efforts undertaken by Christian denominations have also created diasporas, although it can be assumed that after a while the new churches (see **mission, proselytism**) are sufficiently rooted in the local culture to gain selfhood, so that they have lost any self-awareness of being foreign. However, in some cases the foreign character of the new church is cultivated, sometimes in connection with other social, political, historical or theological factors. No country today can claim a total religious homogeneity. The ecumenical dilemma here is, on the one hand, the concern for religious liberty* and cultural identity and, on the other hand, the pursuit of Christian unity* at the local, national and regional levels (New Delhi 1961, document of the Secretariat for Promoting Christian Unity 1975, Common Witness 1981).

Among the various movements of dissemination of the past two centuries, the significance of the Russian emigration to the West cannot be overestimated. It has meant an active ecumenical interaction between the Orthodox tradition and the Latin churches, Roman Catholic as well as Protestant and Anglican. The St Sergius Institute in Paris (founded in 1924) has been a source of spiritual and theological renewal for Orthodox and other churches. The Russian diaspora is not the only one to be taken into account. Other national and/or ethnic minorities originally related to different autocephalous Orthodox churches, or different Orthodox patriarchates emigrated by force or voluntarily to other countries, especially in the West.

The simultaneous presence of various jurisdictions among the Orthodox diasporas in the West creates internal problems which must be faced by the Orthodox themselves. The Preconciliar Pan-Orthodox Conference at Chambésy (1986) decided to put the problem of the Orthodox diaspora on the agenda of the future great synod of the Orthodox churches. The points are, as recalled by Oliver Clément in an influential report (1977), "that there shall not be two bishops in the same town" (first ecumenical council) and "that there shall not be two metropolitans in the one province" (fourth ecumenical council).

The concept of diaspora can be used for

Greek Orthodox War Memorial Church of St Nicholas, near Canberra, Australia (Australian Information Service/Ian Mitchell)

persons and groups of various religions, ideologies and/or ethnic identity. In the current ecumenical language, however, the term "minority" is preferred.

The term "diaspora" became popular in ecumenical reflection on the church* after the tremendous displacements of people in Europe in the wake of the second world war and also in the context of newly established socialist regimes in the German Democratic Republic and other Eastern European states. German theologians like Harald Kruska, Gottfried Niemeier, Werner Krusche, Ernst Lange among Protestants, Karl Rahner and Hans Küng among Catholics, have applied the term "diaspora" to the church in order to highlight the new situation of the church in Germany and in the world generally speaking. The church today, they say, is fundamentally a diaspora.

There are various levels of meaning in this proposition. First, it has to do with the collapse of the *Volkskirche* both as a historical reality and as a national purpose (see **church and state**). The alternative to *Volkskirche* (national church) is *Diaspora-Kirche*. Here church no longer expresses the soul of a nation but has become a social minority of active Christians among a majority of non-believers. This ecclesiological self-awareness is largely a result of sociological studies on the empirical state of the churches in the modern world (see **church and world**). Theologically the concept of diaspora as applied to the church can draw from the OT theology of the remnant, or from the idea of the "little flock" in the NT (Luke 12:32). Another theological undertone is the idea of the church under the cross, facing harassment and oppression from the powers-that-be.

A second level of meaning pertains to the functioning of the church in society.* The church can function in two complementary ways: first as a fellowship assembled before the Lord in worship, and second as a dispersion of believers taking action in society each in a particular place or activity. This may have been the meaning of the oft-quoted definition of the church by the reformer Melanchthon as "the community of the dispersed". This idea applies specifically to the laity.* Actually the Department of the Laity of the WCC developed a strong ecclesiology in this sense. "The whole church shares Christ's ministry in the world and the effective exercise of this ministry must largely be by church members, *when they are dispersed in the life of the world*" (WCC central committee, Galyatető 1956; italics added). A possible theological undertone of this statement is the concept of presence (French *présence au monde*, J. Ellul, 1948).

Modern theology of the diaspora is evidently not a simple concept. It has both a pessimistic, almost sectarian form, and a more optimistic, missionary form.

MARC SPINDLER

O. Clément, "Avenir et signification de la diaspora orthodoxe en Europe occidentale" (ET "The Orthodox Diaspora in Western Europe: Its Future and Its Role", *Sobornost*, 7, 1978) • W. Krusche, "On the Way into Diaspora", *Study Encounter*, 10, 1974 • M. Spindler, *La mission, combat pour le salut du monde*, Neuchâtel, Delachaux & Niestlé, 1967 • L. Ullrich, "Diaspora und Ökumene in dogmatischer (systematischer) Sicht", *Catholica*, 38, 1984 • W.C. van Unnik, "'Diaspora' and 'Church' in the First Centuries of Christian History", in *Sparsa Collecta: Collected Essays*, part 3, Leiden, Brill, 1983 • H.-R. Weber, "Mündige Gemeinde: Einige ekklesiologische Folgerungen aus dem ökumenischen Gespräch über die Laienfrage", *Ökumenische Rundschau*, 9, 1960.

DIBELIUS, OTTO. B. 15.5.1880, Berlin; d. 31.1.1967, Berlin. Dibelius participated in Edinburgh 1910, Stockholm 1925 and Lausanne 1927 and was the first German to be a president of the WCC (1954-61). He was a leader in the Confessing Church,* and signed the Stuttgart declaration* in 1945. Dibelius, a staunch anti-communist, was bishop of Berlin-Brandenberg, 1945-66, and strongly advocated unity in the Evangelical Church in Germany, in spite of the tensions between the FRG and the GDR. He wrote *Ein Christ ist immer im Dienst* (ET *In the Service of the Lord: The Autobiography of Bishop Otto Dibelius*, London, Faber & Faber, 1964). See *Otto Dibelius: Sein Denken und Wollen*, R. Stupperich ed. (Berlin, Christliche Zeitschriften, 1970).

ANS J. VAN DER BENT

DIÉTRICH, SUZANNE de.
B. 29.1.1891, Niederbronn, France; d. 24.1.1981, Strasbourg, France. Diétrich was

Suzanne de Diétrich (WCC/Peter Williams)

a lay leader in ecumenical youth and student movements, founding staff member and associate director (with Hendrik Kraemer) of the Ecumenical Institute in Bossey* (1946-54) and key figure in the mid-20th century "biblical renewal".

Born into an old Alsatian family of metal founders, Suzanne de Diétrich took a diploma in electrical engineering from the University of Lausanne in 1913. While there, she came into contact with the French Student Christian Movement, and in 1914 she decided to devote herself to student work rather than returning to the family foundry. An initial two-year commitment stretched into almost four decades, both in France and in Geneva, where she worked with the World Student Christian Federation* and the World YWCA.*

Despite a lifelong hereditary disability, she travelled on five continents and took part in numerous ecumenical meetings and conferences, including the world youth conference in Amsterdam in August 1939, where she led the Bible studies. During her years in Bossey she organized biblical study seminars and played an active role with her fellow layperson Kraemer in preparing the institute's programmes. Returning to Paris in 1956, she worked closely with the French Protestant

Federation and its aid agency, CIMADE,* which she had helped to create in 1939 and had supported from Geneva during the war.

At the centre of de Diétrich's work stood the Bible as a whole, which she read and taught others how to read, and about which she spoke and wrote. Her books, which were translated into several languages, helped to make the biblically based theologies of her time — including those of Karl Barth, Eduard Thurneysen and Emil Brunner — accessible to laypeople, especially to youth. "No one who heard her expound the Bible", said an associate after her death, "will ever forget her incisive mind, her simplicity of expression and her sense of humour, nor doubt that the Bible is the living word of God for everyone, as it was for her."

After the second world war she organized numerous ecumenical encounters on her estate in Alsace and took up questions of liturgy and worship. In 1950 she received an honorary doctorate from the theological faculty of the University of Montpellier (France).

WALTER MÜLLER-RÖMHELD

Among her books in English are *The Witnessing Community: The Biblical Record of God's Purpose*, Philadelphia, Westminster, 1958; and *God's Unfolding Purpose: A Guide to the Study of the Bible*, Philadelphia, Westminster, 1960 • See also *Reconnaissance à Suzanne de Diétrich*, special issue of *Foi et vie*, May 1971.

DISABLED. Statistics issued by the United Nations in 1989 reveal that 7-10% of the world's population of 5.2 billion (i.e. 5,200 million) have some form of physical or mental disability. Malnutrition, famine, communicable diseases, poor quality of health care, armed aggression, torture, war, accidents (home, traffic and sports) and violation of fundamental human rights are the major causes of disabilities and are the key factors in the increasing number of physically, psycho-traumatically and mentally disabled persons. Many persons with disabilities are denied the right to lead meaningful lives within their families, church and society. Often, they are not given opportunities for education, work and caring social lives and all too often are shut away in institutions, cast out from society. Many people are forced to exist with little or no help, financially, spiritually or emotionally, from either the government, the community or the church. The plight of persons with disabilities in the third world is far worse than that of those in developed countries. Nearly 90% of all resources spent on the disabled are expended in industrialized countries, and yet 85% of persons with disabilities live in developing countries — and only 2% of them receive any services at all.

There are many definitions of the word "disability", and the term itself changes from culture to culture, language to language. In church networks, a disability can be defined as any emotional, mental or physical impairment that can prevent a person from participating fully in life and society. The key word in this statement is "can", for these days many persons with disabilities have the possibilities of leading full lives as valuable and contributing members of society. It is when society itself imposes restrictions and barriers, physical and attitudinal, that they find themselves "disabled". In this connection, it is preferable to say that a person has a disability, a statement which describes a state of being but also gives an implication of wholeness, recognizing that a person still has great potential. To say that someone is "disabled" is to give that person a label that carries with it a much more negative attitude and stigma. As a major instrument of communication, language has great power to change images and attitudes. It can either oppress or liberate, and in many cultures there is a strong movement to use language that will help to free people of past negative stigmas.

This distinction is of particular importance for the churches. Our theological and spiritual roots should bring all people together as one, all in some way whole and broken, rich and poor, weak and strong, laying all we have at the foot of the cross. Many churches, however, look upon persons with disabilities as objects of pity and charity. During the last half of the United Nations Decade on Disabilities, it is hoped that a new attitude is moving into all organizations and the churches in all countries. The churches also have the responsibility of giving the spiritual dimension of wholeness to other more secular perspectives of service in recognizing that persons with disabilities experience suffering (as so many others in the world do), but that often their point of great weakness in fact can

ultimately become their greatest strength. Such is the journey and the mystery of the cross.

In 1971 the WCC began to discuss seriously the disability issue at its Faith and Order* commission meeting in Louvain. At the fifth assembly in Nairobi four years later, a statement was issued entitled "The Handicapped and the Wholeness of the Family of God". Between Nairobi and Vancouver, a consultant was appointed for a year and a half, whose job it was to work with the churches for the International Year of Disabled Persons. In 1983 the issue came into four of the issue groups of the sixth assembly in Vancouver, and persons with disabilities had quite a high visibility in the life and work of the assembly. A full-time consultant was appointed in 1984 to begin to co-ordinate work in the Council and its member churches.

To begin this work, the disability issues were related to the work of each sub-unit, as part of the Council's covenanting for justice, peace and the integrity of creation.* Within the WCC family, it became apparent that each member church or country, if it was doing any work in this issue, had its own starting point, based largely on culture. People's theology as to what causes a person to have or encounter a disabling condition varies tremendously from culture to culture, which greatly affects how that society views and therefore treats someone with a disability. It also has a great impact on the churches, in terms of people with disabilities participating in the life and work of local congregations. Within all this diversity, the WCC acts as a focal point to co-ordinate materials and work, conscientize and mobilize churches and, through all this, emphasize greatly a new and deeper spirituality, transforming and renewing people through new ways of reading the scriptures.

Because of the previous work done and the structures existing denominationally, much has been done ecumenically in North America and parts of Western Europe. Lack of funds and limited human resources often make it difficult for any progress to occur regionally in member churches and even more so on an ecumenical level. But on a local level, more informal ecumenical work and sharing does in fact occur. The challenge for national councils of churches, many of which model their programmes on WCC work, is to incorporate a concern for people with disabilities into their agendas. But again, the problem is often financial and, because the issue is so diverse, it tends to get lost in the list of programme priorities.

LYNDA KATSUNO

DISARMAMENT. Disarmament is a future agenda for humanity. The 1987 intermediate nuclear forces agreement, which could be a first step towards nuclear disarmament, covers only 4% of the world's 55,000 nuclear weapons (*SIPRI Yearbook* 1988, 23). In 1959 the United Nations proclaimed the goal of "general and complete disarmament". The goal of disarmament has in practice been replaced in government thinking by arms control. Efforts towards arms control have not prevented the quantitative and qualitative arms race. The annual global expenditure on arms is now approximately $1 million million. This is more than the income of the poorest half of humanity. Arms spending is over 6% of the world's gross national product. Arms spending in the industrialized world accounts for three-quarters of the global total. In recent years, nuclear disarmament has received much attention. Conventional disarmament and effective measures against the arms trade also need to be addressed.

Disarmament efforts between the two world wars, particularly the work of the League of Nations (see **United Nations**), collapsed in the face of the Nazi threat. However, some of the work done before the second world war has not been superseded. Mention must be made of the 1925 Geneva protocol, which banned the use of chemical and biological weapons, as well as gas warfare. The international community still must achieve a comprehensive ban on chemical weapons, similar in kind to the 1972 biological weapons convention, but with more effective measures for verification.

The period since 1945 is characterized by wars outside Europe (over 120 wars each involving at least 1,000 deaths), the arming of the world and, on the other hand, international efforts towards the foundation of a world peace order. The ecumenical movement has been consistent in its support for the disarmament efforts of the UN, as the then WCC general secretary Philip Potter underlined in his address to the UN Second Special Session in 1982.

Inherent within the UN charter is the paradox which has prevented disarmament. The UN was established "to save succeeding generations from the scourge of war". The Security Council is required "to promote the establishment and maintenance of international peace and security with the least diversion for armaments of the world's human and economic resources" (art. 26). At the same time, however, the UN charter allows for the right of member states to self-defence (art. 51). Arms spending can thus be justified by states as necessary. In spite of the first and second disarmament decades (the 1970s and 1980s) and three UN special sessions on disarmament (1978, 1982, 1988), the most that can be claimed for the results of multilateral and bilateral disarmament efforts is that they are "limited yet significant" (*The United Nations and Disarmament*, 6).

In the early 1960s, the Cuban missile crisis served as a stimulus to the USA and USSR to try to reach agreement. Direct communication in crisis situations, the Partial Test Ban Treaty (1963) and the Non-Proliferation Treaty (1968) were some of the results. It cannot be said that the super-powers or the other nuclear weapon states have fulfilled their commitment "to achieve at the earliest possible date the cessation of the nuclear arms race and to undertake effective measures in the direction of nuclear disarmament". Rather, there is a danger that more countries (Argentina, Brazil, India, Iraq, Israel, Pakistan, South Africa) will join the nuclear weapon states — if some have not already done so. So far, it has not yet proved possible to move on to a comprehensive test ban treaty.

In the 1970s the USA and USSR concentrated particularly on bilateral approaches. In 1971 they agreed upon co-operation in the exploration and use of outer space and later (with Britain and France) prohibited placement of weapons of mass destruction on the seabed and ocean floor. The period of detente was marked by the Anti-Ballistic Missile (ABM) Treaty and SALT I on the limitation of strategic offensive arms (1972). The ABM Treaty, a major achievement of arms control, is most obviously threatened should the USA proceed with deployment of the Strategic Defence Initiative, or "Star Wars", or should the Soviet Union deploy an equivalent system.

Towards the end of the 1970s, the collapse of detente led to the failure by the US senate to ratify the SALT II agreement. However, since the signing of the Helsinki agreement (1975), the Conference on Security and Cooperation in Europe has developed into a forum where European nations, including neutral and non-aligned countries, can exert some influence over the USA and USSR. In March 1989 the Negotiations on Conventional Armed Forces in Europe succeeded the Mutual and Balanced Force Reduction talks.

It is still too early to say whether the 1987 Intermediate Range Nuclear Forces agreement marks the beginning of genuine progress towards nuclear disarmament or merely a break in the upward spiral of the qualitative and quantitative arms race. Consistent with their belief that "nuclear war cannot be won and must never be fought", the USA and USSR agreed in 1988 to notify each other at least 24 hours before launching any intercontinental ballistic missiles and submarine-launched ballistic missiles. But the real test is whether the 50% reduction in strategic arms is carried out in accordance with the statement of intent by the USA and USSR. Significant progress on disarmament requires not only removal of weapon systems but also a genuine shift away from deterrence based on a bipolar view of the world, a clear "enemy-image" and weapons of mass destruction. The Palme commission proposed common security as an alternative to deterrence.

In the world of multilateral negotiations, the UN Conference on Disarmament, the "single multilateral disarmament negotiating forum", established a permanent ten-area agenda in 1979: (1) nuclear weapons in all aspects, (2) chemical weapons, (3) other weapons of mass destruction, (4) conventional weapons, (5) reduction of military budgets, (6) reduction of armed forces, (7) disarmament and development, (8) disarmament and international security, (9) collateral measures including confidence-building measures and verification, and (10) a comprehensive programme of disarmament leading to general and complete disarmament under effective international control.

The UN machinery is only as powerful as the member states enable it to be. A recent focus has been on the connection between disarmament and development. Regional agreements should also be mentioned, such as the Antarctic Treaty (1959), which makes the region a demilitarized zone, the 1967 Treaty of Tlatelolco and the 1986 Treaty of Rarotonga, which declare Latin America and the South Pacific nuclear-free zones. However, it still remains the case that US-Soviet relations are the key to significant progress in disarmament.

From the perspective of the churches, there are clear motivations for concern for disarmament. First, the churches' concern for peace requires disarmament. In particular, in recent years, there has been a growing moral criticism of nuclear weapons, leading to the WCC Vancouver assembly (1983) statement that "the production and deployment of nuclear weapons as well as their use constitute a crime against humanity". This statement is hard to harmonize with the positions of certain church leaders who maintain that nuclear deterrence is still required. The clearest example is that of Pope John Paul II at the UN Second Special Session (1982), who said: "In current conditions 'deterrence' based on balance, certainly not as an end in itself but as a step towards progressive disarmament, may still be judged morally acceptable." The common denominator between these positions is agreement that deterrence based upon weapons of mass destruction must be overcome in the future. Concerns for justice and for the integrity of creation are also hampered by the massive spending and research emphasis devoted to arms.

Second, and most significantly, the churches are increasingly recognizing that the church by its very nature is committed to peace. It seems more and more incongruous if the church preaches reconciliation* between God and humanity and fails to criticize the ever-increasing arms race, which threatens humanity and God's creation. However, the main analytical tool of major church traditions, the just-war theory, gives criteria only for the use of weapons, not their acquisition or threatened use. It is thus seriously flawed and weakens the churches' work for disarmament. An adequate theology of peace today must employ criteria assessing the impact of security policies in terms of justice, ecological impact and peace.

See also **militarism/militarization, paci-fism, peace**.

ROGER WILLIAMSON

F. Solms & M. Reuver, *Churches as Peacemakers? An Analysis of Recent Church Statements on Peace, Disarmament and War*, Rome, IDOC, 1985 • Stockholm International Peace Research Institute, *SIPRI Yearbook: World Armaments and Disarmaments*, annual publication, Oxford, Oxford UP • UN, *The United Nations and Disarmament: A Short History*, New York, UN, 1988 • WCC & Roman Catholic Church, *Peace and Disarmament*, WCC, 1982.

DISCIPLES OF CHRIST. The Disciples of Christ are a worldwide Christian communion whose origins are from the American frontier of the early 19th century. In 1801 Barton W. Stone, a Presbyterian minister, led a revival at Cane Ridge, Kentucky, for a gathering of over 20,000 people. The experience convinced Stone that unity* among Christians was essential for the church's mission,* evangelism* and spiritual renewal. In a landmark document, *The Last Will and Testament of the Springfield Presbytery* (1804), he set forth a vision in which the present church structures would "be dissolved, and sink into the body of Christ at large". Stone and his followers took the name "Christian" for their congregations and members as a sign of inclusiveness and renounced all non-biblical names as they sought to reclaim the faith proclaimed in the New Testament scriptures.

Thomas and Alexander Campbell, father and son, were the primary founders of the second movement, the Disciples of Christ, which joined with Stone's Christians in 1832 to become the Christian Church (Disciples of Christ). Thomas Campbell, a Presbyterian minister from Ireland, came to western Pennsylvania in 1807. He was soon cast out of his denomination for his efforts to remove all "fencing of the table" by use of credal conscriptions and to reconcile the divisions between the various Presbyterian branches whose roots were grounded in the events of 17th- and 18th-century Scotland and Ireland. These divisions made little sense in the context of the American frontier in the early 1800s. In his *Declaration and Address* (1809), Campbell proclaimed that "division among Christians is a horrid evil", and that

"the church of Christ upon earth is essentially, intentionally, and constitutionally one".

The early leaders of the two movements, Christians and Disciples, believed that the realization of Christian unity could be achieved through the restoration of the faith and order of the NT church. Their call was to return to the apostolic tradition of the earliest church, which they identified as the "ancient order of things". They thus rejected all doctrinal formulations when used as "tests of fellowship" and opposed as unscriptural the historic creeds* and authoritarian ecclesiastical government (see **church order**). It was in response to the concept of restoring the unity of the church, based upon the NT witness, that many of the characteristic beliefs and practices of the Disciples of Christ took shape and continue today. These include the weekly celebration of the Lord's supper (see **eucharist**), baptism* by immersion of individuals upon their own profession of the "good confession of faith" (see Matt. 16:16; Luke 9:20), a commitment to the priesthood of all believers, in which lay and ordained share in the ministry of word and sacrament, and an evangelistic zeal in the proclamation of the gospel to the world.

Baptism and the Lord's supper are accepted by Disciples of Christ as sacraments of the church; indeed, they are the primary elements in shaping the Disciples' ethos and identity. Baptism marks entrance into membership in the church universal and is administered "in the name of the Father, Son and Holy Spirit" (see **Trinity**). The Lord's supper, or holy communion, is the central act of each Sunday's worship service; the invitation is always to an "open table" where all Christians are welcomed to share in the eucharistic meal of memorial, sacrifice, and anticipation of the kingdom. For Disciples, Christ is present at each Lord's supper both in the elements as they are received and within the life of the community itself.

Disciples of Christ believe that the church is a sacramental community, a covenantal fellowship brought into being by God's initiative of grace* and sustained in its life by the Holy Spirit.* The church is both *local* (as the congregation of believers are gathered in Christ's name and witness to the power of God's love in each place) and *universal* (as all Christians and Christian communions are bound together to be the community/koinonia* of God's people in all places and at all times).

The movement of the Disciples grew rapidly on the American frontier with its message of freedom, diversity, simplicity of worship, and a reasonable faith, so that by 1900 its membership was over 1.1 million, the largest denomination to be born on North American soil. Its message also spread to Canada, Great Britain and Australia, where the similar themes of Christian unity, restorationism, and the congregation's right to self-governance were already present among different church bodies (often calling themselves by the name "Churches of Christ"). These churches readily acknowledged one another as part of the same worldwide movement.

With the missionary expansion of the churches in the late 1800s and early 1900s, Disciples of Christ communities were established in most regions of the world. Many of these churches have since that time joined with other denominations to form national united churches, e.g. the Church of North India, the United Reformed Church in the United Kingdom, the Kyodan (Japan), the Church of Christ in Zaire.

Disciples of Christ have been prominent in most major ecumenical ventures of this century, including the founding of the WCC and its predecessor bodies, in many national councils of churches, and in giving leadership to continuing efforts in church-union negotiations. In the US, Disciples are currently participating in the nine-communion Consultation on Church Union* and have developed a special ecumenical partnership with the United Church of Christ.

The international body that gives expression to the Disciples of Christ in official church-to-church relationships is the Disciples Ecumenical Consultative Council (DECC). (A second organization, the World Convention of Churches of Christ, is an inspirational, global fellowship for individual members of the Disciples of Christ, who gather every four years at international assemblies.) The DECC has three main purposes: (1) to co-ordinate the appointment of official Disciples representation to international ecumenical events and meetings, (2) to share information on Disciples' ecumenical activities around the world, and (3) to encourage and provide for engaging in international theological dialogue. The three current dialogues of the DECC are with the Roman Catholic Church (1977), the Russian Orthodox Church (1987), and the World Alliance of Reformed Churches (1987). The DECC includes membership of Disciples of Christ churches (and united churches which have former Disciples ties) in Argentina, Australia, Canada, Jamaica, Mexico, New Zealand, Paraguay, Puerto Rico, Southern Africa, the United Kingdom, the US, Vanuatu and Zaire.

ROBERT K. WELSH

K. Lawrence ed., *Classic Themes of Disciples Theology*, Fort Worth, Texas Christian UP, 1986 • L.G. McAllister & W.T. Tucker, *Journey in Faith: A History of the Christian Church (Disciples of Christ)*, St Louis, MO, Bethany, 1975 • K.L. Teegarden, *We Call Ourselves Disciples*, St Louis, MO, Bethany, 1979.

DISCIPLES-REFORMED DIALOGUE.

When Disciples (or Churches of Christ) emerged as a distinct movement in the USA and Great Britain in the early 19th century, many of their early leaders came from a Presbyterian background. Although the adoption of believer's baptism* by immersion marked them off from other Reformed churches, Disciples' theological roots lay in the Reformed tradition. Both Disciples and Reformed have been active in the ecumenical movement nationally and internationally in the 20th century and belong to united churches in Japan, North India, Southern Africa, Thailand, the United Kingdom and Zaire. They are involved in union discussions in Jamaica and were formerly involved in New Zealand; in the USA Disciples are involved in an ecumenical partnership with the United Church of Christ and in united congregations with Presbyterians and UCCs.

Following an initial planning meeting in Geneva in 1984, a consultation between representatives of the World Alliance of Reformed Churches* (WARC) and the Disciples Ecumenical Consultative Council (DECC) took place in Birmingham, England, in March 1987. Four main themes were discussed: the common doctrinal roots of Disciples and Reformed, the sacraments of baptism and communion, ministry, and models of Christian unity. Case studies of Disciples-Reformed relations were presented from Australia, the United Kingdom, the Church of North India, the US, and the United Church of Christ in Japan.

The report of the consultation suggested that "a reconciliation of memories" was needed to overcome past divisions. Common understandings of the church* and the Lord's supper (see **eucharist**) were affirmed. It was noted that both traditions found it easier to relate their understanding of the church to the local congregation and to the church universal than to ecclesial structures of a national or international kind. On baptism it was agreed that neither tradition could be content with a baptismal theology which excluded children from the Christian community, and that the legitimacy of the theological traditions of both infant baptism and believer baptism should be acknowledged. Re-baptism should not be practised because it undermined the once-for-all nature of baptism. Within a general agreement of the nature of ministry, the consultation urged further reflection on the meaning of ordination,* the nature of presbyterial, diaconal and oversight ministry, and the significance of the ordination of women.*

The consultation concluded that there were no theological or ecclesiological issues which needed to divide the two church families and asked the DECC and the WARC to call upon their member churches to say whether or not they could accept this declaration: "The Disciples of Christ and the Reformed Churches recognize and accept each other as visible expressions of the one church of Christ."

DAVID M. THOMPSON

Papers and addresses from the international dialogue between Disciples of Christ and the World Alliance of Reformed Churches, *Midstream*, 27, 2, 1988 • A.P. Sell ed., *Reformed and Disciples of Christ in Dialogue*, Geneva, WARC, 1985.

DISCIPLES-ROMAN CATHOLIC DIALOGUE.
In the USA the Roman Catholic Church and the Disciples of Christ have been engaged in a dialogue since 1962. Although this conversation began at the national level, it was later transferred to the regional level where, in 1987 after 12 years of discussion, the group based in Louisville, Kentucky, published a document entitled

Ministry — the Whole Church for the Whole World.

An international commission was set up in September 1977 with meetings alternating between the USA and Europe. The result of the first series of annual meetings (1977-82) has been the publication of the first report, *Apostolicity and Catholicity*, which discusses "Our Life Together", "Spiritual Ecumenism", "Baptism", "Faith and Tradition", "The Unity We Seek", and "Looking to the Future". In their foreword the two co-chairmen declare that this final report "contains not an agreed statement on points of doctrine but an agreed account, written by those commissioned for the dialogue, to record promising developments. The paper describes some convergence in understanding as well as some of the problems which have yet to be faced."

After the composition of the international commission had been modified in 1983, it began a new series of discussions on the theme "The Church as Koinonia in Christ". In this perspective, the commission has considered the nature of koinonia,* the function of faith* in koinonia, eucharist* and koinonia, apostolic tradition* and koinonia, ministry and koinonia, and the *sensus fidelium* and koinonia (see **consensus fidelium**).

This dialogue follows its own distinctive methodology, which gives precedence to a search for lines of convergence and not for the establishing of agreed formulas. For this reason the results of these discussions have aroused the interest of other groups.

J.-M.R. TILLARD

DISCIPLES-RUSSIAN ORTHODOX DIALOGUE.
The first contacts between the Disciples of Christ and the Russian Orthodox Church came early in the 20th century. Peter Ainslie of Baltimore, Maryland, one of the primary architects of Faith and Order,* attended the historic preparatory meeting at Geneva in 1920, where plans were laid for the first world conference on F&O. While there was no official representative of the Russian Orthodox Church present, the Russian exarch for Western Europe, Archbishop Evlogy of Volynia, attended the conference and expressed Christian love for all the churches in the young F&O movement. In his address at Geneva, Ainslie lifted up the Disciples vision

of a united church that included "the whole House of Christ — Orthodox, Roman Catholic, Anglican and Protestant". This exchange led to a friendship between these early ecumenical pioneers.

Specific contacts and relations between the Disciples and the Russian Orthodox grew after the second world war when the member churches of the National Council of the Churches of Christ in the USA braved the cold war* to join hands with churches in the Soviet Union. One of those delegations was headed by a Disciples lay leader and American industrialist, J. Irwin Miller, then president of the NCCC. In 1973 pastoral relations found deep expression when George G. Beazley, Jr, president of the Disciples' Council on Christian Unity, died in Moscow while on an official visit to the Russian Orthodox Church. In later years leaders of the Disciples have made official visits to the USSR, often with delegations of the NCCC and the WCC. During the mid-1980s, over 200 Disciples regional and local leaders went to the USSR on the church-to-church programme of the NCCC.

Relations reached a new plateau in 1987 when the Disciples of Christ-Russian Orthodox dialogue officially began. Ten Disciples theologians met with leaders in Moscow and with theological faculties at Zagorsk, Leningrad and Odessa. The themes were "Baptism, Eucharist and Ministry" and "The Church's Role in Peace-making" (reports in *The Journal of the Moscow Patriarchate*, 12, 1987, and *Mid-Stream*, 27, 3, 1988). The second dialogue session took place in June 1990, addressing the themes of "The Renewal of Parish Life" and "The Church's Diaconal Ministry in Society".

PAUL A. CROW, Jr

DIVORCE. "... and they become one flesh". This clause in Gen. 2:24 relates not only to couples but to all human beings. It is the complement of Gen. 2:18: "It is not good that the man should be alone." We are all made for companionship, just as our God himself is a God of word, relation, prophecy and, finally, incarnation,* when the Word itself becomes flesh. Thus the universe and our individual lives have their origin in a transport of delight which has become an enduring affection, a single-minded fascina-

tion, consummated as an actual covenant* relationship. This picture has something to say to all human beings of whatever period or family circumstances. Marriage* is only one of the signs — doubtless both the most intimate and the most publicly proclaimed — of this condition which is common to all human beings. It has nothing exclusive about it that might distress or offend those who are not married. For all sorts of reasons, however, living together is difficult: tedium, illicit desires, making comparisons, fear and falsehoods, silence and gossip, suspicions and accusations, all summed up in the ultimate word, *divorce*.

"Divorce" is a very general term. "Fall" would be a much more appropriate word to define the Bible account of events just after its description of the good companionship of human beings and the universe, man and woman, and of course God and human beings. Divorce, separation, exile, disappointment and loneliness are evidence everywhere of the mess made of God's good creation* by human beings (see **sin**). In the Bible that story is only a prologue to the subsequent story of the coming together again of God and human beings (see **reconciliation**). Otherwise, the Bible would be a tragic statement of our fate and not the living history of salvation.*

What happens when war takes the place of peace? Marriage is a secret garden in which creation in its wholeness is re-encountered. A couple living in peace also reflects peace in nature, society and faith (see Hos. 2:18-23). We can live in love, tenderness and truth and can look forward to the future. That being so, the Bible never authorizes divorce as the answer to changes in our feelings. Divorce is always a rupture and an affliction. But the Bible is also realistic. It knows that civil wars are the most cruel and the most exhausting. In the Old Testament, which was written in a patriarchal society, the man could repudiate his wife, provided he gave her a "bill of divorce" (Deut. 24:1), which was a protection for her future. In the time of Jesus there was vigorous discussion among the rabbinical schools on the possible grounds for this repudiation of the wife. Jesus' answer was that "for your hardness of heart Moses allowed you to divorce your wives but", as he recalled, "from the beginning it was not so" (Matt. 19:8).

In the New Testament, separations are also allowed for, where remaining together leads more to conflict than to peace (Matt. 19:9 and especially 1 Cor. 7:15). These are certainly not justifications for divorce but cases of the lesser evil — a preference for separation where life together is impossible. This echoes the mercy of God towards sinners and the unfortunate.

Divorce and the churches. Here too we find an ecumenical split which may be thought of as linked to the theological and liturgical nature of marriage as a sacrament* for some churches and a ceremony of blessing for others. All the churches see in marriage a bond of unconstrained, complete and blissful love which should never cease, just as God never ceased to love his people even — and especially — when at the crucifixion their divorce was at its most complete. All the churches, however, also acknowledge that the separation of the spouses may turn out to be the least bad solution when their shared life has led to their destroying each other; or when one of them deceives, humiliates and contumaciously deserts the other. Peace through separation is then better than daily death through close association.

But the churches take different lines in their evaluation of this separation. For churches that regard the marriage ceremony as a blessing from God on a common life, separation both in religious and civil terms means a total break with the past, however painful and unhappy one's memories may naturally be. It is thus possible also to begin a new future, and justifiable for the church to invoke God's blessing on lives in which trials have been experienced, repentance is felt and a better new start has been made. Why should one not invoke here the God who let David, an adulterer, liar and murderer, have the child — Solomon — who was to become heir to his throne through Bathsheba, the woman with whom he had sinned? And why should we forget also the hard task imposed by Jesus, of forgiving all sinners against society, men first but also and especially women? The church's acceptance of divorced persons is part of that same mercy already referred to.

Those churches which, on the other hand, think of marriage as a sacrament maintain that the sacramental bond remains, even after separation from the common life, for "what...

God has joined together, let not man put asunder" (Matt. 19:6). This enduring nature of the sacrament consequently makes a second sacramental blessing on a new marriage impossible, and so remarried divorced persons find they have become outsiders in the sacramental life of their own church, even if they are now more fully and unreservedly accepted pastorally in this context.

All this explains the misgivings of the "sacramental" churches about what divine element may or may not lie in marriage blessings, and also the fear of churches which bless marriages that the sacrament of marriage may become a legalistic yoke imposed on the partners and on their lives, to the exclusion of possible forgiveness or renewal. Such are the questions we have to ask as regards the theology and practice of marriage in our churches.

Light on ecumenism from the history of the covenant. The situation many societies face is as follows. Divorce is on the increase. There are fewer remarriages of divorced persons. Undoubtedly there is much less hypocrisy than formerly and a great desire to tell each other the unqualified truth throughout life. But perhaps there is also less bearing of each other's burdens, less patience and less hope in terms of what Paul says about love in 1 Cor. 13. At all events, one certainly finds much loneliness, many traumas and frequently one out of two children without the same mother and father to welcome them and go with them throughout their lives.

Here one finds a completely shared ecumenical concern which does not have unfailing remedies of any kind against the present rise in the divorce rate. Three words of first-class importance come to mind to bring light into the lives of couples and families — lives with a story of happiness, losses and mutual re-discovery as long as the story of God's relations with human beings in the Bible. The first word is *truth*. A lie, found out sooner or later, kills trust and establishes itself as an enduring source of shame. Truth is costly. The decision must be taken as soon as possible to tell it. Then there is *equality*, which is often the fellowship of sinners out of which the communion of saints may become possible! We cannot and must not set ourselves up as judges of our partners. Matt. 7:1-5 should be re-read. Finally there is the *love* that is re-discovered but unforced and is not the discharge of a duty but rather both a task and a gift.

See also **family, marriage**.

FRANCINE DUMAS

DODD, CHARLES HAROLD.

B. 7.4.1884, Wrexham, Wales; d. 1973. Facing social and cultural factors in church divisions, Dodd spoke of the "unavowed motives in ecumenical discussions", which had an impact on the preparations of Faith and Order* for Lund 1952. He put forward the much-debated conception of "realized eschatology", i.e. that the Old Testament promises of God's kingdom and Christ's own words about the coming of the kingdom were realized through the incarnation, with definitive consequences for humankind. The most influential figure in British New Testament scholarship during the middle decades of the 20th century, Dodd was a Congregational minister educated at Oxford. In 1930 he became Rylands professor of biblical criticism and exegesis at Manchester, and from 1935 to 1949 was Norris-Hulse professor of divinity at Cambridge — the first non-Anglican to hold a chair there since 1660. His publications include over 20 books and some 70 major articles, essays and lectures. He served as the general director of the New English Bible translation. See *Creative Minds in Contemporary Theology*, P.E. Hughes ed. (Grand Rapids, MI, Eerdmans, 1966), which includes a bibliography of his works.

ANS J. VAN DER BENT

DOGMA.

Dogma refers to communally authoritative truths of revealed faith* essential to the identity or welfare of Christian community. The concept is objective rather than subjective: it points to the faith which is to be believed (*fides quae*), not to the faith by which one believes (*fides qua*). A belief may be a dogma even when it is not recognized or affirmed as such. Thus the term in its theological sense lacks the subjectivism of popular usage, according to which beliefs are dogmas because of the way they are held and asserted, e.g. arrogantly and groundlessly, rather than because of their community-defining character.

Dogma and theology should also be distinguished. Theology refers to reflection on the Christian faith in both its non-dogmatic and dogmatic aspects. Dogmatic theologians focus on the dogmas of Christian community, but even when they agree on what these are, they may differ greatly in their understanding of them. Dogmatic unity is compatible with theological disagreements between individuals and schools of thought.

None of the rare New Testament occurrences of "dogma" fully corresponds to the present-day meaning. The closest is in Acts 16:4, where the decisions of the Jerusalem church in regard to gentile converts are termed *dogmata*. In other passages, the word refers to governmental decrees (Luke 2:1; Acts 17:7) or Mosaic ordinances (Eph. 2:15; Col. 2:14). Later Christian writers often do not use the term at all (e.g. Aquinas) and instead speak of articles, symbols or rules of faith or, most commonly, creeds* and confessions; but these, while containing what are now called dogmas, often include much material of other kinds. The present technical understanding of "dogma" is largely the product of Protestant as well as Catholic developments in the post-Reformation centuries, but it has acquired official status only in Roman Catholicism and chiefly through Vatican I* (1870).

Dogma and Vatican I. For the First Vatican Council, the revealed truths contained in the deposit of faith and transmitted through scripture and tradition are taught in the dogmatic definitions of the church's supreme teaching authority (councils and popes) and in the undefined dogmas of the ordinary magisterium. In addition to the threefold reference to revelation,* community (church)* and teaching authority* that we have already mentioned, Vatican I thus introduces a fourth note, the distinction between defined and undefined dogmas.

Undefined dogmas can be understood as including the *lex orandi*,* the rule of prayer, of which patristic authors spoke. In so far as prayer or worship is the centre of Christian life, the dogmas implicit within it guide the practice of the faith in all its aspects and may also be called the *lex agendi*, the rule of action. Even when they are not explicitly recognized, these undefined dogmas contribute to the shaping of scriptural interpretation, worship, proclamation, pastoral care, and the communal and individual behaviour of believers. Their explicit recognition develops through theological reflection in the face of heresies (such as the Christological and Trinitarian ones of the first centuries) or is stimulated by new forms of action (such as Paul's gentile mission) or of piety (such as Marian devotion, to cite a controverted case). These theological developments may become part of the *lex credendi*, the rule of believing represented by the church's ordinary preaching and instruction, but this is not yet dogmatic definition.

Definitions usually occur only when they are thought necessary for communal unity or faithfulness. They are serious matters, for they mark the boundaries of full ecclesial communion* and can be rightly decided on, as the Jerusalem church acknowledged, only with the help of the Holy Spirit (Acts 15:28). This conviction that God is at work as well as human beings when churches properly decide dogmatic questions is a fifth common element in the understanding of dogma. It has been historically present in various forms in all the major Christian traditions.

Change in dogma? Disagreements about dogma involve different understandings of revelation and of the three criteria for dogmatic definitions: scripture, Tradition, and the teaching authority of the church. In regard to revelation, one view is that the formulations in which dogmatic decisions are expressed are so related to revelation that they cannot be translated into other conceptualities. If dogmas cannot be reformulated, the statement of Vatican I, for example, that dogmatic definitions are "irreformable" means that they can be articulated only in their original terms and in no others.

Among other views, a second one is that irreformability applies more to the decisions than to their formulations, and that formulations may change, even though dogmatic decisions are irreversible. Since Vatican II* (1962-65) this has become the general opinion among those who hold to irreformability: the substance of the faith remains unchanged but not its articulations. A third possible position is that, not only formulations, but dogmatic decisions themselves may in some instances be applicable only in restricted contexts. While irreversible in their original settings, changes in situation may make them unnecessary or no longer binding. Dogmas are thought of in this perspective as confessional

responses to God's revelatory word uttering different directives to his church in different circumstances. Such views are strongest among Protestants but have gained ground everywhere (as has also the second position) with the weakening of the rationalistically propositional understandings of revelation and of truth which characterized early modern orthodoxies, and with the growth of emphases on historicity and contextuality. Whether these changes will make possible an ecumenically acceptable understanding of the irreformability of dogma remains to be seen.

Criteria for dogma. In reference to the three criteria for dogmas, the disagreements on teaching authority are the most clear-cut and perhaps the most intractable. In Eastern Orthodoxy, decisions of ecumenical councils received by the church as a whole have full dogmatic authority. There have been seven such councils, the last of which was Nicea II (787). These decisions are "infallible": believers may confidently affirm that they have been arrived at with the assistance of the Holy Spirit. In Roman Catholicism, not only the councils of the undivided church but also the later Roman Catholic ones are competent to define dogma infallibly when acting together with the pope; and the pope can also exercise this infallibility "with which God has endowed his church" (Vatican I) by himself, under the restricted conditions of ex cathedra pronouncements. Reformation churches do not speak of infallibility: one could perhaps say that they "hope and pray" rather than "believe and affirm" that their community-defining decisions are divinely assisted, are truly dogma. Furthermore, they are not committed to any one form of institutionalization of teaching authority, and communal reception* is proportionately more decisive for them than it has been in Roman Catholicism, though perhaps not in Eastern Orthodoxy. Once again, there has been much theological convergence on these issues of teaching authority in recent times, but it remains unclear how or whether the oppositions can be finally overcome.

In reference to the criterion of Tradition, the historic disputes are perhaps now close to being solved in theological principle, even if not in ecclesial practice. Roman Catholics have generally abandoned the "two-source" theory, according to which tradition is an independent source, supplementary to scripture, of publicly authoritative knowledge of revelation. Reformation Christians, without surrendering the *sola scriptura* in the sense of the supreme authority of scripture, have become much more aware of the inescapable and pervasive influence of Tradition on the communal understanding and use of scripture. They recognize that also for the reformers the traditions of Christ-centred and Trinitarian scriptural interpretation crystallized in the early creeds are essential to reading the Bible as the revelatory word of God — the "cradle of Christ", as Luther put it. Thus theologians of both Roman Catholic and Protestant allegiance now speak, in effect, of a single source of knowledge of revelation in which the scriptural canon, itself the product of tradition, is the centre of the ongoing traditioning process. Distinctive of the Eastern Orthodox is their insistence on the unchanging character of Tradition. Tradition has not changed as much for them as in the West. They have not needed to the same degree as Western Christians to decide dogmatically between new and conflicting traditions such as developed during and after the middle ages and became divisive at the time of the Reformation. Even in Eastern Orthodoxy, however, the continuity of Tradition is being threatened by modernity, and the need for dogmatic decisions going beyond the first seven councils is coming to be recognized.

Such decisions, in the East as in the West, depend chiefly on the Bible, for it, by general agreement, is the primary witness to revelation. The issues here are for the most part hermeneutical (see **hermeneutics**) and cut across the confessional boundaries. Both modern fundamentalist and modern liberal interpretative methods are in disarray, and the retrieval of pre-modern classic ones in combination with historical criticism has not yet progressed to any great extent. Perhaps only by such a retrieval, however, can Orthodox, Roman Catholic and Reformation Christians overcome their respective temptations to exaggerated traditionalism, clerical authoritarianism and biblicism, and thus learn to read scripture together as the primary guide to the dogmatic decisions (such as the recent condemnations of racism*) which will need to be made in the future as in the past.

One major development in the understanding of dogma is especially promising: the recognition of what Vatican II calls the "hierarchy of truths"* or, in language more familiar to Reformation Christians, the acknowledgment that some doctrines are closer to the centre of the gospel than others. At the uniquely authoritative summit and centre, by common consent, are the classic Christological and Trinitarian credal affirmations which define the person of Jesus Christ,* i.e., true God and true man, second person of the Triune deity (see **Trinity**). Those who thus agree on who Jesus is and who God is can join together in what from the beginning of Christianity was the central community-forming acclamation — Jesus is Lord. They can hope to remove the incompatibilities of their dogmatic formulations at lower levels while retaining an enriching diversity. Thus the hierarchy of truths in its Trinitarian and Christological ordering provides a way of understanding and experiencing dogma as primarily unitive, even in the present divided state of the church.

See also **common confession; creeds; ecumenical councils; faith; hermeneutics; infallibility; lex orandi, lex credendi; teaching authority; Tradition and traditions**.

GEORGE LINDBECK

A. Dulles, *The Survival of Dogma*, New York, Doubleday, 1971 • N. Lash, *Change in Focus*, London, Sheed & Ward, 1973 • G.A. Lindbeck, *The Nature of Doctrine*, Philadelphia, Westminster, 1984 • B. Lonergan, *The Way to Nicea*, London, Darton, Longman & Todd, 1976 • G. O'Collins, *Has Dogma a Future?*, London, Darton, Longman & Todd, 1975 • P. Schrodt, *The Problem of the Beginning of Dogma in Recent Theology*, Frankfurt am Main, Lang, 1978.

DU PLESSIS, DAVID J. B. 7.2.1905, South Africa; d. 2.2.1987, Pasadena, CA, USA. Widely known as "Mr Pentecost", Du Plessis was for a generation the leading figure in relations between Pentecostal churches and the ecumenical movement. Born of French Huguenot stock and ordained to the ministry in the Apostolic Faith Mission of South Africa (1928), he emigrated to the US in 1949. He attended several conferences of the International Missionary Council* and numerous WCC consultations and assemblies from

Evanston 1954 (as a staff member) to Vancouver 1983 (as a delegate of the International Evangelical Church). Du Plessis attended the first Pentecostal World Conference (Zurich 1947) and was organizing secretary for several subsequent ones. He preached in more than 50 countries and was a frequent lecturer on Pentecostal issues at theological schools. A catalyst for the denominational charismatic renewal movement which began in the US in the 1960s, Du Plessis was looked on with suspicion and rejection in many Pentecostal circles because of his relationships with the WCC and the Vatican. His contacts with Rome culminated in the Pentecostal-Roman Catholic dialogue, which began in 1972. See David Du Plessis, *A Man Called Mr Pentecost* (as told to Bob Slosser; Plainfield, NJ, Logos International, 1977).

ANS J. VAN DER BENT

DUPREY, PIERRE. B. 26.11.1922, Croix, France. In 1963 Duprey became undersecretary, and in 1983 secretary, of the Secretariat for Promoting Christian Unity* in Rome. Since 1965 he has been a member of the Joint Working Group* between the RCC and the WCC and was liaison officer between the Secretariat for Promoting Christian Unity

and the Commission on Faith and Order,* 1971-83. Since 1970 he has been a member of the international joint commission between the Roman Catholic Church and the Anglican communion. He was also president of the preparatory commission for the theological dialogue between the RCC and the Orthodox churches in 1975, and secretary of this commission from 1980 onwards. He is a member also of the commissions for dialogue with the Lutheran World Federation, the World Alliance of Reformed Churches, and the Pentecostal churches. He is a member of the executive committee of the Ecumenical Institute for Theological Research in Tantur.

After studies with the White Fathers, Duprey was ordained a priest in Carthage in 1950. He received a doctorate in Oriental studies from the Pontifical Oriental Institute in Rome in 1953 and then pursued studies of Arabic language and literature at the Saint-Joseph University of Beirut, 1954-56. He was professor of dogmatic theology and history of dogma at the Saint Anne Seminary of Jerusalem (Jordan), 1956-63. In 1962 he took part in the first session of the Second Vatican Council, serving as theologian/interpreter to the Orthodox observers. In 1990 he was ordained a bishop.

ANS J. VAN DER BENT

E

EASTER. Easter is the annual feast of Christ's resurrection* from the dead — an event that is celebrated on a weekly basis every Sunday, "the first day of the week", when the women discovered the empty tomb (Matt. 28:1; Mark 16:2; Luke 24:1; John 20:1) and the risen Lord appeared to them and to others (also Luke 24:13,36; John 20:19). The annual celebration was at first a unitary celebration of Christ's death and resurrection, a Christian passover, or pasch, corresponding to the fact that Christ's "exodus" (the Greek word in Luke 9:31) for the salvation* of the world had taken place at the time when the Jewish people commemorated their liberation from Egypt. The 4th century saw the development of "Good Friday" as a commemoration of Christ's passion and crucifixion, leaving Easter Sunday and the ensuing 50 days (see **Pentecost**) as the feast of Christ's victory over death. In the 20th century, liturgical and sacramental theology has re-discovered the unitary character of the "paschal mystery" of Christ's death and resurrection, celebrated pre-eminently in the paschal vigil during the night from Saturday to Easter Sunday.

The dating of Easter has been the object of several controversies during Christian history. The serious remaining difference separates the Eastern and the Western churches. While both sides agree to the principle laid down in 325 by the council of Nicea* (Easter falls on the annually variable date of the first Sunday following the full moon after the northern spring equinox), the dates in practice differ because the East dates the equinox by the Julian calendar and the West by the Gregorian calendar (see **church calendar**).

The modern ecumenical movement has seen some modest efforts to consider and achieve the practice of a common date for Easter. An early stimulus came from the League of Nations, which in the 1920s proposed the fixed date of the Sunday after the second Saturday in April. This met with some support in the Life and Work* movement, but the Roman Catholic Church was wary of any semblance of secular control over a religious matter. At Vatican II,* however, encouragement was given to the search for an agreed date for Easter, whether annually variable because dependent on the moon (as at present) or fixed (by the civil, solar calendar); but no change was to be made until the churches reached a common mind. The WCC pursued the matter through a questionnaire to its member churches (1965-67), a Faith and Order* consultation (1970), and a report to the Nairobi assembly (1975). While some churches, particularly Western, would be happy with a fixed date (the most favoured being the one originally proposed by the League of Nations), the Orthodox churches stand by the Nicene principle that makes a variable date dependent on the moon. Ecclesiastically, the best hope for a common date appears to reside in continuing to keep an annually variable date while respecting astronomical exactitude for the equinox, from which the first full moon and the ensuing Sunday are counted.

GEOFFREY WAINWRIGHT

A.A. McArthur, *The Evolution of the Christian Year*, London, SCM, 1953 • D. M. Paton ed., *Breaking Barriers: Nairobi 1975*, WCC, 1976, p.193 • "Report of the Consultation on a Fixed Date for Easter", *The Ecumenical Review*, 23, 2, 1971.

EASTERN CATHOLIC CHURCHES.

These churches originated in very diverse circumstances and live in various situations. Total membership is estimated at around 9 million. What they have in common is full communion* of faith* and sacraments* with the Roman Catholic Church (RCC) around the bishop of Rome, while retaining various Eastern liturgical and canonical traditions inherited from their mother churches from which they were separated by their union with the church of Rome. They were disparagingly called Uniates by the Orthodox or Oriental Churches because of negative memories attached to their origins and to their type of relationship with Rome or with the Orthodox churches of the same traditions.

On the Roman Catholic side, these union attempts were generally founded on the principle of the council of Florence (1438-45): complete respect of the diversity of traditions within the unity of faith. But none of the existing Eastern Catholic churches in fact traces its origin back to this council. In the context of the Counter-Reformation, the awareness of the ecclesial character of the Orthodox churches became blurred in the RCC, and the attempts to restore unity between the two churches slowly gave way to the "return" of individuals or small groups to the Catholic church.

In Eastern Europe, the reunion with Rome of certain communities — at times with their bishops — was strongly influenced by the socio-political situation, especially the changes of frontiers between countries with Catholic or Orthodox predominance. The union of the Ukrainians (Brest-Litovsk 1595-96) was concluded at a time when these regions were under Polish authority. The unions of the Ruthenians (Uzhorod 1646) and that of a group of Romanians (Transylvania 1700) took place in the framework of the Austrian-Hungarian empire. Of lesser importance were the Yugoslavian, Bulgarian, Slovak, Hungarian, Byelorussian, Albanian, Russian and Greek Catholic churches. All belonged to the Byzantine-Slavonic tradition. The Ukrainian (some 3.5 million members), Ruthenian, Byelorussian and Romanian Catholic churches were officially suppressed by force under communist regimes in the late 1940s; they survived only underground in their homelands or outside them, in Western Europe and North America in particular.

In the Middle East the circumstances were very different. The Maronite Church constitutes a special case: originating in the territory of Antioch (monastery of Beit-Marun) in the 4th century, this church claims no historical consciousness of a formal break with Rome; it renewed contact at the time of the crusades; and it has no "Orthodox" counterpart, but belongs totally to the Catholic communion. All the churches of the Middle East lived in very difficult situations; they had become small minorities in the Muslim world, forming ethnic communities with their own separate status. These churches readily welcomed the help offered by Latin religious coming from the West, all the more as most people generally had no vivid awareness of an existing schism* with the Catholic church. The pastoral, intellectual and social activities of these missionaries slowly created, in different places, groups of faithful and pastors favouring union with Rome. When these groups became relatively important, union was proclaimed officially.

Unfortunately, instead of bringing about the union between the Roman Catholic Church and the respective other partners, new divisions resulted, since the majority of the Orthodox generally refused the *fait accompli*. This was the case — with some rather important differences — with all the churches of the Middle East when some of their members became united with Rome: the Eastern Syrian or Nestorian tradition (Chaldeans 1553), the Western Syrian tradition (Syrian Catholics 1662), the Armenian tradition (Armenian Catholics 1740), the Byzantine tradition (Greek Catholics or Melkites 1724). Later on, the passage of individuals to the Catholic church led to the creation of Coptic Catholic (1895) and Ethiopian Catholic (1930) hierarchies.

On the Indian coast of Malabar, attempts by

the Portuguese in the 16th century to impose Latin authority and discipline on the St Thomas Christians resulted in various divisions. Two groups entered into communion with Rome: the Malabar (1599) and the Malankara (1930) churches.

The establishment of canonical ties of all these churches with Rome led to a process of Latinization of their liturgy and their thinking, in varying degrees, as well as to a number of encroachments on their discipline and autonomy as local churches.

Such developments are sometimes interpreted by the Orthodox as a proof that there is no place for a true local church and an original tradition in the Roman Catholic Church. In its Decree on the Eastern Catholic Churches, the Second Vatican Council* insists strongly on respect for their particular traditions and on the necessity for these churches to re-discover their authentic heritage. Vatican II also emphasizes their ecumenical vocation and states explicitly that all juridical dispositions concerning them are of a provisional nature, until the time of full communion with the Orthodox churches.

The Orthodox churches regard the existence of the Eastern Catholic churches as a de facto negation of the ecclesial character of the Orthodox themselves. In their eyes, these churches are also instruments of proselytism* in disguise, aimed at converting to Catholicism ignorant faithful who are unable to recognize the differences. The Eastern Catholic churches are like an open wound in the side of the Orthodox churches, who consistently ask for their suppression. Hence the Eastern Catholic churches cannot act as a bridge between Catholics and Orthodox, as they were sometimes expected to do in the past. The Orthodox churches now want to dialogue directly with the Roman Catholic Church, without the mediation of these churches.

To the Eastern Catholic churches, created by the church of Rome with a view to restoring unity, it is a cause of suffering to be considered still as an obstacle to unity, a "thorn in the flesh" of the dialogue. What could be their future vocation? By faithfully reviving their most authentic Eastern traditions, they could bear witness to the Orthodox church that it is possible to be a real local Eastern church within the Catholic communion around the bishop of Rome. Within the Catholic church, their task is a constant reminder that catholicity* cannot limit itself to the Latin tradition alone but has to remain open to all genuine expressions of the fullness of ecclesial life in Christ.

The official Orthodox-Roman Catholic international commission for theological dialogue (see **Orthodox-Roman Catholic dialogue**), established in 1978 by Pope John Paul II and Ecumenical Patriarch Dimitrios I, began in the mid-1980s to discuss what some on both sides regard as proselytism among vulnerable flocks. The 1990 session had the Eastern Catholic churches on the agenda. What had made the topic most urgent was the sudden 1989 political changes in Eastern and Central Europe which quickly joined the populist demands for full and equal religious freedom for all the churches, including their property rights of places of worship. The new tensions have instigated the holy see in Rome and local Eastern Catholic and Orthodox authorities to begin conversations on what such freedom means in practice for the churches vis-a-vis the governments and between themselves, e.g. in the western Ukraine, Romania, Bulgaria, Czechoslovakia, etc.

The Roman curia has a congregation for the Eastern churches, created in 1862 as part of the Propaganda Fide and made autonomous in 1917. The new 1983 code of canon law has the force of law only for the Latin church, under the pope in his quality as patriarch of the West; the code for the Eastern Catholic churches is still in draft stage, under the pope as pastor of the universal Catholic church.

FRANS BOUWEN

E. Lanne, "Les catholiques orientaux: Liberté religieuse et œcuménisme", *Irénikon*, 63, 1, 1990 ● R.G. Roberson, *The Eastern Christian Churches*, rev. 3rd ed., Rome, Pont. Institutum Studiorum Orientalium, 1990.

EASTERN ORTHODOXY. In recent times, this term has come to be used, particularly in the ecumenical context, to refer to the "Chalcedonian" Orthodox as distinct from the "non-" or "pre-Chalcedonian" churches, known as "Oriental Orthodox churches".*

Eastern Orthodox churches have come to be identified with the East through a series of historical accidents, involving the gradual estrangement between Rome (and Western

Christendom) and the other ancient patriarchates. In reality, Orthodoxy does not consider itself either Eastern or Western. Until the schism* between East and West became a final reality, Eastern and Western Christianity, with tensions from time to time, were one conciliar communion* (with the exception of the pre-Chalcedonians from the 5th century onwards).

The date of 1054, usually given as that of the separation, is that of an exchange of excommunications* between Rome and Constantinople (the "New Rome" since Constantinople I, 381). The process leading to the schism is in fact long and complicated, and in spite of attempts at reunion (councils of Lyons, 1274, and Ferrara-Florence, 1438-39), it still remains unhealed. However, relations have changed considerably in recent decades, particularly in 1965, when Pope Paul VI and Patriarch Athenagoras I mutually lifted the excommunications of 1054. An official international dialogue commission has been at work for some years now (see **Orthodox-Roman Catholic dialogue**).

The Eastern Orthodox claim a direct, unbroken descent from the church of the apostles. This is expressed in their fidelity to the apostolic faith as developed in the seven ecumenical councils* and the patristic tradition (see **apostolic tradition, apostolicity**). Thus, the Eastern Orthodox churches are united in the faith,* and each one has internal autonomy under the primacy* of the patriarchate of Constantinople, the "first among equals".

Orthodoxy also implies a strong attachment to the sacraments,* the most important being the sacraments of initiation: baptism* (by immersion), chrismation* and the eucharist* (communion in both kinds), to which the newly baptized member is immediately admitted, whatever his or her age.

Since the separation from the Christian West, Eastern Orthodox churches have mainly been using the Syro-Byzantine liturgical tradition (see **liturgy**), whose development owes much to the fathers and the great monastic centres (today, Mt Athos is the most important of these). In this liturgical tradition iconography plays an important part (see **icon/image**).

Structurally, Eastern Orthodox churches currently fall under the following classifications. They represent *four out of the five*

 ancient patriarchates which, together with Rome, formed the famous pentarchy, i.e. Constantinople (some 2 million faithful, with only a few thousand in Turkey), Alexandria (about 100,000 faithful), Antioch (primatial see: Damascus; some 450,000 faithful) and Jerusalem (about 50,000).

Orthodoxy includes a number of other *autocephalous churches* (i.e. churches that elect their own primate without reference to another autocephalous church). The largest of all is the church of Russia (about 100 million faithful in 1917; today, probably well over 50 million). Others are the Romanian church (some 14 million); the Serbian church in Yugoslavia (patriarchate in Belgrade; some 8 million); the church of Greece, distinct from the patriarchate of Constantinople since 1833, with its own primate, the archbishop of Athens (about 7.5 million faithful); the Bulgarian church (some 6 million); the church of Georgia, a second autocephalous church on Soviet territory, much more ancient than the Russian church (founded in the 5th century as a result of missionary work by a woman, St Nino, counted as "equal to the apostles" in the Orthodox sanctoral; 2.5 million faithful in 1917); the church of Cyprus (autocephalous since the council of Ephesus, 431; some 450,000 faithful).

A third type are *autocephalous churches which represent a minority among other Christians in their territory,* namely, the Orthodox church of Czechoslovakia (some 350,000 faithful in 1950); the Orthodox church of Poland (about 350,000); the Orthodox church of Albania (about 210,000 faithful in 1944).

Orthodoxy also includes *autonomous or semi-autonomous churches* (i.e. churches that enjoy internal autonomy but whose primate is elected under the aegis of one of the autocephalous churches). Among them are the church of Finland (some 70,000 faithful, under the jurisdiction of Constantinople); the church of Crete (also under Constantinople); the Orthodox church of Japan (about 36,000 faithful, under the jurisdiction of Moscow); the Russian Orthodox mission in China (probably some 20,000 faithful).

Another classification is *missions which are not yet autonomous.* These include the Russian mission in Korea (under the jurisdiction of the Greek Archdiocese of North America) and African Orthodoxy (founded in Uganda by dissidents from Anglicanism, now present also in Kenya, Zaire and Ghana, under the jurisdiction of the patriarchate of Alexandria).

Finally, there is the *Orthodox diaspora.** In the 19th and 20th centuries, many Orthodox emigrated to Western countries for economic and political reasons. As a result, Orthodox are now to be found in most parts of the world.

Although the principle of identifying Orthodoxy with an ethnic group was condemned as a heresy* in 1872 under the name of "phyletism" by a synod held in Constantinople (but received by all Orthodox churches), the present situation resembles a complicated jigsaw puzzle of numerous jurisdictions in most countries of the Western world, where the Orthodox of various origins tend to be claimed by their mother churches according to their ethnicity.*

According to traditional Orthodox ecclesiology, all the Orthodox in a given place, whatever their ethnic origin, should be gathered in one conciliar communion. Such, for example, was the situation in the US until 1917: all the Orthodox were in one diocese (which had grown from the Russian mission among the Aleutian and Alaskan Indians in the 18th century). At the council of Moscow in 1917, Tikhon, the bishop of the American diocese (recently canonized), was elected patriarch. When he was able to send a successor to New York a few years later, the latter found that in the meantime all the mother churches of the Orthodox world had claimed their nationals and created their own jurisdictions. In 1970, the Russian church granted autocephaly to the churches of its old diocese in America, thus creating the Orthodox Church in America. However, finding the solution to the problem of the Orthodox diaspora remains one of the main difficulties of present-day Orthodoxy, one that is high on the agenda of the pan-Orthodox council.

Eastern Orthodox churches have played a part in the ecumenical movement from an early date in the 20th century. Witness the encyclical* letter of the ecumenical patriarch of Constantinople in 1920 to "all the churches of Christ" for "closer intercourse and mutual co-operation". The Orthodox diaspora has also greatly contributed to an encounter with Western Christendom, to better mutual understanding, and to a common renaissance in patristic theological reflection. Most Eastern Orthodox churches have become members of the WCC and have established bilateral dialogues* with most Christian churches. Orthodoxy, however, does include a certain anti-ecumenical strain which is largely due to a suspicion on the part of some that ecumenical dialogue necessarily implies a betrayal of the purity of the Orthodox faith.

Eastern Orthodox churches do not believe in "intercommunion";* in their view, only full communion* has a meaning. This is the main reason why the Orthodox generally have refused to practise so-called eucharistic hospitality. In their conception of the nature of the church,* communion is only possible when the apostolic faith can be fully confessed together. (Some pastors do practise eucharistic hospitality in specific circumstances, but only as a matter of conscience in their personal pastoral responsibility.) For the time being, Eastern Orthodox churches are not prepared to sanction a generalized eucharistic hospitality, not even as a measure of economy.* Indeed, such a step would amount to establishing a *rule*, and the principle of economy is precisely a pedagogical *exception* to a rule which in no way abolishes the existing rule. In the Orthodox perspective, full communion will quite naturally be restored when it is truly possible to confess the fullness of the apostolic faith together.

See also **Orthodoxy**.

NICHOLAS LOSSKY

S. Bulgakov, *The Orthodox Church*, London, Centenary, 1935 ● O. Clément, *L'Eglise orthodoxe: Que sais-je?*, rev. ed., Paris, PUF, 1985 ● P. Evdokimov, *L'orthodoxie*, Paris, Desclée de Brouwer, 1979 ● J. Meyendorff, *The Orthodox Church: Its Past and Its Role in the World Today*, 3rd rev. ed., New York, St Vladimir's Seminary, 1981 ● A. Schmemann, *The Historical Road of Eastern Orthodoxy*, New York, St Vladimir's Seminary, 1977 ● T. Ware, *The Orthodox Church*, Harmondsworth, UK, Pelican, 1963.

ECONOMICS. Economics deals with the production, distribution and consumption of material goods and services. The second assembly of the WCC (Evanston 1954) summarized the ecumenical concern about economic and social issues as follows: "The church is concerned with economic life because of

God's concern for human beings who work to produce goods and services, who use them, and for whom business exists."

The history of the ecumenical debate about economic issues can be divided into four different periods. During the first period, from 1910 to 1933, awareness of the importance of socio-economic issues emerged. The concept of the responsible society played a major role as a criterion for the assessment of economic problems during the second period from 1934 to 1960. In the third period, between 1960 and 1975, the concept of human development* became dominant. The fourth period, which began around 1975, was characterized by the use of two different criteria: sustainability, which expresses a concern for nature and human resources, and solidarity with the poor,* as a key in the struggle against poverty.

Of course this periodization is to a certain degree arbitrary; the elements of one period were present in the previous or continued during the following one. The main aspects which characterized a certain historical period were, in many ways, the result of trends which were already evolving.

First period (1910-33). During this first period the churches manifested a gradual awareness of the importance of socio-economic issues for social ethics. In the 1890s the Roman Catholic Church (RCC) had begun to develop its social teaching, for which Leo XIII's *Rerum Novarum* can be considered as the point of departure (see **social encyclicals, papal**). In this encyclical the concept of the common good plays a key role. This notion was further dealt with by Pius XI in his encyclical *Quadragesimo Anno* (1931), in the context of the rise of fascism. Conservative Protestants, however, approached economic life from a perspective dominated by a sharp distinction between the spiritual and the secular, the eternal and the temporal. The basis of such an approach was provided by the traditional understanding of Martin Luther's theology of the two kingdoms. The social gospel (see **social gospel movement**) was influential in North America, as was religious socialism in Western and Central Europe, mostly in Reformed circles.

The concern for peace and internationalism became a priority for the churches as they realized how much the problems related to social ethics are interlinked. This awareness informed many of the early discussions and reflections of the Life and Work* (L&W) movement, which emerged in this period, with Nathan Söderblom playing a key role. Personalities like Archbishop Germanos of Thyateira and George Bell, then dean of Canterbury and later bishop of Chichester, were also active in the L&W movement.

The first conference of L&W (Stockholm 1925) was an impressive endeavour to create a common basis for discussions on social ethics among Christians of different churches. Although it was not an exclusively Protestant event, it made a meaningful attempt to overcome the over-emphasis on individualism which prevailed in Protestant social ethics at that time. The conference emphasized that industrial activity should not be undertaken only for the sake of personal profit, but that it should provide benefits for the whole community. The human person is a steward in the service of God, whose will embraces the whole of humanity. Therefore private interest and property should be subordinated to social goals.

Second period (1934-60). This second period was particularly creative. The churches had to face enormous challenges, among which were the rise of National Socialism in Germany, the consolidation of Stalinism in the USSR, the consequences of the great depression (1929-33), the gathering power of authoritarian and totalitarian states, the second world war, post-war problems, the cold war between capitalist and socialist states, the birth and development of the world economic order based on the internationalization of capital and labour,* decolonization* and the emergence of independent nations, the emergence of the group of non-aligned countries, the beginning of the period of peaceful co-existence, and the Chinese and Cuban revolutions. The life of the churches was profoundly influenced by these changes. The Confessing Church* in Germany lived through the confrontation with Nazism, and the Barmen confession was issued in 1934.

The second L&W conference met in Oxford (1937) around the theme "Church, Community and State". Plans were underway to establish the WCC, but the implementation was postponed because of the second world war. The WCC held its first assembly in

Amsterdam (1948) and its second in Evanston (1954). Pope John XXIII called the Second Vatican Council, which marked the beginning of the official participation of the Vatican in the ecumenical movement.

Three names from these years deserve special mention: J.H. Oldham, W.A. Visser 't Hooft and Paul Abrecht. Oldham was the first general secretary of the International Missionary Council and the chief organizer of the Oxford conference. He was also the architect of the concept of the responsible society,* which was not an alternative social model or system but a criterion for decisions at the level of social ethics. Visser 't Hooft was executive secretary of the World Alliance of Young Men's Christian Associations* and general secretary of the World Student Christian Federation* before he became general secretary of the WCC. With his passion for the *una sancta*, Visser 't Hooft was also deeply interested in the socio-economic and political problems of the world. Abrecht, who directed the Department on Church and Society of the WCC, introduced into the ecumenical agenda issues related to developing countries like economic growth and development and promoted a contextual and multidisciplinary approach to the kind of problems specific to church and society.

After the second assembly, an international ecumenical study was launched on "The Common Responsibility towards Areas of Rapid Social Change", which culminated in a conference in Salonika, Greece, in 1959. Through this study process the ecumenical movement developed an approach to socio-economic and political matters that was universal as well as culturally and politically pluralistic. Two main lessons were learned. First, it was realized that ecumenical social ethics, in spite of its supranational character, had so far approached economic and political problems from a predominantly Western perspective. The time had come to broaden this perspective to include the concerns of churches and Christians in other parts of the world. This realization marked the beginning of a more inclusive dialogue involving other cultures and also people of other faiths. Second, study of rapid social change demonstrated clearly the inadequacy of the simplistic view of the world as divided between two opposite camps: the liberal-capitalist West and the Marxist-socialist East. This view, which prevailed up to the Evanston assembly, needed to be broadened by including problems related to North-South relationships.

More than ever before, the ecumenical movement paid attention to important issues pertaining to economics, such as migration* (both domestic and international), economic growth, patterns of consumption (see **consumerism**), development co-operation, world poverty,* and trade relations. The overarching key of the analysis was the criterion of social justice and its practical implications. It became evident that there cannot be economic growth and development without structural transformation to bring about justice and democracy. Whereas the first period was characterized by a certain idealism, the second period called for greater realism on the part of churches and Christians: "It is impossible to foresee an ideal pattern of economic development without difficult problems. Some cost in human hardship and misery is inevitable. It will often be necessary to work out proximate goals and least harmful measures. Christians must accept the hard facts of economic life and be ready to take necessary choices and to run the unavoidable risks" (*Dilemmas and Opportunities*, Salonika report, 89). This realism implied that, in spite of the more inclusive approach indicated above, the dominant perspective was still Western — which is no surprise, since the majority of the member churches of the WCC still belonged to the Western world.

Third period (1960-75). Great changes took place in this period, not only for the churches but also at the level of international relationships. As the process of political decolonization continued, more and more independent states emerged in Africa, Asia and the Pacific. Peaceful co-existence was followed by detente, and this new path survived until the end of the 1970s, despite some very difficult situations (e.g. the Cuban missile crisis, 1962; the Vietnam war, 1965-75; the Middle East conflict, 1967, 1973). The gap between the rich industrialized countries in the North and the poor producers of raw materials or semi-manufactured goods of the South continued to widen. The United Nations Conference on Trade and Development was created as a forum to discuss many problems of the so-called third world. A main problem was to see what kinds of national development models and international economic order were required to ensure the real development of the South.

Churches became important partners in this debate. At the end of the Second Vatican Council* (1965), the RCC approved the pastoral constitution *Gaudium et Spes* on the church's presence in today's world. In 1966 the WCC called a world conference on church and society around the theme "Christians in the Technical and Social Revolutions of Our Time". Pope Paul VI published the encyclical *Populorum Progressio* in 1967, stating that "development is the new name of peace". The WCC and the Vatican together organized the conference on world co-operation for development (Beirut 1968). Also in 1968, considerable attention was given to the challenges of the economic world for Christian witness at the third All Christians Peace Assembly of the Christian Peace Conference* (Prague). At the fourth assembly of the WCC (Uppsala 1968), "human development" was identified as a major issue, one that has remained a priority concern for the ecumenical movement. The WCC, jointly with the pontifical commission *Iustitia et Pax*, established the exploratory committee on Society, Development and Peace (SODEPAX*), thus highlighting the importance of issues such as development, peace and human rights for the ecumenical movement. In 1980 this joint venture came to an end.

The criterion of the meaning of the human prevailed in the emerging debate about the quality of life and economic growth. At a consultation on ecumenical assistance to development projects (Montreux, Switzerland, 1970), it was affirmed that human development must be characterized by three main elements: social justice, self-reliance, and economic growth, the last element being one of the means for promoting the first two. This understanding of development reflected prevailing thoughts of third-world economists and social scientists. In the ecumenical movement, this line of thought was strongly promoted by Samuel Parmar, a professor at the Ecumenical Institute of Bossey and later moderator of the working group on Church and Society.

Second, the Montreux consultation proposed to the churches to create an Ecumenical Development Fund (EDF) which would receive money through self-taxation. Churches were asked to contribute 2% of their annual budgets to the EDF. The fund would be used to provide seed money for the launching of development programmes and to support development education aimed at increasing awareness regarding the need for solidarity and human development. The Commission on the Churches' Participation in Development (CCPD) was created, and the administration of the EDF and the connected programmes was one of its tasks. The interest in the development debate was not confined to CCPD alone; other departments of the WCC also took part in it, notably Church and Society, Inter-Church Aid, the Christian Medical Commission, SODEPAX, and later also the Sub-unit on Women.

From 1970 to 1974, the Church and Society programme on "The Future of Man and Society in a World of Science-Based Technology" gave priority to the relationship between economic growth and the quality of life. In the same period the Club of Rome published its report on *The Limits to Growth*, which argued that it is necessary to make an option for a self-imposed limitation to growth in light of our planet's limited physical resources. The programme of Church and Society gave a new impetus to the discussion of science-based technology and the future of humanity. Whereas the reflections about development emphasized social justice as the highest priority, the debate stimulated by Church and Society underlined the importance of sustainability. Social ethics has to deal with both elements, as became particularly clear at the Church and Society conference in Bucharest (1974) on "Science and Technology for Human Development — the Ambiguous Future and the Christian Hope", as well as in the CCPD report *Threats to Survival*, which was approved by the WCC central committee in Berlin (1974).

Another element introduced in the discussion was the experience gained by some churches through their involvement in actions for development, which made them aware that any action in this field demanded an exercise of people's participation in order to be effective. Development matters, as well as orientations concerning the future of humankind, cannot be left in the hands of the powerful and specialists alone. This point was made clear in the report of the WCC general secretary, Philip Potter, to the fifth assembly (Nairobi 1975).

By the mid-1970s, both the international community and the ecumenical movement realized that the eradication of poverty and the transformation of world economic and social structures were far more difficult to achieve than was foreseen earlier. It was hard to implement "human development" and "human economy". Therefore, it was no surprise that a consensus within the churches on economic matters appeared almost impossible to achieve. Nevertheless, the fifth WCC assembly asked for further reflection on a "Just, Participatory and Sustainable Society".*

Fourth period (1976-present). At the special session of the general assembly of the UN in 1974, the non-aligned nations introduced the debate around the New International Economic Order. Powerful groups used this opportunity to manifest their great resistance to proposals for structural transformation in the developing countries. The optimism of the late 1950s and the 1960s concerning the possible transformation of the world economic situation and the development of better patterns of growth at the planetary level was no longer evident. The development of African, Asian, Latin American, and Pacific countries had not occurred. There was economic growth in many cases, but this was achieved at the cost of increased dependency and high social costs, particularly affecting the poor sections of the population. The gathering pessimism was reflected in the report of the Independent Commission on International Development Issues, chaired by Willy Brandt. The process of internationalization of capital and labour, which found its clearest expression in the concentration of decision making in transnational corporations* (TNCs), called for a more careful analysis of the world's economic situation. New technologies created new dynamics — especially in the information industry — which led to a situation demanding special attention to technological developments. Bio-genetic engineering raised new concerns over food and energy production (see **bio-ethics**). The financial instability which marked the beginning of the 1970s was even more evident now and led to complex consequences like the increasing foreign debt

Street scene in Argentina (WCC/R. Salgado, Jr)

of developed and developing countries. The stock exchange crisis of October 1987 was a clear indication of increasing instability. All these developments challenged the churches and the ecumenical movement to the problems of economics from new perspectives.

First, the WCC Sub-unit on Church and Society focused on "Faith, Science and the Future". The conference around this theme (MIT 1979) was a decisive event in this process. It brought out the need of convergence between science and theology, technology and spirituality. The conference itself could not resolve the complex problems science-based technology presented to churches and Christians, but the issues were highlighted, and the promise as well as the threat implicit in them for human society was discerned. The conference underlined the unbreakable link between sustainability, social justice and participation. It declared: "We would strongly argue the need to see the struggle for a just, participatory and sustainable society in coherent terms which will not allow us to dismember the concept and the goal into, for example, justice for the third world, participation for the second world, and sustainability for the first world. We of the human race are all members of one another. We must together struggle to extend participation, develop sustainability and to let 'justice roll down like waters and righteousness like an ever-flowing stream' (Amos 5:24)."

Second, in many parts of the oikoumene, churches and Christian communities were now seriously concerned about the role of TNCs in contemporary economic life. Following indications given by the fifth WCC assembly and the WCC central committee (Geneva 1976), a study programme on churches and TNCs was initiated in 1977 under the responsibility of CCPD. Attention was given to the need for an integral approach to the issue of the transnationality of business as a unique phenomenon, to the power of TNCs and accountability, to the use of technology and its effects on employment and labour, for the need for building up countervailing power, and to the responsibility of churches. A process of consultations was organized, and the report presented in 1982 to the WCC central committee meeting in Geneva.

Third, within the framework of CCPD the Advisory Group on Economic Matters

(AGEM) was established in 1979. A consultation called by Church and Society and CCPD (Zurich 1978) on "Political Economy, Ethics and Theology: Some Contemporary Challenges" emphasized the need to formulate a "new paradigm in political economy". This was outlined in three propositions: (1) the need to re-instate the historical and spatial dimension in economic thought and praxis; (2) the need to have an integrated view on economics through interdisciplinary research; (3) the need for economics again to become political economy in which value judgments play an important role. It was argued that the discussion on limits to inequality in terms of maximum and minimum levels should be central.

In the meantime, the WCC central committee had received the report of the CCPD study programme on "The Church and the Poor", which emphasized that churches should be in solidarity with the underprivileged sectors of society. Building on this perspective, AGEM organized a series of reflections on various political economic issues. The work of AGEM remains one of the most systematic attempts made by the ecumenical movement to deal with economic issues.

Fourth, the contribution of recent Roman Catholic social teaching, notably two encyclical letters of Pope John Paul II, one on human labour (*Laborem Exercens* 1981) and the other on socio-economic issues which challenge the Christian consciousness (*Sollicitudo Rei Socialis* 1987), demonstrates that the RCC shares much the same concern as the member churches of the WCC for social justice and the urgent need for the eradication of poverty. This line of thought was also manifested by the document published by the pontifical commission *Iustitia et Pax* about the problem of foreign debt of many countries (see **debt crisis**), both in the North and in the South (see *At the Service of the Human Community: An Ethical Consideration about the International Debt*, 1987). The pastoral letter of the US Roman Catholic bishops on *The Catholic Social Teaching and the US Economy* (1986) is yet another important contribution to the debate.

Finally, the concern about socio-economic issues in Christian circles in this last period is also manifested by a new wave of research and publications in which the challenges of economic praxis and theory stimulated fresh thinking in Christian theology and social ethics. Some of the most relevant contributions are Franz Hinkelammert, *Las armas ideológicas de la muerte* (1977), *Crítica de la razón utópica* (1983), and *Democracia y totalitarismo* (1987); Arend T. van Leeuwen, *De Nacht van het Kapitaal* (1985); and Ulrich Duchrow, *Weltwirtschaft Heute: Ein Feld für bekennende Kirche?* (1986). Anticipating this wave, Helmut Gollwitzer had written in 1974 *Die kapitalistische Revolution.* All these publications attempt to show how Christian faith is challenged in economic life by false gods and idols, the Molochs and Mammons of our time. Reflected in the ecumenical debate is the call to resist the totalitarianism of the market through confessing the lordship of Christ.

Conclusion. The approach to economics has been multidisciplinary, aiming above all at developing social ethics. In ecumenical thinking, economics has never been dealt with in isolation. The objective has been, and still is, to provide churches, Christian communities, and individual believers with criteria and guidelines for judgment and action in social and economic matters. In so doing, the ecumenical discussion addresses the interests of the churches and the concerns of the international community. Through the process followed by the ecumenical movement, churches have discovered that all ecclesiastical institutions and all religions and ideologies share many common problems. Therefore, no clear distinctions can be made between the agenda of the churches and the agenda of the world when these problems are discussed. Economic matters are ecumenical matters; the economic dimension of life touches the whole inhabited world.

On the other hand, the specificity of the ecumenical dialogue lies precisely in the approach, the values, and the criteria that are applied to the understanding of economics. The ecumenical movement is not called to find one homogeneous and uniform position. What is called for is an intercontextual approach which recognizes that the universality of a given problem needs to be tackled through the diversity of its manifestations in difficult situations. Such an approach demands a multidisciplinary exercise. The ecumenical discussion can be seen as an approach

to economic problems through permanent dialogue. This was clear in the discussion on development and economic growth during the 1960s and 1970s, and the current discussion of the debt crisis.

In the ecumenical dialogue on economic matters, the value of social justice has always been underlined. Social justice was understood as a translation of the commandment of God in Jesus Christ to love one another, and to work for it is therefore a permanent task of the ecumenical movement. Practically, this task has been translated in efforts to eradicate poverty through interchurch channels of cooperation and solidarity.

Another value that has been emphasized is freedom, which, since the beginning of the 1970s, has been understood by some Christian communities as liberation. For the ecumenical movement, freedom has never been an absolute value. For human beings, freedom is a condition in order to be able to act responsibly. The second WCC assembly qualified it as "relative", important for the life of the economic enterprise and the regulating role of the price system. Because freedom is not absolute, it calls for the exercise of stewardship in the administration of property and world resources.

A main question is how to act in order to give substance to the values of social justice and freedom. In this respect, four main criteria have prevailed in the ecumenical debate about economics. First, the concept of the responsible society, which played a key role until the beginning of the 1960s. This concept was based on the understanding of middle axioms,* proposed by J.H. Oldham as a basis for the orientation of Christian witness. These do not exhaust the full content of the commandment of love but are useful in order to interpret it. Middle axioms help to concretize, in a practical way, the truth of Christian beliefs in the context of the ambiguities of history. One of these middle axioms is the responsible society.

Second, since the beginning of the 1960s, the "human" became a prevailing criterion, especially at the time of the world conference on Church and Society in 1966 and the fourth and fifth assemblies of the WCC. The concept of responsible society left room for the practice of a wide humanism. The kind of social ethics which was developed during the 1960s and 1970s did not look for ready-made norms of conduct but were concerned with the biblical imperative to become full human persons. That goal entails the humanization of science and technology and demands the satisfaction of basic human needs. Justice is a prerequisite because people cannot become fully human when they are victims of injustice. Therefore, the goal of the ecumenical movement was not only "economic growth" but above all "human development". The problem is not only of a quantitative nature; the goal is a better quality of life.

Third, this synthesized reflection process culminated in the proposal that the ecumenical movement should strive for a "sustainable society" which can ensure respect for the human as well as respect for nature and the responsibility towards future generations.

Fourth, it has to be noted that the situation which prevailed after the second half of the 1970s did not allow for much hope for the immediate future. The plight of the poor worsened, and the gap between the rich and the poor continued to widen. The foreign debt of many countries in the South, combined with general financial instability everywhere, created conditions favouring the rise of conservative patterns of behaviour. This posed a serious threat to human development, especially because welfare policies were becoming increasingly unpopular. Churches around the world adopted "an evangelical option for the poor", and this choice influenced ecumenical discussions. "Solidarity with the poor" was proposed as a new criterion for economic reflection and action within the ecumenical movement. At its meeting in Geneva in 1980, the AGEM stated: "One of the major political forces of the 1980s is that the poor and the oppressed are rising against the forces of imperialism and political domination. Any future organization of the world must take into account the cultural, social, economic and political priorities of the poor and the oppressed... It is the excluded, the oppressed and the exploited who have paid the highest price for the prosperity and power of the affluent and the mighty, domestically and internationally. A just international order in the 1980s will only come about through a worldwide recognition of the right of the poor and the oppressed to set their own agenda in the light of their socio-cultural experience and

social biography, in a context of human solidarity."

See also **ethics, international order, justice**.

JULIO DE SANTA ANA

K.H. Dejung, *Die ökumenische Bewegung im Entwicklungskonflikt, 1910-1968*, Stuttgart, Klett, 1973 • E. Duff, *The Social Thought of the World Council of Churches*, London, Longmans, Green, 1956 • C. Elliott, *The Development Debate*, London, SCM, 1971 • C.-H. Grenholm, *Christian Social Ethics in a Revolutionary Age*, Uppsala, Verbum, 1973 • M. Lundquist, *Economic Growth and the Quality of Life: An Analysis of the Debate within the World Council of Churches 1966-74*, Helsinki, Finnish Society for Missiology and Ecumenics, 1975.

ECONOMY (OIKONOMIA). The word "economy" (Greek *oikonomia*) means the management of a household, as in Luke 16:2-4. In other New Testament passages, the word refers to divine providence (1 Cor. 9:17; Eph. 1:10, 3:2; Col. 1:25; 1 Tim. 1:4). Beginning in the 3rd century, economy sometimes indicates flexibility in the enforcement of church disciplinary rules. The bishop is to interpret and implement canon law,* and in so doing he can either follow the rules strictly or display flexibility (first council of Constantinople, 381). Departure from strictness is praiseworthy if the attitude has a positive effect on the common good of the church (Cyril of Alexandria). By the middle ages, economy clearly characterizes a departure, made by competent authorities, from strict conformity with a canonical norm.

Strictness *(akribeia)* does not always mean conformity with only written laws, since Eastern canon law never has been a system which provides answers to every kind of problem. Rather, strictness embraces the observance of the church's standards, whether written in canons or not. And internal criteria limit applications of economy.

Thus, economy does not apply to what directly involves doctrines of faith,* such as the basic principles which underlie sacramental theology, church order,* and Christian ethics. But one cannot infer that because economy is impossible in these areas, it is unrestricted in all other cases.

Economy can designate either a decision which departs from a strict norm or, more often, the principle by which one has made such a decision *(kat' oikonomian)*. For example, the council in Trullo (691) dealt with irregular marriages of clergy. While the church of Rome keeps that rule strictly, the church of Constantinople introduces "humanity and compassion" as a principle of economy. The explicit mention of "according to economy" intentionally indicates that an exceptional non-enforcement of a rule does not imply that the rule itself is considered invalid or obsolete.

In Eastern Orthodox church law several canons have sunk into oblivion, either from changes in the life setting or merely from the disappearance of the specific reasons which had provoked their promulgation. The fact that such laws are not enforced has nothing to do with economy, because the use of economy precisely supposes that normally the law is in effect.

But precedents should not simply be ignored; there is "case law" which leads to generalizations based on past decisions. Otherwise, normative canon law would constitute merely a set of theoretical statements which have no real impact on the life of the church. Resorting to economy implies that a rule in effect is purposely not applied.

However, in several occurrences doubts may arise, since limits between legitimate flexibility and transgression of a rule are not always self-evident. Many decisions "according to economy" have been strongly criticized by the upholders of rigorism. For example, it would be impossible to understand Byzantine church history between the end of the 8th century and the beginning of the 10th century without taking into account the continuous existence of two parties: one favoured leniency, the other consistently advocated strict adherence to ecclesiastical law.

The recurrent controversies of that time involved two sensitive issues: remarriages, which the rigorists held as impermissible (this concerns laypeople, since marriage after ordination is not permissible), and acceptance of irregularly ordained clerics into the Orthodox church. To understand how such controversies were possible, one must bear in mind the very nature of canon law in the Eastern church, and the different views of canon law held by the two halves of Christendom from the early middle ages onward.

In the church of the West, rules which do not belong to the province of "natural law" or do not affect "divine positive law" fall within the competency of the supreme authority of the church. Therefore, the pope is entitled either to abolish laws or temporarily to suspend their enforcement. On these grounds, dispensations may be granted. In the church of the East, the situation is completely different: the concept of fullness of power does not exist. Besides, in the East the idea that church authorities might modify ancient laws and customs is not unconditionally admitted. Consequently, in serious matters the church in the West often questions the use of economy by churches in the Eastern tradition. The most thorny questions on the use of economy bear on issues of sacramental theology, because those questions affect ecclesiology.

There are two intertwined reasons for using economy: the good of the church and pastoral concerns. In patristic literature, therefore, one finds the phrase "excellent measure of economy". With regard to penance, leniency is related to the good dispositions of the repentant sinner. This linkage is in canon 102 of the council in Trullo.

That economy has no creative power is a fundamental principle. Economy is inoperative if there is an essential deficiency in the sacramental rite or a serious disagreement over doctrine. For example, the ancient church did not recognize the baptism of the Eunomians, members of an Arian sect, because they did not believe in the Holy Trinity and had purposely altered the baptismal rite (apostolic canon 49). The first ecumenical council (Nicea 325*) did not recognize the validity of the baptism conferred by the Paulianists, although those heretics were using a correct rite. But the Paulianist doctrine on the Holy Trinity was completely at variance with the beliefs of the catholic church. On the other hand, the church did not rebaptize other heretics because their doctrine on the Holy Trinity* — albeit not completely correct — was not basically at variance with the faith of the church (as expressed in the council of Constantinople 381*). Those examples demonstrate that, especially with respect to sacramental theology, one must base the implementation of economy on objective criteria.

It seems that economy which is equated with expediency has wide possibility of application in those matters which are loosely related to doctrines of faith. For example, economy can apply to minor impediments of ordination. It may also apply to impediments of marriage. However, in several cases regarding dispensations for marriage, it would be more appropriate to speak of laxity, not of economy.

Decisions on economy fall exclusively within the competency of the hierarchy. According to the nature of the problems, either the ruling bishop or the synod of bishops makes the decisions (see **episcopacy**). Decisions can be made by a church court whose president is not necessarily the ruling bishop himself, but the bishop needs to confirm them. With respect to procedure, there are two kinds of economy: (1) antecedent economy, where an exemption is canonically requested and granted prior to an act; and (2) retroactive economy, which is granted in order to regularize an already existing uncanonical situation. In all cases, internal criteria and moral justification limit the use of economy.

PETER L'HUILLIER

J.H. Erickson, "Sacramental 'Economy' in Recent Roman Catholic Thought", *The Jurist*, 48, 1968 • F.J. Thomson, "Economy: An Examination of the Various Theories of Economy Held within the Orthodox Church, with Special Reference to the Economic Recognition of the Validity of Non-Orthodox Sacraments", *Journal of Theological Studies*, 16, 2, 1965.

ECUMENICAL ASSOCIATION OF AFRICAN THEOLOGIANS.

Founded in 1977 with offices in Yaoundé, Cameroon, EAAT holds assemblies and consultations: as in 1980, on the word of God and human languages (published in the *African Theology Series*); in 1983, on black theology and liberation in South Africa (published in *Bulletin of African Theology*); in 1984, on dialogue between African and European theologians on the mission of the church today (published in *Bulletin of African Theology*); in 1985, on the liberation of Africa (published in the *African Theology Series*); in 1987, on Africa and the Bible; and in 1988, on inculturation and ecumenical dialogue.

ANS J. VAN DER BENT

ECUMENICAL ASSOCIATION OF THIRD-WORLD THEOLOGIANS.

The idea of an Ecumenical Association of Third-World Theologians (EATWOT) was inspired by young Africans in conversations with Latin Americans and Asians in Louvain, Belgium (1974), and later discussions at the WCC Nairobi assembly (1975). The EATWOT organizing meeting took place in Dar es Salaam, Tanzania (1976); 21 theologians from Africa, Asia and Latin America and a black theologian from the USA participated.

Although many theologians of Africa, Asia and Latin America had already begun to offer challenging critiques of the dominant theology of Europe and the USA, they were not keenly aware of each other's critiques of Western theology and were even less knowledgeable about the creative theological alternatives that each was seeking to provide. Third-world theologians were developing critiques and constructing theological projects in isolation, as if they had nothing to learn from each other. Such isolation existed also among minority groups in the USA and the Caribbean — both were failing to dialogue with each other and also with the peoples of Africa, Asia and Latin America.

The formation of the EATWOT represented an attempt by third-world theologians to end their destructive isolation. As oppressors band together to protect and to expand their privilege, so the oppressed and their supporters on all continents must find ways to unite in a common struggle for justice. When theologians reported on the socio-political exploitation of the poor* in their countries, the religious justifications of it in their churches, and the resistance against injustice by the poor and their supporters, the commonality of the situations of oppression and the struggles of liberation in the third world became increasingly clear to all participants. They recognized the need to continue their dialogue in a facilitating organization.

Three major concerns shaped the development of the EATWOT: (1) the desire to encourage theologians of each continent to work together in order to deepen their analyses of the socio-political and religio-cultural structures in their countries and the need to develop a theology that is accountable to the poor masses; (2) the concern to encourage and assist theologians in Asia, Africa and Latin

America to participate in a joint effort towards the development of a tri-continental third-world theology that all can support; and (3) the hope to develop a creative, challenging dialogue with progressive theologians of Europe and North America which would lead to an interpretation of the faith* that all Christians could embrace as a necessary ingredient of the gospel.

The next three international EATWOT assemblies were held in Ghana (1977), Sri Lanka (1979) and Brazil (1980). Each focused on the theology of the continent where the meeting took place.

In Ghana, African theologians began the process of developing an African theology that emphasized the indigenization of the gospel and the liberation of the people of Africa from the cultural and economic domination of the churches and theologies of Europe and the USA (*African Theology en Route*, 1979). At the Sri Lanka conference, Asian theologians concentrated on the problem of doing theology as a Christian minority amid overwhelming poverty and multifaceted religiosity (*Asia's Struggle for Full Humanity*, 1980). The Brazil conference focused on Latin American liberation theology, the most well known and controversial of all third-world theologies, which emphasizes the role of economic analysis and socio-political transformation in the doing of theology (*The Challenge of Basic Christian Communities*, 1981).

After these four assemblies, the similarities and differences among the theologies of the third world became quite clear. Africans accented indigenization, Asians focused on religious pluralism, and Latins stressed class analysis. Their similarities included a stress on liberation as the central core of the gospel, the need to re-read the Bible in the light of the "hermeneutical privilege" of the poor (see **hermeneutics**), the rejection of the dominant theologies of Europe and the USA, and the identification of theology as an activity subordinate to a commitment of solidarity with the poor.

Because of the uncertainty and debate regarding the meaning of "third world", USA minorities were not included as founding members of the EATWOT. However, they were invited to attend the meetings. The first minority member was invited to join the organization at the Sri Lanka meeting. The

inclusion of US minorities meant that the term "third world" was not limited to geographical space. Theologies of liberation that speak with the voice of the poor and marginated in history have emerged as the central concern of the EATWOT.

Following the three major assemblies, which focused on the distinctive contributions of the theologies of each continent, the EATWOT members held their next assembly in New Delhi, India, in order to begin the process of developing a third-world theology that everyone could support. The task was not at all easy. Centuries of separation and alienation from each other could not be bridged in a few years. Differences remained sharply evident, with each group vigorously defending the unique theme of its theology. But their similarities held them together and enabled Asians, Africans, Latins, Caribbeans, and USA minorities to celebrate their differences as God's gift to humanity (*Irruption of the Third World: Challenge to Theology*, 1983).

After seven years of dialogue with each other, third-world theologians decided that they were prepared to have a dialogue with progressive theologians of Europe and North America. About 40 third-world theologians and an equal number from the first world met in Geneva (1983) in order to assess their mutual concerns about theology and the role of the church in the liberation struggles of the poor. They evaluated the nature of their differences and sought for common grounds for doing theology in a world divided by racism,* sexism* and classism. Like the previous EATWOT conferences, the Geneva meeting represented the beginning of a process in which first- and third-world Christians are seeking to overcome centuries of alienation and separation.

It was clear that the theologians of Asia, Africa, Latin America, and their respective groupings in the USA are no longer prepared to accept the dominant theology of Europe and North America as the authoritative word on the nature and task of theology. Theologies which are shaped in Europe or the USA by privileged groups are grossly inadequate for dealing with the problems of the poor in the third world. If there is to be a theological interpretation of the faith that serves all Christians, then the representatives of all must participate in making it (*Doing Theology in a Divided World*, 1985).

The EATWOT is a male-dominated association. The awareness of the problem of sexism* in the third world and particularly among the theologians of liberation emerged gradually — first at the Ghana and Sri Lanka meetings in a minor way, then in Brazil, and then was vigorously debated at the New Delhi conference. In Geneva, with the presence of first-world women (especially from the USA), the EATWOT was confronted with the problem of sexism in a way it found impossible to ignore. Although third-world women recognized their differences with their first-world sisters, they also acknowledged their mutual solidarity, especially in regard to the deeply rooted sexist attitudes of male third-world theologians.

During the Geneva meeting, the women members of the EATWOT set in motion plans for several national and continental consultations that would lay the foundation for an international assembly of women a week before the general assembly in Oaxtapec, Mexico (1986; see *With Passion and Compassion: Third World Women Doing Theology*). The major concern of the EATWOT is to develop a theology that is committed to, as the women at Oaxtapec said, "total liberation and the achievement of full humanity for all, women and men alike".

JAMES H. CONE

All reports published by Orbis (Maryknoll, NY).

ECUMENICAL CHURCH LOAN FUND.

ECLOF was formed in 1946 as a Swiss non-profit foundation enabling Christians to demonstrate solidarity with the churches of Europe in the difficult times after the second world war. The hardships suffered by those churches prompted Willem Visser 't Hooft to propose setting up an ecumenical fund to help in the rebuilding of churches by providing loans. In 1948 ECLOF was incorporated into the WCC as part of the Division (now Commission) on Inter-Church Aid, Refugee and World Service.

The board of ECLOF, like those of its national committees, is composed of pastors and laypeople with professional training in administration or finance or other fields necessary for analyzing and advising projects. The board has also permanent members from the WCC staff and representatives from member churches and related agencies.

The first countries to belong to the ECLOF network were Germany, the Netherlands, Belgium and Hungary. In the 1960s the German and Dutch national committees repaid their capital to Geneva because the situation in those countries and their churches had improved. With these funds ECLOF was then able to extend its activities to the third world.

ECLOF sets up revolving funds in various countries to finance loans to projects which are screened and recommended by the national committees and ratified by the board or the executive committee. In 1989 there were 59 national ECLOF committees which exercised authority delegated to them from Geneva and were empowered to approve and finance projects up to an amount agreed in advance. Of these 59 committees, 35% are in Africa, 14% in Latin America, 19% in Europe, 15% in Asia, 10% in the Caribbean, and 7% in Australia and Oceania.

In 1970 ECLOF extended its activities by financing development projects other than strictly church-related ones. This wider practical involvement gradually has led ECLOF to realize that its role is not solely financial. Through its working methods ECLOF promotes new attitudes in the churches of the third world and among the popular groups it serves; the loan, plus the process of reflection and the technical assistance that accompany it, helps to avoid or reduce the danger of dependency on donations.

The national ECLOF committees are ecumenical in their composition and activities and provide an opportunity for encounter, discussion and reflection between lay leaders and church ministers. ECLOF's work is of particular importance as a model in the context of the foreign-debt crisis, which affects third-world countries. It would mark an improvement if international banking loans for development were issued on the same conditions as those offered by ECLOF: repayment in local currency, with interest rates below the going market rates and with flexible terms depending on the nature of the project. In this way, the costs of development efforts would be shared between North and South.

FRANKLIN CANELOS C.

ECUMENICAL CONFERENCES.

In the history of the ecumenical movement, major international conferences on various subjects and by various organizations have acquired shorthand titles of identification — the cities in which the meetings were held and the years. This article reviews 36 major conferences held between 1910 and 1990, listing the stated main themes and briefly summarizing the highlights. A separate article deals with WCC assemblies.

Edinburgh 1910 (Scotland), world missionary conference. Eight commissions dealt with (1) carrying the gospel to all the non-Christian world, (2) the church in the mission field, (3) education in relation to the Christianization of national life, (4) the missionary message in relation to non-Christian religions, (5) the preparation of missionaries, (6) the home base of missions, (7) missions and governments and (8) co-operation and the promotion of unity.

This conference marked the climax of earlier gatherings through which Protestants had been drawing together in their purpose to bring the gospel to the world. It was in a succession which began with gatherings held in New York and London in 1854, continued in Liverpool in 1860, in London in 1878 and 1888, and especially in New York in 1900.

The conference did more than build on past achievements in evangelism* and unity:* it prepared for the turbulent years which lay ahead, blazed new trails in Christian fellowship and co-operation, and inspired and enlisted men and women who later were outstanding leaders in the ecumenical movement. The first report emphasized the worldwide mission* of the church. The second stressed the development of what later were called the younger churches and made clear that a leading purpose of the missionary enterprise was to bring into being self-governing, self-supporting and self-propagating churches in every region. The eighth report was ecumenical in both title and intention.

The conference was, however, overwhelmingly Anglo-American. Representatives from Europe were a small minority, and overall there were very few younger church leaders. In consequence, Edinburgh 1910 did not immediately do as much to spread the ecumenical spirit among the churches on the continent as it did in the British Isles and the US and among British and American missionaries. Representatives of the Roman Catholic Church (RCC) and the Orthodox churches were not present at Edinburgh, and indeed had not been invited.

Stockholm 1925 (Sweden), universal Christian conference on Life and Work.* Main subjects were (1) the purpose of God for humanity and the duty of the church, (2) the church and economic and industrial problems, (3) the church and moral and social problems, (4) the church and international relations, (5) the church and Christian education, and (6) methods of co-operation and federative efforts by the Christian communions.

Convened by Archbishop Nathan Söderblom of Sweden, this conference was the fruit of a vision earlier seen by church leaders who agonized over a war-torn humanity and the weakness of a divided Christianity. Although it affirmed in unmistakable terms the responsibility of the churches for the whole life of Christians, it did not produce any ecumenical social creed or solve any controversial problems. Making a rapid survey of the needs of contemporary society, appealing to the conscience of the Christian world and indicating possible lines of advance, Stockholm 1925, in its social idealism, generated a species of optimism which reflected the spirit of the times. Emphasizing the role of the Spirit, it presented a social analysis which could assess the nature of the crisis of post-war Europe. The main achievement of the conference was a fresh discovery of the Christian fellowship which transcends denominational oppositions and national antagonisms. The conference took care not to offend the susceptibilities of the churches by raising divisive confessional issues. Stockholm 1925 went forward under the slogan "doctrine divides, service unites".

The final message, the only official conference statement, expressed penitence for the failure of the churches to do their duty and affirmed the obligation of the churches to apply the gospel "in all realms of human life — industrial, social, political and international". But the message limited "the mission of the church"; it "is above all to state principles, and to assert the ideal, while leaving to individual consciences and to communities the duty of applying them with charity, wisdom and courage".

The presence of a strong delegation from the Orthodox churches, led by the patriarchs of Alexandria and Jerusalem, was of great significance. The RCC was not represented, though it sent a few individual observers. Only six younger churches — from India, China and Japan — sent representatives.

Lausanne 1927 (Switzerland), world conference on Faith and Order.* The sections considered (1) the call to unity, (2) the church's message to the world: the gospel, (3) the nature of the church, (4) the church's common confession of faith, (5) the church's ministry, (6) the sacraments, and (7) the unity of Christendom and the relation thereto of existing churches.

Over 400 delegates from 108 churches participated in this first F&O meeting. The majority were officially appointed representatives of their churches. Africa, America and Europe were well represented, but Asia sent only two nationals and some missionaries. Those to whom a conference of this kind was a novel experience felt a certain bewilderment, in spite of repeated clarifications of the purpose of the meeting by the president Charles H. Brent. It was meant as a forum at which "both agreements and disagreements were to be carefully noted... It is not a conference that aims at complete agreement, still less at a united church." The misconceptions of the aim were at least partly responsible for a marked feature of the latter part of the conference — a series of separate declarations on their position by the members of different communions.

The conference accepted the reports of sections 3-6 without negative votes. The report of section 2, accepted also by the Orthodox members, was destined to play an important role in the whole ecumenical movement. Part of it was incorporated into its own message by the Jerusalem meeting of the International Missionary Council* in 1928, and it was used by the Church of Christ in China in its constitution as its statement of faith. In section 7 some delegates strongly objected to the proposal of collaborating with Life and Work* and the World Alliance for Promoting Friendship through the Churches.* This approach would commit the conference to a conception of ecumenical relations in which interchurch collaboration would be emphasized at the expense of unity in faith and order. The section

report was referred to the continuation committee; the final revision appeared as an appendix to the Lausanne report.

Jerusalem 1928, International Missionary Council* (IMC). Sections dealt with (1) the Christian message in relation to non-Christian systems of thought and life, (2) religious education, (3) the relation between the younger and the older churches, (4) the Christian mission in the light of the race conflict, (5) the Christian mission in relation to industrial problems; (6) the Christian mission in relation to rural problems, and (7) international missionary co-operation.

This meeting marked noteworthy advances beyond Edinburgh 1910. The preparation was carefully developed through seven volumes of comprehensive studies. The growing worldwide threat of secularism to Christianity was given major attention (see **secularization**). Missions were thus seeking to touch life from more angles than in earlier years. The increased place of the younger churches at Jerusalem was partly due to their rapid growth in numbers and leadership. To follow up the concerns of the problems of industrialization, the meeting authorized what came to be known as the Department of Social and Economic Research and Counsel. Its first head, J. Merle Davis, conducted numerous studies in Africa and Latin America and referred to the problem of obtaining an adequate economic basis for the support of the younger churches. From Jerusalem also came the impetus for the creation of the International Committee on the Christian Approach to the Jews, established as a sponsored agency of the IMC in 1930.

Oxford 1937 (England), Life and Work* conference. Sections were (1) church and community, (2) church and state, (3) church, community and state in relation to the economic order, (4) church, community and state in relation to education, and (5) the universal church and the world of nations.

This conference on church, community and state was undertaken with great care and thoroughness. In the face of gathering social crisis, the Stockholm combination of Christian social idealism, spiritual enthusiasm and pacifism had come into question, to be replaced by new tougher trends in Christian thought represented by theologians like Reinhold Niebuhr, Emil Brunner and Karl Barth.

No ecumenically organized reflection on theology and social ethics since Oxford has matched it in quality and thoroughness. Among the theological and ethical insights that emerged were the following. First, the liberal notion of a continuity between history* and the kingdom of God* is to be rejected. History is not redemptive. Evil will persist until the end. Second, a Christian social order is impossible, as is the solution of social problems by a direct application of Christian "moral principles". The Bible offers no direct solutions for contemporary political and social problems. The task of the ecumenical movement and of the churches is to outline tentative or approximate ethical positions (Oxford called them "middle axioms"*) for the encounter of faith* with social issues. Third, one must acknowledge the place of power in the struggle for justice.* The state is necessary, but its dependence on power relativizes its authority. The need for human freedom and the right of the church to resist the state must be emphasized "if obedience would be clearly contrary to the command of God". Fourth, Christians must both critique liberal democracy, without repudiating the democratic principle, and reject atheistic and totalitarian communism, while not joining the Western self-righteous anti-communist crusade. No economic system (capitalism, socialism, communism, etc.) will eliminate injustice; the only recourse for Christians is a pragmatic, discriminating action which maximizes social justice and human welfare within different systems. Fifth, since the church is not *of* the world but *for* the world, its action for social justice (as distinct from the response of individual Christians) differs from that of political and social power blocs that defend particular interests (see also **church and state**).

Edinburgh 1937 (Scotland), Faith and Order.* Four sections considered (1) the grace of our Lord Jesus Christ, (2) the church of Christ and the word of God, (3) the church of Christ: ministry and sacraments, and (4) the church's unity in life and worship.

This second world conference on Faith and Order marked a definite advance upon that held ten years earlier at Lausanne. The advance was due chiefly to two factors. Among the 443 delegates appointed by the churches, 95 had already been at Lausanne. Many delegates of different countries and churches were now meeting as old friends who through their contact had grown in the understanding of confessions other than their own. The other change was due to the theological preparation, a new development in the F&O movement. The delegates of the Orthodox churches reiterated the view they had already expressed at Lausanne: "The general reunion of Christian churches may possibly be hastened if union is first achieved between those churches which present features of great similarity with one another."

Friction arose over the proposal offered by a Life and Work* meeting that a world council of churches be formed. After debate, however, the meeting concurred with the proposal, and ultimately a Committee of 35 was appointed; it met in London in July 1937. The Edinburgh conference appointed a committee of 60 persons to examine and report to it on the proposals of the Committee of 35. After a long and at times heated debate, the recommendation to work towards a world council of churches was carried.

Tambaram 1938 (India), International Missionary Council.* Sections comprised (1) the authority of the faith, (2) the growing church, (3) evangelism, (4) the life of the church, (5) the economic basis of the church, and (6) the church and the state.

Larger in numbers and more representative than Jerusalem (1928), the gathering dramatized the fact that the Christian church had become a truly worldwide company. The representatives of the younger churches constituted slightly more than half of the official delegates. A major emphasis at Tambaram was on the church.* The younger churches, while mostly minorities in their countries, were now strong enough to assume more of the burden not only of their own support and direction but also of the evangelization of their nations. The first section was reinforced by a preliminary book *The Christian Message in a Non-Christian World*, written at the request of the IMC by Hendrik Kraemer. Significant, too, was a large volume, *The Economic and Social Environment of the Younger Churches*, edited by J. Merle Davis. Tambaram provided a sense of Christian unity on the eve of the war soon to break out.

Amsterdam 1939 (Netherlands), world conference of Christian youth. The main theme was "Christus Victor", with seven interest groups: (1) Christian youth in a world of nations, (2) Christian youth in the nation and the state, (3) Christian youth in the economic order, (4) Christian youth and race, (5) Christian youth and education, (6) Christian marriage and family life, and (7) the church: its nature and mission.

This first youth conference was sponsored by the World Christian Student Federation,* the World Alliance of YMCAs,* the World YWCA,* the Ecumenical Youth Commission of Life and Work, and the World Alliance for Promoting Friendship through the Churches.* The age of the 1,500 delegates ranged from 18 to 35, with one-third over 25. The conference faced the growing menace of war. W.A. Visser 't Hooft was conference chairman, R.H. Edwin Espy secretary, H.L. Henriod and Francis House chairman and secretary for worship services, Suzanne de Diétrich chairwoman for Bible study, and Tracy Strong chairman for discussion groups.

The quality of work and reporting varied from section to section. Those who had concentrated on theological preparation and those who had devoted their energies to the study of practical steps found little common ground for sharing. The two great centres of discovery lay in the Bible studies and worship services, although great difficulty was experienced when the problem of different services of holy communion had to be faced. The conference was an adventure in close co-operation among the various Christian youth movements and reflected the geographical extension of the world Christian community and its cultural varieties more clearly than had any previous ecumenical meeting. Many delegates at this conference were to become leaders of the ecumenical movement in the next decades.

Oslo 1947 (Norway), conference of Christian youth. With the main theme "Jesus Christ Is Lord", discussion groups considered (1) freedom and order, (2) Christian responsibility in a secular environment, (3) world order, (4) man and his inventions, (5) the family in community, (6) the Christian congregation's life in the local community, (7) education in the modern world, (8) the Christian faces the situation of the Jew, and (9) the church faces the world.

This second world gathering of young Christians had not quite the same quality of adventure and pioneering which had charac-

terized Amsterdam 1939. It was marked by a new sobriety over the realities of the world situation and the grateful recognition of the lordship of Christ over the whole church and over the world. This conference did not adopt an official message; the delegates themselves were the message as well as the messengers. The very day the meeting began, fighting had broken out between the Netherlands and Indonesia. A joint statement from Dutch and Indonesian youth affirmed "the right of the Indonesian people to liberty and independence". Also the French delegates issued a declaration on the colonial question. Representatives from Great Britain and India rejoiced that India was on the threshold of independence.

Whitby 1947 (Canada), International Missionary Council.* The general theme was "Christian Witness in a Revolutionary World". Subjects treated were (1) partners in obedience, (2) the "supranationality" of missions, and (3) the functions of the IMC.

Even during the terrible period of the second world war, the IMC had been able to maintain to a remarkable degree the fabric of co-operation, especially through the vast programme of support for "orphaned missions". The title of the report of the meeting, *Renewal and Advance*, well indicated the dominant mood of the conference.

It had not yet become clear, however, how drastic the changes were which the world had undergone as a result of the convulsions of the war years. The complete extinction of the colonial pattern, most dramatically in China but also throughout the rest of Asia and Africa, was still in the future. The extent of the spiritual damage which Christianity had suffered could not yet be assessed. Nevertheless, "expectant evangelism" and "partnership in obedience" were the two slogans of the meeting. Representatives of older and younger churches met separately to discuss the devolution of responsibility from mission agencies to churches with their own evangelistic tasks.

Willingen 1952 (Federal Republic of Germany), International Missionary Council.* Major themes were (1) the missionary obligation of the church, (2) the indigenous church — the universal church in its local setting, (3) the role of the missionary society, and (4) reshaping the pattern of missionary activity.

This meeting was widely judged to have

failed in its major task. But subsequent history has shown how significant it really was. Two issues dominated the section which was preparing a statement on the missionary obligation of the church. On the one hand, a sharp attack was launched, primarily by J.C. Hoekendijk of the Netherlands, against the church-centred view of missions which had dominated the thinking of the IMC since Tambaram (1938). On the other hand, and closely related to the first, there was a strong effort made, especially by the North American study group which had prepared for the conference, to relate the missionary task to the signs of Christ's present sovereignty in the secular world. While the Willingen meeting could not achieve an acceptable reconciliation of the theological tensions, its work has proved fruitful in the subsequent years. Its statement "The Calling of the Church to Mission and Unity" echoed much of what the WCC central commmittee had said in 1951.

Lund 1952 (Sweden), Faith and Order.* Section titles were (1) Christ and his church, (2) continuity and unity, (3) ways of worship, and (4) intercommunion.

Already in 1938 and 1939 F&O had appointed three international theological commissions to study the church,* worship* and intercommunion.* Three published volumes provided materials for discussion at this third world conference. The theme of "outward" unity, introduced at Edinburgh in 1937, was further developed. "We agreed", the conference report stated, "that there are not two churches, one visible and the other invisible, but one church which must find visible expression on earth." While the participants differed on whether certain doctrinal, sacramental and ministerial forms are of the essence of the church, they looked forward to a time when all Christians could have unrestricted communion* in sacrament and fellowship. The message to the churches asked "whether they should not act together in all matters except those in which deep differences of conviction compel them to act separately", an approach later called the Lund principle.* For the first time, F&O discussed the social, cultural, political and racial elements and so-called non-theological factors in church divisions and church unity.

Kottayam 1952 (India), Christian youth. The main theme was "Jesus Christ the Answer

— God Was in Christ Reconciling the World unto Himself". Discussion groups studied (1) interpreting the gospel of Jesus Christ, (2) Jesus Christ and the search for personal freedom, (3) the church's witness to Jesus Christ, (4) the claims of Christ in personal and family relationships, and (5) Christ in a world of tensions.

Two-thirds of the 350 delegates from 55 countries and 28 confessions came from Asia, the Middle East and the Pacific. For the first time, youth from other parts of the world worked at ecumenical questions in an Asian and not a Western setting. Participants struggled with the issues raised by the movements for political independence, the renascence of other faiths, the challenge of communism and the need to re-think their understanding of the church.* The meeting emphasized that "the church must become a place where human worth and common responsiblity are actualized. Creative love must express itself not simply in acts of mercy, genuine and important though they may be, but also in attempts to achieve a more just economic and social order." The theme would recur often and would profoundly influence the work of the WCC.

Accra 1958 (Ghana), International Missionary Council.* Group discussions pondered (1) Christian witness in society and nation, (2) the Christian church facing its calling to mission, (3) the Christian church and non-Christian religions, (4) the place and function of the missionary, and (5) what "partnership in obedience" means.

An important item on the conference agenda was the draft plan of integration of the IMC and the WCC which the joint committee of the two bodies had prepared. There were serious reservations about this plan, and a great deal of further discussion was needed. The conference accepted a statement on "The Christian Mission at This Hour" which took as its starting point "the Christian world mission is Christ's, not ours". The statement affirmed that the distinction between older and younger churches was no longer valid or helpful because it obscured the fact that every church, because it is a church, has the same missionary calling. Preparations were made to set up the Theological Education Fund,* which over the years was to bring about a considerable change in the quality and strength of theological education at various seminaries and schools in the third world.

Montreal 1963 (Canada), Faith and Order.* Three sections studied (1) Christ and the church, (2) worship, and (3) Tradition and traditions.

This fourth world conference received the final report of the theological commissions. Section 1 was in two parts, based on a North American and a European contribution. While this report did not contain much that was an advance over previous work, it opened up, through the very disagreements which surfaced in the discussions, new avenues of F&O study. The traditional differences ranged from the insistence on apostolic succession to the view that there is no sufficient New Testament authority to warrant ordination. Increasing consensus on the theological basis of ministry did not lead to greater agreement on matters of order. Section 2 stated that, despite many disagreements regarding holy communion, the churches could agree that the eucharist* is "a sacrament of the presence of the crucified and glorified Christ, until he come, and a means whereby the sacrifice of the cross, which we proclaim, is operative within the church". Lund had not specifically studied the area of Tradition and traditions. The approaches of the North American and European contributions to section 3 at Montreal were different: the first took a more historical perspective, while the second centred on the dogmatic issue of scripture and Tradition. There was nevertheless a large measure of agreement in the final report: "By the *T*radition is meant the gospel itself, transmitted from generation to generation in and by the church, Christ himself present in the life of the church. By *t*radition is meant the traditionary process. The term tradition*s* is used in two senses, to indicate both the diversity of forms of expression and also what we call confessional traditions, for instance the Lutheran tradition or the Reformed tradition."

Mexico City 1963, WCC Division on World Mission and Evangelism.* The sections dealt with (1) the witness of Christians to men of other faiths, (2) the witness of Christians to men in the secular world, (3) the witness of the congregation in its neighbourhood, and (4) the witness of the Christian church across national and confessional boundaries.

This meeting was the first one of the division since the integration of the IMC into the WCC in 1961. With its main theme "Witness in Six Continents", it broke new ground by paying expert attention to the specific problems of mission in Europe and North America. Section 1 did not yield a clear consensus on dialogue with people of living faiths (see **dialogue, interfaith**). Section 4 advocated advance in the direction of more international and ecumenical action in the field of mission. Throughout the meeting there was a vigorous discussion about mission in the context of six continents. The Department on Studies in Evangelism, following the New Delhi assembly (1961), had launched a worldwide study on "The Missionary Structure of the Congregation";* it raised radical questions concerning the nature of the church* and evangelism.* The Department on Missionary Studies had also engaged in several research projects on the missionary situation of the churches in specific areas. Both departments were integrated into the Department on Studies in Mission and Evangelism in 1967.

Swanwick 1966 (England), interchurch aid* (ICA), refugee and world service. The sections were (1) development aid, (2) uprooted people, (3) the role of ICA in the use and training of the churches' manpower, and (4) criteria for interchurch aid projects (the so-called Herrenalb categories of 1956).

With 239 participants from 78 countries, Swanwick was the first large international ecumenical gathering in which representatives of the RCC took part. This world consultation urged the churches to align themselves more closely to governmental and intergovernmental programmes of development aid. The fact that the WCC had more than 200 churches in its fellowship meant a wholly new relationship between the churches themselves. Within the Council, those churches had equal status; requests for aid and offers of aid had taken on a different connotation. There was no more room for paternalistic charity, only for partnership and sharing. Ecumenical diakonia had thus gained significance.

Geneva 1966 (Switzerland), world conference on Church and Society.* Sections considered (1) economic development in a world perspective, (2) the nature and function of the state in a revolutionary age, (3) structures of international co-operation — living together in peace in a pluralistic world society, and (4) man and community in changing societies.

This conference marked the first truly worldwide Christian examination of social issues and responsibility. Under the circumstances, it was bound to have a revolutionary impact on ecumenical social thought, opening up controversy, especially in the Western churches. For the first time, an equal number of participants came from the countries of Africa, Asia, Latin America and the Middle East, and from Western Europe and North America. It was the first gathering to which churches of the Soviet Union and other Eastern European countries made substantial contributions. Also present were a large number of Roman Catholic theologians and laypersons, most of whom had been active in the preparation of the Second Vatican Council's Constitution on the Church in the Modern World (1965). Controversies focused on three ecclesiological points: (1) the right way in Christian social ethics to relate biblical and theological traditions to the fast-changing conditions in modern societies, (2) the ambiguities of the word "revolution"* and the need for a clearer statement of the theological ideas which underlie a positive and critical response to the various demands for revolutionary change, and (3) the different ecclesiologies which surface when the church (or some groups in the church) becomes involved in political and social action. The demand that the ecumenical movement support the revolutionary struggle for justice* in the third world intensified and dramatized this old ecclesiology problem.

Bristol 1967 (England), Faith and Order.* The five sections dealt with (1) creation, new creation and the unity of the church, (2) the eucharist, a sacrament of unity, (3) ministry, church union negotiations, (4) Tradition and traditions, and (5) general faith and order problems.

When the F&O commission met at Aarhus (Denmark) in 1964, it had planned a programme for a new period, in the light of the numerous recommendations and suggestions from Montreal 1963. Bristol 1967 faced the tasks which had grown out of the constant expansion of the ecumenical movement, of relationships with world confessional families, of the progress and problems of national church unions, and of the co-opera-

tion of F&O with other WCC departments. In all these efforts the decisive questions were the understanding of church unity,* of full communion,* and of the theological reflections which can best serve the unity of the church through the most adequate methods. Bristol completed the first stage in the "God in Nature and History" study and authorized the second stage of the "Man in Nature and History" study.

Montreux 1970 (Switzerland), ecumenical assistance to development projects. The working groups discussed (1) the debate about development, (2) policy and procedures for church support to development projects, (3) structure and organization of ecumenical assistance to development projects, (4) technical assistance for church-sponsored development, and (5) the mobilization of funds.

This world consultation emphasized that all Christian development programmes should promote social justice* and the self-reliance of the community. They should help to provide new creative patterns of life for groups and communities whose lives have been disrupted by the effects of economic growth, and help to build bridges between separated groups in the interest of a more integrated society. The consultation recommended co-operation with intergovernmental agencies, especially the UN development system. Such co-operation is not a matter of simply supplying church funds but of involving the participation of local churches in planning and co-operation. The conference appealed to the churches to contribute to the promotion of education for development by changing people's attitudes and by mobilizing public opinion towards fundamental changes in the social, economic and political structures on national and international levels.

Louvain 1971 (Belgium), Faith and Order.* The various committees were (1a) authority of the Bible, (1b) "giving account of the hope that is in us", (2a) catholicity and apostolicity, (2b) worship today, (2c) participation in and methods of Faith and Order, (3a) "baptism, confirmation and eucharist", (3b) "beyond intercommunion", (3c) the ordained ministry, (4a) study on the council of Chalcedon, (4b) common witness and proselytism, (4c) conciliarity and the future of the ecumenical movement, and (5) church union negotiations and bilateral conversations.

Besides studying these themes and concerns, this meeting also concentrated on the comprehensive theme "The Unity of the Church — the Unity of Mankind". Problems related to this theme had already become acute, and the commission decided to provide essential clarifications. It was clear that confessional differences alone no longer called into question the unity of the church. Churches were urged to bring to fruition the fellowship given to them in Christ, amid the debates of the present. Only thus can they become signs of the presence of Christ today.

Lima 1971 (Peru), World Council of Christian Education.* This was the last gathering of an ecumenical federation of national and international bodies involved in Christian education (founded in 1924). After almost ten years of conversations, the union of the WCC and the WCCE was finally consummated. The Lima meeting was in fact dispersed; 17 *encuentros* were held in capital cities of Latin America. The Lima meeting faced the important issue that to educate is not so much to teach as it is to become committed to a reality in and with people, that it is to liberate humankind, under God and his power, from the bonds that prevent the development of God's image.

Bangkok 1973 (Thailand), WCC world conference on mission and evangelism. Under the main theme "Salvation Today", sections considered (1) culture and identity, (2) salvation and social justice in a divided humanity, and (3) churches renewed in mission.

This conference faced the theological theme of liberation,* affirmed the right of every Christian and every church to cultural identity, and urged them to formulate their own response to God's calling in a theology, a liturgy, a praxis, and a form of community that were rooted in their own culture.* The Africans, especially, attacked the West's "imperialism over theology". The meeting drew attention to the indissoluble connection between the individual and social aspects of salvation:* to respond to Christ and his missionary call means to be involved in the struggle for social justice, peace and a fully human life. The conference debated at length the question of the structure of missionary relationships which would reflect genuine equality between partners. Proposals ranged from a temporary moratorium to new forms of co-operation between churches. Bangkok 1973 was undoubtedly one of the most contextual and interdisciplinary ecumenical missionary conferences.

Bucharest 1974 (Romania), Church and Society. The main theme, "Science and Technology for Human Development", was developed in several sections: (1) the significance for the future of pressures of technology and population on environment, and of natural limits to growth, (2) self-reliance and the technical options of developing countries, (3) quality of life and the human implications of further technological change, (4) human settlement as a challenge to the churches, (5) world social justice in a technological age, and (6) the theological understanding of humanity and nature in a technological era.

Organized principally by the WCC Sub-unit on Church and Society, this world conference was the last in a series of ecumenical study conferences which the WCC convened for its five-year study of the "Future in a World of Science-based Technology". The study was launched to evaluate from ecumenical perspective the social and human implications of the modern scientific and technological revolution (see **science and technology**). Bucharest was the first major WCC meeting in a socialist and predominantly Orthodox setting. The conference sought to state clearly some practical ways in which Christians must re-think their societies in this new historical situation. It also laid the basis for a future ecumenical inquiry on the "just, participatory and sustainable society". This inquiry helped clarify issues for later debate, but it was unable to resolve fundamental differences, for example, between those who emphasize the centrality of justice and those who stress the critical importance of sustainability in any responsible society.

Accra 1974 (Ghana), Faith and Order.* The two main themes were giving account of the hope that is within us, and the unity of the church.

The F&O commission had launched a study on the theme of hope* because the churches could overcome their divisions only by starting from the centre of their faith. As long as they continue to deal with inherited differences, they will not be ready to enter the one committed fellowship to which they are called. Only as churches recognize each other as living in and proclaiming the same faith* will they have the freedom to move forward together to become the one Body of Christ within the world's tensions and conflicts.

But what does church unity* require in each region of the world? Theological and ecclesiological debates tend to speak about unity in too general terms, but ultimately, since unity is the committed fellowship of particular people in a particular place, progress can be made only if the specificity of each situation is taken seriously. The conference, finally, discussed the draft statement on baptism, eucharist and ministry (see *Baptism, Eucharist and Ministry*).

Chiang Mai 1977 (Thailand), dialogue with people of living faiths and ideologies. The conference theme was "Dialogue in Community".

This world consultation, sponsored by the WCC Sub-unit on Dialogue, continued the difficult discussion of section 3 at the Nairobi assembly (1975): "Seeking Community: The Common Search of People of Various Faiths, Cultures and Ideologies", which expressed fears about the betrayal of mission* and the danger of syncretism.* The consultation sought to clarify the Christian basis for seeking community by focusing theological reflections on specific issues and particular contexts, to indicate the nature of the Christian community in a pluralistic world and to suggest guidelines which may help Christian communities in pluralist situations to become authentic communities of service and witness without diluting their faith or compromising their commitment to Christ. In 1979, the WCC central committee meeting in Kingston, Jamaica, approved the *Guidelines on Dialogue with People of Living Faiths and Ideologies* and recommended it to member churches "for their consideration and discussion, testing and evaluation, and for their elaboration in each specific situation".

Bangalore 1978 (India), Faith and Order.* Main themes were (1) a common account of hope and (2) growing together into unity. Subjects of discussion groups were (1) the meaning of "conciliar fellowship", (2) towards communion in one faith, (3) growing into one eucharistic fellowship, (4) the discipline of communion in a divided world, and (5) new ecumenical experiences and existing ecumenical structures.

The most significant achievement of the Bangalore meeting was the F&O document "A Common Account of Hope". The debates were not easy. One difference in particular had seemed insurmountable. Some wanted to emphasize the hope* which is above all hopes — Jesus Christ, the risen Lord, who has already overcome the world. But others wanted to state, clearly and strongly, that Christian hope finds expression in concrete human hopes. The final document was seen as doing justice to both positions.

The second theme was intimately connected to the first. The more successful the churches are in giving a common account of their hope in spite of their divisions, the more they will grow in unity.* Bangalore 1978 also faced the fact that unity is not merely a distant goal; however necessary it may be to stress that the churches still have a long way to go, the fact remains that a good stretch of the road is already behind them.

MIT 1979 (Massachusetts Institute of Technology, in Cambridge, Massachusetts, USA), Church and Society. Sections were (1) the nature of science and the nature of faith, (2) humanity, nature and God, (3) science and education, (4) ethical issues in the biological manipulation of life, (5) technology, resources, environment and population, (6) energy for the future, (7) restructuring the industrial and urban environment, (8) economics of a just, participatory and sustainable society, (9) science/technology, political power and a more just world order, and (10) towards a new Christian social ethic and new social policies for the churches.

This world conference on "Faith, Science and the Future" faced a situation that was entirely different from the one faced by the 1966 Church and Society meeting. The issues of science and technology* had become far more complex and controversial, and both church and society were questioning the future of technologically organized and controlled social systems. Science and technology raised those important questions about the relation of faith to science which many churches, in both technologically developed and technologically developing countries, were only beginning to consider. All present political and economic systems have made assumptions about technological and economic planning which now required re-thinking. The scientific-technological world-view had come under challenge and, with it, many previously accepted social goals. Although the 1979 conference highlighted the problems, it could not resolve them. It could, however, help the churches to understand both the promise and the threat posed by modern science and technology and the challenge these present to traditional Christian thinking.

Melbourne 1980 (Australia), world mission and evangelism.* The theme "Your Kingdom Come" was considered in four sections: (1) good news to the poor, (2) the kingdom of God and human struggles, (3) the church witnesses to the kingdom, and (4) Christ — crucified and risen — challenges human power.

The Orthodox churches were involved both in the preparation and holding of this mission conference, and many Roman Catholic theologians, as in the Bangkok conference (1973), participated in the meeting. The main findings were, first, that the kingdom* which Christians pray for is the reign of the One who died outside the gates. Jesus Christ affirmed his centrality by giving it up. He moved towards the periphery in order to seek the marginalized and downtrodden. Second, the poor* challenge missionary criteria. Jesus established a visible link between the coming of the kingdom and the proclamation of the good news to the poor. Third, evangelism* takes place in the midst of human struggles. There is no evangelism without involvement, and no Christian involvement without evangelism. Fourth, at the centre of church life is the eucharist,* pilgrim bread and missionary food, for a people on the march. The eucharist is a powerful example of self-emptying. Finally, unless the pilgrimage route leads the churches to visible unity* in the one God, the one Christ and the one Holy Spirit, the mission entrusted to them will remain incomplete.

Lima 1982 (Peru), Faith and Order.* Sections were (1) the work of F&O, (2) F&O and the WCC, (3) the Latin American context, (4) baptism, eucharist and ministry, (5) towards the common expression of the apostolic faith today, (6) steps towards visible unity, (7) the unity of the church and the renewal of human community, and (8) the community of women and men in the church.

For the first time, the F&O commission met on Latin American soil, where many strands of liberation theology* and new forms of church community have had their origin. Building on the theological convergences formulated in the F&O studies on "Giving Account of the Hope" and the "Common Statement of Our Faith", the Lima conference integrated these understandings in a long-term model for a common affirmation of the faith of the apostolic church, under the title "Towards the Common Expression of the Apostolic Faith Today". The final text of *Baptism, Eucharist and Ministry** was unanimously approved as having reached "such a stage of maturity that it is now ready for transmission to the churches"; it quickly acquired the shorthand title BEM. In deciding to pursue anew the earlier study on "Unity of the Church — Unity of Humankind", the conference agreed to place the classic F&O concern for church unity "on a broadened horizon and to develop its implications for Christian service and mission in the contemporary world".

Stavanger 1985 (Norway), Faith and Order.* The three programme areas were (1) baptism, eucharist and ministry, (2) apostolic faith, and (3) unity and renewal.

The conference reviewed the reception* process of BEM, i.e. how the stated convergences were being received by the churches. The two major projects, "Towards the Common Expression of the Apostolic Faith Today" and "The Unity of the Church and the Renewal of Human Community", were re-examined. Other continuing concerns were F&O and ecumenical spirituality (Week of Prayer for Christian Unity* and Ecumenical Prayer Cycle*), proposals for a fifth consultation of united/uniting churches and church union negotiations, bilateral and multilateral dialogues, and the call to a fifth world conference on Faith and Order. The commission celebrated the 75th anniversary of the F&O movement.

Larnaca 1986 (Cyprus), interchurch aid,* refugee and world service. The theme was "Called to Be Neighbours".

Since the first world consultation on interchurch aid (Swanwick 1966), far-reaching changes had taken place in the world situation. By 1986 the optimism of the mid-1960s about the possibilities of development* had given way to a mood of frustration and an awareness that the people and the churches were losing in the global struggle for justice.* It was against this backdrop that this second world consultation on ICA, refugee and world service took place. There was relatively little discussion of development or projects; rather, discussions centred on the struggle for life and the need to be in solidarity with people. The emphasis was on a comprehensive, preventive and liberating diakonia* in the discipleship of Jesus Christ.

El Escorial 1987 (Spain), sharing of ecumenical resources. The theme was "Koinonia: Sharing Life in a World Community".

This world meeting climaxed a ten-year ecumenical discussion of "resource sharing" that had been initiated by the Nairobi assembly (1975). A central emphasis was that the resources to be shared ecumenically are not only the material wealth and power which a few control but also the churches' rich theological understandings, spiritualities, cultures, expressions through music, prayer, song and dance, and perhaps most important of all, the testimonies of those who are suffering. It raised serious questions about ecumenical relief and development programmes, including those of the WCC.

San Antonio 1989 (Texas, USA), world mission and evangelism.* Under the theme "Your Will Be Done: Mission in Christ's Way", sections studied the topics (1) turning to the living God, (2) participating in suffering and struggle, (3) the earth is the Lord's, and (4) towards renewed communities in mission.

With its great diversity of participants (including, for the first time, consultants of other faiths) and a wide-ranging agenda, San Antonio was planned not to feature authoritative ecumenists instructing the delegates but to create a context in which persons active in mission could address each other. Its two significant trends, said the conference message, were "the spirit of universality (catholicity) of the gathering, and its concern for the fullness of the gospel", holding "in creative tension spiritual and material needs, prayer and action, evangelism and social responsibility, dialogue and witness, power and vulnerability, local and universal". Especially extensive were discussions of the tension between dialogue* and witness* which, a section report said, "we appreciate... and do not attempt to resolve".

Budapest 1989 (Hungary), Faith and Order. A major item on the agenda was the responses to BEM, the 1982 F&O text on baptism, eucharist and ministry. In a statement to the churches on BEM, the commission said the text has "created a new ecumenical situation. It expressed broad convergence on basic Christian affirmations, and revealed sometimes surprising agreements." But, it added, "we still have far to go" in terms of "further growth into unity".

It noted serious disagreements which persist on "the relation of word and sacrament, the understanding of sacrament and sacramentality, the threefold ministry, succession in ministry, the ministry of men and women, the relation of men and women, the relation of scripture and Tradition, and ecclesiology".

The meeting also reviewed plans for the fifth world conference on F&O, projected for 1993, and received a report which suggested, as part of future F&O work, a consultation on "unresolved ecumenical issues concerning ministry, especially the ordination of women", and more attention to "the gifts of the Holy Spirit within the church". Another report urged a major study on ecumenical perspectives on ecclesiology, concentrating on "basic perspectives of unity and diversity" (see **church**).

Seoul 1990 (Korea), world convocation on justice, peace and the integrity of creation.* Coming after regional consultations, the convocation completed the first stage of a process initiated by a decision at Vancouver 1983 "to engage member churches in a conciliar process of mutual commitment (covenant) to justice, peace and the integrity of all creation" (JPIC). A report of the convocation's responses to a preparatory document examining contemporary threats to JPIC and offering a "faith perspective" by which Christians may "reflect upon the world" was not fully covered because of unexpectedly long discussion of its first section. Ten affirmations — on power as accountable to God, God's option for the poor, the equal value of all races and peoples, the creation of male and female in God's image, truth as the foundation of community, the peace of Jesus Christ, creation as beloved of God, the earth as the Lord's, the dignity and commitment of the younger generation, and human rights as given by God — provided a "basic direction" for Christian commitment to JPIC. An "Act of Covenanting" (see **covenant**) provided specific examples of "faithful action" in relation to a just economic order, demilitarization of international relations, preservation of the atmosphere from the threat of global warming, and the eradication of racism* and discrimination.

See also **bibliographies, WCC assemblies**.

ANS J. VAN DER BENT

ECUMENICAL COUNCILS. The English language has only one term to render two different realities designated in other languages by two different terms: *consilium (conseil, Rat)*, and *concilium (concile, Konzil)*. The World *Council* of Churches belongs in the first category; our concern in this article is rather with the second phenomenon.

The idea of an ecumenical council and its fundamental role in the church is deeply rooted in almost all Christian traditions. The best evidence is the constant and regular re-emergence of the ideal of a truly ecumenical council in the contemporary ecumenical movement, as the most significant way to manifest and to seal the unity of all. Considerable differences exist, however, concerning the conditions required for the convening of such a council.

Origin. The fundamental reference for every council remains the Jerusalem assembly of Acts 15, in which the essential elements may be found: representation of the whole ecclesial community, assistance of the Holy Spirit,* and unanimity in the decisions that have to be applied in the life of the church. The special assistance of the Holy Spirit is explained by certain ancient writers with a reference to Matt. 18:20: "Where two or three are gathered in my name, there am I in the midst of them." This reference also suggests a close link between the councils and the liturgical life of the church.

The institution of the ecumenical council as such developed in the framework of the Roman-Byzantine empire. In the presence of grave questions of faith* or church order* that threatened to divide the church* and the Christian world, the emperor took the initiative to convene the bishops of the oikoumene (the inhabited world), identified practically with the empire. This is precisely the origin of the adjective "ecumenical", with the meaning of "universal". Personally or through his delegates, the emperor also supervised the course of the debates, without interfering directly — at least in principle — in the discussions, leaving the theological decisions to the bishops alone; nevertheless the emperor confirmed these decisions and gave them the force of law in the empire.

Conditions. The conditions for a council to be received (see **reception**) as ecumenical were not fixed from the beginning by the councils themselves. They developed gradually in history, sometimes through long confrontations and because of the necessity to refute certain assemblies which claimed to be ecumenical but could not be received as such because of the non-conformity of their decisions with the scriptures and the ancient Tradition. Docility to the Holy Spirit and faithfulness to the word in the scriptures are obviously primary requirements. Only at the seventh ecumenical council (Nicea II, 787), in order to demonstrate the invalidity of the iconoclastic council of Hieria (754), were the following criteria clarified: the presidents of the main churches have to be in agreement, in particular the patriarchs of Constantinople, Alexandria, Antioch and Jerusalem, and above all the bishop of Rome has to collaborate; the decisions should not only be regional, but they should reach out to the ends of the earth and be coherent with previous councils. The participation of the bishops of the (five) principal sees (the "pentarchy") is considered as being necessary to guarantee the representativity of the council, which can be ecumenical only if the whole church is able to identify with it. Representatives of all situations and vocations in the church can be invited to the council, but according to Roman Catholic and Orthodox traditions only the bishops have the right to vote. The Roman Catholic Church (RCC) has strongly emphasized the essential role of the bishop of Rome (see **primacy**): for a council to be ecumenical, he has to convene it, to preside over it (personally or through his delegates) and to approve it (Vatican II*, canon law 1983). But this is a later development that cannot be applied strictly to the first councils celebrated in common by the East and the West. The Orthodox church developed the view that a council is in fact ecumenical only if the whole church accepts its decisions; this is at present the opinion of the majority in Orthodoxy, while others believe that it does not correspond entirely to the self-awareness of the ancient councils. This is also the first reason why the future pan-Orthodox "holy and great council", in preparation since the 1960s, does not want to appropriate the adjective "ecumenical", leaving it to the later judgment of the whole church.

The aim of the ecumenical council is the safeguarding and growth of communion* in the faith* and the sacraments.* Therefore the normal way of proceeding is to seek not a majority vote but as much unanimity as possible. An ecumenical council has reached its final objective only when it results in a strengthening of full communion.

Authority. The authority of the councils is no more than the authority of truth, and truth is guaranteed when it is proclaimed in conformity with the scripture and in accordance with the faith of the whole church, throughout the world and throughout history. For the RCC, Vatican II stipulates that, in the ecumenical council, the college of bishops exercises in a solemn way the supreme power it enjoys over the universal church, in union with the bishop of Rome, its head (Dogmatic Constitution on the Church 22); the emphasis put on the essential and organic role of the pope is characteristic of the RCC. In the Orthodox church the ecumenical council also represents the supreme authority of teaching and decision making: once a council has been received as ecumenical, its authority is final and its decisions are binding for everyone everywhere (see **teaching authority**). For Luther, the only authority belongs to the scriptures, and the councils have no other authority than results from their conformity with the scriptures. For Calvin, the authority of a council depends on its docility to the Spirit, its faithfulness to the scriptures and the fact that it expresses the unity* of the church.

The Roman Catholic and Orthodox traditions speak of the infallibility* of the ecumenical council, as the official expression of the infallibility of the church itself, but it would not be entirely correct historically to project this notion back to the first councils, in which the consciousness of an infallible authority was not explicit; rather, they had the assurance of being in the truth whenever they were united in spirit and heart with the universal church in direct line with the apostolic tradition.* Luther rejects the infallibility of the

ecumenical councils, by virtue of the *sola scriptura*; in his view, councils can err and did err in fact (Leipzig 1519).

List. The first four general councils occupy a privileged place in the consciousness of most of the Christian traditions, because of their importance for the formulation of the Christological and Trinitarian dogmas. Several ancient writers compare them to the four gospels. The first was Nicea I* (325), which condemned Arianism and defined Christ as being of one essence *(homoousios)* with the Father. The second, Constantinople I* (381), proclaimed the divinity of the Holy Spirit. The third, Ephesus (431), condemned Nestorianism and defined the unity of the person of Christ. The fourth, Chalcedon* (451), condemned monophysitism and defined two natures (divine and human) in the one person of Christ. The Apostolic (Assyrian) Church of the East has built its own tradition on the first two councils, ignoring the ones that followed. The Oriental Orthodox churches* (Armenian, Coptic, Ethiopian, Syrian and Indian churches) recognize the first three councils but reject the fourth, mainly for reasons of terminology and political circumstances. Luther (1538) recognizes the special status of these four councils because of their Christological importance, without conceding any other authority than that of their faithfulness to scripture. Calvin writes: "We readily receive the ancient councils like those of Nicea, Constantinople, the first of Ephesus, Chalcedon, and those similar... we honour and reverence them" *(Institutes* 4.9.8), but he is almost completely silent about the councils that followed. The Anglican formularies accept the first four councils.

The churches of the East and West held three other councils together: Constantinople II (553), Constantinople III (680-81), Nicea II (787). The Roman Catholic and Eastern Orthodox churches recognize them unanimously as ecumenical. These seven councils are sometimes called the councils of the undivided church. They are so much part and parcel of the Orthodox consciousness that the Eastern Orthodox church calls itself "the church of the seven ecumenical councils". In the Eastern church no council held after the separation from the West in 1054 received the title "ecumenical".

The Latin church continued to convene

other general councils in the middle ages, and in modern and contemporary times. Afterwards, in the RCC some of them were given the title "ecumenical", but without any official decision being taken to do so: Constantinople IV (869-70), Lateran I (1123), Lateran II (1139), Lateran III (1179), Lateran IV (1215), Lyons I (1245), Lyons II (1274), Vienne (1311-12), Constance (1414-18), Basel-Ferrara-Florence (1431-45), Lateran V (1512-17), Trent* (1545-63), Vatican I* (1869-70), Vatican II (1962-65). Does this not constitute a new obstacle on the road to unity? A possible response may be found in the formula used by Pope Paul VI, in 1974, on the occasion of the seventh centenary of the second council of Lyons: he never used the term "ecumenical" but spoke instead of "the sixth of the general synods held in the West".

The conciliar movement of the late middle ages. At a time of great tensions and profound divisions in the Western church (the so-called great Western schism, e.g., occurred 1378-1417), the conciliar movement gained considerable strength (see **conciliarity**). According to the theory formulated by certain medieval canonists from the 12th century onwards, the general council constituted the supreme authority in the church, and the pope himself was subject to it; nevertheless the principle of the primacy of Rome was not questioned. The general council was considered to be the only authority capable of restoring unity to the church and introducing the radical reforms that had become necessary. The council of Constance (1414-18) proclaimed solemnly that the pope owed obedience to the general council in everything concerning the faith, the extirpation of the schism and the reform of the church; it also fixed a periodic meeting of the councils, which were destined to govern the church in the future. The convocation of the council of Basel in 1431 was partly in answer to this decision, but as a result of the many confrontations between the members of the council and the pope of Rome, the prestige of the council gradually diminished, the extreme positions lost their strength and finally the papacy emerged from it re-inforced. The fifth Lateran council (1512-17) practically marked the end of the movement. The internal quarrels prevented the application of the urgent reforms, while the fear of a resurgence of the conciliar move-

ment made the papacy reluctant to convene a new council. All this had far-reaching consequences for the events surrounding the Reformation of the 16th century.

Towards a "genuinely universal council". In the course of a gradual clarification of the aim of the ecumenical movement ("the nature of the unity we seek"), the WCC's New Delhi assembly (1961) expressed the conviction that the time had come to undertake a new study of the role of the councils in the first centuries and of their methods and influence. During the period 1964-67, Faith and Order* began a study of the nature and structure of the ecumenical councils in the ancient church, and of the significance of the conciliar process in general for the ecumenical movement. The Uppsala assembly (1968) asked the churches "to work for the time when a genuinely universal council may once more speak for all Christians". In 1969 the theme was again raised in the central committee, and F&O organized a consultation on the council of Chalcedon and its reception by the churches, as an exploration of its influence and significance for the present situation. The description of the unity we seek as a "conciliar fellowship", at Nairobi (1975), has to be seen in the same perspective, as it enlarged the New Delhi approach ("all in each place") to a confession of faith and a life of communion on the universal level, regarding conciliarity as an integral part of the essence of the church. After Vancouver (1983) the expression "conciliar process" was used to designate the common commitment to justice, peace and integrity of creation.* But the Orthodox especially objected to the use of the term "conciliar", since for them, as for the Roman Catholics, a genuine council already presupposes unity in faith and must meet some precise criteria. The term was abandoned in official use, but in many places Christian people spontaneously continue to consider the different convocations on the local, regional or global level as provisional stages on the long road to unity. One day they would like to celebrate this unity together in a gathering that would represent them all and would be a visible sign of the communion that unites all churches scattered around the world.

FRANS BOUWEN

B. Botte et al., *Le concile et les conciles: Contribution à l'histoire de la vie conciliaire de l'Eglise,*

Paris, Cerf, 1960 • *Councils and the Ecumenical Movement*, WCC, 1968 • F. Dvornik, *General Councils of the Church*, London, Burns & Oates, 1960 • H. Jedin, *Kleine Konziliengeschichte* (ET *Ecumenical Councils of the Catholic Church: An Historical Outline*, New York, Herder, 1960) • P. Meinhold, *Konzile der Kirche in evangelischer Sicht*, Stuttgart, Kreuz, 1962 • Pro Oriente ed., *Ökumene, Konzil, Unfehlbarkeit*, Innsbruck, Tyrolia, 1979.

ECUMENICAL DECADE OF THE CHURCHES IN SOLIDARITY WITH WOMEN.

Approved by the WCC central committee at its meeting in January 1987, the Ecumenical Decade of the Churches in Solidarity with Women is a long-term framework (1988-98) for action in solidarity with women. Several important events and decisions in the history of the WCC have led to this action.

1948: At the first WCC assembly in Amsterdam, Sarah Chakko, an Orthodox from South India, presented a report from 58 countries on the role and status of women in the church.

1949: The Commission on the Life and Work of Women in the Church was formed.

1954: At the 1954 WCC assembly the Department of Co-operation of Women and Men in the Church was created, headed by Madeleine Barot.

1974: A world consultation on "Sexism in the 1970s" named and recognized sexism* as an oppression, in so far as it refused to allow women their just place in church and society.

1975: The WCC fifth assembly, which coincided with the UN International Women's Year, had a plenary session on women's issues which then were reflected in the WCC reports and recommendations.

1978: As a result of the WCC recommendations, the study process on the Community of Women and Men in the Church* was started.

1981: The study culminated with an international conference held in Sheffield, England, which again highlighted the "web of oppression" in which women are trapped: sexism, racism and classism. Following the conference, the WCC central committee affirmed that equal participation* between men and women should be a goal, starting with the composition of the WCC decision-making and consultative bodies, during and after the Vancouver assembly.

1983: The WCC sixth assembly in Vancouver recommended that "the concerns and perspectives of women should become integral to the work of all WCC units and subunits".

1985: At the end of the UN Decade for Women, the WCC central committee urged member churches to eliminate the teachings and practices that discriminate against women, as a Christian response to the "forward-looking strategies" adopted by the UN Decade and as a follow-up of the Community of Women and Men in the Church study.

1986: A questionnaire was sent by the subunit on Women to all member churches to assess the status of women in the church. The results showed that religious and cultural attitudes militate against social and structural changes and that the higher the decision-making level, the fewer the number of women in leadership positions.

1987: Responding to the findings of the questionnaire, the central committee in January 1987 approved plans to launch the Ecumenical Decade.

The decade was launched in 1988. It is meant for churches, for women specifically at the local level, and for the sub-unit's wider networks of concerned women's organizations and action groups. The objectives are: (1) empowering women to challenge oppressive structures in the global community, their churches and communities; (2) affirming — through shared leadership and decision making, theology and spirituality — the decisive contributions of women in churches and communities; (3) giving visibility to women's perspectives and actions in the work and struggle for justice, peace, and the integrity of creation;* (4) enabling the churches to free themselves from racism, sexism and classism, and from teachings and practices that discriminate against women; and (5) encouraging the churches to take actions in solidarity with women.

The priorities of the decade are the same as the sub-unit's programme emphases: (1) women's full participation in church and community life; (2) women sharing their perspectives and commitments to justice, peace, and the integrity of creation; (3) women doing theology and sharing spirituality.

The decade is a call to the churches to re-examine their structures and to provide for equal sharing of power, so that with fuller contributions of women the life of the church and the community can be enriched. The sub-unit will make a mid-decade assessment in 1991-93 to see how far the goals of the decade have been achieved in the churches.

See also **women in church and society**.

PRISCILLA PADOLINA

ECUMENICAL DEVELOPMENT CO-OPERATIVE SOCIETY. The WCC
established the EDCS in 1975 as "an instrument for the promotion of justice and development among the poor" and as "a proper means of re-deploying part of the investment sources of the churches". By using a model of a just economic order, the churches can play a more concrete role in economic development by mobilizing credit for development in poor areas, which is promoted through loans and investments with co-operative enterprises. The finances originate from churches, religious orders and individuals who support development as a liberating process for economic growth, social justice and self-reliance.

The EDCS has 220 Roman Catholic, Protestant and Orthodox members. As of December 1988 it had mobilized $25 million in share capital; 175,000 people have improved their economic status and self-reliance through participation in enterprises financed by EDCS. Fundings are made to groups unable to qualify for credit because their collateral is insufficient or their repayment capability is unproved; yet the EDCS has had loans outstanding for ten years and has maintained the full face value of the loan fund and shareholders' investments.

The EDCS puts into practice resource sharing: for the poor who share the borrowed capital by repaying it, and for churches and individuals (1) by investing with people normally considered unworthy or too powerless to qualify, and (2) by sharing power. The majority of the board of directors are from developing countries.

DOUGLAS V. BRUNSON

ECUMENICAL DIRECTORY. During
the Second Vatican Council* discussions on the text of the Decree on Ecumenism,* the

Roman Catholic bishops were requesting more detailed directives and guidelines for pastoral practices. After Vatican II, the Secretariat for Promoting Christian Unity* (SPCU; since 1989, a pontifical council [PCCU]) followed a general working procedure of issuing a series of guidelines on specific topics at intervals rather than a thick book of directives at one time.

The *Directory, Part One* (1967) concerned the setting up of diocesan and national ecumenical commissions; the validity of baptisms conferred in other Christian communions; the fostering of "spiritual ecumenism" within the RCC; and the "sharing of spiritual activities", including liturgical worship and occasional eucharistic hospitality. *Part Two* (1969) outlined ecumenical principles and practices for seminaries, colleges and universities. In 1970 the SPCU published reflections and suggestions concerning ecumenical dialogue; and in 1975, a study on forms of ecumenical collaboration at regional, national and local levels. SPCU officers also were consulted for the new norms in mixed (and interchurch) marriages (1970), more specific norms when other Christians may be admitted to eucharistic communion in the RCC (1972), the reception of adult baptized Christians into the RCC (1972), and the celebration of the eucharist for deceased non-Catholic Christians (1976).

Meanwhile, as a new post-Vatican II tradition of ecumenical common witness was developing, the holy see was drafting a new code of law for the Latin church, eventually promulgated in 1983 (as of 1990, the code for the Oriental Catholic churches is still in draft). Many of the canons directly treat ecumenical concerns. It is hoped that by the end of 1990, the PCCU will be able to publish a revised, comprehensive *Ecumenical Directory*. "While fully respecting the competence of local and territorial church authorities, and recognizing that many judgments... can best be made at the local level", the directory "gives general norms of universal application to guide Catholic participation in ecumenical activity", so as to guarantee that it "is in accordance with the unity of faith and discipline that binds Catholics together" (n.7).

The directory presents the Roman Catholic foundations for ecumenical life and action (teaching, attitudes/motivations and spirituality); the ecumenical formation of all the faithful — clergy and laity (studying the word of God in scriptures, preaching, catechesis, liturgy) in various settings (family, parish, schools, seminaries, hospitals, associations and institutes); "spiritual activities" (prayer in common; baptismal celebrations; sharing in sacramental life, especially the eucharist; marriages and mixed marriages; funerals); ecumenical co-operation and common witness (social and cultural life; peace, justice and stewardship of creation); communications media; and structures (college of bishops, bishops' conferences and patriarchal synods, dioceses, religious communities, the PCCU).

TOM STRANSKY

J. Coriden, T. Green & D. Heintschel eds, *The Code of Canon Law: Text and Commentary*, New York, Paulist, 1985 • *Ecumenical Directory*, rev. ed., Vatican, PCCU Information Service, 1990 • T. Stransky & J. Sheerin eds, *Doing the Truth in Charity*, documents of the holy see on ecumenical matters, 1964-80, New York, Paulist, 1982.

ECUMENICAL LEARNING. Ecumenical learning has always been considered an important task, by which Christians and churches, suffering under divisions and their deleterious effect on common witness,* have come together to work towards visible Christian unity* and renewal* of the human community. To discern, admit and, where necessary, overcome existing theological, denominational, historical and cultural differences between Christians and their churches is possible only where comprehensive learning takes place. Therefore, the ecumenical movement has always considered itself a learning movement. Ecumenical learning was long seen as something that happens more or less in all that is done in an ecumenical spirit or context, deliberately or not (in meetings, conferences, visits, joint services, interchurch aid, etc.): "ecumenical learning takes place as an international learning by experience, by a direct encounter and confrontation with situations in a world horizon, with all their shocking and frustrating accompaniments" (Werner Simpfendörfer). But since the mid-1950s there has been a growing awareness of ecumenical learning as a fundamental task and a distinctive programme within the ecumenical movement and its churches.

A statement of the central committee of the WCC in 1957 described ecumenical learning as "fostering understanding of, commitment to and informed participation in, this whole ecumenical process. The vision of the one, missionary church in process of renewal, when it is apprehended by Christians, leads them to an ecumenical commitment, i.e. to participation in the process of letting the churches be more truly the church." Ecumenical learning (or "ecumenical education" or "education for ecumenism", terms which were used at that time) can therefore no longer be limited to the communication of the facts, history, background, structures and functions of the ecumenical movement as part of a curriculum in theological, Christian or religious education. And even imparting information about existing differences between Christians and their churches or about new convergences being achieved covers only one part of a much more comprehensive task of equipping Christians to live as a liberating and reconciling community in a divided world. Certainly, ecumenical learning has to incorporate this kind of information if ecumenism is to be more than a sort of sentimental "being together". Where the Roman Catholic Church took part in the ecumenical discussions about ecumenical learning (e.g. in the Joint Working Group*), it was emphasized that sharing knowledge about others is integral for the formation of priests and laypeople. But equally important for ecumenical learning is the involvement in the deeper levels of ecumenical experience in the life of the Christian community at worship, in service and witness, by sharing life with others, in becoming vulnerable to the suffering of others, and by becoming neighbours to strangers. Ecumenical learning, therefore, has to be described as a dimension rather than a segment of the whole educational task of the church, although it appears also in particular learning projects or programmes, such as development education, education for mission, or education for justice, peace and the integrity of creation.* Its pedagogical approach moves from *teaching about* to *learning together with*.

To describe the task of ecumenical learning more precisely, we must distinguish three elements which determine the understanding of "ecumenical": the *ecclesiological* element, which gives rise to the question of how Christians of different churches, confessions and denominations can move towards more visible unity (see **church**); the *missionary* element, which requires a global awareness and a new understanding of the inter-relatedness of the proclamation of the gospel and social commitment, of evangelism and humanization (see **evangelism, mission**); and the *social-ethical* element, which, by linking the unity of Christians and the renewal of humankind, stresses commitment to the cause of justice, peace and the integrity of creation in a world seen as a dwelling place for all. In a particular learning project, one or another of these three factors may predominate, but none can be completely lacking. Thus ecumenical learning differs from global learning or international learning or multi-cultural learning programmes which have been initiated by UNESCO or other international or national organizations, and which have much in common with ecumenical learning. Since the beginning of the 1960s the call for a theory and for new content, methods and experiments in ecumenical learning has become more distinct, and the need for substantial materials (in terms of curricula for theological, Christian and religious education) which enable children, young people, adults, clergy and laity to understand and to take part in the ecumenical process has become more obvious. First steps towards a learning theory for ecumenical learning were envisaged, and finally Ernst Lange pleaded for an ecumenical didactic, theory and method which enabled people, while remaining rooted in a specific denominational, cultural, historical and socio-political context, to become ecumenically committed and share the experiences of others.

Further discussions led Vancouver 1983 to elevate learning as "a constitutive dimension for the church as church" and helped to develop the following characteristics of ecumenical learning. Ecumenical learning *transcends barriers* — of origin and biography, individual as well as community limitations, because it responds to the exhortation of the word of God* and the far-reaching horizons of God's promise. Ecumenical learning *is action-oriented*. It is not satisfied with information but wants to enable Christians to act in order for them to learn, to be right with God and with one another in word and deed. Ecumenical learning *is learning in community*. People are asked to establish relationships with one another, and also with those who are far away

and with what is unfamiliar. Ecumenical learning *means learning together*. People have to detect the global in the local, the unfamiliar in the context of their own environment, in order to become aware of their own conditions and implications. Ecumenical learning also *means inter-cultural learning*. It seeks to promote the encounter of different cultures, traditions and forms of life because only a widening of perspectives will bring about an experience of the riches of creation* in nature,* history* and culture.* Finally, ecumenical learning *is a total process*: social and religious learning are not separated from one another but constitute a unity.

ULRICH BECKER

Alive Together: A Practical Guide to Ecumenical Learning, WCC, 1989 • S. Amirtham & C. Moon eds, *The Teaching of Ecumenics*, WCC, 1987 • U. Becker, "The WCC and the Concept of Ecumenical Learning", *Education Newsletter*, 1, 1985 • *Christian Education and Ecumenical Commitment*, WCC, 1966 • P.A. Crow, "Unity, Mission, Truth: Education for Ecumenism in the 1980s", *Midstream*, 19, 1980 • E. Lange, *Die ökumenische Utopie* (ET *And Yet It Moves*, WCC, 1979) • W. Simpfendörfer, "Ecumenical and Ecological Education: Becoming at Home in the Wider Household of the Inhabited Earth", *The Ecumenical Review*, 34, 1982.

ECUMENICAL PRAYER CYCLE.

The EPC, a book of prayers for each area of the world, was produced initially in response to a request made by the WCC fifth assembly (Nairobi 1975) that ways be found of deepening spiritual bonds among the churches of the world. The EPC was first published in 1978 under the title *For All God's People*. A subsequent edition was authorized by the central committee in 1984 and, under the slightly revised title *With All God's People*, became available in 1989.

Arising out of the long-standing practice in the Ecumenical Centre in Geneva of praying regularly for member churches around the world, the EPC represents a systematic attempt to make available for wider use a cycle of prayer which ensures that peoples and churches all over the world are prayed for on a regular basis during the course of the 52 weeks of the year. It has been described by one user as "the only satisfying way of praying in this kind of interdependent world".

Consisting of maps, information and appropriate prayers, translated into a number of different languages and in some instances considerably subsidized, the first EPC was welcomed as a significant contribution to ecumenical prayer. It has been used in a variety of different situations: in Sunday worship, in theological colleges, by religious orders, in lay training academies, by Christian councils and by many individuals. It seemed a natural choice for Christians to use in worship in a well-known Indian teaching hospital already devoted to healing and wholeness and in the setting of a church committed to unity. The use of the cycle imparted a sense of support and solidarity to hard-pressed pastors in a particularly isolated part of Africa, and it also provided a focus of intercession in the course of a weekly celebration of the eucharist in a Lutheran parish in New York. It has been available, in a number of different languages, in the chapel of a well-known international airport, giving travellers a global picture of the church, present in every part of the world.

In the second edition, the change in title has certain implications for its contents. There is an increase of prayer material from the regions themselves, thus giving users a better opportunity worldwide to pray *with* their sisters and brothers using, wherever possible, the words they themselves might use on matters about which they would be most concerned to pray. A striking number of concerns such as unity, peace, justice, cities, refugees, young people and unemployment are held in common by Christians nearly everywhere, while others, very specific to an area and situation, call for special understanding and sensitivity. Differences in circumstances and of temperament result in a wide variety of collects, litanies, creeds, lamentations and thanksgivings.

In keeping with the underlying theme of interdependence, the current EPC moves from one yearly cycle to the next with the closing prayer of the Vancouver assembly: "As the earth keeps turning, hurtling through space; and night falls and day breaks from land to land; let us remember people — waking, sleeping, being born, and dying — of one world and of one humanity. Let us go from here in peace."

See also **prayer in the ecumenical movement, spirituality in the ecumenical movement**.

JOHN CARDEN

J. Puls, *Every Bush Is Burning: A Spirituality for Our Times*, WCC, 1985 • J. Puls, *A Spirituality of Compassion*, Mystic, CT, Twenty-third Publications, 1988 • L. Vischer, *Intercession*, WCC, 1980 • *With All God's People: The Ecumenical Prayer Cycle*, WCC, 1989.

ECUMENICAL PRESS SERVICE.

The roots of EPS lie in the little-explored "ecumenical journalism", which began in the late 19th and early 20th centuries. In the wake of the Stockholm conference of 1925, and under the umbrella of the Life and Work* movement launched by that gathering, the International Christian Press Commission began its work. Among other things, it circulated "ecumenical letters" among church leaders and journalists.

Towards the end of 1933, this ecumenical communication activity was named the International Christian Press Information Service (ICPIS). In the 1930s the situation of the church in Germany in the face of Nazism was a major focus of attention. The first in the ICPIS "information series" appeared in March 1934. As such, it probably has the best claim to be the first issue of what is now EPS (the name was changed in 1947).

Aimed at church-related and secular journalists and other communicators, the combined circulation of EPS and its French counterpart, Service oecuménique de presse et d'information (SOEPI), is about 3,000. Church leaders, national staff members and libraries are also on the mailing list.

De facto, the WCC is the institutional sponsor of EPS and SOEPI, though officially EPS is a service of the WCC and three other ecumenical bodies: the World YWCA,* the World Student Christian Federation,* and the World Association of YMCAs.* In the past, two organizations which became part of the WCC (the International Missionary Council and the World Council of Christian Education) sponsored EPS and SOEPI, as did the United Bible Societies.

In a review of its first 50 years, published in a souvenir anniversary issue (July 1984), Lutheran pastor and communications researcher Larry Jorgenson noted trends in EPS coverage over the years. It has, he observed, become "less a house organ and more a press service", less North Atlantic, less interested in "ecumenical greats".

In 1990, after several years of discussion, planning is under way for a new Geneva-based Ecumenical News Service as part of a wider ecumenical news network. ENS could begin as early as 1992, and would be a successor of EPS, SOEPI, and other church-supported news services.

See also **communication in the ecumenical movement**.

THOMAS HARTLEY DORRIS

ECUMENICAL SHARING OF RESOURCES.

For many churches, involvement in sending and receiving personnel and funds for mission,* interchurch aid* and development* has had a considerable effect on their international relationships and ecumenical participation. The WCC in turn has played an active role in the interchurch aid project system, fostered reflection on relationships in mission and promoted sharing of personnel ecumenically. Out of this background, Ecumenical Sharing of Resources (ESR) has emerged as a conceptual framework for new relationships that would free the churches from traditional roles of being either a sending (giving) or a receiving body and enable them to overcome structures of inequality and dependency between rich and poor. In some countries the issues of ESR are often taken up under the term "partnership".

The vision of ESR implies a broad understanding of what is meant by "resources", including spirituality, culture and human resources as well as finance. It calls for just relationships based on equality, which allow for mutual accountability, sharing of power and true interdependence. It requires holding together mission, development and service, which are often treated separately, both in theology and in church organizational structures.

The process. Ecumenical reflection on resource sharing has been a consultative process involving a gradually widening range of participants: first, the church-related agencies for world service and development in the North and churches and national councils of chur-

ches in the South; later, agencies for world mission, regional ecumenical organizations and network groups related to WCC sub-units.

ESR began as a study called for by the WCC central committee in 1976, following the Nairobi assembly, where interchurch aid, mission and development had been discussed in the wake of the debate on the moratorium proposed by some church leaders in Africa and Asia. The moratorium proposal raised fundamental questions about the selfhood of the receiving churches and the self-understanding of churches accustomed to seeing themselves solely as senders or givers. The study was undertaken in an effort to provide an ecumenical platform for reflection. A report was brought to the central committee in 1980, which issued a message to the churches, recommended the study guide *Empty Hands* and endorsed recommendations for WCC programme units. The message and the study guide reflected the basic concept of ESR as described above. In the ensuing period, attention focused on the elaboration of a new "resource-sharing system" for the WCC, implementing the ESR principles. A highlight of this phase was the Glion consultation in 1982.

The sixth assembly (Vancouver 1983) emphasized ESR as one of the priority areas for WCC programmes and insisted on the "comprehensive understanding... as part of a continuing dialogue on the mission and service of the church... to facilitate models... not a heavy, centralized structure".

This comment resulted in a significant shift in the process. A third phase began with the aim to formulate an ecumenical discipline for the sharing of resources, to which all the participants — including the WCC — would be called to commit themselves. One of the main obstacles to ESR has been the difficulty of translating the concept into structural changes of the existing project system and relationships of giving and receiving. This transformation is taking place slowly, and the impact of the ecumenical reflection can be measured only over a long period of time.

The call for commitment. A world consultation on ESR was called by the WCC in October 1987 in El Escorial, Spain, under the theme "Koinonia — Sharing Life in a World Community". It adopted the commitment text "Guidelines for Sharing", together with a set of "Recommendations on Women and Youth". It also formulated a "Common Discipline of Ecumenical Sharing", spelling out its biblical-theological basis and steps for implementing ecumenical sharing locally, regionally and globally. In August 1988 the central committee received the guidelines and recommendations, affirmed the WCC's own commitment and called on the churches to implement the discipline in their own situation. A period of three years was agreed upon to monitor follow-up and to bring the results of the process to the seventh assembly in 1991.

Theologically, ESR is closely linked to the quest for unity.* It belongs to the essence of the local church* to be a sharing community, rooted in the eucharist,* from where it is sent out to be Christ's body, broken and shared in the world. Similarly, the global fellowship of churches engaged in the ecumenical movement should reflect the image of the body. The search for the real meaning of the eucharist as the body broken for the world and for eucharistic unity is therefore closely related to the task of building the ecumenical community of sharing.

ESR has thus been seen as a concept reaching beyond the fellowship of the churches to sharing life with all people. In response to the biblical imperative of compassion and justice, it confronts the injustices of the prevailing world order with its unequal distribution of resources and power, calling for the empowerment of the powerless and for solidarity with the poor.

HUIBERT VAN BEEK

Empty Hands: An Agenda for the Churches, WCC, 1980 • *Sharing Life in a World Community*, WCC, 1989 • *Towards an Ecumenical Commitment for Resource Sharing*, WCC, 1984 • *Towards a New System for Sharing*, WCC, 1983.

EDUCATION, ADULT.

Learning was all-pervasive in communities until it was institutionalized in formal education and ultimately identified with it in the West. That model was exported to other countries during colonial times. In that context, "adult education" was first used for organized learning outside the school system either for adults who had not finished school or for those who needed specific skills for jobs. Education was functional and was clearly linked to development (understood as economic needs).

In the late 1960s a strong movement emerged criticizing the school system. Ivan Illich would later speak of "deschooling society". In the early 1970s, Paolo Freire, a Brazilian known for his work in literacy and author of *Pedagogy of the Oppressed*, a reflection on his experience, was invited to set up the adult education desk at the WCC. From the start, the thrust of the desk was what he called "liberating education" as against "banking" or "domesticating" education. The aim of education was "conscientization", imperfectly rendered by "awareness raising". People should be able to read critically their world, understand their situation in order to transform it through a process of action and reflection. At its core was what would later be called "the option for the poor". Education should enable the poor,* the oppressed, the marginalized to become subjects of their own history* and not objects of the various powers in society. Dom Helder Camara popularized the word "conscientization", and Freire's ideas caught on first in and then outside churches. In Persepolis in 1975, UNESCO recognized the shift in education and came up with the concept of "lifelong learning", which integrated formal, informal and non-formal education and linked literacy with people's participation in decision making. Freire's intuitions inspired quite a number of community-based programmes and accounted at one time, mostly in third-world countries, for much of the practical involvement of churches in education and the struggles for justice, preparing the way for a theology of liberation.

Some of those intuitions expressed in *Pedagogy of the Oppressed* can be summarized as follows: (1) education is never neutral; (2) learners should be involved in selecting the subject matter of the learning; (3) pedagogy should be problem posing and not merely transfer of knowledge from those who know to those who do not; (4) education is not an academic exercise but should contribute to the radical transformation of society so that people should take their destiny in their own hands; (5) learning happens in a dialogue situation.

A wealth of experiences of "adult education" can be found most of all in social movements. Movements of peasants, urban poor, women, and indigenous peoples have affirmed and developed the orientations sensed by Freire. In January 1990, the International Council of Adult Education, presided over by Dame Nita Barrow, a member of the executive committee of the WCC, chose as the theme of its world assembly "Literacy, Popular Education, Democracy: Building the Movement". In March of the same year the World Conference on Education for All, organized by UN agencies, recognized the overall failure of the formal educational systems and the contribution of non-governmental organizations (NGOs) in the creative re-thinking of basic education. For most of these, education must give access to the bases of social power. Several approaches have developed, and adult education is being covered in participatory research, participatory evaluation, participatory training, development education, peace education, environmental education, workers' education, women's education and global education. Many of the pioneering NGOs are either church-based or church-related.

We can say that adult education for lifelong learning today is a process of collective production and diffusion of knowledge involving world-view, vision, values, understanding, attitudes, practices, strategies, skills and tools, as people struggle to survive, to resist oppression and dehumanization, and to build a more human world through communities of solidarity.

PHILIPPE FANCHETTE

P. Freire, *Educaçao como Pratica da Liberdada* (ET *Education for Critical Consciousness*, New York, Seabury, 1973) • P. Freire, *Pedagogia do Oprimido* (ET *Pedagogy of the Oppressed*, New York, Herder 1970) • L. C. Little ed., *The Future Course of Christian Adult Education*, Pittsburgh, PA, Univ. of Pittsburgh, 1959.

EDUCATION, ADULT CHRISTIAN.

Adult education has been important in the life of the Christian church from its beginning. Contemporary Christian adult education includes (1) helping members make meaning of the world in which they live in the light of their faith* by engaging them in a lifelong learning process; (2) learning about Christian belief and action, past and present, worldwide, responding appreciatively and critically; (3) modelling a way of teaching which

shares power and responsibility; (4) providing education in beliefs, values and ethics; (5) promoting two-way traffic by pointing to a theological component in other disciplines and reflecting back to the church discoveries from those disciplines.

Currently there is renewed vigour and interest in adult education inside and outside the church. There has been a shift away from reliance on experts' filling "empty vessels" towards a more collaborative approach which takes account of the learner's skills, experience, motivation and context. In some cases the reasons for this new emphasis may be starkly economic. For example, churches may be at risk if they rely heavily on a small, expensively trained (and probably ordained) leadership. This factor may lead to lay training and thereby a renewed vision of what it means to be the whole people of God.*

The Second Vatican Council gave lay education a new priority and openness. Humanistic psychology — encouraging individuals to identify their own needs, set their aims, help shape their course and evaluate their own progress — has stimulated imaginative adult training programmes in the churches of the USA, Australia, South Africa, Canada and the United Kingdom, so that students travelling from one country to another have been surprised to find the same experiential exercises in use in different areas and churches. Paulo Freire and others, in their emphasis on education among the oppressed, have promoted a new way of looking at social and political issues which transcended church boundaries. The Dutch churches pioneered peace studies on an interchurch basis. Feminist theology* and other radical theologies and therapies have given new life to educational work started earlier by Christian pioneers who were biased towards the education of women and other disadvantaged groups. Ecumenical associations of adult educators at a national and international level have been formed.

Above all, mass media broadcasting has become another means of adult Christian education. In 1986, 57 local radio stations in the UK, for example, combined with the Christian churches on a nationwide Lent course entitled "What on Earth is the Church for?" Probably a million people met in small ecumenical neighbourhood groups with study material and listened to radio transmissions. In the 1990s the churches are challenged by new information technology and in particular by the opportunity to use satellite television (with its option of multilanguage channels) to develop new ways of adult education through distance learning and for interactive conferences and consultations.

See also **laity**.

YVONNE CRAIG

J.L. Elias, *The Foundation and Practice of Adult Religious Education*, Melbourne, Krieger, 1982 • P. Freire, *Pedagogy of the Oppressed*, New York, Herder, 1970 • J.M. Hull, *What Prevents Christian Adults from Learning?*, London, SCM, 1985 • M.J. Knowles, *Modern Practice of Adult Education: From Pedagogy to Andragogy*, New York, Cambridge Books, 1980 • *Rite of Christian Initiation of Adults*, Chicago, Liturgy Training, 1988.

EDUCATION AND RENEWAL.

Education and renewal* have been two aspects of the church's life almost from its beginnings. In 2 Tim. 3:14-17 Timothy is exhorted to "continue in what you have learned and have firmly believed, knowing from whom you learned it and how from childhood you have been acquainted with the sacred writings which are able to instruct you for salvation through faith in Christ Jesus. All scripture is inspired by God and profitable for teaching, for reproof, for correction, and for training in righteousness, that the man of God may be complete, equipped for every good work." Here Tradition* is stressed — what has been learned from forebears and teachers, including in particular the scriptures, which are inspired and are therefore useful in enabling human beings to come to wisdom. Acts 2:42 attests that the earliest Christian community found its unity* inter alia in devoting themselves to the apostles' teaching. Indeed, Luke's task was to pass on the content of the apostles' teaching (Tradition). The church through the ages has been concerned to teach and learn the Tradition for the renewal of the faithful.

Already in the 2nd century A.D. the catechetical school of Alexandria, Egypt, was the focus of the intellectual life of the Christian church as well as for the instruction of candidates for church membership in the principles of the Christian faith.* In the West,

Cassiodorus saw the study of the seven liberal arts as the best preparation for higher studies in Christian theology as well as the best defence against non-Christian attacks on the church. The education of the clergy was very much on the agenda of Emperor Charlemagne, who wanted Christian service, including prayers and rituals, to be correctly understood and properly performed (*Admonitio Generalis*, 789; *De Litteris Colendis*, c.781-91).

Earlier, Emperor Justinian I sought to promote an exclusively Christian form of education, regulating the belief of Christians and removing all traces of pagan philosophy and practices. In 529 he published a decree forbidding pagans to hold positions of public education financed by city councils. Behind such a measure stood two factors: the growing intolerance of the church and the dominance of Constantinople. The result was a narrower focus of the Christian faith, as the emphasis on correct teaching and doctrine served the imperial idea of total mastery.

From the 12th century onwards, scholasticism was the form of theology and theological education. Whereas theology heretofore had been preoccupied with the relationship between Christ and the Father and with the interrelationship of his humanity and divinity, scholastic theology was preoccupied with the relationship between faith and reason and with the nature and attributes of God. In the process, scholasticism became so erudite that it neglected the needs of the churches, and theology became arid. This set the stage for the work of the reformers and thus contributed to the divisions of the church.

The reformers. Martin Luther emphasized education precisely because of his re-discovery of the priesthood of all believers. He promoted adult education because the entire body of Christian believers was called to be intelligent in the faith. Luther himself published the small catechism* for children and the large catechism for adults. Family education received considerable emphasis in his ministry. John Calvin also emphasized education, establishing what eventually became the University of Geneva. Founding educational institutions was rooted in the conviction that there was a necessity for learned ministers who could set forth the true faith, as well as for educated laity.

The reform movement stimulated fresh approaches to education by broadening the base and scope of learning and devising new methods to quicken and train the human mind and spirit. Philipp Melanchthon and John Higenkegin developed *Volksschule* and reconstructed university education. John Amos Comenius (1592-1670) of Unitas Fratrum pioneered an educational theory which influenced the education of the child as a child. Similarly, the Catholic Reformation also produced fresh approaches to education. The Jesuits, for example, developed the *ratio studiorum*. Congregations of women (e.g. the Ursulines) arose to pursue education of the masses (see **religious communities**).

The foregoing history has sought to show that from very early times, education, Christian and theological, was an important element in the renewal of the church and of Christians. Furthermore, such education as was offered was generally to serve the needs of the church and not education just for its own sake. There was a democratic view of education in the sense that it was for all the faithful, not only for the clergy. Thus already in early times we see a foreshadowing of some of the emphases of contemporary ecumenism, i.e. ministry by all God's people (see **people of God**) and the consequent theology by the people.*

The 19th century. In the 19th century there was a distinct change. In Europe education now became the function of the state. Through it the state sought to prepare the youth for service of the state rather than rearing them specifically in the Christian faith. This stage represents not only the distancing of the state from the church but also the distancing of the theology faculty from the church (see **church and state**).

The clergy were often not literate and educated enough in theological matters and therefore could not be trusted to carry on Christian education for the faithful. That was one of the protests of the reformers. Also, to promote Christian education among the young, particularly the unschooled poor, Sunday schools were started. The first was founded by Hannah Ball in the 1760s in High Wycombe, England. In 1780 the Sunday School Movement was pioneered in England by Robert Raikes of Gloucester. It grew around the world, so that in 1889 it was re-named World

Sunday School Convention, with its headquarters in London. Its important work was the production of materials for Sunday schools.

A convention in Rome in 1907 turned it into the World Sunday School Association. In 1924 it became a federation; its board was interdenominational and international, committed to Christian education and to drawing churches together. In 1947 it was re-named World Council of Christian Education* (WCCE), and in 1950 World Council of Christian Education and Sunday School Associations. Its activities included providing resources for effective educational leadership and programmes. It worked on curriculum development for church and day schools. Its distinctive contribution is the development of ecumenical curricula for Sunday schools and religious education in all continents. The WCCE was integrated into the WCC in 1971.

In the 19th century, education was also emphasized by the Christian social action movement. Here education was an element in the concern for human life in society. Under this umbrella, workers in trade unions were educated for political consciousness. The World Alliance for Promoting International Friendship through the Churches* was founded in 1914 to promote education for peace. The Life and Work* movement's 1925 conference in Stockholm included a section on "the church and education". In 1930 the Universal Christian Council for Life and Work was founded. It also had a strong emphasis on education. Indeed it held yearly "ecumenical" seminars in Geneva from 1933 onwards to explore ecumenical education. Its 1937 Oxford conference explored the subject of "Church, Community and State in Relation to Education".

The YMCA* (1855), YWCA* (1894) and WSCF* (1895) addressed matters of faith and the world's agenda through prayer, Bible study and practical missionary and sociopolitical involvement. In their work the lay and youth movements addressed matters of general and Christian education as well as the matter of the renewal of educational institutions and theories.

20th-century developments. A strong ecumenical perspective had developed from 19th-century education, religious and general. Against the background of such consciousness the Ecumenical Institute at the Château de Bossey, Céligny, Switzerland (see **Bossey, Ecumenical Institute**), was founded in 1946. Its expressed aim was the formation of an apostolic type of leadership "which not only aims at changing the life of individuals, but also seeks to achieve a peaceful penetration into the various sections of the community and the various areas of life". The institute, among its diverse undertakings, has been devoted to training laypersons for active involvement in the life of the church as well as service as ambassadors of the church to the world.

Before the integration of the WCCE into the WCC in 1971, the WCC in 1969 had set up the Office of Education. Before that time, the 1954 Evanston assembly had established the Division of Ecumenical Action "to help the churches relate ecumenical thinking to Christian education in all its aspects", a mandate received by the New Delhi assembly in 1961. That responsibility was shared by the Ecumenical Institute, the Laity and the Youth department in collaboration with WCCE. In 1961 a joint study commission on education was formed, in which the Division of Ecumenical Education and the WCCE worked together. Such was the development until the 1969 establishment of the Office of Education. That office had several sub-sections: basic adult education, theological education of the whole people of God, and church education. It included also the education renewal fund, which financed curriculum projects and initiatives in religious education among children and adults. This continues today in the Scholarships Office of the Sub-unit on Education.

One of the basic assumptions of the work in education has been that the whole of life is a learning experience — from birth to the grave and in all its aspects. For that reason there has been a tendency towards the proliferation of the work of the WCC department or sub-unit designated education. Second, an assumption is that attention needs to be paid to the roles of teachers and pupils. For example, what may adults learn from children? What may literates learn from non-literates? What may be learned from peoples with disabilities about true values and the good life? As an unpublished Education sub-unit report put it in 1985: "How can this two-way process of teaching

and learning in a learning community be fostered? What is in such a learning community the specific role of teachers as enablers for learning?" A third assumption is that education in the church context should be not only learning about the faith but also discovering the implications of the faith for personal and social-ethical attitudes and decisions.

Theological education: Theological education has always been part of the life of the church at its best. In the ecumenical movement the Faith and Order* movement has been devoted to tackling matters of theology, which was for educating the churches for renewal and unity. However, it was the International Missionary Council* (IMC) which took steps to structure that concern programmatically. When the missionary movement gathered momentum early in this century, the churches of the North set the agenda for church life, style and theology in the South. But some missionaries, particularly Charles Ranson, missionary to India, convinced themselves that the improvement of the training of indigenous persons was essential for the future of the church. Ranson was tireless in communicating this vision to the IMC, which set up a committee to study theological education in the South. On the basis of that study, the Ghana assembly of the IMC created in 1958 the Theological Education Fund (TEF) not only to promote theological excellence, which at the time was measured in terms of Western standards of theological education, but also to evolve indigenous theological education and creative theological education. The three critical marks of TEF's work were *quality*, which combines intellectual rigour, spiritual maturity and commitment; *authenticity*, which requires critical encounter with each cultural context in the design, content and purpose of theological education; and *creativity*, which leads to new approaches and deepens the churches' understanding and obedience in mission. As a fund, it gave the churches of the South "the completely new possibility of sharing in the decision making about the training of their pastors". When the IMC was integrated into the WCC, TEF became "a service of the Commission on World Mission and Evangelism of the WCC". The location of TEF in CWME expressed the idea that theology and theological education should serve the

Student in open-air school in Chibuto, Mozambique (WCC/Peter Williams)

mission of the church and not be education for the sake of education. When later the TEF was separated from the CWME, the latter too continued to have a desk for education and mission.

TEF went through three mandates until 1977, when it became the Programme on Theological Education (PTE). The particular mandate of PTE is "to assist the churches in the reform and renewal of theological education". The reference to "assisting" highlights the concern for the *churches* to be the principal actors, with whom the WCC through PTE stands to help them achieve their goals. But assistance is also in the sense of playing a catalyst role, challenging churches to reform and renewal of theological education. Besides the churches, PTE's partners include other funding agencies and mission boards and the Associations of Theological Schools.

When the central committee set up PTE in 1977, its mandate included the following: "to relate with and support the churches' efforts to develop creative theological education and adequate ministerial formation in the fulfilment of their mission. In carrying out this responsibility, the sub-unit shall pay attention

to: (1) the influence of the context and culture in theology and ministerial training and practices; (2) the need to liberate theological education and ministerial formation and practices from bondages which hamper faithfulness in their life and witness; and (3) cross-cultural discussion of key aspects of theological education". Following these guidelines two special concerns have been PTE's programmatic emphasis since the Vancouver assembly (1983): theology by the people; spiritual formation and theological and ministerial formation. The former derives from the re-discovery of the church as the people of God. How are the people of God to be formed and equipped for their mission and ministry in today's world? What lessons may be learned from the basic Christian communities, which are actually living the idea of church as the people of God?

The funding of PTE's work supports the following categories: innovative programmes in theological education such as original and contextual reflection in curriculum development, writing, etc.; programmes of associations and regional bodies of theological education; the training of theological educators; the development of alternative models in theological education such as extension education and programmes relevant to the context and responsive to mission and ministry; intra- and inter-regional exchange of students and faculty.

The work of lay academies: Out of the conviction that the church is called to a new and dynamic concern for social welfare, involving the direction of change and growth in human society, lay centres and academies have arisen which stand as signs of a larger renewal of the church's life and structure as a whole. This movement has resulted in a worldwide network of persons and centres gathered up in the World Collaboration Committee for Christian Lay Centres, Academies and Movements for Social Concern (see **academies, lay**). Work on the lay movement has been co-ordinated by the WCC, especially the Sub-unit on Renewal and Congregational Life. But as a worldwide association with regional autonomies, it shows great differences and yet much co-operation and joint action. The Asian chapter emphasizes Christian vigilance; the African chapter emphasizes "learning to change".

The centre of the lay movement seems to have shifted from Europe, and it is now a worldwide network of persons and centres. "The church has seen more clearly its proper location with the poor and disestablished. The focus on laity has yielded to increasing attention to profound reforms in theological education and the continuing education of clergy. Finally, the purpose of collaboration has been more clearly formulated." Its future is tied up with the meaning of mission today.

Basic education: An important work of education has been the adult basic education programme, which is located in the Education sub-unit of the WCC. This operation stands firmly on the churches' "option for the poor". The church's re-discovery of God's preferential option for the poor* has led to an important social change: social groups of the marginalized and dispossessed have been recognized as the effective mediators between the poor, on the one hand, and the political and economic powers, with the poor themselves as subjects in their own right. In this context literacy becomes a weapon for social change, and education the means by which people come to perceive, interpret, criticize and transform their world. Education is not mere socialization; it is as well the tool for enabling people to deal creatively with reality and to participate in the historical process. The most original and influential personality in this area has been Paulo Freire, a Brazilian philosopher of education and a visionary who also has had the capacity for initiating action.

The aim of adult basic education has been "to create or facilitate situations where the poor and oppressed can produce collectively the knowledge which makes them more effective in their everyday life and in their struggles for the practical transformation of society". It thus seeks to generate the learning process through which group leaders and educators become facilitators and bridge-builders who enable the poor to uncover and experience their own expertise. But the educators themselves need to be conscientized. Such an enterprise then necessarily challenges the popular understanding of knowledge, development, politics and the dominant trends in social sciences. The educator tries to locate where learning is already taking place, as well as where the solidarity and community are lived, despite daily conflicts. The educator's

role is to bring "an outer perspective", i.e. helping the struggling groups to discover how the learning is happening, where it is leading and whether it is to the benefit of the most needy.

The programme has been in constant dialogue with ecumenical groups, university centres and governments which are engaged in adult education. The work done in Portuguese and Spanish Africa (Angola, São Tomé, Guinea-Bissau and Cape Verde) and other places helped to develop a cadre of national leaders in the field of adult education.

Women and education: James Kwegyir Aggrey of Africa once said: "Educate a man and you educate an individual; educate a woman and you educate a tribe and a nation." The statement highlights the crucial role of women in the family, the wider community and in the church also. But women have often been discriminated against and marginalized. And, therefore, either through part of laity education or in a separate sub-unit, the WCC has been concerned to raise awareness of women and the churches in regard to the impoverishment of the total community life due to the marginalization of women in the community, the causes of their oppression, and the search for positive action to eradicate the identified root causes. On the local or national level women have been enabled to come together to share their stories of struggle and to analyze their problems. Sometimes they have been enabled to meet with people outside the church, thus promoting the enriching cross-fertilization of ideas and insights, building bridges of understanding and strengthening linkages among groups of women. "Creative communication methods have also been experimented with, such as in biblical and theological reflection through drama, artwork, or just sharing stories. These help much in their learning and help them also develop self-confidence. Shared leadership is also an important feature of women's meetings. In this way they learn from one another, and the process of empowerment takes place. When women are empowered, they also begin to realize that they have a crucial role in the church and community, and they begin to contribute their gifts and talents to enrich the life of the community" (Priscilla Padolina).

Three important publications relating to women must be mentioned: *The Community of Women and Men in Church and Society* (1978) is the end product of a whole process of study on the need to re-capture the place of women in society not as appendages to men but as proper subjects of history; *By Our Lives* (1985) is an attempt to relate the experiences of women today and those in the Bible and thus call people to read the Bible with new eyes; and *New Eyes for Reading* (1986) is a collection of biblical and theological reflections by women from the third world.

Other educational programmes: Another important educational work in biblical studies is the Portfolio for Biblical Studies, established in 1971 to explore ways in which Christians "can more faithfully live, witness and worship in accordance with the scriptures". Since 1976 it has been in the Sub-unit on Education because of the emphasis on the training of Bible-study enablers. That desk has been addressing two questions in particular: How can Bible study become operative for Christian obedience in everyday life? How can Christian believers be enabled to mediate the biblical message in the light of their own personal, political and cultural situation?

In 1978 the Church-Related Educational Institutions Programme (CREIP) was established "to evaluate the role of the church-sponsored schools, colleges, universities and institutions, including their role in human development and nation-building". The programme was an attempt to grapple with such issues as the growing elitism, the influence of governments on Christian education, the relationship between institutional church and private Christian institutions, and racial or religious minorities. CREIP (now discontinued) addressed the subject of the churches' development of leaders for church and society and provided consultancy services to churches in the regions.

An institution like the WCC has to be concerned with ecumenical learning, which seeks "to explore... with the member churches a revision of their curricula and educational programmes so that they promote education for ecumenism, particularly on the local level". This concern necessitated co-operation with other sub-units. For example, to pursue education in a multifaith environment, they had to co-operate with the Sub-unit on Dialogue with People of Living Faiths. But the process of study revealed the necessity of ecumenical education to involve learning through direct experience, in community and involvement even in conflict situations.

While the Education sub-unit was exploring ecumenical learning, PTE with its Vatican counterpart, the Secretariat for Catholic Education, have been exploring ecumenical formation, with its emphasis on the tertiary level of education. This undertaking was under the auspices of the Joint Working Group.* Outside of the WCC's Unit on Education and Renewal, the Commission on the Churches' Participation in Development promotes "development studies and educational programmes". Thus CCPD called a consortium for support of priority programmes of the Ethiopian Orthodox Church, including clergy training centres and the parish council movement.

Education, then, has been a key strand of the ecumenical movement and of its principal arm, the WCC. It has taken different forms but always has emphasized community and the participation of all. Purposeful education not only trains individuals and makes them whole but prepares them to serve the community and the renewal of the church. Such education will continue to be an important aspect of the WCC's work. Prince Thompson, Anglican bishop of Freetown, Sierra Leone, contributing to a 1986 PTE consultation on "Theological Education in Africa: Quo Vadimus?" said: "Theological education is our nerve centre, and our willingness to shoulder it is an indication of our growing maturity in Christ." This was said of theological education in Africa, but it is true of all education in the church and in all regions of the world.

JOHN S. POBEE

P. Freire, *Pedagogy of the Oppressed*, New York, Herder, 1970 • G.T. Haar, "Religious Education in Africa", *Exchange*, 50, 1988 • E.H. Harbison, *The Christian Scholar in the Age of the Reformation*, New York, Scribner's, 1956 • G.E. Knoff, *The World Sunday School Movement*, New York, Seabury, 1979 • H. Kraemer, *A Theology of the Laity*, London, Lutterworth, 1958 • C. Lienemann-Perrin, *Training for a Relevant Ministry*, WCC, 1981 • W. Simpfendörfer ed., *The New Fisherfolk*, WCC, 1988 • *Report of the Committee on the Division of Ecumenical Action*, WCC • *Voices of Solidarity*, WCC, 1981.

ELECTRONIC CHURCH. The electronic church had its origins in the USA during the 1920s, when individual preachers such as Aimee Semple McPherson and Charles E. Fuller discovered the power of radio. In the 1950s Billy Graham brought TV cameras to his mass meetings, and radio healer Oral Roberts brought his tent meetings to the screen. Today's electronic church programmes are syndicated throughout the USA, UK, continental Europe, Latin America, Asia and Africa; they depend on a single highly visible charismatic leader; they exhibit high-budget "slick" production qualities; they consistently solicit money over the air; and they make extensive use of telephone and computerized "personal" letters to contact viewers.

Although "televangelism" represents only a small part of all religious broadcasting, it attracted considerable interest during the 1970s and 1980s. However, in mass media terms, its audience is not large. According to A.C. Nielsen studies, the US viewing public probably peaked around 1978, held steady for a few years, and has been decreasing ever since. The 1985 Annenberg-Gallup study revealed that the total number of US viewers who watch one hour or more of religious programmes per week was about 4.84 million persons, or 2.17% of the population.

The basic message of the electronic church is found not so much in its rhetoric as in its overall images. The programmes are authoritative, built on a strong authority figure (almost always male). They stress the need to change individuals as the key to changing society. They present every issue in simple terms, often as a duality — good versus evil, God versus the devil — and they pose correspondingly simple solutions. They affirm the values of reward for effort, equal opportunity of all to achieve success, and the American free-enterprise system. They pose a concrete eschatology which at once proclaims the imminent end of the world yet endorses symbols of success in this world, and they define success in terms of wealth, power, prestige and beauty — the essence of American secularism.

Electronic church programmes have made some positive contributions to religious outreach. They have identified the alienation of a segment of the population who feel that their local churches have not met their needs. They have met the specialized needs of some people, particularly the ill, the shut-ins, the elderly — those who cannot relate to their community in other ways. And they have made contact with people whom the mainline churches have not been successful in reaching.

There are also serious shortcomings. While televangelists identify with remarkable accuracy the sense of alienation in people, they are all too ready to take advantage of this alienation and to use it to their own advantage. Many televangelists systematically exacerbate and implant viewer self-doubt.

Fund-raising is the central activity. In 1986 Jim Bakker's programme took in $129 million, Jimmy Swaggart $140 million. Pat Robertson claimed in 1985 that the overall operations of his Christian Broadcasting Network (CBN) took in $230 million. In 1983, during a single hour the average televangelist asked the viewer to donate an average of $328.

Several televangelists have been accused of diverting money collected for mission projects to pay ongoing expenses. In 1983 CBN gave less than 8% of its total income to mission ministries, and Swaggart spent more than 80% of his income just keeping his programme on the air.

During the 1980s the televangelists' international influence was considerable. Jerry Falwell generated US political support for the role of Israel during the Palestinian crisis. Robertson's CBN was deeply involved in raising funds in support of the contras during the Nicaraguan war. Swaggart held huge rallies in Latin America and was accused of preaching virulent anti-Catholicism and of starting churches with a promise of funds and staff — which never materialized. Many such evangelists considered their chief mission to be the exportation of American-style fundamentalism overseas.

By 1987 the electronic church encountered serious difficulties. As more televangelists sought a share of the relatively small audience, appeals became more desperate. Several of the leading figures ran afoul of their own puritan ethic. By 1988 the scandals and controversies had caused all the major televangelists to suffer a decline, in some cases by as much as one-third to one-half, of their funding and audience. However, though the phenomenon currently falters, it seems certain that in the future new forms of electronically expressed evangelistic fervour will emerge in broadcasting.

WILLIAM F. FORE

W. Fore, *Television and Religion: The Shaping of Faith, Values and Culture*, Minneapolis, Augsburg, 1987 ● G. Gerbner et al., *Religion and Television: A Research Report by the Annenberg School of Communications, University of Pennsylvania and the Gallup Organization, Inc.*, New York, NCC, 1984 ● P. Horsfield, "And Now a Word from Our Sponsor: Religious Programmes on American Television", *Revue française d'études américaines*, 12, 1981.

ELLUL, JACQUES. B. 6.1.1912, Bordeaux, France. Ellul participated in several conferences of Church and Society and in consultations at Bossey,* and has frequently lectured there. He co-authored *Social and Cultural Factors in Church Divisions* (WCC, 1952). Receiving a doctorate in 1936, Ellul became professor of law at the University of Bordeaux in 1943 and was professor at the Institute of Political Studies in Bordeaux from 1947 until his retirement. Active in the French resistance movement, 1940-44, he was secretary of the regional movement for national liberation, 1944-46. He was a member of the national council of the Reformed Church of France, 1951-70, and of the national synod, and was director of *Foi et vie*. His publications include *Fausse présence au monde moderne* (ET *False Presence of the Kingdom*, New York, Seabury, 1963), *The Technological Society* (New York, Knopf, 1965) and *Ethique de la liberté* (ET *The Ethics of Freedom*, Grand Rapids, MI, Eerdmans, 1976).

ANS J. VAN DER BENT

ENCYCLICALS. An encyclical was originally a circular letter (Greek *enkyklos*) on matters of faith* or church discipline,* usually from a bishop to some Christian local churches* (e.g. 1 Pet.) or to all. In the 2nd century, Ignatius of Antioch, who found it "impossible to write to all the churches", urged Polycarp of Smyrna to bring the far-flung early Christian communities in touch with one another through the exchange of encyclicals. The letter from the Christians of Smyrna on Polycarp's martyrdom was addressed "to all the congregations of the holy

and catholic church in every place". Between the 3rd and 5th centuries, the bishops of Alexandria customarily addressed all the other bishops. It became usual for the Eastern patriarchs to send encyclicals to fellow bishops of "sister churches".*

In modern times, both Constantinople and Rome have issued encyclicals on the restoration of Christian unity* (see **encyclicals, Orthodox; encyclicals, Roman Catholic**). The bishops of Rome have also issued ecumenically significant letters on social questions (see **social encyclicals, papal**).

TOM STRANSKY

ENCYCLICALS, ORTHODOX. The encyclicals and other comparable statements of the Ecumenical Patriarchate of Constantinople dealing with Christian unity* have a pre-eminent character primarily because of the recognition of the patriarch of Constantinople as having a "primacy of honour" among the hierarchs of the Orthodox church. The following statements of the church of Constantinople on ecumenical topics have been especially significant and have been a source of guidance for those Orthodox engaged in interchurch dialogue.

On 12 June 1902 Patriarch Joachim addressed the first encyclical to the other autocephalous Orthodox churches which raised the question of theological dialogue with the West. Following responses to this letter, another encyclical was issued on 12 May 1904. While lamenting proselytism,* the letter expressed the real possibility of discussion with the Old Catholics and the Anglicans, who had already made overtures. The letter concluded by calling for meetings of Orthodox theologians of the various churches and by noting opposition at that time to a change in the calendar (see **church calendar**).

The historic encyclical of January 1920 — addressed "unto all the churches of Christ, wheresoever they be", frequently regarded as one of the founding documents of the contemporary ecumenical movement — called for the establishment of a "fellowship of churches" which would work for charitable co-operation and theological dialogue. Calling for an end to mistrust and proselytism, the letter claimed that rapprochement could begin despite doctrinal differences and listed areas of potential co-operation and dialogue.

On the eve of the establishment of the WCC in 1948, the patriarchate addressed an encyclical to the other autocephalous Orthodox churches on 4 February 1947 soliciting opinions regarding the nature of Orthodox participation. Another encyclical followed on 31 January 1952 in advance of the third conference on Faith and Order. In this letter the patriarchate advocated representation from all Orthodox churches in the WCC, cautious participation in the meetings of F&O, and very prudent participation in ecumenical services of prayer. The letter also urged the Orthodox churches to co-operate in common studies of themes to be discussed by the WCC and to encourage their theologians to examine issues related to ecumenism. Eight Orthodox jurisdictions were among the founding members of the WCC, and Orthodox theologians had been involved in F&O from its beginning.

The patriarchal tome of 7 December 1965 lifted and removed from memory the anathemas* pronounced in 1054 against those who had excommunicated Patriarch Michael. The "Lifting of the Anathemas of 1054" proclaimed in this document by Patriarch Athenagoras and the synod and also in the brief *Ambulate in Dilectione* issued by Pope Paul VI is frequently regarded as the beginning of a new phase in the relationship between Orthodoxy and Roman Catholicism marked by episcopal visits, the return of relics and theological discussions.

In the midst of such dramatic developments, the patriarchate issued the encyclical of 14 March 1967 addressed to bishops of the church of Constantinople. The text affirmed that intercommunion* between Orthodox and other churches did not exist as yet. While commending the progress of the ecumenical movement, the encyclical re-affirmed the view that full sacramental communion* can follow only from doctrinal agreement.

Noting the 25th anniversary of the WCC, a "Declaration of the Ecumenical Patriarchate" was published on 16 August 1973. The text acknowledged the many advances in interchurch relations and commended the activity of the WCC. Note was also taken of the valuable contributions of the Orthodox to the work of the WCC. Mindful of the difficulties of the time, the text also challenged the WCC

to avoid the dangers of "secular ecumenism", to be in service to the churches in their quest for unity, and to remain faithful to its constitution, which emphasized the goal of Christian reconciliation.* The text also called for the full inclusion of the Roman Catholic Church into the WCC.

See also **encyclicals; encyclicals, Roman Catholic**.

THOMAS FITZGERALD

T. FitzGerald, "The Patriarchal Encyclicals in Christian Unity, 1902-1973", *Greek Orthodox Theological Review*, 22, 3, 1977 • V. Istavridis, "The Ecumenical Patriarchate and the Ecumenical Movement", *Greek Orthodox Theological Review*, 9, 1, 1963 • C. Patelos ed., *The Orthodox Church in the Ecumenical Movement*, WCC, 1978 • E.J. Stormon ed., *Towards the Healing of Schism: The Sees of Rome and Constantinople*, New York, Paulist, 1987.

ENCYCLICALS, ROMAN CATHOLIC.

In recent Roman Catholic tradition, an encyclical is a formal papal letter on doctrinal, moral, social or disciplinary matters, written for the universal Roman Catholic Church (RCC) as a means of maintaining unity* of "faith and morals". Such pastoral letters are identified by the opening words, usually in Latin. From the first modern one, Benedict XIV's *Ubi Primum* on bishops' duties (1740), until those of John XXIII (1958-63), the letters were directed to "patriarchs, primates, archbishops, bishops, and other local ordinaries in peace and communion with the apostolic see" (of Rome). With John XXIII's *Pacem in Terris* (1962), recent popes have addressed their social encyclicals on justice and peace not to the church alone but also to "all people of good will".

Although the RCC officially acknowledges that "in writing such letters, the popes do not exercise the supreme power of their teaching authority" (Vatican II, *Lumen Gentium*, 25), one should not generalize about the exact degree of authority* encyclicals bear and about the quality of consent to their contents they require of Catholics. One should evaluate and judge each encyclical and its sections on their individual merits, on what is proposed and how, and all this in the context of Vatican II teachings, other papal pronouncements and theological writings.

In the 19th century popes used encyclicals as one-way appeals "to the Orientals" to reunite with Rome, and they were answered by Orthodox patriarchal encyclicals. Such an appeal in Pius IX's 1848 *In Suprema Petri Apostoli Sede* received the united response of the Orthodox patriarchs of Constantinople, Alexandria, Antioch and Jerusalem; their encyclical defined "papism" as a heresy* and hoped that Pius IX would himself be "converted" to "the true catholic, apostolic and Orthodox church". In 1894 Leo XIII addressed a new appeal to "return" in *Praeclara Gratulationis*. Anthimos, ecumenical patriarch of Constantinople, responded negatively; he envisaged reunion but only on the basis of the undivided faith of the first centuries.

From its side, the Ecumenical Patriarchate of Constantinople in 1920 issued an encyclical to "all the churches of Christ everywhere". It requested that the churches, despite their doctrinal differences, should come closer to one another by "the removal and abolition of all mutual mistrust and bitterness" and in frank exchange of Christian thought and love, "for the preparation and advancement of that blessed union which would be completed in the future in accordance with the will of God". On the part of Rome, Pius XI's *Mortalium Animos* (1928) forbade RCs to participate in ecumenical gatherings and pleaded for "the return of the one true church of Christ of those who are separated from it".

In many ways, the first positive papal response to the 1920 letter of the patriarchate of Constantinople was John XXIII's first encyclical, *Ad Petri Cathedram* (29 June 1959), in which he outlined the ecumenical intentions of the forthcoming Second Vatican Council,* with no appeals to one-way reunion to the see of Rome but a call for the renewal of the RCC as an "example of truth, unity and love". Paul VI's first encyclical, *Ecclesiam Suam* (6 August 1964), greeted all Christians "with love and reverence, in the hope that we may promote together, even more effectively, the cause of Christ and the unity which he desired for his church, in the dialogue of sincerity and love".

In his *Redemptor Hominis* (15 March 1979), John Paul II saw that in "the present situation of Christianity and the world, the only possibility of fulfilling the church's universal mission is that of seeking sincerely, persevering, humbly and also courageously the ways of drawing closer and of union". In fact, in almost every papal encyclical since Paul VI's *Ecclesiam Suam*, the ecumenical dimension of the specific topic is at least mentioned, if not highlighted, as in Paul VI's letter on evangelization, *Evangelii Nuntiandi* (8 December 1975).

See also **encyclicals; encyclicals, Orthodox; social encyclicals, papal**.

TOM STRANSKY

ENERGY. According to Gen. 1:28, humankind has an inescapable responsibility towards keeping its household in sustainable order, comprising all aspects of the use of natural resources, including energy.

The WCC's involvement in energy issues started with a concern about nuclear energy at an international conference held in Bucharest, Romania, in 1974, leading to the Ecumenical Hearing on Nuclear Energy (Sigtuna, Sweden, 1975). This hearing, with the participation of eminent scientists and theologians, was able to demonstrate the inherent theological and ethical issues in the nuclear debate and the need for continued ecumenical dialogue to help resolve the strongly divergent views.

In the year following, the "Energy for My Neighbour" programme was initiated: an action programme intended to sensitize churches about energy problems faced by developing countries and to activate practical steps to ameliorate the energy situation for the less privileged. Many churches took up this challenge. A number of ecumenical consultations were also held on the subject in different developing countries.

The ecumenical study of these two issues continued, culminating at the 1979 conference on "Faith, Science and the Future", held in Cambridge, Massachusetts, USA. Although the conference is best known for its controversial position on nuclear power, it was the first time that the ecumenical movement took a truly global view of energy, as part of the struggle towards a just, participatory and sustainable society. The WCC ideally can provide a forum where scientists and technologists can meet theologians in a constructive debate to identify and discuss the critical issues for the churches.

Several nuclear accidents in the 1980s, including Chernobyl (1986), as well as the growing costs of nuclear installations, lack of significant progress in waste storage and advances in alternative energy production and transmission technologies, led the WCC central committee to mandate a new look at the question. A 1989 consultation in Zaire reviewed the ethics of nuclear energy generation in light of the most recent technology, information, costs and accidents. The published results of this consultation represent not only a contribution to ecumenical discussion but also an attempt to influence public policy formation.

Increasingly, environmental issues are becoming limiting factors to continued material development. Climate change is already taking place. Forests are disappearing due to air pollution in the industrialized countries and to unsustainable overuse in the developing countries. In addition to helping to clarify the related ethical and social issues, the churches also have a responsibility to act. The problem remains, however, what to do, and on what basis?

See also **just, participatory and sustainable society; justice, peace and the integrity of creation**.

JANOS PASZTOR

J. Pasztor ed., *Energy for My Neighbour: Perspectives from Asia*, WCC, 1981 ● K. Shrader-Frechette ed., *Nuclear Energy and Ethics*, WCC, 1991.

ENVIRONMENT/ECOLOGY.

The concern with the issues that underlie present ecumenical discussions on environment/ecology can be traced to the beginnings of the movement early in this century. It can be discerned, for instance, in the 1910 Edinburgh conference, with its motto of evangelizing the whole world in their generation, relating it to the issues of technology* and its possible detrimental effect on the environment, to a secularism that gave such pre-eminence to technological achievement that ethical issues were forgotten or dismissed (see **secularization**). The two world wars added to the problem and at the same time sharpened the issue. The use of nuclear power introduced a new dimension to the ecological crisis. So it is natural that the United Nations and the WCC became international forums for nations and churches to deliberate on the destructive consequences of technology, and irresponsible industrial expansion (see **growth, limits to**) for the sake of profit and the plunder of nature in the third world.

In the WCC, the Church and Society subunit facilitated these deliberations and published significant documentation between 1948 and 1983. At the 1966 Geneva Church and Society conference, the representatives of Africa, Asia and Latin America underlined the need for greater responsibility in relation to environmental issues on the part of the powerful nations, particularly in their industrial and commercial relations in the third world. The 1979 Church and Society conference convened at the Massachusetts Institute of Technology (USA) brought together theologians, scientists, technocrats and political leaders. A section report on "Technology, Resources, Environment and Population" covered the several aspects of the problem and made a number of specific recommendations: although realizing that no general criteria could be established, "we *can* say that God values *all* of his creation and that human redemption involves the redemption of the whole cosmos from 'its bondage to decay'". The WCC programmes on a "Just, Participatory and Sustainable Society"* and "Justice, Peace and Integrity of Creation"* have given continuity in developing these concerns.

The Catholic church has also been concerned for the restoration of ecological balance in the world as a whole. In his letter to priests for Holy Thursday 1988, Pope John Paul II observed that "man has lost the awareness of being the priest for the whole visible world, turning the latter exclusively towards himself". He indicated that the processes of industrialization and urbanization have contributed most adversely to the destruction of ecological balance. It is hoped that lessons from Europe and North America will warn the nations of Africa, Asia and Latin America to be cautiously aware of the environmental and ecological implications of massive, wholesale and uncontrolled industrialization and urbanization.

See also **pollution**.

JESSE N.K. MUGAMBI

EPICLESIS. The word comes from the Greek *epikalein*, meaning "to call upon", "to invoke". In theological language epiclesis is a special invocation asking for the Holy Spirit* to be sent; it can have a place within a variety of liturgical celebrations and more particularly in the eucharistic formulas (see **eucharist**).

The eucharistic liturgy is addressed to the Father and asks for the Holy Spirit to be sent down either upon the elements (the bread and wine) so that they can be transformed into the body and blood of Christ, or on those partaking of the eucharist so that they can be sanctified and united by communion, or on both, with the same results.

In the Eastern tradition this invocation has its place at the end of the anamnesis — the relatively detailed account of the institution of the Last Supper by Christ — which also recalls the main stages in the work of salvation* (cross, resurrection, ascension, etc.). The epiclesis thus represents a conclusion or climax to the anamnesis. In the early documents, especially those from Antioch (end of the 4th century), we find a sequence of this kind.

In the West most of the eucharistic formulas currently in use have two epicleses, in line with a custom attested in a document from Alexandria from the mid-4th century. The first epiclesis, which comes before the words of institution of the supper, asks for the Holy Spirit to be sent down upon the species to transform them; the second, at the end of the anamnesis as in the Eastern documents, asks for it to be sent down upon the members of the congregation to sanctify and unite them.

Controversies have taken place between East and West, mainly from the 14th to the 17th centuries, regarding the part played by the epiclesis and its function in relation to the words of institution of the supper. More recently, this problem has yielded place to an overall view according to which it is the eucharistic anaphora as a whole which among other things has the effect of transforming the gifts and sanctifying those taking part. This idea is more in accord with a view which predated any controversy, since the epiclesis is bound up with the element that precedes it within the eucharistic prayer; it displays the reality according to which every liturgical action is carried out in and by the Holy Spirit.

The place of the epiclesis in the eucharistic prayer as a whole has not changed through the ages, but both the meaning given to that prayer and the theology of the Holy Spirit underlying it have been the subject of clarifying statements.

The controversy about the epiclesis related to whether that prayer was or was not one of consecration, and this prompted the parties in the dispute to look for a particular moment in the anaphora at which it might be said that the consecration of the gifts took place. The polemical atmosphere led them to harden their respective positions, with each defining where they stood in opposition or reaction to the other's position. Thus in the West the words of institution alone, pronounced by the celebrant, were affirmed to have consecrating force. Those in the East then thought it necessary to look for another element in the eucharistic anaphora which would fulfill the same function; they believed they could find it in the epiclesis. The doctrinal disadvantage of such a confrontation lies in its reductionist character: on the one hand, the consecration of the gifts is not the sole aim or effect of the eucharistic celebration, which contains an infinite number of other riches (sanctification of those taking part, re-presentation of the work of salvation, participation in anticipation in the benefits of the coming kingdom, to mention only a few), only in part accounted for in the theological statements (see 1 Cor. 11:26); on the other hand, if we look for a specific moment in the anaphora at which the transformation would be effected, we inevitably fragment the liturgical elements which go to make up this celebration and thus lose the indissoluble link that binds them together.

Thus anamnesis, the recapitulation of the work of the Son, is of no avail without epiclesis, the invocation of the Holy Spirit as the Power which re-presents. The Son has fulfilled the Father's will on earth and has ascended again into heaven (see John 14:31b and 16:5a); since then the Spirit has been at work and will be to the end of the age (Rom. 8:22,26), re-presenting (John 16:13) the work of the Son, which has been accomplished once for all (Heb. 10:12). The process of re-presentation by the Holy Spirit is effected particularly during each eucharistic celebration, and it is the epiclesis which expresses and displays this reality.

The contribution of the ecumenical movement in this field consists first of all in abandoning the controversy about consecration: it appears that most now accept the transformation of the eucharistic species into the body and blood of the Lord as one of the effects of celebrating the eucharist as a whole — but not as the sole effect. The text on the eucharist produced by the Commission on Faith and Order of the WCC (*Baptism, Eucharist and Ministry**) stresses the "intrinsic link" between the words of institution and the epiclesis, as expressing in each celebration the complementary role of the Son and the Spirit. The old idea according to which it was the whole eucharistic prayer that brings about the reality promised by Christ is recalled there as a model to be followed (E14 comm.). The argument about a particular moment for the consecration is thus transcended in this document.

Ecumenical encounters have made it possible to improve the enunciation of the doctrine on the Holy Spirit, a doctrine closely related to the presence of the epiclesis within the eucharistic anaphora. The role of the Holy Spirit makes the work of the Son present in every liturgical celebration; it is the invoked Holy Spirit who guarantees the sanctification,* empowering and unification sought for the congregation meeting together (E17). According to another text, the eucharistic epiclesis exhibits the presence of the Holy Spirit, who through the perceptible gestures and words alone accomplishes an eschatological reality which remains invisible (*Pour la communion des Eglises*, 152-53). This text thus stresses the personal, active character of the Holy Spirit in eucharistic celebration, a character clearly expressed in the petitions of the epiclesis.

See also **eucharist, Holy Spirit**.

ANDRÉ LOSSKY

Baptism, Eucharist and Ministry, WCC, 1982 • *Pour la communion des Eglises: L'apport du Groupe des Dombes, 1937-1987*, Paris, Centurion, 1988 • A. Schmemann, *L'eucharistie, sacrement du royaume* (ET *The Eucharist: Sacrament of the Kingdom*, Crestwood, NY, St Vladimir's Seminary, 1987).

EPISCOPACY. Since the beginning of ecumenical conversations, the episcopacy has proved a difficult topic to tackle, both in theory and in practice. The Lambeth Quadrilateral* of 1888 included "the historic episcopate, locally adapted in the method of its administration to the varying needs of the nations and peoples called of God into the unity of his church". On the other hand, Lutheran churches showed reserve towards restoration of the episcopacy as a condition of unity,* either among themselves or with other churches, because of their commitment to the principle of the one ministry of word and sacrament. Congregationalists, for their part, did not wish to see the episcopacy undermine the autonomy of local congregations. When they eventually entered ecumenical conversations, first the Orthodox churches, and later the Roman Catholic, did so with the presuppositions that the episcopacy is of divine origin and cannot be called into question. This was a stronger position than that of the Anglicans, who wished to retain it in all church unification, without necessarily having to resolve the matter of its doctrinal foundations.

Concrete schemes for the unification of churches of different origins and polity had to decide on what was to be done about the episcopate. The most significant development ecumenically was that of the Church of South India, which united in 1947 after many years of preparation. This plan brought together the local Anglican church and some non-episcopal churches in one episcopal church, but without calling into question the authenticity of the previously exercised ministry of the non-episcopal churches and without demanding re-ordination. A somewhat different plan was followed in North India in 1971. There the mutual recognition of ministries and their assumption into one episcopally structured church involved a mutual laying on of hands. One should also take note of discussions within Lutheran churches about the possible restoration of the episcopacy in synods which did not retain it after the Reformation, both for unification of Lutheran churches themselves and for their communion with other bodies.

The section of *Baptism, Eucharist and Ministry** on ministry may be said to represent the theoretical foundations of these discussions accurately enough and to reflect a widely talked of policy, even if not to the satisfaction of all. It gives precedence to the one ministry over the issue of its structure and gives priority to the apostolic succession of churches over the position of the episcopacy in the church as its sign ("serving, symbolizing and guarding the continuity of the apostolic faith and communion"). In asking for the possible restoration of the episcopacy in churches that have not maintained it, as key to the tripartite form of ministry, BEM presents it as a historical phenomenon of quite early origins and of some significance to the life of the church, rather than as something that dates from the apostles or that is absolutely essential to the church. It also admits a possible diversity in the forms which episcopate could take.

As their respective responses to BEM show, this view fails to meet the position of the Orthodox and Roman Catholic churches, who themselves also issued a joint statement on the sacrament of orders at Valamo, Finland, in June 1988 (see **Orthodox-Roman Catholic dialogue**). There it is bluntly stated that bishops are the successors of the apostles and that the episcopacy is the fullness of the priesthood,* by which the ministry of Christ himself is exercised in the church. At the same time, the statement relates this ministry to the work of the Spirit and sees the apostolic succession of bishops in conjunction with the apostolic succession of churches themselves. The bishops' own apostolic succession is not purely sacramental or juridical in character but includes a succession in teaching and in apostolic witness.

It should not be thought that holding to the necessity of the episcopacy in this way implies historical naivety, for it does not mean that these churches pretend to see the apostles as bishops or to find evidence in the New Testament to say that the apostles themselves ordained bishops. It is rather their position that the eventual form of the episcopacy, as it emerged in post-apostolic times, is an authentic and canonical development of apostolic ministry.

Indeed, all ecumenical discussion on the episcopacy has to be conscious of certain historical realities. The plurality of church structures in NT times is widely admitted, together with the uncertainty about the meaning of the word "episcopos" where it occurs. So is the diversity in the form of the episcopacy in earliest post-apostolic times, as evidenced for example in the difference between the monarchical episcopate noted in the letters of Ignatius of Antioch and the more collegiate form of episcopate practised in Alexandria. It is further admitted, even within the Roman Catholic Church, that there is considerable diversity between the bishop of early times, who was teacher and presider in a eucharistic community, and the medieval bishops, whose principal characteristic was their jurisdictional authority. It was on this account that scholastic theologians often saw the episcopacy as an office rather than as part of the sacrament of order.

Recent studies have also raised the question as to why parts of the Lutheran Reformation rejected or abandoned the episcopacy. It is clear that the fundamental Lutheran commitment was to the one ministry of word and sacrament. It is possible that the episcopacy was let go for practical reasons as much as for reasons of principle. Inasmuch as it was at the time experienced as a hindrance to the gospel ministry, it could not in practice be retained. It was in such a context that the council of Trent* in its decree on order pronounced on the divine origin of the episcopacy and on its superiority over the presbyterate.* Although Trent rejected the liceity of ordinations to ministry within Reformation churches, it did not assert their invalidity. The Anglican communion on its side kept the episcopacy, without any confessional commitment to priesthood or to notions of linear apostolic succession.

Several characteristics of current ecumenical conversations may pave the way for future agreements on the episcopacy. The Roman Catholic position, for example, has re-affirmed the sacramental nature of the episcopacy at the Second Vatican Council (Dogmatic Constitution on the Church, ch. 3) and sees ordination* as a commission, in the power of the Spirit, to the threefold ministry of word, sacrament and pastoral care. More recent statements, such as the joint Orthodox-Roman Catholic one at Valamo, have a much fuller and more ecclesial notion of apostolic succession than that of a linear transmission of power. On the other hand, in some cases of magisterial teaching one could ask for more nuance in referring to the historical origins of the episcopacy, when bishops are spoken of as successors of the apostles. It has also been suggested by theologians within the Roman

Catholic Church, though not officially by church authority, that the episcopacy in a particular church or region could be exercised in a more collegiate form than at present. On the other hand, Reformation and post-Reformation churches appear to be more sympathetic towards the significance of the episcopacy for the communion* of the church through time and space, though they remain sceptical about its factual contribution to greater unity and better communion. BEM speaks of it as "a sign, though not a guarantee, of the continuity and unity of the church" (M38).

In short, agreement on the episcopacy is by no means an ecumenical reality at present. Greater understanding on it has, however, been achieved through conversations, in conjunction with changes internal to participating churches. In the process, some fruitful avenues of further discourse and polity have emerged.

See also **apostolicity; church order; ministry in the church; ministry, threefold**.

DAVID N. POWER

R. Brown, *Priest and Bishop: Biblical Reflections*, Paramus, NJ, Paulist, 1970 • H. von Campenhausen, *Kirchliches Amt und geistliche Vollmacht* (ET *Ecclesiastical Authority and Spiritual Power in the Church of the First Three Centuries*, London, Black, 1969) • *Episkopé and Episcopate in Ecumenical Perspective*, WCC, 1980 • International Dialogue between the Roman Catholic Church and the Orthodox Church, "The Sacrament of Order in the Sacramental Structure of the Church", *Origins*, 18, 1988 • K.E. Kirk ed., *The Apostolic Ministry: Essays on the History and the Doctrine of Episcopacy*, London, Hodder & Stoughton, 1947 • J.H.P. Reumann, *Ministries Examined: Laity, Clergy, Women and Bishops in a Time of Change*, Minneapolis, Augsburg, 1987.

ESCHATOLOGY. Eschatology as logos (discourse) about the eschaton (the end) explicates the doctrine of "the last things". It presents the Christian understanding of future events, such as death (see **life and death**) and resurrection,* the last judgment and the end of the world, eternal damnation (hell) and eternal life (heaven). In scholastic textbooks of theology eschatology was the last chapter of dogmatics, and it stood in a certain discontinuity with its main corpus. Today, a consensus has developed among the various schools of theology that the eschatological perspective is basic to the understanding of the Christian faith, and Christian theology from beginning to end is considered eschatological.

The principal reasons for the contemporary emphasis on eschatology are the rediscovery by biblical scholars of the eschatological nature of the Christian gospel and the philosophical appreciation of the role of hope* in human existence. The recovery of biblical eschatology began in Protestant circles around the turn of the century with the seminal studies of Johannes Weiss and Albert Schweitzer investigating the nature of God's kingdom* in the New Testament. They argued that Jesus' message about the imminent coming of God's kingdom should be understood in continuity with the Jewish apocalyptic world-view, and that Jesus expected the establishment of God's kingdom to take place in the immediate future not as a result of human endeavours but as the final and decisive intervention of God in history.* C.H. Dodd further advanced the discussion on the nature of God's kingdom by examining the time factor in the coming of the kingdom in the teaching of Jesus. He argued that for Jesus the kingdom of God was realized in his own ministry and therefore his eschatology was already "realized". The fact that the kingdom of God was already present in the ministry of Jesus was then recognized by biblical scholarship, but it was also noticed that in some sayings of Jesus and especially in the parables, the coming kingdom of God is both a present and a future event. Joachim Jeremias modified the concept of realized eschatology into "inaugurated eschatology", or eschatology in the process of being realized. This view implied that the salvation* and the judgment already begun in the ministry of Jesus will come to a future climax.

Eschatology as the starting point of all theology inevitably affected the understanding of the Christian gospel and consequently the understanding of the church's nature and mission.* In the context of the ecumenical movement, this influence helped the churches to understand themselves as dynamic communities of God's presence in the world that find their true nature and fulfilment in the coming reality of God's kingdom.

As early as the first conference of the Faith and Order movement (Lausanne 1927), participating theologians urged the divided

Christians to discover their unity* in the future, in proclaiming the coming kingdom of God. Such exhortations were immediately criticized for not giving adequate attention to what the church* had already become through the power of the Holy Spirit and its identification with Jesus Christ. The second world conference on F&O (Edinburgh 1937) tried to synthesize these two views but could not draw any systematic conclusions as to their meaning for divided Christianity. It was agreed that the church, although it intrinsically relates to God's kingdom, cannot be fully identified with it, since the fullness of the kingdom is a future reality. This theme was further developed in the ongoing theological reflections of the WCC, and the biblical image of "the people of God"* was used to describe the eschatological dimension of the church, while the concept "Body of Christ" signified what the people of God had already become through baptism* and participation in the eucharist.*

The third world conference on F&O (Lund 1952) suggested that eschatology could help the churches to change and move from disunity into unity. This belief put eschatology at the centre of WCC theological reflection. The Evanston assembly of the WCC (1954), for which the theme was "Christ — the Hope of the World", invited a detailed study of Christian eschatology in its relation to the unity and the witness* of God's church. In the preparatory documents as well as in the actual proceedings of the assembly, a variety of opinions were expressed on the nature of Christian hope. It was suggested that history should be understood from its relation to its Lord, the crucified and risen Christ. Christian hope was understood as the confident affirmation that God is faithful and will complete what God has begun for the salvation of creation.* There was no speculation or agreement concerning the manner and the time of God's final victory, but it was affirmed that the completion of God's divine will for creation is not an abrogation of history but a redemption.* In Christ people are given a new mode of life which already constitutes the new age in process of fulfilment. It was also suggested that the correct balance of what has been given and what is still expected can be apprehended and experienced only in the Lord's supper. The eschatological and ecclesiological significance of the eucharist received the attention of the F&O commission at Louvain (1971) and reached its climax in Lima (1982). The Lima text, *Baptism, Eucharist and Ministry*,* treats the eucharist as "meal of the kingdom" (E22).

Evanston had further stated that the main task of the church, as the community of those who have identified themselves with Jesus Christ, is to be both the instrument of God's purpose in history and also the first realization of the life of his kingdom on earth. It testifies to the nature of the end towards which its hope is set as the promised climax of what God has done and still continues to do for the created world. From this perspective the oneness of the church is a result of Christ's eschatological and saving presence in the lives of various Christian communities, and it will become visibly manifested when the Lord will return in his glory to judge the living and the dead.

The fact that Christian hope is founded upon God's presence and action in history does not mean that Christians should abandon the world and its problems (see **church and world**). On the contrary, Evanston affirmed that the world, despite its fallen nature, continues to be a world created and sustained by God and that the vocation* of the church is to work for the realization in the world of the basic principles of justice,* peace* and freedom, realities that reflect the grace* of God in history. Concerning the theological significance of these endeavours, the preparatory documents emphasized that all human achievements are fragmentary, all responsibilities are subject to frustration and all hopes based upon human power and wisdom alone are self-defeating. It was emphasized that whatever Christians accomplish in their involvement against the maladies of this world must not be considered as the manifestation of God's perfect world. It is not known exactly how God will use the efforts of his people, or what degree of visible success he will grant to them in any particular project. Through their belief in God's lordship over history, they are secure against despair, for they know that what they commit into God's hands is safe. Thus Christians were challenged never to rest with any existent state of affairs, but rather to press unremittingly onward towards a better and worthier future as it is destined to be by the merciful God.

At Evanston it was also stated that futurist eschatology could help the churches recognize the ambiguity and imperfection of all historical existence and knowledge. Since God cannot be fully identified with any historical institution or event, Christians must live by faith and hope without giving to their historical understandings of truth an absoluteness which will be given to them in the future by God. Orthodox theologians agreed that futurist eschatology could help the churches move beyond their present divisions, but they insisted that it had to be balanced with what God has already done in history for the salvation of humankind. This insight made the churches aware that no escape into the future could heal the church's divisions if it ignored the serious ecumenical problem of lack of a common mind and language by which Christians could discover and express their God-given unity. These concerns were taken seriously and discussed at the fourth world conference on F&O (Montreal 1963). There it was recognized that the Tradition* of the church is Jesus Christ himself, who is known to Christians through their traditions, which are expressions and manifestations in diverse historical forms of the one truth, which is Christ. Yet the churches could not agree whether all traditions which claim to be Christian contain undistorted the totality of Tradition. However, they continued to agree that the church, despite its possession of history and tradition, of settled institutions and abiding forms, is still characterized by an anticipation of the Saviour and the final reign of God. While the churches recognized the transcendental and the temporal aspects of God's kingdom, they continue to be vague or rather uncertain about its exact relation to the church.

After Evanston, eschatology was never ignored in the theological deliberations of the WCC and particularly the discussions of the F&O commission. Either the assembly themes of the WCC and of the F&O commission were eschatological, or their particular subjects were discussed from an eschatological perspective. The Second Vatican Council, with the publication of its Dogmatic Constitution on the Church, affirmed the intrinsically eschatological nature of the church. It is important to note, however, that the WCC carefully avoided developing a systematic view of the church's nature, and therefore we have only occasional, fragmentary and sometimes confessional and repetitive presentations of how eschatology affects the life and the witness of the church and advances the cause of the church's unity. For example, at Montreal the F&O commission, and more generally the WCC at New Delhi and Uppsala, suggested that the structures of the church, conceived eschatologically, are changeable, but this view was not accepted by the Orthodox and other churches which considered the structures of the church sacramentally as divinely given and therefore unchangeable.

A more careful study of such divergence, however, would reveal the emerging ecumenical convergence, which affirms that some elements of the church's life can be considered permanent because of the eschatological significance which they gain as a result of God's grace, through which the church already participates in the eschaton. Although there is no complete agreement among the churches on what elements of the church's life can be considered as permanent because of their eschatological significance, the F&O commission, in agreement with the Vancouver assembly of 1983, considers as prerequisites of the church's unity the confession of the apostolic faith, the mutual recognition of baptism, eucharist and ministry, and the development of structures that make possible authoritative teaching (see **teaching authority**) by the united church. In the studies that F&O has produced towards this goal, the impact of eschatology can be discerned as the common ground of a new theology that makes the church a charismatic institution deriving its existence from the coming reality of God's kingdom. Finally, by making the idea of God's coming kingdom the most appropriate starting point for a theological understanding of the church, the factual inseparability of the church from the life of the world has been affirmed, since the reality of God's kingdom reveals the ultimate destiny of the world intended by God. This combining is reflected in the F&O studies, especially after Uppsala (1968), which deal with the unity of the church and renewal of the world. Note particularly the Bangalore statement "A Common Account of Hope" and the continuing study of "The Church as Mystery and Prophetic Sign".

See also **church, church and world, his-**

tory, hope, kingdom of God, life and death, salvation history.

EMMANUEL CLAPSIS

Anglican-Reformed International Commission, *God's Reign and Our Unity*, London, SPCK, 1984 • *Baptism, Eucharist and Ministry*, WCC, 1982 • E. Clapsis, *Eschatology and the Unity of the Church: The Impact of Eschatology in Ecumenical Thought*, Ann Arbor, UMI, 1989 • G. Limouris ed., *Church, Kingdom, World: The Church as Mystery and Prophetic Sign*, WCC, 1986 • J. Moltmann, *Theologie der Hoffnung* (ET *Theology of Hope*, London, SCM, 1967) • W. Pannenberg, "The Significance of Eschatology for the Understanding of the Apostolicity and Catholicity of the Church", *One in Christ*, 6, 3, 1970 • G. Wainwright, *Eucharist and Eschatology*, London, Epworth, 1971 • J.D. Zizioulas, *Being as Communion*, London, Darton Longman & Todd, 1985.

ETHICS. It is not be surprising that the ecumenical movement has been deeply involved in the consideration of ethical issues. Changes in the relations of production and political organization, new cultural trends and the ideological struggles of the modern world raised a number of questions for which the traditional theological and ethical repertoire of the confessional churches had no ready-made answers and frequently not even the instruments or disposition for understanding. In fact, one could argue that the ecumenical movement developed, in large measure, as a response to the challenges presented to Christians and churches by the complexity of the modern world.

Such a hypothesis is strengthened when we see that some of the early forms of ecumenical encounter that appeared towards the end of the last century and the beginning of ours represent an attempt of individual Christians to tackle problems or respond to opportunities presented by changes in the modern world. Thus the three important youth organizations — YMCA,* YWCA* and the Student Christian Movement (see **World Student Christian Federation**) — born in an evangelical milieu and with an evangelistic concern, were soon engaging in social action and concerns. The International Missionary Council* gathered missionary boards or societies in an effort to co-operate and to avoid the scandal of missionary competition but was soon trying to find answers to the ethical, social and later

political questions raised in transcultural and international relations. More specifically, the World Alliance for Promoting International Friendship through the Churches* and its successors reflected the need to respond to the inevitable and conflictive globalization of human life. While the Roman Catholic Church, except for some individual members, did not participate in the ecumenical dialogue until the mid-20th century, in Leo XIII's *Rerum Novarum* (see **social encyclicals, papal**) of 1891 it developed a social doctrine that was inspired by its traditional theological understanding of humans and society but did so in the face of the same questions that were at the time engaging the attention of the emerging ecumenical movement.

As these trends began to flow together (if not organizationally, at least in dialogue and overlapping of constituencies), and as the churches began to participate institutionally in dialogue and co-operation through the creation of organizations like national councils or the Faith and Order* and the Life and Work* movements, some of the traditional theological and ethical distinctions used by the churches, while retaining a certain analytical value, began to blur. The distinction between individual and social ethics lost all precision in ever more complex societies, where many face-to-face relations became institutionalized and bureaucratized and personal decisions frequently can be reached and implemented only by means of collective action. Social sciences, on the other hand, made clear the social nature of individual life. How should one respond to this new situation? Casuistry would have to include so many variables as to become an impossible game; pure principle ethics has to be worked through infinite mediations, which present their own ethical ambiguities; purely agapaic or situational/contextual proposals seem too subjective. A new discussion of these different directions can make sense only if it begins by recognizing the impossibility of separating an individual and a social ethics.

The 18th- and 19th-century distinction of dogmatics and ethics is also challenged when we realize that there is no ethical decision which does not imply a theological understanding and no dogmatic formulation which is independent of the historical conditions and the actual practice of those who create it.

Moreover, some burning issues, for instance race and nationhood, are indissolubly tied to understandings of creation and redemption. In fact, we discover that certain political or social decisions are in themselves a heresy or a confession of faith (the case of apartheid* or of the Confessing Church* have become typical).

Finally, and in the same direction, the distinction between social issues that belong within the sphere of religious ethics and those that belong to autonomous realms is clearly artificial. Secularization* claims all realms of human life as a field for human debate and decision; faith* claims for the sovereignty of Jesus Christ* all of reality. A distinction between areas where the church has something to say (e.g. public morality, marriage, family, education) and others which must be left as wholly autonomous (mainly politics and economics) is totally untenable. The question becomes one of finding an adequate understanding of how the sovereignty of Christ is exercised in these relatively autonomous realms and how the Christian retains a freedom in obedience.

The sociology of religion, developed mainly since Max Weber and Ernst Troeltsch, also poses critical questions to the churches by showing how they are themselves subject to social conditionings and can act on society only through the mediation of social relations. As Troeltsch put it: "The question of the inward influence of Christianity upon... ethical mutual relationships" can be investigated only in "the concrete effects of its influence in different social groups", and such investigation makes it clear that "great tracts of social life, like that of the economic order, throw a great deal of light upon the general fundamental tendency of Christian sociology". The churches and the ecumenical movement are only slowly and reluctantly incorporating such insights into their self-understanding and action, but some efforts to understand institutionality (see **church as institution**) or the nature of conflict* or to examine the actual praxis of the churches are already part of the ecumenical movement.

This dialogue and co-operation of Christians and churches on ethical questions have revealed coincidences both in relation to concrete questions and on general theological affirmations. At the same time, some of the differences in theological traditions have become visible in their approach to ethical questions. Edward Duff, for instance, finds in the ecumenical discussion a tension between a Catholic ethics of ends, with a more optimistic anthropology and an affirmation of a natural law that reason can know, and a Protestant ethics of inspiration, with a more pessimistic anthropology and a sense of the discontinuity between reason and revelation. C.-H. Grenholm, on the other hand, discerns in the WCC a "pure humanistic ethics", for which the Christian faith does not add any criterion which is not already available in human thought; a "pure theological ethics", for which the Christian ideal of love is specific, only to be known through revelation and totally different from all non-Christian conceptions of love; and a mediating "mixed theological ethics", for which there are certain normative criteria common to all human beings and Christian faith operates as motivation but also as offering some specific insights. Although such distinctions have the approximate character of all typologies, the differences to which they point will be seen in the discussion of specific ethical questions. Different positions on hermeneutical questions concerning the nature of biblical authority for ethical questions and the hermeneutical principles in the interpretation of scripture in this respect are not unrelated to these differences in theological tradition. They can also be discerned in their understanding of eschatology and the role that it plays in relation to ethics. Finally, churches differ in the way they understand the authority of the church on ethical questions and the modes of exercise of such authority, particularly in relation to social and political issues. It is striking that the international bilateral dialogues* should have so far devoted so little attention to ethical questions.

These deep differences, however, should not be seen simply as a liability or a hindrance for ecumenical dialogue and co-operation. They do create tensions and make the road to united witness and action a difficult one. But they also have helped to see the richness of our common Christian heritage, to correct the one-sidedness or misunderstandings of our own traditions as they have developed in particular historical circumstances and to find complementary relations. The frequently quoted slogan "doctrine divides, service unites" proves to be only partially true: service also reveals deep differences, but the urgency for common action leads to a deeper doctrinal unity. Faith and Order and Life and Work are not competitors for ecumenical priority but the necessary presupposition and consequence of each other.

Ethics in the ecumenical movement. When we follow the history of the ecumenical movement in this century, particularly in the tradition that developed in the WCC, we find the points of insertion of the issues that we have mentioned in previous paragraphs. There is both continuity and new developments in that history. It can be developed internally, in the sense of a process that follows the theological and ecclesiastical changes in the churches. But also it can be seen externally as changes in society, geographical expansion of the ecumenical movement and new cultural trends condition the problematics that the churches must assume. We consider here some of these developments, which are dealt with more specifically in the corresponding entries.

The first Life and Work conference (Stockholm 1925), deeply concerned with the question of reconstruction in the aftermath of the first world war, and reflecting the beginning of the crisis of liberal theology and the rise of dialectical theology, centred theologically on the relation between the kingdom of God* and society. Can the relation between them be seen in continuity (and therefore we could discern in history* the signs of the presence of the kingdom), or is the kingdom an eschatological reality which is exclusively God's work and the presence of which in history remains hidden until the end? While the social gospel tradition (the social gospel movement*) and the *Christianisme social* (see **socialism**) moved in the first direction, neo-orthodoxy and the Lutheran tradition were more inclined to emphasize discontinuity. While all would agree that questions of peace* and international order* were fundamental and should engage Christians, the approach to them was seen, in one case, as a form of preparing the way for the kingdom, a co-operation with God's action; in the other, as an act of obedience to the lordship of Christ (more in the Reformed tradition) or of the exercise of love in the secular realm (more in the Lutheran tradition). One of the first

studies carried out by the WCC, even before Amsterdam, dealing with "The Authority of the Bible for Today", culminating in an Oxford meeting in 1949 with some principles of biblical interpretation for social and political issues, hinges on this question and tries to find a common ground that recognizes the autonomy of the worldly realm (a concern of the "two-kingdoms doctrine") as well as the lordship of Christ over both church and world (and therefore the relevance of the testimony of scripture for society).

Twelve years later (Oxford 1937), some things had changed. On the one hand, it had become clearer that Christian concern could not be left to individual Christians alone but had to engage the churches as such. The title of the conference already indicates this: "Church, Community and State". But that title indicates also the new challenge that had emerged with the rise of nationalism in the forms of fascism* and totalitarianism.* The more tragic dimensions of human life became visible. Theologically, the centrality of the lordship of Christ became a main theme that dominated the ecumenical approach to social and political ethics for several decades. It was on this basis that the Confessing Church would carry on its struggle with National Socialism in Germany. But while such an approach was fruitful for a critical position (which after Amsterdam 1948 would be held in the face of both nationalist and communist totalitarianism), it was also necessary to find guidelines for Christian action. What kind of society could Christians envisage in order to define their understanding of the state, economy or political action? The concept of middle axioms* was here introduced as a bridge between a principle ethics which could not find its way into concrete reality and a casuistry that could transform the gospel into a law. For a more liberal tradition, middle axioms could be seen as an encounter between the Christian revelation* and human wisdom and experience; from a more eschatologically oriented theology, they could be understood as "concrete utopia", signs or analogies of the kingdom of Christ. In both, however, the preference for a form of democratic political organization, human rights and freedoms and a mixed economic system was clearly visible.

To provide a vision of society that could give some concrete guidance to Christians in the political and social realm has been a permanent concern of the WCC since its beginning. Its first expression was the responsible society,* seen in Amsterdam 1948 as an instrument for assessing both critically and positively the claims and achievements of both the liberal democratic and the communist ideologies and societies. The dominant Christological approach of Amsterdam was enlarged at Evanston 1954 with an eschatological dimension which had already been explored, from an ethical perspective, in the studies of "Eschatology and Ethics" (Bossey 1951). A global perspective began to appear which increased after New Delhi 1961 with the growing presence of third-world churches, Eastern Orthodoxy and the merger of the International Missionary Council. But the quest for some picture of society, a diacritical instrument, would recur again in the attempt to define the traits of a just, participatory and sustainable society* (after Nairobi 1975) and of justice, peace and the integrity of creation* (since Vancouver 1983).

Between Amsterdam and Vancouver, however, certain fundamental issues had engaged ecumenical interest and enlarged the ethical concerns. Churches from Asia and Africa had raised the political issue of decolonization,* their struggles for liberation* and the problems of nation-building. Theological understandings warned against a confusion of God's kingdom and human struggles, but could not respond to the questions raised by the new peoples and nations, races and classes who, struggling against centuries-old oppressions, began to build their own world. The idea of a responsible society had to be corrected and expanded to include the concern for necessarily revolutionary change (see **revolution**), the concern for rapid social change and development,* the struggle against racism* and the legitimacy of certain forms of nationalism (see **nation**). At the Geneva 1966 conference on Church and Society, a development of the neo-orthodox theology, coming mainly from Latin America, was concerned with the legitimacy of revolution, looking for ways to identify the signs of God's presence in our history, vindicating the positive role of ideologies as the way in which people* define their goals and project their action in the quest for freedom and justice. Some themes had to be explored: on the one hand, the significance

of ideology* for social ethics; on the other hand, the meaning of the humanum as a criterion for Christian reflection.

Struggles against colonialism as well as development and nation-building could not be discussed without taking account of omnipresent economic determinations. Oppressed nations, races and peoples are poor,* economically and therefore also socially. The ethical agenda had to include an understanding of the economic mechanisms of poverty (see **economics**) and a theological as well as a social and political understanding of the poor. Such demands led to programmes on transnational corporations,* questions of investment,* capitalism* and socialism, concrete issues like land reform,* trade unions (see **labour**) and the New International Economic Order. Oppression, however, is also related to political and military situations. Hence issues such as human rights* and militarism/militarization*, the doctrine of national security* and specific repressive policies such as torture* or the ill treatment of refugees* presented challenges which could not be ignored. It has to be admitted, however, that often an immediate response to critical situations has not been followed by a theological reflection that could have enriched the theologico-ethical understanding and critical evaluation of these immediate responses.

Geneva 1966 was concerned not only with the political but also the scientific revolutions of our time. We may not agree with the use of the term "revolution" in this context, but there is little doubt that scientific and technological changes had raised new challenges for the churches. Questions of environment/ecology,* bio-ethics* and genetic engineering, sources and use of energy,* the relation of science and technology,* and pollution* (most of them already mentioned though not developed at Geneva) demanded a practical approach as specific questions, a relational analysis to see them within the total functioning of society and a theological reflection that would undergird and inform the position to be taken by the WCC and the churches on these issues. The 1979 MIT conference was both a gathering point of many studies carried out in the WCC and in many member churches and a point of departure for further theological and practical work. Theologically such issues as our understanding of nature,* and conse-

quently the relation between creation and redemption (see **creation, Trinity**), faith and
science (see **science and technology**), which
in different contexts have been already on the
theological agenda of the ecumenical movement, have now become urgent also from the
point of view of ethical reflection and decision.

The ecumenical movement has not broken
much new ground on ethical issues which
have figured prominently in the ethical concerns of the churches in the past, such as
marriage,* family* and sexual ethics.* The
classical consideration of these subjects under
"orders of creation" or "the mandates" or, in
the Catholic tradition, natural law* was somewhat alien to the Christological perspective
dominant in the ecumenical movement for
many decades. But traditional issues presented now new challenges, partly because of
changes in culture related to social, economic
and political developments, partly because of
new human possibilities opened by science
and technology, both resulting in the erosion
of traditional patterns of behaviour, tacitly or
explicitly accepted and supported by the churches. The struggle of women for a new understanding and experience of their role in church
and society (see **women in church and society, feminism**) required a new discussion of
marriage and family. The debate about
homosexuality,* birth control* and abortion*
could not be postponed. Some traditional issues such as divorce* and euthanasia* demanded new consideration. The ecumenical
movement is far from having developed a
coherent theological approach or clear ethical
criteria for facing such issues, but they will
undoubtedly figure prominently in the future.

An issue traditionally related to what was
seen as "personal ethics" occupied the ecumenical movement in its early stages. The
reflection on the meaning of work* and vocation* was part of the attempt to develop a
theology of the laity* that would enlarge the
understanding of ecclesiology and enrich the
life of the churches. In this context Evanston
1954 (sec. 6) took up a theme raised at Amsterdam, i.e. assuming responsibility in terms
of the struggle for justice, viewing one's
specific place in society as a service (see
diakonia) of love, while respecting the autonomy of the secular realm. Another traditional
Christian concern, that of health and healing,*

has entered the ecumenical agenda (see
health care) and generated a theological reflection of health as wholeness, both in the
personal and communal sense and in understanding healing as much wider than the cure
of specific physical malfunctioning. The consideration of these two classic themes, while
not prominent in the ecumenical movement,
points to an important goal: to recover for
ecumenical thinking areas of human life that
were seen as self-contained and individual and
to insert them in a more holistic approach to
human life in our complex world society without losing sight of the personal centre, where
all these lines converge. Ethical and pastoral
concerns should be seen as intimately related.

Prospects for ecumenical ethics. Ethics
remains a touchstone of ecumenicity, not in
isolation from other concerns, nor as a one-
sided lobby, but as Christian personal and
community praxis, as a doctrine that is aware
of the practice from which it springs and to
which it leads, and as action that acknowledges the doctrine that is implicit in it and its
responsibility to the ecumenical Christian
community in time and space. It has fulfilled
that function to some extent in the period of
our survey. The prospects that we can envisage for the future make it necessary to continue and to strengthen that service.

Ethics makes the ecumenical movement
ever aware of the world in which it operates,
both in the sense of the reality from which it
emerges and of the influence it exerts and
should exert on it. As we stand on the
threshold of a new century, that reality is
rapidly moving: the growing pauperization of
the majority of the human population (both
in third-world countries and in significant
numbers in the "developed" world) reaches a
point where it verges on massive genocide,
while the expansion of economic, scientific-
technological and communication media endeavours to create a homogeneous world market from which the majority will be excluded.
At the same time, the geopolitical and
ideological frontiers of East and West which
defined the world from the beginnings of the
modern ecumenical movement are becoming
fluid in a movement whose direction we cannot anticipate. Such a situation presents to
ecumenical ethics a twofold task. On the one
side, we have the question of priority and
commitment: Will the Christian oikoumene be

simply integrated in this "world market" as its religious legitimation and "accompanying music", or shall it make of the poor of the land the object and subject of its reflection and action? On the other hand, will it engage the rigorous analytical work that is necessary to mediate that fundamental option effectively and to help Christians and churches make the concrete decisions that correspond to it in their different circumstances and possibilities?

Since the 1960s the Roman Catholic Church and the non-Catholic ecumenical movement have entered an ecumenical dialogue in which ethics has occupied a central place, both as an area of co-operation and as a place where differences become explicit. Experiments like SODEPAX* are a good example of both. This dialogue is not easy: there are deep differences in theological tradition, in self-conception, in the understanding of authority and in the role of the magisterium in ethical questions. There are differences of approach to some of the burning issues of today. For all these reasons discussion and, even more, co-operation on ethical questions become at times almost impossible. But there are also other signs. Theologically, Protestants are learning (not so much through theological discussion but by looking at the practice of the Catholic church in certain areas) that notions of natural law and of the common good and classic principles such as solidarity* or subsidiarity* can offer significant guidance for tackling issues and deserve more careful attention than they have usually received. On the other hand, Roman Catholic encyclicals and ethical statements of the last half century have more and more combined the traditional natural-law approach with an appeal to revelation that creatively and carefully incorporates the insights of ecumenical biblical studies of the last half century or more in which Catholics have been active partners. Finally, the increasingly significant presence of Eastern Orthodoxy, of people's base communities of prayer and action and of a growing Pentecostal movement, each with its own approach to ethics deeply related to spirituality, both relativize and correct the more intellectualistic and nomic character of Western Christianity. To make this encounter fruitful for ethics is one of the opportunities opened up for the ecumenical movement.

We have already alluded to the fact that the ecumenical movement has not yet properly developed the theological undergirding of its ethical commitments or profitably developed the theological insights implicit in them. Such shortcomings may be partly due to the pressing nature of the challenges and to the intensity of the commitments that they evoke. But they may also be a result of theological one-sidedness. It seems that the ecumenical movement is led both by the total confessional and geographical scope of participation and by the nature of the global problems that it faces to develop a theological reflection deeply rooted in a Trinitarian faith, responsive to and responsible for the actual praxis of the Christian community in the world and in permanent critical and integrative dialogue with human sciences and ideologies. Such theology could help the churches to be faithful to their mission, not as masters or pioneers of a new world, but as salt in the world that God is creating through human thinking and action and as a permanent reminder of that new earth of promise for which we pray and hope.

See also **church and society, church and state**.

JOSÉ MÍGUEZ BONINO

Ethics and the Search for Christian Unity: Two Statements by the Roman Catholic/Presbyterian-Reformed Consultation, Washington, DC, US Catholic Conference, 1981 • J. Moltmann, *On Human Dignity: Political Theology and Ethics*, London, SCM, 1984 • B. Musschenga & D. Gosling eds, *Science Education and Ethical Values: Introducing Ethics and Religion into the Science Classroom and Laboratory*, WCC, 1985 • O. O'Donovan & R. McCormick, *Studies in Christian Ethics: Ethics and Ecumenism*, vol. 1, no. 1, Edinburgh, Clark, 1988 • R. Preston, *The Future of Christian Ethics*, London, SCM, 1987 • K. Srisang ed., *Perspectives on Political Ethics: An Ecumenical Enquiry*, WCC, 1983 • A.M. Suggate, *William Temple and Christian Social Ethics Today*, Edinburgh, Clark, 1987.

ETHICS, SEXUAL. The basis of any Christian sexual ethics can be Gen. 1:27. It is apparent, not controversial or even "mythical", that the human race comes in two kinds, male and female. Those who believe in God the Creator believe that God intended it so. Sexual ethics is concerned with the interpretation of this fact.

Biology and theology are not at odds in understanding that sexual differentiation is primarily "for" reproduction, nor need science and religion quarrel over the role of the "pair-bond" in the nurturing and protecting of human young through their long childhood. So in Gen. 1:28 human sexuality is immediately linked with procreation and God's blessing upon fertility. The human race has indeed multiplied exceedingly and has filled and subdued the earth, though not always in innocent ways. (The fall is also an evident though not easily interpreted fact about humankind [see **sin**].)

The Yahwist account of the creation of men and women (Gen. 2) is more complex, and anyone who takes it seriously faces questions both of interpretation and of the authority of the Old Testament for today. It may well be characterized, though not of course written off, as a myth. Whatever other meanings can be drawn from it, this story leads up to the key concept of the "one flesh" union. Human pair-bonding is able to transcend its biological function. The Christian churches have been unanimous, both that in the purpose of God men and women are meant to form faithful unions and that human progeny are meant to be brought to birth and nurtured in this context.

Much scope for differences of opinion remains, and from these foundations the argument has gone in diverse and controversial ways. At one extreme is the view (for which Augustine must take some responsibility) that the fall is all-important and that human sexuality has gone so wrong that the only justification for sexual union is the plain intent by a married pair to raise a family. At the other extreme is the view that sexual pleasure is worthwhile for its own sake, is even a human right, apart from any intention of procreation or even of a lasting relationship. Most Christians in all the churches would repudiate both these extremes, though often with some leaning towards one or the other.

Each extreme in turn can be seen as a way of coming to terms with current human common sense. It is fair to point out that in societies without efficient contraception and with high maternal mortality, it is hardly surprising that sexual pleasure should be feared. Nor is it surprising that when, for a few years, the dangers of uncommitted sexual encounters

seemed to be overcome, the view that sex can be just a "healthy form of sport" should come into fashion. Before AIDS* arrived, many Christians were finding the defence of traditional chastity a thankless task, knowing what negative lines the churches have frequently taken.

People expect Catholic Christians to uphold tradition and Protestants to sit loose to it. It has been too easy in the West to see Catholics as rigid, Protestants as antinomian and Anglicans as trying to hold a balance, forgetting the Orthodox meanwhile or drawing upon them belatedly for support. But the arguments are by no means tidily denominational, though two well-trodden controversies, contraception and the divorce issue (see **birth control, divorce**), have lately lent themselves to such oversimplification. Neither Catholicism nor Protestantism is neatly monolithic, especially not Protestantism, which has given rise both to "situation ethics" and to "fundamentalism" as well as to the monumental contribution of Karl Barth. To set, for instance, *Towards a Quaker View of Sex* (1963) against such a Roman pronouncement as *Casti Connubii* (1930) as representatives of the two sides in a straightforward controversy can only darken counsel. Indeed at times the case could be put the other way round, with "puritans" denying the goodness of sexuality in the name of an ethic of respectability, while Roman casuists shocked Protestants by finding ways round moral demands.

Somewhat paradoxically it has been suggested (e.g. O'Donovan) that, after all, there is no great difference between Catholic and Protestant over *sexuality*. Their evident divergence is at least partly a matter of their division over authority.* Protestantism has no clear way of "making up its mind" and may tend to follow public opinion, but Roman Catholicism has great difficulty in publicly changing its made-up mind when understanding develops, as has conspicuously happened over contraception (see *Humanae Vitae* 1968 and the discussions before and since).

There is another way in which a real Catholic/Protestant division can be denied. When Orthodoxy is brought into the picture, the besetting tendency of Western churches towards *legalism*, of which antinomianism is only the reverse image, is shown up. The choice between prohibitions and permissions has more to do with bureaucracy than with the love of God. The Eastern churches in their teaching on sexuality have put more emphasis upon love both human and divine, and this understanding is beginning to be appreciated by Western Christians (e.g. Church of England).

Teaching of Christ in the gospels in fact includes not much about sexuality, but what there is does not let the majesty or the mercy of God be forgotten. In applying his teaching today, we may find it more constructive to look at problems in the light of traditions, rather than traditions in the light of problems. There is convergence for which we may be grateful and outstanding differences about which one must be honest. It has to be said that the ancient Christian emphasis on celibacy as better than marriage* as carried over into Roman Catholicism, whether or not Protestants have been right to consider it an over-emphasis in itself, has had the practical result that unmarried priests have been responsible for Catholic teaching on sexuality, with inevitably unbalanced results.

No doubt the moralist's task would look

Young people in Guatemala City, Guatemala (WCC/Peter Williams)

simpler if sexual relationship and procreation had not been made separable by human skills. The development of first contraception and then in vitro fertilization (see **bio-ethics**) has laid upon human beings the obligation to consider more deeply the meaning of both sexuality and parenthood.

The need is to encourage the expectation that a Christian view will turn out to be, not some arbitrary set of commandments, but the gracious purpose of the Creator for his people. A late-20th-century Christian, respecting tradition and in touch with contemporary developments, will surely be inclined towards an understanding of sexuality which gives great importance to the faithful relationship between a man and a woman. Of course this emphasis is helped, some would say made possible, by greater longevity, smaller families, less pressure simply to keep alive. But, after all, the Christian tradition does have encouragement for such a relational understanding of sexuality, not least in the concept of the "one flesh" union which the Lord picked up and quoted in his teaching on marriage (Mark 10:6-8).

A "relational" understanding of sexuality, at its best, neither belittles procreation nor makes fidelity an optional extra dependent on people's whims. In all the churches there has been an increasing appreciation that physical sexual union can be a kind of human "means of grace" in effecting, developing and sustaining the unity between a man and a woman. The point of permanent fidelity is neither the disgracefulness nor the danger of unlegalized sex but the need for time for real union to develop.

Such a view sheds light on old problems. It is able to honour both marriage and celibacy as particular vocations without setting either up against the other. It can value procreation as truly procreation without making children the rationale of marriage. To believe that human beings are, so to say, relational animals can be a way of talking about natural law* without the finicky legalism of which natural-law theories are suspected. The "hard cases" of this view will be people's real troubles, to be handled with mercy and imagination, rather than artificial dilemmas imposed by recalcitrant theory.

That is not to say that relational views of sexuality are free from difficulties or create no problems of their own. A characteristic weakness is a tendency to idolize "relationship": either permissively, treating relationship, however transient, as self-justifying and as justifying everything done in its name; or smugly, rejecting and blaming people with unsatisfactory relationships. Christians of different persuasions have thought in slogans here and need each other's balance. In particular, "personalism" has become a word with almost contrary moral implications, suggesting to some people truly Christian encouragement of personal fulfilment, but signifying to others the selfish pursuit of atomistic individualism.

An insidious trap for the liberal minded is to allow sexuality to colonize, as it were, all loving relationships. It is true that the contrast between agape and eros has been overworked, but it does not follow that all relationship is what is ordinarily called erotic. It has been too easy, in deploring the so-called puritan tradition of prudery and trying to learn from Freud, to seem to imply that "relationship" just means "sexual relationship", needing and deserving physical expression. So the subtleties of human and Christian love go by default.

The outstanding problem, which is by no means fully resolved, is the right understanding of maleness and femaleness. When procreation is allowed to matter less and relationship more, why do we forbid love-making between members of the same sex, at least as a *faute de mieux*? When women are set free from perpetual child-bearing, can they begin to do everything men can do? If not, why not? (See **homosexuality, feminism**.)

The question of women priests bids fair to be as divisive ecumenically as contraception and more essentially recalcitrant. It is not easily solved one way or the other, partly because of prejudices, but partly because behind it lie deep questions about the meaning of the fact that there are two sexes (see **women in church and society**).

Are men and women "equal", and what would that mean? Are they complementary, without different natures and roles? The more we care about fairness and make them equal, the more we seem to make them merely interchangeable. The more we stress complementarity, the more tendency there is to devalue or patronize women as "the fair sex" or as mother-goddesses, and to be cruel to those of both sexes who cannot or will not conform to stereotype.

The arguments in these matters do not, yet, cut neatly across denominational lines. In other words, Christians are still at an early stage of what could become a fresh and deep schism.* Hindsight may show how too much legalism and too little listening, on both sides, is a recipe for bitterness as the cost of reformation. The silliness of some of the arguments masks the importance of the problem. Women in all the churches are learning not to take for granted the time-honoured assumption that real human beings are all men: pernicious just because it is an assumption, not an argued refutable belief. They are being urged to learn "to say 'I', to accept themselves... as good, whole and beautiful"; and beyond "I" to go on and say "we" (Reinhild Traitler). If only other women listen, the "we" will not be men and women together, but ramifying forms of apartheid between the aggrieved and the complacent. Christians who believe that God made human beings for union must have something better to say than feminism or anti-feminism.

See also **family, marriage**.

HELEN OPPENHEIMER

P. Brown, *The Body and Society: Men, Women and Sexual Renunciation in Early Christianity*, New York, Columbia UP, 1988 • Church of England, *Marriage, Divorce and the Church*, London, SPCK, 1971 • J.M. Gustafson, *Protestant and Roman Catholic Ethics*, London, SCM, 1978 • O. O'Donovan, "Moral Disagreement as an Ecumenical Issue", *Studies in Christian Ethics*, vol. 1, no. 1, Edinburgh, Clark, 1988.

Ancient. St John Chrysostom, *On Marriage and Family Life*, Crestwood, NY, St Vladimir's Seminary, 1986.

Catholic. Pastoral Constitution on the Church in the Modern World, Gaudium et Spes, Vatican II, 1965, part 2, ch. 1, in *The Documents of Vatican II*, W.M. Abbott ed., London, Chapman, 1966 • J. Dominian, *Sexual Integrity: The Answer to AIDS*, London, Darton Longman & Todd, 1987.

Protestant. K. Barth, *Kirchliche Dogmatik* (ET *Church Dogmatics*, III/1.3, IV/1, Edinburgh, Clark, 1981).

Anglican. D.S. Bailey, *The Man-Woman Relation in Christian Thought*, London, Longmans, 1959 • *Homosexual Relationships*, London, CIO, 1979, ch. 4.

Orthodox. P. Evdokimov, *Sacrament de l'amour* (ET *The Sacrament of Love: The Nuptial Mystery in the Light of the Orthodox Tradition*, Crestwood, NY, St Vladimir's Seminary, 1985).

Secular. A. Soble ed., *Philosophy of Sex: Contemporary Readings*, Tatowa, NJ, Littlefield, 1980.

ETHNICITY. The value of patriotism and of ethnic or national identity is assessed in widely varying ways in the text of the Bible and in the course of Christian history. In the Old Testament the Israelites, by virtue of God's special election, constitute "a holy nation" (Ex. 19:6), "a people holy to the Lord... chosen out of all the peoples that are on the face of the earth" (Deut. 7:6). Ethnicity, so far as the Hebrews are concerned, forms part of God's saving plan (see **salvation history**). But, more particularly in later strands of the OT, a place is allowed in the divine purpose for other nations as well. In the last days "all the nations" will come to the temple at Jerusalem (Isa. 2:2); "all the nations" are invited to praise and worship God (Ps. 86:9, 117:1); a guardian angel is assigned to each nation (Dan. 10:13,21; 12:1).

In the New Testament the titles previously applied to Israel are now used to describe the church: "... a holy nation, God's own people" (1 Pet. 2:9). But this implies a transformation of the concept of nationhood, since the church* is essentially universal; within the community of the baptized all ethnic boundaries are transcended, and "there is neither Jew nor Greek... for all of you are one in Christ Jesus" (Gal. 3:27). This supranational approach was evident in the structuring of the early church, which was organized not on a national but on a territorial basis. The term "church" was in no way applied to an ethnic entity but referred to the entire community of the faithful gathered locally in each place for the eucharist, whatever their nationality (see **local church, unity of "all in each place"**). In the ancient canons the powers of each bishop extended not to an ethnic group but to a defined geographical area; all Christians in a given city are under the same bishop.

Yet this did not imply that nationhood lost all meaning within the Christian dispensation. It is symbolically significant that at Pentecost* the Holy Spirit* descended in the tongues of the different nations. Ethnic variety was not obliterated, but it ceased to be a dividing barrier; those present spoke different languages, yet each understood the other (Acts 2:3-11). Nationhood is seen, not just as transitory, but as part of the age to come (see **kingdom of God**): it is not just individuals but "the nations" that enter the kingdom (Rev. 21:24), in all their variety and with their distinctive treasures. In canon 34 of the 4th-century apostolic canons, it is insisted that the "bishops of each nation" are to meet together.

The church of the East Roman or Byzantine Empire was multinational in character, although with Greek culture as the prevailing influence, while in the Roman Catholic West the papacy has always emphasized the supranational, universal nature of the church. But the churches founded by Orthodox missionaries in Bulgaria, Serbia and Russia (9th-10th centuries) possessed from the start a markedly national spirit, and the same was true of the leading Protestant groups at the Reformation. So strong has nationalism proved in modern Orthodoxy that in 1872 the Ecumenical Patriarchate even issued a formal condemnation of the heresy* of "phyletism" (the view that the church should be structured on ethnic, not territorial, principles). But this has had little effect, as the multi-jurisdictional situation of the Orthodox church in the West shows only too clearly.

The ecumenical movement, while combating religious, ethnic and racial intolerance, has always taken as its ideal unity,* not uniformity. Patriotism and ethnicity, while they need to undergo a searching *metanoia*, need not be totally rejected. Within a re-united Christendom there is room for the utmost diversity in styles of theology, ways of worship and forms of church government; likewise, a commitment to world peace does not exclude a strong sense of local loyalty. In the words of the Russian writer Vadim Borisov: "The nation is a level in the hierarchy of the Christian cosmos, a part of God's immutable purpose." "Nations", as Alexander Solzhenitsyn observes, "are the wealth of humankind, its collective personalities; the very least of them wears its own special colours, and bears within itself a special facet of divine intention."

See also **diaspora, nation**.

KALLISTOS WARE

R. Niebuhr, *Moral Man and Immoral Society*, New York, Scribner, 1960 • A. Solzhenitsyn ed., *From under the Rubble*, Chicago, IL, Regnery-Gateway, 1975.

EUCHARIST. "Eucharist" has become the most widely used name ecumenically for the rite which almost all Christian communities believe to have been instituted by Jesus at the Last Supper: "Do this in remembrance of me" (see 1 Cor. 11:23-25; cf. Matt. 26:26-29; Mark 14:22-25; Luke 22:14-20). Coming from the Greek word for "thanksgiving", the name "eucharist" refers to the central prayer in the rite, whereby God is above all thanked for the works of creation* and redemption* accomplished through Christ and in the Holy Spirit. Other names pick up other features or meanings of the complex rite: thus the Lord's supper, the breaking of bread, the holy communion, the divine liturgy, the offering, and the mass (though nobody quite knows the etymology of this last).

The various names carry to some extent particular confessional associations, and differences in the understanding and practice of the eucharist have often been a cause, symptom or result of wider doctrinal and spiritual differences among the churches. In the 16th century, for example, differences over the sacrificial character of the eucharist expressed differences between Catholics and Protestants over the roles of God and the human being in the achievement of redemption and the appropriation of salvation.* Differences among Lutherans, Zwinglians and Calvinists over the presence of Christ at the Lord's supper were connected with differences in Christology as such. Arguments between East and West over the moment and agency of the consecration of the bread and wine — Christ's words of institution and/or the invocation of the Holy Spirit* — reflect controversies over the relations among the persons of the Trinity.* Moreover, participation in the eucharist of other churches, or lack thereof, has usually been the measure of communion among the churches or of its rupture.

The modern ecumenical movement has realized that the restoration of Christian unity* entails a necessary and sufficient agreement in eucharistic doctrine and practice (see **communion**; **intercommunion**). While, on the one hand, what is necessary and sufficient are themselves matters of debate with regard to the eucharist itself, it may, on the other hand, legitimately be hoped that agreements attained in this focal area will have wider consequences for unity in faith and life among the churches. Thus agreeement on the Lord's supper was at the heart of the Leuenberg concordat, which established new relations among the Lutheran and Reformed churches of Europe (1973). Nor is it accidental that several worldwide bilateral dialogues* from an early stage devoted their attention to the eucharist (e.g. the Windsor statement of the Anglican-Roman Catholic International Commission I, 1971; *Das Herrenmahl* of the Lutheran-RC dialogue, 1978; sections of the Denver and Dublin reports of the Methodist-RC dialogue 1971 and 1976; the Orthodox-RC text from Munich 1982, "The Mystery of the Church and of the Eucharist in the Light of the Mystery of the Holy Trinity"). In the international, multilateral Faith and Order movement, the eucharist was never lost from sight between Lausanne 1927 and Lima 1982. The Lima text itself (the "E" of BEM*), the responses of the churches to it, and some directions pointed by the report of F&O in coordinating these responses (*Baptism, Eucharist and Ministry 1982-1990: Report on the Process and Responses*, 1990) may be taken as the measure of eucharistic agreement up to this point.

The meaning of the eucharist. E begins with a Christological and soteriological concentration. In conformity with strong themes in the biblical scholarship of the past two or three generations, Christ's institution of the eucharist is seen to be "prefigured in the Passover memorial of Israel's deliverance from the land of bondage and in the meal of the covenant on Mount Sinai (Ex. 24)", surrounded by the significant meals of Jesus' earthly ministry and after his resurrection, and intended as "the anticipation of the supper of the Lamb (Rev. 19:9)". The eucharist is "essentially the sacrament of the gift which God makes to us in Christ through the power of the Holy Spirit. Every Christian receives this gift of salvation through communion in the body and blood of Christ" (E2).

Lima then expounds the meaning of the eucharist according to a Trinitarian pattern and the fivefold sequences of the ancient creeds, as (1) "thanksgiving to the Father", (2) "memorial of Christ", (3) "invocation of the Spirit", (4) "communion of the faithful", and (5) "meal of the kingdom". In general terms, this arrangement meets with the practically unanimous approval of the churches.

In more detail, (1) is welcomed for its inclusion of creation and its recognition of the cosmic scope of redemption, features which had long been eclipsed in many Western liturgies. All recognize that thanksgiving is the appropriate human response to God's work, but some Lutheran responses fear that an emphasis on "the sacrifice of praise" might obscure the fact that the Lord's supper is first and foremost a divine "benefit" towards humankind.

Regarding (2), the two historically most controversial points have been the mode(s) of Christ's presence in the eucharist and the relation of the eucharist to Christ's sacrifice on the cross. The churches rejoice in the confession of "Christ's real, living and active presence" made in E13, and many responses would remain content with that. But some do not believe that the "convergence [so] formulated" suffices to "accommodate" remaining differences concerning the connection of Christ's presence with the bread and wine (E13 comm.). In particular, Roman Catholic and Orthodox responses want a less-guarded acknowledgment that the elements *become* the body and blood of Christ, while a few Protestant responses ask that precisely some forms of that claim be excluded. This in fact probably remains the single most divisive issue in eucharistic faith, doctrine and theology. The relation to Calvary does not provoke nearly so much comment. There is widespread agreement that Lima adequately protected the uniqueness of the cross; but the Roman Catholic response is doubtful whether the category of Christ's continuing intercession, and the church's participation in it, is sufficient "to explain the sacrificial nature of the eucharist", and several Orthodox responses question whether Christ's sacrifice is sufficiently "actualized" according to the Lima text.

As to the "invocation of the Spirit" (3), the churches welcome this feature as a prayerful recognition that God's gift and the church's action remain entirely dependent on grace.* The traditional Orthodox insistence on the pneumatological dimensions of the Lord's supper has now been largely received by the Western churches, although some Protestant responses continue to question whether the Holy Spirit is appropriately invoked not only on the whole assembly and its action but more particularly upon the bread and wine. The sharpest criticism of Lima's pneumatology

"Last supper", by Napoleon Veloso Abueva, reprinted by permission from Masao Takenaka, "Christian Art in Asia" (Tokyo, Kyo Bun Kwan, 1975), plate 58

comes from some Lutherans who fear for the adequacy of the Word himself and "his promise in the words of institution" (Evangelical Lutheran Church in the Netherlands).

Positively put, there is a very widespread recognition that — even if Lima does not always have the relation quite right — anamnesis and epiclesis (memorial and invocation) do in fact belong together, since Christ and the Spirit belong together in an "indissoluble union" (E14 comm.). The F&O report on the churches' responses suggests that more progress is yet to be made on remaining difficulties over Christ's presence and sacrifice by a deepened reflection, within an acknowledged Trinitarian context, on the biblical realities of "memorial" and "Spirit". Greater development is needed of Lima's recognition that the crucified and risen Christ is the living and active *content* of the memorial in word and meal (E5-6,12), and that the Spirit is "called upon" in order to make the eucharistic event *possible*, *real* and *effective* (E14). In the Holy Spirit, Christ comes to us, clothed in his mighty acts, and gathers us into his self-offering as Son to the Father, in whom is eternal life (cf. Eph. 2:18).

The ecclesiological dimension of the eucharist (4) includes "communion with all the saints and martyrs" (E11). E19 establishes a link between "each local eucharistic celebration" and "the whole church". This is widely acknowledged in principle, but as Old Catholic, Roman Catholic and Orthodox responses to Lima most evidently recognize, this point raises the question of "catholicity"* and the concrete identification of "the church": what does it take to make a eucharist the eucharist, or what constitutes a eucharistic assembly?

Many responses welcomed the association made in E20 between the eucharist and "appropriate relationships in social, economic and political life"; some asked for more precision as to whether "reconciliation and sharing among all those regarded as brothers and sisters in the one family of God" is meant as a *condition* or as a *consequence* of the eucharistic celebration and communion.

Lima's acknowledgment of the eschatological dimension (5) of the Lord's supper finds very widespread approval, whether the accent be placed on joy and hope, or on mission and service, or on the anticipation of the parousia and the feast of the kingdom. The responses of the churches reveal the same tensions between present realization and future consummation as are present in E and as indeed mark the scriptural and traditional material concerning the End and the eucharist's relation to it.

All in all, the reception given to E suggests that the convergence of the churches regarding the meaning of the eucharist is stronger than on almost any other topic of dogma. The United Church of Christ in Japan considers E to be "the best section of BEM and the richest in content"; and the (Anglican) Church of Ireland specifies: "Drawing its inspiration from recent biblical, patristic and liturgical scholarship, it [E] is irenic in approach and successfully transcends the old divisive controversies." It will be important to draw on the agreements here achieved as F&O pursues the wider task of helping the churches "Towards a Common Expression of the Apostolic Faith Today" (see **common confession**).

The celebration of the eucharist. E3 declares that the eucharist "always includes both word and sacrament", and the features which the Lima text (E27) lists as belonging to the "single whole" of the eucharistic liturgy — hymns, prayers and proclamation as well as the action with the bread and wine — correspond remarkably, even as far as detailed

sequence, to the orders now found in the current service books of almost all confessional families (see **liturgical reforms**). Nevertheless, some Protestant respondents have received the impression that BEM "sacramentalizes" worship, to the detriment of "the word". Liturgically speaking, the National Alliance of the Lutheran Churches of France prefers to consider word and sacrament as "two foci of an ellipse". Almost all responses to BEM in fact recognize that it is wrong to *oppose* word and sacrament to each other. The 1990 report of F&O formulates the matter thus: "Using the term 'sacramental' in a general sense, i.e. referring to God's salvific action in history, the proclamation of the word is a sacramental action just as the celebration of baptism and supper are an event of God's word." In its response to BEM, the United Methodist Church (USA) had already declared: "God's effectual word is there [in the eucharistic service of word and sacrament] revealed, proclaimed, heard, seen and tasted."

"As the eucharist celebrates the resurrection of Christ, it is appropriate", declared Lima (E31), "that it should take place at least every Sunday." The principle of "the supper of the Lord every Lord's day" (John Wesley) had in fact been the practice of the whole church in the early centuries. Dating from about A.D. 150, Justin Martyr's classic description records that "on the day called sun-day an assembly is held in one place of all who live in town or country"; "the records of the apostles or writings of the prophets are read"; a sermon is followed by prayers; bread and wine are brought up, and the presider says the prayer of thanksgiving, to which the people assent by their amen; then "everyone partakes of the elements over which thanks have been given". With the mass conversions to Christianity from the 4th century onwards, the frequency of popular communion declined, although in the middle ages, especially in the West, the mass itself came to be celebrated more and more often, with an emphasis on its propitiatory power.

The Protestant reformers stopped the "multiplication of masses", but they were unable to establish the regular weekly communion of the faithful which most of the leaders desired, and so the service of prayers and preaching alone became the normal Sunday fare in their churches. In the 20th century, the Roman Catholic Church has been remarkably successful in increasing the frequency of popular communion; and responses from several Orthodox churches to BEM indicate that they share the same goal, provided adequate spiritual and moral preparation is made. On the Protestant side, the Swiss Protestant Church Federation, for instance, recognizes that "celebration [of the Lord's supper] every Sunday", understood as a service of word and sacrament, "is in line with the biblical tradition"; and the Church of Jesus Christ in Madagascar reports that "at present, thanks to BEM, CJCM accepts the principle of celebrating the eucharist every Sunday". Many Protestant responses express this as a more or less firm desideratum, having attained a greater or less degree of fulfilment.

In the commentary to E28, Lima noted that "in certain parts of the world, where bread and wine are not customary or obtainable, it is now sometimes held that local food and drink serve better to anchor the eucharist in everyday life". The responses of churches in the South Pacific showed most interest in this question, although it is also much discussed in Africa. The Church of South India commented: "The symbol should be obvious and meaningful. We have no problem with any type of bread; but it may be difficult to take the coconut water and say, 'This is the blood of Christ'." The Apostolic Catholic Assyrian Church of the East observes that "the matter of this sacrament Christ ordained to be of wheat and wine as being most fit to represent body and blood". The Orthodox and Roman Catholic churches, as well as responses from some Lutheran and Anglican churches, share that view.

GEOFFREY WAINWRIGHT

J.J. von Allmen, *Essai sur le repas du Seigneur* (ET *The Lord's Supper*, London, Lutterworth, 1969) • A. Heron, *Table and Tradition: Towards an Ecumenical Understanding of the Eucharist*, Edinburgh, Handsel, 1983 • J. Reumann, *The Supper of the Lord: The New Testament, Ecumenical Dialogues, and Faith and Order on Eucharist*, Philadelphia, Fortress, 1985 • G.K. Schäfer, *Eucharistie im ökumenischen Kontext: Zur Diskussion um das Herrenmahl in Glauben und Kirchenverfassung von Lausanne 1927 bis Lima 1982*, Göttingen, Vandenhoeck & Ruprecht, 1988 • A. Schmemann, *The Eucharist: Sacrament of the Kingdom*, Crestwood, NY, St Vladimir's Seminary, 1987 • M. Thurian, *L'eucharistie — mémorial du Seigneur, sacrifice d'action de grâce et d'intercession* (ET *The Eucharistic Memorial*, 2 vols, London, Lutterworth, 1960-61) • M. Thurian & G. Wainwright eds, *Baptism and Eucharist: Ecumenical Convergence in Celebration*, WCC, 1983 • J.-M. Tillard, *L'eucharistie, pâque de l'Eglise*, Paris, Cerf, 1964 • G. Wainwright, *Eucharist and Eschatology*, London, Epworth, 1971 • G. Wainwright, "The Eucharist in the Churches' Responses to the Lima Text", *One in Christ*, 25, 1989.

EUROPE: CENTRAL AND EASTERN.

"Central and Eastern Europe" denotes not only a geographical area from the Elbe to the Ural mountains but also — since the end of the second world war — a political entity consisting of the former socialist societies, which were ruled by Marxist-Leninist parties. The countries are Bulgaria, Czechoslovakia, the German Democratic Republic (GDR), Hungary, Poland, Romania, the Soviet Union, and to some extent Albania and Yugoslavia. These constituted a new entity in world politics, expressed by their economic and military unifying bodies (Comecon, Warsaw pact). However, since 1989 there have been popular uprisings against bureaucratic regimes, seeking a new type of society, and this development has had consequences for the churches in the respective countries.

Ecumenism did not begin in this century. For convenience we could go back to the split in the church initiated by Jan Hus. Some interpret that break with Roman Catholicism as a return to Eastern (for the Slavs, more indigenous) tradition established in Moravia by Cyril and Methodius in 863. Hus was influenced by John Wycliffe, who saw in the papacy a contradiction to the humble Christ.

In the second half of the 16th century Protestantism in Bohemia and Moravia was divided into three churches: Hussite Utraquist, Lutheran (mostly German) and Unity of Brethren. Under the Counter-Reformation of the Roman Catholic Habsburgs, especially through Jesuits, peasants and those who could not emigrate were returned to the RC fold. Through uprisings and other means, the Protestants resisted the re-Catholicization of the Habsburgs and tried to restore religious freedom in the land.

To the end of the 16th century Eastern and Central Europe was very much Protestant, especially in Hungary and Poland — at first

Lutheran and later, after the Geneva reformation, Calvinist. But with the Counter-Reformation Protestantism in Poland was suppressed, although Hungary retained a significant Protestant population. We should distinguish also between the larger churches of the Reformation and the smaller churches such as the Baptists and Methodists, which came much later and have often been discriminated against.

The Catholic push forced the Protestants to forge unity in matters of faith and confession, leading up to the *Confessio Bohemica* (1575) as a common religious programme of Protestants in Czech lands. That *Confessio* combined justification* by faith (the Reformation principle), the "fruits of faith" as applied in daily Christian life (a Hussite emphasis) and a Brethren emphasis on the consistent application of church discipline* and the obedient carrying of the cross among the signs of a true church of Christ. An interesting landmark was the 1609 edict of Emperor Rudolf, who guaranteed to give equal rights to Protestants and the Roman Catholic Church (RCC), a pledge, however, that lasted only for a brief period.

Seventeenth-century church in Suzdal, USSR (WCC/Peter Williams)

The emperor's patent of 1861 made it possible for Protestants to make contacts with foreign Protestant churches, which offered them material and spiritual help, thus providing another stream into ecumenical consciousness. Nevertheless, the churches realized that real ecumenical collaboration begins on home ground. Thus in 1905 there was founded the Unity of Constance, an interchurch society to strengthen interdenominational fellowship and evangelical awareness of a Protestant minority in the predominantly RC nation. Among other things such publications as *The Sparks of Constance* and *Theologica Evangelica* were signs of ecumenical search.

Poland was very much RC, and therefore the dynasty attempted to abolish the "Protestant heresy" and the "Eastern schism". In 1596 the union of Brest inaugurated the Uniate Church of Poland. The ecumenical vision hinged on the search for religious freedom.

The 19th century witnessed much spiritual unrest in Europe. In 1815 the Holy Alliance was formed to re-build political and social life on Christian foundations. The alliance involved Austria (Roman Catholic), Prussia (Protestant) and Russia under Alexander I (Orthodox). But it was also an attempt to re-create unity* of the church on a vision of one Christian nation, with various branches but with Christ as only true sovereign. It was a kind of unity without union, a kind of federation of Christians in one holy nation (see **federalism**). It has been described as utopian ecumenism, a mixture of political scheming and apocalyptic dreaming.

At the end of the 19th century the Russian Orthodox Church and Lambeth (1888) were discussing intercommunion.* Key elements were the unity of faith in the gospel and Rome as their common enemy, as the letter of Archbishop Benson of Canterbury to Metropolitan Platon of Kiev pointed out. The Anglo-Russian student conference at St Albans in England was convened in 1927, sponsored by the Russian Student Christian Movement and Anglican students. That meeting led to the founding of the Fellowship of St Alban and St Sergius* in 1928, a centre of ecumenical experiences organizing annual conferences, courses on Eastern tradition, and student exchange.

The relations of the Protestant and Orthodox churches in Eastern Europe with the ecumenical movement were similar in four respects to those of other European churches up to the end of the second world war. First, the Protestant and Orthodox churches in Eastern Europe participated in the world conferences preceding the foundation of the WCC, including the world missionary conference (Edinburgh 1910) and the meetings of Faith and Order (Lausanne 1927, Oxford 1937) and Life and Work (Stockholm 1925, Edinburgh 1937). At this time the Russian Orthodox Church was present through the church in exile. However, that presence was more fully felt after 1961, when the Russian Orthodox Church formally joined the WCC.

Second, ecumenical conferences took place in this area even before the second world war (Prague 1928, Bucharest 1933, Novi Sad 1933 and 1936, Herzog Novi 1935). In a series of meetings the Orthodox prepared for a pan-Orthodox congress of theologians in Athens in 1936. The significance of this Athens meeting was in the considerable agreement reached among Orthodox theologians on the controversial problem of the mission of the Orthodox church to the modern world. The movement towards unity corresponds to the renewal of interest in the church and theology. An event of significance was the conference in Prague (1928) organized by the World Alliance for Promoting International Friendship through the Churches* (WAPIFC). Ecumenical co-operation among the churches was manifest at three levels: participation in the F&O movement, participation in the L&W movement and co-operation with the WAPIFC.

Third, the Christian youth organizations (WSCF,* YMCA,* YWCA*) were very active in Central and Eastern Europe, preparing the ground for ecumenism.

Fourth, outstanding Christian leaders furthered the ecumenical movement, such as Stefan Zankov of Bulgaria, Josef Hromádka of Czechoslovakia, Vasile Ispir of Romania, and Janos Victor of Hungary. These were regular participants in international conferences and commissions.

After the second world war a new situation emerged. Frontiers were changed, and radically new political and social developments took place. Concerning the Orthodox churches, two important events should be noted. First, the Orthodox and Oriental churches met

in Moscow (July 1948) with the patriarchates of Constantinople and Antioch (the latter representing the patriarchate of Alexandria) and the representatives of the Orthodox churches in Georgia, Serbia, Romania, Bulgaria, Greece, Albania and Poland, with also representatives from the Armenian church. At this meeting it was decided not to join the ecumenical movement, for reasons of dogmatics and politics. Second, contacts between the WCC and the Russian Orthodox Church were established as early as the 1950s, which resulted in the Russian Orthodox Church and other Orthodox churches and the Protestant churches in Eastern Europe joining the WCC at the New Delhi assembly in 1961 and subsequent years.

The participation of Protestant churches in Eastern Europe in the assemblies and decision-making bodies of the WCC can be traced from the constituting Amsterdam assembly 1948 and has been important in several respects.

The tensions of the cold war* (1950-65) were perceivable also in the fellowship of the WCC. This was largely due to the suspicions of the North American and Western European member churches of the WCC regarding the efforts of active church leaders and ecumenical personalities in Eastern Europe as they sought to achieve their place within the new society. These tensions were present already at the Amsterdam assembly, as was clear in the debate between John Foster Dulles and Hromádka. The 1950 Central Committee meeting in Toronto* of the WCC sharpened the tensions (following WCC support for UN intervention in Korea); the WCC position on the events in Hungary (1956) further worsened the situation.

Church leaders like the Hungarian bishop Albert Bereczky and the Czech professor Hromádka warned the WCC of the danger of becoming a tool of the cold war and anti-communism. They were convinced that the identification of the ecumenical movement with a particular political and ideological trend would destroy it. Thus Hromádka's argument helped save the ecumenical movement from falling into the trap of a blind and uncritical anti-communism. On the other hand, leaders of the WCC took their contacts with the churches in Eastern Europe very seriously. Thus the WCC was able to maintain the churches' fellowship at the time of the cold war, even among tensions and bitter arguments. The conviction that the churches living in different societies should maintain their unity in Christ and in prayer became stronger. The presence of Eastern and Central Europe, at the time the worldwide battleground between Russia and the West, prevented the WCC from indulging in a black-and-white reading of the world scene.

The commitment of Eastern European churches to ecumenism has been expressed by their ongoing contributions to all of the WCC assemblies and to many other ecumenical meetings. For example, Hungarian contributions to the following WCC activities were reported in the Hungarian church press: the F&O consultation in Lund (1952), the world conference on Church and Society in Geneva (1966) and all the assemblies.

After the appearance of "contextual theology" beginning in the 1970s, regional meetings were held in Budapest with the participation of member churches in Eastern Europe (1975, 1977, 1980, 1982). The 1975 meeting stated: "It is the duty of the churches living in socialist countries to give their own contribution to worldwide dialogue. A great emphasis was laid on the importance of a clearer position pointing to the future for Christians on great issues facing humankind and on the need for Christian witness in effective deeds." The 1980 meeting "recognizes with gratitude that the WCC provides an open space for encounter in mutual respect and trust". The 1982 meeting declared that "the participants reaffirmed their commitment to the ecumenical cause, which entails the responsibility of the member churches to engage themselves on all levels of church life more intensely in ecumenical endeavours".

Another platform for ecumenical encounter has been the Christian Peace Conference,* founded in Prague in 1958, with the support of all the Eastern European member churches of the WCC.

Radical changes within the socialist countries in Eastern Europe are giving rise to a climate which can bring about increased participation of Eastern European churches in the ecumenical movement and make it possible for them to share more fully in the struggle for Christian unity and the search for justice and peace. The ideological challenge of Marxism has strengthened the churches in their sense of Christian mission and in their belief that the churches can play a positive role in indifferent or even hostile societies. Their membership in the ecumenical fellowship is a source of spiritual power.

Because of the dramatic political changes in Eastern Europe in 1989, the church is looking for a new role in renewing society. The Marxist governments often interfered with church appointments, and consequently some church leaders were compromised as well as their mission. The churches are in some countries divided and themselves need renewal. The ecumenical lines are presently being redrawn, and the ecumenical movement again has a chance to help overcome the division between the churches and society.

See also **Conference of European Churches**.

KAROLY TOTH

Actes de la conférence des Eglises orthodoxes autocéphales, vol. 2, Moscow, Ed. du Patriarcat de Moscou, 1950 • W. Visser 't Hooft, *Memoirs*, WCC, 1987.

EUROPE: NORTHERN. Geographically, Northern Europe extends from Iceland and the Scandinavian peninsula to the northern part of the Ural mountains. Politically, it covers the five Nordic countries: Denmark, Finland, Iceland, Norway and Sweden, including the autonomous areas of Faroe Islands, Greenland and Aland Islands. Northern Europe is a homogeneous ethnological and cultural region with only slight national differences. Although Denmark, Iceland, Norway and Sweden have to a great extent a common ancestry and political history, in most sectors of human life today these countries have developed their own special characteristics.

Christian missions reached Northern Europe in the 9th century, mainly from the West. Only some eastern parts of Finland were Christianized from the Eastern church. By the 13th century even the most remote districts were evangelized. The multiple historical, cultural and ethnological links to Germany brought the Lutheran reformation without delay to Northern Europe. The nationalistic tendencies of the Reformation found a good soil in Scandinavia, where national profiles were emerging. From the very beginning the Lutheran faith thus strengthened the position of the crown and laid the groundwork for the still prevalent state-church system (see **church and state**). Historically, the Scandinavian countries have resisted all non-Lutheran churches and any deviations in the form of their people's worship.

The first part of the 18th century saw some concessions to other faiths and denominations, often for economic reasons. At the end of the 19th century the influence of the French Enlightenment and German Idealism led, on the one hand, to a less dogmatic Lutheranism but, on the other, to a certain alienation between church and culture.* At the same time, strong pietistic revival movements spread through the Nordic countries. National churches could not welcome such movements, especially as they were led by the laity.* Consequently, in Sweden especially, Free congregations and churches were formed. In Finland, Norway and to some extent Denmark, the pietistic tradition entered the Lutheran churches and soon became a spiritual power, which still prevails in large areas of the region.

Northern Europe is one of the most Lutheran areas of the world. In all Nordic countries the Lutheran churches are respected national institutions. The church-going rates are very low, but Christian values are still generally accepted as a foundation for life. Such a setting provides no particular encouragement for ecumenism. Nordic Lutheran churches, however, have traditionally been active in the international ecumenical movement since the conference on Life and Work* in Stockholm in 1925. Called by Archbishop Nathan Söderblom of Uppsala, that event inspired the ecumenical movement in the other Nordic churches. All of the national Lutheran churches in Northern Europe are active members of the Lutheran World Federation* (LWF), the WCC and the Conference of European Churches* (CEC), in most cases from the very beginning. Many of its members have held leading positions. Since the 1920s the Nordic Lutheran churches and the Church of England have organized a series of Anglo-Scandinavian theological conferences, of which the 60th was held in Sweden in 1989. The growing immigration to the region since the 1960s and the recent influx of refugees in Northern Europe have also greatly encouraged ecu-

Church in Norum, Norway (WCC/Peter Williams)

menical attitudes, especially in Sweden but also in Denmark and Norway.

The Nordic missionary societies maintain widespread international relations and have significantly advanced the ecumenical interaction of the Nordic churches, as have the growing church-aid organizations in Northern Europe. As an expression of Scandinavian solidarity in ecumenism, Northern European churches created in 1940 the Nordic Ecumenical Institute (NEI), now located in Uppsala and providing a study and information centre for ecumenical and interchurch activities. Eighteen Nordic churches and national ecumenical organizations are represented on its board of directors.

Denmark. The Evangelical Lutheran Church of Denmark has been established since 1683. Parliament has the sole authority to make statements in the name of the church. This agreement binds the parties together in that the state in its legislation must give the church due consideration. On the church's part, its activities, including its relations with other churches, necessarily involve the state. Since the church has no synods or other ecclesiastic boards, a Danish bishop is the highest church authority of his diocese. Accordingly, the possibilities of local ecumenism differ from area to area. Despite these structural complications, the Danish church has played a growing role in the ecumenical movement.

After long preparation and an intensive debate in both church and society, in 1989 parliament promulgated a law regarding the participation of the church in interchurch work. The new law is of decisive importance for developing both local ecumenism and international relations of the Danish Lutheran church. The law removes obstacles to local ecumenism and establishes diocesan boards for ecumenism.

The Church of Denmark's council on interchurch relations interacts with foreign churches and international organizations such as the WCC and LWF. It is also active in the churches' race programme, development aid and missionary work. The Ecumenical Council of Denmark, founded in 1939, is an active ecumenical organization with members from almost all Danish Christian churches and groups. Its activities are directed towards national and international ecumenism, international development and human rights projects, especially in Latin America and the Pacific.

Ecumenical education is given in the faculties of theology at the state universities of Copenhagen and Aarhus. Connected with the two faculties are voluntary ecumenical centres promoting ecumenism through debate, ecumenical projects and publications. The Nordic Institute for Missionary Research and Ecumenical Research, located in Aarhus, is presently creating a data-base of Nordic missiological and ecumenical bibliographies. It also organizes Nordic joint projects such as one on combating racism.

Finland. As of 1987 the Evangelical-Lutheran Church of Finland composes 89% of the population. The next largest group is the Orthodox, with 1%. Other, much smaller groups include the Covenant church, Roman Catholics, Baptists and Jehovah's Witnesses. Such Jews and Muslims as there are, are mostly descendants of immigrants from Russia in the 19th century. With such Lutheran predominance, ecumenical issues are visible only in the big cities and where the Orthodox are well established.

The responsible body for ecumenical relations of the Evangelical Lutheran Church of Finland is the Council for Foreign Affairs. Its board for theology is responsible for drafting statements and reports on dialogues between churches and ecumenical organizations. The aim has been to maintain a national Lutheran profile in the dialogue with other churches. The position of Finland between East and West has set certain requirements to ecumenical and interchurch relations. One of the main guidelines is to advance peace and to avoid international conflict. Since the 1970s, permanent theological discussions have been conducted with the Russian Orthodox Church. Two books have been published on the talks. In 1989 the two churches started bilateral doctrinal discussions. Negotiations with the Finnish Free Church and the Pentecostal movement in Finland have recently been undertaken.

The growing religious openness in Eastern Europe has revived also the relations with the Lutheran churches in the Baltic countries. The traditional co-operation with the Estonian Evangelical Lutheran Church has recently grown to a nationwide effort to restore the church life of this people closely related to the Finns.

Ecumenical education is given in the University of Helsinki and in the theological faculty of Abo Akademi in Turku. The Ecumenical Council of Finland was founded in 1919. One essential aim of the council is to advance nationally the ecumenical and theological programmes of the international ecumenical organizations. After years of participation as observer, in 1968 the Roman Catholic Church in Finland became a member of the council. This was among the first Catholic memberships in national ecumenical bodies in the world.

Iceland. The Evangelical Lutheran Church of Iceland is predominant with a membership of 93% of the population. Three separate Evangelical Lutheran congregations have some 8,800 members. Other groups, each with less than 1% of the population, include Roman Catholics, Seventh-Day Adventists, Pentecostals, Salvation Army, and several small groups resulting from the charismatic revival of the 1970s.

The Church of Iceland participates in the Scandinavian ecumenical movement through the Nordic bishops conference and the NEI. The church is a member of the main organizations of the international ecumenical movement. Owing to its sheer geographical isolation, the Church of Iceland is genuinely interested in developing Christian information services.

Local ecumenism is rather uncomplicated, as the number of adherents of other churches is very limited. Confessional discussions seldom arise, and ecumenical questions are handled by an unofficial council for promoting interchurch relations, initiated by the Lutheran bishop of Iceland.

Norway. The Church of Norway claims about 90% of its country's population. Other groups, each with less than 1% of the population, include the Pentecostal movement, the Roman Catholic Church, the Evangelical Lutheran Free Church, Methodists and Baptists.

The Church of Norway has been active in the growth of the 20th-century international ecumenical fellowship. Its council on foreign relations co-ordinates ecumenical work at home and abroad. Co-operation between the council and the Norwegian ministry of foreign affairs has been significant, especially in the fields of international social ethics and human rights. The Norwegian contribution to the Southern African liberation movement is internationally acknowledged. Since 1986 the church has been actively involved in work with refugees and migrants. The council on foreign relations is increasing its contacts and support of churches in Eastern Europe directly and in co-operation with the CEC.

Norwegian involvement in ecumenical dialogue has been steadily increasing, both nationally and internationally. Since 1979 a Catholic-Lutheran dialogue group has published statements on the eucharist and the ministry of the church. Several bilateral ecumenical dialogues are in process locally. The Norwegian Theological Dialogue Forum and the Norwegian Theological Council are promoting ecumenism through research and many practical projects. The ecumenical atmosphere is generally open and positive, although it is still resisted by certain smaller Christian groups. Ecumenical education is given at eight institutions, of which the most significant are the free faculty of theology in Oslo, the department of theology of Oslo University and the school of mission and theology in Stavanger.

Sweden. The largest churches represented in Sweden in 1987 were the Church of Sweden, 92%, and, with about 1% each, the Roman Catholic Church, Orthodox and Eastern churches, the Pentecostal movement, and the Mission Covenant Church of Sweden (a member of the World Alliance of Reformed Churches*). Groups with even smaller percentages included the Swedish Evangelical Mission, the Salvation Army, the Örebro Mission, Jehovah's Witnesses, and a recent separatist movement called Livets Ord (The word of life). The fastest-growing group of other religions are the Muslims, now with about 50,000 people (0.5%). This is the result of Sweden's relatively free immigration policy.

Swedish ecumenical history is marked by two outstanding gatherings it hosted. The conference on Life and Work in Stockholm (1925), convened on the initiative of Archbishop Nathan Söderblom, was one of the most significant events in modern international ecumenism. The assembly of the WCC in Uppsala (1968) became the second great landmark of ecumenism and still has its impact on Swedish church life. Among other things, it inspired an ongoing popular series of national ecumenical assemblies which represent a wide range of churches. The latest assembly was held in Örebro in 1989.

The Church of Sweden maintains its international relations through the secretariat of ecumenism. In addition to the current international ecumenical dialogue, many churches in Sweden are involved in several bilateral theological conversations. Among these are the dialogue between the Roman Catholic Church (diocese of Stockholm) and the Church of Sweden, and the joint conversations for deepened unity between the Church of England and the Nordic and Baltic Lutheran churches. Since 1922 the Church of Sweden has enjoyed a special relationship with the Church of England, consisting of an agreement of intercommunion* and mutual attendance at the consecrations of bishops in the two countries. Many of the Swedish Free churches have conducted bilateral talks with the Church of Sweden on doctrinal questions and on issues of practical co-operation at the congregational level.

The Church of Sweden secretariat of research and culture publishes reports in the field of theology, church sociology and ecumenics.

Ecumenical education is given in the faculties of theology at the state universities of Uppsala and Lund and in seven theological seminaries of the Free churches in Sweden. Most denominations are represented in the Swedish Ecumenical Council, founded in 1932.

Since 1972 a development forum of the Swedish churches (Kyrkornas U-Forum) emphasizes the responsibility of the churches for world economic development, peace and justice. The Life and Peace Institute in Uppsala, founded in 1985, is an international centre for peace efforts and peace research on an ecumenical basis. One of its present activities is the "justice, peace and integrity of creation" process. The Swedish Missionary Council coordinates the work of 19 missionary organizations. Other interdenominational organizations include the Swedish Christian Youth Council, the Student Christian Movement, the Swedish Women's Ecumenical Council, the Swedish Fellowship of Reconciliation and the Association for Christian Humanism and Social Concern.

See also **Conference of European Churches**.

KAJ ENGSTRÖM

Annual Report, Helsinki, Finnish Ecumenical Council, 1974- • C.F. Hallencreuz et al., *Missions from the North: Nordic Missionary Council 50 Years*, Oslo, Universitetsforlaget, 1974 • K. Ottosen, *A Short History of the Churches of Scandinavia*, Aarhus, Univ. of Aarhus, 1986 • P. Petursson, *Church and Social Change: A Study of the Secularization Process in Iceland, 1830-1930*, Vaenersborg, Plus Ultra, 1983 • *Studia Theologica: Scandinavian Journal of Theology*, Oslo, 1948-.

EUROPE: SOUTHERN.

The term "Southern Europe" is ambiguous. It certainly includes, from a geographical point of view, the three great peninsulas — the Iberian, the Italian and the Balkan. But the countries ruled by communist parties after the second world war, such as Albania, Bulgaria, Romania and Yugoslavia, are generally considered as belonging to Eastern Europe, even if they are geographically southern. On the other hand, southern France belongs culturally to the Mediterranean world and definitely not to Northern or Central Europe. What the ecumenical circles normally understand today as Southern Europe includes Portugal, Spain,

Italy, Greece and Malta: a fairly artificial classification.

Italy, Spain and Portugal (and to a large extent Malta) have a number of things in common: they have a common Latin cultural heritage; they belong to the Mediterranean world; and they include, to a greater or lesser degree, some of the poorest regions of Europe. Italy experienced, and Spain, Portugal and Greece are now experiencing, the consequences of massive migration from countryside to town and from Southern to Central Europe. The three Latin countries are overwhelmingly dominated by Roman Catholicism, even if some show a large or very large degree of secularization.* Greece is mostly Orthodox, though it is not entirely under the jurisdiction of the Greek Orthodox church; Crete has an autocephalous Orthodox church, and some continental areas and Aegean islands are under the Ecumenical Patriarchate of Constantinople.

In the 16th century the religious ideas of the Reformation reached both the Iberian and the Italian peninsulas, producing a number of groups, congregations and individuals utterly Protestant in their faith. With the exception of the Waldensians, the reformation movement was eventually crushed by the Inquisition. The Waldensians were a medieval movement which joined the Calvinistic Reformation and survived until the 19th century in a tiny area of the western Alps, later expanding to other Italian regions. Otherwise, all Protestant churches in the area under survey (including Greece) are the result of 19th-century missionary endeavours by Methodists, Baptists, Brethren, Episcopalians, Congregationalists, Lutherans and Presbyterians, and by efforts in this century of Pentecostals, Adventists and a number of USA-based denominations. Protestantism remains a tiny minority. Orthodoxy outside Greece is confined to small ethnic groups.

Until the Second Vatican Council and the fall of the dictatorships in Spain and Portugal, Protestantism was (and often still is) considered as something suspicious and alien. The same attitude prevails in Greece to this day. In the wake of Vatican II a large number of works by German- and English-speaking Protestant theologians were translated. Spanish publishers with a large readership in Latin America did much in this line. In Italy the number of interested priests and laypeople was so great that a publisher dared to translate Gerhard Kittel's *Theological Dictionary of the New Testament*. Some exchanges of students and visiting professors among Roman Catholic and Protestant theological seminaries do take place.

Ecumenism has two aspects: among Protestant denominations and between these and the majority church (Roman Catholic or Orthodox). In the Latin countries various federations of Protestant churches represent ecumenical impulses as well as structures of co-operation in areas such as assistance and communications. Fundamentalists seldom belong to them. In Greece there is no ecumenical structure.

In all the countries of the area, with specific peculiarities for each one of them, the minority-majority ecumenism faces several difficulties. First, the mere numerical disproportion (1% or less Protestants) prevents any encounter among churches as equal partners; it is only in special circumstances that partners may have an acceptable degree of equality. Nevertheless on the personal level and occasionally also on the parish level, as well as

The Church of the Holy Family, Barcelona, Spain (WCC/Peter Williams)

within less formal groups, encounters, dialogue, Bible study and common engagement do take place.

Second, the theological and cultural tradition by which the average Portuguese, Spanish or Italian Roman Catholic, lay or priest, and their Greek Orthodox counterparts call their church *the* church and use other names for Protestant churches, appears to imply for these a lesser degree of churchliness. In fact there is no full mutual recognition among all the churches. Along with the numerical disadvantage, this point often makes Protestants feel like some sort of second-class Christians. Such an atmosphere of course makes real ecumenism more difficult.

Third, the issue of proselytism* is especially sensitive for the Orthodox. Everybody is against it, but majority and minority churches understand it differently. Minorities tend to term "proselytism" any bribing or putting psychological pressure on people to lure them into changing allegiances but admit as perfectly legitimate and honest any theologically grounded invitation to join their faith and, consequently, their congregation. Majority churches tend to consider that any invitation to join a denomination different from the one in which the person was baptized — even if it is a totally secularized person — falls under the description of proselytism but do not consider as such the pressure put on members of minority churches by the sociological and cultural weight of their large majority, which is often identified by them, with little ecumenical sensitivity, as *the* religion of the country.

Relationships with the ecumenical movement, with the WCC, with the Conference of European Churches* (CEC) and with other ecumenical organizations vary. In areas where the minorities are not present, it is virtually impossible to have any ecumenism in the sense of dialogue or joint action with people of other confessions or denominations. But dialogues and joint actions exist where circumstances make it possible, e.g. the Italian monthly *Confronti* jointly sponsored by progressive Protestants and Roman Catholics since 1974. The term "ecumenical" appears in the title of several Protestant centres (such as Agape in Italy, Los Rubios in Spain, Figueira da Foz in Portugal — to mention only the older and better-established ones) or organizations such as the secretariat for ecumenical activities, led by Roman Catholic laypeople. The membership of the RC grassroots communities is not very large, but it is with them, as well as with what remains of the "Christians for socialism", that Protestants tend to practise ecumenism, rather than in joint structures or committees with the Roman Catholic hierarchy.

The Vatican pays great attention to the activities of the WCC, sends observers to all major ecumenical events and participates in the Joint Working Group* with the WCC. RC theologians are members of Faith and Order,* but the RCC as such is not a member of the WCC. The Church of Greece is a member of the WCC, the CEC and the Ecumenical Commission for Church and Society (Brussels), as are most traditional Protestant denominations. Several fundamentalist denominations contrast "evangelical" with "ecumenical", considering the latter as inclined to blur unduly the theological discrepancies between confessions, and therefore refrain from participating in ecumenical activities.

Established in 1982, the Ecumenical Forum of European Christian Women promotes ecumenical links and commitment among Protestant, Orthodox and RC women's organizations and groups, especially in the fields of justice for women and of women's theological creativity.

An interesting process is the integration between Waldensian and Methodist churches in Italy. The numerical imbalance (6 to 1) would normally have made traditional church union difficult: either the smaller group would have been absorbed into the larger one, or the larger would have been required to give so many guarantees as finally to lose its identity. Integration implies joint government, joint activities, the same confession of faith, but preserving denominational identity as well as separate fellowship in Christian World Communions.*

Protestant mainline churches in Italy, Spain and Portugal (as well as those of France, Belgium and French-speaking Switzerland) belong to the Conference of Protestant Churches of Latin Countries in Europe (CEPPLE), which up to the 1960s was engaged in the defence of religious liberty* for Protestant minorities in Italy, Portugal, Spain and Belgium. Later on, and for several years, it

developed a keen interest in "diaspora"* issues concerning the problems of Protestant minorities scattered over large areas. It also sponsored seminars for radio preachers. In the three Latin countries of Southern Europe, Protestant churches have developed great efforts in the social field (e.g. with refugees and migrants) and have received financial help from stronger churches.

Besides these institutional ecumenical relations there exists a number of informal movements or groups gathered around themes such as peace, justice, anti-racism, human rights, etc., which are fundamentally ecumenical in nature — they take their inspiration from Christian impulses and forget or largely disregard traditional confessional boundaries. Their number and importance are difficult to assess and are different from country to country and between urban and rural areas.

Events such as the Basel convocation on peace and justice (May 1989) reveal a keen ecumenical commitment by interested groups, even if the follow-up back home is limited. At the Seoul convocation on "Justice, Peace and the Integrity of Creation" (March 1990), the official Roman Catholic delegation was very small, but scores of representatives of Roman Catholic grassroots groups attended at their own expense as journalists, visitors or otherwise, thus showing at the popular level a far greater openness than at the official one.

See also **Conference of European Churches**.

ALDO COMBA

EUROPE: WESTERN. Western Europe for our purposes here comprises Belgium, the British Isles, the Federal Republic of Germany (which, with the German Democratic Republic, has now become one Germany), France, Luxemburg, the Netherlands and Switzerland. Political boundaries have not been the same all the time. For example, Belgium and Holland were united in one kingdom until 1831, when Belgium split off again. In any case, there were kingdoms or nations* such as Alemans, Frisians, Saxons, Angles, Picts, Gauls, etc., which were later to be regrouped into the contemporary geographical boundaries of West Europe.

Christianity was in Europe already by the 2nd century. Church history mentions the martyrs of Lyons, France, in about A.D. 180; the council of Arles met in the same country in 314. In the British Isles Celtic and Roman Catholic missions brought Christianity, the former mostly in Ireland, though from there it went to the Western Isles of Scotland. The synod of Whitby in 664 seems to have settled for Roman traditions. The Celtic tradition has been remembered in connection with the monastic centre of Clonard. Germany, Holland and Belgium were evangelized by Willibrord, later called Clement (739), and Winfrith, later called Boniface (754).

Christianity in West Europe was fairly early backed by rulers. It was, for example, through Queen Bertha, daughter of Charibert of Paris, that Christianity was introduced to Anglo-Saxons. Later still, Justinian I and II and Charlemagne made Christianity their concern, suppressing those who did not oblige.

From the 7th century Islam became a threat. Its impact was not uniform in the world, but it is arguable that the threat contributed to the intensification of monastic life with stress on celibacy, education, copying of manuscripts and the spread of Latin. By the end of the 8th century there was decisive realignment of forces within the Christian world under the impact of Islam. Authority* was divided between secular and religious powers. But the pope exercised independent moral strength.

Although the power of the pope was strong in West Europe until the end of the 15th century and unity seemed to exist, there was very considerable dissidence within the church. The "morning stars" of the Reformation include John Wycliffe (1330-84) and Jan Hus (c.1370-1415). The Reformation* proper (see also **Protestantism**) came with Luther (1483-1546), Zwingli (1484-1531) and Calvin (1509-64). Lutheranism became strong in Germany and the Scandinavian countries. Those of the Reformed tradition came to an agreement, and the Reformed church was strong in Switzerland, Scotland, Bohemia, Hungary and the Dutch Republic. In 1566 Holland saw the Beeldenstorm, or the iconoclastic tempest.

The Reformation took different patterns. For example, in the Holland of the 1570s the Reformation had its impact in the cities, while the countryside was not "purged" until early in the 17th century. In the early 17th century also there were disputes in the Reformed church, leading to the birth of other Reformed groups such as the Mennonites. In any case, the Dutch Reformed Church, which was Calvinist, was a "privileged church" (to be distinguished from the established church) until the French occupation (1795), when Napoleon decided that no denomination should be disadvantaged. But when the privileged church was alive, Catholics and other suppressed Protestant churches were in *hidden* churches.

The Reformation in Holland was not so violent after 1600, and so substantial groups of other churches became signs of a fragmented Christianity which has continued till today. The year 1723 saw the birth of the church of Utrecht, also called the Old Catholic schism.

In England Henry VIII broke with the pope, and his daughter Elizabeth established a religious settlement which brought as many Puritans and Catholics as possible within the Anglican church. All the churches of the Reformation laid stress on the Bible and the vernacular liturgy. The Anglican church also kept the threefold ministry* of bishop, priest and deacon. Attempts at reconciliation* by the Roman Catholic Church failed, as did attempts to bring the churches of the Reformation into a closer unity. This was partly because of the growth of nationalism.

The issue of unity. In the 17th and 18th centuries, people spoke of three parts of the divided church, i.e. Lutheran, Reformed and Roman Catholic. In the 17th century there was a search for the unity* of the church through discussion and theological exploration. The growth of pietism led to a desire for ecumenical exchange of fellowship. Hugo Grotius (1583-1645), for example, saw the connection between ecumenism and mission.* He even tried to organize an ecumenical synod of all churches except the Roman Catholic Church, but failed. Daniel Jablonski (1660-1741) also had a great plan for the unity of the evangelical churches, the cornerstone of which was to be the Brethren biblical orthodoxy and Anglican tradition. This also failed. Believing Europe to be the spiritual centre of humankind, Wilhelm van Leibniz (1646-1716) considered it essential that cultural, political and religious unity should be restored.

Similarly in the 18th century there was a

special search for unity in life, both moral and organizational. The end of the 18th century saw the formation of the German Christian fellowship, a developed idea of the "spiritual society". Once established in Basel, it spread rapidly and gave rise to the Basel Mission House, the Basel Missionary Society and Bible Tract Societies in Switzerland, Germany and Britain. Throughout the 18th century the Society for the Promotion of Christian Knowledge, an Anglican society founded in 1689, kept close contact with the continental Lutheran and Reformed churches. It also supported Lutheran and Reformed ministers in the mission field.

Ecumenical developments in Western Europe. In the 19th century ecumenical interest slowly turned to the area of ecclesiology (see **church**). One reflection of this was the growth of worldwide fellowships of churches with new responsibilities: the first meeting of the Alliance of Reformed Churches (1875); the first Methodist ecumenical conference (1881); the Old Catholic churches of the world joining in the Union of Utrecht (1889); the first Baptist world congress (1905). There were also movements within countries. Friedrich Schleiermacher (1786-1834) stressed the vital theological importance of Christian unity. In 1848 a diet of the churches of Germany was held at Wittenberg, marking the beginning of the moves which gradually led to the Evangelical Church in Germany in 1922.

In Britain the "high church" wing of the Church of England sought closer union with Roman Catholics. The evangelical wing sought better relationships with the non-conformists, and one result of this was the formation of the Evangelical Alliance* in 1846. The "broad church" group sought a "comprehensive church" that would bring in as many nonconformists as possible to a re-constituted Church of England.

The voluntary movements associated with the evangelical awakening in the 19th century also gave fresh impetus to the ecumenical movement. The driving force of these movements was that of mission, which included both evangelism* and social reform. Most churches founded their own missionary societies, but there were also joint ventures such as the British and Foreign Bible Society.

Two great Christian youth movements were founded in England in 1844 and 1855, namely the Young Men's Christian Association* and the Young Women's Christian Association.* The same period also saw the formation of the Student Christian Movements. By 1895 these student movements had coalesced in the World Student Christian Federation.* These three movements nurtured many leaders of the ecumenical movement.

In most nations of Western Europe, national councils of churches* were set up, e.g. the British Council of Churches (founded 1942), the Ecumenical Council of Churches in the Netherlands (founded 1946), the Co-operative Fellowship of Christian Churches in Germany (founded 1822 and re-founded 1948).

In a number of European nations discussions are taking place between the national councils of churches and the Roman Catholic Church. In 1990 the British Council of Churches was re-constituted as the Council of Churches for Britain and Ireland, and it has full Roman Catholic membership. In addition, new national ecumenical bodies were set up in England, Wales and Scotland. The aim of these new instruments is to set a new pattern of ecumenical relationships. It was felt that councils of churches acquired a life of their

Kaiser Wilhelm Memorial Church, Berlin
(Joachim G. Wensch)

own outside the mainstream of churches and the decisions they made were largely ignored. The new ecumenical bodies will have no decision-making powers of their own. All decisions will be made by the relevant bodies in the member churches, which will seek to ensure that there is more genuine ecumenical co-operation at every possible level.

The Christian women's movement in Europe. In the 18th and 19th centuries many Christian women's movements were founded, such as the Mothers' Union (Anglican), the Union of Catholic Mothers (RC) and the Baptist Women's League. In the second half of the 20th century a new phenomenon emerged, the Christian feminist movement with a feminist theology.*

This movement included the Ecumenical Forum of European Christian Women, first discussed in Brussels in 1978. The forum seeks to link together Christian women and Christian women's organizations throughout Europe, both traditional and radical. Its members come from all European churches including Roman Catholic. It seeks to bring about the greater participation of women in church and society and also to promote the unity of the churches and the unity and peace of Europe. The third assembly of the forum was held in York, England, in July 1990, with the theme "From Division to Vision".

New visions for Europe. Ecumenical life in Europe seems to have been at a low ebb for some time. After the early enthusiasm, apathy seemed to have set in. It has been difficult to make any real progress in Christian unity. The year 1989 saw tremendous political change in Europe: one after another of the socialist governments of Central Eastern Europe collapsed. Along with the political freedom came economic collapse and new problems and threats. The WCC, CEC and the Ecumenical Forum of European Christian Women responded to these challenges and possibilities in new ways. A special church leaders meeting was held in Geneva in March 1990 to review the situation, and great emphasis was laid on the mission of the churches in the new Europe. This issue of the mission of the churches in a secularized Europe is one which will dominate the 1990s. Such co-operation could give new life to the ecumenical movement, but there are also dangers to be avoided, such as

fundamentalism, over-simplification of the gospel and the renewed tensions between Orthodox and Catholics over Uniates (see **Eastern Catholic Churches**). In all this ferment in Europe women must be enabled to play a full part, and the Roman Catholic Church has an indispensable role. The unity and peace of Europe can be a great contribution to the unity and peace of the world.

See also **Conference of European Churches**.

JEAN MAYLAND

Churches Together in Pilgrimage, London, BCC and Catholic Truth Society ● H.E. Fey ed., *The Ecumenical Advance: A History of the Ecumenical Movement*, vol. 2: *1948-1968*, 2nd ed., WCC, 1986 ● C.L.W. Halifax ed., *The Conversations at Malines: Original Documents*, Philip Alan, 1930 ● L. Herrin, *The Formation of Christendom*, Princeton, NJ, Princeton UP, 1987 ● S. Herzel, *A Voice for Women*, WCC, 1981 ● J. Matthews, *The Unity Scene*, London, BCC, 1985 ● S. Neill, *The Church and Christian Union: The Bampton Lectures for 1964*, London, Oxford UP, 1968 ● *The Next Steps for Churches Together in Pilgrimage, Including Definitive Proposals for Ecumenical Instruments*, London, BCC, 1989 ● C. Parvey, *The Community of Women and Men in the Church*, WCC, 1983 ● R. Rouse & S.C. Neill eds, *A History of the Ecumenical Movement*, vol. 1, 3rd ed. WCC, 1986.

EUROPEAN UNITY. The continent of Europe, which has its eastern end at the Ural mountains, has always been the home of different peoples and cultures, whether of Greco-Roman, Germanic or Slavonic origin. No single bond has united them more than their adoption of the Christian gospel. In the early Christian era, Rome and Constantinople were influential centres. In their cultural and ecclesiastical spheres these centres represented the different practical expressions of the gospel, with their respective theologies, liturgies, forms of spirituality and structures.

Equally important in each centre, however, is the relationship between church and state,* bishop and monarch. Gradually, the East and West of Europe grew increasingly apart until, in 1054, the formal break occurred in church fellowship. Thereafter, and still in many instances, East and West each has gone its own way — ecclesiastically, politically and culturally. Thus, one can place the boundaries between the East and West of Europe at the point where peoples and countries of Byzantine heritage meet those influenced by Rome. The fact that the political frontiers have long ceased to correspond to the religious and cultural boundaries, and have been pushed far westwards to the advantage of the East, was the result of wars and political manoeuvring.

At the end of the 1980s many changes quickly started to take place in the Eastern bloc. It is yet too early to foresee the future shape of Europe. Following radical changes of direction in Poland, the Baltic states, the German Democratic Republic, Czechoslovakia, Hungary, Bulgaria and Romania, it may be that the political boundaries will once again move closer to the religious and cultural ones. Whatever happens, the Christian churches are challenged to make their own independent contribution to Europe's quest for its identity.

As other continents re-discover their independence and free themselves of European tutelage, Europe has to take stock of its own identity and how to assume in a new way responsibility for itself and towards other continents. The Christian churches, with a significant role to play, are finding it difficult to respond adequately to the high expectations now being made of them. In varying ways the churches have been affected by developments which have weakened their spiritual life and the vigour of their witness. These are: (1) the fragmentation of the Western church into confessional churches and, in the Eastern church, the rivalry between the patriarchates; and (2) the growing secularization,* which is affecting all areas of life as a consequence of the Enlightenment.

The churches in Europe have banded together to fulfill their common responsibility. In 1959 the majority of non-Roman Catholic churches in Europe joined together to form the Conference of European Churches* (CEC). Formally founded in 1964, its self-understanding corresponds to that of the WCC. CEC describes itself as "an ecumenical fellowship of churches in Europe which confess the Lord Jesus Christ as God and Saviour according to the scriptures and therefore seek to fulfill together their common calling to the glory of the one God, Father, Son and Holy Spirit". CEC brings together Reformation and Orthodox churches. Its activities cross all East-West boundaries and make themselves felt in the political as well as in the church

sphere. Europe itself is a central theme in its work. The conference speaks publicly through conferences and documents.

Corresponding to CEC on the Roman Catholic side there is the Council of European Bishops' Conferences (CCEE = Consilium Conferentiarum Episcopalium Europae). The council was founded in 1971 and canonically approved by Pope Paul VI in 1977. Each national bishops' conference sends a representative to the council, which meets in general assembly once a year, as well as organizing other conferences, such as the triennial European bishops' symposium. In general, the tasks of the CCEE resemble those of CEC.

Four joint CCEE/CEC European meetings have been held (Chantilly 1978, Logumkloster 1981, Riva del Garda 1984, Erfurt 1988). Both ecumenically and politically these meetings attracted wide interest. In May 1989 the two bodies sponsored the European ecumenical assembly on "Peace with Justice" in Basel, dealing with the specifically European dimension of these problems.

WERNER LÖSER

I. Fürer, "Die katholische Kirche in Europa", in *Die Römisch-Katholische Kirche*, W. Löser ed. (= *Die Kirchen der Welt*, 20), Frankfurt, Evangelisches Verlagswerk, 1986 • F. König & K. Rahner eds, *Europa — Horizonte der Hoffnung*, Graz, Styria, 1983.

EUTHANASIA. "Euthanasia" derives from a Greek noun meaning a "gentle", or even "happy", death, in which sense Philo of Alexandria was familiar with the term. Central to the public debate of euthanasia in recent years is the question whether or not acts inducing the death of other people are justifiable when performed in a medical context. The problems arising in this connection can be divided into moral (ethical) and legal (judicial) ones. The latter consider the issue of adjusting the law to changing moral attitudes towards euthanasia. The former, which are dealt with here, concentrate on standards of moral justification.

Several definitions and distinctions have been offered to identify the relevant considerations and questions. The term "euthanasia" is most often used to refer to the merciful killing of patients who suffer from incurable illness or from irreparable defects (Singer,

125). Sometimes the patient's supposed interests are taken to be a constituent of euthanasia. Other definitions, however, regard the will of the patients themselves to be a necessary condition, to the effect that killing patients without their voluntary request cannot be considered euthanasia (H. Kuitert). The reason given for this restricted definition is that judgments as to when killing a patient is in his or her own interests are never to be made by doctors or other medical personnel without first being submitted to legal inspection.

Widely accepted are the distinctions between different types of euthanasia (W. Glover, P. Singer, D. Harris). *Voluntary euthanasia* refers to killing a patient at the patient's request, which is confirmed by his or her approval regarding the aspects of its implementation. *Involuntary euthanasia* refers to killing a patient who is unable to express any views, again supposedly in the patient's own best interests.

Moral principles used to justify these various types of euthanasia can be divided into three categories: the principle of the sanctity of life, the principle of autonomy and the principle of beneficence.

The first principle states that human life is intrinsically valuable and therefore not to be taken for reasons other than the defence of human life itself. Thus any justification of euthanasia on grounds of insufficient (actual or possible) value of the patient's life is over-ruled by the sanctity of life as such, regardless of whether this judgment is made by the patient or by others. A theological variation of this argument claims that since matters of life and death* are facts of human existence that are governed by the will of God, the moment of death is not for human beings to decide (Barth, Jüngel).

The problem with this type of moral reasoning is that it entails a duty to intervene medically whenever such efforts would be considered life-preserving, regardless of its effects on the patient's well-being. In order to cope with this problem, additional distinctions are frequently offered, such as between "active" and "passive" euthanasia (allowing the withdrawal of life-prolonging treatment in cases where patients are suffering from incurable illness or irreparable defects) and between "direct" and "indirect" killing (allowing pal-liative treatment which eventually may lead to death as a foreseeable but not necessarily unintended side effect).

The principle of autonomy states that the only reasons capable of justifying the act of killing a suffering patient for whom no cure or reparation is possible are the patient's own reasons. Proponents of the right to autonomy as a prime moral value do not reject the sanctity of life as a principle of medical policy but allow it to be over-ridden by the patient's wish to die. Since, in their view, the patient's ability to make up his or her own mind is considered a necessary condition, it implies that only cases of voluntary euthanasia are morally justifiable. It further implies, however, that actual or foreseeable suffering of the mentally incapable cannot be dealt with under the regime of the principle of autonomy.

In the latter cases, appeal to a principle of beneficence is due, which states that the act of killing a patient should always be judged in the light of the patient's well-being. Two ways can be followed to arrive at this judgment. First, it may be asked what the will of the patients would have been, were they still able to express themselves. This question may provide helpful information when the patients are elderly and mentally retarded individuals. In cases of severely handicapped newborn infants, no information is available, however, other than medically warranted expectations of the patient's capability of well-being, which may be stated in terms of a quality-of-life index.

Euthanasia has not been an object of significant ecumenical debate. The Roman Catholic Church on its part has decidedly rejected euthanasia. Pius XII has made this position clear in addresses in 1947, 1951 and 1957 (H. Denzinger, *Enchiridion Symbolorum*, 2242), although without rejecting the use of medical help to alleviate the suffering of dying people or double-effect drugs that may, as a non-intended effect, cause death. In these cases medical ethical reasons and the will of the patient are the decisive criteria. Other churches have not issued such authoritative, precise pronouncements, although there are indications that they follow a similar direction. There is, however, in all confessions a lively theologico-ethical discussion on an issue that recent developments in medical science turn into an increasingly complex and urgent one. See also **bio-ethics, life and death**.

J.S. REINDERS

K. Barth, *Kirchliche Dogmatik* (ET *Church Dogmatics*, III/4, Edinburgh, Clark, 1961) • W. Glover, *Saving Lives and Causing Death*, Harmondsworth, UK, Penguin, 1977 • E. Jüngel, *Tod*, Gütersloh, Gütersloher Verlagshaus, 1971 • J. Rachels, *Moral Problems*, New York, Harper & Row, 1979 • P. Ramsey, *Ethics at the Edges of Life*, New Haven, CT, Yale UP, 1978 • P. Singer, *Practical Ethics*, London, Cambridge UP, 1979.

EVANGELICAL MISSIONS. In the last third of the 20th century, "evangelical" missions have grown to far surpass "mainline" Protestant missions. This is particularly true in North America, where the overseas missionary personnel of evangelical agencies outnumber those in mainline agencies by a ratio of 10 to 1.

A number of evangelical agencies were founded in the 19th century, often to pioneer in "inland" areas of the non-Christian world: China Inland Mission (1865), Sudan Interior Mission (1893), Africa Inland Mission (1895), etc. From the beginning, such agencies were interdenominational in that they avoided identifying with any one denominational tradition and attracted personnel from across the Protestant spectrum. They typically also were international, though in the limited sense of accepting members from various Western nations. But in recent years these agencies have become international in the broader sense; they include increasing numbers (in some cases almost 30%) of third-world missionaries serving outside their national borders. The Interdenominational Foreign Mission Association (IFMA, 1917) links the North American branches of these agencies.

The Evangelical Foreign Missions Association (EFMA, 1945) links evangelical *denominational* mission agencies in North America, including Pentecostals. One must note, however, that IFMA/EFMA personnel account for less than half the total evangelical missionaries sent from North America; the majority serve in agencies such as the Southern Baptist Foreign Mission Board (1845), Wycliffe Bible Translators (1934), and New Tribes Mission (1942), which belong to no association of mission groups.

In England, India, Europe and elsewhere, similar mission associations serve scores of evangelical mission agencies. The evangelical mission association of West Germany publishes an international newsletter, *IDEA*, which evangelicals follow in many parts of the world.

Two very recent international associations of mission groups reflect the charismatic renewal movement and the growth of mission agencies based in the third world. The Association of International Mission Services (1985) seeks to catalyze new overseas initiatives by charismatic groups. Third World Missions Advance (1988) links third-world agencies. As often as not, the latter undertake cross-cultural mission *within* their national borders. As estimated in 1989, third-world evangelical mission agencies now number more than 35,000 missionaries.

See also **mission, missionary societies**.

ROBERT T. COOTE

EVANGELICAL-ROMAN CATHO-LIC DIALOGUE ON MISSION. In a series of three meetings from 1977 to 1984, theologians and missiologists named by the Vatican Secretariat for Promoting Christian Unity* and evangelical participants from denominations both within and outside the WCC and from para-church mission organizations took part in the Evangelical-Roman Catholic Dialogue on Mission (ERCDOM). The evangelicals did not officially represent any international body, although all were associated with the Lausanne Committee for World Evangelization;* the convener of the ERCDOM evangelicals was the Anglican John Stott, a chief drafter of the 1974 Lausanne covenant.*

The final report is in no sense an "agreed statement" but a record of the ideas shared. It describes some areas in which evangelicals and Roman Catholics (RCs) hold similar views, which "we are able to perceive more clearly as we overcome the stereotypes and prejudiced ideas we have of each other", and other areas on which both sides seriously differ. The method was the placement of all topics around the focal point — Christian mission.*

Here are the topics on which the report outlined both agreement and serious, sometimes contradictory, understandings of biblical teaching: (1) revelation,* the Bible, the formulation of truth; the Bible vis-a-vis the teaching authority* of the church; (2) basis and authority of mission, direct evangelism* and socio-political responsibility; (3) God's workings "outside" the Christian community; (4) the gospel of salvation* and the uniqueness* and universality of Jesus Christ; the role of Mary* in salvation; (5) conversion* and baptism,* church membership and the assurance of salvation; (6) the church* as part, fruit, embodiment and agent of the gospel; (7) the gospel and culture;* (8) our unity* and disunity, possibilities of common witness,* and avoidance of "unworthy witness", or proselytism.*

Evangelicals admit the wide spectrum of their constituencies, from those who appear to regard all RCs as unbelievers in need of conversion to those who desire a very full co-operation with RCs in mission efforts. Since the ERCDOM report, because of the rapid growth of evangelical churches in predominantly RC areas, such as Latin America, the Philippines, Spain and France, the pastoral and missionary issues of worthy and unworthy witness and of co-operation or common witness have become more critical, even more divisive among evangelicals themselves.

More fundamentally, the many points of consensus* are linked with deep differences which focus particularly on the nature and purpose of the church. Further conversations, the report admits, would be required before it would be possible "to arrive at greater clarity and common terms of ecclesiological discourse".

TOM STRANSKY

B. Meeking & J. Stott eds, *The Evangelical-Roman Catholic Dialogue on Mission 1977-1984: A Report*, Exeter, Paternoster, 1986.

EVANGELICALS. The terms "evangelical" and "evangelicalism" had scant use until Erasmus and others derisively aimed them at what they saw as Lutheran narrowness and fanaticism. Luther used the terms for all Christians who accepted the doctrine of *sola gratia*, which he saw as the heart of the evangel, or gospel *(euangelion)*. The treaty of Westphalia (1648) denominated both the Lutheran and the Reformed churches "evangelical". By 1700, on the European continent, the term seems to have become a simple synonym for "Protestant" or, in German-speaking areas, "Lutheran". In Protestant Britain, however, the religious awakening led by the Wesleys and George Whitefield seems to have been called the evangelical revival from around 1750. Slightly later, revival advocates in Britain, whether within the Anglican Church or in the Free Churches, called themselves evangelicals. Their trademarks were deep moral earnestness, commitment to strict personal piety, faithfulness in private and corporate devotion, and vigorous philanthropic enterprise. At the introduction of Protestantism in Latin America during the 1800s, and until the present, its adherents have preferred to call their churches and themselves evangelicals *(evangélicos)* rather than Protestant.

In London, in 1846, some 800 Europeans and North Americans formed the Evangelical Alliance to counter the political and spiritual revival of Roman Catholicism then in progress and, more positively, to co-ordinate various Protestant enterprises in missions, publishing and social reform. Its nine conservative theological tenets summarize the contents of the historic Protestant confessions of faith, but its implicit understanding of Christianity in practice rested on the religious bases developed in early pietism and in the evangelical revival.

In British North America, the first great awakening (1730s and 1740s) had emphasized the necessity for a graciously given personal experience of redemption* in Christ, for personal piety, including social concern, and for confessional orthodoxy. The second great awakening (early 1800s) intensified the experiential element, reduced and simplified dogmatic requirements, slowly institutionalized social concern, and made the revivalistic mode normative for the 19th century. The formation of the American branch of the alliance, in 1867, simply reflected a context already practising the style of Christianity which the alliance advocated.

Between about 1865 and 1900, however, many came gradually to understand the personal evangelical experience that was central

Participants in the evangelical congress Lausanne II (Manila 1989) (idea-bild)

to all evangelical thought and action as a personal moment of spiritual illumination. This understanding encouraged an internalizing of the evangelical experience. The old language remained, but by the 1920s social action and theological reflection were suffering benign neglect among evangelicals. They sought only a "clean heart and right spirit".

By about 1900, American Methodism had divided into three parties, each seeing itself as "evangelical". The liberals, bent on social action and theological modernity, were evangelical but with the accents of the social sciences. The conservatives, including the Holiness movement,* were evangelical in the sense of the word before the civil war. The mainstream insisted on a highly individualistic and private faith,* which meant that traditional terms and doctrines might carry nontraditional connotations. So it was that the Wesleyan tradition as a whole equivocated the very idea of evangelical.

Calvin's American progeny had also divided into three major parties in the late 1800s. The conservative party, with its centre at Princeton, owed much to Charles Hodge and held American evangelicalism, especially revivalism, to be theologically and culturally

suspect. A liberal party, mildly activist, rooted in the work of Nathaniel Taylor at Yale, spoke the language of evangelicalism, but its deeper concern was to reconcile the Reformed tradition and modern thought and culture.* The revivalist party, which claimed the mantle of Charles Finney, Asa Mahan and William Boardman, was led at the end of the century by D.L. Moody, R.A. Torrey and J.W. Chapman. But these later revivalists, who now inherited the name "evangelical", displaced the radical social concern and perfectionism of their predecessors with a very different agenda: "conversion", understood first and last as an internal religious experience; maintaining the authority of the Bible as the inerrant divine revelation;* and restoring evangelicalism as the normative form of Christianity.

From the late 1890s, increasing liberal critiques compelled these evangelicals to explain their position theologically. Here, they found the methods and categories of the conservatives congenial, though they resisted the Calvinist dogmatism and rationalism of the conservatives' systems. A new coalition would soon produce a new definition of "evangelical" among the Reformed.

By the late 1910s, the Reformed tradition fell into civil war, and it drew other traditions in. On one side was the liberal tradition; on the other was the revivalist-confessional coalition, under the names "conservative", "evangelical" and "fundamentalist". The revivalist party became increasingly Reformed and less inclined to revivalism; the conservatives opened up to evangelicalism.

Conservative Wesleyanism, still evangelical in the 19th-century sense, recognized that its theological method and understanding of the Bible had more in common with the spirit of liberalism than with that of the Reformed evangelicals. But certain liberal theological conclusions contradicted their deepest commitments. Often, then, they rejected specific theological insistences of the Reformed evangelicals but joined them in the war against the liberal secularizing of Christ, the Bible and the work of the church. And, little by little, they muted their commitment to social involvement, in part for fear of identification with the social gospel of the liberals. But most also rejected the name "fundamentalist", especially as the theological bases and separatist ethos of fundamentalism became clear (see **fundamentalists**).

In the mid-1940s, Harold J. Ockenga, a Congregationalist evangelical with Methodist roots, criticized fundamentalism for its theological paranoia, its separatism and its contentiousness and led a number of Reformed evangelicals in the creation of an anti-fundamentalist "new evangelicalism". Hence the establishment of the National Association of Evangelicals, Fuller Theological Seminary, and the magazine *Christianity Today*. Doctrinally, the new evangelicals confessed the infallibility of the Bible, the Trinity,* the deity of Christ, vicarious atonement, the personality and work of the Holy Spirit,* and the personal return of Christ; religiously, they revived the coalitional ethos of the early 1900s.

In the 1960s, the Reformed evangelicals debated the meaning of "the infallibility of the Bible" as the question at the heart of their faith. The debate led to a clear separation of new evangelicals from fundamentalists. Also clear was the intention of the former to claim near-exclusive right to the title "evangelical". The large numbers of persons in the Methodist, Baptist and other traditions whose current expressions were more directly rooted in 19th-century evangelicalism than those of the Reformed new evangelicals were simply left off the evangelical map by the new evangelical cartographers.

At the same time, the social dimensions of the gospel were coming under study and were being tested in practice by evangelicals in several traditions. For example, Sherwood Wirt's *The Social Conscience of the Evangelical* and several of the works of Carl Henry called Reformed evangelicals to work actively in the world around them. But works such as Donald Dayton's *Discovering an Evangelical Heritage* revived awareness that the evangelical tradition had originally seen itself as essentially quite radical (although not novel), socially and theologically — a datum somehow lost in the coalitional ethos of new evangelicalism. Dayton and others insist that the (Reformed) new evangelical model, with its primary concern for doctrinal orthodoxy, cannot produce a historically and theologically consistent definition of "evangelicalism". Rather, the model will have to be based on clear and direct lines back to the period 1830-60, the time of the maturing of the second awakening, with its institutionalizing of revivalism and its insistence on a grace-given experience of redemption as the heart of all true Christianity.

On the international scene, those Christians who call themselves evangelicals are among the fastest-growing groups within the Christian family, especially in Latin America. They are finding institutional forums for co-operation, such as the World Evangelical Fellowship* and the Lausanne Committee for World Evangelization,* and those evangelicals among the member churches of the WCC are becoming more articulate in voicing their concerns, especially within the Commission on World Mission and Evangelism.

PAUL MERRITT BASSETT

D.W. Dayton, *Discovering an Evangelical Heritage*, New York, Harper & Row, 1976 • C.F.H. Henry, *Evangelicals in Search of Identity*, Waco, TX, Word Books, 1976 • K.S. Kantzer & S.N. Gundry eds, *Perspectives on Evangelical Theology*, Grand Rapids, MI, Baker, 1979 • G. Marsden, *Fundamentalism and American Culture: The Shaping of Twentieth-Century Evangelicalism, 1870-1925*, New York, Oxford UP, 1980 • C.R. Padilla, *The New Face of Evangelicalism*, Downers Grove, IL, InterVarsity, 1976.

EVANGELISM. One of the main roots of the contemporary ecumenical movement is to be found in the commitment to the evangelization of the world which culminated in the world missionary conference in Edinburgh in 1910. Out of this and other manifestations of God's Spirit, not just within Protestantism, but very specially also in the Orthodox world, there developed a calling to unity* which found its biblical reference and devotional inspiration in the prayer of our Lord "that they may all be one... that the world may believe" (John 17:21).

The WCC basis* is in itself a statement of the gospel message: "The World Council of Churches is a fellowship of churches which confess the Lord Jesus Christ as God and Saviour according to the scriptures and therefore seek to fulfill together their common calling to the glory of the one God, Father, Son and Holy Spirit." As Philip Potter has said: "Evangelism is the test of true ecumenism." To true ecumenism belongs the awareness of being part of the missionary movement of God's own self, who, in the fullness of time, sent the Son to redeem us and sent the Holy Spirit to gather together a people to be the bearers of the revelation* of God's liberating will in Jesus Christ (see **Trinity**).

One of the purposes of the WCC, as laid down in its constitution, is "to facilitate the common witness of the churches in each place and in all places; to support the churches in their worldwide missionary and evangelistic task". This function has been addressed in a wide variety of ways in the course of the WCC's history: studies on evangelism, fusion with the International Missionary Council, conferences on world mission every seven or eight years, publication of the *International Review of Mission* and the *Monthly Letter on Evangelism*, the holding of national or regional consultations on witnessing to the faith* and the publication of *Mission and Evangelism: An Ecumenical Affirmation*. Also, in co-operation with the Bible societies,* the WCC has been associated with the translation, production and distribution of Bibles throughout the world. The worship services and Bible studies which play such an important part in all ecumenical gatherings are ways of reminding people of the gospel and the challenge of its proclamation today.

The responsibility for evangelism and sup-port for common witness* in each place are, then, an integral part of all aspects of the WCC's work. Just as unity is essential to the struggle for justice* in the light of God's promise of reconciliation* in Jesus Christ, so the proclamation of justice and an attitude of service are a testimony to the common faith in Jesus Christ* which has brought together the ecumenical family.

The evangelism debate. Evangelism has been a major subject of discussion in all WCC assemblies and came to a moment of real crisis in Uppsala in 1968, when the notion of mission* was debated in section 2 with the title "Renewal in Mission". The section sought to understand God's own missionary activity in the whole world and the particular role of churches and Christians in accompanying the action of the Spirit of God. Some saw this approach as a secularization* of faith; for others, it was a kingdom (see **kingdom of God**) perspective that challenged them to work for justice and development.*

The Uppsala debate obliged the WCC to concentrate on the substance of the evangelistic message, and that was done first in the world mission conference in Bangkok in early 1973 on "Salvation Today" and later on in the Nairobi assembly in 1975 under the theme "Jesus Christ Frees and Unites". Nairobi affirmed: "The gospel is good news from God, our Creator and Redeemer. On its way from Jerusalem to Galilee and to the ends of the earth, the Spirit discloses ever-new aspects and dimensions of God's decisive revelation in Jesus Christ. The gospel always includes the announcement of God's kingdom and love through Jesus Christ, the offer of grace and forgiveness of sins, the invitation to repentance and faith in him, the summons to fellowship in God's church, the command to witness to God's saving words and deeds, the responsibility to participate in the struggle for justice and human dignity, the obligation to denounce all that hinders human wholeness, and a commitment to risk life itself."

The evangelical congresses. The debate among evangelicals started long before Uppsala. The series of congresses called by the North American evangelist Billy Graham deserves special mention. In 1966 he invited people of evangelical persuasion to a congress in Berlin to consider the situation of world evangelism. This was followed in 1974 by a second congress attended by 4,000 people in Lausanne, Switzerland, around the theme "Let the Earth Hear His Voice". The Lausanne covenant* which was drafted by the congress and signed by the majority of the participants pointed out that "more than 2,700 million people had yet to be evangelized". "The unreached" was an expression coined to refer to all those who have had no chance to hear the gospel of Jesus Christ. "Reaching the unreached" became the main slogan with which to mobilize the church.* Lausanne affirmed evangelism as an independent category related to, but independent of, the demand for social justice: "Social justice is not evangelization, but social justice belongs to our mandate." The awareness of the close relation between these two dimensions of the Christian gospel has been growing in all sectors of the Christian family. So a consultation in Grand Rapids, USA, in June 1982, called by the Lausanne Committee for World Evangelization and the World Evangelical Fellowship, was able to affirm that evangelism and social responsibility, while distinct from one another, are integrally related in our proclamation of and obedience to the gospel. "The partnership is in reality a marriage."

The Roman Catholic understanding of evangelism. The Roman Catholic Church devoted a special synod of bishops in 1974 to evangelization in the modern world. Potter was one of the contributors to that synod. Drawing upon the results of the synod, Pope Paul VI published the encyclical *Evangelii Nuntiandi* (Evangelization in the modern world). It affirmed Christ as the supreme evangelist and the task of evangelizing as the essential mission of the church. It declared that "it is impossible to accept that in evangelization one could or should ignore the importance of the problems so much discussed today concerning justice, liberation, development and peace in the world". It went on to say that the church "re-affirmed the primacy of her spiritual vocation and refused to replace the proclamation of the kingdom by the proclamation of forms of human liberation. She even states that her contribution to liberation is incomplete if she neglects to proclaim salvation in Christ Jesus." In his 1985 encyclical commemorating the 11th centenary of the evangelizing work of Cyril and Methodius, *Slavorum Apostoli*, Pope

John Paul II commended the two saints as authentic precursors of ecumenism and underlined the impact of the gospel on the various cultures of humankind (see **culture**). The encyclical dwells at length on the relation between evangelism and inculturation.

Evangelism and Orthodoxy. Within Orthodoxy,* too, new developments and a reassessment of the church's obligation to render witness (martyria) to Christ have taken place. The Orthodox churches have a long experience of evangelism; through the centuries, they have been telling the story of Jesus Christ through all aspects of family life, and uniquely through the celebration of the liturgy.* Several Orthodox missionary consultations have been organized by the Commission on World Mission and Evangelism (CWME) of the WCC between 1974 and 1982. They have stressed that evangelism is rooted in Trinitarian theology. Christ's sending of the apostles stems from the fact that Christ himself is sent by the Father in the Holy Spirit (John 20:21-23). The Orthodox consultations organized by CWME articulate the evangelistic significance of the liturgical celebration and the priestly role of the congregation interceding for the whole of the human community. The evangelistic experience of the Orthodox churches gives special importance to monastic communities (see **religious communities**) as centres of popular religiosity and of communicative spirituality.*

Mission and evangelism. Years of ecumenical reflection on evangelism culminated in the document *Mission and Evangelism: An Ecumenical Affirmation*, adopted by the central committee of the WCC in 1982. It makes clear that the spiritual gospel and the material gospel are one and the same gospel of Jesus. Liberation, development, humanization and evangelization are all integral parts of mission.

In May 1989, in San Antonio, USA, a world conference on mission and evangelism took place under the main theme "Your Will Be Done: Mission in Christ's Way". This conference confirmed the perspectives of the ecumenical affirmation and was able to say: "We are called to exercise our mission in this context of human struggle, and challenged to keep the earth alive and to promote human dignity, since the living God is both Creator of heaven and earth and Protector of the cause of the widow, the orphan, the poor, and the stranger. To respond to all this is part of our mission, just as inviting people to put their trust in God is part of that mission. The 'material gospel' and the 'spiritual gospel' have to be one, as was true of the ministry of Jesus. Frequently the world's poor are also those who have not yet heard the good news of the gospel; to withhold from them justice as well as the good news of life in Christ is to commit a 'double injustice'."

The contemporary context of evangelism. Today the challenge to evangelism is perhaps even greater, since we have to speak the name of Jesus and show the newness of life offered in him in a world where the vision of reality is measured in billions of years, or where genetic manipulation can condition life itself. This being so, the announcement of the ultimately new at a given time and in a given person comes as an even greater surprise and scandal to the modern mentality. There is something ingenuous about affirming that God was in Christ reconciling the world to God's own self. There is something childlike about pointing to the child of Bethlehem, to the One who was condemned on the cross, as the symbol and centre of a radical transformation of the human condition and of the whole of the universe itself. Yet it is in this story with its ingenuousness and childlikeness that we find the freshness of mind we need to confront the great contemporary perceptions and to testify to a reality that illuminates them and calls for their creative transformation.

The presence of Christians practising liberating diakonia* in the life of society and proclaiming the gospel as they participate in society's search for new models is a concrete announcement of good news. All ethical reflection and social action must be done in constant lively dialogue and interchange between real situations and the gospel history, expressed in theological insights which open up the radiant perspective of the eternal, the "numinous" and the new. It is thus essential that, as we think of the future of the ecumenical movement and its evangelistic calling, we emphasize the need for a greater capacity to relate to the widest possible diversity of churches in local situations, so we can create the links needed to enable the churches increasingly to benefit from and contribute to similar experiences in other parts of the world.

Evangelism in a world of scientific research. To proclaim the gospel of Jesus Christ is to speak a name which rings strangely in the world of genes and mutations and phenomena evolving over billions of years. But the name of Jesus Christ speaks of a historic action in which human limitations, sin* and aggressiveness are not simply accepted as destiny, part of the limits of the human condition, but are actively assumed as a responsibility, assumed as guilt and find historic response in his redemptive death on the cross. In Jesus Christ the new life which is offered is a process of sanctification,* opening the way for the transformation of the whole of reality as a purpose intrinsically present in the creative energies of creation and as a vocational project to which all human beings, scientists and others, are called. The developments in biotechnology call the churches to re-examine the fundamental Christian understandings of the creation and the relationship between God, humanity and the created world (see **bio-ethics**). In the process, the fresh resources of biblical witness and the declaration of the churches' ancient creeds* — all beginning with faith in God as the Creator and Maker of heaven and earth, of all things visible and invisible — must be reaffirmed to give a foundation for addressing the challenges of biotechnology.

If the gospel of love is to permeate all human relations, it is absolutely essential that ecumenical structures maintain a living link between the scholars and the meek of the earth, between the wisdom of the humble and scientific research (see **science and technology**). The affirmation of new life in Christ and of the dimension of spirituality in the middle of a genetic chain that only seemed to be affected by chance but now is subject to the influence of technological power is an evangelizing vocation that challenges Christians and calls for co-operative effort.

Evangelism in a world of faiths and no faith. In fulfilling our calling to preach the gospel, we come into contact with people and organizations of other religious faiths or of no faith. Our meeting with them is witness. In view of the missionary nature of God's message in Jesus Christ, we should approach others in the same spirit of love, sharing and communication as that which rules the life of the man from Nazareth. There is a responsibility of "the part for the whole", the Christian community for the whole human community. This mission is also expressed in service: "As the Father has sent me, even so I send you" (John 20:21). This same spirit of openness and concern for others enables us to describe Jesus in his life as "the one who came to do good" and to see the cross not simply as the manifestation of human evil but fundamentally and above all as total giving of self for the liberation and redemption of others.

The guidelines for our relations with other faiths remind us that it is not just a question of co-existence or pro-existence of the different religious groups. It is also an attitude of dialogue (see **dialogue, interfaith**), an attitude of respect for the neighbour in keeping with that shown by God in Jesus Christ. Consequently, our testimony to our faith should take place in a context not only of respect but of acceptance of the other. Jesus does not hesitate to point to the Samaritan as setting the example of love for his Jewish disciples. In Christ, God offers God's self; God does not impose. The outstretched arms of the cross are perhaps the best symbol of God's attitude towards all humankind — the offering of God's self in an attitude of total powerless-

ness, and from there, from the depths of despair, appealing, inviting to a free decision. The witness we owe to the other is the witness to God's love made manifest in Jesus Christ — a love to which I can testify only in a loving relationship which implies acceptance of my neighbour and co-responsibility for the whole human predicament.

There is also a third level of discussion to the ecumenical debate. An old — yet ever new — question lies ahead of us. At Vancouver a lively debate took place on the theological value to be recognized in non-Christian religious experience. After an extensive debate Vancouver could only state, in terms that left the question open: "While affirming the uniqueness of the birth, life, death and resurrection of Jesus, to which we bear witness, we recognize God's creative work in the seeking for religious truth among peoples of other faiths."

But none of the three levels of our ecumenical experience in the matter of the role and place of other faiths questions the central tenet of our faith: that God was in Christ reconciling the world to God's own self. The spirit of dialogue, friendship and encounter with my neighbour provides the ideal context for wit-

Evangelist in Guatemala City, Guatemala (WCC/Peter Williams)

ness. To accept the questions addressed to us by other religious faiths is to adopt the attitude urged by the apostle Peter: "Always be prepared to make a defence to any one who calls you to account for the hope that is in you" (1 Pet. 3:15). When the apostle Paul affirms his faith and hope in an eschatological understanding of the role attributed to Israel after the coming of Christ, he does so not as an excuse for not bearing witness to his people but out of passionate concern that they should all come to know Jesus (Rom. 9:1-3, 10:1). The missionary conviction of the Christian faith is not called in question but rather is purified, strengthened and deepened when we place ourselves alongside our neighbours of other faiths in an attitude of respect, of listening and appreciation of the cultural and spiritual treasures belonging to them.

The 1989 mission conference in San Antonio summarized the situation very well when it said: "We cannot point to any other way of salvation than Jesus Christ; at the same time we cannot set limits to the saving power of God. At times the debate about salvation focuses itself only on the fate of the individual's soul in the hereafter, whereas the will of God is life in its fullness even here and now. We therefore state: (1) that our witness to others concerning salvation in Christ springs from the fact that we have encountered him as our Lord and Saviour and are hence urged to share this with others, and (2) that in calling people to faith in Christ, we are not only offering personal salvation but also calling them to follow Jesus in the service of God's kingdom.

"We have paid attention to the complex debate about the relationship between witness and dialogue. We recognize that both witness and dialogue presuppose two-way relationships. We affirm that witness does not preclude dialogue but invites it, and that dialogue does not preclude witness but extends and deepens it."

Summing up. The dimension of evangelism is fundamental to the ecumenical calling. Clarity in confessing Jesus Christ as God and Saviour and calling others to faith and Christian discipleship is the guarantee of Christian authenticity and ecumenical work. The only valid theological method for evangelism is conscious participation in the whole of human life and its problems. For the great mass of people, evangelism is a question not of apologetics but of life. Gustavo Gutiérrez has pointed out that in Latin America the people are "poor and believing". Much the same could be said of the vast deprived masses of the world as a whole. The discussion is about explaining the faith in terms of joy, faithfulness, justice and solidarity.

The poor* peoples of the world recognize the gospel message in the solidarity of the Programme to Combat Racism* or in the home the WCC offers to groups fighting for justice, peace and responsible care for the environment in the four corners of the earth. We are called to bear witness to the God of justice, hope, consolation and reconciliation, seeking to identify with the poor and the marginal. Here, too, we have an opportunity to proclaim the good news in situations of oppression and to answer the gospel challenge to manifest the transforming power which the good news of God in Christ brings to every human situation. The San Antonio conference said it very clearly: "In some parts of the world people face a total system of death, of monstrous false gods, of exploitative economic systems, of violence, of the disintegration of the fundamental bonds of society, of the destruction of human life, of helplessness of persons in the face of impersonal forces. We are called to exercise our mission in this context of human struggle... There is no evangelism without solidarity; there is no Christian solidarity that does not involve sharing the message of God's coming reign."

See also **Jesus Christ, mission, salvation, uniqueness of Christ, witness**.

EMILIO CASTRO

I. Bria ed., *Martyria/Mission: The Witness of the Orthodox Churches Today*, WCC, 1980 • E. Castro, *Freedom in Mission: The Perspective of the Kingdom of God. An Ecumenical Inquiry*, WCC, 1985 • *Common Witness*, study document of the Joint Working Group of the Roman Catholic Church and the WCC, WCC, 1982 • J.D. Douglas ed., *Let the Earth Hear His Voice*, Minneapolis, World Wide, 1975 • *Evangelii Nuntiandi*, London, Catholic Truth Society, 1975 • *Mission and Evangelism: An Ecumenical Affirmation*, WCC, 1982 • F. Wilson ed., *The San Antonio Report*, WCC, 1990.

EVDOKIMOV, PAUL. B. 2.8.1901, St Petersburg, Russia; d. 16.9.1970, Meudon,

France. Evdokimov participated actively in the ecumenical movement and in the WCC, particularly as a member of the board of the Ecumenical Institute of Bossey,* 1950-68, where he gave many lectures and was one of the professors of the first graduate school, 1953-54. Teaching at the Orthodox faculty of theology of St Sergius from 1953 onwards, he was also involved in the work of Faith and Order.* He studied in Kiev, at St Sergius, and obtained a PhD in philosophy at the University of Aix-Marseille in 1942. In 1921 he left Russia for Constantinople, and arrived in France in 1923, where he worked night shifts at the Citroën automobile factory to pay for his studies. From 1943 he worked with CIMADE,* an ecumenical organization set up to help displaced persons and refugees, later the interchurch aid organization of the churches in France. He directed a centre for refugees in Bièvres, near Paris, 1946-47, and the CIMADE students hostel in Sèvres and Massy for refugee students from Eastern Europe and later for WCC scholarship students from third-world countries, 1948-68. Evdokimov was also active in setting up Orthodox student movements and meetings for young Orthodox theologians. He wrote *L'Orthodoxie* (Neuchâtel, Delachaux & Niestlé, 1959), *L'Esprit Saint dans la tradition orthodoxe* (Paris, Cerf, 1969) and *Le Christ dans la pensée russe* (Paris, Cerf, 1970).

ANS J. VAN DER BENT

EXCOMMUNICATION. As frequently happens in questions of church order* and church discipline,* practice antedates the emergence of canonical enactments and even the appearance of fixed terminology. The first case of excommunication was pronounced by Paul against a member of the Christian community in Corinth who was accused of sexual immorality. The wording used by the apostle is "be removed from" and pronounce "judgment", or "condemn" (1 Cor. 5:2-3). Paul states that he acts "in the name of the Lord Jesus" (v.4). Later on, Matthew attributes a saying to Jesus, bearing on the procedure of excommunication (Matt. 18:15-17). The concept of exclusion from the community is expressed by a phrasing reminiscent of Palestinian Judaism: "If [the sinner] refuses to listen even to the church, let him be to you as a gentile and a tax collector" (v.17). The verb *aphorizein*, which later on was used to designate the fact of excommunicating, is used for the exclusion of Christians from the Jewish community (Luke 6:22). In patristic literature the verb and the noun *(aphorismos)* are in most cases used with the meaning "casting out". However in the ancient church the concept of excommunication is expressed by several phrases basically conveying the same idea. So, with regard to the first centuries of Christianity, the real significance and seriousness of excommunication has to be inferred from the context in each case.

Taking into account continuing data and canonical materials from both East and West, the various kinds of excommunication can be listed as follows: (1) *minor excommunication* — a temporary deprivation from holy communion; (2) *excommunication with ecclesiastical censure* — a temporary deprivation from holy communion and preventing the guilty party from being involved in communal activities; (3) *major excommunication* — a complete exclusion from the church; and (4) pronouncement of a *break of ecclesiastical communion* with a segment of the church universal as a consequence of serious disagreement bearing on matters of faith* or church order.

Minor excommunication is related to penance,* and as such it is imposed on sinners having committed transgressions which do not require a more severe kind of excommunication. It implies a temporary abstention from holy communion. Since in the early church there was no private sacramental confession, one would have to speak in such cases of "self-excommunication": the sinner was encouraged to abstain voluntarily from holy communion for a short time. It is, for example, the suggestion made by Denys of Alexandria (d.264) in his letter to Basilides. Augustine later expressed the same view throughout his works. Resumption of communion took place without necessarily implying a rite of reconciliation.

During the middle ages, private confession appeared in the church. Thenceforth, minor excommunication was imposed by the confessor, who usually based the terms of excommunication on indications provided by "penitential books". It is noteworthy that from late antiquity onward, there was a continual tendency to relax disciplinary rules regarding penance. In the 3rd and 4th centuries this attitude was opposed by rigorist groups which separated from the church.

The second type of excommunication is an *ecclesiastical censure*, which applies to transgressions including aggravating circumstances. In such cases the sentence is to be pronounced either by the diocesan bishop or by a church court with subsequent approval of the diocesan bishop. In the case of a cleric, the penalty is not excommunication but rather suspension or deposition. Suspension means that a cleric is prevented from exercising his ministry for a determined space of time. Deposition entails a permanent withdrawal from clerical status. A cleric reduced to the rank of the laity can subsequently be excommunicated.

Major excommunication is the most severe penalty which can be imposed on a Christian, regardless of his or her status in the church. Because of its nature and consequences, imposing this censure does not fall within the competency of a single bishop. It must be pronounced or at least confirmed by a synod of bishops. (During the first centuries a bishop had this power. But every bishop acted in close connection with the presbyterium at that time.) From the 4th century, conciliar legislation established the right of appeal. Later on this censure tended to fall within the exclusive competency of synods.

It is difficult to determine to what extent "anathema"* related to major excommunication in the early church. Paul, for example, uses this phrase in order to express a malediction against anyone who "has no love for the Lord" or preaches a different gospel (1 Cor. 16:22; Gal. 1:8-9). In the East during the 4th century, councils pronounced anathematization against groups accused of doctrinal deviations. The council of Nicea (325), for example, took such a stand against Arius and his supporters. Those who disagreed with the Nicene Creed were subject to major excommunication and were no longer considered members of the church.

Sometimes anathematization is simply equated with excommunication. A canon adopted at the first Constantinopolitan council (381) contains the following specification: "By heretics we mean both those who have been previously cast out and those whom we ourselves have anathematized." The ancient church also used to anathematize persons for ethical reasons inasmuch as deviant conduct was based on doctrine at variance with ecclesiastical teaching. So, the council assembled at Gangra (c.340) anathematized those who condemned marriage and social order. However, the members of this council specified that if those sectarians repented and rejected their false doctrine, they would be reinstated to communion in the church. In the ancient church there was only one exception to the canonical principle relating directly or indirectly anathematization with heresy: the council at Elvira in Spain at the beginning of the 4th century (309?) anathematized various categories of sinners.

The fourth kind of excommunication, i.e. the pronouncement of a break of communion with a segment of the universal church, has the most general historical consequences. For example, at the end of the 2nd century, Victor, bishop of Rome, broke communion with the church of Asia Minor because of a disagreement bearing on the date of Easter. In such a case, this kind of excommunication affects all the followers and supporters of the bishops or priests specifically excommunicated and anathematized. It is obvious that such an excommunication does not necessarily imply that a simple follower is excluded from the church in a direct, personal sense. It simply means that such an individual is excluded from church membership because he or she is for the time being a member of a dissident community. In cases of schisms involving no doctrinal issue, the excommunication is automatically lifted if a reconciliation* is achieved at the highest hierarchical level.

See also **anathemas, canon law, church discipline, communion**.

PETER L'HUILLIER

EXEGESIS, METHODS OF.

The modes of interpreting the Bible have varied over the centuries, from the patristic harmonizing interpretation, to the medieval four senses of scripture, to the literal (non-allegorical) interpretation of the Reformation, to the historical-critical method of exegesis today. Though isolated patristic interpreters, such as Origen, Augustine and Jerome, did use primitive forms of historical criticism, the method that is widely used today by Protestants and Roman Catholics traces its roots to the Renaissance, to its "return to the sources", and to the study of the Bible in its original biblical languages — Hebrew, Aramaic and Greek.

Such interpretation of the Bible further developed at the time of the Enlightenment and of the rise of 19th-century Germany historicism. Leopold von Ranke and his "objective historiography" (seeking to present the past "as it really was") affected the interpretation of the Bible. Similarly, the "life of Jesus research" of H.S. Reimarus, F.C. Baur, H.E.G. Paulus, D.F. Strauss, Bruno Bauer and Ernest Renan also gave impetus to that development, as they adopted the methods of historical and literary criticism from classical philology, which had grown from the Renaissance study of Greek and Roman literature.

The historical and archaeological discoveries of the 18th and the 19th centuries likewise contributed to the development of the historical-critical method. The decipherment of the Rosetta Stone (1827, Jean François Champollion) and of the ancient Bisitun Inscription (1835-46, H.C. Rawlinson and G.R. Grotefend) opened the literature of ancient Egypt, Israel's neighbour to the west, and that of ancient Assyria and Babylonia, Israel's neighbours to the east. Thus it became possible to understand the Old Testament against the literary background of such neighbouring cultures. Again, in the 19th century thousands of Greek letters and documents were recovered from the sands of Egypt; they cast unsuspected light on the language of the Septuagint and of the New Testament. Such historical discoveries made it impossible to interpret the Bible as naively as had been done earlier, without regard for the ancient world in which it came into being.

Similarly, in the 20th century, the discovery of Ugaritic, Eblaite, and the Dead Sea Scrolls has made a substantial impact on the historical-critical study of the Bible. Palestinian Judaism of the 1st century is now understood in a way that it had never been known before; this Palestinian Jewish matrix of Christianity cannot be ignored, even if most of the NT writings were composed outside Palestine. All these factors have influenced the understanding of the Bible and have made

the historical-critical method the basic mode of interconfessional interpretation of scripture. Such historical development in the interpretation of the Bible cannot be neglected.

Initially, Roman Catholic interpreters did not use this method, largely because Pope Leo XIII set up a biblical commission to act as a watchdog over biblical interpretation and to guard against the excesses of rationalism associated with that method. *Vigilantiae* was the first word of Pope Leo's apostolic letter (*Acta Sanctae Sedis* 35, 1902-03, 234-38). It set the tone for the activity of the commission in the first third of the 20th century and cast a cloud of fear and reactionism over Roman Catholic interpreters of the Bible. That was changed, however, when Pope Pius XII issued his encyclical *Divino Afflante Spiritu* (*Acta Apostolicae Sedis* 35, 1943, 297-326) and insisted on the study of the Bible in its original languages and according to the forms of ancient literature in which the biblical writings had been composed. Then, in 1964 the biblical commission issued an instruction, "On the Historical Truth of the Gospels" (*Acta Apostolicae Sedis* 56 [1964], 712-18; *Catholic Biblical Quarterly* 26 [1964], 305-12), which explicitly espoused form criticism and recognized the three stages of the gospel tradition (what Jesus of Nazareth did and said [A.D. 1-33], what the apostles and disciples preached about his words and deeds [A.D. 33-65], and what the evangelists culled from such preaching, as they synthesized, explicated, and ordered it in their gospels [A.D. 65-95]). It thus freed Roman Catholic interpreters from their form of fundamentalism, which had been in use for centuries in the post-Tridentine period. On the Protestant side, meanwhile, form criticism in particular called attention to the pre-scriptural life of material that was eventually consigned to the scriptures; it thus enabled scripture to be seen as an internal, though still privileged, part of an older and continuing tradition (see **Tradition and traditions**).

The historical-critical method makes use of two preliminary steps: the consideration of *introductory questions* (authenticity of the writing, its integrity or unity, its date and place of composition, its content or outline, its literary or cultural background); *textual criticism* (the best manuscripts, the best form of the transmitted text, its ancient versions). Along with such preliminary questions, certain forms of criticism affect the historical judgment about a biblical text: (1) literary criticism — the genres or forms of the text; its narrative and rhetorical character, e.g. the use of *inclusio*, chiasmus, catchword bonds, argument; (2) source criticism — origin of often parallel accounts, stereotyped phraseology, documentary differences, synoptic counterparts, all of which affect the historical judgment in an interpretation of a Bible book; (3) form criticism — the kind of psalm; historical, prophetic, apocalyptic, or sapiential writings; sayings, parables, pronouncement stories, miracle stories; poetry, letters, exhortations; (4) redaction criticism — the way in which biblical authors have edited or redacted their sources, or what they have inherited from the tradition before them. All these kinds of criticism are aimed at one goal: to determine the meaning of the text as it was intended by the human author who was moved long ago to compose it. The truth that has been enshrined in the ancient biblical text corresponds to the form adopted, and the historical-critical method teaches us that that text cannot be properly read without an appreciation of the particular form in which the truth is being expressed.

Problems that the historical-critical method have encountered stem not from the method itself (which, being borrowed from classical philology, is basically neutral) but from the presuppositions with which it has often been used. Thus, when it first emerged in full-blown form in the "life of Jesus research", it was linked with a rationalistic, anti-dogmatic prejudice that tainted it. As Albert Schweitzer recognized in *The Quest for the Historical Jesus*, such an approach had sprung not from a purely historical interest in Jesus of Nazareth but from a "struggle against the tyranny of dogma"; he noted that their lives had been "written with hate", not a hate of the person of Jesus, but of "the supernatural nimbus with which it was so easy to surround him". Such an attitude became associated with the method itself and made it suspect in the eyes of many.

Still later, in the 20th century the pioneer NT form critics (K.L. Schmidt, Martin Dibelius and Rudolf Bultmann) used the historical-critical method with still other presuppositions. In Bultmann's case his emphasis on kerygmatic theology (heavily influenced by

Luther's justification* by faith alone) and on Heideggerian existentialism led to demythologization and a lack of concern for the historical Jesus. Again, one realizes that such attitudes coloured the use of the method itself.

Today, the historical-critical method is widely used with other presuppositions. Among Christian interpreters it is recognized that exegesis is not merely philology but "philology plus", and that the "plus" is an empathy of Christian faith* which traces its roots back to the Jesus of history in some fashion. That "plus" reckons with the Bible as the word of God,* as an inspired or authoritative record in which God's revelation* is enshrined, and as a canonical collection (see **canon**). Hence the historical-critical method does not aim merely at analyzing the Bible according to the various forms of criticism that have emerged in the 19th and 20th centuries; rather, all of these must lead to some form of biblical theology.

The historical-critical method is interested, indeed, in the *textual* meaning of words and phrases, but also in their *contextual* meaning in a paragraph, chapter, or book as a whole, and above all in the *relational* meaning of such words, phrases and parts to the complex of theological or religious ideas of the sacred writer. The quest for these meanings must dominate the method itself so that its goal is "biblical theology", the synthetic presentation of the religious teaching of the author, an understanding of how he has enshrined God's word (or revelation) in his composition. If this goal does not dominate the method, then it is not the historical-critical method properly understood or properly used in biblical interpretation.

The method is open to still further minor adjustments, and herein the exegetical techniques that have emerged in recent decades have played a role: the criticisms called canonical, feminist, materialist, narrative, psychological, rhetorical, sociological, semiotic, structural, etc. Although proponents give the impression that some of these aspects have not been part of the method before, these techniques, in fact, help to refine aspects of the existing method. Yet not one of them is or can be a substitute for the basic method that has developed since the Renaissance.

What ultimately lies behind such a critical approach to the Bible in the church is the conviction that God's revelation in Christ took place *in the past* and that the ancient record of that self-manifestion of God is disclosed to the church above all in the Bible, in the word of God couched in ancient human writings, and in the tradition that grew out of them under the guidance of the Holy Spirit.*

Thus the historical-critical method rightly understood and rightly employed (with the empathy of Christian faith) has contributed in a major way to the ecumenical movement of the 20th century. It is used in the interpretation of the Bible in seminaries of all the major Christian churches of the West (Anglican, Lutheran, Methodist, Presbyterian and Roman Catholic). Through it Protestants and Roman Catholics utilize the same mode of interpretation and can agree on the biblical basis of Christian faith or at least dispute an intepretation on more or less agreed principles.

If ultra-conservative groups in each church are sceptical of its use, that is largely because they misunderstand it and fail to see how it can be used with a proper sense of biblical inspiration* and inerrancy. The churches of the East have been slow to adopt the historical-critical method, not because of a suspicion about it, but because their tradition has been more tied to the patristic, harmonizing interpretation, and especially because they did not share the experience of the Renaissance, the Reformation, or the Enlightenment. However, the method is beginning to make its appearance among the Greek Orthodox, some of whose scholars share the experience of the international and interconfessional societies of OT and NT interpretation.

See also **canon, hermeneutics, inspiration, New Testament and Christian unity, Old Testament and Christian unity, scriptures, Tradition and traditions**.

JOSEPH A. FITZMYER

R.E. Brown, *Biblical Exegesis and Church Doctrine*, New York, Paulist, 1985 • R.E. Brown, *The Critical Meaning of the Bible*, New York, Paulist, 1981 • R.J. Coggins & J.L. Houlden eds, *A Dictionary of Biblical Interpretation*, London, SCM, 1990 • T.R. Curtin, *Historical Criticism and the Theological Interpretation of Scripture: The Catholic Discussion of a Biblical Hermeneutic, 1958-1983*, Rome, Gregorian University, 1987 • J.A. Fitzmyer, "Historical Criticism: Its Role in Biblical Interpretation and Church Life", *Theological Studies*, 50, 1989 • R.J. Neuhaus ed., *Biblical Interpretation in Crisis: The Ratzinger Conference on Bible and Church*, Grand Rapids, MI, Eerdmans, 1989 • P. Stuhlmacher, *Historical Criticism and Theological Interpretation of Scripture*, Philadelphia, Fortress, 1977.

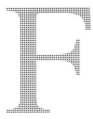

FAITH. Faith has been and is the source, the driving force and the common goal of the ecumenical movement. The latter aims at "visible unity in one faith" (WCC constitution 3.1) and is based on the confession of "the Lord Jesus Christ as God and Saviour according to the scriptures". The churches participating in it are thereby seeking "to fulfill together their common calling to the glory of the one God, Father, Son and Holy Spirit" (WCC constitution 1, the basis). Without faith as a God-given reality, there would not be a Christian ecumenical movement. Without that movement, however, the Christian faith could not find its proper identity.

Though most participants in the ecumenical movement would agree on this general affirmation, they have different and still divisive understandings of the form and content of the Christian faith. Disputes remain about the character of that faith as both gift and task, about the role of the tradition *(paradosis)* of faith (see **Tradition and traditions**) and the authoritative teaching thereof (see **teaching authority**), the relation of personal faith to the faith of the church* community, the intermediary role of scripture, Tradition, sacraments and ministry in the development of faith, the relation of faith and practice, faith and doctrinal formulations, faith and science, etc.

In the older comparative study of the various confessions and churches, such differences were considered to be fundamental differences, a sufficient explanation or legitimation of schisms* and divisions. This debate is still going on. At the same time, however, many contextual factors have caused a radical osmosis of various "models of faith", which are now considered to be more like "modalities" within a legitimate pluralism* of expressions of faith.

Fides qua/fides quae. At a Faith and Order* consultation in Rome (1983) on "The Biblical Roots of the Ancient Creeds", a tentative definition of faith was proposed as follows: "The term faith indicates at the same time a decisive act and a continuing attitude of believing *(fides qua creditur)* as well as a set of beliefs and convictions *(fides quae creditur)*. The Old and the New Testament witness that faith in God is expressed by an existential, personal and communal act and attitude of acceptance, decision, trust, confidence, confessing, hope and obedience. This *fides qua* can never be without or separated from the content of faith *(fides quae)*. Otherwise the act of faith would be an empty or a purely self-generated act. The content of faith is determined by the One towards whom it is directed. This *fides quae* can be expressed in a great plurality of forms, ranging from short biblical affirmations such as 'Jesus is Lord' to massive theological expositions" *(The Roots,* 20).

A personal act or attitude of faith (= confessing, trust in someone or something) can never be without some clear assertion and decision about God and the works of God, as the prophets of Israel and the gospel of Jesus have shown. The Hebrew word for faith *('emunah)* echoes a fundamental trust in God's presence and care, guidance and sovereignty, as becomes clear from the faith of Abraham, Moses and the prophets (see Heb. 11). A confession of faith is never a conceptual statement about the faith only, but always a doxology, involving a personal commitment of life, structuring the consensus* of a community and inviting, persuading others to assent and to adhere. In the words of the Joint Working Group between the WCC and the Roman Catholic Church in *Towards a Confession of the Common Faith*: "The apostolic texts present the faith to us as a vital dynamism by which the whole person (spirit, heart, will), recognizing in Jesus Christ his God and his Saviour, welcomes him through the Holy Spirit and in doing so yields himself to him in all that his mystery admits of and promises. For in giving himself to us, he enables us, always in the Holy Spirit, to give ourselves to him also. Conversion and docility to the Spirit find their source here. And this explains the coming together of the churches in efforts to enable the new creation, of which the Risen Christ is the Lord, to shine forth even now."

Faith and worship. In the words of Faith and Order at Montreal 1963, this faith is transmitted in a process of tradition, "not only as a sum of tenets, but as a living reality transmitted through the operation of the Holy Spirit" (para. 46). In the worship and liturgy, in the prayer and commitment of the church community, this tradition of faith becomes a corporate reality, directly related to the salvific work of Christ and to the actual situation of humanity in nature* and history.* To quote Montreal again: "Christian worship, set forth in baptism and celebrated in the eucharist, is grounded and centred in the historical ministry of Jesus Christ, his death and resurrection, and his exalted and continuing ministry. Such worship always includes the gathering of Christ's people, the preaching of the word of God, participation in Christ's self-offering and intercession for all men, and thanksgiving with joy" (paras 108-09).

The Second Vatican Council* was thinking much along the same lines when it stated in the Constitution on the Sacred Liturgy (1963):

"The church is essentially both human and divine, visible but endowed with invisible realities, zealous in action and dedicated to contemplation, present in the world, but as a pilgrim, so constituted that in her the human is directed towards and subordinated to the divine, the visible to the invisible, action to contemplation, and this present world to that city to come, the object of our quest" (*Sacrosanctum Concilium* 2).

In the tradition of the Orthodox churches, faith as such is enacted within the divine liturgy* and in the eucharistic community of the church. In a study document of F&O on the explication of the Nicene Creed,* the matter is put this way: "The individual's confession of faith, however, is made in communion with the faith of the whole church. Where baptism is conferred within the context of the liturgy of a local church, the community responds: 'This is the faith of the church, this is our faith.' The Nicene Creed is the confession of faith which belongs to the one, holy, catholic and apostolic church. In the Nicene Creed the individual joins with all the baptized gathered together in each and every place, now and throughout the ages, in the church's proclamation of faith: 'We believe in.' The confession 'we believe in' articulates not only the trust of individuals in God's grace, but it also affirms the trust of the whole church in God. There is a bond of communion between those who join together in making a common confession of their faith" (*Confessing One Faith*, paras 2-3).

Faith and practice. The biblical terminology for the act of faith *('emunah, pistis)* implies a faithful practice, even while, in its character as adherence to the living God and participation in divine life (see Vatican II, *Dei Verbum* 1), it transcends the concrete works and deeds of sinful human beings. The old controversy over "faith and (meritorious) works" has been superseded in the modern ecumenical movement by a new awareness of the practical implications of faith. From the Amsterdam assembly onwards, the interrelatedness of faith and hope,* faith and charity, faith and prophetic confession over against all false ideologies has been stressed. The very first sections of the successive WCC assembly reports form a consistent chain of arguments for the unity of faith and practice. "Confessing Christ and being converted to his discipleship belong inseparably together" (Nairobi, 1.13). "Christians witness in word and deed to the inbreaking reign of God. We experience the power of the Holy Spirit to confess Christ in a life marked by both suffering and joy. Christ's decisive battle has been won at Easter, and we are baptized into his death that we might walk in newness of life (Rom. 6:4). Yet, we must still battle daily against those already dethroned, but not yet destroyed, 'principalities and powers' of this rebellious age. The Holy Spirit leads us into all truth, engrafting persons into the Body of Christ in which all things are being restored by God" (*ibid.*, 1.5).

At the F&O plenary meeting in Bangalore 1978, this idea of faith was expressed in a "Common Account of Hope", echoing the worldwide struggle of people for liberation and renewal, as part of their faith. The Vancouver assembly's call for a worldwide conciliar process for Justice, Peace and the Integrity of Creation* and the world convocation on that issue in Seoul in 1990 demonstrate once more the necessity of relating the Trinitarian faith of the church to the problems of suffering humanity and groaning nature.

The Trinitarian basis of faith. Faith is not a mere human form of belief, not an epistemological or ethical "thought-form" or "imperative" only. It refers to the reality of the living God in history and is in fact communion with that God: "Christians believe that 'the one true God', who made himself known to Israel, has revealed himself supremely in the 'one whom he has sent', namely Jesus Christ (John 17:3); that, in Christ, God has reconciled the world to himself (2 Cor. 5:19); and that, by his Holy Spirit, God brings new and eternal life to all who through Christ put their trust in him" (*Confessing One Faith*, para. 6).

The Second Vatican Council declared: "It pleased God, in his goodness and wisdom, to reveal himself and to make known the mystery of his will (cf. Eph. 1:9). His will was that men should have access to the Father, through Christ, the word made flesh, in the Holy Spirit, and thus become sharers in the divine nature (cf. Eph. 2:18; 2 Pet. 1:4). By this revelation, then, the invisible God (cf. Col. 1:15; 1 Tim. 1:17), from the fullness of his love, addresses men as his friends (cf. Ex. 33:11; John 15:14-15), and moves among

them (cf. Bar. 3:38), in order to invite and receive them into his own company" (*Dei Verbum* 2).

This grounding of the faith in the Trinitarian life and communion of God, Father, Son and Holy Spirit (see **Trinity**) through the history of salvation colours the whole of Christian faith, its liturgy, theology and practice. Although Christians still differ about the actual interpretation oι the Trinitarian communion, the ecumenical movement has based itself on the recognition of the glory of Father, Son and Holy Spirit and agrees on the Trinitarian structure of the history of salvation and its narrative functions (see **salvation history**).

Faith and unbelief. Such faith and hope, however, meets with serious challenges in a world which seems to be caught up, at least in the northern hemisphere, in secularization* processes: the rejection of theism and classical metaphysics, the loss of cultural impact on the part of the Christian faith, the quest for human autonomy in a secularized state, in technological advance and scientific freedom, and in heavy criticism of the Christian heritage and the ecclesiastical institutions. Historical criticism and the hermeneutical gap between the faith of the church through the ages and the symbolic universe of people in modern society have made the search for "a common expression of the apostolic faith today" more than timely.

A worldwide reflection on continuity and change in the expressions of faith, resulting in countless new forms of liturgy and prayer, credal statements and confessions of faith, must go side by side with a serious quest to "hand on the faith once received" in the face of those who are inclined to reject it as a hindrance to their autonomy or as an illusory projection of a past state of human development.

Faith and dialogue with other faiths. The Christian faith is rooted in the faith of Israel. But Christians are separated from Jews by a history of anti-semitism, by deep and mutual misunderstandings with regard to the role of Jesus in God's salvific work, and by an essentially different view on the relation between God's covenant* for all peoples and his covenant with Israel. The Jewish-Christian dialogue* within the ecumenical movement has changed our understanding of faith through a serious re-reading of the Jewish scriptures, which belong to the Christian heritage as well, and through a new view on the origins of the church in the ministry of Jesus, as a son of Israel and as a prophet to his people.

Of quite another type is the dialogue with the faith of our Muslim brothers and sisters, Islam, who share with us the patriarchs and prophets of Israel as teachers of our faith. Muslim-Christian dialogue* makes us aware of the wider circles of God's covenant, as the Vatican II Constitution on the Church has put it (*Lumen Gentium* 13-15), but not all Christian churches are ready to share this theological position. For some of them, such views seem to endanger the uniqueness of Jesus Christ,* which is fundamental in Christian faith, they say.

This tension is all the more the case with regard to Buddhist-Christian* and Hindu-Christian* dialogue, though there are many Christians in Asia who are coming nearer to their Asian religious and cultural heritage, without giving up their faith in Jesus Christ. As the Light for the world, Jesus Christ may even be pictured in the New Testament and in Christian iconography as the "cosmic Christ", being present in all stages of creation and being near to all wisdom of old, as it has been delivered in the Asian context through the intermediary of the Asian religions.

The WCC Sub-unit on Dialogue with Living Faiths has taken various initiatives in the past decades for real dialogue and co-operation and has prepared the ground for a wider ecumenism and a more open, respectful and peaceful attitude of faith in most Christian churches today. The WCC's *Guidelines on Dialogue with People of Living Faiths and Ideologies* declares: "It is Christian faith in the Triune God — Creator of all humankind, Redeemer in Jesus Christ, revealing and renewing Spirit — which calls us Christians to human relationship with our many neighbours. It is Christian faith which sets us free to be open to the faith of others, to risk, to trust and to be vulnerable. In dialogue, conviction and openness are held in balance."

Faith as a gift of God and as human response. In the aftermath of Protestant dialectical theology, it became a theological cliché to affirm against liberal theologies that it is impossible for humankind to construct a reasonable faith or to develop a natural theology. It is God who is the one communicating

Elements of faith (WCC/Michael Dominguez)

with us, before ever we could think about him. If we are believers, we know and confess that God loved us, before ever we could love him. He is the God of revelation, inviting us to participate in divine life (*Dei Verbum* 1). Nevertheless, our answer of faith is based on conversion, on a personal decision to confess God as our creator, redeemer and sanctifier, as himself Father, Son and Holy Spirit. We are ourselves involved in the act of faith. In the discussions about the relation of faith and baptism,* faith and sacraments,* this problem has played an important and controversial role. A solution was offered in the Lima text on baptism: "Baptism is both God's gift and our human response to that gift" (*Baptism, Eucharist and Ministry,* B8), a statement that could equally well have been made about faith. In the churches' responses to BEM, however, we find evidence that this problem of the relation of divine and human initiative, of God's grace* and human freedom, of faith as a divine gift and as a human spirituality, is still not solved to the satisfaction of all. Many fear an ungodly synergism. Others, however, stress the anthropomorphic character of the question itself. There is, from the side of God, no competition between God and humans. God does not need force or violence to impose obedience on humans; God rather persuades them, for there is no violence in God (*Epistle to Diognetus* 7.4). It is perhaps this model of a gentle, persuading, strengthening and justifying, reconciling and inviting God, which might renew the Christian faith and inform the ecumenical movement as a movement towards the mercy of God.

Towards a common profession of faith. In an intense and long-term study project ("Towards the Common Expression of the Apostolic Faith Today"), the F&O commission has embarked, since its Bangalore meeting in 1978, on a search for a faithful contemporary explanation of the content of the ancient creeds, for the recognition of the Nicene Creed of 381 by all the churches as the ecumenical creed, and for a common expression of that same faith for today. Thus the commission tried to implement the proposals of the Nairobi assembly: "We ask the churches to undertake a common effort to receive, re-appropriate and confess together, as contemporary occasion requires, the Christian truth and faith, delivered through

the apostles and handed down through the centuries. Such common action, arising from free and inclusive discussion under the commonly acknowledged authority of God's word, must aim both to clarify and to embody the unity and the diversity which are proper to the church's life and mission" (Nairobi, 2.19).

The search for such a common faith and witness inspires the whole ecumenical movement. In 1980 the Joint Working Group between the Roman Catholic Church and the WCC published a document on *Common Witness,** which together with the F&O study on the apostolic faith gives much hope for a growing unity in faith within the one Body of Christ.

See also **Apostles' Creed; apostolic tradition; atheism; catechisms; common confession; common witness; creeds; dialogue, bilateral; dialogue, multilateral; hope; lex orandi, lex credendi; Nicene Creed; salvation history; secularization; teaching authority; Tradition and traditions; Trinity**.

ANTON HOUTEPEN

Common Witness, study document of the Joint Working Group RCC/WCC, WCC, 1980 • *Confessing One Faith: Towards an Ecumenical Explication of the Apostolic Faith As Expressed in the Nicene-Constantinopolitan Creed (381)*, WCC, 1987 • *Guidelines on Dialogue with People of Living Faiths and Ideologies*, rev. ed., WCC, 1990 • H.-G. Link ed., *The Roots of Our Common Faith: Faith in the Scriptures and in the Early Church*, WCC, 1984 • *Sharing in One Hope: Bangalore 1978*, WCC, 1979 • *Towards a Confession of the Common Faith*, WCC, 1980 • G. Tsetsis ed., *Orthodox Thought: Reports of Orthodox Consultations Organized by the WCC, 1975-82*, WCC, 1983.

FAITH AND ORDER. The F&O movement serves the churches by leading them into theological dialogue as a means of overcoming obstacles to, and opening up ways towards, the manifestation of their unity* given in Jesus Christ.

History. Together with the movement for Life and Work* and the International Missionary Council,* the F&O movement shaped the first phase of the modern ecumenical movement between 1910 and 1948. Soon after the 1910 world missionary conference in

Edinburgh, the 1910 convention of the (Anglican) Protestant Episcopal Church in the USA resolved "that a joint commission be appointed to bring about a conference for the consideration of questions touching Faith and Order". Several other churches passed similar resolutions, but the responsibility for preparing the envisioned worldwide conference remained with the newly appointed commission until 1920. In that year a preparatory meeting for the planned world conference on F&O was held in Geneva. Under the leadership of Charles H. Brent, this was a first occasion for the nearly 80 churches represented to exchange their respective positions concerning Christian unity and to create an international and interconfessional continuation committee.

After further preparation the first world conference on F&O took place in 1927 in Lausanne. Over 400 participants, representing 127 Orthodox, Anglican, Reformation and Free churches, assembled under the leadership of Brent "to register the apparent level of fundamental agreements within the conference and the grave points of disagreement remaining". This comparative method was continued at the second world conference (1937) in Edinburgh. Again more than 400 participants, representing 122 churches, met and, under the presidency of William Temple, were able to clarify several concepts of church unity. They also agreed, despite some opposing voices, to unite F&O with the movement for Life and Work "to form a council of churches" — a decision which led to the formation of the WCC in 1948.

After 1948 the tasks of the F&O movement were carried on by the commission on F&O within the WCC. Under the leadership of Yngve Brilioth the new commission held the third world conference on Faith and Order (1952) in Lund, Sweden, and moved from the comparative method to a form of theological dialogue which approaches controversial issues from a common biblical and Christological basis. Oliver Tomkins chaired the fourth world conference in 1963 in Montreal, Canada. After a longer interval a fifth world conference is now planned for 1993.

Structure, method and membership. With its 120 members the commission on F&O, which meets every three or four years, is the most representative theological forum in the world. Its aim is, according to its bylaws,

"to proclaim the oneness of the church of Jesus Christ and to call the churches to the goal of visible unity in one faith and one eucharistic fellowship, expressed in worship and in common life in Christ, in order that the world may believe". The bylaws foresee membership in the commission also of representatives of non-member churches of the WCC, thus underlining the movement character of F&O. The ongoing work of F&O is supervised by a standing commission (30 members) and is carried out by the Geneva secretariat of F&O.

Since 1948 the work of F&O has found its most important expression in the meetings of the commission. There, study projects have been initiated which were carried out through international consultations and smaller study drafting groups. The results of these studies have been received by or formulated at commission meetings. Increasingly churches, ecumenical organizations and commissions and institutes as well as interested individuals have participated in F&O studies and thus have provided a much broader basis and involvement.

The composition of the commission has changed considerably since 1948. The rather small percentage of Orthodox members and representatives of the churches in Africa, Asia and Latin America has increased to over 20% and 40% respectively. Women, who were virtually absent from the commission, represent now nearly 30% of its membership. Since 1968 the Roman Catholic Church has been officially represented with 12 members and participates actively in all F&O studies. Moderators of the commission were Brilioth (1947-57), Douglas Horton (1957-63), Paul Minear (1963-67), H.H. Harms (1967-71), John Meyendorff (1971-75), Nikos Nissiotis (1975-83) and John Deschner (1983-91).

Themes and achievements. Since 1910 the F&O movement and the commission have dealt with a broad spectrum of theological issues: understanding and practice of baptism,* eucharist* and ordained ministry;* the church* and concepts of its unity; intercommunion;* scripture and Tradition;* the role and significance of creeds* and confessions; ordination of women;* influence of so-called non-theological factors on efforts for church unity. Alongside these controversial issues F&O has increasingly taken up themes which are of common concern for the churches or which are fundamental for expressing their already-existing fellowship: worship and spirituality (e.g. the commission prepares jointly with the Pontifical Council for Promoting Christian Unity* the material for the Week of Prayer for Christian Unity*), Christian hope* for today, inter-relation between bilateral and multilateral dialogues* (since 1978 the commission has organized five meetings of the forum on bilateral conversations). Two of the present study projects of F&O also belong to this category of themes: "Towards the Common Expression of the Apostolic Faith Today" and "The Unity of the Church and the Renewal of Human Community". The commission continues to serve united/uniting churches* by organizing regular consultations for them, and it publishes a bi-annual "Survey of Church Union Negotiations". Since 1982 the work of F&O has become more widely known than ever before through the unprecedentedly broad and intensive discussion and reception process in connection with its 1982 *Baptism, Eucharist and Ministry** (BEM) document. This process continues, and F&O will deal with some major critical points raised in the almost 200 official responses of the churches to the so-called Lima text within the framework of a comprehensive study on basic ecumenical perspectives on the nature and mission of the church — a study which formed the integrating centre of F&O work beginning in 1990.

Within the wider ecumenical movement, and as part of the structure of the WCC, the commission on F&O sees its task in a concentrated theological effort to assist the churches in overcoming their dividing doctrinal differences, in sharing their diverse theological insights and forms of life as a source of mutual renewal, and in re-appropriating and expressing their common apostolic tradition.* All these efforts have as their goal the manifestation of the visible unity of the church of Jesus Christ. On the way to this goal the churches are called to become a credible sign and instrument of God's plan for the salvation* and transformation of humanity and all creation. With such a commitment F&O has rendered a significant contribution to the radically changed relationships between the churches and the many steps they have taken to express their full (or at least their growing) unity.

GÜNTHER GASSMANN

Faith and Order Papers, ser. 1, 1910-48; ser. 2, 1948 to date, WCC • *A History of the Ecumenical Movement*, vol. 1, R. Rouse & S. Neill eds, vol. 2, H.E. Fey ed., WCC, 1986 • J. Skoglund & J.R. Nelson, *Fifty Years of Faith and Order*, New York, Committee for the Interseminary Movement of the National Student Christian Federation, 1963 • L. Vischer ed., *A Documentary History of the Faith and Order Movement, 1927-1963*, St Louis, MO, Bethany, 1963.

FAITH AND SCIENCE. The ecumenical movement was slow in catching up with science and technology,* although the latter were rapidly changing the world. The third assembly of the WCC in New Delhi (1961) was notable for a major address on the subject from Joseph Sittler ("Called to Unity"). The unity he called for was a doctrine of redemption* that applied to the larger orbit of the whole creation* as he saw portrayed in Col. 1. The ecumenical movement did not heed his appeal. It seemed afraid that concern about the environment, science and technology would detract it from its major concern with human justice. Sittler repeated his appeal to an ecumenical gathering in the USA (1970) in a lecture entitled "Ecological Commitment as Theological Responsibility". It seemed that the fourth assembly of the WCC at Uppsala (1968) had a change of heart. It became a turning point for ecumenical concern about science, technology and the environment. The presence of Margaret Mead was probably critical in the conference recommendation that "the WCC give particular attention to science and the problems of worldwide technological change in its study programme". This responsibility was handed over to Church and Society in Geneva. From 1970 onwards the ecumenical movement took on this new direction with great vigour and effectiveness. The programme went ahead under the title "The Future of Man in a World of Science-based Technology".

The first step in this new ecumenical venture was a world exploratory conference in Geneva in 1970 on "Technology and the Future of Man and Society". It provided the agenda for years to follow. It indicated how out of touch the churches were with changes in science and technology and their impact on society and how many scientists were concerned to change this situation. An important aspect of the work for the next two decades was the strong involvement of scientists and sociologists in the study programme. Scientists who had dropped out of the church because they saw it as irrelevant came into this programme with enthusiasm. What was achieved came largely as a result of consultations on specific issues such as limits to growth; nuclear energy and alternative energy technologies; genetics and the quality of life; humanity, nature and God; theology, science and human purpose; science, ideology and theology; genetic engineering; and science education.

A method of working included regional consultations in Africa, Asia, Central America and South America which fed into two major world conferences. The first was in Bucharest in 1974 on "Science and Technology for Human Development". This meeting became famous for introducing into ecumenical circles the concept of the ecologically sustainable society. From its ecumenical birth this phrase and the concept it embodies spread around the world. This development resulted in a change in name of the WCC programme to the "Just, Participatory and Sustainable Society",* which was launched at the fifth assembly of the WCC in Nairobi (1975). This was only the second assembly to have a plenary presentation on science and faith. As a result of the new direction, programmes on the ecologically sustainable society were initiated in many countries, linking up with the eco-justice movement in the USA and with serious sociological studies in the Netherlands and elsewhere.

A second critical world conference, on "Faith, Science and the Future", was held at the Massachusetts Institute of Technology in 1979. It was preceded by a preparatory volume, *Faith, Science and the Future*, and the proceedings were published in *Faith and Science in an Unjust World. Anticipation*, the Church and Society journal, published reactions to this conference (27, 1980). These volumes became important resources for the ecumenical movement in churches and theological institutions. A feature of the MIT conference was the division between the developed world and the developing world as to whether science was good or bad and, second,

whether nuclear technology was good or bad. In both cases it was clear that science and technology are not value-free; rather, they reflect the values of the society from which they come.

The sixth assembly of the WCC in Vancouver (1983) saw a change in emphasis with a change in title of the programme to "Justice, Peace and the Integrity of Creation".* The issues now were the tension between war and peace, injustice and justice and industrialization and the integrity of creation. Integrity of creation introduced the subject of the intrinsic value of non-human creatures and the issue of animal rights. This was an ecumenical subject for the first time at a consultation in 1988, reported in the book *Liberating Life* (1990). Just as there was concern in the 1960s that issues of science and technology were a distraction for churches and in the 1970s that environmental issues were a distraction, so too the issue of animal rights is regarded in some ecumenical circles as a distraction from what should be the main concern for the poor.*

In the ecumenical debate on science and faith, the unresolved issues include a theology of nature* and a non-anthropocentric or biocentric ethic. Both go to the heart of what science is and what theology is and the relations between the two. There is a much greater openness on the sides of both science and theology to learn from each other than in 1970, when some theologians argued they should march to different tunes. Instead of simply trying to understand each other better, movement on the frontiers of science and theology is now concerned with ways in which each may become transformed as a result of their encounter.

CHARLES BIRCH

P. Abrecht ed., *Faith, Science and the Future*, WCC, 1979 • P. Abrecht & N. Koshy eds, *Before It's Too Late: The Challenge of Nuclear Disarmament*, WCC, 1983 • P. Abrecht & R. Shinn eds, *Faith and Science in an Unjust World*, vol. 1: *Plenary Presentations*, vol. 2: *Reports and Recommendations*, WCC, 1980 • C. Birch & P. Abrecht eds, *Genetics and the Quality of Life*, WCC, 1975 • D. Gill, *From Here to Where?*, WCC, 1970 • D. Gosling & B. Musschenga eds, *Science Education and Ethical Values*, WCC, 1985 • *Manipulating Life: Ethical Issues in Genetic Engineering*, WCC, 1982 • J. Sittler, "Called to Unity", *The Ecumenical Review*, 14, 1962.

FAMILY. The social group called family is found in every culture from ancient to modern times. The term has described a diversity of social realities from the extended net of relatives, found mainly in agricultural societies, to the contemporary nuclear family, found especially in industrialized urban areas.

Definitions of family are forged culturally. What we call family today probably denotes something very different from what it did to our ancestors. In the northern and western part of the world, where there is a longer experience of the effects of industrialization, the nuclear family tends to be seen as normative. In the southern part of the world, where other modes of production coexist and survival has often depended on the kinship system, "family" has a broader meaning. Thus it is impossible to establish a universal normative definition of the family or its nature, functions and purpose.

What has distinguished a family from other social groups has been its functions: a shared residence, nurture and emotional support, security and economic support, procreation and socialization of the new generations. Some of those properties are now being drastically modified by modern life, especially in the West through social and state institutions like schools, health care, nursing homes, social security and life insurance.

The above-mentioned functions, traditionally ascribed to the family, better describe the tribe, the clan or the extended family. Historically it seems that the human race has not lived in nuclear families, but in bigger social units. Tribes and clans were functional domestic households, genealogically established, where shared interests and divided responsibilities were fairly clear. In the Old Testament, says J.H. Westerhoff, "family" refers to "a 'tribal family' which included a husband, his wives and their children, his concubines and their children, sons and daughters-in-law and their offspring, slaves of both sexes and their children, dependents such as the parentless, the widows and illegitimate children, aliens such as the sojourner passing through and all the marginal folk who chose to live among them" (257). In the New Testament, too, passages dealing with family life (e.g. Mark 1:29-31; Acts 10; Eph. 5:21-6:9) include relatives and servants within the domestic circle.

When human existence increased in its complexity, tribes and clans gave way to the *extended family* and a number of secondary social institutions. The *nuclear family* as such is a later adaptation, emerging along with the process of industrialization. To be sure, the nucleus of man-woman and their offspring existed before the industrial era, but this did not count as "family" apart from a larger net of interwoven familial relations.

In short, "family" today could be regarded as the network of relationships established by marriage, birth and adoption. But the ways in which those relationships are established and the rights and duties attaching to these various roles differ greatly according to culture, class, religion and region.

Studies of the family. Popular books about the family, both secular and religious, often become best-sellers. Over the past 50 years there has also been a tremendous expansion of study and research on the family. Several journals are devoted entirely to this field.

Families have been analyzed from different points of view and disciplines. Cultural anthropologists have seen the family as a privileged place from which to observe and understand a culture. From the sociological standpoint, some have seen it as the basic institution of society* with the amazing capacity of adapting to the demands of the times. Others have seen the family as a historical accident which appeared alongside private property and is destined to disappear when a classless society finally emerges. During the 1980s major revealing shifts in understanding the family took place among social scientists. Studies on world population, migrations, survival strategies among the poor, and domestic work of women and children have brought to light the importance of the family as the nucleus of production and reproduction of life, labour, culture, meaning and ideology. The International Year of the Family established by the United Nations bears testimony that states are recognizing the family as one of the main caretakers of life, health and culture.

Some psychologists have perceived the family as the matrix of all evils and have even announced its demise as humankind matures and finds better alternatives. Others have insisted on seeing it as the fundamental nurturing and socializing space which moulds human life and imprints identity and basic skills for survival. Over the last four decades systemic thinking has contributed to understanding the family as a place of basic and meaningful relationships. Considerable evidence shows that health or disease — physical, mental, social or spiritual — is not only an individual issue but involves a complex exchange of relationships: values, communication patterns, rules and meanings present from generation to generation.

Theologians and pastoralists are trying to reformulate their understanding of family in the light of new knowledge about families worldwide, the challenge of the unprecedented social transformation, the teaching of scripture and of the church. They are realizing, for instance, that the notions of family in the teaching and the practice of the church have been conflated with the understanding of person, couple and household. With the recognition of person and personality, the increasing differentiation of couple from family, the affirmation of women in their personhood as separate from men, and the control over procreation, there is an unavoidable and irreversible process towards clearly distinguishing persons, couples, families and households. This will in turn be conducive to better family pastoral care (see **marriage**).

The family today. To be a family today seems to be more difficult in almost every culture than ever before. More and more families around the globe concentrate most of their energy trying to survive in situations of poverty and exploitation. Families — in the recent past the main transmitters of culture and values — now have to compete fiercely with state agencies, the mass media and the economic system, which impose alien values and behaviours.

However, in spite of the attempts to replace the family with other kinds of social organizations, the family as a nucleus of affection, socialization and nurturing persists. Furthermore, the family has proved to be a very resourceful entity: it designs creative strategies for survival in social strata where income is inadequate to meet the reproduction of life and labour; in most "developing" countries, where developmental programmes, primary health care attention and universal edu-

cation have failed, the family keeps providing — at different levels of proficiency — care, attention, socialization; social scientists, educators and medical doctors are taking a fresh look at the family in order to learn about traditional medicine, popular education and subsistence economics. In the developed world, families have the potential to become emotionally closer in personal ways. Intimacy may rise while authoritarian relations diminish. Equality among sexes may provide solid ground for families to give a better sense of identity and support to the new generations. Procreation, being considered optional rather than essential for family life or group survival, may obtain a much richer meaning.

The church and the family. Churches have traditionally been advocates for family life, in the process sometimes defending very conservative positions. In other instances they have failed to perceive clearly enough that the family belongs to the realm of creation,* not salvation,* or tried to impose Christian values and norms on non-Christian communities — or on the rest of society — without being aware that we live now in a very pluralistic society.

A Christian family surely cannot be identified with any particular social pattern. Churches have often assumed that a Christian family is structured in a particular manner where men, women and children play particular defined roles. But as Westerhoff states: "A Christian family has nothing to do with structures and roles; it has to do with the quality of life together, a quality of life that can assume many shapes and in which persons can play various roles" (254).

Churches are also exploring new pastoral approaches to the havoc created by war, poverty, uprooting and isolation. As Kenyan bishop David Gitari told the 1988 Lambeth conference: "With so many fractured and lonely families in the cities and so many people living alone, the church should see itself as an extended family where every believer finds a home, not just figuratively but literally. The church must work to build strong homes, exploring extended family models, so that each home truly is a church and the church truly a family."

Among churches all over the world there is an increasing awareness about the importance of contextual theological reflection and relevant pastoral care for the family today. To work pastorally requires serious knowledge not only of a particular context and history* but also of the major trends of history and the resources that cultures have to cope with a very changing environment. Besides that, a renewed dialogue with other faiths is demanded to understand better the universality of the family. New research is urgent to determine the limits and the links between persons, couples, families, households, communities and the whole oikoumene.

See also **marriage, society**.

JORGE E. MALDONADO

W. Everett, *Blessed be the Bond: Christian Perspectives on Marriage and Family*, Philadelphia, Fortress, 1985 • L. Hoffman, *Foundations of Family Therapy: A Conceptual Framework for Systems Change*, New York, Basic Books, 1981 • Masamba Ma Mpolo & C. De Sweemer, *Families in Transition: The Case for Counselling in Context*, WCC, 1987 • F.I. Nye, "Fifty Years of Family Research, 1937-87", *Journal of Marriage and the Family*, 50, 2, 1988 • J.H. Westerhoff, "The Church and the Family", *Religious Education*, 78, 2, 1983.

FASCISM. Fascism is a form of totalitarian government (see **totalitarianism**) and organization of society developed by Benito Mussolini in Italy in the early 1920s. Although its ideology* was not too clear, it included some romantic anti-rational elements together with an extreme nationalism. It claimed Georges Sorel and Vilfredo Pareto as ideological influences, built on certain interpretations of Nietzsche's idea of power and continued the nationalist movement of the poet D'Annunzio. The nation* is identified with the state,* conceived fundamentally as a centre of power* that concentrates the totality of the forces and resources of the people and leads it to its goal, the aggrandizement of the nation. The leadership is elitist and concentrated in a charismatic leader (*duce* = leader, conductor) who is always right. Rejecting liberal democracy and proletarian communism, it created a corporate form of government, organizing labour and capital in corporations (professionals, industry, etc.) under the leadership of the government and placing all public servants directly under the direction of the (fascist) party. It led Italy into wars of conquest in Ethiopia and Albania and finally into the alliance with Germany in the second world war.

A number of analogous regimes came to power in several European countries at different times after the first world war (Austria, Hungary, Romania, Spain). Since each of them has its own characteristics derived from historical, sociological and cultural particularities, the word "fascism" becomes a sort of catch-all word and loses precision. This is even more the case when it is extended to third-world countries (e.g. Brazil under Vargas, Argentina under Peron), the geopolitical situation of which defines some fundamental differences. Sometimes the expressions "neo-fascism" or "dependent fascism" have been used for these cases. Even more, "fascist" has become a common word to designate a certain type of reactionary, right-wing or totalitarian attitude of mind which can be found in almost any society.

Although originally anti-clerical, Mussolini's pragmatism led him to seek a recognition by the Roman Catholic Church and a solution to the "Roman question", which culminated in the Lateran treaty of 1929. The totalitarian character of fascism eventually, however, led into conflict with the church, as on the question of the fascist attempt to control the life and education of youth. Pius XII's letter *Non Abbiamo Bisogno* (1931) marked the break between the government and the church.

For the ecumenical movement and Protestant churches, the conflict with fascism was more closely related to German National Socialism (see **Confessing Church, war guilt**). The Life and Work Oxford conference (1937) faced the questions raised by this ideology; and its whole study on church, community and state involved a rejection of this ideology. In this and subsequent WCC meetings (Amsterdam, Evanston), fascism was rejected, implicitly or explicitly, under the label of "totalitarianism" on the basis of its total claim on human life and its tendency to assume an unlimited power.

More recently, the churches are facing this threat in the doctrine of national security.* The ways in which the WCC has portrayed a desirable human society (see **responsible society; just, participatory and sustainable society; justice, peace and the integrity of creation**) espouse forms of democratic organization, people's participation and human rights and responsibilities that radically exclude all forms of fascism.

JOSÉ MÍGUEZ BONINO

FEDERALISM. The word derives from the Latin *foedus*, meaning covenant, alliance (French *alliance*), bond (German *Bund*). In modern ecumenical usage, "federal" relationships have been established within a single country among denominations which, while maintaining their separate identities, desire to collaborate in certain limited areas or for certain limited objectives, especially e.g. in social action or for a combined approach to civil governments. Thus there was the Free Church Federal Council in Britain (1940, after forerunners) and the Federal Council of the Churches of Christ in America (1908, predecessor of the National Council of the Churches of Christ in the USA). Internationally, a federal relationship could link nationally constituted churches of the same confession for consultative or co-operative purposes, though legislative power rested with the individual constituent bodies (thus the World Alliance of Reformed Churches, 1875; the Baptist World Alliance, 1905; the Lutheran World Federation, 1947). The World Student Christian Federation (1895) grouped the national Student Christian Movements that were themselves functionally ecumenical but did not raise any ecclesiological pretensions. The comic potential of federalism is suggested by the secular example of the humorist Garrison Keillor, who claimed that his US radio programme was sponsored by the fictitious "American Federation of Associations".

While federalism has a certain provisional utility, most ecumenists have judged it inadequate as a final model of church unity. John Kent wrote that "Christ is more than the president of a federal republic of Christian associations; he is the Head of the Body which is his church" (*The Age of Disunity*, 1966). The inadequacy of the federal pattern of church unity — what he called denominations "glued together at the edges" — was already perceived by the Episcopalian priest W.R. Huntington (1838-1909), who inspired the Chicago-Lambeth Quadrilateral.* With papal authoritarianism, it constituted the two extremes between which, according to Hunting-

ton, an "organic" alternative should and could be located. Federalism's ecclesiological weaknesses reside in its falling short of a genuinely conciliar capacity for decision making on matters of doctrine and discipline, and in the shallowness of its vision of what is possible and required in a life of koinonia* in the gospel.

It is significant that the Lutheran World Federation in 1990 moved towards a Lutheran "communion" in word and sacrament, a self-understanding as "pulpit and altar fellowship". And in recent "covenantal" plans of church unity between denominations in a single country, the proposed degree of community in doctrine, sacraments, ministry, mission and decision making exceeds the (etymologically equivalent) older idea of a "federation". This was true of the abortive English Proposals for a Covenant (1982), which saw themselves as only an interim step "towards visible unity". It is true also of the current Consultation on Church Union* plan for "Churches in Covenant Communion" (1988), which now nevertheless deliberately renounces "consolidation of organizational structures" among the participant churches.

See also **communion; conciliarity; covenanting; denominationalism; union, organic; unity, models of; unity, ways to**.

GEOFFREY WAINWRIGHT

E.L. Brand, *Towards a Lutheran Communion: Pulpit and Altar Fellowship*, Geneva, LWF, 1988.

FELLOWSHIP OF RECONCILIATION. FOR was founded in Cambridge, England, in December 1914, a few months after the outbreak of the first world war. The founders — Henry Hodgkin, an English Quaker, and Friedrich Siegmund-Schultze, a German Lutheran pastor — had pledged to remain friends and continue to work for peace. The original group saw that for the Christian, answers to the moral questions raised by the war itself lay in pacifist directions and methods. In 1915 FOR had members in the USA.

After the war, the International Fellowship of Reconciliation was inaugurated in Holland in 1919 as a bond between national FOR groups. It determines their right to be affiliated with the international group but does not control or supervise national activities. FOR networks now exist in 27 countries. From its beginning, FOR has brought Roman Catholics into co-operation with the members of other churches.

FOR is composed of those who recognize the essential unity of all humanity and together explore the power of love and truth for resolving human conflict. While it always vigorously opposes war, the fellowship is equally committed to positive efforts for a peaceful world community, with full dignity and freedom for every human being. It denies the right of human-made divisions to sunder the Body of Christ, and it is convinced that the only hope of surmounting the divisions of the human family is in Christ's way. There is also a strong interest in promoting methods of non-violence in race and other conflict situations, chiefly by study groups, personal witness, and widespread literature distribution. FOR's main journal, *Reconciliation Quarterly,* began in 1924. The international headquarters are in Alkmaar.

ANS J. VAN DER BENT

J.A. Donaghy, *Peacemaking and the Community of Faith: A Handbook for Congregations*, Nyack, NY, Paulist, 1983 • L. Stevenson, *Towards a Christian International: The Story of the International Fellowship of Reconciliation*, London, FOR, 1941.

FELLOWSHIP OF ST ALBAN AND ST SERGIUS.

The fellowship of St Alban and St Sergius is an independent society whose aim is to increase understanding and co-operation between Christians of Orthodox and Western traditions. It was founded in St Albans, England, in 1928, by participants in two Anglo-Russian theological conferences organized jointly by the Russian and British Student Christian Movements, and membership was later extended to admit other Christians interested in its work. It takes its name from St Alban, the first martyr of Britain, and St Sergius of Radonezh, patron saint of the Russian theological academy in Paris, with which many of the Orthodox founder members were connected.

In the early years the fellowship worked mainly with theologians and theological students, through conferences and lectures in Anglican and Free Church theological colleges. A key figure in this educational work

was Nicolas Zernov, one of the fellowship's founders and its secretary 1934-47, who, with his wife, Militza, made the development of the fellowship a life's work. Through his talks and writings, he made a great contribution to the knowledge of Orthodoxy* among English-speaking Christians. Early participants in the conferences were predominantly Russians from Paris and members of the Church of England, but gradually they were joined by Orthodox from Romania, Serbia and Greece, Episcopalians from the USA, and Swedish Lutherans. These contacts later led to the formation of branches outside Britain.

In the 1930s and 1940s, an important part of the fellowship's work consisted in providing information on the church in Russia at a time when little or no accurate information on its situation was generally available in the West. The 1930s saw a high pitch of ecumenical enthusiasm in the fellowship, with hopes that a restoration of communion between Anglican and Orthodox churches could be in sight; but the discussions on practical advances in this direction were not continued.

In 1943 the fellowship acquired a permanent base, a house in London dedicated to St Basil the Great. This served as a centre for meetings, hospitality and prayer; its chapel, unique in having both an Orthodox sanctuary and an Anglican altar, was dedicated by Archbishop Germanos of Thyateira in 1949. Fr Lev Gillet, known to many for his retreats, meditations and writings under the name of "a monk of the Eastern church", served as chaplain there until his death in 1980.

After the Second Vatican Council* Roman Catholic participation in the fellowship, never totally absent, showed a marked increase; nowadays, Roman Catholics make up a significant minority of those who join. While this demonstrates that the fellowship's concern is not only for relations between Orthodox and Anglicans, that connection has always been central to the fellowship in the English-speaking world. The inauguration in 1973 of the Anglican-Orthodox Joint Doctrinal Discussions, involving many prominent fellowship members, could thus be seen as official approbation of the work already being carried on unofficially by the fellowship (see **Anglican-Orthodox dialogue**).

Today, fellowship members number over 2,000, with approximately half in Britain and half spread over the rest of the world. Membership is strongest in English-speaking countries, but there are branches which organize local meetings in Greece and Scandinavia as well as North America and Australia. The majority of members are Anglican, with a number of Lutherans and Roman Catholics and some Free Church members; today, a large part of the Orthodox members are converts to Orthodoxy.

The main event in the life of the fellowship is still the annual conference, which brings together clergy and laity, theologians and non-theologians of all ages and from several countries. Another annual event is a pilgrimage to St Albans, where the Orthodox liturgy is celebrated in honour of the saint. Local branches also organize meetings and services, and the fellowship sometimes arranges programmes specifically for theological students. The fellowship headquarters, St Basil's House, provides an important informal meeting place for people from many parts of the world and different Christian traditions.

The fellowship has been responsible for the publication of a number of books reflecting Orthodox and Anglican spiritual life and the points of convergence between the traditions. With the fellowship journal *Sobornost*, founded in 1928, these publications have done much to make Orthodoxy more widely known at a time when very little Orthodox literature was available in English.

Since the first conference, when Orthodox and Anglican eucharists were celebrated at the same altar on alternate days — a revolutionary idea in the 1920s — eucharistic worship has been at the heart of the fellowship's ecumenical work. In fact, a condition of membership is readiness to attend each other's eucharist.* The founders of the fellowship and their successors believed that this both shows the element of real unity, in worship of the same Lord, and reminds Christians of the pain of disunity. Experience of worship is also seen as a vital element in getting to know another Christian tradition; the fellowship has more than once presented to the wider ecumenical movement a plea for common worship according to various traditions rather than mixed services.

Despite great advances in the ecumenical movement since the fellowship's foundation, it still provides a forum unique outside the official bilateral dialogues* for Orthodox and Western Christians to meet on equal terms and address theological issues together, each in the way that arises naturally from their own tradition.

ELIZABETH BRIERE

N. Zernov & M. Zernov, *Fellowship of St Albans and St Sergius: A Historical Memoire*, Oxford, Oxford UP, 1979.

FEMINISM. The word "feminism" has become a key word of the second women's movement, which began in the late 1960s. While the earlier women's movement was chiefly concerned with improving the position of women in society, emancipation, economic independence and work, the issues for the feminist movement of today are replacement of the established patriarchal order, raising awareness of the disastrous effects of the division woman/nature and man/intellect, and the adoption of female rather than male guiding principles. The question of woman's economic, political and social independence from man has thus been joined by that of her psychological independence from him in a male-dominated culture.* This has led to far more radical solutions and utopias.

Feminist groups hold varying standpoints, but common to all is the view that women need their own organizations in order to assert their interests — not as man-hating caucuses, but as self-help groups for women in an overwhelmingly male culture. The conflict experienced by women is today expressed in the word "sexism",* by analogy with "racism" and "classism", and connoting the oppression of one sex by the other which takes various forms — exploitation, expropriation, rejection, persecution and ill-treatment of women.

The church and theology have been a target of feminist criticism from the start. In Paul's commandment that women should keep silent (1 Cor. 14:34), in Bible passages stating that Eve sinned first and must redeem herself through bearing children (1 Tim. 2:11-15), in the works of the church fathers and the reformers, and in dialectical theology (Karl Barth), there is a wide variety of sexist statements declaring women to be weak, inferior, receptive, and passive. In some churches such statements are used as an argument to justify the fact that women have been given a place in the church hierarchy only belatedly or not at all. The predominantly masculine imagery of God and masculine language about God have also served as a religious justification of the oppression of women in society.

On the other hand, there are many examples of Christian groups whose expectation of the kingdom of God* and of the Spirit has encouraged equality between women and men (Cathars, Waldensians, Quakers). In the New Testament there is evidence that men and women were equal in the early Christian communities, though this fact has been glossed over in the course of the patriarchal account of history. Women apostles (Mary Magdalene, Junia), community leaders (Martha, Lydia), and Jesus' vision of a community of women and men not ruled by a father (see Mark 10:29) point to a non-sexist early Christian culture and church which are gradually being re-discovered through the efforts of feminist research and theology. There are many indications that the dichotomy of spirit and nature (body) was unknown in the acts of healing performed by the "Jesus movement" and that women played a prominent role.

The ecumenical movement was ahead of most churches in giving serious attention to the question of the status of women. As early as the 1927 world conference on Faith and Order,* six women presented a statement demanding that the issue be central at the meeting. Before the WCC's first assembly (Amsterdam 1948) a questionnnaire was sent out to obtain information about the the life and work of women in the churches, but the hesitant verbal resolutions made in Amsterdam did not lead to a change in practice. In Evanston (1954) the will clearly existed "to help women find the right balance between their family responsibilities and their professional life" as responsible members of society, but the masculine structure of that society, the "exclusively masculine environment", was taken for granted.

Not until 1974 at the women's consultation in Berlin on "Sexism in the 1970s", in preparation for the WCC's Nairobi assembly, were these structures fundamentally challenged. Sexism, it was said, exists where on the ground of sex individuals or groups are assigned on principle to a subordinate position through attitudes, behaviour or institutional structures. During the consultation, however, women from the third world shifted the problem of sexual oppression to the plane of imperialistic oppression and exploitation, also experienced by men, who, in resignation at their inability to alter their situation, react by adopting sexist behaviour patterns.

Sexism, then, is seen not so much as a struggle between the sexes as a common struggle within the wider struggle for liberation of the oppressed classes. Sexism in the white, middle-class sense of the term was resisted. To the disappointment of some North American women, a demand for the rights of lesbian women was not included in the recommendations made by the consultation.

The first consultation of European Christian women in Brussels in 1978 was able to work out a clearer Christian understanding of feminism: "We realized that it does not mean the same to everyone, but that agreement exists on the following... feminism for us is a strategy, a principle for living which determines our thinking and action. For women in the Western countries of Europe the first important thing is to discover themselves as women. After centuries of being told by soci-

A speaker from Papua New Guinea, at a women's meeting prior to Vancouver 1983 (WCC/Peter Williams)

ety and the church who they should be, what they should and should not do, it is time now to find out who they themselves think they are, what they can do, what they want to do. This process will be linked with a critical examination of the structures of their churches and the society in which they live... The church and theology must be made inclusive, they must be made to see all human beings, including the oppressed... We expressly emphasize that this strategy, this living principle is not directed against men, but should be an encouragement to them to discover in themselves the attributes they have of the other sex. We want to live together in friendship, as allies and partners on the way to liberation."

The problem of sexism within the church was dealt with in greater depth in the following years through the plan, already presented in 1974 at the meeting of the F&O commission in Accra, Ghana, for a study on the "Community of Women and Men in the Church".* A study booklet was presented to the F&O commission in 1978 in Bangalore for comment and approval before being sent to 300 member churches inviting them to participate.

The unique aspect of this study was that its starting point was not what Christian men and women *ought to think* but their own experience and thoughts. Its aim was to discover the reality of partnership between women and men in the different cultures and churches and to invite them to a dialogue. Above all, the aim was to let women speak, and the study was accompanied by regional meetings in Asia, Latin America and Europe. Parallel to this, specialist consultations were held on three subjects: "Ordination of Women in Ecumenical Perspective" (Klingenthal), "Towards a Theology of Human Wholeness" (Niederaltaich, Federal Republic of Germany), and "The Authority of Scripture in the Light of New Experiences of Women" (Amsterdam). Some people felt that the study was organized in such a way as to give prominence to the subject area "church, unity, fellowship", thus blurring the issue of sexism in the church. To women from the Western world in particular, the programme seemed to lack bite, "jumping too quickly to community without taking seriously the deep rifts and the breakdown of communication between women and men in our culture." Others, how-

ever, were relieved that the commmunity study did not have sexism as its theme. From socialist countries came voices saying they did not want a women's study because partnership was already a reality in their countries. Asia and Africa let it be known that their problems were different. And in fact only 20% of the Christian women and men who took part in the study came from outside Europe and North America. Yet the results showed that even in these societies and churches, covert but widespread sexism exists. The aim of the study was not, however, to ignore the problems but to challenge as many people as possible to think afresh about creative ways of working together to build the church and make it into a community of women and men.

At the consultation winding up the study in Sheffield (1981), WCC general secretary Philip Potter spoke of both racism* and sexism as fundamental theological problems that had to be overcome if the world community was to become truly human. But here, too, a focus on Western-style sexism, confined to the personal sphere, was persistently resisted by the third-world countries in favour of recognizing such social manifestations of sexism as sex tourism, child abuse and violence against women. It became apparent at Sheffield that women in the different countries experience different forms of oppression: in South Africa it is racism; in Guatemala, imperialism; in Europe, sexism. Those who begin to fight one form of oppression will also develop solidarity in regard to other forms.

The recommendations from Sheffield were positively received at the meeting of the WCC's central committee in Dresden in the same year, with the exception of those concerning the equal representation of men and women at all levels in the WCC and in all its commissions. Because of protests, mainly from Orthodox delegates, the final action referred, not to quotas for, but to the *principle* of numerically equal representation. In Vancouver at the sixth assembly of the WCC the proportion of women delegates reached 30%, as compared to the 22% at Nairobi (Uppsala 1968 had only 9%). The women held a preliminary conference of their own before the assembly. Both in numbers and in the content of the assembly, their presence was more visible than ever before. A steady infiltration of the ecumenical movement by women and women's issues can be observed.

From the feminist point of view two questions arise: Can the ecumenical movement really represent the interests of women without a Women-Church movement (Elisabeth Schüssler-Fiorenza)? And have the decisive critical questions concerning the destructive effects of patriarchy — "the domination of women by men everywhere in the world, though in quite different forms" (Catharina Halkes) — really been stated radically enough? According to Halkes, this lack of clarity in stating the problems can be seen whenever women are mentioned together as a group with the disabled, children, old people, etc. "If any sex is to be singled out as a problem, then it should be the men. The problem of domination, of the exclusive claim to leadership in the church and church organizations, lies primarily with them." Men's fear of women and of sexuality has in fact appeared only in the margin, although it is the central problem. Only by working through such fear to a liberated relationship to our own bodies and a new body-mind relationship for both women and men will we achieve a credible and growing community of women and men. The church as the Body of Christ composed of the living bodies of women and men could become the new governing principle.

Besides the many other open questions — e.g. inclusive language,* new images of God,* new liturgical forms — the ecumenical movement is here confronted with central theological questions, including the question of women's ordination, as yet unresolved in the Orthodox and Anglican churches. Awareness of such problems should be increased through the deepening and development of feminist theology. The latter has gradually evolved and gained in definition — at the sexism consultation in Berlin it was present only as "liberation theology" and as "holistic theology"; in Brussels it appeared for the first time as a theme; in Sheffield there was little actual mention of it, but it was clearly behind many of the statements and ideas. This gives reason to hope that the psycho-social problems of masculinity and power will be brought out yet more clearly, creating the conditions for a community of women and men who constitute the human and not just the male Body of Christ.

See also **community of women and men in the church; ordination of women; sexism; theology, feminist**.

ELISABETH MOLTMANN-WENDEL

K. Bliss, *The Service and Status of Women in the Churches*, London, SCM, 1952 • *The Community of Women and Men in the Church*, WCC, 1983 • Epd-Dokumentation, no. 25/78 • C. Halkes, "Frauen in der ökumenischen Bewegung", in *Feministische Theologie: Perspektiven zur Orientierung*, M. Kassel ed., Stuttgart, 1988 • E. Moltmann-Wendel, *Das Land wo Milch und Honig fliesst* (ET *A Land Flowing with Milk and Honey*, London, SCM, 1986) • *Sexism in the 1970s*, report of the WCC consultation in West Berlin, WCC, 1974.

FILIOQUE. The filioque clause stands in the version of the Nicene Creed* generally used in the Western churches. It affirms that the Holy Spirit proceeds "from the Father *and the Son*" (Latin "filioque") and seeks in this way to articulate the personal relation between the second and third persons of the Trinity.

The original text of the creed, as approved by the council of Constantinople* (381; the text is *not* that of the council of Nicea, held in 325) and ratified by later ecumenical councils,* stated only that the Holy Spirit "proceeds from the Father". The addition of the filioque came to be accepted in the West, not least under the influence of Augustine (e.g. *On the Trinity* 15.27.29), but was not accepted in the Eastern Orthodox churches. It has remained for more than a thousand years a point of contention between Eastern and Western Christendom, albeit one that has been more eagerly attacked by the East than defended by the West. Not indeed that the West has generally been much inclined to surrender the filioque: the general attitude has been that the filioque is self-evidently correct and that it was not worth troubling to attend much to Eastern objections. In recent decades, however, there have been signs of a change in climate.

The filioque seems first to have been solemnly affirmed as an article of faith* by the synod of Toledo in 589. The occasion was the conversion of King Reccared from Arianism to Nicene Orthodoxy. The filioque served to underline the consubstantiality of the Son with the Father, and the synod had little or no sense of stating anything new or controversial. In the following centuries the filioque became a standard axiom of Western theology. Conflict with the East was provoked in the early 9th century when Charlemagne attempted to impose the filioque on the whole church; he was successfully opposed by Pope Leo III on the ground that the text ratified by an ecumenical council could not be arbitrarily modified. Two generations later Patriach Photius in Constantinople went on the attack with the deliberately opposed formula "from the Father *alone*", but this too remained a private initiative.

In or about 1014 the singing of the Nicene Creed was introduced with papal approval into the liturgy of the mass in Rome, and the form of the creed adapted included the filioque. This contributed to the schism* between East and West and then to notable theological defences of the filioque, e.g. by Anselm and Aquinas. The attempt to reconcile the two sides at the council of Florence (1439), on the principle that the filioque could be interpreted as equivalent to the formula, acceptable to the East, "*from* the Father *through* the Son", foundered on Byzantine resistance. The Reformation brought no change on the matter in the West; the main Protestant churches retained both the filioque theology and the corresponding wording of the Nicene Creed.

Increased contact between East and West began in the 19th century to encourage rethinking on both sides, but it is since more Eastern Orthodox churches joined the WCC in the 1960s that the topic has become important on the ecumenical agenda and that several Western churches have begun to think aloud about deleting the filioque. Specially significant were two ecumenical meetings held at Klingenthal, Alsace, in 1979 and 1980; the report *Spirit of God — Spirit of Christ* states what are still today the chief problems and offers some perspectives on ways forward.

The problems are of considerable complexity. Not only are they not all of the same sort; they tend to appear different from different standpoints in the dialogue. In the eyes of Eastern Orthodoxy, for example, the changing of the wording of the Nicene Creed by any other authority than an ecumenical council is both canonically illegitimate and an offence against Christian community. The very different Roman Catholic view of the locus of authority in the church might concede the second point, but not the first. The attitudes of other churches to these issues naturally vary

according to the degree of their commitment to restoring Christian unity, to their sense of the authority of the early church and the ecumenical councils, and to the role the Nicene Creed plays in their worship.

More substantial, but still more difficult, is the question whether what the filioque affirms is theologically *true* in the context of Trinitarian doctrine (see **Trinity**). This question cannot be settled simply by appeal to biblical texts or to historical tradition conceived as finally authoritative; it is an issue in dogmatic theology, specifically a question of Trinitarian hermeneutics. A major difficulty here is that the tendency and direction of Trinitarian thinking in East and West have been subtly but significantly different since (at the latest) the 5th century; the filioque fits relatively well into the Western scheme, but not into the Eastern.

A further range of issues has to do with possible implications of filioque theology for other fundamental issues. So, for example, the charge has been made that the filioque has led in Western theology to an effectual subordination of the Holy Spirit* not only to Jesus Christ* but also to the church or to the human spirit; the counter-charge in defence of the filioque, advanced in particular by Karl Barth, is that it is an essential bulwark against all kinds of natural theology.

Finally there is the question: if the filioque is abandoned, how can such valid concerns as it sought to defend be upheld? The more distant and more recent past have brought a range of suggestions for alternative formulations, such as "from the Father through the Son" or "who proceeds from the Father and shines forth in the Son". It remains to be seen whether or how far such proposals can deliver the degree of ecumenical theological agreement that is necessary if the filioque controversy is to be relegated to the past.

See also **Holy Spirit, Nicene Creed, Trinity**.

ALASDAIR HERON

A. Heron, "The Filioque Clause", in *One God in Trinity*, P. Toon & J. Spiceland eds, London, Bagster, 1980 • J. Moltmann, *Trinität und Reich Gottes* (ET *The Trinity and the Kingdom of God*, London, SCM, 1981, pp.178-90) • L. Vischer ed., *Spirit of God — Spirit of Christ: Ecumenical Reflections on the Filioque Controversy*, WCC, 1981 • G. Watson, "The Filioque — Opportunity for Debate?", *Scottish Journal of Theology*, 41, 3, 1988.

FISHER, GEOFFREY FRANCIS. B. 5.5.1887, Higham, UK; d. 15.9.1972, Sherborne. Fisher became archbishop of Canterbury in 1945, and the next year he preached an influential Cambridge sermon on reunion. Chairman of the WCC at its inauguration at Amsterdam 1948, he was a president of the WCC, 1948-54. In later years he proposed that the WCC should be transformed into an organization for interchurch aid, which then would present no difficulty for the Roman Catholic Church to join. He met Pope John XXIII in 1960, the first archbishop of Canterbury to go to the Vatican since 1397. In the same year he also met with the Orthodox patriarch of Jerusalem and the ecumenical patriarch of Constantinople. He presided over the Lambeth conferences of 1948 and 1958, which owed their representative character to his careful preparation, especially in America, and to the establishment of new provinces among the newly independent nations. From 1946 onwards he devoted considerable time to the revision of the canon law,* though new canons were not authorized until 1969. He was headmaster of Repton School, 1914-32. He wrote *The Archbishop Speaks* (London, Evans, 1958) and *Touching on Christian Truth* (London, Mowbray, 1971). See W. Purcell, *Fisher of Lambeth* (London, Hodder & Stoughton, 1969).

ANS J. VAN DER BENT

FLOROVSKY, GEORGES VASILIEVICH. B. 28.8.1893, Odessa,
Ukraine; d. 11.9.1979, Princeton, NJ, USA. Florovsky was a universally recognized Orthodox spokesman in the ecumenical movement and the forger of the theological basis for Orthodox participation in that movement. He attended the Faith and Order* conference at Edinburgh in 1937, was a member of the WCC central and executive committees, 1948-61, and in 1950 had a decisive influence on the Toronto statement* "The Church, the Churches and the World Council of Churches". He taught at several institutions in Europe and the US, first as professor of philosophy of law at Prague, 1922-26, and then professor of patristics and later of systematic theology at the St Sergius Orthodox Institute in Paris, 1926-48, professor, and later dean, at St Vladimir's Orthodox

Theological Seminary in New York, 1948-50, professor of theology of religions at Columbia University, New York, 1951-55, professor of history and dogma of the Orthodox Church at Holy Cross Greek Theological School in Brookline, MA, 1955-56, and from 1956 onwards professor of the history of Eastern Orthodoxy at the Harvard Divinity School. He was vice-president of the National Council of Churches of Christ in the USA, 1954-57. Numerous monographs and articles are in the eight volumes so far published of his *Collected Works* (Belmont, MA, Nordland, 1972-). See *Russia and Orthodoxy: Essays in Honor of Georges Florovsky*, 3 vols, A. Blane & T.E. Bird eds (The Hague, Mouton, 1974), and W.A. Visser 't Hooft, "Father Georges Florovsky's Role in the Formation of the WCC" (*St Vladimir's Theological Quarterly*, 1979).

ANS J. VAN DER BENT

FOCOLARE MOVEMENT. The worldwide Roman Catholic movement known as GEN (New Generation), or more popularly as Focolare (Italian for hearth, furnace, hotbed), began in Trent, Italy, in 1943. In the crucible of the most destructive phase of the second world war, Chiara Lubich (b.1920) and a few other young Italian women were convinced that whether they would die or survive, they should daily act out Jesus' command to "love one another, even as I have loved you" (John 13:34) and his will "that they may all be one" (John 17:21) — the Magna Carta of the movement. After the war, the loose association gradually spread among youth, adult men and women (married and unmarried), clergy and religious (who remain members of their orders or institutes), at present in 180 countries. Recognized by Rome as a lay movement in 1962, it has many celibate lay members with private vows.

In the early 1960s, the members, called Focolarini(e), eagerly accepted the new RCC stance towards the ecumenical movement. "Through our love for Jesus, we are able to appreciate the treasures of various other Christians and their churches, grasp their individual qualities and while remaining totally faithful to our own church, feel that we are brothers and sisters of all Christians through our common baptism and mutual love"

(Lubich). The movement then spread among Lutherans, Anglicans, Reformed and other Christians, and received the encouragement of Pope John XXIII, Cardinal Augustin Bea, the Anglican primates, Patriarch Athenagoras and other Christian leaders. Non-Christians are also friend-associates.

The annual meetings in central locations (called temporary cities or citadels) draw thousands of people of every age, occupation and social station. The largest and most famous citadel is the City of Youth at Loppiano in Italy; other large citadels are in Montet (Switzerland), Fontem (Cameroon), O'Higgins (Argentina), Santa Maria near São Paulo, and Tagatay near Manila. In Ottmaring, Federal Republic of Germany, a few Catholic and Lutheran Focolare families live together in the Ecumenical Centre of Life.

TOM STRANSKY

FOOD CRISIS/HUNGER.

Traditionally, churches and Christians have responded to hunger by formulating policies to alleviate the problem. In recent history, churches have channelled foodstuffs worth millions of dollars to places of famine. Nevertheless, attention to root causes has never been absent. For example, the East Asia Christian Conference, meeting in Kuala Lumpur in 1959, saw the solution to the food crisis in connection with the pattern of land ownership. The need for land reform can be found in almost any church statement related to the food crisis.

Another recurring theme in such church statements is the concern about population increase. The WCC central committee meeting in 1967 said: "We recognize that even the most promising combination of measures for increased food production will only postpone catastrophe unless there is a vast increase in responsible family life and planning."

Although carefully phrased, the issue of responsible family life was picked up again during a meeting in Beirut in 1968 of the Committee on Society, Development and Peace (SODEPAX*). The committee stressed that one of the priorities should be to develop "appropriate policies to slow down accelerated population increases". The SODEPAX meeting in Beirut was influenced by the prevailing optimism at that time regarding the problem-solving potential of science and tech-

nology.* It spoke about more fertilizers as a most promising key to higher farm yields, modern techniques and materials, soil and plant research, new strains of wheat, rice, and other food crops, the benefits of modernization and the need for foreign financing and technology.

Fifteen years later, the sixth WCC assembly (Vancouver 1983) adopted a much more critical attitude regarding these factors, saying that the development of technologies of food production which require the use of chemical inputs has in certain instances hampered food production. Transnational corporations and large landowners, which control much of the productive land, were criticized because they prevent farmers, peasants and landless rural workers from participation in decision making.

Some uneasiness about new, sophisticated and capital-intensive technology was expressed at the WCC conference on "Science and Technology for Human Development", held in Bucharest in 1974. Referring to the negative balance of protein exchange between the satisfied and the hungry world, the conference spoke about a "protein empire" that has been built on prevailing trade patterns: "There is something radically wrong about economic systems that result in protein being exported from where it is most needed." The Bucharest meeting sharply criticized the stockpiling of bombs and missiles when not even a start was made to address the urgent need of stockpiling food. The conference concluded that nothing short of a world emergency food programme was urgently needed, thereby echoing similar recommendations made by the WCC conference on Church and Society in Geneva in 1966 and a SODEPAX meeting in Montreal in 1969.

In his message issued in union with the synod of bishops, 1974, Pope Paul VI called upon governments to change their attitude towards the victims of hunger, to respond to the imperatives of justice and reconciliation, and speedily to find the means of feeding those who are without food. In his address to the world food conference in 1974, the pope placed the food crisis in the context of a general crisis of civilization and of solidarity. The reduction of food supplies is at least partially due to certain commercial decisions, according to Paul VI. At the same time he stressed that the world food crisis will not be solved without the participation of the agricultural workers, and this cannot be complete and fruitful without a radical revision of the present underestimation of the importance of agriculture.

A notable example of church co-operation is the Churches' Drought Action in Africa (CDAA), which was formed in 1984 by Caritas Internationalis (Roman Catholic), CIDSE (International co-operation for development and solidarity — Roman Catholic), the Lutheran World Federation and the WCC. Referring to environmental destruction, cash crop production, activities of transnational corporations, and armed conflicts, the CDAA study report of 1985 concludes that multifaceted and complex human arrangements, rather than drought, lie behind the food crisis in Africa. Hunger and famine are symptoms of poverty and underdevelopment, and efforts to eradicate hunger should therefore focus on structures which perpetuate poverty in Africa.

ROB VAN DRIMMELEN

Address of Pope Paul VI to the participants of the world food conference, 9 November 1974 • *The Root Causes of Hunger and Food Insufficiency in Africa*, CDAA, 1985 • "Statement on the International Food Disorder", in *Gathered for Life*, D. Gill ed., WCC, 1983 • D. de Gaspar et al., *World Hunger: A Christian Reappraisal*, WCC, 1982.

FREIRE, PAULO REGLUS NEVES.

B. 19.9.1921, Recife, Brazil. Freire is a Brazilian educator widely known for his use of the term "conscientization" in education, a process by which "both teacher and pupils simultaneously become knowing subjects, brought together by the object they are knowing". He was special consultant to the WCC Sub-unit on Education and professor at the Faculty of Education of the University of Geneva, 1970-80. Earlier (1969-70) he was visiting professor at Harvard University and the Center for Studies in Development and Social Change. During a period of exile, 1964-69, he was consultant to the ministry of education in Chile and to the Institute of Investigation into Agrarian Reform in conjunction with UNESCO. Currently he is professor at the Pontifical Catholic University in São Paulo, director of VEREDA (The Centre

of Studies in Education), and secretary of education of the municipality of São Paulo. He has written numerous books in Portuguese, translated into many languages, including *Pedagogy of the Oppressed* (New York, Herder, 1970) and *Cultural Action for Freedom* (Cambridge, MA, Center for the Study of Development and Social Change, 1970), and, with A. Faundez, *Learning to Question: A Pedagogy of Liberation* (WCC, 1989). See D. Collins, *Paulo Freire: His Life, Works and Thought* (New York, Paulist, 1977) and J. Elias, *Conscientization and Deschooling: Freire's and Illich's Proposals for Reshaping Society* (Philadelphia, Westminster, 1976).

ANS J. VAN DER BENT

FRIENDS/QUAKERS. This prophetic/mystical movement first developed in England around George Fox (1624-91) and his teaching and preaching. His followers first called themselves "children of the light", or simply "friends" — disciples who are called friends by Jesus: "You are my friends if you do what I command you" (John 15:14) — later corporately called "the Religious Society of Friends". "Quakers" was an early derisive nickname, associated with the tremblings of the Friends at their meetings. That title is no longer derisive, and Friends use it also of themselves.

Fox was convinced that the church* had become apostate, and even reformation "in root and branch" could not re-capture the authentic Christian community of the 1st century. So beginning again on early apostolic beliefs, Fox erected a church. It would depend directly on the risen Lord, and its members would function equally without mediation or rite and clergy but with the biblical gifts of the Spirit and the "inward light of Christ" — men and women equally under the direct headship of Christ. Friends' meetings for worship or for business held the holy expectancy that Christ would be in the midst wherever "two or three are gathered" in his name (Matt. 18:20), inspiring them to speak, enabling life to be transformed, and empowering ministries to the world with the same self-giving love that he bore on the cross.

In 1676, Robert Barclay published (in Latin) *Apology of True Christian Divinity*. It has never been displaced as the standard systematic treatment of Quaker theology.

The Quakers' early resistance in England to civil laws of religion that included oaths and marks of civil deference and to military service made the Friends targets of legal and popular oppression, even imprisonment. Many fled to the American colonies. The majority sought refuge in Pennsylvania under William Penn (1644-1718), himself a Quaker. Elsewhere several Friends were persecuted; four were hung for religious dissension in Boston, 1659-61.

Social action is characteristic of the Friends. They "have been more concerned with the here and now than with the hereafter. They have sought in many different ways to improve the societies in which they live — locally, nationally, and internationally." They look to the time when God's kingdom will come and his will be done; in the meanwhile they are summoned "to exhibit to the world a kingdom mind-set, kingdom values, and a kingdom life-style". They are to be "the authentic counter-culture of a better way, the only way that holds true hope and the promise of life for humankind". And they feel "the terrible pull of the unlimited liability for one another which the New Testament ethic lays upon them" (Douglas Steere).

Few Friends have dramatic stories of unusual witness. Most live humbly, barely noticed. Among outstanding role models are some who worked against slavery: John Woolman (1720-72), Anthony Benezet (1713-84), and in the later abolitionist phase, Lucretia Mott (1793-1880). Mott was also active in women's suffrage, along with Susan B. Anthony (1820-1906) and, in the 20th century, in the humane treatment of the mentally ill, Alice Paul. In prison reform Elizabeth Fry (1780-1845) still excels, as do William Tuke (1732-1822), his wife, and grandson.

Friends have worked consistently towards the elimination of war and its root causes in militarism, injustice and economic imperialism. Two Friends received the Nobel peace prize: in 1946 Emily Greene Balch, leader of the international women's movement for peace, and in 1959 Philip J. Noel-Baker, for his 53 years of participation in every international disarmament conference. A third Nobel peace prize in 1947 recognized the humanitarian and reconstruction efforts of the (British) Friends Service Council and the American Friends Service Committee.

For authenticity in all these areas, Friends test "leadings" or "concerns" in a process of group "discernment". One may be way ahead of his or her meeting; the reverse may be true; or there may be a number of correct solutions. Real transformation of society does not come from a programme or an ideology, but from exemplary discipleship. The light, grace, truth, or spirit of Christ are the real inspiration and the agent of transformation, moulding groups and individuals. Quakers follow spiritual disciplines, especially in prayer; a number of their writings have become spiritual classics for Christians.

From the beginning women have had an equal role in all aspects of the Quaker movement. Fox used a whole panoply of biblical texts to support the thesis that "souls have no sex", and that men and women are meant to be "help meets" (Gen. 2:18, King James) rather than antagonists. And Gal. 3:27-28 became the charter not only for equal treatment of women but for the open acceptance of other races and peoples.

Quakers of two varieties (there are four in all, now co-operating closely) were founding members of the WCC. They had an accredited observer at Vatican II (1962-65). Two were delegates to the 1963 Faith and Order* conference (Montreal). Quakers participate in the F&O commission of the National Council of the Churches of Christ, USA. Evangelical Friends are active in the World's Evangelical Alliance* and other evangelical groupings. Most other Quakers participate in local ministerial associations, or in state and national councils.

About half of the 200,000 Quakers comprise 57,000 black Africans, 12,000 Aymara Indians in Bolivia, 2,860 Eskimos in Alaska, 2,700 Taiwanians and 11,000 Latin Americans; and there are very small numbers of Germans, Japanese, Koreans, Scandinavians, Dutch, Middle Easterners, Indians and French-speaking people. The other half are Anglophones.

By and large their impulse to serve still comes from first-hand contact with the resurrected Christ, who is with us "always, to the close of the age" (Matt. 28:20). The basic thrust of all Quaker structure and activities hinges upon George Fox's central dictum, which states (without ruling out Christ's final coming in judgment) that "Christ has come" *again* — as he did again and again to the early church — "to teach his people himself".

DEAN FREIDAY

H.H. Brinton, *Friends for 300 Years*, New York, Harper, 1952 • E. Potts Brown & S. Mosher Stuard eds, *Witnesses for Change: Quaker Women over Three Centuries*, New Brunswick, NJ, Rutgers UP, 1989 • D. Freiday, *The Early Quakers and the Doctrine of Authority*, Quaker Religious Thought, 15, 1, 1973 • L.S. Kenworthy ed., *Friends Face the World: Some Continuing and Current Quaker Concerns*, Kenneth Square, PA, Quaker Publications, 1987 • D.V. Steere ed., *Quaker Spirituality: Selected Writings*, New York, Paulist, 1984.

FRIENDS WORLD COMMITTEE FOR CONSULTATION.

The FWCC was formed by the world conference of Friends in 1927 with an American and a European section, joined in 1971 by an African section. In 1974 the section of the Americas included constituencies in North, Central and South America and in the Caribbean area. The autonomous Friends yearly meetings freely associate themselves with the FWCC. It fosters spiritual life through intervisitation, study, conferences and a wide sharing of spiritual experiences, across all cultures, countries and languages. The FWCC also brings Quaker pacifist and philanthropic concerns to the world's attention. The United Nations recognizes the FWCC as a non-governmental organization with consultative status.

TOM STRANSKY

FRONTIER INTERNSHIP IN MISSION.

FIM, founded in 1960, is an active partnership between regional councils and conferences of churches, the WCC and the World Student Christian Federation.* It has placed nearly 300 interns in projects involving justice and liberation-oriented ministry. Existing focus areas include systemic causes of economic injustice, the resurgence of religion and its relationship to global political conflicts, and the encounter of cultures (interfaith, interethnic, inter-racial) in the struggle for peace with justice. While interns come from within the Christian community, projects are often based within communities of other faiths.

FIM has four principal aims: (1) to serve as a programme of ecumenical leadership formation for interns between 25 and 35 years of age; (2) to provide experiences in new forms of mission in focus areas, including theological, political, economic and socio-cultural issues; (3) to be a tool for community-initiated organizations to extend, augment and supplement their work through the presence of an intern from a similar group in another country; and (4) to be a catalyst for organizational networking, for the creation of new international alliances, and for engagement of interfaith partners in mission through the use of sending and receiving groups for interns. The intern works with a receiving group for two years and returns to his or her sending organization for a minimum one year re-entry period. This ensures a re-integration with the ecumenical movement in the intern's home country.

New styles of decision making, new forms of community organizing, and new methods of political and social analysis form the basis of theological reflection done by every intern. FIM circulates these reflections throughout the year in its publication entitled *Blueprints*.

JOHN BOONSTRA

FRY, FRANKLIN CLARK.

B. 30.8.1900, Bethlehem, PA, USA; d. 6.6.1968, Connecticut. Fry was vice-chairman of the WCC central and executive committees, 1948-54, and chairman of both, 1954-68. He was one of the founders of the Lutheran World Federation* at Lund in 1947, its treasurer, 1948-52, its first vice-president, 1952-57, and its president, 1957-63. Educated at Philadelphia Lutheran Seminary, he was ordained in 1925 and served pastorates in Yonkers, NY, 1925-29, and Akron, OH, 1929-44. Secretary of the Commission on Evangelism of the United Lutheran Church, 1930-38, he was also a member of the Board of American Missions, 1934-42, and in 1942 was elected to the executive board. Fry was president of the United Lutheran Church, 1944-62, and in 1962 became head of the Lutheran Church in America. A leader in the National Council of the Churches of Christ in the USA since its organization in 1950, he was chairman in 1954 of its Policy and Strategy Commission, and director of Church World Service, 1946-50. In 1947 he was president of Lutheran World Relief, and first vice-chairman of American Relief for Korea, 1950-54. See *Franklin Clark Fry: A Palette for a Portrait*, R. H. Fischer ed., *The Lutheran Quarterly* (1972, supplementary number).

ANS J. VAN DER BENT

FUNDAMENTALISTS.

Such major Christian thinkers as Philipp Melanchthon, John Calvin and John Wesley held that certain articles of the Christian faith* are essential, or fundamental, while other statements are matters of Christian liberty. In early 20th-century America, militant Protestant conservatives, or fundamentalists, responded to liberal revisions of doctrines by insisting that certain articles of the faith were essential and thus "non-negotiable" among Christians. For fundamentalists such essential doctrines, already so affirmed at the 1895 Niagara Bible conference, typically included the inerrancy of scripture, Jesus Christ's divinity, his virgin birth, substitutionary atonement, miracle-working power, bodily resurrection, and second coming. Though fundamentalism is primarily an American phenomenon, it has analogues in Great Britain and has been transplanted to other nations by missionary activity. Its roots are in the 19th century, when evolution, biblical criticism, rationalism, and other intellectual currents began to corrode dominant Christian assumptions about the authority of biblical revelation.

Although the terms "fundamentalists" and "fundamentalism" apply generally today to extreme conservatives in any faith (e.g. Islamic or Jewish fundamentalism), they originally were coined in 1920 by the Baptist Curtis L. Laws and harked back to a set of 12 booklets of essays entitled *The Fundamentals*, published and widely distributed free between 1910 and 1915. These essays defended conservative Christianity against liberal views in addressing such topics as scriptural authority and authenticity, Christology, and evangelism. The authors were British and North American conservatives who reflected the traditions of Reformed confessionalism, dis-

pensational premillennialism, and Keswick Holiness theology.

In the wake of the cultural crisis that engulfed America after the first world war, representatives of these various conservative schools united to wage battle against modernists in the Protestant churches and against various cultural changes which were challenging "the fundamentals", e.g. biological evolution and the biblical understanding of creation* and its crown — the human being made in God's image. In the churches, fundamentalists worked to remove liberals, who sought to accommodate traditional doctrines to the increasingly naturalistic assumptions at home and on the mission field. Though the fundamentalist-modernist controversy affected almost all mainline denominations, the battles were most fierce among the Northern Baptists and Northern Presbyterians. By the late 1920s, however, most of the mainline denominations clearly preferred a policy of unity and toleration to exclusion and separation.

In the culture at large, fundamentalists were convinced that a Darwinist "might-makes-right" philosophy had driven Germany into war and now threatened the foundations of American Christian civilization. They sought to prevent the teaching of biological evolution. By the mid-1920s, several southern states had thereby passed legislation which prohibited public schools from teaching the organic evolution of humans. This movement came to a head in the Scopes trial of 1925 in Dayton, Tennessee. There William Jennings Bryan, three-time presidential candidate and the national leader of the anti-evolutionists, debated agnostic lawyer Clarence Darrow. The derison of Bryan in the secular press and Bryan's death a few days after the trial resulted in a gradual decline in the anti-evolutionist movement, at least for the immediate future.

Having lost in many of the mainline churches and in the culture, fundamentalists regrouped in the 1930s. By the 1940s, heirs of this tradition were dividing into two camps: evangelicals,* who were conservative theologically but less militant and separatistic than their forebears, and fundamentalists, who were even more belligerent and separatist than their predecessors. Led by Carl McIntire, some of the stricter fundamentalists established in 1941 the American Council of Christian Churches in self-conscious opposition to the Federal Council of Churches (in 1950, the National Council of the Churches of Christ), and in 1948 set up the International Council of Christian Churches* in opposition to the WCC. In 1942 many of those who eventually became known as evangelicals united in the National Association of Evangelicals. While the fundamentalist organizations forbid their members from participating in any way in the larger ecumenical bodies, the National Association of Evangelicals does allow for individual members to belong to member churches of the NCCC and the WCC.

By the late 20th century many fundamentalists, who had largely eschewed political activity since the 1920s, re-entered the political arena in force. Led most noticeably by the television evangelist Jerry Falwell, fundamentalists began to support a conservative political agenda by stressing patriotism, a strong military, and deregulation of business. They adamantly oppose abortion, homosexual rights, the proposed Equal Rights (between men and women) Amendment, communism and, once again, the teaching of biological evolution in the schools. Fundamentalists'

dispensationalist eschatology leads to strong support of Israel; its existence, they believe, is a sign of the imminent rapture of the church and the return of Christ. In personal discipline fundamentalists typically oppose smoking, drinking, dancing, and movie-going.

The fundamentalist stress on missions and evangelism* resulted in their considerable growth in America and overseas in the years after 1930. By 1980 self-styled fundamentalists in America numbered around 5 million, but this number would be much larger if it included those Southern Baptists who call themselves conservatives. Moreover, many conservative evangelicals share aspects of the fundamentalist heritage and manifest some fundamentalist traits. Nevertheless, differences among fundamentalist bodies often prevent co-operation with each other.

BRADLEY J. LONGFIELD

G. Dollar, *A History of Fundamentalism in America*, Greenville, SC, Bob Jones UP, 1973 • G. Marsden ed., *Evangelicalism and Modern America*, Grand Rapids, MI, Eerdmans, 1984 • G. Marsden, *Fundamentalism and American Culture: The Shaping of Twentieth-Century Evangelicalism, 1870-1925*, New York, Oxford UP, 1980.

G

GARRETT, JOHN. B. 15.7.1920, Sydney, Australia. Garrett was WCC's first director of communication (then information), 1954-60. Previously he was general secretary of the Australian Council of Churches, 1950-54. As Congregational minister (ordained in 1946), he was a delegate of the Congregational Union of Australia and New Zealand to Amsterdam 1948. In Sydney he was church history teacher and college principal, 1960-66. Garrett was a member of the joint commission on church union preparing the union of Congregational, Methodist and Presbyterian churches as the Uniting Church in Australia. He was a faculty member of the Pacific Theological College, Suva, Fiji, 1968-74. He wrote *To Live among the Stars: Christian Origins in Oceania* (WCC and Suva, Institute of Pacific Studies, 1982).

ANS J. VAN DER BENT

GATU, JOHN. B. 3.3.1925, Kianbu, Kenya. A member of the Presbyterian Church of Eastern Africa, Gatu was a sergeant in the colonial army before he was ordained and later served as the general secretary and moderator of his church. He also served as chairperson of the National Council of Churches in Kenya, and with the All Africa Conference of Churches in various capacities. Gatu is most remembered for his call in 1971 for a moratorium* at the Mission Festival at Milwaukee, WI, USA. Moratorium was a plea for complete halt in the sending of missionaries and funds from European and American churches to the churches of Africa, in order to enable African churches to develop their own identity and to define their mission for their time and place. Moratorium, as expounded by Gatu, was a challenge to the assumption that without the large-scale presence of Western missionaries, Christianity could not survive in Africa. The idea of moratorium had been shaped by Walter Freytag in 1958. Gatu also claims the influence of Daniel Berrigan, who thought along the same lines in respect to Latin America.

Gatu served as a member of the WCC's Faith and Order commission (1961-75) and on its executive and central committees. He attended the Montreal Faith and Order meeting (1963), the CWME Bangkok assembly (1973), and Nairobi 1975. He was educated at St Paul's United Theological College, Limuru (1951-55), New College, Edinburgh (1958), Pittsburgh Theological College (1963), and Princeton Theological Seminary (1970-71).

JOHN S. POBEE

GENERATION CONFLICT. This term is used to describe misunderstandings, arguments, hostility and even enmity which can spoil the relationships between older people and the "younger generation".

Some generation conflict is inevitable, for as young people grow into maturity and inde-

433

pendence, they need to claim their own identities as separate from those of their parents, grandparents and older adults. Young people often assert their individuality critically and forcefully, sometimes contradicting and despising the views of their elders. Although this is a natural process, severe or prolonged disruption of relationships between different generations can occur when older people cling to power and use it to negate or attempt to suppress the efforts of the younger generation to contribute to and effect changes in their families.

Generation conflict may arise in Christian congregations, churches and the ecumenical movement when young people become impatient for change and older people, even those who themselves have been effective reformers, resist it. Fear of each other's differing powers — e.g., the vigour of youth vs the experience of age — can fuel natural differences in approach to important issues such as world poverty, global solidarity, militarism, nuclear disarmament, conservation, classism, racism, sexism and ecumenism itself.

Unaware of history, young people may repeat arguments and conflicts that older people thought had been dealt with 30 or 40 years before. This apparent inability to profit from experience so as to build on gains already achieved devalues the life work of those older people whose efforts and sacrifices have brought about substantial change in the past. The consequent hurt to the older generation may cause some of them to use their status and experience against younger people, who lack both.

Another cause of generation conflict is inherent in institutional structures, which are by nature somewhat inflexible so as to safeguard certain traditions and the rights of certain groups. Sometimes young people become impatient with well-established interdenominational doctrines and practices or fret at the constraints of working in systems which are hierarchical in constitution. They may become angry at the apparent unwillingness of individuals and groups to effect necessary reforms, and their anger may lead them to courses of unconventional action which seem antinomian and outrageous to the older generation. These older and more experienced people then attempt to devalue the very people who made them feel undervalued in the first place.

Generation conflict does not always work this way round. Sometimes it is the older generation that wants to effect change and the younger people who resist vigorously. But either way, the vicious cycle of mutual distrust and devaluation can lead to different generations working against each other instead of with each other so as to achieve goals which both in fact desire. This conflict can be overcome only by mutual tolerance and a deepening understanding of how change is often effected in Christian communities through prophetic action followed by a gradual acceptance of the rightness of that action: this in turn leads to structural changes and reforms.

A good example of how this works can be seen in recent times in the ecumenical movement itself. In the early days of the WCC young people were seriously under-represented on its committees, consultations and assemblies. Since the 1970s sustained efforts have been made, either through positive discrimination or through special gatherings of young people, to ensure that their deliberations, recommendations and publications are taken seriously. In this way substantial resolutions are debated and recommendations are often implemented by the older generation. Such efforts build up mutual trust between different generations and must increase mutual respect and strengthen their common effort to proclaim the gospel and bring in God's kingdom on earth.

See also **youth**.

UNA KROLL

GERMANOS (Strenopoulos).

B. 15.9.1872, Silivria, Greece; d. 24.1.1951, London. Germanos was a president of the WCC, 1948-51. He met John R. Mott and Nathan Söderblom at a conference of the World Student Christian Federation* in Constantinople in 1911 and thereafter became actively engaged in the ecumenical movement. He was influential in the publication of the "Encyclical unto all the Churches of Christ", issued by the patriarchate of Constantinople in 1920. Vice-president of the first world conference on Faith and Order (Lausanne 1927), he stressed that from the point of view of Orthodox theology, "unity in faith constitutes a primary condition of reunion of the churches". He was also vice-president of the second world conference on Faith and Order* (Edinburgh 1937) and a member of the provisional committee of the WCC and much involved in its final creation. Educated in Constantinople, Halle, Leipzig, Strasbourg and Lausanne, Germanos was professor of dogmatics and symbolism at Halki, 1908, then dean of the same theological school. In 1922 he was appointed archbishop of Thyateira, with seat in London, and exarch for West and Central Europe in 1922. He contributed to *The Reunion of Christendom* (London, Cassell, 1929) and wrote *Kyrillos Loukaris, 1572-1638: A Struggle for Preponderance between Catholic and Protestant Powers in the Orthodox East* (London, SPCK, 1951).

ANS J. VAN DER BENT

GOD. "Whatever your heart clings to and trusts in, that is really your god," said Luther in his exposition of the first commandment in the large catechism. Unfortunately, the human heart and mind is, as Calvin recognized, a "perpetual factory of idols" (*Institutes* 1.11.8). Phenomenologically speaking, there are therefore "many 'gods' and many 'lords'" (1 Cor. 8:5). But for Christians, the apostle Paul continues, "there is one God, the Father... and one Lord, Jesus Christ" (v.6). To come to the Christian faith is to turn "from idols, to serve a living and true God, and to wait for his Son from heaven, whom he raised from the dead, Jesus who delivers us from the wrath to come" (1 Thess. 1:9-10). Or in Johannine terms: "This is eternal life, that they know thee the only true God, and Jesus Christ whom thou hast sent" (John 17:3).

The Christian doctrine of God is Trinitarian (see **Trinity**). "When I say God", declared Gregory Nazianzus (d.389), "I mean Father, Son and Holy Spirit" (*Oration* 38.8; 45.4). Jesus Christ,* the Son, is "God from God,... eternally begotten of the Father", while the Holy Spirit* "proceeds from the Father" and "with the Father and the Son together is worshipped and glorified" (see **Nicene Creed**). This Trinitarian pattern is profoundly stamped on all Eastern Orthodox liturgy and theology. The classic Western churches are also Trinitarian in creed; but in their theological reflection

they have tended, at least from Augustine (d.430) onwards, to start with the "one simple substance of God" in such a way as to make distinctions among the three persons difficult. From Aquinas (d.1274) onwards, it was for centuries customary for Western dogmaticians to treat "the one God" *(de Deo uno)* before treating "the Triune God" *(de Deo trino)*. Modern Protestantism has stood under the aegis of Friedrich Schleiermacher, who devoted only the last ten pages of his "doctrine of the faith" (*Der christliche Glaube*, 2nd ed., 1830), and then with "unitarian" sympathies, to the doctrine of the Trinity.

The Western situation has changed in the 20th century with Barth's *Church Dogmatics* (1932-67), which begins its doctrine of revelation* in a Trinitarian way that is then maintained throughout the work. And on the Roman Catholic side, Karl Rahner's lengthy article on the Trinity in the encyclopedic *Mysterium Salutis* (Johannes Feiner and Magnus Löhrer eds, 1965-76) has been very influential, especially in its celebrated axiom that "the 'economic' Trinity is the 'immanent' Trinity and vice versa" (vol. 2, 1967, 317-401, in particular 328): God *is* in very being ("immanent Trinity") as God is *self-revealed* ("economic Trinity"), namely, Father, Son and Holy Spirit. In recent years there has been a flurry of books on the doctrine of the Trinity, with varied approaches and different emphases, from across the entire ecumenical board, including Jürgen Moltmann (Reformed), *Trinität und Reich Gottes* (1980, ET *The Trinity and the Kingdom of God*, 1981); Robert Jenson (Lutheran), *The Triune Identity* (1982); Walter Kasper (Roman Catholic), *Der Gott Jesu Christi* (1982, ET *The God of Jesus Christ*, 1984); John Zizioulas (Orthodox), *Being as Communion* (1985); Boris Bobrinskoy (Orthodox), *Le mystère de la Trinité* (1986); and Bruno Forte (Roman Catholic), *Trinità come storia* (1985, ET *The Trinity as History* 1989). The dominant insight has been that God is in very nature the loving communion of three persons. Such Trinitarianism, in its "positive" or "kataphatic" statements, does not impugn but rather recognizes the insights of "negative" or "apophatic" theology concerning the inexhaustibility of God, which must always transcend the knowledge even of redeemed, sanctified and perfected creatures.

The Christian doctrine of God has to be

situated in reference to three developments or ranges of thinking in particular: the revelation embodied in Jesus Christ and the reflection of faith* upon that; philosophical theism and atheism;* and other religions, particularly those which profess faith in "one God".

Revelation and reflection. In the course of its history, Israel came to recognize the absolute uniqueness of the One who bore the revealed name of YHWH, the Lord, the Redeemer of the people and the Creator of all that is: "There is no other god besides me; a righteous God and a Saviour; there is none besides me. Turn to me and be saved, all the ends of the earth! For I am God, and there is no other" (Isa. 45:21-22).

Jesus affirmed the "Shema Israel" (Deut. 6:4-5) as the first and great commandment and the way to eternal life: "Hear, O Israel: the Lord is our God, the Lord alone; and you shall love the Lord your God with all your heart, and with all your soul, and with all your might" (cf. Matt. 22:37; Mark 12:29-30; Luke 10:27). Jesus also regularly addressed this God by the intimate term of "Abba, Father" and himself appears correspondingly as "the Son" (Mark 1:11 and par.; Matt. 11:25-27; John 1:18, 3:16, 14:9; Rom. 8:32; Col. 1:13). The Father and the Son are "one" (John 10:30, 17:11); while remaining distinct, they dwell "in" each other (John 17:21). Jesus Christ is given the name of Lord (Phil. 2:9-10, echoing Isa. 45:23), though only and always "to the glory of God the Father" (Phil. 2:11), who "gives life to the dead and calls into existence the things that do not exist" (Rom. 4:17; cf. vv.24-25).

The New Testament also links the Spirit — "who proceeds from the Father" (John 15:26) — with the Son. At the prayer of the exalted Christ (John 14:16,26, 15:26; Acts 2:33), the Father sends the Holy Spirit into the world, "the other Paraclete" (John 14:16), the Spirit who "gives life" (John 6:63; Rom. 8:11; 2 Cor. 3:6) and guides into all the truth (John 16:13). The triad of Father, Son and Holy Spirit figures together, sometimes explicitly as a threefold name, in many layers of the NT writings, with Matt. 28:19, 1 Cor. 12:4-6; 2 Cor. 13:14, and Eph. 2:18-22 and 4:4-6 among the more notable passages not already cited.

It took at least four centuries for the church, particularly in the intellectual and religious context of the Greco-Roman world, to work out the implications of the Christ-event for belief in "the one God". Against Marcion and the Gnostics it needed to be shown that the Creator and the Redeemer were the same God. Against temptations to a polytheism that would have jeopardized human salvation* by reducing Christ to a demi-god, it needed to be shown that the agent of revelation and redemption was not a "second god" *(deuteros theos)* or a "god by courtesy" *(katachrēstikōs)* but himself "consubstantial with the Father" *(homoousios tō patri)*. Against accusations of tritheism, it needed to be shown that there are "not three gods" (the title of Gregory of Nyssa's refutation of the charge). The decisive dogmatic decisions were taken by the ecumenical councils* of Nicea* 325 and Constantinople* 381.

Among the questions that have remained open for recurrent theological discussion within the church are the implications for God's life and being of the liturgical confession that "One of the Trinity suffered" (recent examples are J.A. Baker's *The Foolishness of God* [1970] and Jürgen Moltmann's *Der gekreuzigte Gott* [1972, ET *The Crucified God*, 1974]), and the precise ways in which the Trinitarian "relations" *(schēseis)* of Father, Son and Holy Spirit are to be described (for a recent discussion see T.F. Torrance's *The Trinitarian Faith* [1988]). Yet since the 4th-century councils it has been the almost unanimous practice among those claiming to be Christians to profess belief in the one God and to confess the name of Father, Son and Holy Spirit. Such Trinitarian faith is required of churches for membership in the WCC (see **WCC, basis of**).

Philosophical theism and atheism. Since its beginnings in ancient Greece, Western philosophy has included a strand of thinking that arrives at "God" (the word is often used as a proper noun) by two main routes: from the contingency of the world (it need not be or have been) is drawn the conclusion of a necessary being, a first cause beyond the internal series of causes; and for the multiplicity of things, a single coherent ground is sought in the One. Despite counter-arguments that are often claimed or considered to be conclusive, "theism" keeps recurring in variant forms throughout the history of Western thought. It hovers around the contemporary search for "meaning" and "purpose". Though preferring to speak of "panentheism", Whiteheadian process theology is a close cousin to "classical theism", as John Macquarrie's preferred term of "dialectical theism" also indicates.

While great difficulties attend the notion of a "proof" of "God", some modern Christian theologians (e.g. Walter Kasper, Macquarrie, Wolfhart Pannenberg) judge the metaphysical quest worth pursuing, even though none would claim that unaided reason could reach the personal knowledge of God granted by the self-revelation of God in Christ. Most would claim that at best the theistic arguments may serve, after the event, to show that belief in the self-revealed God is not irrational, or that the self-revealed God has in fact "answered" the "questions" which serious efforts to reach truth address.

Some Christian theologians, however, are suspicious of the whole theistic route, whether taken *a priori* or *a posteriori*. Thus Eberhard Jüngel argues that theism always makes God "necessary", to ground the world or human self-consciousness (Descartes is a chief culprit). Atheism can then appear as the proper rejection of a "God" in which Christians do not really believe either. Jüngel finds in the God of Christian faith an utterly gracious one who is "more than necessary". Christian faith begins, and must never deviate, from the cross of Christ and the concomitant confession that "God is love" (1 John 4:8). Moltmann dislikes the term "monotheism" on the grounds that, in the history of Christian thought and society, belief in *Eis Theos* (in the eponymous title of Erik Peterson's book of 1926) has too easily gone hand in hand with political oppression and totalitarianism ("monarchism"), whereas a truly Trinitarian doctrine (some would find Moltmann himself to verge on tritheism) is more favourable to a complex and differentiated pattern of human community. None of this, of course, touches the problem of unbelief, whether militant or indifferentist, in face of a Christian message adequately presented.

Other religions. Throughout Christian history there has been a marked tension in attitudes towards the religions of the world. On the one hand, all worship outside of the church may be considered idolatry, directed towards "false gods". On the other hand, elements of truth may be detected in other religions that make them a "preparation for the gospel" *(preparatio evangelica)*.

More along the latter line, monotheism has often been seen as a common factor, especially shared with Jews and Muslims, in so far as they, like Christians, claim a descent from Abraham and intend to worship "the God of Abraham". However, the matter is complex and disputed. For their part, sympathetic Jews have regarded Christians as monotheists, minimizing the significance of the Christian worship of the "mere man" Jesus, which is more strictly idolatry; only rarely have Muslims exempted Christians from the charge of polytheism on account of their belief in "the Father and the Son". (The Qur'an, 112:1-4, is seen as excluding the Trinity and incarnation; cf. 4:171, 5:72-73.) From the Christian angle again, what constitutes the "children of Abraham" is a matter of contention (see Matt. 3:9; Luke 3:8; John 8:33-59; Acts 7:1-60, 13:26-52; Rom. 4:1-25, 9:6-13; 2 Cor. 11:22; Gal. 3:6-18, 4:21-31); in the Christian era it must seem that Jews and Muslims have either refused or altered the revelation of God that has come in Jesus Christ.

Interfaith dialogues are exploring these issues (see **dialogue, interfaith**). It is unlikely that Jews or Muslims can accept the kind of "ranking", however well intentioned, implied in the model of concentric circles found in Vatican II's Declaration on the Relationship of the Church to Non-Christian Religions *(Nostra Aetate)* and in Pope Paul VI's encyclical *Ecclesiam Suam:* the outer edge is no less than the limits of a universal humanity; then come all persons of good will; closer in, we find all who believe in "the one God", people of "the great African and Asian religions", but more particularly Muslims and more particularly yet Jews; finally come Christians and, at the very centre, the Catholic church.

The most liberal modern Christian theologians, whether Catholic or Protestant, have moved towards regarding religions as "equivalent" or simply (in a benign agnosticism) "incommensurable"; but this position is hard to square with scriptural and traditional faith in the unique and universal significance of Christ and hence in the God revealed by him and the events surrounding him (see **uniqueness of Christ, universalism**).

A more characteristically Christian approach to dialogue, let alone evangelism, can find resources in a Trinitarian doctrine of God. This is hinted at in the WCC *Guidelines for Dialogue with People of Living Faiths and Ideologies* (1979): "It is Christian faith in the Triune God — Creator of all humankind, Redeemer in Jesus Christ, revealing and renewing Spirit — which calls us Christians to human relationship with our many neighbours. It is Christian faith which sets us free to be open to the faith of others, to risk, to trust and to be vulnerable. In dialogue, conviction and openness are held in balance." In more academic terms, Karl Rahner's vision provided a valuable Trinitarian framework for many: God is the mystery at the ultimate horizon of human self-transcendence and is constantly pressing upon the human creature in self-communication by word and grace. A more forthrightly biblical account is provided by Lesslie Newbigin in his thoroughly Trinitarian books *The Open Secret* (1978) and *The Gospel in a Pluralist Society* (1989).

If, in conclusion, it were to be asked what picture of God emerges in current ecumenical reflection by those committed to the Christian faith, the Faith and Order* study "Towards the Common Expression of the Apostolic Faith Today" suggests that the following traits at least would be noticeable. The picture will be thoroughly Trinitarian (though with perhaps a blurring at the edges, among those who, under feminist criticism, are attempting the difficult, if not impossible, task of finding alternatives to the name of Father, Son and Holy Spirit). "The Father" and "the Almighty" will be seen as mutually qualifying, with a recognition of the tender qualities of God which may even be designated motherly or feminine. "The Father" will never be without "the Son", or "the Son" without "the Father". It will be stressed, in a recovery of Athanasianism, that the work of Christ in revelation and redemption depends on the Son's being "consubstantial with the Father". Soteriological motifs will be strongly present, with a stress on God's favour towards the poor* and the oppressed. In face of all the difficulties concerning "interventionism" raised by a scientific world-view, God will still be confessed as "acting" in the world. There will be discussion of the work of the Holy Spirit beyond the bounds of the church,* throughout humankind and creation.* The Holy Spirit will be seen in

the church not only as a bond of unity* but also as a principle of diversity. Communion and *perichōrēsis* will be major categories for expressing the inner-Trinitarian relations. The continuing work of God towards the eschatological consummation will figure prominently.

See also **atheism; dialogue, interfaith; faith; grace; Holy Spirit; Jesus Christ; Trinity**.

                                        GEOFFREY WAINWRIGHT

D.B. Burrell, *Knowing the Unknowable God: Ibn-Sina, Maimonides, Aquinas,* Notre Dame, IN, Univ. of Notre Dame Press, 1986 • *Confessing One Faith,* WCC, 1987 • E. Jüngel, *Gott als Geheimnis der Welt* (ET *God as the Mystery of the World,* Grand Rapids, MI, Eerdmans, 1983) • W. Kasper, *Der Gott Jesu Christi* (ET *The God of Jesus Christ,* New York, Crossroad, 1984) • V. Lossky, *La théologie mystique de l'Eglise d'Orient* (ET *The Mystical Theology of the Eastern Church,* London, James Clarke, 1957) • J. Macquarrie, *In Search of Deity,* London, SCM, 1984 • A. Manaranche, *Le monothéisme chrétien,* Paris, Cerf, 1985 • W. Pannenberg, *Metaphysik und Gottesgedanke* (ET *Metaphysics and the Idea of God,* Grand Rapids, MI, Eerdmans, 1990) • K. Rahner, "Theos im Neuen Testament" (ET in his *Theological Investigations,* vol. 1, London, Darton, Longman & Todd, 1961).

GOODALL, NORMAN. B. 30.8.1896, Birmingham, UK; d. 1.1.1985, Oxford. Goodall had great gifts to bring about reconciliation* between churches. He played a leading part both in the re-organization of the London Missionary Society into the Council for World Mission and in the eventual merger in 1972 of the Congregational and Presbyterian churches into the United Reformed Church. He was foreign secretary of the London Missionary Society, 1936-44, secretary of the Joint Committee of the International Missionary Council and the WCC 1955-61, prior to the union of the two in New Delhi 1961, assistant general secretary of the WCC, 1961-63, chairman of a WCC structure committee, and secretary of the International Congregational Council, 1962-68. After studies in Mansfield College, Oxford, he was pastor of a Congregational church in London in 1922 and also was lecturer, broadcaster and author of several publications on ecumenism and mission. Editor of the *Uppsala Report,* 1968, he wrote *The Ecumenical Movement* (New York,

Oxford UP, 1964), *Ecumenical Progress: A Decade of Change in the Ecumenical Movement, 1961-71* (London, Oxford UP, 1972) and an autobiography, *Second Fiddle* (London, SPCK, 1979).

ANS J. VAN DER BENT

GRACE. The concept of "grace", which both in its biblical origins and subsequently was used in the legal realm as well as in the area of human relationships in general, has been applied in a special way to God's relation to human beings. In this form the concept has aroused great passions in the history of Christian theology and dogma, making it one of the central concepts of Christian theology and at times even the quintessence of Christianity as a whole. In Judaism, despite a similarly high estimate of the relevant biblical content, the concept of "grace" has never played the kind of central role it has had in Christianity.

Old Testament. The word "grace" or close synonyms are used to translate a variety of related Hebrew words. The range of meanings includes the formula "to find *favour* in the eyes of the Lord" (Gen. 6:8; Ex. 33:12-13,16-17, 34:9); the statement of God's absolute freedom in his gracious election, "I will be *gracious* to whom I will be gracious, and will *show mercy* on whom I will show mercy" (Ex. 33:19); and something like a general theological formula describing God as *merciful* and *gracious* and as a God of *steadfast love* and *faithfulness* (Ex. 34:6; Joel 2:13; Jonah 4:2; Pss. 86:15, 103:8, 111:4, 116:5, 145:8; Neh. 9:17,31; 2 Chron. 30:9).

It should be observed, all in all, that God bestows his grace freely with no preconditions; he grants it to Israel as a whole. It is a dependable promise, and the individual who in prayer asks to have it can rely on it. Grace is always given precedence over the commandment.

New Testament. In the New Testament the equivalent for the term "grace" is *charis*. Paul's theology is central to the whole NT understanding of grace. The epistle to the Romans is of special importance here. In particular Paul emphasizes God's gracious action in the death of Jesus Christ* on the cross (esp. in Rom. 3-6) and the presence of God's grace in believers (thus Rom. 5:1-11, 6:14;

2 Cor. 6:1; Gal. 1:6, 5:4; Phil. 1:7); the fullness of the various charismata* as gifts of God corresponds to the *charis* bestowed by God and makes that *charis* a reality in the Christian community (thus Rom. 12:3-21; 1 Cor. 1:4-9). In Rom. 3:24f. Paul says that God, through the divine eschatological act in the expiatory death of Jesus, justifies *dōrean* ("as a gift") those sinners who respond in faith.* The *dōrean* explicitly links grace with the corresponding position that "no human being will be justified... by works of the law" (3:20). In Rom. 5:1-11 this eschatological divine act of grace in justification* is equated with the love of God which has been revealed in Jesus' death for sinners. In Rom. 5:12-21 the theme of grace is given expanded treatment. God's grace flows so abundantly that as the righteousness (of believers) it annihilates the power of sin* and will reign victoriously over the power of death in the eternal life of those who are made perfect. Rom. 6 explains how the baptized and justified have died with Christ to sin and are no longer under the law but under grace (v.14) and so have the prospect of eternal life as a gift *(charisma)* of the freely given grace of God (v.23).

Among the synoptic writers, only Luke uses *charis* (e.g. Luke 1:30, 2:40,52, 4:22; Acts 4:33, 7:46, 11:23, 14:3,26, 15:40, 20:24,32). Here Luke speaks of the benefit of grace, "the gospel of the grace of God", the grace that was "upon him (Jesus)", the grace which rested upon the (primitive) Christian community, and of mission* which is represented as a realization of the gracious eschatological act of God. In the Johannine writings we find *charis* only twice (John 1:14-18; 2 John 3); the two conjoined terms "grace and truth" at John 1:14-18 has its own importance, presupposing the incarnation of the Logos where the grace of God exceeds that which was to be found in the law of Moses.

The early church and the middle ages. Right through the history of Christianity up to our own day, the theme of "grace" has been an active and decisive factor in how Christianity understands itself. Theologically and in church politics the theme of "grace" has run alongside the history of Christianity as a whole, finding itself affirmed, re-interpreted, circumscribed, and nuanced, and figuring in disputes and schisms over its own definition and operation. This was especially true in the

Western church, where the doctrine of grace occupied a central position, whereas it did not in the Eastern church.

It is not possible to describe even the Western doctrine of grace since the time of Augustine without reference to the context in which the theme of grace was treated in East and West in the first four centuries. In that period "grace" was discussed in soteriological and ethical contexts, with synergism as a characteristic feature: salvation* is achieved through a conjunction of divine and human action. Here God's action establishes the comprehensive and definitive starting point of the human road to salvation and also provides for the goal, but between start and finish lie human ethics and morals made possible by grace as a life in grace, as the appropriation and demonstration of grace in moral behaviour, and as indispensable for salvation.

The interpretation of the doctrine of grace in terms of salvation history* made it possible for Irenaeus (late 2nd century) to understand the whole existence of human beings as life based on grace: in creation* itself human beings receive an existence based on grace, and as the image of God they are called to a fellowship with God that they cannot attain on their own after the fall. That is why the linking of divine grace with human beings in Jesus Christ is both possible and needed. Christ makes the Holy Spirit* available to human beings (in baptism), and thus human nature is healed through grace — all of which happens in the church.* From the time of Irenaeus onwards it is therefore possible to speak of the original state of grace and saving grace, of nature and grace, and of the church as the place where grace is to be found.

Athanasius, Basil the Great, Gregory of Nyssa and John Chrysostom are important figures from the 4th century. For Athanasius Christ is the mediator in creation and redemption; he is the true image of God and thus the original unity of nature and grace which human beings lost in Adam. To achieve fellowship with God there is a need for the new imparting of grace which takes place in the incarnation* and the subsequent bestowal of the Spirit, which inwardly renews human beings. The connection of grace and Spirit remained significant, especially in Eastern theology (e.g. for Basil the Great). Gregory of Nyssa describes the connection between divine grace and the moral behaviour of human beings in relation to salvation as *synergeia* (synergy), and John Chrysostom puts the main emphasis on grace. The 4th-century reflections on grace remained standard for Eastern theology, particularly in the way it related to pneumatology and was thematically developed.

The situation was completely different for Western theology. It was Augustine who set the course for the whole of the Western Christian world up to the present (drawing on the tradition already available to him, accepting the Christological and pneumatological dogmas of the 4th century, and with particular dependence on Paul). Augustine's own development played an important part in this. In anthropology and ethics he switched under Pauline influence from a Platonic theory of knowledge to an interest in how right action is made possible. By around 396 his doctrine of grace was fully developed *(On Various Questions, to Simplician; Confessions)*. In the controversy with Pelagius it was merely defended and more closely defined (esp. in *The Spirit and the Letter*, 412). Augustine's new understanding of sin, acquired under Paul's influence, is crucial: human beings are intrinsically characterized by sin *(peccatum originale)*, which finds expression in covetousness and greed and in a radical love of self. Only God can open up the self-centredness and self-concern of human beings. This is the work of grace which first enables human beings even simply to will what is good. This latter point is something wholly new in the doctrine of grace; not only the doing of good but even the will to do good is the work of grace. This view corresponds with Augustine's doctrine of everything being effected by God, according to which everything good in God's creatures comes from the Deity. As in Paul, grace is freely bestowed by God without any prior works by human beings.

In the controversy with Pelagius, Augustine's doctrine of grace basically came into conflict with what not only Gregory of Nyssa, John Chrysostom but also Jerome taught about grace. Pelagius rejected a *peccatum originale* as essential to the character of a theological anthropology. The Creator himself had bestowed reason, conscience, freedom of will and the power to will what is good on human nature, which is good. Human weakness results from the seductive power of Adam's sin, which, beyond the merely limited effect of God's grace in the law, is removed through the representation of the grace of God in the incarnation of Jesus Christ and through the moral example he set; and this is made transparent in baptism and makes good and just action possible. Against this less radical conception of Pelagius, Augustine (in *The Spirit and the Letter*) stresses the total incapacity of human beings to turn to God on their own initiative and emphasizes what Paul says in 1 Cor. 4:7: "What have you that you did not receive?" Only grace awakens faith, is the basis of freedom of the will and turns us towards the good. Even the free assent to salvation is a work of grace; it is granted to those God foreknows will give that assent. The resort to predestination is intended to safeguard the complete gratuitousness of the grace of God, which the Deity is not under any obligation to bestow. It is because of God's grace that a life in accordance with the divine will is possible at all: Rom. 5:5 speaks of the love of God poured into our hearts by the Holy Spirit. Spirit and grace are thus interconnected: both are God's gift of love; the Spirit is the Spirit of grace, and grace is the Spirit working as love. It is granted gratuitously. Christology and the doctrine of grace are mediated pneumatologically: contrary to Pelagius, grace is neither nature nor law, but the Spirit who makes us alive. And contrary to Pelagius, Christ is thus not merely a person who works powerfully in history but is present and effective "in the Spirit". The Spirit — purely and simply the gift of God — operates through holy scripture, preaching, the sacraments and the ministry. The Spirit creates love and fellowship, so that the individual partakes in grace in the *communio sanctorum*, in the *ecclesia catholica*. Augustine is not thinking in terms of the church itself as actively mediating grace.

Significant subsequent developments were the church's adoption of Augustine's teaching on grace in a cruder form and the condemnation of Pelagius at the council of Carthage (418). The difficulties arising here are clearly shown by John Cassian and by Vincent of Lérins. They were not supporters of Pelagius but represented traditional synergism. Contrary to Augustine, they were convinced that, despite the fall, the freedom to decide in

favour of conversion* is crucial; grace is not the source of the will to do good but merely re-inforces it. Augustine's doctrine was defended by disciples and supporters of his, first of all Prosper of Aquitaine and then Fulgentius of Ruspe. Finally Caesarius of Arles was able to obtain the condemnation of synergism at the provincial council of Orange in 529. In Gregory I, however, we see how strong it remained: for him, grace starts at the conversion of sinful human beings through faith and the will to do good, it accompanies them after baptism and together with the free will it is the cause of good works. Human co-operation is indispensable for conversion, as it also is for good works. But it also remains clear that there can be no Christian existence without grace. Christian existence is nevertheless bound up with the life of the church. With Gregory I the latter helps — along with quite different approaches — to contribute to the extension of the institutional church's claim to its mediating role in salvation far beyond Augustine's sacramentalism.

Early, high and late scholasticism remained beholden to the Augustinian scheme. The doctrine of grace in the middle ages was characterized in the whole spectrum of its theological schools by systematization and what were plainly hair-splitting definitions, falling back on distinctions which already had a very long history. Early scholasticism interprets grace in the context of ethics and articulates it as the constant principle in virtue. Alongside this it recognizes three other contexts where grace has to be discussed: the doctrine of the sacraments, Christology, and the doctrine of creation and the original state of human beings. Faith ("initial grace", linked to justification) and love are the effect of grace. No good work is possible without grace.

For Thomas Aquinas grace is the creative coming "of the eternal love of God into the centre of the human ego" (O.H. Pesch), with which God rescues us from our natural limitations for a fellowship of love with him and endows us in such a way that we find this possible. Faith, hope and love follow from grace. Although Thomas champions the doctrine of the freedom of the will, human beings make no contribution to justification because freedom in Thomas's sense remains tied to God as its source and is therefore a "freedom that is bestowed". Thomas's concept of merit is not easy to understand; for him the doctrine of merit is an extension of the doctrine of grace. The *meritum de condigno* speaks of the efficacy of the grace of God; only the *meritum de congruo* belongs on the human side because it designates friendship and not a legal right: it is appropriate that God fulfills the request of a friend, but one who is a friend only through the grace of God.

Thomas's whole structure of ideas was bound to give rise to questions, and so it turned out when the crisis in metaphysical thinking made it impossible for the characteristic bracketing of Christian tradition with Aristotelian metaphysics to continue saying what it was trying to say. But as this situation had already begun to arise in the late middle ages, and, alongside a new understanding of freedom, humanism quite generally developed new and different paradigms of language and thought, the by then old linguistic models were bound to suffer a crisis which then led, less inevitably, to the split in the Western church. Both in its classical and its late scholastic form, the doctrine of grace in the 16th century had, not least in view also of the practical situation in proclamation and the cure of souls, come to the end of the road, and so had to be re-thought.

The Reformation. Martin Luther's new reflections on grace were prompted in the nature of the case by the nominalist position that pure love of God was possible for the natural man. Although he was unacquainted with the high scholastic positions, these were by now caught up in the vortex of nominalistic thinking, so that Luther rejected them completely as human self-justification. In a situation where theology and church life had degenerated as a whole, Luther fell back on Paul and took up ideas which were central to Augustine to develop his doctrine of justification, within which grace is an essential constituent. The gospel of Jesus the Christ is grace; it proclaims the gracious God who in Christ has mercy on sinners. In faith human beings "cling" to the Christ who ascends to the Father. God accepts believers who look in faith on Christ and justifies them by grace alone without any merits on their part, vesting them with the righteousness that is God's, since Christ has "drowned" human sins in his death. Justification of sinners is God's act in

Christ. It is actively proclaimed, and they partake of it in faith. All this happens in the Spirit.

In Reformation theology of the Lutheran type, this content is summed up in the four Reformation principles which interpret each other: *sola gratia, solo Christo, solo verbo, sola fide*. Sinners are justified through these. Grace is seen to consist in the forgiveness of sins. It grants fellowship with God together with its effects on the whole of life. In no way is this saying less than what we find in the variations of the scholastic doctrine of grace. Luther's doctrine of grace is a paean to the fact that God is not ours to command and that God alone is efficacious in what he does. In God's sight human beings are always sinners on whom he has mercy in Christ and whom he vests with his righteousness. The Christian is therefore *simul justus et peccator*, righteous and a sinner at the same time. In relation to salvation human beings have — from a strictly theological point of view — no "free will", by means of which they could find the way to salvation apart from and prior to any grace, as this way has already been made smooth for human beings in Christ by God's free will. Even human acceptance of salvation is a work of God's grace, as the believer confesses in prayer.

For Calvin the divine sovereignty in God's gracious acts is decisive. In his *Institutes* it is grace that links the saving work of Christ — which imparts God's grace and salvation — with its consequences in the Christian's life, seen as the "appropriation of the grace of Christ" and as the work of the Holy Spirit. Calvin's doctrine of Christ is marked by its Christological focus and pneumatological explication and acknowledges its permanent indebtedness to the Reformation principle of *sola gratia*.

The council of Trent* was not able to take up the challenges of the Reformation creatively. It carefully avoided taking sides with any of the factions involved in disputes related to the scholastic schools; it sought to counter the situation created by the Reformation pastorally and at the same time to fight the Reformation theologically. The *doctrine* of grace and justification was described in detail in ways which can in fact be harmonized with Reformation teaching: justification was given a Christological basis, and grace was described as the means of obtaining justification. Like the Reformation, Trent subsumes grace in the doctrine of justification.

Despite vigorous controversies on grace in which again, at several centuries' remove, the medieval and Tridentine positions on grace were most violently debated and fanatically defended, the subsequent three centuries after Trent were distinguished in the Roman Catholic Church by a linguistic deficit and the absence of anything more to say, as the systems had lost any real relation to life, society and faith. Thus despite the Reformation, Trent had not been able to settle the medieval disputes; the effect of the biblical and Augustinian position adopted by Trent in the positive doctrinal texts (not in the condemnatory canons) was lost.

The 20th century. All the great 20th-century theological systems or schemes which arose after the destructive violence of the first world war had caused the collapse of the 19th century's optimistic belief in progress, have taken a radical, fresh look at theological thinking. They genuinely recognize their debt to the spirit of the biblical sources and take the greatest trouble to hold on to what is best in each confessional tradition in the light of these, even while they are aware of their indebtedness individually to quite a diversity of philosophical "systems" and even if — like Karl Barth — they deny such connections. Thus Protestant theology in German-speaking countries, in the great presentations of it by Karl Holl (and the Luther renaissance that followed him), Karl Barth, Emil Brunner, Rudolf Bultmann, Paul Tillich, Dietrich Bonhoeffer and others have all in their different ways tried hard to testify to the grace of God in Jesus Christ in faith and in the implementation of faith, thus placing enough "material" in the hands of the subsequent generation (Gerhard Ebeling, Eberhard Jüngel, Wolfhart Pannenberg and many others) for the independent work they are doing. Similarly, however, Protestant theology has also rescued Roman Catholic theology from its lethargy. So far, the only Roman Catholic theology genuinely comparable with the Protestant systems took the form of Karl Rahner's and Edward Schillebeeckx's theologies; nevertheless the earnest attention paid to grace in Latin American liberation theology is worthy of notice (Leonardo Boff).

An interconfessional controversy on grace which would have inevitably meant maintaining division in the churches has been automatically settled. Not least the violent convulsions of our century have played their part, calling theology inescapably to order, as has "acclimatization" to the ecumenical ties of all Christians. When "The Doctrine of Grace" was treated by Faith and Order in the 1930s, W.A. Brown recognized in his synthesis that, despite differences on justification, predestination, the church as locus of grace and the sacraments as means of grace, all bodies of Christians hold to "the conviction that man's welfare and happiness depend in the last analysis upon God and the conviction that God is moved to his gracious activity towards man by no merit on man's part but solely by a characteristic of his own nature which impels him to impart himself in free outgoing love". In 1984 the bilateral dialogue between the Lutheran World Federation and the World Methodist Council entitled its final report "The Church: A Community of Grace" and was able, despite differences of emphasis, to come to what it considered sufficient agreement on "salvation by grace through faith".

Those who, as believing Christians, cast an attentive eye once again over the high scholastic debate, the polemics of the 16th century and the bizarre controversy within the Roman Catholic Church in the 16th, 17th and early 18th centuries will stand ashamed at Christian history and with Paul will want to ask the contention-ridden fathers in the faith: "What have you that you did not receive?" (1 Cor. 4:7). Roman Catholic theology with its high scholastic, late scholastic, Tridentine and post-Tridentine teaching on grace therefore came to the end of the road because it no longer had any relation to reality and because its central concepts such as "preparation", *dispositio, qualitas*, "freedom", "merit", "co-operation", etc. even in their best form (e.g. that of Thomas Aquinas) meant in the linguistic usage of the time the exact opposite of what they normally convey in modern usage. To put the point more clearly, "freedom" in Thomas is the same as what Luther meant by the "bondage" of the will; "merit" in Thomas is not merit at all because it is an effect of grace and therefore no longer can be called merit; "co-operation" is a product of grace and therefore also is not co-operation, and so on.

A "re-reading" of Christian traditions in the light of the statements of holy scripture brings all Christians together before God, who has made himself freely available to us once for all in Jesus Christ. This gift is laid hold of in faith through the Spirit, as we hope for the divine consummation which will be effected at the eschaton and is attested here and now in love — as the work of the grace of God.

See also **redemption**.

JOHANNES BROSSEDER

L. Boff, *A graça libertadora no mundo* (ET *Liberating Grace*, Maryknoll, NY, Orbis, 1979) • A. Ganoczy, *Aus seiner Fülle haben wir alle empfangen: Grundriss der Gnadenlehre*, Düsseldorf, Patmos, 1989 • C. Moeller & G. Philips, *The Theology of Grace and the Ecumenical Movement*, London, Mowbray, 1961 • O.H. Pesch & A. Peters, *Einführung in die Lehre von Gnade und Rechtfertigung*, Darmstadt, Wiss. Buchgesellschaft, 1981 • G. Philips, *L'union personnelle avec le Dieu vivant*, 2nd ed., Louvain, University Press, 1989 • W.T. Whitley ed., *The Doctrine of Grace*, London, SCM, 1932.

GRAHAM, WILLIAM F. (Billy).

B. 7.11.1918, Charlotte, NC, USA. Probably the best-known evangelist of our times, Billy Graham has preached to millions of people around the world in person (during large, mostly urban crusades) and through radio, television and print. Ordained in 1940 by the Southern Baptist Convention, Graham graduated from Wheaton (Illinois) College and was a vice-president of Youth for Christ International when a 1949 evangelistic mission in Los Angeles launched him into national and then international prominence. Besides his evangelistic campaigns, weekly radio broadcast "Hour of Decision" and daily newspaper column "My Answer", Graham and his organization publish the monthly *Decision* magazine (in six languages and Braille), and he has written more than a dozen books, many of them best-sellers. Graham's abandonment of the separatist tradition of much of US fundamentalism — he invites a wide range of churches, including Roman Catholics, to collaborate in his crusades — has cost him support in some quarters. Others have faulted him for his close — and as they see it uncritical —

friendship with several US presidents, particularly Richard Nixon. Among the WCC assemblies and meetings he has attended was a ten-day consultation on "A Theology of Evangelism" at the Ecumenical Institute in Bossey (1958). During the 1980s he was instrumental in sponsoring two large international training conferences in Amsterdam for thousands of "itinerant evangelists", mostly from Africa, Asia and Latin America. Significant biographies of Graham include those by M. Frady (London, Hodder & Stoughton, 1979) and J. Pollock (Minneapolis, World Wide Publications, 1979).

ANS J. VAN DER BENT

GREGORIOS, PAULOS MAR (Paul Verghese).

B. 9.8.1922, Tripunithura, Kerala, India. Orthodox Syrian Church of the East's metropolitan of Delhi, and a president of the WCC, 1983-91, Gregorios was director of the WCC Division of Ecumenical Action and associate general secretary, 1962-67, observer at the Second Vatican Council, 1962-65, member of the Joint Working Group,* RCC-WCC, 1963-75, and of the Faith and Order* commission, 1968-75, moderator of the WCC Working Committee on Church and Society, 1975-83, and chairman of the world conference on "Faith, Science and the Future", MIT, Cambridge, 1979. He has studied in India, at Union and Princeton theological seminaries, Yale University, Oxford University, Gregory of Nyssa Institute, Münster, and at Serampore University, where he received a ThD in 1975. In India he was general secretary of the Orthodox Student Movement, 1955-57. He was personal adviser to Emperor Haile Selassie and executive secretary, Government Committee for Relief Aid, Ethiopia, 1956-59. He led the WCC delegation to UNESCO, 1966, to heads of African states, 1968, and to UN General Assembly special sessions on disarmament, 1983 and 1988. Secretary for Interchurch Relations, Orthodox Episcopal Synod, Gregorios is also principal of the Orthodox Theological Seminary, Kottayam, and director of the Delhi Orthodox Centre. He was joint organizer of the Oriental Orthodox-Eastern Orthodox conversations as well as joint chairman of the Indian Orthodox-Roman Catholic Joint Commission, Orthodox-Mar Thoma conversations and Orthodox-Lutheran conversations. He has been chief editor of the *Star of the East* and *Purohithan*; his publications include *The Gospel of the Kingdom* (Madras, Christian Literature Society, 1968), *The Human Presence* (WCC, 1978), *Science for Sane Societies* (Madras, Christian Literature Society, 1980) and *Cosmic Man* (New York, Paragon, 1988).

ANS J. VAN DER BENT

GROUPE DES DOMBES. The ecumenical Groupe des Dombes (the Dombes group) sprang from the initiative of Abbé Paul Couturier (d.1953), a priest in the diocese of Lyons, France, and a Roman Catholic pioneer of Christian unity, who in 1937 had the idea of meeting for a few days at the Cistercian abbey of Les Dombes, 40 km northeast of Lyon, with a group of Roman Catholic and Protestant friends, mainly pastors and priests, from France and Switzerland. For these men the purpose of meeting was to get to know one another better, by praying together and listening to one another in an atmosphere of love and friendship. Today, after 50 years of existence, the group comprises some 40 members. It meets every year at the beginning of September for three full days. After a long period of alternating between a Roman Catholic meeting place (Les Dombes) and a Protestant one (Présinge, Grandchamp, then Taizé), the group decided from 1971 on to meet every year at Les Dombes. The theological working sessions are interspersed and vitalized every day by three periods of prayer, including a morning eucharist service. These times of prayer are shared with the monks, one of whom participates in the group's theological work.

The life of the group can be divided into three stages. From 1937 to 1955 its members were engaged in getting to know one another and did not address the outside world. In the doctrinal field, they concentrated on comparative theological study (esp. justification* and redemption*), the sacraments* and the church.* They were trying to understand each other's positions better and rid themselves of the caricatures commonly given credence in their respective churches.

The years from 1956 to 1970 marked a second stage. By then the members of the group felt able to publish the results of their conversations in the form of a short series of theses. Thus they shifted from theological confrontation to collaboration. They left comparative theology behind and set about working out elements of a common theology. The subjects chosen were original sin,* the mediation of Christ and the church's ministry, the church* as the Body of Christ, pastoral authority, apostolicity,* the priesthood,* the doctrine of the Holy Spirit,* intercommunion,* the apostolic succession and the communion of saints.*

The third stage began in 1971 as the group's work gathered momentum. With the official entrance of the Roman Catholic Church into ecumenical discussions, and also in view of the urgent questions being asked by young people, the members of the group decided to move away from the rather specialized literary genre of theses presented to a limited audience and to produce instead documents of a wider scope presenting a doctrinal topic on which there was a precise, strong ecumenical agreement. Five brochures of this sort have been produced: *Vers une même foi eucharistique?* (Towards one eucharistic faith?, 1971), *Pour une réconciliation des ministères* (For a reconciliation of ministries, 1972), *Le ministère épiscopal* (The episcopal ministry, 1976), *L'Esprit-Saint, l'Eglise et les sacrements* (The Holy Spirit, the church and the sacraments, 1979), *Le ministère de communion dans l'Eglise universelle* (The ministry of communion in the universal church, 1985). To mark the group's 50th anniversary in 1987, all its output, both theses and documents, was assembled in a single volume under the title *Pour la communion des Eglises: L'apport du Groupe des Dombes (1937-87)* (Towards communion among the churches: The contribution of the Dombes group).

The theological method used by the Groupe des Dombes is based on the spiritual conviction that reconciliation* between the churches can come about only as the fruit of a process of conversion* on the part of the different confessions — converting one another and together being converted to God and his Christ. (The group is at present studying the theological dimension of such conversion in relation to confessional identity.) On this basis, the method used applies the principles of Christological focus (seeking the substance of the gospel in the light of the person of Christ), dogmatic focus (distinguishing the area of necessary unanimity in the faith from that of legitimate pluralism in systematic theology), and lastly, overcoming conflict by refining and combining ("to see together how to do justice to *all* the fundamental and essential demands, in a common truth that is not behind us, but ahead of us, in a Christianity that is spiritually purer and intellectually more demanding, but also more balanced", J. de Baciocchi).

The Groupe des Dombes is an independent group: it has no mandate from anyone, and the documents it produces have no authority apart from what they are able to command by their own worth. This private status enables it, however, to serve the churches as a force for new ideas, able to risk moving forward on doctrinal issues before official commissions are in a position to do so. The group's reputation has thus spread beyond the bounds of the French-speaking world (witness the various translations of its brochures). Its statements have often been picked up in the documents of special commissions, particularly those concerning the eucharist* and ministries. Texts published by the group are also used in ecumenical catechetical classes in parishes and Christian communities. In this way it fulfills its calling to serve ecumenical dialogue creatively in the field of doctrine.

BERNARD SESBOÜÉ

C.J. Dumont, "Eucharistie et ministères, à propos des accords des Dombes", *Istina*, 18, 2, 1973 • "Le Groupe des Dombes", *Unité des chrétiens*, 14, 1974 • Groupe des Dombes, *Pour la communion des Eglises, l'apport du Groupe des Dombes 1937-87*, Paris, Centurion, 1988 • H. Roux, *Interchurch Dialogue about Office: Interdenominational Dialogue in France*, New York, Seabury, 1972.

GROWTH, LIMITS TO. Since the beginning of the 20th century there have been warnings that the pattern of modern economic and industrial development, together with continuing population growth, was endangering the environment — the air, water, soil and living space on which human life depends, and that the wasteful use of natural resources would sooner or later bring "unacceptable consequences". These early warnings did not, however, weaken general confidence in the need for economic and industrial growth.

In the years between the two world wars the main social concerns in the industrially developed countries were justice in the distribution of the increasing wealth and income which economic growth made possible, and the threats to economic prosperity resulting from the periodic downturns in the business cycle, as in the great depression of the 1930s. After the second world war these issues were effectively addressed by the governments of the developed countries, ushering in a long period of prosperity with increasing social security and welfare, sustained by almost continuous economic growth and technological advance. At the same time, it was recognized that the poorer or developing countries needed to grow economically and industrially. The pressures on the environment and raw materials from this worldwide industrial expansion and economic growth led, however, to a new questioning of the assumptions of unlimited growth in a world of finite resources.

Moral theologians and social scientists in the rich countries noted that the emphasis on economic growth arose not only from the desire to meet basic human needs; in their view modern capitalism was creating an acquisitive consumer society based on ever-increasing technological power over nature. The Anglican V.A. Demant, in his book *Religion and the Decline of Capitalism* (1952), maintained that the capitalist system was leading to an unhealthy emphasis on the autonomy of economic life, glorifying the dynamics of individual economic achievement and stifling "the organic growth of human society". While Christian economists like R.H. Tawney and D.L. Munby challenged Demant's understanding of the market economy and the profit system, they agreed that the spirit of dynamic growth tended to become an end in itself: "Dynamism may be a blessing, but it may equally be a curse; outside a proper theological framework, the curse is likely to dominate" (Munby).

In his book *The Costs of Economic Growth* (1967), the English economist E.J. Mishan criticized modern "growth-mania", unchecked by serious regard for the increasing social costs or diseconomies arising from the single-minded emphasis on economic "progress". As a result, life in rural and urban areas was being robbed of its charm and pleasure. "With a hubris unmatched since the heyday of Victorian capitalism and with a blindness peculiar to our own time, we have abandoned ourselves to ransacking the most precious and irreplaceable good the earth provides, without thought to the desolation of the future and the deprivation of prosperity."

Later, other economists, notably E.F. Schumacher, author of *Small Is Beautiful*, also challenged the moral and philosophical assumptions of the liberal capitalist society. "In the excitement over the unfolding of his scientific and technical powers, modern man has built a system of production that ravishes nature and a type of society that mutilates man. If only there were more and more wealth, everything else, it is thought, would fall into place... This is the philosophy of materialism... which is now being challenged by events."

In the early 1970s the "limits to growth" debate entered a new phase when an international group of scientists, economists, engineers and business and political leaders formed the so-called Club of Rome to focus attention on "the Predicament of Mankind", as a global problem resulting from accelerating industrialization, rapid population growth, widespread malnutrition, depletion of non-renewable resources and a deteriorating environment. Drawing on the technical facilities and talent of research centres like MIT, they sponsored studies on *World Dynamics* (1971) and *Limits to Growth* (1972), using the new techniques of computer modelling to estimate the future consequences of present technological and economic trends. Their studies were criticized for making invalid predictions. In fact the book *Limits to Growth* did not predict but extrapolated from present trends, and the extrapolations turned out to be much closer to what has happened than the critics suggested. The book was also criticized for treating the world as one unit. That was rectified in the subsequent book *Mankind at the Turning Point* (1974). These studies did encourage much new thinking about the exponential consequences of economic-growth policies, the urgency of addressing the problems of world pollution, limits to resources, and overpopulation, and the need to challenge a widespread overconfidence in technological solutions to them.

The WCC and its member churches joined in the discussion of these issues in a study programme on "The Future of Humanity and Society in a World of Science-based Technology", begun in 1969. Over the ensuing two decades this resulted in a series of ecumenical studies and findings in which theologians, technologists and scientists offered their views on the moral and spiritual issues posed by (1) the scientific-technological advances in biotechnology and the resulting "manipulation of life", (2) nuclear energy and the over-riding problem of energy for the future, (3) population growth and its impact on the human and physical environment in rich and poor countries, (4) the pollution of the environment and the threat to human life, (5) the social and political implications of limiting growth worldwide and the need to work for the "sustainable society", and (6) the philosophical assumptions of modern science and technology and the critique of these from various theological and ethical perspectives. Ecumenical reflection on these themes was summed up in two international ecumenical conferences: Bucharest (1974) and MIT (Cambridge, USA, 1979). The findings of these meetings presented the churches with new perspectives on the future of society, leading to new agreement and new controversy. From the beginning many Christians from the third world viewed the questioning of modern science and technology and the concern for nature and the environment as deliberate distractions from the problem of social justice, which they perceived as the central issue. There has been disagreement also about the relation of these new concerns to the political and ideological systems which many held to be responsible for the misuse of technology and the natural environment. As one of the early consultations reported on its discussion of the relation of political systems and the use of natural resources (Nemi 1971): "Some say the fault in the current gross inequality is the profit system, which encourages the production of unnecessary items by catering to consumers' whims, and which must be replaced before lasting corrections can be accomplished. Some believe socialist countries are also wasteful as well as being poor contributors to the development of the third world. Some argue that the market mechanism can meet the needs of the developing countries... And some see little hope for substantial progress until international agencies control the allocation of resources."

Ecumenical disagreement on such issues continues today and was in part responsible for the inability of the WCC world convocation on "Justice, Peace and the Integrity of Creation" (Seoul 1990) to arrive at a common understanding either of the "realities we face" or of the "theological and ethical affirmations" which would enable the churches to unite in common Christian witness and action. This failure makes it evident that one of the most difficult challenges for the ecumenical movement in the 1990s will be finding a way to continue reflection and action on these highly complex and contentious issues which continue to divide both church and world.

See also **capitalism, development, economics**.

PAUL ABRECHT

Faith and Science in an Unjust World, report of MIT 1979, 2 vols, WCC, 1980 • D.L. Munby, *Christianity and Economic Problems*, London, Macmillan, 1965 • "Science and Technology for Human Development", report of Bucharest 1974, *Anticipation* (WCC), 19, 1974 • "Three Reports from Church and Society", report of Nemi 1971, *Study Encounter*, 7, 3, 1971.

GRUBB, KENNETH. B. 9.9.1900, Oxton, England; d. 3.6.1980. An Anglo-Irishman, Grubb took great interest in getting to know the unknown lands of Amazonia and the Andes, as well as other areas of Latin America, and wrote several books which were indispensable for missionary policy and work. During the second world war, he was controller of overseas publicity of the British Ministry of Information. From 1946 to 1968 he was chairman of the Commission of the Churches on International Affairs (CCIA).

Grubb was involved as member or officer of numerous bodies in church, mission, business and world affairs, including the Church Missionary Society, Unevangelized Fields Mission, the British Council of Churches, the British and Foreign Bible Society, the United Society for Christian Literature, the Institute of Rural Life at Home and Overseas, the London-based institutes for international affairs, race relations and strategic studies. In the post-war period through the CCIA he

represented the concern of the churches to governments and to the United Nations. On issues of human rights* in Latin America and Europe, he was the chief spokesperson of the churches to governments. He also tackled the issues of the arms race and disarmament on behalf of the churches and helped pioneer the *World Christian Handbook*. In 1971 he published his autobiography, *Crypts of Power* (London, Hodder & Stoughton, 1971).

ANS J. VAN DER BENT

GUTIÉRREZ, GUSTAVO.
B. 8.6.1928, Lima, Peru. Roman Catholic priest and theologian, Gutiérrez is widely honoured as "the father of liberation theology"* — a term he coined in 1968 for the reflection on ministry in solidarity with the poor* which he and other Latin American priests and pastoral workers began in the 1960s. His own seminal work *A Theology of Liberation* was published in Spanish in 1971; its 1973 English translation sold more than 100,000 copies. Though he has been criticized by political and theological conservatives, especially for the Marxist elements in his thought, Gutiérrez, unlike some other controversial contemporary Catholic theologians, has avoided the language and spirit of defiance, agreeing that theology is produced in and for the church* and that there is thus a legitimate function for church authority* in the process. Responding to the critical "Instructions" on liberation theology (1984 and 1986) from the Vatican Congregation for the Doctrine of the Faith, Gutiérrez said that they contained "relevant observations" and stimulated him both to make some corrections and to find phraseology less susceptible to misunderstanding.

Since publishing *A Theology of Liberation*, Gutiérrez's interest in social, economic and political analysis has lessened, and his interest in biblical and theological questions increased — as the title of his 1983 book *We Drink from Our Own Wells* (English, 1984) indicates. His primary concern is not politics or elaboration of a theory, secular or religious: "I am above all a pastor." He serves a poor parish in the historic Rimac section of Lima; he has limited his teaching (at Lima's Catholic University) to students not taking degrees in theology.

ANS J. VAN DER BENT

HARTFORD APPEAL. The Hartford appeal ("An Appeal for Theological Affirmation") emerged from a three-day unofficial ecumenical consultation of theologians at the Hartford Seminary Foundation (Connecticut) in January 1975. Sociologist Peter L. Berger and Richard John Neuhaus initiated the meeting and prepared a preliminary draft for discussion. In its final and thoroughly revised form, the appeal called for theological response to 13 current themes in religious thought that were deemed to be "pervasive, false, and debilitating to the church's life and work". The key problem, said Hartford, is the "loss of transcendence" in religious thought. The rejected themes included the following: "Religious language refers to human experience and nothing else, God being humanity's noblest creation" (no. 3); "Since what is human is good, evil can adequately be understood as failure to realize potential" (no. 7); "The world must set the agenda for the church. Social, political and economic programmes to improve the quality of life are ultimately normative for the church's mission in the world" (no. 10); and "The question of hope beyond death is irrelevant or at best marginal to the Christian understanding of human fulfilment" (no. 13). Among the signers of the appeal were Elizabeth Bettenhausen, William Sloane Coffin, Avery Dulles, George W. Forell, Stanley Hauerwas, Thomas Hopko, George A. Lindbeck, Richard J. Mouw, Carl J. Peter, Alexander Schmemann, George H. Tavard, Bruce Vawter and Robert Wilken.

The appeal received intense popular and scholarly attention, especially in the US and Europe. The general press opined that Hartford might portend "a new reformation", while scholars such as Wolfhart Pannenberg of Munich hailed it as a necessary critique of both fundamentalist obscurantism and liberal secularization. Hartford also provoked a number of counter-statements, notably "the Boston Affirmation", which claimed that Hartford had short-changed Christian social responsibility.

The Hartford signers met again in the fall of 1975 and issued a book of commentaries on the appeal, *Against the World for the World*. In addition to the text of the appeal, the book contains essays by Berger, Lindbeck, Dulles, Forell, Peter, Mouw, Schmemann and Neuhaus. The text of the appeal is available also in *A Documentary History of Religion in America*.

RICHARD JOHN NEUHAUS

Against the World for the World, New York, Seabury, 1976 • E.S. Gaustad ed., *A Documentary History of Religion in America*, vol. 2, Grand Rapids, MI, Eerdmans, 1983.

HEALTH AND HEALING. Many of the laws of the ancient Hebrews dealt with health matters. Healing was a major activity in Jesus' earthly ministry. He sent his disciples out to teach, preach and heal. Christians, since the days of Peter and Paul, have been involved in health ministry in various ways. This ministry figured prominently in the missionary enterprise of the last two centuries.

In modern times two ecumenical consultations in Tübingen, Federal Republic of Germany, organized jointly by the WCC and the Lutheran World Federation, focused in 1964 on medical missions in the third world and in 1968 on the role of the church in healing. The Christian Medical Commission (CMC) was created within the WCC in 1968 to assist the member churches to deal with questions being raised about these subjects and to encourage church-related health programmes to develop ecumenical co-operation.

During CMC's early years emphasis was placed on the promotion of primary health care as a means of redressing the imbalance between sophisticated and expensive institutional medical care for a few and hardly any for the rest. But during the same period growing dissatisfaction with the so-called garage-mechanic approach in modern medicine made Christian groups in many countries begin to search for a health care which more fully addressed the needs of the whole person.

The WCC fifth assembly in Nairobi in 1975 mandated the CMC to "serve as an enabling organization to churches everywhere as they search for an understanding of health and healing which is distinctive to the Christian faith". The central committee in 1976 directed CMC "to set up and develop a means for sustained enquiry, description and reflection concerning the connections between health, being human, the community and the kingdom of God".

In response to this mandate, the CMC embarked on a programme to study "Health, Healing and Wholeness" in 1978. Rather than make the exploration an academic exercise centred in Geneva, CMC took the study to the grassroots. Over the next ten years, ten regional consultations held in Trinidad, Honduras, Botswana, India, Indonesia, Papua New Guinea, Ecuador, USA, Hungary and Japan brought together over 800 pastors, theologians, and health workers to discuss the Christian perspective on health. During the course of the study, presentations were made to the WCC central committee meeting in

Dresden (1981) and the WCC sixth assembly in Vancouver (1983). In July 1989, in Moscow, the final report was presented to the central committee.

The study affirmed clearly that health is not primarily medical. Although the modern "health industry" is producing and using progressively refined and expensive technology, most of the world's health problems cannot be best addressed in this way. The causes of disease in the world are social, economic, political and spiritual, as well as bio-medical. It is an acknowledged fact that the greatest cause of disease in the world is poverty, which is ultimately the result of oppression, exploitation and war. Providing immunizations, medicines, and even health education by standard methods cannot significantly reduce illness due to poverty. The churches were called on to see this as a justice issue to be raised in the centres of power — local, national, regional and global.

Deaths due to armed conflicts and other forms of political violence, and the threat of nuclear annihilation hanging over the entire globe, are also major determinants of illness. Another significant proportion of illness in the world is self-inflicted. What we impose on ourselves individually and collectively — whether out of ignorance, greed, or simply lack of self-control — causes physical, mental, spiritual and ecological damage which is not sufficiently addressed by medical technology.

Most important to health is the spiritual dimension. Unresolved guilt, anger and resentment, and meaninglessness are now being found by medical science to be very potent suppressors of the body's powerful, health-controlling immune system, while loving relationships in community are among its strongest augmenters. Those in loving harmony with God and neighbour not only stay healthier but survive tragedy or suffering best and grow stronger in the process. When we choose the spiritual dimension of life, we opt for the abundant life which is wholeness — life experienced and enjoyed as a gift of God. As persons come to trust in God's unconditional love, they are freed to love each other so they can come together, freely confessing and forgiving, in a healing community.

The development of modern scientific medicine has led to the depersonalization of medical care and an emphasis on curing rather than caring. The impressive achievements of science have led many of the churches to abdicate the Lord's mandate to be in healing ministry. Since wholeness of life is a central issue of the Christian gospel, the churches have an important role to play in leading a movement towards the development of a comprehensive health care system in which all aspects of health have an appropriate place — which is focused not only on saving lives but on wholeness of life.

DAVID HILTON

Healing and Wholeness: the Churches' Role in Health, WCC/CMC, 1990 • J.C. McGilvray, *The Quest for Health and Wholeness*, Tübingen, German Institute for Medical Missions, 1981 • "The Principles and Practice of Primary Health Care", *Contact*, special series no. 1, 1979.

HEALTH CARE. Concern about health care within the ecumenical movement has two main origins: on the one hand, the diakonia* and social service programmes of churches and parishes in the western world, and on the other hand, church-related health care activities that grew out of medical mission programmes, mostly in developing countries. The former have old roots in the command to heal and comprise everything from individual action to large hospitals or institutions for the aged or infirm. Many churches have ministries of deacons and deaconesses (see **diaconate**) as well as lay activities for ordinary parishioners. Health care as part of overseas missionary efforts has mainly been expressed as medical care of the sick in institutions. Training of nurses, doctors and other health workers has played an important role. The underlying concepts of the churches' involvement in health care have varied considerably, and the forms it has taken have been influenced by the prevailing health and social policies in the country of action or, in cases where such activities were initiated by missionaries, in their country of origin.

A natural emphasis on health care as an essential part of the life and witness of every local Christian congregation has often been overshadowed by a preoccupation with larger institutions, which tend to become removed from the day-to-day life of the church and ordinary Christians. Such institutions have nevertheless been an important witness and sign of the kingdom of God* in many societies and countries.

Church-related medical and health services have undergone changes as a result of both theological deliberation and new thinking in health care and medical services. Now there is more interest in developing both health policy per se and also social policy and practice. The ten-year study on "Health, Healing and Wholeness" of the WCC's Christian Medical Commission contributed significantly to this process of reflection. The deliberations have been actively pursued in some churches and congregations.

In addition, new administrative relations and financial difficulties have forced churches to re-think their involvement in health care. An increasing involvement of central and local government in health care has meant in many places relinquishing church ownership, finding different forms of co-ordination and collaboration with the authorities or abandoning former church-related health care institutions. In addition to increased collaboration with different authorities and secular agencies, the new situation has led to increased ecumenical collaboration or at least co-ordination in health care. Ecumenical mechanisms for co-ordination and co-operation have been established on a local, regional or national basis in order to pool and share resources and to develop new activities, or in some instances simply to survive with inherited institutions.

An open mind and relevant response to existing needs, which truly defy all boundaries, have brought about many examples of ecumenical collaboration that have had a positive impact in the areas jointly recognized. Whereas the churches' health care involvement originally focused mainly on the care of the sick, medical care today is supplemented by broader programmes of health education, health promotion and rehabilitation.

The churches' experience in the care of tuberculosis and leprosy patients has influenced not only church-related health care but also more globally important developments in these areas. Many church-related health care programmes aimed at mothers and children in rural areas of developing countries have become models for such activities of other agencies and governments. The churches' involve-

A Roman Catholic nun serving in Brazil (epd-bild/Neetz)

ment in literacy programmes and different types of education has proved the positive effect of education on the health status of people. Care of the suffering and dying has provided examples of a humane approach to areas all too often otherwise neglected or badly handled. Many hospices for the terminally ill have a church relation or are to a large extent staffed by Christians.

The move towards less and less institutional ownership of health care facilities has been more marked in the industrial countries, but there are quite a number of originally church-related institutions run by churches but largely financed by governments. This is true also in socialist and centrally planned countries, where recent developments have opened up new opportunities for church involvement, both within institutions and in the community, e.g. in the care of the elderly. In some developing countries the churches are responsible for the operation of many hospitals of different sizes as well as health centres, clinics and dispensaries, for which the authorities are providing different degrees of support. Similar arrangements for joint ownership or for common support or staffing are made for teaching institutions for nurses, doctors and different levels of other health care personnel.

The churches' role in health care is continuously being discussed and developed as part of the outreach of the church to the community and nation,* i.e. as part of the mission* of the church. A good proportion of the resources available to different interchurch aid agencies goes to health care programmes. This is often done in collaboration with or through the direct use of funds from government aid agencies that favour the use of church-related channels for at least a part of their resources. Some churches readily accept this kind of joint venture, whereas others do not. Health care practice and theological understanding need common reflection and inter-related implementation.

For larger tasks several congregations join together in order to form a broader support base. In the same way several churches can support large institutions if it is considered appropriate for the role and witness of the churches. In many countries church-related co-ordinating agencies support the churches' involvement in health care, and the WCC's Christian Medical Commission has frequently been involved in this area of work.

There are also examples of international

ecumenical action and support programmes, e.g. when several churches and missionary societies in industrial countries join each other to form joint support programmes with and for churches and their health care programmes in developing countries. Many church agencies collaborate with WHO, UNICEF and other international agencies at local, national and global levels in support of health care programmes.

See also **health and healing, life and death**.

HÅKAN HELLBERG

J. Bryant, *Health and the Developing World*, Ithaca, NY, Cornell UP, 1969 • J.H. Hellberg, *Community Health and the Church*, WCC, 1971 • J.C. McGilvray, *The Quest for Health and Wholeness*, Tübingen, German Institute for Medical Missions, 1981 • K.W. Newell, *Health by the People*, Geneva, WHO, 1975 • M. Scheel, *Partnerschaftliches Heilen*, Stuttgart, Verlagswerk der Diakonie, 1986.

HERESY. The word comes from the Greek *hairesis* and, in its original sense, means choice or preference — hence, opinion, party. The Acts of the Apostles often uses it in the sense of sect — that of the Pharisees (15:5), that of the Sadducees (5:17), etc. The apostle Paul, using this word, protests that the Christian church is not a sect but a "way" (Acts 24:14). When divisions begin to emerge in the church (1 Cor. 11:19), he protests, considering heresies as the fruits of sin (Gal. 5:20; Titus 3:10). In 2 Pet. 2:1 we find the sense which was to be generally used in the church: an error which leads to perversion of the faith* and corruption of the Christian life (cf. Matt. 7:15; Jude).

The church was made particularly aware of the idea of heresy by the serious crisis caused by the Arian heresy in the 4th century. Arius, a priest at Alexandria, denied the divinity of Christ and hence also the divine dimension of the church* and the reality of salvation.* He was condemned by the first ecumenical council (Nicea 325*), which recognized the Son of God as consubstantial with the Father, but the Arian heresy initiated a period of controversies and disturbances in the church and in the empire, with sequels which lingered until after the second ecumenical council (Constantinople 381*). As the church experienced several major heresies in the East (Nestorianism,

monophysitism, monothelitism, etc.) and others in the West, Christian doctrine came to distinguish heresy (1) from schism,* which likewise involved separation from the community of the church, a result not of doctrinal disagreement but of problems of discipline, ritual or obedience to hierarchical authority (canon 1 of Basil the Great); and (2) from apostasy,* in that apostates leave the church community, abandoning the name of Christian and all their beliefs. Heretics, however, by remaining or calling themselves Christian yet rejecting certain truths of the faith, injure the unity* of the church by damaging the unity of its doctrine, which is one of its essential marks.

The church has thus traditionally dealt severely with heresy. The second canon of the second ecumenical council declares that heresy is to be punished by excommunication.* Ancient canon law* does not recognize baptism* and ordination* administered by heretics. Marriage with heretics is, in principle, forbidden. A bishop cannot be a heretic; in case of heresy, his people are called upon to withhold their obedience.

The traditional conception of heresy poses a number of problems in the quest for Christian unity and ecumenical dialogue. Are the causes of the division that took place between the churches of East and West in 1054, or that in the 16th century with the Protestant Reformation, to be called heresy or schism? Does the quest for Christian unity mean the restoration of dogmatic unity, or simply reconciliation among the churches? What is to be done in cases where the condemnation of doctrines also involved the condemnation of individuals who have subsequently been canonized by their own communities? This is the problem between the Chalcedonian and non-Chalcedonian Orthodox. Time and theological reflection have reduced many of the Christological divergences between them, but the council of Chalcedon pronounced anathema* against Dioscorus of Alexandria and Severus of Antioch, who are venerated as saints* by the non-Chalcedonians, whereas the latter anathematized Pope Leo the Great, whom both Orthodox and Catholics regard as a great saint and father of the church.

The same problem arises over the question of how heretics are to be received into the traditional churches. In general the baptism received is recognized when administered by a community which recognizes this sacrament, the dogma of the Holy Trinity* and the divinity of Jesus Christ* (the sacrament of chrismation is, however, then conferred on those who have not received that sacrament). The same recognition applies to the sacrament of orders received in communities which have this sacrament and also apostolic succession. But the Pidalion, the official canonical book of the Greek church, and the practice of Mount Athos demand re-baptism for those coming to Orthodoxy from other Christian confessions, which amounts to denying the church status of these communities and poses the problem of the oneness of Christian baptism.

ALEXIS KNIAZEFF

HERMENEUTICS. The question of the interpretation of scripture* has been at the heart of the ecumenical dialogue (see **dialogue, intrafaith**) from the beginning of the modern search for Christian unity.* Ecumenical discussions of issues related to the interpretation of the Bible hold their own with recent developments in philosophical hermeneutics (Hans-Georg Gadamer, Paul Ricoeur et al.), while these developments have in turn shaped the way in which Christian dialogue *with* and *about* scripture has come to be understood (note, for example, the introduction of the terminology of "fusion of horizons"). These reciprocal effects of hermeneutical research and ecumenical dialogue can be seen not only in ongoing discussions of Faith and Order* but also in the internal discussions within Roman Catholicism and Protestantism as well as in the Anabaptist and Orthodox Christian traditions.

Discussions in Faith and Order. In the years following the second world war, many ecumenists were optimistic that the Bible itself could provide the much-desired thematic unity needed for the recovery of unity among the churches. At a F&O conference held in Wadham College, Oxford, in 1949, the influence of "biblical theology" was clearly in evidence. Not only was the thematic unity of the Old and New Testaments presupposed, but this was combined with a confessing theology to underwrite a renewed emphasis on ecumenism.

But within a decade, participants began to realize that the problem was more complex than Wadham had acknowledged. The theoretical consensus proved vulnerable at the point of practical application. Soon scholars again had to contend with the important ways in which ecclesial traditions* served to define biblical interpretation. Subsequent discussions of F&O began to focus on different understandings of the relation of scripture and Tradition, leading up to the report of the fourth world conference on F&O (Montreal 1963) on "Scripture, Tradition and Traditions". The differentiation between the great Tradition (with a capital *T*) and particular ecclesial, confessional or denominational traditions (each with a small *t*) helped make way for the discussion of the diverse expressions of the one gospel. This development in turn made it possible to conceive of a more dynamic view of the relationship of Tradition and scripture. "Tradition" and "scripture" are not two independent entities. Rather, scripture can be understood to be the internal norm of Tradition, and Tradition itself must be seen to be the proper context for reading scripture: "Thus we can say that we exist as Christians by the Tradition of the gospel (the *paradosis* of the *kerygma*) testified in scripture, transmitted in and by the church through the power of the Holy Spirit. Tradition taken in this sense is actualized in the preaching of the word, in the administration of sacraments and worship, in Christian teaching and theology, and in mission and witness to Christ by the lives of the members of the church."

After Montreal, fresh attempts were made in F&O to explore the hermeneutical significance of these new proposals. About the same time, debates about the diversity of the Bible, particularly the diversity of ecclesiologies in the NT (found in the clash between Ernst Käsemann and Raymond Brown at Montreal), led to a deeper sense that the "biblical theology" consensus of Wadham was rather uncritical in its attribution of thematic unity to the biblical witness. Still worse, the interpretative rules of biblical exegesis* which Wadham had confidently announced no longer appeared adequate. The F&O Bristol report on "The Significance of the Hermeneutical Problem for the Ecumenical Movement" (1967) sought to eschew theological presuppositions, emphasizing the literary and *human* character of the Bible as a collection of writings. One of the results of this report was a clear shift in the way inspiration* of scripture is understood; no longer a matter of dogmatic presupposition, the inspiration of scripture comes to be understood as a conclusion of faith* which arises out of the church's experience.

By the 1971 F&O Louvain report on "The Authority of the Bible", the emphasis on diversity resulted in the proposal of "relational" understanding of biblical authority* in place of the earlier claims of a "material centre" (Sachmitte). In keeping with the claims of Montreal, the Louvain report refuses to specify a specific centre of scripture as the hermeneutical key for the interpretation of the whole but instead suggests the idea of a number of "relational centres" (Beziehungs-mitten). These proposals led to speculation about the "prolongation" in the church of the "interpretative process" which can be found in scripture itself: as canonical scripture (see **canon**) itself is the product of fresh interpretations of earlier traditions, so the scriptures invite and require continuing interpretation in the church. By re-opening the issue of the nature of biblical authority, this proposal was also implicitly raising ecclesiological issues: e.g. who is given the authority to interpret scripture?

Discussions of the 1970s and 1980s have focused on four specific issues: (1) "the significance of the Old Testament in relation to the New" (Loccum 1971); (2) the use of scripture in the liturgy* of the churches as well as in the devotional life of Christians (thereby counteracting a one-sidedly intellectualist approach to the Bible); (3) the growing awareness of the experience of Christians in Africa and Latin America, which emphasizes the contemporaneity of scripture interpretation in third-world contexts; and (4) the growing recognition of the greater variety of interpretative strategies, including structuralist literary criticism and the emerging discussion of political hermeneutics, as these in turn raise questions for biblical interpretation.

Hermeneutical developments in representative traditions. It will be helpful to outline separately the recent hermeneutical directions of various Christian traditions.

*Orthodoxy:** The contribution of the Eastern Orthodox communions to the discussion of hermeneutical issues can be seen since 1945. Perhaps nowhere is this more visible than in the discussions of Tradition and the traditions (Montreal 1963). Not so well known is the important contribution to hermeneutics which a new generation of Orthodox biblical scholars, theologians and literary critics is making in "the Orthodox diaspora".

For example, Benedict Englezakis (1972) has called attention to the complex relationship between tradition and prophecy* (as mediated by the Holy Spirit) in the biblical witness. Rejecting a positivist application of historical criticism to the Bible, Englezakis argues that "the 'riddle of the New Testament' can never be solved except in the Holy Spirit.* It is a historical fact that these documents claim to be incomprehensible outside the light of the Spirit, and this is the predicament of the New Testament historian" (*New and Old in God's Revelation*, 1972).

John Breck's *The Power of the Word in the Worshipping Church* (1986) and Thomas Hopko's earlier influential essay "The Bible in the Orthodox Church" (in his *All the Fullness of God*, 1982) both exhibit the importance of the liturgical context for the investigation of hermeneutical issues. As Hopko has noted, it is one of the paradoxes of Orthodox hermeneutics that the revelation of St John the Divine is not included in the cycle of readings for public worship, yet it is indispensable for explicating the liturgical setting of Orthodox worship.

One of the most promising contributions to emerge out of the Orthodox diaspora is that of Anthony Ugolnik. Ugolnik's essay on "An Orthodox Hermeneutic in the West" (*St Vladimir's Theological Quarterly*, 27, 1983) offers a striking account of the literary and theological divergence between Eastern and Western Christian use of the Bible. Contrary to the Western "textualist" tradition of hermeneutics, Ugolnik points to the communal or *sobornost** dimension of Orthodox hermeneutics. In his *The Illuminating Icon*, Ugolnik has extended this line of argument, drawing on the works of Romanian theologian Dumitru Staniloae as well as the literary theories of Mikhail Bakhtin. Ugolnik's explication of the ways in which Tradition "lives" in the present as "dialogue" goes beyond the arguments of the previous generation of Orthodox theologians, even as it also draws on the writings of

Vladimir Lossky, Alexander Schmemann and Staniloae.

A further strength of Ugolnik's study is that he is attentive to the ways in which political ideology (East vs West polarities, etc.) frequently distorts discussions of hermeneutics as well as ecumenism. By calling attention to the problem in this way, Ugolnik moves the discussion of hermeneutics out of the common polarities tradition vs scripture, Tradition vs the traditions, and relocates it in the "politics" of the ecclesial tradition itself. Certainly, Ugolnik's explication of the communal character of Orthodox hermeneutics has great potential for defusing several tired debates in Western hermeneutics.

Roman Catholicism: Since 1970, theological ferment has characterized Roman Catholic discussion of hermeneutics. On the one hand, Joseph Cardinal Ratzinger has urged that "we must learn to read the documents which have been handed down to us according to the hermeneutics of unity". On the other hand, Latin American liberation theologians (Leonardo Boff, Gustavo Gutiérrez) have called for renewed emphasis on the ways in which scripture nurtures political responses to oppression. While fuller explication of both these approaches is needed, it is especially noteworthy that Catholic discussions of hermeneutics have also moved beyond the so-called two sources impasse (scripture vs Tradition). More dynamic categories of analysis also suggest opportunities for renewed hermeneutical investigation within both scripture and Tradition.

Among the most intriguing proposals on the current scene is Nicholas Lash's "performative" hermeneutic as explicated in several essays from his *Theology on the Way to Emmaus.* Lash argues against the stark historical separation of "what the text meant" and "what the text means", preferring a more interactive understanding of exegesis and interpretation. He contends that the "fundamental form of the *Christian* interpretation of scripture is the life, activity and organization of the believing community... Christian practice as interpretative action consists in the performance of texts which are construed as 'rendering', bearing witness to, one whose words and deeds, discourse and suffering 'rendered' the truth of God in human history." Still further, Lash claims that Christian living, "construed as the interpretative performance of scripture", is a *collaborative* enterprise. Lash asserts: "The poles of interpretation are not, in the last analysis, written texts... but patterns of human action: we talk of 'holy' scripture, and for good reason. And yet it is not, in fact, the *script* that is 'holy' but the people: the company that performs the script." Following up this reference with an analogy to *King Lear*, Lash concludes: "There are some texts the fundamental form of which is a full-time affair because it consists in their enactment as the social existence of an entire community. The scriptures, I suggest, are such texts... The performance of scripture *is* the life of the church" ("The Performance of Scripture", 42-44).

Catholic discussion of hermeneutical issues has also been enriched by the growing movement of church base communities* in Latin America, where the use of the Bible among the poor has coincided with the renewal of the church's witness. Ernesto Cardenal's four volumes of *The Gospel in Solentiname* recount the ongoing engagement of the *campesinos* of the village of Solentiname (Nicaragua) with the Bible. While some of the most intriguing discussions of scripture in these volumes arise out of puzzlement of the villagers when they disagree about how to interpret scripture, these volumes also demonstrate that scripture has become a source of unity in the struggle for freedom in Latin America, where Protestant and Catholic alike find themselves victims of oppression. More academically formulated has been the "materialist" reading of scripture associated with José Porfirio Miranda, or (less ideologically phrased) the "socio-economic" interpretation.

Post-Vatican II Roman Catholicism has also been encouraged by a remark of Pope John XXIII: "The substance of the ancient doctrine of the deposit of faith is one thing, and the way in which it is presented is another." In light of this distinction, Roman Catholics have increasingly been willing to extend the range of the hermeneutical question to include post-biblical pronouncements by the councils of the church and other instances of its magisterium (see **teaching authority**). Such re-assessment has in turn evoked new responses from Protestant ecumenists. For example, as a result of his experiences in Roman Catholic-Lutheran dialogue, George Lindbeck was stimulated to propose his ecumenically provocative "rule theory" of doctrine, whereby official dogmas* are to be principally taken as regulating Christian discourse rather than being regarded primarily in terms of their substantive content (*The Nature of Doctrine*, 1984).

Protestantism: A generation ago, the contribution of Rudolf Bultmann ("Is Exegesis without Presuppositions Possible?") preoccupied Protestant hermeneutical discussions. The so-called new hermeneutic of Erich Fuchs, Gerhard Ebeling and James M. Robinson led to increased concern about the relationship of the language of the Bible to the historical character of Christian existence. Bultmann's programme of "demythologization" was also attacked by theologians and biblical scholars influenced by Karl Barth for its lack of "biblical realism" (Hendrik Kraemer) as well as for the existentialist hermeneutic upon which it was built.

More recently, Peter Stuhlmacher has argued that historical criticism itself requires a kind of "hermeneutics of consent" in order to avoid the errors of positivism to which many 19th-century historical critics of the Bible fell prey. Taking Adolf Schlatter as a model and drawing on the insights of Ebeling and Gadamer among others, Stuhlmacher insists upon a "critical dialogue" with the biblical tradition. Such a dialogue will take into account not only the "history of the effects" (Gadamer's *Wirkungsgeschichte*) of the Bible as a text but also the sense in which "the biblical tradition supports, empowers and limits our life at one and the same time". This line of argument has been continued in Stuhlmacher's book *Vom Verstehen des Neuen Testaments: Eine Hermeneutik* (1986). Meanwhile the French Protestant Paul Ricoeur has recalled attention to the multivalence of symbols, which provokes thought ("le symbole donne à penser") and enjoins the "conflict of interpretations".

Along with the renewed sense of the critical task as arising from within the biblical tradition itself, there is in fact a growing awareness among Protestants of the inadequacy of the "modernist" attempt to identify the singular meaning of biblical pericopes. Not only is a case put forward for "The Superiority of Pre-Critical Exegesis" (David Steinmetz, 1980; reprinted in his *Memory and Mission*, 1988),

but there is also more interest among Protestants in overcoming the dichotomous separation of scripture from Tradition, and the gospel from the life of the church. In fact, recent developments point to a renewed awareness of the dialectical relationship of scripture and Tradition among Protestants, suggesting the kind of convergence noted by Cardinal Ratzinger's proposal for a "hermeneutics of unity".

Among several positive proposals worthy of note is Geoffrey Wainwright's discussion of "liturgy as a hermeneutical continuum" (*Doxology*, 1980), within which scripture is rightly interpreted for the life of the church. Wainwright's proposal is noteworthy because he applies the ancient principle of lex orandi, lex credendi in two directions at once: the primacy of scripture remains, but the ecumenical liturgical tradition serves to lend diachronic continuity to the synchronic experience of the church as it gathers to hear the word.

Anabaptism: The contribution of Anabaptist hermeneutics to the ecumenical movement has only begun to be noticed in the 1980s, but since the 1960s the scholarship of the US Mennonite theological ethicist John Howard Yoder and the Canadian historian and NT scholar William Klassen has prepared the way for this recognition. Building on the historical investigations of 16th-century Anabaptists, such as Klassen's study of Pilgram Marpeck, and on his own studies of Balthasar Hubmaier's writings, Yoder has demonstrated how the "rule of Christ" (Matt. 18:15-20) and the "rule of Paul" (1 Cor. 14:29) functioned hermeneutically among 16th-century Anabaptist communities. In so doing, he has also helped to dispel misunderstandings of the Anabaptist tradition while also engaging in ecumenical dialogue regarding the use of scripture in ethics.

Yoder's careful explication of the Anabaptist "hermeneutics of community" arising out of such community-specific practices as the process of "binding and loosing" has also been provocative for theologians outside the Anabaptist tradition, despite the fact that Yoder's emphasis on the synchronic gathering of the ecclesia sometimes appears to call into question the viability of the diachronic dimension of the greater ecumenical tradition. Indeed, Yoder strongly dissents from the cultural model of "Tradition and traditions" which emerged from the discussions of the F&O commission at Montreal (1963). But at the same time, it must also be said that Yoder has called attention to the biblical mandate for visible unity of the church as a political community before the world. Particularly provocative are his proposals for the embodiment of such unity in "sacramental" (not to be confused with what Yoder calls "sacramentalist") practices such as the eucharist, baptism, and the "fullness of Christ" (Eph. 4:13), which exemplifies the gathered ecclesia in ministry.

Summary. As the foregoing summary of developments indicates, given the polyphony of voices which the ecumenical movement comprises, the various ecclesial traditions are nevertheless converging in their awareness of the importance of dialogic unity in hermeneutical investigations. As Ellen Flessemann-van Leer notes: "The ecclesiological counterpart of this renewed emphasis on biblical unity is the insistence that the unity of the churches must find visible expression." This assessment also highlights the source of convergence as well as divergence with respect to the question of hermeneutics.

In the face of continuing disagreements, there are increasing indications of agreement. Among the several noteworthy hermeneutical convergences is the striking fact that the proposals of Lash, Ugolnik, Wainwright and Yoder all have in common an appreciation for the "ecclesial locus" of hermeneutics. Significantly, each of these approaches has gone *beyond* the preoccupation with the "text" of scripture in an effort to understand the interactive dimensions of scripture and liturgy, ethics and ecclesiology, politics and interpretation.

In addition, one can detect a growing sense of convergence among the representative traditions on the relationship of *ecclesial unity* to hermeneutics. Apart from the real differences in orientation in the different traditions in the ecumenical movement, the recent proposals for a hermeneutics of "unity" (Ratzinger), "consent" (Stuhlmacher), "peoplehood" (Yoder), or the Orthodox conception of "sobornost" community (Ugolnik) all presuppose, with varying degrees of emphasis, that the context of the church as a hermeneutical community is crucial. While none of these proposals suggests that all current hermeneutical issues have been resolved, these con-

vergences are serving to re-orient the hermeneutical debate itself towards a dialogue that is *interdisciplinary* as well as interdenominational.

This circumstance also helps to put into perspective the previous shifts in the ecumenical discussion of hermeneutics. The initial discussions of the F&O movement at Wadham College (1949) were primarily nurtured by the contributions of historical-critical scholarship of the Bible. As is widely recognized, the increasing participation of representatives of the Orthodox tradition (Montreal 1963) has led to a more balanced appreciation for Tradition in relation to scripture, but this rediscovery of the ecclesial locus of hermeneutics in the 1980s has gone beyond the contributions of the Orthodox and Anabaptist traditions. In the process, scholars within as well as outside the ecumenical movement have also discovered links between previously disparate disciplines of biblical studies, historical theology, political theory and literary hermeneutics. Through such interdisciplinary studies a renewed awareness of the "unsearchable riches" of the gospel as the source and end of visible unity for the church is emerging.

See also **Bible, its role in the ecumenical movement; church; exegesis, methods of; New Testament and Christian unity; Old Testament and Christian unity; Tradition and traditions; unity**.

MICHAEL G. CARTWRIGHT

E. Cardenal, *The Gospel in Solentiname*, 4 vols, Maryknoll, NY, Orbis, 1976-79 • R.J. Coggins & J.L. Houlden eds, *A Dictionary of Biblical Interpretation*, London, SCM, 1990 • E. Flesseman-van Leer, *The Bible: Its Authority and Interpretation in the Ecumenical Movement*, WCC, 1980 • N. Lash, "The Performance of Scripture", in *Theology on the Way to Emmaus*, N. Lash ed., London, SCM, 1986 • I. Mosala, *Biblical Hermeneutics and Black Theology in South Africa*, Grand Rapids, MI, Eerdmans, 1989 • J. Ratzinger, *Church, Ecumenism and Politics*, Middlegreen, UK, St Paul, 1988 • L. Sanneh, *Translating the Message: The Missionary Impact on Culture*, Maryknoll, NY, Orbis, 1989 • P. Stuhlmacher, *Historische Kritik und theologische Schriftauslegung* (ET *Historical Criticism and Theological Interpretation of Scripture*, London, SPCK, 1979) • A. Ugolnik, *The Illuminating Icon*, Grand Rapids, MI, Eerdmans, 1989 • G. Wainwright, *Doxology*, London, Epworth, 1980 • J.H. Yoder, *The Priestly Kingdom*, ch. 1, Notre Dame, IN, Univ. of Notre Dame Press, 1984.

"HIERARCHY OF TRUTHS". The expression "hierarchy of truths" first appeared in the Second Vatican Council's Decree on Ecumenism (1964): "In ecumenical dialogue, when Catholic theologians join with separated brethren in common study of the divine mysteries, they should, while standing fast by the teaching of the church, pursue the work with love for the truth, with charity, and with humility. When comparing doctrines, they should remember that there exists an order or *'hierarchy' of truths* in Catholic doctrine, since they vary in their relation to the foundation of the Christian faith. Thus the way will be open whereby this kind of 'fraternal emulation' will incite all to a deeper awareness and a clearer expression of the unfathomable riches of Christ (cf. Eph. 3:8)" (no. 11).

The very concept aroused hopes for a more refined methodology in the ecumenical dialogue, for the respectful evaluation of Christian traditions other than one's own, for the enhanced renewal of one's own church's thought and action, and for common witness* of the churches in real but imperfect communion* with one another. But clarifications of the expression and its more detailed implications were urged by W.A. Visser 't Hooft and favoured by John Paul II during the pope's visit to the WCC in June 1984. The WCC/RCC Joint Working Group* issued its sixth report in 1990, which includes an appendix on "The Notion of 'Hierarchy of Truths' — An Ecumenical Interpretation".

The organic nature of faith* affirms that revealed truths are not placed side by side in a static listing of propositions, but they are organized around, and point to, a centre or foundation — the person and mystery of Jesus Christ,* our salvation.* Though equally true, beliefs have greater or less consequence in the measure in which they relate to this foundation. Grace* has more importance than sin,* sanctifying grace more than actual grace; the resurrection* of Christ more than his childhood; the mystical aspect of the church* more than its juridical; the church's liturgy* more than private devotions.

Furthermore, the mystery of Christ is not only that which Christians believe but primarily a life which they share and experience. Differences about the ordering of revealed truths around this central mystery and their expression in the actual life of a church are among the reasons for Christian divisions, either because the legitimate diversity of expression, theological reflections and devotional practices is not acknowledged, or because basic differences are recognized concerning what is revealed or not (see **revelation**).

By better understanding the ways in which other Christians hold, express and live the faith, each confessional tradition can be led to a better understanding also of itself and begin to see its own formulations of doctrine in a broader perspective. The churches together can clarify the foundational content of what, in common witness, should be proclaimed in word and life in a way that speaks to the religious needs of the human spirit.

"In responding to the challenges of the present with an awareness of a 'hierarchy of truths', Christians are encouraged both to draw gratefully on the wisdom of their tradition and to be creative by seeking fresh responses in the light of God's coming kingdom" (1990 report).

TOM STRANSKY

W. Henn, "The Hierarchy of Truths Twenty Years Later", *Theological Studies*, 48, 1988 • G. Tavard, "Hierarchia veritatum", *Theological Studies*, 32, 1971 • WCC/RCC Joint Working Group, "The Church — Local and Universal. The Notion of 'Hierarchy of Truths' — an Ecumenical Interpretation", Sixth Report of the JWG, 1990.

HINDU-CHRISTIAN DIALOGUE.

Contacts between Hinduism and Christianity go back to the beginnings of Christianity. According to an old and honoured tradition, the apostle Thomas preached the gospel in India and suffered martyrdom.* The Thomas Christians were given certain privileges in the Hindu kingdoms of the south in later centuries and formed one of the self-contained communities within Indian society.

The Western "discovery" of India brought about a major missionary effort, first by Roman Catholic and later by various Protestant churches, which led to the formation of new Indian Christian communities along Western denominational lines. The newly converted Indian Christians were taught to break all links with their Hindu past and to consider the religion of their ancestors as inferior, if not as an outright invention of the devil. Similarly many Hindus had a contempt for all non-

Hindus, believing that contact with them would be polluting. When courageous individuals like Ram Mohan Roy and Brahmabandhab Upadhyaya in the 19th century suggested a mutual rapprochement, they were largely ignored or even opposed by their fellow Hindus and fellow Christians.

In the early 1930s philosopher-statesman Sarvepalli Radhakrishnan (1889-1985) persuasively pleaded for a "dialogue of religions". He was perhaps influenced by his teacher and mentor, A.G. Hogg of the Madras Christian College, although Radhakrishnan frequently complained about the negative criticism which Hinduism had received at the hands of other missionary teachers. Only in the early 1960s was the dialogue taken up seriously by Christians. Two Christian scholars deserve special credit: Paul Devanandan, the founder-director of the Christian Institute for the Study of Religion and Society at Bangalore, and Jacques-Albert Cuttat, Swiss ambassador to India 1960-64. Devanandan lectured and wrote about inter-religious dialogue long before the term became fashionable and helped to institutionalize it at the centre and in its bulletin, *Religion and Society*. Cuttat undertook a major lobbying effort among the Roman Catholic Indian bishops to persuade the Vatican to establish what later became known as the Secretariat for Non-Christians (established by Pope Paul VI in 1964). He also assembled what came to be known as the Cuttat group, a gathering of about 20 Christians belonging to different denominations who were united in their interest in Hindu-Christian dialogue. The group was truly ecumenical, and its members in the years to come decisively shaped Hindu-Christian dialogue. Murray Rogers's Jyotiniketan ashram near Bareilly emerged as a kind of central point for dialogue conferences between 1960 and 1970, especially in North India.

Under the leadership of Stanley Samartha the WCC established the Sub-unit on Dialogue with People of Living Faiths and Ideologies in 1971 as part of its Division of Mission and Evangelism. This sub-unit embraced dialogue with all living religions and became a major promoter of Hindu-Christian dialogue through meetings in which Hindus and Christians (besides representatives of other faiths) encountered each other on more or less neutral ground.

While both the Vatican Secretariat for Non-Christians and the WCC Dialogue sub-unit had to contend with a certain amount of opposition from more conservative, traditionally mission-oriented circles within the churches and a certain misunderstanding on the part of Hindus, overall their very existence signalled a new chapter in Hindu-Christian relations. Both initiatives were largely ecumenical, with the Christian side in Hindu-Christian dialogue meetings usually represented by a variety of denominations.

In the 1960s and 1970s the WCC organized several memorable dialogue meetings which also promoted the cause of Hindu-Christian dialogue in a major way. Of special interest were the conferences at Ajaltoun, Lebanon (1970), and in Colombo, Sri Lanka (1974). Meanwhile numerous dialogue centres sprang up in India. Often run by particular Christian denominations, they are nevertheless ecumenical in their approach to Hindu-Christian dialogue.

From the early 1970s onwards a new dimension of Hindu-Christian dialogue developed with the growth and spread of Hindu missions in the West. Whereas the Ramakrishna mission had addressed mainly intellectuals and had propagated a kind of universal religion, with the coming of the Hare Krishna and similar movements a new kind of sectarian Hinduism made its appearance in the West, attracting young people to a life-style rooted in a particular Hindu tradition. Subhananda Das, one of the most active promoters of dialogue, especially on a scholarly level, arranged a memorable three-day seminar in New Vrindaban in 1985. Subhananda is the founder-editor of *Iskcon* review, which also promoted academic dialogue between the Hare Krishna movement and Christianity.

The Christian ashram movement (representatives are the ecumenical Krist-Seva ashram in Pune; Saccidanandashram, founded by Fr Mochanin and Swami Abhishiktananda and now under the guidance of Bede Griffiths in Thanirpalli; Jyotiniketan, founded by Murray and Mary Rogers, now led by Franciscan friars), is essentially dedicated to Hindu-Christian dialogue in an attempt to integrate Hindu *sannyasa* into Christianity. Notable individual efforts to engage in a theological Hindu-Christian dialogue were made by Bishop A.J. Appasamy *(Christianity as Bhak-*

timarga) and Raymond Panikkar *(The Unknown Christ of Hinduism)*. Among the Hindu-Christian dialogue efforts in the West have been the conferences sponsored by Oratio Dominica in Freiburg in the 1970s and several symposia organized by the De Nobili Research Library associated with the Indology department of the University of Vienna, Austria. A Hindu-Christian dialogue conference organized in 1987 by the Calgary Institute for the Humanities led to the foundation of the *Hindu-Christian Studies Bulletin*, which serves as a vehicle for an ecumenical Hindu-Christian dialogue; Harold Coward (North American) and Anand Amaladassa (Indian) are the editors.

Both Hinduism and Christianity are fragmented into numerous denominations and sects. Hindu-Christian dialogue not only leads to an encounter between Hindus and Christians but also acts as a strong incentive to Hindu and Christian ecumenism. By meeting the other, each side is reminded of its own roots and original beliefs, over against which later events and developments leading to fissions and divisions appear relatively unimportant. Such dialogue perhaps will lead to a more essential and more relevant Christianity and Hinduism.

KLAUS K. KLOSTERMAIER

R. Boyd, *Indian Christian Theology*, Madras, CLS, 1976 • P. Devanandan, *Preparation for Dialogue*, Bangalore, CISRS, 1964 • K. Klostermaier, *Hindu and Christian in Vrindaban*, London, SCM, 1969 • S. Radhakrishnan, *Eastern Religions and Western Thought*, Oxford, Clarendon, 1939 • M.M. Thomas, *The Acknowledged Christ of the Indian Renaissance*, London, SCM, 1969 • M.M. Thomas, *Risking Christ for Christ's Sake: Towards an Ecumenical Theology of Pluralism*, WCC, 1987.

HISTORY. The great Abrahamic religions — Judaism, Christianity and Islam — are religions of history *(Geschichtsreligionen)* with a definite direction towards the future, whereas the basic aim of the great religions in the East is to establish an inner and outer equilibrium within nature, society or the human person. Abraham was called by God to leave his home and country and to find a new land, to become a great nation and to be a blessing to many (Gen. 12:1-3). In this primordial and archetypal story are found the basic categories which have created and sustained the Judeo-Christian faith* and which are fundamental for its understanding of history: promise and covenant,* expectation and experience, memory and hope.*

Biblical perspectives. From its earliest to its latest parts, the Hebrew Bible reflects a widening understanding of history, which corresponds to a widening understanding of God's work. The ancient memories of Yahweh's guiding the destinies of the patriarchs came alive in the experience of Israel's liberation from Egypt. The ancient covenants with Abraham, Isaac and Jacob are realized again in Yahweh's covenant with Israel in the revelation of the *torah*. From the book of Joshua to the book of Nehemiah, the story of Israel and its rulers is told. Israel's prophets are Yahweh's witnesses, interpreting, judging and guiding this history. As one follows that witness from Nathan to Daniel, Yahweh is understood not only as the Lord of Israel's history but as the Lord of all peoples. Not least, the creation* accounts and related texts see Yahweh as the maker of heaven and earth, thereby placing the history of the universe under God's rule. Finally, the apocalyptic literature, which appears with Daniel and continues in the intertestamental period, envisages Yahweh as the Creator of a new creation and, therefore, of time beyond this earthly time.

This widening awareness of history is intimately related to Israel's experiencing God as continuously creating, calling, guiding, judging, caring. As a consequence of this experience of God, time is discovered as flowing, moving, unique in its possibilities, not closed in eternally recurrent circles; in short, it is eschatological. Yahweh discloses himself as the sense and meaning of time: I AM WHO I AM or I WILL BE WHAT I WILL BE (Ex. 3:14). This name shows history as the *modus praesentiae Dei*.

History is therefore not simply regarded in terms of a mechanical sequence from past through present to the future but is considered an open, inspired process in which the future holds in store the unfulfilled promises of the past. The present is guided by *experiences* of past events and *expectations* of things to come. Faith moves between memory and hope. Life is shaped by judgment and redemption. Time in its eschatological openness calls forth the categories of the possible and the not-yet, of change and renewal.

Israel's understanding of history as the realm of the living God is not simply linear. In its eschatological character, it also contains elements of a cyclical understanding of time. The *sabbath* is a recurrent time of rest (Ex. 20:10), the *sabbaticals* are years of restoration (Lev. 25:1-7), and the great *year of jubilee* is seen as a time of re-creating the original conditions of life for humanity and nature alike (Lev. 25:11). Since history is seen not as an independent entity (this explains why there is no term for it in the Bible) but as a perspective of God's presence, it is conceived not simply as a fatalistic movement forward but as God's time to create, destroy and regenerate. The land and the people are meant to live in God's own rhythm of working and resting.

Nowhere is Christianity more obviously rooted in the Jewish faith than in its understanding of history. What the New Testament says about God incarnate in Jesus of Nazareth (see **incarnation**) is based on Israel's faith in God's time-creating presence and power. The specific *Christian* contribution to this concept of history is found in the cross and resurrection* of Jesus Christ.* The Christian faith in the resurrected Christ implies an understanding of history as participation in the process of resurrection. Since in Christ the fullness of God is revealed, all creation* shares in the promise of a resurrected life, or life eternal.

So history is placed in the dimension of radicalized eschatology: "Behold, I make all things new" (Rev. 21:5). Christ is not the end of history but the final and decisive revelation of what Israel had learned to believe: God as history's ultimate meaning, God disclosed as love, sacrificial love as warranted by the life and death of Jesus, and love transcending death, as manifested on Easter morning.

The Christ-event is not only a hermeneutical clue in order to find a solution to the age-old question of the meaning of time and of existence. It is at the same time an invitation to participate in it as trustworthy stewards (cf. 1 Cor. 4:1) in the unfolding of God's kingdom.* As history is the realm of God's presence, it is also the realm of discipleship for the believers.

Modern Western civilization. Throughout the early church and the middle ages,
history was largely understood in terms of God's *pedagogia* of humanity. The four-kingdoms concept of the prophet Daniel served as a way of ordering history in a typological sense. The chiliastic concepts of history (as taught e.g. by Joachim de Fiore) follow a similar typological interpretation of past events. Their aim is to proclaim a message for the present; history thus becomes a tool for specific interests, whether political, apologetic or soteriological.

As a discipline in its own right, history takes shape only within the modern civilization, the *Neuzeit*. The origins of this epoch are certainly varied. But it can be safely said that with the Renaissance period a great historical process began which first spread through Europe, and from there to the Americas, before reaching out to all parts of the globe in the 19th and especially in the 20th century. Therefore, it is here called the modern Western civilization. It is a process of unprecedented discoveries, conquests and expansions which led to the formation of great colonial empires and super-powers and, even more significantly, revolutionized the sciences that were known and created new ones. Their results, coupled with new technologies, economic methods and communication skills, have drastically shaped the world of today.

It is within this process — which may justly be called the human project of "dominion over the earth" — that the idea of history has developed and turned into a scientific discipline of its own. And inasmuch as the international connectedness of peoples and cultures became more and more apparent, so history took on a universal scope as *Universalgeschichte*. An impressive example of this is A.J. Toynbee's *A Study of History*, which endeavours to describe the societies and cultures of the earth.

In the modern Western civilization, the human being (in the form of elites, or peoples, or classes) is the subject of history. The world of nature and also the human body are considered mere "resources", objectified and instrumentalized matter to be dealt with at will by the human mind.

Philosophers like Karl Löwith have interpreted this project of *dominium terrae* as the secularized adaptation of the biblical view of history (see **secularization**). Humanity itself is put in the place of God; it sees itself no longer as part of creation but as creator. It is a decidedly *anthropocentric Weltanschauung*. The biblical notion of promise has been replaced by the belief in unlimited progress, eschatological openness by evolutionary necessity.

At the end of the 20th century, however, it becomes apparent that this great project of dominion over the earth, which began 500 years ago, has run into a deep crisis. The economic relationships and structures of the world are marked by deep injustices causing hunger, impoverishment and marginalization in large parts of the earth. The development of nuclear bombs has led to massive overkill capacities which threaten all life with annihilation. The misuse of the natural resources and the contamination of air, water and soil have produced irrevocable ecological damage. Humankind is facing global catastrophes. While attempting to be the maker of its own future, humanity ends up being the possible maker of its death. No wonder, then, that for many people the belief in progress has turned into despair, cynicism or hedonism.

History in the ecumenical movement.

The modern ecumenical movement began in the second half of the 19th century, and young women and men in Western (mostly Protestant) churches took the lead. So this movement is part of what we have called the great project of discovery and expansion. In this case it is the discovery of the oikoumene, the whole inhabited earth, as one great realm of operation. It is the discovery of the church* of Jesus Christ as a global phenomenon, the *una sancta ecclesia*, transcending all denominational lines and limitations. It is the discovery of a universal calling to bring Christ to all the peoples who have not yet heard of him.

The ecumenical movement can thus be seen as presenting a new level of consciousness gaining ground in the churches. There appeared a new perspective in which the histories of the churches led towards the one history of the one church of Christ on earth. This vision was first grasped by young people who formed international organizations such as the YMCA, the YWCA and the WSCF. They provided the generation of leaders who formed the ecumenical movement.

John R. Mott (1865-1955) can be singled out as the most significant of them. Mott was

"The Event", by Glen Bautista, reprinted by permission from Masao Takenaka, "Christian Art in Asia" (Tokyo, Kyo Bun Kwan, 1975), plate 37

keenly aware of the process by which the Western powers of trade, industry, science and technology were opening up the world. But he interpreted this process in biblical terms. Therefore he considered it as God's way to create the providential kairos for the world to hear the good news of Christ. His famous programme of "the evangelization of the world in this generation" reflected his awareness of this unique historical opportunity as an irrevocable moment in God's plan for history. Now was the time to win the world for Christ, lest other faiths, religious or secular, use that kairos. Mott saw clearly that the other great religions were soon to become active in missionary work. But most of all he considered rising communism as the one most dangerous competitor for shaping the course of world history.

While the founding generation of the ecumenical movement shared that great optimism about progress, they understood it in a theological perspective. It was God* leading the histories of the peoples towards one great world history. The discovery of the oikoumene was the discovery of God's purpose and providence.* To work for it was a supreme and timely act of obedience and discipleship. The fervent conviction *Dieu le veut*, "God wills it", transformed itself into three main ecumenical imperatives: the imperative for *mission*∗ (represented in the International Missionary Council*), for *church unity* (represented by the Faith and Order* movement), and for *peace*∗ (represented in the Life and Work movement and the World Alliance for Promoting International Friendship through the Churches*).

From its inception the ecumenical movement has tried to be firmly rooted in the Bible and to follow the Christocentric orientation which appeared as early as the YMCA basis adopted in Paris in 1855: "To confess Jesus Christ as God and Saviour according to the scriptures." This Christocentricity has had a critical influence both in the understanding of the churches' role and in the perception of the world. From the start the ecumenical movement understood itself as a fellowship of believers which was calling their churches to repentance and obedience and approaching the affairs of the worldly powers with prophetic criticism (see **prophecy**). History was conceived not only as the realm of human

activity but equally importantly as the realm in which God was working out his purpose. Hence different concepts of salvation history* played an important part in understanding this relationship.

The first assembly of the WCC (Amsterdam 1948) chose a theme which illuminates this basic orientation: "Man's Disorder and God's Design". This formulation reflects the faith in God's work in history as well as critical awareness of the world's disorders. The Paris basis appears again in the constitution of the WCC (see **WCC, basis of**), and with it the Christocentric orientation was firmly established. Its concept of history was universal. This Christocentric universality can easily be detected in all of the Council's varied activities.

This frame of thought also governs most of the world confessional groupings, such as the Lutheran World Federation* or the World Alliance of Reformed Churches.* But it surfaced most explicitly in the Second Vatican Council* of the Roman Catholic Church. In its Dogmatic Constitution on Divine Revelation, *Dei Verbum*, the Council spells out a linear concept of salvation history. This process of salvation* finds its visible historical expression in the (Catholic) church as the human community of salvation *(Lumen Gentium)*. The other religions of humankind are seen as preparatory approximations to this process of salvation *(Nostra Aetate)*. Finally, Vatican II sets this approach in the context of human history in general. *Gaudium et Spes* speaks of one great organic process leading all history towards its one common goal in God.

If one looks at the theological work of the WCC, one notes that there have been some attempts to clarify the relationship between the mission of the ecumenical movement and the historical awareness of that time. In this context mention must be made of two projects of the F&O commission.

The first, "God in Nature and History" (1967), connects belief in God's providential guidance of history with the modern concept of evolution and tries to integrate the finality of Christ with the universal nature-history process (see **nature**). This study is clearly influenced by visionary thinkers like Pierre Teilhard de Chardin, who considered the coming of Christ the one great telos of the history of the planet earth. Thus the F&O

paper emphasizes the convergent processes in the world and places the ecumenical movement firmly in it. The ambivalence of historical progress, e.g. in the area of medicine, is acknowledged. But that this same ambivalence also pertains to the development of philosophies and theologies of history is not realized.

The second study project was conducted during the 1970s under the title "Unity of the Church and Unity of Humankind". In some ways it was the continuation of "God in Nature and History", but now the attempt was made to look more carefully at the role of the churches in that historic process of increasing global interdependence. The Uppsala assembly in 1968 was so bold as to speak of the church "as the sign of the coming unity of mankind". However, soon after this, interdependence began to unfold its unjust, exploitative and marginalizing character. At the same time the diversity between the churches received more attention, pushing the idea of organic unity into the background. The belief in a positive convergence of all evolutionary processes began to vanish.

By the time of the Nairobi assembly (1975), the key points of the F&O study had changed considerably. The unity of the church, of humankind and of creation were now derived from the faith in the Trinitarian unity of God (see **Trinity**), thus replacing the earlier, more uncritical relation between evolution and salvation.

The Uppsala assembly of the WCC (1968) had earlier formulated a new accent. Under the impact of the growing anguish of large sectors of the world's population (the third world), it sharpened ethical awareness by underlining its option for the poor* and the oppressed. (There is an obvious relationship with the liberation theology* which emerged during those years in Latin America.)

During the 1980s the threefold threat to life on earth led to a further widening of the theological and ethical scope. The call of the Vancouver assembly (1983) for the churches to covenant together for justice, peace and the integrity of creation* marks the end of a merely anthropocentric and social concept of ecumenical ethics. The Christocentric orientation does not imply an anthropocentric concept of salvation. In fact, if Christ is understood in cosmic terms — a dimension already

presented in 1961 to the New Delhi assembly but largely overlooked since then — his saving work extends to all of creation.

In summary, as the ecumenical movement approaches the end of this century, it must realize that the anthropocentric paradigm of modern civilization has come to an end. In view of the threat of an end of history brought about by human beings, it will have to rethink its understanding of history. To deny human responsibility and to resort to a fundamentalist apocalyptic view, as certain churches and evangelical groupings suggest, will not do justice to humanity's unique calling within the whole of creation. Once creation is understood as a community of equal dignity and rights for all living things, human beings will see themselves no longer as the centre of history but as trustees of a history which belongs to the earth.

The tension remains that humanity has entered the stage in which it must assume the responsibility for the future of history, even though the destructive forces set in motion appear to be beyond control. But precisely on that account, the notion of human beings as stewards and trustees of the community of life may help to balance this dilemma, for it reduces them to their proper place in the commonwealth of creation and keeps them accountable to God, who remains the ultimate source of history and its goal.

See also **eschatology, God, prophecy, providence, salvation history**.

GEIKO MÜLLER-FAHRENHOLZ

"Geschichte und Geschichtsauffassung", in *Religion in Geschichte und Gegenwart*, vol. 2, Tübingen, Mohr, 1958 • K. Löwith, *Weltgeschichte und Heilsgeschehen: Die theologischen Voraussetzungen der Geschichtsphilosophie* (ET *Meaning in History*, Chicago, Univ. of Chicago Press, 1949) • G. Müller-Fahrenholz, *Heilsgeschichte zwischen Ideologie und Prophetie*, Freiburg, Herder, 1974 • G. Müller-Fahrenholz et al., *Unity in Today's World*, WCC, 1978 • R. Rouse & S. Neill eds, *A History of the Ecumenical Movement, 1517-1948*, WCC, 1986 • A.J. Toynbee, *A Study in History*, 12 vols, London, Oxford UP, 1935-61 • W.A. Visser 't Hooft, *The Genesis and Formation of the World Council of Churches*, WCC, 1982.

HOLINESS. The church* of the risen Christ, victorious over sin and death, can only be holy. In the Nicene Creed,* holiness is one of the four specific "notes" of the church — "one, *holy*, catholic, apostolic".

The church's holiness is participation in the holiness of God, who is the source of all holiness. The church is "a holy nation, God's own people" (1 Pet. 2:9). The Father so loved the world that he gave his only Son to save it (John 3:16) and made it possible for the church, the "Body of Christ", to share in the communion of the Triune God (see **Trinity**). The church is holy through Christ's righteousness. Jesus, "the Holy One of God" (Mark 1:24; John 6:69), full of the Holy Spirit* (Luke 1:35, 3:22, 4:34; Acts 10:38), is one body with his church (Eph. 5:23). He "loved the church and gave himself up for her, that he might sanctify her... that she might be holy and without blemish" (Eph. 5:25-27). The risen Christ is "a life-giving spirit" (1 Cor. 15:45; cf. 2 Cor. 3:17): through his Spirit the Christians are "a holy temple in the Lord" (Eph. 2:21; cf. 1 Cor. 3:17). Individual Christians are holy through their relationship to God as a member of the church. They are to live a life worthy of their calling (Eph. 4:1-3; Col. 3:12-15). "Holiness" thus defines the church as the redeeming presence of God's holiness in our sinful world (see **sin**), as the call of God to all humankind to that participation in the divine life and love "which is the very mystery of the church" (Cardinal Basil Hume).

The creed relates the holiness of the church to the mission of the Holy Spirit, "Lord and Giver of life". In communion with the Father and Son, the Spirit is the principle of all holiness of, in and through the church. The succeeding articles — communion of saints* (Apostles' Creed), forgiveness of sins, resurrection of the dead and the life of the world to come — make explicit the Spirit's role in salvation.* The holiness of the church, which Trinitarian Christian faith confesses, transcends the concept of the sacred or wholly other, described in such terms as "out of human reach", "awesome" and "fascinating". In the church, God manifests his absolute closeness, shares his "wholly other" life with sinful humans. God is met as love dispelling fear and removing guilt, as Father communicating himself through his Son and his Spirit in our flesh and history.* God's love overcomes sin in his very "enemies": "God shows his love for us in that while we were yet

sinners Christ died for us... While we were enemies we were reconciled to God by the death of his Son" (Rom. 5:8-10).

The church is the place where mortals find holiness and salvation. It is holy in order "that they may have life" (John 10:10). It is the place for proclaiming the gospel, for baptism,* for praying, worshipping, celebrating together, for the forgiveness of sins. It is sign or sacrament* of Christ's and the Holy Spirit's healing and reconciling action through such "means of sanctity" (Vatican II) as scripture, the ministry of the word, sacraments, church structures and discipline. God's sanctifying economy* constitutes the "objective" holiness of the church. Faithful and self-involving response to the gospel makes the church into a communion of "saints", a fellowship of life, love and truth, expecting the resurrection* of the body and the life of the world to come. Many faithful persons whose lives reflected the holiness of the church have been canonized (declared saints) in the course of history. The Second Vatican Council emphasized that "the holiness of the church expresses itself... in a special way" through the monastic life. The saint bears witness to the presence in the world of God's saving power. The "holy" church is recognized in the first place through sanctity in its members.

The church in its pilgrim state is at once holy and, at least in a sense, sinful (see **people of God**). A "subjective" sinfulness of the church can be attributed to its members: "The church herself is sinful, in that her own members are sinners" (Karl Rahner). But also "the church will never lack holiness in her members" (Karel Truhlar). In the early church, various movements such as Montanism and Novatianism refused to reconcile Christians guilty of apostasy,* murder or adultery or to grant penance* more than once in a lifetime. Later, other currents such as the Albigensians, the Waldensians, the Hussites and the extremists of the Reformation times and of Jansenism disputed that sinful Christians remain members of the church. But Christianity on the whole never evolved into a fellowship of the perfect. It also followed Augustine's rejection of Donatist doctrine that sinful ministers do not disperse valid sacraments: sin cannot impair the efficacy of the church's ministry in so far as it is Christ's own saving action. Roman Catholics claim that the fullness of "objective" sanctity is found only in their church. However Vatican II* affirmed the existence of "great holiness" outside it.

The correlation of holiness and sinfulness is constitutive of the very conception of the holiness of the church. "It is precisely through its paradoxical structure of holiness and unholiness that the church is the form of grace in this world" (Cardinal Joseph Ratzinger). Luther saw that such a structure points to Christ's holiness as being our sole holiness and of course the church's holiness. Or in the words of modern Protestants quoted by Yves Congar: "To affirm the holiness of the church is not to exclude sin in it but to proclaim the indissolubility of the union of Christ and the church." As Body of Christ, the church is patterned upon the paradox that Christ has been made sin: "For our sake he made him to be sin who knew no sin, so that in him we might become the righteousness of God" (2 Cor. 5:21). The mystery of the holiness of the church is derived from the primary fact that a man deeply involved in (others') sin is given as the very holiness of God bestowed upon sinners so that they may be freed from sin.

The Reformation* churches rejected the Roman theses on the objective holiness of the church. Protestant theology holds that the church as a fellowship of sinners has no power over the process of sanctification.* There is no proper "sanctifying" capacity of the clergy or even of the sacramental rites as such. Between Roman Catholics who maintain the constitutive role of the church and its ministry, as Body of Christ, in God's sanctifying work and those Protestants who deny the church, as "creature of the word", any "authorship" in salvation, a fundamental difference continues to exist.

Past theological discussions about the holiness of the church demonstrated constantly that to interpret human reality in terms of holiness is fruitful only within the polarity of God's holiness and human sinfulness. Neglect of this specific structure of the topic may lead, for example, to expect from the church an unreal "stainless" purity, a notion of holiness alien to our sinful human condition, wherein we face constantly the destructiveness of sin and also perceive it as lying as heavy as the Crucified's momentous victory over it. The holiness of the church is rooted in this victory of God's holiness over sin, in Christ "made

sin for us", in us, with us sinners. It is as the One who agreed to be "all the sinners" that Christ has become the event of divine holiness, redemptive in the faith of "a holy church of sinners", *ecclesia simul sancta et peccatrix*. Like his "holy" church, Christ has been known and condemned on earth as sinner: but in the Spirit the believer is given an insight into the life of the church "hid with Christ in God" (Col. 3:3).

In today's Christianity the notion of the church's holiness has become controversial on account of the concern for Christian commitment to *justice*.* "There is no holiness without justice" (Paul Tillich). Catholicism has come to admit injustice committed in the past by the Roman church and to acknowledge the need for continual reformation of the church, in the spirit of the Reformed churches' word *ecclesia semper reformanda*. Church bodies come under heavy criticism and are deemed "unholy" wherever they fail to attend to social needs, to appear convincingly committed to active struggle against sin "in the world". The holiness of the church is measured at the present time after the parable of the Good Samaritan and the account of the last judgment in Matthew 25. Even the conception of the church as "congregation of saints" (Augsburg confession) is accused of leaving out the church's function in world history. "The salvation it proclaims is not merely salvation of the soul but also the realization of the eschatological hope of justice" (Jürgen Moltmann).

We thus see today's churches striving to work together for such "worldly" concerns as peace,* freedom, justice and life (see **life and death**). The Christian commitment to secular problems is not always very successful, and not totally without the risk of compromising with sin, as some have argued in the case of the WCC's support of liberation* movements involved in armed violence,* which caused the Salvation Army* to suspend its membership in the WCC. But coming to grips with institutionalized sin through commitment to peace and human rights, through coping with the problems of the people most in need, living as a servant community in the spirit of Jesus — all this has brought to Christianity a fresh understanding of the gospel in the context of a radically changed world. In the experience of holiness given in attending to

Christ's most suffering members, the church witnesses the collapse of many a traditional view about holiness. It realizes and confesses its guilt in much of the injustice in the world, notably for failing to do anything worthwhile to redeem many awful situations, for being indifferent to them. But in Christ made sin, in his epiphany in the socially or politically "crucified" of our times, is revealed God's forgiveness granted to his people in the Son, whom the Father gave up for the sins of the world. The risen Christ, who has buried sin in his death, is the only righteousness of his "body", its life-giving spirit for a new creation. In him is recalled that at human level nothing "just" is spared sinfulness. In his church's struggle, it is Christ who continues to fight "against all ungodliness and wickedness of men who by their wickedness suppress the truth" (Rom. 1:18) — also within the church.

This new gospel awareness owes much to the "discovery" of the Holy Spirit through the ecumenical dialogue with the Orthodox (see **Orthodoxy**). In Orthodox Christianity the Holy Spirit has always been known as the ever-active agent of the holiness of the church. Pentecost* inaugurated an economy of holiness in which sin is not yet totally suppressed but no longer reigns. Through the eucharistic invocation to the Spirit, the church calls upon itself the power that makes it "the icon of the kingdom to come" (John Zizioulas). The Spirit is the one who bears witness in the church to the risen Christ as the eschatological Lord over sin.

Today's deeper understanding of the holiness of the church is prompted by the interaction of the best insights in Western and Eastern Christianity. "The Holy Spirit leads us to understand more clearly that holiness today cannot be attained without commitment to justice, without human solidarity, that include the poor and the oppressed" (Roman Synod on the Laity, 1987). Conversely, the theology of the Crucified makes clear that charisms* are not powers that would allow the church to be, so to say, holy "on its own". Holiness is the church's respiration dependent on the holy breath of Christ, in constant prayer,* the very struggle of life.

The criterion of a "holy" church is this life in the Spirit, not an abstract sinlessness. As long as the process of sanctification is going on in the church, sin remains and calls for

forgiveness; but it is also overcome by this "holiness" which consists in the struggle of Christ's Spirit against evil.

To manifest the church's holiness today is to foster Christian fellowship through inter-church thinking and acting on vital issues, in response to the one undivided gospel of God in Christ. The church's entire reality rests on the holy gospel, whereby God's merciful action is made known and redemptive for our times.

See also **church, redemption, saints, salvations, sanctification, sin**.

DANIEL OLIVIER

J. Ansaldi, *Ethique et sanctification: Morales politiques et sainteté chrétienne*, Geneva, Labor et Fides, 1983 • Y. Congar, "Die heilige Kirche", in *Mysterium Salutis*, IV/1, J. Feiner & M. Löhrer eds, Einsiedeln, Benziger, 1972, 459-77 • K.V. Truhlar, "Holiness", in *Sacramentum Mundi: An Encyclopedia of Theology*, London, Burns & Oates, 1969, 3.

HOLINESS MOVEMENT. The Holiness movement is an agglomeration of individuals and church bodies in the US whose principal purpose is the propagation of what they believe to be the biblical doctrine and experience of Christian perfection. Most Holiness people accept John Wesley's teaching on "entire sanctification" as normative but not absolutely definitive.

The Holiness movement understands Christian perfection to begin in an act of divine grace* in which the already-regenerate recipient, totally submissive to the will of God, is cleansed of original sin,* endowed with perfect love to God and neighbour, and empowered to witness to the saving grace of God in Christ through service. It is received instantaneously by faith.* It is provided for in the atoning work of Jesus Christ* and is wrought by the Holy Spirit.* The Holiness movement distinguishes purity from maturity and insists that while Christian perfection is wholly accomplished at its inception, the sanctified believer will seek to grow in grace and Christlikeness.

Holiness people account themselves strictly orthodox Christians and, with the exception of restorationist elements, accept the creeds,* doctrinal understandings and ethical principles of the ecumenical and undivided church as their own. They also accept as their own the history of the church catholic. They are Protestant, holding stoutly (as basic and essential doctrine) to *sola gratia, sola scriptura*, and the priesthood of all believers. They are Augustinian in their understanding of the human condition apart from saving grace and Arminian in their understanding of universal atonement, free grace and free will, though popular thought has sometimes run to Pelagianism. Currently, some awareness is dawning of affinities with the Eastern Orthodox tradition in the areas of creation and soteriology.

Methodism's Twenty-five Articles of Religion provide the basis for most of the movement's confessional statements. Such statements usually both affirm catholicity* and declare distinguishing tenets.

Beyond the fundamental agreements noted, the Holiness movement bodies vary greatly, as the following differences in sacramental theology illustrate. Most Holiness groups celebrate both baptism* and eucharist,* but the Salvation Army and some Friends congregations celebrate neither. The Church of God (Anderson) advocates the term "ordinances" and celebrates three: baptism, the Lord's supper, and foot washing. The Church of the Nazarene, Wesleyan Church, and Free Methodist Church practise infant baptism; the Church of God (Anderson), Church of God (Holiness), and Missionary Church practise believer's baptism only.

Holiness people have insisted that these and other differences do not divide their witness to the propagation of Christian perfection. The Christian Holiness Association (CHA; formerly National Camp Meeting Association for the Promotion of Holiness and later the National Holiness Association) serves as a co-ordinating and galvanizing agency for that purpose. Serving the same function as CHA for a constituency of perhaps 100,000 in some 30 smaller groups who fear that the mainstream of the movement is spiritually lukewarm, is the Interdenominational Holiness Convention (IHC, 1947). Some persons and groups belong to both CHA and IHC. The Church of God (Anderson) identifies and works with the movement, but as a restorationist body refuses to join either CHA or IHC. Only racial prejudice has kept the Holiness movement from recognizing that Afro-

American Methodism (African Methodist Episcopal, AME Zion, Christian Methodist Episcopal) has historically differed from it not one whit in faith and piety.

The Holiness movement has two major historical roots. By far the larger and more significant of these is the mid-19th century Methodist attempt, largely successful, to revive a flagging commitment to Wesleyan perfectionism. Most significant in the ante-bellum phase of this revival were Phoebe Palmer, George and Jesse Peck, and Nathan Bangs. Immediately after the civil war, these were joined by such persons as Randolph Foster, John A. Wood, and John Inskip. The second major root is that reaching into the perfectionist revivalism of Asa Mahan and Charles Finney, especially its emphases on biblical "proofs" for entire sanctification, "free moral agency", the work of the Holy Spirit as the agent of the sanctifying experience, and spiritual power. Such fundamentalism in method and content as there is in the movement has generally arisen from this latter source, but its Wesleyan roots have kept the movement free of destructive debates concerning such issues as biblical inerrancy and millennialism.

The Holiness movement bears deep commitments to the transformationist social ethic characteristic of its roots in the abolitionism of the Wesleyans and Free Methodists and its primary expression in the Salvation Army. This tradition re-awoke in strength in the 1970s after nearly a half-century of dormancy induced by *embourgoisement*.

The movement has had two periods of denomination-building: roughly 1880-1920 and 1960-80. In the former period, Holiness people formed congregations and associations on the basis of three convictions: that the major denominations did not want them, that those denominations were neglecting the inner cities, and that they needed to nurture those converted and sanctified in their revivalistic ventures. The original congregations and associations quickly entered a period of merger which ended only as the new denominations gained a generation of "tradition" and identity. From 1960 to 1980, a number of groups broke away from older Holiness denominations, usually protesting worldliness and abuse of ecclesiastical power. The 1968 merger of the Pilgrim Holiness Church and the Wesleyan Methodist Church to form the

Wesleyan Church and increasing interdenominational co-operation in such matters as hymnody and materials for Christian education may herald a new period of merger.

Several of the Holiness bodies and a number of individuals belong to the National Association of Evangelicals, in spite of deep concerns on the part of some with the rationalistic style of much of evangelical theology, the supposed emotionalism of the Pentecostals, and the association's programmatic social conservatism. Through the Wesleyan Theological Society, the scholarly commission of CHA, the movement is represented on the Faith and Order commission of the National Council of Churches of Christ in the USA.

See also **sanctification**.

PAUL MERRITT BASSETT

Black Holiness: A Guide to the Study of Black Participation in Wesleyan Perfectionist and Glossolalic Pentecostal Movements, Metuchen, NJ, Scarecrow, 1987 • D.W. Dayton, *Discovering an Evangelical Heritage*, New York, Harper & Row, 1976 • M.E. Dieter, *The Holiness Revival of the Nineteenth Century*, Metuchen, NJ, Scarecrow, 1980 • C.E. Jones, *A Guide to the Study of the Holiness Movement*, Metuchen, NJ, Scarecrow, 1974.

HOLY SPIRIT. The theology of the Holy Spirit, or pneumatology, is not so much one specific chapter of Christian theology as an essential dimension of every theological view of the church and of its spirituality and liturgical and sacramental life. The Holy Spirit, here the object of our research, is first and foremost the Spirit we invoke, the Spirit who presides over the upbuilding and renewal of the church,* the Spirit who infuses everyone that comes into the world with the light of Christ.

Biblical teaching. In the figures of the Old Testament, the link between *dabhar* (word) and *ruah* (wind, breath, spirit) is one of the things which most forcefully heralds Trinitarian theology (see **Trinity**). The Word of God is alive and sanctifies. It is suffused by Spirit and transmitted by the divine breath. This anthropological image suggests the intimate and essential link between the divine persons of the Son and the Spirit.

Gradually the Word achieved greater defin-ition, disclosing its identity and, in some passages from the Psalms, being treated as a person.* The same process of development held good for the Spirit or wisdom. In the post-exilic writings a theology of the Spirit and a theology of wisdom were worked out.

In Gen. 1 the pneumatological prologue is followed by acts of God sustained and signalled by a living Word. But in the work of creation the Word of God is not merely preceded but also accompanied by the Spirit, who ensures that it "carries" and reaches its audience. Thus Word and Spirit go together in the order of creation. Of this the Bible gives evidence in fullest measure (e.g. Ps. 33:6, 147:18).

The entire sacred history of Israel displays God's teaching work as he speaks to this people "whose hearts are hardened", but whom he has chosen for himself and loved. God's hand can be traced in the web of historical events itself, in the summons of the prophets who communicate the word of God. The Spirit of God is always there and suffuses the prophets and fills the poetical writers and the psalmists. The Spirit guides the people and, as it were, ensures the slow rising of sap so that they may become mature and await with increasing impatience and anguish the Saviour and the pouring out of the Spirit in the last days.

The dual presence and action of the Word and the Spirit is pre-eminently embodied and displayed in biblical messianism. Frequently the pneumatological dimension of this messianism has been neglected. If the Messiah can keep the word of the law given by God to Moses and bring about justice on this earth, it is because the Spirit of God rests upon him (Isa. 61:1). If the "Suffering Servant" can "bring salvation to the nations", it is for the same reason. And again if the people as a whole will be able one day to accept the Word in their inmost selves, this is because the heart of each person will be renewed by the Spirit.

The two constants of the Spirit and the Word, of the Spirit and those who are the elect, of the Spirit and the Servant, merge in the anointing of Jesus by the Spirit at his baptism. Here the Elect One of God not only states the Word of God as something outside himself but incarnates and manifests it.

In the period of the incarnation the Holy Spirit is the *Spirit of the incarnation*, in and by whom the Word — the logos — of God breaks into history, the Spirit who prepares a human body for that Word as the temple of its godhead.

The baptism of Jesus by the forerunner in the Jordan is a major stage of the revelation of the Spirit, who proceeds from the Father and rests on the Son, thus accompanying and confirming the witness of the Father. This is a revelation of the eternal movement of the Spirit of the Father, who remains in the Son from all eternity. The Holy Spirit is the Spirit of Jesus, permeating him, revealing him and disclosing him to the world.

Jesus' first words in his public ministry express his awareness of being Christ, that is, of being anointed and permeated by the Spirit (Luke 4:18, 21; Matt. 12:17-18) and even led by him (Matt. 4:1; Mark 1:12). From then on, consecrated by the anointing of the Spirit, who remains in him and sends him, Jesus proclaims the good news to the poor. And in the Spirit he works miracles, heals the sick, raises the dead and expels demons.

All of Jesus' prayers are — or rather the *entire prayer* of Jesus is — in the Spirit (Luke 10:21; John 4:23, 11:33, 41). His praying is something continuous in which the whole being of the Saviour is defined in a constant existential relationship to the Father in the Spirit. Thus the Holy Spirit is the centre, where the indescribable occurs in the exchange of the eternal Trinitarian words "Thou art my Son" and "Abba, Father". From the incarnation* to the ascension the entire earthly life of Jesus is a life filled by the Spirit, moving through the passion, the cross, the supreme impoverishment in which Jesus achieves the ideal of the Beatitudes, of which he is the great and only true example, so that we can paraphrase: "Blessed is he, the One who is poor in the Spirit, for his is the kingdom of heaven" (Matt. 5:3 and 1 Pet. 4:14).

It is indeed in the Spirit that Jesus consecrates himself to the Father (John 17:19) and offers himself to the Father as a sacrifice without blemish (Heb. 9:14) and, according to the passion stories in Luke (23:46) and John (19:30), commits his spirit into the Father's hands and breathes his last. In answer to this definitive gift of the Spirit, the Father raises his Son from the dead by that same Spirit (Acts 2:32-33). Thus henceforward the Spirit is the irresistible force which breaks the seal

"Pentecost", by a Westphalian artist, c. 1380 (Religious News Service, New York)

of the empty tomb, the overflowing joy which fills the disciples and the women who bring spices, the blinding light of the resurrection,* the presence which remained in Jesus himself in death and which hell cannot swallow up.

The Spirit as a person also remains to some extent unmentioned by name and is concealed behind symbols (the finger of God, power, light, cloud, kingdom) and so is inseparable from the living experience of the fruits of the kingdom (peace, joy, gentleness, mercy, wisdom, courage, etc.). This anonymity of the Spirit is confirmed by Paul's words that "in him the whole fullness of deity dwells bodily" (Col. 2:9; cf. John 1:14). In these Pauline and Johannine expressions we have the feeling that the Spirit is hidden and somehow confounded with the gifts of the Spirit, with the energies of the Spirit which radiate eternally from the divine Trinity. These deeply scriptural intuitions were developed in Byzantine and Palamite theology.

The certainty of the coming of the Spirit is affirmed in the preaching of Jesus. We remember the exposition by Jesus himself (cf. Luke 11:13) of the petition in the Lord's prayer, "give us each day our daily bread". All the needs of men and women are signs of the Spirit and an opportunity for proclamation: bread, fire, water, light, etc. (cf. Luke 12:49).

The imminence of the Saviour's passion gives him the opportunity for some final teaching of the most exalted kind on the Holy Spirit on the occasion of the great "words of consolation" which are to be found in the farewell discourse (John 13:31-16:33) and the high priestly prayer (John 17), which are indivisibly part of these words. The promise of the Holy Spirit is given there more solemnly than ever in the setting of Jesus' "departure" (see John 16:7), which acquires its whole meaning as a necessary condition for the coming of the Holy Spirit. Thus because Jesus "is spirit" (John 4:24; 2 Cor. 3:17-18) from all eternity, and "in the days of his flesh" was wholly filled with the Spirit and united with the Spirit to the ineffable core of his being as God-man, he communicates the Spirit to human beings in the unceasing Pentecost* of the church, which is his body and the temple of his Spirit.

The gift of Pentecost is the necessary completion of the mystery of Easter. Christ, being filled with the Spirit, becomes the giver of the Spirit in the morning of Pentecost in the upper room. This is when the church,* baptized and reborn through the blood of Christ, is confirmed and strengthened once for all in the new life which is the life of the Spirit, or life in the Spirit of God.

In the actual life of the early church, the Spirit genuinely is an everyday reality which Christians know from their experience: "Do not quench the Spirit" (1 Thess. 5:19), "be filled with the Spirit" (Eph. 5:18), "be aglow with the Spirit" (Rom. 12:11). Paul describes very fully indeed the experience of the church *in the Spirit:* "God's love has been poured into our hearts through the Holy Spirit which has been given to us" (Rom. 5:5). Rom. 8 sets out the new life of the Christian in the Spirit. At the heart of our renewed personality, our spirit, it is the Holy Spirit himself who acts, speaks, groans and prays (v.26).

Just as much as the New Testament, the patristic writings reflect the church's fundamental confession of faith in Jesus Christ dead and risen, in the certainty of the experience of the Spirit who makes alive. Rather than reflecting *on* the Spirit, the fathers pass on to us an expression of the experience *of* the Spirit in the church.

The Holy Spirit and the church. Christian worship is worship in spirit and in truth (John 4:23-24), both through the strength of the Spirit, who works in the church, and through the purpose of this worship, which is to make us bearers of the Spirit *(pneumatophoroi)*, transformed by and in the Spirit into new people till we attain "the stature of the fullness of Christ" (Eph. 4:13), who both humbled himself in the form he took and was exalted (Phil. 2:6-11).

While Christian worship involves us in the great movement of prayer — in the intercession both on earth and in heaven of Jesus the High Priest — it must also be said that the Holy Spirit is the object and the entire content of that invocation, or epiclesis,* by Christ. The whole of Christian worship thus constitutes an unceasing epiclesis which culminates in the continual Pentecost of the Spirit in the church, which is the temple of the Holy Spirit.

Between the liturgical expression of the eucharist — the continuing Pentecost of the Spirit — and the experience of saints and spirituals, there is a profound connection: in both it is the Holy Spirit who creates the dynamic of the call, the encounter and the transformation of human beings into a temple of God. This sense of the prayer of the Spirit in the human heart is experienced very strongly in the tradition of the Jesus prayer, in which Jesus' name is unceasingly invoked: "When the Spirit comes to dwell in human beings, they can no longer cease from praying, for the Spirit never ceases praying in them" (Isaac of Nineveh).

All the structures of the church are determined by the dual (simultaneous and reciprocal) mediation of the Son in the Spirit and the Spirit in the Son, by that dual, real presence of the Lord Jesus and the Comforter, and in and through them by the encounter with the Father who is the source and term (i.e. the alpha and omega) of the divine fellowship or communion. Thus in the church there is a fundamental balance between the principles of tradition, obedience, order, sacramental, liturgical and canonical forms, on the one hand, and, on the other, the principles of freedom, creativity, personal responsibility, the irreducible integrity of the human person, the local community, the divine grace which gives spiritual content to the forms and structures and which ensures a unique and necessary vertical relation between the individual person and God, between the local congregation and the Master. But this balance is never achieved once for all but must always be renewed. With this in mind, the inspiration* of the Spirit must always be renewed and cannot be codified but becomes incarnated: truth is always live, and never wholly the same as the dogmatic formulas expressing and enshrining it.

The Word — the Logos — is the guarantor that it really is the Spirit that is acting. The Word identifies the Spirit in the gift of distinguishing between spirits. But this does not mean that the Word is subordinating the Spirit to the hierarchy or the institutions. Today the Spirit still creates prophetic gifts or charisms which can come into conflict with the hierarchy, which, though it is established, is not infallible. These charisms may call on the hierarchy to repent or may proclaim God's judgment to it. Prophecy* is just as intrinsic to the very nature of the church as is the royal priesthood, or rather it represents one of the essential, inalienable aspects of the priestly anointing of the church by the Holy Spirit at Pentecost. Prophecy is a characteristic mark of the genuineness of the Spirit and of the Spirit's continuing, sovereign presence. The Spirit is a Spirit of order, but the divine order does not always correspond in everything to that of the established hierarchy in everything.

See also **charism(ata), epiclesis, holiness, inspiration, sanctification, Trinity**.

BORIS BOBRINSKOY

For bibliography, see **Holy Spirit in ecumenical thought**.

HOLY SPIRIT IN ECUMENICAL

THOUGHT. In the reports of major ecumenical conferences prior to the formation of the WCC, reference to the Holy Spirit followed the lines of traditional Protestant thinking and piety of those years. The Holy Spirit was understood mainly as divine power working in the church* and in the life of the individual Christian. While the Trinitarian confession of the faith was acknowledged formally, the affirmation of the Spirit as person* in communion* with the Father and the Son remained largely undeveloped (see **Trinity**).

A new emphasis began to be evident in 1952 at both the world mission (Willingen) and Faith and Order (Lund) conferences. The understanding of the missionary task as participation in the *missio Dei* is based on a Trinitarian conception of the divine oikonomia, the sequence of God's saving acts in the history of salvation.* God has sent his Son to reconcile all things unto himself in order that all people might become one with God through the power of the Holy Spirit. As Jesus Christ* has accomplished his work of salvation, God sent the Spirit — the Spirit of Jesus who assembles people into one body, leads into all truth and enables the church to continue the divine mission. Through the Holy Spirit, the church can both press forward as ambassador and witness to Christ and wait with confidence for his final victory (cf. Willingen's declaration on the "Missionary Obligation of the Church").

In its sections on "Christ and the Church" and "Continuity and Unity", Lund repeated many earlier affirmations about the Holy Spirit. Through the Spirit, Jesus Christ is the head of the church, which is his body, and is present in his church. The continuity of the church in history* is assured "by the constant action of the risen Lord through the Holy Spirit". It is through the "unifying power of his indwelling Spirit" that the organic unity of the Body of Christ is being formed and sustained. However, in describing the inseparable relation between Christ and his church and in speaking of the nature of the church in terms of a double movement (called from the world and sent into the world), Lund recognized the distinct work of the Holy Spirit as the present manifestation of the reign of God. "Through the indwelling of the Holy Spirit the new age of the future is already given to participate in the power of the resurrection." Indicative of the new orientation is the conclusion of the report on "Christ and His Church": "It is of decisive importance for the advance of ecumenical work that the doctrine of the church be treated in close relation both to the doctrine of Christ and to the doctrine of the Holy Spirit."

The WCC's third assembly (New Delhi 1961) made this new orientation clearly visible in several ways. One was the decision to set the Christocentric affirmation of the original WCC basis* into an explicitly Trinitarian setting by adding the doxological formula "to the glory of the one God, Father, Son and Holy Spirit". The preamble to New Delhi's statement on the church's unity, which has served as an ecumenical yardstick ever since, places the understanding of unity* in a Trinitarian setting: "The love of the Father and the Son in the unity of the Holy Spirit is the source and goal of the unity which the Triune God wills for all men and creation. We believe that we share in this unity in the church of Jesus Christ... The reality of this unity was made manifest at Pentecost in the gift of the Holy Spirit, through whom we know in this present age the first-fruits of that perfect union of the Son with his Father, which will be known in its fullness only when all things are consummated by Christ in his glory." Later, the report explains the distinct work of the Holy Spirit in these terms: "The church exists in time and place by the power of the Holy Spirit, who effects in her life all the elements that belong to her unity, witness, and service. He is the gift of the Father in the name of Jesus Christ to build up the church, to lead her into the freedom and fellowship which belong to her peace and joy. For any achievement of a fuller unity than that now manifest, we are wholly dependent upon the Spirit's presence and governance."

A much more fully developed exposition of this Trinitarian approach was found in the plenary presentation to the assembly by Nikos Nissiotis on "The Witness and the Service of Eastern Orthodoxy to the One Undivided Church". Nissiotis stated: "Unity among men in the church is the result, the reflection of the event of the Father's union with Christ by his Spirit realized in the historical church on the day of Pentecost... Unity is not an *attribute* of the church, but it is its very *life*... It includes the act of creation of man by the Logos; the reality of the incarnation of this same Logos in man; man's redemption and regeneration through him, and the participation and consummation of all history in the event of Pentecost — when the Holy Spirit accomplishes the communion of mankind in Christ."

Nissiotis's presentation — the first by an Orthodox theologian at a WCC assembly — marks the official beginning of the full Orthodox impact on ecumenical thought, underscored at New Delhi through the entry of the Russian Orthodox Church in the membership of the WCC.

The period up to the fourth assembly (Uppsala 1968) was characterized by an increasingly clear recognition in ecumenical thought of the work of the Holy Spirit. The fourth world conference on Faith and Order (Montreal 1963) summed up the insights gained so far and provided the stimulation for more detailed analysis and study.

Montreal 1963. Based on the prior study on "Christ and the Church" and the understanding of the church in the context of the history of salvation, the Montreal report on "The Church in the Purpose of God" stated: "The church is founded on the mighty acts of God in calling his chosen people Israel and supremely in his decisive act in the incarnation, suffering, death and resurrection of Jesus Christ, and the sending of the Holy Spirit... The community of the church was founded to proclaim God's saving act to the world through all ages, and to be continually used by the Spirit to make Christ present again and again through the proclamation of the Word and the administration of the sacraments. Through these means Christ is always at work afresh through the Spirit, bestowing his salvation on man and calling him to obedient service."

Tradition: Based again on extensive preliminary study, Montreal affirmed: "We exist as Christians by the Tradition of the gospel testified in scripture, transmitted in and by the church through the power of the Holy Spirit... What is transmitted in the process of tradition is the Christian faith, not only as a sum of tenets, but as a living reality transmitted through the operation of the Holy Spirit." A little later the report adds: "The scriptures as documents can be letter only. It is the Spirit who is the Lord and Giver of life. Accordingly we may say that the right interpretation... is that interpretation which is guided by the Holy Spirit."

Ministry: Stimulated by new interest in the ministry of the laity,* the people of God,* Montreal addressed the difficult issue of a common understanding of the ministry.* All ministry in the church is rooted in the threefold ministry of Christ, which is made effective in the church through the action of the Holy Spirit. "The Holy Spirit dwells in the church. He comes to each member in his baptism for the quickening of faith. He also bestows differing gifts (*charismata*) on groups and individuals. All his activities are to enable men to serve and worship God. All members of the church are thus gifted for the common good." The Spirit equips God's people to live and work in the world; he builds up the Body of Christ in mutual love; and he calls some to the special ministry, which depends entirely on the Spirit's presence and action in the church.

Worship: Within a Trinitarian understanding of worship as "a service to God the Father by men redeemed by his Son, who are continually finding new life in the power of the Holy Spirit", the report addresses in particular the action of the Holy Spirit in the sacraments* of baptism* and the eucharist.* Both sacraments have their central meaning in the participation in Christ through the Holy Spirit. Therefore, the celebration of both sacraments should include an explicit invocation of the Holy Spirit (see **epiclesis**).

Montreal not only brought together the fruits of previous work but initiated a fresh approach. Studies commissioned by F&O at Aarhus (1964) reflected a desire to intensify the dialogue between the Western and Eastern traditions and to explore further the understanding of the work of the Holy Spirit. Thus, a programme of patristic studies from an ecumenical viewpoint was begun which for several years focused on a new reading of the important treatise by Basil the Great on the Holy Spirit. As a follow-up of the Montreal discussion on ministry, a study was initiated on "Christ, the Holy Spirit and the Ministry" which came to a first point of fruition at the commission meeting at Louvain 1971 and served as background for the Lima document on the ministry. Aarhus said the work of the Holy Spirit needed "more thorough and comprehensive treatment than it received in these Montreal paragraphs. In particular it may be noted that the work of the Holy Spirit enabling human response to the word and action of God in Christ would require explicit treatment; but groups may wish to develop much more their understanding of the ministry of the Holy Spirit."

The renewed interest in the eucharist and its ecclesiological significance was pursued in the context of a study on "The Eucharist — a Sacrament of Unity". Among the questions to be given particular attention was the following point: "How is the activity of the Holy Spirit to be understood when the eucharist is celebrated?" The first report on this study, presented at Bristol (1967), devoted a long section to the "anamnetic and epikletic character of the eucharist", which affirms: "It is the Spirit who, in our eucharist, makes Christ really present and given to us in the bread and wine, according to the words of the institution."

But the most significant impulse emerging from Montreal concerned a more conscious exploration of the relationship between ecclesiology and pneumatology. This was pursued through the study on "Spirit, Order and Organization" and through a process of reflection on "The Holy Spirit and the Catholicity of the Church", leading up to section 1 at the Uppsala assembly. Both deserve brief comment.

The outline of the study on "Spirit, Order and Organization", prepared at Aarhus, took its departure explicitly from the New Delhi statement on the unity of the church, with its recognition of the action of the Holy Spirit. "This understanding of the action of the Holy Spirit in guiding Christians towards unity is important and needs to be fully explored in the light of the biblical and historical doctrine of the Spirit." The outline recognizes the Spirit both as the source of continuity in the life of the church and as judging and transforming power.

The reflection on "the Holy Spirit and the catholicity of the church" developed out of a fresh study of the "nature of unity" following Montreal. It was then refocused as a contribution to the preparations for the Uppsala assembly. The report from section 1 at Uppsala was the first WCC assembly document to address explicitly the doctrine of the Holy Spirit. Paragraph 8 provides the fullest summary of ecumenical thinking on the Holy Spirit up to that moment.

But it was not only this section report which made Uppsala a high point in ecumenical thinking on the Holy Spirit. Important plenary addresses by Ignatios Hazim and Hendrikus Berkhof enlarged the traditional Christocentric perspective of ecumenical thought by a fuller exposition of the work of the Holy Spirit. And looking back to Uppsala and the report of section 1, Nissiotis, in a paper on "The Pneumatological Aspect of the Catholicity of the Church", took direct issue with the "Christological universalism" prevalent in ecumenical discussion thus far and urged the inclusion of the Holy Spirit as an essential element in ecumenical reflection about Christ and the church.

The F&O meeting in Louvain (1971) brought together most of the results of the studies initiated following the Montreal conference. Particularly the reports on "The Authority of the Bible", on "Baptism, Eucharist and Ministry", as well as the concluding report on "Spirit, Order and Organization" help to substantiate more fully the insights gained during the previous period into the various dimensions of the work of the Holy Spirit.

An important new aspect was added through a statement on "Conciliarity and the Future of the Ecumenical Movement": "By conciliarity we mean the coming together of Christians — locally, regionally or globally — for common prayer, counsel and decision, in the belief that the Holy Spirit can use such meetings for his own purpose of reconciling, renewing and reforming the church by guiding it towards the fullness of truth and love... The central fact in true conciliarity is the active presence and work of the Holy Spirit. A council is a true council if the Holy Spirit directs and inspires it, even if it is not universal; and a universally representative body of Christians would not become a true council if the Spirit did not guide it." This statement served as the background for the attempt to describe the unity we seek in terms of "conciliar fellowship", which came to its fruition at the Nairobi assembly (1975); it retains its significance in the context of the present "conciliar process of mutual commitment for justice, peace and the integrity of creation" initiated by the Vancouver assembly (1983). Some of the more recent emphases in ecumenical thinking about the Holy Spirit go significantly beyond earlier affirmations.

The Holy Spirit in the confession of the faith. The Nairobi assembly devoted one of its sections to the theme "Confessing Christ Today". The report, speaking about the confessing community as a community in the Spirit, affirms that to confess Christ today means to be led by the Spirit into struggle, to revive the witness of the prophets, to speak and act with concern and solidarity for the whole of creation.

At its meeting in Bangalore (1978) F&O accepted a statement on "A Common Account of Hope" which includes an affirmation of hope* in God the Spirit: "The living God

becomes accessible to us by the *Holy Spirit*, who confirms God's presence in our lives and makes us members of Christ's Body, the church. By the Holy Spirit, we have hope that already our lives can show signs of the new creation... The Spirit sets us free from the powers of darkness, stirs up our spirits, rekindles our energies, gives us visions and dreams, presses us to work for real communion, overcoming the barriers which sin has erected." These last affirmations are taken up again in the statement's later description of Christian hope as "a resistance movement against fatalism": it is the Spirit who sustains people in the struggle against the threats to the integrity of creation, peace and just relationships in human community.

Two special initiatives regarding the Holy Spirit in the confession of the faith may also be mentioned: the study on the ecumenical significance of the "filioque* controversy", and a very tentative discussion of the "maternal office of the Holy Spirit" in the context of the 1981 Sheffield conference on "The Community of Women and Men in the Church".

The ongoing F&O study "Towards an Ecumenical Explication of the Apostolic Faith" enters fully (in its third part) into a discussion of the affirmations about the Holy Spirit in the Nicene Creed.*

The Holy Spirit and the church. This has been the concern most thoroughly considered since the beginning of the ecumenical movement. Here a brief paragraph from the section report on "Confessing Christ Today" of the Nairobi assembly may serve as starting point. "Those who take part in the life of Christ and confess him as Lord and Saviour, Liberator and Unifier, are gathered in a community of which the author and sustainer is the Holy Spirit. This communion of the Spirit finds its primary aim and ultimate purpose in the eucharistic celebration and the glorification of the Triune God. The doxology is the supreme confession which transcends all our divisions."

The Melbourne world mission conference in 1980 underlined two gifts of the Spirit to the community of the church which seldom receive attention — the gift of prophetic discernment and the gift of healing (see **charism(ata)**). According to the report of section 2, "the churches have a prophetic task to discern, in these struggles and in the ambiguities which they represent, where the forces of the kingdom are at work and where countersigns of the kingdom are being established. The church must awaken to exercise anew its prophetic role and itself ask for the gift of the Holy Spirit to establish effective signals of the kingdom of God." The report of section 3 devoted an entire chapter to "the healing community": "It is a healing of the whole person... which is the sign of the kingdom's arrival."

The most important recent contribution to the understanding of the relation between the Holy Spirit and the church is undoubtedly the Lima document on *Baptism, Eucharist and Ministry*.* The sections on baptism and the eucharist both include extensive reference to the Holy Spirit: e.g. baptism as a gift of the Spirit (B5), the eucharist as invocation of the Spirit (E14-18). The statement on ministry, in its introductory part on "The Calling of the Whole People of God", develops a pneumatological understanding of the church: "The church lives through the liberating and renewing power of the Holy Spirit. That the Holy Spirit was upon Jesus is evidenced in his baptism, and after the resurrection that same Spirit was given to those who believed in the Risen Lord in order to re-create them as the Body of Christ. The Spirit calls people to faith, sanctifies them through many gifts, gives them strength to witness to the gospel, and empowers them to serve in hope and love. The Spirit keeps the church in the truth and guides it despite the frailty of its members" (M3).

The Holy Spirit and religious pluralism. Since it began in 1971, the WCC programme on dialogue with people of living faiths has been faced with the task of formulating a Christian theological understanding of religious pluralism. In this context a new, though tentative, emphasis in ecumenical thinking about the Holy Spirit has taken shape.

In his introductory presentation before the central committee meeting at Addis Ababa (1971), Metropolitan George Khodr interpreted the situation of Christianity in a pluralistic world in light of the work of the Holy Spirit. He challenged the traditional understanding of the oikonomia of God, particularly in Western theology, in terms of the history of salvation. "Contemporary theology must therefore transcend the notion of 'salva-

tion history' in order to recover the meaning of *oikonomia*. The economy of Christ cannot be reduced to its unfolding in history; the heart of it is the fact that it makes us participants in the very life of God. It must involve reference to eternity and to the work of the Holy Spirit. For inherent in the term 'economy' is the idea of mystery."

Stanley Samartha, the first director of this programme, has commented: "What we seek here is not so much to extend the work of the Holy Spirit outside the hedges of the church as a more inclusive doctrine of God himself. A more sensitive recognition of the wider work of the Holy Spirit may also help us to broaden our understanding of God's saving activity." The question of the Holy Spirit and people of other faiths, Samartha concludes, "must inevitably lead to the doctrine of God himself and of the Trinity in far more inclusive ways than Christian theology has done before. It must take into account the unknowability, the incomprehensibleness, and the mystery of God and the work of his Spirit among others no less than his revelation in Jesus Christ through the Holy Spirit" (*Courage for Dialogue*, 24, 76f.).

The Holy Spirit and the charismatic renewal. For more than twenty years many member churches of the WCC have experienced manifestations of a charismatic renewal, characterized in particular by instances of baptism in the Spirit, the gift of tongues and of healing. The WCC Sub-unit on Renewal and Congregational Life has given attention to this phenomenon as part of its concern for a renewal of spirituality.

A preparatory paper for a 1980 consultation, "Towards a Church Renewed and United in the Holy Spirit", offered a tentative theological interpretation of the charismatic renewal, distinguishing an ecclesiological, a cosmological, and a sacramental approach to the Holy Spirit. The ecclesiological approach starts from an experience of the church which can be described as a social experience of God. "The Holy Spirit is God 'in between', or 'the go-between God'. His purpose is to establish relationships between us and to produce a common experience among us." The cosmological approach affirms the Holy Spirit as the one who renews creation and bestows fullness of life. "Within the context of this renewal of creation we expect healing of social relationships, healing in our relations with our own human self, healing of bodily sickness." The sacramental approach is based on the experience of conversion as a "once-for-all event which needs constant and repeated renewal and reinforcement by the power of the Holy Spirit". Reference is made particularly to baptism, confirmation* and ordination.*

Such a distinction of approaches to the reality of the Holy Spirit could prove helpful far beyond this particular consultation. The same could be said of the opening remarks by Kilian McDonnell in his presentation on "Church Reactions to the Charismatic Renewal". Commenting on the excessive fear among the churches of an exaggerated doctrine of the Holy Spirit, he said: "A mutuality exists between Christ and the Spirit. Christ sends the Spirit from the Father, but it is only through the Spirit that one can say Jesus is Lord. There is no Christological statement without its pneumatological counterpart. Also the renewal is saying that the Holy Spirit is constitutive of the church. In the West we build up the church in Christological categories and then when it is an already constructed Christological reality we then, in the second moment of her existence, add the Holy Spirit as a vivifier and animator. The second moment is already too late. The Holy Spirit belongs to the first constitutive moment of the church's existence."

A concluding note. What has emerged from ecumenical thinking on the Holy Spirit is much less than a coherent "doctrine". We are left with more indications of important questions perceived than of common answers found. The remarks by McDonnell point to two fundamental challenges the ecumenical movement has only begun to face. Though formulated against the background of the charismatic renewal, they have been raised consistently by Orthodox theology. Since they go to the very core of the inherited "consensus" in the ecumenical movement, enshrined in the Christocentrism of the basis of the WCC and its implications for the understanding of church and world, it has been difficult to meet this challenge.

José Míguez Bonino has also challenged the traditional Christocentric theological framework in the ecumenical movement, calling for a Trinitarian enlargement which interprets "the second article in relation to the first and the third, both creationally and pneumatologically". The theme chosen for the seventh assembly of the WCC, "Come, Holy Spirit — Renew the Whole Creation", opened up precisely this double perspective.

See also **God, Trinity**.

KONRAD RAISER

A. Bittlinger ed., *The Church Is Charismatic: The World Council of Churches and the Charismatic Renewal*, WCC, 1981 • *Come, Holy Spirit* (= *The Ecumenical Review*, 41, 3, 1989) • Joint Commission between the RCC and the World Methodist Council, *Toward an Agreed Statement on the Holy Spirit*, Secretariat for Promoting Christian Unity, *Information Service*, 46, 1981 • G. Khodr, "Christianity in a Pluralistic World: The Work of the Holy Spirit", in *Living Faiths and the Ecumenical Movement*, S. Samartha ed., WCC, 1971 • N. Nissiotis, "The Pneumatological Aspect of the Catholicity of the Church", in *What Unity Implies: Six Essays after Uppsala*, WCC, 1969 • N. Nissiotis, "The Witness and the Service of Eastern Orthodoxy to the One Undivided Church", in *The Orthodox Church in the Ecumenical Movement*, C. Patelos ed., WCC, 1978 • S. Samartha, "The Holy Spirit and People of Various Faiths", in *Courage for Dialogue*, WCC, 1981 • L. Vischer ed., *A Documentary History of the Faith and Order Movement 1927-1963*, St Louis, MO, Bethany, 1963 • L. Vischer ed., *Spirit of God, Spirit of Christ: Ecumenical Reflections on the Filioque Controversy*, WCC, 1981 • W.A. Visser 't Hooft, "The Basis: Its History and Significance", *The Ecumenical Review*, 37, 2, 1985.

HOMOSEXUALITY. In North America and Western Europe (including Britain), increasingly liberal human rights codes are encouraging gays (homosexual males) and lesbians (homosexual women) to demand, and get, their civil and human rights. In significant numbers, men and women are "coming out of the closet" and declaring their orientation and preference for sexual partners of the same sex. More and more acceptance of this life-style, considered by many cultures and most religions to be deviant at best, is found especially in urban areas.

Probably from its beginnings, the church has included, even in its ministry, people oriented to others of the same sex. For centuries it was kept quiet or, if it surfaced, practitioners were quietly removed and sent away in disgrace. Stereotypes of child molestation and the consequent fear within most people of unusual sexual practice doomed most gay and lesbian persons to lives of lonely desperation, denial and fear of being found out. Celibacy was the only legitimate option for such persons. Down through history, the church has persecuted such persons with a vengeance usually reserved for Jews. Indeed, during the holocaust period in Nazi Germany and its conquered territories, homosexuals were the second largest group sent to the gas chambers. Some 500,000 were exterminated, and the pink triangle they were forced to wear for identification has become today a symbol for gay and lesbian liberation.

Even an examination of the issue is enormously painful for churches, where the discussion of human sexuality is usually mired in myth, fear, doubt and guilt. Increasingly, however, the issue of self-declared practising homosexuals and lesbians entering the ordained ministry is becoming a public issue, causing enormous problems in the life of churches which have been forced to face it.

Definitions are difficult. Does orientation necessarily mean practice? Is it a mental and emotional disorder or a physical disease? Is it something one acquires, or is one born with that attraction to members of the same sex? Is it sin or a gift from God? What does scripture say, and how does one interpret the Bible on this issue? Where does the Christian emphasis on family and marriage fit among people who, thus far, have little hope of either? What about the worldwide epidemic of AIDS?*

Medically speaking, most persons who discuss the subject do not classify homosexuality as a mental or physical illness. There is less agreement on how it arises, but again few experts believe that anyone would willingly choose such a life-style, given the persecution and ostracism that almost all societies impose on gays and lesbians. Statistically speaking, the worldwide AIDS epidemic is more common among heterosexuals than homosexuals, although it has devastated the homosexual community in Europe and Northern America. Today the illness is more often found among the poor and ill-educated, who have no access to the "safe sex" information.

But it is in the churches that there is most controversy, which focuses most sharply on the question of ordination. Fundamentalist, Roman Catholic and Orthodox Christians are quite clear: homosexuality is a sin, and its practice is evil. No one openly acknowledging

his or her orientation as anything other than heterosexual could possibly be ordained, even if that one agreed to be celibate. Yet psychologists and sociologists believe that about 10% of adults are considered to be gay or lesbian. If these figures are accurate, then millions of Christians have engaged in homosexual and lesbian practice. It also means that at least a similar ratio of persons exists in the ordained ministry.

Many churches do not discuss the issue or have no stated policy, even though tradition and practice would indicate its unacceptability. A few will ordain, albeit reluctantly and rarely. Many in North America are discussing it and paying a heavy price from members, the vast majority of whom would argue it is unacceptable, especially for ministers and priests, who are seen as role models for children and families.

For the literalistic interpretation of the Bible the question appears quite clear: homosexuality is wrong and is a sin. Scripture passages like Lev. 18:22, Rom. 1:24-32, 1 Cor. 6:9-10 and the Genesis stories (18:20-21 and 19:4-5) seem definite condemnations. But in a contextual interpretation the issue cannot be settled by an appeal to such proof-texts. On the one hand, attention is called to the fact that on other issues (e.g. slavery), positions held by the biblical authors that corresponded to their times would not be today accepted by Christians and churches. One could ask, Why pick certain of the 613 laws in Hebrew scriptures and ignore others? On the other hand, some scholars have argued that in some of the passages cited, the issue under consideration is not homosexuality as such.

Churches have adopted different positions concerning the issue. The United Church of Canada says that all persons, "regardless of sexual orientation", can be received as members of the church and that all members can be *considered* for ordained ministry. Serious conflict has followed this declaration. Anglicans in Canada will ordain persons with a gay or lesbian orientation, but they must remain celibate. Gay or lesbian candidates can be ordained in congregations of the United Church of Christ (USA), but the national church cannot impose the policy on all congregations. Baptist, Lutheran, most Presbyterian and Methodist, as well as fundamentalist,

Pentecostal, Roman Catholic and Orthodox churches will not consider self-declared practising gay or lesbian people for ordination.

The WCC has not directly addressed ethical, theological and ecclesiological issues raised by homosexuality. The sixth assembly (1983) encouraged churches "to examine and study for themselves and with one another the question of homosexuality, with special stress on the pastoral responsibility of the churches everywhere for those who are homosexual". Subsequently, the WCC Sub-unit on Education collected official church statements on this and several other issues in sexual ethics and prepared a study guide to help churches create programmes "in education, pastoral care and advocacy for justice in relation to sexuality and human relations".

The issue, which has created a fierce debate and deep conflicts in most churches, is far from settled and is likely to continue, particularly if societies and cultures in general become more accepting of homosexuality. For the time being, however, gay and lesbian people will likely have to continue to hide their sexuality, become celibate or join one of the small churches, like the Metropolitan Community Church in North America (which has been refused membership in the National Council of Churches), which will accept homosexuals, and indeed is primarily for gay or lesbian people. Homosexuality has the potential to split churches in many ways. For some churches in cultural areas less tolerant to such orientation or more doctrinally inflexible, the debate will be seen as another sign of Western decadence and liberal fuzziness, as a threat to the family or an obsession with genital sex. Others, however, feel that the human dignity of people made in God's image is at stake and therefore it represents a question of justice.

See also **ethics, sexual**.

HUGH McCULLUM

HOPE. The characteristic emphasis in 20th-century ecumenical discussions of Christian hope has been the linking together of hope for church unity,* hope for the healing of human community and hope for the evangelization of the world. As movements representing these hopes joined together at mid-century to create a new World Council of Churches, they posed a large theological question for the second half of the century: What is our "one hope" of which the scriptures speak?

Much occurred, as the century deepened, to test and darken these hopes. Faith and Order's* optimism about "church union" was encountering Amsterdam's acknowledgment of "our deepest difference". Life and Work's* confidence about social amelioration was facing "rapid social change" and a clamour of conflicting ideologies. And as for mission,* it was shaken to its foundations by the realization that the sending and receiving institutions, and the agreements which had served the cause so well, were in need not of repair but of fundamental re-design in a world Christianity whose majority now for the first time lived outside the traditional North Atlantic centre.

Such considerations contributed to the choice of "Christ — the Hope of the World" as the theme for the Evanston assembly (1954), a choice whose vitality and timeliness were attested by the sharp controversy which came with it. An advisory commission of 32 theologians spent three years drafting a 51-page text that offered a profound discussion of the ultimate Christian hope and its relation to the more provisional hopes of our time.

The commission's report makes a sustained effort to view the various basic ecumenical concerns in the light of "Christ our hope". Because his kingdom* is to come, "the pilgrim people of God"* have realistic hope for their unity and their mission. And the rich meaning in this Christian hope for our "earthly tasks" in history* requires us to dialogue with other "hopes of our time": democratic humanism, scientific humanism, Marxism, national and religious renaissance, the hope of the hopeless.

For whatever reasons, this direct excursion into eschatology* did not bring consensus or even convergence in the early 1950s. The more impressive work on what we hope for as churches actually took place in the narrower church unity discussion during these years, especially in the straightforward attempt to define the nature of "the unity we seek" in the famous New Delhi statement of 1961 about "all in each place" seeking communion* with "the whole Christian fellowship in all places and all ages".

But the 1960s brought new dimensions into

this discussion of the unity we hope for. A new third-world majority in the Christian household of faith was urgently asking for an ecumenical vision of hope which was relevant to the rapid social changes in the human community as such. Everywhere there were growing demands that "the unity we seek" deal not simply with confessional divisions but with racism,* sexism* and classism as church-dividing issues. Moreover, weighty new ecumenical voices from Orthodox and Roman Catholic churches brought powerful new momentum and a demand for apostolic depth to this growing discussion about ecumenical hopes.

Indeed, a crucial contribution came from Vatican II's* emphasis upon the sacramentality of the church, and the new light which this ecclesiology brought to the Council's vision of "the church in the modern world" *(Gaudium et Spes)*. In Uppsala (1968) the WCC underwent a parallel development: a fresh perception of the catholicity of the church opened the door to the importance of church unity for human community. "The church is bold in speaking of itself as the sign of the coming unity of mankind."

The F&O study of Christian hope. Against this background, F&O undertook an ambitious study in the 1970s, not only of the relation of church unity to human community, but of the Christian hope which both share. The study was called, after 1 Pet. 3:15, "Giving Account of the Hope That Is within Us". This time the study began not with an international group of theologians but with scores of local study groups attempting to produce "accounts of hope" relevant to their own situations and problems: African statements, Latin American statements, statements from women's study groups, statements from situations of severe poverty, and many others. At Accra (1974) the F&O commission was then charged with attempting, in the light of these particular hopes, to give "a common account". To its credit, this meeting refused to make a universal "a-political, non-ideological" statement. It honestly presented a statement faithful to the local statements and frankly faced the challenge of a conflicting plurality of hopes within the Christian community. "There is only one hope in Christ, but many relevant ways of expressing it."

After four years of further study the attempt to give "a common account" was renewed at Bangalore (1978), where, after 18 days of intense debate and re-drafting, "A Common Account of Hope" was unanimously adopted by the entire commission. The text openly faces the problem: "hopes encounter hopes", yet "we refuse to believe that the hopes of humankind are ultimately contradictory". A Trinitarian confession then spells out "our hope in God", and an ecclesiological section deals with the church* as "a communion of hope" which "provides the possibility of encounter across human barriers". This section also includes some honest confession about "how we in our churches actually look" in spite of our hopes "to establish a credible communion". The statement then turns to hope for the human community. Rather than trying to generalize upon the vast situational diversity in local studies, the account attempts to identify common international threats to Christian hope which F&O itself faces as an international community: excessive concentrations of power, increasing capacity to shape the physical world, growth of armaments, attacks upon human community, assaults on human dignity, the sense of meaninglessness and absurdity. "We believe that each rightful action counts because God blesses it... The Christian hope is a resistance movement against fatalism." And the text concludes with a much-quoted section on "hope as the invitation to risk".

Outworkings. It remains to indicate the influence of this hope study on other F&O studies. The study on hope is more directly related to the studies on "The Unity of the Church and the Renewal of Human Community", where the essential move has been to view both humanity and the church in the light of the kingdom. The kingdom with its judgment and its promise is addressed to the whole of humanity. The church is that part of humanity which receives and affirms the mission of proclaiming the kingdom as its effective sign and instrument. In the perspective of the kingdom it then becomes possible to speak of the relation of church and world* without one-sided distortion. They belong together eschatologically; the church is truly in the world, even if not of it; and their close interrelation shapes the life and mission of the church both as the mystery of the presence of Christ's body among us and as the prophetic sign or instrument of God's grace for the world. On this basis the study then undertakes to face some of the urgent theological issues in the search for justice and in the community of women and men.

The hope study also led intentionally and directly to the major new study of the 1980s, "Towards a Common Expression of the Apostolic Faith Today". "Doctrine divides," said an earlier ecumenical dictum. But it was the experience of the study on hope which encouraged F&O to begin the more difficult project, with its unavoidable questions of apostolicity* and ecclesial teaching authority.*

Finally, the hope study has strengthened the provisional ecumenical hopes invested in the "Baptism, Eucharist and Ministry"* study. The BEM text is completed: a new fact in the ecumenical landscape; it will not, as a text, undergo major revision. The urgent questions about it have to do with the reception among the churches of the apostolic faith to which it bears witness. BEM has thus become a concrete question of Christian hope for the church unity movement. It may also be noted that BEM's claim to be a statement that is a "convergence", not yet a "consensus",* confronts the ecumenical movement with a fresh theme. What, actually, is a convergence? If, as has been claimed, a convergence envisions a point of consensus out ahead of the churches which responsible theological judgment in each church considers attainable in faithfulness to its own confession of the apostolic faith, then a so-called convergence is nothing less than a concrete expression of Christian hope. Bangalore's vision of the church as a communion of hope and of hope as the invitation to risk then becomes directly relevant to the quest for visible eucharistic fellowship among the churches.

See also **eschatology, history, kingdom of God, salvation history, theology of hope**.

JOHN DESCHNER

Faith and Order, Louvain 1971: Reports and Documents, WCC, 1971 • *For the Years Ahead: Programme of the Commission on Faith and Order*, WCC, 1976 • *Minutes of the Meeting of the Standing Commission, 1977, Loccum*, WCC, 1977 • *Minutes of the Working Committee, 1972, Utrecht*, WCC, 1972, and *Minutes of the Working Committee, 1973, Zagorsk*, WCC, 1973 • *Report of the Advisory Commission on the Main Theme of the Second Assembly: Christ — the Hope of the World*, New York, Harper, 1954 • *Sharing in One Hope: Commission on Faith and Order, Bangalore 1978*, WCC, 1978.

HOUSE CHURCH. It could be said that a house church is the oldest form of Christian gathering. New Testament Christians met in prayer, worship and eucharist in private homes (Mark 14:15 and par.; Acts 1:13-14, 20:7-9). Before the building of basilicas and cathedrals began in the 4th century, archaeological evidence confirms that house churches were the usual site of Christian liturgical gatherings. Today, however, the term "house church" is associated specifically with certain kinds of Christian community in China and in Britain.

In China, the term "house churches" refers generally to groups outside the formal structures of the China Christian Council. They range from small fellowship groups regularly worshipping in homes to huge congregations of hundreds of people organized into closely built networks spanning several provinces and running income-generating enterprises. Some have come into being because there are no public churches in the area to serve the aged believers; others are intentional communities seeking freedom of expression from religious and political authorities. During the years of the cultural revolution (1966-75), when all forms of organized religion were suppressed, house churches served as the only means of Christian fellowship and worship. Even then, the number was relatively small. With the modernization policy in the early 1980s, alongside the re-opening of thousands of public churches throughout China, house churches have blossomed in rural areas. By the end of 1988, the China Christian Council reported 20,602 "meeting points", the official name for house churches. House churches in China own no one theological tradition. Generally, it is easy to detect influences from the Jesus Family, the Little Flock, China Inland Mission, and most prominently, a form of Pentecostalism with emphasis on faith healing and exorcism, similar not so much to charismatic non-denominationalism as to Christian animism.

In the Church of England in the 1950s, priests such as E.W. Southcott in Leeds experimented with "house chuches" as sub-units within the parish. In Britain and English-speaking countries (e.g. New Zealand), the term "house churches" is now used of networks of charismatic, non-denominational churches originating from conferences convened by David Lillie and Arthur Wallis in Britain in the late 1950s and early 1960s. Plymouth Brethren ecclesiology and Pentecostal pneumatology combine in house church theology for the "restoration" of the church. Early teachers were largely from these two denominations. In the early 1950s George North ministered "Wesleyan Holiness" in many small home groups, and Sidney Purse at Chard introduced, from the "Jesus Only" Pentecostal movement, deliverance and healing. These, together with a general spiritual hunger for new church life in the country, contributed, along with the charismatic quest, to the movement's rise in the 1960s.

Today "house churches" is a misnomer because many meet in large premises, even church buildings. But the emphasis on local church, charismatic worship and gifts, relationships, a radical discipling (at one time called heavy shepherding, introduced by Ern Baxter from the USA in 1974) is still characteristic. The fivefold ministries of Eph. 4:11 are restored, and groups of churches are led by different leaders who, though divided, yet remain in fellowship and share a common vision for the church and the kingdom (which is primarily for this age). In the early phases evangelism, interchurch relations and social action were low on the agenda. This has now changed. The house churches have been acknowledged as a stimulus and catalyst by many mainline churches.

See also **church base communities**.

RAYMOND FUNG and ROGER T. FORSTER

R. Fung, *Households of God on China's Soil*, WCC, 1982 • A. Walker, *Restoring the Kingdom*, London, Hodder & Stoughton, 1985.

HROMÁDKA, JOSEF LUKL.

B. 8.6.1889, Hodslavice, Moravia, Czechoslovakia; d. 26.12.1970, Prague. Theologian, ecumenist and pioneer of Christian-Marxist dialogue, he was founder of the Christian Peace Conference,* vice-president of the World Alliance of Reformed Churches (1954-64) and longtime member of the WCC central and executive committees.

Hromádka began teaching systematic theology at the John Hus Faculty in Prague in 1920. His outspoken opposition to Nazism put him at risk when the Germans invaded Czechoslovakia in 1938; he then went to the US, where he taught apologetics and ethics at Princeton Theological Seminary until 1947. Returning to Prague after the war, he became dean of the Comenius Faculty of Protestant Theology in 1950, a post he held until 1964. Influenced by the philosophy of T.G. Masaryk and the theology of Ernst Troeltsch, Hromádka took great interest in the role of the church and religion in a secularized world. He studied Roman Catholicism and its re-evaluation in the eyes of Czech Protestants; and in order to understand Orthodoxy, he learned Russian and read Russian literature and theology.

Hromádka's involvement in the ecumenical movement was long and varied. An architect of 1918 unification of Lutherans and Reformed in the Evangelical Church of Czech Brethren, he was also a founder of the Union of Evangelical Churches in Czechoslovakia (1926). Internationally, he attended conferences of the World Alliance for Promoting Friendship through the Churches* (1928) and Faith and Order* (1937), on whose commission he served until 1961. At the WCC's founding assembly in Amsterdam in 1948 (where he was elected to the first of his three terms on the central committee), Hromádka defended the socialist revolution in a famous exchange with US Presbyterian (later secretary of state) John Foster Dulles.

Convinced that "Western civilization" was a spent force in world history, Hromádka emphasized the socialist vision of a society "in which man will be free of all external greed, mammon and material tyranny, and in which a fellowship of real human beings in mutual sympathy, love and goodwill will be established". In 1950 he protested that the WCC's approval of the United Nations action in Korea represented a yielding "to the mood of one side of the present world".

During the late 1950s a number of European theologians began to speak out against the nuclear armament of West Germany. Their platform, under the leadership of Hromádka, led to the founding of the Christian Peace Conference (CPC), of which he was president until shortly before his death. Warning that rigid anti-communism would lead to catastrophe, he devoted much of his attention in the 1960s to Christian-Marxist dialogue, both in his country and abroad, and sought to maintain contacts between Western and Eastern churches by inviting Christians from abroad to travel "behind the iron curtain" (see **Marxist-Christian dialogue**).

When Warsaw pact troops invaded Czechoslovakia in 1968, crushing the "Prague spring" and its effort to build "socialism with a human face", Hromádka wrote to the ambassador of the USSR in Prague that "the Soviet government could not have committed a more tragic error... The moral weight of socialism and communism has been shattered for a long time to come. Only an immediate withdrawal of the occupation forces would, at least in part, moderate our common misfortune." In 1969 he resigned from the CPC.

Though respected for his courage and integrity, Hromádka's views aroused a good deal of criticism, also from his friends in the West. Barth — himself attacked for complaining about the anti-communism of some theologians — wrote to Hromádka in 1962 that he was disturbed "by the arbitrariness with which you not only champion one of the fronts personally but also expect the church and the world to do the same". A successor to Hromádka as ethics professor at Princeton, Charles West, suggested in *Communism and the Theologians* (1958) that Hromádka had a "naive unanalytical picture of social history" and criticized his "silence in the face of flagrant violations of other men's freedom and welfare..., lack of searching critique towards his own society... and acquiescence in government control of the church itself".

In a tribute at his funeral, WCC general secretary Eugene Carson Blake, calling Hromádka "a man of hope... despite his deep disappointments", noted that "many Americans during the cold war supposed he must be a communist and therefore an enemy, while many communists distrusted his loyalty even while for 21 years he was the strongest force in Eastern Europe in persuading his fellow churchmen to support in faith and hope their revolutionary socialist governments and societies. During these same 21 years he was

Josef Lukl Hromádka (WCC photo)

the outstanding moral interpreter to the West of the vision of justice and peace that has inspired the best in the socialist nations."

ANS J. VAN DER BENT

Among Hromádka's books in English are *Doom and Resurrection*, London, SCM, 1945, and *Thoughts of a Czech Pastor*, London, SCM, 1970 ● See also D. Neumärker, *Josef L. Hromádka*, Munich, Kaiser, 1974 ● J. Smolik ed., *Von Amsterdam nach Prag: Eine ökumenische Freundesgabe an Josef L. Hromádka*, Hamburg, Herbert Reich, 1969.

HUMAN RIGHTS. The scholarly formulations contained in many of today's human rights instruments do scant justice to the fact that the driving force behind all of them has been the determination of people demanding respect for their human dignity. The conviction that the human person has inherent worth and dignity is as old as the experience of oppression. The modern term "human rights" derives from the notion that on the grounds of the paramountcy of these values, limits and duties can be placed upon authorities and the community, nationally and internationally, and that these can be codified and guaranteed by law (see **international law**).

The Stoic idea that all human beings have a common nature and the Judaic teaching that all people are created in the image of God are two striking ancient examples of concern for human rights. The Magna Carta, granted more than seven centuries ago, is often seen as the point of departure for modern human rights.

In the wake of the Reformation and the European religious conflicts of the 16th and 17th centuries, safeguards for religious tolerance and civil liberties began to be enacted in law, most explicitly in England with the Bill of Rights of 1689. The rights guaranteed in these documents, however, are tied to citizenship or social class. The American revolutionaries who framed the Virginia Declaration of Rights in 1776 went a step further by ascribing *innate* rights, independent of status within a society or state. This conception was incorporated into the 1789 US constitution by means of the amendments of 1790.

The 1789 Declaration of the Rights of Man and the Citizen, one of the initial documents of the French revolution, was infused with the anti-clerical spirit of the revolution itself. Whereas the American human rights conception was based on Christian enlightenment and natural law,* the French version derived exclusively from rational philosophy. "Human" rights were juxtaposed to the "divine" rights of monarchs, the traditional recipients of the church's patronage. This was a major reason why Roman Catholic and Orthodox teaching as well as most Protestant theology on the European continent rejected the notion of human rights, preferring instead to emphasize human duties.

The profitability of colonialism* and the industrial revolution were prominent factors in the rise to power of the merchant and manufacturing classes, who managed nevertheless to introduce certain human rights into practically all European constitutions during the 19th century. These were almost exclusively what has more recently been termed the first generation of rights, "bourgeois" freedoms guaranteeing the right to personal property* and the free accumulation of wealth. They required of the state a laissez-faire attitude, non-interference in free trade and economic competition.

The granting of civil and political freedoms meant little to the emerging industrial working class, who found themselves in an unprecedented straitjacket of exploitation. Marx and Engels's Communist Manifesto of 1848 inspired a re-thinking of human rights, requiring of the state a positive intervention for the good of the majority. Although many measures for the implementation of these social and economic rights achieved legal expression through the activities of labour unions, it was only following the Russian revolution of 1917 that states began to guarantee such "second-generation" rights as employment and fair working conditions, education, health care and social security (see **labour**).

The 20th-century struggles against colonialism and for independence highlighted human rights which were due more to a collectivity than to individuals. Emerging nations were demanding the right to self-determination and to development, freedom from want and aggression. To these "third-generation" rights have been added newer concepts related to concerns about peace* and the environment, sometimes referred to as the rights of future generations.

The idea of the universality of human rights, with a validity not only independent of the legal constraints of governments but as an international responsibility, gained new respectability in the wake of the wanton disregard for human dignity during the second world war, symbolized by Auschwitz and Hiroshima. At the inception of the United Nations, the Universal Declaration of Human Rights (10 December 1948) linked world peace and the respect for human rights, stressing that "recognition of the inherent dignity and of the equal and inalienable rights of all members of the human family is the foundation of freedom, justice and peace in the world".

To make the contents of the declaration binding obligations of international law, various conventions relating to human rights have been formulated and ratified, the most important of which are the International Covenant on Civil and Political Rights and the International Covenant on Economic, Social and Cultural Rights, adopted in 1966. Regional human rights instruments have also been created, notably the European Convention on Human Rights and Fundamental Freedoms of 1950, the American Convention on Human Rights of 1969 and the African Charter on Human and Peoples' Rights of 1981.

Content. This survey shows that the content of human rights is open-ended, related to the forms of inequality and oppression against which individuals, groups or nations demand their rights. As new expressions of injustice arise, human rights standards must be expanded or refined. Nonetheless, the foundation on which all human rights are constructed has the following basic elements.

Human rights affirm the *inviolability* of the person.* Life, physical and psychological integrity, and privacy of the family, home, correspondence and property are protected against violation, intrusion or dispossession. Human rights uphold *freedom* vis-a-vis illegal restriction, especially on the part of state power. This aspect includes freedom of thought, conscience and religion, of opinion and expression, of movement, assembly and association. Human rights proclaim the *equality* of all persons. This precludes discrimination on the basis of distinctions of any kind. Human rights furthermore postulate *participation* in decisions affecting the life of society, as well as in the production and consumption of society's goods.

The heated ideological debate between proponents of first- and second-generation rights has merely served as a smoke-screen for governments to delay the full implementation of both. If all basic elements of inviolability, freedom, equality and participation are taken seriously, then the question of priorities in human rights becomes a pragmatic matter. Those immediately threatened with death will seek the implementation of the right to life as a priority. Those marginalized by decision-making processes will seek political freedoms.

More useful distinctions can be made with regard to the nature of the obligation involved in the respective rights. Some rights are immediately enforceable, while others involve programmatic aspects that require time and perhaps even systemic social or economic changes for their implementation. Those rights requiring a negative obligation of the state, such as not intruding, interfering or discriminating, are presently demandable no matter what the political system or the level of economic development. When the obligation involved is positive, where the state has to do or to give something as a contribution to the fulfilment of some economic or social right

such as work, education or health care, full implementation will depend on appropriate means and programmes. When these are lacking, the immediately enforceable right to participate in political decision making becomes a high priority.

Theological interpretations. In light of official church opposition to human rights, viewed for much of their history as the product of humanistic philosophy, the claim of a "theological basis of human rights" might be considered somewhat presumptuous. It is only after the second world war that serious theological work related to human rights has surfaced, and even then much of it concentrated solely on the right to religious liberty. In the Roman Catholic Church, human rights received official sanction through Pope John XXIII's encyclical *Pacem in Terris* of 1962 and in the Second Vatican Council's pastoral constitution *Gaudium et Spes*, 1965. Ecumenically, the WCC co-ordinated an interconfessional study project on theology and human rights beginning in 1979, in which Anglican, Lutheran, Reformed, Baptist and Methodist world bodies as well as the preparatory committee of the pan-Orthodox council and the holy see's pontifical commission Justice and Peace participated.

Institutional efforts which for the most part try to derive human rights systematically from traditional theological concepts such as natural law, covenant,* grace,* Christology or redemption* have been criticized for functionalizing theology in order to regain the churches' credibility or to justify Christian engagement in human rights activities. Such an approach differs radically from that adopted by Christians and theologians who are themselves engaged at the forefront of human rights struggles, impelled by their Christian faith, but without an articulated prior justification. Theological literature emanating from Christian reflection on concrete life-and-death* experiences is growing rapidly, especially in regions where the violation of human rights is most severe. Much of this discussion evades or resists systematic classification according to traditional theological categories and is therefore open to controversy, as for example Latin American liberation theology,* Korean minjung theology* or the Kairos document* by South African theologians. The free development of such unorthodox theological approaches has itself become a human rights claim and raises the question as to whether the limits imposed by church hierarchies on theological or ecumenical dialogue are themselves an infringement of human rights.

Ecumenical activities. The ecumenical movement has accompanied and at times led the human rights movement at local, national and international levels. Frederick Nolde, the first director of the Commission of the Churches on International Affairs (CCIA), served as a consultant on religious liberty* and freedom of conscience to the drafters of the Universal Declaration of Human Rights from 1946 to 1948. The WCC's inaugural assembly in Amsterdam (1948) issued a declaration on religious liberty and underlined the importance of the churches' work for human rights. For 40 years the WCC continued to sharpen its concern, highlighting particular violations such as racism (1968), torture (1977), and extra-judicial executions (1982).

While statements were being made regularly over the years in international ecumenical circles, it was the local churches living in situations of oppression which pioneered the methods of effective church activities and underlined the need for international solidarity. At the international level, the churches underwent a learning process that took several decades before a consensus could be reached on the meaning of human rights, the nature of the churches' responsibilities and the strategies for effective action to combat violations.

Highlights in this history are the creation of the Programme to Combat Racism* following the WCC's Uppsala assembly in 1968, the consensus on an ecumenical understanding of human rights arrived at during the Nairobi assembly in 1975, the creation of a WCC Human Rights Resources Office for Latin America following a number of coups in that continent in the mid-1970s, the creation of a Human Rights Advisory Group within the CCIA in 1978 and the creation of numerous regional ecumenical human rights programmes.

Concurrent with increased awareness of the extent and sophistication of current human rights violations, the 1980s have been witness to unprecedented ecumenical engagement at all levels in monitoring, advocacy and public

Human rights office for missing persons, Manila, Philippines (WCC/Peter Williams)

education. Christians of all confessions have suffered imprisonment, torture, disappearance and martyrdom as a result of their human rights activities. The right to be engaged in the struggle for justice and human dignity has itself become a component of religious liberty.

By the end of the 1980s, the realization that effective human rights work requires international ecumenical solidarity has been put into practice through inter-regional exchange programmes among churches and human rights organizations. These experiences have indicated that the ecumenical community will have to achieve far greater political sophistication in dealing with the root causes of human rights abuse, causes which are international in scope and cannot be dealt with by humanitarian approaches within offending countries alone.

See also **Amnesty International, land rights, religious liberty, United Nations**.

ERICH WEINGARTNER

Behind the Mask: Human Rights in Asia and Latin America, WCC, 1988 • J.F. Collange, *Théologie des droits de l'homme*, Paris, Cerf, 1989 • *Forms of Solidarity: Human Rights*, Geneva, International Reformed Centre John Knox, 1988 • H. Hannum, *Guide to International Human Rights Practice*, London, Macmillan, 1984 • M. Reuver ed., *Human Rights: A Challenge to Theology*, Rome, CCIA/IDOC, 1983 • P. Sieghart, *The International Law of Human Rights*, Oxford, Clarendon, 1983 • E. Weingartner, *Human Rights on the Ecumenical Agenda*, CCIA Background Information, 3, 1983 • J. Zalaquett, "The Human Rights Issue and the Human Rights Movement", *CCIA Background Information*, 3, 1981.

HYMNS. Singing is an essentially ecumenical activity, in space and time. We know of no peoples in the world who do not sing as an integral part of their culture,* and according to anthropological experts, singing came into being even before speech in the process of human development.

In individuals singing is one of the most intimate and profound expressions of the human being, coming from the very heart. Sung sound, technically defined as "the musical expression through the voice, of every emotion suggested by thought and imagination" (*Grove's Dictionary of Music and Musicians*), thus becomes an expansion of the singer's

spirit and was recognized as such by the church fathers, who described tunes sung to the word "Hallelujah" as the climax of the believers' praise and prayer, poured out when they could not organize their ideas articulately to express their feelings. Augustine commented insightfully: "In singing we are doubling our prayers."

Group singing: unison. As a tool for both expressing and impressing, singing is most successful in community. First of all, there is the obvious possibility of uniting many voices in a new expression different from each of them individually — in unison, which has a privileged place in most Eastern civilizations as a symbol for joining everyone's spirit in one and as a basic focus for concentration and meditation, i.e. mystical activity with a strong emphasis on the emotions. (See selection 1.)

Unison — chants and psalms: Unison is the sound preferred in the Gregorian chants, which are associated with the papacy of Gregory the Great (1073-85), and the Genevan Psalter, which came into being among those around John Calvin (1509-64) — but for reasons wholly different from those mentioned regarding Eastern music.

Even though the beauty of the Gregorian chant exercised a very strong influence on Eastern music (a fact well documented by musicians of this century), the strict control of its theory and practice, implemented when it was codified at Rome, gave it the character of "official church music", identified with the papacy's attitude of expanding dominance at that period. Unison thus "subjected to rules" came to express the profound cohesion of an ecclesiastical elite and an ecumenism seen as having its centre at Rome. In fact through Gregory's missionary activity the form of singing which bears his name was imposed throughout the known world and sometimes overwhelmed local cultural expressions such as the Ambrosian hymns, which were genuine community forms associated with Ambrose, bishop of Milan (d.397).

The Genevan psalms were sung in unison for yet another reason, though it was stated with the same authoritarian emphasis. Calvin had inherited from Augustine the fear that music would distract the worshippers or lead their minds to nourish emotions the strength of which would obscure the clear sense of the

word. This concern led him to forbid strictly the use of musical instruments as an accompaniment (associated as they also were with secular music) and multipart harmony.

Group singing: polyphony. Polyphony, as a variety of religious music, began in the northern hemisphere in the 12th century as a derivative of the Gregorian chant and exists as a natural form in other parts of the world such as Africa, with its own development and characteristics, independent of European music, which influenced them through the missionary movement in the 18th century, as students of African cultures have shown. At all events, polyphony in the traditions which use it, both in the North and in the South, is regarded as symbolizing the variety of expressions within an integrated, harmonious whole. In Africa, for example, this multiplicity of voices allows a high degree of freedom in individual improvisations alongside the group performance, thus adding a new dimension to the significance of the symbol.

In European Christianity polyphony is synonymous with freedom of expression, especially as to the artist's independence from ecclesiastical direction. Not a few papal bulls and edicts tried to stem its luxuriant, disorderly and fascinating growth in the middle ages. Regulations in extravagant detail indicated what was permitted and what was open to censure, on the basis even of theological arguments, all of which simply stimulated the imagination and subtlety of the composers in this period when polyphony (which in the 18th century became the undoubted height of musical art in the northern hemisphere) had not quite come of age.

Chorales and hymns: One of the most lowly and elementary forms of polyphonic music, called the "chorale" in Germany and "hymn" in England, became the most valuable tool of the churches from the time of the 16th-century Reformation, just because of its simple structure and straightforward, explicit nature. The idea of the priesthood of all believers is accompanied in Lutheranism by clear-cut action tending to encourage active participation by everyone in the worship. The challenge to make the semi-literate masses sing when they packed Germany's cathedrals must have few parallels in the history of liturgy, music and education in general. Luther (1483-1546) and his fellow workers met it by creating the chorale, adapting all kinds of musical expression to a simple form — Gregorian chants (and Ambrosian too, perhaps closer in spirit to Luther, who was of the people and something of a demagogue), folk tunes both religious and secular, popular songs by contemporary authors and, of course, works they themselves produced.

The structure is simple. At times the same musical phrase is repeated several times, vocalization is infrequent, and the original tune is found in the highest part of the harmony (so that it can be easily heard and reproduced), and it is given a lower register which is suitable for all voices. Also the organ sustains the whole force of the singing with its powerful accompaniment, and the choir (which is not abolished but, on the

Germany / Johann Walter 1541 / Harm. 1934

1. All Mor - gen ist ganz frisch __ und ___ neu des
1. Each mor - ning with its new - born ___ light pro -

lan - gen Tag, drauf je - der sich ver - las - sen ___ mag.
have no end; to him our songs of praise __ as - cend.

Her - ren Gnad und gro - ße ___ Treu, sie hat kein End den
- claims the Lord of life __ is ___ great! His faith - ful - ness will

Selection 2. English text by Fred Kaan. English words copyright © 1974 by Hope Publishing Co., Carol Stream, IL 60188, USA. All rights reserved. Used by permission. For all areas outside the USA and Canada, permission to reproduce the English words has been granted by Stainer & Bell Ltd, London, England.

contrary, is encouraged) supports the congregation and also contributes to the final result with its own more elaborate polyphony. (See selection 2.)

Such a musical setting clearly contributes to both impression and expression. The ancient Greek philosophers already recognized the importance of hymns both for memorizing basic contents and for creating appropriate modes of behaviour. And we may be sure that Paul has something of this in mind when in his letter to the Colossians he puts singing (of psalms, hymns and spiritual songs) alongside teaching and exhortation (Col. 3:16). Of

Luther it is indeed said that his enemies complained even more about his songs than about his sermons, thus indirectly acknowledging the enormously educative value of singing together.

We have to look to the 18th century for a second important step in the development of the ecumenical character of liturgical singing. In 1737 John Wesley (1703-91), the founder of Methodism, published the first modern "hymnal", that is, a collection of hymns, psalms and chorales for worship, coming from a variety of traditions — in other words, "ecumenical" (so far as that was possible at that period). Musically the Methodist hymns are completely the opposite of those previously known. They do not have one note per syllable, and they contain tunes with a great range of vocal and rhythmic development, which undoubtedly owed much to the metrical variety of the poems by Charles Wesley, the movement's most prolific author, and to the attitude of John Wesley himself, who, as opposed to Luther, used folk melodies only exceptionally and encouraged instead the adoption of elements from the non-ecclesiastical "classical" music of his day. By his approach, Wesley broke down the church's isolation from secular modes of expression. It should also be noted that he was widely and harshly criticized.

With his hymnal, Wesley thus established the foundations for an ecumenical repertoire in the fields of music and liturgy. It is a highly praiseworthy fact that the churches of the West have been united by a musical inheritance that has cut across all barriers to produce that small yet great miracle by which members of a variety of traditions are surprised to discover that "they sing the same things we do!"

The missionaries were entrusted with the export of these riches to the rest of the world. Unhappily, in doing so — and dazzled perhaps by the splendour of what was in their trust — they did not have the wisdom to see the value in the cultures they found in their tracks and to include them in the treasury of valued Christian riches. Certainly the missionary movement in most instances overwhelmed cultures and divorced the peoples from their own roots.

Third-world hymnody. Two more centuries passed before the nations of the third world achieved awareness and gained enough strength to offer the rest of the Christian world their own expressions of faith on an equal footing with those of others, which till then had been regarded as "universal". The independence movements in Africa and the claims

Selection 3. Reprinted by permission from *Todas las Voces*, Publicaciones SEBILA, San José, Costa Rica [1988], p. 139.

of the indigenous peoples and the blacks in the Americas, in Australia, and elsewhere certainly had something to do with this.

It may be too early to evaluate the contribution by third-world Christians to hymnody, but certain points already stand out clearly: the African musical idiom which contributes so well to the idea of participative spontaneous worship that is in every way expressive, and the texts of the Latin American songs for the strength and poetic imagination with which they state the claim for social justice as an unmistakable sign of the coming of the kingdom. Those from the communities at the base moreover represent genuine expressions of folk culture (e.g. the Salvadorean mass; see selection 3).

Ecumenical hymnody. The panorama of contemporary Christian hymnody is completed by a mention of poets who have given their work a clearly ecumenical focus that goes beyond their nationalities or ecclesiastical origins. From among them two representative figures may be singled out: Fred Kaan, a Dutchman living in England, and Dieter Trautwein, from the Federal Republic of Germany. They worked closely together so that the WCC could put this new innovative tendency in hymnology into practice. Associated in the task on the musical plane were Erik Routley (England), Joseph Gelineau (France) and Doreen Potter (Jamaica). Their efforts culminated in the publication (melody ed. 1974, full music ed. 1980) of the hymnbook *Cantate Domino*. The work had been started in 1924 by the World Student Christian Federation and is certainly the most significant expression of ecumenical hymnody this century.

Also in the European orbit, mention may be made of the unique contribution of the ecumenical community of Taizé* (France), whose prior, Brother Roger, encouraged the creation of much liturgical and popular music, but within the framework of selective traditional European models. Brother Robert and Jacques Berthier, a musician, had the responsibility for this work.

Experimental liturgies. In the WCC assembly at Vancouver in 1983 two things converged: the call of the third-world churches for their forms of cultural expression to be respected, and the innovations to the liturgy in the northern hemisphere. The result has been the start of a new experimental form of liturgy in which music and singing have the following characteristics among others.

New forms: To the traditional hymn with verses has been added the "short liturgical responses", sometimes consisting of merely a single sentence. Among the reasons for their wide acceptance among Christians of the most varied traditions we find the following. First, the shortness of the responses makes it possible to memorize them and thus allows more flexible participation by the congregation. Second, though so short, the content is generally made up of key words ("hallelujah", "kyrie", etc.), a prayer, some imagery, etc., all of which emphasize the emotional rather than the intellectual side of what is being said (e.g. Russian kyrie; see selection 4). Third, repetition, sometimes frequent, creates a degree of "unconsciousness" in which people momentarily cease to focus on their own identity in order to become one with the larger body of the community. They can also stop singing at specific moments without affecting the overall results, because the congregation continues with the repetition. In other words,

Selection 4.   Reprinted from *Jesus Christ — the Life of the World*, p.117.

the community overshadows the individual's participation and appears to be independent of it.

Changed ideas on "sacred music": Identification of certain styles and forms of European music with Christianity has been replaced by acceptance of every kind of rhythm, timbre, and structure of melody and harmony, inasmuch as these represent forms of authentic human expression. Also, the organ has lost its exclusive role for accompanying communal singing, especially with music for which it is not a satisfactory instrument. It is yielding place to instruments (guitar, zither, mbira, percussion, piano, synthesizer, etc.) which are clearly more suitable for interpreting their own styles.

Broadening the idea of vocal technique: Voice production as understood in the West was mainly derived from 17th-century Italian opera and has ceased to be the sole criterion. Now it is not merely thought proper that the community should get closer in its singing to the ways in which the voice is used in other cultures, as an important form of identification — it is specifically encouraged. For instance, just as African Christians were taught to sing German chorales, using a vocal style other than their own (which in its time was also classed as "sacred"), so too German Christians are now being taught to sing the African songs, disregarding the vocal style characteristic of the chorale.

Use of the original languages: With the same purpose of identifying with "the other", with those who are "different", considerable help in overcoming cultural barriers can be given by using the sounds of the original languages of the songs, with a few key words or meaningful sentences which those who do not know them will find easy to pronounce. A pastoral approach which makes it possible to achieve particularly profound levels of communication contributes to overcoming initial reactions of rejection or displeasure.

Theology and doxology. A hymn is a balanced unity of words and music (indissoluble in ideal instances). The music is not a slave to the words, as has sometimes been said in Christian circles, but neither is the word shackled — quite the reverse. Both words and music are liberated by the gospel to attain new levels of expression. More specifically, the hymns which achieve real

recognition ecumenically, i.e. those which overcome the barriers which sometimes so profoundly and artificially keep human beings apart, are seemingly such as express people's deepest and most genuine aspirations. Perhaps the idea will be better understood if put negatively: hymns with texts which represent primarily doctrinal statements of a decidedly academic nature and are resistant to the soaring of the melody generally do not succeed in getting beyond the limits of the community that shares these statements. Neither do hymns which use only parts of the gospel truth and reduce it to the repetition of sentimental adjectives mainly about the person of Jesus, with tunes which merely reflect the dearth of theological content. Examples of these can be found in Christian hymnody of every age.

Finally, in the ideal symbiosis of poetry and music, both undergo change. Among other things, the music takes on meanings beyond "pure" sound and, most important, the poetry is expanded in an ambience where the emotions rather than thought make the sound come across meaningfully. With such hymns it may be possible to stop singing and not be able to repeat the words but yet to experience a very intense and definite emotion. Thus the admonition to sing "paying attention" to what is being sung (i.e. the text) stresses the intellectual aspect of the hymn in an effort to put something in the forefront which has already become secondary because it is united to the music.

The apostle Paul's advice to sing with the spirit and with the mind (1 Cor. 14:15) reflects a certain fear, still present in Christianity, of "unintelligible" forms of expression which may take Christians into regions where emotions cannot always be controlled or at least classified. But the most important contribution of hymns to the Christian world may in any event be the fact that they provide a means of community worship which is easily accessible, and through which brothers and sisters may identify with each other on the basis not of agreements in doctrine but of deeply shared emotions.

What will the future hold for ecumenical music in practice? Experience of the 1980s enables us to suppose that the elements so far noted will stay with us and will certainly continue to be developed more thoroughly. At all events it is clear that while in some fields the ecumenical spirit seems to be declining, the future in regard to music and singing is rather to be seen as already with us and in course of fulfilment.

See also **church music, liturgy, worship in the ecumenical movement**.

PABLO SOSA

Cantate Domino: An Ecumenical Hymn Book, Oxford, Oxford UP, 1980 • F.H. Kaan, *The Hymn Texts of Fred Kaan*, London, Stainer & Bell, 1985 • *Laudamus: Hymnal for the Lutheran World Federation*, Geneva, LWF, 1984 • I-to Loh ed., *African Songs of Worship*, WCC, 1986 • I-to- Loh ed., *Asian Songs of Worship*, Manila, Asian Institute for Liturgy and Music, 1988 • C.S. Pottie, *A More Profound Allejuia! Gelineau and Routley on Music in Christian Worship*, Washington, DC, Pastoral Press, 1984 • E. Routley, *Ecumenical Hymnody*, London, Independent, 1959 • S.J. Savas, *The Treasury of Orthodox Hymnology: An Historical and Hymnographic Examination*, Minneapolis, Light & Life, 1983.

I

IBIAM, FRANCIS AKANU.

B. 29.11.1906, Unwana, Nigeria. First African student at the medical school, University of St Andrews, Scotland (1927-35) and thereafter missionary doctor, Ibiam was founder and director of Abiriba hospital (1936) and doctor at the Church of Scotland mission hospital in Itu (1953). He established SCM Nigeria in 1937, was president of the Christian Council of Nigeria, 1955-58, served on the standing committee of the International Missionary Council,* 1957-61, was chairman of the provisional committee of the All Africa Conference of Churches and AACC representative at the inaugural conference of the East Asia Christian Conference in Kuala Lumpur, 1959. He was a speaker at New Delhi 1961, attended Uppsala 1968, and was present as a guest at Nairobi 1975. He also served as a president of the WCC, 1961-68.

Ibiam was a key figure in national political life also. Britain appointed him as the first indigenous governor of Eastern Nigeria, 1960, from which position he led the churches to host the WCC central committee in Enugu. In the Biafra war, he sided with his people of Eastern Nigeria and consequently had to go into exile near Zurich until he was received back honourably in Nigeria. Identifying with his people, and in protest against British government support of the central Nigerian government against Biafra, in 1967 he renounced knighthood and other honours that Great Britain had bestowed on him. See D.C. Nwafo,

Born to Serve: The Biography of Dr Akanu Ibiam (Lagos, Macmillan, 1988).

JOHN S. POBEE

ICON/IMAGE.

The word "icon" is an adaptation of the Greek *eikōn*, which means "image". Strictly speaking, it covers all forms of representation, but gradually the word came to denote a specific form of sacred painting on wood in the Byzantine tradition. The basic theological principles are the same for all other forms of visual sacred art (frescoes, mosaics, etc.) as for icons.

From early times Christians have used images along with the verbal proclamation of the good news of Jesus Christ. At first, they were mainly symbolic: Christ as the shepherd, the lamb, a fish (Greek *ichthys*, acronym for *Iēsous Christos Theou Hyios Sōtēr* = Jesus Christ, Son of God, Saviour), although according to some traditions, the figurative representation of the holy face of Christ goes back to Christ's own times (cf. the legend of Abgar, king of Edessa, and the "image not made by human hands", as well as the legend of the linen or shroud of St Veronica, a name that means "true image").

From the time Christianity became the official religion of the empire, Christian art played a role in all parts of the oikoumene, with images of Christ, the *theotokos*, martyrs, saints, Old and New Testament scenes playing a part in worship and as objects of veneration for the faithful. Such veneration came under severe attack during the iconoclastic crisis in the 8th and 9th centuries. Iconoclasm (the breaking of images) began in Byzantium in the first quarter of the 8th century with Emperor Leo III the Isaurian and was finally overcome only in 843 under Empress Theodora. During that time, images were destroyed, and many who venerated images were persecuted.

Two aspects of this crisis deserve mention from the ecumenical point of view: the theological issue at stake, and the repercussions in the West. The first was in a sense a continuation of the Nestorian and the monophysite controversies. The adversaries of images started from the question concerning the icon of Christ: which of his natures is represented, the human or the divine? If it is the human, then it amounts to a form of Nestorianism in that it implies two separate persons in Christ; if it is the divine, it is either monophysitism, in that the human is absorbed in the divine, or it is plain blasphemy, since the divine nature or essence is ineffable, invisible, unknowable and therefore cannot be represented. To this was added the argument that the veneration of a material object amounts to idolatry.

The Orthodox, or upholders of the catholic faith (John Damascene, the fathers of the seventh ecumenical council, the second of Nicea in 787, Theodore of Studios), replied to the first set of questions that an icon of Christ represented neither his human nor his divine nature but his divine incarnate Person, or his *hypostasis*. Since the Word became flesh, the uncircumscribed became circumscribed, all matter is assumed in the mysterious process, and the invisible Word who made himself visible can be visibly represented.

In the view of the church expressed in the second council of Nicea, such a theological view is a direct consequence of Christ's incarnation,* and if the incarnation is to be taken seriously, it is by no means a secondary matter, for it concerns the participation of the flesh and the material universe in salvation.* On the charge of idolatry, the texts of Nicea II are very clear. They take up (after John Damascene) a formula used by Basil in the 4th century to the effect that the honour rendered to the image goes to the prototype, so that when an icon is venerated, the honour goes to

Christ, his mother or the saint represented, not to the actual icon. Besides, the texts draw a very clear distinction between the "veneration" of the icon and "adoration", which is due only to God.

When in 843 iconoclasm was finally overcome and the feast known as the triumph of Orthodoxy was appointed to be celebrated on the first Sunday in Lent (it is still solemnized each year in the Orthodox church), the implications were deeply Christological. Liturgical texts show that the veneration of images is the outward expression of taking seriously the consequences of the incarnation.

The repercussions of the iconoclastic crisis in the West were complex. The papacy remained faithful throughout to the catholic faith and practice. Pope Hadrian I sent legates to the seventh ecumenical council, and the council was received in Rome. Meanwhile Charlemagne and his theologians, basing their case on a totally corrupt translation of the acts of Nicea II, attacked it violently and rejected its decisions concerning the veneration of icons in the early 790s. They accused the "Greeks" of enjoining the "adoration" of images (exactly the opposite of what the council had said) and altogether of being heretics. These accusations and rejections are expressed in the *Caroline Books (Libri Carolini)* and were repeated solemnly at the council of Frankfurt in 794.

Although Pope Hadrian I and his successor, Leo III, resisted Charlemagne's requests to reject the second council of Nicea and defended the Greeks' orthodoxy, Carolingian theologians continued to regard the Eastern practice as suspicious well into the 9th century. Vestiges of this suspicion have remained in the Christian West, where the tendency became widespread to accept images, icons, frescoes, mosaics and statues merely as decoration and visual aids for the illiterate. It is of interest ecumenically to recall that some of the Reformation "iconoclasts" referred to the *Caroline Books* to denounce the "superstitions" of the medieval West in the realm of veneration and that the council of Trent* made reference in reply to Nicea II.

In spite of the undeniable diversity due to the peculiar genius of each place and each epoch, there is a striking unity of spirit in the visual sacred art of the Christian church throughout the period between the 3rd and the

Artist working on a fresco in Trinity Cathedral, Zagorsk, USSR (WCC/Peter Williams)

12th centuries. Certain features characteristic of what today tends to be described as Byzantine art (stylized features, figures and landscapes, absence of naturalistic representation, inversed perspective, etc.) are to be found all over Christendom (in the West, until the Romanesque period on the European continent, the Norman period in England). After the separation between East and West, there appeared a tendency in the Christian West to depart from these features and go for more and more "realism" in the naturalistic sense and towards more and more freedom from the theological principles expressed by Nicea II. In the Christian East, the manner of representation of the divine continued unchanged until "decadence" set in roughly in the 17th century. The 20th century has seen a resumption of "traditional" art.

In the ecumenical context, the 20th century is also witnessing a phenomenon whose consequences are yet to be measured. It is a striking fact that icons, which for obvious historical reasons have long been associated with Byzantium and the Orthodox church, have recently tended to be practically omnipresent in Roman Catholic places of worship and many homes. They are also beginning to appear in some Anglican and even Protestant churches, to say nothing of ecumenical gatherings and centres; what is more, they are very often appreciated by non-Christians. Icon painting is being practised both within and outside the Orthodox world.

Whether this is a passing fashion or something which is here to last, no one can say. But from the ecumenical point of view, this trend obviously presents an opportunity to recall what visual sacred art (and sacred art in general) means within the Orthodox context, where it has never completely died (in spite of periods of decline).

Icons in the Orthodox perspective, which strives to be faithful to the seventh ecumenical council, are "theology in colour". In other words, all the responsibility which rests with the theologians, whose service in the church is an endeavour to express for the contemporary world the truth of Jesus Christ "the same yesterday and today and for ever" (Heb. 13:8), rests also and in the same measure with the icon painter (and other artists). Iconography is a liturgical art. It is part of worship where the truth of the kingdom is not only preached but, in a mysterious way, experienced as a foretaste. All visual representation therefore refers to the *transfigured* reality of all things called to salvation. Hence the stylized, non-naturalistic manner of representation.

The decision of Nicea II says that iconography (and therefore sacred art in general) "is in accord with our preaching of the gospel". Therefore there can be no contradiction between the gospel preached (which is true theology) and what the eyes contemplate (and the other senses perceive). More important still for our ecumenical situation is another statement of the council concerning iconography (and sacred art, i.e. liturgy in general): it is "useful to strengthen our faith in the truly real, non-fictitious incarnation of the Word of God".

It is to be hoped that the present generalized use of icons in prayer by many Christians may serve precisely this purpose of a united confession of the true consequences of Christ's incarnation for the whole of creation.

NICHOLAS LOSSKY

F. Boespflug & N. Lossky, *Nicée II*, Paris, Cerf, 1987 • P. Evdokimov, *L'art de l'icône*, Paris, Desclée de Brouwer, 1972 • *Icons: Windows on Eternity. Theology and Spirituality in Colour*, G. Limouris comp., WCC, 1990 • C. Kalokyris, *Orthodox Iconography*, Brookline, MA, Holy Cross, 1985 • L. Ouspensky, *Theology of the Icon*, Crestwood, NY, St Vladimir's Seminary, 1978 • L. Ouspensky & V. Lossky, *The Meaning of Icons*, Crestwood, NY, St Vladimir's Seminary, 1982 • C. von Schönborn, *L'icône du Christ*, Paris, Cerf, 1986.

IDEOLOGY. Although the term "ideology" gained currency only during the 19th century, preoccupation with its central problem — the relation between representation and reality — has a long history. Xenophanes and Plato were critical of those who, like Homer and Hesiod, misrepresented the nature of gods, creating an illusory fiction.

The problem of misrepresentation has continued throughout Western history. It received a more systematic treatment with Machiavelli, who contrasted the use of open force with the use of fraud in the exercise of power. Fraud is efficacious to the extent that the gap between reality and appearance can be widened. Francis Bacon went further by recognizing that the human mind distorted even scientific observations, for it is beset by "idols" that prevent the acknowledgment of truth. Later the notion of prejudice (Etienne de Condillac, Paul-Henri Holbach, Claude Adrien Helvetius) inherited the basic features of Bacon's theory of idols.

The term "ideology" was first used by Destutt de Tracy at the end of the 18th century. Within the context of the French Enlightenment, his *Eléments d'idéologie* (1801) offered a systematic proposal for a new science. Ideas were understood as natural phenomena expressing the relation of the human body with the environment. Ideology is thus the science that recognizes and systematizes the accumulated knowledge of such relation. Auguste Comte extended the meaning of the term further to describe not only the study of the relationship between the human and the environment on the basis of sense perception, but also the ensemble of ideas of an era characterizing the evolving stages of the human mind (theological, metaphysical and scientific).

For these authors the term "ideology" is devoid of critical significance. Napoleon, in 1812, was the first to present "ideology" as a pejorative concept. He attacked the "idéologues" (de Tracy and his followers), his former allies, accusing them of causing the disgrace of France by building a "tenebrous metaphysics" instead of basing knowledge in "the human heart and in the lessons of history". Although Napoleon's attack was political in nature, since the ideologues were legitimate children of the anti-metaphysical convictions of the French Enlightenment, it would become the fundamental insight in the use of the term by Marx, for whom the ideologue was one who inverts and distorts the relation between ideas and reality.

Marxism and ideology. With Marx the concept of ideology is coupled with critical thinking, restoring into it elements of the critique of representations throughout history. The fundamental thesis of *The German Ideology* (1846), which Marx wrote with Engels, asserts the priority of being over consciousness; in their words, "life is not determined by consciousness, but consciousness by life". Since for Marx life is historical existence and history is conditioned by its mode of material production — with the division of labour and the resulting struggle of classes with interests for themselves — the dominant ideas of an epoch, its ideology, are the ideas of the dominant class. Hence for Marx the function of ideology is to veil the contradictions inherent in a historical mode of production in defence of the dominant class, so that those who are dominated will not raise their consciousness to the need to transform reality. At the same time, only revolutionary practice will bring about the possibility of overcoming ideology. An ideology is maintained as long as an economic system produces fetishes which are reifications of real relations, e.g. labour turns into commodity or exchange into money. Ontologically, ideology distorts the real contradictions of a mode of production; epistemologically, it inverts the relationship between theory and practice.

For Marx the critique of ideology is a necessary but not sufficient condition for revolutionary practice. Ideological critique liberates consciousness from the dominant ideology in order to grant space for a new consciousness to emerge out of revolutionary practice. Yet Marx left this problem unsolved: if ideological critique is necessary, though in a negative sense, under what conditions would such a critique be possible?

In the subsequent interpretation of the concept, we find two trends attempting to address this problem left by Marx. One tends towards positivism, the other towards historicism. The former proposes to solve the problem by moving the discussion from the theory-practice frame of reference to the structure-superstructure relationship. Ideology was conceived as a superstructural *reflection* of the structural (economic) relations and forces of production in a society. If a dominant ideology would reflect the interests of the dominant class in order to maintain domination, a competing ideology would emerge as a reflection of the revolutionary interests of the dominated class, the proletariat. Such consciousness does not emerge spontaneously, but as a result of the political and pedagogical work of a group within this class which is conscious of its own historical role, i.e. the party. The party as the conscious vanguard of its class has an ideology radically different from the dominant ideology. Lenin, arguing this view, would recognize that without such an ideology a party would not fulfill its historical role.

Along these lines, a positive assessment of ideology results. Ideologies not only reflect but create the objective world. The resolution of historical conflicts passes through these new ideologies, which are in conflict among themselves. Later development in this interpretation emptied ideology of its Marxian meaning and approached it more generally as an instrument that defines the psychological, social and political project of a class. In Louis Althusser, science is distinguished from ideology in that the latter is only an unconscious expression of the relation of the human to the world, but essential for the ordering of any social formation. Elements of the historical interpretation of the problem that goes through Machiavelli, de Tracy and Comte are here maintained.

The second trend, which recovered Baconian tenets in the assessment of the problem, was developed by the historicist tradition. It is represented by the sociologists of knowledge and is also present in the theoreticians of the Frankfurt school. According to this view, all understanding is socially, culturally and existentially rooted. Knowledge is permeated by social interests. Science itself is ideological, given that it is interest-laden. Karl Mannheim would go so far as to say that there are ideological elements in the process of knowledge which will remain, even after all efforts are made to recognize interest in any proposition. The reading of any socio-cultural fact has to be done from the standpoint of the interests of the actors. To do this systematically is to apply "ideological suspicion". The point of exercising ideological suspicion is not to remove the layers of ideological husk to get to the pure scientific kernel but to achieve a new level of knowledge surpassing subjectivism, without falling into an illusory objectivism. The goal is to relativize ideologies through an open community of intersubjective communication in which conflicting points of view will allow for a permanent recognition of ideologies and their underlying interests.

In Marx the term "ideology" was confined to its pejorative meaning. It was applied both to religious and theological discourse and to the philosophies and critiques of those who attack religious forms and systems (Bruno Bauer, Claude Lévi-Strauss, Ludwig Feuerbach, etc.) with "phrases" instead of doing it through revolutionary practice. Only with Lenin does "ideology" receive a positive assessment. Being different from science, ideologies belong to the superstructure of a mode of production reflecting at the level of ideas the struggle of social classes. The ideological struggle is a function of class struggle. The triumph of the Russian revolution (1917) was then also the triumph of the communist ideology of the proletariat.

Ideology in ecumenical thought. Religious and theological thinking turned itself against such a notion of ideology in the first half of the 20th century. In the ecumenical movement from the 1930s to the 1960s, "ideology" was used exclusively in a pejorative sense, referring primarily to communism as a system of thought competing with Christianity for the spiritual allegiance of humankind. In 1938 the Tambaram conference of the International Missionary Council states (although not using the term "ideology") that "Marxist communism in its orthodox philosophy stands clearly opposed to Christianity". On the Roman Catholic side, Pope Pius XI declared in *Divini Redemptoris* (1937) that "communism is intrinsically wrong".

In the first assembly of the WCC (Amsterdam 1948), the term "ideology" received an expanded meaning. Though still pejorative, it

A conference in Leipzig (July 1989), with the theme "What is man, that thou art mindful of him?" (epd-bild/Neetz)

was no longer used exclusively to attack communism; Amsterdam called on the churches "to reject the ideologies of both communism and laissez-faire capitalism". The Evanston assembly (1954) maintained the Christian rejection of ideologies but recognized the effects which sterile anti-communist rhetoric and practice were producing in many Western societies under the impact of the cold war.

Not until the world conference on Church and Society (Geneva 1966) was the term "ideology" ecumenically assessed in a non-pejorative sense. It was defined as "the theoretical and analytical structure of thought which undergirds successful action to realize revolutionary change in society or to undergird and justify its status quo". It was also recognized that "Christians, like all other human beings, are affected by ideological perspectives". The challenge that came with the world conference was to work out the relationship between faith and ideologies. In 1971 the WCC central committee decided to insert "and Ideologies" in the title of the sub-unit dealing with "Dialogue with People of Living Faiths" (see **Marxist-Christian dialogue**).

An important ecumenical development was the political challenge that Latin American Christians brought to the theological agenda. As a result, the WCC Faith and Order* commission, meeting at Accra in 1974, recognized that Marxism or communism is not the exclusive or even the main reference of ideology, but that all our ideas have material roots and that the conceptions people hold often have an ideological function. The concern shifted from the sheer rejection of ideologies to the need to recognize them and to understand how they function. This was well expressed in the title of the report "Churches among Ideologies" of the Geneva consultation on ideology and ideologies sponsored by the WCC in 1981.

Roman Catholic responses. In the Roman Catholic Church the notion of ideology was also marked by prejudices until the Second Vatican Council. In the Council the concept is understood as the systematic expression of ideas debased by interests of nations or groups. *Gaudium et Spes* regards ideologies as instruments to impose the interests of profit, nationalism or militarism. The building of the Christian community, says *Presbyterorum Ordinis*, implies that priests can never put themselves at the service of any ideology. While the main concern of the Council when dealing with ideology is to reject "systematic atheism" (a concept that includes but avoids an exclusive attack on communism), the final text has a view of ideology that is still negative but more balanced.

A further step on the Roman Catholic side was taken by the third general conference of Latin American bishops, meeting at Puebla, Mexico, in 1979. The bishops defined ideology as a vision of several aspects of life elaborated from the point of view of a determined group in society. It is legitimate if the interests being defended are also legitimate and show respect for the fundamental insights of the other groups of a nation. In this non-pejorative sense ideology functions as mediation for action. Claiming that ideologies have a tendency to absolutize themselves and become idols, the conference defined the three main ideologies of Latin America as capitalist liberalism, Marxist collectivism and the ideology of national security.*

The ecumenical movement, in its approach to the notion of ideology, has moved from sheer rejection of it (in order to affirm faith) to an attitude of tolerance which recognizes it as a psycho-social and cultural phenomenon. But the challenge of the Accra meeting (1974) remains, demanding a further inquiry into the relationship between faith and ideology. It is not enough to examine the material rootedness of ideologies if the spiritual ground of faith is dualistically divorced from it. A critical approach to ideology requires also the examination of the necessity of the faith-ideology relationship. Such an approach will bring the discussion of the relationship between Christian practice and ecclesial teachings into the agenda of Christians in the oikoumene.

VÍTOR WESTHELLE

J. Larrain, *The Concept of Ideology*, Athens, GA, Univ. of Georgia Press, 1979 • K. Mannheim, *Ideology and Utopia: An Introduction to the Sociology of Knowledge*, London, Routledge & Kegan Paul, 1960 • K. Marx & F. Engels, *The German Ideology*, Moscow, Progress, 1976.

IGNATIOS IV (Hazim). B. 1920, Mhardah, Syria. Ignatius, since 1979 patriarch of Antioch and All the East, has been a president of the WCC, 1983-91, a member of the central committee, 1968-83, and president of the Middle East Council of Churches since 1974. Ordained to the priesthood in 1953, he studied philosophy at the American University of Beirut and theology at the St Sergius Orthodox Institute in Paris. He was founder and director of the Annunciation School in Beirut, 1953-62, and principal of Balamand Seminary and School, 1962-70. Elected patriarchal vicar and ordained bishop in 1962, he became metropolitan of Latakia, Syria, in 1965. From 1970 to 1974 he was dean of St John of Damascus Theological Institute, Lebanon. He has published *An Anthology of Homilies*, 2 vols (Beirut, Al-Nour, 1977).

ANS J. VAN DER BENT

IMAGES OF THE CHURCH.

Since biblical times, images have functioned more powerfully than concepts or definitions in shaping the ways in which the church* and its unity* are understood. The images, in so far as they are taken from ordinary human experience, are generally metaphorical; they are predicated only analogously of the church as a mystery of grace.* In ecclesiology, the images serve as models for thinking about the church and its attributes.

In the New Testament the church is described through a number of metaphors taken from spheres of life that range from agriculture, fishing and business to family relations, domestic chores and religious practice. Temple worship, political memories and living organisms furnish material for ecclesiology. Paul Minear, in his classic study *Images of the Church in the New Testament*, considers some 96 analogies. Among the "major images" he lists several taken from the covenant* history of Israel (e.g. people of God, Israel, holy nation, temple), several based on the universal cosmic order (e.g. new creation, kingdom of God,* communion* in the Holy Spirit*), several referring to the mutual union of Christians in the faith (e.g. fellowship of saints,* disciples, household of God) and several pointing up the organic relations between God and his people (e.g. Body of Christ, fullness of God).

Patristic and medieval theology, while exploiting these NT images of the church, tended to enrich them with allegorical interpretations of biblical texts that did not refer literally and immediately to the church. Thus Cyprian, in his treatise on *The Unity of the Church*, speaks of the seamless robe of Christ, of Noah's ark (outside of which no one can escape death) and of the immaculate spouse who cannot be unfaithful to her husband. The Greek fathers show a marked preference for the image of the church as Christ's mystical body, animated by the Holy Spirit, who sustains all the members with the same divine life. Augustine, incorporating material from the Greek fathers, develops the image of the "whole Christ", head and members. He speaks likewise of the church as bride of Christ and as mother of all the faithful. Mining some of the parables of the kingdom, Augustine argues against the Donatists that the church is a mixed society, containing good and evil members, some of whom are not predestined to eternal life.

In the monastic theology of the medieval Western church, the symbolic interpretation of scripture was in great favour. The church was depicted, e.g., as the heavenly Jerusalem, the new ark of the covenant, the new tabernacle, the new temple, the moon, the Samaritan woman, Martha and Mary, and the woman giving birth to a child. In canon law,* ecclesiastical office was discussed in terms of the "power of the keys" conferred upon Peter (Matt. 16:19). The doctrine of the two swords, founded on Luke 22:38, was used to justify the spiritual and temporal powers of the papacy. The scholastic theologians of the middle ages, more sober in their use of metaphor, interpreted the supernatural life and wisdom of the church in Neo-platonic categories, mediated through Pseudo-Dionysius.

Luther and Calvin developed a critical ecclesiology, resistant to what they saw as exaggerated Roman claims. Both of them, in certain texts, distinguished quite sharply between the visible and the invisible church, according greater dignity to the latter. Yet both of them sought to defend, against radical spiritualism, the importance of the visible church as the place where the gospel is preached and the sacraments* are administered. Calvin described the church as the Body of Christ and as the mother in whose womb the faithful are conceived. Lutheranism, with its strong emphasis on proclamation, tended to emphasize the local congregation and to let the universal structures of unity recede into relative neglect. The dominant image of the church in Lutheranism, and in much of classical Protestantism, is that of a herald.

The Catholic theologians of the Counter-Reformation reacted vigorously against the reformers. They tended to prefer categories borrowed from Aristotelian philosophy and Roman law and to interpret the biblical data by means of these categories. Robert Bellarmine, for instance, portrayed the church as a universal society under the government of the legitimate pastors, and especially under the pope as vicar of Christ. This type of ecclesiology was still dominant at the time of Vatican I (1869-70), which defined the powers of the pope as "shepherd and teacher of all Christians". The biblical metaphor of shepherd was still used but was interpreted in juridical and societal terms, with the accent on jurisdiction.

Many Catholic theologians of the 19th and early 20th centuries felt the need to complement the official juridical ecclesiology with a more organic ecclesiology, having a richer biblical and patristic basis. Influenced by the romantic idealism of his day, Johann Adam Möhler (1796-1838) placed the primary accent on the church as mystical communion, drawing abundantly from the Greek fathers. During the ensuing century the theology of the mystical body underwent a notable development. It received official blessing from Pope Pius XII, who in his encyclical *Mystici Corporis* (1943) stated that the expression "the Mystical Body of Christ" was the noblest and most sublime description of the church. Warning against any dualistic spiritualism, the pope went on to insist that the church, as a body, was necessarily visible and that to be cut off from the visible communion of the society was to be placed outside the Body of Christ. In the concluding section of the encyclical, Pius XII called for prayers that straying Christians might receive the grace to "enter into Catholic unity... in the organic oneness of the Body of Jesus Christ".

With Vatican II (1962-65) official Catholic ecclesiology took a new turn. Early in its Constitution on the Church, the Council set forth four mutually complementary sets of biblical images: flock of Christ, vineyard of the Lord, temple of the Holy Spirit, and spouse of the Lamb (*Lumen Gentium* 6). In the following article (7) *Lumen Gentium* went on to expound at some length the image of the church as Body of Christ. Finally, in chapter 2 (arts 9-17), the Constitution on the Church unfolded the mystery of the church as new people of God,* the image that seems to be dominant in Vatican II. But this image cannot be played off against the teaching of Vatican I. Vatican II, rejecting populist models, taught explicitly that the people of God is a hierarchically structured society in which the pope and the bishops in union with him hold the plenitude of power.

In other passages Vatican II developed the idea of the church as sacrament, i.e. as sign and instrument of Christ's redeeming and reconciling activity. The Decree on Ecumenism recognized that the Catholic church, in its present condition, is in some ways deficient and that the sacramentality of the church called for progress towards unity among all Christians. In line with this sacramental ecclesiology, Vatican II muted the rhetoric of "return" and called for a movement forward on the part of all Christians, including Catholics, to the fullness of grace and truth that God wills for the church (*Unitatis Redintegratio* 12).

The complex history of Protestantism over the past four centuries precludes any simple generalizations about its ecclesiological imagery. Some Protestants, such as Paul Tillich, have tended to look on the visible church as a merely human organization having no necessary relation to eternal life. For them the essential is the invisible spiritual community that exists dialectically within the churches. The mainstream of Protestant thought, however, has depicted the church as the place where the saving word of God resounds and is accepted in faith.* Conservative Protestants, adhering to the Reformation emphasis on correct doctrine, magnify the preaching office and the Bible as text. In some 20th-century authors (e.g. Karl Barth, Rudolph Bultmann, Gerhard Ebeling) the church is presented primarily as an event in which the living Lord makes himself present here and now through proclamation. In this ecclesiology little importance is attached to the continuing life of the church from one generation to another or to the overarching structures of unity.

In the ecumenical movement of the 20th century, it is evident how different ec-clesiological images are linked with different visions of unity. At one end of the ecumenical spectrum are those who maintain that the church of Christ (as divine institution, sacrament, or Body of Christ) continues to exist in a single divinely established fellowship of truth and grace. Incorporation in Christ is obtained through sacramental participation in the life of one particular, historically continuous church. This position may be called the catholic concept of ecumenism. It is represented by many Roman Catholics, Orthodox, and members of other sacramental churches. This model can be set forth in a way that acknowledges deficiencies in every church and admits that separated churches may be partial or incomplete realizations of the church of Christ. Indeed both of these points were asserted by Vatican II.

At the opposite end of the spectrum are Christians who hold that the church exists primarily in local congregations where the gospel is faithfully preached and that structures of unity are a matter of human negotiation. Synodical unions, federations and conciliar organizations are seen as beneficial but unessential. This view of unity is often connected with the image of the church as herald or a community of faith.

According to a third view — that of ecclesiological dualism — the unity of the church is in some sense a given; it can be neither constructed nor dissolved by human effort. The church exists as a spiritual, invisible communion of grace within a multiplicity of bodies that are separated from one another on the empirical plane. This theory of unity rests on a vision of the church in which spiritual unity can exist without bodily or external unity. The task of the ecumenical movement, in this perspective, is not to create but to manifest the unity of the *una sancta*.

Still another ecclesiological model has emerged in 20th-century secular theology. The church, according to this view, has the task of pioneering the unity of the larger human society. It sees itself as a servant of the coming unity of the whole human race. In this perspective the internal unity of the church is not a primary consideration. The main focus is on the goals of universal peace,* justice* and solidarity, to which the service of the church is ordered. The unity of Christians may take the form of provisional coalitions for secular goals, such as civil rights.

The various models of union have been intensely discussed within the ecumenical movement in recent years. Distinctions are made between organic union,* corporate union, fellowship through concordats, conciliar fellowship, unity in reconciled diversity, and the like. Upon examination it becomes apparent that a preference for certain models over others is usually a consequence of an option for a particular image of the church. Thus ecumenism must concern itself with images and models in ecclesiology.

See also **church; Jesus Christ; people of God; unity; unity, models of; unity, ways to**.

AVERY DULLES

A. Dulles, *Models of the Church*, Garden City, NY, Doubleday, 1987 • P. Minear, *Images of the Church in the New Testament*, Philadelphia, Westminster, 1960 • L. Newbigin, *The Household of God*, London, SCM, 1953 • Roman Catholic/Lutheran Joint Commission, *Facing Unity: Models, Forms and Phases of Catholic-Lutheran Church Fellowship*, Geneva, LWF, 1985 • G. Wainwright, "Unité confessionelle et confessante des chrétiens", *Irénikon*, 57, 1984.

IMPERIALISM. Traditionally understood as "a policy aiming at the formation and maintenance of empires", imperialism has been re-defined, mainly in the terms of Hobson, Hilferding and Lenin, or of those of third-world nationalisms, as the policy of international capitalism or of powerful "central" states, for control through economic domination, political pressure and, eventually, armed intervention. The term can also refer to the ideological legitimation of such policies.

While the ecumenical movement has seldom spoken of "imperialism", probably to avoid the ideological connotations and emotional resonance characterizing such vocabulary, issues related to imperialism have been the object of ecumenical reflection, pronouncements and action under such rubrics as capitalism,* colonialism,* decolonization,* dependence,* economics,* international order,* liberation* and third world.*

See also **debt crisis; fascism; ideology; investment; justice; liberation, struggles for; militarism; nation; national security; totalitarianism; world community**.

JOSÉ MÍGUEZ BONINO

INCARNATION. The doctrine of the incarnation has been accorded greater or lesser importance at different periods of Christian history. In the theology of the early centuries, both in East and West, it was of fundamental significance. In more recent centuries there has sometimes been a tendency to set "incarnation theologies" over against "redemption theologies", and to trace back these different lines of thought to different emphases in the Johannine and Pauline writings respectively of the New Testament.

While many theologians at the present time would question how far these tendencies are really mutually exclusive, there can be no doubt that in the centuries since the Reformation a certain style of incarnational theology has been characteristic of those theologians who have sought in the theology of the early centuries, particularly in its Greek form, to find a way through some of the impasses of Reformation and Counter-Reformation controversy. This strategy has been followed by a large number of Anglican writers from the 16th century onwards.

The origins of this line of thought in Anglican tradition are to be found in the work of Richard Hooker (1554-1600), the greatest English theologian since the Reformation. In the fifth book of the laws of ecclesiastical polity, Hooker writes: "Forasmuch as there is no union of God with man without that mean between both which is both, it seemeth requisite that we first consider how God is in Christ, then how Christ is in us, and how the sacraments do serve to make us partakers of Christ" (5.1.3). In this way he established a direct connection between the doctrine of the incarnation, the church* and the sacraments.* This line of thought was developed further in the 17th century, and it came to new life in the teaching of the Oxford movement in the middle of the 19th century, particularly in Cardinal Newman and R.I. Wilberforce. A somewhat different elaboration of these ideas is to be found in F.D. Maurice (1805-74), who draws out the social and political implications of such a doctrine of the incarnation and sees in the sacraments models for a more human and participatory ordering of society.

An emphasis on the doctrine of the incarnation is also to be found in the Lutheran tradition, in for example the great Danish churchman N.F.S. Grundtvig (1783-1872). In a different theological style, he also emphasizes the way in which in Christ the original goodness of creation* and humanity, which is masked but not destroyed by sin,* is transfigured and fulfilled. Grundtvig's theology is grounded in a way which is uncommon in the 19th century. His teaching had its effects not only in the world of education but also in that of agricultural production. It provides interesting suggestions for a theology able to respond to the ecological dilemmas of our time.

No Christian theology which is worthy of its name can evade the mystery of the cross, the mystery of Christ's triumph over death by death. But the doctrine of the incarnation, with its affirmation of the Word made flesh, is also vital to a full and balanced presentation of the Christian message. It is particularly important at the present, in that it provides both a way of looking at God's action in the material world and a way of understanding the action of the Word in different cultures and different traditions. In the fourth gospel, as in the epistles to the Ephesians and the Colossians, the Word is seen at work in all things. No part of human experience is altogether alien to him. In the words of one of the greatest of Greek theologians, Maximus the Confessor: "The Word of God, who is God, wills at all times and in all places to work the mystery of his embodiment."

See also **Jesus Christ, resurrection, uniqueness of Christ**.

A.M. ALLCHIN

A.M. Allchin, *The Kingdom of Love and Knowledge: the Encounter between Orthodox and the West*, London, Darton, Longman & Todd, 1979 • N. Anderson, *The Mystery of the Incarnation*, London, Hodder & Stoughton, 1978 • D.M. Baillie, *God Was in Christ*, London, Faber & Faber, 1949 • B. Hebblethwaite, *The Incarnation*, Cambridge, Cambridge UP, 1987.

INCLUSIVE LANGUAGE.
Language which is carefully chosen, ensuring that both vocabulary and content include all people, is known as inclusive language. Inclusive language is important for many people not only because it reflects a change in culture, in particular in the status of women, but also because it may actually effect that change. It encourages people to examine attitudes which may be exclusive and alter them.

By baptism* all people become full members of the Body of Christ, yet the language of theology and liturgy often seems to deny that basic equality. Those who are not male, white, young and healthy find their existence and experience is rarely mentioned. Women have become increasingly aware of, and vocal about, their exclusion. They have observed that language reflects the culture* which has formed it. A language in which a masculine noun or pronoun can be used to denote members of both sexes reflects a culture in which the male is normative. Language which includes only male metaphors for God reflects a culture for which the most sacred is male. Such language has begun to change. As women emerge from subordination, the language has begun to adapt to make them visible.

In the Christian community, especially but not exclusively in the English-speaking world, concern focused initially on language referring to the worshipping community. Many liturgical revisers in Canada, the US, New Zealand and England agree that alternatives should be found for terms such as "men", "sons", "brothers" and "mankind", and for masculine personal pronouns, on the premise that although these words once had a broad meaning, they are now not believed to be inclusive. It is also accepted that the biblical distinction (in Hebrew, Greek and Latin) between "male human" and "human" should from now on be clearly observed in translation.

Recent liturgical writing and hymnody have gone beyond the use of inclusive vocabulary. Drawing on neglected scriptural and spiritual traditions and the reflections of contemporary women, worship can increasingly benefit from the wealth of women's experience now offered in canticle and prayer, reading and blessing. The worship of the people of God* can begin to include the experience of all the people of God. It has been easier to revise language about the worshipping people than language about the One they worship. The scriptures were fashioned in a patriarchal culture. Biblical images for God are predominantly masculine, and although the Christian God is stated to transcend gender and although devotion to a motherly God is well attested within the tradition, there have been strong negative reactions to feminine imagery. The creative use both of non-personal (love, rock, light) and non-gender-specific descriptions (healer, friend, lover, disturber) is inevitably found to be less troublesome.

Close attention to biblical texts has encouraged debate about translation. Some scholars argue that if texts are to be adequately understood, translation must include a considerable amount of interpretation. An inclusive-language translation might refer to Jesus as "child of God" rather than "son of God", as "human one" rather than "son of man", on the assumption that Jesus' humanity is of greater significance than his masculinity. Exclusively masculine descriptions for God might also be modified, "lord" being replaced by "sovereign", "father" by "father and mother". Suggestions such as these test the elasticity of the Christian faith.

While the 1981 central committee mandated the use of inclusive language in all WCC publications, the question of appropriate language for God was a point of growing ecumenical controversy during the 1980s. The 1988 central committee asked for a theological study of this issue. Some Orthodox argue that the scriptural and patristic source of the Trinitarian formula "Father, Son and Holy Spirit" in the WCC basis* means any change in such language has theological implications affecting the foundation of ecumenical fellowship (see **Trinity**). Interim guidelines for worship at the seventh assembly (1991) affirmed adherence to biblical texts and early creeds while recognizing a need to encourage people creatively to express their faith in contemporary language.

See also **sexism, women in church and society**.

VIVIENNE FAULL

D. Cameron, *Feminism and Linguistic Theory*, London, Macmillan, 1985 • Liturgical Commission of the General Synod of the Church of England, *Making Women Visible*, London, Church House Pub., 1989 • C. Milla & K. Swift, *The Handbook of Non-Sexist Writing*, London, Women's Press, 1980 • National Council of the Churches of Christ in the USA, *An Inclusive Language Lectionary*, Philadelphia, Westminster, years A, B, C, 1983,84,85.

INCULTURATION.

Etymologically, "inculturation" means the insertion of new values into one's heritage and world-view. This process applies to all human dimensions of life and development. Within contemporary Christianity, inculturation signifies the movement which takes local cultures and their values as the basic instrument and a powerful means for presenting, reformulating and living Christianity. Within this process effective dialogue between Christianity and local cultures is carried out. Inculturation, therefore, becomes the honest attempt to make Christ and his liberative message better understood by people of every culture,* locality and time.

Inculturation can be traced back to biblical history, which produced an inculturated Bible. From the beginning, Christianity has passed through various stages of inculturation as it moved from the Jewish to Greek, Roman and Germanic cultures. Since the 16th century, however, missionary Christianity became less willing to be truly incarnated within the cultures and world-views of non-Europeans. In the second half of the 20th century, the inculturation movement has reasserted itself, especially in Africa and Asia, following the achievement of political independence, the indigenization of the local churches and the movement for cultural independence.

Inculturation asserts the right of all peoples to enjoy and develop their own culture, the right to be different and to live as authentic Christians while remaining truly themselves at the same time. It makes Christianity feel truly at home in the culture of each people, thus reflecting its universality. It becomes a prophetic and liberative movement which rejects colonial Christianity and proclaims the liberty of all peoples to serve God within their own basic world-view, thus eliminating the constant danger of dualism or dichotomy in their lives. It is not the aim of the movement to create a faulty, separatist, easy, syncretistic or racialist Christianity.

The scope of inculturation extends to the totality of Christian life and doctrine, the central ministry of Christ and all other ministries which derive from it, the manner of witnessing to Christ, proclaiming his message, worship, organization of church, study of the Bible and theology and pastoral methods. There is no area of Christianity that can be considered to be outside the scope of inculturation.

To inculturate Christianity authentically there is a need for a deep knowledge of both Christianity and culture and an intimate link between liberation and inculturation. The people must be fully involved in the entire process in a new way of doing theology. They need the necessary freedom to think, research and experiment, with the co-operation of church leaders at all levels and an adequate catechesis for active participation. Inculturation is best promoted through ecumenical endeavours when all Christian churches within a similar cultural milieu work towards a common goal.

See also **culture; theology, contextual**.

JOHN WALIGGO

M.C. Azevedo ed., *Inculturation and Challenges of Modernity*, Rome, 1983 • A.J. Chupungco, *Cultural Adaptation of the Liturgy*, New York, Paulist, 1982 • *Confessing the Faith in Asia Today*, EACC statement, Redfern, UK, Epworth, 1967 • Proceedings of Symposia of Episcopal Conferences of Africa and Madagascar, 1969, 1970, 1981, 1984 and 1987 • J.M. Waliggo et al. eds, *Meaning and Urgency of Inculturation*, Nairobi, 1986.

INDIGENOUS PEOPLES. While the question of the status, rights and conditions of indigenous peoples was present in the reflection and debates of the missionary movement and is reflected in the meetings of the International Missionary Council, it did not appear directly on the ecumenical agenda until the establishment of the Programme to Combat Racism* in 1969. While to some extent it cannot be separated from the issue of racism,* nor can it be simply identified with it.

A first question is, who are the indigenous? A working definition used by the United Nations Sub-commission on the Prevention of Discrimination and Protection of Minorities is as follows: "Indigenous populations are composed of the existent descendants of the peoples who inhabited the present territory of a country wholly or partially at the time when persons of a different culture or ethnic origin arrived there from other parts of the world, overcame them and, by conquest, settlement or other means, reduced them to a non-dominant or colonial situation."

Certain characteristics mentioned in this definition must be stressed. In the first place, what distinguishes indigenous peoples from national minorities* and other racially oppressed groups is the fact that they are the original inhabitants of the land, before being displaced by an invading group. While indigenous peoples can be a national minority, in some cases they constitute the majority of the population, as in Bolivia, Guatemala or South Africa. There are an estimated 300 million indigenous people in the world, approximately 6% of the total global population. They reside in industrial and non-industrial countries. There are 250,000 Aborigines in Australia, 350,000 Maoris in New Zealand, 80,000 Sami (Lapps) in the Scandinavian countries, 100,000 Inuits (Eskimos) in circumpolar states, 33.5 million indigenous people in Central and South America, and 3.5 million indigenous people in North America (International Work Group for Indigenous Affairs, *Yearbook 1988*). In Asia there are estimated to be over 51 million in India, 67 million in China, 6.5 million in the Philippines, 1 million in Bangladesh, 11 million in Burma, some 1 million in Siberia and the Soviet Far East. The overwhelming majority of these populations are landless, live in desperate poverty and have little or no access to health and education services. It is for this reason that indigenous peoples have remained high on the ecumenical agenda as a priority concern.

In the second place, no matter where they live or what their political or social culture and beliefs may be, all indigenous peoples view *land* as being the basis of their very survival. While other groups suffer from landlessness, they do not have the same affinity to the land as indigenous peoples. For them it is basic not only for economic survival but also for cultural and religious survival. It constitutes a deep-rooted spirituality. Indigenous peoples have three major goals: politically, they seek self-determination or autonomy; economically, they seek control over the resources of their land in order to use them for their development; socially, they seek the right to practise their cultures and religions and struggle against assimilation and integration, which could mean cultural genocide.

After the establishment of the Programme to Combat Racism, the churches turned their attention to the indigenous peoples and the major issue of land rights. Two consultations of anthropologists and indigenous peoples themselves, convened by the WCC in Barbados (1971 and 1977), supported these people's struggles. This position is reflected in the 1982 WCC central committee statement on indigenous peoples and land rights:* "The indigenous peoples' struggle for land rights is challenging the church to be faithful to its gospel of reconciliation and the biblical affirmation of the creation of all human beings in the image of God. The racist denial of indigenous people's identity can only be combatted when the oppressed are empowered spiritually, economically and politically." Previously, in 1981 a WCC team visited Australia to investigate the condition of the Aboriginal people, and this resulted in the Australian churches' returning property to them valued at $250,000.

The issue of indigenous peoples is also connected with the integrity of creation and problems of pollution and ecology. Current efforts of the WCC are likely to further the ecumenical concern and action with indigenous peoples; they include a land rights consultation (1989), a Justice, Peace and the Integrity of Creation* convocation (1990), and the WCC assembly in Australia (1991). In 1992 churches will be forced to face their past and present responsibility in the 500 years of genocide, land theft and cultural destruction that has resulted from the invasion of the Americas. We cannot separate the concern for the preservation of the earth and our interest in indigenous peoples. By engaging our efforts to save them, we will save ourselves.

See also **environment/ecology, ethnicity, land rights, racism**.

JEANE SINDAB

INDIGENOUS RELIGIONS. Indigenous religions have no single founders but seem to have evolved gradually as people reflected on the mysteries of life such as birth and death (see **life and death**), joy and suffering,* the forces of nature* and the purpose of life itself. They are generally integrated into the whole life, and their history is intimately bound up with the history of each people and region concerned.

The term "indigenous religions" covers a wide range of religious traditions around the world. They are referred to as traditional, primal, tribal or native religions, or shamanism, and incorrectly and disrespectfully (generally by anthropologists, missionaries and some scholars of comparative religion from the West) as primitive, ancestral, natural or spiritist religions. No completely satisfactory term has yet been adopted for what we here discuss as indigenous religions.

Distribution. Indigenous religions are found today in Africa, South and Central America, Asia, Australia and the Pacific region. Statistics show that indigenous religions are widely represented among other world religions. In many countries followers of indigenous religions tend to be officially ignored in national censuses. The number of indigenous religions adherents (see table) is no doubt far greater than what available statistics indicate. The total number of adherents is greater than that of Judaism, Sikhism, Confucianism, Shintoism, Baha'ism and many other religions of the world. The presence and impact of indigenous religions are much greater than the statistics might indicate, in terms of their long integration in the history, language, culture* and world-view of the peoples where they have evolved.

Indigenous religion type	1900	1970	2000
		(thousands)	
Tribal religionists	106,340	88,077	100,536
Shamanists	11,341	15,930	9,947
Afro-American spiritists	247	1,777	7,133
Other spiritists	59	1,385	5,606
Total	117,987	107,169	123,222
Total as % of world pop.	7.3	3.0	2.0

Source: Adapted from *World Christian Encyclopedia* (Oxford, Oxford UP, 1982)

Apart from the areas in eastern and northeastern Asia and Siberia, where shamanism has its stronghold, Christianity generally won converts from followers of indigenous religions. To a much lesser extent Islam has also won converts by persuasion and the sword, among adherents of indigenous religions in Africa and regions of Southeast Asia. But converts to other religions do not necessarily abandon altogether their traditional world-views, which tend to surface in situations of stress and in key moments of life like birth, initiation, marriage, sickness and death. Converts bring with them into their new religions a variety of things from their indigenous religions, although statistics speak of them only as adherents of their new religions.

Sources of information. The primary sources for the study of indigenous religions are oral, in the form of stories, myths, proverbs, prayers, ritual incantations, songs, names of people and places, and the secrets of religious personages. To these can be added art, language, ceremonies and rituals, religious objects and sacred places like shrines and altars, ceremonial symbols, and even the so-called magical objects and practices. Indigenous religions have no written scriptures,* though ancient hieroglyphs such as those of Egypt and Latin America may carry religious texts. The traditional art of the Australian Aborigines is unique and tells much about the religious life of the people, going back to their "dream time".

Indigenous religions are tied to the cultures of the peoples concerned. Their adherents do not propagate them to win converts, the way Islam, Christianity and some modern religious movements do. But where sizable numbers of the adherents move to new areas of living, they carry with them their religions and practise them in their new home, with modifications. A good example of this is the transfer and spread of indigenous African religion to the Western hemisphere through the slave trade. Millions of Africans brought with them their religion to the West Indies and the Americas, and it has never totally disappeared.

Cosmology. The various indigenous religions have much in common in their respective views of God, spirits, force, nature and humankind.

God: In many cases, such as among African peoples, cosmological ideas are built around the concept of God as Creator of all things. He is invisible, but his works are evidence of his existence. For some, God is thought to be less involved in daily life of individuals; for others, he is personally involved in the welfare of society, and people speak of him as Father or Mother, Parent, Friend, Saviour, Protector, Giver of life (chil-

dren, health, food), etc. He is good, just and loving to all people. Prayers, sacrifices or offerings are directed to him, either regularly or in times of communal needs. His name is used in pronouncing blessings, making solemn agreements such as covenants and oaths. In some areas priesthood systems have evolved, forming an active link between people and God. The priesthoods (in many cases, carried out by both men and women) are also transmitters of traditional wisdom, theology, history and other cultural values. In some areas temples exist, with priests and priestesses serving in various religious duties. They officiate at religious ceremonies, pray on behalf of their communities, give advice, and in some cases perform health functions.

In other societies there may be a number of divine figures or a plurality of gods, with some of these having specific responsibilities in the universe. Nevertheless, one of these figures is generally regarded as ranking above the others, whether or not people have direct contact with this one. In others (e.g. among some Amerindians), there is no special concern with the origin of the cosmos as such, and this is taken for granted.

Spirits: Many indigenous religions believe strongly in spiritual figures and beings. Some spirits are personifications of natural objects and phenomena, like heavenly ones such as the sun, the moon, the stars and weather phenomena (thunder, lightning, wind, rain) and earthly ones such as oceans, lakes, rivers, waterfalls, mountains, forests, earthquakes, etc. Other spirits are human beings who have died.

In many traditional societies there are active links between the living and the spirits of the departed, so much so that their religion is referred to as spiritism or spirit worship. There is, in any case, a very active relationship between the world of human beings and that of the spirits. Spirits are often involved in matters of health, such as diagnosing the cause and nature of sickness, treatment and healing procedures, measures to prevent or ward off disease and misfortune, spirit possession and exorcisms. Indigenous religions are thus very much aware of the invisible world and its impact upon the world of human beings.

Force: Indigenous religions acknowledge the existence of a force or power in the universe. The Melanesian word *mana* has become current in referring to this force, although it is differently interpreted in different areas. It is often feared and avoided, especially if it is used negatively as magic. Many African societies, for example, concern themselves much with magic and witchcraft, which they see as an explanation of sickness, misfortune, accident and even death. Those who employ this power in the form of magic and witchcraft are hated by society, and in moments of communal crisis the suspects may be beaten or stoned to death.

Within traditional societies, the normal use of this power has always been for the good. It is often used in the treatment of diseases, in divination, in exorcising spirits, in promoting success, in rain-making ceremonies, in protecting against misfortune, in doing abnormal feats like walking on fire or lying down on sharp pieces of metal or pushing nails through the tongue, and even in entertainment (e.g. in conjuring tricks and hypnotizing the audience).

Nature: Indigenous religions have an important place for nature in its various forms. Even though some forces of nature are destructive, the life of the people depends in countless ways on nature — the food, water, air, fields and hunting grounds, fishing waters, herbs and minerals, animals and many insects, and even its infinite beauty. Indigenous religions cultivate nature and generally make friends with it, protect and respect it to the point of even worshipping some natural forces and objects. Certain places and objects, such as mountains, caves, waterfalls, altars, sacrificial pots, certain trees and rocks, masks, drums, rain-making or other ceremonial stones, certain animals and colours, are set apart as sacred. These are held with awe; some are kept as sanctuaries in which no human beings or animals may be killed and where no trees may be felled. People endeavour to have a mystical relationship with nature and to live in harmony with it. Rituals supporting and defending this mystical relationship are found in all societies which practice indigenous religions. People are not destructive masters over nature. Instead, they are one with nature and must be wise stewards of it.

Humankind: Countless myths tell about the creation or origin of human beings. According to some, humans were created at the end of the primal creation. Some depict a creation from clay, others say that humankind (as husband and wife or as two pairs) was created in heaven (the sky) and lowered to the earth. Some say that the creation occurred in a vessel, in water, or in a fruit of some tree.

These creation stories often tell further that the original state of the first people was one of bliss; many say that there was neither sickness nor death. Others tell that the earth was directly linked to heaven (the sky), with God and the human(s) living close to each other. For various reasons the link between heaven and earth got severed, and the two separated. Death came about, and the original bliss also disappeared.

In indigenous religions the life of the individual is marked with a variety of rites, particularly at birth, initiation, marriage and death. Birth and name-giving ceremonies are occasions for rejoicing and expressing gratitude to God, for the living gift of a child. Initiation ceremonies for the youth can be highly elaborate in many places; some may involve undergoing hardships and painful experiences like circumcision, while others may involve periods of seclusion for the initiates, during which they learn a wide variety of matters pertaining to adult life. Some initiations have secrets that are strictly safeguarded.

Marriage is generally a religious duty in indigenous religions. Many customs and ceremonies are connected with marriage, which is primarily a family-to-family arrangement and not simply a private affair between man and woman. The bearing of children is an integral part of family life, and no efforts are spared to make sure that there are children in each family. Kinship plays a crucial role in the life of society, with ties extending to embrace not only the family but in varying degrees the whole tribe or nation. Religious rituals are often performed within the family or community, some of which are intended to strengthen the kinship ties.

Burial and funeral rites are observed carefully. They serve, among other things, to comfort the bereaved, to send off in peace the departed to the spirit world. Some rites are performed many months or years after the death of a person. Belief in the continuation of life after death is held in many places where indigenous religions have evolved. Naturally the views concerning the hereafter vary considerably. As a whole, the next world is pictured as being very much like the present life, even if those who inhabit it are spirits and not humans. They retain their human characteristics. According to some indigenous religions there is neither reward for good life on earth nor punishment for evil life, but others depict a form of reckoning in the hereafter. The departed may appear to their relatives through dreams, in the waking, or through divination. The living remember their departed through various acts, such as naming new children after them, taking care of their graves, pouring libation of various drinks and setting apart bits of food as an expression of sharing meals. In some societies prayers may invoke some departed members of the family, asking them to carry the message further until it reaches God. There is thus a kind of unity between the living, the departed and God (or other spiritual realities).

Ethics and morals. The ethics and morals of indigenous religions are embedded in customs, traditional laws and taboos. God (or some high-ranking spirit) is ultimately the sanctioner and upholder of morality. Custom regulates what ought and ought not to be done in each society. Offences such as stealing, disrespect towards elderly people, sexual abuse, murder and the like are punished through beating, payment of fine, shame, ostracism or even death. Kindness, politeness, generosity, hospitality, hard work, caring for elderly parents, generosity towards others and friendliness are good virtues which earn social respect, praise and admiration.

Community life is a strong feature in indigenous religions, and many values and activities are directed towards promoting, preserving and safeguarding the community of the living, those who are yet to be born, and in many cases those who have departed. The notion of the community extends also to nature as part of the community. In many societies practising indigenous religions, clan or tribal totems symbolize the ties between human community and nature.

Conclusion. Indigenous religions have had contact with other religions of the world, chiefly Buddhism, Christianity and Islam, and with other cultures, especially Western. In many cases their adherents often convert to these religions. Christianity virtually conquered indigenous religions in the Americas, involving, however, the destruction of tribal, national cultures and human lives during this expansion of colonial Christianity. Since the 18th century Christianity began to spread at an ever-accelerating speed in Asia (with comparatively little or no success, except in Korea), Africa, and the Pacific. Indigenous religions have been very accommodating to these other religions and to Western culture with all its positive and negative contributions to modern life. But conversion or accommodation does not mean abandoning the world of indigenous religions. To the contrary, many Christians in Africa, for example, derive spiritual enrichment from indigenous religions. Some Christian values become absorbed in indigenous religions, and in turn some indigenous religions values have been absorbed in Christianity and Islam.

Written studies of indigenous religions in the 19th century (or earlier) were all done by foreigners from the West (or with Western mentality), such as missionaries, anthropologists, colonial rulers and other self-styled experts. On the whole, indigenous religions were negatively presented, often falsely interpreted and blatantly ridiculed by attitudes of racism and a superiority complex. However, from about the middle of the 20th century, a more objective approach has been gaining ground, as indigenous or native researchers and scholars are on the increase. Forms of inter-religious dialogues are also opening up, and some values of indigenous religions are seeping into circles of Christian discussion or even practice. The WCC's dialogue programme has included indigenous religions, especially in Africa and the Americas; apart from holding special meetings to promote dialogue, representatives of indigenous religions are also invited to multifaith dialogue meetings.

JOHN S. MBITI

R.R. Marrett, *The Threshold of Religion*, London, 1914 • J.S. Mbiti, *African Religions and Philosophy*, London, Heineman, 1969 • R.S. Rattray, *Religion and Art in Ashanti*, London, Oxford UP, 1927 • P. Tempels, *Bantu Philosophy*, Paris, Présence africaine, 1959.

INFALLIBILITY/INDEFECT-
IBILITY. In the ecumenical discussions between the Roman Catholic Church and other

Christian communities, the question of infallibility remains one of the areas in which complete agreement appears an impossible achievement. Nevertheless, the final report of the first Anglican-Roman Catholic International Commission (ARCIC) bore witness to a remarkable degree of consensus* with regard to the main issues involved. Even so, the report had to recognize that Catholics and Anglicans differ in their perception of the manner in which infallibility is exercised through the solemn (i.e. ex cathedra) definitions pronounced by the bishop who is "charged by God to maintain the universal church in the unity of faith".

The infallibility of the church of God. The Orthodox churches and the RCC have always affirmed that the people of God,* by virtue of their being God's own people, remain free from error in keeping the faith* (infallibility *in credendo*) through the indwelling presence of the Spirit of the risen Lord (Vatican II, *Lumen Gentium* 10,12). Infallibility is understood, therefore, as the gift of the Holy Spirit.* This gift enables the church,* through its creed* and its living witness, to adhere with unfailing certainty to what God himself has revealed (see **revelation**); and this certainty remains unaffected by any particular reasons or motives which may be advanced as rational vindications of the faith. Handed down through a living Tradition,* this faith is bound to the Spirit of truth and is present in all the local churches.* It is confessed and celebrated in their liturgy* (lex orandi, lex credendi*), explained and defended by their bishops (either preaching individually from their *cathedra* or acting together in a conciliar decree), witnessed by the public and private life of the Christian community, and proclaimed abroad in mission.*

It is worthy of note that in the US, Lutherans and Catholics in dialogue have found themselves in fundamental agreement over the church's perseverance in the truth received from Christ. This steadfastness has its origin in the assistance of the Spirit, who ensures the transmission and safekeeping of all that has been revealed.

The infallibility of the episcopal body and of the primate. When the apostolic community had passed away, the faithful transmission and preservation of the substance of revelation was assured by God in willing the church to possess, in its ordained ministry, an instrument of the Spirit of truth (see **apostolic Tradition**). The RCC speaks of an infallibility of teaching as manifested in certain pronouncements, whether of the episcopal college as such (i.e. united in a communion which the bishop of Rome "watches over") or of the bishop of Rome (in communion with the entire episcopal body). On these occasions a final judgment may be delivered.

It is not a question of introducing any new word by revelation or inspiration but rather of providing a definitive judgment on an essential point of the Christian datum. Where salvation* is concerned, it is necessary to know what to believe and what to reject in the sphere of faith and morals; thus, the final judgment declares and defines what is true and what is false, and in so doing provides the rule of faith for the whole church. The content of revelation remains unaffected, nothing new has been introduced (*LG* 25). But the meaning of revelation, i.e. its underlying truth, is made explicit in the form of a judgment which brings to an end uncertainty and controversy. This judgment is infallible, or in other words, free from error. It eliminates all doubt concerning what it has expressly formulated qua judgment, but not necessarily concerning other related issues. Thus, the judgment of the bishops assembled at Chalcedon defined the authentic meaning of faith in Jesus Christ, true God and true man. It proclaimed the faith that has been revealed from the beginning and celebrated in the local churches, over which the bishops presided; in so doing, it bore witness to the presence of the Spirit of truth, by whom the churches were firmly united to Christ, the one who declared himself to be "the way, and the truth and the life" (John 14:6).

Although definitions of dogma* may be closely linked to a particular historical or cultural environment, they nevertheless express the essential truths of faith and are devoid of error; they remain valid, even though it may become necessary at a later date to complete or perfect them by a change in their formulation. This situation occurred at Vatican II* with regard to some definitions of Vatican I. A further requirement to be noted is that all dogma should be "received" by the local churches, although reception* does not constitute truth. Infallibility in doctrinal judgment, according to the RCC, does not have its source in reception; on the other hand, it is through reception that judgments pass into the life of the ecclesial community in order to become what they are meant to be: living truth, not archival monuments.

The RCC is alone in affirming that, under certain special circumstances and within conditions that are strictly defined and limited by numerous safeguards, the bishop of Rome outside of a council may deliver an infallible judgment. In this he is assisted by the same Holy Spirit who ensures that the people of God dwell in the truth as it has been revealed; in the words of the decree of Vatican I, he is empowered to "exercise the infallibility with which Christ chose to endow the church" (*Pastor Aeternus*, H. Denzinger-A. Schönmetzer, *Enchiridion Symbolorum* 3074).

The bishop of Rome is given this infallibility only for certain very specific judgments. It does not apply to all the pronouncements, decrees, declarations and documents which he issues, nor to all the doctrinal precisions included in his encyclicals* and bulls. Thus, it cannot be regarded as a guarantee which covers all his "magisterial" acts. The divine assistance which guarantees the infallibility of a judgment is given only when the bishop of Rome speaks ex cathedra, i.e. when he specifically invokes the function of the Roman see in its "supreme apostolic authority" over the communion of faith of the churches. This solemn judgment must be directed to the universal church with the intention to elucidate a truth, in the realm of faith and morals, which is essential to salvation. Vatican II (*LG* 25) specifies that it must be "in accord with revelation itself". Of equal importance is the prerequisite that there must be painstaking inquiry into the contents of revelation "by recourse to all the appropriate resources".

A judgment of this kind can be promulgated only when the bishop in so doing is aware of being in communion with the whole episcopal body and therefore with all the local churches; this explains why Pius IX and Pius XII consulted the local churches before defining the two Marian dogmas. The origins of both can be traced back to the important affirmation of Mary as *theotokos*, as defined by the ecumenical council of Ephesus, and both concerned truths which popular devotion had previously "received". These judgments are irreformable

in the sense that they are not subject — as was claimed by the Gallican Articles of 1682 — to adjudication by any higher instance. Moreover, these are judgments issuing from the episcopal college through the one who in his person holds it together in communion: that is, the bishop of Rome. While his definition of a particular truth may not be expressed in precisely the same language which an ecumenical council* might have chosen, the difference is one of terminology and not of truth.

The final report of ARCIC I has clarified the Anglican position. Contrary to Roman Catholics, Anglicans do not accept that the bishop of Rome (keeping within the prescribed regulations) can make an infallible pronouncement; for them the infallibility of his judgment can be recognized only in retrospect. They are also worried by the fact that Pius IX and Pius XII exercised this "privilege" to define two dogmas when the faith was not under threat. To Anglicans this prerogative is of such momentous import that it should be asserted only in cases of extreme urgency or necessity.

The Orthodox churches reprove the RCC because it developed and defined this view of papal infallibility after the separation between East and West; thus it precluded the possibility of discussion and decision by a strictly ecumenical council in which all the apostolic traditions were represented.

See also **church, primacy, teaching authority**.

J.-M.R. TILLARD

P.C. Empie, T. Austin Murphy & J.A. Burgess eds, *Teaching Authority and Infallibility in the Church*, Minneapolis, Augsburg, 1978 • J.T. Ford, "Infallibility: Recent Studies", *Theological Studies*, 40, 1979 • H. Küng, *Infallible? An Enquiry*, Tenbury Wells, UK, Fowler Wright, 1971 • F.A. Sullivan, *Magisterium: Teaching Authority in the Catholic Church*, New York, Macmillan, 1983 • B. Tierney, *Origins of Papal Infallibility, 1150-1350*, Leiden, Brill, 1972.

INSPIRATION. Throughout the history of the Christian church theories of inspiration have used a variety of adjectives: dictational or mechanistic, personal vs verbal, natural or ecstatic vs organic, partial/dualistic/fundamental vs plenary, static vs dynamic, inspiration restricted to the historic event or the book itself vs inspiration including the effective receiving of the message (through the illumination by the same Spirit), dialectical/actual/existential inspiration, and many permutations. In these theories, the same issues occur, but in terms of differing cultural and philosophical contexts: the relationship between human and divine; the Bible's authority* and uniqueness; the role of the Holy Spirit* in interpretation; the role of the church* and therefore tradition in interpretation (see **Tradition and traditions**); the aim and purpose of scripture; its trustworthiness, including its historical and scientific reliability; and the final ground for believers' assuredness.

Especially during post-Reformation orthodoxy, terminology and philosophical ideas were used which led to serious debates during and after the Enlightenment, and these have continued until today. During the 20th century Karl Barth and Karl Rahner made major contributions towards new and positive interpretations of inspiration in their respective traditions.

Although it is too early to speak of an ecumenical consensus,* the last 30 years have evidenced a significant rapprochement between Catholics, (ecumenical) Protestants and the Eastern Orthodox, though many conservative evangelicals still adhere to the essentials of the orthodox Protestant position and strongly debate its nature and implications (esp. the question of inerrancy). The ecumenical convergence is reflected in the Constitution on Divine Revelation *(Dei Verbum)* of Vatican II and some of the documents of Faith and Order.*

At the world conference on F&O in Montreal (1963) a report on "Scripture, Tradition, and Traditions", expressing the common views of Protestant and Orthodox participants, addressed several issues traditionally related to inspiration: the Reformation principle of *sola scriptura* was qualified by the reminder that the Bible is part of Tradition and embedded in tradition; it in fact becomes living Tradition only when correctly interpreted in ever-new situations; Tradition as source of revelation* was qualified by the assertion that it is accessible only in traditions whose trustworthiness must be tested in the light of scripture. The role of confessional traditions in biblical interpretation, the necessity of constant re-interpretation in different cultural contexts, the diversity within the Bible itself and the accompanying difficulties in speaking of "the" biblical doctrine on any particular issue, as well as the theological consequences of critical scholarship were discussed, with direct bearing on authority and inspiration (see **hermeneutics**).

At the F&O meeting in Louvain (1971) a study on "The Authority of the Bible" followed. The authority was seen not as a fixed quality belonging in some way to the Bible but as a "relational concept", present when experienced as the authority capable of leading people to faith,* as the impact of the self-demonstrating biblical testimony, which is ultimately the authority of God himself. While recognizing the importance of the canon,* the report insisted that the dividing line between canonical and non-canonical writings is not hard and fast. It dealt explicitly with inspiration, saying that it cannot be seen, as often in history, as an *a priori* dogmatic presupposition, on which the Bible's authority is based, but rather as a conclusion of faith, acknowledging the powerful activity of the Spirit behind the experienced authority of the biblical message. The report regarded critical distinctions within the biblical materials as necessary, held that different "relational centres" within the Bible were possible, and re-emphasized the ongoing process of interpretation and the role of the present-day situation.

This development shows convergence with *Dei Verbum*, which also affirmed divine inspiration, but in a "depsychologized" way. Repeating the essential teaching of Vatican I,* it depicted inspiration functionally, in terms of the canonical book which was to be the result (ch. 3, paras 11-13). Referring to 2 Tim. 3, it said: "Since, therefore, all that the inspired authors... affirm should be regarded as affirmed by the Holy Spirit, we must acknowledge that the books of scripture, firmly, faithfully and without error, teach that truth which God, for the sake of our salvation, wished to see confided to the sacred scriptures."

Drawing conclusions, *Dei Verbum* dealt with biblical interpretation in a way similar to F&O. Dulles (in McKim) mentions several related points of convergence: the treatment of "without error" (the fundamental idea of inerrancy but not the term, leaving scope for interpretation); the contents of the canon; the "canon within the canon"; the relationship between the two Testaments; scholarly methods of interpretation; and the material sufficiency of the Bible. "The documents... while they do not totally overcome all the historic disputes... go a long way towards reconciliation... It is no longer safe to assume that either Protestants or Catholics adhere to the classical orthodoxies of their own churches, as expressed in past centuries. Protestant and Catholic biblical reflection, since the mid-sixties, has embarked on a common history."

See also **Bible, its role in the ecumenical movement; canon; exegesis, methods of; hermeneutics; Holy Spirit**.

D.J. SMIT

P.J. Achtemeier, *The Inspiration of Scripture*, Philadelphia, Westminster, 1980 • E. Flesseman-van Leer ed., *The Bible: Its Authority and Interpretation in the Ecumenical Movement*, WCC, 1980 • D.K. McKim ed., *The Authoritative Word*, Grand Rapids, MI, Eerdmans, 1983 • W. Vawter, *Biblical Inspiration*, Philadelphia, Westminster, 1972.

INSTITUTE FOR ECUMENICAL AND CULTURAL RESEARCH.

This residential centre for study, research, writing and dialogue was founded in 1967 by Kilian McDonnell, OSB, and the Benedictine monks of St John's Abbey on the campus of St John's University, in Collegeville, Minnesota, USA. It is an independent corporation with its own ecumenical board of directors, most of whom are laypersons. The Benedictine tradition of worship and work, together with the academic stimulation of the university and college, creates the atmosphere for institute activities.

The institute's task — "to dispel religious ignorance and promote better understanding and harmony" — is conceived broadly as the encouragement of constructive thought in historical, literary, artistic, philosophical, sociological, theological and other kinds of research that bear upon the Christian tradition, including the relationship of Christianity to culture. The institute welcomes men and women scholars, together with their families, for one or two semesters of study and writing on their own projects.

During summer months the institute holds invitational conferences to deal with timely ecumenical issues. A feature of these consultations is the insistence that participants speak in the first person; no one comes as an official representative of an ecclesiastical institution. The institute has pioneered in crossing conventional ecumenical lines by including in dialogue persons from traditions that have historically been wary of the ecumenical movement, and by giving such persons an opportunity to name their agenda instead of assuming they will enter into the ecumenical agenda already set by decades of discussion.

The various projects of the institute seek to discern the history, present reality, and future directions of ecumenical Christianity, and to communicate the results of such work to the churches for the sake of their common mission in a religiously and culturally pluralist nation and world.

PATRICK HENRY

INSTITUTE FOR ECUMENICS.

Founded in 1957 in Paderborn (Federal Republic of Germany) by Archbishop Lorenz Jaeger (1892-1975), this Roman Catholic institute pioneered the serious scientific study of Protestant churches and their theologies with objective, non-polemical methods. Originally called the institute "for *Kontroverstheologie*", in 1966 the title changed to "for ecumenics", in recognition that one must study not only the theology but also the total life of other churches, i.e. their liturgies, pieties, disciplines, polities, and that the aim is not articulated differences and counter-statements but acknowledged commonalities, in the light of which one can better understand and evaluate the differences.

In addition to such studies, the institute promotes ecumenical dialogues in the search for visible church unity* in truth and love; arranges lectures, conferences and study days, especially for those who are in pastoral work and who teach religion; trains specialists in ecumenism; builds up a research library in ecumenics (now over 135,000 volumes), open to scholars and students; and publishes studies through the quarterly *Catholica* and a special ecumenical series (over 60 books).

ALOYS KLEIN

INTERCESSION.

"Intercession" literally means "going between" and has come to mean particularly praying for others, caring for them in the presence of God, pleading their cause and offering their need, in what has been called "the prayer of love". There are many biblical examples of intercession. Abraham prays for the righteous remnant in the city of Sodom (Gen. 18:22-33); Aaron carries the names of the children of Israel with him into the holy place (Ex. 28:29); the psalmist prays for the king (Ps. 72); the king prays for the people (1 Kings 8:30-66). In the New Testament the church prays for Peter in prison (Acts 12:5); Paul prays for the church in Ephesus (Eph. 1:15-23); James instructs the elders of the church to pray for the sick (James 5:14). In the Apocrypha there is reference to prayers for the dead (2 Macc. 12:43-45).

The focus of all Christian intercession is the incarnate Christ himself, who, with the Spirit, makes intercession for the whole of humanity (Rom. 8:26,34). He gave to his followers a pattern of intercession in a prayer that is set in the context of asking that God's will shall be done and the rule of his kingdom should prevail. Christ's own intercession for his disciples, for the church and for the world is the great ecumenical prayer that "they may all be one... that the world may believe" (John 17:21).

Intercession itself, while being seen as essential in the liturgy of all churches, has in the past been a cause of dissension between them. Even in the early centuries of Christian history, controversy arose over the question of prayers for the dead, of which there are examples in the catacombs, and which have continued as a permissible custom in some churches in the form of requiem prayers and commemorations. In the medieval church, dissension arose over the invoking of angels, saints and the Blessed Virgin as aids to intercession, a custom strongly attacked by the reformers, who saw in this a threat to their insistence on Christ as the one and only mediator, but defended by Catholics as a way of calling on the prayer offered continually within the communion of saints.*

Though intercession in recent times has come to play an increasingly important role in all forms of Christian worship, there are many diverse ways of engaging in it. Through the ecumenical movement these have been shared across the whole life of the church. Litanies in the Orthodox tradition, bidding prayers from Catholic liturgies and extempore prayers from Protestant usage all find their place now in ecumenical gatherings for prayer, which have during this century become much more frequently observed both in the local and the international scene.

Mary Holliday, a member of an ecumenical community dedicated to a ministry of intercession, writes: "Intercession is inevitably ecumenical, for it involves an openness to the whole of creation, a partaking in divine loving care for the whole inhabited earth and beyond. It is necessary that intercession, ecumenically based, should be well informed. Knowledge leads to concern and ecumenical education leads to intercession. Interconfessional prayer cycles, intercession lists, and ecumenical litanies from many sources are widely used. Local, national and global prayer for others will often be stimulated by knowledge of special initiatives between churches, particular problems of unreconciled factors, sudden emergencies within crucial interchurch processes in many continents, as well as general concern for the needs of the whole world."

Ecumenical intercession is prayer *in* unity as well as prayer *for* unity, shared by people of all traditions, expressing solidarity with all God's creation. In the annual Week of Prayer for Christian Unity,* the material prepared for use in all the churches gives opportunities for intercession that is well informed about the whole ecumenical movement. The World Day of Prayer,* prepared annually by women of different countries, highlights each year the particular needs of the country responsible for the theme. Current ecumenical prayer cycles* enable the churches to pray not only for one another but also with all God's people.

The growing emphasis on intercession in the eucharistic observances of all the traditions is seen as an important part of that growing together reflected in the *Baptism, Eucharist and Ministry** document (BEM, E21,27). Lukas Vischer, in a WCC paper, expresses the belief that the divided churches anticipate unity "by practising mutual intercession" and suggests that it should form an integral part of every celebration of the eucharist. He states the theological implications of this, for "the entire work of Christ can be presented as intercession". He likens it to the "act of blessing", believes that it "entails suffering" and refers to the "prophetic intercession of Jesus as the hallmark of the prayer in John 17". Vischer goes on to state: "As they accept the common bond of mutual intercession, therefore, the churches will also strengthen one another in their freedom for the future and their openness for love."

See also **prayer in the ecumenical movement**.

MARY HOLLIDAY and PAULINE WEBB

J. Carden comp., *With All God's People: The New Ecumenical Prayer Cycle*, WCC, 1989 • Kirchliches Aussenamt der Evangelischen Kirche in Deutschland, *Leiden von Christen in der Welt. Empfehlungen zur Fürbitte*, Frankfurt, Lembeck, 1977 • L. Vischer, *Intercession*, WCC, 1980.

INTERCHURCH AID.

The present understanding of interchurch aid quickly developed in the ecumenical era after the second world war. The concept broadened from the traditional social and economic help that a church of the same communion gives to another (e.g. US Methodist assistance to Ghanaian Methodists) to joint action in Christian solidarity that crosses ecclesiastical as well as geographical boundaries (e.g. different Western churches helping different churches in India) and, finally, to common Christian stewardship towards the human family in assistance to people in need wherever they are, whoever they are.

Even before the war's end, the provisional committee of the WCC had instituted a department of reconstruction and interchurch aid. Headed in Geneva by J. Hutchinson Cockburn of Scotland, it helped to meet the overwhelming immediate needs of the churches in Europe. After the war, the department co-ordinated workers, materials and funds from the "giving" churches (notably in Australia, Canada, Great Britain, New Zealand, Sweden, Switzerland, and the USA) to supply medicine, clothing, foodstuffs, beds, livestock, etc. and to rebuild church buildings, orphanages, hospitals, etc. for the more devastated "receiving" churches on the continent. The department assumed ecumenical responsibilities also for refugees and displaced persons.

In 1948 the WCC incorporated such work as a permanent obligation, now on a world scale, into the Department of Inter-church Aid and Service to Refugees (DICASR), changed at the 1961 New Delhi assembly to Division of Inter-church Aid, Refugee, and World Service (DICARWS). The 1961 WCC assembly gave DICARWS its new mandate: "to express the ecumenical solidarity of the churches through mutual aid in order to strengthen them in their life and mission and especially in their service to the world around them (diakonia), and to provide facilities by which the churches may serve men and women in acute human need everywhere, especially orphaned peoples, including refugees of all categories".

During the 1960s two actions of the United Nations affected interchurch aid projects: the Food and Agriculture Organization (FAO) launched the first Freedom from Hunger campaign (1960-65), and the UN itself named the decade of the 1960s the first Development Decade. To these initiatives the churches and their interchurch agencies responded both nationally and through the WCC. This period marks the rapid expansion of interchurch aid into agricultural, medical, educational and social projects of the churches in the southern hemisphere. As such work became more specialized, so did the agencies which supported it. Support for "traditional" interchurch aid programmes and projects became more difficult as the agencies began to have altered mandates. For some agencies this alteration was necessary because they were receiving government funding, which precluded support to projects which benefited primarily Christians.

The availability of government funding and the growth of specialized agencies in both North and South created tensions within the ecumenical interchurch aid family. In the strenuous efforts to avoid the donors setting the priorities, the WCC's role as a "friendly broker" became increasingly important. The composition of the DICARWS staff changed from being almost exclusively North American and European to reflecting the global nature of its work.

Following the 1968 Uppsala assembly, a conference in 1970 led to the setting up of a more specialized Commission on the Churches' Participation in Development (CCPD). Its work would enable a comprehensive approach to development* questions, including study and research, education, technical and financial assistance. Nevertheless, a development component continued within the programmes and projects of CICARWS. In

1971 a commission linked CICARWS and CCPD and the Programme to Combat Racism* in the new unit on justice and service.

In recent years serious sharing of resources embraces more than financial aid. Interchurch aid efforts continue to find a more just and equitable format for equal partnership in the process. Round tables and country programmes have developed which seek to ensure that not only the most popular programmes and projects receive support but also those which are a priority to the proposers. The interchurch aid process has highlighted the needs and aspirations of marginalized groups, particularly those of women. Interchurch aid is committed through projects to the WCC Ecumenical Decade of the Churches in Solidarity with Women* (1990s). Diakonia 2000, held in Cyprus in 1986 under the theme "Called to Be Neighbours", further developed the interchurch aid thinking on the diaconal task of the churches.

The impact of global political events continues to influence interchurch aid within the WCC and its member churches, just as it did in the 1940s. Among such recent events are the political changes in Central and Eastern Europe in the late 1980s and the development of greater freedom of the churches to play a much more active part in serving their societies, both outside and within those areas. The local churches now have much greater possibilities to develop themselves as the previous strictures on evangelism* disappear. The giving and receiving churches which faithfully pursued interchurch aid for Eastern and Central Europe have contributed to societal and church changes. New challenges in interchurch aid are here for both the local and the international ecumenical family.

PAMELA H. GRUBER

H.E. Fey ed., *The Ecumenical Advance: A History of the Ecumenical Movement*, vol. 2: *1948-1968*, 2nd ed., WCC, 1986 • K. Poser ed., *Diakonia 2000: Called To Be Neighbours, Larnaca 1986*, WCC, 1987.

INTERCOMMUNION. Intercommunion was the slogan around which, for most of the 20th century, the debate took place concerning the point at which churches might properly enter into eucharistic fellowship with one another. The Orthodox rejected altogether the term and concept of *inter*communion — which the Bulgarian and Romanian responses to *Baptism, Eucharist and Ministry** suspect "Eucharist" (E33) of still favouring — on the grounds that there was either "communion"* in the one church or no communion at all. A similar substantive position was held by the Roman Catholic Church (RCC), some Anglicans, some Lutherans and some Baptists, although they differed on what was required for the unity* of which eucharistic communion was or would be the sacramental expression. On the other hand, those churches which accepted a federal model of unity (see **federalism**) used the word "intercommunion" without any pejorative intent or sense of provisionality, in order to describe their sacramental sharing across persisting denominational boundaries. Between these two positions were to be found those ecumenists who had most stake in the notion of intercommunion: they held that at some point along the road to an ever-fuller unity it became possible and desirable for churches to practise intercommunion as both a sign of the unity they already enjoyed and a means towards more perfect unity. Sometimes adopting an eschatological perspective (for the Lord's supper prefigures the banquet of the final kingdom, where a divided fellowship is unthinkable), they argued that the goal of unity could become proleptically effective through its own active anticipation in the sacrament. At the Faith and Order meeting in Lund (1952) T.F. Torrance spoke of the eucharist as "the divinely given sacrament of unity, the *medicine for our divisions*".

In 1963, on the recommendation of the Montreal world conference on Faith and Order, the WCC formalized a procedure that, in order to bear witness to the tensions inherent in the theory and practice of communion in the painful and scandalous situation of a divided Christianity, conferences should include both a celebration "according to the liturgy of a church which cannot conscientiously offer an invitation to members of all other churches to partake of the elements" and one "in which a church or a group of churches can invite members of other churches to participate and partake". In the long-standing custom of an occasional "open" communion at ecumenical events, it was most often the Anglicans who had acted as hosts, since this usually ensured a maximum number of communicants (if only because Anglicans themselves, whatever their churchmanship, were ready to receive at the hands of an Anglican celebrant, whereas they were not sure to do so in the case of a Methodist, Presbyterian or Baptist presiding).

It was probably the official entry of the RCC into the ecumenical movement which did most to shift the terms of the problematic to those of "eucharistic hospitality" (in fact a better description than intercommunion — which implies mutuality — for what took place in many "open" communion services). Vatican II* recognized that other Christians, by virtue of baptism* and faith* in Christ, still or already enjoy "a certain, though imperfect, communion with the Catholic church" (Unitatis Redintegratio 3). On this ground, pastoral provision could be made for non-Catholics "whose eucharistic faith conforms to the Catholic faith" to receive the Catholic eucharist in the emergency circumstances of mortal danger, persecution, imprisonment, or serious spiritual need (Ecumenical Directory of 1967, 55, clarified in further texts of 1 June 1972 and 17 October 1973). An episcopal dispensation also allows non-Catholics to receive Catholic communion at an ecumenical wedding. (In the diocese of Strasbourg for some years Catholics and their Lutheran or Reformed spouses had a continuing permission to receive communion in each other's church, but this was then stopped on the Roman Catholic side.) The RCC would have liked the Orthodox churches — and thereby Rome made a considerable recognition of their ecclesiality — to offer reciprocal hospitality to Roman Catholics in emergency circumstances (Vatican II, Orientalium Ecclesiarum 26-29; Ecumenical Directory of 1967, 39-45); but with the temporary exception of the Moscow patriarchate for some years after 1969, this has not occurred. In 1984, however, Pope John Paul II and Oriental Orthodox* Syrian Patriarch Ignatius Zakka I entered into such a mutual pastoral agreement for the sake of their faithful who had no access to their respective priests. In the case of Protestants, it was clearer that the Roman emergency hospitality would be offered to them as individual Christians, the limited ecclesiality of their own communities being indicated by the fact that Catholics were still expected *not* to communicate in Protestant churches, whose Lord's supper was marred by a "defect" at the level of ordination (*UR* 22).

The largely individual character of eucharistic hospitality is evident in those churches which practise "open communion" or "general admission". Perhaps the Methodists were the first; but at Princeton 1954 the World Alliance of Reformed Churches* recommended the admission to the Lord's table of "any baptized person who loves and confesses Jesus Christ as Lord and Saviour". In 1975 the German Lutheran churches (VELKD) adopted the position that "access to the Lord's table is in principle open to every baptized Christian who comes trusting in Christ's word of promise as spoken in his words of institution"; and the (Lutheran) Church of Norway, in its response to BEM, declares that while it does not "feel that what is stated in the BEM document yet provides an adequate basis for full eucharistic communion between the churches involved", yet it has "long practised the principle of open communion" on the grounds that fellowship around the Lord's table is "a natural expression" of baptismal unity. The common theological thread in the argument appears to be that, in case of ecclesial conflict, the sacraments belong to the Lord *rather than* to the church(es); but this itself is of course only one possible answer to the question of the instrumentality of the church* in the mediation of salvation.*

Beyond and amid the various current disciplines of the respective churches, there are groups of Christians who, on the basis of local advances in ecumenism or in the context of collaboration in significant projects of witness and service, do in fact practise a certain intercommunion. Although an element of self-indulgence cannot always be discounted, these "communions sauvages" are an understandable expression of impatience at the failure of church authorities to enact the degree of unity that is already possible, and they may benevolently be interpreted as prophetic acts.

While the official admission of individuals in pastoral emergencies is charitable, while the ultimate sovereignty of the Lord over his sacraments* must be maintained, and while the flouting of institutional discipline may bring local and temporary relief, yet the question of *ecclesial* relations cannot be evaded. That is why we are driven back to the possibility of, and need for, *communion agreements* between the churches. These have recently come in various kinds: thus the US Lutheran-Episcopalian interim agreement of 1982 requires that a minister from each church preside at a joint celebration, while the 1973 Leuenberg concordat between European Lutherans and Reformed, in its full mutual recognition of members and ministries, allows for the interchangeability of sacramental presidency, as does the "pulpit and altar fellowship" declared in the Germanys in 1987 and 1990 between the Methodists and the Lutheran, Reformed and United churches. Churches have to decide when their relations with particular partners are ripe for a certain kind of agreement and what is the future road they still have to travel together.

Since 1975 the express constitutional goal of the WCC has been to help the churches to advance to "visible unity in one faith and in one eucharistic fellowship". This is an urgent task. In a passionate paragraph, BEM declares: "The eucharist involves the believer in the central event of the world's history. As participants in the eucharist, therefore, we prove inconsistent if we are not actively participating in this ongoing restoration of the world's situation and the human condition. The eucharist shows us that our behaviour is inconsistent in face of the reconciling presence of God in human history: we are placed under continual judgment by the persistence of unjust relationships of all kinds in our society, the manifold divisions on account of human pride, material interest and power politics and, above all, the obstinacy of unjustifiable confessional oppositions within the body of Christ" (E20). An earlier draft said, even more sharply, that such divisions "make a mockery" of the eucharist.

See also **church, church discipline, communion, eucharist**.

GEOFFREY WAINWRIGHT

D. Baillie & J. Marsh eds, *Intercommunion*, London, SCM, 1952 • "Beyond Intercommunion: On the Way to Communion in Eucharist", in *Faith and Order: Louvain 1971*, WCC, 1971 • Church of England Archbishops' Commission on Intercommunion, *Intercommunion Today*, London, CIO, 1968 • W. Elert, *Abendmahl und Kirchengemeinschaft in der alten Kirche hauptsächlich des Ostens* (ET *Eucharist and Church Fellowship in the First Four Centuries*, St Louis, MO, Concordia, 1966) • L. Hodgson, *Church and Sacraments in a Divided Christendom*, London, SPCK, 1959 • G. Wainwright, *The Ecumenical Moment: Crisis and Opportunity for the Church*, Grand Rapids, MI, Eerdmans, 1983, chs 4-5.

INTERNATIONAL ASSOCIATION FOR RELIGIOUS FREEDOM. The IARF was founded by Unitarians in 1900 in Boston (USA) as the International Council of Unitarian and Other Liberal Religious Thinkers and Workers. It held its first congress in 1901 in London. It is the oldest international inter-religious organization in the world. Originally designed to unite Unitarian and related groups and individuals, IARF membership gradually grew to include representatives of a wide variety of faith groups, including Buddhist, Shinto, Hindu, African tribal religion, as well as liberal Christian. It encompasses 54 member groups in 21 countries and holds a triennial congress as well as many other meetings for inter-religious co-operation and dialogue. A social service network provides direct aid and relief, principally in India.

WILLIAM F. SCHULZ

INTERNATIONAL ASSOCIATION OF MISSION STUDIES. The formal organization of IAMS was in 1972 at a meeting held in Driebergen, Holland, though it had been preceded by a meeting in Oslo in 1970. The idea of the association was proposed in a document published in 1951 by Olav Myklebust, then professor and director of Egede Institute, Oslo. Originally the proposal was for an institute rather than an association, but some personnel of the International Missionary Council* objected because they felt it duplicated the activities of its research department.

When IAMS finally took flesh, its aim was "to promote the scholarly study of theological, historical, social and practical questions relating to mission, to promote fellowship, co-operation and mutual assistance in the study, and to relate studies in mission to studies in theological and other fields". IAMS achieves this aim through research, publications, congresses and a journal.

The research activities have been organized principally around Biblical Studies and Mission; Healing; and Documentation, Archives and Bibliography Network, though individuals carry out other pieces of research. The triennial congresses have been held in Frankfurt (1974), San José, Costa Rica (1977), Maryknoll, NY (1980), Bangalore (1982), Harare (1985), and Rome (1988). The list of venues illustrates the desire to expose participants to the varied contexts of mission in the oikoumene. In each case the city chosen related to the theme of the conference.

In its initial stages, IAMS was a Western European and Protestant organization. But it soon grew to include Roman Catholics and peoples from various northern nations. In the 1970s a conscious effort was made to recruit persons from the two-thirds world. When in 1988 it took the other significant step of electing such a person as its first non-northern president, it thereby declared the two-thirds world to be of age in the world of mission and mission studies. The membership of the association in 1990 is over 500 individuals and institutions. As it faces the closing decade of the 20th century, it is conscious of the paucity of women in its ranks. It broke new ground when it elected a woman from the USA as its president for 1985-88, thus giving a face to the many silent and insufficiently acknowledged witnesses to God in the history of the church.

JOHN S. POBEE

INTERNATIONAL CHRISTIAN YOUTH EXCHANGE.

The ICYE grew out of an initiative in 1949 of the Church of the Brethren (USA), in co-operation with the US state department, to bring German youth to the USA to spend a year living with a family, going to school and sharing in church life. In 1957 ICYE was formed by five denominations in the US as an independent church-sponsored agency to continue and expand the opportunities of ecumenical exchange for young people 16-18 years of age. The programme then began sending US high school students abroad for a year and initiated exchanges with other European countries. In succeeding years participation spread to Asia, Latin America and Africa in co-operation with ecumenical youth movements and the WCC Youth department. In 1965 exchanges began among European countries and among regions, not only with the USA. By the late 1960s there were 27 countries involved, and 450 youth participated annually.

At the beginning, the programme was shaped by the urge for reconciliation following the second world war. In the 1950s there was a strong emphasis on the church, Christian commitment and ecumenical education, just as in the churches those were years of church growth and active youth organizations.

Developments in the 1960s were quite different. Religious commitment did not weaken but was interpreted in different ways. In the annual consultations and in the international committee, vigorous discussions took place on how to understand the aims and purposes of ICYE and the meaning of "Christian" in its name. ICYE increasingly reflected the fact that in the US and in Europe especially the decade was marked by turmoil, protest by youth and students, and the demand for international economic justice. There was, moreover, the experience of liberation from traditional ideas and patterns of behaviour.

In 1967 ICYE, the World Student Christian Federation's European section for Student Christian Movement school movements, and the European working group of the WCC Youth department together sponsored a conference for youth with the theme "Revolution: The Struggle for True Humanity". Out of the 183 participants, 115 were ICYE students who had spent a year overseas. Participants were critical of educational systems which ignored the dimensions of social change in a world of economic and political injustice.

The international committee, meeting in Berlin in 1969 and reflecting the questioning of the times and the debate about ICYE's Christian character, stated that "ICYE sponsors the exchange of young people among nations as a means of international and ecumenical education to further Christian commitment to and responsibility for reconciliation, justice and peace in the world. ICYE seeks to enable all participants to discover the common bonds they share with the whole of humanity. ICYE therefore seeks encounter with persons of all convictions and invites participation of those who share its aims and who wish to take part in its programmes."

Organizationally, while still a US-based programme, ICYE early began to make its consultative and decision-making structures representative of the participating countries and churches. Representatives of its national committees in Europe first met in 1959; annual US-European consultations followed. In 1966 the international committee was created to give more organizational reality to what had been a process of informal consultation and to supervise the worldwide programme. The international council for ICYE was formed in 1969 and in 1970 began operating in Geneva; in 1976 it transferred to Berlin.

During the 1970s ICYE faced several crises. The separation of the US programme from the international operation resulted in a precarious financial situation. At the same time, the nature of international exchange and of Christian commitment was called into question. The internal tensions increased, and in 1977 the international council was dissolved and a new federation of national ICYE committees was formed, free to interpret and develop the programme according to their own convictions.

In spite of the difficulties it faced, ICYE retained links with the ecumenical movement. In the years that followed, new thrusts and patterns were developed alongside the traditional one-year school and family programme, including opportunities for voluntary service and community action, independent or group living, special exchanges for youth with disabilities, short-term programmes, and programmes for youth up to 35.

A total of 32 countries in all continents now participate. From its beginning over 12,000 young people from more than 40 countries have participated in this exchange programme, and 20,000 other persons of all ages have been involved as hosts or co-workers.

See also **youth**.

WILLIAM A. PERKINS

INTERNATIONAL COUNCIL OF CHRISTIAN CHURCHES.

Founded in Amsterdam in August 1948, the ICCC grew out of a 1947 appeal by the American Council of Christian Churches for an international body "to give constructive testimony for the Lord Jesus Christ and to stand against the World Council of Churches". Delegates of 58 churches in 29 countries came to the first assembly; by the 12th world congress (1988)

founding president, US Bible Presbyterian Church pastor Carl McIntire, reported 490 churches in 100 countries.

Disavowing "organic union"* in favour of "spiritual oneness" and "unity of mind and effort against all unbelief and compromise with modernism... and against Roman Catholicism", the ICCC's first assembly listed "vital differences" between it and the WCC (founded a week later). These included refusal of fellowship with Orthodox churches, rejection of the idea that "the kingdom of God is a social order to be established by... economic and political processes", and insistence that it is not the church's task "to apply pressure to political bodies". McIntire sharply criticized the "inclusivism" of the ecumenical movement. He said its goal is "one world church", which would lead to the "more universal tyranny" of "a society to which all must belong". That, he said, "is nothing more than the Marxist doctrine".

In 1988 ICCC general secretary J.C. Maris, a pastor in the Christian Reformed Churches in the Netherlands, told an interviewer that "we are still struggling against precisely the same things". Visible evidences of this continuity have been McIntire's frequent appearance, often with a few placard-carrying demonstrators, at WCC meetings and lengthy citation of WCC texts in his magazine *Christian Beacon*.

While the ICCC has been locally divisive, its global influence has been marginal, though McIntire says "exposures by the ICCC" were a major factor behind problems in the US National Council of Churches. Firm statistics about ICCC membership are hard to come by. Many of its members are small breakaway groups (a 1967 list included a Presbyterian congregation in La Paz, Bolivia, with 20 members and no pastor). Among churches to withdraw over the years was Maris's own; a church official faulted the leadership for their tight control of the ICCC and complained of its "almost-political anti-communism".

MARLIN VANELDEREN

J. Reich, *Twentieth Century Reformation*, Marburg, N.G. Elwert, 1969.

INTERNATIONAL ECUMENICAL FELLOWSHIP.

The IEF is an informal

European organization founded in Fribourg, Switzerland, in 1967. Its aim is to develop fellowship between Christians of different denominations and nationalities through regional meetings and an annual international conference. It provides a forum for discussion and an opportunity to share in the worship of different traditions as far as church discipline and consciences permit. Its headquarters is in Belgium, and there are branches in several European countries.

JOSINE HAUTFENNE

INTERNATIONAL FELLOWSHIP OF EVANGELICAL STUDENTS.

The IFES was founded in 1946-47 by leaders of evangelical student movements of ten nations — Australia, Britain, Canada, China, France, Holland, New Zealand, Norway, Switzerland and the USA. Each successive decade has seen the addition of 10-20 new members, so that by 1989 IFES counted about 90 national affiliates, with membership in local student chapters numbering several hundred thousand. Some IFES affiliates have roots going back to the Student Volunteer Movement and the World's Student Christian Federation.* Others arose quite indigenously, while still others owe their origin to the pioneer labours of international IFES staff.

IFES groups identify with conservative evangelical theology and emphasize personal and group Bible study, along with evangelism. Inter-Varsity, as the movement is commonly known (from the name of the British movement at its founding in 1928, Inter-Varsity Fellowship), stresses the principle of student leadership. The chapter at Cambridge University traces its evangelical heritage to Charles Simeon, pastor/mentor of students, in the late 18th century. Cambridge Inter-Collegiate Christian Union has served as a model of Inter-Varsity work around the world.

The two largest affiliates are Inter-Varsity Christian Fellowship-US (founded 1941), represented on some 600 campuses, and Nigeria Fellowship of Evangelical Students (1968), represented in more than 250 schools. Some affiliates have achieved impressive growth without the benefit of national staff (e.g. the Tertiary Students' Christian Fellowship of Papua New Guinea, with several thousand

members). In East Africa several IFES-affiliated groups claim about 10% of the student population in their membership. In 1975 it was estimated that half the pastors of Norway were graduates of the IFES-related Norges Kristelige Student- og Skoleungdomslag.

Over the years IFES has helped identify and nurture a number of third-world Christians now in leadership positions with various missions and international agencies such as the Lausanne movement (see **Lausanne Committee for World Evangelization**) and the World Evangelical Fellowship.* IFES headquarters are in London.

ROBERT T. COOTE

INTERNATIONAL LAW. There are considerable differences between national law and international law. In most states national law has developed as part of a legal and constitutional order with authority attributed to legislative, judicial and executive branches of government. Thus, at the national level institutions exist to enact and to enforce the law. However, the international community does not (yet) have central institutions at the global level vested with authority to legislate, to adjudicate and to enforce the law. The law that governs the relations between nations does not primarily derive its authority from institutions created to enact and to enforce the law but rather from the degree of consent and acceptance on the part of the nations individually and collectively.

The scope of international law has progressively evolved in the course of centuries. The origin of the international community as presently constituted is usually traced back to the peace of Westphalia (1648). The peace treaties signed in the Westphalian towns of Münster and Osnabrück can be considered as the beginning of an international order leading to the modern community of nations. The peace of Westphalia brought about a recognition of the concept of national sovereign states; it initiated a development of making the state independent from the church; and it affirmed a new political distribution of power in a large part of Europe.

The European nations which at that time were expanding their power positions in the world, shaping the content of the law of nations according to their own interests, used to call themselves "Christian nations". Belonging to the community of Christian nations was considered an entitlement to dominate and rule over peoples in other continents who were to be converted and educated. Christian authorities were an important source for determining the nature and the content of the law of nations, as is also evident from the writings of Francisco de Vitoria (*Reflecciones*, 1525-40) and Hugo Grotius (*De jure belli ac pacis*, 1625), two of the founding fathers of the law of nations.

In the 19th century the limited group of Christian nations gradually lost its exclusively Christian character. With a view to maintaining the European "balance of power", the Ottoman empire was invited in 1856 "to participate in the public law and concert of Europe", and thus a clearly non-Christian factor was introduced into the community of nations of that time. Successively Japan, whose military defeated China, was also accepted in the community of nations, which by then was known as the "civilized nations". One of the factors which qualified a nation to belong to the "civilized" world was the capacity to wage war with modern technological equipment. After the war against China a Japanese diplomat observed: "We showed ourselves at least equals in scientific butchery, and at once we are admitted to your council tables as civilized men."

The notion of civilization was very much a guiding principle for the shaping of international law during the later part of the 19th century and the earlier part of the 20th century. For instance, the conclusion of the Congo act at the congress of Berlin (1885), where Western powers divided among themselves spheres of domination over large parts of Africa, was done with the justification of spreading civilization. The law of warfare codified at The Hague in the beginning of the 20th century stated that in the absence of treaty provisions, belligerents were bound to observe "the principles of the laws of nations, as they result from the usages established among civilized peoples, from the laws of humanity and the dictation of the public conscience". The covenant of the League of Nations (1919) referred to the "sacred trust of civilization" as the basis of the mandates system; the statute of the International Court of Justice still contains an echo of the same

notion when it refers to "the general principles of law recognized by civilized nations" as one of the sources of international law (art. 38, para. 1c).

The brutalities of the second world war committed by nations that carried the flag of "civilization" fully discredited this notion. Against this background it is understandable that article 4 of the United Nations charter requires states that wish to become members of the organization to be "peace-loving". The community of nations has lost its exclusive character, which was inherent in the notions of "Christian" and "civilized", and has assumed universal dimensions as presently reflected in the membership of the UN, comprising virtually all nations that have acquired statehood. This development has also a bearing on the nature and scope of international law. Traditional international law was particularly aimed at guaranteeing the liberty of the sovereign state in its relationships with other sovereign states. With the widening of the community of nations into a global society, the claims of the developing nations for more equitable international structures and relationships brought about, albeit in a compromise fashion, new approaches in international law, taking into account the interests of all rather than the interests of the privileged few. Examples of such new approaches can be found in the law of the sea and in the international law of human rights.

An enlightening distinction can be made between the international law of coexistence and the international law of co-operation. The legal system in traditional international law has the essential function of permitting and guaranteeing the coexistence of rival and competing entities, organized in the form of sovereign states, without recognizing a higher authority. The law of coexistence aims at keeping states peacefully apart rather than working actively together. The principles of sovereign equality, self-determination and non-intervention are characteristic of the international law of coexistence. It typically views peace as the absence of war.

On the other hand, the international law of co-operation requires positive measures on the basis of the interdependence of peoples and nations. The international law of co-operation is notably reflected in the UN charter, which provides for international co-operation in the social, economic, cultural and human rights fields. The recognition of common interests and common needs and the understanding that these interests and needs can be adequately met only by collaborative efforts belong to the essence of the international law of co-operation. One of the most obvious present-day threats to the planet and to humanity, the degradation of the environment, can be effectively tackled only by means of international co-operation. And, in fact, since the UN conference on the human environment (1972), some 150 multilateral conventions on a variety of environmental aspects have been concluded, most of them in the framework of international organizations.

The development of the international law of co-operation and the shaping of an international order which upholds the values inherent in peace, justice and the integrity of creation can be realized only through collective efforts in international organizations. In particular the activities of the UN and the specialized agencies are in this respect of crucial importance. They have given impetus to the development of the international law of co-operation.

It is on the basis of this understanding that the WCC, through its Commission of the Churches on International Affairs (CCIA), has always strongly supported the activities of the UN as a forum and instrument of multilateral co-operation. Seeking a substantial role for the UN and demanding effective means of co-operation based on respect for international law are ecumenical endeavours. This is also reflected in the bylaws of the CCIA, whose tasks include encouraging "the development of international law and of effective international institutions".

It should be noted that the WCC in its earlier years referred more often to the development of international law than it has in the last two decades. At its first assembly in Amsterdam (1948) the WCC considered that the authority of law must be recognized and established as much within nations as in their relations with one another. At the same assembly it was also stated that international law requires international institutions for its effectiveness. The Amsterdam assembly regarded international law not only as a means of regulating issues of international concern, such as the use of atomic power, the multilateral re-

duction of armaments, the provision of health services and food for all as well as promoting respect for human rights, but also as a common foundation of moral conviction, "without which any system of law will break down".

This latter notion which linked up international law with principles of morality was echoed at the assembly in Evanston (1954), which stated that the more obvious barriers to a genuine world community were due to the lack of a common foundation of moral principles. Evanston expressed therefore the conviction that the world of nations needs an international ethos to provide a sound groundwork for the development of international law and institutions. And in New Delhi (1961) the WCC again referred to the need for an international ethic and held that a more profound study of the nature and content of the moral foundations of international law and order will help nations of different traditions understand and accept their common allegiance to basic ethical conceptions. This call for an international ethic as a foundation of international law was repeated at the assembly at Uppsala (1968). However, the same notion is not prominent in later WCC pronouncements, which perceived international law more in its concrete function than in its ethical foundation.

The Evanston assembly also advanced a number of considerations relevant to the scope, content and role of international law, among them the principles that all nations should honour their pledged word and international agreements they have accepted (*pacta sunt servanda*) and that international disputes should not be settled by unilateral action but by direct negotiation or by submitting them to conciliation, arbitration or judicial settlement. In the same vein the New Delhi assembly spoke of the need for peaceful settlement of disputes, stating in particular that "so far as possible", legal disputes between nations should be resolved by arbitration and judicial decisions.

The New Delhi report introduced a new and important element in the WCC approach to international law, which reflects the interests, needs and aspirations of peoples and nations not belonging to North Atlantic constituencies, namely, the role of international law as a means to effect just and peaceful changes. New Delhi asserted that the protection of the existing order should be accompanied by the recognition of legitimate demands for its alteration, in so far as these further the maintenance of peace and serve the common good of the international community. The context of this statement was explained by the title of the relevant section ("The Changing Structure of the International Community") and by reference to the peaceful emergence of many newly independent states. At Uppsala the twofold role of international law as a means to preserve *and* to change was again clearly brought out. Uppsala stated that the contribution of law to international order and justice does not consist only in its conserving role. Legal enactments and international treaties reveal a second aspect of law as a force of order and of change and reform.

A constant theme in the WCC support for the development of international law is the call for the strengthening of international institutions — in particular, the UN as an instrument of co-operation and as a centre for harmonizing the actions of nations. Already in Amsterdam the WCC deemed that the purposes of the UN deserved the support of Christians. At New Delhi the universal vocation of the organization was stressed, implying the need for universal membership with special reference to the People's Republic of China. The New Delhi assembly reflected the positive appreciation at that time of the position of the UN by viewing the UN as developing from a conference of national delegations into an organization with an authority of its own, empowered to undertake special responsibilities. In later years, depending on the general political climate, the UN was not always assessed in such optimistic terms, but the support of the WCC for the world organization remained undiminished. Thus, reflecting the mood of that time, the central committee stated in Buenos Aires in 1985 on the occasion of the 40th anniversary of the UN that the world was witnessing a crisis of confidence in international institutions, a growing breakdown in multilateralism and a gradual erosion in the authority of the UN. At the same time, the central committee declared that the strengthening of international institutions for peace and for the respect of international law was more urgent than ever.

The overall position of the WCC with respect to the role and function of international law developed from an ethical and theoretical stand to a more contextual and pragmatic approach to world law. In recent statements the WCC makes hardly any reference to the role of international law as such, but frequent appeals are made to respect existing international agreements or to conclude new agreements relating to disarmament and arms control and to ratify and observe human rights treaties. For instance, the Vancouver assembly (1983) appealed urgently to all governments of the world to adopt and ratify international human rights instruments, to respect the rights included in these agreements and to promote by all means both in law and in practice their fuller realization in every country. Similar appeal was made with respect to international refugee conventions. The WCC also appealed at Vancouver to all nations that they agree and ratify a comprehensive test ban treaty as a necessary step to stopping the further development of nuclear weapons technology. This functional and pragmatic approach to international law and international institutions is clearly not incompatible with the strong conviction that international law and international institutions are indispensable means to promote universal peace and justice and to preserve and enhance the integrity of creation.

See also **human rights, international order, law, nation, state, United Nations, world community**.

THEO VAN BOVEN

A.J. van der Bent, *Christian Response in a World of Crisis*, WCC, 1986 • A. Cassese, *International Law in a Divided World*, Oxford, Clarendon, 1986 • O.F. Nolde, "Ecumenical Action in International Affairs", in *The Ecumenical Advance: A History of the Ecumenical Movement*, vol. 2: *1948-1968*, H. Fey ed., WCC, 2nd ed., 1986 • K. Raiser, "International Affairs: Continuity and Discontinuity", in *Commemorating Amsterdam 1948: 40 Years of the World Council of Churches* (= *The Ecumenical Review*, 40, 1988) • B.V.A. Roling, *International Law in an Expanded World*, Amsterdam, Djambatan, 1960.

INTERNATIONAL MISSIONARY COUNCIL.
The IMC issued from the world missionary conference (Edinburgh 1910). Formally constituted in 1921 in Lake Mohonk, NY, USA, it united the Protestant national missionary councils and councils of

churches in Africa, Asia and Latin America in a federation with Protestant councils of missionary agencies in Europe and North America. Of the original IMC base of 17 members, 13 were Western missionary councils. One cannot understand either the missionary enterprise in the 20th century or the preparatory stages of the WCC without appreciating the IMC's development through its global network of co-ordinated activities, common studies, consultations and conferences, and united action.

In this dictionary the article on mission* chronicles the IMC's main development in thought and activities up until its integration with the WCC in 1961. And the entry on ecumenical conferences* outlines the highlights of major IMC meetings (Jerusalem 1928, Tambaram 1938, Whitby 1947, Willingen 1952, Accra 1958).

This article considers the dynamics of the ecumenical movement which led to the 1961 integration, and issues which caused prior hesitations on both sides. Despite the structural unity within the WCC, these issues still persist, leaving institutional divisions within the missionary enterprise.

If the ecumenical movement is primarily people and not institutions, one notes how the same Christian clergy and laity easily moved through, and gave leadership to, the variety of organizations which were ecumenical in intent. And equally important, these pioneers intentionally discovered, inspired and formed younger talented disciples to stand on their shoulders.

John Mott (1865-1955), for example, a Methodist layman, was intercollegiate secretary of the YMCA (1888), founded the World Student Christian Federation* (1895) and became its general secretary. He chaired Edinburgh 1910 and its continuation committee, helped establish national missionary councils in Asia, chaired the IMC, helped lead the Oxford Life and Work conference (1937), and became vice-chairman of the WCC provisional committee. After the Edinburgh conference Charles Brent (1862-1929), Episcopalian bishop in the Philippines, actively participated in the first Life and Work conference (1925) and organized and became president of Faith and Order (1927). Willem Visser 't Hooft (1900-85), Dutch Reformed, was secretary of the World Alliance of YMCAs* (1931-38),

general secretary of the WSCF (1938), and first WCC general secretary (1948-66). Lesslie Newbigin (1909-) served as a bishop of the Church of South India, became the last IMC general secretary (1959) and, after the integration, the first director of the Division — now Commission — on World Mission and Evangelism of the WCC.

Indeed, the list is quite long of those women and men who came out of the international student movements and the IMC missionary councils, became leaders in Life and Work, Faith and Order (or in both), and formed a network of friendship and shared commitment. The list is very short of those who confined their movements and interests to any one organization. IMC and initial WCC personnel were not strangers to one another. But because of differing constituencies, emphases and organizational demands, IMC as such stood apart from the WCC until 1961.

The IMC Tambaram conference in 1938 discussed the proposed creation of the WCC. It urged co-operation in the formation stage through a joint committee between the two bodies (Mott became its chairman). But most members wanted the IMC to maintain its own "separate organization, autonomy and independence". The IMC preferred to be only "in association" with the WCC-to-be, and to give the WCC time to discover its own role in the ecumenical movement.

After 1948 the IMC and WCC had a number of joint activities, e.g. setting up a single IMC-WCC secretariat in the Far East, meeting refugee and other emergency needs in Asia and the Middle East and integrating the IMC mission research department into the WCC division of studies. But there still was too much overlapping and duplication of energies, time and personnel.

Already in 1945 Samuel McCrea Cavert judged that it would be "a failure of Christian statesmanship to divide the ecumenical forces permanently into two groups". Underlying the logic of events, organizational alignments, and ecumenically committed and talented personnel was a perceived deeper unity of calling and purpose.

The Evanston WCC assembly (1954) set up a joint committee with the IMC to study full integration. In 1956 the committee recommended to the parent bodies the integration possibility, "subject to an adequate safeguarding in any plan... of the distinctive expression of the mission of the church as this has been embodied in the IMC". In the next years the joint committee would uncover hesitation and anxiety on both sides.

Why the IMC hesitation? The 19th-century missionary advances by European and North American Protestants were the work of missionary societies* and mission councils who had organized, educated and financed themselves in varying degrees of independence from the classic Reformation churches. Could one trust these large churches in the WCC, in their slow bureaucratic ways and with safe agendas, to take direct responsibility for world mission, or would that gospel urgency be gradually placed on the margins? Would the direction of missionary strategy be too centralized in Geneva? Would "the greatest achievement of the IMC be put at risk" — a forum of such disparate groups, including those from very conservative theological traditions, which were in no way concerned to promote organizational unity, but "exclusively to serve Christians in the task of preaching the gospel and in advising them on the varieties of experience in this preaching which no group could hope to possess by itself" (Max Warren)?

Thus, many in those IMC member mission councils, especially in Europe, which included vigorous, effective missionary societies organizationally independent of the churches, were reluctant to have close administrative connection with the churches — and this they foresaw would be the case in any IMC-WCC integration.

There was also some anxiety on the WCC side. Would the WCC be altering its character as a council of *churches* if independent mission agencies came aboard the ten-year-old ship? Furthermore, many IMC missionary societies retained an evangelistic theological tradition and practice of direct evangelism to other Christians whom they judged "nominal" or not truly "Bible believing". What one mission group regarded as its true witness in evangelism,* some WCC churches would judge as downright proselytism.* The WCC Orthodox churches, such as those in the Middle East, had direct experience of Protestant missions which built up churches composed almost exclusively of converts from among the Orthodox. Would an IMC-WCC integra-

tion be sanctioning such proselytizing activities and purposes?

The same misgivings were noted by Roman Catholic friends of the WCC, right up to the 1961 integration. The integration, they discreetly suggested, could lend more formal and conspicuous support to what RCs judged to be Protestant proselytism among vulnerable flocks in Latin America, Spain, Portugal, Italy, the Middle East, and elsewhere. The RC critics continued: the integration also could break the WCC trend towards doctrinal catholicity* which F&O was stressing; because of the anti-RC stance and the weak ecclesiologies of so many IMC mission societies, the WCC could easily shift towards a diluted "undenominational" form of Christianity.

On the other hand, the proponents for the integration were pointing out the strong theological currents which wedded mission and church and were emphasizing the missionary nature of the church (see **missio Dei**). The issue, as Visser 't Hooft put it in 1956, was not one of "churchifying mission but of mobilizing the church for its mission". For their own spiritual health, the churches cannot continue to delegate the missionary enterprise to mission societies; these, in turn, should broaden their understanding of the church in their activities. The WCC should bring the missionary task into the very centre of its life, and the missionary councils and agencies should place their studies and activities in an ecumenical perspective that includes not only the mission of the church but also its unity.*

As to fears of proselytism, it was argued that the stronger tradition in the IMC was one of co-operation and unity in mission (see **common witness**) and that in final preparation for approval in the next assembly (1961) was the document "Christian Witness, Proselytism and Religious Liberty in the Setting of the WCC". Furthermore, the issue of proselytism and practical cases in dispute could be more frankly discussed and more practically dealt with in an integrated council than by two separate bodies. The Middle East Orthodox were even "happy with the idea of having Protestant missionaries somewhat controlled through an organization of which the Orthodox themselves were members" (John Meyendorff).

More important, a non-integrated IMC

would still remain a council of councils, and the churches of Asia had been seeking direct links with the WCC rather than with the IMC. In 1961, the majority of the 38 member councils represented the churches in what were formerly called "the mission fields". The integration would offer entrance into the WCC life for many churches that had related to international forums through national councils of churches and missionary organizations. And the integration would introduce mission thinking far beyond the traditional borders of the IMC constituency, e.g. the majority of the Orthodox churches and "independent" third-world churches.

These positive voices in the vigorous discussion (which lasted over four years) won the day. In late 1961 both the IMC and WCC assemblies were held in New Delhi. Integration was approved, with only two IMC dissents: the Norwegian Missionary Council (it feared the submergence of mission in the WCC) and the Congo Protestant Council (it wanted to maintain co-operation with local conservative evangelical bodies which refused WCC membership). A new division (later commission) on world mission and evangelism was created within the WCC.

The IMC history came to an end, but not the fundamental debate. Many mission agencies, para-church groups and non-WCC-member churches of evangelicals* judge that the WCC, especially through the CWME, has *not* been highlighting missionary activity in its thinking, actions and budgets — despite its understanding of church mission and its good intentions to provide "a new frontier, a new dimension of the WCC" (New Delhi). They question even how much the CWME aim remains basically the same as the IMC aim, "to help the churches in the proclamation of the gospel of Jesus Christ in word and deed so that all may believe and be saved". The critics charge that the WCC has so changed the understanding of mission and evangelism that it means almost everything the church is called to do, except direct evangelism — using all available means to reach out to "the two-thirds of humankind yet to be evangelized", so that "every person will have the opportunity to hear, understand, and receive the good news" (see **Lausanne covenant**).

Such WCC critics prefer to rally themselves, their mission societies and their old or new churches around the Lausanne Committee for World Evangelization* and associations of evangelical missions.

In conclusion, there still remain structural divisions in world mission, forcing too many churches, mission agencies and groups to take sides in their stewardship of personnel, funds and energy and in their search for a world forum of fellowship in mission. A sad symbol was spotlighted in 1980, the 70th anniversary of Edinburgh's world mission conference. To celebrate their being the children of Edinburgh and of their prolific offspring (now in six continents), Christians held two large mission conferences, independent of one another — the CWME at Melbourne and the Lausanne committee at Pattaya, Thailand.

TOM STRANSKY

W.R. Hogg, *Ecumenical Foundations: A History of the IMC*, New York, Harper, 1952 • J. Meyendorff, "An Orthodox View on Mission and Integration", *International Review of Mission*, 70, 280, 1981 • L. Newbigin, "Integration: Some Personal Reflections", *International Review of Mission*, 70, 280, 1981 • L. Newbigin, "Mission to Six Continents", in *The Ecumenical Advance: A History of the Ecumenical Movement*, vol. 2: *1948-1968*, 2nd ed., WCC, 1986 • T.F. Stransky, "From Mexico City to San Antonio", *International Review of Mission*, 79, 313, 1990 • M. Warren, "The Fusion of IMC and WCC at New Delhi", *Occasional Bulletin of Missionary Research*, July 1979.

INTERNATIONAL ORDER. Concern for international order has been one of the driving forces of the modern ecumenical movement since its beginnings. The term "international order" here refers to the principles, structures and instruments regulating the relationships between peoples, nations and their governments with the aim of settling disputes, preventing armed conflict and furthering justice and the rule of law. Used initially at the Stockholm Life and Work conference in 1925, it was fully developed at the time of the Oxford conference on "Church, Community and State" in 1937. Present usage speaks in more neutral terms of "international relations", "international affairs" or "international co-operation". The concern for international order is described in the constitution of the WCC, which refers to "the breaking down of barriers between people, and the promotion of one human family in justice and peace". Ecumenical thought and action regarding the establishment of an international order has moved through several phases in close interaction with world political events.

Development of the idea of international order. The early ecumenical movement was to a large extent a response to the international consciousness at the turn of the 20th century. The expanding missionary enterprise, following in the footsteps of European colonialism,* awakened (esp. among the Protestant churches) the sense of the supranational character of the church. The young Nathan Söderblom wrote in 1891: "How glorious it is that Christianity is international." This conviction carried with it the new sense of responsibility for promoting a true international order. The first phase extends from the participation of a Christian delegation in the second peace conference in The Hague (1907), through the founding of the World Alliance for Promoting International Friendship through the Churches (1914) to the large ecumenical meetings in Birmingham (Conference on Christian Politics, Economics and Citizenship [COPEC] 1924), Stockholm (1925) and Jerusalem (1928). The common basis for all these efforts was the conviction that all peoples were meant to form "one human brotherhood" under the "fatherhood of God". Christianity, because of its universal and supranational character, was believed to be the only force that could hold the world of nations together. While the establishment of the League of Nations in 1919 was widely welcomed (see the Orthodox encyclical of 1920), it was felt that its "body" lacked a "soul", that it had to be filled with Christian moral and spiritual principles. This Christian leadership in international life was guided by the ideal of the kingdom of God,* which was to be translated into the social order of humankind.

The hopes for the establishment of a true international order based on Christian principles which would secure justice for all people and eliminate the threat of war were shattered as a consequence of world events from 1929 onwards (world economic and financial crises; emergence of Stalinism, fascism and National Socialism; paralysis of the League of Nations; and finally the second world war). "Man's disorder" (Amsterdam 1948), experienced in the form of growing secularism, aggressive nationalism, totalitarianism and eventually the utter destructiveness of war, became the central preoccupation of ecumenical thinking. Christian realism took the place of the liberal optimism of the earlier phase, but it continued to be rooted in the conviction that there existed a basic moral order willed by God. The highlights of ecumenical discussion during this period were the conferences at Oxford (1937) and Tambaram (1938), the joint decision (1946) taken by the WCC and the IMC to form the Commission of the Churches on International Affairs (CCIA), and the first assembly of the WCC at Amsterdam (1948).

All ecumenical statements about international order during this period were directed towards calling and enabling the churches to be truly the church.* "In a world where disruptive nationalism and aggressive imperialism make [human] brotherhood seem unreal, the church offers not an ideal but a fact, man united not by his aspiration but by the love of God" (Oxford). Therefore, the Christian church has the responsibility of bringing those who exercise power (states, governments) to the recognition of their responsibility before God. This duty means, in particular, challenging power politics by extending the rule of law* into the relations between states, coming to terms with the threat of war and promoting human rights and fundamental freedoms, especially religious liberty.*

The founding of the United Nations in 1945 and the proclamation of the Universal Declaration of Human Rights (1948) re-kindled the expectations regarding international order. However, a number of events (e.g. the Berlin blockade, the Korean war, revolution in China) brought the antagonism between the two super-powers in East and West out into the open which, under the label of "cold war",* marked the whole period from the Amsterdam assembly to the early 1960s (e.g. the Cuban crisis in 1962). The rapidly expanding threat of nuclear weapons placed the efforts to prevent a further world war into the forefront of the concern for international order. At the same time, however, a basic change of perspective began to take place with the emergence of new nations in Africa and Asia (Bandung conference in 1955). Thus, during the 1960s a new discussion about international order took shape crystallizing around the goals of "peaceful co-existence" and socio-economic "development" (the first development decade, formation of UNCTAD 1964). The ecumenical debate received fresh impulses from the integration of the International Missionary Council into the WCC (New Delhi 1961), from the study on rapid social change (beginning in 1954) leading up to the Geneva conference in 1966 and from new openings in the Roman Catholic Church (Vatican II, esp. *Gaudium et Spes* and the encyclicals *Pacem in Terris* [1962] and *Populorum Progressio* [1967]). The new orientation is captured well in this sentence from *Populorum Progressio*: "Development is the new name for peace."

The basic feature of ecumenical thinking about international order during this period is the gradual shift from the earlier static notion of order* towards a dynamic understanding of historical change and its meaning in the providence* of God. Thus, preoccupation with the defence of the order of a "free society" against the threat of totalitarianism and hesitations about the concern for nation-building in Asia and Africa gave way to a dynamic notion of justice* and of the role of states in the framework of a "welfare world". As the historical perspective of formerly dependent people increasingly influenced ecumenical thinking, the breaking down of traditional forms of order as a consequence of rapid social change was interpreted as a positive sign of God's renewing action in history,* preparing the way for the order of God's shalom. This led to a new understanding of the role of the state and of the function of law, not only in preserving order but even more in shaping a new social order.

The extensive re-ordering of international relations was brought to an end through a series of developments in the early 1970s: the end of detente and the re-appearance of aggressive competition between the superpowers, which was now extended into Africa, Asia and Latin America (Vietnam, Chile, the Middle East, Angola, Mozambique); the failure of international development strategies and blocking of the project of a New International Economic Order (note the effects of the oil crisis beginning in 1973); the promotion of a capitalist international order through the trilateral commission and the implementation of the doctrine of national security.*

Within the ecumenical movement this emerging crisis in international relations led to a sharper awareness of the critical issues regarding international order: development,* understood as the promotion of justice through self-reliance, economic growth and people's participation; human and people's rights, especially the right to basic guarantees for life;* racism* as a fundamental denial of justice; a critical analysis of militarism,* of the transnationalization of capital and production and of the power of science and technology.* The earlier emphasis on participation in change gave way to the struggle for justice and liberation. An international order based on the maintenance of the existing political, economic and financial structures was perceived as the main obstacle to true liberation and justice. Thus, ecumenical thought and action have increasingly turned away from the preoccupation with international structures to movements of the people with the aim of building up an "oikoumene of solidarity" over against the "oikoumene of domination". This change in emphasis has found expression in the invitation issued by the Vancouver assembly of the WCC (1983)

United Nations headquarters, New York City (UN photo)

to a "conciliar process for justice, peace and the integrity of creation".

The ecumenical understanding of international order. The concern for an international order has been and is being addressed within the ecumenical movement under a number of different aspects.

Who are the *subjects* of an international order? Traditionally, international affairs are being considered as a matter of organized states and their governments (see **state, nation**). Thus, the ecumenical movement during its early phase and until the mid-1960s focused attention primarily on the responsibility of governments as the primary subjects for establishing and maintaining international order. This emphasis found expression in the efforts to develop criteria and instruments for limiting national sovereignty, especially with regard to war as a means for settling international disputes. Since then the picture has become more diverse. The process of decolonization has given rise to popular liberation movements which challenge the legitimacy of existing governments. Some have been recognized internationally as legitimate representatives of their peoples and thus as "subjects" in terms of international order. Furthermore, since the 1970s large transnational corporations and banks have begun to influence international order, not only in the economic and financial field. Their effective power exceeds that of most governments, yet they have no formal recognition as international "subjects" and escape control or accountability. And finally, in many countries the military has become the primary reference point for international order. As a consequence, ecumenical discussion has progressively moved away from its earlier concentration on states and governments and has begun to address these new "subjects".

The most important *structures* for promoting international order have been the League of Nations and the UN,* with their specialized agencies and organizations. The ecumenical movement has consistently given its support to these structures as the best available, while encouraging their continuous critical review. Most activities of ecumenical agencies regarding international order during the first half of this century were directed towards these intergovernmental structures. Through the CCIA the WCC has enjoyed consultative status with the Economic and Social Council of the UN. A special office for UN relations is maintained in New York. Increasingly, however, attention has been given to regional structures within or related to the UN system, especially the Organization of African Unity. With the emergence of the debt crisis,* the structures maintaining the existing international financial system have come under critical analysis. Very little explicit thinking has been directed towards military alliances as structural elements within the existing international order. However, other structures outside the framework of intergovernmental relationships have become increasingly important for ecumenical efforts regarding international order, such as international federations of trade unions, the International Committee of the Red Cross and the vast network of non-governmental organizations* (e.g. the International Commission of Jurists and the League of Red Cross Societies).

Regarding the *principles* of international order, it has been the conviction within the ecumenical movement from the beginning that international order presupposes bringing the relations between states out of the reign of pure power politics and under the rule of law. This principle is closely related to the modern notion of human rights* as expressed in the preamble of the Universal Declaration of Human Rights. The rule of law refers to all principles, institutions and procedures which protect individuals, peoples and states from arbitrary action and oppression and safeguard human dignity. Much attention was given in earlier decades to the possibilities of further developing the system of international law* based on an international ethic, rooted in principles either of natural law* or of divine order. Already at Oxford in 1937 there was a strong call for an international bill of rights, and through the CCIA the ecumenical movement has actively participated in the drafting of the universal declaration, especially its provisions for religious liberty. Similarly, close attention has been given to the preparation of the other human rights covenants and conventions. More recently, ecumenical concern has focused on the full implementation of accepted human rights standards in view of increasing gross violations. Human rights, both as the rights of individuals and the rights of peoples, have become the elementary criterion of justice. At its assembly in Vancouver (1983) the WCC urged the churches to press governments to "elaborate and ratify an international legal instrument which would outlaw as a crime against humanity the possession as well as the use of nuclear arms".

The main *instruments* available for building up international order are intergovernmental negotiations with a view to agreeing on treaties, conventions, covenants, etc. Such negotiations are taking place either directly between the governments concerned or under UN mandates. Since many international legal instruments of crucial significance still lack ratification by the required minimum number of governments, the WCC has consistently pressed governments to honour their responsibility for international order. Special attention has always been given in the ecumenical movement to the interstate conflicts, e.g. through mediation, arbitration, peace-keeping or observation teams. In recent years the situation in Southern Africa has provoked the call for sanctions as a non-violent means provided for in the Charter of the United Nations (art. 41) in order to force the South African government to comply with resolutions of the UN Security Council or rulings of the International Court of Justice.

The concern for international order constitutes a basic *ethical* challenge. Since international law is still deficient in terms of inner cohesiveness, and in the absence of effective instruments of enforcement, international order is largely dependent on some kind of common ethos of humankind. This issue has been addressed in the ecumenical movement from the beginning. Starting from the conviction that only Christian principles could provide a sound basis for an international ethos, the ecumenical movement has come to recognize that in a religiously pluralistic and increasingly secularized world, neither the appeal to Christian principles nor one to some kind of natural law or so-called orders of creation will be universally accepted. In a world where not only hunger and poverty, wars and violent oppression threaten the lives of millions of people but the very survival of humankind itself is at stake, justice and peace coupled with a caring attitude towards nature have become the central ethical issues in the search for international order. Both justice and peace, however, presuppose recognition of human dignity and respect for it.

While in the early phase of the ecumenical movement the concerns for peace and disarmament and for fundamental human freedoms were paramount, the emerging conflict between North and South has focused attention on the issues of justice and human dignity (poverty, violation of human rights, racism, etc.). In the light of the biblical tradition, justice and peace are inseparable. Yet in concrete situations they frequently enter into tension and conflict. The struggle for justice against structures of oppression often leads to disorder and conflict, including creating threats to peace. Development has been called the new name for peace, yet development inevitably leads into the struggle for justice. This fact brings about the paradoxical situation that struggling for justice and the conflicts it gives rise to must be understood as action that actually is for peace. The ways of achieving a just peace or peace with justice have therefore been at the centre of the more recent ecumenical discussion about international order. This has posed the ethical problem of violence (see **violence and nonviolence**) in terms of both the structural violence of oppressive systems and the actions of violent resistance. By analogy, the traditional criteria of a just war* have received renewed attention. But ultimately both the maintenance of peace and the realization of justice are questions of power, and hence recent ecumenical discussions about political ethics have raised again the question of the different forms of power and their legitimation.

What is the role of the churches regarding international order? Internationally, the Christian churches represent the largest religious community, but they are a minority among minorities. While the Roman Catholic Church through the Vatican enjoys international status and can directly participate in intergovernmental negotiations, the WCC lacks any such international recognition except its consultative status with the UN as a non-governmental organization. Its member churches have very different forms of relationships with their governments. But generally, the power of the churches to influence actions and decisions about international order has been decreasing steadily since the beginning of this century. The World Conference on Religion and

Peace* has been trying to bring the united weight of world religions to bear on the questions of world community. The results have so far been very limited.

The ecumenical understanding of the role of the churches in the search for international order has changed radically since the beginning of this century. Starting from the conviction about the Christian leadership role in holding the community of nations together, through the notion of the church as a "factor" or a "sign and instrument" of the coming unity of humankind, the ecumenical movement has come to the recognition that the churches are meant to live as confessing and witnessing communities among the nations of this world. In their ecumenical solidarity, especially with the poor and the victims, the churches are called to manifest God's unconditional love for humankind (see **unity of humankind**). This task implies both the priestly calling for reconciliation* and the prophetic calling for resistance (see **prophecy**). The relationship between these two dimensions of Christian witness for international order poses the same problems as the relationship between justice and peace. The tension is resolved in the messianic perspective of the witness and praxis of Jesus Christ announcing the presence of the kingdom of God.

KONRAD RAISER

A.J. van der Bent, *Christian Response in a World of Crisis*, WCC, 1986 ● D. Hudson, *The Ecumenical Movement in World Affairs*, London, Weidenfeld & Nicolson, 1969 ● Z.K. Matthews ed., *Responsible Government in a Revolutionary Age*, New York, Association, 1966 ● J.H. Oldham ed., *Foundations of Ecumenical Social Thought: The Oxford Conference Report*, Philadelphia, Fortress, 1966 ● *The Role of the WCC in International Affairs*, WCC, 1986 ● K. Srisang ed., *Perspectives on Political Ethics: An Ecumenical Enquiry*, WCC, 1983 ● E. Weingärtner, "Human Rights on the Ecumenical Agenda", *CCIA Background Information*, 3, 1983 ● *World Conference on Church and Society: Official Report*, WCC, 1967.

INTER-VARSITY CHRISTIAN FELLOWSHIP.

IVCF, a non-denominational movement of evangelical college and university students in the US and Canada, is part of an international movement known as the International Fellowship of Evangelical Students* (IFES). In 1989 IFES counted about 90 national affiliates, of which IVCF-US was the largest.

IVCF is known for evangelism* and discipleship through student-led inductive Bible studies. In the US some 400 staff members minister on more than 600 campuses, offering training, counsel and encouragement. Weekend retreats and summer camps provide evangelistic outreach and leadership training. InterVarsity Press and Twentyonehundred produce Christian literature and video programmes designed to strengthen intellectual foundations and expand horizons for Christian life and service.

IVCF-Canada, in addition to its university-level work (about 150 chapters), also has an extensive high school programme (some 400 groups), which prepares students for Christian life and witness in tertiary schools.

In the late 1940s IVCF launched the triennial Urbana missions convention at the University of Illinois at Urbana. In 1987, during the week between Christmas and New Year, more than 18,000 students attended Urbana, and the majority indicated they would consider overseas mission service.

ROBERT T. COOTE

INTERVOX.

The Uppsala assembly of the WCC (1968) specifically addressed the responsibility of churches regarding the media of mass communication, including radio broadcasting. Noting the exposure of churches everywhere in the world to the effects of mass communication, and the differences in local governmental or other approaches to broadcasting, it said: "The churches would be wise to abandon their traditional suspicion of the media and to accept or seek a firm partnership with those people who are creating, producing, using and evaluating the modern communication systems."

Following Uppsala and the urgent recommendations for churches to be also involved in communication other than print, the central committee of the World Association for Christian Communication (which later merged with the WCC's Agency for Christian Literature Development to form the present WACC) met in Hilversum, Netherlands (1969). The committee discussed the need for an ecumenical radio service. As a result, in February 1970 the communication department of the WCC, within its radio and television section, started Intervox, a multilanguage ecumenical news and feature tape service. Produced in the Council's sound studio, the service was offered to radio broadcasters on a subscription basis.

As a joint enterprise Intervox was initially sponsored by the WCC, the Lutheran World Federation* (LWF) and WACC. The World Alliance of Reformed Churches* became an additional partner in 1971. During the early years, the four organizations shared in some ways in the financial commitment towards the Intervox service, or provided staff participation at different levels. This co-operation was particularly active until the government takeover and subsequent closing of Radio Voice of the Gospel in Addis Ababa in March 1977.

Intervox programming concentrates on signs of renewal in the churches committed to the ecumenical movement. Its aim continues to be the building of bridges between continents. Intervox pays special attention to the churches' involvement in matters of peace, development* and social justice. While it concentrates on issues of interest to the third world, it also hopes to create an awareness of worldwide ecumenical issues among its audiences in industrialized countries of the northern and southern hemispheres.

In 1983 the editorial responsibility for the French version was transferred from the LWF to the WCC News and Information office. The service appears ten times a year in French and English. A multilanguage soundbank, introduced in 1987, offers topical news items to a wide range of broadcasters. The French and English editions of Intervox are used by about 100 stations worldwide.

See also **communication in the ecumenical movement**.

MONIQUE McCLELLAN

INVESTMENT. Worldwide, the number of churches and church-related bodies which have investment capital at their disposal is rather limited. Most of such groups are in the richer countries. Usually investment capital is used to help finance ongoing church activities and programmes or invested in pension funds, etc. For many years, some churches have applied certain ethical criteria for their investments, e.g. in order to avoid investments in companies which produce tobacco or liquor. Investments were not used to influence corporate behaviour. This first model of using investments could be called the "avoidance" strategy.

However, since the late 1960s, there has been a growing awareness that investments can also be used as a tool for actively promoting corporate social responsibility. As shareholders in private companies, churches and church-related agencies can try to exercise their influence by raising questions about social issues, requesting information or asking companies to take specific actions. One way of doing this is through submitting shareholder resolutions at the company's annual meeting of shareholders. The first shareholder resolution from a church investor was filed in 1971 with General Motors by the Episcopal Church in the USA. The company was asked to cease operations in South Africa. Since that time, the corporate-responsibility movement in the US has grown to include churches and public and private pension funds with an estimated total invested portfolio worth in 1990 $500 billion. A major protagonist in this movement is the Interfaith Center on Corporate Responsibility (ICCR), which is a movement sponsored by and related to the National Council of the Churches of Christ in the USA. ICCR is a coalition of institutional investors, including 22 Protestant denominational agencies, pension funds and dioceses and more than 220 Roman Catholic communities, pension funds and dioceses. In 1990, churches in the USA sponsored 219 resolutions to 157 companies on issues related to social justice, military production and environment.

Since the early 1970s, this second model of using investments as a tool to promote corporate responsibility has spread to a number of countries where this model can be applied, e.g. England and the Netherlands. In connection with this, initiatives have mushroomed for establishing alternative investment funds which concentrate on socially responsible activities. This could be seen as a third model of using investments. Investors may have different definitions of what constitutes "socially responsible investment", but in general such investments are seen as those promoting social justice, peace and the protection of the environment. Although the movement for corporate responsibility and alternative investments is much broader than the churches, it is fair to say that some churches and church-related organizations have been and are major protagonists of this movement.

The WCC assembly in Uppsala (1968) recommended that investments in "institutions that perpetuate racism" should be terminated. This recommendation was taken up by the WCC central committee meeting in Utrecht (1972). The committee decided to sell forthwith existing holdings and to make no investments in corporations which were directly involved in investment in, or trade with, a number of countries in Africa, including South Africa. At the same time, all member churches, Christian agencies and individual Christians were urged to use all their influence, including stockholder action and investment, to press corporations to withdraw investments from and cease trading with these countries.

The WCC went beyond merely criticizing certain investment policies. In 1974 the central committee unanimously decided to establish the Ecumenical Development Co-operative Society* (EDCS). The objective of EDCS is to stimulate churches to invest a portion of their investment capital in EDCS as a way to participate in development as a liberating process by financing productive enterprises of poor people. EDCS makes loans to financially viable enterprises, which must comply with a set of social criteria. Regardless of the number of shares held, shareholders have only one vote in the annual shareholders meeting. This is one way in which EDCS highlights new economic thinking by implementing genuine ecumenical sharing of resources, separating power and money. Many thus now realize that through their investment policies, churches can make a visible witness in economic life.

See also **economics**, **Programme to Combat Racism**.

ROB VAN DRIMMELEN

ISRAEL AND THE CHURCH. The theme "Israel (meaning the Jewish people) and the church" poses a truly ecumenical question in two senses. As Karl Barth put it in an address to the Vatican's Secretariat for Christian Unity: "There is finally only one really great ecumenical question: our relations with the Jewish people." The question is also ecumenical in that the churches share a common anti-Judaic tradition, and major differences about recognizing the Jewish people as living Israel appear to cut right across denominational lines. In 1948 at Amsterdam, in the shadow of the Shoah (the Hebrew word for catastrophe, increasingly replacing "holocaust" as the name for the Nazi extermination of 6 million Jews), the first assembly of the WCC received a report in which the churches admitted to a share in preparing the way for the evil of antisemitism and confessed: "To the Jews our God has bound us in a special solidarity linking our destinies together in his design." For the most part, however, the report continued to interpret that solidarity, in agreement with the earlier missionary movement, as grounds for a special concern to convert Jews to Christ.

In view of the supersessionist stance of the church for 19 centuries ("under the new covenant the Christian church has *replaced* the Israel of old") and then the church's conversionist posture ("Jews must become Christian in order to be saved"), the Jewish view of the relationship has been understandably negative. Given the still-unredeemed state of the world, of which the behaviour of the church has been taken to be prime evidence, Jews can hardly believe that the Messiah has come. Yet Maimonides (d.1204) had granted that Christians (and Muslims) had at least helped spread over much of the earth the knowledge of the one God and his *torah*, and in the 20th century, the Jewish philosopher Franz Rosenzweig was the first on either side to develop a positive view of both Israel and the church in God's purposes. In view of the Shoah and the church's hesitation in affirming the Jewish covenant,* however, Jews have been cautious about revising their view of Israel's longest-standing enemy.

On the Christian side, the Second Vatican Council* took an important step ahead in 1965 by speaking (*Nostra Aetate* 4) of the Jews as "very dear to God" and by affirming that "God does not take back the gifts he bestowed or the choice he made". Subsequent Catholic statements have made increasingly clear affirmations of the unbrokenness of God's covenant with the Jewish people.

In 1967 the Commission on Faith and Order of the WCC received a report from the Committee on the Church and the Jewish People which, in the conclusion of the section on theological considerations, presents so clearly the range of Christian understandings of the relationship between the church and Israel, as well as the crucial importance of the issue, that it merits quotation: "Some are convinced that, despite the elements of continuity that admittedly exist between present-day Jews and Israel, to speak of the continued election of the Jewish people alongside the church is inadmissible. It is the church alone, they say, that is, theologically speaking, the continuation of Israel as the people of God, to which now all nations belong. Election and vocation are solely in Christ, and are to be grasped in faith. To speak otherwise is to deny that the one people of God, the church, is the body of Christ which cannot be broken. In Christ it is made manifest that God's love and his promises apply to all. The Christian hope for the Jews is the same as it is for all: that they may come to the knowledge of the truth, Jesus Christ our Lord...

"Others of us are of the opinion that it is not enough merely to assert some kind of continuity between the present-day Jews — whether religious or not — and ancient Israel, but that they actually are still Israel, i.e. that they still are God's elect people. These would stress that after Christ the one people of God is broken asunder, one part being the church, which accepts Christ, the other part Israel outside the church, which rejects him, but which even in this rejection remains in a special sense beloved by God. They see this election manifested specifically in the fact that the existence of the Jewish people in this world still reveals the truth that God's promises are irrevocable, that he will uphold the covenant of love which he has made with Israel. Further they see this continuing election in the fact that God has linked the final hope of the world to the salvation of the Jews, in the day when he will heal the broken body of his one people, Israel and the church.

"These two views, described above, should however not be understood as posing a clear-cut alternative. Many hold positions somewhere in between, and without glossing over the real disagreements which exist, in some cases these positions can be so close, that they seem to rest more on different emphases than to constitute real contradictions. But even where our positions seem particularly irreconcilable, we cannot be content to let the matter rest as it is. For the conversation among us has only just begun, and we realize that in this question the entire self-understanding of the church is at stake."

The WCC's *Ecumenical Considerations on Jewish-Christian Dialogue* (1983) and especially statements by many of its member churches, most notably those of the general synod of the Netherlands Reformed Church (1970) and the synod of the Evangelical Church in the Rhineland (*Zur Erneuerung des Verhältnisses von Christen und Juden*, 1980), have developed even stronger affirmations of Israel and Judaism than the second position outlined in the F&O report of 1967, yet the conclusion of that report still stands: the topic is not only open and disputed in the churches, but "in this question the entire self-understanding of the church is at stake", since it concerns directly the electing nature and purposes of God.

See also **Jewish-Christian dialogue**.

PAUL M. VAN BUREN

P. van Buren ed., *Theology of the Jewish-Christian Reality*, parts 1-3, San Francisco, Harper & Row, 1987-88 • A.R. Eckardt ed., *Elder and Younger Brothers*, New York, Scribner's, 1967 • A.R. Eckardt, *Jews and Christians*, Bloomington, Indiana UP, 1986 • B. Klappert, *Israel und die Kirche: Erwägungen zur Israellehre Karl Barths,* Munich, Kaiser, 1980 • K. Stendahl ed., *Paul among Jews and Gentiles*, Philadelphia, Fortress, 1976 • F.E. Talmage ed., *Disputation and Dialogue: Readings in the Jewish-Christian Encounter*, New York, KTAV, 1975 • *The Theology of the Churches and the Jewish People: Statements by the World Council of Churches and Its Member Churches*, WCC, 1988 • C. Williamson ed., *Has God Rejected His People?*, Nashville, TN, Abingdon, 1982.

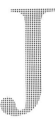

JESUS CHRIST. The constitution of the WCC declares that the council is "a fellowship of churches which confess the Lord Jesus Christ as God and Saviour according to the scriptures" (see **WCC, basis of**), and every major ecumenical conference since the Faith and Order* meeting at Lausanne in 1927 has included in its report some account of Christological fundamentals. However, the apparently straightforward formulation in the constitution (which entered by way of the Faith and Order movement) conceals a number of theological problems. It has become increasingly clear that the unambiguous description of Jesus Christ as "God" can be inadequate and misleading when divorced from the context of a fully stated theology of the Trinity.* If "Jesus Christ" is thought to exhaust the meaning of "God", there is a real risk of what some, especially Eastern Orthodox, theologians have called "Christomonism" — a concentration on the person and narrative of Jesus which ignores the question of how the Holy Spirit* conforms the life of believers in community to the likeness of Christ, and which tends therefore to keep Jesus at a distance from the community.

From Lausanne onwards, care has been taken to minimize this risk: Lausanne's report (para. 11) very clearly associates forgiveness and revelation* with the mission of the Holy Spirit as well as the life, death and resurrection* of Jesus; and Edinburgh 1937 (paras 2,6,7,20) echoes this. Lund 1952 (para. 10)

has a particularly impressive account of Christ's lordship in the church and of the way in which the Spirit makes believers partakers in the suffering and the sovereignty of Jesus. Since 1961 the membership basis of the WCC has itself included a reference to "the glory of the one God, Father, Son and Holy Spirit". However, the phraseology of the constitution remains awkward. More recently, the simplistic equation of God with Jesus has provoked some searching questions from feminist theologians, who have pointed out the implications of identifying God, without remainder, with a male human being. A further problem has been opened up as the churches have considered their responses to the Lima document *Baptism, Eucharist and Ministry** (BEM): the constitution speaks of confessing Jesus "according to the scriptures", but as the 1981 Princeton consultation on the implications of BEM for the project "Towards the Common Expression of the Apostolic Faith" noted, BEM (in common with many other WCC documents) gives no direct attention to the principles of interpretation by which we may draw from scripture material for contemporary faith statements about Christ (see **hermeneutics**). How are we to move beyond the repetition of New Testament idiom to a theology which is critical, challenging and constructive for the churches today?

This question relates to the very serious problem that arose in the 1930s when the German Confessing Church* sought to ensure that it would not be participating in the work of F&O alongside the Reich church. In 1935 Leonard Hodgson, then secretary of F&O, wrote to Dietrich Bonhoeffer that the ecumenical movement could not repudiate *any* body accepting "Jesus Christ as God and Saviour". Bonhoeffer pointed out in reply that the Confessing Church had, in the Barmen declaration of 1934, effectively denied the claim of the Reich church to believe in Christ as God and Saviour: Barmen had condemned as incompatible with the confession of Christ the ascribing of revelatory authority to any other source than "the one Word of God", Jesus Christ, and also the idea that there could be any areas of individual or corporate life not answerable to this authority. The German state church, by accepting the anti-semitic legislation of the Third Reich, had betrayed the Christian faith. It could not be enough to rest content with a mere *verbal* conformity with the F&O definition.

In several respects, therefore, the wording of the WCC constitution requires glossing and putting into context. What is it today to confess Jesus as "God and Saviour according to the scriptures"?

Jesus and the early church. There is no completely unambiguous use of the title "God" for Jesus in the NT (John 20:28 is the nearest; Rom. 9:5 and Titus 2:13 present considerable problems of translation and interpretation). However, it is clear that, within 20 years of the crucifixion (i.e. by the time Paul was writing 1 Cor.), there were Christian communities accustomed to thinking of Jesus as embodying the action of God towards the world, God's "power" and "wisdom" (1 Cor. 1:24). By the end of the 1st Christian century, when the gospel of John was probably written, Jesus could be seen as the one in whom dwelt the creative and mediating logos of God, the divine mind and purpose, the one upon whom the glory of God's tangible presence permanently rested. Jesus has become for believers what the temple was to Israel, the place where God is met, but is also the visible form of the power that makes the world. Both Paul and John suggest that, because Jesus is experienced as inaugurating a new age, a new creation, because he bestows on the believer a new identity in which human life is no longer bound and limited by a past of moral failure and staleness, or self-deceit and

spiritual blindness, the history of Jesus is completely continuous with the infinite resource of divine life which brings all things into reality. Just as in the Jewish scriptures, especially the Psalms and Isa. 40-55, the exodus and the return from exile are seen as images of the creation itself, so now is the formation of the new human race through the history of Jesus. The difference is that here the creative act of God is bound up with a *single* human story as never before and that the scale of the restoration and renewal expands all the time towards the limits of the human world, including all men and women equally. It is inevitable that Jesus, as the one who enacts the saving action of God, should, like the God of Israel, be called Lord and should be seen as the touchstone by which all human events are to be judged, the one who possesses "all authority in heaven and on earth" (Matt. 28:18).

Yet this is only part of the picture. Jesus possesses supreme authority but does not simply stand in the place of the God of Israel. He prays to this God as "Father", "Abba", and interprets his mission and destiny as the fleshing-out of a purpose not his own. His authority is inseparably interwoven with a loving dependence upon the one he worships, a steady "obedience" — i.e. he allows the pressure of God's love for the world to mould his human identity without interruption. Particularly in John's gospel, Jesus is presented simultaneously as entirely and sovereignly free — and as doing nothing from his own human initiative alone. It is this paradox in the way the figure of Jesus is understood in the NT (cf. Phil. 2) that prompts the development of a technical theological account of his person and a new Trinitarian conception of God.* If Jesus' life is entirely moulded by the loving will of God, it makes sense to say that it *is* that loving will "made flesh" (see **incarnation**), that there is no obstacle in Jesus to God's action in renewing the face of the earth.

But the life of Jesus, as we have seen, not simply expresses the outgoing action of God but is also a loving response to God. So the conclusion is slowly drawn that the very life of God — if it is this that is expressed in the life of Jesus — involves *both* the outgoing, generative, creative element *and* the product or issue of that outgoing in the form of total and perfect response, reflection back of the love given. God comes to be conceived as both "Father" and "Son". In the doctrinal controversies of the 4th century, out of which the Nicene Creed* emerged, the crucial point established was that God was never to be thought of as a solitary individual: God is eternally *in relation* and so eternally open to the "other". It is because God is thus that there is no problem about God's will to create: although this is a free action, it is rooted in the divine life itself, whose nature is to generate in love and to generate love. Because of the relation of Father and Son, creation* has access to a share in this movement of creative love: creatures can also be creators. This theme, set forth classically by Athanasius in the mid-4th century, is what lies behind the Eastern Christian understanding of salvation* as *theosis*, sharing in God's life.

Jesus and salvation. The confession of Jesus Christ as God must therefore, if it is to be faithful to the NT witness, involve the belief that through Jesus the renewal of the whole human race has become possible and that all human beings may find in Jesus the good news of their absolution and liberation; through Jesus, all have access to the life he lives, the life of liberty and creativity founded upon complete openness to the divine will for the salvation of women and men. In other words, to confess Jesus as God is to presuppose something about the radical character of the salvation he brings — the "new creation" — and to be committed to the new human race, without barriers of race, sex and status, that has begun to exist as a result of his life, death and resurrection. Bonhoeffer was certainly right in insisting that it is impossible to confess Christ as God and Saviour while refusing to be committed to the hope of an integrated, reconciled humanity: the Christological confession poses clear and sharp questions to our political and social loyalties, to our partial and distorted models of human community.

Remembering Paul's words in 1 Cor. 12:3, "no one can say 'Jesus is Lord' except by the Holy Spirit", we may conclude that to know Jesus as "Lord", to acknowledge him as the Creator and final Judge of the new humanity, and as the one who opens for us the way to a share in the freedom of the Creator, *is* to live in or by the power of God's Spirit. God is "Father" and "Son" but is equally that agency which draws us *into* the relation between the eternal creative source and the eternal creative response — that which realizes in us the possibility established in the history of Jesus Christ and in the coming-to-be of a community committed to Jesus Christ.

Often in the history of theology, the salvation brought by Christ has been analyzed and theorized about without reference to the witness and work of the Spirit. Some have tended to think (as a superficial reading of certain early Christian writers might suggest) that salvation occurs because God, in becoming flesh, transforms human nature by the mere fact of contact with it. Others have stressed that the cross of Jesus alone brings about our redemption,* as a sacrifice or an expiation for our sin, and have refined and developed the language of Paul and the letter to the Hebrews about atonement through sacrifice. Both themes have a significant place in Christian theology. It is essential to see Christ as God's way of pledging absolute faithfulness to our "cause", God's identification with the need and agony of human beings. Salvation does involve a transformation of our situation by God's contact with it. No less is it essential to see the death of Christ as pivotal to the process. Only in the cross do we see clearly the depth of our unfreedom, the way in which our moral, religious and political systems of power fear and reject the life God offers, and strive to obliterate the threatening hope of conversion. Only here do we see the *cost* of our slavery to ourselves and protection of ourselves. To say, as Christians have consistently said, that the cross is God's bearing of this cost may be a metaphor, but it is an untranslatable and irreplaceable one.

However, neither of these themes alone will carry the full weight of what the Bible understands as salvation. For this we need a doctrine of the work of the Spirit actively forming Christ's likeness in us, ceaselessly bringing us to conversion and hope.

We cannot speak of Jesus as God without speaking of him as Saviour; but equally we cannot speak of him as God without speaking of the God he calls Father, and we cannot speak of him as Saviour without speaking of the life in us of God as Spirit. This point is made with admirable clarity in the 1979 document from the Klingenthal consultation on the filioque:* "We are 'christified', 'made christs', in the church by the indwelling in us of the Holy Spirit, who communicates the very life of Christ to us, who in Christ makes us the brothers and sisters of Christ, and strengthens us in our new condition as the adopted children of the Heavenly Father."

The Chalcedonian schism. In the early centuries of the church, Christology proved to be a deeply divisive force at least as much as it was a unifying one. The classic definition at Chalcedon* in 451 of the inseparable co-existence in Jesus of full divinity and full humanity looked back on what was already a complex history of controversy and was itself to fuel further division. The churches that refused Chalcedon did so because some believed it to compromise the necessary distinction between divine and human nature, while others saw it as over-emphasizing the disjunction between the divine Word and the human Jesus.

The 20th century has seen great advances in overcoming the ancient schism. Representatives of Chalcedonian and non-Chalcedonian churches (esp. those of the so-called monophysite tradition — a misleading label — in Egypt, Syria, Armenia, Ethiopia and India) have had candid and fruitful conversations; recent popes have issued joint statements of faith with leaders of the non-Chalcedonian churches (e.g. the joint declaration of Pope John Paul II and the Syrian Orthodox patriarch of Antioch in 1984). There is a growing recognition that terminological confusion and misunderstanding, as well as political and ethnic rivalries, have long embittered what is at heart a disagreement in idiom and emphasis *within* a common faith. Non-Chalcedonians have played an active role in the work of F&O, not least in the recent studies towards an ecumenical explication of the apostolic faith as expressed in the Nicene Creed (381) (the sub-title of the 1987 study document *Confessing One Faith*). These studies have made it clear that a Christology firmly anchored in Trinitarian belief, grounded in a careful, critical and imaginative reading of scripture, and oriented towards the priorities of mission and of proclaiming a shared hope for the human world, remains the fundamental inspiration *and* critique of all ecumenical endeavour. Such an emphasis has increasingly dominated 20th-century reflection on the doctrine of Christ outside the European and North American context.

Jesus Christ in non-Western theologies. As with all theological topics, the doctrine of Christ has largely been explored and developed by theologians from a particular social and cultural world, that of Western Europe and its North American offshoots. Recent years have witnessed the rapid development of theologies whose priorities and criteria do not depend in the same way on a Western tradition moulded by classical Hellenism and the medieval cultural synthesis (what Bernard Lonergan called the world of "classical" thought in the widest sense). Christology is now being written from the standpoint of newer Christian communities, or Christian communities that have only recently discovered a voice of their own, and the insights coming from this burgeoning world of fresh reflection have put some serious questions to aspects of "traditional" Christological thinking in the North Atlantic intellectual world. Asia, Africa and Latin America are all developing distinctive styles of Christological thought, in response to the pressures of being Christian in these diverse environments. What it means to have the life of Christ communicated to us, what, indeed, the divinity of Christ means in terms of critically available images of God in a particular cultural context — these are matters not to be resolved by easy abstractions and generalizations.

Asia: Perhaps the longest tradition of trying to express Christological convictions in non-Western language and thought-forms is to be found in India. Since the middle of the 19th century, a variety of Indian Christian writers have attempted to re-conceive the doctrine of the Trinity in terms of the classical Hindu threefold formula for the absolute: *saccidānanda*, i.e. *sat* (being), *cit* (consciousness), and *ānanda* (bliss). In this perspective, the second person of the Trinity becomes the divine as active and communicative, the exemplar of creation, and, in the remarkable phrase of Keshab Chandra Sen (1838-84), "the journeying God". Jesus is the absolute turned towards relation and love, made particular in the world so as to become the first moment of a new creation in which human beings are enabled to overcome the cycles of karma (the determinism of moral cause and effect, the round of expiation requiring re-birth again and again until the effects of the past are neutralized). These themes are very common in Indian theologians of the later 19th and early to mid 20th centuries (Brahmabandhav Upādhyāya, Pandippedi Chenchiah, etc.); they are sometimes combined with a stress on Jesus' self-emptying, so that he becomes without ego, a "universal person" to whom all without exception can relate (Chandra Sen, V. Chakkarai).

This appropriation of classical Hindu metaphysical and mystical categories, reaching its most sophisticated form perhaps in the early writings of Raymond Panikkar, has not been the only Indian response to Christ. Some Indian Christians (Sundar Singh, A.J. Appasamy) have preferred to underline the native tradition of Bhakti, devotion to a personal "lord", as the entry point for Christian insight. Without necessarily denying the identification of Christ with the relational form of the divine usually referred to as *Isvara*, they concentrate on how that relational form generates individual love and devotion in the believer. There is a rich and little-known heritage of poetry in several Indian languages, especially Tamil and Marathi, expressing this approach, concentrating on the saving work of Jesus, and strongly reminiscent of both Western evangelical piety and the passionate religious poetry addressed in various Indian languages to Krishna or Siva.

More recently, however, Indian writers have become conscious of the difficulties implicit in an approach which privileges either the speculative religion of the higher caste groups or the individualized piety of devotional circles, in a country of acute social divisions and inequality. M.M. Thomas, one of the greatest of Indian Christian writers and a formidably important figure in the history of the WCC, produced an influential book on *The Acknowledged Christ of the Indian Renaissance* (1970), pointing out that Hindu reformers had seen in Christ a stimulus towards the critique of classical Hinduism, a vision of the just social order, even a challenge to the idea of a sacrally validated society. Hindu culture itself is not as static as some Indian speculative theologians seemed to assume. For the first time, Thomas argues, India is discovering a critical dynamic in its life, a sense of the imperative to *make* his-

Crucifix carved from a tree branch, Rwanda (WCC/Michael Dominguez)

tory;* the Jesus who creates a new historical community of human beings in unrestricted fellowship, a new humanity, is the Jesus who must now be preached in India. The interest of some earlier writers in Jesus as Second Adam, as the beginning of the new creation and as the one whose ego does not stand in the way of any other person's full humanity, is here given a more directly political focus. Thomas's work, prolonged in his own *Risking Christ for Christ's Sake* (1987), has been of the first importance in preparing the way for a "liberation" Christology in India, and for engagement not simply with the philosophy of a Hindu elite but with the images, hopes, stories and songs of the working people of India in their search for a fuller humanity. The work of Roman Catholic theologians such as Samuel Rayan and Sebastian Kappen has, in recent years, extended this theme in a dialogue with both popular religions and Marxism.

Elsewhere in Asia, distinctively Christological developments have been less in evidence. The minjung theology* of Korea has moved a little in this direction, identifying the oppressed and marginal peoples of today with those with whom Jesus identified in his ministry; so that the minjung, the marginal and despised classes, become, like the friends of Jesus, an eschatological people, the bearers of God's ultimate distance from and repudiation of worldly power. In this perspective, Jesus becomes not only the fellow sufferer but also the fool, the "clown", wholly free from anxiety about status and dignity, knowing the (divine) truth that God laughs the powerful to scorn. More than one Japanese theologian (Kazo Kitamori, Kosuke Koyama) has found that a theology of the cross, a theology of divine passion and suffering, is a necessary critical tool in confronting both Western abstraction in theology and a Buddhism one-sidedly concerned with overcoming rather than transforming history. Koyama has written of the need to keep Buddhism and Christianity in a close and balanced interaction as two responses to human violence and acquisitiveness — the moment of distance and detachment and the moment of creative and vulnerable engagement, neither making sense without the other. The crucified Jesus once again acts as a challenge to notions of human power and security.

The encounter with Buddhism has gone further still in the work of Aloysius Pieris, a Sri Lankan Jesuit, who has written of "Buddhology" and "Christology" as complementary ways of identifying a particular human being with the non-worldly power of liberation. Both are "crystallizations" of liberating praxis, understood as the movement into the world of final truthfulness and freedom (God for the Christian, the dharma for the Buddhist). Buddhist "gnosis" and Christian agape are both the ways of the divine in the world, and only in mutual relation can they be fully themselves. Pieris's approach has much in common with some of the Indian approaches outlined earlier but is more definitely pluralist in its implications.

Africa: African theology as a whole is still in a fairly inchoate condition, though developing rapidly; it will likely have some very distinctive questions to put to classic formulations from the point of view of a world-picture dominated by a spirituality of *creation*, of continuities with the natural order and with the human past. Gabriel Setiloane, writing from a South African perspective, notes that incarnational language presents few difficulties in a culture for which possession of a human subject by divine spirit is a readily accessible notion; the difficulty comes in understanding what is unique about this. Setiloane gives a hint at an answer in drawing attention to the Sotho-Tswana concept of "flowering" or "coming into vision" (like the sun rising) as a possible "carrier" for traditional doctrinal approaches to conversion in the African context. Jesus' status would be defined, in this perspective, as that of the bringer of a *corporate* "flowering" of the human family in its new unity and communion. Earlier African theologies had debated the question of how far traditional African language about the status and authority of the tribal chief could be used to describe the position of Jesus. An initial enthusiasm for this possibility gave way to caution about borrowing an uncriticized model of political power which in fact carried associations of remoteness in many contexts.

John Pobee of Ghana suggested a middle way, using the Akan idea of the royal spokesman as a metaphor for the role of Christ. It is important to preserve the positive aspects of the chief imagery (the chief as the one who connects the living and the dead, as the one whose word is wholly to be relied on, as the community's priest), while both maintaining the difference between Jesus as the "speaker" and mediator and the real chief, the High God, and also developing a theology of the cross which insists that the metaphor of chiefship, like every other metaphor, stands under the judgment of the sacrificial death of Jesus. It will be noted that both the African writers mentioned here are at best ambivalent about the doctrine of a Trinitarian sharing of the divine substance; the African context more readily assimilates, it seems, a narrative pattern focused on Jesus' relation to the Father, who delegates to him the power of conserving the community and freeing its members from evil and alienation.

Latin America: The liberation theology of Latin America has proved particularly resourceful in the exploration of Christology. Heavy emphasis has been laid upon the humanity of Jesus as the keystone of a theology of liberation; but this stress is meant not as a denial of classic confessions of his divinity, only as a re-locating of that confession. Leonardo Boff has presented this relocation in terms of seeing Christ's divinity in the freedom and the universal accessibility of his humanity. Because the human being Jesus takes his stand beyond the slaveries of history to speak for and from the "utopian" position of God's justice and love for all, he stands in judgment upon the whole of history. Because he offers himself as the focus for an unrestricted human fellowship, he is bound by no local constraint. As the one who proclaims the possibility of a *worldwide* exodus from unfreedom and oppression, he is outside the realm of the merely human. And from the side of God, it can be said that Jesus has and communicates this freedom by virtue of realizing completely the human potential for communion with God; his life, death and resurrection show that to be thus given into God's hands without reserve *is* to be given to the human world without reserve, and so to be the place where all may meet — once they have abandoned their struggles for dominance or privilege. Jesus' self-gift to the Father is of immediate political significance because it is creative of a different social network.

Jon Sobrino shares with Boff the concern to present Jesus as the paradigm of faith as well as its creator and its object; he has linked this understanding with a new and challenging exegesis of the spiritual exercises of Ignatius Loyola, the foundational text for Jesuit spirituality. His contention is that the following of Jesus along the way presented by the gospel narrative is to move from seeing this following as dictated by a logic independent of Jesus (Jesus as a way to arrive in a kingdom whose nature and promise are already known from elsewhere) to grasping that Jesus is to be followed even when there is no correspondence to what we *think* the kingdom should be. This attitude means following Jesus to the "failure" of the cross; walking in the way of justice, exposed to the power of oppression, even where there is no tangible hope of what we would consider a successful issue. *Doing* this, Sobrino argues, is what it means to confess Jesus as Lord and God; it is a praxis which, by putting the following of Christ and the search for the kingdom above and beyond all refutation and undermining by history, sets Jesus himself above the vicissitudes of this world's present order, and so places him with God. Orthodoxy lies in this kind of commitment to the justice of God, to the kingdom, to Jesus crucified.

Latin American theology has also been involved in examining the images of Christ available in its culture. The "official" faces of Christ tend to be either the Man of Sorrows, expressing the helplessness of the sufferer, or the glorified heavenly Monarch. Neither of these provides a vehicle for hope. To do that, an image of Christ must somehow articulate the way in which, because of Jesus' cross and resurrection, human pain is now taken up into the story of God's struggle with human rebellion and alienation, our alienation from our own humanity. Hugo Assmann has argued that practically all images of Christ, like all formulas about Christ, turn a process into a substantive state of affairs; when this happens, the inevitable corruption sets in of identifying the rule of Christ with the prevailing administration of human power, and we lose sight of Christ as the permanent "counterpower". Cross and resurrection must be kept inseparably together in their dialectical relation within the human story of the struggle for humanization — which is the story God has made *his* story.

Liberation Christologies have generally understood the belief in Jesus' divinity to be intelligible only through commitment to the authority of Jesus in social practice. They have thus — without necessarily wanting to deny or set aside the traditional creeds and formulations of faith — drawn our attention back to the origins of Christological confession in the simple acceptance of Jesus as authorized to define the shape of one's human hope and effort, Jesus as judge and prophet. The divinity of Jesus is shown rather than defined, shown in the radicalism of this commitment. Although many liberationists are heavily influenced by a residually liberal conviction about the "natural" utopian aspirations of human beings and hold to a theological anthropology still marked by the influence of writers such as Karl Rahner, their central direction is towards a more austere and cross-centred account of the cost of discipleship.

See also **God; Holy Spirit; salvation; theology, liberation; Trinity; uniqueness of Christ**.

ROWAN D. WILLIAMS

R. Boyd, *An Introduction to Indian Christian Theology*, Madras, CLS, 1969 • A.C. Cochrane, *The Church's Confession under Hitler*, Philadelphia, Westminster, 1962 • *Confessing One Faith:*

Towards an Ecumenical Explication of the Apostolic Faith As Expressed in the Nicene-Constantinopolitan Creed (381), WCC, 1987 • P. Gregorios, W.H. Lazareth & N.A. Nissiotis eds, *Does Chalcedon Divide or Unite? Towards Convergence in Orthodox Christology*, WCC, 1981 • K. Kitamore, *Theology of the Pain of God*, Richmond, VA, John Knox, 1965 • K. Koyama, *No Handle on the Cross*, London, SCM, 1977 • W.H. Lazareth ed., *The Lord of Life: Theological Explorations of the Theme Jesus Christ — the Life of the World*, WCC, 1983 • J. Míguez Bonino, *Faces of Jesus: Latin American Christologies*, Maryknoll, NY, Orbis, 1984 • K.H. Ohlig, *Fundamentalchristologie: Im Spannungsfeld von Christentum und Kultur*, Munich, Kösel, 1986 • A. Pieris, *An Asian Theology of Liberation*, Maryknoll, NY, Orbis, 1988 • J. Pobee, *Toward an African Theology*, Nashville, TN, Abingdon, 1979 • J. Sobrino, *Christology at the Crossroad: A Latin American Approach*, Maryknoll, NY, Orbis, 1978 • M.M. Thomas, *The Acknowledged Christ of the Indian Renaissance*, Madras, CLS, 1970 • L. Vischer ed., *Spirit of God — Spirit of Christ*, WCC, 1981.

JEWISH-CHRISTIAN DIALOGUE.

Increasing awareness of the horror of the Shoah (holocaust) of 1938-45, in which 6 million Jews were exterminated, is bringing about a gradual but radical re-appraisal of the relationship between Christians and Jews. The long history of anti-Judaic sentiment, the systematic teaching of contempt, legal discrimination and pogroms prepared the ground for 19th- and 20th-century antisemitism, which culminated in the Nazi tragedy. A recognition of this history has brought about a determination by all Christian bodies to oppose every form of antisemitism. This was expressed at the first assembly of the WCC at Amsterdam (1948) and even more strongly at the third assembly at New Delhi (1961). The International Council of Christians and Jews (composed of Protestants, Catholics and Jews), meeting at Seelisberg in 1947, published ten points to make such good intentions a reality, including the need to correct distorted images of Judaism and to present the passion of Christ in a way that avoids anti-Judaic references.

The Second Vatican Council* published its historic document *Nostra Aetate* in 1965, and this has revolutionized official Roman Catholic attitudes. Affirming a common "spiritual patrimony", it said that the passion of Christ "cannot be charged against all the Jews" and affirmed that the relationship between Jews and Christians "concerns the church as such". Numerous documents from bodies in the Vatican and conferences of Catholic bishops in the USA and Europe and guidelines for individual dioceses have developed this teaching and sought practical ways of implementing it. However, despite this and the work of *Service international de documentation judéo-chrétienne* in giving detailed teaching on how to avoid negative images of Judaism, it is questionable how much has really changed at the parish level. In Protestant churches, where there is less systematic follow-up, it is likely that despite expressions of good will, even less has actually changed.

Another factor in bringing about a new relationship between Christianity and Judaism is a historical study of the Bible. It is clear that the New Testament was written when the church and the synagogue had already split, and its writings reflect a mutual hostility which need no longer be shared by us. Furthermore, the re-discovery of Jesus as a Jew, against a Jewish background, as much by Jewish scholars as by Christian, shows how important it is for Christian self-understanding to reach a proper appreciation of Judaism.

The WCC at Amsterdam stressed the Christian responsibility to bring Jews to faith in Christ. This is still the view of agencies such as the Church's Ministry among the Jews and the Jews for Jesus movement, who, at the same time, urge that converted Jews should retain their Jewish heritage and identity. In contrast, the Roman Catholic order of the Sisters of Sion, which was founded in the 19th century to convert Jews, has totally changed its role and now works to help Christians to understand Judaism, and vice versa. Similarly, many official church pronouncements, for example that of the synod of the Protestant churches of the Rhineland in 1980, repudiate all attempts to convert Jews to Christianity. This approach emphasizes the one hope for the kingdom, shared by Jews and Christians, the joint mission that God's name be hallowed, and the mutual witness for equal partners in the dialogue. It provides the basis for the growing co-operation of Jews and Christians on social and moral issues.

Behind the disagreements lie unresolved theological questions. There is agreement that the Christian church has not directly replaced or superseded the people of Israel, in any easy sense, and that God remains faithful to those with whom he has made a covenant.* There is not yet a common mind, however, on whether there is one covenant or two and, if two, how they are related. For some, faith in Christ admits to a relationship with God which Jews already enjoy by virtue of their historic faith; and the resurrection* validates belief in the God and Father of Jesus, who was then, and is now, in a loving relationship to Jews.

Jews, for their part, stress that Judaism must be defined in Jewish, not Christian, terms and that Judaism is a living religion, culture and people which has continued to develop through the centuries and should not simply be equated with the religion of the Hebrew scriptures. For most, though not all, Jews, the state of Israel is seen as fulfilling the religious longing of centuries and as providing the political homeland which has been denied them for nearly 2,000 years. The unwillingness of the Vatican to recognize the state of Israel and what is seen as only a grudging recognition of it by other Christian bodies is a source of resentment. Furthermore, the natural sympathy of many church bodies for the Palestinian cause is sometimes a cause of disquiet for many Jews. Despite the real advance that has been made since 1947, great sensitivity is required to avoid the hurts that still continue to be caused, and at a parish level there is still an enormous educational task to be done.

The key documents of the major Christian bodies up to 1983 are collected in *Stepping Stones* and *More Stepping Stones*, listed below. Since then there have been major statements by, among others, the General Assembly of the Presbyterian Church of the USA (June 1987), the Episcopal Church of the USA (October 1987), and the Lambeth conference (August 1988).

The WCC held a consultation in 1988 in Sigtuna, Sweden, where a set of affirmations were made trying to sum up what Christians have learned in the Jewish-Christian encounters during past decades. (1) In God's love for the Jewish people, confirmed in Jesus Christ, God's love for all humanity is shown. (2) Christians share spiritual treasures with the Jewish people. (3) Jesus Christ both binds together and divides Christians and Jews. (4) Christians reject the view that the sufferings

of Jews in history are due to any corporate complicity in the death of Christ. (5) Out of the Jewish community emerged two communities of faith, sharing the same spiritual roots, yet making very different claims. (6) Claims of faith as weapons have been used against the Jewish people, culminating in the Shoah. (7) The Jewish people are not rejected by God. (8) The continuing vocation of the Jewish people is a sign of God's love. Their covenant remains. (9) The Jewish people today are in continuation with biblical Israel.

See also **antisemitism, Israel and the church.**

RICHARD HARRIES

H. Croner comp., *Stepping Stones to Further Jewish-Christian Relations*, London, Stimulus, 1977 • H. Croner comp., *More Stepping Stones to Jewish-Christian Relations*, London, Stimulus, 1985 • *The Theology of the Churches and the Jewish People: Statements by the World Council of Churches and Its Member Churches*, with a commentary by A. Brockway, P. van Buren, R. Rendtorff & S. Schoon, WCC, 1988 • G. Wigoder, *Jewish-Christian Relations Since the Second World War*, Manchester, Manchester UP, 1988.

JIAGGE, ANNIE R. B. 7.10.1918, Ghana. Appeals court judge and then supreme court judge in Ghana, Jiagge was a president of the WCC, 1975-83, and is a member of the Evangelical Presbyterian Church. In 1947 she attended the world conference of Christian youth at Oslo and was one of the speakers at the Kottayam meeting in 1952. She has attended Evanston 1954, Uppsala 1968, Nairobi 1975 and Vancouver 1983 and has served on the WCC committee on the laity and on the Commission on Inter-church Aid, Refugee and World Service. In 1967 she represented the WCC at the RC laity conference in Rome and from 1984 onwards was the moderator of the commission on the Programme to Combat Racism. In Ghana she serves as the moderator of the Commission on the Churches' Participation in Development and as committee member of the Christian Council of Ghana.

ANS J. VAN DER BENT

JOHN XXIII (Angelo Roncalli). B. 25.11.1881, Sotto il Monte, Italy; d. 3.6.1963, Rome. Bishop of Rome and pope from 28 October 1958 until his death, John

XXIII is best known ecumenically for having convoked the Second Vatican Council* (1962-65). Born of peasant farmers on the slopes of the Italian alps, Roncalli was ordained in 1904. After serving as secretary to the bishop of Bergamo, army chaplain during the first world war and national director of missions, with his office in Rome, he began a Vatican diplomatic career in 1925, first with a nine-year tour as apostolic visitor to Bulgaria, where amid the Muslims, the dominant Christians were Orthodox then divided among themselves, and the Catholics were both Latin and Eastern. As part of what he called a "mission of peace", he began his ecumenical apprenticeship in a ministry of charity among the Orthodox laity, clergy and hierarchy. A 1927 visit to the patriarch of Constantinople, Basil III, strengthened his conviction that one can hasten the full unity of the church "by charity... rather than theological discussion".

From 1934 to 1944 Roncalli was apostolic delegate to Turkey and Greece, where he soon became known for his diplomatic skills and practical charity towards various social groups. In diplomacy and humanitarian work, particularly among prisoners of war and refugees, Roncalli tried to be what he wrote in his 1940 private journal: "above all nationalistic disputes" as "a teacher of mercy and truth" with "principles and exhortations from my lips and encouragement from my conduct in the eyes of all — Catholics, Orthodox, Turks and Jews".

In late 1944 he moved to Paris, where he served as apostolic nuncio in post-war France, with a primary task of healing divisions between the victorious followers of De Gaulle and the discredited members of the compromising Vichy regime. He had frequent contacts with Orthodox, Protestant and Catholic promoters of church unity, and was also the first permanent observer of the holy see to UNESCO. In 1953 Pius XII appointed Roncalli to Venice as cardinal patriarch. There he resumed direct pastoral work, especially with the working class, and initiated reconciliation with the socialists.

When the college of cardinals elected the 78-year old Roncalli pope in 1958, it appeared to be a deliberately transitional choice of a relative unknown. But three months into his pontificate, John XXIII announced his intention to convoke "an ecumenical council for the universal church", envisaging the event as "an invitation to the separated communities to seek again that unity for which so many souls are longing in these days throughout the world". He called for the council without prior consultation, claiming that the idea was "an inspiration the spontaneity of which hit us as a sudden and unforeseen blow in the humility of our soul".

John XXIII's own contribution to the Council was his contagious confidence that the Roman Catholic Church needed serious *aggiornamento* (updating) in order to be faithful, his optimism about the action of God in the world as seen in "the signs of the times" and his conviction that the church should "use the medicine of mercy rather than severity".

In 1960 he set up the Secretariat for Promoting Christian Unity,* approved the delegation of official observers to the WCC 1961 assembly (New Delhi) and invited the Orthodox, Anglicans and Protestants to delegate observers to Vatican II. He eliminated anti-semitic expressions in the Good Friday liturgy and placed the Catholic-Jewish relations on the Council's agenda. Although he did not attend the general deliberations during Vatican II's first session, he intervened at a critical point to support the majority's desire to have a new draft on revelation and scripture.

Most noteworthy among his seven encyclicals* were *Mater et Magistra* (1961), on modern social questions in the light of Christian doctrine; *Pacem in Terris* (1962), on peace among all nations based on truth, justice, charity, freedom and the right organization of society; and *Princeps Pastorum* (1959), on updating the missions.

As bishop of Rome, John XXIII restored the tradition of visiting the parishes, hospitals, schools, charitable institutions, and prisons of the city. He convoked, for the first time in Rome's history, a diocesan synod (1960). He died of gastric cancer before the Vatican Council began its second session and was succeeded by Paul VI.

Transparently wide-hearted and affable, humble with his own gifts and limitations, lively and witty, "good pope John" easily won the affection of Catholics and non-Catholics alike and diminished the cult of the aloof pontifical personality. His posthumously published diary reveals the journey of a priest who never felt awkward with his very traditional Italian Catholic piety and who had unshaking trust in divine providence. The "mere transitional pope" had initiated a new age in Roman Catholicism.

John XXIII wrote *Journal of a Soul* (New York, McGraw-Hill, 1965). See also P. Hebblewaite, *John XXIII: Pope of the Council* (London, Chapman, 1984).

TOM STRANSKY

JOHN PAUL II. B. 18.5.1920, Wadowice, Poland. Bishop of Rome and pope from 16 October 1978 to the present, Karol Wojtila laboured in a quarry and chemical plant during the early Nazi occupation. During his Krakow university studies in literature, when he had begun to write poetry and plays and to act on stage, he decided to become a priest and studied in a clandestine seminary (1942). Ordained in 1946, Wojtila was sent to Rome to study for a doctorate in philosophy. Two years later he returned to Krakow for pastoral ministry in parishes and among university students. In 1953 he became professor in ethics and moral theology at Krakow and at Poland's only Catholic university, Lublin. He was named auxiliary bishop of Krakow (1958), later its archbishop (1964) and cardinal (1967).

Wojtila attended the four sessions of Vatican II, 1962-65. He strongly defended the draft on religious freedom, and on other subjects he spoke often in the name of his fellow Polish bishops. He participated in the first five bishops' synods in Rome, whose members repeatedly elected him a European representative on the synod's interim planning committee. After Paul VI's death in August 1978 and then the month-long papacy of Albino Luciani as John Paul I, Cardinal Wojtila was elected pope in October — the first non-Italian in the papal chair since the Dutchman Adrian VI (1522-23), and the first non-Western European since the 8th century (Zachary, 741-52).

Against the background of Vatican II and the papacy of Paul VI, John Paul II intentionally has been trying to pull back in line a church that "threatened to run away" from what he understands were the contents and intent of Vatican II. For some, he is not conservative enough; for some, he is wrongly putting a brake on authentic renewal; for some, he is saving Roman Catholicism from disintegration; for others, the pope has an impossible task, whatever the intent.

Early on in his papacy, he brought Eastern Europe in from the margins of the world's map, judging as "the key fact of our times" that "millions of our contemporaries legitimately yearn to recover those basic freedoms, of which they were deprived by totalitarian and atheistic regimes". Some historians already are tracing the extraordinary government shifts of 1989 in Eastern and Central Europe, with the demise of autocratic communist parties and the legal recognition of the rights of workers, writers, churches, etc., to John Paul II's trip to Poland in June 1987. By his 10th anniversary as pope, John Paul II had made over 50 journeys outside Italy, to over 70 countries in six continents — on the travel road for the equivalent of almost 13 months.

His explicit ecumenical commitment ("irrevocable" for the church and for himself) has been questioned by some, lauded by others. He champions religious freedom and defends all liberties as consonant with strong convictions, yet seems over-restrictive in freedom within the church, especially in the teachings of theologians (e.g. sexual ethics). He supports the strong cautious positions taken by the curial congregations for the doctrine of the faith, for seminaries and institutes of study, and for divine worship.

At the same time, the pope is careful to meet other Christian leaders during his travels (e.g. visiting the WCC offices in Geneva, June 1984) and in Rome. Some observe that despite his contacts with Anglicans and Protestants, he pays far more attention to the healing of the schism between the Church of Rome and the Orthodox. Yet that very interest in the political and ecclesial *Ostpolitik* suddenly proved an objective priority in the delicate post-1989 relations in Eastern Europe between the Orthodox churches and the Eastern Catholic (esp. in the Ukraine).

Nevertheless, Wojtila has frequently expressed his own glimpse into the future. Almost apocalyptic in vision as the pope describes the present battle between good and evil, he believes it cannot be won except with a united church, marching in non-compromising steps towards the year 2000.

TOM STRANSKY

JOINT WORKING GROUP. The JWG is the official consultative forum of the WCC and the Roman Catholic Church to initiate, evaluate and sustain collaboration between their respective organs and programmes. Established by the WCC central committee (Enugu 1965) and by Vatican authorities, the JWG meets annually and submits official reports to its two authorities (1966, 1967, 1971, 1975, 1982, 1990). The JWG seeks to be flexible in the styles of collaboration. It keeps new structures to a minimum while concentrating on ad hoc initiatives in proposing new steps and programmes.

The JWG has facilitated RC membership in the Faith and Order* commission, consultative relations with the Commission on World Mission and Evangelism and with the Christian Medical Commission, and staff visits and consultations between Geneva and Vatican departments. It helped to form the 1968-80 joint committee on Society, Development and Peace (SODEPAX)* and the annual joint preparation of the materials for the Week of Prayer for Christian Unity.* The JWG has sponsored its own studies: of particular note are "Catholicity and Apostolicity" (1968), "Common Witness and Proselytism" (1970), "Common Witness" (1980), "Hierarchy of Truths" (1990), and "The Church: Local and Universal" (1990).

Since 1980 the JWG has structured its agenda around the unity* of the church,* common witness,* social collaboration, and ongoing collaboration. The JWG endeavours to interpret major streams of ecumenical thought and action as well as present successes and obstacles in common witness, relation between bilateral* and multilateral* dialogues, mission* and evangelism,* challenges of youth, Christian women in church and society, education (general and religious), mixed marriages, national and local councils of churches,* ethical issues as new sources of division, human rights* and religious liberty.*

From its beginning the JWG was conscious that despite a shared commitment to common witness within one ecumenical movement, there is a disparity between the two parent bodies which affects the extent, style and content of collaboration. The WCC is a fellowship of churches, and its members do not take direct juridical responsibility for WCC studies, actions and statements; the RCC is one church with a universal mission and structure of teaching and governance as an essential element of its identity.

This RC self-understanding and structure of operation on a world level, which differs from those of the WCC member churches, was offered as a main (but not the only) reason why the RCC in 1972 declined to ask for WCC membership* "in the immediate future" or to co-sponsor such events as the 1990 Seoul world convocation on "Justice, Peace and the Integrity of Creation".

Although the JWG mandate gives priority to encouragement of collaboration on local and national levels, in fact most of JWG's time and energy is spent on relations between Geneva and the Vatican. One observes that the very common ground or basis which the RCC and the WCC, through the JWG, have forged to undergird present collaboration works more naturally and with less strain when the RCC as such and the WCC as such are not directly involved.

TOM STRANSKY

Accounts of collaboration in each quarterly issue of the Vatican Secretariat for Promoting Christian Unity *Information Service* • JWG official reports in *The Ecumenical Review* 18,2; 23,1; 24,3; 28,1; 35,2, and Sixth Report, Geneva-Rome, 1990 • T. Stransky, "A Basis beyond the Basis: Roman Catholic/WCC Collaboration", *The Ecumenical Review*, 37, 2, 1985.

JUST, PARTICIPATORY AND SUSTAINABLE SOCIETY. The search for a just, participatory and sustainable society (JPSS) was a major theme for study and reflection during the period between the fifth WCC assembly at Nairobi (1975) and the sixth assembly at Vancouver (1983). The meeting of the central committee in 1976 identified it as one of the four main programme emphases for the WCC in the ensuing years. As a programme emphasis, JPSS was to be treated as a framework for the coordination of programmes and as an area of concentration for concerted efforts by the different sub-units, especially those involved in the social field. But it was soon recognized that JPSS could also serve another and more important role — to evoke a common vision of a new human society. The need for articulating such a common vision for a new society has been a concern of many in the ecumenical movement for quite some time. The previous attempt to address the issue took place at the first assembly at Amsterdam (1948), where the concept of "responsible society" had emerged. But since then, enormous changes had taken place in world society. Societal issues had become more complex and challenging. Changes had also taken place in the ecumenical movement itself and in Christian social thinking and experience.

The central committee felt that the concept of JPSS might meet this need and therefore initiated a process of enquiry and reflection. The meeting of the central committee in 1977 appointed an advisory committee to stimulate theological reflection on JPSS among the churches, to assist the sub-units of the WCC to intensify their action/reflection programmes towards JPSS and to prepare a document to clarify and elaborate the concept.

The choice of JPSS was not an arbitrary decision. It arose out of the experiences of the churches and the ecumenical movement through the years. Justice, participation and sustainability were three major concerns that were already on the ecumenical agenda. The issue of *justice** had been a central concern of the WCC throughout its history. The promotion of justice was stated as one of the functions of the WCC in its constitution. Since the Church and Society conference in 1966 and the Uppsala assembly in 1968, there was a new urgency in the search for justice. The efforts in combatting injustice became more intense and wide-ranging. Justice was the primary goal of the development concern, a major preoccupation of the WCC and member churches during those years. Systemic injustice had been recognized as the root cause of poverty. The ecumenical concern for peace* also had to include the issue of justice, as situations of injustice posed a constant threat to peace. The re-structuring of society and the elimination of injustice were called for by those engaged in combatting racism,* discrimination against women, and human rights violations. These and other societal issues in which the WCC was heavily involved in the 1960s and early 1970s had revealed the intensity, complexity and universality of the forces of injustice entrenched in the social, economic and political structures.

The issue of *participation** had emerged as a vital concern in the ecumenical discussions on development. People's participation was identified as a major goal of development and the most effective means of promoting development. The emphasis on people's participation was so strong that the Nairobi assembly was led to re-define development as "essentially a people's struggle in which the poor and the oppressed should be the active agents and immediate beneficiaries". Similarly the Commission on the Churches' Participation in Development came to the conviction that "people, the poor and the oppressed, are the subjects and not the objects of the development process". The issue of participation was not confined to the development concern. The right of the people to participate in making decisions that affect their lives was also a guiding principle in many ecumenical concerns, such as decolonization, racial equality, human rights and women's liberation.

The concept of *sustainability** was relatively new in ecumenical discussions. The first major discussion of this issue took place at Bucharest in 1974. The concern arose out of the recognition of several alarming trends in modern society that threaten the lives of people, future generations, all living creatures, and nature itself — environmental deterioration; pollution of water, air and land; deforestation and desertification; depletion of non-renewable resources such as oil and minerals; changes in eco-systems, the atmosphere and the ozone layer, etc. The major source of these threats to survival was identified as the patterns of production and consumption. The concept of sustainability was introduced to challenge the rapidly accelerating growth process pursued in recent years and to recognize the need for selective growth and limits to growth.

Following the discussions and decisions of the central committee on JPSS, a series of consultations were held at national, regional and world levels. The advisory committee on JPSS assisted and monitored these discussions. The committee had two meetings of its own and later submitted a report to the central committee in 1979.

The report identified the search for a just, participatory and sustainable society as the major thrust of the ongoing struggle of the people. The imperative of the churches to strive for JPSS arises from this historical reality, as God's call to the church is a direct response to the cries of God's people, the poor and the oppressed. The report made an attempt to articulate theological perspectives on justice, participation and sustainability. It affirmed the emphasis on justice in the biblical tradition. "Justice is a messianic category. It embraces both God's righteousness and fidelity and his will for a right ordering of human community... In messianic perspective, 'participation' is an essential manifestation of the true koinonia in which there is no domination of one over the other, but where all are mutually accountable to one another...'Sustainability' in the Bible is expressed by the faithfulness of God to his lasting covenant. God blesses continually his creation, preserving it from destruction and leading it to the fullness of life abundant. We have received God's earth as our common inheritance, not as a privilege for some and a source of frustration for others."

Discussion of the report raised some important theological issues, such as the tension between realism and utopianism and the relation between God's justifying righteousness and human justice. The report pointed out the various issues involved in the people's struggle for JPSS and the challenge to the churches; the central committee later approved the recommendations it made to the WCC.

One of the major recommendations for follow-up was a programme of study and reflection on political ethics, i.e. "an examination of structures of power, participation and political organization on local, national and international levels". As a result, an ecumenical consultation was held in Cyprus, the report of which was published under the title *Perspectives on Political Ethics*.

Vancouver 1983 issued a historic call for churches "to engage in a conciliar process of mutual commitment (covenant) to Justice, Peace and the Integrity of Creation". The JPSS programme paved the way for this momentous decision.

See also **justice, peace and the integrity of creation; responsible society**.

C.I. ITTY

JUST WAR. The doctrine of just war constitutes the dominant teaching of the mainline churches concerning war and violence.*

Traceable back to the classical teaching of Cicero (d.43 B.C.), the doctrine appeared in Christian theology through Ambrose of Milan (c.339-97). Subsequent teachers of the church such as Augustine and Aquinas established just-war theory as a part of the Christian ethos, and Luther and Calvin carried it into the Protestant Reformation.

Each of these writers and subsequent scholars have given the doctrine of just war different emphases. These are important variations in the historical tradition of the church, which has at times been firmly in the service of the rulers and at other times struggled to distance itself from oppressive regimes by affirming an alternative liberative tradition. The following are the essential emphases of just-war theory.

Just cause: In order for a war to be regarded as just, the church has traditionally taught that it must be fought for a just cause, although notions of just cause have differed over the years. It is today commonly argued by just-war theorists that it involves the restraint of an aggressor, protection of the innocent, the restoration of rights wrongly taken and the restoration of a just order.

Just end: Perceptions of a just or acceptable end differ vastly, while the price which most communities are prepared to pay for a condoned end is often exorbitant. For those living in extreme situations of oppression, the possibility of future anarchy is often seen (at least at the time) as an end to be preferred to continued oppression. And in most wars legitimated by the church, millions of lives have been expended for only a relative peace. The point of the criteria is, however, that the goal of war ought to be peace and justice, rather than mere vengeance or lust for power.

Just means: Possibly the most difficult of all just-war criteria to put into practice in the heat of battle, this criterion requires restraint in the choice of weapons with a view to minimizing suffering and death. The Geneva convention (1949) and two subsequent Geneva protocols (1977) are, for example, in accordance with this criterion in seeking to prohibit "direct intentional attacks on non-combatants and non-military targets", arguing for the banning of nuclear arms and seeking to prohibit the use of torture.* Using this criterion, some argue that modern military technology has rendered all wars unjust.

Last resort: This is possibly the most important emphasis of just-war theory. All other means of correcting a wrong are to be tried before the resort to arms can be regarded as justifiable.

*Legitimate authority:** The dominant tradition of the church since the time of Constantine has shown a consistent bias in favour of de facto rulers as opposed to armed revolution. In this context the resort to arms was seen to be the sole legitimate function of the king. The church also, however, allowed that a de facto leader is not necessarily a legitimate leader, and the teachers of the church recognized that there comes a time when the tyrant may need to be removed from power. There is little agreement in the church, however, on whose responsibility it is to do so.

Calvin took the first cautious step towards allowing for just revolution.* He recognized that in extreme situations of tyranny it could be the obligation of the magistrate (a recognized leader of the people) to lead the people in rebellion. "In South Africa", said a young black Christian recently, "it is our legitimate community leaders who are required to protect our right and lead us in such actions as may be necessary to ensure that the present unjust rulers are removed from power." Theodore Beza, Calvin's successor in Geneva, went beyond Calvin in legitimating revolution, and in the turbulent religious wars and rebellion that followed, much of the caution of earlier ages was thrown to the wind. The teaching that resulted ranged from Zwinglian notions of legitimate war and the exploits of Thomas Münzer, Karlstadt and the Zwickau prophets, to Oliver Cromwell and John Knox, who insisted that to remain passive in the face of tyranny was tantamount to complicity with the tyrant.

Just-war theory has been abused over the years to legitimate a variety of unjust wars, and there can be a narrow line between the theology of just war and that of holy war or crusade. This distinction makes the challenge of pacifism* a disturbing factor in the church. Not able to affirm pacifism in principle, believing that in extreme situations armed struggle may be the only responsible option available to a suffering people, many committed just-war theorists nevertheless find that the option of non-violence continues to haunt their conscience.

Discussion of this question has been a part of the ecumenical movement from the beginning. While the Stockholm Life and Work* conference (1925) limited itself to expressing its horror of war and its hope for peace, the Oxford conference (1937), on the verge of an almost inevitable conflict, was forced to discuss the issue of Christian participation. The conference recognized the existence of "widely diverging views regarding war", which were then summarized in three positions. Eleven years later, after the second world war had been fought, views had not changed significantly. The three Oxford positions are taken up at Amsterdam 1948: "(1) There are those who hold that, even though entering a war may be a Christian's duty in particular circumstances, modern warfare, with its mass destruction, can never be an act of justice. (2) In the absence of impartial supranational institutions, there are those who hold that military action is the ultimate sanction of the rule of law, and that citizens must be distinctly taught that it is their duty to defend the law by force if necessary. (3) Others, again, refuse military service of all kinds, convinced that an absolute witness against war and for peace is for them the will of God and they desire that the church should speak to the same effect."

The ecumenical discussion on just war has so far produced no larger agreement. The efforts have concentrated on the means and ways to prevent war, a point on which all can agree (see **peace**). Meanwhile, new situations have re-opened the debate, posing the question of "just revolution". It was extensively discussed in relation to the WCC central committee decision in 1970 to establish a special fund to make financial grants available for humanitarian purposes to Southern African and liberation movements in other areas engaged in armed combat against oppressing regimes (see **Programme to Combat Racism; liberation, struggles for**).

The theology of just war was originally written from the perspective of the dominant classes of society. Re-written from the perspective of the poor and oppressed, just-war theory acquires the character of a theology of just revolution. Theological continuity requires that such a theory, like that of just war traditionally intended to limit war, be used only in the same restraining way. Traditionally it allowed that in certain extreme situations war might be justified, even if never entirely "just" or "good"; as a theory of revolution it also allows that revolution, under certain circumstances, might be justified.

See also **justice, pacifism, peace, revolution, violence and nonviolence, war guilt**.

CHARLES VILLA-VICENCIO

JUSTICE. Biblically and historically there have been differing ideas of justice, a lack of common understanding still evident in the ecumenical movement.

Justice in the Bible and in church history. Biblically speaking, justice is a relational concept. It means "behaviour acceptable to the community" (Klaus Koch & Gerhard von Rad). When all relations (between God, human beings and creation) are whole, shalom (peace) prevails (Isa. 32:17). Particularly through the structures by which power is accumulated in highly advanced civilizations, community relations have in practice been endangered or destroyed. In this situation God's judging *(shaphat)* and judgment *(mishpat)* mean the restoration of justice and shalom — God in his mercy hears the cries of the oppressed and liberates them (José Porfirio Miranda). In the light of the sinful structures of unevenly distributed power, justice becomes a term implying struggle. If the oppressors do not repent, God's justice becomes their punishment.

The classic example is Yahweh's liberation of the Hebrews (i.e. the outcasts of the early advanced civilizations) from slavery in Egypt (Ex. 3-15). After their liberation God's people were to act as God himself acts and create an alternative, just society. So God gave them *mishpatim*, ordinances (see Ex. 21:1-23:19 and 20:1-17). When Israel's civilization itself took the form of a monarchy (1 Sam. 8), serving the idol of power (1 Kings 18) and thus dividing into poor and rich (1 Kings 21), Yahweh sent prophets calling for justice (Amos 5:24). Helping the poor* and the weak to obtain justice is identical with the knowledge of God (Jer. 22:16). After the fall of the kingdom, hope grew of God's kingship, the kingdom of God.* Jesus brought this kingdom and his justice and was thus seen to be the Messiah. The poor were encouraged (Luke 4:16-22), small communities of the new righteousness developed (Matt. 5:13-14 and Acts

4:32) and refused to have anything to do with unjust structures of power (Mark 10:42-45). Jesus' resurrection* proved God's power to show that life is produced by suffering* and dying for the sake of justice. Paul saw the righteousness and justice of God in the fact that God calls even the gentiles and the entire creation through the Holy Spirit* and gives them the power to turn away from injustice and perdition and to serve justice (RSV: righteousness) unto eternal life (Rom. 5:21).

Biblically there is no contrast between God's justice and human justice. God's just action calls for the participation of God's creatures. From the human standpoint this means that receiving in prayer is indissolubly bound up with co-operation in the struggle for justice.

In the history of the church, monastic movements and historical peace churches (e.g. Mennonites, Brethren and Quakers) followed the early Christian pattern of resisting injustice and building up an alternative community as (preliminary) signs of the kingdom of God, born of suffering. The majority churches, especially of the West, have developed a different model. After Christianity had been accepted as the official religion of the Roman empire in the 4th century, the church tried to share in power and, when circumstances were most favourable, to tame and limit it. Justice and peace were thus switched from their biblical setting into a Greco-Roman and later a Germanic context. Plato's concept of justice as an ordinance of authority* was taken over — politically in the rule over the artisans by the philosopher-kings assisted by the warriors, and anthropologically in the rule of reason, assisted by the will, over the desires. Thus justice became a virtue.* Aristotle distinguishes between commutative justice (in acts of exchange) and distributive justice (in the distribution of goods). In Roman legal thought justice is "the constant and enduring will to grant their rights to all" (Ulpian, fragment 10).

But in the Roman context "to each his own" means pre-eminently the protection of those with possessions as opposed to the protection of the poor. In the subsequent periods of the middle ages and the Reformation, law* as an order* was understood first and foremost as penal and compulsive (the ordinance of the sword). The participation of Christians and churches in this order was tied to criteria: within a particular society, the order must minister to the common good — to love — and in foreign politics war could be waged only if it was a "just" war.* If compulsion was exercised on Christians to make them sin,* they must refuse to do so (see also, e.g. the Augsburg confession, art. 16).

Classified as the human virtue of mastery over the desires and as the established power of the authorities to exercise compulsion, justice as a human concern ended up in tension with divine justice. Various classifications of the two types of justice were attempted: supremacy of divine justice as the rule of the church over the world (the Curialists), a harmonious graded order (Aquinas), a correlative status (nominalists) and a dialectical relationship (Luther). The theological basis for the correlation of biblical faith* with power structures is the assumption that in the last resort the perspectives of love and reason are one and the same. In the modern bourgeois age there then develops a rigid dualistic opposition between, on the one hand, divine justice for the individual soul and personal relations and, on the other, rigid arbitrary laws in economics* and politics, wholly separated, like the laws of nature, from religion and ethics.* Indeed in economics the question of justice is replaced by market value (first of all in Hobbes). For the most part the majority churches are either helpless to resist this view or come to terms with it.

Not till the 1960s has a third way of "being the church" developed — the liberation church model, which harks back to biblical traditions. The majority church of Constantine's day did not succeed in taming power* in the interests of justice — i.e. of God's will — while the misuse of power in the countries of Asia, Africa and Latin America by this same "Christian" European civilization ran counter to nature and became increasingly violent and destructive in the military sphere. Hence counter-movements have arisen "from below", struggling for liberation (see **liberation, struggles for**). We may cite the people's movements and new social movements and, on the basis of their praxis, liberation theology (Latin America), minjung theology (Asia), black theology (South Africa and North America) and feminist theology (see **theology: Asian, black, feminist, libera-**

tion, and **minjung**). These movements reject "imperial", Constantinian-type civilization and create new participating communities (see **church base communities**). At the cost of suffering, these have been seeking to break up the structures of power and have been building up the counter-power of the people, thus transforming the unjust structures to achieve justice and participation.

Justice in ecumenical discussion. The first major world conferences of the ecumenical movement were entirely under the influence of the majority churches. The crux of the conflict they considered was how to understand the kingdom of God and God's justice in relation to history.

At the world missionary conference in Edinburgh (1910), realization of the kingdom of God meant first and foremost the Christianization of the world, i.e. educating people into the ways of Western civilization, although it undoubtedly also meant criticism of the colonialist policies of the colonial powers. In Stockholm at the first world conference of Life and Work (1925), the German and North American positions clashed violently. The German bishop Ludwig Ihmels, for instance, took the view that the kingdom of God was supramundane, that it had to do with human hearts and that it penetrated only the community life of Christians, and even then never completely, because of sin. On the other hand, Wishart (USA) — in the tradition of the social gospel* — saw a partial realization of the kingdom of God in the League of Nations. Stockholm defined the aim of the movement as "united practical action in Christian Life and Work".

The second world missionary conference (Jerusalem 1928) gave practical shape to the social relevance of the kingdom of God by rejecting in principle the worship of money as the "religion of a capitalistic society". The object of mission* was to shape not merely the life of individual Christians and Christian communities but also social and political life as Christ intended, though here too, of course, no questions were asked about the relevance of the model represented by the positive aspects of Western civilization.

Following these initial and still-tentative attempts to mobilize the biblical perspective of the kingdom of God against modern secularism and the worldwide structures of exploitation in the economic system and in colonialism,* the Oxford 1937 conference on "Church, Community and State" reverted to the medieval and Reformation majority church model of "taming power" by participating in it, thus laying the foundation for ecumenical social ethics in the period till 1966-68. The great world economic crisis and the rise of the fascist totalitarian state (see **fascism**) constituted the background to this "Christian realism", behind which stood theologians like Reinhold Niebuhr, J.H. Oldham and Emil Brunner. Between the line taken by the kingdom-of-God theology (transformation of the worldly orders and resistance on the basis of an alternative Christian society) and resigned accommodation to the worldly orders in privatized piety, the majority at Oxford supported a critical but constructive approach which was intended to contribute to relative justice on the basis of natural law* or the "moral law": "It cannot be assumed that the practice of Christian love will ever obviate the necessity for coercive political and economic arrangements."

Here the conference was explicit in its awareness that this approach was not evolved from the Bible. The criterion for prophetic criticism of the existing orders and for their relative improvement was middle axioms* (Oldham), which could mediate between the absoluteness of Christian love and the realities conditioning socio-economic and political life.

It was on this basis that the founding assembly of the WCC in Amsterdam (1948) developed the idea of a responsible society* as a socio-ethical criterion for assessing all individual questions. This was an attempt to balance freedom, justice and the control of power. Ideologically and politically this position rejects both laissez-faire capitalism* and communism and endorses a kind of social-democratic liberal democracy.

The world conference on Church and Society (Geneva 1966) and the Uppsala assembly (1968) represent the beginning of a new period in the life of the ecumenical movement. This phase was prompted by the participation — which had increased by leaps and bounds since 1961 — of the churches of Africa, Asia and Latin America in the life of the WCC. Central to the change was the shift of orientation from the top (influencing those with the power) to a perspective from below (participation in the actual struggles of the

Residents in Escourt, Natal, protest their threatened expulsion (epd-bild/de Vlieg)

oppressed in their imitation of the suffering Messiah).

In terms of method, this new approach means a switch from studies on "universal" concepts to models of contextual participatory action and reflection (see **praxis**), from "value-free" education to "conscientization" (Paulo Freire) and from aid to committed participation. Spirituality and prayer complement struggle as a second pole in the new approach, and this fact gives expression to the transcendence of the kingdom and justice of God.

The specific struggles for justice in which the liberation-theology approach developed in the WCC were primarily the following: against racism* (Programme to Combat Racism*); against economic exploitation (Commission on the Churches' Participation in Development; Just, Participatory and Sustainable Society; and Urban Rural Mission); countering discrimination against women; and supporting human rights, including socio-economic and political rights. The Vancouver 1983 assembly extended this approach in two ways. First, the inter-related study of justice, peace and the integrity of creation* was placed on the agenda. Second, it became clear that this new approach has profound consequences for the being and understanding of the church. Visser 't Hooft had already said at Uppsala in 1968: "Church members who deny in fact their responsibility for the needy in any part of the world are just as much guilty of heresy as those who deny this or that article of the faith." The two lines of Life and Work* and Faith and Order* came together.

This issue first became acute as a *status confessionis** with the rejection as a heresy* of the structural racism of apartheid* (see **racism**) and of its theological justification (LWF 1977/WARC 1982). But as regards the idol of the transnational economic system and its deadly power, Vancouver 1983 also stated: "The church is... challenged not only in what it does but in its very faith and being" (see **economics, transnational corporations**). In the extreme situations of systematic and flagrant injustice, the approach of the liberation church is therefore linked to that of the "confessing church"* — but also to the Orthodox-inspired understanding of the eucharist* as the sacrament that shapes the life of its participants who have encountered God as move-

ment from death to life (see **life and death**), from injustice to justice, from violence to peace, from hatred to love, from vengeance to forgiveness, from selfishness to sharing, from division to unity.

Where huge and unjust economic power structures are defended by the rich with all the force at their command and are not subjected to any effective political control, and where the poor are increasingly oppressed, it is, besides being biblically justifiable, also realistic not to expect justice simply as a result of prophetic appeals on a rational basis to those with the power. Rather, the church must be alongside those who are suffering in refusing to countenance injustice; the church must itself begin to practise justice in all its forms as a reality in its own life and thus, as a peace church and liberation church, transcend the majority church model. Of course, in so far as the liberation church model seeks, in co-operation with "people's movements", to have a transforming effect on socio-economic and political structures, it must itself develop aims and criteria for change. Thus methodologically it has points of contact with the majority church approaches, e.g. the middle axioms or Roman Catholic social teaching, despite all the differences in content. All approaches remain dependent on the twofold prayer "thy kingdom come, thy will be done."

See also **ethics, peace**.

ULRICH DUCHROW

K.-H. Dejung, *Die ökumenische Bewegung im Entwicklungskonflikt, 1910-1968*, Stuttgart, Klett-Kösel, 1973 • R.D.N. Dickinson, *Poor, Yet Making Many Rich: The Poor as Agents of Creative Justice*, WCC, 1983 • U. Duchrow, *Global Economy: A Confessional Issue for the Churches?*, WCC, 1987 • "Fifty Years of Ecumenical Social Thought", *The Ecumenical Review*, 40, 1988 • J.P. Miranda, *Marx and the Bible: A Critique of the Philosophy of Oppression*, Maryknoll, NY, Orbis, 1974 • K. Srisang ed., *Perspectives on Political Ethics*, WCC, 1983.

JUSTICE, PEACE AND THE INTEGRITY OF CREATION.

Both the title and its initials (JPIC) are shorthand for a fuller statement: "To engage member churches in a conciliar process of mutual commitment (covenant) to justice, peace and the integrity of creation should be a priority for World Council programmes." Originally intended as a programme priority for the WCC by its Vancouver assembly (1983), it was subsequently expanded to include churches that are not members of the WCC, regional and national ecumenical organizations and movements committed to these issues.

In issuing this invitation, Vancouver was not so much initiating a process as responding to a situation. The assembly statement on peace* and justice* reflects this situation. "Humanity is now living in the dark shadows of an arms race more intense and of *systems of injustice* more widespread than the world has ever known. Never before has the human race been as close as it is now to total self-destruction. Never before have so many lived in the grip of deprivation and oppression." It then goes on to state what the Christian response to this situation should be. "The churches today are called *to confess anew their faith* and to repent for the times when Christians have remained silent in the face of injustice or threats to peace. *The biblical vision of peace with justice for all* is not one of several options for the followers of Christ but is an *imperative for our times*." And it repeats what it considers to be the nature of the Christian response at this time. "The foundation of this emphasis should be *confessing Christ as the life of the world* and *Christian resistance* to the powers of death in racism, sexism, caste oppression, economic exploitation, militarism, violations of human rights, and the misuse of science and technology." It sees confessing Christ as the life of the world and Christian resistance to the powers of death not as two separate activities but as one and the same activity.

In taking this position, Vancouver clearly shifted from the position of understanding Christian involvement in world affairs largely as the concern of Christian ethics — to translate the values of the kingdom into achievable social goals (the middle axioms* of the responsible society). Instead, it placed the emphasis on confessing the faith,* which calls for a new understanding of the missionary task of the church at this time. To realize this intention, the assembly envisaged a process that would bring the churches together to take a common stand on the urgent issues concerning the survival of humankind. This is the intention of the phrase "conciliar process of mutual commitment". It expects the process

to lead to a council of the church that will take such a common stand and presumably take the churches to a new stage in the covenant relationship into which they had entered at the inaugural assembly at Amsterdam (1948).

Goals. The JPIC preparatory group, which was constituted by the WCC executive committee to oversee and bring to fruition the process, had to clarify the intention in terms of realizable goals.

A world convocation rather than a council: Except as a general reference to JPIC, the term "conciliar process" had to be abandoned. In the Vancouver call it is used rather loosely to mean a method of churches belonging within a common fellowship or koinonia,* as in the WCC, working together to resolve differences and achieve common goals that are to be given public expression in a council. However, recognizing the differences that persist between the churches, it soon became clear that the time for holding a council in the strict sense of the term had not yet come. Therefore, it was decided to call the first global Christian gathering on JPIC a world convocation. Its purpose, as defined by the WCC executive committee (Istanbul, March 1988), would be "to make theological affirmations on justice, peace and the integrity of creation, and to identify the major threats to life in these three areas and show their interconnectedness, and make and propose to the churches acts of mutual commitment in response to them".

Justice, peace and the integrity of creation: Instead of referring to three separate issues, Vancouver intended these to be viewed as three aspects of one reality: on the one hand, as a vision towards which we work and, on the other, as three entry points into a common struggle in these areas. The addition of the term "integrity of creation" for an understanding of "the biblical vision of peace with justice" was particularly useful. Besides bringing in the issue of the damage being done to the environment and the threat posed to the survival of life, the term also gave a new prominence to the doctrine of creation in ecumenical discussions and the need to re-affirm our Trinitarian faith, beginning with God as Creator and therefore also Liberator and Sustainer.

Covenant for JPIC: At first, the term "covenant"* given in brackets in the JPIC formula did more to confuse than to clarify the meaning of "mutual commitment". At least four difficulties were encountered. First, the term is used in common parlance to refer to pacts and alliances between human partners, so that it is not clear what more is meant when it is used as a theological term in conjunction with "mutual commitment". Second, the Bible mentions several types of covenant, each with its own character and emphasis, so that we cannot assume a common biblical understanding of the term. Third, while the term has ecclesiological significance in some church traditions, it does not in others. This makes the term even more suspect as a way of stating the mutual commitment of all churches to JPIC. Finally, many (if not all) churches understand God's covenant to have been accomplished "once for all" in Jesus Christ. So what does it mean theologically to speak of covenanting?

The way out of this impasse was to use an insight from scripture. Because God is a faithful covenant partner, time and again in times of crisis, the people were called upon to renew their covenant with God, a covenant they had broken, and to reconstitute themselves as a covenant community which is open to the world, especially to the suffering and the destitute. With this basic biblical understanding of covenant renewal, it is possible to speak of covenanting for justice, peace and the integrity or wholeness of God's creation at this time of crisis as a way of working together to resist the threats to life and to seek alternatives that would affirm life in all its fullness for all people and the world.

A continuing worldwide process. The Vancouver call has touched off a worldwide JPIC process. JPIC is the focus of many national, regional and confessional ecumenical initiatives, all of which have contributed to the richness of JPIC and the preparations for the world convocation. To mention only major regional events that have already taken place, there have been conferences or assemblies on JPIC in the Pacific (September 1988), Europe (May 1989) and Latin America (December 1989). There have also been several regional meetings of women on JPIC. Substantial contributions to JPIC have come from several theological perspectives: Orthodox (Sofia 1987 and Minsk 1989), Roman Catholic (Pontifical Council on Justice and Peace, Vatican 1989), World Alliance of Reformed Churches (Seoul 1989). More such meetings are expected.

While JPIC is a fundamental expression of the mission* of the church, it should not be understood as a purely Christian concern. People of other faiths and beliefs are just as concerned and active in this area, and we have to explore ways of working together with all concerned people. Given this plurality of responses to JPIC and the need to achieve in the near future all the commitments made to JPIC, the world convocation that took place in Seoul, Korea (March 1990), should be seen as no more than "an important stage on the road towards common and binding pronouncements and actions on the urgent questions of survival of humankind" (WCC central committee, January 1987).

The convocation was able to make ten affirmations on the following: all exercise of power is accountable to God; God's option for the poor;* the equal value of all races and peoples; male and female are created in the image of God; truth is at the foundation of a community of free people; the peace of Jesus Christ; the creation as beloved of God; the earth is the Lord's; the dignity and commitment of the younger generation; human rights* are given by God. The participants at the convocation also entered into an act of covenanting on four concrete issues: a just economic order and liberation from the foreign-debt bondage; the true security of all nations and peoples and a culture of non-violence; building a culture that can live in harmony with creation's integrity and preserving the gift of the earth's atmosphere to nurture and sustain the world's life; the eradication of racism* and discrimination on all levels for all peoples, and the dismantling of patterns of behaviour that perpetuate the sin of racism. The central committee that met after the world convocation resolved that JPIC will continue to be a primary emphasis in the work of the WCC.

See also **church and world; just, participatory and sustainable society**.

D. PREMAN NILES

U. Duchrow & G. Liedke, *Shalom: Biblical Perspectives on Creation, Justice and Peace*, WCC, 1989 • *The Ecumenical Review*, 38, 3, 1986; 41, 4, 1989; 42, 1, 1990 • D.P. Niles, *Resisting the Threats to Life: Covenanting for Justice, Peace and the Integrity of Creation*, WCC, 1989 • *Now Is the Time*, final document, world convocation, Seoul, WCC, 1990.

JUSTIFICATION. The doctrine of justification can be properly treated only within the wider context of the doctrine of salvation* as a whole. The will of God — Father, Son and Holy Spirit (see **Trinity**) — is to reconcile to himself all that he has created and sustains, to set free the creation* from its bondage to decay and to draw all humanity into communion* with himself. Though we, God's creatures, turn away from God through sin,* God continues to call us and opens up for us the way to find him anew. To bring us to union with himself, the Father sent into the world Jesus Christ,* his only Son. Through Christ's life, death and resurrection, the mystery of God's love is revealed, we are saved from the powers of evil, sin and death and we receive a share in the life of God.

Within the Christian tradition there has always been a great deal of agreement about the doctrine of salvation, including justification, despite some familiar controversies. It has been agreed, above all, that the act of God in bringing salvation to the human race and summoning individuals into a community to serve God is due solely to God's mercy and grace,* mediated and manifested through Jesus Christ in his ministry, atoning death and rising again. Nor has it been disputed that God's grace evokes an authentic human response of faith* which takes effect not only in the life of the individual but also in the corporate life of the church.* Difficulties have arisen in explaining how divine grace relates to human response: (1) the understanding of the *faith* through which we are justified, in so far as this includes the individual's confidence in his or her own final salvation; (2) the understanding of *justification* and the associated concepts of righteousness and justice;* (3) the bearing of *good works* on salvation; (4) the *role of the church* in the process of salvation.

Biblical origins. The biblical terms "righteousness" and "justification" have a rich background and a wide variety of uses. As images they are drawn from juridical, forensic (law court) settings and are employed to describe the right relationship of human beings to God or one another and the mode or process by which such a relationship comes about. The descriptions of the way in which a person is brought to righteousness in the sight of God vary among the Old Testament authors and in the New Testament, especially in the writings

of Paul. When predicated of God, "righteousness" is understood as God's fundamental uprightness; God's triumph(s) in a holy war, in a law-court dispute with Israel, or in legal decisions (Ps. 9:4); but above all, especially in the post-exilic period, as God's gracious salvific activity, manifest in a just judgment (Isa. 46:13, 51:5-8, 56:1; Hos. 2:18-19; Pss. 40:9-10, 98:2).

Clearly in the 30s and 40s of the first century the early Christian community was making use of this OT imagery to express the claim that by Christ's death and resurrection human beings stand righteous before God's tribunal. Inheriting the righteousness/justification language of the OT and its previous applications to Christ, Paul sharpened the meaning, especially, though not exclusively, in Galatians, Romans and Philippians. He related the process of justification to grace and set forth the theme of "justified by faith apart from works of law" (Rom. 3:28), though he also insisted on "the obedience of faith" (Rom. 1:5) and response to the gospel in believers' lives. Justification is not simply a future or past event, but it is an eschatological reality which stretches from the past through the present and into the future. Hence Paul, in writing to the Philippians, can enjoin: "Work out your own salvation with fear and trembling", and then immediately adds: "For God is at work in you, both to will and to work for his good pleasure" (2:12-13). Faith includes for Paul both allegiance to God in Christ and the inescapability of good deeds flowing therefrom. It thus differs greatly from the "faith" dismissed as insufficient in James 2, namely, acceptance of revelation* without corresponding behaviour.

Patristic usage. Historical research has greatly increased our awareness of the degree to which the 16th-century debate over justification was conditioned by a specifically Western and Augustinian understanding of the context of salvation which, in reliance on Paul, stressed the scriptural theme of righteousness. Eastern theologians generally saw salvation within the framework of a cosmic process and stressed the divinizing character of grace. Augustine's intention in developing the doctrine of grace was to protect the absolute priority of God's action over all human endeavour. His distinctions between "operating" and "cooperating", "prevenient" and "subsequent" grace point in this direction. Early scholasticism added further categories such as first grace, grace freely given *(gratia gratis data)* and justifying grace *(gratis gratum faciens)* in order to clarify various stages of the process of the transformation of the individual believer. In view of a growing awareness that the difference between the natural and the supernatural is not simply identical with that between creatures and God, a distinction came to be made between two types of supernatural grace — the uncreated grace *(gratia increata*, i.e. God himself or the indwelling of the Holy Spirit) and the created "habit" or disposition of grace *(gratia creata)*. For some theologians, such as Aquinas, God remained in total command as the initiator and perfecter of the movement from sinner to saint, but for many the insistence on infused grace and on the presence of special assisting graces *(gratiae gratis datae)* was combined with a strong emphasis on the ability of free will to contribute to salvation, not simply on the basis of grace, but independently.

A similar shift can be traced in the expanding thought on merit before the Reformation. Augustine wanted to emphasize God's absolute priority: "When God rewards our merits, he crowns his own gifts." The shift of interest to the role of human nature eventually led to the distinction between "congruous" and "condign" merit. The former in one of its meanings designated the basis for a hope that God "does not deny grace to those who do what is in them". This assertion can be understood as affirming God's priority in the sense that merciful inspiration and direction are necessary for every good action of the human creature. It is in this sense that Aquinas speaks of doing what is in one's power. This formula, however, can also be used in a Pelagianizing sense if "doing what is in one" is thought of as a consideration which on the one hand calls for the conferral of grace but which human beings can and must fulfill by relying on the unaided powers of their fallen nature.

The 16th-century controversies. Instead of a progressive transformation under the power of grace, the imputation of an alien righteousness received in faith implies for Luther an ongoing and paradoxical simultaneity; the justification is complete in the imputing of it, so that the believer is "simultaneously a righteous person and a sinner" *(simul iustus et peccator)*. It is not on the basis of their gifts of infused grace, or inherent righteousness of good works, that God declares sinners just, but on the basis of Jesus Christ's righteousness. For the reformers, the "alien", "extrinsic" justification is the article on which the church stands or falls.

The theological opposition, as indicated by the censures passed in 1518-21 by the theological faculties of Mainz, Cologne, Louvain and Paris, centred not on the doctrine of justification by faith taken by itself but on questions related to free will, the alleged sinfulness of all good works, the role of contrition, confession and satisfaction in the sacrament of penance,* the *ex opere operato* efficacy of the sacraments,* the sinfulness of concupiscence and the value of indulgences.

The council of Trent (1545-47, 1551-52 and 1562-63) dealt extensively with many interconnected topics such as original sin, justification, grace and merit, the sacraments and indulgences. In its teachings on justification the council reaffirmed the unique role of Christ, who died for all and who grants grace "through the merits of his passion" to those reborn in him, and without rebirth in him one can never be justified. The council further taught that "nothing prior to justification, whether faith or works, truly merits the grace of justification".

In a central paragraph the council of Trent expounded the nature of justification with the help of scholastic causal categories. The final cause is the glory of God and of Christ, and eternal life. The efficient cause is the merciful God, who freely cleanses and sanctifies, sealing and anointing by the Holy Spirit. The meritorious cause is Jesus Christ, who by his passion merited our justification and made satisfaction for us to God the Father. The formal cause is "the righteousness of God — not that whereby God is righteous but that whereby he makes us righteous".

Recent history. In the last 400 years both the Roman Catholic and the Lutheran churches have continued to affirm their 16th-century pronouncements on justification. Since the council of Trent and their own Book of Concord, Lutheran theologians have usually claimed that the doctrine is of central importance but have interpreted it in a variety of ways; Roman Catholics, although debating the issues of sin, freedom, nature and grace, have for the most part not made justification itself a primary object of attention. In both cases, furthermore, the discussions have been chiefly within, rather than between, the two communions.

In the 19th and 20th centuries, however, there has been renewed attention to the Reformation doctrine of justification. Especially the growth of dialogue in recent decades between Catholics and the heirs of the Reformation has stimulated research into the interconfessional aspects of justification. Vatican II (1962-65) gave little explicit attention to the theme of justification, but it touched on the subject indirectly in its teachings on matters such as faith, grace, salvation and the ministry of the church. By broadening the definition of faith beyond intellectualistic concepts that had been prevalent in modern scholasticism, the Council left open the possibility that faith might include the entire response of the faithful to justifying grace. In its references to co-operation and merit, the Council showed sensitivity to Protestant concerns and to the need to resist any Pelagianizing tendencies that might exist among Catholics.

The fourth assembly of the Lutheran World Federation (Helsinki 1963) gave particular attention to justification. The Reformation witness to justification was said to have been in a threefold "Babylonian captivity" of "doctrinalization, individualization and spiritualization". The opposition between forensic and transformationist views of justification was questioned: "The old alternative whether the sinner is considered justified 'forensically' or 'effectively' is begging the question, for God's action brings about 'rebirth'". The document "The Gospel and the Church" of the joint Lutheran-Roman Catholic study commission also deals with the question of how the two sides nowadays understand justification. In its Malta report (1972) the commission says: "Catholic theologians also emphasize in reference to justification that God's gift of salvation for the believer is unconditional as far as human accomplishments are concerned. Lutheran theologians emphasize that the event of justification is not limited to individual forgiveness of sins, and they do not see in it a purely external declaration of the justification of the sinner. Rather the righteousness of God actualized in the Christ event is conveyed to the sinner through the

message of justification as an encompassing reality basic to the new life of the believer." Although a far-reaching agreement in the understanding of the doctrine of justification appears possible, other questions arise here. What is the theological importance of this doctrine? Do both sides similarly evaluate its implications for the life and teaching of the church?

A beginning of an answer is given in the document "Justification by Faith" of the US Lutheran-Roman Catholic dialogue group (1983). Lutherans and Catholics wholeheartedly accept the "fundamental affirmation" that their "entire hope of justification and salvation rests on Christ Jesus and on the gospel, whereby the good news of God's merciful action in Christ is made known; we do not place our ultimate trust in anything other than God's promise and saving work in Christ" (paras 4 and 157). They admit that this affirmation is not fully equivalent to the Reformation teaching on justification, according to which God accepts sinners as righteous for Christ's sake on the basis of faith alone; but by insisting that reliance for salvation should be placed entirely on God, their agreed affirmation expresses a central concern of that doctrine. While granting that the principle of justification by faith alone must not be employed to erode the fullness of the apostolic heritage and of the means whereby this heritage is to be mediated in any given time and place, the Lutherans maintain that this principle retains its critical importance. Catholics, on their side, are wary of using any one doctrine as the absolute principle by which to purify from outside, so to speak, the Catholic heritage. While conceding that the church stands under the gospel and is to be judged by it, Catholics insist that the gospel cannot be rightly interpreted without drawing on the full resources available within the church. To speak of "Christ alone" or "faith alone", they contend, could lead, contrary to the intentions of Lutherans themselves, to the position that the grace of Christ is given apart from the external word of scripture, Christian preaching, the sacraments and the ordained ministry.

Here, as on other points such as the imputational or forensic character of justification, the sinfulness of the justified, the sufficency of faith, or questions of merit and satisfaction, there is much common ground, but there are still divergences too. So the Lutherans, e.g., continue to ask whether, even in modern Catholicism, it has been made sufficiently evident that (as the Malta report expressed the Lutheran position) "the rites and orders of the church are not to be imposed as conditions for salvation, but are valid only as the free unfolding of the obedience of faith". They suspect that the papacy and magisterial infallibility remain in need of re-interpretation and restructuring in order to make them unmistakably subordinate to the gospel (see **teaching authority**). Finally, they wonder whether official teachings on Mary and the cult of the saints, despite protestations to the contrary, do not detract from the principle that Christ alone is to be trusted for salvation because all God's saving gifts come through him alone.

A further elaboration of the ecclesiological consequences of the doctrine of justification is given in the agreed statement "Salvation and the Church" by the second Anglican-Roman Catholic International Commission (ARCIC II). The church is itself a *sign* of the gospel, for its vocation is to embody and reveal the redemptive power contained within the gospel. The once-for-all atoning work of Christ, realized and experienced in the life of the church and celebrated in the eucharist,* constitutes the free gift of God which is proclaimed in the gospel. In the service of this mystery the church is entrusted with a responsibility of *stewardship*. The church is called to fulfill this stewardship by proclaiming the gospel and by its sacramental and pastoral life. The church is also an *instrument* for the realization of God's eternal design, the salvation of humanity. The church is therefore — so the ARCIC II texts say — called to be, and by the power of the Spirit actually is, a *sign*, *steward* and *instrument* of God's design. For this reason it can be described as *sacrament* of God's saving work. The church, as the community of the justified, is called to embody the good news that forgiveness is a gift to be received from God and shared with others. Thus the message of the church is not a private pietism

irrelevant to contemporary society, nor can it be reduced to a political or social programme. Only a reconciled and reconciling community, faithful to its Lord, in which human divisions are being overcome, can speak with full integrity to an alienated, divided world and so be a credible witness to God's saving action in Christ and a foretaste of God's kingdom.*

To work out these eschatological perspectives will be a test case for a really ecumenical understanding of the relation of justification and sanctification.* The church participates in Christ's mission to the world through the proclamations of the gospel of salvation by its words and deeds. It is called to affirm the sacredness and dignity of the person, the value of righteous social and political structures and the divine purpose for the human race as a whole; to witness against the structures of sin in society, addressing humanity with the gospel of repentance and forgiveness and making intercession for the world. It is called to be an agent of justice and compassion, challenging and assisting society's attempts to achieve just judgment, never forgetting that in the light of God's justice all human solutions are provisional.

See also **faith, grace, salvation, sanctification, sin**.

MARTIEN E. BRINKMAN

H.G. Anderson, T.A. Murphy & J.A. Burgess eds, *Justification by Faith*, vol. 7 of *Lutherans and Catholics in Dialogue*, Minneapolis, Augsburg, 1985 • H. Küng, *Rechtfertigung* (ET *Justification: The Doctrine of Karl Barth and a Catholic Reflection*, New York, Nelson, 1964) • H. Meyer, "The Doctrine of Justification in the Lutheran Dialogue with Other Churches", *One in Christ*, 17, 1981 • *Proceedings of the Fourth Assembly of the Lutheran World Federation, Helsinki*, 1963, Berlin, Lutherisches Verlagshaus, 1965 • J. Reumann ed., *Righteousness in the New Testament: Justification in the United States Lutheran-Roman Catholic Dialogue*, Philadelphia, Fortress, 1982 • "Salvation and the Church: An Agreed Statement by the Second Anglican-Roman Catholic International Commission, ARCIC II", *One in Christ*, 23, 1987 • G.H. Tavard, *Justification: An Ecumenical Study*, New York, Paulist, 1983.

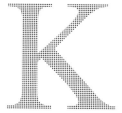

KAGAWA, TOYOHIKO. B. 10.7. 1888, Kobe, Japan; d. 23.4.1960, Tokyo. Social reformer and evangelist, Kagawa in 1928 was in the forefront of an evangelistic campaign — the "Million Souls" movement — which led, with the National Christian Council's nationwide campaign, to the formation of the Kingdom of God movement, 1930-32, of which Kagawa was the central figure. He played a leading role at Tambaram 1938. After the second world war, Kagawa led many Christians in the national penitential movement. He was the president of the Japanese co-operative federation, travelling widely and insisting everywhere that evangelism must be "spiritually motivated, educationally undergirded and industriously demonstrated". His writings had a significant influence on the ecumenical movement and on the development of Asian theology, especially his emphasis on the vital role of lay Christians. He wrote *Meditations on the Cross* (Chicago, Willet & Clark, 1935). See G.B. Bikle, *The New Jerusalem: Aspects of Utopianism in the Thought of Kagawa Toyohiko* (Tucson, Univ. of Arizona Press, 1976) and J.M. Trout, *Kagawa, Japanese Prophet* (New York, Association Press, 1959).

ANS J. VAN DER BENT

KAIROS DOCUMENT. This is a biblical and theological comment on the political crisis in South Africa, first published in 1985.

It arose out of the struggle to discover how to respond as Christians to what the Kairos document calls a situation of death.

The "moment of truth" (kairos) is defined as "the moment of grace and opportunity, the favourable time in which God issues a challenge to decisive action". The document provides a critique of "state theology", which gives theological justification of the status quo. It also critiques "church theology", which in "a limited, guarded and cautious way... is critical of apartheid". The document promotes "prophetic theology" as an alternative, in which biblical teaching on suffering and oppression is considered in relation to a serious social analysis of the structures of oppression in South Africa. Defining the South African regime as tyrannical, the document challenges Christians to participate in the struggle for liberation.

The theological methodology employed in writing the document is as important as the document itself. The document emerged from serious group theological reflection. Frank Chikane (now general secretary of the South African Council of Churches), a formative influence in the production of the Kairos document, has said of the process: "Reflection on experience in faith becomes the word of God. This document is actually a by-product of a process, the process of struggle to remove the apartheid regime. This is the issue, not the document per se."

The writing process began as a group, consisting largely of grassroots black Christians, who met in Soweto to initiate the reflection process. The writing of the document was assigned to different people at different times. These drafts were often rejected by the group as theologically too traditional, failing to reflect their experience of oppression and of faith. The language of the document, severely criticized by some traditional theologians as being too millenarian and apocalyptic, reflects the context out of which the document emerged. Debate on the wording was still vigorously being pursued when it was submitted for publication. "The first publication, therefore," as the preface puts it, "must be taken as a beginning, a basis for further discussion by all Christians in the country." Numerous responses from the international community and from within South Africa led to a second revised edition of the document, published in September 1986.

In South Africa the Kairos document is regarded as a theological watershed. It calls for Christian action against a state which is described as "having no moral legitimacy" and which has become "an enemy of the common good". For the church to be the church, it is required to be "unequivocally and consistently with the poor and the oppressed". Not all Christians or churches in South Africa are prepared to make the choice. The subtitle of the Kairos document — Challenge to the Church — defines its essential intent.

See also **apartheid**.

CHARLES VILLA-VICENCIO

The Kairos Document: Challenge to the Church, 2nd ed., Johannesburg, Skotaville, 1986 • A. Nolan, *God in South Africa*, Cape Town, David Philip, 1988 • C. Villa-Vicencio, *Between Christ and Caesar: Classic and Contemporary Texts on Church and State*, Cape Town, David Philip, 1986 • C. Villa-Vicencio, *Trapped in Apartheid: A Socio-Theological History of the English-Speaking Churches*, Maryknoll, NY, Orbis, 1988.

KING, MARTIN LUTHER, Jr.

B. 15.1.1929, Atlanta, GA, USA; d. 4.4.1968, Memphis, TN. A leader in the mass civil rights movement in the USA from the mid-1950s until his assassination, King won the Nobel peace prize in 1964 for his leadership in applying principles of non-violent resistance to the struggle for racial equality. Educated at Morehouse College, Crozer Theological Seminary and Boston University (PhD, 1955), in 1954 he became pastor of Drexler Avenue Baptist Church, Montgomery, AL, and in 1959 co-pastor with his father of Ebenezer Baptist Church, Atlanta. Involved in the struggle over segregation on buses in Montgomery, in 1955 he organized a boycott by blacks which lasted more than a year. It inspired opposition to discrimination, which resulted in an order of the Supreme Court imposing desegregation on Alabama public transportation. He organized the Southern Christian Leadership Conference, was the leading figure in the march on Washington in 1963, which led to the 1964-65 civil rights acts, and was active in voter registration drives. He arranged further demonstrations in Florida, Alabama, Mississippi and elsewhere. Much influenced by the thinking of Gandhi, he was also committed to the belief that the reconciliation of the black to the white population was as important as that of the whites to the blacks. His success was more marked in the South than in the North, where the black church was less well organized and less discrimination existed. He urged settlement of the Vietnam conflict and admission of China to the United Nations.

He was invited to give the opening sermon at Uppsala 1968, and the reference in the assembly message to "the shock of assassinations" recalls his tragic death three months before the meeting. The WCC established a Martin Luther King memorial fund for reconciliation, rehabilitation and relief, and invited national and regional councils of churches throughout the world to subscribe to a project of the Mississippi Delta Ministry, set up by the National Council of the Churches of Christ in the USA. King wrote *Stride toward Freedom* (New York, Harper & Row, 1958), *Strength to Love* (New York, Harper & Row, 1963) and *Where Do We Go from Here?* (New York, Harper & Row, 1967). Major recent studies of King include D. Garrow, *Bearing the Cross* (New York, Morrow, 1986) and Taylor Branch, *Parting the Waters* (New York, Simon & Schuster, 1988).

ANS J. VAN DER BENT

KINGDOM OF GOD.

The ecumenical movement inherited conflicting historical understandings of the concept "kingdom of

God". When the early church's imminent hope waned, chiliasm (Tertullian, Irenaeus) and spiritualization (Clement, Origen) helped the church to bear with persecution. After Constantine, it became a political category, almost identical with the earthly rule of the *sacrum imperium*, establishing the peace of God within human history (Eusebius). In Augustine's distinction between *civitas Dei* and *civitas terrena* as ideal types, an identification of the kingdom either with the church's rule over society or with a Christian emperor's political rule was rejected. Soon, however, these ideal types were exchanged for identifications of the earthly state with the *civitas terrena* and the institutional church with the *civitas Dei*, with the resulting power struggles of the middle ages between *regnum* and *sacerdotium*, including a loss of the kingdom's eschatological aspect. To settle this struggle, the Western church distinguished between emperor *(potestas)* and pope *(auctoritas)*, both instituted by God, to lead the *christianitas*, the society of church-and-state, to the kingdom, but soon the church claimed identity with the kingdom (Gregory VII, Innocent III, Boniface VIII) against the emperor's religious claims. Repeatedly interpretations were given critical of these identifications of the kingdom of God with church and/or state (for example, by Joachim of Fiore, the Franciscans, mystics, also philosophers, Dante).

Luther spoke of two realms to criticize the claims of the papal church and to see earthly government as autonomous, yet according to God's will. Again, implications and variations included diverse attempts to realize the kingdom immediately in either church or society. Well known was Thomas Münzer's radical political interpretation, with the imminent kingdom to be brought about by divinely elected instruments, through struggle against oppression from the side of the official church, spurred on by the certainty of God's own final victory. Calvinists sought to erect a theocratic society wherein individuals played an active part under God. Catholic theology often identified church and kingdom. After the Enlightenment new interpretations became popular: pietism, linking the coming of the kingdom with individual faith and the winning of souls; utopian visions of a secular kingdom (Thomas More, Campanel-la, but also Marxism), expecting a final state of consummation; religious perversions like Nazi Germany's propaganda; philosophical notions of a realm of ideal human relations on earth, with ideas of development, evolution and material prosperity (Hobbes, Herder, Lessing, Fichte; also Kant, Schleiermacher, Ritschl). Important was the motivation of the kingdom in the social gospel, a practical kingdom theology (Walter Rauschenbusch), and religious socialism (Ragaz, the Blumhardts).

Ecumenism inherited all these occurring tensions: between present and future aspects, between different concepts of power* or rule, between the kingdom and the church, between socio-political and individual interpretations, between views that the kingdom is completely a gift of grace* and that human beings participate in its coming, between gift and responsibility or hope and action, between salvation history* and world history. In the 20th century, important shifts took place: Western theology witnessed a re-discovery of the eschatological dimension, influenced especially by biblical scholarship in German Protestantism, where Johannes Weiss, followed by Albert Schweitzer, rejected the dominant ethical notion of a kingdom to be built.

In ecumenical circles, the concept, although undefined, played a major role in several contexts. Generalizing, one can say that the notion of the kingdom as an ideal society, characterized by equality, justice and freedom, has gradually been accepted. Socio-ethical implications, and conclusions critical of church structures and its life and worship, are often drawn.

Already at Edinburgh (1910), Sloane Coffin, from the social-gospel tradition, said: "Christianity's... ethical ideal is the kingdom of God — a redeemed social order under the reign of the Christlike God in which every relationship is Christlike, and each individual and social group — the family, the trade-organization, the state — comes not to be ministered unto, but to minister, is perfect... and the whole of human society incarnates the love of God once embodied in Jesus of Nazareth." This vision led to controversy. Again, for example at Stockholm (1925), the theological debate of the day between this (evolutionary, ethical) Anglo-Saxon view and (eschatological, a-political) European views was reflected, and in the early ecumenical movement these differences continued.

The WCC Humanum Studies (1969-75) can serve as a typical illustration of the growing use of the concept of the kingdom of God in ecumenical documents. Without definition, it is used to criticize the present state of affairs in church and society, in that full community between human beings is not practised and that "churches are in open and hidden alliance with various exploitative kingdoms of men". Similar use of the concept is made in other places: "Christ — the hope of the world" (Evanston 1954); studies on the community of men and women; several discussions of the eucharist as "paradigm of the kingdom"; etc. More explicit discussions of the concept appeared in the study "Giving Account of the Hope That Is Within Us" (Faith and Order: Accra 1974, Bangalore 1978) and the 1977 Chiang Mai papers on *Faith in the Midst of Faiths*.

A major occasion was the Melbourne world conference on mission and evangelism (1980). "Our theme, 'Your Kingdom Come', has been at the heart of the missionary movement throughout Christian history, and not least in this century" (Philip Potter). The sections discussed good news to the poor,* the kingdom of God and human struggles, the church witnesses to the kingdom, and Christ — crucified and risen — challenges human power. Special emphasis was attached to a vision of the kingdom in which "the gospel is meant for the poor, and Christians and the church must be involved in all the struggles of history, resisting the oppressive realities and oppressive forces of the anti-kingdom".

Another important context is the present F&O study on "The Unity of the Church and the Renewal of Human Community", focusing on "the church as mystery and prophetic sign". Although the project is still only in its initial stages, the concept plays a major role, as "church" and "human community" are related within the broader perspective of the kingdom (Limouris, 58ff.; F&O minutes Madrid 1987, 16-30). Careful distinctions are made in attempts to avoid the misunderstandings inherited from the conflictual history.

In 20th-century Catholicism, the concept has functioned, for example, in Vatican II's *Lumen Gentium* (e.g. 3,9,35ff.) and *Gaudium et Spes* (e.g. 39,72), and in theologies of liberation. During Vatican II,* in spite of some formulations to the contrary, the results of biblical investigations came to the fore. In theologies of liberation, the kingdom serves as central paradigm for the human condition, where all people will participate in God's total salvation* as subjects in freedom, equality and justice; a salvation of which the church must provisionally be an active sign and promise in the divinely qualified kairos of the present situations of death. Discipleship in this kingdom consists in following Jesus' option for the poor in concrete praxis and prophetic criticism. Although the final realization of the kingdom remains God's gift, so that the "eschatological proviso" must remain as a critical instance against all partial realizations, human beings are nevertheless liberated to participate actively in establishing at least signs of the kingdom.

See also **eschatology, salvation history**.

D.J. SMIT

G.H. Anderson ed., *Witnessing to the Kingdom: Melbourne and Beyond*, Maryknoll, NY, Orbis, 1982 • E. Castro, *Freedom in Mission. The Perspective of the Kingdom of God: An Ecumenical Inquiry*, WCC, 1985 • G. Limouris ed., *Church, Kingdom, World: The Church as Mystery and Prophetic Sign*, WCC, 1986 • G. Wainwright, *Eucharist and Eschatology*, London, Epworth, 1971.

KOINONIA. It is noteworthy that from its inception the Faith and Order* commission has perceived the essential nature of the church* as koinonia. The 1927 conference in Lausanne referred to the "communion of believers in Christ Jesus" (sec. 3.17-18) and described this unity* without, however, making use of the term "koinonia". But it was at the centre of discussions at Edinburgh in 1937 on the "communion of saints" (4.52,54,56-58,61; 5.69), and again at Lund in 1952 (1.26-30). The Evanston assembly of 1954 was indebted to the F&O commission for the following declaration: "Thus the fellowship (koinonia) that the members of the church have is not simply human fellowship; it is fellowship with the Father and with his Son Jesus Christ through the Holy Spirit and fellowship with the saints, in the church triumphant" (report, B.8).

The report of the section on unity produced

by the assembly at New Delhi (1961) offers further elucidation: "The word 'fellowship' (koinonia) has been chosen because it describes what the church truly is. 'Fellowship' clearly implies that the church is not merely an institution or organization. It is a fellowship of those who are called together by the Holy Spirit and in baptism confess Christ as Lord and Saviour. They are thus 'fully committed' to him and to one another" (para. 10).

Section 2 (paras 3-7) of the Nairobi report depicted "conciliar fellowship" in terms of the Triune God (see **Trinity**) drawing Christians together, in all their diversity, into a communion in the Spirit around the eucharistic presence of the Lord. It is thus clear that the notion of koinonia has emerged as one of the motivating ideas of the ecumenical movement in this century; it has thus not been by chance that since Lima (1982) the F&O commission has directed a great deal of its attention to this theme.

The concept of koinonia has also come to the fore in several of the bilateral discussions. Often, as in the case of ARCIC I (see **Anglican-Roman Catholic dialogue**), it has arisen in the course of clarifying points of Catholic theology and studying the texts of Vatican II* rather than directly from the work of F&O. Another example is the Munich document involving the Roman Catholic Church and the Orthodox churches; in it koinonia was quite literally the centre around which the whole document was constructed (see 2.1-4, in which the word appears over two dozen times). The theme is equally prominent in the Moscow statement (1976) which followed the Anglican-Orthodox conversations.

The introduction to the final report (1981) of ARCIC I affirmed that reference to koinonia is fundamental to all reflection on the nature of the church and that, in consequence, it is the base on which the whole report rests. The report then proceeded to demonstrate how the eucharist,* episcope (see **episcopacy**) and primacy* are all to be understood in terms of koinonia. Koinonia was also given a predominant place by the 1986 Nairobi report of the Roman Catholic-Methodist International Commission, *Towards a Statement on the Church*. Here there was an endeavour to define the term, which was seen to represent a reality and an experience transcending all other models of union as their

origin and goal. There are several references to koinonia in the opening phase of the conversations between the Disciples of Christ and the Roman Catholics (see the 1981 report, secs 6-7), where "fellowship" is used to translate late *koinōnia*.

In the 1977 final report of the Reformed-Roman Catholic conversations, *The Presence of Christ in Church and World*, both koinonia and *communio* are used in order to emphasize a dual affinity that comes to expression in the eucharist, i.e., the believers' relationship with the Lord himself and with his other followers. The Anglican-Lutheran Pullach report (1972) also interprets koinonia in the same sense of "fellowship".

The ecumenical revival of koinonia is without doubt significant in the sphere of ecclesiology. It is illuminating to observe that the Roman Catholic Church's reconsiderations of ecclesial doctrine at Vatican II were based on the ecclesiology of *communio* (see *Lumen Gentium* 7,9,13,15,18,50, etc.).

The data of revelation. The word "koinonia" is found fairly often within the apostolic writings (Acts 2:42; Rom. 15:26; 1 Cor. 1:9, 10:16; 2 Cor. 6:14, 8:4, 9:13, 13:13; Gal. 2:9; Phil. 1:5, 2:1, 3:10; Philemon 6; Heb. 13:16; 1 John 1:3,6-7). It does not occur in the gospel narratives and is never explicitly used as a synonym of ecclesia. Sometimes it may have no religious significance (as in Rom. 15:16; 2 Cor. 8:4), which is also true of other expressions with the same root.

But we should not be bound by any limitation requiring the use of the actual word "koinonia", for the concept is recurrent throughout the New Testament, implicit in such terms as covenant,* unity, participation,* sharing, and images such as vine, temple, Body of Christ, spouse and so on (see **images of the church**).

The Christian community sees an objective reality which is bestowed by God upon all who accept the gospel: God gives the Holy Spirit,* object of the promise (Rom. 5:5, 8:15-17; Gal. 4:6; Acts 2:33,38, 10:44-47, 11:15; John 7:39, 16:7, 20:22; Eph. 1:13, 2:22, 4:30; 1 Pet. 1:2). This Spirit of the "last days" is, on several counts, a gift of communion.* It is linked to the pardon which restores the *communion* desired by the Creator. It harks back to what Ezekiel described as an interior principle of obedience to the law by a purified Israel once again gathered together in its own land (Ezek. 11:19, 36:26-28, 37:14, 39:29; cf. Jer. 31:31). In Christ this gift acquires a hitherto unsuspected depth. It changes the meaning of our human destiny.

The reality which establishes this koinonia belongs to the mystery of the living God.* For Paul, our koinonia is with the Son of God (1 Cor. 1:9), the one and only Lord (8:6). It has its "sacramental abode" in the communal sharing of the cup and of the one and only broken bread, which is a participation in the blood and the body of Christ in association with his sacrifice (10:14-22). If it leads to an association with Christ's victory (15:12-28; cf. 1 Thess. 4:14-18), it does so by way of real communion with his sufferings (Phil. 3:10 and, without the word "koinonia", 2 Cor. 4:10; Gal. 6:17). In order to explain this union Paul writes: "It is no longer I who live, but Christ who lives in me" (Gal. 2:20; cf. Phil. 1:21).

According to Paul, this is the richness of the divine gift. In taking hold of people, it draws them into what the letter to the Romans calls adoptive sonship: without resort to the term "koinonia", the passage abounds in phrases depicting this intimate relationship to Christ and to God (Rom. 8:15-17). The participation of believers in Christ's relationship to his Father results from koinonia of and in the Spirit (2 Cor. 13:14; Phil. 2:1). It does not distort Paul's intuition to say that koinonia represents the sure substance of God's gospel; it is God's work, his gift (see Gal. 4:7; cf. Rom. 1:1, 15:16).

The beneficiaries of this gift are among themselves in a "state of koinonia". The expression is used to describe their association in the faith* (Phil. 1:5-6), the sufferings endured for the gospel and the consolation given by God (2 Cor. 1:7). More precisely, from now on both Jews and pagans are *sunkoinōnoi* (partners together) because the pagans are to share in the richness which has its "root" in Israel (Rom. 11:17, cf. 4:16; Gal. 3:26-29). The image of the body stresses the bond uniting to Christ and to one another all those who are quickened by the "one and same Spirit" (cf. 1 Cor. 12:11-14; Rom. 12:4-5; Gal. 3:26-29). Unity and diversity are both proclaimed. The latter appears in the multiplicity of ministries and responsibilities

(1 Cor. 12:4-6, 27-31), in the wide range of social conditions (12:13), and in the different rootage in the divine plan and covenant (12:13). There is no question of a simple addition of persons or of a fusion into a *tertium quid* which would eliminate all differences. Out of a diversity which continues to manifest its richness, the indivisible reality of the Spirit brings forth a unity of immeasurable depth.

In directing attention to the association of the gentiles with privileges conferred on the Jews, the letter to the Ephesians (which makes no use of the word "koinonia") develops a Pauline thought (Eph. 2:11-22, 3:4-6). Communion is not to be limited to the personal relationship of each believer with Christ and his Father; it also involves the re-uniting in Christ of the two sections of humanity. The breaking down of the wall of division means that from henceforth "the others" participate in what had been set aside for Israel until the cross. The frequent use of the terms *sunklēronomoi* (inheritors together), *sussōmos* (a body together), *summetochoi* (participating together) and *sumpolitai* (citizens together) clearly points to the same reality — koinonia. And this reality is the church (2:19-22, 3:10).

The first letter of John employs "koinonia" in order to signify in one word the simultaneous union of Christians with the Father and the Son and among themselves (1 John 1:3, 6-7). Similarly, although without making use of "koinonia", John's gospel speaks of the disciples' "being-one" and of this state of oneness finding its source in the "being-one" of the Father and the Son "before the world began" (John 17:5). The disciples are meant to be one just as *(kathōs)* the Father and the Son are one. The word *kathōs* does not imply merely similarity but includes the notion that Christians are taken up into the divine relationship which is the ground of their unity. This relationship is a profound one which not only embraces communion in the Son's mission (17:18) but extends also to the participation in his state of glory (v.24). The Johannine tradition never states that koinonia or "being-one" constitutes the church, but these phrases sum up "the gathering into one of the children of God who are scattered abroad" (11:52), and correspond to what the image of the true vine seeks to convey. The community of

A prayer circle of theologians in Argentina (Prensa Ecuménica/Carlos Salgado)

disciples is far more than the sum of its members.

Koinonia must express itself in a relationship of fraternal communion. This intuition is the basis of Paul's insistence on an authentic agape, which translates in terms of human conduct the meaning of communion with Christ. Or, as the author of the letter to the Hebrews describes it, communion with Christ passes over into human communion, in flesh and blood (Heb. 2:14). Once again it is clear that the reality conveyed by koinonia may be equally well conveyed by other expressions: it is only necessary to read 1 John 3:16-17 and all the passages on agape.

Paul's line of thought is particularly revealing when he was occupied with the collection for the church in Jerusalem. Recalling his meeting with James, Cephas and John (Gal. 2:1-10), he remarked that they had extended to him the hand of koinonia, thus confirming the unity of the mission* to both pagans and circumcised. Here the koinonia thus sealed is bound up with the injunction to "remember the poor" in Jerusalem" (2:10). The way in which Paul repeats and develops this point suggests that he regards it as the concrete expression of the unity between the mother church (Jerusalem) and the gentile churches (Rom. 15:25-26; 1 Cor. 16:15-17; 2 Cor. 8:1-

9,15; Acts 24:17). This is far more than a simple distribution of alms (Rom. 15:25-26). The action of sharing material goods corresponds to a call that is implied in the logic of ecclesial communion; the differences between Jew and gentile, rich and poor are transformed into agape.

In Acts, the summary descriptions of the church at Pentecost are concerned to show the interior unity of a single community (Acts 2:42-47, 4:32-35, 5:12-16). The word "koinonia" and the expression *hapanta koina* (everything in common, 2:44, 4:32) are employed in a cluster of expressions to describe the many facets of communion. To list some of these phrases is illuminating: they were together (Acts 2:44,47), of one heart and one spirit (4:32), devoted to the apostles' teaching and to the temple (2:42,46), holding everything in common (2:44, 4:32), sharing the proceeds from the sale of their possessions according to the needs of each (2:45, 4:34-35), faithful in the breaking of bread and in prayer (2:42), safeguarding the koinonia (2:42). With the restored unity of language as its sign (2:6-11), the church is born by the fire of the Spirit, not simply as a society but as a "communion". At once palpable and deeply hidden, this communion seeks willing hearts prepared to take such practical steps as the sharing of possessions, even to the point of privation. In this context koinonia (2:42) discloses its real meaning, about which exegetes continue to debate. However, one thing is certain: koinonia means more than table fellowship; nor is it simply interior harmony. Rather, it also actively engages people in a communal sharing, the sign of spiritual unanimity expressed within the fabric of daily social life. The terms used in the "summaries", for their true meaning to be understood, must imply a communion in the Lord's own generosity, which may extend when necessary to following him in the total gift of self. This is what Luke stresses in his first book (Luke 14:26-27,33, cf. 12:13-34, 16:1-13, 18:1-30), and probably a similar meaning should be given to koinonia in Heb. 13:16.

The scriptures never provide a precise definition of the church (local or universal). Nevertheless, some texts like 1 Cor. 12:11-28, Col. 1:24 and Eph. 1:22-23 reveal that there was present right from the beginning the awareness of something profound which transcended all of its members and which was established by the binding together of Christians to God and to one another. When 1 Pet. 2:4-10 applies the titles of the *qahal* (assembly) of the old covenant to the church, it transforms the latter into the long-awaited communion between God and his people. Thus, in koinonia is expressed the most profound and all-embracing reality which founds and establishes the *ekklēsia tou theou*, church of God. The church of God is given to participate in the life of the Father, the Son and the Holy Spirit (see **Trinity**) and to manifest this participation in a fraternal koinonia. The ministries, too, are held in this embrace.

The doctrine of the fathers. The Tradition of the early centuries attaches great importance to the reality of koinonia, usually translated in Latin by *communio* or *communicatio*.

The bold identification of God's plan with *communio* was suggested by Irenaeus at an early date. If the mission of the Son brought him into a close *communio* with humanity, this was in order that our *communio* with God in adoptive sonship might be complete (*Against Heresies* 3.18.7, 5.1.1, 5.14.2). Again, if Christ poured out the Spirit of the Father, this was to bring about a true and effective union and *communio* of God and

humankind (5.1.1). Thus, the eucharist, in which we in our human bodily state *communicate* in the risen state of the Lord, is essential (4.18.5, 5.2.2-3). Our whole being must express this *communio* (5.1.1). This view of salvation as koinonia runs through the whole of Tradition and is found in the West, e.g. in Thomas Aquinas (*Against Gentiles* 4.54-55, etc.) and in the East in Nicholas Cabasilas (*Commentary on the Divine Liturgy* 26.4, 36.1, 49.29; *Explanation of Rites* 12).

There was a similar conviction with regard to the bond between eucharist and church. Writers in the early centuries linked 1 Cor. 10:16-22, 12:27 and Eph. 1:22-23 and reasoned that the eucharist "makes" the church. At the dawn of Tradition, Ignatius of Antioch clearly affirmed that the eucharist is the food of the unity that was won on the cross, for "it gathers together all holy and faithful people both Jews and gentiles into the unique body which is the church" (*Letters to the Smyrnaeans* 1.2, *to the Magnesians* 8.1-2, *to the Philadelphians* 4). This unity is of such importance that where division is found, God is not present (*Letter to the Philadelphians* 8.1), and the eucharist ratifies the presence of unity only when it is received in unity. The guarantee of unity lies in communion in the one and only faith, gathered around the bishops with his *presbyterium* and the deacons (*Letters to the Philadelphians* 4, *to the Smyrnaeans* 7.2, 9.1). It is the divine will that "you unite in one and the same faith and in Jesus Christ… obeying the bishop and the *presbyterium*, living in haromony, breaking the one bread, the medicine of immortality" (*Letter to the Ephesians* 20.2). The eucharist is woven into the very fabric of the communion that it establishes.

Very early the *Didache* (9.4) made the connection between the one bread and the "assembling of the church". Cyprian wrote on the same theme in more explicit terms (*Letters* 63.1-4; 69.5.2) and Hilary of Poitiers took it up (*On the Trinity* 8.12.13, 8.16); then liturgies began to incorporate it in the realization that it encapsulated the fruits of the Spirit invoked at the epiclesis* or proclaimed by the post-communion prayers. Several rites such as the *fermentum* and the *commixtio* draw attention to the importance of this association.

Since the documentation is extensive, this discussion will have to remain focused on those fathers whose reflections on this subject are the most fully developed. The most compelling among them is, without doubt, John Chrysostom (above all in *Homily 24 on Cor.* and *Homily 48 on John*): "We are *this* body... not several bodies, but one single body." In a penetrating passage he insists on the indivisible bond uniting the eucharistic body and the koinonia of the afflicted members of the Body of Christ (*Homily on Mat.* 50.2-4). Theodore of Mopsuestia is among the most forceful in proclaiming the unifying power of the eucharist (*Homily* 15, no. 1 on the Mass, 40; *Homily* 16, no. 2 on the Mass, 24). Cyril of Alexandria chose realistic language in order to make clear that in the eucharistic koinonia all, with their individual peculiarities, are formed into a single body, the ecclesial Body of Christ (*Against Nestorius* 4.4-5; *Commentary on John* 11.11, ed. Pusey 735ff.; *On the Trinity* 1).

A place must be reserved here for Augustine; he is the master. In his most important writings on the subject (esp. *Sermons* 71,112,131,227,272; *Denis* 6; *Guelferbytanus* 7; *Treatises on John* 25,26), he explains how the sacramental body and the ecclesial body comprising all communicants are one and the same: "It is to what you are that you respond Amen" (*Sermon* 272); "it is the sacrament of our unity that you behold" (*Guelferbytanus* 7); "it is the Lord alone who bears us all within himself... receive what you are" (*Sermon* 272). However, to receive truly one must already be in unity. This unity is nothing less than the *communio* between Father and Son into which believers are, in the love of God, introduced by the Holy Spirit (*Sermon* 71,12,18). In order to receive the Lord's body, it is necessary to be part of it, most importantly by faith: "It is not what we see but what we believe that nourishes us" (*Sermon* 112.4); "believe, and you have eaten" (*Treatises on John* 25.12). No *communio* without eucharist, no eucharist without *communio*.

Towards the end of the patristic age John of Damascus summarized the position held in both East and West in a passage that has frequent recourse to the terms "koinonia" and *koinonein* (*On Orthodoxy* 4.13; *PG* 94.1153). Other writings from all the early Christian traditions which make use of koinonia and *communio* to signify the act of reception in the eucharist do so only within an ecclesial context.

It was soon understood that to participate (*koinōnein*) at the same eucharistic table was to belong to the koinonia or *communio* which is the church. The next step was to regard exclusion from koinonia as severance from the church, as is clearly stated by Cyprian in *Letters* 55.6, 69.6, 75.14, and this expression came into common use. To be in the church is to be in koinonia (*communio*) and vice versa.

Tertullian insisted on the *communio* of each local church with the apostolic churches (*On the Prescription of Heretics* 21.7, 38.2), and he thereby gave to *communio* all of its ecclesiological dimensions. This overtone comes through at least implicitly in the majority of texts which identify "being in koinonia" (or *communio*) with "being in the church". To be in koinonia, to maintain *communio*, goes further than belonging to the local eucharistic assembly; it involves a close relationship with the whole multitude of churches. No one has expressed this idea more poignantly than Augustine: "As for me, I am in the church, which has for its members all the churches born and established thanks to the labour of the apostles, and all of them together noted down in the canonical writings. With the help which the Lord gives to me, I shall never abandon their *communio*, neither in Africa nor anywhere else. If in this *communio* there are traitors of any kind, show them to me" (*Against Cresconius* 3.35,39). It should be noted that alongside the use of "koinonia" (*communio*) to denote this "being together" of all the churches, in monastic circles the term was applied to the small community inspired by Pachomius. Its members sought to live in accordance with the ideal expressed in the "summaries" in Acts, the invitation being given to "all of you to embrace the common life following the example which was given us in the apostles' time" (*Letters* 295). A similar ideal was set forth by Augustine in his celebrated *regula*.

Conclusion. At the end of this brief survey it should not be difficult to recognize in koinonia the deepest stratum within the church of God on earth, by means of which we are enabled to see God's fundamental gift to humanity. It is not only on the mystical level that a person who has received the Spirit is introduced into the koinonia of

Father and Son; it is also on the practical level that this supreme grace takes form in a community that binds together a common faith, a fellowship of sharing and of service, a common undertaking for the sake of the gospel and common acts of divine worship. In other words, all the biblical images which serve as representatives or models of the church are intended to convey the single reality which is koinonia.

See also **church, communion, communion of saints, eucharist, Trinity, unity**.

J.-M.R. TILLARD

P. Bori, *Koinonia: L'idea della communione nell'ecclesiologia recente e nel Nuovo Testamento*, Brescia, Paideia, 1972 ● J.Y. Campbell, "Koinonia and Its Cognates in the New Testament", *Journal of Biblical Literature*, 51, 1932 ● F. Hauck, "Koinōnós...", *Theologisches Wörterbuch zum Neuen Testament*, Stuttgart, Kohlhammer, vol. 3, 1938 ● P. Neuenzeit, "Koinonia", in *Lexikon für Theologie und Kirche*, vol. 6, 1961 ● H. Seesemann, *Der Begriff* koinonia *im Neuen Testament*, Giessen, Töpelmann, 1936 ● H.J. Sieben, J. McDermott, H. Manzanera, H. Bacht & J.-M.R. Tillard, "Koinonia, communauté, communion", in *Dictionnaire de spiritualité*, Paris, Beauchesne, 1976 ● J.-M.R. Tillard, *Eglise d'églises*, Paris, Cerf, 1987.

KRAEMER, HENDRIK. B. 17.5.1888, Amsterdam, Netherlands; d. 11.11.1965, Driebergen. Kraemer was the first director of the WCC's Ecumenical Institute in Bossey* (1948-55), advocate of the "spiritual mobilization" of laity* in the ecumenical movement (his 1958 book *Theology of the Laity* is a classic in the field) and one of the most influential Protestant thinkers of his time on the question of the relationship of the gospel to the great world religions and cultures.

Assisted by Suzanne de Diétrich, Kraemer taught courses at Bossey to young laypeople from many countries who had lived through the war years and were eager to take part in rebuilding their churches and nations. Afterwards, he was the leading figure of the institute Kerk en Wereld ("church and world") in Driebergen, travelling and lecturing widely and rendering pastoral services to parishes in the Netherlands.

W.A. Visser 't Hooft wrote of Kraemer that his "life work has so many different aspects that anyone who desires to write about him must first select which of Kraemer's varied contributions he will discuss. There is the philologist; there is the expert on Islam; there is the leader of the spiritual resistance against National Socialism; there is the fighter for the renewal of the Netherlands Reformed Church; there is the professor of theology who is really a layman and there is the layman who asks theological questions about modern culture; there is the first director of the Ecumenical Institute who gave shape to that new adventure; and there is, of course, the missionary, or rather the missionary thinker, strategist and statesman."

After studying Javanese at the University of Leiden and Islam at El Azhar University in Cairo, Kraemer worked for the Dutch Bible Society in Indonesia from 1922 to 1937. His experiences there convinced him that the missionary should be a *guru kedewasaan* — a guide to maturity. Only if "mission fields" became indigenous churches would Christians be able to relate the Christian message to their social and cultural environment and be in responsible dialogue with neighbours of other faiths.

Hendrik Kraemer (WCC photo)

In 1937, Kraemer, who had received an honorary doctorate from the University of Utrecht the year before, was appointed professor of sociology of religion at Leiden. Later he was interned in the concentration camp of St Michielgestel for protesting the removal of two Jewish colleagues. After the war, he was a member of the delegation of the churches of the US, UK, France, Netherlands and Switzerland which met in Stuttgart with the new Council of the Evangelical Church of Germany and issued the Stuttgart declaration* of guilt.

In preparation for its 1938 meeting in Tambaram, India, the International Missionary Council* (IMC) commissioned Kraemer to write what became his best-known book, *The Christian Message in a Non-Christian World*, which influenced subsequent decades of missiological thinking. Insisting on "biblical realism", Kraemer argued that "the radical religious realism of the biblical revelation, in which all religious and moral life revolves around one point only, namely the creative and redemptive will of the living, holy, righteous God of love, the exclusive ground of nature and history, of man and the world, has to be the standard of reference". But while this "biblical realism" has been seen as an important contribution to the ecumenical vision of "the whole church with the whole gospel to the whole world", many subsequent missiologists have faulted Kraemer for overemphasizing the exclusiveness of the Christian message and "its radical discontinuity" with other faiths, thus not doing sufficient justice to God's active presence in them (see **uniqueness of Christ**).

Kraemer was also a chief proponent of the plan, taken up by the IMC following its Willingen meeting (1947), of setting up regional study centres at which specialists could devote time to study, research and promotion of dialogue with representatives of living movements of thought outside the church.

ANS J. VAN DER BENT

The Church and the World of Religions and Cultures: Kraemer in Retrospect (= *The Ecumenical Review*, 41, 1, 1989) • C.F. Hallencreutz, *Kraemer towards Tambaram*, Lund, Gleerup, 1966 • A.Th. van Leeuwen, *Hendrik Kraemer, Pionier der Oekumene*, Basel, Basileia, 1962.

KÜNG, HANS. B. 19.3.1928, Sursee, Switzerland. Controversial Roman Catholic theologian who was censured by the Vatican in 1979 for questioning traditional church doctrines, Küng studied at the Gregorian University, the Sorbonne and the Institut catholique in Paris, and in Amsterdam, Berlin, Madrid and London. His dissertation was on "Justification: La doctrine de Karl Barth et une réflexion catholique". Ordained in 1954, he became professor of dogmatic and ecumenical theology at the faculty of Catholic theology and director of the institute for ecumenical research at the University of Tübingen, 1963-80, and afterwards full professor of ecumenical theology in Tübingen. He was co-editor of the series *Ökumenische Forschungen* and *Ökumenische Theologie*, associate editor of *Journal of Ecumenical Studies* and member of the executive editorial committee of *Concilium*. His publications include *Konzil und Wiedervereinigung* (ET *The Council and Reunion*, New York, Sheed & Ward, 1961), *Die Kirche* (ET *The Church*, London, Burns & Oates, 1968), *Fehlbar? Eine Bilanz* (ET *Infallible? An Enquiry*, Tenbury Wells, UK, Fowler Wright, 1971), *Christ sein* (ET *On Being a Christian*, London, Collins, 1977) and *Signposts for the Future* (Garden City, NY, Doubleday, 1978).

ANS J. VAN DER BENT

LABOUR. The labour movement is the product of the 19th-century industrial revolution in the West. To defend their interests and protect themselves from exploitation, those employed in the new manufacturing industries found that they had to organize themselves in political parties and trade unions. These were the means by which they sought to promote social justice and to fight for a fair share of the benefits of economic advance.

Defining the relation of the churches to this movement is complicated by geographical and confessional variations and by the difference between churches with a high proportion of members drawn from the traditional working class and those of predominantly middle-class composition. The influence of the latter on the development of the labour movement has principally been from outside the ranks of those directly involved.

Ecumenical influence on the labour question has been very small. Despite such international ecumenical gatherings as the Oxford conference on Church and Society, immediately prior to the second world war, relations with the labour movement have on the whole been denominational and national.

The most interesting exception to this may be found in the United States, largely because of the more cosmopolitan nature of that society and the widespread church membership within it. The claim that in the US "the ecumenical movement and church support for labour developed hand in hand" could hardly

be applied to any European country. Across the denominational frontiers in the US there developed from the end of the 19th century a powerful concern for social justice. George McClain writes: "With the flowering of the social gospel in the 1890s, the labour question for the first time became also a religious question. Outspoken church leaders such as Vida Acudder, Washington Gladden, Richard T. Ely, George D. Heiron, and Walter Rauschenbusch challenged laissez-faire economics and championed labour's right to organize."

A decline in commitment to the social gospel was due to theological criticism of its too facile optimism about the possibility of establishing the kingdom of God* by human effort, and US churches as a whole retreated from any pretence of being the voice of the labour movement. The most notable exception to this was probably Reinhold Niebuhr, whose early ministry among the workers of Detroit led to his developed theological and political realism: a combination which others have been slow to emulate.

If we assess the involvement of US churches in the labour movement, we have to say that the impetus came from outside the ranks of working people. In European countries where Roman Catholicism has been the dominant form of Christianity, the picture is different. For example, in Italy, France, Spain and Ireland, working people have constituted the majority of those owing some kind of

577

allegiance to the church, but their influence has been severely restricted by the official policy of the hierarchy. This has been due partly to Vatican concern to retain political power and partly to its fear of communism.

Giorgio Girardet identifies different stages in relations between the Italian state and the Roman Catholic Church: "After the crisis of 1870 when Rome was occupied by the Italian army, with subsequent prohibition for Catholics to participate in political life, in 1891 the encyclical *Rerum Novarum* of Pope Leo XII admitted, though paternalistically, the right of the workers to organize. From 1906 to 1914 a Democratic-Christian movement was created, prudently open to workers; and the first Catholic unions were created, without support from or against the will of a more conservatively oriented church."

After the first world war Pope Benedict XV allowed the formation of a new popular party under the inspiration of a Sicilian priest, Luigi Sturzo, who was general secretary of Catholic Social Action. It won over 100 seats in the national assembly and offered promise of playing a leading role in the promotion of working-class interests. However, this movement came to an abrupt end with the concordat between Mussolini and Pope Pius XI in 1929. This meant that conservative views were to prevail in the Vatican; and it was left to more informal groups to advocate social change, without official ecclesiastical support.

Although 80% of the French population is claimed as Catholic, the separation of church and state in 1905 led to the rapid secularization* of national life. But from within the church and among its working-class members, powerful voices have arisen for social justice, despite the conservative orientation of the hierarchy and the majority of its members. To quote Girardet again: "The French Catholic church has manifested from the 19th century a strong concern for what may be called the social question." The most important manifestation of this concern was the movement of worker-priests, identifying themselves with those engaged on the shop floor in industry. Beginning in 1943 with the Mission de France, the movement was brought to an abrupt end in 1954 by the intervention of the Vatican, because of fears that this could lead to too close an alliance

with the then powerful French communist party. Thus the Italian pattern of a hierarchy suppressing identification with working-class aspirations was repeated. Nevertheless, social witness continued through such organizations as Action catholique ouvrière and Jeunesse catholique.

In Latin America, the stream of European immigration, particularly to the Atlantic coast, brought people related to the labour movement in their countries of origin (esp. Italy and Spain), who introduced the trade-union movement in the incipient industrial proletariat of these countries. The churches were not paying much attention to this issue. The RCC had just produced the first declaration on the labour movement (*Rerum Novarum*), and the Protestant missions reflected a liberal view more interested in the entrepreneurial and educated sectors. However, the large percentage of Italian and Spanish immigrants in some missionary churches in Argentina, Uruguay and Chile created a certain sympathy for the labour movement, expressed in their publications in the first two decades of the 20th century.

Since the 1930s the RCC developed Young Christian Workers. Less institutionally related to the RCC but adopting a philosophical and ideological stance based on Catholic social doctrine, the Christian democratic trade unions later organized themselves as the Latin American Confederation of Workers, with its headquarters in Caracas, Venezuela, as an alternative both to the Marxist trade-union organizations and to the Regional inter-American organization of workers, clearly related to the US trade-union movement. Since the 1950s, among the Protestant churches, the sector related to the ecumenical urban industrial mission* has developed a relation to the trade unions.

The British story is very different. The working class has never been identified with the Church of England, and only a tiny minority with the Church of Scotland and the Free Churches. The rise of the labour party in the early years of the 20th century and its dependence on the trade unions, with their leadership drawn from the ranks of the working class, meant that the churches have had only a peripheral relationship to these two arms of the labour movement. There are, however, qualifications to this generalization. In the

A labour centre of the Philippine Independent Church (WCC/Peter Williams)

19th century the Free Churches, particularly the Methodist, were the backbone of the old Liberal party, out of which the Labour party emerged and which it replaced as the main challenge to conservatism. Among its early leaders were a number of free churchmen; and a case can be made for saying that the Labour party was born out of Methodism and its reaction to conservatism and the Anglican church. However, Free Church influence has diminished over the century, despite the continuation of prominent Free Church laymen in positions of leadership. Roman Catholic involvement has closely paralleled that of the continental churches. From outside the ranks of the labour movement significant voices have been raised within the Anglican church to champion the cause of the working class. Most notable of these was the Christian socialist movement of the 19th century, with which the name of Frederick Maurice is primarily associated. And still more significantly in the interwar years, William Temple, later to become archbishop of Canterbury, attacked conservative complacency in public utterances and in his famous paperback *Christianity and Social Order*. With his friend R.H.

Tawney he took a leading part in the workers educational association, and Tawney as an Anglican layman was recognized during these years as the leading theoretician of the labour party, even writing its manifesto for the general election of 1929.

This overview has necessarily been highly selective. In so far as a generalization is possible, it may be said that only Roman Catholicism has had a hold on the working population at large, who have played a passive role, discouraged by a hierarchy entrenched in the perpetuation of its own power structures and fearful of the spread of Marxism. Such influence as other churches have exerted has largely been from middle-class origins.

What is emerging today is an underclass of the underprivileged: the unemployed, one-parent families, ethnic minorities. Churches are beginning to see their fidelity to the gospel in terms of "a bias towards the poor" (see **poor**), thus aligning themselves with the clear emphasis of the WCC and reflecting in a different context the liberation theology* of Latin America and the church base communities* throughout the third world. This is a new agenda with which the traditional labour movement has scarcely begun to come to terms.

See also **capitalism, socialism, work**.

PAUL CLIFFORD

R. Aubert, *Le christianisme social*, actes du XIII congrès international des sciences historiques, Moscow, 1970, Louvain, Publications universitaires, 1972 ● P.A. Carter, *The Decline and Revival of the Social Gospel*, Ithaca, NY, Cornell UP, 1954 ● M.F. Fogarty, *Christian Democracy in Western Europe, 1920-1953*, London, Routlege & Kegan Paul, 1957 ● A. Hastings, *A History of English Christianity, 1920-1985*, London, Collins, 1986.

LACEY, JANET. B. 23.10.1903, Sunderland, UK; d. 11.7.1988, UK. An ecumenical administrator, writer, dramatist and speaker, Lacey produced her first play at the age of 13 with 25 children in the local Wesleyan chapel. She studied at a technical school near Durham and took drama and elocution lessons in a small private drama school. As a young woman she saw poverty in the raw among the Durham miners in the strike of 1926. "I was shattered, and drama did not seem to matter any more." She became a trainee at the Kendal YWCA and learned to be a youth leader. She worked for many years with youth clubs, employing her dramatic talents to help build membership. From 1931 to 1945 she worked in a vast housing estate in Dagenham, Essex, where 200,000 artisans had been uprooted from the East End of London. Later she was secretary of the youth department of the British Council of Churches, where she encouraged youth to be aware of community responsibilities, including the quarter million refugees who had come to Britain. From 1952 to 1968 Lacey was director of Christian Aid, the interchurch aid and refugee service of the British Council of Churches. During these years she built Christian Aid into an internationally recognized organization, raising millions of pounds annually through drama, advertising, films, television, concerts in Trafalgar Square with folk singers and a variety of other innovative techniques.

Lacey was vice-chairperson of the WCC's Division of Inter-church Aid, Refugee and World Service from 1961 to 1968. For Evanston 1954, she wrote a drama called "By the Waters of Babylon". The play was later published in Britain and performed in churches all over the country. For New Delhi 1961, she produced a film for the interchurch aid presentation. She was what she called the "token female" president for the world conference on Church and Society in Geneva, 1966. Again acting as impresario, she arranged for director Patrick Garland to write and produce a play about revolutionaries called "The Rebel", which was performed at the conference.

A layperson, Janet Lacey was the first woman to preach in St Paul's Cathedral, London, and in St George's Cathedral in Jerusalem. Although brought up as a Methodist, she became an Anglican. In the 1950s and 1960s, when women were seldom found in leadership roles in the WCC, she was an exception. Her keen mind, her gifts of diplomacy and courage, and her eloquence earned her a place in the male-dominated structures of the ecumenical movement.

BETTY THOMPSON

LAITY. "Never in church history... has the role and responsibility of the laity in church and world been a matter of so basic, systematic, comprehensive and intensive discussion in the total oikoumene as today" (Hendrik Kraemer, 1961). The rediscovery of the laity was probably the most important aspect of the renewal of the church in the 1950s and 1960s.

Definition. Laypeople are the unordained members of the church.* That is the most common definition of the word "laity". The problem with it is its negative character: laypeople are defined by the lack of ordination,* the lack of training and competence, and thus are seen as being secondary to the ordained members of the church. Indeed, throughout church history the clergy has seen the laity mainly as the objects of its preaching, teaching and pastoral care, and theologians have not developed a positive description of the function of the laity. Very often laypeople have had to assert themselves against the clergy (see **laity/clergy**). Lay movements fought the clericalization of the church in the middle ages and during the early stages of the Reformation. The Reformation proclaimed the biblical concept of the priesthood of all believers (1 Pet. 2:9).

There is no exact equivalent in biblical vocabulary for the word "lay" or "laity". The Greek term laïkos as noun or adjective appears only in the writings of the fathers (Clement of Rome in 95). But the word laos from which it derives has an important place in biblical writing. In the Septuagint (the Greek translation of the Old Testament) it is predominantly used for the people of God,* Israel; in the New Testament it refers to Christians, the people of God including both Jews and gentiles. In the church, therefore, laïkos means "pertaining to the community chosen in Christ" (Hans-Herman Walz). The ecumenical movement uses the biblical concept of the people of God in order to define the laity not by comparison with the ordained clergy, the theologians, the professional church workers, but by a new appreciation of the church in the world (see **church and world**). Laypeople are "those members of the church, both men and women, who earn their livelihood in a secular job and who, therefore, spend most of their waking hours in a 'worldly' occupation". "The phrase 'the ministry of the laity' expresses the privilege of the whole church to share in Christ's ministry to the world" (Evanston 1954).

Towards the re-discovery of the laity.
One of the roots of the 20th-century ecumenical movement was the ecumenical lay movements founded in the 19th century: the Young Men's Christian Association, the Young Women's Christian Association and the Student Christian Movement. John R. Mott, himself a layman and leader in these worldwide movements, called for "liberating the lay forces of Christianity" in order to participate in the missionary task of the church. Also in the Roman Catholic Church there has been a new emphasis on the laity. In 1922 Pius XI, in his pastoral letter *Ubi Arcana*, called on the laity "to participate in the hierarchical apostolate" and proclaimed the foundation of the Catholic lay movement Action catholique.

Another reason for the rediscovery of the laity was the world situation: the breaking down of the corpus Christianum and growing secularization,* as recognized by the Jerusalem meeting of the International Missionary Council in 1928. J.H. Oldham, in preparing the Oxford world conference on "Church, Community and State" in 1937, pointed to the role of the laity as a crucial matter of ecumenical concern: "If the church is to be an effective force in the social and political sphere, our first task is to laicize our thought about it. We stand before a great historic task — the task of restoring the lost unity between worship and work."

Another impulse for bringing the laity onto the ecumenical agenda came from the founding of lay academies* as attempts for rethinking and renewal. Such institutions were founded in both parts of Germany after 1945 and in Sweden, Switzerland, the Netherlands, France, Italy and Scotland. They were centres for dialogue among laypeople of different professions and functions, who tried to understand the relevance of the gospel in their secular activities. Even before the foundation of the WCC, in 1946 the Ecumenical Institute at Bossey near Geneva had been opened, led by Suzanne de Diétrich and Hendrik Kraemer, for a similar purpose: "The laity, men and women, had discovered a new vision of their responsibility for expressing the true nature and task of the church, not only within its own fellowship, but in the world in which the church has been set and their own lives are lived." The German Kirchentag movement, also a post-war phenomenon, initiated by a layman, Reinhold von Thadden-Trieglaff, was another form of church renewal which emphasized the vocation of the laity.

The Laity Department of the WCC. It was in the context of these ecumenical developments that a committee on the "significance of the laity in the church" was appointed at the first assembly of the WCC in Amsterdam in 1948, with Kraemer as its secretary. The report underlines the need for "relevant Christianity" in the modern secularized world: "Only by the witness of a spiritually intelligent and active laity can the church meet the modern world in its actual perplexities and life situations." In 1949 Walz was appointed as WCC staff person responsible for a Secretariat for Laymen's Work. He organized a European laymen's conference in Bad Boll, Federal Republic of Germany (1951), followed by a North American conference in Buffalo (1952), and published a bulletin *Laymen's Work* (1951-55).

This secretariat and the Ecumenical Institute increasingly became the focal point for pioneer thinking and experimentation regarding the ministry of the laity. During the first post-war years the attention was on Europe and North America, but soon it became clear that it was a burning issue in the churches of all continents. When the second assembly of the WCC at Evanston in 1954 was planned, the rediscovery of the laity became one of the six major subjects. The assembly report on it focused on the Christian in his or her vocation* but also made an attempt to define the ministry of the laity and to see its implications for the renewal of the life and structure of the church (see **ministry in the church**).

Evanston also acknowledged the importance of the issue by replacing the provisional Secretariat for Laymen's Work with a regular Department on the Laity, of which Hans-Ruedi Weber became the secretary (1955-61). He edited a new periodical, *Laity* (from 1959 onward co-edited with Madeleine Barot from the Department on the Co-operation of Men and Women), in which laypeople from all traditions and regions discussed and shared experiences. The publication had a wide circulation and considerable impact on the ecumenical thinking of laypeople and church leaders throughout the world. The ongoing studies of the department were reflected in the topics dealt with, which included laity training, the house church, saints in everyday life, Christians in power structures, stewardship concepts, the role of the laity in church history, the world of tomorrow. In 1959 one issue was devoted to Asia and reported on the inaugural assembly of the East Asia Christian Conference in Kuala Lumpur, which decided to establish a standing committee on the witness of the laity.

The increasing influence of the work of the Laity Department was obvious at the New Delhi assembly in 1961, where the ministry of the laity was a central issue in all three sections: witness, service and unity. Under the theme "The Laity: The Church in the World", three laypersons addressed the assembly. And the message from New Delhi contains the sentence: "The real letter written to the world today does not consist of words. We Christian people, wherever we are, are a letter from Christ to the world."

The assembly also decided that the Department on Evangelism should undertake a study on the missionary structure of the congregation, clearly a consequence of the new understanding of the church in the world, with the co-operation of the Laity Department. During the time of the Second Vatican Council the Laity Department co-operated closely with the related Roman Catholic bodies. In 1964 a joint consultation took place in Glion on "The Ministry of the Church".

The ecumenical theology of the laity as the people of God had prepared a new approach to the world as the place of God's action. The emphasis of the Uppsala assembly (1968) was on the dilemmas and hopes of the world, on development,* justice* and peace* issues, and on the participation of Christians in God's renewal of the world. Soon after the assembly new programmes and commissions were created: the Programme to Combat Racism* (1969) and the Commission on the Churches' Participation in Development (1970), of which C.I. Itty, who had worked for several years with the Laity Department, became the director.

In a sense, Uppsala was a turning point. Further consideration of the laity and their self-understanding became less important than the content of their mission and service in the world in the struggle against racial, economic and political injustices. During a restructuring of the WCC in 1971, with the integration of

the World Council of Christian Education, the Laity Department was absorbed in the Sub-unit on Renewal and Congregational Life. The main emphasis of the sub-unit is spiritual and liturgical renewal; it conducts workshops and relates to church base communities and networks. It has a desk for lay and study centres, which functions as a secretariat for the world collaboration committee of academies, laity centres and movements for social concern. The academy movement has spread into many parts of the world, and continental associations have been formed. At a world conference of regional associations from Africa, Asia, Europe and North America in Crete in 1972, the world collaboration committee was founded.

Laity in the Orthodox church. The idea that laypeople have only an inadequate knowledge of their faith* and therefore need the constant help of the ordained ministry is quite alien to the Orthodox tradition. Therefore the Orthodox member churches of the WCC shared readily in the ecumenical rediscovery of the laity. Several Orthodox lay movements like the Russian Orthodox Student Christian Movement in France, Germany and the USA; the Zoe brotherhood and Aktines movement in Greece; and Syndesmos* in the Middle East were related to international lay movements. Orthodox academies were founded in Crete and Finland.

In the Orthodox tradition all members of the church are qualitatively equal in receiving God's grace and in realizing it as a new life. The laity is not unordained according to Orthodox tradition. At baptism* they receive the anointing of the Holy Spirit* in the sacrament of chrismation and participate as members of the Body of Christ in the royal priesthood (1 Pet. 2:9). The important discovery of postwar Orthodoxy was that God is Lord both in the church and in the world. The life of the world itself was seen to be of significance to the gospel. In the eucharist the whole world is presented to God. "The whole church participates in the priesthood of Christ and in his continuing shepherdly ministry in the world" (Paul Verghese, now Metropolitan Mar Gregorios). "The laymen can be, must be and are, by what they say and by the example they give, the best witnesses of Christ to non-Christians and non-believers" (Vitali Borovoy).

The lay apostolate in the Roman Catholic Church. In 1922 Pope Pius XI called the laypeople "to participate in the hierarchical apostolate"; in 1946 Pope Pius XII spoke of the laity as "not only belonging to the church but being the church". Under his pontificate two world congresses on the lay apostolate took place in Rome, in 1951 and 1957. They emphasized the participation of the laity in the apostolate of the church and their calling to be evangelists to their fellow human beings and to humanize the conditions of the world. In 1959 a permanent committee for international congresses of the lay apostolate was formed by Pope John XXIII.

Vatican II approved officially what had developed, and in several statements it underlined the importance of the lay apostolate. The Dogmatic Constitution on the Church (1964), which includes a chapter on the laity, begins by stating that all who are baptized are the people of God, the holy priesthood (1 Pet. 2:4-10), and all of humankind is called to become the people of God. Following a chapter on the hierarchical structure of the church, the chapter on the laity describes the particular

function of laypeople as leaven and salt: "The laity is called in particular to make the church present and effective in those places and circumstances where only through them can she become the salt of the earth" (no. 33).

The Decree on the Apostolate of the Laity (1965) argues that because of the growing autonomy of many realms of human life, the work of the lay apostolate is more important than ever before and needs to be intensified. The church has one mission and many different services. The realms of service — family, community, society, profession and politics — and the different forms in groups, congregations, lay movements and the training for the lay apostolate are outlined. Finally the Pastoral Constitution on the Church in the Modern World (1965) affirms that involvement in cultural, social, economic, political and international affairs is to be seen as a task of the church in the world. "The people of God and the human race in whose midst it lives render service to each other. Thus the mission of the church will show its religious, and by that very fact, its supremely human character" (no. 11). In 1989, following the

Laypersons in the Federal Republic of Germany at work for church renewal (epd-bild/Fechter)

bishops' synod of 1988, Pope John Paul II appealed in a pastoral letter for a clear distinction between ordained and unordained members of the church. The best service of the laity would be performed in obedience to the church and in dependence on the clergy.

Theological concepts of the ministry of the laity. No systematic ecumenical theology on the laity has yet been evolved, but many new theological insights have been gained. Nothing less than a "redefined ecclesiology" (Yves Congar, Kraemer) was required in considering the ministry of the laity as God's action in the world. New insights have come in at least four areas.

The ministry of the laity: "We must understand anew the implications of the fact that we are all baptized, that, as Christ came to minister, so must all Christians become ministers of his saving purpose according to the particular gift of the Spirit which each has received, as messengers of the hope received in Christ. Therefore in daily living and work the laity are not mere fragments of the church who are scattered about in the world and who come together again for worship, instruction and specifically Christian fellowship on Sundays. They are the church's representatives, no matter where they are. It is the laity who draw together work and worship, it is they who manifest in word and action the lordship of Christ over the world, which claims so much of their time and energy and labour. This, and not some new order or organization, is the ministry of the laity" (Evanston 1954).

The church — gathered and dispersed: The church has traditionally been regarded from the aspect of the gathered flock, while the fact that it lives and works mainly as a scattered community is largely neglected. Two biblical images of the Christian community — the salt of the earth and the city on the hill — have been used to illuminate the two poles of the life of the Christian community. The church's function as salt of the earth can be carried out only by the laity. The church is seen in terms not of an established institution but of a "pilgrim people", constantly on the move into the world but also returning to the city on the mountain, where God's people come together for worship (WCC, Galyatetö 1956).

The function of the ordained ministry: Trained theologians and ordained ministers are in a bad position to be evangelists: they are in a good position to be the biblical and theological instructors of the evangelists. "It is not the duty of the laity to help the pastor to carry out his pastoral work, it is the pastor's duty to equip the laity to carry out their work in the world. The work of the laity is not secondary to that of the pastor, but vice versa" (Weber). Laypeople do not leave the church when they leave the church building. They are fulltime Christians just as much as the pastor is.

Christ in the world: God loved the world so much, that he gave his Son. It is the world that matters. "Christ the light did not remain outside the world to illuminate it from above, but entered into human life, conquered the darkness and radiates light from within. This says to us that wherever we are in the world, God is there before us — the light is already there. The responsibility of the laity is to serve as reflecting mirrors or focusing lenses, to beam the light into all parts of the life of the world" (New Delhi).

Consequences of the rediscovery of the laity. The word "laity" has almost disappeared from ecumenical documents. Have the fruits of a worldwide ecumenical learning been lost? The new openness to the world has not been lost, though controversies about a world-directed ecclesiology continue. The threats to the survival of humankind — nuclear arms race, exploitation and impoverishment of millions of people, especially in the third world, the plundering and destruction of the earth — have been understood by the ecumenical movement as challenges to the Christian faith. In a conciliar process for justice, peace and the integrity of creation,* responses to the challenges are sought by the churches together, locally, regionally and worldwide. A new form of lay activities has emerged in church base communities, peace movements, solidarity and ecological groups and the women's movement, often outside traditional church structures, in dialogue or co-operation with non-Christians. What was said about the laity in the churches could be said of these groups too: "The laity are members of God's people, specifically God's people present in the world" (Weber).

See also **laity/clergy**.

ELISABETH ADLER

Y.M.J. Congar, *Jalons pour une théologie du laïcat* (ET *Lay People in the Church: A Study for a*

Theology of the Laity, London, Bloomsbury, 1957)
• M. Gibbs & T.R. Morton, *God's Frozen People*,
Philadelphia, Westminster, 1964 • H. Kraemer, *A
Theology of the Laity*, London, Lutterworth, 1958 •
Laici in Ecclesia, ecumenical bibliography, WCC,
1961 • "The Laity", *The Student World*, 3, 1956 •
Laity Formation, Rome, Arti Grafiche Scalia, 1966
• *The Ministry of the Laity in the World*, a statement
commended by the WCC central committee, Gene-
va, 1956 • S.C. Neill & H.R. Weber, *The Layman
in Christian History*, London, SCM, 1963 • *Signs
of Renewal: The Life of Lay Institutes in Europe*,
WCC, 1956.

LAITY/CLERGY. The semantic field covered by these words is immense, and their
meanings vary, depending both on the
sociologist's analysis of them as an outsider
and on the theologian's interpretation of them
from the inside.

Sociologists note a difference among
church members between those with a function or special status (the clergy) and other
people (the laity). They ask whether that difference is connected with certain professional
qualifications of members of the clergy, with
the exercise of legal or moral authority,* with
the existence of "clergy" as a social group,
and so on.

For their part, theologians raise questions
about whether the nature of this difference lies
in the exercise of some power or "divine
right" or in just serving the community, or
whether it has some symbolic or "sacred"
quality and so on. To a great extent the theory
and practice of the various churches in this
regard are a historical legacy: social positions
and theological arguments have conditioned
each other within it.

For sociologists the variety of models is
more closely bound up with socio-political
situations than with the confessions. The clergy of national churches (paid by the state and
perhaps appointed by the civil authorities) are
on a similar footing in Lutheran Sweden,
Orthodox Greece or (until recently at least)
Roman Catholic Spain — just as elsewhere
the Roman Catholic worker-priest or the
émigré Orthodox priest who works to earn his
living or the Protestant pastor in Japan scarcely count as part of the "clergy".

On the other hand, theologians see a disparity between the great Christian confessions. In
this connection, a significant gulf has come
into existence between the old (Roman

Catholic and Orthodox) churches and most of
the churches which resulted from the Reformation, with the Anglican communion occupying a special position.

Among the Roman Catholics or the Orthodox, developments in the theology of the
ordained ministry led to an accentuation of the
difference between a cleric who has received
ordination* and a layperson, as the sacramental interpretation of ordination leads to its
being understood as inner transformation of
the persons concerned (the theory of *character [indelibilis]* which we find in scholastic
theology). In reaction to this view, the Protestant churches stress the fundamental sameness
of all baptized persons, the difference between ministers and other people being only
an organizational matter, so that it can be said
(etymologically, at least) that ministers are
also laypeople, i.e. one of the people.

During the last few decades the Roman
Catholic Church has again stressed the importance of the idea of the priesthood of all
believers, while some of its theologians have
been warning against improperly ontological
interpretations of "character". In the same
period all the churches have felt the need or
desire for more active participation* by all
baptized persons in the life of congregations
and in the ministry of evangelism.* Thus the
gulf between Roman Catholics and Protestants is in this connection less noticed in
practice than it is emphasized in theory.

For the sake of rather more completeness,
an ambiguous use of the terms within the
Roman Catholic Church must be noted: generally not only ordained ministers but also those
persons described as "religious" (monks, re-
cluses or members of other communities) are
distinguished from those called the "laity". It
should finally be noted that, from a totally
different standpoint, the word "lay" is used in
some countries not to refer to a person's status
within the Christian community but to describe facts or people which are, in a secularized world, alien or even hostile to the
church.

See also **church order, diaconate, episcopacy, laity, ministry in the church, presbyterate, priesthood**.

JEAN ROGUES

Y. Congar, *Jalons pour une théologie du laïcat*
(Lay people in the church), rev. ed., London,
Chapman, 1965 • H. Kraemer, *A Theology of the*

Laity, Philadelphia, Westminster, 1958 • D.N. Power, *Gifts That Differ: Lay Ministries Established and Unestablished*, New York, Pueblo, 1980.

LAMBETH QUADRILATERAL. The so-called Lambeth Quadrilateral is a four-part statement of the basic elements which the Anglican communion* wants honoured in any plans for reunion with other churches. Originally intended as a basis for organic union* within American denominationalism,* the four points were accepted by a general convention of the Protestant Episcopal Church at Chicago in 1886. This church affirmed these elements to be "the substantial deposit of Christian faith and order committed by Christ and his apostles to the church unto the end of the world".

"As inherent parts of this sacred deposit, and therefore as essential to the restoration of unity among the divided branches of Christendom, we account the following, to wit: (1) the holy scriptures of the Old and New Testament as the revealed word of God; (2) the Nicene Creed as the sufficient statement of the Christian faith; (3) the two sacraments — baptism and the supper of the Lord — ministered with unfailing use of Christ's words of institution and of the elements ordained by him; (4) the historic episcopate locally adapted in the methods of its administration to the varying needs of the nations and peoples called of God into the unity of his church."

The 1888 Lambeth conference of the Anglican communion adopted the Chicago Quadrilateral but slightly altered the wording and added the Apostles' Creed* to the second article. The 1920 Lambeth conference incorporated the Lambeth Quadrilateral into its "Appeal 'for Reunion' to all Christian People", though now the fourth article was more cautiously worded: "A ministry acknowledged by every part of the church as possessing not only the inward call of the Spirit but also the commission of Christ and the authority of the whole body."

A "claim" follows that the episcopate alone can meet these criteria. The 1958 Lambeth conference endorsed this form, though the more general use of the phrase "Lambeth Quadrilateral" usually is thought to be including the historic episcopate as a sine qua non

within the text, and not as a lesser commentary on it. In the Lambeth Quadrilateral's role as a clear statement of Anglican desiderata in the reunion of the churches, some have criticized it either as being too minimal or as making too much of the historical episcopate. Arguably, the Lambeth Quadrilateral has served its purpose well, for example, in the coming into being of the united churches of the Indian sub-continent.

See also **Anglican communion**.

COLIN BUCHANAN

J. Draper ed., *Communion and Episcopacy*, Cuddesdon, UK, Ripon College, 1988 • J.R. Wright ed., *Quadrilateral at One Hundred*, Cincinnati, OH, Forward Movement, 1988.

LAND. The stories which we find in the beginning of the Bible point to the inseparable relationships between the three actors that will be central to the whole biblical story: God, Adam (humankind) and the land. The latter, as the solid space and location but also as a determining fact in the development of this history, is created by God on "the third day". Then God creates humankind and commends the land to it as a gift, a responsibility and a task (Gen. 1-2). As the story develops, however (Gen. 3-4), the land and its fruit become an object of temptation and strife for humankind and, as a consequence, a place of suffering and a threat.

Land as promise and gift, as task and demand and as temptation and threat is ever-present in the biblical history of Israel. As promise it accompanies the people as landless sojourners in the desert or as temporary dwellers in slavery in a foreign land. As gift it is appropriated and celebrated in the conquest and occupation of the promised land. As task and demand it occupies a prominent place in the law. As the temptation for greed and injustice and as threat of a new landlessness, it is prominent in the message of the prophets.

The gift of land to Adam (humankind) is not exhausted with the land of Israel. Every people has its land, and as the universality of Yahweh's rule is more clearly perceived, this means that the same God of Israel has brought the peoples to their land (Amos 9:7-15) and determined "the boundaries of their habitation", as Paul would put it (Acts 17:26). Thus, there is in biblical thinking an indissoluble bond between the people and the land.

The land itself can be abused and has to be protected. The Deuteronomic and Levitical regulations prescribe the "rest" that the land should enjoy — what one could call the "rights of the land" — in terms of the rights of the poor* and the question of justice.*

The appropriation, distribution, care and use of the land have taken very different forms through human history but have remained a decisive factor, frequently connected with religious faith, doctrine and ritual. Besides, both in the Bible and in the experience of peoples in the past and present, land has always had a symbolic significance in relation to human life. In our contemporary situation, the churches have had to respond to serious theological and ethical issues related to land. It is understandable but unfortunate that modern theology, both in its confessional and ecumenical expressions, has hardly developed a theology of the land or seriously grappled with the theological dimensions of the concrete issues that it has been forced to face.

See **environment/ecology, land and the state of Israel, land reform, land rights,** for discussion of more particular issues that have been of concern in ecumenical dialogue.

JOSÉ MÍGUEZ BONINO

M. de Barros & J.L. Caravias, *Teología de la Tierra*, Petropolis, Brazil, Editorial Vozes, 1988 • W. Brueggemann, *The Land*, Philadelphia, Fortress, 1977.

LAND AND THE STATE OF ISRAEL.
The return of Jews to Palestine and the establishment of the state of Israel opened a problematic for which the churches were not ready. Since the diaspora, Christianity was used to a Jewish people who were landless and had no universally recognized organization. Christians believed that God's covenant* with Israel was fulfilled in Jesus the Christ: but did that mean "the new covenant" had superseded the old? If the old covenant is still valid, what does it mean for the theological understanding of the return of the Jews to the promised land and the creation of a state? The terrible record of many Christians and Christian churches in relation to Israel loaded each word pronounced by the churches with connotations and overtones that

had to be carefully examined. "We all have to realize that Christian words have now become disqualified and suspect in the ears of most Jews," said the Faith and Order Bristol meeting, 1967 (see **antisemitism**).

Slowly and falteringly, in church pronouncements, ecumenical discussion and dialogue with the Jews themselves, the churches and the ecumenical movement began to hammer out some shared convictions. They saw a continuity between the faith of Israel and that of the church: "The Christian church shares Israel's faith in the one God," said the executive committee of the WCC in 1982. And God's covenant with Israel is still valid: "We believe that God's promise to the people of Israel which he elected is still in force," said the synod of the Evangelical Church of Germany in 1950 (see **Israel and the church**).

The meanings of these affirmations for an understanding of the relation between the land and the state were, however, not so clear. The Roman Catholic Church, in the much-debated declaration *Nostra Aetate*, formulates in a carefully worded sentence the idea of continuity and the validity of the covenant. But it does not include any reference to the question of the land or the state of Israel. In successive dialogues and declarations it has continued to distinguish between the theologico-religious question of "the church and Judaism" and the question of Israel's land and state, which is seen as a purely social and political reality. Other churches, although perhaps less rigorously, have also pointed to the need for proper consideration of this distinction.

In 1970 the general synod of the Dutch Reformed Church made perhaps the first elaborate attempt to face this issue. It recognizes the Jewish people of today as the continuation of the biblical Israel; it argues forcefully for the indissoluble relation of the people to the land. Then it concludes: "If the election of the people and the promises connected with it remains valid, it follows that the tie between the people and the land also remains by the grace of God." It affirms that "anyone who accepts the reunion of the Jewish people and the land for reasons of faith, has also to accept that in the given circumstances the people should have a state of its own". The conditional "in the given circumstances" somewhat qualifies this point; then it further clarifies that the state of Israel is one of the forms "in which the Jewish people appear". In its affirmations and hesitations this statement seems to reflect the state of the question for most churches. Some Christians, however, particularly from the third world and from the Middle East, are radically critical of these views. "We have come to recognize", said Anglican canon Naim A'teeq (St George's, Jerusalem) in 1986, "that God is no longer the God of Israel"; he continues: "God is the God of all people. I understand the Jewish origin, I recognize the Israel of God, but with Jesus Christ the church continues the line that began in the Old Testament."

The war of 1967, the annexation of the new areas and the condition of the Palestinian populations have made this issue even more vexing. The United Methodist statement of 1972 recognizes that "dialogues presently are complicated by... turbulent political struggles such as the search for Jewish and Arab security and dignity in the Middle East." The plight of the Palestinians appears quite strongly in recent ecumenical documents. Perhaps the American Lutheran statement of 1974 best portrays these difficulties when it identifies three positions: *theology of the land*, which recognizes the return of the Jews to the promised land (and consequently the creation of a state) as "a sign of the faithfulness of God towards its people"; a *theology of the poor*, in which concern for the plight of the Palestinians makes a favourable theological statement on the state of Israel quite problematic; and *theology of survival*, which affirms the validity of the state of Israel on "juridical and moral" (rather than theological) grounds. When it concludes: "It seems clear that there is no consensus among Lutherans with respect to the relations between 'the chosen people' and the territory comprising the present state of Israel", it seems to reflect quite faithfully the ecumenical understanding of this issue.

Although it is not a greatly widespread or influential point of view, we must also mention the fundamentalist and millenarian doctrine that the return of the Jews to Palestine is a sign of the imminence of the second coming of the Lord. It is probably in reference to such ideas that the WCC Vancouver assembly warns against "certain theological interpretations [that] have often confused Christians outside in evaluating the religious and political developments in the Middle East".

We are still far from having found an adequate theological hermeneutics* for addressing the issue of "the covenant and the land" as related to present historical and political issues. It seems clear that the attempt to separate the theological and the politico-religious issues and deal with them on "parallel tracks" misunderstands both the biblical teaching and the meaning of land and state for Jews then and today. On the other hand, to deal with the issue on the basis of a one-sided *heilsgeschichtliche* perspective (related to God's choice of Israel and the covenant) leaves us unable to articulate the theological significance of the political situation, the rights of the Palestinians, the complex history of that land and the universal covenant of God with humankind.

A 1984 document of the Presbyterian Church (USA) is probably the most elaborate church pronouncement on this question. After affirming that God's covenant with Israel "included a promise of the land", it goes on to place this promise in the context of God's universal purpose for all peoples. "We understand land to be an earthly, geographical, political place where one can be safe and secure, free from pressure and coercion. It implies a home, a means of life, a source of wealth and a place where individuals can become a people." After briefly developing this theology of the land, it deals with the specific question of "the abiding character of God's promise of a particular land to the Jewish people", noting that it "does not assign fixed boundaries to the promised land" and that "land and political sovereignty are by no means identical". It goes on to discuss the issue of the state of Israel, affirming it but also taking a distance from its concrete operation ("the ways of God... should not be confused with the policies of the state"). It seems that a more Trinitarian approach to the theology of the land and the state would give the churches a clearer basis both for dealing with the undeniable particularity of the promise to Israel and for interpreting it in the context of God's universal covenant and promise to humankind.

See also **Jewish-Christian dialogue**.

JOSÉ MÍGUEZ BONINO

N. A'teeq, *Justice, Only Justice*, Maryknoll, NY, Orbis, 1989 • H. Croner ed., *Issues in the Jewish*

Christian Dialogue, New York, Paulist, 1979 • *The Theology of the Churches and the Jewish People: Statements by the WCC and Its Member Churches*, WCC, 1988.

LAND REFORM. The biblical understanding of "land" as a gift of the deity which humans must preserve and cultivate as a source of life and peace is found, in different ways, in most ancient cultures and raises unavoidably the issue of the possession of the land. For Israel, all land belongs to God and is given to humankind in trust for its use (see **land**). As in many ancient cultures the possession is communal: land belongs to the extended family, is inherited and has to be preserved for the support of the family. This differs from the view of some Near Eastern cultures, in which the land belongs to the king (seen as a representative or almost as a manifestation of the god). The clash of these two understandings appears dramatically in the episode of Ahab and Naboth (1 Kings 21).

Prophets like Isaiah, Amos and Micah never tire of denouncing the greed of "the palace" and its clients, which dispossesses the common people of the land. The Mosaic law, on the other hand, tries to take account of situations that emerge through accident, carelessness or injustice, in which some people lose the family land. A number of measures, particularly the laws of Jubilee, tried to restore the balance, understood as indispensable for the maintenance of peace. We find references to some analogous provisions (sometimes through a royal decree) in neighbouring cultures.

In precapitalist cultures, land is seen as a means of life (to grow the food necessary for life), and the possession of land is a sign of status. With capitalism,* however, land becomes a source of profit. The accumulation of land, therefore, is not merely a form of social prestige but an investment from which the greatest possible profit has to be obtained. This has led to the dispossession of the land in colonized territories (see **land rights**) and to the accumulation of land in the hands of a few people or families (or, more recently, agribusiness companies), creating masses of landless peasants. Land reform laws, which follow different models, aim at redressing these situations. The power struggle related to this

question, which results in many cases in violent confrontation, raises issues of justice* which the churches cannot ignore.

Traditional Christian thinking on this issue rests on a precapitalist view which sees a direct relation between people and land. When Leo XIII, in *Rerum Novarum* (1891), defends private property, it seems clear that his basic presupposition is that of the peasant in his land. But this no longer corresponds to the situation: the relation of people to the land is mediated by the whole economic structure and therefore poses difficult ethical, economic and ecological problems which demand from the churches a greater attention and reflection than they have so far received.

Churches have individually or ecumenically expressed concern for issues related to land possession. The Pastoral Letter on Catholic Social Teaching and the US Economy of the US Roman Catholic bishops devotes an entire section to this issue. In his visits to Latin America, Pope John Paul II has vigorously defended the rights of peasants to own the land. Churches in many countries have worked ecumenically to support land reform, developing in Brazil what is called a "pastoral of the land" *(pastoral da terra)*. Regional ecumenical organizations in Africa, Asia and Latin America have repeatedly denounced situations of injustice in relation to land and identified land reform as an important priority.

A 1989 Lutheran World Federation consultation "Land is Life" concluded that although land problems must be confronted in the light of particular national, historical, cultural and religious contexts, they "are part of many other economic, social and cultural struggles which in turn are inter-related on an international level". Within the WCC, the need for "radical reform of land tenure systems" was first identified (by a 1952 study conference in Lucknow, India) as essential to a "positive programme for social justice" in East Asia.

The WCC has channelled ecumenical support to landless people, notably through its programme on Urban Rural Mission.* URM's advisory group said in a 1979 report that "lack of access to land, though a problem for both urban and rural people, is for the rural poor a threat to their very survival. Land is the key commodity coveted by dominant powers, especially by repressive regimes, large landowners, ranchers and transnational corporations", adding that "dramatic and brutal" repression against the rural poor often goes unnoticed because of their geographical remoteness and lack of access to the legal and pastoral services available in urban areas.

The WCC's sixth assembly (Vancouver 1983) linked landlessness with the "international food disorder": "much of the productive land is controlled by large land-owners and transnational corporations who exploit the land and do not allow the farmers, peasants and landless rural workers to participate in making decisions which would benefit them". "Just sharing of the land" was one sub-theme in the section report on "The Earth Is the Lord's" at the 1989 world mission conference in San Antonio, which said the WCC should "stand in solidarity with landless people in their struggles, organizations and movements to occupy land for their sustenance and survival". But it also called for a global ecumenical strategy "for a genuine land reform programme controlled by its beneficiaries, beginning with the sharing of church lands with the landless and homeless". Land figured in one of the affirmations from the world conference on justice, peace and the integrity of creation (Seoul 1990), again under the heading "The Earth is the Lord's". Participants pledged to resist policies that allow land speculation at the expense of the poor* or prevent "those who live directly from the land from being its real trustees".

See also **land, land rights**.

JOSÉ MÍGUEZ BONINO

M. de Barros Souza & J.L. Caravias, *Teología da terra*, Petropolis, Brazil, Editorial Vozes, 1988.

LAND RIGHTS. Since the earliest days of history, peoples and communities have identified themselves with the land occupied by the group in which they grew up and have defended their right to stay on that land and to nourish themselves from it. Relations between people and land were regulated by social institutions which corresponded to the prevailing political and economic options. Over the centuries, however, aboriginal or indigenous peoples* have as a result of colonization and national development been brutally subjugated. Large-scale genocide was perpetrated in the Americas within de-

cades after its "discovery". Indigenous peoples' title to and use of land were systematically denied, and those who survived were often left without territory.

Underlying this injustice have been racist beliefs that identify indigenous people as sub-human and refuse to acknowledge their spiritual, cultural, social, political and legal values. Thus their land was expropriated (in Mexico, Puerto Rico, Guatemala); they were forcibly re-located (Brazil, Paraguay, Philippines); treaties with them were abrogated (Canada, USA, New Zealand); and they were subjected to ill-conceived and badly administered policies of assimilation (Chile, Australia, Colombia). In the last 30 years the economic value of their land has increased the number and intensity of incursions into areas once considered the exclusive territory of indigenous peoples. Though undertaken in the name of "national development", exploitation of mineral resources, construction of roads, and opening up of forests by logging companies and cattle ranches have often negatively affected the lives and livelihood of indigenous peoples.

The meaning of land for indigenous peoples, of whom there are today some 200 million (4% of the total world population), reflects their conviction that land is given by God to human communities and not to individuals. Thus, the right to occupy land has historically been, and is today, closely related to their social organization. As the land is given by God, the community is connected to God through the land. God-people-land is thus an unbreakable unity embracing the whole of creation.* Since the right to land originates in the will of the Creator, the right to live in a specific place is both symbolized and confirmed by the tribe.

Land, therefore, is not just a primary source of natural resources but a vital element in the balance of nature.* If one of the elements is altered or removed, the balance is disrupted, and all the inhabitants will suffer. This is one of the many reasons why a piece of land cannot be compensated by money or other land. For industrialized societies, however, land is a commodity and thus subject to commercial transactions.

To the native inhabitants, land and its natural resources are a unifying force and a vital element in all aspects of life — an inalienable natural right, essential for survival. For them land *is* life. Therefore, to separate people from their land threatens not only their physical existence but also their identity, and has often led to their extinction.

Indigenous peoples, in defending the legal basis to their traditional lands, have faced major stumbling blocks. With a tradition of collective ownership, they lack clear title to the land they inhabit. Also, their unwritten laws governing the spiritual relation between people and land have rarely been understood by the wider society, whose resistance to oral tradition and customary law draws justification from the fact that it is unwritten. Understanding title deeds requires knowledge of reading and writing, which even today many of them do not have. Governments have often denied and perverted the oral heritage of indigenous peoples.

Even where governments have guaranteed reserves to indigenous peoples, these have generally not included rights to the natural resources of their land. In some countries — Australia, for example — there may be a limited protection of sites of religious or cultural importance; and in the USA, Australia and Canada various agreements about royalty payments and compensation have been made. But governments retain the final decision over whether indigenous peoples' land will be mined and the conditions which will apply. Although indigenous peoples are, in general, opposed to mining on their land, there are cases in the US and Australia where mutually acceptable arrangements have been made. But such examples are rare, and their outcome uncertain.

Today, the industrialization of indigenous peoples' territories is closely linked to the role of transnational corporations* (TNCs) and national security doctrines. The Aboriginals in Australia, Maoris in New Zealand, tribal groups in the Philippines, and Indians in South and Central America all face the same problems with their governments over TNC activities. The latter, equipped with sophisticated legal and economic weapons, weaken or destroy the resistance of the indigenous peoples to acquire their land. National security doctrines often deny the sovereignty of indigenous peoples and their particular socioeconomic and political organizations, attempt to break down their specific cultural traditions, and incite internal divisions among them.

Over the past 15 years, indigenous peoples have organized themselves nationally and internationally to defend their rights — in particular, land rights. Simultaneously, international conferences jointly sponsored by indigenous and non-governmental organizations (NGOs), including the churches, increasingly stress establishing and preserving land rights as the first fundamental step towards ensuring the physical and cultural survival of indigenous peoples. In 1977 the International NGO Conference on Discrimination against Indigenous Peoples of the Americas made extensive reference to historically derived land rights and supported demands for the return or restitution of land to indigenous peoples. Many indigenous peoples are claiming back the right to land illegally taken generations ago, and though a majority may not be seeking formal independence from the states in which they live, almost all are demanding some form of self-determination over their remaining land and resources. In 1981 the International NGO Conference on Indigenous Peoples and the Land declared that the root of the indigenous peoples' crisis is the denial of the right to their land.

The United Nations and several of its specialized agencies have given increasing attention to the protection of indigenous peoples. In 1957 the International Labour Organization (ILO) adopted a convention concerning the protection and integration of indigenous countries and a more detailed recommendation setting out standards for the treatment of indigenous peoples. The convention is the only international instrument which recognizes the right to collective ownership of land. However, indigenous organizations strongly objected to its orientation to "integration" of the indigenous into the dominant society and "development" in the Western sense, and in 1989 the ILO produced a new convention replacing the previous one and bringing it in line with the evolving standards of protection of indigenous rights. Land rights have been a major issue in the debate on the revision of the convention.

The UN itself set up a working group on indigenous peoples in 1982 which would operate in an advisory capacity to the UN Commission on Human Rights. Its task is to provide hearings for the indigenous peoples and draft UN standards. As such it has become a focal point for international action.

Throughout history, churches and missions have been deeply involved in land rights. Colonization made missionary societies owners of land that traditionally belonged to indigenous inhabitants. Missions to these communities often registered land titles in their own names. This created dominance-dependence relationships between them. Geographical concentration of people facilitated the missionary goal of evangelization. Indigenous people reacted either by refusing evangelization and preserving their own cultural patterns, thereby abandoning huge areas of their traditional territories to live in isolation, or by reluctantly accepting evangelization and relocation, thus losing part of their territory. Much of such land was then titled in the name of the mission or church.

Over the last few decades, however, some missions, while continuing to record land titles in their own names, have inserted a clause promising to transfer the land to indigenous communities free of charge when it is legally allowed or viable for them to do this. Churches are working with indigenous peoples to seek legal formulas for their collective ownership of their land and guarantee of their sovereignty. Churches in Brazil have challenged TNCs. The Pastoral da Terra of 1975 is the Roman Catholic Church's response to the plight of the dispossessed rural population of Amazonia. The Australian Council of Churches, Project North in Canada, the Latin American Council of Churches, the Comissão Ecumenica de Documentação et Informação in Brazil and the National Council of Churches in the Philippines are involved in major programmes of support.

The WCC through its Programme to Combat Racism* (PCR) sponsored two symposia, both in Barbados, of anthropologists, ethnologists and representatives of the indigenous peoples, on the situation of the Indian in South America (1971 and 1977). Participants' severe criticism of church and mission activities as interference in the life of Indian societies provoked considerable discussion in some Western mission societies.

In 1979 the WCC central committee meeting received a PCR staff document on "Land Rights and Racially Oppressed Peoples" and requested that information on the issue be made available to WCC member churches and to organizations of the racially oppressed and support groups, particularly in Australia and Brazil, on which the document focused. Through its special fund to combat racism, the WCC supported several groups of indigenous peoples in their struggle for land rights in different parts of the world. The 1980 WCC world consultation on racism* devoted considerable attention to land rights. It considered the issue in relation to the people's right to sources of water, minerals, clean air, and political rights, including the right to self-government.

In 1982 the WCC central committee adopted its first statement on land rights, saying among other things: "Indigenous people claim that the recognition of prior ownership of their traditional territories is fundamental to the issue of land rights. Thus for them, land rights must include the right to political power through self-government and economic power through the right to choose what happens on the land... The indigenous people's struggle for land rights is challenging the church to be faithful to its gospel of reconciliation and to the biblical affirmation of the creation of all human beings in the image of God. Crucial to the Christian understanding of reconciliation between peoples is the demand for justice. In the light of this fact, the church's mission is to express solidarity with the oppressed in all ways compatible with the faith and in recognition of its guilt in the sin of racism. The racist denial of indigenous people's identity can only be combatted when the oppressed are empowered spiritually, economically and politically."

The central committee then recommended that member churches listen and learn from indigenous peoples in order to deepen their Christian understanding, to commit significant financial and human resources to the struggle of indigenous people for land rights, and to become politically involved on the side of indigenous peoples against powers which seek to deny the land rights and human rights of indigenous peoples.

The central committee decisions were preceded by an extensive WCC team visit in 1981 to Aboriginal groups in Australia at the invitation of the Australian churches. The visit was unique in that it was arranged by

Aborigines themselves and the team saw what the Aborigines wanted them to see: the hidden people of Australia.

The issue of land rights was also on the agenda of both the WCC's sixth (1983) and seventh (1991) assemblies, held respectively in Canada and Australia.

The churches and the WCC have spoken out forcefully on the issue of land rights. Involved here is the fundamental question of land ownership as well as economic and social privileges in the biblical and ethical context. In Deuteronomy, the land of Canaan was passed to the people of Israel as the patrimony of God. In the Old Testament, property is seen as a trust given by God and not in terms of private ownership as in Roman law. In Lev. 25, the year of remittance means that all land acquired during the past 50 years shall be returned to the original owner, i.e. to the people, and all slaves shall be set free. The Jubilee year makes clear the OT concept of land ownership; it reflects God's concern for justice and the integrity of creation.

In re-discovering the theological significance of "land", churches would do well to listen and learn from indigenous peoples and their cultures and traditions.

See also **justice, peace and the integrity of creation; land**.

BALDWIN SJOLLEMA

Indigenous Peoples: A Global Quest for Justice, a report for the Independent Commission on International Humanitarian Issues, London, Zed, 1977 • *Justice for Aboriginal Australians*, Sydney, Australian Council of Churches, 1981 • "Land Rights for Indigenous Peoples", *PCR Information Reports and Background Papers*, 16, WCC, 1983 • "No Last Frontier", *Risk*, 13, 2, WCC, 1977 • *The Situation of the Indian in South America: Contributions to the Study of Inter-ethnic Conflict in the non-Andean Regions of South America*, WCC and University of Bern, 1972 • L. Swepston & R. Plant, "International Standards and the Protection of the Land Rights of Indigenous and Tribal Populations", *International Labour Review*, 124, 1, 1985.

LATIN AMERICAN COUNCIL OF CHURCHES.

The Consejo Latinoamericano de Iglesias (CLAI) is an ecumenical body covering the continent and including Latin America and the Hispanic Caribbean. Its consists of 140 churches and ecumenical bodies. The latter are associate or fraternal members. Its headquarters is in Quito, Ecuador.

The Panama conference (1916) is traditionally recognized as the starting point of the ecumenical movement in Latin America. That conference was convened as a Latin American response to the great Edinburgh missionary conference of 1910, at which Protestant missions working in Latin America were not accepted, as it was considered that Latin America was Roman Catholic territory which had already been evangelized. In Panama, Protestant missionaries met to discuss questions of relations and strategies, including evangelizing and mission, secular education and the training of ministers. Since then, over the following decades a number of conferences and consultations have brought Protestant Christians in Latin America and the Caribbean closer together. A number of bodies came into existence for co-operation and study, among them the Latin American Protestant Commission for Christian Education (CELADEC), the World Student Christian Federation in Latin America (FUMECAL), Church and Society in Latin America (ISAL) and the Latin American Union of Protestant Youth (ULAJE). In the 1960s the Protestant "Pro-Unity" Commission in Latin America (UNELAM) came into existence. UNELAM soon saw the need for the Protestant churches to adopt a more realistic position in relation to the ecumenical question and resolved to invite the churches to a continental assembly to decide on the possibility of setting up an ecumenical council. The theme of the assembly was "Unity and Mission in Latin America".

The assembly of churches which met at Oaxtepec, Mexico, in September 1978 approved the setting up of a Latin American council of churches. It also decided that no later than four years afterwards a constituent assembly should be convened to discuss all the ecclesiological and constitutional points relating to this kind of council. CLAI was, therefore, described as being "in formation". That assembly in fact met at Huampani, Peru, in 1982, when the constitution of CLAI was promulgated and its standing orders were approved. The second assembly was held at Indaiatuba, São Paulo, in 1988.

CLAI includes Methodists, Lutherans, Presbyterian and Reformed, Anglicans, Waldensians, Pentecostalists, Baptists, Moravians, united churches, independent and Orthodox churches. In ecumenical fellowship all these churches and the associated or fraternal ecumenical bodies recognize the doctrinal basis of CLAI, i.e. the confession of "Jesus Christ as God and Saviour according to the scriptures". In unity they are trying to "fulfill together their common calling to the glory of God, Father, Son and Holy Spirit" (compare **WCC, basis of**).

The main object of CLAI is to promote the "unity of the people of God in Latin America as a local expression of the universal church of Christ and as a testimony and contribution to the unity of the Latin American people". The ecumenical purpose of CLAI is indissolubly linked with the great political, economic, social and religious problems and the hopes of the peoples of the continent. CLAI is governed by an assembly which meets at an interval of not less than four and not more than six years. Between these meetings the council is managed by a board consisting of a president and 16 members. In this board a balanced denominational and regional representation is sought, including representatives of the neglected sectors (indigenous peoples, women, blacks, young people, etc.).

The various demands coming from the most deprived sections of Latin American society and the churches have determined the priorities for the work of CLAI in the following programme areas: women, children and family; indigenous peoples and blacks; pastoral care, spirituality and human rights; evangelism and worship; and promotion and communication. In looking for a method for ecumenical pastoral work for the continent, CLAI, as a forum for meetings and dialogue, is endeavouring to promote practical participation. With its work centred in the churches, CLAI aims at the training and enabling of leaders, common celebration and dialogue and co-operation among its churches and member bodies.

JUAN SCHWINDT
and SERGIO MARCOS PINTO LÓPEZ

LAUBACH, FRANK CHARLES.
B. 2.9.1884, Benton, PA, USA; d. 11.6.1970, Syracuse, NY. A Congregational educator and evangelist, in 1929 Laubach began an educational project of teaching reading by phonetic symbols and pictures, eventually developing literacy primers for some 300 languages and dialects in over 100 countries and localities in Asia, Africa, and Latin America. As originator of the "each one teach one" concept of adult literacy instruction, he founded Laubach Literacy in 1955, with headquarters in Syracuse, but with branch offices and centres in many parts of the world. He had his education at Princeton and Union theological seminaries and at Columbia University and was a missionary for the American Board among the Lanao Moros in the Philippines. He was professor at the Manila Union Theological Seminary, dean of Union College in Manila, dean of the College of Education at Manila University and director of Maranaw folk schools. Also he served as special counsellor to the Committee on World Literacy and Christian Literature of the Division of Foreign Missions of the National Council of the Churches of Christ in the USA. He wrote *The Silent Billion Speak* (New York, Friendship, 1943) and *Teaching the World to Read* (New York, Friendship, 1947). See D.E. Mason, *Frank C. Laubach: Teacher of Millions* (Minneapolis, Denison, 1967).

ANS J. VAN DER BENT

LAUSANNE COMMITTEE FOR WORLD EVANGELIZATION.
The LCWE came into existence after the International Congress on World Evangelization (Lausanne 1974). The congress, sponsored by the Billy Graham Evangelistic Association, brought together almost 2,500 participants from about 150 nations for ten days of intensive focus on the unfinished task of world evangelization. According to honorary chairman Billy Graham, one main purpose of the congress was to "frame a biblical declaration on evangelism... [and] state what the relationship is between evangelism and social responsibility". This was accomplished in the 15-article Lausanne covenant,* drafted under the leadership of John R.W. Stott and signed by a majority of the participants. Both Graham and the Lausanne covenant challenged "the whole church to take the whole gospel to the whole world".

The congress organizers did not anticipate an ongoing "Lausanne" structure. They let it be known that they did *not* envisage a new version of the International Missionary Council,* which had been integrated into the WCC in 1961. But during the congress it became clear that participants favoured the formation of a vehicle by which the spirit and momentum of Lausanne could be sustained. Thus, a few months later some 50 evangelical men and women, nominated by regional groups around the world, met in Mexico to give shape to the LCWE. In 1989 the committee was almost doubled in size, securing balanced representation from the six continents. *World Evangelization*, a bi-monthly publication, articulates the Lausanne movement's single focus.

Four LCWE working groups, dealing with prayer, theology and education, strategy, and communication, provide international forums and task forces. These units have co-ordinated a series of consultations which has produced more than a score of Lausanne occasional papers and major volumes on themes such as gospel and culture, evangelical life-style, evangelism and social responsibility, Christian witness to the Jewish people, Muslim evangelization, conversion, and work of the Holy Spirit.

To some extent the Lausanne movement is perceived as a meeting ground for mainline and conservative evangelicals who wish to overcome barriers to co-operation in evangelization. In their capacity as individuals (not as representatives of Lausanne), John Stott of England and Vinay Samuel of India have led ad hoc groups of evangelicals into consultations with Roman Catholics and with WCC representatives, thereby helping to enlarge the framework in which the Lausanne movement operates.

An especially large consultation of 800 participants on strategies for reaching various population segments and unreached people groups met in Pattaya, Thailand, in 1980. In July 1989 the LCWE convened at Manila a second International Congress on World Evangelization. Lausanne II drew almost 3,600 participants from about 170 nations. Unlike Lausanne 1974, Manila saw significant participation by representatives of the charismatic renewal. There was also increased attention in the programme and in the Manila manifesto to the social implications of the gospel and its proclamation.

See also **evangelical missions, evangelism**.

ROBERT T. COOTE

LAUSANNE COVENANT. In July 1974 some 2,500 evangelical leaders from about 150 nations met in Lausanne, Switzerland, for the International Congress on World Evangelization, called by evangelist Billy Graham to "frame a biblical declaration on evangelism". Under the leadership of John R.W. Stott, Anglican pastor in London, the Lausanne covenant was discussed and revised during the congress and finally presented for acceptance. While no single document can represent all evangelicals, the covenant is widely acknowledged as a major milestone, reflecting the spirit and stance of the evangelical community in the late 20th century.

In 3,000 words, organized in 15 articles, the covenant articulates the biblical basis of the Christian world mission as its signers understood it. Typical of evangelical hallmarks is article 2. It identifies the Old and New Testaments as "the only written word of God, without error in all that it affirms, and the only infallible rule of faith and practice". This wording prevailed over "inerrancy", a term many conservatives preferred. Other articles addressed "the uniqueness and universality of Christ", "Christian social responsibility" (the covenant expresses "penitence... for having sometimes regarded evangelism and social concern as mutually exclusive"), and "the urgency of the evangelistic task". The last grants that a missionary moratorium "may sometimes be necessary to facilitate the national church's growth in self-reliance and to release resources for unevangelized areas".

Not infrequently the Lausanne covenant is studied alongside of and compared favorably with Pope Paul VI's Evangelization in the Modern World (*Evangelii Nuntiandi*, 1975); with the section report on "Confessing Christ Today" (WCC fifth assembly, Nairobi 1975); and with the 1982 "Mission and Evangelism: an Ecumenical Affirmation", by the Commission on World Mission and Evangelism of the WCC.

The substance of the Lausanne covenant was affirmed and elaborated at the 1989 congress, Lausanne II, in Manila, where Stott again provided leadership in drafting the Manila manifesto, informally affirmed by some 3,600 participants.

See also **evangelicals**.

ROBERT T. COOTE

C.R. Padilla ed., *The New Face of Evangelicalism: An International Symposium on the Lausanne Covenant*, Downers Grove, IL, InterVarsity, 1976 • J.R.W. Stott, *The Lausanne Covenant: An Exposition and Commentary*, Minneapolis, World Wide, 1975.

LAW. The idea of law is an indispensable element and plays an important pragmatic role in the life of individuals and social groups. At the same time it is a concept whose content and basis are far from self-evident. Its obscurity is particularly evident in secularized societies (see **secularization**).

Law and justice. For common sense, what is lawful is confused with what is just; injustice is what fails to conform with the law. For the legal mind, however, law is what is laid down in a set of rules or norms by the political and social authorities in accordance with various procedures. These rules are embodied in codes which govern the relationships and conduct of human beings in society. Known also as laws, these rules are legion. The proliferation of laws is indeed a salient feature of our societies: whenever a new activity is established, new rules need to be formulated. Thus alongside the penal code and the civil code, which apply in principle to every human being endowed with normal mental capacities, special codes have also come into existence: codes for labour, taxation, social security, various professional codes (for doctors, lawyers, journalists, etc.). Given this proliferation and increasing complexity of laws, the principle to which the courts appeal in penalizing breaches of the law (i.e. "ignorance of the law is no defence") becomes inapplicable. A significant difference emerges here between law and morality. An enlightened educated conscience ordinarily manages to distinguish between good and evil. Only with the greatest difficulty, however, is the same conscience able to discern what the law allows and what it forbids. It has to consult the experts (lawyer, solicitor, notary, etc.).

In modern societies, law has come to replace custom and tradition, often retaining many of their elements. But characteristic of law is its attempt to systematize and rationalize and its increasing complexity. The effect of this trend has been to deepen the divide between justice* and law, between morality and law. Behind the constant revision of the system of laws there are, of course, purely technical considerations; but moral considerations also play a part. It has come to be realized that the law was not always just, that it could even generate injustice. In South Africa, apartheid* is built into the law, but who would say that made it just (see the declarations of the WCC assemblies in 1954, 1968 and 1975, etc.)? The Geneva convention is an international law regulating the conduct of war; it outlaws the execution or inhumane treatment of prisoners of war and the wounded, attacks on civilians, etc. But even if these regulations were scrupulously respected, that in itself would not make war a just act.

In the Old Testament the terms for law and justice are in practice interchangeable. But we no longer today have the same situation; we are sometimes obliged to combat this or that provision of a legal code in the very interests of justice.

Does this mean that there is no longer any connection at all between law and ethics? That would be going too far, since many rights recognized by law (the right to life, the right to human dignity, freedom of conscience) are the legal expression of axiomatic moral values. Yet these moral values must also be deeply embedded in custom and be really the expression of majority public opinion. Clearly this is not always the case. Nazism was the subversion at one and the same time both of law and the moral conscience. In the Christian churches themselves, while there may be a certain consensus on the individual right to property,* there is also very vigorous argument over the limits to this right and the possibility of legal expropriation in the name of justice. The relationship between law and morality may be envisaged schematically as that of two overlapping circles with an area common to them both. This common area varies in size depending on the historical epoch and the society in question. Our impression is that today this common area is contracting.

There are several reasons for this partial dissociation of law and morality. One of the most important is the uncertainty in our secularized and specialized societies concerning the *source* of law; another is the uncertainty concerning the *basis* of law.

The source of law: In the Bible, in the Old Testament and in the New, the unique author of law is the holy God, who is just in his judgments and who abhors sin.* God is free to delegate his power to human beings he has chosen: Moses, judges, kings, priests and also prophets who denounce the injustice of rulers and people when they depart from God's laws and who declare the just judgments of God on the failure of one or the other to repent. This justice, however, though it can be extremely severe (note the many examples in the book of the prophet Jeremiah), is always set within a covenant* initiated by God in which he freely chooses his partner (the people of Israel). This covenant is irrevocable, which is why, beyond the threats of dispersion, destruction and annihilation, there shines the hope of re-establishment, the hope of re-integration and a happy future. The law which is the content of this covenant (the ritual code of Ex. 34:10-26; the decalogue in the strict sense, Ex. 20:2-17 and Deut. 5:6-21); the code of the covenant (Ex. 20:22-23); the code rediscovered in the reign of King Josiah (Deut. 1-26); the holiness code of Lev. 17-26; the priestly code, which is scattered throughout the Pentateuch and deals with the respect due to the institutions which are the basis of Israel's identity (i.e. the sabbath and circumcision), is not exclusively repressive, therefore, but is located within a promise of which God is author. It nonetheless fulfills the function of all law, i.e. it regulates the relationships of the people with God, the relationships of human beings with one another, of tribe with tribe. In many parts, moreover, it also focuses attention primarily on those who, in virtue of their weakness or marginal situation, are more likely than most to become victims of injustice: the widow, the orphan, the foreigner. God as the author of law shows himself to be the friend of the weak. This concern for the weak is emphasized again, even more, in the NT.

In our modern secularized societies, which, before being technologized, were strongly influenced not only by the Judeo-Christian tradition but also, and sometimes still more strongly, by the Greco-Roman tradition, the author and guarantor of law has become increasingly a more uncertain, vague and abstract figure. In the Greco-Roman tradition, law has its source in reason or in human nature as subject to reason. The figure of the legislator does not disappear completely. There are many examples of celebrated lawgivers, such as Solon. In accordance with the Judeo-Christian tradition as interpreted by the Catholic church, from the moment it became the official religion of the Roman empire and, above all, from the moment when the church had to take the place of that empire in its decline, God became once more the legislator par excellence. At the same time, however, the church integrated the idea of the natural or rational law into its theology. To be sure, the latter still has God as author. But since God made humanity in his own image and this image, though damaged by original sin, still subsists in humanity, the law which God wills is one which conforms to the nature of humanity; it is in harmony with this human nature of which it is the expression. It is also a rational law, since reason is the human faculty least damaged by sin. But God delegates his power as legislator to the human beings God has specially chosen — and first and foremost to the head of the church, the pope. It can be said that it was the church which was the sole lawgiver in the West in the 12th century and that, thanks to the work of the monk Gratian in compiling what is known as Gratian's Decretum (c.1140), not only the church but society as a whole is ruled by the same canon law.*

This reign of canon law (though it lasted until 1919 in the church) was of fairly short duration, since the temporal lords (emperor, king, prince, free town) claimed the right to publish a civil law more or less independent of canon law. This second source of law explains many conflicts, into which we need not go here, indicating a certain secularization of law. In virtue of their consecration, of course, emperors and kings to some extent share the religious authority. Just as the pope is assisted by the council, so too are temporal lords assisted in their legislative task by assemblies: the diet in the holy Roman empire, the provincial or national "estates" and parliaments in certain kingdoms (England, France, etc.). The breach caused by the Reformation in the corpus Christianum and the constitution of national churches were not unconnected with this development. The two-kingdoms doctrine — formulated in almost identical terms by Luther and Calvin — marks the beginning of the secularization of law. The temporal lord was not to meddle in spiritual matters, and the churches recognized his right to legislate in the temporal realm. In Reformation thought, however, it still remains clear that these two legislative powers (independent but parallel) are both meant to serve the same goal, or rather, different aspects of the same goal — the conservation of creation* and the salvation* of creation — and that both aspects are conjoined in God.

The advent of constitutional monarchies and democracies in the West from the 18th century onwards modified radically the system of law and ended in the establishment of an exclusively civil law. Legislative power was gradually passed to elected assemblies in a variety of arrangements, and in the future, despite the emergence here and there of unchecked dictatorial regimes, the notion of "popular sovereignty" prevailed. The people, holding power directly but more often indirectly through its elected representatives, became the sole author of law. We call that state constitutional whose laws are voted by the majority of the people's representatives, are universally valid throughout the nation and cannot have retrospective force. But what one parliament elected for a limited period has done can obviously be undone by its successor. Another feature of the constitutional state is the separation of powers. Parliament legislates and controls the application of laws though the executive (government), whose power to make rules and regulations is limited to the framework defined by the laws. A third power, independent of the two already mentioned, is charged with the punishment of breaches of the law by individuals, social groups and even the administration itself.

While democracy has in this way made a major contribution to the promotion of human rights (all human beings are equal before the law) and diminished the arbitrary exercise of power by an authority believing itself free simply to do as it pleases, the fact remains that it rests in a morally debatable postulate, namely, that the popular will as expressed in free elections is the sole source of all law. Is it legitimate to affirm as axiomatic *vox populi,*

vox Dei? Laws are rarely passed unanimously. It is the majority which imposes its will. But is it enough to be in a majority to be also in the right? Nothing could be less axiomatic. It is possible for a code of law to be unjust. Who would dare to claim that the code which emerges is always just? Even in a genuine democracy, does it not remain true that the ancient appeal of an Antigone against the law promulgated by the political establishment (Creon) must always remain a possibility? One of the tasks of the Christian church, whether or not it enjoys full freedom within a state, is to oppose the law in the name of justice in certain circumstances and by its influence on public opinion to secure a change in the law whenever the latter violates the dignity of God's creatures and the integrity of God's creation (see the statement adopted by the Uppsala assembly on the role of the churches in the formation of public opinion).

A number of modern democracies have realized the dangers of an exclusive appeal to popular sovereignty. They have therefore provided themselves with constitutions and declarations of human rights* which, placed above the laws voted by parliament, constitute a possible court of appeal against unjust laws. These constitutions and declarations, of course, have themselves also been established by popular suffrage. They nevertheless constitute a sort of self-limitation which checks and balances the power of the legislature, particularly if there are supreme courts or constitutional councils with a mandate to monitor the agreement of laws with constitutional principles. But it is also essential that these institutions should enjoy genuine autonomy vis-a-vis the political establishment. These fundamental texts (e.g. the Universal Declaration of Human Rights) very often contain principles which in a secularized form nonetheless reflect values deriving from the Judeo-Christian tradition.

The content of law: The same uncertainty which overhangs the source of the law is also operative in respect of its content. Lawyers have always distinguished between, on the one hand, a fundamental law or right, often called natural law,* which is in principle unaffected by the hazards of politics and out of reach of modification by political regimes and, on the other hand, a positive law as elaborated by legislative bodies with the aid of experts. Natural law is held in principle to be superior to positive law. Unfortunately, this natural law is often left undefined and of uncertain content, especially at the international level. During the famous Nuremberg trials, international judges had to invent the concept of "a crime against humanity", which had never previously been either defined or recognized. In consequence, whatever the monstrous acts which these judges had to penalize, it is impossible to recall this historic trial without a certain feeling of unease. The Nazi leaders were condemned in the name of a law made retrospective in effect, and this constitutes, from a formal standpoint, a dangerous precedent. True, it is difficult to predict just how far "man's inhumanity to man" may go; some legal minds therefore proposed the notion of "a natural law with variable content", but this, too, is a bastard concept.

As for positive law, because of the proliferation of special codes, it is often difficult to identify its basis. Projects of laws which are submitted to parliamentary vote generally emanate not from the parliament itself or even from the government. The latter may have intuited the existence of a need — or the absence of any need — to legislate on this matter or that. The content of the proposed text, however, has been drafted by specialists, experts and lawyers. A veritable legal technology has established itself in our modern societies. Taught and brought to perfection in the law faculties, it enjoys a real autonomy and is sometimes constructed in accordance with mathematical models. In consequence, the relation between positive law and natural law becomes extremely problematic. The difficulty is not a new one. In the OT, the decalogue, with its very clear profile and perfect intelligibility, was taken in hand by doctors of the law who developed a real casuistry which was hard to understand and already constituted a legal technology. In our modern societies, however, where the need has been felt to develop a fiscal law, a commercial law, an industrial law, etc., legal technology has undergone a considerable scientific development.

The crushing uncertainty which overhangs both the source and content of law in modern secularized and technologized societies and the relationships existing between so-called natural or rational or even universal law and positive law can actually result in a growing gap between law, on the one hand, and justice and equity, on the other. Even in a constitutional state, the law can be unjust. We continue to honour with the name of justice the courts whose business it is to state the law, ensure respect for the law and determine the penalties to be imposed in order to erase infringements of the law and to prevent it from falling into desuetude. But the law which the courts enunciate can be unjust law. In democratic regimes, to be sure, parliaments can always revoke an unjust law and replace it by a more equitable one. But parliaments are inescapably exposed to the pressures of a public opinion which can itself be moved by concerns which have nothing to do with justice. Economic interests, class interests, racial interests can direct the passing of the laws which the courts must implement. The legal and political system of apartheid in force in South Africa is only one extreme example of a law which not only deviates from but manifestly contradicts justice (see particularly the official report of the Nairobi assembly, which specially condemns institutionalized or legalized racism).

Ecumenical discussion. In view of the gap between law, on the one hand, and equity or justice on the other, what attitude are Christians and churches to adopt towards law? The ecumenical movement, especially in its early stages, made several attempts to come to grips with this question. The question of penal theories was discussed at the Stockholm Life and Work conference in 1925, and at Oxford in 1938 the question of law was placed in the context of church-state relations. Since 1945 the study department of the WCC discussed the relationship of law and justice to biblical authority in the modern world. Questions of natural law, law and ethics, and international law and justice were debated at several conferences, as well as the question of a Trinitarian and Christological approach to law and justice. These conferences culminated in the conference in Treysa, Federal Republic of Germany, in 1950 and the publication of *The Biblical Doctrine of Justice and Law* in 1955. This contained the Treysa findings and substantial essays on the theme.

On the basis of our own study and the ecumenical discussion of this theme, the answer to the question may be summarized in the following points. First, Christians and churches must defend the constitutional state, i.e. a state in which each citizen enjoys equality before the law and is not judged according to one's opinions but only according to one's actions measured against a law promulgated prior to these actions. They must therefore resist the opposing dangers of anarchy and tyranny. Revolution may be necessary as a last resort in a situation of flagrant injustice and violation of justice, but the legal vacuum thus created must be speedily filled to avoid the danger of a reign of terror.

Second, Christians and churches must be especially vigilant to point out and denounce as rapidly as possible a growing gap between law and justice as well as violations of justice, a stand taken courageously by organizations such as Amnesty International, the WCC, and Action of Christians for the Abolition of Torture. Christians should strive for a closer approximation of law to justice. Although they should as a rule be reformist rather than revolutionary, revolution can be an *ultima ratio* when all attempts at reform fail.

Third, Christians and churches should constantly re-examine the law established by legislation, not only because it may be unjust, but also because account must be taken of new problems, such as those arising from advances in biology and the human sciences (bioethics,* genetic engineering, euthanasia,* abortion,* etc.). But while recognizing the need for legislation, conscience and responsibility may in certain circumstances set a limit to the intervention of law.

Fourth, Christians and churches regard the word of God* as the norm for their conduct, and this norm holds good whenever a body of law has to be formulated and clothed with authority. But it would be legalistic to look for ready-made answers in scripture to all legal problems. We find in scripture indications, directions and warnings about limits that may not be transgressed, but no possibility of formulating "a Christian legislation". Above all, in Jesus Christ, scripture provides a fundamental inspiration which Paul calls "the law of love".

Finally, the realm of law is not that of love. The law authorizes, forbids and punishes. In the creation of law, however, Christians and churches should do their utmost to ensure that despite its inadequacies the law remains — in the words of Karl Barth — analogous to the order and justice of the kingdom of God. Law is not ethics, but the creation of law is an ethical task which cannot be left either to the political authorities alone or in the hands of the experts. Christians should not try to impose the demands of their Christian faith on all. They are indeed called to promote a law which is universal in scope. They should devote themselves to this task in a way which corresponds to the provisional order of this sinful world.

See also **authority, canon law, international law, justice, natural law, order**.

ROGER MEHL

K. Barth, "Justification and Justice", in *Church, Community and State*, New York, Anchor, 1960 • E. Brunner, *Gerechtigkeit* (ET *Justice and the Social Order*, New York, Harper, 1945) • J. Ellul, *Le fondement théologique du droit* (ET *The Theological Foundation of Law*, Garden City, NY, Doubleday, 1960) • "Recht, Rechtphilosophie", in *Evangelisches Staatslexikon*, Stuttgart, Kreuz, 1966, and in *Lexikon für Theologie und Kirche*, Freiburg, Herder, 1963 • H.-H. Schrey, H.-H. Walz & W.A. Whitehouse, *The Biblical Doctrine of Justice and Law*, London, SCM, 1955.

LEX ORANDI, LEX CREDENDI.

Literally "law of praying, law of believing", this Latin tag is used with varying degrees of precision. Its origin resides in the phrase *ut legem credendi lex statuat supplicandi*, which was long attributed to Pope Celestine I (422-32) but is now considered to come from a lay monk of that time, Prosper of Aquitaine. A disciple of Augustine, Prosper was arguing against semi-Pelagianism that all true faith, even the beginnings of good will as well as growth and perseverance, is from start to finish a work of grace.* In various writings he points out that, following 1 Tim. 2:1-4, catholic churches everywhere, led by the Spirit of God, daily plead the cause of the human race, asking that all categories of unbelievers may be brought to salvation. In this context, the expression then means quite precisely that "the apostolic *injunction to pray* [for all people, which the church obeys in its intercessions, that they may come to the faith] sets the *obligation to believe* [that even the first motions towards faith are themselves a gift of God]".

In more recent use, the phrase has come to represent the more general claim — which may be descriptive and/or normative — that liturgical practice has in historical fact governed, and/or should in theological right govern, what is taught, whether as solemn dogma, official doctrine, catechetical instruction or academic exposition. Historically, it can easily be shown, for instance, that the worship of Christ, the practice already in the first three centuries of addressing praise and prayers to him, helped to establish the Nicene teaching of the Son as *homoousios* with the Father, the dogmatic recognition of Christ's deity. Theologically, it can be argued that the more immediate, spontaneous act of worship rightly possesses priority over the more distanced activity of theological reflection itself, in which believers, as it were, "step back" a little to think about their faith.

From historical research and theological reflection, however, it soon emerges that it is too simple, both descriptively and normatively, to attribute priority to "praying" over "teaching", or at least to see the shaping and controlling influences as flowing only in the one direction; and so the abbreviated phrase "lex orandi, lex credendi" often serves, in a vague but useful way, as a rubric under which to explore, both historically and theologically, the rather complex relationships between worship and doctrine. To stay with the example of Christ's deity: it can only have been by theological reflection — admittedly on the basis of a present experience of salvation* in Christ — that Christians very early came to attribute to him a role in the creation of the world, which they then sang in the hymns from which the apostle in turn quotes in a doctrinal argument (1 Cor. 8:6; Col. 1:15-20); and in its own day, the council of Nicea chose to insert its teaching in a creed,* a form which was used in both catechesis* and baptism* and which before too long found a place also in the eucharistic liturgy. Nor did the Arians, however, hesitate to appeal to the catholic liturgy for evidence of an alleged "subordination" of the Son, which the Nicenes then had the theological task of explaining in an orthodox sense. Clearly there is much historical material here for theological reflection.

Worship and doctrine distinguished. Perhaps the first task is to see how and why worship and doctrine inevitably became and become distinguished and the problems which, with equal inevitability, thereby arise. According to the gospels, the first declaration of the Christian faith can be either a second-person address to its object ("You are the Christ", Mark 8:29) or a first-person proclamation to others concerning him ("We have found the Christ", John 1:41). Transferred to the third person, the confession "Jesus is Lord" (Rom. 10:9; 1 Cor. 12:3) is at once an acclamation, an announcement and an assertion. In the most elemental cases of Christian speech, "liturgy" and "doctrine" thus coincide. However, a diversification of purposes and contexts soon brings a differentiation of linguistic usage.

In its loving address to God, *worship* tends towards exuberance and abandon. In the very act of self-surrender (note "the sacrifice of praise", Heb. 13:15), worshippers will not find it necessary to justify what is taking place, but they will quickly want to sing the praises of their divine Lover before the world.

In *evangelization* Christian preachers have to accommodate to the culture* which is hearing the gospel for the first time. Other languages will be corrected and filled, converted and brought captive to Christ, as their speakers are challenged and changed by the gospel. This process, when successful, will also enrich the linguistic repertoire of the whole Christian tradition.

In *apologetics* the defenders of the faith engage with those who resist, oppose and even attack it. Here language acquires a sharp point, a combative edge. Yet the aim must remain to persuade opponents and win them for God's church and kingdom. Linguistic swords and spears are destined to become ploughshares and pruning hooks.

In its *internal controversies* the church is seeking by argument to clarify the gospel and the faith.* Fine distinctions are drawn. When, after examination and debate, a position is deemed heretical, a doctrinal definition is made that will exclude it. In a combination of positive statement and explicit or implicit exclusion, the definition declares the faith. It thereby sets the rules for other Christian speech on the topic and may even itself get taken up into direct doxological usage.

Signalled by the shifts and variety of linguistic usage, an element of *theological reflection* thus belongs to debate within the church, to the defence and proclamation of the gospel, and even to the Christian worship of God. While such reflection, which also develops its own linguistic style, is in a sense secondary, it is not essentially alien to the faith. Since the gospel is addressed to the whole person and calls for a total response, faith involves the intelligence from the very start. The initial gift and act of faith already contain a moment of understanding, the *intellectus fidei*, whereby God enlightens the heart and mind and enables it to accept the truth of God's own being and history as these are testified in the gospel.

Since Christians speak differently according to these different functions and circumstances just enumerated, there is a danger that they will cease to be substantially consistent. There is a perpetual need to correlate what is said in the several modes in order to ensure that the reference and meaning remain the same. Part of the servant task of reflective theology is to assist in that correlation for the sake of the more primary activities of the church. Yet it is also in reflective theology that critical inquiry and speculative construction may seek to rule and thereby lose touch with the message and purpose. The overriding consideration must, of course, be fidelity to the gospel (lex credendi), so that God may be rightly glorified (lex orandi). That is not the responsibility solely of reflective theology, let alone "professional theologians". The controversial question of *pastoral authority* inescapably arises.

Confessional patterns in controversy. There is a case to be made that differences, both theoretical and practical, in handling the sometimes problematic relations between worship and doctrine have played a part in the maintenance, and perhaps even the origin, of different "confessional identities" within the broader Christian movement. At the unavoidable risk of caricature, three or four types may be sketched by way of example. The purpose of this analysis is to set the background for various efforts already made towards some use of a lex orandi, lex credendi approach in ecumenism, and for some suggestions as to what is further needed.

In *Eastern Orthodoxy* the relation between worship and doctrine is so close that the Reformed theologian Dietrich Ritschl was misled into suspecting that the Orthodox "worship the doctrine of the Trinity" (*Zur*

Logik der Theologie, 1984, 154). Certainly the Orthodox liturgy bears a high dogmatic density, and Orthodox theologians in turn are expected to operate within and for the worshipping community. The Orthodox do not make the sharp distinction between the doxological and the scientific genres that the more critical Westerners make. The heavy reliance upon inherited texts certainly raises hermeneutical problems (see **hermeneutics**); but the writings of an Alexander Schmemann, such as his theological commentary on the rites of initiation (*Of Water and the Spirit*, 1974) and his *The Eucharist — Sacrament of the Kingdom* (1987), show that it is possible to expound the Tradition* from within its own continuum in ways that challenge rather than simply confirm the surrounding culture. Nevertheless, Orthodox theologians rightly owe their Western counterparts an account of the authority* that is accorded to the liturgy, as also of what is happening when the liturgical tradition becomes (as Schmemann admits) distorted in certain particulars, and of the criteria and means of correction.

Roman Catholicism offers some notable examples of devotion leading doctrine. But even here the matter is complex. For while, say, the spontaneous celebration of Mary's holiness marks a starting point, it took many centuries of theological debate — and this in relation to the (itself speculative) Augustinian interpretation of original sin — before Pius IX came in 1854 to the point of declaring her immaculate conception as a dogma,* thereby re-inforcing also the obligatory character of its feast (which it had not enjoyed before the 18th century). The Roman see has in fact a history of increasing doctrinal and pastoral control over the worship of churches in the papal communion, so that Pius XII, speaking magisterially in *Mediator Dei* (1947), could even reverse the ancient maxim to say that "the law of believing must set the law of praying", in the sense that the liturgy "is subject to the church's supreme teaching authority".

The *Protestant* Reformation may be understood, at least in part, as a doctrinal revolt, on the basis of a Bible that was believed to be clear in its own message, against liturgical and devotional practices that expressed false understandings of God, humankind and salvation. In the revised, recast — indeed, newly created — service books, the reformers sought to provide for worship that would be in accord with the pure gospel. In turn, of course, the worship service would function as a teaching instrument, so that it would indeed sometimes acquire such a strongly didactic character that the prayers and sermons sound like courses in dogmatic or moral theology rather than praise and proclamation.

Anglicans, with appeal to a more or less uniform Book of Common Prayer, have often proposed an ostensive definition of their faith: "If you want to know what we believe, look at what we pray" (and *Methodists* have sometimes pointed in a similar way to the Wesley hymns). But, as S.W. Sykes has shown in *The Integrity of Anglicanism* (1978) and *The Identity of Christianity* (1984), this is to be rather disingenuous about the play of forces between scripture, Tradition, experience, reason, culture and church order. As recent liturgical revisions in most Western churches have made clear, all these factors enter into any theologically responsible attempt to shape and reshape worship; and "books" of worship have to be in some way both authorized and accepted within the communities for which they are intended.

Ecumenical efforts and possibilities. In a seminal essay of 1957 on "The Structure of Dogmatic Statements as an Ecumenical Problem", the Lutheran Edmund Schlink observed that a "category shift" takes place when what is expressed in prayer and preaching is translated into the form of dogma. In worship and witness, we face God and our fellow human beings more directly. In dogmatic statements, however, we are *talking about* (the proper way to) worship and witness; we are *teaching about* God, his acts, and the human response. The risk is that the teacher withdraws to "a neutral position from which the encounter between God and man may be observed, described and be cast into didactic formulas". Problems arise when "attention moves away from the experience of salvation which comes through the gospel and is concentrated instead on giving a theoretical definition of the relationship between the divine and human contributions in redemption". Schlink holds that the "structural change" from doxology to doctrine is responsible for some of the most persistent dogmatic problems in Christendom, for it is at the second level that differences show up. Schlink is not so naive as to think that dogma is unnecessary, but it is secondary and subject to marked historical and anthropological conditioning. He proposes an ecumenical concentration upon the primary forms of worship and witness, where (he is persuaded) we shall re-discover an already-existing unity and fullness which differences in doctrinal statements had obscured.

Meanwhile, the Roman Catholic theologian H.J. Schulz in 1976 devoted a substantial book to arguing that an adequate "unity in faith" can be drawn from the ancient eucharistic tradition which the divided churches have retained or restored. The words, actions and celebration of the eucharistic rites, and particularly the great eucharistic prayer or anaphora, provide sufficient expression of Trinitarian faith and of doctrine concerning church, sacraments and ministry. It was to relations between the Roman and the Eastern churches that Schulz gave most attention, but he saw positive prospects also for reconciliation with the churches of the Reformation by this route.

Faith and Order* was already working along somewhat similar lines and across the widest ecumenical range, as the Lima text on *Baptism, Eucharist and Ministry** was to show (1982). The principal source of BEM was the holy scriptures, which are themselves the main liturgical book of the church: much of the material in the scriptures arose in the context of worship or was destined for it; it was their use in worship which helped to establish the canonical status of the biblical writings (see **canon**); and the liturgical assembly remained the chief locus of their preservation, transmission and interpretation. That the scriptures thus used within the continuing Tradition govern BEM is appreciated by the official response of the Roman Catholic Church, which says in part: "The sources employed for the interpretation of the meaning of the eucharist and the form of celebration are scripture and Tradition. The classical liturgies of the first millennium and patristic theology are important points of reference in this text." Or in the words of the response from the United Methodist Church, USA: "BEM deftly unites the truths and testimonies of the New Testament and the ecumenical creeds."

Yet the responses of the churches to BEM

also indicate that there is still some way to go along this liturgical road to fuller unity in faith, order and life. While BEM is found to imply a significant rudimentary agreement in matters of Trinity, Christology, soteriology, ecclesiology and eschatology, most churches still require greater clarification and confirmation of the dogmatic context before unity can be declared. Hence the importance of the more recent and still continuing F&O project "Towards the Common Expression of the Apostolic Faith Today". Here again it is remarkable that the Apostles' and Nicene creeds have been taken as the "theological basis and methodological tool" of the study. For it is the faith learned in catechesis, confessed at baptism and renewed by the eucharist which brings closest together the lex orandi and the lex credendi. It is an encouraging fact that several prominent contemporary theologians have expounded the faith in terms of the creeds: thus Karl Barth's *Dogmatics in Outline* (1947, ET 1949), Joseph Ratzinger's *Introduction to the Christian Faith* (1968, ET 1969), Wolfhart Pannenberg's *The Apostles' Creed in the Light of Today's Questions* (1972, ET 1972), Jan Milic Lochman's *The Faith We Confess — an Ecumenical Dogmatics* (1982, ET 1984).

The popular reception of the Lima liturgy* in many places — even though it was an "occasional" composition which does not enjoy the "maturity" of BEM itself — is at least an indication of the felt need for an instrument whereby a common faith can be confessed, celebrated, proclaimed and taught together. What Yves Congar says of the Dombes Group (see **Groupe des Dombes**) is true of much modern ecumenical work towards doctrinal agreement: "The hallmark of their method is the integration of theological discussion and prayer, and the fecundity of the Group is due to this interaction"; and it is by pressing on in this direction, both theoretically and practically, that divided Christendom may most likely come to a unity in a lex orandi and a lex credendi that are themselves mutually consistent. The mainspring of the ecumenical movement from the start has been the *prayer* of Jesus, into which Christians themselves have entered, that they might be one in order that, through their witness to the faith, the world also might *believe* in the divine mission of the Son (John 17).

According to Paul, our "logical worship" includes the offering of our bodies to God (Rom. 12:1); only as we "live in... harmony with one another, in accord with Christ Jesus" may we "with one voice glorify the God and Father of our Lord Jesus Christ" (15:5-6). Thus the lex orandi and the lex credendi remain incomplete without a corresponding *lex bene operandi*.

GEOFFREY WAINWRIGHT

T. Berger, "Lex orandi — lex credendi — lex agendi. Auf dem Weg zu einer ökumenisch konsensfähigen Verhältnisbestimmung von Liturgie, Theologie und Ethik", *Archiv für Liturgiewissenschaft*, 27, 1985 • P. de Clerck, "Lex orandi, lex credendi: Sens originel et avatars historiques d'un adage équivoque", *Questions liturgiques*, 56, 1978 • K. Federer, *Liturgie und Glaube. Eine theologeschichtliche Untersuchung*, Freiburg, Switzerland, Paulus, 1950 • K. Schlemmer ed., *Gottesdienst — Weg zur Einheit. Impulse für die Ökumene*, Freiburg, Herder, 1989 • E. Schlink, *Der kommende Christus und die kirchlichen Traditionen* (ET *The Coming Christ and the Coming Church*, Edinburgh, Oliver & Boyd, 1967, esp. pp.16-84) • A. Schmemann, *Introduction to Liturgical Theology*, Portland, ME, American Orthodox Press, 1966 • H.J. Schulz, *Ökumenische Glaubenseinheit aus eucharistischer Überlieferung*, Paderborn, Bonifacius, 1976 • C. Vagaggini, *Il senso teologico delle liturgia* (ET *Theological Dimensions of the Liturgy*, Collegeville, MN, Liturgical, 1976) • G. Wainwright, *Doxology: The Praise of God in Worship, Doctrine and Life*, London, Epworth, 1980.

LIBERATION. The word "liberation" has assumed a special significance in ecumenical discussion, providing a touchstone for determining an authentic mode of theologizing and a fundamental guideline for ethical reflection and action.

Broadly defined, liberation is a process by which a subjugated or marginalized section of people, having gained an awareness of their condition of oppression, take control of their destiny and fight to overthrow all the fetters of bondage. This may include several elements: a new social consciousness (conscientization) in a submerged group, appropriation of the means of production by the poor,* freeing the people* from colonialism, liberation movements against racially oppressive and authoritative regimes and organized struggle against all forms of cultural and gender domination. Liberation is the struggle of the marginalized everywhere — blacks, women, dalits, tribal and indigenous people, landless and unorganized workers — for their dignity and justice.

From the perspective of people as subjects of history, not to be manipulated by external forces, sharp challenges are raised to traditional ways of knowledge, ideologies, systems of government and church structures and forms of service. Education that legitimizes the value system of the dominant groups in a given society is rejected for the sake of education for liberation. Social action directed towards a radical alteration of unjust structures is preferred to charitable services which cause no ripples in the existing system.

In three areas of concern, liberation has brought a distinctively new emphasis: development, political movement and theology.

Development. The concept of development* is gradually being replaced by the more dynamic and humanistic concept of liberation. The term "development" does not express the aspirations of the poorer nations and peoples for the simple reason that, even after considerable developmental activities, a wide gap remains between the rich and the poor countries. The pattern of economic growth and the international aid and trade system have made the poorer nations increasingly dependent on the rich countries. The mounting debt problem of the third-world countries is the disturbing consequence of this pattern. It is increasingly realized today that liberation from the domination of economically powerful countries is a prerequisite for the development of countries in the third world. Unless development is placed within the control of international social justice, "development" is an empty word.

Economic development within the third-world countries, which is controlled by a powerful elite with the co-operation of multinationals and external resources, favours the rich and continues to create imbalances between different sections of the people. The bulk of capital investment is concentrated in the industrial or advanced sector in the belief that rapid industrialization will create conditions for wider use of the abundant labour available and reduce inequalities in income distribution. But what in fact happens is that the advanced sector achieves considerably more expansion, leading to the impoverishment of the traditional sector. The gap between the two sectors has widened. In other words, the majority of the population are left outside the development process.

As a critical response to this, it is affirmed that development should become a liberating process. Ecumenical documents, particularly those of the WCC's Commission on the Churches' Participation in Development (CCPD), articulate this perspective forcefully. The central issue is posed as "development by whom and for whom?" Development becomes a liberating process when the oppressed and marginal are able to identify their own needs, mobilize their own resources and shape their future on their own terms. The church is challenged to commit itself to that form of development.

Political movement. The political dimension of liberation is best illustrated in the freedom fights in Asia and Africa that led to the overthrow of the yoke of colonialism (see **decolonization**). Today liberation struggles are being waged on many fronts. Some vestiges of colonialism and forces of neo-colonialism continue to strangle the life of many countries in the third world. Regimes by racial minorities and military dictatorships and other totalitarian systems of governments continue to oppress people.

Even in so-called democratic countries in the third world, the political system is one in which the decision-making process and control are concentrated in the hands of persons or groups whose interests are fundamentally inimical to the well-being of life as a whole. Not only do they keep the masses away from the centres of power, they also fail to resolve the basic problems of mass poverty, glaring inequalities, growing unemployment and rising prices. When any organized effort by the masses to redress their grievances arises, it is brutally suppressed. Imposition of authoritarian and repressive regimes, denial of human rights and excessive dependence on foreign resources are the natural development of the domination by the elite.

The emergence of liberation groups as a countervailing power to unjust systems of government has created many situations of conflict, some of which have turned violent. This raises the question of the nature of Christian presence in the midst of such violent conflicts. Dogmatic renunciation of violence can reduce Christian principles to empty slogans and talk of justice to a mockery. But uncritical acceptance of violence loses the critical edge of our Christian witness to the gospel of love. This issue cannot be settled in academic debate. The church's commitment to violent or non-violent strategies must be evaluated in each situation in the face of its overall commitment to liberation. In any case, the church's commitment to liberation necessarily expresses itself in its solidarity with liberation movements.

Theology. It is in theology that the concern for liberation has brought a distinctly new emphasis (see **theology, liberation**). Latin American theologians challenged the traditional mode of theologizing at every point and unequivocally argued that authentic theology is reflection on faith and praxis for the poor. Living in commitment to liberation is the starting point from which to think through the faith.

The concept of liberation is not new. Various perceptions of it are found in ancient philosophy and in the religions of Asia. But these see liberation primarily as personal and interior and do not envisage any radical change of social structure. The present emphasis situates liberation in the concrete-historical events (see **history**) and arises out of a fresh reading of the Bible (see **hermeneutics**). The God of the Bible is a liberator God, the God of the exodus-experience. The biblical view of liberation is integral. It is not divided into an inner, private or religious realm and an outer, public or secular realm. It is from the beginning a personal and social reality which brings the whole common life to a new fruition. Furthermore, there is a recognition that the poor play a pivotal role in God's liberation.

Asian discussion of liberation has emphasized its cultural and religious dimensions. There, biblical liberation is seen as more than a class struggle. It is a religious experience of the poor. To affirm the biblical faith in the liberator God is to affirm a life in solidarity with the poor. But in a context like Asia, where the majority of the poor are not Christians, to make this affirmation is to enter deeply into the religious and cultural (non-Christian) experience of the poor. The conviction gained is that in the third world, where all religions together face the challenges of enslaving social and cultural systems and the

need to struggle for justice, religions should meet each other exploring and sharing their liberative elements. Inter-religious dialogue should be concerned about what each religion can contribute to human liberation.

See also **colonialism, violence and non-violence**.

K.C. ABRAHAM

N.S. Ateek, *Justice and Only Justice: A Palestinian Theology of Liberation*, Maryknoll, NY, Orbis, 1989 • J. Comblin, *The Holy Spirit and Liberation*, London, Burns & Oates, 1989 • M.H. Ellis & O. Maduro eds, *The Future of Liberation Theology: Essays in Honour of Gustavo Gutiérrez*, Maryknoll, NY, Orbis, 1989 • A.T. Hennelly, *Liberation Theology: A Documentary History*, Maryknoll, NY, Orbis, 1990 • J. Pixley & C. Boff, *The Bible, the Church and the Poor: Biblical Theological and Pastoral Aspects of the Option for the Poor*, London, Burns & Oates, 1989 • V. Wan-Tatah, *Emancipation in African Theology: An Inquiry on the Relevance of Latin American Liberation Theology to Africa*, New York, Lang, 1989.

LIBERATION, STRUGGLES FOR.

The moral and social justification of the role played by the church in the liberation struggles of the peoples of the third world cannot be fully understood outside an understanding of the historical background that necessitated those struggles. The WCC correctly identified the imperatives of these struggles by recognizing that colonialism* and foreign domination were inconsistent with the principle of the right of peoples of any country to shape their own independence and to enjoy freedom from colonial domination and exploitation.

With more than half of the people of the world held in bondage by colonial powers, the church had a moral obligation to identify with the oppressed who were fighting for freedom and basic human rights,* including the right to self-determination. Such identification had to take concrete forms. This is the background against which the financial support of the churches through the WCC (see **Programme to Combat Racism**) to humanitarian programmes of some liberation movements, particularly in Southern Africa, should be understood.

The WCC and the churches cannot assume the authority to determine what methods are proper or improper for the liberation struggles of oppressed peoples. The choice of pacifism* over armed struggle, on which the churches have not been able to find consensus, cannot be invoked to denounce the struggles of the peoples. Rather, the question of the forms of the struggle should be left to the struggling peoples themselves. In Zimbabwe the armed struggle was justified by R.G. Mugabe in the statement: "The justice of our causes is our gun." The WCC has, so far, rightly left the matter of determining the morality of these struggles to the oppressed peoples themselves and has limited itself to recognizing their right to independence and offering help for humanitarian purposes.

It is important for the church, at the same time, to distinguish clearly just and legitimate liberation struggles of entire peoples from secessionist struggles or anti-liberation mercenary campaigns sponsored by foreign powers, as in Mozambique in recent times. The church cannot support such illegitimate struggles; indeed, in some instances their objective is the dismemberment of a nation and the subjugation of its peoples by a foreign power.

See also **just war; theology, liberation**.

CANAAN BANANA

LIBERTY/FREEDOM. The tension between freedom and order* at the ethico-social and political and economic levels represents a dialectics that seems intrinsic to human culture* and that finds expression in one's theology of humankind and of the church.* Although the present article is concerned with liberty as related to theological social ethics in the ecumenical movement, such discussion should not be isolated from the wider cultural and theological context.

Use of the notion of liberty/freedom. At the ethico-social level, the tension has been present in the discussion of development,* reform and revolution* as the relative priorities between justice and order, in the economic debates about planned and market economies and in the consideration of the role of the state* in granting security for the whole society and preserving individual rights and liberties. The effort to find a balanced and dynamic relation of these terms is clearly visible in the attempts to delineate a type or vision of society which can become a criterion for judging and a stimulus for pursuing a social order closer to God's design and human fulfilment. From the beginning of the ecumenical movement, the ideal of freedom/liberty played an important role. It is included in the WCC Unit II's mandate "to assist the churches in combatting poverty, injustice and oppression and to facilitate ecumenical cooperation in service to human need and in promoting freedom, justice, peace, human dignity and world community".* However, the concept of liberty/freedom as a basic element of social organization was never systematically analyzed in WCC studies and discussions. This makes it impossible to provide a neat conceptual or philosophical account of the way in which it has been understood in the ecumenical movement.

The reasons for this situation are manifold: in many different contexts and studies it has been used almost rhetorically, as if its meaning were clear and speaks for itself: freedom of the church itself; freedom within the church; freedom as "freedom for" as opposed to "freedom from"; freedom "through" but also "from" technology; freedom from poverty; freedom "from" but also "for" culture; freedom from racism;* freedom from sexism;* freedom from national-security or law-and-order ideologies. Even when it was used in the theme of conferences, meetings or study groups, it was not necessarily reflected in the documents but almost seen as a generally accepted umbrella term.

Several synonymous terms have been and still are used in ecumenical documents on the structuring of society, e.g. self-reliance, affirming the selfhood of people, self-government, self-determination, defending human dignity, participation, people's power, emancipation. The plural "liberties" was part of the human rights studies, which in itself witnessed a shift from an accent on individual rights and liberties to contextual involvement in the struggles for social rights, especially in third-world situations.

As religious liberty,* it has been an important issue since Oxford's report on church and state (1937). As liberation,* it was introduced in the early 1970s to replace the concept of development (see **liberation, struggles for**).

Freedom in ecumenical history. I highlight here some important events, conferences and documents, indicating a few general periods and trends.

The pre-WCC period (1925-48) can be seen

West Bank demonstration on the second anniversary of the Palestinian Intifada (WCC photo)

as a first phase. The accent of ecumenical social thought was on a commitment to social justice* and peace,* conceived mainly in terms of Western perspectives on justice, human dignity and freedoms.

Stockholm (1925) offered an idealistic vision of Christian action in society. The Oxford conference on "Church, Community and State" (1937) then focused more realistically on the ambiguity of all attempts at achieving social justice, emphasizing among other things economic planning and justice in a "free society". It offered four points of criticism of "the economic order in the industrialized world", as well as a brief criticism of "the actual development of communism". Although reflecting the views of its participants, coming mainly from industrialized democracies and presupposing the existence of dominantly capitalistic economies, it did not identify Christianity with capitalism* or any other system.

During a second phase, the Amsterdam period (1948-61), the first WCC formulations of political and economic policy were made. Now the concept of liberty/freedom was used in important definitions, still from the then-prevailing Western, first-world perspective,

within the context of the search for responsible society.*

J.H. Oldham defended the preference for a "free" or "responsible" society, in the world power struggle of the time, by saying that "two things belong inseparably together — liberty and equal justice". The term "responsible society" was preferable to "free society", which was associated with old-fashioned laissez-faire liberalism. In explaining the principles of this vision, Oldham said: "Christians must stand firmly for the freedom of men to obey God and to act in accordance with their conscience. This is the foundation of a responsible society... To obey God men must be free to seek the truth, to speak the truth and to educate one another through a common search for truth. Only through the freedom of its members to expose error, to criticize existing institutions and to express fresh creative ideas can society advance to fresh levels of life... Political freedom (the freedom of a people to control, criticize and change its government) is the foundation and guarantee of all other freedoms. It is not the source of all freedoms... but so far as freedom in an earthly society is involved, no freedoms are in the long run secure without political freedom."

The assembly's report summarized: "For a society to be responsible under modern conditions, it is required that the people have freedom to control, to criticize and to change their governments, that the power be made responsible by law and tradition, and be distributed as widely as possible through the whole community. It is required that economic justice and provision of equality of opportunity be established for all members of society." The perspective was clear: "A responsible society is one where freedom is the freedom of men who acknowledge responsibility to justice and public order."

Already in the first year after the assembly, the commission on Christian action in society made the vital connection between freedom and social justice even clearer: "Freedom lacks substance unless it is combined with economic justice, and... the quest for economic justice leads to new forms of oppression unless it is united with an insistent concern for political and spiritual freedom."

Through the 1950s, this tension remained, while attention was increasingly focused on worldwide movements for political and economic independence and self-determination, especially in areas of rapid social change. This development, together with the rapidly changing constituency of the ecumenical movement itself, made it urgent that the applicability of ecumenical social thought to the new situations be reviewed.

The years 1962-68 can be regarded as a third phase, "a time of review" (Paul Abrecht). The 1966 Geneva world conference on Church and Society represented the focal point of this process. The report on "Towards Justice and Peace in International Affairs" from Uppsala (1968) clearly reflected the new orientation. The central concerns were no longer freedom and order in the framework of a responsible world society but, rather, social justice and human dignity.

The period beginning in 1969 brought a next phase, that of liberation ecumenism, of impatience with the approach to social ethics of the first three periods, of "increasing pressure to make a more absolute and a more definitive commitment to radical political action for justice and freedom" (Abrecht).

Under the growing influence of voices from the third world, the emphasis shifted to issues of justice in society and to participation in struggles for liberation. Instead of abstract ideals of human freedom(s), the diverse, very specific, historical realities of present-day contexts became important, and therefore very concrete demands for freedom arose in the face of the very real absence of specific freedoms, e.g. affirming people's rights against the dominating and oppressive influence of transnational capital, people's dignity against authoritarian and national security systems, self-reliance in the use of raw materials, as well as seeking solutions to structural unemployment and defending social rights to corporate identity, culturally and spiritually. Action, not merely study, became the new initiative.

During the Nairobi assembly, with its theme "Jesus Christ Frees and Unites", many of these emphases came together. Section 5 linked structures of injustice and struggles for liberation. Section 4 discussed education for liberation and community.

In the programme for a Just, Participatory and Sustainable Society* (JPSS), begun in 1977, the accent on participation* represented this insight that the involvement of all constitutes a necessary condition for the full realization of social justice. Participation called for a recognition of everybody's right to be consulted, heard and understood, whatever their political, economic and societal status may be. Justice will be achieved in a society only where people are regarded as subjects able to transform by their own resources their political, social and natural environment and to establish and maintain relationships of equality with one another. Respect for the civil and social rights of all was seen as an essential condition for justice. In this way, JPSS tried to avoid the dilemma often alleged between social equality and human liberties.

Unresolved tensions: freedom and liberation. During these years, however, conflicts between diverse theological and ethical perspectives in ecumenical social thought became more apparent and difficult to resolve. Especially important was the influence of liberation theology,* challenging the Oxford-Amsterdam understanding of social responsibility as favouring the ideology of liberal capitalist democracy, and propagating a liberation socialist perspective to replace the older liberal capitalist approach, thereby also giving radical new content to the ideal of freedom.

Many insiders experienced this period as one of deep divisions and unresolved tensions in ecumenical social thought. Meanwhile, the JPSS programme was replaced by Justice, Peace and the Integrity of Creation.* The matter of participation, however, has remained an enduring issue.

In the Roman Catholic Church, issues of liberation, liberty and freedom have been important over several decades. The social teaching of the church has been reflected in various documents over these years, also showing the developments and ambiguities seen in the ecumenical movement. Well-known documents on the thinking of liberation theology are those of Medellín and Puebla, from Latin America, as well as the critical and controversial instructions "Certain Aspects of the Theology of Liberation" (1984) and "Christian Freedom and Liberation" (1986), from the Sacred Congregation for the Doctrine of the Faith.

Since its inception in 1976, the Ecumenical Association of Third World Theologians* has concentrated on issues of liberation from different forms of oppression. Its regular conferences and publications reflect this emphasis in many ways and in diverse contexts. In its consultation on religion and liberation in New Delhi (1987), it focused on the liberative potential of religions.

See also **order**.

D.J. SMIT

A.J. van der Bent, *Christian Response in a World of Crisis*, WCC, 1986 • *Church and Society: Ecumenical Perspectives. Essays in Honour of Paul Abrecht* (= *The Ecumenical Review*, 37, 1, 1985) • *The Ecumenical Review*, 40, 2 and 3-4, 1988 • J. Míguez Bonino, *Towards Christian Political Ethics*, Philadelphia, Fortress, 1983.

LIFE AND DEATH. Life and death, unlike such controversial issues as the ordination of women and sacramental doctrine, does not appear on the ecumenical agenda as a discrete item seeking resolution. But the subject is so fundamental to the Christian faith and potentially so all-inclusive that virtually every ecumenical discussion bears upon it in some way. The centrality of life and death has been underscored most recently by the theme of the sixth assembly of WCC (Vancouver 1983): "Jesus Christ — the Life of the World" (John

6:51, 10:10). Studies and reports related to this assembly, as well as other documents, suggest four prominent ways in which the subject enters ecumenical discourse.

Creation, fall and redemption: God has created the world, the assembly proclaims, to share in God's own life, in the loving and eternal communion of Father, Son and Holy Spirit (see **Trinity**). "The glory of God is humanity fully alive," wrote Irenaeus. However, humankind's sinful rejection of God's design for life has brought destruction and death (see **sin**).

Eastern and Western Christianity have viewed the human predicament with different emphases. The East alleges that the West so concentrates on sin, atonement and justification* by faith* that the catastrophe and tyranny of death are not sufficiently confronted by Christ's resurrection* and his bestowal of eternal life through the Spirit (see **Holy Spirit**). The West, in turn, has charged the East with minimizing the gravity of human godlessness and sin by focusing, at the expense of the cross, on incarnation,* resurrection and our *theosis*, or "divinization" (human life made God-like in Christ). Ecumenical discussions have rejected any opposition between a "theology of the cross" and a "theology of the resurrection"; it is not an either-or decision. Both theologies are found in each tradition. Redemption* from sin is placed by the East in the primary context of Christ's victory over death. Anselm, who is often blamed for the West's fixation on atonement, speaks also in *Cur Deus Homo?* of our perfect restoration through the resurrection of the dead. Each charge, when pressed too far, is a distortion. However, the tension between the respective emphases of East and West remains to be faced squarely, both as an ecumenical problem and as a potential source of ecumenical growth.

Christ redeems us from both sin and death; he has come to heal the whole of life, as the theme of Vancouver expresses. In the gospels, Jesus forgives sin, feeds the hungry, raises the dead, releases the captives, befriends the outcast and preaches good news to the poor (Luke 4:18; Acts 10:38). He offers the very life of God to a distressed and dying world (John 5:19-36).

Christian discipleship: Christ's ministry to the world continues through his church.* Baptism* means death to the sinful self and new life in Christ (Rom. 6:3-11; cf. Gal. 2:20; Phil. 1:21). Believers are made members of the one Body of Christ (1 Cor. 12:13). Feeding on the risen Christ in the eucharist,* Christians are to give themselves in loving service to the world, just as Christ gave himself, even to the point of death. In Christ, suffering can be redemptive (Phil. 3:10). The martyr's willingness to die for Christ and neighbour testifies that this life is not an absolute good but is oriented towards and fulfilled in God's kingdom* (1 Pet. 4:13; Rev. 2:10). "The recognition of martyrs already transcends confessional boundaries and brings us all back to the centre of the faith, the source of hope, and the example of love for God and fellow human beings" ("Witness unto Death", in *Sharing in One Hope*, WCC, 1978). Yet the memory of those martyred because of confessional disputes convicts the churches of the seriousness of their division (see **martyrdom**).

As reflected in reports to the Vancouver assembly, the most vigorous ecumenical discussions of life and death today are evoked by the need for a common Christian witness against "the politics of death" practised globally — injustice, poverty,* racism,* sexism,* war and the threat of nuclear annihilation. True life is found in Christ, not in military, cultural or economic dominance. However, the assembly warns, this claim for Christ does not justify Christian intolerance and persecution of non-Christians, but it should foster honest dialogue* with other religions and beliefs. Vancouver was also concerned with the questions posed for Christian discipleship by issues such as abortion,* euthanasia* and the humane use of technology.*

Life everlasting: For a variety of theological and cultural reasons, ecumenical discussion in recent decades has focused more on redeeming the present order than on the life to come, though there are exceptions to this trend (see **eschatology**). Both, however, rightfully belong to the fullness of Christian faith sought by the ecumenical movement and cannot be separated (1 Cor. 15:19). Christ's resurrection has broken the barrier of death. He unites all who belong to him — the living and the dead — in the communion of saints* (Rom. 8:28; Col. 1:12). In their

eucharistic celebrations, the Orthodox and the Roman Catholics invoke the saints and pray for the dead. Anglican liturgies vary on these matters. The abusive practice by the medieval Western church of selling indulgences for the dead in purgatory was a focus of Protestant attacks from the beginning of the Reformation. In the 1978 report of the Joint Roman Catholic-Lutheran Commission on "The Eucharist", there was agreement that Christ's gift of himself in the eucharist must be appropriated through active, believing participation and cannot be transferred from one person to another. Yet Christians may hope that the Lord allows them to share in his saving assistance. All intercessions — for the living and the dead, whether from the saints on earth or in heaven — are completely dependent upon the sovereign love of Christ, and none restricts his freedom (similarly, "The Communion of Saints and the Departed", in the 1984 Dublin statement of the Anglican-Orthodox dialogue*). Still, Protestants are constrained from praying for the dead by doctrinal reticence concerning their state and, in keeping

"The Resurrection", by Murillo, in the Prado, Madrid (Religious News Service, New York)

with the Reformation, reject the invocation of the saints as a denial of the sole mediation of Christ (though the Reformation did not deny their heavenly intercession).

In modern times, individual Protestant theologians have expressed openness to belief in purgatory, and some have even sought to extend it beyond its traditional definition in Catholicism (i.e. a purification of those who died *in Christ*) to include a "second chance" of salvation* for those who in this life rejected Christ. These efforts, however, have never been officially accepted by Protestantism. Historically, the churches have all rejected programmatic universalism* — the notion that God must save all — as an infringement upon both divine and human freedom. Yet many Christians, across the entire confessional spectrum, maintain the *hope** of universal salvation and witness accordingly. In their dialogue report "Together in God's Grace" (1987), theologians from the Reformed and Methodist traditions think their historic conflict over predestination should no longer divide them. Their respective emphases — God's sovereignty in election and the freedom of human response, in unresolvable tension with each other — together constitute the fundamental mystery of salvation, which for both traditions depends upon God's grace* at every point.

Ecumenical discourse has typically stressed that God's wrath and judgment cannot be separated from God's saving deed in Christ (2 Cor. 5:10; John 5:22; Rev. 1:17-18). "[The] Judge is indeed our Deliverer, Jesus, who has already shown in his cross and resurrection that what he desires is our life, not our death" (cf. Ezek. 33:11), writes a group of Protestant, Orthodox and Roman Catholic theologians in *The Report of the Third European Ecumenical Encounter* (WCC, 1985). Final judgment, the report continues, belongs not to humanity but to Christ, friend of sinners and partisan for the dispossessed, when he returns in final glory. The consummation of history can thus be anticipated with joy, trust and good works. The meaning of every human life will be disclosed by the Lord (1 Cor. 4:5), though Christians cannot know now what precise form eternal life will take.

Christian unity: "God's purpose", the Vancouver assembly stated, "is to restore all things into unity in Christ" (see Col. 1:17-20). Through the Holy Spirit, God has called and empowered the church to be the divine instrument of healing and reconciliation.* Yet Christians, in their multifarious divisions, evidence and indeed contribute to the fragmentation of the world. The ecumenical movement, at heart, is a witness to the unifying power of Christ against the divisive forces of sin and death, both in the churches and the world.

This basic purpose is sometimes obscured by the complexity of ecumenical discussions, which by necessity range far and wide. But they all have as their ultimate goal a united offering to the world of new life in Christ, through common doctrine, worship and ministry. The world should be able to see in the church a concrete sign of its own unity restored in God. Commitment to the unity* of the church and concern for its redemptive outreach to humanity are thus inseparable; when one weakens, the other falters. For Christians to acquiesce in disunity would be a denial of Christ's power over sin and death and consequently a legitimation, rather than challenge, of creation's brokenness. Christian unity is essential, not secondary, to the gospel message of life and death.

See also **bio-ethics, creation, redemption, resurrection, salvation**.

ROWAN D. CREWS, Jr

I. Bria ed., *Jesus Christ — the Life of the World: An Orthodox Contribution to the Vancouver Theme*, WCC, 1982 • N. Greinacher, "The Experience of Dying", *Concilium*, 94, 1974 • G. Griffin, *Death and the Church*, East Malvern, Dove, 1978 • B. Hebblethwaite, *The Christian Hope*, Grand Rapids, MI, Eerdmans, 1985 • O. Kaiser & E. Lohse, *Death and Life*, Nashville, TN, Abingdon, 1981 • W. Lazareth ed., *The Lord of Life*, WCC, 1983 • K. Rahner, *Zur Theologie des Todes* (ET *On the Theology of Death*, London, Burns & Oates, 1965) • H. Thielicke, *Leben mit dem Tod* (ET *Living with Death*, Grand Rapids, MI, Eerdmans, 1983).

LIFE AND WORK. The idea of forming a worldwide movement of churches to work for peace* and justice* between the nations had been often discussed in Christian peace movements before the first world war, and during the war the need became far more urgent. Many church leaders began to see that conflict as an immense human and social catastrophe which their national churches had done little to prevent and in which they had too readily participated. Though church leaders from neutral countries instigated attempts to stop the fighting, few churches from the warring powers were prepared to cope with the political and moral problems which this same bold stand would have involved.

At the end of the fighting the churches started plans for a conference which would help work for a just and lasting peace and formulate a Christian response to the economic, social and moral issues in the post-war world. In August 1920, some 90 church leaders, representing Protestant churches in 15 countries, met in Geneva to make plans for such a world Christian meeting. The leading figure was Nathan Söderblom, archbishop of the Lutheran Church of Sweden, a churchman with a deep social concern, a passion for Christian unity,* and remarkable talents as an ecclesiastical statesman and diplomat. Söderblom was determined that this world meeting of churches on social issues should support the idea of an eventual ecumenical council of churches. Accordingly all churches, including the Roman Catholic and the Orthodox, were invited to take part. As chairman of the committee on arrangements, Söderblom instilled his ecumenical vision into this pioneer event — the Universal Christian Conference on Life and Work, in Stockholm, August 1925.

The words "life and work" expressed the organizers' determination to set forth "the Christian way of life" as the "the world's greatest need". The aim was "to formulate programmes and devise means... whereby the *fatherhood of God and the brotherhood of all peoples* will become more completely realized through the church of Christ". This idealistic goal was unfortunately not matched by a realistic estimation of the immense and complex problems facing society in the post-war years. Not surprisingly, the results of the Stockholm conference failed to measure up to expectations.

The spiritual strength of Stockholm was in its insight that "the world is too strong for a divided church"; its weakness was its deliberate avoidance of theological issues, justified in the phrase "doctrine divides while service unites". In fact, the conference became deeply divided on how to relate the Christian hope* for the kingdom of God* to the church's responsibility for the world. The result was vague, with too general statements about "applying the gospel in all realms of life".

The harsh realities of increasing world political and economic disorder in the years 1929-33 and the rise of Hitlerism and other totalitarian systems frustrated the optimistic and idealistic hopes of Stockholm and obliged the movement to engage in deeper analysis and study of the world social and spiritual situation.

Fortunately in these years, new developments in theology at this critical juncture gave fresh spiritual vitality to the Life and Work movement: Barthian theology in Europe, dynamic forms of neo-orthodox theology in North America (esp. in the thought of Reinhold Niebuhr), and a revitalized Orthodox theology in the writing of Russians, such as Sergius Bulgakov and Nicolas Berdyaev. As preparations began in 1934 for the second Life and Work conference (Oxford 1937), new leaders for Life and Work were determined to find more solid theological-ethical foundations for this work. Prominent among these were two English churchmen: William Temple, then the archbishop of York, and J.H. Oldham, secretary of the International Missionary Council. In a determined attack on the theological-ethical problem, seven major theological-ethical studies were published on the themes: *The Christian Understanding of Man; The Kingdom of God and History; The Christian Faith and the Common Life; Church and Community; Church, Community and State in Relation to Education; The Universal Church and the World of Nations;* and *The Church and Its Function in Society.* These volumes were pioneering theological statements, on the basis of which the Life and Work movement reformulated its view of the role of the church in society.

The central theme of the new theological-ethical approach is summed up in a line from Niebuhr in one of these volumes: "It is a dangerous theology... which does not recognize how dialectically the kingdom of God is related to the sinful world in every moment of existence, offering both judgment and a more excellent way in considering every problem of justice."

This preparatory study for the Oxford conference was a remarkable ecumenical and intellectual achievement for the Life and Work movement. It involved contributions of several hundred foremost theological and lay thinkers of that period, and of representatives of all the major denominational and confessional communities. It established Life and Work as a movement which could truly help the churches and the secular world in addressing political and social problems. The conference report on its central theme, *Church, Community and State*, thus represents the first theologically formulated statement on the Christian task in the modern world. Its influence on Protestant and Orthodox thought may be compared with such historic Roman Catholic social encyclicals* as Pope Leo XIII's *Rerum Novarum* (1891) and Pius XI's *Quadragesimo Anno* (1931).

The rapid progress of Life and Work in 1934-37 enabled it to become the dynamic element in the formation of the WCC ("in process of formation") in 1938. In his memoirs, W.A. Visser 't Hooft makes clear that in the merger of the two movements to form the WCC, Faith and Order* was a hesitant and uncertain partner; Life and Work was the motor of advance, seeing in the dangerous and tumultuous social situation of the world the compelling reason for moving decisively towards a dynamic and informed ecumenical council of churches. Only in this way could the churches be helped to do everything within their power to bring the spirit of the living God to a world in great spiritual and social turmoil. And by its emphasis on the contribution of the laity, the Life and Work movement vastly enlarged the field of ecumenical support and endeavour, reaching into the world of the university, government and social life for new talent and new fields of ecumenical advance. In this sense it is fair to say that Life and Work carried the ecumenical movement far beyond the confines which Faith and Order or the International Missionary Council* had set.

From this pioneering movement flows the contemporary ecumenical concern with such issues as international relations, racism,* economic justice* and order,* democracy, human rights,* and religious liberty.*

See also **church and world**.

PAUL ABRECHT

J. Bennett, "Breakthrough in Ecumenical Social Ethics", *The Ecumenical Review*, 40, 2, 1988 • N. Karlström & N. Ehrenström, "Movements for International Friendship and Life and Work: 1910-1925, and 1925-1948", in *A History of the Ecumenical Movement, 1517-1948*, R. Rouse & S. Neill eds, WCC, 1986 • J.H. Oldham & W.A. Visser 't Hooft eds, *The Churches Survey Their Task: The Report of the Conference at Oxford, July 1937, on Church, Community and State*, London, Allen & Unwin, 1937 • B. Sundkler, *Nathan Söderblom, His Life and Work*, Lund, Gleerups, 1968 • W.A. Visser 't Hooft, *The Genesis and Formation of the World Council of Churches*, WCC, 1982 • W.A. Visser 't Hooft, *Memoirs*, London, SCM, 1973.

LIFE-STYLE. A British Council of Churches conference in Birmingham in September 1972 urged Christians "to pledge themselves to a simplicity of life which is generous to others and content with enough rather than excess". About a dozen participants did so pledge, and the Life-Style movement was born. A written commitment was formulated, revised several times since, which about a thousand people have now signed. This "Commitment to Personal Change" contains the following statement: "The Life-Style movement offers a voluntary common discipline to those who are committed to a more equitable distribution of the earth's resources and to the conservation and development of those resources for our own and future generations."

The commitment embodies six points: "live simply that all may simply live; give freely that all may be free to give; avoid wasteful use of resources and show care for the environment; work with others for social justice through appropriate action; enjoy such good things as are compatible with this commitment; share my commitment with others".

Thus the movement seeks to hold together issues of justice* and peace,* of human development and ecological conservation, of political action and personal moderation, of enjoyment of God's gifts and a measure of self-denial. Although its origins are Christian and a survey has shown that some 80% of members profess the Christian faith, the movement is open to people of all faiths or none. To facilitate this openness, care has been taken to exclude from the commitment any reference to religion.

Most members live in the United Kingdom. But they form part of a worldwide trend of some complexity. As long ago as 1978 the

Los Angeles Times reported that "an estimated 45 million Americans are living lives fully committed to the concept of voluntary simplicity, while perhaps twice that many are partial adherents". In Scandinavia Erik Dammann and others founded "The Future in Our Hands" in 1974 with aims very similar to those of the Life-Style movement. This has attracted far more support than Life-Style.

Ecumenical discussion. Global ecumenical reflection on life-style has been rather general, for reasons already apparent in the WCC's first and only major treatment of the subject — at the fourth assembly (Uppsala 1968).

The section "Towards New Styles of Living" declared that "Christian life requires a willingness to be changed and to change the world... Even though we are unable to establish any perfect order for human life in this world, we are convinced that things can be bettered while we wait for the renewal of all things which God himself will accomplish." However, "there is no single style of Christian life"; and the Uppsala report, which limits itself to "proposing some contours of Christian styles of living", also makes apparent several obstacles to going beyond generalities in the global ecumenical discussion.

As political, social, economic and cultural contexts differ from place to place, so do questions of life-style for Christians. Moreover, discussion of life-style invariably elicits tensions between those who emphasize the need to be disciplined by "human rules" and those who emphasize the need to be able to discern through the Spirit the "signs of the times". The report insists that "the problem of rules and of personal responsibility in each situation can only be solved within the framework of community", suggesting that "the moral conduct of each person can benefit from mutual advice and criticism". Churches, too, can learn from one another.

More controversial was Uppsala's acknowledgment that "middle-class people" dominate global church assemblies. What such bodies say about life-style is thus likely to reflect a preference for gradual reform of the existing order and to stress the importance of human relations, family life, material success, efficiency and "interiorized moral standards".

In the late 1970s, an "action/reflection" process on "new life-styles" within the WCC's Commission on the Churches' Participation in Development was rooted in growing concern about the quality of life in view of the ecological crisis and about the perceived discrepancy between the life-style of many churches and the gospel message of "judgment to the rich and hope to the poor".

Several reports adopted by the WCC's sixth assembly (Vancouver 1983) mentioned life-style without elaborating on it. One said that "a more simple life-style and even a life of poverty is laid on the church and Christians as a witness to the poverty of Christ", but added the same qualification made in Uppsala: "Christians and churches, of course, find themselves in very different circumstances." Another report acknowledged that "we have much to learn from one another's spirituality, in prayer, life-style, suffering and struggle".

See also **renewal**.

HORACE DAMMERS
and MARLIN VANELDEREN

A.H. Dammers, *A Christian Life Style*, London, Hodder & Stoughton, 1986 • A.H. Dammers, *Life Style: Parable of Sharing*, London, Turnstone, 1982 • H. Fey, *Life: New Style*, Cincinnati, OH, Forward Movement, 1968 • R. Sider, *Rich Christians in an Age of Hunger*, Downers Grove, IL, InterVarsity, 1977 • J.V. Taylor, *Enough Is Enough*, London, SCM, 1975.

LILJE, HANNS. B. 20.8.1899, Hanover, Germany; d. 6.1.1977, Hanover. One of the pioneers of the ecumenical movement, who helped pave the way for reconciliation between the churches of Germany and those of other countries, Lilje was general secretary of the German Student Christian Movement, 1924-34, and involved in the German church struggle from 1933 onwards. Bishop of the Evangelical Lutheran Church in Hanover from 1947 until his retirement in 1971, he was presiding bishop of the United Evangelical Lutheran Church in Germany, 1955-69, president of the Lutheran World Federation, 1952-57, member of its executive committee, 1947-70, and a president of the WCC, 1968-75. Under the title of Johannes XI, he was the lifetime abbot of the monastery of Loccum near Hanover. Condemned by a people's court in 1944 for preaching "inner resistance" and related to the group which attempted to assassinate Hitler, Lilje was liberated from a prison in Nuremberg by the Allied army. His works include *The Last Book of the Bible* (Philadelphia, Muhlenberg, 1957) and *Memorabilia* (Stein, Laetare, 1973).

ANS J. VAN DER BENT

LIMA LITURGY. The eucharistic liturgy which has come to be known as the Lima liturgy was drawn up by Max Thurian in preparation for the plenary session of the Faith and Order* commission held in Lima in 1982. At the session itself, the text of the liturgy was slightly revised and then used for the first time on 15 January 1982. The presiding celebrant was Robert Wright, an Episcopalian priest. The Orthodox and Roman Catholic members of the commission participated in the service but did not receive communion. The liturgy was used again (with Philip Potter presiding) in Geneva during the meeting of the central committee of the WCC in July 1982. A year later, the celebration of the Lima liturgy was one of the high points of the sixth assembly of the WCC in Vancouver. Robert Runcie, the archbishop of Canterbury, was the presiding celebrant.

The ensuing (and largely unexpected) wide-ranging use of the Lima liturgy is due in part to its having been celebrated at these important points within the most recent life of the ecumenical movement. The reception is also due to this liturgy's being an expression of the convergence reached in *Baptism, Eucharist and Ministry** (BEM) and becoming part of the reception* of this document as a whole — although it has none of its authority.

The Lima liturgy is one possible expression of the eucharistic theology embodied in BEM and, in particular, of a eucharistic liturgy based on the elements outlined in E27. Overall, the Lima liturgy follows a Western pattern of eucharistic celebration, although important inspirations from the Eastern tradition should not be overlooked.

The liturgy of entrance consists of an entrance psalm, a greeting (2 Cor. 13:13), a confession and absolution (taken from the Lutheran Book of Worship, USA, 1978), a Kyrie litany (in analogy of the Byzantine liturgy, but taking up the themes of baptism, eucharist and ministry) and the gloria. The liturgy of the word begins with an opening prayer and makes provision for three scripture readings. These

are followed by a sermon and a time of silent meditation. The confession of the Nicene Creed* uses the text of 381. Intercessions follow, modelled on early Roman usage. The liturgy of the eucharist opens with preparatory prayers (two *berakoth* from the Jewish liturgy and a prayer inspired by the *Didache*). The eucharistic prayer has a fixed preface, followed — after the sanctus — by a first epiclesis, to which there is a congregational response (as is the case at other points in the eucharistic prayer); the institution narrative, the anamnesis and a second epiclesis follow; before the Trinitarian conclusion there is a set of commemorations. The Lord's prayer, the peace, the breaking of the bread and the Agnus Dei immediately precede communion. The liturgy ends with a thanksgiving prayer, a final hymn and a sending with blessing.

The liturgical reception of this rather full liturgy has hardly ever left its texts and structure unchanged but adapted them to a great variety of different situations. This is to be expected, since the Lima liturgy provides only a text (not even rubrics are given) and as such is only the manuscript guiding a specific eucharistic celebration of a specific community of faith.

In the (both critical and enthusiastic) reception of the Lima liturgy, one thing has become clear: there is an obvious desire among the people of God* to see emerging doctrinal convergences become embodied and rooted in the liturgical life of the church. The final locus for doctrinal convergence is not the discussion table but the table of the word and the table of the bread and wine. The Lima liturgy has drawn ecumenical attention to this fact.

See also *Baptism, Eucharist and Ministry*; **worship in the ecumenical movement**.

TERESA BERGER

"The Eucharistic Liturgy of Lima", in *Baptism and Eucharist: Ecumenical Convergence in Celebration*, M. Thurian & G. Wainwright eds, WCC, 1983 • F. Schulz, "Zur Rezeption der Lima-Liturgie", *Studia Liturgica*, 17, 1987.

LITURGICAL MOVEMENT. The term "liturgical movement" denotes the phenomenon of recovering the centrality of worship in the life of the 20th-century church. This movement had antecedents in attempts at liturgical reform and renewal during the Enlightenment and, particularly, in the 19th century. To name but two: the Anglo-Catholic revival brought a renewed interest in liturgical sources as well as liturgical theology and led to a renewal of liturgical life in many Anglo-Catholic communities. Within the Roman Catholic Church (RCC), Prosper Guéranger (1805-75) over-shadows other forerunners of the liturgical movement in the 19th century (such as the Benedictines at the abbeys of Beuron in Bavaria and Maredsous in Belgium). Guéranger, himself a Benedictine, in 1832 re-founded the abbey of Solesmes in France, which quickly became an advocate for the liturgical tradition of the Roman church and in particular for its Gregorian chant.

In the 20th century, the liturgical movement first gained momentum in the RCC. Although this movement can be seen as consisting of different strands of interdependent "liturgical movements", its beginnings are traditionally dated to one event: the address of Lambert Beauduin (1873-1960) at the pastoral congress at Malines, Belgium, in 1909. Beauduin, a Benedictine monk (who in 1925 founded a monastery particularly dedicated to Christian unity, now Chevetogne*), gave the nascent liturgical movement its pastoral orientation. This orientation was shared by a number of other developing centres of the liturgical movement, such as Klosterneuburg in Austria, where Pius Parsch (1884-1954), an Augustinian canon, developed a strong biblical perspective for the liturgical renewal. A pastoral orientation also lay at the heart of the beginning liturgical movement in the USA, where the Benedictine Virgil Michel (1890-1938) of St John's Abbey, Collegeville, in 1926 began to publish a journal with the title *Orate Fratres* (now *Worship*). In France, the Centre de pastorale liturgique was established in 1941 and soon began issuing its journal, *La Maison-Dieu*.

Other emphases were championed by other centres of the liturgical movement. The German Benedictine abbey of Maria Laach, particularly through Ildefons Herwegen (1874-1946) and Odo Casel (1886-1948), gave to the movement a solid foundation of historical and theological research and reflection (see its series *Ecclesia Orans* and its journal *Jahrbuch der Liturgiewissenschaft*). A strong historical

and pastoral orientation also characterized the work of the Austrian Jesuit Joseph Andreas Jungmann (1889-1975). Romano Guardini (1885-1968) worked particularly with groups of intellectuals and with the youth movement. The concerns of the liturgical movement also fell on fruitful ground in many non-Western countries, where the churches had long suffered under the alienation between traditional Roman liturgical life and the worshipping community.

After a time of heightened tensions, Rome gave its stamp of approval to the liturgical movement with Pius XII's encyclical *Mediator Dei* in 1947, although the dawn of official support for the renewal of liturgical life can already be seen in Pius X's motu proprio *Tra le Sollecitudini* of 1903, which introduces "active participation", one of the key themes of the liturgical movement. Liturgical congresses, journals and centres now flourished and opened the way for systematic liturgical reform.

The different strands of liturgical renewal within the RCC find their ecumenically significant parallels within communities of faith stemming from the Reformation. The Lutheran church in Germany, for example, saw a high-church movement form in the 20th century with a keen interest in liturgical life. The Alpirsbacher circle, the Berneuchener circle and the Michaelsbruderschaft re-discovered Gregorian chant and the liturgy of the hours and nourished a revival of eucharistic celebrations and of private confession. The Reformed churches also had their liturgical pioneers both in theology and praxis in the last and in this century: Eugène Bersier, Wilfred Monod and then the Taizé* community in France, Richard Paquier and Jean-Jacques von Allmen in Switzerland, the Mercersburg movement in the US, William D. Maxwell and the Iona community in Scotland. The Anglican communion contributed fine historical scholars to the nascent liturgical movement, among them Walter Howard Frere (1863-1938), who was also involved in the beginning of the ecumenical movement, and Gregory Dix (1901-52). The beginnings of the liturgical movement within the Church of England, however, are often dated more specifically by reference to a book by Gabriel Hebert, *Liturgy and Society*, which was published in 1935. The Methodist churches saw a number of liturgical societies grow up in their midst, such as the Methodist Sacramental Fellowship in Britain and the Order of St Luke in the USA.

It is usually maintained that the Orthodox churches have not known a liturgical movement in the 20th century, since they have not seen the same fundamental liturgical reforms which other churches have witnessed. However, there has certainly been a renewal of liturgical theology (Nikolai Afanas'ev, Alexander Schmemann and others) as well as small steps at liturgical reform which parallel the reforms the liturgical movement initiated in other churches. In some Orthodox churches this century has seen a move to an audible recitation of the eucharistic prayer and a move away from "private baptisms".

The liturgical renewal sweeping through the churches in the 20th century obviously had a strong ecumenical impetus. Liturgical conferences, for example, were soon attended by liturgists from different ecclesial traditions. This implicit ecumenical impetus became an explicit ecumenical programme with the formation of Societas Liturgica, an ecumenical society for the study and renewal of the liturgy. Founded in 1965 by the Netherlands Reformed pastor Wiebe Vos, Societas Liturgica now has over 300 members from all over the world and every major ecclesial communion. The number of members from the so-called two-thirds world and women — not particularly visible in the traditional liturgical movement — is steadily increasing.

One can ask whether the liturgical movement as a historical phenomenon has come to an end with, say, its fruition in the Vatican II Constitution on the Sacred Liturgy (1963) and the ensuing liturgical reforms in the churches. Wherever one decides to place the end of the historical phenomenon known as the liturgical movement, its primary concern — the recovery of the centrality of the worshipping community — is and will remain a central task of the church of every age and place.

See also **Lima liturgy; liturgical reforms; liturgical texts, common; liturgy; worship in the ecumenical movement**.

TERESA BERGER

B. Botte, *Le mouvement liturgique: Témoignage et souvenir*, Paris, Desclée, 1973 • J. Hall, "The American Liturgical Movement: The Early Years", *Worship*, 50, 1976 • A. Haquin, *Dom Lambert Beauduin et le renouveau liturgique*, Gembloux, Duculot, 1970 • J. Hofinger ed., *Liturgy and the Missions: The Nijmegen Papers*, New York, Kennedy, 1960 • T. Maas-Ewerd, *Die Krise der liturgischen Bewegung in Deutschland und Österreich: Zu den Auseinandersetzungen um die "liturgische Frage" in den Jahren 1939 bis 1944*, Regensburg, Pustet, 1981 • R.K. Seasoltz, *The New Liturgy: A Documentation, 1903-1965*, New York, Herder, 1966 • M.J. Taylor ed., *Liturgical Renewal in the Christian Churches*, Baltimore, Helicon, 1967.

LITURGICAL REFORMS. The liturgical reforms which have in varying degrees changed the face of worship in Western Christian churches in recent decades are the fruit of the liturgical movement,* which may be described as one of the great spiritual movements of church history. (The Byzantine East knows no liturgical movement, and only occasional, timid attempts at liturgical reform have been made there.)

Following a predominantly cerebral era in which worship tended to be seen as a marginal aspect of Christian life, members of Western Christian churches began to recover the central importance of the liturgical celebration of the faith* and to initiate reforms to purge it of accretions from various sources. Decisively, an intense new interest in liturgical history focused greater attention on the original intention of the liturgy — on what Vatican II* in its Constitution on the Sacred Liturgy (*Sacrosanctum Concilium*, 1963, hereafter *SC*) called the *norma Patrum* (*SC* 50). This made it easier to differentiate between organic development and accretions distorting the basic norm. For the churches of the Reformation there was the added bonus that research revealed the liturgical intentions of the Reformation's own "fathers".

In the Roman Catholic Church, the liturgical movement, building on tentative efforts during the Enlightenment, arose anew in Belgium in 1909 and spread rapidly to France and Germany. One of its basic insights, and thus a basic impetus to reform, was the re-discovery of the active role in worship of the (hierarchically led) congregation of the faithful. The assembled holy people of God*, led by the presiding priest (see **priesthood**), was seen as the subject of the liturgical and especially the eucharistic celebration (see **eucharist**), contrary to the widely held idea that the priest alone was subject and the faithful "assisted" in his sacred action. On the whole, the reforming aims resulting from this insight, i.e. towards a "democratization" of the RC liturgy (thus Lambert Beauduin, who inaugurated the movement in Belgium) — including the use of the vernacular, tentative at first but then increasingly and eventually universally permitted, even if never with a deliberate exclusiveness — were achieved to a surprisingly generous degree in *SC* and in the revised liturgical books which the "Consilium", the group mandated to implement the constitution, prepared between 1965 and 1970.

These post-conciliar liturgical texts ensured that believers were no longer the "silent spectators" that Pius XI complained (1928) they had become, but once again "fellow actors", responsibly resuming the role originally intended for them in the mass. They are at last seen once again as co-offerers of the sacred gifts on the altar in the mass (*SC* 48). Again they utter the acclamations which in the course of the centuries had come to be assigned to the servers at the altar, i.e. the responses of the people to the celebrant's invitations. Once again, too, they join in the recitation of the Lord's prayer and (where the proposal for its introduction is accepted) in the greeting of peace. In the eucharistic communion, in accordance with ancient church custom, each communicant answers the words of administration with an "Amen!" Here, too, the Council (*SC* 55) pushed open a little the long-closed door excluding the laity from the chalice, and this door has since been opened wide. The turning of the eucharistic celebrant to face the people, recommended and soon generally practised even if never officially prescribed, did more than any other measure of reform to cut the ground from beneath the idea of the mass as an act of the priest at which the faithful piously assisted.

In the daily office, so long mistakenly regarded as a clerical prerogative ("breviary"), the faithful recognize again their ancient rights in a realm of prayer which from time immemorial had been intended and fashioned as a "prayer of the church". In the celebration of the sacraments* they again join with their acclamations in the invocation of the Spirit on the elements and the congregation. The participation of the catechists and sponsors in the rite of admission into church membership (which once again takes place via the three initiatory sacraments of baptism*, confirmation* and eucharist) has recovered its ancient status — wherever the new Order for the Christian Initiation of Adults (1972) is given its chance. That has happened to a very large extent in the USA (in contrast to the German-speaking countries), where, faithful to the intention of this rite, the learning process under the guidance of the clergy has become the lifelong process of growing into the church* (a process of which the indispensable element of "learning" is an organic part).

An outstanding feature of the RC liturgical reform and its popular democratic thrust is the clean break with the anti-Reformation devaluation of the role of the word of God* in RC worship. Of decisive importance here is the statement of the liturgy constitution (*SC* 7) that Christ is also present when the holy scriptures are read in church; and this truth may be extended to the preached word of God in the sermon. Along the same line, the Council directed that sermons should, contrary to previous custom, be preached *ex textu sacro* (*SC* 52) — a measure which has produced lasting changes in post-conciliar RC worship. Finally, the Council spoke of "opening up the treasures of the Bible more lavishly" (*SC* 51) by the transition from a one-year cycle of biblical passages to a three-year cycle for Sundays and feast days, together with a two-year cycle for working days.

While the calendrical reforms cannot be listed here in detail, mention should be made of the radical reform of the paschal vigil (now restored to the night between Holy Saturday and Easter Day), a reform already completed in the decade prior to the opening of the Council (see **Easter, resurrection**).

Further sacramental reforms in the RCC include the return to the original idea of the anointing of the sick* as a sacrament for the seriously ill (not just for the dying) and the decision in the case of infant baptism to take seriously the condition of infancy (parents and sponsors confess their own faith, not that of the child).

The 20th century has also witnessed liturgical reform in the Western churches of the Reformation tradition. Its basis was a similar reconsideration of the importance of worship, but the Protestant churches also noticed the astonishing reform occurring in their once so traditionalistic Roman Catholic sister church, and they were able to appreciate this change all the more in the light of the new ecumenical climate which increasingly prevailed after the Council.

The thrust here could not be (and did not need to be) democratization or the upgrading of the word of God. In the heat of the Reformation controversy, the sometimes exaggerated emphasis placed on the preached and expounded word of God had in places led to a corresponding devaluation of the sacramental dimension, particularly in the Sunday service. Most Protestant churches had also displaced the words of institution from their context in a eucharistic prayer in the style of the *berakah* (as must certainly be presupposed for the Last Supper of Jesus). Contrary to the intentions of most of the reformers, the Lord's supper had largely become an appendix to the Sunday act of worship and was only infrequently celebrated. How anomalous this situation was became clear in the light of the new reflection on the liturgy and prompted liturgical leaders in the Protestant churches to seek a remedy.

The appearance of the first volume of the new service book (Agende I) for the Lutheran churches and congregations of Germany in 1955 was a landmark in the history of the recovery of the eucharistic prayer and the regular (i.e. weekly) celebration of the Lord's supper. This included for the first time, alongside Form A of the Lord's supper, which followed the sequence in Luther's German mass of the Lord's prayer, words of institution (consecration), and distribution, an optional Form B with a broad-ranging eucharistic prayer with an anamnesis and epiclesis such as had been part of the Sunday eucharistic celebration since the beginning of the 3rd century. Alfred Niebergall calls this "a *novum* in the history of recent Protestant service books". It is only an option, to be sure, and even as such still had to clear the hurdle of a regional church decision in each case, which it failed to do in some instances. This modest step in the direction of liturgical reform was nevertheless something of a breakthrough. Niebergall's reference to "increasing agreement and general diffusion" has been con-

Members of the congregation bring forward the elements for the eucharist, Tami inad Theological College, Madurai, India (CMS, London)

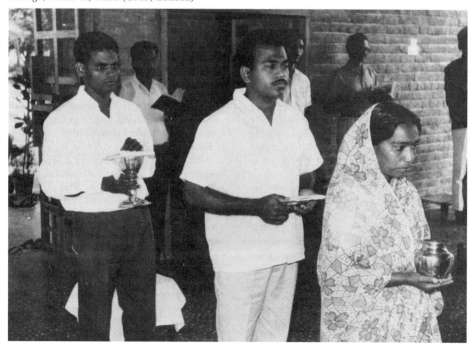

firmed to an astonishing degree in the subsequent decades. One has only to think of the Lima liturgy* of 1982 or of the revised service book (Erneuerte Agende, 1990) of the Lutheran, Reformed and United Churches of both West and East Germany intended as a continuation of the book of 1955. Equally if not more important was the decision made in Agende I, ten years before the Second Vatican Council, to "combine the celebration of the Lord's supper with the preaching service to constitute the evangelical mass".

A similar development took place in the Anglican communion,* here too in the shape of an option. Since 1928, the revised English Book of Common Prayer in its service of holy communion has offered a richer alternative order including an epiclesis. Since 1980 the Book of Common Prayer has had alongside it an official Alternative Service Book in which, as well as a prayer like that of the Lord's supper of 1662, six alternative forms of a full eucharistic prayer are available.

Characteristic of the recent trend in the North American churches in the Reformation tradition is the production by an ecumenical commission of a eucharistic prayer closely related to the fourth eucharistic prayer of the revised Roman missal. This prayer has found its way into the Book of Common Prayer (1979) of Episcopalians in the USA as Form D and into the order of worship (Word-Bread-Cup) of the Consultation on Church Union* as Form III. The re-discovery of the great eucharistic prayer in the churches of the Reformation (which does not necessarily always mean its re-introduction) is therefore not limited to the European scene but is a reality too on the North American continent. (There, as in Britain, the liturgy of the Church of South India of 1963 helped to ease the way.)

This increasingly worldwide trend became spectacularly clear in the Lima liturgy, a classic formulation of the eucharistic prayer including anamnesis and two epicleses (before and after the words of institution), which was produced at the WCC's Faith and Order meeting in Lima, Peru, in 1982. It was intended not as a standard form for the future, to replace the existing liturgies, but as a model. It is highly significant that, whenever it has been used at transconfessional church conferences — in Lima (15 January 1982), Geneva (27 July 1982) and, above all, Vancouver

(31 July 1983) — it has met with an enthusiastic reception on the part of those participating, in spite of all individual reservations; even Catholic and Orthodox delegates who were unable to receive communion accepted roles in the liturgy of the word. For the churches deriving from the Reformation, we have evidence here of a clearly irreversible reform movement in the celebration of the Lord's supper.

Analogously to the RC development, the reforms in the Reformation churches also extend well beyond the central area of the celebration of the Lord's supper, or eucharist. They can only be hinted at here. The order of infant baptism (where it is practised) and the admission of adults to church membership have everywhere been revised. Interestingly enough, in the reform of infant baptism a "countermove" to the corresponding RC reform is observable. While the latter, for the first time in the history of infant baptism, produced an order tailored to the *conditio infantis*, in both the Book of Common Prayer of the American Episcopalians and other Protestant service books, the baptismal order is made the same for infants and adults.

Another universal feature is the reform of the lectionaries: in a number of places in world Protestantism (but not in Germany) the three-year cycle of the post-conciliar RC lectionary has been adopted. Movement is also observable in the re-introduction recently of an optional anointing of the sick (though not as a sacrament) in the North Elbian church, in Germany; the admission of unconfirmed children (sometimes even infants) to the Lord's supper; and a partial return to the use of liturgical vestments where this had fallen out of use.

An era of liturgical reforms — which our century has certainly been for Christian churches across the board — is the appropriate matrix for what has recently come to be called inculturation.* There is a growing realization everywhere that no one should be made to celebrate the liturgy in forms which contradict one's traditional cultural inheritance. The example set in this area at the Second Vatican Council by the RCC, which has always had a reputation for immobility, will in the long run prove fruitful (*SC* 39-40). A quarter of a century after the appearance of the Constitution on the Sacred Liturgy, we find the initial results of an inculturated celebration of the mass in the Zairian mass, to which Rome agreed on 30 April 1988. This mass includes an invocation of the ancestors, a dance around the altar during the gloria, rhythmic movements on the part of the faithful and the use of drums (Evenou). Earlier, an experimental order of mass for India, prepared by the National Biblical, Catechetical and Liturgical Centre at Bangalore and containing much language from the ancient Indian scriptures, had been vetoed by the Vatican.

See also **Lima liturgy, liturgical movement, liturgy, worship in the ecumenical movement**.

BALTHASAR FISCHER

A. Bugnini, *La riforma liturgica (1948-1975)* (ET *The Reform of the Liturgy [1948-1975]*, Collegeville, MN, Liturgical Press, 1990) • A.J. Chupungco, *Liturgies of the Future: The Process and Methods of Inculturation*, Mahwah, NJ, Paulist, 1989 • J. Evenou, "Le missel romain pour les diocèses de Zaïre", *Notitiae*, 264, 1988 • A. Häussling, "Liturgiereform. Materialen zu einem neuen Thema der Liturgiewissenschaft", *Archiv für Liturgiewissenschaft*, 31, 1989 • International Commission on English in the Liturgy, *Documents on the Liturgy, 1963-1979: Conciliar, Papal, and Curial Texts*, Collegeville, MN, Liturgical Press, 1982 • C. Jones, G. Wainwright & E. Yarnold, *The Study of Liturgy*, London, SPCK, rev. ed. 1991 • F.C. Senn ed., *New Eucharistic Prayers: An Ecumenical Study of Their Development and Structure*, Mahwah, NJ, Paulist, 1987 • M. Thurian & G. Wainwright, *Baptism and Eucharist: Ecumenical Convergence in Celebration*, WCC, 1983 • J.-M.R. Tillard, "Liturgical Reform and Christian Unity", *One in Christ*, 19, 1983 • G. Wainwright, "Divided by a Common Language? A Comparison and Contrast of Recent Liturgical Revision in the United Kingdom, the USA and Australia", *Studia Liturgica*, 17, 1987.

LITURGICAL TEXTS, COMMON.
The Second Vatican Council* of the Roman Catholic Church, with its Constitution on the Sacred Liturgy (1963), stimulated an extraordinary reform and renewal of liturgical orders and texts throughout the churches of the Western rites, Catholic and Protestant. Liturgical movements in many of these churches going back a full century had helped prepare for this dramatic development (see **liturgical movement**). Ecumenical contacts, especially in the English-speaking world, facilitated widespread co-operation during and following the

Council. Beginning in 1964, an informal sequence of annual meetings of Protestant and Catholic liturgists in the US took place which resulted in the formation of the (North American) Consultation on Common Texts (CCT). At the same time Roman Catholic bishops in English-speaking lands formed the International Commission on English in the Liturgy (ICEL), with a secretariat in Washington, DC.

The ICEL set about preparing English translations of the new liturgical books of the Roman rite, beginning with the Roman missal in 1969 and finishing with the rite for funerals in 1989. The CCT took upon itself the task of producing English translations of certain important liturgical texts which could be used by a wide variety of churches, such as the Lord's prayer, the Apostles' and Nicene creeds, the ordinary of mass, and office canticles. This effort resulted in the formation of an international ecumenical body corresponding to ICEL known as the International Consultation on English Texts (ICET). Its revision of these texts was published as *Prayers We Have in Common* (1970, 1971 and 1975). During the same decade quite a number of Protestant and Anglican churches produced new service books incorporating these texts as part of rites in modern English.

In addition to this remarkable accommodation in the matter of texts, many of these books included, with some editing, the table of scripture readings for the Sunday mass of the Roman rite, *Ordo Lectionum Missae* (1969). In the US, the Consultation on Church Union* produced in 1974 a consensus version of these denominational adaptations of the Roman *Ordo*. And in 1978 the CCT convened a consultation in Washington, DC, to survey the ecumenical use and acceptability of these adaptations. As a result of this meeting there was formed the North American Committee on Calendar and Lectionary, whose task was to prepare a harmonization of these versions of the Roman lectionary table for submission to churches which were using it in one way or another. This was done in 1983 as *Common Lectionary: The Lectionary Proposed by the Consultation on Common Texts*.

This proposal differs from the Roman table only in that for the Sundays after Pentecost ("Ordinary Time") the Hebrew scriptures lection is no longer chosen for its "typological" relation to the gospel for the day but on the basis of a broader typology wherein for year A, the year of Matthew, the patriarchal and Mosaic narratives are read on a semi-continuous basis; for year B, the year of Mark, the Davidic narrative is read semi-continuously; and for year C, the year of Luke, the Elijah-Elisha narrative is read, together with selections from the minor prophets.

Common Lectionary is finding wide acceptance throughout Protestant and Anglican churches in North America, Australia, New Zealand and South Africa. It has yet to be used in Great Britain due to the ecumenical use there by non-Roman churches of a two-year lectionary system, thematically designed, devised by the Joint Liturgical Group (JLG) and first published in 1967. This system also recasts the traditional annual calendar on a Trinitarian basis, reminiscent of the Peterhead lectionary proposed by A.A. McArthur of the Church of Scotland.

These lectionary developments, as well as some dissatisfaction with some of the ICET texts, brought forth a successor body to ICET known as the English Language Liturgical Consultation, which has met biennially in Boston (1985), Brixen, Italy (1987), and York, England (1989). It is publishing a revision of *Prayers We Have in Common* (ICET, 1975) as *Praying Together* (1989), participating in CCT's evaluation of *Common Lectionary* and encouraging the production of further texts and orders. Its constituent members are CCT, ICEL, JLG, the Australian Consultation on Liturgy, the Joint Liturgical Consultation within New Zealand and the Canadian Churches Co-ordinating Group on Worship.

Such impressive convergences in textual and scriptural use are probably furthest advanced in the English-speaking world. But besides a common Lord's prayer in German, the Arbeitsgemeinschaft für liturgische Texte produced texts of the Apostles' and Nicene creeds, the Gloria in Excelsis, the Sanctus, the Agnus Dei, and the Gloria Patri, which were accepted by both Catholic and Protestant churches; the Arbeitsgemeinschaft für ökumenisches Liedgut produced common versions of over 100 hymns; and there are orders for "ecumenical weddings". The German Bible exists in an "Einheitsübersetzung"; but as yet the German-speaking churches are not agreed on a common lectionary or choice of texts.

The French speakers have a common Lord's prayer and the "Traduction oecuménique de la Bible", as well as a common liturgical psalter (see *La Maison-Dieu* no. 105, 1971, pp.46-65).

HORACE T. ALLEN, Jr

Consultation on Common Texts, *Common Lectionary: The Lectionary Proposed by the Consultation on Common Texts*, New York, Church Hymnal Corporation, 1983 • English Language Liturgical Consultation, *Praying Together*, Nashville, TN, Abingdon, 1989 • D. Gray ed., *The Word in Season*, Norwich, England, Canterbury Press, 1988 • A. Allan McArthur, *The Christian Year and Lectionary Reform*, London, SCM, 1958.

LITURGY. Liturgy, or worship (and the forms it takes), is the public, common action of a Christian community in which the church* is both manifested and realized. From apostolic times, Christians would gather at appointed times for prayer and for the "breaking of bread" (e.g. Acts 2:42,46, 20:7). Numerous references in the New Testament and in early Christian writings amply witness to the importance of these liturgical assemblies. It was precisely such gatherings — criminal in the eyes of the Roman authorities — which led to persecutions. Citizens of the empire could believe whatever they wished, as long as they did not challenge the official state cult. Yet, despite these dangers, Christians continued to assemble, by their actions rejecting the state religion. Nearly 2,000 years later, Christians throughout the world continue to gather at least as frequently as every Lord's day, each time affirming their identity as the people of God.*

Not surprisingly, the vast majority of early Christian literature is liturgical in nature: commentaries on the scripture which was read aloud at the liturgy; instructions on the ordering of the assembly, such as the various church orders; and later, liturgical prayers and hymnography. Even credal formulas were originally used in the context of baptismal celebrations. It was in the liturgy that Christians assembled to become the church, that they came to know the incarnate God and to participate in his very being by sharing in his body and blood. It was also in the liturgy that they learned about the Christian faith,* for it was only much later that theological schools, academic learning or even Sunday schools became widespread. Even today, the vast majority of Christians in the world have contact with the church almost exclusively in the liturgical gathering of the local community.

Liturgy, therefore, embodied the faith of the church. This is the implication of the statement by Prosper of Aquitaine in the 5th century: *ut legem credendi lex statuat supplicandi* — better known in the shorter form: *lex orandi, lex credendi.** As people worship, so they believe. Not surprisingly, the liturgical assembly itself eventually became a source of theology, particularly from the 4th century, when the Christian faith had to be explained to the masses of new converts who flocked to the church after the peace of Constantine. The mystagogical writings of important figures such as Cyril of Jerusalem, Theodore of Mopsuestia, John Chrysostom and Ambrose of Milan are important sources for both liturgy and theology. These and many other sources also reveal the variety which characterized liturgical practice from the very beginning.

In the early centuries, each locality followed its own practices, although there was a remarkable uniformity in the overall structure of worship, as we see already in the "classical shape" of the eucharist described by Justin Martyr in his *First Apology* (c.150). But by the 3rd and 4th centuries, there was in each region a process of unification, a consolidation where local patterns were absorbed into regional patterns. One can by this time speak of the Egyptian, Roman, West Syrian and East Syrian liturgical families, ancestors of our modern rites. Each of these families continued to develop, sometimes in isolation from the others, sometimes strongly influenced by them. At first, the families were distinguished geographically, so that each area or province had its own characteristic practices. But eventually, as the unity of the church was broken by various schisms,* liturgical families increasingly came to be identified with confessional bodies. Each splinter group would develop its inherited liturgical tradition along its own lines, consistent with its own theological, social and political realities. Various political, social and theological factors also played a great role in the growing predominance of certain families, particularly the Roman in the West and the Byzantine in the East. This is the context in which we understand the term "rite" today: it characterizes the total ecclesial tradition, the life, of a particular church or communion. Thus the various rites are invaluable sources for an understanding of the different streams within world Christianity.

Eastern churches. Although there are several different liturgical and theological traditions among the Eastern churches, as enumerated below, it is quite proper to speak of a particular Eastern style, distinct from that of the West. The Eastern approach to reality is more Platonic, not bound by the Aristotelian categories prevalent in the West. For the Easterner, earthly reality is reflective of a higher, heavenly reality which can be communicated. The theology of icons* is a typical example of this approach. The church is perceived not so much as a militant society but as a theophany, the coming of the eternal into time. Spirituality is defined in terms of *theosis*, divinization — grace* is seen as the transforming action of God, not as a means of living in this world. All these differences are reflected in Eastern liturgies. Western worship is generally more austere and simple; its symbols are more direct; there is emphasis on action and involvement. In the East, the liturgy is perceived as an ascent to a higher world, beyond the cares and suffering of this world. This orientation is reflected in the church building — the church is "heaven on earth, where God dwells and moves", says Germanos of Constantinople in his 8th-century commentary on the liturgy. In the liturgy, as in architecture, the emphasis is vertical, transcendental and eschatological. Prayer, particularly liturgical prayer, is seen as the way to be close to God, as true theology. The following are the most significant extant Eastern rites.

Byzantine rite: This rite is used today by all the Eastern Orthodox, who compose the vast majority of Eastern Christians. It is also used, in a somewhat Latinized form, by a significant number of Eastern Catholics, former Orthodox who were absorbed by the Roman church from the end of the 16th century. The Byzantine rite originated in 4th-century Antioch but was later substantially reworked under the influence of Jerusalem, as well as through monasticism. It reached its present form by the 15th century, after which the fixity brought by the printing of books effectively halted its further development. Because it was the rite of Constantinople, the capital of the Eastern empire, it eventually supplanted all other rites among the Orthodox. This rite is perhaps best known for its eucharistic liturgy, ascribed to John Chrysostom. Closely related to the Byzantine is the *Armenian* rite, in use by the non-Chalcedonian church of Armenia.

Syrian rites: The *East Syrian* rite is in use today by the so-called Church of the East, sometimes still called the Nestorian or Chaldean church, as well as by the larger Malabar church in India. This rite derives from the usage of Edessa. The *West Syrian* rite is used primarily by the non-Chalcedonian Jacobite church in Palestine and Syria, as well as by the Malankara church in India. This rite derives from Antiochian and Jerusalem practices, but with Greek (euchologic) and East Syrian (poetic) elements. Also derivative of this tradition is the *Maronite* rite, used by the Maronite Christians, chiefly in Lebanon. This is the only Eastern church totally in communion with Rome. Like the Jacobite rite, this is an Antiochian tradition with significant influence from the usages of Edessa.

Alexandrian rites: The *Coptic* rite of Egypt and the *Ethiopian* rite are the two descendants of the ancient Alexandrian tradition. The respective churches are both non-Chalcedonian, or "monophysite".

Western churches. In the early period, the Western liturgical tradition was quite as rich and varied as the Eastern. The *Roman* rite existed side by side with its close relative, the *Ambrosian* rite in Milan, as well as the more independent *Mozarabic* rite in Spain, the *Gallican* in Gaul, and the *Celtic* in Ireland and Scotland. Gradually, the Roman rite came to predominate, though it absorbed numerous elements from the rites which it supplanted. With the council of Trent, the Roman rite reigned supreme throughout the Latin West, with the major exceptions of only the local Ambrosian rite of Milan and the newly emerging rites of the Protestant Reformation, which derived from Roman practice.

Roman rite: The Roman rite, as indeed all extant Western rites, can be characterized by its brevity and simplicity of expression. Movements, gestures and words are all kept to a minimum. It seems quite austere in comparison to the Eastern liturgies, despite an infusion of more ceremonial and poetic elements from the Gallican and Mozarabic rites during

Syrian Orthodox worship service in Aleppo, Syria (WCC/Peter Williams)

the medieval period. It was to some of these accretions, as well as to excesses in popular piety, that the reformers objected in the 16th century. From the time of the council of Trent, Roman practice has been rigidly controlled by the Congregation for Sacred Rites in Rome, which has tended to suppress all local variation. The new rite promulgated after Vatican II* allows for greater flexibility and the use of the vernacular and even contains elements borrowed from Eastern liturgies. Significantly, the new Roman rite can hardly be distinguished from that of the more conservative churches of the Reformation, particularly the Lutheran and Anglican.

Protestant rites: The various Protestant rites can be categorized by the degree to which each body "reformed" the worship tradition it inherited from a medieval West strongly marked by Rome. Thus the *Lutheran* tradition preserved as much of the Roman rite as it felt was consistent with its theology. Lutheran worship stresses preaching, music, ritual and even the eucharistic sacrament, though the latter until recently played a lesser role due to the influences of pietism and the Enlightenment. The *Reformed* tradition is far less ceremonial and stresses the preaching of the word and the singing of psalms. It has a strongly didactic and penitential bent.

The *Anglican* communion's Book of Common Prayer has in many ways provided a kind of liturgical *via media* among the Western churches. Closely related to the Anglican rite is the *Methodist*, which has also been influential through its rich hymn tradition.

Another strain is the so-called *Free Church* tradition, which bases worship more exclusively on scripture and emphasizes congregational autonomy in the ordering of its liturgy. Tradition is perceived as merely human invention. The *Quakers* abolished all external forms of worship except the act of gathering in assembly for silent meditation. Yet another form of Free Church worship emerged in 19th-century America, which can be categorized as pragmatic. Not tied down to any predetermined order or tradition, each congregation employs whatever forms work, chiefly in attracting converts — much American Protestantism falls into this pattern. The most recent development arising within Protestant worship is the *Pentecostal* tradition, which originated in the US in the early 20th century but has since spread throughout the world. Speaking in tongues is the most visible manifestation of this form of worship, and it is characterized by great spontaneity and the avoidance of any formal order. But even spontaneous forms of worship quickly develop definite patterns which are familiar to regular participants.

Conclusion. Modern Protestantism contains by far the greatest variety of liturgical practice, from "high church" Anglicanism, whose forms of worship are hardly distinguishable from those of medieval Roman Catholicism, to the silent "waiting on God" of the Quakers and the ecstatic glossolalia of the Pentecostals. By contrast, the Eastern rites are remarkably consistent in style and approach, and differences are due more to cultural and historical than to theological or spiritual factors. The Eastern churches have never undergone the trauma of a reformation, and their worship derives from an unbroken, if constantly evolving, tradition.* Liturgical change in the East is not the task of any individual local congregation or even any official liturgical commission; change occurs gradually, almost imperceptibly.

But Eastern worship, just as Western, expresses the faith, culture and spirituality of a given ecclesial body, its understanding of orders, its approach to tradition. Thus a deeper understanding of the various churches' liturgical traditions is a sine qua non for future ecumenical progress.

See also **liturgical reforms, worship in the ecumenical movement**.

PAUL MEYENDORFF

J.J. von Allmen, *Célébrer le salut*, Geneva, Labor & Fides, 1984 ● P. Edwall et al. eds, *Ways of Worship*, New York, Harper, 1951 ● C. Jones et al. eds, *The Study of Liturgy*, London, SPCK, 1978 ● A. Schmemann, *Introduction to Liturgical Theology*, London, Faith, 1966 ● F.C. Senn, *Christian Worship and Its Cultural Setting*, Philadelphia, Fortress, 1983 ● R. Taft, *Beyond East and West: Problems in Liturgical Understanding*, Washington DC, Pastoral, 1984 ● M. Thurian & G. Wainwright eds, *Baptism and Eucharist: Ecumenical Convergence in Celebration*, WCC, 1983 ● J.F. White, *Protestant Worship: Traditions in Transition*, Louisville, KY, Westminster/John Knox, 1989.

LOCAL CHURCH. The various statements on unity* which were approved by the assemblies of the WCC since New Delhi focus on the local church as the basic unit of unity. New Delhi (1961) speaks of a unity which "is being made visible as all in each place who are baptized... and confess... are brought... into one fully committed fellowship... [and] are united with the whole Christian fellowship in all places and all ages". Uppsala (1968) places additional emphasis on "all Christians in all places". Nairobi (1975) sees the one church "as a conciliar fellowship of local churches which are themselves truly united", stressing that "each local church possesses, in communion with the others, the fullness of catholicity". These statements seek to recover the biblical dynamic of "local" and "universal" church as the common origin and background of the various ecclesial structures which have developed throughout history. In the New Testament, *ekklēsia* means both the universal Christian fellowship (Eph. 1:22; 1 Tim. 3:5) and the visible congregation connected to a particular house, city or province (Rom. 16:3-5; 1 Cor. 1:2; 2 Cor. 8:1). The universal church, according to the NT, exists in local churches and in the communion* between them.

As the organization of the church and its various ministries grew more complex, however, the term "local church" lost its unequivocal reference (see **church order**). In early church history, the presence of a bishop and the celebration of the eucharist* clearly marked the identity of a local church. Later, both larger and smaller church structures developed which were also called local. In Orthodoxy, this was the case with the autocephalous church. In Western Christianity, it was the parish which caused complications. For some time, the terms "diocese" and "parish" were largely synonymous. Gradually, however, the term "parish" began to refer to pastoral units, supervised by a priest (presbyter), smaller than the diocese and subordinate to it. This distinction contributed to the emergence of a Rome-centred, pyramidal view of the structure of the church.

In opposition to this, the churches of the Reformation took their point of departure in the parish: the place where the assembly of the faithful under the preaching of the word and the celebration of the sacraments was realized without subordination to supra-local episcopal authority. This territorial point of departure led to the organization of supra-local structures proportionate to political units (nations). Besides this presbyterial approach, an understanding of "local church" emerged in the wake of the Reformation which made it exclusively dependent on the covenant of the faithful.

As a result of all these developments, the term "local church" can refer to dioceses, archdioceses, parishes, national churches and other territorial-ecclesial units, and it can have episcopal, presbyterial and community-centred connotations. In this confusion, the original meaning of both "universal" ("catholic") and "local", as well as the essential significance of the inter-relation between these two, is easily obscured.

In the 20th century, various factors contributed to a re-discovery of more fundamental dimensions. Due to common problems and challenges, Protestant churches experienced the limitation of their national-territorial structures and the need for broader communion and co-operation. At the same time, developments in modern industrial societies relativized the significance of mere territorial givenness of local churches and led to a new emphasis on the missionary quality of church structures (see Uppsala assembly, sec. 2) and to a proliferation of small groups intent upon a creative interaction between church and context. The Roman Catholic Church re-discovered the specific place and function of the laity* and experienced a "re-invention of the church" (Leonardo Boff) in the form of base communities (see **church base communities**). The ecclesiology of the documents of the Second Vatican Council* reflects the implications of this revitalization of the local church and of the growth of "universal" networks of communion and communication. The notions of the "particular church" (*ecclesia particularis*) and of the communion between these churches *(collegialis unio)*, in which the universal church exists (see *Lumen Gentium* 23, *Christus Dominus* 11), revive the insight that episcopal ministry and eucharistic celebration determine the core-unit of the church, rather than specific "local" characteristics. Similarly, the Lima text on the eucharist underlines that "eucharistic celebrations always have to do with the whole church, and the whole church is involved in each local eucharistic celebration" (*Baptism, Eucharist and Ministry,* * E19).

Although ecumenical consensus on the precise meaning of the term "local church" is still lacking, this brief sketch shows a common direction of thought and the possibilities for a re-conception of the local-universal relation. Supra-local church structures are relativized in favour of a dynamic vision of local churches in networks of universal (worldwide) communication. The ecumenical movement provides these networks; it is there that the full implications of the problems of global society become visible, and that the search for common memory and common life in the promise of the unity of humankind takes shape. At the local level this search is translated into the daily life of obedience and witness. The church in its national and regional organization of boards, colleges and synods has the function of keeping alive this interaction between local and global and of making it fruitful in both directions.

See also **church, unity, unity of "all in each place"**.

LIBERTUS A. HOEDEMAKER

L. Boff, *Ecclesiogenesis: The Base Communities Reinvent the Church*, Maryknoll, NY, Orbis, 1986 • *The Church for Others*, WCC, 1967 • "The Church: Local and Universal", *Sixth Report of the*

Joint Working Group Between the RCC and the WCC, WCC, 1990, app. A • *In Each Place: Towards a Fellowship of Local Churches Truly United*, WCC, 1977 • H. de Lubac, *Les Eglises particulières dans l'Eglise universelle*, Paris, Aubier Montaigne, 1971 • E. Schillebeeckx, *Pleidooi voor mensen in de kerk* (ET *The Church with a Human Face*, London, SCM, 1985).

LOCAL ECUMENICAL PROJECTS.

An LEP is the sharing by congregations from different denominations, acting under the supervision of a local, ecumenical body and with the agreement of their respective church structures, of specific aspects of their worship, congregational life and mission. The term refers primarily to an ecumenical form developed in England and in Aotearoa/New Zealand (where they are generally known as co-operative ventures).

LEPs have been recognized as a creative and challenging aspect of the English ecumenical scene since 1964, when the British Council of Churches (BCC) Faith and Order conference at Nottingham called for "areas of ecumenical experiments" to be established "at the request of local congregations, or in new towns and housing areas" to develop ecumenical group ministries, mission, and the sharing of church buildings. A second basic step was the suggestion, in a 1967 Northamptonshire report on "Planning an Ecumenical Parish", that "sponsoring bodies" be developed to oversee both theological and practical aspects of such ventures. The term "experiment" proved difficult, and the phrase "local ecumenical project" was introduced in 1973, the year in which the national LEP co-ordinating body, the Consultative Committee for Local Ecumenical Projects in England (CCLEPE), was established. Staff support for LEPs and CCLEPE has been provided by the ecumenical officer for England of the BCC.

With the failure of the Church of England-Methodist union conversations in 1972, and the covenant proposals in 1982, many felt that the initiative towards church union had passed to the local level. LEPs developed rapidly throughout the 70s and 80s (with 320 recorded in 1978 and 410 in 1985) and were widely regarded as the decisive point of ecumenical growth in England. As of 1990 some 550 LEPs had been registered with the consultative committee, with the number still growing.

An LEP involves congregations from at least two and as many as five or more denominations. The churches most active have been Methodist (as of the last official register, in October 1988, Methodist churches were involved in almost 450 LEPs), Church of England (in some 400), United Reformed Church (in almost 300), Roman Catholic (in 135), and Baptist (in about 115). LEP constituents have also included Brethren, Lutheran, Pentecostal and Assembly of God congregations, as well as Friends meetings.

While LEPs vary greatly from one another, depending on the congregations and denominations involved and on the local ecumenical situation, they are officially registered in one or more of four categories: the *local covenant* (in which the congregations make a basic commitment to common service and mission); those involving a *shared building* (and therefore particular legal obligations); the *shared congregation* (involving "considerable sharing of congregational life", including worship, witness and pastoral care, and possibly common finances); and those involving a *shared ministry* (including certain sacramental services).

Fundamental to LEPs is their accountability both to their "parent" denominations and to the ecumenical community and vision. Internally, each LEP must be based upon a formal written agreement among its constituent congregations; these agreements vary greatly, depending on the extent and level of commitment, from a "sharing agreement" (under the Sharing of Church Buildings Act of 1969) which regulates the joint use of property; to a "declaration of intent" expressing the "essential spirit" of the project and its theological basis; to a written constitution, defining the nature and aims of the project, those involved and the specific commitments which they have made, and procedures for monitoring, evaluation, revision and termination of the project.

Externally, each LEP is responsible to its local sponsoring body, an ecumenical group charged with giving oversight, encouragement, pastoral care and practical advice to existing (and potential) LEPs in its area and serving as both "a buffer and a bridge" between LEPs and their parent denominations. As LEPs have grown, their sponsoring bodies have also grown in extent (as of 1990 there are about 50 in England) and ecumenical significance; typically the sponsoring body for a county will include the Anglican bishop or the provincial moderator of the United Reformed Church, and some have developed into area-wide "ecumenical councils" promoting a range of co-operative activities of ministry and witness. Finally, each LEP is also responsible for complying with the ecumenical canons, or other relevant codes of practice, of each of its constituent denominations.

In facing a wide range of theological and practical problems LEPs have been of creative significance to the whole ecumenical movement. Much creative liturgical reflection and practice has come as LEPs have sought to honour the distinctive gifts and convictions of their various members in their common worship. This has perhaps been most significant in the field of eucharistic sharing (see **communion, intercommunion**); also important has been the development of joint confirmation* services fulfilling the requirements of a wide range of ecclesiological positions. The questions of membership and ministry are perhaps the most enduringly difficult for LEPs. "Multiple membership" (in the several constituent denominations) has been proposed for those who come to the Christian faith within the context of an LEP, but those already baptized when they enter an LEP must continue to identify themselves, at least formally, with one or another of its constituent denominations. There is increasing openness to a "representative" ministry, with clergy from one denomination serving an LEP on behalf of all its constituents. But this often results in the pastor having to fulfill the institutional demands of several denominations at once; and the discipline of some churches, of course, precludes the sharing of certain sacramental functions (see **church discipline, church order**).

Despite such practical difficulties, members of LEPs have strongly affirmed their value, finding through the experience of common worship, life and witness in an LEP a sense of belonging to the whole Christian church rather than to one of its separated denominational parts.

The co-operating ventures in Aotearoa/New Zealand have been distinctively shaped by their commitment to white settler and Maori bi-culturalism, and by delays in the emergence of the United Church of New Zealand after the apparent breakdown of the Negotiat-

ing Churches Unity Council process in 1989. They have included a significant proportion of the membership of some denominations; strikingly, more than 50% of Methodists in New Zealand are said to be in such ecumenical parishes. More sharply than their English counterparts, the co-operating ventures have voiced a challenge to the continuing separation of their parent churches, stating at their most recent national conference (1989) that the present denominational divisions are "increasingly irrelevant for members of co-operative ventures". Thus these ventures pose important questions to the churches and the ecumenical movement in their country.

Within the English situation the genius of LEPs has been their combining of a deep commitment to unity; an insistence upon forging new areas of common Christian experience, confession, witness and mission at the local level; a willingness to experiment; and their readiness to be accountable both to denominational and to ecumenical structures. Through their life and witness they have, in turn, forced the denominations to face the theoretical and practical problems which the divided structures of the churches pose to Christians who seek to confess and witness to their faith together.

See also **covenanting, denominationalism, local church, local ecumenism, unity of "all in each place"**.

THOMAS F. BEST

H. Cross, *A Guidebook for Members of Sponsoring Bodies and Ecumenical Councils*, London, BCC, 1988 • *Local Church Unity: Guidelines for Local Ecumenical Projects and Sponsoring Bodies*, rev. ed., London, BCC, 1985 • *Local Councils of Churches in England and Churches Together in Pilgrimage*, London, BCC, 1989 • *Ministry in Local Ecumenical Projects*, London, BCC, 1985 • *Register of Local Ecumenical Projects and Sponsoring Bodies*, London, CCLEPE, 1988 • *Sponsoring Bodies, County Ecumenical Councils, Metropolitan Councils of Churches, Assemblies, and Ecumenical Councils in England and Churches Together in Pilgrimage*, London, BCC, 1989 • "Venturing Forward: Conference Statement", Wellington, National Review Consultation of Cooperative Ventures, 1989.

LOCAL ECUMENISM. "The ecumenical movement is not alive unless it is local," said the Faith and Order conference at Lund in 1952, and the New Delhi assembly of the

WCC (1961) built this idea into the classic definition of the goal of Christian unity:* "We believe that the unity which is both God's will and his gift to his church is being made visible as all in each place who are baptized into Jesus Christ and confess him as Lord and Saviour are brought by the Holy Spirit into one fully committed fellowship... in such wise that ministry and members are accepted by all and that all can act and speak together as occasion requires for the tasks to which God calls his people."

There is a limitless variety to local situations, to the priorities in the "tasks to which God calls his people" in any one place, to the obstacles to Christian unity, to the social conditions within and for which it is to be sought and to the potential partners for any one group of Christians. There is moreover a wide divergence between the ways different churches envisage the "local unity of the church" and the decision making proper to that. No less important are the particular ways in which churches psychologically understand themselves (e.g. "majority" or "minority", as "of the people" or "international") and their proper relations with other Christian groups in the area (e.g. as rivals or as allies in face of the threat from non-Christians, as newcomers deserving to be welcomed or as nuisances who ought never to come). Local initiatives in, say, Peru will look and feel quite different from those in Korea or Germany.

This variety should not be seen as a problem. Christian unity does not mean uniformity: it is natural and proper that different things should happen in different places, although the people in any one place will have a lot to learn from others. Still more, the chief actor in the striving towards Christian unity, at the local level as on the wider scene, is the Holy Spirit,* who inspires, encourages, cajoles and nudges divided Christians to take the next steps towards and with one another in love for the surrounding world, within an ecumenical movement, a pilgrimage into the fullness and wholeness of what God wants for his people, which has no necessary starting point and which will be completed only in the kingdom of God.*

This article is written chiefly out of experience in Britain, especially England, one of the areas where successive divisions have torn the one church into fragments (each tending to involve people of different social standing, ethnic origin, cultural background, etc.) and yet where Christians have been able to take steps towards reconciliation* and united witness* at the local level.

Milestones on the ecumenical way. By the end of the 18th century and throughout the 19th, when the bitter hatreds of reformation and civil war had been tamed by tolerance and a measure of social stability, Christians in Britain from both the established churches (Anglican in England and Wales, Presbyterian in Scotland) and the various free or nonconformist churches began to come together to promote and undertake certain "good works". There were, for example, foreign missions through the London Missionary Society, the distribution and translation of Bibles through the British and Foreign Bible Society, Sunday schools and other open educational ventures, and youth work through the Young Men's and Young Women's Christian Associations. These specific causes, and so the organizations that served them, were seen as Christian yet not necessarily tied to any one church. Leadership was often given by lay Christians. Friendship, trust and a sense of common purpose could be built up in an open-minded, generally "evangelical" spirit that saw this kind of obedience as "non-denominational", i.e. free from the particular doctrines and requirements of the divided church institutions.

Later in the 19th century the formation of the Evangelical Alliance encouraged Christians to meet locally, especially for united prayer. So also in the 1890s local Free Church councils began to be formed in which the general witness of the free churches could be jointly promoted and a certain sharing of tasks agreed (e.g. hospital chaplaincies). At this same time, the newly formed Christian unions in the universities were open to students from any church background or none for the sake of evangelism in the university and throughout the world. They were thus an "interdenominational" movement, a central part of whose aims was to help the churches overcome division and move towards unity. The Student Christian Movement, whose leaders were instrumental in convening the world mission conference in Edinburgh 1910, was thus foreshadowing the request of the 1952 Lund gathering: "Should not our churches ask themselves whether they are showing sufficient eagerness to enter into conversation with other churches and whether they should not act together in all matters except those in which deep differences of conviction compel them to act separately? Should they not acknowledge the fact that they often allow themselves to be separated from each other by secular forces and influences instead of witnessing together to the sole lordship of Christ who gathers his people out of all nations, races and tongues?" (see **Lund principle**).

The first local councils of churches* in Britain, bringing churches officially into a common framework for joint action and the eventual achievement of full unity, sprang up in Bolton, Manchester and St Albans in 1918-19, under the inspiration of the Edinburgh 1910 conference and in revulsion at the horror of the first world war. They rapidly created a wide range of sub-committees and joint projects, the majority handling major social needs and problems of the time but also involving pulpit exchanges and occasions of common prayer. The great international church conferences of the 1920s and 1930s gave much inspiration to the local level, as did the Religion and Life weeks held in many towns and cities during the second world war, with the active involvement of the Roman Catholic Sword of the Spirit movement. By 1946, two years before the formation of the WCC, there were 126 local councils in association with the British Council of Churches (BCC).

The 1960s saw a new boost in local ecumenical activity. In Britain Christian Aid weeks started in 1957 (a week when church members try to visit every house in their area to collect for the poor and hungry throughout the world); the first British F&O conference was held in 1964; the new openness and enthusiasm of Roman Catholics in many places as a result of Vatican II* led to a particular boost for the January Week of Prayer for Christian Unity;* and the People Next Door campaign of 1967 brought together denominationally mixed small groups in hundreds of neighbourhoods meeting without their clergy and going out to meet and interact with people of other convictions and backgrounds in their area. Since then the BCC has been in touch with some 700 local councils of churches.

Meanwhile the 1964 F&O conference, while issuing a startling appeal for unity in Britain by Easter day 1980, also recommended that the churches establish "areas of ecumenical experiment" where denominational disciplines could be suspended. Progress was slow, but in a number of new housing estates joint churches were built by two or more denominations and jointly staffed, providing a single new congregation, as if the churches concerned were already united. In the 1970s this evolving pattern of Local Ecumenical Projects (LEPs) was adopted also in a number of small towns or self-contained neighbourhoods where the trust and co-operation between congregations of divided churches had become such that they could properly move on into the fuller commitment of a binding "local covenant" (the term used by the Roman Catholic authorities in encouraging their congregations to consider this kind of step forward). Especially in the aftermath of the failure of national covenant plans in England in 1982, but also as part of the developing unity scene in Wales and in Scotland, such LEPs, local covenants and ecumenical parishes have been steadily increasing in the 1980s and are now approaching 600 (see **covenanting**). Their growth, in numbers and in effectiveness, has been helped by the growing network of sponsoring bodies, often now at the level of the county, where denominational leaders and representatives of their synods can give oversight, learn from local experience and explore a measure of common planning.

Many other challenges and inspirations have helped towards significant local initiatives. Two that have been important in Britain in recent years have been the movement of charismatic renewal, releasing many Christians into a spontaneity of prayer and fellowship that has broken down many previous social and denominational barriers, and the Association of Interchurch Families,* in which married couples — one a loyal Roman Catholic, the other from another church — and their children have learned to live out a critical solidarity with both churches and to explore the demands and the joys of the unity they can already anticipate in their "domestic church".

Beyond Britain, New Zealand is one country where local initiatives have in many places forged ahead of denominational leaders in bringing into existence formal anticipations of the united church of tomorrow. More and more countries are experimenting with local councils of churches, the Netherlands and the USA perhaps pre-eminent. Still more important in the long run may well prove the church base communities* of Brazil and other majority Roman Catholic countries. There a new flexibility in the structures of church life in response to the huge challenges of poverty and oppression often includes a new openness to partnership with fellow Christians of other denominations.

Lessons worth learning. This developing pilgrimage at the local level is helpfully seen as moving through some five stages: (1) competition, where each church sees itself as entirely adequate and the others as wrong or in rivalry; (2) co-existence, where acknowledgment is made, more or less explicitly, that Christ is known in other churches, yet where there is little readiness to take positive initiative towards the others; (3) co-operation, where relationships have warmed up enough for churches to be ready to do certain specific projects together, in a real if limited partnership, such as a council of churches; (4) commitment, where mutual recognition as partners within Christ's will for his church has grown to the point that a lasting and deliberately open-ended agreement can be made to do as much as possible within a united framework; and (5) communion,* where it no longer makes sense to speak of divided churches, but earlier division is reconciled and fully common patterns found for the appropriate wholeness and oneness of the Body of Christ in that place.

The goal of the pilgrimage remains that "all in each place who confess Christ as Lord and Saviour are brought into one fully committed fellowship" (New Delhi assembly), or as refined in the 1975 Nairobi assembly: "The one church is to be envisioned as a conciliar fellowship of local churches which are themselves truly united." The spelling out of those compressed phrases always involves seeing the unity of Christians within and for the wider reconciliation, harmony and love of all human beings; the striving for Christian unity belongs with the age-old striving for truth, obedience and the sharing of the good news

and is in no sense a counter or rival movement.

For the actual practice the vital starting point is mutual respect, growing into deeper trust and friendship among those who give leadership, so that whatever the previous experience, relative size or social standing of the churches concerned, there can be a sense that each is taken seriously and on an equal footing. As the movement develops, there must remain a concern both for respecting the actual churches and people as they presently are and for encouraging and enabling those pioneers who are "constrained by the love of God to exert pressure on the limits of our own inherited traditions, recognizing the theological necessity of what we may call 'responsible risks'" (New Delhi). There are many traps and dangers to be avoided on the way, not least those surrounding the role of clergy (see **laity/ clergy**) and other "religious professionals". Almost all the dangers can be traced to half-heartedness and insensitivity in too many of the people whose commitment and awareness are needed if the congregation as a whole is to be able to move ahead.

The relationships between local groups and church authorities (district synod, diocesan bishop, national conference, etc.) are also crucial. High-level initiatives and advances that take place with no thought given to follow-through at the local level are hardly less disillusioning than local efforts and ideas that are blocked by people higher up. For this reason the sponsoring bodies that accompany LEPs have proved such a helpful feature.

The details of any specific place and time are destined to change. What matters in the striving for true Christian unity-in-mission is not the form but the particular next step, since any form or action is best designed precisely for that next step and will give way to what is appropriate for the one after. Ministers' fraternals properly give way to adequately representative local councils of churches, which in turn give way to fuller commitment of a local covenant approved by higher church leaders, itself designed to disappear into the "one church renewed for mission" (1964 British F&O conference). What matters is that as those who seek to follow Jesus Christ in one specific time and place, we can do so in obedience not primarily to the traditions we inherit from earlier quarrels but to the Holy

Spirit, who is preparing the coming of God's kingdom.*

See also **local church; local ecumenical projects; unity; unity of "all in each place"; unity, models of; unity, ways to**.

MARTIN CONWAY

Local Councils of Churches Today, London, BCC, 1971 ● "Ecumenical Collaboration at the Regional, National and Local Levels", London, Catholic Truth Society, 1975 ● *In Each Place: Towards a Fellowship of Local Churches Truly United*, WCC, 1977 ● D. Corbishley, *Local Churches in Covenant*, London, Catholic Services, 1983 ● R. Reardon & M. Finch eds, *Sharing Communion: An Appeal to the Churches by Interchurch Families*, London, Collins Liturgical, 1983 ● A. Birmelé ed., *Local Ecumenism: How Church Unity Is Seen and Practised by Congregations*, WCC, 1984.

LOSSKY, VLADIMIR. B. 8.6.1903,

Göttingen, Germany; d. 7.2.1958, Paris. Lossky's particular contribution to the ecumenical movement was a renewed patristic presentation of Eastern Orthodoxy* to the Western world. His message was an invitation not to repeat or systematize the fathers but to practise their approach to theology for the present day, a theology which is not a speculative intellectual exercise but the expression of the ecclesial experience of God, with the help of the Holy Spirit, who dwells in the heart of the theologian. Expelled from Russia in 1922, he settled in Prague, where he took part in N. Kondakov's seminars and began to read the fathers. In 1924, he started his studies at the Sorbonne in Paris, where he became a disciple of Etienne Gilson and came in close contact with Jean Daniélou, Henri de Lubac, Yves Congar, Louis Bouyer and others. It was in response to this ecumenical challenge that he wrote most of his works, by which he became known as one of the prominent Orthodox theologians of this century. After the war he taught dogmatic theology at the Institut de théologie orthodoxe Saint Denys in Paris. He also played a prominent part in the Fellowship of St Alban and St Sergius* in England. Together with Georges Florovsky he became one of the main speakers at annual summer conferences. He wrote *Essai sur la théologie mystique de l'Eglise d'Orient* (ET *The Mystical Theology of the Eastern Church*, London, Clarke, 1957), *A l'image et à la ressemblance de Dieu* (ET *In the Image and Likeness of God*, Crestwood, NY, St Vladimir's Seminary, 1974), (with L. Ouspensky) *Der Sinn der Ikonen* (ET *The Meaning of Icons*, Crestwood, NY, St Vladimir's Seminary, 1952), *Vision de Dieu* (ET *The Vision of God*, Crestwood, NY, St Vladimir's Seminary, 1983), and *Théologie négative et connaissance de Dieu chez Maître Eckhart*, Paris, Vrin, 1960.

NICHOLAS LOSSKY

LUND PRINCIPLE. On 27 August 1952, the third world conference on Faith and Order,* meeting at Lund, Sweden, agreed on the text of "A Word to the Churches". It was immediately released to the press for worldwide publication. One sentence asked: "Should not our churches ask themselves whether they are showing sufficient eagerness to enter into conversation with other churches, and *whether they should not act together in all matters except those in which deep differences of conviction compel them to act separately?*" (my italics). The italicized final section of that sentence became known subsequently as the Lund principle. Probably this is the most quoted (and sometimes misquoted!) sentence from any F&O document. It has often been misunderstood by being taken as an exhortation rather than, as in its original context, a question to be answered. The original intention was to challenge the churches to talk together so that they could come to act together. Lund was held in the aftermath of the South India union (1947), and hopes were rising for other similar union projects.

Two interpretations of the Lund principle quickly arose which weakened its impact. It became a favourite quotation for ecumenical orators who used it rhetorically, somewhat as a general principle to be stated. Many churches — particularly locally — took it as encouragement simply for limited spasmodic relationships and escaped the full force of the question by thinking in terms of annual celebrations connected with the Week of Prayer for Christian Unity.* The Lund drafters intended quite otherwise. It was a principle to be applied to the ongoing, day-to-day life of the churches. Answered affirmatively, the question was intended to face the churches — whether nationally or locally — with questions of permanent change. There are signs that this is, at last, beginning to happen on a significant scale, particularly in local situations with developing covenant relationships which include a determination to act on the Lund principle. It would appear, therefore, that the Lund question still remains well worth asking.

See also **covenanting; unity, ways to**.

MORRIS WEST

O.S. Tomkins ed., *The Third World Conference on Faith and Order*, London, SCM, 1953.

LUTHERAN-METHODIST

DIALOGUE. The Lutheran World Federation* and the World Methodist Council* conducted bilateral conversations from 1977 until 1984. They concluded with the substantive proposal "that our churches take steps to declare and establish full fellowship of word and sacrament". The process which led to this conclusion was difficult, and at the same time renewing and encouraging. Participants came from every continent, and the internal differences among Lutherans and Methodists were sometimes as striking as the differences between them.

The planning session held at St Simons Island, Georgia, USA, in December 1977 led to the choice of the theme "The Church: A Community of Grace". Sub-topics of special importance for discussion were biblical authority and the authenticity of the church, the gospel of grace, the Holy Spirit in the church, the sacraments of the gospel, and the mission of the church in today's world.

The first regular meeting (Dresden 1979) concentrated on "The Authority of the Bible and the Authenticity of the Church", especially as this related to the auxiliary keys of creeds,* confessions and historical criticism. Representatives exchanged visits in churches in the area. The first service in which bishops of the two denominations officiated together was in the Kreuzkirche on 23 January.

At the second meeting (Bristol, England, 1980) the desired goals of mutual understanding, recognition of oneness in the Body of Christ, and providing theological support for church co-operation and unity according to local needs were all served through the discussion of Christian experience. The difficulties of denoting the meaning(s) of Christian ex-

perience and the diverse emphases found under this theme served to enrich the discussion and the inter-relationships of the two traditions. Justification* and sanctification* were the foci of this discussion, with agreement both that "Christians throughout their whole life are in need of God's forgiving grace" and that "Christian faith is faith that is active in love".

At the third meeting (Oslo 1981) a tentative outline for a common statement was drawn as the discussion focused on the Holy Spirit* and the church* — with special reference to how particular denominational histories have shaped ecclesiology and the understanding of ministry.

The means of grace,* the sacraments* of baptism* and eucharist,* and church order* were the main topics of discussion at the fourth meeting (Lake Junaluska, North Carolina, USA, 1983). The hope was explicitly expressed that the final report would contribute to increased Lutheran-Methodist encounter and co-operation as well as provide theological grounds for official steps towards eucharistic sharing. The final draft constituted the centre of attention along with papers on the Lord's supper and church order.

At Bossey, Switzerland, 1984, the final meeting of the commission was held, with the express purpose of finalizing the report to the sponsoring bodies. The report witnesses to "important agreements and convergences and indicates the ways in which we express our common faith differently". While there is need for further study of certain doctrinal topics (providence, the two kingdoms, aspects of anthropology) as well as of "forms of unity", the report concludes that there is already sufficient agreement for several recommendations to be made: full fellowship of word and sacrament, common work in every place to manifest unity in witness and service, and use of the results of this theological dialogue in seeking the visible unity* of all Christians.

The most concrete result of these consultations so far has been the historic, joint celebration of holy communion in the Lutheran St Lorenz Church at Nuremberg on 29 September 1987 between the Evangelical Methodist Church in the Federal Republic of Germany and the Lutheran, Reformed and United churches of Germany. The text from the bila-

teral consultation was studied by these churches, and their own decision was to establish
an official fellowship of pulpit and sacraments. After the inaugural service in Nuremberg, other services were then held throughout
the FRG. In 1990, a similar relationship was
established in the German Democratic Republic.

THOMAS A. LANGFORD

The Church: A Community of Grace, final report of
the LWF/WMC joint commision, 1979-84, Geneva
and Lake Junaluska, 1984 • Lutherisches Kir-
chenamt, Kirchenkanzlei der Evangelisch-metho-
distischen Kirche, *Vom Dialog zur Kanzel- und
Abendmahlsgemeinschaft*, Hanover & Stuttgart,
1987.

LUTHERAN-ORTHODOX

DIALOGUE. Although Martin Luther expressed an interest in the Orthodox church, it
fell to his colleague Philipp Melanchthon to
establish the first contacts between the Lutheran Reformation and the Eastern church. In
1559 Melanchthon attempted to send a letter
and a Greek copy of the Augsburg confession
to the ecumenical patriarch in Constantinople.
His attempt failed, and contacts ceased for 15
years. Between 1574 and 1581 Patriarch
Jeremiah II and theologians at Tübingen exchanged letters. This correspondence ended
when the patriarch asserted that the Germans
should submit themselves to the teachings of
Orthodoxy.

Official contacts between the Scandinavian
churches and the Russian Orthodox Church
started as early as 1557. The ecclesiastical
reforms of Peter the Great (1672-1725)
brought with them a significant Lutheran presence in Russia. From that time until the early
20th century, however, communication between Lutheranism and Orthodoxy tended to
be more personal than official.

Shortly after his consecration in 1914,
Archbishop Söderblom of Sweden made direct contact with the ecumenical patriarch.
He, the patriarch and other ecumenical leaders
envisaged the creation of something like the
present-day WCC. The archbishop played a
pivotal role in the 1925 conference on Life
and Work* held in Stockholm — a meeting
which brought a significant number of Orthodox to Sweden, including the partriarch of
Alexandria. These early 20th-century events

laid the foundations for the Lutheran-Orthodox bilateral dialogue after the second
world war.

Regional dialogue. Reciprocal visitations
between the Russian Orthodox Church and the
Evangelical Church of the Federal Republic of
Germany began in the 1950s. These visitations set the stage for the Arnoldshain conversations, which have run from 1959 to the
present day. These talks have focused on a
wide range of topics: Tradition,* justification,* the Holy Spirit,* reconciliation,* the
Bible, peace,* baptism,* the eucharist,* and
the offering of Christians.

The Russian Orthodox Church and the
Evangelical Lutheran Church of Finland have
been in dialogue since 1970. These sessions
have dealt with the eucharist, salvation,* justification and *theosis* (see **sanctification**).

After the second world war, Lutherans
from the German Democratic Republic met
with Russian Orthodox Church officials.
From these initial exchanges emerged the
Zagorsk conversations, which began in 1974.
The work has centred on questions relating to
the kingdom of God,* the sanctifying action
of God's grace,* and the life of the church* in
a socialist society. In 1979 dialogue com-
menced between the Lutheran churches in the
GDR and the Orthodox church of Bulgaria.

In 1969 the Ecumenical Patriarchate began
bilateral dialogue (see **dialogue, bilateral**)
with the Evangelical Church of the FRG.
They considered topics such as the Holy
Spirit, salvation of the world, anthropology,*
and the eucharist.

National dialogue. More than 30 sessions
of dialogue have taken place between the
Lutheran and Reformed churches in Romania
and the Romanian Orthodox Church. Unlike
regional bilaterals, these conversations are not
conducted by official church-appointed commissions. They are organized by the two Orthodox theological institutes in Bucharest and
Sibiu and the United Protestant Theological
Institute located in Sibiu (Lutheran) and Cluj
(Reformed). Foci of the dialogue have included ecumenism, church and society, the
active meaning of hope,* the ethics of solidarity, the social aspects of salvation, communion* and intercommunion.*

From 1967 to 1969 a first series of conversations took place between the various Orthodox churches in North America and the

Lutheran member churches of the Lutheran Council in the USA, with scripture and Tradition as topics. Lutherans were joined by the Reformed in 1973 for a three-year trilateral conversation with the Orthodox on "Christian Gospel and Social Responsibility: Biblical and Historical Aspects". A second series of Lutheran-Orthodox dialogues ran from 1984 to 1989. After considering a series of topics (ecumenical councils,* creed* and confession, *imago Dei* and deification, and election and predestination), the commission produced a final report entitled "Christ 'in us' and Christ 'for us' in Lutheran and Orthodox Theology" and a handbook to facilitate Lutheran-Orthodox dialogue at the local level.

World level. At the first pan-Orthodox conference (Rhodes 1961), the Orthodox churches decided that dialogue with the Lutherans should be on the agenda of the Holy and Great Council of the Orthodox. At a similar gathering in 1976 the participants agreed that an invitation should be extended by the ecumenical patriarch on behalf of all autocephalous Orthodox churches, requesting Lutheran churches to engage in global-level dialogue through the Lutheran World Federation.* The Lutherans accepted the invitation in 1977 and appointed Lutheran members to the commission in 1978. The two individual dialogue teams worked separately but on a common agenda from 1978 until autumn 1981, when the first meeting of the joint commission met in Helsinki. The common agenda those years included three major topics: (1) 16th- and 17th-century contacts, (2) regional dialogue results, and (3) the theme for the dialogue. Both sides agreed that the theme would be "Participation in the Mystery of the Church", with the goal of the dialogue being "full communion as full mutual recognition".

After the first five meetings, joint statements reflecting significant convergences of thinking on divine revelation*, scripture and Tradition*, and inspiration* and canon* were prepared for publication in 1991. A new round of work, on "Authority in and of the Church", was scheduled to begin in Moscow in 1991 with a discussion of conciliarity.

DANIEL F. MARTENSEN

E. Benz & L.A. Zander eds, *Evangelisches und Orthodoxes Christentum in Begegnung und Aus-* *einandersetzung*, Hamburg, Agentur des Rauhen Hauses, 1952 • G. Mastrantonis, *Augsburg and Constantinople: The Correspondence between the Tübingen Theologians and Patriarch Jeremiah II*, Brookline, MA, Holy Cross, 1982 • *The Orthodox Church and the Churches of the Reformation: A Survey of Orthodox-Protestant Dialogues*, WCC, 1975 • *Report of the Consultation of Lutheran/ Orthodox Dialogues*, Geneva, Lutheran World Federation, 1975.

LUTHERAN-REFORMED DIALOGUE.

Efforts to bring together the Lutheran and Reformed traditions began early in the Reformation period and have continued through the centuries. While these attempts often have been frustrated, notable achievements have been recorded, especially in our century.

The Marburg Colloquy (1529), which included Luther, Melanchthon, Zwingli and Oecolampadius, achieved agreement on a number of points, but not on the presence of Christ in the Lord's supper (see **eucharist**). Zwingli's formulation came to define the Reformed view for Lutherans, although Luther later expressed appreciation for Calvin's position; and Calvin, who was not at Marburg, stated that he favoured Luther over Zwingli. Colloquies at Maulbronn (1564) and Montbéliard (1586) failed to reconcile differences. The scholastic theology of the 17th and 18th centuries, with important exceptions, widened the gap between the two traditions.

The 19th century produced several instances of convergence. In Prussia, Lutheran and Reformed churches were joined in 1817 by the royal decree of Frederick William III. This controversial "forced marriage" created the Prussian Union, which was largely administrative except in the Rhine provinces and Westphalia, where, in 1835, the two churches were consolidated, the new church retaining both Lutheran and Reformed confessions. In the US, Lutheran and Reformed immigrants from Germany formed a "Kirchenverein" in 1841 which almost 100 years later combined with the German Reformed church to form the Evangelical and Reformed Church, now part of the United Church of Christ (UCC). In Hungary a regional agreement between Lutherans and Reformed established pulpit and table fellowship in 1835, and while the two churches remained separated, the mutual recognition of ministry,* church* and sacraments* became widespread in the 19th century. At the end of the century (1891) the small Lutheran and Reformed churches of Austria formed an administrative union.

The 20th century, however, has registered the greatest achievements, perhaps none more impressive than the European Leuenberg agreement of 1973. The way to Leuenberg was paved by a number of post-war national dialogues, each concluding that continued division is confessionally unwarranted. Reports were issued in the Netherlands (1956), the Federal Republic of Germany (1959) and France (1964), but perhaps the most significant document was the Arnoldshain theses (1957), which express the judgment of some of the most eminent exegetes of the century that the New Testament provides no justification for the eucharistic division of the traditions. Leuenberg was also preceded by European dialogues treating scripture (1957), the presence of Christ (1958), baptism (1959), the Lord's supper (1960), and the important Schauenberg talks (1964-67). The Leuenberg process began in 1969.

Article 7 of the Lutheran Augsburg confession became the critical text for Leuenberg. It teaches that for "the true unity of the church it is enough to agree concerning the teaching of the gospel and the administration of the sacraments". In the first of four sections, the Leuenberg document recalls the common heritage of the Reformation and notes the divisions of the 16th century. The second section articulates the common faith* of the Reformation churches: the centrality of justification* by faith for the preaching, teaching and sacramental life of the church. The third section addresses the difficult issue of the 16th-century condemnations, identifying specifically those raised in article 10 of the Augsburg confession concerning the Lord's supper, Christology and predestination (see **anathemas**). The modern thought-world differs from that of our forebears; the condemnations should be lifted. The Leuenberg agreement concludes by offering itself as an instrument of unity.* Churches signing it thereby declare themselves to be in full communion,* i.e. in table and pulpit fellowship. By autumn 1988, some 80 churches had signed the agreement, including a number in South America.

Only modest results have been achieved in the US, although the first bilateral conversation began in 1962. Its report, *Marburg Revisited* (1966), included studies by a number of prominent Lutheran and Reformed scholars. The conferees could "find no insuperable obstacles to pulpit and altar fellowship" and recommended that the constituent churches "enter into discussions looking forward to intercommunion and the fuller recognition of one another's ministries". No action was taken by any of the sponsoring churches, and a second bilateral met 1972-74. This dialogue produced a short report which concluded that the Leuenberg agreement was not suitable for use in the US, but recommended continuing discussion.

Almost 20 years after the first Lutheran-Reformed dialogue convened, the third and most controversial began its deliberations (1981). Its report, *An Invitation to Action* (1983), builds on the Leuenberg agreement and *Marburg Revisited*. Brief statements on justification, the Lord's supper, and ministry are provided, along with two essays on ministry, a topic of growing ecumenical concern. The report urgently calls Lutheran and Reformed churches to recognize one another's doctrines of church, ministry and the Lord's supper, establish pulpit and table fellowship, and begin a process of reception.

An Invitation to Action stirred heated controversy within the Lutheran ranks. Published shortly before three major Lutheran bodies combined in 1988 to form the Evangelical Lutheran Church in America (ELCA), it sparked debate concerning the ecumenical commitments of the new church. Strong voices in the Lutheran Church in America (LCA) questioned the Reformed understanding of the Lord's supper and ministry, fearing that Lutheran-Reformed fellowship would hinder Roman Catholic-Lutheran convergence. The synods of the American Lutheran Church, Association of Evangelical Lutheran Churches, Reformed Church in America (RCA) and Presbyterian Church USA (PCUSA) adopted the report's principal recommendations and thus were in fellowship until the formation of the ELCA. The LCA, however, declined fellowship, requesting that the new church initiate conversations with the Reformed. ELCA conversations with the PCUSA, RCA and UCC began in October 1988.

Significant progress towards unity has been made in other parts of the world. The Evangelical Lutheran Church in the Netherlands anticipates moving beyond pulpit and table fellowship to formal union with the nation's principal Reformed churches. A union has already been achieved in Ethiopia, where in 1975 the Bethel Church (Presbyterian) became a synod in the Ethiopian Evangelical Church Mekane Yesus. In Indonesia the re-organization of the Communion of Churches in 1984 provided a framework for Lutheran and Reformed churches there to come into full mutual recognition of church, sacraments and ministry.

The first world-level Lutheran-Reformed dialogue was not convened until 1985. Its report, *Toward Church Fellowship* (1989), finds the condemnations of the past no longer applicable, affirms the unity and diversity of the two traditions, and recommends pulpit and table fellowship and growth together in mission.

PAUL R. FRIES

J.E. Andrews & J.A. Burgess eds, *An Invitation to Action*, Philadelphia, Fortress, 1984 • P.C. Empie & J.I. McCord eds, *Marburg Revisited*, Minneapolis, Augsburg, 1966 • W.G. Rusch & D.F. Martensen eds, *The Leuenberg Agreement and Lutheran-Reformed Relationships*, Minneapolis, Augsburg, 1989 • E. Schieffer, *Von Schauenburg nach Leuenberg: Entstehung und Bedeutung der Konkordie reformatorischer Kirchen in Europa*, Paderborn, Bonifatius, 1982.

LUTHERAN-ROMAN CATHOLIC DIALOGUE.

After two years of discussions between the Vatican Secretariat for Promoting Christian Unity* and the Lutheran World Federation,* a Joint Lutheran-Roman Catholic Study Commission first met in 1967 with the mandate to discuss "the gospel and the church". Its statement (1972), commonly called the Malta report, covered a wide range of topics: Tradition* and scripture, justification,* gospel and world, ordained ministry, papacy. Like later Lutheran-Roman Catholic dialogues, the commission noted both "the progressive overcoming of doctrinal disputes" and "structural problems which are largely responsible for continuing to keep our churches divided" (para. 46). Because of the variety of subjects treated, no topic was dealt with at length. The report recognized that growth will be by stages. Despite lack of full agreement on the doctrine of ordained ministry, the commission called for mutual recognition of ministerial office and for official actions making possible "occasional acts of intercommunion as, for example, during ecumenical events or in the pastoral care of those involved in mixed marriages" (para. 73). Of the seven Catholic participants, however, four dissented from the call for occasional intercommunion.*

The achievements and the limitations of the Malta report led to the creation of a second dialogue group, which produced three pairs of documents. First, two documents were occasioned by anniversaries: "All under One Christ" (1980), on the 450th anniversary of the presentation of the Augsburg confession, and "Martin Luther — Witness to Jesus Christ" (1983), on the 500th anniversary of Luther's birth. Second, two documents examined particular doctrinal problems. "The Eucharist" (1978), a topic which had not been discussed in the Malta report, opened with an extensive joint witness, structured by elements common to the liturgies of the two traditions (see **eucharist**). A following section on common tasks described extensive convergence on the presence of Christ in the supper, the latter's relation to the sacrifice of Christ, its communal nature, eucharistic ministry, and eucharistic fellowship. Certain remaining differences over presence and sacrifice were explicitly said to be no longer church-dividing. Nevertheless, agreement could not be reached on a proposed statement on "Reciprocal Admission to the Eucharist".

In "The Ministry in the Church" (1981), the commission agreed that a special ministry is "abidingly constitutive" of the church (para. 18). This ministry stands both within and over against the wider community (para. 23), "with the essential and specific function... to assemble and build up the Christian community by proclaiming the word of God, celebrating the sacraments and presiding over the liturgical, missionary and diaconal life of the community" (para. 31). Despite different formulations, a "consensus on the reality" of ordination* emerged. Greater difficulties arose in relation to episcopal ministry (see **episcopacy**). While the dialogue reached extensive agreement on the tasks of episcopal ministry, agreement on the necessity of a distinct episcopal ministry was stated in a conditional and qualified statement: "*If* both churches acknowledge that for faith this historical development of the one apostolic ministry into a more local and a more regional ministry has taken place with the help of the Holy Spirit and to this degree constitutes something essential for the church, then a *high degree of agreement* has been reached" (para. 49, emphasis in original). The possibility of the mutual recognition of ministries again surfaced but in a more modest form. The commission concluded that "it seems possible" that the *defectus* Catholics find in the sacrament of orders in Lutheran churches "refers to a partial lack rather than a complete absence" (paras 76-77). On this basis, there could be "a mutual recognition that the ministry in the other church exercises essential functions of the ministry that Jesus Christ instituted in his church" (para. 85). Any such recognition, however, must not be "an isolated act" but must be part of "a process in which the churches reciprocally accept each other" (para. 82).

A third pair of documents outlined what such a process would look like. "Ways to Community" (1980) described the ecumenical goal and steps leading towards it. Both goal and path are developed in terms of communion* *(Gemeinschaft)*. Unity* implies "a full spiritual and ecclesial fellowship" (para. 53), "an outward, visible unity which is becoming historically manifest in the life of the churches" (para. 33). "Facing Unity" (1985) described various models of unity (see **unity, models of**) advocated in ecumenical discussions and then outlined a possible process by which Lutheran and Catholic churches could grow together at the diocesan/synodical level. Central to the proposal was the collegial exercise of oversight, based on a mutual recognition "that in the other church the church of Jesus Christ is actualized" (para. 124). Such a collegial episcope would initially imply only the partial mutual recognition of ministry described in "The Ministry in the Church". Through joint ordinations, a common ministry would be created. The gradual creation of a common ministry would replace any immediate full mutual recognition of ministries. Responses to "Facing Unity" from Lutheran churches have been highly cautious. No response has been made

by Catholic bishops conferences or the Vatican.

A third series of international dialogues, begun in 1986, has focused on ecclesiology but has yet produced no texts.

The most extensive national dialogues have been in the US. After discussions of the status of the Nicene Creed* as dogma* of the church (1965) and one baptism for the remission of sins (1966), the dialogue addressed more controversial matters. In "The Eucharist as Sacrifice" (1967), "growing harmony" was reported on the sacrificial character of the supper. In addition, agreement was reached on "the full reality of Christ's presence" in the eucharist, even if that presence is understood in different terms.

Although the following statement on "Eucharist and Ministry" (1970) did not claim full agreement, the Catholic participants saw "no persuasive reason to deny the possibility of the Roman Catholic Church recognizing the validity of (Lutheran) ministry... and, correspondingly, the presence of the body and blood of Christ in the eucharistic celebrations of the Lutheran churches" (para. 54). This recommendation was widely criticized in Catholic circles.

The common statement on "Papal Primacy and the Universal Church" (1973) focused on the "Petrine function", i.e., "a particular form of ministry exercised by a person, officeholder, or local church with reference to the church as a whole" (para. 4). While such a function can be exercised by various persons and institutions, its "single most notable representative... has been the bishop of Rome" (see **primacy**). Legitimate diversity, collegiality, and subsidiarity were the principles for a possible "renewal of papal structures" (paras 23-24). Lutheran churches were asked "if they are able to acknowledge... the possibility and desirability of the papal ministry, renewed under the gospel and committed to Christian freedom, in a larger communion which would include the Lutheran churches" (para. 32). While the Catholic participants noted that the common statement "does not fully reflect everything that we believe concerning the papacy" (para. 34), they nevertheless asked whether "a distinct canonical status may be worked out by which Lutherans could be in official communion with the church of Rome" (para. 38).

The statement on papal primacy did not address questions about infallibility,* which was the topic of "Teaching Authority and Infallibility in the Church" (1978). Significant convergence was reported (Catholic Reflections, para. 1; Lutheran Reflections, para. 18), aided particularly by consideration of the role of reception.*

A greater breakthrough occurred in "Justification by Faith" (1983). Both sides judged the common statement sufficient, without accompanying Lutheran and Catholic reflections. A thematic statement summarized the central agreement: "Our entire hope of justification and salvation rests on Christ Jesus and on the gospel whereby the good news of God's merciful action in Christ is made known; we do not place our ultimate trust in anything other than God's promise and saving work in Christ" (paras 44,157). The dialogue reported "convergence (though not uniformity) on justification by faith considered in and of itself, and a significant though lesser convergence on the applications of the doctrine as a criterion of authenticity for the church's proclamation and practice" (para. 152). The US dialogue also commissioned joint Catholic-Lutheran studies on "Peter in the New Testament" (1973), "Mary in the New Testament" (1978), and "Righteousness in the New Testament" (1982).

Catholic-Lutheran dialogues have also taken place on the national level in other countries, most notably European. Two statements have been produced in Norway ("Communion, the Lord's Supper", 1982; "The Ministry of the Church", 1986) and three in Sweden ("Marriage and Family in the Christian Viewpoint", 1974; "Ecumenical Convergence on Baptism and Church Membership", 1978; and "The Office of the Bishop", 1988). The last Swedish statement is the most far-reaching Catholic-Lutheran agreement on episcopacy.

The only strictly Lutheran-Catholic bilateral dialogue statement from Germany has been "Kirchengemeinschaft in Wort und Sakrament" (1984). Longer than most statements, it discussed confession of faith, sacraments and worship, and ministerial office, all within the context of church and communion. Without minimizing differences, the dialogue questioned whether certain remaining differences are church-dividing, e.g. the sacramental

character of ordination (para. 66). The final paragraph affirmed full communion as the goal of Catholic-Lutheran relations and closed with Luke 9:62: "No one who puts his hand to the plough and looks back is fit for the kingdom of God."

MICHAEL ROOT

Committees of US National Council of Catholic Bishops, "Lutheran-Roman Catholic Dialogue: Critique", *Lutheran Quarterly*, 2, 1987 • W. Kasper, "Grundkonsens und Kirchengemeinschaft: Zum Stand des ökumenischen Gesprächs zwischen katholischer und evangelisch-lutherischer Kirche", *Theologische Quartalschrift*, 167, 1987 • H. Meyer, "Roman Catholic/Lutheran Dialogue", *One in Christ*, 22, 1986 • H. Meyer & L. Vischer eds, *Growth in Agreement: Reports and Agreed Statements of Ecumenical Conversations on a World Level*, New York, Paulist, 1984 • J. Wicks, "Ecclesiological Issues in the Lutheran-Catholic Dialogue (1965-1985)", in *Vatican II: Assessment and Perspectives. Twenty-five Years after (1962-1987)*, R. Latourelle ed., vol. 1, New York, Paulist, 1989.

LUTHERAN WORLD FEDERATION.

Established in 1947 by representatives of Lutheran churches in 23 countries, the LWF in 1990 numbered 105 member churches. It represents approximately 55 million of the estimated 59 million baptized Lutherans in the world; some churches, though not all, which are associated with the Lutheran Church-Missouri Synod remain outside the LWF.

Antecedent organizations include the general council of the Evangelical Lutheran Church in North America (1867), the General Evangelical Lutheran Conference in Germany (1868), and the Lutheran World Convention (1923). The formation of the LWF after the second world war was the extension of such movements as well as a response to post-war needs for reconciliation, relief and service.

The LWF regards itself as a "free association of Lutheran churches" joined together to further united witness in the world, common theological research, ecumenical involvement of Lutheran churches, and common response to issues of human need and social justice. It is ecumenically oriented, working in close cooperation with the WCC. The LWF has also sponsored international bilateral dialogues with official representatives of the Roman

Catholic, Orthodox, Anglican, Reformed, Methodist and Baptist traditions.

LWF assemblies have been held in Lund, Sweden (1947), Hanover, Federal Republic of Germany (1952), Minneapolis, USA (1957), Helsinki, Finland (1963), Evian-les-Bains, France (1970), Dar es Salaam, Tanzania (1977), Budapest, Hungary (1984), and Curitiba, Brazil (1990). LWF's eighth assembly (1990) adopted a new constitution which includes the statement: "The Lutheran World Federation is a communion of churches which confess the Triune God, agree in the proclamation of the word of God and are united in pulpit and altar fellowship." LWF self-understanding is thus built around a theology of communion* (koinonia),* with increased impetus towards confessional unity, joint mission and service, and ecumenical commitment.

The eighth assembly also authorized a new LWF structure. The assembly, which meets every six years, remains the highest legislative authority; a council serves as the governing body. The council, comprising 48 elected members, has a representation of 50% from the so-called Northern churches and 50% from churches of the two-thirds world. Headquarters for the LWF secretariat are in the Ecumenical Centre, Geneva. The new structure calls for three departments: theology and studies, mission and development, and world service. About 100 staff members serve at the LWF headquarters. Approximately 5,000 persons are employed in LWF world service projects throughout the world.

NORMAN A. HJELM

LUTHERANISM. The church reform initiated by Martin Luther in 1517 at Wittenberg, Germany, developed into a movement, became established under political rulers chiefly in Central and Northern Europe, survived elsewhere (in Eastern Europe) until granted toleration, and spread by massive emigration especially to North America but also to Australia, South Africa and Latin America. It also grew by missionary activities in Asia, Africa and Latin America. Early in the 20th century Lutherans (practising infant baptism) were said to number about 80 million baptized, although the ravages of two world wars and the omission of the large

number estimated within the membership of Germany's united churches has reduced the Lutheran total worldwide to a little over a claimed 50 million.

Lutherans have always considered themselves as part of the church* catholic and evangelical, bound to the scriptures and confessing the faith* set forth in the three ecumenical creeds.* Although Lutherans vary among themselves in ways of worship — wherein the Lord's supper is central — and although they differ among themselves in forms of church organization (whether a state church as in Scandinavia, or a free church as in most other parts of the world), Lutherans are doctrinally and legally identified by the same confession of faith as presented by their political protectors to the imperial diet at Augsburg in 1530. To whatever degree professed, the Augsburg confession (also called the Augustana) and Luther's small catechism ("the Bible of the laity") have been the chief symbols of mutual recognition among Lutherans for more than 450 years.

Yet this basic unity has been no guarantee against disunity born of doctrinal debates of ethnic, linguistic, cultural, or other contrasts. Twin developments during the 20th century, however, have fostered Lutheran unity in new ways. One has been the creation of a global and service-oriented confessional fellowship, first through the Lutheran World Convention (LWC, founded in 1923) and then, since 1947, through the Lutheran World Federation* (LWF) — based in Geneva and including most Lutherans. The other has been the Lutheran participation in the ecumenical movement, both in the organizational format of the WCC and in the broader ambience of bilateral dialogues (see **dialogue, bilateral**), especially with the Roman Catholic Church since Vatican II.*

Lutheran teaching presupposes not only "that one holy church is to continue for ever" but also that "for the true unity of the church it is enough to agree concerning the teaching of the gospel and the administration of the sacraments" (Augustana 7) — meaning baptism* and the eucharist.* Guideposts to such agreements have been four: faith alone (justification), grace alone (forgiveness), scripture alone (authority) and Christ alone (Saviour). Tradition and traditions* which are not contrary to scripture have their place in the historical church. The life of the Christian — as forgiven sinner — embodies precepts of the law and promises of the gospel. The interplay of church and society (or state) generally follows Luther's teaching on the two realms: the realm on God's right, the church; and the realm on God's left, the state — both are accountable to God.

Despite Luther's objection, the organized church of his spiritual heirs was called Lutheran and not, as he had preferred, evangelical. By the religious peace of Augsburg (1555) Lutherans were tolerated alongside Roman Catholics on a territorial basis: the religion of the ruler determined the religion of his subjects. Outside Germany, in Denmark (including Norway) and Sweden (including Finland) the change to Lutheran remained. In parts of Eastern Europe (as in Poland) initial gains shrank, and a Lutheran minority survived by toleration. Germany's many territories presented a patchwork of Lutheran and Roman Catholic lands. The entry of Calvinism and the appeal of the Reformed faith to ruling families and territorial princes complicated the confessional situation. Although the principle was that the religion of the ruler determined the religion of his subjects, when the Hohenzollern turned Reformed (1613), the vast majority of his subjects remained Lutheran. When the king of Saxony became a Catholic in order to qualify for the Polish crown (1697), his people continued Lutheran. When Franconia became part of Catholic Bavaria (1803), the Franconians became more Lutheran.

While Scandinavia and Finland remained homogeneously Lutheran, Germany's religious map of Roman Catholic, Lutheran and Reformed territorial churches added the United church in 1817. In that year the administrative (but not confessional) consolidation of a large Lutheran majority and a small Reformed minority became the Evangelical Church of the Old Prussian Union. A common liturgy* and other hallmarks reflected a mainly Lutheran tradition. Other United churches, as in Hesse or the Palatinate, were unions of consensus* which minimized confessional derivation. In Germany as a whole Lutherans and United were about equal in number. Yet, to safeguard their identity, the confessionally intact churches (Hanover, Saxony, Bavaria, etc.) in 1868 formed the General Evangelical

Lutheran Conference (GELC). The aim was to stem an advance of the Prussian Union.

In North America the GELC counterpart, the general council (1868), gathered the confessionally moderate synods of German and Swedish origin. With the older general synod (1820), the council made confessional Lutheranism increasingly active in the anglophone world. What began in 1868 as a loose international linkage of confessional kin intensified, particularly in the wake of the 20th century's world wars. Continental Europe, the Northern countries and North America provided the leaders who formed the LWC and its stronger successor, the LWF.

The North American scene, meanwhile, had come to reflect not only a European diversity but also one created by successive stages of Americanization among Lutherans. On the confessional right stood the Missouri synod and its satellites. On the relative left stood the general synod and its openness towards other Protestants — from before the days of the World's Evangelical Alliance* (1846) and through the early years of the Federal Council of Churches (1908). As to European connections, the Missouri Lutherans treated evangelicals of the Prussian Union, the United, as their traditional enemy; but the general synodists regarded that same body as a friend — thus being charged with unionism by the Missourians. General synod representatives became active in the Faith and Order* movement soon after 1910. Others followed later.

The United Lutheran Church in America (ULCA, 1918) — a merger of the general council, general synod, united synod south — continued the F&O connection. With an eye towards other Lutherans, the ULCA preferred the ecclesial concerns of F&O instead of the more social concerns of the Söderblom-led Life and Work.* German Lutherans and United, however, favoured the latter; they trusted Swedish more than Anglo-Saxon leadership in matters ecumenical. Paradoxically, the Nazi authorities, who resented L&W's decision to side with the Confessing Church* (Fanø 1934), forbade German participation at both the Oxford and Edinburgh (1937) meetings. In that way, Swedish theologians became the leading Lutheran voices ecumenically (Gustav Aulén, Yngve Brilioth, Anders Nygren). At Utrecht (1938), ULCA president

Frederick Knubel proposed to the provisional committee that the new WCC provide for proportional "confessional representation" of Lutheran churches collectively, as had been done for Eastern Orthodox, in the Council's assembly and central committee, a proposal voted upon favourably a decade later at the first assembly in Amsterdam.

In the wake of the second world war, confessional representation as an aim achieved a dual purpose: it helped to rally Lutheran unity internationally, and it opened the way for most Lutheran churches to join the WCC and together to become ecumenically active. The new ULCA president, Franklin Clark Fry, vice-chair of the central committee (under the bishop of Chichester, G.K.A. Bell) 1948-54, subsequently served as its influential chair for two terms (1954-68). Simultaneously, Fry's leading role in the LWF (its president after Nygren, and Hanns Lilje, bishop of Hanover), personified the creative interlinking of confessional and ecumenical realities in the striving for Christian unity.*

In Asia, Africa and Latin America, as earlier in Australia, Lutheran church bodies had been forming slowly since the 1920s. Some, as in Brazil, South Africa or Australia, were mainly gatherings of European immigrants, much as had occurred in the USA and Canada. Other church bodies were the result of mission efforts based in Europe and North America and directed towards peoples of other religions. For Lutherans, the ecclesial autonomy had first developed in the British colonies of North America, then was applied in India, Japan, China, South Africa, and elsewhere.

After 1947, LWF policy was to consolidate diverse enterprises and to achieve one Lutheran church in a given country; the church in Tanzania remains the best example. To be sure, the confessional-ecumenical motif has found various expressions among third-world Lutherans, and instructively so. The pressures to be ecumenical are strong, the need to share from the riches of a confessional heritage is demanding, and the fact of being (usually) a Christian minority amid peoples of other religions has a message for Lutherans in Europe and America.

Of the perhaps 5 million immigrants who arrived in North America as Lutherans from the Old World, an estimated 25% remained in Lutheran churches. Many, upwardly mobile, were gathered into the Episcopalian, Presbyterian, Methodist and other communions, or were lost to the church altogether. The experience of being regarded as fair game for mission from the side of English-speaking Protestants put most Lutheran church bodies on the defensive. Instances of Lutherans and non-Lutherans in occasional pulpit and altar fellowship were denounced by many conservative Lutherans as unionism — mainly on theological grounds, but with sociological implications as well.

Doctrinal agreement, on the basis of the historic confessions (Augustana, etc.), was the prerequisite to fellowship. For some, like the "Missourians", it remains so. The ULCA Washington declaration (1920), however, pointed to great Lutheran union and eventual ecumenical participation. Throughout their history, Lutherans have given prominence to theology, have regarded agreement in doctrine as basic to theology, have emphasized Christology, and have fostered Christian education — also in their missionary outreach.

The gradual indigenization of the Lutheran church in the English-speaking world may be seen as a major development in ecclesial history. This as well as other aspects of the Lutheran legacy have contributed historical depth to the timeliness of the bilateral dialogues in recent years. An early sign in this direction has been the Lutheran Foundation for Ecumenical Research in Strasbourg (1963); its faculty members conduct seminars in all continents. In the USA, too, the common statement on justification by faith (1983) marked 20 years of Lutheran-Roman Catholic dialogue. Within the WCC itself, moreover, Lutherans have participated proportionately and have been a major contributor financially (esp. the Federal Republic of Germany, Sweden and the US). In the ecumenical movement Lutherans, like others committed to Christian unity, act upon the faith "that one holy church is to continue for ever".

E. THEODORE BACHMANN

P. Althaus, *Die Theologie Martin Luthers* (ET *The Theology of Martin Luther*, Philadelphia, Fortress, 1966) • H.T. Neve & B.A. Johnson, *The Maturing of American Lutheranism*, Minneapolis, Augsburg, 1968 • V. Vajta ed., *Die Evangelische-Lutherische Kirche: Vergangenheit und Gegenwart*, Stuttgart, Evangelisches Verlagswerk, 1977.

M

MACKAY, JOHN ALEXANDER. B. 7.5.1889, Inverness, Scotland; d. 9.6.1983, Princeton, NJ, USA. Chairman of commission 5 on "The Universal Church and the World of Nations" of the Oxford conference, 1937, Mackay was a member of the provisional committee of the WCC, 1946-48, chairman of the International Missionary Council, 1947-57, a member of the WCC central committee, 1948-54, chairman of commission 2 on "The Church's Witness to God's Design" of Amsterdam 1948, chairman of the joint committee of IMC and WCC, 1948-54, and president of the World Presbyterian Alliance, 1954-59. He studied at Aberdeen, Princeton and Madrid. He was for a period a missionary of the Presbyterian Church (USA) in Peru. As religious work secretary for the South American Federation of the YMCAs, he lived first in Montevideo and later in Mexico City, 1926-32. He was secretary for Latin America and Africa, Board of Foreign Missions, Presbyterian Church in the USA, 1932-36, and then president and professor of ecumenics at Princeton Theological Seminary, 1936-59. Mackay was founder and editor of *Theology Today*, an editor of *The Westminster Study Edition of the Holy Bible* and contributing editor to *Christianity and Crisis*. He wrote *Ecumenics: The Science of the Church Universal* (Englewood Cliffs, NJ, Prentice-Hall, 1964), and *The Other Spanish Christ* (London, SCM, 1932). See *The Ecumenical Era in Church and Society: A Symposium in Honor of John A. Mackay*, E.J. Jurji ed. (New York, Macmillan, 1959).

ANS J. VAN DER BENT

MAGISTERIUM. "Magisterium" is the term used for the teaching authority* in Roman Catholicism. In the RC church, teaching authority is ordinarily exercised by the bishops (see **episcopacy**) and by other appointed teachers. In extraordinary cases it can be exercised by an ecumenical council,* or even by the pope alone.

See **infallibility, primacy, teaching authority**.

GEOFFREY WAINWRIGHT

Congregation for the Doctrine of the Faith, *Instruction on the Ecclesial Vocation of the Theologian*, Vatican City, 1990.

MAGNIFICAT. The Magnificat, the song of Mary, the mother of Jesus Christ, was highly acclaimed by Luther. Today it serves as a fundamental text in the renovation of Catholic Marian theology (Paul VI, *Marialis Cultus*, n.37; John Paul II, *Redemptoris Mater*, nn.35-37) and as a privileged point of focus among Christians, above all in the third world, and especially in Latin America, where the influence of Mary has always been very strong. This "new woman", servant of God resembling the suffering servant (Isa. 42-53; Phil. 2:7), expresses the spirituality of liberation.

The Magnificat forms a literary unit with the annunciation and visitation (Luke 1:26-56), and its texture is woven with reminiscences of psalms and prophets. The song of Mary, in the mystery of the incarnation* of the Word, is also the song of all the children of God. It is made up of (1) praise and acclamation, at the beginning and end (vv.46-50,54-55); and (2) prophetic announcement, in the central part (vv.51-53).

Current exegesis views Mary as a disciple of Jesus, a prophetess through the power of the Spirit (Luke 1:35) whose message condemns relationships of domination and oppression and announces a new order of justice* and peace,* a new creation. Mary, daughter of Zion, symbolizing the poor* among the children of Israel, sets in motion a "revolution" which will bring about a change of heart (v.51).

Luke, ever insistent on the mercy of God, points out that it is God, Lord and Saviour, all-powerful and holy (vv.46-49), who manifests divine pity by exalting the poor, the weak and the humble and by emptying (and thus disposing them to accept grace*) the rich, the powerful and the arrogant, thus fulfilling the promise made to Abraham.

See also **Mary in the ecumenical movement**.

MARIA TERESA PORCILE SANTISO

MAR THOMA CHURCH.

The Mar Thoma Syrian Church of Malabar, with a membership of around 700,000, is an independent reformed Eastern church. "Mar Thoma" means St Thomas. Much of what is today the Kerala state in India used to be known as Malabar. Christians here were for centuries under the rule of bishops from Syria, and the liturgical language was Syriac; hence the rather misleading epithet "Syrian". The two other major Syrian churches in India are the Malankara Jacobite Syrian Church, which is under the Syrian Orthodox Patriarchate of Antioch, and the autocephalous Malankara Orthodox Syrian Church. A large section of the old St Thomas Church is today part of the Roman Catholic Church, and a much smaller number who joined the Anglican Church are now in the Church of South India (CSI). Up to the 16th century all of them belonged to a single church with one common tradition that traced its origins to the work of the apostle Thomas.

According to that tradition, Thomas landed at the port of Cranganur on the Malabar coast in A.D. 52, established churches in seven places in Kerala, and died a martyr's death in 72 at a place near Madras. While no unambiguous historical evidence supports this tradition, no clear proof exists against it. The tradition is old, strong and an integral part of the self-understanding of the Syrian Christian community. And there is sufficient evidence to support the presence of a thriving Christian community in this part of India from the 4th century onwards. Of how the church was organized and how it lived and witnessed within the Hindu milieu, very little is known. It is often alleged that the Portuguese, in their zeal to keep inviolate the claims of Rome, destroyed the historical records of St Thomas Christians.

The Portuguese came to India early in the 17th century and were welcomed by the Christian community. Largely unaware of the divisions that had crept into the Christian church outside Kerala, by the end of the century the St Thomas Christians allowed themselves to be brought under Roman rule. But disaffection soon set in, both with the Portuguese and with the Roman Catholicism they represented. In 1653 a large number broke away from Rome, re-affirming their centuries-old heritage. The church, however, was now divided and would be further divided in the years to come.

The Mar Thoma Church (MTC) traces its immediate history to a reform movement within the old St Thomas Church. The impetus for reform came from the work of British missionaries representing Anglican evangelicalism. That work, begun in the early years of the 18th century, had led to the translation of the Bible into the local language, Malayalam. Chief among the architects of reform was a parish priest called Abraham Malpan. He translated the liturgy into Malayalam, making changes in it to remove what were perceived as Roman accretions. The reformers were "inspired by the vision of an Eastern evangelical church seeking to comprehend the evangelical faith and experience within the framework of the corporate life and liturgical devotion" of the Eastern tradition. They affirmed the central place of the Bible and encouraged its "open use" in family worship and church services.

They stressed the importance of the sermon in Sunday worship. All this resulted in a search for new standards of conduct and a lived piety and, in course of time, in a recognition of the church's missionary vocation. The Mar Thoma Evangelistic Association was formed in 1889, and it has been active in evangelistic work in and outside Kerala. The week-long annual convention it holds at a place called Maramon attracts over 100,000 people, as well as preachers belonging to a wide variety of church traditions from many parts of the world.

The ecumenical character of the Maramon convention reflects the ecumenical openness of the MTC. The preamble to its constitution affirms that the church, "believed to be founded by St Thomas, one of the apostles of Christ, and called by that name, is part of the one apostolic and catholic church". For decades it has been in communion* with the Anglican church. It maintains special relations with the Episcopal Church. It is a member of the National Council of Churches in India and the Christian Conference of Asia. It has been a member of the WCC from the beginning. Juhanon Mar Thoma, metropolitan at that time, was a WCC president from 1954 to 1961. M.M. Thomas, a Mar Thoma layman, was moderator of the WCC central committee between 1968 and 1976.

Formed in 1978, the joint council of the Church of North India, the CSI and the MTC is "the visible organ of the common action by the three churches, which recognize themselves as belonging to the one church of Jesus Christ in India even while remaining as autonomous churches, each having its own identity of traditions and organizational structures". The joint council has two objectives: to "serve as the common organ of the three churches for working towards a visible manifestation of the unity of these churches and of the whole church of Jesus Christ in India", and to "help the churches to fulfill the mission of evangelization of the people of India and of witnessing to the righteousness of God revealed in the gospel of Jesus Christ by striving for a just society".

The MTC is often described as a bridge church. In its liturgy and in the social life of its community, it retains much of the Eastern tradition. In its theology it has clear affinities with the churches of the Reformation in the West. This synthesis is ecumenically significant. The intrachurch ecumenical dialogue the church embodies is not without tensions and conflicts. But that dialogue is part of the day-to-day life of its members and obtains within a passionate loyalty to the church. In the main the dialogue within the church is about two questions: Did the reform go too far? Did it go far enough? The questions represent distinct ecclesiological and theological stances, but the dialogue itself involves a range of positions between the "high" and "low" emphases. In so far as that ongoing dialogue demonstrates the creative possibilities of ecumenism — such as a new social consciousness, a search for democratic structures for the church, and a new interest in relating issues of faith to questions of life and work — and in so far as the life of the church demonstrates the risks and perils such dialogue entails, the Mar Thoma Church is of importance for the wider interchurch ecumenism.

T.K. THOMAS

G.B. Firth, *An Introduction to Indian Church History*, Madras, CLS, 1961 • K.K. Kuruvilla, *A History of the Mar Thoma Church and Its Doctrines*, Madras, CLS, 1951 • C.P. Mathew & M.M. Thomas, *The Indian Churches of St Thomas*, Delhi, ISPCK, 1967.

MARRIAGE.

I

Love between man and woman is the only real marriage which takes place when they discover each other, delight in each other and cleave to each other, as we read in Gen. 2:23-25 and as Jesus confirms in the gospel (Mark 10:6-9 and par.). Love is what makes marriage, and not the other way round. Love is not legitimized and made to last through formal religious marriage.

The churches eventually became increasingly concerned with preserving marriage, maintaining the civil status of married couples and, through marriage, keeping a hold over private life, emotions and the confession to which the children would later belong. Ecumenism exists because of the relations between the various historic churches with their individual theologies and liturgies. Very often it is precisely when a marriage takes place that a genuine, loyal and respectful ecumenism turns out to be most difficult to put into practice — hence what I have said both about the marvel of human love and the hindrances the various churches can create when it is made official.

While the Bible includes a great many prescriptions for worshipping God and running one's life, neither the Old Testament nor the New contains any rules for the marriage ceremony. Believers live out their marriages exactly as their contemporaries do. In the remote age of the patriarchs, for example, that included polygamy. In a similar way the NT also accepts the manners of its day, when women were subordinate to men and men were responsible for women's honour and happiness. Christians had civil marriages in line with the customs of the civilization and city to which they belonged; there was no specifically Christian marriage during the first three centuries.

The great novelty, however, was that believers practised different customs in the Lord. The God of the people of Israel and of the church of Jesus Christ is in fact a God who joins with humanity in a fervent, patient, strong and elective divine covenant* of love. And it is indeed in human love in marriage that the prophets and apostles of God found the most striking and enduring parable to illustrate the bond God has with us, which is neither a yoke nor a link that lacks warmth but a live exchange. Now at last human marriage for its part stops being an arrangement or a custom and becomes a sharing of everything between two beings who, however, remain quite distinct individuals. They are covenanted in love, one for the other.

Marriage as a church sacrament. By "sacrament" here we must understand a reference to the loving covenant of God with human beings and the church ceremony which alone validates and binds and is therefore as indissoluble as (let us say) God's link with us in Abraham, Isaac, Jacob and Jesus Christ. Through the sacrament marriage establishes an unchangeable state which is strong enough to combat our estrangements, instabilities and infidelities. But marriage as a sacrament also runs the risk of looking like a prison with the church holding the key.

Much interest was devoted to the initial conditions for a valid marriage (the free consent of the partners, the fulfilment of the due conjugal obligations of sex) — more than in

the development of the partners' lives, whereas the whole Bible is simply the story of the high points in the covenant between God and his people. The sacrament becomes the central act, with its conditions and the possibilities for its annulment by a court of the church.

For Roman Catholicism, marriage, clearly defined by the council of Trent,* is one of seven sacraments provided by the church for the salvation of souls. This group of seven sacraments was evolved in the 13th century, in the period of the great cathedrals and scholastic theology. It sanctifies and provides a framework for the subsequent periods of one's life. Marriage is undoubtedly a sacrament in a category of its own. Its biblical roots lie in the Latin translation of the Greek words behind Eph. 5:32 (a profound "mystery"). But does this phrase apply to marriage or to the incarnation of Jesus Christ, who leaves his Father in heaven to cleave to his bride on earth, the church?

It is the married partners who give each other the sacrament. But since Trent the sacrament has to be presided over by a priest, and most frequently the nuptial mass is referred to and the eucharist is celebrated.

"Sacrament" is a strong word. Like baptism, it is not something renewable. But is this word really appropriate theologically, since it is not related here directly to the cross and resurrection of Jesus Christ as in baptism and the eucharist? When situations of spiritual and psychological difficulty and distress will subsequently arise, should people remain sacramentally married, even if they have separated and have no common life? And why should divorce — the failure of marriage — remain the only unforgivable sin?

Anglicans have kept the word "sacrament" for marriage but do not have the seven medieval sacraments. The Protestant churches speak of a "ceremony of blessing" when two partners declare before the whole congregation that they have decided to be joined together in the presence of God and when they make their gratitude public and pray the God of the covenant to go with them and bless them in their future commitments. The word "ceremony" seems more correct theologically than "sacrament" — more firmly rooted in the biblical vocabulary and in the practice of the ancient church. It also makes it possible to

A fisherman and his wife, Lake Titicaca, Bolivia (WCC/Peter Williams)

invoke again God's blessing on those who, having failed, contract a new union. Nevertheless a strong word is needed here too, involving complete commitment, as God entered into a commitment with his people and Jesus Christ did with his church.

Hesitation about marriage: the decision to love. All the churches are faced today with a crisis in marriage. Frequently people are hesitant about marrying, for there are so many divorces. Life in partnership has become considerably longer. Can there be a certainty of getting along well together for so long with truly felt happiness, and not simply because of a vow to be faithful? Also, civil society can very easily come to terms with the fact of unmarried couples and their children, who are by no means looked down on. So then, whether marriage is called a sacrament or a blessing, what does the part played by the churches add or guarantee here?

The ecumenical movement, with its diminishing differences and developing convergences, is in contrast with the past history of our churches. It is the most united possible proclamation of the active goodness of God today. Likewise, marriage means deciding to

live for each other as God decided to live for us in Abraham, David and Jesus Christ, and we in turn decide to live for him. An irresolute love which is always hesitant inevitably becomes weak and gradually disappears. Marriage is the opportunity to decide in love and also to say so in front of witnesses, to make them happy and strengthen us.

This is why the churches certainly do not compel people to marry but rejoice with those who have decided to marry. The happiness of human love on earth makes God happy in heaven. That is what the churches have to say on marriage — and it is a word that is rather more spiritual than moral, psychological or sociological in these days when many are hesitant about making up their minds.

See also **divorce; ethics, sexual; family; marriage, mixed**.

ANDRÉ DUMAS

II

In most parts of the world today, marriage is a voluntary joining of two lives intended to last for the lifetime of the couple. The understanding of marriage has changed dramatically over the centuries from patterns of relationship based on control and subordination to others characterized by mutuality and equality. The transition towards a more personal approach to marriage has not been easy throughout the centuries, but over the last decades the pace of change has tended to increase dramatically.

In every culture there are *laws* which clearly mark the beginning (and the end) of marriage, *rituals* that involve the community (to assure the adequate social transition), and *customs* (norms and rules) for support and encouragement. Thus, the voluntary relationship established between husband and wife is unique to them and to those around them, and is clearly differentiated from the relationship to other relatives, the community and the society at large. In most societies marriages are one of the most important public events in common life.

Marriage has been defined in various ways: as a mystery, a sacrament, a contract, a vocation, a communion, an institution, etc. Each definition corresponds to a specific historical moment and cultural context.

In the West until recently, couples, families and households were part of a whole. To deal with one of them was to deal with them all. In many parts of the world this is still the custom. W.J. Everett affirms: "When a prelate blessed a marriage he also was blessing a family (*matrimonium*) and a household (*patrimonium*). He was also legitimizing the formation of an enterprise central to the economic, social, and governmental welfare of the people as a whole... It is little wonder that today we have such trouble sorting out what the church's concern really was when it got involved with marriage."

The shift from agricultural to industrial economies has had a profound effect on marriage, the family and households all over the world. Economic, cultural and scientific changes deeply affect the understanding of marriage, its nature and goals. Women and men today tend to feel less hesitant about remaining single, and those who choose to marry expect happiness, self-fulfilment, "instant therapy" from the marriage relationship. Procreation is considered an option rather than the inevitable outcome of the marriage union. Married couples share a greater commitment to interpersonal intimacy and are increasingly aware of the equal rights of both sexes.

Longevity and birth control have provided couples with the possibility of looking forward to the time when the marriage will develop into a long-term friendship, independent of procreation and raising children.

Commissions have been appointed in almost every mainline Protestant church to reflect on marriage and to reformulate a Christian approach to it. The Orthodox church is looking afresh into its liturgies of marriage to find theological and pastoral elements to meet new demands. Vatican II developed a new paradigm to describe Roman-Catholic marriages, described by David Thomas as a shift "from viewing marriage primarily as a biological and juridical union to one which is more interpersonal, spiritual and existential".

Marriage in the history of the church. The Bible nowhere records the requirement of a religious ceremony, and in the early church marriage was not a religious matter. Most weddings during the first four centuries were presided over by the father, who joined the hands of the couple. Occasionally bishops were invited to officiate. Late in the 4th century Christian wedding ceremonies acquired sacred character by having a priest or bishop bless the couple, or, more commonly the bride (for fertility). In the 9th century, Charlemagne in the Western church (802) and Emperor Leo the Wise in the Eastern church (895) tried to impose the rule that a priest must officiate at weddings and the church accord its blessings.

In Southern Europe the Roman tradition had long held that the consent (*consensus*) of either the couple or their parents was required, since arranged marriages were a universal practice among all social strata. The Germanic and Frankish traditions of Northern Europe, however, insisted that the key element was consummation (*copula*) after the marriage consent. Since then, these two positions have been part of the church's discussion of marriage, divorce and annulment.

In the 9th century marriages began to be held in the church. This practice was gradually given liturgical form, and by the 12th century, marriage was validly and legitimately contracted in a marriage liturgy, into which the "civil" ceremonies had been assimilated. At the same time theologians began to discuss the sacramental nature of marriage, though it was not until the council of Trent* (1545-63) that official status was given to marriage as a sacrament.

Facing the proliferation of clandestine marriages, the church used the theology of the *sacramentum*, a sacral sign, to defend the Christian marriage, though no saving power was explicitly accorded to marriage. Edward Schillebeeckx asserts: "The idea that sacraments in the strict sense were those of importance for Christian life contributed directly to the inclusion of marriage among the seven, despite the fact that marriage was not regarded at this time as having a power of grace, but only as being a sign of more sublime mystery."

With the Protestant Reformation, sacraments* were questioned. The Reformed churches agreed that marriage as a sacrament and obligatory celibacy were not in accordance with scripture or with the original Christian tradition. Marriage was seen by the reformers as a purely ethical matter to be controlled by the government, rather than a symbolic matter under church jurisdiction. Other concepts were used to characterize marriage, such as "vocation", "covenant", and "communion". In modern Protestantism the covenant* model is very widespread as a protest against the individualistic connotations of contract or the overly naturalistic approaches in hierarchical sacrament models. However, says Georges Crespy, "there is no, in the strict sense of the term, Reformed doctrine of marriage which has been expressed and proposed to Protestant people as a demand or requisite of faith". This does not mean that there is no Protestant theological reflection on the subject nor that marriage has necessarily been secularized. In the Protestant countries marriage still remained within the province of the Christian communities.

Besides re-affirming the sacramental nature of marriage and the church's right to regulate, annul or dissolve it, the council of Trent* resolved that the only valid contract of marriage for baptized Christians was one made in the presence of a priest and two witnesses (though not necessarily liturgically or in church). Marriage, which had always been a secular reality experienced "in the Lord", now seemed to have become an exclusively ecclesiastical affair. Today, despite the above-mentioned new emphasis of Vatican II, the Roman Catholic doctrine and practice of marriage seems frozen in the 16th century.

Points of convergence and divergence. A controversial issue in the Christian understanding of marriage is its ends or purposes. The Roman Catholic point of view has focused primarily on procreation and rearing children and secondarily, as *The Catholic Encyclopedia* (1976) says, "the mutual aid, both material and spiritual, and the overcoming of sexual concupiscence in a legitimate manner".

Most Protestant churches tend to start the list of the purposes of marriage with companionship, without denying the natural effect of sexual intercourse: procreation. Relationship is explained as required for the sake of offspring. The fecundity resulting from the marriage union is a by-product of the union between man and woman, which is valuable for its own sake. "To give relationship priority in importance is not 20th century perversity," says Helen Oppenheimer. "It picks out a strand in our tradition that has always been there (cf. 1 Sam.1:8), though no doubt reliable contraception makes the strand easier to find."

Another point of controversy is related to divorce.* The Roman Catholic Church does not accept divorce, while Protestant and Orthodox churches generally do. Rome, however, holds the "right of the key" to annul a marriage, but excommunicates those who divorce (see **excommunication**). The Orthodox church does not exclude the divorced from communion and in certain cases determines that marriage does not exist, going so far as to bless subsequent marriages when they are entered into with a spirit of repentance. Olivier Clément comments: "The indissolubility of the bond does not promote love. The question of divorce arises when nothing is left to save; the bond declared indissoluble at the beginning is already broken, and the law has nothing that can replace grace. The law can neither heal nor restore to life, nor can it say 'Arise, and walk.'"

On the other hand, most Christians agree on certain characteristics of marriage that claim to be Christian: it is monogamous, holy, based on fidelity and companionship, and intended to last until death. All hold high views of its importance as a divine space, established by God at creation* as a foundation of human society as a blessing for humankind.

Among Eastern churches, the Pauline idea of the church as the bride of Christ exerted an earlier and greater influence. Their liturgies of marriage were inspired in the communion of Christ with the church. More emphasis also has been placed on the mystical meaning of marriage and its spirituality. Besides that, theologians of the Eastern churches had a less pessimistic view of sex and sexuality than the Western church, church fathers and scholars. Marriage, then, is regarded by the church as a miniature where unity (uniqueness, monogamous character, fidelity), sanctity, catholicity and apostolicity (moving towards others) are present.

Conclusion. Theological reflection on marriage, forged throughout centuries to transform a civil contract into a liturgical event, has helped canonists and church jurists to define their field in juridical abstractions, but it has been of scarcely any help in pastoral matters or in the treatment of marriage as an anthropological fact.

A great deal of effort has been invested in defining marriage in its initial stage, the wedding ceremony: how to enter in it, who presides and legitimates, which liturgy is the most appropriate, etc. Proportionately less attention has been accorded the study of marriage as a life-spanning process, comprising stages of growth, dilemmas and pains, crises and challenges. Oppenheimer declares: "In the very ordinariness of the immense claims they make upon each other — the give-and-take of everyday life — married people have a humanly valid mystery which is able to be a model of the grace of God." Never before in the history of humankind has married life been led back in such a remarkable way to its original, authentic shape and form as it has today. It is time to look afresh at marriage from this perspective on the threshold of a new millennium. In doing so, new and creative pastoral understandings and tools may become available to the church, couples and families of today.

See also **marriage, interfaith; marriage, mixed**.

JORGE E. MALDONADO

P. Evdokimov, *Le sacrement de l'amour* (ET *The Sacrament of Love: The Nuptial Mystery in the Light of the Orthodox Tradition*, Crestwood, NY, St Vladimir's Seminary, 1985) • W.J. Everett, *Blessed Be the Bond: Christian Perspectives on Marriage and Family*, Philadelphia, Fortress, 1985 • A. Hastings, *Christian Marriage in Africa*, London, SPCK, 1973 • D. Mace & V. Mace, *The Sacred Fire: Christian Marriage through the Ages*, Nashville, TN, Abingdon, 1986 • H. Oppenheimer, in *New Dictionary of Christian Ethics*, London, SCM, 1986 • E. Schillebeeckx, *Marriage: Human Reality and Saving Mystery*, London, Sheed & Ward, 1978.

MARRIAGE, INTERFAITH. We confront the issue of interfaith or mixed-faith marriage in both the Old and the New Testaments. Joseph, Moses, David and Solomon, for example, married non-Israelite women, and the Bible celebrates the marriage of the Moabitess Ruth to Boaz. On the whole, however, mixed-faith marriages are not favoured in the OT, for fear that faith in the God of Israel would be compromised by the foreign practices introduced by the partner of other faith (Ezra 9-10; Neh. 13:23-29; Mal. 2:10). The clear prohibition and the reason for it are given in Deut. 7:3-4: "You shall not make marriages with them, giving your daughters to their sons or taking their daughters for your sons. For they would turn away your sons from following me, to serve other gods."

In the NT Paul was confronted with the issue in Corinth. Writing on the question of re-marriage where one of the partners had died, Paul allows re-marriage, but "only in the Lord" (1 Cor. 7:39), which is traditionally understood to mean that Paul advocated marriage only among Christians. In the case of a convert where the other partner remained in another tradition, Paul advised against divorce, unless the other partner desired it (vv.12-16).

In the early history of the church there were no uniform practices, although marriage between persons of the same faith was favoured. The first piece of legislation about mixed marriages emanated from the synod of Elvira in Spain at the beginning of the 4th century. It rejected marriage to a person of another faith as "spiritual adultery". In A.D. 314 the synod of Arles repeated the prohibition, adding for the first time the penalty of deprivation of communion for a period to the offenders.

The ecumenical council of Chalcedon* in 451 first issued the injunction that Christians will be permitted to marry a person of another faith, provided the person converted to Christianity and the children are baptized. These stipulations were eventually integrated into the code of canon law of the Roman Catholic Church which came into force in May 1918 and provided the basic policy of marriage to a person of another faith. Where dispensation is given, it is done on the condition that the Catholic partner would continue his or her Catholic practice and would have the children baptized and brought up as Catholics. The marriage had to be celebrated by a Catholic priest according to Catholic rites. Any other religious celebration was forbidden.

Such strict regulations produced insurmountable difficulties for mixed marriages, particularly where the church was in a minority. Often the non-Catholic party in marriage, although willing to be married in church and to allow the Catholic partner to maintain his or her faith, refused to give the written assurance with regard to the upbringing of the children. In other cases, after the marriage was entered into, the promise was not kept, or considerable strain in marriage occurred due to this requirement. Other religious traditions also questioned the unequal treatment of the religious tradition involved and challenged the right of the Catholic side to set the terms.

The Second Vatican Council took up the question and made a thorough evaluation of the situation in different parts of the world. As a result a number of changes were made in the new legislation on mixed marriages. In the first instance, the intention, as far as possible, to baptize and bring up children in the Catholic faith was required only of the Catholic partner. Even though the marriage would take the Catholic form, local bishops were given the authority to allow another suitable form where appropriate and necessary. The penalty of excommunication would no longer be imposed.

The Orthodox tradition, which also holds marriage as a sacrament, insists that it can be undertaken only by two baptized persons.

The Protestant churches have also generally rejected interfaith marriages as contrary to the churches' theology and practice. Often the churches would have nothing to do with interfaith marriages, thus forcing the partners to have a civil ceremony or a ceremony according to the other faith tradition involved. It has also been the practice among some Protestant churches to take disciplinary action against persons who enter such marriages. Often the Protestant churches have demanded that the other party be baptized before a church wedding was permitted.

In more recent years church discipline* has been tempered with pastoral considerations. Some churches provide for a service of blessing in the home if the other partner intends to continue in his or her religion but is willing to go through a Christian ceremony. In a number of Western countries a church wedding is conducted where one partner is a Christian and the other has no objection to the Christian religious rite after a period of instruction on the meaning of marriage.

The question of mixed-faith marriages has also been an issue in other faith traditions. Within the Jewish community, especially in countries such as the USA and Britain, anxiety over mixed marriages has to do primarily with the depletion of the community. In Britain, for example, 30% of Jews are believed to marry outside their faith tradition. Even though Jewish identity is transmitted through the Jewish mother, most Jews feel that mixed marriages in minority situations lead to the loss of the member to the community. It is to be noted that the same fear is shared also by the church leadership in Asian countries, where mixed marriages of Christians with persons of other faiths would eventually lead to the absorption of the church into the larger community.

Traditionally, Islam has permitted the marriage of a Muslim male to a woman of Jewish or Christian faith. There is no obligation for the woman partner from the other faith to embrace Islam, but in actual practice social pressures result in most women becoming Muslim. It is forbidden for Muslim women to marry outside the faith. In some Islamic countries such marriages are invalid in law, and where a Muslim partner converted to another faith, marriage could be automatically dissolved.

Hindus and Buddhists have been more open to mixed marriages, but there is considerable resistance to the Christian and Muslim insistence on conversion,* the use of the Christian or Muslim religious rites for the ceremony and the insistence on bringing up children in the Christian or Islamic faith. Buddhists and Hindus have criticized this requirement as a mark of disrespect for other faiths and as an instance of Christian and Muslim intolerance.

With mixed marriages becoming more and more common, churches in a number of countries have begun to study the issues involved. One of the most significant studies was done in Sri Lanka, where an ecumenical consultation was held on Christian-Buddhist marriages. The official teachings and proposals were considered in the presence of mixed-marriage couples, who shared their own experiences. The discussions were published in the periodical *Dialogue*, issued from Colombo. Guidelines have also been suggested in Britain, France, the USA, Canada, etc., but so far the theological questions remain largely unresolved.

The first cluster of issues has to do with the understanding of marriage itself in the different religious traditions. Related to this is the use of religious rites in marriages and the question of whether it should be regarded as a sacrament, which would make it impossible for persons outside of the faith perspective to participate. Significantly, although religious rites are employed, both Judaism and Buddhism tend to treat marriage as a secular institution.

The second area has to do with sociological issues, especially the question of polygamy. Interfaith marriages where one partner comes from a society or religion that insists on monogamy and the other from societies or religions that accept polygamy have presented problems. The whole issue of monogamy, polygamy, divorce, remarriage, etc. calls for in-depth multifaith, multicultural discussion. Laws of inheritance and the legal rights of partners in marriage and in divorce vary a great deal between communities, and this is yet another area for study.

The religious education and upbringing of children has always been a difficult issue. In some cases, some of the children are brought up in the faith of the mother, while the others follow that of the father. Where one of the partners is indifferent and the other committed, children grow up in the faith of the believing partner. In some situations children are exposed to both traditions in the hope that they will be able to choose a faith when they are adults. In many cases the children grow up without any specific religious commitment. Very often the biggest strain in interfaith marriages relates to the bringing up of the children, often not fully anticipated at the time of marriage. Faith differences are often compounded by cultural differences.

Yet another area of concern is the often-heard accusation that some traditions use marriage as a method of conversion. Since Islam officially allows Muslim men to marry women of other faiths on the understanding that they would embrace Islam, and also tolerates polygamy, both in Africa and in Asia there is the criticism, not always with justification, that Islam uses marriage as an instrument of conversion. The Christian insistence that the partner should convert and that children should be brought up in the Christian faith has also come under similar criticism.

But increasingly the churches have begun to concentrate on the pastoral dimensions of mixed-faith marriages. With greater population movements and increasing urbanization, and as in so many areas of life young people from different religious traditions come together, mixed-faith marriages undoubtedly will be on the increase, and there is greater need to explore more fully the pastoral dimensions of the issue. Since this is a shared concern of all religious traditions, there is also the urgent need for religious traditions to enter into a dialogue on the issues involved and on the impact of their attitudes and practices on mixed-faith couples. Greater dialogue among religious traditions and the removal of mutual suspicion and historical enmities are beginning to help partners in mixed-faith marriages to deal with the guilt complex at the root of most of the crises that arise in these marriages.

See also **marriage, mixed**.

S. WESLEY ARIARAJAH

Dialogue, 5, 2 & 3, December 1978; 6, 3, December 1979 • C. Lamb, *Mixed-Faith Marriage: A Case for Care*, London, BCC, 1982.

MARRIAGE, MIXED. The term refers to marriages between Christians who belong to different denominations, confessions or churches. In English the term "mixed marriage" is widely employed, while "ecumenical marriage" or, better still, "interchurch marriage" is used where both partners are committed Christians who are aware of their differences and who wish to maintain links with their churches. In German, *konfessions-verbindende Ehe* (marriage uniting two confessions) is current, as well as similar formulas which are in themselves already an interpretation. In French, *mariage oecuménique* is little used, still less *mariage interconfessionnel*. The term commonly used for any such marriage regardless of the level of ecclesial and ecumenical awareness of the partners is *mariage mixte* — mixed marriage.

The 1983 new code of canon law* of the Roman Catholic Church (RCC) retains "mixed marriage" for "two baptized persons, one of whom was baptized in the Catholic church or received into it after baptism and has not left it by a formal act, and the other of whom is a member of a church or ecclesial community which is not in full communion with the Catholic church" (canon 1124).

In English, besides "mixed marriage", the term "interfaith marriage" is also used for marriages between Christians and people of other faiths. The RC code calls them technically "disparity of cult" marriages.

History. The position of confessionally mixed households has gradually changed since the middle of the 20th century. Until then, those who contracted a mixed marriage usually brought on themselves the disapproval of their families and almost always of their churches. As a result, one or both the partners would break off links with the church.

The progress made in ecumenism has altered the situation — to a greater or lesser degree, depending on the countries. The discipline of the Reformation churches became more flexible, followed after Vatican II* by that of the RCC (governed by canons 1124-29; for the pastoral aspect, see the 1990 *Ecumenical Directory* of the Pontifical Council for Promoting Christian Unity). Pending the holding of a council, the Orthodox churches have not modified their rules, but practice has become more flexible thanks to what Orthodox call the principle of economy.*

A mixed marriage is no longer considered shameful. It has become quite common — even very common in some regions, such as Switzerland, where the confessional groups are numerically equal, or in the southeast USA, where RCs are a small minority, over 85% of whom are married to other Christians. A mixed marriage exists only where the couple and the churches are determined to respect the confessional allegiance of both

partners — precluding any kind of disingenuous proselytism* and any attempts "to convert" one partner to the other confession.

Progress. Genuine co-operation between the two communities and the two ministers in the *pastoral preparation* of the couple for a mixed marriage is recommended in church documents (at worldwide, regional and local levels) and is fairly widely practised. The details concerning the *celebration* of the ceremony are set out in these documents, in particular the respective roles of the two ministers. Local difficulties are ironed out with the help of specialists — the people responsible for ecumenical relations or ecumenical centres. The RCC recognizes mixed marriages celebrated in the Orthodox church and, provided dispensation from the canonical form has been obtained, those celebrated in a Protestant church. In most cases the Orthodox recognize the validity of marriages celebrated outside their church. Nevertheless, the Orthodox church's insistence that the marriage should be celebrated according to its discipline and liturgy tends to draw the couple and their children towards that church. Couples who are Roman Catholic and Protestant or Anglican are freer to decide which direction they follow.

There are *groups* which provide spiritual support and sometimes a "church home" for couples who are isolated or who feel ill at ease in their parishes. These groups, generally comprising six to ten couples, are run by the couples themselves with the help of ministers of both churches. They organize monthly meetings, weekends and conferences. In the French-speaking countries these groups are linked by the review *Foyers mixtes* (Mixed households, published in France since 1968); in Britain, the US and elsewhere they have formed associations of interchurch families (see **Association of Interchurch Families**).

Publications in various languages exist for engaged couples, married couples and ministers. These range from one-page pamphlets to whole volumes. There are also various periodicals, of which *Foyers mixtes* is typical.

Difficulties. According to the 1983 code of canon law, the RC partner must "do all in his or her power in order that all the children be baptized and brought up in the Catholic church". Such a pledge is often a difficulty, regardless of whether the promise is made orally or in writing. It requires less than the previous formulation of 1917, which required a RC parent to "promise to have the children baptized...", although this important change is very often neglected. Some episcopates have tried to explain that the fulfilment of this promise means taking account of the actual situation, respect for the partner's conscience, no one-sided demands, concern for the harmony of the couple. There is a widely expressed desire that this promise should be suppressed and perhaps replaced by the RC minister's certifying that he has reminded the RC partner of his or her obligations (a suggestion made by the Anglican-Roman Catholic Commission on the Theology of Marriage, no. 71).

Many Protestants want a marriage celebrated in a Protestant church to be automatically recognized by the RCC. The latter maintains the requirement of the canonical form for purposes of pastoral control, because it has some doubts about the doctrine of marriage in some Protestant churches.

Many mixed couples wish the baptism* of their children to demonstrate their ecumenical commitment, with the two churches taking an active part. Ecumenical celebrations of baptism,* in line with ecumenical celebrations of marriage,* have been taking place since the 1970s. In France, a Catholic-Lutheran-Reformed committee (1975) drew up a framework for the preparation and celebration of such baptisms (with the possibility of the child to be registered on the baptismal roll of both churches, as in the case of a mixed marriage). This advance is based on the mutual recognition of baptism, and its ecumenical dimension does not mean some mythical "third church" or a kind of ecclesial no-man's-land, although it does leave open the question of the ultimate church affiliation of the baptized. The proposal of this committee has no authority. In practice the proposal is more often simply ignored than questioned. Outside France there has been no move in this direction, and more often than not the question does not arise.

Ecumenical celebrations of baptism have led to some experiments with *common catechesis.** This form of religious instruction may also be imposed by the state, as in certain

A Catholic-Protestant mixed marriage, Lausanne, Switzerland (CIRIC)

African countries. Any catechesis, even that of a single confession, should be ecumenical in spirit and include a fair presentation of the other churches, a description of the ecumenical movement, an awakening of the desire for unity.* A further step is taken when common instructional material is used or the catechumens work together or the children affiliated with different churches receive common instruction.

Experiments — whether in parishes or outside, in schools or ad hoc groups, but always in relation with church authorities — have so far been confined to a small number of Catholic and Protestant (but not Orthodox) children and young adolescents, not all of them children of a mixed marriage. Generally this involves an introduction to the Bible (for children under 12). In rare cases, older adolescents have received some more doctrinal instruction with, e.g., an explanation of the Apostles' Creed* and have even progressed to common celebration of confirmations* or professions of faith (renewal of the promises of baptism).

At the RC bishops' synod of 1977, Cardinal Willebrands said that common catechesis was "possible, sometimes inevitable, and limited". In his 1979 *Catechesi Tradendae*, John Paul II echoed Cardinal Willebrands's thinking and stressed the need for a RC catechesis in addition to the common one (n.33).

Interconfessional catechetical groups are rare. More common is for the children of mixed households to receive dual instruction, either in parallel or, more often, consecutively. The frequently expressed fear that this could be unsettling for the children or cause confusion has proved in practice to be generally unfounded.

Ecumenical celebrations of baptism and common catechesis are an indication that the children of mixed couples experience a situation very similar to that of their parents: what is often called, no doubt incorrectly, dual membership (of two churches) and which would be better described as dual participation in the life of two churches. The second term does nothing to solve the doctrinal and canonical problems that persist, especially the difficulty concerning the two partners' participation in the eucharist.*

Common participation in the eucharist remains the most serious difficulty for mixed couples and their children. It is not possible when one of the partners is Orthodox. RC doctrine leads to a restrictive discipline, even though, in certain places, the extending of "eucharistic hospitality" in some cases is tolerated rather than accepted (see **intercommunion**). In France, a memorandum from the episcopal commission on unity (1983) defines and governs these exceptions. The Swiss bishops' conference published a considerably more restrictive memorandum (1986). Although practice is sometimes more generous than the legislation, many mixed couples find this situation frustrating and hard to bear. For them it is at the very least a painful trial of conscience.*

Prospects. Despite these difficulties, some mixed couples do continue to follow their own path within the churches. Having acquired a spiritual place thanks to the relaxing of disciplines and the pastoral effort made on their behalf, they are aware of the ecumenical requirement at the very heart of their situation. In their eyes God has turned their necessity into a vocation: being themselves under the spiritual obligation to practise Christian reconciliation in their lives as a couple and with their children, they want to share their convictions and discoveries with the other members of the communities in which they want to be actively involved.

The majority of mixed couples, at least in the northern hemisphere, are indifferent to religion, but no more so than couples of the same confession. On the other hand, the minority of mixed couples who are believers often demonstrate a particularly lively faith and a very active Christian practice as a result of the reflection required in preparation for marriage and the "spiritual emulation" in the couple's life together and with their children. They do not simply practise their faith in a routine manner but seek to anchor it in the essential, which ecumenical dialogue enables them to distinguish from the merely peripheral. Far from falling back on a lowest common Christian denominator, the most thoughtful couples dig down to the very roots and in so doing spontaneously practise Vatican II's "hierarchy of truths".*

Etymology says it all: far from being *fratres sejuncti* (disjoined, or "separated brethren"), they are *conjuncti* (conjoined, conjugal partners). In them and through them, what is elsewhere disjoined is once again joined together. They conjoin the values of two Christian traditions and are able to assimilate the best of each. This is why they have a vocation to bring the Christian communities closer together, to be the bridge over-arching the divisions, the connective tissue drawing together the wound.

Unfortunately this vocation is not sufficiently recognized. Local parishes often do not know how to treat these couples. Churches rarely dare to entrust them with responsibilities in line with their enthusiasm and competence. Sometimes they may be members of interconfessional committees, or in rare cases, they may participate as a couple in parish or diocesan councils.

Nevertheless, in many places, mixed couples or, more often, groups of mixed couples are the driving force of ecumenism. They organize the Week of Prayer for Christian Unity,* help bring together two communities and launch and support interconfessional social and charitable work, ecumenical publications, etc.

See also **interfaith marriage**.

RENÉ BEAUPÈRE

R. Beaupère, "Double Belonging: Some Reflections", *One in Christ*, 18, 1982 • R. Beaupère, "Mixed Marriages at the Synod of Bishops", *One in Christ*, 4, 1968 • R. Beaupère, "L'oecuménisme dans le mariage: Une espérance pour l'Eglise", *Etudes*, 361, 1984 • *Foyers mixtes* (Lyons, since 1968); *Interchurch Families* (London, since 1979); *The Ark* (Louisville, USA, since 1989) • A. Heron, *Two Churches, One Love: Interchurch Marriage between Protestants and Roman Catholics*, Dublin, APCK, 1977 • M. Hurley ed., *Beyond Tolerance: The Challenge of Mixed Marriages*, London, Chapman, 1975 • G. Kilcourse, *Ecumenical Marriage*, Louisville, KY, 1987 • G. Kilcourse, "Ecumenical Marriages: Two Models for Church Unity", *Mid-Stream*, 26, 1987.

MARTYRDOM. Any discussion of the ecumenical significance of martyrdom must begin with Jesus Christ.* The root meaning of "martyr" in the New Testament is "witness" or "one who gives testimony" (Matt. 18:16; 2 Cor. 13:1). Consecrated by God* and empowered by the Holy Spirit,* Jesus is the ultimate witness to the Father; at his trial before Pilate (see 1 Tim. 6:13), he confesses that he has come into the world to bear testimony to the truth of his Father's kingdom (John 18:37). Jesus' witness to God is liberating for all creation. He heals the sick, forgives sinners, and raises the dead. In his ministry, Jesus testifies to the power of his Father to unite the world in love, the same love that he and his Father share in unity with the Holy Spirit (John 17:11).

It was inevitable that Jesus' mission would bring him into conflict with the powers of sin* and evil that enslave and divide humanity. Jesus' witness to the Father took him to the cross, the supreme sacrifice of a life completely dedicated to God and to humanity. Yet, the outcome of Jesus' death was new life for the world (Rom. 5:12-21). For Jesus Christ, "the faithful witness", is also "the first-born of the dead" (Rev. 1:5). In his death and resurrection* Christ has triumphed over the powers that separate humanity from God and divide God's people (Eph. 2:11-22). His martyrdom is thus ecumenical in the profoundest sense: he dies *for the whole of humanity* so that all humanity may be united with God (Eph. 1:9-10; Col. 1:19-20). He suffers death from the divisive forces of the world so that God's creation may be one.

Having ascended to the glory of his Father, Christ draws all people to himself (see John 12:32). He sends the Holy Spirit to his disciples, who are to be his witnesses to the ends of the earth (Acts 1:8). Christ is present through the Holy Spirit in the church* to transform its members into witnesses like him of his Father's reconciling love. In baptism,* believers are united with Christ in his death and resurrection; they share sacramentally in his martyrdom (Rom. 6:3-8). In the eucharist,* the church proclaims the Lord's martyrdom until his final advent in victory (1 Cor. 11:26) and feeds on his spiritual presence here and now. Christ himself is the pattern (Mark 8:34-35) and the power (John 15:5) of all Christian witness.

Christ warned his disciples that their witness to him would evoke fierce and violent opposition, yet he also promised them that the Holy Spirit would inspire their testimony before hostile authorities (Mark 13:9-13). Under the providence* of God, circumstances will sometimes demand that the Christian witness to God take the strongest possible form and become a witness unto death, as was Christ's own witness. The martyrs are those who have resisted sin "to the point of shedding [their] blood" (Heb. 12:4). Only in the period after the NT did the term "martyr" come to refer exclusively to those who had died for the faith, with the title "confessor" honouring those who had been persecuted for their witness but who had survived. Yet, already in the NT there is a close association between witnessing for Christ and sealing this witness with one's death (Acts 22:20; Rev. 2:13, 17:6).

In martyrdom, conformity to Christ is complete. The martyrs are said to have joined Christ in a baptism like his, a "baptism of blood" (cf. Mark 10:38). Ignatius of Antioch anticipates that his martyrdom will "grind" him into one bread with Christ. United to Christ, the martyr becomes transparent to him. "In the martyr, the church discerns Christ himself, the very heart of its faith, beyond all interpretation and division," declares the WCC Faith and Order text "Witness unto Death" (Bangalore 1978), one of the most substantial statements in recent years on the ecumenical significance of martyrdom. The martyr's act of total obedience points the divided churches to Christ their common Lord, in whom alone their unity* lies. Claiming the martyrs of the early church and certain great Christian witnesses of later history as "the common property of all Christians", the statement notes that many churches are already involved in the process of a mutual recognition of the martyrs and calls for an ecumenical anthology of both early and modern accounts of martyrdom.

While the martyr is a most potent witness to Christian unity, there is no more vivid and painful reminder of the seriousness of Christian disunity than the "confessional martyr", Eberhard Bethge's apt term for the victims of the bloody disputes of the Reformation and its aftermath, when Protestants and Catholics killed each other (and Protestants killed Protestants), in contrast to the so-called classic martyrdom of the early Christians, who died at the hands of non-Christians in imperial Rome. Those killed in the course of confessional disputes are a source of both judgment and grace, and a mutual remembrance of them can play a major role in reconciling the churches, argues the Anglican theologian Rowan Williams. "The whole church needs for its wholeness the memory both of its capacity for

Inscription in Brazil commemorating the death of a Jesuit priest who was killed for defending the rights of landless peasants: "The cross which the people planted on 18 October 1976, on the spot where Father João Bosco was martyred" (WCC photo)

violence and of the great witnesses to the risen Christ who have appeared in the midst of it." If the memory of the confessional martyr is not to fuel further hostility and division between Christians, two things are required, says Williams: "that the martyr's community celebrate the martyr's memory in such a way that he or she offers grace and hope to those outside; and that the persecuting body remember the martyr in penitence and thanksgiving."

The Anglican and Catholic martyrs of the English Reformation in the 16th century illustrate well how martyrdom becomes an ecumenical issue. At the canonization of the Forty (Catholic) Martyrs of England and Wales in 1970, aware that some had feared this act would create ill-feeling between the two churches, Pope Paul VI prayed that the memory of these martyrs might rather restore unity between them: "Is it not one — these martyrs say to us — the church founded by Christ?" In a reconciling move, the Anglican church now includes the Catholic martyr Thomas More in its liturgical calendar. One might recall here the forgiveness Christian martyrs throughout the centuries have extended to their persecutors, following the example of Christ on the cross (Luke 23:34) and of Stephen, the first martyr (Acts 7:60).

Ecumenical recognition of the martyrs does not mean re-writing history or disavowing the disagreements. Quite the contrary: that many martyrs have died for an article of faith restricted more or less to their own ecclesial community shows the gravity of specifically doctrinal disputes between the churches and the necessity of resolving them; there can be no doctrinal indifferentism in ecumenical work. The confessional martyr (for that matter, any Christian martyr) points to the truth of Christianity as a whole, though his or her witness was bound by certain historical, cultural and ecclesiological factors. Beyond these particularities, says the F&O statement on martyrdom, it is possible to recognize "the absoluteness of the Christ to whom [the martyrs] desired to bear witness". Indeed, the Christian witness of non-Catholic martyrs was one of the factors which moved the Roman Catholic Church, in the historic ecumenical overtures of Vatican II, to recognize the sanctifying power of the Holy Spirit in non-Catholic communities of faith and to affirm, despite serious differences, a genuine bond between them and itself (*Lumen Gentium* 15).

Precisely *how* to recognize the martyrs and saints* has itself been disputed by the churches and remains a major theological issue on the ecumenical agenda. As early as the 2nd century, the martyrs began to receive veneration. Places of worship were built over their graves, and their relics were used to sanctify altars. Intercessory prayers were made to them. The cult of the martyrs and saints grew to excess and abuse in the middle ages, and became a main target of the Protestant Reformation (though there had been criticism of it all along). Prayer to the saints was judged by the reformers to be a denial of Christ as the sole mediator between God and humanity. Feast days for the saints were virtually eliminated (though the Anglican church retained biblical figures in its calendar), and emphasis was placed on observing the salvation events of scripture. Protestants thus rejected much of the cultic apparatus associated with the martyrs but did not completely disavow the traditional admiration of them.

According to the Augsburg confession (1530), the most influential of all Lutheran confessional writings, saints "should be kept in remembrance so that our faith may be strengthened when we see what grace they received and how they were sustained by faith". The Second Helvetic confession (1566), a widely accepted Reformed text, calls for the saints to be remembered in sermons. Protestant hymns also extol martyrdom. Ecumenical convergence in worship has encouraged some Protestant eucharistic liturgies to renew the ancient practice of commemorating the saints and martyrs as members of the heavenly congregation, whom we join in praise to God, and to pray that we be made like them (see the ecumenical **Lima liturgy**). However, most Protestants still reject prayer to the saints, even though the Orthodox and Roman Catholics have maintained in ecumenical discussions that such prayer is entirely dependent upon Jesus Christ alone and is a proper expression of the communion of saints.*

Some have argued that the classic concept of martyrdom (death as a direct result of an explicit confession of Christ) needs to be expanded to include those killed as the consequence of taking a prophetic Christian stance against oppression for the sake of peace and justice. Martyrdom as a model of non-violent resistance to social evil was affirmed by a 1978 world conference of Mennonites (Wichita, Kansas), who remembered that many of their predecessors were martyred during the radical reformation. The contemporary martyr, humbly identifying with and dying for the poor,* may well be anonymous. Such a witness now crosses denominational lines to form a truly ecumenical partnership in martyrdom. Visible evidence of this is the martyrs' chapel in Canterbury cathedral, England, which commemorates 12 modern martyrs — Anglican, Catholic, Orthodox and Protestant — including Dietrich Bonhoeffer, Martin Luther King, Jr, and Oscar Romero.

The massive suffering of the Orthodox in the East — 1 million Armenians alone were killed or exiled by the Turks during the first world war — led Bishop Stefan of the Serbian Orthodox Church to speak of the Orthodox martyrs as "a precious gift that the church contributes to the universal Christian treasury" (Eastern European consultation on ecumenical sharing of resources, Sofia, 1982). Like the Orthodox, many of the churches have suffered "collective martyrdom" in this century of mass murder. The churches' complicity in such destruction, as in the Jewish holocaust, and their role in fostering and perpetuating repression must also be considered in any account of martyrdom today. The contemporary martyr may well witness *against* the failure of the churches, yet *for* the sake of their greater faithfulness. In the words of the F&O statement, the martyrs "bring us all back to the centre of faith, the source of hope, and example of love for God and fellow human beings".

The phrase *ecclesia martyrum* (church of the martyrs) expresses the true nature of the church. The martyr's self-emptying love reminds the church that its mission* in the world is to offer God's reconciling love in Jesus Christ (see **reconciliation**). The witness of the church and the unity of the church are inseparable; together they arise from and point to the Lord's own witness, his own martyrdom, which united God and humanity. Torn asunder by hatred and destruction, the world should be able to see in the unity of the church a sign of its own unity restored in Jesus Christ. This is the testimony of the martyrs. As Ecumenical Patriarch Athenagoras I of Constantinople said to Pope Paul VI, when the two met in Rome in 1967 to discuss reconciliation between the Orthodox and Roman Catholic churches: "We hear... the cry of the blood of the apostles Peter and Paul, and the voice of the church of the catacombs and of the martyrs of the Coliseum, inviting us to use every possible means to bring to completion the work we have begun — that of the perfect healing of Christ's divided church — not only that the will of the Lord should be accomplished, but that the world may see shining forth what is, according to our creed, the primary property of the church — its unity."

See also **common confession, common witness, witness**.

ROWAN D. CREWS, Jr

E. Bethge, *Bonhoeffer: Exile and Martyr*, London, Collins, 1975 • *The Canonization of the Forty English and Welsh Martyrs: A Commemoration Presented by the Postulators of the Cause*, London, Office of the Vice-Postulation, 1970 • B. Chenu et al., *Le livre des martyrs chrétiens* (ET *The Book of Christian Martyrs*, London, SCM, 1990) • M. Craig, *Six Modern Martyrs*, New York, Crossroad, 1985 • M. Lods, *Confesseurs et martyrs*, Neuchâtel, Delachaux & Niestlé, 1958 • J.B. Metz & E. Schillebeeckx eds, *Martyrdom Today* (= *Concilium*, 163, 1983) • R. Williams, *Resurrection*, London, Darton, Longman & Todd, 1984 • "Witness unto Death", in *Sharing in One Hope*, WCC, 1978.

MARXIST-CHRISTIAN DIALOGUE.

Dialogue between Christians and Marxists, which began in the 1950s and flourished in the 1960s, was the result of a relaxation in the East-West tensions of the cold war. The de-Stalinization campaign in the Soviet Union, the changes in the Roman Catholic Church following the Second Vatican Council,* and the growth of the ecumenical movement all contributed to bringing Marxists and Christians together for serious conversations about critical issues. A large output of literature on the subject appeared in English, French, German, Italian and Spanish. Prominent participants from the Marxist side included R. Garaudy, V. Gardavsky, M. Machovec and E. Bloch; and such Christian theologians as J. Hromádka, A. Dumas, G. Girardi, K. Rahner and J.M. González-Ruiz were involved at one time or another. The Paulus-Gesellschaft, under the leadership of Erich Kellner, sponsored a number of international symposia during the 1960s in the Federal Republic of Germany and Austria, bringing together Marxist and Christian thinkers.

After the Warsaw Pact forces moved into Czechoslovakia in 1968 to suppress the liberation movement led by Alexander Dubcek, the Marxist-Christian dialogue declined swiftly. Although it did not disappear entirely, encounters during the 1970s were less publicized and more widely diffused than earlier ones. In the US, where H. Cox, C. West, P. Lehmann, T. Ogletree, J.L. Adams and others took interest in the dialogue, P. Mojzes continues to chair a task force on the Christian-Marxist Encounter of Christians Associated for Relationships with Eastern Europe, which sponsored recent annual dialogues on the continent.

From the beginning a variety of issues have been on the agenda of many encounters — atheism,* transcendence, death, alienation, the individual and the community, Marxist and Christian eschatology,* the search for the meaning of life, standards of morality. The conversations have succeeded in eliminating a considerable number of prejudices, misunderstandings and false interpretations of each other's positions.

Marxists have openly admitted that religion* is not always the "opiate of the people" and that Christianity in particular has sometimes been and can still be a protest against injustice, oppression and exploitation. They have conceded that socialism is by no means a magical leap from alienation to a de-alienated society. Since the contradictions of human life cannot be erased by some grand act of liberation, Marxists must constantly criticize dehumanizing tendencies in whatever form they arise, and they must seek radical change as a ferment in even advanced socialist societies.

Christians, for their part, have pointed out that Marx and Ludwig Feuerbach, in stressing that God* is an erroneous idea of humanity, ignored the fact that God is a necessary idea, deeply rooted in all human beings. They have expressed their conviction that human efforts at social improvement can never make the gospel superfluous, and even in the most advanced and ideal communist society there would be new questions that would not find answers from within the system. Only the Christian faith provides an adequate response to such new disillusionments and perplexities. How far, they continue to ask, can Christians co-operate with Marxists without embracing communism as the only true vision for human society?

Although the results of the dialogue should not be underestimated, the fact remains that the fundamental Marxist attitude towards Christianity has not changed; the dialogue has never penetrated into the communist parties. Faith in a personal God who reveals himself is still rejected as an antiquated superstition that undermines human autonomy. The attitude of government officials shows that the only real function of dialogue with Christians is to enlist as many of them as possible in the struggle for socialism. It remains to be seen what consequences the loss of state power by communist parties in Central and Eastern Europe will have for future Christian-Marxist dialogues in that part of the world.

Clearly the primary interest of Christians in continuing dialogue with Marxists should be not the mere fact of talking to each other but the higher goal of enhancing human dignity, freedom (see **liberation, struggles for**), creativity and wholeness. What is needed is the increasing humanization of both Marxism and Christianity.

In Latin America and other areas of the third world, the concerns for social change in the criticism and overcoming of oppressive governments and unjust social structures have provided a platform for common action and reflection between many Christians and Marxists. The struggle for liberation in which Marxists and Christians participate is, therefore, a total historical project presupposing a socio-political analysis and proposing a radical change in the direction of a democratic socialist society. A deeper dialogue begins on the basis of the questions emerging from the common praxis that has led some Marxist intellectuals (not only in Latin America but also in Italy, China and even the Soviet Union) to re-open the interpretation of religion and to question some dogmatic Marxist theses concerning the intrinsically reactionary character of the Christian faith. A conversation between Fidel Castro and Frei Betto witnesses to the fact that, while fundamental philosophical differences remain, there is ample basis for common action and serious dialogue.

ANS J. VAN DER BENT

A.J. van der Bent, *The Christian-Marxist Dialogue: An Annotated Bibliography, 1959-1969*, WCC, 1969 ● F. Betto, *Fidel Castro and Religion*, New York, Simon & Schuster, 1987 ● R. Garaudy, *De l'anathème au dialogue* (ET *From Anathema to Dialogue*, New York, Herder, 1966) ● *Journal of Ecumenical Studies*, winter 1978 ● J.M. Lochman, *Christ and Prometheus? A Quest for Theological Identity*, WCC, 1988 ● J. Míguez Bonino, *Christians and Marxists: The Mutual Challenge to Revolution*, London, Hodder & Stoughton, 1976 ● P. Mojzes, *Christian-Marxist Dialogue in Eastern Europe*, Minneapolis, Augsburg, 1981.

MARY IN THE ECUMENICAL MOVEMENT.
Mary the mother of Jesus Christ is mentioned in all four gospels and alluded to by Paul (Gal. 4:4). She is uniquely involved in the life of the Lord. Present at important times in his private and public life, she is with the apostles at the coming of the Holy Spirit.* The New Testament tells the

story of Jesus and the good news of salvation;* there is very little about Mary. She was the Saviour's mother, she was filled with grace and faith, she witnessed her Son's work. This is the foundation of all thought about Mary.

The complex Mariology of the Roman Catholic Church contrasts sharply with the virtual absence of Mary in Protestant evangelical thought. The gulf seemed so wide that Karl Barth wrote: "In the doctrine and worship of Mary there is disclosed the one heresy of the Roman Catholic Church which explains all the rest."

What, then, is the place of Mary in the ecumenical movement today? Ecumenical discussion is necessary precisely because of the bitterness of past arguments, if unity* is to be a real prospect. Rarely the main topic in interchurch discussion, mention of Mary nevertheless brings to the surface a number of controversial issues.

The early church honoured Mary as mother of Jesus Christ. In the patristic period theologians pondered the questions of Mary's freedom from sin* (her own immaculate conception) and the virgin birth in relation to the true nature of her Son. The council of Ephesus, 431, declared Mary *theotokos* — God-bearer, more usually translated "Mother of God". This declaration affirmed the nature of Jesus as true God and true Man. The doctrine of the divine motherhood is entirely Christocentric. John Damascene wrote: "This name — *theotokos* — contains the whole mystery of the incarnation."

Wonder led to devotion and to the celebration of Marian feasts in all branches of the church. Liturgy celebrated Mary's relation to God, to her Son and to the children of God in the church. Mary was the subject of art and popular devotion. The second council of Nicea (787) approved the veneration of images of Mary. The middle ages saw an increase in belief in Mary's maternal influence and powers of intercession with her divine Son on behalf of sinners. Theological controversy continued with varied contributions from Bernard, Anselm, Thomas Aquinas, Duns Scotus and others. But extravagant devotional practices and distortions led to scandal and revulsion, culminating in the need for reform. Late medieval abuses appeared to the Protestant reformers to concentrate too much

on Mary, thus detracting from the Saviour's redemption of humanity. Protestantism rejected development of the Marian doctrine beyond *theotokos* as unscriptural and unnecessary. Luther wrote: "Without doubt Mary is the mother of God... and in this word is contained every honour which can be given to her." Further elaboration was deemed unnecessary, and expression of Marian devotion became unusual in Reformed and evangelical churches. Partly in reaction to this, but also continuing the work of the fathers, Counter-Reformation theologians and Catholic and Orthodox tradition continued to develop Marian theology, spirituality and devotion. Doctrines of the immaculate conception (1854) and the assumption (1950) were defined for Roman Catholics in papal statements.

The Second Vatican Council, in *Lumen Gentium* (1964), restated the Christocentric nature of Marian devotion and its scriptural foundation. It also drew attention to the need to avoid exaggeration and misunderstanding. Mary was placed firmly in the mainstream of theology and recognized as a proper subject for ecumenical consideration. The movement to find what is common to all in the scriptures and in the patristic period has brought increasing trust and willingness among Christians to examine together problems which had long seemed insoluble.

Emphasis in Catholic, Orthodox and Protestant traditions on the meaning of *theotokos* and its centrality to the mystery of the incarnation* has enabled historical suspicions of mariolatry to be dispelled. Many of the visible indications of Marian devotion — like statues, icons, processions and shrines — have been perceived as obscuring its essentially Christocentric direction. The use of language — notably in the titles given to Mary — has too often provoked dissent rather than understanding. Yet, since Vatican II, there is readiness to examine Mary in the context of ecumenism. Christians whose traditions have paid little attention to Mary recognize the antiquity and richness of Catholic and Orthodox liturgies and meditations. At the same time, there is growing realization that some of the disagreements are more than disputes over images, poetry and pious practices. There are significantly different religious perceptions involved.

The underlying theological problems have

been the substance of Marian thought since the patristic period, through the Reformation, right up to the definitions of 1854 and 1950. They concern the nature and action of grace* and the nature of revelation* in the church.

Scripture says that Mary had found favour with God and was chosen to be the mother of his Son (Luke 1:30-31). The annunciation scene stresses both her acceptability to God and her consent to her role in incarnation. Mary is "a model... in the matter of faith, charity and perfect union with Christ" (*LG* 63). The problem is, how can a human being be worthy of God if all humanity is marred by sin? What is the meaning of "full of grace"? Humankind was redeemed only by Christ's sacrifice; Mary could not have achieved a state of grace by her own human action. In Protestant eyes, to call Mary free from sin is to exempt her from the need for salvation. This not only exalts her above other creatures but also belittles Christ's universal saving action. The doctrine of the immaculate conception — the Roman Catholic solution to this problem — teaches that "the most Blessed Virgin Mary in the first moment of her conception was, by the unique grace and privilege of God, in view of the merits of Jesus Christ the Saviour of the human race, preserved intact from all stain of original sin" (*Ineffabilis Deus*, 1854).

In Mary, the Christian recognizes a human person who offers no resistance to the power of God. The use of the word "co-operate" in connection with Mary has led to accusations of elevation of a creature to equality with the Creator. Co-operate can only mean work with, not originate. Grace is God's free gift, but the individual can choose to resist or reject it, or, like Mary, choose to be open to grace. Since the consequence of Mary's personal acceptance of God's grace was to bring the Saviour into the world, where he would free all humankind from sin, she can be considered the channel of grace for all. Some Christians believe that faith alone justifies; others that faith increases as believers struggle to express the action of grace in their lives. In Mary, faith and work were one. She is the human perfected by the Spirit. Both the Marian declarations mean this. The assumption maintains that, by the action of God, Mary did not suffer corruption but was united body and soul with God. She was the first to be saved by the

Redeemer and has gone before us. Prayers are addressed to her, not in worship, but in celebration of the efficacy of grace in one of us. The supplicant prays for encouragement to follow Mary's example. But even when understanding can be reached that Mariology does not contradict other Christian beliefs, many Christians doubt the necessity of this doctrine.

Discussion between Christians can lead to shared insights. Mary is a useful catalyst in ecumenical encounter. Mutual fears have been calmed and common ground identified. But alongside sympathy and toleration, there is refusal to accept dogmatic definitions as essential to faith.

Neither the immaculate conception nor the assumption is mentioned in the NT. Objections can be summed up in Adolf von Harnack's questions "Wann? Wem?" When were these truths revealed, and to whom? This approach provokes arguments about revelation and authority. Some hold that only what is written in the Bible is authentic revelation; others believe that revelation is continued by the Holy Spirit in tradition, in explication and

Madonna in the church at Vester Gausdal, Norway (WCC/Peter Williams)

even in each individual's experience of the Spirit.

There is evidence of patristic development of Marian doctrine. Saving grace and the resurrection* of the body are articles of faith and are in the creeds.* But only the RCC has claimed the authority and seen the need to make declarations and definitions in Marian matters which are binding on the faithful. The Orthodox church, with its strong Marian tradition but having been unaffected by Western disputes provoked by the Reformation, stops short of dogmatic statement. The difficulties these late definitions present to modern ecumenism are, therefore, wider than their Marian content because they call into question authentic revelation and papal authority. The RCC does not doubt them and cannot retract formal definitions; non-Catholic Christians cannot accept that belief in them is necessary for salvation. Thus Mary becomes a crucial test of how far unity can be achieved in the ecumenical movement.

Mary also surfaces in new areas which increasingly come into ecumenical discussion — liberation theology* and feminist theology.* Devotion to Mary is noticeably strong among poorer or oppressed peoples all over the world. The story of the mother rejected by innkeepers, fleeing from violence, quietly raising her Son to manhood, then witnessing his persecution and suffering, yet seeing and sharing in his triumph, offers hope to many. Her song, the Magnificat,* was recognized by Martin Luther for its reversal of the world's values. It is increasingly providing inspiration for Christians. Feminism, too, finds encouragement in Mary as representative of the powerless and as a model of human behaviour. Yet a new criticism of the Marian tradition has begun to emerge. Some see a contradiction between the role of Mary in the incarnation with honour given to her because of it, and the exclusion of women from certain ministries in the church. Reflection on Mary again widens out into discussion about the feminine in the divine and about women in the community. While Mary has always been understood by many to affirm both of these, new accusations have been made that honour of the Virgin Mary and insistence on her perpetual virginity damage the sexuality of all other women (and perhaps men too). Mary invites thought about mothering, about our relations with each other as children of God, and about Mary, mother of the church.

So, is Mary a cause for division or an opportunity for reconciliation? She was certainly the mother of the Saviour and is therefore, at least physically, at the centre of Christianity. Thought about this relationship raises important questions which must be discussed. Mary was the point at which God and the human were united. He; advice to the servants at Cana was to do as her Son told them. John Paul II has written: "Christians know that their unity will be truly rediscovered only if it is based on the unity of their faith" (*Redemptoris Mater*, 1987). Mary, example of faith and unity, can be the hope of all Christians.

RITA CROWLEY TURNER

R.E. Brown, K.P. Donfried, J.A. Fitzmyer & J. Reumann eds, *Mary in the New Testament: A Collaborative Assessment by Protestant and Roman Catholic Scholars*, London, Chapman, 1978 • H. Graef, *Mary: A History of Doctrine and Devotion*, London, Sheed & Ward, 1985 • T.A. O'Meara, *Mary in Protestant and Roman Catholic Theology*, New York, Sheed & Ward, 1966 • A. Stacpole ed., *Mary's Place in Christian Dialogue — Occasional Papers of the Ecumenical Society of the Blessed Virgin Mary*, London, St Paul, 1982 • R.C. Turner, *The Mary Dimension*, London, Sheed & Ward, 1985.

MATTHEWS, ZACHARIAH KEODIRELANG.

B. 20.10.1901, Cape Colony, South Africa; d. May 1968. "Z.K." was educated at Lovedale Missionary Institute (the only high school open to Africans then) and University College of Fort Hare (1918-24). He studied law by correspondence, and later anthropology, first at Yale, then at the London School of Economics under Bronislaw Malinowski. He taught at Adams High School in Natal, and for 24 years at Fort Hare, acting twice as principal. A respected educationist, he served on several committees, including the Royal Commission to investigate higher education for Africans in the territories of Uganda, Kenya, Tanganyika and Anglo-Egyptian Sudan, a signal honour then for an African.

Z.K. was involved with the Council of Europeans and Africans for inter-racial harmony in Durban and with the native Bantu Teachers' Union and developed close association with future African political leaders such as Albert Luthuli and Alphaeus Zulu. He joined the African National Congress (ANC) in 1940 and served on the Native Representative Council. He served as treasurer and president of ANC (Cape). In the latter capacity he addressed the Cradock Congress (1953) of the ANC, at which he proposed "a national convention (of all races), a congress of the people, representing all the people of this country, irrespective of race or colour, to draw up a Freedom Charter for the democratic South Africa of the future". He followed it with a memorandum on the congress of the people and a draft of the freedom charter which was adopted in part by the congress of the people in 1955 and also by the ANC as part of its policy from March 1956. For such activity he was charged with high treason in 1956, but was acquitted in 1962.

Z.K. also contributed to the wider oikoumene. In 1953 while he was Henry Luce visiting professor at the Union Theological Seminary, New York, he was invited to serve on the committee planning the programme for Evanston. He participated in the Cottesloe consultation (1960) and was Africa secretary of WCC's Division of Inter-Church Aid, Refugee and World Service, in which capacity he tackled refugee situations created by Christian-Muslim conflict in the Sudan, and the Congo crisis of 1962-63. His report *Africa Survey* opened the eyes of the United Nations to the extent and gravity of the refugee situation. He was during this period associated with the All Africa Conference of Churches, at whose founding in 1963 he was chairperson of the constitutional committee. Z.K. resigned from the WCC in 1966 and became Botswana's ambassador to Washington and permanent representative at the UN.

JOHN S. POBEE

MEDELLÍN. The first general conference of Latin American bishops, meeting in Rio de Janeiro in 1955, created a permanent body, the Latin American Council of Bishops (CELAM), mainly with a consultative function, for the purpose of "studying the problems of the church in Latin America, coordinating its activities and preparing assemblies of the episcopate". The next conference took place in Medellín, Colombia, in August

1968. In the interim, several important things had happened.

First, CELAM held yearly meetings (with the exception of the years of the Second Vatican Council), organized commissions to deal with central aspects of the life and mission of the church (catechesis, education, family, social issues), and set up a programme of research on social, economic and religious conditions in the sub-continent, with a view to reaching a co-ordinated "pastoral de conjunto" (an integrated approach to the task of the church). Second, through these activities the Catholic church became more clearly aware of the social conditions (extreme poverty, economic oppression and lack of political participation) of large sectors of the Latin American people as well as of the general inadequacy of the religious instruction and pastoral care it was able to provide. Latin America began to be seen by the Catholic church as a field for mission. Third, by different roads Latin American Catholicism came into contact with the renewal movement in European Catholicism: the biblical and liturgical renewal, the new theological trends, and various forms of social action and concern. Finally, and perhaps most important, Vatican II was a decisive experience for most Latin American bishops: they had a unique chance to meet frequently, gathering in groups formally and informally, and discussing their common concerns over a prolonged period of time; they came in contact with the universal episcopate and profited from the experience of the church in other areas of the third world; for many it was also one of their first ecumenical experiences. At the doctrinal and canonical level, the Council gave a strong impulse to the "regional church" and an organic place to "episcopal conferences". The collegial exercise of the episcopal function served as a corrective to the individualist one and the exclusive relation to the Vatican.

The careful preparation of the Medellín conference revealed that it could not merely adapt the Council's documents but had to start from a consideration of the Latin American situation; the purpose of the meeting was thus defined as that of considering "the church in the present transformation of Latin America in the light of the Council". The method therefore had to follow the well-known (Jesuit) pattern: to see, to judge, to act. All the documents produced at Medellín followed this pattern: an assessment of the facts, doctrinal reflection on the Christian understanding of and response to these facts, and a pastoral direction and specific proposals. There was no unanimity on these issues, and a minority clung to a purely conservative position that nothing should be changed. The direction, scope and depth of the transformation which most desired for church and society were at the heart of the debate. A close study of the documents discloses different and at times divergent directions.

In spite of such differences, the main thrust of the conference as a whole and of the impact it had on Latin American Christianity — within and outside the Roman Catholic Church — can be characterized by some key expressions of the "Message to the Peoples of Latin America" issued at the end of the conference. First, the church understands itself as an integral part of the people and commits itself to it: "As Latin Americans, we share the history of our people." Such commitment demands "conversion", "to purify ourselves in the spirit of the gospel, all the persons and institutions of the Catholic church", "to live a biblical poverty that finds expression in authentic manifestations, clear signs for our people". Second, Latin America, in spite of its plurality, must be seen in the unity of "a geographic reality", a common history and "similar problems". The main problem is the continent's intolerable state of underdevelopment, which prevents any possibility of human realization for the large majority of people. Such conditions — which the documents analyze in detail — are called "a situation of sin".

Finally, the church's response is an effort to "discern the signs of the times", to "discover God's plan" and to offer the church that "which is our most peculiar contribution: a global vision of man and humanity and an integral vision of the Latin American man in development". Later in the documents some concrete objectives are mentioned: "to inspire, stimulate and urge a new order of justice", to "dynamize education", "to promote professional organizations of workers" which are "decisive elements for socio-economic transformation", to "encourage a new evangelization and an intensive catechesis", "to renew and to create new structures in the church" in order to promote dialogue, partici-

pation and co-operation, and "to co-operate with other Christian confessions and with all men of good will committed to authentic peace, rooted in justice and love". The 16 documents of the conference elaborate these affirmations and purposes.

From an ecumenical and Latin American point of view, Medellín occupies a decisive place in our recent history. Although there is no specific document on ecumenism, the conference was fully ecumenical: observers from different churches had full access and were invited to participate — even offered eucharistic hospitality. There was a clear "preferential option for the poor", which became the heart of the self-understanding, task and reflection of the church for many Latin American Christians. Medellín has stimulated intense pastoral action and theological reflection and, above all, the extraordinary growth of church base communities across the continent. The third general conference (Puebla 1978) has since confirmed the focus on the poor.

JOSÉ MÍGUEZ BONINO

The Church at the Crossroads: Christians in Latin America from Medellín to Puebla, 1968-1978, Rome, IDOC International, 1978 ● Second General Conference of Latin American Bishops, *The Church in the Present-Day Transformation of Latin America in the Light of the Council*, Washington, DC, US Catholic Council, 1970.

MELITON (Hacis). B. 24.9.1913, Constantinople; d. 27.12.1989, Istanbul. Meliton, metropolitan of Chalcedon, was a member of the WCC central committee, 1961-68, its vice-president, 1968-75, and a member of the committee on Church and Society. As representative of the Ecumenical Patriarchate at the WCC assemblies and the principal collaborator of Athenagoras I and Dimitrios I, he promoted the activities of the Council, was deeply engaged in the pan-Orthodox conferences of Rhodes and Chambésy, and helped with the rapprochement between the WCC and the Roman Catholic Church. He was instrumental in lifting the anathema between Rome and Constantinople in 1965. Meliton studied theology at Halki; in 1938 he was under-secretary of the holy synod, and in 1943, in charge of the Greek parishes in Manchester and in Liverpool, afterwards continuing his studies in Scotland. On the islands of Imbros and Tenedos he promoted religious, cultural and social education and established several schools, a hospital and other institutions of public service.

ANS J. VAN DER BENT

MENNONITE WORLD CONFERENCE.

Mennonite, Brethren in Christ, and related churches form the Mennonite World Conference (MWC). More than 90 conferences in some 50 nations are members. They appoint delegates to the general council, which meets triennially and elects the executive committee. A global assembly — without executive powers and open to anyone who wishes to attend — convenes regularly; Assembly 11 met in Strasbourg (1984), Assembly 12 in Winnipeg (1990). The organization maintains a permanent secretariat, currently based in Strasbourg. MWC promotes unity and Christian discipleship among member churches by providing fellowship, communication and co-operation, as well as interchurch dialogue. Formal conversations began with the World Alliance of Reformed Churches* in 1984 and with the Baptist World Alliance* in 1989.

LARRY MILLER

MENNONITES.

The Mennonites are the closest descendants of 16th-century Anabaptists who espoused non-violence. They take their name from the Netherlands reformer and early influential leader Menno Simons (c.1496-1561).

The Anabaptist-Mennonite movement began in the first half of the 16th century in the southern and northern regions of Germanic Europe. One focal point was Switzerland, where Konrad Grebel and others, who initially followed the Swiss reformer Zwingli, began to practise believers' baptism* in 1525. Another was Holland, where Menno Simons left the priesthood in 1536 and where the Anabaptists became the first organized Reformation movement. Persecution and death followed for many Anabaptists, but dozens of small congregations soon came into existence throughout Germanic Europe.

Migration, due initially to persecution, and mission spread the movement. Migrations of Swiss and South German Mennonites within

Europe continued into the 18th century, while those to North America began in the late 17th century. Dispersion of Dutch and North German Mennonites along the Baltic coast began in 1530 and continued from Prussia to Russia between 1789 and 1870. Other migrations followed, notably within the USSR, and from there to the Americas and, since 1970, to the Federal Republic of Germany. European Mennonites sent missionaries to Asia (1851) and later to Africa (1901). North American Mennonite-related mission, beginning in Asia and Africa at the end of the 19th century, now reaches every continent. Churches in Africa, Asia and South America began to send out missionaries about 1970.

Although Mennonites are non-credal, they have written numerous confessions throughout their history. In spite of significant and perhaps growing diversity, Mennonite confessions continue to reflect a common theological core. At the centre of Anabaptist-Mennonite faith stands Jesus Christ* as Saviour, Lord, and model of life. The church as the Body of Christ continues Christ's life and ministry in the world.

At least three features define the church* in Anabaptist-Mennonite tradition: The church is a *community of believers* who together seek to follow in daily life the teaching and example of Jesus Christ. Believers who voluntarily confess the lordship of Christ receive baptism as the sign of the new covenant* and of their commitment to a life of discipleship. Believers' baptism means also membership in the local community and responsibility for its welfare. The Lord's supper — a memorial to the death and resurrection* of Christ as well as a foretaste of the great messianic banquet — represents solidarity within the community and readiness to live the way of the cross in the world.

Autonomous from the state, the church lives under the *authority of the word of God** as set forth in the Bible, written under the inspiration of the Holy Spirit.* The Old Testament is promise, the New Testament fulfilment. Where the NT gives a new commandment, the old is superseded. Furthermore, the text is best understood in the context of the community of disciples inspired by the Spirit (see **hermeneutics**).

In the Mennonite perspective, both social

and personal ethics in a *life of discipleship* is part of the gospel. The disciple of Jesus Christ lives in the world in order to serve humankind through action and proclamation. This involves a readiness to suffer wrong and injustice rather than to bring harm to others. Love of enemies and rejection of violence are understood as NT absolutes, and they may be the most distinctive ethical emphases of the Anabaptist-Mennonite tradition. Rejection of seeking wealth in favour of economic sharing is frequently emphasized.

By the end of 1987, world membership for Mennonite and related churches surpassed 800,000, in 60 countries. During the 1980s, Central and South America manifested the most rapid church growth (77%), followed by Africa (69%), Asia (53%), and North America (20%). Membership in Europe declined (by 5%).

Although Mennonites profess and live a radical congregationalism, most of them feel unity with all believers who confess Jesus Christ and who seek to live the way of discipleship. Many are open to co-operation with other Christian groups, especially in witness to peace and non-violence or in mission. Occasionally, co-operation is more general, as in the theological conversations with the Baptists and Reformed in the Netherlands (1975-78) or with the Lutherans in France (1981-84). Recently, the Mennonite World Conference* has entered into formal dialogue with the World Alliance of Reformed Churches* (1984) and with the Baptist World Alliance* (1989).

A few Mennonite churches are members of national or world communions of churches. Two North American Mennonite conferences have joined the National Association of Evangelicals. Some Mennonites in the Soviet Union are members in the All-Union Council of Evangelical Christians-Baptists. The Dutch and North German conferences are members of the WCC.

LARRY MILLER

C.J. Dyck ed., *Introduction to Mennonite History*, Scottdale, PA, Herald, 1967 • D.G. Lichdi ed., *Mennonite World Handbook*, Carol Stream, IL, Mennonite World Conference, 1990 • H. Loewen ed., *One Lord, One Church, One Hope, and One God: Mennonite Confessions of Faith*, Elkhart, IN, Institute of Mennonite Studies, 1985 • *Mennonite Encyclopedia*, 5 vols, Scottdale, PA, Herald, 1955-90.

MERCIER, DÉSIRÉ. B. 21.11.1851, Braine l'Allend, Belgium; d. 23.1.1926, Brussels. Educated at Malines and Louvain and ordained to the priesthood in 1874, Mercier became professor of philosophy at the Petit séminaire at Malines in 1877, and in 1882 the first professor of Thomist philosophy at Louvain. In 1906 he was made archbishop of Malines, and in 1907 created a cardinal. He was in many ways a model prelate, ever concerned for the spiritual life of his clergy and people. As primate of Belgium he convoked a Catholic congress in 1909 to co-ordinate religious activity in the whole nation. During the first world war he strenuously upheld Belgian interests against the German invaders and encouraged resistance by his own example. This attitude won for him an enormous prestige in his own country and among the Allied nations, as witnessed by the enthusiastic welcome accorded him in the USA in 1919.

Mercier took a lively interest in the problems of the universal church. Committed to church union, he installed the Institute of the Monks of Union (Chevetogne*) to promote reconciliation with the churches of the Orient. Most important, he presided over the Malines conversations from 1921 to 1925. These conversations had already started earlier under the leadership of Lord Halifax and Abbé Portal and were concerned with the reunion of the Church of England and the Roman Catholic Church. They were private meetings between eminent individuals on both sides. But an official character was given to them when Mercier sought, and received, a letter from Cardinal Gasparri stating that the holy see approved of them. His stand in support of an unpolemical new start was expressed in a pastoral letter in 1924. His actions undoubtedly influenced Pope Paul VI and Archbishop Michael Ramsey in 1966, when they decided to establish an international Anglican-Roman Catholic commission. See C.L.W. Halifax, *Cardinal Mercier's Own Story* (London, Hodder & Stoughton, 1920), and *A Call to Reunion: Arising out of Discussions with Cardinal Mercier* (London, Mowbray, 1922).

ANS J. VAN DER BENT

METHODISM. "Methodist" originated as a pejorative designation by critics of the mem-

bers of the Holy Club in Oxford, but John
Wesley (1703-91), its Anglican leader from
1729 and himself recently converted to serious Christian living (1725), used it to mean
methodical pursuit of biblical holiness.*

Methodism, one of Protestantism's most
influential evangelistic renewal movements,
has become a worldwide communion which
numbers about 55 million members and adherents in about 100 countries. Although the
national churches have their own statements
on doctrinal standards and church order,
Methodism possesses a very real unity* derived from the spiritual heritage which its
principal founder, John Wesley, by his missionary preaching, and his brother Charles
(1707-88), by his colossal output of hymns
and religious poetry, bequeathed to it.

John Wesley's missionary experience in the
English colony of Georgia (1736-37) was in
many ways a failure, but it did provide him
with the setting for shaping his concept of the
small *class* under an appointed leader as the
basic grouping for Bible-centred Christian
nurture, vital to the harmonious growth of the
Methodist movement. With an increase of
dependable collaborators, Wesley later constituted the itinerant pastorate in correlation with
local Methodist societies, each composed of
several classes. The itinerant pastorate still
binds these societies together in a form of
living communion* which avoids both the
danger of fragmentation inherent in congregational church polity and the tendency towards
static centralization in the Presbyterian churches (see **church order**).

Returning to England from Georgia, Wesley experienced a second conversion (24 May
1738). He received the grace* to give up
reliance on his own efforts to attain perfection
and to surrender himself totally, in loving
trust, to the work of God's grace within him.
He thus became the instrument of divine power, which alone accounts for the stupendous
missionary and pastoral achievement of his
remaining 50 years as undisputed head of
Methodism.

The priority he resolutely gave, in the face
of bitter opposition from the establishment, to
the materially and socially underprivileged
coincided with the beginning of the industrial
revolution and the springing up, in England,
of huge industrial cities (still major centres of
Methodism). A century before Karl Marx be-

came a public name, Wesley had brought the
gospel and concomitant social and cultural
betterment to the first working class in the
world.

Against those Anglican-Calvinists who believed in predestination, Wesley taught that
the redemptive love of Jesus excludes no
person; God calls each freely to respond to
that love. Against those Protestants who held
a narrow understanding of "faith alone", he
insisted that free response entails not only an
initial conversion but also continued co-operation with the Holy Spirit,* who sanctifies
and leads one ultimately to the perfection of
love, the ability to triumph over sinful desires and selfish motives (see **sanctification**).
Moreover, the trusting, loving self-surrender
to the Father brought about by God's Spirit
gives one the assurance that the blood of
Jesus is victorious over personal sin (Rom.
8:14-16,38-39). The only requirement for
admission into a Methodist class (10-12
members) was a desire to seek inner holiness
and to live a life of prayer and discipline in
the fellowship of the Spirit. In thus focusing
all his teaching on the doctrine of grace,
Wesley made Anglican credal orthodoxy in-
candescent with the love of Jesus in the
Spirit. Herein lies the heart of the Wesleyan
spiritual heritage.

By inheriting, too, the Wesleyan insistence
on the unity between worship and service,
Methodism improved social relationships,
wherever it took root. The Wesleyan vision of
Christian personhood enables modern Methodist missionaries in recent contact with Latin
American liberation theology* to enter into
that theology's rightful aspirations, while
avoiding theological deviations.

Wesley never intended his renewal movement to separate from the Church of England,
yet a separation was inevitable. Entering the
movement were large numbers of unchurched
people who had no contact with the established church and wanted none. For such
people Wesley created ministerial structures
for their pastoral care, and they could not but
exercise an authority parallel with legitimate
Anglican authority, rather than be subordinate
to it.

Since the American Methodists had been
deprived of episcopally ordained preachers by
the war of independence, pastoral necessity
drove Wesley to ordain his fellow presbyter

Thomas Coke (1747-1814) as "superinten-dent" over "the brethren in America". Wesley sent Coke to the new United States in 1784 with the authority to establish an independent church — which took the name Methodist Episcopal church. The title "superintendent" was changed to "bishop" in 1787.

Wesley's Anglican loyalties made him more circumspect in his dealings with British Methodists. No formal acts of separation from the Church of England were made during his life. But the company of 100 preachers, whom he had made his legal successors by a deed of declaration (1784), inevitably became the governing body of an autonomous church after his death seven years later. British Methodism remained non-episcopal in church order.

The seeds of future dissension were already sown. The plan of pacification (1795) re-versed Wesley's conscientious refusal to al-low itinerant preachers who were not episcop-ally ordained to administer communion, but the plan retained his policy of concentrating pastoral initiative in the preachers' hands, to the eventual detriment of lay participation. Resulting protests gave rise to new denomina-tions in the first half of the 19th century, either by secession or separate foundation. More significantly for Methodism's present ecumenical role, bitter controversy with the Anglican Tractarian movement hastened Brit-ish Methodism's decline from the high theolo-gy and practice of the Lord's supper shared by the Wesley brothers, hardened its non-sacra-mental understanding of the ordained minis-try, and pushed it definitively into the non-conformist camp.

Several schisms* also racked American Methodism — over church polity, required "unworldly" discipline, and public social issues, especially racism and slavery. Already in 1816 and 1820 two black churches were founded — the African Methodist Episcopal and the African Methodist Episcopal Zion. These two, along with the black Christian Methodist Episcopal (1870), number today over 4 million members. In 1844 the Method-ist Episcopal Church itself divided over the slavery question into two separate churches.

This alarming divisioning, however, did not prevent either the growth of the family of Methodist churches or their missionary out-reach. In Great Britain the "connexions" to-talled 800,000 members by 1900. In 1813 the Wesleyan Missionary Society was founded, and in the wake of British colonial expansion, large Methodist churches grew up in Canada, Australia and South Africa, where the church had a large black following, and in other parts of Africa and in Asia. In the USA, the largely white Methodist denominations grew from 2 million in 1900 to 10 million in 1960. Fully integrated into American society, they poured personnel and money into the evangelization of India and China and had a pervasive influ-ence on American Protestantism as a whole.

The Ecumenical Methodist Conference of 1881 brought to London delegates from 30 Methodist bodies in 20 countries. It was a turning point in the healing of Methodist divi-sions at national levels. In Great Britain, by a series of mergers beginning in 1907, the vari-ous Methodist bodies united, until by 1932 almost all had become the one British Meth-odist Church. In the US, the northern and southern branches of the Methodist Episcopal Church united in 1939, and the Methodist Protestant Church, created by secession in 1828, entered the union. In 1968 a merger of this largely white, unified Methodist church with the Evangelical United Brethren formed the United Methodist Church, with over 11 million members. The successful outcome of the Consultation on Church Union,* in which United Methodism, along with other denomi-nations, is in dialogue with the three large black Methodist churches, would heal the most serious rift in the family.

This earnest seeking for a form of unity which is the necessary visible expression of invisible communion in love has taken the Methodist family beyond intraconfessional dialogue. For more than half a century Meth-odist churches have participated in those church unions which transcend confessional barriers. In some of these, Anglican participa-tion has made it possible to overcome the fundamental divide between episcopal and non-episcopal church order (notably in the Church of South India and the Church of North India). But some negotiations involving Methodists have failed. Twice a plan for or-ganic union* between the Church of England and the British Methodist Church was de-feated, in 1969 and 1972. The Methodists approved the plan, but although the Church of England recorded a majority vote in favour, its size was not sufficient for success; the chief problem lay in how Methodism was to acquire the historic episcopacy.* The rejection has been detrimental to Methodism's ecumenical endeavours. Those efforts, however, have found concrete expression, at the world level, in bilateral dialogue with Lutherans, Reformed and Roman Catholics, made possible by the setting up of the World Methodist Council* (WMC) in 1951.

In the ecumenical movement, Methodists such as John R. Mott (1865-1955) and G. Bromley Oxnam (1891-1963) played key roles in the founding of the WCC at the first WCC assembly in 1948. Today 31 national Methodist churches are WCC members. Of the four WCC general secretaries, two have been Methodists — Philip Potter and Emilio Castro.

A statement of the first WMC conference (1951) echoed Wesley's original intention not to found a church but to inspire and organize a movement for church renewal. The WMC rejoiced to see Methodist churches give up separate confessional existence to find new life in the wider community of transconfessional unions. As recent experience shows, however, such unions can remain imprisoned within cultural and national boundaries. Could the WMC, therefore, enable Methodism, without becoming entrenched in a confessional exclusiveness Wesley never intended, to witness to a love which, by being rooted in self-forgetfulness, transcends all human-devised barriers?

FRANCIS FROST

R. Davies, *Methodism*, London, Epworth, 1976 • R. Davies, A.R. George & G. Rupp, *A History of the Methodist Church in Great Britain*, 4 vols, London, Epworth, 1965-88 • N.B. Hamon ed., *Encyclopedia of World Methodism*, Nashville, TN, United Methodist, 1974 • *The History of American Methodism*, Nashville, TN, Abingdon, 1964 • G. Wainwright, *The Ecumenical Moment*, Grand Rapids, MI, Eerdmans, 1983, ch. 11.

METHODIST-ORTHODOX RELATIONS.

At Dublin in 1976 and at Nairobi in 1986, the World Methodist Council* expressed the desire to explore bilateral relationships between Methodism and Orthodoxy, and in 1990 the Ecumenical Patriarchate of Constantinople agreed to set up a small joint group of theologians to explore themes for an eventual dialogue. One promising factor in the situation is the historical influence on Methodism of the theological and spiritual insights which the Wesleys drew from the patristic church, particularly that of the East. At the pastoral level, there exist Orthodox and Methodist diaspora communities in regions where the other body is stronger.

GEOFFREY WAINWRIGHT

B. Frost, *Living in Tension between East and West*, London, New World, 1984 • R.L. Maddox, "John Wesley and Eastern Orthodoxy", *Asbury Theological Journal*, 45, 1990.

METHODIST-REFORMED DIALOGUE.

After two intensive "international consultations" in 1985 and 1987, theologians appointed respectively by the World Alliance of Reformed Churches* and the World Methodist Council* composed a report, "Together in God's Grace", which was immediately welcomed by the executive committees of the sponsoring bodies and transmitted to their member churches for discussion and action. Concluding that "the classical doctrinal issues" on which there has historically been tension between the two traditions "ought not to be seen as obstacles to unity between Methodists and Reformed", the document recommended that Methodist and Reformed churches ask themselves and one another about possibilities for co-operation at local, national, regional and international levels in worship, study, doctrinal commissions, evangelistic outreach and social service; and whether indeed there are more places "in which Reformed-Methodist union negotiations might be initiated". Recognition of "a common gospel" and of "authentic forms of obedience and faithful discipleship" in the partner, such as the theologians believe to be the case, means that "in all places churches in our two traditions are already in a position mutually to recognize membership and ministry", which at the very least entails mutual sensitivity and respect in majority/minority situations and amid differences in relationships to the state and to society at large.

The two traditions have different origins

and have never undergone an active separation. Both "regard the scriptures as the primary authority in faith and practice and confess the shared faith of the universal church expressed in ecumenical creeds and by witnesses to it through the centuries". Specifically, "both testify to the priority of God's grace, the sufficiency of faith, the call to holy living, and the imperative to mission". Yet different secondary authorities obtain in the two traditions; and as between the Reformed confessions of the 16th and 17th centuries and the Wesleyan "standards" of Methodism, there are undoubtedly "differing accounts of the appropriation of saving grace, emphasizing, on the one hand, God's sovereignty in election and, on the other, the freedom of human response".

Wesley stated in his own words his agreement with Calvin on several fundamental matters: "(1) in ascribing all good to the free grace of God; (2) in denying natural free will, and all power antecedent to grace; (3) in excluding all merit from man, even for what he has or does by the grace of God". The 1987 report notes that it is only on this common basis that "the conflicting stances identified as Calvinist and Wesleyan were adopted". Wesley saw as the universal inheritance of Christ's atoning work a prevenient grace* which restores to humankind the lost freedom of choice, while not guaranteeing salvation* to all; Calvinists object that this impugns the divine sovereignty, since it claims that human freedom to deny is greater than God's will to save. When Methodists ask how a predestinarian approach avoids understanding God's freedom as anything more than arbitrariness, and human freedom as anything other than illusion, the Calvinist answer is that since God as Creator is the author of justice* and since God's ways are not our ways, it is a fundamental category mistake to judge God at the bar of human and limited reason. The present report judges that each stance can find scriptural support, but that "both traditions have gone wrong when they have claimed to know too much about [the underlying] mystery of God's electing grace and of human freedom", instead of simply recognizing, receiving and celebrating the mystery.

On the consequent matter of sanctification,* the report again recognizes what Methodists and Reformed hold in common: both "affirm the real change which God by the Spirit works in the minds and hearts and lives of believers. By the sanctifying grace of God, penitent believers are being restored to God's image and renewed in God's likeness... In the two traditions we are taught to strive and pray for entire sanctification." The differences in emphasis are expressed thus: "The Reformed stress on election and perseverance gives believers the confidence that God will keep them to the end. The Methodist preaching of perfection affirms that we may set no limit to the present power of God to make sinners into saints."

In many places, Methodists and Reformed have already entered into close relationships, including both federal and organic unions (see **union, organic**). Examples of unions according to varying models, sometimes including other traditions also, would be Canada (1925), Church of South India (1947), Zambia (1965), Belgium (1969), Church of North India (1970), Zaire (1970), Australia (1977), and Italy (1979). Recognizing that such unions were enacted only "after due doctrinal discussions", the 1987 report "affirms that there is sufficient agreement in doctrine and practice between our two positions to justify such answers to the Lord's call to unity for the sake of mission and our common praise of God". Further rapprochements may therefore responsibly be encouraged: "Our complementary ways of Christian thought and life are built upon a foundation in God's grace, in covenant existence, and in the goal of perfect salvation."

GEOFFREY WAINWRIGHT

I.H. Marshall, *Kept by the Power of God: A Study of Perseverance and Falling Away*, London, Epworth, 1969 • A. Sell, *The Great Debate: Calvinism, Arminianism and Salvation*, Grand Rapids, MI, Baker, 1983 • "Together in God's Grace", *Reformed World*, December 1987 • G. Wainwright, *On Wesley and Calvin: Sources for Theology, Liturgy and Spirituality*, Melbourne, Uniting Church, 1987 • G. Wainwright, "Perfect Salvation in the Teaching of Wesley and Calvin", *Reformed World*, June 1988.

METHODIST-ROMAN CATHOLIC DIALOGUE.

Following the presence of Methodist observers at Vatican II,* the Vatican Secretariat for Promoting Christian

Unity* and the World Methodist Council* (WMC) made provision for an international dialogue to start in 1967. The joint commission between the WMC and the Roman Catholic Church has arranged its work in five-year periods so that its successive reports could be presented to its Methodist principals at the quinquennial gatherings of the WMC. While being simultaneously presented to the Vatican, they have become known by the place and date of the Methodist assembly: Denver 1971, Dublin 1976, Honolulu 1981, Nairobi 1986.

Aimed at "growth in understanding", the first two reports ranged rather widely over the areas of mission* and evangelism,* social concern, moral and ecclesiastical discipline, and (particularly characteristic of this bilateral dialogue*) spirituality: Denver 1971 notes "the central place held in both traditions by the ideal of personal sanctification, growth in holiness through daily life in Christ". The most precisely treated topics were the eucharist* and ministry,* which were contemporaneously occupying also the Anglican-RC and Lutheran-RC dialogues as well as Faith and Order* in the approach to "Baptism, Eucharist and Ministry".* Catholics and Methodists agree that there is "a distinctive mode of the presence of Christ (which) is mediated through the sacred elements of bread and wine, which within the eucharist are efficacious signs of the body and blood of Christ"; and yet a chief point of difference remains over the "change" which Catholics designate transubstantiation. Each party accepts an apostolic ministry of the ordained within the ministry of the whole church, yet "we differ in the account we give of apostolic succession": "Methodists are not in principle opposed to the ministry's being in the threefold form or in the historical succession; but they do not consider either of these to be necessary for the church or for the ministry."

A more concentrated thematization occurred with the third and fourth reports. Honolulu 1981 was entitled "Towards an Agreed Statement on the Holy Spirit". The commission was able to agree on the Trinitarian place of the Holy Spirit* and on the work of the Spirit in justification,* regeneration and sanctification,* recognizing "the Spirit's special office to maintain the divine initiative that precedes all human action and reaction". Perceiving that "the doctrine of the Holy Spirit underlies much of the ecumenical agenda", the commission brought out the ecclesiological dimensions of the doctrine. In particular, it was here that the recurrent question of authority* was located: "The papal authority, no less than any other within the church, is a manifestation of the continuing presence of the Spirit of love in the church or it is nothing."

Nairobi 1986 was entitled "Towards a Statement on the Church". The notion of koinonia* (both communion and community) governs: "Because God so loved the world, he sent his Son and the Holy Spirit to draw us into communion with himself. This sharing in God's life, which resulted from the mission of the Son and of the Holy Spirit, found expression in a visible koinonia of Christ's disciples, the church." Catholics and Methodists "are committed to a vision that includes the goal of full communion in faith, mission and sacramental life". Recognizing that "an ecclesiology shaped in a time of division" cannot be entirely satisfactory, the report draws eclectically on various possible "ways of being one church" in the search for "a model of organic unity". Differences remain over "structures of ministry", particularly over whether a threefold form and a historic succession is necessary — and most particularly of all over a "Petrine office" of primacy,* jurisdiction and authoritative teaching as claimed by Rome. Nevertheless, "Catholics and Methodists are agreed on the need for an authoritative way of being sure, beyond doubt, concerning God's action in so far as it is crucial for our salvation".

The Nairobi report underwent a "doctrinal examination" on the part of the Roman Congregation for the Doctrine of the Faith, which was sufficiently encouraging for the president of the Secretariat for Promoting Christian Unity to support the continuance of the work on the ministry and the teaching office in particular. The current series of meetings, leading to Singapore 1991, is in fact being conducted under the title "The Apostolic Tradition". Employing the key notion of Tradition* as "koinonia in time", the commission is working along two principal lines: "the apostolic faith, its teaching, transmission and reception", and "ministry and ministries: serving within the apostolic Tradition".

When Methodists and Roman Catholics try to characterize their mutual discovery in this international dialogue as well as in national and local dialogues that are taking place at least in Britain, the USA and New Zealand, they often point to the fact that while they find themselves apart, they have never known the bitterness of a direct schism.* Catholics testify to a distinct Methodist "identity". It seems that the two parties come closest when the Wesleyan character of Methodism is sharply profiled, for it is there that a scriptural and credal faith* comes to expression in sacramental life, in the search for personal and social holiness, and in an evangelistic and charitable concern for all humankind.

GEOFFREY WAINWRIGHT

M. Hurley ed., *John Wesley's Letter to a Roman Catholic*, London, Chapman, 1968 • M.S. Massa, "The Catholic Wesley: A Revisionist Prolegomenon", *Methodist History*, 22, 1983-84 • H. Meyer & L. Vischer eds, *Growth in Agreement*, WCC, 1984 (for Denver, Dublin and Honolulu reports) • *One in Christ*, 22, 1986, articles by C. Rand, G. Tavard & G. Wainwright, and the Nairobi report, with comm. by J.-M.R. Tillard • G. Wainwright, *The Ecumenical Moment*, Grand Rapids, MI, Eerdmans, 1983, chs. 10-11.

MIDDLE AXIOMS. The expression "middle axioms" was introduced by J.H. Oldham in the preparatory material for the 1937 Oxford conference of Life and Work,* as "an attempt to define the directions in which, in a particular state or society, Christian faith must express itself". The effort was to provide Christians and churches with an orientation for their participation in the life of society, concrete enough to give direction in specific situations without becoming a rigid law or ecclesiastical casuistry.

Theologically, the quest for such criteria originates, on the one hand, in the crisis of both the natural law* and the "creation orders" foundations for social ethics and, on the other hand, in the crisis of the idealism of the social gospel and the kingdom of God. Oldham locates this criterion in his distinction between an ethics of "ends" and an ethics of "inspiration" which struggles to discern God's marching orders for God's people at particular points in history. Siding with this second line, he tries to combine a strong Christological

orientation on the lordship of Christ — closely bound to the biblical revelation* — and an understanding of the present conditions of society. In this double context he speaks of the church's "discerning the signs of the time and in each crisis of history fulfilling its appointed task". The Oxford conference received these criteria as "intermediate between the ultimate basis of Christian action in community [the law of love] which is too general to give much concrete guidance for action — and the unguided intuition of the individual conscience". Oxford did not elaborate or extensively exemplify this notion. It seems to be used implicitly in the critical assessment of the conditions of the time in relation to the state and the political realm (and to a lesser degree the economic and racial question). Some fundamental dialectics of freedom*/order* or freedom/justice* seem to serve as guide for the discernment of these middle axioms.

Middle axioms (or "concrete utopia", as others preferred to characterize such criteria) found more definite formulations in the context of the responsible society,* developed after Amsterdam. In a significant analogy, they have been compared with anchors and compasses "required for successful navigation. Compasses help those at sea to get their bearings and anchors help to minimize drift in troubled waters." Although there is little reference to these axioms in recent ecumenical discussions, the question which this category addresses is still present, and the distinction and relation which liberation theology establishes between the terms "utopia", "historical project" and "political programme" point, in a different theological context, to an analogous question.

See also **ethics, society**.

JOSÉ MÍGUEZ BONINO

C.-H. Grenholm, *Christian Social Ethics in a Revolutionary Age*, Uppsala, Verbum, 1973 • W.A. Visser 't Hooft & J.H. Oldham eds, *The Church and Its Function in Society*, vol. 1, London, Allen & Unwin, 1937.

MIDDLE EAST. Churches of the Middle East have experienced the reality of an ecumenical movement long before it was known as such. For centuries and in different ways since the emergence of doctrinal or canonical divisions between them, these churches intensely lived "ecumenism before ecumenism". This experience of some 15 centuries can be summed up as follows. Plurality of the Middle Eastern churches preceded certain divisions and has not always been the result of them. The unity* sought for today, therefore, is not tantamount to uniformity and cannot be reached by escaping into simple "co-operationism" between churches. Past centuries of theological debate and dialogue show that, on the one hand, the churches need to go beyond the expression of their legitimate particularism to recover the source of their faith.* On the other hand, they need to face openly and transcend the non-theological reasons for separation. Experience shows that non-theological causes of division have emerged both from within the Oriental churches and their sociocultural and political environment and from abroad, from Western churches and nations.

Proselytism* has been a long-standing threat to the unity of the church in the Middle East. It is also related to the causes of division generated abroad, coming as it does from Western churches. Crusaders supposedly came to rescue the holy sepulchre from the Saracens, but in the process they massacred Eastern Christians, whom they considered heretics and therefore non-persons. Later, Western denominations sent missionaries to the Middle East, often completely ignorant of Christian identity there and seeking only to draw individuals or groups away from the churches of the region. With the mainline Western churches, enormous progress has been made, as reflected in a 1975 document entitled "Church Unity and Witness and Relations with Western Protestant Churches". This first common statement of its kind was issued by representatives of the Oriental and Eastern Orthodox churches together with representatives of the Evangelical and Episcopal churches of the region.

The present danger is the proliferation of neo-fundamentalist evangelical movements, whose extreme variants are premillennialist and dispensationalist, with partisan political agendas considering the modern state of Israel as the fulfilment of biblical prophecies. They project a distorted image of Christianity, frequently provoking violent reactions from other religions.

Three recent developments should be noted. One was the historic meeting in February 1985 of 19 patriarchs and heads of Oriental and Eastern Orthodox, Catholic and Evangelical churches in the region. The second was the meeting on the occasion of the Middle East Council of Churches (MECC) executive committee, 16-19 November 1987, in Cairo, when Eastern and Oriental Orthodox patriarchs met for the first time as heads of their churches and members of the MECC. Their discussions concluded that fundamentally both families of churches have presented the same faith in their Lord Jesus Christ. They further recommended that these discussions be pursued to prepare the way for the eventual full recovery of one communion. Third, Cardinal Jan Willebrands, then president of the Vatican's Secretariat for Promoting Christian Unity,* also paid an official visit to Lebanon and Syria, 13-20 April 1988, to meet with the three Orthodox heads of churches there. The decision was taken to engage in formal negotiations towards full membership in the MECC.

Today renewal* is vital in the current polarized and tragic situation in the Middle East, where each church is being exposed to three different dangers. One is the displacement and emigration of Christians: how can a church be a true community when its members are dispersed over the earth? A second danger is that basic values have become destroyed, spirits perverted and hearts assailed by despair. In a struggle against the powers of darkness, the living churches have to face a radical challenge: faith in the one Christ, the Saviour, hope against all human hope, and above all love that forgives and vivifies. Churches are pushed into evangelical heroism in the purest sense of this concept. Finally, there is the seductive temptation to replace the belonging to a church with the bonds of a sociological community, an ethnic ghetto, a satellite political entity which, at the end of the day, remains precisely as one of the objectives of powers and principalities that confront one another in the Middle East.

Ignatios IV, patriarch of Antioch, stressed in 1987 that the task of the ecumenical movement is not to build unity but rather to discover it. That task calls for repentance and creativity. He notes that in the last few years, the ecumenical movement has been held back by the various confessions' quest for *identity*

— the easiest way of affirming one's identity is to do so against the others, harking back to past grievances. Nevertheless, something of great value may emerge from this difficult stage. While dialogue is called for, to enter into it one has to have a clear idea of one's own identity, provided such clarity is for the sake of the others and not against them. Ecumenical thinking must concentrate on exploring the differences and bringing to the surface the "undeclared items" which give each confession its underlying cohesiveness (see **dialogue, intrafaith**).

But *doctrine*, the patriarch stresses, must never be separated from the *spiritual experience* which it awakens and which in turn feeds it. To Oriental churches, doctrine, spirituality and beauty are but one: holiness, the liturgy and the icon are theologically fundamental. Doctrine transcends its natural limitations by becoming open to the ineffable through the methods of negotiation and antinomy. It is inseparable from poetry and symbol. It demands an asceticism which makes humanity heedful of the revelation of the Wholly Other and of the "Other" as revelation. It is part of the celebration which makes humanity the world's priest, the great celebrant of life.

Ignatios IV underlines that the fullness of love — the language of the Trinity* and of the cross, of *kenosis*, so that the other may *be* — leads to true fullness of life. That is the language of what the Orthodox like to call the divine-humanity, so that nothing that is human in the Western quest and nothing that is divine in the Eastern contemplation may remain foreign to Christians. Indeed, one could say that Christianity has often thought about God to the detriment of humanity, while the approach of modern thought has almost always been to think about humanity to the detriment of God. In other words, as the patriarch puts it, when the Oriental churches learned to see beyond Western power and relations became more fruitful, they discovered the West of knowledge and clear-sightedness, capable of uniting research and intelligence. Now the Orient realizes that it is with Western tools they must define and expound non-Western subject matters so as to make them available to the West itself in its own spiritual quest. Such a process could resolve the tension between the universal and the particular, i.e. by joining the most intense research of the West to that of the

Bishop and priests outside the Syrian Orthodox church in Fuhaila, Syria (WCC/Peter Williams)

Orient's own re-search for identity in its most original sense.

Humanity today seems to be faced with an ultimate choice: either nuclear or ecological suicide or else a kind of spiritual transcendence. The patriarch of Antioch proclaims the urgency of a creative spirituality which alone can overcome the nihilism of the West and its nonchalant cynicism and can respond to the hunger for food and for dignity in so many third-world countries. Contemplation makes action fruitful, and action confirms contemplation. To celebrate liturgically Christ's victory over hell and death is of necessity to struggle against all the forms of hell and death which are scourging culture and society.

Much of this language is not familiar to most Western churches, many of which erroneously believe that that language reflects the reality of the church and the world. But these voices from the Middle East come from churches, many of whose origins go back to the apostolic times. These voices come from Christians in the lands of the Bible, who are today the heirs of rich Christian traditions and who, by remaining indigenous to the areas where Christianity began, link the world church historically to its origins. These voices also come from a church which today faces innumerable dangers, both to its spirit and its physical survival, from a church which, in the words of Ignatios IV, is climbing to Golgotha and making the double and unique drama of Lebanon and Palestine its responsibility in its prayers and its service. It is an unarmed and confessing church, which reminds us that our response to violence should be that of Christ — the cross and, through the cross, the power of resurrection which permits the ministry of reconciliation (2 Cor. 5:18).

It also is a church in a region where religion, transformed more or less into an ideology, covers a multitude of crimes, and where it would like to witness to its anti-totalitarian nature and its power for life and peace. Genuine religion, in fact, is the opposite of totalitarianism when it stresses not a particular sociological form but rather the link between the soul and the absolute that is the irreducible character of the person: the "image of God" in Jewish and Christian tradition, the "helper of God" in Islam. Beyond the opposing ideologies, that church wants to see and foster in Islam both the humble and noble faith of simple people and the high mysticism of the sufis, which so often has a Christological affinity. In Judaism it wants to see and foster its ethical rigour and prophetism.

The church universal can ill afford in today's world to do without the ecumenical contribution, in mutual love and solidarity, of the church of the Middle East.

See also **Middle East Council of Churches**.

LEOPOLDO J. NIILUS

R.B. Betts, *Christians in the Arab East: A Political Study*, Atlanta, John Knox, 1978 • C. Chapman, *Whose Promised Land?*, Tring, UK, Lion, 1985 • J. Corbon, *L'Eglise des Arabes*, Paris, Cerf, 1977 • G. Habib, "Misuse of Religious Sentiments: Religion in Conflict Situations", *CCIA Background Information*, 1, 1987.

MIDDLE EAST COUNCIL OF CHURCHES.

The ecumenical movement was a reality among the churches of the Middle East long before the emergence of the word "ecumenism" in this century. These churches have experienced that "ecumenism before ecumenism" through the centuries before the emergence of doctrinal or canonical divisions between them. The fact of the Christian presence in the Middle East, from apostolic times to our own, is hardly known by the average Western Christian. Yet some 12 million Christians live in the region today as heirs of rich Christian tradition. By remaining indigenous to the areas where Christianity began, they link the world church historically with its origins.

May 1974 marked an important milestone in the history of the conciliar ecumenical movement in the Middle East with the formation of the Middle East Council of Churches at a conference in Cyprus. The MECC is organized along the lines of families of churches rather than on the basis of individual church membership. Three families of churches — Oriental Orthodox, Eastern Orthodox and Protestant/Episcopal — were founding members. During annual synods in 1988, the region's Catholic churches (seven branches from different ethnic and cultural origins, accounting for about one-fifth of Middle East Christians) decided to join the MECC. When the unanimous reception of this fourth family into membership was celebrated at the fifth assembly (Nicosia 1990), virtually all Middle Eastern Christians were represented in the MECC.

The priorities of the MECC reflect those of the Middle Eastern churches. The first concern in the past years is securing the *continuity of Christian presence* in the land in which our Lord was born and lived, and which was sanctified by the blood of apostles, saints and martyrs (see **martyrdom**). All efforts should be made to enable Christians and their churches to live in their lands in freedom in this region and to participate with other communities in developing their nations and their societies.

Spiritual *renewal* is sought in order to enable churches, in the midst of ideological and other conflicts and suffering, to continue their witness to the resurrected Christ. This is done through education, youth work, women and family programmes, church-related schools and schools of theology.

Another priority is *Christian unity**. In a multi-religious and polarized Middle East, the unity of the church is seen not as an end in itself or as a front against any power or group. It is rooted in Christian faith and love. The unity of the church is the prototype of unity and society and a basic requirement of witness and mission.

In the Middle Eastern churches, deep concern has been expressed for *witness** in a multi-religious society where Christians are a minority. It is seen as raising the signs of the kingdom of God* through service and diakonia,* true and positive encounter with other religions and commitment to justice and peace.

International ecumenical relations for better mutual understanding and true solidarity has become an important priority. The Middle East has always been important for the world community and for Christians in particular as the cradle of the revelation of the three monotheistic religions, and the place of the incarnation and resurrection of Jesus Christ. During the last decade the situation has become a focus of attention for the world and a source of concern for world peace.

A particular concern of the MECC in recent years has been the increased activity in the region by Western evangelical and fundamentalist Christians. A number of MECC initiatives seeking to explain misunderstandings caused by the work of these groups and

to open a dialogue with them have received significant response from evangelical leaders. The MECC has been especially critical of the ideology and activities of those groups of Western fundamentalist Christians who refer to themselves as Christian Zionists, in particular the International Christian Embassy in Jerusalem. In 1986 the MECC executive committee condemned "the misuse of the Bible and the abuse of religious sentiments in an attempt to sacralize the creation of a state and legitimate the policies of a government".

The Christians in the Middle East, no less than their neighbours, have been the victims of continuing warfare. An unstable present and an uncertain future have resulted in demoralization and emigration. However, even more fundamental than physical survival is the survival of Christian witness in this region. The Christian affirmation that Christ once and for all overcame death and gave humanity new life based on love to all compels Christians to work for *human dignity, freedom and justice* as prerequisites for peace between people in the Middle East. This motivates the churches to work for human rights and justice in society.

The MECC has maintained its head office in West Beirut, Lebanon, throughout the period of the Lebanese civil war. This has symbolized the council's determination to be a bridge between communities and to emphasize the solidarity of the churches of the region with the people as a whole, irrespective of religion. Liaison offices which facilitate the working together of the churches on the local and national levels are established in Cyprus, Egypt, Syria and Bahrain.

LEOPOLDO J. NIILUS

"Who Are the Christians of the Middle East?", *MECC Perspectives*, 6-7, 1986.

MIGRATION. Whether they have left their country for reasons of economic survival or to escape persecution, migrants are "uprooted" people. After the wrench of parting from their country, they experience the pain of its loss. In most cases they try, singly or in a group, to maintain their identity — so indispensable for facing the future, whether it means adapting themselves to the new society or becoming integrated in it or perhaps preparing for an eventual return.

In 1988 the number of migrants was 80 million, i.e. 1.7% of the world's population. Of this number, 20 million are lawfully employed, and a similar number are members of their families; 20 million others are in an "irregular situation", 16 million are refugees, and 4 million have been displaced within their own country for security reasons.

The main currents of migration affect all the continents, with a certain number of critical points (Brazil, Central America/USA, Haiti, Mozambique, Middle East, Philippines, Mediterranean basin). The main routes for the migrant workers, however, run from South to North, from the poor countries to the industrialized countries.

One has to differentiate between refugees* and migrants. Refugees are migrants who, for security reasons, cannot return home. In virtue of this, they are entitled to an appropriate legal status. Migrants are defined as those who have left their country in search of economic survival, looking for a viable future for themselves and their children. The purpose of migration is no longer to people "empty" territories, as was the case during the first half of the century. At the root of both situations, however, there is always a deterioration of rights, civil and political, economic and social, or even of national rights (e.g. of minorities*).

In theory, economic migrants are moved to migrate for personal reasons. Their departure is said to be "a voluntary choice". In reality, most economic migrations are due to two main factors: (1) the need for a labour force, a demand and sometimes even a search organized more or less clandestinely by the industrial or the industrializing countries; (2) underdevelopment in countries which are "pools of labour" but which offer neither survival nor prospects, nor the decent and full life to which every human being can aspire. The contrast between wealth and poverty and the combination of the "push-pull" effect naturally results in the creation of migratory currents. It is difficult, therefore, to argue that the migrant workers are acting freely.

The economic crisis of the 1970s, the effects of the subsequent re-structuring of enterprises and the use of new technologies have led to severe restrictions on immigration. Yet the need for a compliant, flexible and cheap labour force remains; it engenders an "irregu-

lar" or "illegal" migration and the existence of masses of workers without rights and over-exploited. In addition, the inevitable integration of workers who have put down roots provokes xenophobic and racist reactions in many places. The deliberate achievement of pluri-cultural societies is still difficult.

Whether we like it or not, foreigners constitute a kind of mirror in which societies and churches can see their own reflections. How we behave towards them, individually and collectively, shows clearly how we are actually placed in respect of the principles of equality and justice* and respect for the human person in practice and not simply in theory. Their presence constitutes a call to solidarity, justice and respect for human rights within a profoundly unjust world. They are a challenge to civilization and culture.*

Diakonia* is thus called to recognize a new dimension of service. If it is to be anything more than mere rhetoric, it must tackle the causes of injustice and exploitation. It must demand the universal application of legal and social protection without exception. These are dimensions affecting the economy, collective behaviour and even the political field, for which many Christian communities find themselves poorly prepared.

Some churches and movements, however, have not remained indifferent. The Christian Conference of Asia has called in particular for a struggle against the exploitation of women and support for migrant organizations; the National Christian Council of Japan has decided to support the defence of Koreans against racial discrimination; in Lesotho, the churches have made concerted efforts in favour of the defence and education of exploited mineworkers in South Africa; in the USA, the "undocumented" workers who have crossed the Mexican border are given special legal and social support by certain churches. In Europe, there is a fairly developed conscience within the churches, and efforts are concentrated on three main fronts: legal protection, the struggle against discrimination, and pastoral care.

The study of the WCC's responsibility in this field was recommended by the central committee in 1956. The third assembly (New Delhi 1961) and the Church and Society conference (Geneva 1966) called for special campaigns. This led to the creation of the secretariat for migration within the WCC's Commission on Inter-Church Aid, Refugee and World Service, though without much in the way of means, apart from the publication of a review, *Migration Today*. A European conference likewise created a secretariat for Europe.

The actions undertaken to help migrant workers have not been as effective and appropriate as those in favour of refugees. It is not so easy to separate the two categories today; often they are expelled together because they are "foreign migrants". On the other hand, the resurgence of racism,* often directed against migrants, is an urgent challenge to the churches.

ANDRÉ JACQUES

MILITARISM/MILITARIZATION.

The term "militarism" usually refers to a stockpiling of armaments, a growing role of the military in national and international affairs, the use of force as an instrument of political power, and a dominant influence of the military in civilian affairs. International relations (see **international order**) are increasingly viewed as power relations to be determined militarily, and the influence of the military and the use of force have become more common internally. "Militarism" is used with different connotations in East and West, North and South, and is too often applied in the political debate without precise definition. Historically the term has been used to describe well-known phenomena such as Bonapartism, the rise of the German imperial strength, the ascendancy of Japan or some fascist variants of expansionist regimes. These models are inadequate for a deeper understanding and analysis of contemporary militarism, both in the third world and in the developed countries, capitalist and socialist.

The fifth assembly of the WCC (Nairobi 1975) called upon the churches and the WCC to "raise consciousness about the dangers of militarism and search for creative ways of educating for peace". The consultation on militarism organized by the WCC's Commission of the Churches on International Affairs (Glion, Switzerland, 1977), the first ecumenical consultation specifically on the theme, said: "Militarization should be understood as the process whereby military values, ideology and patterns of behaviour achieve a dominating influence on the political, social and economic affairs of the state and as a consequence the structural, ideological and behavioural patterns of both the society and government militarized. Militarism should be seen as one of the more perturbing results of this process. It must be noted that militarism is multidimensional and varied with different manifestations in various circumstances dependent on historical background, national traditions, class structure, social conditions, economic strength, etc."

While militarism is in no way confined to the third world, the major ecumenical concerns have centred on the spread of militarism there. A number of third-world countries are ruled by military regimes; many others display a process of militarization. Contributing factors to militarism in third-world countries include super-power competition, the creation and maintenance of spheres of influence, the use of the army as the primary agent for modernization, and the failure of democratic governments to provide order* and justice.*

A disquieting trend of militarism in many third-world countries has been para-militarization, which is an intensive and systematic use of civilians for repression. Such groups are formally not part of the army, though they are frequently organized by the army and include military personnel.

The statement on "Peace and Justice" by the sixth assembly of the WCC (Vancouver 1983) said: "Through the Council's work on militarism since the fifth assembly we have come to understand more fully the dire consequences for justice of the increasing reliance of the nations on armed forces as the cornerstone of their foreign — and often domestic — policies. Justice is often sacrificed on the altar of narrowly perceived national security interests."

On the national level, militarization is reflected in political, military, economic, social and cultural domains. Politically it leads to the concentration of power, the weakening of democratic governments, the violation of human rights and the institution of authoritarian rule. Militarily it promotes armaments, including the development, acquisition and deployment of new weapon systems. Economically it tends to give preference to military expenditures, thus impeding efforts for development.

In more than half of third-world countries, military leaders currently hold the reins of political power. Their control is routinely associated with violations of basic human and political rights. In most of these countries extreme forms of repression, including torture, brutality, disappearances and political killing, are used by the authorities.

Demilitarization in countries where the armed forces once enjoyed a dominant and organized political position is often a matter of degree. There is often an attempt on the part of the armed forces to inhibit and constrain the behaviour of the successor government. And the possibility of re-intervention is always present.

There are several problems in the transition from military regimes to civilian governments. While constitutional guarantees and civil rights are re-established in an effort to maintain the new government, which may be still fragile, several of the repressive laws of the former regime are often retained. Human rights* advocates, including the churches, often find themselves in a dilemma because it might appear that too much pressure on the government may bring back the military. This is made difficult particularly because of the unresolved issue of the role of the military in the new context as well as the desire of the military not to be punished for its misdeeds during the previous regime.

Militarization usually proceeds on the national, regional or global level. Lebanon illustrates militarization on a lower level. In the absence of an effective central government and contributing to the further weakening of such authority, militias organized on political and religious lines exercise power. Religious fundamentalism is a primary factor in promoting militarism on this level.

NINAN KOSHY

A. Eide & M. Thee eds, *Problems of Contemporary Militarism*, London, Croom Helm, 1988 • "Report of the Consultation on Militarism, 1977", *CCIA Background Information, 1977* • J.-A. Viera Gallo ed., *The Security Trap*, Rome, IDOC, 1979.

MINISTRY IN THE CHURCH.

Ministry in the church has been a focal point of discussion since the origins of the ecumenical movement. The inability of some communions to recognize the ministerial orders of others has been a principal obstacle in the effort to achieve visible unity.* Dialogue has also raised questions about the structure and practice of ministry in a changing world. Prophetic initiatives and new charisms* have challenged the churches, as has a growing understanding of baptism* as entry into ministry for the whole people of God.* Inquiry concerning ministry, whether lay or ordained, cannot be separated from inquiry into the nature and mission of the church* as such.

Conversations *within confessions or communions* may be ecumenically relevant as they respond to new realities, clarify old positions, or set the stage for wider dialogue. Vatican II,* for example, brought about changes in the Roman Catholic conception of priestly ministry largely through symbolic, but very real, changes in the celebration of the mass: changes which enhance the people's role and thus act out an apparent new conception of the sources and exercise of ministerial authority. Ecumenically significant as well have been conversations on "calling" in the Reformed tradition, debates on *Amt* (office) in German-speaking Lutheranism, and discussions on "episcopacy" and "succession" in Anglicanism.

Ministry has been a central issue in at least eight *bilateral dialogues* at the world level. The aspects considered naturally vary with the history of relationships between the bodies concerned. Texts relevant to the question of ministry may be consulted in Meyer and Vischer as follows: Anglican-Lutheran (24-27), Anglican-Orthodox (52-53), Anglican-Roman Catholic (78-87,93,102-05), Baptist-Reformed (147-49), Lutheran-Roman Catholic (179-84,208-09,248-74), Methodist-Roman Catholic (328-30,356-62), Old Catholic-Orthodox (417-18), Reformed-Roman Catholic (456-61).

Multilateral dialogue on ministry has centred in the Faith and Order* movement. A generation of collaborative work culminated in 1982 in the ministry part of *Baptism, Eucharist and Ministry.* Originally intended as a weaving together of the results of previous ecumenical conversations, this document became a substantially new work in which Roman Catholic and Orthodox participation was added to the original Protestant discussion. The historic threefold ministry* of bishop, presbyter and deacon is re-affirmed, in the context of a strong affirmation of "the calling of the whole people of God". Within the body's multiplicity of gifts, there are those who are "responsible for pointing to its fundamental dependence on Jesus Christ". Scarcely entering the question of the validity of orders, the document acknowledges that the New Testament offers no single pattern of ordained ministry and shows that the development of the threefold pattern has been complex, marked by crises and the indispensable appearance of prophets and charismatic leaders. The threefold ordering is offered as "an expression of the unity we seek and also as a means for achieving it" (M22). Succession in ministry from the apostles onward is *one* of the elements in the apostolicity* of the church, but is not, as thought in some communions, the primary vehicle of apostolicity. Ordination* is a "sacramental sign", embodying many of the elements which have led some communions to interpret it as a sacrament* in the full sense. The apostolic reality is seen not only in the churches which have bishops but in all those which express apostolicity in different ways. The BEM ministry document may be read as picturing the whole liturgical assembly, with the presbyters gathered around the bishop as a "focus of unity", not in terms of higher or lower ranks but on a horizontal plane (M8,20-27,29-30; cf. Vatican II, Constitution on the Sacred Liturgy, para. 41).

In *union negotiations*, the issue of ministry seems most seriously joined when churches of the "catholic" tradition are involved, raising the problem of mutual recognition and reconciliation of ministerial orders. Liturgical acts have been designed, with varying success, to bring about effective unifications of ministry, notwithstanding remaining and acknowledged differences of conception. Many of the more successful unions have been outside Europe and North America, e.g. the South India and North India plans, and the negotiation bringing about the Uniting Church in Australia. Several negotiations have so far not borne fruit, notably in Africa and in Great Britain. A proposal by the Consultation on Church Union (COCU)* in the US would reconcile ministries in "covenanting councils" composed of persons exercising episcopal functions, whether or not designated as bishops, within their own communions. The salient

(but not the only) issue in church union negotiations has been to see to it that all ministers are received and recognized in a way satisfactory to the uniting bodies. Most often this is achieved through a uniting service which includes a mutual laying on of hands seen not as re-ordination but as an act of reconciliation* and of the giving and receiving of a historic sign of apostolicity.*

In these arenas of dialogue a range of issues has emerged which together constitute the current "state of the question". First, what is the distinction, and the relationship, between the ministry of the ordained and other ministries of the church? In what way are the ordained over against the community, and in what way in the community? A gift to the community, or the community's own choice of leadership? The Canterbury statement of 1973 (Anglican-Roman Catholic) says of the ordained ministry that although they share in the priesthood of the whole people of God and represent the whole church in fulfilment of priestly vocation,* "their ministry is not an extension of the common Christian priesthood but belongs to another realm of the gifts of the Spirit".

The theological statement of COCU, speaking of the ordained, says: "Their ordination marks them as persons who represent to the church its own identity and mission in Jesus Christ." The notion of representation appears to break through the classic alternative between seeing the ordained as different from others in *kind* or in *degree*. "Precisely as *representatives* of Christ and his church the ordained ministers are *distinct*, but *what* they represent is not *other* than the character and mission of the whole church" (G. Wainwright).

Second, what is the relation between episcopacy* and other ordained ministries? Is the distinction between the episcopate and the presbyterate* mainly one of jurisdiction among those holding the same order, or is the episcopal order a distinctive and essential one? What ecclesiastical memory predominates: that of the election of a bishop from among the presbyters, or the appointment of local episcopoi by the itinerating apostles?

Third, is "apostolic succession" the sole possession of those who receive it in a "tactile" chain of ordinations claiming to reach back to the earliest times, or does this notion embrace a wider stream of the church's historic life? The Anglican-Lutheran bilateral stated in 1972: "In confessing the apostolic faith as a community, all baptized and believing Christians are the apostolic church and stand in the succession of apostolic faith" (Meyer & Vischer, 24). Is succession in ministry only one of the elements in the apostolic nature of the church, or is it the first and fundamental element?

Fourth, what is the status of the ordination of women?* Many Protestant bodies, particularly in the North Atlantic world, now ordain women, but the Anglican communion is split, while Orthodox and Roman Catholic are firmly against. In some cases, as in the Church of England and in certain dioceses of the Episcopal Church, USA, a decision permitting women's ordination in principle has not been implemented on grounds of conscientious objection by the bishop with jurisdiction, or for fear of schism* in the church. In bodies which have ordained women for some time, there is generally little controversy over the principle. Efforts to achieve greater justice for ordained

Ministry at a home funeral in Munda, Solomon Islands (WCC/Peter Williams)

women in placement and promotion claim the centre of attention. On the other hand, in some churches, notably the Orthodox, the question of women's ordination has only just begun to be faced (Rhodes consultation, 1988). Unrest on the subject exists in Roman Catholicism, but there are no signs of official reconsideration.

The Anglican-Roman Catholic dialogue has sought to isolate the question from gains achieved on a broader front. Women's ordination is a "grave obstacle to the reconciliation of our communions", but the "principles upon which this doctrinal agreement rests are not affected by such ordinations; for it was concerned with the origin and nature of the ordained ministry, not with the question who can or cannot be ordained". Important ecumenical consultations on this subject have been held in Klingenthal (1979) and Sheffield (1981). A statement by F&O may be found in the 1975 document "Baptism, Eucharist and a Mutually Recognized Ministry" (Accra 1974, Nairobi 1975). The BEM document (Lima text, 1982) radically abbreviates this treatment. It recognizes differences among the churches, acknowledges that these differences create obstacles to mutual recognition of ministries, counsels mutual openness and encourages facing, rather than avoiding, the fundamental question.

Fifth, what is the relation between traditional orderings of ministry and the many new, contextually responsive ministries and forms of ministerial practice? This question appears in many guises, e.g. with reference to the Latin American church base communities.* In the face of a general shortage of priests, can the unordained persons who often lead these communities be made eligible to preside at the eucharist?* Are these persons, as Leonardo Boff suggests, not unlike the community-chosen "protestant" pastors at the time of the Reformation? What of those who find ministerial callings in settings not involving sacramental and pastoral leadership of a traditional congregation? What of ministry which is essentially participatory enablement of the people of God in their prophetic tasks?

Finally, what should be the impact of new conceptions of church and ministry on theological education? The WCC Programme on Theological Education is in touch with numerous attempts around the world to find fresh ways to prepare ministers for their callings. Many of these involve departures from the traditional Western connection between seminary education and the culture of the university, turning instead to "theological education by extension", i.e. contextually based, inductive, experiential programmes conducted in the midst of the people and related to problems of faith and witness where they live.

Are there any clear gains? Yes: general agreement that NT patterns in themselves do not settle today's issues; agreement that apostolic succession involves more than continuity of tactile ordination by bishops; awareness that the social context counts and that the meanings of words and practices depend on the culture and usage involved; agreement that actual practices are important and may not always correspond to traditional patterns; agreement that the whole people have a ministry based on their baptism; discovery of the importance of liturgical practice and convergence in the liturgical expression of ordination; movement towards more popular and less restrictive patterns of practice and governance.

One cannot foresee whether these trends will continue, or whether indeed they will prove to have been the important ones for the future of the church. It is difficult to discern, as well, whether local contextuality will triumph over universal convergence or the reverse, or whether possibly a new accommodation between these values will eventually emerge.

See also **apostolicity; charism(ata); church; church order; diaconate; episcopacy; laity/clergy; ministry, threefold; ordination; ordination of women; presbyterate; priesthood; unity**.

LEWIS S. MUDGE

B. Cooke, *Ministry to Word and Sacraments: History and Theology*, Philadelphia, Fortress, 1976 • Groupe des Dombes, *Le ministère de communion dans l'Eglise universelle*, Paris, Centurion, 1986 • F.R. Kinsler, *Ministry by the People: Theological Education by Extension*, WCC, 1983 • H. Meyer & L. Vischer eds, *Growth in Agreement: Reports and Agreed Statements of Ecumenical Conversations on a World Level*, WCC, 1984 • C.F. Parvey ed., *Ordination of Women in Ecumenical Perspective*, WCC, 1980 • D.N. Power, *Gifts That Differ: Lay Ministries Established and Unestablished*, New York, Pueblo, 1980 • E. Schillebeeckx, *Pleidooi voor mensen in de kerk* (ET *The Church with a Human Face: A New and Expanded Theology of Ministry*, New York, Crossroad, 1987) • E. Sigurbjörnsson, *Ministry within the People of God*, Lund, Gleerup, 1974 • G.H. Vischer, *Apostolischer Dienst: Fünfzig Jahre Diskussion über das kirchliche Amt in Glauben und Kirchenverfassung*, Frankfurt am Main, Lembeck, 1982 • G. Wainwright, "Reconciliation in Ministry", in *Ecumenical Perspectives on BEM*, M. Thurian ed., WCC, 1983.

MINISTRY, THREEFOLD. The threefold ministerial pattern of bishops, presbyters and deacons has been and remains a central theme in ecumenical discussion on the nature of the church* and its ministry. Convictions about the necessity or optionality of such a pattern are bound up with different readings of Christian history and with different theologies of ministry and church.

The plurality of church orders in the New Testament communities means that few would now see the NT as warranting in an exclusive way the threefold ministry, especially in its developed form. However, while it is easy in retrospect to over-emphasize the formality and coherence of early Christian institutional life, the threefold order emerges in the 2nd and 3rd centuries as the dominant pattern, largely as a means of securing the church's unity* and continuity. It is also important to bear in mind the influence of secular patterns of social organization on the church as it moves away from local, occasional patterns to more uniform structures.

The content of the threefold form varies considerably. Earlier accounts, as already in Ignatius of Antioch, see the bishop as the president of the local assembly, assisted by presbyters, with deacons as community servants; later, as bishops become regional authorities, deacons' duties are assumed by presbyters, who become the local presiding ministers. The picture is further complicated by the place of the minor orders (lectors, acolytes, etc.) and of the sub-diaconate, sometimes regarded as a minor order and sometimes as the lowest of the major orders. While the Roman Catholic, Orthodox and Anglican traditions have retained the threefold ministry, the churches of the Reformation have generally adopted a single pastoral ministry of word and sacrament, though sometimes with a form of regional authority.

The centrality of the issue in ecumenical debate in the present century was in part ensured by heavy Anglican presence in the nascent ecumenical movement. Anglican conscience on the point derived partly from the 16th-century Anglican ordinals which enshrined the normative status of the threefold order, and partly from the fact that, historically, Anglican identity has frequently been bound up with claims about the validity of Anglican orders and their fidelity to what was construed as the threefold apostolic pattern. Thus the 1927 Lausanne Faith and Order conference recognized dialogue on "the nature of the ministry (whether consisting of one or several orders)" as central to ecumenical advance. The mature fruit of such dialogue is the document *Baptism, Eucharist and Ministry*.* BEM affirms the threefold pattern as an instrument of continuity and order, making modest claims that this ministry "may serve today as an expression of the unity we seek and also as a means for achieving it" (M22). It further asserts that such an order has strong claims to be accepted by churches which have not retained the form, while acknowledging the need for reform of the pattern, especially in the areas of ministerial collegiality and of the profile of deacons.

Churches like the Roman Catholic Church, which regard the threefold order as of the essence of the church, are unlikely to find this a sufficiently strong affirmation of its normative status as a prime instrument of unity, catholicity* and apostolicity,* while churches in the Reformation tradition which have only one basic ministry of word and sacrament may fear that the validity of their patterns of ministry is being undermined if the threefold order is proposed as the generally accepted pattern. A number of other issues also need to be resolved. It remains unclear exactly what the threefold ministry consists of, given the great variety of descriptions of content both of each office and of their inter-relation. The relation of the episcopate (see **episcopacy**) to the presbyterate* has been a matter of debate since the early and medieval periods. Is the episcopate an extension of the presbyterate, or does the presbyterate exist by devolution from the episcopate? How is the distribution between these two orders of functions such as confirmation* or ordination* to be arranged? The recovery of the diaconate* as more than a stepping stone to the presbyterate is a further pressing issue to be worked on both theologically and practically if the threefold order is to be properly *three*fold.

The necessity of clarification and reform in these areas shows that a renewed threefold pattern will of necessity be very different from a re-affirmed medieval pattern of regional episcopate, vestigial diaconate, and presbyterate as the basic local expression of ministry. A further complication is the increasing need to find ways of affirming full-time ministries which have traditionally fallen outside the threefold pattern (such as teachers, evangelists, or men and women of prayer). As it stands at present, the threefold ministry offers little guidance as to how such ministries can be affirmed as genuinely apostolic, permanent characteristics of ministry in the assembly. Work on these issues is most fruitfully undertaken by setting questions of ecclesiastical office in the larger theological context of Christ, Spirit and the people of God,* a context which has so far proved to be immensely fruitful in ecumenical reconciliation.*

See also **church order, diaconate, episcopacy, ministry in the church, presbyterate**.

                                                            JOHN B. WEBSTER

B. Cooke, *Ministry to Word and Sacrament*, Philadelphia, Fortress, 1976 • H. Küng, *Die Kirche* (ET *The Church*, London, Burns & Oates, 1968) • J. Martos, *Doors to the Sacred*, Garden City, NY, Doubleday, 1981 • E. Schillebeeckx, *Pleidooi voor mensen in de kerk* (ET *The Church with a Human Face*, London, SCM, 1985).

MINORITIES. With the creation of nation states (see **state**) as political entities during the last two centuries, many natural ethnic borderlines have been disregarded. As a result of power arrangements, new boundaries were drawn with a variety of consequences, including forced division, forced unity, forced assimilation and marginalization of peoples and groups. These developments, often prompted by political and economic motives, contributed to the emergence and evolution of ethnic, national, racial, religious and linguistic minorities.

No generally agreed definition of "minority" exists, but for present purposes we may refer to a working definition developed by a special rapporteur of the United Nations sub-commission on prevention of discrimination and protection of minorities. He defined a minority as "a group numerically inferior to the rest of the population of a state, in a non-dominant position, whose members — being nationals of the state — possess ethnic, religious or linguistic characteristics differing from those of the rest of the population and show, if only implicitly, a sense of solidarity, directed towards preserving their culture, traditions, religion or language" (see Capotorti).

While in the period between the two world wars a system of protection of minorities was established in the framework of the League of Nations, the members of the UN showed very little willingness to continue that experiment, which was not a great success anyway. Many members of the UN feared that recognition of minorities would constitute a serious threat to the unity and integrity of fragile state structures, and the assumption prevailed that the best solution to the problem of minorities would be to encourage respect for individual human rights. Consequently, efforts by Denmark, Yugoslavia and the USSR to have a provision on minority rights included in the Universal Declaration of Human Rights failed. However, at a later stage a provision on the rights of minorities, albeit very limited in scope and constituting a bare minimum, was accepted as article 27 of the International Covenant on Civil and Political Rights, reading: "In those states in which ethnic, religious or linguistic minorities exist, persons belonging to such minorities shall not be denied the right, in community with the other members of their group, to enjoy their own culture, to profess and practise their own religion, or to use their own language."

It appears that the reluctance of the UN to recognize minority rights had a bearing on ecumenical thinking. The first three assemblies of the WCC were silent on this matter, and it was only the fourth assembly in Uppsala (1968) that produced a substantive statement on majorities and minorities (paras 23-26). This statement underlines the need for protection of minorities and the special responsibility of the church but draws attention also to risks and threats if minority issues are stretched too far. The Uppsala statement reads

in part: "Most nations have ethnic, cultural or religious minorities. These minorities have the right to choose for themselves their own way of life in so far as this choice does not deny the same choice to other groups. Majorities can be insensitive and tyrannical, and minorities may need protection. This is a special responsibility for the church of him who is the champion of the oppressed" (para. 23). The statement continues: "But if pressed too far, the rights of minorities can destroy justice and threaten the stability or the existence of the nation. The frustration of a majority by a minority is as incompatible with justice as the persecution of a minority by a majority" (para. 24).

The tension between minority rights and their misuse which characterizes the Uppsala statement is touched upon in a statement on "Unity and Human Rights in Africa Today" adopted by the WCC central committee in January 1971. On that occasion the central committee stated: "Unity is not an end in itself. National unity must include a recognition of legitimate human rights which also safeguard the basic rights of ethnic minorities."

The ecumenical movement has been particularly supportive of the process which took shape to give concrete expression to the Helsinki Final Act (1975) and has referred in that context to the rights of cultural, linguistic, religious, ideological or ethnic minorities. Thus, Nairobi 1975 defended the rights of minorities in the context of the Helsinki process. Later ecumenical statements, notably also by the WCC central committee at Moscow in July 1989, expressed the same commitment.

THEO VAN BOVEN

F. Capotorti, *Study of the Rights of Persons Belonging to Ethnic, Religious and Linguistic Minorities*, New York, UN, 1979 • F. Ermacora, *The Protection of Minorities before the United Nations*, Recueil des Cours, Hague Academy of International Law 182, p.251 • J. Fawcett, *The International Protection of Minorities*, Minority Rights Group Report No. 41, 1979 • P. Thornberry, *Minorities and Human Rights Law*, Minority Rights Group Report No. 73 • B. Whitaker, *Minorities — a Question of Human Rights?*, New York, Pergamon, 1984.

MISSIO DEI. The expression *missio Dei* (mission of God), usually retained in its Latin form, appeared in the 1950s in the development of a theological basis for missionary activity, especially in Anglican-Protestant circles within the International Missionary Council* (IMC). The concept had been highly refined in Western medieval theology to describe the activities within the Trinity itself which are expressed in God's "outside" mission: the Father sends the Son; the Father and the Son send the Spirit for the redemption of humanity. Already in the 2nd century, Irenaeus wrote of the unfolding of God's inner life in the history of salvation,* and Tertullian refers to "God's own self-distribution" within the saving history, this "economy... which distributes the unity into trinity" — the first known use of the term *trinitas* (*Against Praxeas*, written after 213).

Ever since the Edinburgh world missionary conference of 1910, church* and mission* struggled to discover each other. And by the time of the IMC Tambaram conference (1938), largely because of the dominant presence of mission societies* and councils not directly related to a church or intentionally not a church, Hendrik Kraemer's question to the participants was critical: "The church and all Christians... are confronted with the question, what is the essential nature of the church, and what is its obligation to the world?" If Tambaram was the beginning of an emphasis on the unity and inseparability of church and mission, the theology to support it was not worked out, and it had to be developed in order to satisfy the variety of IMC constituents and to give them a new orientation to the missionary enterprise.

At the Whitby conference (1947), mission representatives proclaimed that "we have entered as never before into the reality and the meaning of the worldwide church", and for the next conference in Willingen (1952), "the missionary obligation of the church" was chosen for the principal theme. The very foundations of the whole missionary movement were in need of re-examination; some even were hearing the death gasps of missions in the traditional sense. Mission and church had met, a new theological understanding of missions was urgent and that must involve a new understanding of the very nature of the church.

But several preparatory papers for Willingen, especially that of the Dutch missiologist J.C. Hoekendijk, as well as conference participants, vigorously criticized the *church-centred* orientation of the missionary enterprise, for missions could easily become narrow in horizon and scope, and the missionary would be defining "the whole surrounding world in ecclesiological categories... The world has almost ceased to be the world and is now conceived as a sort of ecclesiastical training-ground" (Hoekendijk).

The church is not the true centre of gravity towards which one should direct missionary thinking; rather, it should be the self-revelation of the Triune God (see **Trinity**) in Jesus Christ* — the *missio Dei* revealed in the mission of the church, yes, but not only in and through the church. The source of the missionary activity is actually the Triune God: "Out of the depths of his love for us, the Father has sent forth his own beloved Son to reconcile all things to himself, that we and all men might, through the Holy Spirit, be made one in him with the Father in that perfect love which is the very nature of God" (Willingen report).

Thus in *missio Dei* thinking, however closely mission and church go together, so that "the church lives by mission as a fire exists by burning" (Emil Brunner), still "God is, and remains until the last day, the One who alone carries on the missionary enterprise" (William Anderson). In the strict sense, the sending God alone, through the Sent-God, is the sending authority. No church — and even more so, no missionary society with a measure of independence from the church — dare claim "sending authority" for itself.

Roman Catholics and especially the Orthodox welcomed the *missio Dei* expression, in so far as the Trinitarian approach could offset what they judged to be almost Christomonism in much Protestant mission thinking and piety. But the RC and Orthodox understanding of church as sacrament precludes such sharp either-or's: God-sending *or* church-sending. Furthermore, while the term *missio Dei* should not be confined to missionary activity but refers to everything God does for the communication of salvation and, in a narrower sense, to everything the church itself is sent to be and do, the classic terms of "missionary activity", "evangelism" and "witness" are becoming overloaded, beginning to burst and dissipate, so that by meaning too much they end up meaning too little and doing too little.

TOM STRANSKY

W. Anderson, *Towards a Theology of Mission*, IMC research pamphlet 2, London, SCM, 1955 • J.C. Hoekendijk, "The Church in Missionary Thinking", *International Review of Mission*, 43, 1952 • L. Newbigin, *The Relevance of Trinitarian Doctrine for Today's Mission*, London, Edinburgh House, 1963 • G. Vicedom, *Missio Dei: Einführung in eine Theologie der Mission*, Munich, Kaiser, 1958.

MISSIOLOGY. "Missiology" is a word used in two overlapping senses. Considered as the systematic consideration of the nature of the Christian mission,* it is sometimes called theory of mission, theology of the apostolate, or theology of mission. Considered as the whole range of studies appropriate to the understanding of mission, its context and practical application, it is equivalent to the theological discipline "science of mission", or simply "mission studies".

The content of missiology has developed along with the concept of mission. The necessity for study outside the traditional limits of Western theology emerged in the later 19th century as a result of missionary activities. Early missiology naturally focused on missions. Emphasis gradually passed to the mission of the church, especially as the ecumenical movement strengthened the idea of a worldwide church and as Western society was increasingly recognized as a mission field as much as a mission base. Further re-focusing followed, as the heart of mission was seen to lie in the mission of God ("the source of the missionary movement is the Triune God himself", declared the Willingen meeting of the International Missionary Council in 1952). This understanding extended the scope of mission studies to consideration of the whole saving activity of God in the world. The Trinitarian nature of that activity brought questions of environment,* culture* and society,* as well as of the fullness of the church,* within the scope of missiology. Significantly, the *International Review of Missions* changed its last word to "Mission" in 1969. The earlier stress on Christian expansion remains central to some missiologies (e.g. the Church-Growth* and Frontier-Missions schools), but

the former stress on missions in the agency-related sense has gone.

The earliest academic missiological appointment was Alexander Duff's chair of evangelistic theology, established in New College, Edinburgh, in 1867. Gustav Warneck held a similar professorship at Halle, 1896-1908. Chairs of mission science followed in other theological faculties in Germany (Protestant and Catholic), the Netherlands and Scandinavia. A separate development produced professorships of missions in the USA, where K.S. Latourette of Yale introduced a missiological dimension into church history with his monumental *History of the Expansion of Christianity*. The Pontifical Urban University in Rome and the mission-related Selly Oak Colleges in Birmingham provided other bases for missiological scholarship. Teaching was often supported by research institutes, in some cases co-operative, such as the Scottish Institute of Missionary Studies (1967) and the vigorous Inter-University Institute for Missiology and Ecumenics in the Netherlands (1969). Warneck founded the first significant missiological journal, *Allgemeine Missions Zeitschrift*, in 1874; there have been many successors. Missiological libraries developed, such as the Missionary Research Library, New York, and the Day Missions Library, Yale. From its origin in 1912 the *International Review of Mission(s)* has provided a quarterly bibliography on mission studies; the Sacred Congregation for the Propagation of the Faith has produced the massive *Bibliografia Missionaria* for over 50 years.

The oldest major learned society in the field is the Deutsche Gesellschaft für Missionswissenschaft. The American Society for Missiology and the South African Missiological Society bring out notable journals. In 1947 O.G. Myklebust of Norway published a plan for an international organization of missiological scholars. After a consultation of European missiologists (Birmingham 1968), the International Association for Mission Studies came into being in Oslo in 1970, with Myklebust as secretary and H.W. Gensichen as president. It is now fully international in composition, sponsors major conferences, promotes co-operation in research and publishes the journal *Mission Studies*.

Missiology has followed different lines in

different times and places, developing its
frontiers with biblical studies, dogmatics,
church history, practical theology and evangelism, social ethics, ecumenics, history of religions and currently theology of religion
(American missiology has been especially
productive in statistical and cognate data).
Missiology emerged because the resources of
Western theology did not suffice for a world
church in interaction with many cultures. If
the word "missiology" is still not common in
non-Western settings, it is in part because
active and authentic theology in those settings
is itself missiological.

See also **missionary societies**.

ANDREW WALLS

R.C. Bassham, *Mission Theology, 1948-1975*,
Pasadena, CA, William Carey Library, 1979 •
O.G. Myklebust, *The Study of Missions in Theological Education*, 2 vols, Oslo, Forlaget Land og
Kirke, 1955-57 • J. Verkuyl, *Inleiding in de nieu-
were Zendingswetenschap* (ET *Contemporary Missiology: An Introduction*, Grand Rapids, MI, Eerdmans, 1978).

MISSION. We may consider the 20th century in three segments for the purposes of
reviewing the understanding of mission in the
modern ecumenical movement.

1900-21. In the 20th century, mission truly
became an ecumenical priority. The century
began with two significant events. The first
was a meeting of the South India missionary
conference at Madras, India, in January
1900. The nine topics discussed included the
native church, its self-support, self-government and self-propagation; and comity of
missions and co-operation in mission work.
Two convictions about mission were taking
shape. The church* is, by its very nature as
the Body of Christ, called to propagate the
gospel, which it believes and tries to live;
and those coming from afar who attempt to
propagate the gospel in any given place must
act together, or at least they must not act
against each other, for Christ is not divided
(see 1 Cor. 1:13).

The second event was an ecumenical missionary conference held in New York, April-
May 1900, with 2,500 participants and an
attendance of between 170,000 and 200,000.
The conference used "ecumenical" in its title
"because the plan of campaign which it pro-

poses covers the whole area of the inhabited
globe" — in conformity with the literal meaning of the Greek word "oikoumene". But
some participants understood "ecumenical" in
the sense of Matt. 24:14: "And this gospel of
the kingdom will be preached throughout the
whole world (oikoumene), as a testimony to
all nations; and then the end will come."
Mission was not just a campaign from Western Christendom to the rest of the world but
the gospel of God's kingly rule over *all* nations, to be revealed in God's own time of
final judgment. At this conference there was a
detailed survey of the areas of mission both
existing and to be occupied, and the deliberations expressed the need for some international body to co-ordinate and promote the
mission to the world beyond Europe and
North America.

Ten years later, this vision began to find
concrete expression in the world missionary
conference held at Edinburgh (June 1910),
which has rightly been regarded as the beginning of the modern ecumenical movement.
The 1,200 delegates at the meeting placed at
the centre of their prayerful and manifold
work the obligation to make Christ known to
the millions who had not heard the gospel. A
sense of urgency was generated, expressed by
its chairman, John R. Mott, as "the decisive
hour of Christian mission" and "the evangelization of the world in this generation". This
meant that everything must be done so that all
who lived at that time should have an opportunity to hear the gospel and decide for or
against Christ. The climax of the meeting was
the agreement to appoint an international continuation committee which would, in the
words of Mott, be "looking steadily at the
world as a whole, confronting the world as a
unity by the Christian church as a unit".

The first joint effort was the launching in
1912 of the *International Review of Missions*,
which quickly became an effective ecumenical forum for reflections on the continuing
mission of God. The shattering experience of
the 1914-18 world war severely tested the
churches of Europe and North America,
which had assumed the main burden of carrying out the world mission. It became even
more evident that a permanent world body
should be established for co-operative consultation and action. This occurred with the
founding of the International Missionary

Council* (IMC) at Lake Mohonk, New York, in October 1921.

The formation of the IMC was above all the work and achievement of a dedicated band of men and women of many nations who had their apprenticeship in the ecumenical youth and student lay movements — the World Alliance of YMCAs* (1855), the World YWCA* (1894) and the World Student Christian Federation* (1895). They learned to think, pray and study the Bible in an interdisciplinary way and to do so across national, denominational and racial barriers. Thus in their formative years they acquired an insight and conviction that mission was appropriate both at home and abroad and was concerned with the whole of human life and of the life of nations. The Inter-Varsity Fellowship (1910) has also nurtured many soundly committed Christians who have played a significant role in an ecumenical understanding of mission.

1921-61. Two issues were immediately raised for the IMC. The first was clearly stated already in Edinburgh 1910 and now put in the IMC constitution: no statement should be made "on any matter involving an ecclesiastical or doctrinal question, on which members of the council or bodies constituting the council may differ among themselves". In other words, divided churches were carrying out the mission. They were proclaiming the gospel in different and even competing ways and thereby transplanting their divisions in other lands. And yet, Christians fervently believed the prayer of Christ "that they may all be one, even as thou, Father, art in me, and I in thee, that they also may be in us, so that the world may believe that thou hast sent me" (John 17:21). Episcopalian bishop Charles Brent had been convinced since Edinburgh that Christians had to face this contradiction of the one gospel's being proclaimed by the dismembered yet one Body of Christ. His efforts from 1911 were crowned with the formation of the Faith and Order* movement in 1927, concerned with the faith and order of the church and with working for the unity* of the church for a more credible mission to the world.

The other issue for IMC was stated in one of its functions: "to help unite the Christian forces of the world in seeking justice in international and inter-racial relations". This drew attention to the character and scope of mis-

sion, which continues to be debated. The missionary movement from Europe and North America to other continents and islands has been carried out in a context of economic, political and military domination and racist attitudes, and some of these attitudes and behaviour were infecting missionary societies and personnel, in spite of the devoted work they were performing in education, and training in skills, medical and social work, and even advocacy for the rights of the people. The IMC therefore requested its secretary, J.H. Oldham, who had been secretary of the Edinburgh conference, to do a careful study of racism.* In 1924 Oldham produced a pioneering book, *Christianity and the Race Problem*, in which he stated: "As Christ was sent by the Father, so he sends his disciples to set up in the world the kingdom of God. His coming was a declaration of war — a war to the death against the powers of darkness. He was manifested to destroy the works of the devil. Hence when Christians find in the world a state of things that is not in accord with the truth which they have learned from Christ, their concern is not that it should be explained but that it should be ended. In that temper we must approach everything in the relations between races that cannot be reconciled with the Christian ideal."

Mission was thus conceived in the spirit of Ps. 24:1: "The earth is the Lord's and the fullness thereof, the world (oikoumene) and those who dwell therein." Since all persons and all things in the oikoumene belong to the Lord, the task of mission is to manifest the fact that in Christ all peoples are called to be renewed in the image of God, to become what Oldham described, in the words of the American philosopher Josiah Royce, "the universal community of the loyal".

Another ecumenical leader who had a similar vision of God's mission in Christ to the whole oikoumene was the Lutheran bishop in Sweden, Nathan Söderblom. He had consulted Oldham during the early stages of his preparation for the 1925 launching of the Universal Christian Council of Life and Work* (Stockholm), which focused on the issues of social and international justice in Europe and North America and beyond. The good news of Jesus Christ embraced the whole of life.

The first world conference of the IMC was

held in Jerusalem around Easter 1928, ten years after the first world war. This representative gathering discussed as missiological concerns the Christian life and message in relation to non-Christian systems of life and thought, including secularism as a worldwide phenomenon; the ecclesiological question of the relation of "younger" and "older" churches; the Christian mission and race relations, industrialization and rural problems. The heart and centre of mission was expressed in the final message, which was itself influenced by the statements of the 1925 Life and Work conference and the 1927 Faith and Order conference: "Our message is Jesus Christ. He is the revelation of what God is and of what man through him may become. In him we come face to face with the ultimate reality of the universe; he makes known to us God our Father, perfect and infinite in love and in righteousness; for in him we find God incarnate, the final, yet ever unfolding revelation of the God in whom we live and move and have our being... Christ is our motive and Christ is our end. We must give nothing less, and we can give nothing more."

The world was soon caught in turmoil, with economic and monetary depression in 1929; the spread of the monstrous ideologies of fascism* and communism, which made total claims on peoples in the 1920s and 1930s; the Japanese invasion of Manchuria in 1931 and of Shanghai in 1937; the Italian invasion of Ethiopia in 1934-35. In this context two world ecumenical conferences were held in 1937: "Church, Community and State" in Oxford, and Faith and Order in Edinburgh.

All these events affected the next world missionary conference, in Madras, India (December 1938). The report of this conference is notably entitled *The World Mission of the Church*. In response to the world situation and the unfinished evangelistic task, the conference affirmed: "This is the task primarily of the whole church for the whole world... Nothing in the present world situation in any way invalidates the gospel... World peace will never be achieved without world evangelization." The delegates therefore issued a call: "We summon the churches to unite in the supreme work of world evangelization until the kingdoms of this world become the kingdom of our Lord." The church (from *kyriake*, belonging to the Lord) is the sent of God in

Christ through the Spirit. Its true existence is to be the bearer of God's mission to the world in all the dimensions of the world's life. While the Jerusalem conference put the centre of mission in Christ, the Madras conference took the logical step of calling on the whole church, as the Body of Christ, to be through all its members the bearer of the gospel in every place.

The darkness of the second world war, which was but the more devastating continuation of the first world war, put a great strain on mission as the message of Christ, the Light and Peace of the world. But at the end of the war it was discovered that many churches in Asia and Africa had grown, without the benefit of foreign missionaries and resources. These churches had been responding to the call of the Madras conference. So the IMC meeting at Whitby, Canada (1947), summed up its deliberations in the phrase "One world, one Christ." It defined the Christian witness in a revolutionary world: "Evangelism means the proclamation of the cross to a world which is baffled by the tragedy of apparently meaningless suffering; it means the proclamation of Christ's risen life to a world which, athirst for life, seems to be sinking down into death without hope." For this worldwide missionary task, "the first need is the renewal of the inner life of the church by a return to the message of the Bible and to the Lord of the Bible... Total evangelism demands the co-operation of every single Christian." And this co-operation must be a "partnership in obedience" in united action and a sharing of resources in a spirit of "expectant evangelism".

The following year, 1948, the WCC was inaugurated. While the Life and Work and Faith and Order movements combined to create the WCC, the IMC was able at that time only to be "in association with" it. However, the assembly surveyed the situation of the world and of the churches in 1948 and declared: "The evident demand of God in this situation is that the whole church should set itself to the total task of winning the whole world for Christ." Three years later, the WCC central committee made a similar statement and posed a question: "It is clear in the New Testament that the church is called at the same time to proclaim the gospel to the whole world and to manifest in and to that world the fellowship and unity which is in Christ. These

A mission effort in Australia (WCC photo)

two aspects of the calling of the church are interdependent... Can we articulate clearly how these two are related to each other; and can we express in the life of our congregations, our churches, and our ecumenical movements this fundamental unity?"

The IMC continued to promote many aspects of the churches' mission to the world, especially in the development of national and regional councils, such as the East Asia Christian Conference in 1957. It also devoted much reflection on the nature and scope of the Christian mission in a rapidly changing world, and on the relation of mission and unity as constituting the nature and calling of the church. It was a question not of "Why mission?" but of "What is mission?" The 1952 IMC conference in Willingen, Federal Republic of Germany, wrestled with the missionary obligation of the church at a time of East-West and North-South conflicts. With its theme "Mission under the Cross", the conference pointed to the source of mission as the self-revelation of the Triune God (see **Trinity**): "Out of the depths of his love for us, the Father sent forth his own beloved Son to reconcile all things to himself, that we and all

people might, through the Spirit, be made one in him with the Father in that perfect love which is the very nature of God."

At the next meeting of the IMC, in Ghana (December 1957-January 1958), the word that came through most powerfully was "the Christian world mission is Christ's, not ours." In that spirit the IMC decided to integrate into the WCC as its Division on World Mission and Evangelism (DWME). The integration took place appropriately at the 1961 New Delhi general assembly of the WCC, with its theme "Jesus Christ, the Light of the World". The assembly urged "the churches to seek together in each place the help of the Holy Spirit in order that they may receive power to be together Christ's obedient witnesses to their neighbours and to the nations".

1961-90. The new DWME brought much to the WCC as its contribution to the common calling of all the member churches to mission and unity in the name of the Triune God. Its Theological Education Fund, already set up in 1958, helped ecumenically to promote theological education for mission among the third-world churches. This later became the Programme on Theological Education, which serves all the churches around the world. DWME had a programme on Christian literature and was involved in broadcasting (including television and sound radio) through the World Association of Christian Broadcasters. In 1968 the association united with another group of Christian broadcasters to form the World Association for Christian Communication.*

DWME also initiated a process of joint action for mission, an effort by churches in any place who were willing together to survey the mission needs and opportunities and the total material and human resources available to meet them, leading to consultation aimed at securing real and effective deployment of the resources in the light of agreed goals. This concept of joint action for mission has focused the continuing difficult discussion between rich churches, with their traditional mission boards or societies, and the churches which emerged from their missionary activities. Attempts at promoting the ecumenical sharing of resources have so far produced meagre results. All this is complicated by the emergence of church-related funding service agencies which operate within restricted mandates, and also by the activities of certain world confessional bodies. The "implementation of partnership in obedience" is still hardly a reality.

The DWME further launched a series of studies on churches in mission around the world, which have produced several valuable volumes for study and action. It was also involved in the studies and reflections on the missionary structure of the congregation,* which produced two books, *Planning for Mission* and *The Church for Others*.

These and other concerns were reviewed at the first meeting of the DWME in Mexico City (December 1963), with the theme "Mission in Six Continents". The mission is in each place and calls for persons to cross national and confessional frontiers in obedience to Christ and in fellowship with the churches concerned. Of great importance was the presence for the first time of Eastern Orthodox delegates and Roman Catholic observer-participants. This presence had been facilitated by the strong statement of the New Delhi assembly on religious liberty* and proselytism.* This was the period of the Second Vatican Council* of the Roman Catholic Church, which produced decrees on ecumenism, religious liberty, the apostolate of the laity, and the church's missionary activity.

The WCC fourth assembly (Uppsala 1968) was a watershed for the churches' understanding of the many-sided mission of the Triune God in a bustling, broken world. It declared that mobilizing the people of God* for mission today necessitated "a continuing re-examination of the structures of church life at all levels, i.e. the local parish, the denominational synods and conferences, and their agencies, the councils of churches at national, regional and world levels. All these must ask, not 'Have we the right structures for mission?', but 'Are we totally structured for mission?'" The assembly also proposed the following criteria in evaluating priorities for mission: (1) Do they place the church alongside the poor,* the defenceless, the abused, the forgotten, the bored? (2) Do they allow Christians to enter the concerns of others, to accept their issues and their structures as vehicles of involvement? (3) Are they the best situations for discerning with others the signs of the times, and for moving with history towards the coming of the new humanity? These criteria have guided ecumenical approaches to mission in these decades.

In 1968 DWME created the Christian Medical Commission, which grew out of one of the major missionary activities over the centuries — healing and health as expressions of Christ's ministry of salvation. It has promoted community health care, with emphasis on the church becoming a healing, caring community, and has made a strong theological output on "Health, Healing and Wholeness".

The IMC concern about race discrimination and oppression had been taken up at the WCC second assembly in 1954 by a study on racial and ethnic tensions, culminating in 1969 in the Programme to Combat Racism* and its special fund, which received ready support by DWME and its constituent members. Similar support was given by DWME to enable the early functioning of the Commission on the Churches' Participation in Development in 1970. Indeed, DWME itself had a vigorous programme on urban and industrial mission which has later become urban and rural mission. In the 1971 re-structuring of the WCC, the DWME became a commission (CWME).

Of great significance in this period was the

setting up of a secretariat on Dialogue with People of Living Faiths; in 1971 it became a separate sub-unit of the WCC (see **dialogue, interfaith**). This was a new beginning of a 60-year-old central ecumenical missionary concern. The motivation behind this new beginning was that witnessing the Christian faith can be authentic only when we recognize people of living faiths as made in God's image, for whom Christ died, and among whom the Spirit is at work. Our attitude must be one of mutual respect and openness, and the sharing of life with life in the depths of our different faiths. Such an approach calls for a life of constant renewal by the Spirit through the word of God and waiting, interceding prayer. Indeed, a deeper spirituality for witness and service has become today's watchword of the ecumenical movement. This is due, on the one hand, to the wider ecumenical fellowship of Roman Catholics, Orthodox, Anglicans, Protestants, Pentecostalists, etc., as evidenced for example in the WCC-Roman Catholic Joint Working Group document on "Common Witness" (1980, following an earlier document in 1970), and, on the other hand, to Christians being renewed through mission to the poor and the oppressed, and in dialogue with people of other faiths.

But this understanding of mission as the whole church with the whole gospel to the whole person in the whole world has not gone unchallenged. A considerable body of Christians and even churches still conceive of mission as being primarily to those who have never heard the gospel and in what are called non-Christian areas. These Christians emphasize almost exclusively the conversion of people to Christ as their personal Saviour and leave issues of society, economics, race, sex and politics either as of secondary or as strictly consequential to conversion. This different approach takes many forms. It is organized internationally as the Lausanne Committee for World Evangelization,* with meetings from 1974 to 1989. Attempts have been made to have dialogue, mostly on a private basis, between what are loosely and incorrectly called the evangelical and the ecumenical groups.

More serious has been the proliferation of electronic and culturally bound evangelistic groups which have flooded the world, accompanied by funds for charitable projects which some poor, struggling third-world churches find irresistible. There is also a growing aggressive fundamentalism in some of the major faiths, like Islam, which accompanies a strong rejection of consumerist materialism and what is perceived to be the moral decadence emanating from the West.

In such a context the churches have been wrestling with the meaning, scope and goal of mission, as demonstrated by the CWME meetings on "Salvation Today" (1973), "Your Kingdom Come" (1980), and "Your Will Be Done: Mission in Christ's Way" (1989); and by Pope Paul VI's great encyclical on "Evangelization in the Modern World" (1975), following the synod of bishops in 1974. To these must be added the WCC assemblies at Nairobi (1975) and at Vancouver (1983). Most of what has been said at these meetings takes up the missionary concerns of this century. For some 25 years now, mission has been undertaken in terms of proclaiming the good news in word and costly deed to the poor and in liberation of the oppressed. Thousands of base or cell communities have sprung up as living missionary organisms, out of which have emerged new theologies, liturgies and styles of life, which are models for the renewal of churches in mission and for a prophetic witness to the unjust and demonic structures in society.

In an unjust world, mission is the word of judgment and justice spoken by the Lord of history, revealed in the incarnate, crucified and risen Christ. Mission is and has been in its inner core eschatological — concerned to challenge people personally and collectively to encounter their Creator, Redeemer and Judge, who will fulfill history according to the divine purpose.

Besides all that science and technology and economic and military power, in the hands of wilfully self-interested people, can do, there are the vast and rich cultures in which people have been nurtured and sustained. They are encountering each other, with very complex effects, both good and bad. The churches' mission is fundamentally addressed to people within these cultures, which can be transformed by the varied grace and wisdom of God to be the means of human regeneration in interlinked communities of caring and sharing. The history of the missionary movement, especially in this century, has in fact been this encounter with people in their cultures, as evidenced by the determined efforts to translate and communicate the scriptures in the language of the people, even against the policies of the ruling powers. In many instances, especially in Africa, this vital activity has helped to save some cultures from destruction.

With all this in mind, the 1989 CWME conference in San Antonio, USA, on "Your Will Be Done: Mission in Christ's Way" (1989) was drawn to the same Pauline passage which provided the theme for the first WCC assembly in 1948 on "Man's Disorder and God's Design" — Eph. 1:9-10: "[God] has made known to us in all wisdom and insight the mystery of his will, according to his purpose which he set forth in Christ, as a plan (oikonomia) for the fullness of time, to unite all things in him, things in heaven and things on earth." This oikonomia, or economy of God in Christ through the Spirit, is the basis and goal of mission for the whole creation; to it the church as the Body of Christ is called to be the vehicle of the fullness of God, who fills all in all (Eph. 1:22-23).

See also **evangelism, witness**.

PHILIP A. POTTER

The Ecumenical Review, 1948- • H.E. Fey ed., *The Ecumenical Advance: A History of the Ecumenical Movement*, vol. 2: *1948-1968*, 2nd ed., WCC, 1986 • W.R. Hogg, *Ecumenical Foundations*, New York, Harper, 1952 • *International Review of Missions*, 1912-70; *International Review of Mission*, 1970- • S. Neill, G.H. Anderson & J. Goodwin eds, *Concise Dictionary of the Christian World Mission*, London, Lutterworth, 1970 • L. Newbigin, *The Gospel in a Pluralist Society*, WCC, 1989 • R. Rouse & S.C. Neill eds, *A History of the Ecumenical Movement*, vol. 1: *1517-1948*, 3rd ed., WCC, 1986.

MISSIONARY SOCIETIES.

Most Western church historians consider the 19th century "the Great Century" of Protestant and Catholic missions. In world history this period is also pre-eminently the European century, for during it Europe was able to impose much of its will, ideas and power on a large portion of the inhabited world. The economic and imperial upsurge of Europe joined an unexpected Christian pietistic revival, which affected almost every denomination or church in every Western country.

Until that point, the US itself had been a mission field rather than the source of overseas missionaries. But with its mid-19th-century religious revival, the energy and optimism of a "Christian America", wedded to the nation's increasing international prestige, created a climate and image of America as world power and world saviour.

Protestant origins. By 1914, this revival among Protestants in both Europe and North America had given rise to a proliferation of home and foreign missionary societies. The motivation and understanding of mission for the members and supporters of these societies were complex, even as they were being modified from decade to decade. No one prominent motif in theology was all-determinative except that all held that a person who did not believe explicitly in Jesus Christ as Lord and Saviour of every person, everywhere, was in a position of eternal damnation, or at least was living very precariously with God. The pietist influence, in trying to recover the "first love" experiences of the early Christians (cf. Rev. 2:4-5), emphasized personal conversion,* purity of life, and lay initiative. Dominant motives for foreign missions ranged from a strong eschatology* that viewed them as a condition for the second and final return of Jesus the Messiah, to a simple, loving obedience to the Great Commission: Jesus' command to disciple all the nations (see Matt. 28:19-20).

The societies had differing immediate aims: a specific *area* on the non-Christian map (e.g. India, China, interior Africa), a specific *religious group* (e.g. Hindus, Muslims, Jews, Roman Catholics/Orthodox; tribal religions were simply called pagan), a specific *service* (e.g. medical, agricultural development, education, Bible translation/distribution, or all of these).

The European Protestant churches as such, especially if legally tied to the state, were often unable or unwilling to initiate, administer or support foreign missions. So the new mission societies were largely *voluntary* ones: they depended on the initiative of highly motivated individuals (far more laity than clergy, and during the last three decades, half were women, and half of them unmarried); and they relied for financial support on the voluntary gifts of interested Christians. Some societies were explicitly denominational, others were interdenominational or non-denominational, usually agreeing to a fundamental credal statement.

Such societies included Baptist Missionary Society (London, 1792), London Missionary Society (1795), Church Missionary Society (1795), Dutch Mission (1799), British and Foreign Bible Society (1804), London Society for Promoting Christianity among the Jews (1809), American Board of Commissioners for Foreign Missions (1810), Edinburgh Medical Missionary Society (1814), American Baptist Missionary Board (1814), Basel Mission (1815), American Bible Society (1816), and Berlin Society (1824) — the list becomes very long, so that by 1914 every European country, the USA and Canada had such societies. The more successful their work, the more the churches themselves began to collect money for the independent societies; eventually many of the churches began their own directly controlled mission agencies. By 1914 the total personnel of both Protestant types was around 45,000 overseas missionaries.

In the early 20th century, the mission churches, after a measure of stability and self-consciousness, also developed indigenous missionary societies, at first for their own regions. Examples are the National Missionary Society of India (1907) and the Anglican Society in China (1936).

Gradually there developed both "home-based" and "foreign" mission councils or federations of these societies, such as the committee of German Protestant Missions (1885); the Foreign Missions Conference of North America (1893); the Conference of Missionary Societies in Great Britain and Ireland (1913), and in the Netherlands (1915), Finland (1918), Sweden (1920), Norway (1920), Australia (1920), New Zealand (1926) and Switzerland (1944). After the second world war most of these councils became departments of overseas ministries within national councils of churches.

In the "mission fields" before the 1910 Edinburgh world missionary conference, there were a few national field organs, most concerned with comity (the mutual division of areas into spheres of occupation by mission societies, and non-interference in one another's affairs; see **common witness**), e.g. in India (1902), Korea (1905), Japan (1910). The trend increased after Edinburgh, also in

Africa, the Middle East and, with much more difficulty, Latin America.

In the 1920s and 1930s, the development of indigenous leadership and a sense of independent church responsibility prompted these agencies and "younger churches" to form national Christian councils, e.g. in India (1922), Japan (1923), China (1922), Korea (1924), Congo (1924). The major councils became members of the International Missionary Council* (IMC, 1921), which originally was virtually composed of councils of missionaries, then increasingly, also of local councils of churches.

Roman Catholic missions. Overseas mission work by European Roman Catholics, almost exclusively undertaken by religious communities,* had almost collapsed by the 1800s. Rome's suppression of the Jesuits (1773), the paralysis caused by the French revolution, Napoleon's forced removal of the pope from Rome, and the political secularization* and dissolution of religious communities in most of Europe etched a most gloomy picture. Beginning in the mid-1810s, the scene began to change, and a revival of missions eventually became a priority church concern and the focus of large-scale activity under Pope Gregory XVI (ruled 1831-46). The old communities re-organized themselves, such as the restored Jesuits (1814), the Benedictines, Dominicans, Franciscans, Capuchins, Holy Spirit Fathers, Paris Society for Foreign Missions, and Lazarists. And an unexpected number of over 100 new male and female communities arose, specially for mission work, such as the Oblates (1816), Marists (1817), Salesians (1859), Franciscan Missionary Sisters (1859), Scheut (1862), White Fathers and Sisters (1868-69), Franciscan Missionaries of Mary (1896), the last named being the largest women's community in 1990, with over 9,000 members.

Unlike the Protestant structures, these RC societies were composed of clergy, of religious brothers and sisters — all unmarried; assisting them was only a very small percentage of strictly laypeople, married or unmarried. And unlike most Protestant societies, these RC mission groups were not independent of any direct church control. Although most were not dependent on any one diocese, almost all were directly under Rome's Congregation for the Propagation of the Faith, even to the extent that Rome had divided up the whole non-Christian world in mission districts and then assigned them to specific missionary communities. Since several of them were international in membership, one community might have had several nationalities serving a single district.

Protestant policies of comity did not involve RCs. In fact, often the motivation for sending a new group to an area was to offset the work of the other; e.g. the Church Missionary Society and the White Fathers in East Africa, the Presbyterians and Jesuits in Lebanon and Syria, the Methodists and Sacred Heart Fathers in Oceania.

The US, where Protestantism in the latter part of the 19th century produced hundreds of overseas missionaries, was regarded by the RCC as a primary mission field for European societies to labour in. These RC societies sent priests, nuns and other church workers and were generous with money, so that the young unstable American church, bulging with the flood of immigrants, could survive. By 1900, there were fewer than 80 American Catholic foreign missionaries overseas, mostly in the Caribbean and Mexico. In 1907, Propaganda Fide removed most of the USA from the list of mission territories, and the number of US Catholic overseas missionaries, spurred by the first society founded in the US — the Maryknoll Fathers (1911) and Sisters (1912) — reached a peak of over 9,300 in 1966.

Orthodox missions. In the Orthodox church organized missionary activity, understood as the extension of the church by the conversion of previously unreached peoples, was confined almost exclusively to Russian initiatives. The "great captivity" of the ancient churches of the Middle East under the Islamic rule of the Ottoman empire made evangelism impossible. In Russia, the tradition of evangelization by "colonist-monks" (Eugène Smirnoff) was stifled by the strict imperial control, from Peter the Great (ruled 1682-1725) to Catherine II (ruled 1762-96). While not comparable to the Protestant and Catholic missions in the 19th century, the Orthodox saw the revivalistic beginnings of new missionary work, primarily through monastic communities.

In 1828 the holy synod in Moscow called for missionaries to reverse the trend of apostasy to Islam among the Eastern Russians.

Macarius Gloukharev (1792-1847), somewhat marked by German pietism, introduced new mission methods in Central Asia on the model of the London Missionary Society. John Veniaminov (1797-1879), after an extraordinary missionary life with fellow monks in the Aleutian Islands and mainland Alaska, later in Yakutsk and Siberia, became metropolitan in Moscow, and in 1870 he founded the Orthodox Missionary Society. The society collected funds for the support of the missionaries and the construction and maintenance of charitable and educational institutions (although it had no administrative functions, as do the Western mission societies). It was first led by Nicolai Kasatkin (1836-1912), who later returned to Japan to leave behind him a vigorous church with indigenous clergy. The 1917 Russian revolution brought the society's and the missionaries' work to a close.

The world federation of Orthodox youth, Syndesmos,* founded in 1953, places foreign mission work high on its agenda. It has provided recruits for the international Orthodox Missionary Centre in Athens, founded by Anastasios Yannoulatos in 1971, with activity directed primarily to Uganda, Tanzania, Kenya and Sudan. In 1982 Yannoulatos (who also served as moderator of the WCC's Commission on World Mission and Evangelism [CWME], 1983-91) became metropolitan for the East Africa diocese.

Ecumenical perspectives. By the 1960s, the large number of Protestant boards and agencies were accustomed to their cherished independence and flexibility, and this was a chief reason for hesitation in the integration of the IMC into the WCC (the latter not a council of *councils* but a council of *churches*). Despite the abundant positive fruits of integration, there was a vacuum left by the disappearance of the IMC, which had provided a wide forum for voluntary missionary associations, including those who proudly claimed the title of conservative evangelical, whether denominational or interdenominational, whether Western or based in the third world — all focused on direct evangelism, "cross-cultural outreach" at home and abroad.

In the last two decades the vacuum has become more noticeable, since the number of such missionaries sent by old and new missionary societies or voluntary agencies has greatly increased, while those sent directly by WCC-member church mission boards has decreased. The vacuum has become partially filled by a variety of structures, such as the Lausanne Committee for World Evangelization,* non-WCC-related third-world boards and societies, ad hoc Christian leadership mission assemblies, etc.

Since the mid-1960s, the RCC has seen a drastic reduction of male and female vocations to religious communities in Western Europe and North America, but in Africa, Asia and Latin America a steady increase of new members in older communities and new indigenous ones. The sea-change in ecumenical understandings in the RCC owing to Vatican Council II* has developed close co-operation and common witness between large segments of Christian missionaries, exemplified on the world level in the co-operation between Rome's SEDOS* and the WCC's CWME. And despite the anti-RCC stance of many within conservative evangelical agencies, from 1977 to 1984 the Vatican Secretariat for Promoting Christian Unity co-sponsored a series of meetings with evangelicals on mission (see **Evangelical-Roman Catholic dialogue on mission**).

See also **evangelical missions, evangelism, mission**.

TOM STRANSKY

"MISSIONARY STRUCTURE OF THE CONGREGATION".

MSC was the most important WCC study in the theology of mission in the years between New Delhi (1961) and Uppsala (1968) — and is the most fundamental WCC study to date on the renewal of the local congregation (see **local church**). In 1961 the WCC assembly at New Delhi instructed the Department on Studies in Evangelism to carry out the study (see sec. on "Witness", paras 28-37, also pp.189-90).

The question to be raised was what changes in the external structure and self-understanding of the local congregation are needed for it to be able to witness credibly to the message of the kingdom of God* in a secular world of rapid social change. From the outset the study embraced both the expectation that only a departure from a church-centred view of mission could lead to the beginning of a new responsibility of the church for the world, and the conviction that the traditional forms of church life and the inherited principle of territorial parish organization of the church are a hindrance to its missionary presence in all spheres of life.

Among the elements of the context of the study were the external integration of the WCC and the International Missionary Council* (1961) and — connected with this — the internal integration of church and mission (see L. Newbigin, "The Missionary Dimension of the Ecumenical Movement", *The Ecumenical Review*, 1961); the efforts at renewal of the theology of missionary evangelism, which were already beginning in the 1950s (Willingen 1952: "The Missionary Obligation of the Church"; central committee, Rhodes 1959: "A Theological Reflection on the Work of Evangelism"; Johannes Blauw, *The Missionary Nature of the Church*, 1962; D.T. Niles, *Upon the Earth*, 1962); the emphasis on the missionary responsibility of the laity (Evanston, secs 2 and 6; Hendrik Kraemer, *A Theology of the Laity*, 1958; A.A. van Ruler, *Theologie des Apostolats*, 1954); and the rediscovery of the significance of the local congregation ("the fully committed fellowship" in "each place") for ecumenical unity and missionary witness: "The place where the development of the common life in Christ is most clearly tested is in the local situation, where believers live and work. There the achievements and the frustrations are most deeply felt: but there too the challenge is most often avoided" (New Delhi 1961, sec. 3, p.122).

Developments and results. MSC, begun under the leadership of Hans Jochen Margull in 1962, provoked an astonishingly wide interest, especially in North Atlantic countries. A Western European task force, a North American task force and a task force in the German Democratic Republic published in 1966-67 independent final reports (in *The Church for Others and the Church for the World*, 1967). Individual groups also participated in the study of the context in Africa, Asia and Latin America.

The most important results of MSC, documented also in the statement of the committee on studies in evangelism to the central committee in Enugu in 1965 ("Structures for Missionary Congregations") and in the collection of working documents (Margull, *Mission* als *Strukturprinzip* [mission as a structural principle], 1965) are the following:

Mission originates in *God*, not the church. The church is not an end in itself but participates in God's missionary action *(missio Dei*)*, which is valid for the whole world and embraces both church and society (see Willingen 1952, Karl Hartenstein, Georg Vicedom). Instead of the "God-church-world" perspective, we must have "God-world-church" (J.C. Hoekendijk). The church does not *have* a mission, it *is* itself mission. The structure and aim of its missions are legitimate only in so far as they serve God's mission.

The aim of mission is not primarily the quantitative growth of the church but shalom for the world. "Realization of the full potentialities of all creation and its ultimate reconciliation and unity in Christ" is the aim of *missio Dei*. As a witness and pointer to shalom and the messianic gifts of justice, truth, fellowship and peace, the church is essentially a "church for others" (Dietrich Bonhoeffer). The purpose of the church's missionary existence is a credible, symbolic and renewing presence in the world, which makes the presence of God among human beings visible.

The context of the missio Dei is not only the individual or the soul but history, the "world in transformation". The process of secularization* can be understood positively as a "fruit of the gospel" and can be distinguished from its elevation to absolute value in secularism (Friedrich Gogarten). Mission therefore is not to be understood as winning back lost church territory or as the restoration of the corpus Christianum; it is not a counter-attack on secularization but participation in the process of liberation and humanization in society in the name of God, who is at work in the world.

The agents of mission are not first and foremost the ministers or missionaries. The "missionaries of our day" are rather the laity* (as members of the *laos*, the people of God).* A missionary church is a church at the base. As a congregation from below it requires training for the laity and for adults and participation on every level.

The structures of mission are not unchangeable but must be so "flexible, differentiated and coherent" that people in all the many spheres of life (family, profession, leisure, politics) can always be addressed afresh.

Clinging to the parish system as a preferred structure of the church can lead to a "morphological fundamentalism". An effective presence in the various spheres of life calls for a variety of small serving groups, functional arrangements and church ministries which are related to "zonal structures" (i.e. a district in a town, a large-scale concern, a regional structure) and are church structures with equal validity.

On the way to a "church for others", fundamental importance attaches to the serious interest in the "otherness" of the others, a precise (sociological, ecclesiastical and political) analysis of the context of the local congregation, involving congregational questionnaires, the creation of independent committees to look into the congregational structures and a radically renewed practice of worship (ecumenical, with dialogue, fellowship and participation).

Effects. The MSC study was an expression of the redirection of missionary focus back to the traditional "missionary churches" in the North Atlantic area, a direct result of the slogan "mission in six continents" (Mexico City 1963). It contributed decisively to keeping the churches in the Western societies from isolating themselves and withdrawing from responsibility for diakonia* in a social context. It gave an important stimulus to the emergence and development of adult education, urban industrial mission, urban training centres, pastoral work for leisure time and other special forms of church ministry. It substantially influenced the discussion on church reform in the Federal Republic of Germany and the German Democratic Republic in the 1960s. Through the medium of Uppsala the idea of the *missio Dei* and historical theology continued to have an effect in the contextual theologies of Asia and Latin America. The study initiated by the Commission on World Mission and Evangelism (CWME) in 1976 on the "Life-style of the Congregation in Mission" takes the concerns of MSC further. Initiative groups formed in the churches in the mid-1970s and 1980s for justice, peace and the integrity of creation* illustrate what the study called for.

MSC may be criticized from today's standpoint in the sense that the stronger presence of the church in the world has frequently been seen one-sidedly as a professionalizing of services and an expansion of the institutional churches. The optimistic view of the 1960s about the Western process of secularization* temporarily made it difficult to see the profound ambivalences in modernism (with its consumer society, isolation and exploitation). The emphasis has been on structures, to the detriment of the meaning of worship and spirituality for the renewal of congregational life. The pressing problems of congregations in the non-Western context (poverty, relegation to minority status, interfaith dialogue) have still to a great extent remained out of account. The lack of Orthodox and Roman Catholic participation has not so far made it possible to link up the dominant tradition which sees the church in terms of history* and eschatology* with that which has a sacramental view of the church.

The MSC, however, is of lasting significance both because of the basic question it asks — what kind of connection is there between evangelism and modes of existence (mission and structure) for a local missionary congregation which seeks to be "the salt of the earth"? — and because of the fundamental conviction that even the external structure of a church is a factor in evangelism and must serve the *missio Dei*. The missionary renewal of the church begins where people locally do something about the "the world's agenda" in the light of the *missio Dei* and try to be a sign of the kingdom of God* in fellowship, service and worship. If the stimuli for renewal from the ecumenical movement are to register fully down to the level of the local congregation, the unanswered question as to the missionary structure of the congregation must also enjoy high priority in the work of the WCC in the future. The theme of the MSC has been taken up again in, among other things, the joint study project of the Conference of European Churches* and the CWME on "Missionary Congregations in a Secularized Europe", adopted in Stirling in 1986 and supported also in San Antonio in 1989. The task for the future here lies in the deliverance of Christian congregations from their imprisonment within the Western cultural phenomena of consumerism, individualism and apathy, for a prophetic non-conformity in their social context.

DIETRICH WERNER

The Church for Others and the Church for the World: A Quest for Structures for Missionary Con-

gregations, WCC, 1967 ● *Concept*, vols 1-9, WCC, 1962-65 ● W.J. Hollenweger, international bibliography on the "Church for Others", *A Monthly Letter about Evangelism*, no. 7-8, 1971 ● G.W. Webber, *The Congregation in Mission: Emerging Structures for the Church in an Urban Society*, New York, Abingdon, 1964 ● T. Wieser ed., *Planning for Mission: Working Papers on the New Quest for Missionary Congregations*, London, Epworth, 1966 ● C. Williams, *Where in the World?*, New York, NCCCUSA, 1963.

MOELLER, CHARLES.

B. 18.1.1912, Brussels, Belgium; d. 3.4.1986, Brussels. An outstanding intellectual, with deep commitment to ecumenism, Moeller was the first secretary of the Vatican Secretariat for Promoting Christian Unity,* 1973-83. He was ordained to the priesthood in 1937. He studied philosophy and theology at Malines and Louvain and became professor of poetry at the Institut Saint-Pierre in Jette, 1941-54, and then in 1956 professor at the University of Louvain. He was an expert on the theological commission of Vatican II, 1962-65, undersecretary of the Congregation on the Doctrine of the Faith, 1966-73, and rector of the Ecumenical Institute at Jerusalem, 1969-73. A member of the Royal Academy for French Language and Literature in Belgium, he wrote numerous articles in *Irénikon, Revue d'histoire ecclésiastique, Revue nouvelle*, etc. and contributed to *Lexikon für Theologie und Kirche* and to the series *Unam Sanctam*. He wrote *Théologie de la grâce et œcuménisme* (ET *The Theology of Grace and the Ecumenical Movement*, Paterson, NJ, St Anthony Guild, 1969).

ANS J. VAN DER BENT

MORAL REARMAMENT (MRA).

A 20th-century non-denominational renewal movement founded by Frank Buchman (1878-1961). Buchman resigned from the staff of Hartford Seminary (US) in 1922 to undertake a worldwide evangelistic campaign based on divine guidance and moral absolutes. Earlier known as the "Oxford Group" (from its influence at Oxford university), the movement took on the name Moral Rearmament in 1938. With headquarters located in New York, Michigan, Switzerland and Japan, its conferences attracted thousands of people in the

US, England, the Netherlands and South Africa. Strongly anti-communist, MRA was criticized in some quarters for being insufficiently opposed to Hitler and Nazism. Largely Protestant in its origins, MRA later sought to reach out to persons of other than Christian faith. W.A. Visser 't Hooft recounts in his *Memoirs* a visit to a pagoda in Burma which was set apart for the MRA movement, for, as a Buddhist priest told him, "there is no difference between the principles of Moral Rearmament and those of Buddhism". After the death of Buchman and his successor Peter Howard in the 1960s, the movement declined.

MARLIN VANELDEREN

MORATORIUM. "Moratorium" was the name given in the ecumenical movement to a proposal in the early 1970s for a cessation of sending and receiving money and missionary personnel for a period to allow time for the review of the best use of persons and money in response to God's mission and the churches' search for selfhood (see *missio Dei*, **mission**).

John Gatu, then general secretary of the Presbyterian Church of East Africa, first issued the call for a moratorium in 1971. He argued that "the time has come for the withdrawal of foreign missionaries from many parts of the third world, that the churches of the third world must be allowed to find their own identity, and that the continuation of the present missionary movement is a hindrance to this selfhood of the church". Gatu proposed that the problems of third-world churches "can only be solved if all missionaries are withdrawn in order to allow a period of not less than five years for each side to rethink and formulate what is going to be their future relationship". Also in 1971 Emerito Nacpil of the Evangelical Methodist Church in the Philippines said: "The present structure of modern missions is dead. We ought to eulogize it and then bury it... The most *missionary* service a missionary under the present system can do today in Asia is to go home."

In 1972 the WCC committee on Ecumenical Sharing of Personnel (ESP) claimed in a working paper that behind the moratorium call lies "the conviction that in their attempt to respond to God's mission, both sending and receiving churches find themselves caught in a pattern which inhibits rather than serves

mission". Later, in 1974 and 1975, ESP recommended principles and procedures for mutual responsibility and relations in sharing personnel and resources, while commending moratorium "for serious consideration when and where it is appropriate", as "self-discipline, not rejection... for the selfhood and discipline of the churches".

The 1973 CWME conference (Bangkok) recognized that "'partnership in mission' remains an empty slogan" and called for "a mature relationship between churches". It described moratorium as one of the "more radical solutions" that would "enable the receiving church to find its identity, set its own priorities and discover within its own fellowship the resources to carry out its authentic mission. It would also enable the sending church to re-discover its identity in the context of the contemporary situation." While not endorsing moratorium, Bangkok received the report of section 3 that said: "In some situations the moratorium proposal, painful though it may be for both sides, may be the best means of resolving a present dilemma and advancing the mission of Christ."

In 1974 the third assembly of the All Africa Conference of Churches (AACC) called for "a moratorium on the receiving of money and personnel... coming from [the churches'] foreign relationships" as being "the most viable means of giving the African church the power to perform its mission in the African context, as well as lead our governments and peoples in finding solutions to economic and social dependency". This assembly also rejected WCC-ESP proposals for ecumenical sharing of personnel and resources as inadequate.

Numerous African churches, however, soon disassociated themselves from the AACC resolution. Discussion of moratorium reached a high point at the WCC fifth assembly (Nairobi 1975). While allowing that "there may be situations of dependence between churches where, for the sake of the integrity of a church's witness in its own culture, there should be a temporary moratorium on existing dependencies in order to prepare for a more mature independence", the report of section 2 recommended steps "towards a greater degree of joint action and witness".

The outcome of the moratorium debate was greater recognition that the sending and receiving of personnel and funds are joint responsibilities, and that traditional relationships, structures and attitudes which perpetuate dependency had to change for the sake of mission and the selfhood of the churches.

GERALD H. ANDERSON

All Africa Conference of Churches, *The Struggle Continues: Official Report, Third Assembly, Lusaka, Zambia, May 1974*, Nairobi, 1975 • G.H. Anderson, "A Moratorium on Missionaries?", in *Mission Trends*, 1, 1974 • *In Search of Mission: The Future of the Missionary Enterprise*, IDOC Dossier 9, 1974 • *International Review of Mission*, "Moratorium Issue", 254, 1975.

MORAVIANS. The heritage of the Moravian Church is in the so-called first Reformation of the 15th century and in 18th-century German pietism. Its origin can be traced to the Unity of the Brethren (*Unitas Fratrum*), one of the several groups of followers of the Czech reformer Jan Hus (burned as a heretic in 1415). In 1467 they established their own ministry; a visiting Waldensian clergyman ordained the first priests. Although many of the Brethren were assimilated into Lutheran and Reformed churches in Germany, Switzerland, Bohemia and Poland in the course of the 16th and 17th centuries, clandestine groups remained in Bohemia and Moravia. In 1722 some of them, who were in contact with a German pietist convert from Catholicism, were introduced to the Saxon nobleman Count Nicholas von Zinzendorf. During the following years a large number of Brethren immigrated to his domain, forming the Herrnhut settlement. The count took an increasing interest in the group, and in 1727 he drafted a legal contract setting forth their relationship to him and binding them to "walk according to the apostolic rule". This formal revival of the Unity was as an *ecclesiola in ecclesia* within the established Lutheran Church of Saxony. In 1745 the Moravian church re-instituted the ministry of presbyter and deacon alongside its ancient episcopacy.*

Zeal for evangelism* characterized the revived Brethren, and the church spread not only in Europe but also to Greenland, Africa, the Middle East, India, the Caribbean and North and South America. The church today has about 500,000 members in 18 autonomous provinces around the world. Four provinces in Tanzania account for nearly half of the denomination's members. Some of the

provinces, especially in Central America (Nicaragua) and Southern Africa, have lived in the context of ethnic and civil conflict, which has helped to break down the resistance to social and political engagement from the church's pietistic tradition.

Deliberately avoiding the development of its own unique system of doctrine, the church understands itself as a fellowship within the universal church of Christ and accepts the historic creeds and various Reformation confessions as "the thankful acclaim of the Body of Christ", helpful for Christians in formulating their thought, but not binding on believers. Moravians thus have a firm ecumenical commitment, rooted in Zinzendorf's doctrine of the "ways" (*Tropen*) in which God teaches — which places the various Christian confessions on an equal footing in relation to each other. Scripture* is understood as the sole source and guide for faith, teaching and life. Nine of the 18 provinces are members of the WCC; and in 1988 the Moravian Unity Synod (which meets every seven years) urged those provinces which are not members to consider joining, while encouraging all the provinces to promote WCC programmes.

MARLIN VANELDEREN

A.J. Lewis, *Zinzendorf the Ecumenical Pioneer*, London, SCM, 1962.

MOTT, JOHN R. B. 25.5.1865, Purvis, NY, USA; d. 31.1.1955, Evanston, IL. If any one individual could be said to personify the modern ecumenical movement, it would be John R. Mott. In him converged uniquely the varied strands of which the ecumenical movement is woven.

A plausible legend has it that when the young John Mott played with toy trains in the nursery, it was not just with single engines and tracks, but he laid out the toy lines to form a continental railroad system. As a student at Cornell University, Mott passed from agnosticism to faith* and went through the experience of evangelical conversion* after hearing an address by C.T. Studd, one of the famous "Cambridge Seven" — English undergraduate sportsmen who dedicated their lives to foreign missionary service. Shortly after, Mott signed the Student Volunteer Declaration, though his first job was as a travelling secretary of the student YMCA.* In 1895 he participated in

John R. Mott (WCC photo)

the gathering at Vadstena, Sweden, out of which the World's Student Christian Federation* (WSCF) was born.

Students were the lever by which Mott sought to move the world towards God; and the WSCF was perhaps the area in which his most effective work for Christ's kingdom was done. He served it, as general secretary from 1895 and as chairman from 1920, for 33 years, and all his other achievements have their roots in the concerns which the WSCF fostered.

Mott's own missionary vocation found expression in the work leading up to the world missionary conference of 1910, of which he was the chairman. Edinburgh created a follow-up committee (which later became the International Missionary Council*) and Mott was closely associated with the IMC for the rest of his life.

In the cause of world evangelization, Mott was as tireless and as urgent as the apostle Paul — and as careful to follow up initial visits by continuing contact. He travelled repeatedly to Asia and Africa long before air travel made such journeying commonplace. Indeed, there were great advantages in the slower modes of ship and train, for Mott was highly disciplined in the use he made of travelling time. He prepared himself with detailed briefings about the area he was to visit

and wrote voluminous notes on what he had seen and done before he plunged into the next encounter. He often travelled with a heavy trunk with iron bands, stuffed with history books, government reports, biographies and much else relating to his destination, and armed with introductions, carefully sought well in advance, to key people in church and state and other walks of life who could be harnessed, willingly or unwillingly, to the cause of Christ in their own land.

Mott was an exemplar of his own dictum about arranging a visit or a conference: "Plan as if there were no such thing as prayer. Pray as if there were no such thing as planning." Speaking easily no language but his own, he rehearsed with his interpreter (always chosen on careful advice) every important utterance until he was satisfied that every turn of phrase, every illustration, was fully grasped so that it could be accurately translated, while local guidance was sought to make sure there were no gaffes in sensitive political or theological areas. All this, of course, made great demands and grew beyond even his unaided resources.

Mott was not at first particularly a champion of Christian unity,* but his passion for evangelism* made him one. Like Charles Brent, he realized that Edinburgh 1910 implied more than co-operation. His most far-reaching decision arose from his encounter in the WSCF with the Eastern Orthodox churches. There he met Christian student movements which were solidly confessional in character, differing greatly from the often pietistic assumptions of many Western Protestant students. When, at a WSCF meeting at Nyborg in 1925, it was decided that confessional student movements could be corporate members of the federation, the vital distinction between *interdenominational* and *denominational* became part of ecumenism. Mott was fully at home, and played a large part, in the first two world conferences on Faith and Order (Lausanne 1927, Edinburgh 1937).

Equally inevitably, when his friend Nathan Söderblom, archbishop of Uppsala, took the lead in arranging the first world conference on Life and Work* (Stockholm 1925), Mott was among those who saw the value of international Christian witness in issues of peace and social justice. It was not surprising that he should have been awarded the Nobel peace prize in 1946, in recognition of his many contributions to the concord of nations.

At the 1937 Oxford conference of Life and Work (as at the Faith and Order conference in Edinburgh a few weeks later) he was among those who spoke forcefully in favour of the proposal to establish a world council of churches. He was, inevitably, a member of the committee charged with planning the structure of the emergent WCC.

Some ten years later, when the WCC held its inaugural assembly at Amsterdam, Mott, then in his 83rd year, preached at the opening service. "We have entered", he said, "the most exacting period in the history of the church. It will take all the statesmanship, all the churchmanship, all the self-forgetfulness of all of us. But to those who believe in the adequacy of Christ no doors are closed and boundless opportunities are open." At its close the assembly elected him to the unique office of honorary president — a token, at least, of the debt owed to him by the whole ecumenical movement.

OLIVER TOMKINS

Among Mott's books are *Addresses and Papers*, 6 vols, New York, Association Press, 1946-47; *The Decisive Hour of Christian Missions*, New York, Association Press, 1912; *Evangelism for the World Today*, New York, Harper, 1938 • See also C.H. Hopkins, *John R. Mott, 1865-1955: A Biography*, WCC, 1979 • B. Matthews, *John R. Mott: World Citizen*, London, Harper, 1934.

MUSLIM-CHRISTIAN DIALOGUE.

Ever since the dawn of Islam there have been relations between Muslims and Christians with roots springing from the deep soil of Abrahamic tradition. A group of early Muslim refugees found asylum in Christian Ethiopia, while numerous Qur'anic texts provided the bases for a range of attitudes which Muslims could assume with regard to their Christian neighbours. Some verses referred to non-Muslims generally, but others pointed specifically to the followers of Jesus. Among the latter there are both warnings and commendations, leaving successive generations the duty of deciding their own policies and actions according to changing circumstances. Conversely, Christians saw Islam in a similar kaleidoscope of impressions, from regarding it as a heresy* requiring suppression to seeing

it as an estimable rival challenging them to compete with Muslims in good works, so that each faith might be judged by its fruit.

With rare exceptions, the first millennium of Muslim-Christian contact was a dreary series of military campaigns (some of which featured egregious acts of barbarity utterly inconsistent with submission to a merciful God or service to a loving Saviour) and an obstinate theological impasse exacerbated by the sublime triumphalism of both parties. Only in the last few decades has there been any real movement within either community towards constructive exchange on doctrinal questions as well as productive collaboration on common interests of a more practical character.

After a preliminary period of intramural reflection, the WCC, principally through its Sub-unit on Dialogue with People of Living Faiths, sponsored a dozen bilateral meetings between Muslims and Christians on a variety of themes, notably mission and *da'wah* (the Islamic word for mission) (Chambésy, Switzerland, 1976), youth and faith (Bossey, Switzerland, 1980) and diaconic co-operation (Colombo, Sri Lanka, 1982). More recently, the sub-unit has sponsored several regional colloquia on local themes to lay the groundwork for a document about ecumenical perspectives on Muslim-Christian dialogue: Porto Novo, Benin (1986), Kuta, Bali (1986), Kolymbari, Crete (1987), New Windsor, Maryland (1988) and Arusha, Tanzania (1989). Each meeting issued a report; the early discussions were also printed in the anthology *Christians Meeting Muslims*, and a new compendium covering all the WCC-sponsored Christian-Muslim encounters was published in 1989: *Meeting in Faith*.

Roman Catholic institutions, particularly the Secretariat for Non-Christians (now called the Pontifical Council for Interfaith Dialogue), also developed dialogue programmes in the years following the Second Vatican Council.* Apart from one large meeting of Christians and Muslims in Tripoli, Libya, in 1976, however, the Vatican has invested most of its efforts in establishing the principle of dialogue among its own faithful through workshops with local bishops' conferences, academic teaching and research and, especially, topical addresses by Pope John Paul II; the most famous of these was his talk to several thousand young people at Casablanca in 1981. A consultation involving Muslims and Christians from around the Mediterranean at Assisi in October 1988 may indicate a new departure in Vatican activity. Religious orders like the Franciscans and the Missionaries of Africa have fostered sustained intercommunal contacts in several parts of the world, as have a great many regional, national and local ecumenical organizations and several individual churches or confessional federations. A unique phenomenon of prophetic dimensions is the Muslim-Christian research group, which has been working since 1977 with branches in half a dozen centres to develop serious theological reflection in a carefully balanced context.

Dialogic initiatives have not been exclusively of Christian inspiration. In several instances, Muslim organizations have been the hosts of international dialogues, such as those held in Amman under the auspices of the Royal Academy for Islamic Affairs or the ones arranged by the Centre for Economic and Social Research at the University of Tunis. Representatives of the Muslim World Congress, the World Muslim League and the World Islamic Call Society have been meeting regularly with representatives from the Vatican and the WCC for several years to exchange information, encouragement and advice.

In the early stages, most discussions elaborated the theme of dialogue itself, with a few pioneer spirits re-assuring one another that constructive interaction was the worthiest witness to each faith tradition and the surest means to the pluralistic harmony essential to enduring peace. The principal objective of any gathering was the very fact of meeting, although the ancillary benefits of a better awareness and understanding of everyone's beliefs, concerns and hopes made each conversation a new advance in the tentative search for trust. More substantive topics, like mission and *da'wah* (Chambésy 1976) or ethics and development (Beirut 1977) emerged as confidence matured. Also, the circle of enthusiasts gradually widened to embrace a fuller range of theological and social perspectives, affirming the importance of sound relations to both communities and bringing fresh spiritual insights to Muslims and Christians alike. The themes which have recurred in the recent regional colloquia (e.g.

religion and politics, religion and family) have led participants to a stronger commitment to common values and an enhanced respect for each other's particularities. Wider engagement has also spawned a proliferation of continuing associations in national and local settings, addressing specific questions of more direct focus; each of these contributes to the general impetus towards tolerance and exchange.

This tendency for more openness and the increasing numbers of participants in dialogue are not universally accepted among Christians and Muslims. In places, communal suspicions are so ingrained that tension and even armed conflict persist, in spite of the efforts of a valiant few. Many people still hold to narrow missiologies which view interfaith conversations simply as a means of changing the allegiance of their interlocutors, while others have adopted a spiritual isolationism of toleration without communication. Nevertheless, where dialogue was once a daring risk, it is now the preferred form of inter-religious discourse, and Muslims and Christians in every corner of the world are daily building mutual confidence even as they engage in more vital and varied agendas (e.g. ecology, theology and justice, trilateral talks with Jews). Whether we cite examples like the churches' support of the Project for Christian-Muslim Relations in Africa (Nairobi) or the concerns expressed by the Institute of Muslim Minority Affairs (Jidda) on behalf of non-Muslim populations in Islamic countries, today's trend is unquestionably towards wider involvement and deeper commitment.

STUART E. BROWN

M. Borrmans, *Orientations pour un dialogue entre chrétiens et musulmans*, Paris, Cerf, 1981 • *Christian Mission and Islamic Da'wah*, Leicester, Islamic Foundation, 1982 • *The Churches and Islam in Europe*, Geneva, CEC, 1982 • S.J. Samartha & J.B. Taylor eds, *Christian-Muslim Dialogue*, WCC, 1973 • Secretariatus Pro Non-Christianis, *Orientations pour un dialogue entre chrétiens et musulmans* (ET *Guidelines for a Dialogue between Muslims and Christians*, Rome, Ancora, 1969) • J.B. Taylor ed., *Christians Meeting Muslims*, WCC, 1977.

MYSTICISM. The term "mysticism" is linked through its Greek root with the idea of the perception of what is kept secret and protected by silence, the invisible reality. For Paul "mystery" signifies the hidden wisdom of God, the depths of God, the things that no eye has seen and no ear has heard, things beyond the human mind, which can be known only by the Spirit of God (see 1 Cor. 2:6-16). For him the incarnation* of the Word of God was "the mystery hidden for ages and generations but now made manifest" (Col. 1:26).

In a real sense mysticism defies definition, partly because it refers to a very personal experience of God as the transcendent reality, which cannot be formulated in descriptive language or credal formulations. There are many mystical schools, most of them of monastic origin, with a variety of emphases. Mysticism is best described overall as the theory and practice of contemplative life. It is a second kind of faith — contemplation — which deepens the first faith. It has three stages: purification, illumination and perfection, which complement each other.

In the East, mysticism was introduced by Origen of Alexandria (c.185-c.254) in terms of the "mystical" interpretation of the biblical message, which goes far beyond the written text, words and symbols to the unveiled face of the Word of God as person. The most influential mystical writer was Dionysius the Areopagite (c.500), who wrote *The Mystical Theology*. His writings were translated by John Scotus Erigena and circulated in the West in the middle ages. He stresses the epistemological dimension of mysticism, speaking about the "apophatic theology", the negative method of knowledge of the nameless God. For Symeon the New Theologian (949-1022), the only way to praise the ineffable grace of God is through *The Hymns of Divine Love*. Hesychasm is a spiritual stream that originated in Mount Athos (13th-14th centuries) and concentrates on the continual invocation of the name of Christ (an echo of which we find in *The Way of a Pilgrim*, the story of a Russian pilgrim from the mid-19th century who practises the "Jesus Prayer").

In the West, the influence of Dionysius the Areopagite's theory about "divine darkness" is seen in *The Cloud of Unknowing*, a mystical treatise of the 14th century. Meister Eckhart (c.1260-1327), the German mystical writer, developed the idea of the mystical direct vision of God, in a union like light to light. Another German mystical writer, Jacob

Boehme (1575-1624), is the author of *The Way to Christ*. Julian of Norwich (c.1342-1413) and William Law (1686-1761) are among the best-known English mystical writers.

Western spirituality has been enriched by mystics such as St Thomas ("new state of grace"), Ignatius of Loyola *(Spiritual Exercises)*, Francis of Assisi, Theresa of Avila and John of the Cross, Francis Xavier and Catherine of Siena. Cistercian and Cluniac reforms and the Franciscan movement, to take only two examples, owe a great deal to the impact of mysticism.

Two inter-related streams in the mystical tradition may be identified. The first emphasizes *spirituality* as a quality of life and aims at attaining purity of heart through a spiritual pilgrimage towards the fullness of Christ (Eph. 4:13), waging a permanent "unseen war" against all destructive passions through a radical ascetic discipline. (John Climacus, who wrote *The Ladder of Divine Ascent*, exemplifies this emphasis.) The second stream stresses the attainment of divine knowledge, or *gnosis* (Evagrius of Pontus, 346-99). Here the goal is the illumination of the mind, expressed in an existential "negative" language which is beyond names and symbols. The gnosis experience takes the heart to a reality beyond faith, to God himself, to the depth of divine love changing the life of those who receive it: "We all, with unveiled face, beholding [or reflecting] the glory of the Lord" (2 Cor. 3:18).

There are more similarities than differences among the various Christian mystical traditions. When it refers to the nature of the light we see and receive in mystical union, the Eastern Orthodox tradition speaks of the divine uncreated energies of God (e.g. Gregory Palamas of Salonika, 1296-1359), while the West uses the term "created grace". Deification, the transfiguration of persons *(theosis)*, is thus given a different content and intensity. But the goal is the same — to reach out to the ultimate likeness of God: We "are being changed into his likeness" (2 Cor. 3:18). "All human beings are made in God's image; but to be in His likeness is granted only to those who through great love have brought their own freedom into subjection of God" (Diadochos of Photiki, 404-86, *On Spiritual Knowledge*).

Mysticism can have a great significance for the spirituality of our times, especially for personal spiritual growth and renewal movements. It can aid the process of contemplation, even of ordinary contemplation of the created world around us. It can develop the human possibilities in our religious relationships with God (i.e. the anthropological and psychological dimensions of the image of God) and can rid us of illusions and speculations that so often cluster around human natural perfections.

Mysticism is by no means confined to Christianity, and in recent years Christians have been discovering the riches of the spiritualities of other faiths, often steeped in mysticism. A WCC meeting on "Spirituality in Interfaith Dialogue" (Kyoto 1987) explored some aspects of such spirituality and their significance for interfaith relations.

See also **spirituality in the ecumenical movement**.

ION BRIA

P. Agaesse & M. Sales, "La vie mystique chrétienne", in *Dictionnaire de spiritualité*, vol. 10, Paris, Beauchesne, 1980 ● T. Aria & W. Ariarajah eds, *Spirituality in Interfaith Dialogue*, WCC, 1989 ● L. Bouyer, J. Leclercq, F. Vandenbroucke & L. Cognet, *Histoire de la Spiritualité chrétienne*, 4 vols (ET *A History of Christian Spirituality*, 4 vols, New York, Seabury, 1982) ● L. Dupré, "Mysticism", in *The Encyclopedia of Religion*, Mircea Eliade ed., vol. 10, New York, Macmillan, 1987 ● M. Fox ed., *Western Spirituality: Historical Roots, Ecumenical Routes*, Notre Dame, IN, Fides-Claretian, 1979 ● Paulos Mar Gregorios, *Cosmic Man: The Divine Presence*, New York, Paragon House, 1988 ● V. Lossky, *The Mystical Theology of the Eastern Church*, New York, St Vladimir's Seminary, 1957 ● J. Ryan ed., *Christian Spiritual Theology: An Ecumenical Reflection*, Melbourne, Dove Communications, 1986.

N

NATION. The sovereign nation as a structure of the communal life of peoples is now a universal phenomenon. It emerged in modern history under the inspiration and dynamics of the idea of nationalism and is organized politically as the nation state. Today most peoples of the world are organized in nations, with the United Nations an international body composed of representatives of nation states.

Many scholars believe that "the rise of Protestantism coincided with the rise of modern nations" in Europe (Bennett, 93). It would be generally agreed that the Protestant Reformation and modern nationalism together caused the break-up of European Christendom based on the Constantinian idea of tying together universal church and universal empire. As a result the sovereign nation state came into being; and though the churches maintained confessional relations across national lines, they were organized nationally and, formally or informally, became subject to national governments. Inevitably these European national churches were also involved in the expansion of national power in Asia and Africa, and eventually in the conflicts between European nations competing for imperial territories.

The imperialistic rivalry between the major Christian nations of Europe led to the first world war, with the result that the churches began to see that nations had become a law unto themselves and that the supranational character of the church had been lost. The

peace appeals addressed to the churches during and after the war by Swedish Archbishop Söderblom, the 1920 Lambeth (Anglican) appeal to Christian people and the actions of the World Alliance for Promoting International Friendship through the Churches* all presupposed a close relation between international peace* and the unity* of the churches; this growing ecumenical movement posed the challenge of peace to modern sovereign nations. As Wilfred Monod stated it, a spiritual league of churches must become the soul of a moral league of peoples and a political league of nations (R. Rouse & S. Neill, *A History of the Ecumenical Movement*, I, 579).

By the 1930s there emerged in Germany under Hitler a type of nationalism which repudiated all spiritual connections with ecumenical Christianity or Christian values. The Oxford conference on "Church, Community and State" met in 1937 in the context of the struggle of the German Confessing Church* with Nazi paganism, a movement which deified the German *Volk* (nation) as rooted in blood and soil and the will-to-power over other peoples. The 1937 Oxford report on the universal church and the world of nations called upon the churches to maintain their supranational character and provided an ecumenical answer to totalitarian nationalism and its institutionalized idolatry.

During the second world war, the WCC in process of formation worked constantly on post-war peace aims and supported plans to establish the UN. In 1946 the Commission of the Churches on International Affairs was formed to aid the churches in assuming their responsibilities in working for peace and justice between nations.

It was in the International Missionary Council* (IMC) and later in the WCC study of "The Common Christian Responsibility towards Areas of Rapid Social Change" that the ecumenical movement dealt with the growth of nationalism in Asia, Africa, Latin America and the Middle East. In these lands the nationalist movement had its roots in the revolt of the peoples against Western colonial domination and in their awakening to freedom, equality and other values to which Christian missions themselves had made a substantial contribution through their educational and religious work and their critique of traditional societies. The Council was positively inclined to the demand of the younger churches for greater autonomy from mission control, for assuming primary responsibility for the evangelization of their nations, and for building indigenous national churches transcending Western denominationalism in order to make a united witness to awakening nations. This had been the plea of Bishop V.S. Azariah of India at the Tambaram meeting of the IMC in 1938, emphasizing that the churches of Asia and Africa were already organized in national Christian councils within the framework of the IMC. Generally speaking, it may be said that after Tambaram the idea of a united indigenous church for the nation-in-the-making was practically regarded as a theological principle in IMC circles.

In the period after the second world war the WCC's study of rapid social change made an attempt to understand and interpret theologically the politics of nationalism and of nation-building as these emerged in the third world. This became one of the principal points of discussion in the Salonika conference of 1958, which emphasized the danger involved in interpreting nationalism only on the basis of the Western experience. The meeting accepted the need to evaluate positively third-world nationalism, especially in the stage when it expressed the awakening of people to the dignity of their selfhood. Consequently the report of Salonika called on the ecumenical movement to recognize the moral and spiritual justification of nation-building movements, which are means for the emancipation of dependent peoples: "Such emancipation is to be welcomed and encouraged by the Christian church. The concept of the 'responsible society'* implies that people are called to accept responsibility to God and their fellow-men and women for the choices and decisions on which the life of their societies is based; and responsible participation in social and political life can only be achieved where each national group or unit can express itself in freedom. Therefore these nationalisms should not be equated with that aggressive nationalism which seeks to dominate other peoples or an isolationist nationalism which denies responsibility for other peoples. Nevertheless it is necessary to stress the fact that even a legitimate movement of nationalism expressing the urge for political freedom or for nation-making has in it the seeds of perversion" (*Dilemmas*, 57).

In the chapter entitled "The Church and the Conflict of Nationalism and Colonialism", in his book summarizing the rapid social change study, Paul Abrecht gives an overview of the theological debate on this issue. It is evident that many European Christians were not happy with the resurgence of nationalism in third-world countries. Though some, like the

SWAPO supporters in Namibia (epd-bild/Neetz)

German theologian Heinz-Dietrich Wendland, wrote favourably about the "constructive nationalism" of the third world, the general trend was what Abrecht calls "Christian anti-nationalism". Europeans considered it their duty to warn non-Europeans of the dangers of unreasonable outbursts of "exaggerated nationalism". They regretted that the newly formed governments in Asia and Africa "seemed to repeat the mistakes which Europe made in the past" (Abrecht, 97-98).

This warning was in fact absorbed into the Salonika report when it recognized the seeds of corruption in the emerging nationalism in Asia and Africa. What Salonika did in effect was to emphasize not a timeless but a timely interpretation of one phase of the historical phenomenon. But Salonika was also convinced that no self-awakened people in today's world of nations could bypass the stage of nationalism and internationalism, with all their ambiguities, as they struggled towards other and higher expressions of community and selfhood.

Indeed in its assemblies in Bangkok (1968) and Singapore (1973), the East Asia Christian Conference (now called the Christian Conference of Asia — CCA) noted that "nationalism as an ethos" had become inadequate to bring social justice to the peoples of Asia. The Bangkok assembly said that nationalism had become confined to the elite sections of society, an ideology which justified their search for power and affluence. A positive nationalism should motivate the people to make sacrifices as they commit themselves to the development of their country. "But this nationalism can live only from the sense of equality and oneness created by an equal sharing of power by the people" (Thomas, 199-200). Furthermore, nationalism with its emphasis on national security, unity and stability was in many countries giving rise to "an ethos for preserving the existing structures, against change and to justify the suppression of democratic rights and mass action for change" (204). In its later thinking on social action for justice, the CCA emphasized the ethos of the "people"* rather than that of the "nation". In the 1970s in many third-world countries the emphasis shifted from national development to people's liberation, as the ideological dynamic among Christian people concerned with justice.

The UN and WCC studies on transnational corporations* emphasize the universal phenomenon that such organizations, with their centres in the rich nations, are able to recruit the national elite of the poor countries in their community of interests; the national elites are prepared to use their national government and national ideology itself to suppress their peoples' struggles for justice. As the report of the MIT conference on "Faith, Science and the Future" puts it, the UN document on "Multinational Companies and World Development" (1973) implies that today it is the transnational corporations that are the "major agents of imperialism against the nations in the so-called developing world".

Thus the question: what is the combination of alternative technology, social organization and participatory democracy which can bring about a transnational community of people's interests to serve as a counterweight to the transnational community of exploitation? And as the world struggles, in one way or another, to move beyond nationalism, how does the church as a supranational worldwide reality relate itself to this move at national and world levels?

See also **international order, national security**.

M.M. THOMAS

P. Abrecht, *Churches and Rapid Social Change*, London, SCM, 1961 • P. Abrecht & R.L. Shinn eds, *Faith and Science in an Unjust World*, vol. 2: *Reports and Recommendations*, WCC, 1980 • J. Bennett, *Christians and the State*, New York, Scribner, 1958 • *Dilemmas and Opportunities for Christian Action in Rapid Social Change*, WCC, 1959 • M.M. Thomas, *Towards a Theology of Contemporary Ecumenism*, WCC, 1978 • *Towards the Sovereignty of the People. A Search for an Alternative Form of Democratic Polities in Asia: Christian Discussion*, Singapore, CTCCCA, 1983.

NATIONAL SECURITY. The Hobbesian view that society* appears as a means of self-protection in the "war of all against all" is elevated by the doctrine of national security to a universal and all-embracing ideology* and a principle for the state and political life. For Hobbes, such conflict is the natural condition of humanity; the state is a contract through which human beings resign their authority to a sovereign for the sake of being protected from others.

The immediate origin of national security as a doctrine was the organization of national security by the USA after the second world war (e.g. the US's National Security Act, National Security Council, CIA and National War College created in 1947-48). But the ideas go back to romantic ideas of pan-Germanism of people such as Kjellen, who held that "the state can survive only if it practises power politics" because "all civilized life finally leans on power". Nazism made this ideology its own, and at the end of the second world war, several Latin American generals, inspired by it, developed a geopolitical theory built on those assumptions (Golbery in Brazil, Villegas in Argentina, Pinochet in Chile). The amalgam of the "security" idea of the cold war* and the geopolitical dream inspired in many third-world countries the creation of national security totalitarian states.

The doctrine can be summarized in three words — power, state, security — and three strategies — constant growth (expansion), permanent war (internal or external) and total control (totalitarianism). Power is "the ability of the state to make its own will reality"; strategy is the organization of domestic affairs and foreign relations so that power may operate most efficiently in achieving the interests of the state. Total war is a permanent condition on all levels: military, ideological, economic, political. A strong committed elite must hold total power and be able to command all resources. The total war, for example, is against international communism; the enemy is both external and internal (involving infiltration, ideological indoctrination, terrorism and revolution); the military are the only elite capable of facing this challenge. National security, however, becomes an international issue, and the national security states are integrated into the "security system of the West" led by the USA and into the world capitalist economy in its new "world market integration".

In some countries (particularly in the Americas) this doctrine has received also a religious formulation as a war against materialistic atheism* and for the sake of Christianity (witness the New Right in the USA). In Latin America it has sometimes revived the old ultramontane ideology of people like Joseph de Maistre, who said that "war is the normal state of humankind" and that the concentration of authority* was a necessary means for waging such war, since "when the human soul has lost its vigour due to laziness, unbelief... vices... it can only be tempered again by blood". Such bizarre and almost ridiculous ideas have, nevertheless, been used to justify arbitrary repression, human rights violations and genocide in many countries in the third world.

The doctrine of national security has been denounced and condemned by church authorities in Europe, the USA and the third world. The arguments can be summarized in the statement by the Puebla Latin American Third Episcopal Conference (Catholic): "It places the individual at the unlimited service of the total war against the cultural, social, political and economic conflicts and, with them, against the threat of communism. Facing this real or possible permanent danger, all individual freedoms are, as in all emergency situations, limited, and the will of the state is substituted for the will of the people. Economic development and war potential take precedence over the needs of the abandoned masses... It even tries to justify itself... as a doctrine defending Western Christian civilization." The WCC has addressed the problems and issues raised by this doctrine in the studies on militarism/militarization,* human rights,* political ethics and the conditions for genuine global security. "The only security worthy of the name", said the general secretary in 1979, "lies in enabling people to participate fully in the life of their nation and to establish relations of trust between peoples of different nations."

See also **nation**.

JOSÉ MÍGUEZ BONINO

J. Comblin, *The Church and the National Security State*, Maryknoll, NY, Orbis, 1979 • J.-A. Viera Gallo ed., *The Security Trap*, Rome, IDOC, 1979.

NATURAL LAW. In an early study entitled "The Social Thought of the World Council of Churches", Edward Duff pointed to two theological traditions: one he called *catholic* (mainly represented in the WCC by Anglicans), characterized as "an ethic of ends" and based on an optimistic anthropology (all human beings have the ability to distinguish good from evil by means of reason); the other he termed *protestant*, an ethic of "inspiration", supported by a pessimistic anthropology (sin has darkened reason, which is now unable to see the good by itself) and therefore seeing a sharp discontinuity between reason and revelation*. For the first of these two streams the concept of natural law is essential. Some 15 years later (1973) C.-H. Grenholm would still see these main trends but would also speak of a "mixed theological ethics" which would build bridges between the two. The question remains: How is the notion of natural law to be understood, and what place should it occupy in our approach to questions of ethics* (involving the individual and society) and of law* (involving rights and international law)?

Natural law in history. The notion of natural law has a long and complex history. The early fathers received it mainly from the Stoic tradition (witness the frequent quotations from Seneca and Cicero) and conceived it as the order of the universe, perceived by human reason, which participates in the logos that penetrates the whole reality. It is objective and universal. In the effort to relate such law to concrete ethical questions, some were inclined to relate it to biological data, referring to animal life or to "the natural function proper to an organ". Others, such as Irenaeus and, more systematically, Augustine, established a distinction between a primary and absolute right (preceding the fall) and a secondary and derived one (under the conditions of sin*).

Thomas Aquinas, drawing also from Aristotle and the Roman jurists of the empire, conceived a more systematic and flexible concept of natural law, which has remained the basis of Roman Catholic ethics. In a simplified way we can summarize Thomas's view under three headings: (1) a conception of the human person as a psycho-physical unity directed towards a transcendent fulfilment: thus, on the one hand, all crass objectivism is excluded and, on the other, a teleological dimension enters into all ethical questions; (2) a formulation of the distinction between the *primary precepts* of natural law, which Thomas basically identifies in formal terms ("one should do good and avoid evil" or "one should act according to reason") and with some derivations which are attached to it (e.g. self-preservation, conjugal union as necessary

for procreation, sociality and the recognition of God), and *secondary precepts*, which are derived from the primary but involve the mediation of circumstantial knowledge and reflection (things related, for instance, to property or to political decisions); (3) consequently we find in Thomas, in spite of the classical metaphysical conception of human nature, a certain changeability and historicity due to the fallibility of instrumental human reason and to the multiplicity and variety of the elements that have to be considered.

In spite of the criticisms of the Aquinas definition (e. g. by Ockham), it was not until the Reformation that his conception of natural law was seriously challenged. Although the reformers do recognize the value of human reason in discerning the good in everyday human life, they tend to undermine the whole edifice of natural law by their emphasis on the break introduced in human existence through sin and humanity's consequent and absolute dependence on God's self-revelation for knowing God's will. Of course, such a break could not dispense with the question as to how to make ethical decisions both in personal and social life. Here Protestantism has sometimes re-introduced a variation of the natural law concept in the notion of the orders, sometimes radically separated a spiritual and a secular realm, sometimes tried to apply biblical laws, and sometimes looked for a more embracing Christological principle.

Crisis and the validity of the concept of natural law. Since the last century the notion of natural law has undergone a shattering criticism coming from three quarters. Philosophically, positivism and existentialism have rejected the idea of an essential and immutable human nature, or even simply of human nature as such, thus undercutting the possibility of speaking of a universal law rooted in it. Second, the social sciences of anthropology and sociology have corroborated such criticisms by showing that there is nothing that can be called universal in moral precepts, considering the laws and customs of human societies across time and cultures. If we would speak of a "universal moral principle", it would have to be so general ("do the good and don't do evil") that it would have no practical significance. Furthermore, modern science has "historicized" even biological human reality (see **bio-ethics**). Third, the Protestant theological opposition to the idea of natural law has been forcefully and radically expressed by Barth and other theologians with such strictures as "human self-justification" (Dombois) or "arrogance before God" (Schrey), on the basis that "it overlooks God's revelation in Christ" (Barth), that it is "a total interpenetration of creation and sin" (Helmut Thielicke), or that it has an implicitly deist view of a creation which "God, so to say, would have abandoned" (Regin Prenter).

Under such combined criticisms, many have dismissed the notion of natural law. However, some of the questions which this concept answered have not disappeared. "Juridical positivism" (Hans Kelsen etc.) has proved insufficient as a foundation of law. There seems to be an ineradicable human sense of right which protests an unjust law, even when it has been "positively legislated". There is a rebellion against established patterns in the name of some superior justice attributed to the gods, to reason or to human conscience. We can, usually *ex post facto*, find social and economic reasons that explain the objective conditions underlying such appeals. But it would hardly seem intellectually honest to ignore this sense of the transcendence of good and justice.

On the other hand, the Christian community living in the world cannot escape its responsibility to participate in the human effort to distinguish good from evil, to define moral values, to make moral judgments and to establish laws. In so doing, how should one relate the specific vision rooted in God's revelation, attested in scripture and experienced in the church, to the ethical insights (whatever their origin) of the human community? If we hold to the Christian doctrine of creation,* to the universality of the work of Christ, to the eschatological hope of God's kingdom,* are we not forced to establish some relation between God's creative, redemptive and fulfilling activity and the questions raised by human — personal, social, political — life in the world? In the context of these issues we find some theological attempts to re-interpret "natural law" or to find another theological key to give a response to such questions. Some of these attempts have been significant in the ecumenical conversation.

Some thinkers attempt to discover *an anthropological structure* which, avoiding the pitfalls of objectivism, can provide a basis for a reflection on ethics in which Christians and non-Christians can join. Emil Brunner has done so by defining the human in terms of an I-Thou relationship which undergirds the basic category of "respons-ability" as fundamental ethical structure. Building on that foundation, Brunner re-interprets the classic doctrine of "the orders" and develops a critical and constructive dialogue with secular ethical thinking. In a different line, Paul Tillich builds a system of correlation on the basis of the human openness to the transcendent as "an ultimate concern". This expression of being under the conditions of existence (of which Jesus as the Christ is the symbol) makes it possible to discuss ethical issues in their historical form without destroying their transcendent dimension (see Tillich's *Systematic Theology*, vol. 3). Although through a different line of reasoning, this approach is analogous to Karl Rahner's anthropological method, which Johann Metz has continued and transformed as basis for a "political theology" and a theology of praxis. On the Anglo-Saxon scene, and more directly related to WCC definitions, ethicists like John Bennett, John Macquarrie and J.H. Oldham have looked for "middle" ethical fromulations (see **middle axioms**) on which Christians and non-Christians can co-operate and which, although not claiming to derive from some universal and unchangeable natural law, do represent a certain ethical sense or some common "awareness of the desirable good". Concrete utopias like the idea of the responsible society* or, in more recent times, the just, participatory and sustainable society* or justice, peace and the integrity of creation* belong to this category.

A reading of recent *Roman Catholic ethical pronouncements* suggests that, while natural law continues to be a significant element, biblical and theological considerations tend to occupy a privileged place as the basis for ethical definitions, and at the same time, an analysis of social, economic or scientific conditions mediate the more concrete pronouncements. The Vatican II's pastoral constitution *Gaudium et Spes* seems to point to a method which D. Lanfranconi (see his article on "Ley Natural" in *Diccionario Teológico Interdisciplinar*) summarizes in three points: (1) the style is that of dialogue between the church and the world — in which both must give and receive, which means a dialogue with human sciences, cultures and religions; (2) the dialogue engages not only the magisterium but the whole church, laypeople as well as the clergy: therefore "every Christian who thinks and reflects on himself and on the meaning of his own life and activity contributes to the discovery and formulation of the natural law"; (3) in this dialogue the church offers — does not impose — "her vision of man and of the natural law, taken from a higher light: revelation". While the document exhorts a person to enter into his or her own heart, there discerning one's "proper destiny beneath the eyes of God" (a typical Thomist view), there is a strong emphasis on "the dignity of the moral conscience" as the voice of God, "a law written by God" in the heart. The chapter on anthropology culminates in a Christological section in which Christ is seen as the key to the understanding and destiny of the human.

This Christological approach, which in principle would seem to be at the antipodes of natural-law theology, can, however, be seen as offering a fruitful approach to the questions mentioned before. Strongly affirming the unique and universal meaning of Christ's redemption for all humankind, Barth can re-instate a form of humanism in which the dignity of the human person* becomes a fundamental point of departure for ethics, while, by way of analogy, the kingdom of God* which is revealed and enacted in Christ offers a "parable" for thinking about the civil community. The Christological approach has been carried through in Bonhoeffer's tantalizingly incomplete but enormously fruitful ethics, in which the reality of the mandate in which human life takes place is fully honoured in its autonomy, while Christ is seen as the ultimate being for all reality and ethics as "con-formity", Christ "taking shape" in it.

The version of natural law as a universal, immutable law, knowable to all through reason and able to be formulated in specific terms in relation to almost every possible question (as certain rationalists claimed in the 17th century), is certainly impossible. Even classic theorists of natural law (Thomas Aquinas in the first place) already qualified and corrected that view. But it is also clear that an ecumenical ethics cannot avoid today a dialogue with the re-interpretations of natural law in recent Catholic and non-Catholic ethics, not only because it is a dialogue within the Christian family, but because it relates to issues of fundamental importance for a Christian ethics that intends to be relevant to human reality.

See also **anthropology, theological; creation; ethics; grace; law; revelation**.

JOSÉ MÍGUEZ BONINO

D. Bonhoeffer, *Ethik* (ET *Ethics*, London, SCM, 1955) • E. Brunner, *Das Gebot und die Ordnungen* (ET *The Divine Imperative*, London, Lutterworth, 1937) • E. Duff, *The Social Thought of the World Council of Churches*, London, Longmans Green, 1956 • J. Ellul, *Le fondement théologique du droit*, Neuchâtel, Delachaux et Niestlé, 1946 • J. Fuchs, *Lex naturae*, Dusseldorf, Patmos, 1955 • C.-H. Grenholm, *Christian Social Ethics in a Revolutionary Age*, Uppsala, Verbum, 1973 • H. Thielicke, *Theologische Ethik* (ET *Theological Ethics*, Grand Rapids, MI, Eerdmans, 1979) • D. Whitehouse, *Natural Law*, London, SCM, 1946.

NATURE.

I

The English word "nature" (Latin *natura*, Greek *physis*) is used in at least three senses: (1) the constitutive nature of an entity (e.g. "a wolf is by nature cruel"); (2) natural phenomena untouched by humans (e.g. "nature and culture are two distinct but related realms"); and (3) the whole of reality (e.g. "nature has endowed human beings with a very complex brain structure"). The New Testament uses the word often in the first sense ("Jews by birth", Gal. 2:15; "by nature children of wrath", Eph. 2:3; "natural branches", Rom. 11:21,24), i.e. as the structure and constitution with which someone or something is born (see also James 3:6-7; 2 Pet. 1:4; 1 Cor. 11:14; Gal. 4:8). But there is no Hebrew equivalent for this Greek word *physis*.

The second and third senses of *physis* are not in the New Testament or the Old Testament, except in the Hellenistic, apocryphal 4 Macc. 5:5-8 (LXX), where the pagan Antiochus Epiphanes recommends swine's flesh to Eleazar the high priest as a gracious "gift of nature" and says it is wrong to reject "nature's favours".

Etienne Gilson thinks with Malebranche that "*nature* is par excellence an anti-Christian idea, a remnant from pagan philosophy which has been accepted by imprudent theologians". Aristotle and the Stoics used the word *physis* to denote more or less the whole universe with all its creative and regulative powers as a self-existent and self-sustaining whole.

In current usage one finds both the inclusive and the exclusive senses of the word "nature", i.e. including humanity or excluding it. Nature has often been opposed to culture or civilization, especially since Rousseau. One of the several meanings of the word as given by the Oxford English Dictionary (1908 ed.) is "the material world, or its collective objects and phenomena, especially those with which man is most directly in contact; frequently, the features and products of the earth itself, as contrasted with those of human civilization".

Theologians often speak of a process of "historicization of nature" in Israel when the three "nature-feasts" of unleavened bread, first-fruits and booths (Ex. 23:14-17; Deut. 16:1-17) were related to acts of God in history. But the Hebrew OT does not make the distinction between nature and history,* for the Hebrew language does not have words for these concepts as such. The great redemptive act of the exodus was as much an event in "nature" as in "history" (e.g. the burning bush, the ten plagues, the drying up of the sea, the land flowing with milk and honey, the thunder and lightning at the appearance of Yahweh).

The dichotomy between nature and many other entities, like grace, the supernatural, history, humankind, culture, etc., seems peculiar to the Western tradition. The 9th-century European Christian conception of *natura* included God. John Scotus Erigena (c.810-c.877) gave the fourfold classification of nature: (1) nature, creating and not created, i.e. God; (2) nature created and creating, i.e. the Platonic *kosmos noētos*, or world of archetypal or universal ideas generating particular existents; (3) nature created and not creating, in which category Erigena puts humanity, which cannot create *ex nihilo*; and (4) nature uncreated and not creating, a medieval conception of the final *apokatastasis*, or restoration, when all creativity will stop in a static perfection wherein God is all in all.

But medieval thought never conceived a "natural order" which was independent of the "supernatural order". "Nature" in our sense was a dynamic, *contingent, caused* entity. It had its own "natural laws", but God was not subject to these natural laws and could interfere with them and annul them when needed, e.g. in the miracles. God is not bound by nature; nature is bound by God. God can also unbind the laws of nature.

This law-bound nature is active. Nature is an agent. All that happens in the world is caused exclusively by three agents: God, nature and humanity. Everything is an act of God, an act of nature or an act of humanity. When God acts, it is a supernatural act, as distinguished from the last two.

This way of thinking was strange to the Eastern fathers. They spoke about acting according to nature or contrary to nature *(kata physin* or *para physin)*, but they also never spoke about anything *hyperphysikos* (supernatural), except in a poetic sense.

For the Eastern fathers, as for the biblical witness, the act of creation* is the opening phase of God's redeeming work (see **redemption**). Both the book of Genesis and the gospel of John begin with an account of this opening phase. In the prophecies of Deutero-Isaiah we find that the framework of God's redeeming activity is his original act of creation (Isa. 40:21-28, 42:5-9, 44:24-28, 45:12-25, 51:9-16, etc.). Part of God's redeeming act is the restoring of creation (Isa. 41:17-20).

In the debate between the inclusive versus exclusive view of nature, Christians have to be careful not to fall into the trap of including just two entities — humanity and nature. The package has always three "poles" — God, humanity and the world. Neither the second nor the third could exist apart from or independently of the first.

It is important to note here the fundamental tension between certain Eastern religions and the West Asian tradition of semitic religions. The latter prefer to put an almost unbridgeable gap between the world and the transcendent God. Hinduism and Taoism generally have the same ethos as Stoicism in the West, where the world is God and God is the world. Only Buddhism steers clear of this semitic versus South-Asian debate.

By refusing to raise the question of God* altogether and by positing the world and humanity as two inter-related and interacting entities, everything being dependent on everything else and everything in a process of dynamic change, the Buddhist doctrines of causality and dependent origination of phenomena at least avoid the cleavage of transcendence and keep everything together.

In the Indian tradition, the earliest strand, *sāmkhya*, is dualistic. *Prakrti* (nature) is contrasted with *purusha* (person). This is a non-inclusive view of nature, seeing it as devoid of its own consciousness or purpose, composed of various qualities *(gunās)* in mutual interaction. In opposition to this position, Sankara developed the monistic view in which what we call nature, including humanity, is Brahman or the Absolute itself, wrongly perceived as separate from the Absolute. In the Chinese tradition of Tao, the two opposing but complementary principles of yin and yang together constitute all reality, including God, world and humanity.

The Christian teaching prefers the word *ktisis* (creation) to *physis* (nature) to refer to the whole world. The three classic passages in the NT are John 1:1-18, Col. 1:15-20, and Heb. 11:3. In speaking of the created order, the NT always insists that it is held together in and by the second person of the Trinity,* without whom it would be nothing. The biblical tradition not only insists that the created order has its beginning in God but also affirms that without God the world has neither present nor future. The Eastern fathers of the church continued this tradition. The classic patristic writing is Basil's nine homilies on the Six Days of Creation *(Hexaemeron)*. Most of the key doctrines whose origin is wrongly attributed to Augustine in the Western tradition can be found in Basil and Gregory of Nyssa two generations earlier. The world does not begin in time, but in God's will and word *(Hexaemeron,* 1:5ff.). The six days of creation are not 24-hour days (caused by the sun, created only on the fourth day) but long epochs. There is no "three-storey universe" as in Rudolf Bultmann's caricature of patristic teaching. The created order is unfinished, dynamic, moving towards its fulfilment. Heaven is not a place but an order of many-dimensioned reality closed to our senses.

Gregory of Nyssa (c.330-c.395) was more philosophical in his discussion of the created order. Spatio-temporal extension and incessant change are the characteristics of the created as distinct from the Creator. There is both

continuity by participation and discontinuity by transcendence or standing apart, extension between God and world. The created order is a space-time process, or rather a procession, orderly and sequential, journeying through life from something to something. Life is an important aspect of that procession from origin to perfection; it is through the evolution of life that the procession moves forward. Human activity is the key for progress. Human aspiration for the greater good and humanity's free creativity of the good are the factors that make the world meaningful.

In the Byzantine tradition, Maximus the Confessor (580-662) uses the word "nature" only in the first sense, i.e. the constitutive nature of a group or class of entities. For "nature" in the inclusive sense he uses *ktisis* (creation). Its original unity comes by virtue of its common origin both in non-being and in the creative energy of the logos which holds it together. It has also a destined or eschatological unity, achieved by and in Jesus Christ, God-Man, body-soul, who took his body in the ascension to the heavenlies, or eternal realms. Creation is thus inseparable from redemption.

In modern science, nature was often thought of as an objectively existing entity, independent of the Creator and the observing human mind. Today the objective existence of a world can no longer be assumed in science. The world of phenomena can be seen as something emerging in human consciousness and experience, known to be ultimately composed of energy waves operating both in the mind and in the world.

Science persists in the hope that these phenomena can be explained without reference to any Creator outside of it. In science itself there is no basis for the concept of something called nature independent of God and humanity.

The concept of nature as a generic term for reality, whether inclusive or exclusive of humanity, is thus misleading. Christians know only a dynamic created order with a beginning and a destiny as well as a course or path to be traversed from beginning to fulfilment. This created order, which comes out of non-being, has the creative word of God as its original constitutive power and its present sustaining force. Its fulfilled unity is eschatological, to come at the end. This unity is achieved by the

God-Man, body-soul Jesus Christ, who united in himself all things and reconciles them to God as a single offering.

PAULOS MAR GREGORIOS

P. Evdokimov, "Nature", *Scottish Journal of Theology*, 18, 1965 • P. Gregorios, *Cosmic Man: The Divine Presence*, New York, Paragon, 1987 • P. Gregorios, *The Human Presence*, New York, Amity, 1987 • G.S. Hendry, *Theology of Nature*, Philadelphia, Westminster, 1980.

II

A theology of nature is not the same as a doctrine of creation.* They are related, but they have different starting points and serve different purposes.

Belief in God* as Creator declares that all existence has its origin in God, is dependent on him at every instant, stands secure in him and, despite much that is wrong, is to be affirmed as an expression of his loving purpose. In the Bible the doctrine takes shape, not in speculation about the nature of the world, but in the working out of the implications of the sovereignty and power of God who has called and saved his people. The Lord of history* is Lord too of the powers of the world and provides his people with an orderly and stable environment in which they are to live by his laws. The first chapter of Genesis is a declaration of faith in such an environment, all the more remarkable for being made in a world where much was threatening, painful and mysterious.

Deeper insight into the doctrine shows its ultimate basis in God's grace,* an outpouring of love constrained by nothing beyond itself, and finally validated by the revelation* in Jesus Christ.* As God's agent in creation (Col. 1:16-17), Christ sets his seal on its character and points forward to the new creation in which all will be gathered up in himself. Meanwhile the operation of grace entails a certain distancing between God and his handiwork, the creation of a degree of "space" to allow creatures to be themselves and thus to respond freely to the love which is offered them.

Creation includes heaven as well as earth. Here the concept diverges most sharply from that of nature. Whatever is meant by "heaven" in this context — and interpretations have been many and various — it is clear that earth is not the sole sphere of God's concern and creative activity. Creation, in other words, is an inclusive term describing all that is not God in its relation to God, and disclosing a goodness and a purposiveness in things which, because they are gifts of grace, are not to be taken for granted. Such a belief is in theory compatible with very different cosmologies and histories of the universe, and in philosophical terms is directed, not towards detailed scientific explanations, but to the fundamental questions why anything should exist at all, and to what purpose.

By contrast, a theology of nature cannot avoid taking account of the way things are. The term "nature" itself is used in a variety of senses, sometimes referring to the essence of whatever is being described ("human nature"), sometimes to the particular characteristics of a person or thing ("a cruel nature"), sometimes to the world apart from human interference (land* which has "returned to nature"), and sometimes it is simply used as a word for everything, human beings included, as in the phrase "the natural world". These confusions are further increased by the two senses of "natural law".* The first sense, the scientific, refers to the way in which entities and processes of the observable world relate to and interact with one another. The second sense, the moral, refers to the ways in which human beings ought to behave if they had a fully rational insight into their true end as given by God. The common thread in all these meanings is the belief that things are what they are, and that this can in some measure be discerned and described. From a theological perspective the givenness in the ordering of things is seen as deriving from the creative activity of God. If this is further seen as the outworking of a rational and intelligible divine plan, the way is open for the development of natural science, and as a matter of history it was in fact such a Christian belief in creation which made science intellectually possible.

However, such a simple identification between the divine plan and the world as studied by natural science does not do justice to the actual complexities inherent in the concept of nature. Some theologians, for example, would want to emphasize the extent to which the whole natural world is somehow entailed in the fallenness of humanity (Rom. 8:19-21) and thus expresses God's intention only in terms of what it is moving towards, rather than in terms of what it now is. There are doubts too about the extent of human rationality and thus about the ability of the human mind to discern the true nature of things unaided by revelation.

From an opposite perspective, some would bring scientific criticism to bear on theology, questioning whether in an evolving world the belief that there is a fixed nature of things can really be sustained. If everything is in process of change and development, then perhaps it is only the basic laws of nature, rather than any particular forms within it, which represent the orderliness of God's creative activity. The so-called harmony of nature, on this view, results from the complex interaction of many conflicting forces and is not necessarily stable or permanent. The recently developed chaos theory underlines the unpredictability of a great many familiar physical processes and points to a universe with many more degrees of freedom than it has been customary to suppose since the rise of mechanistic physics. In such a fluid and open universe, our human ability to manipulate the natural world for our own ends assumes an even greater significance and places a heavy burden of responsibility on us as possessors of these powers.

Much contemporary discussion of nature centres on the extent to which the natural world is to be seen as resource to be exploited, a God-given reality to be respected and treasured for its own sake, or as a process in which human beings are themselves inextricably involved and in which they have no privileged place. Environmental concerns are leading to the re-discovery of neglected theological emphases, of which the most fruitful is still probably the idea of the responsible stewardship of nature. But there are also emphases, rooted in incarnational theology, which stress the potentiality of the natural world for bearing the image of the divine, and hence provide a theological basis for regarding it as having its own intrinsic worth. A theocentric understanding of nature, derived from the Christian doctrine of creation, might similarly underline the significance of all created things as having their own value in God's sight and therefore as being worthy of respect and protection.

Such thinking represents a radical departure

Philippine landscape (WCC/Peter Williams)

from those Christian traditions in which the natural world was treated as a mere backcloth to human activity, and in which persons were treated as the sole bearers of moral value. It is possible that the reaction against this view may go too far in downgrading the unique significance of the personal. It also needs to be remembered that there is no way in which humanity can survive at present levels of population without massive interference in the natural ordering of things. However, just as in theology grace is said not to destroy nature but to perfect it, ecological wisdom usually lies in learning how to work with the grain of nature rather than against it.

It will be obvious, even from this brief survey of some of the ways in which the concept "nature" is used, that such an ill-defined word can easily generate confusion unless its meaning is carefully specified in particular contexts.

JOHN HABGOOD

R. Attfield, *The Ethics of Environmental Concern*, New York, Columbia UP, 1983 • L.C. Birch, *Nature and God*, Philadelphia, Westminster, 1965 • J.A. Carpenter, *Nature and Grace*, New York, Crossroad, 1988 • J. Moltmann, *Gott in der Schöpfung* (ET *God in Creation*, New York, Harper, 1985) • J. Polkinghorne, *One World*, Princeton, NJ, Princeton UP, 1986 • J. Polkinghorne, *Science and Creation*, London, SPCK, 1988.

NAUDÉ, CHRISTIAAN FREDERICK BEYERS.

B. 10.5.1915, Roodepoort, Transvaal, South Africa. Naudé, first editor of the ecumenical newspaper *Pro Veritate*, has been a strong promoter of the ecumenical movement in South Africa. On accepting the directorship of the Christian Institute, he was discharged from ministry in the Nederduitse Gereformeerde Kerk in 1963. The institute, which he had helped to establish, worked with Christians of all races on issues of church and society in South Africa and was the most outspoken anti-apartheid body in the country. Naudé served the institute for 14 years, till the paper he edited and the institute were both banned by the government in 1977. A banning order for seven years severely curtailed his freedom of movement. Serving as general secretary of the South African Council of Churches, 1985-87, he continued to oppose the policy of apartheid and to counsel various organizations in South Africa which assist disadvantaged people in educational and other spheres. Naudé studied at the University of Stellenbosch, 1932-39, and served the Nederduitse Gereformeerde Kerk, 1940-63, working in seven congregations. He wrote *The Individual and the State in South Africa* (London, Christian Institute Fund, 1975). See *Resistance and Hope: South African Essays in Honour of Beyers Naudé*, C. Villa-Vicencio and J.W. Gruchy eds (Grand Rapids, MI, Eerdmans, 1985); and *Hope for Faith*, by Naudé and Dorothee Sölle (WCC, 1985) for a moving account of his conversion to Christ and involvement in anti-apartheid struggles.

ANS J. VAN DER BENT

NEILL, STEPHEN CHARLES.

B. 31.12.1900, Edinburgh, Scotland; d. 20.7.1984, Oxford. A missionary, church historian, teacher and ecumenical theologian, Neill was associate general secretary of the WCC, responsible for its study programme, 1948-50. He served as principal of a theological college before becoming bishop of the Anglican diocese of Tinnevelly, South India, in 1939. He took a leading part in the movement for church union which later led to the formation of the Church of South India. He was a delegate to the world conference of the International Missionary Council at Tambaram (1938). He was professor of mission and ecumenics at the University of Hamburg, 1962-69, and professor of philosophy at the Department of Religious Studies, University of Nairobi, 1970-73. With Ruth Rouse he edited the important book *The History of the Ecumenical Movement, 1517-1948* (3rd ed., WCC, 1986). For over a decade he was general editor of World Christian Books, a series of short books designed for translation into many languages. His numerous works include: *Anglicanism* (Harmondsworth, UK, Penguin, 1958), *Brothers of the Faith* (New York, Abingdon, 1960), *Christian Faiths and Other Faiths* (London, Oxford UP, 1961), and *The Church and Christian Union* (London, Oxford UP, 1968). He was co-editor of *Concise Dictionary of the Christian World Mission* (Nashville, TN, Abingdon, 1971) and *A History of Christian Missions* (Harmondsworth, UK, Penguin, 1982).

MARTIN CONWAY

NEW RELIGIOUS MOVEMENTS.

The term "new religious movement" (NRM) usually refers to a movement that (1) has become visible in its present form since the second world war, and (2) offers a religious or philosophical world-view or techniques for reaching some higher goal, such as spiritual enlightenment. "Non-conventional religion", "alternative religion" or (often with pejorative overtones) "cult" are terms describing roughly the same miscellany.

Several NRMs provide a distinctive interpretation of the Bible, but NRMs have emerged from all the major religious traditions; some incorporate several traditions. Paganism and occult groups, the "new age and the human potential" movement, offering self-development through, e.g., yoga, meditation, or holistic psychology, are also labelled NRMs — as are some movements that consider themselves part of a mainline tradition but are judged to exhibit certain "cultic" characteristics.

Members of the better-known NRMs in the more developed societies tend, disproportionately, to be materially advantaged young adults; most display high levels of enthusiasm and commitment. But the enormous diversity of beliefs and practices to be found within and between the NRMs cannot be overstressed.

Throughout history, established religions have been suspicious of NRMs, especially when a charismatic leader proclaims a new revelation within their tradition. Since the early 1970s, a number of organizations, some run by ordained ministers and a few supported by mainstream churches, have concentrated on exposing evils allegedly perpetrated by "destructive cults", and on demonstrating that NRMs are not "really" religious or "really" Christian. (In the USA, the Jewish community has been worried about the movement called Jews for Jesus.) Some members of such organizations have advocated the illegal practice of "deprogramming" to rescue adults from NRMs.

Most mainstream churches, however, paid little attention to NRMs until the late 1970s. In 1980 the Lausanne Committee for World Evangelization* tried to come to grips with the problem of distinguishing between "that [NRM] which is truly of the Spirit of God and that which is satanic". In 1986 a consultation organized by the WCC and the Lutheran World Federation* (whose member churches had requested guidelines for appropriate responses to NRMs) produced several recommendations, including one that an ecumenical effort should be made to understand and interact with NRMs. The British Council of Churches also organized a consultation in 1986, which resulted in the Church of England's setting up a nationwide, interdenominational network of advisers in collaboration with INFORM (Information Network Focus on Religious Movements, a charity committed to disseminating objective and balanced information about NRMs).

While generally chary of their beliefs and practices, several churches have forcefully condemned proposals to curtail the activities of NRMs. In Europe, the Dutch Council of Churches, for example, expressed disquiet over the apparent violation of religious freedom and the effect on human rights of a European Parliament motion "concerning the influence of new religious movements in the European Community" and added that it should not be possible to impose obligations on NRMs without a similar imposition on existing churches. In North America, Canadian churches have expressed similar sentiments; and while it found Unification theology incompatible with traditional Christian doctrine, the National Council of the Churches of Christ in the USA has, with other religious bodies such as the American Baptist Churches, filed *amicus curiae* briefs in cases involving the Unification Church and other NRMs, on the ground that arguments presented to the US courts have threatened fundamental principles of religious freedom. In 1986 the Vatican published a preliminary report which, while displaying awareness of various problems, accepted NRMs as a positive challenge to stimulate the church's "own renewal for a greater pastoral efficacy".

As for the NRMs themselves, some apparently embrace an ecumenical mission: the Unification Church (in full, the Holy Spirit Association for the Unification of World Christianity) has sponsored numerous conferences promoting dialogue between Unificationists and other religionists (Christian and other). The NRMs' ecumenical ventures are, however, usually confined to dialogue with established religions; spasmodic attempts to unite (usually over religious liberty) tend to disintegrate, largely because few NRMs wish to be identified with other NRMs. Some NRMs see ecumenism as irrelevant, insisting that one can practise, say, transcendental meditation while being a Methodist or a Roman Catholic. Yet others, such as the London Church of Christ, consider that ecumenism undermines scriptural purity.

EILEEN BARKER

E. Barker ed., *New Religious Movements*, New York, E. Mellen, 1982 • A. Brockway & J. Rajashekar eds, *New Religious Movements and the Churches*, WCC, 1987.

NEW TESTAMENT AND CHRISTIAN UNITY.

"There is one body and one Spirit, just as you were called to the one hope that belongs to your call, one Lord, one faith, one baptism, one God and Father of us all, who is above all and through all and in all." With this imposing summation, Ephesians (4:4-6) sets forth the unity* of Christian faith* and community, grounding it ultimately in one God.* The logic is entirely straightforward: the oneness of God, Jesus Christ,* Christian confession, liturgy,* and eschatology* plainly implies the oneness of the body, the church.* In an apparent allusion to 1 Cor. 12, Ephesians refers to the church as one body (cf. also Eph. 1:22-23, where body and church are explicitly equated).

"Church" (ecclesia) quickly became the generic term for the individual Christian congregation, as well as the congregations as a whole, and so it has remained. Nevertheless, the New Testament has different ways of referring to the Christian community. It is not only the Body of Christ, but the people of God (1 Pet. 2:9-10), God's building (1 Cor. 3:9), the household of faith (Gal. 6:10; cf. Eph. 2:19), God's temple (1 Cor. 3:16-17), the elect lady (2 John 1), etc., so that one may legitimately speak of images of the church* in the NT (Minear). Although these images reflect a healthy variety in the ways the church is conceived in the NT, most of them also convey a sense of its unity.

The emphasis of Ephesians on church unity accurately represents the bearing of the NT as a whole, even if comparable statements are seldom found elsewhere. This emphasis on unity did not, however, exclude diversity, as the wealth of images already suggests. In fact, Paul defends the legitimacy of diverse gifts and functions within the church as the work of the one Spirit (1 Cor. 12); they are necessary, moreover, for the church's well-being.

Paul regards his own ministry as "a priestly service of the gospel of God" (Rom. 15:16), which he relates on the one hand to his collection among the gentile churches of an offering for the Jerusalem church (vv.22-29) and on the other to the praise of God by both Jew and Gentile (vv.9-13). In either case, Paul has in view the unity of the church as God's people (see **people of God**); in the one case in doxology, in the other in a quite concrete act of generosity and helpfulness which had engaged him for some time (cf. Gal. 2:10; 1 Cor. 16:1-3; 2 Cor. chs 8-9). In its own way, Ephesians reflects the successful culmination of Paul's ministry in its emphasis upon the accomplishment of union between Jew and gentile as the very essence of the work of Christ and consequently of the gospel Paul preached (Eph. 2:11-3:6).

Paul's earlier controversy with the so-called Judaizers was a concrete expression of his own sense that the unity of the church is essential to the appropriation of the gospel. Thus the approval of the pillar apostles was of crucial importance to him (Gal. 2:6-10). But the behaviour of Peter at Antioch (vv.11-16) Paul found intolerable, not only because it implied a defective soteriology (vv.17-21), but because it involved a concession to the circumcision party (v.12) that threatened the unity of the church, and therefore the gospel. While Paul did not in principle object to circumcision and observance of food laws among Jewish believers, he insisted upon the unity of the church in its table fellowship and eucharist,* and thus he ran afoul of those who gave such practices priority. The apostolic decree of Acts (15:19-21,23-29) looks like an effort to resolve such problems by laying down minimal food restrictions which all Christians should observe, but whether it was actually published in the time of Paul or at what stage in his ministry is a point of continued dispute among exegetes. In any event, both the controversy of Paul and the apostolic decree were efforts to protect the unity of Christians not only in theory but in practice and particularly in worship.

The gospels, representing for the most part

the generation after Paul, presume the unity of the Christian community, but for the most part do not deal directly with this issue because they are concerned with presenting the earthly Jesus, albeit in light of his death and resurrection.* Yet Mark announces the end of all food restrictions (7:19), and Luke proclaims the universal scope of the gospel (24:47), as does Matthew (28:19). But it is the gospel of John in particular that emphasizes the unity of Christians in one community. In his high-priestly prayer, Jesus prays that his followers may be one so that the world may believe and know that he has been sent from God (17:21-23). Thus the unity of the church is the basis for mission,* and the work of Jesus Christ can be described as the gathering into one of the scattered people of God (11:51-52), "so there shall be one flock, one shepherd" (10:16).

The fourth gospel's emphasis on unity is continued in 1 John, which speaks of fellowship with the Father and Son and among Christians (1:3). "Fellowship" (koinonia*) also means participation and communion* and connotes a close and intimate relationship. Therefore, one is not surprised at the author's abhorrence of schism* (2:18-19). Yet communion must be based on full and right confession; one cannot have fellowship with those who represent the spirit of error or false teaching (1 John 4:1-3; 2 John 9-10). There is one true Spirit, and those who teach what is obviously false cannot lay claim to any valid spiritual authority. The book of Revelation, genuinely if more remotely related to the other Johannine writings, in its graphic portrayal of the new heaven and new earth also presupposes the unity of the people of God in the end time (21:3,22-27). Here is expressed in typically apocalyptic terms the eschatological culmination anticipated in the gospel of John as well (cf. 14:2-3, 17:24).

Belief in the unity of confession, liturgy, community, and eschatology, grounded in the one God and one Lord (Eph. 4:4-6), thus finds wide representation in the NT. The question of the nature of that unity, in what it consists, was debated in NT times, as it is today. Obviously, the earliest churches manifested diversity and discord as well as unity, but while diversity was celebrated, discord and division were not. The NT attests to a primal sense of unity among Christians that is an ingredient of the revelation* of God in Jesus

Christ. The living unity of all Christians, like the unity of Christian faith and confession, remains both a presupposition and a goal in the NT. The contradiction or obstruction of such unity is regarded as intolerable, and its attainment and visible, palpable manifestation as obligatory (see **Old Testament and Christian unity**).

D. MOODY SMITH

P.J. Achtemeier, *The Quest for Unity in the New Testament Church*, Philadelphia, Fortress, 1987 • R.E. Brown, "The Unity and Diversity in NT Ecclesiology", *Novum Testamentum*, 6, 1963 • E. Käsemann, *Exegetische Versuche und Besinnungen*, II, 262-67 (ET *New Testament Questions of Today*, London, SCM, 1969, 252-59) • P.S. Minear, *Images of the Church in the New Testament*, London, Lutterworth, 1961 • R. Schnackenburg, *Die Kirche im Neuen Testament* (ET *The Church in the New Testament*, London, Burns & Oates, 1965) • E. Schweizer, *Gemeinde und Gemeindeordnung im Neuen Testament* (ET *Church Order in the New Testament*, London, SCM, 1961).

NEW ZEALAND. New Zealand, or Aotearoa (in Maori), began its Christian history on two distinct levels — mission church and settler church. Among the indigenous Maori people there were three early competitors: Anglican, Methodist and Roman Catholic. By 1860, mission work was widespread, particularly in the more densely populated North Island. A few of the tribes adopted a single form of Christianity, but many remain deeply divided denominationally to this day.

The mission church was well established before the settler church saw its very uneven beginnings. In the colder South Island, with very few Maoris, denominationally oriented colonies were established — Presbyterian at Dunedin (1848) and Anglican at Christchurch (1851). Elsewhere, settler churches reflected the nationality of the immigrants. Unlike neighbouring Australia, the numerous Scots made the Presbyterians second to the Anglicans, with Irish Roman Catholics third and Methodists fourth. This ratio has been preserved to the present day, although modern-day attendance patterns make the Roman Catholics New Zealand's most active Christians. Presbyterians have drawn closer to Anglicans in participation levels, and Methodists have diminished.

The earliest missionaries were Anglicans,

sent by the Church Missionary Society (CMS) in 1814. Then came the Methodists of the Wesleyan Missionary Society in 1822. The first Roman Catholics came in 1838 and were under a good deal of suspicion, as they were French. In 1835 the British crown recognized a nominal declaration of independence by a group of northern Maori chiefs. The treaty of Waitangi, signed in 1840 by a larger group of chiefs and the crown representative, gave Queen Victoria sovereignty and protected New Zealand from French colonialism. But it also established a bicultural foundation for future New Zealand society.

All three missionary churches sought to build a Maori church, and ministry to the smaller settler community was secondary. From the 1830s, Maori evangelists of all three allegiances took the gospel throughout the land, and the vast majority of Maori conversions were made by other Maoris. Within a short time, the Maori population was more literate and Christian than the European.

As clergy began to arrive for the settler community, competition developed for control of church leadership, especially in light of the valuable land holdings. When national church bodies were established, the Maoris were forgotten. The 1857 constitution of the Anglican church has no Maori signatures, although Maori Anglicans probably represented the majority of New Zealand's Anglicans at the time. It was assumed that the CMS would take care of them. But the settler structures soon found the missionary establishment too threatening, and Maori concerns found little support until well into the 20th century. The first Maori Anglican priest was ordained in 1853, but it was not until 1944 that the Roman Catholic Church ordained its first Maori to the priesthood. A Maori was received into full connection with the Methodist conference only in 1950. As might be expected, tribal concerns soon outweighed those of the denomination. Attempts were made to create indigenized forms of Christianity, two of which survive today. The Ratana Church, emerging from the Methodist tradition under the leadership of a powerful healer and preacher, has gained a central position in Maori political life and remains strong. The more syncretistic Ringatu Church comprises a smaller but often more nationalistic membership.

The Maoris took a major step forward in 1928 with the creation of an Anglican bishopric of Aotearoa — a bishop for all Maoris, although only a suffragan to the bishop of Waiapu. The appointment sought to stem the rising tide of the Ratana movement as much as to respond to an obligation incumbent upon the settler church. In 1978, the Pihopatanga O Aotearoa was created, giving joint jurisdiction of the Maori bishop with each diocesan bishop. The Presbyterian Maori synod was formed in 1954, the Methodist Maori division in 1973, and Te Runanga Hahi Katoriki ki Aotearoa in 1983 by the RCC.

The first major ecumenical effort in New Zealand was the United Peace Committee, bringing together official church representatives in 1927. This led in 1941 to the formation of a National Council of Churches (NCC). For their part, in 1982 the Maoris in virtually all the major churches, including the Roman Catholic, founded a Maori Council of Churches — Te Runanga Whakawhanaunga I Nga Haahi O Aotearoa. This was prepared for in 1945 when the NCC established the NCC Maori section. In the intervening years the Maori population had doubled, Maoris had become leaders in politics, and churches now reflected the nation's growing recognition of the "people of the land".

In 1987, New Zealand Christians launched a new venture, a conference of churches designed to ground ecumenism in the local context. The previous NCC was a product of the worldwide proliferation of such bodies, similar in form to other councils in the Western world and dominated by Protestants and Anglicans, with some Orthodox participation and Roman Catholics only as observers. The new body, the Conference of Churches in Aotearoa-New Zealand (CCANZ), is intended as a truly indigenous expression of the ecumenical journey.

Meanwhile, Anglicans, Associated Churches of Christ, Congregationalists, Methodists and Presbyterians had since 1965 been negotiating a plan of union, but in 1974 and 1976 this narrowly failed to secure Anglican approval, even though the Protestants accepted Anglican insistence on the historic episcopate. A similar fate in 1980 befell the proposal for a covenant and unification of ministries. Many "co-operative ventures" nevertheless sprang up at the local level.

Catholics joined in organizing and funding the new structures. Three NCC members, however, found difficulty in joining the CCANZ — Baptists, Congregationalists, and Associated Churches of Christ. Congregational polity made it impossible for these national unions to accept the CCANZ goals. The Baptists and Congregationalists still remain outside the conference. But the 1988 CCANZ forum created a new "associate membership" to solve this dilemma. Membership is vested in the national body of the denomination on behalf of those congregations which declare their commitment to the goals of the CCANZ. This recognizes the independence of individual congregations and allows the Associated Churches of Christ to seek associate membership.

New Zealand may be described as facing in three directions: towards the WCC, Asia and the Pacific. Five New Zealand churches — Anglican, Presbyterian, Methodist, Associated Churches of Christ and Baptist — are WCC members. On the other hand, the above-mentioned churches together with the Salvation Army, Congregationalists and Quakers are members of the Christian Conference of Asia.*

However, New Zealand is more of a Pacific nation, and indeed, is a buffer between Australia and the Pacific. Yet in reality New Zealand is very much isolated geographically. It maintains its confessional and missionary ties with the Pacific as Presbyterians and Methodists with Polynesia, Anglicans with Melanesia, Roman Catholics with Polynesia. But New Zealand is not involved in any Pacific ecumenical body. Lately, however, there has been some ecumenical activity concerning the Fiji political situation. CCANZ has made statements about the coup d'etat in Fiji (1987) and about the religious extremism which followed it. New Zealand Methodists have tried to be a force for relaxation of tensions within Fiji Methodism. The inter-Polynesian tensions in Auckland (Samoan-Tongan and Maori Islander, in particular) have led to denominational attempts at mediation. Thus far, there has been no islander involvement with CCANZ. The hope has been expressed by CCANZ and by denominational leaders in New Zealand that New Zealand's growing role as a Pacific nation may lead to some

sort of South Pacific ecumenical body in the future.

RAYMOND OPPENHEIM

J. Bluck, *Everyday Ecumenism: Can You Take the World Church Home?* WCC, 1987 • C. Brown, *Forty Years On: A History of the National Council of Churches in New Zealand, 1941-1981*, Christchurch, NCC, 1981 • *Christian Order: Bibliography of Current Literature*, Christchurch, Presbyterian Bookroom, n.d. • *What Happened at Waitangi in 1983?*, Auckland, NCC, 1983.

NEWBIGIN, (JAMES EDWARD) LESSLIE.

B. 8.12.1909, Newcastle-upon-Tyne, UK. In the fields of missiology and apologetics, Newbigin has been an outstanding teacher, and in the practice of church unity an example of total commitment. He began his training for the ministry of the Presbyterian church in Cambridge, England, at Westminster College. He was ordained in 1936 and appointed by the Church of Scotland for missionary service in India. Newbigin began his pastoral ministry in the Madras area where he quickly gained a deep knowledge of Tamil. During the period of the second world war the foundations were being laid for the union of churches in South India, and Newbigin took a major part in the negotiations which led to the establishment of the Church of South India (CSI). At the inauguration of the CSI in 1947, he was appointed bishop in Madurai and Ramnad. Having been a member of the inaugural assembly of the WCC in 1948 and present at many ecumenical gatherings subsequently, Newbigin had become known to a wide circle as an able apologist for the new united churches and a person with great theological insight. In 1959 he was called to become secretary of the International Missionary Council,* based in London. He led that council to the point of integration in the WCC which was completed at the New Delhi assembly. He served as associate general secretary of the WCC and director of the Commission on World Mission and Evangelism till 1965. Invited back to India, he served as the CSI bishop in Madras till he retired in 1974.

From 1974 to 1979 Newbigin was on the staff of the Selly Oak Colleges in Birmingham, lecturing there and in many other places on mission theology. In 1978 he became moderator of the general assembly of the United Reformed Church, and from 1980 to 1988 served as minister of a small local church in the inner city. His ministry continues and the theme of missionary theology remains, the context now being the Western European culture. In this most recent phase of his service, Newbigin has focused on the challenge of the liberal legacy, and this is the theme of several of his books which have had worldwide influence. But there is a unifying focus to all the output over the years, the calling of God to witness to the saving grace we see in Christ, and to do this as a wholly committed member of the Body of Christ, one body in all the world. There is a strongly Trinitarian thrust to all his writing. Three of his recent books have dealt with the confrontation between the claims of Christ and the modern Western culture: *The Other Side of 1984* (WCC, 1983), *Foolishness to the Greeks* (WCC, 1986) and *The Gospel in a Pluralist Society* (WCC, 1989). Among his other books are *The Reunion of the Church* (1948), *The Household of God*, (1953), *Honest Religion for Secular Man* (1966), *The Finality of Christ* (1969), all published by SCM, London, and *Unfinished Agenda — an Autobiography* (WCC, 1985).

Newbigin is a senior statesman of the ecumenical movement. He has seen the WCC develop from its beginnings, and was within that circle of the Student Christian Movement which provided so many pioneers. It is evident that his passion for the missionary engagement has made him a critic of the more liberal theologies which have been influential in recent decades. Yet there is no anti-intellectual conservatism here. Rather we see a restatement for our age of classical positions, close to Hendrick Kraemer, with a worldview and an experience of unity and mission which is of value for all branches of the church.

BERNARD THOROGOOD

NICEA. The first ecumenical council of Nicea (Bithynia) was summoned by the Roman emperor Constantine the Great (288-337) to deal with the heresy* of Arius and other church matters. Though he originally intended the council to take place at Ancyra (the Turkish Ankara of today), and an initial meeting did take place there involving many bishops,

eventually Constantine sent letters to all the bishops of the catholic church inviting them to meet in council at Nicea and promising that expenses for their journey would be paid by the state. The council was officially opened on 19 June 325 and included the presence of Constantine himself. There are different views as to its duration, proceedings and precise number of participants. The official view is that it was attended by 318 fathers (so Athanasius, Hilary, Epiphanius and also later ecumenical councils*); other estimates speak of more than 250 (Eusebius), or about 270 (Eustathius), or 320 (Sozomen), mainly Easterners, with five of them coming from the West. The bishop of Rome was represented by two priests.

The acts of the council have not survived, except the creed,* the council's letter and 20 canons, but there are several reports on it by ancient ecclesiastical authors, historians and theologians. What emerges from all these is that the views of Arius and his supporters, which amounted to a denial of the true godhead of Christ, were condemned and a creed was accepted as the norm of the Christian faith which confessed the godhead of Christ by proclaiming the Son of God to have been fully and truly God, born "from the being of God the Father" and to be "consubstantial" (*homoousios* = "co-existing" or "one in being") with him. This creed included four specific clauses (*anathemas**) which repudiated Arius's main theses. It seems that the creed was based on that used by the church of Jerusalem at the reception of converts to Christian catechism and baptism.* The council rejected a creed by Eusebius of Nikomedia and approved a creed put forth by Eusebius of Caesarea without adopting it for universal use.

The council also resolved other ecclesiastical matters of dispute, including the schisms of Novatianism, Samosatianism, Melitianism and the dispute over the date of the celebration of Easter (see **church calendar**). Canon 8 deals with the return of the Novatianists to the church, and canon 19 with the return of the Paulinianists (the followers of the previously condemned heretic Paul of Samosata), specifying that they should be re-baptized and re-ordained. The case of the schismatic Melitius, bishop of Lycopolis in Egypt, and his followers was dealt with more leniently, as one reads in the council's letter, which has been preserved in Theodoret of Cyrus's *Ecclesiastical History*. Easter was to be celebrated on the first Sunday after the first full moon of the spring equinox. The precise formula of the actual decision has not survived, though there are several reliable sources for it, including the letter of the council and the letter of Constantine to the churches, following the completion of the council, which is preserved in Eusebius of Caesarea's *Life of Constantine*.

The 20 canons issued by the council fathers indicate that there were six areas of church matters that were actually dealt with: the case of the penalties for lapsed Christians at times of persecution and of their restoration (canons 11,12,14), the case of schismatic bishops and clergy (canon 8), the case of the qualifications and conduct of clergy, the case of the precise rights of bishops and presbyters, including the introduction of the metropolitical system (canons 6 and 7), the case of the re-admission of Paulinianist heretics to the church (canon 19), and several matters of procedure and decision. Finally, the fathers accepted Paphnutius's views in rejecting, as we gather from Gelasius's *Ecclesiastical History*, a proposed canon which made celibacy necessary for bishops and presbyters.

See also **ecumenical councils, Nicene Creed**.

GENNADIOS LIMOURIS

W. Bright, *Notes on the Canons of the First Four General Councils*, Oxford, Clarendon, 1882 • C. Luibheid, *The Council of Nicaea*, Galway, Ireland, Officina Typographica Galway University, 1982 • I. Ortiz de Urbina, *Histoire des conciles oecuméniques*, vol. 1: *Nicée et Constantinople*, Paris, Orante, 1963 • V.I. Phidas, *The First Ecumenical Council: Problems Related to the Summoning, Constitution and Operation of the Council*, Athens, 1974 (in Greek) • V.I. Phidas, *The Presidency of the First Ecumenical Synod*, Athens, 1974 (in Greek).

NICENE CREED. The Nicene-Constantinopolitan Creed (381), or simply Nicene Creed (as it is referred to in this dictionary), as its name indicates, is traditionally regarded as an expansion of the original creed of Nicea* (325) and represents the work of the 150 fathers who assembled in Constantinople* in 381 to re-affirm the faith of Nicea. These expansions were necessitated by the various heresies which emerged since Nicea and which included primarily the heresy* of the Pneumatomachians (Spirit-fighters), who denied the full or true godhead of the Holy Spirit,* and, secondarily, the heresies of Apollinaris of Laodicea (denied the integrity of the incarnation*), Sabellius of Ptolemais (denied the Trinity* by putting forth a unitarian theology), Marcellus of Ancyra and Photeinus of Sirmium (denied the eternal generation of the Son and the permanence of the incarnation), Eunomius of Cyzicus (extreme Arianizer who held a tritheist point of view) and Eudoxius of Constantinople (Arianizer who denied the Holy Spirit). All these heresies were condemned by the first canon of the council of Constantinople I (381).

A comparison of the texts of the original Nicene Creed (325) and of the Nicene-Constantinopolitan Creed reveals that the latter consists of the seven clauses of the former with two slight omissions and five new clauses which implicitly repudiate the above-mentioned heresies. The most important additions are "maker of heaven and earth", directed against Marcionites, Manichaeans and especially Hermogenes, all of whom accepted the Greek philosophical view of the eternity of matter and, implicitly, of the world; "before all ages", directed against Sabellius, Marcellus of Ancyra, Photeinus of Sirmium and Eunomius; "from the Holy Spirit and the Virgin Mary", directed against the Apollinarists; "and seated at the right hand of the Father... whose kingdom shall have no end", directed against Marcellus and his disciple Photeinus; and finally, almost the entire eighth article on the Holy Spirit, directed against the various shades of the denial of the godhead of the Spirit and based on 2 Cor. 3:17-18 ("the Lord"), John 6:63, Rom. 8:2 and 2 Cor. 3:6 (the "Giver of life"), John 15:26 combined with 1 Cor. 2:12 (the Spirit of Truth who proceeds from the Father) and 2 Pet. 1:21 ("who spoke through the prophets"). The phrase "who together with the Father and the Son is worshipped and glorified" represents an oblique way of confessing the *homoousion* of the Holy Spirit, an accommodation to the point of view of certain traditionalist bishops who queried the use of non-biblical terms in the creed. The two omissions are connected with the phrases "from the substance (being) of the Father" and "God of God"; the former was probably dropped because, according to certain accredited fathers (Basil the Great, Gregory the Theologian and Gregory of Nyssa), it was contained in the term *homoousios* and could be misleading as having been wrongly used by Sabellians, whereas the latter was redundant in the presence of the phrase "true God of true God".

That this Nicene Creed of Constantinople is in fact an expansion of the original creed of Nicea, or that the faith of Constantinople as summed up in its creed is the faith of Nicea in an expanded form, is stressed in the letter which the 150 fathers addressed to Emperor Theodosius when they completed their deliberations, and in the conciliar letter which was sent by a similar council, summoned in Constantinople in 382. The same point is stressed by many other witnesses, including the 4th-century Pseudo-Athanasian writing *Dialogue between an Orthodox and a Macedonian*, Neilus Ancyranus, alias Sinaita (d. 430), Nestorius of Constantinople (428-31), Flavian of Constantinople and, above all, the fourth ecumenical council of Chalcedon,* which explicitly joins together the two creeds in speaking of the one faith of Nicea, as all subsequent ecumenical councils do. This view has been questioned in more recent times by German and British scholars who have propounded various scholarly hypotheses concerning the precise origins of the Nicene-Constantinopolitan Creed, but none of which has been universally accepted. These hypotheses have primarily concentrated on the assumption that the Constantinopolitan Creed is not an expansion of the original creed of Nicea but a new creed, taken either from Jerusalem or from Constantinople, or newly constructed. Some of these have also argued that there are differences of theological content, especially as far as the understanding of the crucial term *homoousios* is concerned, between the creeds of Nicea and Constantinople, but none of these arguments has so far gained universal acceptance.

The Nicene-Constantinopolitan Creed without the filioque* addition, which was introduced into the eighth article by the Western church much later, still enjoys the greatest universal acclaim among Christians. This is best illustrated in the major study programme of the WCC Commission on Faith and Order on "Towards the Common Expression of the Apostolic Faith Today", which has made it its starting point.

GENNADIOS LIMOURIS

T.H. Bindley, *The Ecumenical Documents of the Faith*, 4th ed. rev. by F.W. Green, London, Methuen, 1950 • A. Hahn, *Bibliothek der Symbole und Glaubensregeln der alten Kirche*, Breslau, Morgenstern, 1897 • J.N.D. Kelly, *Early Christian Creeds*, 3rd ed., London, Longmans, 1972 • I. Ortiz de Urbina, *Histoire des conciles oecuméniques*, vol. 1: *Nicée et Constantinople*, Paris, Orante, 1963 • A. Ritter, *Das Konzil von Konstantinopel und sein Symbol*, Göttingen, Vandenhoeck & Ruprecht, 1965.

NICODIM (Boris Georgivich Rotov).

B. 14.10.1929, Frolovo, USSR; d. 5.9.1978, Rome. Metropolitan of Leningrad and Novgorod, Nicodim was the driving spirit behind the Moscow patriarchate's deciding to join the WCC at the New Delhi assembly in 1961. He led the Russian Orthodox delegation to that assembly and thereafter was an active member of the WCC central and executive committees and, after Nairobi 1975, a president of the WCC. As assistant to Metropolitan Nicolai, head of the department of foreign relations of the Moscow patriarchate, Nicodim accompanied W.A. Visser 't Hooft and his staff team on an extensive visit of the Soviet Union. Head of this department, 1960-72, Nicodim became bishop of Jaroslavl in 1960, archbishop of the same diocese in 1961, and metropolitan of Minsk and of Leningrad in 1963. He consistently promoted better relationships with the Roman Catholic Church and greatly admired Pope John XXIII. Nicodim died suddenly during an audience with Pope John Paul I. Not afraid to face the frequent fierce and bitter attacks against his nation, his church and himself, he was a loyal supporter of the WCC and tireless in promoting the unity of the churches, as evidenced by the many consultations he organized or attended.

ANS J. VAN DER BENT

NIEBUHR, REINHOLD.

B. 21.6.1892, Wright City, MO, USA; d. 1.6.1971, Stockbridge, MA. The older brother of H. Richard Niebuhr, Reinhold was influential at Oxford 1937, at Amsterdam

1948, and also at the world Christian youth conferences in Amsterdam (1939) and Oslo (1947). In many ways he shaped ecumenical social thought both in the US and in the wider Western world. Although influenced by Karl Barth and Emil Brunner, he differed sharply from them in believing that Christianity has a direct prophetic vocation in relation to culture. Stressing the egoism, the pride and the hypocrisy of nations and classes, he argued for a "Christian realism" and supported political policies that carefully delineated the limits of power. A one-time pacifist, he actively persuaded Christians to support the war against Hitler, and after the second world war had considerable influence in the US state department. He regarded as an error attempts to impose US solutions on the new nations that emerged from 1945 onwards, and always attacked American claims to special virtue.

Ordained to the ministry in the Evangelical Synod in 1915, he was a pastor in Detroit, 1915-28, where his exposure to the problems of American industrialism, before labour was protected by unions and legislation, led him to advocate socialism. He broke with the Socialist party in the 1930s. He was professor of applied Christianity at Union Theological Seminary in New York, 1928-60, and one of the most popular preachers in university chapels. He wrote a number of influential books, among them *Moral Man and Immoral Society* (New York, Scribner, 1932), *The Nature and Destiny of Man*, 2 vols (London, Nisbet, 1943-44) and *Pious and Secular America* (New York, Scribner, 1958). See *Reinhold Niebuhr: His Religious, Social and Political Thought*, C.W. Kegley and R.W. Bretall eds (New York, Macmillan, 1956), G. Harland, *The Thought of Reinhold Niebuhr* (New York, Oxford UP, 1960), R. Harries ed., *Reinhold Niebuhr and the Issues of Our Time* (London, Oxford, 1986) and K. Durkin, *Reinhold Niebuhr* (London, Chapman, 1989).

ANS J. VAN DER BENT

NIEMÖLLER, MARTIN. B. 14.1.1892, Lippstadt, Germany; d. 6.3.1984, Wiesbaden. Member of the provisional committee of the WCC, 1946-48, Niemöller was a member of the central and executive committees, 1948-61, and a president of the WCC, 1961-68. His anti-Nazi religious activities and support of the Confessing Church* led to his arrest in 1937 and confinement in the concentration camps of Sachsenhausen and Dachau, most of the time as a "personal prisoner" of Hitler. He was freed by Allied troops shortly before he was scheduled to be executed. He took a leading part in the Stuttgart declaration* of guilt, 1945, and then was head of the foreign relations department of the Evangelical Church in Germany, 1945-56, and president of the territorial church of Hesse and Nassau, 1947-64. A submarine commander during the first world war, he argued after the second world war against German re-armament and for German neutrality. He opposed the creation of the Federal Republic of Germany in 1949, and was also against any crusade against communism and was a vigorous opponent of US involvement in Vietnam. His visits to the Soviet Union did much to bring the churches there into the ecumenical movement. Ordained in 1924 a minister of the Protestant Church in Westphalia, in 1931 Niemöller was appointed pastor at Berlin-Dahlem. His works include *Reden, 1945-1954, 1955-1957* (Darmstadt, Stimme der Gemeinde, 1957-58) and *Reden, Predigten, Aufsätze, 1937 bis 1980* (Berlin, Union, 1980). See *Martin Niemöller: Festschrift zum 90. Geburtstag*, H. Kloppenburg ed. (Cologne, Pahl-Rugenstein, 1982) and J. Bentley, *Martin Niemöller* (Oxford, Oxford UP, 1984).

ANS J. VAN DER BENT

NILES, DANIEL THAMBYRAJAH. B. 4.5.1908, Ceylon; d. 17.7.1970, Vellore, India. D.T. Niles (always affectionately known as "D.T.") was active in the ecumenical movement for four decades and for the last three of these was one of its best-known leaders. He was the son of a distinguished lawyer and the grandson of a much-loved pastor and poet. After school and college in his native Jaffna, he studied theology in Bangalore from 1929 to 1933. He was already much involved with the Student Christian Movement and from 1933 was its national secretary and took part in the meeting of the general committee of the World Student Christian Federation* in Sofia. During this period he also served for a time with the

WSCF staff in Geneva. In 1936 he was ordained to the ministry of the Methodist church and served for three years as district evangelist. He took a prominent part in the International Missionary Council* Tambaram conference of 1938 as a speaker and as secretary of the section on "The Authority of the Faith". Following Tambaram he went to Europe as part of a team bringing the message of Tambaram to the British churches, and then for a year (1939-40) he was in Geneva as evangelism secretary of the World's YMCA.*

Returning to Ceylon, he served from 1941 to 1945 as general secretary of the National Christian Council, the first full-time holder of that office. This introduced him to the arts of interchurch relations, in which he was to become such a master. From 1942 he organized annual theological conferences, which for the first time included Roman Catholics. He was chosen as one of the initial members of the negotiating committee for church union when it was set up in 1945. He was also involved in interfaith dialogue,* having been much influenced by his work at Tambaram with Hendrik Kraemer, "who made me see how essential it was for a Christian to think Christianly of other faiths". In his autobiographical memoir Niles speaks of "the many heart-searching conversations" he had with a Hindu friend as

D.T. Niles (WCC photo)

he tried to work out his beliefs on the relation of the gospel to other faiths.

In 1946 Niles was appointed to his first pastoral charge, which he was to hold for five years, at Point Pedro. During this period he was again to be in Europe for the WCC assembly at Amsterdam, where, with John R. Mott, he preached at the opening service. From 1948 to 1952 he was chairman of the WCC's Youth Department and from 1953 to 1959 he was executive secretary of its Department of Evangelism. Meanwhile in 1950 the Methodist church had transferred him to the Maradana pastorate, and he was also director of the YMCA Bible Study Institute in Colombo. Niles strongly held that those involved in ecumenical work should keep firm roots in the local church,* and while he held the evangelism portfolio in Geneva, he was at the same time superintending minister of St Peter's Church and principal of Jaffna Central College. It is not surprising that even Niles refers to this as "a heavy period".

From 1953 he was chairman of the WSCF and, along with Philippe Maury, planned and carried through an ambitious programme on "The Life and Mission of the Church", with the Strasbourg conference of 1960 as its centre-piece. Meanwhile from 1954 to 1964 he was also chairman of the northern district of the Methodist church while continuing to be heavily involved in the work of the WCC, including the assemblies at Evanston and New Delhi. From 1959 to 1960 he was also Henry Emerson Fosdick professor at Union Theological Seminary, New York.

Meanwhile in 1957 Niles embarked upon what was to be the major work of the last decade of his life. In that year, at Prapat in Sumatra, the decision was taken to establish an East Asia conference of churches, with Niles as its first general secretary. This, the forerunner of other regional bodies, was largely Niles's brain-child, and he was its unquestioned leader. It embodied his conviction about the local rooting of ecumenical work, with a dispersed staff all carrying responsibilities in their churches. Niles's deep commitment to local unity also caused him to be wary of powerful denominational bodies acting on a world scale. This led him, from 1961 onwards, to take an active part in the work of the World Methodist Council,* and he was responsible for the "Niles plan" for a world committee on missionary affairs to guide the council.

In August 1968, he took over the leadership of the Methodist Church in Sri Lanka as the president of the Methodist Conference. In the same year he resigned from his position as general secretary of the East Asia Christian Conference and was made its chairman. His report of the ten years of the EACC under his guidance entitled "Ideas and Services" coupled reporting with envisioning the future of the EACC. It later became the basis for re-organizing the work of the EACC at the Singapore assembly in 1973, when it was re-named the Christian Conference of Asia. He was again asked to preach the opening sermon at the WCC assembly, this time at the fourth assembly (Uppsala 1968). At this assembly he was also elected to the WCC presidium. In 1970 he went to the Christian Medical Hospital in Vellore, India, for treatment and later an operation for cancer, where he died.

Along with this astonishing range of public responsibilities, there was an almost ceaseless succession of journeys to all the six continents to preach, lecture and conduct university missions. The fruits of this labour were made available to others through more than a score of books, including *That They May Have Life* (London, Lutterworth, 1952), *Upon the Earth* (London, Lutterworth, 1962), and *A Testament of Faith* (London, Epworth, 1972). Perhaps the one which will be longest in use, however, is the *EACC Hymnal*, for which he wrote a large number of English verse translations of Asian hymns. He was not, and did not pretend to be, a great theologian, but he had immensely fruitful theological and personal friendships with most of the leading theological thinkers of the time, and these enriched his writing and speaking. He was a great preacher, evangelist and pastor. Above all, he was an expositor of the Bible. His friend Bishop Kulendran has said of him: "He went to the Bible not to pick up a verse but to think with the biblical writers." He was also an ecumenical statesman, a strategist whose long-term planning did much to influence ecumenical development, and also a skillful tactician who could change a situation with a brilliant and unexpected move. He could outwit his opponents, but he did not make enemies. Central to his whole life was the

giving and receiving of friendship. Typical of the man are these words from one of the last sermons he preached: "When I am dead, many things will be said about me — that I held this and that position and did this and that thing. For me, all these are irrelevant. The only important thing that I can say about myself is that I, too, am one whom Jesus Christ loved and for whom he died" (Gal. 2:20). Next to his love of God was the devotion which bound him to his wife, Dulcie, whom he married in 1935. A few months after his death, she followed him.

LESSLIE NEWBIGIN

S.C. Neill, *Brothers of the Faith*, New York, Abingdon, 1960.

NISSIOTIS, NIKOS ANGELOS.

B. 21.5.1925, Athens, Greece; d. 17.8.1986, Athens. On the staff of the Ecumenical Institute, Bossey,* beginning in 1958, and its director 1966-74, Nissiotis was a member of the WCC central committee, 1975-83, and moderator of the Commission on Faith and Order,* 1976-83. He helped design the primary strategy for contemporary ecumenical theological work, including the 1982 text *Baptism, Eucharist and Ministry*.* General secretary of the Student Christian Movement in Greece after the second world war, he was active in the World Student Christian Federation.* He addressed New Delhi 1961 on the role of the Orthodox churches in the ecumenical movement, and was a WCC observer at the Second Vatican Council,* 1962-65. He studied theology in Greece and Switzerland (with Emil Brunner in Zurich and Karl Barth in Basel), received his doctorate from the University of Louvain and was professor in the theological faculty of the University of Athens. As a member of the International Olympic Committee, he lectured frequently on the philosophy of Olympic sport to young athletes. Nissiotis was one of the foremost Orthodox ecumenists and a leading theological spokesperson for the Eastern Orthodox churches. Among numerous contributions in Greek, English, French and German, he wrote *Die Theologie der Ostkirche im ökumenischen Dialog* (Stuttgart, Evang. Verlagswerk, 1968).

ANS J. VAN DER BENT

NON-GOVERNMENTAL ORGAN-
IZATIONS.

The term "non-governmental organization" (NGO) gained popularity in usage only in the second half of the 20th century and refers generally to any special-interest institution which, though it may receive funds from a government, is independent both in policy-setting and administration. Thus, academic institutions, aid agencies, churches, professional organizations and peace and disarmament groups are NGOs. The term has been used to refer to private organizations or voluntary agencies.

The origin of the term is unknown. However, the Charter of the United Nations,* adopted in 1945, made it recognized terminology in international diplomacy. Article 71 of the charter provides for consultative relationship between the UN and the NGOs, especially in the social, economic and cultural fields. Currently over 800 NGOs enjoy this consultative relationship, the nature of which is carefully spelled out in resolution 1296 adopted by the Economic and Social Council in 1968.

Much of the most dynamic international cooperation in recent decades has been provided by NGOs through the Conference of Non-Governmental Organizations (CONGO) in consultative status with the UN. CONGO is run by a bureau of 20 organizations elected triennially and consists primarily of committees dealing with human rights,* disarmament, development,* women, youth,* narcotics, transnational corporations* and decolonization.* These committees are located in Geneva, New York and Vienna.

NGOs recognized by the UN have access to UN premises and meetings and are able to make representation in oral and written forms. They have also organized important parallel NGO activities at several significant UN conferences devoted to food, environment, population, habitat, women, narcotics, crime, disarmament, human rights, new international economic order and the law of the sea treaty.

The WCC has been an important NGO. Represented at the UN through the Commission of the Churches on International Affairs (CCIA), its history of UN involvement began at the UN's founding general assembly in San Francisco, in 1945, where Frederick Nolde, the first CCIA director, was chosen by the NGOs to speak to the general assembly on the significance of article 71 of the charter. For three decades, the CCIA's annual comments on the general assembly's agenda items were popular with diplomats and NGOs alike. Frequently, the UN secretariat seeks information on various political situations from the WCC and requests it to address the UN on behalf of the NGOs. The CCIA staff participate actively in CONGO and its standing committees.

The following organizations within the ecumenical family are among the NGOs in consultative status with the UN: Anglican Consultative Council, Archdiocese of the Greek Orthodox Church in Northern America, Baptist World Alliance, Christian Peace Conference, Church World Service, Conference of European Churches, Friends World Consultative Committee, Lutheran World Federation, Salvation Army, World Alliance of Reformed Churches, World Federation of Methodist Women, World Student Christian Federation, World YMCA and World YWCA.

See also **United Nations**.

VICTOR W.C. HSU

NORTH AMERICA: CANADA.

The Canadian ecumenical movement began before the 19th century. First, the transfer of political authority from France to the United Kingdom (1763) introduced a broad variety of denominational groups into Canada. Most of these derived from older communities in the American colonies or Great Britain. The independence of the USA 20 years later accelerated the pace of settlement in the so-called frontier areas, bringing in thousands of white, black and Amerindian Christians who chose to remain under the British crown. Most new townships had only one or two congregations, and many individuals simply joined the denomination which had first begun to serve in their area. Roman Catholicism and the principal branches of Protestant Christianity quickly established ecclesiastical jurisdictions according to their own models in the zones of more concentrated settlement. Nevertheless, the continuing expansion of the region under intensive cultivation produced a recurrent pattern of regular multidenominational worship in a large number of less populous municipalities.

Around the turn of the 20th century, theological convergence and pragmatic considerations combined to inspire a widespread feeling that the Christian community, or at least the Protestant groups, should unite. Canadian Christians, it was said, ought to overcome the divisions inherited from Renaissance Europe and join in a fellowship of common faith and witness adapted to the special circumstances of their new society. Five major denominations began serious negotiations, but eventually the Anglicans and Baptists withdrew and only Congregationalists, Methodists and two-thirds of the Presbyterians merged to form the United Church of Canada in 1925. This was the very first such union of churches from different ecclesiological traditions in the world.

The United Church declared itself to be open to further combinations, and its representatives have held talks with people from several other churches. Conversations with Anglicans and Disciples came near to agreement in the late 1960s but finally ended without achieving their objective, and only the Evangelical United Brethren and a few independent congregations have joined during the years since the original union. In 1989, the Anglican Church of Canada and the Evangelical Lutheran Church in Canada formally agreed to a mutual sharing of word and sacraments, but with no fusion of structures. No other pluriconfessional mergers or covenants have been realized, although there have been several series of bilateral exchanges involving most of the churches now represented in the country, including the Orthodox.

After the initial wave of ecumenical enthusiasm had achieved the union of 1925, confessional loyalties re-asserted themselves with some force. Gradually, however, interest developed in a conciliar model as a middle option between uncompromising rivalry and corporate amalgamation, until in 1944 leaders of half a dozen denominations met at Yorkminster Baptist Church in Toronto to establish the Canadian Council of Churches (CCC). Representatives of the same groups were among the founders of the WCC in Amsterdam four years later. The CCC has continued to grow, at the end of 1989 comprising 15 full members, including five Orthodox churches. The council's own staff has never become very large, but it has served as a focus for a range of ecumenical activities undertaken directly by the churches or through a number of other institutions.

The ecumenical coalitions are a special feature of the Canadian ecclesiastical scene. Each coalition is supported by the appropriate divisions of a group of church offices or mission societies, and each addresses a particular concern of the Christian community in Canada. Some have a geographic focus, others seek to inform public opinion and influence policy. Yet another type of coalition specializes in economic affairs. Altogether, there are about a dozen coalitions at any given time in official affiliation with the coalition administration committee of the CCC.

The Ecumenical Forum of Canada, whose roots reach back to the early 1920s, operates now as an agency of the CCC. It offers ecumenical training to prospective missionaries and special courses for people returning to Canada after a period of church service abroad. The forum also conducts overseas tours for Canadian theological students, and each year it brings a respected ecumenical personality to visit interchurch groups in several provinces. A more academic sister organization is the Churches' Council for Theological Education, which assists the churches and seminaries in co-ordinating ministerial formation across denominational and geographical obstacles, while the Canadian Association for Pastoral Education has a special interest in the training of hospital chaplains.

The Student Christian Movement (SCM), a major participant in the CCC's youth working group, provides ecumenical leadership on campus and forms vital contacts for the present and future among participating churches in all parts of the country. Another ecumenical organization with an active programme and a long history of working with the CCC is the Canadian Bible Society. Of course, the SCM and the Bible Society both have strong links to their own international federations. The Women's Inter-Church Council, an autonomous network of Christian women's organizations, is the Canadian link in the World Day of Prayer* structure and the touchstone for Canadian involvement in the Ecumenical Decade of the Churches in Solidarity with Women.*

In the quarter-century since the Second Vatican Council, the Roman Catholic Church has become an integral part of ecumenical life in Canada. RC dioceses and orders belong to

Vancouver, site of the WCC's sixth assembly (1983) (WCC/Peter Williams)

most of the coalitions and local interchurch councils, and in 1986 the Canadian Conference of Catholic Bishops became an associate member of the CCC. Relations between the CCC and the Evangelical Fellowship of Canada have been cordial, and at least two churches belong to both. Unlike the council, the fellowship also has individual memberships, and it is still true that the larger denominations in its ranks are reluctant to be too closely associated with the conciliar movement because of perceived differences in theological outlook.

A decline in church attendance and a deterioration in the economy have lately reduced the material resources available to Canadian churches and their ecumenical institutions. It is too early to assume that this trend is irreversible, but the constraints have already brought a bracing challenge to the churches to define and express their ecumenical commitment in terms of the current situation. The mood is one of cautious optimism: the various coalitions are renewing their mandates, the Ecumenical Forum is emerging with fresh confidence from a period of personnel and programmatic transition, and the CCC member churches are seeking to re-draft their agenda of common action. Beyond the vari-

ous forms, the content of ecumenical encounter will in any case remain a vital component of Christian life both locally and nationally, as it has been since there were first churches in Canada.

According to its constitution, the CCC is "a fellowship of churches which confess the Lord Jesus Christ as God and Saviour according to the scriptures and therefore seek to fulfill together their common calling to the glory of one God, Father, Son and Holy Spirit" (see **WCC, basis of**). It began its work in 1944 upon the approval of its letters patent by the parliament of Canada. Gradually, the original small group of Protestant and Anglican churches increased, so that after 45 years of activity the CCC had 15 full member churches and one associate member.

Most of the country's major denominations, in terms of numbers of adherents, are part of the CCC: the United Church of Canada, the Anglican Church of Canada, the Presbyterian Church in Canada, the Evangelical Lutheran Church in Canada, the Christian Church (Disciples of Christ) and the Canadian Yearly Meeting of the Religious Society of Friends are involved in virtually every aspect of the CCC's life. The smaller churches participate in the measure that their resources permit: these include the Baptist Convention of Ontario and Quebec, the Salvation Army in Canada and Bermuda, the Council of Reformed Churches in Canada, the Greek Orthodox Church, the Ethiopian Orthodox Church, the Orthodox Church in America, the Coptic Orthodox Church, the Armenian Orthodox Church and the Polish National Catholic Church. Since becoming the CCC's first associate member in 1986, the Canadian Conference of Catholic Bishops has joined in the work of several of the council's commissions and committees.

The triennial assembly is at once the CCC's principal public manifestation and its supreme authority. Delegates are chosen by the member churches, and representatives of local ecumenical groups and such related bodies as the Student Christian Movement and the Women's Inter-Church Council also attend. Each assembly elects the officers who will serve for the next three years.

Three commissions and four standing committees co-ordinate the CCC's operations. Each commission includes representatives of those denominations wishing to join in its particular agenda, whether or not they are members of the council itself: in this way, the Mennonite Central Committee of Canada, the Christian Reformed Church and other bodies have made valuable contributions to Canadian ecumenical life. The Committee on Justice and Peace sponsors discussions relating to human rights, international affairs and similar concerns. It also oversees the work of the dozen ecumenical coalitions which the Canadian churches have launched at various times to generate public interest and action on specific issues, e.g. the Inter-Church Committee on Refugees, the Inter-Church Committee on Human Rights in Latin America or the Taskforce on the Churches and Corporate Responsibility. This commission plays an important role in co-ordinating the overseas assistance programmes of several churches and church-related organizations.

The commission on ecumenical education and communications issues a newsletter and explores possibilities for increasing interchurch co-operation in the fields of religious education and information. Finally, the commission on faith and witness fosters ecumenical theological reflection, such as the recently completed common catechesis, which will soon be submitted to the churches for internal discussion. The CCC standing committees deal with matters relating to finances, the constitution, nominations and personnel. In addition, the council sponsors an ecumenical committee on Protestant chaplaincy in the Canadian armed forces, and it works with representatives of other bodies on an interfaith committee advising the federal government on matters concerning prison chaplains.

The CCC has never been large or wealthy, but it has consistently played a pivotal role in discerning and realizing the ecumenical agenda in Canada. It has also made a significant contribution to interchurch co-operation on an international scale, both through the structures of the WCC and in direct co-operation with regional and national organizations in every part of the world. As it nears its jubilee in 1994, the council, with its member churches, remains steadfast in its commitment to national and global ecumenical understanding and the quest for a closer unity of Christians everywhere.

STUART E. BROWN

NORTH AMERICA: UNITED STATES OF AMERICA. Bewildering diversity and division have always marked Christianity in the USA. Over 250 different Christian churches exist, some large and some very small, each with its independent authority and organization. Their separations are rooted in different theological, ethnic, social and racial backgrounds.

The reasons for this fragmentation provide insight into the peculiar character of the US church and its struggle for unity:* (1) all the European schisms were transplanted to US soil; (2) a radical individualism and revivalism, especially on the frontier, served the spirit of volunteerism and isolation; (3) religious freedom and the separation of church and state (i.e. no church holds a privileged position) was a fundamental civil doctrine which encouraged the rise of new religious groups; (4) different waves of immigrants brought and continue to bring their diverse ethnic, cultural and national traditions as well as the isolating tensions which these produce. In this milieu a new form of the church, the denomination (see **denominationalism**), became dominant, and the church became identified with partisan names and traditions: Adventist, Baptist, Congregational, Disciples of Christ, Episcopal, Lutheran, Methodist, Moravian, Orthodox, Pentecostal, Presbyterian, Quaker, Roman Catholic, and churches of many other shades and varieties.

The proliferation of divided denominations, however, was countered by an equally dramatic movement towards unity. Already beginning in the early 19th century, US Christianity has been engaged in the struggle between sectarianism and ecumenism, between division and unity. This ecumenical pilgrimage can be described in three categories.

The first approach is association through *voluntary, non-denominational bodies*. Individual Christians, not churches as such, sought common action on particular tasks related to evangelism, religious education, social witness and reform. They did not necessarily envisage the unity of the churches. Those institutions which early drew Christians together for fellowship and mission were the American Board of Commissioners for Foreign Missions (1810), the American Home Missionary Society (1826), the American Bible Society (1826), the American Sunday School Union (1824), the American Peace Society (1828), the American Anti-slavery Society (1833), and youth student movements such as the Young Men's Christian Association (US, 1852), the Young Women's Christian Association (1872), and the Student Volunteer Movement (1886).

Particularly important was the US branch of the Evangelical Alliance (1867), a fellowship within the World's Evangelical Alliance* (London 1846). Its purpose was "to bring individual Christians into closer fellowship and co-operation on the basis of the spiritual union which already exists in the vital relation of Christ to the members of his body in all ages and all countries". The alliance championed Christian unity, religious liberty for minorities in countries where an established church or other religions discriminated against them, the Week of Prayer for Christian Unity,* arbitrations for peace, and international mission. Although it was an association of persons not churches, the Evangelical Alliance was a precursor to later ecumenical bodies in the US and worldwide. The pattern of collaboration among individual Christians in addressing crisis concerns has continued throughout the 20th century in dealing with local and global issues such as hunger, justice, peace, theological education, interfaith dialogue and care for the poor and oppressed.

A second approach to unity in the US is *conciliar co-operation in mission*. The earliest model and pioneer was the Federal Council of Churches of Christ, constituted in 1908 (see **federalism**). Its uniqueness lay in the fact that it assembled churches in official co-operation and federation in order "to manifest the essential oneness of the Christian churches of America in Jesus Christ as their divine Lord and Saviour", by bringing the churches into united service, by encouraging devotional fellowship and mutual counsel concerning the spiritual life and religious activities of the churches and by securing a larger combined church influence on what affects moral social conditions. The Federal Council had no authority to draw up a creed, to propose a common form of worship or church government, or to limit in any way the full autonomy of the member churches. Yet 29 Protestant churches set a new course for ecumenism through their common witness in evangelism, Christian education, mission at home and overseas, and international justice. The majority of the Orthodox churches in the US joined the Federal Council's successors decades later.

In 1950 the co-operative impulse took another major step with the formation of the National Council of the Churches of Christ (NCCC) in the USA. The Federal Council had represented only a segment of co-operative activity between the churches. Other interdenominational agencies pursued common ecumenical work, such as the Foreign Missions Conference of North America, the Home Missions Council, the International Council of Religious Education, and the United Council of Church Women. These agencies formed one inclusive national council, including 29 member churches, confessing "Jesus Christ as the divine Lord and Savior". Operating through what Henry Pitney van Dusen once described as "the most complex and intricate piece of ecclesiastical machinery this planet has ever witnessed", the NCCC's programme for the past four decades has focused on racial inclusiveness and liberation, global mission and international service, through relief and development, Christian education and Bible translations, Christian unity and Faith and Order, stewardship, and international affairs. In 1981 the NCCC changed its mandate and character from "a co-operative agency of the churches" to "a community of Christian communions". Such a deeper covenantal relationship brings potential for the US church to manifest more fully the unity of the churches and to serve God and the world in common mission.

This re-ordering has come with no little tension and conflict over the NCCC's leadership and programmatic implications of being a community of Christian communions. In July 1989, the general secretary resigned, and new directions were pursued that would bring the stronger involvement of the member churches and create a leaner structure of four programme units entitled unity and relationships, international witness and service, discipleship and communication, and prophetic justice. The current crisis of the NCCC is symbolized by reduced contributions from member communions of 50% since 1975 and staff reductions of more than half. In general this is an expression of the crisis within the mainline churches in the US as they face an era of diminished funds and their displacement from being the centre of religious and moral leadership within American culture. The future will require Protestant and Orthodox churches in the NCCC to play a humbler role and to participate more intentionally with conservative-evangelicals and the Roman Catholic Church in a wider ecumenism.

A critical chapter in the conciliar movement was the leadership given by US church leaders in the formation of the WCC. Americans had played key roles in the predecessor movements — the World Student Christian Federation,* Faith and Order,* Life and Work,* and the International Missionary Council.* As the convergence of these movements began to take place in what became the WCC, a small cadre of Americans helped to conceive and give organizational shape to the new world ecumenical body. Among those who played pivotal roles were William Adams Brown, Samuel McCrea Cavert (who first commended the name "World Council of Churches"), John R. Mott, and Henry Knox Sherrill; staff whose untiring efforts served the emerging council were Henry Smith Leiper and Robert S. Bilheimer.

Communion service, Consultation on Church Union, Cincinnati, Ohio (United Methodist Board of Global Ministries, New York/John C. Goodwin)

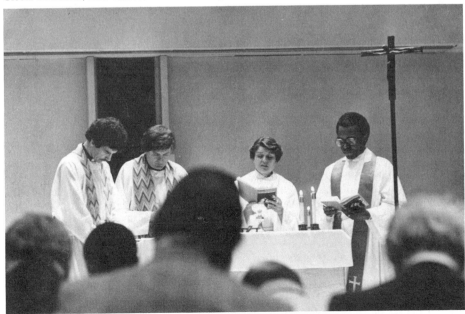

The third approach to ecumenism which marks US church history is the search for *visible church unity*. While federation or co-operation is often thought to be the most dominant form of American ecumenism, it is important to realize that the witness to church union or unity is equally significant. In union — a dynamic, growing concept — the traditions and practices of two or more divided churches are blended into a common identity in faith and brought into a shared ecclesial and sacramental life enriched by diversity. Beginning in the 19th century, four US churches have given special leadership towards visible unity: German and Swiss Reformed, Lutheran, Episcopal, and Disciples of Christ.

Philip Schaff, a Swiss Reformed church historian and immigrant, greatly influenced the ecumenical perspective of the American churches by his prolific writings and by his work in the Evangelical Alliance and other bodies committed to Christian unity. In 1893, he called for "federal or confederative union". Among American Lutherans, Samuel Simon Schmucker brought a wide vision of unity by calling for the formation of the United Apostolic Protestant Church. Its doctrines would be based on the scriptures and a united confession of faith, while its local congregations would retain their worship and practices; unity would be experienced by open communion and a mutual interchange of members and ministry.

The Episcopal Church produced three articulate advocates of the unity of the church. Thomas Hubbard Vail proposed one "comprehensive church", which he defined as the currently constituted Episcopal Church. More irenically, William Augustus Muhlenberg proposed an "Evangelical Catholic" church based on a diversity of worship and discipline and with a common episcopal ministry which all churches would gladly receive. William Reed Huntington offered the Episcopal Church as "the Church of the Reconciliation" and proposed a four-point platform as the basis of all future church union attempts. Later named the Chicago-Lambeth Quadrilateral,* this proposal included: the holy scripture as the word of God, the primitive creeds as the rule of faith, the two sacraments of baptism and the Lord's supper, and the historical episcopate.

The Disciples of Christ* taught the sin of sectarianism and division in the church and articulated a passion for its visible unity. Barton Warren Stone called upon all Christians to make Christian unity "our polar star". His plea for union, contained in the classic ecumenical document *The Last Will and Testament of the Springfield Presbytery* (1804), declares: "We will that this body die, be dissolved, and sink into union with the body of Christ at large." Two Scots-Irish immigrants, Thomas Campbell and his son Alexander, found unbearable the anti-ecumenical teachings and practices of the 19th-century Presbyterians. Reluctantly they formed another church, the Disciples. Pledging to bring about the unity of all Christians based on the simplicity of the biblical faith, Thomas Campbell taught: "The church of Christ upon earth is essentially, intentionally, and constitutionally one" (1809). The churches led by Stone and the Campbells united at Lexington, Kentucky, in 1832, an event which launched the ecumenical leadership of the Disciples within the church universal.

In the 20th-century church, union among the US churches was proposed — but not achieved — by three multilateral initiatives. Between 1918 and 1920, largely under Presbyterian leadership, the American Council on Organic Union sought to bring 19 "evangelical" churches into the United Churches of Christ in America. Although preserving denominational autonomy initially, the plan encouraged collaboration in many mission areas as the first step towards fuller, organic union.* In 1935 the Methodist evangelist E. Stanley Jones called for "union with a federal structure". Modelled upon the US federal-state system, the various denominations would become branches of "the United Church of America". In 1949 the Conference on Church Union offered to unite those churches which were "in sufficient accord in essentials of Christian faith and order", and which "already accord one another mutual recognition of ministries and of sacraments". Important for the future of American Christianity, this plan, called the Greenwich plan, involved both predominantly white churches and black churches, namely the African Methodist Episcopal and the Christian Methodist Episcopal.

In 1962 the most dramatic and far-reaching movement towards church unity in the US was the formation of the Consultation on Church Union.* COCU resulted from a sermon preached two years earlier at Grace Cathedral, San Francisco, by Eugene Carson Blake, stated clerk of the United Presbyterian Church in the USA and later general secretary of the WCC. He called upon the churches to form a united church "truly catholic, truly evangelical, and truly reformed". Future theological commissions and plenaries of the nine COCU churches produced *Principles of Church Union* (1966), *A Plan of Union for the Church of Christ Uniting* (1970), two ecumenical liturgies of word and sacrament (1968, 1984), *The COCU Consensus* (1984) and *The Churches in Covenant Communion* (1989). Far beyond the reconciliation of historic divisions in the church, which centre on baptism, the eucharist and ministry, COCU illustrates a new ecumenism by confronting the divisions of the church and the alienation caused by racism* and classism.

The US churches have participated strongly in interconfessional bilateral dialogues,* a new expression of the ecumenical movement which gained importance in the 1960s largely through the impact of Vatican II. The significance of the bilaterals in the US can be understood only by listing those held in recent decades, many of which are linked to international dialogues: American Baptist-Roman Catholic, Anglican-Roman Catholic, Episcopal-Lutheran, Episcopal-Orthodox, Disciples of Christ-Roman Catholic, Lutheran-Reformed, Lutheran-Roman Catholic, Methodist-Roman Catholic, Reformed-Roman Catholic and Southern Baptist-Roman Catholic. Each bilateral is contributing to the future unity of the church; each is at a different place in the chronology of reconciliation. Undoubtedly the bilaterals and the multilateral conversations (e.g. NCCC and WCC F&O), church unity processes, et al., are making vital contributions to the one ecumenical movement.

PAUL A. CROW, Jr

S.M. Cavert, *The American Churches in the Ecumenical Movement, 1900-1968*, New York, Association, 1968 • S.M. Cavert, *Church Cooperation and Unity in America: A Historical Review, 1900-1970*, New York, Association, 1970 • *Digests of the Proceedings of the Meetings of the Consultation on Church Union*, Princeton, NJ, COCU, 1962-88 • F.S. Mead, *Handbook of Denominations in the United States*, 8th ed., Nashville, TN, Abingdon, 1985 • J.R. Nelson ed., *Christian Unity in North America: A Symposium, Studies after Oberlin, 1957*, St Louis, MO, Bethany, 1958 • R.E. Richey ed., *Denominationalism*, Nashville, TN, Abingdon, 1977 • W.J. Schmidt, *Architect of Unity: A Biography of S. McCrea Cavert*, New York, Friendship, 1978 • W.J. Whalen, *Separated Brethren: A Survey of Protestant, Anglican, Eastern Orthodox and Other Denominations in the United States*, Huntington, IN, Our Sunday Visitor, 1979 • D.H. Yoder, "Christian Unity in Nineteenth-Century America", in *A History of the Ecumenical Movement, 1517-1948*, R. Rouse & S.C. Neill eds, 3rd ed., WCC, 1986.

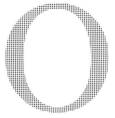

ODELL HODGSON, LUIS E.

B. 28.11.1912, Buenos Aires, Argentina. Odell Hodgson represented his country at the first world conference of Christian youth at Amsterdam 1939. Between the assemblies at New Delhi and Uppsala he was a member of the working committee of the Department on Church and Society and co-operated in various interchurch aid activities. He represented the International Missionary Council* in the joint committee that worked out its integration with the WCC, 1959-61. Lay leader of the Methodist Church in Argentina and Uruguay, and first lay president of the Methodist church in Uruguay, 1973-75, he participated in the initiation of the Latin American Union of Evangelical Youth (ULAJE) in 1941 and was its vice-chairman, 1945-55, was executive secretary of Church and Society in Latin America (ISAL), 1961-68, and contributed to the formation of the Commission for Evangelical Unity in Latin America (UNELAM), 1963-64.

ANS J. VAN DER BENT

OIKOUMENE.

"Oikoumene" is derived from the Greek word *oikein*, to inhabit. With the meaning of "inhabited earth" or "the whole world", the term has been used since Herodotos (5th century B.C.). Since the Hellenistic period the term has been used in *secular* contexts to refer politically to the realm of the Greco-Roman empire or to mark the cultural distinction between the civilized world and the lands of the barbarians.

The *biblical* writings generally follow the secular usage, e.g. taking oikoumene as a synonym for "earth" (Ps. 24:1), yet without giving particular prominence to the term. In the New Testament the political connotation of the term is visible in Luke 4:5-7 (cf. also Luke 2:1; Acts 17:6) and in Revelation (esp. 16:14). The expected reign of God can be called the "oikoumene to come" (Heb. 2:5).

The subsequent, much more widespread *ecclesiastical* use of the term is linked with the extension of the Christian community across the entire Roman empire. By the 4th century the oikoumene had become the "Christian world", with the double (political and religious) meaning of the "Christian empire" and the "whole church". The adjective *oikoumenikos* (Latin *universalis* or *generalis*) refers to everything that has universal validity. Thus, ecumenical is a quality claimed for particular councils and their dogmatic decisions (see **ecumenical councils**), or is used as a title of honour for specific patriarchal sees or for respected teachers of the whole church.

In Roman Catholic and Orthodox tradition, which preserved the memory of the early link between church and empire, the term remained in use, though its meaning became more and more technical. The churches of the Reformation which developed into regional or national entities lost sight of the ecumenical dimension for more than 200 years. The pietistic revival (under Nicholas von Zinzendorf et al.) led to the re-discovery of the worldwide missionary calling of the church as well as to a renewal of the consciousness of Christian unity* and fellowship across the differences of nations and confessions (Evangelical Alliance,* 1846). In both contexts the term "ecumenical" has been reclaimed; the specifically modern meaning, however, refers to a spiritual attitude manifesting the awareness of the oneness of the people of God* and the longing for its restoration (Söderblom).

Present-day usage is largely conditioned by the new reality of the organized ecumenical movement, as represented in particular by the WCC, and the different ways of reacting to this reality. The *WCC* itself, in an early statement by its central committee (1951), gave an account of its understanding of the term "ecumenical". In the light of the original Greek meaning, the term should be used "to describe everything that relates to the whole task of the whole church to bring the gospel to the whole world. It therefore covers... both unity and mission in the context of the whole world." It has proved difficult to maintain the tension built into this definition.

Thus, the *Roman Catholic Church*, after having overcome its very strong initial reservations, accepted the new usage of the term placing the emphasis, however, exclusively on the unity* dimension. The Decree on Ecumenism of the Second Vatican Council* (1964) defines: "The term 'ecumenical movement' indicates the initiatives and activities encouraged and organized... to promote Christian unity."

The *Orthodox churches* have participated actively in the ecumenical movement from the beginning. With a critical accent they defined their understanding of the ecumenical movement as "ecumenism in time": "The immediate objective of the ecumenical search is, according to the Orthodox understanding, a re-integration of Christian mind, a recovery of apostolic tradition, a fullness of Christian vision and belief, in agreement with all ages" (New Delhi 1961).

Among the *churches of the Reformation* there is no common understanding of ecumenism. For many Protestant majority churches "ecumenical" refers to the external relations with churches in foreign countries. For those

living among a diversity of denominations, "ecumenical" means the coming and being together of churches. For many, the ecumenical movement represents the manifestation of Christian concern for a world community in justice and peace. Over against this "worldly ecumenism" conservative evangelicals advocate a "confessing ecumenism" gathering the true believers from among the churches.

Churchly and worldly, spiritual and missionary-social dimensions belong together in a comprehensive understanding of oikoumene. Oikoumene is a relational, dynamic concept which extends beyond the fellowship of Christians and churches to the human community within the whole of creation.* The transformation of the oikoumene as the "inhabited earth" into the living household *(oikos)* of God — that remains the calling of the ecumenical movement.

KONRAD RAISER

W.A. Visser 't Hooft, *The Meaning of Ecumenical*, the Burge Memorial Lecture 1953, London, SCM, 1953 • W.A. Visser 't Hooft, "The Word 'Ecumenical': Its History and Use", in *A History of the Ecumenical Movement, 1517-1948*, R. Rouse & S.C. Neill eds, WCC, 1986.

OLD CATHOLIC CHURCH. The Old Catholic Church (OCC) considers the ideal of the undivided church* of the first centuries to be the focus of unity,* while realizing at the same time that historically the actual existence of such a primitive undivided church is problematic. Therefore this ideal is perhaps even more a task for the future than a givenness of the past. In its active enthusiasm for the ecumenical movement from its very beginning, the OCC demonstrates its belief in the necessity of this task.

The history of the OCC as a separate institution goes back to the troubles of the post-Reformation period in the Netherlands. Since the Protestant rulers had ended the legal existence of the Roman Catholic Church and had forbidden its cult, the central authorities at Rome considered the Netherlands to have reverted to the status of a missionary area. Yet substantial parts of the Catholic church had remained intact and continued to function. Slowly but surely a conflict grew between the missionary ecclesiology of Roman missionaries and the more established ecclesiology of the secular clergy, who obeyed the apostolic vicars who had replaced the pre-Reformation bishops. This conflict was much worsened by accusations of Jansenism hurled at the secular clergy.

The outcome was the deposition, in 1702, of the apostolic vicar Peter Codde. As a consequence, a large part of the secular clergy with their parishes returned to the Roman party. The remaining ones finally chose their own archbishop of Utrecht, Cornelis Steen-oven, who was consecrated in 1723 by a sympathizing French (Canadian) bishop, Dominique Marie Varlet. This meant the confirmation of the Rome-Utrecht schism. The official name of the Dutch Old Catholic church became "Roman Catholic Church of the Old Episcopal Clergy", a name which became more significant when the Roman Catholic Church in the Netherlands restored its hierarchy in 1853.

In 1870 a movement against the proclamation of the infallibility of the pope by the First Vatican Council* arose in Germany, Switzerland and Austria-Hungary (esp. in Bohemia and Moravia). This is where the name "Old Catholic" originates. In 1889 these newly established Old Catholic churches united in the Union of Utrecht. The bishops published a declaration which begins with the motto of St Vincent of Lérins: "Let us hold that faith which has been believed everywhere, always, by all. For that is truly and in the strictest sense Catholic." This motto immediately refers to the controversy around the First Vatican Council. It should be used not so much as a formal criterion of the truth (otherwise nothing can ever change in the church) but rather as an appeal to all Christians to hold the Catholic faith* of all ages, in order that they may all be one in this faith. Until this unity has been achieved, no single church should make one-sided attempts to formulate new Christian dogmas.*

The Old Catholic churches, from their diverse beginnings, have remained episcopal churches (see **episcopacy**). Bishops are chosen in all the churches, and the role of synods and laity is increasingly important for the very identity of these churches. The Polish National Catholic Church of the USA and Canada, and the Polish Catholic Church in Poland, which joined the Union of Utrecht in the 20th century, basically have the same episcopal-synodical structure. Smaller Old Catholic communities in France, Sweden and Italy have their own priests but co-operate with neighbouring countries which have a bishop. In all churches of the Old Catholic communion, clerical celibacy ceased to be an obligation. Recently, women have been admitted to the diaconate.*

From 1870 onwards, intensive ecumenical contacts, especially with the Anglican and Eastern Orthodox churches, resulted in Anglican-Old Catholic intercommunion,* established by the 1931 Bonn agreement (the relationship was termed "full communion" in 1958) and in the Old Catholic-Orthodox dialogue,* 1973-87. In 1965 a concordat of full communion,* modelled after the Bonn agreement, was established with the Spanish Reformed Episcopal Church, the Lusitanian Church (Portugal) and the Philippine Independent Church.

Old Catholic involvement in the ecumenical movement formally began with the participation of two bishops, from Holland and Switzerland, at the Lausanne Faith and Order* conference (1927). This side of ecumenism has always remained a major interest for Old Catholics, who have never missed a F&O conference. Old Catholics also participate in other activities of the WCC and of national councils of churches.* The OCC believes the unity which the ecumenical movement seeks for the churches is one which needs to exist as a reconciled diversity* of all, rooted in the common faith and order of the ancient church of the first ecumenical councils* and their creeds.

MARTIN PARMENTIER

G. Huelin ed., *Old Catholics and Anglicans, 1931-1981*, Oxford, Oxford UP, 1983 • C.B. Moss, *The Old Catholic Movement: Its Origins and History*, London, SPCK, 1948.

OLD CATHOLIC-ORTHODOX DIALOGUE.

The relationship between Old Catholics and Orthodox has developed in five phases. The first phase was *1871-88*. While the Dutch Old Catholic church from the 18th century simply repeated the Roman anathemas* against the Eastern church, the young anti-Vatican movement in Germany began to take initiatives for a serious dialogue. Anglicans and Orthodox were both invited to the Bonn reunion conferences of 1874 and 1875. It was decided that agreement on the faith of the ecumenical councils,* scripture and Tradition,* the office of bishop and the seven sacraments was necessary for unity.* Both the developments which had led to the declaration of papal infallibility* in the Roman Catholic Church and those which in Protestantism had led to discontinuity with the early church were rejected. As for the filioque,* it was agreed that the clause had been inserted wrongly into the creed but that it was possible to explain it in an orthodox way.

The second phase was *1889-1917*, i.e. from the establishment of the Union of Utrecht until the Russian revolution. In this period, dialogue commissions were formed in Rotterdam (Old Catholic) and in St Petersburg (Orthodox). The commissions never met, but they exchanged memorandums on the filioque, the eucharist,* and the canonical validity of Old Catholic episcopal orders. Conservative theologians like Bishop Sergius of Yamburg (later patriarch of Moscow) required that Old Catholics should first of all recognize the Orthodox church as the one true church.* In 1904 Patriarch Joachim of Constantinople wrote an encyclical demanding an official and comprehensive confession of the faith of the Old Catholic churches. Because of communication problems this demand was not received in Utrecht (the demand was reiterated and met in 1970). In 1912 the Russian commission stated, with approval of the holy synod, that all questions put to the Rotterdam commission had been answered satisfactorily.

The third phase was *1920-60*. The initiative now shifted from Russia to Constantinople. Three months after the Anglican-Old Catholic Bonn agreement in 1931, an official Old Catholic-Orthodox conference met in Bonn. No serious dogmatic points of difference were found to remain, but the Orthodox delegates had no power to accept the conference's decisions on behalf of their churches. None of them raised the matter of the recently concluded Anglican-Old Catholic intercommunion.* Later Orthodox criticism of this relationship was disappointing for Old Catholics, as the chairman of the 1931 conference, one of the subsequent critics, was the fully informed Orthodox archbishop in England.

The fourth phase was *1961-75*, i.e. from the pan-Orthodox conference of Rhodes in 1961 and the official delivery by the Old Catholics to the ecumenical patriarch on 21 June 1970 of the *Homologia* (which was first requested in 1904) till the actual beginning of the "dialogue of truth" by the joint commission of Old Catholic and Orthodox theologians in 1975.

The fifth phase comprised the direct dialogue held *1975-87* on the following subjects: (1) the doctrine of God:* divine revelation* and its transmission, the canon* of holy scripture, the Holy Trinity;* (2) Christology: the incarnation* of the Word of God, the hypostatic union, the mother of God; (3) ecclesiology: the nature and marks of the church, the unity of the church and the local churches, the boundaries of the church, the authority* of the church and in the church, the indefectibility of the church, the synods (councils) of the church, the necessity of apostolic succession, the head of the church; (4) soteriology: the redeeming work of Jesus Christ,* the operation of the Holy Spirit* in the church and the appropriation of salvation; (5) sacramental doctrine: the sacraments* of the church, baptism,* confirmation,* the eucharist, penance,* the anointing of the sick,* ordination,* marriage;* (6) eschatology:* the church and the end of time, life after death, the resurrection* of the dead and the renewal of the earth; and (7) ecclesial communion:* conditions and consequences. Between 1975 and 1987 the two sides reached formal agreement on all these points.

With the completion of this dialogue, a sixth phase of the Old Catholic-Orthodox relationship has begun. Now the churches will have to decide what practical conclusions can be drawn from the theological agreement which has been reached. A major point for consideration is the relationship of full communion between the Old Catholic and other churches, and the extent to which in the present ecumenical situation Old Catholic-Orthodox communion could and should be an exclusive one. A remaining task therefore is to relate the positive results of this bilateral dialogue* to the multilateral dialogue* of the churches of the WCC, especially as it develops through the work of the Commission on Faith and Order.*

MARTIN PARMENTIER

U. von Arx ed., "Koinonia auf Altkirchlicher Basis", *Internationale Kirchliche Zeitschrift*, 79, 4,

1989 (suppl. issue) • H. Meyer & L. Vischer, *Growth in Agreement*, WCC, 1984, pp.389-419.

OLD TESTAMENT AND
CHRISTIAN UNITY.

The bearing of the Old Testament on Christian unity merits discussion from several points of view: canon,* lectionary practice (see **liturgical texts, common**), and interpretation (see **hermeneutics**).

It is well known that the OT canon of the Protestant churches agrees with the Hebrew Bible as regards the number of books. But the OT and the Hebrew Bible are not really the same, in view of the Jewish three-stepped canon of Tanakh (law, prophets, and writings). In contrast, the terminology often used in dividing up the Christian OT is somewhat amorphous and even misleading ("historical" books, "prophetical" books, etc.). In Protestant Christianity the influence of Luther has been paramount, although earlier figures such as Jerome also favoured the smaller (Hebrew) canon. In contrast to the Reformation, the Roman Catholic tradition accepted a broader canon (including 1-2 Macc., Jdt., Tob., Sir., Wis., Bar., and certain parts of Dan. and Esth.), and this was officially proclaimed at the council of Trent* in 1546. The position of the Eastern (Orthodox) churches is rather fluid. The general tendency is to accept some of the books generally called apocryphal (e.g., even 3 Macc.).

The adoption of a common liturgical lectionary by the mainline Christian churches in many parts of the world has been a bold and truly ecumenical move. At least Christians might share common biblical passages on Sundays and other holidays, despite their holding separate worship services. It is not a matter of great importance that the translations may differ (thus, for English-speaking Roman Catholics, the *New American Bible* or the *New Jerusalem Bible*, as opposed to the *Revised Standard Version* or the *New English Bible*). In truth there is no "Catholic" or "Protestant" Bible in the vernacular. Translations are done under various auspices, but the translators work from commonly accepted critical texts in the original languages. Differences between them are dictated by technical and scholarly differences of opinion, not by religious beliefs. Such has been the experience of the Catholic and Protestant scholars who have collaborated in some of the English translations as well as the French *(Traduction oecuménique de la Bible)* and the German *(Einheitsübersetzung)*.

For the last two centuries the historico-critical method has dominated the interpretation of the OT by Christians (see **exegesis, methods of**). Despite its limitations, which have been vigorously proclaimed in recent years, this methodology remains a valuable hermeneutical tool — and ecumenical as well. For it has brought together biblical scholars (Protestant, Catholic and Jewish) in a common effort to understand the OT in its historical setting. The accepted results of this scholarship have influenced clerical and lay leadership in these communities. It is the most effective means of correcting certain theological biases and clarifying the theological presuppositions of Christian interpreters. Protestant Christianity, particularly Lutheran, has tended to interpret the OT in the light of the contrast between law and gospel; Roman Catholics and Orthodox have favoured the typological approach. Progress in hermeneutical sophistication has enabled all Christians to hear the OT on its own terms, and not in stereotypes. The gospel (or better, Christian interpretation of the gospel message) needs to be corrected in the light of *torah* piety (Pss. 1, 119), and the eschatology* of the New Testament needs the grim realism of Job and Ecclesiastes if the Christian is to understand the mystery of God.*

Christianity has been able to find its roots in the OT (despite Adolf von Harnack's free advice to the Protestant churches to abandon it, à la Marcion) and to stress continuity with certain ideas ("people of God", etc.). But this selective usage should be broadened by the obvious challenges one Testament offers to the other. Thus, churchly triumphalism deserves to be humbled by the puzzling treatment accorded to the children of Israel as people of God. Or freedom from the law (antinomian strains) needs to be balanced by the emphasis on the *mitzvot* as seen in Deuteronomy. A biblical theology which merely justifies a narrow Christian view contributes nothing to the oikoumene.

The old problem of scripture and Tradition no longer needs to be viewed in an adversarial way. Modern biblical studies have highlighted the role of Tradition in the formation and production of the biblical word (see **Tradition and traditions**). Current hermeneutical theory acknowledges that all texts, including the Bible, have an after-life of their own, in which their meaning is extended. However, there persists in all branches of Christianity a certain fundamentalism which is unwilling to admit the limitations of the word of God* (see e.g. the description of Yahweh, the warrior God, in Joshua). The irony of fundamentalism is that it shares the common traditional concepts about the Bible (e.g. inspiration,* biblical truth), but it proceeds to apply these concepts to the biblical text in a rigid manner. With many fundamentalists the Bible itself replaces the church. The education of Christian readers might profitably begin with the OT, which presents such a wide variety of literary forms and thereby prepares for a more sophisticated approach to the word of God.

See also **New Testament and Christian unity**.

ROLAND E. MURPHY

J. Barr, *Fundamentalism*, Philadelphia, Westminster, 1978 • R.E. Brown, *Critical Exegesis and Church Doctrine*, New York, Paulist, 1985 • R.E. Brown, *The Critical Meaning of the Bible*, New York, Paulist, 1981 • D. Knight ed., *Tradition and Theology in the Old Testament*, Philadelphia, Fortress, 1977.

OLDHAM, JOSEPH HOULDS-
WORTH. B. 20.10.1874, Bombay, India; d. 16.5.1969, St Leonards on Sea, UK. One of the chief architects of the ecumenical movement from the end of the 19th century up to the formation of the WCC in 1938 and its foundation in 1948, Oldham was founder and organizer of more significant ecumenical initiatives than any other Christian of his generation, with the possible exception of John R. Mott. Executive secretary of the world missionary conference in Edinburgh 1910, in 1911 he became the secretary of the continuation committee, and in 1921 the secretary of the International Missionary Council,* which replaced it. From his office in 1912 he launched the *International Review of Missions*, which he edited until 1927. In 1934 he became chairman of the research committee for the Universal Christian Council on Life and Work*, and organizer of its conference on

"Church, Community and State" in Oxford, 1937. In 1938 he prepared with others the meeting in Utrecht which drew up the constitution and made final plans for the formation of the WCC. Not surprisingly he was made an honorary president of the Council at its first assembly in 1948.

When the work of the continuation committee was interrupted by the first world war, Oldham shifted his attention to the problems of German missionaries interned in British colonies. This brought him to the attention of the British colonial and foreign office, where he gained a reputation as a determined and reliable representative of the missionary movement. Already in the war years he was thinking of the future: what should be the pattern of missionary co-operation and the goals of missionary work in the new spiritual, social and political conditions which the war was producing? He addressed these questions in his book *The World and the Gospel* (London, United Council for Missionary Education, 1916).

The wartime exprience had strengthened his conviction that "there is one gospel which is entrusted to Christ's one church, broken though that may be". This church had to find the means to communicate this gospel in a new "one world" context.

In the following years he became deeply involved in the problems of colonial Africa. He took the lead in the missionary struggle against racism* and forced labour. He pressed the colonial governments to give more attention to education, while at the same time working for the preservation of African culture by helping to create the international Institute of African Languages and Cultures, of which he became the administrative director. In 1924 he published what many have called his most influential book: *Christianity and the Race Problem* (London, SCM). This brought him to the forefront of a struggle which would preoccupy the ecumenical movement to the present day.

During the 1930s Oldham's attention was drawn to the development of the modern state, a result of the political and economic upheavals of the time. The preparatory study programme he organized for the Oxford conference on the spiritual-ethical basis of the church's task in the world became a model of ecumenically common study. This brought the Life and Work movement out of its early tendency to-

J.H. Oldham (WCC photo)

wards idealism and utopianism and provided it with carefully thought-out positions on such matters as *The Function of the Church in Society*, *The Christian Understanding of Man*, and *The Kingdom of God and History*. These works greatly clarified and strengthened the world Christian community as it faced the rise of Hitlerism, the threat of the totalitarian state, and the problem of economic justice and order, for which the Oxford conference is now chiefly remembered. Other important works from this period are *The Remaking of Man in Africa* (London, Humphrey Milford, 1931) and *The Resurrection of Christendom* (London, Sheldon, 1940). Throughout the war years Oldham promoted ecumenical study interest, especially among laypersons in English-speaking countries, through his leadership of the Christian Frontier Council and the influential *Christian News-Letter*, which he and Kathleen Bliss edited.

In 1946 he became vice-chairman of the study commission on "The Church and the Disorder of Society" in preparation for the WCC first assembly in 1948. His essay in the preparatory study volume *A Responsible Society* produced the key idea for the assembly's report on social questions. Oldham also pressed hard for more ecumenical attention to the "meaning of work" in modern technologi-

cal society. After 1955 he ceased all active involvement in the ecumenical movement.

He was educated at Edinburgh Academy in Scotland and at Trinity College, Oxford. His plan to enter the Indian civil service was radically altered by his conversion at an Oxford meeting conducted by American evangelist Dwight L. Moody. He later spent a year at the University of Halle, where his teacher was Gustav Warneck, a leading German missiologist. Oldham was never ordained and remained an elder in Free St George's, Edinburgh, until he moved to England in 1921 and became an Anglican layman.

At his memorial service in London, W.A. Visser 't Hooft summarized thus Oldham's immense contribution: "Ecumenical history is full of examples of new development which he started, but which others carried to their conclusion. I have no hesitation in saying that the ecumenical movement owes more to him than to any other of its pioneers."

KATHLEEN BLISS

ORDER. In 20th-century ecumenical discussions on social issues, order and liberty/freedom* have been correlative terms, often representing two major philosophical and political traditions at work, the two major thrusts of social thinking in dialectical tension and even the two major systems of social organization influencing ecumenical actions and concerns. The WCC's constitution includes the following purposes: "To express the common concern of the churches in the service of human need, the breaking down of barriers between people, and the promotion of one human family in justice and peace." This responsibility for participating in a new ordering of human society has largely been the task of the Unit on Justice and Service, although the Council's actions were always closely inter-related. An overview of the history of this involvement shows continuity as well as changes and development.

"Order" in ecumenical social thought. The concept of "social disorder" formed an important backdrop to several ecumenical initiatives of the 19th century. In the development of ecumenical social thought and action in the early 20th century, reflected for example at two Life and Work conferences (Stockholm 1925 and Oxford 1937), this theme became even more apparent. "The forces of evil against which Christians have to contend are found not only in the hearts of men as individuals, but have entered into and infected the structure of society, and there also must be combatted" (William Temple, Oxford conference report).

Before the Amsterdam assembly, J.H. Oldham, W.A. Visser 't Hooft, Reinhold Niebuhr and M.M. Thomas discussed the best term for identifying the church's responsibility in the world. Phrases like "open society", "free society" and "free and responsible society" were considered, before "responsible society"* was adopted. For two decades, this proved to be the key phrase describing the ecumenical vision of the church's role in the social order.

The overall theme of the Amsterdam meeting was "Man's Disorder and God's Design". Sections 3 and 4 specifically dealt with the church and the disorder of society, and the church and the international disorder. A preparatory booklet said: "We see also signs of God's design in the struggles... for economic justice, for political freedom, for a world order that can deliver humanity from war. The results of these efforts will be imperfect and subject to corruption by man's pride and self-interest, but to work for these goals is a responsibility that God lays upon men." In the following years, most of these motifs reappeared repeatedly.

At Evanston, the term "responsible society" was broadened, and its meaning as a guide for action clarified: "Responsible society is not an alternative social political system, but a criterion by which we judge all existing social orders." Sections 3, 4 and 5 dealt with topics related to the question of responsible world order amid disorder and conflict: social questions (the responsible society in a world perspective), international affairs (Christians in the struggle for world community) and intergroup relations (the churches amid racial and ethnic tensions).

After Evanston, a complex and widespread study on "Common Christian Responsibility towards Areas of Rapid Social Change" concentrated on the responsibility of the churches in diverse socio-economic and political contexts, with special emphasis on the "new" nations formulating their concerns and viewpoints. This study laid the foundation for the world conference on Church and Society

(Geneva 1966), on "Christians in the Technical and Social Revolutions of Our Time", addressing economic development in a world perspective; the nature and function of the state* in a revolutionary age; structures of international co-operation — living together in a pluralistic world society; and humankind and community in changing societies. The underlying theme was clearly the responsibility for social action in diverse, rapidly changing, revolutionary contexts, an emphasis far different from that of Oxford and Amsterdam. Several of these issues led to other studies and projects.

In 1968 Uppsala affirmed the positions taken at Geneva. The same year a committee on Society, Development and Peace was constituted by the WCC and the Pontifical Council for Justice and Peace (SODEPAX*). A wide field of issues was addressed at two major conferences (Beirut 1968 and Montreux 1970), in various research documents and in manifold activities.

In 1970 the Commission on the Churches' Participation in Development (see **development**) started its work, confident about the possibilities of transferring technology,* international economic co-operation and infusions of foreign capital. During this process, however, the growth model of development came under heavy criticism, as the emphasis shifted to the people's own struggle for liberation, for justice and economic self-reliance.

A meeting at Bucharest in 1974 concluded a five-year study programme on "The Future of Man and Society in a World of Science-Based Technology" and introduced the long-term concept of a "just and sustainable society", debated at Nairobi and further developed by the central committee (1977) into a "just, participatory and sustainable society" (JPSS)* programme. The search for a just order now found even greater emphasis, with participation and sustainability indicating necessary dimensions of this struggle for justice in the world order.

Again at Nairobi questions of social organization played a major role when, under the theme "Jesus Christ Frees and Unites", the sections, among other things, dealt with seeking community: the common search of people of various faiths, cultures and ideologies (sec. 3); education for liberation and community (4); structures of injustice and struggles for liberation (5); and human development: ambiguities of power, technology and quality of life (6). The official report was published under the apt title *Breaking Barriers*.

After 1977, the JPSS programme formed a very important part of ecumenical social vision and action. An advisory committee delineated the three key concepts, emphasizing a theological interpretation of the people's struggle against unjust powers in the perspective of the messianic kingdom (see **kingdom of God**).

A major development took place when the Vancouver assembly (1983) called on the churches to engage "in a conciliar process of mutual commitment (covenant) to justice, peace and the integrity of creation" (JPIC). It was seen not as a new programme but as a "programme emphasis", affecting all the work being undertaken. In January 1987 the central committee spelled out what this process entails: it is a call to the churches to speak and act together in each place; to do so as a faith response; to base their positions on biblical teachings, Christian traditions and careful analyses of their own situations; to grasp the inter-relatedness of the varying contextual issues and to work on a global response as well; to draw upon available resources, including those of other faith traditions and ideologies.

This call affected almost all activities and became the new overall vision for responsible participation in ordering human society. Several regional meetings have already addressed facets of the process, many discussions have been held, position papers published, and initiatives taken. Representatives of the Vatican Pontifical Council for Promoting Christian Unity and the Pontifical Council for Justice and Peace have already joined the discussions. Precisely because of the truly ecumenical participation, concepts of both "conciliarity" (council) and "covenant" are still problematic, discussed continuously and understood differently.

The Sub-unit on Church and Society is, for example, focusing on concerns related to the churches' role in a world increasingly dominated by science and technology. Especially the integrity of creation (see **justice, peace and the integrity of creation**) has become important, with the insight that "attempts to maintain social and ecological stability through old approaches to development and environmental protection will increase instability, so that stability must be sought through change". A search for a theology and ethics of nature* has become an integral part of the search for responsible social ordering.

A world convocation on JPIC met in Seoul in early 1990, and the Roman Catholic Church participated fully, although not as "co-inviter". This meeting, however, was not the culmination of the process but only an important step along the way.

Threats to a just order. The inter-related global threats responded to in JPIC, namely oppression, militarism* and the destruction of the environment, are all seen in terms of disorder. One aspect of the response against oppression and injustice is the striving for a New International Economic Order (see **economics**). By the end of the 1980s, feelings of frustration and despair replaced the earlier optimism in the global social and economic context. The concept of development as understood in the early 1970s has become extremely suspect. High rates of unemployment in wealthy industrialized countries, a widening gap between rich and poor, volatility in the international monetary system, the concentration of economic power in transnational corporations, the enormous proportions of international debt and repressive measures against popular movements trying to change the impoverishment of a growing number of people in the world all lead to this sense of crisis.

A second aspect of this response is the so-called international food disorder programme. Vancouver made a 13-point call to action in this regard to the member churches, and since then a task force has involved representatives from all three programme units in addressing its implications. The call includes strengthening structures for meeting emergencies, building ecumenical support for long-term solutions, monitoring international policies, providing support for the participation of the poor in food production and distribution; being advocates for farmers and landless rural workers; and denouncing current International Monetary Fund policies. Almost all the sub-units, in their diverse fields, are working on this programme.

An important aspect of the response against militarism is a series of world military order studies, conferences and reports. Especially from the third-world perspective the extent of world militarization and the fact that political and economic decisions are made in terms of military interests, often leading to legitimation of the destructive and unjust order of "law and order" and the violation of human rights, have been pointed out.

Similarly, the three concepts used in JPIC to describe the purpose of the churches' social action can all be seen in terms of order: justice, peace and the integrity of creation — "introducing a sense of wholeness in a fragmented and divided society"; the new idea of "integrity of creation" goes beyond the call for a "sustainable society" precisely in that it "points to an understanding of the wholeness of created life in the world as it is in the plan of God"; the process means that "we must all orientate ourselves to a Word which incorporates the whole created order and is prepared to suffer for its healing".

For order in an ecclesiological sense, see **church order, Faith and Order**.

D.J. SMIT

M. Arruda ed., *Ecumenism and a New World Order*, WCC, 1980 • A.J. van der Bent, *Christian Response in a World of Crisis*, WCC, 1986 • P. Bock, *In Search of a Responsible World Society: The Social Teachings of the World Council of Churches*, Philadelphia, Westminster, 1974 • C. Mulholland comp., *Ecumenical Reflections on Political Economy*, WCC, 1988 • K. Srisang ed., *Perspectives on Political Ethics*, WCC, 1983.

ORDINATION. In ecumenical discussion about ordination, five questions have to be considered: What is the rite of ordination? Who is ordained? By whom is the ordination performed? In what context is this to be done? What rites of unification can be found for a mutual recognition of ministries between churches?

At least since the time of *The Apostolic Tradition*, the church order attributed to Hippolytus, the ancient rite for the ordination of bishop, presbyters and deacons consisted primarily of the laying on of hands, with a prayer for the grace of the Spirit. In other documents, it is apparent that installation of bishops in the cathedra was significant because of their responsibility for apostolic teaching. In Eastern churches, in the ordination of a bishop the imposition of hands was

later complemented by the placing of the gospel on the neck of the ordinand, and in all ordinations by investiture and the acclamation of the people. In Western churches, from the early middle ages, the central rite was first accompanied and then eventually obscured by anointings, investiture and the tradition of instruments. The use of these ceremonies fortified a priestly and sacramental understanding of order.

The 16th-century reformers looked for a ritual that would give priority to God's call to ministry, place the ministry in relation to the common priesthood of all the faithful, and avoid priestly or sacramental interpretations of order. As they acknowledged but one ministry of word and sacrament, so they largely practised but one ordination, doing away with the distinction between presbyter and bishop. For Martin Luther, the service of ordination consisted of the laying on of hands and the recitation of the Lord's prayer, though Lutheran churches did keep other elements of prayer for the ordinand. John Calvin accentuated election and prayer by the congregation and did not deem the laying on of hands to be necessary. Many Reformed churches did keep it, however, or substituted for it the extension of the right hand of fellowship. Though pastors and teachers were the ministers of the word, sometimes elders and deacons were ordained with similar rites.

The Anglican church retained the laying on of hands and the prayer of the people, doing away with the medieval blessing prayers, in which it found elements of the priestly and the sacramental and which had come to be called prayers of consecration. It also retained the offices of bishop, presbyter and deacon (see **ministry, threefold**). Baptists and Congregationalists preferred ordination services which would show the tie to God's call and to the local congregation rather than depict an act of ecclesiastical bestowal of power. In some cases, the laying on of hands was kept as part of such services, linked with prayer for the ordinand by the congregation and forms of recognition of ministry by the local congregation or by a broader fellowship of churches. The extension of the right hand of fellowship was sometimes used instead of the laying on of hands. While ordination was primarily for ministers of the word and the sacrament, at times deacons and elders have been or are installed with similar observances in these churches.

In recent times, the ordination services of the Church of South India have had an influence on Protestant churches generally, and many revised ordination rites have restored the laying on of hands to pride of place. Other factors in new rites include the presentation and examination of the candidate, exhortation, and the prayer of the people. Studies of the ancient tradition pertinent to liturgical reform have had their impact on the ordinal of the Roman pontifical. Though it retains anointings and tradition of instruments, the Roman pontifical now gives clear priority to the laying on of hands and the blessing prayer, incorporating a petition for the gift of the Spirit. This ritual also includes the prayer of the people, presentation and examination of the candidate, and episcopal exhortations. *Baptism, Eucharist and Ministry** has now suggested that all churches restore the laying on of hands as the primary ordination rite, as sign of the gift of the Spirit for ministry. This goes with the suggestion that all churches restore the threefold ministry of bishop, presbyter and deacon. Implementing this idea would entail introducing distinct ordination services in those churches which still prefer ordination to the one ministry of word and sacrament, without ritual distinction of orders.

It is one thing for churches to adopt this ritual of laying on of hands with prayer. It is another for them to agree on its significance and its necessity. For this reason studies of the ancient tradition have become important to ecumenical agreement. It cannot be said without reservation that there is clear evidence of the need for the rite in the appointment of church officers in the New Testament, although a number of texts associate it with a sending for ministry or assignment to community responsibility. The introduction of the rite may have been influenced by a post-baptismal laying on of hands in recognition of the gift of the Spirit in the early church and by a ritual for the appointment of prophets within Judaism. However, as far as historical origins are concerned, it is only in *The Apostolic Tradition* that it is clearly said that bishop, presbyters and deacons are to be appointed with an episcopal laying on of hands and prayer, and that they alone are to

be inducted into office in this way. In some early church orders, deaconesses and widows are included among those who receive the laying on of hands. It is hard to know, however, whether they were intended to be numbered among the clergy (see **laity/clergy**) or even whether such a practice was much followed. The requirement of the laying on of hands for the threefold ministry and its reservation to them did indeed become the universal practice of the church, though not necessarily in all local churches at the same time. Nor was the same weight given to it everywhere, and it did not stand alone without a larger set of observances.

Some idea of the difference in shades of meaning attributed to the laying on of hands can be got by contrasting the use of the Greek word *cheirotonia* with that of the Latin word *ordinatio*. The former means precisely the laying on of hands, and its primary significance is the gift of the Spirit for the service of the church. It is not clear whether at first it meant the actual empowerment for office or a prayer for the guidance of one otherwise designated and installed. It may well be anachronistic to make such distinctions, given that *cheirotonia* and blessing constituted a unity with other actions. These include election or approval of the candidate for ministry by the people, assignment to the service of a particular church within the communion of churches, the participation of other churches, often through their bishops, the prayer of the people as well as of the bishop who ordained, fasting and other forms of preparation, and completion of the rites in the celebration of the eucharist.* On the other hand, while *ordinatio* includes reference to multiple procedures, it does not directly mean the laying on of hands but brings the official assignment to office to the fore and is used also for installation in the lesser orders for which laying on of hands was not employed. While in churches using this term laying on of hands was a normal part of the ordination of bishops, presbyters and deacons, it is advanced as an opinion by some scholars that on occasion, even without the rite, the *ordinatio* might be taken as complete provided a person was legitimately assigned as a member of the clergy.

Such matters obviously affect the ecumenical acceptance of the laying on of hands by a bishop as the common ordination rite. It becomes more acceptable to all, the more it is kept in fuller context, including a link to a particular church and the recognition and prayer of all the people. For some churches, it would be viewed more favourably if it was not invested with a strong sacramental efficacy and if the need for continuity in ministry through episcopal ordination was not deemed indispensable to the validity of ministry. Without such attributions of sacramental efficacy, it could be accepted as indeed a sign of the gift of the Spirit and of the apostolic continuity of the church in which ministry is exercised. On the other hand, the Roman Catholic and Orthodox churches would like to see their own sacramental appreciation of the rite acknowledged. Mutual agreement on this sacramental understanding was formulated in June 1988 by the Joint International Commission for theological dialogue between the Orthodox church and the Roman Catholic Church. As far as mutual recognition of ministries between the churches is concerned, for the RCC issues of validity need first to be resolved, involving episcopal succession and the understanding on which ordinations are performed. For Orthodox churches, recognition of ministry has to occur within the context of recognition of churches. For many Protestant churches, a common faith has to lie at the foundations of such acceptance. Thus the conditions surrounding the adoption of this rite are not the same for all churches, even though there is a growing acceptance of its use and significance.

See also **diaconate; episcopacy; ministry in the church; ordination of women; presbyterate; priesthood; sacrament(s)**.

DAVID N. POWER

J. Lécuyer, *Le sacrement de l'ordination*, Paris, Beauchesne, 1983 • M.B. Pennington, *Called: New Thinking on Christian Vocation*, Minneapolis, Seabury, 1983 • W. Vos & G. Wainwright eds, *Ordination Rites*, Rotterdam, Liturgical Ecumenical Center Trust, 1980 • M. Warkentin, *Ordination, a Biblical-Historical View*, Grand Rapids, MI, Eerdmans, 1982.

ORDINATION OF WOMEN. Some would argue that the move towards the ordination* of women to a ministry of word (see **word of God**) and sacrament* began within the pages of the New Testament. Jesus' treatment of women was revolutionary in the cultural context of his day, and he entrusted to women the news of his resurrection. Women held prominent positions in the early Christian communities and throughout the history of the church have exercised a recognized (though not ordained) ministry as confessors, teachers, theologians and abbesses.

Nevertheless, the twelve apostles were men, the ordered threefold ministry* (of bishop, presbyter and deacon) from its emergence early in the 2nd century was male and, for 19 centuries, the ministry of word and sacrament has been exercised by men. At the Reformation it was a characteristic of the radical movements, especially the Anabaptists, to accept women as ministers.

The movement to ordain women to a full ministry of word and sacrament began in the 19th century in the context of the changing role of women in Western industrializing countries. Women were moving out of the home to work in factories, education and social work. In the church, recognized but not ordained ministries developed. Roman Catholic religious orders for women burgeoned; women were accepted and sent as missionaries; in fast-growing European industrial towns women exercised a ministry as social workers, Salvation Army sisters, Anglican Church Army sisters, Wesleyan class leaders. The order of deaconess, revived among the Moravian Brethren in the 18th century, was instituted in 1836 in Kaiserswerth in Germany in Reformed and Lutheran traditions and spread to Protestant churches all over Europe and eventually to churches around the world.

At the time of the Reformation, churches which had moved away from the threefold pattern were the first to ordain women. The absence of a "catholic" view of the priesthood* of the ministry had its effect. Moreover, since many of these churches emphasized the local or regional church (see **local church**), this development could take place without the formal agreement of a worldwide communion.* For example, the Methodists in the US ordained women in 1956, in England in 1974; among Reformed churches, the Congregationalists of England and Wales ordained women in 1917, the Congregational Union of Scotland in 1929 and the

Eglise réformée in France in 1965. By 1960 Lutheran churches in Germany, Scandinavia (except Finland) and the US had all ordained women. The ordination of women in the Church of Sweden in 1960 marked a significant development in a church which had maintained the historic succession and which had an agreement of intercommunion,* based on the recognition of ministries, with the Church of England, a church which claimed to retain the ministry of the universal church at the Reformation.

A 1970 survey carried out by the WCC found Baptist, Congregational, Disciples, Lutheran, Methodist, Reformed and United churches which ordained women. But many of the churches that ordain women had not taken this move in Africa, Asia and Latin America. Clearly the status and role of women in society in the different continents affect the practice of the ordination of women.

Since 1970 the number of women ordained in churches that ordain women has increased, and the practice has spread in the developing countries. Although no church has reversed the decision to ordain women, there is often resistance to the ministry of women, and positions of responsibility are slow in opening up. Of those churches that did not ordain women in 1970, only the Anglican communion has changed its position. In 1971 Hong Kong became the first of a number of Anglican provinces to ordain women (having already, as an emergency, ordained a woman during the second world war, an ordination subsequently set aside); the USA, Canada, New Zealand, Brazil, Kenya and Uganda followed. In 1990 the Church of Ireland, which is also a province of the Anglican communion, agreed to ordain women. At the Lambeth conference in 1978 the provinces agreed to remain in communion* in spite of their different practices. However, the fact that the priestly ministry of women lawfully ordained in some provinces is not recognized in others means that there is in fact no longer full interchangeability of ministries within the Anglican communion: the communion is thus restricted because there is no longer full interchangeability of ministers.

There have been moves to ordain women in the Old Catholic Church in Germany, while the position in the Roman Catholic and Orthodox churches remains unchanged. An un-

official movement in the RCC has appeared, particularly in the Netherlands, the USA and England. The official Roman Catholic position is stated in *Inter Insigniores*, the 1976 declaration of the Sacred Congregation for the Doctrine of the Faith. The RCC is not free, it is said, to change the unbroken tradition of the universal church on this matter. The Orthodox churches remain opposed: they held a consultation in 1989 in Rhodes to set out their reasons for maintaining the unbroken tradition of the church. Thus the two largest and oldest churches continue to uphold an all-male priesthood.

The movement to ordain women to the full ministry of word and sacrament, especially among the churches springing from the Reformation, has coincided with the movement towards the visible unity* of the church. The one has had an effect on the other. This result is not surprising, for the visible unity of the church involves the recognition not only of all its baptized members as members of a single community of faith but also of those who are called to be ministers of the one communion. As long ago as 1916 Anglican William Temple expressed a view which many committed ecumenists have shared: "I would like to see women ordained;... desirable as it would be in itself, the effect might be (probably would be) to put back the re-union of Christendom — and re-union is more important."

The conflict between the movement to ordain women and the move towards the unity of the church is illustrated by the experiences of uniting churches. The existence of women ministers in the United Church of Canada was one of the reasons why Anglicans did not enter union with that church in 1956. In the Anglican-Methodist scheme for unity in England in the 1960s, the Methodists delayed ordaining women in order that the two churches might consider the matter together. Only after the failure of the scheme did Methodists proceed to ordain women. In the subsequent covenanting* proposals involving United Reformed, Methodist, Moravian and Anglican churches, the ordination of women was once more an issue. In voting on the proposals, the Church of England included a separate motion referring to the recognition of women ministers of the other churches: the motion was defeated in the House of Clergy.

When women were admitted to the full ministry in the Church of Sweden, it was argued that this step would gravely damage relations of intercommunion with the Church of England. Although this did not result, Swedish women ministers are not yet recognized by the Church of England in the same way as their male colleagues are. In 1931 the Old Catholics and Anglicans entered into the Bonn agreement, one of "full communion". The move of some Anglican provinces to ordain women met with grave concern among Old Catholics; the Polish National Catholic Church terminated the agreement. At the consultation of united and uniting churches in 1987, the situation was summed up in this way: "For some churches the ordination of women adds to the hindrances to unity; but the united churches are clear that further union for them is being made a more open possibility by the willingness of those to share that ordination of women which they have found to be a creative element in their common life."

The theological issues involved in the ordination of women have been clarified and developed particularly in the context of ecumenical conversation. The concern was already voiced at the first world conference on Faith and Order (Lausanne 1927) and has been a recurring theme in WCC assemblies, in the work of F&O and in WCC departments responsible for women's concerns. The Council has proved both the most creative but also the most divisive forum in which to face the issue. The churches in the catholic tradition, particularly the Orthodox churches, have felt forced to face a question which was not on their own agenda and which challenged in an unacceptable way their belief that the holy Tradition* is clear and unchangeable.

The 1982 Lima document on *Baptism, Eucharist and Ministry*,* does not treat the ordination of women in the main part of the ministry text but considers the issue in a commentary (to M18), which gives a short description of the positions of those churches which ordain women and those which do not. There is no convergence between the churches on the matter. Behind those short sentences lies a long history of debate and clarification of the issues, not least through the insights of the study on "The Community of Women and Men in the Church", which in 1980 produced

Bishop Barbara Harris preaching at the world convocation on "Justice, Peace and the Integrity of Creation" (Seoul '90) (WCC/Peter Williams)

a book entitled *Ordination of Women in Ecumenical Perspective*.

The contribution of the WCC has been to help the churches to set the discussion within the context of an emerging convergence on the understanding of ministry and priesthood and perhaps, even more important, within the concept of the unity we seek. The studies on the unity of the church and the renewal of human community have enlarged and enriched the perspective of this unity. Some have come to maintain that the churches' ministry must include women in order to show to the world the depths of unity in human community and to make the values of the gospel and the vision of the kingdom credible in a broken and divided world. The unity of the church ought not to be set over against the unity of the human community. In the context of the WCC the challenge has also gone to the churches that "openness to each other holds the possibility that the Spirit may well speak to one church through the insights of another. Ecumenical considerations, therefore, should encourage, not restrain, the facing of this question." The WCC provides the right context for deepening the understanding of the exegetical, doctrinal and pastoral questions which arise in relation to the ordination or non-ordination of women to the priesthood.

Bilateral conversations, particularly those between churches with differing practices, have had to face the issue in a sharp way. Nowhere has this been more evident than in the Anglican-Roman Catholic dialogue.* Just as growth in communion and reconciliation of ministries seemed possible on the basis of the agreed statement on ministry, some Anglican provinces proceeded to ordain women. The pope cautioned that this was a "grave new obstacle" to the movement towards unity. In an official correspondence between the pope, the archbishop of Canterbury and Cardinal Johannes Willebrands (reproduced in *Towards a Church of England Response to BEM and ARCIC*, 1985), some of the central arguments for and against the ordination of women were set out.

They include the question of the representative nature of priesthood and whether women may appropriately represent God in Christ, particularly in the presidency of the eucharist.* The argument relates to the fundamental significance of the maleness of Jesus in the incarnation* and the relation of maleness to the nature of God. It is bound up with the argument, used also by some in fundamentalist and evangelical traditions, for the headship of men and for the "proper subordination of women to men in the order of creation, which also precludes women's ordination". A third argument concerns how decisions are taken on a matter relating to the ministry of the universal church when there is division in the church. Some believe only a truly ecumenical council* would have power to resolve the issue.

The agenda revealed in ecumenical dialogue is crucial, for it touches matters at the centre of faith* regarding what is believed about the ministry, the church, men and women created in God's image and, most crucial of all, the nature and being of God.* Many in the Church of England are reluctant to move on the matter until the Roman Catholic Church finds itself able to accept such a development. Churches committed to unity are forced to face how they may move into deeper communion while remaining divided on the issue.

Until recently developments have concerned the ordination of women to the presbyterate.* The first woman bishop, Marjorie Matthews of the United Methodist Church, USA, was greeted at the 1983 Vancouver assembly of the WCC. More recently, in England for example, women have assumed oversight roles in the Methodist and the United Reformed churches, both non-episcopal churches.

The Lambeth conference in 1988 resolved that, should a woman be consecrated bishop in a province of the Anglican communion, every attempt would be made to maintain "the highest degree of communion" possible, in spite of the fact that the principle of women bishops was not yet agreed. The development would be tested in an open process of reception. In 1989 Barbara Harris was consecrated bishop in the USA and became suffragan bishop in the diocese of Massachusetts. In 1990 Penelope Jamieson was consecrated bishop of Dunedin, New Zealand, the first woman to become a diocesan bishop in the Anglican communion. With these two consecrations women became fully a part of the threefold ministry in the Anglican communion. The development is said by the Roman Catholic Church to make reconciliation of ministries between Anglicans and Roman Catholics more difficult.

See also **ministry in the church, ordination**.

MARY TANNER

M. Hayter, *The New Eve in Christ: The Use and Abuse of the Bible in the Debate about Women in the Church*, London, SPCK, 1987 ● C. Parvey ed., *Ordination of Women in Ecumenical Perspective*, WCC, 1980 ● C. Parvey, "Stir in the Ecumenical Movement: The Ordination of Women", in B. Stendahl, *The Force of Tradition: A Case Study of Women Priests in Sweden*, Philadelphia, Fortress, 1985.

ORIENTAL ORTHODOX CHURCHES.

The five Oriental Orthodox churches — Coptic, Syrian, Armenian, Ethiopian and the (Indian) Malankara — are in communion* with each other and are also called ancient Oriental, lesser Eastern, and pre- or ante-Chalcedonian churches. They are the churches of the first three ecumenical councils* (Nicea,* Constantinople* and Ephesus) and do not accept Chalcedon* (451). The Ethiopian, Coptic and Indian churches have been full members of the WCC since its inauguration in Amsterdam in 1948.

The Syrian church joined at the New Delhi assembly (1961), and the central committee in Paris admitted the Armenian church in 1962. Since the entry of Byzantine Orthodox churches at New Delhi, there have been a number of bilateral consultations between the Byzantine and Oriental churches which have brought them closer to each other, though communion has not yet been achieved (see **Oriental Orthodox-Orthodox dialogue**).

The statement of Nikos Nissiotis at New Delhi that once there is a schism,* both parties are in schism, was objected to by conservative theologians, but it has paved the way for mutual respect in place of the ancient heresy-hunting, which was perhaps a passing and yet necessary stage during the development of dogmas. Whenever the paradoxical mystery of Christology and Trinity* could not be fully appreciated, rationalism erected narrow domestic walls. The Faith and Order* commission of the WCC paved the way for bilateral consultations between theologians of Byzantine and Oriental churches at Aarhus (1964), Bristol (1967), Geneva (1970) and Addis Ababa (1971).

The *Coptic Orthodox Church* traces its history back to St Mark the Evangelist, who founded the church in Egypt. The ancient Egyptian patriarchate of Alexandria represented one of the chief sees of the early church within the Roman empire. The Copts, descendants of the ancient Egyptians, preserved the Coptic language in their liturgy.* Through a long period of persecution since Byzantine times, the Coptic Orthodox Church tenaciously held fast to the "faith of the fathers". One of its chief strengths was in continuing the great ascetic-monastic traditions that originated in the Egyptian deserts. The church has initiated considerable missionary work in other parts of the African continent. The Coptic church has a significant diaspora* in North America, Europe, Australia and the Middle East.

The *Syrian Orthodox Church* traces its history to A.D. 37 and holds the traditions of St Peter's work. The church suffered severe persecution during the struggle against Hellenistic domination at the time of the council of Chalcedon, and later through Mongol invasions and Turkish rule. The patriarchate had to be moved several times until it was established in Damascus in this century. Syrian

liturgical and theological life flourished until the 13th century but steadily declined afterwards. The monastic movement produced many universally acknowledged saints* and contributed enormously to the creation of a rich liturgical tradition. In 1665, the Antiochian church came into contact with the ancient church of St Thomas Christians in India, and the West Syrian liturgy was thus introduced to the Christians in South India. Though the Syrian church is vastly reduced in number because of Muslim domination, it has a considerable diaspora in the US, Australia and Europe.

The *Armenian Apostolic Church:* Armenia, the first nation to accept Christianity as the official religion (in 301), traditionally attributes the beginning of Armenian Orthodox Christianity to the preaching of St Thaddeus and St Bartholomew. Victims of terrible persecution through the centuries, Armenian Christians heroically preserved their apostolic faith. The catholicos of All Armenians resides in Etchmiadzin in the Soviet Union. There are three ecclesiastical centres within the church apart from Etchmiadzin: the catholicate of Cilicia (Antelias, Lebanon), the patriarchate of Jerusalem and the patriarchate of Constantinople. The Armenian church has a very significant diaspora spread out in all the continents. The Armenian national aspirations and the Armenian Orthodox faith are integrally interconnected.

The *Ethiopian Orthodox Church:* An authentically African Orthodox church, the Ethiopian church has a history going back to apostolic times. For long under the tutelage of the Coptic Orthodox Church, the Ethiopian church declared its autocephaly in 1950 and is now governed by its own patriarch in Addis Ababa. The church uses both the ancient language of Geez and modern Amharic in its liturgy. Influenced by a long tradition of monastic spirituality, this church has produced considerable religious literature and has its own iconographic tradition. The Ethiopian church is now gradually emerging from age-old social and economic structures to meet contemporary challenges.

The *Malankara (Indian) Orthodox Church* has always cherished the tradition of St Thomas as the founding father of Christianity in India. The Indian church, now divided confessionally into Roman Catholic, Protestant and Orthodox families, has suffered from Western colonial missions. The church came into contact with the west Syrian patriarchate of Antioch in 1665 and thus inherited the Syrian liturgical and spiritual tradition. The Orthodox church in India declared itself autocephalous in 1912, though conflicts with the Syrian patriarchate continue. With a well-equipped theological college, a mission training centre and many educational and charitable institutions, the church is fully involved in the life of the country. With the catholicos residing at Kottayam, Kerala, the church has 20 bishops and more than 1,000 parishes. It has a diaspora in North America, Malaysia, Singapore and the Gulf countries.

All five Oriental churches have contributed leaders to the ecumenical movement: Aboon Theophilus, patriarch of Ethiopia, was one of the presidents of the WCC from Evanston to New Delhi; Armenian catholicos (Antelias) Karekin Sarkissian was the vice-moderator of the central committee from Uppsala to Nairobi; Paulos Gregorios of the Orthodox Syrian Church (Malankara) has been one of the presidents since Vancouver and was also moderator of the Sub-unit on Church and Society from Nairobi to Vancouver; Patriarch Shenouda and the late Bishop Samuel of the Coptic Church, Patriach Ignatius Zakka of the Syrian Church and V.C. Samuel of the Malankara Church have done signal service for the ecumenical movement; Vasken, catholicos of All Armenia, has hosted a number of ecumenical meetings in Holy Etchmiadzin. The contributions have been greater in the area of Faith and Order than in the other sub-units of the WCC.

GEEVARGHESE MAR OSTHATHIOS

H.E. Fey ed., *A History of the Ecumenical Movement: The Ecumenical Advance,* vol. 2: *1948-1968,* 2nd ed., WCC, 1986, ch. 11 • *The Star of the East,* 4, 3, 1982 • *Wort und Wahrheit,* supplementary issues 1-4, 1972-78.

ORIENTAL ORTHODOX-
ORTHODOX DIALOGUE. The divi-

sion between the Eastern Orthodox and the Oriental Orthodox families of churches can be traced back to the council of Chalcedon* (451). The Eastern Orthodox family (all those churches in communion* with the see of Constantinople) accepted Chalcedon as the fourth

ecumenical council,* while the Oriental Orthodox (ancient churches of Egypt, Syria, Armenia, India and Ethiopia) rejected the council. The main conflict was in the area of Christology — how the divine and the human natures are united in the person of Jesus Christ.* However, strong political, cultural and social factors also played a part. The differences resulted in the breach of communion between these two Eastern families which, in spite of separation, maintain to this day a remarkable unity* in theological approach, liturgical-spiritual ethos and general church discipline.*

The conflict between the Alexandrine and Antiochene theological traditions in the East was a major factor in the Christological controversy of the 5th century. Already in the council of Ephesus 431 the conflict came to a head. Nestorius, the patriarch of Constantinople and a theologian belonging to the Antiochene tradition, was condemned. Cyril of Alexandria's Christology was accepted by the council as the norm of orthodoxy. The council of Ephesus was only the beginning of a long drawn-out controversy which culminated at Chalcedon.

In the Antiochene phrase "two natures after the union", the Alexandrine side suspected the "Nestorian" dividing of natures in Christ. Alexandrine phrases like "from two natures" and "one incarnate nature of God the Word" appeared to the Antiochenes as reflecting the monophysite confusion of natures. Emperor Theodosius tried to reconcile the two factions in 433 through the Formulary of Reunion. But it did not bring about lasting peace. The Alexandrines and the Antiochenes interpreted the terms of the reunion differently.

The issue of Eutychianism can be understood only against that background. Eutyches, an old monk in Constantinople, was accused of denying that Christ was in two natures after the union and that the incarnate Christ was consubstantial with us human beings. He was condemned in 448 in the home synod of Constantinople. Eutyches was not a theologian and probably did not understand the subtleties of the Christological discussion. It is, however, clear that he had strong connections in the imperial court through his nephew Chrysaphius, who was the grand chamberlain of the emperor. The Alexandrine side used his services for political connections at the court.

Meanwhile Pope Leo I of Rome had sent a tome to the East setting forth a Christological doctrine apparently intended to resolve the controversy. Some Antiochene theologians found its Christology similar to their own. The tome brought in the new factor of Western theology to the already muddled situation in the East and further complicated it.

In the second council of Ephesus (449), convened by Emperor Theodosius and presided over by Dioscorus of Alexandria, Eutyches was admitted to communion on the assurance that he adhered to the faith of the fathers as expressed in Nicea* and Ephesus. The contribution of Leo, intended to be read in the council, was ignored.

In the council of Chalcedon 451, these two issues — the admitting of Eutyches to communion and the ignoring of the tome of Leo — were brought up as two principal accusations against Dioscorus I, patriarch of Alexandria 441-51. The council condemned Dioscorus, though his doctrinal orthodoxy was neither examined nor questioned, and at the same time acknowledged the Christology of the tome of Leo as truly Orthodox.

It is noteworthy that the non-Chalcedonian churches which rejected the doctrinal formulations of Chalcedon never adhered to any monophysite or Eutychian doctrine as attributed to them by the Chalcedonians. It is also now recognized that the Chalcedonian churches did not intend any Nestorianism in holding the Christology of Chalcedon. The mutual recognition of this fact is the starting point of the new dialogue. This fact, however, had been already recognized by perceptive theologians in the earlier post-Chalcedonian era. Serious attempts were made to bring together the two sides and to restore the broken communion. But persistent cultural and political factors hindered the attempts at reunion. The dialogue could be resumed only recently, after 1,500 years of separation.

A series of four unofficial conversations took place between 1964 and 1971 at the initiative of Paul Verghese (now Metropolitan Paulos Gregorios) and Nikos Nissiotis, both on the WCC staff at the time. Agreed statements were produced from these conversations, which underline the complete Christological agreement between the two families. The first (Aarhus 1964) declared: "We recognize in each other the one Orthodox faith of the church. Fifteen centuries of alienation have not led us astray from the faith of our fathers... On the essence of the Christological dogma we found ourselves in full agreement. Through the different terminologies used by each side, we saw the same truth expressed." Finding common ground in the formulation "one incarnate nature (*physis* or *hypostasis*) of God's Word", a phrase used by Cyril of Alexandria, the common father of both sides, both traditions re-affirmed their rejection of both the Nestorian and Eutychian teachings.

The fundamental agreement reached in Aarhus was re-inforced in subsequent conversations by agreement in several new areas. "Some of us affirm two natures, wills and energies hypostatically united in the one Lord Jesus Christ. Some of us affirm one united divine-human nature, will and energy in the same Christ. But both sides speak of a union without confusion, without change, without divisions, without separation. The four adverbs belong to our common tradition. Both affirm the dynamic permanence of the Godhead and the Manhood, with all their natural properties and faculties, in the one Christ" (Bristol consultation 1967).

Both sides could affirm together "the common Tradition of the one church in all important matters — liturgy and spirituality, doctrine and canonical practice, in our understanding of the Holy Trinity, of the incarnation, of the person and work of the Holy Spirit, on the nature of the church as the communion of saints with its ministry and sacraments, and on the life of the world to come when our Lord and Saviour shall come in all his glory" (Geneva 1970).

The major difficulties on the way to the restoration of communion identified by these unofficial consultations were the following: (1) the meaning and place of certain councils in the life of the church (the Chalcedonian side accepted seven ecumenical councils, while the non-Chalcedonian family accepted only the first three as ecumenical councils); (2) the respective anathematization or acclamation as saints of certain controversial teachers in the church like Leo, Dioscorus, Severus (patriarch of Antioch), and others; (3) jurisdictional questions related to manifestation of the unity of the church at local, regional and world levels.

It was agreed that councils should be seen

as charismatic events in the life of the church rather than as an authority over the church. The agreement calls for making a distinction between the true intention of the dogmatic definition of a council and the particular terminology in which it is expressed. The latter has less authority than the intention.

As to the anathemas,* it may not be necessary formally to lift them. Nor is it necessary for a church to recognize as saints those who were once condemned by that church. The Addis Ababa consultation of 1971 gave special attention to the questions of anathemas. It advocated the dropping of anathemas in a quiet way. The lifting of anathemas, however, could be formally announced at the time of union. It was agreed that the church has the authority to lift the anathemas which it once imposed for pastoral or other reasons.

The unofficial conversations suggested to their churches, among other proposals, the appointment of an official joint commission to deal with the issues that separated the two families in the past and to consider the mutual agreement reached at an unofficial level so that necessary steps could be taken to restore full unity in eucharistic communion.

Responding to the solid Christological agreement reached by the unofficial consultations and to their suggestions to appoint an official commission, the churches took action and constituted officially a Joint Commission of the Theological Dialogue between the Orthodox Church and the Oriental Orthodox Churches. In the second meeting of this official commission, at the Amba Bishoy monastery in Egypt in June 1989, a historic agreement was signed. Opening a new chapter in ecumenical history, and overcoming 1,500 years of separation, the agreed statement said: "We have inherited from our fathers in Christ the one apostolic faith and tradition, though as churches we have been separated from each other for centuries. As two families of Orthodox churches long out of communion with each other, we now pray and trust in God to restore that communion on the basis of the apostolic faith of the undivided church of the first centuries which we confess in our common creed."

The third meeting of the Joint Commission (Chambésy 1990) re-affirmed the earlier agreement on faith and recommended to local churches in both families that all previous anathemas against each other's councils and fathers should be lifted. Now that both sides have accepted the first three ecumenical councils as their common heritage, the Oriental Orthodox will respond positively to the Orthodox interpretation of the four later councils, in line with the common agreement in all other aspects of faith.

With major theological and historical obstacles to unity now being removed, there is fresh hope that the Orthodox churches will soon take action to restore communion between their two families.

K.M. GEORGE

"Communiqué of the Joint Commission of the Theological Dialogue between the Orthodox Church and the Oriental Churches, 20-24 June 1989, Egypt", *The Star of the East*, 2, 1-2, 1989 ● P. Gregorios, W.H. Lazareth & N.A. Nissiotis eds, *Does Chalcedon Divide or Unite? Towards Convergence in Orthodox Christology*, WCC, 1981 ● Reports of the unofficial conversations between theologians of the Eastern Orthodox and Oriental Orthodox Churches from 1964 to 1971, *The Greek Orthodox Theological Review*, 10, 2, 1964-65; 13, 1968; 16,1 and 2, 1971 ● V.C. Samuel, *The Council of Chalcedon Re-examined: A Historical and Theological Survey*, Madras, CLS, 1977.

ORIENTAL ORTHODOX-ROMAN CATHOLIC DIALOGUE.

The Oriental Orthodox churches are a group of five independent churches — Armenian, Syrian, Coptic, Ethiopian, and Indian (Malankara) — which did not accept the Christological teachings of the council of Chalcedon* (451). This led to a break in communion* with those who accepted the council's teachings. In contrast to the Chalcedonian formula of one person and two natures in Christ, these churches affirmed the formula of Cyril of Alexandria, who spoke of "the one incarnate nature of the Word of God". In the eyes of the Oriental Orthodox, those who accepted Chalcedon held an essentially Nestorian Christology, which, in spite of verbal affirmations, compromised the unity of Christ's person. For Catholics, the "one nature" formula of the Oriental Orthodox seemed indistinguishable from the monophysite position of Eutyches, who taught that Jesus' humanity was totally subsumed into his divinity.

Movement beyond these entrenched positions gained momentum in the late 1960s, in the context of visits by heads of Oriental Orthodox churches to Rome and unofficial meetings of theologians. These contacts have resulted in substantial progress towards resolution of those theological problems which have traditionally divided the two communions. Since 1967 the following heads of Oriental Orthodox churches have met with the pope in Rome: Armenian catholicos Khoren I (Cilicia) in 1967, Armenian catholicos Vasken I (Etchmiadzin) in 1970, Syrian patriarch Ignatius Yacoub III in 1971, Coptic pope Shenouda III in 1973, Syrian patriarch Ignatius Yacoub III in 1980, Ethiopian patriarch Tekle Haimanot in 1981, Armenian catholicos Karekin II (Cilicia) in 1983, Syrian catholicos of India Mar Baselius Thoma Mathews I in 1983, and Syrian patriarch Ignatius Zakka I in 1984. Several of these visits culminated in the signing of an important joint communiqué or common declaration.

Alongside these official visits, five unofficial theological consultations have been held between theologians of both sides under the auspices of the Pro Oriente* Foundation in Vienna. These took place in 1971, 1973, 1976, 1978, and 1988. At these meetings, Christological and ecclesiological issues were discussed, and final communiqués were published stating areas of agreement and continuing disagreement.

The most substantial progress has been in the area of Christology. As early as 1970, in the common declaration signed by Pope Paul VI and Armenian catholicos Vasken I, theologians were encouraged to explore this area. This was precisely the theme of the first Pro Oriente meeting in 1971. The work of these theologians provided a basis for the historic Christological profession of faith signed by Pope Paul VI and Coptic pope Shenouda III in 1973. Avoiding terminology which had been the source of disagreement in the past, this declaration made use of new language to express a common faith in Christ.

The second theological consultation (1973) took up this theme again. In its final communiqué, the group affirmed that while the Oriental Orthodox consider that some of the terms used at Chalcedon can be misleading, both sides agree that the formula can be understood in a correct manner. The heretical Eutychian and Nestorian Christologies were both rejected.

Since 1973, popes and Oriental Orthodox hierarchs have repeatedly asserted that their faith in Christ is the same. In the 1984 common declaration of Pope John Paul II and Syrian patriarch Ignatius Zakka I, which also contained a common Christological profession of faith, it was stated that past schisms and divisions concerning the doctrine of the incarnation* "in no way affect or touch the substance of their faith", because the disputes arose from differences in terminology and culture.

All this makes it clear that the Christological dispute between these two communions has been substantially resolved. We must remember, however, that the Armenian, Ethiopian and Indian churches have not yet been party to such agreements.

Progress has also been made in the area of ecclesiology, but difficulties remain. Both sides have clearly recognized the ecclesial reality of the other and the authenticity of each other's sacraments.* In their 1984 common declaration, Pope John Paul II and Patriarch Ignatius Zakka I even authorized their faithful to receive the sacraments of penance,* eucharist,* and anointing of the sick* in the other church when access to one of their own priests was materially or morally impossible.

The theology of ecumenical councils* and primacy* has been discussed at the Pro Oriente meetings. Although much common ground has been discovered, certain divergences on these issues remain unresolved.

The "Eastern Catholic" churches,* made up of former Oriental Orthodox Christians or their descendants and now in communion with Rome, were discussed at the 1978 consultation. This is a particularly sensitive topic. Oriental Orthodox strongly assert that the existence of these churches is inseparably linked to Roman Catholic proselytism* among the Oriental Orthodox, based upon a denial of the ecclesial reality of their churches. In response to this concern, proselytism on the part of either side had been condemned in the 1973 common declaration of Pope Paul VI and Coptic pope Shenouda III.

The 1988 fifth theological consultation evaluated the results of the first four meetings and called for the establishment of an official theological dialogue between the Roman Catholic Church and the Oriental Orthodox churches as a whole.

Within this complex set of relationships between the two communions, a separate official dialogue between the Roman Catholic and Coptic churches has been in progress since its institution by Pope Paul VI and Pope Shenouda III in 1973. Five meetings have taken place, in 1974, 1975, 1976, 1978 and 1988. Theological experts of the two sides have examined various issues and submitted recommendations to their respective authorities.

Moreover, an official theological dialogue between the Roman Catholic Church and the Orthodox Syrian Church of India began in 1989. This church includes a large part of the Oriental Orthodox faithful in India; the others remain under the jurisdiction of the Syrian patriarchate in Damascus.

Finally, a word should be added about the relationship between the Roman Catholic Church and the Assyrian Church of the East, which, having officially adopted Nestorian Christology in 484, is not in communion with any other church. Although no theological dialogue exists between the Catholic and Assyrian churches, relations improved significantly in the period following the Second Vatican Council.* The present patriarch, Mar Denkha IV, visited Pope John Paul II in Rome in 1984 and participated in the day of prayer for peace at Assisi in 1986.

RONALD G. ROBERSON

R. Roberson, "The Modern Roman Catholic-Oriental Orthodox Dialogue", *One in Christ*, 21, 1985 • The papers presented at the first four unofficial Pro Oriente consultations were published in English in supplements to *Wort und Wahrheit*, nos 1-4, 1972-78. Selected documentation from all four meetings has been published in one volume: *Four Vienna Consultations*, Vienna, Pro Oriente, 1988.

ORTHODOX-REFORMED DIALOGUE.

The first official international dialogue between the Orthodox churches and the World Alliance of Reformed Churches* took place in March 1988 in Leuenberg, Switzerland, with 34 participants from different countries of the world, under the leadership of Metropolitan Panteleimon Rodopoulos (for the Ecumenical Patriarchate) and Lukas Vischer (for the World Alliance). The primary theme considered was the doctrine of the Trinity,* as based on the Nicene Creed.* The second gathering held in Moscow in October 1990 continued discussions on the same subject.

Behind these recent official Reformed-Orthodox dialogues lies a long history of Orthodox and Protestant contacts. The earliest exchange of letters took place between the Lutheran theological faculty of the University of Tübingen and Ecumenical Patriarch Jeremiah II of Constantinople from 1573 to 1581 (see **Lutheran-Orthodox dialogue**). For the Calvinists, the first Orthodox-Reformed discussions centred on the stormy debate over the "unorthodox" confession of faith of Ecumenical Patriarch Cyrill (Kyrill) Loukaris (ruled 1620-38).

Under the influence of Calvin's teachings, Cyrill summarized his reforming beliefs in his published *Eastern Confession of the Christian Faith*. The original document can be seen at the Geneva public library, which has a wealth of materials related to this controversial confession. This confession eventually cost Cyrill his life; to the best of our knowledge this reform-minded patriarch never repudiated his statement, though there have been numerous attempts either to discredit or to dismiss it as a "political" document in the highly volatile polemics between Protestants and Catholics seeking to win the favour of Orthodox believers at that time.

In light of this history, it is necessary for present Orthodox-Reformed dialogues to establish firm grounds on which both traditions can confess the essentials of their Christian faith* in common. Hence the decision for the official international dialogues to focus on the Trinitarian foundation based on the Nicene Creed.

In retrospect, it seems that these official international dialogues have been well prepared for through a series of earlier Orthodox-Reformed consultations initiated in several countries. As early as the 1920s in Romania (Transylvania), discussions between Orthodox and Reformed had started; in the 1950s in Germany, 1968-75 in North America, the 1970s in Hungary (Debrecen) and since 1981 in France and Switzerland.

The themes in these various consultations have ranged widely with studies on Christology, the eucharist,* the role of confession and creeds,* God's saving and sanctifying work through the Holy Spirit,* the meaning of the divine liturgy,* God's revelation* and history,* historical relativism and authority* in Christian dogma,* tradition* and contemporaneity, spiritual values and social responsibility of the church to society, the relationship of creation* and redemption* (nature* and grace*), and practical and pastoral issues such as mixed marriages* and proselytism.*

As each side seeks to interpret faithfully their tradition, we who participate are constantly discovering the common bonding of the Holy Spirit in our midst. Orthodoxy appeals to the tradition of the "undivided church", which preceded the great schism* of 1054 between the Eastern and Western churches, and points to the ecumenical councils* beginning with Nicea* as its norm. The Reformed tradition directs us to scripture and the earliest church for its standards. Dialogue offers the possibility for accepting each other's respective traditions without losing the special gifts each brings to the table of dialogue for our mutual edification and enrichment.

CARNEGIE SAMUEL CALIAN

C.S. Calian, "Cyrill Lucaris: The Patriarch Who Failed", *Journal of Ecumenical Studies*, 10, 2, 1973 • C.S. Calian, *Icon and Pulpit: The Protestant-Orthodox Encounter*, Philadelphia, Westminster, 1968 • J. Meyendorff & J. McLelland eds, *The New Man: An Orthodox and Reformed Dialogue*, New Brunswick, NJ, Agora, 1973 • *The Orthodox Church and the Churches of the Reformation*, WCC, 1975 • T.F. Torrance ed., *Theological Dialogue between Orthodox and Reformed Churches*, Edinburgh, Scottish Academic Press, 1985 • L. Vischer "The Legacy of Kyrill Loukaris: A Contribution to the Orthodox-Reformed Dialogue", *Mid-Stream*, 25, 2, 1986.

ORTHODOX-ROMAN CATHOLIC DIALOGUE.

The schism* between what are now known as the Roman Catholic and Orthodox churches is usually traced back to the mutual excommunications* of Patriarch Michael Cerularius of Constantinople and Cardinal Humbert, the papal legate, in 1054. But in fact this was only a single high point in a long history of strained relations which reached its real culmination only with the crusades and the sack of Constantinople by the Latins in 1204. Although many non-theological factors were at play in this gradual estrangement of Eastern and Western Christians, doctrinal issues were also involved. The

most important of these concerned the eternal procession of the Holy Spirit* (related to the addition of the filioque* to the Nicene Creed* by the Western church), and papal primacy.*

Two major attempts at achieving reunion between the two churches took place at the second council of Lyons in 1274 and the council of Florence in 1438-39. But in both cases, although a formal union was promulgated, it was ultimately rejected by the general Orthodox population. Centuries of mutual isolation and hostility ensued, with each church de facto denying the ecclesial reality of the other.

The situation began to improve only in the 1960s, when important changes in attitude took place within both the Catholic and the Orthodox churches. From the Catholic perspective, the convocation of the Second Vatican Council,* coupled with the presence of Orthodox observers at the Council, marked a greater openness to the Orthodox. A positive evaluation of the Eastern tradition is found in the Council documents (see *Unitatis Redintegratio* 14-18). From the Orthodox perspective, the third pan-Orthodox conference (Rhodes 1964) encouraged the local Orthodox churches to engage in studies preparing for an eventual dialogue with the Roman Catholic Church.

Other events in the same decade exemplified a growing "dialogue of charity" between the two communions and increased the momentum towards a formal theological dialogue. In January 1964 Pope Paul VI and Patriarch Athenagoras of Constantinople met for the first time, in Jerusalem. In a common declaration issued by them on 7 December 1965, the mutual excommunications of 1054 were "erased from the memory" of the church. In 1967 the pope and the patriarch exchanged visits in Rome and Istanbul.

This more positive atmosphere made possible the establishment of a joint commission in 1976 to prepare for an official dialogue. In 1978 it submitted a programmatic document to the authorities of both churches in which the goal of the dialogue was clearly defined as the re-establishment of full communion.* It proposed a methodology according to which the dialogue would begin with the elements which unite Catholics and Orthodox and then move to the more divisive points. The commission recommended that the sacraments* be considered first, especially as they relate to ecclesiology (see **church**).

The official announcement of the beginning of the theological dialogue was made jointly by Pope John Paul II and Patriarch Dimitrios I in Istanbul on 30 November 1979. This new Joint International Commission for theological dialogue between the Roman Catholic Church and the Orthodox church was to include experts representing both churches in equal numbers, the Orthodox side including representatives of all 14 autocephalous and autonomous Orthodox churches. The fact that a large number of members were to be Catholic and Orthodox hierarchs revealed the importance both churches attributed to this dialogue.

The first plenary session took place on the Greek islands of Patmos and Rhodes, 29 May-4 June 1980. This was an organizational meeting which unanimously adopted the plan for dialogue set forth in the 1978 document and chose initial themes for examination. Cardinal Johannes Willebrands, president of the Vatican's Secretariat for Christian Unity,* and Archbishop Stylianos of Australia (patriarchate of Constantinople) were chosen as co-presidents. Three joint sub-commissions were established to produce studies which would then be synthesized into draft documents to be debated at plenary sessions held every two years.

The second plenary session took place in Munich, 30 June-6 July 1982. Here the first agreed text was finalized: "The Mystery of the Church and of the Eucharist in the Light of the Mystery of the Holy Trinity". It describes a common approach to the relation between the eucharist* and the Trinity,* the church* and the eucharist, and the local church* to the universal church.

The Greek island of Crete was the site of the third plenary session, 30 May-8 June 1984. A draft document entitled "Faith, Sacraments, and the Unity of the Church" was discussed. It treated the relationship between the profession of the same faith* and sacramental communion, giving particular attention to the sacraments of initiation. Because of some Orthodox reservations about Roman Catholic practices in this matter, and some technical difficulties, it was not possible to adopt the document at that time.

The fourth plenary took place near Bari, Italy, in two separate sessions one year apart. The first session, 29 May-7 June 1986, was boycotted by several Orthodox churches because of what they understood as both Roman Catholic support for the schismatic Macedonian Orthodox Church and continued Catholic proselytism* among Orthodox Christians. Once these issues were resolved, the plenary met in a second session at Bari, 9-16 June 1987. Here the document that had been discussed at Crete was revised and approved.

The Orthodox monastery at Valamo, Finland, hosted the fifth plenary session, 19-27 June 1988. A third common document was adopted, entitled "The Sacrament of Order in the Sacramental Structure of the Church, with Particular Reference to the Importance of the Apostolic Succession for the Sanctification and Unity of the People of God". It was also decided at this session to establish a subcommission to study the vexed question of the Eastern Catholic churches.* Moreover, the topic of the next document, to be discussed at the 1990 sixth plenary session in Munich, was decided upon: "Ecclesiological and Canonical Consequences of the Sacramental Structure of the Church: Conciliarity and Authority in the Church".

This dialogue is still in its early stages. But, as was envisaged in the 1978 document which set the course of this dialogue, progress is being made in the effort to establish a common foundation, on the basis of which the more difficult issues, especially the role of the church of Rome and its bishop among the local churches, can be most fruitfully discussed.

It should also be noted that the Russian Orthodox Church, while fully participating in the international Orthodox-Catholic dialogue, has also been engaged in separate theological conversations with the Roman Catholic Church since 1967. These conversations have been held at irregular intervals and have been largely restricted to the social teaching of the two churches. Six meetings have taken place, dealing with the following topics: "The Social Thought of the Roman Catholic Church" (Leningrad 1967), "The Role of the Christian in the Developing Society" (Bari 1970), "The Church in a World in Transformation" (Zagorsk 1973), "The Christian Proclamation of Salvation in a Changing World" (Trent 1975), "The Local Church and the Universal

Church" (Odessa 1980), and "The Diaconal Function of the Church, Especially in the Service of Peace" (Venice 1987). These conversations have developed useful contacts between the two sides. Press communiqués, at times substantial, have been released at the end of each session.

RONALD G. ROBERSON

Information Service (Secretariat for Christian Unity), 4, 1968, pp.17-18; 14, 2, 1971, pp.7-8; 22, 4, 1973, pp.10-13; 28, 3, 1975, pp.9-10; 44, 3-4, 1980, pp.112-15; 65, 3-4, 1987, pp.112-14 • E. Kilmartin, *Towards Reunion: The Orthodox and Roman Catholic Churches,* New York, Paulist, 1979 • E.J. Storman ed., *Towards the Healing of Schism: The Sees of Rome and Constantinople: Public Statements and Correspondence between the Holy See and the Ecumenical Patriarchate, 1958-1984,* New York, Paulist, 1987 • The agreed statements are found in *Origins* 12, no. 10, 1982, pp.157-60; 17, no. 44, 1988, pp.743-49; 18, no. 18, 1988, pp.330-40. Also in *One in Christ,* 19, 1983, pp.188-97; 23, 1987, pp.330-40; 24, 1988, pp. 367-77. Both of these publications contain useful ongoing documentation and commentary on the dialogue, as does the French-language journal *Irénikon.*

ORTHODOXY.

"Orthodoxy" means "right opinion" or "right belief" (also "right glorification", as singled out in the Slavonic translation). Consequently, any human community which bases itself on an accepted system of thought, opinions or beliefs will claim "orthodoxy" for its doctrines. Within the Christian context, the term came to be associated with certain sections of Eastern Christendom: the Chalcedonian (or Eastern Orthodox) and non-Chalcedonian (or Oriental Orthodox) churches. In this narrow sense the word will be dealt with here.

Eastern Christians are not united within one communion.* The main divisions appeared in the 5th century. Some did not accept the third ecumenical council (Ephesus 431), and more rejected the fourth (Chalcedon 451).* This non-acceptance was due both to the theological disagreements over the Christological debates and to the reluctance of some, mainly non-Greek or non-Byzantine Christians, to accept the idea that the conciliar dogmatic definitions should be imposed as imperial laws by the capital, Constantinople (see **dogma**). In hindsight after 15 centuries, those theological differences now appear to have

been mainly due to terminological misunderstandings; furthermore, the subsequent displacements of power have suppressed all traces of political imperial domination on the part of Byzantium-Constantinople or New Rome. With the fall of the Russian empire in 1917, the dream of the Byzantine "symphony" has collapsed in the consciousness of the vast majority within the Orthodox world.

Reunion among Eastern Christians has not been yet achieved. But many judge the theological obstacles to be minor, if not nonexistent. The remaining difficulties are only of a practical nature (see **Oriental Orthodox-Orthodox dialogue**).

The gradual estrangement between the Christian East and the Christian West culminated in the split between the two halves of the Roman empire, which most historians include under the terms "Latins" and "Greeks". In fact, the "Latins", though they all used Latin as their liturgical and theological language, included Germanic Franks, Celts and Anglo-Saxons; the "Greeks" or "Byzantines" incorporated the traditions not only of Constantinople but also of Asia Minor, Egypt (Alexandria), Syria (Antioch) and Palestine (Jerusalem).

The date generally recognized as that of the schism,* 1054, was in fact that of an exchange of excommunications* between the legates of Pope Leo IX and the patriarch of Constantinople, Michael Cerularius (these excommunications were solemnly lifted in 1964 by Pope Paul VI and the patriarch of Constantinople Athenagoras I; see **Orthodox-Roman Catholic dialogue**). But the 1054 dating is somewhat conventional: only later did the other three patriarchates of the famous "pentarchy" (Antioch, Alexandria, Jerusalem) break with Rome (universally recognized as the ancient "primatial" see; see **primacy**), and already in the 9th century difficulties had begun (e.g. between Photius, patriarch of Constantinople, and Pope Nicholas I).

The real issues at stake in the eventual schism were doctrinal and ecclesiological: (1) the Western addition of the filioque* ("and from the Son") to the Nicene Creed,* concerning the procession of the Holy Spirit;* (2) the jurisdictional claims of the papacy to a right of universal intervention. In spite of progress made, these two questions still constitute the main obstacles to reunion between the Orthodox and the Roman Catholic churches.

One of the consequences of the Western crusades in the East (1095-1270) was to deepen the breach between East and West. The papal appointment at that time of "Latin" bishops who paralleled existing Orthodox bishops in such ancient sees as Antioch and Constantinople represented in fact an un-churching of long-existing Christian communities. Moreover, the attempts at reunion — the councils of Lyons (1274) and of Ferrara-Florence (1438-39) — not only failed, but in the eyes of the vast majority of the Orthodox, they actually represented a consummation of the schism. After Florence, the two halves of Christendom largely ignored each other.

As a result of this breach and estrangement, the Orthodox world has not experienced the Western crises which resulted in the Protestant Reformation and in the Roman Catholic Counter-Reformation. The Orthodox world had its own crises in the East, as it had to deal with the Reformation and Counter-Reformation, its isolation under Islamic rule, the fall of Christian Constantinople to the Muslims (1453), the rise of nationalisms, etc. But these crises did not affect the essential faith* of the church. Hence, the Orthodox preserved the very strong sense of an unbroken continuity with the faith of the apostles (see **apostolicity**) as interpreted and witnessed to by the seven great ecumenical councils* and the fathers of the church (see **patristics**).

Undeniably, the theology taught in Orthodox schools, particularly in the "Byzantine" or Eastern Orthodox world, came under Western influences, both medieval scholastic and Protestant. However, beyond vestiges of these influences that still survive here and there, Orthodoxy has rediscovered its own proper identity through patristic revivals. These revivals have helped to reveal the common theological spirit of the Eastern and the Oriental Orthodox, the authentic Orthodox theology which refuses the systematizing tendencies of various crystallizations.

The essential theological approach of Orthodoxy consists in an uncompromising adherence to the confession of Jesus Christ* as the incarnate Son of God, second person of the Holy Trinity.* In this perspective, the incarnation* is the most central event in his-

tory,* the only true revolution, because in Jesus Christ and his redemptive work, the personal, Triune God, the living God of Abraham, Isaac and Jacob, not only manifests himself fully but *gives* himself to humanity.

The divine person of Jesus Christ assumed humanity, and he assumed it even to the utmost limits of the human condition, i.e. unto death itself, and death upon the cross, with the agony of the dying person's sense of being forsaken by God. Thus, humanity becomes totally transformed, regenerated in him. This tasting of death by a divine person — what Gregory of Nazianzus calls "the humanity of God" which "sanctifies humanity" — could only result in victory over death, in the destruction of death. This accomplishment necessarily confers a new quality on all life. The sacrificial action of Jesus Christ regenerates, re-creates the whole of creation.* "A few drops of blood remake the whole universe" (Gregory of Nazianzus). This humanity, which Christ assumed and sanctified, has a cosmic dimension. Christ's victory over death grants a new life to the whole of creation. Each human being, called to "put on Christ" (Gal. 3:27), is royally, prophetically and ministerially responsible for the whole universe.

The resurrection* is therefore a cosmic and very central event, and the Orthodox accordingly place great emphasis on the passion-resurrection of Christ, the paschal character of the Christian life. This life is the life offered in Christ through the gift of grace,* which is the breath of the Holy Spirit — the gift of God himself. Salvation,* in the Orthodox perspective, is not restricted to redemption* in the strict sense, i.e. only freeing humanity from sin.* Salvation is viewed in terms not so much of one's justification* as of one's participation in the true destiny of human nature, fully realized in Christ. Salvation is offered to all as a free gift, to be freely accepted by all. The gift of the Holy Spirit enables human beings to become "partakers of the divine nature" (2 Pet. 1:4).

This participation of human beings in the divine life of the Holy Trinity, their incorporation in Christ as adopted sons and daughters through the Spirit of the Son who in their hearts cries "Abba, Father" (Gal. 4:6; cf. Rom. 8:15), is what the Orthodox often express in the famous patristic adage "God became man that man may become God" (Irenaeus et al.). It is also the meaning of the term "deification" *(theosis)*.

Participation in the divine life implies growth in Christ to the dimension of becoming a true person,* i.e. the dimension of cosmic humanity, members of Christ, members of one another, temples of the Holy Spirit (1 Cor. 6:19, 12:12; Eph. 4:25). Christians are co-responsible for the recapitulation of the whole creation for union with God. In other words, the whole of history is their responsibility, and no human situation can possibly be excluded. It is a "eucharistic" view of the destiny of humanity and creation. And the eucharistic offering — the very heart of life — is "for the life of the world" (liturgy of John Chrysostom; cf. John 6:51). Consequently, the eucharist* commits all to participate in history.

The Orthodox conception of salvation leads to the understanding that the church* is not just an institution in a purely human sense, but primarily is a community of "persons" who are built into "a spiritual house". "Like living stones be yourselves built into a spiritual house, to be a holy priesthood, to offer spiritual sacrifices acceptable to God through Jesus Christ" (1 Pet. 2:5). The church is hierarchical, but one views the hierarchy in the larger perspective of 1 Cor. 12 and 13 — within the same Body of Christ, with a diversity of functions, bound together in love and called to witness to this love.

According to the Orthodox teaching on the church, all institutional aspects (hierarchy, discipline, organization, etc.) should be nothing but the expressions of the deep nature of the church as described above. They are all in nature charismatic (see **charism(ata)**), their authority is that of Christ and the Spirit, the "two hands of the Father" (Irenaeus). They are all there to serve the essential and central action of the church: the eucharistic offering for the whole creation in the unity of the one Spirit and in communion with all things visible and invisible ("the whole company of heaven", to quote the liturgy of the Church of England). This eucharistic offering, as the Orthodox like to recall, quoting Chrysostom, does not end in the church building but is there to irrigate the whole of life through the faithful. These should go out into the world as witnesses, every one in his or her own way,

according to the diversity of gifts, to the new life offered to humanity in Christ.

The foundation of Orthodox ecclesiology is the local eucharistic community: the bishop (see **episcopacy**) surrounded by and presiding over the presbyterate* and the community. This local church* or diocese (today often the parish, where the priest fulfills most of the bishop's duties, i.e. preaching of the word of God* and presiding over the celebration of the sacrament*) is not a *part* of the church universal but the *expression* of the church universal — though only in so far as the local church is faithful to the faith of the apostles, the catholic faith of the church, and therefore is in communion* with all the local churches faithful to the same faith.

Consequently, the Orthodox church is, according to its ecclesiology, a fellowship of local churches, in communion of faith and sacrament. But only one local church is entrusted with the duty to "preside in love" over all the churches. Traditionally, this presidency is the responsibility of the church of Rome. Since the split between East and West, the church of Constantinople presides over the Eastern Orthodox churches.

The relations of communion and unity in faith among the local churches constitute what the Orthodox mean by conciliarity.* This conciliar nature of the Orthodox church is sometimes expressed in councils, but it is not restricted to them and is not dependent on their actual meeting. According to Orthodox ecclesiology, every time the eucharist is celebrated, the conciliar nature of the church is expressed. Also the plurality of consecrators of a local bishop is a clear expression of conciliarity: as co-consecrators, bishops from neighbouring local churches witness to the faithfulness to the apostolic faith of the church in which the new bishop will be the guarantor of this faithfulness.

Conciliar relations among local churches through the president, whose role is to be the sign of unity, are well expressed in the 34th of the so-called Apostolic Canons: "Let the bishops of each province recognize the one who is primate among them, let them accept him as their head and let them do nothing without his having expressed his opinion, even though it is incumbent on every one to look to the affairs of his diocese and the dependent territories. But he in his turn must

Russian Orthodox clergy at St Sergius day service of thanksgiving, Zagorsk, USSR (WCC/Peter Williams)

do nothing without the accord of all. Thus concord will reign, and God will be glorified through Christ in the Holy Spirit." The Trinitarian conclusion indicates that the relations among churches are to be based upon the same principles of unity in diversity as those of persons in the church: personhood is in the image of the unity in diversity in the Holy Trinity.

There are, quite naturally, many discrepancies between what Orthodoxy is ideally in its teaching and what the Orthodox churches are in historical reality. There are many distortions of Orthodoxy due to human sinfulness. Thus, for instance, Orthodoxy in the 20th century presents many divisions, in particular of a jurisdictional nature. These have become clearly apparent with the dispersion of Orthodox throughout the world, especially in the Western areas. With the rise of nationalism* in the 19th century, there appeared a tendency to identify Orthodoxy with a particular culture, an ethnic group, a nation in the modern sense of the word. This tendency was condemned as a heresy* in 1872 by a local

council in Constantinople (received by all the other churches) under the name of "phyletism". In spite of this condemnation, the tendency still exists among the Orthodox to substitute in practice a nationalistic ecclesiology for the traditional *territorial* principle, following the apostolic definition ("the church of God which is at Corinth", 1 Cor. 1:2, etc.) which unites all the people (Jews, Greeks, etc.) in one eucharistic community in a given place. The Orthodox who are scattered throughout the world tend to be claimed by their "mother churches" according to an ethnic, cultural, national principle, which leads to a multiplicity of jurisdictions in one place instead of one bishop in each place (see **diaspora**). The debate still goes on; the purity of ecclesiology is at stake.

Another temptation for modern Orthodoxy is the crystallizing of patristic theology into a new form of scholasticism as a system of thought. Instead, there should be ever-renewed efforts to orient each generation to a living sense of union with God. It is a tendency simply to repeat as a rigid catechism what the fathers have said in the past. This practice often leads to a refusal to consider the challenges of history today. Among those who succumb to this temptation, there is sometimes a tendency to reject ecumenism as *the* heresy of the 20th century. Some hold that the unity of Christians can be achieved only through the formal conversion of all to the historical Orthodox church.

Orthodox ecclesiology claims to be eucharistic; the church is the sacrament par excellence. All too often, however, the reality of life belies this understanding of the church. In too many cases, baptism* (as well as marriage*) tends to be a purely social event, and people partake of the eucharist perhaps once a year, if at all. Many churches have indeed reacted against this contradiction within Orthodoxy, but there is still a long way to go. In too many cases, the eucharistic prayers are said in such a way that people cannot hear them. As a result, the laity* tend to regard themselves and are regarded as passive members of the church who are not fully co-responsible in the unity of the one church, not fully co-responsible in the unity of the one Spirit with the presiding minister, and the reality of 1 Cor. 12 and 13 is remote.

The vast majority of Orthodox churches are engaged in the ecumenical movement. With the exception of one or two communities (such as the Russian Church in Exile or the Greek Old-Calendarists), they are all member churches of the WCC. Thus, in spite of all its historical sins, Orthodoxy has a vocation* in the striving towards the recovery of unity among Christians. This vocation is a very special one, since the Orthodox firmly believe that "the Orthodox church is the church of Christ on earth", as Fr Sergius Bulgakov wrote. This conviction, paradoxical as it may sound, can serve the ecumenical search for unity, but of course on certain conditions. Bulgakov expresses the first condition in the very next sentence: "The church of Christ is not an institution but a new life with Christ and in Christ, moved by the Holy Spirit." In other words, the Orthodox community can truly serve Christian unity in so far as they witness to true Orthodoxy and remember that when Orthodoxy is true to itself, it confesses that it does not know the limits of the church of Christ: the Spirit "blows where it wills" (John 3:8). Also, the Orthodox serve Christian unity whenever they remember that one of the essential duties in being an Orthodox consists in one's permanent conversion to Orthodoxy.

NICHOLAS LOSSKY

For bibliography, see **Eastern Orthodoxy**.

P

PACIFIC. The area covers the islands of Melanesia, Micronesia and Polynesia. Christianity was first introduced to the area by Spanish missionaries in Micronesia in the 17th century, but its significant spread began when the London Missionary Society sent missionaries to Tahiti in 1798. From that time the Christian faith moved across the islands until, in the 20th century, it became the faith of all the Pacific peoples except for the Indians of Fiji.

A co-operative spirit prevailed among the Protestant missions from the beginning. Comity agreements provided that different denominations would work in different territories. Only in Samoa did any serious competition develop between Protestant bodies, in this case Methodist and Congregationalist. The usual situation was one of denominational uniformity within each area and complete isolation of each area from the others. The relation to Roman Catholics was another matter. Usually arriving later on the scene than the Protestants, and therefore being a minority, Catholics were regarded with hostility, a feeling which they reciprocated.

The only large-scale contact between the churches of different territories was in the form of missions sent from Christianized islands to unevangelized areas — first from Tahiti to the Cook Islands and Samoa, then from Tonga to Samoa and Fiji, and finally, in large numbers, from Fiji, Samoa, Tonga and the Cook Islands to Papua New Guinea and

the Solomon Islands. This contact, however, did not develop much understanding, since there was a tendency among the islander missionaries to regard those they served as uncivilized and to report them as such to their home constituencies.

Not until 1926 was there any interdenominational conference on church work in the Pacific. Sydney and Auckland were the scenes of two conferences held in connection with the visit of the ecumenical leader John R. Mott. A larger conference was held in Morpeth, Australia, in 1948. But these meetings were for foreign missionaries, not for islanders. The first meeting for island Christians was at Malua, Western Samoa, in 1961. Here the decision was made to form a Pacific Conference of Churches (PCC), a decision put into effect in 1966. The PCC then became the main vehicle of ecumenism in the Pacific.

Another vehicle was the Pacific Theological College in Suva, also founded in 1966 as an international training centre where the future leaders of the churches could study together and come to know each other. It was the first Pacific institution to confer the bachelor of divinity degree and, later, the master of theology. Soon after its establishment, ecumenical associations of theological schools were begun, the South Pacific Association of Theological Schools (SPATS) for schools east of New Guinea, and the Melanesian Association of Theological Schools (MATS) for schools in Papua New

Guinea and the Solomon Islands. The former has had a rather fitful existence, but the latter has been a strong force for co-operative study and advancement.

Christian education has also developed ecumenically. Following the Malua conference, an ambitious plan was formulated for an ecumenical effort to write a complete Christian education curriculum from pre-school to adult grades. This was to be related to island life and was to draw on island culture. Eventually the entire Pacific Island Christian Education Curriculum was completed and published in 28 books.

The establishment of the Pacific island Christian education curriculum and the Pacific Theological College was a result of the Malua meeting. In this the WCC played an important part. The strong presence of the Pacific Conference of Churches also owed a great deal to the enabling role played by the WCC, through bringing together leaders from the Pacific, both from the church and the community, to meet and share common concerns and to be exposed to the wider ecumenical movement.

When these ecumenical agencies were coming into existence during the 1960s an enormous change was taking place in the Roman Catholic Church. With the convening of the Second Vatican Council,* Catholic attitudes in the Pacific Islands went through a profound transformation. Up until this time Catholics had held aloof from contacts with other churches and from the ecumenical organizations. Now they began to get to know their fellow Christians and to consider co-operating with them. Taken together, Catholics made the largest single church in the Pacific, and they constituted the biggest church in New Caledonia and Papua New Guinea. Soon they became one of the strongest ecumenical forces in the Pacific. The Catholic bishops conference joined the PCC in 1976. The Catholic theological schools became members of MATS and SPATS. The central Catholic seminary was established near the Pacific Theological College, promoting co-operative efforts and mutual understanding in theological education. Joint studies and statements on public affairs were made possible when the Catholic office for justice and peace was placed in the headquarters building of the PCC.

All the developments considered thus far

have been on an international scale. National ecumenism came later, reversing the usual order. The slowness in national reconciliation and collaboration may be attributed largely to the effects of the comity maintained by the early missions. Because of comity each country had at first only one church, which regarded itself as the church of the whole people. It looked upon other churches, when they came in, as interlopers. The formation of ecumemical organizations would imply an equal place for all churches, something that the previously dominant bodies were not eager to allow. National councils of churches became strong first in those countries which had no single dominant church, primarily Papua New Guinea and secondarily the Solomon Islands. Papua New Guinea developed the Melanesian Council of Churches, the largest and most active of all the national councils. After some years of remarkable effectiveness on the national scene, with a large staff and close contacts with the government, it passed through a period of financial and personnel difficulties which at times reduced it almost to nothing. The Solomon Islands Christian Association has played a significant

Outside a Roman Catholic church in Western Samoa (WCC/Peter Williams)

role in its country, as has the Tonga Council of Churches. Lesser, but still valuable, bodies have been the Fiji Council of Churches, the Samoa Council of Churches, and the Vanuatu Council of Churches.

Recent years have seen the influx and growth of a large number of non-co-operating churches, which have gradually altered the picture as far as ecumenism is concerned. Most of these churches are of a Pentecostal type, though the largest and most rapidly growing is the Mormon church, which is neither Pentecostal nor new to the region. Small efforts have been made towards developing understanding and possible co-operation with some of these bodies. The most significant of these efforts is that of the Melanesian Council of Churches in its contacts and co-operation with the Evangelical Alliance of the South Pacific, an organization of newer churches and Christian institutions of Papua New Guinea. But in general the separation from these bodies is continuing and represents the greatest challenge to the ecumenical spirit in the Pacific.

See also **Pacific Conference of Churches**.

CHARLES W. FORMAN

J.R. Chandran ed., *The Cross and the Tanoa: Gospel and Culture in the Pacific*, Suva, South Pacific Association of Theological Schools, 1988 • C.W. Forman, *The Voice of Many Waters: The Story of the Life and Ministry of the Pacific Conference of Churches in the Last 25 Years*, Suva, Lotu Pasifika, 1986 • J. Garrett, *To Live Among the Stars*, WCC, 1982 • C. Wright & L. Fugui eds, *Christ in South Pacific Cultures*, Suva, Lotu Pasifika, 1985.

PACIFIC CONFERENCE OF CHURCHES.

The PCC is the regional ecumenical organization for the islands of Melanesia, Micronesia and Polynesia. It was born out of a conference of missions and churches held in Malua, Western Samoa, in 1961. Its official formation took place five years later at the assembly on Lifou Island. Subsequent assemblies were held in Fiji (1971), Papua New Guinea (1976), Tonga (1981) and Western Samoa (1986). The headquarters were first in Samoa, but in 1967 were moved permanently to Suva, Fiji.

The conference grew rapidly under the leadership of two of its general secretaries, Setareki Tuilovoni (1967-74) and Lorine Tevi

(1977-81). It was also much strengthened by the contributions of one of its early chairmen, Sione 'Amanaki Havea (1966-71). New churches joined the PCC fellowship, and membership was also thrown open to national Christian councils. In 1976 the Roman Catholics joined. The conference has always had strong participation from the French-speaking islands of New Caledonia and Tahiti, and they are now fully incorporated into its life, with the provision of simultaneous translation at its meetings and the publication of French versions of its reports and documents. The only countries where it has lost members are Papua New Guinea and the Solomon Islands. Participation by the churches of Micronesia has also been sporadic because of the distance.

The conference has reached out to the churches with a variety of programmes. It has introduced modern methods of Christian education and training for better family life, spreading these through seminars all over the area. It has helped the churches in their communication efforts and in youth programmes. It has tried to raise the place of women by holding regional conferences for women and setting an example itself with the appointment of a woman as chairperson, Fetaui Mata'afa (1971-76), and another as general secretary (Tevi). It has devoted much attention to economic development rooted in the realities of village life. It has taken the lead in dealing with political problems of the region, speaking out against nuclear testing and in favour of national independence.

In 1982 the steady growth of the organization was reversed in a decision, taken under the leadership of the long-time chairman, Jabez Bryce (1976-86), to make drastic reductions in staff and programmes in the hope of decreasing the extreme dependence on foreign funds. Since then programmatic growth has been slower and more selective, but the conference has explored new ways of serving the region. PCC and WCC have close links.

CHARLES W. FORMAN

PACIFISM. The derivation of the word — from Latin *pax* (peace) and *facere* (to make) — establishes an immediate connection with Jesus's statement in the Sermon on the Mount: "Blessed are the peacemakers" (Matt. 5:9). There have been many varieties of pacifism based both on religious and secular philosophies — most notably Buddhism. Within the Christian church, the transition which culminated under the Emperor Constantine changed the church from being a religion whose adherents refused to kill in its first three centuries to being the religion of the empire and the army.

There has always been a minority tradition of Christian pacifism based on the Sermon on the Mount, for example, Francis of Assisi, the left wing of the Reformation (e.g. Mennonites) and the Quakers, founded in the 17th century in England by George Fox. A Quaker, William Allen, founded the Society for the Promotion of Permanent and Universal Peace in 1816. By 1900, there were at least 400 peace organizations. The mood of optimism and belief in progress was punctured by the first world war.

The abolition of war, like the abolition of slavery, had seemed a realizable goal to many at the time of the Hague conferences of 1899 and 1907. War is, historically, almost entirely a male activity. Feminist analyses link the social structures of patriarchy and war closely together. Pacifist women have been strongly represented through peace organizations from the Women's International League of Peace and Freedom (early conferences in 1915 and 1920) through to the Greenham women. Eminent individuals among their number include Bertha von Suttner, Muriel Lester, Maude Royden and Dorothy Day.

In the 20th century, the Sermon on the Mount was returned to the Christian church as practical politics by a Hindu, Mahatma Gandhi (1869-1948). He, in turn, had been inspired by such thinkers as Henry David Thoreau (1817-62) from the US and the unorthodox Russian Orthodox, Tolstoy (1828-1910). Gandhi used pacifist methods, including civil disobedience, in the movement to liberate India from British colonial rule. From Gandhi, the line of influence passes through such struggles as the US civil rights movement, led by Martin Luther King, and black opposition to apartheid in South Africa, with such non-violent leaders as Albert Luthuli in an earlier generation and Allan Boesak, Frank Chikane and Desmond Tutu in the contemporary phase.

Disillusionment after the first world war gave a massive boost to pacifism. Churches had often lent uncritical support to national war efforts. Already before the war, the Fellowship of Reconciliation* was established. During the first world war, conscientious objection led to significant numbers of people being imprisoned, including the atheist philosopher Bertrand Russell in Britain.

Between the two world wars, pacifism became a mass movement under such leaders as Dick Sheppard, founder of the Peace Pledge Union. But as the storm clouds of fascism* darkened in the 1930s, support for pacifism waned. Pacifism as a mass movement was past, and a much smaller core of conscientious objectors refused to serve in the second world war. Nazism proved to be the decisive factor in undermining the popularity and credibility of pacifism. In theological circles, the critique of Reinhold Niebuhr and the example of Dietrich Bonhoeffer proved damaging.

The advent of the nuclear era has made a profound difference to the traditional arguments between pacifists and adherents of the just-war* theory. Since the second world war, with peaks beginning in late 1950s and late 1970s, major "ban the bomb" movements have developed with strong Christian and Christian pacifist involvement. The debate about German re-armament in the 1950s (by Barth, Niemöller, Heinemann, Gollwitzer et al.) and the British Campaign for Nuclear Disarmament set the trend. There was a growing convergence between pacifists and "nuclear pacifists", who argued that strict application of just-war criteria precluded the use of nuclear weapons. The movement beginning in the late 1970s, with strong campaigns in the US and most of Western Europe (particularly Holland and the Federal Republic of Germany), had strong pacifist involvement, particularly through women's organizations and participation. To put it another way, the anti-nuclear campaign converted many Christians to an activist and pacifist expression of their faith.

At the same time, pacifism has been challenged in terms of the right of resistance and how that could be made effective. During the 1950s and 1960s decolonization* proceeded surprisingly peacefully in many countries, but in others armed liberation* movements were formed. The decision of the WCC to support the humanitarian projects of armed liberation movements in Southern Africa created controversy within the member churches. Rejection was strongest in churches not known for a predominantly pacifist position, particularly in the Federal Republic of Germany and Great Britain.

This debate followed the 1968 Uppsala assembly, where Martin Luther King would have preached had he not been assassinated. Prior to his murder, King had taken an unpopular stance and courageously denounced the Vietnam war — a cause which unleashed the mass protests of the 1960s, including much of the 1968 student movement. King also nominated Vietnamese Buddhist Thich Nhat Hanh for the Nobel peace prize.

In Latin America, Brazilian bishop Helder Camara argued that in terms of both principle and practice, active non-violence was the best way to break the "spiral of violence", whereas Camilo Torres, Ernesto Cardenal and others argued that armed resistance could be required. All stressed the primacy of liberation.

Recent events in countries as different as the Philippines and those in Central Europe have shown that mass non-violent movements can bring political transformation (although China serves as a counter example). It can be a costly method, as many of its leaders including King and Gandhi have emphasized. History is not so clear-cut or moral as to guarantee the success of non-violence, and political change often occurs as a result of a mix of non-violent and violent forms of resistance (e.g. in South Africa). What can be said is that many historical examples show that massive levels of state violence in war or repression have a severely declining utility, and that mass non-violent action is increasingly seen as both a moral and a more effective approach. These conclusions also have relevance to the nuclear debate. Related concepts such as civilian defence, non-offensive defence and non-provocative defence are attempts acceptably to implement pacifism — or at least non-aggressive forms of defence — as a substitute for the weaponry of mass destruction. Gene Sharp has done prodigious work in cataloguing the range of techniques below the threshold of violence that people can use.

Ecumenical debate has reflected these shifts in the world political scene. The WCC's first assembly (Amsterdam 1948) stated that "war as a method of settling disputes is incompatible with the teaching and example of our Lord Jesus Christ". From the European context, the final document of the European Ecumenical Assembly (1989) stated: "There are no situations in our countries or on our continent in which violence is required or justified" (61). It is perhaps a measure of the injustice in the countries of the South that there are no comparably clear ecumenical statements from other continents, or at the world level. The WCC's world convocation on "Justice, Peace and the Integrity of Creation"* (Seoul 1990) spoke, however, of the need to overcome the institution of war, and continued the clear denunciation of the possession as well as the use of weapons of mass destruction.

Whereas the major church consensus of the Constantinian era accepted war and state violence, the emerging ecumenical consensus rejects war but does not preclude resistance to tyranny or oppressive government. The peace churches (Quakers, Mennonites, etc.), pacifist fellowships within denominations and interfaith and interdenominational groups such as the International Fellowship of Reconciliation provide the organizational face of Christian pacifism. Churches have campaigned for the rights of conscientious objectors and succeeded in achieving this right in a number of countries — including the German Democratic Republic. The latter was a remarkable achievement in view of the Marxist opposition to pacifism.

See also **just war, militarism/militarization, peace, violence and nonviolence, war.**

ROGER WILLIAMSON

R.H. Bainton, *Christian Attitudes to War and Peace: A Historical Survey and Critical Re-evaluation*, Nashville, TN, Abingdon, 1982 • R.M. Brown, *Religion and Violence*, Philadelphia, Westminster, 1987 • H. Camara, *Spiral of Violence*, London, Sheed & Ward, 1971 • J. Ferguson, *War and Peace in the World's Religions*, London, Sheldon, 1977 • P. McAllister ed., *Reweaving the Web of Life: Feminism and Nonviolence*, Philadelpha, New Society, 1982 • P. Meyer, *The Pacifist Conscience*, New York, Holt, Rinehart & Winston, 1966 • C. Moorhead, *Troublesome People: The Warriors of Pacifism*, Bethesda, MD, Adler & Adler, 1987 • D. Parker & B.J. Fraser eds, *Peace, War and God's Justice*, Toronto, United Church Publ. House, 1989 • J. Wallis ed., *Peacemakers*, Sydney, Harper & Row, 1983 • J. Wallis ed., *Waging Peace*, San Francisco, Harper & Row, 1982 • J.H. Yoder, *He Came Preaching Peace*, Scottdale, PA, Herald, 1985.

PAN-ORTHODOX CONFERENCES.

The pan-Orthodox conferences were inaugurated in 1961 (Rhodes) at the initiative of the Ecumenical Patriarchate of Constantinople, after consultation with all the canonical Eastern Orthodox churches. It was not, however, the first pan-Orthodox encounter. After the great schism between East and West (1054) and the fall of the Byzantine empire (1453), the ecumenical patriarch, in collegial co-operation with all the patriarchs of the East, had convoked several councils in Constantinople (1484, 1590, 1735, 1848, 1872), to deal with canonical and ecclesiological matters, including the elevation of the metropolitan of Moscow to patriarchal dignity (1590).

But behind Rhodes 1961 was the recognition of new Orthodox realities resulting from the establishment in the Balkan peninsula of many national Orthodox churches at the end of the 19th and the beginning of the 20th centuries. In 1923 (Constantinople) and in 1930 (Mt Athos) two inter-Orthodox meetings were held, the first dealing with pastoral and canonical issues, and the second with the preparation of the agenda for a general synod of the Orthodox church. A pre-synod meeting scheduled for 1932 could not be held because of the precarious world situation.

This agenda was finally addressed at the 1961 conference. It included topics of doctrinal, missionary, socio-ethical and ecumenical character. The second and third conferences (Rhodes 1963, 1964) dealt with the issues of bilateral dialogues* with other churches and denominations and attendance of Orthodox observers at the Second Vatican Council. The fourth conference (Chambésy, Geneva, 1968) revised the agenda drawn up in 1961 and established an inter-Orthodox preparatory commission of the Great and Holy Council of the Orthodox church.

The first pre-conciliar pan-Orthodox conference met in Chambésy (1976) and decided upon a ten-point agenda for the council, including ecclesiological, pastoral/anthropological and ecumenical topics: (1) the Orthodox diaspora, (2) autocephaly, (3) autonomy, (4) the diptychs, (5) revision of the calendar, (6) marriage impediments, (7) fasting rules, (8) interchurch relations, (9) the ecumenical movement, and (10) peace and justice. The inter-Orthodox theological preparatory commission is to work out documents on each of the above subjects which, after further elaboration and approval by the pre-conciliar conferences, are to be referred to the future Great and Holy Council for consideration and action.

Of special importance for the ecumenical movement are two documents drawn up by the third pre-conciliar pan-Orthodox conference (Chambésy 1986). The first, dealing with the "Relations of the Orthodox Church with the Christian World", evaluates the bilateral dialogues of the Orthodox church with the Roman Catholic, Anglican, Old Catholic, Lutheran, non-Chalcedonian (Oriental Orthodox) and Reformed churches, and sets guidelines for the dialogues. In the second document, entitled "The Orthodox Church and the Ecumenical Movement", the Orthodox church as a whole, while expressing its commitment to Christian unity, reiterates its readiness to continue to participate in all ecumenical bodies, particularly within the WCC. The document stresses, however, that "the Orthodox church, loyal to her ecclesiology, to the identity of her internal structure and the teaching of the undivided church, while participating in the WCC, absolutely rejects the idea of the equality of confessions and refuses to conceive church unity as an interconfessional re-adjustment. In this sense, the unity sought within the WCC cannot simply be the result of theological agreements."

In addition, the document underlines the necessity of creating within the WCC and other ecumenical organizations the necessary conditions to enable the Orthodox churches to act on the basis of their own ecclesiological identity, in accordance with their own way of thinking and on an equal footing with other churches.

The pan-Orthodox conferences are convoked by the ecumenical patriarch, *primus inter pares* in the Orthodox church, and presided over by the senior delegate of the Ecumenical Patriarchate, which is responsible for the conferences' overall co-ordination. Since 1970 a secretariat for the preparation of the Great and Holy Council has been located at the Orthodox centre of the Ecumenical Patriarchate in Chambésy.

See also **Eastern Orthodoxy, Orthodoxy**.

GEORGES TSETSIS

M. Aghiorgoussis, "Towards the Great and Holy Council, the First Pre-synodal Pan-Orthodox Conference in Geneva", *The Greek Orthodox Theological Review*, 21, 1976 • Damaskinos of Tranoupolis, "Towards the Great and Holy Council", *The Greek Orthodox Theological Review*, 24, 1979 • S. Harakas, *Something Is Stirring in World Orthodoxy*, Minneapolis, Light & Life, 1978 • N. Lossky, "Préparation du concile panorthodoxe", *Etudes*, 1977 • Synodika, 6 vols, minutes of pan-Orthodox conferences, secretariat for the preparation of the Great and Holy Council, Chambésy.

PARMAR, SAMUEL L. B. 7.8.1921, Banaras, Uttar Pradesh, India; d. 29.5.1979, Allahabad, India. Associate director of the Ecumenical Institute of Bossey,* 1964-67, Parmar, a member of the Church of North India, was chairman of the working committee on Church and Society, member of the Commission of the Churches on International Affairs, vice-chairman of the World Student Christian Federation,* vice-chairman of the Student Christian Movement of India, chairman of the Christian Institute for the Study of Religion and Society, Bangalore, member of the executive committee of the National Council of Churches of India, and WCC representative on the SODEPAX committee. He taught international economics at Allahabad University College. A competent economist and knowledgeable on issues of development, he participated in numerous conferences. He was an adviser to the Uppsala assembly, and his contributions helped in shaping the WCC's understanding of the processes and goals of development. He wrote several books in English and Hindi, including *Lift Up Your Eyes: A Layman's Quest for Hope* (Madras, Christian Literature Society, 1972).

ANS J. VAN DER BENT

PARTICIPATION. Participation implies belonging to and involvement in an organization, being an active member of a decision-making body, involved in policy making or participating in the procedures, programmes, staffing or financing of the organization. Within the ecumenical movement there are different levels of participation. For most, attendance at an international ecumenical event is a one-time experience of personal involvement at the world level; for a few, however, that experience will evolve into a more active involvement in the

ecumenical bodies that set policy and make decisions.

Pressure for adequate representation by women, laity, youth, people with disabilities, indigenous peoples — the marginalized — has raised questions about the purpose of WCC gatherings. The very success of the participatory process has brought with it frustrations and problems never envisaged when the original 145 member churches first assembled in Amsterdam in 1948. Enormous difficulties surface today whenever the WCC has to allocate assembly seats, appoint a presidium or central committee, compile sub-unit commissions and working groups or choose staff. The participatory process, demanding that various categories be fully represented, can overshadow the stated aim of the activity or meeting itself. Some of the WCC difficulties stem from failure to recognize that different forms of participation are required by different kinds of events.

Growth of international participation. From the earliest days of the ecumenical movement, outstanding leaders from the so-called younger churches, especially from Asia, had been actively participating in international conferences. The years from the 1940s to the late 1960s found these churches involved in the transition from Western-mission-centred patterns to indigenous leadership. The New Delhi assembly not only met on Asian soil, but the Council moved to be genuinely worldwide with the admission of 11 African churches to its membership. By the time of the world conference on Church and Society in 1966, participants from Africa, Asia and Latin America were in equal numbers to those from the North. Their presence influenced the Council to change priorities and perspectives on world affairs. Concern for development,* for revolution,* for non-violent forms of struggle and for racial justice* became embodied in WCC programmes. But such churches continue to have difficulties dealing with Eurocentric decision-making procedures, pressurized written reports, working in European languages and the lack of genuine consensus* at consultations.

The 1966 conference marked a shift in emphasis for the WCC. For the first time there were more lay participants than clergy at a WCC conference. The Vancouver assembly, with nearly half the participants from the laity, strongly recommended that the churches should encourage the full participation of the laity and ensure that they equip the laity for ministry in the world. However, despite the good intentions, timing of church events and conferences very often exclude those who are bound by the terms of their employment.

The Commission on World Mission and Evangelism conference at San Antonio, Texas (1989), was a highly participatory event leading to "Acts of Faithfulness" which endeavoured to evoke from the participants a sense of active commitment towards the resolutions they made. Stories of involvement in mission* at the local level dominated the conference, requiring a follow-up of reflection and articulation of the theological insights arising from that involvement. Utilizing the gifts of the people of God* leads to tensions, albeit creative, between the participants whose gift is to testify to their experiences through the medium of story-telling, and those with the gift to articulate the ecumenical vision from a theological perspective. Unless both are present, the Body of Christ is not complete.

Participation of non-member churches. At its 40th anniversary in 1988 the WCC was still confronted by the statistic of roughly two-thirds of Christianity not participating in its work for unity* and renewal.* Among those who have not sought closer relationships are churches which oppose the search for worldwide unity on principle, as for example many on the "evangelical" wing of the Protestant churches, as well as members of independent Christian groups and churches. Nor is the Roman Catholic Church (RCC) a member of the WCC.

In contrast to the rather chilly reaction the RCC gave the first assembly at Amsterdam (1948), Roman Catholic observers were present at the third assembly at New Delhi (1961) and in larger numbers at later assemblies. After Vatican II* a whole network of new relationships was established through the Secretariat for Promoting Christian Unity.* Discussions at following assemblies, the work of the Joint Working Group* since 1965, full participation in the Faith and Order* commission since 1968, representation on other commissions and the two papal visits to the Ecumenical Centre in Geneva have underlined a policy of increased collaboration.

At Amsterdam only four Eastern Orthodox churches — the Ecumenical Patriarchate, the Church of Cyprus, the Church of Greece, and the Romanian Orthodox Episcopate of the USA — were represented. By the time of the third assembly in New Delhi, the removal of misunderstandings and the climate of change in East-West political relationships opened the way for the entry of four large Eastern European Orthodox churches into the WCC. But the participation of the Orthodox has meant for them a difficult adjustment to a predominantly Protestant and Western ethos, liturgy,* agenda and style of work. In the succeeding years the Orthodox have made a unique contribution to the ongoing debate on the unity of the church as it is understood theologically and historically.

Participation of various groups. The ecumenical movement has made efforts over the years to increase the participation of several specific groups of people.

Children: While children and their needs have been a focus of discussion within the ecumenical movement since a WCC consultation on children in 1951, their participation has been limited. By 1980 the admission of children to the eucharist* had become a matter for serious debate within the ecumenical movement. This issue was discussed at Bad Segeberg, Federal Republic of Germany, in 1980, followed later that year by another consultation on "Children as Active Partners in the Christian Community", at Evian, France. Apart from a final statement and a "Message to the Children of the World", there were no specific recommendations to the churches.

It was not until the sixth assembly of the WCC at Vancouver in 1983 that the active participation of children became a reality. Prior to the assembly, children from more than 30 countries contributed pictures, poems and stories illustrating the theme "The City of Hope". Recommendations urged the participation of children within church structures, in decision making and in discussions of *Baptism, Eucharist and Ministry.**

The disabled: In the course of the centuries countless Christians have given their lives to the service of people with disabilities, but the question remains as to how much the churches have allowed the disabled to participate fully in their own communal life. Not until the Faith and Order commission meeting at Louvain in 1971 was the participation of the disabled taken seriously. From the fifth assembly of the WCC in Nairobi (1975) came a historic statement on "The Handicapped and the Wholeness of the Family of God". It warned: "The church cannot exemplify 'the full humanity revealed in Christ', bear witness to the interdependence of humankind or achieve unity in diversity if it continues to acquiesce in the social isolation of disabled persons and to deny them full participation in its life."

The Nairobi report brought about a deepened engagement with disabled persons in many churches. Concerns expressed led to a consultation on "The Life and Witness of the Handicapped in a Christian Parish" at Bad Saarow, German Democratic Republic (1978). A statement urged: "Full and unconditional acceptance of the disabled must be made a reality at the very heart of the church's life. It must not be relegated to the circumference nor treated as a separate specialist area of the church's life."

The Vancouver assembly expanded the recommendations of Bad Saarow encouraging local congregations to examine factors which hinder integration and participation by the disabled, and encouraged churches to accept people with disabilities as students and teachers in theological colleges. It was noted for the first time at an assembly that a "small but significant group of disabled persons took part".

The first of three regional consultations of the programme on disabilities was held in Montevideo, Uruguay (1987). The consultation recommended to the WCC that at least 15 persons with disabilities be delegates of churches at the seventh assembly of the WCC in 1991 and that the needs and participation of persons with disabilities be considered as integral components at regional consultations.

Women: Throughout their history both the Young Women's Christian Association* (YWCA) and the World Student Christian Federation* (WSCF) have provided an invaluable training ground for women leaders in the ecumenical movement. Networks formed within the two movements during the second world war were utilized by the WCC in process of formation to circulate a questionnaire about the role of women in the church. Replies from 58 countries provided a basis for

study and discussion at a conference on "The Life and Work of Women in the Church" prior to the first assembly of the WCC in Amsterdam. Despite only a 6% representation of women, the assembly supported the suggestion that a permanent commission on the life and work of women in the church be formed.

Beginning in the 1960s the developing world was preoccupied with questions concerning marriage and family* life. Regional assemblies in Asia and Africa in the early 1960s provided a catalyst for a series of seminars involving large numbers of women throughout each region. These were followed by an equally enthusiastic participation of churches in the Pacific and throughout Europe. Bridging the 1960s and 1970s was a growing relationship with Roman Catholic women.

Some 160 women from 49 countries met in Berlin in 1974 to study "Sexism in the 1970s" and to challenge the churches to recognize them as equals and partners in the work of the church. The participants in Berlin urged that, beyond the fifth assembly, a special project be established called "Education for Participation", regionally based, funded and staffed by women. Participants pledged to work together to raise financial support to send women from their home churches as official delegates to the Nairobi assembly in 1975. As a result women made up a conspicuous 22% of the assembly. The document "The Community of Women and Men in the Church" was recommended for a three-year study by the churches. From 1978 to 1981 the study programme enjoyed the most extensive grassroots participation of any such project within WCC history, culminating in a consultation at Sheffield in 1981. Among many recommendations, Sheffield urged that 50% of all members elected to sub-units and committees of the WCC be women. The Vancouver assembly provided proof of the effectiveness of Sheffield, as 30% of the delegates were women.

Over the years participation by Orthodox women in ecumenical activities had been slow to receive official encouragement from their churches. At the conference for Orthodox women in Agapia, Romania, in 1976, at least half of the 45 women present had studied theology, and several were active in ecumenical affairs. The high profile of Orthodox

Speaker at a WCC central committee meeting, Buenos Aires, Argentina (WCC/Peter Williams)

women at Vancouver led to a heightened desire for more information about the Orthodox church.

In 1988 the WCC initiated an Ecumenical Decade of the Churches in Solidarity with Women, calling on the churches for full participation by women in church and community life.

Young people: Youth* can trace the genesis of their participation in the ecumenical movement to the middle of the 19th century. The Young Men's Christian Association* and the YWCA, founded in 1844 and 1855 respectively, were comparatively little concerned about their relationship to the churches prior to the first world war. The Student Christian Movements which came into existence between 1890 and 1910 almost from the first took up the cause of Christian unity. All three movements nurtured future leaders with an ecumenical outlook. Both world wars provided opportunities for the movements to work among the armed forces, with young women in munitions factories and to provide students. Work with prisoners of war was later followed by involvement with refugees and displaced persons.

The first great worldwide gathering of Christian youth was held in Amsterdam in 1939, just prior to the outbreak of war. After both world wars, the International Fellowship of Reconciliation* organized work camps for young people in Europe in order to promote reconciliation and peace through service. By 1950 work camps were taken into the programme of the newly formed Youth department of the WCC. Thousands of young people have been able to experience at first hand a living, working, worshipping fellowship lasting from three weeks to one year in countries around the world. The Ecumenical Institute at Bossey* provided youth with a centre for discussion and study of ecumenical concerns.

Some 1,700 young people gathered in Lausanne in 1960 from all parts of Europe. Lausanne, like the simultaneous Strasbourg conference of the WSCF, saw the beginnings of a radical re-interpretation of the ecumenical task. Regional youth assemblies followed elsewhere, reflecting the post-colonial world's call to revolution. The 1960s saw the rise of denominational youth movements with many young people trying to participate on equal terms in local churches.

From 1965 a series of encounters was held between younger Orthodox and Protestant theologians and later joined by the Roman Catholics in 1970. A total of 127 young people attended the pre-assembly youth conference prior to the fourth assembly of the WCC at Uppsala (1968), in a confident and defiant spirit. The meeting issued a statement declaring that youth were anxious to participate in the assembly to the fullest possible extent. Youth argued for full participation of youth concerns within all departments of the WCC.

By the 1970s many youth deeply involved with crucial issues within their own societies experienced alienation from the churches and a growing disenchantment with the ecumenical movement. Each year a growing number of young people gathered to participate in discussion and worship with the Taizé* community in France. This was the time of new religious movements, including the Jesus movement, which many young people saw as a celebration of their own culture.

The WCC Youth programme received a particular lift from the Vancouver assembly, where 13.5% of the delegates were youth, compared with 9% at Nairobi. Major ecumenical meetings provide a unique opportunity for youth to learn about and to participate in the ecumenical movement by attending as stewards.

The International Year of Youth in 1985 with its theme "Participation, Development and Peace" saw inter-regional conferences which strengthened the international network of ecumenical youth. In 1986 the WCC youth working group met at Iloilo City in the Philippines. It was a landmark for the global ecumenical youth movement, confirming as it did clear solidarity platforms for inter-regional action.

Rural youth programmes have developed networks which take initiatives to remedy rural problems in developing countries. In Asia the young detainees' programme seeks to support youth who have been imprisoned for their commitment to the poor and oppressed. Through world youth projects, 40 projects and programmes are supported worldwide. Opportunity is also given for youth to serve as interns with the WCC and regional youth offices. By 1987 the main thrust was towards strengthening networks and fostering solidarity rather than arranging conferences or co-ordinating structures.

Philip Potter shared with the Vancouver assembly his hope that the "churches should be a fellowship of participation". If this vision is to become a reality locally and internationally, far more creative effort needs to be made to open up channels through which that participation can be experienced. Locally, participation is often hampered because ecumenical activity is seen as an optional extra to the programmes of individual churches rather than as an integral part. Internationally, the number who can participate is limited by finance. Wider and more representative participation calls for an active moving beyond the inner circle in the selection process and a genuine commitment to enable as many people as possible to participate for their own enrichment and the enrichment of the ecumenical movement.

DOROTHY HARVEY

S. Herzel, *A Voice for Women: The Women's Department of the World Council of Churches*, WCC, 1981 • G. Müller-Fahrenholz, *... And Do Not Hinder Them: An Ecumenical Plea for the Admission of Children to the Eucharist*, WCC, 1982 • G. Müller-Fahrenholz ed., *Partners in Life: The Handicapped and the Church*, WCC, 1979 • D.M. Paton ed., *Breaking Barriers, Nairobi, 1975*, London, SPCK, 1976.

PARTIES, POLITICAL. Politics is, in one sense, ideas and aims around which citizens in a country unite in order to influence and govern their country. Political parties are tools for achieving political goals. The parties represent various socio-economic, cultural, religious and ethnic backgrounds. They may be based on class, economic group interests, regional concerns, or various ideologies — such as communism, state capitalism, or free-market economies.

A special case is parties based on religion.* In principle, in Islam it is impossible to make a distinction between religious and political issues because both are expressions of one and the same Islamic world order. Occasionally this may lead to political conflicts such as the civil war in Sudan, which is partly based on conflicts of interest between Muslim Arabs and black Africans in the north, and mostly Christians or followers of African Traditional Religions in the south. In Christianity a similar identification underlay the crusades.

Political parties in Europe and Latin America bearing the title "Christian" in their names can in most cases be defined as conservative or right-wing. On a personal level, there is today a wide differentiation in Christian involvement in political parties, and not a few active Christians seem to be more active in parties to the left of those so-called Christian parties.

Political parties ideally are tools or channels through which citizens can co-operate for the common good. However, sometimes they become ends in themselves or even dictatorships based on class, group interests, religion or interests of an individual person. To avoid such developments and secure a democratic system, there is need for checks and balances. Competition between parties and free elections have turned out to be the best means to that end. The WCC Commission of the Churches on International Affairs consultation on human rights and Christian responsibility (St Pölten 1974) states: "There is a right to dissent which preserves a community or system from hardening into authoritarian rigidity."

In Western societies political parties tend to rely too much on shallow information and the influence of mass media. Thomas Jefferson's dictum, "a democracy cannot be ignorant and free", still holds true. Political parties have the twofold duty of maintaining an open, free dialogue with the citizens and providing information to the citizens about their aims and actions.

The churches' relation to politics and political parties seems often to reflect a separation of sacred and secular, in which God's concern is understood as limited to the church, and to be unrelated to the experience and activity of tens of thousands of active Christians in governments, parliaments and political parties. Or they are concerned with political life only when the churches' specific religious activities or ecclesiastical interests seem to be at stake. Many of the concerns of churches and ecumenical organizations — for justice,* human dignity, and welfare and peace* — are universal goals which require that Christians see as their opportunity and duty to co-operate, without any feeling of religious superiority, with political parties of different religious and/or ideological persuasions.

See also **church and state; religious liberty; theology, political.**

OLLE DAHLÉN

PATON, WILLIAM. B. 13.11.1886, London, UK; d. 21.8.1943, Kendal, UK. William Paton was the "fourth man" of post-1910 British ecumenism, somewhat overshadowed by Temple, Bell and Oldham. "If he had been an Anglican, he would have been an archbishop," said Cyril Garbett. He was the indispensable diplomat and bureaucrat behind the creation of the WCC.

Paton was educated at Whitgift School, Pembroke College, Oxford, and from 1908 to 1911 at Westminster College, Cambridge, under John Skinner. From 1911 to 1921 Paton served his apprenticeship with the Student Christian Movement, being secretary of the Student Volunteer Missionary Association, and for a year was secretary with the Indian YMCA. In 1917 he was ordained in the Presbyterian Church of England. The Indian YMCA re-called him in 1921 as its secretary, and he later served, with K.T. Paul, in the re-formed National Christian Council of India, Burma and Ceylon. He had a formidable reputation as a missionary strategist foreshadowing Indian independence and the Church of South India. Paton thus belonged to the generation shaped by John R. Mott and Edinburgh 1910 — he parodied Mott's slogan "the

evangelization of the world in one generation" as "the moon turned to blood in one generation".

Direct evangelism* began to move into dialogue, and books such as J.N. Farquhar's *The Crown of Hinduism* greatly influenced Paton. After 1927, when he succeeded J.H. Oldham as secretary of the International Missionary Council,* the first of the three "prongs" of the post-Edinburgh ecumenical initiatives, Paton's key task was organizing the missionary conferences at Jerusalem (1928) and Tambaram (Madras, 1938). Jerusalem was typified by a more liberal approach to missions. Christianity seemed the "crown" or fulfilment of the great world faiths. Paton's policy of encouragement of full participation of the so-called younger churches was highly significant. For Tambaram, preliminary reading (sponsored by Paton) included Hendrik Kraemer's *Christian Message in a Non-Christian World*, with its assertion of the centrality of Christ in human history, downplaying all "religion", including Christianity. Since the second world war some of the emphases stemming from Jerusalem have come to the surface again.

Paton's diplomatic and organizing skill came into full prominence when, with W.A. Visser 't Hooft, he became associate general secretary of the provisional WCC in 1938. He was also deeply involved in the British scene with Jews, refugees, internees and peace aims, where he was an ally of Bell and Carter.

Paton was awarded the DD by Edinburgh University in 1939. Among his books, reflecting the ecumenical modes of his day, are *Jesus Christ and the World's Religions* (London, Church Missionary Society, 1916), *A Faith for the World* (London, Edinburgh House, 1929), *The Faiths of Mankind* (London, SCM, 1932), *World Community* (London, SCM, 1938), *The Message of the Worldwide Church* (London, Sheldon, 1939) and *The Church and the New Order* (London, SCM, 1941). *A Life of Alexander Duff* (London, SCM, 1923) revealed his lifelong interest in missionary education, which had full scope in his work for the Lindsay report on Indian higher education (1931) and editorship of the *International Review of Missions*. Almost his last published article ends: "Behind all the holding of conferences and making of organizations there has grown up a reality of

William Paton

personal trust and friendship together with a minimal organization. It is impossible for any Christian mind to doubt that the drawing together on the part of the churches just at the time when political hopes of peace grew darkest was no less than the act of God training and fitting us for what was to come" (W. Temple ed., *Is Christ Divided?*, 1943, 23).

A rock-like character, he was the "Admirable Crichton" of the formative years of the ecumenical movement. This and his work in India reveal him to be a man of greater stature than is often realized. His theology moved from the missiology of the era of J.R. Mott to the more confessional ecumenism of the age of Kraemer and Barth. See E.M. Jackson, *Red Tape and the Gospel: A Study of the Significance of the Ecumenical Missionary Struggle of William Paton* (Birmingham, Phlogiston Publishing & Selly Oak Colleges, 1980), and M. Sinclair, *William Paton* (London, SCM, 1949).

JOHN MUNSEY TURNER

PATRISTICS. "Patristics" or "patrology" is a term which designates the academic discipline dedicated to the study of the fathers. In the Old Testament, the concept of paternity was often used as a reminder of the continuity of the people of Israel, going back to Abraham, Isaac and Jacob, the "first fathers" (or "patriarchs"). God was often designated as the "God of the fathers", pointing at the genetic continuity of the "holy nation", chosen by God.

It is in this biblical context that Jesus commands his disciples, "call no man your father on earth" (Matt. 23:9), since membership in the people of God "in Christ" is not created genetically by "the will of man" (John 1:13), but by a new birth "of water and the Spirit" (John 3:5), God himself being the only "heavenly" Father (Matt. 6:9) of those who have received adoption in his Son, Jesus.

However, human beings are assuming ministries which are actually accomplishing the work of God, e.g. Simon becomes "a stone" (John 1:42; cf. Matt. 16:18), whereas Christ is the true "rock" of Israel (1 Cor. 10:4); or a "shepherd" (John 21:15), although God is the "shepherd of Israel" (Ps. 23:1). Thus Paul claims to have "begotten" the Corinthians in Christ (1 Cor. 4:15), and spiritual fatherhood becomes associated with presidency at sacramental functions and is assumed by bishops or presbyters. By extension, with the rise of spiritual direction by monastic elders, the title of father or mother is also attributed to holy monastics beginning in the 4th century. The general usage designates as fathers those who — after the time of the apostles — have secured the continuity of the apostolic message by teaching the true faith and thus assuring the "spiritual birth" of Christian generations (see **apostolicity**). Writing in the 2nd century, Irenaeus declares: "When any person has been taught from the mouth of another, he is termed the son of him who instructs him, and the latter is called his father" (*Against Heresies* 4.41.2).

Particular concern for the study of patristics, i.e. the life and writings of "fathers", is understandably emphasized in connection with the idea of Tradition,* which implies continuity and consistency in the teaching of the church at all times. The role of patristics in shaping theology necessarily depends upon the authority* attributed to Tradition. In the Orthodox church the patristic legacy provides the main authoritative direction for understanding and interpreting the content of scripture (see **hermeneutics, teaching authority**). In Roman Catholicism, patristic authority is also emphasized, but the existence, in the modern church, of a more clearly defined

magisterium* tends to make references to the
fathers less essential in practice. This magisterium has adopted four qualifications for
those to be generally regarded as fathers of the
church: orthodoxy of doctrine, holiness of
life, ecclesiastical approval and antiquity. The
title of "doctors of the church" is attributed to
those who lack the last qualification, i.e.
those who lived after the 8th century. This
category includes the great scholastics who
determined the direction of Western theology
since the middle ages. The Orthodox, although they do sometimes insist upon the
particular traditional authority of the period of
the ecumenical councils,* which coincides
with the "classical" patristic period, would not
consider such chronological limits as absolute
and would accept the authority of many
fathers who lived in the second millennium of
Christianity.

Another concept important both for Orthodox and Roman Catholics in their approach
to patristic authority is the notion of patristic
*consensus.** Since it is obvious that, on the
one hand, no single individual can be seen as
an exclusive interpreter of Tradition and that,
on the other hand, there are contradictions on
individual issues between otherwise very authoritative fathers, the real content of transmitted truth should be sought where there is
unquestionable consensus. Sometimes the
consensus is easier to define in terms of
theological methodology or a general approach to issues, rather than in actual theological formulations. One speaks then of the
"sense of the fathers".

The overall insistence of the reformers of
the 16th century on the Bible as the unique —
or at least a very privileged — source of
divine revelation* removed patristics from the
basic curriculum of most Protestant theological schools. It should be noted, however, that
Calvin, Luther and particularly Melanchthon
looked at the fathers with great respect as
authoritative commentators on scriptural
texts.

There is a further problem related to the
question of authority: any academic course in
patristics today includes the study of authors
who do not qualify as either fathers or doctors
of the church. Indeed, it is impossible to
understand the historical development of
Christian thought without considering the entire contents of early Christian literature,
which includes persons who were formally
condemned by ecclesiastical authority either
during their lifetime (Nestorius) or after their
death (Origen, Theodore of Mopsuestia).
There are also very influential authors whose
true identity is unknown because they wrote
under a cover name (Pseudo-Dionysius the
Areopagite). Secular historians of Christian
doctrine would include such authors in their
survey without hesitation, whereas Orthodox
or Roman Catholic theologians would attempt
to qualify their position in reference to the
mainstream of Tradition.

Early Christian literature, which is generally studied under the general name of patristics, has come to us in Greek, Latin and
Syriac, with additional texts available in Coptic, Ethiopian, Armenian, Arabic, Georgian
and sometimes Slavonic versions. Their publication in printed form began in the 16th
century. Some publications involved interesting ecumenical concerns. For instance, the
French Benedictines of St Maur — a congregation founded in 1618 in Paris — worked
with the generous support of King Louis XIV,
who was interested in finding in early Christian literature some support for his Gallican
sympathies. "Maurist" editions are being used
in a reprinted form today. Similarly, the publication in Venice in 1718 by Nikodemos the
Hagiorite of the famous *Philokalia* — a large
anthology of Greek patristic texts on the
spirituality of "mental" prayer — would have
been impossible without the editor's Western
contacts. (He also published a modern Greek
paraphrase of the *Spiritual Exercises* of Ignatius Loyola.) In 1882 Adolf von Harnack
began the famous series of *Texte und Unter-
suchungen zur Geschichte der altchristlichen
Literatur*, as a source for the study of early
Christianity on the basis of his own Protestant
approach.

The most widely available collections of
Greek and Latin texts — the *Patrologia Grae-
ca* and the *Patrologia Latina*, by the French
priest J.-P. Migne (d.1875) — are also in their
own way an ecumenical witness. Migne was
as comprehensive as he could be, including
texts of various Christian theological tendencies (even Greek anti-Latin polemics, e.g.
Patriarch Photius). He also reprinted the Orthodox *Philokalia*. Furthermore, his Greek
patrology ends with A.D. 1453, whereas the
Latin one stops at the works of Innocent III

(1160-1216). Paradoxically, the editor seems to imply that the patristic tradition continued longer in the East than in the Latin West.

The texts printed by Migne are often superseded by new series, with more critical editions. The French series of *Sources chrétiennes* was started in Paris in 1941 by Henri de Lubac and Jean Daniélou as a conscious attempt to restore the traditions of the early church within Catholicism, thus making ecumenical dialogue easier. This same ecumenical concern earlier dominated the so-called Oxford movement within Anglicanism. The famous *Library of the Fathers*, containing the English translations of major patristic texts, was edited by Edward Pusey, John Keble and Cardinal Newman and laid the basis for the "Anglo-catholic" revival (45 vols, Oxford, 1838-88). It was often reprinted and complemented by other English editions, including the more recent series initiated by Roman Catholics. As a result, works written by Greek or Latin fathers available in English are much more numerous than French or German translations. In 19th-century Russia, patristic translations were initiated by the leader of modern Russian theological scholarship, Metropolitan Filaret (Drozdov, 1782-1867). It is important to note that Filaret's patristic interests were inseparable in his mind and activities from biblical research: in particular he was a zealous promoter of a new Russian translation of the Bible.

The obvious importance of these great enterprises of editing and translating the writings of the fathers resided in the concern, in each case, to grasp the mind of the Christian community *before* the occurrence of historical schisms,* splits or other crises. The result, more often than not, was a better understanding of what is absolute and permanent in the Christian faith,* and what is of relative importance, determined by passing historical factors. Not that *all* the approaches to patristic research were always successful: e.g. in spite of great scholarly achievement, the liberal 19th-century school, symbolized by Harnack, hardly succeeded in its attempt to prove that, starting with the 3rd century, Greek Christian thought was "Hellenized" to the point of becoming instrinsically unfaithful to original "Paulinism". The achievements of the Oxford movement were more lasting. It did not swing the entire Anglican communion to "catholic"

principles, but it became very influential in establishing the thoroughly *biblical* content of patristic thought, as it developed in the classical period of the 4th century.

The revival of patristic studies in France and Germany after the second world war represented attempts, among Roman Catholics, to understand the Christian traditions as independent from medieval scholasticism, which had appeared to many as stale and unhelpful in the framework of the prevailing new "existential" approach to theology. Furthermore, on the patristic basis, the dialogue with other Christians, particularly the Orthodox, was becoming easier. Some basic methodological achievements, linked to the patristic revival, seem to be universally accepted today: e.g. the existence of two distinct models of Trinitarian theology in the 4th century — the Augustinian in the West and the Cappadocian in the East — which explains the divisive issue of the filioque* addition to the creed; the impossibility of understanding the later development of the Roman papacy without first admitting the predominance in early Christianity of an ecclesiology of the local church,* etc.

If one avoids the temptation of making the notion of a "return to the fathers" into a slogan or a conservative panacea, there is no doubt

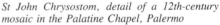

St John Chrysostom, detail of a 12th-century mosaic in the Palatine Chapel, Palermo

that the entire problem of Tradition, as it stands before divided Christians today, cannot be approached without reference to patristics, its methodology and its achievements. Unless one accepts a blind doctrine of *sola scriptura* — which very few Protestants would uphold today — one cannot discover the *mind* of Christianity without referring to the fathers, recognizing that the specific authority of scripture is enhanced rather than diminished when one studies the ways in which it was read and understood throughout the centuries.

JOHN MEYENDORFF

J. Meyendorff, *Living Tradition*, Crestwood, NY, St Vladimir's Seminary, 1978 • J. Pelikan, *The Christian Tradition: A History of the Development of Doctrine*, vol. 1: *The Emergence of the Catholic Tradition*; vol. 2: *The Spirit of Eastern Christendom (600-1700)*, Chicago, Univ. of Chicago Press, 1971, 1974 • J. Quasten, *Patrology*, 4 vols, Utrecht-Brussels, Spectrum, 1950-87.

PAUL VI (Giovanni Battista Montini).
B. 26.9.1897, Concesio, Lombardy, Italy; d. 6.8.1978, Rome. Bishop of Rome and pope from 21 June 1963 until his death, Paul VI presided over the last three sessions of the Second Vatican Council.* He was the first modern pope to travel outside Italy. Several of his trips were ecumenical landmarks, including his visit to the WCC in 1969.

Born into an upper-class family, Montini was ordained in 1920, after which he went to Rome for graduate studies in philosophy, canon law and literature, then entered the Vatican's curial service where he remained for 22 years. In the secretariat of state he also became chaplain to students at the University of Rome, set up a weekly newspaper to develop a Catholic intellectual elite, and organized seminars from which leaders of the Christian Democratic Party emerged after the world war. In 1939 Pius XII entrusted to Montini a variety of duties: directing the holy see's extensive relief work, settling displaced persons and hiding political refugees.

Montini remained responsible for the ordinary affairs of the church until 1954, when (to the surprise of many) he was appointed archbishop of Milan, one of the church's largest ecclesiastical jurisdictions. In Milan, Montini quickly revealed his organizational skills and pastoral sensitivity in concern for social needs

and the role of the laity. Calling himself the "archbishop of the workers", Montini gave priority to winning back to the church the labouring class in the communist strongholds of Milan.

He was active in the central preparatory commission for the Second Vatican Council and a prominent leader among the bishops at its first session (1962), especially in his urging a new document, one that eventually would become "The Church in the Modern World". After John XXIII died Montini was elected his successor. As Paul VI he immediately promised to continue the Vatican Council, to further efforts for justice and peace among peoples and to strive for the unity of all Christians.

Paul VI described the simple objective of Vatican II as "to make the church of the 20th century ever better fitted for proclaiming the gospel to the people of the 20th century". If John XXIII had conceived and given spirit to the Council, Paul VI helped give the event its flesh and blood.

Within the Roman curia, he established offices to implement new concerns: secretariats for promoting Christian unity,* for non-Christians, for non-believers; the council for the laity, the commission for justice and peace, the office of mass communications, etc. He diminished the Italian influence in the curia, internationalized the college of cardinals, instituted the synod of bishops representing the various episcopal regions and convoked five of them (1967, 1969, 1971, 1974, 1977). His travels took him to South America, Africa, India, Australia, Oceania, the United Nations in New York, the Holy Land, Geneva and Constantinople.

Paul VI judged that the distrust and rivalries among the churches produced a "strange, absurd situation", one of Christianity's and humanity's "gravest problems". He considered ecumenism an obligatory "mysterious" part of his papal ministry, though he admitted that many other Christians regard the papacy as an ecumenical "stumbling block". He met with Anglican and Protestant leaders, addressed ecumenical groups, reminded RC bishops of their ecumenical responsibilities and gave a yearly update on his ecumenical observations during the January Week of Prayer for Christian Unity.*

After he embraced the Ecumenical Patriarch Athenagoras in Jerusalem as "two pilgrims with eyes fixed on Christ" (in 1964), both agreed solemnly to "remove from the memory and from the midst of the church the excommunication of 1054" (7 December 1965). Paul VI visited Athenagoras in Istanbul in July 1967, and the patriarch returned the visit in Rome in October. Common declarations were promulgated. The same was done when the pope received also the heads of the Armenian Orthodox (1968), the Syrian Orthodox (1971), and Coptic Orthodox (1973) churches.

Called "progressive" for his appeals for social justice in the evolution of developing countries (*Populorum Progressio*, 1967), for his teaching on urbanization, racial discrimination, environment and the evolution of Marxism (e.g. *Octogesima Adveniens*, 1971) and evangelization of the modern world (*Evangelii Nuntiandi*, 1975), Paul VI was just as loudly dubbed "conservative" on the eucharist (*Mysterium Fidei*, 1965), artificial birth-control (*Humanae Vitae*, 1968), priestly celibacy (*Sacerdotalis Caelibatus*, 1967) and non-ordination of women (1977).

As revisionist history moves in the 1990s, with a more objective look at Pope Paul's personality and the tasks he could not avoid and did face head-on, one hears, in the evaluation of the nine modern popes since Leo XIII (1878-1903), Montini's name as "the greatest of them all".

TOM STRANSKY

E.J. Stormon ed, *Towards the Healing of Schism: Public Statements and Correspondence between the Holy See and the Ecumenical Patriarchate, 1958-1984*, New York, Paulist, 1987 • T.F. Stransky & J.B. Sheerin eds, *Doing the Truth in Charity: Vatican and Papal Statements on Ecumenism, 1964-1980*, New York, Paulist, 1982.

PAX CHRISTI. Pax Christi (Peace of Christ), an international Roman Catholic peace movement with headquarters in Antwerp, Belgium, was initiated in March 1945 by a small French group led by Bishop Pierre Théas of Lourdes. The group's original purpose was to promote reconciliation between the French and Germans, especially but not exclusively RCs, through the exchange of prayers. In December 1950 Pax Christi was re-organized and recognized by the holy see in

Rome as an international federation of European national sections, and it has since spread to North America and third-world countries. Its objective is "the unity and pacification of the world through the promotion of a new international order based on the natural law and on the justice and charity of Christ". It publishes the monthly *Pax Christi*.

Pax Christi tries to establish a broad coalition among RCs of different political stances. It supports prayer crusades, propagates papal statements on justice and peace, and supports studies on sociological, psychological and spiritual conditions of peace, e.g. Christian alternatives to violence and "de-militarizing" Catholic education. The movement promotes opportunities for discussions among all groups, especially youth. In the USA, for example, Pax Christi since 1973 has supported whatever can establish "peace-making as a priority for the American Catholic Church". International Pax Christi has constant contacts with similar groups in other churches, and with ecumenical and inter-religious organizations such as the WCC, the Christian Peace Conference* and the World Conference on Religion and Peace.*

TOM STRANSKY

PAX ROMANA. Founded in Switzerland in 1921, Pax Romana is an international movement of Roman Catholic students, with a section (since 1946) for graduates and professionals — International Catholic Movement for Intellectual and Cultural Affairs (in French, MIIC). Under the umbrella of "Christian presence and evangelization of culture", Pax Romana's concerns and priorities include the search for more humane means of scientific development, promotion of intercultural dialogue, joint actions with the poor and oppressed for the defence of their culture and human dignity, and re-inforcement of human rights in all political regimes.

As an international community of RC laity,* Pax Romana gathers together 69 federations and over 30 contact groups from some 80 countries in all six continents. With its headquarters in Geneva, its specialized secretariats are distributed elsewhere: secondary school teachers (Vienna); engineers, agronomists and industry officials (Paris); jurists (Barcelona); Christian artists

(Munich); and scientists (Boulogne-sur-Seine, France).

Already in 1887, Baron George de Montenach and Count Albert de Mun tried to organize French and Swiss RC students through a meeting, eventually held two years later in Fribourg. But from this and similar efforts sprang no organization until after the first world war. Although in its beginnings Pax Romana was kept aloof from ecumenical co-operation, it began such in 1955, with Vatican permission, sponsoring a conference on the university, culture and human community, jointly organized with the World Student Christian Federation* (at the WCC Ecumenical Institute, Bossey). One of Pax Romana's most innovative leaders in ecumenical activities was the Australian laywoman Rosemary Goldie. As former Pax Romana staff member in Fribourg, in 1952 she left for a top position in Rome. There she organized large international and regional congresses of the lay apostolate, including the post-Vatican II congress of laity in Rome (1986), which included active participation by lay representatives of other churches. She helped initiate contacts with the WCC, the WSCF, YWCAs and YMCAs after she had become a general secretary of Pope Paul VI's newly created Council for the Laity (1967).

Besides its publication of seminar and conference reports, Pax Romana issues a newsletter in English, French, and Spanish and a journal *Convergence* (since 1989 also with the International Young Catholic Students and the International Movement of Catholic Students).

TOM STRANSKY

Memory and Hope: Pax Romana, 1947-1987, Geneva, Pax Romana, 1989 • G. De Weck, *Histoire du mouvement des étudiants catholiques vers la fondation d'une confédération internationale (1887-1925)*, Fribourg, 1926.

PAYNE, ERNEST ALEXANDER. B. 19.2.1902, London; d. 14.1.1980, London.

Vice-moderator of the WCC central committee, 1954-68, and a president of the WCC, 1968-75, Payne was general secretary of the Baptist Union of Great Britain and Ireland, 1951-67, vice-president of the United Society for Christian Literature and of the British and Foreign Bible Society, and chairman of the executive committee of the British Council of Churches, 1962-71. He studied in London, Oxford and Marburg and was ordained in 1928. Trained in church history and the history of denominationalism, he influenced the discussion on the "non-theological factors in the making and unmaking of church union" and played an important role in the revision of the basis of the WCC in 1954. In a rare recognition for a free churchman, a memorial service for him was held in Westminster Abbey, London. He wrote *The Free Church Tradition in the Life of England* (London, SCM, 1944), *The Growth of the World Church* (London, Edinburgh House, 1955) and *Thirty Years of the British Council of Churches, 1942-72* (London, BCC, 1972). See W.M.S. West, *To Be a Pilgrim: A Memoir of Ernest A. Payne* (London, Lutterworth, 1983).

ANS J. VAN DER BENT

PEACE. The Hebrew shalom designates not only the reduction of conflict but rightness, wholeness — not only peace but justice.*

The same root is properly translated as liberation,* salvation.* It denotes things as they should be and shall be in the divine purpose. The vision of Isa. 2 and Micah 4 promises that peoples will "no longer learn war" because "the oracle of Yahweh will go out from Jerusalem".

That this shalom is fulfilled in the work of Jesus Christ* is what the apostles called good news. "Peace on earth" was promised by the angels of Luke 2:14. That the inauguration of God's rule is at hand was the promise of John, as it was of Jesus. In the light of this beginning, the seventh beatitude calls peacemakers "God's children". The fulfilment of the law by a "higher righteousness" (Matt. 5) reveals that it is by loving one's enemies that disciples are like their heavenly Father. Eph. 2:14 says that Christ is "our peace" because by reconciling Jew and gentile he has created "one new humanity". That expresses itself in the harmonious interaction of the many ministries in the body (Eph. 4, and par. in Rom. 12, 1 Cor. 12) and in formal procedures of conflict resolution (Matt. 18:15-17; 1 Cor. 6:5-6). Effective reconciliation* is a real experience in the believing community, and its extension to the ends of the earth is a concrete social project.

The peace-making function of the church*
as community is undergirded theologically by
the confession of Christ's lordship, which
refuses to let the present rulers of the world
sacralize its oppressive and divisive structures. The primitive Jewish denunciation of
idolatry unveils the pretensions of any who
would claim the right to sacrifice lives to their
causes.

The re-alignment which began in the 4th
century abandoned the universality of the gospel vision in favour of an alliance of the
bishops with the Roman empire, yet it did
promote a vision of peace in the earthly city.
Pax romana, now externally Christianized,
was not the Hebraic vision of a global right
order* but rather the relative tranquillity of a
very large but not worldwide empire. Constantine's support for the churches was seen as
prefiguring and furthering the kingdom of
God.* Augustine re-defined the peace of God
as belonging in heaven or in the human heart.
It no longer called for loving the enemies of
the empire or for empowering underdogs.

Medieval bishops and synods worked for
the pax terrena, seeking to restrain local wars
by proclaiming "the truce of God" and "the
peace of God", or by intervening between
princes as mediators. Gradually canon law*
(Gratian) and then academic theologians
(Francisco de Vitoria, Francisco Suarez) developed the "justifiable war" or "just war"*
tradition as a "concrete utopia". The notion
that wars could be evaluated in the light of
criteria of authority, cause, intention, means,
etc. projected an unrealistic but not irrelevant
hope that the violence of rulers might be
restrained by respect for due process and the
rights of the victim. Jurists like Hugo Grotius
formulated these visions of restraint in the
language of international law. Treaties (culminating in those at The Hague, 1899, 1907)
committed governments to respect rules safeguarding the rights of prisoners and occupied
populations. Thus the usage was re-inforced
that "peace" refers to reducing unrest and
damage, under the control of the present regime, including the use of violence in a
"police" function. The term still is so used in
the political rhetoric of major powers, to describe the balance of terror between the blocs
and the internal stability of each of them.

As nationalism undermined the vision of
"Christendom" and technology* increased

war's destructiveness, other kinds of utopia
arose as well. Visions of world order were
projected by philosophers like Kant, later
taken over by popes and politicians. The first
world war was supposed to "end war"; anti-
militarists spoke of outlawing war. In the
Kellogg-Briand pact (1927) governments dis-
avowed "war as an instrument of national
policy". Vatican social teaching (see **social
encyclicals, papal**) posits such a world order
as the way to eliminate war. "Peace" here
means a reversal of Augustine's relegating to
heaven the promise of a new righteous order;
the hope has continued to be that the present
regimes could be called on to carry it out.

The other critical vision came to be called
pacifism.* Rooted historically in the radical
renewal vision of the historic peace churches, recovered in the 19th century by Tolstoy, Garrison and others and in the 20th by
the Fellowship of Reconciliation,* pacifism
rejects on moral grounds all war, even for
causes purported just. Ever since the Oxford
Life and Work conference (1937) ecumenical statements have recognized the unresolved tension between just war and pacifism as moral positions. There has been less
responsible theological attention directed to
the fact that in many cases the military
activities in which Christians have served
their governments cannot stand up to
scrutiny under just-war principles, and
would not have been acceptable if there had
been such testing.

Without resolving the tension, numerous
areas of common witness* have been found.
Just-war and pacifist reasoning agree in rejecting war waged for unjust causes, or the use of
means unable to respect the criteria of discrimination, proportion, and non-combatant
immunity. These criteria found expression in
the work of the WCC study commission on
Christians and the prevention of war in a
nuclear age (1955-57), which rejected any all-
out use of nuclear weapons. This insight
amounts to a condemnation of the policies of
both the super-powers.

The question of war had been present in
WCC assemblies since the creation of the
WCC. Amsterdam 1948 (sec. 4) included
such affirmations as "war is contrary to the
will of God", "peace requires an attack on the
causes of conflict between the powers", but
could not find agreement in answering the

Rally in Madrid of "Christians for Peace" (WCC/Peter Williams)

question: "Can war now be an act of justice?" Evanston 1954 emphasized the relation of peace and justice at the national and international levels and encouraged "a continuing effort to reach agreement on outstanding issues, such as the peace treaties and disarmament" and "readiness to submit all unresolved questions of conflict to an impartial international organization and to carry out its decisions". Uppsala 1968 drew on earlier work and stated: "The concentration of nuclear weapons in the hands of a few nations presents the world with serious problems: (a) how to guarantee the security of the non-nuclear nations; (b) how to enable these nations to play their part in preventing war; and (c) how to prevent the nuclear powers from freezing the existing order at the expense of changes needed for social and political justice." But not until Vancouver 1983 was the all-out rejection of nuclear weapons to find expression in assembly documents. It has not yet found expression in concerted policies of political opposition to the super-powers or in personal resistance.

The two stances agree as well to call on present governments and international agencies to make the most of present possibilities

for peaceful change and the reduction of hostilities. Thus the WCC (in process of formation) in 1946 created the Commission of the Churches on International Affairs to monitor the state of international relations and to testify at those points where a common witness is possible.

A further commonality between just war and pacifism became visible as well in the 20th century. Whereas pacifism, as represented from the age of Francis of Assisi and the Waldensians until that of Tolstoy and Garrison, was at first held by persons and small groups with no political weight and seemed to call only for abstention from involvement in violence, possibilities for effectively achieving political goals through non-violent direct action have become visible. Mohandas K. Gandhi and Martin Luther King, Jr, have been among the architects and protagonists of this development, whose presence and potential are far wider than currently recognized. This fact was confirmed in an exploratory way by the WCC study on "Violence, Non-Violence, and the Struggle for Justice" (1971-73), which took cognizance of the growth of peace studies as a branch of political science and of conflict resolution as a social skill. War and police violence are no longer self-evidently the ultimate means of restoring peace and achieving justice.

Further common concerns support the struggle against racism* (since Uppsala) and against militarism* (since Nairobi). The Programme to Combat Racism* heightened the awareness that in places where no war is going on, human dignity is nonetheless being violated. The militarism studies made it clear that, not only in classic dictatorships but also in the "national security state", where the might of the armed forces is directed within their own borders, both peace and justice are ill served by "preparedness".

The world Christian community, especially as visible in the new missionary movements of the last two centuries and the ecumenical relationships developed still more recently, represents an agency of peace-making in ways often under-estimated. The mere fact of being a transnational, polycultural community is peace action. Missionary service and international diakonia* educate those who send and pray, those who travel, and those who receive, in cross-cultural awareness of the believing community as a global fellowship, first-fruits of a global humanity. Interchurch reconciliation develops models for possible interdependence between nations and blocs. World Christendom brings prophetic judgment to bear on injustices occurring in regions whose rulers do not want the "peace" of their regime disturbed, and it supports Christians in a posture of resistance. People-to-people relationships develop international understanding from below, as support and corrective for the less redemptive internationalisms of diplomacy, trade, tourism, sport and entertainment.

As ecumenical thought became less Eurocentric, the equation of peace with tranquillity under the present regime was increasingly questioned. The usage arose of yoking the concepts "justice" and "peace" in dialectical tension. Some meant by this that neither justice nor peace is possible without the other. Others meant that justice (defined in terms of a particular contemporary political programme) must come first, thereby retrieving in a new form the just-war tradition. To this binary formulation has been added since Vancouver (1983) "the integrity (or safeguarding) of cre-

ation", recognizing that neither tranquillity nor structural change can suffice without the underlying resources of ecology, economy and culture.* This broadening of the leitmotif coincided with the call for a new kind of conciliar process which should work somehow "from below". The present system of co-operating and competing confessional bureaucracies cannot adequately channel the energies and the shared commitments which such a restored vision of the wholeness shalom demands.

See also **disarmament, international order, justice, militarism/militarization, pacifism**.

JOHN H. YODER

R. Bilheimer & T.M. Taylor, *Christians and the Prevention of War in an Atomic Age*, London, SCM, 1981 • J.S. Conway, "The Struggle for Peace between the Wars", *The Ecumenical Review*, 35, 1, 1983 • D. Durnbaugh ed., *On Earth Peace*, Elgin, IL, Brethren, 1978 • D. Gill, "Violence, Non-Violence and the Struggle for Justice", *The Ecumenical Review*, 25, 4, 1973.

PENANCE AND RECONCILIATION.

The forms for the remission of sins committed after baptism* have undergone some surprising changes in the course of church history. The 1st and 2nd centuries knew various and even divergent practices. The Pauline literature appears to exclude reconciliation* after baptism (1 Cor. 5:13; see also Heb. 6:4-6), while Matthew already foreshadows an ecclesial procedure (18:15-17); several texts allude to a kind of general confession (James 5:16; 1 John 1:8-2:2; *Didache* 14:1).

The 3rd century saw the development of a "canonical penance". In the East, the *Epistola Canonica* of Gregory Thaumaturgus distinguishes four successive stages through which penitents must pass. In the West, canonical penance, which could be undergone only once in a lifetime for the serious sins of murder, adultery and apostasy, is a sort of partial excommunication* and comprises three steps: the entry into the order of penitents (at the beginning of Lent, from the 4th century onwards), the *actio paenitentiae*, or (long) period of amendment, and finally the celebration of reconciliation (on Holy Thursday) presided over by the bishop, when the entire community prays for the penitents, now re-instated into full ecclesial communion.*

By the 5th century, the East placed more stress on the therapeutic aspect of penance; confession was tied to spiritual guidance, and often the penitent confessed to a monk. From the 7th to the 11th centuries, the West acquired from Irish monks a "tariff penance", whereby sins were penalized according to degrees of gravity specified in the Penitential Books. Its abuses led to yet another form, namely "confession", which is characterized by four parts: contrition, confession made to a priest, satisfaction (all three being acts of the penitent), and absolution. At the end of the middle ages, a "devotional confession" had developed, which sometimes became more frequent than communion.

The reform of the 16th century. In practice, the rejection of confession was not always as clear-cut as the theological principles of the Protestant Reformation might require. Luther was acquainted with confession, even though, from 1520, he no longer counted it as a sacrament.* The Augsburg confession refers to confession in article 12, and to penance in article 13; the Apology for the Augsburg confession lists penance among the sacraments (art. 13). Calvin strongly criticized the "power of the keys" attributed to the priest but did not minimize the place of forgiveness of sins in the church (*Institutes* 3.4). The Anglican Book of Common Prayer provided for auricular confession and also for a general confession of sins during the eucharist and the office; the 16th article of religion provides for the forgiveness of sin after baptism. The other reforming movements were more radical, usually retaining only a general confession of sins during worship and occasionally forms for confession in small groups.

Contemporary tendencies. Today theological reflection on penance and reconciliation is done within the context of soteriology, notably by means of the Pauline concept of reconciliation. This solid theological framework allows one to go beyond confessional controversies and to bring into focus the essential theological question, i.e. the reality of salvation* (reconciliation) in the church. A good example of this re-thinking is provided in the beginning of the introduction to the Roman *Ordo Paenitentiae* (1973).

Along the same lines, current theology grounds reflection on penance and reconciliation in baptism, notably by recalling their historic origin as *paenitentia secunda*. This reflection is concerned with the forgiveness of sins, those committed before baptism, as well as those committed subsequently. In this context the questions of the sacramentality of penance and of its minister may also be reformulated.

Theologians are divided on the importance of confession in penance. Some attribute to it a great importance, renewed today by psychology and the need people have to be "heard" in the midst of secularized society; they stress the therapeutic aspect of the process. Others prefer to emphasize its ecclesial dimension, the subsequent reconciliation among members of the community and, at the extreme, its aspect of church discipline.* In this respect, the choice of terminology (whether penance, confession or reconciliation) is not neutral. Attempts are made to take into account the social and collective aspect of sin.* But theologies of penance are as yet too little in touch with psychoanalysis, sociology, and even the moral theology of sin.

The most ecumenical aspect of the question is that of the reconciliation of the churches themselves. Today, many consider the ecumenical endeavour as a true ministry of reconciliation. The unions realized among various churches offer material for reflection.

There is now a diffusion of diverse forms, contrary to the standard forms for so long used in auricular and in general confession. Thus, the Roman *Ordo Paenitentiae* of 1973 offers, first of all, a revised ritual for individual confession and then two forms for community celebration, the first with individual, and the second with communal confession and absolution (with canonical restrictions for the latter one). In Western Catholicism, one witnesses a decline in the practice, or perhaps more precisely, a passage from frequent confession to a rhythm of a few celebrations per year.

Orthodoxy has very diverse practices. In some Greek- and Arabic-speaking churches, confession has almost entirely disappeared, while in the Slavic churches, the most traditional forms of confession are still maintained. In Anglicanism there is a certain reassertion of the value of confession, attested in the revision of liturgical books. Thus, the

American Book of Common Prayer (1979) includes "The Reconciliation of a Penitent", as does the Canadian Book of Alternative Services (1980). The same tendency is manifest in some currents of Lutheranism, where pastors invite the people to a community celebration during penitential seasons such as Lent.

These issues have been little discussed within the ecumenical movement, perhaps because of the sacramental quality attributed to penance and reconciliation by the Catholics and the Orthodox, which is troublesome for the Protestant churches. If that is the only cause, recent theological tendencies are bound eventually to remove the obstacle.

See also **reconciliation, redemption**.

PAUL DE CLERCK

E. Bezzel, *Frei zum Eingeständis: Geschichte und Praxis der evangelischen Einzelbeichte*, Stuttgart, Calwer, 1982 • H. Karpp, *Die Busse*, Zurich, EVZ-Verlag, 1969 • *Studia Liturgica*, 18, 1, 1988 • M. Thurian, *La confession* (ET *Confession*, London, SCM, 1958).

PENTECOST. The term derives from *pentēkostē* (lit. fiftieth), the Greek name for the Jewish Feast of Weeks at the close of the grain harvest 50 days after Passover and Unleavened Bread (see Tob. 2:1). In the early church, Pentecost at first designated the whole period of 50 days from Easter;* only later did it refer particularly to the 50th day, which became a feast in its own right.

The 50 days celebrating Christ's resurrection* were the "most joyful season" (Tertullian), one "great Sunday" (Athanasius); there was no kneeling for prayer, but only standing (to mark the heavenly location of believers in Christ, in anticipation of the general resurrection); and there was no fasting (a foretaste of the heavenly banquet with the messianic bridegroom). In the 4th century, the 50th day was regarded as the seal of the period, with Christ's ascension and the Spirit's descent as its twin themes. At the turn into the 5th century, the two distinct feasts emerged of Ascension (40 days after Easter; see Acts 1:1-11) and Pentecost (see Acts 2:1-4). The vigil of Pentecost became a baptismal occasion, and the white robes of the baptized account for the English "Whitsunday".

First in sectarian Judaism in the intertesta-mental period, and then in rabbinic Judaism by the 2nd and 3rd centuries of the Christian era, the Feast of Weeks has become associated with the law-giving and covenant* of Sinai. Sermons at the feast of Pentecost by Christian preachers of the 5th century relate the new covenant of the Spirit to the old covenant of the law. Furthermore, the gift of the Holy Spirit* for apostolic preaching is considered as a reversal of Babel, bringing unity* and catholicity* to the church* and its mission.* An ancient Latin collect prays: "Make the peoples dispersed by the division of languages to be joined by your heavenly gift in the united confession of your name."

In the modern ecumenical movement, Pentecost became a time of special prayer for Christian unity. The preparatory conference of Faith and Order* at Geneva in 1920 appealed for an annual week of prayer for the unity of the church, ending with Whitsunday. In 1941 F&O changed its dates to the 18-25 January octave, but the Pentecost time remains favoured in some parts of the world (see **Week of Prayer for Christian Unity**). The presidents of the WCC send a Pentecost message to member churches every year.

See also **Easter, Holy Spirit**.

GEOFFREY WAINWRIGHT

R. Cabié, *La Pentecôte: L'évolution de la cinquantaine pascale au cours des cinq premiers siècles*, Tournai, Desclée, 1965 • J. Gunstone, *The Feast of Pentecost: The Great Fifty Days in the Liturgy*, London, Faith, 1967.

PENTECOSTAL-ROMAN CATHOLIC DIALOGUE. Unique among the international dialogues, the Pentecostal-Roman Catholic conversations began with official Roman Catholic representatives but only with Pentecostal and other Protestant charismatics whom the co-chairman, David Du Plessis, had recruited. The impetus had come from contacts Du Plessis had made as guest of the Secretariat for Promoting Christian Unity* to observe Vatican Council II;* from initiatives of Ray Bringham, an American charismatic; and from the Vatican's acceptance of the fast-rising charismatic movement within the Roman Catholic Church. From the beginning of the dialogue in 1972, Kilian McDonnell, US Benedictine priest, has been co-chairman.

The dialogue has been organized in five-year periods, with one session per year. During the first period (1972-76) the Pentecostal team included also charismatics from Protestant churches, who presented the majority of the papers. The topics concentrated on the Holy Spirit's* role in Christian initiation, the Spirit and the church,* and the Spirit's role in prayer and worship.

For the second period (1977, 1979-82), the Pentecostals decided to exclude charismatics from other churches. Du Plessis's efforts to get official denominational backing, especially from the large American Assemblies of God, met constant rebuff, but he secured participation by smaller Pentecostal groups. Topics addressed faith* and experience, biblical hermeneutics,* speaking in tongues, healing, the church as communion* in worship, scripture and tradition, Mary,* and ministry in the church.*

The three-year gap between the second and third quinquennia (1985) partly reflected the Vatican's concern that the dialogue receive more backing from Pentecostal denominations. For this third series, David Du Plessis (d.1987) was replaced as Pentecostal co-chairman by his younger brother, Justus, who is the ecumenical officer for the Apostolic Faith Mission of South Africa. The third quinquennium has seen more Pentecostals participate, often as observers, with the backing of their denominations, in a more international team. The importance of this dialogue may lie primarily in assisting a largely anti-ecumenical movement slowly to re-evaluate its attitudes and positions. In this process the prophetic role of David Du Plessis and the respect for him shown by most Pentecostal leaders have been key factors.

PETER HOCKEN

A. Bittlinger, *Papst und Pfingstler: Der römisch katholische-pfingstliche Dialog und seine ökumenische Relevanz*, Frankfurt, Lang, 1978 • J. Sandidge, *Roman Catholic/Pentecostal Dialogue (1977-1982)*, Frankfurt, Lang, 1987.

PENTECOSTAL WORLD CONFERENCE.

The PWC is a continuing, non-legislative body providing a forum in which leaders of Pentecostal churches around the world can exchange ideas, share information and participate in fellowship. Organized in 1947 in Zurich, Switzerland, the conference meets in convention every three years, electing a 25-member advisory committee to supervise the conference's work and plan the next meeting. Pentecostal ecumenist David Du Plessis was active in organizing several of the early conferences. The 1989 PWC meeting in Singapore drew 3,800 delegates from about 40 countries. Estimates at that time were that the worldwide membership of Pentecostal bodies represented in the conference had grown from about 10 million in 1947 to about 60 million in 1989. The conference also publishes the quarterly *World Pentecost*.

MARLIN VANELDEREN

PENTECOSTALS.

The 20th-century Pentecostal movement affirms a post-conversion work of the Holy Spirit.* This work is designated baptism in the Spirit, generally understood as empowerment for mission* and ministry,* and is said to represent the restoration of the spiritual gifts listed in 1 Cor. 12:8-10 (see **charism(ata)**). Of these gifts, speaking in tongues has particular significance for most Pentecostals as the initial evidence of baptism in the Spirit.

First-generation Pentecostals saw the Pentecostal movement as a revival with distinctive characteristics. It was the latter rain, a downpour of Holy Spirit in the last days before the parousia, comparable in power only to the spring rain of the New Testament church. It was the full gospel, completing the restoration of the gospel established by the Reformation and furthered by Wesleyan sanctification.* It was the "foursquare gospel", manifesting Jesus as Saviour, Healer, Baptizer in the Holy Spirit, and Coming King. It was the apostolic faith, identical with the supernatural faith of the first Christians. It was Pentecostal, because in baptism in the Spirit each believer experiences a personal Pentecost, with God restoring the divine endowments of the church poured out at Pentecost* but lost through later apostasy and unbelief. These terms have influenced the name of many Pentecostal denominations.

Most Pentecostal histories hold that the Pentecostal movement stems from the ministry of Charles Parham, around 1900-01 in the US; he first linked baptism in the Spirit with glossolalia. The movement's explosion beyond a local Holiness revival in Kansas and Texas resulted from the multiracial Azusa Street revival in Los Angeles, 1906-09, under the black pastor William J. Seymour. Further impetus came from Parham's mission in Zion City, Illinois, in late 1906. Within two years of the Azusa Street outbreak, the Pentecostal movement had centres throughout the US, in many Northern European countries, in India, China, and in West and South Africa. The following years saw its establishment in Latin America, especially in Brazil and Chile, and more missions in Africa and Asia.

The Pentecostal movement initially had a strong eschatological orientation (see **eschatology**). It emphasized that Pentecost had to be preached throughout the world before the imminent return of the Lord. Many evangelicals denounced the Pentecostal movement for unbridled emotionalism, spiritual deception and the subordination of scripture to experience. Strongest opposition was among Holiness groups. They had been a matrix for Pentecostal concepts and provided most Pentecostal recruits in North America and Europe.

Despite this evangelical rejection, the Pentecostal movement in America and Europe has steadily adopted conservative evangelical doctrine, pre-millennial eschatology and a fundamentalist approach to biblical exegesis. In the USA this process was cemented by white Pentecostal membership in the National Association of Evangelicals, from its founding in 1943.

The Pentecostal movement's rapid spread has been accompanied by Pentecostal denominations and independent ministries. We can distinguish four categories: (1) Holiness churches which add baptism in the Spirit as a third blessing after regeneration and sanctification, e.g. the black Church of God in Christ (1907), the Church of God of Cleveland, Tennessee (1907), and the Pentecostal Holiness Church (1911); (2) two-stage Pentecostals, mostly from a Reformed background, who profess baptism in the Spirit as a "second blessing", e.g. the Assemblies of God (1914), the Pentecostal Assemblies of Canada (1919); (3) the Oneness Church, which rejects the Trinity,* affirms a modalist Christology, and baptizes only in Jesus' name, e.g. the United Pentecostal Church (origins in 1914, formed in 1945);

and (4) churches which restore the offices of apostle and prophet on the basis of Eph. 4:11, e.g. the Apostolic Church (1918).

Other major figures in the Pentecostal movement were Lewi Pethrus of Sweden, who strongly defended the autonomy of each assembly; Smith Wigglesworth, an itinerant British evangelist; Aimee Semple McPherson, American evangelist; Donald Gee, British educator; and Nicholas Bhengu, an African prophet. Missionary heroes include the American Lillian Trasher in Egypt, the Swedes Daniel Berg and Gunnar Vingren in Brazil, the Canadian C. Austin Chawner in Mozambique, and the English William Burton and James Salter in the Congo.

The Pentecostal movement has flourished among the poor and uneducated (hence the title of R.M. Anderson's study *Vision of the Disinherited*). It appeals through its oral-gestural character, involving less conceptual forms of communication, such as hand-clapping, raised arms, dance, visions, dreams and prophecy, and through its participatory patterns, which characterize especially the earliest phases of the movement. Consequently, Pentecostal churches begin as bodies of fervent believers who exalt spiritual experience and wisdom over formal education. Bible colleges and educational institutions have followed only in the third and fourth generations.

The Pentecostal movement has spread rapidly in the third world, faster than in those controlled by foreign mission boards. In Latin America, Pentecostals now account for 80% of the Protestants, far outstripping the numbers in older Protestant missions and churches. Worldwide Pentecostals now number more than 128 million Christians.

The first Pentecostal world conference was held at Zurich in 1947, the second in Paris in 1949. These early conferences saw fierce opposition to attempts to form a representative body that could speak for the entire Pentecostal movement. Now held every three years, they are largely celebratory occasions which centre on worship, testimonies and inspirational preaching, without any forum for public debate.

Pentecostals have generally been hostile to the ecumenical movement, which they perceive as embracing the apostate and stigmatize as merely human efforts to organize institutional unity. This opposition has been less marked in the third world, with two Chilean Pentecostal churches joining the WCC in 1961, followed in 1969 by the larger "O Brasil para Cristo" church of Manoel de Mello. The vision of baptism in the Spirit promoting Christian unity has been found among some early Pentecostals. It has been kept alive especially by David Du Plessis (see **charism(ata)**. He attended all the WCC assemblies from Evanston to Vancouver and constantly laboured to gain official denominational support for the international Catholic-Pentecostal dialogue. Local theological dialogues involving Pentecostals have begun in Finland, the Netherlands and South Africa. Some American Pentecostal scholars have participated in the Faith and Order* study on the apostolic faith and reflect those more open attitudes which are developing within the Society for Pentecostal Studies, formed in 1971. The Pentecostal movement today faces the dilemma of how to be less sectarian without becoming too cerebral and thus losing its power and appeal.

PETER HOCKEN

D. Dayton, *Theological Roots of Pentecostalism*, Metuchen, NJ, Scarecrow, 1987 • W.J. Hollenweger, *The Pentecostals*, Minneapolis, Augsburg, 1972 • *One in Christ*, 23, 1-2, 1987 • A.C. Piepkorn ed., *Profiles in Belief*, vol. 3, New York, Harper & Row, 1979.

PEOPLE. The term "people" is an elusive word that changes meanings and connotations as it moves through time and space and across linguistic, national, cultural and ideological lines. Theologically, it is significant in the ecclesiological use as "people of God",* in the biblical references to people and also in the modern social, economic and ideological meanings and connotations.

Biblical usage. The biblical vocabulary related to the subject presents some problems. The two basic Hebrew terms, *'am* and *goi*, usually translated "people" and "nation" respectively, are sometimes used interchangeably, but as a rule the former designates relations of consanguinity, family and consequently extended family and people as "a consanguineous body" (Ephraim Speiser). *Goi*, on the other hand, usually designates land and political organization. The two

terms are applied both to Israel and to other peoples, but the first is preferred for Israel, whereas *goy(im)* is more used for the other nations. The word *'am* is used in many composite names with the name of God, while *goi* is not used in this way. In this sense we could say that Israel is a "people" that becomes a "nation". But we cannot separate too much these two dimensions of Israel's life and calling (see **land rights**). Variations, however, also include social conditions within Israel. Perhaps the most interesting is the expression *'am ha 'erets* (the people of the land), which in pre-exilic times designates either "the men" or more frequently the higher sectors of society (landowners, propertied people, authorities) and after the exile is used for the non-Jewish (e.g. Samaritans) living within or around the borders of the returned exiles. Finally, by extension, it designates in the times of Jesus "the people who do not know (or do not observe) the law", the despised *ochlos*, for whom Jesus felt compassion.

The New Testament vocabulary is also complex. *Laos* is used in at least four ways: as a number of peoples without any definite identity, as a specific people having definite particularities, as "the common people" over against the rulers or the "upper classes" and as "the chosen people", the eschatological community, the people of the covenant.* Luke seems to prefer the popular meaning (as crowd or population), while Pauline literature leans to the figurative meaning (the Christian community). In this connection it is interesting to note the use of *ochlos* (usually translated "crowd"), which the gospels tend, with some exceptions, to use for "the common people" who came to Jesus, those despised by the higher classes and the religious authorities, almost synonymous with the *'am ha 'erets*.

Even this cursory review points to at least three significant theological issues: the relation of people to God, which appears in different linguistic constructions and finally becomes a technical term, "people of God"; the "internal" constitution of the people: the relation between the different sectors of the people — full citizens, leaders, common people — and the relation between people in consanguineous relations and as structured in a political body; and, finally, the relation between "the people" (Israel, the church) and the other peoples ("the nations", or *ta ethnē*).

Ecumenical usage before the second world war. For the modern ecumenical movement, one might see as significant for the understanding of the notion of people the discussions in the missionary movement of "the religions of the peoples", but usually this was posed as the relation between the revelation in Jesus Christ and the non-Christian religions (see **revelation, mission**). The issue has re-appeared lately as part of the claims of marginalized peoples (native populations, black) or traditional cultures to recover their own cultural identity, including their religious symbols and traditions.

A more direct challenge for the ecumenical movement was the ideological use of the concept of people by totalitarian movements such as fascism* and Nazism. Extraordinary claims for a particular people are not new. However, the ideology of "pan-Germanism" with all its political connotations, developed in Romanticism and incorporated in different organizations and associations since the last decades of the 19th century, assumed political and religious proportions that presented the church with an unavoidable challenge. The Oxford conference (1937; see **ecumenical conferences**) was partly dominated by the need to respond to it. The problems had to do with three inter-related issues. First, by identifying people and nation, the mystical attributes related to the *Volk* (in its romantic and even some pietistic tendencies) were transferred to the political ambitions, policies and decisions of the state. Second, since this *Volk* was also considered a superior race (a myth of consanguinity and soil, *Blut und Boden*), the idea of "purity of the people" unleashed ethnic persecution (see e.g. **antisemitism**). Third, in different ways and to different degrees a certain "revelational" and even "salvific" significance is attached to people: a claim that goes from the extremes of elevating a supposedly original Germanic religion to the rank of exclusive and superior revelation and rejecting Christianity as a corruption (Alfred Rosenberg), through degrees of identification of Christianity with this Germanic religion to more modest claims of some special and unique identity and role for the German (or Germanic) people.

The issue posed serious problems both at Edinburgh 1937 and Oxford 1937. In previous meetings of the executive committee of the Life and Work movement at Novi Sad (1933) and Fanø (1934), there were critical affirmations, particularly in relation to the freedom of the church in Germany and the discrimination against the Jews. In the ecumenical conferences the criticism found expression in declarations which some German delegates found unacceptable; one of these delegates spoke of "the national resurrection of the German people as a manifestation of God's concern". In fact, the Oxford statements allude to the three issues mentioned above: a totalitarianism that denies "the sovereignty of Christ and the freedom of the church", the persecution of minorities on the basis of race and colour, and "the deification of one's own people", which is "a sin against God". This last sentence could only be understood as a response to an affirmation of Theodor Heckel early in 1937, stating positively that "fundamentally National Socialism *is* the *Volk*. At its heart is the unique life-style of the (biologically) homogeneous *Volk* and its rich store of creative values."

Beyond these more specific declarations, the quest for a social and political ethics based on the notions of justice and freedom, "a responsible society", can be understood as an attempt to build, on a Christological basis, a response to the challenge of totalitarianism. The relation between the Confessing Church* and the WCC was strengthened during the war and led to actions like the Stuttgart declaration.* The warning against the dangers of a "people's ideology" led the WCC and many member churches in the 1940s and 1950s to a definite mistrust of all nationalist claims, a fact that is reflected even in the names for the churches that avoid genitives of the land, preferring forms like "church in..." and other more neutral expressions.

Third-world contributions. With the participation of third-world churches, a different perspective appeared on questions of "people" and "nationalism". Peoples that had just reached their independence or were in the midst of liberation struggles against colonial or neo-colonial domination saw their commitment to the nation as a legitimate expression of a Christian's commitment to justice and freedom (see **decolonization, nation**). Thus, "people" gains a positive meaning. Moreover, mainly in Asia and Latin America, where local economic and political minorities or military regimes, frequently allied to foreign interests, held control, the struggle for emancipation brought the people — now in the social sense of the common people, the poor,* the peasants — against the power elites. In Asia and Latin America, reacting to the restiveness of growing populations, governments became totalitarian and mercilessly curtailed civil liberties and violated the human rights of their peoples. As a consequence, people's movements irrupted all over Asia and Latin America, and the more perceptive elements of the churches stood in solidarity with the people and took up their cause. Their sufferings are perceived as a powerful cry to the God of justice, who, in mysterious ways, introduces a dynamics in history which judges, liberates and transforms society as a whole.

In secular history, the visible initiator and bearer of this historical dynamics is the people. People, therefore, are not the objects of history but the subjects of their own history. God is perceived as being genuinely incarnate in people's struggles for justice and humanity because justice belongs to the very nature of God. But God's identification with the poor, the oppressed, and all victims of injustice is not because of some ontological or ethical quality of goodness which the people possess but because of their actual historical condition as victims of injustice. Needless to say, this understanding of "people" holds enormous revolutionary potential, and the most articulate practitioners have been involved in different kinds of movements for socio-political transformation. A good number have been incarcerated, tortured and murdered because their thought and action are perceived to be subversive of the interests of the state. In such contexts ancient creeds and primeval symbols once more become energizing and inspiring.

This struggle has made possible a new exploration of the biblical and theological as well as political dimensions of the concept of people. Asian theologians point out that the Bible itself enshrines this understanding of people. Recent biblical scholarship indicates that the people of God referred to in the Bible is not a single tribe but a motley group of marginalized, powerless, disenfranchised people who were bound by a common experience of oppression and injustice, and by a common yearning for justice and freedom (Norman Gottwald, *Tribes of Jahweh*). The Old Testament prophets confronted tyrannical rulers and corrupt wielders of religious authority with God's judgment. In much of the New Testament, Jesus is portrayed as an iconoclast who champions the cause of the poor, the powerless, the oppressed. He associated himself with the poor, prostitutes, drunkards, the sick — a segment of society that the official theology of the time considered outside the pale of God's kingdom. For Jesus there is a linkage between the people and the kingdom of God,* and this linkage is the focus of many Asian theologians today.

The Christian Conference of Asia* has organized a number of consultations and seminars to explore in a systematic way the implications of a people-centred theology in the areas of Christology, ecclesiology and soteriology. A new openness has emerged towards such groups, seen as being of a piece with the corpus Christi in some essential way. And soteriology is being given a socio-political dimension, in which a person's liberation is linked with his or her actual solidarity with the poor and oppressed. Such theologians do not romanticize people, for they know only too well that people can and do embrace false values, can be swallowed up by the psyche of the mob and can give rise to and follow demagogues; but as victims of injustice they yearn for God's justice and righteousness. In other words, the theological understanding of people is consistent with the theology of grace which runs through the mainline theological thought: people are the bearers of God's grace* because as victims of injustice they are the ones God seeks to be in solidarity with. And God does not merely liberate people from injustice; God also seeks to express God's image in them, to transform them and make them agents of God's liberating grace.

While there is substantial agreement among third-world theologians and communities on this understanding of people, peculiar social, political, cultural and religious differences lead to different emphases. In Latin America in the 1960s and 1970s the concept of people received mainly a socio-economic-political connotation along the lines of class differentiation. Usually the understanding of "people" was defined by three concentric circles: the poor and oppressed, the marginalized majorities (peasants, workers, sub-proletariat); those who become aware of themselves and their condition and assume the cause of their liberation (who could be seen as an avantgarde or a force within the larger poor population); and those who, without belonging to the marginal, make an option for them and unite themselves with them in their historical pilgrimage. On the other hand, their belonging by right to the "people of God" was not theologically problematic, since these majorities are almost totally Christian. The acceptance of the Christian faith and the potential liberating significance of its doctrines and symbols could therefore be taken for granted (see **church base communities; theology, liberation**).

At both points, however, corrections had to be made. In the first place, the experience of participation in the life of this people led theologians to realize the importance of ethnic and cultural factors in the self-understanding of the people and the meaning of such factors in the struggles for liberation. Culture and race could not be seen as a secondary or

Meeting of a community housing association in Novo Marotinho, Brazil (Christian Aid/Derrick Knight)

peripheral dimension but as belonging together with the social and economic condition for any significant understanding of people. Culture, tradition and ethnic belonging are inseparable from religion, particularly among native and black populations.

In Asia and Africa, on the other hand, these dimensions have been prominent since the beginning. In Asia, the theological efforts to recover and re-read the religious and cultural tradition, as expressed in folklore, dance, language, customs and gestures (see **culture**), can be seen in much theological production in India, Korea (see **theology, minjung**) and the Philippines. The biographies and stories of the people are one of the main sources from which theology must be derived. Thus, the people are seen not as recipients of a theology elaborated elsewhere but as the subject of theology. In Latin America, Bible reading in the church base community takes this character of theological reflection, a hermeneutics* born from the experience of the people in contact with the biblical text.

Current ecumenical initiatives. Several WCC programmes are related to the role, the condition and the struggles of "the people", particularly in the meaning indicated in the last paragraphs. At the political level, the defence of human rights* and the Programme to Combat Racism,* the support of land rights claims of native populations are all part of the people's struggles. The Commission on the Churches' Participation in Development programme of the church in solidarity with the poor and the work of the sub-commission on rural and industrial mission have related to people's movements. In 1985 the Programme on Theological Education organized a consultation in Mexico on theology by the people. The concern was twofold: on the one hand, to seek new ways of doing theology in community; on the other, to see that an active commitment to justice and peace become an integral concern of the theological enterprise. Though the consultation was very much aware of theological (as well as political) dangers present in an uncritical populism, and attention was called to the need for a certain *distanciamiento* in any rigorous reflection, it strongly affirmed a theology that positively recognizes and assumes its organic relation to the people and the historical and cultural conditions which, frequently unacknowledged (and therefore uncritically incorporated), are present in all theological work.

See also **nation**.

CYRIS MOON and LEVI V. ORACIÓN

S. Amirtham & J. Pobee eds, *Theology by the People*, WCC, 1986 • K.Y. Bock ed., *Minjung Theology: People as the Subjects of History*, Singapore, CTC-CCA, 1981 • K.Y. Bock ed., *Towards the Sovereignty of the People*, Singapore, CTC-CCA, 1983 • G. Castillo-Cardenas, *Liberation Theology from Below*, Maryknoll, NY, Orbis, 1987 • I.M. Fraser, *Reinventing Theology as the People's Work*, Madurai, Unemployed Young People's Assoc., 1985 • G. Mathew ed., *Struggling with People Is Living with Christ*, Hong Kong, CCA, 1981.

PEOPLE OF GOD. In the Old Testament, "people of God" designates the calling and mission of Israel as the people chosen by God from among all the peoples (Ex. 6:7, etc.). In the New Testament the term serves to describe the self-understanding of the Christian community (1 Pet. 2:9). The Christian community is the "true" people of God of the end times, founded by the self-offering of Christ and united by the Spirit of God. Through faith* in Christ and baptism* into him, Israel and all peoples are made into the one new people of God, which takes concrete form in the local church. This claim of the primitive Christian community raised the problem of the respective places of Israel and the church* in the history of salvation (see **salvation history**), which already in the patristic literature was reduced to a metaphoric opposition between Israel as the prototype of infidelity and sin* and the church as the prototype of salvation* (see **Israel and the church, Jewish-Christian dialogue**).

In the 20th century the biblical term received fresh attention as part of the renewal of ecclesiology. The way was prepared by exegetical studies and by a more general shift in the approach to ecclesiology, involving now also the historical character of the church and the role of Christology and eschatology. At Vatican II "people of God" appears in *Lumen Gentium* as a second central concept in ecclesiology alongside "sacrament" (i.e. the church as a sign and instrument of salvation; *LG* 9-17). The category there serves as a basis for the unity of laity* and clergy in the church as the one messianic people of God. Towards

humankind as a whole, which is the people of God in the broadest sense and diversely related to the church, the church acts as the sign and the instrument of salvation and unity.* The existence of the church is determined by the hope that all humankind may be integrated into the messianic people; until this unity is finally achieved, the church's existence remains a "pro-existence", i.e. for the sake of the world. The church moves towards this consummation as the pilgrim people of God. Within the Roman Catholic Church, the formulations of *LG* were particularly taken up by liberation theology and linked with the idea of a "people's church". The church as the people of God goes hand in hand with the acquisition of (political) peoplehood by oppressed social groups.

In ecumenical work on ecclesiological questions, "people of God" has likewise been adopted as an image of the church. In *Baptism, Eucharist and Ministry** (1982), the understanding of ministry* is developed on the basis of the opening declaration that "God calls the whole of humanity to become God's people" (M1). The mission* of the church to proclaim the kingdom of God* in the world is founded on this calling (M1-4; cf. also the final "perspectives on ecclesiology" in *BEM, 1982-1990: Report on the Process and Responses*, 1990).

In comparison with other descriptions of the church, "people of God" has the following advantages as an ecclesiological image. It does not allow the nature of the church to be separated from its concrete historical form. The nature of the church is determined by its relation to the kingdom of God. As the people called by God, the church lives under God's direction until the kingdom comes. At the same time, the church plays a part in the history of salvation by acting, in faithfulness to its vocation,* as a sign of hope in every particular situation. The image of the people of God presupposes the active participation of all members of the church, while also pointing to the unity of the church and finally of all humankind. Besides the danger of a politicization of the concept (which is present in liberation theology), other open questions remain in connection with the Jewish-Christian dialogue and the dialogue with other living religions (see **dialogue, interfaith**), as well as in the matter of the concrete structures required by the church in fulfilment of its calling.

See also **images of the church; kingdom of God; laity/clergy; ministry in the church; people; theology, liberation; Vatican II**.

URSULA GIESEKE

L. Boff, *E a Igreja sa fez povo* (partial ET *Ecclesiogenesis*, Maryknoll, NY, Orbis 1986) • E. Käsemann, *Das wandernde Gottesvolk*, 2nd ed., Göttingen, Vandenhoeck & Ruprecht, 1957 • M. Keller, *Volk Gottes als Kirchenbegriff*, Zurich, Benziger, 1970 • G. Lindbeck, "The Church", in *Keeping the Faith*, G. Wainwright ed., Philadelphia, Fortress, 1988.

PERSON. The Latin word for person, *persona*, derives most probably from the Greek word *prosōpon*, which refers to the "mask" an actor wore in the theatre. Both the Latin and Greek words for person were associated with the "role" one took upon oneself either as a part of the Greek theatre or as a member of the Roman state. In neither case was the concept of a person determinative of the essence of someone (i.e. who one really is), a concept expressed in Greek as *hypostasis*, and in Latin as *substantia*.

The notion of person has a crucial place within early Christian Trinitarian and Christological discussions. These early debates sought formulations which would witness to the church's confession of biblical monotheism as well as the divinity of the Son and the Spirit. Yet one of the results of the early debates and councils was that the concept of person no longer simply meant the role one takes, but was now indicative of one's being, one's essence. Exactly how this change took place is not actually clear; however, it was the arguments within Eastern and Western churches concerning the relation of the Father, Son and Spirit which brought the notion of person to the centre.

The church in the East and the West realized that the central challenge was to speak of God* in such a way as to respect both the divine unity or oneness and the eternal expressions of God as Father, Son and Spirit. Eventually, the church agreed that the most appropriate formulations would have to affirm that God is one divine reality in three eternal manifestations. Western theological formulations, following

the lead of Tertullian and the suggestions of Augustine, spoke of God as one substance or essence in three persons, *una substantia, tres personae* (Tertullian, *Against Praxeas*, 11-12; Augustine, *On the Trinity*, books 1-7). In basic agreement with the West, the East, following the Cappadocian fathers, spoke of God as one divine nature or being, *mia physis*, or *ousia*, in three persons, *treis hypostaseis* (Basil, *Letter 38*, 2). Unfortunately, some terminological confusion resulted from the fact that the East used *hypostasis* for what is three, while the West used *substantia* for what is one (and *persona* for what is three).

By using the concept of person (*hypostasis* or *persona*), the church was able to affirm that God is not the sum of three divine parts; rather God is Father, Son and Spirit, indicative of one essence. Yet the use of "person" also revealed a subtle but crucial difference between Eastern and Western theological formulations. This difference stems not from any overarching theological dispute between East and West, but most probably from perceived theological dangers within their somewhat different philosophical contexts.

In fear of tritheism, the West placed emphasis on the unity of the Father, Son and Spirit in the divine essence. It was better to think of God first as one essence in three persons, because everything that can be said of God can be said equally of Father, Son and Spirit. This meant that "person" was basically a limiting term which prohibited the exchange of divine names (e.g. the Son is not the Father, etc.).

Attempting to rework Aristotelian and Neoplatonic categories, the East placed emphasis on the unity of the Father, Son and Spirit in the person of the Father. It was better to think of God as the Father, who is the source of the Son by generation and of the Spirit by procession, because there is no naked divine substance which exists without the divine persons. This meant that "person" was fundamentally a positive term which constitutes the divine nature or essence. The divine nature consists in the fact that God is the persons of Father, Son and Spirit in communion.

This subtle difference in the use of "person" meant that the West was able to guard itself more carefully than the East against any accusations of tritheism. Western theologians were able to say that it was the relations of

Father, Son and Spirit in the divine essence which made them persons. Thus the divine persons were defined as three relationally distinct ways of existing in one essence (Thomas Aquinas, *Summa Theologiae*, 1a.29.4). While the East was in basic agreement with the West that the divine persons are constituted by their relationships, the West was unable to grasp the break the East had made with the general doctrines of essence or substance. Such a break meant that the divine essence does not precede but is constituted by the Father's begetting of the Son and sending forth the Spirit. As John Zizioulas states, God is Trinity "because the Father as a person freely wills this communion" (44).

Person and individualism. Western theologians, for the most part, have been more uncomfortable than their Eastern counterparts with the notion of person. The West perceived the notion as inadequate because, even with the important qualifications, it was difficult to see how the divine persons could suggest real relations without also suggesting three distinct beings. The danger of God's being thought of as three distinct beings was based not only on the continuing acceptance of substance-essence categories but also on the acceptance, in some measure, of the Boethian definition of person, which placed incommunicability, substantiality, and intellectuality as fundamental to being a person (Boethius, *Treatise against Eutyches and Nestorius*, 3; see Fortman, 161ff.).

The idea of person was made more problematic with the addition of the attributes of personality and self-consciousness. With the inclusion of these attributes, generated by the advent of the Enlightenment, most Western theologians now saw the notion of person as an obstacle to be overcome in elaborating the doctrine of the Trinity as well as in explaining the relation of God as person to the human person (Barth, 35ff.). If a person could be defined as a self-conscious individual with intrinsic rights who was able to reason and pursue the perceived good, then God could not actually be three persons (but possibly was one person).

Theological reflection in the West has had to contend with the ideology of individualism, which defines the person according to essential attributes and rights. Such persons are the building blocks of community and society;

thus the protection of the wills and rights of the individual becomes our greatest task. Against this perspective, some theological circles in the West have attempted to return to the Trinitarian persons and their relations as the basis upon which we understand ourselves as persons. Thus Walter Kasper has argued that persons are defined not by their individual essence or attributes but by their relationships (285ff.; cf. Hill).

Although this return in the West to the doctrine of the Trinity signals an attempt to overcome "substance" definitions of personhood, the West has still not fully appreciated the break Eastern theologians have made with essence-substance presuppositions. It was the necessity that Father, Son and Spirit fully partake in the non-corporeal divine essence that was overturned by the Eastern theologians (Zizioulas, 40ff.; cf. Lossky, 111ff.).

Eastern theologians have wanted to push the West beyond simply saying that "God is not a substance because God's existence is prior to God's essence", towards seeing that God as the person of the Father (who in love begets the Son and sends forth the Spirit) constitutes God's essence. Thus the movement of the persons towards each other in love is the mode of God's existence (Zizioulas, 46). For the East, individualism can be overcome only by overcoming the notions of divine or human essences applied to the idea of person.

Person and Christian community. Theologians in the East and West recognize that the Trinitarian concept of person should serve as the basis of our definitions of personhood. They also recognize that to understand fully what it means to be a person, one must enter into communion* with the Triune God through the sacramental life of the church.* In and through the life of the church, we partake in the divine life in which the Son by the Spirit turns us towards the Father. The church must stress that in Jesus Christ we enter into a new understanding of personhood. We are persons not because of any essential national, racial or biological necessities but because we live in response to the love of God. The church accordingly must remember that true unity and healthy human community take place only as we enter into fellowship with the Triune God (John 17).

See also **anthropology, theological; Trinity**.

WILLIE J. JENNINGS

K. Barth, *Kirchliche Dogmatik* (ET *Church Dogmatics*, I/1, Edinburgh, Clark, 1936) • E.J. Fortman, *The Triune God: A Historical Study of the Doctrine of the Trinity*, Grand Rapids, MI, Baker, 1972 • W.H. Hill, *The Three-personed God*, Washington, DC, Catholic Univ. of America Press, 1982 • W. Kasper, *Der Gott Jesu Christi* (ET *The God of Jesus Christ*, New York, Crossroad, 1986) • V. Lossky, *A l'image et à la ressemblance de Dieu* (ET *In the Image and Likeness of God*, Crestwood, NY, St Vladimir's Seminary, 1974) • J.D. Zizioulas, *Being as Communion: Studies in Personhood and the Church*, Crestwood, NY, St Vladimir's Seminary, 1985.

PLURALISM. Pluralism has engaged the attention of such philosophers as William James (*A Pluralistic Universe*, 1909), who argued against monistic metaphysical systems in defence of the multiformity of nature,* and of political scientists who have contended for the diversity of social organization over against the monopoly of an absolute state. Ecumenically, pluralism became an issue at a comparatively late stage. While some at the first Life and Work* conference (Stockholm 1925) saw in the League of Nations the potential nucleus of a worldwide Christian commonwealth, by the time of the Oxford Life and Work conference (1937) the tune had changed, in view of what was regarded as the danger of the disintegration of Christian culture under the forces of neo-paganism.

Secularization* and the renascence of cultural and social diversity demonstrated two things. First, the ideal of a monolithic corpus Christianum and its attendant privileges had to be abandoned. Christians were becoming a minority in the world, and in any case "return" to an integrated Christian commonwealth made no sense for non-Western churches, which had never had a share in the authority of Western Christendom. Within the Roman Catholic Church, Vatican II* emphasized the recognition of a universal plurality, replacing compulsion by intellectual and political freedom.

Second, ecumenical discussion of the issue should be informed by a distinction between existing *plurality* and *pluralism* (in the sense of diversity as a value in itself). It should avoid the extremes of exclusiveness (ignoring plurality in order not to succumb to pluralism) and inclusiveness (transferring the fact of plurality into pluralism), for neither does justice to the need for peaceful relations in the "global village" and the right of people freely to live a meaningful life in society.

The ecumenical movement has pioneered in demonstrating that an approximation to Christian unity* is possible with converging church structures and theological traditions alongside continuing diversity of theological reflection and plurality of life-styles. As Christian co-operation transcends historical frontiers, the question inevitably arises whether similar processes are possible within the plurality of religions in the world. On the whole, the ecumenical movement has refused to countenance introverted and exclusivist Christianity which ignores the existing plurality of religions and ideologies, while not endorsing the pluralist view that all religions are so many paths to one divine reality (see **uniqueness of Christ**).

As new channels of dialogue between people of different faiths open up (see **dialogue, interfaith**), many ecumenically initiated, the relevance of an enlightened understanding of religious plurality becomes clearer. Respect for and co-operation with others can disclose commonalities among people of different faiths. What is held in common serves as a basis for understanding what is different and vice versa. The freedom for worship which one group expects must be granted to others. Thus it is one of the outstanding ecumenical tasks to articulate a Christian theology of religion* which can promote and undergird a responsible dialogue with people of different faiths. A number of attempts are currently being made to work out fresh approaches to such a theology, and the WCC's sub-unit dealing with dialogue has significantly contributed to it. For example, in January 1990 the sub-unit brought together in Baar, Switzerland, an ecumenical group of prominent theologians from Protestant, RC and Orthodox churches to explore the basic issues of religious plurality. The Lutheran World Federation* convened a similar meeting in 1986.

HANS GENSICHEN

C. Braaten, "Who Do We Say That He Is?", *Occasional Bulletin of Missionary Research*, 4, 1980 •

H. Coward, *Pluralism: Challenge to World Religions*, Maryknoll, NY, Orbis, 1985 ● J. Hick, "Religious Pluralism", in *Encyclopedia of Religion*, 12, New York, Macmillan, 1987 ● L. Newbigin, *The Gospel in a Pluralist Society*, WCC, 1989 ● J.P. Rajashekar, *Pluralism and Lutheran Theology*, Geneva, LWF, 1988 ● W.A. Visser 't Hooft, "Pluralism — Temptation or Opportunity?", *The Ecumenical Review*, 18, 1966.

POLLUTION. The technologized world has generally failed to control the hazardous byproducts of its industries, with the result that water, soil and air are polluted around and beyond heavily industrialized areas. The effects of such pollution vary, but the consequences for human health and the delicate balance of our ecosystem are increasingly recognized as being profound and, in some cases, irreversible. Thus, for example, acid rain caused by the burning of fossil fuels destroys marine and plant life; nuclear waste from military and, to a lesser extent, civil nuclear establishments has long-term effects on health and the functioning of human reproductive processes; and dangerously high levels of lead in fumes produced by motor vehicles can accumulate in the bodies of people continuously exposed to them, causing retarded brain development. Pollution is often unevenly distributed, with the result that certain vulnerable population groups which do not benefit from the positive benefits of industry are nevertheless exposed to its hazardous byproducts.

Governments and non-governmental organizations have been aware of the problems caused by pollution for many years, and during the last decade significant progress has been achieved in reducing the production of environmentally harmful pollutants — but much more remains to be done. The final report of the World Commission on Environment and Development called for a form of sustainable industrial development according to which governments first need to establish clear environmental goals and "enforce environmental laws, regulations, incentives and standards on industrial enterprises". Among the various recommendations of the commission are proposals that no new chemicals be placed on international markets until the health and environmental impacts have been tested and assessed, that plant workers be provided with full information and relevant training relating to the products and technologies they handle, and that standards be established for liability and compensation for any damage caused by pollution across national borders.

During the 1988 meeting of the central committee of the WCC in Hanover, concern was expressed over the manner in which certain countries violate existing international agreements by deliberately dumping toxic waste on others. In response to this concern the working group of the WCC Sub-unit on Church and Society subsequently urged that the churches take action on this issue via the following five channels: (1) support for the efforts of the United Nations* to establish international legislation dealing with all aspects of the production, movement and storage of hazardous substances; (2) the affirmation that the export of industrial waste to developing countries is both ethically and politically unacceptable, since it attempts to solve the problem of the rich industrialized countries by creating new problems and dangers for countries which are economically poorer and less developed industrially; (3) the promotion of awareness that there is a substantial difference between the cost incurred in waste treatment in industrialized nations and the price that is offered to developing countries for the disposal of wastes, which makes these operations so attractive for the companies involved, and the consequent need for effective legislation at the local, national and international levels to prohibit this practice; (4) the encouragement of governments and other responsible bodies to fund research into methods of production which eliminate or at least minimize toxic waste, and where this is impossible, to ensure the safe handling, recycling and storage of such substances; and (5) the encouragement of governments to consider the need for their long-term responsibility for the disposal of toxic wastes, especially in relation to the development of social audit systems by industries and corporations that take into account social and environmental as well as economic costs.

See also **environment/ecology**.

DAVID GOSLING

World Commission on Environment and Development, *Our Common Future*, London, Oxford UP, 1987.

POLYGAMY. Polygamy is a plural marriage in which there is more than one spouse simultaneously. It includes polyandry (one woman married to more than one man) and polygyny (one man married to more than one woman).

From fairly early in its history, Christianity taught that monogamy is the paradigm of marriage. But that history was in part shaped by Greco-Roman cultures. The idea of Christian marriage shows the influence of Roman law at several points: consent is essential for marriage; its purpose is procreation; and impediments to marriage include impotence, consanguinity, and disparity of cult. The idea that marriage is indissoluble and monogamous perhaps owes something to the Greco-Roman traditional pagan "religion of the hearth". The indebtedness to the Greco-Roman tradition regarding marriage was well articulated by Augustine when he wrote: "Now, indeed in our time, and in keeping with Roman customs, it is no longer allowed to take another wife, so as to have more than one wife living" (*The Advantage of Marriage* 7).

However, the Christian theologian also deduced views of marriage from the New Testament, where marriage acquires sacramental significance (see *ibid.* 21). But that was a "baptism" the church made of the Roman understanding of marriage.

The missionary church took this Romanized understanding of marriage, including a negative view of polygamy, to the ends of the world. On the few occasions polygamy was tolerated, it was because, as Pope Gregory II wrote in 726 to Boniface, missionary to the Germanic peoples of Northern Europe, the people lacked "high ideals", or because it was expedient to wean primitive people gradually from rude practices.

In those earlier times polygamy was not discussed as a missionary and pastoral problem; it was always debated in apologetic and theoretical terms, especially trying to deal with the embarrassing fact that the Old Testament patriarchs had more than one wife. Against this background the council of Trent* condemned the pastoral proposals of the 16th-century reformers Martin Luther and Philipp Melanchthon, who justified the polygamous marriages of Henry VIII of England and Philip of Hesse.

When Roman Catholic missionaries went to Africa, they demanded that polygamists divorce all but one of their wives. In the process great pain was brought on wives who went into the relationship innocently before becoming Christian. That approach was based on Pope Paul III's constitution *Altitudo* (1537). Pope Pius XII went further in enunciating a canonical regulation by which the pope had the power to dissolve valid marriages between non-Christians, neither of whom intended to receive baptism.

On the Protestant side there has been a slightly more liberal attitude which includes several variations: (1) women and children may be baptized, but not the polygamous husband; (2) the husband may be baptized if he divorces all other wives but the first one; (3) the husband may be baptized if he sticks only to the preferred wife; (4) the entire family may be baptized in clear understanding that subsequent plural marriages are forbidden; and (5) on the testimony of their faith alone, anyone in a polygamous marriage may be baptized with no other previous conditions. On the whole, on the Protestant side, polygamy was seen as a missionary issue, though the seemingly liberal approach was tinged with an anthropology* that left much to be desired, ethnocentrism and rather questionable exegeses of scripture.

The Anglican Lambeth conference of 1888, responding to the debate in Africa, especially in the diocese of Natal at the time of Bishop John Colenso, faced the matter. Only 21 of the 104 bishops were prepared to accept polygamists, and 34 opposed any concessions, even to the wives of polygamists. But in spite of some concessions, it declared "polygamy is inconsistent with the law of Christians concerning marriage". It was only at the Lambeth conference of 1988 that the official position was revised to allow polygamists to be received into the church, provided they promised not to take any more wives. They were not to be compelled to put away their wives. The consent of the local Anglican community was also to be sought (resolution 26). Similarly, the Bremen mission, in its church rules for 1976, opted for monogamy as "the true marriage according to God" but still allowed the admission of polygamists to baptism* and communion* (para. 62).

Today African Instituted Churches are a mark of buoyant Christian life in Africa. They are divided over the issue of polygamy. The evidence suggests that their positive acceptance of polygamy is a significant factor behind their growth. But for such a stance, such AICs have been excluded from ecumenical fellowship, for allegedly not upholding authentic Christian faith.

Several basic issues are at stake in the discussion of polygamy. First, is it right for the law of monogamy to be allowed to become a criterion of Christian faith and a mark of the true church?* There is room for debate. Second, the issue may no longer be discussed as an academic, theological one; whatever the theological position, it must be in dialogue with the evidence from social scientists. Otherwise, the church's position may be irrelevant and unpastoral. Third, it is important not to make a caricature of a particular people's marriage customs. Not infrequently, polygamy is treated as a sign of loose living. But in Africa, for example, social traditions have encased polygamous relationships in strict morality.

In any case, two issues need separate responses: first, what to do with the polygamist who desires to join the church, and second, what to do with a Christian who decides to become a polygamist for whatever reason? The first question is one of pastoral practice. Is it sensible for the church to refuse membership on grounds of polygamy when others who commit serious sins are not unchurched? The second question is the more difficult one of theology. Although churches have typically formulated laws against polygamy, it is worth asking here whether the law of the church equals the law of Christ.

JOHN S. POBEE

D.S. Bailey, *The Man-Woman Relationship in Christian Thought*, Toronto, Longman, 1959 • "The Committee of Churches of Dar es Salaam on the Government's Proposals for a Uniform Law of Marriage", *Tanzania Standard*, 28 November 1969 • A. Hastings, *Christian Marriage in Africa*, London, SPCK, 1973 • E. Hillman, *Polygamy Reconsidered*, Maryknoll, NY, Orbis, 1975.

PONTIFICAL COUNCIL FOR PROMOTING CHRISTIAN UNITY.
In 1989, this pontifical council superseded the Secretariat for Promoting Christian Unity,* the title generally used in this volume.

POOR. The ecumenical concern for the poor during four decades after Amsterdam 1948 moved from an overview approach to becoming a pivot around which the dogmatic task as a whole might turn.

The concordance view: "The unequal distribution of the blessings of life is not ideal in the sight of God" *(Westminster Dictionary of the Bible)*. Such a premise led to a lining up of biblical data for a bird's-eye view of the poor. Usually the Mosaic law functioned as bedrock of the biblical notion of the poor, especially in regard to equality in ownership of the land. A Jubilee every 50 years seemed the proper recourse, ensuring that injustices accrued in land ownership would be corrected (Lev. 25:13-25). From here the wide range covered by these dynamics would be visible: widows, orphans and strangers in the land enjoy what we might call the protection privilege of the poor (e.g. Ps. 9:18). It is common knowledge that the prophets frequently speak up for the poor (e.g. Isa. 1:23; Mal. 3:5). Within this framework it seems obvious why Jesus shows special concern for the poor (Matt. 11:5; Luke 14:21-23). No wonder the early church was strongly committed to care for its own poor and also other poor. So everywhere in the Bible, the conclusion runs, the implication is that God wants us to help the poor.

The liberation view: With the 1968 Medellín* conference the ecumenical image of the poor changed. Now God was viewed as doing more than just expressing displeasure with the unequal distribution of material blessings. Here the poor were seen as a major agent in the working out of the divine purposes in history.* But it took an awakening of the church of an entire continent to give the poor so crucial a role. In the Medellín documents the Roman Catholic Church in Latin America discovered its inescapable solidarity* with the poor, so it could envision its future as the church of the poor protesting poverty. The word "poor" now became less sentimental: "The 'poor' person today is the oppressed one, the one marginated from society, the member of the proletariat struggling for... basic rights;... the exploited and plundered social class, the country struggling for its liberation" (Gustavo Gutiérrez).

The God of the poor: Since Medellín, Latin American theology has moved towards assessing the reality of God* itself in the light of the poor. In Jon Sobrino's terms: "The present history of the world is the ongoing history of the suffering of God." Therefore the theodicy question will be answered in a new way (see **suffering**). Now theological discourse is more dialectical than analogical. In terms of the analogy of being, the divine was known more in terms of its likeness to created reality. Now the stress is on the unlikeness: dialectical cognition knows things in their dissimilarity. The theological will here "be known... from its contrary, from the negative structures of reality, the structures of oppression as lived experience" (Victorio Araya). Encounter with God is thus mediated through oppression and injustice as these realities point to the utterly different: liberation,* life (see **life and death**) and justice.* Black theology and other minority theologies say the same.

The poor God: As the debate moves towards a new dogma of the character of God, we realize that ultimately God is known not in the sheer point/counterpoint of merely human discourse dialectics but in the work of Jesus manifest in the eucharist,* living the proclaimed word. In the body language of this life God personally appears as despised and rejected by human beings, a refugee child, a rejected prophet, a crucified Messiah. Encounter with God is mediated through these very distinct negativities unlocking *God's* liberating struggle for justice in all of creation.

See also **people; poverty; theology, liberation; theology, minjung**.

FREDERICK HERZOG

V. Araya, *God of the Poor*, Maryknoll, NY, Orbis, 1987 • C. Boerma, *The Poor Side of Europe*, WCC, 1989 • J.H. Cone, *Black Theology and Black Power*, New York, Seabury, 1969 • G. Gutiérrez, *Teología de la liberación* (ET *A Theology of Liberation*, Maryknoll, NY, Orbis, 1973).

POPULATION EXPLOSION.
Ecumenical interest in population questions began in the late 1950s, after demographers called attention to the world "population explosion", to the social and economic implications of overpopulation and to the need to check population growth. These problems had arisen in part as a result of the decline of the death rate especially in Africa, Asia and Latin America. Faced with the prospects of a doubling of the world population by the end of the century, national governments and the United Nations were beginning to explore means to cope with growing population pressures.

Richard M. Fagley, then on the staff of the WCC's Commission of the Churches on International Affairs (CCIA), was the first to address these issues from an ecumenical perspective. On his urging, the officers of the WCC and the International Missionary Council convened an international ecumenical study group on "Responsible Parenthood and the Population Problem" (Oxford 1959). Fagley's book *The Population Explosion and Christian Responsibility* analyzed the moral and social issues facing the churches in the discussion of world population policy.

The population issue was also addressed in the WCC study on the "Christian Responsibility towards Areas of Rapid Social Change" (1955-62). In his concluding volume for the study on *Man in Rapid Social Change* (1961), Egbert de Vries pointed to the unique historical character of the population explosion in Africa, Asia and "other areas of rapid social change". He mentioned five critical features: (1) the dramatic drop in death rates in a few decades, (2) the absence of empty continents into which to spill any excess population, (3) the difficulty of achieving rapid increases in food supply in the short run, (4) the lack of purchasing power to buy, on a large scale, imported food, and (5) the cultural and social obstacles to a rapid reduction of the birth rate through various forms of family planning or other methods of birth control. The fourth WCC assembly in Uppsala (1968) was the first to address the challenge of the population problem, emphasizing the enormous task facing the world: by the end of the century, world population would have doubled, hence "food supplies need to be doubled; twice as many habitations must be built as have been built during man's entire history". The assembly called on the churches to support the needed action and to resolve their differences about certain methods of population control.

In 1971, in the context of the ecumenical study of limits to growth, environment and use of resources, the central committee authorized an international study of the related problems of population policy, social justice and the quality of life. Their report was presented to the central committee in 1973, which commended it to the churches "for study, comment and suitable action". It was later submitted as the WCC's contribution to the UN-sponsored world population conference in Bucharest, Romania (1974).

The 1973 study challenged the tendency to put the chief responsibility for the population crisis on the developing nations. Both developed and developing countries have an obligation to meet the needs of growing populations. In developed countries "the main stress needs to be on reducing the wasteful use and, in the long run, the per capita use of the world's resources". In the developing countries, concern for population problems "should lead to a re-examination of the fundamental nature of their economic objectives".

The report stressed the role of the churches in helping to promote "the acceptance and practice" of responsible parenthood by both husbands and wives, involving also the right of parents to "the means of family planning acceptable to them in conscience". With regard to state programmes to limit births which go beyond family planning, the report recommended "non-coercive procedures", stressing the need for churches to examine carefully all coercive proposals.

This 1974 report remains the only major WCC statement on the population issue. Neither Nairobi (1975) nor Vancouver (1983) did much more than mention the problem in relation to economic development or the sustainable society.

PAUL ABRECHT

R.M. Fagley, *The Population Explosion and Christian Responsibility*, New York, Oxford UP, 1960 • *Population Policy, Social Justice and the Quality of Life*, WCC report to the UN third world population conference, 1974.

POTTER, PHILIP A. B. 19.8.1921, Roseau, Dominica (West Indies). Third general secretary of the WCC (1972-84), Potter devoted a long career in church service to mission, ecumenism and work with youth and students. Besides 24 years on the WCC staff, he was a missionary to poor and mostly illiterate Creole-speaking people in Haiti, president of the World Student Christian Federation and a staff member of the Methodist Missionary Society in London.

In 1944, after leaving a job as assistant to Dominica's attorney general to become a Methodist lay pastor on the island of Nevis, Potter began ministerial training at Caenwood Theological Seminary in Jamaica (later he did post-graduate work in London University). Jamaica Student Christian Movement representative at the world conference on Christian youth (Oslo 1947), he was spokesperson for youth at WCC assemblies in 1948 and 1954; and from 1954 to 1960 he worked in the WCC youth department in Geneva.

As a Methodist Missionary Society overseas secretary, he was active in the International Missionary Council during integration with the WCC; and in 1967 he became director of the WCC Division of World Mission and Evangelism, though he had looked forward to spending the rest of his career as a theological teacher. Named to succeed Eugene Carson Blake as WCC general secretary in 1972, he led the Council until the end of 1984, when he finally took up the challenge he had felt earlier to return to the Caribbean to work with students at the University of the West Indies, though he continued some international travel and ecumenical involvement.

A central committee resolution honouring Potter on his retirement identified some main thrusts the WCC owed to his leadership: "the insistence on the fundamental unity of Christian witness and Christian service which the gospel commands and makes possible, the correlation of faith and action, the inseparable connection between the personal spiritual life of Christian believers and their obedient action in the world". An eloquent and forceful speaker and leader of Bible studies, Potter received numerous honorary degrees and awards. Tributes from 14 colleagues, including a personal portrait by Pauline Webb, are in *Faith and Faithfulness* (WCC, 1984); for a bibliography, see *The Whole Oikoumene*, comp. Ans J. van der Bent (WCC, 1980).

POVERTY. In her celebrated book *The Idea of Poverty* (1984), Gertrude Himmelfarb observes that by the middle of the 18th century in England, it was not possible to speak categorically about "the poor", despite the intensive debate about "the poor" and "poverty" which had been going on at least since the Elizabethan poor laws, enacted in 1597-98. "In the period of only a century, circumstances conspired to create a highly differentiated poor. This was not a matter of raising or lowering the poverty level. The changes affecting the poor were changes in kind as well as degree, in quality as well as quantity, in ideas, beliefs, perceptions, values. They were changes in what might be called the 'moral imagination'." The notion of poverty had become so complex that it was difficult to define poverty and to develop a coherent strategy to reduce it.

Ecumenical literature of the last 50 years reflects the same diffuse and changing understanding of poverty. This is not surprising in view of the diverse cultural assumptions, social situations and groupings of the poor reflected in the ecumenical debate. Given this complexity, it is useful to identify common denominators in an ecumenical understanding of poverty and to examine why poverty occurs and how to alleviate it.

The ecumenical discussion focuses on poverty which is generalized (widespread, affecting 40-50% of a nation's population), persistent (rather than cyclical), and systemic (rather than poverty which results from indolence, incapacitation, etc.). Other types of poverty are important, but destitution as a generalized and persistent phenomenon is so universal, central and demanding that the ecumenical debate centres on systemically induced poverty. Most ecumenical literature on poverty centres on broad discussions of social justice, socio-economic development, a "responsible society",* a "just, participatory and sustainable society",* capitalism, communism, a New International Economic Order.

A corollary of this emphasis on a systemic analysis means that poverty is a historical (social, economic, political) issue rather than a natural one. Generalized poverty is not perceived as resulting primarily from the shortcomings of individuals, natural laws such as the survival of the fittest, the pre-ordained ordering by God of social divisions, ineluctable laws of supply and demand exacerbated by population (as in Malthus), or even a defective and ungenerous natural environment. Poverty is usually perceived as a direct result of the failure, intentional or otherwise,

of political and economic organization to satisfy the legitimate rights of all people for a dignified and equitable life. Furthermore, these are perceived as rights which should be expected and demanded from any social system, rather than reliance upon charity or benevolent paternalism. It is assumed that defective systems can be corrected to meet basic human needs.

An ecumenical perspective on poverty is not limited to an exclusively economic understanding, although economic criteria are crucial. In recent years the notion of poverty has expanded from questions of mere subsistence to include a wide range of human and social rights. Marginalization from political processes, denial of opportunities for education or job, denial of speech and assembly, etc. are seen as integral to deprivation and poverty.

This view is illustrated in Julio de Santa Ana's influential *Towards a Church of the Poor* (1979), which defines poverty as "unfulfilment of basic human needs required to adequately sustain life free of disease, misery, hunger, pain, suffering, hopelessness and fear, on the one hand, and the condition of defenceless people suffering from structural injustices on the other. Such a life would not be limited to the satisfaction of basic human needs but would include an existence with dignity, based on the exercise of justice, participation and freedom." The definition of poverty has become blurred, but it is clearly more than a matter of lacking material weal.

Because poverty is understood as primarily systemic, produced by inadequate political, economic and social organization, today's global interdependence of these systems makes poverty dependent upon a constellation of forces which transcend national boundaries and policies. Those peoples who are culturally, technologically, economically and politically powerful globally re-inforce their own (and one another's) power, at the expense of the half to three-quarters of the world's people living in poverty. An adequate analysis of poverty and an effective strategy to diminish it have to be conceived globally. Thus the ecumenical debate is immersed in such issues as transnational corporations, third-world indebtedness, trade and tariff policies, transfers of capital and technology, a New International Economic Order.

Poverty is perceived as both absolute and relative — absolute because there are minimum conditions essential for sustaining life itself; relative because poverty is partially defined by what levels of existence are possible in a particular society, what levels are enjoyed by other members of that society and what levels have come to be defined as necessary. Two objective economic criteria have increasingly found their way into ecumenical conversations: physical quality of life index (measured by infant mortality, literacy and life expectancy); and equality index (measuring the relative economic conditions of the different quintiles of the population). Composite indices of economic well-being, such as average caloric consumption and gross national product, are generally considered irrelevant or inappropriate indices.

Much ecumenical literature suggests that the poverty of the many is a direct result of the undue affluence of a relatively few. There exists an enrichment/impoverishment relationship, a zero-sum situation, in which the increased material well-being of some automatically entails diminished weal for others. This analysis of the relationship between wealth and poverty has not been endorsed in any ecumenical conference, but it has grown in prominence in less formal statements. It tends to become a simple class analysis.

An intriguing change in terminology has occurred in the WCC's discussions of poverty. From 1948 to 1974 there was emphasis on "poverty", a term to reflect structural analyses of why people are destitute and marginalized. There was an economically defined "subclass" of people, oppressed and marginalized, below an identified material poverty line. The vast majority of the poor were poor because of structures of oppression.

In the early 1970s a terminological shift occurred. Instead of referring to poverty, it became fashionable to talk about "the poor".* Several reasons could be adduced for this change. The term "poverty" seemed too impersonal and abstract. "Poverty" too easily assumed that structures are benign and reformable, ignoring the power realities against which the poor struggle tooth and claw. "Poverty" seemed to miss non-economic, and especially political, aspects of deprivation and alienation. To some, "poverty" seemed to treat the poor and marginalized as a homogeneous entity, when actually there are differences and controversies among them.

The analysis of poverty's causes remained, but strategies to cope with it changed. Perhaps the major reason for changed terminology was a growing conviction that the remedy for poverty was not top-down reforms but changes of structure emanating from among the poor, acting as agents for their own emancipation. What has emerged is an implicit tension between those who emphasize changing international structural relationships (e.g. debt policies, transnational corporations' policies), and those who stress the need for people's movements to define and fight for their own destiny. To some extent, these two analyses and strategies are both competitive and complementary and are reflected in the language of "poverty" and "the poor".

Ecumenical literature is highly critical of every economic system; none can be identified with the Christian gospel. In the 1950s and 1960s, the WCC's literature was careful to point out the failure of both capitalism and communism. An alternative "third way" has been a constant theme. In the 1950s the concept of a responsible society* was formulated to point towards this third way, emphasizing political and economic freedom and responsibility. By the mid-1970s, a "just, participatory and sustainable society"* was advocated, highlighting material well-being, political participation and ecological sanity. The ecumenical position, especially as it has been defined in the WCC and in regional and national Christian councils, increasingly criticizes laissez-faire capitalism.* There is an expressed conviction that some form of socialism, not equated with communism, is the system most likely to overcome poverty.

Notwithstanding allegations to the contrary, ecumenical views on poverty are rooted in biblical-theological arguments. Convinced that a passion for social justice is essential to a Judeo-Christian understanding of covenant,* current ecumenical literature argues that God makes a "preferential option for the poor". This option for the poor is evident in the calling of a slave people, in the denunciation by the prophets of the amassing of and reliance on wealth, and in Jesus' calling of a noname band of disciples. This option for the poor is not only an emotional attachment to the vulnerable. It is based upon the relative

La Esperanza ("The Hope"), a fast-growing slum in Guatemala City, Guatemala (WCC/Peter Williams)

freedom of the poor to eschew the securities and prestige of this world; they think they do not need the present structures, so they can be relatively free to challenge them. While all people are called to be agents of liberation,* the poor are most fully free to receive the gospel and thus to be agents of new possibilities. Their location in society gives them a perspective on reality different from how things appear "from the top". This perspective is sometimes referred to as the epistemological privilege of the poor. Much current ecumenical literature stresses that historically the poor have played this creative role, and that because of their social position they can play that role again today. The possibilities for social transformation are linked closely with the capacity of the poor to achieve their own emancipation, the liberation of the rich and the healing and wholeness of even non-human nature.

Finally, this emerging vision of the roots and character of poverty has led to significant alteration in understanding the role of the churches in overcoming poverty. In broad strokes one can trace differing stages in the churches' understanding of how they should promote justice and overcome poverty. First,

poverty is an expression of the "laws of nature", of divine will. The churches' task is to respond to the most egregious and destructive consequences of this poverty through charity, without changing the system. Second, poverty is the result of unpredictable and unfortunate forces in one's environment, but that environment is basically sound. Again, the churches' task is to offer relief. Third, poverty is a result of moral or character failings of the poor. The church should urge regeneration of the sinful. Fourth, poverty is a consequence of humanly devised social systems which need improvement. The churches' task is to bring a prophetic judgment and constructive presence to the reform of social structures, usually through top-down evolutionary reform. Finally, poverty is a result of social structures which express and perpetuate the vested interests and egoism of the powerful, reluctant to relinquish privilege. The churches' main task is to identify with and support those groups of the poor struggling to win their own and others' liberation and dignity. Such support means taking seriously the goals and strategies of those engaged in the struggle for justice.

This enumeration is not an airtight typology

or a description of a linear evolution of ecumenical thinking about poverty. What is abundantly clear, however, is the complex, creative and emergent character of ecumenical reflection on poverty. This debate rests on differing assumptions and analyses; it is a sociological, anthropological, political and economic debate. But in the final analysis, ecumenical literature reveals that the issue of poverty ultimately entails a theological, moral and spiritual debate as well.

See also **development, economics, poor**.

RICHARD D.N. DICKINSON

C. Boerma, *The Poor Side of Europe*, WCC, 1989 • C. Elliott, *Comfortable Compassion*, London, Hodder & Stoughton, 1987 • G. Gutiérrez, *The Power of the Poor in History*, London, SCM, 1983 • H.L. Perkins, *Roots for Vision: Reflections on the Gospel and the Churches' Task in Re-Peopling the De-Peopled*, Singapore, CCA, 1985 • *Poor in the World Economy*, WCC, 1989.

POWER. Power is not only the self-expression of a subject, whether divine, human or natural; it expresses a relation between a subject and an object. Recovery of this insight, in which Christian theology and the ecumenical movement have played a significant role, has been one of the outcomes of 20th-century ideological struggles.

Power in the modern age. The issue was posed for the modern age by the vast expansion of human control over the forces of nature. The conversion of coal, oil and most recently the nucleus of the atom into energy to drive machines has changed the very meaning of the word in the popular mind. Power has come to mean first a natural force at the service of endlessly expanding human needs and desires. The implicit assumption has been that there is no determinate limit to its expansion and that the meaning of human life consists in the freedom to enjoy it.

The older meaning of the word did not disappear, however. Rather, political-social power was compounded with technological-economic power in new unstable ways. Forces of production, often anonymous, have created new power elites who have sought political influence in various ways. At the same time a revolution of rising expectations has empowered masses of people in both the benefits of an expanding economy and the

political power that gives it direction. It is not surprising that other masses, powerless for centuries, are rising in revolutionary action to claim their share.

Reinhold Niebuhr was the first to grasp this modern complex of issues theologically. Human power, he wrote, is good, as the response of human vitalities to their Creator. It is also the source of evil in the world as "the will to live becomes the will to power", which knows no limits to its desire for domination. The first task of human society, therefore, is to avert the judgment of God and human destruction by balancing power against power so as to achieve a relative justice.* This justice is always unstable, however. The balance of power on which it rests will break down unless it is set under the inspiration and judgment of higher levels of mutuality, ultimately that of the saving grace* of God in Jesus Christ. It is itself subject to judgment by the Lord of history, whose ultimate mercy and character is revealed on the cross. In Niebuhr's view, history will be, until the final judgment, the story of various forms of power — political, economic, religious, popular and military — struggling to achieve tentative forms of order which express a relative justice but also a new form of domination subject to further protest and change, challenged and humbled by the mercy of God in the servanthood and sacrifice of Christ.

Niebuhr's great contribution was to overcome both the simple continuity between divine and human power in liberal Christianity and the dualism of traditional orthodoxy, with a dialectical understanding of sin* and grace in the human power struggle. In this he provided a foundation for the ecumenical movement.

The Amsterdam assembly of the WCC in 1948 (sec. 3) identified "vast concentrations of power", both political and economic, and a technical society having a "momentum of its own" rooted in human creativity and power struggles but subjecting human beings to its laws while destroying community and deepening injustice throughout the world. The assembly sounded a note of triumphant hope in its message: "There is a word of God for our world. It is that the world is in the hands of the living God, whose will for it is wholly good, that in Jesus Christ his incarnate Word who lived and died and rose from the dead,

God has broken the power of evil once for all and opened for everyone the gate into freedom and joy in the Holy Spirit." The task of living this message, however, meant subordinating and humanizing these powers, finding a way between the absolutes of communism and laissez-faire capitalism to create just and satisfying ways of life for "little men in big societies" and of decentralizing power into responsible decision-making communities (sec. 3 report).

The ecumenical debate: Amsterdam to Geneva. Amsterdam set the agenda of the ecumenical movement in dealing with power for the next two decades. It had three levels.

A practical theological understanding of the power of God in Christ: Niebuhr posed it in speaking of the transcendent yet ever-relevant presence of the crucified Christ in a world of human power struggles. Karl Barth re-defined it as the reality of God who is not abstract omnipotence: "To possess the power to do everything without distinction would be a limitation or rather the removal of his power and not its extension. Possessing that power, he would not be God." Rather "God's omnipotence is the omnipotence of his free love", of the perfection of his "grace, holiness, mercy, justice, patience and wisdom" in Jesus Christ (*Church Dogmatics*, II/1, 490-608). Dietrich Bonhoeffer in his immensely influential *Letters and Papers from Prison*, against the background of his own life and death, gave the theme an urgent social relevance: "Man's religiosity makes him look in his distress to the power of God in the world...; the Bible directs man to God's powerlessness and suffering; only the suffering God can help. To that extent we may say that the development towards the world's coming of age... which has done away with a false conception of God opens up a way of seeing the God of the Bible, who wins power and space in the world by his weakness."

The power of God in the serving, crucified and risen Christ to save the world from its own powers became a dominant theme of the ecumenical movement in the period following Amsterdam. It was central to the messages of the assemblies at Evanston 1954 and New Delhi 1961. The World Alliance of Reformed Churches* took as the theme of its assembly in Brazil in 1959 "The Servant Lord and His Servant People". Its combination of repentant humility with action and confidence in the power of the word (see **word of God**) permeated missiological reflection, as mission practice during this period moved from its centre in the West to being a worldwide enterprise.

Biblical reflection on the nature of power: "We do not find the Bible claiming to be a book of philosophy or science or history. It does not speak to us *of* God but *in the name of God*... Each of [God's] words is an act. For this reason we can refer interchangeably to the Bible as the word of God or as the book of the acts of God." With these words Suzanne de Diétrich set the tone of ecumenical Bible study which she herself helped to guide for nearly 30 years (see **Bible, its role in the ecumenical movement**). The biblical God is a God who acts, a God of power, a God who creates, who calls, who binds himself to us in covenant,* who is faithful when we are faithless and who redeems the world in Christ. This describes not so much a particular biblical theology as an attitude towards the Bible which has characterized the ecumenical movement from its formation. Hendrick Kraemer called this attitude "biblical realism" in his challenge to the world mission of the church in 1937. It is active encounter with the power of God, through which the churches are constantly called to repentance in their relations with the world and with one another, and re-discover together their ecumenical mission.

This encounter has also had another dimension: a fresh study of the relation between the power of Christ and the principalities and powers of the world in the New Testament. Several writers from various traditions have contributed to this discussion. In each case the question was raised how these powers operate in the world today. At least one such power, the political, is clearly identified in the NT (Rom. 13). If Mammon is taken seriously, there are also economic powers. Albert van den Heuvel suggests, citing Col. 2, that "public opinion, the pressure of conformity, moral rules and religious observances, philosophies and ideologies" are also among them.

In any case, ecumenical study has made certain points clear. First, the powers are created by God and have their meaning in God's purpose and plan. Second, the powers are rooted in human desires and actions, in human idolatries and false absolutes, but in their structure they transcend human beings

Namibian workers at May day rally (John Liebenberg)

and have power over them. We are responsible both for them and for their victims. As such they are destructive and rebellious against God. Third, Christ on the cross was the victim of these powers. In his resurrection* he is Lord over them. Fourth, the church* is witness in a world dominated by the powers of Christ's victory and coming reign. This role involves conflict against the powers (Eph. 6:12) and witness to them of their true purpose in the economy of God (Eph. 3:10). This leaves the continuing question of identifying the powers in modern society which need to be resisted and redeemed, and of the strategy of this conflict and this witness.

Guidance for Christian responsibility amid the powers of the contemporary world: The term "responsible society"* was coined at Amsterdam to indicate both a style of Christian action and the form of a society towards which that action would aim. "For a society to be responsible under modern conditions, it is required that people have freedom to control, to criticize and change their governments, that power be made responsible by law and tradition and be distributed as widely as possible

throughout the whole community, [and] that economic justice and provision of equality of opportunity be established for all the members of society" (sec. 3). Theologically, the concept found its deepest roots in Dietrich Bonhoeffer's "Structure of Responsible Life", lived concretely for the neighbour in the world of political and social forces, ready to accept the guilt of impure but necessary action in the power struggle, a life guided but not dominated by conscience and the law, bearing witness in the human struggle to the presence and coming judgment and mercy of Christ (*Ethics*, ch. 6).

The form which this responsibility took in the ecumenical witness varied with time and place. The Bangkok (1949) and Lucknow (1952) conferences of the churches in Asia emphasized fundamental social revolution beset by ideological conflicts as the basic power at work in their world. They called for "the proclamation of the word of God with a profound sense of its relevance to the ideological and political conflicts of the Orient" (Bangkok) and in that context for democratic transformation of the social order, for freedom of religion and other human rights, for effective land reform and full development of natural resources, for common sharing of the national wealth and responsible development of human community.

The WCC's Evanston assembly (1954) made a discriminating analysis of state* power as not the source but the guardian of social justice, of economic power in concrete terms which went beyond the labels of "capitalism"* and "socialism",* and then explored the differing particular responsibilities of the church in the Western world, the communist world and the economically underdeveloped regions of Asia, Africa and Latin America. The Salonika conference on "Christian Action in Rapid Social Change" (1959) emphasized (1) the powers of technology,* (2) nationalism,* and (3) the dynamics of economic development,* and called for Christian action towards new forms of human community to cope with the first, discriminating participation in nation-building to bring out the creativity and counter the idolatry of the second, and the right use of the world's resources to promote "the widest possible participation in the planning process and in the execution of plans" for progress in the midst of the third.

The Geneva conference on Church and Society (1966) said bluntly that "in seeking a responsible society we need to discover the operations of power, unveil the hidden centres of power and hold all power accountable to men and God... Since man fulfills his God-given potential only by exercising power and by sharing in making the decisions that affect his life, we believe that maximum participation in authentic decision making must characterize the systems where technologies are shaped and employed." This means workers as well as experts and managers in an industry, and an informed general public, organized perhaps in advocacy groups to bring countervailing power to bear where it is needed. It also means the state, which the report said should not be the only repository of power but should nevertheless have the means of controlling other centres in the public interest.

Beyond this understanding, however, consensus in the Geneva conference broke down. There was no agreement as to the degree to which the state should exercise its controlling and managing power, about the way in which participation in state power by conflicting groups and interests among the people should be organized, or even about the role of law* vs the powers of revolutionary change. Behind such differences lay a deeper dispute about the nature of power itself, which challenged the context of previous ecumenical debate.

This challenge had many sources in social experience and ideology.* But whether it grew out of the cause of black power in the US or South Africa, the class struggle of the poor in Latin America or the rising self-consciousness of peoples in Asia, the theme was the same: the experience of living in the midst of a struggle against the dominant and oppressive powers in society is basic to humanity, to faith* and to theology. To be aware of oneself as a human being, to be conscientized, is to find oneself already in the midst of struggle against the structures of class domination. In the midst of this praxis and this theoretical awareness, one discerns also one's relation to the power of God.

The ongoing debate. This starting point and this stance have had three consequences for the ecumenical debate about power.

First, a profound *suspicion of the ideological bias* in previous ecumenical theology and social ethics, and a demand that solidarity with the oppressed, whether with the poor* in class terms, with the blacks in terms of race, or with "the people" as culturally defined, be the starting point for all theological and ethical action and reflection. "God's word of reconciliation means that we can only be justified by becoming black," wrote James Cone in the US situation. "Theology to be authentically Asian must be immersed in our historic-cultural situation and grow out of it. Theology which should emerge from the people's struggle for liberation would spontaneously formulate itself in religio-cultural idioms of the people." So wrote the Asian participants in an ecumenical conference whose report appears in *Towards a Church of the Poor*. One could multiply the examples. Only from a particular position and engagement in the world power struggle can truth about God be known.

Second, the demand that *action in the form of engagement* on the right side of social conflict be the test of faith and the form of Christian obedience. The WCC, representing the churches of the world, must therefore also be so involved. This is the motivation behind the Programme to Combat Racism,* and it defines the difference in emphasis between interchurch aid and the Commission on the Churches' Participation in Development.

Third, a theology of *continuity between the human struggle for liberation and the saving work of God in Jesus Christ*. "The historical-political liberating event *is* the growth of the kingdom and *is* a salvific event; but it is not the coming of the kingdom, not *all* of salvation. It is the historical realization of the kingdom and therefore it also proclaims its fullness." So wrote Gustavo Gutiérrez in his now-classic work *A Theology of Liberation*. Christ is identified with the human power struggle of the poor and completes it with his work.

The issue at stake in all three points of this challenge is not the empowerment of the poor and the oppressed to achieve their just participation in society. This has been a theme of ecumenical ethics from the beginning. Nor is it the healthy reminder that the theology and ethics even of Christian people can be distorted and biased by their political and economic interests and allegiance of the power structures in which they feel secure. This, too, has been an ongoing discovery of churches in mission and in ecumenical encounter, a cause for continual repentance and renewal of life.

The fundamental question is rather that of the relation between divine and human power. Can the world be redeemed by replacing the principalities and powers that now dominate it with others representing the people and the poor? Is the justice achieved by human struggle itself subject to the judgment of God and the correction of further struggle for the corruption which is present in its relative goodness? Are there resources in the Christian community to empower believers in their struggle against injustice while at the same time believing in and praying for divine forgiveness and transformation of us all? Will we learn in this light that human power is more ambivalent and more complex than we now imagine? Much work remains to be done in internal ecumenical struggle to clarify the relation of God's power in Christ to our own.

A final word must be said which qualifies this whole discussion. During the past 20 years, the awareness has been forced upon the world that human power over the non-human creation, or nature,* although without deter-

minate limits, can defeat itself and lead to our destruction. The discovery of nuclear power is only the most obvious example. Synthetic chemical compounds that do not degrade, pesticides that also poison people, energy-producing fuels that pollute the air and change our climate — these are only a few examples of the consequences of human power that has not learned to live within the limits of God's creation.

The problem in this area is that nature cannot rise up and liberate itself. Future generations who will bear the consequences of our technology and industry cannot vote in our elections or struggle against our exploitation of them. Instead, we must muster the restraint and discipline to respect the integrity of creation, although we have the power to destroy it for our immediate profit. "The Christian hope sets science and technology in the open-ended process of God's history with his creation," says the report of the WCC conference on "Faith, Science and the Future" in 1979. Human beings cannot renounce their power. Their task is to discern the promise of nature in partnership with humanity. This too is ecumenical agenda for the future. It is intertwined with the struggle for justice, in that no ecological policy will succeed which is not secured by shared access for all to the resources of the earth and just distribution of the products made from them.

The power of God, as has been said above, is self-limited by covenant with the people of God, implicitly with the whole creation as well. It is an open-ended covenant filled with promise, a covenant redeemed even when human beings in their power struggles seek to destroy it. Under the risen Christ and looking to his coming, it is a promising covenant fulfilled in the service of one another and appreciative use of the creation around us. The exercise of power in this responsibility is an ecumenical art we are only beginning to learn.

See also **order, society, state**.

CHARLES C. WEST

K. Barth, *Kirchliche Dogmatik* (ET *Church Dogmatics*, II/1, Edinburgh, Clark, 1957) • H. Berkhof, *Christ and the Powers*, Scottdale, PA, Herald, 1962 • D. Bonhoeffer, *Ethik* (ET *Ethics*, London, SCM, 1955) • J. Cone, *Black Theology and Black Power*, New York, Seabury, 1969 • A. van den Heuvel, *These Rebellious Powers*, London,

SCM, 1966 • R. Niebuhr, *The Nature and Destiny of Man*, vol. 1, London, Nisbet, 1943 • J. de Santa Ana ed., *Towards a Church of the Poor*, WCC, 1982 • H.-R. Weber, *Power: Focus for a Biblical Theology*, WCC, 1989 • C.C. West, *The Power to Be Human*, New York, Macmillan, 1971.

PRAXIS. The Western reception of the notion of praxis should undoubtedly be traced back to Aristotle's distinction between pure contemplation *(theōria)*, production *(poiēsis)* and a human moral action which expresses the intention of the agent, the value of which cannot be separated from the agent *(praxis)*. While some ascetics and mystics shared the Neo-platonic contempt for praxis as contaminated by the material world in which it operates, many church fathers, including Clement of Alexandria, saw it as an expression of Christian love. The word does not necessarily appear, but the form of human expression that it designates is present in scholastic theology, although always second to theory. The theological significance of human purposeful action inspired by love has never been denied, even if it is differently valued. A whole theological tradition has extolled it over against a purely intellectual and propositional theology. The tradition of "practical Christianity" has been a powerful component of the ecumenical movement from the very beginning. It even finds polemical expression in the slogan "doctrine divides, but action unites". Such vindication, however, does not attach to praxis any epistemological or methodological significance in dogmatic thinking. "Theoria" may or may not be liked, but it remains — even when directed to "religious experience" — the only muse of dogmatics.

It was left to Marx to invert the Aristotelian paradigm and assign to praxis the place of privilege. It is in the human beings' purposeful transformation of the world that they create themselves as well as the world around them. To be sure, they cannot do it capriciously or arbitrarily but according to the laws of the material world (of which they are part) — not as a purely mechanical operation *(poiēsis)* but as *human* work, an intention through which one affirms one's freedom.* It is this dialectics that Antonio Gramsci tries to capture when he re-baptizes Marxian materialism as "the philosophy of praxis".

It is probably this overshadowing influence of Marx in the modern recovery of the notion of praxis that rendered it suspicious when contemporary political and liberation theology re-introduced it, not only in the realm of ethics but as an instrument of knowledge, a methodological principle and a form of verification in dogmatics. Thus in the Vatican "Instruction on Certain Aspects of the Theology of Liberation" (1984), the use of praxis in some currents of that theology is criticized for its relation to "the materialist conception of history to which praxis is linked", for its political contents centred on class struggle and it made revolutionary praxis a criterion of truth.

It is therefore important to characterize more precisely the place attributed to praxis in these (liberation and political) theologies. In a more general sense we can say that the act of knowledge is never a purely passive contemplation of abstract truth but is an act involving the totality (psychological, social, historical) of the human reality of the knower, including his or her intentional relation to the world. Praxis cannot be conceived as independent from theory. In fact, theory is reached by a process of abstraction on the basis of praxis; a specific practice, as a concrete form of human praxis, always has an implicit theory. Thus, praxis cannot be understood as mere pragmatic action. This relation between praxis and its theoretical content is a mutual one in which each element supports, tests and corrects the other. Since praxis signifies an active relation to the world, it necessarily affects its subject; persons are thus modified by their praxis as they modify the world by it.

More specifically, in the theologies mentioned usually some elements are underlined. First, the contents of the Christian praxis envisaged is defined by "an option for the poor": it thus points to a location (which is both social and spiritual) in history and society which defines a "horizon of knowledge". Second, it is a praxis of faith,* which is therefore controlled by the object of that faith, Jesus Christ* — his person, his message, the kingdom which he announced and inaugurated. Third, it is a communal praxis, lived and acted out and critically revised within the community of faith. Fourth, it verifies the Christian message in so far as it makes it a reality in human history.* One could say that it enacts the presence of the kingdom, although in the limited and imperfect form of a sign which participates in the reality it signifies but does not render it perfectly present. Finally, since the Spirit of God is present in history, Christian praxis is an act of discernment and, therefore, a form of knowing (see John 7:17) with dogmatic significance. It is in this sense that Gustavo Gutiérrez can say that "theology is a critical reflection on Christian praxis in the light of the word".

Praxis as a word has not entered the WCC vocabulary in any significant way. But the "action-reflection" model which is operative in several programmes and activities of the WCC is inspired by analogous concerns, although it has not developed a methodological rationale for praxis.

See also **theology, liberation; theology, political**.

JOSÉ MÍGUEZ BONINO

C. Boff, *Theology and Praxis: Epistemological Foundations*, Maryknoll, NY, Orbis, 1987 • J.B. Metz, *Faith in History and Society: Toward a Practical Fundamental Theology*, New York, Seabury, 1979.

PRAYER IN THE ECUMENICAL MOVEMENT.

Ecumenical prayer was anticipated by Jesus in the "Our Father", focused upon his followers in the great prayer for unity* in John 17 and then widened out again to embrace all human beings in the spread of the gospel since Pentecost.* It is prayer offered for the unity of Christ's universal church* and the well-being of the world he came to save. Although this vision has never been wholly lost sight of in divided Christendom, it was, however, left mainly to a few discerning souls in every tradition to recognize their unity of spirit with those otherwise separated from them and to travelling Christians of one kind or another to promote a cross-fertilization of prayer and devotion across confessional and national boundaries. It was not until the turn of the 19th century and through an awakened concern for mission* and unity and a growing experience of the interdependence of the whole human family that the deeper implications of such prayer began to be more widely known and available.

The first modern movement to be inspired by our Lord's high priestly prayer "that they may all be one" arose from two quite separate sources and resulted eventually in what is now well known as the Week of Prayer for Christian Unity.* Today this week is observed either in January or at Pentecost, according to local preference, and has continued to give many local Christians an experience of ecumenical prayer. As an extension of the week of prayer, many religious communities follow the practice of lighting a candle week by week — the Thursday candle — accompanied by the prayer: "Grant that in you, who are perfect love, we may find the way that leads to unity, in obedience to your love and your truth."

Described in the Orthodox Easter prayer as "the myrrh-bearing women", the ministering-praying women of the New Testament have been followed and identified with the countless Christian women who, as part of families, congregations, religious orders and positions of leadership, have played a vital part in healing the bruised and broken Body of Christ. Over the last 100 years two women's organizations have made a particularly important contribution to ecumenical prayer.

The World Day of Prayer,* founded in the USA in 1887 in response to needs following the civil war and for prayer for missions overseas, has developed over the years into a worldwide movement, composed mainly of women, who engage in "informed prayer and prayerful action" on behalf of the needs of the whole world. The second such movement, conceived in 1956, was the brainchild of the Asian Christian Women's Conference. Focusing on the smallest coin of each country's currency, offered with prayer for peace, the Fellowship of the Least Coin continues to draw a response from women all over the world.

More recent participation of women in ecumenical prayer and decision making has led to a demand that the language of prayer itself should be revised to do justice to the place and activity of women within the church and to acknowledge the feminine attributes of God. Ecumenical prayer is currently being greatly enriched along these lines: "O God whose word is life and whose delight is to answer our cry, give us faith like the Syro-Phoenician woman, who refused to remain an outsider; that we too may have the wit to argue and demand that our daughters be made whole, through Jesus Christ, Amen" (*All Desires Known*, Janet Morley, 1988).

A third and arguably the most significant contribution to the growth of ecumenical prayer has been the quickening of concern for the renewal and mission of the church, which led to the inception of the modern missionary movement and to its fruit in the suffering, praying, growing churches around the world today.

Originating in a series of humble "concerts" of prayer for the renewal of the church in Scotland in the late 18th century, the movement eventually spread to other countries and played an important part in the programme of the newly formed mission agencies and subsequently in their great conferences. Attributing much of the success of the 1910 world missionary conference in Edinburgh to the fact that it had been the focus of wide intercession, John R. Mott wrote: "The heart of Edinburgh was not in its speeches but in its periods of prayer." Seventy years later the same was to be said of another important and more representative gathering of Christians, the sixth assembly of the WCC (Vancouver 1983) — that its heart was in its prayer and worship.

In the early years of the modern missionary movement, first by necessity and later by desire, co-operation developed between the different missionary groups, accompanied by prayer and consultation and later common action, and eventually, in some places, by plans for church union. Thus it was that united prayer among missionaries of different denominations grew, much of it directed towards the renewal and evangelistic outreach of the newly established churches. Such prayer, however, was not without its critics among local Christians, many of whom were excluded from early missionary assemblies and who came to feel that prayer itself only too easily became an instrument of paternalism. Moreover, many local Christians resented imported denominationalism* and imposed forms of worship and sought freedom to address God in their own way and in the mode of their own culture. A prayer used at a later Asia youth assembly expressed what many were feeling at a much earlier time: "O Lord,

World Day of Prayer for Peace, Assisi, Italy, 1986 (Foto Felici)

lead us not into imitation." It was a prayer which was already being answered as early dependency and denominationalism gave way to autonomous churches and eventually, in some areas, to the formation of united churches whose liturgies have contributed in a special way to ecumenical prayer.

The fourth and central strand in the development of ecumenical prayer emerges from the well-known early student gatherings in Europe and North America, where young men and women met together for prayer, to read the Bible and to face the challenge of service overseas. It was in such prayer and meeting that impatience with denominational differences was generated; and to meet the needs of these young people, organizations like the Young Men's and Young Women's Christian Associations and the Student Christian Movement came into being. Between them they produced the earliest books of ecumenical prayer and worship. Now somewhat dated and limited in the range of their material, they were nevertheless pioneers in their field and gave many of the future leaders of the missionary and ecumenical movement their first taste of ecumenical prayer. The presence of such student groups at Edinburgh 1910 and subsequent ecumenical gatherings, and the concerns which they voiced, along with those of representatives of an ever-widening circle of churches, were to form the milieu of the WCC. Many of those present at the WCC's first assembly (Amsterdam 1948) spoke of the moving moment when, after hundreds of years of confessionalism and division, representatives of many different churches and nationalities were for the first time able to say the Lord's prayer together, each in his or her own tongue.

The worship of the early assemblies, however, remained fairly traditional as the various church leaders shared their own denominational treasures. Those earlier years were marked by an over-optimistic internationalism, which regarded the kingdom of God* as attainable in a relatively short period of time. This was to be severely challenged, along with the patterns of prayer which went with it. The reality of the ever-changing world situation demanded a realignment of prayer and theology which provided the theme for a particularly formative WCC assembly at Uppsala in 1968.

Work camps and student conferences and the changing needs of young people produced more informal acts of worship and new approaches to intercession. A growing number of churches from a wide spectrum of traditions, including members of the Orthodox family, African Independent, Pentecostal and black American churches, and with an ever-increasing representation from third-world countries, officially entered the ecumenical movement, bringing with them both ancient liturgies and new insights into prayer and worship. Many of these challenged what was held to be an overly cerebral approach to worship and pointed to new dimensions of prayer in the form of symbols, music and movement more meaningful to the vast majority of the world's Christians.

In addition, the wide-reaching changes initiated at Vatican II* have allowed greater participation of Roman Catholics in ecumenical prayer, and the revitalization of many traditional Christian practices and acts of devotion has been reflected in a renewed interest in a specifically Christian life-style, in the use of silence, in pilgrimages and in the observance of vigils and fasts. Similarly the hurt and pain experienced by Christians in many places and situations has forced ecumenical prayer back to its biblical roots and to the crying and questioning of the people of God in the Old Testament, producing many contemporary lamentations. A more sympathetic approach to those of other faiths has brought with it an awareness that they, too, are people of prayer and have much to offer in this and other ways.

Meanwhile in response to various WCC assembly themes from Uppsala onwards, the Council's mandate and ecumenical vision have been widening considerably, and this has been mirrored in the content of its prayer. The programmes of development* and those to combat racism, to promote peace and health and the good of the environment; the ever-growing recognition of social justice as a spiritual commitment; and the decade of churches in solidarity with women have all had their implications for ecumenical spirituality. While in an increasingly one-world culture there are still significant differences of need between different peoples, there are also an increasing number of concerns held in common across the world. But unity continues unchanged as a central theme of all ecumenical prayer, although perhaps nowadays directed less towards organized schemes of union and more towards the ending of the shame and scandal of divisions at the local level, in addition to that between peoples and races divided from one another. To respond to all such needs the concept of solidarity is one which has been fostered in recent years to express a relationship which is to be deepened between different churches and peoples of the world, and in which prayer and the sharing of spiritual resources is held to play a very important part. To this end an ecumenical cycle of prayer has been produced.

If the widening out of its concerns over the years has led some to refer, disparagingly, to the WCC as "the United Nations at prayer", it is a title which is nevertheless welcomed by some, especially when it comes to finding ways of identifying with those many people around the world who, often in situations of desperation, relate their prayers to the realities of their lives as they use one of the most ecumenical of all prayers: "Maranatha: come, Lord Jesus, come, soon."

See also **intercession, spirituality in the ecumenical movement, Week of Prayer for Christian Unity, worship in the ecumenical movement**.

JOHN B. CARDEN

A.J. van der Bent, "The Concern for Spirituality: An Analytical and Bibliographical Survey of the Discussion Within the WCC Constituency", *The Ecumenical Review*, 38, 1, 1986 • J. Carden comp., *With All God's People: The New Ecumenical Prayer Cycle*, 2 vols, WCC, 1989 • E. Castro, *When We Pray Together*, WCC, 1989 • D.J. Fleming, *The World At One in Prayer*, San Francisco, Harper, 1942 • M.A. Thomas, *About You and Me*, Madras, CLS, 1974.

PRESBYTERATE. This is the term given to the second order of ministry from the time when the three orders of bishop, presbyter and deacon were clearly distinguished. The words *presbyteratus* and *presbyter* are still used in the Latin version of the Roman pontifical, though they are usually translated in other languages as "priesthood" and "priest". *Baptism, Eucharist and Ministry** has the traditional distinction between bishop and presbyter in mind when it suggests the universal adoption of the threefold ministry (see **ministry, threefold**).

Ecumenically what is at stake is the distinction between the ministry of the bishop and that of presbyters within the one pastoral ministry, as well as the importance of adopting an episcopal church structure which places a second order of pastors, called presbyters, under the supervision of the episcopacy.* At the world conference on Faith and Order* in Lausanne in 1927, there seemed to be some acknowledgment of the three kinds of church structure going under the names of episcopal, presbyterian and congregational (see **church order**). In the responses to BEM, some churches have asked why this has now been dropped, so that a presbyterian structure with only one order of pastors and a supervisory presbytery should be expected to give way to an episcopal structure that appears to favour distinct roles of bishop and presbyter within the pastoral ministry. Others have asked why there is no reference to the role of elder, as distinct from pastor, as practised in some Reformed churches.

Calvin allowed for only one ministry of word and sacrament, without internal distinction of orders. In the church structure of Geneva he assigned this place to pastors, but he also had elders (this term translates the Greek *presbyteroi*), teachers and deacons, since he found these offices in the New Testament. Elders were not pastors and had no part in the ministry of word and sacrament, but they had a role in church governance. With some differences in how the office is envisaged and in how elders are designated, many churches today believe that elders are part of the church structure indicated in NT texts. Ecumenically, the question arises whether adopting a distinction between bishop and presbyter within the pastoral ministry introduces an unnecessary ranking within that ministry and also whether so doing suppresses an office distinct from it that is, however, pertinent to the good of the church.

It is in fact not easy to draw any clear conclusions about bishops and presbyters in NT writings. The church in Jerusalem seems to have been governed by a group of presbyters, or elders, under the presidency of James, adopting a pattern found in Jewish communities (Acts 11:29-30, ch. 15; Gal. 2:9). This pattern carried over into some churches of Asia Minor (Acts 14:23). In other churches, leaders are called bishops and deacons

(Phil. 1:1). There is no great precision about the ministry of any of these roles. The pastoral letters mention both bishops and presbyters. Some exegetes take the titles as synonymous.

In the post-apostolic period, there is reason to believe that some churches, such as Rome and Alexandria, were governed by a presbyterium, or group of presbyters, one of whose number exercised the sacramental and presidential ministry in the community. In the letters of Ignatius of Antioch there is clear mention for the churches of Asia Minor of the tripartite ministry of bishop, presbyters and deacons. This is the pattern clearly adopted in the ordination* ritual of *The Apostolic Tradition* attributed to Hippolytus and the one that subsequently prevailed until the Reformation.

Despite the clear distinction of names, there is no great clarity in the evolution of the presbyterate as a distinct office and ministry. From writings such as those of Hippolytus and Cyprian of Carthage, there is reason to see that the office was by very nature collegial and that the main role of the presbytery was to advise and act with the bishop in matters of church government, such as the purchase and disposal of church property, the selection of ministers, the healing of conflicts within the community, and the excommunication* and reconciliation* of sinners. Their part in teaching and in sacramental ministry appears to have been at first one of substitution for the bishop. It was with the expansion of the church and the separation of local churches into diverse communities that presbyters assumed as normal the presidency of smaller communities, and a sacramental and teaching ministry. Indeed, by the 4th or 5th century the ordination of presbyters was to this pastoral office rather than to membership in the collegial presbyterate, though traces of this are to be found in church order and canon law* down through the ages. Such was the evolution that in time the sacramental ministry and priesthood* were predicated primarily of the presbyterate rather than of the episcopacy, which was taken by many medieval theologians to be a divinely instituted jurisdiction rather than a sacrament. Thus the words *sacerdos* and *presbyter* became practically synonymous. In English, the word "priest" is related etymologically to *presbyter* but has assumed a sacerdotal meaning.

At the Second Vatican Council,* the Roman Catholic Church clearly affirmed the sacramental nature of the episcopacy.* At the same time, it affirmed that ordination to the presbyterate is ordination to the comprehensive ministry of word, sacrament and pastoral care, rather than only to sacrament. In allowing this ministry to both bishop and presbyter, it attributed a supervisory and magisterial role to the bishop and retrieved something of the collegiate sense of the presbyterium from early centuries, applying it to the exercise of the full ministry. If one abstracts the sacerdotal and hierarchical factors in Roman Catholic teaching, this appears to correspond in a general way to the suggested adoption of the threefold pattern in ecumenical discussions. While the adoption of the episcopacy would be a sacramental expression of the church's apostolicity* and would provide for a link between churches beyond local boundaries, the existence of a group of presbyters sharing in the pastoral ministry would allow for its collegiate nature in the particular church. The risk is that the collegiate would be swallowed up in the hierarchical and that the equation of presbyterate with pastoral ministry would suppress the participation of the church membership in the ordering of church life through its representative elders.

An examination of the simple word "presbyterate" thus uncovers a number of valid ecumenical questions. Is it not important to maintain a collegiate responsibility, even on the local level, for pastoral ministry? Does the distinction between bishop and presbyter allow for this, and how is it to be maintained if this division is adopted? On the other hand, is it not important to keep open a collegiate responsibility for church governance which includes the members not appointed to the pastoral ministry (i.e. the laity)? Can this now be allowed for through the office of elder, and does the equation between presbyterate and pastoral ministry of word and sacrament not obscure this part of church heritage?

See also **collegiality; episcopacy; ministry in the church; ministry, threefold; priesthood**.

DAVID N. POWER

J.L. Ainslie, *The Doctrines of Ministerial Order in the Reformed Churches of the Sixteenth and Seventeenth Centuries*, Edinburgh, Clark, 1940 • R.E. Brown, *Priest and Bishop: Biblical Reflections*,

Paramus, NJ, Paulist, 1970 • H. von Campenhausen, *Ecclesiastical Authority and Spiritual Power in the Church of the First Three Centuries*, Stanford, CA, Stanford UP, 1969, pp.76-123 • D.N. Power, *Ministers of Christ and His Church: Theology of the Priesthood*, London, Chapman, 1969 • P.S. Wright, *The Presbyterian Elder: Based on the Books of Order, 1985-86 Presbyterian Church (USA)*, rev. W.B. Lane, Philadelphia, Westminster, 1986.

PRIESTHOOD. As a cultic term, connected with the offering of sacrifice, the use of this word is problematic in ecumenical discussions at the point where the theology of ministry* intersects with the theology of the eucharist.* The Roman Catholic and Orthodox churches teach a ministerial priesthood that is exercised in the celebration of the eucharist and that is distinct from the common priesthood of all the baptized exercised in the pursuit of a life according to the gospel and culminating in the act of worship. The first is indeed related to the second and is intended to bring it to fruition, but it is particular inasmuch as it means an exercise of sacramental ministry and offering performed in the person of Christ. Without the power given to the ordained ministry to perform this service, the common priesthood could not be nurtured or expressed in the service of the eucharistic sacrifice.

With the teaching of the Second Vatican Council* on the laity,* the Roman Catholic Church began to give much more prominence to the active role of the baptized in teaching, apostolate and worship than it had done for some centuries, but it continues to give some preference to the use of the word "priesthood" in speaking of the sacramental powers and ministry of the ordained and to teach a difference in kind rather than in degree between common priesthood and ministerial priesthood. This understanding of the term therefore remains a point of tension in the dialogue between the Roman Catholic Church and the Protestant churches, although the tension has been eased somewhat by reason of the agreements formulated on the nature of the eucharistic sacrifice, when this is seen in its proper sacramental relationship to the sacrifice of the cross. Nonetheless, it continues to be disputed whether priesthood in the New Testament sense is to be used only of the baptized and of the church as a body, or whether it has a more particular meaning in the case of the ordained.

The roots of the dispute are found in the early Christian assumption of sacerdotal terminology to speak of the church and the faithful, and later of its worship and ministries. The initial tendency of NT writers was to eschew any direct use of priestly terms, so as to contrast the gospel with the older covenant.* Even in the case of Christ's death, formal use of sacrificial language is low key, the principal purpose of any reference to it being to indicate that this redeeming death is the fulfilment of the Old Testament types, including the sacrificial ones such as the paschal lamb and the covenant sacrifice. It is the letter to the Hebrews which deliberately writes of Jesus Christ* as priestly mediator and of his death and heavenly intercession as priestly. Whenever a cultic term is used in the NT in reference to the church,* it is to designate a life according to the gospel, acts of mutual service, and the ministry of apostolic preaching. In a more general way, the church as a body is called a living sacrifice, a royal priesthood, a temple of God's Spirit, for in its obedience to the gospel true worship is rendered to God, and the glory of God is made manifest to all. Some Catholic exegetes believe that this usage is a legitimate foundation for the language of ministerial priesthood, but the point is controversial.

In the post-apostolic church, sacrifice and priesthood began to be used of the eucharistic prayer, or more generally of the eucharistic celebration, by way of such OT texts as Mal. 1:10, or by way of contrasting this one sacrifice of praise and thanksgiving with the religious sacrifices of the Jews and of the pagans. With 3rd-century writers like Hippolytus and Cyprian, the bishop began to be called a priest because of his presidency of the eucharist, where he offers the gifts. Subsequently this is said also of presbyters who join the bishop in this ministry or take his place (see **presbyterate**). When writers such as John Chrysostom made a formal link between the action of the bishop and the heavenly liturgy of Christ the High Priest, sacerdotal language was the natural way of expressing that relation. Hence, in the use of sacerdotal terminology the relation of the minister to Christ came more into the forefront than did his relation to the people. Medieval and scholastic theology then related the priesthood of the minister to his action *in persona Christi* and gave the ministerial priesthood decided priority over the common priesthood. In face of the problems of the reformers, the council of Trent* formally taught the priesthood of the sacrament of order and its connection with the eucharistic sacrifice.

Many of the dialogues which have taken place between the Roman Catholic Church and other churches since the Second Vatican Council have found some reconciliation of differences in the new accent on the priesthood of the church as such, both common and ministerial; in the sacramental and memorial understanding of the eucharistic sacrifice; in the clear relationship of the ministerial priesthood to the common priesthood, both in worship and in the church's obedience to the gospel; and in the clear subordination of both to the one priesthood of Jesus Christ. Thus *Baptism, Eucharist and Ministry** states: "Ordained ministers are related, as are all Christians, both to the priesthood of Christ, and to the priesthood of the church. But they may appropriately be called priests because they fulfill a particular priestly service by strengthening and building up the royal and prophetic priesthood of the faithful through word and sacraments, through their prayers of intercession, and through their pastoral guidance of the community" (M17).

The statement in BEM is quite irenic, but of course it glosses over the particular sacramental relation to Christ which the Orthodox and Roman Catholic churches predicate of the ordained bishop and presbyter. Thus other dialogues, such as that between the Vatican Pontifical Council for Promoting Christian Unity and the Lutheran World Federation,* note a continuing divergence in the use of priestly predicates and in sacramental practices, highlighting the sacrifice of the ordained minister, sanctioned by the Roman church but found unsatisfactory by the Lutheran. For its part, in response to the ARCIC (see **Anglican-Roman Catholic dialogue**) statements on eucharist and ministry, the Vatican Congregation for the Doctrine of the Faith found the priestly and sacrificial nature of both eucharistic action and ordained ministry underdeveloped. Clearly the precise relation between ministerial and common priesthood is still a concern for ecumenical discus-

sion, especially in regard to the relation of the former to Christ.

See also **episcopacy, sacrament(s)**.

DAVID N. POWER

B. Cooke, *Ministry to Word and Sacraments: History and Theology*, Philadelphia, Fortress, 1976, pp.525-657 • R.J. Daly, *Christian Sacrifice: The Judaeo-Christian Background before Origen*, Washington, DC, Catholic Univ. of America Press, 1978 • J.H. Elliott, *The Elect and the Holy: An Exegetical Examination of 1 Peter 2:4-10 and the Phrase basileion hierateuma*, Leiden, Brill, 1966 • W. Lazareth, "Priest and Priesthood", in *The Encyclopedia of the Lutheran Church*, 2, 1964-66 • J.-M.R. Tillard, "What Priesthood Has the Ministry?", *One in Christ*, 9, 1973 • A. Vanhoye, *Old Testament Priests and the New Priest according to the New Testament*, Petersham, MA, St Bede's, 1986.

PRIMACY. Primacy is one of the burning issues in the ecumenist's file. The difficulty springs from two sources: first, the biblical texts which speak of Peter's special role within the apostolic community make no reference to a succession in the fulfilling of this function; and second, the subsequent functioning of the Roman primacy has raised problems to do with prestige and power that have frequently seemed intractable. The issue of primacy was central to the separation between East and West and, within the West, to the division at the Reformation.

Primacy in ecumenical dialogues. The achievements in this area that have followed the entry of the Roman Catholic Church into the ecumenical dialogue are significant: there has been convergence and even agreement on some points. This is particularly evident in *The Final Report* of ARCIC I (1981) (see **Anglican-Roman Catholic dialogue**). It is there recognized that the New Testament references apply to Peter and not to his successors. However, a broader interpretation of the way in which God in his providence (i.e. in the patristic sense of this term) acts on behalf of his church* permits the affirmation that the primacy is in accord with God's plan. Indeed, the care of the churches, with their need to remain visibly united in their confession of faith,* sacramental life and mission,* requires a ministry of this nature. The only episcopal see that lays claim to this office is Rome, the city which preserves the witness of Peter and

Paul, who were martyred there (*Final Report*, Authority I, nos 22-23; Authority II, nos 2-9,33). Nevertheless, the form in which the primacy is exercised continues to be problematic. Nor was it possible to reach full agreement on an understanding of infallibility* (Authority II, nos 29,31).

The Methodist-Roman Catholic* joint commission has paid equal attention to this question (Nairobi report, 1986, nos 39-75). Agreement was achieved with regard to the role attributed to Peter in the NT (nos 39-47) and to the need for a ministry of authority* (no. 48), but the matter of the Roman primacy raised difficulties when it was faced concretely. While the idea of primacy remains alien to Methodists (no. 37), they admit that it could be useful (no. 58). The Catholic viewpoint is objectively presented in this report; but the Methodists declare that, if they should some day come to accept some degree of primacy and leadership from the bishop of Rome, their reasons might differ from those affirmed by the Roman Catholic Church today.

In the USA the Lutheran-Roman Catholic* group has examined the problem in depth (*Lutherans and Catholics in Dialogue*, vols 5-6). For the sake of unity* and the universal mission of the church, the Lutherans are prepared to accept an authentic Petrine office (5.28,30). However, it would have to be purged of the aberrations condemned by the Reformation, become pastoral rather than juridical, respect evangelical freedom, submit to the authority of the word of God* and safeguard the spiritual inheritance of the Lutheran tradition. Infallibility wisely construed, which would be concerned with the faith and refrain from the oppressive use of authority, could be of service to the Spirit in guiding the church towards the fullness of truth.

These conclusions are close to those of the French Dombes Group. Its document of 1985 on *Le ministère de communion dans l'Eglise universelle* (*Documentation catholique*, no. 83, 1986) proposed that the Petrine office should be at the service of a universal communion,* acting primarily as an arbitrator between churches, as a guide discerning new directions for the future, and as the bond and promoter of visible unity (nos 152-62). But a primacy of power and centralized authority is not acceptable (nos 136,153).

There has as yet been no statement on this subject from the Orthodox-Roman Catholic* commission. However, it is clear that as a result of the warm exchange of words and gestures between Paul VI and Athenagoras (see *Tomos Agapes: Vatican-Phanar, 1958-70*), Orthodoxy is changing the way it looks at the primacy of the bishop of Rome. The harsh stance taken by the encyclical of the four patriarchs in response to Pius IX's invitation (*In Suprema Petri Sede*, 6 January 1848) is no longer that of Athenagoras, who describes the ancient see of Rome as first according to honour and order. But the Orthodox churches would find it difficult to accept a Roman primacy which differed from that of the first few centuries, even if some Orthodox sense the need for a ministry of unity in a form different from the one presently exercised by the patriarch of Constantinople.

Primacy in the historic Roman church. From a historical perspective the primacy of Rome is that of a local church* in the city where the witness of Peter and Paul was fused by their martyrdom into an indivisible confession of faith. In Peter, this faith is linked to the preaching of Jesus and the memory of the Twelve, who represent Israel and the privileged witnesses to the life, death and resurrection of the Lord. In Paul, the newness of the faith, its universal mission and its radical openness are revealed. Because the church located in Rome is thus the guardian of this apostolic witness (see **apostolic tradition, apostolicity**), its directives are to be followed in order to preserve unity. In looking to Rome in times of crisis, the other churches remain, or should remain, free from any interference in their own internal affairs, because the Roman primacy is not based on domination.

Each bishop is the representative of his local church; the bishop of Rome is thus present as guardian and instrument of the primacy of the church of Peter and Paul. He continues the function of leadership exercised among the apostles by Peter, who had particular concern for the faith both before and after Pentecost,* first as spokesman for the apostolic group and then later as its leader. It is in this context that the words "strengthen your brethren" (Luke 22:32) and even "you are Peter" (Matt. 16:18-19) should be applied to the bishop of Rome. This background provides the basis of the conviction that through the bishops of the see of Rome the primacy entrusted to Peter survives as the bond of communion with the authentic apostolic tradition.

However, it is a primacy which is an integral part of, and inseparable from, the episcopal body (see **episcopacy**). The point of departure was "Peter himself, a single person" (Cyprian, *On the Unity of the Catholic Church*, 4-5), but with him it is the whole *collegium* that becomes involved. As Augustine explained: "If Christ spoke to one person alone, it was in order to emphasize unity" (*Sermons* 295.2-8; *Letters* 53.2; *Homilies on the Gospel of John* 124.5). Primacy must be understood within this framework.

Until the intervention of Leo the Great (440-61) at Chalcedon,* ecumenical councils* were in communion *with* Rome without being *under* its authority. The element essential to these assemblies was their communion in faith and spirit, a requirement to which the Eastern church adheres to this day. Before Leo there was no submission to a primacy of jurisdiction. A turning point came when Leo asserted his sense of the rightful authority* he had as bishop of Rome. This was the meaning of his intervention at Chalcedon, where his legate occupied the chief seat beside Patriarch Anatolius. He also intervened when the rights of some episcopal sees were being infringed. His function was one of service.

The exercise of the prerogatives of Rome was remarkably balanced under Gregory the Great (590-604), but this gradually gave way to an increasing claim to absolute power. Gregory VII laid down regulations for the functioning of this power in *Dictatus Papae* (1075), and Innocent III (1198-1216) went to the length of saying that the ancient patriarchal churches had received their privileges from the church of Rome. The rupture with the Eastern churches, followed by the conciliar controversy (see **conciliarity**), led to a further hardening of attitudes in the West and resulted in the view of a church governed by a pontiff who looked on the other bishops as his vicars rather than as brothers.

Against the background of these later developments, Vatican I's* constitution *Pastor Aeternus* sounds moderate. In it the raison d'etre of the Roman primacy is viewed as the close unity of the bishops and the koinonia*

of all Christians (H. Denzinger-A. Schönmetzer, *Enchiridion Symbolorum*, 3050-52). Vatican I made it clear that the primacy belongs to the *church* of Rome and that it takes effect in the *bishop* of Rome through the exercise of a genuinely episcopal authority (*DS* 3060) that does not restrict the authority of other bishops over their own flock (*DS* 3061). The Roman primate is bishop of Rome, but he is not bishop of any other local church. Nevertheless, he does have over the faithful of other local churches a power which is "immediate" (i.e. does not *necessarily* pass through any intermediaries) and "ordinary" (i.e. is not delegated but is given by virtue of his function).

Vatican II and primacy. Vatican II* did no more than re-read *Pastor Aeternus* by placing it within the totality of Tradition.* In this way it opened itself to the challenge brought by the Orthodox churches. According to Vatican II the bishop of Rome is a member of the episcopal college which, *as such and in its entirety*, inherits all that is transmissible of the functions which pertained to the apostolic group. The Roman primacy is that of the head *within this college*. Yet, for the college as such to have the full and supreme power over the whole church, it is necessary that it be united with its head, the bishop of Rome. He, however, may not consider himself as above the college even when, by virtue of his special responsibility, he uses his freedom to intervene.

Since Vatican II the Catholic conscience has become more aware that this primacy is, by its very nature, a ministry of communion. The diversity of traditions, circumstances and peoples is the concrete expression of the local churches; and the safeguarding of their communion is the charge of the bishop of Rome acting in accordance with Christ's will which was first affirmed in the vocation of Peter.

Koinonia is not confined to a mere "being-together". It requires unanimity in the profession of faith despite diversity of expression. On major points, it requires someone to point out the errors to be avoided. It needs information to be passed to all the churches concerning the ways some of them seek to resolve common problems. Finally, it calls for the admonition of any groups which seriously depart from the common faith and practice.

These are the hallmarks of the mission of the bishop of Rome.

J.-M.R. TILLARD

N. Afanassieff, N. Koulomzine, J. Meyendorff & A. Schmemann, *La primauté de Pierre dans l'Eglise orthodoxe* (ET *The Primacy of Peter*, Leighton Buzzard, UK, Faith, 1973) • J.J. von Allmen, *La primauté de l'Eglise de Pierre et de Paul: Remarques d'un protestant*, Fribourg, Ed. universitaires, 1977 • Arbeitsgemeinschaft ökumenischer Universitätsinstitute eds, *Papsttum als ökumenische Frage*, Munich, Kaiser, 1979 • R. Brown, K.P. Donfried & J. Reumann, *Peter in the New Testament*, Minneapolis, Augsburg, 1973 • J.-M.R. Tillard, *L'évêque de Rome* (ET *The Bishop of Rome*, Wilmington, DE, Glazier, 1983).

PRO ORIENTE. Founded in 1964 by Cardinal Franz König of Vienna, Pro Oriente promotes ecclesial relations between the Roman Catholic Church (RCC) and the Orthodox, pre-Chalcedonian and pre-Ephesian Eastern churches through research, publications and visits which contribute to a better understanding of the Christian East.

Pro Oriente's first meeting, in 1974, between Roman Catholics and Byzantine Orthodox theologians helped lead to the official theological dialogue between the RCC and the Orthodox local autocephalous churches, with the aim to "advance towards the re-establishment of full communion between the Catholic and Orthodox sister churches" (Patriarch Dimitrios I and Pope John Paul II, 1979).

Pro Oriente sponsored five Vienna consultations between Roman Catholic theologians and those of the Oriental Orthodox churches (Coptic, Syrian, Armenian, Ethiopian and Syro-Indian), in 1971, 1973, 1976, 1978 and 1988. One can regard these as the first dialogue between the RCC and whole family of Oriental Orthodox churches since the schisms, especially through the agreed statements on Christology, which avoided the disputed definition of the council of Chalcedon* (451).

A further Pro Oriente task was to initiate relations with the Romanian Orthodox Church by inviting Romanian bishops to ecumenical symposia and conferences and by the visits of Cardinal König to Romania (1967) and of the Romanian patriarchs Justinian (1968) and Teoctist (1987) to Vienna. Pro Oriente has contributed to improve relations between the Ethiopian Orthodox Church and the RCC. Ethiopian Orthodox theologians participated in the five consultations, and Patriarchs Tekle Haimanot (1981) and Merkorios (1990) visited the RCC in Austria. Cardinal König was in Ethiopia in 1983.

Pro Oriente has organized 57 ecumenical symposia in Vienna, eight theological conferences, two symposia (St Methodius and the Rus' Millennium) and two exhibitions of icons; published 28 volumes on ecumenical, theological and historical subjects; and provided several stipends for Orthodox students.

ALFRED STIRNEMANN

Wort und Wahrheit, supplement issues 1-5, 1972-88 (papers and minutes, five Oriental Orthodox-RCC consultations).

PROGRAMME TO COMBAT RACISM.

Racism* is denounced as incompatible with the Christian doctrine of the human being and the nature of the church of Christ. But for over 40 years (between the 1925 Stockholm Life and Work conference and the 1968 Uppsala assembly) the churches within the ecumenical movement were not sure exactly how to combat it. In those years over 30 statements had been issued, condemning racial discrimination and racism. But despite some humanitarian programmes to help the victims of racism, there continued to be a great distance between word and deed in actually tackling the problem at its roots.

In the 1960s eminent Christians like Martin Luther King, Jr, Albert Luthuli and Eduardo Mondlane deeply influenced the racism debate, and King's assassination only weeks before he was to address the WCC's Uppsala assembly in 1968 gave the matter an urgent focus. The assembly urged the WCC to "embark on a vigorous campaign against racism" and to undertake "a crash programme to guide the Council and member churches in the matter of racism".

More pressure came in 1969 from a WCC-sponsored world consultation on racism held in Notting Hill, London. In an emotional and often confrontational meeting, representatives of the racially oppressed demanded, among other things, a boycott of all institutions supporting racism, a fund for the payment of "reparations" for the injustices suffered over

the centuries, and support for the armed struggle of oppressed blacks in situations where all
other means had failed. Though these demands were not met, they certainly influenced
the recommendations to the WCC central
committee, which set up the Programme to
Combat Racism. Out of a heated and emotional debate a five-year mandate was adopted for
the programme. This was renewed in 1974.

PCR's scope and focus was to deal with
racism as a worldwide problem. However, the
coincidence of an accumulation of wealth and
power in the hands of white people, as a result
of their historical and economic progress during 400 years, made it necessary to give
special attention to white racism in different
parts of the world. The member churches
were called upon to confess their involvement
in the perpetuation of racism and to allocate a
significant portion of their total resources,
without employing paternalistic mechanisms
of control, to organizations of the racially
oppressed and those supporting the victims of
racism.

PCR's mandate stipulated five major emphases: (1) white racism, which in its many
forms is by far the most dangerous form of
present racial conflicts; (2) institutionalized
racism, as reflected in social, economic, and
political power structures which use racism to
enhance their power; (3) the need for a re-
distribution of social, economic, political and
cultural power from the powerful to the powerless as an essential aspect of combating
racism; (4) absence of a single, universally
appropriate strategy for combating racism; (5)
the need to analyze and correct the churches'
complicity in benefitting from and furthering
racism.

A commission on the PCR was appointed to
guide its work and to make specific policy and
programme recommendations to the central
committee. PCR became a sub-unit of WCC's
programme unit II, on Justice and Service.
The new sub-unit developed a list of programmatic categories for its work, ranging
over the many aspects of worldwide racism,
initiated research and published material on
different forms of racism and the struggle of
the oppressed. It also became responsible for
the administration of the WCC special fund to
combat racism, from which annual grants are
made to racially oppressed groups and organizations supporting the victims of racism.

From 1970 to 1990 a total of more than
US$9.2 million was distributed.

Much of PCR's attention and energy has
been focused on Southern Africa. As a result
of research and recommendations, beginning
in 1972 the central committee made policy
decisions on: (1) a withdrawal of investments
from Southern Africa, (2) an end to bank
loans to the South African government, (3) a
break in WCC relations with banks doing
business with South Africa, (4) a halt to white
emigration to Southern Africa, (5) a rejection
of South Africa's bantustan policy, (6) a man-
datory arms embargo and a halt to nuclear
collaboration with South Africa, and (7) comprehensive sanctions against South Africa.

In addition, PCR has sponsored a number
of important consultations between church
and liberation movement leaders, as in Lusaka
1987 and Harare 1988, which helped to chart
the course of international church support for
the struggle against apartheid.* In 1989, an
eminent church persons group visited a
number of countries that have a high level of
economic ties with South Africa.

As changes began to come to South Africa
in 1989 and 1990, PCR supported preparations for the historic National Conference of
Churches in South Africa (Rustenburg*
1990). PCR director Barney Pityana was one
of two co-ordinators for this meeting, 30 years
after the Cottesloe* consultation, the
watershed in WCC relationships with Afrikaner churches and the South African government.

While Southern Africa has remained a
priority, PCR has also focused on the struggle
of indigenous people and land rights* in general. A 1989 land rights consultation, held in
Darwin, Australia, affirmed the inherent right
of indigenous peoples to self-determination
and control of their territories, as well as the
establishment of their governments and the
maintenance of their traditional cultural and
religious practices.

Furthermore, PCR developed a programme
on women under racism, designed to give
visibility to issues and concerns of women
who suffer from triple oppression: racism,
sexism* and classism. In 1986, a world consultation was held on the issue in Geneva.
Emphasis is placed on indigenous and dalit
women (in India) and on the issue of race and
tourism, its impact on the rights and the digni-

ty of women as well as the effects on indigenous values and culture.*

In 1990 PCR was significantly involved in discussions about the resurgence of racism in Europe; it prepared a new programmatic category of its work to support dalit emancipation in India and extended its support work with minority groups in Asia and South America. The dramatic increase in institutional and community racism in the USA has meant new PCR efforts in that country also.

Over the years, PCR has given considerable attention to racism in education. In 1978 a study was made on racism in school textbooks, while in 1990 PCR organized a consultation in Toronto on racism in education and the media, with emphasis on North America.

PCR, from its beginning, has been one of the most controversial among WCC initiatives. While there was strong support from many member churches, there was also criticism, especially over its support of liberation movements in Southern Africa. Some of those movements are now legitimate governments, and the WCC and PCR's vision and commitment have been vindicated. Indeed PCR is now often pointed to as one of the ecumenical success stories. All WCC units and sub-units were forced to deal with racism as it affected their respective mandates. Member churches were challenged in an unprecedented way to take a stand and to become actively involved in racial issues. The WCC would never be the same again: it had taken sides with the racially oppressed. Charity was being replaced by solidarity. The WCC became more relevant to the majority of Christians and even to people of other faiths. Concrete action against racism had severely tested the ecumenical fellowship, but it was not broken.

See also **apartheid, racism**.

BALDWIN SJOLLEMA

E. Adler, *A Small Beginning: An Assessment of the First Five Years of the PCR*, WCC, 1974 • *Link*, a PCR bimonthly newsletter • J. Mutambirwa, *South Africa: The Sanctions Mission*, WCC/Zed Books, 1989 • *PCR Information*, reports and background papers • B. Rogers, *Race: No Peace without Justice. Churches Confront the Mounting Racism of the 1980s*, WCC, 1980 • B. Sjollema, *Isolating Apartheid. Western Collaboration with South Africa: Policy Decisions by the WCC and Church Responses*, WCC, 1982 • J. Vincent, *The Race Race*, London, SCM, 1970.

PROPERTY. Definitions of what constitutes property as well as attitudes towards ownership vary with different cultures and epochs. Property is what is owned, but all theories on property depend on the respective economic systems and ideologies (from Proudhon's "property is theft" to the libertarian "taxation is theft", to limitations on water rights, mineral rights, intellectual property, trademarks, design, copyright, etc.).

The basic biblical criteria and attitudes towards property are relevant and valid in any society, but there are various interpretations of the biblical statements. Because God is the absolute owner of all things, no individuals or groups have absolute ownership of property, but all human beings are responsible to God as stewards (Ps. 24:1). Limitations are found in the prescriptions of the sabbatical year (Ex. 21:2, 23:10; Deut. 15:12) and the year of Jubilee (Lev. 25:10). The prophets of the Old Testament revealed God's bias in favour of the oppressed and the poor, widows, orphans, slaves and foreigners, who need solidarity and help.

Jesus underlines the perils of wealth, although he does not condemn the possession of property or denounce ownership of land, house or money. While there is no condemnation of rich people as such, Jesus does point out the danger of accumulating earthly treasures (Matt. 6:19-21). Jesus lays down the principle that life does not consist in the abundance of possessions (Luke 12:15). The kingdom of God* has to come first; everything else is secondary and subsidiary (Matt. 6:33).

Property must be shared with others. As God's stewards, we are at the same time everyone's neighbours. Stewardship does not imply mastery over nature, economic forces and society. This would be corruption of neighbourliness. Both the New Testament letters and the history of the early church present examples of sharing (e.g. Acts 4:31-35; 2 Cor. 8:1-5; Phil. 4:10-20; Gal. 6:1-10).

Property is closely related to power.* The rich have power over the poor because of their economic strength. Although article 17 of the Universal Declaration of Human Rights (1948) underlines the right of property as an individual and personal right, ownership also means social responsibility, and as a social right it must be socially justified in respect to its acquisition, its effect on the owner and its consequences for the rest of the nation or the world. Here, the question of scale is decisive. As the ownership of property increases (up to the level of the transnational corporation), so responsibility increases for the right use of power.

The ecumenical movement has from its beginning urged the Christian churches to work for greater justice in the distribution of the world's resources, in order to narrow the yawning gap domestically and globally between rich and poor (see various WCC conferences, for example Geneva 1966 on Church and Society, and MIT 1979; Justice, Peace and the Integrity of Creation, Seoul 1990; see also the Lutheran World Federation studies "Christian Ethics and Property", 1981-87, "Christian Ethics and Land", 1985-90; and the US Catholic bishops' pastoral letter on "Catholic Social Teaching and the US Economy").

The findings of the ecumenical studies can be summarized as follows: (1) the churches need prophetic critics of all social, economic and political systems, of personal or systemic injustices; (2) the churches are called to represent their biblical concern for the poor and suffering of this world; (3) the churches should have a concern for life-styles that are simpler and involve less consumption, for ecology of "spaceship earth" as common property of humankind in longer-range planning, and for community and balance of private rights to property and responsibility to the world of nations and to the public good.

BÉLA HARMATI

H. Brattgaard, *Im Haushalt Gottes* (ET *God's Stewards*, Minneapolis, Augsburg, 1963) • M. Hengel, *Eigentum und Reichtum in der frühen Kirche* (ET *Property and Riches in the Early Church*, Philadelphia, Fortress, 1974) • O. Hirmer, *Marx-Money-Christ: An Illustrated Introduction to Capitalism, Marxism and African Socialism, Examined in the Light of the Gospel*, Harare, Mambo, 1981 • J. Míguez Bonino, *Toward a Christian Political Ethics*, Philadelphia, Fortress, 1983 • National Conference of Catholic Bishops, "Catholic Social Teaching and the US Economy: Pastoral Letter", Washington, DC, 1986 • R. Shinn & P. Abrecht eds, *Faith and Science in an Unjust World*, WCC, 1980.

PROPHECY. Prophecy is found in many religions, but it has occurred most significantly in religions of history* such as Judaism, Islam and Christianity.

In the biblical tradition prophets are messengers of God in times of crisis — of ambivalent and eschatological openness. They act out of a deeply felt personal relationship with, and obligation to, God. For their witness (martyria) they often pay with their lives (see **martyrdom**). They claim to have received special revelations from God ("Thus says the Lord" is a typical beginning of their message) which offer a radical alternative to existing beliefs, ethical standards or established structures, whether religious, societal or political. Since these structures are represented by priests and political leaders, prophets tend to stand in marked opposition to such figures. They are easily accused of being "false prophets", a fact which indicates that prophecy cannot avoid the ambiguities of any partisan involvement in a critical moment of history.

As messengers, prophets belong to God. It is God's glory, righteousness, anger or mercy which they proclaim. They act in the name of the God who is coming, who is ready to do new and unheard-of things. In the light of the advent of God, prophets proclaim and predict new historical developments. According to the nature of the crisis, these may be times of judgment and doom or of comfort and renewal. Prophets are not interested in forecasting doom; they are endowed with the Spirit to see through, to disclose the future impact of present evils in order to call people to conversion. Therefore, prophecy has always a salvific dimension.

Jesus placed his ministry in the line of the great prophets before him, such as Moses, Elijah and Isaiah (e.g. Luke 4:17-21; Matt. 17:2). The early Christians were convinced that prophecy is a gift of the Holy Spirit* (a charisma*) as important as teaching, oversight (episcope), or healing (1 Cor. 12:27-28 and elsewhere). Consequently, the Christian churches have always maintained the view that the prophetic element is essential for the well-being of the church. But owing to the nature of prophecy, it could never be defined or instituted as a constitutive part of the churches' ministry. It was mostly in hindsight that churches have come to acknowledge some of their servants and martyrs who had been much contested at their time as true prophets of God.

In the same manner some of the leading persons in the ecumenical movement have been acknowledged as prophetic. Laypersons such as John R. Mott, Robert Gardiner or Joseph Oldham, or clergy such as Nathan Söderblom, Charles Brent, Dietrich Bonhoeffer or Oscar A. Romero are now revered as prophetic servants of the universal church in times of trial and persecution.

However, whether the ecumenical movement as such should be called prophetic is open to debate. Certainly it has the role of reminding the churches of their shortcomings (such as lack of unity,* sharing and solidarity*). In this way some messages and actions of the WCC have had all the characteristics of prophetic witness.

The Faith and Order* study on "God in Nature and History" (published in 1967) expressed the hope that the WCC would be able, if necessary, to "pronounce the right prophetic words in the name of the churches". The 1968 assembly of the WCC placed itself under a markedly prophetic word: "Behold, I Make All Things New". Its decision to embark on the Programme to Combat Racism* was greeted by some as prophetic, discarded by others as too worldly. As none dare to call themselves prophets unless they are prepared to carry the terrible burden of such a calling, so no one dare designate or label from outside who or what is prophetic. Prophecy is something to be awaited in prayer and to be followed in discipleship.

As the churches grow together in their common calling to serve the world and each other, they also owe to each other the elementary charism of prophecy. But to identify this charism with a particular institution or movement is incompatible with the nature of prophecy. It appears more appropriate to describe the role of the ecumenical movement in the words of one of the WCC general secretaries, Philip Potter, who wrote in 1981: "We... are called to be paracletes, to comfort and counsel one another. We are called to be beside each other, helping, exhorting, consoling, strengthening. That is what fellowship within our congregations and churches and between the churches around the world is all about."

See also **revelation, witness**.

GEIKO MÜLLER-FAHRENHOLZ

L. Boff, *Igreja, Carisma e Poder* (ET *Church, Charism and Power*, London, SCM, 1985) ● J.E. Corbett, *Becoming a Prophetic Community*, Atlanta, John Knox, 1980 ● G. Müller-Fahrenholz, *Heilgeschichte zwischen Ideologie und Prophetie*, Freiburg, Herder, 1974 ● P. Potter, *Life in All Its Fullness*, WCC, 1981.

PROSELYTISM. In the New Testament, the word *prosēlytos* refers to a convert to Judaism (Acts 2:10). To induce someone towards such conversion* is to proselytize, and organized efforts to do so are proselytism. Ecumenically, the term has acquired the negative connotation of the perversion of witness* through secret or open improper persuasion such as bribery, intimidation, or external coercion.

Proselytism became a major interchurch problem through Roman Catholic (RC) and Protestant missionary work in countries where other Christian churches were already present — for example, among the Orthodox in the Middle East, Ethiopia and India, and among the RCs in Latin America. Since 1552 the activities of RC mission orders had helped to form Uniate churches (in union with the papal see in Rome), whose members had previously been part of the Orthodox church (see **Eastern Catholic churches**). They became Armenian Catholic, Greek Catholic, Chaldean Catholic, etc. In some areas, converts from Orthodox and Roman Catholic background formed Protestant churches. The mother community regarded the formation of these churches as an act of proselytism; the missionaries saw them as the inevitable consequence of witness to the gospel.

Agreement on the distinction between true witness* and unacceptable proselytism has thus become an issue of mutual ecclesial acceptance. Significantly, proselytism was studied around the time of increasing Orthodox involvement in the WCC, the integration of the International Missionary Council,* and Vatican II.* The WCC third assembly (New Delhi 1961) received and commended the document on "Christian Witness, Proselytism and Religious Liberty". In 1970 the Joint Working Group* between the Roman Catholic Church and the WCC (JWG) issued a study document on "Common Witness and Proselytism".

Both documents point to the contrast between true witness and proselytism. The New

Delhi statement affirms that mutual witness is an essential part of the ecumenical fellowship. It includes witness to Christians who have lost contact with their own church and renewal carried from one church into another. It may even lead to a witness against the doctrine and practice in another church believed to be contrary to truth (see Toronto statement* of 1950). Equally, the right to change church affiliation on grounds of conscience is affirmed as part of religious liberty.*

The perversion of witness into proselytism depends on the intention and the means used. Every intention to divide another church or to draw members from it constitutes proselytism. To offer material or social advantages is to proselytize.

The 1970 JWG document continues along these lines, though in greater detail. Proselytism includes "exploitation of the need or weakness or of the lack of education of those to whom witness is offered". The condemnation of proselytism among non-Christians is added, including "unjust or uncharitable reference to the beliefs or practices of other religious communities".

If a wide ecumenical consensus condemning proselytism in principle has been achieved, the distinctions are not so easily drawn in practice, especially under circumstances such as intermarriage, competing congregations, immigrant and migrant contexts. The memory of some of the traumatic experiences of the past persists; and not all groups consider themselves bound by the ecumenical consensus.

PAUL LÖFFLER

"Common Witness and Proselytism", *The Ecumenical Review*, 23, 1971 • *A Monthly Letter on Evangelism*, nos 4-10, 1988 • Revised report on "Christian Witness, Proselytism and Religious Liberty in the Setting of the WCC", in *Evanston to New Delhi*, WCC, 1961.

PROTESTANTISM.
Just as the disciples of Christ were only belatedly called Christians, so too those who supported the Reformation were called Protestants only from 1529 onwards. This was the date of the second diet of Speyer, when five princes of the holy Roman empire and 14 free cities "protested" against the decision taken three years earlier which had granted the princes (or

cities) the right to decide as sovereigns what the religion of their subjects should be. In support of their stand they affirmed: "In matters which concern the honour of God and the salvation of our souls, every individual must stand alone before God and give an account." Until then the Protestants had been called by different names — Lutherans, Evangelicals, Huguenots (this in France). The term "Protestantism" has more than a negative side to it. Rather, it is an affirmation of the freedom* of faith.*

One might think that Protestantism arose out of a challenge to the abuses of the Roman Catholic Church, such as the sale of indulgences, the second-rate quality of the lower clergy, and the dissolute life-style of the higher clergy. But these had been denounced already for over a century. Hence, the Reformation would have been original only in succeeding, at least partially, where others had failed. But at a more profound level, the Reformation criticized the importation of the Roman tradition into the gospel, such as the doctrines of purgatory, Mariology, the veneration of saints and the power of the clergy. Even here Protestantism is not wholly original, for it owes something to humanism, which commended a return to the primary documents — in this case, the holy scriptures. Many humanists, however, did not become Protestants; the most famous example was Erasmus (1467-1536).

The real originality of Protestantism lies in a fresh reading of the Bible. This led Martin Luther (1483-1546), an Augustinian monk and theologian, to claim that Christians are "justified", that is, they become righteous in the sight of God, not by their works and the merits which derive from these, but by God's grace* alone, received in faith and not by means of works (see **justification**). Even if human beings or the individual conscience approve these works, God in his holiness cannot accept them as righteous, for human beings are radically sinners through and through, and their works are evil (see **sin**). Only the redeeming work of Christ is pleasing to God, and in his grace God "reckons to us" the righteousness of Christ. Our righteousness is therefore external *(forensis)*, for we are not its source, but this does not mean that it is unreal, for God does accomplish what he tells us and promises to us in his creative word.

Having become good trees, by grace alone, we bear good fruits, in so far as we continue to have faith in Christ crucified and raised. In turn, this faith is not a work; it is a gift of God, awakened in us by the Holy Spirit.*

Protestantism thus developed a new understanding of faith. Faith is not primarily intellectual assent to doctrines which the church,* its councils and the pope formulate. First and foremost, faith is a personal bond of trust in Christ and recognition of the rightness of the judgments which God pronounces on sinful human beings. At least in the beginning, Protestants unanimously recognized the ancient ecumenical symbols or creeds,* and even drew up their own doctrinal confessions of faith: Augsburg confession (1530), confession of La Rochelle (1559 and 1571), Scots confession (1560), second Helvetic confession (1560), Westminster confession (1646), etc. But these confessions are not standards with absolute authority. Only holy scripture — in so far as, in Luther's words, it is the bearer of Christ — has the force of the ultimate standard or court of appeal *(norma normans)*; the confessions are standards only to the degree that scripture confirms them *(norma normata)*.

Polemics naturally accused the Reformation of moral laxity because of its claim that works do not save. This censure is unfounded. While works cannot produce salvation,* they are nonetheless an essential to demonstrate that we have not received the righteousness of Christ in vain — or as the Heidelberg catechism (1563) says, to give evidence to God of our gratitude. This is the true basis of a rigorous Protestant ethic.

This ethic is all the more rigorous in that while Roman Catholic tradition progressively reduced good works to prayer, pilgrimages, charitable gifts, etc., Protestantism for both Luther and Calvin re-established the dignity of work* in the world. Hence Luther's struggle against monastic vows, in which he saw a flight from Christian responsibilities in the world, the city and the family. Hence also Calvin's doubtless bolder initiatives to encourage trade and industry. Calvin's exegesis of Old Testament passages clearly shows that these condemned loans at exorbitant interest rather than loans at interest that were intended to increase production. The clerical profession has no pre-eminent status for Christians: those who work to ensure a livelihood for their family, the prosperity of their town and help for the deprived are as worthy of respect as the minister entrusted with the proclamation of the word of God. One's trade, according to Luther, is also one's calling or vocation.*

This rehabilitation of secular work led certain sociologists and historians, especially Max Weber in his *The Protestant Ethic and the Spirit of Capitalism* (1904-05), to look for the origins of the capitalist quest in the Protestant ethic. But one must note, as Weber explicitly does, that it was the puritan spirit which above all provided the religious foundations and created the necessary mental attitudes for capitalist enterprise, at least in its beginnings. This thesis continues to find critics, but they introduce only slight differences and further details into a thesis which in its essentials retains its full value.

Protestantism sought to reform the church from within but failed in this respect because of the intransigence of popes and the holy Roman emperor. The Protestant churches were compelled to constitute themselves as separate churches. But even before the schism* was completed, they evolved an ecclesiology different from Rome's. For a start they asserted that the pope and even councils could be mistaken, that scripture remains the supreme arbiter, that it has a clarity of its own and that its obscure parts are clarified by its more self-evident passages. This was in embryo the modern idea — accepted by Protestantism and in large measure by Roman Catholic theologians today — that there is a canon within the biblical canon.*

Furthermore, while the Roman Catholic Church maintained that there is no church except where there are priests ordained by a bishop who is within the apostolic succession and in communion with the pope as the successor of Peter, the Reformation maintained that the church is wherever the word of God* is rightly proclaimed and where the sacraments* instituted by Christ (i.e. only the two sacraments of baptism* and the Lord's supper or eucharist*) are administered in agreement with the gospel. The church is a community of sinners who have been forgiven and, prompted by the Spirit, are brought together by the word of God.

Patently in its definition of the church, Protestantism gave pride of place to the event by which the people are brought together through the word, as compared with the institution as a socio-historical phenomenon. This is not to claim that Protestantism rejected all ecclesial institutions. As the schism moved towards its completion, it adopted a variety of institutional forms in its various denominations, but all of these institutions were marked by their collegial character and by the increasing role of the laity* in the government of the church (see **church order**).

Defining faith as a relation of personal trust in the Lord meant depriving the church of its power as an institution. No longer did the church mediate and dispense salvation, even as a secondary cause. Its one role is to proclaim and bear witness to the salvation which God effected in Christ, and to do so in the most varied ways — by preaching, administering the sacraments, and declaring forgiveness (no longer itself doing the forgiving), and by mutual aid, service and the care of souls. Thus the church was made subordinate to the redeeming work of Christ, and ecclesiology depended on Christology. The church is a second reality. But it is not a secondary one, for it is and remains the Body of Christ, and all whom God has justified are brought into the church (in particular, by baptism); and this body is called to grow in unity* and holiness.* Though the church has a divine foundation, it is not in itself a divine reality, and as an earthly institution it has its limitations. God alone knows who the true believers are; it is not up to the ecclesiastical institution to decide this. This explains why the practice of excommunication* eventually lost a great deal of its significance in the churches of the Reformation.

The ecclesiastical dispute with Rome is naturally accompanied by a profound difference in regard to the ministry (see **ministry in the church**). That the ministry is an essential is not disputed in churches which resulted from the Reformation. But pastors are not priests, in that they have no special character or power which would distinguish them from laypeople. In principle, although pastors are ordained to their ministry, laypersons can carry out the same activities if the occasion arises and if they are called upon to do so by the constituted authorities. Already in 1520 Luther framed the Protestant doctrine of the priesthood of all believers. He said that all

baptized Christians "can pride themselves on already being priests, bishops and pope". But he added, "though it is not appropriate for each person to fulfill the same office", because of his concern for order and his respect for each person's calling.

The question of the nature of the ministry continues to be a stumbling block in the ecumenical dialogues begun some decades ago between the Protestant churches and the Roman Catholic and Orthodox churches. Difficulties over the mutual recognition of ministries remain a serious barrier in the quest for unity. The three confessions have been able to reach agreement on recognizing baptism, which in any case may be validly administered by a layperson, according to the Roman Catholic Church. But in regard to the Lord's supper (or eucharist), there is no such recognition. According to present Roman Catholic teaching, there are certain values in the Lord's supper celebrated in the Protestant churches, but the Lord's supper is defective because it is not presided over by a minister considered validly ordained in the apostolic succession. Hence intercommunion* and *a fortiori* intercelebration are not possible. Rome does extend, within certain limits, eucharistic hospitality to baptized Protestants, but this is a one-way hospitality.

The current stage of the problem is found in connection with the 1982 WCC Faith and Order document *Baptism, Eucharist and Ministry,** prepared by Protestant, Orthodox and Roman Catholic theologians. This document clearly shows that there has been some convergence on questions of ministry, but some responses still see a continuing deadlock: Protestantism cannot give up its concept of the priesthood of all believers, nor can it acknowledge that its ministers have an intrinsic power to effect sacraments.

To sum up so far, one can define Protestantism in the three classic formulas: *sola gratia* (grace alone), *sola fide* (faith alone), *sola scriptura* (scripture alone) — to which Calvin liked to add *soli Deo gloria* (to God alone be glory).

International communications were not easy in the 16th century, yet the expansion of Protestantism was extremely rapid. Theologians and the clergy, and merchants too, were significant agents of that expansion. But it was checked by the wars of religion, persecutions (the Inquisition in Spain and Italy, the repressiveness of the monarchy in France, etc.) and the application of the principle in the (German) holy Roman empire that the sovereign in each region would decide the religion of his people, but also by the internal divisions in Protestantism between Lutherans, Calvinists, Zwinglians, especially in regard to the way Christ is present in the Lord's supper.

Nevertheless, Protestantism in its Lutheran form conquered central and eastern Germany, the Rhineland area of Germany and south of the River Main, the Baltic lands and Scandinavia. In its Calvinist form the Reformation spread in France (around 1560 nearly a third of the kingdom was Protestant) and in Switzerland, though there, especially at Zurich, it was also in a Zwinglian mode. In the Netherlands it took a Calvinist and also a Mennonite form.

England is a special case. The break with Rome was the result of a conflict between King Henry VIII and the pope, who refused to annul Henry's marriage with Catherine of Aragon. The schismatic Church of England (1534) was however quickly penetrated by Reformation ideas under the influence of Archbishop Thomas Cranmer of Canterbury, and of the Strasbourg reformer Martin Bucer, as the 1552 prayer book and the articles of religion show. In Jean Baubérot's words, the Church of England is "a theologically Protestant church with an ecclesiastical structure which has remained close to Roman Catholicism", while the Church of Scotland was and remained resolutely Calvinist. Protestantism was making headway also in the direction both of Bohemia, where the Bohemian Brethren had already prepared the ground, and of Hungary. The old church of the Waldensian valleys in northern Italy rallied behind the Reformation.

In general terms, at the beginning of the 18th century confessional boundaries were more or less fixed, choices had been made, and the period of consolidation had begun which favoured both the emergence of denominational orthodoxies and a growing inflexibility on their part. This general comment finds two major exceptions: the (seeming) elimination of Protestantism in France by the revocation of the edict of Nantes (1685), and the progressive and continued growth of Protestantism in North America.

The Anglicans landed in Virginia in 1607 and converted certain Indians and blacks. The Anglican church they founded also established itself in the two Carolinas and, in the 18th century, in Georgia. But Protestantism's great triumph in North America was the work not of the Anglicans but of Puritan and Congregationalist non-conformists from the Netherlands and from England, followed by the Baptists and the Methodists. While no religion is constitutionally "established" there, many in the US saw their country as a great Protestant nation. Despite significant later immigration by Roman Catholics, the election of a Roman Catholic president (John F. Kennedy) and the establishment of diplomatic relations with the Vatican, have continued to be problematic.

But Protestantism became divided. The above has highlighted the reasons for the divisions of the large Protestant churches which stem directly from the Reformation. But from the 16th century onwards, further divisions arose. The Mennonites,* which continue to this day, reject infant baptism, adopt a principle of non-violence, and assume an ascetic approach to the world. Anabaptism also rejected infant baptism and re-baptized adults but exhibited too a variety of forms, pacifist on the one hand, violent on the other. The latter tendency gave it an affinity with the movement of Thomas Münzer (1489-1525). He originally was a disciple of Luther but later became his opponent. While commending a spiritualized form of Christianity, Münzer supported the peasants' revolt and died with those who took part in it. One can see in him a distant ancestor of present theologies of liberation.

Through the 17th to 19th centuries, movements of renewal or awakening came into being also in the historic Protestant churches. Some evolved within the church, such as pietism. Others, either by accident or design, ended up in schisms and in the founding of new churches which claim to be Protestant.

The first is the Baptist movement, with origins at the beginning of the 17th century. It is in fact the heir to Anabaptism, for it rejects infant baptism and considers as members only persons baptized after they make a personal confession of their faith and give signs of their conversion. The Baptists are a church of those who personally profess their faith, as opposed to those churches of the masses which directly emerged from the Reformation. Fundamentally the Baptist movement is congregationalist. Only the local congregations are called churches, and they enjoy a great deal of independence. They are linked by conventions. Considered as a sect in many European churches, where they are a very small minority, the Baptists represent large, powerful conventions of churches in some other countries. In the USA, the Southern Baptist Convention is the largest Protestant denomination.

Then comes Methodism, initially a movement of awakening which John Wesley (1703-91) led within the Church of England. But his para-church structures eventually led to separation from the national church, while in the newly independent USA Methodism became an autonomous church in 1784. In English-speaking countries Methodism became a strong, powerful and well-organized family of churches. Methodist churches of the American branch retained the episcopal system.

Many more small churches and denominations derive indirectly from the Reformation and maintain some links with the historic Protestant churches.

Despite — or sometimes because of — its divisions, Protestantism, from the end of the 18th century to our own day, has been distinguished by intense missionary activity. Some dates illustrate the vitality of these missions, which had for their main fields of activity Africa and Madagascar, India, Southeast Asia, the Pacific islands and China: in 1792 the Baptist Missionary Society of London was founded; in 1795 the London Missionary Society; in 1799 the Dutch Mission at Rotterdam; in 1799 the (Anglican) Church Missionary Society; in 1810 the American Board of Commissioners for Foreign Missions (initially a joint undertaking, then Congregationalist) at Boston; in 1813 the Wesleyan Methodist Missionary Society at London; in 1814 the American Baptist Mission at Boston; in 1815 the Basle (Switzerland) Mission; in 1822 the Société des missions évangéliques de Paris (Paris Evangelical Missions Society). Many other missionary societies, often fundamentalist in type and of American origin, came into existence during the 19th and 20th centuries.

All these missions had considerable success. For example, French Protestantism, with only 1 million members, started missions in Africa, Madagascar and the Pacific, and brought 1.2 million converts to Christian faith. But they transferred overseas both a very Westernized form of Christianity and their own confessional divisions — with disastrous results. To put an end to this competition, the world missionary conference (Edinburgh 1910) launched an appeal for unity. This conference is conventionally reckoned as the start of the modern ecumenical movement and explains also Protestantism's significant role in the organization and personnel of both Life and Work* and Faith and Order* and in the creation of the WCC. To a greater degree than Eastern Orthodoxy, which had little overseas mission activity, Protestantism (including Anglicanism) was for long the vanguard of ecumenism.

In the European homelands, Protestantism has made little evangelistic progress. Since the end of the 16th century, confessional barriers between Protestantism and Roman Catholicism have, it seems, become fixed. There were of course, and still are, many individual conversions in both directions, but they are not statistically significant. Besides, since industrialization and urbanization made their appearance, neither Protestantism nor Roman Catholicism really has succeeded in reaching the de-Christianized masses, despite the numerous efforts which still continue. Thus, one cannot claim an expansion of Protestantism in Europe, except for the Baptists in the USSR, with 1 million members there.

On the other hand, Protestantism has remarkably expanded in South America, traditionally Roman Catholic. In this vast continent there were only around 120,000 Protestants in 1920. Today they number more than 10 million. In general, the evangelizing was not the work of the great historical churches but of the Pentecostals;* offshoots of both Congregationalism and Methodism, they began in North America in the early 1900s. Most often, the more intense Protestant evangelization has been in the small, conservative, often fundamentalist evangelical churches, rather than in the great historic churches, which are firmly established and highly institutionalized.

In 1985 there were about 278 million Protestants, i.e. 5.8% of the world's population. In 1900 there were only some 103 million, but they were 6.4% of the population. This considerable growth in actual numbers is due to the population increase, especially in the third-world countries, and also to the mission activity there. It should be borne in mind that the churches do not all record their numbers in the same way. Most include children in their statistics, but churches opposed to infant baptism, such as the Baptist, count only baptized adults. Statistics project that Protestants will number close to 350 million towards the year 2000, but will represent only 5.5% of the world's population. Theologically and sociologically linked with the Protestantism of the Reformation as it is, the Anglican communion numbered 51 million members in 1985, i.e. 1.1% of the world's population. In the year 2000 it should have about 61 million members. (All these figures are from the *World Christian Encyclopedia*, ed. David B. Barrett.)

Thus Protestantism represents a relatively significant body of people in a world where Christianity is itself a minority. But the Protestant churches are divided, although they have a very substantial common theological basis and closely related forms of worship. How long will they remain so? This question is hard to answer. The great majority of the Protestant churches belong to the WCC, and the large confessional families such as the World Alliance of Reformed Churches,* the Lutheran World Federation,* the Anglican communion,* the Baptist World Alliance* and the World Methodist Council* increasingly undertake common activities and dialogues with a view to unity. These dialogues have made particular progress between Lutheran and Reformed Christians. In Europe most Lutheran, Reformed and United churches approved the Leuenberg agreement (1973), which established a complete "table and pulpit fellowship". In the USA, the Consultation on Church Union* has been under way for over 25 years. Finally, in many countries most Protestant churches are members either of a federation or of a national or regional Christian council, to which they delegate responsibility for taking certain common measures in ethics or socio-political life, and even, as in France, for some pastoral ministries and chaplaincies (prisons, hospitals, army).

In addition to the various unions of Protestant churches already effected between Reformed and Congregationalist bodies, Re-

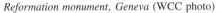

Reformation monument, Geneva (WCC photo)

formed and Methodists, etc. (of which the first was the United Church of Canada in 1925), other unions may take place before the year 2000. Many past disputes have been overcome, and as a general rule a clear distinction is drawn in Protestantism between those increasingly fewer problems which still justify a separation of churches and those which reveal a legitimate diversity of theological trends. These latter, moreover, often cut across confessions, and for their part do not justify retention of the boundaries between the churches.

The legal position of Protestantism in secular society varies greatly, from situations where there is a church-state agreement in the strict sense of the term "concordat" (with church ministers as state officials) to total separation of the churches and the state (see **church and state**). Between these extremes are systems which are semi-concordats and forms of separation which do not exclude co-operation with the state and the allocation of various subsidies to the churches. In West Germany, for instance, church and state are separate, but the state collects a church tax which is proportional to general taxation and passes it on to the churches. To be excused payment of this church tax, one must give official notice that one has left the church. In addition, regional subsidies (from the *Länder*) can be allocated to the work of the churches, and they support the university faculties of theology. In the USA church and state are separate, but problems such as prayers in the public schools are solved in different ways depending on the decisions of the supreme court and of individual states. In the Scandinavian countries the sovereign is in theory head of the Lutheran church, but in practice the churches enjoy a very great deal of freedom. In the Church of England the monarch is legally "governor" of the church, and parliament retains a residual veto in matters of worship and doctrine. In France, to eliminate the grip of the Roman Catholic Church on the schools, a free compulsory secular primary school was established in 1881 (though confessional schools were not abolished), and in 1905, in an atmosphere of violent anti-clericalism, a law separating the churches and the state was passed. Protestants had no difficulty in accepting this law, but until 1923 the Roman Catholics did not accept it. Since then

relations have become less strained, and through social and medical work, etc. the state indirectly subsidizes the churches.

In the states of the communist bloc the churches enjoy much less independence in relation to the state, even where they are separate from it, as in the USSR, or where by contrast legal and financial ties subordinate the church to the state, as in Czechoslovakia. But since the several revolutions in Eastern Europe during 1989-90, greater freedoms have been legalized for the churches.

Generally, Protestantism favours a legal arrangement under which it enjoys full autonomy from civil authorities not merely for preaching and teaching but also for its internal organization. This preference takes it back to its deepest roots. The Lutheran doctrine of the two "regiments" or kingdoms (the spiritual and the temporal, which are parallel but essentially independent of each other) is a doctrine which Calvin fully adopted; in fact, it represents an initial form of secularity, clearly designed to be compatible with the political organization of Christendom at the time. When the political authorities and lay society were secularized, it was normal, in Protestant eyes, for secularity to take on new forms to ensure full freedom for the preaching of the gospel. This acceptance of a secularization* of state, institutions and public life in no way means that Protestantism had given up playing a part in society and withdrawn into itself for the sole task of saving individual souls. Of course this temptation existed, but today it seems to have been removed.

Protestantism has recognized that a human being created by God is a whole, that the body is part of the person, that everyone has a social and community dimension, and that the salvation promised in Jesus Christ relates to the whole human being. Under the influence of movements like the social gospel,* social Christianity, religious socialism, Life and Work, and finally the WCC, Protestantism, for the most part, sees that social justice, fair sharing of wealth and resources, the preservation of peace, and ecological balance in a world entrusted by God to human beings and preserved with a view to future salvation are not secondary tasks but in fact integral to preaching the gospel. This realization has been clearer and quicker in the churches that came directly out of the Reformation than in the individualistic type of evangelical churches, although the latter are beginning to open up towards these concerns.

At all times, indeed, the Protestant churches have pressed their members to practise charity, but they have seen that this personal activity was too limited to be really effective. Hence the emergence, especially from the 19th century onwards, of large charitable diaconal and nursing institutions, etc. Many of these are still active today and seek to equip themselves with modern technological aids. But while these bodies contribute to healing certain wounds inflicted by industrial and urban society and by wars, they have not tackled the roots of the evil. Initially the Protestant churches paid special attention to preventing these evils, for instance by setting up, even before states thought of it, organizations such as welfare centres and holiday camps for young people, and structures for social workers. Several of these services then became models which inspired the state and lay society. Later on, these same churches thought they ought to contribute to creating a public opinion which would exercise pressure on the state to change unjust laws, encourage industrial concerns to undertake better sharing of profits, give their employees a share of power in decision making and more effectively combat unemployment — that menace of the third industrial revolution.

Yet many Protestant churches played a far from negligible part in combating the proliferation of nuclear weapons, in stopping nuclear test explosions — in fact supporting denuclearization. The Protestant churches are not alone in these struggles. They co-operate with other churches, political parties, trade unions, etc. But they have sometimes been a driving force in all these movements, either directly or through groups within the churches. And when co-operating with other social forces, the churches have almost always been concerned to preserve their own identity and not to let themselves be taken over by political parties whose ideology they refuse to accept.

Many qualifications of this description might be made. Members within the Protestant churches are not all of one mind, even on limited individual issues, when it comes to deciding on matters relating to the economy, politics or disarmament. Motions, even when approved by synods with a very large majority, do not have compelling power in Protestantism. Nevertheless, there is a general trend: the Protestant churches must exercise a watchful politico-social and if possible prophetic ministry, but without succumbing to a politicization which would be disastrous both for the unity of the ecclesial community and for the gospel message itself. Protestantism thus treads along a narrow ridge from which it is hard not to stray. What matters is that Protestantism should, in agreement with scripture (esp. Rom. 12:1-2), remain a power for renewal and for changing the world and not be conforming to it.

Protestantism will make a success of this task only in so far as its theologies are well rooted in scripture, well worked out, and capable of giving substance to its preaching. In no way need these theologies be uniform. A great part of this century, from the 1920s to 1960, has been inspired by great theological systems — of a Karl Barth, a Reinhold Niebuhr, a Rudolf Bultmann, a Paul Tillich, a Dietrich Bonhoeffer, not to mention the vast amount of work done by Old and New Testament exegetes. In this last field Protestant scholars, who were the vanguard, are now joined by their Roman Catholic colleagues, and the work of exegesis* is now being carried on ecumenically. The great Protestant theological renewal, which eclipsed the traditional conflicts between orthodox, liberal and pietist thinkers, has temporarily come to a halt, as if to draw breath. Many theologians are concentrating on more limited fields. Their work is preparing the way for the very necessary renewals of tomorrow, for the theologies which relate to the indigenization of Christianity are still in their infancy, and the so-called liberation theologies (which are not specifically Protestant) are exciting ethical calls which must be listened to, but perhaps because of their one-sidedness they have not really succeeded in renewing Protestant thinking.

ROGER MEHL

D.B. Barrett ed., *World Christian Encyclopedia*, New York, Oxford UP, 1982 • G. Casalis, "Protestantism", in *Encyclopaedia Universalis*, Paris, Encyclopaedia Universalis, 1968 • H. Harms, H. Krüger & G. Wagner eds, *Die Kirchen der Welt*, vols 2,4-11, 14-17, Stuttgart, Evangelisches Verlagswerk, 1970-77 • F.H. Littel & H.-H. Walz eds,

Weltkirchenlexikon, Stuttgart, Kreuzverlag, 1960 • R. Mehl, *Traité de sociologie du protestantisme* (ET *The Sociology of Protestantism*, London, SCM, 1970) • G. Thils, *Histoire doctrinale du mouvement oecuménique*, Louvain, Warny, 1955 • R. Winling, *La théologie contemporaine (1945-1980)*, Paris, Centurion, 1983 • H. Zahrnt, *Die Sache mit Gott* (ET *The Question of God: Protestant Theology in the Twentieth Century*, London, Collins, 1969).

PROVIDENCE. Providence means God's ordering and caring activity through the history of creation. Providence comprises God's upholding the creatures against nothingness, co-operating with their created creativity and directing the worldly events to the fulfilment of their inner aims and God's eternal purpose of salvation.* Thus, cosmology and soteriology interpenetrate.

In the scriptures, the word "providence" (Greek *pronoia*, Latin *providentia*) is found only in Wis. 14:3, 17:2. Traditionally, the concept has been discerned also in Gen. 22:8 (Vulgate *Deus providebit*). Nevertheless, the idea of providence is central in the Old Testament: God is the Lord of history* — Israel's and all nations' (e.g. Deut. 4:19; Amos 9:5-7; cf. Gen. 9:8-17). What God plans will be effected (e.g. Isa. 46:9-11). After the exile this idea of God's fore-knowledge and all-directing reality was extended to the individual (e.g. Jer. 1:5; Ps. 139; cf. Gen. 50:20) and furthermore generalized (Wis. 8:1). Beside the idea of God's global providence in history, we find the notion of God's design for the local moment (kairos). God has made everything to suit its time (Eccles. 3:1-8), and human beings are called to act with timing, according to the God-given moment (Isa. 28:23-29; Prov. 15:23, 25:11; Sir. 4:20).

In the New Testament God's active omnipresence in creation* provides the cosmological background for soteriology (John 5:17; 1 Cor. 12:6; Acts 17:27). God takes care for the lowest creatures, and even more for human beings, good and bad alike. Again, this statement of fact invites humans to participate in the praxis of faith: living without anxiety and loving without respect of persons (Matt. 5:45, 6:25-34, 10:29-31).

The soteriological interest is predominant in the NT. God's eternal plan (*prothesis*, e.g. Rom. 8:28; Eph. 3:11) extends to the universe

as a whole (Rom. 8:19-23; Eph. 1:10; Col. 1:20). Although God's hidden purpose is revealed to the elect (Eph. 1:7-9), God's "multicoloured wisdom" (Eph. 3:10) exceeds all understanding (Eph. 3:18-19). The faith that God in everything co-operates for good with those who love him implies no mere optimistic *Weltanschauung* but means rather that no fate or fortune can separate from the love of Christ (Rom. 8:28,31-39; cf. Luke 13:1-5).

In the early church, the fathers very soon (1 Clement 20) elaborated the doctrine of providence by assimilating certain cosmological ideas of Plato, the Stoics, and later Platonism. The polemics against the Epicurean doctrine of accident and fortune is unanimous from Justin Martyr (*First Apology* 28) onwards, and the charge of Epicureanism was raised also against the Gnostics (Irenaeus, *Against Heresies* 3.24-25). Stoic ideas of a ruling world-soul were corrected, in so far as they denied human freedom (Origen, *On First Principles* 3.1.6) and the dependency of fate on the purpose of God (Augustine, *The City of God* 5.8). Nevertheless, providence was generally considered to be accessible to the minds of pious pagans.

Beside the problem of evil, the reconciling of God's omniscience and omnipotence with human freedom* was essential to the doctrine of providence. Among the Greek fathers, we find the idea of providence as part of divine pedagogy: God does not determine the particular course of events but awaits patiently the appropriate response of human freedom (so Origen, *On First Principles* 3.20). After the Pelagian controversy, the outcome of human free will was generally taken to be predetermined: the will of the human person is embedded in a causal order, fixed by God; but the will does not act under external pressure, but according to its inner compulsion and thus is phenomenologically free (Augustine, *The City of God* 5.9-10). Boethius formed a theory of perspective: seen from the point of view of eternity, God's knowledge is not a fore-knowledge of future events, but is a co-knowledge with any creature, being simultaneous with past, present and future time (*Consolation of Philosophy* 5.6). This theory was later adopted by Anselm and entered through Thomas Aquinas into Protestant dogmatics up to this day.

In scholastic theology, providence was normally considered as part of God's eternal knowledge and connected with predestination. Protestant dogmatics, inspired by nominalistic voluntarism, underlined the activity of God's providence. Consequently, the doctrine of providence was treated under the heading "creation". According to Luther, God co-operates with any creature (*W.A.* 18,752-54), using it as his "mask" (e.g. *W.A.* 31/I,436). Likewise, Calvin declared any creature to be God's instrument (*Institutes* 1.16.2). Both denied the intelligibility of providence to human reason. In Protestant orthodoxy, the Thomistic distinction between first cause (God) and second causes (the created order) was adopted. Thereby, especially the Lutherans stressed the relative independency of the created order, whereas many Reformed rejected the idea of God's "permission" of things happening. Since Karl Barth (*Church Dogmatics* III/3) this difference has no controversial importance between Lutherans and Reformed.

From early Enlightenment to Romanticism, providence had a double locus. It was part of dogmatics and devotional literature, and part of natural theology. In natural theology, providence was interpreted in the light of an optimist this-worldly teleology, leaving out the eschatological reservations of classical doctrine. Newton regarded the continual presence in creation of an active Spirit as necessary to explain the order reigning between otherwise unrelated atoms. Gottfried Leibniz, on the other hand, conceived the world as a pre-established harmony, leaving no reason for God to intervene in a world created once for all as perfect.

In our time, the concept of providence has been vigorously challenged. Scientific determinism, culminating 1850-1920, left no room for God in nature.* The sense of the tragedies of history since the world wars divested any optimistic immanent teleology of its plausibility. And the abuse of the term "providence" for national and racial chauvinism among South African Boers and in Nazism caused traditional theologians to abandon the concept (e.g. Carl Heinz Ratschow).

Dialectical theology, if not attacking the concept, interpreted providence Christologically, as the paradox of God's gospel in creation (so Regin Prenter). After Vatican II,* the Catholic church, too, has interpreted providence in the light of the history of salvation (cf. *Lumen Gentium* ch. 7), although the earlier assertion of the intelligibility of providence by human reason alone is still upheld (so *Humani Generis*, H. Denzinger-A. Schönmetzer, *Enchiridion Symbolorum* 3875).

Almost consensually, modern theology refuses to think God's plan as fixed in details beforehand. God's creation is seen as God's self-limitation, making room for created creativity. History being open-ended, God always communicates with human freedom throughout the contingencies of history. This has recently given rise to the new interpretations of providence, sensitive to the ambiguities of history, asserting God as the source of human freedom and novelties in the cosmos, and re-discovering the practical dimension of the Christian faith in providence.

The majesty of God has been interpreted in terms of future rather than in terms of past: God is the attractant power of the future (Pierre Teilhard de Chardin), and the comings of the kingdom of God* are manifestations of God as the power of future (Wolfhart Pannenberg, Jürgen Moltmann). Process theology perceives God's presence in history in terms of God's offering still new possibilities to the self-creative agents of the world, persuading them to take over voluntarily God's (objectively best) proposals as their own aim. This Whiteheadian idea of God's luring has been received by Langdon Gilkey, while transforming the Pelagian tendency of self-creativity into the idea rather of created freedom. In the light of science, chance has been re-evaluated as God's providential means to let the matter explore its created, inbuilt possibilities (Arthur Peacocke, David J. Bartholomew, John Polkinghorne).

Paul Tillich concretized the idea of providence with reference to historical kairoi: situations pregnant with destiny, which nevertheless demand decision (*Systematic Theology* 5.2). Through his struggle with the Nazist Emanuel Hirsch, Tillich realized the necessity of a Christological criterion for reading the signs of the times (Matt. 16:3). Tillich may have inspired the idea of kairos as a God-given time of prophetic critique and resolute action in the South African Kairos document* against apartheid* (1985). Likewise, Latin American liberation theology* stresses that God's will has to be "enfleshed in history".

But God is more than a provident God in general; he takes sides with the poor* and invites anybody to follow him (Gustavo Gutiérrez, Ronaldo Muñoz).

See also **creation, God, history, nature, salvation history**.

NIELS HENRIK GREGERSEN

L. Gilkey, *Reaping the Worldwind: A Christian Interpretation of History*, New York, Seabury, 1981 • J. Polkinghorne, *Science and Providence: God's Interaction with the World*, London, SPCK, 1989 • J. Walsh & P.G. Walsh eds, *Divine Providence and Human Suffering: Message of the Fathers of the Church*, vol. 17, Wilmington, DE, Glazier, 1985.

R

RACISM. Racism has been a matter of concern to the Christian church from early times. It was J.H. Oldham, however, who in his *Christianity and the Race Problem* (1924) pioneered a systematic theology against racism. Racism as an issue definitely entered the agenda of the fledgling ecumenical movement at the Jerusalem conference of the International Missionary Council in 1928, and then again in Oxford (1937).

The inaugural assembly of the WCC in Amsterdam in 1948 was very much alive to the issue of racism. It identified "prejudice based upon race or colour and from practices of discrimination and segregation as denials of justice and human dignity". Amsterdam argued that the church must take action against racial prejudice: "if the church can overcome the national and social barriers which now divide it, it can help society overcome those barriers".

Building upon the reports of the world conference on Church and Society (Geneva 1966), the fourth assembly (Uppsala 1968) produced a conceptual and analytical framework for the elimination of racism. More particularly, Uppsala stated that "racism is linked with economic and political exploitation" and then went on to define racism as "ethnocentric *pride* in one's own racial group and preference for the distinctive characteristics of that group; belief that these characteristics are fundamentally biological in nature... strong negative feelings towards other groups who do not share these characteristics, coupled with the thrust to discriminate against and exclude the outgroup from full participation in the life of the community".

A similar definition of racism had come from the committee of experts commissioned by UNESCO, who produced their Statement on Racism and Racial Prejudice in 1967. But Uppsala went further and made special mention of white racism as lying at the root of white domination and privilege.

On the basis of such understandings, the WCC central committee in 1969 mandated the establishment of a Programme to Combat Racism* (PCR) within the WCC. PCR was formed to undertake the churches's crusade against racism. The central committee firmly stated that "racism is not an unalterable feature of human life. Like slavery and other social manifestations of man's sin, it can and must be eliminated." It went on to assert: "There can be no justice in our world without the transfer of economic resources to undergird the re-distribution of political power and to make cultural self-determination meaningful."

In recent years an effort has been made to distinguish between racialism and racism. One can understand racialism to be the use of racial or ethnocentric characteristics to determine value or access or participation and, by the same token, to exclude others from such. Racialism may not necessarily be value-laden as such. It does not say that one person is better than another because of race but simply

The Ku Klux Klan, persistent white racist organization in the US (United Methodist Missions, New York/Ken Thompsen)

that one chooses not to associate with people on account of their race. But racism has become a political ideology, on the basis of which the social reality is being interpreted and political and economic decisions made. In essence a racist ideology attaches value to ethnocentric characteristics and seeks to maintain deterministic relations between biological characteristics and cultural attributes. However, one must not lose sight of the fact that, ultimately, racism is about power. As an ideology* it is the means whereby the dominant group, as determined by racial characteristics, imposes its will upon others so as to exclude them from effective participation in decision making and to exploit them for economic gain.

Some fundamental questions have been raised about the relationship between race and class. It is necessary to understand that the pattern of inequality at work in the world arises fundamentally from economic exploitation. That analysis must attempt to make sense of the fact that a combination of economic power and racial or cultural characteristics of the dominant group leads to racism. The valuation of the class factors in racism is

not to make Marxist analysis a determinant as such but to point to an adequate understanding of racism and the means necessary to develop action to eliminate it. A. Sivanandan argues that it is necessary to maintain this dual consciousness if one is to address the structural inequality on which racism is based. And so he says that the fight against racism must not be reduceable to "the fight against prejudice, the fight against institutions and practices and to a fight against individuals and attitudes".

The second cluster of issues which is now being challenged is that the focus on white racism obscures other and dominant forms of racial ideologies like tribalism, language and caste, which are at the root of many conflicts in the world today. In any event ethnocentrism is not universally an adequate way to characterize a racial ideology, as so many people who are victims of racism have characteristics which are hardly distinguishable from those who maintain hegemony over them.

These nuances have been reflected in the work of the PCR. The emphasis on the elimination of white racism can be seen in PCR's support for the liberation movements and in other struggles for decolonization. PCR has become best known for its campaigns against apartheid* in South Africa and the consequences thereof in the Southern African region. The programmes of PCR have, however, extended to the support for the land and cultural rights of the indigenous peoples the world over, including the racial minorities in Asia and the Pacific who are victims of race and caste oppression. The programme on women under racism focuses on the twin oppressions of racism and sexism.

PCR's method of operation has been radical. It seeks to get to the roots of this structural inequality. Unfortunately, one of the consequences of this approach has been to push the racially oppressed to the periphery of action for justice without acknowledging them as pro-actors in their struggle. Meanwhile, those who have the means, and may even be responsible for the racism, can be indifferent, paralyzed by guilt or a sense of powerlessness. A new and effective approach seems necessary — one which encourages partnership for effective action.

N. BARNEY PITYANA

E. Adler, *A Small Beginning: An Assessment of the First Five Years of the Programme to Combat Racism*, WCC, 1974 • A. van der Bent ed., *Breaking Down the Walls: Statements and Actions on Racism (1948-85)*, WCC, 1986 • *International Review of Mission*, 49, 235, 1970 • B. Rogers, *Race: No Peace without Justice*, WCC, 1980 • B. Sjollema, *Isolating Apartheid: Western Collaboration with South Africa, Policy Decision by the WCC and Church Responses*, WCC, 1982 • J.J. Vincent, *The Race Race*, London, SCM, 1970.

RAHNER, KARL. B. 5.3.1904, Freiburg im Breisgau, Germany; d. 30.3.1984, Innsbruck, Austria. One of the most influential contemporary Roman Catholic theologians, especially in German-speaking countries but also among Latin American liberationists. Rahner made original contributions to the ecumenical dialogue from his particular Catholic theological perspective. Together with Heinrich Fries he published *Unity of the Churches: An Actual Possibility* (New York, Paulist, 1984). His concept of "anonymous Christian" depends on the offer of grace and salvation to all men and women throughout history. He believed that ecumenism is an achieved reality at the level of ordinary people, though it continues to be discussed and debated at the higher rungs of church authority. He held that, with Vatican II, the church gained a truly universal consciousness. His re-interpretation of doctrines such as the inspiration of the scriptures and human subjectivity as spirit in the world gave them a radical and global perspective. His literary and philosophical idiom was largely influenced by Martin Heidegger, under whom he studied in Freiburg. He joined the Jesuit order in 1922 and was ordained in 1932. He was appointed professor of dogmatic theology — in Innsbruck in 1949, and then at Munich in 1964. He was a main editor of Denzinger's *Enchiridion Symbolorum* (1952), of the new *Lexikon für Theologie und Kirche* (10 vols, 1957-65) and of the six-volume encyclopedia *Sacramentum Mundi* (1968-70), which was strongly influenced by his outlook. See R. Bleistein, *Bibliographie Karl Rahner*, 1924-69, 1969-74 (Freiburg, Herder, 1969, 1974).

ANS J. VAN DER BENT

RAMSEY, ARTHUR MICHAEL. B. 4.11.1904, Cambridge, UK; d. 23.4.1988, Oxford. Archbishop of Canterbury, 1961-74, and a president of the WCC, 1961-68, Ramsey (as did his predecessor, Archbishop Fisher) promoted church union negotiations between the Anglican church and other churches in the third world. In 1962 he visited Patriarch Athenagoras I in Constantinople, and he received Patriarch Alexis in London in 1964. He met with Pope Paul VI in the Sistine chapel in Rome in 1966. He was greatly disappointed by the failure of the Church of England in 1969 and 1972 to approve the plans for reunion with the Methodist church. Educated in Cambridge and ordained in 1928, Ramsey was canon of Durham cathedral and professor of divinity at Durham University, 1940-50, Regius professor of divinity, University of Cambridge, 1951-52, bishop of Durham, 1952-56, and archbishop of York, 1956-61. His numerous works include *The Gospel and the Catholic Church* (2nd ed., London, Longmans, 1956), *From Gore to Temple* (London, Longmans, 1960) and *Canterbury Pilgrim* (London, SPCK, 1974). See O. Chadwick, *Michael Ramsey: A Life* (Oxford, Clarendon, 1990).

ANS J. VAN DER BENT

RANSON, CHARLES WESLEY.

B. 15.6.1903, Northern Ireland; d. 13.1.1988, Lakeville, CT, USA. From 1929 to 1945 Ranson served as a missionary in India, principally in the Madras area. He was secretary of the National Christian Council of India, Burma and Ceylon from 1943 to 1945, and general secretary of the International Missionary Council* from 1948 onwards. In 1958 he became director of the Theological Education Fund, and was president of the Methodist Church in Ireland, 1961-62. From 1968 to 1972 he was professor of theology and ecumenics at the Hartford Seminary Foundation. He wrote *The Christian Minister in India* (London, Lutterworth, 1945), *Renewal and Advance* (London, Edinburgh House, 1948), *That the World May Know* (New York, Friendship, 1953) and *A Missionary Pilgrimage* (Grand Rapids, MI, Eerdmans, 1988).

ANS J. VAN DER BENT

RECEPTION. During the past 25 years of the ecumenical movement, "reception" has become a new key-term for the gradual and mutual acceptance by the churches of the results of ecumenical dialogues (see **dialogue, intrafaith**). As a technical term it was, however, used much earlier in canonical discussions and regulations regarding the authority or authentication of councils and synods, the validation of legislative action in and among churches, the validity or validation of baptism,* eucharist* and ordination* as practised within heretical communities. And, rather recently, it has appeared in the theoretical context of the history of law, of literature and ideas in general, with regard to the impact and spread of customs, formulas or ideas in a certain cultural field. So one can speak of the reception of German law into Roman law from the 6th century onwards, or of the reception of the work of Freud in America.

Reception in its explicit theological meaning, derived from the biblical vocabulary of *lambanein/apolambanein, dechesthai/apodechesthai*, points to one of the main characteristics of faith* itself. We believe that we receive our existence as creatures from God,* our salvation* as redemption* through Jesus Christ,* a new life as "anointed ones" in the Holy Spirit.* We receive the word of God* and the sacraments* as signs of the new covenant.* We receive the mission* to be disciples and ministers, prophets and teachers of the community through the laying on of hands in the Spirit. Such inheritance, handed down through the ages, was received with differences of form and manner, owing to diversities of genius and conditions of life. Therefore only mutual exchange and reception of various traditions within one communion* could build up the unity* and catholicity,* the holiness* and apostolicity* of the early church.*

In that context, the process of reception of conciliar decisions by the local churches was more than a process of legitimation alone. It implied the testing and appropriation of such decisions in the life of the churches. The same would be true for the results of the ecumenical dialogues of the last 25 years, even if their canonical weight cannot be compared with the conciliar decisions of the church.

Discussion on reception within the ecumenical movement started in the context of the Second Vatican Council* (1962-65) through a collection of essays edited by Hans Jochen Margull, *Die ökumenischen Konzile* (Stuttgart, 1961; ET *The Councils of the Church*, Philadelphia, 1966). The WCC's New Delhi assembly (1961) requested Faith and Order* to undertake a study on "Councils and the Ecumenical Movement", the result of which was published in 1968. The final report on "The Importance of the Conciliar Process in the Ancient Church for the Ecumenical Movement", adopted at the F&O meeting in Louvain (1971), describes reception as follows: "Reception represents the process by which the local churches accept the decision of a council and thereby recognize its authority. This process is a multiplex one and may last for centuries. Even after the formal conclusion of such a process and the canonical reception of a council's doctrinal formula, usually through a new council, the process of reception continues in some way or other as long as the churches are involved in self-examination on the basis of the question whether a particular council has been received and appropriated properly and with justification. In this sense we can say that *in the ecumenical movement the churches find themselves in a process of continuing reception or re-reception of the councils*" (*Louvain 1971*, WCC, 1971, p.29, italics added).

Such a wider idea of reception as a spiritual process of appropriation and mutual critical testing of the traditions along the lines of "the faith of the church through the ages" was explicitly discussed further in F&O consultations at Crêt-Bérard 1977 ("Towards an Ecumenical Consensus on Baptism, the Eucharist and the Ministry"), at Odessa 1977 ("How Does the Church Teach Authoritatively Today?"), and at the third and fourth forum on bilateral dialogues* (1980 and 1985). In several bilateral dialogues paragraphs on reception urge the churches to take the results of the dialogues seriously and to deal with them at all appropriate levels of authority and of the involvement of their members. A most remarkable test case of reception in this sense was the invitation to the churches to respond to the Lima text on *Baptism, Eucharist and Ministry*,* sent to the churches in 1982. Over 190 churches responded, which marks a new stage within the ecumenical movement indeed, by involving nearly all churches in a reception process, both at the level of "the widest possible involvement of the whole people of God" and of "the highest appropriate level of authority" (*BEM*, p.x).

ANTON HOUTEPEN

A. Houtepen, "Reception, Tradition, Communion", in *Ecumenical Perspectives on Baptism, Eucharist and Ministry*, M. Thurian ed., WCC, 1983 • U. Kühn, "Reception: An Imperative and an Opportunity", in *Ecumenical Perspectives on BEM*, M. Thurian ed., WCC, 1983 • W.G. Rusch, *Reception: An Ecumenical Opportunity*, Philadelphia, Fortress, 1988 • M. Thurian, *Churches Respond to BEM*, 6 vols, WCC, 1986-88.

RECONCILED DIVERSITY. Reconciled diversity, or, more exactly, "unity in reconciled diversity", is one of today's concepts of church unity.* It goes back to two conferences of representatives of Christian World Communions* (CWCs) in 1974 (Geneva). A year before, the Faith and Order* commission had elaborated its concept of "conciliar fellowship" (Salamanca 1973), requesting at the same time the CWCs engaged in bilateral dialogues* "to clarify their understanding of the quest for unity by co-operating with the WCC". Responding to this request, the CWCs felt unable simply to endorse the F&O "conciliar fellowship" concept and, in-

stead, developed the concept of "unity in reconciled diversity".

Its guiding principle is that "the variety of denominational heritages [is] legitimate" and "remains a valuable contribution to the richness of the life in the church universal". Therefore, church unity does not necessarily demand the surrender of denominational convictions and identities, as often advocated and usually implied in the concept of organic union.* Rather, denominational traditions and confessional convictions can have a continuing identifiable life within the one church, provided that in a process of dialogue, of living encounter and mutual correction, they have lost their denominational exclusiveness and divisive trenchancy and have thus been transformed into a "reconciled" diversity.

The concept of reconciled diversity condenses into a concise formula concerns which have always been voiced in the ecumenical movement. It is an expression of one of the two legitimate and not mutually exclusive tendencies in the search for unity, the one "whose primary stress is upon the necessity for faithfulness to the truth as it has been confessed in the past and as it is embodied in the received traditions" (Nairobi 1975).

Reconciled diversity in its developed sense includes all essential elements required for unity: a shared faith;* mutual recognition of baptism,* eucharist* and ministry;* and agreed ways of deciding and acting together. It should, however, be admitted that the last aspect may be the weak point of the concept. Any application of the reconciled diversity concept should show that genuine Christian unity can only be a fully committed fellowship in life, witness and service and that, therefore, reconciliation of diversity must lead beyond mere peaceful co-existence.

The sometimes heated debate about concepts of unity during the years following 1974 seems, at least on the level of ecumenical theory, to have come to a conclusion in the course of 1978. It was acknowledged that the reconciled diversity concept intends neither to rule out the concept of organic union nor to be a counter-concept to conciliar fellowship, inasmuch as "conciliar fellowship presupposes organic union" (Accra 1974). Its point of divergence from these concepts is the basic conviction that not only contextual (cultural, ethnic, etc.), but also confessional, diversity can be a "legitimate diversity" compatible with and even necessary for the true unity of the church. At the first forum on bilateral dialogues (Bossey 1978), as well as at the F&O commission meeting in Bangalore (1978), it was affirmed that the concepts of unity under discussion, especially the organic union and the reconciled diversity concepts, are "not to be seen as alternatives. They may be two different ways of reacting to the ecumenical necessities and possibilities of different situations and of different church traditions" (Bangalore).

In many circles the reconciled diversity concept has been very positively received. In 1977 the Lutheran World Federation* endorsed it as a "valuable help in the present phase of the ecumenical movement". In other instances at least its basic intention was strongly affirmed, or equivalent concepts were developed (e.g. the vision of the one church as a "communion of communions" or as a communion* of different ecclesial *typoi**).

See also **communion; conciliarity; reconciliation; unity; unity, models of; unity, ways to**.

HARDING MEYER

G. Gassmann & H. Meyer, *The Unity of the Church: Requirements and Structure*, LWF report 15, 1983 • H. Meyer, "Einheit in versöhnter Verschiedenheit" — "konziliare Gemeinschaft" — "organische Union", *Ökumenische Rundschau*, 27, 1978.

RECONCILIATION. Reconciliation is the renewal of relationship with the Triune God (see **Trinity**) accomplished for us in Jesus Christ* and offered to us in word and sacraments through the church.* The reality of this reconciliation is what the church proclaims to the world. It decisively shapes the way the church understands itself and its service to Christ. Reconciliation has been understood as (1) a biblical-traditional category of ecclesial discourse, (2) a principle which guides Christian life and service, and (3) a standard which calls the church to unity* and energizes ecumenical activity.

Central to the biblical witness is the notion that humanity has been reconciled to God by a sheer act of God. This activity of God finds its locus in Jesus of Nazareth (2 Cor. 5:18-21)

and its antecedent in the cultic history of the people of Israel (Lev. 16). At the heart of this history is the motif that God has made a covenant* with Israel, and despite their unfaithfulness, God acts to restore covenant. Reconciliation is first the renewal of covenant with the people of God through Jesus the Messiah of Israel.

Jesus Christ has overcome the enmity between God and humanity and has thereby restored our fellowship with God (Rom. 5). The church, which understands its own existence to be grounded in the ministry, death and resurrection of Jesus, has seen in the scriptures various themes which help illumine the work of Christ. Thus closely related to the concept of reconciliation are the themes of redemption* and atonement. These themes, which are understood to indicate the objective condition of our restored relationship with God, re-inforce the fact that salvation* is based on God's own initiative in Jesus Christ. He is our reconciliation, and humanity is called to be reconciled to God.

The church lives as the reconciled community. This means that the life of the church should display the proper response of humanity to the work of God. To be reconciled to God means to enter into reconciliation with all peoples, nations, and tribes (Eph. 2). Therefore the church acts as an agent of forgiveness and love both within and outside its community (John 20:22-23; 1 John 4:7-12). To those outside its community the church proclaims the restoration of all things in Christ and therefore the end of divisions and war and the invitation to live reconciled lives (Col. 1). The church offers the means whereby its members can live personally reconciled to God. For those who have fallen away it provides means to re-enter into fellowship. The renewal of fellowship, made possible by the presence of the Spirit of Christ in the church, is the ground for the activity of repentance and the repeated gift of forgiveness. Reconciliation issues in sacramental activities in the church because the church lives within the *pax Dei* (the peace of God).

The fact that there is division in the church stands over against the message of reconciliation that the church is called to proclaim. However, the church can remove the breach in its own life if it allows God to work fully through the word of God* and the sacraments of baptism,* eucharist* and penance* (or reconciliation). Through the word and sacraments, the church can partake in the life of repentance it offers to the world. This means that when Christians rightly celebrate the eucharist and practise their baptism, they have already entered into a fellowship which should move them to acts of reconciliation with their sisters and brothers.

Entering into actions of reconciliation witnesses to a common commitment to live in obedience to the reconciling God and therefore opens the actors to the posssibility of entering into the reality of the healing power of the Holy Spirit. Such sacramental acts are the "medicine of the church" by which the church can let itself be healed and offer to the world the healing that is inherent in fellowship with God.

See also **penance and reconciliation, redemption, salvation, unity**.

WILLIE J. JENNINGS

D. Bonhoeffer, *Gesammelte Schriften*, Band 4 (ET *Christ the Center*, New York, Harper & Row, 1978) • J.M. Lochman, *Versöhnung und Befreiung* (ET *Reconciliation and Liberation*, Philadelphia, Fortress, 1980) • T.F. Torrance, *Theology in Reconciliation*, Grand Rapids, MI, Eerdmans, 1975 • G. Wainwright, "The Reconciliation of Divided Churches: A Witness to the Gospel", *Studia Liturgia*, 18, 1988.

REDEMPTION. The central biblical theme of salvation* is broached in the Bible in a number of images, one of which is redemption (Greek *apolytrōsis*), other major images being justification,* sacrifice and reconciliation.* Every image is a partial truth, highlighting a particular aspect of a greater whole. Redemption is an image from captivity and therefore has the merit of highlighting the captivities from which redemption is offered. Redemption is from legalism and self-sufficiency (Rom. 8:34; Gal. 3:10), sin,* death and the cosmic powers (Eph. 6:12; Rom. 8:35). In the history of the church these captivities have tended to be spiritualized. It has been the merit of the ecumenical movement to recall the churches to relate these captivities to everyday realities and situations. Thus, for example, sin is not only personal but also corporate, relating also to institutional structures. Cosmic powers are also a kind of or-

ganized disobedience to the will of God, taking the form of self-aggrandizement and independent pride, appearing in political, social, economic, personal and corporate matters.

The image of captivity also highlights the costliness of the act of redemption. It is at the cost of the life of Jesus Christ* (1 Cor. 6:20, 7:23). To that extent redemption is a present reality, almost equivalent to the forgiveness of sins (Col. 1:14). It is, however, not a *fait accompli*, nor is it possessed in its fullness yet (Eph. 1:14, 4:30; Rom. 2:5).

The larger ecumenical question is this: if redemption is in the name of Jesus Christ, then what will be the fate of those who have never had Christ preached to them and those who belong to other faith traditions such as Buddhism, Hinduism, Islam, or African Traditional Religions? Karl Barth's distinction between religion* and Christian faith* has long dominated theological thinking: religion, "the concern of the godless man", according to him is abolished through Jesus Christ, who justifies the sinner. However, there is also the idea that it is impossible to have faith without religion because revelation,* including the Christ-event, is apprehended through the coloured glasses of culture,* context and people as they are. Other scholars argue for intimations of Christ in other religions, seeing Christian faith as continuous with insights of the *mysterium tremendum et fascinosum* found in other faith traditions — hence such ideas as the "anonymous Christ", or certain developments in African or Asian theologies. The basic question in ongoing ecumenical debate is whether God's continuing self-disclosure in the constantly widening experience of human beings can still be rightfully described as "in Christ" (see **uniqueness of Christ**).

If the death of Christ is the means of redemption, then has the church* a place in it? The church itself is founded on the new covenant* at Calvary and commissioned to go and preach that offer of redemption in Christ (see **mission**). The ecumenical debate around the role of the church in Christ's saving work as well as the value of good works and religious practices has been addressed by the statement "Justification by Faith" agreed on in 1983 by the Lutheran-Roman Catholic consultation in the USA, and the Anglican-Roman Catholic International Commission's statement "Salvation and the Church" (1987). By and large, the emerging position seems to be that salvation may not be restricted to any established institution, not even the church (over which God exercises sovereignty), and that there is Christ without Christianity. Christ's presence transcends the boundaries of Christendom, even though there can be no Christianity without Christ.

Redemption is not only "deliverance from", it also highlights "freedom for". In this regard there were two ancient paradigms: the Greco-Roman practice of sacral manumission, a legal and religious rite by which a slave by purchase price became a devotee of a deity in return for his freedom; and the exodus experience of the Hebrews. Redemption, positively speaking, is for a new life of freedom,* which is not the same as licence to perform according to self-will. God's action of redemption is to be matched by human beings' keeping their part of the covenant relationship, involving needed changes in the social, economic and political life of human beings.

See also **dialogue, interfaith; reconciliation**.

JOHN S. POBEE

H.G. Anderson, T.A. Murphy & J.A. Burgess eds, *Justification by Faith: Lutherans and Catholics in Dialogue*, Minneapolis, Augsburg, 1985 • ARCIC II, *Salvation and the Church*, London, SPCK, 1987 • F.W. Dillistone, *The Christian Understanding of Atonement*, London, SCM, 1984.

REFORMATION. The ecumenical understanding of the Reformation has been dominated by a re-assessment of Martin Luther. In large part the concentration on Luther has been prompted by Roman Catholic historians, who, far more than their Protestant counterparts, have identified the origins of the Reformation with Luther's religious crisis and subsequent career. While Catholic historians like Alexandre Ganoczy, Kilian McDonnell and Jacques Pollet have made substantial contributions to the study of Calvin and Zwingli, the principal energies of Catholic historians engaged in the study of Protestant origins have traditionally been devoted to an evaluation of Martin Luther.

Until the end of the 19th century Catholic historiography was dominated by the essentially negative portrayal of Luther drawn by the Catholic polemicist Johannes Cochlaeus in his famous book *Commentary on the Acts and Writings of Martin Luther* (1549). Since medieval Catholic theology taught that heresy* is more a matter of will than intellect, more a defect of character than a failure of understanding, Cochlaeus attempted to account for Luther's heresy by identifying the defects of his character that prompted his apostasy from Rome. As Cochlaeus saw matters, Luther was a proud and self-centred man, driven by his appetites and utterly lacking in religious seriousness.

The attack on Luther's character was not altogether abandoned by Catholic historians in the early 20th century, as the writings of Jacques Maritain and G.K. Chesterton demonstrate. Nevertheless, the traditional picture of Luther's religious development was modified by the work of two Catholic scholars, Heinrich Denifle and Hartmann Grisar. In 1904 Denifle, a medieval historian then serving as an archivist in the Vatican library, published a two-volume study of Luther's early theology entitled *Luther and Lutheranism in Its First Development*. Luther had claimed that he had been taught to regard the righteousness of God described in Rom. 1:16-17 as the punishing righteousness with which God justly punishes sinners. As Luther later recounted it, his theological breakthrough occurred when he realized that the righteousness of God in this passage refers, not to God's punishing righteousness *(iustitia activa)*, but to the righteousness with which God makes sinners just *(iustitia passiva)*.

Denifle examined a wide range of medieval commentaries on Rom. 1 and concluded that Luther's claim about the medieval exegetical tradition could not be sustained. Even though Luther alleged that all of his teachers identified the righteousness of God in 1:16-17 with God's punishing activity, Denifle could not find a single Catholic commentator who did so. Without exception they identified the *iustitia Dei* with God's reconciling gift to the sinner. It seemed therefore to Denifle that Luther's critique of Catholic theology rested in large measure on his ignorance of the very tradition he presumed to criticize.

Although Denifle had introduced the question of theological causes for the Reformation, he was not inclined to press his point in such a way as to mitigate the traditional

Catholic attack on Luther's character. On the contrary, Denifle was only too happy to catalogue what he regarded as Luther's besetting sins: pride, spiritual negligence, intemperance and unchastity. He was even willing to accept the scurrilous rumour that Luther, like Francis I, was a victim of syphilis. "Luther," Denifle cried, "there is nothing divine in you!"

Unlike Denifle, the Jesuit historian Hartmann Grisar was less interested in Luther's theological development than in his psychological profile. Grisar argued that Luther was psychologically unbalanced, haunted by an abnormal hatred of good works. The doctrine of justification* by faith alone, codified in the confessional books of the Reformation churches, originated out of Luther's compelling inner need to offer a theological rationalization for his uncontrolled lechery, drunkenness and gluttony. What Cochlaeus and earlier Catholic critics had attributed to flaws in Luther's character, Grisar was inclined to attribute to abnormalities in his psychological composition.

A new era in the ecumenical re-evaluation of the Reformation was inaugurated by the publication in 1939-40 of the two-volume study *The Reformation in Germany* by the Roman Catholic historian Joseph Lortz. Lortz broke decisively with the older Catholic tradition of scholarship that blamed the Reformation on flaws in Luther's character. He accepted the view, advocated by Luther himself, that, as an Augustinian friar, Luther had been a morally upright and decent man who had followed in scrupulous detail the rules and regulations of his order. Lortz was even willing to defend, against Catholic critics like Denifle, the unpopular proposition that Luther was a profoundly Christian theologian, whose theology of the cross and doctrine of assurance touched on deep themes in the gospel. From Lortz's perspective the tragedy of the Reformation could not be traced to moral grounds, as traditional Catholic historiography had argued, but to theological causes.

Lortz regarded the theology of Aquinas as the finest flowering of the medieval Catholic tradition. Unfortunately for 16th-century Europe, Luther was not trained at Cologne in the authentically Catholic theology of Aquinas, but at Erfurt in the "fundamentally uncatholic" theology of William Ockham.

Luther studied the commentaries and writings of Gabriel Biel and Pierre d'Ailly, disciples of Ockham, whose theology, Lortz believed, reflected the unclarity and confusion that marked the later middle ages. Luther correctly perceived many of the problems inherent in Occamist theology and made a genuinely Catholic protest against its distortions of the Catholic theological tradition. However, because Luther was not schooled in the theology of Aquinas, he went to what Lortz regarded as unwarranted extremes in his theological critique of Occamism and so lapsed into heresy. Nevertheless, even as a heretic, he was not guilty of moral turpitude, as Cochlaeus had argued, but only of theological subjectivity. From Lortz's perspective, the schism* in the Western church might have been avoided if only Luther had studied the balanced, Augustinian theology of Aquinas.

A new note in the Catholic re-appraisal of Luther was sounded by Otto Pesch in his massive study of the doctrine of justification in the theology of Aquinas and Luther. Unlike Lortz, who bemoaned the absence of the stabilizing impact of the theology of Aquinas on Luther, Pesch argued that Luther and Thomas held very similar understandings of grace.* They differed not so much in what they said as how they said it. Thomas wrote sapiential theology that described in an objective and detached way the unfolding of the creative and redemptive acts of God, whose being conditions, but is unconditioned by, the things he made. Luther wrote existential theology from the perspective of an engaged believer who stands in the presence of a living God of grace and judgment, who has called the believer by name. In Pesch's opinion, differences in theological style and method have led historians to over-estimate the differences between Luther and Thomas and to misunderstand and misjudge their substantial agreements. To recover an understanding of the theological agreements between Luther and Thomas, often hidden beneath the real, but far less significant, disagreements in style, would itself represent an important ecumenical step forward for Protestants and Roman Catholics.

Protestant historians have, with some notable exceptions, made fewer contributions to the study of Catholic reform in the 16th century than Catholic historians have to the study of Protestant origins. While Protestant historians have engaged in their own wide-ranging re-assessment of the major Protestant reformers, their principal contribution to the ecumenical re-assessment of the Reformation has centred in their re-evaluation of the theological and religious situation in the Western church on the eve of the Reformation. No longer content with a confessionally biased description of religious life in the later middle ages, Protestant historians from Reinhold Seeberg and Adolf Martin Ritter to Bernd Moeller and Heiko Oberman have attempted to reconstruct a more accurate picture of the milieu in which the Reformation was born. Especially important in this re-assessment has been the study of late medieval scholastic and mystical theology from Ockham and Thomas Bradwardine to Biel and John of Paltz.

Over the last two decades an approach to the Reformation has developed that is neither Protestant nor Catholic, though supported by a wide spectrum of Protestant, Catholic and secular historians. This newer approach regards the Reformation, not as a single unified movement to which a second unified movement, the Counter-Reformation, reacted, but as a complex series of interdependent religious, social and political movements. On this reading, Luther's reformation was one of many reformations occurring before 1600 and may even have been the most important. But the 16th century was marked by multiple religious reformations — Lutheran, Reformed, Erasmian, Anabaptist, Catholic, Erastian, anti-Trinitarian, Chiliastic, Epicurean — that interacted with each other in an intricate pattern of dependence and independence. The principal task of Reformation historians is to understand and explain the originality, individuality and interdependence of these multiple movements of religious reform. The older view that equated the beginnings of the Reformation with Luther's religious experience has now been replaced by a view that situates Luther within the context of his own age, a period impatient with the status quo and stirred by new longings and aspirations. Only within this broader context, Reformation historians now feel, can the achievements and limitations of Luther's Reformation be properly assessed.

Scholarly re-assessments of the Reformation have begun to reach the level of the official ecclesiastical leadership. This was apparent in the speeches of Pope John Paul II during his visits to the Federal Republic of Germany in 1980 and 1987. The 1990 report of the Reformed-Roman Catholic* international dialogue commission sought to re-read the history of the 16th century with a view to "the reconciliation of memories".

See also **justification**.

DAVID STEINMETZ

F. Büsser, *Das katholische Zwinglibild*, Zurich, Zwingli Verlag, 1968 • A. Ganoczy, *Le jeune Calvin, genèse et évolution de sa vocation réformatrice*, Wiesbaden, Steiner, 1966 • K.G. Hagen, "Changes in the Understanding of Luther: The Development of the Young Luther", *Theological Studies*, 29, 1968 • H.A. Oberman, *Luther: Mensch zwischen Gott und Teufel* (ET *Luther: Man between God and the Devil*, New Haven, CT, Yale UP, 1989) • S.E. Ozment ed., *Reformation Europe: A Guide to Research*, St Louis, MO, Center for Reformation Research, 1982 • O.H. Pesch, "Twenty Years of Catholic Luther Research", *Lutheran World*, 13, 1966 • D.C. Steinmetz, *Luther in Context*, Bloomington, Indiana UP, 1986 • G. Tavard, "Reassessing the Reformation", *One in Christ*, 19, 1983 • G. Wainwright, "Is the Reformation Over?" *TSF Bulletin*, 7, 1984.

REFORMED ECUMENICAL COUNCIL.
The REC is a council of 30 Reformed and Presbyterian churches located in 18 countries. Its member churches, which represent about 5 million Christians, have come together for closer fellowship on the basis of a shared confession of faith.*

The REC was formerly called the Reformed Ecumenical Synod. Founded in 1946 by ethnically Dutch churches in the Netherlands, North America and South Africa, it was created out of a desire to speak of God's grace* to a fragmented, post-war world. The adopted confessional unity* was the basis on which the founding churches established their witness* to each other and to the world. Other churches that desire to build ecumenical relations on this Reformed confessional basis have joined the founding members.

The REC meets in general assembly every four years. Between assemblies, an interim committee makes decisions on council matters. A permanent secretariat handles the daily business of the council. Other committees focus on special areas of ministry, in theology, mission, youth work, and study projects.

The REC has a number of publications, mostly arising from its conferences, committees and official meetings. Through three periodicals, *News Exchange*, *Theological Forum*, and *Mission Bulletin*, the council communicates to its members and other churches outside the council.

The REC regularly sends delegates to other Christian ecumenical meetings. It has held bilateral meetings with the WCC, the World Alliance of Reformed Churches,* and the Seventh-day Adventists.*

RICHARD L. VAN HOUTEN

REFORMED/PRESBYTERIAN
CHURCHES. Although the word "reformed" is often used generally, with reference to all churches which were shaped by the Reformation of the 16th century, there were already by the end of that century *ecclesiae reformatae* which distinguished themselves under that name from the Lutheran churches; the distinctions were both in doctrine and in form of church government.

These churches were often described as Zwinglian or Calvinist, names the churches themselves resisted, declaring that they sought to be reformed according to the word of God.* While grateful for the witness of the reformers, they were convinced that a reformed church is also *semper reformanda*, "always to be reformed" in accordance with the divine purpose.

When the Swiss reformation spread to Scotland, great emphasis came to be laid upon achieving a polity which was both scriptural and effective for continuous reformation (see **church order**). Presbyterianism was held by many to be such a polity, while courageous minority groups opted for a Congregational order, over against the authority of either bishop or council. From this historical development there emerged the churches of continental Europe called Reformed and those of Great Britain and Ireland called Presbyterian or Congregational/Independent.

Along the paths of exile and in the settlements of trade and empire, the European movement steadily expanded throughout the world. The World Alliance of Reformed Churches* represents 175 churches with about 70 million members and adherents in 84 countries.

The distribution of these millions around the world is very uneven. By country, the centres of strength, in numbers over a million, are in Australia, Canada, the Federal Republic of Germany, Hungary, Indonesia, the Netherlands, the Republic of Korea, the Republic of South Africa, Scotland and Switzerland. Yet strength is not only in numbers, and minority churches have a proud record. In Mediterranean countries, in Latin America, in Asia, Africa, the Caribbean and the Pacific, churches with total membership of thousands rather than even tens of thousands have endured under persecution and repression, and often at length won the respect of other Christians and of the surrounding community. One of the frequently used symbols of Reformed/Presbyterian churches is the burning bush, which, though burning, was not consumed.

Theology. These churches did not intend at the Reformation or in their more recent foundings to begin a new church* or to teach any new doctrine. They commonly affirm the doctrines of the Apostles'* and Nicene* creeds; their confessions are attempts to expound the central themes of the scriptures. They have disagreed among themselves about the use of creeds* and confessions to test the orthodoxy of members and ministers, but they have always emphasized the importance of declaring the truth through word and sacrament.

Main emphases of Reformed teaching have been the sovereignty and authority of God,* the lordship of Jesus Christ* as the divine Saviour, and the centrality of scripture* as the rule of faith and life. It is in relation to these positive doctrines of divine rule and revelation* that many theologians of this tradition have also emphasized the total dependence of created humankind upon God, the utter lostness and depravity of sinners, and the consequent need of a saving action by God which by prevenient grace* draws the sinner back to a right relationship with the Creator and Redeemer. If these emphases are then taken as a basis for logical extrapolation of doctrine, there can emerge a harsh predestinarian view of salvation* and damnation. The developments within the Reformed family of churches have tended towards a return to the primary emphases on divine lordship and grace, but past doctrinal controversies are by no means over. They are often revivified when ecumenical discussion takes place.

Polity. The polities of the Reformed churches were consciously developed to enable a return to what was held to be the discipleship of the early church. The main features of the Presbyterian polity are the parity of ministers, the participation of all members in church government, and the authority of councils (see **conciliarity**).

While exceptional needs call for the exercise of a special authority, as in the case of the first apostles, the regular ministry of word and sacrament is exercised by ministers who have an equality of standing. If one of them (or indeed a layperson) presides over a meeting or a council, it is as a moderator elected for a fixed period of service. In meetings of the local church* or councils of representatives of local, regional or national churches, the ministers are conjoined with lay elders; the voting is not carried out in separate groups of ministers and laity. In the local church some meetings are open for the participation of every member. Regional and national leadership and decision making belong to councils, not to individuals.

This polity is open to considerable variations. Three are frequent enough to require mention. The most important is that which produced Congregationalism* by a fusion of elements from the Reformed tradition and from the radical wing of the Reformation. Here the wider councils are only advisory to a local church, in which the presence of the risen Christ gives full authority to the deliberations of the church meeting. A second variation affects the relation between ministers and elders in terms of the New Testament offices: are only ministers presbyters with elders as helpers and administrators (see 1 Cor. 12:28), or are both ministers and elders presbyters, some being preachers and teachers as well as ruling (see 1 Tim. 5:17)? Third, there may be additional offices, e.g. church professors of theology, deacons in community service and, in the Hungarian-speaking churches, bishops with a permanent role of presidency and oversight.

Reform, unity and division. From their beginnings Reformed churches have had a vision of a reconstituted Christian unity.* In the view of the Reformed leaders, the failure to achieve consensus* with the Lutherans was a tragedy, which Lutheran-Reformed dialogue* in the 20th century has sought to overcome. Calvin and Farel succeeded at least in turning three Protestantisms into two by the historic consensus of Zurich (1548) with the Zwinglians. In succeeding centuries such very different men as Richard Baxter in England and Friedrich Schleiermacher in Germany have struggled to realize a unity based in reform.

It is, however, sadly evident that Reformed churches have also shown a tendency to division. It is difficult even to draw a chart of the many divisions among Presbyterians in countries as varied as Scotland and Brazil. Admittedly there are comings together as well as fallings apart to complicate the charting, but the overall impression is of a splitting trend.

Those who have anxiously considered the reasons for this trend have found them both in features accidental to the church's life, such as national characteristics of stubbornness or impetuosity, and in negative consequences of the positive features of Reformed doctrine and polity. To stress the right of all to ponder the scriptures, each in their own language, may lead to dispute over interpretations; to give to all a participation in church government may turn dispute into schism,* when a defeated minority leaves a council to establish a purer reform in its own assembly. The conviction that God's truth is to be known is turned into the belief that a particular church or group or individual knows it better than anyone else.

Within their own life and through their interchurch relations, the Reformed churches have often been notably self-critical. This process of self-assessment before God has often included penitent recognition of the divisive tendencies just described. This, coupled with the vision of unity inherent in scriptural reformation, has led Reformed churches in the modern era to make a strong contribution to the ecumenical movement.

Ecumenical contribution. The foundation of Presbyterian (1875) and Congregational (1891) worldwide confessional bodies was seen by the participant churches as a step towards wider relationships. At its formation, the Alliance of Reformed Churches throughout the World holding the Presbyterian System declared: "In forming this alliance, the Presbyterian churches do not mean to change their fraternal relations with other churches, but will be ready, as heretofore, to join with them in Christian fellowship." This policy has been repeatedly endorsed by subsequent gatherings of the alliance and of the International Congregational Council.

Reformed churches were among the first to respond to the initiatives which led to the founding of the movements which later came together in the WCC. While many of the conservative churches grouped in the Reformed Ecumenical Council* have distanced themselves from the WCC, the majority of Reformed churches have continued to be deeply involved in ecumenical developments. Most united churches (see **united and uniting churches**) have had a Reformed church among those which formed them.

As churches of Presbyterian and Congregational polity sought union, in 1970 the 11th assembly of the International Congregational Council and the 20th general council of the Alliance of Reformed Churches united, to form the World Alliance of Reformed Churches* (Presbyterian and Congregational).

MARTIN H. CRESSEY

S. Louden, *The True Face of the Kirk*, London, Oxford UP, 1963 ● J. Moffatt, *The Presbyterian Churches*, London, Methuen, 1928 ● M. Pradervand, *A Century of Service: History of the World Alliance of Reformed Churches, 1875-1975*, Edinburgh, St Andrew, 1975 ● L. Vischer ed., *Reformed Witness Today: A Collection of Confessions and Statements of Faith by Reformed Churches*, Bern, Evangelische Arbeitsstelle Ökumene Schweiz, 1982.

REFORMED-ROMAN CATHOLIC DIALOGUE.

After long hesitation the Reformed churches in 1968 followed others by engaging, especially through the World Alliance of Reformed Churches,* in international, interconfessional conversations of the bilateral kind (see **dialogue, bilateral**). Their policy had previously always been to favour multilateral conversations, in particular those conducted through the WCC (see **dialogue, multilateral**). They nevertheless decided to take this new step in order to avoid duplications on the national level, or indeed to make up for the lack of dialogue there, but above all with the worldwide constituency of the Roman Catholic partner in mind. It was on this authoritative level that they sought to achieve dialogue, and their aim was effective common witness.*

Reformed-Roman Catholic dialogue, however, did not await the outcome of Vatican II and the changes it introduced before making a start in several European countries and the US and Australia. Over the centuries very few dialogues were undertaken, such as the Poissy Colloquium in France (1561) or the correspondence between Bossuet and Leibniz in the 17th century, but these failed because of the intolerance of the times, such as the wars of religion or the revocation of the edict of Nantes (1685). Not until the rise of the ecumenical movement were talks revived on a fresh basis, particularly by pioneers such as Yves Congar or Paul Couturier, who organized the Groupe des Dombes* as far back as 1937. Bilateral dialogue was not so much a deliberate choice as a convergence of various historical circumstances. On the European continent the Reformation had primarily produced only the two major traditions — Lutheran and Reformed — with their churches covering more or less distinct geographical areas, and this led to bipolar confrontations between Roman Catholicism, on the one hand, and either Lutherans or the Reformed on the other.

Doctrinal divergence on the nature, place and role of the church* in relation to God and to the world had been a cause of Reformed hesitation to enter into dialogue with the Roman Catholic Church, which appeared to have a different set of priorities. The question of the central position of the church or its displacement from such a position determined the theme of the first series of bilateral conversations on "The Presence of Christ in Church and World" (1970-77), and this was to be tested out in the parallel and trilateral conversations, bringing in also the Lutherans, on "The Theology of Marriage and the Problem of Mixed Marriages" (1971-77). This was before embarking on the second phase of the bilateral dialogue with the Roman Catholic Church "Towards a Common Understanding of the Church" under firmly Trinitarian colours (1983-89).

The first series of conversations in the bilateral Reformed-Roman Catholic dialogue resulted not so much in the working out of a consensus* as in the listing of points of agreement and divergence which had been noted while it was proceeding. The final report goes no further than to follow the sequence of the successive phases of the dialogue and the themes tackled in them: "Christ's Relationship to the Church" (1970), "The Teaching Authority of the Church" (1971), "The Presence of Christ in the World" (1972), "The Eucharist" (1974) and "On the Ministry" (1975).

The following salient points may be highlighted. First, importance was attached to hermeneutical problems, as regards scripture, the relation between the Testaments and covenants, the status of the canon, the relation of scripture and Tradition, the meaning of metaphors for the church in the New Testament, the diversity of models for the church in the NT, the recognition of the normative among relativities, the universal in the particular, the importance of the confession of faith, the nature of interpretative authority in the church, and the role of the Holy Spirit as both giver and gift in the church. Second, the dialogue accorded real value to the world and its history as being the immediate object of the saving plan of God in Christ through the Holy Spirit and the ethical domain of a church which is itself a historical entity endowed with the gifts or charisms of the Holy Spirit and appropriate structures for its missionary work. Third, Christ is in the world and in the church, which witnesses to him and points to him; Christ is present because of his lordship as the glorified and risen One: the church as guide, model and herald of the coming kingdom for the world proclaims and celebrates him in that world. Hence, ecclesiology is one of the "pilgrim people", whose eucharistic memorial bears witness to a communion with the glorified Christ through the Holy Spirit, a communion founded on fellowship with Christ in his glory rather than on the substitutionary nature of his expiatory sacrifice on the cross, which is seldom referred to. The resultant ecclesiology is along the lines of the true presence of Christ as Lord in the Holy Spirit and not of continuous incarnation. Fourth, an ecclesiology of service to the world takes shape implicitly, fluctuating between a more "ontological" Roman Catholic and a more "relational" Protestant conception (André Birmelé), between the idea of a church which is a sanctifying sacrament and of a church which is a sign and a witness. Finally, there are still the questions which relate primarily to the ministry — to its form and scope, the conditions for its fullness and mutual recognition, its character as a sacra-

mental sign, the internal relation between ministry and charism and between order and power, and the primacy of the legal or the liturgical sphere.

The same facts and questions were noted in the dialogue on marriage and mixed marriages in the pastoral and practical fields and were set out in the same way. This dialogue took into consideration an extra partner, at least in the West: secularization,* which raises questions about what circumstances make a church marriage indissoluble and sacramental. The ecumenical question remains about the sacramental nature of marriage and the conclusions to be drawn for pastoral work, especially as to marriages which fail or are renewed (remarriage of divorced persons). Is marriage in the same category as baptism, with its unrepeatable character as an avowal of God's enduring covenant, or is it like the condition of the sinner who is forgiven? Is marriage sanctified because of the inherent sacramental nature of the mystery of salvation or the extension of forensic justification through grace and faith?

Under the title "Towards a Common Understanding of the Church", the 1990 report of the international dialogue between Reformed and Roman Catholics is a more mature and cohesive document than the product of the first phase. The first chapter aims to serve a "reconciliation of memories" which may become possible through new and self-critical perspectives on the separate and mutual histories of the two communities over the past 450 years. Then a "common confession of faith" by the dialogue commission shows what is already taken to be agreed Christologically, soteriologically and ecclesiologically: Christ is the only mediator between God and humankind, and his work reveals that he is the Son within the Trinity; justification is received by grace through faith, "a faith embraced with a freedom restored to its fullness", so that the justified "can henceforth live according to righteousness"; and the church is confessed as the community of all who are called, redeemed and sanctified through the one mediator and in the one Spirit.

In the more directly ecclesiological third chapter, there is a reconsideration of the relation between the gospel and the church as the chosen "place, instrument and minister" of the grace it receives in the sovereign liberty of

God. Difficulties reside largely in different understandings of the relationship between what is *confessed* concerning the church and the concrete forms of its historical existence. Two rival conceptions of the church are discerned to be potentially complementary: the church is both "the creation of the Word" and "sacrament of grace"; the church is the servant of Christ's unique mediation, but never either its source or its mistress. Yet divergence, incompatibility, or at least tension appears to remain on the questions of continuity and discontinuity in church history, of the visible and invisible nature of the church, and (in these contexts) of the forms and significance of ecclesial structures and ministerial order.

In pointing the way forward, the fourth and final chapter envisages that increasingly common testimony, joint action and mutual challenge should become part of a deepening fellowship as remaining differences are settled or accepted (there remains a difference about what issues are serious enough to be church-dividing), and as exploration is made of the kind of unity needed for the ultimate goal of full communion in one faith and one eucharistic fellowship.

ALAIN BLANCY

A. Birmelé, *Le salut en Jésus Christ dans les dialogues oecuméniques*, Paris, Cerf, 1986, pp.255-76 and 331-43 • A. Blancy & M. Jourjon eds, *Pour la communion des Eglises: L'apport du Groupe des Dombes, 1937-1987*, Paris, 1988 • "Consensus oecuménique et différence fondamentale", reflections and proposals of the joint RC-Protestant committee in France, in *La documentation catholique*, 1931, 1987 • N. Ehrenström & G. Gassmann eds, *Confessions in Dialogue*, WCC, 1975, pp.49-52 and 120-23 • H. Meyer & L. Vischer eds, *Growth in Agreement: Reports and Agreed Statements of Ecumenical Conversations on a World Level*, WCC, 1984, pp.279-306 and 433-63 • "The Presence of Christ in Church and World: Evaluation Session of the Roman Catholic-Reformed Dialogue", *Reformed World*, 36, 1980-81 • L. Vischer & A. Karrer eds, *Reformed and Roman Catholic in Dialogue*, Geneva, WARC, 1988.

REFUGEES. Refugees have been on the agenda of the WCC from the very outset. During the second world war when the WCC was still "in the process of formation", Jewish and other refugees received ecumenical assist-

ance to escape Nazi persecution. By the time the WCC was officially constituted, the ecumenical refugee programme was already well established. It was further developed into the WCC's largest single operation. Though the initial focus was on Europe, a 1960 report of the WCC refugee service refers to a field staff of 500 persons working in 70 countries. Since then, however, there has been a gradual transfer of operational responsibilities to regional, national and local churches and ecumenical agencies. When the refugee situation seriously worsened in the 1970s and 1980s and took on a global dimension, the WCC refugee service developed into a worldwide network of churches and ecumenical partners working closely together for the protection and assistance of refugees.

In 1981 the WCC central committee adopted a public statement on "The Churches and the World Refugee Crisis". The introductory paragraph states that refugees, as victims of social, economic and political injustice and armed conflicts, who are struggling for survival and for the recognition of their human dignity, "have a natural claim on the churches". It is this claim which constantly challenges the churches to express solidarity with refugees, whatever their creed, race, nationality or political convictions.

Refugees fleeing their home country are in need of protection and assistance. The creation in 1951 of the Office of the United Nations High Commissioner for Refugees (UNHCR) provided an important instrument for the international protection of refugees and the promotion of durable solutions. The statute of UNHCR and the 1951 UN Convention on Refugees define refugees as persons who have left their countries because of well-founded fear of persecution for reasons of race, religion, nationality, membership of a particular social group or political opinion. The 1951 refugee convention also stipulates that contracting states shall not expel or return refugees to territories where their life and freedoms would be threatened for the reasons mentioned above. In addition to the refugees defined in these international instruments, other categories of persons finding themselves in refugee-like situations have in the course of the years come within the concerns of UNHCR.

Despite this positive development, millions

of refugees fall outside the scope of UNHCR's mandate, including internally displaced persons. For those refugees, the churches, which are not bound by official definitions of who is a refugee, carry particular responsibility.

As part of their diaconal task, the churches have a long history of extending spiritual and material assistance to refugees. Apart from emergency aid to help people survive, efforts have been geared to finding lasting solutions through voluntary repatriation, local integration and resettlement. Those solutions, which in the past met the needs of many refugees, now are applicable in only a limited number of cases. Co-operation on every possible level is more essential than ever and has proved fruitful for the ecumenical movement. Often churches in remote areas have had their first contact with the ecumenical movement through their work with refugees. Growing co-operation with Catholic churches on refugee concerns led in 1986 to the formation of an international ecumenical consultative group on refugee protection, a forum for joint reflection and analysis. The fact that most refugees today are of non-Christian religious traditions has opened up new ways for dialogue.

The vast majority of today's 15 million refugees live in countries of the South. Consequently, countries which can least afford it carry the main burden in hosting and helping refugees. As the refugee problems are recognized as an international concern which must be tackled through international solidarity, poor asylum countries repeatedly stress the need for greater burden-sharing.

In recent years a growing number of refugees from the South have found their way to countries of the North to seek asylum. Though their number is small compared to the masses of refugees in the South, governments in northern countries have introduced restrictive policies for the admission and recognition of those who seek asylum. As a result, the question of international protection, formerly the prerogative of UNHCR, has become an important issue for the churches. This has required from the church a sharper awareness of the root causes of refugee situations, more effective advocacy on behalf of the rights of refugees, alertness with regard to xenophobic and racist trends, sharing of credible information and, in some cases,

the granting of sanctuary to refugees. In particular it has required and continues to require that the churches and the ecumenical fellowship meet the challenges of the refugees in the context of the WCC's call for justice and peace. Only in that way will they do justice to the cause of refugees.

See also **sanctuary**.

GEERTRUIDA VAN HOOGEVEST

RELIGION. Religion is a phenomenon which is experienced directly. No people or tribe is without it, however variously it finds expression and even if it has not been specifically identified by name. It has not everywhere been defined by a special term because it has permeated the whole life of a group. There is no such thing as "religion" in abstraction. We can experience it only in religions that actually exist. But these go back to the appearance of a God or the breaking through of transcendence — of the "holy" — in meditation and ecstasy. Human beings respond to this experience in worship and ethics; they give it form and make it reproducible. Three types of religion can be distinguished.

Tribal religions: The worship of such religions focuses on the cycle of the year and on the life-cycle. Rites take the form of festivals covering hazards and high points in everyday life. They emphasize worship and not doctrine. In many instances ancestor worship is central, linking together tradition, identity and tribal unity. The piety made available in them continues to underlie all other religions, especially ethnic ("folk") religions which have actually been founded and have superimposed themselves on this piety and adapted themselves to it.

Religions with a founder: Here the new element is that these religions originate in historical times and have a rigorously ethical approach which claims worldwide validity. Doctrine is central in such religions. The rites of the existing tribal religion are mostly integrated in the new cult but are symbolically reinterpreted in accordance with the latter's own doctrine (e.g. the Christmas festival in Christianity and pilgrimage in Islam). New festivals are introduced, and these focus on the life of the founder or on other important historical events.

Mysticism: Often this type of religion is not

at all sympathetic to ritual. Mysticism* can break through the distinctive features of religions and seeks to lead them back to the unity behind them which is accessible in meditation and ecstasy.

Every religion carries within it the germ of its own degeneration or perversion. This is why soothsayers, prophets or reformers appear, to take a religion back to its origins or to change it by leading it forward to something new. Thus criticism of religion is actually inherent in it. But in our own day this criticism has taken on a new dimension in that it stands outside religion, and seeks to triumph over it as a whole.

Christians believe that God as Jesus' Father, the Creator, stands behind all religions and that through them God wants to protect human beings in their life and in their humanity. Religions are thus part and parcel of God's work of preservation in the world. To what extent they are also part of God's saving activity is variously answered in Christian churches and teachings. But there is no lack of unanimity in the conviction that God's saving activity in Christ is for all human beings and must be made accessible to all (see **uniqueness of Christ**).

See also **dialogue, interfaith; God**.

THEO SUNDERMEIER

J.P. Asmussen, J. Laessde & J.C. Colpe eds, *Handbuch der Religionsgeschichte*, 3 vols, Göttingen, Vandenhoeck & Ruprecht, 1974 • M. Eliade, *Patterns in Comparative Religion*, London, Sheed & Ward, 1958 • W. James, *The Varieties of Religious Experience*, New York, Longmans Green, 1923 • W.L. King, *Introduction to Religion: A Phenomenological Approach*, New York, Harper, 1968 • G. Van der Leeuw, *Phänomenologie der Religion* (ET *Religion in Essence and Manifestation: A Study in Phenomenology*, 2 vols, New York, Harper, 1963) • R. Otto, *Das Heilige* (ET *The Idea of the Holy*, London, Oxford UP, 1926).

RELIGIOUS COMMUNITIES.

The first steps towards monasticism and other forms of religious communities were the special ways, in the 2nd century, by which many virgins and widows were leading city lives. Then in the deserts of Egypt and Syria, hermits (anchorites) followed a strict asceticism, and gradually most of them gathered around a master, such as Anthony of Egypt (c.251-c.356). In Upper Egypt Pachomius (c.290-

346) developed this experience into a stable common life (cenobitism), and Basil of Caesarea (329?-379) wrote a rule for his several monasteries in Cappadocia. The council of Chalcedon* (451) provided the first official church recognition of religious institutes, by that time well flourishing in cities and rural areas.

Theodore of Studius (759-826) wrote that a monk is one "who looks only towards God, who is drawn to God and is close to God, desiring to serve, being in peace with God and becoming an instrument of peace with other human beings". Renouncing marriage, family and profession, the monks devoted themselves to prayer and contemplation and to such activities as painting and making religious articles and serving others by medical aid and teaching. Monasticism began as a movement of laypeople but gradually was transformed into a more official calling, so that only monks could become bishops in later Byzantium.

In the West, John Cassian (c.360-435), after a monastic life in Bethlehem and Egypt, established in Marseilles (France) a monastery for men and another for women. Later in Italy Benedict of Norcia (480-546), considered the founder of Western monasticism, constructed several autonomous monasteries. His rule gives absolute priority to worship, around which work and study revolve almost inseparably. It became the guide for Benedictine monks and nuns and for those in several similar communities. To them more than to any other groups one can credit the preservation of Greco-Roman culture and the missionary advance, establishment and consolidation of the church in Northern and Central Europe.

The 13th century saw the rise of mendicant orders, such as the Franciscans, Dominicans and Carmelites; by rule they were freed from the monastic obligation of stable residence for the sake of more flexible apostolic activities. At the dawn of the Reformation, new orders arose, such as the Jesuits (1540). Then appeared congregations of women and of men who took no vows and dedicated themselves to education, health care and foreign missions, such as the lay fellowship, the Brothers of the Christian Schools (1680).

Foreign missions in the 19th century attracted dozens of new Roman Catholic communities founded solely for that work, such as the Mill Hill (1866), Verona (1867), and White Fathers and Sisters (1868). The same period saw two new RC communities for explicit ecumenical work, as that was then understood: the American Paulist Fathers (1858) and the Franciscan Atonement Friars (1890).

In the 20th century, one more RC model of consecrated life developed, called secular institutes: by private vows and promises, men and women — single and married, lay and ordained — live "in the world", alone, in families, or in groups; they strive for the perfection of charity and work for the sanctification of the world. Such is the Grail (1921) for women.

The Second Vatican Council (see **Vatican Councils**) urged all these forms of religious life to renewal and adaptation by a continuous return to the sources of Christian life, especially the study and meditation of the gospel, and to the original inspirations that brought the communities into being. Vatican II asked all religious institutes to make their own "the ecumenical initiatives and objectives of the Council".

The Reformation and Protestant communities. One of the many listed causes of the Reformation is the loss of monastic integrity in too many religious houses and the immoral lives of too many monks and nuns. Martin Luther entered the Augustinians in 1505, in his belief that this vocation would most nearly assure salvation. In 1519 he commended vowed celibacy as a good exercise of one's baptismal pledge of lifelong struggling with sin. But by 1521 he rejected vows as tantamount to seeking righteousness and salvation outside of Christ and faith. John Calvin was far harsher in his condemnations; for him monks were papal minions who represented idleness, pride, hypocrisy and ignorance.

Although the reformers rejected religious vows and suppressed monasteries, in northern Germany six communities of nuns did survive in the Lutheran tradition. And some forms of religious life as attempts to replicate the first Christian community in Jerusalem (see Acts 2:42-43) revived in the Moravian Brethren and in the German Pilgrimhuts (1700s); the many Lutheran deacon and deaconess "charity communities" in Germany (1800s); the (Reformed) Sisters of Charity in France and, in the USA, the Society of the Women in the

Wilderness and the Ephrata cloister (1800s); the Swedish Lutheran Society of St Bridget, the Danish Theological Oratory, and the Norwegian Order of the Cross (early 1900s).

In Europe after the first world war, Lutheran and Reformed brotherhoods and sisterhoods gathered men and women, theologians and laity, around a common spiritual rule and discipline as they continued to live single or family lives "in the middle of the world", e.g. the Humility Order (1925) and Michaelsbrotherhood (1931). In India the Christian ashram movement began, and in the USA, the Koinonia farm.

In the Church of England, Elizabeth I (ruled 1558-1603) finally suppressed all religious orders. During the next three centuries some Anglican religious houses were established, but none survived. The modern Anglican revival began in 1845 (Sisterhood of the Holy Cross, London). By the 1960s there were in Great Britain and Ireland over 100 female communities, for teaching, charitable and social work or for contemplative prayer in cloistered life; during this same time, 40 Episcopalian sisterhoods were active in the USA. Male communities are less numerous. The most noted are the Society of St John the

Brothers of the Franciscan order in Brisbane, Australia (Church Scene/Sue Williamson)

Evangelist (1866; Cowley Fathers), now in England, USA and Canada; the Nashdom Benedictines; and the Society of the Holy Cross (1881, USA). Anglican communities of men and of women, with foreign and indigenous members, are in Africa, Australia, New Zealand, India, Japan and elsewhere.

After the second world war a more obvious revival took place in new Protestant communities such as the Marian Sisterhood of Darmstadt (1947), the Swedish Sisterhood of Mary (1954), and the Sisters of the Church of South India (1964). The Taizé community* in France was originally composed only of Reformed brothers (1949), but now has also Anglican and Roman Catholic members.

Since the mid-1960s in Western Europe and North America, male and female vocations* to most forms of structured religious life have been drastically fewer, whether in the Roman Catholic or Orthodox, Anglican or Protestant communities. One finds it impossible to generalize the complex reasons for the swift reduction. But elsewhere, especially in Africa and Asia, there has been a sharp increase of new members in older communities and in new indigenous ones.

Ecumenical witness. Despite aberrations and extravagances, monasticism, in East and West, preserves two truths for all Christians: without discipline there can be no holiness,* and discipline which costs nothing (which lacks renunciation in any form) is valueless. For the monks themselves, renunciation is neither condemnation nor denial of the world, but in Christ God reveals the glory of the coming kingdom, and in its light "the image of this world passes". The road of every disciple of Christ is the narrow road of struggle, tested until death, for "you... must be perfect as your heavenly Father is perfect" (Matt. 5:48; see also **sanctification**).

The monastic approach to theology has developed recognizable characteristics. It stresses a contemplative unity between scriptures, patristics and liturgy, and a union between spiritual reflection and experience. The word of God* is prayed and experienced more than analyzed and systematized. This authentic core of monastic theology and spirituality is finding a home in the ecumenical arena.

By his writings and personal spiritual pilgrimage, the Trappist monk Thomas Merton (1915-68) introduced thousands of Christians to the relation of contemplation to social justice ("solitude and solicitude"), helped them to see "the monk in each of us", and reached out to other monastic traditions, especially the Buddhist.

Cloistered communities of contemplatives give quiet witness by using their monasteries and convents also as retreat centres, where clergy and laity of all communions can participate in regular liturgies and meditation and can seek spiritual counsel. Most RC, Anglican and Protestant religious communities regard an ecumenical spirit as essential to their vocation of prayer, study and activities; in fact, they are usually more ecumenical than the general clergy. Taizé in France and Benedictine monasteries, such as Chevetogne* and St John's (Collegeville, USA), are praying, intellectual centres for ecumenical gatherings. In the early 1980s an ecumenical council of religious began to network RC and Anglican communities, holding that the promotion of Christian unity is "an integral part of our life and mission".

Some pronouncements from the monasteries of Mt Athos seem to be "anti-ecumenical", reflecting a fear that Orthodoxy may be compromised and the churches may be too accommodating to the vagaries of modern times. Other monks have been active bridge-builders, in their witness of prayer and dialogue, such as the Armenian Orthodox in Jerusalem and the Russian Orthodox at Zagorsk (Moscow). Many Orthodox leaders in the ecumenical movement, both bishops and others, come out of the monastic tradition.

TOM STRANSKY

F. Biot, *The Rise of Protestant Monasticism*, Baltimore, Helicon, 1963 • T. Gannon & G. Traub, *The Desert and the City: An Interpretation of the History of Christian Spirituality*, Chicago, Loyola UP, 1984 • D. Knowles, *From Pachomius to Ignatius*, Oxford, Clarendon, 1966 • A. Schmemann, *Historical Road of Eastern Orthodoxy*, Crestwood, NY, St Vladimir's Seminary, 1977 • *A Spirituality for Our Times: Report of a Consultation on Monastic Spirituality*, WCC, 1987.

RELIGIOUS LIBERTY. The Universal Declaration of Human Rights (UN, 1948) states: "Everyone has the right to freedom of thought, conscience and religion: this right includes freedom to change his religion or belief, and freedom, either alone or in community with others and in public or private, to manifest his religion or belief in teaching, practice, worship and observance." Its first draft had said only: "There shall be freedom of conscience and belief and of private and public religious worship"; the redrafting largely followed the work of the Commission of the Churches on International Affairs (CCIA) on the basis of the International Missionary Council-WCC Declaration on Religious Liberty.

The first assembly of the WCC (Amsterdam 1948) described freedom of religion as an essential element in any good international order. "This is an implication of the Christian faith and of the worldwide nature of Christianity." Amsterdam laid down four basic principles: (1) the right to determine one's own faith and creed; (2) the right to express one's religious beliefs in worship, teaching and practice and to proclaim the implications of those beliefs for relationships in a social or political community; (3) the right to associate with others and to organize with them for religious purposes; and (4) the right of every religious organization, formed or maintained by action in accordance with the rights of individual persons, to determine its policies and practices for accomplishing its chosen purposes.

As Philip Potter once pointed out: "Just as theology was long considered the 'queen of the sciences', religious liberty was in the early years of the World Council of Churches a sort of 'prince of human rights'." Ecumenical concern for human rights emerged from the missionary stream of the Christian tradition. Much of the ecumenical action on human rights was focused on establishing international standards through the United Nations. There was a juridical, philosophical and theological orientation to such concern and action, within which religious liberty was considered the cornerstone of the entire edifice of human rights.

The statement on religious liberty adopted by the third assembly of the WCC (New Delhi 1961) is significant in various respects. "Holding a distinctive Christian basis for religious liberty, we regard this right as fundamental for men everywhere." It further said: "Christians see religious liberty as a consequence of God's creative work, of his redemption of man in Christ, and his calling of men into his service. Accordingly human attempts by legal enactment or by pressure of social custom to coerce or eliminate faith are violations of the fundamental ways of God with men. The freedom which God has given in Christ implies a free response to God's love and the responsibility to serve fellow men at the point of deepest need." While thus the WCC has over the years explained and professed that religious liberty has a distinctive Christian basis, there was no suggestion that religious liberty should be seen exclusively as a Christian concern or that religious liberty is an exclusive Christian privilege.

The WCC has often maintained a distinction between the internal aspects of religious freedom and the external manifestations. The internal aspects mean the realm of the mind and of conscience.* It is clear that the internal aspects of religious freedom must not be subject to coercion or to limitations. The external manifestations, however, may come into conflict with other human rights or with the religious freedoms of other people. The WCC has distinguished and emphasized four types of such external manifestations: worship, teaching, practice and observance. The New Delhi statement said: "Freedom to manifest religion or belief includes freedom to practise religion or belief whether by performance of acts of mercy or by the expression in word or deed of the implications of belief in social, economic and political matters, both domestic and international." This is a significant aspect of religious freedom for Christians, especially in their understanding of the demands of the gospel.

From the 1970s some new perspectives on religious liberty have been developed by the WCC within the broader framework of Christian responsibility and human solidarity. The CCIA consultation on "Human Rights and Christian Responsibility" (St Pölten 1974) stated: "The WCC has frequently declared that religious liberty is a basic human right. This right is required so that the full responsibilities of Christian faith may be undertaken. This right is not a privilege or an exclusive freedom for the church. Human solidarity demands that we should be aware of the inter-relatedness of all rights, including the rights of those of other faiths or no faiths... The right to religious liberty exists in order to serve the community according to the commands of the gospel." The fifth assembly of the WCC (Nairobi 1975) based its statement mainly on the insights from the St Pölten consultation. "This right should never be seen as belonging exclusively to the church. The exercise of religious freedom has not always reflected the great diversity of convictions that exist in the world. This right is inseparable from other fundamental human rights. No religious community should plead for its own religious liberty without active respect and reverence for the faith and basic human rights of others. Religious liberty should never be used to claim privileges. For the church this right is essential so that it can fulfill its responsibilities which arise out of the Christian faith. Central to these responsibilities is the obligation to serve the whole community." The WCC has, while affirming certain fundamental principles of religious liberty, agreed that the content and definition of religious

liberty will vary with different cultures and ideologies and with the theological presuppositions of different churches and religions.

A study paper on religious liberty (prepared by the CCIA for the 1980 central committee of the WCC) outlined the various contexts in which religion functions. Churches operate in accordance with their teaching, tradition and practice in countries undergoing radical social transformation, including often a total secularization of state and society. There are situations and problems encountered by Christians and people of other faiths in countries struggling for liberation and self-determination. In several societies, with different political systems and social backgrounds that grossly violate basic human rights, an increasing number of churches and Christians have become actively involved in struggles for justice and human rights based on their sincere understanding of the gospel of Christ.

The Roman Catholic Church. From the beginning the WCC was concerned about "discrimination and repression exercised by dominant religious majorities against

Demonstration of Ukrainian Catholics for the re-opening of their churches (WCC/Peter Williams)

minorities". In Toronto (1950) the central committee spoke of "serious infringements of religious freedom in certain countries in which the Roman Catholic Church is the dominant religion and in regions in which the Muslim faith is the dominant religion".

One of the issues was proselytism.* The third assembly (New Delhi 1961) report on "Christian Witness, Proselytism and Religious Liberty in the Setting of the WCC" described proselytism as the corruption of witness by subtle or open "cajolery, bribery, undue pressure or intimidation".

By the mid-1960s there was a perceptible change in the Vatican's understanding of religious liberty and human rights. The WCC central committee in 1966 welcomed Vatican II's* Declaration on Religious Freedom "with its clear statement proclaiming full, civil, religious freedom, both individual and collective, for everybody everywhere". The second report of the Joint Working Group* between the RCC and the WCC in 1967 concluded that "though the theological justification may still differ from one church to the other, there is basic agreement on what the principle of religious liberty requires in practice".

Vatican II's declaration on religious freedom is contained in the document *Dignitatis Humanae*. This was probably the most bitterly disputed question which the Council tackled. The Council limited itself to clarifying one particular, but vital, aspect of freedom: religious freedom in civil society. The declaration therefore speaks more at a juridical than at a theological level — and is addressed to society as a whole.

The declaration states that every person has a right "to immunity from coercion" in religious matters. The church itself utterly repudiates coercion in religion. Christians must respect religious freedom even more conscientiously than others. The human response to God in faith* must be free, no one is to be coerced into faith, nor can one be coerced into not leaving the church. The Council admitted that these principles have often not been followed by the church. The declaration also speaks of the church's right to freedom. If the church has a unique authority* among people, a unique mission* from God and a unique duty to fulfill that mission, it certainly has a uniquely well-grounded right to preach everywhere.

It is interesting to note that recent statements from the Vatican on religious freedom are very similar to the views expressed by the WCC in earlier times. The message of Pope John Paul II for the World Day of Peace (1 January 1988) said: "In the first place, religious freedom, an essential requirement of the dignity of every person, is a cornerstone of the structure of human rights. It follows that the freedom of individuals and of communities to profess and practise their religion is an essential element for peaceful human existence." The uniqueness of religious liberty and its place in the international order (cf. the Amsterdam declaration) are emphasized in the message.

The UN on religious liberty. In statements on religious liberty from the early days of the WCC (Amsterdam 1948, Evanston 1954, and to a certain extent New Delhi 1961), the UN was part of the frame of reference. In 1981 the UN adopted the Declaration on the Elimination of All Forms of Intolerance and of Discrimination Based on Religion or Belief. The declaration was preceded by 20 years of intensive discussion in various organs of the UN. With the declaration, the general assembly reminded the nations of the world that it is in the higher interests of humankind to put an end to persecution based on religion or belief and to manifestations of prejudices that exist in this connection. In some respects, however, the declaration constitutes a reduction rather than an enlargement of existing standards. The freedom to change one's religion or belief (which is in the Universal Declaration of Human Rights) is no more explicitly included in the declaration. Also the notion of religious practice, as it was understood by the WCC (cf. the New Delhi statement), is conspicuously absent in the declaration. The types of manifestations covered by the declaration mainly belong to the internal functioning of religious organizations and the internal structures of religion rather than to questions of translating the implications of religion or belief in public and social life.

The declaration proclaims that religion or belief, for those who profess them, is one of the fundamental elements in their conception of life, and therefore freedom of religion or belief should be fully respected and guaranteed. It declares that freedom of religion or belief should also contribute to the attainment of the goals of world peace, social justice and friendship among peoples.

The UN Human Rights Commission has a tentative mechanism (a special rapporteur) to monitor the implementation of the declaration. It is significant to note that governments feel greater accountability now to the international community regarding religious tolerance in their countries. There is a proposal to have a more binding instrument such as a convention.

Some current trends. Current trends that substantially influence the situation regarding religious liberty are mainly three: religious resurgence with a growing climate of fundamentalism and fanaticism; changes in the policies of many socialist states, especially the Soviet Union, regarding religion; increasing conflict between religion and politics over the social and political manifestations of religion.

There is an amazing resurgence of religion in many parts of the world. In several countries this has resulted in inter-religious tension and the introduction of laws based on the tenets of the majority religion, leading in turn to infringement of the religious liberty of minorities. The introduction of Islamic sharia is a clear example.

There appears to be a relaxation in the attitude of the socialist states towards religion, as evidenced by developments in countries like the USSR and the People's Republic of China. It is not yet clear whether there is a fundamental change in the policies, but the current developments seem to provide for greater religious liberty.

The social engagement of churches and Christian organizations is interpreted by many governments as subversive political activity. While this is not entirely new, the greater involvement of churches and related groups in struggles for the defence of human dignity has led to curtailment of religious liberty in some countries.

See also **human rights, liberty**.

NINAN KOSHY

A. F. Carrillo de Albornoz, *The Basis of Religious Liberty*, London, SCM, 1963 ● *Freedom of Religion and Belief, Basis of Peace*, Washington, DC, International Religious Liberty Association, 1984 ● F.H. Littell ed., *Religious Liberty in the Crossfire of Creeds*, Philadelphia, Ecumenical Press, 1978 ● J.C. Murray ed., *Religious Liberty, an End and a Beginning. The Declaration on Religious Freedom: An Ecumenical Discussion*, New York, Macmillan, 1966 ● *Religious Freedom: Main Statements by the WCC, 1948-75*, WCC, 1976 ● *Statements on Religious Rights and Related Rights from 1937 to 1955 Made by the Commission of the Churches on International Affairs and Related Ecumenical Agencies*, WCC, 1955 ● L.J. Swidler ed., *Religious Liberty and Human Rights in Nations and Religions*, Philadelphia, Ecumenical Press, 1986.

RENEWAL. The post-1945 religious world referred to such topics as biblical renewal, liturgical renewal and renewal in mission, but the word "renewal" itself did not come into vogue in ecumenical circles until the publication of W.A. Visser 't Hooft's book *Renewal of the Church* (1956). Visser 't Hooft argued that "renewal" was not a new word in the life of the ecumenical movement and listed six ways he saw it manifested, but the argument itself confirms the novelty of the expression.

One of the first official ecumenical consultations on renewal was held in 1957 in New Haven, Connecticut (USA), under the sponsorship of the WCC Departments of Laity and the Co-operation of Men and Women in Church and Society. The 123 participants dealt mainly with the renewal of the life and mission of the church.

"The Missionary Structure of the Congregation", an influential WCC study programme arising out of the New Delhi assembly (1961), struck chords with those who were committed to renewal. Many of them found a fertile field in the work of the Young Men's Christian Association and, more especially, the World Student Christian Federation. Much of this interest in renewal was articulated at the global youth assembly in Lausanne (1960) and in regional youth meetings in the following years.

During the 1960s the impact of the charismatic renewal was also being felt in many churches, and the outcome of the long years of liturgical study and renewal became crystallized in many new liturgical texts and revisions (see **liturgical reforms**). Within the WCC, the magazine *Risk*, founded in the Youth department in 1965, became an instrument of explanation and discovery in the context of the renewal agenda. Over the years, its issues on a range of subjects — from develop-

Youth council at Taizé (WCC/Wendy Goldsworthy)

ment* to liturgy,* from black theology* to cinema — were widely read. In 1978 it became a series of short paperback books tackling major topics on the ecumenical agenda from the point of view of a single author.

Renewal was given greater ecumenical currency in the 1960s by the use of the term in Roman Catholic circles. Pope John XXIII's use of the word *aggiornamento* (lit. "bringing up to date") in calling the Second Vatican Council was echoed in the documents of the Council as renewal: "In this assembly, under the guidance of the Holy Spirit, we wish to enquire how we ought to renew ourselves, so that we may be found increasingly faithful to the gospel of Christ," said the message of 20 October 1962. Earlier, Hans Küng, in his book *The Council as Reunion*, had set an agenda for the council with renewal as its theme.

The theme of the WCC's fourth assembly (Uppsala 1968) — "Behold, I Make All Things New" — foreshadowed considerable ecumenical attention to renewal in the subsequent decade. This newness was the subject of much debate. Some spoke of "new situations, demanding new forms of life and new structures for the church", while others backed

away from such radical calls for reformation. Style and substance were given to the ecumenical idea of renewal by stories of renewed communities in many parts of the world, particularly abundant in the 1960s and 1970s (e.g. Corrymeela, Taizé, East Harlem Protestant Mission, Emmaus House). Theological insights grew out of the work on the missionary structure of the congregation and of such widely read authors as Jürgen Moltmann (*Theology of Hope*, 1962), George W. Webber (*God's Colony in Man's World*, 1960), Colin Williams (*Where in the World?*, 1963, and *What in the World?*, 1964) and Mark Gibbs and Ralph Morton (*God's Frozen People*, 1965).

The Orthodox churches never felt comfortable with the radical style of renewal in and (esp. in the late 1960s) on the fringes of the Western churches. Orthodoxy claimed a holistic view of renewal, of recovery of the valid Tradition* and experience. On such terms, renewal had a certain ambiguity about it. It need not be about a response to rapid change but rather the recovery and re-endorsement of the basic and ancient truths of Christianity.

A similar aura of recovery and restitution

seemed to attach to Taizé* as an ecumenical community in the context of a Reformed church. Only when Brother Roger summoned the council of youth did the remote village in eastern France begin to become a mecca for thousands of young people searching for a more spiritual texture to ecumenism.

With the restructuring of the WCC in the early 1970s, attention to renewal centred on Unit III, Education and Renewal. Consultations in the period between the Uppsala and Nairobi assemblies (1968-75) reflected the renewal theme, with sharp tension between those who advocated active and radical participation in the post-1968 student groups and youth movements and those who believed that renewal is essentially a churchly matter for the edification and nurture of congregational life. The essence of much of the most stimulating renewal activity was its transience; as a plurality of "theologies" developed, the legitimacy of any single spirituality became more and more questioned.

The provisionality of many of the ecumenical meetings on renewal in the 1970s, the lack of coherence and the apparent futility of seeing any continuing programme definition, was the subject of often unproductive and sometimes bitter debate. There were questions about whether the notion of renewal was adequate to accommodate the growing sharpness of issues high on the ecumenical agenda: development, the insights of Paulo Freire on education and "conscientization", political and liberation theologies, and increasingly articulate feminist theology.

Concern for renewal also lay behind the formation of centres for ecumenical dialogue and education which sprang up around the world after the second world war, using the German lay academy as a model. Notable among these was the Christian Institute for the Study of Religion and Society in Bangalore, India. These centres have often stimulated debate and created experiences that have helped churches and church people to discover an appetite for renewal themselves.

A workshop on spirituality* at the WCC's fifth assembly (Nairobi 1975) tried to identify some useful criteria for spiritual renewal. The term "spirituality for combat", coined by M.M. Thomas, enjoyed some currency. But in recent years, a re-invigorated retreat movement, rediscovering techniques of Ignatian

spirituality, for example, has become even more influential. More and more writers are exploring the question of a style for contemporary spirituality — in which ecumenism is almost taken for granted.

By its very nature, the work on spirituality does not lend itself to general treatment in large conferences, but specific aspects of spiritual life have been explored in more intimate WCC workshops, such as the one held on the theme of monasticism in 1986. The role of iconography and of symbolism in nurturing spirituality was explored in a workshop held in 1987 at the time of the celebration of the 1200th anniversary of the seventh ecumenical council (Nicea II), which in the Orthodox tradition restored the veneration of icons* after a period of iconoclasm. And in the growing dialogue with people of other faiths, experiences are shared across the faiths of the insights of mysticism and ways of contemplative meditation.

For many people who were at the Vancouver assembly in 1983, the abiding memory has been that of the tent which became the spiritual home to many of the delegates, where daily ecumenical worship* took on a new and vibrant quality. Like an incoming tidal wave, the influence of that worship has since flowed into the life of many local congregations across the world, renewing their own worship life. As a consequence, worship workshops have been held in several regional centres, which have encouraged the exchange and circulation of local music and lyrics, and substantial international collections of such liturgical materials have been published. A worship resource centre has been established at the ecumenical centre in Geneva. Thus, worship shared across the traditions and cultures becomes an element not only of renewal but also of experiential ecumenism.

Other forms of Christian renewal at the local level have profound ecumenical implications. The growth of church base communities,* of house churches* and of charismatic groups can be ways of bringing renewal to church congregations, but it can also become a stumbling block in the way of a fuller ecumenism. In recent ecumenical visits to such local groups, questions have been raised as to how wide their ecumenical vision is and how far their insights are helping to renew the whole life of the churches. In 1989 a WCC team visit to Brazil published its report under the title "Renewal from the Roots" and described the base communities as "providing a model of grassroots ecumenism".

In all such processes of ecumenical renewal, the laity* have a key role to play. In 1987 the synod of the Roman Catholic bishops took up the theme of the ministry of the whole people of God* as one of the great potentially renewing factors in church life today. The ecumenical network of lay centres across the world continues to keep laymen and women from a variety of secular ministries in their daily work in living communication with one another and with the whole institutional church. The question remains, however, whether ecumenical experience today can be part of a spiritual renewal, and whether a renewal of spirituality in Christian communities will lift ecumenism to a new level of experience and achievement.

REX DAVIS

A.J. van der Bent, *From Generation to Generation: The Story of Youth in the WCC*, WCC, 1986 • S. Crose, *The Grassroots Church: A Manifesto for Protestant Renewal*, New York, 1966 • R. Davis, *Locusts and Wild Honey: The Charismatic Renewal and the Ecumenical Movement*, WCC, 1978 • J.C. Hoekendijk, *De kerke binnenste buiten* (ET *The Church Inside Out*, Philadelphia, Westminster, 1966) • *Renewal* (=*Risk*, 5, 3/4, 1969).

RESPONSIBLE SOCIETY. Within the ecumenical movement there has been widespread unanimity regarding "the responsible society" as a goal for political action. This social-ethical criterion made possible a critical evaluation of both communism and capitalism.* Amsterdam 1948 defined the concept as follows: "A responsible society is one where freedom is the freedom of men who acknowledge responsibility to justice and public order, and where those who hold political authority or economic power are responsible for its exercise to God and the people whose welfare is affected by it."

The "responsible society" was regarded as a free and democratic society, where all citizens are guaranteed freedom and where those holding political authority are responsible to the electorate. It was also regarded as a society where the individual and the state aspire to social and economic justice.* The Amsterdam

assembly stated that the responsible society was to be neither communist nor capitalist. Communism was criticized as guaranteeing neither political nor economic freedom, and capitalism was criticized because the state does not take responsibility for a just distribution of welfare.

The WCC assembly in Evanston (1954) emphasized that the responsible society is not a specifically "Christian" social system, constituting a third alternative to communism and capitalism. It is rather "a criterion by which we judge all existing social orders and at the same time a standard to guide us in the specific choices we have to make". However, the responsible society was regarded to be a democratic society with both private ownership and public economic initiative.

During the Rapid Social Change study (1954-59), the responsible society was given as a social idea for the developing countries. At the world conference in Salonika in 1959, the aim of social change in developing countries was stated to be a society where "men are called to accept responsibility to God and their fellow men for the choices and decisions on which the life of their societies is based; and responsible participation in social and political life can only be achieved where each national group or unit can express itself in freedom". The responsible society now included a demand for the national independence of developing countries and their liberation from the colonial powers.

As a social ideal, the responsible society has been based on two different theological traditions. The Barthian tradition is represented by J.H. Oldham, W.A. Visser 't Hooft and Roger Mehl. They advocate a "pure theological" social ethics, according to which the criteria for a right political action can be known only through revelation in Christ. Their ethics is *deontological*, i.e. the criterion for a right action is not good consequences but the will of God. The natural-law* tradition is represented by William Temple, John C. Bennett and Heinz-Dietrich Wendland. They advocate a "humanely grounded" social ethics, according to which we can understand what is right independently of revelation* in Christ. Their ethics is *teleological*, which means that an action is right if it produces better or less evil consequences than alternative actions.

According to Oldham, who introduced the

concept of the responsible society (see **middle axioms**), an action is right if it is carried out as a response to the guidance of God. Human beings are "responsive persons", in the sense that they should act in response to the call of God in every new situation, and society ought to be formed in such a way that every human being can be responsive in this sense. A responsible society is a free society, where human beings, by their freedom to control, criticize and replace the government, are respected as responsible persons with freedom to obey God.*

According to Bennett, there are moral convictions which could be embraced by both Christians and non-Christians. The responsible society is a social ideal which is universally human in this sense. It is a democratic society, where the government is controlled by those governed. It is also a mixed economy, where a market economy is combined with both public and private ownership of the means of production. This political and economic system is desirable, since it promotes such intrinsic values as freedom, justice and welfare.

The responsible society was used as a social-ethical criterion at the WCC assembly in New Delhi (1961) and at the Church and Society world conference in Geneva (1966). However, in Geneva this social ideal was also criticized, mainly by theologians from the third world. The alternative was regarded to be a socialist society with both political and economic democracy. In the 1970s the responsible society was replaced by other ecumenical social ethical criteria, such as "the just, participatory and sustainable society".*

See also **society**.

CARL-HENRIC GRENHOLM

C.-H. Grenholm, *Christian Social Ethics in a Revolutionary Age: An Analysis of the Social Ethics of John C. Bennett, Heinz-Dietrich Wendland and Richard Shaull*, Uppsala, Verbum, 1973 • J.H. Oldham, "A Responsible Society", in *The Church and the Disorder of Society: Man's Disorder and God's Design*, Amsterdam Series, vol. 3, London, SCM, 1948 • *The Responsible Society. "Christian Action in Society": An Ecumenical Inquiry*, WCC, 1949.

RESURRECTION. Though beliefs about the resurrection were certainly vital to the Christological and Trinitarian dogmas of the early councils, the resurrection itself has never been comparably defined. We find instead what Gerald O'Collins calls "a living consensus" grounded in the New Testament witness to the resurrection and maintained by the common creeds of the churches.

Yet, in the midst of this ecumenicity, there has also been controversy, primarily over the relationship of the resurrection to the cross. It has often been asserted that the East worships the risen Christ, the West the crucified Christ. This generalization is unfair to both traditions, but it does point to a historic tension between them. The resurrection, writes Kallistos Ware of the East, "fills the whole life of the Orthodox church". The Orthodox see the cross from the perspective of the empty tomb. Even in his suffering, Jesus is "indestructible life" (Heb. 7:16), the Incarnate One of God who vanquishes the power of death by his death. "On the tree he triumphed over the powers which opposed him," proclaims the Orthodox baptismal liturgy. Orthodox hymnology exalts the cross itself as "life and resurrection" and "life-bearing".

For the West, the cross is more a sign of human godlessness. That we would crucify the Lord of glory shows the extent to which we have fallen in sin.* Yet it also reveals the depth of God's love: God sacrifices his own Son so that we sinners may be reconciled to God. Since Luther, Protestant theology has considered the cross to be the standard of all Christian preaching: only through the crucified Christ does God save us (1 Cor. 1:18-25). The West fears that the East does not allow the cross to stand on its own horrific terms but too easily subsumes it under the triumphant glory of the resurrection. The Orthodox reply that Christ offers not only forgiveness of sin but new life, prefigured by his resurrection, for all creation. In their view, the West has not sufficiently appreciated the cosmic scope of salvation* achieved by Christ but has focused too narrowly on the justification of the sinner.

These contrasts need not be divisive. There are numerous points of contact between East and West for constructing a common faith. The Eastern fathers hardly neglect the forgiveness of sins as part of Christ's total work, sometimes even speaking of the cross, like the West, in juridical and penal terms. Anselm, who is often charged with focusing the West on atonement, understands the ultimate end of the cross to be the resurrection of the dead, when God will perfectly "complete what he began with human nature" (*Cur Deus Homo?* 2.4).

Most important, however, the liturgical movement* of this century has helped to recover the unity of Christ's death and resurrection found in the paschal celebration of the early church. The Jewish passover (Hebrew *pesach*, from which is derived the Greek *pascha*) remembered the central saving event of the old covenant,* God's deliverance of Israel from Egyptian bondage. The Christian pasch celebrated a new exodus, God's redemption of humanity from sin and death through Jesus Christ (1 Cor. 5:7-8). The service originally proceeded as an all-night vigil from Saturday evening to Easter* morning. Through a series of lessons and psalms, Christ was proclaimed as the fulfilment of Old Testament salvation history.* Then, at dawn, the darkness of the cross yielded to the light of the resurrection, and fasting and expectation gave way to joy. Worshippers passed with Christ from death to life, as in the words of Paul: "We were buried with him, and lay dead, in order that, as Christ was raised from the dead... we shall also be one with him in a resurrection like his" (Rom. 6:4-5, NEB). In one continuous service, ending appropriately with baptism* and eucharist,* the paschal celebration kept together cross and resurrection, suffering and victory. Only later, around the 4th century, did this unitive celebration start to divide, with eventually Good Friday commemorating the cross, and Easter the resurrection.

There is now a growing ecumenical consensus that the paschal mystery prohibits any opposition or competition between a "theology of the cross" and a "theology of the resurrection". The two cannot be isolated from each other or from the great sweep of salvation history remembered in the pasch. While some modern theologians have sought to deny the centrality of the resurrection or reduce it to the genesis of faith in the life of the disciples, the paschal mystery asserts the fullness of resurrection belief in unity with the cross: God's act in raising the crucified Jesus from the dead re-creates the whole of creation — personal, social, historical, cosmic. Dying

and rising with Christ is the mystery of redemption* itself. The old, sinful life is crucified with Christ; new life comes through the risen Lord's gift of the Spirit.

All Christians, Eastern and Western, can claim the paschal celebration of the early church as their common heritage and theological norm. The ecumenical significance of the paschal mystery cannot be overstated. Through it, Christ would purify and renew his church for service to God and to the world. Indeed, the paschal mystery is the very means of our union with Christ and, as we faithfully struggle to overcome our divisions, the basis of our union with each other.

See also **Jesus Christ, life and death**.

ROWAN D. CREWS, Jr

O. Casel, *Das christliche Kultmysterium* (ET *The Mystery of Christian Worship*, Westminster, MD, Newman, 1962) ● F.X. Durrwell, *La résurrection de Jésus, mystère de salut* (ET *Resurrection*, London, Sheed & Ward, 1960) ● V. Kesich, *The First Day of the New Creation: The Resurrection and Christian Faith*, Crestwood, NY, St Vladimir's Seminary, 1982 ● W. Lazareth ed., *The Lord of Life*, WCC, 1983 ● G. O'Collins, *What Are They Saying about the Resurrection?*, New York, Paulist, 1978 ● P. Selby, *Look for the Living*, London, SCM, 1976.

REVELATION. The 20th century has witnessed the slow reconstruction of the doctrine of divine revelation in the aftermath of the Enlightenment. In particular it has been realized again that God* is not simply another being in the universe whose existence, essence and self-expression may be assessed on purely naturalistic or intra-mundane grounds. This rediscovery is not complete, and in fact progress towards it has been marked as much by the raising of new perplexities as by the resolution of old ones. Nevertheless, a refinement of revelation theories is discernible.

The doctrine of divine revelation begins (as do all doctrines) with an observation concerning human beings: we are open to experiences which disclose God. The God thereby revealed is thus not solely the object of the experience but is in fact the very ground of its possibility (i.e. the gracious self-revealer). Thus the doctrine of divine revelation is primarily concerned not so much with *what* is revealed or discovered about God as it is with *how* any such self-transcending revelatory discovery is possible in the first place. We shall return to this description after summarizing the major features of 20th-century discussion of the doctrine.

Regardless of how one defines "20th century" in this context, by all accounts its fundamental Protestant expression begins with Germanic neo-orthodoxy's rejection of theological subjectivism, the idea that knowledge of God was immanent within creation and thus fully accessible to the human rational subject. "General revelation", it appeared, had largely done away with the need for any "special" revelation ("additional" revelatory acts of God necessitated by human sin*). But now, with Protestant neo-orthodoxy, we find the complete (Karl Barth) or virtually complete (Emil Brunner) rejection of the possibility of general revelation and hence of natural theology.

For Barth, divine transcendence means that God is wholly other than human beings and as such is utterly unknowable by humans except through the self-disclosing acts of the preached word, the biblical word and the living Word (Christ). Were any sort of degree of knowledge of God possible apart from these acts, each would be attenuated. Specifically, this means that no genuine (much less saving) knowledge of God is discoverable within creation itself by means of human reason. Barth insisted that the two realms or categories of the divine and the created are mutually exclusive, hence only dialectically related. Human finitude, radically compounded by and ultimately indistinguishable from human sinfulness, completely annihilates the possibility of discovering God from below. God's self, identical with Christ, can be revealed only through Christ (see **Jesus Christ**).

Brunner maintains the distinction between the divine and the created realms as seriously as Barth in all areas except for personal encounter. The God of the Bible clearly desires personal encounters with sinful human beings and brings them about. For this to be possible, there must be something in pre-saved human nature that in and of itself can receive the divine initiative and thus complete the divine intention of human salvation.* Apart from some such postulate, there could be no way to distinguish between human beings, whose efforts towards God *(ex hypothesi)* always fail, and animals, who make no such efforts at all.

In particular there could be no way to distinguish their respective responsibilities towards God, especially for the person who really believed Barth and consequently gave up even trying to think about God. Instead, Brunner said, God's sovereign transcendence is shown in the operations of the human conscience,* whose accusing and excusing functions point beyond themselves precisely to God, who both judges and pardons. And it is in the encounter with the personal God, seen most clearly in the special revelation of Jesus Christ, that humans become confident that God would rather excuse than accuse. Contrary to Barth, Brunner held that sin *is* a form of relationship with God, albeit a negative one. From that ground, then, God encounters human beings in grace* and redemption.*

Germanic neo-orthodoxy culminated as an ecumenical expression in the 1934 Barmen declaration (see **Confessing Church**). Barmen rejected the historical immanentism of Nazi theology, in particular its identification of Nazi policies with the kingdom of God.* In place of such theology, it advocated a return to a supernatural and Christocentric revelation as the only sufficient guide for personal faith* as well as social morality. But some in the Confessing Church nevertheless stopped short of Barth's dialectical brick wall, preferring instead Dietrich Bonhoeffer's axiom that "God is the beyond in our midst".

Roman Catholic theories of revelation during the 20th century tended, not surprisingly, to focus more on the corporate encounter with God than on the individual one, which eventuated in the reduction of revelation to salvation in much Protestant thought. This is said without ignoring Catholics such as Pierre Teilhard de Chardin, whose notion rested ultimately upon "contact between two centres of consciousness" rather than any form of external verification such as reason, miracle, ecclesial authority or the like.

In general Roman Catholic theories have followed, and at times provoked, the evolution from Vatican I's *Dei Filius* (1870) to Vatican II's *Dei Verbum* (1965). In the former, the Roman Catholic Church saw itself as the sole and terminal sign of revelation, in that it alone bears the verifiable marks of unity,* holiness,* catholicity* and apostolicity* in their concrete entirety. This self-description resulted historically in the anti-modernist entrenchment of the early 20th century, whose internal characteristic was rejection of the critically new and whose external characteristic became virtual ecclesial sectarianism. More particularly, anti-modernism insisted that revelation is transcendental as well as immanent, that it proceeds from miraculous divine intervention, that it has a predominant doctrinal or intellectual aspect and that it is gracious and hence not naturally present within the human person. The traditionalists in this controversy were eventually impressed with the incompatibility of their theology, according to which God continues to be revealed to and through the church* within history,* with their historiography, according to which the meaning of history is found in its primitive and pristine origins. The first official recognition of this incompatibility is found in Pope Pius XII's encyclical *Divino Afflante Spiritu* (1943), whose signal effect was to allow Roman Catholic biblical scholars to resume their use of historical criticism in exegesis because it was no longer perceived as a necessary threat to divine revelation (see **exegesis, methods of**).

Dei Verbum made the church rather the *sacrament** of revelation. This modification located the concept of revelation in a historical rather than a strictly dogmatic context, seeing it as both word and deed, dynamically creative, universal as well as particular, calling for obedience by all (including the magisterium), and finally as critically grounded within scripture rather than fully parallel to it.

Among contemporary Protestants, Wolfhart Pannenberg also affirmed, as Brunner and Bonhoeffer had done, encounter as the mode of divine revelation. For Pannenberg, though, the encounter is with God through history rather than through conscience, in particular the qualitative "end" of history brought about in the resurrection* of Jesus. The resurrection of Jesus certifies our own future resurrection and reveals God by showing that both private and corporate history depends for its fulfilment upon the God "who gives life to the dead and calls into existence [i.e. everlasting life] the things that do not exist [i.e. the dead]" (Rom. 4:17). *What* is revealed here is God's power and love, first for Jesus and thus for us as well. This makes the death and resurrection of Jesus, and reflexively his historical life, salvific and not merely exemplary. The faith which estimates the resurrection in this way lives today in view of the ultimacy of the kingdom of God,* which in turn both testifies to God's presence in the revelation and helps to bring about that kingdom in history. But because this revelation is of God's own self, only the Christ-revelation is directly valid; all other "revelations" are but indirect divine "manifestations". Hence Pannenberg rejects as fatally circular the concept of salvation history,* according to which a determinate segment of history critically evaluates the remainder by means of an ongoing tradition of partial self-disclosures culminating in Christ. Both the presupposition (a super-revelatory word-disclosure guaranteeing the critical distinctiveness of *salvation* history) and the effect (all other history is merely profane) of this concept are unsatisfactory. Pannenberg prefers instead a *universal* history in which the whole is evaluated, proleptically yet rationally, by the singular and climactic resurrection-disclosure.

The Roman Catholic Avery Dulles objects to Pannenberg's theory of "revelation as history" because it posits events, rather than words, as primary to divine revelation. This is unsatisfactory because events are by definition meaningless apart from interpretation, and interpretation is by nature cognitive or verbal. We should instead view revelation as both deed and word. Dulles suggests the use of "symbolic revelation" as a proper category here, in that symbols are cognitive entities (words) which have evocative and hence participatory effects (events) within human life and history. "Word and deed thus participate in one another. Speech is at once an operation of the intelligence and a motor phenomenon."

It is not entirely surprising to discover Pannenberg's preference for history over word affirmed within liberal (or ethical) Protestantism, represented here by F. Gerald Downing. Downing contends on biblical grounds that the category of revelation is subservient to that of salvation, that it was largely unknown to the biblical authors because it implies a full and complete personal disclosure which *ex hypothesi* we cannot expect of God, and that the term is fraught with ambiguity because its primary modern usage is epistemological rather than religious (i.e. it served as the warrant for theological argumentation against those who thought such a possibility simply incoherent, rather than serving for actual saving encounters with God). Therefore, says Downing, the only "revelation" of interest to the Christian community is what will come at the end. What the biblical tradition has instead of present revelation is salvation, a form of "commitment [which] is essentially love in response to... the 'myth' of the prior love of 'real God in Christ'". What counts here is not the historical verifiability of the myth but rather the agapic quality of the obedient commitment which flows from it.

The notions of revelation within liberation theologies resist easy systematization, at least in part because liberationists are not much concerned either with denominational borders or traditional methodologies. Generally they fall within this same ethical or praxis-oriented construct. Central to all is the insight that Christ's death revealed God precisely as victim. Hence God's word reaches us today as a summons to participate in the struggle to liberate today's victims. Gustavo Gutiérrez says: "History is the scene of the revelation God makes of the mystery of his person. His word reaches us in the measure of our involvement in the evolution of history."

For Karl Rahner, revelation is the self-disclosure of *God*, not in an extrinsic (and especially propositional) sense, but instead as the loving and hence radically personal mystery presupposed by the existence of material beings capable of loving self-transcendence (i.e. human beings). Transcendentally considered, revelation is the dynamic ground of the coming-into-being of humans, in that humanity constitutes the "other" which God lovingly posited as the ultimate possibility of the acceptance of self-transcending divine love. Historically considered, revelation centres in Jesus of Nazareth, in that he was the obedient and receptive person by whom God's love (ultimately inseparable from God's self) was accepted and thus became most fully evident within the conditions of history. Far from being a mere communication of propositional information from heaven to earth, far from being an encounter between persons of merely different ontological value, divine revelation is seen by Rahner as the condition absolutely presupposed by the existence of humanity. And since humanity does exist precisely as material reality capable of spirit, i.e. the dynamic exchange of self-transcending love

(one notes the difference between this and Downing's agapic or uni-directional love), then the divine self-communication must be its ground both in particular and in general. Jesus Christ is at once the real God as communicated, the fully human acceptance of this communication, and the historically definitive manifestation of this offer and its acceptance.

Because (still according to Rahner) there is no *human* being who is not essentially constituted by the dynamic love of God, divine revelation is universal in scope (see **universalism**). What were traditionally considered its outer limits are better thought of as demarcating the boundary between explicit and implicit reception of God's self-communication. This position better accounts both for the universality of the notions of faithfulness and sin, and for the presence of genuine truth among the various world religions and philosophies. Apart from some such expression of universality within revelation theories, it is impossible to say with precision either how sin is against *God*, or how truth can exist within non-biblical religions.

Rahner's transcendental method has been criticized as overly psychological, hence insufficiently relational or communal. This weakness may be met by further clarifying his notion of spirit as the fundamental locus of dynamic self-transcendence. The activities of spirit may be specified as knowing, loving and hoping. Each of these shows the human person in self-transcendence, historically and incrementally progressing beyond ignorance, autonomy and anxiety. Each is grounded within the dynamic category of goodness, which functions as a power beckoning the human spirit from ignorance to knowledge, from autonomy to love and from anxiety to hope. Furthermore, each is communal, necessarily relating the spiritual subject with other such subjects in the common pursuit of their goals. Finally, especially in view of the latter, these activities are collectively grounded within the Triune God: Father as mysterious ground of knowing, Son as object of the Father's love and hence the prototype of human love and Spirit as creative appropriation of this love and thus the possibility of dynamic intentionality and progress (see **Trinity**).

This account of divine revelation overcomes two characteristic weaknesses within many traditional ones: first the uncritical presumption of the meanings of "God" and "human beings" in theories which intended to relate them, and second the seclusion of divine revelation within the biblical religions. But it does not fail to address their intentions, especially those relating to the possibility of a relationship between God and humans, on the one hand, and the gracious (i.e. inescapably responsible and ultimately good) character of that relationship and consequent possibility of sin, on the other.

The doctrine of divine revelation addresses the very heart of what it means to be human. Narrowness and sectarianism are especially invalid here. Christian expressions of God's self-communication must draw upon an ever-wider number of revelatory experiences in order to understand the meaning of God's work of creation more richly, wherein history is precisely the medium of the gracious offer of salvation to all human beings as well as the setting within which that offer is concretely grasped and made personal (see **person**). As the third millennium approaches, we may look to this doctrine as the ground of increasingly fruitful ecumenical relations both within and beyond the Christian tradition.

See also **God, grace, history, kingdom of God, salvation, salvation history, Trinity**.

KERN ROBERT TREMBATH

J. Baillie, *The Idea of Revelation in Recent Thought*, New York, Columbia UP, 1956 • K. Barth, *Kirchliche Dogmatik* (ET *Church Dogmatics*, II/1 and II/2, Edinburgh, Clark, 1957 and 1964) • B.A. Demarest, *General Revelation*, Grand Rapids, MI, Zondervan, 1982 • A. Dulles, *Models of Revelation*, Garden City, NY, Image, 1985 • R.P. McBrien, *Catholicism*, Minneapolis, Winston, 1981, ch. 7 • W. Pannenberg ed., *Offenbarung als Geschichte* (ET *Revelation as History*, New York, Macmillan, 1968) • K. Rahner, *Grundkurs des Glaubens* (ET *Foundations of Christian Faith: An Introduction to the Idea of Christianity*, New York, Seabury, 1978, part 1 and part 5).

REVOLUTION. "Revolution" is a term with many meanings, each of which includes the idea of radical change, the overthrow of an old order and the introduction of a new. Usually it means abrupt, self-conscious change, although occasionally historians will discover, in retrospect, a "silent revolution" that took place over a period of time. A revolution is not necessarily violent, but most of the famous revolutions of history have been violent, either because revolutionaries attacked an old order or because the old order sought violently to repress the new movement.

Traditionally the term, used in both astronomy and human history, referred to the restoration of an order* that had been disturbed. Just as the heavens made their apparent annual revolution around the earth, human history moved to restore a given order. In ancient China, for example, when evil rulers violated "the mandate of heaven", a revolutionary movement was justified in overthrowing the past regime and re-establishing an order that could again claim the mandate.

But in societies influenced by the Bible, revolution often aimed to introduce a genuinely new era. The God of scriptures was capable of "doing a new thing" (Isa. 43:19). That belief had many expressions. In the late middle ages and Renaissance, it took on a broad historical meaning. The Franciscan monk Joachim of Fiore (c.1135-1202) developed the doctrine of the three ages (of the Father, Son and Holy Spirit) and contributed to a vivid expectation of the future. The Enlightenment secularized the theme. The 17th-20th centuries saw the English, American, French, Soviet and Chinese revolutions, along with many revolutions against colonial powers. Fascists and Nazis claimed to be revolutionary, partly to avoid the stigma that went with identification as "counter-revolutionary".

The earliest of the modern revolutions were avowedly political, although economic factors were important, too. In Marxist revolutions the economic role got primary emphasis, but politics, although theoretically subordinated to economics, played a major part. The vocabulary of revolution extended to art, architecture, and much of cultural life — but it remained for Mao Zedong to popularize the term "cultural revolution" in a total sense.

Theology and revolution. Historically, religion* often functions to legitimize existing structures of power.* Most rulers have claimed some kind of divine right or sanction for their authority.* All who object are then put in the position of resisting divine order. A priest-king can combine religious and military power against foes domestic or foreign. When offices of king and priest are separate, the two parties may work out a partnership convenient to both.

But religion may criticize the existing order in the name of a transcendent God* who judges all human systems. In the biblical record Moses confronted Pharaoh, demanding freedom for a people. Later, Nathan challenged David, Elijah challenged Ahab. In a classic confrontation the priest Amaziah tried to stifle the prophet Amos, telling him to leave Bethel, which was "the king's sanctuary", but Amos refused to be silenced (Amos 7:14-17). These cases are not quite revolutions, because old orders persisted, but the revolutionary impulse is clear.

Three contemporary theological meanings of revolution may be distinguished: (1) *metanoia*, the New Testament term usually translated repentance, has been described by theologian H. Richard Niebuhr as "permanent revolution", the ceaseless transformation of faith and ethics; (2) in the NT the Magnificat* testifies that God puts down the mighty from their thrones and exalts those of low degree; the beatitudes of Jesus portray the kingdom of God* as a revolutionary reversal of existing society, bringing blessing to the poor,* the meek, the persecuted; (3) revolution most commonly means an organized political movement overthrowing an oppressive government.

Theology almost universally recognizes the kingdom of God as a radical transformation of historical societies. But in much of Christian history that kingdom has been located in an other-worldly heaven or at the end of history, where it has little meaning for present political and economic life. Thus Christendom could be understood as a divinely ordained social order (often with reference to Rom. 13) — certainly imperfect, but God's will for a sinful world.

However, protests were possible. John of Salisbury in the 12th century and Thomas Aquinas in the 13th recognized a carefully qualified right of tyrannicide in extreme cases. John Wycliffe (d.1384) and Jan Hus (d.1415) joined biblical fervour and the cry for social change.

Karl Mannheim in *Ideology and Utopia* saw a decisive turning point in modern history at the point when the expectation of the imminent kingdom of God "joined forces with the active demands of the oppressed strata of society". Thomas Münzer (d.1525) identified NT eschatology with social revolution, earning the enmity of political rulers and of Roman Catholic and Protestant church leaders. Martin Luther, who had earlier called on the princes to recognize the just demands of the peasants, responded in furious anger to Münzer's revolutionary theology.

Yet Luther late in his career called on the princes to resist the emperor, "even though it mean a revolution". Calvinists and Puritans (including Thedore Beza, John Milton and others) more frequently justified revolutionary acts against kings. Many modern revolutions have invoked some religious or theological vindication. The American Declaration of Independence (1776) appealed to "the laws of nature and of nature's God". But all these examples diverge from Münzer's identification of eschatology* and revolution.

The contemporary situation. Social revolution has become a frequent, if controversial, theme in ecumenical theology. On a world scale Christians have supported many revolutions of peoples seeking self-government and independence from colonial powers (see **colonialism, decolonization**). Ironically, the prior colonization had often claimed Christian sanction; and in some revolutionary conflicts (most conspicuously in South Africa), both sides have given theological justifications, although the world church has resolutely opposed apartheid.*

In the anti-colonial revolutions of this century, the chief actors have been people of many faiths. Some have been Christians, specifically guided by theological concerns. For example, T.B. Simatupang, a hero of the Indonesian struggle for independence and later a president of the WCC, acknowledged the influence of Reinhold Niebuhr in his own participation in the revolution (*The Ecumenical Review*, 1985). Niebuhr, who worked out his theology of conflict primarily in relation to the Nazi threat, characteristically found justification for coercion in a sinful world, both to maintain government against anarchy and to resist tyranny. The break-up of the old imperial systems has not always brought freedom.* People have continued to struggle against oppression by national despots and by foreign powers (nations and business corporations) that maintain economic dominance, often called neo-colonialism.

In the 1960s revolution broke into ecumenical discussion on a new scale. Several events were important. In 1966 the WCC called a conference in Geneva, on the theme "Christians in the Technical and Social Revolutions of Our Time". The addresses and discussions showed a wide recognition of a revolutionary spirit in the Bible and a revolutionary ferment in the contemporary world. Some speakers called for a "revolutionary theology". There was recognition of vast injustice in the world and the need for some kind of social revolution. The report of section 2, "The Nature and Function of the State in a Revolutionary Age", urged non-violent methods of change but raised the question "whether the violence which sheds blood in planned revolutions may not be a lesser evil than the violence which, though bloodless, condemns whole populations to perennial despair" (para. 84).

In 1965, Vatican II* produced its pastoral constitution *Gaudium et Spes* (The Church in the Modern World), with its attention to large-scale social injustices. In 1967 Pope Paul VI, building on Vatican II and prior papal teachings (esp. of Leo XIII, Pius XI and John XXIII), issued his encyclical *Populorum Progressio* (On the development of peoples). It pointed to grave social ills, including the economic bondage of some newly independent nations. The pope advocated "a new humanism", with property rights subordinated to justice* for all peoples, freedom from imposed servitude, land re-distribution, international debt relief, and international re-distribution of wealth. While warning against illusory messianism and "totalitarian ideologies", he said: "A revolutionary uprising — save where there is manifest, long-standing tyranny which would do great damage to fundamental personal rights and dangerous harm to the common good of the country — produces new injustices, throws more elements out of balance and brings on new disasters" (para. 31). That statement was noteworthy, both for the warnings against revolution and for the exception that justified revolution.

In 1967, some 16 bishops of the third world (from Latin America, Africa, Asia, Eastern Europe and Oceania) issued a statement, "Gospel and Revolution". They affirmed that revolutions are part of history, not always good, but sometimes necessary and productive of good fruits. Christians, they said, "should know how to recognize the hand of the Almighty in those events that from time to time put down the mighty from their thrones and raise up the humble, send away the rich empty-handed, and fill the hungry with good things" (para. 12).

In 1968, the fourth assembly of the WCC (Uppsala), receiving the report of the Geneva conference of 1966, authorized restructuring of some programmes. Coincidentally, 1968 was the year of the assassination of Martin Luther King, Jr — a reminder that revolutionary activity, even when committed to non-violent methods, may meet violence. The next year the WCC launched the Programme to Combat Racism,* one that led to controversies when it made grants for non-violent educational activities to organizations that in other activities might resort to violence (or counter-violence against existing violence).

In 1968, the Latin American bishops' conference (CELAM) at its historic second meeting in Medellín, Colombia, issued landmark statements on justice and peace.* It held that both liberal capitalism and the Marxist system "militate against the dignity of the human person". It called for political and economic reforms, for liberation from neo-colonialism. It affirmed that justice is a prerequisite for peace. It strongly urged non-violent change but pointed out the reality of "institutionalized violence" in existing systems.

The next decade saw an outpouring of "theologies of liberation", including Latin American (both Roman Catholic and Protestant), feminist, and black theologies. Although these include great variety in detail, all can be called revolutionary in the broad sense of the term.

The story is far from finished. The non-violent protests of Chinese students, crushed by government troops in 1989, evoked expressions of support in Chinese churches. The people's movements of Eastern Europe in 1989-90, predominantly non-violent, marked revolutionary protests against purportedly revolutionary entrenched governments. All signs are that the age of revolution is not ended.

Ecumenical theological-ethical issues. The theological appraisal of revolution is complex, because conflicting values are involved. The biblical tradition recognizes that some kind of government and order are essen-

Protest by farm labourers who have occupied land in Cusco, Peru (Salgado Jr)

tial to social life and well-being but does not sanctify every system of authority. The records of the exodus and the crucifixion are testimonies that governments can do criminal acts. Cries for justice often demand radical social change. But not every discontent with government is an occasion of revolution.

The first theological-ethical issue raised in most discussions is usually violence.* And all Christians can be reluctant to engage in violence. But the objection to violence involves, in many cases, a pseudo-argument. Since most people, including most Christians, justify violence on at least some occasions, even though with regret and restraint, the special rejection of revolutionary violence requires explanation. In situations of radical injustice, enforced by violence, it is hard to refute the argument that revolutionary violence is more justifiable than the institutional or systematic violence it opposes. The Russian Orthodox theologian Nicholas Berdyaev maintained that class war is an "irrefutable fact", that the greater violence is exercised by the privileged, that war may sometimes be "a good" — even though the church should seek to "spiritualize" the struggle.

But other theological-ethical issues remain.

Is revolution, in intention and action, truly aimed at justice? Some revolutions, like most coups d'état, are simply grabs for power. They substitute one oppressor for another. The proverbial statement — that revolutions devour their own children — provokes some hard thoughts. Even well-intentioned revolutionaries may, in the exercise of power and the fanaticism of struggle, betray their aims and become tyrants.

Does the revolution maximize the possibilities of non-violent action and restrain violence as far as possible? Just as the classic doctrine of just war* imposes restraints on violence, a doctrine of "just revolution" must do the same. In the heat of conflict, these restraints are often forgotten, but they remain ethical responsibilities. Guerrilla warfare, one characteristic form of revolutionary war, has special temptations. Juan Luis Segundo has pointed out that such war is especially destructive of what he calls the social ecology.

How does ideology* impinge on theology? In every social order, the privileged are likely to value the existing order and magnify the perils of change. The oppressed are likely to depreciate the order and magnify the benefits of change. Thus ideology influences theology and ethics. The Bible often says that the poor and humble are more likely to recognize reality than the rich and haughty. That is a help in correcting ideological bias. It does not of itself tell us that every proposed overthrow of the social order is good.

How does the revolutionary relate eschatology and ethics? Thomas Münzer, as noted above, virtually merged revolutionary ardour with apocalyptic expectations. Most contemporary Christians agree with CELAM's Medellín document that temporal progress and the kingdom of Christ are not the same. But they may also agree that the kingdom of Christ requires action for justice in the temporal sphere. Christians are called simultaneously to distinguish between their ultimate loyalty to God and their immediate political causes, yet to keep a lively relation between the two.

Only an idolatry of the status quo can discourage all revolution. Yet revolution can itself become an idol. The distinction between God and idols is a constant issue for the ecumenical church throughout its history and as far ahead as anyone can see.

See also **power, totalitarianism**.

ROGER L. SHINN

N. Berdyaev, *Christianity and Class War*, New York, Sheed & Ward, 1933 • C. Brinton, *The Anatomy of Revolution*, rev. ed., New York, Random, 1938 • M. E. Marty & D. Peerman eds, *New Theology No. 6: On Revolution and Non-Revolution, Violence and Non-Violence, Peace and Power*, New York, Macmillan, 1969 • Z.K. Matthews ed., *Responsible Government in a Revolutionary Age*, New York, Association Press, 1966 • J. Míguez Bonino, *Doing Theology in a Revolutionary Situation*, Philadelphia, Fortress, 1975 • Paul VI, *Populorum Progressio*, Tablet, 221, 1967 • R.L. Shinn, "Liberation, Reconciliation and 'Just Revolution'", *The Ecumenical Review*, 30, 4, 1978.

ROMAN CATHOLIC CHURCH.

Where one begins the history of the Roman Catholic Church (RCC) is itself a matter of theological judgment, fraught with serious ecumenical implications. Is Roman Catholicism (RC) a post-Reformation phenomenon, or is it the original form of the church?* Is "early Catholicism" to be found already in the New Testament, or is it an entirely post-biblical development? Catholic scholars, even those with a very liberal label, such as Hans

Küng, insist that Catholicism is present from the beginning, that the history of the RCC has its starting point within the NT rather than in the post-Reformation period.

If, indeed, one holds that RC is not simply a denomination within Christianity but its original expression, how does one deal with the historical fact that the earliest community of disciples gathered in Jerusalem, not in Rome? Indeed, the see, or diocese, of Rome did not even exist at the very beginning, nor did the Roman primacy.*

For many Catholics, the adjective "Roman" tends to obscure rather than define the reality of Catholicism. For them, the history of the Catholic church begins with Jesus' gathering of his disciples and with the eventual post-resurrection commissioning of Peter to be the chief shepherd and foundation of the church. Accordingly, it is not the *Roman* primacy that gives Catholicism its distinctive identity within the family of Christian churches but the *Petrine* primacy.

History. For the Catholic tradition, the classic primacy texts are Matt. 16:13-19, Luke 22:31-32 and John 21:15-19. Given their symbolism, the conferral of the power of the keys on Peter suggests an imposing measure of authority.* On the other hand, it is an authority that was not to be exercised in any absolute way, since from the beginning Peter is presented as consulting with the other apostles (see **apostolicity**) and even being sent by them (Acts 8:14), and he and John act almost as a team (Acts 3:1-11, 4:1-22, 8:14). Nevertheless, the biblical images concerning Peter (fisherman, shepherd, elder, proclaimer of faith in Jesus, rock) continued in the life of the church and were enriched by additional ones: missionary preacher, great visionary, destroyer of heretics, receiver of the new law, gatekeeper of heaven, helmsman of the ship of the church, co-teacher and co-martyr with Paul.

According to tradition Peter was martyred and buried in Rome, the centre of the empire and eventually the centre of the RCC. During the first five centuries the church of Rome gradually assumed pre-eminence among all the churches. It intervened in the life of distant churches, took sides in theological controversies, offered counsel to other bishops on doctrinal and pastoral questions and sent delegates to distant councils. The see of Rome came to be regarded as a kind of final court of appeal as well as a focus of unity* for the worldwide ("ecumenical") communion* of churches. The correlation between Peter and the bishop of Rome became fully explicit during the pontificate of Leo I (440-61), who claimed that Peter continued to speak to the whole church through the bishop of Rome.

In the view of some other Christian communities, the RCC has its origin in the Edict of Milan (in 312, also known as the Edict of Constantine), whereby the church, now free from persecution, came to enjoy the status of an imperially protected and favoured religion. Thus we have the term "Constantinian Catholicism".

By the beginning of the 5th century, German tribes began migrating through Europe without effective control. This movement has been called, somewhat inaccurately, the barbarian invasions. The movement was to last some 600 years. It changed the institutional character of Roman Catholicism from a largely Greco-Roman religion to a broader European religion. The influence of Germanic culture on Catholicism was especially pronounced in the areas of devotion, spirituality and organizational structure. Church office became more political than pastoral, and imagery for Christ, the church and its leaders became increasingly militaristic.

When, at the beginning of the 8th century, the Eastern emperor proved incapable of aiding the papacy against the Lombards in northern Italy, the pope turned for help to the Franks. This new alliance led to the creation of the holy Roman empire, climaxed in 800 with the crowning of Charlemagne. The line between church and state,* already blurred by the Edict of Milan, was now practically erased.

With the collapse of the Carolingian empire, however, the papacy fell into the hands of a corrupt Italian nobility. Only with the reformist pontificate of Gregory VII (1073-85) was the papacy's reputation restored. Papal prestige was even more firmly enhanced during the pontificate of Innocent III (1198-1216), who fully exploited the Gregorian teaching that the pope has supreme, even absolute, power over the whole church.

By the middle of the 13th century the classic papal-hierarchical concept of the church had been securely established, and the pope's power was said to embrace both church and state alike (the so-called two-swords theory). Newly elected popes were crowned like emperors, a practice that endured until suddenly discontinued by Pope John Paul I in 1978. Emphasis on the juridical, over against the communal, aspects of the church did not significantly subside, however, until the Second Vatican Council (1962-65).*

The historical bond between the church of Rome and the church of Constantinople came apart through a series of gravely unfortunate and exceedingly complex political and diplomatic manoeuvres, starting with the excommunication* of Michael Cerularius, patriarch of Constantinople in 1054, and culminating in the fourth crusade (1202-04) and the sack of Constantinople by Western knights. Two attempts at bringing the two sides back together — at the council of Lyons in 1274 and at the council of Florence in 1439 — did not have lasting results. Indeed, the climate began to change for the better only with the election of Pope John XXIII in 1958, with the Second Vatican Council and then with the historic pilgrimage of Pope Paul VI in 1964 to meet Ecumenical Patriarch Athenagoras in Jerusalem, the patriarch's home territory.

By the beginning of the 14th century other events had introduced a period of further disintegration of unity, reaching a tragic climax in the Protestant Reformation of the 16th century (see **Protestantism**). The confrontation between Boniface VIII and Philip the Fair over the latter's power to tax the church opened a wide breach between the papacy and the imperial authority. Then there were the scandalous financial abuses during the subsequent Babylonian Captivity of the papacy at Avignon, France (1309-78). There followed a rise in nationalism and anti-clericalism in reaction to papal taxes, and then papal authority itself came to be challenged on theological grounds by Marsilius of Padua and others. Conciliarism rose as a challenge to the prevailing monarchical concept of the church.

The Western schism* of 1378-1417 (not to be confused with the more serious and more enduring East-West schism between Rome and Constantinople) produced at one point three different claimants to the papal throne. The council of Constance (1414) turned to the new principle of conciliarism to bring the schism to an end, by asserting that a general council, not the pope, is the highest ecclesiastical authority. One claimant was deposed, a second resigned, and a third eventually died. Martin V was elected on St Martin's Day, 11 November 1417.

There were other, more immediate causes of the Reformation of the 16th century: the corruption of the Renaissance papacy of the 15th century, the divorce of piety from theology and of theology from its biblical and patristic roots, the negative effects of the Western schism and the rise of the national state — not to mention the powerful personalities of Luther, Calvin and Zwingli. The Reformation itself took different forms, so different in fact that one should perhaps speak more precisely of reformations in the plural. The reformers of the right (Lutherans and Anglicans) retained essential Catholic doctrine but changed certain canonical and structural forms. The reformers of the left (followers of Zwingli and the Anabaptists) repudiated much of Catholic doctrine and sacramental life. The reformers nearer to the centre (Calvinists) modified both Catholic doctrine and practice but retained much of the old.

The Roman Catholic response, belated but vigorous, was given at the council of Trent* (1545-63), which was itself part of a broader movement known as the Counter-Reformation, conducted principally under the leadership of Pope Paul III (1534-49). The council proved to be the single most important event in the history of the RCC from the time of the Reformation until the Second Vatican Council, a period of some four centuries. By and large, the post-Tridentine RCC emphasized those doctrines, devotions, and institutions that were most directly attacked by the Protestants: veneration of the saints,* Marian piety, eucharistic adoration, the authority of the pope and the bishops (see **episcopacy**) and the essential role of ordained priests in the sacramental life of the church (see **priesthood, sacraments**). Other important elements tended to be downplayed precisely because of their favourable emphasis by the Protestants: the centrality of Christ in theology and spirituality, the communal and participatory nature of the eucharist* ("priesthood of all believers") and the responsibility of the laity* in the life and mission* of the church.

Because of the Reformation, Catholic mis-

sionary activity was reduced in those countries where Protestantism began to flourish, but Catholicism was carried abroad by Spain and Portugal, who ruled the seas and who sought new gains for the church to offset losses throughout Europe. Religious orders such as the Dominicans, Franciscans and Jesuits were instrumental in bringing the Roman Catholic faith to India, China, Japan, Africa and the Americas. The Congregation for the Propagation of the Faith was established in 1622 to supervise all of these new missionary undertakings.

By the beginning of the 17th century the church faced another crisis from within. Jansenism, an Augustinian-inspired movement in France that emphasized the corruption of human nature, generated a new form of Catholic life that was excessively rigorous, even puritanical. When Rome moved against Jansenism, many in France saw Rome's action as a threat to the independence of French Catholicism. Gallicanism, by which this nationalistic reaction was to be known, held that all papal decrees are subject to the consent of the entire church, as represented in a general council. This view was later condemned by the First Vatican Council* (1869-70), which declared, against Gallicanism, that the infallible teachings of the pope are irreformable, that is, not subject to the subsequent consent and approval of any other ecclesiastical body or authority, including a national church.

In the 18th century it was the Enlightenment that offered the next challenge to the RCC. Exalting reason at the expense of authority and the natural at the expense of the supernatural, the Enlightenment touched RC primarily in the Catholic states of Germany, stimulating advances in historical and exegetical methods (see **exegesis, methods of**), combatting superstition, inspiring liturgical and catechetical reform and promoting popular education for clergy and laity alike. Although the Enlightenment did not influence Catholicism (so much of which flourished in southern Europe) as early or as profoundly as it did Protestantism, it did mark the beginning of the end of an unhistorical, classicist Roman Catholic theology.

The French revolution (1789) had a much more immediate and decisive impact on the RCC, bringing about the definitive end of medieval Catholicism. The feudal, hierarchical society of the middle ages was simply swept away. And so was Gallicanism, as the Enlightenment uprooted the clerical system upon which it had been based.

In France and Germany the Enlightenment produced a counter-reaction in the form of Romanticism, a movement that extolled RC as the mother of art and the guardian of patriotism. Thousands of European intellectuals returned to the church with new enthusiasm. With few exceptions (Cardinal Newman's work being a shining one), Roman Catholic theology at this time was restorative rather than progressive — restorative not of the biblical and patristic witnesses but of a scholasticism of a generally decadent kind. There developed in France a rigid traditionalism, the forerunner of the post-Vatican II movement led by the excommunicated Archbishop Marcel Lefebvre. The practitioners and partisans of traditionalist theology were said to look "beyond the mountains" (the Alps) to Rome for papal direction and support. Thus did the movement get the name Ultramontanism. The popes of these decades, Gregory XVI and Pius IX, were entirely sympathetic with this new reactionary trend, and nowhere was this papal defiance of modern developments more sharply stated than in the latter pope's *Syllabus of Errors* (1864).

The 19th century also witnessed the rapid development of industrialism and of concomitant social problems. Marxism provided one answer to the new challenge, taking advantage of the growing alienation of the workers not only from the fruits of their labour but also from their Roman Catholic heritage. The church's response, however belated, came in the form of an encyclical letter of Pope Leo XIII in 1891, *Rerum Novarum*, which defended the rights of workers to unionize, to receive a just wage and to work under humane conditions.

By the first years of the 20th century the RCC faced yet another major problem. A new ecclesiastical movement known as modernism proposed that dogmatic truths (see **dogma**) as well as truths contained in the Bible are neither absolute nor unchanging, but they are affected and shaped by historical conditions and circumstances. Pius XI condemned modernism in 1907. That action was to affect profoundly Catholic biblical and theological scholarship until just before the Second Vat-

ican Council. The anti-modernist spirit in the RCC intimidated particularly seminary faculties, but not even bishops were immune from unsympathetic scrutiny; one suspect was the future Pope John XXIII. Some of the positions that had once been denounced as modernist, however, were later embodied in the teachings of the Second Vatican Council and even in certain decrees of the Roman curia as they touched upon such controverted topics as the historical truth of sacred scripture and the development of dogma.

The period between the two world wars was especially important for RC if only because many of the developments occurring then were to find fruition at Vatican II: the liturgical movement,* the biblical movement, the social action movement, the lay apostolate movement, the missionary movement and, finally, the ecumenical movement. The last, however, had the most difficult path to follow, given the negative tone of Pope Pius XI's encyclical *Mortalium Animos* (1928) and assorted curial directives against any kind of participation by Catholics in ecumenical conferences. But even against this official resistance, pioneering Catholic theologians were ecumenically alive. For example, Yves Congar, OP, prepared the way for Vatican II's Decree on Ecumenism by his hundreds of lectures, articles and books, including his classic *Divided Christendom* (1937).

No other person or event more profoundly affected modern RC, however, than Pope John XXIII and the Second Vatican Council that he conceived and called. Given his own diplomatic and pastoral background in such countries as Bulgaria, Greece and Turkey, Angelo Roncalli entered the papacy in 1958, at age 78, as a man thoroughly prepared for, and completely committed to, the ecumenical apostolate, not only between Roman Catholicism and Protestantism but also between the churches of East and West. His first major encyclical was devoted to the problem of unity, *Ad Petri Cathedram* (1959), in which he greeted non-Catholics as "separated brethren".

In June 1960 John XXIII established the Secretariat for Promoting Christian Unity* and in December he received Archbishop Geoffrey Fisher of Canterbury. The next year he dispatched envoys to Istanbul to greet Ecumenical Patriarch Athenagoras, and he also exchanged greetings with Patriarch Alexis of Moscow. At the same time, the pope approved the sending of five official observers to the WCC assembly in New Delhi (1961). In addition, he removed words offensive to Jews from the Good Friday liturgy, and on one celebrated occasion he introduced himself to a group of visitors: "I am Joseph, your brother."

The Second Vatican Council that he called taught, in the Dogmatic Constitution on the Church and the Decree on Ecumenism,* that the church is the whole people of God* and that it includes non-Catholic Christians as well as Catholics, all united by a common baptism* and a common faith in Jesus Christ and his gospel. Christian unity, the Council declared, requires on the part of all sides renewal and reform, both institutional and spiritual. Indeed, the disintegration of Christian unity was a tragedy for which all involved parties must accept blame.

The Council's landmark Declaration on Religious Freedom declared that no one is to be forced in any way to embrace the Christian or the Catholic faith, and the Declaration on the Relationship of the Church to non-Christian Religions insisted that God speaks and works also through other religions. The church, therefore, should engage in dialogue and other collaborative efforts with them (see **dialogue, interfaith**). The Jews, finally, have a special relationship to the church, one that should not be soured by the false belief that the Jewish people bear blame for the death of Jesus.

Vatican II adjourned in December 1965. The history of the RCC since the council — through the pontificates of Paul VI (1963-78), John Paul I (1978) and John Paul II (1978-) — has been a story of the church's efforts to come to terms with the various challenges, opportunities and crises that the Council generated, directly or indirectly. The principal challenge remains the same as it has always been: how can the church be faithful to its historic identity and mission and at the same time adapt itself to each new social, political and cultural milieu?

Theology, doctrine and spirituality. As the name "catholic" itself suggests, the RCC is characterized in principle by a radical openness to all truth and to every authentic value (see **catholicity**). It is comprehensive and all-

St Peter's Square, Rome (Foto Felici)

embracing. It is not linked with any one culture, nation or region. It is as African as it is European, as Slavic as it is Latin, as Mexican as it is Irish, as Indian as it is Polish.

There is no list of "Catholic fathers" or "Catholic mothers" which does not include the great theological and spiritual writers of the period before as well as after the division of East and West and then the divisions within the West. Irenaeus and Gregory of Nyssa are as much Catholic fathers as are Augustine and Thomas Aquinas. Catholics continue to read Ignatius of Antioch and Clement of Alexandria, Athanasius and Cyril of Jerusalem, Gregory of Nazianzus and Augustine, Anselm of Canterbury and Bernard of Clairvaux, Abelard and Hugh of St Victor, Aquinas and Bonaventure, Robert Bellarmine and John Henry Newman, Karl Rahner and Hans Urs von Balthasar.

The RCC is open to *The Cloud of Unknowing* and the *Introduction to the Devout Life*, to the way of Francis of Assisi and of Bernard of Clairvaux, to Ignatius Loyola and John of the Cross, to Abbot Marmion and Thomas Merton. Catholics are guided by the council of Nicea* as by Vatican I,* by Chalcedon* as by Lateran IV, by Trent* as by Vatican II. They read Gregory the Great as well as Paul VI, Clement of Rome as well as Leo XIII, Pius XII as well as John XXIII.

The RCC is characterized by a both/and rather than an either/or approach. For the Roman Catholic tradition, it is not nature* or grace* but graced nature; not reason or faith* but reason illumined by faith; not law* or gospel but law inspired by the gospel; not scripture* or Tradition* but scripture as both the product and norm of Tradition; not faith or works but faith issuing in works and works as an expression of faith; not authority or freedom but authority in the service of freedom; not unity or diversity but unity in diversity. Holding this all together in a theologically creative tension are three central Roman Catholic principles: sacramentality, mediation and communion.

Sacramentality: In its classic (Augustinian) meaning, a sacrament* is a visible sign of an invisible grace. Pope Paul VI provided a more contemporary definition: "a reality imbued with the hidden presence of God". A sacramental perspective is one that "sees" the divine in the human, the infinite in the finite, the spiritual in the material, the transcendent in the immanent, the eternal in the historical. God is present to people, communities, movements, events, places, objects, the world at large, the whole cosmos. The visible, the tangible, the finite, the historical — all these are actual or potential carriers of the divine presence. Indeed, for the Roman Catholic it is only in and through these material realities that God can even be encountered. The great sacrament of encounter with God is Jesus Christ,* and the church is the sacrament of encounter with Christ.

For the Roman Catholic the world is essentially good, though fallen, because it comes from the creative hand of God (see **creation**) and continues to be sustained by God's providential presence (see **providence**). The world, though fallen, is redeemable because of the redemptive work of God in Jesus Christ (see **redemption**). The world, though fractured and fragmented, is capable of ultimate unity because of the abiding presence of the Holy Spirit.*

Over against this sacramental vision is the view, strengthened by memories of past excesses, that God is so "totally other" that the divine reality can never be identified with the human, the transcendent with the immanent, the eternal with the historical. The abiding Protestant fear is that Catholics take the sacramental principle to the point where they are just short of, if not actually immersed in, idolatry.

Mediation: A kind of corollary of the principle of sacramentality is the principle of mediation. A sacrament not only signifies; it also causes what it signifies. For the Catholic, God is not only present in the sacramental action, as an object of faith. God actually achieves something in and through that action (*ex opere operato*, the council of Trent taught). Thus, created realities not only embody the presence of God, they make that presence effective for others. The encounter with God is a mediated encounter.

Catholicism's commitment to the principle of mediation is evident, for example, in the importance it has always placed on the ministry of the ordained priest and on the intercessory role of the saints, especially of Mary, the mother of Jesus. Again, the Protestant raises a word of caution. Just as the principle of sacramentality edges close to the brink of idolatry, so the principle of mediation moves one along the path towards magic.

Communion: Finally, the RCC affirms the principle of communion:* our way to God, and God's way to us, is not only a mediated but a communal way. The encounter with God is a communal encounter. For the Christian it is an ecclesial encounter. The word is proclaimed by the church, and we respond within the church.

And that is why, for the RCC, the mystery of the church* has always had so significant a place in its theology, doctrine, pastoral practice, moral vision and devotional life. The church is the sacrament of Christ, mediating saving grace through sacraments and various ministries. It is the people of God* and the Body of Christ, an integral part of the communion of saints.* Indeed, it is here, at the point of RC's understanding of itself as church, that one comes to the heart of the distinctively Roman Catholic understanding and practice of Christian faith. For in ecclesiology we find the convergence of those three principles that have always been so characteristic of the RCC: sacramentality, mediation and communion.

The Protestant again raises a word of caution. If we emphasize too much the principle of communion, we run the risk of endangering the freedom of the individual. If sacramentality can lead to idolatry, and mediation to magic, the principle of communion can lead to a collectivism that suppresses individuality and an authoritarianism that suppresses freedom of thought.

But that, of course, is what the ecumenical encounter is all about. It is only through dialogue based on mutual respect that each tradition, including the Roman Catholic, can come to know itself better, purify itself of imperfections and distortions, and contribute finally to the fullness of unity for which Jesus prayed.

RICHARD P. McBRIEN

Y. Congar, *Chrétiens désunis* (ET *Divided Christendom: A Catholic Study of the Problem of Reunion*, London, Geoffrey Bles, 1939) • Y. Congar, *Neuf cents ans après* (ET *After Nine Hundred Years: The Background of the Schism between the Eastern and Western Churches*, New York, Fordham UP, 1959) • L.S. Cunningham, *The Catholic Faith*, New York, Paulist, 1987 • F. Cwiekowski, *The Beginnings of the Church*, New York, Paulist, 1988 • L. Gilkey, *Catholicism Confronts Modernity: A Protestant View*, New York, Seabury, 1975 • H. Küng, *Strukturen der Kirche* (ET *Structures of the Church*, New York, Crossroad, 1982) • G.A. Lindbeck, *The Future of Roman Catholic Theology*, Philadelphia, Fortress, 1970 • H. de Lubac, *Catholicisme: Les aspects sociaux du dogme* (ET *Catholicism: A Study of the Corporate Destiny of Mankind*, New York, Sheed & Ward, 1958) • R.P. McBrien, *Catholicism*, San Francisco, Harper & Row, 1981.

ROMAN CATHOLIC CHURCH AND PRE-VATICAN II ECUMENISM.

The organizers of the 1910 Edinburgh world missionary conference (see **ecumenical conferences**) had intentionally not invited the Roman Catholic Church (RCC) and the Orthodox. But the commission of the Protestant Episcopal Church in the USA, which initiated the efforts to bring about a conference on Faith and Order* questions for "all Christian communions throughout the world which confess our Lord Jesus Christ as God and Saviour", invited the holy see. In December 1914 Cardinal Gasparri, the secretary of state to Pope Benedict XV (ruled 1914-22), answered with neither a final acceptance nor a rejection of the invitation. But after the first world war, the same pope met a delegation of the same US commission (May 1919) and told it that because of the RCC understanding of "the unity of the visible church of Christ", the RCC could not take part in such a congress. The pope promised his prayers that, "if the congress is practicable, the participants may, by God's grace, see the light and become re-united to the visible head of the church, by whom they would be received with open arms". In 1921 Benedict XV also declined an invitation to the first conference on Life and Work.*

The 1917 Roman Catholic (RC) code of canon law forbade "Catholics from holding disputations or meetings, especially public ones, with non-Catholics, except with permission of the apostolic see or in urgent cases, with the local ordinary" (canon 1325). Shortly after the first Faith and Order conference (Lausanne 1927), Pius XI (ruled 1922-39) promulgated *Mortalium Animos*, on "fostering the religious union". By "participation in assemblies of non-Catholics", both RCs and others would easily have confirmed that one religion or church is as good as another, that ecumenical gatherings were negotiations of revealed truths through compromise, and that the RCC would be tacitly accepting some of the Protestant ecclesiologies of the day. The very foundations of the Catholic faith would be "subverted by the desire of other Christians to treat the Catholic church as one among many churches". Therefore, if Catholics were allowed to give encouragement or support to such gatherings, "they would be countenancing a false Christian religion quite alien to the one true church of Christ". The pope concluded: "There is only one way in which the unity of Christians may be fostered, and that is by promoting the return to the one true church of Christ of those who are separated from it; for from that one true church they have in the past unhappily fallen away."

For the RCC, the reunion of all Christians was one-way — the return of those who were not already RC to the RCC, because it believed it was co-extensive with the one church of Christ and would compromise witness to this self-understanding by mixing with others who were not clear on what the ecumenical movement was, or where it was to move.

The shift in RC evaluation and policy began in the 1950s. The holy office letter *Ecclesia Sancta* (20 December 1949) positively evaluated the ecumenical movement "among those who are dissident from the Catholic church" and "believe in Christ the Lord" as derived from the inspiration of the Holy Spirit,* and thus "for the children of the true church a source of holy joy in the Lord". Other Christians do care deeply for church unity,* and RCs must take their efforts seriously, in charity and in prayer. And under strict conditions, RC experts, approved by the hierarchy, can participate in discussions "on faith and morals" with other Christians, but all religious indifferentism should be avoided. Even though the RCC then stood firmly in its ecclesiology of "return", it now accepted the idea of a dialogue-in-fellowship.

The WCC Toronto statement* in 1950, aided in its formulations by a small group of RC theologians, recognized that membership "does not imply a specific doctrine concerning the nature of church unity" or that "each church must regard the other member churches as churches in the true or full sense of the word". This clarification made easier RC unofficial contacts with the WCC.

In 1952 was held the first annual meeting of the Catholic Conference for Ecumenical Questions,* with the Dutchman Johannes Willebrands as secretary. The conference, which lasted until 1969, enlisted the interest of European Catholic theologians, historians, biblicists, liturgists and missiologists in taking seriously Protestant and Orthodox ecumenical efforts, especially WCC Faith and Order issues. W.A. Visser 't Hooft, WCC general secretary, met frequently with Willebrands, and the latter reported in Rome annually to Pius XII's designated contact person, the Jesuit Augustin Bea. Many in this unique fraternity later were drafters of Vatican II documents, e.g. Yves Congar, Charles Moeller, Gustave Thils, Edward Stakemeier and Karl Rahner. And John XXIII in 1960 appointed Bea and Willebrands as the president and the secretary of his newly created Secretariat for Promoting Christian Unity.*

See also **encyclicals, Roman Catholic**.

TOM STRANSKY

ROMERO Y GALDAMES, OSCAR ARNULFO. B. 15.8.1917, Ciudad Barrios, El Salvador; d. 24.3.1980, San Salvador. As archbishop of his nation, Romero fearlessly condemned the violent activities of government armed forces, right-wing groups, and leftist guerrillas involved in El Salvador's intense civil conflict. A champion of the poor and a strong advocate of human rights,* he was nominated for the 1979 Nobel peace prize by a number of US congressmen and many members of the British parliament. He courageously denounced the regime of the dictator General Carlos Humberto Romero (no relation) and the brutal activities of the national guard, and refused to support the military-civilian junta that replaced the deposed dictator. There were repeated threats to his life. In February 1980 a bomb destroyed the archdiocese's radio station. Before his assassination at the hands of an unknown assailant, Romero had declared: "I am prepared to offer my blood for the redemption and resurrection of El Salvador. If God accepts the sacrifice, I hope it will be a seed of liberty and a sign of hope." Works published posthumously include *Assassiné avec les pauvres* (Paris, Cerf, 1981) and *The Church Is All of You* (Minneapolis, Winston, 1984). See

J.R. Brockman, *The Word Remains: A Life of Oscar Romero* (Maryknoll, NY, Orbis, 1983).

ANS J. VAN DER BENT

RURAL AGRICULTURAL MISSION.

The concern of the churches and missionary agencies for rural societies, leading to their separate and diverse activities on behalf of those societies, came particularly on the ecumenical agenda at the fourth assembly of the WCC in Uppsala (1968). At that assembly the concern was given an ecumenical dimension in view of the rapid social and economic changes which were adversely affecting rural communities. Consequently, the Division on World Mission and Evangelism (DWME) was asked to "consider ways in which the member churches and councils can be assisted in mission to the world's rapidly changing rural societies".

Following extended discussions between DWME (particularly the Urban Industrial Mission office) and the WCC's Commission on the Churches' Participation in Development, an office for Rural Agricultural Mission (RAM) was established within DWME in 1973.

RAM's mandate was "to stimulate member churches to pay particular attention to rural areas; to facilitate ecumenical co-operation in the prosecution of rural mission; to encourage regional/local groups that will be responsible for training animators; to encourage churches to re-examine and re-construct their lay and ministerial training schemes and programmes with a proper orientation towards rural mission; and to select one or two places for an experiment in intensive integrated rural mission". The RAM office had close relations with Agricultural Missions, Inc. (which sponsored the RAM staff position), of the National Council of the Churches of Christ in the USA, and with the Vatican's permanent representative to the Food and Agriculture Organization in Rome.

The renewed emphasis (articulated by the Urban Industrial Mission [UIM] advisory group in Kyoto in 1970) on the "urban-rural nexus" was singled out for special attention. "Rural" was taken to include not just peasants but "all those human communities that are separated from centres of urban power; it includes fishermen, mining communities, landless farm labourers and others".

The 1973 Bangkok conference on world mission and evangelism saw urban and rural as a joint enterprise. It was agreed that UIM's known style of operation — attempting to respond to local initiatives — provided a useful basis for work with rural communities. Therefore in 1978 RAM merged with UIM to become the Urban Rural Mission office.

See also **urban industrial mission, urban rural mission**.

KENITH A. DAVID

RUSTENBURG DECLARATION.

The Rustenburg Declaration emerged from a consultation of churches in November 1990. The most representative such event in South African history, the conference was attended by representatives of the African Independent Churches, evangelical churches, the Gereformeerde Kerk, the Nederduitse Gereformeerde Kerk (NGK), the Roman Catholic Church, member churches of the South African Council of Churches, and observers from the WCC and other ecumenical partners. The Nederduitsche Hervormde Kerk and Afrikaanse Protestante Kerk, which broke away from the NGK in 1986, declined an invitation to attend.

At the heart of the declaration stands a confession of guilt, acknowledging the different ways in which different churches have legitimated and supported apartheid. It rejects the theological support of apartheid as a heresy and sin, and calls for concrete forms of restitution.

Facing pressure from the various constituencies represented, a key sentence of the declaration reads: "Some of us are not in full accord with everything said in this conference, but on this we are all agreed, namely the unequivocal rejection of apartheid as sin." A press statement after the conference by the moderator of the NGK re-affirmed this church's confession of guilt, while disassociating it from some aspects of the declaration. The Rustenburg Declaration has brought the churches in South Africa into a closer relationship than ever before. Full ecumenical unity has, however, not yet emerged. "We have started a process," said SACC general secretary Frank Chikane. "I only hope the NGK will be able to move ahead with us. Time will tell whether they can."

CHARLES VILLA-VICENCIO

SACRAMENT(S). Differences over the understanding and practice of sacraments can be the cause, symptom or result of some of the deepest and most stubborn divisions among churches. Knowledge of centuries-long developments in conceptuality and religious sensibilities will help to clarify persistent difficulties encountered in ecumenical dialogue concerning sacraments.

Almost all the various Christian churches know a number of sacramental rites which represent the continued work of the Saviour in his church.* "Sacrament" is the name given to actions by which believers receive a share in the salvation* effected by God in Christ. Each of these actions (see the individual sacraments) has some substantive basis in the biblical revelation, although in the Bible they are not covered by any generic term. This happens only much later.

Christendom managed for a whole millennium without a general doctrine of the sacraments, even if the foundations for such a doctrine were laid in the patristic period. As is made sufficiently clear by the New Testament accounts relating to baptism* and the Lord's supper (see **eucharist**), but also to the laying on of hands, anointing with oil and the giving of the Spirit, this does not mean there were no sacraments in the earliest church.

There are divergences of opinion on the development of sacramental thinking in the early church. Jewish and Hellenistic influences certainly cannot be excluded. Bap-

tism and the Lord's supper, as Paul shows in 1 Cor. 10:1-22, were already given parallel status in the primitive church as saving events, against the background of the Old Testament mediations of salvation. And Rudolf Schnackenburg sees the emergence of "sacramental" ideas, not uninfluenced by Hellenistic modes of thought, in the conception that eternal salvation and life were mediated by a material element and word (cf. Eph. 5:26) and by earthly gifts bestowed by the Lord (John 6:53-58), and that in these rites the mystery of a regeneration (Titus 3:5; 1 Pet. 1:23, 2:2; John 3:3-8), a sanctification (Heb. 12:9-11) and permanent union with the Lord (John 6:56-57) took place (Schnackenburg, "Sakrament", in *Lexikon für Theologie und Kirche*, 1964).

Subsequently such saving rites were given the general description of "sacred actions". Generally baptism and the Lord's supper were acknowledged as being of outstanding importance, and baptism also included chrismation* or confirmation.* Nevertheless, individual churches laid different emphases on the value they attached to the other so-called sacred actions.

God's saving work in the sacred actions is directed through the church to believers. God's saving power makes use of specific material elements such as water, oil, the altar, church buildings. As the means of salvation have been entrusted by Christ to the church, they are normally administered by church functionaries specially authorized to do so. This authorization in many churches rests on a corresponding ordination,* which then likewise counts as one of the sacred actions.

In view of the mysterious working of God's grace,* the sacred actions have been described as *mystēria*. In the LXX *mystērion* simply means something hidden and refers neither to the Greek mystery religions nor to any rite. In the NT, *mystērion* is used for God's eschatological purpose, now revealed in Christ, and stretching beyond Israel to include the nations (Mark 4:11; Rom. 11:25, 16:25-27; Col. 1:25-27, 2:2-3, 4:3; Eph. 1:9-10, 3:1-12, 6:19; Rev. 10:7). The apostolic ministry is to be "servants of Christ and stewards of the mysteries of God" (1 Cor. 4:1).

From the standpoint of the Greek church fathers, each *mystērion* is a reflection of the prototype; it is an *antitypon*. "This is called a mystery because we look at one thing and believe another" (John Chrysostom, *Homilies on 1 Cor.*, 7.1). In Neo-platonic thinking, which left its imprint very clearly on early Christianity and still affects the Eastern churches today, the *mystēria* represent a link between Creator and creatures, between the prototype and the antitype, the former being mysteriously present in the latter and effective in it. The *mystēria* are therefore symbols which efficaciously represent realities.

As Tertullian translated the term *mystērion* by *sacramentum*, the Western interpretation subsequently changed considerably. *Sacramentum* actually meant not only an act of consecration but also the oath taken by soldiers and confirmed by an outward sign. In the Latin regions, instead of the symbolic and representational character intrinsic to the word *mystērion*, what now came into prominence was the "sacrament" as a *sign*.

It was above all Augustine who placed emphasis on the sacrament as a visible sign. "A sign is a thing which, over and above the impression it makes on the senses, causes something else to come into the mind as a consequence of itself" (*On Christian Doctrine* 2.1). For this reason the invisible God too has in the course of salvation history* revealed himself constantly to human beings by means of signs (visible *significationes*), and these visible signs *(signa)* point to an invisible divine reality *(res)* to which they bear a resemblance. "Signs... are called sacraments when they are applied to divine things" (*Letters* 138). But as the visible sign does not have a saving effect without being linked to the word of God,* Augustine stated that "the word is added to the element, and there results the sacrament as if itself also a kind of visible word" (*Homilies on the Gospel of John* 80.3).

Although he too was still quite attached to Neo-platonic ideas, the shift of emphasis from mystery to sign, which began in Tertullian, has already acquired its theoretical basis with Augustine. But into the second millennium the Western church continued to use *sacramentum* in the two senses of "sacred sign" and "mystery". Likewise there was still no rigorous restriction of the term to "the seven sacraments" listed by the council of Lyons in 1274. So long as the Neo-platonic idea of prototype and antitype was followed, it was clear that the former was present in the latter. When, however, in the West from the 9th century onwards, the old Latin idea established itself of a pictorial representation which regarded the antitype as no more than a *similitudo*, something with a similarity to the prototype, then the question began to be more and more pointedly raised how the real presence of Christ was to be explained. Thus the issue of *causality* was raised.

To the extent that the emphasis in the West was definitively shifted in early scholasticism to the *sign*, the *mystery* forfeited importance, and the Eastern and Western views of the sacrament began to diverge. In the West, the view of Berengarius of Tours (d.1088) was that Christ was represented in the eucharist "only symbolically", and it may in fact have been the need to respond to this heretical view that prompted the development of a *doctrine of the sacraments*.

The decisive definitions were already provided by Hugh of St Victor and Peter Lombard. Hugh of St Victor (d.1141) proceeded from the natural symbolism of a corporeal reality which, when dispensed by a recognized officiant, becomes a sign of grace on the basis of an institution by Christ (which for the 12th century as yet raised no problems). The defect of this definition lay in the fact that not all sacraments contain a material sign. Peter Lombard (d.1160) therefore stated that the specific character of a sacrament lay in its efficacy (causality), thus paving the way for a new shift of emphasis away from the sign and on to the nature of sacramental efficacy. "For that is properly called a sacrament which is a sign of the grace of God and a form of invisible grace, so that it bears its image and works as its cause" (*Sentences* 4.1.2). It was Lombard who fixed the number of the sacraments as seven (which is the usual number in the Roman Catholic Church).

Then came the distinction between the action of the officiant *(opus operantis)* and the action accomplished *(opus operatum)*. The sacrament is a work of God's, not of the officiant's, and it therefore causes grace by the work performed *(ex opere operato)*. But this conclusion does not leave out of account the subjective frame of mind of the officiant and the recipient. If someone does not intend to administer a sacrament or to receive one, then no sacrament is administered and received!

To the second half of the 12th century belongs also the formulation of the doctrine of sacramental character. Already in William of Auxerre (d.1231 or 1237) there is a hint of the view that baptism, chrismation (confirmation) and holy orders give the soul an ineradicable character by which those so marked out are united for ever with God or Christ and are distinguished from those who do not possess this character.

The appropriation of Aristotelian thought by the high middle ages also continued to affect the further development of the doctrine of the sacraments. From the 13th century onwards the outward sign of the sacrament is defined by the concepts of "matter" and "form". And at the same time a clear description is now provided for causality in the sacramental event.

Thomas Aquinas (1225-74) classifies the sacraments as sacred signs. He thinks human beings, as spiritual and corporeal creatures, can attain to knowledge of supersensory things only through those that are sensory (*Summa theologiae* 3.60.4). Because of their ambiguity the sensory objects have to be more closely defined by the word — more precisely, by God's word — because the sacraments are for the sanctification* of human beings, and God alone disposes over sanctification and therefore also over the means of sanctification. And this is where the Aristotelian distinction between matter and form comes into play. "In the sacraments the words are as

the form, and sensible things are as the matter. Now in all things composed of matter and form, the determining principle is on the part of the form which is as it were the end and terminus of the matter" (*ibid*. 3.60.7). According to Aquinas, therefore, the word (which is an interpretative sign) has precedence over the visible element in terms of significance. For Aquinas the sacraments are not only vessels of salvation but instruments of grace in the hand of God, and they have an effect independently of the worthiness of the officiant or of the recipient. "The sacraments of the new law are both cause and signs; hence, too, is it that, to use the common expression, *they effect what they signify*" (*ibid*. 62.1.1).

In the Reformation the development that began when scholasticism was at its zenith is taken to its strictly logical conclusions by consistent absolutizing of the significance of the word (i.e. the word of God). For Luther the sacrament was already closely linked with the word of God, but on the basis that the same effect properly belonged to the sacrament as to the word proclaimed in preaching. Both were vehicles of grace leading to the forgiveness of sins, the indwelling of Christ and finally eternal life.

Luther considered not the nature of the sacraments as such but the way they related to believers. So there are three elements which for Luther constitute a sacrament: God's word of promise, the sacramental sign, and faith.* Since such a word of promise from God can be directly derived from holy scripture only in the case of baptism, the Lord's supper and penance, Luther finally accepted only two sacraments, the Lord's supper and baptism (to which he subordinated penance as its renewal). Luther derived the efficacy of the sacraments from the divine word of promise. For him the sacraments are indeed genuine means of grace, but the sacramental sign can never lead to faith or salvation without the word of promise. The real object of faith is not the sign but the word of promise, for which reason the importance of the sacramental sign diminishes.

This tendency can be seen even more markedly in Zwingli and Calvin, because in their view God's effective work of salvation becomes accessible only through preaching. For Zwingli the sacraments have meaning only as

Worship in Orthodox church, Fuhaila, Syria (WCC/Peter Williams)

symbols relating to Christ and the saving events of the past, and they are of service to believers as a memorial action or a public confession in the community. Accordingly they depict but do not bestow salvation (see F. Blanke, "Zwinglis Sakramentsanschauung", *Theologische Blätter*, 1931).

Calvin occupies an intermediate position between Luther and Zwingli. For him the sacrament is "a testimony of divine grace towards us, confirmed by an outward sign, with mutual attestation of our piety towards God" (*Institutes* 4.14.1). The sacramental signs receive a new definition and meaning through the word of God without becoming the vehicles of a spiritual power. They are only a concession by God to human nature, which depends on the senses, a figurative expression of the divine promise; in this way they undergird faith.

The council of Trent* reacted in 1547 with 13 canons which were directed primarily against Luther. Canon 1 postulated seven as the number of sacraments. Relatively often the view is taken today in Roman Catholicism that the number seven does not relate to something fixed in numerical terms but is to be understood as pointing to the completeness of

all the means of salvation taken together. It is striking that none of the other Christian churches agrees completely as to the number of the sacraments, apart from baptism and the Lord's supper. In canon 2 Trent admitted that there is an order of precedence among the sacraments. Originally all the sacraments flowed into the central event of the eucharist and were therefore also administered within its context.

New approaches to a theology of the sacraments do not appear till around the middle of the 20th century. With the Second Vatican Council* the ecclesial dimension of the sacraments was again brought into the foreground in the Roman Catholic Church, as opposed to the more individualistic and seemingly "objectifying" view of them. This we owe to theologians like Henri de Lubac, Otto Semmelroth, Edward Schillebeeckx and Karl Rahner. In the dogmatic constitution *Lumen Gentium* we read that "the church, in Christ, is in the nature of sacrament — a sign and instrument, that is, of communion with God and of unity among humankind" (*LG* 1). From the Christ-church relationship Rahner drew the conclusion that there is also a church-sacrament relationship. By founding the church, Christ established a primal or basic sacrament and so also its actualization in the seven sacraments. For wherever the church meets human beings in a specific salvation situation, it actualizes the appropriate sacrament of the seven.

Protestant theologians express reservations about a view of the church as the primal sacrament. For Eberhard Jüngel, Christ himself is the sacrament of the church, and baptism and the Lord's supper are the two ways of celebrating this sacrament (see Jüngel & Rahner). In both Roman Catholicism and Protestantism there is now a quest for new approaches aided by an interpretation in terms of salvation history and by anthropological and semiotic criteria.

Generalizing, we may give the following description of the differences between the major Christian confessions as to their view on the sacraments — differences originating in the Western departure from the idea of *mystērion*:

First, following the tradition of the ancient church, the Orthodox and Oriental churches stress the mysterious saving action of God in the sacred actions, which they describe as *mystēria*.

Second, in the sacraments, the Roman Catholic Church emphasizes seven means of salvation which are efficacious as signs, but it regards the church as the primal sacrament.

Third, the Protestant churches (which have no uniform concept of the sacraments) place the accent instead on the divine word of promise and limit the sacraments to baptism and the Lord's supper, understood in different ways as symbolic actions.

Some of these characteristic differences continue to be manifested in the churches' responses to the Lima text *(Baptism, Eucharist and Ministry*)*. Several Orthodox responses, for example, find the use of the term "sign" inadequate in connection with the sacraments, understanding it as a "pointer" to something external rather than as embodying the reality itself. Or again, many Protestant responses reject any mediatory role for the church in the communication of divine grace to believers. In its 1990 report on the churches' responses to BEM, however, the Faith and Order commission offers a clarification that takes up positive suggestions from the churches and that sets "sacra-

ment" within a context that is fully Trinitarian, Christological, anthropological, soteriological and eschatological:

"In the incarnation, life, death and resurrection of Jesus Christ, God has communicated effectively the mystery of his saving love to the world. Through the power of the Holy Spirit, the risen Christ continues this saving action of God by being present and active in our midst. ѓor this purpose God continues to act through human persons, through their words, signs and actions, together with elements of creation. Thus God communicates to the faithful, and through their witness to the world, his saving promise and grace. Those who receive in faith and trust this gracious action of God are thereby liberated from their captivity to sin and transformed in their lives. Those who receive this gift respond to it in thanksgiving and praise and are brought into a koinonia with the Holy Trinity and with each other and are sent to proclaim the gospel to the whole world. Through this divine action, communicated through words, signs and actions, this community, the church, is called, equipped and sent, empowered and guided by the Holy Spirit to witness to God's reconciling and re-creating love in a broken world. And so all who in faith long for fullness of life in Christ may experience the first-fruits of God's kingdom — present and yet to be fully accomplished in a new heaven and earth" *(Baptism, Eucharist and Ministry 1982-1990*, 143f.).

ROBERT HOTZ

W. Beinert, "Die Sakramentalität der Kirche im theologischen Gespräch", in *Kirche und Sakrament*, J. Pfammatter & F. Furger eds, Zurich, Benziger, 1980 ● L.-M. Chauvet, *Symboles et sacrement: Une relecture de l'existence chrétienne*, Paris, Cerf, 1987 ● N. Clark, *An Approach to the Theology of the Sacraments*, London, SCM, 1956 ● R. Hotz, *Sakramente im Wechselspiel zwischen Ost und West*, Zurich, Benziger, 1979 ● E. Jüngel & K. Rahner, *Was ist ein Sakrament?*, Freiburg im Breisgau, Herder, 1971 ● E. Schillebeeckx, *Christ and the Sacrament of Encounter with God*, London, Sheed & Ward, 1963 ● E. Schillebeeckx & B. Willems eds, *The Sacraments in General*, New York, Paulist, 1968 ● G. Wainwright, "Word and Sacrament in the Churches' Responses to the Lima Text", *One in Christ*, 24, 1988 ● G. Wenz, *Einführung in die evangelische Sakramentenlehre*, Darmstadt, Wissenschaftliche Buchgesellschaft, 1988 ● J.F. White, *Sacraments as God's Self Giving*, Nashville, TN, Abingdon, 1983.

SAINTS. At the beginning of his epistle to the Romans, Paul wrote: "To all God's beloved in Rome, who are called to be saints: Grace to you and peace from God our Father and the Lord Jesus Christ" (1:7). This is a particular name given to the members of the first Christian communities (e.g. Eph. 1:1). It may signify the Christians who constitute the "church of God" in a particular place (2 Cor. 1:1; Heb. 13:24-25; Col. 1:2). It may signify the whole Christian people (Eph. 1:1; 1 Cor. 1:2). Its most frequent equivalent is "brothers", as in Col. 1:2: "To the saints and faithful brethren in Christ at Colossae" (cf. Phil. 4:21-22). Saints form a new community coming both from the Jewish community in Jerusalem (Acts 9:13; Rom. 15:25) and from gentile Christianity (Rom. 1:7). The apostle is one of them: "To me, though I am the very least of all the saints" (Eph. 3:8). Later, they were called Christians (Acts 11:26).

Saints and the mystery of the church. The notion of saints should be seen as part of the mystery of the church,* "those sanctified [i.e. the holy people] in Christ Jesus" (1 Cor. 1:2), the people of the New Testament. It includes certain basic affirmations.

"One only is holy, One only is the Lord, Jesus Christ, to the glory of God the Father." This is a very ancient liturgical exclamation which echoes the hymn of the Lamb (Rev. 15:3-4), acclaimed as Kyrios (Eph. 4:5; Phil. 2:11) and as "the Holy One of God" (John 6:69; cf. Luke 4:34). Jesus Christ* is holy both as the Son of God and as bearer of the Spirit when at the baptism the Holy Spirit* descended on him (Luke 3:22). It is with this authority and power that he destroyed the unclean spirits (Luke 4:33-37). The Christians "have been anointed by the Holy One" (1 John 2:20), being called to become "a temple of the Holy Spirit" (1 Cor. 6:19). The identity itself of the saint is to be bearer of the Spirit.

The faithful are called saints because of their participation in the holiness of God, who is holy by his own nature (Isa. 6:3). Christians are saints in God's holiness (1 Pet. 1:15), in Christ (Phil. 4:21). They are "God's chosen ones, holy [or saints]" (Col. 3:12). One aspect of the mystery of the church is this new consecration in Christ of a "kingdom of priests", "consecrated nation", "royal priesthood" (Ex. 19:6; Isa. 43:20-21; 1 Pet. 2:9) which is not exclusive or restricted. An essen-

tial criterion of the new people is: "You are no longer strangers and sojourners, but you are fellow citizens with the saints and members of the household of God, built upon the foundation of the apostles and prophets, Christ Jesus himself being the main cornerstone" (Eph. 2:19-20).

It is part of the mystery of the church to be the manifestation of God's glory and holiness: "[God] has blessed us in Christ with every spiritual blessing in the heavenly places, even as he chose us in him before the foundation of the world, that we should be holy and blameless before him" (Eph. 1:3-4). He presents to himself a glorious church "without spot or wrinkle or any such thing, that she might be holy and without blemish" (Eph. 5:27). Christ sacrificed himself for her to make her holy (Eph. 5:25). Christ made the church his body, in spite of the sin* of its members. Hence, the church must always be in a state of renewal, of repentance.

Scripture refers also to the communion* of saints, the friends and fellow heirs of Christ (see Eph. 4:1-6), the "inheritance among all those who are sanctified" (Acts 20:32). He will come "to be glorified in his saints, and to be marvelled at in all who have believed" (2 Thess. 1:10). The kingdom of God* is promised to them and includes "the riches of his glorious inheritance in the saints" (Eph. 1:18). The book of Revelation recalls those who, having finished their earthly pilgrimage, enjoy God's presence in the heavenly city (Rev. 7:9-17). "To be 'in Christ' is to be in his body, a member of a fellowship which transforms the local neighbourhood, which overleaps boundaries of nation and race and whose own boundaries are lost to sight in the infinite horizons of the eternal communion of saints" (Oliver Tomkins, *Youth in the World-Church*, 1947).

Belonging to a community is a sign of the new condition (see 1 John 2:19). Conversion* means, then, "to share in the inheritance of the saints in light" (Col. 1:12). It implies equally "the service of the saints" (1 Cor. 16:15).

As a holy people, the church has the capacity to discern, to sort out, to reveal the light that "darkness has not overcome" (John 1:5). The church of God received the power to bind and to loose (see John 20:23) and the power to judge (1 Cor. 6:2).

The vocation of saints. Saints' vocation* is to hallow the name of God: "The name of God is in its own nature holy, whether we say so or not; but since it is sometimes profaned among sinners, according to the words, 'through you, my name is continually blasphemed among the Gentiles' (Rom. 4:24), we pray that in us God's name may be hallowed; not that it becomes holy from not being holy, but because it becomes holy in us, when we become holy; and do things worthy of holiness" (Cyril of Jerusalem, *Mystagogical Catechesis* 5.12).

"You shall be holy, for I am holy" (1 Pet. 1:16). This verse teaches that the saints have their own way of life, a distinctive spirituality — a radical orientation of life, not in a legalistic sense, but in an incarnational sense: "Put on the new nature, created after the likeness of God in true righteousness and holiness" (Eph. 4:24). The emphasis is here on the cleansing of the inside so that the outside may also be clean (Matt. 23:26).

The life of a saint is the most valid exposition of Christ himself. The disciples can speak of "Christ who lives in me" (Gal. 2:20) or of Christ "speaking in me" (2 Cor. 13:3). In fact, the saints gain later the special connotation of those who reflect the likeness of Christ (2 Cor. 3:18), who have "become partakers of the divine nature" (2 Pet. 1:4), and who develop into "mature manhood, to the measure of the stature of the fullness of Christ" (Eph. 4:13).

In the saints' experience, Christ comes to offer the gifts of his kingdom, and they themselves become the first-fruits of it. "I chose you and appointed you that you should go and bear fruit and that your fruit should abide" (John 15:16). The saints worship God by offering their living bodies as a holy sacrifice (Rom. 12:1). In fact, the discipline of the saint implies a continuous ascetic combat. The struggle of the saint is primarily not to lose sight of Jesus, who leads us into our faith and brings it to perfection (Heb. 12:2).

Saints and the ecumenical community. The theme of saints has its own value for ecumenical concerns. For ecumenical spirituality, e.g., one cannot separate or confuse sanctification and social transformation. Those who are more active socially do not have the right to exclude those who place a special emphasis on conversion, renewal, holiness — and vice versa. Both disciplines should be experienced and preserved in their distinctiveness. Therefore "[let] the righteous still do right, and the holy still be holy" (Rev. 22:11).

The theme of saints is also essential in order to keep the search for visible unity* deeply rooted in the life of prayer, of mutual intercession among the churches. The practice of continued intercession for one another, and for *all* the churches, keeps before every Christian something of the catholicity* of the church of Christ. It enables the churches to see one another not with the eyes of confessional appraisal and historical assessment but as joint petitioners before the throne of God. It opens one not only to give but also to receive within the fellowship of prayer and service.

In the ecumenical community, the churches bring their particularities of life, worship and witness. From the "saints" tradition, we learn about the extraordinary power of the Christian life ("holiness as witness"), for the proclamation of the gospel. The churches have arrived at a more active appreciation of what we might call the common priesthood of all the baptized (see 1 Pet. 3:15; Rev. 1:6, 5:9-10), of the gifts of grace, vocations and ministries found in the communities; they devise new life-styles which commend the gospel in today's world; they have reconsidered the *lives of saints, martyrs and mystics* as real spiritual nourishment for the communities.

It is highly important for today's ecumenical spirituality and liturgical renewal to recognize the saints as encouraging examples on the pilgrim journey and as symbols of the church universal: "Confessing the apostolic creed in our worship, we affirm our belief in the community of saints. Thus we are reminded that we live together with the martyrs of all times. Christians who give their lives for the sake of the kingdom are martyrs. We remember them in our worship as encouraging examples. They are symbols of the total church. They give us inspiration as to how 'worship and work must be one'. We have learned that the unity between worship and daily Christian life needs urgently to be recovered" (*Gathered for Life*, 1983). Commemoration of all saints and martyrs of the church universal is observed on the first Sunday after Pentecost in the Orthodox churches and on 1 November in the Western tradition.

Saints and the liturgy. The tradition of mentioning the names of saints before God and of making intercesssion for each other is apostolic (see Eph. 1:15-23). The commemoration of saints is a liturgical act. There are saints who are venerated only in certain places, in certain local churches. The names of other saints are in the calendar of the church universal.

"We worship him, the true Son of God. We honour our martyrs as teachers and followers of the Lord" *(Martyrdom of Polycarp)*. The second council of Nicea (787) made the distinction between the true worship due to God *(latreia)* and proper devotion accorded to the sacred images and to the saints. (The council also decided that each new church should contain a relic of a saint on the altar table.) The veneration given to the saints in the Roman Catholic and Orthodox tradition goes to the only Holy One, Jesus Christ. In the liturgy of this tradition, Christians invoke saints as intercessors and protectors, not as mediators. Saints make supplication for the pilgrim church (Eph. 6:18). They render thanks to God for those who enter the glorious church. The saints do not cease to intercede and to offer prayers for the historical church.

"The church has always believed that the apostles, and Christ's martyrs who had given the supreme witness of faith and charity by the shedding of their blood, are quite closely joined with us in Christ. She has always venerated them with special devotion, together with the Blessed Virgin Mary and the holy angels. The church too has devoutly implored the aid of their intercession. To these were soon added those who had imitated Christ's virginity and poverty more exactly, and finally others whom the outstanding practice of the Christian virtues and the divine charisms recommended to the pious devotion and imitation of the faithful" (Vatican II, Constitution on the Church, 50).

Owing to some excesses in the reverence of saints in the development of the liturgy, Protestants in particular felt that the uniqueness of Christ as mediator was threatened. This fear led to reactions against the invocation of saints and the suppression of their commemoration in the liturgy and the liturgical calendar. In today's ecumenical context, it is perhaps necessary to beware of excesses leading to deviations in Christology and at the same time to pay serious attention to the presence in some Protestant liturgies of the notion of the "communion of saints". It is also necessary to consider seriously what it means to be a saint in today's world, in the light of the Christian belief that the Spirit "blows where it wills" (John 3:8).

See also **communion of saints, holiness, martyrdom, sanctification**.

ION BRIA

O. Procksch, "*Hagios* in the New Testament", in *Theological Dictionary of the New Testament*, G. Kittel ed., vol. 1, Grand Rapids, MI, Eerdmans, 1976.

SALVATION. The Old Testament view of salvation appears in passages which recount events of deliverance and liberation* and speak of blessings granted and promised, of peace and life. Two basic features set the pattern here.

First, salvation is not only deliverance and peace* for the individual. Primarily it affects the people as a whole. The fundamental paradigm is to be found in the exodus from Egypt and the entry into the promised land so that life can be lived without hindrance in the service of Yahweh. Here we have a total process which directly includes both physical and social well-being. In particular, the idea of all-embracing shalom gives the OT view of salvation its character.

Second, the issue is one of promises and fulfilments occurring within the existing world and therefore not oriented as a rule to the Beyond. Only in late OT passages — and especially in apocalyptic texts — do we find evidence of a vision of salvation that goes beyond the bounds of this world, characterized as it is by death (e.g. Isa. 25:6-8).

In its various groups of writings, and in varied terminology, the New Testament also sees salvation (*sōtēria*, e.g. Acts 4:12) as an act of deliverance and consequently as the condition of a fulfilled life into which deliverance leads. Such a deliverance, however, is now wholly and exclusively bound up with the name and person of Jesus Christ* (as the deliverer — the Saviour *[sōtēr]*, e.g. Luke 2:11). Essentially such a deliverance through Jesus Christ is from the powers of sin* and death (see **life and death**), and primarily each individual participates in such a deliverance or salvation on the basis of repentance, conversion* and faith.* Salvation is ultimately a future event in which death will be overcome (Rom. 8:23-24; Rev. 21:4-7), but at the same time it is a gift granted and obtained in the present (Luke 17:19; Rom. 5:1-5; John 5:24-26), though accompanied by the continuing challenge from sin, suffering* and dying. But it would be a mistake to attribute a purely individualistic view of salvation ("the salvation of souls") to the NT. Instead, it takes up OT promises which describe salvation in physical and social terms (e.g. Luke 4:18-19).

The cures Jesus performs epitomize and point to his saving activity. The individual and his or her salvation are bound up with the community of those welded together by baptism* into the congregation of the new covenant* of salvation (Acts 2:38-47; Gal. 3:27-28; Eph. 2:19-22). The salvation which is yet to come can be described as eating and drinking in fellowship in the kingdom of God* (Luke 22:30). And we hear of a new heaven and a new earth, the new city of God (Rev. 21:1-5). Paul thinks of the whole creation* waiting for redemption* (Rom. 8:19-21).

The NT also describes salvation in a variety of images. In Jesus' preaching, the message about the kingdom of God — as a religious and communal, individual and social, present and future reality — has pride of place. After Easter the saving work of Jesus Christ is interpreted as reconciliation,* redemption, priestly ministry, sacrifice, etc. This kind of salvation coming from Jesus Christ is encountered by the individual as liberation, justification,* renewal,* sanctification,* light, life and so on. The different NT writings and groups of writings thus prepare the way for the many ideas and conceptions of salvation that have been subsequently worked out in the history of theology and the church.

Aspects relating to the history of dogma. In the history of theology the meaning of salvation has primarily been considered in regard to the person and work of Jesus Christ. Following Gustav Aulén, we may distinguish three fundamental types of interpretation.

The first was given its shape in the early church and still determines the way salvation is viewed in the Orthodox churches. In it, Christ appears as the one who frees human beings from the power of death and sin. Basically this happens through God's assumption

of full humanity in the incarnation* and the healing work of God accomplished thereby. But it happens also through the victory of the risen Christ over the power of death and of the Prince of this world (see **resurrection**). Thus through Christ we are granted salvation in the sense of being restored in the image and likeness of God *(theosis)*.

As opposed to this basic type, a second view of salvation received its imprint in Western theology and particularly in the Latin middle ages, focusing especially on the interpretation of Christ's death, which it understands as an expiation of human sins. Anselm of Canterbury (1033-1109) in his teaching on satisfaction — the most famous example of this type — interpreted the death of Jesus as the destiny (originating in God) of the God become flesh, through which God's honour, offended by human sin, is satisfied, thus making reconciliation, justification and forgiveness possible. The reformers in particular remained committed to this model of how salvation is to be understood.

Third we find — above all in modern European theology — an interpretation of Jesus Christ's saving activity which turns our attention wholly to the person of the earthly Jesus — his preaching, action and religious attitude. Thus the Protestant theologian Friedrich Schleiermacher (1768-1834) identified what was special in Jesus of Nazareth as the strength of his awareness of God. Thus human salvation results in so far as human beings let themselves be embraced in Jesus' basic religious attitude, sharing in the self-surrender he made for them and thus following him.

While the first type of understanding continues to characterize the Orthodox churches' view of salvation, the Latin type has been more at home in the Roman Catholic and large Protestant churches. This difference, however, has never caused division in the churches but indicates rather a legitimate diversity of descriptions — foreshadowed in the NT — of the one mystery. In fact, in the belief held by all the churches on salvation, we find elements of all three paradigms for interpreting Christ's saving activity. Common to all three models of interpretation is the fact that Christ is regarded as the one who has come "for us" (in the two senses of "in our stead" and "for our sake"). They also share the understanding this gives of God* as the One who from his very nature is active on behalf of us human beings. This view was worked out in the Trinitarian idea of God, according to which the Father is at work for our salvation through the Son in the Spirit (see **Trinity**). Because of the crisis in metaphysics and the rise of historical awareness, the third type of interpretation strikes a chord in present-day thinking and can therefore be found in a wide variety of modern theologies — including the theology of liberation, which has discovered the liberating, subversive Jesus of Nazareth.

The controversies of the Reformation period produced opposing views of (the appropriation of) salvation, which caused division in the church. Central to the controversy was the teaching on justification inherited from Paul: How do human beings profit from the salvation made available in Christ? The Roman Catholic theology which derived from the middle ages saw justification as a supernatural pardoning of the sinner, implying his or her re-creation as a person who has been dedicated to God in faith, love and hope* and has been freed in principle from the dominion of original sin. The Reformation feared that this was a wrong way of defining the freedom* and intrinsic worth of human beings in God's sight and that it directed them into the path of good, pious, meritorious works, thus robbing them of their true consolation. "Justification by faith alone", on the other hand, was understood by the reformers to mean the sinner's acquittal by grace* (salvation as the speaking of a word), an acquittal received in trusting faith, which also results in good works. But here the justified sinner exists in a tension between the sin which remains and the righteousness which results from the acquittal *(simul justus et peccator)*. On the Roman Catholic side it was feared here that due justice would not be done spiritually and theologically to the power of the re-creating grace of the Holy Spirit* (as in Rom. 8).

Ecumenical discussion. In contemporary ecumenical discussion the question of salvation is being pursued primarily in three directions.

Re-thinking of the 16th-century controversies: Analysis has been undertaken showing that we no longer have to regard these controversies about how salvation was to be viewed as ecclesiastically divisive. In its final report, the second world conference on Faith and Order* (Edinburgh 1937) produced joint statements on the significance of grace, on justification and sanctification, and on God's action and human responsibility in regard to the sovereignty of God's action. Justification and sanctification, God's action and the human will, are not alternatives but are necessarily complementary in the description of the process of salvation.

The 16th-century's contrasting views of salvation have more recently been the subject first and foremost of Lutheran-Roman Catholic dialogue,* in which many insights from research in the history of dogma and of theology have found a place. Alongside the results of the North American dialogue (*Justification by Faith*, 1985) may be mentioned in particular the document *Lehrverurteilungen — kirchentrennend*? (Mutual condemnations of doctrine: Do they still divide the church?, 1986), produced in the Federal Republic of Germany. The way is prepared for specific comments on the theme by hermeneutical reflections (e.g. on the time-bound nature of certain statements of the problems and modes of expression, or on the significance of a common understanding of the biblical witness). No premature harmonization of general ideas is made, but the consolation of the sinner and the re-creating power of the Spirit of God are two parallel concerns, formulated in the 16th century as opposites, each of which is necessary, although they cannot be reduced systematically to a single formula. References to this state of the discussion have also found a place in the F&O document "Towards the Common Expression of the Apostolic Faith Today", on which work is still being done. The Orthodox concept of *theosis* as the epitome of God's saving activity should be brought more fully into this discussion.

The idea of salvation as for today: Completely new dimensions of a possible contemporary understanding of salvation began to emerge at the beginning of the 1970s, when salvation, in the slogan "Salvation Today", was the theme for an entire ecumenical conference — at the world conference on mission in 1973 in Bangkok, which reacted to the promptings from the WCC assembly at Uppsala in 1968. It is stressed that "salvation for the whole person" is meant, as in Luke 4:18, and especially also a new social justice* and liberation from oppression and exploitation: Christ shows us the unity of body and soul, individual and society, humanity and creation. God's all-embracing salvation for the whole person frees us for our own total salvation. By our commitment to liberation from the oppression and exploitation of others, we procure "in fear and trembling" the salvation bestowed by Christ. In the European theology of the 1960s (e.g. that of Jürgen Moltmann) and at the same time perhaps in Latin American liberation theology,* it was increasingly recognized that salvation is a total event which embraces society and social structures too. Here history as a whole is seen as a process of salvation (see **salvation history**),and the OT idea of shalom plays its part as a prospect of hope. The world conference on mission in Melbourne in 1980, with "Your Kingdom Come" as its theme, also clearly stressed the social dimension of salvation (especially with regard to the world's poor).

This highlighting of the horizontal and social dimension of salvation did of course also provoke contradiction in various churches (e.g. in the Russian Orthodox Church and among evangelicals). In the WCC it was felt necessary to talk in more nuanced, balanced terms, without abandoning the horizontal trend (see M.M. Thomas's speeches at the meetings of the central committee and the Nairobi documents, 1975). It proves necessary to distinguish between (earthly) well-being and (eschatological) salvation. Does holy scripture not record situations of outward well-being which are nevertheless devoid of saving grace? And conversely, must not the reality of salvation be proclaimed where earthly, social well-being has not yet been achieved? In this context mention must be made of discussion on the meaning of mission,* which also regards the simple equation of salvation and earthly well-being as problematic.

Salvation for non-Christians? A third cluster of questions has been brought into ecumenical discussion by the documents of Vatican II,* which raise the question of salvation for non-Christians. The constitution *Lumen Gentium* spoke of the grace of God even among members of other faiths and even among unbelievers; but at the same time it

"Exodus", by Kim Cung Sook, reprinted by permission from "Christian Art in Asia" (Tokyo, Kyo Bun Kwan, 1975), plate 9

underlined the relation of such grace to its centre in the (Roman Catholic) church of Christ. Since then, the possibility of the salvation of non-Christians has also been discussed in various ways in Protestant theology and within the WCC's programme of dialogue too, in regard to other faiths and world-views (see the Chiang Mai consultation, 1977). Some theological models (which naturally also meet with hesitant reactions) suggest an implicit or "anonymous" Christianity. The possibility of the salvation of non-Christians is thus combined with the tying of salvation to Jesus Christ in line with the witness of the NT (see **uniqueness of Christ**). Here again the question of the meaning of mission is on the agenda. On this point the reality and problem of salvation require considerable thought at a deeper level.

See also **liberation, mission, reconciliation, redemption, sin**.

ULRICH KÜHN

G. Aulén, *Den christna försoningstanken* (ET *Christus Victor*, London, SPCK, 1931) • *Bangkok Assembly 1973*, WCC, 1973 • A. Birmelé, *Le salut en Jésus Christ dans les dialogues oecuméniques*, Paris, Cerf, 1986 • F.W. Dillistone, *The Christian Understanding of Atonement*, London, SCM, 1984 • K. Lehmann & W. Pannenberg eds, *Lehrverurteilungen − kirchentrennend?*, vol. 1, Freiburg, Herder, 1986 • J.M. Lochman, *Versöhnung und Befreiung: Absage an ein eindimensionales Heilsverständnis* (ET *Reconciliation and Liberation: Challenging a One-dimensional View of Salvation*, Philadelphia, Fortress, 1980) • J. Matthey ed., *Your Kingdom Come: Report on the World Conference on Mission and Evangelism, Melbourne, 1980*, WCC, 1980 • P. Potter ed., *Bangkok Assembly 1973*, WCC, 1973.

SALVATION ARMY. The Salvation Army (SA) movement began in 1865, when William Booth founded The Christian Mission. Originating in Booth's revival meetings in the slums of London's East End, the mission quickly spread throughout the British Isles by the effective use of recent converts to evangelize others in a language familiar to them. In 1878 the name "The Salvation Army" was adopted. Expansion in Great Britain immediately leapt forward.

The SA speedily took root overseas, first in the US and then Australia (1880), followed by France (1881), Canada, India, Switzerland and Sweden (1882) and so on. When in 1912

William Booth died (in SA terminology, "was promoted to Glory"), the Army was established in almost 50 countries. The SA now operates in no fewer than 90, using 129 languages in preaching the gospel. It has 14,397 corps (churches) and 25,000 officers (full-time ministers).

The objects of the SA are "the advancement of the Christian religion... of education, the relief of poverty, and other charitable objects beneficial to society or the community of mankind as a whole". Salvationist doctrines, following mainstream Christian beliefs, include acceptance of the scriptures of the Old and New Testaments as "the divine rule of Christian faith and practice"; belief in the Triune God (see **Trinity**), the atoning work of Christ, the necessity for repentance and faith* in claiming salvation;* and the call to live a holy life. Every SA soldier is required to subscribe to an 11-point statement of doctrines. SA worship is non-liturgical. Extemporaneous prayer, personal testimony of members and preaching of the word by the leader are important features. Often a brass band leads the singing.

Salvationists are taught that they are "saved to serve" — they are soldiers in their spare time, without remuneration. Officers, trained in SA training colleges, devote their whole lives to the cause and receive a modest salary. All Salvationists are expected to live a disciplined life of high moral standards, including abstinence from alcohol and tobacco.

From the beginning the SA was involved in schemes to help the poor. From simple soup kitchens to feed the starving of London's East End, the movement's social work has evolved to meet modern needs with modern methods. Centres for the homeless, the alcoholic, and deprived children cater annually for thousands of people. Hospitals and clinics provide healing and hope. Schools and institutions provide education. All is done in the name of Christ. No Salvationist believes that people can be made whole by the ministry to the body and mind alone.

The SA claims to be an "integral part and element of the Great Church, a living fruit-bearing branch of the True Vine". The SA was a founding member of the WCC, but since 1978 the Army has been in the revised status of fraternal relationship. This status is more suited to the Army's polity of a single representative for all its worldwide constituents. The SA continues to play a significant role in the WCC, as well as in other movements such as the Lausanne Committee for World Evangelization.*

The SA has one international leader, the General, elected by the movement's leading officers who form the High Council. The General directs all SA operations from the world headquarters in London, though he or she spends much time in necessary travel, reviewing the work, preaching the gospel. The SA is led at present by General Eva Burrows, elected in 1986, and the movement's second woman leader. From its earliest days the Army has given equal opportunities to men and women.

WILLIAM CLARK

F. Coutts, *No Discharge in This War: The History of the Salvation Army*, 6 vols, London, Nelson, 1947-68 • F. Coutts, *The Weapons of God*, London, Hodder & Stoughton, 1986 • *The Handbook of Doctrine*, St Albans, UK, Campfield, 1969 • E.H. MacKinley, *Marching to Glory*, San Francisco, Harper & Row, 1980.

SALVATION HISTORY. Christians believe that God* is at work in history.* Hence this divine work has its history. Since salvation* is a historical reality, the notion of salvation history presents itself as an appropriate way to perceive and interpret history.

This approach can be found in the Bible. The covenant* tradition in the Hebrew Bible, for instance, affirms the particular history of God with the people. The testimonies of the Hebrew prophets are connected with different readings of Israel's history. Similarly, when Luke writes his gospel and the Acts of the Apostles, his aim is to give an account of God's saving work in and through Jesus Christ,* which continues in the ministry of the apostles. Throughout the history of Christianity efforts have been undertaken to interpret the past in terms of salvation history, i.e. to show that the present is in line with God's all-embracing design and purpose.

It is not surprising, therefore, that the emergence of the ecumenical movement should have been accompanied by attempts to place this new historical phenomenon in the perspective of God's great purpose. The founding fathers of the modern ecumenical movement were convinced that God willed them to struggle for this new task. They saw the past history in terms of divine preparation. John R. Mott, for example, firmly believed that God had in many ways prepared the way for "the evangelization of the world in this generation". Referring to Mott, George Bell, Eivind Berggrav, Donald Baillie and others, W.A. Visser 't Hooft declared in 1961: "They felt constrained to work for the unity of the church of Christ, simply because that unity is an essential part of God's design."

It is not surprising either that a similar tone was struck at Amsterdam 1948. Its theme, "Man's Disorder and God's Design", reflects a salvation-history approach. This is clearly evidenced in the section 1 report, which states: "God's redeeming activity in the world has been carried out through his calling a people to be his own chosen people. The old covenant was fulfilled in the new when Jesus Christ, the Son of God incarnate, died and was raised from the dead, ascended into heaven and gave the Holy Ghost to dwell in his body, the church. It is our common concern for that church which draws us together, and in that concern we discover our unity in relation to her Lord and Head."

We can see here a three-stage concept of salvation history: (1) God's story with Israel; (2) God's story with Jesus Christ; (3) God's story with the churches leading up to the one church* universal. In the oikonomia of God the oikoumene has a providential place (see **providence**).

The third assembly of the WCC (New Delhi 1961) underscored and widened this approach. Christ, the "light of the world", is proclaimed in cosmic dimensions (see the contributions of Joseph Sittler and Paul Devanandan). Under the world-ruling Christ there can be but one church and one history of salvation, into which all histories of the world must ultimately flow.

The Second Vatican Council* (1962-65) takes a similar approach. It describes the history of our globe through its evolutionary stages as God's creative history leading to God's self-disclosure in the Son. It regards the world's religions as agents in humanity's search to grasp the meaning of this great history but affirms that the real meaning is revealed through Christ in the Holy Spirit* to the (catholic) church as that sacramental institution in which God's purpose is most adequately manifested. This approach was also significantly influenced by the work of Protestant scholars, most of all by Oscar Cullmann.

The Bristol document "God in Nature and History" of the Faith and Order* commission (1967) can be regarded as a summary of ecumenical thinking on history. It seeks to combine secular evolutionary thinking with the notion of salvation history. It describes the global evolutionary process as God's creation history, which culminates in Christ's ministry and finds its fulfilment in God's ultimate reign (see **kingdom of God**).

With the Uppsala assembly (1968) a shift from reflection to action takes place. God is confessed as the Lord of change and renewal.* Hence the church is called to be an agent of change and renewal. Since God is at work, his disciples must work also. Salvation history is not something to think about but something to work out in concrete solidarity for the poor* and oppressed. This approach comes very close to the affirmation of the Latin American Roman Catholic bishops conference at Medellín (1968) concerning God's "preferential option for the poor". Since then salvation history has been looked at less in terms of a hermeneutical clue to *understand* history but as a prophetic tool to *change* it.

In both versions, however, the concept of salvation history remains ambiguous. Care should be taken to understand the character of such thinking. Salvation history is a way in which faith* sees and interprets the vast expanse of history. It can never be anything else than a claim of faith. It should never be mistaken for an objective account of what history is. Properly understood, salvation history has a *doxological* meaning, i.e. it is a way of celebrating God's creative and redemptive presence in this world. It will at times also have a *prophetic* meaning, i.e. it will have to elucidate ethico-polical options and challenges (see **prophecy**). Whenever this limited perspective is overlooked, systems of salvation history stand in danger of harmonizing the deep contradictions of history, of simplifying the mystery of Christ's cross and resurrection, and thus of turning into triumphalism.

GEIKO MÜLLER-FAHRENHOLZ

H. Berkhof, *Christus de zin der geschiedenis* (ET *Christ the Meaning of History*, London, SCM,

1966) • O. Cullmann, *Heil als Geschichte* (ET *Salvation in History*, London, SCM, 1967) • "God in Nature and History", *Study Encounter*, 1, 1965 • G. Müller-Fahrenholz, *Heilsgeschichte zwischen Ideologie und Prophetie*, Freiburg, Herder, 1974.

SAMARTHA, STANLEY JEDIDIAH.

B. 7.10.1920, Karkal, South India. First director of the WCC Sub-unit on Dialogue with People of Living Faiths and Ideologies, 1970-81, Samartha was able to secure wide acceptance for dialogue as an important ecumenical concern. He studied at Madras University, United Theological College, Bangalore, Union Theological Seminary, New York, and Hartford Seminary Foundation (PhD), and did post-graduate studies at the University of Basel, 1951-52. From 1947 to 1960 he was connected with the Basel Mission Theological Seminary (later Karnataka Theological College), Mangalore, from 1947-49 as lecturer, from 1952 as principal. Ordained to the ministry in 1952, he became principal of Serampore College, West Bengal, and consultant to the Christian Institute for the Study of Religion and Society, Bangalore. Samartha is visiting professor at the United Theological College, Bangalore, and also connected with the South Asia Theological Research Institute. Among his books are *The Hindu Response to the Unbound Christ* (Madras, Christian Literature Society, 1974) and *Courage for Dialogue* (WCC, 1981). See *Dialogue in Community: Essays in Honour of Stanley J. Samartha*, C.D. Jathanna ed. (Mangalore, Karnataka Theological Research Institute, 1982).

ANS J. VAN DER BENT

SAMUEL, BISHOP.
B. December 1920, Cairo; d. 6.10.1981, Cairo. Bishop Samuel attended Evanston 1954 and afterwards was a member of the WCC central committee. An interpreter of the Coptic church to the churches in the West, he helped in establishing a basis of understanding and dialogue with the Roman Catholic Church. He was instrumental in theologically reconciling the different Orthodox churches. Educated in Cairo and at Princeton University, in 1949 he chose the monastic order known as Makary El Souriany.

Consecrated as bishop in 1962, he served

many villages in Egypt, explaining the Bible, starting a group for Coptic education, and establishing the rural diakonia. He was director of the churches' department of social studies. Appointed by President Anwar Al-Sadat to administer the church in terms of its state relationships, he was among those assassinated together with the president.

ANS J. VAN DER BENT

SANCTIFICATION. The Christian faith* includes the confidence that God wills the sanctification of all who are one body with Christ (see **holiness**). "Partakers of the divine nature" (2 Pet. 1:4), disciples are to lead holy lives. "As he who called you is holy, be holy yourselves in all your conduct" (1 Pet. 1:15). All Christian traditions teach sanctification, with various emphases.

Eastern Orthodox Christianity understands participation in the life of the risen Christ as "divinization" *(theosis)*, which transforms not only the human person but the whole cosmic order. In the West, the Augustinian spiritualization and individualization of the "new creation" prevented sanctification from being seen in the framework of a cosmic process of divinization. Sanctification became a progressive cleansing of the person from sinfulness, by the gift of grace.* Medieval theologians taught the power of human nature to cooperate with grace. Notwithstanding our total need of grace in regard to salvation* and the absolute priority of God's sanctifying initiative, they stressed the compelling call to grow in sanctity through meritorious works.

"Perfection" in the sense of sinlessness was the prevailing outlook on sanctification when Luther's despairing conscience found relief in the gospel of justification* by faith, "without the works of the law". Justification as imputation of Christ's righteousness to the sinner through faith makes all notions of growth in sanctity irrelevant: Christ's righteousness is imputed totally as the Holy Spirit* works faith in the soul. Christ alone is the holiness of his disciple, who is "simultaneously a sinner". Roman Catholicism fosters more optimistic views of righteousness: "We are truly called just, and we are just" (council of Trent*). According to Vatican II,* faith, hope and charity equip us "to bear increasingly rich fruit of the Holy Spirit".

Following the Reformation breakthrough on the issue of justification, new patterns of sanctification arose, opposing (1) the idea of the persistence of sin in the righteous, and (2) Luther's idea of "faith alone", which seemed to ignore the role of moral conversion. German pietism saw justification as the beginning of "rebirth", with an emphasis on the growth of the "new man". Calvin related sanctification to God's election. For him, the fear of God's judgment, in firm reliance upon his mercy, leads to a life obedient to divine law and church discipline. In Methodism, "Christian perfection" (entire sanctification) is the goal of initial conversion: penitents who are forgiven for their sins retain a "residue of sin within" which calls for a "second work of grace". In discipline, methodical devotion, avoidance of worldly pleasures, "growth in grace" and victory over sin are then sought and may be achieved. The international Methodist-Roman Catholic dialogue* was able to reach extensive agreement on the sanctifying work of the Holy Spirit (Honolulu report, 1981). Contemporary holiness movements* value the personal experience of the Spirit, including "baptism in the Holy Spirit", which gives power to live an effective Christian life.

The yearning for sinlessness in today's discussions about eschatological transfiguration, in the Roman Catholics' insistence on the "objective" agency of the church's ministry and sacraments in salvation, and in the Protestant concern for ethical righteousness, makes it worth recalling the rich man's lesson (Mark 10:17-22): sinlessness avails little, God alone is good, and holiness comes through following Christ. Forgiveness of sins, rather than sinlessness, is God's truth for sanctified sinners.

See also **holiness, Holy Spirit.**

DANIEL OLIVIER

R.N. Flew, *The Idea of Perfection in Christian Theology*, London, Oxford UP, 1934 • *Histoire des saints et de la sainteté chrétienne*, Paris, Hachette, 1986 • C. Lindberg, *The Third Reformation? Charismatic Renewal and Lutheran Tradition*, Macon, GA, Mercer UP, 1983 • J. Meyendorff & J. McLelland, *The New Man: An Orthodox and Reformed Dialogue*, New Brunswick, NJ, Angora, 1973 • K. Ware, "Salvation and Theosis in Orthodox Theology", in *Luther et la réforme allemande dans une perspective oecuménique*, Chambésy, Eds du Centre oecuménique, 1983.

SANCTUARY. Sanctuary is traditionally offered by the church as a protective community to refugees whose basic human rights are being violated. It is a faith practice which reaches back to the earliest memories of the people of Israel, and a movement of the ecumenical church in response to the current plight of refugees thoughout the world. At the present time there are more than 15 million refugees scattered over the face of the earth. They are crossing borders without documents to flee war and persecution, or they are displaced within their own country. In all cases these are the most vulnerable and suffering people imaginable.

The name "sanctuary" has been given in the USA to the movement for the protection of refugees from Central America whom the US government has been sanctioning or deporting since 1980, claiming that they were not bona fide political refugees but had crossed the borders for economic reasons. A number of Catholic and Protestant churches have challenged this interpretation of the 1980 refugee act and have organized themselves for the transportation, reception, protection and relocation of these refugees in what has been called (recovering a term from the times of slavery) "the underground railroad" and declared themselves as "sanctuary churches". The US government has arraigned and indicted a number of people involved in these actions. The ethical and legal debate and the processes continue. Churches and individuals engaged in this task have made explicit the theological, biblical and ethical grounds of their action.

The Bible is replete with stories and instructions on sanctuary, asylum and the treatment of refugees. Most often these stories are told from the perspective of the refugee. The Hebrews, displaced from their own land by famine, are enslaved in Egypt. God hears their cry and liberates them from their suffering and bondage. Therefore, Israel is to remember that they were once aliens or sojourners and that special care must be taken for the stranger in their midst (Lev. 19:33-34; Deut. 10:18-19). The God who saved Israel from bondage is the protector of the poor and suffering (Ps. 145; Num. 35:9-11).

Within the Old Testament we find both the tradition of cities of refuge and altar sanctuary, both for the purpose of saving human life from blood vengeance until judicial safeguards can be employed. Jesus begins life as a refugee child fleeing from Herod. He identifies with the poor and persecuted (Matt. 25:43). The early church is instructed to receive the stranger (Heb. 13:2).

The community of faith often affords the only possible protection to people fleeing for their lives. Seeking safe haven from death squads, arbitrary arrest and detention, torture, or conditions of war, desperate people thoughout history have sought the church as a place of sanctuary. This is true of those fleeing internal persecution in their own countries as well as those who find themselves to be strangers in a strange land. When one has nowhere to turn, the door of the church is a beacon of hope and refuge in a dark and desperate world.

The practice of sanctuary is again emerging as a movement within the ecumenical church, which assumes responsibility for the non-violent protection of human rights. Sanctuary is more than a matter of individual conscience. It is the church entering into communion with the violated and oppressed and building together a community of solidarity and love. The refugee becomes a gift from God, the presence of Christ to the sanctuary church. The refugee becomes not the object of charity or paternalistic ministry but, rather, the spiritual guide for congregations to help the protective community read the Bible as much of it was written — through the eyes and hearts of refugees.

When the protective community of faith adds a public witness to its practice of sanctuary, then the state is held accountable for its violations of human rights and the church becomes prophetic. Often the church must practise sanctuary in silence in order to protect those who need refuge. But even in these instances, the church provides documentation of human rights abuses so that the truth can be spoken with authority at a later time. When a church cannot speak publicly of severe repression, it must depend on other communions within the international community to assume the prophetic role. Documentation of violations of human rights is prophetic witness in the world.

Refugees who cross international borders without documents, exposing the root causes of their flight into exile, can become a part of the witness of the sanctuary church. Refugee rights are directly linked to issues of military intervention, pacification, low-intensity conflict, arms sales, foreign-aid programmes and police training.

As more and more countries adopt highly restrictive policies to prevent the admission of refugees, prophetic witness may risk aiding refugees to cross borders safely. Many nations are trying to deal with the refugee problem by closing borders to applicants for asylum, intercepting boats at sea, and requiring individual proof of refugee status under more restrictive terms. The public resistance of faith communities to these violations of human rights has extended the prophetic role of the church across national borders.

In many instances, the refugee becomes the prophetic voice within the faith community, speaking truth to political powers about the causes of their suffering and exile. In the case of internally displaced people, the church is often the only voice documenting gross violations of human rights, torture, bombing or starvation of civilian populations in counter-insurgency military strategies. It is through this solidarity and communion with the suffering and violated that the sanctuary church becomes one Body in Christ.

See also **refugees**.

JOHN FIFE

I. Bau, *This Ground Is Holy: Church Sanctuary and Central American Refugees*, New York, Paulist, 1985 • P. Golden & M. McConnell, *Sanctuary: The New Underground Railroad*, Maryknoll, NY, Orbis, 1986 • J. Schaeffer ed., *Sanctuary and Asylum: A Handbook for Commitment*, Geneva, World Alliance of Reformed Churches, 1990.

SCHISM. The word comes from the Greek *schisma*, meaning split, rent, division. In the New Testament it refers to divisions and quarrels of all kinds which had developed in the church.* Later, the word came to be used solely for divisions of a lasting nature which had developed within the church, not over questions of doctrine but because of disagreements over questions of discipline. Schismatics therefore were people who, though still agreeing with dogmas, split away from the church, refusing to obey its hierarchical authorities because of differences of opinion over questions such as the legitimacy

of this or that hierarch, or a particular disciplinary measure, or problems concerning rites or organization (see canon 1 of Basil the Great).

One of the most famous schisms in the ancient church was that created by Donatus (d.355), the bishop of Casae Nigrae, in Numidia, against the bishop of Carthage, whom he accused of having surrendered the holy books during the persecutions. He led a schismatic church in opposition to the latter, drawing on the support of the rural Berber population. Attacked by Augustine, Donatism was finally condemned at the council of Carthage. Mention may also be made of the schism at Antioch caused by the banishment of the bishop of Antioch, Meletius, and the consecration of Paulinus as bishop against canon law (363).

The church suspends eucharistic fellowship with schismatic groups. But, according to canons 10 and 11 of the council of Carthage, the priest who creates a schism is liable to excommunication.* Canon 33 of the council of Laodicea forbids prayer with schismatics. However, canon 1 of Basil prescribes that baptism* received among schismatics be recognized.

Other schisms have likewise left their mark on the history of the church. One of these was the schism between the East and the Roman West which culminated in 1054. As a result of this, Roman theology characterizes the Orthodox as schismatics because of their refusal to recognize the universal authority and jurisdiction of the pope. Another schism that should be mentioned is the great schism in the Western church which divided the Roman Catholic Church from 1378 to 1417, when there were two popes at the same time, one in Rome and one in Avignon; in 1409 there was even a third pope in Pisa before the council of Constance (1414). The election of Pope Martin V (1417) put an end to the division.

One should not forget the schism of the Old Believers (Raskol), which has divided the Russian Orthodox Church since the second half of the 17th century. This was caused by the stubborn opposition roused by the reforms introduced by Patriarch Nikon, making changes in the service books and in ritual. The adherents of the old ways were condemned and excommunicated at the great council of Moscow of 1666-67 (condemnations which were lifted at the council of Moscow in 1971).

Their movement continued, however, divided into sects, and still counts its followers in the millions.

This latter schism highlights the dangers of hasty and abrupt liturgical reforms. It also shows that schisms arising out of disagreements over questions of rite or discipline can in the long run engender heresies* in matters of faith* and doctrine, opening the way for ecclesiological errors and quarrels over the sacraments,* the nature of the church* and even the means of salvation.* Schisms as well as heresies obviously represent serious obstacles to the unity* of the Christian world.

ALEXIS KNIAZEFF

SCHMEMANN, ALEXANDER.

B. 13.9.1921, Revel, Estonia; d. 13.12.1983, Crestwood, NY, USA. Professor of church history and liturgical theology at St Vladimir's Orthodox Theological Seminary, Crestwood, 1951-83, Schmemann was dean of the seminary, 1962-83. Earlier he was professor of Byzantine church history at the St Sergius Orthodox Institute in Paris, 1945-51, vice-chairman of the WCC Youth department and member of the Faith and Order commission. He lectured as adjunct professor at Union Theological Seminary, General Theological Seminary and Columbia University. His theological world-view was shaped during his studies at the St Sergius Institute, 1940-45. Under his guidance St Vladimir's became the centre of a liturgical and eucharistic revival and was an academic institution much respected in ecumenical circles. He favoured Orthodox unity in the USA and the establishment of the autocephalous Orthodox Church in America in 1970. Editor of St Vladimir's *Theological Quarterly*, he wrote *The Historical Road of Eastern Orthodoxy* (New York, Holt, Rinehart & Winston, 1963), *Church, World, Mission: Reflections on Orthodoxy in the West* (Crestwood, NY, St Vladimir's Seminary, 1979) and *The Eucharist, Sacrament of the Kingdom* (Crestwood, NY, St Vladimir's Seminary, 1988).

ANS J. VAN DER BENT

SCHUTZ-MARSAUCHE, ROGER.

B. 12.5.1915, Provence, Switzerland. Brother Roger is the founder and prior of the ecumenical community of Taizé,* near Cluny, in France, counting 90 brothers today. In 1940 he arrived alone in Taizé and was joined in 1942 by a few brothers. In 1949 seven brothers took monastic life vows. In 1952 he wrote the *Rule of Taizé*. When the *Office of Taizé* was published in 1962, its careful balance of old and new aroused the attention of many who were concerned for the renewal of Christian worship around the world. In 1958 he was received in audience by Pope John XXIII and later was an observer at the Second Vatican Council. In 1970 he announced a worldwide council of youth (which opened in 1974) and in 1982 led to a "pilgrimage of trust on earth" which includes European meetings (20,000 youth each year in a European capital), intercontinental meetings (Madras, India) and East-West meetings (Yugoslavia). He received the Templeton prize (1974), the peace prize in Germany (1974), and the UNESCO prize for peace education (1988). He wrote *Le dynamique du provisoire* (ET *The Dynamic of the Provisional*, London, Mowbray, 1981), *Violence du pacifique: Etonnement de l'amour* (ET *Afire with Love*, New York, Crossroad, 1982) and *Fleurissent les déserts du cœur* (ET *And Your Deserts Shall Flower*, London, Oxford, Mowbray, 1984).

ANS J. VAN DER BENT

SCIENCE AND TECHNOLOGY.

In 1926 the philosopher Alfred North Whitehead described science and religion* as "the two strongest general forces" that influence human life. Inevitably, then, the ecumenical movement has had an interest in science.

Historians frequently make the case that the development of science owes something to the biblical tradition. Polytheism and animism discourage efforts at unified explanations of nature,* and religions that teach the unreality of the physical world devalue scientific exploration. Belief in divine creation implies a unity and authentic reality to all nature, the presuppositions for most scientific inquiry. Even so, scientific discoveries have often clashed with traditional beliefs and have threatened ecclesiastical authority,* leading to sporadic, sometimes dramatic conflicts between science and theology.

In the ancient and medieval church the

clashes were usually not severe. Christians understood that no human language was adequate to the mystery of God and that much of the Bible was to be read symbolically. Scientists were a small elite, and scientific methods had not come to dominate culture.* Platonism diverted human attention from nature (a shadow-world) to the eternal "real" world, and Aristotelianism assumed a teleology in nature that theologians could relate to their understanding of divine creation. So it was not until the great modern advances of science that the problems of relating science and theology became critical for society at large.

Catholicism met the challenge of new scientific cosmologies by condemning Galileo (1633). Learning from that event, it did not make a similar mistake with the scientific doctrine of evolution. Protestantism sometimes rejected evolution, insisting that Gen. 1-3 gave a literal and accurate account of creation — a belief that still causes conflicts in public education in some parts of the world (see **creationism**). A quite different Protestant response, typical of some liberal theology, was to make a theology of development and progress out of evolution. Today theologians are engaged in new efforts to relate contemporary scientific cosmologies and evolutionary concepts to Christian belief.

Technology has often been a quite different enterprise from science. Science seeks understanding. Its motivation is both intellectual and aesthetic; it loves a comprehensive and "elegant" theory. It is a work of imagination joined with realism. It traces connections of cause and effect; its methods include observation, development of theories that explain the evidence and verification of those theories by further observation and experimentation, thus expanding the boundaries of knowledge. Technology seeks to cope with and sometimes control physical nature and society. Its motivation is practical. It is less concerned with grand theories, more concerned with effectiveness. In some cases technology is the application of science; thus the scientific theories of Albert Einstein led to the technology of nuclear energy and weapons. But technology has also preceded science; the lever, the wheel, the first ancient steam engine and the magnifying glass probably came long before the theories that explain them.

In some societies, including the ancient Greek, science was mainly an interest of intellectuals, who disdained physical labour and therefore technology. Both class structure and metaphysics separated theory from practice, science from technology. Christian faith,* remembering the carpenter of Nazareth, drew the two closer. Monasteries, though often unsophisticated intellectually, became the centres for the preservation of scientific knowledge and the development of crafts and technologies. The Benedictine monks have been called the first intellectuals to get dirt under their fingernails.

In the modern world science and technology are interdependent, sometimes almost indistinguishable. Ever since Francis Bacon (1561-1626) declared that "knowledge is power", the sharp separation between science and technology has been blunted. In pragmatic theories of knowledge, in which all inquiry is problem solving, science and technology are closely akin. Contemporary science often leads to technological innovations; just as often its experimentation depends upon elaborate technological apparatus. Frequently it is funded by government and industry interested in military and economic pay-offs.

Even so, the distinction between science and technology remains important. Science with its understanding of the world presents issues to theology concerning the truth claims of Christian faith. Technology presents issues to ethics, as its new powers require human direction and evaluation.

Ecumenical attention in the 20th century. The WCC from its beginnings has taken an interest in the social impact of scientific technologies. The first assembly, meeting in Amsterdam in the aftermath of the second world war (1948), called attention to the relation between technology and modern secularism and to the ways in which technology acquires a momentum of its own that has a powerful effect on society (see **secularization**). It warned against the technological depersonalization of life and its wasteful exploitation of natural resources. However, delegates from Asia and Africa (a very small minority in the WCC at that time) saw the potential of technology to "lessen the burden of toil and alleviate poverty". They thought the Europeans and North Americans were overly pessimistic about technology.

The second assembly (Evanston 1954)

launched a study project on the "Christian Responsibility towards Areas of Rapid Social Change", with special attention to Africa, Asia, Latin America and the Middle East. The discussions emphasized political, economic and cultural change, but with constant awareness of the impact of technology on all these. The climax of the project was a conference in Salonika (1959) on "Christian Action in Rapid Social Change: Dilemmas and Opportunities".

The third assembly (New Delhi 1961) brought major changes in the WCC. The merger of the WCC and the International Missionary Council, along with the entrance of the Russian Orthodox and other churches from Africa, Asia and Latin America, changed the predominantly Western European-North American character of the WCC's earlier years. The Asian setting influenced the assembly's concern for the responsible uses of technology.

The years 1962-65 were the years of the Second Vatican Council.* Pope John XXIII, who had authorized the presence of Roman Catholic observers at New Delhi, invited Protestant and Orthodox observers to Vatican II. Roman Catholicism had a strong legacy of papal encyclicals* and addresses dealing with the modern political-economic world, including its technologies. These usually endorsed the benefits of technologies, urged believers to use them in accord with Catholic moral teachings and warned against the depersonalizing effects of modern social change. If these documents sometimes showed nostalgia for medieval Christendom, Vatican II changed that — above all, in its Pastoral Constitution on the Church in the Modern World, *Gaudium et Spes*.

This influential document recognized the importance of industrialization and urbanization in shaping the modern world. It acknowledged the impact of the physical and human sciences upon the understanding of the world and upon human self-knowledge, and it took account of the technology that it saw "transforming the face of the earth". It addressed issues of marriage* and family,* culture,* economic organization, political life, world peace and the community of nations — seeking to understand all these in their scientific as well as their moral aspects. It welcomed science and technology when these are directed

towards human dignity and equality, while warning against their dehumanizing effects when ethical issues are neglected.

During Vatican II, the WCC was making plans for a world conference on "Christians in the Technical and Social Revolutions of Our Time" (Geneva 1966). This was the first major WCC conference devoted solely to issues of social ethics. It was in many respects an heir of the Oxford conference of the Life and Work movement (1937), prior to the organization of the WCC. But Oxford had been a conference of church leaders, mostly clergy and mostly from Western Europe and North America. At Geneva a majority of the 420 delegates were laypeople, and a majority came from outside the old geographical nexus. Roman Catholics had prominent roles as speakers and observers.

The conference had a wide impact. Its four preparatory volumes of essays were studied around the world. It was the first global platform for emerging Latin American and African theologies of liberation. Its findings won major attention among member churches and among critics of the WCC.

The delegates, when they addressed the topic of the conference, were more adept at talking about social than technological revolutions. Despite some major addresses on technology, the conference centred its attention on political, social and cultural issues, and it considered technology primarily as a form of power with social impact. Some of the participating scientists objected that their concerns had been neglected, and the report of the conference contained recommendations that the WCC find ways for continuing work involving scientists and technologists.

Following Geneva, the WCC and the Vatican co-operated in the founding of the committee on Society, Development and Peace (SODEPAX*), which for a few years pursued vigorously some of the concerns shared by Vatican II and Geneva. Within the WCC, the department of Church and Society carried out the recommendations for continued work involving co-operation of scientists and technologists with theologians.

This process took an unexpected direction when the issues of ecology leapt into prominence in several parts of the world. The Geneva reports had stated: "The churches should welcome the development of science and technology as an expression of God's creative work. They should also welcome the economic growth and social development which it makes possible." That confidence was balanced by warnings that technological power can be an instrument of injustice. But the new accent, neglected at Geneva, was on the destructive consequences of present technologies and economic development, as they consume unrenewable resources, pollute the environment and endanger human life and ecosystems. Some scientists involved in the programme of the WCC made this point with great power. The fifth assembly of the WCC (Nairobi 1975) endorsed continuing work on the theme, and the central committee adopted a programme emphasis on the struggle for a "Just, Participatory and Sustainable Society".*

Within the WCC there was some resistance to the new theme. To nations suffering poverty, a warning against economic growth seemed to be a message of despair. Others feared that well-intended people, weary of strenuous conflicts for justice, welcomed a turn to a gentler environmental interest. Ecologists answered that if the dream of overcoming the gap between rich and poor by

At the public hearing on nuclear weapons and disarmament, Amsterdam (WCC/John Taylor)

making everybody rich was illusory, the concern for distributive justice was all the more urgent. They also pointed out that existing patterns of economic growth usually widen the gap between rich and poor and that pollution harms the poor far more than the rich. The department of Church and Society, often gaining the co-operation of eminent scientists, sought to define the kinds of economic growth and distribution that are not destructive. It sponsored regional conferences in Africa, Asia and Europe. It gave special attention to problems of energy and justice in a world in which the poor societies that lack fossil fuels are especially disadvantaged. On another front, it arranged international conversations on the new genetics and the ethical issues it presents (see **bio-ethics**).

In 1979 the WCC convened a world conference on "Faith, Science and the Future" at the Massachusetts Institute of Technology (see **ecumenical conferences**). About half of the 405 delegates (including 91 students) were physical scientists and technologists; the other half were church leaders, theologians, social scientists, people from government and industry. In recognition of the worldwide nature of the issues, the conference heard Buddhists and Muslims, as well as Christian theologians, speak out of the insights of their faith. Other speakers, chosen for their technical competence, included Christians, Jews and agnostics. Two of the ten sections dealt specifically with themes of science and faith, one with science and education, seven with various aspects of technology and Christian ethics.

The major surprise of the conference came when some of the physical scientists asked to change the agenda in order to give more attention to the issue of war and nuclear weapons. Original plans had not given adequate importance to the topic, only because of another WCC programme on militarism.* The scientists argued persuasively that any understanding of contemporary technology is radically incomplete without attention to weapons. One recommendation of the conference was that the WCC sponsor an international hearing on nuclear weapons. That took place in Amsterdam in 1981.

The preparatory book and the two volumes coming out of the MIT conference had wide distribution and influenced theological education and programmes of churches in various nations. Spin-offs from the conference include further programmes in many parts of the world. Some of the themes of the conference entered into the programme of the sixth assembly of the WCC (Vancouver 1983) and are integral to the present WCC programme on Justice, Peace and the Integrity of Creation.*

Continuing issues. Out of this ecumenical history have emerged several issues that continue to engage the churches. Five of them are listed here. In keeping with the historical record, these centre more directly on technology and ethics than on science and theology. The reason is that the issues of science-theology permit extended discussion; the issues of technology-ethics often require urgent decisions. Ecumenical Christianity can choose to move slowly on some theological issues rather than foreclose discussion by premature decisions, but on many ethical issues it must throw its weight into the struggle or stand by and watch others direct the course of history. Even so, all the ethical issues mentioned here have theological grounding and implications.

Humanity within God's creation: The report of Geneva 1966 includes these words: "Christians believe God expects man to exercise dominion over the earth, to name the creatures and to cultivate the garden of the world... Man is both the master and the steward of nature. His dominion over nature, considered as God's creation, is that of a keeper and transformer, not of a conqueror."

The delegates who formulated and adopted those sentences could not guess how great a controversy would soon arise over the concept of human dominion. A few months later medieval historian Lynn White, Jr, delivered an address to the American Association for the Advancement of Science on "The Historical Roots of Our Ecological Crisis". White, himself a Christian and later a participant in the programme of the WCC, charged that Christianity, especially in its Western form, had destroyed the sacral quality of nature* and encouraged its predatory exploitation to a degree that now threatened the integrity of nature and of humankind. A little later Arnold Toynbee made similar accusations. But whereas Toynbee advocated a return to a pre-Christian pantheism, White asked for a recovery of the insights of Franciscan Christianity. Others found resources in Eastern Orthodoxy.

At New Delhi in 1961, Joseph Sittler had urged a theological concern for "the realm of nature as a theatre of grace". But other Christian writers were exulting in Christianity's "desacralization" of nature and the secularization of society. There was even bold talk of the "humanization" or "hominization" of the universe. White, without mentioning these writers, took up their challenge and condemned exactly those elements in the Christian tradition that they had acclaimed.

The growth of ecological consciousness has made humanity more aware of its dependence on a nature that it did not create. Geneva 1966 emphasized both dominion and stewardship. Human beings survive and build civilizations by modifying the course of nature; they immobilize or eradicate some forms of life (the polio virus and smallpox bacillus) for the sake of human values. But in stewardship they are caretakers of an earth that was created before them. Furthermore, the mystery of creation extends far beyond human dominion or stewardship, as Job and some of the prophets knew well. The Pleiades and Orion were surely not created for human convenience.

At what point does the human use of nature become both irreverent and destructive to human aims? At what point do new biological sciences including genetic engineering become irreverent intrusions? When does a God-given "dominion" become an arrogant exercise in "playing God"? The ecumenical discussion continues.

Evaluations of technology: A closely related issue is the contrasting evaluations of technology. Some welcome technology as a product of human creativity, a force that liberates people from poverty and drudgery. Others, notably Jacques Ellul, the French lawyer-sociologist-theologian, see it as a dehumanizing power that subjects persons to an impersonal fate that is remarkably similar in all social systems. A third group see it as a neutral force that can be used for good or evil, depending on the purposes of its users or the social system in which it functions. The telephone, for example, is quite indifferent to the good or bad messages it transmits. A fourth group see it as inherently ambivalent, as all power is ambivalent. Power* is not evil; the purpose of much Christian action is the empowerment of people. Yet in a sinful world power is almost inevitably misused (see **sin**).

Power and inequality: Technology increases some human powers to cope with and make use of nature. But as C.S. Lewis pointed out, the new powers that people win over nature become powers of some people over other people. There are exceptions to that generalization: the victory over smallpox has been a human victory. But most technological advances, obviously in weapons and almost as obviously in economic productivity, enhance the power of some people to dominate other people.

The unequal distribution of technologies accentuates inequality. UNESCO data, often discussed within the WCC, show that 97% of the expenditures on research and development occur within the "developed nations", only 3% within the "developing nations", where the majority of people live. Research is directed primarily towards the projects of the rich and powerful, only slightly towards the problems of the poor. The international transfer of technologies, even when it purports to help the poor, often serves the interests of wealthy corporations and governments.

Similarly technology enhances the power of elites who understand and control it. The participatory society, often advocated by the WCC, may be frustrated when wise decisions depend on expert skills possessed by a few, who can use those skills for their own advantage.

High risk: Scientists sometimes estimate that the human race is living in an era of higher risk than at any time since people first established their precarious existence in the face of hostile animals and natural forces. Through the centuries of history, people have exercised new powers in a trial-and-error method. They built upon experiments that succeeded; they abandoned experiments that failed. The new situation is that the failure of some experiments could mean disaster for humankind. The most obvious risk is the use of weapons that could destroy civilization. Less immediate is the risk of changing the climate of the earth through human interventions in the ecosystem. To cease experimentation would be to cease to be human; but rash experimentation is more portentous than in past eons.

The increase in risk comes at a time when political organizations are inadequate to cope with the issues. Acid rain, nuclear radiation, fluorocarbons, atmospheric carbon dioxide and a host of similar concerns have no respect for national boundaries. The unity of humankind,* long a matter of Christian faith, has new programmatic implications for science and technology.

Unprecedented ethical questions: In a world of high technology, individuals and societies face ethical decisions for which there are no direct precedents. The Bible, the theological tradition and the philosophical tradition have no commands: thou shalt (or shalt not) re-arrange DNA, prolong the lives of permanently comatose patients, use nuclear energy, contribute to vast climatic change by burning fossil fuels. The contemporary world must develop new ethical codes to deal with new problems and possibilities. Technology itself does not answer questions about the evaluation and direction of technology. Scientists frequently talk of problems for which there is "no technical fix"; but we must recognize there is likewise "no moral fix" in the sense of simply repeating rules from the past.

The ecumenical movement is developing methods of ethical inquiry in which people of diverse skills (technological, theological, cultural), diverse social situations and diverse ideologies can interact in assessing unprecedented ethical issues. The agenda extends far into the future.

See also **bio-ethics, creation, nature, scientific world-view, technology**.

ROGER L. SHINN

P. Abrecht ed., *Faith, Science and the Future: Preparatory Readings for the 1979 Conference of the World Council of Churches*, WCC, 1978 • P. Abrecht & N. Koshy eds, *Before It's Too Late: The Complete Record of the Public Hearing on Nuclear Weapons and Disarmament Organized by the World Council of Churches*, WCC, 1983 • C. Birch & P. Abrecht eds, *Genetics and the Quality of Life*, Oxford, Pergamon, 1975 • R.L. Heilbroner, *An Inquiry into the Human Prospect, Updated and Reconsidered for the 1980s*, New York, Norton, 1980 • E.F. Schumacher, *Small Is Beautiful: Economics As If People Mattered*, New York, Harper & Row, 1973 • R.L. Shinn, *Forced Options: Social Decisions for the 21st Century*, New York, Pilgrim, 1985 • R.L. Shinn & P. Abrecht eds, *Faith and Science in an Unjust World: Report of the World Council of Churches' Conference on Faith, Science and the Future*, vol. 1 (ed. Shinn): *Plenary Presentations*; vol. 2 (ed. Abrecht): *Reports and Recommendations*, WCC, 1980.

SCIENTIFIC WORLD-VIEW. The term "scientific world-view" represents an imprecise but influential concept, arising from the modern revolutionary scientific developments originating in Western Europe and spreading throughout the world. It is associated with such famous figures as Copernicus (1473-1543), Galileo (1564-1642), Descartes (1596-1650), Newton (1642-1727), and Darwin (1809-82). Their discoveries do not, of themselves, constitute a world-view, but the cultural reverberations of their work have contributed to a widespread and comprehensive understanding of reality.

There is no single scientific world-view, but the more ambitious formulations include some or all of the following propositions: (1) the universe can be understood as a mechanism of matter in motion, acting by strictly causal laws or some combination of causality and chance; (2) accurate understanding requires quantification of evidence; qualitative distinctions can be reduced to quantitative; (3) the earth, rather than being the centre of the universe, is only a satellite of one star within one of innumerable galaxies; (4) geographical and astronomical evidence shows that the earth is billions of years old; (5) the human race is the result of an evolutionary process, operating through random variations of genetic material and survival of the fittest; (6) persons are mechanisms; freedom, soul and responsibility are illusory, (7) many ethical principles, once thought to be immutable, are in fact cultural habits, rooted in particular histories.

Historically the rise of the scientific world-view had various implications for theology. It presented obvious difficulties for those theologies that understood the Bible as a literal, scientific account of the world and history. But it then took several directions. *Deism*, popular in the 18th century, accepted God* as the first cause of the universe, now remote and irrelevant to human affairs. *Pantheism* understood God as equivalent to nature* or (as in Spinoza) the basic rational principle in nature. *Atheism** took science to be a refutation of God. *Radical agnosticism* found the idea of God irrelevant, as in the astronomer LaPlace's reply to Napoleon that he had "no need of that hypothesis". *Positivism* defined truth in terms of empirical verification and found all propositions about God, metaphysics and ethics to be neither true nor false but meaningless and nonsensical.

The modern scientific world-view is not entirely new. Ancient astronomers had rejected the geocentric view of the solar system. Democritus had taught that the world is constituted of matter and motion, operating deterministically according to causal laws. Epicurus added to the materialism of Democritus a factor of chance — a curious anticipation of modern theories of indeterminacy. But modern scientific world-views involved new comprehensive syntheses, influencing not only intellectual elites but also popular culture.

Theology responded in a variety of ways. Christians showed that exegetes through the ages had rarely interpreted all of scripture as a literal, scientific record. Kantians and neo-Kantians accepted science as an account of phenomena but not of the deeper noumenal reality of selfhood and God — a position akin to Platonic and some Oriental philosophies. Others, accepting the theological significance of science, have held that no world-view can be complete if it ignores such obvious elements of human experience as the ethical, the aesthetic and the religious. They have moved to a revision both of theological traditions and of science — a move helped by scientific developments that emphasize the relational character of all scientific understanding.

A 20th-century controversy about the scientific world-view centres in the work of Rudolf Bultmann, who argued that modern science requires a radical revision (a "demythologizing") of the Bible and traditional doctrine. Accepting a "scientific philosophy", he reinterpreted Christian faith as an expression of the Christian experience of freedom, anxiety, and faith, eliminating "objective" and metaphysical interpretations. The Swiss philosopher Karl Jaspers replied that science "does not provide a total world-view" and that much of the scientific world-view is simple "modern scientific superstition".

Both the Vatican and the WCC have given attention to the implications of science for theology. In general they have endorsed scientific endeavours and affirmed the verified findings of science, while challenging some aspects of various scientific world-views and asking for further inquiry into others.

See also **science and technology**.

ROGER L. SHINN

P. Abrecht ed., *Faith, Science and the Future*, WCC, 1980 • W.M. Horton, *Theism and the Scientific Spirit*, New York, Harper, 1933 • J. Monod, *Chance and Necessity*, New York, Knopf, 1971.

SCOTT, EDWARD WALTER.

B. 30.4.1919, Edmonton, Canada. Scott became primate of the Anglican Church of Canada in 1971 and from 1975 to 1983 was moderator of the WCC central committee. Educated at the University of British Columbia and the Anglican Theological College in Vancouver, he became active in the Student Christian Movement, of which he was for five years the general secretary at the University of Manitoba in Winnipeg. In 1960 he became director of social service for the diocese of Rupert's Land and priest in charge of Indian work. He was associate secretary of the National Council for Social Services until elected bishop of Kootenay in 1966. As an active supporter of ecumenical concerns, with pastoral gifts for prayer and reconciliation, he strongly believes that Christians must work across denominational lines on a variety of issues, although in no way denying the right of self-determination. See E.S. Light ed., *Man of Faith, Man of Action: Edward Scott* (Toronto, Anglican Book Centre, 1981).

ANS J. VAN DER BENT

SCRIPTURE.

Scripture is for Christians the Bible, containing the Old and New Testaments. From the viewpoint of the history of religions, the Bible may be compared for content and function with the scriptures* of some other faiths. Within Christianity, scripture is normally taken as the permanent written witness to God's history with the world and humankind, particularly with the elect people of Israel, and more particularly still with Jesus confessed as the Christ, Son of God and Lord — these particularities opening up again to the universal perspective and ultimate prospect of God's kingdom and the completion of the human calling in it.

In the context of some such broad general agreement, many important issues concerning scripture have been the object of controversy within Christianity: the precise limits of scripture; the understanding of its divine inspiration; the methods of its interpretation; its relation to oral, practical and institutional tradition; its authority and use in the life of the church. The state of the ecumenical discussion on these questions is reflected in several articles in this dictionary.

See **Bible, its role in the ecumenical movement; canon; exegesis, methods of; hermeneutics; inspiration; New Testament and Christian unity; Old Testament and Christian unity; Tradition and traditions; word of God**.

GEOFFREY WAINWRIGHT

SCRIPTURES.

Written texts, believed to be of supernatural revelation and preceded by oral traditions of varying lengths, are found in the major historical religions. The scriptures are used in public and private rituals and are interpreted by professional priests or scholars, providing standards of faith. A canon* (or "rule") indicates the books accepted as authoritative.

Christianity is unique in incorporating in its Bible the scriptures of its parent religion, Judaism, as an Old Testament or covenant preparatory to the New Testament. It is also unusual in providing detailed accounts of the life of its founder (in the four gospels) in its sacred canon. The earliest Christians were Jews, but the NT was written in Greek, and its authors normally used the Greek Septuagint version of the OT. Partly in response to 2nd-century Marcionism, which rejected the OT and some of the Christian writings which had already gained authority, the church established a NT canon, with as kernel the gospels and 13 epistles of Paul, but there were doubts for some time of books such as Hebrews and Revelation. Reading of the scriptures has always formed part of public worship, with law and prophets alongside epistle and gospel in the liturgy.* Readings in the West long continued in Latin, even when the modern languages had developed. At the Reformation, many vernacular translations were made, and public and private

Fragment of a Dead Sea scroll, part of a commentary on Habakkuk; reprinted by permission from "New Atlas of the Bible" (Garden City, NY, Doubleday, 1969), p. 136

Bible study flourished. Today there are portions of the Bible in more than 1,900 languages.

Jews usually prefer to speak of the Hebrew Bible, rather than the OT, Hebrew being the language in which all except a few chapters were written. The canon traditionally consists of 24 books, but with sub-division such as the "minor" prophets there is a total of 39. These fall into three sections: *torah*, "teaching" or "law", also called the Pentateuch, or "five books"; *nevi'im*, "prophets", including early historical books and major and minor prophets; *ketuvim*, "writings", including Psalms, Proverbs, Job, and some later history. It is an article of faith among Orthodox Jews that the Torah was written by Moses, but liberal Jewish and Christian writers see it as coming from various hands and dates. The written Torah was sole authority for priestly Sadducees, but Pharisees used an oral Torah to complement it, and this was developed in the Mishnah, "repetition", and vast commentaries of the Talmud, "instruction", revered and studied next in importance to the Bible. The Bible, especially the Torah, is read in Hebrew in public worship, with some use of the vernacular today.

The Qur'an ("recitation") is the basic scripture of Islam, in 114 *suras*, or "chapters". After an opening prayer these are arranged roughly with the longest first (similar to the Jewish arrangement of the prophets or the Christian ordering of the Pauline epistles). The Qur'an is regarded as the very word of God (Allāh), and commentators quote it as "God said". Fiqh Akbar II, a creed of the 10th century, declared that

"our pronouncing, writing and reciting the Qur'an is created, whereas the Qur'an itself is uncreated". It is believed that the Qur'an was revealed to the prophet Muhammad by the angel Gabriel from A.D. 610 to 632 in Mecca and Medina, that the prophet was illiterate, and that the book was written down later from "scraps of parchment and leather... and the breasts of men". The Qur'an recognizes that Moses received the Torah from God, David the Zabūr or Psalms, and Jesus the Injīl or Evangel, but while there are many biblical stories in the Qur'an it is held that the latter versions are perfect and final. Recitation of verses from the Qur'an in Arabic forms the basis of five ritual daily prayers *(salāt)* required of all Muslims, and in communal mosque worship, especially Friday prayer. The Qur'an contains religious and moral teachings, but biographies of Muhammad came much later and are not canonical. Next to the Qur'an are Hadīth, lengthy "traditions", providing guidance for many aspects of life but debated today, while the Qur'an remains uncriticized.

The Bahā'īs also recognize that previous revelations were given to Moses and Jesus, and Zoroaster and Buddha, but by placing their own leaders as prophets after Muhammad they aroused fierce persecutions from Muslims, and again recently in Iran. Bahā'ī scriptures comprise Arabic and Persian writings of the Iranian Bāb (1819-50) and Bahā' Allāh (1817-92) as verbally inspired revelations, followed by infallible commentaries of "Abd al-Bahā" (1844-1921). Much remains in manuscript, but short selections have been translated into many languages for this missionary religion.

Zoroastrianism, from Iran but chiefly now represented by small communities of Parsees in India, had a long tradition of oral texts, but like the Hindus, they were loath to use the alien art of writing for sacred purposes. The dates of Zoroaster (Zarathushtra) are debated, perhaps before 1000 B.C., and the Avesta scriptures were set down in a special alphabet about the 5th century A.D. All the Avesta are anonymous except for 17 hymns attributed to Zoroaster himself, called Gāthās, "songs". The texts have long been employed as mantras, "sacred words", used in prayers and rituals five times daily. Zand (or Zend) commentaries on the Avesta are secondary. Many texts have been translated, but some translations need revision.

Hindu scriptures are vast and amorphous, after the manner of Indian religion itself. Ancient texts were composed and recited by a Brahmin priestly elite but, like the Zoroastrian, not written down for over a millennium, and there were masses of other works. Distinction was made between *shruti*, "heard" by sages from gods (i.e. direct revelation), and *smriti*, "remembered", traditional religious and legal teachings. The oldest texts were hymns of the Vedas, "knowledge" — Rig, Sama, Yajur and Atharva — followed by Brahmanas with priestly rituals and myths. Important philosophical speculations followed in Upanishads, "sessions", which are Vedānta, "Veda's end". This title is also applied to one of six schools of philosophy which includes great thinkers like Sankara and Rāmānuja who clinch arguments by quoting Vedic texts as "scripture declares". Then came two great epic poems, Rāmāyana and Mahābhārata, the latter including the short Bhagavad-Gītā, "Lord's Song", the revelation of Krishna, best known of all translated Hindu texts in the West. Priests performed rituals three times daily, with recitations of mantras, and for other Hindus there are countless texts and hymns for communal and private worship. Vedas and epics are in Sanskrit, and other texts are in many Indian languages, small portions of which have been translated into European languages.

The Sikhs, "disciples" of the Indian Guru Nānak and his successors, have as scriptures the Adi Granth, "first book", or Guru Granth Sahib, "revered book". This comprises religious teachings in metrical form of the ten Sikh Gurus, "teachers", the first collection made by the fifth Guru Arjan in 1604 and the last recension by the tenth and last Guru, Gobind Singh, in 1706. The Adi Granth includes verses of some Hindu and Muslim teachers of comparable outlook, but not from Hindu Vedic scriptures. Lives of the ten gurus are in later hagiographies but are popular. A Dasam Granth, "book of the tenth (Guru)", includes teachings and legends. The Adi Granth is written in Gurmukhi, the script of modern Punjabi; it is chanted in temples by congregations led by musicians and is read in homes daily.

Numerically small but ancient, the Jains of India have extensive canonical scriptures differing between the Shvetāmbara, "white-clad" Jains, and the Digambara, "sky-clad". The former claim 45 collections, and the Digambara have two older texts and dispute the language and form of the canon. Of the 45 texts eight have been translated into European languages. Jain monks and nuns recite texts and engage in study, meditation and physical discipline, while the laity take part in communal worship and pilgrimages.

Buddhism was roughly contemporary with Jainism, also arising in India in the 5th or 6th century B.C. and rejecting Hindu scriptures. Among innumerable schools and texts broad distinction is made between Theravāda, "doctrine of the elders" (also called Hīnayāna, "small vehicle", by opponents), and Mahāyāna, "great vehicle"; these roughly correspond to the geographical regions of southern and northern or eastern Asia. The Theravāda canon is in "three baskets", Tri-pitaka (or Ti-pitaka); the first is Vinaya, "discipline", and the third is Abhi-dhamma, higher "dhamma", or doctrine of philosophical analysis. The second "basket" is the most important and popular, comprising the Sutta, "texts", long discourses about the Buddha and other subjects, of many dates, but with no detailed life of Gautama Buddha. Mahāyāna canons, in China, Korea and Japan, include versions of the Tri-pitaka with many other texts from different schools. Most famous is the Lotus Sutra (Saddharmapundarika), which has been called "the gospel of half Asia", and whose 24th chapter of devotion to a personal lord is recited by Zen and Nichiren adepts even when they reject other scriptures. Tibetan Buddhism has two great canonical collections, translations of Indian works, and an enormous corpus of its own, much untranslated and unpublished.

Buddhism so entered Chinese and Japanese life that its scriptures provided texts for many occasions, notably funerals. Of native Chinese writings there was a canon of five so-called Confucian Classics, though the teachings of Confucius were mostly in a short work, the *Analects* (Lun Yü). The Classics were for centuries the basis of Confucian learning, and examinations on them gave entrance into official positions. After modern revolutions the *Little Red Book* of Mao Tse-Tung (Zedong) has been used with almost religious awe by his followers. A Chinese Taoist canon of sacred texts served for ritual and festal purposes, as well as for exorcisms and alchemy. The Lao Tzu, or Tao Te Ching, inspired thinkers, and its short 81 chapters have been widely translated.

Japanese native Shinto had ancient mythology, but it was not written down till the 8th century A.D., and then in Chinese, the Kojiki and Nihongi. These were not canonical scriptures comparable to the Tri-pitaka or Classics, so that in Neo-Shinto in the 19th century attempts were made to canonize not only the oldest annals but also ancient hymns and prayers. New Shinto groups also, such as Tenri-kyo, produced modern scriptures for use in worship, and these are widely popular.

In cultures where writing was unknown, there were nevertheless traditional rituals accompanied by oral verses which often dated back centuries, and some have been rescued and preserved in modern studies. To some extent religious art was a form of scripture, representing beliefs and hopes.

Scriptural religions have great advantages: canons of texts, ancient history, and international influence. This partly accounts for the modern success of Christianity and Islam, in particular in Africa, and to a lesser extent of Hindu and Buddhist thought in Europe and America.

See also **dialogue, interfaith**.

GEOFFREY PARRINDER

J. Barr, *The Bible in the Modern World*, London, SCM, 1980 • E. Conze, *Buddhist Scriptures*, Harmondsworth, UK, Penguin, 1959 • J.R. Hinnells ed., *A Handbook of Living Religions*, Harmonds-worth, UK, Penguin, 1984 • J.S. Mbiti, *The Prayers of African Religion*, London, SPCK, 1975 • W.M. Watt, *Bell's Introduction to the Qur'an*, Edinburgh, University Press, 1970 • R.C. Zaehner, *Hindu Scriptures*, London, Dent, 1966.

SECRETARIAT FOR PROMOTING CHRISTIAN UNITY.

The SPCU originated as a preparatory organ of Vatican II,* then functioned as a Council drafting body, and now is the office of the Roman curia which deals with the pastoral promotion of the church's participation in the one ecumenical movement. After the Council, Paul VI confirmed the SPCU as a permanent office of the holy see (3 January 1966). Until 1989 it was called a secretariat; thereafter it has been a pontifical council.

On 5 June 1960, John XXIII created the SPCU to enable "those who bear the name of Christians but are separated from this apostolic see to find more easily the path by which they may arrive at that unity for which Christ prayed". He appointed Cardinal Augustine Bea (1881-1968) to be the SPCU president; Johannes Willebrands (1909-) became its secretary and, after Bea's death, its president until December 1989.

The SPCU began official contacts with leaders in the Anglican, Orthodox and Protestant churches. It evaluated their suggestions for the Council themes and, where necessary, used these for its own draft work or passed them on to other preparatory commissions. The SPCU negotiated with the world confessional bodies, e.g. the Lambeth conference of bishops (Anglican), for the participation of their delegated observers to the Council.

The SPCU was responsible for the promulgated pastoral documents *On Ecumenism; On Religious Freedom; On the Relation of the Church to the Non-Christian Religions;* and *On Divine Revelation,* co-drafted with the theological commission.

After the council, Paul VI confirmed the SPCU as a permanent office of the holy see (3 January 1966), and he later specified its structure and competence in the re-organization of the Roman curia (15 August 1967).

The SPCU's contacts with other Christian communions had initiated the personal and organizational relations which in the post-council period led to the active presence of

SPCU-delegated observers at confessional and interconfessional gatherings and to a variegated series of international and national bilateral dialogues.* The SPCU has been co-sponsoring international theological dialogues with the Lutheran World Federation (1965), the Anglican communion (1966), the World Methodist Council (1966), the Old Catholic churches of the Union of Utrecht (1966), the World Alliance of Reformed Churches (1968), the Pentecostals (1972), the Disciples of Christ (1977), the evangelicals (1977), the Orthodox church (1979), and the Baptist World Alliance (1984).

In 1966 was held the first annual meeting of the Joint Working Group* between the RCC and the WCC. This group recommends to the parent bodies both the agenda and the means of collaboration in studies and action.

Since Vatican II the SPCU has been issuing norms and guidelines on specific topics. Of major import has been the *Directory, Part 1* (1967), on diocesan and national ecumenical commissions, on mutual recognitions of baptisms,* and on sharing "spiritual activities", including liturgical worship. *Part 2* (1969) covers ecumenical principles and practices at the university and seminary levels. In view of the 1983 code of canon law, an updated directory was promulgated in 1990.

In bearing responsibility for the holy see's dealing with Jewish religious concerns, the SPCU formed, with the International Jewish Committee for Interreligious Consultations, the Catholic/Jewish International Liaison Committee. In 1974 Paul VI set up the Commission for Religious Relations with the Jews; its president is ex officio the SPCU president. In 1975 the commission issued "Guidelines and Suggestions" for implementing Vatican II's statement on the Jews, and in 1985, notes on the Catholic presentation of "Jews and Judaism in Preaching and Catechesis."

In John Paul II's 1989 re-structuring of the Roman curia, the SPCU became one of the pontifical councils. The new council (PCPCU) retains all the SPCU's original post-conciliar mandates; among them, "to interpret correctly ecumenical principles" and "to apply with opportune initiatives and activities the ecumenical duty to restore unity among Christians". All curial offices are juridically equal, but they must submit documents which "touch on doctrines as to faith and morals" to the

Congregation for the Doctrine of the Faith for its judgment prior to publication. One understandably questions, in the post-Willebrands era, how the two bodies will resolve differences on the content, for example, of multilateral and bilateral dialogues in which PCPCU is a partner through its designated members, including its staff.

TOM STRANSKY

"An Historical Sketch of the SPCU", in *Doing the Truth in Charity,* Vatican ecumenical documents, 1964-80, T. Stransky & J. Sheerin eds, New York, Paulist, 1982 • SPCU, *Information Service,* Vatican City, 3-4 times a year • T. Stransky, "The Foundations of the SPCU", in *Vatican II by Those Who Were There,* A. Stacpoole ed., London, Chapman, 1986.

SECTS. The word "sect" (Latin *secta,* from *sequi,* to follow, i.e. a teacher or teaching; a translation of the Greek *hairesis,* originally a choice — see **heresy**) has acquired a special meaning and force in Christian language, particularly in the context of ecclesiology. From the outset, although it sometimes meant simply a particular school or party (see Acts 5:17, 24:5, 26:5) without conveying disapproval or stigma, its dominant reference was to a group which either broke off from the church* or formed independently as a separatist body within the traditional Christian world, in opposition to the church.

Sects were accused — and the accusation still clings to the word — of falsifying the gospel, apostasy from the church's faith, separation from the Body of Christ, arrogance, and leading souls astray, even to damnation. In countries where Christianity became dominant, "sectarians" were accused also of endangering the unity of the nation and of undermining prevailing standards. Thus the term is clearly negative. Those who belong to a sect have been written off in church and society, especially in Europe. The accusatory term should no longer be used, however, especially by Christians and churches which consistently advocate freedom of belief, civil religious liberty, and the unrestricted formation of religious groups.

The sociology of religion has tried to employ the term in a neutral sense, e.g. to refer to a relatively small religious group which has split off from a larger one; a new lively community as opposed to an inactive traditional community; a voluntary association of individuals with a personal faith, as opposed to the church as an establishment for salvation into which one has been born (Max Weber, Ernst Troeltsch); an alternative group as opposed not to the church but to society as such (Gerardus van der Leeuw). These sociological attempts, however, remain within the academic sphere. They carry little conviction, because none of these terms can do justice to the variety of phenomena. But above all, one cannot disregard the history of the term; it carries such heavy negative connotations that it cannot again be understood in a neutral sense.

Historians of religion look at secondary formations of religious groups within the sphere of influence of a dominant religion and should choose a general term such as "religious communities". These groups are then differentiated according to their origins, age, size, influence; their relation to the parent religion, to other religious groups, and to the surrounding culture which sustain them; and their effects on individuals and society. In all these points groups may change throughout their history and then must be assessed differently.

A "sect" is not simply removed from the world because of changed terminology. Phenomenologically, one can speak of a sectarian attitude and mentality (Joachim Wach) also within the churches. The marks of such a sectarian mentality are: some traditional articles of faith are so over-emphasized that they squeeze Christ and his gospel out of the central place in the faith; new doctrines and forms of belief, which are beyond the Bible and church tradition, acquire central importance and they become a means of distinguishing the members from all the other Christians; the religious and spiritual horizon is narrowed. The sectarians are detached from the world and exclusive, and their group-related self-understanding makes church fellowship impossible and often creates social isolation. Accordingly, the "sectarian" and the "sectarian group" is a *type* of religious adherence.

In the context of ecumenical ecclesiological studies, the following distinctions should be drawn (allowing for overlaps and constant changes): (1) churches in the Christian tradition which have more or less fellowship with each other: the historical churches, those in

traditionally Christian countries that have detached themselves from the dominant (often a state) church, and "mission" or "young" churches; (2) Christian denominations and congregations which have separated from the church fellowship or have newly come into existence alongside the churches and live independently or as separatist groups (e.g. Adventist, Apostolic and many Pentecostal communities, African Independent Churches); (3) groups whose approach to faith and whose doctrines and practices are alien to the biblical Christian tradition and in some circumstances are directed against it (e.g. spiritualist and gnostic-esoteric communities and those which believe in a new revelation, as the Latter-Day Saints [Mormons]); (4) syncretistic formations where the non-Christian element predominates (e.g. Christian Science, communities of Christians characterized by anthroposophy) and tends to the establishment of new religions.

Religious groups which originate outside the Christian tradition do not count as "sects" but as offshoots from other religions. In the USA the term "cult" has appeared in the last few decades for those new groups with a high conflict potential which stand outside the mainstream of Christianity and are in fact hostile to the prevailing society and its cultural values. All in all, one notices an increasing religious pluralism even in countries with an established Christian tradition, and this trend is obliging the churches to strengthen their efforts for giving a Christian response as they encounter other types of belief.

HANS DIETHER REIMER

K. Hutten, "Seher, Grubler, Enthusiasten", in *Das Buch der traditionellen Sekten und religiösen Sonderbewegungen*, Stuttgart, Quell, 1982 • J.G. Melton, *The Encyclopedia of American Religions*, Wilmington, DE, McGrath, 1978 • H. Turner, *Bibliography of New Religious Movements in Primal Societies*, 2 vols, Boston, Hall, 1977-78.

SECULARIZATION. The Latin word *saeculum* denotes a limited but extended period of time: a human generation, a century (French *siècle*), or simply an age. It is still so used, e.g. in speaking of the secular appearance of a comet or the secular cooling of the earth.

The word entered Christian vocabulary as

the consistent Vulgate translation of the Greek New Testament word *aiōn*, age (sometimes confusingly translated "world"), in all the variety of its meanings. It is this age, created by God (Heb. 1:2), when we marry and are given in marriage (Luke 20:34), in which we are to do good to our neighbours (1 Tim. 6:17), but whose cares can steal our minds from the promise of God (Mark 4:19). It is an age ruled by powers blind to God's promise in their false wisdom (1 Cor. 2:6-8), to whose values and standards we are not to be conformed (Rom. 12:2) and which will end in the judgment of God (Matt. 24), to be followed by an age to come in which the faithful will have eternal life (Luke 18:30). The *saeculum* in the NT is the history* which God has created, the time in which God works in judgment and grace.* It is also the history of human sin* and rebellion, of powers that exalt themselves, of wisdom that is ephemeral because it is not rooted in faith* and obedience. But the kingdom* to which the faithful look forward, and according to which they live, is also a *saeculum*, a redeemed, everlasting *(aiōnios)* age to come, but still an age.

The Vulgate, however, did not so translate. The Greek *aiōnios* became the Latin *aeterna*, obscuring its relation to the word "age". Justification for this translation could be found in Plato's *Timaeus*, where *aiōn* means not time but timelessness, the unchanging reality of true forms, with an eye to which imperfect things of this world have their time *(chronos)* and decay.

Subtly, never completely but nevertheless dominantly, the *saeculum* came to be identified with the temporal, and the eternal with the timeless and unchanging. The *saeculum* was no longer the sphere in which discipleship could be most fully learned and practised; that was reserved for the religious discipline of the monastery. It was no longer the historical time that lived in expectation of the coming of the Redeemer, realizing the promise of that coming in the events of the present age. Rather, in medieval Christendom, a hierarchical relation developed between secular estates of human life and work, affirmed as God's good creation, and the religious life in the service of the church, whose goal is the eternal contemplation of God.

This distinction is preserved in the Roman Catholic Church to this day. The code of canon law reserves the term "religious life" for those who "profess the evangelical counsels of poverty, chastity and obedience by vows or other sacred bonds" and who live "in institutes of consecrated life canonically erected by competent church authority" (canon 573). "Secular" clergy serve the church in normal parish situations while still practising a religious discipline. For the rest, secular activities are commended to the laity as their mission (canon 225) and strictly forbidden to clergy as "unbecoming to their state" (canon 285). Secularization is mentioned only once: unfrocking of a priest for due cause. The *Catholic Encyclopedia*, however, uses the term also for the removal of property or of functions, in themselves quite secular (lands, schools, hospitals, orphanages, et al.), from the control of the (Roman) church.

In Latin America the term has been used in this sense, particularly in the 19th century, when liberal governments, with the support of freemasons, positivists and Protestant minorities, challenged the control of the Roman Catholic Church in the field of education and certain civil functions (like the record of births and the celebration of marriages). This was understood by Protestants as a struggle for religious freedom and equal rights for all, and the debate about some still-remaining limitations (chaplaincies, eligibility for some public offices) still gives rise to tension and continues as a subject of dialogue in ecumenical relations.

The process. The meaning of "secular" for the present time, however, is determined by two other factors: the mid-20th-century discovery of how deep and broad the process of secularization has become among not only structures and powers of the common life but also methods of thought and ways of perceiving reality, and the theological recovery of the biblical meaning of the word as a context of the work of God and the mission* of the church.*

Dietrich Bonhoeffer described secularization, in a letter from prison in 1944, as a movement "towards the autonomy of man, in which I would include the discovery of the laws by which the world lives and deals with itself in science, social and political matters, art, ethics and religion". The world has reached adulthood; it no longer needs the working hypothesis "God" to make sense of reality and to solve the problems of human life. Secularization is, in the words of an Ecumenical Institute (Bossey) report in 1959, "the withdrawal of areas of life and thought from religious — and finally also from metaphysical — control and the attempt to understand and live in these areas in the terms which they alone offer".

Secularization is not a world-view but a process. Its essence is a change in the method of human thought and action. Total coherence is no longer sought. Various sciences concentrate on specialized areas in which their findings can be experimentally validated. Various technologies aim at the working effectiveness of their operations (see **science and technology**).

Universal structures of meaning, whether religious or otherwise, are irrelevant to this enterprise. Human beings no longer live in embracing communities that determine their values and judge their actions; rather, they live in the anonymity of the city (Harvey Cox), where they are free to move about, to choose their own associations and the direction of their lives. Even religion,* where accepted, is validated by its usefulness for social coherence (Emile Durkheim), for psychological health or for good human relations.

The ideology. Secularization is a habit of mind and a way of life, a trend of human events, not a philosophy. Not surprisingly, however, it has been accompanied by repeated efforts to give it a world-view which would show its powers and tendencies to be hopeful and liberating and which give them a particular direction (see **ideology**). These forms of secularist humanism have been many and varied, ranging from idealism to pragmatism to materialism; from economic liberalism to revolutionary Marxism to anarchism. One such philosophy defined by the British writer G.J. Holyoake took the name "secularism". It was a system of ethical principles based on four premises: (1) primary emphasis on the material and cultural improvement of humanity; (2) respect for and search for all truth, from whatever source, which can be tested in experience as leading to human betterment; (3) concern for the improvement of this world and not for another; (4) an independent rational morality.

Utilitarian in its ethics, idealistic in its optimistic view of human nature, and pragmatist in its radical epistemological relativism, Holyoake's secularism was a moral-humanist reaction against the Christianity of his time. It was a good example of the secularism which concerned the Jerusalem conference of the International Missionary Council in 1928, defined there by Rufus Jones as "a way of life and an interpretation of life that include only the natural order of things and that do not find God or a realm of spiritual reality essential for life or thought". The Jerusalem conference treated secularism as one of the religions of the modern world with many positive values — freedom, idealism and devotion to the common good — which needs to find its fulfilment, as do all other religions, in the spirit of Jesus Christ.

But this theology of continuity between humanist ideologies and Christian faith ran counter both to the insights of dialectical theology (Emil Brunner, Karl Barth, Hendrik Kraemer) and to the process of secularization itself. Bonhoeffer recognized that his non-religious colleagues in the struggle against Hitler retained no humanist illusions. Confidence in natural human morality and progress has been undermined by the success of science and technology itself in releasing nuclear energy and in manipulating the human environment. Political economic formulas for human salvation, both socialist and capitalist, have lost credibility by their performance in power. Secularized methods of thought and action produce phenomena that defy all attempts — religious or secularist — to incorporate them into a total system of meaning and hope.

The theology. By what faith and in what hope, then, can secularization be endured without falling into nihilism (Helmut Thielicke) or into a practical polytheism (H.R. Niebuhr)? Some maintain that this is not possible. "Secularization, as religionless neutrality, exists not as an end product but only as a process, that is, only in contrast to Christian religion or in its reflected light. If the latter is lacking, a vacuum arises which sucks in religious or pseudo-religious powers" (Wilhelm Hahn). Barth is ambivalent on the subject. On the one hand, his critique of human religion (*Church Dogmatics* I/2) and his affirmation of secular inquiry concerning both nature and humanity outside the context of faith, just in so far as it does not erect new world-views (III/2), seem to affirm secularized existence in the context of divine grace. On the other hand, Barth explicitly rejects Bonhoeffer's understanding of humanity as mature in its secularity apart from faith *(The Humanity of God)*.

A clear positive theology of secularization owes its origin to Bonhoeffer and to Friedrich Gogarten. For Bonhoeffer, Christ confronts the world not in its weakness and dependency on religious or other world-views but at the strong points of human health and responsibility. "It is not the religious act that makes the Christian but participation in the sufferings of God in the secular life. That is *metanoia*, not in the first place thinking about one's own needs, problems, sins and fears, but allowing oneself to be caught up in the way of Jesus Christ." Bonhoeffer is clear that a sinful, godless world must still be brought to repentance and new life in Christ, but sins of which it must repent are first of all those of its powers and vigour amid the responsibilities where human problems are faced and dealt with. Christ, the ultimate reality of the world, takes form in the world in order that the world, in its penultimate secularity, may move towards its ultimate redemption in him *(Ethics)*.

Gogarten links secularization directly to the faith of the Reformation. Justified by grace alone, the Christian is free to participate in the sonship of Jesus Christ. This is the manner of human creatureliness, and with it human beings receive the world to rule over responsibly. In Christ the world is known not in the wholeness of its structure and destiny but historically, in the promise of its participation in God's creative and redemptive work. The church's secular attitude in faith "knows the limits of its reason yet does not give up the question which God has planted in the human mind about the wholeness of all things. It lives in expectant relativity." The scientific technological development of modern times is not only acceptable in God's sight; it is in its relativity called to strive for wholeness under God's blessing, threatened with God's judgment when it erects its own myth or ideology, but affirmed in its secularity.

The ecumenical influence of this theology has been widespread. In 1959 a conference of university teachers at the Ecumenical Institute examined the process of secularization in various disciplines of the university — philosophy, the physical sciences, sociology, and the humanities — in an effort to discern the form of Christian responsibility and theological insight with relation to them. One interesting fruit of this conference was testimony from Japan and from India that secularization is also a phenomenon in those religious contexts as it is most radically in China.

The implications of this fact for the mission of the Christian church are large. They were given full expression by A.T. van Leeuwen in his *Christianity in World History* (1964). In van Leeuwen's view, the whole of Western and now of world history should be understood in terms of the historicizing impact of Christian mission rooted in the biblical history which preceded it. The rule of structures of being (ontocracies), whether mythological or rationalistic, which understood the world as divided between eternal order and shifting time, has been continually challenged by God's choice of a people with a secular message of redemption and fulfilment for the world. The historical promise of ˙the gospel continually breaks through sacred structures, Christian and non-Christian, which limit human history and hope. It foments revolution against these structures in the name of the promise of God. Western history, and now world history, in van Leeuwen's view, is the story of this interaction. Thus the gospel of the kingdom both judges and inspires secular history with its promise. Cox in his immensely popular *Secular City* presented the same message in the US. Ecumenical studies in evangelism were preoccupied in the 1960s with the question of the form of the church as witness to the secular promise of God.

Recent events raise questions to van Leeuwen's confident prediction that secularization, challenged and inspired by the gospel, is the wave of the future. Religious revivals of varying intensities have arisen in reaction to the ongoing technological logic and power of the secularizing process. Ideologies have become more popular as rallying cries, even as their power to explain reality disintegrates. Theologically, however, the question bequeathed to us by the NT text itself, properly understood, remains: what is the significance of the *saeculum* — of this age — as the time and place of God's revelation in Christ? And then, what is its relation to the age to come?

See also **church and world, unity of humankind**.

CHARLES C. WEST

D. Bonhoeffer, *Widerstand und Ergebung* (ET *Letters and Papers from Prison*, London, SCM, 1972) • J.F. Childress & D.B. Harned eds, *Secularization and the Protestant Prospect*, Philadelphia, Westminster, 1970 • H. Cox, *The Secular City*, London, SCM, 1965 • F. Gogarten, *Verhängnis und Hoffnung der Neuzeit* (ET *Despair and Hope for Our Time*, Philadelphia, Pilgrim, 1970) • A.T. van Leeuwen, *Christianity in World History*, London, Edinburgh House, 1964 • L. Newbigin, *Honest Religion for Secular Man*, London, SCM, 1966 • R.G. Smith, *Secular Christianity*, London, Collins, 1966 • C.C. West, *The Meaning of the Secular*, Ecumenical Institute, Bossey, September 1959.

SEDOS. Servizio de Documentazione e Studi (Documentation and research centre) organizes over 70 Roman Catholic religious and missionary institutes of men and women to combine their resources to serve the church more effectively in its missionary activity. With its permanent secretariat in Rome, SEDOS was founded after Vatican II (1966) by superiors general whose communities are committed to mission work, e.g. Jesuits, Society of Divine Word, Society of African Missions, Franciscan Missionary Sisters, Medical Mission Sisters, Christian Brothers.

SEDOS maintains an ample documentation library on trends and experiences in mission, organizes research seminars and study sessions, collaborates with other research centres and international agencies specializing in missiology and related disciplines, and publishes a monthly bulletin on mission issues. SEDOS and its member communities closely collaborate with the Pontifical Council for Promoting Christian Unity and the WCC Commission on World Mission and Evangelism, e.g. in preparation for and follow-up of the CWME Melbourne (1980) and San Antonio (1989) conferences and in inviting CWME representatives to major SEDOS seminars. In Rome it receives Anglican, Protestant and Orthodox mission leaders.

See also **missionary societies**.

TOM STRANSKY

SEVENTH-DAY ADVENTIST CHURCH. The SDAC is the largest Adventist denomination which came out of the early 19th-century advent awakening in North America. Though their immediate roots are found in Millerism and its emphasis on the second coming of Christ, SDAs see themselves as being in apostolic succession with the doctrines and message of the New Testament church and in harmony with the basic principles of the Protestant Reformation.

The SDAC is a conservative Christian movement, largely evangelical in doctrine and professing no creed but the Bible. Nevertheless, SDAs affirm 27 fundamental beliefs; many they share with other Christians, such as the Trinity,* salvation by faith in Jesus Christ alone, and the unconditional authority of the Bible. They also observe the biblical seventh day of the week as the sabbath. They practise believer's baptism by immersion and include foot washing as part of the communion service (Lord's supper). They also believe in eternal life as the gift of God. The saved receive immortality at the time of the resurrection, which takes place at the second coming of Christ, prior to the millennium. Adventists believe also in the priesthood of Jesus as Intercessor and Judge.

Because the body is the temple of the Holy Spirit, SDAs believe they are to care intelligently for both their spiritual and physical health. In aiming at the most healthful diet, they abstain from unclean flesh foods, alcoholic beverages and other drugs, including tobacco. The modern packaged breakfast-cereal industry owes its origin to the SDAC and its emphasis on health.

In its polity, the SDAC has a blend of representative and congregational forms of government. The local church* determines membership, and delegated authority passes up from one level of church constituency to another. Several churches in an area form conferences (or missions), several conferences form unions, and the almost 100 unions form the SDA General Conference.* Between constituency meetings (every three or five years), the church on each level is administered by executive committees, officers and departmental directors.

The latest SDAC statistics indicate a baptized membership of almost 6 million (88% outside of North America) in some 30,000 local churches, 420 conferences, 5,200 schools (elementary through university), 530 health-care institutions, and organized church work in 184 countries or political areas. To support their worldwide pastoral ministry and evangelistic outreach, SDAs give free-will offerings and practise tithing, although it is not a test of fellowship.

Though the SDAC is not a member of the organized ecumenical movement, it recognizes those church agencies that lift up Christ as a part of the divine plan for the evangelization of the world and holds in high esteem fellow Christians in other communions who are engaged in winning souls for Christ. The SDAC is regularly represented through observers or advisors at WCC and other church meetings. For many years, a SDA has been a member of the WCC Faith and Order* commission in a personal capacity. The SDAC has participated in dialogues with the WCC and various religious bodies and since 1968 has been represented at the conference of secretaries of Christian World Communions.* More recently, the SDAC has been represented at the annual conference of US church leaders. Christian World Communions and various churches have responded to the SDA invitation and sent observers to the quinquennial general conference sessions.

Seventh-day Adventists recognize that true religion is based on conscience and conviction. No selfish or traditional tie should hold any church member to one's communion, except the belief that in this way he or she finds true connection to Christ. Because of its understanding of the gospel commission's mandate, the SDAC acknowledges the rights of all religious persuasions to operate without geographic restrictions. The SDAC wishes to preach the "everlasting gospel" to every nation and people in the spirit of Christian courtesy, frankness and fairness.

BERT B. BEACH

B. Beach, Ecumenism — Boon or Bane?, Washington, DC, Review & Herald, 1974 • Seventh-day Adventist Encyclopedia, Washington, DC, Review & Herald, 1976 • Seventh-day Adventists Believe, General Conference of SDA, 1988.

SEVENTH-DAY ADVENTIST GENERAL CONFERENCE. The general conference is the world administrative body of the Seventh-day Adventist Church,* headquartered near Washington, DC, with a staff of about 700. The general conference was organized in 1863 when the total church membership was 3,500. It operates through 12 division branch offices.

The conference meets every five years. Delegates (now approximately 2,600) come from every part of the world. This meeting "synthesizes and implements church organization on a world scale" and elects conference and division officers and departmental directors for the ensuing period. Only the sessions can change the general conference constitution and the Church Manual, which includes the fundamental beliefs, standards of church membership and matters regarding the operation of local churches.

BERT B. BEACH

W.R. Beach & B.B. Beach, Pattern for Progress: The Role and Function of Church Organization, Washington, DC, Review & Herald, 1985.

SEXISM. This term was introduced into the ecumenical debate mainly through the 1974 consultation in West Berlin on "Sexism in the 1970s: Discrimination against Women". Long before — and even more after — that time, women (and men) in the ecumenical movement have addressed the problem of sexism as it presents itself within the churches and the WCC. Sexism is seen as an ideology* of male supremacy and superiority which deprives women of their equal status with men. It is defined as discrimination of a person on the basis of sex (as racism* discriminates on the basis of skin colour). Some controversy exists within the women's movement about the inter-relationship of sexism and other forms of oppression like racism or classism ("Is sexism more fundamental than racism or classism?" "How do white middle-class women express solidarity with black poor women?"). But it is clear that sexism combined with racism or classism puts women at the lowest end of the social ladder and subjects them to double or triple oppression. Women themselves can also act as agents of oppression of other women.

Sexism is a manifestation of patriarchy, a system in which highest value is given to the father. All others are subordinated to a hierarchical order: men-women-children-slaves-animals-nature. Women are seen as weaker than and inferior to men, needing male protection and (esp. spiritual) guidance ("paternalism").

In a process of growing awareness women discovered that sexist thinking is created, supported and maintained by law,* culture* and religion.* Sexist thinking is also deeply ingrained in many women's self-perception as helpless, incapable and weak. Feminist scholarship "discovered" that the Bible was written within the patriarchal context of Palestine and the Roman empire. The Judeo-Christian tradition is accused of, consciously or unconsciously, perpetuating sexism by its symbol systems (e.g. an all-male Trinity: Father, Son and [male] Holy Spirit), its patriarchal structure (headed only by male popes and bishops); its teaching, language, art and so on. All of these elements imply women's inferiority or unworthiness. This critique emerged in a systematic way beginning only in the middle of this century since the time women gained access to learning and teaching theology in the universities and theological colleges.

Sexism has raised several objections to patriarchal theology. The Bible, being itself shaped by patriachal values, has over the centuries been interpreted exclusively by men, i.e. from the male perspective. Female participation in shaping cult and theology has been marginalized, suppressed, even denied altogether in church history, although the role of women was prominent in the Jesus movement and the early church. From the early church fathers to this very day, women are presented as possessing less of the image of God than males (note that they were created only from "Adam's rib"), therefore they are non-normative, belonging to the realm of nature or flesh over against the realm of the spirit. Patriarchal theology has blamed women for the first sin and justified their subordination under men as God-given punishment. It has stressed women's bodily impurity in menstruation and childbirth and equates women with sexual temptation ("eternal Eve"), while Mariology presents Mary as an unobtainable role model ("Virgin mother"). The church has excluded women from the representation of the Divine and Christ in the leadership of the church and thus perpetuated male superiority and male power. It has barred women's access to the ordained ministry. It has excluded women from the language of liturgy, confessions, hymns and prayers (referring to "men", "fathers", "brotherhood" only) and has encouraged women to be "silent in the church" and rendered them invisible in church history. The church has given women no access to theology and spiritual formation and has discriminated against girls in baptismal rites (in some Orthodox churches the baby boy is laid on the altar, not the girl). It re-inforces subordination of women through marriage liturgies and has applied Christian values like humility and self-denial mainly to women. Finally, the church sustains stereotyped role models for women by stressing their subsidiary role as "helpmate", commonly appealing to Martha (Luke 10:38-40).

The most radical critique from post-Christian feminists accuses the churches of being the ideological backbone and stronghold of sexist practices ("If God is male, then the male is God", Mary Daly). Against such accusations and in the interest of restoring the truth of the gospel as expressed in Gal. 3:28 ("there is neither Jew nor Greek, there is neither slave nor free, there is neither male nor female; for you are all one in Christ Jesus"), many programmes and initiatives have emerged within the WCC: the women's forum in the fifth assembly (Nairobi 1975); the "Community of Women and Men in the Church"* study and the Sheffield consultation (1981); the strong participation of women in all areas of the sixth assembly (Vancouver 1983) as drafters, speakers, preachers, leaders, and the preassembly women's meeting; the Ecumenical Decade of the Churches in Solidarity with Women.*

In all these meetings and programmes it was stressed that sexism in the churches needs to be eradicated through (1) advocacy for women's full access and participation in the leadership of the churches; (2) the ordination of women* to the priesthood (which is not accepted mainly by the Orthodox member churches of WCC); (3) elimination of sexist language and practices; (4) re-reading of the Bible and the Tradition from women's perspective; (5) equal opportunities for women in all fields of life (employment and pay, education and health, esp. within the structures of the churches).

The discussion about the extent of sexism

in the churches and its abolition, however, has proved to be one of the most controversial issues in the present ecumenical movement. The ordination of the first black woman as Episcopalian bishop (Barbara Harris of the USA in 1989) was welcomed by many women in all denominations worldwide as a historic breakthrough; at the same time, some interpret it as endangering the ecumenical dialogue between Anglicans, Orthodox and Roman Catholics.

Sexism touches deeply the matrix of the churches' existence. But it will not go away by itself. Many women leave the churches, as they see no signs of change. There is the danger that the churches will lose their most faithful members if they do not deal seriously, self-critically and creatively with the challenge.

See also **feminism**.

BÄRBEL von WARTENBERG-POTTER

J. Becher ed., *Women, Religion and Sexuality*, WCC, 1990 • E.S. Fiorenza, *In Memory of Her: A Feminist Theological Reconstruction*, New York, Crossroad, 1983 • C. Parvey ed., *The Community of Women and Men in the Church: The Sheffield Report*, WCC, 1983 • R. Ruether, *Sexism and God Talk: Towards a Feminist Theology*, London, SCM, 1983 • *Sexism in the 1970s: Discrimination against Women*, WCC, 1975.

SIMATUPANG, TAHI BONAR.

B. 20.1.1920, Sidikalang, Sumatra, Indonesia; d. 1.1.1990. A WCC president, 1975-83, and central and executive committee member, 1968-75, Simatupang was educated at the Dutch royal military academy. After Indonesia's proclamation of independence (1945), he was involved in organizing the war to defend the Republic of Indonesia and later in the peace negotiations with the Netherlands. After early retirement from the post of chief of staff of the armed forces, he was active in the ecumenical movement at regional, national and world levels. He was president of the Christian Conference of Asia, 1973-77, and president of the National Council of Churches in Indonesia, 1967-84. For a number of years he wrote regularly for the influential Indonesian newspaper *Sinar Harapan*. He wrote numerous books and articles on political, military and ecumenical concerns in Indonesia, some of which have been trans-

lated into English, Dutch, German and Japanese.

ANS J. VAN DER BENT

SIN. Anthropology (see **anthropology, theological**) and soteriology (see **salvation**) are interwoven in the doctrine of sin. It is common Christian teaching that God originally created human beings in his image and likeness. This nature enables them to reveal, but also to betray, their Creator, because it gives them the opportunity of suppressing the distinction between Creator and creature (creation*) and of dangerously identifying themselves with, or mistaking themselves for, God (see Gen. 6:1-4, 11:1-9). The worship of God the Creator turns into self-worship and demonic idolatry. The Bible depicts this mistake as sin, thereby using a vocabulary (*hata'* and *hamartanein*) and an imagery that stresses the failing in and falling short of one's intention, the missing of the mark. Because human beings in their failing and pride are prevented from establishing the communion with God and one another to which they are originally called, sin can also be defined as the destruction of the totality, the breaking of positive relations — indeed, of the human community — revolt against and violation of covenant,* alienation between God and humankind. To this effect the Old Testament denounces sin as idolatry and interprets it as adultery against Yahweh. On the other hand, the prophets also vehemently condemn social injustice as sin and take sides in the struggle for the weak and poor against the mighty and powerful. The New Testament continues this line of thought when expounding sin as the human attitude and act directed against Christ and the Holy Spirit* and at the same time emphasizing the failure to exercise love towards one's neighbour as sinful. In the last analysis, sin results in death (Rom. 6:23; see **life and death**). In short, the Bible as a whole reprobates any human approach and any mentality directed against God and humankind as sinful transgression of the boundaries and limits inherent in divine creation and human createdness.

This sin (singular) against God becomes concrete in the sins (plural) against his creatures. The alienation between God and God's creation is, however, part of the human condition, from which we cannot escape (Rom. 3:23). Humankind does not just act sinfully; it *is* sinful. This teaching is meant when Christian tradition throughout the centuries has spoken of original sin. This doctrine expresses the conviction that sin, though universal, is not necessary, holding human beings, who have committed the breach of solidarity with their Creator and one another, paradoxically responsible in united solidarity of sin and guilt. It prevents us from misinterpreting sinfulness in moralistic terms and qualifies it as having primarily to do with human relation to God and only derivatively with interhuman contacts. It asserts the idea of a free will, inherent in humankind's being created in the image and likeness of God, as the necessary prerequisite for individual and collective responsibility for sin, while at the same time claiming that human beings cannot but be sinful (Rom. 7:18-19), because they fall victims to the temptation to be like God and thus lose the freedom that they were from the beginning destined to enjoy. The free will implies, negatively as it were, the possibility of distorting the likeness with our Creator into its demonic contrast and the potentiality of orienting ourselves towards the idols, whom we, treacherous to God and ironically enough, serve in an unending faithfulness. We commit adultery with other gods and distrust our own Creator. Thus sin can basically be understood as unbelief.

Because this radical faithlessness draws humankind away from God, the gospel calls it back to communion with God by urgently inviting conversion and promising redemption* and forgiveness of sins. This offer is made possible because Jesus Christ* on the cross took upon himself the guilt of humankind and was punished in its place. In spite of its failure and betrayal, God remained in solidarity with his creation, and his Son's death on the cross brought reconciliation* between God and the world. Christ did what human beings ought to have done — bore the divine condemnation merited by human sin — and thus through dying in their place he won the righteousness required from them. Through faith* in Jesus Christ humankind now participates in his justice, bestowed upon them and sealed in the sacrament* of baptism.* Through faith, believers have developed from having been instruments of and slaves to sin-

fulness into becoming instruments of and slaves to righteousness (Rom. 6:12-13). Out of sheer grace* God declares them righteous and accepts them as his sons and daughters; as a consequence, they leave death behind and start to walk in newness of life. The baptized are cleansed of their past sin and are from now on expected to live in purity of heart, although this does not mean that sinfulness has been totally overcome and that post-baptismal transgressions are unknown.

From the angle of *justification* by *faith*, this view of sin seems theologically awkward but is nevertheless an empirical fact. Every human being is *simul iustus et peccator*, at once righteous and a sinner. This (originally Lutheran) phrase is interpreted in a somewhat different way in the various confessions and even within the Lutheran tradition itself. The Reformation churches normally stress that justification does not only imply the forgiveness of sins but also brings a person into the newness of life. On the one hand, God *declares* a person to be righteous (forensic, imputative justification); on the other, God *makes* him or her righteous (effective justification). Justification and sanctification* imply one another, the latter always being the result of and never the prerequisite for the former. Because believers, therefore, *are* just, they do good works, which, however, can never form the basis for their justification and redemption. People can never be saved on account of their works; on the other hand, it is as certain that without these works they perish (Formula of Concord, solid declaration 3).

But justification does not protect the justified person from still committing sins, because his or her righteousness remains a *iustitia aliena (iustitia extra nos)*, righteousness of another (righteousness outside of us). Through justification the attitude of a sinful person to God has been, to be sure, totally changed, but the person has not at all changed ontologically (on a Lutheran view) and therefore remains, though totally justified, what he or she ever was, i.e. totally a sinner. Yet Martin Luther himself can also speak about the faithful as *partially* sinful and *partially* justified, so that sanctification is seen as an ongoing learning process and the factual situation of the person as not being changed all at once. But from the beginning, Lutheran theology has indisputably tended to over-em-

Dance around the Golden Calf, Kirchentag 1987, Frankfurt (epd-bild/Neetz)

phasize the *simul iustus et peccator* in terms of a paradox indicating that the human person is totally righteous and totally sinful and that post-baptismal sin is inevitable. This view may under unhappy circumstances prepare the way for antinomianism and ethical indifference and thus neglect the importance of good works as the necessary fruits of faith.

This is exactly the point on which Roman Catholic criticism intervenes and attacks. Because the Reformation so strongly underlines the unconditional divine grace as the sole agent of justification, it runs the risk of rejecting the transforming and creative power of that same grace and is exposed to underestimating sanctification. The council of Trent* maintains that when God justifies, sinners not only are declared to be justified but are ontologically changed, so that from now on they are a new creation (2 Cor. 5:17; Gal. 6:15). As such, they are no longer totally sinners, although their righteousness flows from God *propter Christum* (because of Christ) and in this sense also in the Catholic tradition can be seen as a *iustitia aliena*. On the other hand, individuals are still living in the realm of sinfulness and under the impact of original sin. They are prone to sin and hence in the last analysis uncertain of their own salvation and

totally thrown upon God's grace, which makes a growth in sanctification possible and allows an interpretation of the justified believer as *both* righteous *and* a sinner.

The Western polemic as described here has never really touched the Eastern Orthodox tradition, in which the theological point of departure is taken in the incarnation* rather than in justification. God "became man that we might become divine" (Athanasius, *Incarnation* 54). God's incarnation is interpreted to imply the deification of humankind *(theosis)* and thus the final reconciliation between Creator and creation.

Today the traditional controversy between Rome and the Reformation churches may be said to be overcome to the extent that the Lutheran concern for the *promissio Dei* (promise of God) and the Catholic interest in the *meritum ex gratia* (merit according to grace) can be regarded as compatible; but tensions still remain, not least with regard to the understanding of the human person and the radical character of sin (Lutheran-Roman Catholic dialogue,* Malta report, 26; Justification by Faith [USA Lutheran-Roman Catholic dialogue], 112). In ecumenical texts of recent decades the issue of sin is mostly debated in a rather traditional manner (e.g. the

Leuenberg agreement [Lutheran-Reformed dialogue*], 10-12; The Presence of Christ in Church and World [Reformed-Roman Catholic dialogue*], 49,87), though there are also quite a few examples of dogmatically and ethically actualizing the reality of original sin that draw conclusions to the sinfulness of unjust, venial and selfish structures and institutions (Dublin report [Methodist-Roman Catholic dialogue*], 18, and numerous documents from the socio- and economico-political discussion in the WCC and related bodies). Recent trends such as liberation theology* and political theology* show an unprecedented tendency to give more weight to the issue of structural and institutional sin, as they describe sinful economic, social, political structures. It can also be maintained that the whole ecumenical movement is nurtured by the basic insight that ecclesiastical and confessional divisions are sinful violations of inalienable Christological principles (see John 17:21; 1 Cor. 1:10-13). This sin of disunity (see **unity**) demands reconciliation that expresses itself in eucharistic sharing, which in turn represents a constant and radical challenge to "all kinds of injustice, racism, separation and lack of freedom" (*Baptism, Eucharist and Ministry*, E20). Thus all individual and structural sin is overcome by Jesus Christ, giving himself to his followers in the eucharist* as the meal of reconciliation.

See also **anthropology, theological; faith; grace; justification; reconciliation; redemption; salvation; sanctification**.

PEDER NØRGAARD-HØJEN

G. Freund, *Sünde im Erbe: Erfahrungsinhalt und Sinn der Erbsündenlehre*, Stuttgart, Kohlhammer, 1979 • R. Niebuhr, *The Nature and Destiny of Man: A Christian Interpretation*, New York, Scribner, 1942 • W. Pannenberg, *Anthropologie in theologischer Perspektiv* (ET *Anthropology in Theological Perspective*, Philadelphia, Westminster, 1985) • P. Schoonenberg, "Der Mensch in der Sünde", in *Mysterium Salutis*, vol. 2, Einsiedeln, Benzinger, 1975.

SKYDSGAARD, KRISTEN EJNER.

B. 15.11.1902, Fünen, Denmark. Skydsgaard was a member of the commission on Faith and Order, 1952-68, and in 1957 was appointed to the commission of ecumenical research of the Lutheran World Federation* (LWF). Actively involved in the creation of the Institute for Ecumenical Research at Strasbourg, and in its programme for several years, he was vice-president of its board, 1964-74. He was an observer for the LWF at the Second Vatican Council* and, as representative of the non-Catholic observers, spoke on the need to examine Christian doctrine in its historical dimension. He participated in the long ecumenical debate on the relation between scripture and Tradition and made a contribution to the Roman Catholic-Protestant theological dialogue. He was also a member of the official group of dialogue between the Lutheran churches and the Roman Catholic Church. He wrote *One in Christ* (Philadelphia, Muhlenberg, 1957) and edited *Konzil und Evangelium* (Göttingen, Vandenhoeck & Ruprecht, 1962).

ANS J. VAN DER BENT

SOBORNOST. The term made its appearance on the ecumenical scene in the course of the 1920s. The closest English equivalent is perhaps "conciliarity"* or "ecumenicity"; the dictionary defines *sobornost* as "the principle of spiritual unity and religious community based on free commitment to a tradition of catholicity interpreted through ecumenical councils of the Eastern Orthodox church".

In the first flush of the post-revolutionary Russian emigration to Western Europe, there was no reluctance among host nations to accept an untranslated Russian word like this. At the Faith and Order* conference of 1927, Sergius Bulgakov (1871-1944) tantalized his audience with the thought that "Russian theology expresses the fundamental essence of church unity in a word for which no other language has the equivalent". *Sobornost* was a neologism born out of the 19th-century Slavophile movement, and in particular out of the writings of Aleksey Khomyakov (1804-60).

Not that Khomyakov necessarily coined the term himself. For it makes its first appearance in print only in a posthumous translation of that author's *Lettre au redacteur de l'Union chrétienne* (1860), and even there only once. The *Lettre* itself involved a polemical defence of a related term, *sobornaia*, the medieval Slav translation of "catholic" in the Nicene Creed. It was a translation to which the Russian Jesuit priest Gagarine had recently taken exception (1859).

Both Khomyakov and his successors were convinced that *sobornaia* was not only a correct translation but one that enhanced and enriched the original, proceeding as it did beyond the quantitative aspect of catholicity* and universality to an emphasis on quality, on the idea of a love-inspired "unity in multiplicity". For the root of the Slavonic word *(sobor)* relates to gathering together, togetherness, mutuality. Furthermore, noted Khomyakov, the root, taken by itself, implies assembly and is the very word for "council". But this in turn points beyond councils and assemblies proper, important as they are. Khomyakov held that the church possesses an essential togetherness over and above any actual gathering; "her very essence consists in the agreement and unity of the spirit and life of all the members who acknowledge her throughout the world". Such can exist even "without [their] formal reunion".

The abstract noun *sobornost* therefore pointed beyond the hierarchical and formally conciliar nature of the church.* In 1932, in his work *L'Orthodoxie*, Bulgakov ventured the translation *conciliarité*. But he also offered *symphonicité* and *unanimité*. Such were the ineffable attributes of the body as a whole, whose truths were ultimately guarded by "the totality, by the whole people of the church", terms which Khomyakov had eagerly adapted from the encyclical of the Eastern patriarchs to Pope Pius IX (1848). All the more eagerly did he borrow them, since they were so congruent with the ecclesiology of Johann Möhler (1796-1838), a Roman Catholic theologian whom he had undoubtedly read and admired.

Even when the church did gather in council, however, such unity* should as much or even more abundantly prevail. Conversely, it could be argued that in the absence of a properly constituted council, *sobornost* might well be at risk, and so the integrity of the body as a whole. Such was the concern of those who prepared for the long-delayed council of the Russian Orthodox Church in the early 1900s. Vladimir Zavitnevich's article of 1905 "On the Restoration of Sobornost in the Russian Church" was one of many to express it. The article was firmly based on Khomyakov, to whom the author devoted an extensive study (1902). At no stage was this restoration

nearer or more needed than at the turbulent time of the council itself (1917-18).

The very constitution of this all-important council demonstrated that any serious restoration of *sobornost* had to involve a re-assertion of the importance of the laity* in Orthodox church life. It was all the more natural for Bulgakov (himself a member of that council) to stress that "the laity, no less than the clergy, has its place and value in the church as a whole" when he came before the Faith and Order conference of 1927.

No doubt this position eased the mind of many a Protestant in his audience, faced with what had been expected to be a highly clericalist body. But the apparent lessening of rigorous canonical standards and demands which the concept of *sobornost* seemed to herald in debates between Orthodox Russians and their fellow Christians in the nascent ecumenical movement served only intermittently and superficially to further interchurch convergence. The very vagueness of the term could lead so seasoned an ecumenist as Oliver Tomkins to associate it in due course with "charity of the Spirit" as an essential mark of the church ("an idea that is perfectly expressed in the untranslatable Russian word for catholicity, *sobornost*"); this comment in turn conjured up the vision of an obscure partner to the historical Orthodox church, "a charismatic church in which the Holy Spirit of love constitutes members of those who are outside the canonical church" itself (1964).

In the event, no more than a small and decreasing number of ecumenists were to labour under such illusions, nor did each and every Russian Orthodox theologian help to provoke them. A fertile ground for would-be promoters of *sobornost* in the furtherance of Christian unity was provided — under the aegis of Bulgakov and the direction of his follower, Nicolas Zernov (1898-1980) — by the Anglican-Orthodox Fellowship of St Alban and St Sergius, founded in 1928. The very journal of the fellowship was renamed *Sobornost* in 1935.

The subject of its conference in the preceding year had been "The Church of God", and this was duly furnished with a paper on "Sobornost: The Catholicity of the Church". It was delivered by Georges Florovsky (1893-1979), and the second part of the title was addressed in an exemplary way. But the first part was studiously ignored. Indeed, *sobornost* was not even mentioned once. Thus did Florovsky turn his back on post-Khomyakovian Russian religious thought, the better to address himself instead to a perceived pan-Orthodox tradition and to its patristic base.

In subsequent ecumenical debate Florovsky's bypassing of the use of *sobornost* generally prevailed. Nevertheless, largely in Russian circles, the term *sobornost* still commands respect. When he addressed the inter-Orthodox symposium on "Baptism, Eucharist and Ministry" (1985), Archbishop Kirill of Smolensk took it for granted that members of the Orthodox church invariably "maintain the principles of conciliarity *(sobornost)*". He invoked *sobornost* to justify the substance and the spirit of the statutes he had drafted for the Russian church in its millennial year (1988).

See also **catholicity, conciliarity, unity**.

SERGEI HACKEL

S. Bulgakoff, "One, Holy, Catholic and Apostolic", *Journal of the Fellowship of St Alban and St Sergius*, 12, 1931 • S. Hackel, *One Holy Catholic and Apostolic: The Problems and Limitations of Language*, London, 1989 • B. Plank, *Katholizität und Sobornost*, Würburg, Augustinus, 1960 • N.V. Riasanovsky, "Khomyakov on Sobornost", in *Community and Change in Russian and Soviet Thought*, E.J. Simmons ed., Cambridge, MA, Harvard UP, 1955.

SOCIAL ENCYCLICALS, PAPAL.

Encyclicals,* or solemn letters which popes write for the universal Roman Catholic Church, have been the major means by which the modern papacy has directly proposed and developed Roman Catholic teaching on social-ethical issues, beginning with Leo XIII (ruled 1878-1903). Although the RCC has never elaborated a complete doctrinal system in social matters but has responded in rapid succession to issues as they have arisen and to the religious and secular controversies surrounding them, in hindsight one can detect a developing unity of papal social teaching. The Second Vatican Council's* magisterial "The Church in the Modern World" (*Gaudium et Spes*) could not have been promulgated without the previous encyclicals and their generative influence on the interdisciplinary reflection and activities of Catholics. Nor could Paul VI and John Paul II have written their social encyclicals without *Gaudium et Spes*.

Among the over 100 papal social documents, including encyclicals, from Leo XIII to John Paul II, we highlight only a few here.

Leo XIII's *Libertas* (1888) and *Rerum Novarum* (1891) outlined the fundamental principles regarding the nature of the modern state, relations between church and state;* the right of the church to be free in exercising its mission;* the right of peoples to determine their own form of government; and rights and duties of management, workers and the state, in the context of the wage economy that was emerging in Europe and North America after the industrial revolution. Leo XIII began the papal teaching tradition of protecting the worker against exploitation and of promoting the right of workers to receive just wages and to organize themselves for group protection and representation.

In issuing *Quadragesimo Anno* in 1931, Pius XI (1922-39) developed these principles by emphasizing the common good of society and the state's responsibility to promote the temporal well-being of every segment of society. He introduced the concepts of social justice* and social charity as essential to the reconstruction of society, with stress on the role of the Christian laity* in such an apostolate.

The *Summi Pontificatus* (1939) of Pius XII (1939-58) called the denial of the unity and solidarity* of the human race one of the major modern heresies. In later writings he saw that a juridically established international organization would be a necessary condition for international peace.

His successor, John XXIII, issued *Mater et Magistra* (1961) and *Pacem in Terris* (1962). The first developed papal social doctrine since Leo XIII regarding property, union organizations, co-operatives, rural and urban life, and the balance between state-regulated activities and the freedom of individual and group enterprises. True prosperity is not only total national wealth but its just distribution. The encyclical was noted for its treatment of international concerns, including the imbalance between wealthy industrial nations and less-developed ones, and for its call to richer nations to aid the others but not to impose their way of life or attempt political advantages, which would be "another form of colonialism". *Pacem in Terris* advocated human freedom* and dignity as the basis for world order* and peace and proposed that a proper philosophy of law* be based on the necessary conformity between human legislation and the laws of God. The pope pleaded for the ceasing of the arms race, the banning of nuclear weapons, and the negotiating of a general disarmament.

Paul VI's *Populorum Progressio* (1967) expressed the social conscience of the RCC in regard to poverty and wealth. It dealt with "development of those peoples who are striving to escape from hunger, misery, endemic disease, and ignorance; of those who are looking for a wider share in the benefits of civilization and a more active improvement of their human qualities; of those who are aiming purposefully at their complete fulfilment." Denouncing "the scandal of glaring inequalities not merely in the enjoyment of possession, but even more in the exercise of power", Paul VI declared that "the superfluous wealth of rich countries should be placed at the service of poor nations... The new name for peace is development."

The eclipse of the development* theme, dominant in the 1960s, began in the 1970s with the strong emergence of human rights* issues, so that John Paul II would say in 1979: "After all, peace comes down to respect for man's inviolable rights" *(Redemptor Hominis)*. John Paul II's *Laborem Exercens* (1981) reflects the pope's extended, critical dialogue with Marxism. Labour* is the key for understanding people's historical vocation* and societal projects; through labour people create their social world, and in so doing they in some sense create themselves. The pope offers a critical analysis of Western capitalism* and Eastern collectivism by spelling out the principle of "the priority of labour over capital". If capital does not serve the whole of working society, the economic system will generate injustices, exclude some from the very wealth they produced, and create hardships among the majority. The violation of the principle of labour over capital is the reason for the crises of unemployment, inflation, insecurity and growing poverty, both in the Western and Eastern societies.

The uniqueness of John Paul II's social writings is his entering into the Marxist perspective of understanding society and history largely in terms of human labour, but he insists that for the unity of nations one must move "from class war to solidarity". "By applying certain Marxist insights and some Christian ones at the points where Marxism is weak, he explodes Marxism, or better he transcends Marxism from within — but not in the direction of political theories popular in capitalist countries" (Gregory Baum).

In papal teaching, the centre of society is the human person,* who is divinely created a social being and raised to an order of existence that transcends nature. Persons "are necessarily the foundation, cause and end of all social institutions" (John XXIII).

Authority,* required by moral law with its God-given power, must strive for the respectful recognition and caring promotion of the individual's basic rights in the context of the common good — the total of those conditions of social life whereby persons are enabled more fully to achieve their own authentic fulfilment. Justice demands respect for human rights, but rights are always relative; they can be neither specified nor understood apart from the web of social interdependence, which involves mutual duties and responsibilities. Solidarity and mutuality in truth, justice, love and freedom regulate human relationships, whether economic, social, cultural or political.

This more positive understanding of justice is rooted in the RC traditional acceptance of the Aristotelian and Thomistic view of the essentially social nature of persons, and this is joined to a Christian morality of love or mutuality — the willing acceptance, support and promotion of the other's selfhood and freedom. Though love does not substitute for justice, without love justice becomes a lifeless theory and can neither be adequately conceptualized nor effectively realized in action. "True co-operation will be possible for a single common good when the constituent parts of society deeply feel themselves members of one great family and children of the same heavenly Father" (Leo XIII).

By appeals to rational reflection and to natural law,* RC tradition has specified human rights, such as the right to life, to food, to housing, to assembly, etc. But past exaggerated claims to identify concrete demands of justice with precision have more recently brought about an "epistemological humility" in RC statements. Paul VI observed that

Christian social ethics "no doubt will see its field restricted when it comes to suggesting certain models of society, while its function of making critical judgment and of taking an overall view will be strengthened by its showing the relative character of the behaviour and values presented by such and such a society as definitive and inherent in the very nature of man".

In fact, this very RC caution in being precise in "official answers" to modern social problems and to political and economic crises is causing tensions in relations between the RCC and the WCC, when various WCC bodies tend to be more precise in proposing Christian analyses and solutions.

See also **encyclicals; encyclicals, Roman Catholic.**

TOM STRANSKY

G. Baum, "John Paul II's Encyclical on Labor", *The Ecumenist*, 20, 1, 1981 • J. Gremillion ed., *The Gospel of Peace and Justice: Catholic Social Teaching since Pope John*, Maryknoll, NY, Orbis, 1975 • D. Hollenbach, "Modern Catholic Teachings concerning Justice", in *The Faith That Does Justice*, John C. Haughey ed., New York, Paulist, 1977 • P. Pavan, "Social Thought, Papal", in *New Catholic Encyclopedia*, vol. 13, 1966 • J. Schasching, "From the Class War to the Culture of Solidarity", in *Vatican II: Assessment and Perspectives*, R. Latourelle ed., vol. 3, New York, Paulist, 1989.

SOCIAL GOSPEL MOVEMENT. This American Protestant movement sought to Christianize social, economic and political institutions as well as the family and individual life. Convinced that the kingdom of God* embraces the whole of human life, social gospel proponents believed the church's* task is to be the conscience and guide for "the Christian transfiguration of the social order".

Stimulated by ideas from England and Europe, the movement originated in the 1870s. But advocates were unable to arouse the Protestant churches to it broadly until 1907-12, when denominations and the new Federal Council of the Churches of Christ in America (1908) endorsed it. The ecumenical body adopted the Social Creed of the Churches (1908), which symbolized Protestantism's commitment to social responsibility and expressed its social conscience. Early emphasis on economic conditions of workers expanded to family life, urban problems and social justice. The most significant impact of this clergy-dominated movement occurred between 1907 and 1917.

Primary leadership was provided by Baptists Walter Rauschenbusch and Shailer Mathews, Congregationalists Washington Gladden and Josiah Strong, Episcopalians W.D.P. Bliss and Richard Ely, Methodists Frank Mason North and Harry Ward, and Presbyterians Charles Stelzle and John McDowell. Gladden has been called the father of the social gospel, but Rauschenbusch became its most famous advocate.

Much of the social gospel's success resulted from its strong ecumenical commitments and co-operation. The Federal Council of the Churches' commission on the church and social service became the social gospel's most active agency. Through it, denominational leaders were able to avoid competition, effectively use limited funds, and develop mutual programmes and publications. By this means the cause exerted disproportionate influence, although it never found more than a minority in denominations. The Federal Council always was at the core of this Protestant social service.

Theologically, the social gospel was a product of pre-first world war liberalism. Its biblical basis emphasized the Hebrew prophets and the social teachings of Jesus. Inveterately optimistic about human potential and social possibilities, the movement found its "spiritual centre and unity in the idea of the kingdom of God on earth" (Rauschenbusch). Its doctrine of God recognized divine activity in all of creation,* not just in the church, which led proponents to regard reforms advocated even by muck-raking journalists and progressive politicians as redemptive. Consequently, social gospel leaders interacted with other movements for reform and social improvement. The two most influential books which represent this theology are probably Rauschenbusch's *Christianity and the Social Crisis* (1907) and *A Theology for the Social Gospel* (1917).

Social gospel theology aroused negative responses from divergent Protestant wings. Fundamentalists attacked its assumptions that God's kingdom could be attained on earth prior to the millennium and that the church should become directly involved in politics.

Neo-orthodox writers criticized the movement's naive understanding of human nature and social change. With the combined impact of these attacks, the economic depression, and the second world war, the optimism inherent in the cause crumbled. However, a more realistic social action took its place, revised and sustained by permanent boards for social action in denominations and the National Council of Churches (1950). By such means the basic social responsibility expressed in the social gospel continues to work in the church today.

DONALD K. GORRELL

D.K. Gorrell, *The Age of Social Responsibility: The Social Gospel in the Progressive Era, 1900-1920*, Macon, GA, Mercer UP, 1988 • R.T. Handy ed., *The Social Gospel in America, 1870-1920*, New York, Oxford UP, 1966 • W.A. Visser 't Hooft, *The Background of the Social Gospel in America*, St Louis, MO, Bethany, repr. 1962.

SOCIALISM. A term of disputed and decreasingly precise meaning, "socialism" refers to a socio-economic formation which exists for the benefit of most members of a society, particularly working people. Perhaps the most definite characteristic of socialism is the collective ownership of at least the major means of production in a society operated by workers in the interest of the entire society. Another useful approach is to see socialism as an alternative social theory or system to capitalism* and exaggerated individualism, in which existing class antagonisms would be gradually resolved. Currently one can distinguish so many types of socialism that it is necessary to add qualifiers — e.g. utopian, scientific (or Marxist-Leninist or communistic), democratic, nationalist, really existing, developed or advanced, Eurocommunist, Latin American, Arab, African, religious (Christian), or "socialism with a human face". The many ideological conflicts, including among socialists, have often emptied the term of concrete content, making it a valuative slogan rather than a descriptive term, something which is assessed as good or evil depending on the user of the term.

Both socialism and communism are pre-Marxian concepts upon which a definitive Marxist interpretation was stamped. Pre-Marxian thinkers (Thomas More, François-Noël Babeuf, Saint Simon, François-Marie-Charles Fourier, Pierre-Joseph Proudhon, Robert Owen and Wilhelm Weitling) criticized the evils of the industrial revolution and laissez-faire capitalism and proposed or organized idealized communities in which the interest of all members of the community would be respected and oppression and exploitation removed. These authors were inspired by their understanding of the message and mission of Jesus and considered these socialist projects as "the expression of true Christianity of Jesus".

Such schemes were resolutely rejected as "utopian socialist" by Marx and Engels. In order to make socialism "scientific" they combatted all other interpretations of socialism, which they regarded as unreal, and thus gradually promoted the Marxian understanding of socialism as "the necessary outcome of the struggle between the two historically developed classes — the proletariat and the bourgeoisie" (Engels). The notion of the objective nature of Marxism as a scientific world-view allowed for little discussion not only about the inevitability of socialism but also about its constitutive elements. Socialism came to be seen as a transition between capitalism and communism, marked by the state as a revolutionary dictatorship of the proletariat, but in which such conditions would exist that would erode the need for the state. In socialism the distribution of abundant material goods produced by everyone's unselfish contribution is supposed to correspond to a person's contribution to society. In communism, consumption would be based entirely on one's "real" needs. Taking his clues from the experiences of the Paris Commune (1870), Marx believed that socialism would bring about the free association of producers who would take power into their hands by revolutionary, though not necessarily violent, means, first in the most advanced capitalist countries in which labour is already sufficiently socialized to be able to carry out this takeover effectively.

While Marx believed that religion* would wither away along with many other superstructures of class society, he was not overly concerned about its existence in socialism, though he believed that freedom of religion and separation of church and state* would be a feature of socialism. The financial support of churches would be based upon the unpressured commitment of believers.

Marx's relation with his contemporaries, the Christian socialists, was conflictual. Generally he was scornful of Christianity and the churches, and they reciprocated this animosity. The French socialists Félicité Robert de Lammenais, Louis Blanc and Etienne Cabet were all believers and did not get along with Marx's atheism.* The socialist divorce with religion resulted from Marxist materialist metaphysics; hence only a small number of Christians espoused socialist ideas and engaged in organizing the working class. These were people or organizations such as Friedrich Naumann, Christoph Blumhardt, Hermann Kutter, Leonard Ragaz, Keir Hardie, the Society of Christian Socialists, the Church Socialist League, and Pope Leo XIII's support to the organizing of Catholic labour unions. Basically, the relation between Marxian socialists and Christian socialists was one-directional: Christian socialists used a fairly large number of Marxist concepts, though their struggles were less conspiratorial and violent; Marxists rarely adopted Christian insights.

After the death of Marx and Engels the socialist movement gradually split into two antagonistic movements, democratic socialist and Leninist (or Bolshevik). The differences between them are numerous, but the fundamental one is that the democratic socialists believed it was possible to take control of the state apparatus by legal means, namely the ballot, while the Leninists became convinced that power could be wrested from the capitalists only by revolution, such as the great October revolution of 1917.

Unanticipated by Marx and Engels, the first country to become socialist was Russia, a country more feudal than capitalist. Vladimir Ilich Lenin not only succeeded in gaining control of the dissatisfied masses who brought about the revolutionary uproar but also gave Marxism his own stamp, hence Marxism-Leninism. Originally the Bolsheviks and their sympathizers expected world revolution, but they were later satisfied to hold power in one country, the Soviet Union. This situation lasted until the end of the second world war; after that, other countries became socialist. In the Soviet Union the building of socialism entailed central political and economic state monopoly, nationalizing of industry, collectivization of agriculture and an increasing grip by the communist party not only on politics but also on culture, education, recreation and spiritual life. The dictatorship of the proletariat became the dictatorship of the communist party.

Under Lenin's successor, Joseph Stalin, the process of concentrating power continued until the dictatorship of the party was replaced by dictatorship of the central committee, then of the politburo and finally of the general secretary, Stalin himself. The transformation of the Soviet Union into a socialist country was exceedingly bloody, and the demand was made that the socialist movement around the world blindly conform to the dictates from the Kremlin. The state became nearly all-powerful; hence this form of government is statist and totalitarian. In the name of the working class, a new bureaucratic ruling elite monopolized power internally and dominated the communist movement internationally.

Not until the 1950s, and in many instances much later, did any communist party develop an alternate road into socialism. While many splinter movements arose within this branch, they were combatted relentlessly. Bolsheviks promoted the impression that no other form of socialism was legitimate. In those countries in which a communist take-over was successful, there was at the outset a slavish copying of the USSR model. The Soviet Union, to distinguish itself from other Marxist socialist countries, declared itself to be a country of developed or advanced socialism, even proclaiming that it had reached the communist stage of socialist development. The other countries declared themselves as countries of "really existing socialism".

The greater diversity that emerged in the 1950s was primarily in the form of nationalistic socialism, such as the Titoist mould in Yugoslavia, Chinese Maoism which later, like Yugoslavia, transformed into a reformist socialism, socialism with a human face during the Prague spring of 1968 in Czechoslovakia, the Polish model, Castroism, and Sandinista socialism in Nicaragua. Under Gorbachev, such variants have finally been accepted by the Soviet Union, which is attempting a restructuring (perestroika) and liberalization of its own form of socialism. By the late 1980s a large number of socialist countries experienced a profound economic, political, social and ideological crisis which caused a number of unanticipated but profound changes affecting these countries internally and internationally. It appears that the proponents of perestroika prefer co-operation to confrontation and are willing to do away with many dogmatic cliches as they seek to reject the legacy of Stalinism.

The Leninist and Stalinist approach to religion is almost uniformly restrictive and oppressive. Instead of waiting for religion to wither, administrative means are employed to root it out. Actual religious policies vary according to the contingencies of the moment, leading sometimes to tactical co-operation, greater degrees of toleration and manipulation of churches, but the overall strategy and expectation is that religion will die out. Generally it was asserted that religion always plays a "reactionary" role. Only a small group of humanistic Marxists from socialist countries asserted the usefulness of a dialogue with Christians and other religious people (see **Marxist-Christian dialogue**), but only since the 1960s has there been a grudging official admission that religion is capable of motivating some people for "progressive" goals. In some socialist countries (e.g. Poland, Czechoslovakia, Yugoslavia, Hungary and the German Democratic Republic), a Marxist-Christian dialogue took place, mostly among a small but relatively influential group of intellectuals.

Originally the churches opposed the communist take-over, and many Christians remained in passive opposition. But gradually other forms of relations have developed. Christians often become passive objects to the processes of socialization, and some churches attempt to find a non-confrontational niche in socialism. A small but vocal minority of Christians become advocates of socialism and attempt a Marxist-Christian synthesis. The most creative response seems to be those attempts in which Christians define themselves as being a "church in socialism", seeking to be loyal yet critical in their attempt to contribute to building the kind of socialism which respects human and moral values rather than destroys them.

It was different with democratic socialists, and even with the so-called Eurocommunists (primarily communists of Italy and Spain), in the West. The totalitarian and repressive practices of Leninism, Stalinism and Maoism were criticized and rejected. A commitment was made to preserve and advance the humanistic heritage. Socialistic political parties entered the political arena, sometimes won elections and influenced their society by establishing policies for the welfare and protection of the rights of workers and of the entire society. They committed themselves to pluralism* in society, parliamentary democracy and a mixed economy. These developments took place in nearly all Western European countries.

A number of Christian theologians in the 20th century sharply criticized advanced capitalist forms of human denigration but also distanced themselves from the terror in Marxist-Leninist socialism. The most prominent figures in the earlier part of the century were Walter Rauschenbusch, Karl Barth, Paul Tillich, Reinhold Niebuhr, Jaques Maritain, Emmanuel Mournier, Josef Hromádka, and former Russian Marxists exiled in the West, such as Nicolas Berdyaev, Sergius Bulgakov and Pyotr Struve. Of the theologians active in the second half of the century, Karl Rahner, Charles West, Jan Lochman, Johann Baptist Metz, Jürgen Moltmann, Giulo Girardi and Dorothee Sölle are particularly significant. Their response to socialism and to Marxism varies considerably, but they all take Marxism and socialism seriously and believe it to be a Christian responsibility to espouse those values which are common to both Christianity and socialism.

The WCC became concretely involved with the issue of socialism because its member churches operated in both socialist and nonsocialist countries. But in a more general sense socialism influenced the ecumenical movement on account of its striving for social justice and equality. From the beginning the ecumenical movement was concerned with the issues raised by socialism. "Christian socialists" participated actively at the Stockholm Life and Work conference (see **ecumenical conferences**). Amsterdam 1948 tried to steer an independent course by rejecting "the ideologies of both communism and laissez-faire capitalism" (see **capitalism**), as if "these two extremes were the only alternatives". The notion of a responsible society* was offered as a tool for assessing both the values and shortcomings of various social systems. Evanston 1954 deplored the totalitarian practice of communism, while also rejecting sterile anti-communism. The Church and Society Geneva conference (1966), influenced by third-world concerns, was the first to give a positive meaning to ideology* as a mobilizing force and to raise the revolutionary challenge to the level of a Christian option. The Sub-unit on Dialogue with People of Living Faiths has concentrated on inter-religious and not inter-ideological dialogue. But emphases like "the church and the poor" (see **poor**) or the Pro-gramme to Combat Racism* have raised fun-damental issues of economic and social conflict which could not ignore the socialist challenge.

Liberation theology, a Latin American Christian movement starting in the late 1960s, took a favourable attitude towards revolution and socialism. Here a number of theologians such as Gustavo Gutiérrez, Camilo Torres, José Míguez Bonino, José Porfirio Miranda, Leonardo Boff, Enrique Dussel and Hugo Assmann, as well as grassroots movements such as Christians for Socialism, made use of Marxist tools for social analysis and were optimistic about helping the masses of Latin America and the rest of the third world to end the poverty and domination caused by capital-ism. An alliance with Marxists is favoured, but the Christian (especially Catholic) reli-gious element remains pronounced. Libera-tion theologians are not uncritical towards Marxism but seek a positive re-interpretation of Marxism which would foster a socialism friendly to religious concerns. While the Cu-ban socialist experiment is not negligible, greater interest was manifested in the brief experience of building socialism in Chile and in the Nicaraguan Sandinista socialism.

Other forms of liberation theology can be found in the Philippines, Sri Lanka and South Korea, where various attempts have been made, both independently and under Latin American influence, to create Asian liberation theologies. Similarly in Africa (e.g. in Tan-zania, Zimbabwe, Senegal and South Africa), some theologians are espousing African so-cialism or else more specifically Tanzanian or Zimbabwean socialism.

The nature of much of third-world social-ism is highly unclear. The rhetoric is often Marxist, but the content is frequently tradi-

tional local collectivism coupled with the de-sire for development* and independence. Socialism and Marxism have a manifest ideological role in the movements for national liberation.

Over the centuries Christians have adjusted to, justified, and endorsed various socio-economic ideas and systems. This is also true of socialism. Socialism, however, is both di-visive and uniting for Christians. It is divisive because many Christians clearly favour it and even claim that of all social systems it is the most Christian, while others vehemently op-pose it. It is uniting because there is a tenden-cy of Christians to collaborate across denomi-national, theological, and other lines of separation when it comes to working together in supporting or opposing socialism. Thus, socialism is a serious ecumenical concern.

In the second half of 1989, encouraged by the process of democratization and restructur-ing fostered by Mikhail Gorbachev, a mostly bloodless (except in Romania) revolution took place in Eastern Europe and many other socialist countries which many equate in im-portance with the Bolshevik revolution. Some trends of that revolution are democratic socialist, but others are frankly anti-socialist. While the end result is not discernible, at a minimum it represents the dismantling of Stalinistic communism and the enthusiastic acceptance of the idea of multi-party democ-racy. Many of the classical features of Marx-ist-Leninist socialism are being abandoned even by political parties that previously em-braced such concepts dogmatically. Some Communist parties practically collapsed and many changed their name to a socialist var-iant. The impact of those monumental changes are not yet clear in the third world. For the churches in Marxist socialist countries the changes presented the probability of true religious freedom and a rehabilitation of reli-gion as a social factor. In at least some of the countries religious people were in the fore-front of the movement for democratization. The world ecumenical movement is adjusting to these profound transformations of socialism whose final outcome is quite unclear.

See also **capitalism, economics, labour, property**.

PAUL MOJZES

M. Buber, *Paths in Utopia,* London, Routledge & K. Paul, 1949 • S.N. Bulgakov, *Sozialismus im*

Christentum, Göttingen, Vandenhoeck & Ruprecht, 1977 • H. Desfosses & J. Levesque eds, *Socialism in the Third World*, London, Praeger, 1975 • *L'Eglise et le socialisme*, Paris, Nouvelles Editions Latimer, 1972 • W.H. Friedland ed., *African Socialism*, Stanford, Stanford UP, 1964 • W. Huber & J. Schwerdtfeger, *Frieden, Gewalt, Sozialismus*, Stuttgart, Klett-Verlag, 1976 • A. Pfeiffer ed., *Religiöse Sozialisten*, Olten, Walter, 1976 • W. Sombart, *Sozialismus und soziale Bewegungen*, Jena, G. Fischer, 6th ed. 1908 • L.P. Wallace, *Leo XIII and the Rise of Socialism*, Durham, NC, Duke UP, 1966.

SOCIETAS OECUMENICA.

Societas Oecumenica, the European Society for Ecumenical Research, was founded in 1978 and represents various Roman Catholic, Protestant and Orthodox ecumenical institutes and centres and professors of ecumenics at European theological faculties and seminaries. Its meetings (1980, 1982, 1984, 1986, 1988, 1989) have debated ecumenical themes, sometimes supplementing and deepening ongoing WCC theological programmes. It publishes *Signalia*.

ANS J. VAN DER BENT

SOCIETY. To the despair of sociologists, the term "society" is variously used in Christian literature on social ethics as synonymous with world, culture,* civilization, community,* political and economic life — a shorthand label for the fabric of social phenomena in general. However, this general use also reveals the broad range of ethical, ideological and historical forces and processes which arouse Christian interest and which draw the churches into encounter with every facet of "society", with practically all the social sciences and, increasingly, with the physical and natural sciences.

Since New Testament times, there has been a continuous Christian reflection on issues of society, used in this general sense, as the transcendent claims of the faith* have encountered the historical contingencies and changes of organized society, illustrating what H. Richard Niebuhr called the "enduring problem of Christ and culture". The Christian response has ranged from "Christ against culture", as expressed by 1st- and 2nd-century Christians and the millennialist Christian sects of all ages, to "Christ the Transformer of culture",

as interpreted by such diverse theologians and disciples as Augustine of Hippo and the Christian socialists of more recent times.

In his pioneering historical study *The Social Teaching of the Christian Churches*, Ernst Troeltsch concluded that, alongside the extreme, though not uninteresting, social ideas of the Christian sectarians and the Christian mystics, there were only two main historical church teachings about social order: (1) the social philosophy of medieval Catholicism, based on the institutions of family, guild and class, on personal relations of authority and reverence in the relatively simple pre-capitalist economy, and the old solidarities involved in being bound to the soil or linked to some ancient family; (2) the social philosophy of ascetic Protestantism, resulting from a kind of Free Church pietistic Calvinism, inwardly related to modern utilitarianism and rationalism, which glorified work as a calling and developed links with political democracy and liberalism; it was able to neutralize the ethically dangerous ideas of modern life (in utilitarianism and liberalism) by the religious ideas of individual and communal responsibility and by heroically "serving the cause of Christ all over the world".

By the 18th century, however, the churches had to face the "entirely new" situation created by the rise of modern science and liberal ideas of the Enlightenment with its rational secular criticism of the state and other institutions of society. The new situation posed the problem of capitalism* and the new industrial classes it created, rapid technological change and enormous growth in material productivity, the rise of revolutionary social protest movements (especially Marxism), the growth of giant militaristic and bureaucratic states, the enormous increase in population, the spread of European colonialism and New World outlooks linking up and mobilizing the whole world for the purpose of trade. In these circumstances, the two main types of Christian social teaching were impotent despite the development of new forms of diakonia.

Troeltsch's analysis opened the way for a new approach to Christian social thinking, combining the Christian ethical concern for justice and community with the insights of scientific social inquiry (his impact on non-German-speaking Christianity came only after 1931, when his book was translated into English). He was extremely critical of the Christian moral idealism which prevailed at the end of the 19th century: "Nowhere does there exist an absolute Christian ethic, which only awaits discovery; all that we can do is to learn to control the world situation in its successive phases just as the earlier Christian ethic did in its own way. There is also no absolute ethical transformation of material nature or of human nature; all that does exist is a constant wrestling with the problems which they raise. Thus the Christian ethic of the present day and of the future will also only be an adjustment to the world situation, and it will only desire to achieve that which is practically possible... Only doctrinaire idealists or religious fanatics can fail to recognize these facts" (1013).

Church and society in the ecumenical era. The first world war and the worldwide economic crisis of the 1930s aroused the Western churches to the need to re-examine their witness to society. An "ecumenical approach" was necessary to overcome the nationalist outlook which dominated Christian political and social thought. Inspired by church leaders like Archbishop Söderblom of

Sweden and challenged by social movements like Christianisme social in France, the social gospel in the USA and Christian socialism in the UK, Protestant and Orthodox churches gathered for the first "Universal Christian Conference on Life and Work" (Stockholm 1925). This meeting, however, lacked the theological and social insight to analyze developments in the modern world and was unable to resolve theological-ethical differences among its members.

In these years the churches were also baffled by the growth of secularism (see **secularization**), to which attention had been called in a much-debated paper on "Secular Civilization and the Christian Task", presented by the American philosopher Rufus Jones to the world missionary conference in Jerusalem (1928). He argued that the advance of secular culture, "a fruit of modern science", was the principal world rival of Christian faith.

The second Life and Work conference (Oxford 1937) considered the theme "Church, Community and State". Aided by the theological renewal which had taken place in

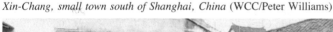

Xin-Chang, small town south of Shanghai, China (WCC/Peter Williams)

Western Christianity in the intervening years, it produced creative new approaches to these and other pressing social issues. Theologians like Karl Barth, Reinhold Niebuhr, Emil Brunner, William Temple and Nicolas Berdyaev (and other Russian Orthodox theologians in exile in Paris) addressed the social and political crisis from their different theological-ethical perspectives, but all generating new Christian concern for what was happening in society. The Oxford conference was particularly successful in suggesting new approaches in three key areas.

First, in considering the function of the church in society, it provided a new methodology (an approach using so-called middle axioms*) for Christian witness in relation to contemporary social issues, going beyond the affirmation of general ethical principles while avoiding the churches' becoming identified with particular economic and political programmes (Visser 't Hooft & Oldham, 209-10). This method also emphasized the need for the churches to depend less exclusively on clerical leadership and to draw upon their "best lay minds" with knowledge and experience in social affairs. The model continues to have the support of many contemporary social ethicists and moral theologians (Preston).

Second, in its concern for economic order, the conference identified the points at which modern capitalism and communism challenged the Christian understanding of life. This analysis and understanding would in the post-war years become the basis of Christian support for the welfare state* and social democracy.

Third, the conference clarified the principles which should guide Christian thinking about church and state* (see also **state**), especially in view of "the widespread tendency of the state to control the totality of human life". The conference declared: "Since we believe in the holy God as the source of justice, we do not consider the state as the ultimate source of law but rather as its guarantor. It is not the lord but the servant of justice. There can be for the Christian no ultimate authority but very God" (report, 67).

The second world war interrupted but also intensified Christian reflection on these issues, emphasizing the need in the post-war world for increased social security and social democracy for the populations of modern industrial societies.

Christians and the conflict between capitalism and communism. After the defeat of Hitler the conflict between the capitalist and communist systems intensified, leading to the cold war (see **capitalism, socialism**). This conflict provided the first test of the ecumenical movement — how to help its member churches transcend the rival claims of two self-righteous political-economic systems. At the first assembly (Amsterdam 1948), the newly established WCC addressed this "disorder of society" and proposed the idea of the responsible society* as the criterion by which churches in communist and non-communist countries should determine their responsibility in the East-West conflict. This idea was substantially re-affirmed and expanded in a second statement adopted by the second WCC assembly (Evanston 1954), emphasizing the need of churches in all societies to examine critically their ideological assumptions. Evanston said: "Responsible society is not an alternative social political system, but a criterion by which we judge all existing social orders and at the same time a standard to guide us in the specific choices we have to make. Christians are called to live responsibly, to live in response to God's act of redemption in Christ, in any society, even within the most unfavourable social structures." The assembly also stressed the importance of maintaining dialogue between churches in the communist and non-communist countries.

"Rapid social change" in Africa, Asia and Latin America. After the second world war, the churches largely supported the decolonization* process, one that involved revolutionary social change as well as new ethical problems. The concern was how to encourage nation-building and rapid economic and technological development without further weakening the traditional societies and cultures of these lands. In this context it was first suggested that the churches needed a "theology of revolution" (Keith Bridston, 1956) to explain the immense cultural and social consequences of the rapid secularizing-modernizing process which accompanied decolonization and nation-building, a process all the more disturbing because it was so largely guided by Western secular ideas of nation-building, economic development, education and social welfare.

Ten years later at the world conference on Church and Society (Geneva 1966), the WCC debated the same term, but on this occasion (as presented by Richard Shaull) insisted that the churches should be more active in promoting a worldwide revolutionary opposition to the capitalist political and economic system being imposed on the new nations by the Western industrial countries, which was leading to new types of colonialism and oppression.

Geneva 1966 was the first genuinely "world" Christian conference on social issues, including equal numbers of representatives from the so-called first, second and third worlds and a large group of observers from the Roman Catholic Church. The discussion of the theme "The Christian Response to the Technical and Social Revolutions of Our Time" produced many new ideas on economic justice, political responsibility, racism,* the relation of men and women in community, and the problems of rapid technological change. The attempt to define a pluralist approach to the three competing economic systems and ideologies (market economy, mixed economy, and centrally planned economy) did not satisfy those who believed that the basic conflict was between Western capitalism and proposals for a revolutionary new political and economic order in the world.

A follow-up consultation on theology, social ethics and revolution (Zagorsk 1968) confirmed the refusal of the 1966 conference to provide a theological endorsement of a specific revolutionary ideology. However, Christian opinion was increasingly divided on this point, and after the fourth assembly (Uppsala 1968), the new WCC action-oriented programmes on economic development,* racism and problems of rapidly growing cities in the developing countries tended to support proposals for revolutionary change. Throughout this period there was increasing co-operation with Roman Catholic scholars in relation to social questions, and the publication of the report by Vatican II on the "Church in the Modern World" (1965) showed that the social thought of the WCC and the Roman Catholic Church was on converging lines.

The search for a new ecumenical consensus on social responsibility. In the continuing debate about the theology of revolution, re-defined in 1971 by Gustavo Gutiérrez

as liberation theology,* its advocates have maintained that earlier ecumenical social thought had been based on the capitalist system and its supporting economic and political rationale. They held that in the new situation of political and social oppression and the need for solidarity with the poor,* the churches should accept the Marxist world-view and its "scientific" explanation of world economic injustice and the need for new economic structures. This view was accepted by many Christian groups throughout the 1970s, as the cultural revolution in China, Vietnam's victory over the USA and the various national revolutions in Southern Africa seemed to provide the criteria and a model for the kind of radical socio-political change needed not only in the third world but also in North America and Western Europe.

Since 1979 this view has seemed less credible. The collapse of Maoism, the serious economic and political problems confronting socialist countries and a variety of other factors have diminished hope in worldwide revolutionary change. The increasing mastery of modern technology and capitalist methods of production and trading by many developing countries, especially in East Asia but also in Latin America, suggests the need for a new, updated Christian analysis of the contemporary world economic situation (see **economics**).

Another factor upsetting the calculations of both socialist and capitalist promoters of change has been the new awareness of the limits of world resources and the impact of modern science and technology on the natural and human environment. Many churches and the ecumenical movement have shown concern for issues of faith, science and the future (the theme of the 1979 WCC world conference at MIT, USA). But ecumenical efforts to integrate this new concern with the older themes of social justice and social democracy (participation) have proved difficult. A first attempt, the WCC study programme on the "Just, Participatory and Sustainable Society"* (1976-79), failed to find an agreed theological-ethical basis for such an integration. In accordance with a call from Vancouver 1983, the WCC launched a programme emphasis on "Justice, Peace and the Integrity of Creation",* which included a 1990 world consultation in Seoul, South Korea.

Since 1975 increasing attention has been given to the issue of sexism,* which has resulted in a large new WCC programme on the role of women in church and society, undergirded by a substantial development of feminist theology* in many member churches. The larger implications of this programme for Christian social thought are already apparent but have yet to be spelled out in detail and in relation to other ecumenical views on issues like contrasting economic and political systems.

Clearly it is difficult for Christians to agree today on a common theological and ethical approach to society. The surge of new "theologies" fostered by these new social concerns adds to the problem. Theologies of liberation, theologies of the "radical" right, theologies of feminism, theologies of people's participation, theologies of ethnic and racial justice, new theologies of nature — all tend to vie for pride of place. As John Cobb has pointed out, all these "theologies of" make claims to be complete theological systems, offering more than Christian ethical doctrines on one particular human or social problem. This may help to explain why the WCC's post-Vancouver effort to achieve "a vital and coherent" theological basis for ecumenical witness and action in society made little progress.

At a time when so many Christian groups are confident that they have the only theological-ethical answer to the horrendous problems of modern society, it may be sobering to recall an observation of an earlier ecumenical prophet, Ernst Lange. Reflecting on a Faith and Order conference (Louvain 1971), Lange made this judgment on the large claims of the churches to work for their own unity and the unity of humankind: "Stored up in the realities of [world social] interdependence is a potential for conflict of such grotesque dimensions that any large claims for the church simply die on our lips" (*And Yet It Moves*, 95).

Today the main task facing churches in their relation to society may be to encourage these many confident new social theologies to undertake a more incisive dialogue with each other. Its aim would be to clarify common theological perspectives and more effectively to relate their varying perceptions of peace, justice, social order, and the natural creation and also to clarify the methods and strategies

Christians may use in the struggle for human betterment and reconciliation.*

See also **church and world**.

PAUL ABRECHT

"Fifty Years of Ecumenical Social Thought", *The Ecumenical Review*, 40, 2, 1988 ● R. Mehl, *Traité de sociologie du protestantisme* (ET *The Sociology of Protestantism*, London, SCM, 1970) ● H. R. Niebuhr, *Christ and Culture*, New York, Harper, 1951 ● R. Preston, *Church and Society in the Late Twentieth Century*, London, SCM, 1983 ● M.M. Thomas, *Christian Participation in Nation Building*, Bangalore, Christian Institute for the Study of Religion and Society, 1960 ● E. Troeltsch, *Die Soziallehren der christlichen Kirchen und Gruppen* (ET *The Social Teaching of the Christian Churches*, London, Allen & Unwin, 1931) ● W.A. Visser 't Hooft & J.H. Oldham, *The Church and Its Function in Society*, London, Allen & Unwin, 1937.

SODEPAX. The joint committee on Society, Development and Peace — transcending languages by its acronym SODEPAX — was from 1968 to 1980 the sole co-responsible agency between the Roman see (through the Pontifical Commission on Justice and Peace, established in 1967) and the WCC (through the 1968 Commission on the Churches' Participation in Development, then in 1970 through the more embracing unit on Justice and Service). Jointly announced as "an ecumenical experiment" with three-year mandates, SODEPAX had a sufficient number of charter documents to support it: from the WCC church and society conference (1966) and the WCC Uppsala assembly (1968); John XXIII's social encyclicals* on Christianity and social progress (*Mater et Magistra*, 1961) and on peace (*Pacem in Terris*, 1962), Paul VI's on development (*Populorum Progressio*, 1967), and above all, Vatican II's document on the Church in the Modern World (*Gaudium et Spes*, 1965).

A WCC/RCC-sponsored conference on development* in Beirut (1968) brought together theologians and church leaders from "developed and developing" countries, representatives from international organizations, and leading experts in world politics and economics. The success of this interdisciplinary conference and its widely circulated report were a major impetus to the formation of SODEPAX.

Headquartered in Geneva with competent

staff and generous funding from foundations and trusts, SODEPAX quickly responded to the widespread local and national initiatives by helping them to set up their own SODEPAX groups. It launched six programmes: social communication, education for development, mobilization for peace, development research, theological reflection, and working with people of other faiths. It organized several large international conferences, notably on the theology of development (1969), on the communications media in the service of development and peace (1970), on peace and the international community (1970), on the churches' role in the development of Asia (1970), and on peace in Northern Ireland (1973). In 1976 SODEPAX launched a programme of encouraging local and national ecumenical collaboration on the issues of the New International Economic Order, the church and the poor, the environment. Its quarterly *Church Alert* (1973-80) published the positions of the holy see and the WCC, and stimulating articles on development, peace and human rights.

Within a decade SODEPAX became the victim of its own vigorous successes. It needed more staff to respond to demands from so many areas but found less outside funding. The parent bodies were under pressure to bear almost all the costs, at the very time when they were worrying about SODEPAX becoming an almost independent third entity because of the somewhat diffuse character of its programmes and its free style of operation. And SODEPAX was coming up against the limits of the whole relation between the RCC and the WCC — a world-organized church with central authority, and a council of churches which is one step removed from the decision-making structures of the member churches.

By 1980 the two most effective, visible symbols of RCC/WCC collaboration were the full RC participation in Faith and Order and SODEPAX, and the latter even more so because of its close contact within the network of similarly structured national and regional organizations. Many on both sides interpreted the demise of SODEPAX (31 December 1980) as a weakening or even a withdrawal from a shared commitment to active collaboration. On the contrary, the WCC/ RCC Joint Working Group* (JWG) emphasized that what "ultimately matters... is

the will to work together effectively" and to find realistic, visible, "flexible forms of collaboration on the international as well as on the national and local levels"; for example, in common witness for peace, for the defence of human rights, including the right to religious freedom (JWG fifth report, 1983). But current visible WCC/RCC joint structures have so far failed to replace the original aims, activities and studies of SODEPAX. Even the post-SODEPAX joint consultative group for social thought and action (1982), composed of staff from related offices in Geneva and the Vatican, collapsed in 1989.

TOM STRANSKY

Church Alert, October-December 1980 • P. Land, "SODEPAX: An Ecumenical Dialogue", *The Ecumenical Review*, 37, 1985 • J. Lucal, "SODEPAX," in *Ökumene Lexikon*, Frankfurt, Lembeck, 1985 • Vatican Secretariat for Promoting Christian Unity, *Information Service*, 44, 1980.

SÖDERBLOM, NATHAN.

B. 15.1.1866, Trönö, Sweden; d. 12.7.1931, Uppsala. Archbishop of Sweden, historian of religions and pioneer of the 20th-century ecumenical movement, Söderblom did more, according to George Bell, than any other Christian leader or teacher of his time "to unite Orthodox and evangelical churches of all nations and communions in a common fellowship".

Söderblom grew up in a pietistic parsonage, and he remained rooted in its deep revivalist spirit throughout his entire life, even if his scientific investigations and encounter with liberal Protestant theology allowed him to grow far beyond it. After studying theology in Uppsala, Söderblom served as chaplain to the Swedish legation in Paris from 1894 to 1901. There he received a doctorate in theology with a dissertation on ancient Persian religion. He was professor of the history of religion in Uppsala from 1901 to 1914 (and simultaneously in Leipzig from 1912 to 1914). His numerous writings in this field earned him an international reputation.

Involvement in the student movement had brought him early contacts and experiences with Christians from other churches and continents. Already at the age of 24, while attending the 1891 Northfield student conference in the US, Söderblom had written in his diary

Nathan Söderblom (WCC photo)

words that could well stand as the motto for his entire life: "Lord, give me the humility and wisdom to serve the great cause of the free unity of your church."

His surprising choice as archbishop of Uppsala in May 1914 (he was third on the list of three presented to the king) gave him unexpected scope for exercising such responsibility, and this came to expression in the first instance in his repeated initiatives for peace during the first world war. To be sure, his appeal "for peace and for Christian fellowship" at the beginning of the war — signed only by churches in neutral countries — turned out to be as unsuccessful as the three efforts (in 1917 and 1918) to bring church leaders in the belligerent countries together in an international church conference (which also in the end drew participants only from several neutral countries).

Söderblom's renewed efforts after the war at founding an ecumenical council of the churches, which would seek to bring Christian principles to bear on international relations and social, industrial and economic life while deferring consideration of differences of doctrine, issued eventually in the Universal Christian Conference on Life and Work,* held in Stockholm in 1925. The successful

preparation and follow-up of this milestone in ecumenical history were due almost exclusively to Söderblom's personal initiatives and surpassing breadth of vision. After Stockholm 1925, it was no longer possible to ignore the fact of common Christian responsibility for humanity living together in peace, freedom and justice.

Although working out the consequences of the Life and Work conference was Söderblom's most urgent priority, he also took part in the parallel Faith and Order* movement. In 1927, at its first world conference in Lausanne, he chaired the important section on "the unity of Christendom and the relation thereto of existing churches".

His life work was given worldwide recognition and honour in 1930 when he was awarded the Nobel peace prize.

HANFRIED KRÜGER

C.J. Curtis, *Söderblom: Ecumenical Pioneer*, Minneapolis, Augsburg, 1967 • B. Sundkler, *Nathan Söderblom: His Life and Work*, Lund, Gleerup, 1968.

SOLIDARITY. In the main, two basic conceptions of solidarity can be distinguished in present-day discussions of this term: solidarity as (comprehensive) interdependence and solidarity as covenant* or alliance.

In Roman Catholic social doctrine the term "principle of solidarity" denotes a basic conception of political order* regarded as opposed both to middle-class individualism and to social collectivism, and as emphasizing not only that the individual is dependent on other human beings but also that society exists for people. Opinions are divided as to what importance the principle may still be thought to have for contemporary discussions of social theory and practical politics. While some regard it as serving as a critical corrective, others point to the problems raised by its appeal to neo-scholastic arguments of natural law and its consequently abstract character. On this account, it is said, the principle is not sufficiently relevant to situations of oppression and threat. While this principle of solidarity is based entirely on a conception of solidarity as mutual interdependence, the papal encyclicals of recent years (e.g. *Sollicitudo Rei Socialis*) increasingly refer also to a conception of solidarity as alliance (with the poor*), though apparently without linking the two conceptions.

In view of the growing awareness of worldwide problems affecting everyone, in particular the nuclear and ecological threats, a concept of *universal solidarity* is becoming increasingly important, emphasizing general involvement in the sense of global interdependence. This view of solidarity complements an increasingly popular conception of politics that transcends the limits of the nation state, analyzing particular problems in the perspective of wider contexts.

The theory and practice of *party* or *partisan solidarity* were promoted in particular by the labour movement. Such solidarity denotes, on the one hand, the coming together of people suffering under the same unjust structure in order to campaign against it and the interest groups defending it and, on the other hand, the practical action of other people who join in active sympathy with the victims and their fight for liberation. Party solidarity has become a major historical driving force, channelled by people's awareness that they themselves can shape their social conditions.

A specific danger of party solidarity is clearly that of pressure or coercion to conform within the group. In situations of conflict, outspoken self-criticism often looks like treason. To that extent, morally re-inforced party solidarity needs to be counterbalanced by deliberately cultivated openness and participation.

The phrase *solidarity with the poor* may be taken to sum up the comprehensive challenge which confronts Christian churches at the present time. At the same time it expresses an outlook strongly influenced by the traditions of party solidarity (solidarity as self-organization by the poor and as a challenge to the churches, esp. those of the first world, to join in and help).

It is theologically explosive to adopt the Old Testament covenant theme, according to which God made an alliance with the poor as a defence against their adversaries, thus assigning the poor a special role in the history of redemption. To stand in solidarity by their side is not merely an expression of a faith already constituted beforehand but concerns the essence of faith,* church* and theology.

This solidarity has a universal tendency because it extends to all who are poor. In a certain sense it even goes beyond normal solidarity, in that the latter envisages the individual in his or her immediate social environment (e.g. in a particular state). Solidarity with the poor goes beyond this towards a solidarity with those who are outsiders in terms of existing societies.

In a somewhat modified sense *solidarity with others* means those who are culturally different, especially people of other ethnic groups. This attention to people of other cultures is of recent date in the churches. If in face of the threat from a standardized Western civilization, poor people and people who are different come together, the nature of such a solidarity must not be overlooked. In so far as it includes differences, it possesses an inherent corrective to the pressure for uniformity stemming from party solidarity. The tenacity of cultural difference and its claim to full respect can protect solidarity with the poor from degenerating into a one-dimensional conception of liberation.

See also **subsidiarity**.

PETER ROTTLÄNDER

M. Lamb, *Solidarity with Victims*, New York, Crossroad, 1982 • J.B. Metz, *Glaube in Geschichte und Gesellschaft*, Mainz, Matthias Grünewald, 1977 • O.v. Nell-Breuning, *Baugesetze der Gesellschaft*, Freiburg, Herder, 1968 • A. Pieris, "A Theology of Liberation in the Asian Churches", *Japan Missionary Bulletin*, 40, 1986.

SOLOVIEV, VLADIMIR.

B. 16.1.1853, Moscow; d. 31.7.1900, Uzkoe, near Moscow. Theologian, philosopher, mystic, poet, journalist and ecumenist, Soloviev thought that the essence of Christianity consisted in the union of God and the human being in the incarnate Word, but that Eastern Orthodoxy neglected the human being, while Western Christianity tended to forget God. He pleaded for the reunion of the Orthodox church and the Roman Catholic Church. In 1889 he published *La Russie et l'Eglise universelle*, which met a very hostile reception in Russia. The holy synod forbade him to write further on religious topics. In 1896 he made a profession of faith, confessed to a Catholic priest and received holy communion. He hoped to see all human beings united religiously in Christianity, which would be in practice a theocracy under the pope, and politically under the czar. Afterwards he became more pessimistic, and more concerned with the problem of evil and of the antichrist. On his deathbed he received the last rites from a Russian Orthodox priest. Since he believed that Roman Catholicism and Orthodoxy remained mystically united despite their outward separation, he considered intercommunion* justifiable. In his philosophy he was influenced by J. Boehme, F.W.J. Schelling and G.W.F. Hegel. He sought to combine their pantheism with the Christian doctrine of the incarnation.* Dostoyevsky fashioned the character Alyosha in *The Brothers Karamazov* after Soloviev. Several of Soloviev's works were translated into English, including *Russia and the Universal Church* (London, Bles, 1948) and *God, Man and the Church* (Cambridge, James Clarke, 1937). See E. Munzer, *Solovyev, Prophet of Russian-Western Unity* (London, Hollis & Carter, 1956) and D. Stremoukhoff, *Vladimir Soloviev and His Messianic Work* (Belmont, Nordland, 1980).

ANS J. VAN DER BENT

SOUTH AMERICA: ANDEAN REGION.

Peru, Bolivia and Ecuador as part of the vice-royalty of Peru and Chile as a Capitania General were early areas of the colonial system and the colonial Catholic church. Lima, the capital of the vice-royalty, was an important centre where several synods took place during the colonial period. It was also a see of the Inquisition where a number of foreigners (mostly British or French) were condemned for "Lutheran heresy" (a general term used for all suspected of Protestantism). No religious liberty* existed in the colonial period. Foreign non-Catholics, however, enjoyed a certain tolerance after emancipation. With the protection of liberal governments, the Scottish colporteur and educationist James Thomson introduced the Bible and the system of Joseph Lancaster in Chile (1821), Peru (1822) and Ecuador (1824). Other colporteurs and missionary pioneers established a Protestant presence towards the end of the century. When the first pan-American missionary conference took place in Panama in 1916 (see **Latin American Council of Churches** [CLAI]) Protestant churches had been established in all the Andean countries but their numbers were still small. The missionary agreements reached in the 1914 Cincinnati meeting were perhaps the first "ecumenical" decision affecting the churches in this region insofar as it determined which churches would be present in the different parts of each country. A policy of bitter polemics and accusations characterized relations with the majority Roman Catholic Church. Intra-Protestant relations soon developed their own problems and the region suffered from denominational divisions and theological conflicts imported from abroad and from local division owing to leadership conflicts between missionaries and nationals or within each of the two groups. Under the influence of the co-operation committee created by some missionary societies and boards and through the friendship developed among not a few local leaders, different forms of co-operation and joint action developed, particularly since the 1920s.

Missionaries in the field established "associations" or "fellowships" for consultation, practical co-operation and sometimes comity agreements. In Bolivia a regional conference for Bolivia was created in 1917, followed by the Conference of National Evangelical Workers in 1935 and the attempt in 1941 to create an Evangelical Council of Bolivia, inspired by the Panama conference. Some evangelical churches created ANDEB (National Association of Evangelicals of Bolivia) in 1966, which was joined by most Protestant churches in the country. Four Bolivian churches are members of CLAI. In Ecuador an Association of Evangelical Churches of Ecuador was created in 1949 by several evangelical churches, and in the same year an Inter-mission Fellowship was organized, but both disappeared in the 1960s and the Confraternidad Evangélica Ecuatoriana took their place in 1963, mostly concerned with the defence of religious liberty. Five Ecuadorian churches are members of CLAI. A national council of churches was organized in Peru in 1940 on the basis of the Evangelical Alliance that had existed for some years. An interconfessional committee of religious leaders, including the Jewish community and the Roman Catholic Church, has been recently organized with the participation of some of the member churches of the council and not in competition with it. The Centro Cristiano de Promoción y Servicios (CECPS) is perhaps the most active ecumenical organization in the area of human rights and pastoral studies and publications. Four churches are members of CLAI. A council of churches was created in Chile in 1941 with 22 member churches. It has gone through several crises. In the crisis created by the military regime (1973-90) a group of leaders legitimizing the regime organized themselves with government support as "Consejo de Pastores", while the "Confraternidad Cristiana de Iglesias", representing a larger number of churches, ecumenically carried out evangelistic, social (SEPADE), human rights (FACIT) and theological (Comunidad Teológica Evangélica) tasks. Fifteen churches are members of CLAI. In all of these cases the membership of councils include a variety of Protestant families — Pentecostal, Holiness, Evangelical and Protestant churches — although the composition varies from country to country and withdrawals and admission of new members are not infrequent.

There are ecumenical seminaries in Chile and Peru and denominational seminaries often have interdenominational enrolment and faculty. Latin American ecumenical or transconfessional bodies such as CONELA, the Student Christian Movement, the Theological Fraternity, CELADEC (Christian Education) and the Latin American Association of Theological Education are active in the region. CLAI has an Andean region programme based in La Paz (Bolivia). The Indian majority of the population in all these countries, the growth of poverty* and marginalization as a result of the economic "adjustment plans", the violation of human rights* and the escalating violence* in some areas (particularly in Peru), together with the growing numerical strength and public visibility of the Protestant churches, pose great challenges and offer opportunities that call for a greater ecumenical solidarity and a testimony of unity from all the churches in this area.

JOSÉ MÍGUEZ BONINO

W. Browning, *The West Coast Republics*, London, World Dominion, 1930 • J.B. Kessler, *A Study of the Older Protestant Missions and Churches in Peru and Chile*, Goes, Costerbaan & Le Cointre, 1967 • C.P. Wagner, *The Protestant Movement in Bolivia*, Pasadena, CA, William Carey, 1970 • W. Padilla, *La Iglesia y los Dioses Modernos: Historia del Protestantismo en el Ecuador*, Quito, Corporación Económica Nacional, 1989.

SOUTH AMERICA: BRAZIL. The history of the ecumenical movement in Brazil has been marked by the pan-Protestant spirit which characterized the modern missionary movement and by the impact made on Brazilian Protestantism by denominationalism,* the conferences of Edinburgh (1910) and Panama (1916), the foundation of the WCC (1948), conservative and fundamentalist propaganda, and the Second Vatican Council (1962-65).

In a way, the reformers laid the foundations of Christian denominationalism by refusing to identify the church with any type of institution, declaring that the church is to be found wherever there are believers and that the continuity of the church in time is equivalent to the continuity of the faithful to the extent that they maintain the true faith. On the other hand, when the various Calvinist tendencies produced in England the Westminster confession of faith and its catechisms (1643-49), those foundations were re-inforced by the thesis of freedom of conscience and of the presence of the individual churches within the universal church. Although this theological position favours both the principle of unity and that of diversity, the development of Protestantism in Brazil, due to a large extent to North American missions, promoted the very strong denominational spirit which characterized Christianity in the US in the 19th century. The principles of strict separation of church and state and of voluntary association, together with the ecclesiastical traditions of the Old World and the ethnic origins of the waves of immigrants flowing from Europe in the 19th century, tilted the balance towards diversity and predominance of the denominationalist spirit.

As well as denominationalism, however, the missionaries also brought the pan-Protestant spirit developed by evangelicalism and by the Calvinist heritage, modified in the direction of the Arminianism of the Methodist movement, a fairly common theology strongly influenced by the great revival that occurred in the US in the first part of the 19th century. In consequence, Protestantism in Brazil, although having developed apart from the churches of European origin, maintained a common theological inheritance, and this fact should have promoted the ecumenical spirit. Nevertheless the denominationalist principle prevailed and has had considerable influence on the ecumenical movement in this part of the world.

If denominationalism developed in the US for specific economic and cultural reasons, in Brazil it can be explained only by the fact that the missionaries reproduced their own denominations as a duty imposed by the respective missionary societies which sent and maintained them. On the other hand, the need for strong assertion of identity in face of the dominant religious majority of the country encouraged attachment to specific doctrines and a spirit of opposition to Roman Catholics. In this last respect, a notable paradox resulted from the impact of the congress of Panama (1916) on the Brazilian Protestant mentality. The congress, called in reaction to that of Edinburgh, which had excluded Latin America from its organization, displayed remarkable ecumenical spirit, not only by its pan-Protestantism, but especially by regarding the Roman Catholic Church as Christian and recognizing its evangelizing work in Latin America as legitimate. Thus Protestant evangelism was to go to those areas not reached by the RCC, co-operating with it in the common Christian mission.

The spirit and attitude of the congress, however, produced an irremediable split in Brazilian Protestantism and, though it meant well, compromised the future of the ecumenical movement in Brazil. It did so in the first place by weakening pan-Protestantism itself, for while some people accepted the spirit of the congress, others did not, thus opening up a source of internal distrust. In the second place, it re-inforced anti-Catholicism, producing a sort of united front against the RCC. In fact most of those Brazilians who had been Catholic found the reasons for their conversion to Protestantism would have been undercut by the attitude of the congress and its followers. It is against this background that one must understand the development of the ecumenical movement in Brazil.

As an expression of reaction against the Edinburgh conference, the conference on missions in Latin America, held in New York in 1913, created the Committee on Co-operation in Latin America, which in its turn planned and held the congress of Panama in 1916. In Brazil, the Brazilian committee on co-operation was established for the purpose of encouraging joint Protestant-Catholic theological, Christian and secular educational work, demarcation of missionary territories, etc. The committee pushed on with those projects, although some of them, such as the united seminary in Rio de Janeiro, did not manage to survive the denominationalist spirit. Nevertheless the committee, whose activities continued from 1920 to 1932, included the Sunday School Union, the Young Men's Christian Associations, the Evangelical Schools Federation and the above-mentioned seminary. The great leaders of the co-operation movement were the Presbyterian Erasmus Braga (1877-1932), whose ideas were expressed in his book *Pan-Americanismo — Aspecto Religioso* (Pan-Americanism — its religious aspect), 1917, and his disciple, also a Presbyterian, Epaminondas Melo Amaral (1893-1962), who defended views which openly favoured union in his book *Magno Problema* (Great problem), 1934. Melo Amaral was the first secretary general of the Evangelical Confederation of Brazil (CEB), which was founded in 1934 as a successor to the Brazilian committee on co-operation.

As well as stimulating internal co-operation by means of congresses, publications and representation of churches in their dealings with government authorities, the CEB maintained international relations with the World's Sunday School Association, the International Missionary Council* and the Stockholm movement (Life and Work*). However, the confederation never had close relations with the WCC, which was taking shape in embryo in those organizations. The confederation undoubtedly paid the price exacted by its inclusion of the hostile forces mentioned earlier, just as it could not represent all Brazilian churches, since the Baptists did not form part of it, while some of the numerous Lutherans joined only later (1958), through the Evangelical Church of Lutheran Confession in Brazil. Although the confederation served Protestantism in Brazil well, it could not survive its own internal ambiguities and the pressures of the changes that were taking place in the churches, both nationally and internationally, and in the early 1960s it entered on a process of decline. The lack of representation resulting from the demise of the CEB encouraged the rise of various other associations of churches and institutions expressing the different tendencies found within the ambit of Brazilian Protestantism.

The foundation of the WCC polarized the various tendencies mentioned, chiefly because at a time when the churches were examining their positions in face of a new state of affairs, the preaching against the WCC unleashed by Carl McIntire and his International Council of Christian Churches* (ICCC) all over the world, and especially in Brazil in 1949, divided Protestantism in Brazil into three camps in regard to ecumenism: the fundamentalist, radically opposed to it; the conservative, representing a position midway between the WCC and the ICCC; and finally the openly ecumenical, composed of churches that gradually joined the WCC. In practice, however, the three attitudes reduce to two, because churches which opted for the middle position very frequently have assumed attitudes hostile to the ecumenical movement in general and the WCC in particular.

On the other hand, growing awareness of the socio-political crisis led the CEB to organize its final and perhaps most significant expression of pan-Protestantism. Through its social responsibility of the church sector, in 1962 the confederation organized and held the conference of the northeast in Recife. Under the heading "Christ and the Brazilian Revolutionary Process", Protestant theologians and sociologists presented theses on the church's responsibility in regard to a society in profound crisis. For the first time also, non-Protestant sociologists and economists, such as Gilberto Freyre, Celso Furtado and Paulo Singer, were invited to help analyze the actual economic situation in Brazil. It seems, however, that this conference played a decisive part in the almost total extinction of the CEB, for the conservative wing of the churches came to regard with even greater mistrust any expression of concern for social problems. And so, while pan-Protestantism was disintegrating, a growing radical movement agitated church circles, giving rise to a period of persecutions, exclusions and schisms. Socio-political instability, both continental and national, as well as the constant pressure from conservative and fundamentalist sources, often coming from outside the country through "faith missions", created a marked increase in suspicion and mistrust of the ecumenical movement, which was often regarded as in complicity with socialism.

The Second Vatican Council for its part, with its openness to ecumenical dialogue, rekindled the old problem of Protestant anti-Catholicism in Brazil, now embittered by propaganda inspired by the ICCC; those of a more liberal and open tendency (who were in the minority) were favourably impressed by the broader spirit in the RCC. However, these various forces operating in the religious field of Brazilian Protestantism are responsible for divisions, antagonisms and the closed self-centredness of some churches and make the ecumenical journey in Brazil increasingly difficult. An anti-socialist attitude which identifies socialism with atheism still persists, as does a lingering anti-Catholicism, now perhaps as a vestige of the need for Protestant self-identity.

The present situation of the ecumenical movement in Brazil, then, mirrors the conflicts and changes referred to above. It is not easy to discern in the panorama of Brazilian Christianity the currents and focal points of

A young mother with her two children in Quixeramobin, Brazil (WCC/Peter Williams)

ecumenism because of the ambiguous attitudes that some churches seem to have towards it. It is a fact that some — e.g. the Baptists and Congregationalists — openly declare themselves opposed to ecumenism, not to speak of the fundamentalist Presbyterian groups. Consequently some, though participating in pan-Protestantism, still have reservations about the presence of the RCC. This internal indefiniteness in the religious field has not prevented the presence of an ecumenical mentality and spirit among individuals within most churches, a fact that explains the emergence in recent years of numerous ecumenical service organizations which operate outside the churches and endeavour to maintain good relations with them, not merely fraternally co-operating but, wherever possible, supporting and sharing in projects.

The ecumenical movement in Brazil at the present time includes both an ecclesiastical and a para-ecclesiastical ecumenism. The former is represented by the National Council of Christian Churches (CONIC), characterized by sincere and broad ecumenism, for it includes the RCC through the national bishops conference of Brazil (CNBB), as well as the Latin American Council of Churches (CLAI), Brazil region, which also represents pan-Protestantism, since it includes only evangelical churches. Other members of CONIC in addition to the CNBB are the Evangelical Church of Lutheran Confession in Brazil, the Methodist Church, the Reformed Christian Church, the Reformed Evangelical Church, the Episcopal Church of Brazil and the United Presbyterian Church of Brazil. Members of CLAI, Brazil region, are the Methodist Church, the Independent Presbyterian Church of Brazil, the Evangelical Church of Lutheran Confession in Brazil, the Episcopal Church of Brazil, the Christian Reformed Church, the Arab Evangelical Church and the Congregational Evangelical Church of Brazil.

Para-ecclesiastical ecumenism includes numerous agencies, the chief being the Ecumenical Centre of Documentation and Information, the Institute of Religious Studies, the Ecumenical Services Co-ordinating Agency, the Brazilian Evangelical Centre for Pastoral Studies, the Ecumenical Centre for Evangelism and Popular Education, the Ecumenical Institute of Postgraduate Studies

in the Religious Sciences, and the Ecumenical News Agency.

The internal conflicts within Protestantism and its historical attitudes in regard to Catholicism have unfortunately held back the progress of the ecumenical movement in Brazil. However, the support given by para-ecclesiastical ecumenical institutions, the advance of CONIC and the broad ideals of CLAI make it possible to predict a promising future for ecumenical projects and dialogue in Brazil.

See also **Latin American Council of Churches**.

ANTONIO G. MENDONÇA

P.E. Pierson, *A Younger Church in Search of Maturity: Presbyterianism in Brazil from 1910 to 1959*, San Antonio, Trinity UP, 1974 • D.A. Reilly, *História Documental do Protestantismo no Brasil*, São Paulo, ASTE, 1984 • J. de Santa Ana, *Ecumenismo e Libertação*, Petrópolis, Editora Vozes, 1987.

SOUTH AMERICA: RÍO DE LA PLATA REGION.

The present ecumenical situation in the River Plate region is the product of a historical process in which for nearly four centuries (16th to 19th) the Roman Catholic Church had a religious monopoly. In the middle of the 19th century Protestantism arrived with English and Scottish, and later other European, immigrants. Orthodox churches also came, with waves of immigrants — Armenians, Syrians, Greeks, Russians, etc. — and devoted their attention primarily to their own ethnic groups. At the end of the 19th century and beginning of the 20th, the Protestantism which grew out of the work of missionaries was characterized by strong antagonism towards the RCC, and this continued until the 1940s.

The development of the churches and of interchurch relations has also been marked by the different roles played by the state in Argentina and Uruguay in the sphere of religion. In Uruguay the state has always been secular and has maintained the religious tolerance typical of liberalism. In Argentina, although the constitution affirms freedom of worship, the state has always maintained a special relationship with the RCC. Indeed, in different periods and provinces of Argentina compulsory RC religious education came to be established. At present the state maintains a more neutral position.

Within these various contexts relations between the churches and with the community have developed along parallel lines, and it is possible to identify various dimensions of ecumenical activity which are not necessarily mutually exclusive: ecumenism as a dialogue and as a co-operation among the Protestant denominations; ecumenism as an interconfessional dialogue between Roman Catholics, Protestants and Orthodox; ecumenism as encounter, commitment and action in relation to the community in general.

In these various types of ecumenism a decisive influence has been exercised by the worldwide ecumenical movement organized round the WCC, the Latin American Evangelical Union (UNELAM) in the 1950s and 1960s, and the Latin American Christian women's movements in the same decades. Young people's and students' organizations such as the Student Christian Movement and the Latin American Union of Evangelical Youth Movements have been involved in the problems of Latin America, and groups such as Church and Society in Latin America have been concerned with the relations between the church and society. Similarly, the Second Vatican Council contributed significantly to interconfessional openness and dialogue.

Ecumenism among the Protestant denominations. Denominations with an ecumenical calling such as the Waldensians, the Methodists and the Disciples of Christ reached the River Plate region around the turn of the century. At the end of the 19th century the Waldensians and Methodists began theological training of their ministers in Uruguay (1884), and the Disciples of Christ joined them in this task (1917), leading up to their constituting the Evangelical Faculty of Theology in 1935. Since 1970 the Argentine Evangelical Methodist Church, the Anglican Church, the Reformed churches, the United Evangelical Lutheran Church, the Christian Church (Disciples of Christ), the Evangelical Waldensian Church, the River Plate Evangelical Church (of German origin) and the Presbyterian Church have constituted the Instituto Superior Evangélico de Estudios Teológicos (ISEDET = Higher evangelical institute for theological studies), which provides an ecumenical academic training. Common educa-

tion was also an emphasis in Protestant mission, which led to the foundation of many schools. For instance, in 1913 the Colegio Ward was founded under the sponsorship of the Methodists and the Disciples of Christ.

Later in the 1960s catechesis* for children and young people led to the establishment of the United Council for Christian Education. Encounters gradually began to be organized between the ministers of the various churches. In these encounters, prayer, work experiences and biblical reflection were shared. Through these activities, other organizations were taking shape, leading initially to the Confederation of Evangelical Churches of the River Plate in 1935. This confederation was later to divide into two national bodies, the Federation of Evangelical Churches of Uruguay (1956) and the Argentine Federation of Evangelical Churches (1958). At present the former has 4 member churches and the latter has 28. Both federations also sponsor projects of service to the marginal sectors of society such as the poor people on the periphery of Montevideo and those who have had to leave home because of natural disasters in two provinces of Argentina. The main aim of the dialogue and co-operation among the Evangelical churches is to foster closer co-operation in contrast to the generally accepted image of a movement of churches which are very much divided and heterogeneous.

Various Protestant churches in the region are searching for unity in doctrine and liturgy and for mutual recognition of membership and ministry and organization. Examples include: (1) the process towards unity between the Evangelical Methodist Church of Argentina and the Disciples of Christ (the main points of agreement between them were affirmed by their respective assemblies of 1987); (2) signing of the Leuenberg agreement by the Evangelical Waldensian Church, the River Plate Evangelical Church, the United Evangelical Lutheran Church and the Reformed Churches (1986-87); (3) declaration of ecclesial communion* between the Evangelical Waldensian Church and the River Plate Evangelical Church as a result of both churches' signing the Leuenberg agreement (the declaration embraces mutual recognition of membership, mutual recognition of ordained ministry, recognition of intercommunion in word and the sacraments); (4) the pro-

Students at ISEDET, Buenos Aires, Argentina
(WCC/Peter Williams)

cess of mutual recognition of ministries which began in 1984 between the churches participating in ISEDET; (5) the formation of a consultative council with the participation of the presidents (bishops, moderators, presidents) of all Argentine churches in full or associate membership of the WCC.

Both in Argentina and in Uruguay the women of different Protestant — and in some cases also RC and Orthodox — churches have been in dialogue and have been celebrating unity in Christ on various special days and in mutual training campaigns. The Argentinian and Uruguayan Leagues of Protestant Women came into being in the 1930s. More recently ecumenical women's groups have come into existence in Buenos Aires and Montevideo. The latter have affinity with the theologies of liberation.

Ecumenism in interconfessional encounters. Since 1960 leaders of the RC and Armenian Orthodox churches and various branches of the Protestant churches have begun to meet particularly to celebrate the great Christian festivals (Advent, Christmas, Holy Week) and days of prayer for peace and unity. These op-

portunities for interconfessional encounter call for commitment to witness to unity in reflection and spirituality, overcoming the prejudices arising out of the historical involvement of the churches in the region. On the local level, too, there are groups of ministers, priests and lay leaders meeting periodically for prayer and reflection on the word. Various bodies in the River Plate region are promoting courses on ecumenism and liturgical and pastoral encounters such as the Christian Ecumenical Centre at Córdoba (Argentina), the Institute of Ecumenical Relations (Argentina), the Ecumenical Institute (Montevideo) and the Centre for Christian Studies, etc.

Ecumenism in relation to the community. Not merely various Christian churches but also secular groups with a commitment to the claims of the poor* take part in this field of ecumenism. This type of ecumenism revolves round the commitment to the struggle for justice.* Consequently, the churches' and groups' encounters, activities and reflection focus on various levels relevant to very practical social issues such as the indigenous population, the protection of refugees,* help for the victims among them, condemnation of violations of human rights,* defence of migrants, women and abandoned children. The River Plate Evangelical Church, the Reformed churches in Argentina, the Evangelical Methodist churches in Argentina and Uruguay, the Church of God, the Christian Church (Disciples of Christ), the Evangelical Waldensian Church in Argentina and Uruguay, the Anglican Church and some dioceses of the Roman Catholic Church have joined forces in the struggle for justice and full life for all.

Argentine ecumenical organizations most representative of this commitment to action include Ecumenical Movement for Human Rights, Argentine Commission for Refugees, Ecumenical Social Action Centre, Urban New Parish Centre, and United Board of Missions. In Uruguay, the Ecumenical Re-integration Service is active.

To sum up, it may be said that the ecumenical movement in the River Plate region has as its main concerns the struggle for justice and the protection of life, and dialogue among the different Christian positions, with the aim of bearing witness to unity, showing solidarity and the mercy of Jesus Christ in the midst of the people's struggles.

See also **Latin American Council of Churches**.

MABEL FILLIPINI

Informe Relatado de los Programas y Actividades Año 1980, Comisión Ecuménica Popular Argentina, 1980 • J. Míguez Bonino ed., *Polémica, Diálogo y Misión: Catolicismo Romano y Protestantismo en la America Latina*, Rio de la Plata, Centro de Estudios Cristianos, 1966 • O.D. Santagada, "Chronicle of the Argentine Second National Session on Ecumenism", *Journal of Ecumenical Studies*, 10, 1973.

SPIRITUAL ECUMENISM.

Spiritual ecumenism arises out of the gospel's being confronted with two phenomena which blossomed fully in the 19th century: the competition in which the missionaries of the various Christian confessions indulged and their frequently difficult encounters with the local cultures. In his high priestly prayer, Jesus on the eve of his death prayed that his disciples might be one. But this was not an end in itself. They had to be one "so that the world may believe" (John 17:21). Spiritual ecumenism consists in identifying with Jesus' prayer so that through the action of his Spirit he himself can raise up from within each people a reconciled church capable of proclaiming the good news to all.

Spiritual ecumenism was affirmed at the Edinburgh missionary conference in 1910. Historically it takes the form of a refusal to identify the proclamation of the gospel with any one culture.* On the contrary, the Christian life and message are to be incarnated in the various cultures, making use of elements belonging to those cultures. Thus spiritual ecumenism can be understood in practice as an effort of the separated Christians to create "a new unity and communion, not only within the cultures in question but also within the church universal".

Spiritual ecumenism as affirmed from 1910 onwards may thus be defined functionally as a gospel requirement which is prior to practical and theological ecumenism, as expressed in the conferences of Life and Work (1925) and Faith and Order (1927), and which justifies and co-ordinates them. It is the foundation on which the WCC was built (1948).

In the Roman Catholic Church spiritual ecumenism has been affirmed since the 1930s, with some forerunners preparing the way for the changes made by Vatican II. Mention may be made of the priests from Lyon: Paul Couturier, who organized the world Week of Prayer for Christian Unity;* and Jean Monchanin, who went to India in 1938 and founded an ashram there — a place for prayer and encounter for Christian and Hindu forms of spirituality. The fundamental intuition of these two priests was that "union will be the concern of all those who pray". In 1940, a dark year of war, Roger Schutz and Max Thurian established the Taizé community in Burgundy, in a spirit of fellowship with all who suffer. This community has been one of the first to provide a stable setting for Protestants, Anglicans, Orthodox and Roman Catholics to unite in prayer. With spiritual ecumenism taking root, an ecumenical translation of the Bible became necessary. The French version was completed in 1976 with the support of the Roman Catholic, Protestant and Orthodox leaders and has been distributed since 1977 by the United Bible Societies in a smaller version and with notes, for use of the general public.

The success of common translations of the Bible and of prayer communities like Taizé* (which continues to attract many young people from all over the world) shows that spiritual ecumenism answers a real need among many Christians, whether they identify with a church body or not. It enables them to witness in common to their faith, even while the prospect of theological agreement seems to be receding with the crisis of identity from which many churches are suffering. It also helps to prevent practical ecumenism from being carried along by ideological currents just when the ideology which since 1917 has chiefly mobilized — or immobilized — a large part of humanity is crumbling. And it makes it possible to combine the duty of evangelism* with respect for religious liberty* and the diversity of cultures. It is a risk and a hope, a reflection of the faith itself.

See also **Bible, its role in the ecumenical movement; prayer in the ecumenical movement; spirituality in the ecumenical movement**.

RÉGIS LADOUS

SPIRITUALITY IN THE ECUMENICAL MOVEMENT.
The ecumenical movement, which brings together Christians from diverse confessional and cultural tradi-

tions, is also a meeting-place of many different forms of spirituality. Some of these strands (e.g. Orthodox worship life, the monastic tradition, contemplative orders, Reformation spiritualities) have stood the test of time over many centuries. Others (e.g. the "spirituality for combat", liberation spirituality, feminist spirituality, renewal movements, new communities and the development of lay ministries) have arisen relatively recently.

Defining spirituality. Against the background of these and other diverse spiritual traditions and disciplines, two questions help us define an ecumenical spirituality: What would characterize the church* if it were indeed one church for the whole world? What kind of lived discipleship would incarnate that vision? If the church is called to be the one church for the whole world, it is inclusive, incarnational, universal, and sent in mission.* Such a renewed church will necessarily enlarge an understanding of Christian discipleship.

Spirituality has come to be seen as a more integrated and integrative dimension of the life of faith* as a result of several influences. A more holistic approach to theology, new emphases in biblical studies, a greater awareness of the need for meditation disciplines, the interface of many religious traditions and cultures, a sense of the needs of separate identities together with a realization of global interconnection and the impetus of many renewal movements have all led to the concept of spirituality as a whole way of life. However, the use of the term to contrast "the things of the spirit" with "material things" persists; in both English and French, the connotation of "devotion", "piety" or the "inner life" remains. Dogma* and theology are seen as rational and intellectual; spirituality is often taken to refer to their experiential counterparts.

This article builds on a simple definition of spirituality as the endeavour to live in obedience to the gospel — in a word, in discipleship. "Who do you say that I am?" (Matt. 16:15), Jesus asked his first disciples. The lived response to that question is the disciple's spirituality.

The vocation of the disciple has many dimensions. Obedience demands that Christians discern the voice of the Spirit (see **Holy Spirit**) in the world, make the gospel live in their own culture,* help in the transformation of the world, find meaning in life's struggles and participate in the life of exchange that is basic to human existence. The whole of life is to be placed at the disposal of the gospel. Spirituality, then, is the way people take to be Christian, to fulfill their Christian vocation. It embraces ministry and service, relationships, life-style, prayer and response to the political and social environment.

Historical context. The relationship between prayer and the birth of the modern ecumenical movement has been well documented. The slow dawning of inner questions relating to discipleship is illustrated in the various prayer movements of the 18th and 19th centuries, which discovered that there must be not only prayer for unity but prayer for unity by people of different traditions praying *together*. In the early years of the WCC, common worship emerged as an important question (see **worship in the ecumenical movement**). *How* can we pray and worship together? Work began on a new hymnology that expressed the search for a relevant discipleship (see **hymns**).

The 1960s were a significant decade for spirituality in the ecumenical movement. By 1961 virtually all of the Orthodox churches had entered the WCC, bringing along their own rich tradition of worship. Many of the third-world churches that joined the WCC in the 1960s brought political questioning of the status quo. At the same time, a wave of secularism in Europe and North America brought attempts inside and outside the church to put greater energies into social issues (see **secularization**). These forces sharpened what is often called the ecumenical-evangelical divide. At the heart of this tension lie perceptions about the meaning of discipleship and obedience to the gospel (on the one hand, a community which stresses engagement for the world and expresses impatience with what it regards as pie-in-the-sky mentalities; on the other, a community which testifies to salvation* by grace* and is committed to leading others to this experience). The hardening and institutionalization of this division is a tragic example of the fragmentation of Christian discipleship.

Vatican II's* contributions to a renewed church began in the 1960s, and are still taking root. Among these are the re-discovery of the

Bible as belonging to the people, renewal of worship (see **liturgical reforms**), updating of religious life and responsibility for social engagement.

By the 1970s, many of those engaged in the struggles for social justice were disillusioned, and there was hunger for more spiritual nourishment and undergirding. The charismatic and Pentecostal movements provided healing for individuals but also made their own ecumenical breakthroughs. At the WCC's fifth assembly (Nairobi 1975), where the dominant motif was the struggle of peoples in a broken and divided world, a band of enthusiasts ran a spirituality workshop which was in effect a side-show to the main meetings.

In the 1980s the growing search for a more integrated discipleship became a serious concern on the ecumenical agenda. Liberation theology* in Latin America, with its rich blend of worship and struggle, prayer and politics, posed an influential challenge to Western efforts to divide these. After 20 years the Orthodox concern for the centrality of spirituality and worship was at last being heard. The challenge of the evangelical groups continued. The fruits of Vatican II and the vitality of Roman Catholic encounter with other Christians in most parts of the world added to the pressure on mainstream Protestantism to take a fresh look at the quality of its discipleship. The Vancouver assembly of 1983, where worship was central and testimony and prayer invaded the plenary sessions, was a convincing sign of a deeper ecumenical concern for spirituality and a new willingness to put back together what belongs together in the life of the Spirit.

One of the four major emphases for the post-Vancouver work of the WCC was spirituality. This found its programmatic expression in a series of small meetings where people from the frontiers of lived discipleship shared their stories and tried to perceive what the Holy Spirit was bringing to birth in our times.

One, holy, catholic and apostolic. We consider here four key dimensions of Christian spirituality.

Spirituality and unity: Unity* is one of the truest and deepest aspirations of humankind. Spirituality is a binding force on the journey towards unity. Jesus' words and example address the way Christians are to live and to relate in the new order he initiated. Holiness and discipleship are not sectarian, not denominationally determined. Christians recognize the mystery of life lived in faith and overcoming the obstacles of sin and selfishness. Christians hear the call to live in obedience, to reconcile the broken fragments of life and of human community. No one person or church has reached the fullness of life in Christ. Spirituality links simple believer and erudite theologian, laity and clergy, various denominational traditions, different religious views of the world, history* and culture.

As a world community, Christians have the opportunity to engage in a mutually beneficial exchange of gifts and charisms.* Spirituality draws Christians into a common discipleship and affirms the truth of the search for unity and growth in community. The aim is inner transformation and common freedom so as to communicate to the world this message of conversion and liberation.

Concentration on historical splits and on dogmatic and doctrinal debate has long been challenged by a vision of unity as the reconciling of creation, which "has been groaning in travail" (Rom. 8:22). The real interface of the theological debate about unity and the unity of creation is in the realm of discipleship and spirituality.

A section from *Baptism, Eucharist and Ministry** illustrates: "The eucharist embraces all aspects of life... All kinds of injustice, racism, separation and lack of freedom are radically challenged when we share in the body and blood of Christ... The eucharist involves the believer in the central event of the world's history. As participants in the eucharist, therefore, we prove inconsistent if we are not actively participating in this ongoing restoration of the world's situation and the human condition" (E20). Here doctrine and discipleship combine, and the ecumenical movement is an inspiration for the unity sought by Christians at every level. Here it becomes manifestly clear that division over the eucharist contradicts the discipleship which the eucharist implies.

A church which is one is inclusive. Laity and clergy, women and men, black and white, poor and rich — all find a valued place within it. Ecumenical spirituality calls all to hospitality, to participation, to a sense of partnership in service and in decision making. "No one is outside the church, because there is no longer an outside, because no one is outside the reality of God and the risen Christ" (L. Boff, *Church, Charism and Power*, 1985).

The call to be holy (see **holiness, sanctification**): There is a shift in much current understanding of spirituality towards a greater emphasis on the incarnational. Old understandings of holy as "consecrated", "set apart", "purified" find new fulfilment in a perception of the God-givenness and potential holiness of all of life (see **life and death**). The church which celebrates God's creation in its totality and inter-relatedness will begin to be healed of the splits which have deformed much of Western Christendom — between sexuality and spirituality, public and private spheres, piety and politics, to name a few. New energies are released when old splits are healed. Values and creeds* are incarnated. The church's new perception of the largeness of God's purposes sets people free to be disciples in the fullness of their daily lives, not only during Sunday worship. Thus a new integrity and authenticity emerge.

The call to be catholic (see **catholicity**): Christian discipleship is situated within a church which is both local and universal, which strives to live its obedience locally as well as in relationship to the worldwide church, which recognizes the interconnectedness of reality, both for good and for ill. "If one member suffers, all suffer together; if one member is honoured, all rejoice together" (1 Cor. 12:26).

The gospel is always communicated and received in concrete situations. But it is the same gospel and the same Spirit that inspires all to create shalom (peace), to live in the fellowship of faith, hope and love. An ecumenical spirituality immerses people in their local settings, but with a global consciousness and an awareness of the connections which make all mutually dependent. In fact, it enables people to live those connections as they make choices, build relationships, respond to their milieus, enter into mission, hold one another in prayer. The challenge is to believe that the church is essentially in its local expression part of the church universal, and to be faithful to the implications of sharing one faith, one baptism,* one mission. It demands a conversion, a dying to attitudes and traditions that separate and divide.

The call to be apostolic (see **apostolicity**): The church is sent into all the world. It exists for mission, to fulfill God's purposes in the world. Discipleship which takes seriously the call to be apostolic will constantly be sensitive to the Holy Spirit's promptings to go forward into the new and unexpected. Key images are the servant church, the pilgrim church and the prophetic church. Implicit in each is a willingness to be poor, to reach out, to die, to follow the Spirit.

The discerning of this call to be in mission is one in which each part of the church may offer help and mutual correction: solidarity in struggles, mutual intercession, sharing and relief of pain, combat with principalities and powers. The church places itself at the disposal of a God who is co-opted by no political system and contained by no single set of beliefs, the time-scale of whose purposes is beyond our compass. Yet each act of obedience, each martyr's lonely suffering (see **martyrdom**), is woven into God's redemptive activity for the world. To be one, holy and catholic is to be set free and formed to be apostolic.

Implications and new explorations. In

Joint worship service of three congregations in Ruhuha, Rwanda (WCC/Michael Dominguez)

the classic arena of spirituality, prayer and worship, there are breakthroughs where risks are being taken that point the way. The context in which praise and thanksgiving are offered, the scope of confession and the extent of commitment are all indications of how ecumenical a person's or a church's prayer life has become. Intercession* is a litmus test. The personal and corporate intercession of Christians shows the range of their concern. Many churches still design their prayer calendars to pray only for their own denominational or confessional groupings. The Ecumenical Prayer Cycle* is an appeal for prayers for the world and the church in the world. If its work is to be successful, it must result in the deepening and broadening of prayers of intercession. To pray for one another involves engagement, the offering of something. All worship should connect to life and send people out into life, the "liturgy after the Liturgy".

The record of eucharistic inhospitality is still a painful scandal in the ecumenical movement. Many testify today, though, of the rich blessing they have received when breakthroughs have happened. In some parts of the world intercommunion* exists between Protestant and Catholic, but it is still a breach of discipline. In some places the great spiritual centres of the past, the cathedrals, are becoming ecumenical centres, places of pilgrimage for many who had given up on the faith.

Failures in building and living in community are evident in continuing exclusions and excommunications,* separations and divisions, in the alienation of many potentially vital members. But the ecumenical movement is also experiencing a re-discovery of community and of its fruits: covenants,* church base communities,* renewed religious life, ecumenical communities and projects, feminist solidarity, etc. Walls are coming down, sometimes in spite of the attitudes and decisions of the official church.

Today's widespread hunger for a deeper, more integrated way of living manifests itself in different ways: as a questioning of the idols of our times, as an emptiness or lack of meaning, as escapes into self-destructive behaviour, as a search for relevant worship, as a yearning for solidarity and sustenance in the struggle with evil powers and in a commitment to the poor and oppressed. Movements are emerging worldwide that strive to connect prayer and politics, reflection and action, and to make the church a more inclusive, participatory community. The underlying initiative in both this search and this rebirth is God's. God is at work in the world, if we will but discern and co-operate. The church has been entrusted with God's own mission. Fidelity to that task will be costly, requiring an enlarged vision, discerning spirits, a willingness to witness regardless of the risks. Churches and individual Christians are called to an ongoing conversion and an ongoing process of formation and renewal. Communal relationships will serve as discipline and mutual correction as well as offer solidarity in efforts to build the kingdom (see **kingdom of God**). It is within and because of a community of faith, prayer and celebration that strength and hope for discipleship are found.

Ecumenical spirituality, therefore, is common discernment of the direction in which the Body of Christ, the church, is being led. It is the common Christian vocation of enfleshing the gospel and co-operating with the Spirit so that through a transforming spirituality the servant church becomes truly one, holy, catholic and apostolic.

See also **faith, holiness, Holy Spirit, prayer in the ecumenical movement, sanctification, spiritual ecumenism, worship in the ecumenical movement.**

GWEN CASHMORE and JOAN PULS

T. Arai & W. Ariarajah, *Spirituality in Interfaith Dialogue*, WCC, 1989 • L. Bouyer, *La spiritualité du Nouveau Testament et des pères, La spiritualité du moyen âge, La spiritualité orthodoxe, protestante et anglicane* (ET *A History of Christian Spirituality*, 3 vols, New York, Seabury, 1982) • *Christian Spirituality*. I: Origins to the Twelfth Century, B. McGinn & J. Meyendorff eds; II: High Middle Ages and Reformation, J. Leclercq, F. Vandenbraicke & L. Bouyer eds; III: Post-Reformation and Modern, L. Dupré & D.E. Saliers eds; New York, Crossroads, 1985-89 • M. Fox, *Western Spirituality, Historical Roots and Ecumenical Routs*, Notre Dame, IN, Fides/Claretian, 1979 • C. Jones, E.J. Yarnold & G. Wainwright eds, *The Study of Spirituality*, New York, Oxford UP, 1986 • *Monastic Spirituality: A Spirituality for Our Times*, WCC, 1988 • J. Puls, *Every Bush Is Burning*, WCC, 1985 N.J. Ryan ed., *Christian Spiritual Theology, an Ecumenical Reflection*, Melbourne, Dove, 1976 • L. Swidler ed., *Ecumenism, the Spirit and Worship*, Louvain, Duquesne UP, 1967 • *With All God's People: The New Ecumenical Prayer Cycle*, WCC, 1989.

STATE. In the 20th century, Christian thinking about the state has reflected both the multiplicity of religious traditions and the shaping influence of theological and political movements. Not surprisingly, therefore, the term "state" has no single definitional or conceptual meaning in theological discourse today. It is used to refer to a particular territory, the administrative apparatus of the society, the government, the nation,* the body politic, the nation state, the polis, or the organization and monopoly of power* or violence* in a given society.

The differences in meaning often reflect cultural and linguistic differences, or the confusions of speaking at times descriptively, at times normatively. The historicity of the concept itself is a factor in the problem of definition. Many writers contend that the term is a fairly modern one, perhaps no earlier in usage than Machiavelli's early-16th-century reference to "lo stato". Dietrich Bonhoeffer, by contrast, sees the origin of the state in pagan antiquity, but argues that the concept is foreign to the New Testament, where its place is taken by the concept of government. The dynamic character of the reality to which the term points also invites the blurring of distinctions. Thus Luigi Sturzo speaks of the "trend towards unification in the modern state", referring thereby to the (totalitarian) tendency of centralizing power to draw all other social and individual realities into itself and redefine them in its image.

Jacques Maritain distinguishes among nation, body politic (or political society), people and state and refers to the last term as "that part of the body politic especially concerned with the maintenance of law, the promotion of the common welfare and public order, and the administration of public affairs. The state is a part which *specializes* in the interests of the *whole*." This distinction and its accompanying definition are very useful and are widely shared, but they do not cover all the varying nuances and theological slants and the differences in empirical reference.

Theological interpretations. Theological writings on the state are not always theologies of the state. A theological understanding may be implicit rather than explicit, and the method of inquiry non-theological. Aware of the menace of Hitler's totalitarianism,* the Oxford conference on "Church, Community

and State" (1937) addressed the issue directly. The Amsterdam assembly of 1948 addressed it more indirectly through inquiry into the "responsible society"* and comparisons of capitalism* and communism. Subsequent conferences dealt with the state in relation to liberation movements and prospects for a "just, participatory, and sustainable society"* and explored the questions more social-scientifically than theologically. Latin American liberation theology* committed itself methodologically to the priority of social-scientific investigation.

Theological interpretations of the state fall mainly into two types, although a third type has been recognized and advanced in this century by Barth and Bonhoeffer. The state is represented as being grounded either in human nature as created (see **creation**) or in sin* (see also **anthropology, theological**). The former view is characteristic of Roman Catholic and Anglo-Catholic interpretations but is also consonant with some liberal Protestant interpretations. The latter view predominates in churches and theologies of the Reformation traditions.

Where the state is understood to be grounded in sin, it is referred to frequently (esp. in the Lutheran tradition) as an "order of preservation". Its primary function is to serve as a barrier to sin-induced chaos — to maintain order,* enforce the law,* defend against enemies, protect the innocent, punish the wicked. It is also to serve justice, but "justice" often is defined in terms of provisions of the legal order. With this view of the state, it has been difficult — although certainly not impossible — to expand the notion of justice* into a dynamic concept, challenging established orders of privilege and power and requiring the state to take on broader responsibilities for the welfare of all the people. Where the state is understood to be grounded in original human nature, it is recognized as an "order of creation" with functions that include those of order and defence, but within a more flexible and comprehensive concept of "common good".

In the third type, the state is understood to be grounded in Christ and to have the redemptive function of assuring time, space and order for the proclamation of the word of justification.* Barth intended this Christological interpretation of the state to provide a theologi-

Children of the Pioneers movement, Volgograd, USSR (WCC/Peter Williams)

cal basis for church criticism of the Nazi state, and both Barth and Bonhoeffer saw it as an alternative to the Lutheran two-kingdoms concept. Neither theologian developed this view into a systematic theology of politics.

Christian theologies of the state in this century have been influenced by other considerations in addition to the theories of origin. A principled commitment to the priority of justice in the order of political values yields an activistic approach to the role of the state in social transformation. The optimistic understandings of human nature generated by the Enlightenment allow possibilities for popular control of political power and for social change that brush aside the warnings of more negative views of human nature and historical expectation and that promise the engineering of an end to war, poverty and oppression, and the transformation of the state system of international politics into a world society with a democratic government committed to the advancement of the human rights of all peoples. Proletarian movements, informed by Marxist interpretations of society and history, consign the state to the role of instrument of class power and imagine a time prepared by revolution and socialist governance when the state as

an administrator of persons will wither away and be replaced by an institution commissioned solely for the administration of things.

All theologies of the state insist that its functions and authority are merely temporal and that it has no sacramental, sacerdotal, doctrinal or other ecclesiological functions. These limitations are basic to all theories of church-state relationships, however much they may differ otherwise.

Forms of the state. Christian political thought in the 20th century generally has agreed that no particular form of the state is theologically necessary. Nevertheless, it has tended to show a distinct preference for some form of democracy. Most of the major theologians who wrote on political questions — Reinhold Niebuhr, Karl Barth, Emil Brunner, Jacques Maritain, John Courtney Murray, Luigi Sturzo, Jürgen Moltmann and others — have argued the case for democracy. Democracy was endorsed also in the encyclical *Pacem in Terris* of Pope John XXIII. Most ecumenical documents on political issues have been democratic in tendency if not explicit commitment, through their emphases on equality,* freedom,* participation* and human rights.* The arguments in German theology of the 1930s for an autocratic and hierarchical state grounded in the *Volk* as a natural order did not survive the collapse of Nazism. Post-war German theology is explicitly democratic in its treatment of political questions.

The principal arguments over the form of the state have pertained to the presuppositions and structure of democracy itself. Democracy could not survive the severe tests put to it by movements and situations of the 20th century with an excessively optimistic view of human nature, a social theory based on contractarian individualism, and a definition of governmental responsibilities limited primarily to protection of life and property. The main thrust of much democratic theologizing therefore was to re-equip the notion of democracy with a view of human nature that acknowledged its sinful and demonic tendencies as well as its capabilities and creativity, with a relational understanding of society as persons-in-community and with an expanded vision of state responsibilities that placed protection of life and property in the context of a more comprehensive commitment to the "general welfare", especially to the welfare of the poor, powerless and oppressed members of the society.

The structural goal of this reformulation was a state with sufficient power to carry out its expanded responsibilities, yet with constitutional limitations of sufficient efficacy to restrain the oppressive tendencies of central power. Doubting the possibility of restraining a state with comprehensive welfare and educational functions, Helmut Thielicke argued instead for a minimal state. Liberationists, rejecting the notion of improvement within the context of the bourgeois state, argue for radical transformation of the property* and political systems and accept the risk of the constitutionally unrestrained power of a revolutionary government (see **revolution**).

The authority of the state. Major issues of political authority* include the following five. First, is the authority of governors from God* or the people? Pope Leo XIII (*Diuturnum*, 1881) stated that elections may designate rulers but God confers their authority. Protestant writers asked whether a theological prescription (Rom. 13) for an autocratic state could be applied to the modern democratic state and answered that in a democracy the people themselves were the fundamental

"governing authorities" (v.1). Second, the secularization* of politics aggravated the problems posed by popular sovereignty, further attenuated the relevance and viability of the Rom. 13 tradition, encouraged the turn towards non-theological modes of authorization and opened the way to absolutist claims and solutions. Third, the emergence of totalitarian systems in the third and fourth decades of the century tested the limits of a theologically grounded obligation to obey. Fourth, revolutionary movements denied the legitimacy of bourgeois and autocratic states but opened questions of the authority of revolutionary leadership and revolutionary governments. Fifth, the new internationalism called in question the authority of particular nation states without resolving problems of transferring their authority to a world government. Helmut Thielicke insisted that sovereignty is an essential and constituent attribute of states, that states therefore must be plural and that in consequence it is impossible to conceive of a single world state. Maritain insisted that sovereignty is neither essential to nor constitutive of states, that particular states can and eventually will transfer their "sovereign" authority to a world political society and that such transfer will manifest the logic of the common good, the principle of subsidiarity* and the perfect society in its process of becoming.

The pathology of states. Far-reaching questions concerning the pathology of states overshadow persistent issues of the corruptive tendencies of politics and power. Totalitarian movements and systems suggest that under the conditions of modernity, states tend inevitably to discard the limits of power, put themselves in the place of God, destroy or absorb all other institutions and thereby make themselves the source and centre of meaning and existence. Liberation theologians argue that the state in capitalist civilization is not a potentially neutral if somewhat corrupt institution but a "national security state" (see **national security**) — an armed instrument of international capitalism, serving the expansion and consolidation of capitalist power. Both totalitarianism and liberation theory call in question the viability of the liberal democratic state. The conditions which lead to totalitarianism also call in question whatever might replace the liberal democratic state, including any proposed revolutionary successor to the "national security state".

To establish the terms under which a state can be just, stable and peaceful, it is necessary to probe the perennial questions of human nature and historical expectation. Is it true that "man's capacity for justice makes democracy possible; man's inclination to injustice makes democracy necessary" (Niebuhr)? Or is the ambiguity of human nature and politics to be resolved towards radical pessimism or optimism? Also, is it possible to understand the nature of states from the particularity of states, or ultimately only in the context of international society? Finally, does it suffice to understand the state theologically in terms of creation and the fall, or must we not continue the Christological project of Barth and Bonhoeffer, exploring the power, promise and limits of the state in the light of the reconciling work of God in Christ?

See also **church and state, fascism, law, nation, national security, revolution, society, totalitarianism**.

THEODORE R. WEBER

J.C. Bennett, *Christians and the State*, New York, Scribners, 1958 • J. Comblin, *The Church and the National Security State*, Maryknoll, NY, Orbis, 1979 • J. Maritain, *Man and the State*, Chicago, Univ. of Chicago Press, 1950 • R. Niebuhr, *The Children of Light and the Children of Darkness*, New York, Scribners, 1944 • L. Sturzo, *Church and State*, Notre Dame, IN, Notre Dame UP, 1962 • L. Sturzo, *The Inner Laws of Society*, New York, P.J. Kennedy, 1944 • H. Thielicke, *Theologische Ethik* (ET *Theological Ethics*, vol. 2: *Politics*, Philadelphia, Fortress, 1969).

STATUS CONFESSIONIS.

The term (Latin for "situation of confession") has only recently entered the ecumenical vocabulary with a measure of common acceptance. Derived from Reformation contexts, *status confessionis* came to make its way in ecumenical language in connection with the Barmen declaration (1934) and its aftermath (see **Confessing Church**).

The Barmen declaration, with its six short theses, sought to give the church guidance in the critical moments of an incipient totalitarianism in Germany, fighting the inroads of the so-called German Christians, who wanted to make the church a tool of the state. Defining this as a *status confessionis* means that this

was a moment for the church to confess its faith* in the face of idolatrous powers. In more recent times, apartheid in South Africa has been seen as calling for a similar response. W.A. Visser 't Hooft connected apartheid* and *status confessionis* for the first time in 1964. More recently Eberhard Bethge, Jürgen Moltmann and Ulrich Duchrow have made effective use of the term in their work in regard to nuclear weapons or the global economy, for example. Although there is no commonly accepted working definition of the term, Duchrow cites Dietrich Bonhoeffer's twofold test for a *status confessionis*: "firstly, whether the state is going beyond its own mandate and trespassing on that of the church ('too much' state) and, secondly, whether the state falls short of its mandate ('too little' state)". This latter criterion clearly comes into play when the racist South African government systematically deprives not just a minority but the majority of its citizens of their human rights by an indefensible constitution.

Besides Barmen, Medellín (1968) is the other great 20th-century "synod" in the church that models compellingly the *status confessionis*, i.e. the need for confession in the face of the destruction of human life. Confronted by the millions of the world's poor, the Roman Catholic bishops of Latin America at Medellín stressed discipleship as part of the necessary Christian witness, not as a catch phrase but as an attitude that embraces all of life.

While there is a genuine appreciation of Barmen in both Americas today, there is also a sharp criticism of expectations that any new confession would have to be modelled on Barmen. That critique focuses on two concerns at least: First, declarations do not eliminate the need for discipleship. "Barmen was flawed ecclesiologically. If the doctrine is right, the rest will follow... It is not true biblically, statistically, or in terms of social science theory that the verbal proclamation of a theologically impeccable message will automatically renew the church, without attention to any other measures of discipleship and discipline" (John H. Yoder). Second, the experience of a persecuted church in parts of the Americas and the witness of martyrdom* precede a formulated confession: "The church first undergoes the fires of persecution and disappearance, torment and death. Out of that experience comes a new and vital theology" (Daniel Berrigan).

FREDERICK HERZOG

U. Duchrow, *Global Economy: A Confessional Issue for the Churches*, WCC, 1987 • *Katallagete*, 10, 1-3, 1987 • J. Moltmann ed., *Bekennende Kirche wagen, Barmen 1934-1984*, Munich, Kaiser, 1984.

STUDY AS AN ECUMENICAL METHOD.

Early in the Life and Work* movement, ecumenical encounters brought forth such a variety of divergent and conflicting views on all subjects that some method and form of organized reflection and research was necessary on those issues which were dividing Christians into opposing camps.

Already the first Life and Work conference (Stockholm 1925) had emphasized the need for continuing research on social issues, but only in the preparation for its second conference (Oxford 1937) did a systematic rationale for ecumenical study emerge. In a preparatory volume, *The Church and Its Function in Society*, W.A. Visser 't Hooft and J.H. Oldham presented the need for organized reflection and discussion of the issues facing the churches in the modern world. Oldham is generally regarded as the pioneer of the study method. He wrote that the church must be seen not only as a community of worship and love but also as "a community of thought". He summed up the method of study in a famous sentence: "In the fulfilment of its task, the church must call to its aid the best minds that it can command." This includes laity* from all areas of public life as well as theologians and church leaders.

Critics later challenged this emphasis on "the best minds" as academic and elitist. But Oldham had been careful to point out: "The clearer understanding of the significance of Christian faith for the actual life of our time... is not primarily a matter of scholarship and learning. It is rather the fruit of spiritual insight and understanding, and we must never allow ourselves to forget that the realities of the spiritual world may be hidden from the wise and prudent and revealed to babes." In Oldham's view this qualification does not diminish the need for serious intellectual work by the churches. The church as a community of thought has to broaden its understanding of the organic structure of life, the "law of things", the laws of institutions, the role of the nation and the state, and the sources of social evil.

With Oldham as the chairman of its preparatory committee, the 1937 Oxford conference became the first ecumenical "study" conference on social issues, involving large numbers of theologians and laity in preparatory studies and in the conference itself. For the first time the non-Roman Catholic churches addressed, in a substantial way, economic, political and ideological problems.

In view of the Oxford achievements, it is not surprising that the 1938 organizational plan for the new WCC churches included a "study department" as one of its four principal offices. In 1954 it became the Division of Studies, comprising the departments of church and society, evangelism, missionary studies, and the Commission on Faith and Order. This office was responsible for study programmes in these fields and for the organization and preparation of the four WCC assemblies between 1948 and 1968 (Amsterdam, Evanston, New Delhi and Uppsala).

The emphasis on study proved particularly helpful in these years as a way of easing churches into the examination of controversial issues which needed ecumenical attention but found no consensus. The 1966 world conference on Church and Society was the most notable of a series of ecumenical study conferences on the urgent social issues facing the churches in this period.

After the fourth WCC assembly (Uppsala 1968) there was increasing tension between the tradition of ecumenical study and a growing demand for ecumenical action. In 1969 the WCC instituted new action programmes to mobilize the member churches for the struggle against racism* and world poverty.* And older WCC sectors were stimulated to become more action-oriented, for example, through the programme on the Co-operation of Women and Men in Church and Society.

The 1972 plan for restructuring the WCC emphasized the need to integrate study and action, without proposing ways to do so. Some action programmes discovered the need to reflect, which led to the formula "action-reflection". This did not resolve the substantial differences of methodology and ideology which underlay the "study-action" debate.

Since 1969, alongside the new action programmes the traditional discipline of ecumenical study continues in such sub-units as Faith and Order, and Church and Society, and in the programme on Dialogue with People of Living Faiths. It has proved its role in such new ecumenical programmes as the study of the future of humanity and society in a world increasingly dominated by science and technology. The conflicts and disagreements which confront the churches and the world in the 1990s on the issues of freedom, justice and order would seem to validate a fresh emphasis on imaginative ecumenical study.

PAUL ABRECHT

R. Rouse & S. Neill eds, *A History of the Ecumenical Movement, 1517-1948*, WCC, 1986, ch. 12 • *The Ten Formative Years, 1938-1948*, report to the first WCC assembly, Amsterdam 1948 • W.A. Visser 't Hooft, "Oldham's Method in Abrecht's Hands", *The Ecumenical Review*, 37, 1, 1985 • W.A. Visser 't Hooft & J.H. Oldham, *The Church and Its Function in Society*, London, Allen & Unwin, 1937, part 3.

STUDY CENTRES. Within ecumenical circles, the term "study centre" refers to ecumenical or denominational centres which are engaging in special areas of research and dialogue particularly from an ecumenical perspective. Their common aim is to assist the churches and congregations in their total task of witness and service in various cultural, social and religious contexts. They should be distinguished from ecumenical institutes in Europe, which are also in a sense study centres but are engaged more in academic research and less in dialogue.

The study centres are often known as "dialogue centres" or "institutes for religion and culture". Most of them concentrate on research and dialogue in areas of religion and culture or on social and cultural analyses for renewal in mission. Some of them also hold conferences and undertake other programmes. Many of them are members of regional associations of "lay academies" (see **academies, lay**). Most of these centres publish periodicals in order to share their findings with churches.

Consultations on the role of study centres were held in Kandy (1967), Hong Kong (1971) and Singapore (1980) in co-operation with the WCC. A Fellowship of Study Cen-

tres was organized in 1980, and exchange of information among them is co-ordinated by the WCC's Sub-unit on Renewal and Congregational Life.

TOSH ARAI

Directory of Study Centres, WCC, 1982 • *Inter-religio*, a periodical magazine of the network of study centres in Eastern Asia, Nagoya, Nanzan Institute for Religion and Culture, 1987- • *The Role of the Study Centres*, WCC, 1981.

STUTTGART DECLARATION. Led by W.A. Visser 't Hooft and the provisional leaders of the Evangelical Church in Germany — bishops and leading representatives of the Confessing Church such as Hans Asmussen, Otto Dibelius, Hanns Lilje, Wilhelm Niesel and Martin Niemöller — an ecumenical delegation met in Stuttgart from 17 to 19 October 1945. The common purpose was to prevent German Protestantism from isolating itself from the other churches and to find ways to help the German people, who had been spiritually, politically and economically shattered. An admission of guilt was expected from the Germans for the crimes that had been committed during the National Socialist regime and had become fully known only in the summer of 1945 (see **war guilt**). This expectation found the German theologians and church leaders ready to reflect self-critically on the behaviour of the Protestant church in relation to the temptations of a totalitarian state and to re-examine the church's political responsibilities.

In August 1945 the German Roman Catholic bishops conference had deplored the crimes committed by Germans before and during the war and demanded the punishment of the guilty. The Stuttgart declaration of 18-19 October goes a considerable step further, confessing the church's guilt in the sight of God and humanity: "We accuse ourselves for not witnessing more courageously, for not praying more faithfully, for not believing more joyously and for not loving more ardently."

This confession was also made by men who had been persecuted in the Third Reich or had offered resistance to it, thus admitting their own share of guilt and resisting the temptation to set victims and evil-doers over against each other. It is then also impossible for them to draw up a balance-sheet of what human beings have done to each other. A people's "shared suffering" also means their "shared guilt". It must be stressed that this was a theological conclusion and was not limited to the idea that no one in a state built on injustice can in the long run remain innocent.

The Stuttgart declaration applies the formula of the confession of guilt used in public worship to a politically disastrous situation. Both elements — the theological character and the joint responsibility for the future direction to be taken by the German people — constitute a unity, but even at that time that unity met with vigorous resistance. The declaration was misunderstood (which frequently happened abroad too) as a quasi-legal admission of the collective guilt of all Germans. On the other hand, many church members resisted attempts to use this confession — made to God who judges and reconciles — to criticize earlier political aberrations and new developments of a problematic nature.

GERHARD SAUTER

G. Besier & G. Sauter, *Wie Christen ihre Schuld bekennen: Die Stuttgarter Erklärung 1945*, Göttingen, Vandenhoeck & Ruprecht, 1985 • M. Greschat ed., *Im Zeichen der Schuld: 40 Jahre Stuttgarter Schuldbekenntnis*, Neukirchen, Neukirchener Verlag, 1985 • M. Greschat, *Die Schuld der Kirche: Dokumente und Reflexionen zur Stuttgarter Schulderklärung vom 18./19. Oktober 1945*, Munich, Kaiser, 1982.

SUBSIDIARITY. According to a dictionary definition, subsidiarity is the theory that "functions which subordinate or local organizations perform effectively belong more properly to them than to a dominant central organization". This principle has played an important part (1) in the social teaching of the Roman Catholic Church, especially in the papal encyclical *Quadragesimo Anno*; (2) in German Roman Catholic social philosophy and in Christian social sciences, especially where these have a neo-scholastic slant; (3) in the socio-political debates of the 1950s and 1960s in the Federal Republic of Germany, where it was used as the basis for arguments by RC associations and charitable organizations involved in these discussions and where it gained a new relevance; (4) in the political debates of the 1980s in the FRG, where local

left-wing groups claimed the right to autonomy and self-assertion against bureaucratic tendencies, the dominance of large-scale social organizations and legal limitations on the responsibility and rights of small, more manageable social units.

The significance of the principle of subsidiarity can be understood only from the context in which it arose — German RC social metaphysics. In that context subsidiarity, along with the principles of the person and of solidarity, is the third principle for the creation of social order. The other two principles define the right to life of the individual, who is always also linked to the community, and the common good, which represents the content, aim and meaning of human community and is the necessary guarantee of the former right. In subsidiarity, on the other hand, we have a principle that goes beyond the person's right to life and stresses individuals' basic, general responsibility for maintaining themselves, achieving their own well-being and developing their natural potential.

In this relative adaptation of the idea of autonomy, subsidiarity as a principle also has a certain affinity to bourgeois liberalism. In terms of this principle, the private initiative of the free person as an economic agent can be regarded as primary, as opposed to the economic activity of the state. Negatively, subsidiarity rejects the authority of social institutions when they supplant or eliminate the individual's responsibility for action, a view that seems to coincide with liberalism.

The fundamental contrast between the two models of order becomes clear when we consider the metaphysical status of subsidiarity as a principle. It is an *ontological* statement — about what the person fundamentally is and what responsibility can be allotted to the person — but not a description of empirical reality. If individual persons are essentially responsible for themselves, this always implies the ethical imperative that they should actually be in a position to guarantee each other self-fulfilment, or that conditions must be created to that end. Thus subsidiarity as an ontological statement concerning independent human responsibility means that human beings cannot in fact simply be left to themselves in a laissez-faire way. In situations of physical or any other kind of need, when individuals, social groups or classes are actually incapable of providing for themselves, a society must act to help, in order to fulfill the over-riding claim of the right to life.

On the one hand, one's incapacity to be what by nature one should be may be *temporarily* lost (through illness, inability to work, etc.). If there are personal reasons for this incapacity, then help must be granted in the interests of restoring responsibility. If social structures and mechanisms are responsible for it (through unjust distribution of goods, oppression or unemployment), then a society, which is the frame of reference for independence and self-realization, must provide a remedy by transforming itself.

On the other hand, the actual incapacity for independence may be *permanent* (through disability, old age, etc.). Even when for individuals and groups the discrepancy between the natural right to exercise responsibility and their actual situation remains so serious that outside help is a condition of survival and is necessary for the achievement of the greatest possible well-being of the person, the principle of subsidiarity can never be adduced to justify euthanasia or the like, but rather lays an obligation on the community to help.

The principle also applies when certain phenomena in highly complex industrial societies are taken into account. In some wealthy societies, for instance, health care may become so technological, bureaucratic and scientific that individual persons or small compact units (such as a village or small town) no longer have access to such care. This real incapacity is not temporary but permanent. In this context the principle of subsidiarity offers a justification for the exercise of responsibility by larger units (e.g. the states of the Federal Republic of Germany).

It has been objected that the principle of subsidiarity is too static to cope with the dynamism of capitalistic industrial societies, that it idealizes rural societies with a low standard of welfare and production and is suitable as a principle of order only where the pace of development is slow. In reply, it may be said that subsidiarity as a principle necessarily requires accurate knowledge of the actual circumstances of human beings and their relationships so that development and change can occur.

The subsidiarity principle likewise assumes that there is an unimpaired, general moral subject who is able to create social order and to react to any demonstrated incapacity of human beings to live with dignity in their own strength. What tells against such an assumption, which is essential to the significance of the subsidiarity principle, are experiences of anonymous and subjectless mechanisms which have catastrophic effects and for which no individual person can be blamed. Also, in the light of experiences which involve an overall destructive agent (say, in the Nazi regime's extermination camps), it is clear that the right of human beings to life clearly is not uniformly accepted and cannot be assumed in the kind of thinking appealing to natural law, which lies behind the principle of subsidiarity.

For these reasons, the reservations against the principle of subsidiarity voiced by Protestant theologians and others gain in force. In an ethic guided by Protestant theology, the standards and norms for social activity, the rights and duties of individuals, are seen as having their basis in God's justifying action towards human beings and in his saving word. In particular, if we insist on the human capacity for guilt in social contexts, and especially where the rights to life are denied, it becomes extremely urgent for RC social proclamation, too, to ask whether socially relevant Christian practice can be clarified and defined exclusively in terms of natural reason and the principles that can be derived from this, or whether, in the light of the actual denial of human rights, Christian praxis must be motivated first and foremost by the content and requirements of faith.

In recent RC discussions of ecclesiology, subsidiarity has also been introduced in a derivative way as a category for help in determining the respective competences of the parish, the diocese, the national bishops conferences, the universal church, and the papacy.

See also **solidarity**.

OTTMAR JOHN

C. Cordes, "Kann evangelische Ethik sich das Subsidiaritätsprinzip, wie es in der Enzyklika 'Quadragesimo anno' gelehrt wird, zu eigen machen?", *Zeitschrift für evangelische Ethik*, 3, 1959 • F. Klüber, *Katholische Soziallehre und demokratischer Sozialismus*, Bonn, 1979 • O. v. Nell-Breuning, *Gerechtigkeit und Freiheit: Grundzüge der katholischen Soziallehre*, Munich, Olzog, 1980.

SUFFERING. Human suffering is an ecumenical theme par excellence. All churches and religions participate in responding to the challenge it presents, and even non-religious ideologies need to deal not only with its causes but with the meaning of unremovable suffering to the human being as well.

The specific contribution of Christian spirituality and theology to the theme occurs within the tension between *outrage* and *acceptance*, both voiced most clearly in the Book of Job. Throughout the history of the church there is outrage, protest and fighting against avoidable and unnecessary suffering, grounded in "the power of anger in the work of love" (Beverly Harrison), but there is patience, independency and inner freedom as well in those who bear the unbearable burden. Church history shows that mostly one of the two elements prevails in a given historical situation. But if one part of the dialectical tension between outrage and acceptance is completely lost, the other will degenerate as well. A church, for example, that preaches submissiveness and acceptance of God-given suffering to women has betrayed Christ's active and passionate work for freeing and redeeming all of God's children. Social activists, on the other hand, untrained in endurance and lacking revolutionary patience, will rather break under the burden and easily can become bitter.

These two spiritual-ethical responses are coded in the Christian symbol systems of sin,* cross and the city of God. These are interpretative figures that Christian tradition has offered in response to the questions that arise with the suffering of the innocent, such as: Is suffering God's will or not? Is God the source of evil as well as of good? Does God permit suffering that comes from other sources? Do we have to choose between God's love and God's omnipotence?

The Judeo-Christian tradition does not emphasize the tragic unsolvable depth of suffering that is caused by natural defects or events. It places suffering in its historical context and, starting at the very first mythical narratives of origin, "ethicizes" the question why humankind has to suffer.

Sin. Suffering is the result of separating oneself from God's life-giving love to the other, and it is caused by the lack of care for others. In response to God's question, Cain's answer "Am I my brother's keeper?" (Gen. 4:9) is a rejection of our connectedness to each other. Sinners tear down the web of life, and in separating themselves from the giver of life, they inflict suffering on others. Even brutal natural sufferings, such as an earthquake, challenge the community of bystanders and ask them to become the keeper of their siblings. Even more so, brutal sufferings caused by human actions point to the reality of sin. The two-thirds of today's human family who lack adequate food, water, shelter, health care, education and work suffer as the victims of sin — namely, an economic world order of injustice. The concept of sin is a key to make us understand human suffering in the light of ecumenical responsibility for the sufferers. It is misused when seen as punishment for those who suffer (see John 9:2). The biblical God asks two questions which belong together: "Where are you?" (Gen. 3:9) and "Where is your brother?" (Gen. 4:9). By denying the second call, we suppress the first one and fall, especially as citizens of the industrialized world, into the normal secular response to human suffering, which is denial and suppression: "Take a pill!" By embracing apathy as one of the prevailing spiritual patterns of white middle-class churches, we avoid listening to both questions of God. The technological avoidance of suffering cuts us off from living. Natural secular persons take suffering not as what they inflict upon others but exclusively as their own shortcomings; we remember our being hurt, not our hurting.

In biblical understanding, suffering follows not from God's good creation but from human freedom misused. The Christian teaching of sin and responsibility maintains the unity of the human family. We are one in Adam and shall be one in Christ (see **unity of humankind**). This teaching precludes racism,* sexism,* class-divided societies, and other forms of structural injustice where some people seem to be children of a lesser God. From an ecumenical perspective the Body of Christ is one. "If one member suffers, all suffer together" (1 Cor. 12:26).

God is not the source of evil, nor does God "permit" other powers to punish or treat humans in the manner of a sadist. God does not make us suffer but suffers with us. God fighting and suffering for freedom makes us fighting and suffering as well. Not the one who causes suffering but only the one who suffers can answer Job's despair and ours. Living after the holocausts of Auschwitz and Hiroshima, contemporary Jewish and Christian theologians (Abraham Heschel, Hans Jonas, Rabbi Kushner, Dietrich Bonhoeffer, James Cone, most feminists) have shifted the Enlightenment's question of theodicy — How can God almighty permit evil to happen to "good people"? — to two more modest ones: How can God the co-sufferer abide with those who suffer? And, how long will *we* permit evil to happen to the poor?

Cross. The cross of Christ embodies an understanding of human suffering close to God's pain, in which we may participate. The cross, used as a torture instrument by the imperial power, is the ultimate response of "this world" and its powers to those who fulfill the will of the Father. Christ fulfills God's lifegiving will. "I came that they may have life, and have it abundantly" (John 10:10). For that, Christ was sentenced to death. To share life, to make justice come true, to feed the hungry necessarily leads those who try into conflicts with authorities,

breaks from friends and family, losses in career, wealth and health, to name just the mild forms of the cross. Persecution for the sake of truth and the kingdom of God* has been in many periods of history a criterion of the church.* In today's liberation struggles, Christians give their lives, risk torture and death, and suffer with Christ "in order that we may also be glorified with him" (Rom. 8:17). Those martyrs touch the deepest meaning of human suffering, which is to become "heirs of God and fellow heirs with Christ" (Rom. 8:17; see 2 Tim. 3:12).

In ecumenical gatherings Christians from the poor countries have reminded those from the "developed" world of the situation of the early Christians in the New Testament, which has many similarities to their own. Being a minority under an imperium of blood and tears, or even being a disempowered majority under repression, seems to be the normal status of the Christian church. Resistance and endurance are to be learned. Even in the first world, the Christian churches, if they commit themselves to Christ's way of sharing life, are to expect more suffering, more discrimination, loss of prestige and income, more con-

Human rights office for the disappeared, in Manila (WCC/Peter Williams)

flicts with the state. When we avoid suffering with Christ, we will have to be "the devil's martyrs" (Thomas Münzer), who suffer under the contradictions of necrophilic societies. Suffering with Christ is a call to resistance against the powers of death. Love has its price.

"Rivers of blood may have to flow before we gain our freedom, but it must be our blood" (Martin Luther King). King insisted on the teaching of Jesus and Gandhi that unearned suffering is redemptive. The willingness to suffer is the utmost expression of human freedom. We then leave the technocratic illusion of a suffering-free life and join Christ's option for justice, peace and the integrity of creation.*

Christian faith is not a complete and perfect ideology* that solves all problems. The mystery of inequity, of nature's cruelty and indifference, is not to be solved on a dogmatic level. We miss Christ's point with our readymade explanations of the tragic aspects of human life in reducing them to God's masterplan of either punishment for the past or education for the present.

City of God. The pastoral task is to throw the light of Christ's suffering on those seemingly meaningless pains we have to endure. We need to learn to integrate our losses and pains into God's pain over the world. Outrage and endurance, then, come together. Plunged into the mighty river of justice, we may hand over even our most intimate griefs and pain into the hands of the co-suffering and wait with Christ for the radical transformation of the heavens and the earth. "I will rejoice in Jerusalem and be glad in my people" (Isa. 65:19). We understand God's annunciation only when we hear the tears in God's voice. The God who "will wipe away every tear from their eyes" (Rev. 21:4) weeps in us.

See also **liberation, struggles for; martyrdom; salvation**.

DOROTHEE SÖLLE

A.A. Boesak, *Comfort and Protest: The Apocalypse from a South African Perspective*, Edinburgh, St Andrews, 1987 • J. Bowker, *The Problem of Suffering in the Religions of the World*, London, Cambridge UP, 1975 • G. Gutiérrez, *Hablar de Dios desde el Sufrimiento del Inocente* (ET *God Talk and the Suffering of the Innocent*, Maryknoll, Orbis, 1987) • K. Kitamori, *Theology of the Pain of God*, Richmond, VA, John Knox, 1965 • D. Sölle, *Suffering*, Philadelphia, Fortress, 1975.

SUSTAINABILITY. Beginning in 1971, the ecumenical discussion of "limits to growth" and the concern for humanity's long-range future led to much lively debate over the kind of society and the attitude to science and technology* which these implied. "Limits to growth" seemed a negative term, expressing an anti-progress and anti-technology approach which would be dangerous to apply globally. It was generally agreed that poor countries would need to grow economically and technologically over the foreseable future, whereas rich countries would need to reduce their material expansion, both contributing in this way to a global increase in the quality of life. How might this concept of a balanced future growth based on equitable and tolerable levels of resource use be defined?

The term "sustainable society" was first used in the report of a working group of demographers, physical scientists, economists and theologians at the WCC world conference on science and technology for human development, in Bucharest, Romania, in 1974. The group concluded that to promote quality of life in the future, humanity must begin to strive for development* which could be sustained, economically and environmentally, over the long run, making sure that the use of non-renewable resources would not outrun the increase in resources made available through technological innovation. This would also require a stable population and some limits on material wealth per person: in fact a society actively pursuing quality of life in basically non-material dimensions.

The report resulted in ecumenical study and discussion on such practical issues as sustainable energy systems and specifically on the nuclear option. It also started a dispute within the WCC constituency between, on the one side, natural scientists and environmentalists, who insisted that sustainability was an important new criterion for measuring social welfare and, on the other side, many third-world Christians, who believed that the ecumenical preoccupation with sustainability would detract from the "primary concern for justice", despite the Bucharest report's emphasis on a "sustainable *and* just society".

This issue was presented to the fifth assembly of the WCC in Nairobi (1975), which accepted the concept of a sustainable society as an important addition to ecumenical social thinking, and in 1976 the WCC authorized a follow-up study of "the Just, Participatory and Sustainable Society". While the term "sustainable society" was abandoned by the WCC at the sixth assembly in Vancouver (1983) in favour of the phrase "integrity of creation", in a new enlarged study programme on "Justice, Peace and the Integrity of Creation", it continues to be used widely by churches and environmental economists as a useful concept. In 1987 the UN-sponsored World Commission on Environment and Development (the Brundtland commission) firmly established the concept of "sustainable development" as the basis for an integrated environmental-economic approach to government policy-making in this field. The term "sustainable development" has since been adopted in various official environmental research programmes, most notably in the UK.

See also **just, participatory and sustainable society; justice, peace and the integrity of creation**.

PAUL ABRECHT

D. Meadows et al., *The Limits to Growth*, New York, Universe, 1972 • D. Pearce et al., *Blueprint for a Green Economy*, London, Dept. of the Environment, 1989 • J. Randers, "The Future of the Global Environment", *Anticipation*, 8, September 1971 • Report of the World Conference on Human Development, Bucharest, Romania, June 1974, *Anticipation*, 19, November 1974 • World Commission on Environment and Development, *Our Common Future*, London, Oxford UP, 1987.

SYNCRETISM. The term "syncretism" in its negative meaning came into common parlance in the modern ecumenical movement at the meeting of the International Missionary Council* (IMC) at Tambaram, South India, in 1938. H. Kraemer's *Christian Message in a Non-Christian World*, the conference study book, defined syncretism as "illegitimate mingling of different religious elements" (203).

Kraemer recognized that from the standpoint of naturalistic and monistic religions, any mingling of different religions or religious elements is regarded as legitimate. Their approach to all religions is relativistic and pragmatic. But for the "prophetic religion of biblical realism" (210), the reference point is a unique historical revelatory event. Any indis-

criminate mixture, amalgamation or harmonization of that revelation* with elements from other religions is illegitimate.

In this theologically negative sense Kraemer rejects as syncretistic the call to Christians by the 1928 Jerusalem meeting of the IMC to appropriate "values" of different religions because, as he puts it, "the argument of value does not coincide in any way whatever with that of truth" (106) and because "every religion is a living, indivisible unity" (135). No part of it — a dogma, a rite, a myth, an institution, a cult — can be separated from the faith-apprehension of the whole. Furthermore, the uniqueness of the Christian revelation in Jesus Christ* does not permit Christians "to consider undiscerningly the glimpses of revelation and the religious institutions of mankind as a preceding and preparatory stage for the full revelation in Christ" (123).

Nor, Kraemer argues, is there theological justification for considering non-Christians like Gandhi, Tagore and others who have assimilated Christian ideals and ideas as "unbaptized Christians", as Friedrich Heiler does. Nor, for that matter, is it permissible to consider reforms in other religions under the influence of Christianity as producing "an embryonic Christianity" leading to the church of Christ. William Hocking's missionary approach in terms of "sharing religious experience" is also regarded as illegitimate. Any approach where a decision for Christ is not taken as marking a radical break with one's religious past is a denial of biblical realism and is syncretistic (291, 296).

Kraemer, however, speaks of "adaptation" as a positive way of utilizing concepts and practices from other religions to "translate" and "interpret" the gospel of Jesus Christ in the world of non-Christian religions and cultures, and a legitimate way for Christians to relate to elements in other religions. He defines it thus: "Adaptation in the deepest sense does not mean to assimilate the cardinal facts of the revelation in Christ as much as possible to fundamental religious ideas and tastes of the pre-Christian past, but to *express* these facts by wrestling with them concretely, and so to present the Christian truth and reveal at the same time the intrinsic inadequacy of man's religious efforts for the solution of his crucial religious and moral problems" (308). He refers to the ways Paul and John used

Jewish and Hellenistic categories of thought to controvert Jewish legalism and Hellenic monism and to express the truth and meaning of the Christian gospel, leading to new embodiments of Christianity.

Western forms of Christianity are the result of similar adaptations. Since they are foreign to Asian and African cultural milieus, "in principle and for reasons of history, new incarnations and adaptations of Christianity in the concrete Asiatic and African settings are natural and legitimate" (313). But Kraemer warns that this practice has always been associated with syncretism. The attempts to use what he calls "foreign tongues" in the past to express the gospel "have served as much to distort and falsify the revelation in Christ as to express it" (327). Some modern enthusiasts for the indigenization of Christianity in non-Western churches, he argues, "mistake cardinal and essential elements of the Christian revelation for cultural idiosyncrasies of the West" (319).

Visser 't Hooft, in his book *No Other Name: The Choice between Syncretism and Christian Universalism*, follows much the same line. He distinguishes between a negative syncretism and a positive approach, which he calls "accommodation" rather than "adaptation" (123). His survey of syncretism covers all history and all continents. It recognizes illegitimate amalgamations of Christianity not only with traditional religions but also with modern paganism finding expression in political ideologies (see **ideology**).

Syncretism has continued to be a subject of controversy in the ecumenical movement. The argument has not been primarily on the substance of what Kraemer and Visser 't Hooft were saying, but on the question of whether the fear of syncretism has not stopped the Christian church from entering into relationships with non-Western or modern religions and cultures, which alone can lead to new, legitimate incarnations of Christianity. In fact, as Lesslie Newbigin has pointed out, at the Tambaram conference of 1938 a red light stopped the traffic between Christianity and other religions; it never turned to green, and so the traffic was halted for a long time. Any attempt at dialogue between Christianity and other religions was frowned upon as syncretistic.

The Faith and Order consultation of the East Asia Christian Conference (Hong Kong 1966) on "Confessing the Faith in Asia" recognized that the Asian churches in the past were too inhibited by an idolatrous absolutization of Western confessional formulations and by a fear of syncretism to venture into confessing Christ in relation to religious renaissance and social revolution in Asia *(Asian Christian Theology: Emerging Themes)*.

This inhibiting fear of syncretism was also evident in the reaction of a section at the WCC Nairobi assembly (1975) to the first report from the group dealing with "Seeking Community: The Common Search of People of Various Faiths, Cultures and Ideologies". It is in this context that an effort has been made in many centres in the ecumenical movement to affirm that the legitimate and illegitimate relations of Christianity to other religions and quasi-religious ideologies are two possibilities within the same process. There is historical warrant to use the word "syncretism" in its neutral character, accepting the possibility of true and false forms of syncretism.

Peter Latuihamako of Indonesia takes up the history of Balinese Christianity (in whose creation Kraemer played no small part) and says that what we call adaptation, amalgamation and the like seem to stem from the same spiritual source as syncretism. He calls the Christian approach "creative syncretism": "If ultimate Truth is the criterion, then there is no compromise and no syncretism. But still, the incarnation has happened. Logos has become flesh. Jesus Christ has become a fact in history. Is his earthly presence not seen as a kind of syncretism, a peaceful syncretism if you will, or maybe creative syncretism?"

John Carman, who studied a village church in South India, speaks of "a higher syncretism" evident among new converts from Hinduism to Christianity. He writes: "Syncretism may be regarded either as the same person's participation in both Christian and Hindu worship, or, more rarely in India, an attempt to combine the two. Yet there is also what I would like to call a higher syncretism, something close to what Hocking calls 'creative reconception', but not carried on by theologians. It is rather the faith, the ritual forms, and the patterns of living of lay Christians, sometimes new 'converts' to Christianity, who manage to clothe their new faith in the forms of the old, not merely the external language, but also something of the inner intent of the old faith and thereby create a genuine 'Hindu Christianity'" (93).

Among theologians closely related to the WCC in recent times there is a tradition of defining syncretism as a neutral or even as a very positive process. In Pannenberg's view, the growth in understanding of the biblical figure of God has "actually the form of a syncretic process". In his estimation, "Christianity affords the greatest example of syncretic assimilative power; this religion not only linked itself to Greek philosophy but also inherited the entire religious tradition of the Mediterranean world" (*Basic Questions in Theology*). Moltmann characterizes the religion of Israel as itself the product of a syncretic process: "Israel achieved a syncretism between the religion of the nomad and of the Canaanite peasant through historicizing the latter in struggle." The Orthodox theologian Demetrius Constantelos writes: "After all, it was a syncretic approach that won Christianity its followers in the first five centuries."

If an attempt is made to keep the purity of the gospel of Christ through isolation from other religions and secular ideologies, it will lead to a conception of the uniqueness of Christ which will militate against the universality of Christ. As the Willowbank consultation report of the Lausanne Committee for World Evangelization puts it: "Indeed perhaps the most insidious form of syncretism in the world today is the attempt to mix a privatized gospel of personal forgiveness with a worldly (even demonic) attitude to wealth and power." Raymond Panikkar characterizes Western Christianity as "ancient paganism, or to be more precise, the complex of Hebrew-Hellenic-Greek-Latin-Celtic-modern religions converted to Christ more or less successfully".

Since all conversions are "more or less" and require continued struggle for the transformation of the unconverted elements, any new form of Christianity, like the old, will have to continue to fight within itself against thought-forms and life-practices which betray the universal lordship of Christ. Therefore, the decision for Christ which makes a person or culture or religion Christian is the dominant intention and goal of the conversion process. This is more so in the modern pluralistic world in which we all live with fragments of culture, philosophy and cult drawn from different religious and secular ideological tradi-

tions. "All Christians are pagan in parts. More so today. Synthesis is a long way away, it is almost 'eschatological'. Syncretism with a sense of Christian direction is all that we can now realize" (Thomas, 392).

See also **dialogue, interfaith; religion; uniqueness of Christ**.

M.M. THOMAS

L. Boff, *Church, Charism and Power,* London, SCM, 1985, ch. 7 • J. Carman, "Continuing Tasks in Inter-religious Dialogue", in *Living Faiths and the Ecumenical Movement,* S.J. Samartha ed., WCC, 1971 • D. Elwood ed., *Asian Christian Theology: Emerging Themes,* Philadelphia, Westminster, 1980 • H. Kraemer, *Christian Message in a Non-Christian World,* London, Edinburgh House, 1947 • J. Moltmann, *Theology of Hope,* London, SCM, 1967 • W. Pannenberg, *Grundfragen systematischer Theologie* (ET *Basic Questions in Theology,* vol. 2, Philadelphia, Fortress, 1971) • R. Panikkar, *Christian Revelation and World Religions,* London, Burns & Oates, 1967 • M.M. Thomas, "The Absoluteness of Jesus Christ and Christ-centred Syncretism", *The Ecumenical Review,* 37, 4, 1985 • W.A. Visser 't Hooft, *No Other Name: The Choice between Syncretism and Christian Universalism,* London, SCM, 1964.

SYNDESMOS. Syndesmos, the World Fellowship of Orthodox Youth, was founded in 1953 at the initiative of Orthodox involved in the work of the WCC Youth department. Its name is the Greek word for "uniting bond" (see Eph. 4:3). Syndesmos is a federation of youth movements and theological schools within local Eastern Orthodox churches. Oriental Orthodox youth movements can join as associate members, and new forms of partnership have been explored with them. In 1989 it had 49 member movements in 23 countries in Europe, the Middle East, Asia, Africa, North America and Latin America. As the only worldwide Orthodox organization, Syndesmos requires all member movements to be officially endorsed by the local hierarchy.

The problems of "diaspora"* — Orthodox living in countries without traditional Orthodox presence — have always been high on the Syndesmos agenda. It took significant initiatives in foreign mission in the 1950s and again in the early 1980s, and the African region has grown to be a significant one in the fellowship. Orthodox participation in the ecumenical movement was a high priority for Syndesmos in the two first decades and again in the late 1980s, with fraternal relationships developing with the WCC youth network, the World Student Christian Federation,* the Ecumenical Youth Council of Europe, the Middle East Council of Churches* and others.

Several Syndesmos assemblies have taken initiatives to improve international means of communication and information among the Orthodox, but because of very limited finances, little has been achieved. Syndesmos has always been financially dependent on ecumenical support, and severe financial restrictions have required reliance on volunteer work.

The role of laity* in the life of the Orthodox church has been an important topic throughout Syndesmos's existence, but with more focus in recent years on its social and ecclesial implications. Rapprochement and co-operation with Oriental Orthodox youth has been a growing concern since the 1960s, with significant steps taken in a slow pace. By the time of its 1989 assembly in Boston, Syndesmos had established links of communication and co-operation with movements from all Oriental churches, with Oriental representation in all Syndesmos meetings as a rule.

Although Western European groups were the most active in beginning Syndesmos, there has been official Greek, Middle Eastern and Finnish representation from the outset. The role of Greek student movements with an ecumenical outlook grew stronger in the late 1950s, with the increasing presence and influence also of the Lebanese and Syrians of the patriarchate of Antioch. As an important area of diaspora, with several youth movements, North Americans became members officially in the 1960s.

With the 1964 amendment of the constitution to include theological schools as affiliated members, Eastern European members were able to join, since youth work as such was not permitted in most socialist countries. Their number grew slowly but steadily in the 1980s, as did the participation of youth movements of local dioceses in Greece and North America.

After a period of low activity in the early 1970s, Syndesmos was able to take new initiatives in the late 1970s and through the 1980s in all of the areas mentioned above. Besides general assemblies (approximately every three years), Syndesmos has organized three international festivals of Orthodox youth, with thematic discussions on current challenges facing the Orthodox church, and four consultations of Orthodox theological schools, including those in Leningrad in 1986 and in Suprasl, Poland, in 1989.

The Syndesmos office is usually hosted by the church and youth movement of the general secretary, thus giving them a prominent role in the fellowship for that period, providing a strong local base and practical and financial support.

See also **youth**.

HEIKKI HUTTUNEN

TAIZÉ COMMUNITY. The ecumenical community of Taizé was founded by Brother Roger in 1940. Alone for two years during the second world war, in the small village of Taizé in eastern France, he gave shelter to political refugees, mainly Jewish people. In 1949, seven brothers took monastic vows for life. Today, the brothers number 90 and include Catholics, Anglicans and others from various Protestant backgrounds from 20 countries, some of them living in small "fraternities" in poor regions of the world. The community lives exclusively from its work and refuses donations. Brother Roger's aim was to create a monastic community that would be a "parable of communion" among divided Christians.

The community is in constant contact with church leaders. Pope John Paul II, Archbishops Ramsey and Runcie, Metropolitan Nikodim of Leningrad and countless pastors and church leaders have visited Taizé. The brothers, as guests of Pope John XXIII (who once said of Taizé: "Ah! that little springtime!"), were present throughout the Second Vatican Council.* They have participated in several assemblies of the WCC and have been associated with the work of WCC commissions. In 1988 Brother Roger was invited to take part in the celebrations of the millennium of the Russian Orthodox Church.

Since 1958, Taizé has welcomed hundreds of thousands of young people from around the world for weekly meetings. They participate in the community's common prayer three times each day, study the Christian sources of faith and reflect on inner life and human solidarity. Refusing to create a movement, the community encourages participants to return to their local churches and parishes. Taizé is also a place of retreat for many ministers and priests.

In 1982, to stimulate reconciliation and trust in the world, a "pilgrimage of trust on earth" was undertaken, leading Taizé not only to the major capitals of Europe but to other continents as well. The European meetings, always prepared with parishes, bring together each year thousands from both Eastern and Western Europe, from all denominations. Two Asian meetings were held in Madras, India, and several large gatherings have taken place in North America.

The pilgrimage of trust has also led Brother Roger to meet twice with Javier Perez de Cuellar, the secretary-general of the United Nations (1985 and 1988), to express the hopes of the young for the UN to become a creator of trust between the peoples of the earth.

BROTHER ÉMILE

J.L. Balado, *The Story of Taizé*, 3rd ed., London, Mowbray, 1988 • K. Spink, *A Universal Heart*, London, SPCK, 1986.

TAKENAKA, MASAO. B. 1925, Peking. Takenaka has been active in the WCC and the Christian Conference of Asia. He has addressed major ecumenical gatherings, including New Delhi 1961, and has delivered lectures on ecumenical topics from an Asian perspective at various universities. A graduate of Doshisha University in 1950, he received a PhD degree in social ethics from Yale University in 1955. He became professor of Christian ethics and sociology of religion at Doshisha University in 1962, and was visiting professor at Union Theological Seminary, New York, 1962-63, at Yale University, 1973, and at Harvard University, 1981-82. In 1986 he became director of the Centre for American Study at Doshisha University. He has written *Reconciliation and Renewal in Japan* (New York, Friendship, 1967), *Christian Art in Asia* (Tokyo, Kyo Bun Kwan, 1975), and *God Is Rice: Asian Culture and Christian Faith* (WCC, 1986).

ANS J. VAN DER BENT

TANTUR ECUMENICAL INSTI-TUTE. Located in Jerusalem, Tantur sprang from an urgent suggestion in 1963 to Pope Paul VI from the official Anglican, Protestant and Orthodox observers to the Second Vatican Council: someone, somewhere, should establish an international, intercultural institute where Christian scholars and teachers could experience a community life of prayer, study and dialogue. The main focus would be "Christian reflection on the mystery of salvation as revealed through the sacred scriptures and the teachings of the early, undivided church, and as expressed in the experiences of the diverse Christian communions throughout the ages".

Upon Paul VI's return from the holy land in January 1964, where he had met Ecumenical Patriarch Athenagoras, he decided that Jerusalem should be the place for the centre. "There Christ founded in the Spirit the one, undivided church, and today Christians of all communions, one yet sadly divided, find other 'peoples of the book', Jews and Muslims." The Vatican purchased the Tantur property, and an interconfessional advisory board authorizes the institute's programmes and personnel.

Since Tantur's opening in 1972, over 2,500 Christian scholars, teachers, parish clergy and other church workers have participated in its programmes. Besides the programme for young and senior scholars on sabbaticals, three-month sessions in continuing education and spiritual formation are so designed that one can concentrate on biblical studies and field trips in historical geography; biblical spiritualities; the Eastern churches; Jewish and Islamic spiritualities; the bases and practices of ecumenical and inter-religious relations; the social, political and religious situation in the Middle East; and human rights and conflict resolution.

Tantur also serves as a forum of discourse among local Christians, and between them and the Jewish and the Muslim communities.

TOM STRANSKY

TAYLOR, JOHN VERNON.
B. 11.9.1914, Cambridge, UK. Taylor was bishop of Winchester, UK, 1975-85. Earlier he was research worker for the International Missionary Council,* 1956-59, Africa secretary of the Church Missionary Society, 1959-63, general secretary of CMS, 1963-74, and vice-chairman of the Theological Education Fund, 1968-74. He was a speaker at the Ecumenical Institute, Bossey, in 1955 and 1957 and was a delegate to the IMC Ghana assembly (1958), New Delhi 1961 and Uppsala 1968, and the Bangkok 1973 and Melbourne 1980 conferences. He studied theology at Oxford 1938 and was warden of Bishop Tucker Theological College, Uganda, 1945-54. His writings include *The Growth of the Church of Uganda* (1958), *The Primal Vision* (1965), *The Go-Between God* (1972), *Enough Is Enough* (1975) and *A Matter of Life and Death* (1986), all published by SCM, London, and *Weep Not for Me: Meditations on the Cross and the Resurrection* (WCC, 1986).

ANS J. VAN DER BENT

TEACHING AUTHORITY. Although the issue has not been dealt with explicitly in ecumenical discussions until recent years, many aspects of the problem of "teaching authority" lie behind the history of church division, schisms* and lack of Christian unity.* From its very beginning within the Jewish community of faith, which was characterized in Jesus' time by a pluralism of at least four main teaching traditions, Christianity wrestled with three decisive questions: *What* is the normative and unifying content of the Christian faith* (the *regula fidei*) which could guide the re-reading of the Jewish scriptures in light of the Christ-event? *Who* are the authoritative witnesses and teachers in the new-born communities of the church?* *How* should the community and its leaders proceed in order to safeguard the content of faith and the way of life according to the gospel of Christ, to unite the church members and the scattered communities within one bond of love, and to guide them in committed confession to that faith amid the challenges of the surrounding world?

The New Testament writings reflect this foundational struggle over the original *kerygma* of the gospel *(euangelion)*, the *didachē* (teaching) of Jesus and the apostles, the *exousia* (authority) of the Lord sent forth upon the community, and the *parrēsia* (boldness) and *martyria* (testimony) of the witnesses. Amid all the diversity, the NT has also kept in mind the factors of unity and *homologia*: early confessional formulas, the authority of "the Twelve" and of the first missionaries like Paul, the collection of gospel narratives and apostolic correspondence themselves, a common sacramental practice of baptism* and the eucharist,* a common discipline of life (e.g. on marriage, on public life within the Hellenistic context), a practice of excommunication* and reconciliation,* a conciliar form of decision making about divisive issues (Acts 15) and, in a later stage of development, a more common pattern of ministry* and its orderly transmission.

Initially there was no need for formal legitimation of the action of the bearers of the *kerygma*, as they could speak with the *exousia* and *parrēsia* of the Lord (see Matt. 28:18-20; Luke 10:19; John 1:12, 18:20; 2 Cor. 10:8, 13:10; Acts 4:29,31, 9:27, 18:25, 28:31), i.e. unlike the scribes and without mandate (Matt. 7:29), but rather like "uneducated, common men" (Acts 4:13), yet "in the Spirit" (Acts 2; 1 Cor. 12:3-11) and "in the name of Jesus" (Acts 4:10), as messengers of the gospel, sent by Christ (Rom. 1:1) and as (eye)witnesses of his life, death and resurrection (Acts 1:21-22).

But already in Paul's writings, and much more in the pastoral epistles and in 2 Peter and Jude, some formal structures of a teaching authority can be discerned: apostolic authority and episcope (1 Cor. 1:10-17, 4:1-6; Acts 15:2,22,28; 1 Pet. 1:1, 5:1-4; 2 Pet. 1:12, 3:1-2), a deposit of faith (2 Tim. 1:14), a canon* of apostolic writings (2 Pet. 1:20-21, 3:15-16), a finished *paradosis* (Jude 3), the truth laid down in a rule of faith (1 Tim. 1:15, 2:5-6; 2 Tim. 2:11-13), which must be defended against false teachings and myths (1 Tim. 4:4-7; 2 Tim. 2:18; Titus 1:13-14; 2 Pet. 2:1-22, 3:17; Jude 4,8).

This rather early development of a rule of faith, a common discipline of life and common structures of authoritative teaching and decision making, was further elaborated during the first four or five centuries through councils, through the appeal to patriarchal sees, especially the bishop and see of Rome, and through episcopal authority in general to protect the apostolicity* and catholicity,* the unity and the holiness* of the church. But we have to wait until the middle ages before a more formal idea of magisterium developed in the West.

From that time on, it has been marked by juridical overtones, with a shift from charismatic and traditional to legal authority (Max Weber), from original *auctoritas* to present *potestas* (Yves Congar), from *traditio* to *discretio* (Karl Morrison). Teaching authority is founded upon the civil ideas of investiture, representation and licence and becomes part of ministerial jurisdiction. Here originate the disputes between conciliar and papal jurisdiction (see **conciliarity**), which lie behind the Western schism, as well as the origins of the theory of papal infallibility* (Brian Tierney). Even the Reformation and Counter-Reformation can be viewed to a large extent as a theological struggle over the right "hierarchy of authorities" with regard to the teaching of the church. The challenges of the European Enlightenment and the contextual and inculturation problems of the Christian faith in the 20th century have added to the urgency of an ecumenical debate about the authoritative and faithful teaching of the church. A common authoritative teaching today would become possible and credible only if on this matter the controversies and censures from the past could be overcome.

It was to this end that the Accra meeting of the Faith and Order* commission in 1974 started an "ecumenical inquiry" on "the ways in which the various churches decide or define or proclaim basic teaching about Christian faith and morals in the contemporary situation". As reasons for the study are given: the factual pluralism of authoritative teaching organs or "instances" and hermeneutical procedures (see **hermeneutics**), the crisis in church teaching authority in an era of rapid change, a strong sense of the historicity and contextuality of all church teaching, the challenge of modern linguistic philosophy, hermeneutical insights and, last but not least, the division of the churches itself, which seems to be caused not only by the content of their teaching but also by the authoritative procedures leading to the reception* of such teaching in various churches. "No church", it is said, "can be satisfied until the fullness of the truth attested by its own authoritative doctrine and promised through its own living teaching office is perceived and appreciated by the whole people of God."

The WCC assembly at Nairobi in 1975 warmly welcomed the project "How Does the Church Teach Authoritatively Today?" A small consultation in Geneva in 1976 prepared a working paper (*One in Christ*, 12, 1976), which was followed by reports from Italy, Greece, Holland, the FRG and the GDR. In 1977 a F&O consultation took place in Odessa (report in *The Ecumenical Review*, 31, 1979). It concluded: "As the churches engage in the ecumenical movement, they need to re-examine deliberately their ways and modes of teaching. Consensus and communion in conciliar life can be reached only if the ways of teaching become more and more capable of common decision making."

The report reflected especially on the divergences and convergences among the various traditions, the varieties of actual situations, and the search for new patterns of credibility, and it offered examples of common teaching today within the ecumenical movement. At the Bangalore plenary meeting of the F&O commission in 1978, due attention was paid to the results of the study thus far, but a decision was taken to give priority to the *content* of the apostolic faith, before pursuing further the study on common ways of decision making and teaching authority.

By doing so, Bangalore postponed the issue of ecumenical hermeneutics, on which F&O had prepared various studies in the 1960s, like

those on "The Hermeneutical Significance of the Councils" and on "The Authority of the Bible". The theme of teaching authority was also left aside in the Lima text on ministry (see **Baptism, Eucharist and Ministry**). The importance of the subject was, however, recognized and perhaps even overstated by repeated reminders (Lima 1982, Vancouver 1983, Stavanger 1985, Budapest 1989) that the unity of the church depends on three main elements or conditions: a common understanding of the apostolic faith, full mutual understanding of the apostolic faith, *agreement on common ways of teaching and decision making*.

In the responses to the Lima text *Baptism, Eucharist and Ministry*, several churches asked for continuation of the study on decision making and teaching authority. The Budapest meeting of F&O in 1989 decided to include such a study on teaching authority in its programme for a study on "Common Perspectives for an Ecumenical Vision of the Church", to be prepared for the fifth world conference on F&O, scheduled for 1993.

Meanwhile, the topic had been further discussed in some bilateral dialogues,* e.g. in the Reformed-Roman Catholic report on "The Presence of Christ in Church and World" (1977), in the Anglican-Roman Catholic International Commission's Venice (1976) and Westminster (1981) reports on "Authority in the Church", in the Disciples-Roman Catholic dialogue (1981), in the Lutheran-Roman Catholic report on "Ministry in the Church" (1981), in the Methodist-Roman Catholic Commission's Denver (1971), Dublin (1976) and Honolulu (1981) reports (see the respective **dialogues**). In most of those dialogues the issue of the specific claims of the papal magisterium was treated to some extent, though far from resolved.

To quote just two of these reports: "There is no disagreement that the church has authority to teach. In the church, the revelation of God in Christ comes to us through scripture, and to maintain God's people in the truth is the loving work of the Spirit in the church. But this maintenance is not a matter of mere repetition of formulae. The Spirit moves the church to constant reflection on the scriptures which he himself inspired and on their traditional interpretation, so that she may speak with undiminished authority to men in different times and places, in different social and cultural settings, facing new and difficult problems. This is not of course to question the abiding importance of credal statements and such conciliar pronouncements as the Chalcedonian definition. The enduring validity of these does not restrict the power of the Spirit to speak in new ways to the church, whose living voice never speaks in isolation from its living past. It stands under the living word of God. The old oppositions of scripture and tradition have given way to an understanding which we share, that scripture in witness to the living tradition from which it arose has a normative role for the total tradition of the church as it lives and is guided still by the Spirit of truth... The papal authority, no less than any other within the church, is a manifestation of the continuing presence of the Spirit of love in the church or it is nothing. Indeed it should in its exercise be preeminently such a manifestation. It was declared at Vatican I to be 'for the building up and not the casting down of the church' — whether of the local church or the communion of local churches" (Methodist-Roman Catholic Honolulu report, paras 34-35).

"The church exercises teaching authority through various instruments and agencies at various levels. When matters of faith are at stake, decisions may be made by the church in universal councils; we are agreed that these are authoritative. We have also recognized the need in a united church for a universal primate who, presiding over the koinonia, can speak with authority in the name of the church. Through both these agencies the church can make a decisive judgment in matters of faith and so exclude error. The purpose of this service cannot be to add to the content of revelation, but is to recall and emphasize some important truth; to expound the faith more lucidly; to expose error; to draw out implications not sufficiently recognized; and to show how Christian truth applies to contemporary issues...

"The church's teaching authority is a service to which the faithful look for guidance especially in times of uncertainty; but the assurance of the truthfulness of its teaching rests ultimately rather upon its fidelity to the gospel than upon the character or office of the person by whom it is expressed. The church's teaching is proclaimed because it is true; it is

not true simply because it has been proclaimed" (ARCIC, final report, paras 26-27).
                                    ANTON HOUTEPEN

Y. Congar, "Pour une histoire sémantique du terme 'magisterium'", and "Bref historique des formes du 'magistère' et de ses relations avec les docteurs", *Revue des sciences philosophiques et théologiques*, 60, 1976 • Congregation for the Doctrine of the Faith, *Instruction on the Ecclesial Vocation of the Theologian*, Vatican City, 1990 • Faith and Order: *Minutes Accra 1974*, WCC, 1974 • "How Does the Church Teach Authoritatively Today?", *The Ecumenical Review*, 31, 1979 • K.F. Morrison, *Tradition and Authority in the Western Church, 300-1140*, Princeton, NJ, Princeton UP, 1969 • *Sharing in One Hope: Bangalore 1978*, WCC, 1978 • F.A. Sullivan, *Magisterium: Teaching Authority in the Catholic Church*, Dublin, Gill & Macmillan, 1983 • B. Tierney, *Origins of Papal Infallibility, 1150-1350: A Study on the Concepts of Infallibility, Sovereignty and Tradition in the Middle Ages*, Leiden, Brill, 1972.

TECHNOLOGY. Although derived from the Greek *technē*, meaning simply "art" or "craft", "technology" is increasingly a word with associated value. To some it is a promise for a better future, to others a present source of human exploitation and damage to the environment. The word has therefore developed different meanings in different societies and social groups within them. Always it is used to convey some sense of action, of altering the environment or the ways in which things are done.

Three main approaches to technology may be identified. The first, tool-based, is directed towards the environment and human social life; e.g. tools for fishing, coping with hostile climates, producing energy for cooking, creating music and jewellery. Second, technology can be viewed as a pool of practical knowledge and experience to design systems to accomplish more with less effort; e.g. the modern systems for communication, power and water. A third approach identifies how human institutions and social structures become dependent upon, and integrated with, technology; e.g. the transport and supply of food in cities and of oil for light, cooking, etc.

The promise of technology is that it increases possibilities for those who have access to it, whether in extending human life, gaining more food by new agricultural practices, seeing further into space or into the nucleus of an atom or simply by increasing the amount and range of goods and services available to a consumer society. The current wave of mistrust of the use of advanced technology arises, however, from a recognition that it frequently increases the benefits for a few, or for certain societies, at the expense of others. To take three examples: some ways of organizing technology require debilitating human labour and exclude those who cannot afford to participate in the benefits. Those privileged with access to new technology limit possibilities for others, as occurred in the imposition of inappropriate technologies in many parts of the world, especially the third world. Commerical global application of technology, e.g. chlorofluorocarbons and destruction of rain forests, may have irreversible effects on the earth's environment.

The churches' response to technology. When the churches were influential through Western Europe, their pedagogic role gave them a strong link with the teaching of technology. This role diminished during the 18th century, and other human institutions were formed to develop technology in the light of new scientific discoveries (see **secularization**). Since then the churches have largely ignored the social implications of technology. Through the ecumenical movement, the churches have begun to realize how people in the world are differently affected by technology and how the environment is affected globally. From around 1970 the churches have been increasingly concerned about the social and environmental implications of technology.

From 1970, the WCC's Church and Society conferences and the Club of Rome report *Limits to Growth* (1972) focused on the effect of new science-based technologies. The need for reconsideration of the churches' role in relation to the pervasive influence of scientific-technological developments led to a concentration of the Church and Society sub-unit on themes of science and technology.

Debate between the churches about the use of technology emerged most pointedly in 1979 at the Massachusetts Institute of Technology. In that Church and Society conference on "Faith, Science and the Future", representatives from Asia, Africa and Latin America accused the North of seeking to limit their possibilities for development by restricting access to nuclear technology. Nuclear

scientist David Rose and ecologist Charles Birch at the earlier Nairobi assembly were major contributors to the re-awakening of environmental concern in the context of unequal opportunity. This shift of emphasis was reflected in the quest for a just, participatory and sustainable society* and the process of covenanting for justice, peace and the integrity of creation* initiated by the 1983 Vancouver assembly.

Themes and methodologies. The main themes that have been studied by the churches have emerged in three ways: (1) through having been on the political agenda as a result of international negotiation, economic need and public demand, e.g. pollution* and energy* requirements; (2) as a response to events, e.g. nuclear and chemical accidents, such as Three Mile Island, Chernobyl and Bhopal; and (3) for philosophical and theological reasons, e.g. the role of Christianity in relation to the domination of nature.* Consequently, the churches' debate has been oriented towards energy issues and human use of the environment (including land*). These create most disharmony between regions in the world and so between the churches. There are also similar debates within each nation in which the following questions are frequently raised: whether or not it is legitimate for the churches to be concerned about technology and to make specific suggestions about its use; whether the churches should identify with or criticize the preference of their nations (see **nation**) which may want to maximize their own possibilities; how to assess the validity of different and conflicting theological interpretations which are shaped by environments created by technology.

Ecumenical debates over technology have been sharpened and aggravated by virtue of their expert-oriented, high-tech northern focus. Recent Church and Society analyses have attempted to shift the emphasis towards *in situ* interdisciplinary regional case studies, e.g. "New Technology, Work and the Environment" (Manila 1986). The themes, however, have been limited, and although there has been much questioning, detailed analyses have been restricted to few areas and have had little theological and social influence as yet. There are, however, growing signs that churches are increasingly recognizing the limitations of their societal futures as influenced by

CERN (European Organization for Nuclear Research), Geneva (WCC/Peter Williams)

technology and their potential role in creating alternative futures.

One illustration of the themes and the new role of churches in presenting alternative futures for society emerged at the Church and Society working committee meeting in Tambov, USSR, in 1988. There was a new public recognition of the seriousness of the Russian Orthodox theological contribution to vital environmental issues which the Soviet Union is facing. Consequently there was a real engagement of various theologies, exploring such questions as the different approaches to science and theology to our understanding of the natural world.

Recent developments and future concerns. While the main concern continues to be with the human threat to nature, there is a growing awareness of technologies that directly affect the human world. Many technologies are being shown to have a more pervasive but hidden effect on humans and social structures than had been thought hitherto, e.g. the different effect of pollutants and of unemployment owing to new technologies on sections of a society (in these cases children, mothers and the disadvantaged). Genetic engineering as a rapid way of creating new types

of organisms raises ethical questions as to who will benefit and how far species should be changed. The same techniques could be applied to the species homo sapiens, giving rise to further concern about the risks and benefits of the developments (see **bio-ethics**). Computerization lies behind many current technological developments in facilitating research and design, enabling large organizations to run bureaucratically, altering working patterns and jobs and changing financial handling throughout the world. All these make it imperative that the churches examine the risks, benefits and speed of change.

Technology is increasingly global in its operation and impact. Not only is it spread worldwide, but all areas of life are influenced more and more by the introduction of new technologies. The fulfilling of Isaiah's and Micah's vision that everyone should reap the benefit of their labour in peace seems to be made more difficult by the global interdependence of the technological-economic-political structures which have less concern for each individual than for some particular groups. The challenge for Christianity is to find ways in which technology can be used to promote justice between all people in a manner which recognizes the interdependence of the whole of creation.*

See also **creation, environment/ecology, science and technology.**

DAVID J. PULLINGER

F.V. Carino & D. Gosling eds, *Technology from the Underside*, Manila, National Council of Churches in the Philippines, 1986 • J. Ellul, *Le bluff technologique* (ET *Technological Bluff*, Grand Rapids, MI, 1990) • B. Jenner ed., *Future Conditional*, London, Methodist Church, 1983 • S.V. Monsma ed., *Responsible Technology*, Grand Rapids, MI, Eerdmans, 1986.

TEMPLE, WILLIAM. B. 15.10.1881, Exeter, UK; d. 26.10.1944, Westgate-on-Sea, Kent, UK. William Temple was the most prominent British ecumenist in the period from the Student Christian Movement (SCM) conference at Matlock in 1908 and the Edinburgh conference of 1910, at which he was a steward, to the creation of the British Council of Churches (BCC) in 1942.

Temple was the son of Beatrice and Frederick Temple, bishop of London, who later (1896-1902) became archbishop of Canterbury. William thus came from the heart of the English establishment. He attended Rugby School and Balliol College, Oxford, where he received first-class honours in classics, ancient history and philosophy. He had the unconscious, effortless superiority of the Balliol scholar but combined this with a winsome humanity and humility, tempered by chronic ill health.

Temple taught philosophy at Queen's College, Oxford, 1907-10, and was ordained, though not without some doubts from his bishop (Paget) over doctrinal issues. From these early wrestlings stems Temple's theology expressed in *Mens Creatrix* (London, Macmillan 1917), *Christus Veritas* (London, Macmillan, 1924) and *Nature, Man and God* (London, Macmillan, 1934). Here — Caird was the great influence — is the last theological flowering of Oxford neo-Hegelianism before the era of logical analysis. Temple links matter, life, mind and spirit but insists at the same time on the historicity of the incarnation.* It was this which made Christianity "the most avowedly materialist of all the great religions", for the coming of the Logos into the created world was seen as the fulfilment of

God's immanence. Rejecting any kenotic theory, Temple did not foresee the difficulties which philosophers and theologians were soon to discover.

Temple quickly put theology into practice as president of the workers' education association, 1908-24, a lifelong concern for the underprivileged he shared with Frances Anson, whom he married in 1916. After four years as headmaster of Repton school (1910-14), Temple became rector of St James', Piccadilly, London, throwing himself with vigour into the mission of repentance and hope and also the life and liberty movement, which aimed at securing greater self-government for the Church of England. Temple's hopes were partially fulfilled in the Enabling Act of 1919, which set up the church assembly.

From a canonry at Westminster, Temple was appointed bishop of Manchester in 1921, then archbishop of York in 1929, becoming archbishop of Canterbury from 1942 to 1944 — arguably the sharpest mind in that see since Anselm, and the most popular archbishop of modern times.

Temple was in the line of Anglican social thinkers running back through the Christian social union to F.D. Maurice. He combined

William Temple (WCC photo)

an incarnational theology with an acute social conscience. He was a moderate, if idealistic, radical. Chairmanship of the Conference on Christian Politics, Economics and Citizenship at Birmingham in 1924 was his first significant ecumenical foray. COPEC foreshadowed much of the thinking which came to legislative fruition in the "welfare state" (that phrase was popularized by Temple) created by Clement Attlee's administration, 1945-50. Temple searched for "middle axioms", i.e. statements which offer working guidelines between fundamental Christian theological statements and the complexities of both legislation and industrial problems. *Christianity and Social Order* (Harmondsworth, Shepheard-Wolwyn & SPCK, 1976; orig. ed., 1942) is a foreshadowing of much social thinking in the era of consensus in Britain from 1945 to 1979. Freedom, fellowship and service were characteristics of the approach to the common good stated in an Anglican form at Malvern in 1941. A stress on corporate sin* was learned from Reinhold Niebuhr.

Temple came into international ecumenical prominence at the Jerusalem missionary conference (1928). He drafted the statement of the conference, revealing extraordinary gifts of penetration and empathy that enabled him to synthesize diverse views. He was prominent at Lausanne in 1927, drafted the final statement at Oxford 1937 and was chairman of the Faith and Order conference at Edinburgh in 1937. It was there by 122 votes to 19 that the plans for a world council of churches were laid. Temple embodied the inevitable link between faith and action, both stemming from the absolute allegiance to Christ as Lord. At the first meeting of the provisional committee at Utrecht on 13 May 1938, Temple was elected chairman. His dream came true, not in 1941 as planned but after the cataclysm of war in 1948. It was in 1942 at his enthronement at Canterbury that Temple pointed to the "worldwide fellowship of Christians" stemming from missions as the "great new fact of our era".

In England Temple dominated two decades, though disappointed at the follow-up to the Lambeth Appeal of 1920 and at the failure of Lambeth 1930 to live up to its promise. Temple himself, though consistently backing the South India negotiations, became rather more "Catholic" on church order but must be

given credit for Anglican initiatives, without which there might have been no religion and life weeks, unprecedented co-operation with Cardinal Hinsley, or a BCC inaugurated in 1942 with the inevitable sermon from Temple, who became president.

In the world of ecumenical scholarship Temple was a paradox. If his theology became unfashionable in the decades of Hitler and Barth, his devotional writings were widely read. *Readings in St John's Gospel* (London, Macmillan, 1939) helped many, though it was out of key with critical scholarship. Temple also had the ear of students to an extraordinary degree, especially through the SCM, which was a vital ecumenical seedbed for Christian leaders. Many trace the renewal of Christian apologetic among students to the Oxford Mission of 1931 led by Temple. His biographer recalls 3,000 student voices at that mission whispering the words of the hymn "When I Survey the Wondrous Cross". Perhaps that was his greatest hour. Temple's death was a great shock to a war-stricken nation.

JOHN MUNSEY TURNER

Besides Temple's works cited above, see *Christianity and the State* (London, Macmillan, 1928) • See also F.A. Ironmonger, *William Temple, Archbishop of Canterbury: His Life and Letters*, London, Oxford UP, 1948 • R.H. Preston, *A Future of Christian Ethics*, London, SCM, 1987 (ch. 6: "Church and Society: Do We Need Another William Temple?") • A.M. Ramsey, *From Gore to Temple*, London, Longmans, 1960 • A.M. Suggate, *William Temple and Christian Social Ethics Today*, Edinburgh, Clark, 1987).

THEOLOGY, AFRICAN. African theology is the articulation of the Christian faith* by African theologians or Christians. They ask themselves what the Christian faith means, and they try to understand and explain it within the context of their history* and culture* and of the contemporary issues they face. They look at it through their reading and understanding of the Bible. They bring into it the rich cultural heritage which has evolved over many generations. They sing it in their own liturgies or express it through art, drama and song.

The phrase "African theology" is used mostly of the contemporary developments in theology in Africa. But of course the early church attests to the impressive theological developments in Roman North Africa and Egypt. Augustine of Hippo, Cyprian of Carthage and Athanasius of Alexandria are among the great names from the early years.

Currently one of the problems of doing theology in Africa is the issue of language. Africa has some 2,000 languages, not counting dialects. In order to communicate beyond one's ethnic and language setting, one is forced to use a foreign language, chiefly English or French. Theologizing in a foreign language imposes limitations. One question is how far a given language that has been exposed to Christianity for only 50 or 100 years can fully assimilate, sustain and articulate Christian concepts. How does one talk about the Trinity, the incarnation, transubstantiation, or "Towards a Just, Participatory and Sustainable Society"?

Sources of theology in Africa. The first and foremost source is the *Bible*, of which there were in 1989 about 580 translations in African languages. Second is *Christian heritage*, which has come down the centuries through Hebrew, Greek, Roman and later European and American cultures. It has been wrapped in the dresses of those cultures, and it is rich in spirituality, theological concepts, art, music, liturgies, symbols, etc.

Third is *African culture*, particularly African religion, world-view and values. African religion, which at many points resembles the religion of the Old Testament, has been the most influential force in shaping the African world-view. It is still strong today, especially in times of crisis. African religion is grounded on the conviction that God* exists and is the Creator of all things. The main and new element in the teaching of missionaries was the naming of Jesus Christ.* The vocabulary used in the churches, the spirituality of the Christians, and the translation of the Bible are all heavily coloured by African religion.

The fourth source is *African history*, which we primarily divide into pre-colonial, colonial and post-colonial periods. Contemporary history in Africa includes rapid social, economic and political change, for better or for worse, with mass media, modern technology and contact with other nations playing increasingly important roles.

Main issues in African theology. In reality, African theology addresses itself to all aspects of the Christian faith. But here we mention the items which get more attention than others.

African religion and the Christian faith: The encounter between these two began the very moment the first missionaries preached the gospel in Africa. Is the God of the Bible the same God who is acknowledged and worshipped in African religion? African theologians themselves generally answer yes, affirming that God's revelation is not limited to the biblical record (see Matt. 5:17; Heb. 1:1-2).

Furthermore, the theologians are discussing in what ways the gospel comes to fulfill our religious longing and yearning. The question is being raised: What contributions does African religion make to the life of the church, in terms of, for example, sensitivity to the spiritual realities, harmony with and respect for nature* and creation,* in the evolving of relevant forms of liturgy* and worship? Worship in African tradition utilizes the whole body through singing, dancing, clapping, yelling, shouting and moving rhythmically, so that the whole person (body and spirit) is rejoicing, giving thanks to God and calling upon God.

The growing consensus of African theology is that African religion has said yes to the gospel. The gospel has also said yes to African religion. Consequently, African theology is taking up this inter-religious dialogue seriously. Many theologians have done research in African religion to understand it better and to relate it to the Christian faith, for example: the late Harry Sawyerr (Sierra Leone), E. Bolaji Idowu (Nigeria), Engelbert Mveng (Cameroon), Vincent Mulago (Zaire), Gabriel Setiloane (South Africa), A.B.T. Byaruhanga-Akiiki (Uganda) and Samuel Kibicho (Kenya).

A few theologians, however, are saying that such a discussion is nothing but a form of syncretism and should not be undertaken. Some do not see any continuity between biblical religion and African religion.

Christology: The question of who Jesus Christ is receives various answers from African theology. In the theology of liberation (e.g. T.A. Mofokeng) Jesus Christ is taken as the fighting God, the Liberator who is on the side of the poor* and oppressed. The footprints of Jesus in his suffering appear today in Southern Africa in the torture chambers, imprisonments, beatings and cries of the oppressed. Africans are being driven to the cross of Jesus, to the God who hears the cries of the oppressed, and not to the God of the oppressor.

Some, like Mveng, see Jesus Christ as the Master of initiation because he has gone through the main stages of life according to African tradition and has survived death, the hardest of them all (see **resurrection**). He has risen again and has, therefore, the qualifications to be Friend-Master, to show us the way of life in its fullness and to win our respect, confidence and love.

Jesus Christ is being experienced in African Christianity as the great Chief, the Ancestor, the Healer, the One who exorcises troublesome spirits, the One who protects against magic and sorcery, the One who enables childless women to bear. This image of Jesus Christ in particular is being experienced in the African Independent Churches (AIC), many of which emphasize healing.

It could be asserted that the religious thinking of the AIC is in reaction to what was perceived as unsatisfactory theology and practices of the historic churches, which have to some extent failed to operate at the wavelength of Africans. But as AICs broke away from historic churches, they also retained some of the theology and practices of the historic churches.

Women's theology: As they do in all countries of the world, women constitute the majority in the church in Africa. Yet, power is in the hands of the men. African women are waking up to this form of injustice. There is a growing stridency in women's theological voices in Africa which deserves attention. Mercy Amba Oduyoye, for example, on the basis of the Genesis creation story, emphasizes creation and the continuity of human life in the womb of the woman. Unfortunately there are not yet many women theologians. In 1989 the first convocation of African women theologians was held in Accra, Ghana; it brought together some 80 African women theologians.

The theology of liberation: This theology is prevalent in Southern Africa, where oppression is rampant and Africans have been denied their human rights by the minority European settlers. Among the African theologians of liberation are Desmond Tutu, Allan A.

Boesak and Zephania Kameeta. The first major book on the subject was published in 1972, but the South African government banned it before it was put on the shelves. A year later it was published in London and New York as *Black Theology: The South African Voice,* edited by Basil Moore, an Englishman. In this book of essays, one hears the cry of the oppressed "in revolt against the spiritual enslavement of African people... It is a theology of the oppressed, by the oppressed, for the liberation of the oppressed."

In 1985 appeared the Kairos document,* which took up the issues of liberation theology and exposed the false theology of the state, which justifies the government's committing violence against Africans, under the guise of keeping law and order. The document identifies God as being on the side of the oppressed people and urges Christians to stand against oppression.

Church and state: The relation between church and state* is a main concern in many areas. For example, in socialist countries like Ethiopia, Angola and Mozambique, the freedom of the church has to a certain degree been curtailed, and the state is (at least theoretically) committed to an ideology of atheism.* In predominantly Muslim countries like Egypt, Sudan and the others in the northern one-third of Africa, the church has little freedom, and Christians sometimes live under pressure if not persecution. Many African countries are or have been under military regimes. Here, too, situations of conflict arise, and churches have sometimes been faced with difficulties, as was the case in Uganda at one point during the regime of Idi Amin (1971-79). Most African Christians, however, live in countries where the state and the church enjoy a high degree of co-operation, as for example in Zaire, Zambia and Zimbabwe.

Other themes in African theology include biblical studies, the nature and mission of the church, the liturgical life of the church, Christian art and drama, the ecumenical movement, the church itself and the relation between human life and nature at large.

Conclusion. African theology is in its early stage. Much of it is expressed orally, through art, singing, sermons and prayers. Written theology is the privilege of a small number of theologians, and these are often forced to express their thoughts in languages not native to them. But African theology is raising issues which are relevant to the living situation of the church in Africa. At the same time, it is in touch with theologies from other parts of the world.

There has been an explosion of Christianity in Africa in the 20th century, and African theology is taking shape in this process. Whereas there were only 10 million Christians in Africa in 1900 (9% of the total population), by the year 2000 the number is expected to reach 394 million, or 48% of Africa's total population. Within less than 100 years the southern two-thirds of Africa has become predominantly Christian, while the northern one-third remains predominantly Muslim. African theology is thus at a very exciting period in the history of Christianity in Africa.

See also **anthropology, African**.

JOHN S. MBITI

K. Bediako, *Jesus in African Culture*, Accra, Asempa, 1990 • K.A. Dickson, *Theology in Africa*, London, Darton, Longman & Todd, 1984 • K.A. Dickson & P. Ellingworth eds, *Biblical Revelation and African Religions*, London, Lutterworth, 1968 • J.S. Mbiti, *Bible and Theology in African Christianity*, London, Oxford UP, 1986 • T.A. Mofokeng, *The Crucified among the Crossbearers*, Kampen, Kok, 1983 • M.A. Oduyoye, *Hearing and Knowing*, Maryknoll, NY, Orbis, 1985 • J.S. Pobee, *Toward an African Theology*, Nashville, TN, Abingdon, 1979.

THEOLOGY, ASIAN. A living theology is one that addresses itself to the questions, aspirations and sufferings of a people in a given situation. When Asian churches begin to relate their theology to their context, there emerges a distinctive Asian theology. In the past the Asian churches, by and large a product of Western missions, were content with repeating, without reflection, the confessions of faith evolved by the Western churches. A creative theology in Asia began to emerge in the 19th century when the churches started relating their faith to the questions and concerns peculiar to Asia. This theological encounter continues as the church faces new problems and challenges.

The relation between Christian faith and the major Asian religions continues to be a dominant theme of Asian theology. The worldviews and doctrines of traditional religions exercise a profound influence in moulding the

sensibilities of the people of Asia. In the days of aggressive evangelization and colonization, the missionaries were not prepared to see any value in Asian views. Most of them considered the religions in Asia to be discontinuous with Christian faith.

A new awareness of the spiritual values embedded in them surfaced as a result of the objective study of these religions and a closer contact with the votaries of these faiths. Still basing their approach on a theological framework that drew a sharp distinction between Christ and religions, the missionary theologians began to interpret Christ as the fulfilment of the deepest yearnings in the religions of Asia. J.N. Farquhar's *The Crown of Hinduism* (1919) is perhaps the best-known expression of this view. During this period there were bold attempts on the part of Asian theologians to use concepts and doctrines of other faiths for the church's apologetic task. The Hindu concept of *avatar* was used to interpret the Christian doctrine of incarnation,* or that of *sat-chit-anand* (being, consciousness, bliss) for explaining the doctrine of the Trinity.* In all these, the superiority of Christian faith was affirmed but with a sympathetic, even if somewhat condescending, view of other faiths.

A new stage was set when Asian theologians like D.T. Niles (1908-70) acknowledged the incognito presence of Christ in Asia's history and religions long before the missionaries came to Asia. A cogent interpretation of this view is provided by P.D. Devanandan (*The Gospel and Renascent Hinduism*, 1964). Writing on the same theme, M.M. Thomas affirmed a more recognizable presence of Christ in renascent Hinduism, as the title of an influential book of his suggests, *The Acknowledged Christ of the Indian Renaissance* (1975).

In other parts of the region writers tried to integrate gospel and culture.* Buddhist experience of nirvana and the reality of the kingdom of God* were brought together by writers in Sri Lanka. Christ assumed a cultural face in China. Chinese Christ was the man who was also the Tao in the writings of Chang I-Ching (b.1871) and Chao Tzu-ch'en (1918-56). For Pandipeddi Chenchiah (1886-1959), an Indian theologian, Christ was the cosmic Christ, whose birth brought a new creative energy into the biosphere. An admirable work of this genre was Kazo Kitamori's *Theology of the Pain of God* (1946). Its main theme of pain *(itami)* was very familiar to people in Japan, who had suffered much during the war.

Theology at this time emerged from an active interaction between the gospel and the religious philosophies of Asia. Concepts, doctrines and symbols of other religions were used freely and critically by Asian churches to deepen their experiences of Christ and to interpret the Christian faith. With this there was a vigorous search for an Asian face of Christ, dismantling the foreignness of Christianity. Profound was their recognition that the Christ reality was greater than formal Christianity and that the Christ was present but unacknowledged in the religions and cultures of Asia.

A second stream in Asian Christian theology has its beginning in the churches' encounter with the socio-political realities of their context. Early beginnings of this emphasis are found in the life and writings of Toyohiko Kagawa (1888-1960) of Japan. He had questioned the "spatially extensive evangelism" and attempted to relate the gospel to the social realities of his people, especially to the labour situation in Japan. In reflecting on the experience of colonialism and the freedom movements, many Asian thinkers discovered a vital link between the gospel and the aspirations of their people for a freer and better social and political order. A profound analysis of the Asian revolution from the perspective of the gospel is provided by M.M. Thomas in a number of his writings. According to him, colonization, though ruthless and exploitative, has been the bearer of an ambiguous process of humanization in Asian societies, especially through technology* and industry and liberal ideas of freedom* and justice.* Christ, the promise of a new humanity, he argued, should be confessed as the transforming and judging presence of God.*

The East Asia Christian Conference provided the forum for Asian thinkers to reflect more deeply on the events of the gospel in the social and cultural contexts of Asia. They affirmed that confessing faith in Christ meant constructive participation in revolution and in the building of nations based on justice and freedom. The methodology governing their theology is that of contextualization (see **inculturation; theology, contextual**). The late Shoki Coe of Taiwan, who contributed significantly to the growth of Asian theology, indicated that this process is a dynamic interaction between the text and the context. Contextual theologians also proposed a critical Asian principle as a method for doing theology in their situation.

In recent years, the theme "people"* has assumed a special significance in the discussions of Asian theology. Korean theologians focused their attention on minjung (see **theology, minjung**), the neglected and suffering people who gain their selfhood through struggles. The irruption of people's histories and cultures into Asian consciousness has brought a critique of the elite-oriented theologies and philosophies of religion.

The minjung (not all of whom are Christians) are the theological actors or subjects of theology in the measure in which they struggle against domination. The place of theology therefore is the human community striving for liberation* and life, in which the Spirit is at work. Minjung theology expresses itself in people's stories — mostly unwritten, articulated in symbols, folk songs, poems, myths, dance and celebration.

The method of doing theology with people's symbols and images holds great promise. Indications are that if this project is pursued, there will emerge a distinct voice in theology that comes out of the deepest yearnings of the people of Asia. Choan-Seng Song of Taiwan has made important contributions in this area. (*Theology from the Womb of Asia*, 1986, is one among many volumes.) Mention must also be made of the work of Kosuke Koyama (*Mount Fuji and Mount Sinai*, 1984) and Masao Takenaka (*God Is Rice*, 1986).

Even when the end product and the mode of theologizing are new, the presuppositions of this theology may raise a serious challenge to traditional formulations on the scriptures, revelation* and Christology. An Asian report presented to a conference of the Ecumenical Association of Third World Theologians* (EATWOT) poses this challenge in these words: "Could a live historical process and spiritual quest be ruled for ever by fixed texts born of particular limited experiences of one ancient group of people? Is it not the witness of the scriptures that God is present not in books but among the people and in their struggles for justice and dignity?" The same statement concludes: "The task of theology is to recognize the embodiments of the Word in the history of freedom; the passion of Jesus in the struggles of the people; and the resurrection in their growing emancipation and fellowship" (excerpts from unpublished records of the Oaxtepec conference of EATWOT, 1986).

This is people's theology; this is Asian theology.

K.C. ABRAHAM

D. Elwood ed., *Asian Christian Theology*, Philadelphia, Westminster, 1980 • E. Nacpil & D. Elwood eds, *The Human and Holy*, Maryknoll, NY, Orbis, 1980 • S.J. Samartha, *The Search for New Hermeneutics in Asian Christian Theology*, Bangalore, BTE-SSC, 1987.

THEOLOGY, BLACK. Black theology is the attempt of so-called black people to articulate the word of God* out of their own experience. It implies a dissatisfaction with theology done by people of the North, what is often called "white theology". It is found among blacks of the USA and of Southern Africa, particularly the Republic of South Africa. Its high priests include James H. Cone, Gayraud Wilmore and Cornel West from the USA and Itumeleng J. Mosala, Takatso Mofokeng, Simon Maimela and Allan Boesak from the Republic of South Africa. A point not to gloss over is that on the South Africa side some of the pundits of black theology are white, such as Albert Nolan and C.F. Beyers Naudé. In the African continent, black theology is one expression of African theology; in the US black theology is an expression of liberation theology.

"Black" qualifying theology is not about pigmentation of the skin but is about black experience, out of which the reflection on God's word emerges. The black experience in practical terms has been synonymous with poverty, ignorance, terror, insult, being exploited by others, being relegated to the periphery of humankind. By contrast, "white" is the symbol of lordship, mastery of history and of the gospel, power, being automatic heirs of the chief seats in the great parliament of humanity. The difference between white and black experience is thus of epistemological relevance. Unlike black experience, white experience has been accommodated to, if not

co-opted by, the white power structures and ideology with its hallmarks of racism, capitalism, white nationalism (e.g. Afrikaner nationalism) and the ideology of national security.

In so far as these hallmarks of white experience are functional factors of domination, they become a formative factor in the articulation of black consciousness and of black theology. The point to underline is that the elements of the power structure are not only political and social but also theological issues, because they relate to the integrity of the gospel, to the credibility of the Christian and church witness in the world and to the confession of Jesus as Christ and Lord. Therefore, four key words of black theology are idolatry, heresy, sin and blasphemy, which are used in its analysis of the white power structure. By the same token, there is a truth claim in the black experience which has been described as the epistemological privilege of the poor,* i.e. truth is often suppressed in the context of oppression and may therefore be more accessible to the oppressed.

This overview of black theology suggests an epistemological break with traditional theology. In Western theology it is often assumed that ideas such as revelation, reason, nature, and church doctrines are the points of departure. On the contrary, black theology in the tradition of liberation theology chooses for its departure point social relations, particularly the cry of the oppressed. Black theology's epistemology is one from below and is counter-hegemonic, rejecting any assumption that all people, irrespective of experience, can perceive reality in the same way and, therefore, reflect theologically in the same way.

Because social relations have been identified as the starting point of theologizing, social analysis is an important tool of theology. Social analysis is "a mediation between the black experiences and the theological reformulation", attempting to clarify contrasting experiences. In this regard structural analysis is seen as being fully as important as attitudinal analysis. Structural analysis interprets the black experience with reference to a global structure, very much related to European expansion. The black experience is explained in terms of the inter-relation between economy and the symbolic structure of society. Boesak develops this point theologically as follows: "Racism is an ideology of racial domination that incorporates beliefs in the cultural or inherent biological inferiority of a particular ethnos. It uses such beliefs to justify and prescribe unequal treatment of that group. In other words, racism is not merely attitudinal but structural. It is not merely a vague feeling of racial superiority, but a system of domination, furnished with social, political and economic structures of domination" (*Black and Reformed*, 110-11). In that light repentance must include the structural change of the society so as to overcome the negative black experience, especially racism.*

Black theology's insisting on perspectives from below has sometimes sounded like a Marxist theory of knowledge. Some black theologians have even used Marxist terminology. There is, however, a difference between the two because black theology insists on the cultural creativity of the oppressed. Intellectuals such as theologians are convincing only in so far as they are willing to learn from the poor, those on the underside of history. Here black theology risks becoming the voice of the privileged and not taking seriously enough the experience of the poor.

Opponents of black theology criticize it for being simply politics using a vocabulary of religion and theology. But in point of fact black theology is concerned to address a fundamental dysfunction in spiritual life. It promotes speaking responsibly about God in the modern world, social relations based on love and justice, a sense of Christian identity which eschews alienation and upholds true humanness, and making real the gospel of hope, which is threatened by the idols which are death-dealing and oppressive, (i.e. political ideologies such as racism, economic theories such as capitalism).

The emphases of black theology include creation faith, pointing to the God who created all humanity in his own image and likeness and to the black person's identity in that creation* and in the company of fellow believers; wholeness of life, seeing politics, economics, and all of human life as based on a relation to God, life being the arena where God meets humankind with his gifts, and therefore sacramental; wholeness of life as an ecclesiological postulate, requiring reconciliation, when blacks and whites live in community in which equality and justice are central values.

The similarity between black theologies from the USA and Southern Africa leads some to suggest that the former influenced the latter or even that the latter derives from the former. Influences may not be denied, but South African black theology is rooted in the black consciousness, an integral part of black power, in which religion and politics interact. Black consciousness is concerned with affirming black identity and not so much with maintaining an anti-white posture; it is concerned with an egalitarian society in which there is no racial differentiation.

Black theology is a reminder that all theology is contextual, addressing concrete issues, especially of a political nature. To describe it as hermeneutics belonging to the preaching and therefore not dogmatic discipline is to fail to see that all theology is contextual. Indeed, black theology represents an inter-relation of dogmatics and social-ethical issues.

Two personal comments may be made. First, black theology is in danger of not taking seriously enough the grassroots communities. As Bonganjalo Goba puts it: "So many of us are remote from the everyday experiences of our black people. There is a gap between the black elite and the ordinary black man. We have allowed our acquired intellectualism to separate us from the ordinary people. Today when we speak of the black consciousness movement, we immediately think of students in South African students organizations and a few clerics. The rest of the people are not involved... Does black theology really play a liberating role in our situation in Southern Africa? Are we able to measure the contribution of the black theology of liberation to the struggle of the oppressed masses in South Africa? Or is it just an intellectual exercise for the benefit of the black theologian to enhance his/her position in the academic world?" This indeed is the danger facing all theologians: they should be articulate intellectuals in the womb both of the church and of the community. Second, black women — always at the bottom of the heap — have not received enough attention, even though they are more than half of the people of God.

See also **theology, liberation**.

JOHN S. POBEE

J.A. Banks & J.D. Grambs, *Black Self-Concept*, New York, McGraw Hill, 1972 • A. Boesak,

Farewell to Innocence, New York, Orbis, 1977 •
A. Boesak, *The Finger of God*, Maryknoll, NY,
Orbis, 1982 • J.H. Cone, *Black Theology and Black
Power*, New York, Seabury, 1969 • B. Moore, *The
Challenge of Black Theology in South Africa*, At-
lanta, John Knox, 1973 • I.J. Mosala & B. Thlagale
eds, *The Unquestionable Right to Be Free*, New
York, Maryknoll, 1986 • A. Nolan, *The Service of
the Poor and Spiritual Growth*, London, CIIR,
1985.

THEOLOGY BY THE PEOPLE. The
phrase has been associated with the WCC
since the Vancouver assembly (1983), which
made it a major thrust of the Programme on
Theological Education and, to some extent, of
the Commission on the Churches' Participation in Development. The phrase continues
the emphasis of the earlier focus on "ministry
by the people of God".

These slogans arise from the re-discovery of
the church as the people of God. For too long
clericalization of the church had been the model. Ignatius, bishop of Antioch (A.D. 110-17),
said: "Where the bishop is, there is the
church"; i.e. the bishop guarantees the harmony of the people of God when they are
gathered around him in eucharistic celebration.
Through the centuries this idea developed into
the practice of a clergy-centred church, which
did not take seriously enough the place of the
people — i.e. all who are united to God and
one another by faith* and baptism.*

Two recent documents have helped to elevate the idea of the people of God: *Lumen
Gentium (LG)* (esp. 2), which came out of the
Second Vatican Council* in 1964, and the
WCC's Faith and Order document *Baptism,
Eucharist and Ministry** (BEM, 1982). These
documents did not invent the idea of the
people of God, but they reflect a new sensitivity to the strand of biblical tradition represented by 1 Pet. 2:9 — that the church is "a
chosen race, a royal priesthood, a holy nation,
God's own people, that you may declare the
wonderful deeds of him who called you out of
darkness into his marvellous light". *All* the
faithful, not only specialist theologians and
the clergy, are called to give an account of the
faith and to exercise ministry in God's name
on behalf of the world. Thus the equipping of
the whole people of God to exercise ministry
has been a particular concern of the ecumenical movement.

There is a continuing debate on who the
people are in the phrase "theology by the
people". Some have used it in the sense of the
whole people of God, i.e. all the baptized, all
Christians. Others use "people" to mean the
poor, i.e. the oppressed, the marginalized, the
suffering (see **theology, minjung**). In Latin
America, "people" is used in a still more
specialized sense of the people in whom popular power is constituted and established as the
collective will.

Theology, or talk about God, has for long
been the preserve and preoccupation of the
specialist. In a scholarly way it articulates the
revelation of God and a holistic Christocentric
world-view. The revelation of God thus came
to be seen as first and foremost a body of
doctrines.

The starting point of talk about God, however, should be the gospel, the good news.
Theology is not to be erudition for its own
sake but a clarifying of the word of God* so
that it can be experienced by people as good
news. Theology by the people recalls theologians and others to a missiological emphasis.
People's hopes and fears must be addressed
by theologians, from within a community of
faith.

The preposition "by" in this phrase, while
not denying that the source of theology is the
word of God, suggests that the perceptions,
hopes and fears of the ordinary people are also
an important factor in the theological task and
that the specialist must speak only from the
midst of the people, the poor, who seek God's
salvation.* We must see that "poor people are
the very origin of the theological discussions".

The phrase "theology by the people" carries
some assumptions and implications. First, if
holy scripture* is the source of revelation, it is
also claimed that people's experiences can be
a source of revelation. While a relevant and
authentic theology may reflect a particular
temporal horizon, it must retain the biblical as
well as the transcendental dimensions as a
framework of reference.

Second, since theology is concerned with
good news, it cannot only be an intellectual
activity; it must involve a life-style which acts
to bring good news to the poor, makes sacrifices on behalf of the poor and the weak in
whom Christ meets people (Matt. 25:31-46).
Theological education must produce people

with commitment to the values of the kingdom. The vitality of theology may be judged largely by its relevance to the life and tasks of the people of God. Theology should seek to motivate the people of God and through them all humanity to be redemptively involved in the world. Therefore, those in theological training must be involved in the realities of daily life of the people and society in which they live.

Third, people have an ecclesiological significance (see **church**). Particularly the poor are part of the Body of Christ and must be respected and given due recognition. Teaching the word of God and encouraging one another becomes a community task that always must aim at human transformation. For that very reason dialogue becomes a mark of theology by the people.

Fourth, if the theological task of the church belongs to the whole people of God, then traditional elitist theological education practices are inadequate for the task. Numerically the schools cannot cope. This calls for alternate models of theological education — preeminently, theological education by extension.

See also **church base communities, poor**.

JOHN S. POBEE

S. Amirtham & J.S. Pobee eds, *Theology by the People*, WCC, 1986 • E. Cardenal, *The Gospel in Solentiname*, Maryknoll, NY, Orbis, 1976 • F. Castillo, *Theologie aus der Praxis des Volkes*, Munich, Kaiser, 1978 • F.R. Kinsler ed., *Ministry by the People*, WCC, 1983 • *Minjung Theology*, Singapore, CCA, 1983.

THEOLOGY, CONTEXTUAL. Many people view theology as absolute: it is the queen of the sciences, a scientific discipline to be studied with the same methods — philological, historical, psychological, sociological, philosophical, etc. — as any other subject in the humanities. And theology, especially as carried on in the North, has been based on a universalism which holds that every human being, from whatever region, class or circumstance, may perceive reality and reflect theologically in the same way.

In recent times there has been some questioning of these assumptions, particularly by theologians from the South. The attempt to harmonize the understanding of social realities in one place, let alone at a universal level, is suspect. Besides, there is new awareness that theology's formative factors include experience, God's self-exposure (otherwise called revelation*), scripture,* Tradition,* culture* and reason. The facts of experience and culture ensure that there can never be only one theology; any particular theological construct represents the confluence of a number of variant factors, some of which may be labelled context. Furthermore, in so far as Christianity claims to be gospel, the good news of the Christ-event, Christian theology may not start from a body of church doctrines, lest it become insensitive to the situation around it, the context from which it speaks. Theology's starting point cannot be an idea such as revelation, reason, nature, or church doctrine; rather, its point of departure should be the specific social relations, the hopes and fears of people — the context. For precisely that reason social analysis is a vital aspect of contextual theology. Liberation theology* of Latin America therefore sometimes has used Marxist critique as a tool for social analysis.

The word "context" and its cognates "contextuality" and "contextualization" were thrust into the centre of theological debates by the work of the Theological Education Fund, a service of the WCC's Commission on World Mission and Evangelism. Its director reputedly coined the term in regard to theological education. "Context" means the interpenetration of subject and object, signalling the willingness and concern to live with specifics rather than generalities, particulars rather than universals. Shoki Coe wrote: "By contextuality we mean the wrestling with God's word in such a way that the power of the incarnation, which is the divine form of contextualization, can enable us to follow his steps to contextualize" (*Theological Education*, 11, 1974).

Contextual theology, then, represents a declaration for relativities in theology. This, however, does not mean doctrinaire relativism, that every item of faith is negotiable. Second, it signals that in a Bible study (as in chemistry), the inductive method at the best yields probabilities rather than necessities. Therefore, contextual theology is concerned to bring together faith and life, the Bible and one's respective context and the different ways in which people's context or consciousness of their context influences their understanding or appreciation of the Bible. Thus contextual theology seeks to direct attention to the task of communicating the gospel in terms of what really is happening now in the cultures with which the church is involved. Naturally, contextual theologies (e.g. feminist theology, narrative theology, cultural theology) are wide-ranging and diverse.

Contextualization has become a slogan of third-world theology, referring to a kind of theology which starts from the problems of the community and attempts to formulate the Christian message accordingly. Contextual theology thus not unexpectedly often reads like a programme, a crusade rather than a gospel.

JOHN S. POBEE

R.O. Costa ed., *One Faith, Many Cultures. Inculturation, Indigenization and Contextualization*, Maryknoll, NY, Orbis, 1988 • *Learning in Context: The Search for Innovative Patterns in Theological Education*, London, New Life, 1973.

THEOLOGY, ECUMENICAL. Theology begins when the believer becomes conscious of his or her faith* and finds it necessary to reflect upon it mainly for reasons of communication. Theology is therefore a necessity for the transmission of the faith, for the sharing of the experience of belief, for the edification of the community of believers.

Within the Christian community, theology has always been present in the preaching of the good news, in the confession of faith and in liturgical prayer. From the very start, one of the main concerns in the Christian community has been maintaining the unity* of the church,* expressed in the confession of the one faith. This unity has always been endangered by the difficult theological problem of announcing the good news of Jesus Christ* in the context of ever-new contemporary challenges. Theology therefore is not only the private reflection of believers upon their individual faith. It is the concern of the church as a community constantly striving to express its faith in a manner which preserves the shared experience of God by the witnesses of all times from the apostles onward and which guards against deviations affecting the truth of God and the salvation* offered by God. This is what councils (see **ecumenical councils**) sought to achieve. They have thus contributed

to the development of an ecclesial theology, a theology belonging to the church.

In their effort to maintain the purity of the apostolic faith, i.e. in doing church theology, Christians have been conscious of acting, thinking, debating, preaching in the light of Christ's words about the "Spirit of truth" who "will guide you into all the truth" (John 16:13; see **Holy Spirit**). Church history is nevertheless full of examples of failure to achieve unanimity in the one Spirit who testifies to Jesus Christ (John 15:26); as confessions and confessionalism developed, theology has tended to become defensive and often divisive (see **schism**).

This divisive character of theology springs from different roots. The most obvious cause, of course, is the difficulty which constantly arises among Christians about the interpretation of revelation* as witnessed to by the scriptures and the apostles.

There are also dangers inherent in "private" theology, i.e. an individualistic reflection pursued in isolation from the community, from the church. This practice often begets a tendency to single out one aspect of the revealed mystery and to systematize the whole in the light of this over-emphasized aspect. This form of divisiveness is due to the human temptation to substitute one's own private spirit for the Holy Spirit.

Another form of divisive theology springs from the temptation to use theology and the church of God for "non-theological" ends, such as political domination or imperialism, which arises from the human tendency to self-assertiveness, misuse of power, authoritarianism. This approach tends to substitute the spirit of this world for the Holy Spirit.

Theology also tends to become divisive when it consists in a pious conservatism which misinterprets tradition* to mean a rigid adherence to past formulas with a total failure to be attentive to history* as a dynamic process. This attitude leads to a blindness to the signs of the times and encourages defensive, if not aggressive, theology. The church in this perspective is seen as free from any responsibility for the world.

The reaction to such theology, however, can be just as divisive in its own tendency to identify theology with the immediate, narrow historical context. This reaction may lead to a Christology which loses sight of the full implications of the incarnation* and the announcement of the coming of the kingdom.* Christ's message becomes purely human or rather humanistic in the negative limiting sense. The transformation of humanity through its assumption by the second person of the Trinity* tends to disappear, and theology becomes yet one more political ideology.*

In so far as the ecumenical movement is a reaction against a passive, complacent or even self-righteous acceptance of divisions among Christians, its ultimate goal is the reunion of all in one eucharistic community — the one, holy, catholic and apostolic church. Consequently, it necessarily involves theology. And because the ecumenical movement involves theology, it is an invitation to react against all forms of divisive theology and to recover a theology of unity, a theology of the church.

It must be emphasized immediately that in this context unity does *not* mean uniformity. Conciliar unanimity, the unity in the one Spirit, should not be confused with generally imposed conformity. When Paul speaks of our being "all one in Christ Jesus", after stating that "there is neither Jew nor Greek, there is neither bond nor free, there is neither male nor female" (Gal. 3:28), he does not mean that Christians are an indistinct, neutral, sexless company of beings united in a kind of middle-of-the-road compromise, but that the categories enumerated do not represent a limiting characterization of each; they are the expression of a unity in diversity.

Does this mean that ecumenical theology consists simply in placing side by side diverse, sometimes contradictory, if not conflicting, expressions of faith in Jesus Christ and declaring that their co-existence is legitimate? Such a form of pluralism* would not be conducive to the unity in the one Spirit, any more than would authoritarian uniformity. Theology, as a necessary means of communication, especially with a view to re-establishing broken unity, necessarily implies finding out the meaning that each gives to the same words.

After a period of confrontation, of comparing notes, of discovery of each other, Christians in the ecumenical movement have begun to work in a form which tends towards an ecumenical type of theology: in statements such as those produced by bilateral dialogues* (both at an official level and among such less

formal parties as the Dombes Group*) or by multilateral work such as the *Baptism, Eucharist and Ministry** text or the explication of the Nicene Creed* in course of elaboration by the WCC's Faith and Order commission.

These statements or texts are attempts to say together what can be said to express agreement or convergence in particular on divisive questions. And in some areas, the progress made in the last 50 years is extraordinary. However, the spirit of suspicion is not dead within the divided Christian communities: behind each word, suspicious readers tend to see the old "heresies"* of the other party or parties. Yet it is not impossible to overcome these historical stumbling blocks and arrive at statements which represent doctrinal agreement and even consensus.*

The difficulties of ecumenical theology lie elsewhere. First of all, it implies taking very seriously the words of the WCC basis* about confessing "Jesus Christ as God and Saviour" and about the churches' vocation to glorify the Trinity.* Taking these words seriously means that the sole criterion for ecumenical theology is God himself, Jesus Christ, image of the Father, bearer of the Spirit who reveals Christ and cries "Abba, Father" in the hearts of all the baptized.

Ecumenical theology implies total humility and intellectual honesty; it implies being prepared to be guided into all truth by the Spirit of truth (see John 16:13). This stance is a permanent crucifixion for the intellect. All philosophical categories are to be used critically, with constant awareness that none can comprehend or circumscribe the fullness of the mystery of Christ. Ecumenical theology implies readiness to be guided into recognizing the presence of the Truth, i.e. Christ himself, in forms of expression which may be unfamiliar or even "alien" at first sight.

Perhaps the greatest difficulty for ecumenical theology is the fact that if it is relatively easy to agree about doctrinal problems in the light of a common acceptance of Jesus Christ as the sole criterion of truth, it is much harder to reach a common mind about the reading of the historical context in which theology, the gospel message, the good news of the kingdom, is to be expressed. Jesus Christ is "the same yesterday and today and for ever" (Heb. 13:8), whereas the ethnic, cultural, political,

regional conditions are so complex, conflictual and divisive as to represent an almost insuperable obstacle to an intellectually unified
view. The permanent temptation is therefore
either to be content with the formulations of
the past and disregard the concrete conditions
of today, of the here and now, or to consider
only these latter and disregard or reject the
past, the formulations of our predecessors.

Ecumenical theology can be neither blind to
the variety of contexts of the present world
nor deaf to the witnesses of all times to the
apostolic faith. It must needs be a theology of
the church, the one church whose unity is as
absolute as its diversity, in the image of the
Holy Trinity; it is to be worked out within the
communion of saints.* It is therefore no mere
intellectual exercise. It implies a permanent
intensification of the relation of each one
engaged in this process with the one Lord
Jesus Christ in the Holy Spirit for the glory of
the Father. In other words, it is prayerful and
doxological, as well as intellectual. It is a
permanent re-discovery of the church as the
heart of the world, of creation.* It is a renewed awareness of the church's responsibility for all, in that it exists "for the life of the
world" (liturgy of John Chrysostom). That is
why the unity of the church is closely linked
with the unity of humankind and why no
human problem can be disregarded by ecumenical theology.

See also **theology in the ecumenical
movement**.

NICHOLAS LOSSKY

Y. Congar, *Diversités et communion* (ET *Diversity
and Communion*, London, SCM, 1984) • W.M.
Horton, *Christian Theology: An Ecumenical Approach*, New York, Harper, 1955 • J.M. Lochman,
Das Glaubensbekenntnis (ET *The Faith We Confess: An Ecumenical Approach*, Philadelphia, Fortress, 1984) • E. Schlink, *Ökumenische Dogmatik*,
Göttingen, Vandenhoeck & Ruprecht, 1983 • G.
Wainwright, *Doxology*, London, Epworth, 1980.

THEOLOGY, EUROPEAN. Theology
in the years between the two great European
wars was largely dominated by concerns arising out of the German intellectual tradition.
The war had hastened the decline of liberal
Protestantism, with its confidence in the re-
concilability of Christ and culture;* and the
rise of National Socialism in Germany

prompted a strong reaction against any notion
of a revelation apart from the word of God*
uttered in Jesus and witnessed to in scripture.*
This approach, associated above all with the
name of Karl Barth, had great influence in all
the European Protestant churches, though it
certainly did not go without criticism (and had
relatively little impact at first in the Anglo-
Saxon world). Barth's own involvement in the
ecumenical movement also meant that his
insights and arguments were influential outside the Reformed tradition: the important
Russian emigré theologian Georges Florovsky
was able to integrate some of Barth's ideas
into the framework of Orthodox thinking,
combining Barth's insistence on revelation*
with a rather fuller sacramental theology.

Within the ecumenical movement itself,
considerable tensions developed during the
1930s between those like Barth and Bonhoeffer who insisted on extremely rigorous standards of theological integrity, appropriate to
the apocalyptic dimensions of the German
struggle, and English and North American
voices, more inclined to pragmatism and the
maintenance of dialogue. The dominance of
Barthian language and ideas in ecumenical
circles is probably most marked in the era
immediately after the 1939-45 war, in a
period when the rhetoric of divine judgment
and human impotence answered a deep need
for a theology of corporate repentance.

Barth had derided theologians who admitted a concern with philosophy or with theories
of history and culture. Related to, but distinct
from, the Barthian influence was the radical
New Testament exegesis of Rudolf Bultmann
during this period, sharing Barth's scepticism
about natural theology and rejecting any attempt to ground Christian faith in history, by
using the philosophy of Martin Heidegger as a
tool for re-interpreting the Lutheran commitment to justification* by faith alone.

In the post-war years, theologians in Germany began increasingly to challenge the
dominance of Barth's anti-philosophical and
Bultmann's anti-historical prescriptions, and
the face of European theology changed substantially as various writers made attempts to
reclaim history and culture. The group associated with the young Wolfhart Pannenberg at
Munich in the early 1960s developed a theology in which history, including intelligible history, was itself revelation: the events of scrip-

tural history were not to be seen as different in kind from other historical happenings, and the rationality of faith required a foundation in such authentic occurrences. Pannenberg went on to produce a very influential essay in Christology *(Jesus: God and Man)*, and a programmatic study of the foundations of the philosophy of science in relation to Christian theology; and more recently he has written extensively on ethics and on the doctrine of human nature *(Anthropology in Theological Perspective)*. He has not substantially deviated from his early commitment to a theology which can justify itself in the realm of "public" intellectual discourse, by criteria that are not special to theology alone.

A different path has been followed by Jürgen Moltmann. Closer to Barth, and more particularly to Bonhoeffer, he produced, again in the 1960s, an important book entitled *Theology of Hope*, conceived as a kind of dialogue with the Marxist philosophy of Ernst Bloch. Christian faith is presented as a living under the judgment of God's future: that judgment is made concrete in our history by the raising of the crucified Jesus from the dead, the sign and promise that God does not let go of the humanly lost, the oppressed and murdered, the despairing, the "godless". This theme is taken up in Moltmann's perhaps most influential book, *The Crucified God*, where this account of Christian belief and identity is developed in close engagement with the unhealed and unhealable memory of the holocaust. Later works have discussed the theology of the church *(The Church in the Power of the Spirit)* and have presented a novel and provocative version of Trinitarian theology, underlining the idea that God's very being is lived out in suffering and the transformation of suffering *(Trinity and the Kingdom of God)*. Most recently, major studies towards a theology of the material environment have appeared *(God in Creation)*.

Moltmann has maintained an important dialogue with political trends in Europe and, increasingly, in the third world as well. Although his passionate commitment to the centrality of Jesus in the process of making sense of the human and material world still echoes Barth, his wide-ranging and often speculative engagement with politics and philosophy sets him very definitely apart. He has been — as has Pannenberg — an influential presence in

the ecumenical scene; both theologians have manifestly developed in unexpected and fresh directions through their participation in the work of the WCC from time to time, and it is no longer as true as it once was that so-called mainstream European theology is totally indifferent to movements in the rest of the Christian world.

Moltmann represents one flowering of the movement among several of Barth's pupils and followers towards a politically literate and critical theology. Helmut Gollwitzer, one of Barth's most loyal disciples, has been a prophetic voice on many issues in Germany over the last few decades: he and an older associate of Barth's, Ernst Wolf, were prominent in demanding a theological critique of German re-armament in the 1950s and in arguing that the possession of nuclear arms was a matter on which the church should make a "confessional" stand, as it had in opposition to the Third Reich. Gollwitzer has continued to write on the responsibilities of Europe to the poorer nations and on questions of war and peace and has directed several significant pieces of doctoral research into the borderlands of theology and politics.

Other figures in Germany have developed Barth's legacy in rather different ways. Less overtly political have been Eberhard Jüngel's monumental efforts in re-examining the meaning of the word "God"* against the background of the history of European atheism* *(God as Mystery of the World)*: he shares with Moltmann the conviction that only the theology of the cross can meet atheist charges against an indifferent ruler of the cosmos and is equally prepared to speak of suffering in God, even of death "in God"; but he is less interested in ecclesiology than is Moltmann and has not developed the theology of God's identification with the suffering into a programme of Christian solidarity with the oppressed to the same extent as Moltmann.

Roman Catholic theology in the 20th century in Europe offers a story of enormous upheavals and divergences. In the 1920s and 1930s, there were the beginnings of a new look at the theology of grace,* searching for a more personal and less mechanical understanding. These explorations, however, were conducted more in the sphere of philosophy than in that of theology. The French Jesuit Joseph Maréchal is probably the most important figure here, and his work was to bear fruit by way of its considerable influence on the great Karl Rahner, whose mature writing in the post-war period was one of the major formative elements in the thinking of the Second Vatican Council. Rahner's thought pivots around the conviction that the structure of human being as knowing and loving is intrinsically oriented to the divine, so that God is to be encountered wherever humanity is becoming authentically human. Christ is less the great interruption of the order of the human world than the fulfilment of the human subject's potential for union with God. The possibilities opened up in Rahner's work for dialogue with other faiths and ideologies have been eagerly taken up by a good many Catholic theologians working in non-Christian contexts.

Rahner was also much influenced by the "new theology", or *théologie nouvelle*, which developed in France in the post-war years. This represented a re-discovery of early Christian thought, especially the Greek fathers, as a source of theological wisdom more fertile for the 20th century than the rigid categories of medieval scholasticism. Typical of this school (whose leading names were Jean Daniélou, Henri de Lubac and Yves Congar) was a profound concern with the church* as an organic, living community, rather than an institution with members and hierarchy standing in a quasi-legal relation. The *théologie nouvelle* greatly influenced many writers in the Anglican tradition and opened new possibilities for conversation with Eastern Orthodox Christians; the entry of the Roman Catholic Church (RCC) into fuller involvement with international ecumenism, especially through the many bilateral dialogues now in process, owes an incalculable debt to this theological movement.

The two decades following Vatican II have seen more and more variety in Roman Catholic theology in Europe (let alone other continents). Hans Urs von Balthasar produced several multivolume works setting out an integral vision of theology as the contemplation of the paradoxical beauty of the work of God in Christ crucified; his concerns form a counterweight to those of Rahner, emphasizing the priority of revelation and repentance, as well as the central significance of the aesthetic dimension in religious understanding. Edward

Schillebeeckx, after writing important studies on the philosophical foundations of faith, much marked by the critical social philosophy of the Frankfurt school, and immensely influential studies in the theology of the eucharist,* has more recently published substantial books on Christology and some radical essays in the theology of Christian ministry, which have already had great impact outside the RCC itself (where they have been received with some hostility). Hans Küng, author of one of the earliest Catholic studies of Barth, has become well known as a critic of the present practice of papal authority and as a prolific writer on Christian themes for a general educated public. His views on ordained ministry are close to those of Schillebeeckx and have had similar reception inside and outside the Roman Catholic Church.

A fuller account of European theology would need to include more detail on the evolution of Eastern European thought, both Protestant and Orthodox. The experience of churches in a nominally socialist and often anti-religious atmosphere has generated some very different theological priorities and, in particular, the theology of the church as servant, popular in Romania in the 1970s, had an impact on the wider thought and language of the ecumenical movement. In recent years, some of the impetus towards a deeper engagement with the theological issues raised by the nuclear question has come from Eastern European churches, especially in Hungary and East Germany. Peace* has become a major concern for many European theologians in the past decade, and there now exist several international networks to further this discussion. The WCC's 1981 public hearing "Before It's Too Late: The Challenge of Nuclear Disarmament" included some pertinent material (for example, an article by Schillebeeckx on theology and disarmament). A broader discussion has opened out of this in the WCC project on "Justice, Peace and the Integrity of Creation",* picking up the themes which Moltmann and others had begun to treat connected with our theological perception of our belonging in the world, as both creatures and co-creatures. As European politics comes to be more and more attuned to "green" issues, there will be more and more need for this area to be explored by theologians.

A final area of development which must be

noted is a growing theological sensitivity in Europe to the complex questions arising from the growth of multicultural social patterns. These questions range from considerations of the theology of work (in connection with the issues of migrant labour) to the urgent issue of racism and the need for a more consistent and far-reaching theological critique, to the problems associated with interfaith dialogue.* It is a time of rapid movement and diversification in European theology; there seems little chance in the foreseeable future of any one systematic perspective emerging as dominant or claiming the kind of authority that was once attached to single names or schools.

See also **theology in the ecumenical movement**.

ROWAN WILLIAMS

D. Ford ed., *The Modern Theologians*, Oxford, Blackwell, 1989 • A. Heron, *A Century of Protestant Theology*, London, Lutterworth, 1980 • R. McBrien, *Catholicism*, London, Chapman, 1984 • A. McGrath, *The Making of Modern German Christology*, Oxford, Blackwell, 1986 • K. Rahner, "Aspekte europäischer Theologie", in his *Schriften zur Theologie*, vol. 15, Zurich, Benziger, 1983.

THEOLOGY, FEMINIST. The term "feminist theology" refers to a way of doing theology which takes seriously the criticism and conclusions of contemporary feminism.* It entails the self-conscious adoption of a critical feminist hermeneutic which is then applied to any, and all, of the individual disciplines which together compose "theology". Under the heading of feminist theology is to be found work on scripture, church history, doctrine, philosophy of religion and ethics. It is a theological method, then, rather than a branch of theology or area of study. Nor does the term refer simply to theology "done by women", as some women theologians would not consider themselves to be feminists, nor would they adopt this methodology. Alongside of this, it could be argued that if men can be feminists, then men can do feminist theology in so far as it involves a critique of the patriarchal underpinning of church and theology. The overwhelming majority of feminist theologians, not surprisingly, are women.

While the term "feminist theology" is a modern one, it is by no means a new phenomenon in that women have consistently challenged patriarchal presuppositions about their role and status within the church. In more recent times the work of the 19th-century American feminists Elizabeth Cady Stanton *(The Women's Bible)* and Matilda Joslyn Gage *(Woman, Church and State)* can be seen as a precursor to the kind of material being produced by contemporary feminist theologians. The origins of the modern movement are to be found in the US, during the 1960s, when scholars such as Mary Daly, Rosemary Radford Ruether and Judith Plaskow found an eager and receptive audience for their work. The development from these beginnings into an ecumenical and worldwide network of systematic scholarship has been rapid. This is no doubt due to the fact that feminist theology has been experienced by so many Christian women and men to be a liberating force in their lives. It has enabled them to make sense of their previously un-named sense of unease experienced within their church community.

The ecclesiological dimension of this work has clear implications for the modern ecumenical movement. Not only has received historical tradition about patterns of ministry and leadership been challenged by feminist scholars (and has obvious relevance to the debate within some churches regarding the ordination of women*), but there is also a creative re-visioning of what it is to *be* church.* While the work of some feminist theologians will clearly reflect the concerns of the particular church community to which they belong, the whole tenor of this scholarship is ecumenical. The tendency has been to extend and create networks of shared experience, knowledge and community. This has involved creative dialogue between women from different socio-political contexts; in the USA between white women and Afro-American women (who are developing what they term "womanist theology"); between Asian and African women and Western women, as well as dialogue between Christian women and women from other religious traditions, as is being encouraged by the WCC Sub-unit on Dialogue with People of Living Faiths. Groups such as the women's commission of the Ecumenical Association of Third World Theologians* clearly embody the guiding principle of modern ecumenism that "partners in dialogue should be free to define themselves".

A central concern of feminist theology is

the question of the use of language: the twin issues of inclusive language* and, perhaps more critically, of the language chosen to present images of God. The recovery of female images of the divine from scripture and tradition has been a first stage. The second is to ask the question why male images and language have been deemed more appropriate. Whereas traditionally Western theology has used philosophy, and liberation theology sociology, it may be that feminist theology (in asking psychological questions about human self-understanding) will use psychology as one of its major conceptual tools. Do women and men experience, and make sense of, the world in different ways? If so, do they experience God differently too? Has Christian theology been the record of only male "faith seeking understanding"? What would a doctrine of God based on women's experience be like? How far would this conform to what is generally perceived to be traditional Christian theology? And so on. Dealing with such questions leads contemporary feminist theology to be one of the most dynamic and creative fields of scholarship within theology today.

See also **women in church and society.**

DIANE M. BREWSTER

C.P. Christ & J. Plaskow eds, *Womanspirit Rising: A Feminist Reader in Religion*, San Francisco, Harper & Row, 1979 • V. Fabella & M.A. Oduyoye eds, *With Passion and Compassion. Third World Women Doing Theology. Reflections from the Women's Commission of Third World Theologians*, Maryknoll, NY, Orbis, 1988 • R. Ruether & E. McLaughlin eds, *Women of Spirit: Female Leadership in the Jewish and Christian Traditions*, New York, Simon & Schuster, 1979 • E. Schüssler Fiorenza & M. Collins eds, *Women: Invisible in Church and Theology* (= *Concilium*, 182, 1985).

THEOLOGY IN THE ECUMENICAL MOVEMENT.

Theological currents have been clearly shaping the ecumenical movement from its beginnings, and the emergence of the movement has been influencing developments in theology. Attempts to clarify the understanding of theology and its specific function in the movement are meagre. With diverse theological traditions and various methods of doing theology, one cannot easily reduce "theology" to a single definition, even a very general one. For the purposes of this article, however, I define "theology" as *that*

human activity by which the Christian community accounts for its faith.

To unfold this general formula, note that (1) theology is *human* reflection and must be distinguished from divine revelation;* (2) it takes place in the midst of, and is supported by, a Christian *community* of faith (see **church**): the theologian remains accountable to the community; (3) it can develop into a specialized, academic discipline, but this should not be considered as the norm; (4) it is related to doctrine (dogma*) but is not bound by it: as a living *account*, it responds to questions from within and from outside the community; and (5) theology is meaningful only on the basis of a *commitment of faith* which is not itself the result of theological argument.

These mainly descriptive, clarifying terms point to a number of critical issues or relationships: the relationship of theology and doctrine/dogma, or the issue of the *magisterium*, that is, teaching authority;* the relationship between theology and philosophy/secular sciences, or the issue of *methodology*; and the relationship between theology and church, or the issue of the *freedom* and the autonomy of theology.

The ambiguities which have developed around the Christian usage of the term "theology" can be traced to its origins in classical Greece. The Greek word *theo-logia* — literally, God-talk — has carried a double meaning since its emergence in the 5th century before Christ. It refers (1) to the act of religious and cultic proclamation through which the myths about divine reality are being passed on; and (2) to the critical, rational reflection about religious talk, subjecting its truth claims to certain basic rules.

The Christian reception* of the term "theology" began to spread from the 3rd and 4th centuries onwards (Origen, Eusebius of Caesarea). It is an expression of the Christian victory over pagan religion and is much less the result of the Hellenization of Christianity. Thus, theology is used primarily to refer to proclamation, confession or doxology with regard to God* (God-talk in the literal sense). This is distinguished from oikonomia, i.e. knowledge and teaching about the events of salvation.

The Eastern Orthodox understanding of theology remained close to this patristic tradition: theology is experiential rather than intellectual; it is mystical rather than rational; it is "apophatic", i.e. it respects the inaccessibility of God to human knowledge and therefore speaks of God in negative terms. The appropriate setting for theology in this tradition has remained the monastic community.

The specific Western, Roman understanding of theology emerged together with the development of the European university and the reception of Aristotelian philosophy (Aquinas). Theology now becomes the methodical exposition of revealed truth through rational argument. Scholastic theology appropriated philosophical categories to unfold the sacred doctrine of the faith. In this tradition, theology and the magisterium have remained closely linked.

The Reformation strove to liberate theology from the rigid, scholastic framework by recovering its existential character and by re-establishing its biblical framework. The specific profile of Protestant theology emerged only in the encounter with the Enlightenment and the rise of secular science and philosophy. Its characteristic features are the distinction between theology and religious praxis (spirituality), the distinction between historical and dogmatic theology, and the strong sense of autonomy vis-a-vis the institutional church. The academic community has become the general context for theological work.

Theological influences upon the ecumenical movement. The theological profile of the ecumenical movement has undergone several significant changes. The period before the first world war was shaped by the theology of the evangelical revival, a dominating non-intellectual lay theology. The WCC basis,* confessing "the Lord Jesus Christ as God and Saviour", comes out of this tradition and the concern to preserve and affirm the essential evangelical truths over against the spread of religious indifferentism. At the same time, the programme for the Edinburgh world missionary conference (1910) deliberately excluded questions of doctrine or theological issues which could become divisive. This non-denominational attitude is rooted in the affirmation of the Bible as the principal source and norm of Christian faith.

The second phase covered the period up to the years of crisis, 1929-32. It presents a very different profile. Ecumenically, this phase is marked by the emergence of the main branches of the ecumenical movement: the International Missionary Council* (IMC), the World Alliance for Friendship through the Churches,* and the two movements Faith and Order,* Life and Work.* Theologically, this period is shaped by a broad current of liberal theology with a strong sense of social responsibility (the so-called social gospel*) on the one hand, and on the other, by a more conservative, confessional theology of Lutheran or Anglo-Catholic persuasions. Strong tensions erupted between different theological orientations at the conferences of Life and Work at Stockholm (1925) and of the International Missionary Council at Jerusalem (1928). Within this diversity, the influence of liberal Protestantism remained dominant.

The third phase lasted up to the end of the second world war. It bears the mark of the increasing influence of dialectical theology (Karl Barth, Emil Brunner, Paul Tillich and others), known in the USA also as neo-orthodox theology (Reinhold Niebuhr). The main features which influenced the development of the ecumenical movement were the radical criticism of the liberal convictions of the preceding period and the struggle for the independence of theology from cultural patterns by affirming its dependency only on divine revelation through holy scripture.

Joined to this critical theological mood were a renewal of the tradition of Reformation theology, a fresh encounter with Orthodox and particularly with patristic theology through Russian theologians-in-exile (Nicolas Berdyaev, Sergius Bulgakov, Paul Evdokimov and Georges Florovsky) and in all of this, a re-discovery of the integrity of the church in confrontation with secular ideologies.*

Never before had a similar effort to draw academic theologians into ecumenical work been made as that undertaken by J.H. Oldham for the Oxford Life and Work conference in 1937. This conference and those of F&O (1937) and of the IMC (1938) came closest to developing a "recognized theology" of the ecumenical movement.

This close identification of the ecumenical movement with the prevailing theological orientation in theology faculties and seminaries continued through the fourth phase, until the early 1960s. Building on earlier foundations, the profound crisis of the world war was overcome by a re-discovery of the Bible and its relevance in opening up a new understanding of God's purposes in history* ("salvation history"*). Biblical theology became the common framework of orientation. It affirmed the unity of the Bible as the faithful and uncorrupted witness of God's history of salvation.* Jesus Christ* as the centre of the history of salvation also became the central point of reference for the interpretation of the entire Bible. This Christocentrism was accepted as the undisputed principle of theological orientation in the ecumenical movement, as can be seen in the various intensive theological studies carried out within the WCC during these years.

The years immediately after the war also saw a new departure in Roman Catholic theology, which in fact prepared the ground for the later openings towards the ecumenical movement through Vatican II.* The so-called *théologie nouvelle* (1945-50), with its centre in France (Yves Congar, Henri de Lubac and others), broke through the limitations of scholasticism and appropriated the re-discovery of patristic theology and of the church (see **theology, new**). The *théologie nouvelle* could build on the earlier RC movements for liturgical and for biblical renewal, as well as on the lay movement (Action catholique, since 1923). The encyclical *Humani Generis* (1950) put a provisional stop to this advance, but during these years contacts between theologians were established in France, the Netherlands and Germany, and their efforts bore fruit at Vatican II. This council marks the high point of theological influence on the church and the ecumenical movement.

The fifth phase began in the early 1960s. The close relationship between theology, Bible and church began to break up. The "systematic theologies" of Barth, Tillich, Niebuhr and others, which had formed the minds of a whole generation of ecumenical leaders, were slowly losing their dominating influence. Just as the Montreal F&O conference (1963) marked the crisis of "biblical theology", so the 1966 Geneva conference on Church and Society marked the re-discovery of the prophetic tradition of theology by discerning the signs of God's "revolutionary" action in history.

More and more, the search for a relevant, living theology (black, political, liberation) began to influence the ecumenical agenda. The advocates of an inductive, dialogic way of "doing theology" were challenging classical deductive approaches. Since the early 1970s "contextualization" has become the focus of this new theological orientation in the ecumenical movement (see **theology, contextual**). Contextualization accepts, but goes beyond, the claim that relevant theology must be rooted in a given historical and cultural setting. "Authentic contextualization always is prophetic" (Shoki Coe). Growing out of a genuine encounter between gospel and culture,* it aims to challenge and transform the given historical situation, guided by the vision of the reign of God. Around these convictions the Ecumenical Association of Third World Theologians,* formed in 1976, has begun to influence the ecumenical movement.

While the inculturation* of theology has been promoted mainly by academic theologians, contextualization challenges theology to re-insert itself into the life of the Christian community. Thus, the quest for new ways of doing theology leads to the new discussion about practical ecclesiology; that is, the appropriate community base from which a relevant and living theology can grow and to which it remains accountable. The formula "theology by the people" expresses this new theological consciousness.

While these developments have opened fresh perspectives for theology, the growing diversity which goes along with contextualization has become a challenge, if not a threat, to the inner coherence and unity of the ecumenical movement. While the movement certainly needs the challenge of a critical and prophetic theology which presses for radical renewal and a re-assessment of inherited tradition, it also needs the assurance of a theological coherence which provides for a sense of continuity. Therefore, the call by the 1983 WCC Vancouver assembly for a "vital and coherent theology" remains timely and appropriate.

Ecumenical influences on theology. Eight decades of the growing ecumenical movement have left their mark on theology — on its self-understanding and its praxis. Four significant themes show the influence of this movement upon theology.

First, *all theology must be rooted in the biblical witness*. This is not a new criterion for doing theology but has been recognized since the time of patristic theology. For a long time in the Western traditions, however, theology had accepted the constraints of philosophical logic. The ecumenical movement has helped to liberate theology from this captivity. The lively debates about biblical authority, the relationship between scripture* and Tradition,* as well as between context and tradition — in short, the whole hermeneutical debate during 1950-80 — makes sense only as long as one accepts the criterion formulated above. Thus, the most notable ecumenical advance in theology has been the broad co-operation between theologians from different traditions in the area of biblical translation and interpretation (note the French *Traduction oecuménique de la Bible* and the various series of biblical commentaries which are written and published ecumenically).

As the Bible is being liberated from dogmatic captivity, it is being read with new eyes and is beginning to challenge theology. Traditional theology does have a sharpened historical consciousness of the fact that the meaning of the Bible is only in the reading, and the reading itself is conditioned by the experience of a given, present reality. But traditional theology has difficulties in responding to the challenges that are emerging from the new readings of the Bible which are taking shape among Christian communities in Asia, Africa and Latin America. What these communities expect from theology is not primarily translation, analysis and interpretation of a biblical "text" but rather mediation between the biblical story and the life story of peoples today. Reading, in the sense of entering into dialogue with the Bible, is in itself an encounter of life with life. Theological reflection about different readings of the Bible thus becomes a paradigm for the ecumenical dialogue of cultures.

Second, *all theology is being shaped by and is accountable to the life of the Christian community*. There is no entirely autonomous theology. The validity of theology, in the end, depends on its spiritual reception* in the community of faith. A fruit of the ecumenical movement and the inspiration it has provided for the re-discovery of the church is that most acknowledge the inseparable linkage between theology and the church. The dynamics of this

A man studying at his home in Western Samoa (WCC/Peter Williams)

relationship, however, give rise to passionate discussions within and between the different churches and traditions. The positions range from the classical RC stance, which subjects theology to the magisterium of the church, entrusted to the bishops — together with and under the pope — to the radical Protestant affirmation of the critical task of theology vis-a-vis the church, which presupposes that theology should be free from hierarchical control. There are many positions in between these two extremes; however, each position carries with it an implicit ecclesiology which one should openly acknowledge.

To affirm the linkage between theology and the life of the Christian community is to call in question the current separation of academic theology from spiritual praxis. In fact, one of the crucial ecumenical discoveries is that the first act of theology is doxological.

Third, *all theology is contextual; there is no universal theology*. This is perhaps the most far-reaching change in the perception of theology which the ecumenical movement has brought about. Over against a tradition of theology which has accepted a metaphysical, timeless framework of universally valid propositions, the ecumenical movement is requiring theology to face up to the radical historicity of human existence. Theology, as a human activity, is subjected to the limitations of space and time. The ecumenical movement makes us recognize that we live in the same space, on the same earth, but not in the same time. A universal theology presupposes simultaneity, but only oppression and domination could achieve that.

The affirmation that there is no universal theology seems to undermine one of the very purposes of the ecumenical movement, i.e. to bring about the unity of the church by way of agreements on the essential truths of the Christian faith. To the extent that the intensive theological dialogues between the churches lead to growing agreement, even beyond the essential truth, it becomes apparent that quite a number of the original reasons for separation were "non-theological", that is, contextual. The same is true for those factors which prevent the churches from entering into full communion with one another.

Contextual theology is "local" theology. It is in danger at any time of falling into theological provincialism, of becoming self-

sufficient. Confessionalism in theology is the result of an earlier process of contextualization which has turned rigid. The contextual character of theology calls for mutual accountability in dialogue. Dialogue is the proper mode of doing theology in the ecumenical movement, over against the apologetic defensiveness of traditional theology.

Finally, *theology belongs to the whole people of God*.* With this affirmation the survey has come full cycle. The ecumenical movement began in a setting which was characterized by an evangelical, non-academic understanding of theology; it was far removed both from the cathedral and the faculty. Some generations later, theology had gained a prominent place in the ecumenical movement. The theological experts and specialists were put in the centre of the ecumenical discussion. At the same time, the ecumenical movement began to re-discover and affirm the role of laypeople. Meanwhile, there is growing recognition that theology not only arises from the people but belongs to them — not a theology for the people, but a "theology by the people". True, there may be agreement that theology is the continuous effort to account for the faith in response to questions and challenges. But the decisive issues then become: Where do the challenges come from? What are valid questions which merit a theological response?

For a long time the questions and challenges which theology took up arose from within the intellectual, academic community. The ecumenical movement has helped in broadening the basis beyond the seminaries, colleges, faculties and professionals. The basis now includes groups and networks which are involved in theological reflection in the context of social and political conflicts. Important as this opening of the traditional understanding of theology may be, it is at best a half-way step towards implementing the programmatic stance of theology by the people.

What, then, is the role of academic theology in the ecumenical movement? It has the indispensable function of working out and enforcing the rules and the criteria which are needed to keep the dialogue between different contextual theologies alive, to keep theological activity authentic. Academic theology is not an end in itself; it is meant to serve and support the theology by the people. The partner and addressee of theological reflection should, therefore, be much less the non-believing, secular person than the person who is involved in the struggle for human dignity. At this critical point the ecumenical movement most disturbs academic theology.

See also **Bible in the ecumenical movement; church; theology, ecumenical**.

KONRAD RAISER

S. Amirtham & J. Pobee eds, *Theology by the People: Reflections on Doing Theology in Community*, WCC, 1986 • E. Flesseman-van Leer ed., *The Bible: Its Authority and Interpretation in the Ecumenical Movement*, WCC, 1980 • *The Humanum Studies: 1969-1975*, WCC, 1975 • *Ministry in Context*, London, Theological Education Fund, 1972 • "Reflections on the Methods of Faith and Order Study", in *Minutes Accra, 1974*, WCC • "Theological Issues of Church and Society", *Study Encounter*, 4, 2, 1968 • W.A. Visser 't Hooft, "Teachers and the Teaching Authority: The Magistri and the Magisterium", *The Ecumenical Review*, 38, 2, 1986.

THEOLOGY, LIBERATION. Although "liberation"* is a correct translation of the biblical vocabulary of salvation*/redemption,* only very recently has it found a significant place in theological vocabulary. Its basic concerns, however, have been present in different forms throughout Christian history. As a general designation, liberation theology refers to several contemporary expressions of theology which intend to reflect on the presence and power of God* in the life and struggles of oppressed people (women and certain races, classes and groups) in the light of God's redemptive purpose manifested in Jesus Christ.* Since oppression is a many-sided phenomenon, such struggles have economic, political, cultural and spiritual dimensions. Liberation theologies, trying to be faithful at the same time both to God's purpose of a fullness of life that integrates all these dimensions and to the particular conditions of the context, have taken different characteristics as feminist, black, African or Asian theologies (see the relevant **theology** entries), while recognizing their basic unity and engaging in a dialogue which has found one important institutional form in the Ecumenical Association of Third World Theologians.*

In the singular, liberation theology is generally identified with its Latin American expression, which has used this name since Rubem Alves's and Gustavo Gutiérrez's books of 1971, the second of which was entitled *Theology of Liberation: Perspectives*. The origins of this theology in Latin America can be traced to the growing participation of Christian priests, ministers and laypeople in the life and struggles of the large poor* majorities to overcome the condition of marginalization, poverty and oppression. Such participation generated a deep spiritual commitment to the poor, an awareness of the destructive nature of their conditions, an admiration for the solidarity, depth and resourcefulness which these people manifested and a need to understand better the social, economic and political structures which caused such situations.

Theologically, the biblical and theological developments in European theology emphasizing the historical nature of God's revelation* and the relevance of fundamental biblical categories like justice,* shalom and eschatology* for social change influenced some younger theologians. For Roman Catholic ones, these influences found expression in Vatican II;* for Protestants they were received through the ecumenical movement, and specifically the Church and Society commission of the WCC. Between 1960 and 1980 a number of theological essays explored methodological questions for the articulation of a Latin American liberation theology: the use of social analysis and therefore the need for an interdisciplinary dialogue with the social sciences (Hugo Assmann, Julio de Santa Ana, Franz Hinkelammert, Joseph Comblin, Juan Luis Segundo), the need for a hermeneutics* in the use of scripture and Tradition (Segundo, José Croatto, Pablo Richard), the significance of praxis both as epistemological instrument and as verification principle (Gutiérrez, Clodovis Boff). But at the same time certain theological themes demanded particular attention: Christology (Leonardo Boff, Jon Sobrino, Segundo, Raul Vidales), ecclesiology (Segundo, Sobrino, L. Boff), the doctrine of God (Victorio Araya, L. Boff, Ronaldo Muñoz). The collection entitled *Teología y Liberación* tries to respond more systematically to this need.

There is little doubt, however, that the strength of this theology rests particularly on the expansion of the church base communities* throughout Latin America, from which the theology receives inspiration and insight and to which it contributes. In this sense the question of a spirituality related to the quest for liberation is of fundamental importance. The songs, prayers and liturgical and sacramental celebrations are at least as important as the formal theological articulations for an understanding of liberation theology.

Liberation theology is ecumenical in its origin, expression and intention, while it remains closely related to the life of the churches. The Vatican Congregation for the Doctrine of the Faith has issued two instructions concerning liberation theology, the first as a warning against the danger of "certain liberation theologies" becoming forms of reductionism or ideologization; the second, establishing some principles for a right understanding of freedom and liberation. In a letter to Brazilian bishops, Pope John Paul II stated that a theology of liberation is "both necessary and opportune". Although the WCC has never explicitly discussed liberation theology, the general concern for liberation has been present in different forms and especially in the Nairobi assembly's theme: "Jesus Christ Frees and Unites". Latin America liberation theology was discussed at the Christian education meeting (Lima 1971), and references to black theology appear in Bangkok 1973 and to feminist theology in Berlin 1974 in a way that is affirmative but not developed. It has nevertheless been implicitly present in such WCC programmes as "The Church and the Poor" and the political ethics consultation of Cyprus (1981) of the Commission on the Churches' Participation in Development, in the Human Rights Resources Office for Latin America and in the Programme to Combat Racism.

JOSÉ MÍGUEZ BONINO

C. Boff & L. Boff, *Introducing Liberation Theology*, Maryknoll, NY, Orbis, 1987 • G. Gutiérrez, *A Theology of Liberation*, Maryknoll, Orbis, NY, 1988 • J. Míguez Bonino, *Doing Theology in a Revolutionary Situation*, Philadelphia, Fortress, 1975.

THEOLOGY, MINJUNG. Minjung theology is an indigenous theology of politics and culture* that has developed in South Korea in recent years. "Minjung" is a Korean word for people,* mass, or the masses of people, but it refers specifically to the oppressed vis-a-vis the oppressors, or to the poor* over against the rich and powerful. Thus, minjung theology may mean a theology by the people, for the people, and of the people. It emerged out of Christian concern for and solidarity* with the economically exploited, politically oppressed and socially marginalized peoples in South Korea in the 1970s. It is a theological endeavour by the whole people of God.*

Minjung theology developed out of the political struggle of Korean Christians. In the 1970s, Korea's oppressive military dictatorship silenced nearly all of its political opposition, denying the people their fundamental human rights. In addition, the regime imposed a "development" ideology upon the people, which created a wide gap between the rich and the poor in the country, denied the people's right to form labour unions, and created massive poverty in both the industrial urban and rural areas of the nation. Many Korean Christians resisted the dictatorship and the ideology thus imposed. This was especially the case with student activist groups such as the Korean Student Christian Federation and the Ecumenical Youth Council, as well as the Urban Industrial Mission, Church Women United and the Human Rights Commission of the National Council of Churches. These groups organized Christian movements which entered into solidarity with the urban and rural poor in the struggle for justice and democratization in Korea. Minjung theology is a faith reflection of, by and for the people in their struggle against oppression; it is a political theology of liberation developing from the people's struggle towards and within the kingdom of God.*

Out of the experiences of suffering* and struggle against oppressive powers, and with the eyes of the poor, minjung theologians read and interpret the Bible. For minjung theology, God is working in human history to liberate the suffering people of God. Jesus himself was of the minjung and a friend of the minjung; he suffered, died, and was raised with and for the minjung. Of central importance to minjung theology is this minjung Jesus who is on the side of the poor and oppressed for their liberation. The gospel and the Jesus-event are interpreted from the perspective of the poor and oppressed, and in turn the Jesus-event interprets the struggles of the minjung. Thus the history of the liberation struggle of the minjung is seen from the perspective of the presence of God in and through the person and work of Jesus.

As minjung theologians struggle with the people for their liberation, they also identify with and reflect upon events in the history of the Korean poor which highlight the peoples' quest for freedom and dignity. One such event was the student revolution of 1960, which toppled the corrupt political regime of President Syngman Rhee. Other events include the independence movement of 1 March 1919 against Japan's harsh imperial rule, and the 1894 Donghak farmers' rebellion against the brutal feudal bureaucracy imposed by the Confucian kingdom of Chosun. In minjung theology, the irrepressible struggle of the people for their liberation in history is viewed as a movement of the Holy Spirit* and a source of power, which names the minjung as the true subjects of history.

In addition to history, minjung theologians also perceive that culture is a source of power for people's liberation. The Korean minjung express and celebrate their life in music, drama and masked dances which are distinct from those of the rulers and the Confucian aristocrats, particularly in the minjung farm dances, where the music is rhythmic and throbbing and where it calls forth dynamic and often frenzied dancing steps and motions, and the minjung mask dance, which gives satirical expression to the people's sublimated grief, anger and frustration *(han)* over against their oppressors. In attempting to give theological understanding to these various expressions, minjung theologians perceive that they are indigenous forms of "confessing", resistance and empowerment; they are Spirit-infused cultural expressions of the minjung for their liberation from oppression.

Minjung theology, therefore, is an indigenous theology deeply rooted in the culture and religions of the Korean people, and it takes the Bible very seriously. It takes seriously the developments in Latin American liberation theology and uses openly the language of that theology, for example, "God's preferential option for the poor", the hermeneutical "sus-

picion", and "Jesus the liberator". In addition, minjung theology follows Latin American liberation theology in its limited use of Marxist analysis of political economics, and gives its own critical analysis of the ideologies of militarization and economic development, which are the principal "idols" oppressing the people in contemporary Korea. It has links also with the liberation theologies that have developed in other Asian countries and has had a certain ecumenical impact, chiefly through the work of the Christian Conference of Asia.*

Minjung theology has made story-telling an indispensable part of its hermeneutics,* and in that sense it differs from Latin American liberation theology. Minjung theologians originated the phrase "socio-biography of the minjung", and they have made the stories of the minjung — their suffering, their *han*, their struggles against oppressive powers — central to their theological methodology. Minjung theology in this sense is essentially narrative theology; it is a vehicle through which the stories of the joy and the grief, failure and success, laughter and tears of the minjung are faithfully gathered, told and interpreted, as a means for their liberation.

Minjung theology takes seriously the feminist liberation movement; Korean feminist theologians argue that Korean women are the "minjung of minjungs". Minjung theology condemns the sexist exploitation of the poor and the patriarchal systems which discriminate against women, whether in the church or society. It is now being developed in minjung church movements among labourers, the urban poor, and farmers, confessing faith in Jesus Christ who is in solidarity with the people in their daily struggles for economic and political rights against the present oppressive regime.

Minjung theology is in the vanguard of those addressing the tragic division of Korea between the North and the South, the consequence of decisions imposed on the Korean people by super-powers following the second world war. It defines the Korean people forced to live under the present divided structures of government and ideology as minjung. The theologians are active in the movement for peace and re-unification in Korea, and minjung theology articulates a theology of peace and re-unification, of justice and reconciliation.

See also **liberation, struggles for; people**.

DAVID KWANG-SUN SUH

Y.B. Kim, *Minjung Theology: People as the Subjects of History*, Singapore, CCA, 1981 • J.Y. Lee ed., *An Emerging Theology in World Perspective: Commentary on Korean Minjung Theology*, Mystic, CT, Twenty-Third Publications, 1988 • C. Moon, *A Korean Minjung Theology: An Old Testament Perspective*, Maryknoll, NY, Orbis, 1985.

"THEOLOGY, NEW" (Roman Catholic *théologie nouvelle*).

The expression *théologie nouvelle* came into existence in (French) Roman Catholic circles, mainly in the 1940s, in an attempt to discredit the renewal of theological methods using history, exegesis, patristics and liturgy at the expense of a rigid scholastic methodology. The term occasioned a public controversy which developed after the appearance of the book by Henri Bouillard, SJ, entitled *Conversion et grâce chez saint Thomas d'Aquin: Etude historique* (Conversion and grace in St Thomas Aquinas: A historical study, 1944).

This "new theology" was never an organized movement, even if an article by Jean Daniélou on present trends and religious thought ("Les orientations présentes et la pensée religieuse", *Etudes*, 1946) has sometimes been represented as a kind of manifesto. The expression appeared in an article by Monsignor Parente, definito of the holy office, in the *Osservatore Romano* of 9-10 February 1942. This article, entitled "Nuove tendenze teologiche" (New theological trends), condemned criticism of scholastic theology and put it in the same category as modernist trends. Also, an article by M. Cordovani in the *Osservatore Romano* of 22 March 1940 had prepared the way by its criticism of a supposed "theological renewal" relating to ecclesiology, ecumenism and ethics. These various criticisms came to a head with the publication of the encyclical *Humani Generis* in 1950, which afforded Réginald Garrigou-Lagrange a further opportunity to write one of his many articles in which he lumped this theology together with modernism, sentimental Romanticism, empiricism, Kantianism, scepticism, Pierre Teilhard de Chardin and even heresy.* This controversy, then, though indeed limited both in time and geographically, clearly epitomized the polemics hurled by the "official theologians" at the "theological renewals" of that time.

This controversy was limited to a few main centres: on the one hand Rome, supported by St Maximin and the *Revue thomiste*, and on the other Fourvière and Louvain with certain Jesuits, and Le Saulchoir with some Dominicans. One of the immediate issues was the interpretation of "Thomism", which had been established as an official theology. By showing a development in Thomas's thought on the question of grace,* Bouillard seemed to be relativizing a deductive, narrowly rationalist scholastic method in which the role of the fathers and of scripture was simply to provide a more effective confirmation of a hidebound, authoritative theology. But there was something immoderate in these polemics, and so the main surviving witnesses now tend to play down the arguments of that period, the more so since the theologians who were referred to at the time were to a great extent those who inspired Vatican II (M.-D. Chenu, Bouillard, Henri de Lubac, but also Daniélou and Hans Urs von Balthasar). Also, some prelates, especially the cardinals of Paris and Toulouse, had officially come to their defence in and after 1946. And while Pius XII on 17 and 22 September 1946 had expressly condemned the "new theology" in addresses to the Jesuits and the Dominicans, Monsignor Parente was to rehabilitate them publicly in a speech given at the Urbaniana University in Rome on 11 November 1967.

This controversy, however, still has a highly symbolic significance because it points clearly to the great biblical, patristic, liturgical and historical renewals which were to be legitimized at Vatican II in the Roman Catholic Church. For far from being an argument primarily of the French among themselves (on both sides of the Alps), this discussion indicated the limits of post-Tridentine thinking and Roman Catholic authoritarian centralism both in France and also beyond the Rhine and in Belgium. This centralism was challenged in regard to its methods of justifying theological positions by recourse to the fathers, the liturgy, scripture and the historical method. It is not by chance that Monsignor Parente in 1942, in his criticism of the "new

theology", also evoked the name of Johann Adam Möhler (the 19th-century Roman Catholic church historian), whose work was published by Yves Congar in the series *Unam Sanctum* immediately after *Chrétiens désunis* (Disunited Christians) in 1937, the same year as Chenu's book.

But conversely Monsignor Bruno de Solages came to the defence of theological pluralism just at the time when a group of Jesuits, in reply to attacks made on them, wrote in the *Recherches de science religieuse* of 1946 that the Christian revelation is not first and foremost "the communication of a system of ideas" but "the revelation of a person" and that "the church has always in the past accepted the freedom of theological schools within the same orthodoxy". Certain notes had already been struck which were to be strongly sounded by Vatican II — especially the Constitutions on Revelation, on the Church, and on the Liturgy, the Decree on Ecumenism, and the affirmation of the "hierarchy of truths".*

BERNARD LAURET

G. Alberigo, M.-D. Chenu, E. Fouilloux, J.-P. Jossua & J. Ladrière, *Une école de théologie: Le Saulchoir*, Paris, Cerf, 1985 • A. Avellino Estaban, "Nota bibliográfica sobre la llamada 'Teología Nueva'", *Revista española de teología*, 1949, pp.303-18 and 527-46 • R. Winling, *La théologie contemporaine (1945-1980)*, Paris, Centurion, 1983.

THEOLOGY, NORTH AMERICAN.

Today there is a division developing between those who write the history of North American theology (here limited to the US, and largely to Protestants) as success story and those who write it self-critically. North American theology in the critical mode is becoming distinct in the ecumenical movement, for example, on account of its examination *theologically* of conquest and colonialism.* Initially evoked by black theology,* but also influenced by other ethnic theologies (Native American, for example), and especially by feminist theology,* the critical mode is now expressing the strong hope for a new oikoumene.

As the story of North American theology is usually told, it moved from Puritanism with Cotton Mather (1663-1728) and Jonathan Ed-

wards (1703-58) to Unitarianism with William Ellery Channing (1780-1842); from neo-Puritanism with Nathaniel William Taylor (1786-1858) and liberalism with Horace Bushnell (1802-76) to the social gospel* with Walter Rauschenbusch (1861-1918). Through it all one can discover, among a wide variety of specifically North American concerns, a major anthropological interest, with Edwards already stressing the power of reason to discover truth, even the truth of God. Unitarianism moved the intellect into close proximity to the divine perfections. With neo-Puritanism we are close to the rejection of the dogma of original sin. From then on, it was usually free game for a celebration of the anthropological emphasis, though the social gospel was followed by neo-orthodoxy and a revival of orthodoxy with fundamentalist and "evangelical" ramifications. In recent times the Niebuhr brothers stand out in influence and stature, Reinhold Niebuhr (1892-1971) re-issuing ideas of Luther, and H. Richard Niebuhr (1894-1962) re-stating partly the work of Friedrich Schleiermacher in combination with ideas of Ernst Troeltsch and Karl Barth. Paul Tillich (1886-1965) had a vast influence. But he too ultimately centred on anthropological dimensions of faith. For many, though, the peculiarly North American achievement would be the retention of a measure of Constantinian orthodoxy under long-standing conditions of religious pluralism.* In this view, liberalism functions widely as a kind of modified orthodoxy.

More or less within this conventional framework a number of North American theologians have in recent decades made significant contributions to ecumenism on the world scene. Georges Florovsky, Alexander Schmemann and John Meyendorff have proved invaluable in mediating Eastern Orthodoxy to the Western churches. J.C. Murray was influential in the treatment of religious liberty* at Vatican II,* while his fellow Jesuit Avery Dulles has helped to re-shape Roman Catholic thinking on the church* in such books as *Models of the Church* (1974), *A Church to Believe In* (1982), and *The Catholicity of the Church* (1985). Protestant contributions to Faith and Order* range from the ecclesiological studies of J.R. Nelson (*The Realm of Redemption*, 1951) and P.S. Minear (*Images of the Church*, 1960), through the

work of Albert Outler on scripture and Tradition* around Montreal 1963, to the part played by Geoffrey Wainwright in the BEM (see **Baptism, Eucharist and Ministry**) process and his advocacy of the ecumenically healing potential of a doxological approach to doctrine (*Doxology*, 1980). Harvey Cox epitomized many themes of the 1960s in *The Secular City* (1965).

In the middle of the 19th century Phillip Schaff observed that North American church history, with the exception of a few insignificant sects and the obviously influential idea of the separation of church and state, "had not produced anything original that could be viewed as church-historical event". This is still very much the case. The more academic theologies at least initially perpetuated European models of thought. Popular theology, however, soon tried to legitimate the conquest of the continent, sanctioning the genocide of the Native American. It was continued in a slave-holder theology summed up in 1850 by Iveson I. Brookes of South Carolina: "Next to the gift of his Son to redeem the human race God never displayed in more lofty sublimity his attributes, than in the institution of slavery." North American popular theology has always curried favour with the successful. The modern televangelists are obvious examples. And yet academic theology often has not been lagging far behind. The new effort demands research in the history of US academic theology in view of the deep chasm between the gospel and North American religious reality. Since the publication of Martin E. Marty's *Righteous Empire*, it is no longer possible to overlook the difference between theologies of the American empire and a self-critical approach.

The present situation is characterized by a deep struggle over the character of God* and the reality of Jesus either as ultimately untouched by the reality of poverty and injustice or as uncompromisingly struggling against it. This debate involves the most radical struggle over the authority of the Bible the 20th century has seen in the US.

FREDERICK HERZOG

S.M. Cavert, *Church Cooperation and Unity in America: A Historical Review, 1900-1970*, New York, Association Press, 1970 ● R.W. Jenson, *America's Theologian: A Recommendation of Jonathan Edwards*, New York, Oxford UP, 1988 ● G. Marsden ed., *Evangelicalism and Modern America*, Grand Rapids, MI, Eerdmans, 1984 ● M.E. Marty, *Righteous Empire*, New York, Dial, 1970.

THEOLOGY, PACIFIC. Pacific theology is a contextual theology, growing out of the Pacific soil and waters; it is concerned to bring the gospel of Jesus Christ to bear on contemporary sociological, political, environmental and religious events as well as on the future of the region. It seeks to put faith,* gospel and religion in the local Pacific soil and context so that these may exist meaningfully in the local climate.

For 150 years the Pacific has been described as a mission field — missionaries came from the North to "the ends of the earth", the periphery of the world, to proclaim the good news. They came with such theology as they knew in their context, a Western theology conditioned by their history, culture and circumstances. Now Pacific islands are independent nations, and the churches are autonomous. Missionary trends have changed; the Pacific is no longer the periphery for "sending churches" to evangelize, and foreign missionaries are no longer the major personnel; now Pacific islanders are missionaries to themselves. Since the Pacific islanders can never be like the Western missionaries, Pacific churches desire that the revelation* of God in the history* and cultures of peoples shall also be good news in the history and culture* of the Pacific region.

The effectiveness of Christ's birth in Bethlehem, his crucifixion at Calvary and the descent of the Spirit at Pentecost* in Jerusalem was immediate and simultaneous to every part and every people of the world. Indeed, the good news was present in the Pacific before the missionaries' arrival. The missionaries from the North came to enable the Pacific to re-discover and name what was already there. Pacific theology then illustrates, in the light of the gospel and from the Pacific history, culture and customs, what God is like and is doing in revelation and salvation.*

In going about this task, they follow the principle of what Christ did, using his environment (e.g. animals of Palestine, mustard seed, fish, farmers) to contextualize the

ecumenicity and catholicity* of the gospel. Pacific theology uses the ever-present environment of coconut, kava, betel nuts, hibiscus, orchids, yams and taro — Pacific delicacies — to articulate the good news of Jesus Christ, hence such designations of Pacific theology as betel nut theology (in Papua New Guinea) or coconut theology (in Fiji and Tonga). These are varieties in a genus. They may be limited in so far as the symbols are from a regional context, but the applied theology is universal and ecumenical.

Pacific life is characterized by celebration. The life-cycle of birth, puberty, marriage and death is marked by feasting and celebration, which also refurbishes the sense of community. A community is so by virtue of co-operation of its members, inclusiveness of the extended family, sharing, and caring, particularly for the aged. The symbol of Maori tiki is three fingers, representing their solidarity and their unity, in which happiness is found. Characteristic of Pacific theology, then, are the emphases on solidarity and unity, very much the opposite of the individualism of Western theology.

Two statements of coconut theology with regard to Christology and eucharist* should illustrate Pacific theology. The coconut is the key Christological image because the coconut is the life of the Pacific. The tree has many potentialities as drink and food, its branches for shelter, housing and fuel, its raffia for mats. To drink it is to draw nourishment by "kissing" it. It falls from the tree only in the fullness of life. Thus the image of the coconut encapsules biblical Christology: the virgin birth and the incarnation* are in the coconut. The full potential of new life is in the coconut, and when it is ready (fullness), the new life breaks through its sprouts and is rooted in the soil, growing towards heaven. The glimpses of death and resurrection* are also present because "a seed must die in order to live". At the final end, the world powers forced him to the earth's womb, intending to keep him there with the Roman seal and to say "the end has come". But instead of the expected end, the shell cracked and the resurrection took place; a new full-grown coconut came to its own.

In the earliest eucharistic celebration Jesus used unleavened bread and wine, the very common elements in society. In the Pacific these elements are not only expensive and difficult to come by but also very foreign. To use coconut for eucharistic celebration is more relevant because it is to bring the common and the familiar into the orbit of the Holy Spirit in the ritual act. Besides, the coconut is both drink and food from the same fruit, even as the blood and flesh are from the one and same body of Christ.

With other third-world theologies, Pacific theology claims that the eternal Word of God* seeks an encounter with every people as they are and that no group may be assimilated to another group. Pacific theology is the symbol that the islanders have taken their place among the "great multitude which no one could number, from every nation, from all tribes and peoples and tongues, standing before the throne and before the Lamb... crying out with a loud voice, 'Salvation belongs to our God who sits upon the throne, and to the Lamb'" (Rev. 7:9-10).

Pacific theology is in the process of creation, and most of it is in oral form. But it is a reality which can be ignored only to the detriment of the fullness of the ecumenical movement.

SIONE 'AMANAKI HAVEA

C. Forman, *The Island Churches of the Pacific*, Maryknoll, NY, Orbis, 1982 • J. Garrett, *To Live among the Stars*, WCC, 1982 • J.D. May ed., *Living Theology in Melanesia: A Reader*, Goroka, Papua New Guinea, Melanesian Institute for Pastoral and Socio-Economic Service, 1985 • G.W. Trompf, *The Gospel Is Not Western*, Maryknoll, NY, Orbis, 1987.

THEOLOGY, POLITICAL. Political theology arose in Europe in the 1960s and 1970s in reaction to the privatizing tendencies in existentialist interpretations of Christianity that emphasized personal encounter as the appropriate framework within which to understand the Christian gospel. Political theology sought to make clear the public nature of the eschatological message. What is promised is not just a new self-understanding for the individual but a new society. Even when addressing the individual, the fact remains that the person is embedded in a social milieu which must be addressed at the same time, if one is to speak to the real situation. For human existence is by nature political. Moreover, the God of the Bible is not "apolitical" (Jürgen

Moltmann), a neutral observer of the human situation, but a partisan in the struggle against the forces of injustice. It follows that there is no apolitical theology. A theology which is not calling for change is in effect legitimating the status quo, whether it intends to or not.

Discernable in the thought of the leading representatives of political theology, Johann Metz and Jürgen Moltmann, is the influence of the Frankfurt school of critical sociology (Jürgen Habermas, Max Horkheimer, Theodor Adorno) and the philosopher Ernst Bloch's exploration of utopian thinking. Political theology does not seek to "mix religion and politics" but disavows the alliances of the past between the political order and the church in which theology served to legitimate and give divine sanction to those in power. Instead, political theology calls for the church to function in a consistently critical mode, analyzing existing conditions by the plumbline of the kingdom of God* and the "dangerous memory" (Metz) emerging out of the Hebrew-Christian past of the suffering of the people, on the one hand, and the intervention of God to free them, on the other. God's self-identification with those who suffer poses a permanent threat to all attempts to link God with the forces of wealth and power. This insight parallels the "preferential option for the poor" in Latin American theology.

Political theology grounds its critical stance in the divine commandment prohibiting idolatry and in the hope for justice* conveyed by the eschatological promise of the kingdom of God. The first supplies the "secularizing" impulse in political theology, its critical examination of political and ideological loyalties to determine whether they are claiming for themselves a devotion that belongs to God alone. The second, the vision of the kingdom, makes the theory-praxis dialectic an integral part of the position. Every historical realization is questioned in the light of that which still remains to be actualized.

The consistently critical stance has caused objections to be raised by Latin American theologians. While acknowledging their own indebtedness to political theology and the kinship they share, Latin Americans complain that an approach which only critiques ignores the necessity in the practical world to form alliances and to be committed to concrete, less-than-perfect alternatives in order to achieve proximate justice. Theology must take the risk of being partisan (José Míguez Bonino), rather than simply the critic, if it is to mobilize the disenfranchized to secure their rights. From the Latin American perspective, therefore, political theology's revolutionary critique looks more like a Cartesian revolution of systematic doubt than a practical one (Juan Luis Segundo), a theoretical principle and method that assure the thinker a position above the fray rather than committing one to the movements that bring about change.

Political theologians counter that theology responds to the concrete situation in which it finds itself. In the social democracies of Europe, where there is hope for change through normal political processes, criticism of existing conditions may be the most important contribution the church can make. In other contexts, where fundamental changes are required before justice is a possibility, commitment to a single political alternative may be necessary. Theology's goal in either case is to make clear God's identification with the disenfranchized, who have no one to speak for them, and to bring about those reforms necessary to ensure their full participation in society.

See also **theology, liberation.**

THEODORE RUNYON

R. Chopp, *The Praxis of Suffering*, Maryknoll, NY, Orbis, 1986 • J. Metz, *Glaube in Geschichte und Gesellschaft* (ET *Faith in History and Society*, New York, Seabury, 1980) • J. Moltmann, *On Human Dignity*, Philadelphia, Fortress, 1984 • K. Srisang ed., *Perspectives on Political Ethics*, WCC, 1983 • S. Wiedenhofer, *Politische Theologie — Politische Ethik*, Stuttgart, Kohlhammer, 1976.

THEOTOKOS. This is a Greek term meaning "God-bearer", one given officially to Mary the mother of Jesus by the ecumenical council of Ephesus in 431. The expression is, however, older. It appears in a papyrus from the end of the 3rd century, and it was used for Mary very frequently throughout the 4th century.

Christians at that time were very much aware that this expression was fundamental to discussion of the incarnation* of the second person of the Trinity.* It was to culminate in the Chalcedonian formula in 451: "Jesus, very God and very man" (see **Chalcedon**), contrasting with the philosophy of the first few centuries, for which the incarnation of God remained a scandal. If a woman gives birth to God, does that make her his mother? "When the time had fully come, God sent forth his Son, born of woman" (Gal. 4:4).

Polemics at Ephesus were lively. Nestorius proposed the expression *Christotokos* (Christbearer), but the council adopted *theotokos* (she who brings God into the world) as its formula, for Mary gives birth to Jesus of Nazareth, the Son of God. "The child to be born will be called holy, the Son of God" (Luke 1:35). It is Mary, a woman like all other women, but a virgin chosen by God, who writes the divine Word into the human family tree.

This designation was joyfully welcomed by the church and has remained a title uniting the majority of Christians up to the present. In the 16th century, even though Calvin refused to use the word, Luther and Zwingli for their part continued to mark the Marian feasts (the annunciation, visitation, incarnation, presentation and dormition) by sermons stressing Mary's unique place in the history of the human race: "Let Mary be held in honour and the Lord be worshipped!"

The Orthodox church remained faithful to the doctrinal judgments of the ecumenical councils; in hymnology and iconography moderate veneration of the *theotokos* continued.

In the last few centuries, however, Christian tradition in the West developed extremely polarized positions. On the Protestant side, the churches of the Reformation like to speak of Mary as an "example of humility, prayer and faith" for believers; "the woman" in the book of Revelation represents the church. On the Catholic side, the Roman dogmas of 1854 and 1950 laid down as an essential affirmation "the immaculate conception of Mary" by her parents, and her "assumption" instead of her dormition.

For some decades, thanks to the breadth and openness of ecumenical dialogue, we have been able to tell each other where the differences between us lie and to ask each other how Mary, whom the angel called "full of grace", is to be venerated without that veneration becoming worship of the "queen of heaven" as a supposed co-mediatrix alongside Jesus. Today the expression *theotokos* may

help the church to re-discover the true place for Mary, who sang the Magnificat.*

See also **Mary in the ecumenical movement.**

ELISABETH PONTOPPIDAN

B. Bobrinskoy, *Le mystère de la Trinité*, Paris, Cerf, 1986 • A. Dumas & F. Dumas, *Marie de Nazareth*, Geneva, Labor & Fides, 1989 • J. Feiner & L. Vischer, *Neues Glaubensbuch: Der gemeinsame christliche Glaube* (ET *The Common Catechism*, London, Search, 1975) • V. Lossky, *Théologie mystique de l'Eglise d'Orient* (ET *The Mystical Theology of the Eastern Church*, London, Clarke, 1957) • G. Miegge, *La Vergine Maria* (ET *The Virgin Mary*, Philadelphia, Westminster, 1955).

THIRD WORLD. The term "third world" is generally understood as synonymous with developing nations. Of course the term "developing nations" itself merits definition. The term "third world" is used more commonly than the terms "first world" and "second world"; more recently the term "fourth world" also has come into use.

By the first world is usually meant the leading industrialized countries mainly of Western Europe and the USA and other countries of comparable economic development. The second world consists of the rest of the industrializing nations, mainly the Soviet Union and other East European countries. The third world is the rest of the world, in particular the developing countries of Asia, Africa and Latin America.

There are several difficulties with the term "third world". It has a negative connotation. There is the impression of a hierarchy in the world order. The term may appear to some to be derogatory. The countries of the third world have very little in common. Even in terms of industrial growth, which is one of the criteria for classification, there are countries in the third world which may not belong there. Some would prefer to use the term "two-thirds world".

The quotation given below from Shiva Naipaul *(The Myth of the Third World)* gives strong expression to the reservations about the term: "The third world is a form of bloodless universality that robs individuals and societies of their particulars. Blandly to subsume, say, Ethiopia, India and Brazil under the one banner of third-worldhood is absurd and denigrating. A third world does not exist as such... The idea of a third world, despite its congenial simplicity, is too shadowy to be of any use." However the term is widely used not only in the media but also in academic circles.

It is believed that the term "third world" was first used in 1952 by the French writer Alfred Sauvy in an essay on "Trois mondes, une planète" (Three worlds, one planet). During the period of the cold war* it clearly referred to the non-aligned world. It was also a world of poor countries. The use of "third world" originally expressed ideas of neglect, exploitation and revolutionary potential. It may be argued that it is the very condition that the developing nations find themselves in that separates them from the former colonial powers.

The use of the expression became part of the development* debate, especially in the 1960s. The rich countries began to be called developed countries. The poor countries were then called backward or under-developed. On the global level in addition to the East-West confrontation there was the North-South confrontation, the great majority of the poor countries lying in the southern hemisphere. The first world became the rich nations, the second the industrialized or industrializing, centrally directed socialist countries. The term "fourth world" was added only much later to denote the least developed and chronically poor countries. The third world came to represent the developing nations. The so-called theory of dependence* developed in the 1960s by people like Samir Amin in Africa and A. Gunder Frank, O. Sunkel, Celso Furtado and others in Latin America, saw under-development as a process related to the development of the "central countries". The third world, therefore, can also be seen as the dependent "periphery" of that integrated "international division of labour".

Even the term "developing nations" is a case of diplomacy by terminology. As the membership of the United Nations expanded with the addition of "under-developed" countries, the term began to be regarded as derogatory and was gradually dropped first in favour of "less-developed" and then "developing".

The WCC gives major attention to the issues of the third world. This is sometimes a point of criticism against the Council. The expansion in the membership of the Council, especially in the 1960s, with a large number of churches from developing nations, a preferential option for the poor* and an action-oriented approach to issues naturally make the Council deeply involved in the third world. In the 1950s and 1960s the Council conducted a long and impressive study on "The Common Christian Responsibility towards Areas of Rapid Social Change", coming to grips with the significant developments of newly independent countries in Asia, Latin America and Africa.

In the Roman Catholic Church, Paul VI's *Populorum Progressio* (1967) is the first document devoted to this question, although John XXIII had already called attention to the condition of under-developed peoples. The joint WCC/RCC SODEPAX* commission worked extensively on this theme, recently underlined again in John Paul II's *Sollicitudo Rei Socialis*.

See also **dependence; poverty; social encyclicals, papal.**

NINAN KOSHY

British Churches and the Third World, London, BCC, 1979 • T. Draisma, *Underdevelopment Continued?,* Rotterdam, Ecumenical Research Exchange, 1984 • V. Samuel, *Evangelism and the Poor: A Third World Study Guide,* Bangalore, Partnership in Mission-Asia, 1983 • W.R. Schmidt ed., *Catalysing Hope for Justice: Essays in Honour of C.I. Itty,* Singapore, CCA, 1987.

THOMAS, M.M. (Madathilparampil Mammen). B. 15.5.1916, Kerala, India. "M.M.", a pioneering Asian ecumenical thinker and layman, active in the ecumenical movement for many years, was moderator of the WCC central committee, 1968-75. Earlier he was chairman of the working committee of the Department on Church and Society and of the world conference on Church and Society at Geneva in 1966. He helped to organize and spoke at the world Christian youth conferences — Oslo 1947, Kottayam 1952 and Lausanne 1960. He was also a main speaker at New Delhi 1961 and Uppsala 1968. He organized a series of ecumenical study conferences in Asia on social questions, which provided the basis for social reflections during the early years of the East Asia Christian

Conference: Bangkok 1949, Lucknow 1953 and Kuala Lumpur 1959. Secretary and later vice-chairman of the World Student Christian Federation,* 1947-53, he was secretary of the Youth Christian Council of Action, Kerala, and afterwards youth secretary of his own church, the Mar Thoma Syrian Church of Malabar, and later director of the Christian Institute for the Study of Religion and Society in Bangalore, 1962-75.

He studied for a year at Union Theological Seminary in New York on a WCC fellowship. He has lectured extensively in North America, Europe and Asia on Christianity and social problems and on the dialogue between Christianity and other faiths. He was visiting professor at Union Theological Seminary, at Princeton Theological Seminary, and at Perkins School of Theology. In 1990 he was appointed governor of Nagaland in India. His numerous publications include *The Christian Response to the Asian Revolution* (London, SCM, 1966), *The Acknowledged Christ of the Indian Renaissance* (London, SCM, 1970), *Salvation and Humanisation* (Bangalore, Christian Institute, 1971), *Risking Christ for Christ's Sake* (WCC, 1987), and *My Ecumenical Journey* (Trivandrum, Ecumenical Publishing Centre, 1990). See T.M. Philip, *The Encounter between Theology and Ideology: An Exploration into the Communicative Theology of M.M. Thomas* (Madras, Christian Literature Society, 1986).

ANS J. VAN DER BENT

THURIAN, MAX. B. 16.8.1921, Geneva, Switzerland. Since 1949 Thurian has been engaged in ecumenical study and research in the service of the Commission on Faith and Order* and has attended all its major conferences. From 1970 onwards he was instrumental in preparing the document on *Baptism, Eucharist and Ministry*,* adopted by the WCC in 1982, and afterwards was editor of six volumes of official responses of the churches to the convergence document: *Churches Respond to BEM* (WCC, 1986-89). He also edited *Ecumenical Perspectives on Baptism, Eucharist and Ministry* (WCC, 1983) and, together with Geoffrey Wainwright, *Baptism and Eucharist: Ecumenical Convergence in Celebration* (WCC, 1983). Thurian studied

theology in Geneva and, after meeting Roger Schutz in 1942, became the theologian and liturgist of the Taizé community*. With Brother Roger he was personally invited by Pope John XXIII to be an observer at the Second Vatican Council and has had private audiences with Pius XII, John XXIII, Paul VI and John Paul II. In 1987 he became a priest of the Roman Catholic Church in Naples, Italy. His other works include *Mariage et célibat* (ET *Marriage and Celibacy*, London, SCM, 1959), *L'unité visible des chrétiens et la tradition* (ET *Visible Unity and Tradition*, Baltimore, Helicon, 1962), *Marie, mère du Seigneur, figure de l'Eglise* (ET *Mary, Mother of the Lord*, London, Faith, 1963) and *Le mystère de l'eucharistie* (ET *The Mystery of the Eucharist* (London, Mowbray, 1983).

ANS J. VAN DER BENT

TING, K.H. (Ding Guangxun). B. 29.9.1915, Shanghai. Ting was secretary of the YMCA, 1938-46, secretary of the Student Christian Movement in Canada, 1946-47, secretary of the World Student Christian Federation,* 1948-51, and general secretary of the Christian Literature Society, Shanghai, 1952-53. In 1953 he became principal of Nanjing Theological Seminary, and in 1979, vice-president of Nanjing University. Since 1981 he has been president of the China Christian Council and the National Three-Self Movement. In 1983 he was made a member of the standing committee of the National People's Congress. He became president of the Amity Foundation in 1986 and vice-moderator of the National People's Consultative Conference in 1989. Educated at St John's University, Shanghai, and Union Seminary and Columbia University, New York, he was ordained as Anglican priest in 1942, and as bishop in 1955. His publications include *The Study of the Bible* (Shanghai, China Christian Council, 1982), and *Christian Witness in China* (Kyoto, Doshisha UP, 1985).

ANS J. VAN DER BENT

TOMKINS, OLIVER S. B. 9.6.1908, Hankow, China. Anglican theologian and church leader, Tomkins was associate general secretary of the WCC, in charge of its London office, 1945-53. He also was assistant secretary of the Faith and Order* continuation committee, 1945-48, secretary of the Commission on Faith and Order, 1948-53, chairman of the Faith and Order working committee, 1953-67, a member of the central committee, 1968-75, and a member of the WCC-Roman Catholic Joint Working Group,* 1968-75. He was active in the British Student Christian Movement and in the World Student Christian Federation.* He graduated from Cambridge University and was bishop of Bristol, 1953-75. His publications include *The Church in the Purpose of God* (London, SCM, 1950) and *A Time for Unity* (London, SCM, 1964).

ANS J. VAN DER BENT

TORONTO STATEMENT. This statement was received by the 1950 meeting of the central committee of the WCC gathered at Toronto — from whence it takes its name. Its full title is "The Church, the Churches, and the World Council of Churches". It carries an explanatory sub-title: "The Ecclesiological Significance of the World Council of Churches". In retrospect, to attempt so comprehensive a statement on so potentially divisive a subject so soon after the first assembly in Amsterdam in 1948 may seem to be, at one and the same time, both foolhardy and courageous. Subsequent ecumenical history has shown that the risk was worth taking.

That the ecclesiological question had to be faced so soon after Amsterdam was the result of critical and fundamental questioning of the implications of Council membership for the member churches' concepts of the nature of the church and of what it meant to relate to churches with concepts which differed on ecclesiology. Among the questioners, interestingly enough, were some Roman Catholic ecumenists. In September 1949, a group of ten WCC representatives met with a like number of Roman Catholics at the Istina centre in Paris. This meeting helped the WCC leaders to realize that, even at this early stage, it was essential to try to define more clearly what the WCC was and what it was not. The Istina meeting was an important stage in the preparation of the Toronto statement. Oliver Tomkins of Great Britain was then secretary of the Faith and Order* commission, and he, together with W.A. Visser 't Hooft, drafted a statement on the ecclesiological significance

of the WCC and sent it to theologians for comment. Out of this consultative process came the draft of the Toronto statement.

Content. The statement, as finally agreed, begins by quoting the Amsterdam resolution on "the authority of the Council" and goes on to indicate that a further statement is needed, both to prevent misunderstandings and to indicate the provisional nature of any WCC utterance. In the light of this stated intention the statement begins with a series of five disclaimers headed "What the World Council Is Not". These are followed by eight assumptions which, it is claimed, underlie the WCC. The disclaimers have proved particularly significant in the history of the WCC as providing sufficient safeguards to encourage membership applications by churches for whom ecclesiology is the crucial test of relationship. The five disclaimers are as follows: (1) the WCC is not and must never become a super-church; (2) the purpose of the WCC is not to negotiate unions between churches, which can only be done by the churches themselves acting on their own initiative; (3) the WCC cannot and should not be based on any one particular conception of the church; it does not prejudge the ecclesiological problem; (4) membership of the WCC does not imply that a church treats its own conceptions of the church as merely relative; (5) membership of the WCC does not imply the acceptance of a specific doctrine concerning the nature of church unity.

The positive assumptions underlying the WCC speak of belief that all relationships must be based upon the headship of Christ; belief in the New Testament view that the church is one; recognition that membership of the church of Christ is more inclusive than any one church body; recognition that in churches other than one's own there are elements of the true church; a willingness to consult together to learn the will of Christ; an acceptance of a solidarity to assist each other; a resolve to enter into spiritual relationship for the purpose of mutual instruction, help and renewal.

One assumption requires fuller quotation, as it provoked lively and difficult debate in its drafting and final reception and carries with it ecclesiological implications for the WCC. It states: "The member churches of the World Council consider the relationship of other churches to the holy catholic church which the creeds profess as a subject for mutual consideration. Nevertheless, membership does not imply that each church must regard the other member churches as churches in the true and full sense of the word."

The commentary immediately following goes on: "There is a place in the WCC both for those churches which recognize other churches as churches in the full and true sense, and for those who do not." The debate on that fourth assumption and the following commentary has been described by Visser 't Hooft as "one of the most heated we have ever had in the World Council". It reflected the different presuppositions of the founding fathers of the Council. One group assumed that the churches in membership gave full and unreserved recognition to each other. Others believed that membership did not mean that any church had to give up its convictions about the nature of the church, but rather that each member church was ready to enter the relations of fellowship and dialogue with other churches with the hope that it would lead to full recognition and full unity. If the first group had had its way, membership of the Council would have become virtually impossible for those holding the second view. Far more was at stake than sentences in a document. The Orthodox churches, in particular, regarded the other churches as *essentially* incomplete. Others acknowledged that they did not consider their own church as a full, true and complete church and were not afraid of being told the same thing by others. As the statement was finally received at Toronto, it reflects the very originality of the WCC in that it sought to create a fellowship between churches who were not yet able to give full recognition to each other.

Beyond Toronto. There is little doubt that at Toronto in 1950 the WCC so early in its life was at a crisis point. But it proved to be a "crisis unto life". From then on, the member churches recognized not only that they had a deep discernment of the differences between them but also that they had to live with them and work through them as the Holy Spirit led them on into deeper relationships. Unity was developing through admitted and acknowledged diversity. The existence of the Toronto statement has enabled a number of churches to become members of the WCC. Vitaly Borovoy has commented on the statement: "For the

Orthodox it is the great charter of the WCC." It has also facilitated developing relationships between the RCC and the Council.

Not surprisingly, since 1950 the ecclesiological issue relating to membership has been handled cautiously by the Council. The New Delhi assembly in 1961 confirmed the statement but pleaded for further clarification of the issues raised. "We learn what the Council is by living together." But hopes for theological reflection on the meaning of that life remained, on the whole, unfulfilled. The world Faith and Order conference at Montreal in 1963 asked again that the WCC should devote further attention to the question of its ecclesiology. The fourth assembly at Uppsala (1968) spoke of the Council as a fellowship of churches seeking to express catholicity. By the time of the Nairobi assembly in 1975, the concept of the Council as "a conciliar fellowship of local churches which are themselves truly united" had developed. But the meaning of "conciliar" was and is still awaiting clear and agreed definition. The Vancouver assembly in 1983 sought to develop the perspective of such conciliar fellowship by considering practical steps in the churches' life and relations with one another.

At the present time, the Toronto statement still remains as basic. It has rightly been described as more of a milestone than a stumbling block. It has served the churches well for 40 years. It remains still generally relevant though many feel it needs revision. Any revision can now be undertaken in the light of walking together for a generation and of convergence and growing consensus on issues which are, at root, ecclesiological. Among these are baptism, eucharist and ministry; mission in Christ's way; justice, peace and the integrity of creation. But those undertaking the revision will need the wisdom of Solomon, the patience of Job, and the grace of the gospel and, beyond all, the guidance and presence of the Holy Spirit.

See also **church, World Council of Churches**.

MORRIS WEST

Text of Toronto statement in *Documents on Christian Unity*, 4th series, 1948-57, G.K.A. Bell ed., London, Oxford UP, 1958 • V. Borovoy, "The Ecclesiastical Significance of the WCC: The Legacy and Promise of Toronto", *The Ecumenical Review*, 30, 3-4, 1988 • H.E. Fey ed., *The Ecumeni-*

cal Advance: A History of the Ecumenical Movement, vol. 2: 1948-1968, 2nd ed., WCC, 1986 • W.A. Visser 't Hooft, The Genesis and Formation of the World Council of Churches, WCC, 1982 • W.A. Visser 't Hooft, Memoirs, London, SCM, 1973.

TORTURE. Practised in nearly half of the countries of the world, torture today has become more scientific and hence more destructive. At the same time, it has never been so universally denounced as it is today. The struggle against it is in the forefront of the human rights* question.

Christian communities have not always had the same attitude to torture. Early Christians were persecuted for their refusal to accept the divine claims of political powers. Later on, however, in new conditions, Christians allowed or at least acquiesced in the practice of torture, from positions of influence in political relationships and organizations. During the Inquisition in Europe, the conquest of America and the era of colonial expansion, torture was widely practised.

Used to obtain confessions and to increase the punishment of criminals, methods of torture often become methods of governing, as political authorities terrorize entire populations by systematically resorting to torture to suppress all kinds of dissidence. Physical suffering caused by beating, weapons, electric shock, rape and sexual brutality, the inhuman treatment of children, mock executions, forced labour, the use of drugs and psychologically destructive procedures, sensual deprivation and destabilizing prison routines, harassment and perpetual menace are all so many acts of cruelty aimed at breaking the free will of the victim and sometimes of an entire population.

The diversity and universality of the methods of torture practised today contrast with the unanimity of its prohibition. Article 5 of the Universal Declaration of Human Rights of 1948, the international pact on human rights of 1966, the 1984 international convention (UN) against torture, the European and inter-American conventions on human rights, the African charter, and numerous national laws absolutely forbid the practice of torture. An international committee against torture (UN) examines cases and appeals; a recorder files an annual report denouncing torture at the Commission on Human Rights; the European Convention for the Prevention of Torture invites a group of acknowledged experts to visit places of detention so that states can install mechanisms designed to prevent torture in places of high risk. All the countries of the world have promised to abolish torture, yet nearly half of them still practise it.

The pressure exerted by non-governmental organizations often brings the facts to light, protects victims by publicizing their cases and shows states that the practice of torture can undermine their international standing. People from all parts of the world write letters to support a victim. Public attention has to a large extent shattered the isolation and silence that torturers need to hold and break their victims. Individuals are no longer alone. They know that others are working for them. At the same time, the torturers have discovered that they too are being watched and must eventually account for their actions.

Torture can be prevented by educating the public about human rights and by providing special training for law enforcement agents in every country. We need to build up a network of solidarity to unite the numerous anti-torture groups to make their efforts more effective.

The theological undergirding of the struggle against torture is not difficult to find: the dignity of the human person, the reality of our common humanity, God's universal concern for men and women, Christ's presence in the "little ones" that suffer — all these speak clearly against all abuse of the human person. With regard to torture, Pope John Paul II said to the International Committee of the Red Cross (1982): "From their childhood Christians hear the story of Christ's passion. The memory of Jesus stripped naked, beaten, derided, nailed to the cross, should make them refuse to see similar treatment meted out to other human beings. The disciples of Christ reject, spontaneously and absolutely, any recourse to such means which nothing on earth can justify and which destroy the dignity of both the tortured and the torturer."

In 1977 the WCC gave expression to its permanent concern on this question: "Torture is endemic, breeds in the dark, in silence. We call upon the churches to bring its existence into the open, to break the silence, to reveal the persons and structures of our societies which are responsible for this most dehumanizing of all violations of human rights." The WCC has made a number of concrete proposals to the churches to participate in the struggle against torture and initiated specific programmes in which churches could be involved. Many Christians have joined non-confessional organizations such as Action of Christians for the Abolition of Torture, created in France in 1974.

The flare-up of the phenomenon of torture reveals a profound sickness that has stricken humanity. Torture is indeed the product of several causes. The economic injustice that rules in some countries and which results from the pursuit of international business can only cause reactions of violence and repression. When the personalization of power is pushed to the limit, the dictator feels justified in torturing those who would not submit. Similarly, when ideologies leave no place for the mystery, for humankind's higher state, they become totalitarian and crushing. Deviants become easy prey for those who impose their singular and total truth. Christian churches themselves learned this sad lesson: when they transformed faith in Jesus Christ into an ideology at the service of a temporal power, they justified the use of torture.

GUY AURENCHE

TOTALITARIANISM. Totalitarianism as a form of government and a society where there is no individual freedom and where all aspects of personal and social life are subordinated to the authority of a centralized government has existed in various forms throughout history. But in modern times it was Benito Mussolini who used the term "totalitarianism" *(totalitario)* to define the fascist project (see **fascism**): "All within the state, none outside the state, none against the state." Mussolini's Italy, Stalin's Soviet Union and Hitler's Germany have usually been seen as typical forms of totalitarianism.

The basic characteristics are easily recognized: a strong central rule that controls all aspects of life through coercion and repression, usually exempt from all legal or political control, the control or suppression of social institutions and political organizations (political parties, trade unions, religious, social, cultural and even sports institutions), and the attempt to replace or subordinate all relations of allegiance (family, friendship, religious loyalty) to the ties of loyalty and obedience to the state.

Totalitarianism can be distinguished from dictatorship, despotism and tyranny by two characteristics. On the one hand, it usually eliminates all existing political institutions, laws and traditions and replaces them with new ones. On the other hand, it claims that this is done in pursuing some absolute goal, such as national expansion, race purity or theocratic rule. All opposition must be eliminated at whatever cost. Usually some group, internal or external to the country, is denounced as the main enemy (the Jews in Nazi Germany is a paramount example) and targeted for destruction. In these circumstances large-scale and organized violence is permissible and often necessary. Government is exercised by an elite, conceived as of superior intelligence, moral integrity and willpower and sometimes claiming divine sanction. The economy rests in the hands of such elite, allegedly for the sake of the superior end, and frequently simply for the profit and enjoyment of its members.

Totalitarianism has been repeatedly condemned as an ideology* by most Christian churches (see **Confessing Church**), although groups of Christians and even churches have sometimes supported such governments and even tried to justify them theologically. The WCC has emphatically rejected totalitarianism, ever since the Oxford conference (1937). The word had been used by J.H. Oldham in a preparatory document, and Oxford took over with slight modifications his definition, speaking of "totalitarian societies" as reflecting "the widespread tendency of the state to control the totality of human life in its individual and social aspects, combined with the tendency to attribute absolute value to the state, to the national community, to the dominant class". The theological rejection of such claims is based on the affirmation of the sovereignty of God and on the understanding of what it is to be human. Totalitarianism becomes a species of idolatry by claiming for the state, the nation or the race an absolute allegiance that is owed to God alone; it reduces the person,* created in the image of God, to a mere particle in a total whole; and it prevents the participation of people in the building of society, thus denying a fundamental right of all human beings and a demand that God makes of them.

Amsterdam 1948 confirmed the rejection of totalitarianism. It is easy to see that the opposite to such a totalitarian society is the "responsible society", an idea developed by the ecumenical movement between Oxford and Evanston, which can be used as a criterion against some claims of liberal capitalism and, more often, of communist regimes. Although the notion of responsible society came later under serious criticism, the definition and rejection of totalitarianism in most ecumenical documents have been based on similar arguments. Only at Nairobi 1975 is the element of "economic domination" included as a significant aspect of totalitarianism. It is also significant that, from Oxford onwards, the criticism of totalitarianism was also applied to the churches' temptation (actualized in practice in many cases) of claiming for themselves such absolute character, trying to control the whole of society and preventing participation and responsibility in their own internal life.

JOSÉ MÍGUEZ BONINO

TOURISM. Ecumenical concern about tourism grows out of the recognition that its effect on the economies, cultures and lifestyles of third-world countries is a crucial issue of justice and development. WCC attention to tourism emerged in the late 1960s in the context of a Department on the Laity study of "Changing Concepts of Work and Leisure". Following a 1969 conference on leisure-tourism in Tutzing, Federal Republic of Germany, the issue was studied under the rubric of "Participation in Change", one of five major WCC programmes between the fourth and fifth assemblies. Visits to the Middle East assessed the impact of leisure travel on Arab-Jewish relations. A chaplaincy at the Munich Olympics (1972) sought to evaluate the effect of such sporting occasions on international relationships.

In the early 1970s a conference in Nairobi explored tourism in East Africa. Black Africans in the tourist business pointed out that almost all the profits from tourism went to white tour operators and their partners in Europe, with minimal spin-off for the country that provided the surf, sand, scenery and ser-

vice. Tourism was the subject of one of the five preparatory consultations that led to the founding of the Caribbean Conference of Churches in 1973. Researchers gathered advertisements for Caribbean tourism in North American periodicals; in every case, black people were shown serving whites.

In Asia, concerns expressed at ecumenical workshops in Penang, Malaysia, in 1974 and in Manila in 1980 led in 1982 to the formation of the Ecumenical Coalition on Third World Tourism (ECTWT), with its headquarters in Bangkok. Its member organizations — both Roman Catholic and groups related to the WCC — are from Africa, Asia, the Caribbean, Latin America, the Middle East and the Pacific. ECTWT has links with the European Ecumenical Network on Third World Tourism (TEN) and the Center for Responsible Tourism (NANET) in San Anselmo, California.

ECTWT co-operates with organizations in destination countries that challenge tourist policies and practices and encourage codes of tourist ethics and alternative forms of tourism. International industry promotions have been used as occasions to present dissenting views that expose political and economic imperialism, racism,* sexism* and human rights* abuses in the tourism industry.

In seeking to call attention to the injustices of the tourism industry, ecumenical programmes have investigated the role of the transnational corporations controlling travel and resort facilities and the collaboration with them by third-world governments. Foreign currency earned by a tourist-destination country is about 15% of the travel, hotel and entertainment costs. Little technology or management skill is transferred. Environmental destruction often accompanies resort construction. Loss of fishing rights and farming areas aggravates the drift to city squatter areas.

The ecumenical programmes seek to defend the rights of those who suffer human rights abuses, cultural desecration, loss of livelihood and destruction of life-style. People are encouraged to express and to organize themselves in resort areas. A particular concern is sex tourism, including child prostitution, which may enslave children as young as three years old. Ecumenical programmes have indicated the evils of prostitution, the threat of AIDS* and other sexually transmitted diseases, the link with drugs and the exploitation of "bar hostesses" in conditions of virtual slavery. Other programmes focus on alternative approaches to tourism which enable tourists to see the actual life-style and cultural traditions of people and to avoid the debasement of "cultural performances" for tourists, dependence on foreign hedonism to make a living and inculcation of servile attitudes and consumer values.

National and international groups have also worked on the theological basis of ecumenical concern for tourism — for example, seeing travel as a pilgrimage of humble discovery of the human face of God in the peoples, maximizing the inter-relationship of people. They have emphasized that humanity's creation in the image of God implies the preciousness of human life and the importance of human relations. Liberational approaches to theology have helped to focus on victims of tourism so as to arouse new consciousness and point to new structures for more just relationships.

IAN FRASER and HARVEY PERKINS

I. Fraser, *Leisure and Tourism: Threat and Promise*, WCC, 1970 • R. O'Grady, *Third World Stopover: The Tourism Debate*, WCC, 1981 • *Tourism: An Ecumenical Concern*, Bangkok, ECTWT, 1988.

TRADITION AND TRADITIONS.

"Tradition" is used in a variety of senses, some wide-ranging and others more restricted. (1) In an inclusive sense it designates the whole of Christian faith* and practice — not only doctrinal teaching but worship, norms of behaviour, living experience, sanctity — as handed down within the church* from Christ and the apostles down to the present day. Understood in this comprehensive way, Tradition is not to be contrasted with holy scripture* but seen as including it; scripture exists within Tradition. (2) In a narrower sense Tradition may be distinguished from scripture, and taken to mean the teaching and practice of the church, not explicitly recorded in the words of the Bible, but handed down from the beginning within the Christian community. (3) More narrowly still — especially when used in the plural, "traditions" — the term may refer, often in a pejorative sense, to a belief or custom which cannot claim any divine or apostolic origin.

Although different Christian bodies differ widely in their estimate of Tradition in sense (2), it is obvious that no religious body could exist without some kind of tradition. Even the decision to dispense altogether with Tradition and to rely solely on the authority of scripture would itself constitute a "tradition".

Tradition in the New Testament. The key passages occur in 1 Corinthians. "I received from the Lord", says Paul, "what I also delivered to you, that the Lord Jesus on the night when he was betrayed took bread..." (1 Cor. 11:23). Here the noun "tradition" *(paradosis)* does not occur, but Paul uses the related verb *paradidonai,* "hand on". Two points are noteworthy in this text: Tradition is regarded as derived from Christ (cf. Gal. 1:12); and it is directly connected with the institution and celebration of holy communion. This second point acquires particular significance when seen in the context of contemporary "eucharistic ecclesiology". The church, in the view of many present-day theologians, both Roman Catholic and Orthodox, is essentially a sacramental organism, which becomes itself through the celebration of the eucharist;* and so Tradition is best understood not primarily as a collection of facts and propositions, whether recorded in writing or preserved orally, but rather in terms of a communal action and a living presence. Tradition means the eucharistic Christ; to live within the Tradition signifies above all to "eat this bread and drink the cup", proclaiming the Lord's death "until he comes" (1 Cor. 11:26).

Paul also links Tradition not just with the eucharist but more broadly with the total ministry of Christ. After stating, "I delivered to you... what I also had received", he goes on to refer to Christ's death "for our sins" and, more particularly, to his resurrection* (1 Cor. 15:3-4). But tradition in the Pauline writings can also carry a much more restricted meaning, denoting a custom such as the veiling of the head by women during prayer (1 Cor. 11:2,5-6).

While in these passages the word "tradition" and its cognates bear a favourable sense, elsewhere in the NT the attitude is more ambivalent. Paul, for instance, refers to the "traditions of my fathers" (Gal. 1:14), Jewish customs which he himself observes but which he does not consider obligatory upon all believers. Elsewhere he makes an emphatic contrast between the truth which is "according to Christ" and mere "human tradition" which is to be rejected (Col. 2:8). In the synoptic gospels Jesus draws a similar distinction between the "tradition of the elders" and the "commandment of God", and he accuses the scribes and Pharisees of "making void the word of God through your tradition which you hand on" (Mark 7:5-13).

The NT attitude towards Tradition and traditions is therefore one of critical discernment. Traditions require to be continually tested; as the Russian Orthodox theologian Vladimir Lossky (1903-58) observes, Tradition represents "the critical spirit of the church". Seen in this way, Tradition is not only a protective, conservative principle but primarily the principle of growth and regeneration. Christians do not remain "in" the tradition simply through passive inertia or mechanical repetition. There has to be an unceasing effort to discriminate between "Tradition" and "traditions", between the essential gospel of salvation in Christ and what is simply accidental and historically conditioned. "The Lord said, I am truth. He did not say, I am custom" (council of Carthage, A.D. 257).

Tradition in the early church. Since, so far as we know, Christ did not commit his teachings to writing, the church depended at first entirely on oral tradition. After the composition of the books of the NT, oral traditions continued for a time to circulate in the Christian community and are cited by 2nd-century authors such as Papias and Hegesippus; but from A.D. 200 onwards little use is made of these unwritten traditions. The Gnostic appeal to a secret tradition independent of the recognized scriptures was firmly rejected by Irenaeus (d. c.200), who insisted that the Christian faith is based on the Bible and on the public teaching, in full agreement with the Bible, which is handed down by the succession of bishops in each Christian centre. Clement of Alexandria (d. c.215) appealed like the Gnostics to esoteric tradition, but here Origen (d. c.254) adopted a significantly different standpoint, holding that all tradition must be based ultimately on the Old and New Testaments. Writers in the late 2nd and early 3rd centuries, such as Irenaeus, Tertullian, Origen, Hippolytus and Novatian, refer to a summary of Christian teaching which they term the "canon" or "rule of faith" *(regula fidei)*, but the contents of this turn out to be entirely biblical; it is regarded, not as something supplementary to the Bible, but as identical with scripture and confirmed by it (see **canon**). The same is true of the primitive baptismal creeds,* and of later conciliar statements of faith such as the Nicene Creed* (381) and the Chalcedonian definition (451); these again are intended simply as re-affirmations of the fundamental biblical message concerning Christ.

One of the most explicit patristic statements concerning unwritten Tradition occurs in Basil of Caesarea (d. 379): "Some things we have from written teaching, and others we have received handed down to us in a mystery from the tradition of the apostles. Both traditions have the same value for piety" (*On the Holy Spirit* 27 [66]). This passage has sometimes been used to support a "two-source" theory of divine revelation. When Basil goes on, however, to give examples of the things "handed down to us in a mystery", these involve not points of doctrinal teaching but various practices in Christian worship such as the sign of the cross, turning to the east during prayer, the invocation (epiclesis*) over the gifts at the eucharist, and threefold immersion in baptism, all of which he considers apostolic in origin, although not explicitly mentioned in scripture. Thus for Basil unwritten Tradition, while important for liturgical prayer, does not seem to represent a second source of doctrine, independent of the Bible. In this text, as in 1 Cor. 11:23, we note the connection between Tradition and the eucharist.

For patristic authors in general, then, Tradition does not constitute a supplementary source of information about Christ alongside scripture, but it denotes simply the manner in which scripture is interpreted and lived by successive generations within the church.

The Reformation debate. The relationship between scripture and Tradition (in sense 2) has figured prominently in controversy between Roman Catholics and Protestants since the 16th century. The council of Trent (session 4, 8 April 1546) drew a distinction between "written books" *(libri scripti)* and "unwritten traditions" *(sine scripto traditiones)*. It was probably not the intention of the bishops at Trent to commit themselves specifically to a "two-source" doctrine, whereby revelation is handed on partly in scripture and partly in living oral tradition, but this was in fact the prevailing view among the Roman Catholic theologians from Trent until Vatican II. Tradition was usually treated as distinct from scripture, and it was held that teachings not contained in the Bible may be gathered from Tradition alone. On such a view Tradition becomes something added to the biblical testimony, so that scripture and Tradition form two parallel and complementary elements that together make up a larger whole, the totality of revealed truth.

"Two-source" language, similar to that employed by Roman Catholics, frequently occurs in Orthodox texts from the 17th century onwards. The statement in the Orthodox confession of Peter of Moghila (1643) is typical: "The articles of faith have received their authority and approbation partly from holy scripture and partly from ecclesiastical Tradition... The dogmas of the church are of two kinds, some being committed to writing... and the others handed down orally" (1.5).

On the Protestant side, the Reformers carefully distinguished between apostolic and post-apostolic Tradition, accepting the first as divine revelation,* while regarding the second as human teaching, to be received only if it agrees with the Bible. Scripture was proclaimed as the sole and final test by which all traditions were to be judged. The *principle* of Tradition was not denied, but its *applications* were rigorously submitted to the sovereign criterion of scripture, and any notion of two parallel "sources" of revealed truth was repudiated. Thus the Westminster confession of faith (Presbyterian: 1646) states that "all things necessary... for man's salvation" are to be found "expressly set down in scripture", or else may be deduced from it, "unto which nothing at any time is to be added, whether by new revelations of the Spirit or traditions of men" (1.6). But approval is then given to such traditional statements of faith as the Nicene Creed and the Chalcedonian definition. The Lutheran Augsburg confession (1530) and formula of Concord (1576), while affirming the primacy of scripture, similarly endorse the ancient creeds (the Apostles', the Nicene and the Athanasian), together with the other conciliar

decisions that have the "unanimous consent" of the undivided church.

The same position is adopted in the Thirty-Nine Articles of the Church of England (1562). Here it is stated as a basic principle: "Holy scripture containeth all things necessary to salvation" (art. 6). The "three creeds" are to be received, since they agree with scripture (art. 8), but the decisions of "general councils" do not possess authority unless "it may be declared that they be taken out of holy scripture" (art. 21); "traditions" may be changed (art. 34). Tradition is thus accepted, on the Protestant and Anglican view, only in so far as it represents the true interpretation of scripture, and it can never constitute a parallel authority, independent of scripture or supplementary to it.

In modern ecumenical discussions concerning Tradition, the 16th-century categories with their sharp polarity have been largely superseded. The "two-source" language, while still found occasionally in Roman Catholic authors, is no longer generally prevalent. Tradition is now commonly understood, by Catholics and Orthodox alike, in an inclusive manner (sense 1 rather than sense 2); there is, in other words, one source and not two, so that Tradition and scripture must be always taken together and never treated separately. Many Anglicans and Protestants today are willing to recognize the need for Tradition, viewed in this comprehensive way, so long as the primacy of scripture is safeguarded.

In the context of multilateral ecumenism, the statement on "Scripture, Tradition and traditions" made by the fourth world conference on Faith and Order at Montreal 1963 marked an incipient convergence: "We exist as Christians by the Tradition of the gospel (the *paradosis* of the *kerygma*) testified in scripture, transmitted in and by the church through the power of the Holy Spirit. Tradition taken in this sense is actualized in the preaching of the word, in the administration of the sacraments and worship, in Christian teaching and theology, and in mission and witness to Christ by lives of the members of the church." Yet Montreal could as yet do no more than recognize the hermeneutical problem of the relation between scripture and authoritative ecclesial traditions or between those traditions and Tradition (i.e. the transmission of the gospel as a whole, including scripture). Montreal offered no criteria but simply asked questions: "How can we distinguish between traditions embodying the true Tradition and merely human traditions? How can we overcome the situation in which we all read scripture in the light of our own traditions? Does not the ecumenical situation demand that we search for the Tradition by re-examining our own particular traditions?" The Montreal convergence made the production of *Baptism, Eucharist and Ministry** possible. But the unresolved questions re-emerge in the responses of the churches to BEM, particularly in connection with the first question put by the Lima document: How far can your church "recognize in this text the faith of the church through the ages?" (see *Baptism, Eucharist and Ministry, 1982-90*, WCC, 1990, 131-42).

The shift in Roman Catholic opinion was strikingly apparent at Vatican II (1962-65). In the original draft of the Dogmatic Constitution on Divine Revelation, the first chapter was entitled "Two Sources of Revelation", but such language was firmly eliminated from the final version. While "sacred Tradition and sacred scripture" continue to be mentioned as co-ordinate elements, the integral connection between the two is constantly emphasized: together they "form one sacred deposit of the word of God" (para. 10). But the constitution also specifies: "It is not from sacred scripture alone that the church draws her certainty about everything which has been revealed" (para. 9). While this statement is bound to prove disturbing to Protestants, it does not exclude the opinion, held in fact by many at the Council, that all revelation is indeed contained in scripture, albeit at times only in an obscure and implicit fashion. Since Vatican II most Catholic theologians have taken the view that Tradition and scripture, while different in form, are identical in content, so that Tradition is only formally, but not materially, independent of scripture. But this is not actually stated in the Constitution on Revelation; Vatican II deliberately left the question open.

In its Decree on Ecumenism Vatican II invoked the important concept of "an order or hierarchy of truths" (para. 11), which makes possible a more flexible approach towards the nature of Tradition (see **"hierarchy of truths"**). Certain elements in Tradition are nearer than others to the central message of

salvation; Tradition is not to be viewed in strictly monolithic terms. Whereas at Vatican I* (1869-70) Tradition was closely associated with the pronouncements of the magisterium,* after Vatican II increasing emphasis has been placed on the role of the *sensus fidelium*, the conscience or consciousness of the people of God as a whole, in preserving and expressing Tradition (see **consensus fidelium**). This understanding too has served to re-inforce a more inclusive and flexible understanding of Tradition.

The developing ecumenical convergence on Tradition and scripture is evident in the agreed statement adopted by the Anglican-Orthodox Joint Doctrinal Commission at Moscow in 1976. Here Tradition is taken in a comprehensive sense: it is "the entire life of the church in the Holy Spirit" (para. 10). Interdependence is stressed: "Any disjunction between scripture and Tradition such as would treat them as two separate 'sources of revelation' must be rejected. The two are correlative... Holy Tradition completes holy scripture in the sense that it safeguards the integrity of the biblical message" (para. 9). The primacy of scripture is asserted, but in qualified terms: scripture is styled, not "the only criterion", but "the main criterion whereby the church tests traditions" (para. 9). The Moscow statement concludes with some optimism that the agreement reached on scripture and Tradition "offers to our churches a solid basis for closer rapprochement" (para. 12).

Yet difficulties remain. A notable instance is the belief in the bodily assumption of the blessed Virgin Mary, proclaimed as a dogma* by the Roman Catholic Church in 1950. On the Protestant side it can be objected that the assumption is nowhere mentioned in the NT, either directly or indirectly, while the earliest specific references to it in ecclesiastical authors do not occur before the late 4th century. In what sense, then, can the doctrine be regarded as present, even in an obscure fashion, within scripture or apostolic Tradition? For this very reason the 1950 definition has also aroused misgivings among the Orthodox. While affirming the assumption in their liturgical worship, they feel that because of the absence of early evidence it should not, and indeed cannot, be proclaimed as a dogma. In Lossky's words, it is a mystery "which the church keeps in the hidden depths of her inner consciousness... not so much an object of faith as a foundation of hope".

Living Tradition. Recent writing on Tradition is marked by a strong preference for dynamic rather than static categories. Tradition is not so much a "deposit of doctrine" as a shared style of living; not primarily an accumulation of documents and testimonies but the life of Christ and the Holy Spirit in the church. For the French Catholic Yves Congar, Tradition is "the church's life in the communion of faith and worship... the setting in which the Catholic sense is fostered and finds expression"; for the Romanian Orthodox Dumitru Staniloae it is "not a sum of propositions learned by heart, but a lived experience". In any contemporary discussion of the topic, what needs to be said first of all is that the only true Tradition is living, critical and creative, formed by the union of human freedom with the grace* of the Holy Spirit.*

However, this vision of Tradition as dynamic and developing is by no means exclusively modern. Gregory of Nazianzus (329-89), for instance, envisages a progressive revelation in three main stages: "The Old Testament preached the Father clearly, but the Son only in an obscure manner. The New Testament revealed the Son, but did no more than hint at the godhead of the Holy Spirit. Today the Spirit dwells among us, manifesting himself to us more and more clearly." So, "by gradual additions and ascents, advancing from glory to glory", the people of God grows in its apprehension of the truth (*Oration* 31.26-27). Significantly Gregory uses the words "more and more" of the Spirit's self-disclosure; the Paraclete's manifestation is not completed at Pentecost,* but it develops with an ever-increasing clarity in the continuing life of the church.

A dynamic understanding of Tradition was re-affirmed during the 19th century in Catholic Germany by Johann Möhler and the Tübingen school, and in Orthodox Russia by Aleksey Khomyakov. Möhler described Tradition as "the living gospel... this vital, spiritual force, which we inherit from our fathers and which is perpetuated in the church". Cardinal Newman discussed the subject more systematically in his seminal *Essay on the Development of Christian Doctrine* (1845). His views, although never officially adopted by the Roman Catholic Church, have proved widely influential and received at least partial confirmation in the Dogmatic Constitution on Divine Revelation at Vatican II: "This Tradition which comes from the apostles develops in the church with the help of the Holy Spirit. For there is a growth in understanding of the realities and the words that have been handed down" (para. 8). But many Orthodox, while wholeheartedly endorsing a dynamic view of Tradition, are unhappy about the phrase "development of doctrine", preferring to speak rather of a "development in the expression of doctrine".

As living and dynamic, Tradition is essentially communal. It is transmitted not by isolated individuals but by persons* in relation — by the total ecclesial community, especially when gathered for the celebration of the eucharist. While, in the Catholic and Orthodox view, the apostolic succession of bishops plays a central role in the transmission of Tradition, it is handed down equally through the succession — which also may be termed "apostolic" — of holy men and women in the church, through what Symeon the New Theologian (959-1022) called the "golden chain" of the saints extending from Christ to our own day (see **apostolic Tradition**). Tradition involves the transmission not just of doctrine but of sanctity and spirituality. And, alongside the bishops and the saints, all the baptized without exception are active and responsible guardians of Tradition. In the words of Paulinus of Nola (d.431): "Let us hang upon the lips of all the faithful, for the Spirit of God breathes upon every one of them."

While Tradition is indeed the dynamic movement of God in history,* it is to be seen also in a metahistorical or eschatological perspective. It is not so much a long line stretched out in time as the gathering of time itself into God's eternity, the irruption into this present age of the eschaton, or age to come (see **eschatology**).

See also **apostolic Tradition, scripture**.

KALLISTOS WARE

Anglican-Orthodox Dialogue: The Moscow Agreed Statement, London, 1977 • *Commission on Faith and Order: The Report of the Theological Commission on Tradition and Traditions*, WCC, 1963 • Y. Congar, *La Tradition et les traditions* (ET *Tradition and Traditions: An Historical and Theological Essay*, London, Burns & Oates, 1966) • R.P.C. Hanson, *Tradition in the Early Church*, London, SCM, 1962 • V. Lossky, "Tradition and traditions", in *In the Image and Likeness of God*, Crestwood, NY, St Vladimir's Seminary, 1974 • P.C. Rodger & L. Vischer eds, *The Fourth World Conference on Faith and Order: Montreal 1963*, London, SCM, 1964, 50-61.

TRANSNATIONAL CORPORATIONS.
Corporations with activities in one or more foreign countries have existed for a long time. After the second world war, however, when transnational corporations (TNCs) expanded at an unprecedented rate, a strong interest in the phenomenon developed.

According to the United Nations Centre on TNCs, the most important actors in the world economy today are TNCs. The biggest ones have sales which exceed the aggregate output of most countries. For some countries, between 80 and 90% of their exports is associated with TNCs. World production is concentrated in the hands of a decreasing number of these corporations, and this trend is likely to continue in the future.

An important concern for the ecumenical movement is the fact that corporate concentration and power are rising at a more rapid pace than the capacity of individual governments and the international community to monitor, regulate and control TNC activities. The conference on "Church, Community and State" (Oxford 1937) noted: "The earlier stage of competitive capitalism has been gradually replaced by a monopolistic stage, and this economic change has brought with it corresponding political consequences." The original ideal of modern democracy has therefore become increasingly difficult to achieve, since "centres of economic power have been formed which are not responsible to any organ of the community and which in practice constitute something in the nature of a tyranny over the lives of masses of men".

In 1955, the WCC central committee identified the need for critical study and evaluation of the impact of private trade and enterprise in the "economically under-developed nations" of the world. Concern about the effects of TNC activities in developing countries was also expressed at the meeting of SODEPAX* in Montreal, 1969. Whereas a SODEPAX meeting in Beirut one year earlier had expressed optimism about the beneficial effects of TNCs,

the Montreal meeting said that the Beirut report did not give adequate attention to certain questions regarding the ambiguity of private investment in the under-developed countries. The international corporation within the next decade will have control over an enormously increased productive capacity. Hence the need for international regulation and study of the circumstances under which private investment would lead to a net gain in welfare.

Criticism of the exploitative nature of TNCs and the need for effective control on their power also came during the assembly of the WCC Commission on World Mission and Evangelism in Bangkok 1973, and at the WCC conference on science and technology for human development in Bucharest 1974. The criticism culminated in a sharp statement of the fifth WCC assembly in Nairobi, 1975: "TNCs are a typical example of the ways in which capitalist forces in the international and national sphere join together to oppress the poor and keep them under domination."

It was recommended that a study programme on TNCs be initiated. The WCC executive committee in Zurich (1978) approved a number of guidelines for this programme, which was to help raise awareness through action and reflection and to be undertaken from a perspective of solidarity with victims of TNC operations. A report on the lessons learned through the TNC programme was given to the WCC central committee in 1982.

Reactions of churches to the phenomenon of TNCs are diverse. Some churches see TNCs as catalysts to world economic growth and as carriers of technological progress. Some try to use moral authority or investments they might have in TNCs to change certain aspects of their behaviour, e.g. through share-holders' actions. Some churches publicly denounce specific TNC activities, e.g. in relation to corporate investments in South Africa or the irresponsible promotion of baby food. Certain churches are actively promoting codes of conduct for TNCs, and yet others are involved in boycott campaigns against certain TNCs. Despite the variety of church positions regarding this subject, there seems to be a general consensus that TNCs should be rendered more accountable to society and their power constrained.

There is no frequent reference to TNCs as such in Roman Catholic social teaching.

However, in the apostolic letter to Cardinal Maurice Roy, 1971, Pope Paul VI mentioned multinational corporations, "which by the concentration and flexibility of their means can conduct autonomous strategies which are largely independent of the national political powers and therefore not subject to control from the point of view of the common good. By extending their activities, these private organizations can lead to a new and abusive form of economic domination on the social, cultural and even political level. The excessive concentration of means and powers that Pope Pius XI already condemned on the fortieth anniversary of *Rerum Novarum* is taking on a new and very real image."

ROB VAN DRIMMELEN

Churches and the Transnational Corporations: An Ecumenical Programme, WCC, 1983 • *Transnational Corporations in World Development: Trends and Prospects*, New York, UN Centre on Transnational Corporations, 1988.

TRENT, COUNCIL OF. The first of the three modern Roman Catholic councils, named after the imperial city in the Italian Alps, the council of Trent (1545-63) is noted for its response to the Protestant Reformation.

Already in the late 1400s, strong church leaders, clergy and lay, were beginning to cry out for a general council to reform the Western church "in head and members". Disagreement on the agenda and participation (esp. the selection of political delegations) and opposition by vested interests of papal courts, powerful bishops, emperor and king kept the dream from becoming reality. Even Rome's fifth Lateran council (1512-17), with only a few besides Italian prelates present, produced superficial decrees. Finally, spurred by the growth and influence of the Protestants, Pope Paul III (1534-49) was able in 1544 to convoke the council with three stated goals: the healing of the schism* in the West, the reform of the church, and a Christian coalition against the European encroachment of the Ottoman Turks.

Because of political upheavals, poor attendance and even outbreaks of disease, the council had three separate periods, lasting through four papacies. The first period (1545-48) gave the Catholic answer to the Protestant principle "faith alone, grace alone, scripture alone". The council listed the books of the Old and New Testament canon,* insisted on the reverent role of Tradition,* addressed original sin* and justification,* and explained the seven sacraments.* The second session (1551-52) failed to have the intended Lutheran representation, with equal voice and vote. By the word "council", the two sides meant different assemblies, and Trent could not serve both. The session defined the eucharist,* with the real presence of Christ described by transubstantiation, and clarified the sacraments of penance* and the anointing of the dying. The third session (1562-63) gave reasons for denying the chalice to the laity, explained the mass as sacrifice, and declared the priesthood* to be truly a sacrament.

Although the reform of church practices was dividing the council fathers, Trent legislated seminary training for all priests; moral and intellectual qualifications for cardinals, bishops and priests; norms for admission in religious orders; and the prohibition of clandestine weddings, with procedures for valid marriages. Within a decade of the council's close, the popes published new editions of the breviary, the Roman missal, and a general catechism or manual of Catholic instruction for parish clergy.

As an answer to the Protestant Reformation, Trent had limited success. The council distinguished essential elements of the faith* from theological opinions and made room for the continued debate of those opinions. It tried to understand the various Protestant confessions first-hand and, unlike previous councils, it did not condemn persons but only errors (see **anathemas**). It initiated at least some serious ecclesiastical reforms. But the council of Trent failed to heal the schism within the Western church between Catholics and Protestants. In hindsight, one sees that both had limited visions of what should be entailed in a true church reformation of teaching and practice. Trent gave birth to what is called Counter-Reformation Catholicism. The church leaders and theologians of the next four centuries became far less irenic in spirit and acts than Trent itself had displayed and intended.

TOM STRANSKY

O. Chadwick, *The Reformation*, London, Penguin, 1972 • H. Jedin, *Geschichte des Konzils von Trient* (ET *History of the Council of Trent*, 2 vols, London, Nelson, 1957-60).

TRINITY. Although there is no developed or systematic doctrine of the Holy Trinity in the Bible, yet the holy scriptures, especially the New Testament, bear witness to the self-revealing mystery of God the Father, the Son and the Holy Spirit as distinct and yet inseparable persons acting for the life, salvation* and glorification of all humanity and of all creation.* In this respect, all the individual biblical references to God,* the Creator of heaven and earth, to his eternal Word and his eternal Spirit, from the beginning of the book of Genesis till the end of the book of Revelation, find their coherence and focus in the mystery of the incarnation* of Jesus Christ* (1 Tim. 3:16) and in its ultimate goal: the participation of the whole creation in God's kingdom* (Rev. 21:1-3). The mystery of the cross of Christ and of his resurrection* is the window and light through which the church* experiences the mystery of the divine Trinity as eternal love and sees the inner coherence and unity of the otherwise apparently diverse biblical witnesses related to the mystery of the Triune God.

Shortly before his crucifixion, the incarnate Word of God gives account to his eternal Father of his mission in the world, telling that he revealed to his disciples the very name of God, i.e. Father, and the eternal love of the Father for his only-begotten Son (John 17:6-26, also 1:14), with whom the Father shares the same glory before the existence of the world (John 17:5). It is for the Father's eternal Son and through him that the world was created (John 1:1-3; Col. 1:15-20) and the church comes into existence (John 17:9-26; Eph. 2:19-22, 4:9-16; Col. 1:17-18). The very purpose of the Son's incarnation was to reveal to the world not only the love of God for his eternal Son but also God's love for the whole creation, and to inaugurate its participation in the eternal life of God (John 3:16), liberating the world from sin* and death (Matt. 26:28; John 6:51-58; 1 Cor. 15:20,26). The incarnate Son reveals also the identity of the Holy Spirit* as an eternal person distinct not only from the Father, from whom he proceeds, but also from the Son, to whom he bears witness (John 14:26, 15:26). On the other hand, the Father and the Holy Spirit not only confirm the very identity of Jesus Christ as being the only-begotten, eternal Son of the Father, upon whom rests the Holy Spirit (Matt. 3:16-17 and

par.; John 1:29-34), but they are also united with the Son, co-operating permanently with him, being present in him even in or since the very moment of the Son's incarnation, although the Son alone became man (Luke 1:35).

This differentiated yet indivisible action of the three distinct and inseparable divine persons revealed through the mystery of the incarnation of Christ is in fact present in the whole economy of salvation and consequently in the whole life of the church, pointing to the kingdom of God as being the kingdom of the Father, Son and Holy Spirit. This life and activity of the Holy Trinity is an eternal and perfect communion* of love, a permanent movement of mutual and fully free self-offering of each person* to the others and of all of them to the world (John 10:17-18, 17:4; Phil. 2:6-11; Heb. 9:14). The Trinitarian revelation shows that ultimately the truth, life and unity in God are identical with koinonia*/communion.

The Father and the Son sent the Spirit into the world (Luke 4:18) in order that the Son may reveal to the world the love of the Father for it and the future action of the Spirit, who by his personal dwelling in the believers enables them to participate in the eternal love and glory which unite the Father and the Son (John 14:15-26, 15:26, 16:14-15). It is precisely by the dwelling of the Holy Spirit in those who believe in Christ that they can truly confess Jesus Christ as Lord (1 Cor. 12:3) and call God "Abba, Father" (Rom. 8:15-16), for the Spirit alone knows and declares all that the Father possesses and has given to the Son (John 16:13-15).

There is no confusion or subordination among the persons of the Holy Trinity, but only mutual self-giving, each person glorifying the others. In fact the unity of the Trinitarian life lies in the movement of perfect mutual self-giving. This Trinitarian unity affirms the communion and distinctiveness of the persons.

The fact that the Holy Spirit proceeds from the Father (John 15:26) and rests upon the Son or is received by the Son from the Father (John 1:32; Luke 4:18; Acts 2:32-33) allows him to be called the Spirit of God the Father (1 Cor. 2:12, 3:16) and the Spirit of his Son or the Spirit of Christ (Gal. 4:6; Rom. 8:9). Since the Holy Spirit proceeds *from* the

Father, he is called the Spirit of God, but he is also called the Spirit of the Son, since he is received by the Son and sent by the Son from the Father or by the Father in the name of Christ and at the request of Christ (John 14:26, 15:26). Being in a distinct manner the Spirit of the Father and the Spirit of Christ, the one Holy Spirit bears witness to the other two distinct persons in their irreducible distinctiveness: the Father and the Son.

At the same time, the Holy Spirit enables those who believe in Christ to be baptized in the koinonia of the one body of Christ, while preserving their unique identity (1 Cor. 12:13) and helping them to have access to the Father (Eph. 2:18) and to live within the world as adopted sons and daughters of the Father, receiving the same glorious gifts which the risen Jesus Christ received from the Father (Rom. 8:14-18). These gifts of the Father are communicated by the Spirit to those who believe in Christ in order that they may become like his Son, so that the Son should be the firstborn among many brothers and sisters (Rom. 8:29). Those who receive the Holy Spirit know the love of the Father as the Son knows it (John 17:25). In this way the Holy Spirit builds up church life and unity* through the participation of human beings in the life and koinonia of the Holy Trinity. Therefore all sacramental life of the church is accomplished through the action of the Holy Spirit and bears witness to the saving presence of the kingdom of the Father, Son and Holy Spirit within the world, thus preparing believers to long for the revelation of the glorious freedom of the children of God, for which in fact the whole creation is longing (Rom. 8:18-25).

For this reason, the apostolic church early identified baptism* with sharing in the mystery of the cross and resurrection of Christ (Rom. 6:3-4), and in the eternal Trinitarian communion of the Father, Son and Holy Spirit (Matt. 28:19). The same church experienced in the whole ecclesial celebration both the distinctiveness and the indivisibility of the divine Trinitarian love for humankind (2 Cor. 13:14: "the grace of the Lord Jesus Christ and the love of God and the fellowship of the Holy Spirit"). To early Christians, this experience of the living presence of the Holy Trinity in church life was so deep and self-evident that they could easily grasp the fact that "the church is full of Trinity" (Origen).

"Icon of the Holy Trinity", by Andrey Rublyov, 15th century (Hermitage National Museum, Leningrad, USSR)

The Trinity in church history. The fact that the sharing in the Trinitarian communion of life and love was the centre and focus of the new life of the Christians is particularly attested by the baptismal creeds* and rituals of the church but also by its whole sacramental and liturgical life in the first millennium after Christ (and especially in the Eastern and Oriental churches). The Christological and pneumatological controversies of the 4th and 5th centuries were in fact a challenge for the church to express and defend in more conceptual ways the permanently lived mystery of the divine Triune communion revealed in Christ and communicated by the Spirit to the church.

The doctrine of the Trinity as formulated by the fathers of the church in the Nicene* (325) and Constantinopolitan (381) creeds and in the Chalcedonian council (451; see **Chalcedon**) was in fact a great effort to preserve the unity of God, not as an abstract arithmetical or quantitative kind of unity which makes of God an eternal solitude, but precisely the Trinitarian unity as the eternal, indivisible and life-giving communion of the three consubstantial, equal and yet distinct persons, avoiding any separation, confusion and subordination among them. It is precisely the uniqueness of the Trinitarian unity that crucifies the human discursive (or linear) way of thinking.

The dogmatic formula of the council held in Chalcedon in 451 ("one person in two natures") is not primarily an explanation of the mystery of the incarnation of Christ but rather an effort to preserve the fullness of the divine-human communion accomplished and revealed in Christ, in which humanity fully and eternally participates in the life of the Trinity, without confusion or separation between God and humanity. In fact the Chalcedon formula protects the faith of the apostolic church, which recognized and confessed the risen Christ as being at the same time the only-begotten Son of God (John 1:14) and "the firstborn among many brethren" (Rom. 8:29). To Greek philosophy or any human way of thought which is inclined to confound or separate God and humanity in order to obtain artificial unity, the church, inspired by the Spirit of truth (John 15:26) and of communion (2 Cor. 13:14) and faithful to the revelation, opposed a real and authentic theology, i.e. that of the saving and deifying communion.

The Trinitarian unity as mutual self-giving and total sharing of life, love and glory, accomplished through the *mutual dwelling* of each person in the others *(perichōrēsis)*, becomes both the supreme model and the ultimate source of church unity (John 17:21-23) and points to the final unity in the glorious kingdom of God,* when all of creation will be renewed and united in God (Rev. 21:1-4). In the light of this unity revealed by Christ to his disciples and communicated to the church by the outpouring of the Holy Spirit, the fathers of the church took the mysterious plural of the book of Genesis — "Let *us* make man in *our* image after *our* likeness" (1:26) — as a project of God which anticipates the eschatological unity of all humankind in God. In this respect the patristic doctrine of the Trinity, as expressed in the formulas of the ecumenical councils* and in the sacramental life of the patristic church, has a permanent ecumenical significance precisely because it bears witness to the living apostolic faith that continues throughout the centuries, representing in itself a praise directed to the Trinitarian communion present in the church catholic universal.

The Trinity in the modern ecumenical movement. The understanding of the Trinity, after many centuries of ecclesiastical polemics and theological controversies, offers a new climate and basis for re-discovering the mystery of the Holy Trinity as the source, model and goal of Christian unity and as the basis for a deep renewal of Christian theology and spirituality. Although the doctrine of the Trinity has not yet been the object of an organized and systematic ecumenical reflection, the ecumenical interest in a common understanding of the centrality of the mystery of the Holy Trinity for the life of the church, and particularly for Christian unity, can be detected in many significant ecumenical events.

Particularly at the demand of the Eastern churches, the Christocentric affirmation of the Amsterdam basis (1948; see **WCC, basis of**), i.e. "a fellowship of churches which accept our Lord Jesus Christ as God and Saviour", was placed at New Delhi 1961 into a Trinitarian setting: "to the glory of the one God, Father, Son and Holy Spirit". The ecumenical vision of unity formulated at New Delhi is also marked by a Trinitarian perspective: "The love of the Father and Son in the unity of the Holy Spirit is the source and goal of the unity which the Triune God wills for all men and creation... The reality of this unity was made manifest at Pentecost in the gift of the Holy Spirit, through whom we know in this present age the first-fruits of that perfect union of the Son with his Father, which will be known in its fullness only when all things are consummated by Christ in his glory."

This Trinitarian perspective concerning the unity of God and church unity also marked to a certain extent the efforts of the Second Vatican Council* (1962-65) in its teaching on revelation and the mystery of the church. At the same time, the Faith and Order* conference in Montreal (1963) displayed interest in a Trinitarian perspective, in its understanding of worship as a "service to God the Father by men redeemed by his Son, who are continually finding new life in the power of the Holy Spirit". Later on, when the "conciliar fellowship" model of unity was discussed at the fifth assembly of the WCC at Nairobi in 1975, it also appeared necessary to place the deep theological and spiritual understanding of conciliarity in a Trinitarian setting.

Furthermore, the study of the F&O commission on the ecumenical significance of the so-called filioque* controversy ended in 1979 with the recommendation that the meaning of faith in God, Father, Son and Holy Spirit, be more fully explored "so that the Holy Trinity may be seen as the foundation of Christian life and experience". Another study of the F&O commission, namely the project "Towards an Ecumenical Explanation of the Apostolic Faith as Expressed in the Nicene-Constantinopolitan Creed (381)", has been to a certain extent an ecumenical effort to understand the apostolic faith in the Holy Trinity in the light of contemporary challenges (human responsibility for the integrity of creation, women's emancipation in church and society, dialogue with people of other living faiths, etc.). Again, in their evaluation of the Lima document on *Baptism, Eucharist and Ministry,** many churches expressed their appreciation of the fact that baptism and eucharist are approached in BEM from a Trinitarian perspective.

At the same time, an increasing interest in deeper ecumenical understanding of the significance of the faith in the Holy Trinity for church unity and life in the world is also displayed in many bilateral dialogues. Some examples are the Orthodox-Roman Catholic* international dialogue with its first theme "The Mystery of the Church and of the Eucharist in the Light of the Mystery of the Holy Trinity" (1980-82), or the Orthodox-Reformed* and Anglican-Orthodox* dialogues in which common agreement on the faith in the Holy Trinity appears as a necessary presupposition for a common vision of church unity.

To promote an ecumenical ecclesiology of communion based on an ecumenical reflection on the very nature of the church appears today to be one of the most urgent ecumenical tasks. It calls all churches to re-discover together that the mystery of the Holy Trinity is the very heart of any authentic Christian theology and spirituality. Since, from the Christian point of view, the unity that really matters is a saving and liberating divine-human communion, the ecumenical prayers, the ecumenical theological efforts and the practical actions have a lasting value when they help us recover the early Christian experience according to which the "church is full of Trinity" amid a creation that is ultimately moving towards the glorious reign of the Father, Son and Holy Spirit.

See also **communion, filioque, God, Holy Spirit, Jesus Christ, unity.**

DANIEL CIOBOTEA

B. Bobrinskoy, *Le mystère de la Trinité*, Paris, Cerf, 1986 ● L. Boff, *La Trinidad, la Sociedad y la Liberación* (ET *Trinity and Society*, Maryknoll, NY, Orbis, 1988) ● British Council of Churches, *The Forgotten Trinity*, (1) report of study commission, (2) study guide, London, BCC, 1989 ● R.W. Jenson, *The Triune Identity*, Philadelphia, Fortress, 1982 ● W. Kasper, *Der Gott Jesu Christi* (ET *The God of Jesus Christ*, New York, Crossroad, 1984) ● H.-G. Link ed., *One God, One Lord, One Spirit: On the Explanation of the Apostolic Faith Today*, WCC, 1988 ● J. Moltmann, *Trinität und Reich Gottes* (ET *The Trinity and the Kingdom of God*, London, SCM, 1981) ● L. Newbigin, *The Open Secret*, Grand Rapids, MI, Eerdmans, 1978 ● J. L. Segundo, *Nuestra Idea de Dios* (ET *Our Idea of God*, Maryknoll, NY, Orbis, 1974) ● W.A. Visser 't Hooft, "The Basis: Its History and Significance", *The Ecumenical Review*, 38, 2, 1985 ● A.W. Wainwright, *The Trinity in the New Testament*, London, SPCK, 1962 ● J. Zizioulas, *Being as Communion*, Crestwood, NY, St Vladimir's Seminary, 1985.

TUTU, DESMOND MPILO.

B. 7.10.1931, Klerksdorp, Transvaal, South Africa. Tutu, recipient of the 1984 Nobel peace prize and known worldwide for his efforts against apartheid in South Africa, was a speaker at Vancouver 1983 and earlier was assistant director of the Theological Education Fund of the WCC, based in Bromley, Kent, UK, 1972-75. He was general secretary of the South African Council of Churches, 1978-85, and in 1987 became president of the All Africa Conference of Churches. He received his theological education at St Peter's Theological College, Rosettenville, Johannesburg, and was ordained an Anglican priest in 1961. He was a member of the chaplaincy staff of the University of Fort Hare, 1967-69, and lecturer in the department of theology of the University of Botswana, Lesotho and Swaziland, 1970-72. He served as dean of Johannesburg, 1975-76, bishop of Lesotho, 1976-78, bishop of Johannesburg, 1985-86, and since 1986 has been archbishop of Cape Town. He has written *Crying in the Wilderness* (London, Mowbray, 1982) and *Hope and Suffering* (Grand Rapids, MI, Eerdmans, 1984). See E. Adler, *Desmond Tutu* (Berlin, Union, 1983).

ANS J. VAN DER BENT

TYPOI. The notion of *typoi*, or types (singular *typos*), adopted from sociology, has been used in ecumenical research to describe each of the particular forms that may be taken by a variety of Christian communities or churches within the visible fellowship of the one church.* Various people have spoken of "typologies" within a single ecclesial allegiance (Bernard Lambert 1962, Emmanuel Lanne 1967), but the notion of *typos* really caught on after an address given by Cardinal Johannes Willebrands in 1972. On the basis of two Vatican II* texts (*Unitatis Redintegratio* 14 and *Lumen Gentium* 23) concerning the different forms which the churches of the East and the West had from the start given to their ecclesial life within the communion* of the one, undivided church, Willebrands offered this description of a *typos*: "Where there is a long coherent tradition commanding men's love and loyalty, creating and sustaining a harmonious and organic whole of complementary elements, each of which supports and strengthens the other, you have the reality of a *typos*." He went on to indicate certain distinctive elements of a *typos*: a theological method and approach, a liturgical expression, a spiritual and devotional tradition, a canonical discipline.

Whereas the components of universal communion must be the same in all the churches, that is, communion in the faith,* sacraments* and ministry,* the characteristic elements of the *typoi* vary from one to the other. According to the Vatican II Decree on Ecumenism, this variety of forms, subsequently called *typoi*, contributes to "giving ever richer expression to the authentic catholicity and apostolicity of the church". The idea of *typoi* described by Willebrands was taken up in the Lutheran-Roman Catholic dialogue* (*Facing Unity*, 1984, nos 42-43) as one of the models for unity in diversity. The Methodist-Roman Catholic* *Towards a Statement on the Church* (1986) lists it as one "model of organic unity in the koinonia of the one Body of Christ": the notion of *typos* "implies that within the one church in which there is basic agreement in faith, doctrine and structure essential for mission, there is room for various 'ecclesial traditions', each characterized by a particular style of theology, worship, spirituality and discipline".

See also **unity, models of**.

EMMANUEL LANNE

P.A. Crow, Jr, "Ecumenics as Reflections on Models of Christian Unity", *The Ecumenical Review*, 39, 1987, esp. pp.400-401 ● J. Willebrands, address in Cambridge, England, January 1972, in *Documents on Anglican/Roman Catholic Relations*, vol. 1, Washington, DC, US Catholic Conference, 1976.

U

UNA SANCTA MOVEMENT.

The USM comes from the ecumenical awakening in Germany during the National Socialist period (1933-45) and after the second world war. Both Roman Catholic and Protestant ministers and laity participated. The USM should be distinguished from other worldwide currents of the ecumenical movement (without Roman Catholic participation) in the prehistory of the WCC, and from those which emerged in German Protestantism out of the *Hochkirchliche Vereinigung* (High Church Union), which sought to re-structure church worship on medieval lines and to go back to Luther. Yet the USM was not in isolation from them. Every effort to overcome confessional divisions is of service to the church, which the ancient creed characterized as being *una* (one) and *sancta* (holy) in its essence (see **unity, holiness**). Already in 1937 the world church conferences in Oxford (Life and Work*) and Edinburgh (Faith and Order*) re-awakened the *una sancta* idea in the ecumenical movement.

Roman Catholics prepared the way for the USM by various movements for church renewal after the first world war, together with a critical awareness of the inadequate nature of catholicity* in terms of the gospel within the actual history of the RCC. The Bonn theologian Arnold Rademacher and the dean of Paderborn cathedral, Paul Simon, became spokesmen for a "catholicity not constricted by a narrow idea of catholicism" in an effort for the reunion of the Christian churches. They were in fact supporting Yves Congar, a French Dominican, who in his 1937 *Chrétiens désunis* claimed: "That... which the separation of our brethren has... realized and actualized" outside the "visible borders" of the Roman Catholic Church "is a loss... to its actual and effective Catholicity."

At the same time, the church historian Joseph Lortz revised the traditional RC interpretation of the Reformation* and of Martin Luther's person and chief concerns. These suggestions gained wide publicity, so that "in every region of our country and beyond, circles of earnest Christians from the various Christian communities came together privately, working quietly and humbly to fulfill — completely independently of each other at the start — the last wishes of the Lord" (Matthias Laros).

Seizing upon this increasing readiness for ecumenism, Max Josef Metzger (1887-1944) produced effective work in addresses and short articles and in personal contacts. In 1928 he established the "House of Christ the King" and the Society of Christ the King, at Meitingen-bei-Augsburg. This was the focal point of the USM, initially called the Una Sancta Fraternity as an expression of the re-awakened self-awareness of "fraternity in Christ across all barriers". In 1939 Metzger organized the first Meitingen ecumenical dialogue. The USM task was to break down misunderstandings and prejudices, to create awareness of common elements in the faith, to test in open encounter and discussion between Roman Catholics and Protestants how far contrasts might be reconciled, but above all in common prayer to provide a sign of "hope against all hope". The Nazis executed Father Metzger for high treason, April 1944.

Out of USM circulars developed the journal *Una Sancta*, in co-operation with the Benedictine abbey of Niederaltaich, Federal Republic of Germany. There, since 1946, the abbot, Emmanuel Heufelder, has held regular encounters of RC and Protestant Christians. In 1935 the abbey also began relations, in studies and contacts, with the Eastern churches, based upon Pope Pius XI's 1924 letter to the confederation of Benedictine monasteries. In 1946 a Una Sancta meeting centre (since 1962, the ecumenical institute) was established at Niederalteich for such work.

The experiences which Protestants and Roman Catholics shared in the period of National Socialism and the second world war, the upheaval in the post-war distribution of the German population, and the resulting far larger number of interconfessional marriages brought about a new atmosphere of co-existence. In many places new Una Sancta circles were founded. But the USM was also exposed to a variety of criticisms: among the Protestants, that it was disguised proselytism; among the Roman Catholics, that it promoted religious indifferentism. A Vatican *monitum* in 1948, warning RCs about participation in ecumenical conferences and services, sharpened the tone of the USM vetoes. According to Vatican Radio, this warning should be a safeguard against a rank, uninhibited growth of the USM. The Vatican's later instruction (20 December 1949) was more positive and gave more exact rules for ecumenical gatherings, which were even encouraged. The biennial *Katholikentage* (German RC laity congresses) and the Protestant *Kirchentage* of the 1950s, and especially the Una Sancta event at the eucharistic congress of 1960 in Munich, made clear how far the ecumenical idea had caught the imagination of the grassroots in the church on the eve of the Second Vatican Council.

After Vatican II, the USM merged largely into new ecumenical bodies. To some extent the USM continues in the Council of Ecumenical Groups (Arbeitsgemeinschaft ökumenischer Kreise), co-founded by Niederaltaich and by the ecumenical centre of the German Churches' Ecumenical Institute.

GERHARD VOSS

M. Laros, *Schöpferischer Friede der Konfessionen: Die USB, ihr Ziel und ihre Arbeit*, Recklinghausen, Paulus, 1950 • L. Swidler, *Bloodwitness for Peace and Unity: Life of M.J. Metzger*, Denville, NJ, Dimension, 1977 • L. Swidler, *Ecumenical Vanguard: The History of the Una Sancta Movement*, Pittsburgh, PA, Duquesne UP, 1966.

UNDA. Unda (Latin for wave, here applied to radio waves) is an international Roman Catholic association for radio and television, with its headquarters in Brussels. Its purpose is to co-ordinate and stimulate the professional and apostolic activities of Roman Catholics in radio, television and related audiovisual means of communication, with a view to proclaiming the gospel and serving human development.

The association was first formed at Cologne in 1928, when a bureau was set up which organized "International Catholic Radio Congresses" at Munich (1929), Breslau (1932), Prague (1934) and Hilversum (1936). In 1947, after the disastrous interruption caused by the war, links were re-established at Fribourg in Switzerland and took account of the birth of television. It was then that the association took the name Unda.

Unda relies in the first instance on national sections (24 of them in 1947, around 110 in 1990), which meet each year in their respective continents. Every three or four years a world assembly is held (Manila 1980, Nairobi 1983, Quito 1987, Bangkok 1990). The president of Unda is appointed by the assembly and is a member of the Pontifical Council for Social Communications in the Vatican.

The media have unique advantages for ecumenical co-operation, in which Unda's main partner is the World Association for Christian Communication* (WACC). The latter association is Protestant in origin but accepts members of any Christian confession. Co-operation between WACC and Unda is particularly close in Latin America. In Europe, attempts which were initially parallel (beginning for Unda in 1958 at Monte Carlo) led to the creation of an "International Christian Television Week", for which Unda-Europe and

WACC share responsibility. Held once every two years, the tenth such week was at Hilversum in May 1989.

ANDRÉ BABEL

UNEMPLOYMENT. Mass unemployment became a serious issue after the industrial revolution, when the relative importance of agriculture and other forms of self-employment declined. The great depression of the 1930s triggered worldwide concern with the welfare implications of widespread unemployment. The United Nations charter acknowledges such concern, as it calls on governments to take action to promote the achievement of full employment.

The International Labour Office (ILO) reported in 1984 that while industrial societies have seen their unemployment triple over the past decade, 15 times as many people in developing countries are today without paid work or are grossly under-employed, a total of some 500 million. By the year 2000 the world's job-seekers are expected to increase by another 750 million, nearly nine-tenths of them in so-called developing countries.

There is no single universally accepted definition of unemployment. National statistics are not uniform and cannot easily be compared or added. Besides definitional problems, there is the difficulty of measuring under-employment, work done in the so-called informal sector, and clandestine employment.

The results of unemployment are distributed very unequally among population groups. The hardest hit are those who suffer ill health and disabled, younger and older workers, women and ethnic minorities.

The issue of unemployment has been on the agenda of the modern ecumenical movement since its beginning. The Anglican Conference on Christian Politics, Economics and Citizenship (COPEC), which was held in England in 1924 and behind which William Temple was the driving force, called unemployment morally unacceptable and said that the causes should be removed. The COPEC was organized in preparation for the universal Christian conference on Life and Work,* held in Stockholm in 1925, which also spoke about the "tremendous question of unemployment". The message of the conference was sent to the workers in the world "in the name of the Son of Man, the Carpenter of Nazareth". The Life and Work movement established the International Christian Social Institute in Geneva. Close links were established with the ILO. Its first major research project was a study of unemployment, a widespread problem during the great depression. A series of national study conferences was organized leading up to an international conference in Basel. This resulted in a pressing appeal to the churches to combat unemployment and to alleviate the distress of those most deeply afflicted.

The great depression also influenced the world conference on "Church, Community and State", which took place in Oxford in 1937. The message from this conference speaks about unemployment, which saps people's strength of body, mind and spirit. The conference report points to the progressive mechanization of industry, which has periodically thrown large numbers of workers into long periods of unemployment. The threat of unemployment "produces a feeling of extreme insecurity in the minds of masses of the people. Unemployment, especially when prolonged, tends to create in the mind of the unemployed person a sense of uselessness, or even of being a nuisance, and to empty his life of any meaning. This situation cannot be met by measures of unemployment assistance, because it is the lack of significant activity which tends to destroy his human self-respect."

Probably because of the relatively high employment levels, the issue of unemployment received less ecumenical attention during the post-second world war period. This situation changed when the world economy plunged into a deep recession which started in 1979. The WCC Sub-unit on Church and Society and the Commission on the Churches' Participation in Development organized consultations and published reports on the issue of unemployment seen from a global perspective. Many WCC member churches and related ecumenical bodies put the issue high on their agendas, organized consultations, published reports and suggested policies to combat rising unemployment. Most of the churches' activities in this field are based on the conviction that involuntary unemployment is a basic injustice against each person and family suffering from it, that it is an obstacle to the fulfilment of Christian vocation,* and that work is both a right and a need of all persons.

Roman Catholic social teaching has always been very emphatic about labour issues and the rights of workers. In *Gaudium et Spes* (1965) and "The Church and Human Rights" (Pontifical Commission Iustitia et Pax, 1974), work is regarded both as a duty and as a right. The encyclical of Pope John Paul II, *Laborem Exercens* (1981), stresses the centrality of "suitable employment for all who are capable of it". According to John Paul II: "The opposite of a just and right situation... is unemployment, which in all cases is an evil, and which when it reaches a certain level can become a real social disaster." The pope also stressed "the principle of the priority of labour over capital", stating that "capital, the whole collection of means of production, remains a mere instrument" (see **social encyclicals, papal**).

The United States bishops' "Pastoral Letter on Catholic Social Teaching and the US Economy" (1986) is also unequivocal about the place of labour* and employment in society. According to the US bishops, "people have a right to employment". Full employment is the foundation for a just economy: "Work with adequate pay for all who seek it is the primary means for achieving basic justice in our society."

ROB VAN DRIMMELEN

Advisory Group on Economic Matters, *Labour, Employment and Unemployment: An Ecumenical Reappraisal*, WCC, 1987 • H. Davis & D. Gosling eds, *Will the Future Work? Values for Emerging Patterns of Work and Employment*, WCC, 1985 • *Unemployment: A Case Study on Contemporary Christian Social Responsibility*, Geneva, LWF, 1984 • *Unemployment: Work for the Churches: A Survey of Church Resolutions, Publications, Projects and Initiatives in the United Kingdom, Western Germany and the Netherlands*, MCKS, Netherlands, 1986.

UNIAPAC. The Union internationale chrétienne des dirigeants d'entreprise (UNIAPAC = International Christian Union of Business Executives) comprises 25 national associations of Christian business people and managers, principally in Western Europe and Latin America, but also in Africa and Asia. Founded in Rome in 1931 by a small Roman Catholic group of Belgian, French and Dutch

employers, it expanded and in 1962-63 included other Christian executives. The network is committed to studying and spreading the ethical principles of Christian social teaching in economic and social life, particularly at the level of business and management.

From its general secretariat in Belgium, UNIAPAC issues occasional socio-economic papers on e.g. Latin American business investments, the ethical climate in companies, integration of young people into business, the churches and transnational corporations,* and ethical approaches to the international debt question (see **debt crisis**).

TOM STRANSKY

UNION, ORGANIC. As the Body of Christ, the church* is an organism "joined and knit together by every joint with which it is supplied when each part is working properly" (Eph. 4:16). Its unity* is therefore properly described as organic. All churches accept and use this biblical language with reference to their own inner life. The debate about organic union arises when churches seeking closer unity have differing views of the way in which unity and diversity are related to each other in the Body of Christ. Churches with similar polities have had little difficulty in entering into organic union. Scores of such intraconfessional unions have taken place in the present century.

The world missionary conference (Edinburgh 1910) debated the respective merits of organic and federal types of union and found strengths and weaknesses in both. Some delegates, notably Charles Brent, Episcopal bishop of the Philippines, were convinced that practical co-operation was not enough and that only a united church could offer a credible invitation to adherents of the great religions of the East. From his initiative came the first call for a world conference on Faith and Order,* and at the initial meeting of those churches which had responded to the call (New York 1913), it was agreed that "while organic unity is the ideal which all Christians should have in their thoughts and prayers", the immediate task was not to propose such unity but to explore patiently the reasons for disunity.

It was no accident that this initiative came from Anglican sources. The movement for co-operation in missions had been, prior to 1910, an affair of Protestant churches of an evangelical persuasion, with the assumption that the questions of faith and order which divided their churches were of small account compared to the task of evangelism.* Anglicans of a Catholic churchmanship could not accept this assumption. As far back as 1870, the American Episcopalian W.R. Huntington had proposed a plan for organic union among the American churches on the basis of what was to become the Chicago-Lambeth Quadrilateral:* scripture,* the ancient creeds,* the sacraments* of baptism* and eucharist,* and the historic episcopate (see **episcopacy**). In the country of its origin this vision was to be swept aside by the federal ideas which were to lead to the creation of a council of churches (see **federalism**), but it provided the basis for the appeal to all Christian people issued by the Lambeth conference of 1920. The vision offered in this appeal was of "an outward, visible and united society, holding one faith, having its own recognized officers, using God-given means of grace, and inspiring all its members to the worldwide service of the kingdom of God".

This appeal and Anglican initiatives flowing from it occupied centre stage in unity discussions for the next 40 years. Its proposal of the historic episcopate as the visible centre around which unity could be restored was both its strength and the stone of stumbling for churches not episcopally ordered.

When the first world conference on F&O met in Lausanne in 1927, the only section which was not able to produce a report acceptable to the whole conference was section 7 on the unity of Christendom and the relation thereto of existing churches. Anglican members of the conference held that the report gave too much emphasis to co-operation in practical tasks and not enough to unity in faith and order. The second F&O conference (Edinburgh 1937) discussed the issue under the three headings: co-operative action, intercommunion,* and corporate union. The last is described as "the final goal" but also as the most difficult.

The formation of the WCC in 1948 created a new situation in which it became immediately necessary to assure member churches (esp. the Orthodox) that by joining the Council they had not committed themselves to any particular conception of union. This assurance was given in the Toronto statement* of the central committee (1950), which affirmed that the Council was a forum for the discussion of this question but did not prejudge the outcome. In the following decade there was intense discussion of the nature of the unity we seek, leading to the formulation of the New Delhi statement of 1961 (see **unity of "all in each place"**). This statement does not use the term but expresses what has generally been understood as "organic union". At no point before or after this has the WCC committed itself so explicitly to the goal of organic union.

But by the time this statement was made, changes were afoot which would alter the terms of debate. At New Delhi the Orthodox churches of the Eastern bloc, hitherto outside the Council, became full members exercising increasing influence in all its thinking. None of these had been involved in discussion of organic union with non-Orthodox churches. At the same time the Second Vatican Council* brought the Roman Catholic Church for the first time into full participation in the discussions of faith and order. Its immense influence, and its character as a single supranational church, shifted the focus away from local moves for organic union and towards the relations of the World Confessional Families with Rome and with one another. The suggestion of Cardinal Willebrands that the aim should not be organic union but rather the co-existence of different "types" of church life was widely canvassed (see **typoi**).

In the ensuing years, while intraconfessional unions of an organic type continued to occur, the only area in which the Lambeth appeal led to organic union between episcopal and non-episcopal churches was the Indian sub-continent. Numerous attempts in other parts of the world failed. And (perhaps partly because of wider political changes) the Anglican communion no longer played the leading role in initiating moves for union which it had played earlier in the century. Moreover, movements in biblical scholarship eroded the assumption which lay behind the Lambeth appeal, namely that our task is to restore an original organic unity which has been lost. Much New Testament scholarship claims to show that such unity did not exist in the primitive church. And meanwhile the growth of para-church organizations and of church base communities* in many parts of the world has strengthened the tendency to bypass the issues of faith and order which divide the great communions and to concentrate on practical issues of peace* and justice.* Organic union does not appear urgent.

It would seem, however, that as long as churches continue to use and to cherish the language of scripture about the Body of Christ, the issue of organic union can never be ignored. The periodic conferences of united and uniting churches* continue to bear witness to the fruitfulness of unions among churches of different polities. However difficult the way, it is hard to believe that anything can be the final goal except the organic unity of one body. But, as Stephen Neill remarks at the end of his survey of unions achieved and contemplated: "The final and terrible difficulty is that churches cannot unite unless they are willing to die" (*A History of the Ecumenical Movement, 1517-1948*, 495).

See also **unity; unity, models of; unity, ways to.**

LESSLIE NEWBIGIN

G. Gassmann, *Konzeptionen der Einheit in der Bewegung für Glauben und Kirchenverfassung*, Göttingen, Vandenhoek & Ruprecht, 1979.

UNIQUENESS OF CHRIST.

If Jesus Christ* is not unique, then it must be that either the Word of God has become personally incarnate in others also (which would be a highly unusual position in Christian thinking), or else Jesus himself is something less than the incarnation of the second person of the Trinity* (an opinion which would be definitely heretical). Some seek to evade the ontological problem by denying that the (divine) salvation* of humankind requires such a "metaphysical" basis, or by softening the question of uniqueness to one of degree rather than kind, a relative rather than an absolute matter.

Of those who question that Jesus Christ is "the saviour of the world" (John 4:42; or "the light of the world", "the life of the world", "the hope of the world", to cite the attributions made at several WCC assemblies*), while still holding to the possibility of human salvation, the most radical are those who consider that salvation may come by other routes (whether such routes pluralistically in-

clude the way of Christ or Christ is excluded in favour of another path). While, by definition, no Christian can espouse the second possibility (the denial of any saving value to Christ), some who claim to be Christian theologians have recently argued for the first, namely that Christ is (simply, and perhaps not even pre-eminently) one access to salvation (see, for instance, Hick & Knitter). Evangelism,* if practised at all, will not have much urgency in this perspective. The problem, however, is whether salvation means the same thing when the saviours are different; and whether different saviours mean different "gods" (see **God**).

Hitherto Christians have held that human salvation depends *in some way* on Christ. From the beginning of Christianity, Christians have had to face the question concerning people who lived before the time of Jesus. With regard to the righteous in ancient Israel, the answer was reached quite quickly: they had believed in the same God, who would later reveal himself in the incarnation* of the Son and the pentecostal gift of the Spirit. Abraham's faith was reckoned to him for righteousness (Rom. 4:3); Abraham and Isaiah had "seen" Christ's "day" and his "glory" (John 8:56, 12:41). With regard to the pagans, Justin Martyr held that the good Greeks who had lived "according to the Logos" (which "enlightens every man", John 1:9) were Christians *avant la lettre* (*Apology* 1.46). Perhaps the same principle can be applied, even in the Christian era, to those who never hear Christ preached. For pagans, according to Paul, have "what the law requires written on their hearts" (Rom. 2:15), and they may "do by nature what the law requires" (2:14), and in the divine judgment there will be "glory and honour and peace for every one who does good" (2:10; cf. 2:16; 2 Cor. 5:10). By virtue of the Logos (which became personally incarnate in Jesus Christ, John 1:14) or the law (for, according to Justin Martyr, Christ himself was the fulfilment of the promise of "an eternal law and a new covenant for the whole world", *Dialogue with Trypho*, 43, cf. 11,51,122; see already 1 Cor. 1:30), a reference to Christ is here maintained.

A modern version of this position is the "anonymous Christians" of Karl Rahner. Although those so designated may reject the designation for various reasons (for example, considering it to be "Christian imperialism"), some such accounting seems from a Christian standpoint to be both *necessary* ("No one comes to the Father, but by me", John 14:6; cf. Matt. 11:27) and *possible* ("And I, when I am lifted up from the earth, will draw all men to myself", John 12:32), if salvation is already to be found outside the historic Christian community; it allows Christians to discern, rejoice in, and be grateful for "signs of Christ" beyond the bounds of the institutional church. Thus M.M. Thomas envisages a "koinonia in Christ" that includes not only those who acknowledge "the *person* of Jesus as the Messiah" but also, at different levels, "people of different faiths inwardly being renewed by their acknowledgment of the ultimacy of the *pattern* of suffering servanthood as exemplified by the crucified Jesus" and, even more broadly, people engaged in "the power-political struggle for new societies and a world community based on secular or religious anthropologies *informed by* the agape of the cross" (*Risking Christ*, 119). Ontologically, this would seem to imply the *saving presence* of Christ among and with all such people. Or if a similar vision is phrased in terms of the Spirit, then it will be remembered that in Christian teaching the Holy Spirit is never separated from the Son — who was incarnate in Jesus Christ. In such a perspective, evangelism will be seen as the effort to bring people to an *explicit* faith in Christ and a *deliberate* discipleship to him.

Other Christians remain doubtful about the notion of "anonymous Christians" or a vision such as that of Thomas. They will appeal to Acts 4:12: "There is salvation in no one else, for there is no other name under heaven given among men by which we must be saved", and see this "name" to require confession that "Jesus is Lord" (Rom. 10:8-13) to the point of receiving baptism* in the Triune name (Matt. 28:19-20; Mark 16:15-16). The preaching of the gospel will then be regarded as an act of rescue towards those who are otherwise perishing (Rom. 10:14-17; John 3:18,36).

Doxologically, Christians have always affirmed the uniqueness of Christ in a strong sense, attributing the gift of salvation to him and ascribing him universal significance, all in closest association with the Father and the Holy Spirit. In what appears to be liturgical language, all things are said to be made "through him" and "for him" (John 1:1-3,14; 1 Cor. 8:6; Col. 1:15-20; Heb. 1:1-3). Because he has been given "all authority in heaven and on earth", he can instruct his followers to "make disciples of all nations, baptizing them in the name of the Father and of the Son and of the Holy Spirit" (Matt. 28:18-19). An early hymn looks to the time when "at the name of Jesus every knee [will] bow, in heaven and on earth and under the earth, and every tongue confess that Jesus Christ is Lord, to the glory of God the Father" (Phil. 2:10-11). A "great multitude... from every nation, from all tribes and peoples and tongues" will cry: "Salvation belongs to our God who sits upon the throne, and to the Lamb" (Rev. 7:9-10). Meanwhile, God's blessings descend, and our prayers ascend, "through Jesus Christ our Lord", while "Father, Son, and Holy Spirit" are worshipped and glorified together. The doctrinal account of this doxology is given in the dogma* of the Trinity, which is epistemologically grounded in the history of Jesus (incarnation, life, death, resurrection, exaltation), which itself rests ontologically on the reality of the Triune God.

How, or whether, all will finally, by God's grace* and with God's help, be saved, is not yet given to human knowledge (see **universalism**).

See also **dialogue, interfaith; Jesus Christ; mission; redemption; revelation; salvation; Trinity.**

GEOFFREY WAINWRIGHT

J. Hick & P.F. Knitter, eds, *The Myth of Christian Uniqueness*, Maryknoll, NY, Orbis, 1987 • L. Newbigin, "The Christian Faith and the World Religions", in *Keeping the Faith*, G. Wainwright ed., Philadelphia, Fortress, 1988 • L. Newbigin, *The Gospel in a Pluralist Society*, WCC, 1989 • J. Ries, *Les chrétiens parmi les religions: Des Actes des Apôtres à Vatican II*, Paris, Desclée, 1987 • M.M. Thomas, *Risking Christ for Christ's Sake*, WCC, 1987.

UNITARIAN UNIVERSALISM. Unitarian Universalism is an amalgamation of two religious traditions: the Unitarian, which derives its name from its belief in the unity of God (as contrasted with a Trinitarian view); and the Universalist, which holds to the doctrine of universal salvation,* in the conviction

that a loving God could never condemn human beings to the fires of hell (see **universalism**).

Unitarianism generally traces its roots to *On the Errors of the Trinity*, a book written in 1531 by the 20-year-old Michael Servetus, who found no sound basis in scripture for the doctrine of the Trinity* (Servetus was burned at the stake by Calvin in 1553). Unitarian ideas, including the belief that Jesus saved human beings not by dying for them but by setting an example for them to follow, were spread widely throughout Poland by Faustus Socinus (1539-1604) and the so-called Polish Brethren. As an organized movement, however, Unitarianism first received official recognition in 1569 when the only Unitarian king in history, John Sigismund (1540-71) of Transylvania, issued his act of religious tolerance and freedom of conscience.

The first Unitarian congregation in England was formed in 1774 by Theophilus Lindsey (1723-1808), and in the USA in 1782 by James Freeman (1759-1835). But the movement in the USA did not become organized and coherent until after William Ellery Channing (1780-1842) had preached his Baltimore sermon, "Unitarian Christianity", in 1819; he added to traditional Unitarian views a rational approach to the interpretation of scripture and opposition to the Calvinist doctrine of original sin.* The following years witnessed the division of New England Congregationalism into Trinitarian and Unitarian branches. The American Unitarian Association was founded in 1825.

While universalist views of salvation had spread widely in England in the late 17th and early 18th centuries, Universalism as an organized movement was principally a US phenomenon, founded by John Murray (1741-1815). In his *Treatise on Atonement* (1805) Hosea Ballou taught a Unitarian view of God and argued that the Bible ought to be interpreted in the light of reason. The Universalist Church of America traces its formal beginnings to 1793.

A growing commonality of belief resulted in the formal institutional merger of the two North American movements in 1961 with the formation of the Unitarian Universalist Association* — a creedless denomination which encourages its members to seek religious truth out of their own reflection and experience.

While Unitarian (Universalism) is found in its largest numbers in North America, Unitarians still practise their faith around the globe from Transylvania to India, Nigeria to Japan.

Unitarian (Universalism) teaches tolerance and respect for other religious viewpoints. Unitarians were the founders in 1901 of the oldest continuing international interfaith organization in the world, now known as the International Association for Religious Freedom.

WILLIAM F. SCHULZ

UNITARIAN UNIVERSALIST ASSOCIATION.
The UUA resulted from a 1961 merger between the American Unitarian Association (1825) and the Universalist Church of America (1793). It consists of approximately 1,000 congregations located principally in the US and Canada with about 185,000 members. All Unitarian Universalist congregations are congregationally governed.

While not permitted on doctrinal grounds to be a member of the WCC or national councils of churches, the UUA is an official observer of the National Council of the Churches of Christ in the United States, a founding member of the International Association for Religious Freedom, and a co-operating organization with the International Ethical and Humanist Union.

UUA headquarters are in Boston, Massachusetts, USA.

WILLIAM F. SCHULZ

UNITED AND UNITING CHURCHES.
In broadest definition, united churches are national or regional churches (as distinguished from union parishes or congregations) formed by the union of two or more previously separated denominations. These may be churches within the same confessional family, such as the United Methodist Church (USA) or churches from different confessional traditions, such as the Church of South India (CSI), which in 1947 brought together Anglican, Methodist, Reformed and Congregationalist streams. While intraconfessional unions can be both ecumenically significant and difficult to achieve, it is the transconfessional churches that have attracted most ecumenical attention; this article focuses on these.

There is no typical united church, but the following characteristics generally hold true. First, united churches have achieved "organic" or structural union (see **union, organic**) in the sense that they can make common decisions of faith and order,* mission* and the use of their own resources. This distinguishes them from relationships of "full communion" between still-separate churches (see **communion**). Second, they are worshipping faith communities, with their own patterns of authorized ministry (see **ministry in the church**). This distinguishes them from councils (see **councils of churches**) or federations (see **federalism**) of churches. Next, they seek to give theological expression to the gospel in the context more of the present ecumenical movement than of inherited confessions. Fourth, while they certainly do not abandon the vision of universal Christian fellowship, they are committed to manifest the unity of the church in their particular nation, region or culture* (e.g. the United Church of Christ in the Philippines or the Church of North India). Finally, their self-understanding is, to a considerable extent, shaped by an intentional act of "uniting" through which a new churchly identity has been assumed.

Beyond this, united churches manifest great diversity. Most are the result of decades of negotiation and planning, but others came quickly into being, e.g. the United Church of Christ in Japan (Kyodan), formed as a result of governmental mandate in 1941. A few are episcopally ordered (see **episcopacy**), usually because Anglicans have been involved in the union; others have a basically connectional polity, having been formed by the union of Reformed (Presbyterian), Methodist, Congregationalist, Disciples, Baptist or Brethren churches (see **church order**). In most cases, the confessional identities of the negotiating churches are superseded by the identity of the united body (though distinctive ways of worship or confessions of faith from the parent traditions may well be preserved), but others (e.g. the Church of Christ in Zaire) understand themselves as united while allowing the previous denominations to continue as identifiable communities within the new church structure.

Most churches which think of themselves as united are products of the 20th-century ecumenical movement; the Evangelical Church of the Union (EKU), however, which stems from early-19th-century efforts in Prussia to heal the division between Lutherans and Calvinists, is a central participant in gatherings of united churches. The majority of united churches have originated since the second world war in formerly colonized nations where confessional divisions have little historical significance and where the need for a common Christian witness is intensely felt (see **colonialism**). The first major union of the modern ecumenical movement, however, was that of the United Church of Canada in 1925.

The difficulty with definition also makes it hard to determine the precise number of united churches. According to the "Survey of Church Union Negotiations", compiled by the WCC's Faith and Order staff and published biennially in *The Ecumenical Review*, 18 transconfessional united churches, representing more than 60 former church bodies, have come into existence since the second world war, and several of these (e.g. the United Protestant Church of Belgium and the United Reformed Church in the United Kingdom) have undertaken more than one union process. A conservative estimate is that over 20 million Christians belong to churches which identify themselves as having united across confessional boundaries.

Advocates of church union often defend their vision with various arguments. First, the New Testament speaks positively of the church in different places (e.g. Rome or Corinth) but not of different "types" (e.g. Apollos or Paul [1 Cor. 1]). Second, confessional labels seem to undermine the Christian claim to be a reconciled and reconciling people (see **reconciliation**) and thus damage their witness to Christ, especially in places where Christians are a minority. Third, for unity to be meaningful, it must make a difference to the way Christians live their lives in local communities; it must find visible, structured embodiment through which Christians take direct, active responsibility for one another. Fourth, united churches, by avoiding duplication and competition, are better stewards of resources; they are also able to bring these resources to bear on new issues of witness and service in a concentrated way. Fifth, those who have undergone union generally testify that, while painful, it has led to enrichment and renewal. They would agree with these sentences from the WCC's New Delhi assembly (1961): "The achievement of unity will involve nothing less than a death and rebirth of many forms of church life as we have known them. We believe that nothing less costly can finally suffice."

United churches may be called "uniting" in the sense that they generally view themselves as but a stage in the process of seeking the unity of "all in each place". At least one united church, the Uniting Church in Australia, has incorporated this understanding into its name. The term "uniting churches" is also used, however, with reference to churches that are currently participating in conversations which intend church union. The 1986 F&O "Survey" identifies 14 transconfessional church union negotiations in 12 countries.

Church-union committees often report that questions of polity (esp. the reconciliation of ministries) and the fear of losing a sense of ecclesial identity are the most stubborn obstacles to union. The socio-political context can also be a very important factor. A proposed union of Anglican, Methodist and Presbyterian churches in Nigeria was postponed in 1965 due to legal challenges. Two months after postponement, a military coup overthrew

the civilian government and led to civil war and the abandonment of plans for a united church. In Sri Lanka, decades of careful preparation were left unfulfilled by litigation and ethnic violence.

Recent trends. The creation of united churches through structured, "organic" union was, for much of this century, a favoured strategy for ecumenical advance. The New Delhi assembly, which spoke of the unity we seek as a "fully committed fellowship" of "all in each place", contributed to an unprecedented surge in union activity. Between 1965 and 1972, united churches were born in Zambia, Jamaica and Grand Cayman, Madagascar, Ecuador, Papua New Guinea and the Solomon Islands, Belgium, North India, Pakistan, Bangladesh, Zaire and Great Britain.

During this same period, however, mounting criticism was directed against the idea of church union. Many church leaders, especially in developing countries (where the call to united churches had been so prominent), began to argue that overcoming confessional differences through corporate union should not be their primary agenda. The major challenges before the church, they maintained, are political and social injustice or

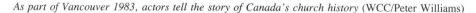

As part of Vancouver 1983, actors tell the story of Canada's church history (WCC/Peter Williams)

threats to peace; and the deepest source of division between Christians is not their denominational identity but their differing responses to such issues. The tremendous effort expended on uniting would thus be better spent on the struggles against racism* or hunger or nuclear weapons.

The 1960s also marked the official entry of the Roman Catholic Church into the ecumenical movement. This development quickly transformed discussions about what unity entails and how it is to be realized. The idea of union which develops a new identity among churches in various regional or national settings is at odds with Roman Catholic ecclesiology. From the RC perspective, preferable are "bilateral dialogues" (see **dialogue, bilateral**), which seek the reconciliation of theological differences between globally organized Christian World Communions* (CWCs, e.g. the Lutheran World Federation). These conversations, far from undermining confessional identity, have tended to strengthen it. They have also helped to shift the ecumenical spotlight away from national-level church union. (This shift is occurring, despite the accepted understanding of unity as a "conciliar fellowship of local churches which are themselves truly united", articulated by the WCC Nairobi assembly [1975], which reinforced the work of united churches.)

Such challenges have contributed to several new developments in the search for church union. Union negotiations are increasingly unwilling to talk about unity across doctrinal and structural barriers apart from issues which divide the human community (e.g. racial discrimination or poverty). It is now widely affirmed that inclusive community and greater sensitivity to the needs of mission are not simply the byproducts of union. As authentic marks of what it means to be the church, they must be central to the uniting process itself.

There is broad agreement that visible unity must be realized "in stages". Several union efforts (e.g. the Commission of the Covenanted Churches in Wales and the Consultation on Church Union* [COCU, USA]) have established or are trying to establish "covenants" (involving such agreements as the mutual recognition of members, mutual recognition or reconciliation of ministries, regular eucharistic sharing and common mission) as a way of moving towards deeper fellowship

(see **covenanting**). Church union, in other words, is viewed not as an all-or-nothing, one-time achievement but as a process of gradual growth that allows the churches to strengthen their commitment to each other through interim steps. There seems to be less preconceived adherence to a particular "model" of union (e.g. "the CSI plan") than in the past. The COCU, for example, in its 1988 text (*Churches in Covenant Communion*), speaks of its proposed covenant as an expression of unity in its own right (though one which must deepen and expand) and not simply an interim stage.

In line with the previous point, churches in various parts of the world are now exploring federation models while yet identifying themselves with the basic vision of united churches. A good example is the joint council of the Church of North India, the Church of South India, and the Mar Thoma Church. For some time these churches have had relationships of full communion.* The current joint council seeks to give visible expression to their "organic oneness" while still maintaining denominational autonomy and identity (see **denominationalism**). In Italy the Waldensians and Methodists refer to their covenant as a united church, although both keep their specific identities. In 1984, the 54 member denominations of the Council of Churches in Indonesia redefined their relationship under a new name — the Communion of Churches in Indonesia. Unity, they contended, will not come by the negotiations of official representatives but gradually through the common will and actions of "all the church members of all levels... and in all places".

This quotation indicates a fourth trend: less interest in developing national plans of union and more attention to building relationships at the grassroots level. Indeed, in such places as England and New Zealand "local ecumenical projects"* (united or co-operating parishes) seem to be exerting the greatest pressure for church unity.

United churches and church union negotiations are attempting to relate their work and vision more deliberately to the wider ecumenical picture, including the bilateral conversations between CWCs and the multilateral efforts of F&O (e.g. *Baptism, Eucharist and Ministry*). Recent meetings of united churches speak frequently of the dangers of a competitive ecumenism which polarizes the search for unity (e.g. union with Protestants *or* closer relations with Rome, international theological dialogues *or* national union conversations).

Many of these developments have received focused attention at a series of F&O consultations which involve representatives from united and uniting churches around the world. Five such meetings between 1967 and 1987 exchanged information, sought solutions to common problems, lifted up the vision of church union and strengthened relations between these churches. Of particular interest is the relationship of *Kirchengemeinschaft* ("full communion", involving mutual recognition and accountability) between the Evangelical Church of the Union in Germany and the United Church of Christ in the US.

Ecumenical significance. The debate between united churches and the CWCs is a useful framework for describing the contribution of united churches to the wider ecumenical movement. For example, the CWCs acknowledge the importance of unity "in each place", yet they tend to emphasize that the church is a universal fellowship which transcends national and cultural boundaries. On the other hand, united churches affirm that unity must be "in all places", yet they see their task as witnessing to the need for a visible, embodied fellowship in each particular location. They remind the ecumenical movement that the church can manifest catholicity by its ability to give common witness in a variety of cultural settings.

The CWCs frequently stress the historical continuity of the church's faith and life, especially as this finds expression in the various confessional traditions. Advocates for church union insist that, while continuity is important, the presently divided church will also need to be transformed if it is to show forth more fully its given unity in Christ. They remind the ecumenical movement that the search for unity is never without cost.

The bilateral dialogues carried on by CWCs emphasize the need for extensive theological consensus as a prerequisite for consideration of structured commitment between church families. United churches, while by no means ignoring the importance of theological work, have stressed that the building of trust and commitment through structural forms of interaction is at least as essential to the search

for unity as theological agreement. They remind the ecumenical movement that one must not minimize "non-theological factors", such as fear of change and institutional inertia. These churches also affirm that unity grows as much after union as before it. As a result, many united churches leave the development of constitutions, statements of faith, and worship materials to the period after the new church is inaugurated.

United churches may be the place where the ecumenical vision of Christ's one Body is most concretely tested and experienced. Visible unity often seems, at best, like a distant goal. Yet every week millions of Christians, once divided at the Lord's table, break bread together within communities that have made a deliberate decision to grow beyond past separations. This can be an important sign of hope.

See **church; church order; denominationalism; federalism; local church; union, organic; unity; unity of "all in each place"; unity, models of; unity, ways to.**

MICHAEL KINNAMON

T.F. Best ed., *Living Today towards Visible Unity: The Fifth International Consultation of United and Uniting Churches*, WCC, 1988 • N. Ehrenström & W.G. Muelder eds, *Institutionalism and Church Unity*, New York, Association, 1963 • M. Kinnamon ed., *Unity: In Each Place... In All Places: United Churches and the Christian World Communions*, WCC, 1983 • M. Kinnamon & T.F. Best eds, *Called to Be One in Christ: United Churches and the Ecumenical Movement*, WCC, 1985 • "Survey of Church Union Negotiations", *The Ecumenical Review*, 1954 and every two years.

UNITED NATIONS. The United Nations was established in 1945 "to maintain international peace and security", "to develop friendly relations among nations", "to achieve international co-operation in solving international problems" and for "promoting and encouraging respect for human rights and fundamental freedoms".

During the second world war it was realized that a universal organization dealing with collective security after the war could no longer be the League of Nations, which had been established in 1920. The league, of course, was the first world organization created for maintaining peace* and development of international co-operation. Before the first world war the system for limiting international conflict and avoiding war consisted mainly of certain generally accepted principles of international law, supported by certain understandings as to spheres of influence and by alliances to maintain balances of power, as a means of discouraging any nation from dominating the world.

The system broke down with the first world war, and at the end of the war the League of Nations was established. The basic concept of the league was that its members should be protected by collective action from aggression. The number of league members varied. At the beginning, in 1920, there were 42 states, and in 1939 there were 58 members. In the 20 years of the league's activity, events did not fulfill expectations. The support its members gave to the league was halting and reluctant, and certain states, dissatisfied with the post-war arrangements, were determined to destroy it.

On 2 February 1946, after the establishment of the new universal organization, the UN General Assembly set up the Negotiating Committee of the UN for League of Nations Assets and required the secretary-general to take over formally some of the functions, activities, obligations and property of the league. Many international agreements which came into being under the league remain valid.

The UN charter was drawn up by the representatives of 50 countries at the UN Conference on International Organization, which met at San Francisco from 25 April to 26 June 1945. The UN officially came into existence on 24 October 1945, when the charter had been ratified by China, France, the USSR, the UK and the USA and by a majority of other signatories at the conference. As of 1989 it has a membership of 159 nations.

The principal organs of the UN are the General Assembly, the Security Council, the Economic and Social Council, the Trusteeship Council, the International Court of Justice, and the Secretariat. The General Assembly is the main deliberative organ, the only one composed of all the UN member states. The Security Council's task is to promote international peace and security. The Economic and Social Council promotes world co-operation on economic, social, cultural and humanitarian problems. The Trusteeship Council has

supervised the UN Trust Territories through the administering authorities to promote the political, economic, social and educational advancement of the inhabitants towards self-government or independence. The International Court of Justice is the principal judicial organ of the UN.

The secretariat consists of the secretary-general and the staff. The secretary-general is the chief administrative officer of the organization, elected for a five-year term by the General Assembly on the recommendation of the Security Council.

The Security Council has five permanent members: People's Republic of China, France, USSR, the UK and the USA. The remaining ten members are elected by the General Assembly for two-year periods.

The UN charter (1945) has remained unchanged. The charter therefore largely reflects perceptions about international relations which pre-date the second world war and the nuclear age. It does not adequately represent the realities today. However any attempt to change the charter is likely to face enormous difficulties.

The objective of the UN is stated in article 1 of the charter: "to maintain international peace and security". The constraints the charter itself puts on the UN in fulfilling its mandate should be taken into account in assessing its achievements and failures. Of fundamental importance is the doctrine of national sovereignty. Article 2 of the charter declares: "The organization is based on the principle of sovereign equality of all its members." The doctrine of national sovereignty is reflected in several provisions of the charter, for example, "the domestic jurisdiction provision" in article 2 and the inadequate provisions regarding the jurisdiction of the International Court of Justice and the enforcement of its judgments. Closely linked to this is the tendency on the part of the major powers — who are also members of the Security Council — to protect and expand their spheres of influences. It is therefore evident that general improvement in relations among the major powers, especially between the super-powers, enhances the capacity of the UN in fulfilling its mandate.

It should be said to the credit of the UN that it has helped to keep peace in many conflicts and has successfully resolved disputes in some important instances. Its efforts at peace-keeping have been more successful than those for peace-making. UN peace-keeping forces have been able to end hostilities and enforce cease-fire and truce agreements. The secretary-general establishes and maintains channels of contact and negotiations with states, thus providing for eventual settlements of disputes. There are many failures and evident inadequacies in the system of the UN and its functioning. Lack of consensus among major powers on important issues has greatly inhibited co-operative action.

The accomplishments of the UN in humanitarian, development and cultural fields are commendable. UN bodies and agencies like the UN High Commissioner for Refugees (UNHCR), the UN Children's Fund (UNICEF), the UN Development Programme, the Food and Agriculture Organization, the UN Educational Scientific and Cultural Organization (UNESCO) and the World Health Organization have made substantial contributions in alleviating human suffering and in laying the foundations for development in many countries. Notwithstanding the exceptional efforts of the past years, which have registered substantial achievements, it is necessary to strengthen the capacity of the UN system for anticipating and responding to major problems of a humanitarian nature.

One of the important objectives of the UN is to promote respect for human rights and to address fundamental human problems. The Commission on Human Rights is the main forum where member states consider the practical application of the charter, the Universal Declaration of Human Rights and the instruments codified through the organization. Non-governmental organizations play an important role in providing information to the commission on violations of human rights in different parts of the world. The Centre for Human Rights is the principal secretariat organ in charge of following up matters related to human rights.

The UN provides several facilities for the promotion of disarmament. It is a unique public forum for the articulation and debate of proposals of disarmament before the world community. It provides a practical negotiating forum in the Conference on Disarmament in Geneva. The UN also has the capacity to monitor or manage arms-limitation agreements.

The WCC's Commission of the Churches on International Affairs (CCIA), which has consultative status with the Economic and Social Council of the UN (and with all major specialized agencies), represents the WCC in the UN system. It played a significant role in the formulation of the article on "religious liberty" in the Universal Declaration of Human Rights and in the establishment of the UN Commission on Human Rights. The forms of involvement of the WCC in the UN system through the CCIA include formal interventions and submissions to UN bodies, contacts and discussions with the secretariat and agencies, facilitation of access of churches, national councils of churches, etc. to the UN, participation in UN meetings and dissemination of information on the UN. The WCC's Christian Medical Commission has a special relationship with the World Health Organization and the Commission on Interchurch Aid, Refugee and World Service works closely with the UNHCR.

The WCC has supported the UN from the very beginning. Secretary-general Dag Hammarskjöld made a speech at the second assembly of the WCC (Evanston 1954). On the occasion of the 40th anniversary of the UN, the central committee (1985) re-affirmed support for the UN "as the principal organization of the world community in defence of the common good of humankind". The Vatican as a non-member state has a permanent observer status at the UN.

NINAN KOSHY

Basic Facts about the United Nations, New York, UN, 1987 • *Everyone's United Nations*, New York, UN, 1986.

UNITY. Christians confess the church* as "one, holy, catholic and apostolic" (Nicene Creed,* 381). Even where this creed is not in official use, the oneness of the church of Jesus Christ is affirmed. Thus the unity of the church, while it is a goal yet to be realized in history,* has as its essential presupposition the already-given oneness of the church. The ecumenical task, then, is to manifest this oneness, to make it visible and effective.

Both this indicative and imperative are grounded in biblical witness. The New Testament writings refer in a great variety of ways and images to the oneness or unity of the church as one of the fundamental characteristics of its nature and mission (see also **New Testament and Christian unity, images of the church**). This unity, as well as the very being of the church, is grounded in and reflects the unity of the Trinity.* As there is only one God,* one Lord (see **Jesus Christ, uniqueness of Christ**), one Holy Spirit* and one communion* among them, there can be only one church: the one people of God,* the one Body of Christ, the one temple of the Holy Spirit. This God-given unity is constantly sustained by the proclamation of the one gospel, the celebration of the one baptism* as incorporation into the one body, and the eucharistic communion (see **eucharist**) with Christ in the Holy Spirit and with one another. It becomes visible in the koinonia* within and between Christian communities, in their confession of the same faith,* in spiritual and sacramental fellowship, in mutual love, in the common service of the multiple gifts of the Spirit given to all, in the upbuilding of each community and of their communion with each other through a common apostolic ministry (see **ministry in the church**). It becomes effective in the world through common service (see **diakonia**) and witness* in continuing the mission of Christ. These basic lines of the biblical witness were expressed not as a theoretical system but in direct relation to the emerging early Christian community, and they are often formulated as exhortations and challenges addressed to communities whose internal unity or whose bond of unity among them was threatened from within or outside.

The struggle for unity. From New Testament times church history has been deeply marked by the tension between the confession of the given oneness of the church of Jesus Christ and the historical reality of division within Christianity (see **schism**). The implications of these divisions for the oneness of the church of Christ as confessed in the creed have been and still are interpreted differently by the different Christian traditions. Some claim that the one church is preserved in their own tradition, others have seen in the divided Christian traditions "branches" of the one tree, while yet others have come to the recognition that the divisions break up the Body of Christ and are therefore to be regarded as sinful (see **sin**). Yet, whatever the explana-

tions, there was a growing general recognition before and even more so after the turn of this century that the reality of a divided Christianity is a counter-witness against the confession of the one church and thus contradicts the gift, will and prayer of Jesus Christ. This recognition brought about the modern ecumenical movement, which sought to reverse church history from a history of division to a movement towards unity.

With the establishment of the WCC in 1948, the aspirations and efforts for unity received a new and effective instrument. Accordingly, the first constitutional function of the WCC is "to call the churches to the goal of visible unity in one faith and in one eucharistic fellowship expressed in worship and in common life in Christ, and to advance towards that unity in order that the world may believe". This commitment finds its central expression in the work of the WCC Commission on Faith and Order,* with the understanding that all the diverse activities of the WCC should help the churches to live effectively their already-existing fellowship and to move on towards full visible unity. Since 1948 the WCC has helped churches to enter into radically changed relationships with each other, to reach agreements and convergences in basic issues of faith and order, and to develop forms of solidarity, co-operation and common witness.* With the official entry of the Roman Catholic Church into the ecumenical movement at the time of the Second Vatican Council,* the efforts for unity have been decisively broadened and now include all major Christian traditions.

Concepts and models of unity. Already in the early stages of the F&O movement, discussion on particular church-dividing issues inevitably raised questions like: What are the constitutive elements of the unity we seek? How much (and in what form) is agreement necessary in such elements? How much diversity is possible and legitimate? In what form is unity to be expressed? Some Protestants emphasized the already-existing spiritual unity as a sufficient basis for mutual respect and for co-operation in mission and service. Others went one step further and pleaded for general agreement on some basic convictions of faith as a basis for forming federations of churches (see **federalism**). Anglicans and some others consistently argued for the goal of organic or corporate unity/union (see **union, organic**), which would be realized in the coming together of hitherto independent churches in one, united church.

The concept of organic unity received a certain pre-eminence in the F&O movement and in the work of the WCC after 1948. This is clearly seen in the way the WCC at the 1961 assembly in New Delhi formulated for the first time the goal of unity: "We believe that the unity which is both God's will and his gift to his church is being made visible as all in each place who are baptized into Jesus Christ and confess him as Lord and Saviour are brought by the Holy Spirit into one fully committed fellowship, holding the one apostolic faith, preaching the one gospel, breaking the one bread, joining in common prayer, and having a corporate life reaching out in witness and service to all, and who at the same time are united with the whole Christian fellowship in all places and all ages in such wise that ministry and members are accepted by all, and that all can act and speak together as occasion requires for the tasks to which God calls his people."

The 1968 assembly in Uppsala further developed this concept by emphasizing its universal and conciliar dimension and by the call to the churches "to work for the time when a genuinely universal council may once more speak for all Christians and lead the way into the future". The 1975 Nairobi assembly reaffirmed the basic statement of New Delhi and combined it with the Uppsala emphasis on the conciliar and universal dimension of unity: "The one church is to be envisioned as a conciliar fellowship of local churches which are themselves truly united. In this conciliar fellowship each local church possesses, in communion with the others, the fullness of catholicity, witnesses to the apostolic faith, and therefore recognizes the others as belonging to the same church of Christ and guided by the same Spirit... Each church aims at maintaining sustained and sustaining relationships with her sister churches, expressed in conciliar gatherings whenever required for the fulfilment of their common calling." This concept of a conciliar fellowship met with wide approval in all Christian traditions.

At the time of the Nairobi assembly the bilateral dialogues* between Christian World Communions* were already increasing in number, and in their context the question of the goal of unity was also raised. Because worldwide communions were undertaking these dialogues, the significance of entire confessional traditions for the search and expression of unity was given more attention than in multilateral dialogues.* Accordingly concepts of unity like "unity in reconciled diversity", full communion between "sister churches"* or "a communion of communions" were developed which seek to preserve (changed and reconciled) confessional identities as an element of future structures of church unity. Here the idea of a union, a merger of churches leading to a united church, is no longer seen as the only structural expression of organic unity. But in their description of the essential conditions of unity, these new concepts agree fully with the perspectives expressed in the New Delhi and Nairobi statements including the idea of a "conciliar fellowship".

Realizations of unity. For a long time now, ecumenical language has used the expression of an already-existing, though imperfect, fellowship between the churches to indicate that the churches are on their way from division to unity. This fellowship is expressed in new relationships with one another, forms of common prayer and worship, convergence on dividing theological differences, common witness and service. The WCC and the regional, national and local councils of churches* are both expressions and instruments of this already-existing fellowship. But there are also more direct expressions of unity or steps towards it.

Churches of the same confession in a particular country have united. Different denominations have come together to form united churches, e.g. the United Church of Canada as early as 1925, the Church of South India (1947), the Churches of North India and Pakistan (1970), the United Reformed Church in the United Kingdom (1972), the Uniting Church in Australia (1977). Lutheran, United and Reformed churches in Europe have declared full church fellowship (Leuenberg agreement 1973; see **Lutheran-Reformed dialogue**). Methodist churches in East and West Germany have agreed with their Lutheran, United and Reformed partners to establish sacramental fellowship and forms of cooperation (see **Lutheran-Methodist dialogue**). Lutherans and Episcopalians in the

USA have agreed on "interim eucharistic sharing" as a first step towards fuller communion (see **Anglican-Lutheran dialogue**). In fact, most Reformation and Free Churches practise today, whether officially declared or generally permitted, what is called eucharistic hospitality (see **communion, intercommunion**). All these forms manifest a commitment to move beyond mutual respect and friendly co-existence.

Methods and common orientations. In ecumenical endeavours one of the fundamental and continuing questions has been whether it is theological dialogue or rather common missionary and social action that leads the churches into unity. Today many are agreed that this is not a true alternative, since efforts for unity require a comprehensive approach involving both the doctrine and the life of the churches. Another question where differences remain concerns the degree of consensus* or convergence required for unity and the forms in which agreement should be expressed — whether by mutual recognition that each already holds the same faith or by new consensus texts. All agree that theological agreements and convergences need to be "received" by the churches on all levels of their life in order to facilitate steps towards unity (see **reception**). The spiritual dimension of unity (prayer, sharing in each other's joys and sufferings) is affirmed by all; and at the same time the role of so-called non-theological factors in facilitating or preventing closer fellowship is also generally recognized. There is also general agreement that the goal of visible unity, however defined structurally, can be reached only by intermediary steps and forms on the way.

Among the common fundamental orientations which have emerged in the course of ecumenical history, the following are of special importance. First, the unity confessed in the creed and to be manifested by the churches is not merely a spiritual, invisible reality but must be visible. Sacramental communion is one basic element of this visibility, but there must also be additional forms of visible and effective expression. Second, unity is not to be regarded as uniformity but must allow for a diversity of theological expressions and forms of ecclesiastical life. Positive heritages of different Christian traditions should be preserved, and the "rootedness" of churches in

various social and cultural contexts must be respected. Third, unity can be achieved only through renewal* of the life of the churches. Such renewal is necessary in order to overcome antagonistic positions and constitutes at the same time an enrichment of thinking and life. Fourth, unity is not aimed at for its own sake but in order that the world might believe, i.e., for the sake of the salvation and renewal of all humanity according to God's purpose. Finally, all forms of unity are provisional. They are first-fruits of that eschatological fulfilment when God will unite and complete all things in the perfect communion of his heavenly banquet (see **eschatology**).

See also **apostolicity; catholicity; church; holiness; united and uniting churches; unity of "all in each place"; unity, models of; unity, ways to.**

GÜNTHER GASSMANN

G. Gassmann & H. Meyer, *The Unity of the Church: Requirements and Structures*, Geneva, LWF, 1983 • C.S. Song ed., *Growing Together into Unity*, Madras, CLS, 1978 • G. Wainwright, *The Ecumenical Moment: Crisis and Opportunity for the Church*, Grand Rapids, MI, Eerdmans, 1983 • *What Unity Requires*, WCC, 1976.

UNITY, MODELS OF. Models of unity are statements of the nature and form of the full visible unity* of the church,* which is the final goal of the ecumenical movement. The term is normally used of the classic visions of church unity associated either with the united churches and the multilateral discussions of the Faith and Order* commission of the WCC (organic union,* conciliar fellowship) or with the bilateral discussions of the Christian World Communions (reconciled diversity,* communion of communions). Without claiming the precision and predictive power of their mathematical or scientific counterparts, these "models" have fostered discussion among the churches and focused the issues, options and fundamental choices facing them in their search for visible unity.

The various models should not be regarded as competitive; their value is in helping the ecumenical movement define a form of unity which enables all Christians, in their proper diversity, to experience themselves (and to appear to the world) as belonging to the one Body of Christ, and which enables them to speak and act as one on issues of faith* and life.

Organic unity, the historical goal of the F&O movement, envisions "a church so united (that) the ultimate loyalty of every member would be given to the whole body and not to any part of it". This unity would be that "of a living organism, with the diversity characteristic of the members of a healthy body" (Edinburgh 1937). The third WCC assembly (New Delhi 1961) emphasized that the institutional price of such unity would "involve nothing less than a death or rebirth of many forms of church life as we have known them". This has meant the end of denominational identities (see **denominationalism**) and the creation, in their stead, of new "local" (i.e. national) churches expressing the fullness of Christ's body in that place. Though no such local union has yet encompassed all churches in any one place, this vision has been most fully embodied in the some 60 united churches which have come into being over the past 175 years, in all regions of the world.

Conciliar fellowship, defined at the fifth WCC assembly (Nairobi 1975, drawing upon F&O discussions at Salamanca 1973), is not itself a model but a vision of how organic unity might be realized among the various local united churches. Though separated by "space, culture, or time", they would periodically express their unity through "councils of representatives of all the local churches at various geographical levels" (see **conciliarity**). In this view, legitimate Christian diversity is not based on historical factors (e.g. confessional and denominational divisions) but is rooted in the cultural and geographical diversity of the whole people of God and arises from the indigenization of the gospel in the diverse regions and cultures of the world.

Reconciled diversity begins from "the legitimacy of the (present) confessional differences and therefore the need to preserve them", though not as ends in themselves but as "points of reference" within a larger Christian identity. Thus, as stated at the Lutheran World Federation* (LWF) sixth assembly (Dar-es-Salaam 1977), these differences and unique confessional identities are not "simply preserved and maintained unaltered" but "lose their divisive character and are reconciled to each other". Furthermore, a church so united

would be "ordered in all its components in conciliar structures and actions" (LWF seventh assembly, Budapest 1984).

In the *communion of communions* proposed in 1970 by Cardinal Willebrands, secretary of the Pontifical Council (then Secretariat) for Promoting Christian Unity* of the Roman Catholic Church, the confessions would continue within the framework of a larger ecclesial allegiance (with a common dogma,* sacraments,* and basic ordering of ministry*), each confession (with its characteristic expression of theological emphasis and method, discipline, liturgical life, and spirituality) embodying a distinctive *typos* (see **typoi**) of the one faith: "the confessions should be the form and expression of ecumenicity" (Karl Rahner and Heinrich Fries). The bishop of Rome would exercise within the one church a unique ministry in the service of unity.

The various models embody important differences in the approach to unity, particularly in the role which they foresee, in a future united church, for the present confessional identities and denominational divisions. Proponents of organic unity doubt that a model (reconciled diversity) beginning from the present divisions of the church — however unquestioned their historical and theological importance — can ever inspire a compelling vision of future unity. Thus the Anglican-Reformed dialogue,* although itself "bilateral", has refused to seek "a modus vivendi between two globally organized denominations which would continue their separate though reconciled existence". On the other hand, proponents of reconciled diversity claim that recent failures of some church union schemes (Ghana 1983), and the rejection of institutional merger as the goal of others (Consultation on Church Union,* 1988), illustrate the need to maintain denominational identities. They ask whether many united churches do not often appear, only a few years after their creation, as just "another denomination".

The discussion of models is presently being enriched in two important respects. First, recent calls for a unity "in solidarity" (Jon Sobrino and J.H. Pico) and a unity "marked by shared suffering" (Paul Crow) are challenging all models to remember that church union is not an end in itself; each model must be judged as to how well it enables and empowers the church in its mission,* witness* and service (see **diakonia**) in the world. Second, it is increasingly recognized that the structural unity of the church must empower the renewal* of its life and enable the proper participation of all the people of God,* at all levels, especially the local congregation (see **local church**). Otherwise, as stated at the fifth international consultation of united and uniting churches* (Potsdam 1987), "union without renewal only continues the sin of division — not institutional division, but divisions between Christians (now within one church) of different races, economic levels, sexes".

Further work on models of unity is essential, with five related areas requiring special attention: (1) the structural form of a future united church, including the inter-relation of the various levels of its life (congregational, national, regional, global; it is striking that all models envision some type of conciliar structure, but no model is sufficiently clear about its form); (2) the nature of authority* within the future one church, and how authority will be exercised for the maintenance of unity (the question of authority awaits adequate discussion in the ecumenical movement); (3) the proper balance between unity and diversity within a future united church (here it should be remembered that the word "organic" in organic unity was intended to guard precisely the rich diversity of Christian faith and church life); (4) new ecumenical thought on the nature of the church, particularly the concept of koinonia* (communion*); (5) the relationship between the visible unity of the church and the renewal of its life, witness, mission and service.

See also **unity, ways to**.

THOMAS F. BEST

T.F. Best, "Models of Unity", *One World*, 132, 1988 • P.A. Crow, Jr, "Reflections on Models of Christian Unity", in *Living Today towards Visible Unity*, T.F. Best ed., WCC, 1988 • H. Fries & K. Rahner, *Einigung der Kirchen — reale Möglichkeit* (ET *Unity of the Churches: An Actual Possibility*, Philadelphia, Fortress, 1985) • H. Meyer, "Einheit in versöhnter Verschiedenheit" — "konziliare Gemeinschaft" — "organische Union": Gemeinsamkeit und Differenz gegenwärtig diskutierter Einheitskonzeptionen", *Ökumenische Rundschau*, 27, 1978 • L. Newbigin, "What Is 'a local church truly united'?", in *In Each Place: Towards a Fellowship of Local Churches Truly United*, WCC, 1977 • *What Kind of Unity?*, WCC, 1974.

UNITY OF "ALL IN EACH PLACE".

At the first WCC assembly in Amsterdam, provision was made for meetings of the World Confessional Families but not for representatives of united churches (see **united and uniting churches**). The latter met in an extra-curricular exercise. The assembly's report did not discuss local unity except for a brief commendation of the "courage and enterprise" which had inspired "some notable unions" of churches (*The Universal Church in God's Design*, 125).

Immediately following the first assembly there was sharp debate about the ecclesiological significance of the formation of the WCC. Did it commit the member churches to specific models of unity (see **unity, models of**)? Would it press churches to unite? Would it become a "super-church"? At the meeting of the central committee in Toronto (1950), these questions were squarely faced, and a statement was issued which has remained determinative of subsequent development (see **Toronto statement**). Membership in the WCC committed churches to the quest for unity but did not imply acceptance of any particular model of unity. There were in fact many different models on offer — re-integration into the Orthodox church, organic union* on the lines suggested by the Lambeth Quadrilateral,* a federal relationship between the world confessional families (see **federalism**) — and for some the WCC itself represented the desirable form of unity. The WCC could not espouse any of these but continued to show an interest in local unions of churches by publishing regularly surveys of such unions or plans for unity in many parts of the world.

The Lund Faith and Order conference (1952) and the Evanston assembly (1954) followed their predecessors in omitting discussion of the local schemes of union from their agenda, but after each of these meetings there were unofficial consultations of representatives of united and uniting churches in which leading personalities in the WCC participated. The representatives at Lund of younger churches involved in united or uniting churches felt obliged to counter the suggestion that their eagerness for unity might be "mistaken for a by-product of Asian nationalism" (Lund report, 130). But in the debates which centred on the Toronto statement, it was made clear that, while the WCC could not propose the acceptance of a particular model of unity as a *condition* of membership, member churches, if serious in their quest for unity, could not remain permanently uncommitted to one model or another. In a lecture at the time of the Evanston assembly, the writer of this article affirmed that "the proper form of the church's unity" required "first that it must be such that all who are in Christ in any place are, in that place, visibly one fellowship; and secondly that it must be such that each local community is so ordered and so related to the whole that its fellowship with all Christ's people everywhere, and with all who have gone before and will come after, is made clear" (published in *The Journal of Religion*, 35, 1, 1955).

These phrases were to be further refined in the following five years. The impetus to do so came partly from a conference of North American churches on "The Nature of the Unity We Seek", partly from a WCC central committee request for F&O comment on the Toronto statement and partly from the appointment of a committee on the future of F&O. In 1958 that committee presented a report advocating a "churchly" model of unity, in contrast to a model which appeared to call only for co-operation. The next year the F&O working committee submitted to the central committee a report which contained the following sentences: "We believe that the unity which is both God's will and his gift to his church is one which brings all in each place who confess Christ Jesus as Lord into a fully committed fellowship with one another through one baptism into him, preaching the same gospel and breaking the one bread, and having a corporate life reaching out in witness and service to all; and which at the same time unites them with the whole Christian fellowship in all places and all ages in such wise that ministries and members are acknowledged by all and that all can act and speak together as occasion requires for the tasks to which God calls the church."

After further discussion this statement was adopted by the third assembly in New Delhi with small modifications — one of which was to remove the semicolon which divided the "local" and "universal" parts to make it one single sentence. In spite of this attempt to hold the two parts of the statement together, it was

the "local" emphasis which captured attention. The fourth world conference on F&O at Montreal (1963) gave much attention to the local church.* It affirmed that "the proving ground of unity is the local church" (80) but was concerned that new forms of the local church might in fact be forms of schism.* It was no doubt by inadvertence that the Montreal report put a comma at the crucial point from which a semicolon had been removed! It followed that the fourth assembly at Uppsala (1968) thought it necessary to recover a balance which had been tipped one way. It emphasized the global dimension of unity and expressed the hope that "the members of the WCC, committed to each other, should work for a time when a genuinely universal council may once more speak for all Christians" (*The Uppsala Report*, 17).

This vision of a "genuinely universal council" was taken up at the next meeting of the F&O commission (Louvain 1971). In a statement entitled "Conciliarity and the Future of the Ecumenical Movement", a vision of unity was sketched in the form of a "conciliar fellowship of churches". There were factors which favoured this shift of emphasis. Movements for local organic union which had seemed promising ten years earlier were faltering. The growing role of the Orthodox churches in the life of the WCC was giving wider recognition to the role of ecumenical councils* in the history of the church. And (most importantly) the massive presence of the Roman Catholic Church in the ecumenical movement from the 1960s onwards had shifted emphasis from local schemes of union to bilateral dialogues* between world confessions. It was obvious that the RCC as a single world communion should find its partners in the world confessional families. These thus assumed a much more prominent role than in the preceding decades. "Conciliar fellowship" seemed to be a more attractive (and less costly) way to unity than the sometimes traumatic experiences of organic unions in which churches surrendered their separate existence to form new bodies. By the middle of the decade a WCC publication was able to list almost 50 of these bilateral conversations between world confessional bodies (*Confessions in Dialogue*, 1975).

The relation between these two approaches to unity was discussed at a conference in

Offering collection at joint Baptist-Episcopal service, Rwanda (WCC/Michael Dominguez)

Salamanca (1975), and its findings were taken up by the fifth assembly at Nairobi in the same year: "The one church is to be envisaged as a conciliar fellowship of local churches which are themselves truly united. In this conciliar fellowship, each local church possesses, in communion with the others, the fullness of catholicity, witnesses to the same apostolic faith, and therefore recognizes the others as belonging to the same church of Christ and guided by the same Spirit" (*Breaking Barriers: Nairobi, 1975*, 60).

The acceptance of this formulation led naturally to the question: What is a "local church... truly united"? At New Delhi it had been recognized that the word "place" did not have a simple unambiguous denotation. It affirmed that the unity among Christians "must be found in each school where they study, in each office or factory where they work, and in each congregation where they worship" and, furthermore, that "place" may imply not only local communities but also wider geographical areas such as states, provinces or nations (*The New Delhi Report*, 118). A consultation called by the WCC in December 1976 sought to clarify the issues. It noted that by using the term "place" for all

levels of the church's life, the third assembly (New Delhi) avoided a clear definition. It affirmed that "the church cannot even be conceived apart from the reality of places" (*In Each Place: Towards a Fellowship of Local Churches Truly United* [WCC, 1977], 4).

It considered the missionary obligation to relate the gospel to the specificity of particular groups in changing situations and affirmed that "a place is not merely a geographical area which can be identified on the map. It has temporal dimension as well" (5). It attempted a definition of the term "local church"* as follows: "The term refers to an area where Christians can easily meet and form one committed fellowship in witness and service. Every local church will normally gather in one eucharistic service. The conditions of the area may be such that there is need for several separate services. Even then it must be made evident that these communities understand themselves as one eucharistic fellowship" (8).

Common language is widely recognized as legitimate grounds for forming a distinct congregation. But "is it proper to recognize distinct eucharistic assemblies in the same area on the basis of distinct language, race, culture and other factors?... There is no agreed answer to these questions" (9-10). It is agreed, however, that in the course of its missionary outreach into new cultural groups, "as a provisional measure, there must be room for the formation of a congregation within [the] receiving culture, speaking its language and sharing its style of life, through which the full riches of that culture may be brought into the life of the universal church" (10). In a final section, which suggests the direction for the future, the consultation noted that "in many places small groups and fellowships have grown around common concerns and interests" and that in many cases "their commitment to the unity of the church leads them to anticipate the communion of the future" (11). These discussions about the nature of "local unity" need to be continued. The sixth assembly (Vancouver 1983) re-affirmed the Nairobi statement and sought to develop it further through a search for a common understanding of the apostolic faith, through mutual recognition of baptism, eucharist and ministry (see *Baptism, Eucharist and Ministry*), and through common ways of decision making. The WCC has also sponsored consultations of united and uniting churches by themselves, and with the Christian World Communions* including the Roman Catholic Church and representatives of the Orthodox churches.

See also **church; conciliarity; eucharist; union, organic; united and uniting churches; unity; unity, models of; unity, ways to**.

LESSLIE NEWBIGIN

E. Benignus, *All in Each Place*, Cincinnati, Forward Movement, 1966 • W.B. Blakemore, "All in Each Place", *Midstream*, 3, 2, 1963-64 • A.H. Dammers, *All in Each Place*, London, BCC, 1964 • M.B. Handspicker, "All in Each Place", *Study Encounter*, 1, 79, 1965 • M. Kinnamon ed., *Unity in Each Place... in All Places...: United Churches and the Christian World Communions*, WCC, 1983 • L. Newbigin, "What is 'a Local Church Truly United'?", *The Ecumenical Review*, 29, 2, 1977.

UNITY OF HUMANKIND.

Although the concern to relate church unity* and social problems has characterized 20th-century ecumenism from the start, the phrase "the unity of humankind" appears to have become an explicit theme in ecumenical discussions in the early 1960s. The nerve of this discussion has been the attempt to discern how divisions in the human community are becoming problems of church unity today, and likewise how the quest for church unity might be a sign of promise for the healing of these broken human communities as well.

Vatican II's* concept of the sacramentality of the church ("the church is a kind of sacrament or sign of intimate union with God, and of the unity of all mankind") provided a powerful impulse for developing this theme. That insight then became the basis for the Pastoral Constitution on the Church in the Modern World, addressed to "the whole of humanity". The parallel development in the WCC echoes Vatican II with an eschatological accent: "The church is bold in speaking of itself as the sign of the coming unity of mankind" (Uppsala 1968).

Faith and Order* straightway launched a major local, regional and international study on "The Unity of the Church and the Unity of Mankind" and built much of its programme at Louvain (1971) around an attempt "to view our historic theme of church unity in a new context, specifically in the context of human, not simply denominational divisions": in the struggle for justice,* encounters with living faiths, the struggle against racism,* in relation to the handicapped (see **disabled**) in society and church, and to differences in culture.* And a concern developed that the method of such studies should not be simply "contextualization", but "intercontextualization", whereby the two contexts reciprocally provide the interpretative frame for each other. Subsequent discussion revealed large problems about anthropology (see **anthropology, theological**), ambiguity in the notion of "the unity of mankind", the comparability of "the two unities", the abstractness of the perspective from which such "unities" could be discussed, among others.

Accra (1974) attempted to clarify the language of the theme: "human inter-relatedness" refers to an inescapable fact of modern global life (e.g. air travel) which has both positive and negative aspects; "the just interdependence of free people" refers to the kind of utopian visions of human community which animate movements of liberation; "the unity of humankind", on the other hand, is a theological term for the eschatological promise of the coming kingdom of God.*

The first phase of studies reached its provisional conclusion in a comprehensive report entitled *Unity in Today's World* (1978). Almost immediately a powerful impulse for renewed study came from the Sheffield conference on "The Community of Women and Men in the Church" (1981). And in 1982 at Lima, F&O launched a new (and as of this writing continuing) major study on "The Unity of the Church and the Renewal of Human Community". This study concentrates on explicating "the church as mystery and prophetic sign"; on probing two specific major problems as issues of church unity: the community of women and men, and the search for justice; and on promoting a considerable number of local study groups around the world. A comprehensive progress report was approved by F&O in 1989 for publication in 1990 and submission to the WCC's Canberra assembly (1991).

Although "Baptism, Eucharist and Ministry"* has been more noticed by the churches, it is this 20-year study of church unity and human community which has been most closely followed by the central organs of the WCC, for this study addresses as no other the constitutive concerns which brought the WCC into being, and the question about the unity of the ecumenical movement itself.

See also **universalism**.

JOHN DESCHNER

T.F. Best ed., *Beyond Unity-in-Tension: Unity, Renewal and the Community of Women and Men*, WCC, 1988 ● *Church and World: The Unity of the Church and the Renewal of Human Community*, WCC, 1990 ● *Faith and Order, Louvain 1971: Study Reports and Documents*, WCC, 1971 ● M. Kinnamon ed., *Towards Visible Unity: Commission on Faith and Order, Lima 1982*, 2 vols, WCC, 1982 ● G. Limouris ed., *Church, Kingdom, World: The Church as Mystery and Prophetic Sign*, WCC, 1986 ● G. Müller-Fahrenholz, *Unity in Today's World: The Faith and Order Studies on "Unity of the Church — Unity of Humankind"*, WCC, 1978.

UNITY, WAYS TO. Ways to unity are the various processes, and practical steps, through which the churches seek the full visible unity* of the church,* which is the final goal of the ecumenical movement. Effective ways to unity are rooted in the conviction that because God wills the church to be one, it is the state of church *union* which is normal, and the present state of church division abnormal

and requiring correction. The sharing of this conviction with others — however separated by boundaries of confession and Christian conscience — in common prayer and commitment to overcome all that divides us is "spiritual ecumenism".* Nurtured in personal contacts and through programmes such as the Week of Prayer for Christian Unity,* this is the source and power of all the more visible and practical ways to unity.

The various ways to unity differ principally in their estimation of (1) the specific elements of Christian faith* and practice upon which agreement is required for unity, and (2) the degree of agreement (which may be different for differing aspects of the church's faith and life) necessary for unity to be achieved.

The most dramatic "way" to unity is unity itself, an approach exemplified by the united churches. Their constituent denominations, on the basis of not necessarily complete but "sufficient" agreement on essentials of the apostolic faith and on sacramental practice (esp. the areas of baptism,* eucharist* and ministry*), have committed themselves to common decision making and mutual accountability within a single unified structure. Considerable diversity may remain, for example, in the form of baptismal practice, within congregations or from one congregation to another. Through experience of, and continuing dialogue about, such differences the church grows in its common faith and life more effectively, it feels, than had the union been postponed until full agreement in all areas had been reached. The united churches have experienced this process as a dying to old confessional identities and a re-birth to a new and richer identity: "No schemes of union have come about," said D.T. Niles about the Church of South India in a memorable comment, "the churches have united."

Active negotiations towards union continue (for example in New Zealand), and there have been recent important intraconfessional unions (among Presbyterians in the US and among Lutherans in the US). But there is a growing tendency to focus rather on proximate goals, such as intense sharing in life and witness with another church (the Disciples of Christ-United Church of Christ "partnership"), or marking a present "stage" towards unity (the "covenant"* sought in Wales). Significantly, these immediate steps are no longer always seen as intermediate: the "covenanting" language of the Consultation on Church Union* in the US now specifically excludes structural union, as traditionally sought by the united churches, as its final goal.

Another important approach understands full agreement in faith as a necessary precondition of union. This way to unity lies through slow, patient work towards full common understanding in matters of faith and practice; until these exist, any thought of institutional union is premature. In particular, sharing in sacramental life must be the fruit of unity rather than a means towards it (see **intercommunion**). In the Roman Catholic view, "the common celebration of the eucharist must be the sign of an already-existing ecclesial unity" (Swiss bishops' statement, Einsiedeln, June 1986); for the Orthodox, "intercommunion must be considered as the crowning act of real and true reunion which has already been fully achieved by fundamental agreement in the realm of Faith and Order and is not to be regarded as an instrument for reunion" (statement by the representative of the ecumenical patriarch of Constantinople to the second world conference on F&O, Edinburgh 1937).

Where churches bear a burden of bitter historical conflict, the way to unity must lie through a "reconciliation of memories", a process exemplified in the Leuenberg agreement reached in 1973 between Reformation churches (Lutheran and Reformed) in Europe. Despite "the condemnations pronounced (against each other) by the Reformation confessions of faith" in the areas of the Lord's supper, Christology, and predestination, the agreement affirms that, in their present common understanding of the gospel, these churches consider that these ancient accusations and actions "are no longer an obstacle to church fellowship". Some differences still persist among the churches, but these are not judged to have divisive force, and thus a state of pulpit and altar fellowship can be declared.

The healing power of this approach lies in its courageous facing of past wounds. Often this frees the churches to transcend the theological language of their ancient disputes — language formulated precisely to distinguish one church from others, if not to prove them heretical — and to discover new language adequate to their present common convictions.

An effective and widespread way to unity is participation by churches in the life of councils at the city, national, regional and global levels (see **councils of churches**). Councils provide opportunities for common programming in mission,* witness* and service (see **diakonia**), and accustom the churches to working together rather than apart or in competition. In councils, the bilateral dialogues* of pairs of churches or confessional families can be set in a much wider, multilateral framework, and insights tested and enriched by the experiences and convictions of many churches (see **dialogue, multilateral**). Such reflection on issues of faith, previously neglected within councils (with the important exception of the F&O commission of the WCC), is increasingly pursued in councils at city, national and regional levels.

While the councils cannot be confused with their member churches, there is a growing awareness that they fulfill some ecclesial functions. In reflecting, sharing, speaking and acting together, the churches within councils experience themselves, as described at the most recent global gathering of national councils of churches (Geneva 1986), as "both instruments and signs of unity", as expressing a growing koinonia of confession, of worship and of common witness and action.

Clearly no single way to unity is sufficient in and of itself; it is the responsibility of Christians to pursue the search for visible unity through all ways open to them, and with all the energy and ingenuity at their command.

See also **union, organic; unity, models of**.

THOMAS F. BEST

T.F. Best ed., *Instruments of Unity: National Councils of Churches within the One Ecumenical Movement*, WCC, 1988 • M. Kinnamon, *Truth and Community: Diversity and Its Limits in the Ecumenical Movement*, WCC, 1988 • H. Meyer & L. Vischer eds, *Growth in Agreement: Reports and Agreed Statements of Ecumenical Conversations on a World Level*, WCC, 1984 • S.C. Neill, "Plans of Union and Reunion, 1910-1948", in *A History of the Ecumenical Movement, 1517-1948*, R. Rouse & S.C. Neill eds, WCC, 3rd ed. 1986 • "Survey of Church Union Negotiations", every two years in *The Ecumenical Review* • L. Vischer, "Drawn and Held Together by the Reconciling Power of Christ", in *What Kind of Unity?*, WCC, 1974.

UNIVERSALISM. In its strongest sense, universalism designates the view that all intelligent, moral creatures (angels, humans, devils) will certainly be saved in the end. In 543 the emperor-theologian Justinian anathematized the view that the punishment of devils and the wicked is only temporary, so that they would be included in a final "restoration of all things"; and such an *apokatastasis* appears to have been part of the "Origenism" subsequently condemned at the second ecumenical council of Constantinople in 553. Continuing proponents of universalism appeal to God's love, power, patience and mercy. In the 20th century, such prominent figures as Karl Barth and Hans Urs von Balthasar have stopped only just short of the universalistic conclusions implicit in certain tendencies in their theology. Since so many humans appear to die in their sins and unbelief, universalism seems to imply opportunity for repentance and conversion after death.

All opponents of universalism hold that it does not take seriously enough moral evil and sin:* "Deeds that cry out to heaven also cry out for hell" (Peter Berger). Some opponents of universalism think that it does not respect the freedom* humans have to reject God; but others hold that such a view of human freedom impugns God's sovereignty, and that the biblical hell will be peopled by those whom God has "passed over" for salvation* and deliberately predestined to condemnation.

A middling view notes that "God *desires* all to be saved" (1 Tim. 2:4) but reckons that, while God will continue resourcefully to elicit an opening to himself and to others, the self-closure of the sinner to love and life (*cor in se incurvatum*, "the heart turned in upon itself") may finally entail self-extinction. Thus there would be no subject left to endure an eternal hell.

In a weaker sense, universalism denotes the global scope of the activity of the one true God,* the God of Israel and of Jesus Christ.* (Linguistic clarity might be furthered if "universality" could be used instead of "universalism" in this case.) Echoing the ancient promise that all the families of the earth would find blessing in Abraham (Gen. 12:3), later prophets proclaim that, after judgment, the survivors of the nations will turn to the Lord, the Sovereign of all creation and history, and join in the salvation granted to the remnant of Israel (see, for example, Isa. 25:6-9, 45:1-25; Zech. 14:1-21). According to the New Testament, the risen Christ sends his apostles to "make disciples of all nations, baptizing them in the name of the Father and of the Son and of the Holy Spirit" (Matt. 28:19), and missionary witness to him will be borne "in Jerusalem and in all Judea and Samaria and to the end of the earth" (Acts 1:8). The universality of the Christian mission is grounded in the "mystery" of God, i.e. the divine design, long hidden but now revealed in Jesus Christ, to include both Jews and Gentiles in salvation (Rom. 16:25-27; Eph. 1:9-10, 3:1-6; Col. 1:24-28; 1 Tim. 3:16).

Christian theologians have differed as to whether salvation is to be enjoyed only by those with explicit and confessed faith in Christ (see Mark 16:15-16; John 3:16-18,36; Acts 4:12; Rom. 10:8-21), or whether also by those who follow Christ "anonymously", by virtue of the "law written in their hearts" (see Rom. 2:14-16; 2 Cor. 5:10), or whether salvation is possible even without reference to Christ at all (but this would run counter to John 14:6 and 12:32).

Whether discussion involves universalism in the stronger or in the weaker sense, many would recognize the wisdom of the Lutheran Paul Althaus (1888-1966): "What believers hope for themselves in their own assurance of faith, they hope also for all their fellow humans. The grace which has been directed towards believers is not grounded in a preference for their own persons; rather it is unconditioned, groundless grace. Therefore they may not think of it as other than comprehensive."

See also **salvation, salvation history, uniqueness of Christ**.

GEOFFREY WAINWRIGHT

B.E. Daley, "Apokatastasis and 'Honorable Silence' in the Eschatology of Maximus the Confessor", in *Maximus Confessor*, F. Heinzer & C. Schönborn eds, Fribourg, Editions universitaires, 1982 • G. Müller, *Apokatastasis pantōn: A Bibliography*, Basel, Missionsbuchhandlung, 1969.

URBAN INDUSTRIAL MISSION. At the third assembly of the WCC in New Delhi (1961), considerable attention was given to the concerns and issues surrounding industrialization and urbanization. Although several national churches and agencies had already given the phenomena some attention, this was the occasion on which the twin concerns first became part of the global ecumenical agenda. Masao Takenaka (Japan) addressed the assembly on the theme "The Service of the Church in the Changing World Today", ending with these words: "What we need today is to accept this decisive service of Christ and to make the decisive change within ourselves. We need a revolutionary renewal both in ourselves and in the structure of our churches to respond to the transforming and redemptive power of God which is going on in our changing world today."

The programmatic responsibility for these concerns within the WCC was assigned to the newly formed Division (later Commission) of World Mission and Evangelism (DWME, later CWME). Paul Löffler (FRG), then responsible for the DWME service of laymen abroad programme, began the investigations into how the church could respond with "strong organs of thinking and action".

Shortly after the world mission conference in Mexico City (1963), an informal group met to discuss "urban industrial evangelism". By 1964 the DWME executive committee realized that many efforts at urban industrial evangelism are being made in many parts of the world, "but it is convinced that these efforts need co-ordination and cross-fertilization leading to a common approach, and that all members of the WCC should engage actively at the front line of the work". Thus the first meeting of the DWME advisory group on urban and industrial mission (1965, later known simply as Urban Industrial Mission — UIM) articulated the goal: "to involve the total church in all continents in the ecumenical task of urban industrial evangelism and so to promote greater co-operation and a common understanding of its goals". Flexibility and a decentralized form of co-operation, with a minimum organization at the top, were to be among the guiding principles.

By 1966, spurred on by concrete actions in many countries, the question of securing social justice came firmly on to the agenda: "In developing countries the basic aim is to try, by entering into the conflict between the power structure and its victims, to see if justice and peace can be achieved." And again: "We need to define the meaning of

power." In UIM's first major public document, "Becoming Operational in a World of Cities: A Strategy for Urban and Industrial Mission" (presented to and adopted by the WCC's fourth assembly in Uppsala), there was a strong call for the churches to "involve themselves more deeply with the new groups — the new poor, the workers, the new marginal groups — and become a servant church among them".

Subsequent UIM advisory group meetings were held in Limuru, Kenya (1969); Kyoto, Japan (1970); San Juan, Puerto Rico (1971); Cartigny, Switzerland (1972); Rome (1973); Tokyo (1975); Vancouver (1976); and Mexico City (1977). Each of these meetings — now representative of five major regions of the world — reflected on the implications for contemporary Christian obedience of an increasing number of community and national struggles for justice and dignity. During this period, churches, communities and groups involved in actions for justice gradually became knit together in a loose fellowship of solidarity and common understanding. Staff travel and inter-regional visitations helped forge common bonds and directions.

As the fellowship encompassed increasing numbers of groups and communities, so did the annual WCC "askings list" for financial support for various programmes. These nationally and regionally approved requests were brought to the UIM advisory group for validation prior to approval by the CWME. With its longer history and its structural integration within the Christian Conference of Asia, Asia dominated both the annual askings list and the global UIM discussions.

In 1978, after consistent pressure from the continents of the South to bridge the apparent gap between "urban" and "rural", the CWME decided to merge its UIM and Rural Agricultural Mission offices into Urban Rural Mission.

See also **rural agricultural mission, urban rural mission**.

KENITH A. DAVID

URBAN RURAL MISSION. In 1978 the Commission on World Mission and Evangelism (CWME) merged its Urban Industrial Mission and Rural Agricultural Mission desks into Urban Rural Mission (URM), in recognition of the reality of the urban-rural nexus.

The period 1978-82 was characterized by escalating militarization and violence in many parts of the world, increasing exploitation of people by governments and transnational corporations, and the widespread denial of human rights and dignity. People's struggles proliferated; some were won — most were ruthlessly crushed. URM had the opportunity of reflecting theologically and politically on many of these struggles at CWME-URM advisory group meetings in Newark, New Jersey, USA (1979), Melbourne, Australia (1980) and Washington, DC (1982), as well as at the 1980 world mission conference in Melbourne and the 1981 Christian Conference of Asia assembly in Bangalore.

From 1983, with a Latin American moderator of the CWME-URM advisory group, a deliberate attempt began through staff and inter-regional visitations to recover URM-related activity in Africa and Latin America. Also, a process of re-organization was undertaken in North America and Western Europe. In 1988 the Middle East began to take its place within URM circles.

Throughout this period, the primary method employed in URM's commitment to local action was organizing for empowerment the victims of oppression and marginalization in local communities, enabling them to participate in the decision-making processes which affect their lives. Such community organizing activities within national and global liberation perspectives, undergirded by leadership development, training, documentation and information exchange, were comp-lemented by theological reflection, leading to reports such as "A URM Perspective on Mission", "Resistance as a Form of Christian Witness", and "The Church: a URM Perspective" (on the ecclesiological implications of community organizing).

A high point of URM activities and reflections was reached in 1987 with the "Celebration and Challenge" event in Manila, which brought together 120 community organizers and others from all regions of the world to mark the 25th anniversary of URM concerns within the WCC. Subsequently the advisory group met in Belfast (1988) and Bangkok (1989).

It was as a result of the concerns, actions and experiences over three decades that URM agreed on the following self-description: "Urban rural mission is primarily a movement of men and women rooted in the Christian faith who are called, along with others, to the mission of God to participate in the struggle of the exploited, marginalized and oppressed for justice and liberation... URM is involved in concrete situations of human suffering where people are victimized in the process of rapid social change caused by modernization and industrialization, and exploitative economic and political systems... URM has been committed to work with slum-dwellers, the unemployed, industrial and women workers, indigenous peoples, fishworkers, rural poor and landless labourers, migrant workers, etc."

See also **rural agricultural mission, urban industrial mission**.

KENITH A. DAVID

V

VATICAN COUNCILS I & II. St Peter's basilica within the Vatican witnessed the 20th (Vatican I) and 21st (Vatican II) of the general councils which the Roman Catholic Church (RCC) counts in its long history.

Vatican I (1869-70). In June 1868 Pope Pius IX formally convoked the Council for bishops, abbot-presidents, and generals of male religious orders. During the Council itself 774 Council fathers participated, mostly European in birth. The number was double that of the previous council, Trent* (1545-63). In September 1868 the pope invited also the patriarchs of the Armenian, Coptic, Syrian and Greek Orthodox churches. Because of the invitation's wording, all declined. A public papal appeal to "Protestants and all non-Catholics" to return to the only true fold also received resentful refusals.

The preparatory committees had prepared 51 drafts or schemata, but the Council discussed only six and then promulgated only two dogmatic documents: *Dei Filius:* God the Creator, the human possibility of knowing God and the human need for revelation,* and the nature of faith* and its relation to reason; and *Pastor Aeternus:* the institution, continuation and extent of the papal primacy* of the bishop of Rome, and the extent and limits of papal infallibility.* This statement re-cast two later chapters of the lengthy draft on the church; the entire draft was never discussed. Because of the outbreak of the Franco-Prussian war in July 1870 and the Italian occupa-

tion of the papal states in September, Pius IX abruptly suspended Vatican I in October.

Vatican II (1962-65). During the 90 years after Vatican I, people became aware that every frontier of personal and communal experience was changing — social, cultural and scientific, economic and political, intellectual and psychological. In both positive and negative responses to these changes, biblical, liturgical, missionary and ecclesiological renewal* movements were becoming steady but hesitant streams in the RCC, especially after the second world war. Although encouraged by Pope Pius XII (ruled 1939-58) through lengthy papal letters (encyclicals*), such movements needed more affirming integration.

Three months after his papal election (28 October 1958), John XXIII, dubbed a mere transitional pope because of his 78 years, announced his intention to convoke "an ecumenical council for the universal church" (25 January 1959, at the conclusion of a prayer service for church unity*). In various speeches the pope gradually clarified his intention and hopes: the Council would be a new Pentecost* and means of spiritual and apostolic renewal, an updating (*aggiornamento*) of the church in modern times, and a service to the unity of the church. The Council would not be a "re-union" gathering of all Christian churches, but a Catholic event — "the first gathering together once more of the whole mystical flock of our Lord".

During 1959-60, the Vatican solicited for

the Council agenda "wishes and desires" from more than 2,800 bishops, 156 superiors general of male religious communities, 62 theological and canonical faculties of Catholic universities, and the offices of the Roman curia. The collated results of over 9,300 proposals, 9,520 pages in 15 volumes, were handed over to 11 commissions which began to shape drafts into 119 booklets. These, in turn, had been whittled down to 20 projects by the time the Council fathers assembled for the first session in October 1962.

One of the preparatory drafting groups was Pope John's newly created Secretariat for Promoting Christian Unity.* It was responsible also for negotiations with other world confessional bodies to delegate official observers to the Council's public and closed sessions.

From October 1962 to December 1965, the bishops (from 2,100 to 2,540 at any one time) gathered for debate during four long autumn sessions — 168 plenary working meetings and 10 public assemblies during 36 weeks, with continuous re-drafting between and during each yearly session.

With one-fifth of the bishops from Latin America, and over one-third from the local churches of Asia, Africa and Oceania, Vatican II marked the transition of the RCC to a worldwide basis. The majority of RCs were no longer found in the Northern Atlantic regions. Unlike Vatican I, Vatican II did not hear Europe as the all-controlling voice.

In his opening talk to the bishops, John XXIII set the pastoral tone which pervaded the deliberations. He chided "those prophets of doom who are always forecasting disaster, as though the end of the world were at hand". God is leading us "to a new order of human relations" in a world which expects "a step forward towards doctrinal penetration and the formation of conscience". This must be "in conformity with ancient doctrine", but "the deposit of faith is one thing, the way it is expressed is another". The church demonstrates the validity of its teaching not by condemnation or severity but with "the medicine of mercy". The pope emphasized the church's duty to work actively for "the full visible unity in truth" among all Christians in a "fullness of charity" which should extend also to non-Christians.

Present at the first session was the first group of 38 delegated observers from almost all the world confessional families. By the Council's end, 186 had participated for longer or shorter periods. Their most active presence, including their suggestions to the drafters, became a fact and a symbol of RC ecumenical need.

John XXIII died on 3 June 1963, after the first session; canonically the Council was suspended. His successor, Paul VI (1963-78), quickly announced that Vatican II would continue according to the spirit and direction of John XXIII. Under Paul VI's presidency, the last three sessions produced 16 statements. With over 100,000 Latin words, this body of material far outstripped all previous general councils in its wide-ranging agenda. The Council covered every major dimension of personal and communal renewal, organizational life, missionary and service outreach. The themes included divine revelation, the church, the liturgy, bishops' pastoral office, the ministry and life of priests, priestly formation, the laity, Christian education, religious life, Eastern Catholic churches, the church in the modern world, missionary activity, ecumenism, non-Christian religions, religious freedom, and the communications media.

Vatican II used the church as the fulcrum or vital centre around which all *aggiornamento* themes organized themselves. The result were the two key documents, identified by their opening Latin words: the Church (*Lumen Gentium*) and the Church in the Modern World (*Gaudium et Spes*). But the other 14 statements also throw light on the RC understanding, in the 1960s, of what God, in Christ and through the Spirit, has promised to do and is doing in the midst of humanity through God's pilgrim people.

Without taking account of the debates and resolutions of Vatican II, it is impossible to understand the modern RCC. The church's current consensus and its dissents — its confidence and its hesitations in theology, pastoral and missionary activities, social and political involvements, ecumenical and inter-religious concerns, and understanding of its own structures — are a result of the Vatican II deliberations and of the subsequent debates about what they meant and intended.

TOM STRANSKY

C. Butler, *The Vatican Council, 1869-70*, London, Collins, 1962 • A. Flannery ed., *Vatican II: The*

Conciliar and Post-conciliar Documents, Col-legeville, MN, Liturgical Press, 1975 • A. Hastings ed., *The Second Vatican Council and Its Influence across 25 Years*, London, SPCK, 1990 • R. Latourelle ed., *Vatican II: Assessment and Perspectives Twenty-five Years After*, New York, Paulist, 1989 • H. Rondet, *Vatican I*, Paris, Lethielleux, 1962.

VIOLENCE AND NONVIOLENCE.
The need for clearer understanding of the churches' responsibility in an often violent world helped shape the early years of the modern ecumenical movement. It gave rise to the Life and Work* movement and inspired the formation of other Christian organizations, international in membership and ecumenical in vision, in the period between the two world wars.

Prior to 1960, however, the moral dilemma of violence was considered almost exclusively in terms of international conflict between sovereign states (see **state**). No easy consensus was forthcoming. "Can war now be an act of justice?" asked the WCC's founding assembly in 1948, concluding reluctantly that "we cannot answer this question unanimously" (see **just war**). Its second assembly (1954) affirmed that Christians should search for new approaches to peace, "taking into account both Christian pacifism as a mode of witness and the conviction of Christians that in certain circumstances military action is justifiable".

Against this background, in which Christian pacifism played a significant but not predominant role, the churches in the 1960s were drawn into serious reflection on violence as a reality in the struggle for social justice. Hints of the new discussion appeared at the WCC's third assembly (1961), which went on record exhorting those in power to refrain from using violence and to avoid provoking it. In a carefully phrased statement, the 1966 world conference on Church and Society asked "whether the violence which sheds blood in planned revolutions may not be a lesser evil than the violence which, though bloodless, condemns whole populations to perennial despair". Rejecting the view that absolute nonviolence is binding on all Christians, it warned nevertheless against evils inherent in any resort to arms and said violence could be justified only as an ultimate recourse.

During this period, Roman Catholic documents began to comment on the same issue. Emerging from Vatican II, *Gaudium et Spes* praised those who renounced the use of violence in the movement for social justice. In 1967, *Populorum Progressio* noted the "temptation to violence" and warned that revolutionary uprisings generally produce far more harm than good. This emphasis has continued, in Vatican teaching, to the present.

The WCC's fourth assembly (1968) was painfully aware of the violence issue. Martin Luther King, scheduled to preach at the opening service, had been assassinated three months previously, and the assembly's dominant concern for justice sharpened the question of how social change should be advanced. A resolution of the assembly, encouraging churches to bring King's example to the attention of their members, asked the WCC's central committee to promote the study of nonviolent methods of achieving social change.

Unprecedented debate on the subject was catalyzed within and beyond the churches when, in September 1970, the WCC executive committee approved a first set of grants from the special fund of the new Programme to Combat Racism,* some of which were to support humanitarian projects of liberation movements engaged in armed struggle in Southern Africa. A notable aspect of the ensuing controversy was the way in which many pacifists felt able to give full endorsement to the WCC's action, while the strongest objections were raised within traditionally nonpacifist churches. Another element complicating the debate was the confusion of meanings associated with terms such as "violence", "power", "force", "nonviolence" and "revolution",* particularly when discussion ranged across different cultural, linguistic and ideological lines.

Meeting a few months later, the central committee (Addis Ababa 1971) pointed out that the grants should be seen not as the WCC identifying itself with any political movement but as tangible support for the cause of racial justice. The Council, it added, could "not pass judgment on those victims of racism who are driven to violence as the only way left to them". In a related action, the department on Church and Society was asked to undertake a study aimed at furthering the churches' reflec-

tion on the ethical dilemmas posed by violence and nonviolence in the struggles for
justice and peace, and contributing to the
search for strategies of action that might
minimize the sum total of violence in conflict
situations.

The two-year study project engaged people
from a wide spectrum of viewpoints and experience: theologians from historic peace
churches and leaders of denominations in the
"just war" tradition, activists involved in
armed struggle and experts in nonviolent
strategies and tactics, sociologists and local
pastors, biblical scholars and authorities on
constitutional law — all of them from extra-
ordinarily diverse local situations. It included
a consultation at Cardiff, Wales (1971), to
explore the potential of nonviolent strategies
and culminated in a major report entitled
"Violence, Nonviolence and the Struggle for
Social Justice" that was presented to the central committee in 1973. After debating the
matter at length and appending some comments of its own, the central committee commended the statement to the churches for
study, comment and action.

The statement attracted considerable interest from the media and was well received by
member churches. As it remains the most
substantial piece of work the WCC has done
on this subject, its main points are worth
noting.

After observing that the problem of Christian responsibility in a world of force and
violence is as old as the church itself, the
document speaks of Christian hope* and the
promise of the kingdom* as the context within
which the church must try to elaborate guidelines for its social thought. The statement, in
carefully crafted words, offered just such
guidance. "We believe that for our time, the
goal of social change is a society in which all
the people participate in the fruits and the
decision-making processes, in which the centres of power are limited and accountable, in
which human rights are truly affirmed for all,
and which acts responsibly towards the whole
human community of mankind, and towards
coming generations. Such a society would not
be the kingdom of God, but it might reflect
within the conditions of our time that subjection of the powers of this world to the service
of justice and love, which reflect God's purposes for man."

Under God, governments have a legitimate
and necessary function to restrain private
power, assure human rights* and serve the
public good. To this end they use force governed by law. All human powers, however,
are tempted to misuse and exceed their authority. No wielder of power is perfect, and a
government may become so tyrannical and so
hostile to its own people that citizens feel
obliged to try to overthrow it. Then, says the
statement, the goal should be not the destruction of the enemy but a more just social order
in which contending groups are reconciled
and enabled to participate in decisions affecting the community as a whole.

Without taking a stance itself, the document lists three distinct points of view about
methods of resisting oppression. The first
understands nonviolent action as the only way
consistent with obedience to Jesus Christ. The
second sees violent resistance as a Christian
duty in extreme circumstances, constrained by
criteria similar to those traditionally applied to
assessing a just war. "Not only must the cause
be just and all other possibilities exhausted,
but also there must be reasonable expectation
that violent resistance will attain the ends
desired, the methods must be just and there
must be a positive understanding of the order
which will be established after the violence
succeeds." The third point of view recognizes
violence as a seemingly unavoidable element
in certain situations in which nonviolence
simply does not appear to present itself as an
option.

While unable to reduce the three viewpoints
to agreement, the statement goes on to register
several important convictions on which there
was consensus. It identifies some forms of
violence in which Christians may not participate and which the churches must condemn:
"Violent causes — the conquest of one people
by another or the deliberate oppression of one
class or race by another — which offend
divine justice... Violent means of struggle —
torture in all forms, the holding of innocent
hostages and the deliberate or indiscriminate
killing of non-combatants for example —
which destroy the soul of the perpetrator as
surely as the life and health of the victim."

It calls the churches and action groups to
give more attention to the techniques of non-
violence. "There are vast possibilities for preventing violence and bloodshed and for

mitigating violent conflicts already in progress, by the systematic use of forms of struggle which aim at the conversion and not the destruction of the opponent and which use means which do not foreclose the possibility of a positive relationship with him. Nonviolent action represents relatively unexplored territory..."

It challenges widely held misunderstandings of nonviolence. "Nonviolent action is highly political. It may be extremely controversial. It is not free of the compromise and ambiguity which accompany any attempt to embody a love-based ethic in a world of power and counter-power, and it is not necessarily bloodless. Moreover, most struggles for freedom — and most government actions — have been, as a matter of fact, mixtures of violent and nonviolent action."

With a warning that Christians should be wary of handing out gratuitous advice on behaviour to people living in distant and different situations, the document notes that those near the top of the world's socio-economic pyramid must be particularly sensitive to the limitation their affluence places on their giving moral counsel to others less well placed.

Sharp questions are posed to all parties in the debate: those prepared to use violence, advocates of principled nonviolence, those who by whatever means work to bring down an existing power structure, the defenders of institutions that are under challenge, and Christians in countries where government is relatively responsive to pressures for change. Yet the most important question, says the statement, is raised not by any one of these groups to any other but by all of them together to the whole church, which is challenged to become wiser and more courageous in translating its commitment to Jesus Christ into effective engagement in the struggle for social justice.

A decade later, in preparation for the WCC's sixth assembly, the 1973 statement was reviewed at a small consultation held at Corrymeela, Northern Ireland. Its report, *Violence, Nonviolence and Civil Conflict*, affirms the main thrust of the earlier work but notes a major change in the international scene and highlights significant shifts in the ecumenical debate.

In many places, says the Corrymeela document, optimism about the struggle for justice and peace has turned into something ap-

Rubber bullets collected by residents of Shatti refugee camp, Gaza (Rick Reinhard)

proaching despair. "For the churches, the question becomes how to articulate the gospel in such a way that we may be delivered both from the illusion of facile optimism and the paralysis of faithless pessimism." Both pacifism and the just-war theory are feeling their inadequacies in the developing ecumenical debates about militarism,* weapons of mass destruction and revolutionary conflict. Indeed, the violence/nonviolence dichotomy of the 1973 statement now seems a trifle simplistic, suggesting instead a broader focus on the variety of ways in which power is exercised and the constructive possibilities inherent in each.

See also **just war, pacifism, peace**.

DAVID GILL

Violence, Nonviolence and Civil Conflict, WCC, 1983 ● "Violence, Nonviolence and the Struggle for Social Justice", *The Ecumenical Review*, 25, 4, 1973.

VISCHER, LUKAS. B. 23.11.1926, Basel, Switzerland. From 1961 onwards Vischer was a staff member of the secretariat of the WCC's Commission on Faith and Order,* and its director, 1965-79. He was a WCC observer at the Second Vatican Council,* 1962-65, and was moderator of the theological department of the World Alliance of Reformed Churches,* 1982-89. He studied history and theology at the Universities of Basel, Strasbourg, Göttingen and Oxford and received a D.theol. from the University of Basel in 1952. Ordained to the ministry in 1950, Vischer became pastor of the Reformed church in Herblingen, an industrial town near Schaffhausen. He wrote *The Common Catechism* (with J. Feiner; London, Search, 1975), *Ye Are Baptized* (WCC, 1961), *A Documentary History of the Faith and Order Movement, 1927-63* (St Louis, MO, Bethany, 1963) and *Überlegungen nach dem Vatikanischen Konzil* (Zurich, EVZ-Verlag, 1966).

ANS J. VAN DER BENT

VISSER 'T HOOFT, WILLEM ADOLF. B. 20.9.1900, Haarlem, Netherlands; d. 4.7.1985, Geneva. Visser 't Hooft was the first general secretary of the WCC and a leading figure in the 20th-century ecumeni-

cal movement. Like many others, he had his formative ecumenical experience in the Student Christian Movement (see **World Student Christian Federation**). As chairman of the relief committee of the Netherlands student organization during his student years in Leiden, he attended several ecumenical conferences in Europe. In 1924, after finishing his theological examinations, he accepted a position on the Geneva staff of the world committee for the YMCA.* His introduction to the wider ecumenical movement came the following year, when the YMCA named him an alternate delegate to the Stockholm Life and Work* conference (where he was the youngest participant).

During the 1926 YMCA world conference in Helsinki, he served as personal assistant to John R. Mott — learning, he wrote later, "the art of running a complicated world conference". The previous year, during a visit to the US to prepare for the Helsinki conference with Mott, he had become interested in the social gospel movement;* and in 1928 he wrote a critical study of it as his Leiden doctoral dissertation. Though trained in theology and subsequently ordained a minister in the National Protestant Church of Geneva and the Netherlands Reformed Church (his own background was in the smaller Remonstrant Brotherhood Church in Holland), Visser 't Hooft never considered himself a theologian; and he described his own writings on theological subjects as "interpretations across confessional and linguistic frontiers of thoughts which I have picked up from the theological path-finders".

Appointed general secretary of the World Student Christian Federation in 1932, he made his first trip to Asia in 1933 to help organize Christian students there. Visser 't Hooft attended both of the 1937 global ecumenical conferences where it was decided to form a world council of churches — the Oxford Life and Work meeting as part of the steering group, and the Edinburgh Faith and Order conference as a member of the executive committee. At the 1938 meeting in Utrecht, where the WCC was formed, he was named general secretary of its provisional committee. At its first assembly (Amsterdam 1948) he assumed the general secretaryship, continuing in that post until his retirement in 1966.

Visser 't Hooft chaired the steering committee for the world conference of Christian youth (Amsterdam 1939), the last major international ecumenical event before the war. After the war broke out, he worked actively from Geneva to assist refugees from Nazi Germany and maintain liaison between churches in occupied territories and the outside world.

Beginning in 1948, his tenure as WCC general secretary (in an organization for which there were, as he said, no precedents) involved him in endless travel around the world, making a vast number of personal contacts, lecturing and speaking on behalf of the Council and attending hundreds of meetings large and small.

He himself described the job as one of administration (coping with a rapidly expanding programme and budget), policy-making (helping the churches to find better ways to define and fulfill their "common calling"), liaison (between the WCC's staff and its member churches and governing bodies), "external affairs" (building relations with non-member churches, especially Eastern Orthodox, Roman Catholic and African churches, and with inter-governmental and non-governmental organizations), interpretation (including editorship of *The Ecumenical Review*, weekly meetings with the department of information and annual lectures to the graduate school at Bossey*) and serving as chief of a large staff of men and women from many different national and confessional backgrounds.

Central to all this activity was Visser 't Hooft's unwavering commitment to the unity* of the church.* "The ultimate aim of the movement", he once observed, "is not dialogue, but true unity. Our Lord did not pray 'that they may all enter into conversation with one another'; he prayed that they all may be one." This did not mean building something which had not existed before: "all ecumenism that is worthy of the name is a movement of concentration, a return to the sources, or still better a return to the *centre*. The ecumenical movement is Christocentric, otherwise it cannot exist at all." Critical of "underground" and "private" ecumenism, he stressed the importance of linking the movement to enduring manifestations of the church through the ages.

Following his retirement, the WCC's fourth assembly (Uppsala 1968) elected him honorary president. Visser 't Hooft remained in

Willem Adolf Visser 't Hooft (WCC photo)

Geneva, which had made him an honorary citizen, staying active in the WCC until the 1980s, contributing to debates in nearly every meeting of the central and executive committees. Until shortly before his death he was a regular visitor to the ecumenical centre, where he was often joined in conversations by WCC staff and others over afternoon tea in the cafeteria.

Concluding his *Memoirs* with a reflection on how the ecumenical scene of the 1970s differed from that of the early days, Visser 't Hooft affirmed what he described as a shift in orientation from a certain "institutional preoccupation" to service to all of humanity. "When the World Council gives high priority to the issues of worldwide development, or when it takes very concrete steps in the fight against racism, it is certainly not denying the mandate which it has received. When we study the problems of church unity in the light of the unity of mankind, we are not changing our course altogether, but seeking to bring together two dimensions which had always been there but which had not been sufficiently related to each other." At the same time, he insisted that the church's task was more than "the agenda of the world", for "if the church is the church of Jesus Christ, it knows only one destination: the kingdom of God. And all human goals must be critically analyzed in the light of the information which we have received about the nature of that kingdom and the road that leads towards it."

Visser 't Hooft, who had suffered from emphysema for several years, died in Geneva in July 1985. Three days earlier he had given a radio interview to a German journalist and had completed the second draft of a long survey of WCC-Roman Catholic relations since the 1920s.

The recipient of numerous awards and honorary degrees from around the world during his lifetime, he received a vast number of tributes at the time of his death — not only from leaders of WCC member churches and ecumenical organizations but also from the pope and the queen of the Netherlands. Five *Festschriften* were published in Visser 't Hooft's honour, the first on his 60th birthday. His own literary output was staggering — including an estimated 50,000 letters. Among the more than 1,500 items to appear under his name in printed or duplicated form were some 15 books in several languages. His 1973 *Memoirs* and his 1982 *Genesis and Formation of the WCC* are invaluable sources of information about the origins of the ecumenical movement.

A close associate on the WCC staff during Visser 't Hooft's tenure has written of his personal energy — which "characterized everything from his entry into a room, to conversation, to his ultimate commitment, always expressed by the words 'calling' and 'common calling'" — and his capacity of discernment. "He did not engage in long analyses, nor did he listen to them patiently. His mind grasped the essential point — whether of world historical developments, proposed departmental programmes, or drifts in the central committee or the life of the member churches — with immediate clarity and penetration. It was a capacity that made him unable to suffer fools gladly."

Another person who worked with him for many years wrote after his death that without Visser 't Hooft's "combination of gifts the WCC might never have existed. No other person in the leadership of those days possessed the acumen, imagination, statesmanship, experience, daring, energy and languages necessary to bring it into being."

ANS J. VAN DER BENT

Among Visser 't Hooft's best-known books are *Memoirs*, 2nd ed., WCC, 1987 • *No Other Name: The Choice between Syncretism and Christian Universalism*, London, SCM, 1963 • *The Pressure of Our Common Calling*, New York, Doubleday, 1959. See also A. van der Bent, *Voices of Unity: Essays in Honour of Willem Adolf Visser 't Hooft on the Occasion of his 80th Birthday*, WCC, 1981 • A.M. Chirgwin, *These I Have Known: William Temple, William Paton, W.A. Visser 't Hooft, Martin Niemöller*, London, Missionary Society, 1964 • F. Gerard, *The Concept of Renewal in the Thought of W.A. Visser 't Hooft*, dissertation, Hartford Seminary Foundation, 1969 • J.R. Nelson ed., *No Man Is Alien: Essays on the Unity of Mankind*, Leiden, Brill, 1971 • *Willem Visser 't Hooft, Eugene Carson Blake* (= *The Ecumenical Review*, 38, 2, 1986).

VOCATION. Christian churches agree that God* takes the initiative in calling people to faith* and glory. Humans themselves have not decided that it would be good to enjoy eternal life; they have been *called* to a life of glory by a God who freely desires to share everlasting life and love. The vocation of every human being is the attainment of life with God (see **salvation**).

If the Christian churches consistently hold that God takes the initiative, they also maintain that God's call reaches us through Jesus Christ.* Jesus comes at the appointed time and preaches conversion and the kingdom: "The kingdom of God is at hand; repent, and believe in the gospel!" (Mark 1:15). Those who hear the good news and have a change of heart enter the realm of God and look forward to eternal glory.

The New Testament speaks in terms of universal salvation: "God our saviour... desires all to be saved and to come to the knowledge of the truth" (1 Tim. 2:3-4). This passage seems to imply that everyone is called; everyone has a heavenly vocation. But some Christian thinkers have found other passages which seem to narrow the call to eternal life. Paul's letter to the Romans contains one of these passages: "Those whom [God] foreknew he also predestined to be conformed to the image of his Son, in order that he might be the first-born among many brethren. And those whom he predestined he also called; and those whom he called he also justified; and those whom he justified he also glorified" (Rom. 8:29-30).

Augustine, Calvin and Luther understood this and similar passages in terms of a special election on the part of God. In inscrutable freedom God chooses some to receive the effective grace of Christ and so to attain eternal glory; others are not elected and do not receive the power of conversion.* Today almost all churches in their contemporary statements agree that God does not appoint some persons for glory and others for damnation. The call and the power of conversion are present for everyone, but the individual is able to thwart the call.

The scriptures bear witness to the call to individuals such as Abraham, Jeremiah, John the Baptist, and Paul. They were called to perform a task. The same may be said of Jesus; he was called for a mission, and his commitment to the kingdom became clear in his baptism and preaching.

All Christian believers are called to holiness and perfection, but not all are called to the same ministries. The Holy Spirit* provides an abundance of gifts, and believers become recipients of multiple charisms* and ministries (e.g. teaching, administering, encouraging and consoling).

All churches recognize the need for a variety of ministries, but they are not in agreement on the way in which the ministries are ordered or arranged (see **ministry in the church, church order**). They recognize that all believers are called to perform tasks in the church, but they differ in their understanding of the ministries: their variety, performance, dignity, rank, etc. Many churches, for example, distribute most of the ministerial tasks to the offices of bishop, priest and deacon. Other churches exclude or minimize these offices in favour of a more general priesthood or at least a less distinctive office of service.

All believers are called to a life of conversion and holiness* (see **sanctification**); this includes discipline of the body and of the mind, self-sacrifice, generosity, etc. The NT churches promoted a life of poverty, self-giving and prayer (see Acts 2:42-47). In the late 3rd century and the beginning of the 4th, some Christians desired to live the Christian life intensely by following what came to be called the monastic movement: a life alone or in community; the discipline of celibacy, prayer, simplicity, common use of goods, and obedience to a spiritual master. Anthony of Egypt stands as the foundational figure: he heard the call of the gospel (Matt. 19:21), took it quite literally, gave away his property, and went into the desert to pray and to lead an ascetic life.

The church, especially the medieval church, acknowledged and was marked by the monastic and religious life. But its promotion also had the effect in many circles of downgrading the regular Christian life of ordinary labour and marriage. The 16th-century reformers were generally critical of the religious life and discouraged or forbade it in their churches. They emphasized the goodness of the daily life of labour and marriage. Today one notes again an interest in monastic and religious orders in the Reformation traditions, e.g. the community of Taizé* and the Anglican Benedictines. Vatican II* (1962-65) both maintained the special place of religious life in the church and generally emphasized the goodness of the created world and the labours that sustain human life.

The churches today exist in a global situation in which freedom, equality and community are the cry. They cannot avoid the ferment of liberty and equality as they consider their vocation as a whole. The ferment affects the understanding of God's call: it must not appear arbitrarily or capriciously selective, and it must go out to all peoples; in some way or other the call must be received by everyone, preferably through the church but in other ways as well (the call of conscience,* the call of equal rights, etc.).

The ferment also affects the understanding of the people who are called to be one people of God;* they are called to holiness in Jesus Christ. Distinctions in tasks and ministries are appropriate, but access to the love of God (to a divine vocation) is present for all. God calls people, one and all, to conversion, holiness of life, and the joy of everlasting glory.

JEROME THEISEN

WAR GUILT. After the second world war the leaders of the Protestant church in Germany made the confession that Christians in Germany had been implicated in the crimes committed by the National Socialist government, including the world war (Stuttgart declaration,* 19 October 1945). The declaration acknowledges the guilt in relation to God. "We accuse ourselves for not witnessing more courageously, for not praying more faithfully, for not believing more joyously and for not loving more ardently." The confession was made in the presence of delegates of the WCC in process of formation, which was a helpful step for re-integrating the Germans into the ecumenical communion. However, there were no comparable acknowledgments of guilt in the victorious countries, although Visser 't Hooft and other church leaders had suggested taking into account the fact that a total war involves many nations in guilt.

There were declarations in Hungary deploring political errors of the church (especially its commitment to nationalism) and demanding a new course in politics as well. In a similar way, leaders of the Confessing Church* in West Germany, the Bruderrat, suggested a new political approach to reconciliation and social justice (Darmstädter Wort 1947). In 1948 anonymous voices in Czechoslovakia blamed the political impotence of the government on the moral and spiritual weakness that had already been manifested in the expulsion of Germans in 1945; the church had been implicated in this lack of resistance to inhumanity. In 1966 the synod of the Protestant church in Germany declared that the whole German people were liable for the consequences of the war. Praying for God's forgiveness of guilt, the church expected reconciliation with the nations of the Eastern bloc.

At least two Japanese churches have made similar statements. The United Church of Japan issued its "Confession of Responsibility for World War II" in 1967, and the Japan Baptist Convention adopted a "Statement on War Responsibility" at its 42nd annual meeting in 1988.

In these confessions of guilt, every church also claimed to speak for its own nation. The confessions become a political sermon, even without always pursuing political purposes. Here we find a mixture of the recognition of guilt, which calls us to repentance, and the discernment concerning wrong developments and faults, a discernment demanding a new beginning and a new course. The horror of the second world war, with its terror and destruction of moral values, prompts the question whether war *as war* is always sin,* justifiable under no circumstances.

Is it possible to describe "war guilt" in terms of the causes which produced the conflict? In the 20th century the League of Nations and the United Nations organizations have been established to determine and to condemn such guilt beyond any national interest. Since The Hague peace conferences

(1899 and 1907) there have been endeavours to appoint international courts of arbitration, which should give also a moral judgment of military conflicts. But often the protection of the struggle for human rights* and human values (freedom and justice) are given as reasons for interventions. It is often difficult, however, to distinguish such justification from the mere will to power.*

GERHARD SAUTER

WEBER, HANS-RUEDI. B. 21.3.1923, Ruchwil, Switzerland. Weber was director of the WCC Department on the Laity, 1955-61, associate director and professor at the Ecumenical Institute, Bossey,* 1961-71, and director of biblical studies at the WCC, 1971-88. Ordained a pastor of the Swiss Reformed Church in 1947, he served as a missionary in Central Celebes and East Java. In 1966 he received a ThD from the University of Geneva. Since retirement from the WCC in 1988, he has been teaching at the Pacific Theological College in Suva, Fiji. He wrote *The Communication of the Gospel to Illiterates* (London, SCM, 1957), *The Militant Ministry* (Philadelphia, Fortress, 1963), *On a Friday Noon* (WCC, 1979), *Experiments with Bible Study* (WCC, 1981), *Immanuel* (WCC, 1984) and *Power, Focus for a Biblical Theology* (1989).

ANS J. VAN DER BENT

WEDEL, CYNTHIA CLARK.
B. 26.8.1908, Dearborn, MI, USA; d. 24.8.1986, Alexandria, VA. Wedel was a president of the WCC, 1975-83. She received a PhD in psychology from George Washington University, Washington, DC. She was associate general secretary of the National Council of the Churches of Christ (NCCC) 1960-69, and president, 1969-72, as well as director of the Centre for a Voluntary Society, and executive director of the Church Executive Development Board until her retirement in 1973. President of Church Women United, 1955-58, she was moderator of the NCCC broadcasting and film commission from 1955 to 1960. Wedel served as observer at the Second Vatican Council* and also was a member of the WCC commission on the co-operation of men and women in church, fami-

ly and society, 1952-61, and of the committee on the laity, 1961-68.

ANS J. VAN DER BENT

WEEK OF PRAYER FOR CHRISTIAN UNITY. This widely observed annual programme of ecumenical prayer for Christian unity is celebrated 18-25 January (more rarely at Pentecost* or, in the southern hemisphere, in July). Based on the conviction that common prayer is fundamental to the search for the visible unity of Christ's church, the Week of Prayer for Christian Unity (WPCU) is one of the oldest and most enduring institutionalized expressions of "spiritual ecumenism".*

The WPCU unites earlier streams of prayer for unity. Anglican (later Roman Catholic) Paul Wattson proposed in 1908 a "church unity octave", held between the feasts of St Peter (18 January) and St Paul (25 January). Roman Catholic in orientation, this was broadened by Abbé Paul Couturier's call in 1935 for a Universal Week of Prayer for Unity, a unity to be achieved "as Christ wishes and by the means which he desires". Since 1926 the Faith and Order* movement (involving Protestants and Orthodox) had published "Suggestions for an Octave of Prayer for Christian Unity", celebrated around Pentecost. From about 1957 a common WPCU text was prepared through informal co-operation between the WCC F&O commission and the Roman Catholic ecumenical agency Unité chrétienne (Lyons, France). Since 1966 the WPCU has been a joint project of the F&O commission and the Pontifical Council for Promoting Christian Unity (formerly the Secretariat for Promoting Christian Unity*) of the Roman Catholic Church.

The WPCU text for each year is developed by an international Protestant, Orthodox and Roman Catholic team of liturgists, biblical scholars and pastors working from draft materials prepared by a local ecumenical group. Each year's theme is based upon a biblical text; for example, "The love of God casts out fear: 1 John 4:18" (1988, based on material by Waldensians and Roman Catholics in Italy), and "Building community: One body in Christ: Rom. 12:5-6a" (1989, based on material from the Canadian Council of Churches). The text includes sub-themes, additional biblical readings, commentary and prayer intentions for the eight days of the observance; an ecumenical worship service (the most widely used part of the material); additional prayers and information from the local group; and suggested ecumenical activities for use throughout the year.

The WPCU text is distributed, and observances organized, through WCC member churches and Roman Catholic bishops conferences, as well as national councils of churches,* ecumenical institutes, etc. The principal languages are English, French and German, with translations into many others reported, including Urdu and Fijian. Local adaptation of the material is strongly encouraged. It is estimated that many millions of persons participate annually in WPCU observances in some 75 countries throughout the world.

See also **prayer in the ecumenical movement**.

THOMAS F. BEST

T.F. Best, "The Week of Prayer for Christian Unity: Promise and Problems", *Ecumenical Trends*, 14, 1, 1985 • E. Castro, "The Ecumenical Significance of the Week of Prayer", *Ecumenical Trends*, 17, 1, 1988 • H.-M. Steckel, "Gebetswoche für die Einheit der Christen", in *Ökumene Lexikon*, H. Krüger, W. Löser & W. Müller-Römheld eds, Frankfurt-am-Main, Otto Lembeck-Josef Knecht, 1987 • L. Vischer, "The Ecumenical Movement and the Roman Catholic Church", in *The Ecumenical Advance: A History of the Ecumenical Movement*, vol. 2: *1948-1968*, H.E. Fey ed., WCC, 2nd ed. 1986 • J. Willebrands, "Prayer for Christian Unity", *Ecumenical Trends*, 17, 1, 1988.

WELFARE STATE.

The term "welfare state" is used to describe the acceptance by a state of collective responsibility for the well-being of all of its members. The state* provides, from its central financial resources, services to meet the welfare needs of individuals or families.

The antecedents of the welfare state are to be found in the political philosophies and economic doctrines which emerged in some developed countries in the 19th century. It was realized that many people were confronting economic or social hardship which they could not overcome alone. It was often the example and influence of Christians and the churches which led to a greater public awareness of human needs and of how they could be met. This was based on the recognition that the extent of social need was greater than voluntary effort could provide.

By the early 20th century the scale of economic growth in some developed countries made it possible for the state to direct financial support to alleviate hardship. Help was made available to the very poor, the sick or the unemployed in the form of payments for social security or social assistance. By the 1920s many countries, whether having centralized or federal structures, had begun to develop a range of inter-related public welfare services paid for primarily by taxation.

Such developments were affirmed by William Temple (1941) when he said: "In place of the conception of the power state we are led to that of the welfare state." In the UK, as elsewhere, the aims of the social policy which provided the legislative basis for the welfare state were (1) to support or compensate those who were disadvantaged; (2) to help all people to achieve their personal potential; and (3) to create a social environment which offered communal benefits and helped eliminate sources of tension within communities.

These services, whether administered on a national or local basis, typically made provision for social security, health, education, personal social services and housing. In some countries, employment and training services were also seen as welfare provision. Together these major services constitute the components of a welfare state, ideally intended to be comprehensive in scope and universally available to citizens.

In communist and socialist countries the state has assumed a central and directive role in policy matters and in the provision of welfare services. In other countries private (commercial) provision, for example in health, education or housing, has co-existed with public welfare services. Furthermore in many nations, there has been a significant non-governmental sector, sometimes with governmental financial support, of which churches and religious organizations form an essential part.

The welfare state was originally based upon assumptions of consistent economic growth. It is argued that welfare expenditure in many countries is now very high and this itself has placed limits on economic development.

When financial resources are limited, services cannot respond to any increase in demand, and they may have to be provided on a selective or means-tested basis.

In recent decades there has been public concern about the effectiveness of the welfare state. From the political right the promotion of welfare rights and entitlements has been questioned, and welfare-dependency alleged. The high cost and apparent bureaucratization of the system have been criticized. New emphasis has been placed by politicians upon the moral responsibility of individual citizens to care for themselves and their families. It is claimed that the welfare state represents a form of social engineering. State involvement in welfare should therefore be restricted to those in greatest need, within clearly defined priorities.

From the left it is affirmed that the continuing problems of poverty,* unemployment,* ill-health or inadequate housing require the welfare state to be reformist and radical rather than ameliorative: to tackle the causes of disadvantage and deprivation. Political, demographic, social and cultural changes raise questions about the basis of policy formulation and accountability within the welfare state.

Hence, there are two contrasted sets of values: those of individualism, free enterprise and market systems; and those of mutuality, equality and collective security. Debate now centres on whether the state should itself be the institution which provides, or funds, welfare services on an extensive basis. If not, what residual role should it play if individual initiatives, family self-help or non-governmental services break down? The problem that faces countries which created a welfare state is how to achieve an economy which can sustain a major programme of public welfare services. One view is that, because of the prevalence of market capitalism,* some kind of social market system for welfare is almost inevitable. However, if a mixture of governmental, private and non-governmental welfare services emerge, what action can be taken to ensure that citizens will gain access to the choice thus afforded? How can they participate by both contributing and receiving in the communal, caring society?

Individual Christians may be at any point in their country's political spectrum. Churches take a particular stance on matters of national social policy, based on their beliefs, traditions and the social structure of which they are a part. Within a formalized welfare state or the mixed welfare society, they will expect to perform a serving role and an interpretative one, seeking to influence the course of social and economic policy, in a manner that makes known God's purpose for his creation.

The WCC, in view of its social concerns, was naturally favourably inclined towards the welfare-state policy. Although it seldom refers to it explicitly, the discussions of the "responsible society"* in the early 1960s tend to favour this conception of the role of the state. In the New Delhi (1961) assembly this appears in a more explicit way. However, some criticism developed in the late 1960s concerning the limitation of its perspective to the national scene (Evanston 1954 already called for a shift from "a social state" to a "social world" understanding of welfare, and this perspective dominated Uppsala 1968). The Geneva conference on Church and Society (1966) criticized the reformist perspective. At the Montreux consultation (1970) Samuel Parmar summarized the distinction between the WCC and the welfare-state approach to the question of development and social justice, indicating that the latter, "based on enlightened self-interest of owning classes", is "essentially a class doctrine, though considerably tamed and civilized by the increasing role played by the state in assuring a more equitable sharing of wealth". The crisis of the welfare state in the 1980s has deepened this discussion within the ecumenical movement.

RAYMOND T. CLARKE

WILLEBRANDS, JOHANNES GERARDUS MARIA. B. 4.9.1909, Bovenkarspel, Netherlands. Secretary in 1960 and president from 1969 of the Secretariat for Promoting Christian Unity,* Willebrands established official contacts with many representatives of Christian churches and communities, and with international organizations such as the WCC. He took a major role in the work of the secretariat during the Second Vatican Council* and was responsible for receiving the non-Catholic observers to the Council and for drafting the documents on ecumenism, religious liberty, the relation of the church to non-Christian religions, and a

substantial part of the Dogmatic Constitution on Divine Revelation. In 1969 he was named cardinal and in 1975 archbishop of Utrecht, but continued as president of the secretariat. He is also a member of the Congregations for the Doctrine of the Faith, for the Oriental Churches, for the Sacraments, for the Evangelization of Peoples, for Catholic Education, and of the Pontifical Commission for the Revision of the Code of Oriental Canon Law. After serving as chaplain to the Begijnhof church in Amsterdam, 1937-40, in 1940 he became professor of philosophy at a seminary in Warmond, and in 1945 its director. In 1951 he was organizer and secretary of the (European) Catholic Conference for Ecumenical Questions. He received his doctorate from the Angelicum in Rome and has written *Oecuménisme et problèmes actuels* (Paris, Cerf, 1969), as well as many other works.

ANS J. VAN DER BENT

WILSON, LOIS MIRIAM. B. 4.8.1927, Winnipeg, Canada. A president of the WCC, 1983-91, Wilson was president of the Canadian Council of Churches, 1976-79, and moderator of the United Church of Canada, 1980-82 (the first woman in both positions). She has been associated with the work of several WCC sub-units. Ordained a minister of the United Church of Canada in 1965, she shared pastorates with her husband in Ontario, 1965-80. She was visiting lecturer on mission and evangelism in several theological colleges in Canada, and at the Ecumenical Christian Centre in Bangalore in 1975. Wilson has done extensive work in voluntary sectors such as Amnesty International* and has promoted interfaith dialogue* on the local level. She has written *Like a Mighty River* (Winfield, BC, Wood Lake, 1981).

ANS J. VAN DER BENT

WITNESS. The WCC's New Delhi assembly (1961) considered *witness*, together with *unity** and *service* (see **diakonia**), as the primary concerns of the ecumenical movement. In the attempt to clarify missiological vocabulary in its ecumenical setting, "witness" has come to mean the total evangelizing presence and manifestation of the church (see **evangelism**).

The most original New Testament usage of witness (martyria) is in the gospel of John. The incarnation* of the Word relates to the revelation* and knowledge of God.* "For this I was born, and for this I have come into the world, to bear witness to the truth" (18:37). Jesus speaks the words of God with authority* because "he who comes from above... bears witness to what he has seen and heard" (3:31-32). "We speak of what we know, and bear witness to what we have seen" (3:11). Jesus as the Word incarnate speaks out of his communion* with God, and therefore through him the disciples hear directly the word of God: "I have manifested thy name to the men... Now they know that everything that thou hast given me is from thee; for I have given them the words which thou gavest me, and they have received them and know in truth that I came from thee; and they have believed that thou didst send me" (17:6-8).

Jesus Christ, the faithful witness. Indeed, the heart of the NT is Jesus Christ,* the unique and decisive witness of God, "the faithful and true witness" (Rev. 3:14), "who in his testimony before Pontius Pilate made the good confession" (1 Tim. 6:13); "he sealed the new covenant with his blood" (see Heb. 9:24-28) by becoming "obedient unto death, even death on a cross" (Phil. 2:8). The faith,* glory, thanksgiving and worship of the church converge in front of the throne and in front of the Lamb (Rev. 7). The Lamb is given glory because he has been slain (Rev. 5:9). The relationship between cross and resurrection,* suffering servant and eschatological glory, is fundamental to the whole NT.

The witness of Christ — who sums up in his person the testimony borne by all prophets of the Old Testament and by all God's messengers — is the foundation of the church, which at Pentecost* bears witness to the resurrection. Any speculation about the essential role of martyrdom* in the mission of the church, without recognizing Jesus Christ as the one witness of God, has no biblical foundation.

In common biblical use, "witness" refers to bearing witness to the world, proclaiming and making known that Jesus Christ is the Saviour and Lord of all humankind and of all creation.* Jesus Christ himself commissioned the disciples to be his witnesses (Acts 1:8). The Holy Spirit* comes upon the faithful and

Prison worship in Wiesbaden, Federal Republic of Germany (epd-bild/Neetz)

makes them witnesses of Christ. The epistles describe some of the ways in which the early Christians testified to the resurrection of Christ. There are certain essential dimensions of the Christian witness: we have an apostolic-missionary commission (Matt. 28:19-20); without love such a witness is only "a noisy gong or a clanging cymbal" (1 Cor. 13:1); in bearing this witness Christians are committing themselves to the diaconal service of others, for it is the good news of God they are bringing (Acts 13:32-33); the kingdom of God,* whose coming they have to proclaim in word and deed, consists in "righteousness and peace and joy in the Holy Spirit" (Rom. 14:17); witness includes the work of reconciliation* of people with God coming together under the one Head, who is Christ (Eph. 1:10); the church has to be ready to witness also before the principalities and powers of this world (Eph. 6:12; cf. Rom. 8:38-39); the Christian witness draws its power and nourishment from the word and sacrament.

Eucharist as an act of witness. For the apostolic community the celebration of the eucharist* is a proclamation of the Lord's death until he comes (1 Cor. 11:26). "Especially in difficult circumstances, the very cele-

bration of the eucharist can constitute an act of witness. In 'impossible' situations, it proclaims that God alone creates a saving future. When it cries 'maranatha', the eucharistic community is calling for the overthrow of all that is opposed to God; it is praying for the final coming of God's kingdom: 'Let grace come: let this world pass away' (*Didache* 10). This hoped-for future is already prefigured in the fact that the eucharistic community itself includes pardoned sinners, reconciled adversaries, and the desperate restored to life: all are welcomed by the Lord at his table of justice, peace and joy in the Holy Spirit (cf. Rom. 14:17)" (*Sharing in One Hope*, 198).

Cloud of witnesses (Heb. 12:1). The book of Revelation was written to increase the hope* and determination of the church in a period of disturbance and bitter persecution. Thus, the book emphasizes the *martyrs*, those faithful disciples who live in conformity with the Lord to the point of death. They "had been slain for the word of God and for the witness they had borne" (Rev. 6:9).

In the post-apostolic period Christians defended the gospel and established the church by the witness of their whole life; in certain circumstances, others bore this witness to the point of surrendering their lives in martyrs' deaths. Church tradition holds that most of the apostles were martyred. At the beginning of the second century, Ignatius of Antioch considered that his martyrdom would "grind" him into one bread with Christ. New local churches often followed where the first evangelists or disciples had suffered martyrdom. Liturgical altars were built over the tomb of martyrs. "The blood of the martyrs is the seed of the Christians," wrote Tertullian.

Indeed, the ancient church venerated the Christian martyr as a strong witness to the living God and to the coming of his kingdom. But it never absolutized those "prophetic" acts and attitudes. It recognized a diversity of choices and possibilities. Christians are called to bear witness also through their active daily involvement in the world.

The witness of the monastic life takes up again in the church the witness of the martyrs of the early centuries. By striving to be unattached to worldly possessions or to family and to be available for God and one's fellow human beings, the monk or nun bears witness to the eschaton inside the church and thus exercises a truly prophetic ministry in showing forth the gospel's way of the kingdom (see **religious communities**).

Common witness. The witness of the community as a whole has the same value and quality as the confession of those who followed the path of Christ in difficult or dangerous situations. But that witness has been undermined by the historical divisions among Christians and the churches. They are called nevertheless to give common witness* to those divine gifts which they already share.

Common Christian witness cannot, of course, replace the theological debate searching for the unity in a common faith. But it can help Christians to realize, through their unity in evangelism and mission,* the visibility of their incomplete universality. Common witness therefore gives a possibility of having a vision of catholicity* and of detecting a possible historical and pastoral universality in the midst of the existing doctrinal and ecclesiological divisions.

ION BRIA

Common Witness, WCC, 1982 • *Mission and Evangelism: An Ecumenical Affirmation*, WCC, 1981 • *Sharing in One Hope: Bangalore 1978*, WCC, 1978.

WOMEN IN CHURCH AND SOCIETY.

It could be argued that the first ecumenical encounter was the meeting between Adam and Eve. The man had to learn how to live with another human being like but unlike himself, without whom he could not survive in one household of diversity and unity. The affirmations of scripture that both male and female are made in the image of God and that in Christ both are incorporated into the one body, the church, form the basis of the fundamental Christian conviction that men and women are of equal worth and have complementary and essential contributions to make within the life of the whole community.

In the church, the leading role in priesthood,* liturgy, policy-making and scholarship has in almost all denominations traditionally been reserved to men. But there is a long history throughout the church of the lay ministry of women (see **laity**), of women in religious orders, diaconates (see **diakonia**) and missionary service, and of the strength of women's movements within congregational life. In secular society, the 20th century has been one of accelerating change for women. Profound questioning of their traditionally subordinate role has led to a struggle for their full rights as citizens, for equal opportunities in employment and for a fuller partnership with men in all aspects of family and community affairs.

By the beginning of the 20th century such movements as the Young Women's Christian Association (YWCA),* the Women's World Day of Prayer,* the various auxiliaries for the support of women missionaries and sisterhood movements were pioneering ecumenical relations across the denominations. At the 1910 International Missionary Conference, though the representation of women was minuscule, the issue of women's work came on the agenda; and a study on "The Place of Women in the Church in the Mission Field" published in 1923 carried the recommendation: "What we ask is that the church keep pace with the other agencies that are according to woman a new status and new opportunities for development and achievement. The church, because of her own conservatism and lack of vision, is allowing trained, talented, spiritual women to slip away from her into other lines of activity."

By the time the WCC was in process of formation, the international network of women drawn together through the YWCA was already conducting research into the place of women in the church throughout the world. Through that work the WCC was itself encouraged to give systematic attention to evaluating the worldwide ministry of women, in a study which became the subject of one of the addresses at the first assembly in Amsterdam (1948). The address was given by Kathleen Bliss, whose subsequent book *The Service and Status of Women in the Churches* was a well-documented account of the work of women in all the major denominations except the Roman Catholic Church. It became the formative resource book for the permanent commission set up by the Amsterdam assembly on the life and work of women in the church. Speaking of its mandate, Willem Visser 't Hooft commented: "The significance of this commission must be regarded in the light of the ecumenical movement, which seeks to foster the wholeness of the church and to work for its renewal. Unless women are given more responsibility in the life of their local churches, that renewal cannot be achieved. The work of the commission may meet with some nervousness. People may fear that we are going to make an onslaught on the whole tradition of some churches or interfere with their life. The commission will need an immense amount of tact in getting its ideas across."

Those diplomatic words proved prophetic. In the second half of the century the concern about women's participation in the whole life of the church, including holy orders, has become a focus of ecumenical controversy. But parallel to that debate has been the growing awareness of the distinctive gifts of women, of feminist insights in theology and liturgy and of the mutual enrichment that comes through full partnership in ministry and service in both family and community.

The emphasis on partnership was echoed in the new title adopted by the Evanston assembly (1954) for the department dealing with what had been thought of as women's concerns within the WCC. It was now to be called the Department on the Co-operation of Men and Women in Church and Society. Madeleine Barot, the department's first executive secretary, developed relations with secular organizations, such as the United Nations, which were also increasingly concerned about the status of women. At the same time, she emphasized the need for the churches to reflect theologically on the status accorded to women within their own traditions. In a January 1955 article in *The Ecumenical Review*, she appealed for a blending of male and female spiritual insights which would result in a theology to which women could more fully respond.

A subsequent theological consultation was held at Herrenalb in 1956 which examined in detail the question of the relationship between the sexes as reflecting a divinely ordained order. An important paper by André Dumas explored the concept of mutual submission in the context of common obedience to the authority* of the kingdom of God.* A further consultation, sponsored jointly with the Department on the Laity, recognized closer co-operation between men and women as an essential part of the renewal of the church and of the whole *laos*, the people of God.*

At the foundation of the All Africa Conference of Churches* in 1963, the women of the churches were invited to a preliminary gathering to prepare for their full participation in the new ecumenical body, an invitation they accepted with alacrity. In Asia, immediately preceding the New Delhi assembly (1961), a consultation was held in Madras on "Changing Patterns of Men/Women Relationships", which prepared the way for the enlargement of the women's department's mandate to include questions specifically relating to family life.

Within the Roman Catholic Church it has traditionally been in the context of family* life that women's responsibilities have been most frequently discussed. The Second Vatican Council* made scarcely any other specific references to the work of women, except in the final drafting of the documents concerning the lay apostolate, which included the sentence: "Since in our times women have an ever more active share in the whole life of society, it is very important that they participate more widely also in the various forms of the church's apostolate." One of the chief advisers to the Vatican on the lay apostolate, Thomas Stransky, strongly recommended the formation of a women's ecumenical liaison group so as to create a network between Catholic, Orthodox and Protestant women. At a consultation in Taizé in 1967 on "The Christian Woman: Co-Artisan in a Changing Society", Lydia Symons, a Dutch Roman Catholic professor of theology, stressed that the church's vocation in humanizing the world requires full co-operation between male and female: "Above all, we need a form of spiritual care which will help women to live as adults in Christ, liberated from all subjugation to obsolete structures which have been maintained too long in many church circles."

The women's ecumenical liaison group was given personal encouragement by Pope Paul VI, who, in an audience with its representatives, stressed "the importance of women not only in the home, but in society generally and in the church". But the structure of the group was to prove short-lived, as the Vatican became more cautious about the creation of joint bodies developing an identity of their own. The official mandate of the group came to an end after only four years. The participation of Roman Catholic women in WCC consultations on all matters relating to women has continued on an informal and personal basis ever since.

Shortly before the Uppsala assembly (1968) Barot's indefatigable leadership of the department came to an end, and her place was briefly taken by Rena Karefa Smart of Sierra Leone and then for over a decade by Brigalia Bam of South Africa. At Uppsala attention was specifically directed to the low level of representation of women within the official delegation of the churches (less than 9%). It became apparent that the sexual discrimination endemic in society prevailed in the church too. The new word coming into vogue to describe such discrimination was "sexism",* a word used in the title of an all-women's consultation held by the WCC in Berlin in 1974 to prepare the churches to participate fully in the International Year for Women, designated by the UN in 1975, a year which expanded into a decade as concerns about the injustice, poverty and abuse of which many women were victims throughout the world became urgent matters for the international agenda.

The Berlin consultation on "Sexism in the 1970s" gave a dynamic impetus to the women who later attended the WCC assembly in

Meeting of Latin American women theologians, Buenos Aires, Argentina (Prensa ecuménica/Carlos Salgado)

Nairobi (1975), where for the first time a whole plenary session was given to the concerns of women. It was resolved to pursue issues of social justice* as they concerned women and to undertake further theological exploration and biblical studies in the light of feminine insights and experience. The resulting recommendations led to the launching of a new worldwide study process on "The Community of Women and Men in the Church", under the joint guidance of Faith and Order* and the Sub-unit on Women in Church and Society. The study was given a full-time director, Constance Parvey, an advisory committee and a four-year mandate. The preliminary study material had an unprecedented popular reception, involving more local groups in discussion and response than any other study initiated by the WCC. The responses were collated and formed the basis of an international conference held in 1981 in Sheffield, England, a conference whose message to the churches proved to be both controversial in its challenge to the long tradition of male domination, and formative in its encouragement to both women and men to seek the mutual enrichment coming through fuller partnership.

In that same year Pope John Paul II addressed an apostolic exhortation on the theme of the community of the family, in which he spoke specifically of the many forms of degradation and discrimination from which women suffer and the high esteem Jesus had always shown towards women and the responsibilities he had entrusted to them. The pope underlined the equal dignity and responsibility of women with men, which, he said, fully justifies women's access to public functions. "On the other hand," he went on to say, "the true advancement of women requires that clear recognition be given to the value of their maternal and family role, by comparison with all other public roles and all other professions."

The question of women's equal opportunity and participation in all spheres of life had by this time become a frequent matter of debate in both secular and ecclesiastical circles. The sixth assembly of the WCC at Vancouver (1983) gave clear evidence that the process begun by the study on the "Community of Women and Men in the Church" had prompted widespread concern for fuller representation of women in all the deliberative councils of the churches and for women's

voices to be heard on all the major issues. Under the leadership of Bärbel von Wartenberg, who had succeeded Brigalia Bam as director of the women's desk, a conference for women was held preparatory to the assembly. During the assembly itself 12 of the speakers in main plenary sessions were women, and the worship, debates and whole corporate life were all influenced by the lively participation of women. In the official policy-making bodies elected by the assembly, the proportion of women elected rose to 29%.

The sixth assembly resolved that still further emphasis must be given to the needs and the contribution of women. It was decided by the central committee of 1987 that there should be a special decade during which the churches would demonstrate their solidarity with women. The decade was launched on Easter day 1988, under the leadership of WCC women's desk director Anna Karin Hammar. Its focus is on empowering women at all levels to participate more fully in the decisions that affect their destiny, to be partners with men in shaping the lives of their families and their societies and to be equipped for ministry in the churches in the full fellowship of the people of God.

See also **anthropology, theological; Ecumenical Decade of the Churches in Solidarity with Women; feminism; ordination of women; participation; sexism; theology, feminist**.

PAULINE WEBB

K. Bliss, *The Service and Status of Women in the Churches*, London, SCM, 1952 • J. Crawford & M. Kinnamon eds, *In God's Image*, WCC, 1983 • S. Herzel, *A Voice for Women*, WCC, 1981 • M. Oduyoye, *Who Will Roll the Stone Away?*, WCC, 1990 • C.F. Parvey ed., *The Community of Women and Men in the Church*, WCC, 1981 • *Sexism in the 1970s*, WCC, 1974 • B. Thompson, *A Chance to Change: Women and Men in the Church*, WCC, 1982.

WORD OF GOD. God* acts through his word, which is not only a means of communication and instruction but also a creative power (Gen. 1; John 1:3). Through his word God created the universe; through the preaching of Jesus (see **Jesus Christ**) the kingdom of God* came into this world; and through the Holy Spirit* this word is at work today. God does not carry out any fundamental work without his word, and without it nothing can be identified as coming from God.

Biblical data. The Old Testament emphasizes the power of the word of God. God "spoke, and it came to be; he commanded, and it stood forth" (Ps. 33:9). The "word that goes forth from my mouth... shall not return to me empty, but it shall accomplish that which I purpose, and prosper in the thing for which I sent it" (Isa. 55:11). It is fulfilled in creation,* salvation history,* the law* and prophecy.* The history of Israel is understood as election and salvation by and under the word of God. The decalogue is called "the ten words" (Ex. 34:28), and Deuteronomy identifies the law with the word spoken (Deut. 4:2, 15:15, 28:14). In the word of the prophet, God himself speaks to his people. The dynamic character of the word is accompanied and given emphasis by the meaningful acts of the prophet. The word proclaims the devastating judgment which follows from the people's unfaithfulness (Isa. 1-3; Amos 1-9; Hos. 4) and then the new life and re-establishment of the covenant,* the sign of God's faithfulness (Ezek. 37; Jer. 31:31-34; Isa. 54). These various forms of the word of God complement and interpenetrate each other. They express God's revelation* in the law and in history* and show the difference between God and idols (Isa. 41:4).

In the New Testament the use of term "word of God" corresponds to what we find in the OT and means both scripture* and God's self-communication in the Holy Spirit. The word of God involves more than a form of knowledge. It effects salvation when it is received in faith.* It is the word of life (Phil. 2:16), of salvation (Acts 13:26), of reconciliation* (2 Cor. 5:18-25) and of truth (Eph. 1:13) and is "living and active, sharper than any two-edged sword" (Heb. 4:12). "Word of God" thus becomes a synonym for "gospel".

What is new in the NT lies in the close link there is between the word of God and the person of Jesus. In the synoptic gospels the word of God is the saving message of God which Jesus proclaims and with which he identifies himself; the proclamation of the kingdom of God and what Jesus does are one and the same reality (Luke 17:21). The word of God is the message of salvation effected in Jesus Christ. For John's gospel, Jesus is the logos, and logos defines the actual person of

Jesus (John 1:1-14). Because he is the word of God by which God has been expressing his will since the beginning of the world, the words, life and works of Jesus reveal him as the source of true life and as the final and saving word of God for humanity (see **uniqueness of Christ**).

From the NT period onwards, the question of the authority and interpretation of the OT has been raised. This problem sets Jesus over against the Pharisees (Mark 2:23-28, 3:1-6; Matt. 5:21-48; cf. also the parable of the sower, Mark 4:1-9). Paul states this problem in the form of the dialectical relationship of law and gospel. The OT law is holy, just and good (Rom. 7:12), but it cannot be imposed on gentile Christians (Gal. 1-4). The law cannot purchase justification in the presence of God, nor can it purchase salvation. It enables us only to become aware of sin (Rom. 3:20, 8:2). In and by the cross of Jesus Christ, the law has itself been abolished (Gal. 3). Jesus Christ is the fulfilment and the end of the law (Rom. 10:4). This gospel of Jesus Christ is the sole source of life (see **life and death**), the word which sanctifies and regenerates (1 Tim. 4:5; 1 Pet. 1:23). Paul and the young Christian church emphasize that the power of the word of God lies in its proclamation (Rom. 10:17; Eph. 6:17). The ministry entrusted with spreading this word is a divine institution (Matt. 28:18-20; Acts 20:24; 2 Cor. 5:18-20). In the word of the apostle, the word of God lets itself be heard and acts (1 Thess. 2:13-14). The word of those who are sent is the word of Jesus Christ, who is the sender (Luke 10:16; Rom. 10:15-16; Titus 1:2-3; see **apostolicity**).

Historical developments. The ancient church, in its opposition to Gnosticism and the movement of "enthusiasm" (Montanism), first narrowed down the idea of the word of God through the identification of holy scripture (the canon*) and the word of God (revelation). But there was also an expansion of its meaning. In the East the Greek understanding of the logos (reason) was set alongside the logos Christology. Origen insists on the unity of the word of God in the flesh, in scripture, in the eucharist* and in reason. The literal and moral interpretations of scripture must be supplemented by the spiritual meaning derived from the logos. This view was to remain essential for the Orthodox churches, which emphasize the complementary nature of real inspiration* (God as the author of the scriptures) and of passive inspiration (internal illumination of the reader's mind for true knowledge of the word of God).

The West separates more clearly the word of God (*kerygma* and *logos*) and the revelation of God in reason (Tertullian, Cyprian), while seeking not to restrict the word of God to scripture. For Augustine, God himself is the eternal word who gives himself to us in the sacrament* as the visible word and in the written and proclaimed word as an audible sacrament. To discover the fullness of the word of God in scripture, the latter must be interpreted in a fourfold way: literal or historical meaning, allegorical or doctrinal meaning, tropological or moral meaning, and anagogical or eschatological meaning (Augustine, John Cassian). The correctness of the interpretation of scripture as the word of God is vouchsafed through its being linked to the church* and to the dogmatic decisions (see **dogma**) of the councils of the church (see **ecumenical councils**).

The middle ages took up again the great Augustinian options while again restricting the word of God to scripture. It stressed the need for the dogma and tradition* of the church as a guarantee for the interpretation of scripture as the authentic word of God (Vincent of Lérins, Gregory the Great). Scholastic theology regarded holy scripture and Tradition as norms of the revelation and of the word of God (Anselm of Canterbury, Thomas Aquinas). In response to the Reformation, the council of Trent* (1545-63) specified that scripture and the traditions are dictated by Christ or the Holy Spirit (H. Denzinger, *Enchiridion Symbolorum [DS]*, 1501) and that scripture cannot be interpreted contrary to the doctrinal tradition of the church (*DS* 1507).

For the 16th-century Reformation and especially for Martin Luther, understanding the word of God is central to theology. Scripture is the only true basis for faith (*sola scriptura, norma normans non normata* — scripture alone, the criterion which sets the criteria and is not itself subject to a criterion) and is its own interpreter. Under the working of the Holy Spirit, scripture becomes the word of God when it is proclaimed and interpreted in the light of the sinner's justification* before God. The word of God is also given in the

sacraments, which like scripture are means of salvation.* The word of God comes to us as a summons and judgment (law) and as a liberating and creative word (gospel). John Calvin insists on the "internal witness of the Holy Spirit", which makes scripture the word of God.

By its stress on the literal inspiration of scripture, Protestant orthodoxy (16th-17th centuries) identifies scripture and the word of God. But the word of God goes beyond scripture as such, as the eternal word of God (Trinity*), the incarnate word of God (Christology), the preached word of God (preaching) and the visible word of God (sacrament). This literalist view of inspiration was criticized in the Enlightenment, and then in pietism and by Friedrich Schleiermacher, with their view that the word of God is at work also in human experience.

In the 20th century, the Reformation concern was taken up again and developed in the theology of the word of God put forward by Karl Barth. He called for a return to the witness of scripture and rejected any other basis for faith. The presupposition for every theology lay in the fact that God has spoken. The written word of God cannot be verified either by historical research or by human experience. Human knowledge of God is based on the revelation of the Trinitarian God. By analogy with the Trinity the word of God comes in a threefold form as the revealed word of God, the written word of God and the proclaimed word of God. This word of God is at one and the same time the communication, work and mystery of God. It is one and is given definitively in Jesus Christ. Exegesis must show "how the words relate to the word *in* the words" (see **exegesis, methods of**).

In Roman Catholic theology a new slant is given by Vatican II* and its Dogmatic Constitution on Divine Revelation, *Dei Verbum (DV)*. Vatican I's statement that the magisterium of the church is the positive norm for scripture, which is therefore subordinate to it (*DS* 3007), is no longer used. Scripture "firmly, fully and without error" teaches the truth of God, the word of God which "shines forth in Christ, who is himself both the mediator and the sum total of revelation" (*DV* 11 and 2). The word of the church is the proclamation of the word of God *as* the word of scripture. The magisterium and doctrinal tradition of the church are fundamental but come from "the same divine well-spring" (*DV* 9); the witness of scripture is normative for the later tradition (*DV* 10,24).

Theological and ecumenical issues. The ecumenical dialogues of the last few years have revealed significant convergences among the various Christian families in their understanding of the word of God.

The Montreal conference (Faith and Order 1963) made it possible to have a common re-definition of the relation between scripture and Tradition. The word of God which has to be passed on is itself the Tradition (with a capital *T*), "God's revelation and self-giving in Christ, present in the life of the church" (Montreal, 45-46). Holy scripture is the written form of this (50). Tradition (with a small *t*) is the transmission of the Tradition: "tradition can be a faithful transmission of the gospel, but also a distortion of it" (48). And finally, traditions (plural) "are the expressions and manifestations in diverse historical forms of the one truth and reality which is Christ" (47).

The bilateral dialogues* took up this convergence, which for the transmission of the word of God stresses the role of Tradition and the normative nature of the biblical witness (see Anglican-Orthodox dialogue, Moscow, 1976, 24-42; Reformed-Roman Catholic dialogue, "The Presence of Christ", 1977, 24-42; Lutheran-Roman Catholic dialogue, Malta, 1972, 14-25, and "Ways to Community", 1980, 62-65; Methodist-Roman Catholic dialogue, Honolulu, 1981, 34; all in *Growth in Agreement [GA]*). The question still open is that of the criterion for the faithfulness of the tradition and traditions to the Tradition, especially the role of the church and its magisterium for determining what is the word of God (Anglican-Roman Catholic, Authority II, 1981, 23-33, in *GA*).

A corollary of this convergence is the distinction between holy scripture and the word of God. This is not something that separates them. The word of God is fully attested in scripture, which is essential for the church (Baptist-Reformed 1977, 1-3; ARCIC 1981, E1.2), but it cannot be reduced to scripture (Reformed-Roman Catholic 1977, 27). Under the influence of the Holy Spirit, scripture itself must become the word of God, the gospel, in which is transmitted the salvation God gives to the world in Jesus Christ. The

task of interpreting scripture arises out of this distinction. No external datum can guarantee it. "Neither the *sola scriptura* nor formal references to the authoritativeness of the magisterial office are sufficient. The primary criterion is the Holy Spirit making the Christ-event into a saving action" (Lutheran-Roman Catholic dialogue, Malta, 18).

This broader understanding of the word of God finds expression in the word-sacrament relationship, even if more dialogue is called for with a view to the exact definition of the sacrament. Word and sacrament cannot be set against each other (Methodist-Roman Catholic dialogue, Dublin, 1976, 54-58, in *GA*); by them God approaches human beings and gives his salvation. Following Vatican II (*DV* 21 and *Sacrosanctum Concilium* 7), Roman Catholicism insists on the efficacy of preaching and the unity in the sacrament of word and sign and accords a dominant role to the sacrament of the eucharist (Orthodox-Roman Catholic dialogue, Munich, 1981, 1-6; cf. also BEM,* E1). For the Lutheran, Anglican, Methodist and Reformed traditions, salvation is fully offered in the word of God whether in the form of preaching or in that of the sacraments (cf. Augustine). The separating character of the difference between Roman Catholics and these Protestants has here been overcome. This resolution is still not so for certain traditions which consider the word of God to be given in the preaching and hearing of scripture, the sacrament being more a response of the believer and of the community to the word of God.

The question of extending the term "word of God" to cover other things besides preaching and sacraments remains more difficult. What is the value of what we find in nature*? of the order of creation? of the witness of other religions? Can the word of God be discerned there as law? as gospel? Different traditions give different answers, and so far these questions have not been central in the dialogues. A reflection on the word of God and revelation, and on law and gospel, is necessary with regard to the ethical issues of the moment.

All the traditions agree in saying that the word of God, the gift of salvation, must be proclaimed throughout the world (Matt. 28:19-20; 1 Pet. 2:9-12). The word of God calls on Christians to display signs of love

(Acts 6:1-6; 1 Thess. 4:9). The church lives on the promise that God himself is working in his word, and that this never remains without a response (Isa. 55:11).

See also **Bible in the ecumenical movement; canon; exegesis, methods of; hermeneutics; inspiration; revelation; teaching authority; Tradition and traditions.**

ANDRÉ BIRMELÉ

K. Barth, *Kirchliche Dogmatik* I/1-2 (ET *Church Dogmatics*, I/1 and I/2, Edinburgh, Clark, 1936 and 1956) • A. Birmelé, *Le salut en Jésus Christ dans les dialogues oecuméniques*, Paris, Cerf, 1986 • G. Ebeling, *Wort und Glaube* (ET *Word and Faith*, London, SCM, 1963) • E. Lohse, "Deus dixit — Wort Gottes im Zeugnis des AT und NT", in *Die Einheit des NT*, 2nd ed., Göttingen, 1976 • H. Meyer & L. Fischer eds, *Growth in Agreement*, WCC, 1984 • Vatican II, Dei Verbum, in *Documents of Vatican II*, A. Flannery ed., Grand Rapids, MI, Eerdmans, 1975 • G. Wainwright, "Word and Sacrament in the Churches' Responses to the Lima Text", *One in Christ*, 24, 1988.

WORK. Two dimensions of work are revealed in Genesis. Work is a joyful task, a divinely appointed stewardship of the earth; and work is a punishment for sin,* a painful duty, a heavy burden. Christian theology must take both aspects seriously.

Since the Bible was produced in an agricultural society, the biblical texts respect manual labour. Today certain writers have been critical of the creation story because in it humans are appointed "to subdue" the earth and exercise "dominion" over the animals. These writers claim that since the Bible presents humans as exploiters of the natural environment, Christianity is partially to blame for the present ecological crisis. Yet since Genesis was written for an agricultural people, possibly a people just settling down after a nomadic existence, subduing the earth and exercising dominion referred to ploughing, sowing and harvesting, and the taming of animals. Responsible for the ecological crisis is the maximization of production, derived from the logic of industrial capitalism.*

In the Bible, manual work was honourable. By contrast, the Greek intellectual tradition, originating in a society based on slave labour, despised manual work. Labour was assigned to women and slaves. Man, or the free male citizen, was defined as an intellectual being. This cultural current was not without influence on Christian thought.

Writing in a feudal society, Thomas Aquinas praised work as a source of personal satisfaction and service to the community. The church had ritual blessings for fields, stables, tools and workshops. Yet even for Thomas, it was the rational soul that represented the image of God in human beings. Thus thinking and contemplating was the most honoured human engagement.

In the Reformation, work came to be looked upon as obedience to God, as a discipline and an achievement. This new ethos corresponded to the economic needs of the emerging modern society. Still, the modern philosophies continued to define humans in terms of their rationality. The Enlightenment thinkers, members of the bourgeoisie, had little respect for peasants and workers.

Karl Marx revolutionized philosophical thinking on labour.* He defined the human being as worker. Humans differed from the animal world because they alone had to produce the conditions of their survival (food, housing, clothing, etc.) by labour. Marx recognized the two aspects of labour specified in the Bible. He distinguished "creative labour", defined as the way of human self-realization, from "alienated labour", brought about by the exploitation inflicted on slaves, serfs and, in modern times, the working class.

In the bourgeois age, Christian theologians were slow to recognize the need for a theology of work. Only in recent decades have Protestants and Catholics seriously wrestled with this issue.

A good number of theologians, in critical dialogue with Marxism, have defined human beings created by God as workers and stewards. *Laborem Exercens* (1981) developed such a theology of work (see **social encyclicals, papal**). Humans produce their world (the "objective dimension" of labour), and in doing so, they also realize their own potentialities (the "subjective dimension" of labour). The subjective dimension, human self-realization, has priority over the objects produced. Labour becomes alienated whenever the subjective dimension is subordinated to purely objective concerns.

Thus workers are meant to be "the subjects" of production. They are entitled to participate

Women at work in Bangladesh (WCC photo)

East European socialism, the urgent task now is to scale down industrial production. Defining humans as workers, these Christians argue, only supports the present orientation towards industrial growth.

Another question in regard to the theology that defines humans as workers is raised by some Christians living in non-Western cultures. Is Western-style hard work really necessary? Is it human? In warm climates, they argue, human needs are quite limited; they could be met by a modest economy that relies on relatively simple tools and does not demand constant labour. Should the whole globe become Westernized? Or is there to be room for alternative cultures, based on subsistence economies, where people live lives that are materially modest yet culturally and spiritually rich?

GREGORY BAUM

Christians in the Technical and Social Revolutions of Our Time, WCC, 1967, pp.62-64 • *Dilemmas and Opportunities*, WCC, 1959, pp.81-84 • J. de Santa Ana, *Towards a Church of the Poor*, WCC, 1982 • M. Volf, *Zukunft der Arbeit – Arbeit der Zukunft*, Munich, Kaiser, 1988.

in the decisions regarding the organization of labour and the use of the product of their hands. *Laborem Exercens* argues that in capitalism and in communism, workers are excluded from these decisions and hence have become "objects" of production. Since justice* demands that workers be the subject of production, workers are destined to become the co-owners of the giant work-benches at which they labour.

Following this theology of work, many churches have denounced unemployment* as a social evil and called for public policies of full employment. Yet defining humans as workers has been seriously questioned by other churches. They say that since unemployment is becoming a permanent feature of automated, computerized society, Christians should define the human essence and human dignity independently of work and on the political level demand a guaranteed annual income for all.

Ecologically concerned Christians have also questioned a theology that defines humans as workers. Since the ecological crisis is produced by the maximizing impulse of capitalism, reflected to some extent even in

WORLD ALLIANCE FOR PROMOTING INTERNATIONAL FRIENDSHIP THROUGH THE CHURCHES.

In the early 1900s several church leaders were convinced of the need to apply Christian principles to international relations, to promote mutual understanding between nations, and to develop and strengthen international law. Two members of the British parliament, Quaker J. Allen Baker and Anglican Willoughby H. Dickinson, were prompted by the two peace conferences at The Hague (1899 and 1907) to promote peaceful relations between the churches in Great Britain and Germany by a large-scale exchange of visits between church representatives. A German church delegation, led by Friedrich Siegmund-Schultze, visited England in 1908, and the next year an English delegation went to Germany. Both delegations included Roman Catholic clergy and laity. Charles S. Macfarland, general secretary of the Federal Council of the Churches of Christ in the USA (founded in 1908), also played an important role in work for closer understanding between the US and European churches. In 1914, Protestant,

Roman Catholic and Jewish organizations founded the Church Peace Union. It received $2 million from the industrialist Andrew Carnegie, and this money served to finance most of the future activities of the World Alliance.

The first world war erupted on 1 August 1914, and the very next day in Constance (Switzerland) the World Alliance was founded. On 3 August the delegates quickly left for their homes, but Christians had formed an association for peace among the nations — an ecumenical pioneer movement to face international problems. The World Alliance post-war conference in 1919 (The Hague) helped lead to the first conference on Life and Work* (Stockholm 1925). The World Alliance would function through national councils in the US, Canada, India, Japan and several European countries.

A 1929 peace conference of 500 delegates at Prague climaxed World Alliance history. The World Alliance held that it was "a paramount duty of the Christian church to strive for the mental and moral disarmament of the people in all countries and to lead them at the same time to insist upon a rapid and universal reduction of armaments and the adoption of methods of arbitration and mediation in the settlement of all international disputes". The World Alliance further encouraged the churches to support wholeheartedly the work of the League of Nations.

From 1931 to 1937, the World Alliance and the Universal Christian Council for Life and Work were closely related through common offices in Geneva, a joint general secretary, joint youth work, and a common bulletin *(The Churches in Action)*. However, it decided in 1938 to remain "an autonomous movement which serves the churches" rather than to join with Faith and Order,* and Life and Work, in forming the WCC.

During the second world war most World Alliance national councils in Europe were dissolved, and the Church Peace Union stopped its financial support of World Alliance. Attempts to re-establish it internationally after the war proved unsuccessful; a particular point of disagreement was whether it should be a Christian or an interfaith organization. Meanwhile, in 1946 the International Missionary Council and the WCC in process of formation created the Commission of the Churches on International Affairs. This con-

tinues to be the ecumenical agency within the WCC for advocating peaceful resolution of conflicts, disarmament and international reconciliation.

ANS J. VAN DER BENT

C.S. Macfarland, *Pioneers for Peace through Religion*, New York, Revell, 1946 ● R. Rouse & S. Neill eds, *A History of the Ecumenical Movement, 1517-1948*, 3rd ed., WCC, 1986 ● World Alliance for Promoting International Friendship through the Churches, *Handbook*, London, WAPIFC, 1916, 1919-38.

WORLD ALLIANCE OF REFORMED CHURCHES.

Founded in 1875, WARC presently includes 175 churches in 84 countries, with an estimated 70 million communicant members. Nearly two-thirds of the churches are in Africa, Asia and Latin America; most are minority churches.

Already in 1877 the WARC, then composed primarily of North American and Anglo-Saxon churches of the Presbyterian tradition, defended the rights of Native Americans in the US. Since then, WARC has repeatedly expressed its commitment to human rights, usually on behalf of small, persecuted churches of any denomination. In recent decades, global human rights problems have become as great a concern as that for individual churches.

Ecumenism has also shaped the work and witness of the alliance. Broadly speaking, the Reformed ethos considers that every church is a particular expression of the one universal church of Jesus Christ; each community of faith contributes to the life of the whole. This underlying principle has led succeeding executive committees and staff to promote ecumenism and church unity wherever possible. WARC fully supported the growth of the WCC, participates in annual conversations with other Christian World Communions,* and since the late 1960s has organized and welcomed bilateral and multilateral dialogues with Christians of other traditions and people of other faiths.

The major contribution of the Reformed tradition to Christianity has often been its deep interest in theological reflection. In the 1970s WARC published works on the theological basis of human rights and, in cooperation with the Roman Catholic Church and the Lutheran World Federation, on a theology of marriage and the ecclesial and pastoral problems of mixed marriages. With the Reformed, theology also usually involves the biblical concept of covenanting. In 1983, the alliance initiated the WCC programme on "Justice, Peace and the Integrity of Creation", with its study on covenanting for peace and justice. In Seoul in 1989 the general council directed the staff to begin theological reflection on the moral legitimacy or illegitimacy of governments, echoing a historic debate for the Reformed: relationships between church and state.

In 1970, the International Congregational Council and the Alliance of Reformed Churches holding to the Presbyterian tradition merged to become the World Alliance of Reformed Churches. Since then, WARC focus began to broaden and in some ways to blur the details of Reformed identity. Ecclesiastical as well as hermeneutical and theological differences now range from John Calvin's Consistoire of Geneva to the united Church of North India and the Uniting Church of Australia, mixing various ecclesiological understandings of ministry. Some churches are guided by one or two early Reformed confessions, while others revise their confessions as they believe the times and the Holy Spirit dictate. While most, if not all, of the member churches would agree that scripture is the final authority on matters of faith and practice, their interpretations vary from a nearly literal reading of the text dictated by the Spirit of God to the authors, to a view of the Bible as a series of editors re-writing and re-editing to suit the needs of the addressed community.

Such pluralism also incorporates wide cultural differences, further complicated by the fact that most of the member churches are minorities, not only religiously but also culturally and ethnically. The challenges which the alliance faces to celebrate diversity and unity, particularly in a world where political and economic realities preclude stability and are rife with injustice, will demand of WARC much flexibility as well as a firm grip on the helm of the Reformed dictum: the Reformed being reformed. The work and witness of the WARC at least in the next decade will be to discern the essence of this Reformed heritage in the midst of astounding change.

JILL SCHAEFFER

WORLD ASSOCIATION FOR CHRISTIAN COMMUNICATION.

The origins of the WACC go back to 1950, to a meeting in Chichester, England, of Christian broadcasters from many of the national broadcasting corporations of Europe. The meeting was organized by Edwin Robertson, at that time head of religious broadcasting at the BBC. Bishop George Bell of Chichester had encouraged him to organize an informal international conference on Christian broadcasting. That first meeting led to a statement of aims and methods of Christian broadcasting. The following years saw European agencies meeting with missionary societies from the US which culminated in a World Committee for Christian Broadcasting, founded in Königstein, Federal Republic of Germany, in 1956.

In 1963 a new constitution was drawn up at a meeting in Limuru, Kenya, setting the ground rules for a new World Association for Christian Broadcasting (WACB). Five years later, in 1968, another group, the Coordinating Committee for Christian Broadcasting, merged with the WACB in Oslo, to form the WACC. Its concerns now included all forms of media to proclaim the gospel and their relevance to life and the promotion of a just society.

The WACC continued to develop and to cooperate with other organizations involved in Christian communication. In 1975 the Agency for Christian Literature Development (ACLD), a programme of the Commission on World Mission and Evangelism (CWME) of the WCC, was merged with the WACC. Developing out of the CWME-sponsored Christian Literature Fund, the ACLD aimed to provide literature which would be addressed to people in their total environment, speaking in the idiom of contemporary society.

Combining print media with electronic media determined to a large extent both the work and structure of the new organization. Apart from providing fellowship among Christian communicators, the WACC's main task became the development and evaluation of projects, particularly in the third world. Around 150 projects are supported every year, such as audiovisuals, video, radio, book publishing, news services, communication education, journalism, music and others. The WACC's project work is mainly in those sectors of society which have limited resources.

During the 1970s, however, there was a great deal of debate on the problems of international communication, most of which was spurred on by the non-aligned movement and communication specialists working for non-governmental organizations. This resulted in the call for a new international information order, which greatly influenced the "new WACC". In parallel, the WACC closely followed the international discussions on the relationship between communication and socio-economic development.

The WACC promotes its policies and principles through studies (e.g. theology and communication, women's issues), training, and publications: a quarterly journal, *Media Development*, offers articles on topics of interest in the area of communication, and *Action*, a monthly newsletter, carries news of events and trends in communication worldwide, with an occasional supplement *Communication Resource*. The WACC also sponsors the publication of books by subsidizing researchers and authors, especially from the third world.

The majority of members and almost all the partner organizations which support the WACC are deeply rooted in the ecumenical movement as it has developed in the Protestant and Orthodox families of churches. It is primarily these churches which have provided the vision and inspiration for the WACC throughout the various phases in its history. For this reason, the WACC has given priority to ecumenical work. It seeks to maintain close contacts with the WCC and denominational families at the international level, like the Lutheran World Federation. Likewise, the WACC emphasizes close ecumenical relationships on the regional and local levels. The WACC has a long tradition of close relationships with Roman Catholic institutions at various levels, such as the Centre for the Study of Communication and Culture (London), the Catholic Media Council (Aachen), a joint publishing agreement with Ediciones Paulinas (Argentina), and the Asian Social Institute and the Communication Foundation of Asia (both in Manila).

Speakers and writers of other faiths have sometimes participated in the WACC's forum work, giving new insights and contributing to dialogue in the sphere of international communication. The WACC has made a provision in its guidelines for applicants to the small-projects fund "whose work reflects Christian values" and who wish to address themselves to "crucial issues facing people and communities", while expressing "an ecumenical vision that recognizes the oneness of all people regardless of race, sex or religion". This ecumenical openness with respect to people of other faiths also applies to secular groups which share the WACC's understanding of communication.

The WACC divides the world administratively into seven regions, each establishing its own priorities and work structure in order to meet the needs each defines. World headquarters are in London. The WACC currently comprises some 600 corporate (e.g. church agencies and communication institutions) and individual members. Some 500 people from 70 countries attended the WACC's first world congress (Manila 1989), considering the theme "Communication for Community".

Praxis and reflection have shaped the profile of the WACC over the years. The understanding of communication and the churches' mission in it have been the basis for the WACC's self-criticism as well as the incentive to renewal and greater commitment, all in the service of communication which is participatory and liberating, and which is prophetic, creates community and respects culture.

CARLOS A. VALLE

WORLD CATHOLIC FEDERATION FOR THE BIBLICAL APOSTOLATE.

The WCFBA is an international association of Roman Catholic organizations which promote the use of the Bible in the pastoral and evangelization life of the church.

Vatican II* (1962-65) demanded "easy access to holy scripture for the Christian faithful" (On divine revelation, 22). In 1966 Pope Paul VI entrusted to the Secretariat for Promoting Christian Unity* (SPCU) the task of contacting both RC episcopal conferences about the needs and possibilities of Bible translation, and the United Bible Societies about possibilities of RC collaboration in the translation, publication and distribution of biblical texts. In 1967 the SPCU contacted all RC biblical organizations, and in 1969 their directors founded the WCFBA, under SPCU patronage.

The WCFBA responds to the needs of local churches through mutual support and financial aid. It has been active in translation, production and distribution of Catholic or interconfessional Bible editions; compilation of instructional materials; formation of Bible animators and catechists; organization of small Bible groups; use of the Bible in theatre, music, audiovisual media, etc.; celebration of national Bible weeks; and co-operation with organizations of other Christian churches active in Bible ministries.

The WCFBA is represented in 90 countries. Its headquarters are in Stuttgart, Federal Republic of Germany. It publishes the quarterly *Dei Verbum*, in English, French and German.

TOM STRANSKY

WORLD COMMUNITY. The term "world community", coined in the ecumenical movement during the 1960s, relates to the unity of humankind. The Vatican II* decree *Nostra Aetate* (1965) emphasized that "in her task of fostering unity and love among individuals, indeed among nations, the church considers above all what human beings have in common and what draws them towards fellowship". Leslie Cooke appealed to this idea in remarks he made to the Swanwick interchurch aid consultation in 1966: "We have to press on beyond co-operation to community... The overwhelming compulsion to move from co-operation to community derives from the fact that it is clear that many of the problems which face mankind can be solved only by the building of a world community. Perhaps the most significant contribution the churches can make is in manifesting that they are a world community, that they in fact share a common life in the Body of Christ." The 1968 WCC Uppsala assembly stated: "The church is bold in speaking of itself as the sign of the coming unity of mankind", but "secular society has produced instruments of conciliation and unification which often seem more effective than the church itself". Section 2 of the 1975 Nairobi assembly, "Seeking Community: The Common Search of People of Various Faiths, Cultures and Ideologies", pointed out that "almost

everywhere Christians live together with neighbours of other faiths and we are all part of the world community. We live in one world and have a common calling to work for its survival and betterment."

A 1974 WCC-sponsored multifaith dialogue (Colombo, Sri Lanka) had the theme "Towards World Community". It spoke of a "world community of communities", rather than of "world community", and warned that the term should not be understood "as a move towards a homogeneous unity or a totalitarian uniformity". World community is neither an attempt to build a super-organization nor the search for a world religion. "The primary responsibility towards the task of living together as a world community is to seek for all a higher and more just quality of life."

"The Unity of the Church and the Unity of Humankind" has been on the agenda of the Faith and Order* commission since 1971. In 1981 the theme was changed to "The Unity of the Church and the Renewal of Human Community". The methodological approach has been intensively debated, but there is wide agreement that the study can succeed only if it is both intercontextual and interdisciplinary.

ANS J. VAN DER BENT

WORLD CONFERENCE ON RELIGION AND PEACE. The 1968 International Inter-religious Symposium, held in New Delhi to commemorate the centennial of Mahatma Gandhi's birth, recommended that a "world conference on religion and peace" (WCRP) be held. The first world conference took place in Kyoto, Japan (1970). Among the founders were President Nikkyo Niwano, leader of the lay Buddhist movement Rissho Kosei-Kai; Dana McLean Greeley, a US Unitarian; Angelo Fernandes, Roman Catholic archbishop of Delhi; and R.R. Diwakar, chairman of the Gandhi Peace Foundation. The first secretary-general was Homer Jack, a US Unitarian, who served until 1983.

World assemblies have been held at Louvain, Belgium (1974); Princeton, USA (1979); Nairobi (1984); and Melbourne (1989). Fernandes was the president until 1984; then a joint presidium of religious leaders from a variety of world faiths was elected, so far including Christians from the USSR, France, South Africa, India, Australia and the

UK; Muslims from Pakistan, Indonesia and Cameroon; Buddhists from China and Japan; Hindus from India; Sikhs from Kenya and India; a Jew from the USA; a Shintoist from Japan; and a Unitarian from the USA.

From the international organization a growing network of regional, national and local bodies has developed. Regional headquarters are in Singapore, Tokyo and Nairobi; the international offices in New York and Geneva serve regional concerns in the Americas and Europe. These national and regional chapters provide delegates for periodic world assemblies. At the WCRP in 1989, some 300 delegates, including 35% women and 15% youth, represented 14 religions.

The WCRP has consultative status with the United Nations as a non-governmental organization. It has been especially active in monitoring issues of disarmament and human rights. It engaged in various inter-religiously funded and executed humanitarian projects, such as among Vietnamese boat people 1976-78, among Khmer refugees 1979-81, and among victims of drought in Africa 1984-86.

The organization attracts delegates and funding not only from individuals but from established religious bodies such as episcopal conferences, Christian councils of churches, confessional organizations and world confessional bodies, and from peace movements, women's organizations, etc. in the worlds of Islam, Buddhism, Judaism, Hinduism and other religions. The WCRP has been active in promoting struggles for peace and justice in the social and political fields and in encouraging the coming together of peoples of various faiths to pray for peace, each in their own tradition.

See also **peace**.

JOHN B. TAYLOR

WORLD COUNCIL OF CHRISTIAN EDUCATION.

In 1889 more than 900 Sunday school leaders registered for the first convention of what soon became the World Sunday School Association. More than 400 came from Great Britain and Ireland and almost an equal number from the US and Canada. These leaders represented a lay movement (only 54 of the North Americans at the convention were ordained ministers) that had originated in England around 1780 to provide some elementary schooling for urban youngsters, who were increasingly present and troublesome in the cities. The movement spread rapidly to North America, and mostly through the Free Churches into much of Europe.

What started as a school to teach reading, writing and arithmetic to wayward children soon developed into a school for the churches. It became an evangelistic activity to bring children into contact with the church and the Christian message. It also provided nurture that substituted for and complemented religious training in the home and gradually included more and more children of church members.

Missionaries from "sending churches", chiefly in Great Britain and North America, developed Sunday schools which in many lands served as forerunners of formal education systems that developed later. Sunday schools constituted a major strategy of the world missionary movement. It is claimed that "Jesus Loves Me", the "song of the Sunday school", became the best-known hymn throughout the Christian world.

The Sunday school depended on lay volunteer teachers who used curriculum materials produced by church or religious agency publishers. It provided a significant place for the leadership of women. In many places it offered classes for adults. The official church organizations often gained control of the movement, although its identification with children and women continued to limit its stature within many churches.

In the late 1940s the change of name to World Council of Christian Education (WCCE) symbolized its expansion into youth activities and other field services. Reports of its work in different nations were made to its regular world meetings. From 1889 to 1958 the WCCE sponsored 14 world conventions, all but the first two registering more than 1,000 delegates; they were held in London (1889 and 1898), St Louis, Jerusalem, Rome, Washington, Zurich, Tokyo (1920 and 1958), Glasgow, Los Angeles, Rio de Janeiro, Oslo and Toronto. World assemblies and institutes followed until the final assembly in 1971 in Peru, when years of co-operative work, frustrating relationships, and negotiations led to a vote to integrate with the WCC. General responsibility for continuing its work was lodged in the newly established Office of Education of the WCC.

WILLIAM B. KENNEDY

W.B. Kennedy, *The Shaping of Protestant Education: An Interpretation of the Sunday School and the Development of Protestant Educational Strategy in the United States, 1789-1960*, New York, Association Press, 1966 ● G.E. Knoff, *The World Sunday School Movement: The Story of a Broadening Mission*, New York, Seabury, 1979.

WORLD COUNCIL OF CHURCHES.

This article deals with the origins, basis, nature and purpose, functions, organization and structures of the WCC. Several other entries deal with the developments in ecumenical thinking and activities which the WCC has initiated and fostered through its programmes and personnel.

Origins. The WCC was formally constituted at the first general assembly (Amsterdam) on 23 August 1948. It became the most visible international expression of varied streams of ecumenical life in the 20th century. Two of these streams — Life and Work* (L&W) and Faith and Order* (F&O) — merged at the first assembly. A third stream — the missionary movement, as organized in the International Missionary Council* (IMC) — was integrated at the 1961 third assembly (New Delhi). And a fourth stream — Christian education — entered with the 1971 merging of the World Council of Christian Education.*

Each of these movements is wider and deeper than any one of its structured expressions, including the WCC fellowship of churches. "Applied" or "practical" Christianity, for example, had been institutionalized not only in the L&W movement but also in the World Alliance for Promoting International Friendship through the Churches* (1914). Some world missionary bodies, such as the Lausanne Committee for World Evangelization,* still carry out many of the original aims of the IMC. The WCC youth department could never replace the YMCAs,* the YWCAs,* or the World Student Christian Federation.* And no one would claim that F&O can gather and focus the whole bewildering variety of biblical/theological thinking.

In 1920, the Church of Constantinople (the Orthodox Ecumenical Patriarchate) became the first church to appeal publicly for a permanent organ of fellowship and co-operation of "all the churches" — a "League of Churches" *(Koinōnia tōn Ekklēsiōn)* similar to the proposal after the first world war for a League of Nations *(Koinōnia tōn Ethnōn)*. Also calling for the same in the 1920s were such individual church leaders as Archbishop Nathan Söderblom (Sweden), a founder of L&W (1925), and J.H. Oldham (UK), a founder of the IMC (1921).

In July 1937, on the eve of the world conference of L&W at Oxford and of F&O at Edinburgh, representatives of the two movements met in London. They decided to bring the two together and to set up a fully representative assembly of the churches. The proposed new organization "shall have no power to legislate for the churches or to commit them to action without their consent; but if it is to be effective, it must deserve and win the respect of the churches in such measure that the people of greatest influence in the life of churches may be willing to give time and thought to its work". Also involved should be laypeople "holding posts of responsibility and influence in the secular world", and "a first-class intelligence staff". S. McCrea Cavert (USA) suggested the name "World Council of Churches".

Both Oxford and Edinburgh accepted the proposal and appointed seven members to a Committee of 14 to form the WCC. Meeting in Utrecht in May 1938, it created a provisional committee responsible for the World Council of Churches "in process of formation". William Temple (archbishop of York, later of Canterbury) was named chairman, and W.A. Visser 't Hooft (the Netherlands) general secretary. The provisional committee established a solid foundation for the WCC by resolving constitutional questions concerning its basis, authority and structure. In October-November 1938, it sent out formal invitations to 196 churches, and Temple wrote a personal letter to the Vatican secretary of state.

At Tambaram (India) in 1938 the IMC expressed interest in the WCC plan but decided to continue as a separate body. A number of missionary societies in its constituency did not want to come under the control of the churches, and there was fear that the churches of North America and Europe would not give to the younger churches elsewhere the place they deserved. Nevertheless, the IMC helped facilitate the eventual entrance of these churches into the WCC, "associated" with it in 1948, and eventually integrated in 1961.

In 1939 the provisional committee planned the first WCC general assembly for August 1941, but world war intervened, and the period of formation lasted for another decade. Between 1940 and 1946, the provisional committee could not function normally through its responsible committees, but its members and others did gather in the USA, England and Switzerland. Under the leadership of Visser 't Hooft in Geneva during the war, several activities contributed to the supra-national witness of the church: chaplaincy service, work among prisoners of war, assistance to Jews and other refugees, relay of information to the churches, and the preparation through contact with Christian leaders on all sides for post-war reconciliation and interchurch aid.

After the war the provisional committee met in Geneva (1946) and at Buck Hills, Pennsylvania (1947). The committee could affirm that the tragic war experience increased the churches' determination to manifest their fellowship. By 1948, 90 churches had accepted the invitation to join the WCC.

Second thoughts on representation and WCC membership* resulted in careful regard for numerical size and adequate confessional and geographical representation. The principal membership requirement was agreement with the basis upon which the council would be formed; other requirements specified the autonomy of a church, its stability and appropriate size and its good relationship to other churches. Although some favoured a council composed primarily of national councils of churches or of world confessional families (e.g. Lutherans, Orthodox, Baptists), the argument prevailed that the WCC should be in *direct* contact with national churches and thus should comprise the Methodist Church of Great Britain, the Methodist Episcopal Church, USA, the Methodist Church of Southern Africa, etc. World confessional bodies, national councils of churches and international ecumenical bodies could be invited to send representatives to the first assembly but would have non-voting observer status.

When the inaugural assembly convened on 22 August 1948, there were 147 churches from 44 countries ready to participate in the WCC. All confessional families within the

Christian world, except the Roman Catholic Church, were represented in some way. On the following day the assembly accepted the constitution of the WCC, and the newly organized fellowship of churches issued its message: "Christ has made us his own, and he is not divided. In seeking him we find one another. Here at Amsterdam we have committed ourselves afresh to him, and have covenanted with one another in constituting the World Council of Churches. We intend to stay together."

Amsterdam defined the WCC tasks in a general way in its constitution and more specifically in its decisions concerning policies, programmes and budget. The assembly authorized the WCC to make common pronouncements to the churches and to the world, but clearly defined the nature and limits of such pronouncements.

Basis. The 1948 inaugural assembly declared: "The World Council of Churches is a fellowship of churches which accept our Lord Jesus Christ as God and Saviour" (see **WCC, basis of**). Soon this formulation gave rise to questions, and requests for a clearer definition of the Christ-centredness of the churches' common calling, a more explicit expression of the Trinitarian faith and a specific reference to the holy scriptures. The result was the re-formulation, adopted by the third assembly (New Delhi 1961), which still stands: "a fellowship of churches which confess the Lord Jesus Christ as God and Saviour according to the scriptures, and therefore seek to fulfill together their common calling to the glory of the one God, Father, Son and Holy Spirit."

Less than a confession of Christian faith and more than a formula, the basis serves as a point of reference for WCC members, a source or ground of coherence. Since the WCC is not itself a church, it passes no judgment upon the sincerity or firmness with which member churches accept the basis or upon the seriousness with which they take their membership. Thus, the basis itself comes under William Temple's formula: "Any authority the Council will have consists in the weight which it carries with the churches by its own wisdom."

Nature and purpose. In 1948 the member churches understood that the WCC was not a church above them, certainly not the church universal or incipient "world church". They understood the council to be an instrument whereby the churches bear witness together in their common allegiance to Christ, search for that unity which Jesus Christ wills for his one and only church, and co-operate in matters which require common statements and actions. The assembly acknowledged Visser 't Hooft's description of the WCC: "an emergency solution, a stage on the road,... a fellowship which seeks to express that unity in Christ already given to us and to prepare the way for a much fuller and much deeper expression of that unity".

What was not clear in 1948 was how this spiritual nature of the fellowship should relate to member churches' understanding of the nature and limits of the WCC, and their understanding of their ecclesial relation to other members. In short, did membership of a church in the WCC have any implications for the "self-understanding" or ecclesiological position of that church?

To clarify positions, the WCC central committee in 1950 adopted the Toronto statement* on the church, the churches, and the World Council of Churches. It was forged in "a debate of considerable intensity" (Visser 't Hooft), even though its contents "defined a starting point, and not the way or the goal" (Lesslie Newbigin). According to this statement, the WCC "is not and must never become a super-church". It does not negotiate union between churches. It "cannot and should not be based on any one particular conception of the church". Membership does not "imply that a church treats its own conception of the church as merely relative" or accepts a "specific doctrine concerning the nature of church unity". Nevertheless, the common witness of the members "must be based on the common recognition that Christ is the divine head of the body", which, "on the basis of the New Testament", is the one church of Christ. Membership of the church of Christ "is more inclusive" than the membership in one's own church body, but it "does not imply that each church must regard the other member churches as churches in the true and full sense of the word". Yet common WCC membership implies in practice that the churches "should recognize their solidarity with each other, render assistance to each other in case of need, and refrain from such actions as

are incompatible with brotherly relationships".

While debates still continue on the apparently unchangeable status of both the basis and the Toronto statement, the functions and purposes of the WCC and its organs are changing, in statement and in fact. The present list of functions, approved by the 1983 sixth assembly (Vancouver), reveals far less neutrality in the ecclesiological understandings of the churches than an impartial reading of the basis and of the Toronto statement would suggest, even if the functions are not binding upon the member churches.

A clear example of this shift is from the vague WCC purpose "to carry out the work of the world movements for Faith and Order and Life and Work" (1948) to the much more specific call to the churches to pursue "the goal of visible unity in one faith and in one eucharistic fellowship expressed in worship and in the common life of Christ, and to advance towards that unity in order that the world may believe" (Nairobi 1975). It would be hard to describe this change as harmonious with Toronto's conclusion that "membership does not imply the acceptance of a specific doctrine concerning the nature of church unity". The churches may now be taking for granted what they might not have in 1948. Or are their representatives at assemblies only being swept up into verbal approvals while in fact their constituents back home hold different self-understandings?

This question itself may support the judgment that in many ways the Toronto statement is out of date. Many of its affirmations about what the WCC is *not* or about what WCC membership does *not* imply are indeed still valid and need re-affirmation. But one cannot expect a 1950 "emergency solution", crafted in the nervousness of an infant taking its first steps, to do justice to the collective ecumenical and missionary experience of the churches in six continents over more than 40 years. A clearer identity and profile for the WCC and its future requires a clearer identity for the ecumenical movement.

What do the churches today perceive as their "common calling" (or basis)? What do the churches today see as the future of the ecumenical movement, in vision and in fact? What are the visions or images that are really alive in the member churches when one talks of "ecumenism"? Are the visions and images the same in non-member churches? Is the WCC the natural framework and context of witness in fellowship for the member churches, in particular in congregational thinking and acting? If not, why not? The present questions about the WCC's identity and role in the ecumenical movement are not simply repeating those of 1950. Renewal of the WCC as such cannot come about simply by re-arranging programmes and Geneva offices. Thus, many church people are calling for a comprehensive, realistic analysis of the development, standstills and setbacks of the ecumenical movement in the churches since 1948. They are asking for some updated form of an articulated synthesis and "common ground" affirmation, such as, "the ecumenical movement, the church and the churches, and the WCC".

Organization. Amsterdam defined the WCC tasks in its constitution and in its decisions concerning policies and programmes. WCC programmes are a service in the name of the member churches and a service to all the churches, members or not. The WCC discharges its legislative and executive functions through the assembly, the central committee and the executive committee, and through the officers and subordinate bodies of the general secretariat.

The *assembly* is the supreme legislative body which determines WCC policies and reviews their implementation in its programmes. Meeting every seven or eight years, it is composed of voting delegates elected by the member churches. It elects the six (or seven) WCC presidents, who form the presidium, and members of the central committee.

The central committee allocates the assembly seats to the member churches on the basis of numerical size, confessional representation and geographical distribution. The following table gives an idea of the growing participation in the assemblies.

Assembly	Delegates	Churches
1. Amsterdam 1948	351	147
2. Evanston 1954	502	161
3. New Delhi 1961	577	197
4. Uppsala 1968	704	235
5. Nairobi 1975	676	285
6. Vancouver 1983	847	301
7. Canberra 1991	842	317

The rapid decolonization* of the post-war world began in Asia with India and Pakistan becoming independent in 1947, and in Africa with Ghana's independence in 1957. The subsequent growth of the national churches and the rise of indigenous clerical and lay leadership within them, and the increased number of Orthodox churches, are reflected in the regional representation at the assemblies. In 1948 the large majority of the 351 delegates of the 147 churches were in fact Western European and North American. At Vancouver 1983 the regional breakdown of the 847 delegates was much more balanced, with North America sending 158 delegates; Western Europe, 152; Eastern Europe, 142; Africa, 131; Asia, 114; the Middle East, 53; Latin America, 30; Australia and New Zealand, 26; the Pacific, 22; and the Caribbean, 19.

This geographical spread indicates a shift that is affecting the ecumenical movement as a whole. The traditional centre, which in 1948 embraced the areas of the North Atlantic, Eastern Europe and the Mediterranean, is fading in its dominant influence over those centres in the southern hemisphere that are no longer mere passive recipients — Africa, Asia, the Caribbean, Latin America and Oceania.

As both a geographical and a historical repositioning, these areas are becoming the new centres of theological articulations, personal and social ethical stances, spiritualities, church disciplines, artistic expressions and interchurch co-operation in common witness. As R.D. Paul of the Church of South India said in 1954 at the Evanston assembly to the churches of the West: "You have taught us how to think, but now that we are mature we are trying to think the message of Christianity out for ourselves. We can now be trusted to look after our own affairs. We have become your partner in the great mission of the church to the world." Whether in the WCC assemblies or in its programmes, all voices have begun to receive an equal hearing. The "contexts", no matter what their variety, still have the theatre of God's one church in God's one world as *the* context.

The more recent strong recommendations and negotiations (not always successful with some churches) to have an adequate cross-section of men and women, adults and youth, clergy and lay have produced changes in the composition of recent assemblies, as the following table shows.

Assembly	Percentage of delegates who were		
	Women	Under 30	Lay
Uppsala 1968	9	4	25
Nairobi 1975	22	9	42
Vancouver 1983	30	13	46

The delegates form the core of an assembly but in fact do not by themselves shape the milieu. Already at Amsterdam far more numerous than the delegates were alternates, consultants, accredited visitors, and youth delegates and stewards (two categories that were traditional breeding grounds for ecumenical leaders: e.g. Temple had been a steward at Edinburgh in 1910, and Philip Potter, later WCC general secretary, was a youth delegate at Amsterdam). At the Evanston assembly 646 press people were accredited, 144 more than the number of delegates. A rough estimate of the total number of direct participants at Vancouver was around 2,500; this figure does not include the crowds that were present for a variety of activities and for worship (as many as 4,500 a day).

The *central committee* is the main continuation body between assemblies. Ordinarily meeting each year, alternately in Geneva and elsewhere, it implements assembly policies by approving and reviewing programmes and determining priorities among them, adopts the budget and secures financial support, and elects the 14-16 non-ex-officio members of the *executive committee* (which normally meets twice a year). The central committee has grown from 90 members in 1948 to the present 145. The executive committee now has 27 members.

The general secretary is the chief WCC executive and heads the staff comprising those who conduct the continuing operations. He or she is elected normally for a term of five years by the central committee and is accountable to it. The first general secretary was W.A. Visser 't Hooft (1948-66), the second Eugene Carson Blake (1966-72), the third Philip A. Potter (1972-84) and the fourth Emilio Castro (1985-).

Structures. For some committed ecumenists, there has been too much post-war preoccupation with structures in the churches and in the ecumenical movement, at first both reasonable and proper but over the years becoming "dangerously neurotic" (Max Warren, 1976). Since 1948, they claim, far too much time and energy has been spent on "tinkering". Other critics, over the 40 years, have been calling for a more radical appraisal of the total WCC structure.

Most take for granted that effectiveness in church life, as in the world of business, requires that scarcely a decade pass without important organizational changes. Others judge that in fact the predominant "business management model" for churches and the WCC has hurt and dimmed more than fostered and expressed their nature and tasks. All agree there is no "right and perfect" WCC as an organization and that any decisions about WCC structures, old or new, should be pragmatic ones.

The 1948 assembly had to enflesh the WCC fellowship by assisting the churches not only to stay together but also to live and grow together. Amsterdam set up 12 departments bodies, well aware that the structural experiment would need constant, thorough evaluation. The 12 were Faith and Order, Study, Evangelism, Laity, Youth, Women, Interchurch Aid/Refugees, International Affairs, Ecumenical Institute, Publications, Library and Finance.

Most of the offices were in Geneva, at an old home on the route de Malagnou (at present a museum of watches and clocks), then in 1964 in a new building at Grand-Saconnex, Geneva. An office for maintaining closer relations with the North American member churches was established in New York, and in London an East Asia secretariat, in co-operation with the IMC.

For all these departmental activities the first assembly had authorized an executive/programme staff of only 36; the total payroll staff in January 1949 was 98. In fact the top staff of 36 never reached that number before the Evanston assembly (1954). Several churches had made available the services of their own paid people to strengthen the official staff for shorter or longer periods. Some posts vacated by resignations were deliberately not filled until Evanston could work out a new plan for the structuring and functioning of the Council. The experience of six years showed the necessity of more effective co-ordination of the various departments. The Evanston as-

Opening worship service of the WCC central committee meeting, Moscow 1989 (WCC/Peter Williams)

sembly provided the WCC with four divisions, each with departments: (1) *Studies* — Faith and Order, Church and Society, Evangelism and Missionary Studies; (2) *Ecumenical Action* — Youth, Laity, Men and Women in Church and Society, Ecumenical Institute; (3) *Interchurch Aid/Refugees and International Affairs*; and (4) *Information*.

The post-Evanston model continued through the New Delhi assembly (1961). The IMC-WCC integration in itself had brought about sufficient alterations. The large Eastern European Orthodox Churches of USSR, Romania, Bulgaria and Poland had just become members. More drastic changes would not be wise. But New Delhi did call for a re-examination. A 1964-67 structure committee reported to the 1968 assembly, which authorized the new central committee to study and implement its findings.

The central committee in 1972 put into effect the re-organization for "simplification and co-ordination". It tried to reflect the WCC's main constitutional functions in three flexible administrative units with broad mandates. The units would overcome the noticeable separation between study and action and would encourage greater participation by vari-

ous segments of the WCC constituency through sub-units with specific programmes. The several sub-units were deliberately placed into positions of "creative tension". Each unit had a committee of members from the central committee and from the governing bodies of the various sub-units. With minor changes, the overall structure instituted in 1972 remained in place at the time of the seventh assembly (Canberra 1991).

Finances. The WCC financial situation is symptomatic of the health and vitality of its programmes and relationships, but it also mirrors world financial trends, such as recessions, debt crises and inflation. Since the 1970s wide fluctuations in exchange rates of other major currencies against the Swiss franc (in which the WCC must purchase most of its goods and services) have created problems, since even when churches increase their giving from one year to the next, the value of this income in Swiss francs may actually decline.

Where does the money come from? About 75% of the income is given by member churches and their mission and aid agencies, and about 96% of that comes from 13 countries. Although only a small percentage of the total income comes from third-world churches, many of these contribute more per capita than do first-world churches. There is no fixed membership fee. Churches are to make annual contributions "commensurate with their resources". Yet one-third of the members take no financial responsibility for the WCC.

The WCC receives money both to cover its operating budget and to be channelled to ecumenical programmes and projects around the world (these latter "trust funds", administered without cost by the WCC, totalled about US$50 million a year between Vancouver and Canberra). The income for the WCC is either "undesignated" for the WCC's flexible use or "designated" by the giver for a specific programme or sub-unit. The undesignated portion is steadily declining, from 30% of WCC funds in 1981 to 16.5% in 1989.

Where does the WCC money go? The Amsterdam assembly had budgeted $386,000 (then SFr. 1.6 million) for the first year, but it was not completely spent. The first five years of expenditures totalled around $1.4 million (then SFr. 7.0 million). Between Vancouver and Canberra (1983-89) the programme budget expenses were SFr. 307.5 million. Nearly two-thirds of the 1989 total was staff-related costs, and one-third of it was for "participation", i.e. the involvement of member churches through travel, meetings, consultations, translation and communication.

In 1972 began a systematic internationalization of the Geneva staff and a salary structure based on non-discriminatory justice. The 1990 payroll for the 359 people on the total staff was around SFr. 26.4 million.

Relationships. Structure charts and budget sheets do not in themselves capture the new or growing demands over two decades for effective functioning of relationships between the WCC and member churches, non-member churches and groups, and other ecumenical bodies. Pertinent facts include the following. *Membership* has more than doubled since Amsterdam, from 147 churches to 311 at Canberra. *National Christian councils* in association with the WCC now total 35; a further 46 are affiliated with the Commission on World Mission and Evangelism, and still another 35 are in "working relationships". *Regional councils*, non-existent in 1948, have been established in Africa, Asia, the Caribbean, Europe, Latin America, the Middle East, and the Pacific.

The 12 *world confessional* structures have become more active, with larger scopes, as have other international organizations, such as the YMCAs, YWCAs, WSCF, and United Bible Societies. The *Roman Catholic Church*, though not a member, affects most of the WCC programmes (see **Joint Working Group**). The RCC is a full member of over 30 national councils and of the Caribbean, Middle East, and Pacific regional councils, and it has close working relations with the other national and regional councils.

Most of the fastest-growing churches are in the conservative *evangelical* and *Pentecostal* families. Most of these groups are not WCC members. Some are in dialogue with the WCC, others are explicitly anti-WCC or strangers to it. Many of the Pentecostal (and Independent) churches are quite small, with very informal administrative structures.

The numerical increase and geographical spread of this WCC constituency in the widest sense does not in itself provide an answer to the question: What is the quality of fellowship? A greater cross-section of the churches' life is found in the representative participation in the work and decisions of the WCC constitutional bodies. Yet there are calls for greater involvement of more member churches in creating and reviewing WCC policies and programmes. There are also calls for "more deliberate use of staff travel and church visits, in order to listen to the needs and concerns of the churches, to share in their life, and to represent the Council as a whole and interpret its programmes and concerns" (central committee, 1989), and to "enable creative relationships" with the broader range of ecumenical partners: non-member churches, new ecclesial communities, specific transdenominational movements (e.g. the charismatic movement) and action groups, as well as local, national and regional councils of churches, Christian World Communions, etc.

WCC programmes reveal a vast extension of activities in the last two decades, with a large breadth of concerns and interests. The sub-units have a variety of histories, methods of work, even ways of receiving funding. The focus of some sub-units is quite distinct; for others there is considerable overlap in the issues or constituencies. Few programmes have had built-in clauses for termination. Most want more staff and funding. New

interest groups ask for new programmes.

The member churches themselves vary
widely in their own structures and personnel
to receive WCC services — ranging from one
person handling all communication with the
WCC to the efficient communication within
the appropriate constituency of a church and
its follow-up by responsible study and action.
And those churches which are seriously committed to the WCC are also ecumenically
engaged in local and regional activities or
organized fellowships and bilateral dialogues;
they often find too much on their ecumenical
plates to digest. An overload of WCC programmes in service to the churches could thus
be contributing to the headache of reception,
i.e. the process of disciplined digestion and
ownership at all levels of the churches' life,
thought and practice.

In conclusion, the very success of the WCC
in carrying out its various purposes over more
than four decades has more clearly uncovered
failures and weaknesses in both the WCC and
member churches. Quite aware of this, the
July 1989 central committee began to face the
"programmatic re-organization" of the WCC
in the context of the ecumenical movement as
a whole, and realistically to consider any proposals in the face of expected financial resources.

TOM STRANSKY

And So Set Up Signs... The WCC's First 40 Years,
WCC, 1988 • A.J. van der Bent comp., *Rules, By-
laws, Mandates and Programmes of the WCC*,
WCC, 1987 • R. Bilheimer, *Breakthrough: The
Emergence of the Ecumenical Tradition*, WCC,
1989 • *Commemorating Amsterdam 1948 (= The
Ecumenical Review*, 40, 1988) • H.E. Fey ed., *The
Ecumenical Advance: A History of the Ecumenical
Movement*, vol. 2: *1948-1968*, WCC, 2nd ed. 1986
• M. VanElderen, *Introducing the World Council of
Churches*, WCC, 1990 • W.A. Visser 't Hooft, *The
Genesis and Formation of the World Council of
Churches*, WCC, 1982.

WCC ASSEMBLIES.

WCC ASSEMBLIES. Constitutionally, an
assembly — held approximately every seven
years — is the "supreme legislative body" of
the World Council of Churches. Delegates are
appointed by member churches, with the
number to which each church is entitled determined by size (every member church may
send at least one delegate). Allowance is
made in the allocation of delegates for balanc-

ing confessional, cultural and geographical
representation.

Member churches are urged to select their
assembly delegates in a way that will ensure
good distribution of church officials, parish
ministers and laity, men and women and persons under the age of 30. Moreover, to improve balance or provide special knowledge
and experience, up to 15% of the delegates
may be persons proposed by the WCC central
committee, which then asks their churches to
name them as additional delegates.

Also present at each assembly is a wide
range of non-voting advisers, representatives
and observers from non-member churches or
other ecumenical organizations and guests (including, since the fifth assembly, persons of
other faiths). An assembly usually draws several hundred press and media persons; and in
recent assemblies, extensive programmes
have been arranged for visitors.

Assemblies are too large and infrequent to
make detailed decisions. Rather, they look at
the wider ecumenical picture: evaluating what
the WCC has done since the previous assembly, seeking a common assessment of current
issues demanding ecumenical attention and
specifying broadly what the Council should
focus on until the next assembly. They elect
the WCC presidents and, from among delegates present, members of the central committee.

This entry offers a brief overview of each of
the WCC's seven assemblies.

First assembly: "Man's Disorder and God's
Design"; Amsterdam, Netherlands, 22 August
to 4 September 1948; 351 delegates, from 147
member churches.

Sections: (1) the universal church in God's
design, (2) the church's witness to God's
design, (3) the church and the disorder of
society, (4) the church and the international
order.

Central committee moderator: George Bell;
vice-moderator: Franklin Clark Fry; *presidium:* Marc Boegner, Geoffrey Fisher, T.C.
Chao (from 1951 Sarah Chakko), G. Bromley
Oxnam, Germanos of Thyateira (from 1951
Athenagoras of Thyateira), Erling Eidem
(from 1950 Eivind Berggrav); *honorary president:* John R. Mott.

The WCC's first assembly marked the assumption by the churches of responsibility for the ecumenical movement, as its message made clear: "Here at Amsterdam we have... covenanted with one another in constituting this World Council of Churches. We intend to stay together." Those constituting this world body, however, were largely from North America and Western Europe — only 30 of the founding churches came from Africa, Asia (including 5 from China) and Latin America. Although the term "younger churches" was often used for the latter bodies, they in fact included some of the oldest (Church of Ethiopia and Orthodox Syrian Church of Malabar); and among Western churches were some of the youngest (Old Catholic Church and Salvation Army).

Amsterdam said clearly that the churches had decided to come together in accordance with the will of the Lord of the church. Where this common way would lead them could not be foreseen. "We acknowledge", the report of section 1 emphasized, "that he is powerfully at work amongst us to lead us further to goals which we but dimly discern."

The first assembly adopted the WCC constitution (revised at successive assemblies), laid down conditions for membership, outlined programmes, discussed relationships with other ecumenical bodies and addressed a message to the churches — a practice repeated by succeeding assemblies. The "nature of the Council", defined in an assembly statement, would be further elaborated on by the statement "The Church, the Churches and the World Council of Churches", adopted by the central committee at Toronto in 1950 (see **Toronto statement**).

Section 2 expressed the indissoluble connection between unity* and inner renewal: "As Christ purifies us by his Spirit we shall find that we are drawn together and that there is no gain in unity unless it is unity in truth and holiness." Evangelism* was seen as the common task of all the churches, and the present day as "the beginning of a new epoch of missionary enterprise". Mission* and evangelism belong together and condition one another; and the distinction between "Christian" and "non-Christian" nations must be discarded. The question of the training of the laity* was examined by a special committee, which took as its starting point the experience of the already established Ecumenical Institute at Bossey.

In section 3 emerged the ecumenical concept of the "responsible society",* as opposed to both laissez-faire capitalism and totalitarian communism. "Each has made promises which it could not redeem. Communist ideology puts the emphasis upon economic justice, and promises that freedom will come automatically after the completion of the revolution. Capitalism puts the emphasis upon freedom, and promises that justice will follow as a by-product of free enterprise; that, too, is an ideology which has been proved false. It is the responsibility of Christians to seek new, creative solutions which never allow either justice or freedom to destroy the other." It was also agreed that since "no civilization, however 'Christian'", can escape the radical judgment of the Word of God, none is to be accepted uncritically.

Section 4 was able to encompass such divergent views as those of the Czech theologian Josef L. Hromádka and John Foster Dulles (later US secretary of state). While this showed the strength of the fellowship in the newly formed Council, it also put that strength to its first test. Two points in this section were significant for the future: (1) rejection in principle of war as "contrary to the will of God", but inability to endorse such rejection unanimously; (2) concern that every kind of tyranny and imperialism calls for opposition, struggle and efforts to secure basic human liberties for all, especially religious freedom.

Second assembly: "Christ — the Hope of the World"; Evanston, IL, USA, 15 to 31 August 1954; 502 delegates, from 161 member churches.

Sections: (1) our oneness in Christ and our disunity as churches, (2) the mission of the church to those outside her life, (3) the responsible society in a world perspective, (4) Christians in the struggle for world community, (5) the churches amid racial and ethnic tensions, (6) the laity: the Christian in his vocation.

Central committee moderator: Franklin Clark Fry; *vice-moderator:* Ernest Payne; *presidium:* John Baillie, Sante Uberto Barbieri,

Otto Dibelius, Juhanon Mar Thoma, Michael (from 1959 Iakovos), Henry Knox Sherill; *honorary presidents:* John R. Mott (d.1955) and George Bell.

If "staying together" was the motto of the Amsterdam assembly, Evanston's was "growing together". A deep sense of belonging together enabled the assembly to tackle its extremely difficult and controversial theological theme. A previously published report on the main theme, on which two dozen eminent theologians had worked for three years, acknowledged "sharp differences in theological viewpoint" in the discussions. The concept of Christian hope* among European churches tended to be eschatological, whereas North American churches stressed hope for the here and now. A reference to the hope of Israel (Rom. 9-11) introduced a discordant note and was omitted after a heated debate; many did not wish to recognize that the Jewish people occupy a special place in the history of salvation.

Evanston defined more clearly than Amsterdam the phrase "responsible society". It did not indicate "an alternative social or political system" but "a criterion by which we judge all existing social orders, and at the same time a standard to guide us in the specific choices we have to make". Like Amsterdam, Evanston addressed itself to "The Church in Relation to Communist-Non-Communist Tension". Priority in sections 3 and 4 went to "social and economic problems in the economically underdeveloped regions", a question to which the WCC was giving increasing attention. The assembly affirmed responsibility for Christian peace and justice and urged governments to ban all weapons of mass destruction and abstain from aggression. There were statements on religious liberty* and "intergroup relations", insisting on racial equality. Continuing the Amsterdam discussion, Evanston stressed even more strongly the missionary task of the laity, which "bridges the gulf between the church and the world" and "stands at the very outposts of the kingdom of God".

The so-called younger churches (except those in China, which had suspended their WCC participation in the wake of the Korean war) were much better represented than at the first assembly. Their presence was felt in many ways, especially in their impatience

with the disunity of the churches. The accent on the missionary dimension of the churches' task, so characteristic of Amsterdam, was missing at Evanston. But the assembly did show that the Council was centred on the word of God, theologically alert and becoming better equipped to help the churches to discover their common heritage.

Third assembly: "Jesus Christ — the Light of the World"; New Delhi, India, 19 November to 5 December 1961; 577 delegates, from 197 member churches.

Sections: (1) witness, (2) service, (3) unity.

Central committee moderator: Franklin Clark Fry; *vice-moderators:* Ernest Payne and J. Russell Chandran (1966-68); *presidium:* A. Michael Ramsey, Francis Ibiam, Iakovos, David G. Moses, Martin Niemöller, Charles C. Parlin; *honorary president:* Joseph H. Oldham.

New Delhi's theme was again Christocentric, but the discussion now included the issue of other world religions. The theme, however, was not given the same prominence as at previous assemblies, and served mainly as a sort of guiding principle. The International Missionary Council* was integrated into the WCC, becoming the Division on World Mission and Evangelism. The assembly approved an extension of the WCC basis* by adding the phrase "according to the scriptures", and the Trinitarian formula.

Of the 23 churches welcomed into WCC membership at New Delhi, 11 were African, 5 Asian and 2 South American. Only 5 were from Europe and North America. Two Pentecostal churches from Chile formed a bridge to evangelical churches. The presence of the large Orthodox churches from Eastern Europe was regarded as an opportunity to ensure "a real spiritual dialogue" between Eastern and Western churches. "If we accept this opportunity our ecumenical task will not become easier, but we shall surely be greatly enriched." Out of the estimated 400 million Christians who belong to WCC member churches today, almost 140 million are Orthodox.

Section 1 faced the theological problem of understanding other religions in the light of Jesus Christ (a still-unresolved problem). Another issue was how to distinguish Christian service from mere philanthrophy. Discussion in section 2 of the problems of political, economic and social change was largely oriented to the third world. In section 3, the unity* of the church was conceived as "one fully committed fellowship, holding the one apostolic faith, preaching the one gospel, breaking the one bread, joining in common prayer, and having a corporate life reaching out in witness and service to all and who at the same time are united with the whole Christian fellowship in all places and all ages..."

New Delhi took a renewed stand on religious liberty, adopted a resolution on antisemitism, clarified the churches' views on the international crisis and issued a message to Christians in South Africa and an "Appeal to All Governments and Peoples". The WCC had by now assumed increased responsibility for relief to people in distress, refugees and victims of catastrophes all over the world. In Amsterdam the churches committed themselves to stay together; in Evanston they affirmed their intention to grow together; and now they were eager to assume new tasks together.

Fourth assembly: "Behold, I Make All Things New"; Uppsala, Sweden, 4 to 20 July 1968; 704 delegates, from 235 member churches.

Sections: (1) the Holy Spirit and the catholicity of the church, (2) renewal in mission, (3) world economic and social development, (4) towards justice and peace in international affairs, (5) worship, (6) towards new styles of living.

Central committee moderator: M.M. Thomas; *vice-moderators:* Pauline Webb and Metropolitan Meliton; *presidium:* Patriarch German, Hanns Lilje, Daniel T. Niles, Kiyoko Takeda Cho, Ernest A. Payne, John Coventry Smith, Alphaeus H. Zulu; *honorary presidents:* Joseph Oldham and W.A. Visser 't Hooft.

Uppsala, the WCC's most activist and politically oriented assembly, can be seen as ending an era in the ecumenical movement and marking a new beginning. Typifying this was the vigorous presence of youth,* whose demonstrations made it clear that they were not satisfied with the role given them at the assembly.

Uppsala set the unity* and catholicity* of the church squarely within the sphere of God's activity in history. Stating that "the church is bold in speaking of itself as the sign of the coming unity of mankind", the assembly admitted that secular "instruments of conciliation and unification... often seem more effective than the church itself". Therefore, "churches need a new openness to the world in its aspirations, its achievements, its restlessness and its despair". All church structures, from local to world level, must be examined to see whether they enable the church and its members to be in mission. More dialogue with the world and more effective proclamation of the good news are equally needed. For the first time the idea of "a genuinely universal council", able to speak for all Christians, was articulated.

In his assembly address the Jesuit Roberto Tucci referred to the possibility of the Roman Catholic Church joining the WCC — a challenge that was seriously discussed in the following years. Closer WCC relations with national and regional councils of churches was also high on the agenda.

The reality that the rich were becoming richer and the poor poorer dominated Uppsala's socio-political and economic discussions. The assembly recommended that the churches set aside 1% of their total income for development aid and appeal to their governments to invest the same percentage of their gross national product. The central issue in development is the criterion of the human. Public opinion must be persuaded to support deep changes in both developed and developing nations.

Uppsala's discussion of worship* called on Christians to be open to learn from the practices of worship of other Christians. Describing worship as "ethical and social in nature" and thus "orientated towards the social injustices and divisions of mankind", the assembly specified that segregation by race or class in Christian worship must be rejected. It recommended "that all churches consider seriously the desirability of adopting the early Christian tradition of celebrating the eucharist every Sunday".

The assembly also grappled with how Christians make faithful ethical decisions. Social and cultural differences make a single style of Christian life impossible. Refusing to choose between "contextualism" and "rules", the gathering pressed for the position that individual moral choices can be made only in Christian community which is held together by biblical insight and the communion table.

In the wake of Uppsala several new programmes were added to the WCC: the Programme to Combat Racism* (PCR), the Commission on the Churches' Participation in Development, the Christian Medical Commission, Dialogue with People of Living Faiths and Ideologies, and the Sub-unit on Education. Unit II, Justice and Service, became from 1971 onwards the largest unit in the Council.

Fifth assembly: "Jesus Christ Frees and Unites"; Nairobi, Kenya, 23 November to 10 December 1975; 676 delegates, from 285 member churches.

Sections: (1) confessing Christ today, (2) what unity requires, (3) seeking community, (4) education for liberation and community, (5) structures of injustice and struggles for liberation, (6) human development.

Central committee moderator: Edward W. Scott; *vice-moderators:* Jean Skuse and Karekin Sarkissian; *presidium:* Annie R. Jiagge, José Míguez Bonino, Nikodim (from 1979 Ilja II of Georgia), T.B. Simatupang, Olof Sundby, Cynthia Wedel; *honorary president:* W.A. Visser 't Hooft.

Nairobi has been described as an assembly of consolidation, providing theological undergirding for much that surfaced in Uppsala. It declared that faith in the Triune God and socio-political engagement, conversion to Jesus Christ and active participation in changing economic and social structures belong together and condition one another.

Among contentious discussions was that of interfaith dialogue:* the section report on this subject was referred back for reconsideration before a plenary vote. Some delegates in the West thought the report was weak and susceptible to interpretation as a spiritual compromise. Asian representatives, on the other hand, stressed that dialogue in no way diminishes full commitment to one's own faith. Far from leading to syncretism, it safeguards against it.

Debate on evangelism related spirituality* to involvement. As unity requires a commonly accepted goal, a fuller understanding of the context and companionship in struggle and hope, section 1 asked the churches to respond to the three agreed statements on *Baptism, Eucharist and Ministry** (BEM), compiled by the Commission on Faith and Order.

The assembly resisted efforts to weaken the PCR and its special fund, but strove to understand this commitment to action on behalf of the oppressed in a more deeply theological way. The search for a "just, participatory and sustainable society" became a major theme. Programmes on faith, science and technology, militarism and disarmament, ecology and human survival, the role of women in church and society, and renewal and congregational life received a new emphasis. Concern for sharing of resources entered ecumenical discussions.

The assembly's programme guidelines committee approved four "programme thrusts" until the next assembly: (1) expression and communication of our faith in the Triune God; (2) search for a just, participatory and sustainable society; (3) unity of the church and renewal of human community; (4) education and renewal in search of true community.

Sixth assembly: "Jesus Christ — the Life of the World"; Vancouver, Canada, 24 July to 10 August 1983; 847 delegates, from 301 member churches.

Issue groups: (1) witnessing in a divided world, (2) taking steps towards unity, (3) moving towards participation, (4) healing and sharing life in community, (5) confronting threats to peace and survival, (6) struggling for justice and human dignity, (7) learning in community, (8) communicating credibly.

Central committee moderator: Heinz Joachim Held; *vice-moderators:* Chrysostomos of Myra and Sylvia Talbot; *presidium:* Nita Barrow, Marga Bührig, Paulos Gregorios, Johannes W. Hempel, Ignatius IV, W.P. Khotso Makhulu, Lois M. Wilson; *honorary president:* W.A. Visser 't Hooft (d. 1985).

At Vancouver, some observers said, Amsterdam and Uppsala appeared to come to terms with each other. It was a "re-integrated" assembly. Great emphasis in this most representative gathering in ecumenical history fell on participation,* and up to 4,500 people a day took part one way or another in the assembly. Of voting delegates more than 30% were women, more than 13% youth (under 30) and more than 46% laypeople. Leadership by women was prominent as never before. Canada's cultures and concerns made a strong impact on the gathering.

Daily worship services in a large tent drew thousands of people. The celebration of the eucharist according to an order of worship (the Lima liturgy*) reflecting the Faith and Order convergence statements on BEM was a memorable event, as was the night-long vigil to mark the anniversary of the atomic bombing of Hiroshima and Nagasaki.

Churches were requested to respond officially to the BEM document by the end of 1986. The assembly received the fifth report of the WCC-RCC Joint Working Group,* with an outline of future work. In evangelism, wide attention was drawn to Christian witness in the contexts of culture, worship, the poor, children and religious pluralism.

On Christian education, the assembly pressed member churches "to take seriously the ecumenical dimension of learning and include it in all educational activities and programmes". In emphasizing the central importance of language and culture in ecumenical education, the assembly urged churches to experiment with alternative forms of communication.

A recommended WCC priority was the engagement of member churches "in a conciliar process of mutual commitment (covenant) to justice, peace and the integrity of all creation", whose foundations were "confessing Christ as the life of the world and Christian resistance to the demonic powers of death in racism, sexism, caste oppression, economic exploitation, militarism, violations of human rights, and the misuse of science and technology".

Seventh assembly: "Come, Holy Spirit — Renew the Whole Creation"; Canberra, Australia, 7 to 20 February 1991; 842 delegates, from 317 member churches.

Sections/sub-themes: (1) Giver of life — sustain your creation!, (2) Spirit of truth — set us free!, (3) Spirit of unity — reconcile your people!, (4) Holy Spirit — transform and sanctify us!
Central committee moderator: Aram Keshishian; *vice-moderators:* Soritua Nababan and Nélida Ritchie; *presidium:* Anne-Marie Aagaard, Vinton Anderson, Leslie Boseto, Priyanka Mendis, Parthenios of Alexandria, Eunice Santana, Shenouda of Alexandria, Aaron Tolen.

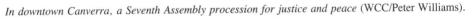

In downtown Canverra, a Seventh Assembly procession for justice and peace (WCC/Peter Williams).

As at Vancouver, delegates from member churches made up only about a fifth of those present in Canberra; other participants included 10 guests from other faiths, about 1500 visitors and over 200 observers from non-member bodies.

In two respects Canberra's theme was a departure from earlier assemblies: its formulation as a prayer and its reference to the Holy Spirit. The theme was at the heart of daily and special worship services, carefully prepared to draw on the rich variety of traditions in the WCC. But frequent remarks in assembly sessions showed that while the pneumatological emphasis opens up new perspectives in relating theology and experience, it can also kindle controversy. Many argued the need for discernment and for maintaining the link between Jesus Christ and the Holy Spirit.

War in the Gulf broke out just three weeks before the assembly began. Discussion about a statement on the war revealed the deep differences within the WCC over classic questions about the justifiability of war. The way in which the Gulf war overshadowed consideration of other situations of conflict and oppression in the world highlighted growing tension within the ecumenical family between global and local concerns.

The venue gave a high profile to indigenous people, especially Aboriginal Australians. An assembly statement committed the WCC to support and monitor "a treaty process" between Aborigines and the Australian government, and called on churches to "return land unjustly taken" from the Aborigines.

Despite significant ecumenical theological convergence in recent years, assembly discussions and worship made clear that eucharist, ordained ministry and views about the nature of the church remained painful stumbling blocks to full communion. An open letter from Orthodox participants insisted that the WCC's main aim must be restoration of church unity, and asked that faith and order be given greater prominence. But obstacles to unity were also manifest in pleas that certain groups must be better represented within WCC structures. In particular, member church delegations fell considerably short of the target of 20 per cent youth. Even more than at previous assemblies, trying to achieve all mandated "balances" on governing bodies led to sometimes bitter debate.

Christians from mainland China attended a WCC assembly for the first time in over 30 years; and the China Christian Council (seen as a united church in the process of formation, rather than as a council of churches) was one of seven churches welcomed as new members. Another milestone was the presence of observers from the (white) Dutch Reformed Church in South Africa (NGK), a first since it left the council in the 1960s.

ANS J. VAN DER BENT

Harold E. Fey ed., *The Ecumenical Advance: a History of the Ecumenical Movement*, vol. 2: *1948-1968*, WCC, 1986, has extensive bibliographies on the first six assemblies of the WCC.

WCC, BASIS OF. According to the WCC constitution, "agreement with the basis upon which the Council is founded" is a precondition for membership. The first general secretary, W.A. Visser 't Hooft, considered the basis as defining the Council's nature.

The original basis, adopted by the inaugural assembly in 1948, was formulated at the 1938 meeting in Utrecht, where the Committee of Fourteen appointed by the Life and Work* (L&W) and Faith and Order* (F&O) conferences, together with a group of church leaders, drew up a constitution for the proposed WCC. It read: "The World Council of Churches is a fellowship of churches which accept our Lord Jesus Christ as God and Saviour."

The expression "fellowship of churches" had by then become part of ecumenical terminology. The 1920 encyclical of the Ecumenical Patriarchate of Constantinople had proposed "a koinonia of churches". L&W had often been described as a koinonia. Although the English word "fellowship" lacks some of the rich biblical nuances of the Greek original, it nevertheless affirms the reality of a unity that is "given" and "previous", and not just constituted by human decisions.

The second part of the Utrecht formula — "which accept our Lord Jesus Christ as God and Saviour" — met some controversy. Some claim that the source of this part of the basis is the 1855 Paris basis of the YMCAs:* "The Young Men's Christian Associations seek to unite those young men who, regarding Jesus Christ as their God and Saviour, according to the holy scriptures, desire to be his disciples in their faith and their life, and to associate their efforts for the extension of his kingdom amongst young men." But the formulation can be traced more directly to the F&O movement; invitations to its first world conference were addressed to churches "which accept our Lord Jesus Christ as God and Saviour".

Some in both liberal and conservative circles expressed dissatisfaction with the phrase "Jesus Christ as God and Saviour". Unitarians, and even the Society of Friends, did not want to be committed to a definite doctrinal formula. To the more orthodox the term appeared to be doctrinally unsound in so far as it did not adequately affirm the humanity of Christ. Thus for William Adams Brown "this phrase 'God and Saviour' has a heretical flavour which would have led to its rejection by any one of the ecumenical councils" *(Toward a United Church)*.

In his explanatory memorandum on the WCC constitution, William Temple, who had chaired the Utrecht meeting, drew out the two main implications of the basis as formulated. First, the fact that the WCC is a fellowship, not a federation, of churches means that it cannot exercise any constitutional authority over the member churches. Second, while the Council stands on faith in Jesus Christ as God and Saviour — in essence "an affirmation of the incarnation and the atonement" — the churches will have freedom to interpret that faith in their own way.

From Utrecht on, some have argued against the adoption of a basis. Any basis, they feared, would undermine the koinonia by introducing an element of ecclesiastical judgmentalism. Others would rather accept the Nicene* or Apostles'* Creed as the basis.

The Amsterdam assembly viewed the basis as "adequate for the present purposes" of the WCC. Nevertheless, in response to criticisms before and at the assembly, it endorsed the need "for clarification or amplification of the Christian faith" as set forth in the basis. The assembly passed on that task to the central committee, on the clear understanding that changes in the basis would be incorporated within the Christological framework which the assembly had affirmed. A sub-committee considered the suggestions from churches and individuals but concluded that there was no need to change the basis, though it was necessary to explain its meaning and also make

clear that the incarnation* and the Trinity* were implicit in it. Accordingly the second assembly (Evanston 1954) accepted a description of the purpose and function of the basis: "less than a confession" but "much more than a mere formula or agreement". The basis showed the nature of ecumenical fellowship, provided an overall orientation for the Council's work, and indicated the general range of fellowship which the member churches sought to establish.

Between Evanston and New Delhi (1961) a new sub-committee worked on the issue, receiving suggestions from a number of theologians. A new basis drawn up by the central committee in 1960 was presented at the assembly, which resolved to adopt it with 383 votes in favour, 36 against and 7 abstentions. It reads: "The World Council of Churches is a fellowship of churches which confess the Lord Jesus Christ as God and Saviour according to the scriptures and therefore seek to fulfill together their common calling to the glory of the one God, Father, Son and Holy Spirit."

The basis, thus reformulated, incorporates five significant changes. The word "accept" is substituted by "confess", a word which suggests commitment and emphasizes the experience of togetherness in fellowship. "Our Lord Jesus Christ" now reads "the Lord Jesus Christ", a less restrictive formulation that points to the universality of Christ's lordship. The addition of the familiar confessional phrase "according to the scriptures" to an extent meets the criticism that the earlier version tended towards Docetism or monophysitism and, at the same time, affirms the place of the Bible in the ecumenical fellowship. "And therefore seek to fulfill their common calling" adds a dimension of dynamism to the understanding of fellowship and also underlines the ontological priority of what God in Christ has already accomplished. The final doxological formula, by setting "the Christocentric affirmation in a Trinitarian setting", besides making the basis totally acceptable to the Orthodox, adds a celebrative element to the fact of and aspiration for unity.

The New Delhi assembly affirmed the new basis. Most of the delegates who took part in the discussion were of the opinion that it is in full agreement with the Trinitarian doctrine as formulated by the first two ecumenical councils* and in the Nicene Creed, and that it makes more explicit the evangelical and scriptural rationale of the ecumenical movement. But there were also critical voices. One feared that, in going beyond mentioning the essential Christological criterion for membership, the WCC was moving in the direction of confessionism. Another was afraid that any expansion would set a precedent for still further additions until the basis became "a burdensome doctrinal statement". Yet another was of the view that the new basis would block any future revision and leave uncorrected "the one-sided monophysite character of the original basis".

The basis has endured. Any future attempt to revise it is likely to go in one of two disparate directions. And both would have consequences for membership. On the one hand, the activist image the Council has projected in recent years may require a kind of theological undergirding which the present basis does not provide. The network of action groups and people's movements may well want to find in the basis a more explicit recognition of the humanity of Christ. The emerging theologies of interfaith dialogue may also be more comfortable with a stronger emphasis on God's involvement in and identification with all human beings in their struggles and search. On the other hand, the doctrinal convergence being discovered through the work of the F&O and the ecumenical experience of member churches through their participation in the Council's life, together with the relatively new ecumenical openness in other churches, notably the Roman Catholic, may make it necessary to seek a basis beyond the basis, going beyond "a neutral ecclesiological stance towards the ecclesial implications" of the basis itself.

If a new ecclesiology emerges out of the interpenetration of these two trends, for example through the F&O study on "The Unity of the Church and the Renewal of Human Community", that of course can lead to a different kind of basis.

T.K. THOMAS

The Ecumenical Review, 37, 2, 1985 • H.E. Fey ed., *The Ecumenical Advance: A History of the Ecumenical Movement*, vol. 2: *1948-1968*, 2nd ed., WCC, 1986, ch. 2 • W. Theurer, *Die trinitarische Basis des Ökumenischen Rates der Kirchen*, Frankfurt, Gerhard Kaffke, 1967.

WCC, MEMBERSHIP OF. Churches which agree with the WCC basis* are eligible to apply for WCC membership. Applications may be approved at an assembly by two-thirds of the member churches or, between assemblies, by two-thirds of the central committee (unless objection from one-third of the member churches is received within six months).

A prospective member must evidence "sustained independent life and organization" and "constructive ecumenical relations" with other churches in its country. Ordinarily, member churches have at least 25,000 members (churches with at least 10,000 members may be associate members, eligible to participate in all WCC activities but not to vote in the assembly).

WCC rules state that becoming a member signifies a church's "faithfulness to the basis of the Council, fellowship in the Council, participation in the life and work of the Council and commitment to the ecumenical movement as integral to the mission of the church". There is no membership assessment, but "an annual contribution to the general budget and programmes of the WCC, commensurate with their resources", is listed among membership responsibilities.

History and statistics. In Amsterdam in 1948 representatives of 147 churches, mostly European and North American, constituted the WCC. By each subsequent assembly the number had increased — 161 at Evanston (1954), 197 at New Delhi (1961), 235 at Uppsala (1968), 285 at Nairobi (1975), 301 at Vancouver (1983), and 311 at Canberra (1991). The churches come from about 100 countries all over the world.

Only a few churches have withdrawn, notably the Presbyterian Church of Ireland and the Salvation Army; both objected to grants from the Programme to Combat Racism* to armed liberation movements in Southern Africa, although the Salvation Army also noted the difference between its organization and that of most member churches and has remained an active participant in a number of WCC activities. Four Chinese churches were founding members; but there was little WCC contact with China after the Korean War (1950-53). In the mid-1980s, after Chinese Protestants entered a "post-denominational" period following the cultural revolution, they renewed many contacts with the WCC but did not resume membership. The number of member churches may drop due to a union of two or more member churches — perhaps creating discontent if the newly united church is allowed fewer delegates than its constituting churches were.

Churches calculate membership on different bases, ranging from those which count only adult confirmed members to those which include all inhabitants of their country except persons who explicitly indicate otherwise. Thus there is no precise answer to the question of how many people are members of WCC churches. Commonly used numbers range from 350 to 450 million.

Membership issues. The WCC faces various interesting issues of membership within (and without) its fellowship.

National churches as the "building block": Nearly all of the member churches are organized bodies of local parishes or congregations, usually within the boundaries of a single nation, where they exist alongside other similar organizations of local congregations. They are often described as "denominations", although not all of them would accept this designation.

During early discussions of a WCC constitution, some favoured a council composed either of regional councils of churches* or of World Confessional Families; but the argument prevailed that it was essential for the WCC, as a body without its own canonical authority, to be in direct touch with the national churches. In turn, the WCC takes account of confessional and regional representation in its governing bodies. Moreover, national councils of churches, regional ecumenical organizations, Christian World Communions and other international ecumenical bodies are normally invited to send non-voting representatives to assemblies and central committee meetings.

WCC regulations and Orthodox canon law* make it likely that new member churches will be Protestant, thus reducing the proportion of the Orthodox voice in the WCC and (some have argued) in effect rewarding the Protestant tradition for the schismatic and divisive tendencies which the WCC is intended to overcome. To help counter this, the WCC ensures a certain percentage of seats to Orthodox representatives.

Roman Catholic membership: The first WCC assembly after the Second Vatican Council (Uppsala 1968) raised strong hopes of RC membership. In 1969 Pope Paul VI said the membership question "contains serious theological and pastoral implications. It thus requires profound study and commits us to a way that... could be long and difficult." A 1972 report on membership, from the WCC/RCC Joint Working Group,* concluded that there were no insuperable theological, ecclesiological or canonical objections to membership. But the holy see made its prudential judgment not to apply "in the near future".

Were the RCC to apply, two difficulties would be considerable, if not insuperable. Given that representation on WCC governing bodies must give "due regard" to size and that there are perhaps twice as many RCs as members of all the WCC member churches combined, the consequences for achieving balanced representation would be enormous.

Moreover, since the RCC understands itself as a family of local churches with and under the bishop of Rome — "a universal fellowship with a universal mission and structure" — RC representation would come from both the holy see and the local churches. What would happen if within the RCC there was public dissent among the RC episcopal, clerical and lay representations, and between some of them and the contingent of the holy see, especially on important ecclesiological and personal and social ethical issues?

Although not a member, the RCC does participate in various ways in almost all WCC programmes.

Other non-member churches: The limited nature of WCC authority enables it easily to involve a range of people from non-member churches in its conferences and consultations, studies and other activities. Some judge, however, that many small national churches, particularly those in a minority situation, are unfairly excluded from the benefits of belonging to the WCC because they do not have enough members to be eligible for it. Others note that the WCC does not take sufficient account of the interests of diaspora* Christians — those in a smaller ecclesiastical jurisdiction of a church with its headquarters in another country.

A more wide-ranging challenge is raised by statistical projections of the growth of independent, Pentecostal and evangelical churches outside the WCC's membership; most have little or no knowledge of or contact with the WCC or are in principle against the WCC. By the turn of the 21st century, some project, fewer than half of the non-Roman Catholic and non-Orthodox Christians in the world will be members of WCC churches; this imbalance will have serious implications for the understanding of the WCC as an instrument of the worldwide ecumenical movement.

MARLIN VANELDEREN

T. Stransky, "RC Membership in the WCC", *The Ecumenical Review*, 20, 1968 • WCC/RCC Joint Working Group, "Patterns of Relationships", *The Ecumenical Review*, 24, 1972.

WORLD DAY OF PRAYER.

The World Day of Prayer is a movement initiated and carried out by women in 170 countries from all regions of the world. Each year on the first Friday of March, women and men in countless villages, cities, and towns gather together to pray, using a common theme and worship service translated into hundreds of languages.

The World Day of Prayer was begun in 1887 at the initiative of Mary Ellen James, president of a US Presbyterian women's home mission board. Concerned about the plight of immigrants, she called on women to release the power of prayer in a day of prayer for home missions "when there shall be confession of individual and national sins with offerings that fitly express the contrition".

Other women who were denominational leaders of that day were also stirred by what they saw around them and began to join in an annual day of prayer focused on justice and human dignity for all. In 1890 two remarkable Baptist women, Helen Barrett Montgomery and Lucy Peabody, sent out a call for a day of prayer for foreign missions. Through missionaries, other world travellers and world mission conferences, the idea spread rapidly across all continents and islands. In 1927 this Day of Prayer became in name what it already was in fact, a World Day of Prayer.

In response to the growth of the World Day of Prayer, an international committee was formed to carry responsibility for this movement. Since 1967 representatives of national committees have met every four years in a different region to share experiences of the World Day of Prayer and select themes and writers for forthcoming services in the light of world realities. The motto of the World Day of Prayer is "Informed Prayer and Prayerful Action". The logo adopted in 1982 is from a design sent by women of Ireland when they wrote the worship service. National committees of the World Day of Prayer continue the tradition begun by James in insisting that the offerings gathered from the annual celebration be used to further humane change and support the improvement of the conditions of life and persons everywhere.

EILEEN KING

WORLD EVANGELICAL FELLOW-SHIP.

The WEF began to cluster several evangelical persons and groups after the second world war. A number of European evangelicals had been linked since 1846 by the World's Evangelical Alliance,* but the alliance was limited to a loose affiliation of regional fellowships, based on membership of individuals rather than ecclesial units.

US evangelicals formed the National Association of Evangelicals in 1943. They wanted means of responding to overseas national churches that had resulted from US conservative evangelical missions and that now sought support in an international network of like-minded Christians.

In August 1951, in response to a call for an international convention of evangelicals, 91 participants from 21 countries formed the World Evangelical Fellowship (Woudschoten, Netherlands). The WEF statement of faith echoes the Evangelical Alliance statement of 1846, except for the addition of "infallible" in the article on the divinely inspired scripture and a reference to Christ's "personal return in power and glory". The European Evangelical Alliance was organized the following year (1952), in objection to WEF use of the term "infallible". Only in 1968 did the European evangelical community join the WEF.

From the outset the WEF took a low profile; it encouraged evangelicals of other nations without pressing for their membership. By the mid-1970s, when the WEF began to enjoy the service of full-time general directors, there were about 50 member nations; in 1989 the WEF counted 60 national evangelical fellowships, 80% of them from the third world. Several internationally constituted commissions spearhead WEF programmes. Consultations and general assemblies and various publications give voice to the concerns of the WEF's worldwide constituencies.

Two persistent issues on the WEF agenda — which also occupied the founders of the Evangelical Alliance — are theological liberalism and unreformed Catholicism. Contacts in the late 1970s by WEF leaders with Roman Catholic representatives were not well received by some WEF members (see **Evangelical-Roman Catholic dialogue**). The breach created was healed only by the 1986 adoption of a position paper critical of traditional Catholicism; in some parts of the world, evangelicals find Roman Catholicism to be little affected by the reforms of Vatican II or by the biblical/charismatic renewal movement.

A 1989 consultation on evangelism* involved representatives of the WEF, the Lausanne Committee for World Evangelization,* and the WCC. The WEF took issue with an Ecumenical Press Service report that "what unites us is greater than what divides us". Divergent stances on the uniqueness* and finality of Jesus Christ* for salvation,* on the role of interfaith dialogue,* and on the doctrine of inspiration* continue to be sources of tension between the WEF and the WCC.

Noting the loss of focus on world evangelization due to the integration of the International Missionary Council* in the WCC, the WEF at its sixth general assembly (1974) created a missions commission. The commission seeks to promote greater world mission, particularly by supporting emerging third-world missions, and to facilitate co-operation between mission agencies and associations.

See also **evangelical missions, evangelicals**.

ROBERT T. COOTE

WORLD METHODIST COUNCIL. In
1881, some 400 delegates from 30 Methodist bodies, primarily British and North American but including some mission-related churches, attended the first ecumenical Methodist conference in London. It continued to gather every ten years. At the eighth conference, in 1951, the name World Methodist Council was adopted. It agreed the WMC would meet every five years.

The WMC is a worldwide association of 64 member churches; 8 are united churches with some roots in the Wesleyan tradition. It embraces 25 million full members (i.e. baptized, confirmed and in good standing) among a total Methodist community of about 55 million (including young children and adult sympathizers).

The policy-making body is a 500-member council of persons appointed by member churches. WMC functions are co-operative. It has no legislative authority over the churches but tries to serve them and harmonize their witness and activities. It surveys programmes, transacts business, organizes committees and convenes the quinquennial World Methodist Conference, an inspirational gathering which draws thousands of delegates from churches in 90 countries. The WMC urges member churches to be involved in union negotiations and in councils of churches at every level. It is almost always represented at major WCC meetings. Since 1967 it has been in bilateral discussions with the Roman Catholic Church. Recent international dialogues with the Lutheran World Federation and with the World Alliance of Reformed Churches have already led to practical results in some countries. First steps have been taken towards conversations with Orthodox and Anglican churches.

Its permanent secretary has offices in Lake Junaluska, North Carolina (USA), and a Geneva secretary works out of the Ecumenical Centre there. While the paid staff is small, several hundred volunteers do effective work as members of the executive and of 15 other committees and related organizations. The official WMC publication is *World Parish*.

RALPH C. YOUNG

WORLD STUDENT CHRISTIAN
FEDERATION. The WSCF is a federation of national ecumenical student movements, most of whom are called Student Christian Movement (SCM). Such movements affiliated to the WSCF are found in 61 countries. Some 24 denominational student and youth movements and organizations have associate status. Both affiliate and associate movements

participate fully in the programmes and work of the WSCF, but only affiliate movements have voting rights.

The WSCF was established in 1895 at Vadstena Castle, Sweden, by students and student leaders from ten North American and European countries. Key founders included John R. Mott (USA) and Karl Fries (Sweden). There is a close historical connection between the WSCF and the Young Men's and Young Women's Christian Associations. Mott, for example, was a leader of the YMCA, and with the help of YMCA colleagues he developed the vision and strategies for forming an international federation of autonomous and self-directing ecumenical student movements. Much of the subsequent work of establishing and linking SCMs was done with the assistance of YMCAs and YWCAs.

The WSCF was a primary pioneer of the modern missionary and ecumenical movement. It encouraged and inspired students in the late 19th and early 20th centuries to engage actively in the work of spreading the gospel by committed discipleship. It provided a forum for students to meet and work closely with those of other national and denomina-

tional backgrounds. Its ecumenical vision and commitment emphasized the importance of mutual communication, co-operation, and challenge with the mainline institutional churches. The WSCF worked for unity in the church and in the world.

The WSCF was instrumental in the formation of the International Missionary Council* (1921) and the WCC (1948). The federation provided for these ecumenical bodies the leaders who had found their training and inspiration in the free atmosphere of the federation. For example, Mott became honorary president of the WCC, and W.A. Visser 't Hooft moved from being WSCF general secretary to become the first WCC general secretary. William Temple, Madeleine Barot, Suzanne de Diétrich, Valdo Galland, T.Z. Koo, Robert Mackie, D.T. Niles, K.H. Ting, M.M. Thomas, Philip Potter and many other ecumenical leaders of the 20th century began their ecumenical career with the WSCF.

The exclusively European and North American representation at the first gathering in 1895 reflects its first-world origins. Immediately afterwards, Mott toured through Southern Europe, the Middle East and Asia.

Early WSCF meeting, at Bossey, near Geneva (WCC photo)

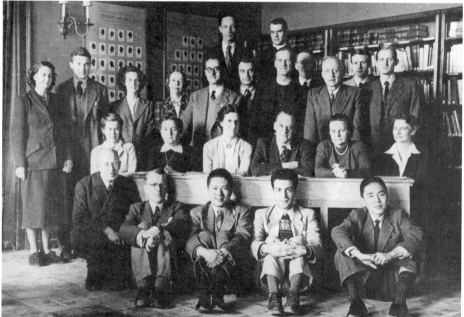

His journeys led to the federation membership's extension to India, Ceylon (Sri Lanka), Australia, New Zealand, China and Japan. Today there are member movements on every continent and in the islands. Eastern Europe, the Caribbean, and the Pacific are regions where the federation has been striving to strengthen its work in recent decades.

Until the late 1960s, the international staff of the WSCF were based in Geneva. A major structural change in 1972 decentralized the WSCF into six regions: Africa, Asia/Pacific, Europe, Latin America, Middle East and North America. The Geneva headquarters became the inter-regional office. Programmatic and decision-making work shifted to the regions, reflecting the new mood of self-determination in third-world countries and the search for contextualization in theology and politics. The WSCF continues to examine critically its structures, both politically and administratively, especially as its constituency is now looking for ways to strengthen programme and solidarity links that go beyond the regional boundaries.

In its long history, the WSCF has lived through several phases, influenced by both internal and external developments. In the early years, mission and ecumenism were the federation's raison d'etre and these still serve as the basis of identity, though their manifestations continue to change with the times. From 1895 to 1910, WSCF member movements were, in most countries, the only Christian organization run by students and for students in educational institutions. In 1910 the Inter-Varsity Fellowship broke away from the British SCM on theological and political grounds, and this split led to the formation in 1947 of the International Fellowship of Evangelical Students* (IFES). Accordingly, in many countries an unfortunate polarization developed between Christian students on the basis of an artificial distinction between "ecumenical" and "evangelical".

During and after the world wars, the WSCF played a key role in refugee work in Europe and strove to keep communication and solidarity links open between Christians divided by nationalism and war. After the first world war, the WSCF established European Student Relief. For four years, students of 42 nations provided over £500,000 for the relief of starving students in 19 countries. At that time close

working relationships developed with Pax Romana, the student organization of the Roman Catholic Church. In 1926 European Student Relief became an autonomous body, International Student Service, later to be called World University Service, which continues to this day. During the second world war, women leaders of the WSCF and YWCA played a major role in creating CIMADE,* which worked with refugees.

When the WCC was formed in 1948, it was decided not to incorporate the WSCF into its structures; the federation should maintain a degree of autonomy from institutional church structures, as this was an important ingredient of its creativity. However, as the WCC now embraced the missionary and ecumenical goals, the WSCF focused more sharply on its role in educational institutions and its analysis of education. The WCC included a youth department in its structures which became a natural working partner for the WSCF, though its establishment also introduced some areas of overlap in constituency.

In the 1960s and 1970s, WSCF movements, especially in North America and Europe, were closely involved with the radical political movements. Their political solidarity and their critique of education convinced them that the mission field was no longer in educational institutions but on the streets and in the villages. The theme of the WSCF in the 1970s — Christian Witness in the Struggle for Liberation — sums up the political commitment of the WSCF at the same time it moved to a regional structure. The political debates in the WSCF were painful, at times divisive.

The commitment to justice* and peace* issues remains strong in the WSCF and indeed has influenced the mainline churches to rethink their own missionary policies and political analyses. Some WSCF people in some parts of the world have become martyrs (e.g. Dietrich Bonhoeffer). Member students in South Korea, Philippines, El Salvador and Sri Lanka continue to suffer arrest, imprisonment and death. The WSCF is often called upon to use its extensive solidarity networks. The worldwide fellowship provides a key support and inspiration for students who face unjust powers.

By the 1970s the organizational base of SCMs in many countries had become critically weak, and even disappeared completely in some countries, such as the USA. This decade saw the rapid rise of conservative evangelical (at times, fundamentalist) groups on campuses around the world, such as Campus Crusade for Christ and Inter-Varsity. These groups emerged in critical periods in both the first and third worlds. In the first world, cynicism and disillusionment followed the "political 1960s", and the student population became increasingly conservative, preoccupied with jobs and security. In the third world, students living under increasingly militarized and repressive governments were disillusioned when hopes for justice and peace failed to materialize under "independent" governments. The soil was ripe for more conservative evangelical and fundamentalist groups to flourish, backed by big money and glossy publicity and with the support of governments and business. The SCM's organizational base was not strong enough to provide an alternative to these groups in many cases. Also some mainline denominations, sensing the vacuum left on campuses where SCMs have diminished or disappeared, and spurred on by their own anxiety about the fundamentalist groups, started their own campus ministry organizations.

Hence in the late 20th century the WSCF lives in a much more complex environment in the educational institutions, and this poses a new challenge to its missionary and ecumenical task. Its member movements have been consolidating their presence in educational institutions again, giving specific attention to conveying the unique ecumenical character of their work and life. As a result, some movements that almost disappeared in the 1970s have re-established their organizational base. However, many movements remain vulnerable, with little financial support and strong competition from conservative groups.

There is a strong, renewed interest in theological work, honouring the contextual theologies as well as seeking global visions. Leadership-development programmes form the basis of most WSCF regional programmes. The 1980s saw a marked increase in women's leadership at the international level. Women from all regions are half of the executive committee. In 1986 the posts of general secretary and associate general secretary were replaced by two co-secretaries general, one man, one woman. Women's programmes exist in most regions, and women's pre-assemblies precede general assemblies.

The ecumenical vision and practice of the WSCF is also under continuing scrutiny. Since its inception, the WSCF has drawn most of its membership from Protestant students. Roman Catholic students have also been members, especially in Latin America and some parts of Asia. In 1911 Orthodox students joined the federation as a result of a conference in Constantinople. This paved the way for the involvement of the Orthodox churches in wider ecumenical relations. Bilateral relationships have remained healthy between the WSCF and Roman Catholic student organizations, particularly Pax Romana, and also Syndesmos* (world fellowship of Orthodox youth). Within the WSCF itself, the impact of Orthodox students in particular continues to challenge the predominantly Protestant ethos of worship and world-view. The WSCF continues a good degree of co-operation with its historical ecumenical partners — the World Alliance of YMCAs, the World YWCA, and the WCC Youth sub-unit.

The WSCF inter-regional office is housed within the Ecumenical Centre in Geneva. Regional secretaries are based in Nairobi, Hong Kong, Amsterdam, Quito and Beirut. The North American regional structure is currently in abeyance, pending developments in ecumenical student work in the USA.

CHRISTINE LEDGER

S. de Diétrich, *Cinquante ans d'histoire: La Fédération universelle des associations chrétiennes d'etudiants (1895-45)*, Paris, Semeur, 1948 • C. Howard Hopkins, *John R. Mott*, Grand Rapids, MI, Eerdmans, 1979 • R. Rouse & S. Neill eds, *A History of the Ecumenical Movement, 1517-1948*, WCC, 3rd ed. 1986 • R. Rouse, *The World's Student Christian Federation: A History of the First 30 Years*, London, SCM, 1948 • W.A. Visser 't Hooft, *Memoirs*, WCC, 1973.

WORLD VISION INTER-NATIONAL.
Founded as an American Protestant evangelical agency in 1950 to help Korean war orphans, World Vision International (WVI) today is thoroughly international in its leadership, staff, contributors and ministry. A number of factors are responsible.

As it grew and expanded its work throughout the third world, the agency established autonomous support offices in other countries — first in Canada, then Australia, New Zealand, South Africa, United Kingdom, Federal Republic of Germany, Austria, Switzerland, Hong Kong, Singapore, Netherlands, Finland and, in 1987, Japan. Only about half of the total funds used for overseas programmes now come from the USA.

In 1978 the support offices established the WVI as the co-ordinating body that conducts field operations and that represents WVI globally. The supporting "partners", who remain autonomous, are represented on the WVI international board and on the international affairs committee, which decides key issues and recommends plans and budgets to the board.

In the 40 years since its founding, the WVI has grown into one of the world's largest private voluntary organizations. Total income and commodities to the WVI from all support entities in 1990 was $230 million for some 6,400 projects in more than 80 nations. Total permanent staff numbers around 5,200, of which 98% are nationals.

The agency's initial sponsorship scheme for Korean orphans has changed over the years, evolving into a child-focused development programme that assists 980,000 children (1990) in 52 nations. The agency also supports relief and rehabilitation projects; community development involving agricultural, educational, medical, nutrition and vocational training; Christian leadership training, evangelism and mission challenge (in recent years, field countries, such as Korea, Taiwan, Brazil, are also being challenged to give). More often than not, aspects of child care, development, leadership training and evangelism are integrated into every project. The agency is continually seeking a holistic approach to all its ministries.

More than 80% of all WVI projects are carried out through partner agencies (mission agencies and local churches) of all denominations. For 1990, approximately $100 million was channelled through nearly 200 partner agencies. Outreach and evangelism programmes are therefore contextualized within each culture; by WVI board policy, proselytism is opposed. The WVI also works with United Nations groups such as UNICEF and the High Commissioner on Refugees and has consultative status with WHO and the UN Economic and Social Council.

RICHARD L. WATSON

WORLD YOUNG WOMEN'S CHRISTIAN ASSOCIATIONS.

The YWCA, the oldest international women's movement, was first a Christian response in mid-19th-century Great Britain to the radically altered social conditions caused by the industrial revolution: massive shifts of rural populations to cities, and the exploitation of the poor and working-class women, men and children. The YWCA attributes its origins to two sources: the prayer unions of Emma Roberts, which regularly gathered groups of young women for prayer and support; and the network of homes and institutions under the patronage of Lady Kinnaird. The first home was established in London in 1855, a residence for young Christian working women.

The movement spread rapidly in Great Britain and elsewhere, e.g. in the USA by 1858, providing in the homes Bible studies, discussion and companionship. In 1894, the World's YWCA united similar movements in France, Germany, Norway, Switzerland and Sweden. In 1898 it adapted for eligible membership the YMCA* 1855 Paris basis: to unite those young women who regard "Jesus Christ as their God and Saviour according to the holy scriptures... and desire to associate their efforts for the extension of (God's) kingdom among all young women by such means as are in accordance with the word of God". Headquartered in London, it held its first world conference in 1898, with 326 delegates. By then there were almost 500 YWCA missionaries in different Protestant churches and 50 missionaries directly under YWCA sponsorship. National secretaries travelled widely, and many YWCA leaders came out of the Student Christian Movement (see **World Student Christian Federation**), itself internationally oriented.

Although the basis of the World Alliance of YWCAs was not exclusively Protestant, in most countries it developed the impression that it was such. Leadership in predominantly Eastern Orthodox countries (Russia, Bulgaria, etc.) or in Roman Catholic environments (Latin America, Philippines) or where Protestants were a small minority of the Christians (Middle East) was urging the YWCA to clearly state its position on its relations in working with non-Protestant Christians. In 1928 the alliance faced a serious division by formally admitting Roman Catholics to membership; at this juncture Finland and South Africa withdrew their YWCAs. That same year the papal encyclical* *Mortalium Animos* warned RCs against participation in "pan-Christian" activities, and YWCA Catholic leaders thereafter found themselves often in conflict with their church authorities.

Especially after the first world war, YWCA programmes developed a new emphasis on social action, for example, in urging national associations to support those standards for working women that had been adopted by the International Labour Conference.

In 1930, following discussions with the YMCA World Alliance and the World Student Christian Federation, the World YWCA moved its general offices to Geneva. This location re-inforced its image as an international, interconfessional movement. In 1939 a world conference on Christian youth, co-organized with the YMCA, brought together 1,500 young people from 70 countries. Many became leaders in the ecumenical movement after the second world war.

In 1951 the World YWCA held its council meeting in Beirut, where the membership was predominantly Catholic and Orthodox. The basis, aims and principles were revised and by 1955 clearly marked an advance in the official YWCA position: members "of different Christian traditions" joined in a "worldwide fellowship through which they may grow as Christians, participating in the life and worship of their church and expressing their faith by word and deed". The present constitution states: "believing that unity among Christians is the will of God, and desiring as a lay movement to make a contribution towards that unity... "

Working in 92 countries, the World YWCA has a federated structure of 79 national affiliates which in turn direct thousands of local branches or clubs. It has consultative status with the United Nations and its specialized agencies, and co-operates with many ecumenical and non-governmental organizations.

World YWCA-sponsored programmes have helped women obtain the skills to generate much-needed income, to improve the health and nutrition of their families, and to help build a solid base for their children's educational growth. Generations of women around the world have been trained by YWCA programmes to gain the skills and confidence needed to assume leadership roles within their communities. Women who had been trained by these programmes have emerged as prominent leaders struggling for women's rights, for peace and for development with justice for all.

See also **women in church and society**.

ELAINE HESSE STEEL
and KITTY STRONG

A. Rice, *A History of the World's Young Women's Christian Association*, New York, Women's Press, 1947 • M.S. Sims, *The Natural History of a Social Institution: The Young Women's Christian Association*, New York, Women's Press, 1936.

WORLD'S EVANGELICAL ALLIANCE.

In August 1846, some 800 evangelicals from Britain, Europe, and North America, representing a variety of Protestant traditions, met in London to form the Evangelical Alliance. (The British branch was incorporated decades later as the World's Evangelical Alliance.) Based on membership of individuals rather than of churches, the Evangelical Alliance was "the first society formed with a definite view to Christian unity" (Stephen Neill). The founders identified a core of evangelical belief which includes: the inspiration and authority of scripture, the unity and Triune nature of the godhead, the fallenness of human nature, the incarnation and atonement of Jesus Christ, justification by faith alone, and resurrection and final judgment.

When the American delegates in 1846 balked at barring slave-holders from membership, the Evangelical Alliance's founders dropped the quest for an international organization and settled for loosely affiliated national fellowships. Units quickly formed in England, Canada, India, Sweden and Turkey. Later Spain, Portugal and the USA were added.

The alliance strongly encouraged co-operative missionary work and facilitated "comity" and "non-interference" agreements among mission groups. The Evangelical Alliance annual week of prayer became, at the urging of missionaries in India, the Universal Week of Prayer. The periodical *Evangelical Christendom* articulated Evangelical Alliance concerns for more than a century, notably world mission and solidarity with Christians who were suffering persecution. The alliance sponsored several missionary conferences, which were precursors to the 1910 world conference in Edinburgh.

In the USA, due to tensions over the social gospel, theological liberalism, and the drive towards institutional unity (realized in the Federal Council of Churches in 1908), the US alliance movement ceased to function after 1900. The British and several European alliances have continued to this day. When evangelical forces began to coalesce in the USA in the 1940s, the historic alliance network was ready to give birth to the World Evangelical Fellowship.*

ROBERT T. COOTE

WORSHIP IN THE ECUMENICAL MOVEMENT.

The subject of worship has been on the agenda of the ecumenical movement since its beginnings, although it did not really come to the fore until the concurrently growing liturgical movement* had also gained strength among the divided churches. Both movements show a near-parallel development; Vatican II* recognized them respectively as "movements of the Holy Spirit through his church" and as "the work of grace of the Holy Spirit".

Ways of Worship. All of the references to worship in the report of the first world conference on Faith and Order at Lausanne in 1927 are more or less incidental. The report of the second world conference on F&O (Edinburgh 1937), however, suggested a study of patterns of worship characteristic of different churches. A theological commission on worship began to study the relevance of worship for the divided churches. Not until 1951 did the commission publish its report, together with selected papers: *Ways of Worship*. The material provided the basis for discussion at the third world conference on F&O (Lund 1952).

The work of the theological commission on worship is the first definite indication of the impact of the liturgical movement on the ecumenical movement. Although in the end this liturgical renewal would contribute significantly to the striving towards unity, early WCC documents tend to see worship as the focal point of existing divisions. This is probably due to the widely differing liturgical traditions then represented by the member churches.

In Lund ecumenical reflections on worship concentrated on the fact that in worship "disunity becomes explicit and the sense of separation most acute". The conference maintained: "In worship we meet the problem, nay, rather the sin of the disunion of the church in its sharpest form." This judgment is not surprising in light of the commission's primarily descriptive and comparative work. Since worship was explicitly on the agenda of an ecumenical discussion for the first time, a basic overview of the different patterns of worship in the churches was necessary. Part 1 of *Ways of Worship* therefore described and compared "The Elements of Liturgy", and part 2 dealt slightly more theologically with the "Inner Meaning of Word and Sacrament". In both sections, members of the different churches outlined the essential features of the worship of their own community. The aim was not so much to attempt a common approach but to describe actual patterns of worship in the churches. Part 3 treated "Liturgy and Devotion", concentrating on the question of Mariology. (The 1950 promulgation of the Roman Catholic dogma of the Assumption of Mary influenced the agenda here.)

The report of the commission reflected, ecumenically and theologically, on the different contributions. On the one hand, it tried to sketch important distinctions, such as eucharist-centred versus preaching-centred worship, and, on the other hand, to assess the unifying impact of the liturgical movement. The report mentioned especially the growing sense of the corporate aspect of worship, the re-discovery of its sacramental character and the return to primitive patterns of worship.

All in all, *Ways of Worship*, with its basically descriptive and comparative orientation, was a necessary starting point for the ecumenical discussions about the nature of worship. Lund explicitly recognized that the commission's work "has strengthened the conviction that worship, no less than Faith and Order, is essential to the being of the church".

Lund 1952 was a first attempt to formulate both the existing agreement and the unsolved problems as to the meaning and practice of worship. The formulation of agreement appropriately and convincingly begins with the Trinitarian basis (see **Trinity**) and pneumatological context (see **Holy Spirit**) of worship. "We worship one God, Father, Son and Holy Spirit, the Triune God, by whose Spirit all true worship is inspired and unto whom all Christian worship is offered." The agreed statements which follow concern anthropological questions (worship involves the whole person), liturgical questions (a drawing together of the common elements observed in *Ways of Worship*), sacramental questions (the appreciation of both word and sacrament*) and ecclesiological questions (worship always takes place within the communion of saints*). Also mentioned is a theme that would be stressed repeatedly in subsequent ecumenical documents on worship: "However we view the church's worship, we are unanimous that its setting is the church's mission to the world." The section on unsolved problems takes up more specific questions (e.g. the precise relationship between word and sacrament and the place in worship of saints and the departed).

Lund's recommendations to the churches focus on unity* as the aim of all the studies on different patterns of worship. Some recommendations re-appear in future documents, indicating that in the meantime the member churches have not taken them seriously enough. For example, the inclusion in the curricula of theological colleges of courses on worship in an ecumenical setting is as relevant today as it was at Lund.

Theological approaches: Montreal and Uppsala. This worship commission, working between Lund and Montreal (1963), consisted of three regional sections: Europe, East Asia and North America. Each had quite different approaches. The European section left behind the method of comparative study and concentrated on the theology of worship in the Bible ("creation and worship", "redemption and worship", "new creation and worship"). This starting point yielded a definitely Christocentric understanding of the nature of worship: "Jesus Christ as the culmination of the mighty saving acts of God forms the living centre of all worship." The biblical approach also drew attention to the genuine variety of types of worship in the New Testament (e.g. sacra-

ments, preaching of the word, prayers), but these were not systematized or evaluated as different forms over against each other. This variety may suggest the possibility of a unity among the different patterns of worship existing today.

The East Asian section concentrated on understanding worship as a response to God's creative and redemptive activity and on the indigenization of worship. This was the first time that an Asian report was included in such a theological commission on worship; it soon became clear, especially at the Uppsala assembly (1968), how important the insights and correctives from this Asian perspective were for ecumenical reflection on worship.

The North American section had a dual focus: the matrix of worship in the scriptures and the matrix of worship in contemporary North American churches. The group came to a parallel conclusion to that of the European section: a purely descriptive and comparative approach to the question of worship does not sufficiently advance the unity of the church; liturgical questions have to be seen within the wider context of biblical and systematic issues.

The fourth F&O world conference (Montreal 1963) reacted to the above work of the theological commission on worship. Its report, *Worship and the Oneness of Christ's Church*, shifted from the differing patterns of worship to a firm commitment to unity in and through worship. This was a shift in the evaluation of the place of worship itself. While Lund had maintained that worship is no less essential to the church's life than faith and order, Montreal called worship "the central and determinative act of the church's life" and pressed for the study of worship as one of the main tasks facing the ecumenical dialogue. Some fundamental agreements are enumerated. As in Lund, the Trinitarian perspective is the starting point of the interpretation of the nature of worship: "Christian worship is... a service to God the Father by men [and women] redeemed by his Son, who are continually finding new life in the power of the Holy Spirit." The next point of agreement is the ecclesiological aspect, not the anthropological one as in Lund: "Worship... is an act formative of Christian community..., an act... which represents the one, catholic church." This statement clearly recognized the fundamental ecclesiological relevance of worship. The importance given here to worship as a fundamental act of the being of the church* exceeds anything said about worship before, and one may ask whether subsequent ecumenical discussions have ever taken these statements seriously enough.

Other aspects of worship often stressed are the interdependence of public liturgy and private devotion, the links of worship with creation* and the new creation, the Christocentric groundings of baptism* and the eucharist* and the eschatological perspective of worship (see **eschatology**). Special sections of the report were devoted to worship, mission and indigenization and Christian worship in the world today. The latter foreshadows the central concern of subsequent ecumenical debates on worship. The focus shifts from examining different patterns of worship in the churches and its underlying essence and unity to considering the crisis of worship in the modern world, with "authenticity" as the new key word. The mandate from Montreal, however, still concentrated on the newly discovered importance of worship in the ecumenical dialogue and the need for "a fresh approach... to the relation between theology and worship, so that,... as a definite step beyond current practice, our entire theological work may be informed by a fresh sensitivity to the demands and problems of Christian worship". It soon became obvious that this vital concern was not maintained. The whole discussion narrowed down to specific problems of worship, losing sight of the importance of worship for theological work as a whole.

The crisis of worship today. After Montreal, the subject of worship was important enough to constitute one of the six sections at the WCC's fourth assembly (Uppsala 1968). Of the Uppsala report on worship, one of its contributors has written: "I do not see how one could fail to be disappointed on reading the report" — especially after Montreal, one might add. (The challenge to see positively the fact of a WCC assembly officially treating worship, over against the "respectable obscurity" of F&O, does not seem convincing in the light of what was achieved.) Several factors were responsible for this disappointment. Because of the general theme of the Uppsala assembly, "Behold, I Make All Things New", the working group for the section on worship had to focus on the current theological crisis in the life of the church, i.e. the problems connected with the secularization* debate.

The section's original title was "The Worship of God in a Secular Age". This wording was criticized both by the churches in countries where secularization did not (yet) seem to be the main problem facing the churches and their worship and by the Orthodox churches, who feared that worship was being surrendered to secularization. In the end, a very limited agreed statement was published as a "starting point". It bears few traces of the former agreed statements concerning the Trinitarian and ecclesiological essence of worship and concentrates instead on the crisis of worship and the positive and negative possibilities of secularization. Lengthy justifications of worship are repudiated: "Worship needs no more justification than does love." Recommendations to the churches are included under the cautious title "Helping People to Worship", but they do not go beyond anything already said before. Despite its overall disappointing character, one positive thing seems worth pointing out: behind the emphasis on the need for authentic worship in a secular age lies the important conviction of the fundamental link between liturgy and life, a subject to be stressed in most subsequent documents on worship.

A 1969 F&O consultation in Geneva took up the subject of worship again, very much within the perspectives set by the 1968 assembly. Although its title was "Worship in a Secular Age", the report dropped the reference to secularization, since this term did not seem universally applicable. The report was simply called *Worship Today*, a fitting characterization of the content if the stress is put on the word "today". The consultation agreed to begin with an analysis of the present situation and then to face the question whether authentic worship was still possible under the analyzed circumstances. The answers were as varied as the analyses. Equally divergent opinions became apparent in facing liturgical reforms;* merely changed forms of worship cannot resolve the crisis of worship.

The Uppsala report on worship and *Worship Today* constitute a significant shift from the fairly continuous line of development evident in the earlier ecumenical documents on worship. One cannot deny that the two reports faced very real (and by no means solved) problems, but one may ask whether they would not have gained — especially as far as their lasting interest is concerned — from greater continuity with former ecumenical thinking on worship.

Ecumenical convergence. After these reports of the late 1960s, the ecumenical movement has had difficulties in picking up the lines and expressing itself on worship again. Since then, worship as a subject in its own right has not been on the agenda of a major WCC forum. The theme was not entirely forgotten, but interest shifted from the nature of worship as such to detailed consideration of emerging convergences in the areas of baptism* and eucharist.*

Liturgical reforms: In some senses ecumenical reflection on worship since the late 1960s has been overtaken by the ecumenical convergence in worship patterns, which has taken place largely as a result of thorough-going liturgical reforms among the divided churches. One of the most remarkable liturgical reforms is certainly that within the Roman Catholic Church. Even if its liturgical renewal was not initiated as an ecumenical enterprise, the ecumenical ramifications were quickly perceived as considerable. The uniformity, rubricism and centralization which characterized Roman Catholic worship after the liturgical reforms of the council of Trent* set it apart from the worship patterns of many other Christian communities. But the Second Vatican Council reforms returned to earlier (and common!) liturgical patterns. The change in the liturgical language from Latin to the vernacular, the clearer structure of the liturgical rites, the more prominent place given to the scriptures and the sermon, the emphasis on an active participation of the laity, the eucharistic celebrations facing the people, the openness to liturgical inculturation (see **culture**) — all these characteristics of the Constitution on the Sacred Liturgy and the subsequent liturgical reforms brought about a much greater affinity between worship patterns of the divided churches. Protestant liturgical reforms also based largely on a return to common origins have supported this ecumenical convergence. The pro-

grammatic beginning of the Constitution on the Liturgy has found a fulfilment: "It is the goal of this most sacred Council... to nurture whatever can contribute to the unity of all who believe in Christ."

Confessions in dialogue: In 1972 a survey of bilateral conversations among World Confessional Families was published under the title *Confessions in Dialogue*. It included a section on "Worship and Bilateral Dialogue". Rather than theoretical reflections or agreed statements, this section is a series of observations, by persons involved in bilateral dialogues,* about worship as a topic and matrix in these conversations. Most contributors stressed the importance of a worshipping fellowship during the conversations. One very attractive notion is that of the bilateral dialogues as a continuous act of thanksgiving. But one contributor also admitted that there had not been much worship in his group at all.

Theologically, the most interesting contribution is undoubtedly Edmund Schlink's. He tries to make clear the methodological significance of worship for ecumenical conversations. He argues that dogmatic and canonical statements of different churches cannot simply be compared in order to reach agreement. Instead, they may have to be translated back into the elementary functions of church life and worship, where they have their true source and meaning. Schlink's suggestion, if taken seriously, would have important consequences for the basis and form of any emerging consensus* among the churches. It is not without justification, however, that in the context of these important reflections on worship and ecumenical dialogue, the following sentence also occurs: "The centrality of worship in Christian life and consequently also in the search for unity is an inalienable ecumenical conviction — though perhaps honoured more with the lips than in acts." *Confessions in Dialogue* confirms this statement in both directions.

"The Worship of the Congregation": In 1978, the WCC Sub-unit on Renewal and Congregational Life held a workshop in Crete on "The Worship of the Congregation". Its report in a way reunites the threads of earlier WCC documents on worship and the problems and challenges faced during the debates on secularization. Although there is no affirmation of the Trinitarian perspective of wor-

The worship tent at Vancouver 1983 (WCC photo)

ship, its Christocentric, pneumatological, ecclesiological and eschatological aspects are
clearly stated. Important is the repeated emphasis on the connection between liturgy and
life, and a definition which sees worship as
something larger than what takes place in
church: "The new temple is the Body of
Christ, and wherever one encounters another
in the power of the Spirit of the risen Christ,
there true worship takes place." The report
further deals with questions of faithfulness
and creativity, worship and culture (with a
positive, anthropologically justified emphasis
on symbols) and worship and social engagement. It is interesting to note that the report
speaks not only of the challenges which today's world implies for worship but also of
the "radical challenges" brought by worship to
today's world — clearly an important re-
adjustment after the one-sided focus of the
secularization debate.

*The Lima liturgy:** The eucharistic liturgy
prepared for the plenary session of the F&O
commission meeting in Lima in 1982 and its
subsequent (unexpected) enthusiastic reception have indicated a deep-felt need for a
liturgical expression paralleling any emerging
doctrinal agreement. The need for one ecu-

menical liturgy par excellence should not
lightly be discarded, even if it may be doubtful that the Lima liturgy in the long run can
fulfill this need. In any case, the task which
some people seem to have considered solved
with the eucharistic text of Lima is still before
us: to give the emerging doctrinal agreement
liturgical expression(s) (see **lex orandi, lex
credendi**).

The celebration of the Lima liturgy was one
of the high points of the sixth assembly of the
WCC in Vancouver (1983), which has been
described as "the most liturgical of all the
assemblies". Maybe here, too, reflection on
worship was overtaken by the actual experience of worship by the participants. One feature worth particular mention, characteristic
of thinking about and acting in worship since
the fifth assembly in Nairobi in 1975, is the
greater appreciation and use of indigenous
material in the liturgy (such as hymns, lyrics,
vestments, gestures, art). There is a growing
awareness not only of the liturgical richness of
other denominational traditions but also of
other cultural-linguistic communities. Although the question of liturgical indigenization has been part of the ecumenical reflections on worship ever since Montreal, it is

now being faced with heightened enthusiasm and urgency.

Conclusion. Montreal (1963) and the consequent decision to put the subject of worship on the agenda for the Uppsala assembly of the WCC (1968) were the peak points of ecumenical interest in the question of the nature of worship. After that, the crisis of worship seemed more fascinating and threatening than did the privilege of worship. Then, in the 1970s and 1980s, discussion of the nature of worship was swallowed up by the all-absorbing work on *Baptism, Eucharist and Ministry*.

The subject of worship is, however, reasserting itself as part of the ecumenical agenda due to the growing importance which almost all the churches are placing on liturgical life. More attention must therefore be devoted to worship in future discussions. Fortunately, the ecumenical movement will not have to start over from the beginning. Some fundamental and important ground has already been covered by the WCC documents, and some basic agreements have been reached. These are foundations which can and should be built upon. A worthwhile aim to

strive for seems to be the statement made by one of the contributors to *Confessions in Dialogue:* "Doxology is at the beginning and at the end of all striving for unity. It also accompanies it at every stage of the way."

See also **hymns; lex orandi, lex credendi; Lima liturgy; liturgical movement; liturgical reforms; liturgical texts, common; liturgy; prayer in the ecumenical movement; sacraments; spirituality in the ecumenical movement**.

TERESA BERGER

T. Berger, "Unity in and through Doxology? Reflections on Worship Studies in the WCC", *Studia Liturgica*, 16, 1986-87 ● H. Davies, *Worship and Theology in England*, vol. 4: *The Ecumenical Century, 1900-1965*, Princeton, NJ, Princeton UP, 1965 ● P. Edwall, E. Hayman & W.D. Maxwell eds, *Ways of Worship: The Report of the Theological Commission on Faith and Order*, London, SCM, 1951 ● P.W. Hoon, *The Integrity of Worship*, Nashville, TN, Abingdon, 1971 ● "Worship and the Oneness of Christ's Church", in *The Fourth World Conference on Faith and Order at Montreal*, P.C. Rodger & L. Vischer eds, London, SCM, 1964 ● "Worship and Secularization", *Studia Liturgica*, 7, 2-3, 1970.

YOUNG MEN'S CHRISTIAN ASSOCIATIONS.

The first association known as the YMCA was founded in London in 1844 by 22-year-old George Williams to provide young men with a Christian atmosphere for spiritual and educational development, especially through Bible classes and prayer meetings. The movement rapidly spread to different countries of the British empire. The first North American branch was in Montreal in 1850, and the second in 1851 in Boston. Similar associations began to flourish on the European continent. Two of their main characteristics were mission at home and overseas and a will to move towards greater unity among Christians.

Jean-Henri Dunant in Geneva (later the founder of the Red Cross) and others had pressed for a world movement of the YMCAs, and in 1855 the first world conference was held in Paris. It adopted what has become known as the "Paris basis", which sets out the fundamental principle of the world alliance: "The Young Men's Christian Associations seek to unite those young men who, regarding Jesus Christ as their God and Saviour according to the holy scriptures, desire to be his disciples in their faith and in their life, and to associate their efforts for the extension of his kingdom among young men."

Under the Paris rules only active members of evangelical Protestant churches were eligible for YMCA membership; this rule was re-affirmed in 1914 but relaxed in the 1920s.

Nevertheless, the formula of the Paris basis to bring together those who regard "Jesus Christ as their God and Saviour according to the holy scriptures" was later used as a basis for the World Young Women's Christian Associations* (1894), the World Student Christian Federation* (1895), and the WCC (1948). YMCA leaders helped to shape the events after the 1910 Edinburgh mission conference, which led to the WCC formation and founding.

After the first world war the YMCA extended its work to Eastern Europe and reached agreements with leaders of the Eastern Orthodox churches. After the second world war, the World Alliance continued its contacts with the Orthodox churches through the ecumenical patriarch of Constantinople.

During the same period, important YMCA developments took place also in countries that were predominantly Roman Catholic. Work with prisoners of war during the second world war presented many opportunities for service to Catholics. In 1950 the alliance held a world consultation which involved Protestants, Eastern Orthodox, Roman Catholics and Copts from 27 countries, for whom this truly ecumenical fellowship was an "encouraging indication that Christians of the three confessions are drawing closer together" (C.P. Shedd).

In 1962 a consultation on ecumenical policy and practice for lay Christian movements was held jointly by the World Alliance of YMCAs and the World YWCA. The introduction to its report states that "it was one of the rare occasions in recent times when members of Orthodox, Protestant and Roman Catholic churches — both laymen and women and members of the clergy — have been privileged to join informally and intimately in prayer, Bible study and discussion on questions of ecumenical policy".

The Second Vatican Council opened new opportunities in the area of the YMCA's relationship with the Roman Catholic Church. During the Council and its aftermath, Sir Frank Willis often travelled to Rome as a representative of the world alliance and maintained friendly contacts with the staff of the Vatican Secretariat for Promoting Christian Unity (SPCU). In 1970 the YMCA special commission to re-evaluate the Paris basis had as one of the consultants Basil Meeking, a SPCU staff member.

Since then, YMCA contacts and working relationships have been developed not only with the SPCU but also with the Vatican offices for the laity, for inter-religious dialogue, and for justice and peace. Two consultations have been held between world alliance and SPCU representatives (1984, 1989). Catholic representatives have participated at local, national and regional levels in YMCA events concerning human rights and interfaith dialogue.

The over 26 million YMCA members in 96 countries comprise almost all Christian confessions and denominations and in some places include also people of other faiths or none. Particularly at local levels the YMCA works with, besides its members, millions more people of different social and cultural origins. Recently the YMCA has increasingly sought to address some of the inter-related core issues which affect all peoples, such as justice and development, peace and human rights. This is based on the conviction that involvement in these issues is an integral part of the Christian character of the YMCA.

In the late 1980s, the world YMCA, as a lay organization in the context of contemporary social realities, has been involved in searching for a deeper understanding of its Christian mission, through action-oriented studies related to justice and peace. There were also concentrated efforts to deepen understanding of the YMCA's ecumenical task in a climate of religious pluralism and secularization.

ERIKA TYSOE-DÜLKEN

C.P. Shedd, *History of the World Alliance of YMCAs*, London, SPCK, 1955 • SPCU *Information Service*, 61, 1986, and 69, 1989.

YOUTH. Youth participation in the ecumenical movement began in the YMCA* and YWCA,* the World Student Christian Federation (WSCF),* the World Alliance for Promoting Friendship through the Churches,* and the Life and Work* movement. The Ecumenical Youth Commission (later to become the World Christian Youth Commission — WCYC) organized the world conference of Christian youth, in Amsterdam in 1939. A global partnership of the generations was committed to a visible Christian community witnessing around the world. The Amsterdam theme "Christus Victor" would carry them through the difficult years of war.

After the end of the second world war, the need for leadership training and the call for another world youth conference led to the forming of the Youth department of the WCC, which, with its partners in the WCYC, organized the second world conference of Christian youth (Oslo 1947). In the post-war situation, the conference was marked by reconciliation and solidarity under the theme "Jesus Christ Is Lord". A world Christian youth community was now a reality. A year later at the first WCC assembly in Amsterdam, a strong youth delegation, made up of men and women in equal numbers from 48 countries, called the churches to overcome their disunity; study the issues of communism, liberalism, colonialism,* racism,* human rights* and atomic power; and commit themselves to ecumenical obedience.

Post-war priorities for the Youth department became reconstruction in Europe, revitalization of church youth work and encouragement of ecumenical youth work around the world. Major emphases were training and conferences for youth leaders, Bible study, ecumenical work camps and other voluntary service programmes, world youth projects (for financial support of youth work). A joint youth committee of the WCC and the World Council of Christian Education (WCCE)* made it possible to reach out to more young people around the world; the WCC focused mainly on youth aged 18-30, and the WCCE on those under 18. In 1952 the third world conference of Christian youth met at Kottayam, Travancore, India. The last of the world youth conferences organized by the WCC, it signalled a shift to more regional work.

An important world study on church youth work published in 1951 on behalf of the WCC, the WCCE and the International Missionary Council (IMC) showed a new consciousness of the needs of youth and an awareness that these needs were not being met by much of traditional church life. This insight was helpful to the WCC in its work of reminding the churches of their responsibility for youth and their responsibility to the ecumenical movement. The Youth department continued to press for maximum youth participation in all major ecumenical gatherings. Special relationships with Orthodox youth led to the creation of the Orthodox youth organization Syndesmos* in 1953.

Following the Evanston assembly in 1954, the integration of youth in the life and mission* of the church became the theme for WCC youth work. Work camps, voluntary service and world youth projects continued as forms of ecumenical education and service, but concern was expressed that so many young people left the church after confirmation and that youth participating in ecumenical activities often felt out of place in their churches. Already in 1957 the rapid and radical changes in society were cited as partially responsible for this situation. Consultations were held on baptism* and confirmation*, holy communion and other Faith and Order concerns, including one which challenged the member churches on their rules of communion discipline and their effect on ecumenical gatherings (see **church discipline, intercommunion**).

At the European ecumenical youth assembly in Lausanne in 1960, the delegates were strongly critical of the fact that they could not together participate in the holy communion. They challenged the selfish acquisitiveness of Europe and called on the churches and the youth to commit themselves to third-world development. It had become clear that youth were a disillusioned lot, more interested in "critical participation" than in integration in

the church. Adult leadership was challenged. For the first time in ecumenical gatherings, official representatives were present from Eastern European churches and from Roman Catholic youth movements.

The Lausanne assembly presaged the tumultuous developments of the 1960s. Its impact was felt in other parts of the world as regional youth movements which had developed with WCC/WCCE support responded to their own situations. Although WCC youth work had inevitably concentrated on Europe in the early years, it soon developed relationships elsewhere and began to encourage other national and regional ecumenical initiatives, many of which had been stimulated by the world conferences. National and regional ecumenical youth movements developed during the 1950s, often in co-operation with the WSCF and the IMC, alongside the developing regional ecumenical structures and often furthered by WCC staff travel.

Beginning in the 1950s the WCC enabled training courses and ecumenical work camps in Africa. The All Africa Conference of Churches* (AACC) in 1958 pointed to the situation of youth caught between two civilizations. Drawn into the political preoccupations of their nations, they sought guidance for the future. The AACC set up a youth commission in 1963, and an all-Africa Christian youth assembly was held in Nairobi in 1962. Among other things, it pointed to the need for church structures and worship to reflect present needs and African styles. For many years the struggle for development and against colonialism and racism was central to the work of the AACC youth department.

Asian youth were eager to meet and discuss the tasks confronting them as Christians in their nations. The East Asia Christian Conference appointed a youth secretary in 1961 to succeed the WCCE Asia youth secretary; publications, ecumenical work camps and training institutes helped build up a regional movement. Special attention was given in later years to the needs of rural youth. The first Asian Christian youth assembly in the Philippines (1965) introduced a new generation of leadership to the ecumenical movement. The 1984 Asian youth assembly was sponsored by the Christian Conference of Asia, the WSCF and the International Movement of Catholic Students.

Latin Americans who had attended the Amsterdam conference in 1939 formed the Union of Latin American Evangelical Youth (ULAJE), which held regional conferences beginning in 1941. An ecumenical team of youth leaders visited 13 countries in 1956-57. Work camps and training courses were conducted as part of ULAJE's programme. As ecumenical relations became more open, relations among the churches and with the WCC became closer; ULAJE became the Union of Latin American Ecumenical Youth with Roman Catholic participation in 1970. Its priorities have been community organization for rural and urban youth and participation in the process of people's liberation.

In the Middle East, ecumenical work camps as well as two important meetings brought together Orthodox and Protestants — a youth leaders' consultation in 1955 and a youth and student conference in 1964. A secretary for youth and student work worked for the WCC and WSCF. The youth department of the Middle East Council of Churches* has emphasized the concern for regional political issues and youth's identity vis-a-vis their own churches, other Christian communities and nations.

In North America interdenominational youth work began in the 1930s, and for 20 years large conferences were held. The activities of the United Christian Youth Movement paralleled those of interdenominational student movements. North American initiatives were responsible for the development of world youth projects and the ecumenical work-camp programme. The WCC/WCCE gave young people in the USA and Canada opportunities to cultivate relationships with youth in other parts of the world. The North American ecumenical youth assembly (Ann Arbor, Michigan, 1961) challenged churches and participants to face up to the realities of the church in the contemporary world, especially the North American situation. Ecumenical youth work in the USA and Canada has depended on the denominations and national councils of churches, since there is no regional structure, although in the 1980s Young Christians for Global Justice was formed to fill this void. A 1987 North American consultation of ecumenical groups and denominational youth bodies expressed new commitment to ecumenical co-operation.

In Europe the annual consultations of ecumenical youth leaders begun by the WCC in 1947 led to the formation of the Ecumenical Youth Council in Europe (EYCE) in 1968, which has worked closely with the WCC, WSCF, the Conference of European Churches and other European youth and church organizations, and serves as a forum for dialogue and encounter. Quadrennial conferences sponsored by the EYCE were significant encounters for church youth bodies and action groups from East and West Europe.

Regional youth work started late in the Caribbean and the Pacific, but in both areas the regional conferences of churches have addressed themselves to youth concerns. Caribbean emphasis has been on self-reliance and self-development and the struggle against racism and cultural deprivation. The Pacific Conference of Churches* is especially concerned about a nuclear-free Pacific and the ambiguities of tourism. A Pacific youth convention was held in January 1980.

The period between the New Delhi and Uppsala WCC assemblies (1961-68) was marked by dramatic developments in the ecumenical movement, in society and especially among young people. The emergence of third-world nations and churches, the internationalization of economic-justice issues, the war in Vietnam, the US civil rights movement, the youth and student revolts against accepted value systems, the entry of the Roman Catholic Church into the ecumenical movement — all had consequences for church youth work. Youth-led movements replaced adult-led organizations; churches had to rethink what they were doing "for" youth, and much church-centred youth work disappeared.

The WCC was called to interpret what was happening to the churches and to be a liaison between youth and the leadership of the ecumenical movement. Emphasis shifted from the teenager to the young adult. Youth were less interested in churchly ecumenism than in common ecumenical action in response to crying needs. Disappointed with the institutional inertia of the churches, they sought unity and renewal in the struggle for an authentic Christian presence and action in the world. Powerless and voiceless in the past, youth became aware and active, vocal and politicized.

Concerns taken up by the Youth department in the 1960s included evangelism and the missionary structure of the church, communion and intercommunion, youth in a complex society, confessionalism and the ecumenical movement, youth in rapid social change, international economic justice, new hymns and worship material. Growing contacts with Roman Catholic youth movements led to consideration of the problems of youth in industry, rural youth and those whose needs were not met by any organized activity.

During these years the WCC co-operated with other organizations and movements. Originally initiated by several US churches, the International Christian Youth Exchange provided a year-long ecumenical experience for teenagers. The German Kirchentag attracted many youth seeking a place where urgent questions of conviction and commitment and burning issues of the time could be dealt with honestly. The Christian Peace Conference brought together church leaders from Eastern and Western Europe to consider issues of peace and justice. The ecumenical community in Taizé in France was attracting increasingly large numbers of youth seeking spiritual renewal.

Work camps continued (17,000 young people had participated over 20 years) but developed new forms — smaller teams, longer terms of service and a variety of service projects responding to social as well as material need; the programme was renamed Ecumenical Youth Service. World youth projects were an accepted form of interchurch aid.

A major document was prepared for the Uppsala assembly entitled "Youth in God's World". It acknowledged the tension between the generations that had become evident in the 1960s and suggested the need for the education of adults; pointed out that youth need to find identity and responsibility without having it offered to them; and affirmed that youth ministry should never become "a nervous effort to keep young people in or win them for the church". The youth delegation at Uppsala expressed its distrust of institution and bureaucracy in protests throughout the assembly, calling the churches to practise a common service and common eucharist, communicating their concerns effectively, although with-

Youth delegates at San Antonio 1989, world conference on mission and evangelism (WCC/Peter Williams)

out visible results in the decisions of the assembly.

From 1969 to 1973 the WCC Youth department staff was greatly reduced, and it was expected that youth concerns would be taken up by all departments, but the *Uppsala to Nairobi* report said that "youth as a constituency was obscured and seemed to become the object of benign neglect", although progress was made in involving youth in some WCC committees. Programmes for youth diminished, in spite of some useful consultations and publications. This development paralleled similar changes in church youth work itself and a growth of youth activities outside the churches.

The Nairobi assembly (1975) saw a renewed commitment to youth and a renewed task for the WCC: "to bring the presence and concerns of youth fully into the life of the ecumenical movement". Major areas of concern in the following years were youth and education, youth and theology, and youth and social justice. Priority was given to developing a network of Christian youth leaders around the world. The regional youth bodies became primary partners with the WCC in implementing its work in Ecumenical Youth Service, world youth projects and consultations with a strong emphasis on faith and justice issues. An important inter-regional conference was held by the European, Middle East and African regional youth bodies in 1980. Youth-to-youth team visits were organized during International Youth Year (1985) in all regions to strengthen the youth network and build global solidarity.

Youth participation as stewards in assemblies and central committee meetings had become an established practice, and in the 1970s special efforts were made to increase youth participation in WCC conferences and committees. Youth under 30 were 4% of the voting delegates at Uppsala, 9% at Nairobi, 11% at the Vancouver assembly (1983); the goal for the Canberra assembly (1991) was 20%.

The close co-operation now developing among the WCC, YMCA, YWCA, WSCF, Syndesmos and Roman Catholic youth organizations could give rise to a more inclusive movement. Dialogue and co-operation with evangelical youth movements have been initiated in certain countries and regions. Current emphases of the WCC Youth sub-unit are continued advocacy for youth within the WCC and in relation to the churches, the strengthening of a global ecumenical youth movement and exploration of a Christ-centred spirituality. Local, national and regional movements are key partners in the work. There is a new solidarity emerging in common struggles for justice and peace. Seminars, training courses, action projects and other ecumenical events are supported together with service programmes in Ecumenical Youth Action. Thus, a new vision of the ecumenical movement is seen in the light of the needs of today's youth.

See also **generation conflict**.

WILLIAM A. PERKINS

A.J. van der Bent, *From Generation to Generation*, WCC, 1986 ● A. van den Heuvel ed., *The New Creation and the New Generation: A Forum for Youth Workers*, New York, Friendship, 1965 ● *Risk*, vols 1-13, WCC, 1965-77 ● "Youth and God's World", in *Work Book for the Assembly Committees, Uppsala, 1968*, WCC, 1968.

ZERNOV, NICOLAS. B. 9.10.1898, Moscow; d. 25.8.1980, Oxford, UK. Greatly influential in analyzing and evaluating the ecumenical relations between East and West Europe, Zernov was an advocate of ecumenism in the Orthodox churches. He was secretary of the Russian Student Christian Movement in exile, 1925-32, and was honorary area secretary of the youth commission of the World Alliance for Promoting Friendship through the Churches* and the Life and Work* movement, with the Orthodox countries as his special field, 1934-39. Secretary of the Fellowship of St Alban and St Sergius, 1933-47, and lecturer at the School of Slavonic Studies in London, 1936-39, he was also professor of Eastern Orthodox culture at the University of Oxford, 1947, and later was associated with an Orthodox college in Kerala, India, 1953-54. Zernov's numerous works include *Moscow, the Third Rome*, 2nd ed. (London, SPCK, 1944), *The Russians and Their Church* (London, SPCK, 1945), *The Reintegration of the Church: A Study in Intercommunion* (London, SCM, 1952) and *Sunset Years* (London, Fellowship of St Alban and St Sergius, 1983).

ANS J. VAN DER BENT

ZULU, ALPHAEUS HAMILTON. B. 29.6.1905, Nqutu, KwaZulu, South Africa; d. 29.2.1988, Ulundi, KwaZulu. Zulu was a president of the WCC, 1968-75, and a member of the executive committee of the Christian Council of South Africa, 1945-58, of the South African Institute of Race Relations, 1943-84, and of the African National Congress (ANC), 1942-60. He was director of the KwaZulu Development Corporation, 1978-85 (chairman 1981-85). In 1939 he entered St Peter's Anglican theological college in Johannesburg and was ordained a priest in 1942. Zulu was appointed assistant curate at St Faith's mission in Durban in 1940, where he stayed for the next 20 years. In 1960 he was consecrated assistant bishop of St John's diocese in the Transkei, and in 1968 he became bishop of Transkei. His spiritual mentor was Albert Luthuli, with whom he developed a strong fellowship. He refused to condone any form of violence. His decision to break with the ANC in 1975 and to accept office as national chairman of Inkhata ye Nkululeko Yesizwe (arm of the freedom of a nation) and to remain a member of the national council led to much rejection and criticism. He had a profound influence on the life and work of his people and devoted all his energies and talents to promoting a spirit of self-help and self-reliance in all aspects of their life. He wrote "The Dilemma of the Black South African" (*Study Encounter*, 9, 3, 1973).

ANS J. VAN DER BENT

Index of Subjects

Index of Names

Abbreviations

In most cases, the full form of an abbreviation is spelled out in each article in which it appears. The following abbreviations are those most widely used in the articles as well as those commonly used in English texts and bibliographies.

AACC	All Africa Conference of Churches
ann.	anniversary
app., apps	appendix(es)
ARCIC	Anglican-Roman Catholic International Commission
art., arts	article(s)
b.	born
BCC	British Council of Churches
BEM	*Baptism, Eucharist and Ministry,* WCC, 1982 (individual sections referred to as B12, E2, M31 comm., etc.)
c.	*circa,* about
CBC	church base community
CCA	Christian Conference of Asia
CCC	Caribbean Conference of Churches
CCIA	Commission of the Churches on International Affairs
CCPD	Commission on the Churches' Participation in Development
CEC	Conference of European Churches
CELAM	Latin American bishops' conference
cf.	*confer,* compare
ch., chs	chapter(s)
CICARWS	Commission of the Churches on Inter-church Aid, Refugee and World Service
CLAI	Latin American Council of Churches
CLS	Christian Literature Society
CMC	Christian Medical Commission
COCU	Consultation on Church Union (USA)
comm.	commentary
comp., comps	compiler(s)
CWCs	Christian World Communions

CWME	Commission on World Mission and Evangelism
d.	died
ed., eds	editor(s), edition(s)
e.g.	*exempli gratia,* for example
esp.	especially
ET	English translation
et al.	*et alii,* and others
etc.	*et cetera,* and so forth
F&O	Faith and Order
FRG	Federal Republic of Germany
GDR	German Democratic Republic
GNP	gross national product
hom.	homily
ibid.	*ibidem,* in the same place
i.e.	*id est,* that is
IMC	International Missionary Council
JPIC	Justice, Peace and the Integrity of Creation
lit.	literally
L&W	Life and Work
LWF	Lutheran World Federation
LXX	Septuagint
MECC	Middle East Council of Churches
MIT	Massachusetts Institute of Technology
n., nn.	note(s)
NCCCUSA	National Council of the Churches of Christ in the USA
NEB	New English Bible
no., nos	number(s)
NT	New Testament
OT	Old Testament
p., pp.	page(s)
par.	parallel(s)
para., paras	paragraph(s)
PCC	Pacific Conference of Churches
PCR	Programme to Combat Racism
PhD	doctoral degree
PTE	Programme on Theological Education
RC	Roman Catholic, Roman Catholicism
RCC	Roman Catholic Church
RCL	Renewal and Congregational Life
repr.	reprinted
rev.	revised
RSV	Revised Standard Version
SCM	Student Christian Movement
sec., secs	section(s)
SODEPAX	Committee on Society, Development and Peace
SPCK	Society for Promoting Christian Knowledge
TNCs	transnational corporations
UK	United Kingdom
UN	United Nations
UNCTAD	United Nations Conference on Trade and Development
UNESCO	United Nations Educational, Scientific and Cultural Organization

univ.	university
UP	University Press
US, USA	United States of America
USSR	Union of Soviet Socialist Republics
v., vv.	verse(s)
vol., vols	volume(s)
WARC	World Alliance of Reformed Churches
WCC	World Council of Churches
WCFs	World Confessional Families
WMC	World Methodist Council
WSCF	World Student Christian Fellowship
YMCA	Young Men's Christian Associations
YWCA	Young Women's Christian Associations

Books of the Bible

Gen.	1 Sam.	Esth.	Lam.	Jonah
Ex.	2 Sam.	Job	Ezek.	Micah
Lev.	1 Kings	Ps.	Dan.	Nahum
Num.	2 Kings	Prov.	Hos.	Hab.
Deut.	1 Chron.	Eccles.	Joel	Zeph.
Josh.	2 Chron.	S. of S.	Amos	Hag.
Judg.	Ezra	Isa.	Obad.	Zech.
Ruth	Neh.	Jer.		Mal.

Matt.	1 Cor.	1 Thess.	Philemon	1 John
Mark	2 Cor.	2 Thess.	Heb.	2 John
Luke	Gal.	1 Tim.	James	John
John	Eph.	2 Tim.	1 Pet.	Jude
Acts	Phil.	Titus	2 Pet.	Rev.
Rom.	Col.			

States of the United States of America

AK	Alaska	ID	Idaho
AL	Alabama	IL	Illinois
AR	Arkansas	IN	Indiana
AZ	Arizona	KS	Kansas
CA	California	KY	Kentucky
CO	Colorado	LA	Louisiana
CT	Connecticut	MA	Massachusetts
DC	District of Columbia	MD	Maryland
DE	Delaware	ME	Maine
FL	Florida	MI	Michigan
GA	Georgia	MN	Minnesota
HI	Hawaii	MO	Missouri
IA	Iowa	MS	Mississippi

MT	Montana	RI	Rhode Island
NC	North Carolina	SC	South Carolina
ND	North Dakota	SD	South Dakota
NE	Nebraska	TN	Tennessee
NH	New Hampshire	TX	Texas
NJ	New Jersey	UT	Utah
NM	New Mexico	VA	Virginia
NV	Nevada	VT	Vermont
NY	New York	WA	Washington
OH	Ohio	WI	Wisconsin
OK	Oklahoma	WV	West Virginia
OR	Oregon	WY	Wyoming
PA	Pennsylvania		

Contributors

K.C. Abraham (Church of South India) is director of the South Asia Theological Research Institute, Bangalore, India. *Caste; liberation; theology, Asian.*

Paul Abrecht (American Baptist Churches in the USA) was on the staff of the WCC from 1949 to 1983, and was director of the Sub-unit on Church and Society from 1972 to 1983. *Consumerism; growth, limits to; life and work; population explosion; society; study as an ecumenical method; sustainability.*

Elisabeth Adler (Evangelical Church in Berlin-Brandenburg) was director of the Lay Academy of Berlin-Brandenburg, Berlin, German Democratic Republic. *Laity.*

A.M. Allchin (Church of England) is director of St Theosevia Centre for the Study of Spirituality, Oxford, UK, and honorary canon of Canterbury. *Communion of saints, incarnation.*

Horace T. Allen, Jr (Presbyterian Church (USA)) is assistant professor of worship, Boston University School of Theology, and co-chair of the English Language Liturgical Consultation, USA. *Liturgical texts, common.*

Gerald H. Anderson (United Methodist Church) is director of the Overseas Ministries Study Center, New Haven, CT, USA. *Moratorium.*

Tosh Arai (United Church of Christ in Japan) is secretary for lay and study centres in the WCC's Sub-unit on Renewal and Congregational Life. *Asia: Northeast; Christian Conference of Asia; study centres.*

S. Wesley Ariarajah (Methodist Church of Sri Lanka) is director of the WCC's Sub-unit on Dialogue with People of Living Faiths. *Dialogue, interfaith; marriage, interfaith.*

Guy Aurenche (Roman Catholic) is a former president of the international Action of Christians for the Abolition of Torture, Paris, France. *Torture.*

André Babel (Roman Catholic) was president of Unda-Europe from 1983 to 1989, based in Geneva, Switzerland. *Unda.*

E. Theodore Bachmann (Evangelical Lutheran Church in America) was secretary for publications with the Lutheran World Federation in Geneva, Switzerland, from 1973 to 1978. *Lutheranism.*

Canaan Banana (Methodist Church in Zimbabwe), president of the Republic of Zimbabwe until 1988, is honorary professor of theology at the University of Zimbabwe, Harare. *Liberation, struggles for.*

Eileen Barker is reader in sociology with special reference to the study of religion at the London School of Economics, University of London, UK. *New religious movements.*

Paul Merritt Bassett (Church of the Nazarene) is professor of the history of Christianity at the Nazarene Theological Seminary, Kansas City, MO, USA. *Evangelicals, Holiness movement.*

Gregory Baum (Roman Catholic) teaches at the Faculty of Religious Studies of McGill University, Montreal, Canada. *Work.*

Bert B. Beach (Seventh-day Adventist Church) is director of the council on interchurch relations of the General Conference of Seventh-day Adventists, Washington, DC, USA. *Seventh-day Adventist Church, Seventh-day Adventist General Conference.*

René Beaupère (Roman Catholic) is director of the Centre Saint-Irénée, Lyons, France. *Marriage, mixed.*

Ulrich Becker (Evangelical Lutheran Church of Hanover) is professor of theology and religious education at the University of Hanover, Federal Republic of Germany. *Catechesis, children, ecumenical learning.*

Huibert van Beek (Swiss Protestant Church Federation) is secretary for Ecumenical Sharing of Resources with the WCC. *Ecumenical sharing of resources.*

Inga M. Bengtzon (Church of Sweden) is president of Diakonia and director of parish education in Uppsala, Sweden. *Diakonia.*

John C. Bennett (United Church of Christ) is president emeritus, Union Theological Seminary, New York, USA. *Cold war.*

Ans van der Bent (United Church of Christ), was on the staff of the WCC from 1963 to 1989, as director of the library from 1963 to 1986, then as ecumenical research officer from 1986 to 1989. *Several biographies; bibliographies, Christian World Communions, Ecumenical Association of African Theologians, ecumenical conferences, Fellowship of Reconciliation, Marxist-Christian dialogue, Societas Oecumenica, World Alliance for Promoting International Friendship through the Churches, world community, WCC assemblies.*

Teresa Berger (Roman Catholic) is assistant professor of ecumenical theology at the Divinity School, Duke University, Durham, NC, USA. *Catechisms, Lima liturgy, liturgical movement, worship in the ecumenical movement.*

Thomas F. Best (Christian Church (Disciples of Christ)) is an executive secretary in the WCC's Sub-unit on Faith and Order. *Councils of churches: local, national, regional; local ecumenical projects; unity, models of; unity, ways to; Week of Prayer for Christian Unity.*

Charles Birch (Uniting Church in Australia), a fellow of the Australian Academy of Science, is retired Challis professor of biology and head of the School of Biological Sciences, University of Sydney, Australia. *Faith and science.*

André Birmelé (Evangelical Church of the Augsburg Confession Alsace and Lorraine) is research professor at the Institute for Ecumenical Research, Strasbourg, France, and professor at the faculty of theology at Strasbourg University. *Word of God.*

Alain Blancy (Reformed Church of France) is ecumenical officer for his church, Lyons, France. *Bossey, Ecumenical Institute of; Reformed-Roman Catholic dialogue.*

Klauspeter Blaser (Reformed Churches in Switzerland) is professor of systematic theology at the University of Lausanne, and professor of missiology at the University of Basel, Switzerland. *Confessing Church.*

The late Kathleen Bliss (Church of England) was involved throughout her life in ecumenical work, and in the WCC from its founding. She was a member of the WCC's central committee from 1954 to 1961. *Oldham, Joseph Houldsworth.*

Boris Bobrinskoy (Orthodox Church, Ecumenical Patriarchate of Constantinople) is professor of dogmatic theology at the Orthodox Theological Institute of St Sergius, Paris, France. *Holy Spirit.*

Clodovis Boff (Roman Catholic) is professor at the Franciscan Theological Institute of Petropolis and the Faculty of Theology in Sao Paulo, Brazil. *Church base communities.*

John Boonstra (United Church of Christ, USA), formerly director of Frontier Internship in Mission, Geneva, Switzerland, is executive director of the Washington Association of Churches, Washington, DC, USA. *Frontier Internship in Mission.*

Frans Bouwen (Roman Catholic) is editor of *Proche orient chrétien*, Jerusalem, and a member of the WCC's Commission on Faith and Order. *Churches, sister; Eastern Catholic churches; ecumenical councils.*

Theo van Boven (Netherlands Reformed Church) is professor of international law at the State University of Maastricht, Netherlands. *International law, minorities.*

Diane M. Brewster (Religious Society of Friends) is tutor in religious studies and women's studies in the Department of Extra-Mural Studies, Birkbeck College, London University, UK. *Theology, feminist.*

Ion Bria (Romanian Orthodox Church) is director of the WCC's Sub-unit on Renewal and Congregational Life. *Mysticism, saints, witness.*

Elizabeth Briere (Russian Orthodox Church) was formerly secretary of the Fellowship of St Alban and St Sergius, London, UK. *Fellowship of St Alban and St Sergius.*

Martien E. Brinkman (Reformed Churches in the Netherlands) is on the staff of the Interuniversity Institute for Missiological and Ecumenical Research, Utrecht, Netherlands. *Justification.*

Johannes Brosseder (Roman Catholic) is professor of systematic theology at the University of Cologne, Federal Republic of Germany. *Grace.*

Stuart E. Brown (Anglican Church of Canada), formerly executive secretary for Christian-Muslim relations with the WCC's Sub-unit on Dialogue with People of Living Faiths, is now general secretary of the Canadian Council of Churches, Toronto, Canada. *Muslim-Christian dialogue, North America: Canada.*

Douglas V. Brunson (Presbyterian Church (USA)) is general manager of the Ecumenical Development Co-operative Society, Amersfoort, Netherlands. *Ecumenical Development Co-operative Society.*

Colin Buchanan (Church of England) was suffragan bishop of the diocese of Birmingham, UK. *Anglican communion, Anglican Consultative Council, Lambeth Quadrilateral.*

Paul M. van Buren (Episcopal Church in the USA) is honorary professor of systematic theology at the University of Heidelberg, Federal Republic of Germany. *Israel and the church*.

Carnegie Samuel Calian (Presbyterian Church (USA)) is president and professor of theology at Pittsburgh Theological Seminary, PA, USA. *Orthodox-Reformed dialogue*.

Franklin Canelos C. (Evangelical Lutheran Church in Ecuador), formerly on the staff of the WCC's Ecumenical Church Loan Fund, is community development service secretary for Latin America and the Caribbean, Lutheran World Federation, Geneva, Switzerland. *Ecumenical Church Loan Fund*.

Kathleen Cann (Church of England) is archivist at the headquarters of the United Bible Societies, London, UK. *Bible Societies*.

John B. Carden (Church of England) was a missionary in Pakistan and later served as a priest in the diocese of Jerusalem. *Ecumenical Prayer Cycle, prayer in the ecumenical movement*.

Michael G. Cartwright (United Methodist Church) is assistant professor in the Department of Philosophy and Religious Studies, Allegheny College, Meadville, PA, USA. *Hermeneutics*.

Gwen Cashmore (Church of England), director of the WCC's Sub-unit on Renewal and Congregational Life from 1983 to 1986, is now co-director of the British Council of Churches' Centre for Ecumenical Spirituality in the UK. *Spirituality in the ecumenical movement*.

Emilio Castro (Evangelical Methodist Church in Uruguay) has been general secretary of the WCC since 1984. *Evangelism*.

Daniel Ciobotea (Romanian Orthodox Church) is archbishop of Iasi and metropolitan of Moldavia. *Trinity*.

Emmanuel Clapsis (Greek Orthodox Archdiocese of North and South America/Ecumenical Patriarchate) is professor of dogmatic theology at the Holy Cross Greek Orthodox School of Theology, Brookline, MA, USA. *Eschatology*.

William Clark (Salvation Army) is secretary for international external relations and Salvation Army representative with the WCC, London, UK. *Salvation Army*.

Raymond T. Clarke (United Reformed Church in the UK) chairs the United Reformed Church's national Forward Planning Group. *Welfare state*.

Olivier Clément (Orthodox Church, Ecumenical Patriarchate of Constantinople) is professor of theology at the Orthodox Theological Institute of St Sergius, Paris, France. *Athenagoras I.*

Paul de Clerck (Roman Catholic) is director of the Higher Institute of Liturgy, Paris, France, and professor at the Centre for Theological and Pastoral Studies, Brussels, Belgium. *Penance and reconciliation*.

Paul Clifford (Baptist Union of Great Britain) is a former president of the Selly Oak Colleges, Birmingham, UK. *Labour*.

Aldo Comba (Waldensian Church, Italy) is a part-time pastor in the National Protestant Church of Geneva, Switzerland. *Europe: Southern*.

James H. Cone (African Methodist Episcopal Church) is Briggs distinguished professor of systematic theology at Union Theological Seminary, New York, USA. *Ecumenical Association of Third-World Theologians*.

Martin Conway (Church of England) is president of the Selly Oak Colleges, Birmingham, UK. *Bonhoeffer, Dietrich; local ecumenism; Neill, Stephen Charles.*

Robert T. Coote (American Baptist Churches in the USA) is assistant to the director of the Overseas Ministries Study Center, New Haven, CT, USA. *Campus Crusade for Christ, evangelical missions, International Fellowship of Evangelical Students, Inter-Varsity Christian Fellowship, Lausanne Committee for World Evangelization, Lausanne covenant, World Evangelical Fellowship, World's Evangelical Alliance.*

Yvonne Craig (Church of England) is national adult education adviser at the General Synod Board of Education, London, UK. *Education, adult Christian.*

Martin H. Cressey (United Reformed Church in the UK) is principal of Westminster College, Cambridge, UK. *Baptist-Reformed dialogue, Reformed/Presbyterian churches.*

Rowan D. Crews, Jr (United Methodist Church) is an ordained elder in the North Carolina Conference and pastor of a church in Norlina, NC, USA. *Life and death, martyrdom, resurrection.*

Paul A. Crow, Jr (Christian Church (Disciples of Christ)) is president of the Council on Christian Unity, Indianapolis, IN, USA. *Covenanting; Disciples-Russian Orthodox dialogue; North America: United States of America.*

Olle Dahlén (Mission Covenant Church of Sweden) was moderator of the WCC's Commission of the Churches on International Affairs from 1971 to 1982. *Parties, political.*

Horace Dammers (Church of England) was dean of Bristol and founder of the Life-style Movement. *Life-style.*

Kenith A. David (Church of the Province of Southern Africa — Anglican) is co-ordinator of Urban Rural Mission in the WCC's Commission on World Mission and Evangelism. *Rural Agricultural Mission, Urban Industrial Mission, Urban Rural Mission.*

Kortright Davis (Church of the Province of the West Indies — Anglican) is professor of systematic theology at Howard University Divinity School, Washington, DC, USA. *Caribbean.*

Rex Davis (Church of England) is subdean of Lincoln cathedral, Lincoln, UK. *Renewal.*

Volkmar Deile (Evangelical Church in Berlin-Brandenburg) is general secretary of Amnesty International for the Federal Republic of Germany, Bonn, FRG. *Amnesty International.*

John Deschner (United Methodist Church) is Lehman professor of Christian doctrine at the Southern Methodist University, Dallas, TX, USA, and moderator of the WCC's Commission on Faith and Order. *Hope, unity of humankind.*

Richard D.N. Dickinson (United Church of Christ) is president of Christian Theological Seminary, Indianapolis, IN, USA, and moderator of the WCC's Commission on the Churches' Participation in Development. *Development, poverty.*

Thomas Hartley Dorris (Evangelical Lutheran Church in America) is editor of the WCC's *Ecumenical Press Service. Ecumenical Press Service.*

Rob van Drimmelen (Reformed Churches in the Netherlands) is executive secretary for socio-economic programmes in the WCC's Commission on the Churches' Participation in Development. *Food crisis/hunger, investment, transnational corporations, unemployment.*

Ulrich Duchrow (Evangelical Church of Baden) is regional secretary for mission and ecumenism of his church, Heidelberg, Federal Republic of Germany. *Justice.*

Avery Dulles (Roman Catholic) is professor emeritus of theology at the Catholic University of America, Washington, DC, USA. *Communion, images of the church.*

André Dumas (Reformed Church of France) was professor of philosophy and ethics at the Protestant Faculty of Theology, Paris, France. *Birth control, marriage.*

Francine Dumas (Reformed Church of France) was national secretary of the "Young Women" (Jeunes femmes) movement, and director of studies at the school of social service "Faith and Life" (Foi et vie) in Paris, France. *Divorce.*

Suzanne Eck (Roman Catholic) is Dominican sister at Weesen, Switzerland. *Asceticism.*

Brother Emile (Roman Catholic) is a member of the Taizé community, France. *Taizé community.*

Kaj Engström (Church of Sweden) is director of the Swedish Ecumenical Institute, Sigtuna, Sweden. *Europe: Northern.*

Philippe Fanchette (Roman Catholic) is executive secretary for adult basic education in the WCC's Sub-unit on Education. *Education, adult.*

Vivienne Faull (Church of England) is an Anglican deacon and chaplain at Clare College, Cambridge, UK. *Inclusive language.*

John Fife (Presbyterian Church (USA)) is pastor of a Presbyterian church in Tucson, AZ, USA, and a leading figure in the US sanctuary movement.

Mabel Fillipini (Evangelical Methodist Church of Argentina) is executive secretary of the Centre for Christian Studies, Buenos Aires, Argentina. *South America: Río de la Plata region.*

Balthasar Fischer (Roman Catholic) was director of the Liturgical Institute, Trier, Federal Republic of Germany. *Liturgical reforms.*

Thomas FitzGerald (Greek Orthodox Archdiocese of North and South America/Ecumenical Patriarchate) is associate professor of religious studies and history at Hellenic College — Holy Cross Greek Orthodox School of Theology, Brookline, MA, USA. *Encyclicals, Orthodox.*

Joseph A. Fitzmyer (Roman Catholic) is professor emeritus in the Biblical Studies Department, Catholic University of America, Washington, DC, USA. *Exegesis, methods of.*

William T. Flynn (Lutheran Church (Missouri Synod)) is assistant professor of church music and liturgy at Emory University, Atlanta, GA, USA. *Church music.*

William F. Fore (United Methodist Church) has served as president of the World Association of Christian Communication, and assistant general secretary for communications with the National Council of the Churches of Christ in the USA. *Electronic church.*

Charles W. Forman (Presbyterian Church (USA)) was professor of missions at Yale Divinity School, New Haven, CT, USA. *Pacific, Pacific Council of Churches.*

Roger T. Forster is the leader of Ichthus Christian Fellowship house-church movement in Great Britain. *House church.*

Ian Fraser (Church of Scotland) is research consultant to the Scottish Churches Council, Edinburgh, UK. *Tourism.*

Dean Freiday (Religious Society of Friends) is a member of the Christian and Interfaith Relations Committee of Friends General Conference, Philadelphia, PA, USA. *Friends/Quakers*.

Albert H. Friedlander (Jewish) is dean of Leo Baeck College and minister of Westminster synagogue, London, UK. *Antisemitism*.

Paul R. Fries (Reformed Church in America) is professor of theology and academic dean at New Brunswick Theological Seminary, NJ, USA. *Lutheran-Reformed dialogue*.

Francis Frost (Roman Catholic) is lecturer at the Ecumenical Institute, Bossey, Switzerland. *Methodism*.

Raymond Fung (Hong Kong Baptist Convention) is secretary for evangelism in the WCC's Commission on World Mission and Evangelism. *Asia: China; house church*.

E. Clinton Gardner (United Methodist Church) is professor of Christian ethics, Candler School of Theology, Emory University, Atlanta, GA, USA. *Abortion*.

Günther Gassmann (Evangelical Lutheran Church of North Elbia) is director of the WCC's Sub-unit on Faith and Order. *Faith and Order, unity*.

Hans Gensichen (Evangelical Church in Baden) is professor emeritus of the history of religions and missiology at the University of Heidelberg, Federal Republic of Germany. *Pluralism*.

K.M. George (Malankara Orthodox Syrian Church) is lecturer at the Ecumenical Institute, Bossey, Switzerland. *Oriental Orthodox-Orthodox dialogue*.

Ursula Gieseke (Evangelical Church of the Rhineland) is assistant at the University of Heidelberg, Federal Republic of Germany. *People of God*.

David Gill (Uniting Church in Australia) is general secretary of the Australian Council of Churches, Sydney, Australia. *Violence and nonviolence*.

Alec Gilmore (Baptist Union of Great Britain) is director of Feed the Minds, London, UK. *Christian literature, Christian Literature Fund*.

Donald K. Gorrell (United Methodist Church) is professor of church history at the United Theological Seminary, Dayton, OH, USA. *Social gospel movement*.

David Gosling (Church of England), director of the WCC's Church and Society Sub-unit from 1984 to 1988, is on the staff of Great St Mary's University Church, Cambridge, UK. *Pollution*.

Niels Henrik Gregersen (Evangelical Lutheran Church of Denmark) is associate professor of dogmatics at the University of Aarhus, Denmark. *Providence*.

Paulos Mar Gregorios (Malankara Orthodox Syrian Church) is metropolitan of his church for Delhi and the North, and head of the Delhi Orthodox Centre, New Delhi, India. *Nature*.

Carl-Henric Grenholm (Church of Sweden) is university lecturer in ethics at the University of Uppsala, Sweden. *Responsible society*.

Aloys Grillmeier (Roman Catholic) is professor emeritus of dogmatics and the history of dogma at the Jesuit Faculty of Philosophy and Theology, Frankfurt, Federal Republic of Germany. He was a consultant at Vatican II. *Chalcedon*.

Jeffrey Gros (Roman Catholic) is director of the Commission on Faith and Order of the National Council of the Churches of Christ in the USA, New York, USA. *Creeds*.

Pamela H. Gruber (United Reformed Church in the UK) is secretary for the international and development affairs committee of the Board for Social Responsibility, General Synod of the Church of England, London, UK. *Interchurch aid.*

Charles W. Gusmer (Roman Catholic) is professor of sacramental theology and liturgy at the Immaculate Conception Seminary, Seton Hall University, South Orange, NJ, USA. *Anointing of the sick.*

John Habgood (Church of England) is archbishop of York, UK. *Nature.*

Sergei Hackel (Russian Orthodox Church) teaches at Sussex University, UK, and works at the BBC world service. *Sobornost.*

Theresia Hainthaler (Roman Catholic) is research worker at the institute for the history of dogma and the councils, the Jesuit Faculty of Philosophy and Theology, Frankfurt, Federal Republic of Germany. *Chalcedon.*

Douglas John Hall (United Church of Canada) is professor of Christian theology in the faculty of religious studies, McGill University, Montreal, PQ, Canada. *Creation.*

Béla Harmati (Lutheran Church in Hungary) is bishop of his church in Budapest, Hungary. *Civil religion, property.*

Richard Harries (Church of England) is bishop of Oxford, UK. *Jewish-Christian dialogue.*

Elizabeth J. Harris (Methodist Church of Great Britain) is researcher at Tulana Research Centre, Kelaniya, Sri Lanka. *Buddhist-Christian dialogue.*

Susannah Harris-Wilson (Episcopal Church, USA) is principal of the Lahore College of Arts and Sciences, Pakistan. *Chakko, Sarah.*

Dorothy Harvey (Presbyterian Church of New Zealand), an ordained minister, has worked at the Christian Conference of Asia and the World Council of Churches. *Participation.*

Josine Hautfenne (Roman Catholic) is secretary general of the International Ecumenical Fellowship, Brussels, Belgium. *International Ecumenical Fellowship.*

Sione 'Amanaki Havea (Methodist Church in Tonga) is president of his church, based in Nuku'alofa, Tonga. *Theology, Pacific.*

Håkan Hellberg (Evangelical Lutheran Church of Finland), formerly on the staff of the WCC's Christian Medical Commission, is editor-in-chief of the leading Swedish language daily paper in Finland. *Health care.*

Patrick Henry (Christian Church (Disciples of Christ)) is executive director of the Institute for Ecumenical and Cultural Research, Collegeville, MN, USA. *Institute for Ecumenical and Cultural Research.*

Alasdair Heron (Reformed Church in North-Western Germany and Bavaria) is professor of Reformed theology at the Evangelical-Theological Faculty, University of Erlangen, Federal Republic of Germany. *Filioque.*

Frederick Herzog (United Church of Christ) is professor of systematic theology at Duke University, Durham, NC, USA. *Poor; status confessionis; theology, North American.*

Henry Hill (Anglican Church of Canada) is Anglican co-chairman for Anglican-Oriental Orthodox relations. *Anglican-Oriental Orthodox dialogue.*

David Hilton (United Methodist Church, USA) is associate director of the WCC's Christian Medical Commission. *Health and healing*.

E. Glenn Hinson (Southern Baptist Convention) is David T. Porter professor of church history at the Southern Baptist Theological Seminary, Louisville, KY, USA. *Church order*.

Norman Hjelm (Evangelical Lutheran Church in America) is director of the Department of Communications, Lutheran World Federation, Geneva, Switzerland. *Lutheran World Federation*.

Peter Hocken (Roman Catholic) is a member of the Mother of God Community in Gaithersburg, MD, USA. *Charismatic movement, Pentecostal-Roman Catholic dialogue, Pentecostals*.

Libertus A. Hoedemaker (Netherlands Reformed Church) is professor of ecumenics, missiology and Christian ethics at the State University of Groningen, Netherlands. *Church and world, local church*.

David R. Holeton (Anglican Church of Canada) is professor of liturgics at Trinity College, Toronto, Canada. *Chrismation, confirmation*.

Mary Holliday (Methodist Church of Great Britain) was head of the Farncombe Ecumenical Community, UK, and chaplain to the Swanwick 1987 "Not Strangers but Pilgrims" conference of the interchurch process. *Intercession*.

Ludger Honnefelder (Roman Catholic) is professor of philosophy and director of the Institute for Philosophy, University of Bonn, Federal Republic of Germany. *Conscience*.

Geertruida van Hoogevest (Dutch Reformed Church) was co-ordinator of the WCC's refugee service from 1975 to 1986. *Asylum, refugees*.

Robert Hotz (Roman Catholic) works in the department for Eastern affairs at the Institute for Philosophy and Theology, Zurich, Switzerland. *Sacraments*.

François Houtart (Roman Catholic) is professor of sociology at the Catholic University of Louvain, and director of the international journal for socio-religious studies *Social Compass*, Louvain, Belgium. *Colonialism*.

Richard L. van Houten (Christian Reformed Church in North America) is general secretary of the Reformed Ecumenical Council, Grand Rapids, MI, USA. *Reformed Ecumenical Council*.

Anton Houtepen (Roman Catholic) is director of the Interuniversity Institute for Missiological and Ecumenical Research, Utrecht, and professor of fundamental theology at Erasmus University, Rotterdam, Netherlands. *Common confession, faith, reception, teaching authority*.

Victor W.C. Hsu (Presbyterian Church (USA)) is director of the East Asia/Pacific Office of the National Council of the Churches of Christ in the USA, New York, USA. *Non-governmental organizations*.

Heikki Huttunen (Orthodox Church of Finland), director of the WCC's Sub-unit on Youth from 1985 to 1989, is now a parish priest of his church in Helsinki, Finland. *Syndesmos*.

Nat Idarous (Evangelical Lutheran Church in Tanzania) is acting director for administration at the All Africa Conference of Churches, Nairobi, Kenya, and director of the department of church co-operation and interfaith dialogue. *All Africa Conference of Churches*.

C.I. Itty (Malankara Orthodox Syrian Church) was for many years on the staff of the WCC, from 1970 to 1979 as director of the Commission on the Churches' Participation in Development. *Just, participatory and sustainable society*.

André Jacques (Reformed Church of France) is president of ACAT — Action of Christians for the Abolition of Torture, Paris, France. *Barot, Madeleine; CIMADE, migration.*

Willie J. Jennings (Independent Bermuda Baptist) is lecturer in theology and black church studies at the Divinity School, Duke University, Durham, NC, USA. *Person, reconciliation.*

Ottmar John (Roman Catholic) is professor at Wilhelms University of Westfalia, Münster, Federal Republic of Germany. *Subsidiarity.*

Lynda Katsuno (United Church of Canada) is special adviser on issues of disabilities with the WCC's Sub-unit on Education. *Disabled.*

William B. Kennedy (Presbyterian Church (USA)) is professor of practical theology, religion and education at Union Theological Seminary, New York, USA. *World Council of Christian Education.*

Eileen King (Roman Catholic) is administrative secretary for the international committee for the World Day of Prayer, New York, USA. *World Day of Prayer.*

Michael Kinnamon (Christian Church (Disciples of Christ)) is dean and associate professor of theology and ecumenical studies at Lexington Theological Seminary, KY, USA. *United and uniting churches.*

Aloys Klein (Roman Catholic) is director of the Johann-Adam-Möhler Institute for Ecumenics, Paderborn, Federal Republic of Germany. *Institute for Ecumenics.*

Klaus K. Klostermaier (Roman Catholic) is professor and head of the Department of Religion, and director of the Asian Studies Centre, Faculty of Arts, University of Manitoba, Canada. *Hindu-Christian dialogue.*

Alexis Kniazeff (Orthodox Church, Ecumenical Patriarchate of Constantinople) is rector of the Orthodox Theological Institute of St Sergius, Paris, France. *Apostasy, heresy, schism.*

Ninan Koshy (Church of South India) is director of the WCC's Commission of the Churches on International Affairs. *Asia: South; militarism/militarization; religious liberty; third world; United Nations.*

Una Kroll (Church of England) is a deaconess and a medical doctor. *Generation conflict.*

Hanfried Krüger (Evangelical Church in Germany) is professor of ecumenics at the University of Mainz, Federal Republic of Germany. *Söderblom, Nathan.*

Ulrich Kühn (Evangelical Lutheran Church of Saxony) is professor of systematic theology at the Theological Seminary of Leipzig, German Democratic Republic, and at the University of Vienna, Austria. *Salvation.*

Régis Ladous (Roman Catholic) is professor of modern history at the University of Lyons III, France. *Spiritual ecumenism.*

Thomas A. Langford (United Methodist Church) is W.K. Quick professor of theology and Methodist studies at Duke University, Durham, NC, USA. *Lutheran-Methodist dialogue.*

Emmanuel Lanne (Roman Catholic) is a monk at the Benedictine monastery of Chevetogne, Belgium, and a member of the WCC's Commission on Faith and Order. *Apostles' Creed, apostolic tradition, baptism, conciliarity, typoi.*

Bernard Lauret (Roman Catholic) is on the staff of Editions du Cerf publishing house, Paris, France. *"Theology, new"*.

Christine Ledger (Anglican Church of Australia) is co-secretary general of the World Student Christian Federation, Geneva, Switzerland. *World Student Christian Federation*.

Peter L'Huillier (Orthodox Church in America) is archbishop of New York, and professor of canon law, St Vladimir's Seminary, Crestwood, NY, USA. *Economy (oikonomia), excommunication*.

Gennadios Limouris (Orthodox Church, Ecumenical Patriarchate of Constantinople) is an executive secretary in the WCC's Sub-unit on Faith and Order. *Constantinople, first council of; Nicea; Nicene Creed*.

George Lindbeck (Evangelical Lutheran Church of America) is Pitkin professor of historical theology, Yale University, New Haven, CT, USA. *Dogma*.

Jan Milic Lochman (Swiss Protestant Church Federation) is professor of systematic theology at the University of Basel, Switzerland. *Atheism*.

Paul Löffler (Evangelical Church of Hessen and Nassau) is director of the Board of Mission and Ecumenical Relations of his church in Frankfurt, Federal Republic of Germany. *Conversion, proselytism*.

Bradley J. Longfield (Presbyterian Church (USA)) is a visiting assistant professor in the history of American Christianity at the Divinity School, Duke University, Durham, NC, USA. *Creationism, fundamentalists*.

Sergio M.P. López (Methodist Church in Brazil) is regional secretary for Brazil of the Latin American Council of Churches. *Latin American Council of Churches*.

Werner Löser (Roman Catholic) is professor of dogmatics at the Jesuit Faculty of Philosophy and Theology, Frankfurt, Federal Republic of Germany. *European unity*.

André Lossky (Orthodox) is assistant at the Institute of Biblical Sciences, Faculty of Theology, University of Lausanne, Switzerland. *Epiclesis*.

Nicholas Lossky, editor. *Eastern Orthodoxy; icon/image; Lossky, Vladimir; Orthodoxy; theology, ecumenical*.

Denton Lotz (American Baptist Churches in the USA/Southern Baptist Convention) is general secretary of the Baptist World Alliance with headquarters in McLean, VA, USA. *Baptist World Alliance, Baptists*.

Steven G. Mackie (Church of Scotland) is lecturer in practical theology and Christian ethics, University of St Andrews, Scotland. *Church as institution*.

John Macquarrie (Church of England) is Lady Margaret professor emeritus of divinity, Oxford University, England. *Anthropology, theological*.

Jorge E. Maldonado (Covenant Church of Ecuador) is executive secretary for the programme on family education in the WCC's Sub-unit on Education. *Family, marriage*.

Jonathan M. Mann (Jewish), until recently director of the global programme on AIDS, World Health Organization, Geneva, Switzerland, is now director of the International AIDS Centre at Harvard University AIDS Institute, Cambridge, MA, USA. *AIDS*.

Daniel F. Martensen (Evangelical Lutheran Church in America) is associate director of the Office for Ecumenical Affairs of his church, Chicago, IL, USA. *Lutheran-Orthodox dialogue.*

Melanie A. May (Church of the Brethren) is ecumenical officer for her church, Elgin, IL, USA. *Brethren.*

Jean Mayland (Church of England) is president of the Ecumenical Forum of European Christian Women, UK. *Europe: Western.*

Ali A. Mazrui is Albert Schweitzer professor in the humanities, State University of New York at Binghamton; professor at the University of Michigan, Ann Arbor; and Andrew D. White professor-at-large, Cornell University, Ithaca, NY, USA. *Decolonization.*

John S. Mbiti (Church of the Province of Kenya), director of the Ecumenical Institute, Bossey, from 1974 to 1978, teaches Christianity and African religions at the University of Bern and is pastor in Burgdorf, Switzerland. *Indigenous religions; theology, African.*

Richard P. McBrien (Roman Catholic) is chairman of the department of theology at the University of Notre Dame, IN, USA. *Roman Catholic Church.*

Monique McClellan (Presbyterian Church (USA)) is press officer and audio producer with the WCC's Department of Communication. *Intervox.*

Hugh McCullum (United Church of Canada) is head of information, Southern African Research and Documentation Unit, Harare, Zimbabwe. *Homosexuality.*

Kevin McDonald (Roman Catholic) is a delegate at the Pontifical Council for Promoting Christian Unity, Vatican City. *Anglican-Roman Catholic dialogue.*

Roger Mehl (Reformed Church of Alsace and Lorraine) is emeritus professor of ethics and sociology of Protestantism at the Faculty of Protestant Theology, University of Social Sciences, Strasbourg, France. *Law, Protestantism.*

Gerhard Meier (Roman Catholic) is secretary general of Caritas Internationalis, Vatican City. *Caritas Internationalis.*

Antonio G. Mendonça (Independent Presbyterian Church of Brazil) is professor of the sociology of religion at the Ecumenical Centre for Postgraduate Studies on Religious Sciences, Sao Bernardo do Campo's Nucleus, Brazil. *South America: Brazil.*

John Meyendorff (Orthodox Church in America) is dean of St Vladimir's Orthodox Theological Seminary, Crestwood, NY, USA, and professor at Fordham University, Bronx, NY, USA. *Patristics.*

Paul Meyendorff (Orthodox Church in America) is assistant professor of liturgical theology at St Vladimir's Orthodox Theological Seminary, Crestwood, NY, USA. *Liturgy.*

Harding Meyer (Evangelical Lutheran Church of Hanover) is research professor at the Institute for Ecumenical Research, Strasbourg, France. *Dialogue, bilateral; reconciled diversity.*

José Míguez Bonino, editor. *Conflict; ethics; fascism; imperialism; land; land and the state of Israel; land reform; Medellín; middle axioms; national security; natural law; praxis; South America: Andean region; theology, liberation; totalitarianism.*

Larry Miller (Evangelical Mennonite Churches in France) is executive secretary of the Mennonite World Conference, Strasbourg, France. *Mennonite World Conference, Mennonites.*

Gerald F. Moede (United Methodist Church), now a pastor in Wisconsin, was general secretary of the Consultation on Church Union, Princeton, NJ, USA. *Consultation on Church Union.*

Paul Mojzes (United Methodist Church) is professor of religious studies at Rosemont College, Rosemont, PA, USA, and co-editor of the *Journal of Ecumenical Studies*. *Socialism.*

Elisabeth Moltmann-Wendel (Evangelical Church in Württemberg) is a writer on the church and feminist theology living in the Federal Republic of Germany. *Feminism.*

Cyris Moon (Presbyterian Church of Korea) is director of the Hanmi Christian Academy, Palmdale, CA, USA. *People.*

Lewis S. Mudge (Presbyterian Church (USA)) is dean and professor of theology, San Francisco Theological Seminary, and professor in the doctoral faculty, Graduate Theological Union, Berkeley, CA, USA. *Ministry in the church.*

Jesse N.K. Mugambi (Church of the Province of Kenya — Anglican) is lecturer in philosophy and religious studies, University of Nairobi, Kenya. *Environment/ecology.*

Geiko Müller-Fahrenholz (Evangelical Lutheran Church of North Elbia) is professor of peace ethics, University for Peace, Escazu, Costa Rica. *History, prophecy, salvation history.*

Walter Müller-Römheld (Evangelical Church of Germany) is director of the publishing house Verlag Otto Lembeck, Frankfurt, Federal Republic of Germany. *de Diétrich, Suzanne.*

Roland E. Murphy (Roman Catholic) is G.W. Ivey professor emeritus of biblical studies at Duke University, Durham, NC, USA. *Old Testament and Christian unity.*

Owen Nankivell (Methodist Church of Great Britain) is executive director of the Hinksey Centre, Oxford, UK. *Capitalism.*

J. Robert Nelson (United Methodist Church) is director of the Institute of Religion, Texas Medical Centre, Houston, TX, USA. *Bio-ethics.*

Richard John Neuhaus (Roman Catholic) is director of the Institute on Religion and Public Life, New York, USA. *Hartford appeal.*

Peter Neuner (Roman Catholic) is professor of dogmatics at the Catholic Faculty of Theology, University of Munich, Federal Republic of Germany. *Anathemas; dialogue, intrafaith.*

Lesslie Newbigin (United Reformed Church in the UK) was for many years a missionary and bishop in the Church of South India, and director of the International Missionary Council from 1959 to 1961. *Niles, Daniel Thambyrajah; union, organic; unity of "all in each place".*

Leopoldo J. Niilus (United Evangelical Lutheran Church of Argentina) is representative of the Middle East Council of Churches at the Ecumenical Centre, Geneva, Switzerland. *Middle East, Middle East Council of Churches.*

D. Preman Niles (Christian Church (Disciples of Christ)) is director of the WCC's programme on Justice, Peace and the Integrity of Creation. *Justice, peace and the integrity of creation.*

Peder Norgaard-Højen (Evangelical Lutheran Church of Denmark) is professor of dogmatics and ecumenical theology at the University of Copenhagen, Denmark. *Sin.*

Mercy Amba Oduyoye (Methodist Church in Nigeria) is a deputy general secretary of the WCC. *Anthropology, African.*

Daniel Olivier (Roman Catholic) is professor of Luther studies at the Catholic Institute, Paris, France. *Holiness, sanctification.*

Milan Opocensky (Evangelical Church of Czech Brethren) is general secretary of the World Alliance of Reformed Churches, Geneva, Switzerland. *Christian Peace Conference.*

Raymond Oppenheim (Church of Aotearoa/New Zealand) is ecumenical officer for his diocese. *New Zealand.*

Helen Oppenheimer (Church of England) is a writer on Christian ethics and a member of several Church of England commissions on marriage. *Ethics, sexual.*

Levi V. Oración (United Church of Christ in the Philippines) is executive secretary for theological studies in the WCC's Commission on the Churches' Participation in Development. *Asia: Southeast; people.*

Nicolas Ossorguine (Orthodox Church, Ecumenical Patriarchate of Constantinople) is professor of liturgy at the Orthodox Theological Institute of St Sergius, Paris, France. *Church calendar.*

Geevarghese Mar Osthathios (Malankara Orthodox Syrian Church) is metropolitan at Niranam and teaches at the Orthodox Theological Seminary, Kottayam, India. *Oriental Orthodox churches.*

Priscilla Padolina (United Methodist Church) is programme secretary for women and rural development in the WCC's Sub-unit on Women in Church and Society. *Ecumenical Decade of the Churches in Solidarity with Women.*

Martin Parmentier (Old Catholic Church of the Netherlands) is lecturer in early church history, patristics and the history of dogma at the Roman Catholic Theological University, Amsterdam, Netherlands. *Old Catholic Church, Old Catholic-Orthodox dialogue.*

Geoffrey Parrinder (Methodist Church of Great Britain) is professor emeritus of the comparative study of religions at the University of London, UK. *Scriptures.*

Constance F. Parvey (Evangelical Lutheran Church in America) was director of the WCC's Community of Women and Men in the Church study, and is now pastor of a church in Jericho, VT, USA. *Community of Women and Men in the Church.*

Janos Pasztor (Reformed Church in Hungary) is programme officer responsible for energy, UN Environment Programme, Nairobi, Kenya. *Energy.*

Harvey Perkins (Uniting Church in Australia) served both the WCC and the CCA in the area of development and service. *Tourism.*

William A. Perkins (Episcopal Church — USA) is executive secretary for assembly administration in the WCC's seventh assembly office. *International Christian Youth Exchange, youth.*

Arturo Piedra (Federation of Evangelical Churches in Costa Rica) is professor of church history at the Latin American Biblical Seminary, San José, Costa Rica. *Central America.*

N. Barney Pityana (Church of the Province of Southern Africa — Anglican) is director of the WCC's Programme to Combat Racism. *Racism.*

John S. Pobee, editor. *Africa; African Instituted (Independent) Churches; All Africa Conference of Churches; education and renewal; Gatu, John; Ibiam, Francis Akanu; International Association of Mission Studies; Matthews, Zachariah Keodirelang; polygamy; redemption; theology, black; theology by the people; theology, contextual.*

Elisabeth Pontoppidan (Reformed Church of France) is prioress of the Community of Pomeyrol, St-Etienne-du-Gres, France. *Theotokos.*

Maria Teresa Porcile Santiso (Roman Catholic) is professor of biblical theology and Mariology at the Theological Institute of Uruguay, Montevideo, Uruguay. *Magnificat.*

Philip A. Potter (Methodist Church in the Caribbean and the Americas), general secretary of the WCC from 1972 to 1984, teaches at the United Theological College of the West Indies, Kingston, Jamaica. *Covenant, mission.*

David N. Power (Roman Catholic) is professor of systematic theology at the Catholic University of America, Washington, DC, USA. *Episcopacy, ordination, presbyterate, priesthood.*

David J. Pullinger (Church of England) is director of the Society, Religion and Technology Project of the Church of Scotland, Edinburgh, Scotland. *Technology.*

Joan Puls (Roman Catholic), a Franciscan sister, has written extensively on spirituality, and is co-director of the British Council of Churches' Centre for Ecumenical Spirituality. *Spirituality in the ecumenical movement.*

John A. Radano (Roman Catholic) is delegate for the Western section of the Pontifical Council for Promoting Christian Unity, the Vatican. *Baptist-Roman Catholic international conversations.*

Konrad Raiser (Evangelical Church in Germany), a former deputy general secretary of the WCC, is professor of systematic theology and ecumenics at the Faculty of Protestant Theology, Ruhr University, Bochum, Federal Republic of Germany. *Holy Spirit in ecumenical thought, international order, oikoumene, theology in the ecumenical movement.*

Ruth Reardon (Roman Catholic) is secretary of the Association of Interchurch Families, Haywards Heath, UK. *Association of Interchurch Families.*

Hans-Diether Reimer (Evangelical Church in Germany) is a theologian at the Protestant Central Agency for Religious and Ideological Issues, Stuttgart, Federal Republic of Germany. *Sects.*

J.S. Reinders (Reformed Churches in the Netherlands) is professor at the Faculty of Theology, Free University, Amsterdam, Netherlands. *Euthanasia.*

Russell E. Richey (United Methodist Church) is associate dean for academic programmes at the Divinity School, and research professor of church history, Duke University, Durham, NC, USA. *Denominationalism.*

Cecil M. Robeck, Jr (Assemblies of God) is associate dean for academic programmes and associate professor of church history, Fuller Theological Seminary, Pasadena, CA, USA. *Charism(ata).*

Ronald G. Roberson (Roman Catholic) is on the staff of the Pontifical Council for Promoting Christian Unity, the Vatican. *Oriental Orthodox-Roman Catholic dialogue, Orthodox-Roman Catholic dialogue.*

Jean Rogues (Roman Catholic), formerly professor of ecumenical theology and director of the Higher Institute for Ecumenical Studies at the Catholic Institute of Paris, France, is parish priest of Notre-Dame-des-Champs, Paris, France. *Laity/clergy.*

Michael Root (Evangelical Lutheran Church in America) is research professor at the Institute for Ecumenical Research, Strasbourg, France. *Lutheran-Roman Catholic dialogue.*

Peter Rottländer (Roman Catholic) works in theological research at Misereor, Aachen, Federal Republic of Germany. *Solidarity.*

Theodore Runyon (United Methodist Church) is professor of systematic theology at Candler School of Theology, Emory University, Atlanta, GA, USA. *Theology, political.*

William G. Rusch (Evangelical Lutheran Church in America) is executive director of the Office for Ecumenical Affairs of his church, Chicago, IL, USA. *Athanasian Creed, Baptist-Lutheran dialogue.*

Horace Russell (Jamaica Baptist Union), formerly principal of the United Theological College, Kingston, Jamaica, is now teaching at the Eastern Baptist Theological Seminary, Philadelphia, PA, USA. *Caribbean Conference of Churches.*

Saïd Elias Saïd (Roman Catholic Church, France, and Maronite Church of Saïda, Lebanon) is anesthesiologist, theologian and canonist. *Canon law.*

Julio H. de Santa Ana (Evangelical Methodist Church in Brazil) is director of the Ecumenical Centre for Evangelism and Popular Education, and professor of the sociology of religion at the Ecumenical Centre for Postgraduate Studies on Religious Sciences, Sao Paulo, Brazil. *Debt crisis, dependence, economics.*

Gerhard Sauter (Evangelical Church in the Rhineland) is professor of systematic theology and director of the Ecumenical Institute, Faculty of Protestant Theology, University of Bonn, Federal Republic of Germany. *Stuttgart declaration, war guilt.*

Jill Schaeffer (Presbyterian Church (USA)) is an executive secretary in the World Alliance of Reformed Churches, Geneva, Switzerland. *World Alliance of Reformed Churches.*

William F. Schulz is president of the Unitarian Universalist Association of Congregations, Boston, MA, USA. *International Association for Religious Freedom, Unitarian Universalism, Unitarian Universalist Association.*

Juan Schwindt (Evangelical Church of the River Plate) is regional secretary for the River Plate region of the Latin American Council of Churches, Argentina. *Latin American Council of Churches.*

Alan P.F. Sell (United Reformed Church in the UK) holds the chair of Christian thought at the Department of Religious Studies, University of Calgary, Canada. *Anglican-Reformed dialogue, congregationalism.*

Bernard Sesboüé (Roman Catholic) is professor of theology at the Faculty of Theology of Centre-Sèvres, Paris, France. *Authority, Groupe des Dombes.*

Wilbert R. Shenk (Mennonite Church) is director of the missionary training centre, Associated Mennonite Biblical Seminaries, Elkhart, IN, USA. *Church growth.*

Roger L. Shinn (United Church of Christ) is Reinhold Niebuhr professor emeritus of social ethics at Union Theological Seminary, New York, USA. *Revolution, science and technology, scientific world-view.*

Werner Simpfendörfer (Evangelical Church of Württemberg) was executive secretary of the Ecumenical Association of Academies and Laity Centres in Europe, Bad Boll, Federal Republic of Germany. *Academies, lay.*

Jeane Sindab (Progressive National Baptist Convention) is an executive secretary with the WCC's Programme to Combat Racism. *Indigenous peoples.*

Baldwin Sjollema (Netherlands Reformed Church) was the first director of the WCC's Programme to Combat Racism, then co-ordinator of the anti-apartheid programme of the International Labour Office. *Land rights, Programme to Combat Racism.*

Jean Skuse (Uniting Church in Australia), general secretary of the Australian Council of Churches 1976-88, is national co-ordinator for the WCC's seventh assembly in Canberra, 1991. *Australia.*

D.J. Smit (Dutch Reformed Mission Church) is professor of systematic theology and ethics at the University of the Western Cape, Bellville, South Africa. *Inspiration, kingdom of God, liberty/freedom, order.*

D. Moody Smith (United Methodist Church) is George Washington Ivey professor of New Testament at Duke University, Durham, NC, USA. *New Testament and Christian Unity.*

Dorothee Sölle (Evangelical Lutheran Church of North Elbia) is a theologian and writer living in Hamburg, Federal Republic of Germany, and visiting professor of systematic theology at Union Theological Seminary, New York, USA. *Suffering.*

Choan-Seng Song (Presbyterian Church in Taiwan) is professor of theology and Asian cultures, Pacific School of Religion, Berkeley, CA, USA. *Culture.*

Pablo Sosa (Evangelical Methodist Church of Argentina) is professor of music and liturgy at the Higher Evangelical Institute of Theological Studies (ISEDET), Buenos Aires, Argentina. *Hymns.*

Marc Spindler (Netherlands Reformed Church) is professor of missiology and ecumenics at the State University of Leiden and the State University of Utrecht, Netherlands. *Diaspora.*

Peter Staples (Church of England) is senior lecturer in contemporary church history and ecumenics at the University of Utrecht, Netherlands. *Apostolicity, catholicity.*

Elaine Hesse Steel (Church of England) is general secretary of the World YWCA, Geneva, Switzerland. *World Young Women's Christian Associations.*

David Steinmetz (United Methodist Church) is A.R. Kearns professor of the history of Christianity and director of the Center for Medieval and Renaissance Studies at Duke University, Durham, NC, USA. *Reformation.*

Alfred Stirnemann (Roman Catholic) is general secretary of the Pro Oriente Institute, Vienna, Austria. *Pro Oriente.*

Tom Stransky, editor. *Beauduin, Lambert; Catholic Conference for Ecumenical Questions; Chevetogne; CIDSE; collegiality; common witness; Congar, Yves; criticism of the ecumenical movement and of the WCC; Decree on Ecumenism; Ecumenical Directory; encyclicals; encyclicals, Roman Catholic; Evangelical-Roman Catholic Dialogue on Mission; Focolare movement; Friends World Committee for Consultation; "hierarchy of truths"; International Missionary Council; John XXIII; John Paul II; Joint Working Group; missio Dei; missionary societies; Paul VI; Pax Christi; Pax Romana; religious communities; Roman Catholic Church and pre-Vatican II ecumenism; Secretariat for Promoting Christian Unity; SEDOS; social encyclicals, papal; SODEPAX; Tantur, Ecumenical Institute; Trent, council of; UNIAPAC; Vatican Councils I and II; World Catholic Federation for the Biblical Apostolate; World Council of Churches.*

Kitty Strong (United Church of Christ) was a staff member of the World YWCA. *World Young Women's Christian Associations.*

David Kwang-sun Suh (Presbyterian Church of Korea) is professor of theology at Ewha Womans University, Seoul, Korea. *Theology, minjung.*

Theo Sundermeier (Evangelical Church of Baden) is professor of comparative religion and missiology at the University of Heidelberg, Federal Republic of Germany. *Religion.*

Masao Takenaka (United Church of Christ in Japan) is professor of Christian ethics, Doshisha University, Kyoto, Japan. *Art in the ecumenical movement.*

Mary Tanner (Church of England) is theological secretary of the Board for Mission and Unity, General Synod of the Church of England, London, UK. *Ordination of women.*

John B. Taylor (Methodist Church of Great Britain), director of the WCC's Sub-unit on Dialogue from 1980 to 1983, is secretary general of the World Conference on Religion and Peace, Geneva, Switzerland. *World Conference on Religion and Peace.*

Rudolf Teuwsen (Roman Catholic) is assistant professor of philosophy at the Institute for Philosophy, University of Bonn, Federal Republic of Germany. *Conscience.*

Jerome Theisen (Roman Catholic) is abbot of St John's Benedictine Abbey, Collegeville, MN, USA. *Vocation.*

M.M. Thomas (Mar Thoma Syrian Church of Malabar), moderator of the WCC central committee 1968-75, is governor of the state of Nagaland in India. *Nation, syncretism.*

T.K. Thomas (Mar Thoma Syrian Church of Malabar) is publications editor in the WCC's Department of Communication. *Christian Conference of Asia; Mar Thoma Church; WCC, basis of.*

Betty Thompson (United Methodist Church) is director of public relations for the General Board of Global Ministries of her church, in New York City, USA. *Lacey, Janet.*

David M. Thompson (United Reformed Church in the UK) is lecturer in modern church history at Cambridge University, UK. *Disciples-Reformed dialogue.*

Bernard Thorogood (United Reformed Church in the UK) is general secretary and clerk of the general assembly of his church, London, UK. *Newbigin, James Edward Lesslie.*

Max Thurian (Roman Catholic) is canon of the cathedral of Naples, Italy. *Baptism, Eucharist and Ministry.*

J.-M.R. Tillard (Roman Catholic) is professor at the Dominican Faculty of Theology, Ottawa, Canada. *Consensus fidelium, Disciples-Roman Catholic dialogue, infallibility/indefectibility, koinonia, primacy.*

Oliver S. Tomkins (Church of England) was bishop of Bristol, UK. *Mott, John R.*

Karoly Toth (Reformed Church in Hungary), a former president of the Christian Peace Conference, is a bishop of his church. *Europe: Central and Eastern.*

Kern Robert Trembath (Episcopal Church) is professor of systematic theology at the University of Notre Dame, IN, USA. *Revelation.*

Georges Tsetsis (Orthodox Church, Ecumenical Patriarchate of Constantinople) is permanent representative of the Ecumenical Patriarchate to the WCC, Geneva, Switzerland. *Pan-Orthodox conferences.*

John Munsey Turner (Methodist Church of Great Britain) is superintendent minister of the Bolton circuit, Lancashire, UK. *Bell, G.A.K.; church and state; Paton, William; Temple, William.*

Rita Crowley Turner (Roman Catholic) is a writer and broadcaster living in England. *Mary in the ecumenical movement.*

David Tustin (Church of England) is bishop of Grimsby and co-chair of the Anglican-Lutheran International Continuation Committee, UK. *Anglican-Lutheran dialogue.*

Erika Tysoe-Dülken (Evangelical Church in Germany) was secretary for communication at the World Alliance of YMCAs, Geneva, Switzerland. *Young Men's Christian Associations.*

Carlos A. Valle (Evangelical Methodist Church of Argentina) is general secretary of the World Association for Christian Communication, London, UK. *World Association for Christian Communication.*

Marlin VanElderen (Christian Reformed Church in North America) is editor of the WCC's monthly magazine *One World. International Council of Christian Churches; life-style; Moral Rearmament; Moravians; Pentecostal World Conference; WCC, membership of.*

Charles Villa-Vicencio (Methodist Church of Southern Africa) is professor of religion and society at the University of Cape Town, South Africa. *Apartheid, Cottesloe, just war, Kairos document, Rustenburg declaration.*

Lukas Vischer (Swiss Protestant Church Federation), director of the WCC's Sub-unit on Faith and Order from 1966 to 1979, is professor of ecumenical theology at the University of Bern, and director of the ecumenical commission of his church. *Consensus.*

Gerhard Voss (Roman Catholic) is director of the Ecumenical Institute, Niederaltaich Abbey, Federal Republic of Germany. *Una Sancta movement.*

Geoffrey Wainwright, editor. *Anglican-Methodist relations; canon; church; church discipline; dialogue, multilateral; Easter; eucharist; federalism; God; intercommunion; lex orandi, lex credendi; magisterium; Methodist-Orthodox relations; Methodist-Reformed dialogue; Methodist-Roman Catholic dialogue; Pentecost; scripture; uniqueness of Christ; universalism.*

John Waliggo (Roman Catholic) is professor of history at the Catholic Higher Institute of Eastern Africa, Nairobi, Kenya. *Inculturation.*

Andrew Walls (Methodist Church of Great Britain) is director of the Centre for the Study of Christianity in the Non-Western World, University of Edinburgh, Scotland. *Missiology.*

Kallistos Ware (Orthodox Church, Ecumenical Patriarchate of Constantinople) is bishop of Diokleia and lecturer in Eastern Orthodox studies at the University of Oxford, UK. *Ethnicity, Tradition and traditions.*

Bärbel von Wartenberg-Potter (Evangelical Church in Germany), director of the WCC's Sub-unit on Women in Church and Society from 1980 to 1985, teaches at the United Theological College of the West Indies, Kingston, Jamaica. *Sexism.*

Richard L. Watson (Episcopal Church) is assistant to the president/public relations, World Vision International, Monrovia, CA, USA. *World Vision International.*

Pauline Webb, editor. *Communication, intercession, women in church and society.*

Hans-Ruedi Weber (Swiss Protestant Church Federation), director of biblical studies with the WCC from 1971 to 1988, was visiting lecturer at Pacific Theological College, Suva, Fiji, until 1990. *Bible, its role in the ecumenical movement.*

Theodore R. Weber (United Methodist Church) is professor of social ethics, Candler School of Theology, Emory University, Atlanta, GA, USA. *State*.

John B. Webster (Anglican Church of Canada) is associate professor of systematic theology at Wycliffe College, Toronto, Canada. *Ministry, threefold*.

Erich Weingärtner (Evangelical Lutheran Church in America), formerly on the staff of the WCC's Commission of the Churches on International Affairs, is a free-lance writer living in Canada. *Human rights*.

Robert K. Welsh (Christian Church (Disciples of Christ)) is vice-president of the Christian Church Foundation, Indianapolis, IN, USA. *Disciples of Christ*.

Dietrich Werner (Evangelical Lutheran Church of Oldenburg) is assistant in ecumenical theology at the Ecumenical Institute, Bochum, Federal Republic of Germany. *"Missionary structure of the congregation"*.

Charles C. West (Presbyterian Church (USA)) is S.C. Colwell professor of Christian ethics at Princeton Theological Seminary, NJ, USA. *Power, secularization*.

Morris West (Baptist Union of Great Britain) was principal of Bristol Baptist College, and special lecturer in theology, University of Bristol, UK. *Lund principle, Toronto statement*.

Vítor Westhelle (Evangelical Church of Lutheran Confession in Brazil) is professor of systematic theology at the Lutheran faculty of theology, Sao Leopoldo, Brazil. *Ideology*.

Teresa J. White (Church of England) is editor and administrator of *Distinctive Diaconate News* and *Distinctive Diaconate Studies*, London, UK. *Diaconate, diakonia*.

Glen Garfield Williams (Baptist Union of Great Britain) was general secretary of the Conference of European Churches from 1967 to 1987. *Conference of European Churches*.

Rowan D. Williams (Church of England) is Lady Margaret professor of divinity at the University of Oxford, UK. *Jesus Christ; theology, European*.

Roger Williamson (Methodist Church of Great Britain) is researcher at the Life and Peace Institute, Uppsala, Sweden. *Disarmament, pacifism*.

Hugh Wybrew (Church of England) is vicar of St Mary Magdalen, Oxford, UK. *Anglican-Orthodox dialogue*.

John H. Yoder (Mennonite Church) is professor of theology at the University of Notre Dame, IN, USA. *Conscientious objection, peace*.

Ralph C. Young (United Church of Canada) is Geneva secretary for the World Methodist Council, Geneva, Switzerland. *World Methodist Council*.